Central & Eastern

Anmatyerr to English DICTIONARY

Published by IAD Press in 2010
PO Box 2531, Alice Springs NT 0871
phone + 61 8 8951 1334
facsimile + 61 8 8951 1381
email sales@iad.edu.au
website www.iadpress.com

National Library of Australia Cataloguing-in-Publication data

Central and Eastern Anmatyerr to English dictionary
compiler, Jenny Green (Jennifer Anne)

ISBN 978 1 86465 080 8

Anmatyerre language – Dictionaries – English
English – Dictionaries – Anmatyerre language

499.15

Cover painting by Lena Pwerl, *Goannas* (detail), 1980, batik on silk, 232 x 88 cm,
National Gallery of Victoria, Melbourne
Cover photography by National Gallery of Victoria, Melbourne
Design and typesetting by Bruderlin MacLean Publishing Services
Map by Brenda Thornley
Illustrations by Christine Bruderlin, Felicity Green and Jenny Green, with additional illustrations by Faye Alexander, Julie Jones, Gary Prior, Jenny Taylor and Brenda Thornley
Printed in Australia by Ligare Pty Ltd

Australian Government
Department of the Environment, Water, Heritage and the Arts

This activity is supported by the Australian Government under the Maintenance of Indigenous Languages Program of the Department of Environment, Water, Heritage and the Arts.

Australia Council for the Arts

The Institute for Aboriginal Development Incorporated is assisted by the Australian Government through the Australia Council, its arts funding and advisory body.

IAD Press acknowledges the funding provided by the Australian and Northern Territory Governments through the Intergenerational Transfer of Indigenous Ecological Knowledge Program.

Central Land Council

Natural Resource Management Board (NT) Inc.

Northern Territory Government

Contents

Preface

This is the first dictionary of the Anmatyerr language, and it is the result of many years of work in Anmatyerr bush communities and in Alice Springs. The project has taken almost a decade to complete, and during this time a large number of Anmatyerr people have been involved in documenting their language. This dictionary follows in the tradition of dictionary making which began at the Institute for Aboriginal Development (IAD) in 1984, when the Arandic Languages Dictionary Program was first established. In the years since that program started several major dictionaries of central Australian Aboriginal languages have been published, such as the *Alyawarr to English dictionary*, the *Eastern and Central Arrernte to English dictionary* and many smaller language publications — picture dictionaries, learner's grammars, and word lists. Each new work reflects some of the achievements of those that preceded it.

This dictionary includes Anmatyerr from all of the Anmatyerr region, even though there are some significant differences between Central Anmatyerr — spoken at Ti Tree and in communities as far west as Mt Allan — and Eastern Anmatyerr, spoken at Stirling and in some Sandover communities. After much thought and discussion we decided to make one dictionary for Anmatyerr rather than two. Because it is a large region and there is lots of variation it has been difficult to balance the contributions from all Anmatyerr communities, and to those who may feel that they have not been involved sufficiently I extend my apologies. Whenever new words came up I tried to check them in a range of Anmatyerr communities, but this process could not go on forever and the dictionary had to be completed.

This dictionary contains over 8000 entries and sub-entries, and over 8500 example sentences. It includes a wealth of cultural information, some grammatical notes, a discussion of the Anmatyerr kinship system, and an English to Anmatyerr finder list. However, this dictionary will by its nature have mistakes and shortcomings. There will be Anmatyerr words that have been left out, and some of the complexities of the meanings of words will be either absent or misconstrued. It is not a grammar, and a thorough treatment of Anmatyerr grammar is yet to be published. What is true for all languages also holds true for Anmatyerr — the meaning (and the pronunciation) of some words changes over time. All of these issues provide challenges for those who may compile future editions of the Anmatyerr dictionary.

The many people who have contributed to the making of this dictionary are acknowledged in the next section, and I thank them for their enthusiasm and patience over the years. The sustained effort required to make dictionaries would not be possible without the support of colleagues, friends and family. In particular I would like to thank the Anmatyerr people for their commitment to the long process of making the dictionary, and for their generosity in teaching me about Anmatyerr. Thanks also go to the schools and the school staff in the Anmatyerr region, and to the Anmatjere Council. I am also indebted to colleagues who provided linguistic and other kinds of support. I thank Robert Hoogenraad, Gavan Breen and David Strickland for their detailed and thoughtful comments on drafts of the dictionary; the staff at IAD Press and at the IAD Language Centre; and Mark MacLean and Christine Bruderlin for their meticulous editing, and elegant design. In particular I thank Myfany Turpin for her support throughout the project, especially during the many wonderful times we spent working on dictionaries in the bush together.

I hope that this dictionary will assist Anmatyerr people who want to become literate in their own language, learners of the Anmatyerr language, educators, translators and others with an interest in Anmatyerr, and that it will help keep the Anmatyerr language strong for the future.

Jenny Green
April 2006

Acknowledgements

Anmatyerr contributors

Mt Allan (Yuelamu)
Lilly Stafford Penangk
Rosie Patterson Pengart
Elaine Quinn Penangk
Janie Briscoe Mpetyan
Roslyn Quinn Kemarr
Linda Quinn Kemarr
Caroline Stafford Pwerrerl
Cheryl Briscoe Peltharr
Lisa Cook Mpetyan
Rosina Stafford Pwerrerl
Susie Stafford Pwerrerl
Jack Cook Ngal
Anne Cook Ngwarray
Banjo Patterson Kemarr
David McCormack Penangk
Rowena Larry Ngwarray
Billy Stafford Kemarr
Anne Cook Ngwarray
Andrew Collins (dec)
Old Peter Stafford Pwerrerl (dec)
Brenda Morton Penangk (dec)

Pulardi (Desert Bore)
Teddy Briscoe Mpetyan
Veronica Gorey Pwerrerl
Brenda Lynch Ngwarray

Pine Hill
Teddy Ngwarray (dec)
George Ngwarray (dec)

Ti Tree
April Campbell Pengart
Janie Long Pwerrerl
Billy Woods Mpetyan
Tiny Ross Pengart (dec)
Aileen Pwerrerl
Clarry Long Kemarr
Doris Nelson Pengart
Archie Mpetyan
Janie Woods Ngal
Peggy Martin Pengart
Jacqueline Woods Ngal
Patch Price Mpetyan (dec)
Paddy Willis Kemarr
Simon Gorey Mpetyan
Jimmy Haines Ngwarray
Seraphina Presley-Haines Pengart
Willy Long Pwerrerl
Peterson Stuart Pengart
Don Presley Pengart
Rosemary Tilmouth Kemarr
Alice Pwerrerl (dec)

Alice Springs
Margaret Heffernan Pengart
Johnny Leo Kemarr
Katie Briscoe Penangk (dec)
Morris Briscoe Penangk (dec)
Barbara Briscoe Kemarr (dec)

Laramba (Napperby)
Nancy Long Pwerrerl
Mary Ngal
Connie Ngal (dec)
Kitty Gibson Peltharr
Rita Ngal
Rita Peltharr
Amy Stafford Peltharr
Beryl Gorey Kemarr
Kitty Kakatew Peltharr
Sandra Leo Pwerrerl
Loretta Abbott Ngal
Janice McMillan Pwerrerl
Veronica Tilmouth Kemarr
Amarantha McMillan Pwerrerl
Ronnie McNamara
Lena Ngal (dec)
Rosy Ngal (dec)
Elsie Mpetyan (dec)
Topsy Pengart (dec)
Jillery Dixon Peltharr (dec)
Nancy Mpetyan (dec)

Derwent Bore (Town Bore)
Dick Lechleitner Penangk (dec)
Kangaroo James (dec)
Jim Lawless (dec)

Stirling
Hilda Price Pwerl
Weetji Mpetyan
Gracie Mpetyan
Norman Price Pwerl
Fanny Mpetyan
Michael Price Tyapeyarte
Christopher Tyaname
Janie Mpetyan
Jacob Petyarr
Lucy Price Kemarr
Elizabeth Inkamala
Lowie Pwerl (dec)

Utopia
Lena Pwerl
Lena Skinner
Myrtle Petyarr
Gloria Petyarr
Violet Petyarr
Joy Petyarr
Wendy Purvis Mpetyan (dec)
Nancy Petyarr (dec)
Emily Kam Ngwarray (dec)
Jedda Ngwarray
Maureen Ngwarray
Jennifer Ngwarray
Kathleen Kemarr
Rosie Pwerl
Helen Kunoth
Glory Ngal (dec)

Other acknowledgments

Principal researcher/compiler
Jenny Green

Other consultant linguists
Gavan Breen, David Strickland, Myfany Turpin, Robert Hoogenraad, Bernard Schebeck, Gail Woods, David Wilkins

Scientific advisers
Peter Latz, Dave Albrecht, Melinda Hilley, Nick Gambold, Mike Gillam

Proofreaders, draft checkers
Gavan Breen, David Strickland, Robert Hoogenraad, Christine Bruderlin, Mark MacLean

Funding and assistance
This dictionary was funded by the Aboriginal and Torres Strait Islander Commission (ATSIC) until 2005, then by the Office of Indigenous Policy Coordination. The Institute for Aboriginal Development (IAD) and IAD Language Centre also provided financial support. IAD Press acknowledges the funding provided by the Australian and Northern Territory Governments through the Intergenerational Transfer of Indigenous Ecological Knowledge Program.

The dictionary also benefited from other small projects on Anmatyerr such as those funded by the Australian Institute for Aboriginal and Torres Strait Islander Studies, by the Language Access Initiatives Program of ATSIC and by the School of Australian Linguistics. Thanks also to the Max Planck Institute for Psycholinguistics, in Nijmegen, the Netherlands, for the use of a fieldwork vehicle.

Introduction

The heart of Anmatyerr country is several hundred kilometres north of Alice Springs, right in the middle of Australia. There are no hard and fast geographical boundaries to Anmatyerr country, but the region extends roughly from Mt Allan in the west to some of the Sandover outstations in the east, and from Stirling in the north to around Native Gap in the south (see map overleaf). Neighbours of the Anmatyerr are the Warlpiri to the west, Alyawarr to the north-east, Kaytetye to the north and the northern Arrernte to the south. Some of the main communities where Anmatyerr is spoken are Yuelamu (Mt Allan), Laramba (Napperby), Pulardi (Desert Bore), Ti Tree, Ti Tree Six Mile, Stirling, some of the outstations on Utopia (the Angarapa Land Trust), Mulga Bore and Adelaide Bore. Many Anmatyerr people also live in regional centres, such as Alice Springs, and in other communities, such as Yuendumu and Engawala (Alcoota).

Anmatyerr is one of a network of closely related languages and dialects which include different kinds of Arrernte — such as Western Arrarnta, Eastern and Central Arrernte and Lower Arrernte — and Pertame, Alyawarr, and Kaytetye. This group is sometimes referred to as the 'Arandic group', and altogether there are probably around 5500 speakers of these languages. Within the Anmatyerr language itself there are significant variations. These include some differences in sounds, in vocabulary, and in the use of various grammatical constructions. Although it would have been possible to make two dictionaries of Anmatyerr — one for the Central dialect (spoken in communities including Ti Tree and those to the west) and one for the Eastern dialect (including Stirling and the Sandover communities) — after extensive discussions with Anmatyerr speakers it was decided that both varieties of the Anmatyerr language would be put into one dictionary. One of the reasons for this was that it seemed artificial to separate the language into two when, in reality, the differences in the language are spread over the region. The difference between the Anmatyerr spoken on the edges of Anmatyerr country — in the far west and the far east — is the greatest, and in the middle the Anmatyerr spoken shows some of the features of both the Central and Eastern dialects. The other reason was that, in spite of differences, there would have been a great deal of overlap if there were two separate dictionaries of Anmatyerr.

Some may be puzzled by the name 'Central Anmatyerr' for the type of Anmatyerr spoken in the central and western parts of Anmatyerr country. Although at times this has been referred to as 'Western Anmatyerr' the choice to call it 'Central' was made by senior Anmatyerr people from that area at the time the *Central Anmatyerr Picture Dictionary* was published. They were, in part, taking into consideration the naming of the Central Anmatjere football team, but their choice also reflects their view of their position in the Anmatyerr world. As there is so much variation in Anmatyerr, this dictionary marks the dialect of each word, and the example sentences are usually annotated to show which community they came from.

There is also an older type of Anmatyerr, known to some as 'Kal Ntheyelkwer' or 'Ntheyelkwer', which is spoken in the western part of Anmatyerr country, but there is little specific information about this in this dictionary.

The earliest known written records of Anmatyerr words were those of NB Tindale who recorded a list of 230 words at Cockatoo Creek, near Mt Denison, in 1931. In the late 1950s and 1960s Ken Hale recorded a range of Arandic languages, including Anmatyerr at Napperby. More recent work includes that by Avery Andrews at Ti Tree and by Bernard Schebeck, and the Anmatyerr word lists compiled by Gavan Breen (1988, 1996) and by Purle, Green and Heffernan (1981). The *Central Anmatyerr Picture Dictionary* was published in 2003, and some other bilingual Anmatyerr books have been completed during the course of the dictionary project (see the list of further readings on page xxvii).

This dictionary is the result of work that began intensively in the mid 1990s. It is based on extensive fieldwork in the main Anmatyerr communities — in particular Mt Allan, Napperby, Ti Tree, Stirling and the Sandover — resulting in well over 250 hours of tape-recorded language, and in other field notes and Anmatyerr materials. Over the years almost one hundred Anmatyerr people were involved in the dictionary work, and for all of us it was a pleasurable and rewarding experience. Many of these Anmatyerr people were senior people, involved

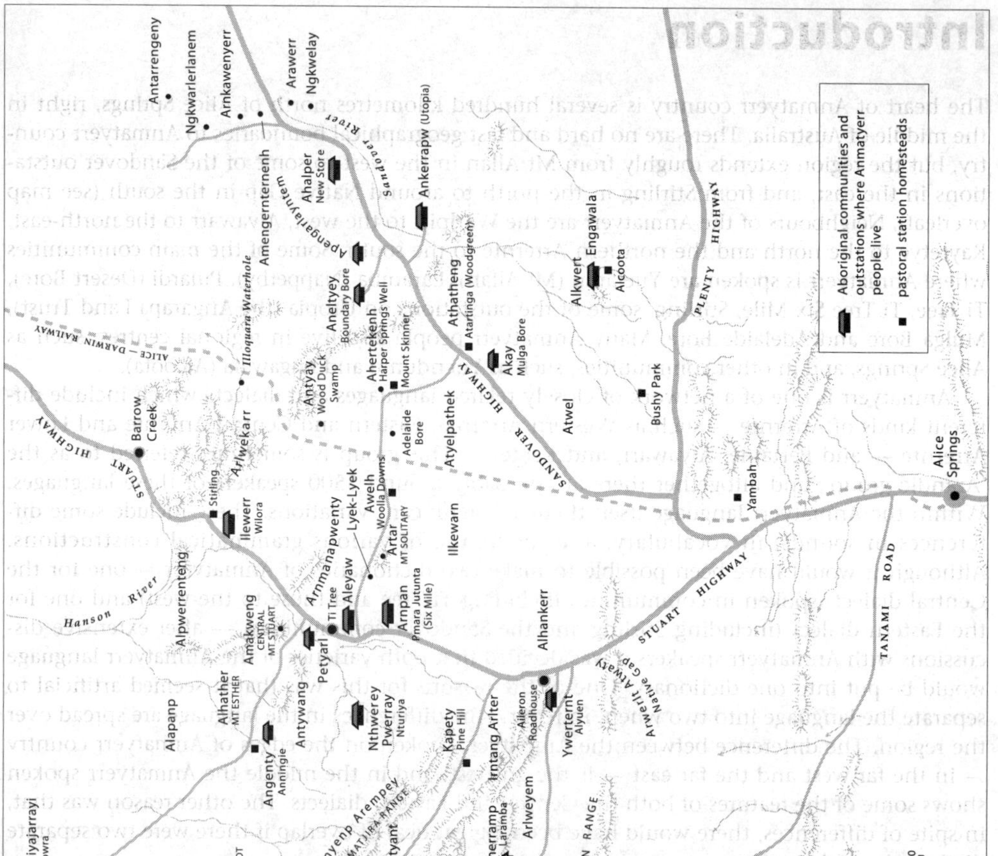

Location of the main communities where Anmatyerr people live, and some places in the Anmatyerr region.

because of their deep knowledge of Anmatyerr language and culture. Younger people, in particular those working to teach language and culture in Anmatyerr schools, were also involved in the making of the dictionary.

The methodology of the Central Australian Dictionaries Program team was to try to make the maximum use of pre-existing work on Anmatyerr and on the other Arandic languages which are related to it, and to recognise and utilise the multilingual skills of language speakers. We often worked in groups, and we used other Arandic languages as a source of words to check against Anmatyerr, as all of these languages have much in common (see Green & Turpin 2001 for detailed discussion).

The audio tapes of the language work recorded in the bush communities were transcribed and entered into a database in which all the Anmatyerr language material for the dictionary project is kept. The database allowed us to keep careful track of who said what, when and to whom, and of variation in Anmatyerr pronunciation. It also tracks the processes of identifying plants and animals and all the myriad bits of information that go into making a dictionary. The original tapes are archived at the Australian Institute of Aboriginal and Torres Strait Islander Studies in Canberra and copies are kept at IAD in Alice Springs. The example sentences for the dictionary were chosen from this database, but of course there are many many more for which there was not enough space in the dictionary. The example sentences in the dictionary reflect spoken language rather than written language simply because there were almost no written Anmatyerr texts in existence before the dictionary project came into being.

Anmatyerr spelling, pronunciation and grammar

Although written records of Anmatyerr go back to the 1930s, the language has only recently been written down systematically for word lists, dictionaries and other language publications. An example of the consequences of *not* writing things down systematically is clearly shown in the following spellings of the word Anmatyerr itself: Anmatyerre, Anmatjirra, Anmajirra, Anmatjera, Anmadjara, Anmatjara, Nmatjera, Imatjera, Unmatjera and Urmitchee. All of these spellings have, at some time or other, appeared in documents mentioning Anmatyerr language or Anmatyerr people.

Spelling system and pronunciation

The spelling system adopted in this dictionary is the result of years of work with Anmatyerr speakers, many of whom expressed their views about which letters to use for which Anmatyerr sounds. In 1998 Anmatyerr people also made decisions about spelling at a big Arandic-language spelling workshop in Alice Springs, and consultations continued in communities as the dictionary project progressed. Having said this, the dictionary team recognises that the spelling system is not perfect, and it may well be modified at some time in the future.

Many of the sounds of Anmatyerr are different to those found in English and so it is not possible to simply spell Anmatyerr words the way they 'sound' in English. In the spelling system used for Anmatyerr and other languages in the Arandic group, English letters, or combinations of two or three letters, are used to represent the sounds of the language. Thus, each Anmatyerr 'sound' is expressed in a unique way. Once this system has been mastered it is possible to predict the way an Anmatyerr word sounds from the spelling, unlike English, which has many inconsistencies and idiosyncrasies. (Consider words such as 'through', 'bough', 'cough' 'enough' and 'bought', in which the sequence of letters 'ough' stands for quite different sounds.)

Consonants

Table 1 (overleaf) shows how the letters used to spell Anmatyerr consonant sounds can be arranged so that similar groups of sounds appear in the same row or column. The sounds in the columns are arranged according to the part of the mouth they are made with, and those in the rows according to the way they are made. Those in the shaded columns and rows are the additional consonant sounds found in the Eastern Anmatyerr region but not in the central or western part of the region. The technical linguistic names for these types of sounds appear in column 1 and row 1.

Table 1: Central and Eastern Anmatyerr consonants

	Labial	Lamino Inter-dental	Apico-Alveolar	Retroflex	Pre-palatal	Palatal	Velar
Stop	*p*	*th*	*t*	*rt*	*yt*	*ty*	*k*
Nasal	*m*	*nh*	*n*	*rn*	*yn*	*ny*	*ng*
Pre-stopped nasal	*pm*	*tnh*	*tn*	*rtn*	*ytn*	*tny*	*kng*
Lateral		*lh*	*l*	*rl*	*yl*	*ly*	
Flap/trill			*rr*				
Approximant	*w*			*r*		*y*	*h*

In Anmatyerr there is no distinction between 'p' and 'b', between 't' and 'd', and between 'k' and 'g', so don't be surprised to hear a word spelled with a *p* pronounced as a 'b', or a word with a *t* in it pronounced as 'd'. In English these pairs of of consonants contrast with each other because of voicing — the vibration of the vocal cords, and aspiration — the little puff of air that escapes from the mouth with some pronunciations of 'p', 't' and 'k'. These differences in sound are not important in Anmatyerr and so the distinction between 'p' and 'b', 't' and 'd' and 'k' and 'g' is irrelevant to Anmatyerr ears. For Anmatyerr spelling the letter 'k' was chosen instead of 'g', the letter 'p' instead of 'b' and 't' instead of 'd'.

Anmatyerr does not have the sounds represented in English by 'v', 's', 'f', 'z' and 'sh'. When words with sounds in them that are not normally in Anmatyerr are borrowed into Anmatyerr they are replaced by the closest Anmatyerr equivalent. So, for example, an English word like 'bicycle' might sound, in Anmatyerr pronunciation, like *patyekel* or *pathekel*.

The Anmatyerr sounds written on their own as *k, l, m, n, t* and *w* sound similar to those sounds in English:

kapert	head
ilep	axe
mern	food (vegetables and fruits)
anert	stomach
item	cook
warl	house

Anmatyerr has a set of three sounds that are spelt using the letters *th, nh* and *lh*. These are inter-dental sounds and they are pronounced with the tongue touching the back of the upper front teeth, and sometimes with the tip of the tongue protruding slightly between the teeth. To Anmatyerr speakers, these sound completely different to the apico-alveolar sounds *t, n* and *l*. For example, the word *alem* 'liver' sounds different to the word *alhem* 'go', and the word *aterr* 'cicada' sounds different to *atherr* 'two'.

atherr	two
nhenh	here
alhem	go

There is another group of sounds called retroflexes. They are made with the tip of the tongue higher in the mouth than for the regular *t, n,* and *l*, and curled right back so the bottom of the tongue tip touches the roof of the mouth. These sounds are hard for English speakers to hear and produce properly and they have a 'heavier' sound than non-retroflex sounds. For example, *rt* sounds a bit like the way some Americans pronounce the 't' in 'water'. The sound spelt with a single *r* is also made in this way, and sounds much like the English 'r'.

kwert	smoke
arnem	cry

arley	emu chick
arem	see, look

The sounds spelt *ty*, *ny* and *ly* are produced by putting the tongue forward so that its tip touches the backs of both sets of teeth, while the blade of the tongue rests against the palate. The *ty* sound is pronounced in a somewhat similar (but subtly different) way to the 'ch' in '**ch**ur**ch**', or the 'j' and 'dg' sounds in '**j**u**dg**e'.

tyap	edible grub
pe**ty**em	come

The *ny* sound is pronounced a bit like the sound in the middle of words such as 'onion', 'senior' and 'canyon'.

a**ny**ent	one
i**ny**em	dig

The *ly* sound is pronounced a bit like the sound in the middle of 'million'.

a**ly**ap	honeyant nest
lyep-**ly**ep	part of intestines

The *ng* sound is pronounced like the 'ng' in English words such as 'sa**ng**' and 'lu**ng**', but not like the 'ng' in 'fi**ng**er' (where the 'ng' sound is followed by a hard 'g' sound) or in the word 'da**ng**er'. This sound is common at the beginning of Anmatyerr words and some English speakers may have trouble hearing or pronouncing it in this position as it is not found at the beginning of English words.

ngangkar	traditional healer
a**ng**enty	soakage

The *h* sound is a difficult sound not found in English, and found in only a few Anmatyerr words. It sounds a bit like the Scottish pronunciation of 'ch' in the word 'lo**ch**', or a bit like the 'w' in '**w**onder', but without rounded lips. Anmatyerr children and some young adults tend not to pronounce this sound, substituting a long vowel instead, and Anmatyerr people on the west tend not to use this sound at all. For example, younger people often drop the sound written as *h* in words such as *aherr* 'kangaroo', and so it sounds a bit like *aarr*. Words like this are still written with the *h* whether it is actually pronounced or not.

a**h**err	kangaroo
a**h**enty	throat

The *rr* sound is a hard, rolled, tapped or trilled sound, a bit like that used in Scottish English. It can be made with a quick flick of the tongue against the ridge behind the teeth, or it can be a rolled or trilled sound made by several quick flicks of the tongue. It is quite different from the *r* sound mentioned above.

a**rr**akert	mouth
a**rr**ke**rr**	barn owl

The *y* sound is similar to the 'y' sound in the word '**y**es', but not like that in 'by', 'hymn' or 'silly'.

yanh	that, there
yerr	ant

All the consonants — except for *w* and *h* — have another form in which they are pronounced with rounded lips. This is written with a *w* following the consonant:

***pw**erlep*	'shoulder'
***mw**ekart*	'hat'
***thw**errem*	'rub skin off bush onions'
***nhw**em*	'bite'
***lhw**elk*	'blue-tongue lizard'
*a**tw**em*	'hit'
*a**nw**erl*	'barking spider'
***lw**ernp*	'kingfisher'
***rrw**elty*	'kindling wood'
***rtw**ekert*	'heart'
***rnw**ang*	'water dish'
***rlw**ang*	'forehead'
***rw**ang*	'fire'
***tyw**enp*	'perentie'
***nyw**err*	'mountain devil lizard'
***lyw**ang*	'shade'
***yw**errem*	'get lost, disappear'
***kw**art*	'egg'
***ngw**ely*	'dog'

In Eastern Anmatyerr there is an additional set of consonant sounds that are written as *yt, yn* and *yl*. The examples below show how they sound when they are preceded by *a*, by *e* (in the middle of a word) or by *i* at the beginning of a word.

ayt sounds like 'ate'	*atnyem**ayt*** 'witchetty grub'
ayn sounds like 'ain' in 'pain'	***ayn**tem* 'lie down'
ayl sounds like 'ale'	***aylayl*** 'boomerang'
eyt and *iyt* sound like 'eat'	*arrk**eyt*** 'yellow'; ***iyt**eny* 'flirtation'
eyn and *iyn* sound like the 'een' in 'been'	*atw**eyn**em* 'keep on hitting'; ***iyn**teng* 'rotten'
eyl and *iyl* sound like 'eel'	*arr**eyl*** 'cheek'; ***iyl**aw* 'munyeroo'

Eastern Anmatyerr also has pre-stopped nasal sounds, written as *pm, tnh, tn, rtn, ytn, tny* and *kng*. These are made by combining two sounds that are made in the same part of the mouth but by different mechanisms. For example, when making a *pm* sound both the *p* and the *m* parts of it are made with the lips, but *m* is a nasal sound. These two sounds really work as one, and sound a bit like the 'pm' in the English word 'to**pm**ost'. The sound *tn* is made with the tongue touching the ridge just above the upper teeth, and sounds a bit like the 'tn' in the word 'chu**tn**ey'. In the pair of words *anem* 'sit' and *atnem* 'digging stick' the difference between the sounds *n* and *tn* is the significant difference between the two words. This distinction does not exist on the western side of Anmatyerr country, and there the words for 'sit' and 'digging stick' sound the same. In the east it seems that younger people may not pronounce these pre-stopped sounds, which could reflect a general change away from pre-stopping in Arandic languages.

These additional Eastern Anmatyerr consonants — the pre-stopped consonants and the pre-palatal consonants — also have a rounded form which is written with a 'w' following the consonant. These are spelt as *pmw, tnhw, tnw, rtnw, ytnw, tnyw, kngw, ytw, ynw,* and *ylw.*

Vowels

The vowel sounds in Anmatyerr words are heavily influenced by the consonant sounds in the word, and this is especially true of *e*. However, *e* will often sound like the second vowel sound in 'bord**er**':

mern	'food (from plants and trees)'
mer	'country', 'place'

Following rounded consonants (discussed above), *e* sounds like 'oo' in 's**oo**t':

kwert	'smoke'
pwerlep	'shoulder'

The Anmatyerr *a* is pronounced like the 'a' in 'f**a**ther' or, at the beginning of words, like the 'a' sound in '**a**lone':

*arr**a**kert*	'mouth'
*kw**a**ty*	'water'
***a**mak*	'elbow'

Remember that many Anmatyerr words start with *a*, but that this *a* is often dropped without the meaning of the word changing.

The letter *i* is generally only used at the beginning of words and at the beginning of some word endings (following a hyphen). It may sound a bit like the 'i' in '**in**' or '**ill**', or even like the second vowel sound in 'bord**er**':

***i**ntey*	'cave'
***i**ngkang*	'foot'
***i**rrety*	'eaglehawk'
*arrken-**i**rrem*	'play', 'have fun'

There are a handful of words where *i* is used in the middle, for example, *ampinem* 'stalk, track someone or something'.

The letter *u* is only used at the beginning of some Eastern Anmatyerr words when the 'rounding' is heard at the beginning of the word. It sounds a bit like the 'u' sound in 'p**u**t'. Equivalent words in Central Anmatyerr tend to have this rounding pronounced later in the word — that is, after a consonant — and this is shown by a *w* following the consonant. The following examples show differences in pronunciation and spelling between some words in Eastern Anmatyerr (in the first column) and the Central Anmatyerr (in the second column):

***u**ra*	***rw**a*	'fire'
***u**ntyey*	***ntyw**ey*	'corkwood'
***u**rrpety*	***rrpw**ety*	'three', 'a few'
***u**rrtyirrem*	***rrtyw**errem*	'tell a lie'

Stress

Another thing that is important when pronouncing words properly is knowing which part of the word you emphasise, or stress. For example, in English the correct pronunciation of the word 'ignorant' is '**ig**norant' rather than 'ig**nor**ant'. A difference in stress can make a word sound weird and in some cases, such as the difference between the two words 'per**mit**' (I allow you to do it) and '**per**mit' (a licence to do something), a difference in stress can change the meaning of the word. In Anmatyerr the stress is usually on the first vowel after a consonant or consonant cluster:

*arr**a**kert*	'mouth'
*ant**e**therrk*	'carpet snake'

Stress usually goes on the vowel at the beginning of a word if the only other vowel is right at the end of a word. For example:

***a**lhwa*	'blood'

Note that in the central and western part of the Anmatyerr area people usually add *+ang* to these short words so ***alhwa*** 'blood' would become *alhwang*, and ***ra*** 'he', 'she', 'it' becomes *rang*. Thus the stress shifts to after the first consonant.

Spelling rules

No spelling system of any language in the world is perfect, and the Anmatyerr one is no exception. Besides, people have different opinions about what makes a good spelling system. It generally takes a bit of effort to master the spelling systems of other languages, as they rely on different conventions or pairings of orthographic symbols with sounds.

One of the big challenges in making a dictionary of a language with a sound system very different to English is striking a balance between making it easy to find words in the dictionary and then, once they have been found, making them easy to spell and read. In the Anmatyerr region there is a lot of variation in the pronunciation of words, some of which are closely related even though they may not seem so at first hearing. This is due to some differences in the sound system within the region and to variations in the way individuals pronounce words. This is the case in any language; for example, there is an enormous variation in the way some words in English can be pronounced.

In this dictionary I have tried to reflect some of this variation while at the same time standardising spellings as much as possible. It would not be wise to put all of the variations in the dictionary, just as it would not be useful to leave most of them out. Thus the entries in the dictionary aim both to give guidance about spelling and to help people to find words that they don't know how to spell.

What follows is an outline of the principles applied when making these decisions about which of the various spellings to put in and which to leave out. It is early days for writing Anmatyerr and, as more people become literate, it is probable that speakers of Anmatyerr will refine the spelling system as it appears in this dictionary. For example, the rules for hyphenating words may change over time as more people get used to reading and writing Anmatyerr.

Vowel sounds at the end of a word

You may hear variation in the vowel sound at the end of a word, or hear no vowel sound at all, and so this sound (or lack of sound) is not represented in the Anmatyerr spelling system. Thus, *e* is not written on the end of Anmatyerr words, unlike the Eastern and Central Arrernte and the Kaytetye spelling systems. For example, the word *ilep* 'axe' is written in Anmatyerr without the final *e*, even though it sounds the same as the word spelt *ilepe* in Arrernte and *elepe* in Kaytetye.

Short words have *a* on the end, such as *ra* 'he, she, it', *ntwa* 'you,' *tha* 'I', *atwa*! 'hit (him, her it)! and *ana!* 'sit!'. As mentioned before, in the Central dialect of Anmatyerr short words often have *+ang* on the end of them, for example, *rang* 'he, she, it', *ntwang* 'you,' *anang*! 'sit!'. Longer imperative verbs also have *a* on the end, for example, *ntert-irra*! 'be quiet!'.

Vowel sounds at the beginning of a word

You will notice that many Anmatyerr words begin with *a*, though they may not be pronounced with this *a* all the time. In fact, more than half of the entries in this dictionary begin with *a*! The meaning of a word is not usually affected by including *a* on the front of the word or leaving it out, though some speakers of the language may prefer to pronounce the word in one way or the other. Note that there are some words that never begin with *a*, for example, *kwaty* 'water'. In this dictionary we have not included all possible variations, but rather chosen the pronunciation which seems to be the most frequently used. This is not to say that other pronunciations are 'wrong'. The reader is encouraged to learn that words with an *a* vowel at the beginning may sometimes drop the *a*. For example, *atanthem* 'to spear' may also be pronounced as *tanthem* — that is, without the *a* on the front, and without the meaning changing.

There is also some variation between the way that different Anmatyerr speakers pronounce other sounds at the beginning of words. For example, the word for 'bird's crest' may be pronounced both as *irrkarlp* and *arrkarlp* and the word for 'ear' may be heard as both *irlpang* and *arlpang*. Some of these differences are very noticeable when comparing the speech of older speakers of Anmatyerr with young ones.

Rounded sounds

One feature of the Anmatyerr language is the mobility of the rounded sound, indicated in the spelling system by *w* following a consonant. This rounding may 'move about' the word. For example, there are variations in pronunciation such as that between ***angw**ayak* and *angaya**kw*** 'hungry', *a**rrw**engak* and *arrenga**kw*** 'on the other side'. An Anmatyerr speaker may pronounce these words in these different ways at different times, and all of these pronunciations are equally correct. In this dictionary we have decided only to write one of these possible pronunciations, and the choice has been made based on the most frequent pronunciation. The Eastern Anmatyerr pronunciations — where the rounding is at the beginning of the word (and spelt as *u*) — come under a separate entry. For example, the word for 'you' appears twice in the dictionary — as *ntwa* (W,T) and as *unta* (E). These are cross-referenced to each other in the dictionary entries (see page xxvi for an explanation of these abbreviations).

Retroflex-initial words

The difference between *rt* or *t*, *rl* or *l* and *rn* or *n* at the beginning of words does not seem to be important in Anmatyerr when the following vowel is *a* or *e*. In this dictionary most words that could begin with a retroflex sound (*rt*, *rn*, *rl*) followed by either of these vowels are written as beginning with the 'plain' sound — *t* rather than with *rt*, *n* rather than *rn* and so on — although both variations may occur in ordinary speech. There are corresponding cross-references from the retroflex-initial words to the main entry.

Some words that seem to be most commonly heard as starting with the retroflex sound are written this way, with a cross-reference to the plain ('*r*-less') sound. For example 'windbreak' appears in the dictionary under *rt* as *rtak* but with a cross-reference from *tak*. There are a few words which are written beginning with the retroflex sound (e.g. *rtety* 'tooth') because they can have an alternative pronunciation with a vowel on the front (*irtety 'tooth')*, so it seems that the retroflex sound is there even if it is often hard to hear.

*Retroflex followed by **w***

Where a retroflex sound at the beginning of a word is followed by a *w* — for example, ***rlk**werrp* 'froth' or ***rl**weth* 'in half' — the retroflexion is written, even though it may not always be heard. One reason for doing this is that the equivalent forms in other dialects often have an initial vowel followed by a retroflex consonant such as, ***urlk**errp* (E), ***urle**th* (E). There are a few pairs of words in which this particular sound does make a difference, such as the difference between ***rl**wakem* 'dislocate kangaroo's leg joints before cooking' and ***l**wakem* 'chase'.

Variation in pre-stopping

For many speakers of the Eastern dialect of Anmatyerr there may be a significant difference between the sounds written as *n* and *tn*, *pm* and *m*, *kng* and *ng*, *tnh* and *nh*, *tny* and *ny*, *rtn* and *rn*, and *ytn* and *yn*. There is also variation, and some speakers do not pronounce the pre-stopping at all. The word without this 'pre-stopping' appears first in the dictionary entry because it appears to reflect the way younger people are pronouncing the words, and there are cross-references from one form to the other. This variation in pre-stopping has been written in example sentences when it was heard.

*Word-initial **iy***

Eastern Anmatyerr words beginning with *iy* followed by a consonant — for example, *iyt*, *iyn*, or *iyl* — are often also pronounced as if they started with *irt*, *irn*, or *irl* respectively. For example, *iyltem* 'break or crack something open' may sound like *irltem*. Generally only one of these options appears in the dictionary.

Another example of variation is found in the following pronunciations of the word for 'beefwood': *ltyenty*, *iyltenty*, *irltenty*. Although all are correct we have decided only to include *ltyenty* and *iyltenty* as the form with the retroflex (*rlt*) is a predictable variation in words like this.

Pre-stopping in consonant clusters
The *rrkng*, *rrtny*, and *rrpm* sounds are written as *rrng*, *rrny*, and *rrm*, as the pre-stopping (the *k*, *t* or *p* sounds) in these consonant clusters is predictable.

Hyphens
Many Anmatyerr words are made up of lots of different parts or endings and so can be quite long. Hyphens are put between the parts of words to break them up in order to make it easier to read them. For example, *Arrwekarenyehenh* 'belonging to the people from Coniston' is broken up into *Arrwek-areny-henh*.

Hyphens are used to break up doubled up words such as *kwaty-kwaty* 'watery' or *rnter-rnter* 'red'.

They are used before most, but not all, long endings. For example, *mer* 'camp', plus the ending *-warn* 'towards', is written as *mer-warn* 'to the camp'. The word *tyerrty* 'people', plus the ending *-henh* 'belonging to', is written as *tyerrty-henh* 'the people's'.

Anmatyerr verbs can be made up of several verbs joined together, particularly using the verbs stems *alh* 'go', *atw* 'hit', *alp* 'go back' and *int* 'lie'. Hyphens are used to break up long verbs that have *alh, alp, atw* or *int* as part of them, as in *arlkety-**alh**em* 'go and sing out', *angety-**alp**em* 'get something and go back; go back and get something'.

If a short word is followed by an ending, the *a* on the end of the short word is dropped and the ending begins with a vowel. For example, *rwekwenh* 'without fire' (*rwa* 'fire'+ *-kwenh* 'without') instead of *rwakwenh* or *rwa-kwenh* and *rwakert* 'with fire' (*-akert* 'having') instead of *rwa-akert*. If the beginning part of a word is short, hyphens are not used to separate this part of the word from the next part. For example, if the ending *+arl* is added to the pronoun *ra* it is spelt as *rarl*.

Grammar and word building

At the time of this dictionary's publication, no learner's guide or grammar of Anmatyerr had been written. It is not within the scope of this dictionary to provide comprehensive grammatical notes; however, there are several aspects of the grammar worth mentioning.

The first of these is a brief description of the types of words found in the Anmatyerr language. The entries for most words in the dictionary are followed by an abbreviated code that shows the part of speech of the word. The main part-of-speech categories are as follows:

- *n.* — 'Nominals' include words for things, people and places, but also include words that in English would be thought of as adjectives.
- *n.kin* — 'Kin nominals' are words for family and relations. As their grammar is distinct from other nominals (for example, they take endings that other nominals can't), they have their own part-of-speech label. They include a few words that English speakers may not expect to find in this category, such as *altyerr*[1] 'dream', 'Dreaming'.
- *prn.* — 'Pronoun'. Anmatyerr has a lot of pronouns, and these have special bits added to them which show kinship categories — how people are related to each other. Pronouns are discussed properly in Appendix 1.
- *vt.* — 'Transitive verb'.
- *vi.* — 'Intransitive verb'. A discussion about the differences between these types of verbs appears below.
- *adv.* — Anmatyerr adverbs almost always occur with verbs, and typically they express the way that things are done; for example, *artangaty* 'doing things together', *apelkel* 'doing something without reason', *arwengkel* 'doing something sneakily or secretively' and *ywarn/uyarn* 'being unable to do something, doing something in vain'. They also show such things as the orientation of the verb action (*ntywem/untyem* 'facing or moving away' and *lwarr/ularr* 'facing or moving towards') and the degree to which an action continues or is repeated (*aweth* 'again' and *akwet* 'still, always').
- *part.* — Particles are words which cannot have the main Anmatyerr grammatical endings on them and which do not need to be with a verb in a sentence. Particles include

interjections and exclamations (*mpa* 'let's go', *ma* 'here!, there!, take it!', *yekay* 'Oh!'), words which show the speaker's attitude to what they are saying (*apek* 'maybe, might, perhaps', *akwel* 'supposedly, apparently' and *kwenh* 'really, definitely'). Other particles include *anem* 'now, and then', *kel* 'OK' and *kenh*[2] 'whereas, on the other hand'.

ending Many Anmatyerr words are made up of lots of smaller parts, or consist of a word with a series of endings. These endings show things such as direction, location, the absence of something, kin relationships, resemblance to things, the number of participants in an action, and the tense of verbs. Most of these go on the end of the word, although some may appear in the middle. Appendix 2 on page 751 lists these endings and the types of words that they typically go on. In the main part of the dictionary *n.ending* (goes on nominals), *v.ending* (goes on verbs), *prn.ending* (goes on pronouns) and *k.ending* (goes on kin terms) are all distinguished. As discussed on page xvi, longer endings are generally hyphenated onto the end of a word, and shorter ones are not. Small endings appear in the body of the dictionary preceded by a '+' sign and longer ones by a '–' sign. However, there are a few 'endings' that have been written as separate words. One example of this is *arlka*[2] 'too, also, as well as'. At a later time Anmatyerr speakers may well decide to write some other endings as separate words (or conversely other 'separate words' as endings).

It is important to remember that the above categories of words are not hard and fast ones, and some Anmatyerr words really belong to several categories at once. For example, some words which have been classified in this dictionary as nominals may also be regarded as adverbs because they do not take the range of endings that most nominals do. These include temporal nominals — words such as *amwerrk* 'yesterday', *lyet* 'today' and *ngwenp/ngwenth* 'tomorrow — and some spatial words such as *akern* 'high, on top' and *kwen* 'inside, in, down, under'.

There are also some adverbs that behave a bit like particles because they can stand on their own without a verb. For example, the word *mwanty* goes with verbs to show that the action is done carefully or slowly, but it can also be used on its own as a command: *Mwanty!* 'Be careful!' The word *parrp* goes with verbs to show that the action happens quickly, but on its own (often with emphasis) it means 'hurry up!'. Some words that are called 'adverbs' in this dictionary are called 'pre-verbs' in other Aboriginal language dictionaries.

Verbs

Mastering the use of Anmatyerr verbs is one of the most important things to do when learning the language, as the verb carries much of the important meaning in a sentence — you can't say much without them. There are two types of Anmatyerr verbs: transitive and intransitive. Transitive verbs are those where an action is typically being done *by* someone *to* someone (or something) or the action directly affects something; for example, 'eating', 'hitting', 'cooking'. Intransitive verbs are generally ones where there is no recipient of the action, or the action of the verb does not directly affect something and is related only to the subject of the sentence. Examples are verbs like 'sitting', 'going', and 'lying'.

Some transitive verbs:

awantem	'feed someone'
atanthem	'write', 'spear something'
antywem	'drink'
awem	'listen', 'hear'

Some intransitive verbs:

alyelhem	'sing', 'sing yourself'
anarnpem	'get down from something'
itirrem	'think'
mwerr-irrem	'get better'

There are two important differences between sentences with a transitive verb in them and those with an intransitive verb. The first thing that happens in a sentence with a transitive verb is that the actor in the sentence, or the one that is performing the verb action, is marked by the ending *+el*[1] (unless the actor is represented by a pronoun). Secondly, the pronoun meaning 'I' is *tha* or *thang* in transitive sentences and in intransitive sentences it is *ayeng*. The pronoun meaning 'you' is *ntwa*, *ntwang* or *unta* in transitive sentences and *nga* in intransitive ones. These are exceptions, and for all other pronouns the form is the same regardless of whether the verb is transitive or not.

Verbs can also become very complicated, with many 'bits' or 'endings' added to the stem of the verb to extend its meaning. In this way many things can be shown about the action, such as when the action happened: whether it happened in the past; is about to happen or is happening now; whether more than one individual was involved in the action; and whether or not the action was completed. For example, here is the verb stem *arlkw* 'eat' with some of the more common endings:

Present	*arlkw**em***	'is eating'
Past	*arlkw**ek**/arlkw**eh***	'ate'
Habitual past	*arlkw**etyart***	'used to eat'
Future	*arlkw**etyenh***	'will eat'
Negative	*arlkw**etyakenh***	'not eating', 'did not eat' etc.
Imperative	*arlkw**a**/arlkw**ang***	'eat!'
Negative imperative	*arlkw**etyal***	'don't eat!'

If the event is happening now, is ongoing, or almost certainly will happen, the present tense (*+em*[1]) is used, and if it is over and done with the past tense (*+ek*[1]/*+eh*) is used. If it is a future event which will probably happen the future ending (*+etyenh*) is used, and so on. In this dictionary all verbs appear with the *+em*[1] (present tense) ending as the citation form.

Word order

Anmatyerr is one of those languages in which the order of words in a sentence is relatively free, unlike English. In English the sense of who is doing the action is shown by the order of the words, but because the order of words in Anmatyerr is relatively free there has to be some other way of showing who is doing what. Endings on the words, rather than the word order, tell you such things as who is the actor in a sentence, and who the action is being done to. Take the following examples:

*Artw**el***	*aherr*	*arem*
man-actor	kangaroo	look

'The man is looking at the kangaroo'

Aherr	*artw**el***	*arem*
kangaroo	man-actor	look

'The man is looking at the kangaroo'

Both of these sentences mean the same thing even though the word order is different, and it is the *+el* on the end of *artwa* that shows us that the man is doing the looking.

If, however, *aherr* (the kangaroo) is marked with *+el* , rather than *artwa* (the man), the meaning changes:

Artwa	*aherr**el***	*arem*
man	kangaroo-actor	look

'The kangaroo is looking at the man'

In this case the *+el* on the end of *aherr* shows us that the kangaroo is doing the looking.

Doubling words up

Apart from making words by adding endings to them, Anmatyerr also makes new words by doubling up existing ones. The doubled-up words do not usually mean the same thing as the original, although there are clear patterns of meaning change when this process happens. For example:

ampeny	'deserted', 'empty'
ampeny-ampeny	'scraps', 'leftovers'
kwern	'bad', 'no good'
kwern-kwern	'not very good', 'so-so'
aperl	'father's mother', 'a woman's son's child' etc.
aperl-aperl	'father's mother', 'a woman's son's child' etc. (Affectionate or respectful way of talking about one's *aperl*.)

There are also many occasions when the meaning of the doubled-up word does not bear an obvious resemblance to the original word, although in some cases it reflects cultural issues to do with kinship, Dreamings and the country where the Dreamings come from:

Mpetyan	'one of the skin names'
mpetyan-mpetyan^1	'yellow or white seeds from the bean tree'
mpetyan-mpetyan^2	'young bush turkey'

Anmatyerr words with more than one meaning

As in English, many words in Anmatyerr have more than one meaning. When this is the case, and the meanings are in some way related, they are numbered within the entry. For example: **rwa, rwang** 1. fire 2. firewood 3. matches 4. a general word that goes before things to do with fire 5. battery (of car).

Other words may sound the same yet have distinctly different meanings, and when this happens they are listed as separate entries with a superscript number. For example: **kwep-kwep**^{1} 1. caustic vine, milk bush, milk vine (*Sarcostemma viminale* ssp. *australe*) 2. caustic weed, mat spurge (*Euphorbia drummondii*); **kwep-kwep**^{2} desert spadefoot toad (*Notaden nicholl-si*); **kwep-kwep**^{3} stalked puffball (*Podaxis pistillaris*). Deciding whether or not meanings are related (and so should appear within a single entry in the dictionary) or whether they are different (and so should appear as separate entries) is not a straightforward matter. In the above example it may be argued that **kwep-kwep**^{2} really belongs with **kwep-kwep**^{1} as the two plants and the desert spadefoot toad all exude a milky substance. Their meanings could be linked in some way. To really clarify the number of meanings particular words have (from the Anmatyerr point of view) and how these relate to English meanings of similar words is very complex and requires a great deal of time.

There are many instances of words being used to build up new words. In some cases these related words appear in a single, long entry, and in others they are separate, even though they are related in some way. The decision to do this was based on an attempt to keep entries at minimal length to make them easier to read, and on the rules of alphabetical ordering.

A note about translations

As is common for most dictionaries of Aboriginal languages in Australia, the Anmatyerr dictionary is bilingual — it has definitions and/or glosses in English for Anmatyerr words, the example sentences are translated into English, and there is an English to Anmatyerr finder list in the back of the dictionary. But how do non-native speakers know that they are getting it right — that the Anmatyerr words are matched to the English accurately? This is of course one of the central tasks in making a dictionary, and requires many approaches. When working on the Anmatyerr dictionary we often worked in groups, checking words many times, and getting a range of opinions about the meanings and use of words. We tried to understand the meanings of words in context, both in texts and stories and in the context of their use in communities and in the bush. We went bush and looked for plants and animals in order to more precisely identify them and match the Anmatyerr taxonomy to the whitefella one. We caught ants and put them in little bottles to show the scientists so that we could get the scientific names for them. We talked about Anmatyerr in Anmatyerr and used the partial equivalences of the words in neighbouring languages as a way of trying to pin down the meanings of Anmatyerr words. We only used English as a tool for communication about the meaning of words if all else failed, as a last resort.

The majority of the translations of example sentences were done by myself, partly because in the bush we were concentrating on talking about Anmatyerr in Anmatyerr, and partly because many senior Anmatyerr people have little English at all. Younger Anmatyerr speakers with good English certainly helped out with the hard words and sentences, but even for them matching hard Anmatyerr words with English words is a very difficult task.

The punctuation of Anmatyerr written sentences, and the alignment of this with that in the corresponding English ones, raises some interesting issues. Every attempt has been made to keep the two close. However, in some cases particular grammatical features of Anmatyerr, and the way that the sentences were expressed in the original spoken language, make one-to-one correspondence hard to achieve.

It is now commonly accepted that the English words 'Dreaming' and 'Dreamtime' are capitalised, as are words such as 'God', 'Jesus' and the proper names of planets and stars. Where possible this convention is followed in the Anmatyerr example sentences in this dictionary. However, as some of the Anmatyerr words that these English translation equivalents are based on are complex, it is not always a straightforward matter to apply such a principle. For example, some meanings of the words *altyerr* and *anengkerr* express religious concepts (Dreaming, Dreamtime), whereas other phrases containing these words — such as *altyerr arem* and *anengkerr arem* 'to dream' — would not normally be capitalised. To simplify matters these headwords and their derivatives are not capitalised, but where their use in context clearly requires a capital letter in English the Anmatyerr follows suit. For example, *Anengkerreng-ntyel* is capitalised if the translation reads 'from the Dreaming'.

English words in Anmatyerr

As the example sentences are mostly from spoken language rather than written language they do include some English words and some English words that have been borrowed into Anmatyerr (people tend to be more 'careful' about what they are saying when they write things down and may use less English). Some Anmatyerr speakers prefer that English words which have good Anmatyerr equivalents do not appear in the example sentences in this dictionary; in these cases the original spoken sentences have been modified slightly and so are a bit different from the original spoken version. There remain, however, some English words in the example sentences, and when this happens they are styled differently to clearly distinguish them from Anmatyerr. One of the reasons for leaving some of these in is that there is not necessarily agreement about what is borrowed from English; over time some words have become thoroughly 'Anmatyerrised', even though the historical records will show us that a word originally came from English. They have taken on Anmatyerr sounds and, in some cases, the meaning has changed slightly from the original word that was borrowed. Over time this connection is forgotten. A good example is *lwethep* 'matches', which is from the English 'lucifer' (an old type of match). Another is the word *parrik*, which originally comes from English 'paddock', but in contemporary Anmatyerr means 'fence' as well. These words, that have been thoroughly borrowed and have taken on Anmatyerr sounds, have their own distinct entries in the dictionary and are not distinguished in example sentences by a different font style.

English verbs can also be made into 'Anmatyerr' ones by adding *+em-ilem* (to make transitive verbs) or *-irrem* (to make intransitive ones). This can often happen for verbs that do not have really good Anmatyerr equivalents, for example, the English verb *push* becomes *pwetyem-ilem*, and the verb *buy* (or *pay*) becomes *payem-ilem*.

Other Anmatyerr communication systems

This dictionary is obviously about words and spoken language, and as it is a 'paper dictionary' sound and moving images cannot be included (although at some time in the future we may well make a multimedia version). However, there are other Anmatyerr communication systems that are used as well as speech, or in some cases instead of speech. People use gesture and sign to accompany spoken language, and drawn symbols can accompany spoken language (as in, for example, traditional sand drawing). There are also special subsystems of spoken language that are used in particular contexts.

Hand signs

In Aboriginal Australia rich systems of hand signs have developed, particularly for use by bereaved kin during extended periods of mourning, but also in hunting, in certain types of restricted ceremonies, and in other situations where speaking is inappropriate. Many of these hand signs are clearly iconic, that is to say that their action (the shape of the hand or the way it moves) resembles in some way the concept or idea that is being communicated. For example, hand signs for various animals may be based on a symbolic representation of the shape of their tracks or their movement; those for particular plants based on the distinctiveness of their smell; or on a mimicking of the hand action involved in processing plant foods; and those for kin relations may be based on the way that particular relations are expected to behave towards each other, such as 'turning away' from restricted or 'avoidance' kin.

Respect language

The Anmatyerr kinship system (see Appendix 1, page 741) has rules and conventions about marriage and about behaviour towards particular kin. In Anmatyerr society, verbal communication (speech) and close contact is avoided between particular people. Traditionally, one of the strictest of these avoidance relationships is that between men and women who are in a mother-in-law/son-in-law relationship to each other. There is an auxiliary language, or a set of specialised vocabulary, that is used for talking about these relations. I use the term 'respect' for this language because this kind of language is used in other situations as well as those involving kin in avoidance relationships to each other. The respect language has a set of words that replace ordinary ones when a person is speaking in a way that shows respect. Many of these are included in the dictionary and they are marked thus: [RESPECT LANGUAGE]. The examples below show the difference between a sentence in ordinary language (the first sentence) and a sentence in respect language.

Ker tha anthem.	'I am giving the meat.'
Tyety-ayerr tha urrem-ilem.	'I am giving the meat [e.g. to my son-in-law].'

In the above example *tyety-ayerr* replaces *ker* 'meat' and *urrem-ilem* replaces *anthem* 'give'.

There are also some grammatical markers that go onto ordinary words to turn them into respect words. For example, the ending ***+erlentyarr*** goes in the middle of ordinary verbs to turn them into respect verbs. So the verb *apernem* 'rub on something' can be changed to *aper**nerlentyarr**em* 'rub on something [RESPECT]'. The ending ***-ayerr*** turns ordinary nominals into respect-language words. For example, in everyday language you say *ilep* for 'axe'. If a woman wants to talk about her son-in-law's axe she might say *ilep-**ayerr***, use the replacement respect words *alenyakenyak* or *nyerlp,* or alternatively use the phrase *iylpwer arternenh* — which literally means 'that which is used for chopping out hollow trees'. Particular oblique or roundabout ways of saying things also convey the message of respect.

Anmatyerr has a small set of kin terms that are used when a speaker wants to convey sympathy or respect. For example, the everyday word for 'mother' is *amey* and a sympathetic one is *artakw*; the ordinary word for 'father' is *angey* or *anywek* and the sympathy one is *arrawel.*

Another set of kin terms take several perspectives at once, and the speaker may use these terms either when they are in a respect relationship to the person being referred to or when the person they are talking to is in such a respect relationship. For example, when a woman is talking to her daughter's child about her (the child's) father she uses the term *urrer* rather than the ordinary word for father (as the person being referred to is the woman's son-in-law). A woman uses the term *ngwarr* to refer to her daughter's husband (again the woman's son-in-law) rather than the word *anew*.

***Ngwarr**engkw*	*ahanenhek*	*nthenhenty-angkwerr?*
husband-your	go-past	where-in which direction

'Which way did your husband go?' (said by a woman to her daughter)

Baby talk

Another way of talking is the way that adults talk to young children. In this way of speaking there are some special words, and some words that are almost like their ordinary counterparts except that some of the sounds have been changed slightly. For example, the word *katyerr* 'desert raisin' becomes *katy* in baby-talk style. Another way of making baby-talk words is by basing them on the sound that the thing being referred to makes. For example, *mpwempew* is the baby-talk word for 'car' (based on 'brm brm'). In the dictionary these words are marked thus: [BABY TALK].

The *kwementyay* rule

There are some words in this dictionary that are not used in some communities because a person with the same name or a similar-sounding name has passed away. In such cases the substitute word *kwementyay* is used instead. When we were working on the dictionary we took note of words affected by this tradition, but after discussion Anmatyerr people decided to include words that are *kwementyay* in the dictionary. Most people agreed that these words should still be in the Anmatyerr dictionary because they will not be *kwementyay* forever.

Anmatyerr place names

There are many, many more named places in the Anmatyerr region than those included in this dictionary. It has been beyond the scope of the project to locate all the places mentioned accurately, so in many cases the location given is approximate. Where Anmatyerr names refer to station bores, wells and rivers, it is often the case that the Anmatyerr name will actually refer to a soakage or another natural feature in the vicinity of the place with a whitefella name. Some whitefella names for mountains, creeks and bores and so on are based on the proper Anmatyerr name for a place in that area, and as such reflect the early contact history of the Anmatyerr region.

Many place names are based on, or named after, other words in the Anmatyerr language, often because the place is the location of significant events in the creation time, involving various named Dreamings or ancestors. These appear as sub-entries following the entry for the word on which the place name is based.

Using the dictionary

If you have trouble finding an Anmatyerr word you can look it up in the English to Anmatyerr finder list at the back of the dictionary. Remember, however, that this finder list is not meant to be a fully-fledged English to Anmatyerr dictionary. It does not have all English equivalents for Anmatyerr words and it should only be used as a guide to help you find the main entry for a word; here you will find fuller explanations of the meaning and use of the word, example sentences and such like.

If you have difficulty in finding a word that seems to begin with an *a* it is a good idea to look up the word under the first consonant that you hear. For example, the word *mern* 'food' can be pronounced as *amern* with the initial *a*, but appears in the dictionary as *mern*.

Many Anmatyerr words are long and made up of several parts. The verbs in particular can be very complex. Consider *nakelhety-alpem* 'go back and skite', which is really made up of the parts *nak+elh+ety+alp+em*. It is not possible to have separate entries for every possible verb form or every possible combination of words and endings. If you hear a word that is long and probably made up of several parts it may be helpful to start breaking off the endings from the right-hand end of the word with the assistance of the list of endings in Appendix 2.

The following groups of sounds may be easily confused, especially by English speakers, and so if you think you hear one of these sounds and cannot find the word in its appropriate place in the dictionary it is a good idea to look it up under one of the alternative sounds:

rt / t
rn / n / nh
rl / l / lh
rr / r
nk / rnk / ngk
np / rnp / mp

Layout of a dictionary entry (see diagram page xxv)

1. Main Anmatyerr word, or 'headword'. The main words are listed in English alphabetical order, and appear set out to the left of the rest of the entry. Verbs all appear in the present tense, that is, with the *+em*[1] ending. Headwords preceded by a hyphen (-) are endings which are hyphenated in the text unless they are preceded by a short word, in which case there is no hyphen used. Headwords preceded by a plus sign (+) are endings that are not hyphenated in the text. Where there are several alternative pronunciations (and thus spellings) of a word these follow the headword in bold typeface. The alternatives also appear independently in the alphabetical listing, with a short gloss and 'SEE UNDER . . . ' indicating that the reader should refer to the main entry for definitions and examples etc.
2. Words or expressions built from the main word appear in bold but slightly smaller typeface than the headword. They are indented.
3. Parts of speech, for example, *'n.'*, *'vt.'* or *'vi.'* (See list of abbreviations page xxvi. These appear in italics.)
4. The raised number or superscript distinguishes words that sound and are written the same but have distinctly different meanings.
5. A code in brackets following the headword shows the region where the Anmatyerr word is used. Words that have no dialect code after them are used throughout the Anmatyerr area. (W) means those communities west of the Stuart Highway, including Mt Allan, Laramba (Napperby) and Desert Bore; (T) means Ti Tree; (E) means the Eastern Anmatyerr communities of Stirling, and the Sandover outstations (see list of abbreviations, page xxvi).
6. Bracketed information [RESPECT LANGUAGE], [BABY TALK] shows that the word belongs to the respect register or the baby-talk register.
7. Bracketed information [SENSITIVE LANGUAGE] following a headword shows that the word is regarded by some as being potentially offensive in some contexts. (Really offensive words were left out of the dictionary if Anmatyerr speakers requested it, and every attempt was made to check that the words that appear in this dictionary should appear in a public document).
8. If a word has the note [SOME SPEAKERS] after it then it means that there is not agreement between everybody as to whether or not the word is used or how it is used; however, it is included in the dictionary because some Anmatyerr people use that word.
9. Definition and glosses, or lists of words that may be used for translating the Anmatyerr word into English. Short descriptions of plants, grammatical notes, and some other types of cultural or further information are also included in this field.
10. Different senses of headword. If there is more than one meaning of the headword, this is indicated by a number before each definition within an entry.
11. Scientific names appear in italics and are used for plants and animals in order to identify the particular genus or species.
12. If a word or phrase is made up of a few different words then these constituent parts appear in brackets with their gloss. For example, the phrase *artep nyerr* 'shamefully' is made up of *artep* 'back' and *nyerr* 'shame'.
13. If a word is borrowed from another language (e.g. English) the original form and its origin is shown in brackets.
14. Where the meaning of a group of words or a phrase is not immediately clear from the

meanings of the individual words that make it up, then the literal meaning is given in brackets. For example, *arlta pwerrk*, meaning 'Sunday' is made up of the words which literally mean 'tired day' or 'day of rest'.)

15. Example sentences appear in plain font and after the symbol '◆'. The community where the example sentence came from is usually marked by a bracketed code (see list of abbreviations on page xxv). English words in the Anmatyerr sentences are in italics.

16. Translations of example sentences appear in italics. Anmatyerr words in the translations are in plain font.

17. Synonyms are words which we think have the same meaning or meanings as each other. These are preceded by an '=' sign. Some words that are cross-referenced using a slightly heavier '=' sign are not synonyms but alternative spellings for words that differ substantially in sound across the Anmatyerr region and hence have their own entry and example sentences. For example, Eastern Anmatyerr words that have the rounding at the beginning of the word and are thus spelt with an initial *u* are cross-referenced to their Central Anmatyerr counterparts using this heavier '**=**' sign.
Note: If the cross-reference is only to the sense of a word immediately above it then it is preceded by a '•' symbol and it does not start on a new line.

18. Cross references to words with related meaning. These are preceded by the words 'SEE ALSO . . . '.
Note: If the cross-reference is only to the sense of a word immediately above it then it is preceded by a '•' symbol and it does not start on a new line.

19. Cross references to other words which sound similar to the headword, and so might be confused. These appear in the following form: 'CAN SOUND A BIT LIKE . . . '
Note: If the cross-reference is only to the sense of a word immediately above it then it is preceded by a '•' symbol and it does not start on a new line.

20. For many entries about flora and fauna the broad Anmatyerr categories that they fall into are indicated. For example, *aherr* 'kangaroo' is also referred to as *ker aherr* (*ker* 'meat'), and *mamp* 'honey made by a lerp insect living under the bark of the river red gum' as *ngkwarl mamp*. These broad categories are often, but not always, indicated in the dictionary entry.

21. Punctuation in definitions is a difficult matter and it is hard to be consistent. In general, lists of single-word glosses that are more or less equivalent are separated by commas. Semicolons are used to separate definitions that have several distinct parts that seem to have slightly different meanings, and to separate off more general definitions from glosses. Otherwise the comma is used for punctuation in the definitions.

See 'Layout of a dictionary entry' on page xxiii for more detailed information.

aharlparrengk[1] (E), **aharlparingk** (E) *n.*
big male red kangaroo ◆ Aharlparingk wenh atwek. (St) *[They] killed a big male red kangaroo.*
SEE ALSO ampelaherr, yawerrang, artar

aharlparrengk[2] (E) *n.*
whirlwind, willy-willy

akapweley (T,E), **akepweley** (E) *n.*
bald (lit. 'baldy head') (from English 'baldy')

angwerl *n.*
cool
angwerleny *n.* = **angwerl** ◆ Lywel angwerl-irrerl-alhem, kel angwerlenyem alhem. (TT) *Cool down in the shade, and then go on when [you're] feeling cool.*

ayenp *n.*
1. bark; skin of fruits
= arntap
SEE ALSO rltimp[1]
2. skin (of a person or animal)
◆ Ayenparl akernengan. Ayenp nhenh apetyem amwelteng arlka. Kenh alhwarl kweneng *run*-irrerl-anem, ingkewarn-athek, iltyewarn-athek, alakenh kapert-warn-athek. (TT) *Skin is on the surface. For example, there is skin all the way along the arm. Whereas blood runs on the inside, towards the feet, the hands and to the head.*
arna ayenp
bark (of a plant) (arna *'plant', 'tree'*)

ayep *n.*
tar vine (*Boerhavia schomburgkiana*). A creeping herb with stems trailing up to 1 m along the ground. ◆ Ayep, alewatyerrel arlkwerl-apem, anter angerr mparelhetyek. *Goannas eat tar vine to make themselves fat.*
= irlperleny
CAN SOUND A BIT LIKE yep *'umbilical cord'*

ayepel-irrem *vi.* [RESPECT LANGUAGE]
1. sit ◆ Ngwarrengkw nhakw ayepel-irretyel. (Sa) *Your husband is sitting over there [said by a woman to her daughter].*
2. sit down, be seated
3. be, am, is, are, were, be (in a particular way)
4. live, stay (in a place)

1. headword
2. words or expressions based on headword
3. part of speech
4. raised number indicates two or more words with the exact same sound, but different meanings
5. dialect code
6/7/8. type of language
9/10. definition/s
11. scientific name
12. breakdown of word or phrase
13. borrowed word
14. literal translation
15/16. example sentence and translation
17. synonym
18. words with related meaning
19. words with similar sound

Abbreviations

(?) There is a degree of uncertainty about a word, a definition or a translation etc. If a (?) follows a translation then it indicates uncertainty about its accuracy. If it follows a definition, such as '*alemerr* water-holding frog (*Cyclorana platycephalus*) (?)', this shows uncertainty about the English (and scientific) identity of the *alemerr* frog. In the finder list a (?) following an Anmatyerr word shows that we are not certain that it is equivalent to the English word or words it is paired with.

(SP) Only used by some speakers.

Dialects

(E) The Eastern Anmatyerr communities: Stirling, and the Sandover outstations

(T) Ti Tree

(W) Those Anmatyerr communities west of the Stuart Highway, including Mt Allan, Napperby (Laramba) and Pulardi (Desert Bore)

Communities

(M) Mt Allan

(N) Napperby (Laramba)

(P) Pulardi (Desert Bore)

(Sa) Sandover region communities

(St) Stirling

(T) Ti Tree

Parts of speech and other

adv. adverb

excl. exclusive marker on pronouns (see Appendix 1)

incl. inclusive marker on pronouns (see Appendix 1)

k.ending kin-term ending

n. nominal

n.ending nominal ending

n.kin kin nominal

part. particle

pers. person marker on pronouns

pl. plural

prn. pronoun

prn.ending pronoun ending

sp. species

spp. species (plural)

ssp. subspecies

v.ending verb ending (includes verbal infixes)

vi. intransitive verb

vt. transitive verb

Jenny Green
April 2006

Further reading

Breen, JG 1988, 'Western Anmatyerr draft thesaurus word list', Institute for Aboriginal Development, Alice Springs.

Breen, JG 1996, *Anmatyerr wordlist for Aniltji*, Institute for Aboriginal Development, Alice Springs.

Cook, J & Green, J 2007, *Anengkerr angkety: Dreaming stories*, Batchelor Press, Batchelor Institute of Indigenous Tertiary Education, Batchelor.

Green, J (comp.) 1992, *Alyawarr to English dictionary*, IAD Press, Alice Springs.

Green, J 1994, *A learner's guide to Eastern and Central Arrernte*, IAD Press, Alice Springs.

Green, J 1998, 'Kin and country: aspects of the use of kinterms in Arandic languages', unpublished MA thesis, University of Melbourne.

Green, J 2000, *Alherramp-areny Angkety Arelh-kenh: women's stories from Laramba*, IAD Press, Alice Springs.

Green, J 2003, *Anmatyerr Ayey arnang-akert: Anmatyerr plant stories*, IAD Press, Alice Springs.

Green, J 2003, *Central Anmatyerr picture dictionary*, IAD Press, Alice Springs.

Green, J & Turpin, M 2001, 'Common sense: continuing in the comparative tradition', in J Simpson, M Laughren, D Nash, B Alpher & P Austin (eds), *Forty years on: Ken Hale and Australian languages*, Pacific linguistics, Australian National University, pp. 89–111.

Hale, K nd, 'Arandic word list', unpublished typescript, 25 pp, AIATSIS Ms738.

Henderson, J & Dobson V (comps.) 1994, *Eastern and Central Arrernte to English dictionary*, IAD Press, Alice Springs.

Kendon, A 1988, *Sign languages of Aboriginal Australia: cultural, semiotic and communicative perspectives*, Cambridge University Press.

Latz, P 1995, *Bushfires and bushtucker: Aboriginal plant use in Central Australia*, IAD Press, Alice Springs.

Purle, C, Green, J & Heffernan, M 1981, *Anmatyerre word list*, Institute for Aboriginal Development, Alice Springs.

Tindale, NB 1974, *Aboriginal tribes of Australia: their terrain, environmental controls, distribution, limits, and proper names*, University of California Press.

Wilkins, DP 1989, 'Mparntwe Arrernte (Aranda): studies in the structure and semantics of grammar', PhD thesis, Australian National University, Canberra.

Woods, G 2006, 'The anarchic adverb: investigating the adverb class in Anmatyerr', upublished honours thesis, University of Melbourne.

Central and Eastern Anmatyerr *to* English
Dictionary

Aa

+a *v.ending*
an order or command (goes on the end of verbs to show that a person or thing is being told to do the action) ◆ Arrpwarnt-arey alherl-wa! Ayeng angkep intetyeh kwenh! (T) *You noisy mob leave! I want to go back to sleep!* ◆ Ampa akelyek ilem, 'Ahentey-ahentey-warl alha!' (St) *You tell a child, 'Go to your father-in-law!'* ◆ Pwertay iyntwarr-iyntwarr ana! (Sa) *Look out! Shift a bit further away!*
SEE ALSO +aw, +ang, +ay, +erl-anerr^2, +errirr

aha, ahang (W,T) *n.*
1. anger, angry, aggression, aggressive ◆ Akaty-akaty anep-anem ayeng. Ahekety apek, angkemarl-kety apek, akaty-akaty anep-anem. (St) *I'm not frightened. I'm not frightened of [people's] anger, or what they might say.* ◆ Arengk yanh ahakertel arrpwernepwernem. *That dog is aggressive and it's growling.*
2. trouble, a fight

ahel *adv.*
angrily, in anger, aggressively ◆ Warrernem arrkenel. Ahel apek unta apek angkep-angkem, wal ayeng angkep-angkem *same* way akin — warrernepernem tha ngenh. (St) *Imitating for fun. You might talk in an angry way, and then I talk the same way again — I copy you.*

ahel-ahel *adv.*
a bit aggressively, a bit angrily

ahangerr, ahakngerr (E) *n.*
dangerous, savage, bad-tempered, aggressive, violent, cruel, 'cheeky' (liable to cause harm) (angerr^1 *'big', 'large', 'lots of'*) ◆ Ahangerr yanhanaw! (St) *That one is really aggressive!* ◆ Arengk yanh ahangerr. Tyerrty yanh ahangerr. (T) *That dog is aggressive. That person is dangerous.*

ahelengkw (E) *n.*
1. dangerous, savage, bad-tempered, aggressive, cruel, 'cheeky' (liable to cause harm) ◆ Arlety akwek urrperl, wal ra ahelengkwarl, tyerrty utnhemel wangkem anem ra. (St) *The* arlety *ant is small and dark in colour. It is aggressive, and if it bites a person then they will swell up.* ◆ Arriperan ahelengkw artelhampwarl. Irrewalyekan akenh-akenh arriperan ahelengkwarl. (Sa) *Western brown snakes are really dangerous and big. They are deadly and their bite can be fatal.* ◆ Intwerrker weth mantarr-warlarl aylperreman. Arraper ahelengkw akin, *same one* akin, arraper ahelengkw arrpemarl. (Sa) *That curly wire grass gets stuck in clothes. The* arraper *grass is another 'cheeky' one, the same as the curly wire grass.*
2. strong or biting in taste, something with a bite or a kick to it

ahelengkw-ahelengkw (E) *n.*
a bit aggressive, a bit dangerous ◆ Ahelengkw-ahelengkw arengk yanhan. *That dog is a bit aggressive.*

ahekweny, ahekwenh (W,T), **ahel-kweny** (W,T), **ahang-kweny** (W,T) *n.*
quiet, non-aggressive, calm (-kweny *'without'*) ◆ Ahekweny mwerrarl yanhan, ahelengkw anetyakenh. (St) *That one is not aggressive, not dangerous.* ◆ Ahekweny aneyaw, ahel angketyal aneyaw! (St) *Sit down and stop being angry, don't talk angrily!* ◆ Ahang-kweny aneyaw! (T) *Sit down and don't be angry!*

ahel-irrem *vi.*
get angry, growl, talk angrily, tell someone off, speak roughly or rudely (-irrem *'become something'*) ◆ Tyerrtyek arrpenhek ahel-irrem, iltem renh ahel-irremel. (St) *Getting angry with another person and swearing at them.* ◆ Tyerrty yanh ahel-irrem kereng. (T) *That person is getting angry over meat.* ◆ Tyerrtyek ahel-irrem angwely arrpenh. Angwely atherr nhwerrem ahel-irrem anem angwely arrpeh. (T) *Another dog growls at a person. Two dogs are fighting*

each other and one growls at the other.
SEE ALSO arlelty-irrem, rrwampem, urrampem, yerrng-irrem, ngkwanty-irrem
ahel nhwerrem (W,T), **ahel utnherrem** (E)
fight, argue (nhwerrem *'fight'*, *'argue'*)
ahel-ahel akerrem (E)
fight with each other, argue with each other

ahakey *n.*
1. bush plum, native currant, native citrus (*Psydrax latifolia*). A shrub up to 3 m high, with broad, deep green leaves, small white flowers and fruit which ripens to a black colour.
2. the fruit of the bush plum, native currant, native citrus ◆ Ahakey ilkwang-amparr anem. Ahakey irntang anem anem. (T) *The native currant has flowers first of all. Then it has fruit.* ◆ Ahakey rwerrkem, ahelh-warnan lernelhem ahakey *seed* map. Renh anem kwetyerl-anem. (T) *[You] shake the native currant tree so that the fruits fall to the ground. Then you go along and collect them.* ◆ Mern ahakey inerl-alpek arntap-warn. *Not billycan*-warn anwa inetyart — arntap-warn. Anetyart anwern arntap-warn inetyart inetyart pwel-irretyart. Arrpenh-warn alhemel aweth arntap arrpenh inemel angerretyem inem aweth, pwel-iletyart anwern pwel-iletyart anwern pwel-iletyart. (N) *We collected the native currant fruits in bark containers. Not in billycans — in bark containers. We used to fill the bark containers and then go on to another tree and then fill another container. We used to fill them up.*
= arrarntenh, artapaly, antyern-angerr
SEE ALSO yernt

Ahalper (E), **Aharlper** (T,E) *n.*
the name of a place and of a country/estate in the New Store area (Angarapa Aboriginal Land Trust). The community store itself, Arlparra, is named after this country. See map p. viii.

ahalyepweng (E) *n.*
a type of small lizard with pretty markings

ahamwerrk (E) *n.* [RESPECT LANGUAGE]
yesterday ◆ Ahamwerrkel ahanenhek. (St) *[They] went yesterday [said by someone in a respect relationship to one of those who went].*
= ilamwerrk
SEE ALSO amwerrk

ahanem *vi.* [RESPECT LANGUAGE]
go. A special word for 'go' used by a mother-in-law about her son-in-law, or by a man about his mother-in-law. ◆ Ahanang anewengk-warn. (M) *Go to your husband [said by a mother to her daughter].*
SEE ALSO alhem
ahanenhem, ahaneynem (E) *vi.* [RESPECT LANGUAGE]
go back ◆ Kwey ahanenha, ngwarrengkw ahanety-alperl-wek. (St) *Go back daughter, your husband has come back.*
SEE ALSO alpem
ahanety-alpem, ahanenty-alpem (E) *vi.* [RESPECT LANGUAGE]
come back ◆ Yanh ahanety-alpem lyweny-penh. (T) *That one is coming back after hunting [said by someone in a respect relationship to the one who is coming back].* ◆ Yanhenty anem kel ahanerlentyarrety-alperl-wek, yanhenty-anyeman. Wethenty-antey ahanety-alpek. (Sa) *That one has come back. That one has already come back [said by someone in a respect relationship to the one who has come back].*
SEE ALSO apety-alpem
ahanelh-ilem *vt.* [RESPECT LANGUAGE]
take something somewhere ◆ Ahanelh-ilenherr-areyay tyety-ayerr yanhentyakay. Weyapelek-uthek tyety-ayerr ahanelh-iley. 'Weyapel' ap ilem 'angayakw'. (Sa) *All of you take the meat to that one over there. Take it to the one over there [e.g. my son-in-law] who is hungry. 'Weyapel' is what is said [in respect language] for 'angayakw' [hungry].*
ahanety-alhem, ahanenty-alhem (W) *vi.* [RESPECT LANGUAGE]
come
SEE ALSO arlwety-irrem, apetyem, apety-alhem
ahanintyem (E) *vi.* [RESPECT LANGUAGE]
come towards

ahang (W,T) anger, aggressive SEE UNDER **aha**

ahangey (T,E) father's father and his brothers and sisters SEE UNDER **angang**

ahanterr (E) father-in-law SEE UNDER **ahenterr**

ahanthem (E) *vt.*
eat or drink greedily or quickly, eat everything up ◆ Ahantherrek mern atyenh, ingkerrek-antey. Tey atyenh impen ingkerrek ahantherrek. Ahantherrek ingkerrek innga. Ker atyenh uyerrek, angayakwarl apetyarr-alherrek. (Sa) *All of my food has been eaten, the whole lot. The only tea I have has been used up. Absolutely everything has gone. All of my meat has run out, eaten up by the hungry people who came.*
SEE ALSO nyant arlkwem, arnterr arlkwem, ankeyel arlkwem, nwanthem, arrwer-ilem, arlkwem

ahap-irrem (E) *vi.*
die, pass away
SEE ALSO ilwem, arrangkw-irrem, uyerrem, ywerrem, alyent-artek-irrem

aharl *n.*
heap, pile
SEE ALSO antyakwer, thalh
aharl-wem, **aharl-iwem** (E) *vt.*
heap something up, put things in a pile ◆ Rwang map arrernem aharl-iwem, keram ampem. (N) *The firewood is heaped up and then the meat is cooked.* ◆ Arnang arrwelty aharl-way, rwang itetyek. (T) *Heap up the firewood so that we can light the fire.*
= aharl arrernem
SEE ALSO lyernt arrernem, mpwer tywenem, ayak-arrernem, antyakwer-wem, antarr-arrernem
aharl arrernem (E) = **aharl-wem** (arrernem *'put'*) ◆ Aharl arrernetyeh mern renh. (N) *Heap the food up into a pile.*

aharlkwerr, **ahelkwerr** (E) *n.*
underground cave ◆ Altyerr tha arek aharlkwerr-areny. *In a dream I saw the inhabitants of the underground caves.* ◆ Atham-areny ahelkwerr-areny. (Sa) Atham-areny *spirits live in underground caves.*
= yalkwerr

aharlparrengk[1] (E), **aharlparingk** (E) *n.*
big male red kangaroo ◆ Aharlparingk wenh atwek. (St) *[They] killed a big male red kangaroo.*
SEE ALSO ampelaherr, yawerrang, artar

aharlparrengk[2] (E) *n.*
whirlwind, willy-willy ◆ Aharlparrengk-kety apetyay, urntety kwenh. (Sa) *Run here quickly, away from the whirlwind.*
= awerantyerrng, rrwep-rrwep

Aharlper (T,F) the name of a place and of a country/estate in the New Store area (Angarapa Aboriginal Land Trust) SEE UNDER **Ahalper**

aharlperr angkem (T,E), **arlperr angkem** *vi.*
speak loudly, talk loudly in public (angkem *'talk', 'speak'*) ◆ Ayeng aharlperr akin angkem arelh ampwekan. Anerl-anetyek ayeng aharlperr angkerl-anem awetyek-areny ra. (St) *I talk loudly to the old woman. I keep on talking loudly to her so that she can hear.* ◆ Aharlperr angkem mer ingwer-theyarl apetyemel, arrpenhek-arey. (St) *You talk loudly to people that are coming from another place, to other people.* ◆ Terangk yanh aharlperr angkem ahel. 'Rntert aneyaw, aharlperrarl angkem-kety.' (T) *Those drunks are talking loudly and angrily. 'Sit down quietly, because people are talking loudly.'*
SEE ALSO arlperrepwenty

aharraty (T) dry, waterless country SEE UNDER **aherraty**

aharretyepwer (E) fruit of bush bean, *angerak* SEE UNDER **aherretyepwer**

ahat hot SEE UNDER **ata**[2]

ahatyerr (W,T) *n.*
a crack in the ground caused by a tuber or root underneath
= urrper, karnt[1]
ahatyerr-wem (W,T) *vt.*
(tubers or roots) cause the ground crack and lift up
= urrper-wem, karnt-wem
SEE ALSO antwerlperlp-wem

ahaylem (E) *vt.*
do something first (before others do it) ◆ Kwaty ahaylemaw, atyeng ahaylerl-aynaw kwatyaw. (Sa) *Drink some water, before I do.* (?)
SEE ALSO arnang-ilem[1]

ahayleng (E) a place which is avoided SEE UNDER **ahileng**

ahaylengkeyler (E), **aheylangkeyler** (E) *n.*
a type of blind snake (*Ramphotyphlops endoterus*) ◆ Rtetyant ra arlkwem ahaylengkeyler, akwek, rtety ra arlkwem altywer-ilemel. Pwengarl ra aretyangarl akeng. Irrpenhemap ra ahernek anem. (St) *The* ahaylengkeyler *bites into your teeth and makes holes in them. They are blind and can't see. They burrow into the ground.*
= rtety arlkwenh-arlkwenh, arranyenganyeng

ahaytn (E) non-Christian SEE UNDER **aheyen**

ahekwenayt (E), **ahekwen** (E), **weken** (E) *n.*
edible grub found in the ground at the base of the river red gum, *aper*. This is possibly the larvae of the cicada beetle (*Tropha* sp. (?)). ◆ Ahekwenaytan ahern-areny, aper intert-utek — *not* artekerrel — arwa ahernel aylpem. Artekerr-angkwerr anperel ayntenhem, alhwengan ikwerenh. (Sa) *The* ahekwenayt *grub lives in the ground at the base of the river red gum tree — not in the roots — they just live underneath the ground. Their holes are found around beside the roots of the tree.*
SEE ALSO mpaty[2], ingweneng

ahelh *n.*
1. earth, ground, dirt ◆ Marl nhenhel ahelh panthel inyem. (N) *This woman is digging the ground with a wooden scoop.* ◆ Amelel ra intep-intemarl aherr, angernem ra wal ra

interl-anem ahelh kwerel irrerntel anem, amel angernem. *A kangaroo lies in the cool earth, digs out a hole and then lies there in the cool earth.* ◆ Atek arnamel anenty-angerr. Atek arrtyanem arnam arrpenh-warn, ahelh-angkwarr. (N) *The button quail is a grass dweller. The quail runs across the ground from one clump of grass to another.*
2. country, region, land ◆ Alker arrpenh-arenyarl yanhanaw, ahelh arrpenhengarl apetyek. Alker arrpenh-they. (St) *That person is from another place, they've come from another country. From another 'sky'.*
3. the Earth
= ahern
SEE ALSO mer
ahelh-ahelh *n.*
1. brownish in colour, the colour of the earth
2. woma, sandhill python (*Aspidites ramsayi*)
• = ahenenh, nwey, uney

ahelkwerr (E) underground cave SEE UNDER **aharlkwerr**

ahen (W,T) non-Christian SEE UNDER **aheyen**

ahen-ilem (W) *vt.*
become responsible for a person through a ceremonial relationship, become boss for someone ◆ Thang ahen-ilek artwang akwerrk yanh. Thang renh arntarntarem — ra arntarnt antem arem ayengenh. (M) *I became boss for that young fella. I look after him — and he looks after me as well.*
SEE ALSO alkwertek-ilem, mayeth, pwath

ahenenh, aheneny (T,E) *n.*
woma, sandhill python (*Aspidites ramsayi*) ◆ Amwang ahenenh apwertel anem. (T) *The woma snake lives amongst the rocks.* ◆ Ker ahenenh angkwey ina arlkwetyart. (T) *They used to eat the woma snake in the olden days.*
= nwey, uney, ahelh-ahelh
SEE ALSO arrwerrperl, ankwepenh

ahengey (E) father's father and his brothers and sisters SEE UNDER **angang**

ahenp, ahinp *n.*
long ago, a long time ago
SEE ALSO arrul, angkwey, arrwekel
ahenpeny, ahinpeny *n.*
a long time ago, from a long time ago, old ◆ Ker yanh impa ahinpeny anert akeng-irrekerr. (T) *Leave that old meat in case [you] get an upset stomach.* ◆ Angka lyeteny anetyakenh — ahinpenyant nhenh. (St) *This language is not from nowadays — it's olden-time language.* ◆ Mer ahinpeny — antyerrk-antyerrk weth-lkwer anemel artelhemel, antyerrk irreman waly — ahinpenyarl. (St) *Old camps — those ones where the branches are going dry — they are from a long time ago.*
= arruleny, angkweyeny, arrwekeleny

ahenterr (E), **ahenterrey** (E), **ahanterr** (E) *n.kin*
1. mother's mother's mother; great-grandmother ◆ Ahanterr nhakw anyent — *Mum*-kenh anyanyikw-ant. *Mum*-kenh anyanyant ahanterr. (Sa) *I have only one* ahanterr *over there — my mother's granny. My mother's granny is called* ahanterr.
2. father-in-law (?)
3. man's son-in-law and daughter-in-law (?)
SEE ALSO ampaty-ampaty, ampwek, arnemerr, maly, maly-maly, rtwalty
ahenterr-ahenterr (E) *n.kin*
mother's mother's mother, great-grandmother etc. ◆ 'Ahenterr-ahenterr arerl-wa angayakw anerl-anem.' Nyanyelikw ilanthem. (Sa) *'Go and see your great-grandmother who is sitting there hungry.' Her granny might send her [to her mother].*
ahenterraty (E) *n.kin*
my/our *ahenterr*
ahenterrengkw (E) *n.kin*
your *ahenterr*
ahenterrikw (E) *n.kin*
his/her/their *ahenterr*
ahenterr-nheng atherr (E) *n.kin*
a person together with his/her *ahenterr* ◆ Ahenterr-nheng atherr apety-alpem. *The person and their great-grandmother are coming back.* ◆ Ahenterr-nheng-rnem alherl-iwem mernek apek, irrer. (Sa) *The grannies and their great-grandchildren are going hunting.* (?)
ahenterr-nheng (E) *n.kin*
a group of two or more people related to each other as *ahenterr*
= ahenterr-intyerr
ahenterr-intyerr (E) *n.kin* = **ahenterr-nheng**
ahenterr-nheng-arey (E)
a group of more than two people related to each other as *ahenterr*
ahenterr-ankethenh (E) *n.kin*
1. having a close *ahenterr* still alive
2. someone who is always with their *ahenterr*
SEE ALSO -ankethenh

ahentey-ahentey (E) *n.* [BABY TALK]
great-grandmother ◆ Ampa akelyek ilem, 'Ahentey-ahentey-warl alha!' (St) *You tell a child, 'Go to your great-granny!'*
SEE ALSO ahenterr

ahenty[1], **antya** (W) *n.*
1. throat ◆ Ahenty akeng-irrek, iterlaretyakenh apek ayeng, ahentyarl akeng-irrekarl, nhenh akwerrng ingkerr. (St) *My*

throat is no good, and I'm not sure about things, my throat is feeling no good and my brains, everything. ◆ Anyem antywem ahenty tywen-akertel. (St) *You can drink the witchetty bush leaf mixture if you have a sore throat.*
2. voice ◆ Ahenty irrkay angketyakenh, inkwerr-penh. (Sa) *[Your] voice fades and you can't talk, from having a cold.*
3. opening leading down to a honeyants' nest
CAN SOUND A BIT LIKE antya1 *'worm found in kangaroo's stomach'*; antya2 *'snake venom'*
ahenty mwelper *n.*
windpipe (mpwelper *'windpipe'*)
ahenty ahenpem (W)
choke or strangle somebody or something; wring somebody's or something's neck (ahenpem (?))
= ahenty twerl-akem, ahenty ltwakem
ahenty twerl-akem (W) = **ahenty ahenpem** (twerl-akem *'choke someone or something'*)
ahenty ltwakem (W,T), **ahenty ultakem** (E) = **ahenty ahenpem** (ultakem *'break'*) ◆ Arelhel ahenty ltwakem ker rapet. (T) *The woman is wringing the rabbit's neck.* ◆ Kwer atherr arrkenel ltwakerrem ahenty. (M) *The two kids are pretending to strangle each other.*
SEE ALSO alyernem, awerrkem, itutnhem
ahenty kwen
soft voice, low voice (kwen *'low', 'inside'*)
= ahenty akwek
ahenty akwek = **ahenty kwen** (akwek *'small'*)
ahenty angerr
loud voice (angerr1 *'big'*)
ahenty amern-amern (E)
Adam's apple; the lump on the front part of the throat of some men (amern-amern *'lump' or 'gall'*) ◆ Mwelper nhenh-lkwer, 'ahenty amern-amern', *lump*-arl wangkem. *Round about where the windpipe is there is a lump called* 'ahenty amern-amern'.
ahenty arrkay-irrem
fade (voice) (arrkay-irrem *'fade', 'become faint'*)
ahentyel-intenh (W,T) *n.*
neckband made of hairstring (lit. 'that which is lying around the neck') ◆ Ahentyel-intenh arrernem kwer-warl. (M) *The neckband is put on the boy.*
= ahenty-henh
SEE ALSO itepenh
ahenty-henh (W,T), **ahenty-kenh** (E) *n.* = **ahentyel-intenh** (-henh, -kenh *'belonging to'*)

ahenty2, antya (W) *adv.*
1. liking or wanting something, liking to do something
2. desiring, fancying or wanting someone
ahenty-kwenh (W,T) *adv.*
disliking somebody or something, not wanting to do something ◆ Parrkemarl artenyemarl anerl-anem merel kwenh! Nthwety ahenty-kwenh, ingkarl arekar-irrem-akert, nthwenty-penh nthwenty-penh. (N) *[I] am tired and I'm going to stay home! I don't want to go walking around because my feet are hurting from walking everywhere.*
ahenty-penh (W,T) *n.*
the one you like or fancy; lover, boyfriend, girlfriend ◆ Anngwenhem marl yanhel rrwey yanhew, artwang kwerenhan anngwenhem, ahenty-penh kwerenh. (T) *That girl is getting jealous over that boy, over her boyfriend.* ◆ Ahenty-penhel arrilem kwer ahenty-anetyek. *The one who desires her sings her to make her like him.*
SEE ALSO anew, anew-anew, mert, mert-mert
ahenty-irrem, antyirrem (W) *vi.*
1. want to do something ◆ Ahenty-irrem alhety mpa, anwengkerr alhety kwenh lyweny, lyweny alhetyew. Kerwep inay. (N) *I want to go, let's go, all go hunting. Get the crowbar.*
2. like or want someone or something, fall in love with or desire (someone) ◆ Arelh yanh ahenty-irrem rrwey yanhek. (T) *That woman likes that bloke.* ◆ Arelh Ngwarray ahenty-irrem artwang Ngal anew aketyek. (T) *Ngwarray women like to marry Ngal men.*
= ahenty-anem
SEE ALSO alherrem2, iyteny-irrem
ahenty-anem, antyanem (W) *vi.* = **ahenty-irrem** ◆ Ankwa intetyek ayeng ahenty-anem, pwerrkarl awelhem. (St) *I want to go to sleep, because I'm feeling tired.* ◆ Ayeng ahenty-anem marl yanh kwer. (T) *I like that girl over there.* ◆ Ker atyeng anthay — ayeng ahenty-anem! *Give me some meat — I want some!* ◆ Ahenty-anemam artwang yanhan atyeng. (T) *That man over there likes me.*
ahentyel-arem (T,E) *vt.*
be unable to do something ◆ Ahentyel-arem tha mern — angwenhel atyeng *help*-em-ilem? 'Kel menty anem aney kwenh.' (St) *I am unable [to carry] the food — who is going to help me? 'Oh just leave it.'* ◆ Arwengalker tha ahentyel-arem akern akngerr. Menty anem arerl-alhem. (St) *The sugarbag is too high up and I can't get it. I'll just leave it and go.*
ahentyel-akem (T,E) *vt.*
feel disappointed or let down (by someone) ◆ *Family* atyenh tha ahentyel-akem, ayenh arntety-akert akngetyakenh. (St) *I am disappointed in my family because they didn't*

take me when I was sick. (?) ◆ Yay kwerenhel ahentyel-akem, kwer-warn lhetyakenh. (T) *Her older sister is disappointed that [they] didn't go to her.* ◆ Ahentyel-akem tha ngenh, unta atyeng apetyetyakenh. (St) *I feel disappointed because you didn't come to see me.*

ahenty-ahenty[1] (E) *n.*
part of the upper back between shoulder-blades

ahenty-ahenty[2] (W,T) *n.*
make a thumping or thudding noise; sound of someone or something running away or coming; sound of footsteps; a rattling or rustling noise ◆ Nantew arrtyanem ahenty-ahenty werrk-angkwerr. (T) *The horse is making a thudding noise as it gallops through the scrub.*
= rrmwangk-rrmwangk, anenty-anenty, twerlepwelh-pwelh

ahenty-ahenty-irrem (W,T) *vi.*
make a thumping or thudding noise, make a rattling or rustling noise

aheny (E) *n.*
mosquito ◆ Ahenyel ankwa-kweny-ilem. (Sa) *Mosquitos stop you from sleeping.*
= weny, angeylk, kewenyeweny

ahepet (E) *n.*
dry, waterless country; place where there is no vegetation; drought-stricken country
= aherraty, arrangketh, urrepert

ahepet-irrem (E) *vi.*
dry up (of country) ◆ Mer ahepet-irrem atherrkeny anetyang. (Sa) *The country is drying up and there isn't any green grass.*
= aherraty-irrem, antyerrk-irrem

aher *adv.*
fast, quickly, in a hurry ◆ Tyerrty alenh aher angerram alhep-alhem kwenh — *no* arternp apek alhem kwenh. (M) *That person is going along really quickly — they're not going slowly.*
= parrp, arrengker, uremeny
CAN SOUND A BIT LIKE aherr *'kangaroo'*

ahererr (E) *n.*
an open or clear place, open space ◆ Tha ahererr arem, alpetyek anem ayeng werrk-kety. (St) *When I see an open place in the scrub I will go back [through it].*

ahererr arem (E)
look for an open or clear place (arem *'look', 'see'*)

aherlkem *vi.*
dawn, get light, rise (sun) ◆ Aherrk arratem aherlkemel. (T) *The sun comes up and it gets light.*

aherlkenty, aherlkentyel *n.*
early in the morning, daybreak, dawn, daylight (about 6 o'clock in the morning) ◆ Aherlkentyel akem-irrem, tey apek mern item. (T) *At daybreak [you] get up and boil tea and cook food.*
SEE ALSO ingwelem

aherlkenty-aherlkenty *n.*
very early in the morning (about 4 o'clock in the morning), predawn, before daybreak ◆ Ayeng akem-irrerl-alhek aherlkenty-aherlkentyel. (St) *I got up and went before daybreak.*

aherlkenty alhem
rise or come up (sun or moon) (alhem *'go'*) ◆ Atay aherlkenty alhem. (T) *The moon comes up.* ◆ Kweny amparr anem, wal aketh-aketh-irrentyem, an aherlkentyem alhem. (M) *It's dark at first, and then it gets light and the sun rises.*

aherlkelh-ilem *vt.*
make the daylight come, make the sun come up ◆ Nyarew angkerl-anem rlpwerel, rlpwerel arnerl-apem, arnang antarlkwel apek. Kwenyel *all night* angkerl-anem nyarew, aherlkelh-ilem nyarewel. (N) *The* nyarew *cuckoo sings out from hollow trees, or maybe from a forked branch. The* nyarew *sings out all night, and makes the daylight come.*

aherlkey (W,T) *n.*
white-headed, grey-haired ◆ Kapert aherlkey. Aywarl ingkerr ampern. (M) *White-headed. All the hair has just gone grey.* ◆ Ankerr yanh aherlkey anem. (T) *That emu is white in colour now.*
SEE ALSO mperlker

ahern *n.*
1. earth, ground, dirt ◆ Ahernel anwengkerr anep-anem, ananther. (N) *We are all sitting on the ground.* ◆ Mern atwakey apek alyempelhem, ahinpenyarl irrek alyempelhem, antyerrk-irrem. Antyerrk anem ra, atnyem ahern-warl. (St) *A wild orange might shrivel up, when it gets old and dry. It gets dry and then it falls to the ground.*
2. country, region, land
3. the Earth ◆ Kwerraly anyem ahern-warn. (T) *The star is falling to the Earth.*
= ahelh
SEE ALSO mer
CAN SOUND A BIT LIKE aheyen *'non-Christian'*

ahern ata (E) *n.*
a lump of dirt, mud

ahern-ahern *n.*
brownish in colour

ahern-areny (E) *n.*
western bower bird (*Chlamydera guttata*) (-areny *'belonging to', 'inhabitant of'*)
= akerrk

aherr *n.*
red kangaroo (*Macropus rufus*). Also referred to as *ker aherr.* ◆ Aherran akem-irremel arrtyanek itetheh. (M) *The kangaroo stood up and ran for its life.* ◆ Artwa map apety-alpek ker aherr arlka akert. *The men came back, with kangaroo meat as well.*

CAN SOUND A BIT LIKE aher *'fast'*

aherr rrwey (W,T)
male kangaroo (rrwey *'male'*)

aherr artar
young male kangaroo

aherr purl (E)
old male kangaroo

aherr ampelaherr (E)
old male kangaroo
= aherr purl

aherr marl (W,T)
female kangaroo, doe kangaroo (marl *'female'*)

aherr aympa ampwerrk (E)
young female kangaroo (aympa *'pouch'*; ampwerrk *'whole', 'unopened'*)

aherr areperrk (T,E)
female kangaroo with joey

aherr alkeperr (T,E)
old female kangaroo

aherr-anwerlk (T,E), **aherr-atnwerlk** (E) *n.*
fat from the lower back or rump of the kangaroo (anwerlk *'rump of an animal'*) ◆ Atnwerlk anter tha arlkwetyek kwenh. *I'm going to eat some fat from the kangaroo's rump.*
SEE ALSO anter

aherr arem, aherr-aherr arem *vt.*
imagine something; have a vision of someone or something; think you see something but be not sure ◆ Aherr-aherr arep-arem tha. Wal mer arrpenh-warl anem ra alhek. Ingkern aherr-aherr arep-arem. Arraty-artekarl arep-arem. (St) *I am seeing a vision of her. She went to another place. Later on I see a vision of her. It seems as if it's real.*
SEE ALSO ywer-ywer arem

aherr-aherr *n.*
native lemon grass, scented oilgrass (*Cymbopogon ambiguus*). A grass about 1 m high that usually grows in rocky areas. ◆ *Medicine* irntareny. *Medicine* nhel alhewetyart lweren, aherr-aherrel. Mernt alhewelhetyart, tyerrty. Arnngelhewarretyart, tyerrty ingkerr. Lpwelemel, lpwelem lpwelem irntel apek lpwelem lpwelem arrernetyart. Lpwelemel, *boil*-irretyartey *milk*-art irretyartey. (N) *The native lemon grass is a medicine that grows in the hills. People used to wash themselves with it if they were sick. It was used to clean the whole body. The grass was smashed up on a rock and then it was boiled so that it went like milk.*
= areng-areng

aherr-arlweth (T,E), **aherr-arleth** (E) *n.*
kangaroo balls vine (*Austrobryonia centralis*) (arlweth, arleth *'testicles'*). A creeping vine that has small yellow flowers and bitter green fruit. Used as medicine.
SEE ALSO lkwart-lkwart

aherrantyerr (E) *n.*
an old, weak person ◆ Arelh aherrantyerr anerl-anem, ampwirrekarl. (Sa) *The woman is really weak and old.*

aherrantyeyantyeng (E) kangaroo's sleeping hole SEE UNDER **arrantyeyantyeng**

aherraty, aherrety (E), **aharraty** (T), **awerraty** (E), **aherrty** (E) *n.*
dry, waterless country, country with little or no vegetation ◆ Kwaty-kwenyelap aherrety. Aherrety-angkwerr anantherr alhem wal angkethel-irreman. (St) Aherrety *is where there is no water. If we go through the waterless country then we'll get thirsty.* ◆ Arrangkw kwenh — kwaty anetyakenh aharraty lpway aharraty — kwaty kwenh. (T) *There's nothing — a creek with no water is* aherraty *— no water.* ◆ *No* atherrk, kwaty apek urntetyakenh, mer aherrety. (St) *Country is* aherrety *when there is no grass, when there hasn't been any rain.*
= ahepet, arrangketh, urrepert, rrwepert
SEE ALSO antyerrk

aherraty-irrem, aherrety-irrem (E) *vi.*
dry up (country or vegetation), wither (vegetation) ◆ Aherraty-irrem kwaty-kwenyel. Wal, interrkel arlka anem arna renh arlkwem. (T) *Without water it dries up. Well, then the termites eat the tree.*
= ahepet-irrem, antyerrk-irrem

aherraty-anywertangey (E), **aherraty-atnywertangey** (E) *n.*
a type of mouse or rat (?)

aherrepweng (E) a type of rain cloud SEE UNDER **awerrepweng**

aherrety (E) dry, waterless country SEE UNDER **aherraty**

aherretyepwer (T,E), **aharretyepwer** (E) *n.*
fruit of bush bean, *angerak* (*Rhyncharrhena linearis*)
= awerretyepwer
SEE ALSO werrp

aherrk *n.*
1. sun ◆ Aherrk irrpenhem angwerr-angwerr. (St) *In the afternoon the sun goes down.*
2. heat of the sun ◆ Aherrkel ampem. (St) *The heat of the sun is burning.*
SEE ALSO twern

aherrkel *n.*
daylight, daytime, in the daytime
◆ Aherrkelem alpeyaw mer-warl. *Before that sun go down* — ingwirrek ra anem. (St) *Going home in the daylight — before the sun goes down and it gets dark.*

aherrk akern
midday (akern *'high'*)
= irntar

aherrk angerr, **aherrk akngerr** (E)
midday (angerr[1] *'big'*)

aherrk mpep (E)
midday (mpep *'middle'*)

aherrkelam aherrkel (E)
1. all day, all through the day ◆ Aherrkelam aherrkel alherl-anetyek, ingwirrek-irrem-athath. (St) *Going around all day, right up until it gets dark.*
2. in the daytime ◆ Aherrkelam aherrkel alpey kwenh, mer-warl. (St) *Let's go back home in the daytime.*
= uternek uternek

aherrk arrpanenh (E)
every day, frequently (arrpanenh *'each'*, *'every'*)

aherrk aylpenhem (E)
set (sun), go down (sun) (aylpem *'go in'*)

aherrk irrpem, **aherrk irrpenhem**
set (sun), go down (sun) (irrpem *'go in'*)
◆ Aherrk irrpem altwerl-atheh. Ingerreng apetyem aherrk anenty-alhem, altwerl-atheh irrpem. (N) *The sun goes down in the west. It rises in the east and goes down in the west.*

aherrk tyerrelhem (T,E)
rise or come up (sun) (tyerrelhem *'come out'*)
◆ Aherrk tyerrelhentyem, twernel anem ampem. (T) *The sun comes up and then it gets hot.*

aherrk itenty-alhem (W) = **aherrk tyerrelhem**

aherrkenety-alhem (E) = **aherrk tyerrelhem**

aherrk anintyem (T) = **aherrk tyerrelhem**

aherrk iltya (T), **aherrk iltyem-iltyem** (E)
the rays of the sun (iltya *'finger'*, *'hand'*)
◆ Aherrk iltyel-rwek ayeng arety-kwenh. (T) *I can't see anything because of the rays of the sun.*

aherrk iltyem-anem (E)
set (sun), go down (sun) ◆ Angwerr-angwerr aherrk iltyem-anenhem, irrpenhemel. (St) *In the evening the sun sets, goes down.*

aherrk aketh-irrem
become daybreak, get light (aketh-irrem *'become clear'*, *'light'*) ◆ Aherrk aketh anem irrintyem. (St) *It's daylight now.*

aherrk ney-ney, **aherrk tney-tney** (E)
daybreak (ney-ney *'daybreak'*)

aherrk parrk-irrem (W,T), **aherrk pwarrk-irrem** (W,T)
wane (moon) (parrk-irrem *'get tired'*) ◆ Aherrk nhak pwarrk-irrem. (T) *The moon is waning.*
= atay parrk-irrem

aherrty (E) dry, waterless country SEE UNDER **aherraty**

ahert deaf, heedless SEE UNDER **arert**

ahert (T,E) *n.*
bilby, rabbit-eared bandicoot (*Macrotis lagotis*)

◆ Ker ahert alhweng-areny. Kerarl. Tyapap renh arlkwerl-anem, tyap anyemayt. Tyap anyemaytek angernem angernem angernem, kel ra arwerl-rnem akemel akemel, arlkwem anem tyap tyerremel. Ikwerel-antey. Arrakertel angernemel, iltyel. (Sa) *Bilbies live in burrows. They are edible. They go along eating witchetty grubs. They dig and dig and then break the roots, then pull the grubs out and eat them. Like that. They dig with their mouths, and their feet.*
= angkay, artnangk

Ahert-kenh (T,E) *n.*
Harper Springs (lit. 'belonging to the bilby'). See map p. viii. ◆ Mer Ahert-kenhel anwantherr arety-inkwern, *Harper Springs.* Ikwerel arlkwerretyart atnyemayt ahertel. Tyap renh iytnetyart, tyerremel arlkwemel. (St) *And we used to see them at Ahert-kenh, Harper Springs. That's where the bilbies used to eat the witchetties. They used to dig up the grubs and pull them out and eat them.*

ahert-ahert[1] (T,E) *n.*
smoke bush (*Ptilotus obovatus*). Soft plant with greyish green leaves and small white and pink flowers. Grows to about 60 cm.
SEE ALSO rlkwetherlkweng
CAN SOUND A BIT LIKE arert-arert *'mad'*, *'silly'*

ahert-ahert[2] (W) *n.*
pygmy mulga monitor (*Varanus gilleni*)
= arwangk, arin

ahertety[1] (E) *adv.*
bouncing or skidding along the ground
ahertety-iwem (E) *vt.*
throw something so that it slides or skids along the ground ◆ Aylayl ahertety-iwem ahern-angkwerr, kel artwa ilpelherleng alkwertel. (Sa) *Throwing the boomerang so that it skids along the ground, as the man is protecting himself with the shield.* ◆ Atnem ahertety-iwem, arlewatyerr apek wemel. (St) *The digging stick is thrown at the goanna, and it skids along the ground.*
= irrepereperr-wem
SEE ALSO ankert-wem, arnpakem

ahertety[2] (E) *n.*
leaf or sprouts of bush banana, *alangkw, parl* (*Marsdenia australis*) ◆ Altyey akwerrk lyapem, wal ahertety renh ilem. (St) *The young bush banana leaves grow, well they are called* ahertety.
SEE ALSO altyey, unelh

ahety-ilem (W,T), **ayety-ilem** (W) *vt.*
winnow seed (rapid sideways movement of coolamon); yandy. When winnowing seed the coolamon is also shaken in a vertical motion referred to as *ilpem*[1]. ◆ Arelh ampwang nhenhel ahety-ilem mamperrk. (N) *This old woman is winnowing* mamperrk *seeds.* ◆ Arnwety. Atherl-apemel. *Grandmother*-rlpwerel. Ahety-iletyam. Altywart. Ahety-iletyam yerrelarl arrernetyam *heap* arrernetyam yerrel. Twetyam wetyam wetyam antyakem iletyart akemel panth-warn lernetyam ahety-iletyam athetyem angernetyam. Awantyetyam altywart. (N) Altywart *is a seed that is ground up. All our grandmothers used to winnow the* altywart *seeds. They winnowed the seeds that the ants had heaped up. They pulled the seeds off the grass into wooden dishes, winnowed the seeds and then ground them up and took them back to eat.*

SEE ALSO aympernem, ilpem[1]

ahetyem (W), **aheytem** (E) *vi.* [SENSITIVE LANGUAGE]
move backwards and forwards against someone or something in a sexual fashion
= uripem

ahey *n.*
breath
ahey-angkem, wey-angkem (E)
1. breathe; pant (dog); breathe heavily (angkem *'speak', 'talk'*) ◆ Uyarn ahey-angkem ayeng, alhepenh apek. (St) *I am breathing with difficulty after going along.* ◆ Nhenh iteth-antey ahey-angkerl-anem. (M) *This one is still alive and breathing.* ◆ Arengk apek ahey-angkem, angkethel artnerl-anem arnterr ahey-angkem, parretyek. (St) *A dog might pant, breathe heavily when it's thirsty and perishing for water.* ◆ Ahey-angketyakenh-irrem. (M) *[They] are not breathing.*
2. beat (heart), pulse (blood) ◆ Parrp-parrp ahey-angkerl-anem rtwekert. (T) *The heart is beating rapidly.* ◆ Rtwekert-akertarl parrk-irrem. Rtwekert ahey-angkentyeh rrwem *shaking* antem, kel renh parrp *medicine* anthem, wal mwerram antem. (N) *With heart disease a person gets tired. Then their heart beats fast. If they are given medicine quickly then they get better.*
ahey-ahey-angkem *vi.*
pant, breathe heavily

ahey-ahey (W) *n.*
fontanelle, the soft spot on top of a baby's skull
= atek-kenh, iylpwerr-iylpwerr, kapert thelty, kapert ahey-ahey, thelty-thelty, kwerrk-kwerrk[1]

aheyen (W,T), **ahen** (W,T), **aheytn** (E), **ahaytn** (E) *n.*
non-Christian (maybe from English 'heathen') ◆ Aheyen maparl arrpenhan, arrpenh mapan Pep-arenyarl Kerretyen maparl. Aheyenan anem Pep-areny-kweny, pepek irrpetyakenh. (T) *Some people are non-Christians and others are church-goers, Christians.* Aheyen *are people who are not Christians, those who haven't become Christians.*
SEE ALSO Kerretyen, Pep-areny, Kerretherreng
CAN SOUND A BIT LIKE ahern *'ground'*

aheylangkeyler (E) a type of blind snake SEE UNDER **ahaylengkeyler**

aheyleng (E) a place which is avoided SEE UNDER **ahileng**

aheynem (E) dig SEE UNDER **ahinem**

aheytem (E) [SENSITIVE LANGUAGE] move backwards and forwards against someone or something in a sexual fashion SEE UNDER **ahetyem**

aheytn (E) non-Christian SEE UNDER **aheyen**

ahileng (T,E), **aheyleng** (E), **ahayleng** (E) *n.* [RESPECT LANGUAGE]
a place which is avoided, such as a woman's son-in-law's camp or a man's mother-in-law's camp. Also referred to as *mer ahileng.*
◆ 'Aheyleng-ketyaw!' Alanh angkem, mwerekikwenh mer-kety. (Sa) *'Look out for your son-in-law's camp!' That's what is said about her son-in-law's camp.* ◆ Mer 'ahayleng' ilem

mwerekikwenh. 'Ahayleng-ayerr-kety ayeng nhenhentyel ahanem. Ahayleng yanhentyak-kety.' (Sa) *'Ahayleng' is what her son-in-law's camp is called. 'I am going this way because of my son-in-law's camp. Because of my son-in-law's camp over there.'* ◆ Ahileng-kety, talkw alhem. (T) *You go around the side way because of your son-in-law's camp.*
SEE ALSO tyangkay, irrewatyent
3. the place where a woman's or man's son went through the ceremonial business during which he became a young man ◆ Ikwerenh *son*-arl tyarl-iwem, wal 'aheylengarl' akem mer ikwer. 'Meran' inewetyan. (Sa) *The place where her son has been released [in ceremonial business] is called* 'aheyleng'. *It's not called* 'mer' *[place].*
4. a place where people have passed away
5. the traditional country of someone who has passed away
SEE ALSO mer

ahimperr-wem (E) *vt.*
make a mark on the ground or a blaze on a tree to show where you have gone
SEE ALSO thwerremp-irrem, arlkeny-wem, mpaty-ilem

ahinem (E), **aheynem** (E) *vt.*
dig ◆ Tyap tha aheynetyekay. (Sa) *I'm going to dig some witchetties.* ◆ Mern arlatyey ipertek aheynem. (Sa) *Digging the pencil yams out of the hole.*
SEE ALSO angernem[1], inyem

ahinelhem (E), **aheynelhem** (E) *vi.*
scratch yourself
= angernelhem, arreynelhem, irrkernelhem

ahinp long ago SEE UNDER **ahenp**

ahiwelhem (T) *n.*
horn (of animal) ◆ Ahiwelhem arrerlp angerr kwenh, atwekety kwenh. (T) *Look out for those long sharp horns.*
SEE ALSO napey, rewelyerr, yarwelyem, yerewelyek

+ak[1] (E) *n.ending*
Goes on a nominal to indicate an extra thing; something else or someone else, other people, and, as well as. ◆ Mern**ak** inerl-alha, tey**ak** inerl-alha. Tyampit**ak** inerl-alha. (Sa) *Go and get the food, and the tea as well. Go and get the billycan as well.*

+ak[2] *prn.ending*
Goes on the end, or in the middle, of dual and plural pronouns and shows that the people being referred to are in the same patrimoiety and different generation moiety. For example, a person or persons along with their father, brother's children, son-in-law, or mother-in-law. See Appendix 1. ◆ Ilak alherretyek awenh-nheng atherr. (T) *We two are going, auntie and niece (or nephew).* ◆ Arra**k**erram alherrirra awenh-intyerr rwang inetyeh. (T) *You all go and get wood, all the aunties and nieces.*
SEE ALSO +anth, ingkerr[2]

aka *n.*
head. This 'shortened' or base form of the more usual word for head — *kapert[1]* — often appears in compound words which have something to do with the head. For example, ***ak****alyer-alyer* 'bald', ***ak****amer* 'the crown of the head', ***ak****alangkw-alangkw* 'matted or knotted hair'. ◆ **Ak**el angem, kapertel angem. (St) *Carrying it on the head.*
SEE ALSO kapert[1]

akak-atwem[1] (E) *vt.*
bang something in (e.g. post) (atwem *'hit'*)
SEE ALSO kanth-atwem

akak-atwem[2] (E), **akek-atwem** (E) *vi.*
nod head in agreement or shake head in disagreement (atwem *'hit'*) ◆ Akak-atwerl-alhem ra alhetyek, anetyek apek, arlkwetyek apek ra akak-atwem. (St) *She is nodding her head in agreement about going or staying, or eating.*
= tyek-tyek-irrem

akakwem *vt.*
bite something, chew something
= karlkwem

akakwerrng (E) brain SEE UNDER **akwerrng**

akal-atwerrey (T,E) red-capped robin SEE UNDER **akarl-atwerrey**

akalangkw-alangkw (E) *n.*
matted or knotted hair (aka *'head';* alangkw-alangkw *'matted'*)
= irrkety-irrkety, akaylep-aylep
SEE ALSO kelh-kelh

akalangkw-alangkw-irrem (E) *vi.*
become matted or knotted (hair) ◆ Alta apernelherl-anem ker anterel apek, akalangkw-alangkw-irretyam. (St) *The hair got matted and knotted after being rubbed with fat.*
SEE ALSO kelh-irrem

akalapantherrty (T) *n.*
bean tree flowers, (*inernt, atywerety*) (*Erythrina vespertilio*)
SEE ALSO akenty

akalk *n.*
1. separate, on one's own
2. (do something) oneself ◆ Tha akalkel atwek. *I shot it by myself.*

akalkew-akalk, **akalk-akalk** (E) *n.*
separate, apart, spread apart ◆ Arrpenhem akalk anetyel, ikngwer-arey akalk akin anerl-anem. Ingwer-rnem *self* akin anerl-anem.

Akalkew-akalk, *self*-ek-*self* inngart. (Sa) *Some are living on their own, and others are on their own as well. Others are separate too. They are separate from each other.*

akalk-irrem *vi.*
scatter, split up, become separate, disperse, go in different directions ◆ Tyerrty yanh map akalk-irrem *meeting*-penh. (T) *Those people are splitting up after the meeting.*
= irrarnp-irrem
SEE ALSO alperrty-irrem

akalk-ilem *vt.*
divide something up, separate something out from other things, split something up
= akalkelh-ilem

akalkelh-ilem *vt.* = **akalk-ilem** ◆ Manter apek ker apek akalkelh-ilem arrpenhek anthemel. (St) *Divide up the clothes and the meat to give to someone else.* ◆ Artwang atherr atwerrem, an arelhel akalkelh-ilem renh-atherr. (T) *Two men are fighting each other, and the woman splits them up.*
= irrarnpelh-ilem

akalker anem (E) *vi.*
sit with legs curled back or bent

akalt (E) *n.*
hair (aka *'head'; alta 'hair'*)

akalthem (E) *vt.*
1. cut, split, chop ◆ Akaltherlentyarreyaw amely-aketyek keraw, akaltheyaw. Kwey ngwarrekengkw akaltha. (Sa) *Cut up the meat to eat. Daughter, cut up the meat for your husband [said by the daughter's mother].*
2. pick fruit, collect or gather things
3. be in pain, hurt (?)
SEE ALSO akem1

akaly (W,T) *n.*
soft honey or sweet gum ◆ Akaly yanh arlkweyaw. (M) *Eat that soft gum.*
SEE ALSO rnpwa

akalyer (F), **akalyer-alyer** (E) *n.*
bald ◆ Akalyer-alyeran *no* alta. Akalyer-alyer *is no hair.*

akalyer kwart (E)
bald (kwart *'egg'*)
= kapert ather-ather
SEE ALSO aka, kapert aketh, akeperleyn, akepweley

akamer (E), **akapmer** (E) *n.*
top of the head, crown of the head (aka *'head'*; mer *'place', 'camp'*)
= akampwep

akamp (W,T), **akampw** (E) *n.*
liquid honey, nectar or sap
SEE ALSO rnpwa

akampamp (E), **akampep** (T,E) top of the head
SEE UNDER **akampwep**

akamperrng (E) *n.* [RESPECT LANGUAGE]
head ◆ Kweth-kwethek akamperrng ulpakek. (St) *[My son-in-law's] head was hit until it bled.*
SEE ALSO aka, kapert1, ayepert

akampw (E) liquid honey SEE UNDER **akamp**

akampwep (W,T), **akampep** (T,E), **akampamp** (E), **akempep** (E) *n.*
top of the head, crown of the head (aka *'head'*; mpep, mpwep *'middle'*) ◆ Akampamp-angkwerr arem kwementyayek. (St) *You look around the crown of the head for* kwementyay *[lice].* ◆ Kwer akwek thelty akampwepel-ayel. (T) *Little babies have a soft part on the crown of the head.*
= akamer

akampwerr (E) *n.*
short hair (i.e. that has been cut in mourning)
= ampwerr

akampwerr-ilelhem (E) *vt.*
cut one's hair (in mourning)
= urlpat-ilelhem
SEE ALSO arrtyelhem, itelhem, anker-athek-irrem, aka

akampwerrk (E) *n.*
ignorant, not knowing about something. Especially said of someone who is ignorant of country and business or Law (perhaps just said of men) (aka *'head'*; ampwerrk *'whole', 'not opened'*) ◆ Law iterlaretyakenh akampwerrk anem. (St) *Somebody who doesn't know the Law is* akampwerrk. ◆ Akampwerrkarl yanh — iterl-aretyakenh apmer. (St) *That person is* akampwerrk *— they don't know about country.*

akaneng (T,E) *adv.*
going off with another lover (?), being sneaky (from English 'cunning' (?))
SEE ALSO iyteny-irrem

akangkem *vi.*
like someone or something; want or like to do something; feel happy about something; be pleased ◆ Atnertinp ayeng akangkem. (St) *I really like it.* ◆ Ayeng akangkem mer arrpenh-warn alhetyenh. (T) *I would like to go to another place.* ◆ Mikwarl akangkem. 'Mwerr kwenh ampa yanh kwerlek irrperl-anem atyenh.' Wal ra akangkem anem, anyikw then. Amikw arrpenh apek ikwer akangkem. (T) *Her mother is pleased. 'It's good that my child goes to school.' Well she's happy, and the father is too. And the child's aunties are pleased about it too.*
SEE ALSO inkwerelhem, ilkelhem, ahenty-irrem, anyerrkem, irrngerney-irrem, kwak-irrem

akangkenty *n.*
kind

akangkwerrem (W,T) *vi.*
take notice, listen to someone, pay attention, obey ◆ Artwang atherr akangkwerrem, arelhelarl ilem. (T) *The two men are listening to what the woman is saying.* ◆ Kwer map, akangkwirrerrirray kwerl tetyekay! (T) *You kids, pay attention to the school teacher!* ◆ You *got to* akangkwerrerl tyerrtyel ngenh apawenherl — *not* rntert anerl-anety unta. Tyerrtyel ngenh apawenhetyenheng, 'Iwenh-apert apek ntwa akarntemel anep-anem? Akangkwerretyeh — irlpel awemel.' (N) *You have to pay attention to what people are asking you — you shouldn't sit there silently. Or the person will ask you, 'Why are you sitting there quietly? Pay attention — listen with your ears.'* ◆ Akangkwerrenty itya, kwer kwerl-areny map — maneyekant angkerl-anem, maney akwel ngkwelty anthetyeh. (N) *The school kids don't pay attention — apparently they just ask for money, ask to be given coins.*
SEE ALSO awelhem

akanthwek-anthwek, **akanthwel-anthwel** (W,T) *n.*
head dripping or pouring with blood ◆ Akanthwek-anthwek thelelhem marl arrpenhelarl atwek kweterel. (T) *Her head is pouring with blood because another woman hit her with a nulla-nulla.*
akanthwek-anthwek-ilem, **akanthwel-anthwel-ilem** (W,T) *vt.*
make someone's head bleed
akanthwek-anthwek atwem, **akanthwel-anthwel atwem** (W,T)
1. hit someone so that their head bleeds
2. hit someone so that they bleed [SOME SPEAKERS]
◆ Iltya apek atwemarl tyerrtyel, wal tyerrty arrpenhel ilem, '*Eh*, akeweny akanthwel-anthwel atwek iltyang yanh kwenh'. (T) *A person might hit someone's hand, and another person says, 'Hey, the poor thing, their hand has been hit till it bleeds'.*
SEE ALSO aka, anthwek-anthwek

akantyer (E) *n.*
thick rain cloud

akap (E) *n.*
no good, lumpy or uneven (of food) ◆ Mern tamp akap — mern mwerr athetyakenh. Ipert-ipert, mern akaparl athep-athem nhel, mern mwerr apek athetyakenh. (Sa) *This damper is no good — it wasn't kneaded well. It's lumpy and uneven because it wasn't made properly.*

akap-rlwem (W,T), **akap-irlwem**, **akap-iylwem** (E) *vt.*
uncover or peel off something that covers or is around something else; take off clothes; take inner tube out of a tyre; undo something that is tied around something else ◆ Mantarr akap-rlwem. (M) *Take off the clothes.* ◆ Arnantey akap-irlwem rltimp apek. (St) *Peel the bark off the tree.* ◆ Nantheng akap-irlwang *hobble* yanh. (T) *Take that hobble off the horse.* ◆ Rlwelty tamp-arteh intem. Akap-rlwem rlwelty renh, kwaty antywetyenheng. (T) *The ice is [solid] like a damper. You peel the ice [off the water] and then drink the water.* ◆ Ayenp akap-rlwem, arternemem renh — anem renh — kwer-penh arrerlpem ilem aneman alenh, arternenty-penh. (N) *The bark is stripped off and then [the stick] is straightened — the digging stick — and then after it has been straightened the digging stick is sharpened.*
SEE ALSO lywem[1], rlwem, iyltem
akap-rlwelhem (W,T), **akap-irlwelhem** *vi.*
peel something off self; shed bark or skin ◆ Arnang ayenp akap-rlwelhem. (T) *The bark is peeling off the tree.*

akapmer (E) top of the head SEE UNDER **akamer**

akapw (E) *n.*
dry (of damper or seed mixture) ◆ Akapw-antey nhenhanaw, kwaty theley-antey. Tampan akapw, wal thelem kwaty, kwaty theley akwek. (St) *This damper [mixture] is dry so you have to tip some water in. If the mixture is too dry then you tip a little bit of water in.*
akapw-akapw (E) *n.*
a bit dry (of damper or seed mixture)
akapw-irrem (E) *vi.*
get dry (of damper or seed mixture)

akapweley (T,E), **akepweley** (E) *n.*
bald (lit. 'baldy head') (from English 'baldy') ◆ Inngan ilem akapweley. Ampa apek ilem, ampa alerl lyapetyenh weth-lkwer alta lyapetyenh, 'Akapweleyay'. 'Akapweley' arrpantey ilem ampa kelyan. (Sa) *You call a person bald. You might call a child whose hair is yet to grow 'baldy'. You might just pretend and call a child 'baldy'.*
= kapert ather-ather
SEE ALSO akalyer-alyer, kapert aketh, akeperleyn, aka

akarem *vt.*
1. wait for someone, wait with someone
2. look after someone, mind something
◆ Angwelyel akarep-arem rlkert intep-intemel. (M) *The dog is lying down looking after the sick man.* ◆ Arntety tha akarep-arem. Ngkwengan

ayeng uyarnarl iwerr arelhepelhem, atherrel akaretyek, arntety nhenh. (St) *I am looking after the sick person. I watched the road in vain for you to come so that the both of us could look after this sick person.* ◆ Tyerrty rlkert nhenh thang akarem. (T) *I am looking after this sick person.*

akarelhem (W,T) *vi.*

wait for someone or something, wait around ◆ Ayeng ngkweng akarelhem. (T) *I am waiting for you.* ◆ Akarelhem tyerrty alerteh, mpwelherl-anem, tywempelherl-anem, akwetarl aywerreperremeh. Anemel anemel arerl-anem arerl-anem arerl-anem, ilenger rang arratenty-alpetyenh kwenh. (N) *I am waiting for that person, waiting for the person that disappeared for a long time. Sitting and watching for the time when they turn up.*

= tywempelhem, mpwelhem[1]

akarl-atwerrey (T,E), **akal-atwerrey** (T,E) *n.*

1. red-capped robin (*Petroica goodenovii*)

2. crimson chat (?) (*Epthianura tricolor* (?)) (aka *'head'*; twerrem *'hit each other'*) It is said that the red on the heads of these birds is from the blood that flowed after they hit each other. ◆ Akarl-atwerrey kapert rnter-rnter. Altyerreng rnter-rnter anem. Mwerr-angker *pretty* ikwerenh. (Sa) *The red-capped robin has a red head. It's red from the Dreaming. It's really nice and pretty.*

SEE ALSO kapert rnter-rnter, alywerr-alywerr, uneng atyetyek

akarl-wem (W,T) *vt.*

1. throw water over someone, wet someone ◆ Thang ngenh kwatyel akarl-wem, nywerrpel. (M) *I'm throwing water at you, because we're in opposite generation moieties to each other.*

2. start to rain (the first drops), shower (rain), sprinkle (rain) ◆ Kwaty irnmerr war, akarl-wem. (T) *It's just starting to sprinkle, starting to rain.*

SEE ALSO anhem

akarl-welhem (W,T) *vi.*

wet oneself to cool down ◆ Kwatyel akarl-welhem anhelhem. Angwerleny mparelhemel. (T) *[You] wet yourself with water to cool yourself down.*

= irrpelh-ilelhem, anhelhem

akarlarlw (E) kneecap, knee joint SEE UNDER akarlwarl

akarlety, akarley (E) *n.*

1. northern wild orange (*Capparis umbonata*). Shrub up to 3.5 m high, with rough dark bark, white flowers and yellow or reddish fruits which hang down on stalks.

2. edible fruits of the northern wild orange. Also referred to as *mern akarlety.*

= ngarntatyarr

akarlwarl (E), **akarlarlw** (E) *n.*

kneecap, knee joint

SEE ALSO kelkert, amper alkwert-alkwert, itelh, kelkert tyelh, kelkert ngkwern, tyelh, amper[2], ampweth

akarnkw (W) *n.*

white-coloured seed heads of bush onion, *yerrakwerr, yalk* (*Cyperus bulbosus*)

SEE ALSO akenty

akarnng[1] (E) *n.*

skull. Also referred to as *akarnng ngkwern.*

SEE ALSO aka

kapert akarnng

back of the head (kapert[1] *'head'*)

akarnng[2] (W) *n.*

something that blocks the throat or makes someone choke (?) ◆ Rnpwang antyerrk arlkwek kwer rang. Wal kwer akarnng antem anek, akwernetyakenh itya antem, nheng irlkang kwenh irrek, rnpwang ra kwerel-arleng atanelhek. (M) *The boy ate some* alalherrk *sweet that was too dry. But he was unable to swallow the dry sweet and the lolly got stuck in his throat so that he couldn't breathe.*

akarntem[1] (E) *vi.*

have a headache (aka *'head'*; arntem *'ache'*)

akarntem[2] *vi.*

be quiet, sit down quietly and thoughtfully; worry about something [SOME SPEAKERS]

◆ Akarntemel anep-anem, rntert-irremel weth-lkwer anerl-anem. Akarntemel ra anep-anem. Itirremel apek anep-anem ker apek arlkwetyek. (St) *Sitting down quietly. She is sitting down quietly, maybe thinking about eating meat.* ◆ Akarntem ayeng, alharrp apek. (T) *I'm sitting down quietly, maybe because I'm sad.* ◆ Kwer nhenh iwenheh akarnteparntem? (M) *What is that kid sitting down and thinking about?* ◆ Akarntemel anem iwenh-apert anemay? Iwenhengay? (N) *Why are you sitting down quietly? What's happened?* ◆ War akarntemel ayeng anep-anem angayakw kwenh. (N) *I am just sitting down quietly because I'm hungry.*

akarntel anem (W,T)

sit quietly and thoughtfully; think about something ◆ Akarntel anem alharrp, *might be* tyerrty apek rlkert intem-arleng, anetyem. (T) *Sitting down quietly because [you're] sad, maybe about someone who is sick.*

akarnterrng (T,E) *n.*

1. young girls when their breasts are just

starting to develop.
2. the shape of breasts when they are starting to develop. Also referred to as *werlaty akarnterrng* or *paty akarnterrng*. ◆ Werlaty akarnterrng, akwekarl lyapem. (St) *Breasts that are* akarnterrng *have just grown a little bit.*
• = alhwetepwet, alhwemperemper, paty arrwert
kwey akarnterrng (T,E)
young girl, teenage girl ◆ Kwey awenk akarnterrng. (St) *A young teenage girl.*

akarntety-arntety (E) *n.*
a type of gecko (sand-plain or northern spiny-tailed) (*Diplodactylus stenodactylus* (?), *Strophurus ciliaris* (?)) (lit. 'aching head'). Lives amongst the bark on trees. ◆ Akarntety-arntety pelh-iwenh-iwenharl akarntety-arntety. Pelharl iwem ampwileman, *skinny one* mpwaremel. Pelhel apek ran iwem, akarntety-arntetyel. Akarntetyek. Kapert arntetyek. (Sa) *The* akarntety-arntety *lizard is a spitter. It spits and makes people skinny. The* akarntety-arntety *lizard spits and gives people a headache.*
= pelh iwenh-iwenh, rltimp-areny
SEE ALSO arlwer, irnar, aka

Akarntey (W) *n.*
Rembrandt Rock, in the south-west of the Anmatyerr area

akarr (T,E) *n.*
1. liquid honey ◆ Ngkwarl untyeyamp akarr-akert nhenh. (St) *This corkwood has liquid honey.*
SEE ALSO ngkwarl
2. meat juice [SOME SPEAKERS] ◆ Awerrp akarr antywem. (T) *Drinking the meat juice.* • SEE ALSO awerrp1
CAN SOUND A BIT LIKE karr *'awake'*

Akarr *n.*
1. language name. An Arandic dialect spoken to east of the Plenty River area, and in the Harts Range area.
2. Akarre people
= Karrwerlereny
SEE ALSO Kityarr

akarr-irrem (T,E) *vi.*
meet together, gather together, come together in a group, swarm (ants) ◆ Map akarr-irrem, akngerr akarr-irreperrem, angkerretyek apek. (St) *Lots of people get together, maybe to talk.*
SEE ALSO arraw-irrem, anyent-irrem
CAN SOUND A BIT LIKE karr-irrem *'wake up'*
akarr-ilem (T,E) *vt.*
1. sweep or gather things together
2. gather people together (?)
SEE ALSO arraw-ilem, arlwelem
akarrelh-ilem (T,E) *vt.* = **akarr-ilem**

Akarralwereny (E) Karrwerlereny language SEE UNDER **Karrwerlereny**

akartemarl (W) pillow, headrest SEE UNDER **akertemarl**

akarternem (W,T) *vi.*
change form, metamorphose, turn into a moth or butterfly ◆ Anyematy akarternem. (M) *The witchetty grub changes form.*
SEE ALSO irrarl-irrem, rlwarlp-irrem, urlaylp-irrem, ngkekern-irrem
akarternenty (W,T) *n.*
1. the metamorphosed form of a grub ◆ Anyematy akarternenty interl-anem kwenel arnel. Rnkem, thepemey alhem arlpakert rnkenty-penh. (M) *The witchetty grub lies in its metamorphosed form inside [the root] of the tree. Then it gets wings and it emerges and flies away as a moth.*
SEE ALSO irrarl
2. the 'pipe' through which the witchetty grub (and other grubs) emerge from the ground ◆ Irrarl 'akarternenty'-angkwerr tyerrelherl-alhem. (T) *The metamorphosed grub emerges out through the pipe called an 'akarternenty'.* • = akartw, impakwert

akartw (E) *n.*
the 'pipe' through which the witchetty grub (and other grubs) emerge from the ground ◆ Urlaylp tyerrelhem akartw-angkwerr, kel ra alhem intelyapelyap anem. (St) *The witchetty grub comes out through the* akartw, *and then it flies around as a moth.*
= akarternenty, impakwert

akartwernem (E) *vi.*
lie with knees up
= tyakwert intem

akat *n.*

munyeroo, pigweed, purslane (*Portulaca oleracea*). Fleshy herb that spreads along the ground, has small yellow flowers, pinkish stems and small black seeds. ◆ Akat anterrng anwern awantyerl-apek, athemel. Panth-warn, atwerl-apek, rrpwerl anthwerr kwenh. Ahety-ilem ahety-ilem, rlkwank-ilem alakenh arrernem clean. (N) *The munyeroo is a seed that we went along eating, after grinding it up and putting it in the wooden dish. It's really black in colour. We winnow the seed and separate it out and then put the clean seed to one side.*

= iylaw
SEE ALSO ngkweytek

akatemarengk *n.*
hands clasped behind head; supporting head with hands ◆ Artwa irnerl-anem akatemarengk, kapwert arntwerrkelhemel. (T) *The man is standing with his hands clasped behind his head, holding his head.*
SEE ALSO aka

Akateny (W) *n.*
the name of a waterhole west of Mt Allan community

akatwem (E) *vt.*
hit or beat something ◆ Ntang artety apek akatwetyek, katyerr apek, arwerlel akatwem. (St) *Mulga seeds or desert raisin fruits are beaten with a stick [to separate husks or stems].*
SEE ALSO atwem

akaty-akaty *adv.*
feeling safe or protected from something; fearless, not frightened, without a care ◆ Akaty-akaty anep-anem ayeng. Ahekety apek, angkemarl-kety apek, akaty-akaty anep-anem. (St) *I'm not frightened. I'm not frightened of people's anger, or what they might say.* ◆ Arelh yanh akaty-akaty anerlanem lywel twern-kety. (T) *That woman is sitting under the shade, protected from the hot sun.* ◆ Warl kwenel anem akaty-akaty, kwaty angerr irlkakerteng. (T) *Sitting inside the house, safe from the big storm and the wind.*
SEE ALSO akwenpeny, rrkwanth

akawer (E) *n.*
a big head (aka *'head'*; awer *'big'*). Also referred to as *kapert awer.*
kapert angerr

Akay (E) *n.*
Mulga Bore. Location of a small outstation. See map p. viii.

akay *adv.*
wailing or crying in mourning (women) ◆ Arelh akay arrangkem ayey anetyarl awekarl. (T) *The woman is wailing after hearing bad news.*
SEE ALSO wartay2

akayel arnem, akayel artnem (E)
wail or cry in mourning (women) (arnem *'cry'*) ◆ Akayel artnem ampek apek. Arnetheyarl atnyek apek. (St) *Maybe [someone is] crying over a child that has fallen from a tree.*
SEE ALSO wartay-irrem

akayak *n.*
restricted, not allowed, out of bounds
SEE ALSO kwerert, mwekeny, amek-amek, tikeley

akayak-ilem *vt.*
tell someone they are not allowed to do something; tell someone to keep away from private belongings; stop someone doing something; warn somebody about something ◆ Thang akayak-ilem atyenenyeng. (M) *I tell [them] to keep away from other people's things.* ◆ Kwer nhak akayak-ilay, arnang inehety! (T) *Stop that kid from getting that thing!* ◆ Akayak-ilem urel ampekerr. (T) *Warning [someone] that the fire might burn them.* ◆ Thweker akayak-ilem, arneng apek anyekety — arnekarl antyem tenteyek, aperek apek. Wal akayak-ilem, 'Unta anyekety kwenh'. (T) *I might warn him about falling from the tree — when he is climbing up onto the overhanging branch, maybe of a river red gum. Well then I warn him, 'You'll fall down'.* ◆ Mern apek arlkwekerr arnterr, akayak-ilemel arrpenhel. (St) *In case they eat too much, another might tell them not to do it.*
SEE ALSO angernt-wem, arnpakem, arrngert-wem, ayakem, apatel-anthem

akaylep-aylep (E) *n.*
matted or knotted hair (aka *'head'*; aylep-aylep *'matted'*)
= akalangkw-alangkw, aylep-aylep, kapert kelh-kelh

akek-atwem (E) nod head in agreement or shake head in disagreement SEE UNDER **akak-atwem2**

akekw (E) *n.*
southern boobook (?) (*Ninox novaeseelandiae* (?))
= kwerrkwerrk
SEE ALSO kwekew, arntep

akel-intenh (T), **akel-ayntenh** (E), **akel-anenh** (E) *n.*
women's headdress (lit. 'that which is on the head') ◆ Alpeyt anem arrernetyam akarl-ayntenh-warl. Arelh-kenh. Ker artnangk weth — ahert. (St) *The white bilby tail tips were put in the women's headdresses. That bilby —* artnangk *or* ahert.
SEE ALSO akwelty, itepenh, aka

akelawerl-wem (E) *vt.* [RESPECT LANGUAGE]
go and get something, save something for someone ◆ Ikwenty-ayerr atyeng akelawerl-wa, awakerl-wa. (Sa) *Go and get me some ashes for chewing tobacco [from someone I am in a respect relationship to].*
= awakerl-wem
SEE ALSO inem

akeleraperap-irrem (E) *vi.*
become silly in the head, get a headache, be driven mad ◆ Akeleraperap-irrerl-anem amper-irrerl-anem, ampa apek, tyerrty then arert-arert mpwarerrerl-anem. (Sa) *Maybe a child will go silly in the head and go round and*

round in circles, driving everybody mad.
= raperap-irrem

akeley-akeley (T,E) *n.*
life-saver burr, teddy bears arsehole (*Sida platycalyx*). Soft herb with large yellow flowers. Fruits are doughnut-shaped and prickly when dry. ◆ *Comb*-arrpantey akwel akunyel *use*-em-iletyart akeley-akeley renh. Arwerl-warl akwernemel. (Sa) *The poor old things used to use the life-saver burr seeds as a kind of comb. They threaded them onto sticks.*
= ingka-mwerney, kwem, anmang

akelty (E) *n.*
old woman, mature woman
akelty ampwa (E) *n.*
old woman (ampwa '*old*')
= arelh ampwa

akely (E) *n.*
1. little, small
2. a bit of something, a small amount of something
3. child, young (animal) ◆ Atwety akely, akwek-amperl alhelth-angem ra, aympel, melikw. (St) *The little joey, its mother carries the little thing in her pouch.*
= akwek
akely-akely (E) *n.*
little, small, smallish ◆ Arlpenty arnterrarl anwerlarr, artelhampw tyelpetyerrem. Aylpa ra akely-akely, arlatyey-kenh aylpa awer-rnem. Pertipelawan *yellow one* ratherr atherr-antey. (Sa) *The* anwerlarr *yam is really long, and the big ones are pulled out. It has smallish leaves, whereas the* arlatyey *yam has big ones. Both of them have similar looking yellow flowers.*
= akwek-kwek
akely-amperl (E) *n.*
really small, really little, tiny
◆ Arengkatwepatwetyenh *Dreaming* angwely-kenh. Angwelyarl anngampelh-ilem. Angwely akely-amperl. *Dingo* akwek anngampelh-ilem annga. (N) *The* arengkatwepatwetyenh *plant is a Dreaming for dingoes. It makes the little dingoes open their eyes.*
= akwek-amperl, akwek-antyey
akely-awaty (E) *n.*
a small amount, something smaller, a little bit
= akwek-awaty
ampa akely (E)
baby, small child
= kwer akwek, ampa akwek

akem[1] *vt.*
1. cut, slice, break a piece off something
◆ Mer-warn alpem itna ker aketyek. *They return to the camp to cut up the meat.*
2. pluck or pick (fruit) ◆ Mern katyerr aketyek alhey. *Let's go and pick desert raisins.*
3. bite someone or something ◆ Arengkel akem — arengk ahelengkwelan akem. 'Arengk yanhel akekerraw!' (Sa) *Dogs bite — aggressive dogs bite. 'Look out or that dog over there will bite you!'* • = nhwem
akerrem *vi.*
1. cut each other
2. bite each other; fight (dogs)
3. fight (people), argue ◆ Ahel-ahel akerrem. (Sa) *Fighting with each other.*
akelhem *vi.*
1. cut yourself ◆ Artwa akelhem alety lyweper alhwarrp. (St) *Men cut themselves on the thigh when they are in mourning.* ◆ Amarr ra akelhem ampa akely apekan utyen anentyek, kel apernemel ra ikwerel amarrel. Arelh akelhem, amarr akelhem, kel alhwa thelelhemel, kel annga anem ikwerel aperneman, utyen, annga utyen-irrenty. (Sa) *She cuts herself on the arm and then rubs a child who has sores with the blood. Women cut themselves and then the blood seeps out and then they used the blood to rub on the eyes, eyes that have got sore.* ◆ Artwa akelhem alety lyweper alhwarrp, artnemel inngart. Tyerrty artwekenhantarl aletyarl akelheman. Arelhan arrangkwarl. Arelhan kapertant atanthem atnemel — alety-kweny. *The man cries and cuts himself on the thigh in sorrow. That's just men's business — to cut yourself. Women don't do that. Women just hit their heads with a digging stick — they don't cut themselves.*
2. break down, fall apart ◆ Mwetek akelhekaw! (St) *The car broke down!*
3. clear up (rain)

akem[2] *vt.*
call someone by a kinship term; describe someone as a relation ◆ Thang arelh Pwerrerl nhenh marley akem. (T) *I call this Pwerrerl woman here great granddaughter.*
akerrem *vi.*
call each other a particular kinship term; describe each other as relations
◆ Mpwernikwan ateyant-atherrel akerrem. 'Pantyey' inngart 'mpwerney'. *Not* arelhel athew — arelhant-atherr arntengantarl akerrem. (Sa) *Only men call each other* mpwernikw *[brother-in-law]. 'Pantyey' is the same as* 'mpwerney'. *Women don't — they call each other* arnteng *[sister-in-law].* ◆ Yanh atherr altyel akerrek, *two cousins — sister and brother*-kenh. (T) *Those two are full cross-cousins*

for each other — belonging to a sister and a brother.
SEE ALSO anpernerrem

akem-irrem *vi.*
1. get up, wake up ◆ Aherran akem-irremel arrtyanek itetheh. (M) *The kangaroo stood up and ran for its life.* ◆ Arelh anentyemarl-penh akem-irrem. (T) *The woman is getting up after sitting down.*
2. be revived
akem-ilem *vt.*
stand something up; make someone or something get up ◆ Kwer yanh akemelh-ilay mer-warn alpetyeh. (M) *Get that kid up so that [we] can go home.*
akemelh-ilem *vt.* = **akem-ilem**
akem-arrernem (E) *vt.*
lift up someone who is old and infirm (arrernem *'put'*) ◆ Tha arelh ampwa akem-arrernetyek *wheelchair*-warl. (St) *I am lifting the old woman up to put her in the wheelchair.*

akementhwerlk (W) *n.*
hairless, without hair
SEE ALSO aka
Akementhwerlk (W) *n.*
name of a place south of Mt Allan community

akempep (E) top of the head SEE UNDER **akampwep**

aken, akin *part.*
as well, also, and, (do something) again, (something happens) again (from English 'again') ◆ Ayteyaty, 'Angkwer-nheng-arey alheyaw anwingkerr'. Ayeng angkem. Ra angkem alanh akin, angka anyent. *My younger sister, I might say to her, 'Let's go, all of us sisters together'. And she might talk like that as well, say the same thing.* ◆ Arengk akwerrk map anngerlkem akin, pweng-penh, akwerrkarl aneman. *Puppies open their eyes as well, after being blind at first, as little puppies.* ◆ 'Amek-amek' akin ilem Anmatyerrel — marl alhety-kweny itya. (M) *In Anmatyerr you say 'amek-amek' as well — where women aren't allowed to go.*
aweth aken
once again, another time, (do something) another time ◆ Weth ina alhetyam mern ywerretyamam aweth akin ina kwarrety renh, nheng yerrelarl arrernem akethek. Arrernerl-apem, wal arerlapetyam, 'Nhenhey arrernek kwenh — atyeng-apenh kwenh', inelhalhetyam. Weth alhetyam arrpenhem *find*-em-iletyam. (N) *When the food ran out they used to go again for* kwarrety *seeds, where the ants had heaped them up in the open ground. They'd see that and say, 'Here's where the ants have heaped up the grass seeds — these are mine.' They'd go and collect them and then go looking for more.*

akeng (T,E) *n.*
1. bad, no good, wrong, inappropriate ◆ Ikwa akeng atherr. (Sa) *Those two are the wrong skin for each other.* ◆ Ikirrenty anetyakenh yanh alhewer alhem, mey-mey kwerenh, rtwalty kwerenh-angkwarr. Akengarlaw. (St) *That person does not respect the avoidance rules and just goes anywhere, near her son-in-law. It's really bad.*
2. no good, useless, dysfunctional ◆ Arrwekeleny mapel mern awerant anaty arlkwerretyart. Ararr arlkwetyakenh. 'Ararran' akeng *light one*-arl, *can't eat*-em. Angayakw akweteth anerl-anem. (Sa) *The olden-time people used to eat just substantial foods such as bush potatoes. They didn't eat 'light' foods. 'Ararr' are light ones — they are no good and if you eat them you'll always be hungry.*
3. sick, unwell
= kwern, anety
akeng-akeng (T,E) *n.*
not too good, not very good, so-so, a bit unwell, a bit useless ◆ Arwerl apek tha akeng-akeng yanh-lkwer lyapek, tyerretyek tha, tyerremel iwetyek. (St) *If I have grown some useless plants or that sort of thing, then I'll pull them out, pull them out and chuck them away.* ◆ Warleng-anyimp atyenh, akeng-akeng artelhepelhem. (St) *My house is sub-standard — it wasn't built very well.* ◆ Iltelhey, akeng war alhep-alhem lthel-lthel war, mantarr akeng-akeng-akert iltelhey-iltelhey alhep-alhem. Aternng-aternng mantarr atyenh *clean* anetyakenh. Iltelhey akeng wararl alhep-alhem alhewelhetyakenh. (St) *I am just going along with raggedy, dirty clothes on. My clothes are dirty — they're not clean. I'm a bit scruffy — I haven't had a wash.*
= kwern-kwern
akengenty *adv.*
wrongly, badly ◆ Ra akengenty alhek. *He went the wrong way.*
= anetyengwerl
akengenty angkem
talk the wrong way; say inappropriate things (angkem *'talk', 'speak'*) ◆ Tyerrty arrpenhek akengenty angkem. (St) *Saying the wrong thing to another person.* ◆ Artwang yanh akengenty angkern. (T) *That man over there just said the wrong thing.*
akeng-irrem (T,E) *vi.*
1. go bad or go off, become damaged or

spoilt, get wrecked, break down
2. get sick ◆ Mwetekay akeng-irrek ultakelhelk. (Sa) *The car is useless — it broke down.* ◆ Tyelk ingkerrek ayeng akeng-irrek *pain*-angketyarr, arlkwemarl. Tyelk ingkerrek ayeng arlkwem. (St) *My whole body is no good — the whole lot is hurting. All of my body is hurting me.* ◆ Irrkerlanty-kety arrwert artelhemel, amparl, arrwert akeng-irrekerr, irrkerlerrk anekerr. (Sa) *Young boys cover their chins if they see a falcon — otherwise their beards will not grow very well — they'll be thin and sparse.*
= kwern-irrem, anety-irrem

akeng-ilem (T,E) *vt.*
1. wreck something, damage something, spoil something
2. make someone sick ◆ Arrwengkelth yanhel akeng-ilek. Arrwekeleny map *clean*-arl ina anek, *no* arrwengkelth ina atnyenek *disease* apek *nothing*. (St) *That disease made him/her sick. The olden days people were free of disease, they didn't have any sickness.*
= kwern-ilem, anety-ilem

akengentyeny (E) *n.*
someone who has married the 'wrong' way ◆ Akengentyeny atherr anep-anem, Ngal then Kemarr then. (St) *Those two people are married the wrong way, a Ngal and a Kemarr.*
SEE ALSO alem atherrk-atherrk, alem iyterrk-iyterrk, atherrk-atherrk, atna iyterrk-iyterrk

akenh but, and, whereas, on the other hand SEE UNDER **kenh**[2]

akenp (T,E), **akinp** (E) *n.*
newly ripened fruit of bush plum, native currant, native citrus (*Psydrax latifolia*) ◆ Akenpan atyet-irremant, urrek-antey. (St) *The* akenp *fruit has just turned ripe and it's not quite ready [to eat].*
SEE ALSO ahakey

akent-wem (E), **akent-iwem** (E) *vt.*
1. sort through things to find something ◆ Manterr mwerrek akent-wetyel, terreth mwerrek. Tha akent-wetyel. (Sa) *I am sorting through to find good clothes, a nice dress.* ◆ Mer irranyent-iwem arengkel. Mern, ingkerr arlkwerrek. Mernek akent-werreperrem irranyent-iwetyel. (Sa) *The dogs have gone through the place and messed everything up. They've eaten all the food. They've gone through everything looking for food and messed everything up.*
2. uncover something, turn something over
SEE ALSO irrkerem, ilkakem

akenty (W,T), **akeynt** (E) *n.*
1. flower of wild onion, onion grass, nalgoo, *yerrakwerr, yalk* (*Cyperus bulbosus*)
2. bean tree flower, *inernt, atywerety* (*Erythrina vespertilio*) • = akalapantherrty
3. crest of Major Mitchell's cockatoo, *angkwen*

akepenh *n.*
1. something that is given to another person to 'square them up'; something given reciprocally or in return
2. promised wife (?) ◆ Artwek anthem, arelhelarl alhilek-penh, *promise*-arl anek-penh akepenh anem. Akwekarl ikwerenh anek, renh anem anthem — 'akepenh'. (St) *After the wife has been promised to the man, she is given to him. She was his [promised wife] when she was little, and then she is given to him — that's 'akepenh'.* ◆ Mwey-mweyek akepenh antheyaw. (T) *The promised wife is given [by the mother] to her son-in-law.*
3. (doing something) back to someone; doing an action reciprocally
SEE ALSO alhelenty, rlwerrker, urlerrker

akepenh anthem
give reciprocally (anthem *'give'*)

akepenhek-akepenh (E) *adv.*
giving reciprocally; giving something to each other ◆ Akepenhek-akepenh anthetyek ker *or* mern. (St) *Giving each other meat or food.*

akeperleyn (E) *n.*
bald (lit. 'plain head') (English 'plain')
SEE ALSO kapert aketh-aketh, akalyer-alyer, kapert aketh, aka

akepitelh (E), **akepityelh** (E), **akepityenh** (E), **akepityely** (E) *n.*
fat from kangaroo's kneecap and leg ◆ Aherr-kenh arlkwem akepityely. (St) *The fat from the kangaroo's kneecap is edible.*
SEE ALSO ulyelatanenh, anter tyelh, apertaynp, iylpernk, itelh

akepweley (E) bald SEE UNDER **akapweley**

aker-aker-ilem *vt.*
ask for things all the time; talk all the time ◆ Akwet aker-aker ilemel angkerl-angkerl-iletyal — *don't* akwet aker-aker-ilerl-anerl. (N) *Don't keep asking for things and talking all the time — don't ask all the time.*
SEE ALSO arnterr angkem, arlelty angkem, arrkwertep-irrem, tyety angkem

aker-aker-ilerrem (W) *vi.*
argue over something, fight over something ◆ Angwely atherr aker-aker ilerrem ker ngkwerneng. (M) *The two dogs are fighting over the bone.* ◆ Rrwey atherr marleng aker-aker-ilerreperrem. (M) *Two men are arguing over a woman.*
SEE ALSO nhwerrem

-akerl+ *v.ending*
doing an action down or along something; do an action from one end to the other; right along, down. Preceded by *+ety* ending. ◆ Apwert-angkwerr anarnpety-**akerl**em. (St) *Going down the hill.* ◆ Tyerrty alhekarlan ampinety-**akerl**em. Aley ran alpekey, ampinem, *right up find*-em-ilety-alhemel. (Sa) *Following the tracks where the people went. Following the tracks right along where they went, right up till you find them.* ◆ Anyent arrpantey atywekel-iwerrem, ingkatyel-iwerrem, anyent arrpantey anem alhemel. Anyent arrwekel alhem, ingwer ra ingkernel irrkaty ingka ikwerenhel akin. Ingkatyel-werrety-**akerl**em. (Sa) *Stepping in someone else's footsteps to make it look as if only one person is going along. One person goes in front, and the other goes along behind. Stepping in the same foot tracks.*

akerlak (E) *n.*
the back of the neck (where the neck joins the shoulders); upper back ◆ Artep akerlakarl ayeng arntem. (St) *The back of my neck is aching.*

akerlkem *vi.*
1. sparkle or shine, glisten ◆ Ngkwarl yerrekeyerr akerlkeperlkem, arlter-irrem. Ngkwarl aperelty apek akerlkem. (St) *The sweet stuff called* yerrekeyerr *sparkles, goes white. The white substance, made by the lerp-scale insect from the river red gum tree, shines.* ◆ Ntewal arrkernk-areny akerlewarranem. (M) *The flowers from the bloodwood tree shine.*
SEE ALSO **mperlkem**
2. have feathers or eaglehawk down put on the head (initiate's mother-in-law during ceremony). The brothers of the initiate (young fella) put feathers on the head of the initiate's mother-in-law. ◆ Mwerikw akerlkem artwek. Marl ikwer anthem anem akerlkenty-penhel, kwey akwekan ikwer anthem awenk. Akerlkekarl mwerekikw. (T) *The mother-in-law has feathers put on her head for her son-in-law. Later the girl [her daughter] is given to the man. The young teenage girl is given to him.*
= **akerlkelh-ilem**
3. cover self with ashes (in mourning or sorry business) ◆ Arnmenyel apek marl yanh akerlkem. Tyerrty anengk apetyem kel arrwekel akerlkem ra. (T) *That woman is covering herself with ashes. Lots of people are coming so she covers herself first.*

akerlkelh-ilem *vt.*
put feathers or eaglehawk down on the head of the initiate's mother-in-law during ceremony ◆ Antethel renh akerlkelh-ilem marl renh. Akerlkelh-ilenty-penh marl anem ikwer anthem (T) *The woman has the feathers put on her head. Then later her daughter is given to her [the woman's] son-in-law.*

akerlkemerlkwerr (E), **akerlkwelmelkerr** (E) a type of plant SEE UNDER **akwerlkerrmwerlkerr**

akerlpangkwarl (T), **akerlpankwel** (W,T) bush coconut, bloodwood apple SEE UNDER **arrkipangkwarl**

akerlperr (W,T) *n.*

1. dogwood (*Acacia sericophylla*). Tree to 6 m high, with long grey-green leaves, pale yellow flowers and long twisted pods.
2. the edible seeds of the dogwood. Also referred to as *mern akerlperr.* ◆ Mern akerlperr. Anngang renh. Akem akem kik-wemel arlkwem alakenh. (N) *The dogwood seeds are edible, the seeds. They are picked and then peeled and then eaten, like that.* ◆ Rwel item. Akemel walyel-ayel, item, alkakem, mern arlkwem, kik-werl-anemel mern arlkwerl-anem, ntyerrp renh. Rwel itemel arlkwem. (N) *They are cooked in the fire. The seeds are picked along with the branch, and then the seeds are eaten, after peeling the shell off. The seed is called 'ntyerrp'. They are cooked in the fire and then eaten.*
= **awenth**
SEE ALSO **ntyerrm**

akern, akertn (E) *n.*
1. high, on top ◆ Atwayntenhem akern-antep kel tharew ilenhem anem, kwenelak. (Sa) *Climbing up to the top then facing downwards again.* ◆ Arna akernek ayeng antyetyek, arlewatyerr tha akernek atwetyek. (St) *I am going to climb to the top of the tree so that I can kill a goanna.* ◆ *Not* akern *jump*-irretyeh ahelh-warl ngkwern ultakelh-kety. (N) *Don't jump high or you'll [fall] to the ground and break your leg.*
SEE ALSO **irrwerl**
2. on the surface, just near the surface ◆ Ayenparl akernengan. Ayenp nhenh apetyem amwelteng arlka. Kenh alhwarl kweneng *run*-irrerl-anem, ingkewarn-athek, iltyewarn-athek, alakenh kapert-warn-athek. (T) *Skin is on the surface. For example, there is skin all the way along the arm. Whereas blood runs on the inside, towards the feet, the hands and to the head.* ◆ Inkwareny kwaty-rlwer anwern akern war inyem. (M) *In the rain-time we dig up honeyants just near the surface.*
3. shallow

SEE ALSO aketh

akerneng-ampeny, akern-ampeny, akertn-ampeny (E) *n.*
on top, high up

akern-antep, akertn-antep (E) *adv.*
1. going upwards; moving upwards ◆ Kwer map akern-antep antyem apwert-warn. Kwer map kwenelak anarnpem. (T) *The children climb up the rocks. Then they go down again.*
2. facing or pointing upwards ◆ Kwer yanh akern-antep intem. (T) *That child is lying facing upwards.*
SEE ALSO kwenelak

akernelak = akern-antep

akern-antep intem
lie on back
= impalkert intem
SEE ALSO ulperr intem, arlkarlkar intem

aherrk akern
midday (aherrk *'sun'*) ◆ Aherrk akernel apety-alpek. (St) *[They] came back at midday.*

akern-irrem *vi.*
get up, move upwards

akern-ilem *vt.*
raise or lift something up ◆ Yerramparl akern-ilep-ilem perrpantywerlel. (St) *The black-faced woodswallow is what makes the honeyants come up [closer to the surface of the ground].*
◆ Ilewerr. Kwatyek-athen arem ilewerrelarl akern-ilem. (St) *The mirage. You see where the mirage raises it [the earth] up and you mistake it for water.*

akerrk *n.*
western bower bird (*Chlamydera guttata*)
◆ Akerrkel arwengkel inerl-apem mern ararnt. (N) *The bower bird goes along stealing native tomatoes.*
= ahern-areny

akerrng (E) *n.*
young shoots of native tobacco plant (*Nicotiana* spp.) ◆ Lyetant lyapek akerrng-rnem. Kwatyel atherrk alyapelh-ilem. (Sa) *The young shoots of the native tobacco have just grown. The rain has made the green shoots grow up.*
= ngerrng, antyanp2, rrngwaly, ngkwerlp akwerrk

akert1 (T,E) *n.*
1. the end or edge of something; the point of something; outskirts of town ◆ Antyam iwemel, wal akert anem interl-anem. (St) *Throwing out the swag and lying down on the end of it.* ◆ Ankwa ayeng intetyek akertel ayeng intetyek. Mpepel apek arrpenh-arey intey, ayengan akertelarl interleng. (T) *I'm going to sleep on the edge. The others can sleep in the middle while I sleep on the edge.*
SEE ALSO iter, kanty1
2. short, abbreviated ◆ Angkety akert war thang ilem. (T) *I am just telling a short story.*
3. part of something

-akert2 *n.ending*
1. with something, having (something); holding or carrying something; equipped with something; having a particular part or physical feature ◆ Angkwey anetyam aherr akwerrk-**akert**. Kel yatherr alherrek atherrk arlkwetyeh menheng. (M) *A long time ago there lived a kangaroo with her baby. They used to go together to eat grass.* ◆ Tyap-**akert**arl arlperr, artekerrel intem. Arreyn-**akert** ra tyap 'arlperrenhayt'. (St) *The whitewood tree has grubs that live in the roots. The name of the grub is* 'arlperrenhayt'. ◆ Mantarr apek altywer-altywer; altywer-**akert** anem ra anem, iwem anem renh. (St) *Clothes might be full of holes; when they get holes in them then you throw them away.*
2. having a feeling or emotion; having a particular state of mind or physical state
3. having something wrong with a particular part of the body ◆ Arlenty-**akert** ayeng arrernelhey, arlentyarl arlkwem. (T) *I'm going to sit myself down, because I've got a sore hip.*
4. using something to do an action; with ◆ Arelhel atwek arn**akert**el angwely yenh. (M) *A woman hit the dog with a stick.* ◆ Artwel anenem ker aherr irntang arlter-**akert**el. (T) *The man guts the kangaroo with the stone knife.* ◆ Kwer marlel arlkeny-wem twererr way-**akert**el. (T) *The girl is making designs on the music sticks with a wire.*
5. with someone, accompanied by someone ◆ Aleraty-rnem-**akert** ayeng alhek. Atyenh-akwerrk. (Sa) *I went with my nieces and nephews. My family.*
6. Following a word that identifies a person, refers to their husband or wife.
7. Shows the thing that a story, conversation or meeting is about.
SEE ALSO -arleng2

irrtyart-akert (E) *n.*
1. baby boy
2. a respectful word a father uses to refer to his son (irrtyart *'spear'*) ◆ Irrtyart-akert apetyay. (St) *Come here little boy.*
SEE ALSO atnem-akert

atnem-akert (E) *n.*
baby girl (atnem *'digging stick'*)
SEE ALSO irrtyart-akert

artep-akert *n.*
having backache (artep *'back'*) ◆ Artep-akert intem, arteparl arekar-irrerl-anem. (N) *Lying down with a backache, a back that is hurting.*

akert-arraty *n.*
in a straight line or path; one after another in a straight line (arraty *'straight', 'correct'*)
akert-arraty-irrem *vi.*
go along one after another; go along in a straight line ◆ Pwelek kwaty-warl akert-arraty-irrintyem, kwaty antywetyek. (St) *The cattle are coming this way, in a straight line, to drink water.*
akertarreng-irrem (E) *vi.* = **akert-arraty-irrem** = arraty-irrem

akertang (T,E) *adv.*
half, partially ◆ Akertang antywetyek, arnang-iletyek. Akertang atyeng antyway, arlkwetyek apek. (St) *Drinking half of it (before someone else drinks). Drink or eat some of it before I do.* ◆ Akertang arlkwa, atyeng anthetyenheng. (T) *Eat half of it and then give me some.*
SEE ALSO artang-ilem

akertemarl (W,T), **akartemarl** (W) *n.*
pillow, headrest; something used to rest the head on (aka *'head'*; temarl, rtemarl *'back of head', 'pillow'*)
= rtwenk
SEE ALSO temarl, aka

akerter *n.*
1. someone who is not allowed to talk (especially because of bereavement) ◆ Marl yanh kwenh *sorry* anem akerter. *Don't* apawenherl kwenh. (T) *That woman is not talking because she is in mourning. Don't ask her [anything].* ◆ Angketyakenh, akerter. Arrularl anetyam akerter. *Not* arert — awemarl kel — angketyakenh akerter. *Son* ikwerenh apek *lose*-em-iletyam, akerter ra anetyam. Anewikw apek *lose*-em-iletyam, akerter ra anetyam, iltyirretyam war. Kel ra mern anthetyam kel renh angkakert iletyam. (St) Akerter *is not talking. In the olden days people were not allowed to speak. They were not deaf — they could hear all right — but they didn't talk. Maybe they lost their son, and then they didn't speak. If they lost their husband or wife, then they didn't speak and just used handsigns. Then [somebody] gave them some ceremonial food and then they were allowed to speak again.*
SEE ALSO kertemwengk
2. unable to speak (because of physical impediment), mute • SEE ALSO apap, aleny apekap, angka apekap

akertn (E) high, on top SEE UNDER **akern**

akerurrurr (E), **akerurrerurr** (E), **akerurew** (E) *n.*
yellow stage of the witchetty grub, *anyematy* (*Xyleutes bipartii*), before it goes black
SEE ALSO irrarl

aketh *n.*
1. outside, in the open ◆ Arratemel alhay, aketh-warn! *Go out into the open!* ◆ Aketh-warl alhay! Aketh-warl alherl-wa kwenh amparey! (St) *Go outside! All you kids go outside!*
2. a clear or open space ◆ Ahelh akethel anetyek. (St) *Sitting on the clear ground.*
3. clear (water) ◆ Kwaty aketh-penh. *Clear water.*
4. daylight, break (of day), with the sun out
5. bald, hairless • = kapert aketh
6. bare ◆ Ingka aketh alhem, alakenh untarl anem artek ingka aketh. (St) *Going about bare-footed, like you do with bare feet.*
7. out in the open, not restricted ◆ Awely aketh-akert, awely aketh war anwa alyelherl-anem — *not* kwen intem, itya. Aketh-akert anwa ananem, arreny-akert, awely-akert. (N) *We are singing our* awely *ceremony out in the open — we are not keeping it secret. We are still keeping our ceremony and song that goes with it.*
aketh-aketh (T,E) *n.*
1. clear (sky)
2. early in the day; daybreak, when it is just getting light ◆ Ingwa aketh-aketh anem irrintyem, ingwan alpem anem. (St) *It starts to get a bit light and then the night is over.*
aketh-irrem *vi.*
1. clear up (rain)
2. become daybreak, get light (sky) ◆ Akethamarl irrentyem perempeth arlkwerremel anwern rwang item mern item tey item mernam arlkwerrem. (N) *As it gets light we light the fire, boil tea and cook, and eat breakfast.* ◆ Aherrk aketh anem irrentyem. Tyerrelhenty aketh anem irrentyem, ingwelarl anek penh. (St) *Then the sun comes up. It comes out and then it gets daylight, after the night.*
3. come out into the open ◆ Aherrk aketh-irrek, matayelarl artek-penh. (St) *The sun came out after it had been covered with clouds.*
4. come out into the open (after ceremonial business)
aketh-aketh-irrem *vi.*
get light, break (day), come out (sun) ◆ Kweny *early* irrenty-alhemel aketh-aketh-irrentyem, aketh-aketh rntwarr-amparr. (M) *Very early in the morning it gets a bit light, gets light in the distance at first.*

SEE ALSO alker-irrem[1]

aketh-ilem *vt.*

1. clear something, clean up; uncover something; grade a road ◆ Apmer nhenh tha aketh-ilem, arnam-kety. (St) *I am clearing this place, because of all the grass.* ◆ Ra [*grader*] akethel alhem. Aketh-ilenhem ra. Ahern aketh-ilenhem. Arna apek. (St) *The grader goes along clearing the ground. It grades the ground and the vegetation.* ◆ Thenkarr-kety aketh-ilem kerwepel. (T) *Using a crowbar to clear the ground of prickles.*

SEE ALSO antarr-wem

2. make something light or clear

3. bring a young man out into the open (after ceremonial business)

kapert aketh

bald, bald headed (kapert[1] *'head'*)

akety-irrpenem (E)**, akety-urrpenem** (E) put a curse on someone (so that they get very sick or die), cause someone to have 'bad luck'

SEE UNDER **akwety-irrpenem**

akew (W,T), **akiw** (E) *n.*

bush camp, men's business camp, ceremonial camp (for young men) ◆ Akiw-warl alpek artwa mapant. *Only all the men have gone back to the bush camp.*

= yelk

SEE ALSO apwelh, anmanty

akeweny (W,T), **akuny** (T,E) *n.*

An expression of sympathy; 'Poor bugger', 'Poor thing', 'Dear thing'. This word can also be used on its own. ◆ Akeweny tyerrty yanh arerrirra, mantarr akeng-akeng-akertarl apetyekek, akeng-akeng-akert. Akewenyek mantarr antheyaw, mantarr *new one* apek akewenyek anthey mantarr ra irrpetyek. Kel kwer anthem antem, kel ra irrpem antem. (T) *Look at that poor thing has come along with raggedy clothes. Give the poor thing some new clothes to put on. Then you give them some and then they put them on.* ◆ Mern antheyaw akewenyek angayelarl anem-arlek. (T) *Give some food to the poor thing who is hungry.* ◆ Marl yanhan apetyem akeweny lthanam, antywekarl-penh. (T) *That poor woman coming there is just skin and bone from drinking grog.*

SEE ALSO -amperl, -angwel-angwel, -angwen-angwen, -apenh, -awern, inaty, inaty-amperl

akeweny-amperl (W,T), **akuny-amperl** (T,E) *n.*

= **akeweny** ◆ Akuny-amperl angayakw wantetyang alhetyel ampa akely. (Sa) *That poor little kid is hungry and nobody has fed him/her.*

akeweny-apenh (W,T) *n.* = **akeweny**

-akey *prn.ending*

In Anmatyerr society there are two patrimoieties. In one are Pwerrerl/Pwerl, Kemarr, Ngal, and Mpetyan people and in the other are Penangk, Pengart, Ngwarray and Peltharr/Petyarr. The ending *-akey* goes on some dual and plural pronouns to form words which refer to patrimoiety divisions. The most commonly used of these are *alak-akey* 'they (people in the opposite patrimoiety as me or us)' and *ilernak-akey* 'we (people in the same patrimoiety as each other)'. Others forms that occur are *inakerr-akey, ilak-akey, ilern-ingkerr-akey, anwern-akey, anwernakerr-akey, anakerr-akey* and *mpwelak-akey*. Not all Anmatyerr speakers agree about these forms. Although more work is needed to establish the precise way these words are used, it seems that even though a word such as *alak-akey* is based on the pronoun *alak* 'they two' it can refer to 'they (more than two)'. In a similar way *mpwelak-akey* is based on *mpwelak* 'you two', but can refer to both 'you (singular)' or 'you (plural)'.

SEE ALSO -apakwey

-akey 'Is that so?' SEE UNDER **akwey**

akey-irrem (E) *vi.* [RESPECT LANGUAGE]

cry ◆ Yanhentyal akey-irrem. Yanhentyak akey-irrerliwerretyel. (Sa) *Those people over there [who I am in a respect relationship to] are crying.* ◆ Mernekarl akey-irrerliwerretyel aweyapelek-uthek apek. Kwetyakw-rnem yanhentyak atyewey-rnem akey-irrem arntwalyek apek. (Sa) *They are all crying out for food. For goodness sake — the little [sons-in-law] over there are crying out for water.*

SEE ALSO arnem

akeyarr (E) *n.*

dried tobacco (native tobacco plant)

◆ Akeyarrant yanh tha arerl-alpek, arleny-irrekarl. Kwatyelant irrkaty aken lyapelh-ileynemel. (Sa) *I went there and all I saw was dried tobacco. When it rains it will make it grow back the way it was.*

akeyarr-irrem (E) *vi.*

go dry (native tobacco plant)

akeynt (E) flower of wild onion, *yerrakwerr, yalk* SEE UNDER **akenty**

akikart (E) sulky SEE UNDER **kekart**

akin as well, also, and SEE UNDER **aken**

akinp (E) newly ripened fruit of bush plum, native currant, *ahakey* SEE UNDER **akenp**

Akityarr (T,E) *n.*

1. Kityarr language. An Arandic dialect spoken in the Plenty River area.

2. Kityarr person or people
SEE ALSO Akarr, Karrwerlereny

akiw (E) bush camp, ceremonial camp (for young men) SEE UNDER **akew**

akiwarr (T,E) sulky, bad-tempered SEE UNDER **kewarr**

akngakem (E) pick out, sort things out SEE UNDER **angakem**

akngarnem (E) originate or come from (a place) SEE UNDER **anganem**

akngart (W,T) native pine SEE UNDER **anngart**

akngelhem (E) move self or part of self SEE UNDER **angelhem**

akngem (E) carry someone or something SEE UNDER **angem**

akngerr (E) big, large (in size) SEE UNDER **angerr**[1]

akngerrakw (E) east SEE UNDER **angerrakw**

akngetyem (E) bring something, get something SEE UNDER **angetyem**

akngey (E) father SEE UNDER **angey**

akngirnem (E) take or bring something back SEE UNDER **angernem**[2]

akngwelern (E) east SEE UNDER **ngwelernety**

akngwelerneyt (E) east SEE UNDER **ngwelernety**

akngwely (E) dog SEE UNDER **angwely**

akngwerrel-penh (E) east SEE UNDER **angwerrel-penh**

akngwert (E) large, dark-coloured bush potato tuber (?) SEE UNDER **angwert**

akngwethek (E) type of frog SEE UNDER **angwethek**

akngweyep-akngwey (E) not taking notice, preoccupied SEE UNDER **angweyep-angwey**

akuny (T,E) an expression of sympathy; 'Poor thing' SEE UNDER **akeweny**

akutn (E) ignorant SEE UNDER **akwen**

akwa, **akwang** (W,T) *n.*
1. arm, forearm ◆ Nhenh akwa pwerlep akwa inteynem, amak-warl-athek. *Here the upper arm goes along towards the elbow.*
2. the bones of the arm
3. the front leg or foreleg of some animals
SEE ALSO amwelt

akwang anety (W,T) *n.*
1. left-hand, left arm (anety *'bad', 'no good'*)
2. left-handed
= **akwang alyeng**
SEE ALSO anety, akwang arraty

akwang alyeng (W,T), **akwa alyeng** (T,E)
= **akwang anety**

akwang arraty (W,T), **akwarraty** *n.*
1. right-hand, right arm (arraty *'straight', 'correct'*)
2. right-handed
SEE ALSO akwang anety, arraty

akwengkwern (E) *n.*
wrist (ngkwern *'bone'*)
= amwelt anngang, anaynenh, iltya ngkwern

akwelayntenh (E) *n.*
armband (lit. 'that which lies on the arm')
= akwelty

akwerrem (W,T) *vi.*
wave or signal to someone ◆ Akwerrerl-anem akwerrem akwerrem antangkem, 'Apetyang kwenh!' (N) *Waving and waving and calling someone over, 'Come here!'*
= iltyerrem

akwangeny-ayerr (E) *n.* [RESPECT LANGUAGE]
left-handed (note Western Arrernte *kwangeny* 'left, left-handed') ◆ Ngwarrengkwan akwangeny-ayerr. (Sa) *Your husband is left-handed [said by a woman to her daughter].*
SEE ALSO alyeng

akwanth-ilem (E) *vt.*
take aim at something; get ready to strike; threaten to strike ◆ Arlewatyerr apek atwetyek akwanth-ilem, arwerlel apek akwanth-ilem atnemel apek. Kel atyengety urntemarl ra. (St) *Taking aim and getting ready to hit the goanna with a stick or a digging stick. Then it runs away from me.*
SEE ALSO angkarr arem

akwanth-akwanth *adv.*
taking aim; getting ready or threatening to strike
CAN SOUND A BIT LIKE kwanth-kwanth *'bleed (a lot)'*

akwek *n.*
1. small, little ◆ Kwer nhenh amangkety-kwenh itya — akwek-antey anep-anem. (M) *This child has not grown — it is still small.* ◆ Arelhel alparrel rrkwerl-anem kwer akwek. (M) *His wife is holding the little baby in the coolamon.*
2. a bit of something, a small amount of something ◆ Mern akwek anthay, ampeny. (M) *Give me a little bit of food, the leftovers.*
3. child, young (animal) ◆ Amangkep-angkem lyet-atheh Pwerrerl akwek. (T) *Little Pwerrerl is growing up these days.* ◆ 'Kwelyalp kwelyalp kwelyalp.' Alakenh angkerl-anem irrety akwek an angerr *too*, amwek kwer-artwey. (M) *'Kwelyalp kwelyalp kwelyalp.' That's the sound that baby wedge-tailed eagles, and bigger ones too, make for their mother.* ◆ Arley, akwek map angernerl-apem pap kwerenhel, aperrk arlkwerl-apem lpway-angkwerr, rltar-rltarel arlka wanterl-apem, aperelty arlka, atyankern arlka. (N) *The father emu takes the little ones [emu chicks] along, eating charcoal along the creek, and feeding them on rattlepod fruits,*

mistletoe fruits and white substance made by the lerp-scale insect from the river red gums.
= akely
ampa akwek (E)
baby, small child (ampa '*child*')
= kwer akwek, ampa akely
kwer akwek (W,T) = **ampa akwek** (kwer '*child*')
akwek-akwek *n.*
small, smallish
= akely-akely
akwek-antyey (W), **akwek-antywey** (W,T) *n.*
really small, really little ◆ Arathap akwek-antywey. (T) *A really little baby.* ◆ Arnapar akwek-antyey anngampelh-ilem. (N) *[It] makes the little dingo pups open their eyes.*
= akwek-amperl, akely-amperl
akwek-amperl (T,E) *n.* = **akwek-antyey**
akwek-awaty (T,E) *n.*
a small amount; something smaller; a little bit ◆ Akngerr-awaty ineyaw, arna apek akngerr-awaty yanh inay, akwek-awaty apek inetyek. (St) *Get that bigger branch over there, or maybe a smaller one.*
= akely-awaty
akwek war
(do something) a little bit ◆ Akwek war rntwarr-irray! (M) *Move just a little bit!*
akwek-ilem *vt.*
make something smaller ◆ Ker urleth atwem akwek-ilemel, akwek anem arlkwetyenheng. (T) *Cutting the meat up into bits and making it smaller, and then eating the smaller bits.*

akwel *part.*
supposedly, so they say, reportedly, apparently. Used when the speaker is not sure if what they are saying is true or accurate, and when they are not talking about their own personal experience or knowledge, but rather reporting what they have been told by others. *Akwel* can show that the speaker is a bit sceptical about the truth of what is being said. ◆ Yerr mapel akwel nyetempwer kwetyerl-apem. (N) *Supposedly ants collect the* nyetempwer *seeds.* ◆ Akangkwerrenty itya, kwer kwerl-areny map. Maneyekant angkerl-anem, maney akwel ngkwelty anthetyeh. (N) *The school kids don't pay attention. Apparently they just ask for money, ask to be given coins.* ◆Irrkwentyel ilpernem-antey, ilpernek apek irrkwentyel ayenh, tharl akwel inek. (St) *The police blamed me, supposedly because I took it.* ◆ Ampengamp amarrkel angerl-wetyel ampel-rnem, *nappy*-akert. Amparrpantey. *Bottle* angetyel ampa akwel *baby* akwel kwerenh, ampengamp. (Sa) *All the children carry the dolls, with nappies, around on their hips. They are pretend babies. They carry bottles and supposedly they are their babies.*

akwelty *n.*
men's armband (decoration) ◆ Akwelty arrernelhem mwerr angerr aretyenheng. (T) *[Men] put armbands on themselves so that they look really good.*
= akwel-ayntenh, akel-intenh
SEE ALSO akwa

akweltyayt (E) *n.*
grub found on mistletoe (*Amyema* spp.) ◆ Akweltyayt arlkwem tyap. Rwel renh item, war ampem aperrkel, wal irrnyiwelhem anem. (St) *The grub from the mistletoe is edible. It's cooked in the fire, just cooked on the coals, and then its skin peels off.*
SEE ALSO arraltyaltyen, atyankern, amar, ngartangkern, peketyalkwarr, ngkwerrm

akwely-akwely (E) *n.*
samphire, brown-head glasswort (*Halosarcia indica*)

akwem *vt.* [BABY TALK]
eat ◆ Meny akway. (St) *Eat [this] food.*
SEE ALSO arlkwem

akwemp-akwemp (W,T) *n.*
froth on floodwater, froth on lips ◆ Kwaty rewel-ayeng akwemp-akwemp anenhem. (M) *The froth is on top of the floodwater as it goes along.*
SEE ALSO rlkwerrp

akwemper (T) *n.*
young fruit of bush banana, silky pear (*Marsdenia australis*)
= amwernt, mwemper, twemper[1], ngwemper
SEE ALSO parl, alwerremp
CAN SOUND A BIT LIKE kwemper '*sharp pointy hill*'

akwen, **akwetn** (E), **akutn** (E) *n.*
ignorant, not knowing about something, unknowing, unaware, inexperienced with something ◆ Ayeng akwen, *no* tha awek ayey. (T) *I don't know, I didn't hear the story.* ◆ Ayeng akutn iterlaretyakenh. (St) *I am ignorant — I don't know.* ◆ Ayengan akwen, arety-kwenh. War than awek antem kwenh. (M) *I don't know about it, I didn't see it. I just heard about it.* ◆ Ayeng akwen iterlaretyakenh — apal war anep-anem. Anngelant thang arerl-anem, akwenel, akwen-akwen ayeng. (N) *I don't know about it — I'm just sitting down unaware. I'm just watching what's going on, but I don't know much about it.*
= akwerrp
SEE ALSO kalty
CAN SOUND A BIT LIKE kwen '*inside*'; kwern '*bad*'

akwengerr-werl-alhem *vt.*
roll or pack up possessions such as swags and clothes ◆ Rnwanenty ngkwengenh nta akwengerr-werl-alhem ngkwengenh rnwanenty map apek, nheng *fold*-em-ilemel *swag roll*-em *up* ilemel. '*Eh* yanhel akwengerram werl-alhem ingkerr kwenh.' Alakenh ilem. (M) *You pack up all your things, fold your clothes up and roll up your swag. 'Hey, that person is packing everything up.' That's what they say.* ◆ Alhwengkelty akwengerr-werl-alhem, alethel apek alhetyek. (St) *Packing up all the bits and pieces to go on a trip.*

akwenp *adv.*
not taking notice of anyone; without shame, not paying attention, not knowing about something, ignoring someone, minding one's own business, keeping on doing something regardless of anything, being unconcerned about others ◆ Angwely arrpenhek anem angwely atherr anem nhwerrem *properly* anthwerr ratherr nhwerrem, kel pwath *one*-el renh-atherr atwem atwem kenh akwenpel atherr nhwerreperrerleng. (T) *The two dogs are really fighting each other hard, and then the boss of the dogs belts them and they keep on fighting each other regardless, ignoring him.* ◆ Akwenp ayeng alhey nyerr-irretyal. (St) *I'll just go anyway, without getting shamed.* ◆ Akwenp ayeng angketyek tyerrty yanhek, nyerr-irretyal. (St) *I won't get shamed, I'll just talk to that person over there regardless.* ◆ Akwenp ayeng anem, menty tha awerl-anemel akwenp ayeng anerl-anem. (St) *I am sitting and not taking much notice, just sitting and half listening to what is being said.* ◆ Ampa nhenh *naked* anwekantherr akwenpel alhem — arlkant-akert. (St) *This kid is just wandering around naked and not taking any notice of us — just their naked body.*
SEE ALSO alhewer, alanty, atanty

irlpa akwenp
1. not hearing or paying attention (irlpa *'ear'*)
2. ear wax, blocked ear

akwenp-akwenp (T) *adv.*
not taking notice of anyone etc.

akwenpety-akwenp *adv.*
not taking notice of anyone etc. ◆ Iyterrkel arlkwep-arlkwem yanhel anthetyakenhel, akwenpety akwenpel. (St) *That person is greedily eating and not giving anything to others, without caring a bit.* ◆ Arnkaty anerl-anem akwenpety-akwenp. (T) *Sitting down fearlessly and not taking any notice of anyone.*
SEE ALSO angweyep-angwey, anngwa

akwenpeny *adv.*
not thinking about anything or anybody; sitting down quietly, lost in one's own thoughts; ignoring or not paying attention to things ◆ Kwerenharrp ra *think*-irrerl-anem akwenpeny anerl-anem. (M) *She is sitting there just thinking about private things and not taking notice of anyone else.* ◆ Alarterl-anem arelh lywel. Kwentyel alarterl-anem, mern arlkwerl-anemel ananem arelh ingkerrek, akwenpeny alarterl-anem, alhetyakenh. (N) *The women are sitting in the shade. All of them are sitting eating food, sitting in one place without thinking of anything else and not going anywhere.*
SEE ALSO ankwaty

akwenpeny-ilem *vt.*
distract someone, keep someone occupied, put someone at ease

Akwenyemp (W) *n.*
the name of a place in the Yuelamu (Mt Allan) area, south of Crown Hill

akwepenh (T,E) *n.*
blood taken from the arm and used by men as a medicine (akwa *'arm'*; -penh *'from'*) ◆ Akwepenhan anthetyam arntetyek, mwerr-iletyam. (St) *Blood from the arm was given to sick people, to make them better.*
SEE ALSO amarr

Akweranty (T,E) *n.*
1. name of the Hanson River in the area round Ti Tree
2. name of a place near Elkedra
SEE ALSO Alarnenty

akwerl *n.*
long (of hair) ◆ Akwerl akngerr arelh yanh, alta arlpenty alta akngerr. (St) *That woman has really long hair, lots of long hair.*

kapert akwerl (W,T)
long hair, having long hair (kapert[1] *'head'*) ◆ Kapert akwerl angerr yanh. (T) *That person has long hair.*

akwerl-akwerl (W,T) *n.*
desert fringed lily (*Thysanotus exiliflorus*). A plant about 25 cm high, with long shiny green leaves, purple lily-like flowers, and swollen roots. ◆ Akwerl-akwerl nyerrirretyart nhenh tyampet-warlam arrernewarretyart kwaty-warl wal kapert lpwel-iletyart, lpwelem lpwelem lpwelem wal alakenham kapertam apernelhem akwerl-akwerl nhenhey. Alta angerr irretyenheng mwerr angerr. Angkwey anwa apernelhetyam angerr-irremel akwerl-akwerl nhenh renh. (N) *The desert fringed lily was dug up and put in a billycan with water and then used to rub on the head. It makes the hair*

grow nice and long. In the olden days we used to rub it on our hair to make our hair grow long.
= arrwelth-arrwelth

akwerlkerrmwerlkerr (E), **akerlkwelmelkerr** (E), **akerlkemerlkwerr** (E) *n.*
a type of plant. Has white flower and grows in swampy areas.

akwerlp *n.*
1. riverbank, creekbank ◆ Akwerlp arrpenh-warl alhetyek. (St) *Going to the other riverbank.*
SEE ALSO twemper², arnkarr, twerr
2. slope (of hill, etc.), top of hill ◆ Irntang akwerlp-angkwerr alhem akin, arerlapetyeh ngkerlpeh. (M) *Going along the slope of the hill looking for wild tobacco.*
SEE ALSO urterrp

Akwerlp (W,T) *n.*
the name of a place north of Yuendumu (note Warlpiri *Wakurlpa, Wakurlpu*). *Irrety* 'eaglehawk' Dreaming. See map p. viii.

akwernem *vt.*
1. put something inside something else, fit something into something else ◆ Yakwetheh akwernetyeh. (M) *[I am] going to put it in the bag.* ◆ Irrtyart akwernek amirr-warn ker aherr atanthetyek. *The spear was fitted into the woomera to spear a kangaroo.*
2. swallow something ◆ Akwernem anwern artapaly akwernem anwern — *not* anwern iwem athew, akwernem athew. *Not* arlkwem athew. Akwernem war. (N) *We swallow the bush plums — we don't spit them out, we just swallow them. We don't 'eat' them [i.e. chew them].*
3. plant something ◆ Akwernemek-amparr renh ahern-warl, ahernel renh artem, lyapem anem ra *wet*-penh. (St) *You plant them in the ground, cover them with earth, and then they grow after rain.*
4. bury something
akwern-akwern-wem (E) *n.*
eat fast, gobble food up ◆ Ankey-kety tha akwern-akwern-wem. (St) *I'm eating fast in case someone asks me for some.*
ipertek akwernem
bury something; put something in a hole (ipert *'hole'*)

akwerr¹ (E) *n.*
on the edge or the side of something
= itep, kanty¹, iter, arrethaker
SEE ALSO akert¹
CAN SOUND A BIT LIKE kwerr *'girl'*
akwerreny (E) *n.*
smallest or youngest child ◆ Ampa aletharr akwerreny. (Sa) *The youngest child.*
SEE ALSO ingkerneny, ingkerney
iltya akwerreny (E)
little finger (iltya *'finger', 'hand'*)
ingka akwerreny (E)
little toe (ingka *'foot'*)

akwerr² *n.*
desert bandicoot (*Perameles eremiana* (?))
◆ *Like* pek-pek arteh. Angwely mapel *can't* akwerr renh *catch*-em-ilerl, *tricky-tricky* alakenh war alhetyart alakenh war alhetyart. *But* arnang intertel yang *live*-irretyart meran kwerenh — ahern ipert angernekarl an arnamem ya arrernetyart. Tyey apel kwerenh angerr *like* nheng aherr nheng tyey anem-arteh, nheng lywang arrpenh-warl. Yenh *catch*-em-ilem ankwang angerr-warl — intyerrenty angerr aken ra intetyart. (M) *They are a bit similar to pigs. Dogs can't catch the bandicoot because they are very tricky in the way they move about. They make their nests at the bottom of trees — they dig a hole and line it with grass. Their paths that go from shade to shade are wide, like those of kangaroos. They can be caught when they are fast asleep — they snore a lot.*
SEE ALSO rtway, lkwameny

akwerremp *n.*
a lot of game, a large 'kill' ◆ Akwerremp-akert ina apety-alpem. Map-akert. (T) *They are coming back with a large 'kill'. With lots [of meat].*
akwerremp-ilem *vt.*
kill lots of something (game), wipe out (animals) ◆ Ker aherr akwerremp-ilem, arwenth anthwerr atwem, an ker arlewatyerr atwem akwerremp-ilem. Kel akwerremp anem ingkerrek angetyetyenh *bag*-el apek. (T) *Killing lots of kangaroos, a real lot, and killing lots of goannas. Then they come back with the kill, maybe in a bag.*
SEE ALSO iltatwem, althinem, akwetyerretyerr-ilem, arlperreh atwem

akwerrerteth (E) *n.*
native truffle, desert truffle (*Choiromyces aboriginum* (?)). These are white and juicy when young, and yellow and wrinkled when older. Found in spinifex country. Also referred to as *mern akwerrerteth*.
= irrkwenng, pwerlantar
SEE ALSO kwerrart

akwerrk¹ *n.*
1. young person or animal, child ◆ Angkwey anetyam aherr akwerrk-akert. Kel yatherr alherrek atherrk arlkwetyeh menheng. (M) *A long time ago there lived a mother kangaroo with her baby. They used to go together to eat grass.*

◆ Angeyel arntarnt-arem ankerr akwerrk map. (M) *The father looks after the baby emus.*
2. newly grown (of plants), seedlings, young tuber of the bush potato, young bush banana ◆ Anaty akwerrk. (T) *Young bush potato.* ◆ Anaty akwerrk anthal. Mern anthal-penh anaty akwerrk anem renh ilem. (St) *A young bush potato tuber. After the bush potato is small [called* anthal*] it is then referred to as* akwerrk.
3. newly made native bees' hive ◆ Alhang akwerrk. (M) *Newly made native bees' hive.*
4. the beginning of seasons

akwerrk iltyelhek (W)
become lots of (children), have lots of children (?) (iltyelhek (?)) ◆ Kwer atyengenh akwerrk iltyelhek nhel-antey. (M) *I had lots of kids in this place here.*

tyerrty akwerrk (W,T)
young person (tyerrty *'person'*)

arelh akwerrk (W,T)
young woman (arelh[1] *'woman'*)

utern akwerrk (T,E)
the beginning of summer (utern *'sun', 'summer'*) ◆ Utern akwerrk anintyem. (T) *The hot weather is coming.*
= utern urla, aherrk akwerrk

aherrk akwerrk
beginning of summer (aherrk *'sun'*)
= utern akwerrk

alhwerrp akwerrk
the beginning of winter (alhwerrp *'winter'*)
= alhwerrp urla

anyenty akwerrk (T,E), **atnyenty akwerrk** (T,E)
new moon (anyenty *'moon'*) ◆ Atnyenty akwerrk anem, kel atnyenty atarlanenty anem anem. (St) *There is a new moon, and then there is a full moon.*
= atay akwerrk, anyenty akwerrk

atay akwerrk (W,T)
new moon (atay *'moon'*) ◆ Atay akwerrk kel apety-alpekew. (M) *The new moon is already back.*

kwaty akwerrk (E)
rain cloud (kwaty *'water', 'rain'*) ◆ Kwaty akwerrk arrernenhelhety-alhem urntetyek *ready*. (Sa) *The rain clouds are covering [the sky] and it's about to rain.*

akwerrk-penh (E) *n.*
promised wife ◆ Akwerrk-penh anthekarl — mikwel anthek rtwalty ikwerenhek. (St) *The woman was promised from when she was a baby — her mother gave her to her [the mother's] son-in-law.*

-akwerrk[2] *prn.ending*
family, relation. This ending goes on all dative and possessive pronouns (?) (see Appendix 2). ◆ Atyeng-**akwerrk**an arwenth, nhenh anem. (St) *I have lots of family here.* ◆ Ikwer-**akwerrk**. (St) *His family.* ◆ Ngkweng-**akwerrk**-artey? (St) *Where's your family?* ◆ Arrekantherr-**akwerrk**-warl arrantherr alperleway. (St) *You can all go back to your family.*

akwerrk-akwerrk (W,T) *n.*
unable to hear, silly (note Warlpiri *kurrka-kurrka* 'senseless, unconscious') ◆ Arertarl apant-irrem — akwerrk-akwerrk, ampa arert. (T) *That mad child is getting lost — that silly child.*
SEE ALSO arert

akwerrng (T,E), **akakwerrng** (E) *n.*
1. brain ◆ Kapertan arlkwemarl. Ker tyelkant weth-lkwer arlkwem akwerrng apek. *The head is eaten. Just the fleshy parts, and maybe the brain.* ◆ Ahenty akeng-irrek, iterlaretyakenh apek ayeng, ahentyarl akeng-irrekarl, nhenh akwerrng ingkerr. (St) *My throat is no good, and I'm not sure about things, my throat is feeling no good and my brains, everything.*
2. mind ◆ Akwerrng ayengan theley-anetyang, *idea*-akert. (Sa) *My mind is not silly, I've still got ideas.*
= kampely[1]

akwerrp (E) *n.*
1. ignorant, not knowing about something; unknowing; unaware ◆ Pweltak pang inngekarelh, arreynelhetyek mpwarem *scratch*-em ilelhem. Ayengan akwerrp pweltak ikwer *clean*. Arrulan angerrirretyart pweltak. Petherr ra. (Sa) *The* pweltak *louse is found on people, and they make people scratch themselves. I haven't had much experience with lice, I'm clean. There used to be a lot of* pweltak *lice a long time ago. They are also called* petherr.
2. an 'abstainer', particularly said of non-drinkers and non-smokers
= akwen

akwerterrp (T,E) *n.*
a short-cut
= ntwertety

akwerterrp alhem (T,E)
take a short-cut ◆ Akwerterrparl ayengan alhem, arleng-arlentyarl alhem-kety. (St) *I am taking a short-cut so that I don't have to go too far.*
= ntwertety alhem

akwerteyteng (E) *n.*
rainbow snake, water-snake monster. A large mythological snake that lives in waterholes.
= kwelay, kwelernarr

akwet *adv.*
(something) keeps going for a while or stays the same way for a while; still, always, forever. This word can also occur in sentences without verbs. ◆ Ayengan rlkert akwetam. (M) *I am still sick.*
◆ Itya, mpwank akwet. *No* ina arratek. (M) *They are still away. They haven't turned up.*
◆ Kel arnkwert-arnkwert kweny arraty akwet alhem kwenh. (Sa) *Don't go crooked — keep going in a straight line.* ◆ Anmatyerr anyent akwet anem. Kartety arlka Alyawarr arlka anem *self* akin. Kenh anwern Anmatyerr akwet. (M) *There is still one Anmatyerr. Kaytetye and Alyawarr are separate. But we are all still Anmatyerr.*
= aleth
itya akwet (W,T)
nothing yet, (there's still) nothing (itya *'no', 'nothing'*) ◆ Thang arltwarem, itya akwet. (T) *I see nothing, nothing yet.*
= arrangkw akwet
anyent akwet
something is the same as something else, the same thing (anyent *'one'*) ◆ Anemarraty marlew-alyey-alyey, anyent akwet. Arnang war. Atherrk. (N) *The* anemarraty *plant is the same as the* marlew-alyey-alyey. *Just a plant. A grass.* ◆ Kwer akwek rant-atherr, inngerr anyent akwet. (T) *These two kids are similar to each other, their faces are alike.*
akwetant *adv.*
for good, forever ◆ Unta apekarl alhek akwetant. (St) *It seems like you went for good.*
= twem, intem[2]
akwet-antey *adv.*
still (doing an action), keep on (doing an action), (do something) for good ◆ Anwernan akwet-antey ananem, alhetyakenh. (T) *We are still living here, we haven't gone.*
akwet-ilem (T,E) *vt.*
hit someone or something without stopping ◆ Arnterrarl atwem akwet-ilemel. Atwem, akwet anem renh ilem. (St) *Hitting someone really hard without stopping.*
akwet-irrem (T) *vi.*
stay in one place
SEE ALSO antarl-irrem, amarn-irrem
akweteth *adv.*
1. all the time, always, often, frequently. This word can also occur in sentences without verbs. ◆ Nhenhan akwetetharl angkep-angkem. 'Rntert anay!' (T) *This person is always talking. 'Sit down and be quiet!'* ◆ Akweteth ngang alhalhem. (M) *You're always travelling around.*
2. permanent, usual ◆ Nga akenh akweteth. Nga ampwelpampw-irrek yanh-angkwerr. (St) *Whereas you are permanent. You've got older and older in that area.* ◆ Kwaty yanh ywerretyakenh, akwetetharl interl-anem. (St) *That water never runs out — it's permanent.*
◆ *Drink* akweteth. (T) *[That person] is always drinking.*
• SEE ALSO amelerr, amperreny, irrkaty, marany
mer akweteth
1. staying in one place; not moving anywhere or travelling a long way from home; staying at home all the time (mer *'country', 'place'*)
◆ Ntwam mer akweteth ananem. (M) *You always stay at home.* ◆ Unta mer akweteth anerl-anem, arleng alhetyakenh. (St) *You are always staying at home, and not going far away.*
2. a type of spirit [SOME SPEAKERS]. These spirits live in particular places in the country and do not travel far. ◆ Mer akwetethel anety-ilem tyerrty. (M) *The spirits make people sick.*
• = melarlp, irrernt-areny, atham-areny

akwet-akwet *n.*

spotted nightjar (*Eurostopodus argus*) ◆ Akwet-akwetel kwart arrernem arnamek. (St) *Spotted nightjars lay their eggs in the grass.*
= angkertakwertak, arrthwarrthw
akwet-akwet-irrem *vi.*
(spotted nightjar) sing or make an *akwet-akwet* sound ◆ Tyerrtyel awem akwet-akwet-irremel wal arengkek akwel ra angkem, arengk akwerrkek. Uternek anem ra angkem. Utern akwerrkarl anem, utern urla. (St) *When people hear the spotted nightjar singing, well they know that supposedly the nightjars are singing to the puppies. They are singing to the summer, to the beginning of summer.*

akwetelh (E) *n.*
1. lukarrara (a type of grass), desert sedge (*Fimbristylis oxystachya*). A grass about 30 cm high.
2. the edible seeds of this grass
SEE ALSO taty-taty[1], arlepenh, kwarrety, nyetempwer, yakerr

Akwethakw (T,E) *n.*
the name of a place on Stirling Station

akwetn (E) ignorant SEE UNDER **akwen**

akwety-irrpenem (T,E), **akety-urrpenem** (E), **akety-irrpenem** (E) *vt.*
1. put a curse on someone (so that they get very sick or die); cause someone to have 'bad

luck' ◆ Akwety-irrpenem. Tyerrty yanh apek ilem, akwety-irrpenem ilwetyek rarrp. (St) *Putting a curse on someone. Putting a curse on that person and then they die themselves.* ◆ Arengkel akety-urrpenetyel, mer angernemel. (Sa) *The dog is bringing bad luck for people by digging up the ground.*

2. bring 'bad luck' on yourself by breaking certain laws or social conventions. Fighting with one's *atyew, thampartey* or *ntyangkwelkng* is an example of this. ◆ Mwer-mwer kwerenh atwarekerr, akety-irrpenekerr. (Sa) *Don't go up to your son-in-law's [things] in case you bring bad luck upon yourself.* ◆ Altwerl-athek intetyalay, akwety-irrpenekerr unta. (St) *Don't sleep with your head to the west, or you'll have bad luck.* ◆ Ntyangkwelkng-penh atwerretyakenharl anem akwety-irrpenekerr. (St) *Women who are related to each other as* ntyangkwelkng *aren't supposed to fight each other or it will bring bad luck.*

SEE ALSO mawenng, mamety, akwetyerretyerr, artarrernem, artimperr-wem, pew-ilem, rltwatyel atwem, urltatyel atwem

akwetyakw (E) *n.* [RESPECT LANGUAGE]

small ◆ Akwetyakw-ayerr yanhentyak angwely-ayerr yanhentyak irrepetheyaw. (Sa) *Go and get that little dog over there [from someone I am in a respect relationship to].*

SEE ALSO akely, akwek

akwetyerr (T,E) *n.* [RESPECT LANGUAGE]

a woman's young son-in-law ◆ Mey-mey akely akwetyerr ilem. (St) *A young son-in-law is called* akwetyerr. ◆ 'Akwetyerr akwek yanh atyengety alhey.' Mwerikwarl ilem. (T) *'My little son-in-law is going over there to avoid me.' That's what his mother-in-law says.* ◆ Ahanerlentyarretyel akwetyerr yanh. Akwetyerr, ahanenh nhakw-angkwerr. Ampa akely mwerikw akelyan ilem 'akwetyerr'. (Sa) *That young son-in-law of mine is going over there. A young baby son-in-law is called* 'akwetyerr'.

SEE ALSO ngkwernerrp, ngwenyarr, mwer

akwetyerretyerr (T,E) *n.*

1. certain behaviour that will bring bad luck, for example, sleeping with one's head to the west ◆ Akwetyerretyerr kapert altwerl-athek intetyal akwety-irrpenekerr. (St) *Don't sleep with your head facing to the west or it will bring bad luck.*

2. something a hunter says when beating a goanna against the ground to kill it. If the goanna bites its tongue then the hunter believes that she or he will be successful and find another goanna (i.e. bad luck will come to other goannas). ◆ Arelhel arlewatyerr kanty-they inemel, ntewem anem renh, 'Akwetyerretyerr akwetyerretyerr'. (St) *A woman grabs the goanna by the tail and then beats it against the ground, saying,* 'Akwetyerretyerr akwetyerretyerr'.

SEE ALSO akwety-irrpenem

atna akwetyerretyerr (E)

'You're cursed' (atna *'arse'*) ◆ *Might say* atyeng apek, 'Atna akwetyerretyerr'. Kwety-irrpenemel. *Might anytime pass away* irrem, ilwekerr apek. (St) *Someone might say to me, 'You're cursed'. They're cursing me. And then I might pass away anytime.*

SEE ALSO akwety-irrpenem, animampel

akwetyerretyerr-ilem, akwetyerretyerr atwem *vt.*

get lots of game (meat) (lit. 'bring bad luck on the animal') ◆ Arlewatyerr nta apek atwerl-apem anyenteng amparr nta *start*-irrem atwerl-apem atwerl-apem, wal tyerrty alenhel arnarem ilem ilek, '*Eh* nta akwetyerretyerram nhenh ingkerr ilek kwenh'. Anengk-iperram, anengk nheng angetyem tyerrtyel, perrap anengk anthwerr apek. Wal 'akwetyerretyerrarl ilem' ilem. (M) *You might go along and kill a goanna — one at first, and then you go along killing and killing them. Well a person watches you coming along and says, 'Hey, you've killed the whole lot.' When a person gets lots of meat, a real lot, then that's called* 'akwetyerretyerr-ilem'.

SEE ALSO arlperreh atwem, akwerremp-ilem, iltatwem

akwey, akey *part.*

1. Used in making questions or in indicating uncertainty. Shows that you are not sure about the truth of what you are saying; 'Is that so?' ◆ John-el akey renh atwek? *Was it John that hit him?* ◆ Werlaty-angketyarrarl ahekwenayt, werlaty-akert. Werlaty akely-rnem, werlaty-artek ilenngem **akwey** ikwerenh. (Sa) *The* ahekwenayt *grub has lots of 'breasts'. Little breasts. They are like — what-d'ye-call-it — like breasts.* ◆ Atherr-areng ayeng alhem. Atherr-areng **akwey** unta alhemay? (St) *I am going for two days. Are you going for two days?* ◆ Iwenham ngan iterreperremay? Alhety akey? Nthenh-warn ntwa alhetyenh? (N) *What do you reckon? Are you going? Where to?*

2. Provides emphasis to what is being said (?). ◆ Tyerrty yanh akey arelh then yanh apetyemarl arrantherr alhengkem ara kwenh, yanharl apetyepetyem atherr kwenh, yatenh atherr kwenh. (N) *Look at those people there, that woman and the other one that are coming there — you'll all recognise them, those two that are coming.* ◆ Ayeng arengk anyent-arteh anerlanem. Tyenem akey ayeng irrek. (M) *I was sitting down on my own like a dog. Then my family came back and I felt better.*

angwenh-akwey (W,T) *n.*
Something said when the speaker is not sure of the name of something or has temporarily forgotten it; 'What's-his-name', 'What-d'ye-call-it', 'Thingummybob', 'Thingummyjig' (angwenh *'who?', 'what?'*). ◆ Ker ikarl. Ker ikarl kwaty iterelarl aylpem. Angwenh-**akwey**-apeny, atneth-akert-apeny. (Sa) *Yabbies. They burrow into the sides of creeks. They are like what-d'ye-call 'em — scorpions.*
SEE ALSO thakey[1], tyakey

ala *prn.*
they (two). This pronoun is used in the subject part of the sentence (i.e. representing the 'doers' of the verb action) when the two people are both in the same patrimoiety and the same generation moiety, such as a person together with their sister or brother, or their father's father. See Appendix 1.
SEE ALSO alengkerr, alak, alanth
CAN SOUND A BIT LIKE ila *'we two'*; arla[1] *'opening to ant's nest'*; arla[2] *'without'*; arla[3] *'stem'*

alenh *prn.*
them (the two of them). This pronoun is used in the object part of the sentence (i.e. representing those the verb action is done to).

aleh (W,T), **alek** (E) *prn.*
for them, to them (the two of them)

alehenh (W,T), **alekenh** (E) *prn.*
their, theirs (belonging to the two of them)

alaltyerr *n.*
his or her son-in-law; his or her mother-in-law (closely related ones whose mothers come from the same country) ◆ Kwey alaltyerrap nhenh itnarey altyerrak anyent. (Sa) *This girl is their 'sibling' because they all call one country* altyerr.
SEE ALSO -altyerr

alak *prn.*
they (two). This pronoun is used in the subject part of the sentence (i.e. representing the 'doers' of the verb action) when the two people belong to the same patrimoiety and different generation moiety, such as a person together with their father or father's sister. See Appendix 1. ◆ Alak alherrek awenh-nheng atherr. (T) *Those two went, auntie and nephew or niece.* ◆ Alak alherrek. Mwer-nheng atherram. (P) *Those two went. Son-in-law and mother-in-law.*
SEE ALSO ala, alengkerr, alanth
CAN SOUND A BIT LIKE ilak *'we two'*

alenhak *prn.*
them (the two of them). This pronoun is used in the object part of the sentence (i.e. representing those the verb action is done to).

alehak (W,T), **alekak** (E) *prn.*
for them, to them (the two of them)

alehakenh (W,T), **alekakenh** (E) *prn.*
their, theirs (belonging to the two of them)
SEE ALSO alak-akey

alak-altyerr *n.*
his or her son-in-law; his or her mother-in-law (closely related ones whose mothers come from the same country)
SEE ALSO -altyerr

alak-akey *n.*
they (people in the opposite patrimoiety) ◆ Alak-akey-kenh ayerrer-thayt. Angerrakw-thaytarl alak-akey ingwerek-areyenh, aylernak-akeyenh altwerl-thaytarl. (St) *The north side belongs to people from the other moiety, and the east side belongs to another group of people from the opposite moiety to us. The western side belongs to people from the same moiety as us.*
SEE ALSO -akey, ilernak-akey, inakerr-akey
CAN SOUND A BIT LIKE ilak-akey *'we (belonging to the same patrimoiety as each other)'*

alakaper collared sparrowhawk (?) SEE UNDER alekaper

alakatey (W,T) *n.*
someone who sits down in one place doing nothing, someone who never moves

alakenh *n.*
like that, in this way; thus, 'this is how' (while showing someone) ◆ Kwer-penh artwang alakenh angkek. (M) *After that the man spoke like that.* ◆ Mern akerlperr, anngang renh. Akem akem kek-wemel arlkwem alakenh. *The dogwood seeds are edible, the seeds. They are picked and then peeled and then eaten, like that.*
= alanh

alakenh-irrem *vi.*
do something like that; do something in that particular way; go like that (while showing someone) ◆ Ampel arlkan aretyart, arrkenel-arleng alakenh-irreperrem. Arrpenhem alyerl-anem, arrpenhem rntertarl anerl-anem, arrpenhem rlpwerrng atwerl-anem. (St) *Children used to watch for fun as well, watch people going in for the* althart *ceremony, enjoying themselves doing it like that. Some*

would sing, others would sit quietly, and others would beat the rhythm on their laps. ◆ Aympelh atherr ap alakenh-irrerl-anem, ker arerl-anemel, kaperl apek, alyalkarr apek. Renh anem inenhem alakaperel. (St) *The sparrowhawk's two wings go like that, while it is looking out for the lizards, the* kaperl *or the* alyalkarr. *Then it gets them.*
= alanh-irrem

alakenh-ilem *vt.*
do something to something in a particular way ◆ Lweren arlka nheng arrwekeleny mapelam atwetyart. Nheng alpety alakenh-iletyeh, nheng kwer-tayem. (N) *That's why the olden-time people used to kill them. So that they could use the bilby tails like this [swing them around] during initiation ceremony time.*
= alanh-ilem

alakenh-anyem (E)
in that particular way; that's how (something is done)
= alanh-anyem

alakenty *n.*
this/that many; this/that much (while showing how many)

alakenty-ingar *n.*
this/that, that many times ◆ 'Nthakenty-ingar nga alhemay?' *You might* ilem, *'Four days* apek. Alakenty-inger ayeng alhem atherr-atherr.' (St) *'How many days are you going for?' And you might say, 'Maybe for four days. That's how many days I am going for.'* ◆ Arengk iltya akert. Alakenty iltya — iltya atherr ingka atherr. *A dog has front paws. That many front paws — two front paws and two back paws.*
SEE ALSO nthakenty

alal-wem *vt.*
1. make camp, find a place to camp, find a good spot to camp ◆ Mer alal-wem, rtakw arterl-alhemel, mer apek atnhwerrelh-ilem, ura anem arrernerl-alhem, ura amperl-anetyek. (Sa) *Making camp, building a windbreak, and clearing the ground, and heaping up the wood to make a fire.* ◆ Inwekel mer mwerr arem alal-wetyek-alhem tha, rtakw arlka mpwarem. (St) *If I'm going out camping for a night I find a good place to make camp and I make a windbreak as well.*
SEE ALSO anhwerrem
2. shift camp
3. leave things in a place (like a dinner camp) while going out hunting ◆ Mer apek aremel mwerr apek, alal-wem anem kwerenh rnwanenty. (St) *If she sees a good spot, then she leaves her things there.* • SEE ALSO rwanenty-wem

alalherrk (W,T), **arlalherrk** (W,T) *n.*
Coonavittra wattle (*Acacia jennerae*). A shrub about 4 m high, with bluish green leaves and yellow flowers. ◆ Alalherrk rnpwang nhenh-lkwer arlkwetyart, larlart rnpwang. Awantyetyart larlarl awantyem-artek. Lwerenart. Intertelarl anem. (N) *We used to eat the sweet resin from the Coonavittra wattle, like a lolly. We used to suck on it just like you suck lollies. It's found in the base of the tree.* ◆ Alalherrk anwern rwel arlkwetyart atyerretyart, mern rwel itemel anwa arlkwetyart kik-wemel, kwer mapel arrken. (N) *As kids we used to enjoy cooking the Coonavittra wattle seed pods in the fire, and then peeling them open and eating the seeds.*

alamarr lame, crippled SEE UNDER **arlamarr**

alanenty (E) *n.* [RESPECT LANGUAGE]
everything, everybody ◆ Ingkerr-antey alanenty-ayerr mwarlenth ahanenherl-wek. (Sa) *All of them, all of the married couples went [including my daughter and her husband].*
SEE ALSO kewerrewerr, ingkerr[1], angerr[1]
CAN SOUND A BIT LIKE arlanenty *'big river'*

alangkw *n.*
1. bush banana, silky pear (*Marsdenia australis*). A winding vine which climbs other trees and shrubs. It has creamy flowers and oblong edible fruits.
2. the edible fruit of the bush banana plant ◆ Rlkwantyek-amparr ra anem, kel alangkw akwerrk anem ra anem, amwernt akwek ra anem, kel alangkw akngerr anem ra irrem. Altyey-akert alangkw an rlkwanty-akert. Kel alangkw anem anem akernel. (T) *At first there are the bush banana flowers, then the baby bush banana fruits, and then they grow into big bush banana fruits. The bush banana plant has [leaves called]* altyey, *and [flowers called]* rlkwanty. *Then the fruit is found up high.*
= parl, alkwarrer
SEE ALSO ilkwanty, altyey, amwernt
CAN SOUND A BIT LIKE arlangkw *'bloodwood'*

alangkw-alangkw (E), **arlangkw-arlangkw** (E) *n.*
matted hair or knotted hair, unwashed hair
= akalangkw-alangkw, werrp-werrp, irrkety-irrkety, akaylep-aylep
SEE ALSO kelh-kelh

alanh *n.*
like that, in this way; this is how (while showing someone); that's what (is done) ◆ Ayteyaty — 'Angkwer-nheng-arey alheyaw anwingkerr'. Ayeng angkem. Ra angkem alanh akin, angka anyent. *My younger sister — I might*

say to her, 'Let's go, all of us sisters together'. And she might talk like that as well, say the same thing. ◆ 'Mey-mey ngkwenh aray!' Alanh ilem ampa akelyek. (Sa) *'Look at your* mey-mey*!' That's how you talk to a small child.*
= alakenh, lweren

alanh-irrem *vi.*
do something like that; do something in that particular way; go like that (while showing someone)
= alakenh-irrem

alanh-ilem *vt.*
do something to something in a particular way ◆ Iylwem kwenh alyatywereng, ingka atherr alanh-ilem. Alyatywereng ahelhek-arlek iylwem. (Sa) *The woollybutt grass seed is husked, and your feet go like that, husking the woollybutt grass seed on the ground.*
= alakenh-ilem

alanh-anyem (E) *n.*
in that particular way; that's how (something is done) ◆ Alanh-anyem akwel rarey arrken-irretyart — wirarl awetyart kwa atha. (Sa) *Supposedly that's how they used to play — I just heard about it.*
= alakenh-anyem

alanth *prn.*
they (two). This pronoun is used in the subject part of the sentence (i.e. representing the 'doers' of the verb action) when the two people belong to different patrimoieties, for example a person together with their husband or wife, their sister-in-law or their cross-cousin. See Appendix 1. ◆ Alanth alherrek menheng atherr. (T) *Those (two) went, mother and child.*
SEE ALSO ala, alengkerr, alak
CAN SOUND A BIT LIKE ilanth *'we two'*

alenhanth *prn.*
them (the two of them). This pronoun is used in the object part of the sentence (i.e. representing those the verb action is done to).

alehanth (W,T), **alekanth** (E) *prn.*
for them, to them (the two of them)

alehanthenh (W,T), **alekanthenh** (E) *prn.*
their, theirs (belonging to the two of them)

alanth-apakwey *n.*
they (who are in the opposite patrimoiety and generation moiety to the speaker)
◆ Akengentyeny-rnem 'alanth-apakwey'. (Sa) *'Alanth-apakwey' are wrong for me [i.e. I shouldn't marry people like them].*
= nywerrp
SEE ALSO -apakwey, -apatherr, arrantherr-apakwey, ilernanth-apakwey, anwernanth-apakwey, anantherr-apakwey

alanth-apatherr (T) *n.* = **alanth-apakwey** (E)

alanty *adv.*
(doing something) without taking notice of others; anyway, despite, heedless, regardless
= atanty
SEE ALSO akwenp
CAN SOUND A BIT LIKE arlanty *'type of lizard'*

alanty-alanty *adv.*
doing something while others are waiting
= atanty-atanty

alanty anem
wait for someone while they are doing something; wait with someone, keep someone company ◆ Unta atyeng alanty anep-anem. (St) *You are waiting for me.*
◆ Ntwarrp alhay, ayeng alanty anerl-anemeng. (M) *You go yourself, I'm going to wait here.*
= atanty anem

alanty alhem
go without caring about others or without waiting for others, leave someone behind, go away from someone, move or walk away from something not liked, go regardless of what people say (alhem *'go'*) ◆ Alanty alhem ayeng yanh-kety. Ra angkerl-aneyamel alanty alhem, ayakenty angerr-kety, alanty alhem ayeng. (St) *I am going regardless of what that person says. She can talk and try and stop me but I am going anyway.* ◆ Ngkwengety ayeng alanty alhem. (T) *I'm going to walk away from you.* ◆ Tyel angkep-angkem, alanty alhetyek anem ayeng — *I don't want* awerl-anetyek akwet. (St) *That person is running [me] down so I'm going to go off — I don't want to keep listening to them.* ◆ Angketyakenh alanty alhem ayeng. (St) *I'm going away without saying anything.*
= atanty alhem

alanty anthem
give something to someone without taking notice of others (anthem *'give'*)
= atanty anthem

alanty arlkwem (E)
eat without sharing, eat while another is waiting, eat greedily (not caring about others) (arlkwem *'eat'*)
= atanty arlkwem

alanty angem
take something away from someone (without asking) (angem *'take'*) ◆ Warek-amparr tha alanty angey ngkwenh? (St) *Can I just take this thing of yours for a while?*
= atanty angem

alanty angkem (E)
1. say something in spite of what others say, talk to someone regardless of what others think (angkem *'talk', 'speak'*)
2. talk to someone on behalf of someone else, do the talking for someone else ◆ Ayeng apek alanty angketyek arrpenhek. Ahel apek ra irrekerr. (St) *I am going to talk to the other person [for her]. In case they get angry.*
= atanty angkem
alanty arem (E)
watch while someone else does something (arem *'look', 'see'*) ◆ Tha alanty arem menty — rarey angkep-angkemarl. (St) *I am just watching — that mob can talk.*
= atanty arem

alany (E) *n.*
fighting hook or pick
= walarnp

Alapanp (T) *n.*
place name, Anningie Station area. See map p. viii.

Alarnenty (T,E), **Alartnenty** (E) *n.*
part of the Hanson River (in the Ti Tree area)

alart *n.*
point or sharp piece on the end of a spear ◆ Irrtyart alart-akert akin an arrwemper alart-akert akin. (T) [Irrtyart] *spears have a point on the end, and so do shovel spears.* ◆ Arrerlp nhenh irrtyartek arlka arrernerl-anem, alartarl. (T) *The sharp thing that is put on the end of a spear is called* alart.
SEE ALSO aparr

Alart *n.*
Wallaby Bore (Stuart Bluff Range area)

alartem (W,T) *vi.*
sit together, sit (plural) (?); stay somewhere, be somewhere ◆ Kwatyelam anhem, kenh map kenh irrperl-irrperlem-ilem kwenem alartem. Irnmerr arlka thelelhem antyweng. (N) *It rains and everybody goes inside and sits down. The drops of water fall down from the shelter.* ◆ Arreny-akert ingkerr anem, arreny-akert ingkerr tyerrty map alartem. Peltharram arreny ayeng anem. (N) *All of them have skin names, all the Aboriginal people have skin names. My skin name is Peltharr.* ◆ Alarterl-anem arelh lywel. Kwentyel alarterl-anem, mern arlkwerl-anemel ananem arelh ingkerrek, akwenpeny alarterl-anem, alhetyakenh. (N) *The women are sitting in the shade. All of them are sitting eating food, sitting in one place without thinking of anything else and not going anywhere.* ◆ Tyerrty map alarterl-anem ahelhel. (N) *People are sitting on the ground.* ◆ Alarterl-atherr-anem. (M) *Lots of people sitting down.*
SEE ALSO anem[1]

Alartnenty (E) part of the Hanson River (in the Ti Tree area) SEE UNDER **Alarnenty**

alatyeyt (E) *n.*
soft spinifex (*Triodia pungens*). A grass that grows in hummocks 0.5–2 m high. It has a sticky resin covering/coating.

Alawenng (W) *n.*
rockhole near Centipede Dam, east of Mt Allan community

alay[1] *n.*
a large expanse of water; sea, sea water; flood ◆ Alakenh anem ilety-alpem arrpel, 'Kwaty alay kwenh alhep-alhem yanh'. (T) *Another comes back and tell the others something like this, 'There's a big flood running there'.*
SEE ALSO rew, urew, awarr, anyerr, ulamp

alay[2] *part.*
an exclamation used when warning someone; 'Look out!', 'Watch out!'
= pwertay

alekaper, alakaper *n.*
collared sparrowhawk (?) (*Accipiter cirrhocephalus* (?)) ◆ Thep alekaperel intelty arlkwem. (T) *The sparrowhawk eats grasshoppers.* ◆ Aympelh atherr ap alakenh irrerl-anem, ker arerl-anemel, kaperl apek, alyalkarr apek. Renh anem inenhem alakaperel. (St) *The sparrowhawk's two wings go like that [vibrate as stays still in the sky], looking out for the lizards, the* kaperl *or the* alyalkarr. *Then it gets them.*
SEE ALSO lyentyelyeng

Alekareng (T,E) *n.*
the name of a community approximately 170 km south-east of Tennant Creek. Was known as Warrabri. (from Kaytetye aleke *'dog'*; arenge *'pertaining to'*). Also spelt Ali Curung.

alekw (E) *n.*
mimosa bush (*Acacia farnesiana*). Shrub up to 5 m high with fern-like leaves which have a sharp spine at the base.
= irnker
SEE ALSO arlketyerr

alem *n.*
1. stomach area, belly, abdomen ◆ Alem anety antew-irrem. (M) *Vomiting because of an upset stomach.*
2. liver
3. edible liver of some animals. Also referred to as *ker alem*.
alem altywer (W,T)
feeling sad or sorry (altywer *'open'*) ◆ Kwer

atyengenheh wart ayeng alem altywer awelhem. (M) *I am feeling sad about my child.*
= anert altywer

alem iyterrk-iyterrk (T,E)
someone who has married the 'wrong' way (iyterrk-iyterrk *'someone who marries the wrong way'*) ◆ *Wrong way* anew akerrenty ap atna iyterrk-iyterrk. Alem iyterrk-iyterrk. (Sa) *Someone who marries the 'wrong' way is referred to as* atna iyterrk-iyterrk. Alem iyterrk-iyterrk.
= atna iyterrk-iyterrk, alem atherrk-atherrk, akengentyeny

alem atherrk-atherrk (T,E) = **alem iyterrk-iyterrk** (atherrk-atherrk *'someone who has married the "wrong" way'*)

alem-penh, **alem-pwenh** (E) *n.*
a woman's child or a person's sister's child; nephew, niece (-penh[1] *'from'*) (lit. 'from the stomach') ◆ Atyeng-warn alem-penh apetyem, akeweny. (T) *My nephew/niece is coming to me, poor thing.*
= anert-penh, rnwepenh
SEE ALSO ampaty-ampaty, arrarn-penh

alemeh (W,T), **alemek** (T,E) *n.*
for the taste; sweet; something eaten after the main meal (lit. 'for the stomach') ◆ Ngkwarl alemek arlkwetyek, arwengalker. (Sa) *Sweet things, such as sugarbag, are eaten for the taste.*
SEE ALSO ikwa, kwang, ikwemey

alem-alem (T,E) shiny, sparkling SEE UNDER **alenm-alenm**

alemerr (E) *n.*
water-holding frog (*Cyclorana platycephalus*) (?). Some speakers say that this is Alyawarr.
SEE ALSO alyeyamp, angwethek

alemey (E) father's father and the father's father's brothers and sisters (respect term) SEE UNDER **ilemey**

alemp (W,T), **alimp** (W,T) *n.*
skewer used for closing the belly cavity of certain animals before cooking them ◆ Artwel alimp arrernem ker aherrek. (T) *The man is putting the skewer in the kangaroo.*
= interlp, rltimp[2]

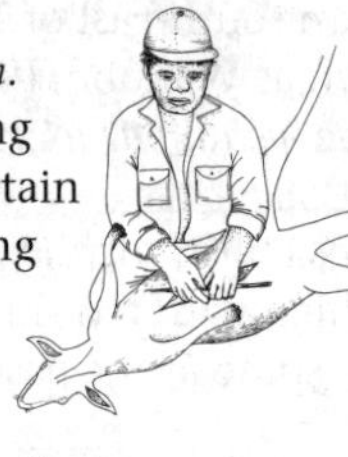

alengk-wem, **alengk-iwem** (E) *vt.*
hide something ◆ Man apek tha atyenh alengk-wem, atyeng ankeyel inekerrel. (St) *I might hide my money in case someone comes and asks me for it.*
CAN SOUND A BIT LIKE alhengk-awem *'understand'*

alengk-welhem, **alengk-iwelhem** (E) *vi.*
hide yourself ◆ Ayeng apek alengk-welhemer ngkweng-kety, warrk-kety apek. (St) *I might hide myself from you, or hide myself from work.* ◆ Alengk-welhem ayeng tyerrty yanh-kety iwenhek apek apay-unhekerr. (St) *I am going to hide from that person in case they ask me for something or other.* ◆ Kwer map alengk-welhem werrkel-ayel. (M) *The children are hiding in the scrub.*

alengk-alengk-welhem, **alengk-alengk-iwelhem** (E) *vi.*
play hide-and-seek ◆ Alengk-alengk-welhepelhem amparey arrkenel-arleng. (St) *The children are enjoying themselves playing hide-and-seek.*

alengkerr, **alingkerr** *prn.*
they (two). This pronoun is used in the subject part of the sentence (i.e. representing the 'doers' of the verb action) when the two people are both in the same patrimoiety and the same generation moiety, such as a person together with their sister or brother or their father's father. See Appendix 1. ◆ Alengkerr alhem, nyany-nheng apek. *They are going, maybe grandmothers and grandchildren together.*
= ala

alengkerrenh, **alingkerrenh** *prn.*
them (the two of them). This pronoun is used in the object part of the sentence (i.e. representing those the verb action is done to).

aleh-ingkerr (W,T), **alek-ingkerr** (E) *prn.*
for them, to them (the two of them)

aleh-ingkerrenh (T), **alek-ingkerrenh** (E), **alengkerr-henh** (W,T) *prn.*
theirs, their (belonging to the two of them)

alenh (W,T) *n.*
that, there (not close) ◆ Tyerrty alenh tha arep-arem merlpengel. (M) *Shading my eyes with my hand, I can see that person over there.* ◆ Apal nta arrernelhem, wal rlpwerrkem tyerrty alenh. (M) *If you sit yourself down without thinking or looking properly then you'll squash that person.* ◆ Kwaty alenh arrarntwer angerr apetyem. (M) *There is a big thunderstorm coming there.*
= alert[1], alertenh, nhakw
SEE ALSO nhetenh, yatenh, rntwarr, aley[2]

alenm-alenm, **alem-alem** (T,E), **alim-alim** (E), **aleynm-aleynm** (E), **alinm-alinm** (E) *n.*
shiny, sparkling ◆ Mwetekay yanh alenm-alenm apetyem kwenh. (M) *There's a shiny car coming along there.*
SEE ALSO amparrkey

alenm-alenm-irrem *vi.*
shine, sparkle ◆ Tyampet apek kelath apek alinm-alinm-irrerl-anem, amparrkerl-anem.

Tin or glass shines, sparkles.
SEE ALSO amparrkem
alenm anyem
shine, sparkle
SEE ALSO arlkerrk-wem

aleny *n.*
1. tongue ◆ Aleny arratem, mern arlkwetyew, alakenh arratem angayakw, ngayel. (N) *The tongue goes out to eat the food, the hungry person's tongue goes out to eat.*
2. Goes before other words that refer to ways of speaking.
3. flame • SEE ALSO anngenth, anngenenty, lherrm, lyenenty
CAN SOUND A BIT LIKE arleny *'dry'*
kwaty aleny
the front part of floodwater, head of the flood (kwaty *'water'*) ◆ Kwaty rew ilem 'aleny'. (T) *Floodwater is called* 'aleny'.
SEE ALSO kwaty urew
aleny kanty
1. tip of the tongue (kanty *'tip'*) ◆ Aleny kanty war arratem. (St) *Just the tip of the tongue comes out.*
2. speaking in a high tone of voice, speaking deceitfully (?) ◆ Aleny kanty wararl angkep-angkem. *Might don't like* apek atyeng, mwerr-arrpantey, ra *still* ilkelhetyakenh apek. *Just speaking a bit deceitfully. Maybe the person doesn't like me, and they pretend to say the right things, but they don't like me all the same.* (?)
aleny akngerr (E)
middle of the tongue (akngerr *'big'*)
aleny apekap
being unable to speak properly (apekap *'being unable to speak properly'*) ◆ Aleny apekap angkem, aleny ywarn angketyek. War apekap-irrek aleny. *Might* tywen-akert apek. (St) *Unable to speak properly, the tongue having difficulty in talking. Maybe there is a sore on the tongue.*
− angka apekap
SEE ALSO akerter
aleny iter
side of the tongue (iter *'side'*)
aleny-aleny-irrem (W,T) *vi.*
burn high, flare up (fire) ◆ Rwang aleny-aleny-irrem — aleny arratem rwang. Rwang angerr ampem. Aleny-aleny-wem. (N) *The fire flares up — the flames come out. A big fire burns. It flares up.*
aleny-aleny-wem (W) *vi.* = **aleny-aleny-irrem** (M)
alenyenp-wem (T,E), **alenyenp-iwem** (E) *vt.*
poke out tongue, flick tongue out
◆ Alenyenp-iwem — aleny arratem. 'Alenyenp-wetyelarl-kety yanh-ketyaw!' Urnemel alenyenp-iwetyel. (Sa) *Flicking the tongue out — the tongue comes out. 'Look out [for that thing] that's flicking its tongue out!' Snakes flick their tongues out.* ◆ Kwer mapel alenyenp-wem ngkwantyel. (T) *The children are cheekily poking out their tongues.*

alenyakenyak *n.* [RESPECT LANGUAGE]
axe ◆ Ilepan ilem mwerehekwenh, kerremel, 'alenyakenyak'. (M) *In respect language [you] call your son-in-law's axe* 'alenyakenyak'.
= nyerlp, iylpwer arternenh
SEE ALSO ilep¹

alep (T,E) *n.*
firestick. Also referred to as *ura alep*. ◆ Ura alep, alep-akert alhep-alherl. Kel nthilety-alhemel ura urrelty anem akety-alhemel. (T) *Going along with a firestick. Then collecting kindling wood and lighting the fire.*
= kep¹, rwang kep, rwang lyenenty, uralep
alep-ilem (T,E) *vt.*
light a fire with a firestick ◆ Mwantyel ina aperrk angetyart, arrernerl-alhetyart, panth-warn, mwar-warn apek, angetyart, aherr-kenh atna inety-alhemel nthilety-alhetyek. Alep-iletyam, angetyam alep-ilemel anyer. (St) *They used to carefully carry the coals, put them in a wooden dish to carry them, and go and get [dried] kangaroo shit to make the fire ignite. They lit the fires, using the supplejack wood.*
= kep-ilem
alep-irrem (T,E) *vi.*
catch alight (fire) ◆ Rwang nhenham kel alep-irrern. (T) *This fire has just caught alight.*
= altherrem, antant-irrem, lherrm-irrem

alepenh (E) desert Flinders grass SEE UNDER **arlepenh**

aleper-ankwerl-wem (E) *vt.* [RESPECT LANGUAGE]
go and get something
= ankwerl-wem

aleperenty (E) *n.*
a type of female spirit ◆ Aleperenty tham-areny ilem. Ankwa ayntenty-warl antarl ap ra arratem, utnengan arratem ankwa ayntenty-warl ilerl-anem. Kel *story* apek ilerl-anemel. Ilety-alhem. 'Nhakw alherl-wek, aretyek ayeng apetyekaw.' Alanharl angkemel, ingwel, ankwarl ayntetyerlek. Ankwepenh akem-irrentyem inngek-athen. (Sa) Aleperenty *is what the* tham-areny *spirits are called. They only come out when someone is asleep, and they come to the sleeping person to tell them things. They might come and tell a story. 'They went over there, and I've come to have a look.' That's how they talk, in the night, when people are sleeping. When the people wake up they think*

that is was a real person.
SEE ALSO athan-areny, melarlp, irrernt-areny, awerreng-iylpwer

alepey (E) *n.*
fat-tailed antechinus (*Phascogale macdonellensis*) (?)
SEE ALSO thakwer

aler, alerey (E) *n.kin*
1. child (a man's child); what a man calls his son or daughter
2. a person's brother's child; niece, nephew
3. particular relations with the same skin as your *aler*
4. a person's father's father's father and his brothers and sisters; great-grandfather, great-grandmother, great-uncle, great-aunt
= pap aywa
5. the hairs on a woman's chin which symbolise her nieces and nephews ◆ Aleraty ayeng tyerrelhem. (St) *I am pulling out the hairs [my* aler*] from my chin.* • SEE ALSO arrarn-penh, arrwert-penh

aler-aler *n.kin*
child (man speaking); what a man calls his son or daughter, a person's brother's child; niece, nephew etc. This may an affectionate or respectful way of talking to or about one's *aler.* ◆ Rernem ayenh awenh-awenh akem, than aler-alerarl akem renh. (Sa) *They call me* awenh-awenh *[auntie] and I call them* aler-aler *[niece, nephew].* ◆ Arrwertan lyapeman. Marl arrpenhemant arrwert-akert, aler-aler. *The beard grows. Some women have beards — called* aler-aler *[nephew or niece].*

aleraty *n.kin*
my/our *aler* ◆ Arrwertel netyel aleraty. Aleraty nhenh netyel. Impenarl ap nhenhey, arrwertel netyel. (Sa) *The hairs on your chin are your* aler. *Here is where your nephews and nieces are [pointing to chin]. The hairs on your chin are very important.*

alerengkw *n.kin*
your *aler*

alerikw (E), **alereyekw** (E) *n.kin*
his/her/their *aler*

alerekw (W,T) *n.*
1. your *aler*
2. his/her/their *aler*

aler-nheng *n.kin*
a group of two or more people who are related to each other as *awenh* and *aler* or as *angey* and *aler* (as aunties and nephews and nieces or as father and child etc.)

aler-intyerr *n.kin* = **aler-nheng** ◆ Aler-intyerr alhekarl, aywa kwer-arleng. (P) *All the daughters went, with the old man [their father].*

aler-nheng-arey *n.kin*
a group of more than two people who are related to each other as *awenh* and *aler* or as *angey* and *aler* (as aunties and nephews and nieces or as father and child etc.)

aler-nheng-atherr *n.kin*
a person together with one of their *aler*

aler-ankethenh *n.kin*
1. having a close *aler* still alive
2. someone who is always with their *aler*
SEE ALSO -ankethenh

aleraperap (E) *n.*
peregrine falcon (?) (*Falco peregrinus* (?))
SEE ALSO kaperl-kaperl

alerey (E) child (a man's child) SEE UNDER **aler**

alerl (E) *adv.*
1. for a while, in a while, soon; by and by; just a minute; (something) has not yet happened. This word can also occur on its own as a command. ◆ Antyanp ngkwerlp akely atherrk lyapem, aketyakenh-antey alerl. Antyanp *are the small green shoots of the native tobacco plant that haven't been picked yet.* ◆ Inngan ilem akapweley. Ampa apek ilem, ampa alerl lyapetyenh weth-lkwer alta lyapetyenh, 'Akapweleyay'. Akapweley arrpantey ilem ampa kelyan. (Sa) *You call a person bald. You might call a child whose hair is yet to grow, 'baldy'. You might just pretend and call a child 'baldy'.*
2. 'Wait on', 'Wait a minute', 'Wait a while' ◆ Alerl, tha mernt arlkwerl-alhey. *Wait on, I'll eat first before I go.* ◆ Alerl athek-irrerl-iwerretyang arternpeng anenherr-arey. Mern arlkwetyek athek-irrerlarr-anetyang — yanhan atyenharl. (Sa) *Wait, don't you all get excited and rush in — sit down quietly. Don't get over-excited about eating — that's my food.*
= urrek, rrwek

alerl-mernt (E) *part.*
'Wait on', 'Wait a minute', 'Wait a while', 'Hang on a moment'
= rrwek-mernt

alerl-antey (E) *adv.* = **urrek-antey, rrwek-antey**
= alerl-mernt

alernem[1] *vt.*
shine (sun); shine a light on something
◆ Aherrkel alernetyel. *The sun is shining.*
= alhenem
CAN SOUND A BIT LIKE lernem *'shake something out'*

alernenty *n.*
a light
= alhenenty

alernem[2] (T,E), **alertnem** (E) *vt.*
1. poke or push into something ◆ Lyekel ingka alernepernem. (T) *The prickle is poking into [my] foot.* ◆ Alertnem irrtyart kerel-arleng apek, ker aherrel-arleng, atanthekarl. Tyerretyakenh. (St) *The spear might be sticking out of the kangaroo that was speared. It hasn't been pulled out yet.*
2. rest something against something; prop something up on something else ◆ Maketek annga akwernem, thak yanhan alernem pwerlep-warl, kel atyerrem anem. (St) *You put the bullet in the gun, rest the stock against your shoulder and then shoot.*
CAN SOUND A BIT LIKE lernem *'shake something out'*
alernelhem (T,E), **alertnelhem** (E) *vi.*
lean on something for support; lean up against something; press down on something ◆ Alernelhemel ayeng ngkwengeng-arleng. (St) *I'm leaning on you.* ◆ Ayeng arwerlel alernelhem. (St) *I'm leaning against the tree.* ◆ Iltyel alernelhemel alhem. Iltyel arrernelhemel. *Going along, leaning on your hands.*
SEE ALSO ampekernem, rlpwerrkem, rrwethem, kerrk-welhem
CAN SOUND A BIT LIKE lernelhem *'fall down', 'scatter'*

alernkem (T) *vi.*
gather together, build up (clouds) ◆ Kwaty akwerrk alernkem, kwaty rntwetyek-anngernt. (T) *The clouds are building up and then it's going to rain.*

alert[1] (W) *n.*
there, that there (someone or something in sight but not close) ◆ Tyerrty alert-hety ntwa rakem. (M) *You are taking [things] off that person.*
alertenh (W,T) *n.* = alert[1]
◆ Tyerrty alertenh artwangel atwem. (M) *The man is hitting that person.* ◆ Tyerrty alertenh apetyem. (M) *That person is coming.*
= alertekwenh, alenh
SEE ALSO nhetenh
alertekwenh *n.* = alert[1]
◆ Alertekwenh rntwarram alhem. (T) *Something/somebody is going along in the distance there.*
= alertenh
SEE ALSO aley, nhetenh

alert[2] (E)
ankwa alert (E)
fast asleep (ankwa *'sleep'*) ◆ Ra ankwa alertarl intem kwenh — awelhetyakenh anem intyerrem. (St) *He is fast asleep — he can't hear a thing and he's snoring.* ◆ Ankwa alert intep-intem. (St) *[That person] is fast asleep.*
SEE ALSO ankwa[1], ankwa angerr, pelp

alerterrperterrp *n.*
grey shrike-thrush (?) (*Colluricincla harmonica* (?)) ◆ Alerterrperterrp arnang akerneng angkerl-apem. (N) *The shrike-thrush goes along singing from high in the trees.*

alertnem (E) poke or push into something SEE UNDER **alernem**[2]

aleth *adv.*
for a long time, for good, forever ◆ Aleth akwet ayeng alhem. (T) *I am going away for good.* ◆ Aleth ankwayntetyel, aylpmerretyel. (Sa) *[That person] is sleeping for a long time.*
= twem, intem[2]
SEE ALSO akwet
CAN SOUND A BIT LIKE arleth *'testicles'*
aleth alhem
go away, go for a trip, go away for some time (alhem *'go'*)
aleth-antey *adv.*
continuing to do something for a long time; doing something for good (permanently) ◆ Aleth-antey ayeng alhem — weth apety-alpetyakenh. (St) *I am going for good — I'm not coming back.* ◆ Aleth-anteyelarl ntwan arreylpepeylpem. Akwet-antey arlkwep-arlkwem arreylperl-anem aleth. (Sa) *You keep on chewing and chewing. You're always eating and chewing.*
SEE ALSO akwet-antey
aleth-irrem, alethek-irrem (T,E) *vi.*
go away for good; move to another place ◆ Aleth-irrem, alhetyek alhem alethel. Ayeng aleth-irrem, kwetant. (St) *Going away for good, for a long time. I'm going away for good.*

alethang *n.*
stranger, traveller, visitor ◆ Mer arrpenh-they apetyek alethang. Nyerr apek irrem ulereny-irrepirremarl yanh-ketyaw. Angketyakenh. (St) *A stranger came from another place. [People] were shy of him and didn't say a word. They didn't say a word* ◆ Altwerl-penh apetyem tyerrty alethang apek. (M) *A stranger might come from the west.*
SEE ALSO lwereny, ulereny

aletharr (T,E) *n.*
eldest sibling ◆ Ayengan arrwekeleny aletharr. (St) *I am the eldest sibling.*
SEE ALSO arrwekeleny, itep-penh, kantyeny, ingkerneny
aletharr-ilem (T,E) *vt.*
make a child the eldest (by having another one) (?) ◆ Aletharr-ilem ayenh yanhel. (St) *Now that I have a younger sibling I have been made the eldest.* (?)

alethayerr *n.*
a type of grub found on mulga trees
= kepartart, artetyayt
SEE ALSO arrpayerr

Aletheperreng *n.*
Alice Springs (from English 'Alice Springs')

alety *n.*
cut, wound ◆ *Knife*-el-arl akerrem-penharl aletyarl anewem. Alety *is what you call a wound from a knife.* ◆ Ilepel atwenhek, tyarrp-ilelhek ingka, aletyarl tyarrp-ilelhek. (St) *The axe cut the foot and split it open [the person split their foot open with the axe].*
SEE ALSO urrma, tywen, utyen

alety-akem *vt.*
wound something ◆ Ker alety-ilekarl, ker aherr — angwerrelarl alety-ilenty-alpek wal alheyaw, ingka aremel ampinetyek, irrtyartelarl atanthek-penh. Alety-ilek. (St) *The kangaroo has been wounded — well let's track the kangaroo that was wounded in the evening, the one that was wounded with a spear.*

alety-ilem (E) = **alety-akem**

alety-akelhem *vi.*
cut yourself (of men in mourning) ◆ Artwa akelhem alety lyweper alhwarrp, artnemel inngart. Tyerrty artwekenhantarl aletyarl akelheman. Arelhan arrangkwarl. Arelhan kapertant atanthem atnemel, alety-kweny. *The man cries and cuts himself on the thigh in sorrow. That's just men's business, to cut yourself. Women don't do that. Women just hit their heads with a digging stick, they don't cut themselves.*

-alew[1] (E), **-arlew** (E) *ending*
'Where is (someone or something)?', 'What about (someone or something)?'
◆ 'Arrawelengk-**alew**?' 'Nhak alhek.' (Sa) *'Where is your father?' 'He went over there.'*
= -artey

alew[2] (W,T), **alew-alew** (W,T) *part.*
'Truly?', 'Oh yeah?', 'Is that right?'
SEE ALSO arraty-akey

alewal (W,T) *adv.*
doing things separately (because of kinship restrictions) ◆ Alewal ratherr anem. Ikerrenty ratherr anem. *Can't* ker arlkwerl mwerewekenh. (M) *Those two are separate. They are in an avoidance relationship to each other. [A woman] is not allowed to eat her son-in-law's meat.*
SEE ALSO rlwerrkerek-rlwerrker

alewarr (W,T) *n.*
all of something, the whole thing, the whole lot ◆ Ker alewarr nhenh-warn angetyeh, anwern nhenhel tyep-iletyeh. (T) *Bring all of the meat here so that we can cut it up here.* ◆ Alewarr apek nta mern apek angerl-apem anthetyakenhel — alewarr akwet nta angernerl-apem, ker apek. (M) *You are going along with all of the food or meat and not giving it to anyone — you just go along keeping it to yourself.*
SEE ALSO antyaper

alewatyerr sand goanna SEE UNDER **arlewatyerr**

alewatyerr-alewatyerr (T,E) yellow-faced whip snake (?) SEE UNDER **arlewatyerr-arlewatyerr**[1]

alewatyerr-alewatyerr broom bush SEE UNDER **arlewatyerr-arlewatyerr**[2]

aleway (W,T) Stimson's python (?) SEE UNDER **ileway**

Alewer (E) *n.*
Laura Yard, south-east of Wilora (Stirling) community

alewerr (W) *n.*
full, entire, uncut ◆ Apwert lyerl-warl akwernek ker alewerr antey. (M) *[The man] had put the entire kangaroo carcass in a cave.*

aley[1] *n.*
coolibah seed (*Eucalyptus coolabah* ssp. *arida*). This seed is edible.
SEE ALSO ankerrmern, ankwerrern

aley[2] (T,E) *n.*
1. there, that (person or thing) there ◆ Aley apek angkep-angkem, 'Urrek tha rlterrk-iley.' (St) *That person might say, 'Wait while I tighten it.'* ◆ Akayel aley artnep-artnem. (St) *That person there is wailing in grief.* ◆ Anwantherr anep-anem nhenh ingkerrek, kel anwantherr alperrety-irrerl-alhem. Alpetyenh anemarl aley atherran, anwantherr alperrty-irremel anem alperl-anem. (St) *All of us are here, and then we'll all split up and go back home. Those two will go back and we'll all scatter and go home.*
2. now, nowadays ◆ Arrulant tnyetyam — aleyan arrangkw anem aley. Inpa anem — aretyakenh anem. Mern iylpar arrwekelenyel antarl arlkwerrek. (Sa) *[They] used to dig it up a long time ago — nowadays there's none left. We don't know — we haven't seen them. Only the olden-time people ate the* iylpar *yam.*
SEE ALSO alertekwenh, alenh

aley anem (T,E)
'Just now', 'There it is' ◆ Kwer akwek alyerremey, aley anem alhep-alhem kwenh. (T) *There is that gorgeous little kid going along there now.* ◆ Ilkewem tha, *might* arem, arlewatyerr-kenh nhenh. Arrpenh-angkwarr tha ilkewem, ilkewetyek tha, '*Oh* akengarl nhenh arrangkw.' Atnemel apek angerneynerl-anem, ilkeweynerl-anem. Altywer anem irrenhem, ker aley anem. (St) *I might poke around in the burrow, in the*

goanna's hole that I've seen. I'll poke round on the other side, 'Oh, this one is no good — there's nothing here.' I might dig along with a digging stick, poking at the hole. It gets opened up, and there's the animal.

aley-antey (T,E) = **aley anem**

aley-anyem (T,E) = **aley anem**

aleyak *n.*
a woman who has not had children ◆ Aleyak arelh awenk, kwer-kweny. Aleyak *is a young woman without children.*

Aleyaw (T) *n.*
place name, Ti Tree town. See map p. viii.

aleynm-aleynm (E) shiny, sparkling SEE UNDER alenm-alenm

alha[1], **alhang** (W,T) *n.*
1. nose, snout ◆ Alhang irtakert. (M) *A snotty nose.* ◆ Alha ayeng urltaty-irrem alethangek, alethang tha arnarem, arrer ra anem, yalengarl apetyem. Alha ayeng rltwar-irrem — urltaty-irrem. (St) *I have a feeling in my nose about a stranger, and then I see a stranger coming, and they come closer, from over there. My nose clicks — I have a premonition.*
2. entrance to native bees' hive or sugarbag ◆ Alhang, ya martelhenty anem, kel twern anentyem. Lwerenel altywer anem ilem. Tyalangk renh akap-rlwem. Kel yerr akwek akwek ra apem antem *outside*. Kel tyerrtyel arety-alhem, '*Oh* nhenh kwenh ngkwarl *sugarbag* apem, altywer nhenh kwenh alhang.' Kel atwem antem. (T) *The opening to the native bees' hive is closed up, and then the summer comes along. Then it opens up. The wax [plug] is peeled off. Then the little bees go outside. Then people come along and see it and say, 'Oh here are the sugarbag bees flying around — here's the opening, the* alhang.*' Then they chop [the sugarbag].*

alha altywer
nostril, nasal cavity (altywer '*opening*', '*hole*')
SEE ALSO alhalker

alha arrenpenp (W,T)
nostril

alha kanty
tip of nose (kanty '*tip*')

alha ngkwern
the bony part of the nose (ngkwern '*bone*')
SEE ALSO intyengintyerl, urleynterr[1]

alha nthat (T,E)
blocked nose (nthat '*blocked*')

werlaty alha (T,E)
nipple (werlaty '*breast*')
= paty alha

arwengalker alha (T,E)
entrance to native bees' hive (arwengalker '*native bees' hive*')
= rltwamp alha

alhakwerrk (W,T), **alhang akwerrk** (W,T) *n.*
newly made native bees' hive (akwerrk[1] '*young*', '*newly made*')

alhangkwarr *adv.*
going right in front of somebody (too close) (-angkwarr '*by way of*') ◆ 'Alha kwenh rntwarr, alhangkwarr alhetyal!' Tyerrty apek. *Two fellas might talk* ingkerneny *tickley-*irremel. 'Iyntwarr-angkwerr alha kwenh!' (St) *'Go further away, don't go right in front of me!' People talk like that. Later those two people might get annoyed with each other. 'Go further away!'* ◆ Unpakert alhangkwarr alhetyal! (St) *Don't go right in front of me — you smell!* ◆ *Don't* alherl alhangkwarr — ayeng artwek-artey akin anem. Unta antem artwek-antey. Rntwarr-angkwarr alherl. (T) *Don't go right in front of me — I've got a husband as well. You've got a husband too. You've got to go further away.*

alhel arem (T)
have a premonition about someone coming (have a feeling in nose) (arem '*look*', '*see*') ◆ Thang alhel-arem, tyerrty apetyem. (T) *I can feel that someone is coming.*
SEE ALSO rlkwem, rltwaty-irrem, urltaty-irrem, alhirrkem

alha[2], **alhang** (W,T) *n.*
dry fruit of desert raisin (*Solanum centrale*) ◆ Alha anem renh akemel. 'Mern alhirrekarl aketyek alheyaw!' (Sa) *And then the dried fruits of the desert raisin are picked. 'Let's go and pick the fruit that has dried!'*
= tweny
SEE ALSO kwart, katyerr

alhirrem, **alherrem** (W,T) *vi.*
go dry or shrivel up (desert raisin fruit) ◆ Alherrem, kwartarl anenh-penh, wal alherrem anem, katyerr ra. (T) *After being unripe the fruit of the desert raisin dries up.*
SEE ALSO arleny-irrem

alhalhek (E) *adv.*
without feeling shamed; not feeling restricted ◆ Ayeng alhalhek alherl-anem mer arrpenh-angkwerr. Alhalhek angkerl-apem. (St) *I can go to different places without restriction. I can talk [to people] without feeling shamed.* ◆ Nyerr-irretyakenh ayeng alhep-alhem — alhalhekarl ayeng alherl-anem, *anyway* angkenh-angkenh. (St) *I don't get shamed — I can go anywhere and talk to anyone.*
SEE ALSO alhewer

alhalker (E) *n.*
a hole made through the septum of the nose;

a hole through rock
SEE ALSO alha altywer
Alhalker (T,E) *n.*
the name of a place and of a country/estate on Mt Skinner Station and Utopia (Angarapa Aboriginal Land Trust)

alhamp, alhampw (T,E) *n.*
orphan; someone whose mother or father (or mother's brother or father's sister) has died. This term can occasionally be used when a person becomes bereaved of some other family member or relation. Some speakers also use it to refer to animals whose owner has died. ◆ Alhampw atnyenetyek mwanty kwenh. (St) *Look after the orphan carefully.* ◆ Alhamp anem ayeng anem, akeweny. Atyeng-artweyarl tha aparlp-ilerneng. (T) *Poor old me is an orphan now. Because I just lost my parents.*
SEE ALSO rrkwern, amatheng, kwetyenty
alhamp-irrem, alhampw-irrem (T,E) *vi.*
become an orphan, become bereaved or bereft, lose a family member or relation ◆ Ayeng alhampw-irrek, mamek, akngeyek, atyemeyek, nyanyek, awenh-awenhek. Kemarrek awenh-awenhek alhampw-irrek ayeng. (St) *I lost my relations — my mother, my father, my mother's father, my mother's mother and my auntie. I lost my auntie, Kemarr.* ◆ Alhampw-irrek, amarl-kweny irrek — *no* amarley. (St) *I became bereaved — I've got no uncle [mother's brother].*
= rrkwern-irrem
alhamp-alhamp, alhampw-alhampw (T,E) *n.*
without family, orphaned ◆ Akwek alhamp-alhamp akeweny atwerrirretyalaw — menty anem aney. (T) *Don't fight with the poor little orphan — leave her alone.*

alhang (W,T) nose, snout SEE UNDER **alha**[1]

alhang (W,T) dry fruit of desert raisin SEE UNDER **alha**[2]

alhang irrkem (W,T) have a premonition SEE UNDER **alhirrkem**

alhanker (E) *n.*
silver witchetty, pirli (*Acacia cuthbertsonii* ssp. *cuthbertsonii* (?)). Shrub up to 3 m high, with silvery leaves and cylindrical flowers.
SEE ALSO perley, lywey
alhankerayt (E) *n.*
grub from the silver witchetty. Also referred to as *tyap alhankerayt*.

Alhankerr (T) *n.*
name of a swamp east of Aileron Roadhouse. See map p. viii.

alhap *n.*
1. shut, blocked off
2. bung-eye, blocked nose ◆ Annga alhap-irrem amengelarl atwem, atherrkeny apek. (St) *Eyes become bunged up when flies bite them, in the green time.*
SEE ALSO nthat
alhap-ilem *vt.*
block something up
alhap-irrem *vi.*
become blocked or closed up ◆ Alhang alhap-irrem. (M) *The nose is blocked up.* ◆ Anngang alhap-irrem ameng-penh. (M) *Eyes get closed up from [being bitten by] flies.*
alhapelhem (W) *vi.*
swell up
SEE ALSO wangkem, arlwar-irrem, amwerenthenng-irrem

alharlkwem *vt.*
hunt or chase someone or something away; send someone away, get rid of someone ◆ Alharlkwemarl alpem. Ntwa apekarl ayeng alharlkwem, mern-they apek ayeng alharlkwek. (St) *Hunting someone away and sending them back home. You might hunt me away because of food.* ◆ Alharlkwem, ayeng aneyameng. 'Ankey-akert alpeyaw!' Alharlkwem tha ikngel tha arlkweyameng. (St) *Chasing [someone] away so that I can sit down then. 'Go back you bludger!' I hunt them away so that I can eat by myself.* ◆ Arengk alharlkwem rntwarr irnetyek. (T) *Hunting the dog away so that it stands further away.*
= aywepem, anpwem
alharlkwelhem *vt.*
1. chase or hunt someone or something away from yourself, tell someone to go away and leave you alone ◆ Thang alharlkwelhemel anpwem arengk, tyerrty apek atyengety. (T) *I am chasing the dog, or the person, away from me.* ◆ Ngenh apek tha alharlkwelhem, ankeyarl apetyemeng. (St) *I'm hunting you away from me, because you're coming and asking for things.* ◆ Alhetyeh ahenty-kweny apek nta alharlkwelhem, 'Alhay — ayeng alhetyeh ahenty-kwenyengay. Ayeng ankwa apek intetyenheng.' (M) *If you don't want to go somewhere you might tell someone to go away. 'Go away — I don't want to go. I might have a sleep.'*
= ayepwelhem, anpwelhem
2. give something up, refuse something ◆ Alharlkwelhem, ngkwarl antywetyek. '*No* menty anem kwenh.' Menty, alharlkwelhemarl ra. Antywetyakenh anem

ra. Imelhem anem. (St) *He refuses to drink grog. 'No, I don't want any.' He refuses to drink. He has given up now.*

alharrenty *n.* [RESPECT LANGUAGE]
devil, monster, snake, creepy crawly
◆ Alharrenty-ketyaw, mwerrenganty apek. (St) *Be careful and look out for snakes.* ◆ Kwep-ana atyeweyay alharrenty-ayerr yanhentyak-kety, paytey-kety. (Sa) *For goodness sake, sing out and warn them [respect kin of speaker] about that creepy crawly, that 'bitey'.*
SEE ALSO arrenty

alharrkem *vi.*
1. flash (lightning) ◆ Kwaty akngerr alharrkem, akngerrarl apetyem, ingwemernt irremel, alharrkenty-alpem. Mperlkemel ap alharrkenty-alpem arlter. (St) *There is a big thunderstorm, and it gets dark, and the lightning flashes. The lightning flashes white.*
2. flutter, tremble or quiver (wings or others parts of the body)
= ngkwarrkem
SEE ALSO arrkem, angap-angap-irrem, arraly-arraly-irrem

alharrkw (E) *n.*
dust haze seen after rain
= alhek unmernt

alharrp (W,T), **alhwarrp** (T,E) *n.*
worried, sad, depressed, lonely ◆ Alharrp apek tyerrty apek rlkert intemeng. (T) *Feeling sad about someone who is sick.* ◆ Arnem, alharrpelam arnemam, tyerrtyarl ywerremeng. *Feeling sorry and crying because somebody has passed away.*
= altarrp
alharrp-alharrp (W,T),
alhwarrp-alhwarrp (T,E) *n.*
a bit lonely or sad ◆ Arelh yanh alharrp-alharrp anem ker kwerenharl arlkwek-arleng arengkel. *That woman is a bit sad because the dog ate her meat.*
= altarrp-altarrp
alharrp-irrem (W,T), **alhwarrp-irrem** (T,E) *vi.*
feel sad, sorry or lonely ◆ Angwely ap ilwemarl kwa, alharrp-irrem angwely-artey mapel alharrp-irrem. 'Angwely akeweny atyengenh kwenh, akeweny angwely. Rtwek-rtwek. Alharrp anetyakenham arrantherr kwenh.' (N) *If the dog dies, then the owners of the dog feel sad. 'My poor dog, my poor dog. Poor dog. You mob aren't sorry.'*
= altarrp-irrem, atham-irrem

Alhather (T) *n.*
Mt Esther. See map p. viii.

alhek nmwernt (W,T), **alhwek nmernt** (W,T), **alhek unmernt** (T,E) *n.*
dust storm (before rain) (nmwernt *'dust'*)
◆ Awenhelikwek-amparr artem alhek ulpmerntel. *After that* kwaty anem urntetyenh. Arrwekelenyel iletyam alakenh-anyem. (St) *The olden-time people used to say that the dust storm was the 'auntie of the rain' and that first of all it covers [everything] over. Then after that it rains. That's exactly what the old people said.* ◆ Alhek nmwerntel arltwintyem, alhek nmwerntel arltwem ingkerr, ahelh ingkerr. Lwerenarl alker-irrenhem ingkerr anam-irrerl-alhem alhek nmwernt ran. (N) *The dust storm comes this way and covers everything over, all of the ground. Then it all clears up and the dust storm moves on.*
= alharrkw

alhelem (W,T), **alhilem** (T,E) *vt.*
1. promise (to give something to someone)
◆ Mern alhilem, ker apek alhilem, anthetyek. Mwetek apek tha alhilem, anthetyek nhakwek, ngkweng apek. (St) *Promising to give food, or meat [to someone]. I might promise to give a car to that person over there or to you.*
◆ Maneh apek nta alhelem ikwer. (M) *You might promise them some money.*
2. promise someone in marriage ◆ Tharl alhilekaw nhakwek rtwalty atyenhek, mey-meyek atyenh, *daughter* atyenh tha alhilekarl. Rtwalty atyenhek tha alhilekarl tha anthetyek. (St) *I made a promise to that one over there, to my son-in-law. I promised my daughter. I made a promise to my son-in-law that I would give my daughter to him.*
3. ask for something on someone else's behalf
alhelenty (W,T), **alhilenty** (T,E) *n.*
a promise, someone or something that is promised to someone (e.g. wife) ◆ Alhelenty atyengenh. Ra inem anem artwa alenhel. (T) *My 'promised' one. Then that man gets her.*
SEE ALSO akepenh

alhelp (W,T) *n.*
1. blue mallee (*Eucalyptus gamophylla*). Tree about 3 m high, with bluish green leaves. Grows in spinifex country.
= uleperr
2. bastard coolibah (*Eucalyptus intertexta*)
3. Normanton box (*Eucalyptus normantonensis*). Tree about 4 m high, with pale yellow flowers and small, hard nuts.
• = alywelp

alhelth-angem (T,E), **alhelth-akngem** (E) *vt.*
carry (a baby animal) in pouch (angem *'carry', 'take'*) ◆ Atwety akely, akwek-amperl alhelth-

angem ra, aympel, melikw. (St) *The little joey, its mother carries the little thing along in her pouch.*
= aympel angem
SEE ALSO peth, aympa

alhem *vi.*
1. go, go along, travel ◆ Awerr atherr alherl-aperretyam. (M) *Two boys were going for a walk.* ◆ Arelh alhem yatyarr arlweker-warn. (T) *The woman is going to the single-women's camp for a visit.* ◆ Lyweny alhem. *Going hunting.* ◆ Marnteng alhem, lyweny apek, apety-alpem, altywer-ilety-alpem, anarnpenty-alpem. (N) *We might go for a day trip in the bus, come back, open it, and get out.* ◆ Ayeng anyentarl alhem. Atherr alherremarl. Anwantherr alherl-wem. *I am going, myseslf. Two are going. We are going.*
2. flow (water) ◆ Ilerrty alhem kwaty alhem ikwerel, ulpay angerr-warl lher angerr-warl anem ra anyent-irrem. (St) *The water flows along the small watercourse and then it joins in with the big river.*
SEE ALSO apem[1], nthwem

alhenem *vt.*
shine (sun); shine a light on something ◆ Mwetekay *light* alhenenhetyem. (Sa) *The car light is shining as it comes towards us.*
= alernem
CAN SOUND A BIT LIKE lernem *'shake something out'*; alernem *'lean against something'*

alhenenty *n.*
a light
= alernenty

alhenelhem (T,E) *vi.*
get warm, warm oneself ◆ Uternel ayeng alhenelhetyek. (St) *I am warming myself in the sun.*
SEE ALSO arrtyenem

alhengerr (E) *n.* [RESPECT LANGUAGE]
good, well
SEE ALSO mwerr, mwenkerr

alhengerr-irrem (E) *vi.* [RESPECT LANGUAGE]
get better
SEE ALSO mwerr-irrem

alhengk-arem *vt.*
1. recognise someone or something; know someone; know about something (arem *'look', 'see'*) ◆ Ngenh tha alhengk-arem. (St) *I recognise you.* ◆ Tyerrty yanh akey arelh then yanh apetyemarl arrantherr alhengkem ara kwenh, yanharl apetyepetyem atherr kwenh, yatenh atherr kwenh. (N) *Look at those people there, that woman and the other one that are coming there — you'll all recognise them, those two that are coming.* ◆ Ingkerneny, alhengk apek aretyenheng tywerreng mer arreng-kenh angey-kenh. Kalty apek anetyenheng. (M) *The next generation might know about sacred things and about their grandparent's and father's land. Maybe they'll get to know about it.* ◆ Alhengk-arem war peltyant, kenh lwereny akenh apalarl arem. (N) *[I] only recognise friends, whereas I don't recognise strangers.* ◆ *Knife* atyengenh tha alhengk-arem. (M) *I recognise my knife.*
2. take notice of someone; pay attention to someone ◆ Ntweth-ntweth ayeng ananem tyerrtyel alhengk-aretyakenh — ntweth-ntweth ingareny war anyent-areny-iperr ananem. (M) *I am feeling neglected, and nobody is taking any notice of me — I'm all on my own.* ◆ Alhengkey ayeng anep-anem. Tyerrtyel alhengk-aretyakenh, alhengkey. (St) *I am not wanted. People don't take any notice of me.*

alhengk-arelhem *vi.*
recognise yourself (in someone else) (arelhem *'look at self'*) ◆ Ampa akwek aremel tha, alhengk-arelhekarl ayeng. 'Ayeng-artekarlaw nhenh.' (St) *Looking at the little baby, I recognised myself in her. 'Hey, this one resembles me.'*

alhengk-awem *vt.*
understand; recognise sound of someone or something (awem *'hear', 'understand'*) ◆ Angka tha alhengk-awem. *I know that voice.* ◆ Nhakw apekarl angkerreperrem, alhengk-awemarl tha, tyerrtyarl angkerremarl. (St) *Those people talking over there, well I know the sound of their voices, of those people talking.* ◆ Thwengk awerl-anem, angkety yanh angkerl-anerleng, alhengk-awep-awem. (N) *I can understand you, what you are saying, I can understand.*
CAN SOUND A BIT LIKE alengk-wem *'hide something'*

alhengk-awelhem *vi.*
hear something about yourself, hear the sound of your name (awelhem *'hear self'*) ◆ Unta apekarl iltep-iltem ayenh, alhengk-awelhem ayeng. (St) *You might swear at me and I know that you are talking about me.* (?) ◆ Arreytn atyenh alhengk-awelhemarl ayeng. (St) *I hear my name being said.*

alhengkem (T,E) *vt.*
growl at someone (?); really swear at someone; pick on someone; hunt someone away, get rid of someone
SEE ALSO iltem, alhengkey

alhengkelh-ilem (E) *vt.* = alhengkem

alhengkey *n.*
1. someone who is not wanted ◆ Alhengkey war anep-anem. *Might* ayeng tyart akeng-akeng akert ra apek alhengkey-alhengkey anep-anem.

Alhengkey ayeng anep-anem. *Might* tyerrty arrpenh apek atyeng *don't like.* Alhengkey kwenh ayeng anep-anem. *I am just sitting down feeling neglected. I, or she, might have a raggedy shirt on. I'm not wanted. Perhaps other people don't like me. I'm feeling really rejected.* ◆ Alhengkey ayeng anep-anem — tyerrtyel alhengk-aretyakenh, alhengkey. (St) *I am not wanted — people don't take any notice of me.*
2. raggedy, neglected, untidy
SEE ALSO alhengkem
alhengkey-ilem *vt.*
make someone feel not wanted; reject someone ◆ Alhengkey-ilemarl ayenh iltep-iltem rarey. (St) *They are growling and making me feel not wanted.*
SEE ALSO alhengk-arem

alhepalh (E) *n.*
waxy wattle (*Acacia melleodora*). Shrub to about 2.5 m high, with grey-green leaves with a whitish crust and edible seeds.
= ilkwernarr
SEE ALSO patwert
alhepalhayt (E) *n.*
grub from the waxy wattle. Also referred to as *tyap alhepalhayt.*
= ilkwernarrayt

alheramp (W,T) *n.*
Main's frog (*Cyclorana maini* (?)). Also referred to as *ker alheramp.* ◆ Alheramp anem ahelh lpwayel kwen. Arrwekeleny mapel arlkwetyart alheramp. (M) *The* alheramp *frog lives under the sand in the creek. The olden-time people used to eat them.*
SEE ALSO alyeyamp, kalyeyamp
CAN SOUND A BIT LIKE Alherramp *'Laramba community'*

Alherarrpant (W) *n.*
the name of a waterhole south of Mt Allan community

alhernter *n.*
1. white person, white people, European person
2. any non-Aboriginal person (lit. 'red nose') ◆ Alhernter nyerrek akutn — alhewer war angkerl-anem. (St) *Whitefellas don't know about being shamed — they just talk anyway, without restriction.* ◆ Alhernter yanh anpway, merarl irrpem-arleng. (M) *Tell that white person not to go into my house.* ◆ Alhernter-rnem uneng-akert arrma — uneng rlterrk-akertarl ikwer-areyenh. (Sa) *White people have a spirit as well — their spirits are strong.* ◆ Alha apekarl rnter-rnter war anem. (St) *Maybe they [white people] just have red noses.*
= warlpal
SEE ALSO arlter, kartey, mperlker, tyerrty arlter, tywelker

Alherramp (W,T) *n.*
Laramba community (located on an excision from Napperby Station). See map p. viii.
CAN SOUND A BIT LIKE alheramp *'type of frog'*

alherrem[1] (E) *vt.*
1. rub, chafe or scratch something ◆ Arwerlel ayenh alherrek utyen mpwaremel. *The stick rubbed me and made me sore.*
2. peel off skin or bark ◆ Rltimp alherrem atnemel apek, kel arrerlp-ilerl-anem anem. Rltimp tha alherrem. (St) *Peel the bark off the digging stick and then sharpen it. I am peeling the bark off.* ◆ *Orange* alherrem, ayenp ap alherrem *orange.* (St) *Peel an orange, peel the skin off an orange.*
SEE ALSO angernem[1], irrkem, alterrem, arreynem, irrkernem

alherrem[2] (W,T), **alhirrem** *vi.*
1. really like or want something ◆ Ayeng rnwanenty mwerreh alherrem. (M) *I really want those nice clothes.*
2. fancy someone, desire someone, lust after someone ◆ Artwek apek alherrem. Alherrenty mpwaremel, kel ratherr alherrem antem. Kel angem antem renh, akwetant angem. (T) *Desiring that man. Then two of them go off together. Then he/she takes the other for good.* ◆ Artwang nhenh alherrem arelh nheteh, ahenty-anem. (M) *This man really fancies this woman, wants her.*
= iyteny-irrem
SEE ALSO ahenty-anem, ahenty-irrem, mpweny

alhewal (W,T) *adv.*
fighting over someone or something ◆ Merneng apek alhewal atwerrem. (T) *Fighting over food.* ◆ Arengk atherr alhewal nhwerrem kereng. (T) *The two dogs are fighting over meat.*

alhewem *vt.*
wash something ◆ Mantarr atyenh tha alhewetyek. (St) *I've got to wash my clothes.* ◆ Rnwanenty alhewetyenheng kel lherek apek atek arrernetyenheng. (T) *I'm going to wash my clothes and then lay them out to dry in the creek.*
alhewelhem *vi.*
bathe oneself, wash oneself ◆ Kapert ayeng alhewelhetyek, tyerrty arlka ayeng alhewelhetyek, arlkarl-ilelhemel. (St) *I'm going to wash my head and my whole body to cool myself down.*

alhewer *n.*
1. without feeling shamed or restricted;

confidently, without (social) restrictions ◆ Alhernter nyerrek akutn — alhewer war angkerl-anem. (St) *Whitefellas don't know about being shamed — they just talk anyway, without restriction.* ◆ Alhewer ayeng alhetyek, mey-mey atyenh-angkwerr, ampatyey-angkwerr apek. Alhewer ayeng angkem. War ayeng angketyek, nyerr-irretyal. *I just go anyway, to my son-in-law or my father-in-law. I just talk [to them] without getting shamed.* ◆ Ikirrenty anetyakenh yanh alhewer alhem, mey-mey kwerenh, rtwalty kwerenh-angkwarr. Akengarlaw. (St) *That person does not respect the avoidance rules and just goes anywhere, near her son-in-law. It's really bad.*
SEE ALSO nyerr
2. without restriction, variable, any sort of thing ◆ *Lizard* akely, alyelkarl ap ra, urnem-apeny, *quiet. Colour*-an alhewer — *yellow one*, arlkeny-arlkeny *batik one batik one.* (Sa) *A little lizard, a smooth one like a snake, quiet [not aggressive]. They have any sort of colour — some are yellow and they have markings and patterns like batik.*
SEE ALSO alhalhek

alhilem (T,E) promise (to give something to someone) SEE UNDER **alhelem**

alhingk (E) *n.*
mulga snake, king brown snake (*Pseudechis australis*)
= ikwelengk, atetherr arlkwenh, arreperlp, kantharlkw, tyamparl

alhirrel (E) *n.*
many, a big mob, a lot ◆ Anewart alhirrel ap yanh-rnem, anewartewart. Artwernem urrpety, arelh-rnem urrpety anewart-rnem. (Sa) *There's lots of couples there, husbands and wives. A few men and a few women, husbands and wives.* ◆ Ampernem alhirrel alherl-wek. (Sa) *Lots of kids went.* ◆ Akngerr weth arey apwertel. Arwerl weth tnenherretyel alhirrel, ilpey-ilpey. (Sa) *There are lots of those [trees] in the hills. Lots of those* ilpey ilpey *trees grow there.*
SEE ALSO map, anengk[1], angerr[1], arnkengeny, ingkerr[1]

alhirrem really like or want something SEE UNDER **alherrem**[2]

alhirrkem, alhang irrkem (W,T) *vi.*
have a premonition; have a twitching or itching feeling in the nose that makes you think about somebody, or about something that is about to happen (alha[1] *'nose'*; irrkem *'itch'*) ◆ Alha ayeng irrkem ngkweng, unta apekarl iterrek atyeng ngkwelty anthetyek. (St) *I have a feeling about you, that maybe you thought about giving me some money.* ◆ Alhekarl apek ayeng wal unta apekarl alhirrkem apety-alpem apek. Arrwekel ngan alhirrkem — urltaty apek nga irrem. (St) *I might have gone away, and then you have a feeling that I'm coming back. Beforehand you have a premonition about it — you might have a twitching feeling in the nose.* ◆ Arrpenharl alethang apetyemek, wal alhirrkem. Atwerrem-arlek apek alhirrkem ayeng. (T) *I have a feeling that a stranger is coming. Or I might have a feeling about people fighting.*
SEE ALSO rlkwem, rltwaty-irrem, urltaty-irrem, alhel arem

alhur (E) soft inside part of fruits or damper SEE UNDER **alhwer**

alhurrp (E) winter SEE UNDER **alhwerrp**

alhwa, alhwang (W,T) *n.*
blood ◆ Alhwa irrert-irrem, arnelarl atanthem-penh. (St) *The blood flows out from where the stick pierced.* ◆ Alhwa ikelh-irrem tywen-penh, rlterrk-irremel. (St) *Blood from a sore solidifies, gets hard.* ◆ Alhwa pwelap-ilelhemel awerrpan antywemarl. (Sa) *[You] drink kangaroo blood to make your blood plentiful.* ◆ Tyerrtyel rrkwem alhwang. (T) *The body has blood.*
alhuntem (E), **alhwentem** (E) *vi.*
bleed (untem *'run', 'flow'*) ◆ Alhwarl alhuntem. (Sa) *It is bleeding.*
= arrnguntem
alhwa thelelhem, alhwang thelelhem (W,T)
bleed (thelelhem *'pour out of'*) ◆ Amarr ra akelhem ampa akely apekan utyen anentyek, kel apernemel ra ikwerel amarrel. Arelh akelhem, amarr akelhem, kel alhwa thelelhemel, kel annga anem ikwerel aperneman, utyen, annga utyen-irrenty. (Sa) *She cuts herself on the arm and then rubs a child who has sores with the blood. Women cut themselves and then the blood seeps out and then they used the blood to rub on the eyes, eyes that have got sore.*
= arrnguntem

alhwarrp (T,E) worried, sad, lonely SEE UNDER **alharrp**

alhwek nmernt (W,T) dust storm (before rain) SEE UNDER **alhek nmwernt**

alhwemperemper (E) *n.*
small (of breasts), breasts that are just starting to grow
= paty arrwert
SEE ALSO akarnterrng, parray, alhwetepwet

alhweng *n.*
hole where animals live; burrow, nest
◆ Kweleynterreynterrel alhweng ra angernem

baby anem ra mpwarem kwer-antey alhweng kwer-antey. Kel arraterl-alhep-alhem arlewatyerr-artek. Arnam arrernem kel akwerrk map anem ra mpwarem. (St) *The rainbow bee-eater digs a burrow and then it has its babies there in the burrow. Then it comes out and goes around just like a goanna does. It puts grass there in the burrow and then it has its babies.* ◆ Mpwenyerlpel mpweny iytarr-iytarr arrwekety, marl ikwerenh anewikw. Marlarl iytarr akngem ra, alhwengek akwernety-alpem. (Sa) *The* mpwenyerlp *mouse drags the female — its mate — off to have sex with her. He drags the female off and puts her in the burrow.*
SEE ALSO arleytarr, arwerr, antywa, atharlkw

alhwengkelty *n.*
bits and pieces of things; fragments of something; all sorts of (things); anything; everything ◆ Alhwengkelty kwer nhenhel inerl-anem iwenh arrpanenh. (M) *This kid is getting everything.* ◆ Thep alhwengkelty. (T) *Every sort of bird.* ◆ Alhwengkelty atyenh-arey tha akngemarl. (St) *I'm going to take my bits and pieces.*
SEE ALSO ngkwelty
alhwengkelty angkem (W)
say all sorts of inappropriate things, say things you shouldn't say
SEE ALSO ywetherrk angkem

alhwengkengk (W) *n.*
nasal bone (soft part inside nose)

alhwer (E), **alhur** (E) *n.*
1. soft inside part of fruits or damper
2. white inner skin of the bush banana, silky pear (*Marsdenia australis*)
SEE ALSO alwerremp, antweth, alangkw, parl

alhwer-alhwer *n.*
swollen or puffed up (eyes or other parts of the body) ◆ *Might* nga apek *fat one* apek irrek, anter angerr irrek, *me might say* arrkenel, 'Alhwer-alhwer anem yanh. Alhwer-alhwer-irrek nga'. *Maybe you will get fat, get really fat and I might say for fun, 'That one is swollen, you've swollen up'.*
alhwer-alhwer-irrem *vi.*
swell or puff up (eyes or other parts of the body) ◆ Alknga alhwer-alhwer-irrek ayeng. (St) *My eyes have swollen up.*
SEE ALSO wangkem

alhwerrk (E) *n.*
muddy or dirty water ◆ Kwaty alhwerrk altyiwetyek. (Sa) *Tip out the dirty water.*
= ulpert
SEE ALSO aternng, alkwemp-alkwemp, altelhey
alhwerrk-alhwerrk (E) *n.*
a bit dirty or muddy (water) ◆ Kwaty alhwerrk-alhwerrkek-amparr thelelhem kwaty angenty-they. (St) *First of all the muddy water comes out of the soakage.*
= ulpert-ulpert
alhwerrk-irrem (E) *vi.*
get dirty or muddy (water)
SEE ALSO aternng-irrem
alhwerrk-ilem (E) *vt.*
make water dirty or muddy ◆ Pwelekel alhwerrk-ilek kwaty. Aternng anem ra anetyel. (Sa) *The cattle muddied the water. Now it's dirty.*
SEE ALSO aternng-ilem

alhwerrkert *n.*
1. speaking in a way that is mixed up or is difficult to understand ◆ Awetyakenh, Irrkwerteth angwenh apekarl angkep-angkem, Tyapaney apek, angkep-angkem awetyakenh — alhwerrkert. (St) *[I] can't understand, Italian or Japanese or whatever they're talking — it sounds all mixed up [to me].* ◆ Alhwerrkert angketyalay! Arnterr-artek angkay! (T) *Don't talk in a mixed up way! Speak clearly!*
SEE ALSO aperrpert, tetherrp-tetherrp, irrkwerteth
2. talking in an inappropriate way, maybe saying something untruthful or harping on about something from the past; saying things that will upset people
SEE ALSO tyel angkem

alhwerrp, **alhurrp** (E) *n.*
1. winter, cold weather ◆ Arlewatyerr rlwelth arrernelhem alhwerrpel. (M) *The goanna hibernates in winter.* ◆ Kwer akwek akert alhwerrp-rlwer anay, kwen anay. (T) *You've got a little kid, so sit down inside, in the winter time.*
2. cold wind (from the east (?)) ◆ Atnengk tnek, alhwerrp-kweny. Atnengkel ampemaw, alhwerrp anetyakenhel. (Sa) *It's calm and there's no wind. Because there's no wind [we] are getting hot.* ◆ Kernt anthwerr kwenh anwern alhwerrpelant apem — alhwerrp angerrarl anemeng. *We are really cold because the cold wind is blowing — now that it's the middle of winter.* ◆ Akngerrakw-they alhwerrp pwetyel. (Sa) *The* alhwerrp *wind blows from the east.*
SEE ALSO irrernt, alyangkw, rlka
alhwerrp urla, **alhwerrp rlwang** (W,T)
the beginning of winter, start of the cold weather (urla *'forehead', 'front part of something'*) ◆ Alhwerrp urla, irrernt anem irrem. (St) *It's the beginning of winter and it's getting cold now.*
= alhwerrp alhang, alhwerrp akwerrk

alhwerrp alhang (T) = **alhwerrp urla** (alha *'nose'*)
alhwerrp akwerrk = **alhwerrp urla** (akwerrk[1] *'young', 'newly formed'*)
alhwerrp mpank (T) = **alhwerrp urla** (mpank *'(something) that hasn't happened yet'*)
alhwerrp mparnt, **alhwerrp mpwarnt**
the middle of winter (mparnt *'middle'*)
◆ Alhwerrp mpwarnt mpepel anem, alhwerrp mpep anem irrenhem, mpep. *Really cold.* Mpwarnt. (St) *The middle of winter, when it's really cold, is called* mpwarnt.
= alhwerrp mpep, alherrrp rlkwerr, alhwerrp artep
alhwerrp mpep (E) = **alhwerrp mparnt** (mpep *'middle'*)
alhwerrp rlkwerr (W,T) = **alhwerrp mparnt** (rlkwerr *'middle'*)
alhwerrp artep (T) = **alhwerrp mparnt** (artep *'back'*) ◆ Alhwerrp angerr artep. Alhwerrp angerrarl apetyem, 'Alhwerrp angerr kwenh artep apetyem'. (T) *Right in the middle of winter. When the middle of winter comes [people say], 'The* alhwerrp artep *is coming'.*

alhwerrp akely-akely (E), **alywerrp akely-akely** (E), **lyerrp akely-akely** (E) *n.*
a type of lizard (akely-akely *'very small'*)

alhwet (E) *n.*
burrowing bettong (*Bettongia lesueur*) (?). Also referred to as *ker alhwet.* ◆ Ker alhwet arlkwerretyart arrwekelenyel-rnem. (Sa) *The olden-time people used to eat the bettong.*
SEE ALSO rtway, awert[2]

alhwetepwet (T) *n.*
girl's breasts when they are just starting to develop ◆ Marl awenk yanh apetyem alhwetepwet. (T) *That young teenage girl coming along there has small breasts.*
= akarnterrng, paty arrwert
SEE ALSO alhwemperemper

Ali Curung SEE UNDER **Alekareng**

alim-alim (E) shiny, sparkling SEE UNDER **alenm-alenm**

alimp (W,T) skewer used for cooking SEE UNDER **alemp**

alingkerr they (two) SEE UNDER **alengkerr**

alinm-alinm (E) shiny, sparkling SEE UNDER **alenm-alenm**

alkakem (W,T) open or uncover something, spread something out SEE UNDER **ilkakem**

alkamp (E) *n.*
large flat rock ◆ Apwert alkamp akngerr. Alkampan apwert ather akngerr. *A big flat rock. An* alkamp *is a big flat rock.*
= ather

alkaper (W,T) *n.*
a type of plant (possibly a type of yam)
SEE ALSO arlatyey

alkaperr (E) old female animal SEE UNDER **alkeperr**

alkart (W,T) *n.*
1. kalkardi (*Acacia colei*)
2. Halls Creek wattle (*Acacia cowleana*)
3. a type of acacia (no common name) (*Acacia elachantha*). Shrubs up to 7 m high, with large, sickle-shaped leaves and cylindrical yellow flowers. ◆ Alkart anterrng antem, arlkwenh-arlkwenh. Alkart, rwel antem atyerretyam ina alkart yanh kwa. Rwel itenh-itenh, awantyenhantyenh, athenh-athenh. Athetyamarl awantyetyamarl, Anengkerr-penh wart. (N) *The* alkart *seed is edible as well. They cooked the* alkart *seed in the fire. It's cooked in the fire and then ground up and eaten. It comes from the Dreaming of course.*
SEE ALSO ilkert

alkent (E) *n.* [RESPECT LANGUAGE]
moon, moonlight (note Alyawarr *alkent* 'moon') ◆ Ngwarrenhengan alkentel anem anerlanerrem. (Sa) *My daughter and her husband are sitting down in the moonlight.*
SEE ALSO anyenty

-alkenty SEE UNDER **+ant-alkenty**

alkeperr, **alkaperr** (E) *n.*
1. female dog that's had pups; old female animal ◆ Arengk alkeperr ahinpeny apek. (St) *An old female dog.* ◆ Arlewatyerr alkeperr, kwart-penh. Alkeperr ampwan. (St) *An old goanna, that's had eggs. An old goanna.*
SEE ALSO areperrk
2. old woman [SOME SPEAKERS]

alker *n.*
1. sky, clear sky ◆ Irrety angap-angap-irrem alkerel akern. (St) *The eaglehawk is fluttering [its wings] high up in the sky.*
2. country, place
alker arrpenh-areny
someone from a different country; someone from overseas (lit. 'something associated with another sky') ◆ Alker arrpenh-arenyarl yanhanaw, ahelh arrpenhengarl apetyek. Alker arrpenh-they. (St) *That person is from another place, they've come from another country. From another 'sky'.*
alker tyelk
high in the sky (where something is hardly visible) (tyelk *'body', 'the inner part of things'*)
◆ Alker tyelkel alhem akern. Akernarl alhem

aretyakenh, *that's* 'alker tyelkel alhem'. *Might see*-em ywarn anem. *Might* alker tyelkel nhakw ra alhem akwek-amperl. *Really high.* (St) *[Something] going along very high up in the sky. Going high up where it can't be seen is going along in the* 'alker tyelk'. *It is hardly visible. Something might be going along high up in the sky and it looks really small.*

alker anert, alker atnert (E) *n.* = **alker tyelk**
(anert '*stomach*') ◆ 'Alker anert' anwern ilem akern alker. (M) *'Alker anert' is what we call the high part of the sky.*

alker-areny *n.*
bird or aeroplane (-areny '*inhabitant of*')

alkerel alhenh
aeroplane (lit. 'something which travels in the sky')

alker-alker, alkerey-alkerey (E) *n.*
1. eggwhite, albumen. Also referred to as *mern alker-alker.*
2. white of the eye
SEE ALSO athwenter

alkerelhem (E) *vi.*
1. eyes fade or whiten over
2. clouds clear up; clear up (rain)

alkerek-irrem *vi.*
to fly ◆ Alkerek-irrem mer arrpenh-warl ayeng alhetyek. *Might* alkerel apek alherl wenhel apek *aeroplane*-el apek. (St) *I'm going to fly to another place. I might fly in an aeroplane.*

alkerel alhem
to fly ◆ Thip map alkerel alhem aterel anthem tyerrtyel. Tyerrty alherl-apem angwelyarl apek. (N) *Birds fly when people give them a fright. People going along or maybe dogs.*

alker-irrem[1] *vi.*
clouds clear up; clear up (rain) ◆ Alker anem irrem kwatyarl urntek-penh. (St) *It is getting clear now after the rain.* ◆ Kwaty ankert-penh alker-irrem. (M) *After the rain clouds [have covered the sky] it is clearing up.*

alker-irrem[2] *vi.*
to fly ◆ Thepan alker-irrem alker-irrem arrernelhem. (N) *Birds fly along and then they land.*
SEE ALSO antyan-akelhem

alkeramp, alkerampw *n.*
resin from mulga (*Acacia aneura*) ◆ Ngkwarl athengarlperl-artek weth anem artetyel. Arem renh alkeramp nhenh arlka ngkwarl anem, wenh-warl apek pmwar-warl apek akemel — akngerr apek aremel. Athengarlperl-artek. (St) *There is a sweet stuff that is similar to the ironwood resin and it grows on the mulga. If you see this mulga resin you can pick it and put it in a wooden dish — that's if you see a lot of it. It's similar to the ironwood resin.*
= artetyaywerrk
SEE ALSO artety, athimpangkwarl, athengarlperl

alkerr (E) *n.*
swamp, water from a swamp. Also referred to as *kwaty alkerr.* ◆ Kwaty alkerr antywem. (Sa) *Drinking the water from the swamp.*

Alkerreylp (E) *n.*
Mars
SEE ALSO Awelh, Arwenpeng

Alkerreylp (T,E) *n.*
name of a place in the Delmore Downs area

alkewerr (T) avoidance of certain relatives SEE UNDER **alkiwerr**

alkey[1] (W,T) *n.*
long, tall ◆ Kapert arratyeny arrpenhem, akwerl alkey. (T) *Some have straight hair, long straight hair.* ◆ Rrwerleng ap mern ngkwarlarl, alkey angerr *anyway* twakemel lywernkel arlka akerrirretyart. (N) *The honey grevillea tree has edible honey, and we used to just pull the branches of the tall trees down with a hooked stick and break them off.*
= arlpenty
SEE ALSO karteng

alkey-alkey (W,T) *n.*
longish, a bit tall
= arlpenty-arlpenty

alkey-irrem (W,T) *vi.*
grow tall, get longer ◆ Tyerrty alkey-irrem akwek-penh, angerr-irrem. (M) *A person grows tall after being small, grows up.*
= arlpenty-irrem

alkey[2] (E) *n.*
room to go (absence of restriction caused by the presence of certain relations, restricted places etc.) ◆ *No* alkey, mwey-mwey apekarl anep-anem-kety, ngwarrenheng, *daughter* atyenh then. (St) *There is no room to go there because my son-in-law is there, my daughter and her husband.*
SEE ALSO alkiwerr

alkey-kweny (E) *n.*
'no room'; lack of social space caused by the presence of certain relations that a person should avoid direct contact with, in particular a man's mothers-in-law and a woman's sons-in-law (-kweny '*without*')
= alkiwerr-kweny

alkiwerr (E), **alkewerr** (T) *n.*
avoidance of certain relatives whom a person is not supposed to go near (iwerr '*path*', '*track*') ◆ Alkiwerr kel atyeng arnang-ilek anem, iwerr altywerel anem ayeng alhetyek.

Kel mey-mey atyenh arnang-irrenhek-arleng. Iwerr arlpawel anem inngart ayeng alhetyek, apetyetyek apek warl-warl. (St) *He went first and avoided me, and then the path was clear for me to go. Because my son-in-law had already gone before me. Then the path was open for me to go, or to come to the house.* ◆ Iwerr-kety alkiwerr rarrp alheyam-kety, arneng-irremel. Mwerikw ap alheyam arnang-irrem. (Sa) *Because he should be avoided. Because there is no room, he has to go first and do whatever. Her son-in-law goes first.* ◆ Ayengan alkiwerr-ayerr-kety ayepel-irretyel nhel-antey. Yanhentyak antey ayepel-irrerl-iwerretyel-kety. (Sa) *I'm sitting down here because I can't go near [him]. Because [all my sons-in-law] are sitting over there.*
SEE ALSO alkey[2]

alkiwerr-kweny (E) *n.*
'no room'; lack of social space caused by the presence of certain relations that a person should avoid direct contact with, in particular mothers-in-law and sons-in-law ◆ Alkiwerr-kweny, alhetyakenharl ayeng, mey-mey atyenh-kety. Alkiwerr-kwenyarl yanh. (St) *There's no room there and I can't go, because of my son-in-law. There's no room [for me] there.*
= alkey-kweny

alknga (E) eye SEE UNDER **annga**

alkngampem (E) open eyes SEE UNDER **anngampem**

alkngangem (E) delay or stop someone from doing something SEE UNDER **anngangem**

alkngaparek (E) someone who stares a lot SEE UNDER **anngaparek**

alkngarem look back SEE UNDER **anngarem**

alkngarenty uncooperative, someone who doesn't want to do something SEE UNDER **anngarenty**

alkngarlp (E) pelvic bone (?), hipbone SEE UNDER **anngarlp**

alkngarnpelh (E) eyelash SEE UNDER **anngarnpelh**

alkngarnt (E) eyebrow SEE UNDER **anngarnt**

alkngarr-ilem (T,E) warn somebody about something SEE UNDER **anngarr-ilem**

alkngaympelh (E) eyelash SEE UNDER **anngarnpelh**

alkngayt (E) brow bone SEE UNDER **anngayt**

alkngenth (E) flame SEE UNDER **anngenth**

alkngerlkem (E) open eyes SEE UNDER **anngerlkem**

alkngernt (E) naughty, mean, argumentative SEE UNDER **anngernt**

alkngerurrk (E) ankle SEE UNDER **anewerrk**

alkngetherr (E) (doing something) right in front of someone SEE UNDER **anngetherr**

alkngeyner (E), **alknginer** (E) cicada SEE UNDER **anngener**

alkngirrem (E) be 'found' or spiritually conceived in a particular place or country SEE UNDER **anngirrem**

alkngwa (E) not paying attention SEE UNDER **anngwa**

alkngwelty (E) tears SEE UNDER **anngwenty**

alkngwenhem (E) be jealous of someone or over something SEE UNDER **anngwenhem**

alkwa (E) *n.*
1. plum bush, wild plum (*Santalum lanceolatum*). Shrub to 3 m high, with drooping bluish green leaves, white flowers and purplish-black fruit.
2. the fruit of the plum bush
= ankwerlay

alkwarrer (E), **alkwarrey** (E) *n.*
1. bush banana, silky pear (found in sandhill country, especially growing on red-mallee) (*Marsdenia australis*). A winding vine which climbs other trees and shrubs. It has creamy flowers and oblong edible fruits.
2. fruit of the bush banana, silky pear
= parl, alangkw

alkwarrer-arrpwernenh (E) *n.*
pallid cuckoo (*Cuculus pallidus*) (arrpwernem '*sing out to someone to get their attention*') ◆ Alkwarrer-arrpwernem apek ra, *hunt*-em *away*, aywepemarl-artek. Awem renh alkwarrer-arrpwernenh, kwaty angerrarl urntentyenh. (St) *They sing out to the bush bananas, as if chasing them away. When you hear them, the pallid cuckoos, then there'll be a lot of rain.* ◆ Mern akngerr ilem alkwarrer alkwarrer-arrpwernenhel. (Sa) *The pallid cuckoos make lots of bush bananas.*
SEE ALSO lyalth, lyweketweretwer, alkwarrer, arrpwernem

alkwarrey (E) bush banana SEE UNDER **alkwarrer**

alkwemp *n.*
1. no good, gutless; someone who doesn't stick up for themselves ◆ Ahel utnherretyakenh, akeng-akengarl anep-anem — alkwemp. (St) Alkwemp *is someone who doesn't fight or stick up for themselves — a bit gutless.*
2. useless, raggedy, tattered
SEE ALSO mwenyent

alkwemp-alkwemp *n.*
dirty, 'rubbish one', raggedy, tattered ◆ Alkwemp-alkwemp akeng war tha anyenepenem *rubbish-rubbish* [*swag*]. (St) *I've got a really useless rubbish swag.*
SEE ALSO alther, aternng, altelhey

alkwererlp (T), **alkwerilp** (E), **alkwereylp** (E) *n.*
open country, plain country ◆ Arna kweny aketh, alkwereylp anem arem — arna arlka aretyakenh. Alkwereylp-angkwarr ayeng

alhem, arlewatyerrek urntetyek aketh-angkwarr. *An open place with no trees, that's where you see open country — you don't see any trees. I'll go through the plain country looking for goannas out in the open.*
SEE ALSO aketh, perlern

alkwernem *vi.*
1. wait (while others go); wait for someone to go and come back ◆ Ayeng alkwernem *David*-el inerl-alhetyeh *Coniston*-warn. (T) *I'm waiting for David to take me to Coniston.*
◆ Alkwernemel ayeng anep-anem nhak-warl alhekek. (St) *I'm sitting down and waiting for that one who went over there.*
2. let someone do something first; give others a chance to do something first ◆ Arrpenhel-areyek-amparr inetyek arlkwernem. Arrpenhel-arey inemel ra anem irrpemel, arlkwernerl-anenty-penh anemel. (St) *She is letting the others get things first. The others will get theirs and then she will go in, after sitting down and waiting for them to go first.*
◆ Arrpenh mapeng-amparr *doctor*-el aremeng, ilern apety-alperrek alkwernemel anetyeh. (T) *We two returned to sit down here while the other mob went first [to the doctor].*
SEE ALSO mpwelhem[1]
CAN SOUND A BIT LIKE arlkwenhem *'fill something up', 'fill up a container'*

alkwert *n.*
1. shield ◆ Artwel mpwarem alkwert arnang inernt-penh, alyang-kety ilpelhetyek. (T) *Men make shields from bean tree wood to protect themselves from boomerangs.* ◆ Rrmwarl-wem, alkwert-warn. (M) *Make fire [by rubbing a piece of wood] on the shield.*

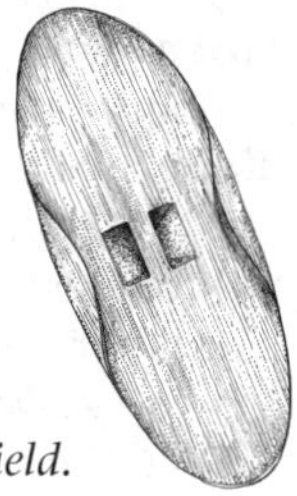

2. someone who talks up front or who talks strongly; boss ◆ Alkwert ilem, pwatharl *block*-em ilem-arteh. Alakenh ilelhem alkwertan. *Shield*-elarteh ilpelhem. Wal artwang aywang kenh alkwertem. *If someone* apek ahang apetyem, kenh alkwert-arteh anantherr arrernem artwang aywang yenh arrwekel irnetyeh. Arelh apek. (T) *'Alkwert' is what we call a boss who protects us. They are like a shield and they put themselves up to protect us from things in the way that a shield does. An old man who is like that is called a 'shield'. If there is someone coming looking for a fight, then we put the old man or woman up there in the front, like a shield.*

Alkwert *n.*
the name of a place in the Alcoota Station area. The name of a site close the community of Engawala. The station name 'Alcoota' is derived from this name. See map p. viii.

alkwerteng-alkwert *n.*
pretend shield, toy shield ◆ Ampa mapel mpwaretyam alkwerteng-alkwert arrkenel, arntap-warl, arnan anem arrernetyam alkwert-arrpantey. Arntapel ina mpwaretyam, ankerrmern-penh apek iyltemel ilwemp, aper apek, alkwerteng-alkwert anem ina mpwaretyam arrkenel-arleng. (St) *Children made toy shields from bark for fun. They made sort of pretend shields from bark. Maybe they'd strip bark from the coolibah tree, the ghost gum or the river red gum and then enjoy themselves making toy shields.*
SEE ALSO irrtyarteng-irrtyart, alyaper

alkwertek-ilem (W) *vt.*
form a ceremonial relationship between men who are in the father–son relationship to each other
SEE ALSO ahen-ilem

alkwert atwenh (E) *n.*
rabbit (lit. 'one that hits the shield') ◆ Ipert apek ra atweynerl-anem rltar-irrerl-anem alhwengek kwen, alkwert atwerl-anem, rapet, rltar-irrerl-anem kwen alhwengel. 'Alkwert atwenh'. Itnan. 'Pet-pet' an 'alkwert atwenh', atherrarrp. 'Rapet' arrekantherrenh, arlter map-kenh. (Sa) *The rabbit makes a banging and rattling noise from inside its burrow. It bangs its shield inside the burrow. That's its name —* 'alkwert atwenh'. *It has two names —* 'pet-pet' *and* 'alkwert atwenh'. *'Rabbit' is yours, whitefellas' [language].*
= pet-pet, rapet, mwetyernk, metyernk

alkwert-alkwert *n.*
1. collarbone
2. shoulder-blade [SOME SPEAKERS]
SEE ALSO anirnterrm-irnterr, kwaty-kwaty[2]

amper alkwert-alkwert (T)
kneecap (amper *'knee'*)

alng SEE UNDER **alkng**

alpalth (E) *n.*
lame, having a gammy leg, dragging a leg
◆ Ayeng alpalth alhep-alhem, ingka ntewemel, irrtyart apekarl atanthek. (St) *I am going along lame, dragging my foot, perhaps from being speared.*
SEE ALSO arlamarr, rnwerr

alpalyel angem, alpwalyel angem, alpwalyel akngem (E) *vt.*
carry something (especially kangaroo) slung across or over shoulder ◆ Ker alpalyel angem, atanthekarl, kel aketheh wety-alhem. (N) *The*

kangaroo that has been speared is carried on the shoulder and then thrown down onto the open ground. ◆ Artwel alpwalyel angem ker aherr. (M) *The man carries the kangaroo round the back of his shoulder.*
SEE ALSO untyel angem, intwerl anem, intarlp angem, ntwarlp angem, anhwert angem, aylpwar angem, anhwert

alpangwerr (W) *n.*
black-headed monitor, freckled monitor (*Varanus tristis*)
= altywekerr, kweny-areny, kwenyel alhem, pwer rrpwerl

alpar *n.*

1. rat-tail goosefoot, green crumbweed, kalpari (*Dysphania kalpari*)
2. rat tails, alpara (*Dysphania rhadinostachya*). Sticky herbs about 25 cm high with flowers forming erect spikes, and with tiny, shiny, black edible seeds. The nice-smelling leaves are used as a bed for children. The *arrerlang* plant is said to be the elder sister and *alpar* the younger sister. ◆ Ntang atherretyart ap yanh, apwertel athemel awantyemel — arlpar then arrerlang then. (Sa) *That is a seed that used to be ground up, ground up with a stone — the* alpar *and the* arrerlang.
SEE ALSO parntentyarlp, mwelyeparnt-parnt, arrerlang

alparr[1] (W,T) *n.*
1. large wooden dish, coolamon ◆ Arelhel alparrel rrkwerl-anem kwer akwek. (M) *His wife is holding the baby in the baby-carrier.* ◆ Inernteng alparr twem. *Wooden dishes are made from bean tree wood.*
= panth, lengarr
SEE ALSO atywekal, urety, kwerlintyerr, lwengkart[2], irrkwely[2], irrkwa, rnwa, urna
2. the tray of a ute or truck

alparr[2] *n.*
cloth, material or fabric that hasn't been sewn ◆ Atanthetyakenh an alparr, terreth alparr war. Alparr yanh atyeng antheyaw. (St) *Cloth that hasn't been sewn up yet is* alparr. *Give me some of that material.*
SEE ALSO awer[1]

alparr-alparr (E) *n.*
light, flimsy (of fabric) ◆ Ilterrelhekarl alparr-alparr. (Sa) *The light [fabric] ripped apart.*

alparrantyey native tomato SEE UNDER **alperrantyey**

alpayerr grub from the tar vine SEE UNDER **arrpayerr**

-alpem SEE UNDER **+ety-alp+**

alpem *vi.*
1. go back, return, go home ◆ Tweperr alpem ayeng. (M) *I'm going back for good.* ◆ Mer-warn alpem itna ker aketyek. *They are returning to the camp to cut up the meat.* ◆ Ker-kweny-antey ina artwep-irremel. Artwep-irremel ina alpem, rlkert-akert — artwepelh-ilem arelh merntel. (N) *They are turning back although they still haven't found any meat. They are turning back because they have a sick person with them — the sick woman made them turn back.*
2. go away ◆ Lywa angerrakw-athek anem alpep-alpem anwekantherr-kety. (St) *Now the shade is going towards the east, away from us.*
3. flow (water) ◆ Lher akngerr, alpep-alpem lher akngerr yanh. (St) *There is a big river flowing along there.*
SEE ALSO apety-alpem, alhem
4. Combines with other verbs to show that an action is done before going back, or that the 'doer' of the verb action goes back somewhere and then does the other verb action.
SEE ALSO +erl[2], +ety-alp+

alpent-alpent (W) *n.*
fast, really fast ◆ Tyerrty alpent-alpent alhem. (M) *The person is going really fast.*
SEE ALSO inangkal

alpent-wem (E) lever something up SEE UNDER **ilpent-wem**

alpent-wem (T) *vt.*
1. tell stories, spread a story around, broadcast a story ◆ Thang kel angkety atyenh ngkweng alpent-wek-arleng. (T) *I already told you my story.*
2. spread seeds, sow seeds, scatter seeds ◆ Artety-areny apek alpent-wetyek lyapelh-iletyek. (T) *Spreading the mulga seeds around so that they grow.*

alperl *n.*
pubic covering (traditional)
= pely
CAN SOUND A BIT LIKE arlperl *'lerp scale on mulga'*

alperr (E) *n.*
leaf, leaves
= arlpa[2]
SEE ALSO waly
CAN SOUND A BIT LIKE aylperr *'fish';* arlperr[2] *'whitewood'*

alperr-ayerr (E) *n.* [RESPECT LANGUAGE]
playing cards ◆ Alperr-ayerrel yanhentyak arrken-irrerlentyarretyel-rnem apwert-ayerrek. (Sa) *They [respect kin] are all playing cards over*

there, for money.

alperr-wem (T,E) *vt.*
scatter things around; tip things out; strew things about ◆ Ampel apek arnkely-irremel alperr-wem. (St) *The kids are sulkily tipping [things] out.* ◆ Rapety arengkel anem alperr-wem ingkerrek. (T) *The dogs are scattering all the rubbish around.*

alperrantyey, alparrantyey *n.*
1. native tomato, potato bush, wild gooseberry (*Solanum ellipticum* var. *Foothills GJ Leach 1145*)). Plant, about 30 cm high, with velvety grey leaves, purple flowers, and edible fruits that are green with purplish stripes at first and then pale yellow when ripe.

2. the fruit of the native tomato ◆ Alparrantyey, ararnt, arlelyek. *Different* ingkerr. Ararntek-arneng. Alparrantyey. Ntyer-areny. Alparrantyey apwertelarl arlka *mixed up* akwel anenh-anenh. Mwerr anthwerr theweyet anthwerr. (N) *Alparrantyey,* ararnt *and* arlelyek *are all different —* alparrantyey *is closely related to the* ararnt, *and it's found in the floodout country. It also grows in the hills as well. It's a really sweet food.*
= ararnt
SEE ALSO manyem, rrwarlp[1], arlelyek, katyerr

alperrty (T,E) *n.*
everywhere, scattered, all over the place, spread out

alperrty-alperrty (E) *n.*
messy or knotty hair
SEE ALSO alyep-alyep[2]

alperrty-irrem (T,E) *vi.*
split up, spread out, scatter in all directions, go in different directions ◆ Anwantherr anep-anem nhenh ingkerrek, kel anwantherr alperrty-irrerl-alhem. Alpetyenh anemarl aley atherran, anwantherr alperrty-irremel anem alperl-anem. (St) *All of us are here, and then we'll all split up and go back home. Those two will go back and we'll all scatter and go home.* ◆ Akwekarl ra pwerrk-pwerrk akely, atnek irrpem aherrek apek, alperrty anem irrerl-anem. (St) *The* pwerrk-pwerrk *beetle is small, and it burrows into kangaroo dung and makes a mess of it.*
SEE ALSO irrarnp-irrem

alperrty-ilem (T,E), **alperrtyelh-ilem** (T,E) *vt.*
split or divide things up, spread things out, share things out ◆ Mantarr apek atyenh alperrty-ilem. (St) *Dividing up my clothes.* ◆ Ampeny yanh renh kel alperrtyelh-iletyek, kel itnek anthemel anem. Ampeny anthem, arrpenhek-arey. (St) *The belongings of the deceased are split up, and then given to other people. The dead person's things are given to other people.*

alperrty-wem (T,E), **alperrty-iwem** (E) *vt.*
scatter things around, scatter things all over the place ◆ Mern atyenh alperrty-iwek arengkel. (Sa) *The dogs scattered my food all over the place.*

alpert (T) white tail tip of the bilby SEE UNDER **alpety**

Alpert-alpert (W) *n.*
name of a hill and soakage in Mt Denison Station area

alpety (W,T), **alpeyt** (T,E), **alpert** (T) *n.*
1. white tail tip of the bilby ◆ Ker angkay alpert-akert, mperlker-akert. (T) *The bilby has a white tail tip.* ◆ Lweren arlka nheng arrwekeleny mapelam atwetyart, nheng alpety alakenh-iletyeh, nheng kwer-tayem. (N) *That's why the olden-time people used to kill them, so that they could use the bilby tails like this [swing them around] during initiation ceremony time.*
2. blossom, flower
SEE ALSO anteth, angkay, ahert

alpety-alpety (W,T), **alpeyt-alpeyt** (T,E) *n.*
blossom, flower ◆ Ngkerlp anmakert, alpety-alpety anem ra irrem. *The native tobacco plant has buds and then it blossoms.*

alpety-alpety-irrem (W,T), **alpeyt-alpeyt-irrem** (T,E) *vi.*
to flower or blossom

Alpety amenheng (W) *n.*
place name; small cave near Bean Tree Dam, Mt Denison. Bilby Dreaming.

alpeyart-alpeyart (E) *n.*
1. spiny-cheeked honeyeater (*Acanthagenys rufogularis*)
2. singing honeyeater (*Lichenostomus virescens*)
= arrakwerakwer, arrety-arrety

alpeyt (T,E) white tail tip of the bilby SEE UNDER **alpety**

alpiwem (E) *vi.* [RESPECT LANGUAGE]
move away (?) ◆ Ngwarr-nheng atherr alpiwetyek, tawert ingwer-warl anem akwel, *change*-ek. (Sa) *The married couple are going to move back to another camp, for a change.*
SEE ALSO iwem

alpiwerl-alpem (E) *vt.* [RESPECT LANGUAGE]
take someone back, drop someone or something off ◆ Nhak anem akwel tawert

nhakwarl anem alpiwerl-alpem, iwerl-alpem. *That one [respect kin] is being dropped off at that camp over there now.*
SEE ALSO iwerl-alpem

alpma (T,E), **ama** (T,E), **anma** (T,E), **atnma** (E) *n.*
1. bud or flower of native tobacco (*Nicotiana* sp.) ◆ Ngkerlp anmakert, alpety-alpety anem ra irrem. *The native tobacco plant has buds, and then it flowers* ◆ Alpmakert anem irrek nhenhan ngkwerlp. (St) *This tobacco plant has flowered.*
SEE ALSO alpety, anteth
2. orange-coloured outgrowth on the dogwood seed (*Acacia sericophylla*). Also referred to as *ngkwarl alpma.*
SEE ALSO ntyerrm, apal[1], kertaty
3. yellow substance found in sugarbag, or native bees' hive. Some people say that *ama* from the sugarbag is not edible, but rather is used as a rubbing medicine for itchy skin and sores. ◆ Arrwengkelth-akert renh arlkwem akin renh, kel renh mwerr-ilem. (St) *If a person is sick they can eat it [the* ama*] as well, and it will make them better.*
• SEE ALSO arrem, arwengalker, rltwamp

alpmangkem (E) go yellow (native tobacco) after being put in ashes SEE UNDER **atnmangkem**

alpment (E), **atnment** (E) *n.* [RESPECT LANGUAGE]
1. fire
2. firewood ◆ Alpment-ayerr ineyaw, irrepethey, tyety-ayerr ampernetyek. (Sa) *Go and get some firewood [from respect kin], so that the meat can be cooked.*
SEE ALSO rwa, ntyangkwenng, anyengk

alpment-irrem (E), **atnment-irrem** (E) *vi.* [SOME SPEAKERS] dance for son-in-law (women) The woman holds the ceremonial firestick called *ntyangkwenng.* ◆ Arelh alpment-irrem mwerekikw. (Sa) *The woman dances for her son-in-law.* (?)
SEE ALSO ntyangkwenng-irrem

alpment-penh (E), **atnment-penh** (E) *n.* [RESPECT LANGUAGE]
a person with whom you are in a special relationship because of their role during an initiation (young man) ceremony; a woman's son-in-law or a man's mother-in-law (-penh[1] '*from*') ◆ Alpment-penh atyenh yanhenty-antey ayepelirretyel. (Sa) *My son-in-law is sitting over there.*
SEE ALSO rtwalty, ntyangkwenng, ntyangkwenng-penh

alpwaly (carrying something) slung across or over the shoulder SEE UNDER **alpaly**

alpwarternem (E) *vt.*
lever something up (in order to remove it); dig something out ◆ Nhenh tha alpwarternem. Arna apek arrerlp nepenem, wal alpwarternem anem renh. Atnemel apek. Ingkekety apek, mwetek apek atanthekerr *tyre* apek. Alpwarterney urrek tha. (St) *I am levering this out. If there is a sharp stick there, well I'll dig it out with a digging stick. In case it hurts someone's foot or skewers a tyre. Wait while I lever it out.*
= arwakem, ilpent-wem

alpwely *n.*
1. loose, deflated, slack
2. shrivelled up
SEE ALSO arlwar, alyemp-alyemp[1]

alpwely-irrem *vi.*
1. go flat, limp or slack; deflate ◆ Tyelk alpwely-irrem, ampwerremel. (T) *When [a person] gets old their flesh gets loose or saggy.* ◆ Alpwely-irrem wangkekarl-penh. Atnert apekarl pwelap arrpenhel anep-anem, wal alpwely anem irrem anem, angayakw-irremel. (St) *Deflating after being swollen. Somebody might have a full swollen stomach and then, as they get hungry, their stomach goes flat.* ◆ Werlaty alpwely-irrem antywekarl-penh. (St) *The breasts have gone slack from [the baby] drinking.*
SEE ALSO ampwerrem, alyempelhem
2. shrivel up, become dry (of plants) ◆ Mern arlatyey apek alpwely-irrekaw, mern altyey apek, alpwely-irrek. (St) *Pencil yams, or the leaves of bush bananas might have shrivelled up.* ◆ Atwakey alpwely-irrem, antyerrk-irremel. (T) *The wild orange [fruit] shrivels up and dries.*
3. feel sad or homesick, feel deflated ◆ Alharrp apek alpwely-irrem, *happy*-arl anek-penh alpwely-irrerl-weman. Alharrp. (St) *Feeling sad is* alpwely-irrem. *After feeling happy [you] feel deflated. Sad.*

alpwerrem (W,T) go rotten SEE UNDER **lpwerrem**

Alpwerrenteng (T) *n.*
name of a rockhole in the Hanson River area north-west of Ti Tree town. See map p. viii.

alpwertek-alpwert (E) *n.*
grey butcherbird (*Cracticus torquatus*)
= arrpwerek-arrpwer

alta, **altang** (W,T) *n.*
1. hair (on body as well as head); hair or fur of an animal ◆ Alta arlwerr-arlwerr. *Curly hair.* ◆ Alta alyep-alyep-irrem, urlpepenh apek, urlpelarl apernelhek, anter *mix up*. (St) *Hair might get matted after being rubbed with ochre, with ochre and fat.* ◆ Arengk irrkerlerrk yanh

aywepeyaw. Alta anetyakenh *naked one.* (Sa) *Hunt that naked hairless dog away.* ◆ Ker altang nthek-weyew! (M) *Singe the fur off the animal!*
2. feathers, down ◆ Artewan akerarlam. Altang althem altang althem kwer-penh ker renh atyerrem. Rlweth akem amwelt atherr an kapert rlweth akem. (N) *Bush turkey meat is edible. The feathers are plucked out and then after that the meat is cooked. The two legs and the head are split open.*
CAN SOUND A BIT LIKE arlta[1] *'day';* arlta[2] *'part of emu's guts'*
lhenp alta
armpit hair (lhenp *'armpit'*)
alteperety (E) *n.*
unwashed or messy hair

altalt (W,T) pubic hair SEE UNDER **antalt**

altang (W,T) hair SEE UNDER **alta**

altarrp (W,T) *n.*
sorry, lonely, sad, worried, depressed, unwell
= alharrp
altarrp-irrem (W,T) *vi.*
feel sad, sorry or lonely ◆ Altarrp-irrem angwely atyeng rang twerrirrern akeweny, altarrp-irrem akewenyew. (N) *I am feeling sorry for my dog that was in a fight, the poor thing.*
= alharrp-irrem
altarrp-altarrp (W,T) *n.*
a bit lonely, sad, sorry ◆ Altarrp-altarrpam tyerrty yanh map anep-anem. (M) *Those people are feeling a bit sad.*
= alharrp-alharrp
altarrp awelhem (W,T)
feel sad or sorry; feel homesick, lonely or sick ◆ Ayeng altarrp awelhem mer-warn alpetyeh. (M) *I am feeling sad and I want to go home.*

Altatwem (W) *n.*
the name of a place to the north of Mt Allan community

altelhem *vi.*
become scruffy, fall out (hair or fur) ◆ Yanh aywepeyaw — altelhekarl, iltelheyaw. Arengk yanh aywepey, alpetyek ra arleng-warl. (Sa) *Hunt that dog away — its hair has fallen out. Chase that scruffy dog away so that it goes a long way away.*
altelhey (W,T), **iltelhey** (T,E) *n.*
1. dirty, raggedy, scruffy, messy ◆ Iltelhey, akeng war alhep-alhem lthel-lthel war, mantarr akeng-akeng-akert iltelhey-iltelhey alhep-alhem. Aternng-aternng mantarr atyenh *clean* anetyakenh. Iltelhey akeng wararl alhep-alhem alhewelhetyakenh. (St) *I am just going along with raggedy, dirty clothes on. My clothes are dirty — they're not clean. I'm a bit scruffy — I haven't had a wash.*
SEE ALSO alther, alkwemp-alkwemp, aternng, nywet-nywet[2]
2. mangy, without hair ◆ Arengk altelhey, tywen-akert, altarl altelhem ingkerr. (M) *That mangy dog has got sores, and all its hair has fallen out.*
SEE ALSO arrkenty[1], rtety-rtety, mentyey
3. lots of hair (of a dog) • SEE ALSO lthel-lthel
iltelhey-iltelhey (T,E) *n.*
a bit dirty, raggedy, scruffy, messy

alterrem, ilterrem (E) *vt.*
tear something, rip something open ◆ Tyart atyenharrp tha ilterrem. (Sa) *I'm tearing my shirt myself.*
= tyep-akem
CAN SOUND A BIT LIKE altherrem *'burn away', 'catch alight';* ilterrem *'swear at each other'*
alterrelhem, ilterrelhem (E) *vi.*
become ripped or torn ◆ Mantarr atyenh apek alterrem, atanthetyek kwenh tha, alterrenty, alterrelhem-arleng kwenh. (St) *My clothes are ripped and I've got to mend them, mend the tear where they ripped.*

+alth, +elth *n.ending*
Goes on certain nominals to describe someone or something that characteristically behaves in that way.
nyerralth
timid, shy (nyerr *'shame'*) ◆ Lyetant kaltyirretyel, ampa nyerralth. *The timid child is just starting to learn things (at school).*
ateralth
fearful, frightened (ater *'fear'*) ◆ Kwer yanh ateralth-kwenyel. (T) *That child is not frightened.*
arwengkalth
a thief (arwengkel *'sneakily'*) ◆ Angank arwengkalth — arraty. Nyennngel arlkwerl-anem akweteth akweteth ateram arrtyanetyenheng, pwerlt-irrem. (N) *Crows are robbers — that's true. They always sneak around and steal food to eat and then when they are frightened they fly off, clear out.*

altha (E) *n.*
messed up or obscured with footprints ◆ Nhenhan altharl-kety, altha ingkerrek, ingka apapeth. Mpwankeny anem aretyek alhetyek. (St) *There's too many footprints here, footprints all over the place. [We'd] better go and look for a fresh place.*

althalth, althwalth (T,E) *n.*
light (not heavy), crumbly, powdery, raggedy, broken down, rotten (wood), flimsy, insubstantial ◆ Ura nhenh althalth tha tyarrp-ilem. (St) *I'm going to split up this light*

wood. ◆ Interrkelarl arlkwek, interrk, 'Oh althwaltharl nhenhaw, interrkelarl arlkwek-penh'. (St) *If the white ants have eaten it, 'Oh this one is rotten because the white ants have eaten it'.* ◆ Mwetek althwalth-akert yanh alhemaw, akeng-akert althwalth-althwalth-akert, althwalth akeng weth-lkwer akelhekarl, *raggedy one.* (St) *That person is driving round in a broken-down car, a useless car that has broken down.* ◆ Rwang akem, 'Althwalth nhenh menty kwenh. Rwang angerr-warn rrwek ayeng alhey kwenh'. (T) *Cutting firewood, 'Leave this light stuff. Wait while I go and get some big bits'.*

SEE ALSO althekalth, arrmaly-arrmaly, artaly-artaly, atyet[1], twer

althalth-irrem, althwalth-irrem (T,E) *vi.*
lose weight, become light or flimsy, become light in the body ◆ Althwalth-irremel untem, alwerrng ikwerenh atywaty-irremel. *That person is running around to stretch their legs and make themselves feel lighter in the body.*

althalth-ilem, althwalth-ilem (T,E) *vt.*
make something crumble up or break into bits ◆ Arna arlkwenh-arlkwenharl ra — arna anem interrkel arlkwerl-anem althalth-ilemel. (St) *The white ants eat trees — they eat trees and make them break up into bits.*

althart *n.*
a type of ceremony. This is a 'public' ceremony, attended by men, women and children. ◆ Ampel arlkan aretyart, arrkenel-arleng alakenh irreperrem. Arrpenhem alyerl-anem, arrpenhem rntertarl anerl-anem, arrpenhem rlpwerrng atwerl-anem. (St) *Children used to watch for fun as well, watch people going in for the* althart *ceremony, enjoying themselves doing it like that. Some would sing, others would sit quietly, and others would beat the rhythm on their laps.*

althekalth *n.*
able to move easily, free, loose
SEE ALSO althalth

althekalth-irrem *vi.*
1. stretch yourself, loosen up ◆ Althekalth-irrey ayengaw, urrek. Artep apekarl ayeng arntem. Althekalth-irrey. (St) *Wait while I stretch myself. Maybe my back is aching. I'll stretch myself.* ◆ Ayeng althekalth-irrem, alhekarl-penh, anemel ayeng althekalth-irrem, kel ayeng alhem anem althekalth-irrenty-penh. (St) *After walking round I'm going to sit down and stretch myself, then after stretching I'll go off again.*
SEE ALSO arternelhem, atywaty-irrem[1]
2. be able to move easily; flow freely (blood) ◆ Alhwa althekalth-irremel alherl-anem — mwerr, rew-ilemel. (St) *The blood flows easily [when] you move around — it's good, making it flow.*

althekalth-ilem *vt.*
1. heal or cure somebody, use healing massage to loosen someone up ◆ Mernt-penh tyerrty yanhan althekalthelhek. Ngangkayel renh althekalth-ilek. (T) *That person got better after being sick. The traditional healer cured him.*
SEE ALSO mpwarem, mwerr-ilem, iteth-ilem, tangkelh-ilem
2. release someone (from jail); set someone free [SOME SPEAKERS]

althem *vt.*
1. pluck feathers from a bird ◆ Artwel althem ker artew itetyenheng. (T) *The man plucks the bush turkey and then cooks it.*
2. clear away grass; strip foliage from plants ◆ Apmer althem, arnel apek atnemel althem. Arnam renh iwemel, akethel ilemel inteyameng. (St) *Clearing the grass away from the camp, with a stick or a digging stick. Throwing away the grass and clearing it so that you can sleep there.* ◆ Menyeynterlel arwerlarl altheynerl-anemel, antywer anetyangarl ileynem. Akngerrel altheynerl-anem alanh alpep-alpem. *The locusts are the ones that go along stripping the trees, go along wiping out the grass. Lots of locusts go along like that, stripping the foliage.*

althelhem *vi.*
1. have a shave ◆ Artwang map arralt althelhem. (T) *Men shave their beards.*
2. fall out (hair or fur) ◆ Kapert althelhem, kapert alta ingkerrek anyem. (M) *The hair falls out, all the hair falls out.* ◆ Angwely alta althelhem *mangy* apek. (M) *The dog's fur falls out if it has got mange.*
SEE ALSO ltheley

althenem (T,E) kill lots of something (game) SEE UNDER **althinem**

alther (T,E) *n.*
1. a feeling of sadness, loneliness or homesickness
SEE ALSO irrar
2. without anything ◆ Ker-kweny kwenh ra alther apety-alpem. (T) *He is coming back without any meat, with nothing.*
3. dirty ◆ Alther alherl-anem mantarr akeng-akert. (Sa) *She is going around in dirty raggedy clothes.*

alther-irrem (T,E) *vi.*
feel lonely, homesick or alone; miss someone or something; long for something; pine for someone or for something ◆ Alther-irrem ayeng alpetyek anem mer atyenh-warl apety-alpetyek. (St) *If I'm feeling homesick then I'll have to go back to my country, come back to my country.*
= irrar-irrem

altherrem *vi.*
burn away, catch alight; fire spread out of control ◆ Awely-awelyel ultewem arnang, rwang anem altherrenhem. (T) *If the lightning hits the tree then the fire will catch and burn away.*
SEE ALSO alep-irrem, lherrm-irrem, antant-irrem

altherrng (E) *n.*
holey, having holes ◆ Kwaty irrert-irremel akngem *billycan* altherrng-they apek, altywer akert-they. (St) *As you go along water leaks out from a billycan with a hole in it.*
SEE ALSO altywer

altherrp *n.*
having just a few hairs of the head. Also referred to as *kapert altherrp.*

althinem (T,E), **althenem** (T,E), **althitnem** (E) *vt.*
kill lots of something (game) ◆ Arlewatyerr tha althinem, map. Arlewatyerr ker althinem, ker aherr apek althinem. Ankerr arlka. (St) *I am killing lots of goannas. Lots of goannas or kangaroos or emus.* ◆ 'Ntwa antem althenek alewatyerr anengk kwenh, tha kenh atherrarl atwek.' *'You've killed lots of goannas, whereas I only killed two.'*
SEE ALSO akwerremp-ilem, iltatwem

althwalth (T,E) light (not heavy) SEE UNDER **althalth**

althwerrk (W) *n.*
hole ◆ Mantarr nhenh althwerrk-akert. (M) *This dress has holes in it.*
SEE ALSO altywer

altwerl, **alturl** (E) *n.*
west
SEE ALSO ayerrer, antekerr, ingerr, angerrakw

altwerl-altwerl *n.*
1. north-west
2. in a westerly direction, roughly west ◆ Altwerl-altwerl nthwerl-apem lyweny. (T) *Going hunting in a westerly direction.*

altwerl arraty, **altwerl arratyeny** (T)
due west (arraty *'correct', 'straight'*)

altwerleng (W,T) *n.*
from the west ◆ Rlkang altwerleng apetyem aretharr. (M) *The* aretharr *wind comes from the west.*

altwerleny (W,T) *n.* = **altwerleng**

altwerl-penh, **altwerl-pwenh** *n.*
1. west, in a westerly direction, to the west ◆ Kerek untherl-anetyek, antekerr-pwenh, altwerl-penh apek. Altwerl-penh uyelp-uyerrenhem irrer. Altwerl-pwenh-they apety-alpek. (Sa) *Looking round for meat in the south or in the west. Going hunting and disappearing to the west. And then returning from the west.* ◆ Ayeng altwerl-penh alhem. (T) *I am going to the west.*
2. from the west, from a westerly direction ◆ Altwerl-penh apetyem tyerrty alethang apek. (M) *A stranger might come from the west.*

altwerl-iperr (T,E) *n.* = **altwerl-penh** ◆ Ayeng altwerl-iperr alhek. (T) *I went to the west.*

altwerlernety (W),
altwerlerneyt (E) *n.* [RESPECT LANGUAGE]
west ◆ Altwerlerneyt ahanenhek tyety-ayerrek, nyewel-areny apek aretyek, arrep-iletyek. (St) *He has gone hunting to the west, looking for euros [said by a woman about her son-in-law].*

altwerlenety-athek (W),
altwerlerneyt-athek (E) *n.* [RESPECT LANGUAGE]
in a westerly direction
SEE ALSO altwerl, aywelernety, antwekenety, ngwelernety

altya *n.*
close relations, family. For Anmatyerr people the concept of 'close family', or *altya,* extends well beyond immediate or biologically related kin. ◆ Altyang map anwern anem. (M) *We are all family.* ◆ Altyernem amikw anyent-kenh *mother* anyent-kenh-rnem altyernem. Rernem-antey, altyernem. Angkwer-intyerr. (Sa) *'Family' are children who have one mother — they are close relations. They are 'altya', just them, all the sisters.* ◆ Altyant-amperl akngerrerretyel, altyernem anetyel. (Sa) *Just all the family are living there.* ◆ Aleraty-arey altyarey. Altyarey anteyarl ipmenhaty-arey. Arrengaty-areyan altyarey anteyarl. Anherraty-areyan altyarey antey. (St) *My nephews and nieces are close family. My daughter's children are family as well, and my son's children are family. My sons' wives are family too.*
SEE ALSO arlalty, pelty
CAN SOUND A BIT LIKE iltya *'hand', 'finger'*

altyarey, **altyernem** (E) *n.* = **altya**
(-arey, -rnem *'plural'*) ◆ Anwengkerr angkwer-intyerr anem altyarey. Amer anyent-kenh map anwengkerr anem — altyarey. (T) *We are all sisters, family. We are belonging to one country — close family.*

SEE ALSO arlalty-arey
altyirrem *vi.*
feel happy, particularly about one's family ◆ Ayeng altyirrem atyenh angkwerekarl apetyem. (T) *I am happy that my sister is coming.*
SEE ALSO pelty-irrem, tyen-irrem, akangkem
CAN SOUND A BIT LIKE iltyerrem *'wave'*

altyarrernem (T) turn or tip something upside down SEE UNDER **altywarrernem**

altyart (W,T) native millet SEE UNDER **altywart**

altyek-altyek *n.*
wrinkled, furrowed
SEE ALSO alyemp-alyemp[1]
altyek-altyek-irrem *vi.*
get wrinkled; skin sag or go slack or loose ◆ Tyerrtyarl altyek-altyek irrem — tyew-irremelarl altyek-altyek anem irrem. (St) *A person gets wrinkly — when they lose weight they become wrinkled.* ◆ 'Keweny altyek-altyek-irrek ntwa kwenh.' 'Yaw kwenh. Ayeng ampwerrek angerr anthwerr kwenh.' (T) *'You poor thing, you've become really wrinkly.' 'Yeah. I've really aged a lot.'*
= alyemp-alyemp-irrem
altyekelhem *vi.*
1. get wrinkled; skin sag or go slack or loose
2. frown or screw up your face
= alyempelhem

altyel, **altyeley** (T,E) *n.kin*
1. female cross-cousin (father's sister's or mother's brother's daughter)
2. particular female relations with the same skin as your *altyel* ◆ Arelhel ilem 'altyeley' arelh arrpekw. (T) *A woman calls another woman* 'altyeley'. ◆ 'Mpa altyeley aylanth alherrey kerek arlewatyerrek untherl-anetyek.' Arelhant-atherr. (Sa) *'Come on cousin, let's go and look for goannas.' Just two women.*
altyel-altyel *n.kin*
female cross-cousin (father's sister's or mother's brother's daughter) etc. This may be an affectionate or respectful way of talking to or about one's *altyel*, or it may be a way of talking to children about their *altyel*.
◆ Peltharr tha 'altyel-altyel' anpernem. Artwel *too.* Kwerel apek ilem, 'Altyel-altyelay, kwaty apek antha mern apek antha'. (P) *I call Peltharr people* 'altyel-altyel'. *Men do too. They might say, 'Cousin, get me some water or some food'.*
altyelaty *n.kin*
my/our *altyel*
altyelengkw *n.kin*
your *altyel*
altyelikw, **altyeleyekw** (E) *n.*
his/her/their *altyel*
altyelekw (W,T) *n.kin*
1. your *altyel*
2. his/her/their *altyel*
altyel-nheng *n.kin*
a group of two or more people who are related to each other as *altyel* ◆ Altyel-nheng alhek lyweny. (P) *The cousins went hunting together.*
altyel-intyerr *n.kin* = **altyel-nheng** ◆ Marl Pengart then, rrpwety apekarl alhekarl, 'Altyel-intyerr alhek. Altyel-nheng alhek mern apek inetyeh, arlatyey-warl apek'. (P) *Some Pengart women, a few on them that have gone, 'All the cousins together went. All the cousins went to get food, or to get pencil yams'.*
altyel-nheng-arey *n.kin*
a group of more than two people who are related to each other as *altyel*
altyel-nheng atherr *n.kin*
a person together with their *altyel* ◆ Altyel-nheng atherr alherrekaw, lyweny alherrek. (P) *Two cousins went, went hunting.* ◆ Mpetyan, marl Mpetyan an marl Peltharr, altyel-nheng atherr. (P) *A Mpetyan woman and a Peltharr woman are related as cousins.*
altyel-ankethenh *n.kin*
1. having a close *altyel* still alive
2. someone who is always with their *altyel*
SEE ALSO -ankethenh
altyel-parety *n.kin*
respectful or 'sorry' way of talking about someone's *altyel*
SEE ALSO -parety
amikw altyeley (E)
mother-cousin (lit. 'mother cousin')
altyel akerrem (W,T)
be full female cross-cousins to each other (daughters of a brother and a sister) ◆ Yanh atherr altyel akerrek, *two cousins — sister and brother*-kenh. (T) *Those two are full cross-cousins for each other — belonging to a sister and a brother.*
SEE ALSO ankel akerrem, rnwek-werrenty, urnek-iwerrenty

altyel-altyel (E), **altyeley-altyeley** (E) *n.*
a type of plant (?). Has a white flower and edible seeds.
= arrwekety-arrwekety[1]

altyerr[1] *n.kin*
1. dream ◆ Altyerr tha arek kel ingwepenh alheyaw aretyek anem ker apek arlewatyerrek apek. (Sa) *I had a dream [about hunting] and then in the morning I'll go and then I'll see kangaroos or goannas.* (?)
2. Dreaming, totem, ancestral being

3. God, Jesus ◆ Altyerr anarnpety-anek nhenh-thayt, Ntwerrperl-thayt — Ntwerrperl anthwerr. Tyerrty anengk anetyam arrwekeleny map. Wal wenh arek, 'Amwang apetyem kwenh'. Ingkart *Isew*-arl apetyekarl, anarnpety alenheh. Wal ngangkayel ltewek ltewek, *well he been go* Ntharey anthwerrem ra anarnpek, Kwerrperrely yang mpwarenh. Altyerr-henh kwaty Kwerrperrely. Aterel-anthek ina, arrwekeleny map, *myall* mapel, Anmatyerr mapel. Ingkart *Isew* nheng Altyerr, *no* ina iterlarek — itya apalekalek ina arrwekelarl anek. Aterel-anthek ina, akeweny. (M) *Jesus came down to earth on this side, Ntwerrperl side — right there at Ntwerrperl. There were a lot of olden-time Aboriginal people there. When they saw him they said, 'A snake [a monster] is coming'. That was what happened when Jesus came to earth. Well the traditional healers threw [spears] at him and then he went on to Hermannsburg and came down to earth there and made Kwerrperrely. That water there at Kwerrperrely is God's water. The olden-time Anmatyerr people frightened him away [from their country]. They didn't know anything about Jesus or God — they were ignorant about those things in the early days. They frightened him away, the poor thing.* ◆ Mwerr anetyek Altyerrel ilem. Altyerr iterlaremel, itirrenty anemel, Altyerr. *No* atwerretyek, *no* ilterretyek, *no* ilerretyek, urrtyel ilerretyek, urrtyirretyang — mwerr akwet anetyek. Altyerr iterlarenty anem, mwerr anetyek, ingkart *way* anetyek. Atnert irrernt, arlka irrernt anetyek, altyerrant iterlaremel, ingkartant iterlaremel angerrirretyek. (Sa) *God tells us to be good. To know God and live with this knowledge. No fighting, no swearing, no telling lies, no lying — being consistently good. Knowing God and living well, in God's way. Being good to each other and not getting angry [lit. 'being with a cool stomach and cool body'], just thinking of God.*

4. a person's mother's country ◆ Mer nthenh untan altyerr akek? Untap altyerr akek Alhalker. (Sa) *Where is your mother's country? Your mother's country is Alhalker.*

5. the Dreamings or totems that come from a person's mother's country

6. story, television [SOME SPEAKERS] ◆ Altyerr aretyek alha, amparey alhenherr-arey aretyek, *television* yanh. Arrken aretyek altyerr. (Sa) *Go and watch* altyerr, *all you kids go and watch television,* altyerr. *Go and watch for fun.*

SEE ALSO **anengkerr**

altyerraty (T,E) *n.kin*
my mother's country; the Dreamings or totems from my mother's country ◆ Altyerraty-warn alhey, arerl-alpetyek. (T) *I'm going to go and have a look at my mother's country.*
Also referred to as *amer altyerraty.*

altyerrengkw (T,E) *n.kin*
your mother's country etc. Also referred to as *amer altyerrengkw.*

altyerrikw (E), **altyerreyekw** (E) *n.kin*
his or her mother's country etc. Also referred to as *amer altyerrikw.*

altyerr-ankethenh (E) *n.kin*
be related to a place or Dreaming through mother and uncles (mother's brothers) ◆ Ayengan altyerr-ankethenh anetyel mer Atarrkertek. Atarrkertap atyenh altyerraty. Altyerraty-areny. (Sa) *I am related to Atarrkert through my mother. Atarrkert is my* altyerr *country.* ◆ Altyerr-ankethenh ayeng anem mer Ipertek. (St) *I am related to Ipert through my mother.*

SEE ALSO **-ankethenh**

altyerr-penh (E) *n.*
something from the Dreaming or creation time = **anengkerr-penh**

altyerreng (E) *n.*
creation time, Dreamtime ◆ Altyerrengarl anek kwenh kel iterlarem. Ker apekarl altyerreng anek. (Sa) *[We] know about the things from the creation time. The different sorts of animals that were in the creation time.*

altyerr iylkwem (E)
make someone have a predictive dream (iylkwem *'foretell'*) ◆ Altyerr iylkwerl-alhek yanhel ayenh. (St) *That person made me dream about them.*

altyerr arraty
1. the right, true or correct story (any story) (arraty *'correct', 'straight'*)
2. the right, true or correct Dreaming story

altyerr ampety (E)
birthmark ◆ Altyerr ampetyarl nhanyeman, kerarl atwek. Aherrarl atwekan impelty anerl-anem urrperl. Ulta apekarl atyerrek, ulta apekarl atanthek irrtyartel, wal impeltyarl anerl-anem, ampan. *Mark*-akert anem anerl-anem, urrperl. (Sa) *This is a birthmark on the child from where the animal [associated with the child's place of quickening, or where the child was 'found'] was shot. Where the kangaroo was shot is a dark-coloured mark. If it was shot in the side, or speared in the side, well there is a corresponding mark there on the child. The child*

has a dark-coloured mark.

altyerr arem

dream, have a dream (arem *'look', 'see'*) ◆ *Might something* apek — *mother* atyenh-kenh, *uncle* atyenh-kenh *country* apek arem, '*Oh* mer kwerenh iylkwek, altyerr iylkwerl-alhek'. Ankwa apek ayeng intem wal tharl altyerrarl arem. Kel arratemarl ra. (St) *I might see something — my mother's or my uncle's country, and I'd say, 'Oh I've predicted something about the country [or the relations] through the dream'. I might have been lying asleep and had a dream. Then [that person] really turns up.*

= anengkerr arem

altyerr ilem

tell Dreaming stories (ilem *'say', 'tell'*) ◆ Altyerr ilerreperrem ahelhek, arrernepernem, arnwer-irrep-irrerl. (St) *Telling the Dreaming stories on the ground, putting the story on the ground, and singing along.*

= anengkerr ilem

SEE ALSO tyepety[1]

altyerr akem

be related to a place or a Dreaming through your mothers and uncles (mother's brothers) (akem[2] *'call someone a relation'*) ◆ Arnkam tha 'altyerr' akek, maty-henh, kamern-henh. (T) *Arnka is the place that I call* 'altyerr', *that I am related to through my mothers and mother's brothers.* ◆ Antarrengeny tha 'altyerr' akek. Antarrengeny altyerr ap ayeng — math-kenh. (Sa) *Antarrengeny is the place that I call* 'altyerr'. *I am Antarrengeny* altyerr — *my mother's country.* ◆ Altyerrarl akek-warn alhetyek, maty-kenh, tha aretyek, mer iwenh-artek kwenh. (T) *I want to go and see my mother's country to see what it's like.*

= anengkerr akem

altyerrel arem (W)

'Really, truly, true to God', 'Cross my heart' (lit. 'God will see [it]')

= ngkartel arem

altyerr-altyerr *n.*

sleep talk, nightmare ◆ Nga apek angkem altyerr-altyerr, *when you fast asleep. Me might* angkety-ayntem ikwer altyerr-altyerr akin — atherrerl-anem angkerl-anem then, *talk talk.* (St) *When you are fast asleep you might talk in your sleep. I might talk to her in my sleep as well — laugh and talk and talk.* ◆ Altyerr-altyerr angkep-angkem yanh. Thamtheng atham-arenyelarl altyerr-altyerr mpwarek. Marl arrpenh ankwethey angkerl-anem altyerr-altyerr. (Sa) *That person is talking in their sleep. Something or other, the* atham-areny *spirits, made them talk in their sleep. Another woman is talking in her sleep.*

= anengkerr-anengkerr

altyerr-altyerr arem *vt.*

have a bad dream or a nightmare (arem *'look', 'see'*)

= anengkerr-anengkerr arem

altyerr-altyerr angkem *vi.*

talk in one's sleep (angkem *'talk'*)

altyerreng-altyerr *n.*

stories that are told for fun ◆ Altyerreng-altyerr ina mparerl-anem kwerel, kwer marl mapel awenk mapel, arrkenel-arleng. (M) *The children just tell stories for fun, the young girls and the teenage girls.*

altyerreh arlkwem (W,T), **altyerrek arlkwem**

have breakfast, eat something (including tobacco) or drink upon waking (arlkwem *'eat'*) ◆ Altyerrek ingwepenh arlkwetyek, 'Altyerrek tha arlkwetyek nthay atyeweyay — angayakw, atnertarl arrerlkart urntem'. (Sa) *Eating breakfast in the morning, 'Give me something to eat for breakfast for goodness sake — I'm hungry, my stomach is burning with hunger'.* ◆ Kwaty altyerrek antywetyek, altyerr yanh iylkwetyek, pewetyem altyerr. (St) *Drinking water first thing in the morning, to push that* altyerr *down.* ◆ Ngkwerlp apek altyerrek arlkwem. (St) *I'm chewing some tobacco first thing in the morning.*

= anengkerrek arlkwem

altyerreh antywem (W,T), **altyerrek antywem**

drink something for breakfast (antywem *'drink'*) ◆ Altyerreh thang tey antywetyeh kwenh. (M) *I am drinking some tea for breakfast.*

= anengkerrek antywem

altyerrinp (E) *n.*

hungry (not having had breakfast) (+inp *'having'*) ◆ Altyerrinp-antey ayeng apetyek. Akem-irrek ayeng, altyerrinp-antey. (Sa) *I came without having any breakfast. I got up, and I still haven't had breakfast.*

altyerrakw (E) *n.*

hungry (not having had breakfast)

-altyerr[2] *prn.ending*

Combines with pronouns to form a word which refers to closely related sons-in-law or mothers-in-law. This compounding of *-altyerr* seems to be possible with all forms of dual and plural pronouns, with the notable exception of the forms with *+anth* (opposite patrimoiety). These are logically impossible, as these compound forms of *-altyerr* refer to kin relations within one's own patrimoiety, rather

than in the opposite one. See Appendix 1.
SEE ALSO ilern-altyerr, mpwel-altyerr, mpwelak-altyerr, alaltyerr, alak-altyerr, arrengkerr-altyerr, arrakerr-altyerr, anwernakerr-altyerr

altyerrper (E) *n.* [RESPECT LANGUAGE]
1. spear
SEE ALSO irrtyart
2. digging stick ◆ Mey-mey-ketyarl ilem 'altyerrper'. (St) *The word 'altyerrper' is used because of [your] son-in-law.* • SEE ALSO anem[3]

altyewem, altyiwem (E) *vt.*
1. throw or tip something out, spill something out ◆ Ampeny-ampenyan altyewem arlkwekarl-penh. (St) *After eating, the leftovers are thrown out.* ◆ Kwaty ulpert altyiwem. (St) *Dirty water is thrown out.*
2. turn something upside down (so that the back part is facing up and the hollow part down) ◆ Ampa apek ilem, 'Altyiway, arengk-kety kwenh!'. *You might say to a child, 'Turn it [cup] over, because of the dogs!'.* • SEE ALSO altywarrernem

altyewelhem, altyiwelhem (E) *vi.*
spill out, get spilt ◆ Arengk nhwerrem kwaty-angkwerr. Kwaty altyewelhem. (T) *The dogs are fighting near the water. The water spills.*

altyey *n.*
leaf of the bush banana, silky pear, *alangkw, parl* (*Marsdenia australis*) ◆ Mern altyeyel anwern amangketyam, parl. Altyey arlakey kwerenh. Altyey arlkwem akin anteth-akert. Pertipelaw kwer-penh anem alangkw angwerrm-irrem. Lyapem, akwerrk antem. (N) *We grew up on bush banana leaves and on bush bananas.* Altyey *are the leaves. We eat the leaves and the flowers as well. After the flower the bush banana is found. It grows into a small fruit.* ◆ Mern altyey artaper-wemel altyey kwer-penharlam ayernetyam *roll*-em *up* ampetyam atyerretyam. (N) *The leaves of the bush banana are rolled up and then cooked.*
SEE ALSO unelh, ahertety[2]

altyiwem (E) throw or tip something out SEE UNDER **altyewem**

altywarrernem, altyarrernem (T) *vt.*
1. turn or tip something upside down (so that the back part is facing up and the hollow part down) ◆ Tyampet altywarrernetyeh kwenelak angwelyel awantyeh-hety. (M) *Turn the tin upside down in case the dog licks it.*
2. make someone bend over; turn someone over ◆ Impalkertarl intep-intem yanh altywarrernay, *cough*-arl irremeng. (St) *Turn that person that's lying on their back over, because they're coughing.*
= artep arrernem
SEE ALSO angart-wem, altywernem, altyewem

altywart, altyart (W,T) *n.*

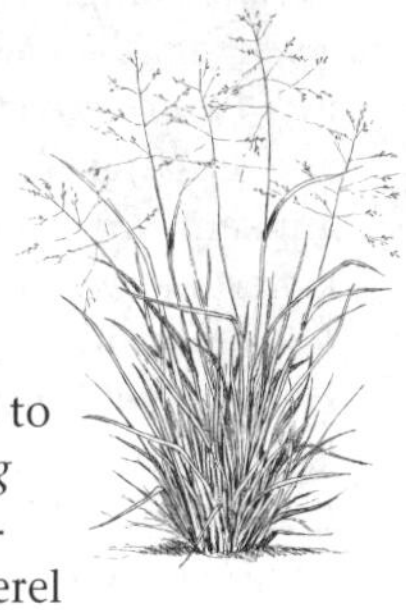

1. native millet (*Panicum decompositum*). A grass about 70 cm high with bluish green leaves, and large seed heads.
2. the edible seeds of the native millet. Also referred to as *arnwety altywart* or *ntang altywart.* ◆ Arnwety, atherl-apemel. *Grandmother*-rlpwerel ahety-iletyam altywart. (N) *This is a seed that is ground up. All our grandmothers used to winnow the native millet seeds.* ◆ Ahety-iletyam yerrelarl arrernetyam *heap* arrernetyam yerrel. Atwetyam wetyam wetyam antyakem iletyart akemel panth-warn lernetyam ahety-iletyam athetyem angernetyam. Awantyetyam altyart. (N) *They used to winnow the seeds that the ants had heaped up. They winnowed the seeds and then ground them up and took them back to eat.*

altywekerr, altywekarr *n.*
black-headed monitor, freckled monitor (*Varanus tristis*). Also referred to as *ker altywekerr.* Black in colour, it lives in hollow trees. ◆ Ker altywekerr tnepetnem atwerl-ayneyaw. Anter innga. (Sa) *Quickly kill that* altywekerr *lizard that's standing there. It's really fat.*
= alpangwerr, kwenyel alhem, kweny-areny, pwer rrpwerl

altywen (W) *n.*
a permanent soakage; a very old soakage. Also referred to as *kwaty altywen.* ◆ 'Altywen' ilem kwaty Anengkerr-penh. (M) *'Altywen' is what a permanent soakage is called [one from the Dreaming].*
SEE ALSO angenty

Altywep (W,T) *n.*
1. Brooks Well, north of Tilmouth Well
2. Hardons Soak

altywer *n.*
1. hole, a hole in something; the opening to something ◆ Kwaty thelelhem tyampet altywereng. (T) *Water is pouring out from the hole in the tin.* ◆ Alhweng altywer yanh-lkwer, *well* 'arlarl'. Arlethey tyerrelhem yerr. (St) *'Arla' is the opening of the ants' nest. The ants come out of the opening in the nest.*
2. open (not closed) • SEE ALSO althwerrk, ampwerrk, martelhenty
kapert altywer
1. someone who is clever or knowledgeable

(kapert[1] *'head'*) ◆ Kapert ayeng altywer-irrem tharl iterlarem. Kapert ayeng altywer, wal tha iterlarem ingkerrek. (St) *My head has become 'open' and I know things. If my head is 'open' well I know everything.* ◆ Urrem-urremel angkep-angkem, akengentyarl angkep-angkem. Arraty-anteyarl angkep-angkem kapert altywer. (St) *Talking in a silly way, talking the wrong way. Someone who is knowledgeable talks the right way.* ◆ Arelh yanh kapert altywer anthwerrem. Pep *read*-em ilenh-ilenh. (T) *That woman is really knowledgeable. She can read.*
2. being unwell or sick in the head (?) ◆ Kapert altywer, kapert mwerr anem ilek renh, altywerarl-irrek. Rlka aretharrel, rlka altwerlengarl apetyernel. Aretharrel renh akeng-ilek kapert, altywer-ilek. Mwerr anem ilemel interrenty-irrek. (T) *His head was no good after being opened up by the west wind, but now it is better. The west wind was the thing that made his head no good, opened it up. Now it's been healed and it has closed over.*
SEE ALSO kapert wetyerretyerr

anert altywer, atnert altywer (E)
1. feeling sorry or sad (and empty); feeling as if something is wrong (anert *'stomach'*) ◆ Anert altywer ayeng awelhem. (T) *I am feeling sorry.*
2. feeling hungry; feeling empty (stomach) (lit. 'open stomach') ◆ Atnert altywer awelhem angayakw. (Sa) *I'm hungry and my stomach feels empty.*
= anert arltwang, alem altywer

alha altywer, alhang altywer (W,T)
1. nostril (alha *'nose'*) ◆ Alha altywer kwert apek tha intyernetyek. (St) *I'm smelling the smoke with my nostrils.*
2. a hole in the nose

kart altywer (W,T), **atna altywer** (E)
anus, arsehole (kart, atna *'shit, excrement'*)

altywer-altywer *n.*
1. full of holes, holey ◆ Mantar apek altywer-altywer — altywer-akert anem ra anem, iwem anem renh. Iwem anem renh altywer-akert wart. (T) *Clothes might be full of holes — if they get holes in them then they are thrown out. They are thrown out because they've got holes.*
2. a small opening

altywer-ilem *vt.*
1. open something (up); make a hole in something ◆ Rtetyant ra arlkwem ahaylengkeyler, akwek, rtety ra arlkwem altywer-ilemel. Pwengarl ra aretyangarl akeng. Irrpenhem ap ra ahernek anem. (St) *The ahaylengkeyler [blind snake] bites into your teeth and makes holes in them. They are blind and can't see. They burrow into the ground.* ◆ Ntyerlarl akwernetyart arrwekel, alharlan altywer-ilem, kel ntyerl anem arrernem. Arelhel inngart. (Sa) *In the old days they used to put a nosebone there. After making a hole in the nose, they'd put a nosebone in the hole. Women did it.* ◆ Kwart-they arratemel, wal altywer-ilem akwek, iyltemarl ra kwart. Iyltepeyltem kweneng, kel arratenhem anem. (St) *[The chick] comes out of the egg, making a little opening. It cracks the egg open from inside and then hatches out.*
2. cash a cheque ◆ *Cheque* ampwerrkarl apetyekan altywer-ilem. Altywer-ilem kel *money* anem tyerrem. (Sa) *The full cheque that came is cashed. Cashed and then the money is taken out.*
3. turn on a light or a tap

altywer-irrem *vi.*
open up, become open ◆ Arraperel tyart ingkerr mwernetyenheng atanthetyenheng altywer-altywer irremel. (N) *The kerosene grass will stick into your shirt and pierce it, and the shirt will get full of holes.* ◆ Irlpang atherr ntwa altywer-irretyakenh kwenh. (N) *Your ears aren't open [i.e. you're not listening].*

altywernem *vi.*
1. bend over, crouch down, lie curled up ◆ Angwely map altywernerl-anem antyamel. (M) *The dogs are lying curled up on the bed.* ◆ Mwer-kety apek ayeng altywernem. (St) *I am crouching down because of my son-in-law.* ◆ Tyampet altywernem. (Sa) *The tin is upside down.*
2. be or lie (of hills) ◆ Irntang angerr altywernerl-anem. Iter-angkwerr anwern alhem arlewatyerrek. (T) *There is a big hill there. We go along the side looking for goannas.*
SEE ALSO altywarrernem

altywernelh-ilem *vt.*
incubate or hatch out eggs ◆ Angey ikwerenhel anem altywernelh-ilerlanem kwart renh, iltewetyek-atwety akngey ikwerenhel. Kel renh akngey inerl-alpem akwerrk rernemarl ikwerenh inenhem ra. (Sa) *The father [emu] comes and he sits on the eggs until they hatch. Then the father takes all his baby chicks along.*

Aluraty (E) Luritja person or people SEE UNDER **Alweraty**

alurr (E) split-jack SEE UNDER **alwerr**

alurremp (E) green seeds inside the fruit of the bush banana *alangkw, aparl* SEE UNDER **alwerremp**

alurrng (E) sinew, tendon SEE UNDER **alwerrng**

alwepay (W,T) *n.*
a type of mouse (?)
SEE ALSO ilkwenng, thakey[2], thakwer, aherraty-anywertangey

Alweraty, Aluraty (E) *n.*
1. Luritja person or people
2. Luritja language

alwernem *vt.*
chase someone or something ◆ Arengk yanh alwernay kerek-arrngel. Kerarl arlkwerl-alherneng. Alwernemel atway! (St) *Chase that dog away, because it's just gone and eaten the meat. Chase it and hit it!*
= rlwakem
CAN SOUND A BIT LIKE ilwernem *'extinguish'*
alwernerrem *vi.*
chase each other round ◆ Atwerremel, atwemel-arrpantey arrkenel, nyetyeng-anyety-they. Alwernemel, alwernerremel. Alwernemel anem ampa ingwer atnem-akertel, atnem akely-akertel alwernemel. Urrtyirremel, arrkenel-arleng. (Sa) *Hitting each other, pretending to hit each other for fun, in the cubbyhouses. Chasing each other around. One kid chasing another with a digging stick. Just pretending, for fun.*

alwernp (W) *n.*
native currant fruit that is just getting ripe (*Psydrax latifolia*)
SEE ALSO ahakey
CAN SOUND A BIT LIKE rlwernp *'red-backed kingfisher'*

alwerr, alurr (E) *n.*
1. split-jack (*Capparis lasiantha*). Shrubby vine with small white flowers and oval yellow fruit which splits when ripe.
2. the edible fruit of the split-jack. Also referred to as *mern alwerr.* ◆ Alwerr tyarrp-irrem angwarlp-irremel an angwarlparl-irrem. Ampeng anem ra irrem, tyarrp anem ra irrem. Arlkwem. (St) *The split-jack fruit splits open as it ripens. When it is ripe it splits open. It's eaten.*

alwerrem, alwirrem (E) *vi.*
run away from someone or something; escape ◆ Artwang alenh alwerrem aneweh-kety mwetekay-akert. (M) *This man in the car is running away from his wife.* ◆ Ker arlewatyerr apek atyengety alwirremel untem. (St) *The goanna is running away from me.* ◆ Tyerrty alenh alwerrem *hospital*-eng. (M) *That person is running away from hospital.*
SEE ALSO arrtyanem
alwerrelh-ilem *vt.*
make someone run away ◆ Artwang yanhel arelh awenk alwerrelh-ilem. (T) *That man is making that young girl run off with him.*
alwerrerl-angem *vt.*
run off with something; take (someone's things) ◆ Arengkel ker alwerrerl-angem arelh yanh-kety. (T) *The dog is running off with the woman's meat.*

alwerremp (W,T), **alurremp** (E) *n.*
green seeds inside the fruit of the bush banana, silky pear, *alangkw, aparl* (*Marsdenia australis*) ◆ Alwerremp inemel alkakemel parl renh. Mern renh arlkwem akin, alwerremp. (N) *The bush banana is split open and the green stuff inside is eaten, the* alwerremp.
= antweth
SEE ALSO twemper[1]

alwerrng, alwerrkng (E), **alurrng** (E) *n.*
1. sinew, tendon ◆ Alwerrngel mpwarem irrtyart, alwerrng aherr-penhel. (T) *Sinews from the kangaroo are used to make spears.*
2. edible sinews or tendons (?). Also referred to as *ker alwerrng.*
3. vein, artery, blood vessel ◆ Alhwang thelelhem alwerrng-angkwarr. (M) *Blood flows along the veins.* ◆ Alwerrng nharlkarl intep-intemarl alwerrng war — alhwekenhan aleyarl. Alakenh anpem, rlkertarl intetyam, wal nhenh anpetyam, *old people.* (St) *The* alwerrng *that are here are just tendons — these ones [pointing to the pulse] are the ones associated with blood. People used to feel it, if someone was sick — they used to feel here [the pulse]. That's what the old people did.*
4. telephone, phone (after the telephone line or wire)
alwerrng angkenh-angkenh (E)
telephone, phone (lit. 'the sinew for talking')
SEE ALSO terlepawen, arrakert-kenh, irlpekenh

alwerrpent (W), **alwerrpaty** (W) *n.*
grub from the emu bush, *lhwek-lhwek* (*Eremophila longifolia*). Also referred to as *tyap alwerrpent.*
SEE ALSO lhwek-lhwek, unerrengayt

Alwerrpent (W), **Ngarlwerrpernt** (W) *n.*
Ngalurbindi hills, in the Mt Allan area

alwirrem (E) run away from someone or something SEE UNDER **alwerrem**

alya, alyang (W,T) *n.*
boomerang ◆ Artwel arrwekelenyel ker aherr alyangel ltewetyam. (M) *The men in the early days used boomerangs to hunt kangaroos.* ◆ Artwel mpwarem alkwert arnang inernt-penh, alyang-kety ilpelhetyek. (T) *Men make shields from*

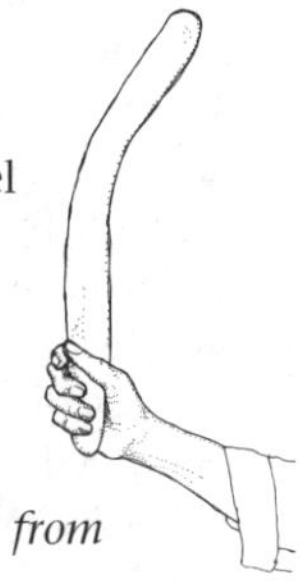

bean-tree wood to protect themselves from boomerangs.
= kayl, aylayl
CAN SOUND A BIT LIKE **alyeng** *'left-hand'*
alyang-alyang (W,T), **alyeng-alyeng** (W,T) *n.*
toy boomerang
= kayleng-kayl
alyang rlkwang (W,T)
1. hooked boomerang, number 7 boomerang ◆ Artwangel alyang rlkwang mparem artety-penh. (N) *Men make hooked boomerangs from mulga wood.*
= kayl iylkwa, aylayl iylkwa, rlkwa
2. Seven Sisters star constellation (?)
alyang lyweper (W)
a type of boomerang (curved shape) (lyweper *'thigh'*)
= kayl ulyeper

alyakw *n.* [RESPECT LANGUAGE]
man. This word is used between men who have a particular ceremonial relationship to each other. The word may also be used by women as a respectful word for 'man'. ◆ Ankelikw ikwerenhel ilem *private one*-el, 'Alyakw anert akeng-irrek-akert-ketyaw, rlkert-irrek-kety'. (Sa) *His close cousin says, 'The man [my cousin] has got a stomach ache, has become sick'.* ◆ Arelhel ilem, 'Alyakw-ketyaw!' (St) *The women say, 'Look out for the men!'*
SEE ALSO **artwa, perlawel, thampartey, antewarety, arlwety-penh, arlwety[2], anyent arrpenh**

alyalk-alyalk (T) *n.*
the noise of lots of people talking; buzz, hubbub ◆ Alyalk-alyalk angkerremaw! Tyerrty alhernter. *The whitefellas are talking loud, making a lot of noise.*

alyalkarr (T,E), **alyalkerr** (E) *n.*
a type of skink (*Ctenotus schomburgkii* (?)) ◆ *Lizard* akely, alyelkarl ap ra, urnem-apeny. *Quiet. Colour*-an alhewer — *yellow one*, arlkeny-arlkeny *batik one batik one*. Ingka-akert, ingka iltya, alha anem ikwerenh. Urnemek-athen ikwerety ater-irrem. (Sa) *A little lizard, a smooth one like a snake. Quiet. They have any sort of colour — some are yellow and they have markings and patterns like batik. They have front legs and back legs and noses. [We] get frightened of them if we mistake them for snakes.*
= lyengkarr, lyangkay-lyangkay
SEE ALSO **ikwarr**

alyaly (W) *n.*
dry seeds (especially of the dogwood) (*Acacia sericophylla*)
SEE ALSO **kertaty, tartaty, lyarr, ntyerrm**
alyaly atwem (W)
crush seeds with a round rock (atwem *'hit'*). Particularly said of *artety* (mulga), *akerlperr* (dogwood) and *arlep* (acacia bush). ◆ Akerlperr alyaly atwetyart, irntel apwertel atwerl-anek. Anterrng *milk*-arteheeey *nice one*. Athemem athetyartem mwerr angerr anthwerr. *The dogwood seed used to be smashed up with a rock. It goes like milk and tastes really really good. It is ground up with a rock.*

alyalyarr (E), **alyalyerr** (E) *n.*
small green seed pods of the kurrajong tree (*Brachychiton gregorii*)
SEE ALSO **apeng, ngkweyang, artwengarr, arlpetharlp**

alyang (W,T) boomerang SEE UNDER **alya**

alyangkw (E) *n.*
cold weather, winter ◆ Interrk weth-rnem alyangkwek-arelh-rnem. Alyangkwek rernem arraly-irretyel. (Sa) *Those Seven Sisters stars are associated with winter-time. They shine in the winter.*
SEE ALSO **alhwerrp, irrernt**

alyap *n.*
honeyant nest or hole ◆ Alyap kwerel irrperl-anem yerramp map. (M) *The honeyants go into the nest.*
SEE ALSO **yerramp, inkwareny, inkwa**

alyaper *n.*
toy boomerang, made from the bark of the river red gum or the ghost gum ◆ Alyaperel wererrl-anem wey map arrkenel, ampa mapel. Arntap iyltemel kel alyaper mpwaremel werremel. (St) *Young boys throw the* alyaper *at each other for fun. They peel bark off trees and then make* alyaper *to throw at each other.* ◆ Alyaper kwer mapel mparem alyeng-alya. Alyel anem akwel ina ltewerretyenh. Arrken-kenh war. (T) *The* alyaper *is a sort of toy boomerang that the kids make. Then they throw them at each other. It's just for fun.*
SEE ALSO **kayleng-kayl, alyang-alyang, lwekatat**
alyaper-warn (E) *n.*
elder brothers or sisters of initiate (young man), who look after him at *apwelh* ceremony time ◆ Ayeng alyaper-warnek arlkerl-anetyek, 'Pay pay pay', alakenh. (St) *I sing out to my* alyaper-warn *like this, 'Pay pay pay'.*
SEE ALSO **anyent arrpenh, thampartey, perlal, ntwerleng, ntyangkwenng, rteyepertey, alyey[2], ywerlperr**

alyarrp, **lywerrp** (E) *n.kin* [RESPECT LANGUAGE]
a respectful term used by a woman to refer to her son-in-law's brother

alyarrpengkw, lywerrpengkw (E) *n.kin*
your *alyarrp* ◆ Alyarrpengkw nthenh ntwa atwarek? (M) *Where did you see your* alyarrp*?*
alyarrpikw (E), **lywerrpikw** (E) *n.kin*
his/their *alyarrp*
alyarrpekw (W,T) *n.kin*
1. your *alyarrp*
2. his/their *alyarrp*
alyarrp-nheng, lywerrp-nheng (E) *n.kin*
a group of two or more brothers (said by a woman if one of them is her son-in-law)
SEE ALSO kenheng
alyarrp-intyerr, lywerrp-intyerr (E) *n.kin*
= **alyarrp-nheng**
alyarrp-nheng atherr, lywerrp-nheng atherr (E) *n.kin*
two brothers together (said by a woman if one of them is her son-in-law) ◆ Alyarrp-nheng ahanenhek tyety-ayerrek. (St) *My son-in-law and his brother went hunting for meat [said by a woman].* ◆ Akenheng atherrarl. 'Alyarrp-nheng atherr kwenh.' Mwerikwek angkem, 'Alyarrp-nheng atherr ahanenhem kwenh'. (St) *That's two brothers together. 'Those two brothers went.' That's what you say to the mother-in-law [of one of the brothers], 'Those two brothers went off together' [using* alyarrp-nheng atherr *instead of* kenheng atherr*].*
SEE ALSO kenheng atherr
alyarrp-ankethenh, lywerrp-ankethenh (E) *n.kin*
1. having a close *alyarrp* still alive
2. someone who is always with their *alyarrp*
SEE ALSO -ankethenh
alyarrp-parety, lywerrp-parety (E) *n.kin*
respectful or 'sorry' way of talking about someone's *alyarrp*
SEE ALSO -parety

alyartey (W,E) green seed pods of the Georgina gidgee (*Acacia georginae*), *rrwenyenk/urrenyenk*
SEE UNDER **ilyartey**

alyatywereng (E) *n.*
1. woollybutt grass (*Eragrostis eriopoda*). A grass about 35 cm high with a white woolly substance at the base of the plant.
2. the edible seeds of the woollybutt grass. Also referred to as *ntang alyatywereng*. ◆ Ntang alyatywereng ingkel ulthem ipert-warl. (Sa) *The woollybutt grass seed [is husked] by treading on it in a hole.*
= antyey[1]

Alyawarr *n.*
1. Alyawarr language
2. Alyawarr person and people

alyeleng (E) gap left in front teeth after a tooth has been knocked out (ceremonial)
SEE UNDER **alyeneng**

alyelk *n.*
1. slippery, smooth, slimy ◆ Arna alyelk atetywemel anem antyem, arntarlkw anetyakenh. (St) *[You] cut footholds to climb a smooth tree that has no forks in it.* ◆ *Lizard* akely, alyelkarl ap ra, urnem-apeny. *Quiet. Colour*-an alhewer — *yellow one*, arlkeny-arlkeny *batik one batik one.* (Sa) *A little lizard, a smooth one like a snake. Quiet. They have any sort of colour — some are yellow and they have markings and patterns like batik.*
2. salty, bad-tasting; a sort of smell or taste that makes you feel sick ◆ Kwaty mwerr-warn ayeng urrek alhey, alyelk-kety. (St) *I'll go to the good water later, because this water is salty.*
3. tasteless, bland ◆ Ker ikwakert. *Shop*-areny alyelk. (Sa) *[Bush] meat has taste. The meat from the shop is tasteless.* • SEE ALSO anetywek
4. without cultural identity ◆ Ikwek arrangkw ikwa anpernerrenty anetyakenh — ikwek arrangkw 'alyelk'. Alhernter mapan ikwek arrangkw — 'alyelk'. (Sa) *Not having a skin name is like not being related — not having a skin name is* alyelk. *Non-Aboriginal people don't have skin names — they are* alyelk *or 'without identity'.* ◆ Anpernerretyakenharl *Alice Springs*-areny — kwaty-artek alyelk ingkerr. (Sa) *The Alice Springs people don't follow the kinship Law — they are* alyelk, *like water.*
5. just starting to grow ◆ Ngkerlp akwerrk alyelk mpank. (M) *The native tobacco is just starting to grow.*
alyelk-alyelk *n.*
1. smooth, slippery ◆ Alyelkelhekerr, alyelk-alyelk yanh-kety. (St) *Watch out or you'll slip on that slippery surface.* ◆ Irntang alyelk-alyelk. (M) *A smooth/slippery rock.*
= arler-arler
2. nauseating • SEE ALSO antewek-antew, alyew-alyew, kaly-kaly[2]
alyelkelhem *vi.*
1. slip over; slip out of something; slide on something; skid ◆ Ampa yanh alyelkelhekerray alyelk yanhel. (St) *Look out, that child might slip on that smooth surface.*
= arler-irrem
2. vomit, throw up, spew (?) ◆ Alyelkelhek atyeng-they mern. (St) *I vomited the food up.*
• = antew-irrem
alyelk-irrem *vi.*
1. slip over; slip out of something; slide on something; skid
= arler-irrem

2. feel nauseous or sick; get nauseous (from something eaten or drunk, or the smell of something) ◆ Atnert alyelk-irrem antew-irretyenh, atherrkenyel, antew anem irrem. (St) *In the green time [your] stomach feels nauseous and then you'll vomit.* ◆ Atnert alyelk-irrem, war, kerarl arlkwek-penh, ker arntert apekarl arlkwekarl alyelk-irrem. (St) *After eating meat, rotten meat, [you] feel sick in the stomach.* ◆ Anert alyelk-irrem antew-irretyeh. Ngkerlp-kwenyel alyelk-irrem. (T) *Without tobacco [to chew] you feel sick in the stomach and want to vomit.*
3. become a bit fat or plump, put on weight ◆ Arengk alyelk-alyelk-irrem, anter anem irremel. (St) *The dog is putting on weight and becoming fat now.*

alyelk-ilem *vt.*
make something smooth ◆ Yarr-wem, atnem pek tha arterrp-ilemel yarr-werl-alhem alyelk-ilemel. Apwertel apek, apwert ilep-arrpantey *knife*-arrpanteyel. *Knife*-el anem lyetarr yarr-wepewem. (St) *I am scraping the digging stick to make it smooth. I might scrape it with a stone, or with a stone axe or some sort of knife. Nowadays people use knives to scrape things smooth.*
SEE ALSO yarr-wem

alyelyek banana-flavoured bush tomato SEE UNDER **arlelyek**

alyem, **aylem** (E) *vt.*
1. sing ◆ Anmanty alyem. (M) *Singing the young man ceremonies.*
SEE ALSO ayatwem, alyelhem
2. 'sing' someone or something with supernatural powers or magic. The use of songs for this purpose may have a positive or negative effect on the person who is 'sung'. ◆ Alyem awely arntety apek mwerr-irretyek. Anter warel tha alyem, apernelhetyek ra mwerr-irretyek, irrernt-irretyek. (St) *A sick person is sung with* awely *to make them better. I just sing them with the fat, so that they can rub themselves with it and get better, cool down.* ◆ Anter alyem. (M) *Singing over the healing fat.* ◆ Rlkert apek tyerrty alyem awelyel. (M) *A sick person is sung with* awely *ceremonies.* • SEE ALSO arrilem, arrilenty-ilem, artimperr-wem, arrwengkelthel alyem

alyerrem, **aylerrem** (E) *vi.*
1. make a noise; sing, hum
2. sing each other with supernatural powers or magic ◆ Arrwengkelth yanhel akeng-ilek. Arrwekeleny map *clean*-arl ina anek — *no* arrwengkelth ina atnyenek *disease* apek *nothing*. Perrap *clean*, *only* artwekenhant arrwengkelthant ina alyerretyart. Alhernter maparl apetyek-tayman *worse* anem. (St) *That disease made him/her sick. The olden-days people were free of disease — they didn't have any sickness. They lived a clean life and didn't have any sickness or disease. They just used to sing each other with men's things and with traditional* arrwengkelth. *When white people came things got worse.*

alyelhem, **aylelhem** (E) *vi.*
1. sing ◆ Kwer map kwerlel alyelhem. (T) *The children sing in school.* ◆ Ayeng alyelhem irrararl irrem alpetyek mer-warn. (T) *I am singing about how I am homesick and want to go home.* ◆ Tyerrty war alyelherl-anem arrkenel nheng *happy* mpwarelherl-anemel alyelherl-anem, merel anerl-anemel. (N) *People just sing along to make themselves happy when they are sitting round at home.* ◆ Ilpenty alyelhem. (M) *Singing a love song.*
2. sing yourself with supernatural powers or magic ◆ Ayeng alyelhem artwang tha inetyek. (T) *I am singing myself so that I can get a man.*
SEE ALSO alyem

alyemp-alyemp[1] *n.*
wrinkled, shrivelled, limp, hanging loose ◆ Marl apek tywenap-tywenap irrem, ngkwern-kweny-irrem alyemp-alyemp, artwel akwel renh aretyek, tywenap-irrem. (St) *The girl might be showing off, acting flirtatiously and making her legs go all limp, so that the man can see her showing off.*
SEE ALSO altyek-altyek

alyempelhem *vi.*
dry up, shrivel up, go slack, become wrinkled ◆ Mern atwakey apek alyempelhem, ahinpenyarl irrek alyempelhem, antyerrk-irrem. Antyerrk anem ra, atnyem ahern-warl. (St) *A wild orange might shrivel up, when it gets old and dry. It gets dry and then it falls to the ground.* ◆ Akeweny alyempelhem, tyerrty ampwerremarl. (T) *That poor thing is getting wrinkled, as she ages.*
SEE ALSO alpwely-irrem

alyemp-alyemp-irrem *vi.*
become wrinkled or limp; skin sag or go slack or loose ◆ Alyemp-alyemp anem ra irrem angerr-pat-irremel. (T) *The poor thing is getting wrinkled now that she's getting old.*
SEE ALSO altyek-altyek-irrem

alyemp-alyemp[2] (W) *n.*
greedy ◆ Alyemp-alyemp apel nhenh, kwer apek *or* tyerrty angerr apek. (M) *This person is greedy, a child or an adult.*

SEE ALSO ankerl

alyempetayt (E) *n.* [RESPECT LANGUAGE]
1. witchetty bush (*Acacia kempeana*)
SEE ALSO anyem2
2. witchetty grub (*Xyleutes biarpiti*) • SEE ALSO anyematy

alyeneng (T,E), **alyeleng** (E) *n.*
gap left in front teeth after a tooth has been knocked out (ceremonial) ◆ Alyeneng, nyanyel ayeng atwek. (St) *My granny knocked my front tooth out.*
= arrimper, tyekerr
alyeneng atwem (T,E), **alyeleng atwem** (E)
remove a front tooth (ceremonial) (atwem *'hit'*) ◆ Arntek atwaty-ilem alyeleng atwek. (Sa) *A tooth was knocked out to make a gap in the teeth.*
= arrimper atwem

alyeng, ayleng (E) *n.*
1. left-hand, left-handed ◆ Alyengel-thaytel mpwarem. Ayengan akwarraty. *Making things with the left-hand. I am right-handed.*
2. left-hand side, left side
SEE ALSO arraty, akwarraty, akwang arraty
CAN SOUND A BIT LIKE alyang *'boomerang'*
akwang alyeng (W,T), **akwa ayleng** (E)
left-handed (akwa *'hand', 'arm'*)
alyeng-ampeny, ayleng-ampeny (E) *n.*
left-hand side, left side
alyeng-angkwerr, ayleng-angkwerr (E) *n.*
to the left, on the left-hand side ◆ Alyeng-angkwerr ampa akwekan angem, panthel, panthel ap ra angep-angem. *Carrying the small baby on the left side, carrying him/her along in the coolamon.*

alyent atwem (W,T) *vt.*
beat seed pods with a stick to make the seeds dislodge from the pod (especially said of mulga and dogwood) (atwem *'hit'*) ◆ Arnangel apek atwem alyent-atwem alyent-atwem, *seed* map arratetyeh *tent*-warn apek. Arna artety renh akemel alyent-atwem. (M) *A branch is used to beat the seeds so that they all come out [of the pods] and fall onto the swag sheet. The branches of the mulga tree are picked and then beaten to get the seeds to fall.*
alyent arrernem (W,T)
lay seed pods out so that they can be beaten (arrernem *'put'*)

alyent-artek (E) *n.* [RESPECT LANGUAGE]
in mourning, bereaved ◆ Alyent-artek ahern anengkan anwantherr pwernkel aney. Pwernkel aney anwantherr lyent-artekel. (Sa) *We are sitting down in mourning.* (?)
alyent-artek-irrem (E) *vi.* [RESPECT LANGUAGE]
pass away, die ◆ Arengk atyenh alyent-artek-irrekaw. (Sa) *My dog died.*
SEE ALSO arrangkw-irrem, arremangkw-irrem, anengkan-irrem, ilwem

alyenteng-ayerr (E) *n.* [RESPECT LANGUAGE]
playfully
SEE ALSO arrken
alyenteng-irrem (E) *vi.* [RESPECT LANGUAGE]
have fun, play ◆ Akwetyerr-ayerr alyenteng-irretyek ahanenherrarey arleng-warlay, arlewent-warl nhak-ampeny perlern-warl — alyenteng-irrerl-ayntetyek. (Sa) *All my little sons-in-law, go off and play a long way away, in the distance there over on that plain — go off and play there.*
SEE ALSO arrken-irrem

alyep1**, aylep** (E) *n.*
1. hairstring belt or strap; string made from fur of animal
SEE ALSO irrkety, antingkar, antyarn, arlpalh, antay
2. head ring (used for carrying things on). This can be made from plants such as *arratherrk* 'snake vine'. ◆ Alyep arrernem kapert-warn kwaty angernetyek. (T) *The head ring is put on the head to carry water back.*
3. snake vine (*Tinospora smilacina*) [SOME SPEAKERS]. A woody vine that climbs trees and shrubs, has leaves like a bush potato, and inedible red fruits. • = arratherrk, anwerl
alyep mpwarem, aylep mpwarem (E)
spin hairstring (mpwarem *'make'*)
= irrkety-wem
alyepel angem, aylepel angem (E)
carry something using a carrying strap (angem *'carry', 'take'*)
= urtatyel angem, antayel angem
alyep-alyep1**, aylep-aylep** (E) *n.*
matted or knotted hair ◆ Alta alyep-alyep-irrem, urlpepenh apek, urlpelarl apernelhek, anter *mix up.* (St) *Hair might get matted after being rubbed with ochre, with ochre and fat.*
SEE ALSO akaylep-aylep
alyep-alyep-irrem1**, aylep-aylep-irrem** (E) *vi.*
become matted or knotted (hair)
alyepelengkw, aylepelengkw (E) *n.*
young male who is going through initiation (young man) ceremonies
alyepengantay (W,T), **alyepelentenh** (W) *n.*
carrying strap made from hairstring and used to carry things over the shoulder
◆ Alyepengantayel rwang inetyam angkwey. (M) *In the olden days people collected wood with a carrying strap.*
SEE ALSO antay, rtwaty

alyep2 (W) *n.*
emu intestines

alyep-alyep[2] (W,T), **alywep-alywep** (T) *n.*
tired ◆ Ayeng rrkwapekarl rrkwapekarl ayeng alyep-alyep antem anem. Alyep-alyep anem ayeng awelhemel anem. Alyep-alyep kel irrek kwenh ayeng. (T) *I worked and worked and then I got tired. Now I feel tired. I've got tired.*
alyep-alyep-irrem[2] (W,T),
alywep-alywep-irrem (T) *vi.*
get tired
alyep-alyep-ilem (W,T),
alywep-alywep-ilem (T) *vt.*
make someone tired ◆ Alywep-alywep-ilerrerlanetyal akwet kwenh, aneyaw! (T) *Don't keep making [me] tired, sit down!*

alyer smooth, slippery SEE UNDER **arler**

alyer (E) *n.*
small grinding or pounding stone. Also referred to as *apwert alyer.* ◆ Intyerrm apert-atwemel apwert alyerel, mern apeng-areny weth-lkwer, ngkweyang, alyer. (Sa) *The dogwood tree seed is crushed with a grinding stone called* alyer, *and that edible seed from the kurrajong tree,* ngkweyang, *is as well.*
SEE ALSO tyeng, ather, artwert[1], pwerl

alyerlk-alyerlk (W), **arlerlk-arlerlk** (T) *n.*
Sandover lily, desert lily (*Crinum flaccidum*). A plant with shiny leaves, white flowers and a large, inedible onion-like bulb. ◆ *Onion*-artek kwa wal arlerlk-arlerlk. Ina akwel alhewelhetyart yanh perrap *medicine* akin akwel yanhey. Arlkwenh-arlkwenh kwenyarl, arlerlk-arlerlk. (T) *It is like an onion, that Sandover lily. Supposedly, they [olden-time people] washed themselves with it and it was used as a medicine. The Sandover lily is not edible.*
= lyelkenng, iylelty

alyernem, **aylernem** (E) *vt.*
1. twist or wring something out ◆ Mantarr *wet* alyernem ra, kel kwaty thelelhem, kel tekem arrernem. (T) *Wringing out the wet clothes, then the water runs out from them, then the clothes are hung out to dry.*
2. choke something, wring or screw something's neck, strangle someone
SEE ALSO twerl-akem, ahenty ltwakem, ahenty ultakem, ahenty twerl-akem, ahenty ahenpem, awerrkem
CAN SOUND A BIT LIKE ayernem *'tie something up'*
alyernelhem, **aylernelhem** (E) *vi.*
wind something round yourself; twist yourself up in something

alyerr (W) *n.*
nice, lovely ◆ Mern alyerr, mern ingkety. (M) *Really lovely food.*

alyerremwey, **alyerremey** (T) *n.*
1. nice-tasting, lovely (of food or water); something that you really crave for ◆ Mern anaty tnyetyek alherrewey. Kerwep anetyangel ayeng-amperlan anem, mern anaty alyerremwey-kety. (Sa) *Let's all go and dig bush potatoes. Poor bugger me hasn't got a crowbar to get those lovely bush potatoes.* ◆ Kwaty alyerremwey nthenhek anwantherr antywey kwenh? (T) *Where are we going to get some nice-tasting water to drink?*
2. gorgeous, lovely (of a person) ◆ Kwer akwek alyerremey, aley anem alhep-alhem kwenh. (T) *There is that gorgeous little kid going along there now.*
3. quiet, non-aggressive ◆ Alyerremwey anwengkerr aney mwerr atwerr-kety. (T) *We'll all sit down quietly and not fight.*
SEE ALSO alyerr

alyetyepengalyety (W), **lyetyepengalyetyep** (W), **angetyepengangety** (W) *n.*
cubbyhouse ◆ Anwantherr arrken-irremel kwer map alyetyepengalyetyeng. (N) *Us kids play in the cubbyhouses.*
= nyetyep
SEE ALSO mereng-amer, arnkentyeng-arnkenty, antyweng-antyweng, arlwekereng-arlweker, mey-mey[2]

Alyew *n.*
1. Spring Range, east of Stirling Station
2. name of spring in the west Mt Allan area

alyew-alyew (E) *n.*
salty or bad-tasting, nauseating ◆ Kwaty alyew-alyew uyarnel tha antywem, alywer-irretyang arnterr antywetyakenh. (Sa) *I can't really drink this salty water, I can't drink much of it and quench my thirst.*
SEE ALSO alyelk-alyelk

alyey[1] (W) *n.*
grinding stone. Also referred to as *irntang alyey.*

alyey[2] *n.kin*
1. ceremonial relationship between men who have been through ceremonial business together, co-initiate
SEE ALSO atyew, anyent arrpenh, thampartey, perlal, ntwerleng, ntyangkwenng, rteyepertey, alyaper-warn, ywerlperr
2. place where initiation (young man) ceremony is held
3. people who grew up together or were born at around the same time; people of the same age-group, age-mate • SEE ALSO alyey-alyey, atyew, pelty
alyeyaty *n.kin*
my/our *alyey*

alyeyengkw *n.kin*
your *alyey*
alyeyikw (E) *n.kin*
his *alyey* ◆ Alyeyikw yanh. Aylekarl renh atherrenh anyentek-antey. Aylekarl renh atherrenh anyentek-antey apwelhek. *That is his* alyey *over there. The two of them went though the business together. They were both sung at the same time, at the same* apwelh *ceremony.*
alyeywek (W,T) *n.kin*
1. your *alyey*
2. his/their *alyey*
alyey-nheng *n.kin*
a group of two or more people who are related to each other as *alyey*
SEE ALSO atyew-nheng
alyey-nheng atherr *n.kin*
a person together with their *alyey*
SEE ALSO atyew-nheng atherr
alyey-tayem *n.*
the time when initiation or young man ceremonies are held ◆ Mern arlpwerr ngkernetyek alyey-tayem. Anthep-irremel. Mern arlety *dish*-elayeth. (Sa) *During the young man ceremony the* arlpwerr *food is put out. When people are dancing. Uncooked flour in a dish.*
= kwer-tayem

alyey-alyey (W,T) *n.*
1. men's spirit friends who look after them at ceremony time
2. caustic bush, desert spurge (*Euphorbia tannensis*). A small plant that grows along the ground, with milky sap and small flowers and fruit. • = anemarraty, marlek-alyey-alyey
3. lamb's tail, pussy-tails, pink mulla mulla (*Ptilotus exaltatus*). Plant about 60 cm high with smooth green leaves and pink flowers. • = mernteparn, awerreh-alyey-alyey, urreyek-alyey-alyey
SEE ALSO alyey2

alyeyamp (E), **kalyeyamp** (T) *n.*
Spencer's burrowing frog (*Limnodynastes spenceri*). Also referred to as *ker alyeyamp*.
SEE ALSO larrangkern, mpwelengk, antyetyerr, atweynterl, terrenth
alyeyampel (E), **kalyeyampel** (T,E) *adv.*
swimming or paddling ◆ Ntwa apek kalyeyampel pwerlp-irrenhem. (St) *Maybe you are diving into the water and swimming along.*
alyeyampel alhem (E), **kalyeyampel alhem** (T,E) *vi.*
swim, paddle or stroke along (in water)
alyeyamp-irrem (E), **kalyeyamp-irrem** (T,E) *vi.*
= aleyampel alhem ◆ Akernarrp alhem alyeyampel. Arengkan alyeyamp-irrem akernarrp war iltyel atherrant atwelhem. (St) *Paddling a long on the top [of the water]. Dogs paddle along on the top, just paddling with their paws.*

alywek *n.*
stone knife or scraper ◆ Alywek yanh atyeng anthay, tha akety-alhetyeh ker alenh. (M) *Give me that stone knife, I'm going to go and cut that meat.* ◆ Alywek mpwaretyam, *knife* arrwekeleny mapel. Ankeram arrernemel ina, kel ker renh aketyam, *something* ina aketyam. Tyerrty then akerretyam, alety apek akelhetyam. (St) *The olden-time people used to make stone knives. They fixed [the blade to the handle] with spinifex wax and then they used them to cut up meat or something. People cut themselves with stone knives as well, wounded themselves [in mourning].*
SEE ALSO inkwartety, antha2, apwert antha, kartamp, irntarlter, irntang arlter, werlamp

alywel (E) *n.*
buttocks, bum, backside ◆ Atna alywelel-ayeth anep-anem, akem arlka irretyakenh. (St) *Sitting on [your] backside and not getting up.*
= anwerlk2, anaynp, artelh2

alywelenhem (E), **alyweletnhem** (E) *vt.*
scrape out inside of a tuber; scrape kurrajong roots; scrape food to make soft ◆ Alywelenhetyam anaty apek mern antyalkenh apek, *scrape*-em *out. Spoon*-artekarl ina mpwaretyam alywek kwer. Alywelenhetyam, arlkwetyam. Alywelenhemel arlkwemel. (St) *They used to scrape the inside out of the* anaty *and* antyalkenh *tubers. They used to make a tool like a spoon, called* alywek, *to do it with. They'd scrape the flesh out and eat it.*
SEE ALSO tewem, alywek

alywelp *n.*
Normanton box (*Eucalyptus normantonensis*). Tree about 4 m high, with pale yellow flowers and small, hard nuts. ◆ Alywelpel-ayel yerrekeyerr perrap kelh anthwerr, an perrap theweyet anthwerr. Akemel akemel akemel kel mer-warn angety-alpetyenheng theweyet anthwerr. (T) *There is a substance made by the lerp-scale insect on the* alywelp *tree that is in lumps, and it's really sweet. It is picked and this really sweet stuff is taken back to camp.*
SEE ALSO alhelp, yerrekeyerr

alywep-alywep (T) tired SEE UNDER **alyep-alyep1**

alywer1 (T,E), **aylwer** (E) *n.*
1. young seed pods of the dogwood (*Acacia sericophylla*)
SEE ALSO ntyerrm, apal1, artwengarr, awenth

2. emu chick ◆ Anywekelam angetyem alywer akwek map. Alywer akwek map wantem, anywelek. (T) *The father emu takes the young baby emu chicks around. The father feeds them.*
• = ankerr akwerrk, ankerr akwek, artelh[1]
CAN SOUND A BIT LIKE arlwer *'gecko'*

alywer[2] *n.*
full (stomach after having a drink) (?)
SEE ALSO anhwerlk, anerteng, nthat

alywer-irrem *vi.*
quench thirst; fill stomach up (with water); drink (to quench thirst) ◆ Alywer-irrem kwatyel, irrer-penh apek alywer-irrem, ahentyarl *dry*-irrekarl apety-alpem, ahenty antyerrk-irrekarl. Alywer irrem anem, anert arlkarl-ilemel. Angkethelarl apety-alpek, mern perlap arlkwenty-penh, ker arlewatyerr arlkwenty-penh, angkethel-irrem. Antywety-alpem alywer-irrem anem. (St) *When you come back from hunting and your throat is dry you quench your thirst with water. This quenches your thirst and makes your stomach cool. You might come back thirsty, perhaps from eating conkerberries or eating goanna meat. You come back and drink and then you feel full [of water].* ◆ *Cool drink*-el alywer-irretyakenh arrangkwarl, wararl antywem, *just* theweyet war antywem. Kwatyarl *main one*, alywer-irremel antywetyekarl. (St) *You can't quench your thirst with cool drink, you just drink that for the sweetness. Water is the main thing to drink to quench the thirst.* ◆ Kwaty arwekel antywetyeh alhetyeh alywer-irretyeh. (M) *Drinking water to quench the thirst.*

alywer-ilem *vt.*
quench thirst (W)

alywerlp (W) *n.*
a type of hawk (?)

alywerr (E) *n.kin* [RESPECT LANGUAGE]
A respectful way of referring to the mother's mother and the mother's mother's brothers and sisters of a person whom the speaker is in an avoidance relationship to. For example, a woman may use *alywerr* to refer to her son-in-law's mother's mother, or a man may use *alywerr* to refer to his mother-in-law's mother's mother. The term may also be used by a man to refer to his male cross-cousin's wife. ◆ Anewikw ankelekikwenh 'alywerr' akem, artwel. (Sa) *A man calls his cross-cousin's wife* 'alywerr'.
= inkely (?)
SEE ALSO ipmenh, nyany[2]

alywerraty (E) *n.kin*
my/our *alywerr*

alywerrengkw (E) *n.kin*
your *alywerr*

alywerrikw (E) *n.kin*
his *alywerr*

alywerr-nheng (E) *n.kin*
a group of two or more people related as grandparents (mother's mothers or mother's mother's brothers) and grandchildren (daughter's children or a person's sister's daughter's children). This is said by a woman if one of them is her son-in-law, or by a man if one of them is his mother-in-law.

alywerr-nheng atherr (E) *n.kin*
a grandparent (mother's mother or mother's mother's brother) together with their grandchild (daughter's child or a person's sister's daughter's child). This is said by a woman if one of them is her son-in-law, or by a man if one of them is his mother-in-law.

alywerr-ankethenh (E) *n.kin*
1. having a close *alywerr* still alive
2. someone who is always with their *alywerr*
SEE ALSO -ankethenh

alywerr-parety (E) *n.kin*
respectful or 'sorry way' of talking about someone's *alywerr*
SEE ALSO -parety

alywerr-alywerr (W,T) *n.*
red-capped robin (*Petroica goodenovii*)
= akarl-atwerrey, kapert rnter-rnter, uneng atyetyek

alywerrp akely-akely (E) a type of lizard SEE UNDER **alhwerrp akely-akely**

+am[1] (W,T), **+em** (W,T) *ending*
1. Goes on the end of words to add emphasis to that word. ◆ Rrtywerremel**am** arengk nhenh arlkwerrp-nhwerrerreperrem. *These dogs are always barking at nothing.* ◆ Atwek yatherr twewarn-perr. Ywarn**em** angelhetyam. (M) *They killed it properly, so it was not moving at all.*
2. Often used to form questions. ◆ Angwenh-henh**am** angwely yanhan? (M) *Whose dog is this?* ◆ Angwenh**am** yanhan? Ayeng**am**. (M) *Who is that? It's me.* ◆ Angwenh-apatherr ntw**am**? (M) *What skin are you?*

+am[2] *n.ending*
Goes in the middle of doubled-up words that describe number or amount to show that something happens gradually or in stages; bit by bit, one at a time, two at a time etc. ◆ Tha impen-impenel arlkwep-arlkwem anyent**am**-anyent impen-impen. Arrpenhek apek anthetyang. (St) *I'm greedily eating it, bit by bit, without sharing it or giving it to another.*

◆ Anyentam-anyent *chips* arlkwep-arlkwem, pep nhek-arlek. Anyent anem tyerremel arlkwep-arlkwem. (St) *Eating the chips from the paper one by one. Then pulling another one out and eating it.*
atherram-atherr (E) *adv.*
two at a time, in pairs, two each
SEE ALSO anyentam-anyent

ama (W) *n.*
milk
SEE ALSO paty, werlaty

ama (T,E) bud or flower of native tobacco etc. SEE UNDER **alpma**

amak *n.*
elbow ◆ Ananthcrr amak atherr anyenem. (T) *We have two elbows.*
amak annga (W,T) *n.*
point of the elbow (annga *'eye', 'seed', 'round thing'*)

amakw (E), **apmakw** (E) *n.*
the back of the emu
= warr
Amakweng, Apmakweng (E) *n.*
Central Mt Stuart. See map p. viii.

amakwernem (W,T) *vt.*
(native bee) put pollen in native bee nest (?) ◆ Lwerlkerel amakwernem *sugarbag*, akwernem akwernem akwernem amakwernem amakwernem rlpwer-warl. Pertipelaw anteth-penh amakwernem. (T) *The native bee puts the pollen inside the native bee nest, puts it in the hollow tree. It puts the pollen from the flowers in the hollow tree.*

amangkem *vi.*
1. grow up, be brought up in a place ◆ Ayeng mer nhel amangkek. (St) *I was brought up in this country.*
2. grow bigger, grow up ◆ Arna nhenh amangkek angerr. (M) *This tree has grown big.* ◆ Kwer nhenh amangkety-kwenh itya. (M) *This child hasn't grown.*
3. grow up on something (e.g. food) ◆ Mern tywerrkel anwern amangkek, arlkwerl-apekarl, ampeng-irremarl. Arnkang arerl-alhem mentyel. '*Ah* ampeng-irrekam nhenh kwenh, anwengkerr mern arlkwerl-aney kwenh.' Inerl-alhemel iltyel inerl-alhemel arlkwem anemarl. Lwerenarl yanh mern tywerrk, kwerel anwern amangkelhekarl. (N) *We grew up on wild figs, going along and eating them when they were ripe. If we saw unripe ones we'd leave them. 'Ah, this one is ripe, let's eat these ones', we'd say. We'd pick them by hand and them eat them. That's what it's like, the wild fig that we grew up on.*
SEE ALSO angerr-irrem[1]
amangkelh-ilem *vt.*
grow someone up; bring up a child; raise someone or something up ◆ Tha akwek nhenh map amangkelh-ilek. Akwekeng-ntyel tha amangkelh-ilek. (P) *I grew these kids up. I raised them from when they were little.*
= kwetyakw-ilem

amankethenh SEE UNDER **amey** 'mother etc.'

amany-irrem, apmany-irrem (E) *vi.*
sigh or take a deep breath because of tiredness, fear, sorrow or relief ◆ Amany-irrem, 'Aaaaaaaa'. (M) *Sighing deeply and going, 'Ahhhhhhh'.* ◆ Apmany-irrem ayeng ngkweng, mwerr nga anetyenh. (St) *I am sighing with relief and in the hope that you will be better.*

amar *n.*
1. types of mistletoe (*Amyema* spp. and *Lysiana* spp.)
2. edible mistletoe fruits. Also referred to as *mern amar.*
SEE ALSO peketyalkwarr, akweltyayt, ngkwerrm, pweralhem, atyankern

amaralty-anem (E) *vi.*
swing from something ◆ Kwey amaralty-anem arwerlel. (Sa) *The girl is swinging from the branch.*
SEE ALSO arlparernem

amarl, amarley, apmarl (E), **apmarley** (E) *n.kin*
1. uncle (mother's brother) [SOME SPEAKERS]
2. particular male relations with the same skin as your mother
3. a woman's daughter's daughter's children; great-grandchild
4. male cross-cousin's son
5. mother's mother's mother and her brothers and sisters; great-grandmother, great-grandfather
6. father's cross-cousin
7. senior father-in-law
SEE ALSO ahenterr, arnemerr, ampwek, ampaty-ampaty, maly, kamern
amarl-amarl, apmarl-apmarl (E) *n.kin*
uncle (mother's brother), father's cross-cousin, senior father-in-law, etc. This word is particularly used for senior *amarl.* ◆ *Father* ngkwengenh ankelekw, wal 'amarl-amarl' akem nta. (M) *You call your father's male cross-cousin* 'amarl-amarl'. ◆ Aywang intert map amarl-amarl. (M) Amarl-amarl *are the senior men.* ◆ *We call*-em 'amarl-amarl' *uncle Fred*-arey Pwerl. Amarl-amarl atyenh. *He calls me* ampaty. Ampaty ikwerenh yay ikwerenh-kenh. (Sa) *We call them* 'amarl-amarl', *uncle Fred and the others, Pwerl. He calls me* ampaty.

I am his ampaty *because I am his elder sister's child [Petyarr woman talking].*
amarlaty, apmarlaty (E) *n.kin*
my/our *amarl*
amarlengkw, apmarlengkw (E) *n.kin*
your *amarl*
amarleyekw (E), **apmarleyekw** (E) *n.kin*
his/her/their *amarl*
amarlekw (W,T) *n.kin*
1. your *amarl*
2. his/her/their *amarl* ◆ Yanhan marl yanhkenh amarlekw. (T) *There is that woman's father-in-law.* ◆ Angey ngkwengenh *cousin* amarlekw akem. (M) *[You] call your father's cross-cousin* amarlekw.
amarl-nheng, apmarl-nheng (E) *n.kin*
a group of two or more people, one or more of whom are called *amarl* by the others
amarl-intyerr, apmarl-intyerr (E) *n.kin*
= **amarl-nheng**
amarl-nheng-arey *n.kin*
a group of more than two people, one or more of whom are called *amarl* by the others
amarl-nheng atherr, apmarl-nheng atherr (E) *n.kin*
a person together with their *amarl*
amarl-ankethenh, apmarl-ankethenh (E) *n.kin*
1. having a close *amarl* still alive
2. someone who is always with their *amarl*
SEE ALSO -ankethenh

amarleyarr (W) *n.*
young man who has just been initiated (note Warlpiri *marliyarra*)
SEE ALSO alyepelengkw, awerrty, arwekert, lyaty, arleyarr, tyakwertekwert, lwekerleny, antingkar

amarn, apmarn (E) *n.*
still, quiet, motionless
amarn-irrem, apmarn-irrem (E) *vi.*
1. stay in one place; be quiet or still, be immobile or 'rooted' to the spot (because of fear or shyness) ◆ Amarn-irrem, antarl anerlanem, alhety ahenty-kweny. (M) *Staying in one place, because [you] don't want to go.* ◆ Tyerrty alenhel atwehety amarn-irrem. *He is frightened and doesn't want to move because that person might hit them.*
2. quieten down, freeze (of animal); become motionless because of cold or fear ◆ Ker aherrek *sneak up*-irrem wal amarn-irremel anem ker aherr. Arem ra, wal ra amarn-irremel kwen-irremel kapert kwen-irremel. Arem ra. Kerel arnarem, nheng kwer aperterlek, *sneak up*-irrerlek. (T) *When [a person] is sneaking up on a kangaroo, the kangaroo becomes motionless with fear. It looks and then stays still, putting its head down. The animal watches the person who is sneaking up on it.* ◆ Apmarn-irrek-arlaw ayeng — yanh menty angketyam rarrp. (St) *I've gone quiet — that person can do the talking themself.*
amarn-ilem, apmarn-ilem (E) *vt.*
quieten something down (kangaroo or euro); cause an animal to become mesmerised or 'freeze' ◆ Ker aherr apek amarn-ilem tyerrty alenh apetyepetyemel, *rifle*-akert. Amarnem anem ker aherr. Amarn-ilem tyerrtyel. *One place no move.* Apetyem *rifle*-akert, atyerrem renh. (M) *The person coming along with a rifle makes the kangaroo 'freeze' in fear. The kangaroo stays rooted to the spot. The person makes it immobile with fear. It stays in one place and doesn't move. The person comes with the rifle and shoots it.*

amarr *n.*
1. the blood which comes from small cuts made on the upper arms and breasts and used by women for healing ◆ Amarr ra akelhem ampa akely apekan utyen anentyek, kel apernemel ra ikwerel amarrel. Arelh akelhem, amarr akelhem, kel alhwa thelelhemel, kel annga anem ikwerel aperneman, utyen, annga utyen-irrenty. (Sa) *She cuts herself on the arm and then rubs a child who has sores with the blood. Women cut themselves and then the blood seeps out and then they used the blood to rub on the eyes, eyes that have got sore.* ◆ Amarr antywetyam, amarr apernelhetyam. (St) *Drinking the* amarr *blood and using it to rub on yourself.*
2. scars on women's upper arm and breasts
SEE ALSO urrma, akwepenh

amarrkel angem, apmarrkel angem (E), **amarrkel rrkwem** (W,T) *vt.*
carry something on the hip (angem '*carry*', '*take*'; rrkwem '*hold*') ◆ Ampengamp amarrkel angerl-wetyel ampel-rnem, *nappy*-akert. Ampanpantey. *Bottle* angetyel ampa akwel *baby* akwel kwerenh, ampengamp. (Sa) *All the children carry the dolls, with nappies, around on their hips. They are pretend babies. They carry bottles, and supposedly they are their babies.* ◆ Amarrkel rrkweperrkwem amwelek kwer rrwey. (M) *His mother is carrying the baby boy on her hip.*

Amarteng (W), **Amartenng** (W) *n.*
the name of a hill east of the Mt Allan community

amatheng (E), **apmatheng** (E) *n.*
orphan

= alhamp, rrkwern

amatheng-amatheng (T,E), **apmatheng-apmatheng** (E) *n.*
black-faced cuckoo-shrike (*Coracina novaehollandiae*)
= matyekwel

amaty my/our mother etc. SEE UNDER **amey**

amayernem (E) *vi.*
a hand movement made by women when calling out to particular relatives during a ceremony

amek-amek *n.*
sacred place, restricted place ◆ Amek-amek ilem, nthakenh arelhel atwaretyakenh. (Sa) Amek-amek *is a place that women aren't allowed to approach.* ◆ 'Amek-amek' akin ilem Anmatyerrel, marl alhety-kweny itya. (M) *In Anmatyerr you say* 'amek-amek' *as well, where women aren't allowed to go.*
SEE ALSO kwerert, mwekeny, tikeley, akayak

amek-arem *vt.*
1. avoid close contact with particular kin (such as mothers-in-law or sons-in-law) ◆ Mey-mey atyenh tha amek-arem. (St) *I avoid my son-in-law.*
2. avoid something ◆ Tyampet atyenh nta unmely-ilem, amek-aretyakenhel. Ingkel ulthemel ap atyenh unmely-ilek nta tey-kenh impen. (St) *You squashed my billycan, you didn't avoid it. You trod on and crushed my special tea-making billycan.*
3. be blocked or stopped by something, be unable to do something or go somewhere because of something ◆ Kwaty urew, tharl amwerrk amek-arety-alhern kwaty urew, ulpayek. *Shopping*-ek alhek, amek-arerl-alpek. (St) *Just yesterday I went and was blocked by the flood water in the creek. I went to go shopping and I was blocked off and came back.* ◆ *Road* arrngert-wekarl, anwantherr amek-arek, amek-aremel, twep-twep anem apety-alpek, ilety-alpem arrpenhek-arey. (St) *Something was blocking the road, and we went and were stopped by it, so then we turned round and came back to tell the others.* ◆ 'Kwaty tha amek-arerl-alpek angerr.' Ilelhety-alpem ingwerek-arey. (Sa) *'I saw lots of water blocking the way.' That's what I went back and told the others.*

amek-arenty (E) *n.*
rules about avoiding particular kin, for example mothers-in-law or sons-in law

amek-arenty-penh (E), **amek-arenty-iperr** (E) *n.*
a person who is of an age when they have to follow avoidance rules ◆ Amek-arenty-iperr yanhaw, ampa yanh. (St) *That child now has to avoid particular relations.*

amel[1] *n.*
wet or damp dirt or sand used for covering people when they are out in the bush a long way from water; a shallow hole dug for cooling down in; a cool place that a kangaroo digs out to lie in; a hole for putting fruits (such as *anakety*) in to keep them soft and green. ◆ Alerlaw, amel tha angerney. Amelel ayeng artelhetyek, irrernt ilelhemel. Angkethel anem ayeng. (St) *Wait while I dig a hole to cool off in. I'll cover myself with damp earth to make myself cool. I'm thirsty.* ◆ Amelel ayeng rlkwerr intety-alhek kwaty-kwenyel. (M) *Because I haven't got any water, I'm going to lie down half way there in the damp earth.* ◆ Amelel ra intep-intemarl aherr, angernem ra wal ra interl-anem ahelh kwerel irrerntel anem, amel angernem. *A kangaroo lies in the cool earth, digs out a hole and then lies there in the cool earth.*

+amel[2] (E) *v.ending*
(the verb action) will happen soon ◆ Ikngwetyek alhem tyerrty arrpenh, kel apety-alpeyamel antey. (St) *Going and asking the other person, then coming back again soon.* ◆ Urrek atyeng mpwelhay. Ayengek-amparr mantarr *clean*-ek apek terrethek apek irrpelh-ileyamel. (St) *Hang on, wait for me. I'm going to put on a clean dress first.* ◆ Alkngwanngw-ilem tha arengk nhenh-arey, ker apek antherl-anem, tyerrty yanh alheyamel. (St) *I'll distract these dogs by giving them some meat and then these people can go.*
SEE ALSO +etyenh, +etyenheng

amel-rrkwem (W,T), **amel-irrkwem** (W,T) *v.t.*
1. hug, embrace or put your arms around someone (rrkwem *'have', 'hold'*) ◆ Amel-irrkwem kwer akwek kwerenh. (T) *[She] is hugging her child.*
2. hold or embrace someone in an expression of mourning ◆ Yanh kwenh ngkweng anyent-irretyek anep-anem mal-malek kwenh. Nta amel-irrkwerl-apetyem mal-malel kel mal-malel irrkwetyem amel-irrkwerrem antem. (T) *Those people are all gathered together for the sorry business. You come and embrace people to express your grief at the sorry camp.*

amel-rrkwerrem (W,T), **amel-irrkwerrem** (W,T) *vi.*
hug or embrace each other ◆ Lyetantarl apetyem, wal amel-irrkwerrem. *'Ah atyengenh kwenh atyengenh kwenh.'* (T) *If somebody who has just arrived, well they hug*

each other. 'Ah, [you're] mine, you're mine.' ◆ Anewart atherr amel-rrkwerrem. (M) *The husband and wife are hugging each other.*

amelerr (T,E), **apmelerr** (E) *n.*
permanent, same, usual, something or somebody who is always there ◆ Arelh yanh amelerr anep-anem, merek-artwey. (St) *That woman is the owner of the place and she's always there.* ◆ Kwaty apmelerr intep-intem, uyerretyakenh. (St) *That water is permanent, it never runs out.* ◆ Amelerrant akeweny apetyem. (T) *It's just that same old person that's coming, poor thing.*
SEE ALSO akweteth, irrkaty, marany, amperreny

ameleth *n.*
1. harmless, quiet, timid, unthreatening, not dangerous
2. not able to do something (from English 'harmless') ◆ Artwel wem — arelhan ameleth. (St) *Men spin hairstring — women aren't able to do it.*
SEE ALSO anik, angwang, apertap, ahelengkw, ahangerr

amely-wem *vt.* [RESPECT LANGUAGE]
1. eat ◆ Amely-wetyek tyety-ayerr amely-wetyek, urrem-iletyek tyety-ayerr. Mwerelikw ilanthem amely-wetyek. Ahanelh-ila, yanhek-antey amely-wem ratherr, arlkwetyek. (Sa) *Eat the meat, give [them] the meat to eat. His mother-in-law sends meat over for them to eat. Take the meat for those two to eat [her daughter and her husband].* ◆ Amely-wem, urrekatyakenh-antey. (Sa) *Wait while [I] eat.*
2. drink
3. take medicine
amely-akem (E) *vt.* [RESPECT LANGUAGE]
1. eat ◆ Tyety-ayerr amely-akerrey, weyapelek-uthek. (Sa) *You two will eat the meat, hungrily.*
2. drink ◆ Arntwaly-ayerr amely-aketyek, mern then ker then. (Sa) *Drinking water and eating bread and meat.*
SEE ALSO arlkwem, antywem

ameng *n.*
1. fly (insect), bush fly (*Musca vetustissima*) ◆ Amengel anngang tywen-ilem. (T) *Flies make your eyes sore.* ◆ Alkngewarl akarr-irrem ameng. (Sa) *Flies gather around your eyes.*
2. sugarbag bee, native bee
ameng irrkwenh-irrkwenh, ameng irrkweny-irrkweny (T,E) *n.*
a type of skink (?) (lit. 'fly holder')
Amengernternenh (E) *n.*
name of a place on the Alyawarra Aboriginal Land Trust area, west of the Sandover Highway (rnternem *'spearing'*). Location of the Urapuntja Medical Service. See map p. viii.

ameng ulpma (E), **ameng iylpmwa** (E) *n.* [RESPECT LANGUAGE]
1. mouth
2. story (ulpma *'language', 'word'*)
SEE ALSO arrakert, ayey

amenheng SEE UNDER **amey** 'mother etc.'

amenheng-arey SEE UNDER **amey** 'mother etc.'

amenheng-atherr SEE UNDER **amey** 'mother etc.'

amenhengart SEE UNDER **amey** 'mother etc.'

amenty-ilem (T,E) *vt.*
hit someone or something by mistake, accidentally hit someone ◆ Apalel tha ngenh amenty-ilek. (St) *I hit you by mistake.*
= aperrpert-ilem

ameparety SEE UNDER **amey** 'mother etc.'

ameram-irrem *vi.* [RESPECT LANGUAGE]
1. speak, talk ◆ Ntert-irrerlentyarr merrkwernerl ameram-irrerlanetyakenh kwarrernerliwerrekerr. (Sa) *Be quiet, and don't say anything, it's shameful for those family to hear you [i.e. in-laws might hear].*
2. sing out, yell out ◆ Ngwarrengkwarl kwey nhak ameram-irretyel. (Sa) *Daughter, it's your husband that is singing out over there.* ◆ Ngwarrekengkw ameram-irrem angayel-they, weyapel-they. (St) *Your husband is singing out because he is hungry and wants food [said by a woman to her daughter].*
SEE ALSO kwep-anem, angkem, arlkem

amerl-amerl arrernem (W,T), **ameyl-ameyl arrernem** (E) *v.i.* (?)
vibrate or shake the legs when getting ready to fight (women). This action accompanies a shuffling or hopping step used in preparation for ritual fights. ◆ Arrtyel alhem, kel amerl-amerl arrernem, kwaty-artek ngkwern atherr arrewem. (T) *[The woman] skips along, then shakes her legs, and her two legs vibrate like water.*
= anwerntem
SEE ALSO arrtyernem

amern-amern (E) *n.*
lump or gall on a tree ◆ Arrkernk amern-amern, ulemp amern-amern, artelhampw-irrem, akweteth amernelhetyel. (Sa) *Bloodwood trees have lumps on them, and ghost gums have them — they get very big and swollen up.*
= mwenth
SEE ALSO ankerl
ahenty amern-amern (E)
Adam's apple (ahenty *'throat'*) ◆ Mwelper nhenh-lkwer, 'ahenty amern-amern', *lump*-arl wangkem. *Round about where the windpipe is*

there is a lump called 'ahenty amern-amern'.
SEE ALSO kwaty-kwaty[2]

amernelhem (E) *vi.*
become twisted or swollen ◆ Artep amernelhem !twakelhenty. (Sa) *[His] back is twisted from being broken.* ◆ Ingka ayeng alhetyang amernelhem. (Sa) *My foot is swollen and I can't walk.*
SEE ALSO wangkem
CAN SOUND A BIT LIKE imernelhem *'show self'*; mwernelhem *'get stuck'*

amernt (E) young fruit of the bush banana SEE UNDER **amwernt**

amernt (E) (do something first) SEE UNDER **mernt**[2]

amernt-ayerr (E) *n.* [RESPECT LANGUAGE]
bush banana (note Alyawarr *amernt* 'young fruit of the bush banana') ◆ Amernt-ayerr akwel ngwarr-nhengel irrepethenherr-atherr atyeng. 'Atyeng awakerl-alpetyek kwey untay, ngwarr-nhengel.' (Sa) *My daughter and her husband are supposed to be getting me some bush bananas. 'Daughter, save me some and bring them back, you and your husband.'*
SEE ALSO alkwarrer, alangkw, parl

amerr woomera, spear-thrower SEE UNDER **amirr**

Amerraketyart (T) *n.*
the name of a rockhole east of Ti Tree town

amerrelhem (W) *vi.*
be arrogant or big-headed, set yourself apart from others, have a 'swollen head' ◆ Tyerrty alenh kapert amerrelherl-anem. *Don't* like map-warn apetyeh. (M) *That person has a 'swollen head'. They don't want to associate with the others.*

Amerrengerreng (W) *n.*
name of a waterhole/swamp east of Mt Allan community

amerrk[1], **apmerrk** (E) *n.*
young boy about 10 to 12 years old; teenage boy (before young man ceremonies), pre-initiate ◆ Ampa apmerrk amparrarl anemeng inngart *man* anem irreyamel. (St) *The young boy is an* apmerrk *at first, and then he becomes a man.*
amerrk-irrem, **apmerrk-irrem** (E) *vi.*
become a teenage boy (before initiation ceremonies) ◆ Awey apmerrk — akwek-penh ra apmerrk-irrek anem. (St) *The teenage boy — after being a small boy he turns into a teenager.*

amerrk[2] (E), **apmerrk** (E) *n.*
hot earth or ashes (used for cooking or healing) ◆ Apmerrkel item ker apek, tyap apek. *Cooking the meat or the grubs in the hot earth.*
= awerrth, rtwap
SEE ALSO arnmeny, arlpa[1], atnmanth, ntyerlp[1]

amerrkwernem (E) *vt.* [RESPECT LANGUAGE]
sing, sing someone or something ◆ Amerrkwernerliwerretyel yanhentyak-antey. (Sa) *They [respect kin] are singing over there.*
SEE ALSO alyem
amerrkwernelhem (E) *vi.* [RESPECT LANGUAGE]
sing, sing a song
SEE ALSO alyelhem

amey *n.kin*
1. mother ◆ Ameyan amwekek ilem, amwek-irrwengerr antey ilem anyent-antey ilem. Amam-kenh amwek ilem *sister* amey akin. *Mothers are called both* amwek *or* amey *— that's what they are called. Your mother's sister is called* amey *as well.*
2. mother's sister; aunt
3. a woman's daughter's daughter's child; great-grandchild
4. male cross-cousin's daughter. Sometimes referred to as 'young mother', or 'little mother'.
SEE ALSO mam
amaty *n.kin*
my/our *amey*
amwengk *n.kin*
your *amey* ◆ Nhel apek ilem ngkwengay, 'Mwengk ngkweng-artey alhekaw'. *This person might say to you, 'Your mother has gone'.*
amikw[2] (E), **ameyekw** (E) *n.kin*
his/her/their *amey*
iltya amikw (E)
thumb (iltya *'hand', 'finger'*)
amwek (W,T) *n.kin*
1. your *amey*
2. his/her/their *amey* ◆ Amwek ngkwengenh. (M) *Your mother.* ◆ Ngkweng-artwey alhekarl amwek. (M) *Your mother went.*
amwek-amwek (W,T) *n.kin*
1. your *amey*
2. his/her/their *amey* ◆ Amwek-amwek-warl alherrirra! Intetyehem ankwang. (M) *Go back to your mother! Go to sleep.*
amenheng *n.kin*
a group of two or more people who are related as mother and child or as mother's sisters (aunties) and nephews and nieces
CAN SOUND A BIT LIKE menhenheng *'a group of two or more people who are related as granny and grandchild'*
amenhengart (W,T) *n.kin* = **amenheng**
◆ Amenhengart rrpwety alhem lyweny kerek. *A few people went hunting for meat, mothers and children together.*
amenheng-arey (E) *n.kin* = **amenheng**
amenheng atherr *n.kin*
a person together with their *amey* (a woman

together with her child; a person together with their mother's sister; a woman together with her nephew or niece (sister's children)) ◆ Menheng atherr war alhem amwek an kwer kwerenh. *They go as* menheng atherr, *a mother and her child.*
CAN SOUND A BIT LIKE menh-nheng atherr *'a person together with their granny'*
ameparety *n.kin*
respectful or 'sorry way' of talking about someone's *amey*
SEE ALSO -parety
amankethenh, **amenkethenh** *n.kin*
1. having *amey* (still alive)
2. someone who is always with their *amey* ◆ Kwer yanh amankethenh angerr. (T) *That kid is always following its mother.* ◆ Amankethenh angerr kwer nhenh. (M) *This kid is a real mummy's girl.*
SEE ALSO -ankethenh

ameyl-ameyl arrernem (E) vibrate or shake the legs when preparing for a fight (women) SEE UNDER **amerl-amerl arrernem**

amikw[1] (E), **apmikw** (E) *n.*
native pine (*Callitris glaucophylla*). Tree to 6 m high with rough bark, blue-green leaves and woody fruit. Grows in hilly country. ◆ Apwert-areny apmikw — apmikw-rnem tnenherretyel. *Medicine.* Renh rltimp akem, apert-atwemel anter, rltimp iylwem. Irrnyiwemel. (Sa) *The native pine grows in the hills — that's where you find the native pine trees. It's a medicine. You collect the bark and smash it up with fat. The bark peels off.*
= rlwek, anngart

amikw[2] SEE UNDER **amey** 'mother etc.'

amirr, **amerr** *n.*
woomera, spear-thrower ◆ Artwel irrtyart arrernetyam amirr-warn ker atanthetyek. (T) *The man put the spear in the woomera to spear the kangaroo.*

-amp, **-ampw** *n.ending*
Goes on the end of nominals (usually plant names) to refer to the types of sweet resin or honey often found on that plant.
anyerampw, **atnyerampw** (E) *n.*
edible gum from the supplejack tree, *anyer (Ventilago viminalis)*
ntyweyamp, **untyeyamp** (E) *n.*
honey from the northern corkwood, *ntywey/untyey* (*Hakea chordophylla*)
alkeramp, **alkerampw** (E) *n.*
resin from mulga (*Acacia aneura*)
yerramp *n.*
honeyant (yerr *'ant'*)
rltwamp (W,T) *n.*
sugarbag, native beehive

ampa *n.kin*
1. child (a general word for a child)
= kwer[1]
2. child (of a woman)
3. a person's sister's child; niece, nephew
4. particular relations with the same skin as a person's *ampa*
5. the word a father uses for his daughter
6. a general word for child that goes before other words for children ◆ Artwa *daddy* ikwerenhel renh akem, 'Ampa atyenh' — alerikw kwerenh. 'Ampa apety-alpa.' (Sa) *Her father calls her 'My* ampa*' — that's his daughter. 'Come back daughter.'*
SEE ALSO alem-penh, anert-penh, rnwepenh
ampaty *n.kin*
my/our *ampa* ◆ Ampaty atyenh rrpwety. *I have three children.*
ampatyey (E) *n.kin*
child (of woman); sister's child; niece, nephew etc. ◆ Untan 'ampatyey' akem Ngwarray. (St) *You [Kemarr] call Ngwarray people* 'ampatyey'.
ampengkw *n.kin*
your *ampa* ◆ Yanhan ngkwengenh ampengkwam. (T) *There is your child.*
ampikw (E), **ampeyekw** (E) *n.kin*
his/her/their *ampa*
ampwek (W,T) *n.kin*
1. your *ampa*
2. his/her/their *ampa*
3. father in law (if young) • SEE ALSO ahenterr, arnemerr, amarl
ampenkethenh *n.kin*
1. having *ampa* (still alive)
2. someone who is always with their *ampa* ◆ Ampenkethenh ayeng — ampaty atyenh *there.* (St) *I have a child — my child is there.*
SEE ALSO -ankethenh
ampa akwek (E)
baby (akwek *'small'*)
ampa alhenty-iperr (E)
child just starting to walk (alhem *'go'*; -iperr *'after'*)
ampa rlternt (E)
newborn baby
= ampelyerrk
ampengamp (E), **ampeng-ampeng** (E) *n.*
doll, pretend baby ◆ Nyetyep-nyetyep, ampa akwek anetyart ampeng-ampeng-akert. Panthel angernepernel. (St) *Little kids used to be*

in cubbyhouses with their dolls. They would carry the dolls around in wooden dishes.
◆ Ampengamp amarrkel angerl-wetyel ampelrnem, *nappy*-akert. Amparrpantey. *Bottle* angetyel ampa akwel *baby* akwel kwerenh, ampengamp. (Sa) *All the children carry the dolls, with nappies, around on their hips. They are pretend babies. They carry bottles, and supposedly they are their babies.*
= kwereng-akwer

ampak-irrem (W,T) *vi.*
1. rush in and grab things ◆ Ampak-irretyal anang! Rwa atyengarl anem! Irrernteng ayeng rwel intenh-intenh. (T) *Don't try to take my firewood! That's my firewood! In the cold I want to sleep by the fire.* ◆ Tyerrty map ampak-irrem ker anyentek. (T) *The people are all rushing in and grabbing the one piece of meat.*
2. gang up on a person ◆ Tyerrty anyenteh ampak-irrem map anthwerr. (M) *Lots of people are ganging up on one person.* • SEE ALSO artangatyel atwem

ampakem *vt.*
tear (meat) apart; cut or break food up ◆ Atnwenth ampakemel arlkwem, ampakemel arlkwem. Lyetant *knife* ant akngerr anemel ampakemel arlkwetyek. *Knife*-akwenyel ampakemel arlkwarlkwerl-wem. (St) *Meat is ripped apart and eaten. Nowadays knives are used to divide up the meat. If there is no knife the meat is torn apart and eaten quickly.* ◆ Ker ampakem arrakertel. (T) *Tearing the meat up with your mouth.* ◆ Ker ampakem arrengkerel, arlkwety arlkwetyew. (M) *Hungrily tearing the meat apart to eat.* ◆ Larl twerr angerr ywarn ampakerl-anem. (T) *It is difficult to break up hard lollies.*
SEE ALSO ltwakem

ampakelhem (W,T) *vi.*
1. break part of youself, injure yourself
2. break, fall down
3. turn away from people; walk away from someone; go off in your own direction ◆ Tyerrty yanh ampakelhemel alhem. (T) *That person is going their own way, turning away from people.*
4. stop what you are doing, leave off (e.g. hunting) ◆ *Family* aremel rang ampakelhemel arrernelhety-alpek. (T) *Seeing his family he quit what he was doing and went back and stayed with them.*

ampangkem (T,E) *vi.*
groan, moan, or cry out in pain ◆ Tyerrty arntety ampangkem, arengk apek. (St) *A sick person, or a dog, might cry out in pain.*
SEE ALSO arrangkem, arnem, apangkem, arlkwatelhem, kwatem, anpelhem

ampap-ampap (E) *n.*
tall, slender or thin (of people)
SEE ALSO lyerrer

-amparr, -amperr (W) *ending*
(do something) first (before some other action); (someone does something) first (before doing something else); initially. In the Eastern dialect of Anmatyerr this ending is always preceded by *+ek*. ◆ Angerr renh arrawelhiletyam walyel-**amparr**. (T) *First of all lots [of things] were gathered together with a branch.* ◆ Ahakey ilkwang-**amparr** anem. Ahakey irntang anem anem. (T) *At first the bush plum has flowers. Then it has fruit.* ◆ 'Atyeng-**amparr** wetyay — atyeng-**amparr**!' (N) *Throw me some first — me first!'* ◆ Maney anetyakenh **amparr**. *No money* — arrangkw. (N) *There wasn't any money at first. No money — nothing.* ◆ Urrek atyeng mpwelhay. Ayengek-**amparr** mantarr *clean*-ek apek terrethek apek irrpelhileyamel. (St) *Hang on, wait for me. I'm going to put on a clean dress first.* ◆ Antywantywerl-wey urrek, teyek-**amparr** tha antywantywerl-wey, urinp nhenh. (St) *Wait while I drink this quickly, I'll quickly drink this hot tea first.* ◆ Ntw**amparr** alha, alhetyenheng ingkernangkwerr ayeng. (M) *You go first, and I'll go along behind later.* ◆ Ntw**amparr** arlkwa ker. (M) *You eat the meat first.*

amparrkem *vi.*
flash, shine, glint, sparkle ◆ Ilewerr arem kwaty-artek amparrkerlek. (Sa) *You see the mirage sparkling like water.* ◆ War thelelherlanem irnmerr renh war amparrkerl-anerlek arerl-anem, arna anyent kwerel antem. Arlperl artety kwereng antem war thelelherlanem. Renh-iperr arraw-ilemel walyel arrawilemel rnpwang arrernetyam, kelh arrernetyam. (N) *It just drips from the mulga tree and you can see it like drops of water sparkling on the branch of that particular tree. The* arlperl *just drips from the mulga tree. Then it is gathered together with a branch and the sweet stuff made into a lump.* ◆ Mwetekay apek amparrkenty-alhem yanh arerr apetyemel. (T) *The car is shining as it is coming closer.*

amparrkey, amparrkey-amparrkey *n.*
shiny, sparkling, pretty ◆ Lyerteny mwetekayaw. Amparrkey-amparrkey. (St) *This is a new car. It's shiny.*
= alenm-alenm

amparrkerl-wem (E) *vt.*
flash at something (like a camera flashes)

ampatherr (W) *n.*
emu fat (from belly). Also referred to as *ker ampatherr*.

ampaty-ampaty *n.*
1. a person's sister's child; nephew, niece
2. woman's father-in-law (especially young ones), and his brothers and sisters. Relations that are called *ampaty-ampaty* are especially respected, and direct contact is avoided.
◆ Atnert ayeng altywer, *might be son*, ampaty-ampaty atyenhek apek. *Like sorry you know*, lhwarrp-irrem ayeng. (St) *I am feeling sorry, maybe for my son or a nephew or niece. I'm feeling sorry.*
SEE ALSO ampa, ampwek, maly, amarl, ahenterr, arnemerr

ampay (W) *n.*
hot ◆ Ampayel ayeng alhem aketh-warn. Anyatwetyeh irlkel. Antyey angerrarl irrem-arleng. (M) *I'm hot and I'm going outside, so that I can cool down in the wind. I'm sweating too much.*
ampay-irrem (W) *vi.*
cool down (?) ◆ Ampay-irremel ayeng intem akethel anyarteyel, *hot*-eng. (M) *I'm going to lie down outside in the open so that I can cool down, because it's so hot.*
SEE ALSO tyenelhem[2]

ampekernem *vi.*
stand leaning against someone or something (irnem, rnem '*stand*') ◆ Arnel-arleng ampekernem. (M) *Leaning on a stick.* ◆ Apeng intertel ampekernep-rnem. (Sa) *Leaning against the base of the kurrajong tree.*
ampek-intem *vi.*
lie leaning against someone or something (intem[1] '*lie down*') ◆ Ampek ayeng intem lyweperel-ayel. (M) *I am lying down, leaning on the [person's] thigh.* ◆ Kwer ampek-intem amwekel-ayel. (N) *The child is lying leaning on his/her mother.* ◆ 'Mernt-irremarl kwenh. Ayeng ampek-intey ngkwengel-ayel kwenh? Rtwenkarl arrernekarl-arleng ayeng ampek-interl-anem.' (N) *'I'm sick. Can I lie leaning on you? I'll lie down resting against the pillow that I put there.'*
ampek-anem *vi.*
sit leaning against someone or something (anem '*sit*') ◆ Arelh atherr ampek-anem pwetewel inetyenheng. (T) *The two women are leaning against each other to have their photo taken.*
ampek-arrernem *vt.*
put something on something else (arrernem '*put*') ◆ Arelh yanhel ampek-arrernem iltyang mpaty ahernel-ayel. (T) *The woman is putting hand prints on the ground.* ◆ Kwer akwek ampek-arrernem arnewarn. (T) *Putting the child into the tree.*
ampek-welhem *vi.*
lean on something ◆ Kwer ampek-welhem artepel-ayel. (T) *The child is leaning on the [mother's] back.*

ampelaherr (E), **ampelawerr** (E) *n.*
large male kangaroo ◆ Thanh atnhwert akngetyang wethan ampelaherr. Artelhampw weth-lkwer. (Sa) *That large male kangaroo is so big it's impossible to carry it around your neck.*
SEE ALSO aherr, yawerrang, aharlparrengk[1]

ampeltyey (W,T) *n.*
diarrhoea, 'gutsache' ◆ Kart ampeltyey ingkerr kwer nhenh map. *All of these kids have got guts-ache.*
SEE ALSO atnelth
ampeltyey-irrem (W,T) *vi.*
have diarrhoea or 'guts-ache' ◆ Kwer akwek ampeltyey-irrem uternek apek, ampemarl. (T) *The little kids get 'guts-ache' from being in the hot sun.*
= atnelth-irrem
ampeltyem *vi.*= **ampeltyey-irrem** ◆ Ayeng ampeltyem, anertarl ltwakem. (M) *I've got diarrhoea and my stomach is hurting.*
= atnelth-irrem

ampelyerrk *n.*
newborn baby ◆ Kwer ampelyerrk intem panthel-ayel. (T) *The newborn baby is lying in the coolamon.*
= ampa rlternt
SEE ALSO arathap, iylker, arlkarl[2], ampa

ampelyetyerrker (E) *n.*
banded lapwing (*Vanellus tricolor*)
◆ Ampelyetyerrker angkem, 'Tyelkatherather tyelkatherather'. (St) *The banded lapwings sings out like this, 'Tyelkatherather tyelkatherather'.*
SEE ALSO interrk-atherather, tyelkatherather, tartarrp

ampem[1] *vt.*
burn something; make something hot; (sun) beat down on something. ◆ Ingkan ampemarl uternek, ahernel alhentyan ingka aketh, ampem. (Sa) *In summer, if you walk about on the ground with bare feet your feet will get burnt.* ◆ Uternel ampemaw, urinp anem ayeng irrek. (Sa) *The sun is beating down on me and I've got very hot.* ◆ Ntywey arrernetyart, akem renh arrernetyart, twernel ampetyeh. Twernel ampetyek, akerl-anek akerl-anek ahern arrernerl-alhetyart. *Jam*-arteh am irrety-alhem. (N) *We used to pick the corkwood flowers*

and lay them out in the sun to heat up. We'd lay them on the ground in the heat of the sun. Then the honey would go like jam.

ampem2 *vi.*

1. cook, heat up ◆ Ker aherr ampem aperrkel. (T) *Kangaroo is cooking in the coals.* ◆ Arlpa ipert-ileyew mern ampetyek. *Make a hole in the hot ashes to cook the damper.* ◆ Altyey artaper-wem, mern ampem anem artaper anem. (St) *Bush banana leaves are rolled up and then cooked in a bundle.*

2. be burning ◆ Rwang ampem. (T) *The fire is burning.*

3. become hot, agitated or angry

4. go grey (hair), go white-headed ◆ Aywangem ntwang ampey! (T) *Old man, you're going grey!* ◆ Kapert ampem. *Go grey (hair).* • SEE ALSO aywa

anert ampem

feel angry or sick; have a burning feeling in the stomach (anert '*stomach*')

ampeng *n.*

cooked, ripe, ready to eat ◆ Kel ker ampeng anemew. (M) *The meat is cooked now.* ◆ Arlkwerl-apem mern angelth *anyway* war, ampeng, arnka, arnkang arlkwerl-apem. Tyerrty angety-alpem arrpenh, rwewarl. (N) *[You] can go along eating the fruits of the native pear however you want, cooked or raw. People take some of them back to cook.*

SEE ALSO arnka

ampeng-ilem *vt.*

1. cook something

2. make something ripe

ampeng-irrem *vi.*

1. get cooked ◆ Ker ampeng-irrek, kel ampeng anem arlkwetyek. (St) *The meat is cooked and now we can eat it.*

2. get ripe ◆ Mern tywerrk. Mern tywerrkel anwern amangkek, arlkwerl-apekarl, ampeng-irremarl. (N) *Wild figs. We grew up on wild figs, going along and eating them when they got ripe.* ◆ Irntang mpank ahakey — ampeng-irretyakenh. (M) *The bush plum fruit is not ready — it hasn't ripened.*

ampeny1 *n.*

1. leftovers, the remains of something, food that is leftover after a meal ◆ Nhenhan ampenyarl ingkerrek arrantherr arlkwekarl. Ampenyant anem ngkernek. (Sa) *You mob have eaten everything, all the leftovers. There's only a little bit [of food] left.* ◆ Altyiwem tha teyan ampenyarl irrem, tey ampeny-ampenyan iwem anem ra. (St) *I am throwing out the tea that is left over.* ◆ Mern akwek anthay, ampeny. (M) *Give me a little bit of food, the leftovers.*

2. empty, deserted, abandoned (place or camp) ◆ Mer ampenyam thang arety-alpek. (M) *I came back and saw that the place was empty.* • SEE ALSO arramperrty, ingkeny, arltwa

3. personal belongings of the deceased; a collection of possessions that are divided up and given to certain relatives after someone has passed away ◆ Ampeny yanh renh kel alperrtyelh-iletyek, kel itnek anthemel anem. Ampeny anthem, arrpenhek-arey. (St) *The belongings of the deceased are split up, and then given to the others. The dead person's things are given to other people.* • SEE ALSO tempety, waly-waly

ampeny-ampeny *n.*

1. leftovers, the remains of something ◆ Ampeny-ampeny an altyewem arlkwekarl-penh. (St) *After eating, the leftovers are thrown out.* ◆ Ker ampeny-ampeny angety-alpek mer-warn. (M) *The leftover meat was taken back to camp.*

2. a woman's son-in-law's camp [SOME SPEAKERS]

ampenyel alhem

1. go along behind others and not get anything (when hunting) ◆ Ker-kwenyel alhem, ampenyel, itya. (M) *Going along behind, [I] got no meat, nothing.* ◆ Arrpenhem arrwekel alherl-wem wal ayeng ampenyel ant alhep-alhem. (St) *Others are going ahead, and I'm just going along behind [and not getting anything].*

2. not see anyone (when you arrive at a place) ◆ Ayeng ampenyel alhek ingkern, tyerrty maparl alhek-arleng. (T) *I went to the camp and no-one was there.* ◆ Ampenyam ampenyam alhek, uyarenhek ampeny, innga kweny. (Sa) *I went there to look for them and there was no-one there, not a single person.*

-ampeny2 *n.ending*

side, area, region, in the vicinity of (some thing or some place), on that side. Generally goes on words for cardinal directions, locations or place names. ◆ Ilkewarn-**ampeny**ek akngeyek ayeng alkngirrek. (St) *I was 'found' [spiritually conceived] in the Ilkewarn area, in my father's place.* ◆ Ikngerr-**ampeny**-kenh 'yalkw' — anwern-kenh 'yerrakwerr'. Kik-wemel arlkwerl-apem inelhapemel. *The word 'yalkw' belongs to the people from the eastern region — our word is 'yerrakwerr'. We go along picking them and peeling them and eating them.*

SEE ALSO -thayt

arrwekel-ampeny (E) *n.*

in front, first (arrwekel '*in front*')

rlkang-ampeny (W,T) *n.*
with head to the prevailing wind (often east); to the wind-side (rlkang *'wind'*) ◆ Rlkang-**ampeny**el intetyeh. (M) *Sleeping with [your] head to the wind [facing east].*
iter-ampeny *n.*
at the side (iter *'side'*)
angath-ampeny *n.*
this side, close (angath *'this side'*)

amper[1] (E) *n.*
flower of the acacia bush, elegant acacia, bramble wattle (*Acacia victoriae* ssp. *arida*)
SEE ALSO arlwep

amper[2] *n.*
knee
= kelkert, ampweth
amper irrertety anem (T,E)
sit on heels or haunches (irrertety *'supported on something'*; anem *'sit'*)
= ampwethel-ayeth anem
amper alkwert-alkwert (T)
kneecap (alkwert *'shield'*)

amper[3] (E) *n.*
around, in a circle
amper-amper *n.*
crooked, bent, round, winding, not in a straight line ◆ Atnem atyenhan ap amper-amper. (Sa) *My digging stick is crooked.* ◆ Amwang amper-amper alhem tyerrty-kety ater. (T) *The snake is going in a crooked path because it's frightened of the people.* ◆ Arnang amper-amper menty impey — arratyeny nhenh atwey. (T) *Leave that bent tree — chop this straight one.* ◆ Iwerr amper-amper. (St) *A crooked track.*
= arnkwert-arnkwert, iylwerl-iylwerl, irrkert-irrkert, liw-liw, rtapety
amper-irrem (E) *vi.*
1. go around and around, spin around
2. go around someone or something ◆ Irrety amper-irrerl-anem. *The eaglehawk is circling around.* ◆ Urtalty-kety amper-irraw! (Sa) *Go round and avoid your son-in-law!* ◆ *Law*-akert ilkwarl ayengan, ikanelheyarl mwey-mwey-ketyarl. Arlengel amper-irrerlanetyek mwerekaty, ikanelhem. (Sa) *I've got that important Law, and I avoid my son-in-law. I avoid him and go the long way round.*
= artwep-akelhem
SEE ALSO irrep-akelhem
amperelhem (E) *vi.*
go in a crooked line or direction (?) ◆ Arratyek-amparr anem, wal amperelhem anem ra. (St) *She went straight at first, and then she went in a crooked line.*
amperelh-ilem (E) *vt.*
go around something ◆ Amperelh-ileynemel artekerr yanh arey akerl-apek kerwepel, angernerl-anemel. (Sa) *Going round [the tree] and digging those roots up with a crowbar.*

-amperl (E) *n.ending*
1. an expression of endearment or sympathy; 'Poor thing', 'Poor bugger', 'Dear thing' ◆ Altyernem amikw anyent-kenh *mother* anyent-kenh-rnem altyernem. Rernem-antey, altyernem, angkwer-intyerr. Altyant-**amperl** akngerrerretyel, altyernem anetyel. (Sa) *'Family' are children who have one mother, they are close relations. They are* altya, *just them, all the sisters. Just all the dear old family are living there.* ◆ Thang impern Caroline kartel-ayeng kwenyel akeweny-**amperl**. (M) *I beat poor old Caroline at cards last night.* ◆ Akuny-**amperl** *too* ayeng anep-anem iknga. *No* ilkwatherr. Arengk-artekarl iwerrek. (Sa) *Poor me, I am all on my own. I have no company. They abandoned me like a dog.*
SEE ALSO -angwel-angwel, -angwen-angwen, -apenh, -awern, keweny-amperl
2. really, extremely ◆ 'Mmmmm hmmmmm' athew ra angkerl-anem atek. Ker akwel inarl arlkwetyart. Akely-**amperl**, atek. (St) *The button quail makes a 'Mmmmm hmmmmm' sound. Supposedly they [people] used to eat them. They are tiny little things, button quails.*

ampernem (E) *vt.*
cook something ◆ Mern tha ampernem. (Sa) *I am cooking some food.*
SEE ALSO ampem[1], item, atyerrem[1], arrtyem, ampeng-ilem

-amperr (W) (do something) first (before some other action) SEE UNDER **-amparr**

amperr (W,T) *n.*
not want to do something, not want or like something ◆ Ayeng amperr anem ahenty-kweny. (M) *I've had enough, I don't want it.*

amperreny (E) *n.*
usual, same ◆ Mantarr amperrenyek ayeng irrpepirrpem. (St) *I'm getting into the same old clothes.* ◆ Amperrenyarl ayeng anetyel, nthakenh alhetyang. (Sa) *I'm staying in the usual place — I'm not going anywhere.* ◆ Arelh amperrenyarl apetyepetyemarl. (Sa) *It's the same woman that is coming.*
SEE ALSO amelerr, akweteth, irrkaty, marany

ampeyamp senior son-in-law or mother-in-law [SOME SPEAKERS] SEE UNDER **ampweyampw**

ampeyamp (E) *n.*
a type of bird (possibly the spotted harrier, *Circus assimilis*)

ampinem (E) *vt.*
stalk, track someone or something (follow tracks) ◆ Arlewatyerr ampinem, kel renh alhwengkek arety-alhemel atwety-alhem. (St) *Tracking the goanna, and then finding it in its hole and killing it.* ◆ Ingka ampinem, alhirremarl alhek inngan. Tyerrty alhekarlan ampinety-akerlem. Aley ran alpekey, ampinem, *right up find*-em-ilety-alhemel. (Sa) *Following the tracks where the people went. Following the tracks right along where they went, right up till you find them.*
SEE ALSO ingkantem, apentem

+ampw Goes on the end of nominals (usually plant names) to refer to the types of sweet resin or honey often found on that plant. SEE UNDER +amp

ampwa, ampwang (W,T) *n.*
1. skinny, thin, lean ◆ Ker arlewatyerr ampwa iwey apek menty. Anter anetyakenh menty iwey. (St) *[I'll] leave that skinny goanna. Throw it away because it hasn't got any fat.* ◆ Ker aherr nhenh ampwang. (M) *This kangaroo is thin.*
2. middle-aged, old (of persons or animals)
3. old (said jokingly to babies)
ampwerrem, ampwirrem (E) *vi.*
1. get thin, lose weight, get skinny ◆ Intyerrm ampwirremarl ilem *no* anter. Intyerrm anem irrem. Ankerr ra ampwirrenty intyerrm. Arwerl ikwerenh inngart ratherrarl akngenek mer anyent ikwerel. Ankerr ampwirrenty, intyerrm renh ilem. (St) Intyerrm *is what you call an old, thin emu — no fat. An emu that has got old is* intyerrm. *That's the emu's tree [the dogwood] — in the creation time they both came from the same place. [So] an old emu is called* intyerrm.
= tyew-irrem, utyew-irrem, ngkwern-ngkwern-irrem
SEE ALSO alpwely-irrem, ampweyampw-irrem
2. grow old, age ◆ Arelh ampwirremel apek arert-irrem. (St) *When a woman gets old she might go silly.* ◆ Mern arlatyey apek alpwely-irrekaw, mern altyey apek, alpwely-irrek. Tyerrtyan alpwely-irrem anteyarl, *old people* irremel wart — ampwirremel artwa ampwirremel apek, alpwely-irrek. (St) *Pencil yams or the leaves of bush bananas might have shrivelled up. People 'shrivel up' as well, as they get older — as a man gets older [the skin] goes slack.*
ampwelem, ampwilem (E) *vt.*
make someone thin or skinny, make someone lose weight ◆ Akarntety-arntety pelh-iwenh-iwenharl akarntety-arntety. Pelharl iwem ampwileman, *skinny one* mpwaremel. Pelhel apek ran iwem. Akarntety-arntetyel. Akarntetyek. Kapert arntetyek. (Sa) *The* akarntety-arntety *lizard is a spitter. It spits and makes people skinny. The* akarntety-arntety *lizard spits and gives people a headache.*
arelh ampwa, arelh ampwang (W,T)
old woman, senior woman (arelh[1] '*woman*') ◆ Arelh ampwang nhenhel ahety-ilem mamperrk. (N) *This old woman is winnowing* mamperrk *seeds.* ◆ Arelh ampwang anngang pweng arnerrerl-apem. (M) *The old blind woman is crawling along.*
= akelty ampwa
SEE ALSO ngayekety
artwampw (E) *n.*
old man, senior man (artwa '*man*') ◆ Akuny-amperl kwenh artwampw-amperl akuny kwenh. Artwampw-angwel-angwel apetyem, akuny. (St) *The poor thing, the poor old man. The poor old man is coming.*
= artwang aywang
SEE ALSO aywa

ampwatem (W) *vt.*
split something; chip flakes off a rock
SEE ALSO peltyem, iyltem

ampwengamp *n.*
happy, lively, energetic, hard working ◆ Ampwengamp awelhem rlkert-penh. (T) *Feeling lively after being sick.* ◆ Ampwengamp awelhem alhetyeh lyweny. (M) *Feeling happy about going hunting.*
SEE ALSO irrngerney, arwekar, atyep-atyep
ampwengamp-irrem *vi.*
feel lively, energetic ◆ Ampwengamp-irrem anem ayeng irrer ayeng alhetyek. (St) *Now I'm feeling lively and I'll go hunting.*

ampwerr (E) *n.*
short hair (that has been cut in mourning). Also referred to as *kapert ampwerr.* ◆ Kapert anem ratherr ampwerr anem anetyel. Ampwerr ratherr anem, ratherr arrtyelhekarl atherr alta akelhemel. Aka perlern ilelhemel. Arrwekelenyan antywerel arrtyelherl-anemel, alakenh. (Sa) *Then both of them sit down with short hair. They have short hair because they have cut their hair off in grief. They have made themselves bald. In the old days they used to burn their hair off with grass.*
= akampwerr
SEE ALSO arrtyelhem, itelhem, anker-athek-irrem

ampwerrk *n.*
1. full, whole, unopened ◆ Ker aherr ampwerrk angernem, merelant tyep-iletyeh. (M) *Take the whole kangaroo back, and then just*

cut it up back at camp. ◆ Tyampet ampwerrk. (St) *An unopened tin.*
SEE ALSO mpank
2. fat, solid, a fat person ◆ Arlewatyerr ampwerrk, anter akngerr. (Sa) *A really fat goanna.* ◆ Tyerrty ampwerrk. (M) *A fat person.* • SEE ALSO anter, anter angerr, awek, angerrety-pwek, artelhampw, awer[1]
ampwerrk angerr
fat person, something that is really big and solid ◆ 'Ampwerrk angerr' tyerrty angerrem ilem. (M) *'Ampwerrk angerr' is what [you] call a fat person.*
ampwerrk-ilem (E) *vt.*
1. fill something in ◆ Atha ahern ampwerrk-ilem, ipertarl angernek arengkel. (Sa) *I am filling in the hole that the dog dug.*
2. make someone fat, fatten someone up
ampwerrk-wem (E) *vt.*
fill something up
ampwerrk-ilwem (E) *vi.*
laugh really hard; kill yourself laughing (ilwem '*die*') ◆ Ilekek nhenheyan atherreperrem ampwerrk ilwep-ilwem atyewey-rnem? Ilek ra nhengey? (Sa) *Why is [this person] killing themself laughing? What's it about?*
SEE ALSO arnterr atherrem
ampwerrty (E) *n.*
edible gum from the witchetty bush, *anyem* (*Acacia kempeana*). Also referred to as *anyemampwerrty*.
= anyemangkwarl, anyemaywerrk
SEE ALSO anyem[2]
ampwert (E) *n.*
1. mulgara (native rat) (?) (*Dasycercus cristicauda*)
2. ampurta (?) (*Dasycercus hillieri*)
SEE ALSO artekw, alepey
ampweth (E) *n.*
knee
= amper[2], kelkert
SEE ALSO akarlwarl
ampwethel-ayeth anem (E) *n.*
kneel
= amper irrertety anem
ampweth-ampweth (E) *n.*
a type of plant (no common name) (*Stylobasium spathulatum*). A shrub about 2 m high, with hard, brown nuts about the size of a pea. The nuts of the *ampweth-ampweth* plant are used to make necklaces.
= arleyakwerr, warrangkwer
ampwetyampw (E) *n.*
1. old ◆ Irrernngel-arey iletyam arrwekeleny, ampwetyampwel irrernngel-arey. (St) *Those who have since passed away said that, the olden-time people, all the old women [who have since died].*
2. thin, skinny
ampwety-ampweyneng (E), **ampwey-ampweyneng** (E) *n.*
old man or woman, old people ◆ Arelh ampwety-ampweyneng anetyel. *The old woman is there.*
SEE ALSO akelty ampwa, ampwa, ampwerrem, ampeyamp
ampwey (E) *n.*
1. kurapuka, scrub wattle (*Acacia stipuligera*)
2. velvet hill wattle (*Acacia acradenia*). Shrub up to 3 m high with broad leaves and cylindrical yellow flowers. The seeds are cooked and eaten.
ampweyampw, ampeyamp *n.*
1. senior son-in-law or mother-in-law [SOME SPEAKERS] ◆ Ampweyampwel arntwerrkerlantyarreh alkwert. (M) *[My] son-in-law is holding a shield.* ◆ Ampeyampelarl atyeng rrwem-ilern thang mely-wern. (M) *I just ate the meat that my son-in-law gave me.*
2. senior mother-in-law [SOME SPEAKERS] ◆ Akngerr-patan ilem ampweyampw, mwey-mwey. (St) *A senior mother-in-law is called* ampweyampw.
SEE ALSO angerr-pat, mey-mey[1], ilern-altyerr, urtalty, rtwalty
3. thin, skinny [SOME SPEAKERS] ◆ Ampa urrey ampweyampw arntety-penh. (St) *The little boy is skinny from being sick.*
SEE ALSO ampwa
ampweyampw-irrem (E) *vi.*
get thin, lose weight ◆ Arntety-penharl apekarl ampwerrek ampa akwek, ampweyampw-irrek. (St) *Maybe the little child lost weight from being sick.*
SEE ALSO ampwerrem, utyew-irrem, alpwely-irrem
amult (E) arm, forearm SEE UNDER **amwelt**
amwa[1], amwang (W,T), **apmwa** (E) *n.*
1. snake (a general word for snake) ◆ Awerr atherr alherl-aperretyam anyerrkentyem mer-warn, amwang yatherr atwekarl-penh. (M) *The two boys went home happy because they had killed a snake.* ◆ Apmwekety yanh-kety! (St) *Look out for that snake!*
2. a general word for snake that goes before the name of a particular type of snake
= urnem
amwang mpaty (W,T)
snake track (mpaty '*track*')
= urnem arlkeny
amwa[2] (E), **apmwa** (E) *n.*
bad, no good, wrong, dangerous, awful

SEE ALSO akeng, kwern
amwirrem (E), **apmwirrem** (E) *vi.*
go off, turn bad
SEE ALSO akeng-irrem, kwern-irrem

amwek, amwek-amwek SEE UNDER **amey** 'mother etc.'

amwekel-amwekel[1] (E), **amwekel** (E) *n.*
1. caustic weed, milk weed, mat spurge (*Euphorbia drummondii*). A ground-hugging herb that has small flowers and leaves and milky sap.

= merterr[1]
2. caustic vine (*Sarcostemma viminale* ssp. *australe*). Shrub with leafless tangled branches, pale green flowers and milky sap. Very poisonous.
= kwep-kwep[1]

amwekel-amwekel[2] (E) *n.*
Spencer's burrowing frog (*Notaden nichollsi*)
SEE ALSO kwep, atweynterl, kwep-kwep[2], pwerreparnt

amwelt, amult (E) *n.*
1. arm, forearm ◆ Amult akeng. *Weak arm.* ◆ Ngangkarel amwelt atherr angkwerr-wem, arlka ingkerr angkwerr-wem atheperr-ilemel. (Sa) *The traditional healer massages both of the arms, and all of the body to make it cool.* ◆ Amwelteng arntwerrkem mpweny inem. (Sa) *Grabbing [the person] by the arm to race off with them.*
SEE ALSO amak, akwa
2. the forelegs or front legs of animals, legs of some animals ◆ Artewan kerarlam. Altang althem altang althem kwer-penh ker renh atyerrem. Rlweth akem amwelt atherr an kapert rlweth akem. (N) *Bush turkey meat is edible. The feathers are plucked out and then after that the meat is cooked. The two legs and the head are split open.*
amwelt anngang (W)
wrist
= anaynenh, akwengkwern, iltya ngkwern

amwely *n.*
cadney lizard, central bearded dragon, carney, jew lizard (*Pogona vitticeps*). Also known as *ker amwely*. ◆ Amwelyan atnemelarl atwem, karlkwemel arntekel arlka. Ker anter angerr atherrkeny-iperr. (Sa) *The cadney lizard is hit with a digging stick, and then bitten [on the back of the neck]. The lizards are really fat when the country is green.*

= ankert[2]
SEE ALSO pwelkanty
CAN SOUND A BIT LIKE mwely *'squashed'*

amwengk SEE UNDER **amey** 'mother etc.'

amwer (E), **apmwer** (E) *n.*
mint bush (*Prostanthera striatiflora*). Shrub to 2 m high, with shiny green leaves (which smell nice when crushed), and white flowers. ◆ Apmwer, *medicine*-arl mpwarem renh apmwer, antyerrk-ilemel anem renh apmwer mpwarem anterel-arleng. Apernelhem tyerrty ingkerrek. (T) *The mint bush is made into a medicine. It's dried and then mixed with fat. It is used to rub over the whole body.*
SEE ALSO ngkwern rnter-rnter

amwerenthenng (E) *n.*
swollen
amwerenthenng-irrem (E) *vi.*
swell up ◆ Amwerenthenng-irrek atnerurrk nhenh. (Sa) *This ankle swelled up.* ◆ Artweker amwerenthenng-irrek. (Sa) *The boil swelled up.*
SEE ALSO wangkem

amwernt (T,E), **amernt** (E) *n.*
young fruit of the bush banana, silky pear, *alangkw, parl* (*Marsdenia australis*). Edible.
= akwemper, mwemper, twemper[1], ngwemper

amwerrk, amwerrkel, apmwerrk (E) *n.*
yesterday, a few days ago ◆ Apmwerrkel anwantherr angkern. (Sa) *We spoke just yesterday.*
= ngwerrew
SEE ALSO ingwepenh, lyet, ahamwerrk
amwerrkel arrpenh-ingar (E), **apmwerrkel arrpenh-ingar** *n.*
the day before yesterday
= ngwerreh arrpenh
amwerrkarr (E), **apmwerrkarr** (E) *n.*
yesterday
amwerrkeny (E), **apmwerrkeny** (E) *n.*
from a few days ago; from yesterday; not recent or fresh ◆ Amwerrkeny ulpirrekarl, iweyaw, ulpirrekarl amwerrkeny — tyelkarl ulpirrek, iynteng-irrek. (Sa) *Throw out the meat from yesterday — it's gone off and the flesh has gone rotten.* ◆ Ingka apek arem apmwerrkeny. (St) *[You] might see tracks that are not fresh, those from yesterday.*
= angwerreweny
SEE ALSO lyeteny

an[1], **ant** *part.*
and (from English 'and') ◆ Arnang atherr yatherr inek, an irntang atherr yatherr inek. (M) *Then both of them took a stick each and a stone each.* ◆ Rtak angerr yatherr arrernek an

rwang yatherr itek. (M) *They had made a big windbreak and lit the fire.*

+an² (W), **+arn** *ending*
Provides emphasis or focus ◆ Arelh**an** ankweperr intep-intem awetyakenh. (M) *The woman that is asleep doesn't hear a thing.*
◆ Nhenh**an** kwer akwek. (M) *This is a small child.*

ana, anang (W,T), **atna** (E) *n.*
1. faeces, shit, excreta, droppings, poo
◆ Mwantyel aperrk angetyart, arrernerl-alhetyart, panth-warn, mwar-warn apek, angetyart, aherr-kenh atna inety-alhemel nthilety-alhetyek. Alep-iletyam, angetyam alep-ilemel anyer. (St) *[They] used to carefully carry the coals, put them in a wooden dish to carry them, and go and get kangaroo shit to make the fire ignite. [They] lit the fires, using the supplejack wood.*
2. guts, intestines, innards
3. A general word for guts that goes before a particular term for part of the guts. ◆ Atna atherrk 'anthwerrk' anem akem. Kapert *headache* apek apernelhem. (St) *The green stuff [in the kangaroo's stomach] is called* 'anthwerrk'. *If you have a headache you can rub it on your head.*
= kart¹
atniwem (E) *vt.*
gut (an animal); take its innards out (iwem '*throw away*') ◆ Ker atnarlt artew-kenh kwen, anertel. Inem renh, arlkwem renh, atniwemel. (St) *The edible* atnarlt *meat is inside the stomach part of the bush turkey. You get it and eat it, after cleaning out the guts.*
atna rltwar-rnkem (E)
fart (rltwar-rnkem '*burst out of something*')
= kart inkem, kart ltwakem, atnernkem
atnernkem (E), **atnengkem** (E), **atna anengkem** (E) *vi.*
fart ◆ Atnertengel atnert rltar-rnkem — atnernketyel. (Sa) *[If a person] is full in the stomach then they make a noise — they fart.*
◆ Atnernkem atnerteng, mernarl arnterr arlkwek. (St) *Farting when [you are] full after eating a lot of food.*
= kart inkem, atna rltwar-rnkem, kart ltwakem
SEE ALSO rnkem
atna altywer (E)
anus, arsehole (altywer '*opening*', '*hole*')
atna ulhem (E)
defecate, have a shit (ulhem '*defecate*') ◆ Atna ulhem arengk atnerteng. (St) *The dog's stomach is full and it's having a shit.*
atnerlayeth (E) *n.*
sit not moving, sit on one's 'arse'
◆ Atnerlayeth ngan anerl-aynta akngantyakenh — aletharl arrernelhek atnerlayeth. (Sa) *You are sitting on your arse and not moving — you have settled yourself down and you're not moving.* ◆ Atnel-ayeth unta anetyel arrpenhek mpwelherl-anemel. (Sa) *You are sitting on your arse and waiting for other people [to do things].*
atnel-ayel (T) *n.*
sit not moving, sit on one's 'arse'
atna ateralth (E)
frightened, scared 'shitless' (ateralth '*frightened*', '*cowardly*') ◆ Atna ateraltharl untep-untem yanh. (St) *That [person] is running away, scared shitless.*
atna ankerl-ankerl (E)
someone who has married the 'wrong' way (ankerl-ankerl '*someone who has married the "wrong" way*')
SEE ALSO ankerl, tyerrk, anapert

anakapeltharr (E), **anakapeltherr** (E) a type of cricket (insect) SEE UNDER **anwengkapeltharr**

anakerr, anwakerr (T,E) *prn.*
we (more than two). This pronoun is used in the subject part of the sentence (i.e. representing the 'doers' of the verb action) when the people belong to the same patrimoiety and different generation moiety; for example, a person together with their fathers or father's sisters. The person being spoken to is included in the group. See Appendix 1. ◆ Anakerr alhem lyet lyweny, awenh-intyerr. (T) *We are all going hunting today, all the aunties.*
SEE ALSO anwa, anwengkerr, anantherr, anwern, anwern-ingkerr, anwernakerr, anwernantherr
anenhakerrenh, anwenhakerrenh (E) *prn.*
us (more than two). This pronoun is used in the object part of the sentence (i.e. representing those the verb action is done to).
anehakerr (W,T), **anekakerr** (E), **anwekakerr** (E) *prn.*
for us, to us (more than two)
anakerrenh, anehakerrenh (W,T), **anwekakerrenh** (E) *prn.*
ours (belonging to more than two)
anakerr-akey (T,E), **anwakerr-akey** (T,E) *prn.*
we (people belonging patrimoiety as each other)
SEE ALSO -akey, ilernak-akey, ilak-akey, ilern-ingkerr-akey, anwern-akey, anwernakerr-akey

anakety *n.*
1. bush tomato (*Solanum chippendalei* (hill form)). Plant about 80 cm high (though it may grow to 1.5 m) with purple flowers and

fruits which are pale yellow when ripe. The seeds inside the fruit are inedible and are thrown away.
2. the fruit of the bush tomato ◆ Mern anakety akem arrernem *clean*-em-ilem arna 'tyepal' nheng-lkwerel alakenhel *clean*-em-ilem *seed* renhan antarram wemel *clean* anthwerr mparem. Atanthem atanthemel wem kart renh *clean*-em mern aperrk war arrernem arlkwemem. *Clean*-em ilenty-penh *clean* anthwerr antem renh arlkwem. (N) *The bush tomato is picked and then the seeds are cleaned out using a stick called* 'tyepal'. *All the seeds are cleaned out and thrown away and then the fruits are cooked on the coals and eaten. They are eaten after they are cleaned properly.*
SEE ALSO antyewarl, unemangkerr

anal (E), **atnal** (E) *n.* [RESPECT LANGUAGE]
house ◆ Atnal-ayerr-warl ingketharrp-kety ahaneynerl-aynta, alyakw-kety. (Sa) *Go over there to the house and stay there, because the man [my son-in-law] is on his own.*
SEE ALSO warl

analharr (E), **atnalharr** (E) *n.*
yellow fat from the emu's stomach. Also referred to as *ker atnalharr*. ◆ Ker atnalharr yanh tha arlkwerl-aynetyek. Ker atnalharr yanh antheyaw kely tha kerl-aynemel arlkwerlanetyek. (Sa) *I'm going to eat some emu stomach fat straightaway. Give me some of that* ker atnalharr *so that I can cut a bit off to eat.*
SEE ALSO arnwa

analpenty (E), **atnalpenty** (E) *n.*
a type of spirit ◆ Analpentyel awely alyemel inngek, ankwa aynterl-anentyek. Awely renh alyerl-anemel. 'Alanh alanh kwenh arrekantherr aney.' Analpentyel alyerl-anem, kel arlkeny arlka ingkwernelhemel. Alyemel kel inngel anem alyemel. Innga anem ingkwernelherl-anem. (Sa) *The* analpenty *spirits sing* awely *ceremonies to people while they are asleep. They sing the* awely. *'This is how you've all got to do it.' The* analpenty *sing and then they paint themselves with ceremonial designs as well. Then the people sing and paint themselves up.* ◆ Atnalpenty rap atham-areny. Atham-arenyarl atnalpenty ilem. Atnalpentyarl ingwer, atham-arenyarl ingwer. Atherr *name*. (Sa) Atnalpenty *is the same as* atham-areny. Atham-areny *is called* atnalpenty. Atnalpenty *is one and* atham-areny *is another. Two names.*
= atham-areny
SEE ALSO irrernt-areny, melarlp, arnamarwengk, arnam-areny

analty arem (W) *vt.*
see someone coming ◆ Tyerrty apek ingka apetyerl, analty arem tha. (M) *A person is coming on foot, and I see them coming.*

anam *adv.*
1. doing something for someone else or for someone who is unable to do things for themself ◆ Kwer akwek anam wantem amwelek. (T) *The mother is feeding the little child.* ◆ Anam anwern anthep-anthem mern ikwer, ra apek rlkert angerr. (T) *We feed him, because he is very sick and he can't feed himself.*
2. waiting for someone else to do things for you ◆ Anam theletyek arelh yanhek angkep-angkem. Anam war anthetyek renh. (St) *That woman is talking about someone else pouring it for her. About someone else giving it to her.* ◆ Anam-aney tha ngkweng antherl-anetyek. (St) *Sit down and wait and I'll give it to you.*
CAN SOUND A BIT LIKE arnam *'grass'*
anam-kenh (T,E), **anam-henh** (W,T) *n.*
a lazy person, someone who does not do anything for themselves or expects others to do things for them; someone who waits for someone else to do things for them (-kenh *'belonging to'*) ◆ Arelh arrpenhel iterl-anem, kel ra anerl-anem arelh arrpenh, antyamel. Kel ilem, 'Untam anam-kenh anep-anem kwenh. Mern itetyakenh unta anam-kenh anep-anem kwenh. Atyengem unta mpwelherl-anem kwenh'. (T) *One woman is cooking, and the other woman is sitting on the blanket. And then [she] says, 'You are sitting down lazily. You're sitting down and not doing any cooking and waiting for me [to do the work]'.*
anamek (T,E) *n.*= **anam-kenh**
◆ Unta anamek anep-anem tha ngkweng inelherl-anetyek kwaty arlka mern arlka. (St) *You're sitting down and waiting around for me to go and get you water and food.* ◆ *Painting* apek mpwaretyakenh nhenhan anamek anep-anem. (St) *This one hasn't done any painting, they're just waiting for others to do it.*
anam-athek (T,E) *n.*= **anam-kenh**
◆ Anam-athek amernt arelh nhenh anep-anem kwenh. 'No nta *self*-el apek item. Anam-athekarl nta anep-anem kwenh.' (T) *This woman is sitting down really lazily. 'You don't cook your own food. You just sit down waiting for others to do things for you.'*

anam-irrem[1] *vi.*
move over, shift away, move on, move out of

the way ◆ Anam-irray, ayeng anetyenheng. (M) *Move out of the way so that I can sit down.* ◆ Antyakwer inep-inem yanhel, mer arrpenh-warn apek ra anam-irrem. (St) *That person is collecting their things into a bundle, maybe because they are shifting to another place.* ◆ Alhek nmwerntel arltwintyem, alhek nmwerntel arltwem ingkerr, ahelh ingkerr. Lwerenarl alker-irrenhem ingkerr anam-irrerl-alhem alhek nmwernt ran. (N) *The dust storm comes this way and covers everything over, all of the ground. Then it all clears up and the dust storm moves on.*
= arnang-irrem
anam-ilem *vt.*
move someone or something out of the way; shift something
= arnang-ilem2, arnangelh-ilem, rntwarr-ilem
anamelh-ilem *vt.* = **anam-ilem**

anam-irrem2 (W,T) *vi.*
get cramped ◆ Iltyang anam-irrem anerl-anemel. (T) *Sitting down with cramped hands.*

anampart-wem (W,T) *vt.*
push someone or something, push something over, tip something over ◆ Kwer angerrel anampart-wem kwer akwek. (T) *The big kid is pushing the little kid.* ◆ Nhenh artwel anampart-wem mwetekay ltwakelhenty. (T) *The man is pushing the car that has broken down.* ◆ Kwer akwek-akert *pram* anampart-werl-apem. (T) *Pushing the little baby along in the pram.* ◆ Apalel anampart-wem. (M) *Pushing something by mistake.*
= ankert-wem
SEE ALSO pewetyem-ilem, ilatwem
anampart atwem (W)
give someone a punch, punch someone or something
= palty atwem, apar atwem

anang (W,T) faeces, shit SEE UNDER **ana**

Anang (W) *n.*
name of soakage north of Arlpatyant (Coniston area)

Anangker (T,E), **Atnangker** (T,E) *n.*
name of place and of country/estate in the Utopia (Angarapa Aboriginal Land Trust)/Mt Skinner Station area

anantherr, **anwantherr** (E) *prn.*
we (more than two). This pronoun is used in the subject part of the sentence (i.e. representing the 'doers' of the verb action) when the people belong to different patrimoieties; for example, a person together with their sisters-in-law or their cross-cousins. The person being spoken to is included. This form of the pronoun is also used when the kin relations are not specified or in a group where there is a range of kin relations. See Appendix 1.
SEE ALSO anwa, anwengkerr, anakerr, anwern, anwern-ingkerr, anwernakerr, anwernantherr
anantherrenh, **anwantherrenh** (E) *prn.*
us (more than two). This pronoun is used in the object part of the sentence (i.e. representing those the verb action is done to).
anehantherr (W,T), **anekantherr** (E), **anwekantherr** (E) *prn.*
for us, to us (more than two)
anantherrenh, **anwekantherrenh** (E) *prn.*
ours (belonging to more than two)
SEE ALSO +anth
anantherr-apakwey, **anwantherr-apakwey** (E) *prn.*
we (belonging to the opposite patrimoiety but the same generation moiety as each other)
SEE ALSO -apakwey, -apatherr, nywerrp, alanth-apakwey, arrantherr-apakwey, ilernanth-apakwey, anwernantherr-apakwey

anapert (T,E), **atnapert** (E) *n.* [SENSITIVE LANGUAGE]
larrikin, promiscuous person
SEE ALSO ana, annga atherrk-atherrk, mpweny angerr, mpwenyartw-mpwenyartw

anaraty (W,T), **aneraty** (T,E), **atneraty** (E) *adv.*
1. feeling happy about something or about someone doing something
2. uncaring, oblivious, unconcerned, just letting someone do something without intervening ◆ Ayeng atneraty anerlanem-ketyaw, atneraty-irremel, mpwelhemel mernek arlka. (Sa) *I am not concerned, I'm just sitting round waiting for food and things.* ◆ Atneratyel unta arep-arem. *Never* ilterl, iletyakenh unta ampa ngkwenh, ankeyel inerlenty angep-angem. (St) *You just watched without intervening. You didn't growl at your child that was taking things.*
anaraty-irrem (W,T), **aneraty-irrem** (T,E), **atneraty irrem** (E) *vi.*
1. feel confident or happy about something happening or someone doing something; feel happy or relieved ◆ Tyerrty arrpenh apety-alpem ker-akert, anaraty-irrem ra. (M) *Another person comes back with some meat, and then that person gets happy.*
SEE ALSO anyerrkem, akangkem
2. be uncaring, oblivious or unconcerned; just let someone do something without intervening ◆ Arelh yanh atyeng anaraty-irrek — thang wantem kwer kwerenh. (T) *That woman couldn't care a less about me — I'm*

feeding her child. ◆ Atneraty-irrem, yanhelarl iltemek. Anerlanetyek akwenp. (St) *I don't care if that person is swearing at me. I'm just going to sit down and not take any notice.*

3. agree, let someone go ahead with something (?)

anaraty-ilem (T,E), **aneraty-ilem** (T,E), **atneraty-ilem** *vt* (E).

say you will do something ◆ Mernek atneraty-ilem, 'Tha ngkweng anthety-alpeyamel'. (St) *I am saying, 'I'll give you back the food'.* ◆ Rtwaltyek atneraty-ilem, kwey anthetyek apek. Alerl ra *wait*-irrerl-anem. (St) *She tells her son-in-law that she will give him her daughter. So then he waits [till she does].*

SEE ALSO alhilem

anarlt, **atnarlt** (T,E) *n.*

track, pad or path of a kangaroo or euro

SEE ALSO iwerr, terarl

CAN SOUND A BIT LIKE atnarlt *'part of bush turkey's guts', 'crop of a bird (?)'*

anarnkw, **atnarnkw** (E) *n.*

in a group or bunch (of particular fruits) ◆ Alangkw atnarnkw lyapem. (St) *The bush bananas are growing in a bunch.* ◆ Parl nhenh anarnkw arlparernem. (M) *These bush bananas are hanging in a bunch.*

= iltyingk

SEE ALSO rlkwangk, arlpar athwenkarr

anarnkw-ilem, **atnarnkw-ilem** (E) *vt.*

gather things into a pile or bunch

anarnpem, **atnarnpem** (E) *vi.*

1. jump down from something ◆ Kwer rrwey anarnpem arnang akerneng ahelh-warn. (M) *The boy is jumping from the top of the tree to the ground.*

2. descend, get off something, get down from something, climb down from something ◆ Mwetekeng anarnpa, ntwa anyekerr. Arnethey anarnpa, ntwa anyekerr. (St) *Get down from the car, in case you fall. Get down from the tree, in case you fall.* ◆ Anarnpenhem kwenelak, an akernelak intyernem. (M) *Going downwards and climbing upwards.* ◆ Lher-angkwerr atnarnpenhem. (St) *Go down across the river.* ◆ Ker aherr anarnpenhem, akern-antep antyenhem. (N) *The kangaroo goes down and then climbs upwards.*

3. fly out (sparks) ◆ Ntyeth anarnpem. (M) *The sparks are flying out.*

anarnpelh-ilem, **atnarnpelh-ilem** (E) *vt.*

unload something, get or bring something down from somewhere

SEE ALSO rwelh-ilem

anarnperl-alhem, **atnarnperl-alhem** (E) *vi.*

jump over something

anarnperl-apem, **atnarnperl-apem** (E) *vi.*

jump along, hop along

anarrk (E), **atnarrk** (E) *n.*

part of kangaroo guts (stomach or large intestine) (?) ◆ Atnarrk ipem, atherrk iwemel, item anem renh. (St) *The green stuff inside the* atnarrk *is cleaned out and thrown away, and then the* atnarrk *is cooked.*

= arrka

SEE ALSO ana

anarrkenelhem (W,T) *vi.*

rush all over the place ◆ Anarrkenelhem kwer anengk. (M) *Lots of kids are rushing all over the place.* ◆ Angwely irrert map anarrkenelhem — mpaty anwern arem. (M) *The dingo pups are running around — we can see the tracks.* ◆ Angank map akern yanh ina anarrkenelhem (T) *The crows high up are flying around all over the place.*

anartelh (W) *n.*

upper part of kangaroo tail. Also referred to as *ker anartelh.*

Anartelh (W), **Arnartelh** (W), **Anartely** (W) *n.*

the name of a place in the Mt Denison area. See also Kakatew. See map p. viii.

anarteng, **atnarteng** (E) *n.*

the base or bottom of something ◆ Antyelty atnartengel anem, apeng rltwel. (Sa) *Sitting at the base of the big kurrajong tree.*

SEE ALSO intert

Anatakerl (W) *n.*

the name of a place west of Coniston

anatem *vi.*

not know what is going on; feel bored, not know what to do with yourself ◆ Anatemel anem, angketyakenh, arrpenh-arey alherl-iwem-arleng. (Sa) *I don't know and I'm not saying anything, the others can go.* ◆ Iy! *Somewhere* ra alhek. Ayeng anatem. (T) *I don't know! He went somewhere. I don't know.*

= apatem

anath (W,T), **atnath** (T) *n.*

unable to walk, handicapped, paralysed, crippled ◆ Anatharl ilem, apetyakenhan anatham ilem, kel interl-anem antyamel interl-anem. Anath akeweny intety-alhem, interl-anem pwerrkarl awelhem intem. (T) *Someone who can't walk is called 'anath', and they lie on the blankets. The poor thing goes and lies down, lies down feeling tired.* ◆ Anatharl anerl-anem, apety-kwenh. (T) *Sitting down paralysed, unable to walk.*

SEE ALSO anenyirrp irrkweynar, apekap, apertap,

arlamarr, arlwemeny, lim-lim, lyer, rnwerr, rnwerr-rnwerr, rtapety, yer

anaty *n.*
1. bush potato, desert yam (*Ipomoea costata*). A shrub to 1 m high, with branches that creep along the ground, big, pink trumpet-like flowers and large tubers.
2. the edible tuber of the bush potato plant ◆ Anaty arelhel inyem anemel. (N) *The woman digs for the bush potato tubers with a digging stick.* ◆ Urrper-iwem kwenh mern apekarl urrper-iwem tyap apek, *crack*-arl irrem an urrperarl iwem. Mern anaty apek urrper iwem. 'Urrper-iwek yanhan kwenh!' Arlatyeyan arrangkw — *only* anatyant urrper-iwenh-iwenh. (St) *Certain types of food or grubs make the earth swell up, make the earth crack and swell up. Bush potatoes make the earth raise up. 'There's where the earth has risen up!' Pencil yams don't make that happen — only bush potatoes do it.*
= anek
SEE ALSO antyalkenh

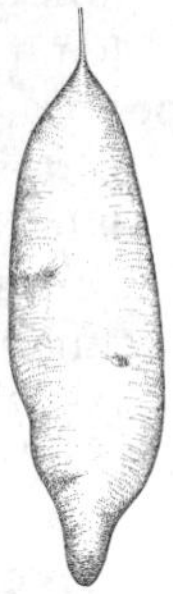

anatyelepwerray (E) *n.*
1. Horsfield's bronze-cuckoo (?) (*Chrysococcyx basalis*)
= nyarew
SEE ALSO urrempen urrempen
2. black-eared cuckoo (?) (*Chrysococcyx osculans*) ◆ Itniwelhem rantey, *name* ikwerenh, 'Anatyelepwerray, anatyelepwerray'. (Sa) *It's named after itself, the way it sounds, '*Anatyelepwerray, anatyelepwerray*'.*

anawerr *n.kin*
1. father's elder brother or sister; auntie, uncle
2. younger brother's child; nephew, niece. If somebody calls someone *anawerr* then they call them *anawerr* back. ◆ Kakey ngkwenh-kenh unta 'aler' akem. Kenh atyeyaty ngkwenh-kenh unta 'anawerr' akem. (Sa) *You call your elder brother's [children]* 'aler'. *Your younger brother's children you call* 'anawerr'. ◆ Ker atyeng antheyaw anawerray. (Sa) Anawerr, *give me some meat.*
SEE ALSO pap aywa

anawerraty *n.kin*
my/our *anawerr*

anawerrengkw *n.kin*
your *anawerr*

anawerrikw (E) *n.kin*
his/her/their *anawerr*

anawerrekw (W,T) *n.kin*
1. your *anawerr*
2. his/her/their *anawerr*

anawerr-anawerr *n.kin* [BABY TALK]
1. father's elder brother or sister; auntie, uncle
2. younger brother's child; nephew, niece ◆ Anawerr-anawerr ilem ampa akelyek. Ampa akelyek, 'Anawerr-anawerr ngkwenh aray'. Anawerrikw-rnem. (Sa) Anawerr-anawerr *is what is said to little kids. To kids you say, 'Look at your* anawerr-anawerr*'. All his or her uncles/aunties.*
= anawey

anawerr-nheng *n.kin*
a group of two or more people, one or more of whom is called *anawerr* by the others

anawerr-nheng atherr *n.kin*
a person together with their *anawerr* ◆ Irrer alherrek anawerr-nheng atherraw. *Those two went hunting, uncle and nephew together.*

anawert, atnawert (E) *n.*
native willow, apricot tree (*Pittosporum angustifolium*). Tree to 7 m high, with drooping leaves, pale yellow flowers and orange fruits which have sticky red seeds. ◆ Apetyem ampa akwek apek awenk werlaty-kweny apetyem, wal atnawert yanh aremelan artelhemarl. Ra werlaty akert aneyamel, kenh arrangkwan-kety. (St) *A child coming along, or a young teenage girl who hasn't got any breasts yet, well when they see the native willow they cover themselves. That's so that their breasts will grow — whereas if they don't then their breasts won't grow.*
= welterr

Anawert (W) *n.*
name of a rockhole east of Arrangkey

anawey, anawey-anawey (E) *n.* [BABY TALK]
father's elder brother or sister; uncle, aunt etc. ◆ Ampel ngenh ilem alerelengkw 'anawey-anawey' akem. (Sa) *Your young nephew or niece calls you* 'anawey-anawey'.
= anawerr-anawerr
SEE ALSO anawerr

pap anawey (W)
father's elder brother; uncle (pap '*father*')

anaweylker (E) cockatiel, quarrion SEE UNDER aneweylker

anaynenh (E), **atnaynenh** (E) *n.*
wrist. Also referred to as *iltya anaynenh*.
= amwelt anngang, akwengkwern, iltya ngkwern

anaynp (E), **atnaynp** (E), **atnaymp** (E) *n.*
buttocks, bum, backside ◆ Atnaympel-arleng anetyek. (St) *Sitting on [your] bum.* ◆ Atnaynpel-arleng ayeng anemaw. (St) *I am*

sitting on my backside.
= anwerlk, alywel

anek (W,T) *n.*
1. bush potato, desert yam (*Ipomoea costata*). A shrub to 1 m high, with branches that creep along the ground, big, pink trumpet-like flowers and large tubers.
2. the edible tuber of the bush potato plant ◆ Anek inyetyek nhel tyer-wem kwenh. Tyer-wem, wal inyem, angerrety apek. (N) *To dig the bush potatoes you poke around with the digging stick. Then you dig, and maybe get a big one.*
= anaty

anekapeltherr (E) a type of cricket (insect) SEE UNDER **anwengkapeltharr**

anel-ayeth anem (E) *vi.*
sit with knees up

anelhem (T,E), **atnelhem** (T,E) *vt.*
1. frighten or chase something away; give something a fright ◆ Arengk-rnem untarl atnelhek, aterarl anthem. (Sa) *You frightened all the dogs away, gave them a fright.* ◆ Ker aherrarl atnelhekaw, ampa akelyel angkerl-apemel. Rntert anetyakenh. (Sa) *The little kids gave the kangaroo a fright, by talking as they were going along. They weren't quiet.*
2. let something go ◆ Atnelhem tha ra apekarl *yard*-el apek nantew apek rnepernem, kel tha atnelhem anem *gate* altywer-ilemel. (St) *The horse might be standing in the yard, and then I let it go by opening the gate.*
SEE ALSO aywepem, aterel-anthem
CAN SOUND A BIT LIKE anhelhem *'tease'*

aneltyem (W) *vt.*
clean out guts or innards (especially said of *aneperrk* 'fat-covered intestines of some animals') ◆ Kart map aneltyem. Aneltyem aneltyem aneltyem altywer-ilerl-apemel, kart nhenh map, atnarl arlwepwelem nheng map. Kel ipenhem ipenhem kel *finish clean*-em angem. (N) *Cleaning the intestines out. Cleaning the intestines and opening them out and cleaning out all the round pieces of shit. Then squeezing the shit out along the intestines and then, when it's finished, taking the clean intestines [back].*
SEE ALSO ipem, anenem

Aneltyey (E), **Atneltyey** (E) *n.*
name of a place and the location of an outstation (Boundary Bore) west of Sandover River in the Utopia (Angarapa Aboriginal Land Trust) area. Also spelt as Aniltji. See map p. viii.

aneltyey-irrem (E), **atneltyey-irrem** (E) *vi.*
have diarrhoea or 'guts-ache' ◆ Atneltyey-irrem ayeng. (St) *I've got diarrhoea.*
= ampeltyey-irrem

anely-pwet (E) *n.*
a type of plant (?)

anem1 *vi.*
1. sit ◆ War akarntemel ayeng anep-anem angayakw kwenh. (N) *I am just sitting down quietly because I'm hungry.* ◆ Ayeng angwerleny-irretyek lywel anemel, twernelarl ampem-arleng. (T) *I am going to sit under the shade to cool down because I was so hot in the sun.*
2. sit down, be seated
3. be, am, is, are, were, be (in a particular way)
4. live (in a place), stay (in a place)
◆ Urlepety-antey ayengan anep-anem, apmer arrpenh-kenh-warl alhetyakenh. (St) *I keep stopping in one place, I haven't been to other people's country.*
CAN SOUND A BIT LIKE arnem *'cry'*; irnem *'stand'*

anerl-anem *vi.*
stay somewhere, be somewhere ◆ Arelh awenk map anerl-anem arlwekerel angkety angkerrerl-anemel. (T) *The teenage girls are sitting around in the women's camp telling stories.* ◆ Atnwernt-irrem, arrpenhelarl ikngwem, 'Mpa alhey kwenh irrer'. 'No, ayeng anerl-anemarl kwenh atnwernt-irrem.' (St) *Refusing, when another asks you, 'Come on, let's go hunting'. 'No. I don't want to go and I'm staying.'*
SEE ALSO alarterl-anem

anem2 *part.*
now; and then (something happens); shows a changed or new situation ◆ Kel antyerrk anem irrek aker. *And then the meat dried up.* ◆ Kweleynterreynterrel alhweng ra angernem *baby* anem ra mpwarem kwer-antey alhweng kwer-antey. Kel arraterl-alhep-alhem arlewatyerr-artek. Arnam arrernem kel akwerrk map anem ra mpwarem. (St) *The rainbow bee-eater digs a burrow and then it has its babies there in the burrow. Then it comes out and goes around just like a goanna does. It puts grass there in the burrow and then it has its babies.* ◆ Anwantherr apek ilwemarl wal alkngirrenty anem anem. (St) *Well, if we die we will be spirits then.* ◆ Apwert ather, ikwer-warl apert-atwemel ntang, ntyerrm arlka apert anem ulpilemel, kel aympernem anem. (Sa) *The seed is crushed on the grinding stone, and dogwood seed is ground up as well, and then it's winnowed.*
SEE ALSO antem

CAN SOUND A BIT LIKE arnem *'cry'*; irnem *'stand'*

anem3, atnem (E) *n.*

1. yam stick, digging stick ◆ Arelh map alhetyart anem-akert mern arlatyey nyetyek. (T) *The women used to go with their digging sticks to dig up pencil yams.* ◆ Atnem atyenhan ap amper-amper. (Sa) *My digging stick is crooked.*
2. group of stars near the Seven Sisters constellation (?)

atnem-akert (E) *n.*
1. baby girl (-akert *'having'*) ◆ Marl akwek 'atnem-akert', angwerrm-irrek — 'atnem-akert'. Alakenharl iletyam. *Granny* kwerenh then mern akert apetyam, altywernetyam math kwerenh *grandmother* kwerenh, irrparlerrp-wetyam, war nheng *rub*-em, uneng-warl anem. Ampa akwek nhenh, iylpa atherr pewelhetyam. (St) *A little girl 'atnem-akert' was found [born] — 'atnem-akert'. That's what they used to say. Her granny came with food and her mother and granny crouched down and rubbed their chests against each other. They blew in the little baby's ears.*
2. respectful word a father uses to refer to his daughter
= atnem-kenh
SEE ALSO irrtyart-akert
CAN SOUND A BIT LIKE arnem *'cry'*; irnem *'stand'*

atnem-kenh (E) *n.*
baby girl (-kenh *'belonging to'*)
= atnem-akert

anem atherr-akert (W) *n.*
scorpion (lit. 'having two digging sticks')
= aneth-akert

anemangkarr (E), **anemangkerr** (T,E) bush tomato SEE UNDER **unemangkerr**

anemarraty (W,T), **atnemarraty** (W,T) *n.*
caustic bush, desert spurge. (*Euphorbia tannensis*) (lit. 'straight digging stick'). A small plant that grows along the ground, with milky sap and small flowers and fruit. Referred to as women's spirit friend.
◆ Anemarraty marlew-alyey-alyey, anyent akwet — arnang war, atherrk. *The* anemarraty *is the same as* marlew-alyey-alyey *— just a plant, a grass.*
= marlek-alyey-alyey
SEE ALSO alyey-alyey

anemel pweyntengeynteng (E), **atnemel pweyntengeynteng** (E) *n.*
a type of beetle. This beetle emits a foul smell if you touch it.
SEE ALSO iynteng-iynteng, lengarr-lengarr, anwengkapeltharr

anenem (W,T), **aninem, atninem** (E) *vt.*
gut or take innards out of (an animal) (ana *'guts'*; inem *'get'*) ◆ Artwel anenem ker aherr irntang arlter-akertel. (T) *The man guts the kangaroo with the stone knife.*
= atniwem

anengant (W) *n.* [RESPECT LANGUAGE]
behind, going after
= atneyarnteng
SEE ALSO ingkern

anengk1 (W,T), **atningk** (E) *n.*
many, lots of things ◆ Kwer map irnep-irnem, anengk anthwerr. (T) *The children are standing there, really lots of them.* ◆ Atningk apetyem angketyek. *Lots are coming to talk.*
= map
SEE ALSO angerr1, alhirrel, arnkengeny

anengk-ilem (W,T), **atningk-ilem** (E) *vt.*
make a lot, make bigger, make more, increase the number of something

anengk-irrem (W,T), **atningk-irrem** (E) *vi.*
get together in a large group, increase in number, multiply ◆ Tyerrty anyent anetyamarl-penh anengkem-irrek. (M) *After there was only one person there, there are lots now.*
= map-irrem
SEE ALSO anyent-irrem

anengk2 (E), **atnengk** (E) *n.*
calm, windless, no wind ◆ Atnengk tnek, alhwerrp kweny. Atnengkel ampemaw, alhwerrp anetyakenhel. (Sa) *It's calm and there's no cold wind. Because there's no cold wind [we] are getting hot.*
SEE ALSO teraty

anengk-irrem (E), **atnengk-irrem** (E) *vi.*
become calm (wind), die down (wind) ◆ Iylka atnengk-irrekaw, iylka anetyakenh. *The wind has died down, there is no wind.*
= teraty-irrem

anengkan (W,E), **atnengkan** (E) *n.*
arriving somewhere too late for something ◆ Atnengkanel ayeng alhek. (St) *I got there too late [the business was over].* ◆ Ayeng alhek *shop*-warl, martelhek. Atnengkan martelhek arrwekel-antey. (St) *I went to the shop and it was closed. I was too late and it had closed before I got there.*

ahern anengkan (E), **ahern atnengkan** (E)
being in mourning (?), feeling sorry (ahern *'ground'*) ◆ Ahern atnengkanel ayeng anerlanem, irrarel warel. Alther anem irrep-irrem (St) *I am sitting down feeling sorry, a bit homesick. Feeling lonely.* ◆ Alyent-artek ahern anengkanel anwantherr pwenkel aney. Pwenkel aney anwantherr alyent-artekel. (Sa)

We are sitting down in one place in mourning. (?)
anengkan-irrem, **atnengkan-irrem** (E) *vi.*
pass away, die (respectful way of talking)
SEE ALSO ilwem, alyent-artek-irrem, arremangkw-irrem
anengkerr (W,T) *n.*
1. a dream ◆ Altyerr akin anwern ilem, wal *that's why* anwern ilem anengkerr. Altyerr *Jesus* anwern ilem, wal anengkerr anwern ilem, ankwang intemel aremel anengkerr, anengkerr apek *something* arem. *Too much* Altyerr [*Jesus*]. Wal Altyerr *too much Jesus* Altyerr akin anem-arleng wal anengkerr anwern ilem, Anmatyerrel. Arrwekeleny ina Altyerr iletyart — *myall* mapel kwa. (M) *We say* altyerr *as well [as* anengkerr*], well that's why we say* anengkerr *[for dreams]. We call Jesus* Altyerr, *and when we are lying down sleeping and we see something — we call that* anengkerr. *The word* Altyerr *is used for Jesus. In Anmatyerr we have to use the word* anengkerr *[for dreams] because the word* Altyerr *means Jesus as well. The olden-time people used to say* altyerr *[for dream] — they were myall [a bit ignorant].*
2. a Dreaming, a person's Dreaming or totem ◆ Arelhel ingkwernem Anengkerr kampeth-warn. (T) *The woman is painting Dreamings on the canvas.* ◆ Tyepety-wem arnarnk-warn arelh Anengkerr kwerenh ra rntwetyek kwer akwekek. (T) *The woman is being painted up on her chest with her Dreaming designs so that she can dance for the little kids.*
3. the Dreaming or creation time
4. a person's mother's country ◆ Anengkerr atyenh mer alenh. (M) *That country over there is my mother's country.*
5. the Dreamings or totems that come from a person's mother's country
6. birthmark
SEE ALSO altyerr[1], anganenty
anengkerr penh (W,T) *n.*
(something) from the Dreaming or creation time ◆ Alkart anterrng antim, arlkwenh-arlkwenh. Alkart, rwel antim atyerretyam ina alkart yanh kwa. Rwel itenh-itenh, awantyenhantyenh. Athenh-athenh. Anengkerr-penh wart. (N) *The* alkart *seed is edible as well. They cooked the* alkart *seed in the fire. It's cooked in the fire and then ground up and eaten. It comes from the Dreaming of course.*
= altyerr-penh
anengkerreng (W,T) *n.* = **anengkerr-penh**
◆ Alhernter kwenh anpernerrenty itya, kenh tyerrty akenh Anengkerreng-ntyel anpernerrem. Anengkerrel anpernek Anengkerreng-ntyel anpernerrem kenh alhernter akenh anpernenty ityarl. Apal wararl alhernteran. (M) *White people don't have a skin system, whereas Aboriginal people get their skin system from the Dreaming. The Dreaming named everyone as relations, and people got the way of calling each other as relations from there. White people don't have a skin system. White people don't know.*
anengkerr arem (W,T)
dream, have a dream (arem *'look', 'see'*)
◆ Anengkerr arerl, ankwa intemel. Wal arraty ina apetyem. (T) *Dreaming [about them] while lying asleep. Then they really come.*
= altyerr arem
anengkerr akem (W,T)
be related to a place or a Dreaming through your mothers and uncles (mother's brothers) (akem[2] *'call someone as a relation'*) ◆ Nhak antekerr-thayt tha anengkerr akem kwenh. (T) *That place to the south is the one that I'm related to through my mother.*
= altyerr akem
anengkerr ilem (W,T)
tell Dreaming stories (ilem *'tell', 'say'*)
◆ Ankwang intetyeh, kwer Anengkerr-ilem angerr-pat mapel, *just like Dreamtime stories.* (T) *Old people tell children Dreaming stories to make them go to sleep.*
= altyerr ilem
anengkerr-anengkerr (W,T) *n.*
sleep-talk, nightmare, dream ◆ Kwer map apek anengkerr-anengkerr ankwang intemel angkem. (M) *The children are talking in their sleep.*
= altyerr-altyerr
anengkerr-anengkerr arem (W,T) *vt.*
have a bad dream or a nightmare
= altyerr-altyerr arem
anengkerr-anengkerr angkem (W,T) *vi.*
talk in sleep
= altyerr-altyerr angkem
anengkerr-anengkerr-irrem (W,T) *vi.*
dream; have a dream ◆ Anengkerr-anengkerr-irrem, 'Tyerrty map apetyemarl kwenh'. Kel kweny-itwek arety-ayntem yanh kel apetyewarrem, tharl anengkerr-anengkerr arek-penh. (T) *Having a dream, 'The people are coming'. And then, during the night, seeing the people that you dreamt about coming.*
anengkerrek antywem (T)
drink something for breakfast (antywem *'drink'*)
= altyerrek antywem

anengkerrek arlkwem
eat something for breakfast (arlkwem *'eat'*)
= altyerrek arlkwem
Anengkerrant-alkenty (W,T)
Dreaming story, from the Dreaming or creation time (?)
anenperetyarr (W) *n.*
a type of bird (possibly mulga parrot) (*Psephotus varius*)
SEE ALSO urimpering
Anenth (E) *n.*
name of place near Millionaires Well, south-east of Wilora (Stirling) community
anenty (W,T) *n.*
risen (sun, star, moon) ◆ Aherrk kel anenty. (M) *The sun has already risen.*
anenty-alhem (W,T) *vi.*
rise (sun, star, moon) ◆ Aherrk anenty-alhem. (M) *The sun is rising.*
anenty-anenty *n.*
a thumping or thudding noise; sound of running or of footsteps
= ahenty-ahenty², rrmwangk-rrmwangk, twerlepwelh-pwelh
aneny *n.*
hip (of animal or person) ◆ Ampa angart-wemel aneny arntetyeng. (Sa) *A child with a sore hip is turned over.*
SEE ALSO anngarlp
ker aneny
hip-meat of an animal
= ker antywantyw
anenyerr, atnenyerr (E) *adv.*
1. avoiding or staying away from trouble (ana *'arse'*; nyerr *'shame'*) ◆ Ayeng anenyerr alhem terangk map-kety kerek apawenhem-hety. (T) *I am walking away from the drunks in case they ask me for meat.* ◆ Anenyerr ayeng alhem ngkwengety, ntwa ayenh ahel-ahel akek, ntwa rntert-irreyaw, *cool down*-irreyaw ntwa. (St) *I am going to keep away from you, after you growled at me, so that you can quieten down, cool down.*
2. being shamed because you know you have behaved badly; trying to get out of doing something ◆ Ntwem atyengety anenyerr alhek ker arlka itety-kweny kwenh, mern arlka. (T) *You walked away from me, shamed because you hadn't cooked any meat or damper.*
3. having an appropriate degree of modesty or shame ◆ Anenyerr anetyakenharl nga, nyerr-irretyakenh. Iy! (Sa) *You haven't got any shame, you don't get shamed. That's terrible!*
anenyerr-irrem, atnenyerr-irrem (E) *vi.*
walk away from a fight, retreat, keep away from somebody or something, avoid trouble
SEE ALSO nyerr-irrem
anenyerrel angem, atnenyerrel angem (E)
1. take something off someone (because you don't like what they have done with it or they might do with it) ◆ Thang ilep yanh angetyek anenyerrel, ntwang atyeng ngkwarl rltwamp angetyety-kwenh. (T) *I am going to take that axe off you because you didn't bring me any sugarbag.* ◆ Terangk yanh-kety *knife* tha angetyek anenyerrel, tyerrty atanthekerr. (T) *I'm going to take the knife off that drunk in case they stab someone.*
2. take someone out of the way of trouble
aneperrk, atneperrk (E) *n.*
fat-covered intestines of some animals. Also referred to as *ker aneperrk.* ◆ Tha arlkwetyek parrp amperneyaw atneperrk. (Sa) *Cook those intestines quickly so that I can eat them.* ◆ Aneperrk kart twer map-akert iperl-apem. (T) *The intestines have solid bits of shit in them that are squeezed out.*
SEE ALSO lyep-lyep
anepetheng-irrem, atnepetheng-irrem (E) *vi.*
go backwards, reverse
= aneyangketh-irrem
anepetheng-ilem, atnepetheng-ilem (E) *vt.*
reverse something, make something go backwards
anepeywenp (E), **atnepeywenp** (E) *n.*
a big perentie, *ilkwert* (*Varanus giganteus*) ◆ Ker urlkert atnepeywenp. Ultewek renh atnepeywenpek-anternenh. (Sa) *The big perentie. They hit the great big perentie with something.*
anepwart, atnepwart (E) *n.*
a type of big louse
= pweltak
SEE ALSO arrem, nya¹
aneraty (T,E) feeling happy about something SEE UNDER **anaraty**
anerlpem *vi.*
make a thudding noise (kangaroo) ◆ Aherr anerlpemel arrtyanem. (M) *The kangaroo makes a thudding noise as it runs away.* ◆ Ker aherr yaleng anerlpentyarr arrtyanem kwenh, arengkelarl alwernern werrk-warn. (T) *The kangaroos over there are making a thudding noise as they run away from the dogs that are chasing them into the scrub.*
anerlpewem *vi.*
take no notice of others, go off regardless ◆ Akwenp kwenh alhem anerlpewerl-alhemel. Nhenhel apek ayenh ayakem uyarn anem. (St) *Going off regardless. This [person] is unable to*

stop me from going. ◆ Rlkertel apek anerlpewem akwet, akem-irremel alhem. (T) *Even though she's sick she gets up and goes.* ◆ Anerlpewemel ayeng alhemaw, 'Menty angkerlana, ayeng alhemarl-kety'. (St) *I'm going anyway, 'You can all keep talking, but I'm going'.*
SEE ALSO akwenp
anerlpewemel alhem = anerlpewem
◆ Alenhan anerlpewemel alhek, ywarn arnpakek tha. (M) *That person went off without taking any notice and I tried in vain to stop them.*

anerrk-ilem (W) *vt.*
miss something when trying to spear or shoot it ◆ Thang ker aherr alenh anerrk-ilern. (M) *I just missed that kangaroo.*

Anerrwelty (E) *n.*
name of hill on Mt Skinner station (Mt Skinner (?))

anert, atnert (E) *n.*
1. stomach area, belly, abdomen ◆ Urinp-irremarl atnert ayengaw, rlkert. Atnert urinp-irrem. (St) *My stomach is getting hot and I am sick. My stomach is burning* ◆ Ngangkay-akertel kwer aretyenh anert arlka ingkerreny. (M) *The traditional healer will look at him all over, even the stomach.*
2. guts, innards
SEE ALSO mwerlk[1]
3. the middle or centre part of something ◆ Lher anert. *The middle of the river.*
anert anety (W,T)
1. stomach-ache, feeling sick in the stomach (anety *'bad'*) ◆ Ayeng anert anetyam irrek. *I got sick in the stomach.*
2. feeling sorry
anert akeng (E), **atnert akeng** (E) **= anert anety** (akeng *'bad'*)
anert angayel, atnert angayel (E)
feeling hungry (angayel *'hungry'*)
anert ampem, atnert ampem (E)
feel angry or sick; stomach burn from hunger or thirst (ampem[2] *'heat up'*) ◆ Anert ayeng ampem rwarteh. (M) *My stomach is burning like fire.* ◆ Atnert ayeng ampemaw angkethakw. (Sa) *My stomach is burning from thirst.*
anert anhwerlk (W,T)
have a full stomach, be full (of food), feel satisfied (from eating)
anert-anert, atnert-atnert (E) *n.* [SENSITIVE LANGUAGE]
pregnant
anert-anert-irrem, atnert-atnert-irrem (E) *vi.* [SENSITIVE LANGUAGE]
be pregnant
anerteng (E), **atnerteng** (E) *n.*
being full (of food); feeling satisfied (from eating) ◆ Arnterr tha arlkwek, ker apek mern apek, atnerteng anem ayeng, intetyek anem ayeng ankwa. (St) *I ate a lot, food and meat, and now I'm full and I'm going to go to sleep.* ◆ Angayakwel atnert arrerlkart urntek, atnerteng anem. (Sa) *I was really hungry and now I'm full.*
SEE ALSO anhwerlk, nthat, alywer[2]
anert-penh, atnert-penh (E) *n.*
a person's sister's child; nephew, niece (-penh[1] *'from'*)
= alem-penh
anert altywer, atnert altywer (E)
1. feeling sorry or sad and empty, feeling as if something is wrong (lit. 'open stomach') (altywer *'open'*) ◆ Atnert ayeng altywer, *might be son,* ampaty-ampaty atyenhek apek. *Like sorry you know,* alhwarrp-irrem ayeng. (St) *I am feeling sorry, maybe for my son or a nephew or niece. I'm feeling sorry.* ◆ Anert altywer ayeng awelhem. (T) *I am feeling sorry.*
2. feeling hungry ◆ Atnert altywer awelhem angayakw. (Sa) *My stomach feels hungry.*
= anert arltwang, alem altywer
anert arltwang (W,T)
1. feeling sorry or sad (and empty); feeling as if something is wrong (lit. 'empty stomach') (arltwang *'empty'*)
2. feeling hungry
= anert altywer
iltya anert, iltya atnert (E) *n.*
palm of the hand (iltya *'hand'*)
ingka anert, ingka atnert (E)
bottom of the foot, sole of the foot (ingka *'foot'*)
lher anert, lher atnert (E)
1. the middle of a creek (lher *'creek', 'river', 'sand'*) ◆ Lher anerteng alperl-anem. (Sa) *Going back along the middle of the creek.*
2. the sand in the middle of a creek ◆ Lher atnertel ingka ampem ayeng uternelaw. Aper-warl iparrp alhey, ingkarl ampem-kety lherel. (Sa) *The heat of the sand in the middle of the creek is burning my feet. Let's go quickly to [the shade of] the river red gum because my feet are being burnt by the sand.*
alker anert, alker atnert (E) *n.*
high in the sky, clear sky (alker *'sky'*) ◆ 'Alker anert' anwern ilem akern alker. (M) *'Alker anert' is what we call the high part of the sky.* ◆ Aherlkelarl ampetyel, alker atnert-they — aketh, *no* kwenpay. (Sa) *The sun is shining from*

high up in the sky — it's clear, no clouds.
= alker tyelk

anert-wem (E) *vt.*
lean on someone ◆ Ayeng anert-wetyal, rntwarr-artek atyengety ana. (Sa) *Don't lean on me, move a bit further away from me.*
anert-iwelhem (E) *vi.*
lean yourself on something ◆ Anert-iwelherl-anem arwerlel-arleng. (Sa) *I am leaning against a tree.*
SEE ALSO ampekernem

aneth-akert, atneth-akert (E) *n.*
scorpion ◆ Aneth-akertel tyerrty nhwem, kwaty-taym. (T) *Scorpions bite people during the rainy time.*

= anem atherr-akert

anety (W,T) *n.*
1. bad, no good, wrong ◆ Mpwel anety atherr. (M) *You two are wrong way for marriage.* ◆ Arrantherr anety map kwer-intyarr. (M) *All of you kids are no good.*
2. useless, dysfunctional ◆ Lterr anety. *A bad leg.*
3. bad-tasting ◆ Tampewenh yanh anety tyekert, irrkertey kwa. Arrakert itenh-itenh. (N) *The* tampewenh *melon is no good, bitter-tasting. It burns the mouth.* ◆ Kwaty apek arlepewem, anety apek. (M) *Try the water, it might be no good.*
4. sick, unwell
= kwern, akeng
anety-anety (W,T) *n.*
not very good, not too good, a bit useless ◆ Angwely yanh nhwenh-nhwenh-kweny anety-anety. (M) *That dog is a bit useless, it doesn't bite.*
= kwern-kwern, akeng-akeng
anety-irrem (W,T) *vi.*
1. go bad, get wrecked, become useless, go off, become damaged or spoilt, break down ◆ Mwetek apek mpwep angwenh-irrem, anety-irrem, *somewhere*-warl apek alhem-arleng. *Or something*, ker arlkarl arrernerl-alhem *plastic*-elayeng, wal ingkern anety-irrem. (P) *The car might, whatever, break down while on the way to somewhere. Or something such as meat that's left behind in plastic, well after that it goes off.*
2. get sick ◆ Anert anety-irrem rlkert. (M) *[My] stomach is no good and I'm sick.*
= kwern-irrem, akeng-irrem
anety-ilem (W,T) *vt.*
spoil something, wreck something; make someone sick ◆ Arrwengkelthel anety-ilek tyerrty. (M) *The disease made the person sick.*
= akeng-ilem, kwern-ilem
anetyengwerl (W) *adv.*
wrongly, badly ◆ Anetyengwerl atherr anem — mwer-nheng atherr. (M) *Those two are the wrong way for each other — they are related as mother-in-law and son-in-law.* ◆ Anetyengwerl angkem. (M) *Talking the wrong way.*
= akengenty
anety-wem (W,T) *vt.*
throw rubbish away (such as when cleaning husks from seeds)

anetyerrkernem (W,T) *vi.*
burp, hiccough. Traditionally, grass was put on top of the heads of babies to stop them hiccoughing. Their foreheads and stomachs were also rubbed with the burnt bark of the corkwood tree, *ntywey aperrk*. ◆ Ngkerlp-penh anetyerrkernem. (M) *Burping after chewing tobacco.* ◆ Anetyerrkernem ker arlkwenty-penh. (T) *Burping after eating meat.*
= arltarrernem, arnenthernem, artekernem, anterrk angkem
anetyerrk-irrem (W,T) *vi.* = **anetyerrkernem**

anetywek (W) *n.*
1. bad-tasting, not sweet, tasteless ◆ Katyerr akem, arlepewem. 'Anetywekam nhenh kwenh menty aney kwenh.' Menty imperl-alhem. Mern mwerrant akerl, mern mwerr theweyetant. (M) *[You] pick some desert raisins, and taste them. 'These ones don't taste too good, leave them.' Then you leave them and go on. You just the pick the good fruits, the ones that are sweet.*
SEE ALSO alhengkety, alyelk
2. marrying 'wrong way'; marrying, sleeping with, or acting flirtatiously towards inappropriate kin (i.e. someone who is not related in the proper way under Aboriginal Law) ◆ Ankerl tyerrk, anetywek atherrarl inerrek. Arrwemp-nheng apek mwer-nheng, amenheng apek inerrek, tyerrk. (M) Tyerrk *is when two people marry the wrong way. Maybe they get married with their brother or sister, their son-in-law or mother-in-law, or people related as mother and child get married.* • SEE ALSO tyerrk, ankerl

anew *n.kin*
1. spouse, wife, husband, boyfriend, girlfriend, lover
2. wife's sister or husband's brother; sister-in-law, brother-in-law ◆ Mpwernatyan ilem artwelant athew, kenh anewekarl ilem marlel. 'Artwang yanhan anewaty.' (T) *'Mpwernaty' [my brother-in-law] is only said by men, whereas,*

on the other hand, women call [their brother-in-law] 'anew'. 'That man is my brother-in-law.'
3. particular relations with the same skin as your *anew*

anew-anew[1] (E) *n.kin*
boyfriend, girlfriend
CAN SOUND A BIT LIKE anew-anew *'brave', 'fearless'*

anewaty *n.kin*
my/our *anew* ◆ Anewaty apety-alpa. Unterl-unterl-wetyal. Merel arternp-irremel anetyek. (Sa) *My wife/husband, come back. Don't run round all over the place. Sit down quietly in camp.*

anewengkw *n.kin*
your *anew*
CAN SOUND A BIT LIKE newingk *'cockatiel'*

anewikw (E), **aneweyekw** (E) *n.kin*
her/his/their *anew*

anewek (W,T) *n.kin*
1. your *anew*
2. her/his/their *anew*

anewart *n.kin*
husband and wife, married couple ◆ Anewart atherr alherraw — ker atwerl-alperraw. (Sa) *You two, husband and wife — go off and shoot some kangaroos.*
SEE ALSO +art

anewart atherr *n.kin*
husband and wife, married couple

anewartewart *n.kin*
a group of husbands and wives, a group of married couples, a husband and his wives ◆ Anewartewart-rnem alherl-iwepiwem. Anewart nhel-arey ker anthetyangarl. Ayengan arrarenty — anewart nhek-arey arraretyel. (Sa) *All the husbands and wives are going along. These couples didn't give [me] any meat. I missed out — I wanted them to give me some but I missed out.*

anewart-rnem (E) *n.kin* = **anewartewart**

anew-ankethenh *n.kin*
1. having *anew* still alive ◆ Anew-ankethenh alhay! (T) *Go away, you've got a husband [i.e. don't hang around me]!*
2. someone who is always with their *anew*
SEE ALSO -ankethenh

anew-anew[2], **atnew-atnew** (E) *n.*
1. brave, fearless, confident ◆ Ahelengkw iyterrtyarl atwarem, atnew-atnewel, ater-irretyakenh. (Sa) *[That person] is confidently facing the other, without getting frightened.* ◆ Atnew-atnew ayeng alhem mwetekay mpwaretyek — iterlarem tha. (St) *I'm happy to go and fix the car — I know how to do it.* ◆ Atnew-atnewel tha mpwarem tharl iterlarem-angkwerr. (St) *I'm confident and I know what I'm doing.*
2. pleased with yourself, arrogant, don't care what people think ◆ Anew-anew anthwerr artwang angkety-alhem, arnkarr apek angkety-alhem — terangkel wart. (M) *That man really thinks he's smart, and he comes up and argues, and just about hits [the person] — he's drunk of course.*
= arnkaty

anew-anew-irrem (W) *vi.*
be argumentative ◆ Tyerrty arrpenh alenh atwetyeh anew-anew-irrem. (M) *Getting argumentative and going to fight that person.*
SEE ALSO irrpelth-irrem

anew-irrem (T,E), **atnew-irrem** (E) *vi.*
1. get excited or happy about something but then be let down, be tricked by someone ◆ Atnew-irrek ayeng, atyengarl akwel anthekek-athen. Ra rrtywekelarl anthek. (St) *I was excited because supposedly she was going to give me something. But she lied about it.* ◆ Ayengarl ngkweng atnew-irrek, apetyarl-alpekek-athen. Nga urrtyirrern. Urrtyirrek aleth-antey nga alhek. (Sa) *I was excited about you coming back. But you lied. You lied and went away for good.*
2. disbelieve or mistrust someone who breaks promises or does not keep their word ◆ Ayeng itya yanheh anew-irrem. (T) *I thought you had already gone but you're still here.* ◆ Ayeng ngkweng anew-irrerl-alhern anem. Akwet nta arraty anthernek-athen atyeng kwenh. Ker apek *money* apek. Wal anew-irrerl-anem ayeng ngkweng. (T) *I don't believe you now. You were supposed to give me money or meat, but you didn't. Now I don't believe you.*
CAN SOUND A BIT LIKE anewerrem *'say each other's names'*

anewel anthem (T,E), **atnewel anthem** (E) *vt.*
pretend to give something to somebody (then take it back) ◆ Maney atnewel antherl-anetyang. Arraty anthay. (Sa) *Don't just pretend to give me money. Really give it to me.*
= ulang anthem, tywerengk anthem

anewem[1] (W,T), **inewem** (T,E), **itnewem** (E), **itniwem** (E) *vt.*
name something, call somebody or something by a name, say the name of someone or something (ina[2] *'name'*) ◆ Arreny ayeng inewetyalaw. (Sa) *Don't say my name.* ◆ *Knife-el-arl akerrem-penharl* aletyarl anewem. Alety *is what you call a wound from a knife.*
SEE ALSO arreny
CAN SOUND A BIT LIKE arnewem *'throw hot soil or ashes at someone'*

anewerrem (W,T), **inewerrem** (T,E), **itniwerrem** (E) *vi.*
say each other's names, call each other's names ◆ Tyerrty atherr arreny anewerrem. (M) *The two people are saying each other's names.*
CAN SOUND A BIT LIKE anew-irrem *'be tricked'*
anewelhem (W,T), **inewelhem** (T,E), **itniwelhem** (E) *vi.*
call something after yourself, say your own name ◆ Itniwelhem rantey, *name* ikwerenh, 'Anatyelepwerray, anatyelepwerray'. (Sa) *It [the bronze-wing cuckoo] is named after itself, the way it sounds,* 'Anatyelepwerray, anatyelepwerray'.

anewem² (T) *vt.*
let something go ◆ Irrkwentyel tyerrty nhak anewek. (T) *The policeman let the person go.*
CAN SOUND A BIT LIKE arnewem *'throw hot soil or ashes at someone'*

anewerrk, **atnerwerrk** (E), **anurerrk** (E), **atnurerrk** (E), **alkngerurrk** (E), **atnerurrk** (E) *n.*
1. ankle
2. heel [SOME SPEAKERS]
SEE ALSO anwar

aneweylker (E), **anaweylker** (E), **areweylker** (E) *n.*
cockatiel, quarrion (*Nymphicus hollandicus*) ◆ Kapert an *yellow one*, arreyl atherr, arrkaylp kel arratem antarl ra. Arrkaylp akwek renh, *grey* tyerrty, anngayt atherr *yellow one*. *Rock pigeon*-artek weth. *[It] has a yellow head and cheeks, and a small crest standing up. The body is grey and the two temples are yellow. It's a bit similar to those rock pigeons.*
= newingk, kanaweylker, arew-arew

aneyangketh-irrem (E), **atneyangketh-irrem** (E) *vi.*
go backwards, reverse, turn round and go back ◆ Mwetekay aneyangketh-irrem. (Sa) *The car is going backwards.* ◆ Aterarl ra aneyangketh-irreynem. Aneyangkethel-antey alpem. (Sa) *He is turning round and going back because he is frightened.*
= anepetheng-irrem, angkep-irrem, urtep-irrem, anwengentyengenty-irrem, tyenelhem¹
SEE ALSO pert-irrem
aneyangketh-ilem (E), **atneyangketh-ilem** (E) *vt.*
reverse something, make something go backwards

+ang (W,T) *ending*
This ending goes on the end of most short words used in the western and central parts of the Anmatyerr region. Sometimes it is used on the end of the imperative or order form of the verb. When other endings are added to short words, *+ang* may be dropped (e.g. *artw**ang** anem* 'the man is sitting', *artwel atwem* 'the man is hitting') ◆ Rw**ang** angerr amperl-anem kwer rlkerteh. (M) *A big fire is burning for the sick man.* ◆ Antyam w**ang**! (M) *Spread a groundsheet out!* ◆ Alh**ang** irtakert. (M) *A snotty nose.* ◆ Iltyel anpem ankarrelh-ilemel, ankw**ang** alenh intep-intem, alakenh ankarrelh-ilem iltyel, 'Kem-irr**ang** kwenh!' (N) *Somebody is lying there sleeping, and you wake them up by touching them with your hand, by passing your hand over their face, and saying, 'Get up!'* ◆ Nmwernt r**ang** apety-alhem aterel anthety-alhem tyerrtyan. (N) *The dust comes along and gives people a fright.* ◆ Alt**ang** rlpwat-ilang. (M) *Singe the hair/fur off.* ◆ Artwel arrwekelenyel ker aherr aly**ang**el ltewetyam. (M) *The men in the early days used boomerangs to hit kangaroos.* ◆ Artw**ang** ampw**ang**el rrkwem alkwert irlkwatherr. (N) *The old man has a shield to protect himself.*

angakem, **akngakem** (E) *vt.*
1. pick out, sort things out, choose things, divide things up ◆ Arrpenh atyeng angakang anyent apek. (M) *Pick another one out for me, maybe one.* ◆ Akeng iwemel, mwerrant angakem. (M) *You throw the rubbish away and just keep the good stuff.* ◆ Akngakemel than atyenh iney, ingkerr arlkwerrerl-anekerr? (Sa) *Can I pick some out for myself in case everybody eats the lot?* ◆ Tha angakem mantarr. (M) *I'm picking out some clothes.*
2. cut or draft out (e.g. bullock from a mob)
SEE ALSO urrarem, urlanem
angakelhem, **akngakelhem** (E) *vi.*
separate self out from other people (e.g. after a family fight) ◆ Angkwer-nheng-arey akngakelhem alhem. Akngakelhem — *cut*-em out from another people. (Sa) *All the sisters separate themselves out from the others and go.* Akngakelhem — *separate themselves out from other people.*
angakelh-ilem, **akngakelh-ilem** (E) *vt.*
separate a person from another, cut one out from the others
= urlanem
SEE ALSO akalkelh-ilem, alperrty-ilem, ingekelh-ilem

angalthen (E) *n.*
younger sister of a man. If a male calls somebody *angalthen* then they call him *arrwemp* or *kak*. ◆ 'Angalthen' akem kakey kwerenhel, kakey kwerenhel 'angalthen' akem kwey, ayteyikw. Kenh ra renh akem

'kak'. *Her elder brother calls her* 'angalthen' — *her elder brother calls the woman, his younger sister,* 'angalthen'. *And she calls him* 'kak'.
SEE ALSO atyey, arrwemp, kak, angkwer, yay

anganem, akngananem (E) *vi.*
1. originate or come from (a place), be created (in the Dreaming), come into being, 'belong to' (a place) ◆ Ahalper nhel akngananekarl ayeng. (Sa) *I came from Ahalper here.* ◆ Akngananekarl ayeng ikwerel apmerel. Apmer atyenhel ayeng akngananek — Arlwekarrel. Tyaparl anganek ikwerel atnyemayt, tyap irrarl anem weth atnyemayt-penharl ra irrarl anem irrem. (St) *I came from there, from the place. I came from my country — Arlwekarr. The witchetty grub came into being there, the chrysalis phase of the grub.* ◆ Ker akngwethek anwekakerrarl akngananek. (St) *The* akngwethek *frog was created for us.* ◆ Mern aperelty. Mern arlkwenh-arlkwenhap aperelty anthwerr — anganekarl, mern aperelty akerl-apemel. (N) *The white substance made by the lerp-scale insect from the river red gum tree is edible — it's a traditional practice, going along and collecting* aperelty. ◆ Anganek ayeng *Napperby*-thayt. Waram apety-alpek angey-henh mer-warn. (M) *I came from over Napperby side. I just came back to my father's country.*
2. be 'found' or spiritually conceived in a particular place or country. An Anmatyerr person has a special connection to the place where they are 'spiritually conceived' and to the Dreamings from that place. This refers not to the baby's actual conception or birth itself but rather to the moment of 'quickening' when the entry of an ancestral spirit into a woman animates the unborn child.
SEE ALSO anngirrem, angwerrm-irrem

anganenty, akngananenty (E) *n.*
1. the country where a person comes from or where they came into being (the place of quickening); a person's traditional country. Also referred to as *mer anganenty*. ◆ Atnangker akngananentyarl ayeng. (Sa) *The country where I came from is Atnangker.* ◆ Akngananentyel anetyel, mer akngananentyel. Mer Altyerrengarl akngananekarl anetyel. (Sa) *Living in the country where [we] came from. The country that was created in the Dreaming time.*
2. particular groups of kin that are related to a place, especially through their father's father
3. Dreaming, totem ◆ Ker apek aherr atwenty, atyerrenty — wal amparl alkngirrem. Mern ikwerel akngananekarl, akngananenty. Kerarl arlkwem, aynikwel, wal ra alkngirrenty anem. Ampa anem. (Sa) *From the killing of a kangaroo, the shooting of a kangaroo — well a child might come from that. That's the food, the Dreaming, that the child originates from. The child's father kills the kangaroo and eats it, and then the child is 'found' there.*
SEE ALSO altyerr[1], anengkerr, anganty

angang (E), **angey** (T,E), **ahangey** (T,E), **ahengey** (E), **ayengey** (E) *n.* [BABY TALK]
father's father and his brothers and sisters; grandfather, grandmother, great-uncle, great-aunt ◆ Ahangey ngkwenh. (St) *Your grandfather.*
SEE ALSO arreng
CAN SOUND A BIT LIKE angey *'father'*

angank *n.*
the little crow (*Corvus bennetti*) ◆ Angank mer-warn apetyem arwengkel inerl-alhem mern. (N) *The crow comes into the camp and steals food.* ◆ Angank arwengkalth. Arraty. Nyenngel arlkwerl-anem akweteth ateram arrtyanetyenheng, pwerlt-irrem. (N) *The crow is a robber. True. Crows always steal food to eat and then fly away frightened, bolt off.*
= angep, angerl, kway-kway, kaw-kaw

Angank (W) *n.*
Wangala hills, Mt Allan area (note Warlpiri *wangarla* 'crow')
= Wangerlakwerlang

anganty (W,T) *n.*
1. sacred place, restricted place. Also referred to as *mer anganty*. ◆ Mer anganty, *not allowed* ikwer-angkwerr alhetyeh arelh. *Boy*-ant war anganty ikwer-angkwerr alhem. (T) *Women are not allowed to go close to the restricted places. Only the men can go to the* anganty *places.*
2. Dreaming, totem ◆ Iwenham angantyam nta? Ankwareny anganty apek? (M) *What Dreaming are you? Maybe honeyant Dreaming?*
SEE ALSO amek-amek, anganenty, altyerr[1], anengkerr, anger

angap-angap-irrem (E) *vi.*
flutter (wings) ◆ Irrety angap-angap-irrem alkerel akern. (St) *The eaglehawk is fluttering [its wings] high up in the sky.* ◆ Intelyapelyap angap-angap-irrerl-anem. (St) *The butterflies are fluttering.*
SEE ALSO alharrkem, arraly-arraly-irrem

angapanty (E) *n.* [RESPECT LANGUAGE]
1. eye
2. blind ◆ Angapanty aweleth aparrng-irrek. (St) *He went blind in one eye [said of respect kin].*
= parerr
SEE ALSO aparrng, annga, apal-apal[2]

angapety-iwem (E) *vt.*
turn something over, turn something around

◆ Angapety-iwem renh arlety-angkwerr anem ra ampetyek. (St) *Turn it [the meat] over so that it can cook on the raw side.*
= angart-wem
angapety-iwelhem (E) *vi.*
turn yourself over, turn yourself around
= angart-welhem
angarak (W,T) bush bean vine SEE UNDER **angerak**
angart-angart (W) *n.*
really flash, really dressed up ◆ Angart-angart anthwerr anetyam, tyerlarr-akert, arlkeny-akert, anmanty-warn ina atwetyam, an irrkarlp-akert. Angart-angart anetyam. (M) *[They] were really flash and they had feather headdresses and ceremonial designs on for the* anmanty *ceremonies. They were really dressed up.*
angart-wem, angart-iwem (E) *vt.*
1. turn something over; turn something around ◆ Keran angart-wem, mern angart-wem. Ampa angart-wemel aneny arntetyeng. (Sa) *Meat is turned over and food is turned over. A child with a sore hip is turned over.*
= angapety-iwem
2. translate, interpret ◆ Anwern Arrernteng angart-iwem Anmatyerr-warn. (T) *We're translating from Arrernte into Anmatyerr.*
angart-welhem, angart-iwelhem (E) *vi.*
1. turn yourself over; turn yourself around ◆ Impalkertem intem, kwer-penh aweth angart-welhem. (N) *Lying on your back, then, after that, turning over again.* ◆ Aneny impelhenty akngart-iwelhem. (Sa) *Turning yourself over if your hip is cramped.*
2. turn into (something), change into a different form
= angapety-iwelhem
angath *n.*
1. this side of something or somewhere (on the speaker's side) ◆ Aneltyeyeng angath-ampenyarl Apengarlayntem. (Sa) *Apengarlayntem is this side of Aneltyey.*
2. close, nearby ◆ 'Ilwengar mer itwek-irretyenh?' 'Angathemam', nta ilelhem. 'Angathem kwenh, *close now*.' (M) *'When will the place get close [to us]?' 'It's close', you say. 'It's really close now.'* ◆ Arlengel anetyang — angath yanhel anay. (Sa) *Don't sit a long way away — sit there close.*
SEE ALSO itwa, arrer, rntwarr
angath-angath *n.*
a bit close, a bit closer ◆ Angath-angath anay, paytey akely yanh-kety. (Sa) *Sit a bit closer, because of those biting things.*
angath-ampeny *n.*
this side of something or somewhere (on the speaker's side)
angath-irrem *vi.*
come close; move closer to something ◆ Kwey angath-irray. (T) *Girl, move closer.*
angath-ilem *vt.*
move something closer
angay (W) *n.*
cat
= nyarrapeng, mangw, pwethekat, rlwatert
SEE ALSO annga atherrk, meyaw-meyaw
angayakw *n.*
1. hungry ◆ War akarntemel ayeng anep-anem angayakw kwenh. (N) *I am just sitting down quietly because I'm hungry.* ◆ Anert urrelp-urrampem angayakw, arrerlkart ulthem, *right out* mernek angayakw, arlkwetyek anem arlkwem mern arnterr anem anert pwelap-ilelhemel. (Sa) *My stomach is starting to burn from hunger, I'm really starving, hungry for food so that I can eat a lot and fill my stomach up.*
2. feel like eating, or drinking something such as tea
= angayel
angayakw-irrem *vi.*
feel hungry ◆ Angayakw-irrek anemarl ayeng. (Sa) *I'm hungry now.* ◆ Alpwely-irrem wangkekarl-penh. Atnert apekarl pwelap arrpenhel anep-anem, wal alpwely anem irrem anem, angayakw-irremel. (St) *Deflating after being swollen. Somebody might have a full, swollen stomach and then, as they get hungry, their stomach goes flat.*
= angayel-irrem
angayakw-uthek (E) *n.*
hungry ◆ Ngka — tha angayakw-uthekel arlkeyam angayakarl alhep-alhem — tha angayakw-uthekel arlkweyam-kety. (Sa) *Give me some — I'm hungry and I want to eat because I'm going round hungry — I'm hungry and I want to eat.*
SEE ALSO weyapelek-uthek
angayel *n.*
1. hungry ◆ Angayelemap awelhem. (M) *[I'm] feeling hungry.* ◆ Ngkweng ayeng akiwarr-irrem, angayelek apek ayeng ngkweng akiwarr-irrek, ngkweltyek apek, ker apek anthetyakenh, ngkwelty apek anthetyakenh. (St) *I am in a bad mood with you because I am hungry, and over money, because you didn't give me any meat or money.*
2. feel like eating, or drinking something such as tea
= angayakw
3. a respectful word for native currant

(*ahakey*) fruit (*Psydrax latifolia*) ◆ 'Angayel' akem ahakey renh, 'mern' aketyakenh. Angayelantarl renh akem. (St) *The fruit of the* ahakey *is called* 'angayel' *— you don't call it* 'mern' *[the general word for food]. You only call it* 'angayel'.

angayel-irrem *vi.*
feel hungry ◆ Ayeng angayelem-irremew — alpey mern-warn, mern arlkwetyek. *I'm really hungry — let's go back home to eat.*
= angayakw-irrem

angelhem, akngelhem (E) *vi.*
move self or part of self, move around, fidget ◆ Yanharl akngelhetyel-kety, aley akngelhetyel. Yanh akngelhepelhem werrkel. (Sa) *Look out, there's something moving there. There's something moving there in the scrub.* ◆ Tyampernem ayeng, kwereng rlkerremelhem, ingkang angelherl-anem alakenh. (N) *I am lying with my knees up, and after that I stretch, move my legs like that.*

angelh-angelh-ilem, akngelh-akngelh-ilem (E) *vt.*
rock (baby in arms); move something backwards and forwards
= arrew-arrew-ilem

angelth *n.*
1. native pear (*Cynanchum floribundum*). Shrub up to 1 m high, with twining branches and milky sap. Usually grows near watercourses.
2. the edible fruit of the native pear. Also referred to as *mern angelth*. ◆ Mern angelth, arlkwerl-apekarl, akerl-apemel, *roll*-em *up*-ilemel itemel. Inemem, arlkwemem, ampengem, ampengem arlkwem. (N) *The native pear was picked and then rolled up in leaves and cooked in the fire. Then, when it's cooked, it's eaten.*
= tywekerl[1]

angem, akngem (E) *vt.*
1. carry someone or something ◆ Alyeng-angkwerr ampa akwekan angem, panthel, panthel ap ra angep-angem. (St) *Carrying the small baby on the left-hand side, carrying him/her along in the coolamon.* ◆ Kwaty rewel angem anthwelk. (N) *The floodwater carries dead leaves and sticks along.* ◆ Mwantyel ina aperrk angetyart, arrernerl-alhetyart, panth-warn, mwar-warn apek, angetyart, aherr-kenh atna inety-alhemel nthilety-alhetyek. Alep-iletyam, angetyam alep-ilemel anyer. (St) *They used to carefully carry the coals, put them in a wooden dish to carry them, and go and get kangaroo shit to make the fire ignite. They lit the fires, using the supplejack wood.*
2. take someone or something somewhere ◆ Mereng-amer ina mer mparem, pelangket an *all there* ina angem, *billycan*, tey apek angem, tey itemel, merel anerremel mereng-amer kwerel. (P) *They make cubbyhouses and they take blankets and all there, billycans and tea. They sit in the camp and make tea, in the cubbyhouse.*
SEE ALSO angelhem, angernem[2], angetyem

angemang (W,T) *n.*
quiet, non-aggressive ◆ Angemang anay! (T) *Sit down quietly!*

angemang-irrem (W,T) *vi.*
settle down (after argument or fight) ◆ Angemang-irremel anwengkerr aney, ahel ilterretyal. (M) *We'll all settle down and not argue with each other.*

angent[1] (T,E) *n.*
mirage, heat haze ◆ Angent, akern-ilem kwaty-artek anem renh arem Ilewerr yanh. (St) *The mirage raises it up [the ground] and then you see that salt lake [Ilewerr] looking as if it's water.* ◆ Apwert arleng-areny arrerelh-ilemel angentel. (Sa) *The mirage makes distant hills appear closer.*
= merawarr, ilewerr

-angent[2], -anngernt (T) *ending*
1. (something happens) before the verb action, before, awaiting. On nominals, it follows the *+ek*[2] or *+eh* ending. ◆ Kwaty yanh impang tha antywety-**angent**. *Leave that water for me, I'll drink it after.* ◆ *Right story* kwenh ina ilek arrwekeleny mapel akewenyel map, ywerretyeh-**angent**el. (M) *They told the right stories before they passed away, the poor things.* ◆ Iyterlarr arrernelhem awelyek-**angent**, anthep-irretyek-**angent**. (St) *Putting the headdress on before the* awely *ceremonies, before dancing.*
2. for, on behalf of ◆ Manterr yanh impay, marl akwekeh-**angent**. *Leave those clothes for the little girl.* ◆ Anwern *wait*-irrety-alhem lpway-warn arelh map apetyety-**angent**. (M) *We'll go to the river and wait for the women to come.*

angent-wem (W,T) step in to stop a fight SEE UNDER **arrngent-wem**

angenty *n.*
1. soakage, temporary waterhole, soak. Also referred to as *kwaty angenty*. ◆ Angenty angernetyel kwaty antywetyek angkethakwel. (Sa) *Thirsty and digging a soakage to get a drink of water.* ◆ Kwaty angenty antywetyek. (Sa) *Drinking soakage water.*

= arnwengk
SEE ALSO altywen, ayay
2. water found in the hollow trunks of some trees • = unthарr
angenty-ilem (E) *vt.*
dig a soakage
= arnwengk-ilem
angenty arrernem (E) = **angenty-ilem** (arrernem *'put'*)

Angenty (T) *n.*
the name of a place and of a country/estate in the Ti Tree and Anningie Station area. See map p. viii.

angep *n.*
the little crow (*Corvus bennetti*)
= angank, angerl, kway-kway, kaw-kaw

anger (W) *n.*
birthmark
SEE ALSO anganenty, altyerr[1], anengkerr

angerak, **angarak** (W,T), **angwarak** (W) *n.*
1. bush bean vine (*Rhyncharrhena linearis*). Climbing vine with long, green bean-like pods. Often found on mulga trees.

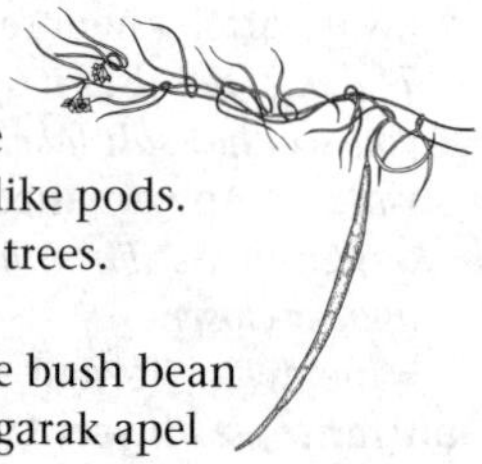

= werrp
2. the edible fruit of the bush bean [SOME SPEAKERS] ◆ Mern angarak apel akwerrk arlkwerl-apem. Awerretyepwer anyent renh. 'Angarak' akenh arlparl, kenh mern 'awerretyepwer'. *The young pods of the bush bean are eaten. That's the same thing as* awerretyepwer. *'Angarak' is what the leaves are called, and the edible part is called 'awerretyepwer'.* (N) ◆ Mern angwarak lpwayel irnem. Arlpenty angerr. Altyeyart akin angwarak. (N) *The bush bean grows in the creeks and it's a tall bush. It is similar to the bush banana vine.* • = awerretyepwer, aherretyepwer, werrp

angerak-angerak (W) *n.*
tickweed, mustard bush (*Cleome viscosa*). A sticky herb about 40 cm high with yellow flowers.

angerl (E) *n.*
the little crow (*Corvus bennetti*)
= angank, angep, kway-kway, kaw-kaw
angerl-irrem (E) *vi.*
go black ◆ Artapaly apek rrpwerl-irrek, angerl-irrekarl. (Sa) *The bush plums have gone black.* ◆ Mern tamp atyenh angerl-irrek-ketyaw! (Sa) *My damper has gone all black!*
SEE ALSO rrpwerl-irrem

angerl-angerl (T,E) *n.*
uvula (the small fleshy appendage that hangs down at the back of the throat). Also referred to as *ahenty angerl-angerl.* ◆ *Eh,* angerl-angerl akeweny ngenh atanth-kety kwenh *something* apek akwernemel. (T) *Hey, you poor thing, something might stab you in the uvula when you swallow.*
= ngarlaleny

angernem[1] *vt.*
1. dig with hands or with a scoop; dig into something ◆ Rtwep angernem. (M) *Digging a cooking hole.* ◆ Iltyel angernem an arlatyey inemem. (M) *Dig with the hands and then get the pencil yam out.* ◆ Kwaty angenty ipert angernem. (T) *Digging a hole for a soakage.*
2. dig something up ◆ Mern anaty angernem, yerramp angernem akin. (Sa) *Digging up bush potatoes and digging up honeyants.* ◆ Thang angernem ahelh alewatyerreh. *I'm digging in the ground for a goanna.*
SEE ALSO inyem, ahinem
3. scratch someone ◆ Ayenh angernay, artep ayenh angernay! (Sa) *Scratch me, scratch my back!* • SEE ALSO alherrem[1], arreynem, irrkernem
angernelhem *vi.*
scratch yourself ◆ Angernelhetyel. Arengk yanh angernelhetyelarl ayepweyaw. (Sa) *Scratching itself. Hunt away that dog that is scratching itself.* ◆ Arengk angernelhem mentyey-akert. (T) *The mangy dog is scratching itself.* ◆ Ayeng angernelhem wenyelarl nhwek. (T) *I'm scratching myself because the mosquitoes bit me.*
= arreynelhem, ahinelhem, irrkernelhem
SEE ALSO irrkem, alherrem[1]

angernem[2] (W,T), **akngirnem** (E) *vt.*
take or bring something back somewhere ◆ Artwangel rwang irrwelty mer-warn angernem. *The man is taking the kindling wood back to camp.* ◆ Mern apmer-warl akngirnem. (St) *Taking the food back to camp.* ◆ Ker aherr ampwerrk angernem, merelant tyep-iletyeh. (M) *Take the whole kangaroo back, and then just cut it up back at camp.* ◆ Alangkw, mern aparl akerl-apek, mern akwerrk akerl-apek, akerl-apemel akerl-apemel. Rwewarn antem angernem, rwel ap itetyam, mern aparl apel, rwel itetyam. (N) *The young fruits of the bush banana were picked. Then they were taken back to the fire to be cooked.*
SEE ALSO angem, angetyem, +ern[1]

angerr[1], **akngerr** (E) *n.*
1. big, large (in size) ◆ Ahakeyan arlpang angerr. (N) *Bush plum trees have big leaves.* ◆ Kwer angerrel anampart-wem kwer akwek. (T) *The big kid is pushing the little kid.* ◆ Nwernengk arrakert angerr lthel-lthel an

annga angerr. (M) *The tawny frogmouth has a big hairy beak and big eyes.*
2. many, lots of (something) ◆ Tyerrtyel ltewem artetyerretyerr kwaty angerrem anhem. (M) *If a person throws something at the willie wagtail then there will be a lot of rain.* ◆ Mern angerr arlkwep-arlkwerl ayert angerr irrek. (St) *He'd eat lots of food and that's how he got really fat.* • SEE ALSO map, anengk[1], alhirrel, arnkengeny
3. very, really, extremely ◆ Mern angwarak lpwayel irnem. Arlpenty angerr. Altyeyart akin angwarak. (N) *The bush bean grows in the creeks and it's a very tall bush. It is similar to the bush banana vine.* ◆ Mwerrem artwang anep-anem rlkert angerr-penh. *The man is all right now after being very sick.* ◆ Nhenhan ker ampwang-awaty — nhenhan ker anter angerr-awaty. (T) *This meat is a bit lean — this meat is a bit fattier.* ◆ Twer angerr ayernay! *Tie it up really tight!* ◆ Ingway-ingway anemarl irrem. Ingwel anem lyet artety-alhetyenh ingwa angerrel, ingwa angerr. (St) *It's got a little bit dark now, and soon it will be really dark.*
4. important, significant
5. senior, mature (of a person)
SEE ALSO awer[1], ilkwa[2], rltwa, rltwang, urlta, artelhampw, artelh[3], akwek, akely, +enty-angerr

iltya angerr, **iltya akngerr** (E)
1. thumb
2. large fingers (i.e. not little finger) (iltya *'hand', 'finger'*)

ankwang angerr (W,T)
deep sleep, fast asleep (ankwang *'sleep'*)

angerr-pat, **akngerr-pat** (E) *n.*
1. elder, senior person ◆ Anwernenh *show-em*-iletyart angerr-pat mapel. Lweren anwern arek arek arek awenkel. (N) *All the old people used to show us [about bush food]. That's what we saw all the time when we were teenagers.* ◆ Ankwang intetyeh, kwer Anengkerr-ilem angerr-pat mapel. (T) *Old people tell children Dreaming stories to make them go to sleep.*
2. eldest (in a family group or a group of siblings) ◆ Kakey angerr-pat. (M) *Older brother.* ◆ Marl angerr-pat atyengenh arrwekeleny. (M) *My eldest daughter, the first one.*
SEE ALSO ingkerneny

angerr-pat-irrem, **akngerr-pat-irrem** (E) *vi.*
grow old ◆ Alyemp-alyemp anem ra irrem angerr-pat-irremel. (T) *The poor thing is getting wrinkled now that she's getting old.*

angerrety, **akngerrety** (E) *n.*
1. elder, eldest, senior, grown up ◆ Angkweraty angerrety. *My eldest sister.*
2. a respectful word for mother's brother (used by men); uncle [SOME SPEAKERS] ◆ 'Kamern' akem kwerelant, kenh artwel akenh renh 'angerrety' ilem. 'Angerrety apetyay, nhenh-warlay.' 'Angerrety' akem, *he don't* 'kamern' anpernerl. (M) *Only children use the term 'kamern', whereas on the other hand men call [their mother's brother]* 'angerrety'. *'Come here* angerrety, *come here.' They call them* 'angerrety', *not 'kamern'.* • SEE ALSO kamern
3. big, solid, heavy ◆ *Choke*-em-iletyart anwern 'kwep' angerrety, arrernetyart *billycan*-warl. (N) *We used to choke those big frogs called 'kwep', and put them in a billycan.* ◆ Mantarr atyenh angerrety-penh pwarn-irrek, atewatelarl alhewek. (T) *My clothes, that used to be big, have shrunk after being washed in hot water.*

angerrety-iteng (E), **akngerrety-iteng** (E) *n.*
middle-aged, senior

tyerrty angerrety (W,T)
1. a big person
2. senior person (tyerrty *'person'*)

atay angerrety (W,T)
full moon (atay *'moon'*)

angerrety-pwek (W,T) *n.*
a fat person or thing, a very large thing ◆ Angerrety-pwek marl yanh apetyem. (T) *That big fat woman is coming.* ◆ Rnwek-anternenh angerrety-pwek, kel antayelant angetyam. (T) *A really big water dish, that could only be carried with a carrying strap.* ◆ Ankerrmern-areny tyapek-anternenh atwerl-apekarl. Atwerl-apek perrap perlatyart angerrety-pwek antem. (N) *We went along chopping out the big fat grubs from the coolibah tree. They were really large, like the grubs from the river red gum.*

angerr-angerr *n.*
a bit big, largish; quite a lot (of something) ◆ Kwak-irrem mernarl akemeng. Arrpenhel ingweyameng 'Kwaty-kwenyel alpem, mer-warn'. 'No, urrek nhenhek-amparr tha akeyaw mern, angerr-angerr.' *[I] am really enjoying picking the bush foods. Another person might ask me, 'Let's go home, we haven't got any water'. [And I'll say] 'No, wait, I'm going to pick these fruits first, there's quite a lot of them.'*

angerr-ingar, **akngerr-ingar** (E) *n.*
many times, a lot of times ◆ Akngerr-ingarel aynterl-alpem. (Sa) *Going away for many days.*
SEE ALSO -ingar

angerr-irrem[1], **akngerr-irrem** (E) *vi.*
1. grow up, get bigger, increase in number ◆ *Baby one*-an arrakert arrangkwarl-areny,

arntek anetyakenh. Ampa angerr irrem arntek-akert anem irrem, arratem apek, lyapem apek. (St) *Babies have empty mouths, they don't have any teeth. When they get bigger they get teeth, the teeth come out or grow.* ◆ Artwa angerr-irremel irrpentyem marl-warn. (T) *When the man grows up he gets a wife.* ◆ Kwentarreng alewatyerr akwek, kwart-penh, nheng kwart-penh lyetantarl arratem. Angerr anetyakenh. Ilanthem rarrp angerr-irretyeh. Akwek anthwerr *can't* atwerl, akwek, akely-amperl. Ilanthem, ker angerr-irretyeh. (N) *A* kwentarreng *is a small goanna that has just hatched out of the egg, that has just come out of the egg. They are not very big. You leave them so that they grow up themselves. You can't kill the little ones, the tiny little ones. You send them off, so that they can grow bigger.*
SEE ALSO amangkem
2. sit in a group, live (in a place) ◆ Arelh nthakentyel yanhan angerr-irretyel? *How many people are there?* ◆ Nhenh anem anwantherr urrpety ap angerr-irrep-irrem. Ingwek-atwety anwantherr angerr-irretyel urrpety ap nhenh-arey. (Sa) *There's only a few of us sitting here. A few of us are sitting here until it gets dark.*
angerr-ilem, akngerr-ilem (E) *vt.*
1. make something bigger, increase the number of something
2. make bush plants and animals abundant by performing ceremonies
3. make up stories, exaggerate a story (?)
SEE ALSO arrmernem, intety-iwem

angerr-irrem2 (W,T) *vt.*
take something somewhere or to someone (plural) ◆ Tyerrty mapel angerr-irrem tyerrty yanh rlkert ngangkay-warn. (T) *All of those people are taking the sick person to see the traditional healer.* ◆ Mapel ker angerr-irrem-arleng. (M) *Those people are taking the meat.*
SEE ALSO angem, angernem2

-angerr2 *n.ending*
Goes on the end of words to show that there is a lot of of that thing, characteristic or quality. ◆ Artwang yanhel reng-reng arrernepernem ker aherr map, ker anter-**angerr**, ker ampwang map. *That man is sorting out the kangaroo meat, the fatty meat and the lean meat.*
= -angker
kwen-angerr (T,E) *n.*
deep (water)

angerrakw, akngerrakw (E), **ikngerrakw** (E) *n.*
east ◆ Akngerrakw-they alhwerrp pwetyel. (Sa) *The cold wind blows from the east.* ◆ Alak-akey-kenh ayerrer-thayt. Angerrakw-thaytarl alak-akey ingwerek-areyenh, aylernak-akeyenh altwerl-thaytarl. (St) *The north side belongs to people from the other moiety, and the east side belongs to another group of people from the opposite moiety to us. The western side belongs to people from the same moiety as us.*
= ingerr
SEE ALSO antekerr, ayerrer, altwerl
angerrakw-angerrakw, akngerrakw-akngerrakw (E) *n.*
south-east
angerrakw-ampeny, akngerrakw-ampeny (E) *n.*
on the eastern side
angerrakw arraty, akngerrakw arraty (E)
due east
akngerrakw-penh (E) *n.*
east
= angwerrel-penh

Angerretyalarteh (W) *n.*
the name of a cave in the Mt Allan area

angert (W,T) a barrier SEE UNDER **arrngert**

angert-irrem (W,T) *vi.*
go somewhere to bring someone back ◆ Ayeng ngkweng angert-irrerl-alpek mer arrpenheng. (T) *I went to bring you back from another place.*
= angety-alpem

angerterrk (E) *n.*
1. gidgee wild orange, narrow-leaf bumble (*Capparis loranthifolia*). Shrub to 3 m high, with rough bark and creamy flowers.
2. the edible fruits of the gidgee wild orange
= iwerrarrkw
SEE ALSO akarlety, atwakey

angetyem, akngetyem (E) *vt.*
bring something, get something ◆ Ker thalh angetyem. Ker ampeng thalh. Ker aherr apek thalh angetyem. Ker arlewatyerr thalh angetyem. (N) *Bringing a load of cooked meat. Bringing a load of cooked kangaroo meat. Bringing a load of cooked goanna meat.* ◆ Marl mapel waly akem akem akem, angetyem antyepanty-wem waly renh antyepanty-wem. (N) *The women cut lots of leafy branches and then they bring them and spread them out.* ◆ Tey arlpelh yaleng angetyay. (M) *Get me those tea-leaves from there.* ◆ Ilewerr angetyay ker kwemey mpwaretyeh. (M) *Bring some salt to make the meat tasty.*
angety-alpem, akngety-alpem (E) *vt.*
bring something back, take something back somewhere ◆ Arlkwerl-apem mern angelth *anyway* war, ampeng, arnka, arnkang

arlkwerl-apem. Tyerrty angety-alpem arrpenh, rwewarl. (N) *[You] can go along eating the fruits of the native pear however you want, cooked or raw. People take some of them back to cook.* ◆ *Toyota* nhenh war tha arlenthek, angety-alpem atyeng. (St) *I just lent this Toyota, and you'll bring it back to me [later].* ◆ Ker-kenh rerrk akweteth. Aherr apek akngety-alpem rerrk anyent yanh ikwerel iterl-anetyek, ipert anyentel iterl-anetyek. (St) *A* rerrk *is a permanent cooking place. You might bring the kangaroo back to that one place to cook it, to cook it in the same hole.*
SEE ALSO angem, angernem[2]

angetyepengangety (W) cubbyhouse SEE UNDER **alyetyepengalyety**

angey (T,E) father's father and his brothers and sisters [BABY TALK] SEE UNDER **angang**

angey, akngey (E) *n.*
1. father. If you call someone *angey*, then they call you *aler* (in most cases). ◆ Angey atyenharl athew anetyam arementyel, an atanthetyam ankerr. (M) *My father sat in the hide, and speared emus.*
2. father's brothers; uncle
3. particular male relations with the same skin as your *angey*
SEE ALSO anya[1], anyenheng[1], arrawel
4. God, Jesus [SOME SPEAKERS] ◆ Akngey-warl angkeyaw arntarnt-aretyekaw. (Sa) *Praying to God so that he looks after you.*
CAN SOUND A BIT LIKE ahangey *'father's father', 'father's father's sisters etc.'*

angeylk (E) *n.*
mosquito
= aheny, weny, kewenyeweny

angka[1] (E) *n.*
1. word, the meaning of a word ◆ Alharlkwem, aywepemarl kel angka anyent ra. (St) Alharlkwem *and* aywepem *have the same meaning.*
2. language ◆ Ilek angkarl untan? *What language do you speak?* ◆ Angka lyeteny anetyakenh — ahinpenyant nhenh. (St) *This language is not from nowadays — it's olden-time language.* ◆ Antelhemel angkay, angka atyenh-warl Anmatyerr-warl. (St) *Follow me and say what I say, in my language, Anmatyerr.*
3. message, story ◆ Angka tha ilanthek. (St) *I sent a message.* ◆ Ilek unta angka ilerl-wek ikngwerek? (Sa) *What story did you go and tell the other person?*
4. voice ◆ Angka tha alhengk-awem. *I know that voice.*
5. Goes before the name of a particular language, e.g. *angka Anmatyerr* Anmatyerr language.
= angkety, ulypma
SEE ALSO angkem

angka ilem (E)
tell a story (ilem *'tell'*)

angka ilanthem (E)
send a message, pass on a message (ilanthem *'send'*)
= ulpma ilanthem

angka angkem (E)
speak an Aboriginal language (angkem *'speak'*)
= ulpma angkem, angkety angkem

angka apekap (E)
being unable to speak properly (apekap *'being unable to speak properly'*)
= ulpma apekap, aleny apekap

angkakert-ilem (E) *vt.*
release a person from speech taboo or ceremonial ban on speaking (lit. 'make someone have speech')
= ulpmakert-ilem, angkeparr-ilem

angka ultakem (T,E)
interrupt someone who is talking, stop talking, break up an argument (ultakem *'break'*) ◆ Angkarl ultakem-ketyaw, atwetyekarl angkerrem-ketyaw — angka ultakem, atwetyekarl angkerremeng. (Sa) *Break up the argument, because they are talking about fighting — break it up.*

angkek-angkek-ilem (E) *vt.*
make someone talk, ask someone to tell a story ◆ Ilekek unta angkek-angkek-ilety-alpek? Ayenhan arlan. Ayengarrparl anep-anem. (Sa) *Why did you go and try to make me talk? I've got nothing to do with it. I'm just sitting here minding my own business.*

angka[2] (E) *n.*
1. upper part of back. Also referred to as *artep angka.*
2. emu heart. Also referred to as *ker angka.*

angkangk iytarr-inenh (E) *n.*
the vestigial wings of an emu (iytarr-inem *'drag or pull something out of something'*). These have a small hook on the end which the emu uses for pulling down certain of its foods, such as corkwood and grevillea honey, and mistletoe berries.
= perlap tyarr-inenh, perlap arrawelenh

angkarl *n.*
1. rain cloud (white before turning dark). Also referred to as *kwaty angkarl.* ◆ Kwaty angerr apetyem, kwaty angkarl. (T) *There are lots of rain clouds coming.*
2. cloud of smoke

angkarr-angkarr, arnkarr-arnkarr *adv.*
aiming at something, making out as if to strike or hit someone, showing that you are ready to fight someone
angkarr arem, arnkarr arem
take aim; be ready to strike with a weapon such as a nulla-nulla, spear, boomerang or gun; threaten to strike; make out as if to strike or hit someone; be about to hit someone; brandish a weapon ◆ Yanh ampel arnkarr aretyel lyet rtemarl atwetyek. (Sa) *That kid is threatening to hit [someone] on the back of the head.*
SEE ALSO akwanth-ilem, rtwely inem, arrang-arem
angkarr atwem, arnkarr atwem
make out as if to strike or hit someone, threaten to strike or hit someone

-angkarreny (W,T), **-angkerreny** (W) *ending*
1. more (of a quality). Goes on the end of describing words to show something has more of this quality. Similar to the English ending '-er' in 'bigger'; better, good quality, really ◆ Ker yanh atyeng anthay, thelty-**angkarreny**. (M) *Give me that meat, it's softer.* ◆ Inngenyel-**angkerreny** alewatyerr atwerl-alpek. (T) *The really clever hunter went and killed a goanna.* ◆ Kapert altywer-**angkerreny** angkay. (T) *[You] talk because you're very knowledgeable.*
2. in spite of the fact that . . ., even though . . ., contrary to expectations ◆ Metheth yanh ntwang arem? Alhernter-**angkarreny** rang rntwem tyerrty mapel-ayel. (M) *Can you see that white woman over there? Even though she's white she's dancing with the Aboriginal women.* ◆ Tyerrty yanhel mwetek mparek, anetyel-**angkarreny**. (M) *That person fixed the car, even though he's sick.*

angkawelhem *vi.*
1. ask for permission to do something ◆ Ayeng angkawelhem ngkweng, ngkwengel-ayel ayeng alhetyek. (T) *I'm asking you if I can go with you.*
2. tell someone what you are doing, explain yourself to someone, give people notice of what you are doing ◆ Ayeng kel ngkweng-warn apetyek angkawelhetyeh. Ayeng alhem inwekel atherr-inger interl-alpetyeh, atherr-inger-penh apety-alpem. (T) *I've come to tell you I'm going. I'm going to sleep out for two nights and after that I'm returning.* ◆ Ayeng alhetyeh angkawelhem, ayeng ngkwengel-ayeng *Coniston*-warn alhetyeh. (T) *I'm explaining that I want to go to Coniston with you.*
SEE ALSO angka[1], ilelhem, awelhem

angkay (W,T) *n.*
bilby (*Macrotis lagotis*) ◆ Angkayel inyemel arlkwem anyematy. (N) *Bilbies dig up and eat witchetty grubs.*
= ahert, artnangk

angkel *n.*
uncle (from English 'uncle')
SEE ALSO amarl, kamern

Angkeleth *n.*
English (from English 'English') ◆ Ilanthem apek, *grandmother*-el apek, *mother*-el apek, 'Alhang kwenh, kweray kwenh. *Don't* anngarenty-irrerl-anerl kwenh, ayerrp ilelhemel kwenh. *You* kwerl-warl alherl kalty-irretyeh unta kalty-irretyeh kwenh, Angkeleth unta kalty-irretyeh kwenh'. (N) *Their grandmother or mother might send them, 'Go child! Don't behave as if you don't want to and avoid it. You've got to go to school to learn, to learn English'.*

angkem *vi.*
1. say, speak, talk to someone ◆ Mentyel awem, arrpenh nhakw apekarl atyeng angkem wal mentyel tha awem, rarrp angketyek. (St) *That person over there might talk to me, but I'm not taking any notice, she can just talk herself.*
2. speak (a particular language) ◆ Angkety Anmatyerr angkem. (M) *Speaking Anmatyerr language.* ◆ Angka irrkwerteth wararl angkep-angkem. *Might* Arlper apek awetyakenh angkerl-anem, irrkwertetharl angkep-angkem tha awetyakenh, *German* apek. Irrkwerteth-irrkwertetharl angkem. *They just keep on speaking a different language. They might speak Warlpiri, which I don't understand. You can't understand [some] other languages. German, for example. Those people speak a language that is not understandable to me.*
3. make the noise that a particular animal or thing usually does; sing (birds), thunder (storm), make a noise (car or engine) ◆ Thep angketyel. (Sa) *The birds are singing.* ◆ Thep rantem angkem, 'Apetyepetyem apetyepetyem'. (M) *Then the bird sings, 'Apetyepetyem apetyepetyem'.* ◆ Kwaty angkem, awely-awelyan tnem. (St) *There is thunder and lightning.* ◆ Kwaty arrer angkenhetyem — wakek aylpeyaw. (Sa) *The noise of thunder is coming closer — go inside the shelter.*
4. pray
SEE ALSO ilem
iltyem iltyem angkem
signal with hands, use handsigns (iltya *'hand'*,

'finger')
SEE ALSO akwerrem, iltyerrem
ahey-angkem, wey-angkem (E) *vi.*
breathe, pant (dog), breathe heavily
atemart angkem (E)
stamp feet, make a knocking or thudding noise
angkerrem *vi.*
1. talk to each other ◆ Ulengerek-ulengerek angkerreperrem, ilak apek angketyek. Unta apek atyeng angkem, ayeng ngkweng angkem, ulengerek-ulengerek angkerrem. Arratyant-arey weth-lkwer angkerrem alknga arerrem. (St) *Talking face-to-face. The two of us might talk. You might talk to me and I might talk to you, talk to each other face-to-face. Talk straight to each other, looking each other in the eye.*
2. talk (a group of people), tell stories ◆ Arelh awenk map anerl-anem arlwekerel angkety angkerrerl-anemel. (T) *The teenage girls are sitting around in the women's camp telling stories.*
angkelh-ilem, angkelh-angkelh-ilem *vt.*
1. make someone talk, get someone to talk ◆ Angkelh-angkelh-ilem marl nhenh uyarn. Angketyek ra. (St) *It's hard to get this woman to talk.*
2. start something up (e.g. a car or an engine) ◆ Mwetek angkem akin. Mwetek kel angkelh-angkelh-ilem anem ra, aywerr anem. Angkelh-angkelharl-ilem anem artweyelikw. (Sa) *Cars make a noise as well. When the car is started then it makes a noise. The owner of the car starts it up.* ◆ Ywarn angkelh-angkelh-ilek. (St) *[The car] wouldn't start.*

angkep, ingkep *adv.*
back, returning, backwards ◆ Angkep-antey apety-alpem. (Sa) *Coming back again.* ◆ Kwer akwek nhenhey arlelty-irrem. Inang nhak angkep anthety-alpangaw! Kwer arlelty-irremek. (T) *This little kid is crying. Give those things back to him! To the kid who's crying.* ◆ Arrpwarnt-arey alherl-wa! Ayeng angkep intetyeh kwenh! Arrantherr alhetyeh, ayeng intetyeh kwenh! (T) *You noisy mob leave! I want to go back to sleep! Go away so that I can sleep!*
angkep-irrem, ingkep-irrem *vi.*
go backwards
= aneyangketh-irrem, anepetheng-irrem, anwengentyengenty-irrem, tyenelhem[1], urtep-irrem
SEE ALSO pert-irrem
angkep-ilem, ingkep-ilem *vt.*
make something go backwards, reverse something
angkepelh-ilem, ingkepelh-ilem *vt.*
= **angkep-ilem**
angkep-athek, ingkep-athek, ingkep-atheh (W,T), **ingkep-athep** (E) *adv.*
1. backwards
2. back (go back) ◆ Ingkep-atheh arnarnpenhetyeh. (N) *Climbing back down.*
angkep arem, ingkep arem
look back, look behind
angkep-athek arem, ingkep-athek-arem, ingkep-atheh arem (W)
look back, look behind ◆ Angkep-athek anngarelhemel arem. (T) *Looking back over [your] shoulder.*
= anngarelhem, artepeng arelhem

angkeparr (W,T) *n.*
1. type of duck (?) ◆ Angkeparr aperl-apem kwatyel-arleng akwerrk map akertel — *line up* irrerlapetyenh, aperlapetyenh aperlapetyenh. (N) *The* angkeparr *duck swims along in the water with its ducklings — they go along in a line.*
2. black-tailed native-hen (*Gallinula ventralis*) • SEE ALSO narremantyerr, karlayteng-ayteng, kart-irrkwely-irrkwely

angkeparr-ilem (E) *vt.*
release a person from speech taboo or ceremonial ban on speaking ◆ Angkeparr-ilem, arrpenhel artwel apek angkeparr-ilem arelh *mother*-an akerterel anetyel *family*-ketyeng. Kel renh angkeparr-ilemel marlel artwel. Angkemel anem anerl-anem. (Sa) *Another person, maybe a man, frees her so that she can talk, after she has been sitting down and not talking out of respect for the family. The man frees her to talk, and then she talks.*
= arrakert-ilem, ulypmakert-ilem, angkakert-ilem
SEE ALSO angka, angkep

-angker (E) *n.ending*
Goes on the end of words to show that there is a lot of of that thing, characteristic or quality. This ending most commonly goes on the word *mwerr* 'good' to form *mwerr-angker* 'really good, fantastic'.
= -angerr[2]

-angkerreny (W) better, good quality, really SEE UNDER **-angkarreny**

angkert rain cloud (white) SEE UNDER **ankert**[1]

angkertakwertak (W,T), **ankertwakertwak** (W) *n.*
1. spotted nightjar (*Eurostopodus argus*)
= akwet-akwet
SEE ALSO arrthwarrthw
2. the sound made by the spotted nightjar ◆ Angkertakwertak kwenyel angkerl-anem, 'Angkertakwertakwertak'. (T) *The spotted nightjar sings out in the night like this,*

'Angkertakwertakwertak'.

angket-angket (E) *n.*
a type of dragon lizard (*Tympanocryptis tetraporophora* (?)) ◆ Kaperl artek akwek angket-angket ra. Intetyeng-intety atnertangey akwek. (St) *The* angket-angket *lizard is similar to the* kaperl. *It's got spots on its stomach.*
= apwet-apwet
SEE ALSO kaperl

angkethakw (T,E) *n.*
thirsty, thirstily ◆ Angenty angernetyel kwaty antywetyek angkethakwel. *Thirstily digging a soakage to get a drink of water.*
◆ Antywerretyart angkethakwel. Apeng-areny artekerr. Lyetarr kwatyant anem antyweynerl-wetyel. Kwatyant anem antyweynetyel. (Sa) *They used to drink the liquid from the roots of the kurrajong tree when they were thirsty. Nowadays they just go along drinking [any sort of] water. They just drink water.*
= angkethel, arwekel, arrangketh

angkethakw-irrem (T,E) *vi.*
get thirsty
= arwekel-irrem, parrety-irrem

angkethek-uthek (E) *n.* [RESPECT LANGUAGE]
thirsty ◆ Angkethek-uthekek ahanenh-ilenh-areyay atyeweyay, parrety-ayerrek. (Sa) *All of you, take [some water] to the one [respect kin] who is thirsty.*
= wangkethel, weng angkethel

angketharrp (E) alone, on your own [RESPECT LANGUAGE] SEE UNDER **ingketharrp**

angkethel (E) *n.*
thirsty, thirstily ◆ Alerlaw, amel tha angerney. Amelel ayeng artelhetyek, irrernt ilelhemel, angkethel anem ayeng. (St) *Wait while I dig a hole to cool off in. I'll cover myself with damp earth to make myself cool because I'm thirsty.*
◆ Angkethel tha antywetyek. (St) *I'm going to drink because I'm thirsty.* ◆ Alknga ipert-irrek angkethel. (St) *When [the person] was thirsty their eyes sank back in their head.*
= angkethakw, arwekel, arrangketh, parrety

angkety *n.*
1. word ◆ Pep-warn intelh-ilem angkety yanh ingkerr. (M) *Writing all those words on paper.*
◆ 'Mpetyan', 'Kemarr' — angkety anyent akwet *use*-em-ilem. *'Mpetyan' and 'Kemarr' — [we] still use both words.*
2. language ◆ Angkety Anmatyerr angkem. (M) *Talking Anmatyerr language.* ◆ Anmatyerr anyent akwet anem. Kartety arlka Alyawarr arlka anem *self* akin. Kenh anwern Anmatyerr akwet. (M) *There is still one Anmatyerr. Kaytetye and Alyawarr are separate. But we are all still Anmatyerr.*
3. message, story ◆ Arelh awenk map anerl-anem arlwekerel angkety angkerrerl-anemel. (T) *The teenage girls are sitting around in the women's camp telling stories.* ◆ Tha angkety ilanthem tyerrty arrpenhel-ayeng ayeng inety apetyetyeh. (M) *I'm sending a message with someone else to tell someone to come and pick me up.*
4. voice
5. Goes before the name of a particular language.
= angka[1]
SEE ALSO angkem

angkety angkem (W,T)
speak an Aboriginal language (angkem *'speak'*)
= angka angkem, ulypma angkem

angkety ltwakem (W,T)
interrupt someone who is talking; stop talking (ltwakem *'break'*)
= angka ultakem

angkety kertemwengk (W,T)
1. a short version of a story, a summary of a story (kertemwengk *'indirect way of talking'*)
◆ Artwangel angkety akwek war ilem, angkety kertemwengk, kwer mapel iterlaretyek. (T) *The man is just telling the children part of the story, so that they will know it.*
2. not the full story, not the real story

-angketyarr (E) *n.ending*
1. Goes on the end of nominals to show that there is plenty of, lots of, or an abundance of (that thing). ◆ 'Apanterrekerr apety-alpa kwenh melarlp-**angketyarr**-kety!' (Sa) *'Come back in case you get lost, there's lots of* melarlp *spirits there!'* ◆ Werlaty-**angketyarr**arl ahekwenayt, werlaty-akert. Werlaty akely-rnem, werlaty-artek ilenngem akwey ikwerenh. (Sa) *The* ahekwenayt *grub has lots of 'breasts'. Little breasts. They are like — what-d'ye-call-it — like breasts.* ◆ Tyelk ingkerrek ayeng akeng-irrek *pain*-**angketyarr**, arlkwemarl. Tyelk ingkerrek ayeng arlkwem. (St) *My whole body is no good — the whole lot is hurting. All of my body is hurting me.*
2. a place where there is lots of a particular thing ◆ Ulemp-ulemp, ulemp-**angketyarr**el alhetyek. (St) *Going through the place where there are lots of ghost gum trees.*

angkeway *n.* [RESPECT LANGUAGE]
1. creek, river ◆ Angkeway-warl ahanenherl-wek untyerrek anem. (St) *[He] has gone to the river for water.*
2. creek, river (word used if someone has

passed away there) ◆ Angkeway yanh-angkwerr alhetyal kwenh. (M) *Don't go along that creek [because someone passed away there].*
= ngkwerlpay-ayerr
SEE ALSO lher, ulpay

angkeyawarr (E) *n.*
thunder ◆ Angkeyawarr kwaty-ketyaw. (St) *Look out for the thunder.*
SEE ALSO kwaty angkem, awely-awely

+angkw your relation SEE UNDER **+engkw**

-angkwarr by way of, through something SEE UNDER **-angkwerr**[2]

angkwelk (E), **angkwerlk** (E) *n.*
good solid shade, thick shade, bushy plants ◆ Arwerl angkwerlk ulya. Angwerlk weth-lkwer ulya mwerr, atherrk. Angkwerlk, irreltyenng anetyang. (Sa) *A nice shady tree.* Angkwelk *is nice green shade. Not sparse or thin shade.*
= angwarlp
SEE ALSO irreltyenng, lywa

angkwelk-ilem (E), **angkwerlk-ilem** (E) *vt.*
make something grow thick or bushy ◆ Uterrp-areny ap arrwelth-arrwelth. Mern kweny akeng, arnam ant. Alhewelhemel kwatyel, alta angkwelk-ilelhemel, alta angerr ilelhemel, alta awer anetyek arlpenty. *The desert fringed lily grows in the sandhills. It's not edible — it's just a plant. Mixed with water and used to wash yourself, it makes your hair thick, makes it grow long and thick.*

angkwelk-irrem (E), **angkwerlk-irrem** (E) *vi.*
grow thick or bushy (hair or plants), grow long (hair)
= angwarlp-irrem

angkwely-angkwely (W) *n.*
light soft feathers from the emu. These are used to make *memp* 'feathers hats', and kurdaitcha shoes.
= awenth-awenth
SEE ALSO artarr, apwa

angkwen *n.*
Major Mitchell's cockatoo (*Cacatua leadbeateri*) ◆ Thep angkwen rlpwerel anenh-anenh. (M) *Major Mitchell's cockatoos live in hollow trees.*
SEE ALSO kakepewey

angkwer[1], **ankwer** (E) *n.*
back of porcupine; meat from the back of the porcupine. Also referred to as *ker angkwer.* ◆ Ker angkwer arlkwetyek, ngkwernant. (St) *Eating the meat from the back of the porcupine, just the bone.*
SEE ALSO inarleng, inap, lyek

angkwer[2] (W) *n.*
a type of duck (?). Also referred to as *ker angkwer.*
= awengker
SEE ALSO tyepelyakw

angkwer[3], **angkwerey** (E) *n.kin*
1. elder sister
2. mother's elder sister's daughter or father's elder brother's daughter; female cousin
3. particular (senior) relations with the same skin as your *angkwer.* Whether or not a person is a junior or senior sibling to another can be calculated in terms of the relative ages of the parents. If person A calls person B *angkwer,* then person B calls person A *atyey,* or *arrwemp* back (?).
= yay
SEE ALSO atyey, arrwemp

angkweraty *n.kin*
my/our *angkwer* ◆ Ayengarl angkem ikwer, 'Angkweratyay, ayla alherrey'. (Sa) *I say to her, 'Elder sister, let's us two go'.*

angkwerengkw *n.kin*
your *angkwer* ◆ *Mother*-el ilem, 'Angkwerengkw ntwa arekay?' 'Yew, Arek tha angkweraty.' (Sa) *The mother says, 'Have you seen your elder sister?' 'Yes, I saw my elder sister.'*

angkwerikw (E), **angkwereyekw** (E) *n.kin*
his/her/their *angkwer*

angkwerek (W,T) *n.kin*
1. your *angkwer*
2. his/her/their *angkwer*
3. my/our *angkwer* [SOME SPEAKERS]

angkwer-angkwer *n.kin*
elder sister, etc. This form may be a respectful word used for senior *angkwer.*

angkwer-nheng *n.kin*
a group of two or more people who are related to each other as *angkwer* and *atyey* (elder sister and younger sibling)

angkwer-intyerr *n.kin* = **angkwer-nheng**
◆ Angkwer-nheng-arey arrengkerr alhek? Yew. Ingkerr anwingkerr apety-alperrek angkwer-intyerr. (Sa) *Have all of you sisters gone? Yes. All of us came back, all the sisters together.*

angkwer-nheng-arey *n.kin*
a group of more than two people who are related to each other as *angkwer* and *atyey* (elder sisters and younger siblings)

angkwer-nheng-atherr *n.kin*
a person together with their *angkwer*

angkwer-ankethenh *n.kin*
1. having a close *angkwer* still alive
2. someone who is always with their *angkwer*

◆ Angkwer-ankethenh atyenhan akngerr. *I have lots of elder sisters.*
SEE ALSO -ankethenh
angkwer-parety *n.kin*
respectful or 'sorry way' of talking about someone's *angkwer*
SEE ALSO -parety

-angkwer[4] (E) *prn.ending*
Goes on third person pronouns (he, they, them etc.) to show that the speaker is in a respect relationship to the people referred to. See Appendix 1. ◆ Alengkerr-**angkwer** ahanenhek. (St) *Those two went [including someone in avoidance relationship to speaker].*

angkwerey-angkwerey (E) *n.*
ant lion (*Neuroptera* spp. (larvae of))
= kwatyarl ntyeny-ntyeny
SEE ALSO mamerweterwet

angkwerlk (E) good solid shade SEE UNDER **angkwelk**

angkwerr[1] (T,E) *n.*
a type of ceremony ◆ Angkwerrek urnteyaw. Arelh-rneman arlperrng atwelhemarl, angkwerrekan urntem-arlek. Artwerneman urntemek angkwerr ikwer. (Sa) *Dancing the* angkwerr *ceremony. The women beat the rhythm on their laps while the men dance the* angkwerr *ceremony.*
SEE ALSO thayengarr
CAN SOUND A BIT LIKE inkwerr *'bad cold'*

-angkwerr[2], **-angkwarr** *ending*
1. Goes on nominals to show the path or direction something goes along; by way of, through something, this way, in the direction of, along a particular line or path, across, via. ◆ Ananther alhem lpway-warn-athek *road* nhenh-**angkwerr**. (M) *We are going along this road towards the creek.* ◆ Anngang arrkwerelhem arem, altywer akwek-**angkwerr** arerl-anem. (M) *Peeping through a little opening.* ◆ Kwer map arrew-**angkwerr** arrtyanem. (T) *The children are running through the door.* ◆ Arelh anyent anper alhem atyeng-**angkwerr**. (T) *A woman is going past me.* ◆ Urlaylp tyerrelhem akartw-**angkwerr**, kel ra alhem intelyapelyap anem. (St) *The witchetty grub comes out through the pipe in the ground, and then it flies around as a moth.*
2. with someone or something, close to someone ◆ Angwely intep-intem tyerrty rlkert-**angkwerr**. (M) *A dog is lying beside the sick man.* ◆ Pwethekateh angkek, 'Ayeng rlpwerel-arleng ngkweng-**angkwerr** intey?' (M) *He went to the wild cat and said to him, 'Can I sleep in the hollow with you?'*
3. Used in making comparisons between things; compared with, in comparison to.
4. Goes on verbs and indicates that the action happens in a particular way, manner or fashion. ◆ Atnew-atnewel tha mpwarem tharl iterlarem-**angkwerr**. (St) *I'm confident and I know what I'm doing.*
arrpenh-angkwerr *n.*
in a different way, on another side, to another person, with another, through another ◆ Ntwang *don't* alhetyek arrpenh-**angkwerr**, rlkertarl intep-intem-**angkwerr**. (T) *Don't you go over to other people, people who are sick.* ◆ Alkngarlp ayeng arntem, ayeng arrpenh-**angkwerr** anem intetyek, alkngarlp arrpenh-**angkwerr** anem. *My hip is aching so I'll lie on the other side, on the other hip.*
alyeng-angkwerr (W,T),
ayleng-angkwerr (E) *n.*
to the left, on the left-hand side

angkwerr-wem, angkwerr-iwem (E) *vt.*
use healing massage to cure or heal someone ◆ Ngangkarel amwelt atherr angkwerr-wem, arlka ingkerr angkwerr-wem atheperr-ilemel. (Sa) *The traditional healer massages both of the arms and all of the body to make it cool.* ◆ Pwentyel artarrernem, urlaylpel apek artarrernem, urlaylpel apek artarrernem pwenty yal, kel arntety-irrem ra ikwer-penh. Kel ngangkerelant angkwerr-iwem. (Sa) *The kurdaitcha might send the sickness onto someone, and then they get sick after that. Only the traditional healer can cure them with the healing massage.*
= parr-iwem
SEE ALSO tyew-tyew-ilem

angkwey (W,T), **ingkwey** (E) *n.*
1. old
2. a long time ago, from a long time ago, in the olden days ◆ Alyepengantayel rwang inetyam angkwey. (M) *In the olden days people collected wood with a carrying strap.* ◆ Angkwey anetyam aherr akwerrk-akert. Kel yatherr alherrek atherrk arlkwetyeh amenheng. (M) *A long time ago there lived a mother kangaroo with her baby. They used to go together to eat grass.* ◆ Angkwey inang ker pwethekat arlkwetyart. (T) *In the old days they used to eat cats.*
SEE ALSO ahenp, arrwekel, arrul
angkweyeny (W,T), **ingkweyeny** (E) *n.*
old, from a long time ago ◆ 'Mern angkweyeny unta anert anety-irrekety impaw.' (T) *'Leave that old food alone in case you get a bad stomach.'* ◆ Mwetekay angkweyeny yanh impa anem kwenh. (T)

Leave that old motor car. ◆ Anwern anetyart nhenhel merel angkweyeny, angkweyarl anwern anetyart. (T) *We used to live at this place a long time ago.*
= arruleny, arrwekeleny, ahenpeny

angkwey-antey (W,T), **ingkwey-antey** (E) *n.*
a long time ago

angkweyeny-irrem (W,T), **ingkweyeny-irrem** (E) *vi.*
grow old, get old ◆ Angkweyenyem irrem tyerrty apek. (M) *The person might grow old.* ◆ Mwetek nhenh angkweyeny-irrem — angkweyel inekarl wart. (M) *This car is getting old — well, we did get it a long time ago.*

angwang *n.*
1. forgetful, oblivious
2. harmless, gentle, mild, not looking for trouble, not dangerous, non-aggressive ◆ Rang angwang anthwerr anem. Rang itya *trouble* mpwarem *family* kwerenheh apek, *family* arrpenhek apek. (T) *He's a really quiet man. He doesn't make trouble for his family or for anyone else.* • SEE ALSO anik, apertap, ameleth

angwang-irrem (T) *vi.*
forget about something ◆ Tyerrty terangk atherrem atwerrem. Angwang-irrem arrpenh. Arrpenhelant iterlarem. (T) *Two drunk people have a fight. One forgets all about it and only the other remembers.*
SEE ALSO anngwa, anik, parlk

angwang-ilelhem (W,T) *vi.*
make yourself forget about something ◆ 'Rrwek ayeng angwang-ilelherlaney kwenh.' Kel ra nekeleth apek atanthem, wal angwang-ilelherlanem ra. *'Wait while I make myself forget.' Then she burns holes in seeds to make necklaces, so that she can make herself forget about it.*

angwarak (W) bush bean vine SEE UNDER **angerak**

angwarem *vt.*
1. copy someone or something, imitate someone ◆ Unta ayenh angwaremel iylteynepeynem, angka atyenhel ant unta angwareparemel angkep-angkem. (St) *You are swearing at me and copying what I say, you are just saying what I say.* ◆ Ina angwaremel akin arlkeny yanh arrernepernem. Nhenh unta atyenh arep-arem angwareynepeynem. Unta ayenh angwareparem, angwaremel anteyarl atyenh arlkeny nhenh angwaremel unta mpwarep-arem. (St) *They copy designs as well. You might look at mine and go along copying it. You are copying me, copying my designs and painting them.*
2. want something (similar to the thing you see) ◆ Manterr nhenh-lkwer apek angwaremel angkem, 'Atyeng anthay kwenh, mantarr mwerr kwenh!' *[If you] see a really nice dress and you would like one like it you might say, 'Give it to me, give me that lovely dress!'* ◆ Mwetek yanh angwareparemel tha. (St) *I want a car just like that one.*
3. catch something (a disease); become infected with sickness or disease ◆ Tharl angwarek arrpenh-kenh tywen. (T) *I became infected with another person's sores.* ◆ Rlkert arrpenh rlkert-irrerleng angwarem arrpenhel. (Sa) *One person catches the sickness that the other person has.* ◆ Not angath anetyeh, ngwenh angwaretyenh. (M) *Don't sit close or you'll become infected.*
= warrernem, arlepewem
SEE ALSO antelhem, atwarem

angwarlp (T,E) *n.*
good solid shade, thick shade, lush growth ◆ Ulya angwarlp yanh-warl alheyew angerr-warl. (St) *Let's go to that thick shade over there.*
= angkwelk, yar-yar

angwarlp-irrem (T,E) *vi.*
grow thick or bushy (hair or plants), grow long (hair) ◆ Angwarlp-irrek nhenhan kel arna yanh-arey atyenh, kwaty-penh. (St) *After the rain these plants of mine have grown lush.* ◆ Alta angwarlp, akekarl-penh apek, arratyarl anek ap alta, akelhekarl penh — renh anem angwarlp-irrem. (St) *The hair is thick, maybe after being cut, after being straight — then it grows thick.*
= angkwelk-irrem

-angwel-angwel (E) *n.ending*
An expression of sympathy or endearment; 'Poor thing', 'Poor bugger', 'Dear thing' ◆ Akuny-amperl kwenh artwampw-amperl akuny kwenh. Artwampw-**angwel-angwel** apetyem, akuny. (St) *The poor thing, the poor old man. The poor old man is coming.* ◆ Arengk ampw**angwel-angwel** atyenh apetyem. Akuny-amperl. *My poor old dog is coming. Poor thing.*
SEE ALSO -angwen-angwen, akeweny, -amperl, -apenh, -awern

angwely, akngwely (E) *n.*
dog ◆ Angwely map altywernerl-anem antyamel. (M) *The dogs crouched on the bed.*
= arengk

-angwen-angwen (T,E) *n.ending*
An expression of sympathy or endearment; 'Poor thing', 'Poor bugger', 'Dear one', 'Dear thing' ◆ Arengk apek atyenh ampw**angwen-angwen** atyenh arrangkw-irrekarl arengk-**angwen-angwen**. *My poor old dog died.*

SEE ALSO -angwel-angwel, akeweny, -amperl, -apenh, -awern

angwenh *n.*

1. 'Who?', 'Which person?' ◆ Angwenhel renh tey itek kwaty-kwaty — *no tea leaf* anengk arrernek, *strong* mpwaretyek? (T) *Who made this weak tea — not putting lots of tea-leaves in to make it strong?* ◆ Angwenhan yanhan angwelyel arlkwerrpel-nhwerrerreperrem? (M) *Who were the dogs barking at?*

2. 'Whatever', 'What-d'ye-call-it', 'What's-his-name' (said when the speaker is not sure of the name of something or has temporarily forgotten it) ◆ Rlterrp atwem angwenh, kayl apek, alakenh akin ilem, althartek apek. (St) *[They] rattle the what's-his-name, the boomerangs, at the* althart *ceremony.* ◆ Tha awetyakenh, Irrkwerteth angwenh apekarl angkep-angkem, Tyapaney apek — angkep-angkem awetyakenh, alhwerrkert. (St) *I can't understand, Italian or Japanese or whatever they're talking — it sounds all mixed up to me.*

SEE ALSO wenh, ilek, nthakenh, nthanh

angwenhant angwenh *n.*

whoever, whichever people, various people ◆ Angwenhant angwenhant apetyek. (St) *Various people came.*

angwenh-irrem *vi.*

become 'whatever', go or become a certain way (said when the speaker is not sure how to express what they mean) ◆ Mwetek apek mpwep angwenh-irrem, anety-irrem, *somewhere*-warl apek alhem-arleng. (P) *The car might, whatever, break down while on the way to somewhere.*

angwenh-akwey, angwenh-akey (W,T) *n.*

Something said when the speaker is not sure of the name of something or has temporarily forgotten it; 'What's-his-name', 'What-d'ye-call-it', 'Thingummybob', 'Thingummyjig' ◆ Kwerenh angwenh-akey, mwer — rarl ilem 'ampweyampw'. (P) *Her what's-his-name, son-in-law — he's the one that says 'ampweyampw'.* ◆ Anwerneh mpwaretyam alakenh amangkelh-ilek alakenhel-iperr, arnwety angwenh-akeyel-iperrel athep-atherl. *Not* mern perlawel, itya. (N) *[They] made it for us like that and that's how we grew up, from grinding those what's-his-name seeds. We didn't grow up on flour, not at all.*

= wenh-akwey

angwenh-athew (W,T)

'What is it?', 'What's its name?' (when trying to remember something) ◆ Urrek, ayeng iterrey amparr. Angwenh-athew? Angwenh-athew? (M) *Wait while I think first. What is it? What is it?*

= wenh-athew

angwenh-apatherr (W,T) *n.*

1. 'What skin?', 'What is [a person's] skin name?' ◆ Angwenh-apatherr ntwam? (M) *What skin are you?*

2. 'Whatever it is', 'What's-his-name'

= wenh-apatherr

SEE ALSO angwenh

angwenh-penh *n.*

from whatever (said when the speaker is not sure of the name of something or has temporarily forgotten it) ◆ Arrwekelenyel mapelarl atnyenek itepenh, angwenh-penh, akekarl-penh, alta-penh. *Rabbit*, tyerrty-kenh apek alakenh. (St) *The olden-time people had necklaces made from whatever, from hair. Rabbit hair or human hair.*

SEE ALSO -penh[1]

angwenh-iperr *n.* = **angwenh-penh**

SEE ALSO iperr

angwenm (W) something that is found in a place SEE UNDER **angwerrm**

angwenthangw *n.* [RESPECT LANGUAGE]

'Who?' This word is used when a person is not sure of the identity of a person or group of people, and they want to ask respectfully in case they are in an avoidance relationship to any of them. ◆ Angwenthangw anetyepetyemay? Angwenthangw ahanety-alhetyelay? (Sa) *Who is that there? Who is that going?* ◆ Yalengarl apetyewarrern angwenthangw kwenh? (M) *Who are those people who just arrived?*

SEE ALSO angwenh, wenh, ilek

angwenthangwek (E) *n.*

'Who for?', 'To whom?' [RESPECT LANGUAGE] ◆ Angwenthangkwek-arleng ntan angkepangkem? (St) *Who are you talking to?*

angwerl *n.*

cool

SEE ALSO irrernt, kernt, anyartey, anyel, arlkarl[1], atheperr

angwerleny *n.* = **angwerl** ◆ Lywel angwerl-irrerl-alhem, kel angwerlenyem alhem. (T) *Cool down in the shade, and then go on when [you're] feeling cool.*

angwerl-irrem *vi.*

get cool, cool down (food) ◆ Anwenth angwerl amparr irrem — walyel-ayel arrernem angwerl-irretyeh. (N) *The meat cools down first — it is put on the branches to cool down.*

= anyartey-irrem

SEE ALSO irrernt-irrem

angwerleny-irrem *vi.* = **angwerl-irrem** ◆ Ayeng angwerleny-irretyek lywel anemel, twernelarl ampem-arleng. (T) *I am going to sit under the shade to cool down because I was so hot in the sun.* ◆ Menty, mpwank angwerleny-irrey aketyeh-anngernt. (T) *Leave it to cool down before you cut it.*

angwerl-ilem *vt.*
make something cool, cool something down ◆ Angwerl-iletyeh kwaty kerntel tey. (N) *Cool the tea down with cold water.*
SEE ALSO irrernt-ilem
CAN SOUND A BIT LIKE ngwelh-ilem *'ask someone to go with you'*

angwerleny-ilem *vt.* = **angwerl-ilem** ◆ Mern yanh angwerleny-ilek waly-warn arrernemel. *That damper was put on the leaves to cool it down.*

angwerr *n.*
mid afternoon (about 3 o'clock) ◆ Angwerr anem irreynepeynem. (St) *Now it's getting later in the day.*

angwerrel, ingwerrel *n.*
in the mid afternoon (about 3 o'clock) ◆ Angwerrel anem anwantherr alpey. (St) *Now we'll go back in the mid-afternoon.*
= atwerrp

angwerr-irrem, angwerrel-irrem *vi.*
set (sun), get late in the day ◆ Aherrk angwerrel-irrem, an ankwem intem aherlkentyem alhem. (M) *It gets late in the day, and then [you] go to sleep when the sun goes down.*
= atwerrp-irrem

angwerr-angwerr *n.*
late afternoon, early evening ◆ Rntwetyart rntwetyart anwern akwek map rntwetyart rntwetyart rntwetyart, angwerr-angwerrek-artwety. (N) *Us little ones used to dance and dance and dance until evening.* ◆ Aherrk angwerr-angwerr anem aherrk irrpetyek anem, angwerr-angwerr. (St) *When it gets late in the day the sun goes down.*

angwerr-angwerr-irrem *vi.*
become late in the afternoon; become evening ◆ Angwerr-angwerr-irrem lyet war. (T) *Soon it will be late afternoon.*
= atwerrp-irrem, ngway-ngway-irrem

angwerrel-penh (E), **akngwerrel-penh** (E) *n.*
east ◆ Akngwerrel-penh-they, akngerrakw-they ayeng apety-alpek. (St) *I came back from the east.*
= ingerr, angerrakw

angwerrm, angwenm (W) *n.*
1. something that is found in a place ◆ 'Ngka, pwelertek, annga anthetyek, urrpety apek.' Kel renh inerl-alhem. Ker angwerrm atwety-alheyamel. (T) *'Give me a few bullets.' Then he gets them and goes off. Then he goes and shoots the game that he finds.*
2. be somewhere ◆ Nthenhem alhekay? Tyerrty angwerrm anemaw! (T) *Where's he gone? That person's right here!* ◆ Wal anwern angkenty-alpem mapek, *'Eh,* aywang nheng angwerrm anep-anem kwenh'. (P) *Well we go back and tell everybody, 'Hey, that old man is sitting down right here'.*
3. body, uncut carcass, game (animal) ◆ Atwek ina, kwart arlka ingkerrek ina angernek, angwerrm an *all*, ina apek atyerremel arlkwek. (M) *They killed it, and then they took all the eggs and the carcass back to cook and eat.*

angwerrm-irrem *vi.*
be 'found' or spiritually conceived in a particular place or country, come from a particular place or country, be born in a particular place. An Anmatyerr person has a special connection to the place where they are 'spiritually conceived' and to the Dreamings from that place. This refers not to the baby's actual conception or birth itself but rather to the moment of 'quickening' when the entry of an ancestral spirit into a woman animates the unborn child. ◆ Arelh Pwerrerlel anew akem artwang Penangk. Kwer kwer-atherrenh angwerrm-irrem Pengart map. (T) *A Pwerrerl woman's husband is Penangk. Their children will be born Pengart.* ◆ Ayeng angwerrm-irrek mer atyenhel. (M) *I came from my country.* ◆ Anngirrekek-amparr, angwerrm antem irrek kel pepey akwek akethel anem angernem. (T) *At first the baby is 'found', then after being spiritually conceived the little baby is brought out into the world.*
SEE ALSO anngirrem, anganem

angwerrm-ilem *vt.*
1. 'find' a child in a place (spiritual conception) ◆ Ampa nhenhel angwerrm-angwerrm-ilek, alkngirrek, *Stirling*-el angwerrm-angwerrm-ilek-arey, wal itna alpetyakenh Atnangker-warl. (St) *The children who were 'found' here, the ones that were found at Stirling, well they didn't go back to Atnangker.*
2. find something, come across something ◆ Lyelyer-wem kwaty anem angwerrm-ilem. 'Kwaty angernem nhenh, kwaty akernarl lyelyer-wem tha.' (St) *Poking around for water and then finding some. 'I'm digging the water*

here, that I found close to the surface.'
◆ Ngkerlp angwerrm-ilek nhenh-antey atyenh. (T) *I found my tobacco here.*
angwerrmelh-ilem *vt.* = **angwerrm-ilem**

angwert (E) *n.*
large, dark-coloured bush potato tuber (?)
◆ Mern anaty angwert, urrper-wemarl ra. (St) *The large bush potato makes the earth lift up and crack.*
SEE ALSO anthal, urrper

angwethek (T), **akngwethek** (E), **apmwethek** (E) *n.*
water-holding frog (*Cyclorana platycephalus*) (?). Also referred to as *ker angwethek*. ◆ Ker akin akngwethek, iylpek arlka thelem, iylparl arwengk-irremel, arert-irreman, iylpel arlkwep-arlkwem, wal iylpewarl thelem annga apek mwerr-ilem. Mpwa kwerenh. (St) *The* akngwethek *frog is edible as well, and it's also used if your ears are aching or if you can't hear properly. Well you pour some of its urine into your ears. That can also be used to make eyes better as well.*
SEE ALSO mpwelengk, mpwekenh, alemerr

angwey-ilem (E) *vt.*
cook something [RESPECT LANGUAGE]
SEE ALSO irrkwertem, irrkertem, ulerrtyem, arntampernem, item, arrtyem, ampernem, ampem

angweyep-angwey, akngweyep-akngwey (E) *adv.*
not taking notice, not hearing what is said, preoccupied, not thinking about anything apart from your own immediate concerns, not worried about anything or anybody else
◆ Angweyep-angwey nhenh arelh anep-anem itirretyakenh. (M) *This woman here is not taking any notice, not thinking.* ◆ Iwenh-apert unta angweyep-angwey anep-anem? Apal war unta anerl-anem iwenh-apert? *No* unta arlkep-arlkem ampa ngkwenhek apek. (T) *Why are sitting down preoccupied and not thinking about anyone else? What's up? You don't even sing out to your own children.*
SEE ALSO anngwa, akwenp-akwenp, akwenpety-akwenp

anhamp-anhamp (T) soft and squishy (of food)
SEE UNDER **anhwemp-anhwemp**

anharrel alhem (T) *vi.*
follow somebody

anhelengkw-ayerr (E) *n.*
emu [RESPECT LANGUAGE] (note Alyawarr *anhelengkw* 'emu') ◆ Anhelengkw yanhentyak tha amely-aketyek (Sa) *I want to eat that emu meat [belonging to respect kin].*
SEE ALSO ankerr, arnwa

anhelhem *vi.*
be rude or mean, be cruel or nasty ◆ Ampa arrpenhek apek anhelherl-anem atwerl-anem ampa akwek arrpenh anhelherl-anem, anhelhepelherlek atantherl-anemel, *tease*-em. *Going along being nasty to another little child, hitting them and poking them and teasing them.*
◆ Kwer anhelhem kwer arrpenheh. (M) *A child is being mean to another.*
CAN SOUND A BIT LIKE anelhem *'to frighten'*
anhelhenty *n.*
naughty, mean, rude, cruel, nasty
◆ Arrarletyel tha iltem arelh nhenh anhelhenty angerr. Iltek anem tha arrarletyel akuny-amperl. (St) *I am growling and swearing at this nasty woman. I swore at the poor thing.*
SEE ALSO ngkwanty, anngernt, ltyernt

anhem, anhwem (W,T), **atnhem** (E) *vt.*
fall (rain); rain (to rain) ◆ Kwatyel anhem. (Sa) *It's raining.* ◆ Tyerrtyel ltewem artetyerretyerr kwaty angerrem anhem. (M) *If a person throws something at the willie wagtail then there will be a lot of rain.* ◆ Kwatyelam anhem, kenh map akenh irrperl-irrperlem-ilem kwenem alartem. Irnmerr arlka thelelhem antyweng. (N) *It rains and everybody goes inside and sits down. The drops of water fall down from the shelter.*
SEE ALSO urntem, anyem1, kwaty arrwerelhem
anhelhem *vi.*
wet oneself to cool down ◆ Kwatyel anhelhem tyerrty ingkerr twernelarl ampem. (M) *Wetting the whole body with water to cool down after getting hot in the sun.*
= akarl-welhem
SEE ALSO irrpelh-ilelhem

anherr, anherrey (E) *n.kin*
1. woman's mother-in-law
2. woman's daughter-in-law
anherr-anherr *n.kin*
woman's mother-in-law, etc. This may be a more affectionate or respectful way of talking than using *anherr*. Some speakers use this word for either 'woman's mother-in-law' or 'woman's daughter-in-law' rather than for both.
anherraty *n.kin*
my/our *anherr*
anherrengkw *n.kin*
your *anherr*
anherreyekw (E), **anherrikw** *n.kin*
her/their *anherr*
anherrekw (W,T), **anherrek** (W) *n.kin*
1. your *anherr*
2. her/their *anherr* ◆ Yanhan ngkwengenh

anherrekwam, artwang ngkwengenhel-arlengarl anem. (T) *There is your daughter-in-law, who is married to your son.*
anherr-nheng *n.kin*
a group of two or more people who are related to each other as *anherr*
anherr-intyerr *n.kin* = **anherr-nheng**
anherr-nheng-arey *n.kin*
a group of more than two people who are related to each other as *anherr*
anherr-nheng atherr *n.kin*
a person together with one of their *anherr*
anherr-parety *n.kin*
respectful or 'sorry way' of talking about someone's *anherr*
SEE ALSO -parety
anherr-ankethenh *n.kin*
1. having a close *anherr* still alive
2. someone who is always with their *anherr*
SEE ALSO -ankethenh

anhwem (W,T) fall (rain) SEE UNDER **anhem**

anhwemp-anhwemp (W,T), **anhamp-anhamp** (T) *n.*
soft and squishy (of food) ◆ Mern anhwemp-anhwemp. (M) *Soft food.*
SEE ALSO alyemp-alyemp[1]
anhwemp-anhwemp-irrem (W,T) *vi.*
get squashed, break into bits
anhwemp-anhwemp-ilem (W,T) *vt.*
squash something ◆ Kwerel anhwemp-anhwemp-ilek mern atyengenh, akerneng anetyam. (M) *The child sat on top of my bread and squashed it.*

anhwerlk (W,T) *n.*
satisfied (after being hungry), full (stomach). Also referred to as *anert anhwerlk.*
= anerteng
SEE ALSO nthat, alywer[2]
CAN SOUND A BIT LIKE anwerlk[2] *'buttocks'*
anhwerlk-irrem (W,T) *vi.*
feel satisfied from eating, become full (stomach)
anhwerlk-ilem (W,T) *vt.*
feed someone or something, feed someone up
anhwerlk-anhwerlk-ilem (W,T) *vt.*
feed someone or something, feed someone up

anhwerrem, atnhwerrem (E) *vt.*
clear (the ground for a camp or to collect bush foods such as *ahakey* plums); grade a road; make ground level ◆ Ankwa ayntetyek atnhwerrem. Ipert-ilemel anem anenyek akwel. (Sa) *Level the ground so that [we] can sleep. Make a hole for the hip.* ◆ Apmer aketh-ilemel atnhwerrem, thenkarr-kety. *Clear the camp, because of the prickles.*
SEE ALSO aketh-ilem, iylperrem, alal-wem

anhwerrm-anhwerr (W) *n.*
cracked
anhwerrm-anhwerr-irrem *vi.*
get cracked ◆ Mern nhenh anhwerrm-anhwerr-irrern rwel. (M) *This damper became cracked in the fire.*

anhwert, atnhwert (E) *adv.*
folded up, in a bundle (?)
SEE ALSO antyakwer, artaper
anhwert angem, atnhwert angem (E)
carry something slung across shoulders (angem *'carry', 'take'*) ◆ Aherr apek atnhwert akngem untyel. Ker arlety atnhwert akngem, untyel. (St) *Carrying the kangaroo slung across the shoulders. Carrying the uncooked carcass, across the shoulders, across the back of the neck.* ◆ Ker aherr atnhwert akngem, arrengey atyenhel-arey *all day* atnhwert akngetyam. Arrpenh akngetyam nhenh-angkwerrarl interl-apem atnhwert interlapetyek. Kapertel arrpenh. (St) *All my grandfathers always carried kangaroos slung across their shoulders. Some were carried lying across [here], lying curled up as they went along. Others were carried on the head.*
SEE ALSO ntywel angem, alpalyel angem, intarlp angem, ntwarlp angem, intwerl angem, aylpwar angem
anhwert-ilem, atnhwert-ilem (E) *vt.*
roll something up, bundle something up, make something into a bundle ◆ Atnhwert-ilem. War ayernem, *string*-el apek, arratherrkel apek, ker aherr, akngetyek anem. (St) *Roll the kangaroo up. Just tie it up with string or with snake vine and then carry it back.*
SEE ALSO artaper-ilem, artaper-wem, ayernem, akwengerr-werl-alhem, rwelemap-ilem
anhwert inem (E), **atnhwert inem** (E)
lift someone or something up (inem *'get'*)

anik (E), **atnik** (E) *n.*
1. quiet, non-aggressive, harmless, not dangerous, timid ◆ Ahelengkw anetyang untarl anikarl. (Sa) *You're not aggressive, you're harmless.* ◆ Arengk atnik, ahelengkw anetyakenh. (Sa) *A quiet dog, not aggressive.*
2. someone who isn't good at hunting or collecting food
atna anik (E), **atna atnik** (E)
scared, cowardly (atna *'arse'*)

Aniltji SEE UNDER **Aneltyey**

animampel (T,E), **atnimampel** (E) *n.*
someone who is cursed, someone who is going to get into trouble or get very sick (ana, atna *'arse'*). A swear word. ◆ 'Animampel alherlana kwenh!' Atywetyekarl ra alhem

akwenp. (T) *'Off you go and get into trouble — you're cursed!' And they just head off to fight regardless.*
SEE ALSO akwetyerretyerr

aninem gut (an animal) SEE UNDER **anenem**

aningkerr (E) we (more than two) SEE UNDER anwengkerr

anirnterrm-irnterr (E), **atnirnterrm-irnterr** (E) *n.*
collarbone
= alkwert-alkwert
SEE ALSO kwaty-kwaty2

anka, **ankang** (W,T) *n.*
1. raw, uncooked ◆ Kwaty thelem mern ankangeh. (M) *Pour the water into the uncooked mixture.* ◆ Ker ankang rrkwerl-anem, an kelant itetyenheng ampeng-ilemel. (T) *[You] have raw meat, and you just cook a little bit.*
2. raw, green, unripe ◆ Arlkwerl-apem mern angelth *anyway* war, ampeng, anka, arnkang arlkwerl-apem. Tyerrty angety-alpem arrpenh, rwewarl. (N) *[You] can go along eating the fruits of the native pear however you want, cooked or raw. People take some of them back to cook.*
SEE ALSO arlety2, ampeng

ankarr (T,E) *n.*
juice of native citrus or bush plum fruit, *ahakey* (*Psydrax latifolia*); liquid honey from corkwood flowers, *ntywey/untyey* (*Hakea chordophylla*) ◆ Untyeyamp rrpwerl-akert aken, ankarr-akert. Kwaty-artek irremel ankarr thelelhemel. (T) *The corkwood flower has dark-coloured honey,* ankarr, *as well. It goes like water and the* ankarr *drips down.*
SEE ALSO akarr, ntyweyamp, ntyweyangkwarl, tyan
CAN SOUND A BIT LIKE arnkarr *'riverbank'*

ankel1, **ankeley** (E) *n.kin*
1. male cross-cousin (father's sister's or mother's brother's son)
2. particular male relations with the same skin as your *ankel*

ankel-ankel *n.kin*
male cross-cousin (father's sister's or mother's brother's son) etc. Some speakers say that this is a way of talking to children but others say that *ankel-ankel* is the word a woman would use to talk to or about her male cross-cousins. ◆ Ankel-ankel ampa akelyek ilem. 'Ankel-ankel ara kwenh.' (Sa) Ankel-ankel *is what is said to a little kid. 'Look at [your] cousin.'*

ankelaty *n.kin*
my/our *ankel*

ankelengkw *n.kin*
your *ankel*

ankelikw (E), **ankeleyekw** (E) *n.kin*
his/her/their *ankel*

ankelekw (W,T) *n.kin*
1. your *ankel*
2. his/her/their *ankel*

ankel-nheng *n.kin*
a group of two or more people who are related to each other as *ankel*

ankel-intyerr *n.kin* = **ankel-nheng**

ankel-nheng-arey *n.kin*
a group of more than two people who are related to each other as *ankel*

ankel-nheng atherr *n.kin*
a person together with one of their *ankel* ◆ Ankel-nheng atherr alherrek. (P) *Two cousins went.*

ankel-aparety *n.kin*
respectful or 'sorry way' of talking about someone's *ankel*
SEE ALSO -aparety

ankel-ankethenh *n.kin*
1. having a close *ankel* still alive
2. someone who is always with their *ankel* ◆ Ankel-ankethenh ayengan apetyek mernek. (Sa) *I came with my cousin to get food.*
SEE ALSO -ankethenh

ankel akerrem
be full male cross-cousins to each other (sons of a brother and a sister) ◆ Ankel-nheng atherr alhek — ratherrarl ankel akerrek atherr-antey. (St) *Two male cross-cousins went — both of them are full cross-cousins.*
SEE ALSO urnek-iwerrenty, altyel akerrem

-ankel2 (E) *n.ending*
when, in that time, at that time. ◆ Awenk-**ankel**. *At the time when [you] were a young girl.*

Ankelehenh (W) *n.*
Buggy Hole, in the Coniston/Napperby area

ankeley (E) male cross-cousin SEE UNDER **ankel**1

Ankemal (W) *n.*
name of place near Yippee dam, south of Mt Allan community

anker1 (E) *n.*
1. spinifex wax, spinifex resin (*Triodia pungens*) ◆ Anker anem renh ikelh mpwarem, aywert-penh. (St) *The spinifex resin from the spinifex is made into a lump.*
= tyalangk
SEE ALSO arletyety
2. adze with handle joined on with spinifex wax • SEE ALSO kantyengarr, kwempalth
3. lump of wax or resin-like substance at the base of the native bees' hive • SEE ALSO alpma, arwengalker
4. batik wax

ankerel-irrem (E) *vi.*
become bereaved or mourn (especially for son

or daughter) ◆ Amikw ankerel-irrem ampekikw, atwek-arlek. (Sa) *The mother is mourning for her child that was killed.* (?)

anker-athek-irrem (T,E) *vi.*
become bereaved, become bereaved of a son or daughter ◆ Anker-athek *daughter* apek *lose-*em ilek, anker-athek-irrek yanh. *Like* ankerel anem atwelhemarl ra. Ankerel ra atwelhek. *When him lose-*em *daughter son* apek, *well* ankerelarl akuny atwelhem. (St) *She has lost her daughter. She hits herself with the [lump of] spinifex resin. When she loses a daughter or a son the poor thing hits herself with the* anker.
= ywerlt-irrem
SEE ALSO inpert-irrem, warlekwert-irrem, itelhem, arrtyelhem

anker[2] (E) *n.*
unripe fruit of the split-jack (*Capparis lasiantha*)
SEE ALSO alwerr, arlety

anker-anker[1] (E) *n.*
Eurasian coot (*Fulica atra*)

anker-anker[2] (E), **atnker-atnker** (E) *n.*
1. a type of spinifex (*Triodia triaristata* (?))
2. curry wattle, spine-leaf wattle, flying-saucer bush (*Acacia spondylophylla*). A sticky shrub to 1 m high which grows on rocky slopes and has leaves with a curry smell.

3. type of sedge, ankar-ankar (*Cyperus ixiocarpus*). A sticky medicinal grass to 0.5 m high which grows in creeks and has black seeds. ◆ Anker-anker ikwerel alhewelhetyek. (Sa) *You wash yourself with the* anker-anker.

ankerl *n.*
1. someone who has married the 'wrong' way; marrying, sleeping with, or acting flirtatiously towards inappropriate kin (i.e. someone who is not related in the proper way by Aboriginal Law) ◆ Ankerl nhenh — mwerewek anew, arrwempewek anew apek. (M) *This person is* ankerl — *they've married their son-in-law or their brother.*
SEE ALSO iyterrk
2. greedy; not giving things to other people ◆ Ankerlel arlkwep-arlkwem, tyerrkel, arrpenhek anthetyakenh. (St) *That person is eating greedily and not giving anything to anyone else.* ◆ Tyerrty nhenh ankerl apelay, ywarn angkem nheng mern apek ker. 'Ker anthay.' 'No.' Ankerlam tyerrty nhenh. (M) *Everybody knows that this person is really greedy and [you] ask them in vain for bread or meat. 'Give me some meat.' 'No.' That person is greedy.*
3. stubborn, uncooperative, keeping on doing something ◆ Ampa akwek ankerl artnep-artnem. (St) *The little kid keeps on crying.*
4. lump or gall on a tree, a knot in wood; wart. Warts are believed to be caused by the calling of a son-in-law or mother-in-law's name, or by the marrying of inappropriate kin. ◆ Arnel-arleng anem ankerl. Iltyel-arleng anem ankerl. (St) *There are lumps on trees. Warts are on the hand.* ◆ Arnang ankerl-akertan ilem. Arnang irnem, wal ankerl angerr-akert. (M) *It is said that trees have* ankerl. *Some trees have lots of lumps on them.* ◆ Ankerl lyapem mey-meyarl atnewem-penharl ankerl lyapem. *Or* mey-mey apek anew akem alerekikw apek anew akem, wal ankerlarl. (St) *People get warts growing on them from saying the name of their mother-in-law or son-in-law. Someone who has married their mother-in-law or son-in-law or their son or daughter is* ankerl.
SEE ALSO mwenth
CAN SOUND A BIT LIKE ankel[1] *'male cross-cousin';* ankel[2] *'when', 'in that time'*

ankerlewarr *n.*
someone who has married the 'wrong' way ◆ Ankerlel anem, tyerrk-warl nta irrpek kwenh. Ankerlewarr ntan kwenh, Mwerekwarl kwenh. (T) *You have married the wrong way. You are* ankerlewarr *because you have married your son-in-law.*

ankerl angerr (W) = **ankerlewarr**

ankerl-irrem (W,T) *vi.*
1. be stubborn or uncooperative, refuse to do something ◆ Kwer apek nta ilem *something* inetyeh, *and he* akangkwerrerl itya. *Him* ankerl anthwerr irrerl. (M) *You ask the child to go and get something, and he doesn't take any notice. He gets really stubborn.*
SEE ALSO anwernt-irrem, mwernt-irrem, arlelty-irrem
2. be greedy
3. marry the 'wrong' way

ankerl-ankerl *n.*
1. being wrong for marriage, being the wrong skin for someone ◆ Nheng mpwenyel apek angem ra. Wal arrpenh mapel apek ina iltemer. 'Ankerl-ankerlam ntwan *wrong skin-*ek ntwa angwenhek-irrerl-anetyek, alperl-anetyek.' (P) *He might race off with her. Well then other people might growl at him. 'You are the wrong skin, you're doing whatever, going off with someone who is the wrong skin for you.'*

2. stubborn, not wanting to move
3. lumpy, covered in knots or lumps ◆ Arna ankerl-ankerl-warl antyetyek, arntwerrkemel. (St) *Climbing up the lumpy tree, holding onto it.*
atna ankerl-ankerl (E)
someone who has married the 'wrong' way

ankerr *n.*
emu (*Dromaius novaehollandiae*) ◆ Ankerrel arlkwerl-apem mern atyankern, mern ngkwerrm. (M) *The emu goes along eating mistletoe fruits.*
= arley
ankerr akwek (W,T)
emu chick (akwek *'small'*)
= alywer[1], artelh[1]
ankerr akwerrk (W,T) = **ankerr akwek**
(akwerrk[1] *'young animal'*)

Ankerrapw (T,E) *n.*
the name of a place near the location of the old Utopia Homestead (Angarapa Aboriginal Land Trust area) (apwa *'emu feathers'*). See map p. viii.
SEE ALSO ankerr, apwa
ankerr-ankerr (W) *n.*
1. heavy-soil handflower, tobacco handflower (*Goodenia lunata*). A herb about 10 cm high with yellow flowers and leaves shaped a bit like an emu's foot.
= ankerringk, ntywenart
2. type of solanum (?) (*Solanum orbiculatum* ssp. *orbiculatum* (?))
ankerringk (T,E) *n.*
heavy-soil handflower, tobacco handflower (*Goodenia lunata*) (ankerr *'emu'*; ingka *'foot'*). A herb about 10 cm high with yellow flowers and leaves shaped a bit like an emu's foot.
◆ 'Ankerringk' ap ra, ngkwerlpek-athen, ngkwerlp anem rarey ngkwerlp-kwenyel renh arlkwetyart, arnmenyel. Urrelty akemel anyem, renh itetyart. Arlkwetyart anem ina. (St) *It's called 'ankerringk' and it could be mistaken for tobacco. They mixed it with ashes and used it as a tobacco when they didn't have other sorts of tobacco. They cut the witchetty bush twigs and cooked them to make ashes and then chewed it.*
= ntywenart
SEE ALSO ankerr-ankerr

ankerrayt (T,E) *n.*
grub from the coolibah tree, *ankerrmern* (*Eucalyptus coolabah* ssp. *arida*)
= anwerrngaty
SEE ALSO ankwerrern

ankerrmern, ankerrmen, atnkerrmern (E) *n.*
coolibah (*Eucalyptus coolabah* ssp. *arida*). Tree to 12 m high, with creamy white flowers and small seed capsules. Has edible seeds.
◆ Arntap iterl-anem arnmeny akin, arnmeny ngkerlp-kenh antyerrkarl irrek arnmeny. Ankerrmern atanthem atanthem atanthem rwel item arnmeny mparem. (N) *The bark is burnt to make ashes for tobacco. The dry bark is used for ashes. The bark is stripped from the coolibah tree and then burnt to make ashes.*
◆ Tyap ankwerrern, ankerrmern inetyenheng tyap renh arlkwetyenheng. Anyematyart akin ankwerrern. Lywenkel tyarr-inetyart. (N) *The grub called 'ankwerrern' is collected from the coolibah tree and eaten. It is similar to a witchetty grub. We used to pull it out [from the hole in the trunk] with a grass hook.*
SEE ALSO ankwerrern, ankerrayt

ankert[1], angkert *n.*
rain cloud (white). Also referred to as *kwaty ankert*. ◆ Kwaty arrwerelhem ankerteng. (M) *The rain is falling from the clouds.* ◆ Ankert amparr anem, mperlker amparr anem, mperlker-penh rrpwerlem irrem, wal anhemem kwatyel. (M) *At first there are the* ankert *clouds, white at first, and after that the clouds darken and then it rains.*
SEE ALSO kwenpay, aperler, awerrepweng, mwekelengk, rlweyang, kwaty akwerrk, kwaty angkarl

ankert[2] (W,T) *n.*
cadney lizard, central bearded dragon, carney, jew lizard (*Pogona vitticeps*). Also referred to as *ker ankert*. ◆ Ankertel arerl-anem kwaty ankert. (N) *The bearded dragon lizard looks out for* ankert *clouds.*
= amwely

ankert-wem, ankert-iwem (E) *vt.*
1. push someone or something, roll something along, tip something over, turn something over ◆ Tyerrty apek alakenh, 'Iyntwarr apek irray'. Ankert-ankert-wem. Arengk apek iyntwarr artek intetyek, ankert-wemarl yanh. (St) *A person might say this, 'Move out of the way'. [Then they] give them a bit of a push. [You] might push the dog out of the way so that it sleeps further away.* ◆ Mwetek mwerr unta ankert-iwek. (Sa) *You rolled a good car.* ◆ Tha ankert-wemel atwek. (St) *I hit them and pushed them over.*
SEE ALSO pewetyem-ilem
2. trip someone up ◆ Arwerlel ayenh ankert-wek. (Sa) *The branch tripped me up.*
SEE ALSO ahertety-iwem, arnpakem, anampart-wem

ankert-ankert-wem (E) *vt.*
give something a bit of a push

ankertwakertwak (W) spotted nightjar SEE UNDER **angkertakwertak**

-ankethenh *k.ending*
1. Goes on the end of kin terms to show that the speaker, or the person being referred to, still has that particular close kin relation (i.e. that relation is still alive). This ending may sometimes sound like *+enkethenh*, particularly when it goes on short forms of kin terms such as *k+* 'elder brother' or *m+* 'mother'. ◆ Arreng-**ankethenh**-kweny irrek ayeng. (St) *My grandfathers are no longer alive [lit. 'I became someone without an alive grandfather'].* ◆ Amp**enkethenh** ayeng, ampaty atyenh *there.* (St) *I have a child, my child is there.* ◆ Anherrey-**ankethenh** ayeng angerr. (St) *I have lots of daughters-in-law.* ◆ **Menkethenh** kweny. *Mummy*-ek alhampw. Mam uyerrekeng. *No* m**enkethenh** arey *no mum*, alhampw. Alhamp ayeng. *No* ayn**enkethenh**. Akngey ingwerel arey ap ayenh arntarnt-aretyang. *No* nyany-**ankethenh**. Arrangkw. Aperley anetyang, *no* aperl-**ankethenh**. Perley atyenh uyerrek. *My mother is not alive. I've lost my mother. She's passed away. I have no mother and no father still alive. My other fathers don't look after me. I have no granny left. Nothing. My father's mother is not still alive. My father's mother passed away.*
2. Goes on the end of kin terms to show that the person being referred to is together with that particular relation all the time. ◆ Kwer yanh awenh-**ankethenh**. *That kid is always with her auntie.* ◆ **Mankethenh** angerr kwer nhenh. (M) *This kid is a real mummy's girl.*

ankety, arnkety *n.*
scarf, headscarf (from English 'handkerchief') ◆ Anketyel kapert ayernelhem. (M) *Tying the headscarf round [your] head.*

ankey *adv.*
asking for something; begging for something; wanting something from someone; bludging off someone ◆ Ayeng ankey alhem ngkweng-warn, ayeng alhemem ankey, angayelarl awelhem. Ayeng alhem ankey ngkweng-warn. (T) *I'm going to go to you and ask for something because I am feeling hungry. I'm going to go and bludge off you.* ◆ Ankey ayeng alhem mernek, ngkwerlpek apek, ankey inerl-alhetyek. (St) *I'm going to go and bludge some food and tobacco off someone.*
SEE ALSO rnter

ankey inkem
ask someone for something, demand something off somebody (inkem *'ask for something'*) ◆ Ngkwerlpek ankey inkety-alhem. (St) *[I'm] going to go and ask [that person] for tobacco.*
SEE ALSO aparelhem

ankey angkem (W)
challenge someone to fight with you (angkem *'talk'*) ◆ 'Arelh tyerrelhety-alhay, ilern atwerretyeh.' Ayeng ankey angkek. (M) *'Come out here and fight with me.' I asked that woman to fight with me.*

ankeyel arlkwem
1. ask if you can eat (?) (arlkwem *'eat'*) ◆ Thang ankeyel arlkwety-alhem kwer-henh mern. (M) *I'm going to go and ask if I can eat some of the kids' food.*
2. eat greedily, eat secretively, eat food that you have taken without asking ◆ Ankeyel arlkwem ipmengel anthetyakenh ra. (St) *That person is greedily eating and not giving anything to anyone else.*
SEE ALSO ankerl

ankeyalth *n.*
a greedy person; someone who is always asking for something or someone who helps themself to things without asking ◆ Ankeyalth nhenh arrernelhety-alhek. Ankeyalth-kety tha akarerl-anem. (St) *That person has come to help themself to things. I've got to look after my things because of her.*

ankey-irrem (E) *vi.*
ask someone for something; be demanding, demand something off somebody ◆ Angayakw, ankeyarl irrem, arlkwetyek. (St) *That person is hungry and is demanding something to eat.*
SEE ALSO rrngwerrty-irrem

ankey-ankey-irrem *vi.*
make a particular dancing movement and hand gesture (women) when a young initiate is brought back from seclusion in the bush ◆ Arelh map ankey-ankey-irrem artwang mapel kwer angerr angetyemeh. (M) *The women dance and gesture to the men who are bringing all the young initiates [back from the bush].*

ankwa[1], ankwang (W,T) *n.*
sleep, asleep ◆ Kwer-penh ankwem yatherr interl-anem. (M) *Then the two of them were tired and went to sleep.* ◆ Ankwa aynterlanetyang — atyek-irraw, akem-irraw! (Sa) *Don't go to sleep — wake up, get up!*
SEE ALSO karr, atyek

ankwang intem (W,T), **ankwa intem** (E), **ankwayntem** (E)
go to sleep (intem[1] *'lie down'*)
ankwang angerr (W,T), **ankwa angerr** (E), **ankwa akngerr** (E)
deep sleep, fast asleep, sound asleep (angerr[1] *'a lot'*)
ankwa alert (E)
deep sleep, fast asleep, sound asleep
ankwang arralkem (W,T)
to yawn
ankwek-irrem (E) *vi.*
get sleepy, fall asleep
ankwerrem *vi.*
get sleepy, fall asleep
ankwelem, **ankwilem** (E) *vt.*
send someone to sleep, make someone sleepy, get someone to sleep ◆ Kwer akwek ankwelem. (M) *Sending the child to sleep.*
ankwathenem *vt.*
lay (baby) down to sleep, send someone to sleep (athenem *'lay someone or something down'*) ◆ Arrew-arrew-ilemel ankwathenem ampa akely inngart ankwathenem artnerl-anenty. (Sa) *Rocking a little crying baby to make it go to sleep.*
ankwapaperr (T,E) *n.*
half asleep, half awake, sleepless ◆ Ankwarl intem-penh wal ra ankwapaperr akem-irrenhem. (T) *After being asleep she gets up sleepily.*
ankwakel (E) *n.*
sleepless, insomniac, doing something all through the night ◆ Ankwakel untetyel awenkan. Ankwakel ankwa ayntetyakenh, arternp ayntetyakenh. (Sa) *The teenage girl is walking around all night without sleeping. She is not settling down, just walking around sleeplessly.* ◆ Arengkan arrpwarntarl angkem, arrpwarnt angketyel ankwakel. (Sa) *The dogs are barking all through the night.*
SEE ALSO irrkaw
ankwang (W) *n.*
a type of lizard (*Morethia* sp. (?))

ankwa[2], **ankwankw** (E), **rnkwang** (W,T), **ngkwank** (W) *n.*
glands inside mouth or under jaw ◆ Ankwa wangkem arntety-irremel, tyerrtyarl arntety-irrem, wangkemarl ra. (St) *When a person gets sick the glands inside the mouth swell up.*

ankwang (W,T) the chamber or shelf in a honeyant nest SEE UNDER **inkwa**

ankwankw (E) glands inside mouth or under jaw SEE UNDER **ankwa**[2]

ankwarn (E) 'sleep' (in the eyes when you wake up), pus SEE UNDER **arnkwarn**

ankwaty (W,T) *n.*
in a daydream, in a world of one's own, not thinking about anyone else, not doing anything ◆ Ankwaty kwenh anerl-anem rarrp akwenpeny anerl-anem. (M) *[That person] is sitting there in a world of their own, just themself, not aware of anything else.* ◆ Kwer atherr apek atwerrekety nta kwenh ankwaty anerl-anem. *No* nta apalenthwem kwereh. (M) *The two kids might be fighting but you're in a world of your own. You don't go looking for the child.*
SEE ALSO akwenpeny, ankwa[1]

ankwepenh (E) *n.*
a type of large yellow snake

ankwer (E) back of porcupine SEE UNDER **angkwer**[1]

Ankwerl (T) *n.*
1. name of a big hill west of Aileron
2. name of a place and location of an outstation on an excision from Woodgreen Station

ankwerl-alhem (E) *vi.*
go and get something [RESPECT LANGUAGE] ◆ Ankwerl-alhay rwa alep yanhenty anyem. (Sa) *Go and get that firestick from over there [from respect kin].*
SEE ALSO inerl-alhem
ankwerl-wem (E) *vt.*
go and get something for someone [RESPECT LANGUAGE] ◆ Ankwerl-waw mperlker-ayerr atyeng tha thetyek. (Sa) *Go and get me some flour so that I can make some damper.*
= aleper-ankwerl-wem
SEE ALSO inerl-wem

ankwerl-inem (W,T) *vt.*
take sides in a fight, help someone in a fight, fight on behalf of someone ◆ Ankeley atyengenh thang ankwerl-inem. (T) *I'm helping my cousin in the fight.* ◆ Arrpenh apek kwer-atherr atwerretyek, ratherr anem ankwerl-inerrem. (T) *Somebody might come to fight those two, they help one another.*
SEE ALSO irrpem
ankwerl-atwem (W,T) *vt.* = **ankwerl-inem** ◆ Thang ankwerl atwem artwang yanh, ngwenharl atwek. (T) *I'm going to fight that bloke that hit you.*
SEE ALSO artengel-arem

ankwerlay (W,T), **ankwerley** (T,E) *n.*
1. plum bush, wild plum, sandalwood (*Santalum lanceolatum*). Shrub to 3 m high, with drooping bluish green leaves, white flowers and purplish-black fruit.

2. the edible fruit of the plum bush. Also referred to as *mern ankwerlay*. ◆ Arntap-warn anwa ntywerrketyart, arntap-warn. Awantyetyart anwern, *seed*-an wetyartan. Mpank, perrap rrpwerl anthwerr akin ahakeyart. Ankwerlay. (N) *We used to mash it [the* ankwerlay *plums] up in water in the bark containers. Then we sucked on the juice, discarding the seeds. The* ankwerlay *plum is a really black colour like the* ahakey *plum.*
= alkwa

ankwernem (W,T), **rnkwenem** (W) *vt.*
1. take sides in a fight, help someone in a fight, fight on behalf of someone ◆ Artwa atherr wenh nhwerrem, *might be* artwang ankelekw apek atwem artwang anywek ankelekw. Kenh artengel-arerleng *might be* kelekw apek — *that's* ankwernem. Yatherr anem atwerrem. (M) *Two men might be fighting each other, maybe a man is fighting with his cousin or his cousin-father. And then his brother might step in and back him up, take his side — that's* ankwernem. *The two of them fight then.*
2. hit someone back, pay them back, 'square' someone back ◆ Ntwan atwentyeyam renh, ankwernang, ngenharl atwekarl-penh. (T) *You go and hit him, pay him back after he's hit you.* ◆ *Jail*-eng arratem rang, *policeman*-el apek angety-alhem renh *community* antyaper-warl *like Yuendumu* arlka kwer-warl, wal mapel renh atanthem irrtyartel. Irrtyartel atanthem ankwernem renh, tyerrty irrewalyek apek atwekeng. Ankwernem ina renh, artwang renh ina atwem. Alakenham angkety Anmatyerr anwa ilem. (M) *He comes out of jail, and the policeman might bring him back to whichever communities, to such places as Yuendumu and all, and then all the people spear him with spears. They spear him to 'pay him back', to pay back the person who has killed someone. They beat the person who did it, to pay him back. That's how we talk about it in Anmatyerr.*
= unkil-ilem

ankwernelhem (W,T) *vi.*
submit yourself for 'payback' or traditional punishment ◆ Tyerrty yanh anwern angem ankwernelhetyek. (T) *We are taking that person for payback.*
SEE ALSO anthelhem, unkilelhem

ankwerrern (T, E), **ankwerrernayt** (T) *n.*
1. edible grub from the trunk of the coolibah tree, *ankerrmern*. Also referred to as *tyap ankwerrern* or *tyap ankwerrernayt*. ◆ Tyap ankwerrern, ankerrmern inetyenheng tyap renh arlkwetyenheng. Anyematyart akin ankwerrern. Lywenkel tyarr-inetyart. (N) *The* ankwerrern *grub is collected from the coolibah tree and eaten. It is similar to a witchetty grub. We pull it out [of the hole in the trunk] with a grass hook.*
= ankerrayt, anwerrngaty
SEE ALSO perlanty
2. edible seeds from the coolibah. Central Anmatyerr speakers use the word *ankwerrern* to refer to the grub, and Eastern Anmatyerr speakers use it to refer to the seed of the coolibah.
SEE ALSO aley[1]

ankwetyankw (E) *n.* [RESPECT LANGUAGE]
sleep ◆ Ankwakel ankwetyankw-kweny ayepel-irrep-irrem. (St) *They [respect kin] are staying up all night without sleeping.*
SEE ALSO ankwa

anma (T,E) bud or flower of native tobacco etc. SEE UNDER **alpma**

anma (W,T), **anmang** (W,T) *n.*
hairstring skirt (men's and women's)
= matyart

anmang (W) *n.*
life-saver burr, teddy bears arsehole (*Sida platycalyx*). Soft herb with large yellow flowers. Fruits are doughnut-shaped and prickly when dry.
= ingka-mwerney, akeley-akeley, kwem

anmanty (W,T) *n.*
young men's ceremony, initiation ceremony ◆ Anwern alhem anthep-irretyek anmanty-warn. (T) *We'll go and dance in the young men's ceremony.* ◆ Anmanty-warn tyerrty map arraw-irrem rntwetyek. (T) *Aboriginal people gather together to dance at the young men's ceremony.* ◆ Ayang map alyelhem anmanty. (T) *The old men sing the* anmanty *ceremony.*
= apwelh

Anmatyerr, Anmatyarr *n.*
1. an Anmatyerr person, Anmatyerr people. Also spelt as Anmatjara (see page ix). ◆ Anmatyerr anwern anem. Anmatyerrelem anwern *born*-irrek — angey-henh, arreng-arreng-henh. Arreng-arreng Anmatyerr anek, aperl-aperl anek anwern-henh — Anmatyerr akin. Kenh Arlper akin inehenh-thayt. *Self* akin Arrernt, *self* akin Kartety. (T) *We are Anmatyerr. We were born Anmatyerr — from our fathers and our fathers' fathers. Our grandfathers were Anmatyerr, and our fathers' mothers — they were Anmatyerr as well. Whereas Warlpiri [language and people] is over on their side. Arrernte is separate, and Kaytetye*

is separate as well.
2. the Anmatyerr language ◆ Antelhemel angkay, angka atyenh-warl Anmatyerr-warl. (St) *Follow me and say what I say, in my language, Anmatyerr.*

anmernem (W) hold increase ceremony to make bush plants and animals abundant SEE UNDER **arrmernem**

anmerrem (W,T) *vi.*
die down (flames) ◆ Rwang anmerrem. Rwang item, anmerrem, arelh atanty anem rarrp amperleng. (N) *The fire is burning down. The fire is lit, and then the woman waits for it to burn down itself.* ◆ Rrwek rwang nhenh amperr anmerrey ker arlewatyerr itetyenheng. (T) *Wait till the flame dies down and then you can cook the goanna.*
SEE ALSO ilwem

annga, anngang (W,T), **alknga** (E) *n.*
1. eye, eyesight ◆ Nwernengk arrakert angerr lthel-lthel an annga angerr. (M) *The tawny frogmouth has a big hairy beak and big eyes.* ◆ Annga alhap-irrem amengelarl atwem, atherrkeny apek. (St) *Eyes become bunged up when flies bite them, in the green time.* ◆ Ingwemernt ap ayeng anngan arrkay-irrenhemel an ingwemernt anem irrenhem, *can't look much now.* (St) *I can't see much now and everything looks dark because my eyesight is fading.*
2. fruit, seed, bulb (of a plant) ◆ Annga arratepatem kwenh, mern anem anetyenheng. (T) *The plant seeds and then there is the fruit.*
3. small round things; bullet ◆ Iylpwer yanh-warl akwernetyek, ker atwetyek. Annga tha akwernetyek iylpwer-warl annga. (St) *[You] put the bullet in the gun to shoot game. I am putting the bullet in the gun.* • SEE ALSO pwelert
CAN SOUND A BIT LIKE irnnga *'worm', 'maggot'*

anngang atyerrenherrenh (T)
bullet (atyerrenherrenh *'shooter'*)
= pwelert

annga kwart, alknga kwart (E)
eyeball (kwart *'egg'*)

annga rrpwerl (W,T), **annga urrperl** (E), **alknga urrperl** (E)
iris, pupil (of eye) (urrperl *'dark-coloured'*)

annga artep, alknga artep (E)
eyelid (artep *'back'*)

annga tyelk, alknga tyelk (E)
fleshy part of the eyelid (tyelk *'flesh'*)

annga urreyt (E), **alknga urreyt** (E), **alknga urretyeny, alknga urreyteny** *n.*
eyebrow (urreyt (?))

annga iylpwer (E), **alknga iylpwer** (E), **alkngeylpwer** (E) *n.*
eye socket (iylpwer *'hollow'*)

annga anyent-irrem, alknga anyent-irrem (T,E)
wink, blink (anyent-irrem *'become one'*) ◆ Alknga anyent-irrerl-alhekaw, mpweny ra alknga anyent-irrerl-alhek, mpweny, nhakw akwel alhetyek. (St) *He went and winked, making eyes at someone, suggesting that they could race off together.*

annga arrkay, alknga arrkay (E)
poor or faded eyesight (arrkay *'faded'*) ◆ Arrkay tha arem arlengan. Alknga arrkay, *can't* tha arleng arerl. (St) *I can't see properly in the distance. My eyesight is poor and I can't see a long way.*

annga pweng, alknga pweng (E)
1. blind (pweng *'blind'*) ◆ Pweng aretyakenh. Alknga pweng aretyakenh. (St) *[I] am blind. I can't see.*
2. eyes shut ◆ Ankwepenh apek pwengek-amperr intep-intem kel alkngerlkenty alhem. *After being asleep [you] lie there with your eyes closed and then you open them.*
3. 'blind one', said as a joke to some relatives (when they are not really blind)

annga pweng-irrem, alknga pweng-irrem (E)
blink, close eyes, go blind

annga ipert, alknga ipert (E)
sunken eyes (ipert *'hole'*)

annga ipert-irrem, alknga ipert-irrem (E)
(eyes) sink back in head ◆ Alknga ipert-irrek angkethel. *When [the person] was thirsty their eyes sank back in their head.*

annga alhap (E), **alknga alhap** (E)
1. bung-eye (alhap *'blocked'*)
2. Chinese person

annga alhwer-alhwer, alknga alhwer-alhwer (E)
bung-eye (alhwer-alhwer *'swollen or puffed up'*) ◆ Alknga ayeng alhwer-alhwer-irrek nhanyem amengel apekarl utnhek. *This eye of mine here has bunged up, probably because flies bit it.*

annganthwerr-anthwerr (W,T) *n.*
weepy, dirty or pussy eyes ◆ Kwer nhenh annganthwerr-anthwerr. (M) *This child has pussy eyes.*

annga lthwem (W,T), **annga ulthem** (E), **alknga ulthem** (E)
have heavy eyes, get sleepy (lthwem *'press down on'*) ◆ Ankwel ayenh annga ulthem. (St) *Sleep is making my eyes heavy.*

annga rnter-rnter, alknga rnter-rnter (E)
red eyes (rnter-rnter *'red'*)

annga alker-alker (T,E), **alknga alker-alker** (E)
cross-eyed; eyes that have whitened over with cataracts
annga alkerelhem, alknga alkerelhem (E)
feel dizzy, black out, eyesight fade
annga ingwemernt-irrem, alknga ingwemernt-irrem (E)
feel dizzy, black out, eyesight fade (ingwemernt-irrem *'go dark'*) ◆ Alknga ingwemernt-irrem, aretyakenh ayeng. (St) *My eyesight is fading and I can't see.*
SEE ALSO therrert-irrem
annga therrert-irrem (E), **alknga therrert-irrem** (E)
be unable to see, feel dizzy ◆ Alknga therrert-irrem ayeng angayakw. (Sa) *I am feeling dizzy and I can't see properly because I'm hungry.*
annga kwenengeneng (T,E), **alknga kwenengeneng** (E)
looking at something with narrowed eyes, looking downwards
annga intyemel arem, alknga intyemel arem (E) **alkngintyem** (E)
look sideways, look out of the corner of your eye
annga atherrk, alknga atherrk (E)
cat (atherrk *'green'*)
SEE ALSO rlwatert, mangw, nyarrapeng, pwethey, pwethekat, angay, meyaw-meyaw
annga atherrk-atherrk, alknga atherrk-atherrk (E)
1. eyes that are a blue-green in colour
2. a promiscuous person • SEE ALSO anapert, mpweny angerr, mpwenyartw-mpwenyartw
anngel arrernem (T,E), **alkngel arrernem** (E)
witness something; see someone do something (?) (arrernem *'put'*) ◆ Alkngel arrernek tha — *might someone* ankey apek inerl-alhek, than arek, *murder*-em apekarl ilek. (St) *I saw [them] do it — maybe I saw someone come and greedily take something, or murder someone.*

anngampem, alkngampem (E) *vi.*
open eyes ◆ Kel anngampek, pwengarl intetyeh arengk akwek map. (T) *The puppies have opened their eyes after being blind at first.* ◆ Ankwiperr apek ayeng alkngampety-ayntem. (Sa) *After sleeping I open my eyes.*
= anngerlkem
anngampelh-ilem, alkngampelh-ilem (E) *vt.*
make someone or something open their eyes ◆ *Dreaming* angwely-kenh. Angwelyarl anngampelh-ilem. Angwely akely-amperl. *Dingo* akwek anngampelh-ilem annga. Arengkatwepatwetyenh angwely akwerrk anngampelh-ilem, annga. Arrken-irrem anem angwely akwek ra. Anngakert antem. (N) *This plant is a Dreaming for dingoes. It makes the little dingo pups open their eyes. The* arengkatwepatwetyenh *plant makes the pup open its eyes and then it starts to play. It can see then.*
= anngerlkelh-ilem

anngang (W,T) eye SEE UNDER **annga**

anngangem (E), **alkngangem** (E) *vt.*
delay or stop someone from doing something, keep someone waiting ◆ Alkngangem, alhetyek *ready* ayeng alheyam, alkngangelhetyal. Ampa yanh arntirrkway, alkngangetyal. (Sa) *I'm ready to go, don't stop me. Hold onto that kid so that they don't delay me.* ◆ Arengkel alwernenty angerrel alkngangepangemaw. (St) *The dogs who chase people all the time are stopping us from doing something.*
SEE ALSO arlkem

anngaparek (T,E), **alkngaparek** (E), **anngaparwek** (E) *n.*
someone who stares a lot ◆ Marl apek anngaparwek, arnterrarl arerl-anem. (St) *A woman might be* anngaparwek, *someone who stares really hard.*

anngarem, alkngarem (E) *vt.*
look back at something
anngarelhem, alkngarelhem (E) *vi.*
1. look behind, look over your shoulder ◆ Ayeng alkngarelhey urrek. *Wait, I'll look back.* ◆ Tyerrty arrpenharl apetyemek anngarelhem. (T) *Looking behind for the other person that's coming.*
= artepeng arelhem, angkep arem, angkep-athek arem
2. be older than someone, be the older brother or sister of someone ◆ Ayeng alkngarelhek yanhek. *Second* atyenharl yanh. (St) *I am older than that one. She's second to me.*
CAN SOUND A BIT LIKE anngarr-ilem *'warn someone about something'*
anngaremp-anngar, alkngaremp-alkngar (E) *n.*
looking over your shoulder all the time, one who is always looking over their shoulder ◆ Alkngaremp-alkngar untem ararerl-alpem artepeng arelhemel. (Sa) *You are going along, always looking back over your shoulder.*

anngarenty, alkngarenty (E) *n.*
1. uncooperative, someone who doesn't want to do something
2. woman who doesn't want to get married or go with a man ◆ Anngarenty ananem ayeng, artwang yanh-kety. (T) *I don't want to go with*

that man. ◆ Arelh anngarenty arrtyanem pwerlt-irremel, alwernerl-apem rrweyel. Ra akenh arrtyanerl-apemarl, arelh rang anngarenty. Awenk wart anngarenty — *no* arrwekel ra artwa arek, artwa aretyakenh-penh, lyetantarl amangkek. (N) *The* anngarenty *woman runs away, and the man chases after her. The* anngarenty *woman keeps on running away. Of course young girls are* anngarenty — *they haven't seen men before, and they haven't much experience with men, because they've just grown up.*
SEE ALSO ankerl, anwernt
CAN SOUND A BIT LIKE anngirrenty *'type of spirit'*

anngarenty-irrem, alkngarenty-irrem (E) *vi.*
not want to do something; not want to go with a man ◆ Ilanthem apek, *grandmother*-el apek, *mother*-el apek. 'Alhang kwenh, kweray kwenh! *Don't* anngarenty-irrerl-anerl kwenh, ayerrp ilelhemel kwenh. *You* kwerl-warl alherl kalty-irretyeh unta kalty-irretyeh kwenh, Angkeleth unta kalty-irretyeh kwenh.' (N) *Their grandmother or mother might send them. 'Go child! Don't behave as if you don't want to and avoid it. You've got to go to school to learn, to learn English.'* ◆ Anngarenty-irrem, ahenty-kwenh artweh. Marl alwernemel alwernemel alwernetyam ityantey. Marlek ikwerenh arrtyanep-anem. Arrtyanetyam marl ikwerety rwernelhemel. 'War anerl-anerray, anngarenty-kweny.' (N) *[She] doesn't want to go with the man because she doesn't like him. [The man] keeps on chasing the girl but she doesn't change her mind. The girl runs away from him and hides herself from him, behind something. 'Just sit down, don't be* anngarenty.*'*
SEE ALSO anngarem, anwernt-irrem, annga

anngarlp (T,E), **alkngarlp** (E) *n.*
pelvic bone (?), hipbone ◆ Alkngarlp ayeng arntem, ayeng arrpenh-angkwerr anem intetyek, alkngarlp arrpenh-angkwerr anem. *My hip is aching so I'll lie on the other side, on the other hip.*
SEE ALSO arlenty

meth anngarlp (T)
rib (bone) (meth *'rib'*)

anngarnpelh, alkngarnpelh (E), **alkngaympelh** (E), **anngaympelh** (E) *n.*
eyelash (annga *'eye', 'seed', 'round thing'*; arnpelh *'wing', 'feather'*)

anngarnt, alkngarnt (E), **anngaty** (W,T) *n.*
eyebrow
SEE ALSO annga

anngarnt alta, alkngarnt alta (E) *n.*
eyebrow (alta *'hair'*)

anngarnt rrpwerl (W,T) *n.*
stalked puffball (*Podaxis pistillaris*) (rrpwerl *'dark-coloured'*). Grows to about 10 cm high, on a long stalk. Powdery purplish black spores inside. ◆ Anngarnt rrpwerlel kwer map apernelhem artwarteh apernelhem. (M) *Kids use the puffball to paint themselves and make themselves look like men.*
= pwek-pwek, kwep-kwep³, arrekwep-kwep, arrepweng-pweng, pweng-pweng

anngarr-ilem, alkngarr-ilem (T,E) *vt.*
warn somebody about something ◆ *Might* nhenhel ilety-alhemer, alkngarr-ilety-alhek ayenh, *might someone* apekarl apetyepetyem atwetyek atyeng. Alkngarr-ilety-alhek anherrey atyenhel. (St) *Maybe this one went and told me, went and warned me that somebody was coming to fight with me. My daughter-in-law warned me.* ◆ Alkngarr-ilek ayenh yanhel. (St) *That person warned me.*
= ateng-ilem
CAN SOUND A BIT LIKE anngarelhem *'look behind'*

anngarrkwer (W,T) *n.*
bush cat, feral cat
SEE ALSO arrkwer-ilem, annga

anngart (W), **akngart** (W,T) *n.*
native pine (*Callitris glaucophylla*). Tree to 6 m high, with rough bark, blue-green leaves and woody fruit. Grows in hilly country.
◆ Akngartel walyel alhewelhem arlpelhel, anngartel, rlwek. Apwertel irnerl-apem, nhak irnem map. Arreny atherram — anngart, rlwek. Renh-lkwerel anngang apernelherl-apek alhewelherl-apek arnang yanh kwerel, rlwek yanhel mwerrarl ilem *clean*-em ilelhem annga — *everything* alhewelhem artwengkenng-apertem mernt apert, iteth-ilem. (N) *The leaves and branches of the native pine are used as a washing medicine. The trees grow in the hills. It has two names —* anngart *and* rlwek. *That's what was used as a washing and rubbing medicine, that tree now. The native pine was used to wash eyes and clean them and make them better — to wash everything and make people better after they had a cold or were sick.*
= rlwek, amikw¹

anngatherr (T) to one's face, (doing something) right in front of someone SEE UNDER **anngetherr**

anngaty (W,T) eyebrow SEE UNDER **anngarnt**

anngaympelh (E) eyelash SEE UNDER **anngarnpelh**

anngayt (E), **alkngayt** (E) *n.*
brow bone
SEE ALSO annga

anngener, **alknginer** (E), **alkngeyner** (E), **anngeyner** (E) *n.*
cicada. Also referred to as *tyap anngener.* ◆ Tyap anngener. Arlkwenh-arlkwenh, ingweneng-artek. *The cicada is edible, like the grub from the river red gum.* ◆ Anngener aperel-ayeng angkerl-anem twern-rlwer. (M) *Cicadas sing in the river red gums in the summer time.*

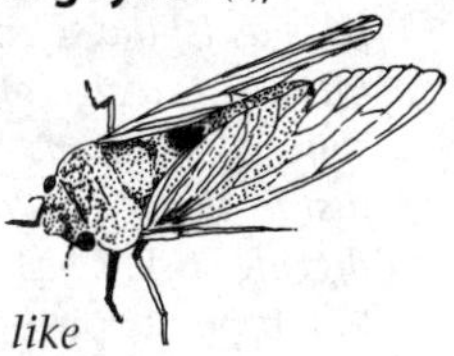

= aterr, arrey-arrey
SEE ALSO ingweneng

anngenth, **alkngenth** (E) *n.*
1. flame ◆ Rwang anngenth ampem. (T) *The flame is burning.* ◆ Anngenth nhenh akwek-irrem, kwen-irrem — lwerenelarl nthekemarl wem rrweyel. (N) *When the flame becomes smaller, dies down — that's when the boy singes the hair off the animal.*
2. light (car light, etc.) ◆ Mwetek anngenth-akert, *light* amperl-apem. (T) *The car has lights, lights shining as it goes along.*
= lherrm

anngenth-ilem, **alkngenth-ilem** (E) *vt.*
light a fire ◆ Alkngenth-ilem, pew-ilem tha, alkngenth ampem. (St) *I am blowing the fire to make it catch alight, so that the flames burn.*
= antant-ilem, lherrm-ilem, nthilem
SEE ALSO lyenenty

anngenenty (T) *n.*
flame
= lyenenty

annger (W) *n.*
without food, not having any food ◆ Annger ayeng anep-anem, mern anetyakenh, ker anetyakenh. (M) *I'm sitting down with nothing, no bread and no meat.*

anngerlkem (T,E), **alkngerlkem** (E) *vi.*
open eyes ◆ Lyetant *born* pwengek-amparr intcp-intcm, kel ra alkngerlkem anem alkngerlkenty-alhep-alhem. Amangkemel an alkngerlkem anemel. (St) *Something that is just born is blind at first, and then it opens its eyes. As it grows up its eyes are open.* ◆ Ankwepenh ayeng alkngerlkem. *I open my eyes after sleeping.* ◆ Arengk akwerrk map anngerlkem akin, pweng-penh, akwerrkarl aneman. *Puppies open their eyes as well, after being blind at first, as little puppies.*
= anngampem
SEE ALSO annga

anngerlkelh-ilem (T,E), **alkngerlkelh-ilem** (E) *vt.*
1. make someone or something open their eyes
= anngampelh-ilem
2. stare at someone, not take your eyes off someone or something ◆ Ahel tha ngenh alkngerlkelh-ilemarl. (St) *I am staring at you because I'm wild at you.*

-anngernt (T) (something happens) before the verb action SEE UNDER **-angent**

anngernt (T,E), **alkngernt** (E) *n.*
naughty, mean, argumentative
SEE ALSO anhelhenty, ltyernt

anngernt-irrem (T,E), **alkngernt-irrem** (E) *vi.*
pick a fight with someone, be naughty, tease someone, misbehave, tell someone off
◆ Arelh alkngernt-irrem arelh arrpenhek, mern-they angkemel, alkngernt-irremel anem angkem. (St) *One woman picks on another women, maybe she growls at her over food.*
◆ Kwer nhek anngernt-irrem kwer arrpenhek. (T) *This child picked a fight with another one.*
◆ Tyerrty arrpenh apek apal anerl-anem wal *he might* angkerl-anerl ilterl-anemel. 'Alkngernt-irrek kwenh, alkngernt-irrekarl yanhan atyeng.' *One person might be sitting there just minding their own business and another comes and growls at them. 'That person picked on me.'*
= ltyernt-irrem
SEE ALSO anhelhem, iltem

anngerrem be 'found' or spiritually conceived in a particular place or country SEE UNDER **anngirrem**

anngerrenhem (W) go along together (?) SEE UNDER **angerrenhem**

anngetherr, **anngatherr** (T), **alkngetherr** (E) *adv.*
to one's face; (doing something) right in front of someone; doing something out in the open or in public ◆ Ngenh alkngetherr tha ilem. (St) *I am telling you straight to your face.* ◆ Atyeng alkngetherr anem angka. Tha awerleng. (St) *Say it straight to my face. I'll listen to you.*

anngetherrek-anngetherr, **alkngetherrek-alkngetherr** (E) *adv.*
facing each other; face to face
◆ Alkngetherrek-alkngetherr atwerretyek ulanengek-ulaneng. (St) *[They] are fighting face to face.* ◆ Alkngetherrek-alkngetherr atwerretyek ulanengek-ulaneng. Kenh ayenh apek ina atwetyek alpay, marl yanheng atwep-atwem, kel tha atwemel-alpem renh. (St) *Fighting each other face to face. Maybe they hit me, and then I hit them back.*
= ularrek-ularr, lwarrek-lwarr
SEE ALSO ulanengek-ulaneng, annga

Anngewaneny (E) *n.*
the name of a place near Bean Tree Bore

anngey-anngey *n.*
1. desert broom bush (*Anthobolus leptomerioides*)
2. (the) tall saltbush (*Rhagodia eremaea*)
3. mulga native currant, narrow-leaved native currant (*Psydrax suaveolens*) [SOME SPEAKERS]. A shrub up to 3 m high, with narrow leaves, small white flowers and fruit which ripens to a black colour. • = ngkwernelyerr, ngkwernateylp, antenh-antenh, anwengk-anwengk

Anngeyerr (W) *n.*
the name of a hill in Mt Wedge/Tilmouth Well roadhouse area

anngeyner (E) cicada SEE UNDER **anngener**

anngirrem, anngerrem, alkngirrem (E) *vi.*
be 'found' or spiritually conceived in a particular place or country; come from a particular place or country. An Anmatyerr person has a special connection to the place where they are 'spiritually conceived' and to the Dreamings from that place. This refers not to the baby's actual conception or birth itself but rather to the moment of 'quickening' when the entry of an ancestral spirit into a woman animates the unborn child. ◆ Mer nhenh-ampenyel anngirrek ayeng. (M) *I came from round this area.* ◆ Ayengan mer yanhel anngirrek Ankerrapwel. (Sa) *I was 'found' over there at Utopia.* ◆ Ayeng alkngirrek, Ilkewarn ampenyek akngeyek ayeng alkngirrek. (St) *I was found in the Ilkewarn area, in my father's country.* ◆ Ker apek aherr atwenty, atyerrenty, wal amparl alkngirrem. Mern ikwerel akngAnekarl, akngAnenty. Kerarl arlkwem, aynikwel, wal ra alkngirrenty anem. Ampa anem. (Sa) *From the killing of a kangaroo, the shooting of a kangaroo, well a child might come from that. That's the food, the Dreaming, that the child originates from. The child's father kills the kangaroo and eats it, and then the child is 'found' there.*
SEE ALSO angwerrm-irrem, anganem

anngirrenty (E), **anngerrenty** (E), **alkngirrenty** (E) *n.*
1. the spirit of a person, which comes from their conception place — the place of quickening or the place where they were 'found' ◆ Rnwem apek atwem, ampa ranteyarl ap renh atweman, alkngirrenty. Ampa rantey ap impelty anem ra anerl-anem atwekarl atnemel apekarl rnwem. Impelty anem urrperl-irrerl-anem. Urrperl anem irrerl-anem. Ampan. (Sa) *If a snake is killed [by the parents to be], then [it is as if] the spirit of the unborn child itself is hit — it is a sign of the place where the child's spirit comes from. And the child will have a mark, just as the snake does from being hit with the digging stick. The child will have a dark mark.* (?)
2. a type of spirit or ghost ◆ Anwantherr apek ilwemarl wal alkngirrenty anem anem. (St) *Well, if we die we will become spirits then.* ◆ Alkngirrentyarl tha lyet altyerr arek, arwemarl-irrekaw. Thampethengek alkngirrenty arwem-irrekarl tharl altyerr arek-ketyaw. Mwanty akngerr-irrey. Apetyemarl-kety alkngarr-ilety-alhek alkngirrentyel. (Sa) *I had a dream about a spirit today. Look out because it appeared in my dream — for some reason the spirit appeared in my dream. You mob had better be careful. The spirit came and warned me about something.*
3. skin and bone; skeletal ◆ Iteth pwelek ra alhem alkngirrenty, ngkwernant — *no* anter *no* tyelk *no* alhwa. (St) *The bullock goes around alive, just skin and bone — no fat, no flesh and no blood.*
SEE ALSO uneng2, kwerrern, lthan, tywetyerrng, aleperenty
CAN SOUND A BIT LIKE anngarenty *'uncooperative'*

anngwa, alkngwa (E) *adv.*
not paying attention; not seeing or noticing something; being oblivious to what is going on ◆ Alkngwa ayeng anetyam aretyakenh, tyerrty talkw-irrerlek aretyakenh. (St) *I was not paying attention and I didn't see them, I didn't see the person who went across.*
SEE ALSO apal2, akwenp-akwenp, akwenpety-akwenp, angweyep-angwey

anngwerrem (W,T), **anngwirrem** (E), **alkngwirrem** (E), **akngwirrem** (E) *vi.*
1. forget something ◆ Ngkweng angketyek alkngwirrek ayeng. (St) *I forgot to talk to you.* ◆ Ngkweng thang iletyek anek, ayeng anngwerrek. (T) *I was going to tell you, but I forgot.* ◆ *Family* atyenh ayeng anngwirrek, alhekarl apek iyntwarr. Ayeng-kweny itnarl alhekarl, ayeng anngwirrek anem. (St) *I forgot about my family because they went a long way away. They went without me, and then I forgot [about them].*
2. leave something behind ◆ Arna atyenhek anem ayeng anngwirrerl-alhek merek-antey. Kel ayeng alpemel inetyek anem inerliwek anem. (St) *I left my things behind at camp. So I went back to pick them up.*
3. become distracted; not pay attention to someone or something ◆ Alkngwerlpalkngw-

irretyek nga, tha ngenh alkngwanngw-ilem, kel ayeng alwirremel ngkweng-kety. (St) *I keep on distracting you so that you'll start to lose attention, and then I'll run away from you.*
= iylpel-irrem
SEE ALSO aparlp-ilem

anngwanng-ilem, **alkngwanng-ilem** (E) *vt.*
distract someone; take someone's attention away from something; settle someone down ◆ Alkngwanng-ilem tha arengk nhenh-arey, ker apek antherl-anem, tyerrty yanh alheyamel. (St) *I'll distract these dogs by giving them some meat and then these people can go.* ◆ Ampa akely alkngwanng-ilem amikw alwernekerr. Alkngwanng-ilemel atnyenerl-anem, arteny. (Sa) *[You] distract a child in case it runs after its mother. You distract it and hold onto it, keep it at home.*
SEE ALSO aparlp-parlp-ilem, aparlp-ilem, arternp-ilem, arternpelh-ilem, kwart-wem

anngwelem, **alkngwilem** (E) *vt.*
= **anngwanng-ilem**

anngwanng-ilelhem, **alkngwanng-ilelhem** (E) *vi.*
take your mind off something, make yourself forget something, distract yourself ◆ Rrwek ayeng anngwanng-ilelhem, nekeleth mpwarerlanemel. (T) *Wait while I take my mind [off it] by making some necklaces.*

anngwelty (T) tears SEE UNDER **anngwenty**

anngwenhem, **alkngwenhem** (E) *vt.*
be jealous of someone or over something ◆ Mantereng anngwenhem arrpenh yalelarl anthemeng, arrpenh yal anngwenhemarl. (St) *Somebody might get jealous with a person who gave clothes to someone else.* ◆ Marl yanhel alkngwenh-kerr ayenh, anewikweng, artwa yanhek-arrngel. (St) *That woman over there might get jealous of me, over her husband, over that man there.*
SEE ALSO arwelth, arwelth-rnem, mayel anngwenhem, tyaleth-irrem

anngwenherrem, **alkngwenherrem** (E) *vi.*
be jealous of each other ◆ Artweng apek anngwenherrem. Artwa anyenteng apek ratherr anngwenherrem. Kel ratherr atwerrem antem. (T) *They are getting jealous with each other over a man. The two of them might be jealous over one man. Then they fight each other.*

mayel anngwenhem, **imayel alkngwenhem** (E)
be jealous over someone or something

anngwenty (W,T), **arrngwelty** (E), **alkngwelty** (E), **anngwelty** (T), **ngwenty** (T) *n.*
tears, watery eyes ◆ Anngwelty thelelhem anngangeng. (T) *Tears are falling from the eyes.* ◆ Akuny-amperl alkngа arrngwelty-arrngweltyekarl atwerliwerreperremarl. Arrngwelty yanh irrarlkey. (St) *The poor thing was beaten till the tears came. Wipe the tears away.*
SEE ALSO annga

anngwenty-anngwenty, **arrngwelty-arrngwelty** (E) *n.*
watery (eyes), teary ◆ Alknga arrngwelty-arrngwelty, arrngweltyarl thelelhetyel utern-penh. (Sa) *The eyes are all watery and they are streaming from the hot sun.*

Anngwenyenp (W,T), **Ngwenyenp** (W,T) *n.*
name of a large hill in the Pine Hill area. See map p. viii.

Anningie SEE UNDER **Angenty**2

anpaty-irrem (T) *vi.*
separate or fan out while hunting
= anpert-irrem

anpelhem (E) *vi.*
moan or groan in pain ◆ Ayeng anpelhemel artnem rlkert. (Sa) *I am moaning in pain and crying because I'm sick.*

anpem *vt.*
feel something; touch someone or something ◆ Anpem tha ngenh. (St) *I am touching you.* ◆ Ayenh anpetyalaw! (Sa) *Don't touch me!* ◆ Iltyel anpem ankarrelh-ilemel, ankwang alenh intep-intem, alakenh ankarrelh-ilem iltyel, 'Kem-irrang kwenh'. (N) *Somebody is lying there sleeping, and you wake them up by touching them with your hand, by passing your hand over their face, and saying, 'Get up'.* ◆ Rrwey nhenh anewek anpem, kemelh-ilem renh, 'Kemirray! Ilanth alperretyekay!' (N) *The man touches his wife to wake her up and says, 'Get up! We two are going back!'*
= lyarnem

anper1 *adv.*
passing (by someone or something); being beside (someone or something)
◆ Ahekwenaytan ahern-areny, aper intert-utek — *not* artekerrel — arwa ahernel aylpem. Artekerr-angkwerr anperel ayntenhem, alhwengan ikwerenh. (Sa) *The* ahekwenayt *grub lives in the ground at the base of the river red gum tree — not in the roots — they just live underneath the ground. Their holes are found beside the roots of the tree.* ◆ Ayeng anperel arrernenhem, rnwanenty, alkwert apek. (N) *I am going to leave my clothes, or maybe my shield [there] as I go past.*

anper alhem
pass by (someone or something); go past

◆ Tyerrty alenh anper akwet alhem. (M) *That person went straight past.* ◆ Rlkwerr nta arem tyerrty, wal nta anper akwet alhem. (M) *If you see someone halfway, well you should go straight past them.* ◆ Arelh anyent anper alhem atyeng-angkwerr. (T) *A woman is going past me.*

anper² (W,T) *n.*
really good, fantastic, great, superior ◆ Ker arlpaty akwerrk anwern inerrirretyart rlpwereh, atwemel anwern inetyart *full* anwern atwetyart. Thewetam yanh perrap anper akin, atetherrart. (N) *We used to get baby ringneck parrots from the hollows in trees, kill them and collect lots of them. The meat is really lovely and sweet, like budgerigar meat.*
SEE ALSO mwerr
anper anthwerr (W,T)
really good, fantastic (anthwerr *'really'*)
◆ Anper anthwerr *story* nhenh anwern ilep-ilem. *Olden time* renh anwern *story* nhenh ilep-ilem anper. Mwerr angerr — kerarl atanthetyam, kerelarl wantetyam. (N) *This is a really good story that we keep on telling. It's the olden-time story that we continue to tell. It's really good — about the kangaroos that were speared, and the meat that we were fed on.*
◆ *Painting* anper anthwerr mpwarek ntwa. (T) *You painted a really fantastic painting.*
= mwerr anthwerr

anpernem *vt.*
call someone or something a particular relation ◆ Thang amey anpernem. (M) *I call [that person] mother.* ◆ Tha apek ngenh anpernem nyany — Mpetyan then Kemarr uthen apek. Nhenh apek anherrey apek tha anpernem. (St) *I might call you granny — a Mpetyan and a Kemarr. I might call this [person] daughter-in-law.*
anpernerrem *vi.*
call each other particular relations; be related to each other in a particular way ◆ Kenh tha ngenh apawenhem, 'Ntwa iwenharl kwenh?' 'Kemarrarl ayeng kwenh.' Ntwan ilelhem. Alakenh anpernerremarlan. Wal, nyany-nheng anpernerrem. (St) *And then I ask you, 'What skin are you?' 'I am a Kemarr.' That's what you say. That's how people call each other as relations. Well, we are related as granny and grandchild.*
SEE ALSO akerrem
anpernenty *n.*
skin name or subsection name. See Appendix 1. ◆ 'Iwenharlam ntwan anem anpernenty ngkwengenh arreny?' 'Ngwarray,' arlka war ilelhem — anpernenty ra kwa, arreny. (N) *'What is your skin name?' [The person] might just say 'Ngwarray' — that's the skin name.*
anpernerrenty *n.*
1. skin name or subsection name ◆ Alhernter kwenh anpernerrenty itya, kenh tyerrty akenh Anengkerreng-ntyel anpernerrem. Anengkerrel anpernek Anengkerreng-ntyel anpernerrem kenh alhernter akenh anpernenty ityarl. Apal wararl alhernteran. (M) *White people don't have a skin system, whereas Aboriginal people get their skin system from the Dreaming. The Dreaming named [everyone] as relations, and people got the way of calling each other as relations from there. White people don't have a skin system. White people don't know.*
2. the rules about how people are related to each other; skin system, kinship system
SEE ALSO ikwa

anperr (E) *n.* [RESPECT LANGUAGE]
single-women's camp
◆ 'Ampweyampwekarety. Ampweyampw-ayerr yanhentyakel ayepel-irrerl-iwerretyel anperrel.' Ampwelan mwerikwan ilem arelh. Ateyelap ilem. (Sa) *'Mother-in-law. The women [including my mother-in-law] are sitting in the single-women's camp.' That's what a man says of his old mother-in-law.*
SEE ALSO arlweker, irrewatyent, arnkenty, ahileng, arramenty, ngwemay

anpert-irrem (T) *vi.*
separate or fan out while hunting
= anpaty-irrem

anpeth (E) *n.*
point or top of the shoulder
SEE ALSO pwerlep, pwerlep annga, arety

Anpetyety (W) *n.*
Leichhardt Bore

anpwem (W,T) *vt.*
hunt someone or something away; chase someone or something away, get rid of someone ◆ Alhernter yanh anpway, merarl irrpem-arleng. (M) *Tell that white person to go away, because they are going into the house.*
= aywepem
SEE ALSO ilanthem, ilhem, alharlkwem
anpwelhem (W,T) *vi.*
chase someone or something away from yourself ◆ Ayeng anpwelhem arrenty-kety, *pray*-irremel. Altyerrek ayeng *pray*-irrem wal arrenty anpwemarl. (T) *I pray to keep the devil away. I pray to God and then the devil is chased away.* ◆ Rrweyeng anpwelhemeyay. Rrwey ahenty kweny anerl-anetyenh. Anem, *olden time* anpwelhetyam, ahenty-kwenh, *self*

anetyeh, *self* anerl-anetyeh. (N) *Chasing the men away. So that if you don't like men you can sit down without them. In the old days, if you didn't like them, then you'd hunt them away and you'd sit down without them.*
= aywepelhem
SEE ALSO alharlkwelhem

ant and SEE UNDER **an**[1]

+ant *ending*
only, just, just that and nothing else, only this and nothing else, precisely, particularly, exclusively ◆ Lyet**ant** kalty-irretyel, ampa nyerralth. (St) *He's just started learning things [at school] lately, he's very timid.* ◆ Akangkwerrenty itya, kwer kwerl-areny map. Maneyek**ant** angkerl-anem, maney akwel ngkwelty anthetyeh. (N) *The school kids don't pay attention. Apparently they just ask for money, ask to be given coins.* ◆ Atyankerney-apenh angetyetyart warntapel**ant** mern atyankern arrwekeleny mapel. Aperl-aperl-rrpwerelaty menh-menh-rrpwerel arlka atyemeyel-rrpwer. *The olden-time people used to get mistletoe berries, just in bark containers. All my grandmothers used to do it.* ◆ Angka lyeteny anetyakenh — ahinpeny**ant** nhenh. (St) *This language is not from nowadays — it's olden-time language.*

akwetant *n.*
for good, forever ◆ Unta apekarl alhek akwet**ant**. (St) *It seems like you went for good.*
SEE ALSO akwet

lyetant *n.*
just now (after a time), now for the first time in a long time
SEE ALSO lyet

+ant-alkenty *ending*
1. everybody ◆ Atningk**ant**-alkenty apetyarralhekaw. (Sa) *Everybody came.*
2. Provides emphasis; really. ◆ Anmatyerr**ant**-alkenty kwenh ayeng anem. (M) *I really am Anmatyerr.*

anengkerrant-alkenty (W,T) *n.*
Dreaming story, something from the creation time ◆ Story Anengkerr**ant**-alkenty ilep-ilem. (T) *Telling a Dreaming story.*

arratyant-alkenty (W,T)
really, truly ◆ Arraty**ant**-alkenty apelay ina *win*-em-ilek — tha arekay kwenh. (T) *It's really true that they won — I know for a fact because I saw them.*
SEE ALSO arraty

mwerrant-alkenty (W,T)
really good, better ◆ Tyerrty nhenh mwerr**ant**-alkenty ananem. (T) *This person is really better now.*
SEE ALSO mwerr

+ant-atherr *n.ending*
just the two of them, those two in particular ◆ Akengentyeny**ant**-atherr, mwer-nheng atherr menh-nheng atherr. Akengentyeny atherrarl anerretyelarl atyeweyay, mwer-nheng atherr, *wrong one* atherr! (Sa) *Those two are wrong way for each other, mother-in-law and son-in-law, or grandchild and granny. For goodness sake! Those two are wrong for each other, related as mother-in-law and son-in-law.* ◆ Mpa altyeley aylanth alherrey kerek arlewatyerrek untherl-anetyek. Arelh**ant**-atherr. (Sa) *Come on cousin, let's go and look for goannas. Just two women.* ◆ R**ant**-atherr ratherr atwerrek. *Just those two fought.* ◆ Arraper arreylp-arreylp-akert ap ra. Mantarrek mwernelhem akin. Intwerrker then *same one-***ant**-atherr. Ratherr arreylpant-atherr. (Sa) *The curly wire grass has sharp spines. They get stuck in clothes as well. Both of them are the same, the* arraper *and the* intwerrker *grasses. They are both prickly.* ◆ Anewart arraty**ant**-atherr anerretyel. Kemarr uthen Petyarr uthen. (Sa) *The husband and wife are right [skin] for each other. Kemarr and Petyarr.* ◆ Mpwernikwan atey**ant**-atherrel akerrem. *Not* arelhel athew. Arelh**ant**-atherr arnteng**ant**arl akerrem. (Sa) *Only men call each other* 'mpwernikw' *[brother-in-law]. Women don't. They just call each other* 'arnteng' *[sister-in-law].*

+ant-arey (T,E) *n.ending*
just the group of them, those in particular ◆ Thakeman pwert**ant**-arey anwern warrk-irretyart. (T) *We used to work together as stockmen.* ◆ Marl**ant**-arey alhem urlart, marl map, urlart-antey alhem marl**ant** angerr. (St) *Just all the women are going, just lots of women.* ◆ Artw**ant**-arey 'mpwerney' akerrem. 'Anewikw' marlelan ilem (Sa) *Only the men call each other* 'mpwerney' *[brother-in-law]. Women use the term* 'anewikw' *[her brother-in-law].*

antalt (W), **altalt** (W,T) *n.* [SENSITIVE LANGUAGE]
pubic hair
= intywa
SEE ALSO alta

antangkem *vt.*
call someone over; send a message for someone to come ◆ Antangkem, 'Apetyay teyekay, mern nhenh inerl-alpetyekay!' Antangkeyay tha kenh ngkweng. (N) *Calling you over, 'Come for tea, come and get this food to take back!' I am calling you over.* ◆ *Cheryl*-eh

antangkay apetyetyek. (M) *Tell Cheryl to come.* ◆ Akwerrerl-anem akwerrem akwerrem antangkem, 'Apetyang kwenh!' (N) *Waving and waving and calling someone over, 'Come here!'*
antangkelhem *vt.* = **antangkem**
SEE ALSO arlkelh-ilem

antant-ilem (W,T) *vt.*
light a fire, ignite a fire ◆ Rwang inety-alpem antant-ilety-alpem. (N) *Get the firewood and take it back to light the fire.* ◆ Rwang antant-ilem rrmwarl-wemel. (N) *Lighting the fire using a firesaw.*
= nthilem, anngenth-ilem
antant-irrem (W,T) *vi.*
catch alight (fire)
= alep-irrem, lherrm-irrem

antarl (W,T) *adv.*
staying home, staying behind, not going anywhere ◆ Antarl anetyeh merel. (M) *Stopping home and not going anywhere.* ◆ Rlwepety antarl merel anerlanetyeh. (M) *Staying in one place, at home.*
SEE ALSO artenyem-arteny, arteny[1], rlwemp, urlemp, rlwepety, urlepety
antarl-irrem (W,T) *vi.*
stay home, stay behind, not go anywhere ◆ Ntwang alhay! Ayeng antarl-irrem. (T) *You go! I'm stopping here.*
SEE ALSO akwet-irrem, amarn-irrem

antarlkw, arntarlkw *n.*
1. V-shape, forked tree or stick ◆ Arna arntarlkw anetyakenh, alyelk-alyelk. Tetyep-wemel anem antyeynepeynem tety-wemel. (St) *The tree has no forks, it is smooth. Steps are cut [for a person] to climb up.* ◆ Antarlkw-warn tywenem ker aherr. (T) *Putting the kangaroo meat in the fork of the tree.* ◆ Arelh yanhel arnang arntarlkw akem mer mpwaretyek. (T) *The woman is cutting forked branches to make a shelter.*
2. cross (Christian cross) • SEE ALSO ntwerlk
antarlkw-irrem, arntarlkw-irrem *vi.*
split, fork out (tree), branch out (tree) ◆ Arntarlkw-irrekarl yanh athimp yanh apek. (St) *That ironwood tree has forked out.*

antarlperrk (sitting) cross-legged SEE UNDER **arntarlperrk**

antarr-wem, antarr-iwem (E) *vt.*
clean up; push something out of the way; throw something out of the way, discard something ◆ Arnam yanh map antarr-way anantherr akethel anetyenheng. (T) *Clean the grass so that we can sit on the clear space.* ◆ Arelh yanhel mantarr antarr-wem rapety-warn. (T) *That woman in throwing her clothes in the bin.* ◆ Mern anakety akem arrernem *clean*-em-ilem arna arrert nheng-lkwerel alakenhel *clean*-em-ilem. *Seed* renhan antarram wemel *clean* anthwerr mparem. *The bush tomato is picked and then the seeds are cleaned out using a tool called* arrert, *with a thing like that. All the seeds are cleaned out and thrown away.*
SEE ALSO iwem, altyewem, intyalp-wem, arrarlp-wem
antarr-arrernem *vt.*
push things to one side; put things into a heap ◆ Kwaty rewel antarr-arrernek anthwelk. (M) *The floodwater has left all the flood refuse in a heap.*
SEE ALSO aketh-ilem, aharl arrernem, aharl-wem, lyernt arrernem, mpwer tywenem, ayak-arrernem, antyakwer-wem

Antarrengeny (E) *n.*
name of place and outstation west of the Sandover River on the Alyawarra Aboriginal Land Trust. See map p. viii.

antay (T,E) *n.*
rope of hairstring; carrying strap made from hairstring ◆ Rwa tha inerl-alpem antayel. (St) *I am carrying the firewood back with a carrying strap.* ◆ Rnwek anternenh angerrety-pwek, kel antayelant angetyam. (T) *A really big water dish, that could only be carried with a carrying strap.*
SEE ALSO alyep[1], antingkar, antyarn, arlpalh, irrkety, alyepengantay, rtwaty
CAN SOUND A BIT LIKE arntay *'deep water'*
antayel angem (T,E), **antayel akngem** (E)
carry something using a carrying strap (angem *'carry'*, *'take'*)
= urtatyel angem, alyepel angem

antay-wem (W,T) *vt.* [SENSITIVE LANGUAGE]
commit sexual indecency; commit adultery
SEE ALSO arlkwer-irrem[2]

antek (T,E) *n.*
wide, spread out ◆ Apwenan arlpa akely-rnem. Areyawarran apwen arlpa ilperr-ilperr-awern, antek-awern, apwen yanh-lkwer arlpenty-antey. (Sa) *The* apwen *bush has small leaves. The* areyawarr *has flattish leaves, a bit wider, whereas the* apwen *leaves are longer.*
SEE ALSO arlpaw
CAN SOUND A BIT LIKE arntek *'tooth'*
antek-irrem (T,E) *vi.*
spread out ◆ Kwaty-penh amangkemel antek-irrem atherrk map lyapemel. (T) *After rain the grass grows up and spreads out.*
antek-ilem (T,E) *vt.*
make something wide, spread something out

◆ Mer rtakw antek-ilemel artem. (Sa) *Building the windbreak a bit wider.*

antekerr *n.*
south
antekerr-penh (W,T), **antekerr-pwenh** (E) *n.*
1. south ◆ Antekerr-penh ayeng alhek. (St) *I went to the south.* ◆ Kerek untherl-anetyek, antekerr-pwenh, altwerl-penh apek. Altwerl-penh uyerlp-uyerrenhem irrer. Altwerl-pwenh-they apety-alpek. (Sa) *Looking round for meat in the south or in the west. Going hunting and disappearing to the west. Then returning from the west.*
2. from the south ◆ Antekerr-they ayeng apety-alpem, antekerr-penh-they. (St) *I came back from the south.*
antekerreng (W,T) *n.*
1. from the south ◆ Rlkang pwenty-alhem antekerreng. (N) *The wind is blowing from the south.*
2. south wind
antekerreny (W,T) *n.*
south wind
antekerr altwerl
south-west (altwerl *'west'*)
antekerr ikngerr (E)
south-east (ikngerr *'east'*)
antekerr-antekerr
south-west, more or less south, southerly
antekerr arraty
due south (arraty *'straight'*, *'correct'*)
antekerr-ampeny *n.*
on the southern side, in the southern area

antelh-ilem (T,E) *vt.*
fill a container up with something (such as food, petrol); collect things together (one by one, bit by bit) ◆ Mern perlap antelh-ilem tha, antelh-ilemel utnhem, panth-warl apek. Mern akngerr-ilemel panth-warl. (St) *I am picking the conkerberries and filling the wooden dish with them. I am gathering a lot of food until it's full up.* ◆ Lyeteny antelh-ilem *billycan*-ekarl arrernem, kenh arrwekeleny panthekarl arrernetyam, antelh-iletyam, mern pwelap. (T) *Nowadays people fill up billycans, whereas in the old days people used to put the food in wooden dishes, fill them up with food.* ◆ *Petrol tank*-ek thelem, antelh-ilem. (T) *Pouring the petrol into the tank to fill it up.*

antelhem *vi.*
1. follow someone (usually when they don't want you to); hang around someone (?); latch onto someone; attach yourself to someone ◆ Kwer nhak antelhem artwa mapel-arleng. (T) *That child is following the men.* ◆ Antelhey ayeng yanhel-arleng. (St) *I'm going to follow that person.* ◆ Tyerrty-warl antelhem ilka, ra angernelhem anem. (St) *Ticks attach themselves to people, then the person scratches themself.*
2. follow or copy what someone is doing ◆ Antelhemel angkay, angka atyenh-warl Anmatyerr-warl. (St) *Follow me and say what I say, in my language, Anmatyerr.* ◆ Antelhemel tha mpwarerl-anem *painting*, angwaremel tha mpwaretyek. (St) *I am making a painting and following what that person is doing, copying them.*
3. catch or become infected with sickness or disease ◆ *Cup* alenheng nta antywem wal ngwenh antelhem akin *bad cold* arlka. (M) *If you drink from that cup you might become infected with a bad cold or something like that.* ◆ Paniken yanh atyenh *wash*-em-ila, nta antywernepernem — artwengkenng-akert ra. Rlkert-akert kwenh antywern, paniken atyenhel, atyeng antelh-hety. (M) *Wash that cup of mine that you've been drinking from — it's got germs on it. You are sick and you drank from my cup and I might catch that sickness.*
SEE ALSO angwarem, apentem, ingkantem, yel-irrem

antelyapelyap, **intelyapelyap** (E) *n.*
butterfly, moth. Also referred to as *thep antelyapelyap.* ◆ Antelyapelyap kwer mapel arrkenel atwem. (N) *The children hit at the butterflies for fun.*
Antelyapelyap Arneng (W) *n.*
name of waterhole east of Mt Allan community

antem (W,T) *part.*
Used when there are a series of actions; then (something else happens), subsequently (something else happens), shows a changed or new situation. ◆ Yenper arternetyam, *clean* antem yarr-wetyam, arrerlp-iletyam. (N) *The spearwood was scraped and cleaned and then straightened and sharpened.* ◆ Mern inyem inyem inyem kel urel anem item, kel ampeng antem arlkwem. (T) *Dig and dig and dig for the food, now cook it in the fire, and then eat it when it's cooked.* ◆ Akeweny tyerrty yanh arerrirra, mantarr akeng-akeng-akertarl apetyekek, akeng-akeng-akert. Akewenyek mantarr antheyaw, mantarr *new one* apek akewenyek anthey mantarr ra irrpetyek. Kel kwer anthem antem, kel ra irrpem antem. (T) *Look at that poor thing that has come along with raggedy clothes. Give the poor thing some new clothes to put on. Then you give them some and then they put them on.* ◆ Thep rantem

angkem, 'Apetyepetyem apetyepetyem'. (M) *Now the bird sings, 'Apetyepetyem apetyepetyem'.* ◆ Rtwekert-akertarl parrk-irrem. Rtwekert ahey-angkentyeh rrwem antem, kel renh parrp *medicine* anthem, wal mwerram antem. (N) *With heart disease a person gets tired. Then their heart beats fast, and if they are given medicine quickly then they get better.*
SEE ALSO -anem2

antenh *n.*
common brush-tailed possum (*Trichosurus vulpecula*) ◆ Antenh arnewarn antyerl-apem. (M) *The possum goes along climbing trees.*
= rrpwamper, pathem

antenh-antenh (E) *n.*
1. mulga native currant, narrow-leaved native currant (*Psydrax suaveolens*). A shrub up to 3 m high, with narrow leaves, small white flowers and fruit which ripens to a black colour.
2. the edible fruits of the mulga native currant
= ngkwernateylp, ngkwernelyerr, anwengk-anwengk
SEE ALSO anngey-anngey

-antep *n.ending*
(up)wards, (down)wards
akern-antep *n.*
1. (going) upwards (akern *'high', 'on top'*) ◆ Atwayntenhem akern-**antep** kel tharew ilenhem anem, kwenelak. (Sa) *Climbing upwards and then facing downwards.*
2. (facing or pointing) upwards ◆ Kwer yanh akern-**antep** intem. (T) *That child is lying facing upwards.*
kwen-antep *n.*
facing or going downwards (kwen *'inside', 'in', 'down'*)
SEE ALSO kwenelak, -akerl, -athek

anter *n.*
1. fat, oil, butter, grease ◆ Alewatyerr anterel apernelhem kapert rwernparl-irrem. (T) *If your head is hot you can rub yourself with goanna fat.*
2. fat, in good condition, plump (of a person) ◆ Ayeng alhetyek atherrkenyel anem, arlewatyerr apek tha atwetyek, ker arlewatyerr ampwarl anek-penh, anter anem. (St) *I'm going hunting for goannas in the green time because the goannas are fat now after being skinny.*
3. Goes before the name of a particular type of fat.
ker anter
edible fat (ker *'meat'*) ◆ Ker anter aherr yanhel ampem. (St) *The kangaroo fat is cooking over there.*
anter angerr
1. very fat, fatty (of meat or an animal) (angerr1 *'lots of'*) ◆ Ker aherr nhenh anter angerr. (M) *This kangaroo is fat.* ◆ Nhenhan ker ampwang-awaty, nhenhan ker anter angerr-awaty. (T) *This meat is a bit lean, whereas this meat is a bit fattier.*
2. fat, in good condition, plump (of a person) ◆ Karteng anter angerr weth apetyepetyem. (St) *That short fat [person] is coming.*
SEE ALSO ampwa
anter-irrem *vi.*
get fat, put on weight
SEE ALSO ampwerrem

anterernp, anterirlp *n.*
1. a type of very strong bush tobacco (?) (*Nicotiana* sp. (?)) ◆ 'Anterernp' anwern ilem, ngkwerlp-arteh akwek ra. Anmatyerrel. Artwa ayang mapel arlkwetyart ngkwerlpeh *starving*-irremel. Renhem ina akemel arlkwetyart. Irntang-areny. Ahangerr. (M) *'Anterernp' is what we call the plant that is like a bush tobacco plant. In Anmatyerr. The old men used to chew it when they were starving for bush tobacco. They used to pick that and chew it. It grows in the hills. It's very strong.* ◆ Anterirlp arlkwenh-arlkwenh-kweny. Arlkwenh-arlkwenh anetyakenh ngkwerlp-artek nheng-lkwer. (St) *That* anterirlp *plant that is similar to the native tobacco is not chewable.*
2. rock isotome (*Isotoma petraea*). A small plant about 30 cm high with soft green leaves and pale blue flowers. It grows around rocks and in caves. It is very poisonous and can cause blindless. Some people say that small amounts were chewed along with native tobacco to increase its potency. • = pitherr

anterl (T,E) *n.*
1. handle
2. a star constellation; the Saucepan (part of Orion) (from English 'handle')

anternem *vt.* [SENSITIVE LANGUAGE]
have sex with someone

-anternenh *n.ending*
very big, enormous, huge. Usually preceded by *+ek* or *+eh* ending. ◆ Rnwek-**anternenh** angerrety-pwek, kel antayelant angetyam. (T) *A really big water dish, that could only be carried with a carrying strap.* ◆ Ankerrmern-areny tyapek-**anternenh** atwerl-apekarl. Atwerl-apek perrap perlatyart angerrety-pwek antem. (N) *We went along chopping out the big fat grubs from the coolibah tree. They were really large, like the grubs from the river red gum.* ◆ Arelh arrpenhel ilem, *'Oh,* rtwarnp angerr

yanhey, arelh yanh apetyepetyem. Rtwarnpek-**anternenh**'. (T) *Another woman says, 'Oh, that woman coming along there has a really big paunch. An enormous paunch'.*

anterrk angkem (E) *vi.*
hiccough, burp (angkem *'talk', 'speak'*) ◆ Ampa akwek anterrk angkem akin, *milk*-penh apek — anterrk angkem atnerteng. (St) *A child might burp as well, after drinking milk — it burps when it's full.*
SEE ALSO anetyerrk-irrem, arnenthernem, artekernem

anterrng *n.*
1. edible seed ◆ Anterrng arrwekelenyel athetyam, apwert arlkwartekarl athetyam. (T) *The olden-time people ground seeds up on flat rocks.* ◆ Akat anterrng anwern awantyerl-apek, athemel. Panth-warn, atwerl-apek, rrpwerl anthwerr kwenh. Ahety-ilem ahety-ilem, rlkwank-ilem alakenh arrernem *clean.* (N) *The munyeroo is a seed that we eat, after grinding it up and putting it in the wooden dish. It's really black in colour. We winnow the seed and separate it out and then put the clean seed to one side.*
2. A general word that can go before the name of a particular type of seed. In the Anmatyerr way of classifying foods most fruits and vegetables are known as *mern,* sweet things as *ngkwarl,* seeds as *anterrng, arnwety* or *ntang,* meats as *ker* and edible grubs as *tyap.*
= ntang
SEE ALSO arnwety

anteth *n.*
1. flower, blossom ◆ Parl twemper, twemper akwek. Anteth-penh akwek twemper irrem, angerrem ra irrem. (N) *A small bush banana. After it flowers the small fruit develops, then the fruit gets bigger.* ◆ Anteth atherrk yanh-lkwer atwem, aherrkek-amparr iwem, antyerrk anem ulpilem. Althartek, artwekenh urntetyek. (St) *Beat the green blossoms, and put them out in the sun first and then, when they are dry, crush them up. They are used for* althart *ceremonies, for men to dance with.*
SEE ALSO alpety
2. feather (down) ◆ Irrety anteth-akert, anteth kwerel wantelhem artwa. (N) *Eaglehawks have down, and it's with that down that the men decorate themselves.*

anteth-anteth (W) *n.*
types of daisies, including Tietkin's daisy (*Rhodanthe tietkensii* and other *Rhodanthe* spp.). The blossoms are used for decoration in ceremonies.

antetherrk, arntetherrk *n.*

carpet python, diamond python (*Morelia spilota* ssp. *bredli*). Also referred to as *ker antetherrk.* ◆ Arntetherrkan aper-areny, aper iylpwerelarl anerl-anem. (Sa) *The carpet python lives in the hollows of river red gum trees.*

antew *n.*
vomit, spew

antew-irrem *vi.*
to vomit, throw up, spew ◆ Ayeng antew-irrem, atherrkarl tha antyernemel. (St) *I am vomiting from smelling the green grass.* ◆ Alem anety antew-irrem. (M) *Vomiting because of a bad stomach.*
SEE ALSO alyelkelhem

antewek-antew (T) *n.*
nauseating
SEE ALSO alyelk-alyelk, alyew-alyew, kaly-kaly[2]

antew arrernem (W,T) *vt.*
tell a story (said of the *lyweketweretwer* 'pallid cuckoo') (arrernem *'put'*) ◆ Thep yanhel antew arrernety-alhem ilem alethangarl apetyem. (T) *That bird [the pallid cuckoo] went and told everyone that a stranger is coming.*

antewarety *n.*
A respectful word for 'man' used by women to refer to some relations, especially sons-in-law. ◆ Rtwalty apekarl akem 'antewaretyan'. 'Artwa' aketyakenh, antewarety. (St) *A son-in-law is called* 'antewarety' *[by a woman]. They are not called* 'artwa' *[the ordinary word for man].* ◆ Ampa akelyek apek ilem anngernt-irrerl-anetyal ilanthem, 'antewarety'. *Not* 'mwey-mwey'. (Sa) *[When you] are telling a little child not to be naughty, and sending them off, you say* 'antewarety'. *Not* 'mwey-mwey'. ◆ Antewarety yanh ahanety-alhang kwenh. (M) *Go and see that man over there [said by a woman in referring to respect kin].*
SEE ALSO mey-mey[1], ampeyamp, alyakw, arlwety-penh, arlwety[2]

-antey *ending*
1. Emphasises that an action or state of affairs has continued for some time; always, again, still, yet, keep on (doing action). ◆ Yanh-**antey** ran. *'He's still there.'* ◆ Urlepety-**antey** ayengan anep-anem, apmer arrpenh-kenh-warl alhetyakenh. (St) *I keep stopping in one place, I haven't been to other people's country.* ◆ Anwernan akwet-**antey** ananem, alhetyakenh. (T) *We are still living here, we haven't gone anywhere.* ◆ Ahakey nhenh anthwerrk-**antey**, alherl atyet-irretyenh

rrpwerl-irremel. (St) *This* ahakey *plum is still unripe, wait till it gets ripe and black.* ◆ Ampa akwek atyet-atyet alhem. Atnyem ra, kel akem-irrerl-alhem kel alhem-**antey**arl ra, atnyem-**antey**arl ra. (St) *The small child toddles along. She falls then gets up and goes, then keeps going, then falls again.* ◆ Nthenh-angkwerr nga uyerreperrem. Ayengarl ngkweng uyarn-**antey** ayeng mpwelhek, untan alhep-alhemant, uyerreperremarl nga. (St) *Where did you get to? I kept waiting for you in vain and you kept going, disappeared.*
2. With negative verbs, emphasises that an action hasn't yet happened. ◆ Antyanp ngkwerlp akely atherrk lyapem, aketyakenh-**antey** alerl. Antyanp *are the small green shoots of the native tobacco plant that haven't been picked yet.*
3. Emphasises the similarity between things; too, as well, also, is similar to. ◆ Rewelyek-akert nanekwet. Yep-yep rewelyek akert-**antey**. (St) *Goats have horns. Sheep have horns as well.*

rantey (E) *prn.*
1. something is similar to or the same as something else
2. emphasises that someone did an action themselves ◆ **Rantey** pewelhek terangk apekarl irrek. (St) *He brought trouble on himself by getting drunk.*
SEE ALSO ra

aleth-antey *adv.*
continuing to do something for a long time; doing something for good
SEE ALSO aleth

rrwek-antey (W,T), **urrek-antey** (T,E)
'Wait on', 'Wait a minute', 'Wait a while'
= alerl-antey
SEE ALSO rrwek

ingkerr-antey *n.*
all, the whole lot, all of them
SEE ALSO ingkerr[1]

+anth *prn.ending*
1. Goes on the end or in the middle of dual and plural pronouns and shows that the people being referred to are in opposite patrimoieties. For example, a person or persons, along with their spouse, cross-cousins, father's mother or mother's father. See Appendix 1. ◆ Rrwey nhenh anewek anpem, kemelh-ilem renh, 'Kemirray! Il**anth** alperretyekay!' (N) *The man touches his wife to wake her up and says, 'Get up! We two are going back!'*
2. Goes on the end or in the middle of plural pronouns when the kin relations are not specified or in a group where there is a range of kin relations. ◆ Apmer iwenhel arr**anth**err anep-anem? (St) *Where do you all live?* ◆ Arr**anth**err irrkwaperl-anenhareyay ayengan anyent irrkwapepapem-kety. (Sa) *All of you do some work, because I am working on my own.*
SEE ALSO +ak

antha[1] (E) *n.*
mud. Also referred to as *ahern antha.*
SEE ALSO urta, antha[1], anthwerrng, ata[1], tert
CAN SOUND A BIT LIKE ntha *'give'*

antha[2], **anthang** (W) *n.*
stone point in handle of woomera; stone knife. Also referred to as *apwert antha.* ◆ Apwert antha, ker-kenh, ker akemelarl arlkwetyart aherr tyep-ilemel apwert antha yanhel. (St) *The stone knife is used for meat — that stone called* 'antha' *used to be used for cutting up kangaroo meat to eat.*
SEE ALSO kartamp, inkwartety, irntarlter, irntang arlter, werlamp, ipa
CAN SOUND A BIT LIKE ntha *'give'*

anthakem (E) *vt.*
1. interrupt someone to try to get their attention ◆ Tha anthakem ngenh *stop*-emilemel. (Sa) *I am trying to get your attention to make you stop.*
2. cut across someone when they are trying to do something ◆ Ilekek unta anthaketyelan — ayengarrp alhetyel anay kerek urek unthep-untherl. (Sa) *Why are you interrupting me — sit down while I go myself for meat and firewood.*

anthakemel angkem (E)
talk across someone, talk over the top of someone, interrupt
SEE ALSO atnalth-ilem

anthal (T,E) *n.*
young white tubers of the bush potato or desert yam (*Ipomoea costata*) ◆ Mwarel angernemel anaty anthalek, anthal then urrper then. (Sa) *Digging with the wooden scoop for the bush potato tuber, for the* anthal *and the* urrper.
SEE ALSO anaty, anek, akwerrk[1], lyelyerr, urrper

anthang (W) stone point in handle of woomera; stone knife SEE UNDER **antha**[2]

antharr (E) *n.*
desert death adder (*Acanthophis pyrrhus*)
= mantharr

anthelk[1], **anthwelk** (W,T) *n.*
tree litter, flood refuse, dead leaves and sticks (left by floodwater) ◆ Anthwelk lpway-angkwerr intem. Anthwelk kwatyel antarr

angem an arrernenhem iterehem, kwatyel anthwelk. *The flood refuse lies along in the creek. The water carries it along and leaves it along the sides of the creek.*
SEE ALSO nthat, inthwerey

anthelk[2] (E) *n.*
'Poor thing' (an expression of sympathy or fondness) ◆ Aperlaty. 'Akem-irrey. Nyany anthelk akem-irrey. Ingkerrek anwantherr.' *My grandmother. 'Get up. All my poor old grannies get up. We've all got to get up.'*
SEE ALSO akeweny

Anthelper (W,T), **Antherlper** (W,T) *n.*
Morning Star, Daylight Star, Venus ◆ Anthelper angerr anenty-alhem, kweny-itweh. (N) *In the night the big Morning Star comes up.*
= Arwenpeng, Awelh, Kwerraly Angerr, Kwerraly Rltwa, Kwerraly Urlta
SEE ALSO kwerraly

anthem *vt.*
give something to someone ◆ Nhenhan tha ngkweng anthem arnam ntyenty angerr ngwenh mwerr-iletyek. (T) *I am giving you this scented herbal grass to make yourself better.* ◆ Akangkwerrenty itya, kwer kwerl-areny map. Maneyekant angkerl-anem, maney akwel ngkwelty anthetyeh. (N) *The school kids don't pay attention. Apparently they just ask for money, ask to be given coins.*
antherrem *vi.*
give things to each other; swap things ◆ Ulengerek ulengerek anthem — unta ayeng mern akwek anthem, tha ngenh anthem. Ulengerek ulengerekarl antherreperrem. (St) *Giving things backwards and forwards to each other — you give me a bit of food and I give you some. Giving things to each other.*
anthelhem *vi.*
give yourself up for payback (traditional punishment) ◆ Atwerrenty-penh anthelhem, tyerrtyel renh atwetyek. 'Anthelhay! Rem ngwenh atwetyeh!' (T) *After a fight, a person gives himself up, so someone can punish him. 'Give yourself up! He wants to hit you!'* ◆ Menty ngenh atwetyek anthelhay. (Sa) *Just give yourself up so that they can hit you.*
war anthem
lend something to someone ◆ War thwengk anthern, angety-alpang antey. (M) *I just lent it to you and you can bring it back later.*
kalty-anthem, kaltyel-anthem (E)
teach (kalty '*knowledgeable*')
paty anthem (W,T)
breastfeed (paty '*breast*')
= werlaty anthem

anthep (T,E) *n.*
women's dance at initiation (young man) ceremonies
anthep-irrem (T,E) *vi.*
to dance (women) ◆ Awelyek anthep-irreperrem anwantherr. (St) *We are dancing* awely *ceremonies.* ◆ Anwern alhem anthep-irretyek anmanty-warn. (T) *We'll go and dance in the young men's ceremony.*
SEE ALSO rntwem

anthep-anthep (E) *n.*
nankeen kestrel (*Falco cenchroides*)
= lyentyelyeng, lyentyelyaw, warakeparleparl, ulpmerr-atwenh
SEE ALSO nyengk-rnternenh

Antherlper (W,T) Morning Star, daylight star, Venus SEE UNDER **Anthelper**

antherrty *n.*
steep rockface or cliff; steep-sided mountain. Also referred to as *irntang antherrty* or *apwert antherrty*.
= arnka, apwert arnka

anthety (E) *n.*
young man, young fellow. Also referred to as *artwa anthety*.

anthetyingk (T,E) *n.*
fatty meat. Also referred to as *ker anthetyingk*.
SEE ALSO anter angerr

anthim-ilem (T,E), **anthipm-ilem** (E) *vt.*
smash or crush something (with stone axe or rock)
SEE ALSO ulpilem, apert-atwem, mwely-mwely, mweltyem

anthurrk (T,E) the green, unripe fruit of the native currant SEE UNDER **anthwerrk**[1]

anthurrng (E) mud SEE UNDER **anthwerrng**

anthwek-anthwek *n.*
wet (clothes); dripping, drenched or soaked (with blood or another liquid) ◆ Anthwek-anthwekek atwem alhwant anem irrem, anthwek-anthwekarl atwek. (St) *[He] was hit until the blood started pouring out, till he was drenched with blood.*
SEE ALSO kanthwek-anthwek, lthangkw
anthwek-anthwek-ilem *vt.*
drench or soak something ◆ Mantarr atyenh anthwek-anthwek-ilek kwenh. (St) *My clothes have got soaked.*

anthwel (T,E) *n.*
soft (of food)
SEE ALSO ampeng, apely
anthwel-irrem (T,E) *vi.*
go soft from cooking ◆ Mern anaty anthwel-irrem. Ker apek rlterrkarl aneman anthwel-

irrem-antey. (St) *Bush potatoes go soft from cooking. Meat that is tough goes soft as well.*
anthwel-ilem (T,E) *vt.*
make something go soft by cooking it
◆ Anthwel-ilemel item awerrthel. (Sa) *Cook it in the hot ashes to make it soft.*
CAN SOUND A BIT LIKE anthwelh-ilem *'squeeze something out of something'*

anthwelk (W,T) tree litter, flood refuse SEE UNDER anthelk[1]

anthwely-anthwely (T) *n.*
plenty of food
anthwely-anthwely-ilem (T) *vt.*
collect plenty of food ◆ Ker thwen mern arwenth inang anthwely-anthwely-ilek. (T) *They collected plenty of meat and food.*

anthwem (T,E) *vi.*
seep or ooze out of something; leak out; weep (of wounds) ◆ Anthwemarl ankwarn utyen-they. Utyenengarl anthwem. (Sa) *The pus seeps out of the wound.* ◆ Athengarlperl apek anthwem, lyetant arratepaterl, wal anthwem anem irrert-irrerl-anem ahern-warl. (St) *The ironwood tree gum seeps out of the tree, comes out and then drips to the ground.*
SEE ALSO thelelhem
CAN SOUND A BIT LIKE unthem *'walk around'*
anthwelh-ilem (T,E) *vt.*
squeeze something out from something, e.g. pus from a boil ◆ Kwarnarlelhetyel arnterrarl awangkek anthwelh-ilem. Nga mwerr anem untherl-ayntetyek anthwelh-ilemarl yanh-lkweran. Anthwelh-ilenh-ilenhan artwekeran. (Sa) *[If] you are in a great deal of pain from a large swelling, then you'll feel better if you squeeze things like that [to get the pus out]. Boils are squeezed.*
SEE ALSO antyelp-ilem
CAN SOUND A BIT LIKE anthwel-ilem *'make something go soft by cooking it'*

anthwerr (W,T) *part.*
very, really, completely, totally ◆ Ampeng anthwerr. (M) *[It's] really cooked.* ◆ Ngkwarl anyemaywerrk akin anem, rnpwa akin perrap theweyet anthwerr inenhem. Anyem-areny. Anyemangkwarl. (N) *There is also a sweet resin from the witchetty bush called* 'anyemaywerrk' *or* 'anyemangkwarl'. *We collect that and it's really sweet.* ◆ Thwengk apawenhem mern apek ker apek kwenh, angayel anthwerr kwenh. (N) *I am asking you for bread or meat because I am really hungry.* ◆ Akat anterrng anwern awantyerl-apek, athemel. Panth-warn, atwerl-apek, rrpwerl anthwerr kwenh. Ahety-ilem ahety-ilem, rlkwank-ilem alakenh arrernem *clean.* (N) *The munyeroo is a seed that we eat, after grinding it up and putting it in the wooden dish. It's really black in colour. We winnow the seed and separate it out and then put the clean seed to one side.* ◆ Aperrk atyerrem rwel arlatyey map an arlkwemem ampeng mwerr anthwerr patartart. (N) *The pencil yams are cooked in the coals and then eaten and when they are cooked they taste really nice, like potatoes.*
mwerr anthwerr (W,T)
really good

anthwerrk[1] (T,E), **anthurrk** (T,E) *n.*
the green, unripe fruit of the native currant, native citrus (*Psydrax latifolia*) ◆ Ahakey nhenh anthwerrk-antey, alherl atyet-irretyenh rrpwerl-irremel. (St) *This* ahakey *plum is still unripe, so wait till it gets ripe and black.*
SEE ALSO ahakey, irnta

anthwerrk[2] (T,E) *n.*
green, watery contents of a kangaroo's stomach. Also known as *atna anthwerrk, ana anthwerrk* or *ker anthwerrk*. This was used to squeeze over the head in the hot weather to cool oneself down. ◆ Atna atherrk 'anthwerrk' anem akem. Kapert *headache* apek apernelhem. (St) *The green stuff [in the kangaroo's stomach] is called* 'anthwerrk'. *If you have a headache you can rub it on your head.*

anthwerrng (W,T), **anthurrng** (E) *n.*
mud. Also referred to as *kwaty anthwerrng*.
◆ Mwetek atanelhem lherel, anthwerrngel. (M) *The car is getting bogged in the creek, in the mud.* ◆ Perrpantyel irntelarl anem, wal anthwerrng akin arrernem, antywang akwek kwer artem, inteyel. (M) *Black-faced woodswallows live in the rocks and they make mud nests in caves.*
SEE ALSO antha[1], tert, urta, ata[1]

anthwerrng-irrem (T) *vi.*
1. feel upset about something (women)
◆ Marl atherrel atyeng anthwerrng-irrek merneng. (T) *Two women got upset with me over food.*
2. feel sad or upset over men (women); pine for (?) ◆ Marl arrpenh-warnarl alhemeng marl yanh kwer anthwerrng-irrerl-anem, arnerl-anem kwer. Arnerl-anemel anthwerrng-irrerl-anem kwer, marl arrpenh-warnarl alhemelarl iwerl-alhem. Wal, antherrng-irrerl-anem kwer marl arrwekel-penh kwerenh. (T) *If he goes off with another woman then she feels upset and sits there crying for him. She cries and pines for him, because he has gone off and left her for*

another woman. Well, the woman who was his first wife gets very sad.
SEE ALSO arnem

antingkar (E) *n.* [RESPECT LANGUAGE]
1. hairstring belt or strap
SEE ALSO antyarn, antay, arlpalh, irrkety, antay
2. young man who is going through initiation (young man) business ◆ Antingkar nhak alhek-kety. (St) *[Watch out] for the young business men who went over there.*
SEE ALSO alyepelengkw, awerrty, arwekert, lyaty, arleyarr, amarleyarr, tyakwertekwert, lwekerleny

antwekenety (W), **antwekeneyt** (E), **antweken** *n.* [RESPECT LANGUAGE]
south ◆ Antweken atyety-ayerr-warl ahanenherl-wek ngwarrengkw. (St) *Your husband went off hunting, to the south [mother talking to her daughter].*
SEE ALSO antekerr, aywelernety, ngwelernety, altwerlernety
antweken-athek *n.* [RESPECT LANGUAGE]
in a southerly direction, to the south

antwenharr (E), **nthwenharr** (E) *n.*
a type of cloud (after rain has finished) ◆ Alker-ilenhem antwenharrel. (St) *The* antwenharr *clouds clear the rain up.* ◆ Kwaty ankert-artek-anteyarl antwenharr anem, wal ra alheparl alhem, kwaty-iperr ampeny. (St) *The* antwenharr *clouds are a bit like* ankert *clouds, but they move along, left over after the rain.*
SEE ALSO akwerrk[1], urrarl, urrartn

antweparr (W) *n.* [RESPECT LANGUAGE]
water
SEE ALSO kwaty

antwerlperlp (W,T) *n.*
1. ground that is swollen and raised up because of a tuber or a swollen root underneath ◆ Antyalkenyarl anyenem-artek, antwerlperlp. Antwerlperlp anem anyenem. Anatyel arlka artek. (T) Antwerlperlp *is like what the* antyalkeny *yams have. They make the earth swell up. And like the bush potatoes do.*
2. the sound that the ground makes when there is a tuber or a swollen root underneath and it is tapped with a crowbar or digging stick
SEE ALSO urrper, akarternenty
antwerlperlp-wem (W,T) *vt.*
make a hollow sound (when there is a tuber or a swollen root underneath and the ground is tapped with a crowbar or digging stick) ◆ Antwerlperlp-wem, nta apek atanthem alakenh, ahelh apek nta atanthem anemel, anyematy apek, 'Nhenh-iperr antwerlperlp-wernay'. (M) *You might be poking or tapping the ground with a digging stick to listen for the sound that tells you there is a witchetty grub underneath, and then you say, 'Here is where the ground made that hollow sound'.*
= arntwangkem
antwerlperlp arrernem (W,T)
make the earth swell up (by a swollen root or tuber underneath) ◆ Mern anatyel antwerlperlp arrernem ahern. (T) *The bush potato is making the earth swell up.*
antwerlperlp-antwerlperlp (W,T) *n.*
fat, particularly around the legs and stomach area ◆ Arelh antwerlperlp-antwerlperlp terawath-akert apem — arelh ampwerrk angerr. (T) *The woman with the really fat legs and stomach is wandering round in trousers — the really fat woman.*

antwerrem (T,E) to growl (dog) SEE UNDER **arntwerrem**

Antwerrepenh *n.*
the name of a rockhole near where the Pine Hill road intersects with the Stuart Highway

antwerrkem hold something SEE UNDER **arntwerrkem**

antwerrkenh (W,T), **antwerrkeny** (T), **intwerrkenh** (W) *n.*

black-headed python (*Aspidites melanocephalus*). Also referred to as *ker antwerrkenh.*
◆ Antwerrkenh arlewatyerr-kenh alhwengel anem. (T) *The black-headed python lives in goanna holes.* ◆ Ker antwerrkenh, tyerrtyel arlkwem. Arrwekeleny mapel arlkwetyart. (M) *People eat the black-headed python. The olden-time people used to eat them.*
= arrwerrperl, rwayerrp, urayerrp

Antwerrpel (T) *n.*
the name of a place in the Pine Hill area

antweth (E) *n.*
white silky substance inside fruit of bush banana, silky pear, *alangkw, parl* (*Marsdenia australis*)

antya (W) throat SEE UNDER **ahenty**[1]

antya (W) like or want something SEE UNDER **ahenty**[2]

antya[1] (E) *n.*
worm found in kangaroo's stomach
◆ Ngangkar ikwerenh, 'antya' anem renh ilem. Anertel-arleng, atherrkel-arleng. (St) *The [kangaroo's] traditional healer is called 'antya'. It's found in the stomach, in the green grass in the stomach.*

= ultyitywelty
SEE ALSO ngangkar
CAN SOUND A BIT LIKE ahenty¹ *'throat'*; ahenty² *'desire'*

antya² (T,E) *n.*
snake venom, snake poison ◆ Apmwa antyakert, arntekelarl anyenem. Wal, apmwa antya anem arrep-wem. (St) *Snakes have venom that they keep in their teeth. Well, the snake spits the venom out.*
CAN SOUND A BIT LIKE ahenty¹ *'throat'*; ahenty² *'desire'*

antyakem *vt.*
uproot something (such as grass); pull seeds or resin off plant; loosen and break something ◆ Rwarr angerrel arna antyakem. (St) *The big wind uproots the trees.* ◆ Arnwety. Atherl-apemel. *Grandmother*-rlpwerel ahety-iletyam altywart. Ahety-iletyam ayerrelarl arrernetyam *heap* arrernetyam yerrel. Twetyam wetyam wetyam antyakem iletyart akemel panth-warn lernetyam ahety-iletyam athetyem angernetyam. Awantyetyam altyart. (N) Altywart *is a seed that is ground up. All our grandmothers used to winnow the* altywart *seeds. They winnowed the seeds that the ants had heaped up. They pulled the seeds off the grass into wooden dishes, winnowed the seeds and then ground them up and took them back to eat.*

antyakwer (E) *vt.*
a bundle or heap ◆ Antyakwer inep-inem yanhel, mer arrpenh-warn apek ra anam-irrem. (St) *That person is collecting their things into a bundle, maybe because they are shifting to another place.*
SEE ALSO artaper, anhwert, aharl, thalh

antyakwer-wem (E) *vt.*
make something into a bundle; throw things into a heap ◆ Antayel ra akngety-alpem antyakwer-wemel ura apek — ura antyakwer inentyem antayel. (St) *She is bringing the firewood back in a carrying strap and then throwing it into a heap — the bundle of wood that she has collected in the carrying strap.*
SEE ALSO artaper-wem, aharl arrernem, aharl-wem, lyernt arrernem, mpwer tywenem, ayak-arrernem, antarr-arrernem

antyalkenh (T,E), **antyalkeny** (W,T) *n.*
1. type of bush potato, yam (*Ipomoea* sp. *Stirling PK Latz 10408*). A shrub to 1 m high, with branches that creep for up to 4 m along the ground, big pink trumpet-like flowers and large round tubers. Only grows around the Arnmanapwenty area, to the east of Ti Tree.
2. the edible tuber of this bush potato ◆ Mern antyalkenh, mern anwernekantherr akngankekarl. (St) *The* antyalkenh *yam is a food that was created in the Dreaming for us.* ◆ Mer *Long Range*-el anem mern antyalkeny *too much, pumpkin*-artek. (M) *At Long Range [*Arnmanapwenty*] there are lots of* antyalkeny *yams, and they are like pumpkins.*
SEE ALSO anaty, anek, arlatyey

antyalyerrkwereny (E),
antyalyerrkwenenh (E) *n.*
a type of ant

antyam *n.*
something that is used to cover the ground; groundsheet, bedding, blanket, swag, mat ◆ Antyamel intem. (St) *Lying on the blanket.* ◆ Antyamel anerl-anem anantherr. Antyam-kweny arrwekelenyan anek, war arnam arlperlpelant. (T) *We are sitting on the blanket. There weren't any blankets before and [people] just used* arlperlp *grass to sit on.* ◆ Angwely map altywernerl-anem antyamel. (M) *The dogs are curled up on the swag.*
SEE ALSO antyepanty, pangkarr, panty, rnwananty, urnanenty, thewak, pelangket

antyam-wem, antyam-iwem (E) *vt.*
spread out a bed, blanket or groundsheet; spread out leaves to cut meat on ◆ Than antyam-iwem alerl. Arengk arey atwey tha antyam-iweyameng. (St) *Wait while I spread the blanket out. Hunt the dogs away so that I can spread the blanket.*

antyan-akelhem (W) *vi.*
1. climb up something ◆ Tyerrty antyan-akelhem akern antem ngkwarl atwetyeh. (M) *The person climbs up the tree to chop the sugarbag.*
2. take off into the air, ascend ◆ *Aeroplane* antyan-akelhem lyetant kwenh. (M) *The aeroplane is about to take off.* • SEE ALSO alker-irrem², alkerek-irrem

antyanp¹ (E) *n.*
a small wooden shovel or scoop made from a hollow branch and used for handling hot coals, cooking food, or getting a damper out of the fire ◆ Anterrng alyatywereng map itetyam antyanp ikwerel. Mwar-artek akwek, panth-artek akwek. Aperrk akernek arrernem antyanpel. (St) *The* alyatywereng *seeds were cooked in the* antyanp. *The* antyanp *is like a little wooden scoop or dish. The coals are put on the top of it.*
= tyerrker
SEE ALSO mwar, panth

antyanp² (T,E) *n.*
young shoots of native tobacco (*Nicotiana* spp.) ◆ Antyanp ngkwerlp akely atherrk

lyapem, aketyakenh-antey alerl. Antyanp *are the small green shoots of the native tobacco plant that haven't been picked yet.*
= ngkwerlp akwerrk, rrngwaly, akerrng, ngerrng
SEE ALSO ngkwerlp

antyaper, **intyaper** (T) *n.*
1. all (of something), the whole thing; full, uncut, entire ◆ Mer antyaper. (T) *Every place.* ◆ *Australia* antyaper. (T) *All of Australia.* ◆ Iltya antyaper. (M) *The whole hand.*
SEE ALSO ampwerrk, alewarr
2. lots (of people), all of the people ◆ Tyerrty antyaper anem. *There's lots of people there.*

antyarlk (E) *n.*
a type of caterpillar, elephant grub ◆ Antyarlkan arlkwerretyart, arrwekelenyel-arey ipetyartan arlkwerretyart. Antyarlkan artelhampw. (Sa) *People used to eat the* antyarlk *caterpillars, the olden-time people used to squeeze the guts out of them and eat them.* Antyarlk *are really big.*
SEE ALSO arrpayerr, unerrengayt, ayep

antyarlk ngkwern (T) *n.*
pelvis, hipbone

antyarlkw (E) *n.*
a nest in a burrow (?) ◆ Antyarlkw, thakwerel apekarl arrernem antyarlkw, antyam kwerenh, arnamarl ra ulpilekarl. Alhweng-warl kwen antyarlkw ra arrernem. (St) *Mice make nests of grass, their beds, out of the grass that they have broken up into bits. They make them inside their burrows.*
SEE ALSO antywa

antyarn (E) *n.*
hairstring, hairstring belt or strap
= irrkety
SEE ALSO alyep

antyarrp-ilem (E) play a joke on someone SEE UNDER ayntarrp-ilem

antyatar-antyatar, **antyater-antyater** *adv.*
(walking) quickly, purposefully and resolutely (often with intent to fight); (hopping or skipping along) showing intention to fight. Only used of women. ◆ Kweter-akert yanh apety-petyem antyater-antyater. (T) *That woman with the nulla-nulla is coming [striding] along resolutely/purposefully.*
antyatar-irrem, **antyater-irrem** *vi.*
walk quickly, purposefully and resolutely (often with intent to fight); hop or skip along showing intention to fight
SEE ALSO anwerntem, apeyarr-irrem, rrwernter, arrtyernem

Antyay (T,E) *n.*
Wood Duck Swamp, on Mt Skinner Station. See map p. viii.

antyekanty (T,E) *n.*
mantis, stick insect (*Eurycnema osiris*). This insect is poisonous to cattle.
= kapert atwenh
Antyekanty-atherr (E) *n.*
Magellanic Clouds (atherr[1] *'two'*)

antyelp-ilem (E) *vt.*
make something burst or bust; burst something that has liquid inside, such a boil or pimple ◆ Utyen tyapinp antyelp-ilem. (St) *Squeezing a boil.* ◆ Antyelp-ilek anem tha apalel. Kel inem alakenh arwakemarl renh artekerr. Tyap antyelp-ilek atha. (St) *I mistakenly busted it. Levering up the root, I burst [the witchetty grub].*
= aterlk-ilem
SEE ALSO ipelhip-ilem, anthwelh-ilem
CAN SOUND A BIT LIKE ntyerlp-ilem *'stoke up a fire'*
antyelp-irrem (E) *vi.*
burst ◆ *Balloon* apek antyelp-irrekaw, alpwely-irrek anem. (St) *A balloon might burst and then go flat.*
= aterlkem
SEE ALSO atem, rltwar-rnkem, urltar-rnkem

antyelty (E), **intyelty** (E) *n.*
1. tree, bush, plant ◆ Antyelty atnartengel anem, apeng rltwel. (Sa) *Sitting at the base of the big kurrajong tree.*
2. stick
3. thing (any sort of thing)
4. A general word that can go before the word for a particular type of tree or plant.
= arwerl, arna

antyem *vi.*
1. climb up something ◆ Arnang akern antyem, arnang kwerengam anyem, kwer. (N) *The child climbs to the top of the tree and then falls down.* ◆ Amwek arlkety-alhem, 'Iwenham nta arna renh antyantyam akernan kwenh? Nhenham arertarl-irrek ntwa antyerl-anetyeh arna akerneh kwenh. *You want to* anerl-anerl arna antyetyal kwenh!' (N) *The mother sings out, 'What are you climbing that tree for? You must have gone mad to want to climb to the top of the tree. You should sit down and not climb trees!'* ◆ Arnkarr antyem, akern anthwerram antyenhem, akern anthwerrelam aperl-apem aperl-apem. (N) *Climbing the bank of the creek, climbing right to the top, and then going along the very top.*
2. ride; mount or get on or into something such as a car, horse or bicycle ◆ Kwer rrwey antyem patyekelek. *The boy is riding the bike.*
SEE ALSO nganem, atwayntem, antyan-akelhem

antyerl-alhem *vi.*
get into something and go ◆ Mwetekayek antyerl-alhaw! (St) *Get into the car and go!*

-antyem SEE UNDER **+ety-aynt+**

antyen angerr (T) bush plum SEE UNDER **antyern angerr**

antyeny (T,E) *n.*
1. old person, grey-headed person ◆ 'Antyeny' ilem artwa ampwa — *old people.* Or tyerrty arrpenh apek, 'Antyenyay!' (St) *'Antyeny' is what you call an old man — old people. Or you might call out to another person, 'Antyenyay!'*
2. dear person, dear old thing ◆ Antyeny apetyepetyemaw, akeweny. (T) *The dear old thing is coming, the poor thing.*
3. that dear person (one known to the speaker or to the person being spoken to) • SEE ALSO wemey
CAN SOUND A BIT LIKE ntyeny *'red mallee'*

antyepanty (W,T) *n.*
blanket, groundsheet ◆ Anwengkerr antyepantyel anem, yerreng arlka, nhwekerr. (T) *We are sitting on the blanket because of the ants, in case they bite us.*
= antyam

antyepanty-wem (W,T) *vt.*
lay or spread something out; spread out leaves to cut meat on ◆ Marl mapel waly akem akem akem, angetyem antyepanty-wem waly renh antyepanty-wem. (N) *The women cut lots of leafy branches and then they bring them and spread them out.* ◆ Antyepanty-wetyam pelangket anetyakenh arnam war, antyepanty-wem arnam arlperlp, arlperlpel akwet intetyam antyamel. (N) *If [we] haven't got any blankets we just spread out grasses, such as the* arlperlp *grass, and then sleep on a blanket of grass.*
= antyam-wem

antyepey (W,T), **antyeper** (T,E), **antyiper** (E) *n.*
1. type of bat ◆ Iylpwer-arenyap antyiper. Ahelengkw, utnherl arlka. (St) *The bat lives in hollow trees. They are aggressive and they'll bite as well.* ◆ Antyepeyel thakey inerl-alhek kwenyel arlkwetyek. (T) *At night bats go and get mice to eat.*
2. buds of the bloodwood (*Corymbia opaca*) (?)

antyer (W) *n.*
a type of grass. Has edible seed.

antyern angerr (T), **antyen angerr** (T) *n.*
1. bush plum, native citrus (*Psydrax latifolia*). A shrub up to 3 m high, with broad, deep green leaves, small white flowers and fruit which ripens to a black colour.
2. the edible fruits of the bush plum ◆ Anwengkerr alhey lyweny, antyern-angerr-warn. Antyern-angerr anantherr akwernetyek. (T) *Let's go hunting and get some bush plums to eat.*
= ahakey, arrarntenh, artapaly

antyernem[1] (W,T) *vi.*
1. be in pain; hurt ◆ Artep-akert alakenh intem, arteparl antyernem-akert. Artep antyernem rlkertel. (N) *Lying down with a sore back, with your back hurting. Feeling sick and having a sore back.*
2. feel funny or cold in the stomach after eating fatty meat, meat cooked in fat, or drinking cold water; feel queasy or nauseous ◆ Anter arlkwemel anert ayeng antyernem. (T) *My stomach feels queasy after eating fat.*
SEE ALSO atnerteng

antyernem[2] (T,E) *vt.*
cool something down ◆ Iylkel antyernem, irrernt-irremel. (St) *The wind cools [you] down.* ◆ Kwatyel antyernety-alhem, irrernt-ilety-alhem, antyelpantyernety-alhem. (St) *The water cools [you] down, making you cool.*
SEE ALSO irrernt-ilem, wernelhem

antyernem[3] (W) *vt.*
wet the ground (water), water soak into the ground ◆ Kwatyel antyernem ahelh. (M) *The water is soaking the ground.*

antyerr (E), **antyirr** (E) *n.*
spiny-tailed monitor (*Varanus acanthurus*)
= kerr-kerr

antyerrk *n.*
dried (of food, vegetation); withered, not green (of vegetation) ◆ Lyetantarl antyerrk-irrerl-anem, arlpa, waly. Antyerrk-irremel anem anyem ahern-warl. (St) *The leaves and branches are just drying up lately. They dry up and then they fall to the ground.* ◆ Mern atyenh antyerrk, iwetyek tha arengkek. (St) *I'm going to throw my dried-up food to the dogs.*
= arleny

antyerrk-irrem *vi.*
dry up, get dry, wither ◆ Aleny ayeng antyerrk-irrek, kwaty-kwenyel. (St) *Without water, my tongue has gone dry.*
SEE ALSO aherraty-irrem, ahepet-irrem

antyerrk-ilem *vt.*
make something dry, dry something

antyert *n.*
keep something with you all the time; always be together with someone ◆ Anyent apek ra akngem irlkwatherr ikwer, atherr apek ra ikngwerl-alhem — wal, antyert-akert alhem anem ra. (St) *He might take one person with him as company, or he might ask two people to go*

with him — well, then he goes with them. ◆ Bag akenh tha antyert akngenhepenhem atyenh, mantarr tha antyert akngem, ankey-kety antyert akngem. (St) *I carry my bag with me, and I keep my clothes with me, in case someone asks for them.* ◆ Arwengk-wety thang antyert angenherl-anem yakweth ngkerlp-akert. (M) *I carry the bag with the tobacco in it along with me in case someone steals it.*

antyet-antyet (T,E) *n.*
wet
antyet-antyet-ilem (T,E) *vt.*
wet something ◆ Kwatyel lernemaw, antyet-antyet-ilemel. (St) *The rain is falling and making things wet.*
SEE ALSO anthwek-anthwek-ilem

antyetem (E) *vt.*
satisfy hunger or thirst, eat or drink quickly, really get stuck into food or drink ◆ Angayel tha antyetetyek atyeweyay. (Sa) *I'm really hungry and I'm going to get stuck into it [the food].* ◆ Angkethakwel tha antyetetyek. (Sa) *I'm thirsty and I'm going to drink [a lot] to satisfy my thirst.*
= arrwer-ilem[1]

antyetyerr *n.*
tree frog (*Litoria* spp.) ◆ Kwaty-kwenyel *too* ra angkerl-anem 'Aaaaaang aaaaaaang aaaaaaang'. *Baby*-artek ra artnem. (St) *When there is no water it sings out 'Aaaaaang aaaaaaang aaaaaaang'. It cries like a baby.*
= larrangkern, karlarrangkern
SEE ALSO alemerr, atweynterl

antyewarl (T,E), **intyewarl** (E) *n.*
1. a type of bush tomato plant (*Solanum chippendalei* (hill form) (?)). Plant about 80 cm high (though it may grow to 1.5 m) with purple flowers and fruits which are pale yellow when ripe. The seeds inside the fruit are inedible, and are thrown away.
2. the edible fruit of this bush tomato plant
= ngantyewarl
SEE ALSO anakety, unemangkerr

antyey[1] (W,T) *n.*
1. woollybutt grass (*Eragrostis eriopoda*). A grass about 35 cm high with a white woolly substance at the base of the plant.
2. the edible seeds of the woollybutt grass ◆ Arnwety antyey akin anwernarl awantyetyart. Panth-warn arrernem, ahety-ilemel, panthel. Ahety-iletyam angkwey kwa. *The woollybutt grass is another seed that we used to eat. We'd put it in the wooden dish and yandy the seed. In the olden days we used to yandy it.*
= alyatywereng

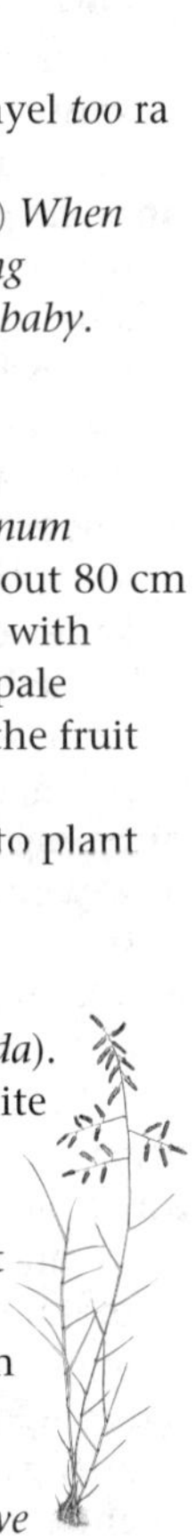

antyey[2] *n.*
perspiration, sweat
antyey iylpem (E)
to sweat, perspire ◆ Ayeng antyey iylpemarl-kety, uternelarl ampem antyey iylpem. (St) *I am sweating, sweating from the heat of the sun.*
SEE ALSO awempem
antyey-irrem *vi.*
to sweat, perspire ◆ Arelh antyey angerr irrem twern-penh. (T) *The woman is sweating a lot from the sun.*

antyey-antyey (W) *n.*
a type of grass

antyiper (E) bat SEE UNDER **antyepey**

antyirr (E) spiny-tailed monitor SEE UNDER **antyerr**

antywa, antywang (W,T) *n.*
1. humpy, shelter ◆ Thang antywang artem kwaty-kety. (T) *I am building a humpy because of the rain.* ◆ Antywa tyerrtyel mpwarem kwerel, thipelarl mpwarem-artek anteyarl, thipel tyewaketyel apek. (St) *People make humpies there, just like birds, such as babblers, make nests.*
= wak, iltha
2. nest ◆ Thep antywel anerl-anem kwartel-arleng. (M) *The bird is sitting on eggs in the nest.*
SEE ALSO antyarlkw

antyweng-antywa (T,E), **antyweng-antyweng** (W) *n.*
cubbyhouse ◆ Nyetyepel arrken-irrem ampekenh antyweng-antyweng ina mpwareparem. Arrkenel-arleng antywa akwek apek mparem. Nyetyep. *Children make cubbyhouses to play in. They enjoy themselves making humpies. Cubbyhouse.*
= mereng-amer, nyetyep
SEE ALSO arnkentyeng-arnkenty, arlwekereng-arlweker

Antywang (T) *n.*
name of a hill north-east of Ti Tree town

antywantyw (E) *n.*
hipbone
SEE ALSO anenty
ker antywantyw (E)
meat from the hip of an animal ◆ Ker antywantyw yanh antheyaw, antywantyw tha arlkwetyek urinp-awaty. (Sa) *Give me that hip meat there, so that I can eat it while it's still a bit warm.*
= ker aneny

antywekelywekely *n.*
feeling unwell or in pain; really sick ◆ Ayeng uternarl antywekelywekely-irremel ampek. Aherrkel ayeng ampek antywekelywekely-ilek tyerrty ayenh. (St) *The sun burnt me and made me feel really sick. The heat of the sun made my body feel unwell.* ◆ Warrk-penh antywekelywekely-irrem, artep apek. (St) *[The person] feels unwell, maybe from work, maybe their back hurts.*
SEE ALSO arekwenth-kwenth

antywekelywekely-irrem *vi.*
feel unwell or in pain; (feel) pain all over ◆ *Mattress*-kweny ayeng intek akethel wal ayeng antywekelywekely-irrek. (St) *I slept outside without a mattress, and that made me feel unwell.*
SEE ALSO arekwenth-kwenth-irrem

antywekelywekely-ilem *vt.*
make someone feel sick or in pain ◆ Kwer yanh atwem antywekelywekely-ilemel. (T) *Hitting that kid and making him sick.*

antyweleny (T,E) *n.*
1. whipstick wattle (*Acacia adsurgens, Acacia tenuissima* (?)). Shrub about 3 m high with narrow leaves and cylindrical yellow flowers. The leaves are crushed, mixed with fat and used as a medicine.
2. edible seeds of the whipstick wattle ◆ Antyweleny anterrngarl aketyam wal renh awantyetyam akin, arrwekelenyel. (T) *Olden-time people picked the seeds of the whipstick wattle and ate them as well.*
= ateyepenh

antywem *vt.*
1. drink something, have a drink ◆ Anyem antywem ahenty tywen-akertel. (St) *You can drink the witchetty bush leaf mixture if you have a sore throat.* ◆ Arengkelarl antywem-penh, altyewa! (T) *Chuck it out, the dog's been drinking it!*
2. take (drink) medicine ◆ Mwerr anem awelhem *medicine*-arl antywem-penh. (T) *I feel better now after taking the medicine.*
3. drink alcohol
CAN SOUND A BIT LIKE ntywem[1] *'warm self'*; ntywem[2] *'facing away'*

kwert antywem
smoke a cigarette (kwert *'smoke', 'cigarette'*) ◆ Arrpenhemel ngkwerlp arlkwem, arrpenhemel kwert antywem. (St) *Some people chew tobacco and others smoke cigarettes.*

paty antywem (W,T)
drink from the breast (paty *'breast'*)
SEE ALSO awantyem, arrantywem

antywemp (T,E) *n.*
western brown snake (*Pseudonaja nuchalis*) (?). This is a very poisonous snake.
= arriper
SEE ALSO tyamparl, arreperlp

antywer[1] (T,E) *n.*
1. bushfire
2. smoke from bushfire in distance. Also referred to as *ura antywer.* ◆ Ura antywer, arnam-they akem-irrem antywer anem. (St) *The smoke in the distance rises up from the [burning] grass.*
SEE ALSO kwert

antywer[2] (E) *n.*
1. grass ◆ Antywer urlpat-ilemel kel kwert anem arratem. Antywer *that one* ampem. 'Nhakweyay, antywer arleng ampem kwenh.' (St) *When the grass is burnt the smoke rises up. That's the grass burning. 'Over there in the distance, the grass is burning.'*
2. Goes before the name of a particular type of grass.
= arnam
SEE ALSO atherrk

antywer iper (E)
feather-top spinifex (*Triodia schinzii*). Spinifex grass with feathery seed heads. Grows in sandy areas.

antywerreng (E) *n.*
possum's track or path ◆ Ker antenh, rarl alhep-alhem iwerr kwerenh — wal, 'antywerreng'. (St) *Where the possum goes, its track — well, that's called* 'antywerreng'*.*
SEE ALSO antenh, iwerr, tyey[1], atnarlt

antywert (W,T), **intywert** (W) *n.*
lower back of a person; lower back part of a kangaroo. Also referred to as *ker antywert.*
= urteth, atheng-atheng

antywetenty (E) a type of plant that grows in swamps SEE UNDER **intywetenty**

antywey (W,T), **antyey** (W) *n.*

akwek antywey (W,T), **akwek antyey** (W,T)
something really small or little (akwek *'small'*) ◆ Arathap akwek antywey. (T) *A little baby.* ◆ Arnapar akwek antyey anngampelh-ilem. *[It] makes the little dingo pups open their eyes.*

anurerrk (E) ankle SEE UNDER **anewerrk**

anwa *prn.*
we (more than two). This pronoun is used in the subject part of the sentence (i.e. representing the 'doers' of the verb action). See Appendix 1. ◆ Mangarray arrkernkel-arleng anem altywernem anyent, alakenh anem. Akemem renh tyarrp-aketyenheng. Tyap-akert akwel akwek-akert nhenh, rnpwa

akert. *Nice one.* Anwa arlkwetyart akwel. (N) *The bloodwood gall grows on the bloodwood tree. We pick them and then split them open. They have a little grub inside, a nice-tasting one that we used to eat.* ◆ Rrwarlpan irntareny. Mern akin an tyekert. Ampengant arlkwenh, wal tyekertarl yanh, mentyel anwa aretyart. (N) *The native tomato grows in the hills. It has a fruit but it is bitter and we only eat it if it's ripe. If it was bitter we used to just leave it.*
SEE ALSO anwengkerr, anakerr, anantherr, anwern, anwern-ingkerr, anwernakerr, anwernantherr
anwekenh (E) *prn.*
ours (belonging to more than two)

anwakerr (T,E) we (more than two) SEE UNDER **anakerr**

anwalty (T,E), **atnwalty** (E) *n.*
1. part of guts (of kangaroos or cattle). Also referred to as *ker anwalty*. ◆ Ker anwalty, ker lyep-lyep, ker ingka, ker aneperrk apek apakerl arlkwem. (St) *The guts, the intestines and the feet are eaten first, before the main meal.*
SEE ALSO atnarrk, arrka, lyep-lyep, aneperrk
2. a person with a big belly

anwantherr (E) we (more than two) SEE UNDER **anantherr**

anwar (E), **atnwar** (E) *n.*
heel
SEE ALSO atnerwerrk

anwek (W,T) *n.*
(do something) overnight; camp out for a night or for a few nights; go and stay somewhere for a night or a few nights ◆ Anwek atherr-ingar ayeng alhem. (T) *I'm going for two nights.*
= **unek** (E)
anwekel (W,T) *adv.*
overnight; camping out
= **unekel** (E)

anwekepeltharr (W,T) a type of cricket (insect) SEE UNDER **anwengkapeltharr**

anwekert, atnwekert (E) *n.*
bent over, bent
anwekert-anwekert, atnwekert-atnwekert (E) *n.*
a bit bent
anwekert-anem, atnwekert-anem (E) *vi.*
sit bent over (anem *'sit'*) ◆ Atnwekert anem akem-irrerl-anem. (St) *Sit bent over and then get up.*
anwekerternem, atnwekerternem (E) *vi.*
stand bent over (irnem, rnem *'stand'*) ◆ Weth katyerr ilern akeynepeynem amwerrk atnwekert-atnwekertel atnwekertel rneynepeynerl akeynerreperrem atnwekertel anem akeynerreperrerl. (St) *When we were picking desert raisins yesterday we went along picking them, bending over.*

anwematy (W), **arnwematy** (W) *n.*
mallee fowl (*Leipoa ocellata*). This bird is probably now extinct in the region. They make a large round nest and lay lots of eggs, which were covered over during incubation.

anwengentyengenty (W,T) *n.*
backwards
anwengentyengenty-irrem (W,T) *vi.*
go backwards, reverse
= anepetheng-irrem, aneyangketh-irrem, tyenelhem[1], angkep-irrem

anwenger (E) *n.*
on the other side of something (to the speaker); behind something; on the back side of something ◆ Anwenger ayeng alhetyek. Alhetyek ayeng aketh-warl irremel. (St) *I'm going to the other side. I'm going outside.*
= arrwengak, irrweper
anwenger-irrem (E) *vi.*
move to the other side of something (from the speaker); be on the other side of something
= arrwengak-irrem

anwengk[1] (E), **atnwengk** (E) *n.*
a type of wallaby or bettong (?). No longer found in the Anmatyerr area.
SEE ALSO kwarlp, arrwa

anwengk[2] *n.*
pituri, wild tobacco (*Nicotiana excelsior*). Fleshy herb about 50 cm high and found growing in hills.

anwengk-anwengk (E), **atnwengk-atnwengk** (E) *n.*
1. mulga native currant, narrow-leaved native currant (*Psydrax suaveolens*). A shrub up to 3 m high, with narrow leaves, small white flowers and fruit which ripens to a black colour.
2. the edible fruits of the mulga native currant
= ngkwernateylp, ngkwernelyerr, antenh-antenh
SEE ALSO anngey-anngey, yernt, ahakey, artapaly

anwengkapeltharr (W,T), **anwekepeltharr** (W,T), **anakapeltherr** (E), **atnakapeltherr** (E), **anekapeltherr** (E), **atnekapeltharr**, **anekapeltherrey** (E) *n.*
a type of cricket (insect). Associated with kurdaitcha. ◆ Anekapeltherrey atherrkenyel anetyel, uthep weth. (Sa) *The* anekapeltherrey *is that flying thing that lives in the green grass.*
SEE ALSO ltywelty, anemel pweyntengeynteng

anwengkerr, anwingkerr, aningkerr (E) *prn.*
we (more than two). This pronoun is used in the subject part of the sentence (i.e. representing the 'doers' of the verb action) when the people are all in the same patrimoiety and the same generation moiety; for example, a person together with their sisters or brothers, their father's fathers or their mother's mothers. The person being spoken to is included in the group. This form of the pronoun is also used when the kin relations are not specified or in a group where there is a range of kin relations. See Appendix 1. ◆ Anwengkerr alhem lyet lyweny, awenh-intyerr anwengkerr alhem. (T) *Today we are going hunting, all of us aunties together.* ◆ Angkwer-nheng-arey arringkerr alhek? Yew. Ingkerr anwingkerr apety-alperrek angkwer-intyerr. (Sa) *Have all of you sisters gone? Yes. All of us came back, all the sisters together.*
SEE ALSO anwa, anakerr, anantherr, anwern, anwern-ingkerr, anwernakerr, anwernantherr
anwengkerrenh, anwingkerrenh, aningkerrenh (E) *prn.*
us (more than two). This pronoun is used in the object part of the sentence (i.e. representing those the verb action is done to). ◆ Anwengkerrenh iltep-iltem. (M) *[They] are growling at us.*
anweh-ingkerr (W,T), **anwek-ingkerr** (E), **anek-ingkerr** (E) *prn.*
for us, to us (more than two)
anweh-ingkerrenh (W,T), **anwek-ingkerrenh** (E), **anek-ingkerrenh** (E) *prn.*
ours (belonging to more than two)

anwenth, atnwenth (E) *n.*
1. meat, flesh, game ◆ Angayel apetyam mern-kweny ker-kweny. (M) *He had no meat and no food. He walked around starving.* ◆ *Salt*-arl anwern inetyart *sell*-em-iletyart, an pwelekam *salt*-em-iletyart anwenth pwelekem. (N) *We used to get the salt and sell it to make salted bullock meat.* ◆ Anwenth angwerl amparr irrem — walyel-ayel arrernem angwerl-irretyeh. (N) *The meat cools down first — it is put on the branches to cool down.*
2. edible animal, bird or reptile; an animal's prey
3. A general word that can go before the name of a particular type of edible meat. In the Anmatyerr way of classifying foods most fruits and vegetables are known as *mern*, sweet things as *ngkwarl*, seeds as *anterrng*, *arnwety* or *ntang*, meats as *ker* or *anwenth*, and edible grubs as *tyap*.
= ker
SEE ALSO tyelk

Anwenthenh (W) *n.*
name of place near Star Creek, to the east of Mt Allan community

anwer (E), **atnwer** (E) *n.*
dry kangaroo droppings, dry kangaroo shit ◆ Atnwer aherr-kenh. Urrmarl-wetyek, kwert intem anem ra, kel atnwer renh arrernem arnam-warl anem pew-iletyek anem. Ampem anem ra. Arrwekelenyel kwa. (St) Atnwer *is kangaroo's [droppings]. When you are using a firesaw to start a fire, it starts to smoke, then you put the kangaroo shit and the grass there, and blow on it. Then [the fire] starts to burn. That's what the olden-time people did.*
SEE ALSO ana
CAN SOUND A BIT LIKE arnwer *'dingo'*

anwerl (E), **atnwerl** (E) *n.*
snake vine (*Tinospora smilacina*). A woody vine that climbs trees and shrubs, has leaves like a bush potato, and inedible red fruits. ◆ Atnwerlel kapert ayernelhetyek kapert arntenty. (Sa) *You bind your head up with snake vine stems if you have a headache.*
= arratherrk
SEE ALSO alyep[1]

anwerl (W,T) barking spider SEE UNDER **inwerl**

anwerl-anwerl (E), **atnwerl-atnwerl** (E) *n.*
emu's intestines or guts. Also referred to as *ker anwerl-anwerl.* ◆ Ker atnwerl-atnwerl renh arlkwem apakek-amperr, ilep then. (St) *The emu's intestines and liver are eaten first as a snack.*
SEE ALSO arlta[2]

anwerlarr (E), **atnwerlarr** (E) *n.*
1. pencil yam (narrow leaf variety) (*Vigna lanceolata* var. *filiformis*). Creeping plant with bright green leaves, yellow flowers and edible roots.
2. the edible root of the pencil yam ◆ Arlpenty arnterrarl anwerlarr, artelhampw tyelpetyerrem. Aylpa ra akely-akely, arlatyey-kenh aylpa awer-rnem. Pertipelawan *yellow one* ratherr atherr-antey. (Sa) *The* anwerlarr *yam is really long, and the big ones are pulled out. It has smallish leaves, whereas the* arlatyey *yam has big ones. Both of them have similar looking yellow flowers.*
SEE ALSO arlatyey, katywetarr, arnamp

anwerlkel anthem[1] (W,T) *vt.*
say you will give someone something and then not do it (anthem *'give'*) ◆ Arelh nhenhel ayeng anwerlkel anthek terrethek. (T) *This woman said she was going to give me a*

dress, but she didn't.
SEE ALSO anew-irrem

anwerlk[1], **atnwerlk** (E) *n.*
fright, fear ◆ Anwerlkel angkem ayeng. (M) *I am speaking fearfully.*
CAN SOUND A BIT LIKE anhwerlk *'satisfied (after being hungry)'*
anwerlkem, atnwerlkem (E) *vi.*
jump in fright, get a fright or shock ◆ *He can* artep-warl irrem, artep-warl irrem, ingkern-thayt-warl irrem *kidney* renh nheng anwerlkemarl. (M) *It can go towards the back, the kidney can go towards the back if [the person] gets a fright.* ◆ Anwerlkel anthem ntwa ayenhaw. *Like you might asleep*, arrpenh *might wake-em up*. *'Oh,* anwerlkelh-ilep-ilem ayenh. Atnwerlkel anthem ntwa ayenh.' Ayeng atnwerlkem. (St) *You are giving me a fright. Like you might be asleep and another might wake you up. 'Oh, someone is giving me a fright. You are giving me a fright.'*
anwerlkel anthem[2], **atnwerlkel anthem** (E)
give someone or something a fright or a shock (anthem *'give'*) ◆ Tyerrty yanhel anwerlkel anthem ingkern-angkwarr aperlapemel. (M) *That person is giving [me] a fright by coming along behind [me].*
anwerlkelh-ilem *vt.* = **anwerlkel anthem**[2]
SEE ALSO ilkwem

anwerlk[2], **atnwerlk** (E) *n.*
1. buttocks, bum, backside; the rump of an animal ◆ Thep arrernelhem anwerlk-arleng, antywel-arleng. (N) *The bird settles down on its rump in the nest.* ◆ Anwerlkel-arleng anerl-anem. (M) *Sitting on your arse [lazy bugger].*
= anaynp, alywel, artelh[2]
2. fat from lower tail and scrotal area of kangaroo
3. insides of some edible grubs
CAN SOUND A BIT LIKE anhwerlk *'satisfied (after being hungry)'*
aherr anwerlk (T,E), **aherr atnwerlk** (E)
fat from lower tail and scrotal area of kangaroo (aherr *'kangaroo'*)
SEE ALSO anter, urtarnp (St)

anwern *prn.*
we (more than two). This plural pronoun is used in the subject part of the sentence (i.e. representing the 'doers' of the verb action). It does not include the person being spoken to. This form of the pronoun is used when the kin relations are not specified or in a group where there is a range of kin relations. See Appendix 1.
SEE ALSO anwa, anwengkerr, anakerr, anantherr, anwern-ingkerr, anwernakerr, anwernantherr
anwernenh *prn.*
us (more than two). This pronoun is used in the object part of the sentence (i.e. representing those the verb action is 'done to'). ◆ Rntwetyart anwern, mer nhenh kwerel anwern rntwetyart kalty-anthetyart akngerr-pat mapel anwernenh. (N) *We used to dance, at this place here we danced, and the elders used to teach us.* ◆ Awenk apel anwern rntwetyartel akwekeng-ntyel anwernenh apernetyart, apernetyart anwernenh. (N) *When we were teenage girls we used to dance — from when we were small they used to paint us up.*
anwerneh (W,T), **anwernek** (E) *prn.*
for us, to us (more than two)
anwern-henh (W,T), **anwern-kenh** (E) *prn.*
ours (belonging to more than two) ◆ Ikngerr-ampeny-kenh 'yalkw' — anwern-kenh 'yerrakwerr'. Kik-wemel arlkwerl-apem inelhapemel. *The word 'yalkw' belongs to the people from the eastern region — ours is 'yerrakwerr'. We go along picking them and peeling them and eating them.*
anwern-akey (T) *prn.*
we (people belonging to the same patrimoiety as each other)
SEE ALSO -akey, ilernak-akey, ilak-akey, ilern-ingkerr-akey, anwernakerr-akey, anakerr-akey

anwern-ingkerr *prn.*
we (plural, same skin). This pronoun is used in the subject part of the sentence (i.e. representing the 'doers' of the verb action) when the people are all in the same patrimoiety and the same generation moiety; for example, a person together with their sisters or brothers, or their father's fathers. The person being spoken to is not included in the group. See Appendix 1. ◆ Anwern-ingkerr angkwer-intyerr alhem anwekel. (T) *All of us, all the sisters, are going camping out.*
SEE ALSO anwa, anwengkerr, anakerr, anantherr, anwern, anwernakerr, anwernantherr
anwernenh-ingkerrenh *prn.*
us (more than two). This pronoun is used in the object part of the sentence (i.e. representing those the verb action is 'done to').
anwerneh-ingkerr (W,T), **anwernek-ingkerr** (E) *prn.*
for us, to us (more than two)
anwerneh-ingkerrenh (W,T), **anwernek-ingkerrenh** (E), **anwern-ingkerrenh** (E) *prn.*
ours (belonging to more than two)

anwernakerr *prn.*
we (more than two). This pronoun is used in

the subject part of the sentence (i.e. representing the 'doers' of the verb action) when the people belong to the same patrimoiety and different generation moiety; for example, a person together with their fathers or father's sisters. The person being spoken to is not included in the group. See Appendix 1. ◆ Anwernakerr alhem intetyek anwekel, awenh-intyerr. (T) *We are going to camp out, aunties and nieces together.*
SEE ALSO anwa, anwengkerr, anakerr, anantherr, anwern, anwern-ingkerr, anwernantherr

anwernenhakerrenh, **anwernenhakerr** *prn.*
us (more than two). This pronoun is used in the object part of the sentence (i.e. representing those the verb action is 'done to')

anwernehakerr (W,T), **anwernekakerr** (E) *prn.*
for us, to us (more than two)

anwernehakerrenh (W,T), **anwernekakerrenh** (E) *prn.*
ours (belonging to more than two)

anwernakerr-altyerr *n.*
our son-in-law; our mother-in-law (closely related ones, whose mothers come from the same country) ◆ Anwernakerr-altyerr anepanem atherr, atherrarrp — mer anyentarl altyerr akek atherr. (Sa) *Our two sons-in-law are there — their mothers are both from the same country as ours.*
SEE ALSO -altyerr

anwernakerr-akey (W) *n.*
we (people belonging to the same patrimoiety as each other)
SEE ALSO -akey, ilernak-akey, ilak-akey, ilern-ingkerr-akey, anwern-akey, anakerr-akey

anwernantherr *prn.*
we (more than two). This pronoun is used in the subject part of the sentence (i.e. representing the 'doers' of the verb action) when the people belong to different patrimoieties; for example, a person together with their sisters-in-law or their cross-cousins. The person being spoken to is not included. See Appendix 1.
SEE ALSO anantherr

anwernantherrenh, **anwernenhantherr** *prn.*
us (more than two). This pronoun is used in the object part of the sentence (i.e. representing those the verb action is 'done to')

anwernehantherr (W,T), **anwernekantherr** (E) *prn.*
for us, to us (more than two)

anwernehantherrenh (W,T), **anwernekantherrenh** (E) *prn.*
ours (belonging to more than two)

anwernantherr-apakwey (E), **anwernanth-apakwey** (E) *n.*
we (belonging to a different patrimoiety but the same generation moiety as each other)
SEE ALSO -apakwey, nywerrp, anantherr-apakwey, alanth-apakwey, arrantherr-apakwey, ilernanth-apakwey

anwernt, **atnwernt** (E) *n.*
stubborn, uncooperative, not wanting to do something, refusing to do something ◆ Arelh atnwerntel anep-anem mpweny-kety. Mpweny inep-inem uyarn anem ran atnwernt akwet anep-anem. (St) *The woman doesn't want to go off with [the man]. [He] has tried in vain to race her off, but she keeps refusing.*
SEE ALSO anngarenty

anwernt-irrem, **atnwernt-irrem** (E) *vi.*
not wanting to go anywhere, do anything or cooperate; be stubborn or uncooperative; refuse to do something ◆ Uyarn tha ikngwerl-alhek, ra atnwerntarl irrek. Anerl-anem akwel ra. (St) *I went and tried to ask her, but she doesn't want to go. She must want to stay.* ◆ Atnwernt-irrem, arrpenhelarl ikngwem, 'Mpa alhey kwenh irrer'. 'No. Ayeng anerl-anemarl kwenh atnwernt-irrem.' (St) *Refusing, when another asks you, 'Come on, let's go hunting'. 'No. I don't want to go, I'm staying.'* ◆ Artwa apek atnwernt-irrem arelhel mpweny inenty. (Sa) *A man might refuse to go with a woman who tries to race him off.* ◆ Ilanthem renh. 'Ilekety nga atnwernt-irrep-irrem — inetyek lhay. Atnwernt-antey irrerl-anetyang.' (Sa) *Sending her off to do it. 'Why are you being uncooperative — go and get it. Don't keep refusing.'*
SEE ALSO mwernt-irrem, ankerl-irrem, mwernt-irrem, arlelty-irrem

anwerntem (W,T) *vi.*
vibrate or shake legs when preparing for a fight (women)

anwerntenty alhem (W,T)
go along vibrating or shaking the legs when preparing for a fight (women). This action accompanies a skipping or hopping step used in preparation for ritual fights. ◆ Arelh yanh anwerntenty alhem. Anantherr apal anep-anem arety-kweny kwenh. (T) *That woman is going along, shaking her legs and getting ready to fight. We are just sitting here and we don't know about it.*
= amerl-amerl arrernem
SEE ALSO arrtyernem

anwerreng (W) *n.*
emu bush (*Eremophila longifolia*). Shrub to

4 m high, with green drooping leaves and red flowers with pink inside. Leaves used as a washing medicine and for 'smoking' babies.
= lhwek-lhwek
= **unerreng** (E)

anwerrng, atnwerrng (E) *n.*
1. yellow fatty substance inside witchetty grubs
2. wet dough made by mixing boiling water with flour. Also referred to as *mern anwerrng.* ◆ Mern ankey ina arlkwerl-anem anwerrng, tamp ina atherl-anem. Anwerrng inarrpelam arlkwem. (N) *When they are looking around for food they eat the doughy mixture made from flour, when they are making damper. They eat some of the mixture themselves.* • = mern thwep-thwep
SEE ALSO urrnga

anwerrngaty (W) *n.*
grub from the coolibah (*Eucalyptus coolabah* ssp. *arida*)
= ankerrayt
SEE ALSO ankerrmern, ankwerrern

Anwerrp (W) *n.*
name of spring west of Kapety (Pine Hill area)

anwerrtyem (E), **atnwerrtyem** (E), **anwerrty-irrem** (E), **atnwerrty-irrem** (E) *vi.*
[RESPECT LANGUAGE]
dance ◆ 'Atnwerrty-irretyel alhirrel', artwel ilem. Mwerikw kwerenhel ilem, 'Yanhentyak antey ampweyampw-rnem atnwerrty-irretyel yanhentyak antey'. (Sa) *'Lots of people are dancing', says the man. Her son-in-law says, 'Over there all the mothers-in-law are dancing'.*
SEE ALSO anthep-irrem, urntem

anwingkerr (E) we (more than two) SEE UNDER **anwengkerr**

anya[1], **ayna** (E) *n.kin*
1. father
2. father's brother; uncle
3. particular male relations with the same skin as your *anya*. If person A calls person B '*anya*', then person B calls person A '*aler*' (in most cases). Some forms of this word sound the same as forms of the word *anyey* 'cousin-uncle'.
SEE ALSO angey

anyaty, aynaty (E) *n.kin*
my/our *anya*

anyengkw[1] (W,T), **aynengkw** (E) *n.kin*
your *anya* ◆ Aynengkw arerl-wa. (Sa) *Go and see your father.*

aynikw (E), **ayneyekw** (E) *n.kin*
his/her/their *anya*

anywek (W,T) *n.kin*
1. your *anya*
2. his/her/their *anya* ◆ Anywek ngkweng-artey alhek. (P) *Your father went.*

anywek-anywek (W,T) *n.kin*
father's brother; uncle ◆ Anywek-anywekel angetyek, kwer akwek nhenh arrangkemarl. (T) *The uncles can take this crying child.*

anyenheng[1], **aynenheng** (E) *n.kin*
a group of two or more people who are related to each other as *anya* and *aler* (father and child or father's brothers and nephews and nieces)

anyenheng-nheng, aynenheng-nheng (E) *n.kin* = **anyenheng**[1] ◆ Aynenheng-nheng alherl-wem kerek apek. (Sa) *The father and his children are going hunting.*

anyenhengart (W,T) *n.kin* = **anyenheng**[1]

anyenheng atherr[1], **aynenheng atherr** (E) *n.kin*
a person together with their *anya* (a man together with his child or a person together with their father's brother) ◆ Aynenheng atherr alhem atherrarrp ratherr. *Father and son are going, just the two of them.*

anyankethenh, anyenkethenh, aynenkethenh (E) *n.kin*
1. having *anya* (still alive)
2. someone who is always with their *anya*; 'daddy's baby'; someone who adores their father
SEE ALSO -ankethenh

anyeparety, ayneparety (E) *n.kin*
respectful or 'sorry way' of talking about someone's *anya*
SEE ALSO -parety

anya[2] (W,T), **anyang** (W,T) *n.*
louse, lice (in head hair), nits ◆ Tyerrtyel-ayel anem anya. (M) *Lice live on people.* ◆ Anyang kapert arlkwenh-arlkwenh arntert, anya, kwartarl ampenem wal tyerrtyel atantherrerl-anem alakenh. (N) *Lice are no good and they burrow into the head and lay eggs, which people crack.*
SEE ALSO petherr, arrem
CAN SOUND A BIT LIKE inyang *'sick'*; nya *'almost dead'*

anyang kwart (W,T)
louse egg, nits (kwart '*egg*') ◆ Anyang kwart atanthem. (T) *Cracking nits.*

anyanelhem, aynanelhem (E) *vi.*
make a fuss of someone; be affectionate to someone; feel pleased or excited
◆ Anyanelhem ampa akwekek. Akwek yanhek lyet anwern anyanelhern-artek. (St) *Making a fuss over a little baby. Like that baby that we*

just made a fuss over today. ◆ Anyanelhem artweyekikw arengk-arey, ahenparl alpetyam anyanelhety-ayntem. (St) *All the dogs are excited about their owner who has come back after going away a long time ago.*
SEE ALSO inkwerelhem, anyerrkem, kwak-irrem

anyang (W,T) louse, lice (in head hair) SEE UNDER **anya**[2]

anyartey (W,T), **anyartwey** (W,T) *n.*
1. cold, cool ◆ Anyartey apel tey arlka, kwaty arlka anyartey. (T) *Tea, and water as well, can be cold.*
2. something cold (such as ice-cream) ◆ Kwaty anyarteyel anyatwem. (M) *Cooling [yourself] down with cold water.*
SEE ALSO irrernt, kernt, irrernt, angwerl, angwerleny, anyel, arlkarl[1], atheperr
anyartey-irrem (W,T), **anyartwey-irrem** (W,T) *vi.*
cool down ◆ Tey anyartwey-irrem, nta antywemarl renh anyartwey. (T) *The tea cools down, and then you can drink it when it's cool.*
anyartey-ilem (W,T), **anyartwey-ilem** (W,T) *vt.*
cool something down ◆ Kwaty irrernt anem thelemel tha anyartey-ilem. (T) *I am pouring some cold water in to cool it down.*

anyatwem (W,T) *vi.*
get cool, feel cold ◆ Anyelel anyatwem ayeng. (M) *I am feeling cold.* ◆ Alhwerrp rlwa amparr nhenh anywatety-alhem, angerr warl-atheh. Alhwerrp angerr warl-atheh. (T) *At first it gets cold, at the beginning of winter, and then it's cold right up until the middle of winter.*
anyatelhem (W,T) *vi.*
make yourself cool ◆ Anyatelhem tyerrty kwaty irrerntel. (T) *The person is cooling themself down with cold water.*
SEE ALSO anhelhem

anyaty SEE UNDER **anyey** 'cousin-uncle'

anyaty SEE UNDER **anya**[1] 'father'

anyel (W,T) *n.*
cold ◆ Anyelel arrewem. (M) *Shivering with cold.* ◆ Rlwelty ikwerety ater-irrem anyelel arrewem. (N) *Frightened of the frost and shivering in the cold.* ◆ Iltyang arlerlp-irrem anyelel. (T) *In the cold [your] hands cramp up.*
= irrernt
SEE ALSO kernt, anyartey, irrernt, angwerl, angwerleny, arlkarl[1], atheperr
anyel-irrem (W,T) *vi.*
get cold, cool down
= kernt-irrem, angwerl-irrem, irrernt-irrem

anyelk (E), **anyelkng** (E) sneakily, secretly SEE UNDER **anyenng**

anyem[1], **atnyem** (E), **aynem** (E), **aytnem** (E) *vi.*
1. fall off something ◆ Kwer anyekew, arneng. *The kid fell from the tree.* ◆ Atwakey kel atnyem akin arna akern-they — arna akern-they atnyep-atnyem ahern-werl. (St) *The wild orange falls as well, from the top of the tree — from the top of the tree it falls to the ground.*
2. drop down; fall down, fall (rain) ◆ Kwaty anyem. (T) *The rain is falling.* ◆ Kwerraly anyem ahern-warn. (T) *The star is falling to the earth.* ◆ Ankwang interleng map, wal lwelty anyem nta lweltyem arem, pelangketel nheng mperlkerel. (M) *When people are asleep, and there is a frost [lit. frost falls] you'll see the white frost on the blankets.* ◆ Ngkwarl rnpwang yanh anyerleng-penh anyem pertipelaw kwer-penh *red one* kwer-penh anyem, renh-iperr arraw-ilem arraw-ilemel arlkwetyam. Awantyem akwel arlkwem arlka. Rnpwarl inem renh antyerrkel-ayel anyek tampart anemel arrawelh-ilemel inem, arrernem, renhem arlkwerl-anem akerl-anemel nheng arna alakenh awantyem amparr arlkwemem, anteth. (N) *The honey drips from the flower on the* anyerleng *bush and we gather it together and eat it, suck it and eat it. We collected the honey that has fallen with the dry flowers and has gone like a damper. We suck on it and then eat it, the flowers.*
SEE ALSO urntem, anhem, arrwerelhem
anyenhem, atnyenhem (E), **aynenhem** (E), **aytnenhem** (E) *vi.*
fall over (as going along)
anyelpanyem, aynelpaynem (E) *vi.*
stagger about (as a drunk)
anyelh-ilem, atnyelh-ilem (E), **aynelh-ilem** (E), **aytnelh-ilem** (E) *vt.*
drop someone or something ◆ Anyelh-ilem rnwanenty kwerenh apek, kwer akwek apek, mantar apek anyelh-ilem. (M) *She might drop her things, or a baby or clothes.* ◆ Ker tha kwer anthek arrpenh yanhek wal atnyelh-ilekarl ran. 'Ker atnyelh-iletyalaw kwenh!' (St) *I gave some meat to that person there and they dropped it. 'Don't drop the meat!'*
CAN SOUND A BIT LIKE nyely-ilem *'show something'*

anyem[2], **atnyem** (E) *n.*
1. witchetty bush (*Acacia kempeana*). Shrub up to 4 m, with broad leaves and flat, papery pods.

◆ Anyem arety-alhem, wal tyer-wety-alhem. Tyer-wem, kel arntwa yanh renh, inyemel akem akem *right up* akenhem kel *finish.* Aweth arrpenh artwep-akemel akenhem akenhem

akenhem, *right round* akem akem akem tyap renh kel akemem-irremel arrernem *billycan*-warn. Kel akem akem irrenhem. Artekerr kwenel kwel. (N) *We go and look for the witchetty bushes and poke about with the digging stick. When we find a place where the ground makes a hollow sound we dig up [the witchetties] and then go around to the next one and dig that and keep going right round the tree filling up the billycan with grubs. They are found in the roots of the witchetty bushes.*

2. a mixture made from the witchetty bush leaves mixed with water and used as a medicine ◆ Anyem antywem ahenty tywen-akertel. (St) *You can drink the witchetty bush leaf mixture if you have a sore throat.* ◆ Anyem apel antywem merntel, antywem *tea leaf* akwek arrernemel. *Stir*-em *up* ilemel item renh, *mixed up* ampemey kel antywemem. (N) *Witchetty bush leaf mixture is drunk by sick people. The small leaves are put in water and stirred up and cooked, and then the liquid is drunk.*

anyematy, atnyematy (T), **atnyemayt** (E), **anyemayt** (T, E), **anyemart** (T) *n.*
witchetty grub larva (*Xyleutes bipartii*) ◆ Inyemel arlkwetyek tyap atnyemayt. (St) *Witchetty grubs are dug up and eaten.*

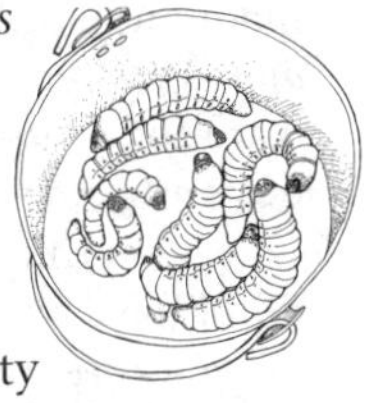

anyemaywerrk (W) *n.*
edible gum from the witchetty bush ◆ Ngkwarl anyemaywerrk akin anem, rnpwa akin perrap theweyet anthwerr inenhem. Anyem-areny. Anyemangkwarl. *There is also a sweet gum from the witchetty bush called* 'anyemaywerrk' *or* 'anyemangkwarl'. *We collect that and it's really sweet.*

anyemangkwarl (W) *n.* = **anyemaywerrk**

anyemampwerrty (E) *n.* = **anyemaywerrk**
◆ Ngkwarl athengarlperl-artek anem, anyemampwerrty. (St) *The* anyemampwerrty *is similar to the sweet resin from the ironwood tree.*

-anyem³ (E) *n.ending*
just, exactly, precisely. Goes on end of the words *nhenh* 'here', *yanh* 'there', 'that', *alakenh* 'like that', and *alanh* 'like that'. ◆ Awenhelikwek-amparr artem alhek ulpmerntel. *After that* kwaty anem urntetyenh. Arrwekelenyel iletyam alakenh-**anyem**. (St) *The olden-time people used to say that the dust storm was the 'auntie of the rain' and that first of all it covers [everything]. Then after that it rains. That's exactly what the old people said.* ◆ Alhernteran arntety-irrem arrmel wethey pwenty-penh. Pwenty alanhel-**anyem** angetyetyel aretharrel atwenhem, kel ra arntety-irremel angkwerr-wenty apek ra mwerrarl-irrem. (Sa) *White people get sick as well from that disease. It's the* aretharr *wind that brings that sickness. Then the person gets sick, and they get better after being treated with traditional massage.* ◆ Mern nhenh-lkwer-**anyem** mwerr arlkwey? (Sa) *Is this particular sort of food all right to eat?*

anyem anteth (E), **atnyem anteth** (E) *n.*
part of guts (kangaroo)
SEE ALSO atnarrk, aneperrk, lyep-lyep, anwalty

Anyem Kwaty, Atnyem Kwaty (E) *n.*
Ryans Well (anyem '*witchetty bush*'; kwaty '*water*')

Anyem-anyem (W) *n.*
the name of a hill in Mt Wedge/Napperby roadhouse area

Anyemamern (E), **Atnyemamern** (E) *n.*
Goofy Bore, near the Sandover River on Mt Skinner station

anyemilparr (E), **anyemeylpar** (E), **atnyemilparr** (E), **atnyemeylpar** (E) *n.*
south wind ◆ Atnyemeylpar anem wernem iylkel — rtakw artey. (St) *The south wind is blowing — we'll build a windbreak.*
= aretharr

anyemp unhem (E), **anyemp utnhem** (E) *vt.*
make something really well; make something flash (especially said of wooden tools) ◆ Anyemp unhek kweter mpwaremel — alyelk mpwarekarl anyemp unhek. (Sa) *[She] made a really flash fighting stick — really smooth.*

anyemwerr *n.*
1. good, nice ◆ Anyemwerr tha arern, talkw-irrerlek. (St) *I Just saw a good place as I went across.* (?)
2. lush, green (after being dry)
3. a plentiful hunt, (being) happy about a hunt (?)
4. meat (especially emu) ◆ Anyemwerr-akert arratem aker-akert. Kerek anyerrkem, akangkem. (T) *He's happy coming back with emu meat.*
SEE ALSO mwerr

anyemwerr-ilem (T,E) *vt.*
make country green and lush; clean a place up; visit a place and make it better ◆ Anyemwerrarl ilek, therrkeny apek anyemwerr-irrem kwaty-penh weth atherrk anem. Anyemwerr anem ra irrem atherrkenyel. (St) *The country is green and lush after rain and there's green grass. The country*

has become green. ◆ Merel anetyel anywemerr-ilemel. Merel anetyel merek-artwey. (Sa) *The owners of the country are living there and making it good.* ◆ Mer ingkeny anek, inngek arrangkw. Tha anyemwerr-ilemel ayeng anety-alpek. (Sa) *The place was empty, with no people living there. I came back to live there and make the place good again.*

SEE ALSO mwerr-ilem, atherrkeny-ilem

anyemwerr-irrem (T,E) *vi.*

become green and lush (country)

SEE ALSO mwerr-irrem, ilkelhey-irrem, atherrkeny-irrem

anyenem (T,E), **atnyenem** (E) *vt.*

1. hold onto something, carry something ◆ Warn anyenem arrakertel. (St) *The tobacco wad is carried in the mouth.* ◆ Iylpa nhenh artepel, wal ngkwerlparl arrernem, ngkwerlp atnyenem akngerl-anem nhenh kwerel, iylpa artepel. (St) *Here at the back of the ear, well that's where you put the tobacco wad, and you hold it there and carry it along there behind your ear.* ◆ Aylper ra atnyenem, *bag* apek, iltyel aylper atnyenepenem. (St) *She is carrying the bag, dangling from her hand.*

2. own or have something ◆ Yakweth apek mantarr apek atnyenem tha. (St) *I have a bag, or maybe some clothes.* ◆ Anantherr anyenem ngkelthel iltyangel-ayel. (T) *We have fingernails on our fingers.*

3. keep something (in a particular place) ◆ Tha atnyenepenem yakwethel, yakweth akwek nhel tha atnyenepenem ngkwerlp atyenh. (St) *I keep my tobacco in this little bag here.*

4. hold (a meeting or ceremony) ◆ *Meeting* atnyenetyek apetyem. (St) *[They] are coming to hold a meeting.*

= rrkwem

anyengk (W) *n.* [RESPECT LANGUAGE]

1. fire

2. firewood ◆ Anyengk angetyem rwang alenh, amwehek apek. (M) *She brings that firewood, perhaps for her mother.*

SEE ALSO rwa, alpment, ntyangkwenng

anyengkw[1] SEE UNDER **anya**[1] 'father'

anyengkw[2] SEE UNDER **anyey** 'cousin-uncle'

anyenheng[1] SEE UNDER **anya**[1] 'father'

anyenheng[2] SEE UNDER **anyey** 'cousin-uncle'

anyenheng-atherr[1] SEE UNDER **anya**[1] 'father'

anyenheng-atherr[2] SEE UNDER **anyey** 'cousin-uncle'

anyenhengart SEE UNDER **anya**[1] 'father'

anyenng, anyelkng (E), **anyelk** (E) *adv.*

(doing something) without asking or behind someone's back; sneakily, secretly, furtively, dishonestly ◆ Atnem impen ngkernek anyelk-kety. (Sa) *[I] put my only crowbar somewhere in case someone steals it.*

anyenngel, anyelkngel (E), **anyelkel** (E) *adv.*

= **anyenng** ◆ Angank arwengkalth — arraty. Nyenngel arlkwerl-anem akweteth akweteth ateram arrtyanetyenheng — pwerlt-irrem. (N) *Crows are robbers — true. They always sneak around and steal food to eat and then when something gives them a fright they fly off — they bolt.*

= arwengkel

anyenngalth, anyelkngalth (E), **anyelkalth** (E) *n.*

a thief, robber ◆ Arelh nhenh anyenngalth. (St) *This woman is a thief.*

= arwengkalth

anyenngel inem, anyelkngel inem (E), **anyelkel inem** (E)

steal something, take something without asking (inem *'get', 'take'*) ◆ Anyenngel inem unta atyenh, atyenh apek apwert unta inek anyenngel. (St) *You might steal my things, maybe you stole my money.* ◆ Mwetek atyenh anyenngel inerl-alhek. (St) *[Someone] came and took my car without asking.* ◆ Anyenngel tha inem mern arlkwetyek angayel. (St) *I'm hungry and I'm going to sneak some food.*

= arwengkel inem

anyenng artem (T), **anyelk artem** (E)

hide something from others, say that you don't have anything (when you do have) (artem *'cover something over'*) ◆ Mern anyelk artem, ingwerekarety, 'Arrangkwarl ayeng'. Arrangkw-arrpantey. (Sa) *Hiding the food from the others. 'I haven't got anything.' Pretending to have nothing.*

anyenng artelhem (T), **anyelk artelhem** (E)

deny having something (that you have stolen) (artelhem *'cover self over'*) ◆ 'Ayeng anyelk-kweny arrangkwarl, ayeng anyelkel inetyang arrangkwel.' Nga anyelk artelhetyel, anyelkel nta inerl-alpek-penh. (Sa) *'I didn't steal anything, I didn't steal a thing.' You deny it after stealing something.*

anyent *n.*

1. one ◆ Rtety-kwenh arrimper-akert. Rtety anyent atwekarl, arrimper mpwarek. (T) *Teeth have a gap in the front. One tooth is knocked out to make the gap.*

2. hardly any, one or two ◆ Arnam-angkwerr apal untherl-apek mern-kwenh itya. Mern arlatyey apek anyent arety-alhek. (N) *[I] looked around in the scrub and I didn't find any food, nothing. All I saw was one or two pencil yam plants.*

3. on one's own, solitary, alone ◆ Arrantherr irrkwaperl-anenhareyay ayengan anyent irrkwapepapem-kety. (Sa) *All of you do some work, because I am working on my own.*
4. that particular thing, the same thing ◆ Mern angarak apel akwerrk arlkwerl-apem. Awerretyepwer anyent renh. 'Angarak' akenh arlparl, kenh mern 'awerretyepwer'. (N) *The young pods of the bush bean are eaten. That's the same thing as* awerretyepwer. *'Angarak' is what the leaves are called, and the edible part is 'awerretyepwer'.* ◆ War thelelherl-anem irnmerr renh war amparrkerl-anerlek arerl-anem, arna anyent kwerel antem. Arlperl artety kwereng antem war thelelherl-anem. (N) *It just drips from the mulga tree and you can see it like drops of water sparkling on the branch of that particular tree. The* arlperl *just drips from the mulga tree.*
anyent-areny *n.*
on one's own; someone who is on their own, a loner (-areny *'associated with'*) ◆ Anyent-areny ayeng alhek. (St) *I went on my own.*
= ingareny
anyent-irrem *vi.*
1. unite, meet, get together; get together (sorry business) ◆ Ilerrty alhem kwaty alhem ikwerel, ulpay angerr-warl lher angerr-warl anem ra anyent-irrem. (St) *The water flows along the small watercourse and then it joins the big river.* ◆ Tyerrty map anyentek-irrem anyent-warl. (St) *The people are getting together in one place.*
2. join up with something else; join together
SEE ALSO anengk-irrem, pwety-irrem
anyentelh-ilem *vt.*
mix or stir things together; join something together ◆ Kwaty, tey-warl tha anyentelh-ilem thelern. (St) *I just poured some water into the tea.*
= intwerelh-ilem
SEE ALSO pwetyelh-ilem, arrakwernem^1
anyent-ingar, anyent-inger (E) *adv.*
1. once ◆ Thew-warn alhay anyent-ingar anem — map-ingar alhetyal. (T) *Go to the store once — don't go lots of times.*
2. all at once ◆ Tey anyent-ingar war antywerl-wem. (St) *Just drink the tea all at once.*
3. in one day, for a day ◆ Anyent-ingar ayeng interl-alhem, kel ayeng alhem mer arrpenh-warl. (St) *I'm going to go and camp for a night and then go to another place.*
anyent-areng (E) *adv.* = **anyent-ingar** (?)
anyentam-anyent *adv.*
1. every now and then, sporadically, occasionally, only a few ◆ Anyentam-anyent katyerr apek arlkwerl-anem. Anyentam-anyent anem anemaw, arrangkw anem. (St) *Every now and then we'd eat bush raisins. Now there's only a few, hardly any.*
2. one at a time, not all at once, one by one; one each ◆ Anyentam-anyent *chips* arlkwep-arlkwem, pep nhek-arlek. Anyent anem tyerremel arlkwep-arlkwem. (St) *Eating the chips from the paper one by one. Then pulling another one out and eating it.*
SEE ALSO +am^2
anyentek-anyent *adv.*
one each; one at a time
= anyentam-anyent
anyentak (W) *n.*
being one-sided, not sharing things with others ◆ Atyengenh akwet ntwa ywerrelh-ilem anyentak akwet, tey apek mern apek. (M) *You're still using up all of my tea and food, and not sharing it.*

anyent arrpenh *n.*
A respectful term used to refer to particular people who have a special role in men's ceremonies. Close relations of the 'young fella' or initiate who is going through the Law will call these people *anyent arrpenh.* It is not polite to go near these kin nor to say their names. The name *anyent arrpenh* is used instead. ◆ 'Anyent arrpenh' renh ilem, *son* ikwerenhek ntwerleng-irrek, wal 'anyent arrpenh' renh akem. (St) *Someone who has become* ntwerleng *for his/her son is called* 'anyent arrpenh'. ◆ Anyent arrpenh-kety alhetyang anem. Arreytn iletyal. Mey-mey-artek akin. (St) Anyent-arrpenh *are a bit similar to sons-in-law in that you don't go near them and you don't say their names.*
SEE ALSO perlawel, ntyangkwenng, thampartey
anyent arrpenh-irrem *vi.*
become *anyent arrpenh* for someone ◆ Anyent arrpenharl irrem artwa. Arelhan ntyangkwelkng irrem. (St) *Men become* anyent arrpenh. *Women become* ntyangkwelkng. (?)
SEE ALSO ntyangkwenng-irrem

anyenty (T,E), **atnyenty** (E) *n.*
1. moon, moonlight ◆ Atnyenty akngerrakw-they apetyem. (St) *The moon rises in the east.* ◆ Anwern atnyentyek alhek kerek apek, ker inapek apek. (St) *We went hunting in the moonlight for meat and for porcupine.*
= atay^1
SEE ALSO atarlanenty
2. month

anyentyel (T,E), **atnyentyel** (E) *n.*
in the moonlight
= parrtyel
anyenty ngkarlt (E), **anyenty ngkaylt** (E)
new moon (ngkarlt '*new moon*')
anyenty tamp (T,E) *n.*
full moon (tamp '*damper*')
anyenty anert angerr (E)
full moon (anert '*stomach*'; angerr '*big*')
anyenty akwerrk (T,E), **atnyenty akwerrk** (E)
new moon (akwerrk[1] '*young*', '*newly formed*') ◆ Atnyenty akwerrk anem, kel anenty atarlanenty anem anem. (St) *There is a new moon, then there is a full moon.*
= atay akwerrk
anyenty anyent (T,E), **atnyenty anyent** (E)
one month (anyent '*one*') ◆ Atnyenty anyentel alhem kel atnyenty arrpenh tnety-alhem, urrpety-ingar, atnyenty urrpety apek. (St) *Going for one month, then another month passes, or several months.*
anyenty atherr (T,E), **atnyenty atherr** (E)
two months (atherr[1] '*two*') ◆ Unta alhem. Atnyenty atherrel unta anem, kel unta apety-alpem. (St) *You are going. You are going for two months and then you'll come back.*

anyenty-anyenty (E), **atnyenty-atnyenty** (E) *n.*
small white grub, the larva of the Christmas beetle (lit. 'moon moon'), cockchafer larvae (*Anoplognathus olivieri* sp.) ◆ Atnyenty-atnyentyan alhemey kel tyerrtyel apek anpem, alakenh rtapety anem irrerl-alhem. (St) *The* atnyenty-atnyenty *grub goes along and, if a person touches it, it curls up.*
= atay[2]

anyer, **atnyer** (T,E) *n.*
supplejack, suplejack (*Ventilago viminalis*). Tree to 5 m high, with intertwined trunks, drooping green leaves and winged seeds.
anyerampw, **anyeramp** (W), **atnyerampw** (E) *n.*
edible gum from the supplejack tree. Also referred to as *ngkwarl anyerampw*.
anyerangkwarl, **atnyerangkwarl** (E) *n.*
= **anyerampw** Also referred to as *ngkwarl anyerangkwarl*.

anyerleng, **atnyerleng** (T,E) *n.*

1. turkey bush (*Eremophila latrobei*). A shrub to 1.5 m high, with bright red flowers.
2. sweet honey found in the flowers of the turkey bush. Also referred to as *ngkwarl anyerleng*. ◆ Ngkwarl rnpwang yanh anyerleng-penh anyem pertipelaw kwer-penh *red one* kwer-penh anyem, renh-iperr arraw-ilem arraw-ilemel arlkwetyam. Awantyem akwel arlkwem arlka. Rnpwarl inem renh antyerrkel-ayel anyek tampart anemel arrawelh-ilemel inem, arrernem, renhem arlkwerl-anem akerl-anemel nheng arna alakenh awantyem amparr arlkwemem, anteth. (N) *The honey drips from the flowers on the turkey bush, from the red flowers, and we gather it together and eat it. Suck it and eat it. We collect the honey that has fallen with the dry flowers and has gone like a damper. We suck on it and then eat it, the flowers.*
Anyerleng (W) *n.*
name of hill east of Mt Allan community

anyerr (E), **atnyerr** (E) *n.*
running water, floodwater
SEE ALSO rew, urew, awarr, alay[1]

anyerrkem, **anyirrkem** (E) *vi.*
1. feel happy, excited or pleased ◆ Tyerrty arrpenharl apetyemek anyerrkem. (T) *[We] are pleased that the people are coming.* ◆ Mern ahakey inerl-alpek arntap-warn. Anetyart anwern arntap-warn inetyart inetyart pwel-irretyart. Arrpenh-warn alhemel aweth arntap arrpenh inemel angerretyem inem aweth, pwel-iletyart anwern pwel-iletyart anwern pwel-iletyart. Anyerrkemel. (N) *We went and collected the native currant fruits in bark containers. We used to fill up the bark containers. Then we'd move on to another tree and fill another container — we filled them up. We enjoyed doing it.*
2. wag tail (dog); be excited or pleased (dog) ◆ Arengk anyirrkem artweyekwek, pwath kwerenhek. Apety-alpem artweyekw, anyirrkem anem ra, tayl. (St) *The dog is wagging its tail excitedly for its boss. Its boss comes back and the dog wags its tail.*
SEE ALSO akangkem, inkwerelhem, anyanelhem, kwak-irrem, ahenty-irrem, irrngerney-irrem

anyey, **atnyey** (E) *n.kin*
'cousin-uncle' (particularly referring to a close mother's brother's son or father's sister's son). If person A calls person B '*atnyey*', then person B calls person A '*ankel*' [male cross-cousin] back. Some forms of this word sound the same as forms of the word *anya* 'father'.
SEE ALSO amarley
anyaty, **atnyaty** (E) *n.kin*
my/our *anyey* ◆ *Cousin* ikwerenharl 'atnyaty'. Awenhekikwenharl ap 'atnyaty' akem, *cousin* ikwerenh. 'Anyatyay apetyaw, aylanth

alherretyek.' Atey atherr — artwant-atherr anyaty akerrem. *His cousin is called* 'atnyaty'. *His father's sister's child is called* 'atnyaty', *his cousin. 'Come here cousin, let's go, the two of us.' Two men — just men call each other* 'atnyaty'.

anyengkw[2], **atnyengkw** (E) *n.kin*
your *anyey*

anyikw (E), **atnyikw** (E) *n.kin*
his/her/their *anyey*

anyenheng[2], **atnyenheng** (E) *n.kin*
a group in which at least two people are related to each other as *anyey* and *altyel* or *ankel* (cousin-uncle and cousin)
SEE ALSO amarlenheng

anyenheng atherr[2], **atnyenheng atherr** (E) *n.kin*
a person together with their *anyey* (cousin-uncle and cousin)
SEE ALSO amarlenheng atherr

-anyimp SEE UNDER **+eng**[1]

anyirrkem (E) feel happy, excited or pleased SEE UNDER **anyerrkem**

anyurr-irrem (E) be rude to someone SEE UNDER **anywerr-irrem**

anywek SEE UNDER **anya**[1] 'father'

anywek-anywek SEE UNDER **anya**[1] 'father'

anywerr-irrem, **anyurr-irrem** (E) *vi.*
show someone that you don't like them; be rude to someone, give them a dirty look; talk about someone behind their back or run someone down; dislike someone or something ◆ Nywerr-irrenty angerr arrantherr. (M) *You mob are really rude.* ◆ Iwenhekarl unta tyerrty arrpenhek anywerr-irrem? (T) *Why are you being rude to that other person?* ◆ Atyeng anyurr-irrepirrem arelh yanh. Anyurr akngerr kwenh arelh yanh. (St) *That woman is giving me dirty looks. She's really rude.*
SEE ALSO yerrng-irrem, tyweker-irrem, tyel angkem

anywerr-anywerr, **anyurr-anyurr** (E) *n.*
showing someone that you don't like them; being rude to someone etc. ◆ Alknga anyurr-anyurrarl yanhan alhep-alhem, *don't like.* Anyurr-anyurrarl arem. (St) *That person is going round giving people dirty looks. They don't like [those people] and they give them dirty looks.*

+ap *ending.*
Gives emphasis to what is said; shows the main thing in a sentence; really, actually, very, of course. This ending may be written as a separate word. ◆ Mern aperelty. Mern arlkwenh-arlkwenh**ap** aperelty anthwerr, anganekarl. Mern aperelty akerl-apemel. (N) *The white substance made by the lerp-scale insect on the river red gum tree is edible — it's a traditional practice — going along and collecting* aperelty. ◆ Ilpetyel**ap** ra item ker, anwernt-irretyakenhel, ilpetyarl ra. (St) *She cooks the meat really quickly, without bailing up or sulking, she is helpful.* ◆ Iylpwer-areny**ap** antyiper. Ahelengkw, utnherl arlka. (St) *The bat lives in hollow trees. They are aggressive and they'll bite as well.* ◆ Anwantherr-artek**ap** arremparreng ra. (St) *The* arremparreng *are like us.* ◆ Uterrp-areny **ap** arrwelth-arrwelth. (Sa) *The* arrwelth-arrwelth *is a plant from the sandhills.* ◆ Aylayl arrak, aylayl**ap** ra arnkwert-arnkwert, arrak. Artwekenh**ap** ra. (Sa) *The* arrak *is a crooked type of boomerang. It belongs to the men.* ◆ Lher-arenyarl **ap** ra ker arwemay. Alhweng-areny arlewatyerr-artek antey. (St) *The* arwemay *lizard lives in the creek. They live in burrows like goannas do.* ◆ Ratherr **ap** anganekan Atnangkerel. (Sa) *Those two come from Atnangker.* ◆ Tyap-akert**ap** ra areyawarr. (Sa) *The* areyawarr *plant has edible grubs.* ◆ Rrwerleng **ap** mern ngkwarlarl, alkey angerr *anyway* twakemel lywernkel arlka akerrirretyart. Tek-arrernem akin renh. (N) *The honey grevillea tree has edible honey, and we used to just pull the branches of the tall trees down with a hooked stick and break them off. They were spread out in the sun as well.* ◆ Uthipel**ap** irrkerlanty rnternerl-anem thip akely nyingk apek. Nyingkek unthemel atanthenhemel. Mperlker**ap** ra. *The falcon actually goes along hunting small birds such as zebra finches. It looks for zebra finches and grabs them with its claws. They [falcons] are white in colour.*
SEE ALSO +ay[1], +aw, +eyay

apa (W,T) *n.* [BABY TALK]
water
= akwek
SEE ALSO kwaty

apak, **apwak** (W) *adv.*
(eating something) before the main meal, having a snack (?) ◆ Ker anwalty, ker lyep-lyep, ker ingka, ker aneperrk apek apakel arlkwem. (St) *The guts, the intestines and the feet are eaten first, before the main meal.* ◆ Apakek amparr tha tey antywey arlkweyamel. (St) *I might drink some tea first then I'll eat later.* ◆ Apak amparr thang arlkwem ker lyep-lyep. (T) *I'll eat the intestines first.* ◆ Anwern ingkang arlkwetyart apwak-amparr ker alenh amperleng. (N) *We used to eat the feet first to satisfy our hunger while the meat was cooking there.*

-apakwey *prn.ending*
Shows whether or not people are in the same

or in the opposite generation moiety to the person speaking. In Anmatyerr society there are two generation moieties. In one generation moiety are Kemarr, Peltharr (Petyarr), Pengart and Mpetyan people and in the other Ngwarray, Pwerrerl (Pwerl), Ngal and Penangk. The ending *-apakwey* goes on some dual and plural pronouns (referring to people not in the same patrimoiety) to form names which refer to generation moiety divisions. Some forms that occur are *ilernanth-apakwey, anwernantherr-apakwey, anantherr-apakwey, arrantherr-apakwey* and *alanth-apakwey*. When the ending *-apakwey* goes on words that mean 'we' it forms words meaning 'we who are in the same generation moiety as each other', and when it goes on words meaning 'you' or 'they' it forms words that mean 'you, who are in the opposite generation moiety to me' or 'they, who are in the opposite generation moiety to me'. Not all Anmatyerr speakers agree about these forms. Although more work is needed to establish the precise way these words are used, it seems that even though a word such as *alanth-apakwey* is based on the pronoun *alanth* 'they two' it can refer to 'they (more than two)'. ◆ Aylernanth-apakwey pwelty iwemel aylernanth-apakwey arrpenh-warl. Alanth-apakwey antwerrkemel mpep-they. (St) *We of the same generation team throw the ball towards the others in our team [i.e. people in the same generation moiety as us]. The others [those in the opposite generation moiety] get hold of the ball in the middle.*
SEE ALSO -akey, +anth, -apatherr

apal[1] (E) *n.*
1. ripe seeds of the dogwood tree, *awenth, akerlperr* (*Acacia sericophylla*)
2. sweet milky drink made from the dogwood seeds. Also referred to as *ngkwarl apal.*
SEE ALSO ntyerrm, artwengarr, anma[1], kertaty

apal[2] *adv.*
wrongly, in ignorance, mistakenly, accidentally, without knowing, not properly ◆ Apal alhemel therrert-irremel anem, iwerr ingwer-angkwerr anem. Iwerr ayeng alhetyek alhek ikwer-angkwerr kweny anem apal anem alhek. (Sa) *Going the wrong way and then getting lost, going along another track. I went to go on the track, but I went the wrong way.* ◆ Apal apek tha aretyang. Apal aremel ayeng alhern [mey-mey apek]. (T) *I didn't see properly. I went [close to my son-in-law] without looking properly.* ◆ Apal tha ngenh awek. (St) *I didn't hear you properly.*
SEE ALSO apalekalek, apant

apal-apal[1] *adv.*
wrongly, in ignorance, mistakenly, accidentally, without knowing, not knowing what to do

apalel *adv.*
wrongly, in ignorance, mistakenly, accidentally, without knowing ◆ Apalel ayeng ngkweng angkern. (Sa) *I just told you the wrong thing.*

apal-wem, apal-iwem (E) *vt.*
throw something mistakenly or in the wrong direction ◆ Pelh apalel tha ngkweng-warn werl-alhern. (T) *I just accidentally spat in your direction.* ◆ Ahelh apal-iwek ngkweng-warl anem. Atyeweyay ngkweng-warl tha iwek. (Sa) *I mistakenly threw the dirt at you. For goodness sake, I threw it at you.*

apal-arem *vt.*
not recognise someone or something ◆ Thang alhengk-arem war peltyant, kenh lwereny akenh apalarl arem. (N) *I only recognise friends, whereas I don't recognise strangers.*
SEE ALSO uyemem, ayemem, yem-irrem

apal angkem
say the wrong thing, speak wrongly ◆ Apal ayeng angkek ngkweng. (St) *I said the wrong thing to you.*

apal-apal[2] (E) *n.* [RESPECT LANGUAGE]
1. eye ◆ Apal-apal-ayerrek ahaneynaw, ngwarrekengkw. Parerrarl atnerrk-irrerlentyarrekek. (Sa) *Go [and have a look] at your husband's eye. Your husband's eye is no good [said by a woman to her daughter].*
2. blind
SEE ALSO annga, aparrng, pweng, parerr, angapanty

apalekalek *adv.*
being unable to see what you're doing; wrongly; mistakenly; not knowing what you are doing; not knowing what to do; being confused ◆ Apalekalek anem ayeng alhep-alhem, *torch*-em *on*-ilem anem tha. (St) *I'm going round and I can't see what I'm doing, so I'm going to turn the torch on.* ◆ Apalekalek arlkerl-apem tyerrty yaleng. Irrer apekarl alhem. 'Nthenh-angkwerr rarey alhek kwenh?' (T) *That person is going along singing out because they don't know what they're doing. Maybe out hunting. 'Where did the others go?'*
SEE ALSO apal[2]

apalekalek-irrem *vi.*
become lost or confused; not know what to do ◆ Apalekalek-irremel anem ra arlkerl-

apem, 'Nthenh-angkwerr arrantherr alhek kwenh?' (T) *She is singing out, confused, 'Which way did you all go?'* ◆ Apalekalek-irrem ngkwarl antywem, apalekalek anem apant-irrerl-apem alherl-apem, ngkwarl antywenty-penh. (T) *Drinking grog and getting confused, then wandering round drunk, lost and confused.*
SEE ALSO therrert-irrem

apalenthwem (W,T), **apalunthem** (T,E) *vi.*
search for something, look for something (nthwem, unthem *'look around for something'*) ◆ Uyarn anwern apalenthwek tyerrty ikwer. (M) *We searched in vain for the person.* ◆ Ngkerlpek apalunthem arelh, aparlp-ilekarl. (T) *The woman is looking around for the tobacco that she has lost.* ◆ Apalenthwety-alhay, arnang nheng ntwarl *lose*-em-ilekarlekay. (M) *Go and look for that thing that you lost.* ◆ Arnam-angkwerr ayeng apaluntherl-apem mern-kwenh itya. Mern arlatyey apek anyent arety-alhem. (N) *I looked around in the scrub and I didn't find any food, nothing. All I saw was a few pencil yam plants.*

apangkem (W,T) *vi.*
yelp, bark, moan, groan ◆ Atwemem renh, angwely renh atwem atwem atwem. Apangkenhem apangkenhem *everywhere* rang anwenth kwereng atwem alwernemel. (N) *Belting the dog, over and over. It goes off yelping after you've chased it and beaten it because of the meat.* ◆ Rlkert kwenh apangkerl-anem, artwa apek arelh apek. (T) *The man or the woman is sick and moaning in pain.*
= parlkwem, ampangkem
SEE ALSO anpelhem

apanp *adv.*
everywhere, all over the place ◆ Ker aherr apanp war anem. (St) *There are kangaroos everywhere.* ◆ Nhenh kwenh apanp alhalhem. (M) *This person goes all over the place.*
SEE ALSO apawerr, apapeth

apanp arem (T,E)
look everywhere, be able to see all over the place (arem *'look', 'see'*) ◆ Pwengarl anek-penhel, wal tha apanp anem arep-arem. (St) *After being blind, I can see all over the place.*

apanp-irrem *vi.*
spread out, get scattered all over the place

apant (W,T) *adv.*
wrong, wrongly, not properly, mistakenly ◆ Angkety apant ntwa angkerl-apem. Arraty-ila. (M) *You're going around telling the wrong story. Straighten it out.*
SEE ALSO apal[2]

apant-irrem *vi.*
get lost, lose your way, go the wrong way ◆ Ayeng apant-irrek werrkel-ayeng. (M) *I got lost in the scrub.* ◆ Tyerrty arert-arert apant-irrem, apant-irremel alherl-apem. (N) *A person who is a bit silly in the head gets lost, gets lost as they go along.* ◆ Apant-irremel arlkerl-apem, 'Nthenh tyerrty mapay? Pay! *Might* ayeng apant apek irrek kwenh.' (N) *Getting lost and singing out, 'Where is everybody? Here I am! I might be lost.'*
= therrert-irrem, aperrpert-irrem
SEE ALSO aparlp-irrem

apant angkem (W,T)
speak wrongly, say the wrong thing (angkem *'speak'*) ◆ Apantarl angkem. *No* arraty angkem nta kwenh, apant nta angkem atyeng *wrong* kwenh. (T) *Talking the wrong way. You aren't telling it the right way, you are telling me the wrong thing.*

apantel anthem (W,T)
give wrongly; give something to someone by mistake (anthem *'give'*)

apantantenh (W) *adv.*
the wrong way ◆ Apantantenh alhem. (M) *Going the wrong way.*

apap (W) *n.*
unable to speak (because of physical impediment); dumb ◆ Angkety-kwenh apap — irlpelant awem. (M) *Unable to speak — only able to listen.*
SEE ALSO akerter, apekap, alhwerrkert, tetherrp-tetherrp, aperrpert

apapeth *n.*
all over the place, everywhere, spread out ◆ Warl apapeth artelhem. (T) *There are houses built all over the place.* ◆ Tyerrty akngerrarl anem, maparl anep-anem weth-lkwer, tyerrty apapeth. (St) *When there are lots of people there, people all over the place.*
– apawerr
SEE ALSO apanp

apapeth-irrem *vi.*
1. go all over the place; spread out ◆ Yerr apapeth-irrem. Ker aherr-warl yerr apapeth-irrem. (St) *The ants are going everywhere. The ants are crawling all over the kangaroo meat.*
2. crowd in on someone, push in ◆ Unta apapeth-irretyal ayenh alhay, rntwarr nta alhetyek ker aherr tha arlkwetyenheng atyenh tha arlkwetyenheng. *Can't* ngkwengant antherl-anerl. Ntwang apapeth-irremel ingkerrek rakerlapem atyeng unta. (St) *Go away and don't crowd in on me, you've got to go further away so that I can eat my own meat*

myself. I can't just give it to you. You are crowding in on me and you're going to grab the lot.

apar atwem (T,E) *vt.*
give someone a punch, a smack or a whack (atwem '*hit*')
= palty atwem, anampart atwem

aparelhem (T,E) *vi.*
ask someone for something; bludge off someone; hang round waiting for someone to give something to you ◆ Angayel anwantherr aparelhetyek arelh mapek. (St) *We are hungry and we're going to wait around for the women [to give us something].* ◆ Iwenhek unta atyengan aparelhepelhem kwenh? *No* unta nhakw alhem kwenh. Atyengarrp untam aparelhepelhem kwenh. (T) *Why are you always asking me for things? You don't go over there [and ask the others]. You are always bludging off me.* ◆ *No* unta apek rntwarr alhek. Atyengant akwet untang aparelherl-anem kwenh. Thwengk anthetyeh-atwety unta aparelherl-anem. (T) *You didn't go any further. You always bludge off me. You wait around until I give you something.*
SEE ALSO ankey

aparew (E) *n.*
rainwater, puddle, fresh water ◆ Kwaty alker-penh aparewel intem. (St) *Rainwater lies in puddles.* ◆ Angkethel tha antyweyam kwaty aparew lyeteny. (Sa) *I'm thirsty and I'm going to drink fresh rainwater.*
SEE ALSO kwaty lyeteny, narwep, narengk

aparlp-ilem *vt.*
1. leave something behind; forget something, lose something ◆ Arna atyenh tha aparlp-ilek. Manek ayeng untherl-alpeyam arna atyenh tha aparlp-ilekek. (St) *I left my things somewhere. I'll go back and look for my money where I left my things.* ◆ Artwep-irremel ayeng alpem kwenh ngkwerlp atyenharl aparlp-ilern kwenh. (N) *I'm going to turn back because I've just lost my tobacco.* ◆ Thangey aparlp-ilern atyengenh. (M) *I've just lost my thongs.*
2. lose a family member, become bereaved ◆ Mwerrem aneh rlkert-penh akeweny atyengenh. Tharl aparlp-ilety anek. (N) *That poor old relation of mine is better now after being sick. I nearly lost him.*
3. make someone confused; distract someone, create a disturbance, interrupt (?) ◆ Aparlp-ilem ayenh ampel, arrpenh tha awetyakenh. Aparlpelh-aparlpelh-ilem, awetyakenh, aparlpelh-aparlpelh-ilem ampel. (St) *The kids are distracting me and I can't hear the other person. The kids are interrupting and I can't hear.*

aparlp-irrem *vi.*
get lost, lose your way ◆ Werrk-angkwerr alhemel an aparlp-irrem. Arrpenhek apek arlkerl-anem, aparlparl-irrek, kel arrpenh tyerneman. (St) *Getting lost going through the scrub. Singing out to another person and then the other person answers.*
= apant-irrem
SEE ALSO anngwirrem

aparlpelh-ilem *vt.*
make someone confused; distract someone, interrupt (?) ◆ Aparlpelh-ilerrem ampel awetyakenh ilemel. (St) *The kids are interrupting and making it so that I can't hear.*
SEE ALSO apatel-anthem, apatelh-ilem, lpwertelh-ilem, ulpertelh-ilem

aparlp-parlp-ilem (W) *vt.*
settle someone down, distract someone
SEE ALSO anngwanng-ilem, arternp-ilem, arternpelh-ilem

aparr *n.*
extra piece of wood added to the butt end of a spear to make it longer
SEE ALSO alart

aparrng (E) *n.* [RESPECT LANGUAGE]
blind ◆ Aparrng-ayerr anem apal-apal-ayerr anem arrep-iletyang anem. (Sa) *He [my son-in-law] is blind now and his eyes can't see any more.*

aparrng-irrem (E) *vi.* [RESPECT LANGUAGE]
go blind
SEE ALSO pweng

aparrty (E) *n.*
bean tree, bat's-wing coral tree (*Erythrina vespertilio*). Tree to 10 m high, with bright red flowers and shiny red and yellow seeds in clustered pods.
= atywerety
SEE ALSO inernt

apatem *vi.*
1. not know (about something); be confused; not know what to say; not understand something; not recognise something, be unable to do something, be at a loss as to what to do ◆ Nthenh-angkwerr ayeng alhetyek — wal, ayeng apatem. (St) *Which way should I go — well, I don't know.*
2. feel homesick, lonely or displaced ◆ Apatemel anerl-anem, ikngа anerl-anemel apatem. (Sa) *I'm sitting on my own feeling lonely.* ◆ Nheng mer arrpenh apek nta alhem, *different country*-warl, wal nta apatem. Apatem nta irrar-irremel. Apatem nta mer-warn nta alpetyeh, mer *country* ngkwenh-henh. (M) *If you go to another place, to a different country,*

well you feel homesick and displaced. You feel homesick. You want to go back to your own country. ◆ Alpetyek anem apatem. (St) *I want to go home because I'm lonely.*
= anatem
SEE ALSO irrar-irrem
apatelh-ilem *vt.*
distract or confuse someone, interrupt, stop someone from doing something, create a disturbance or make a noise ◆ Kwer atherrarl atwerrem, wal apatelh-ilem. (M) *There might be two kids fighting, well you stop them doing it.*
SEE ALSO lpwertelh-ilem, ulpertelh-ilem, aparlp-ilem, aparlpelh-ilem
apatel-anthem (T,E) *vt.* = **apatelh-ilem** ◆ *Paint*-ek apek, *paint* ingkwern kel ingwerel apatel-anthenhety-alhek, ra akeng-ilemel anem apatem. (Sa) *When someone is painting, and another person goes past them and interrupts them, then they make a mess of it then.* ◆ Ayengarl apatel-anthemeng artwa nhenhel. Ayeng apatemel alhetyeh mer arrpenhel intetyeh. (T) *This man is hassling me. I'm at a loss to know what to do; I'll go to another place to sleep.*

-apatherr *n.ending*
1. An ending used when asking a person what their skin name or subsection name is. Goes on the end of question words *iwenh, ilek* 'what' and *angwenh* 'who'. ◆ Ilek-**apatherr** untaw ikwan ngkwenh? (Sa) *What is your skin name?* ◆ Iwenh-**apatherr** nga? (St) *What skin are you?* ◆ Angwenh-**apatherr** ntwam? (M) *What skin are you?*
2. Something said when the speaker is not sure of the name of something or has temporarily forgotten it; 'What's-his-name', 'What-d'ye-call-it', 'Thingummybob', 'Thingummyjig'. ◆ Mer iwenh-**apatherr**? (M) *What's the name of that place?*
3. With pronouns shows whether or not people are in the same or in the opposite generation moiety to the person speaking. See Appendix 1. • SEE ALSO -apakwey
ilern-apatherr (E)
we who are in the same generation moiety as each other ◆ Thang ilem, 'Ilern-apatherr alherretyeh, lyweny apek'. Mpetyan arrpaty, 'ilern-apatherr' ilem. (T) *I'll say, 'We in the same generation moiety will go hunting'. I call someone who is Mpetyan like me* 'ilern-apatherr'.
alanth-apatherr (T)
they (who are in the opposite patrimoiety and generation moiety to the speaker)
= alanth-apakwey

apatwem (E) *vt.*
bump something
SEE ALSO ankert-wem, aperrpert-ilem
apatwerrem (E) *vi.*
bump into each other, collide ◆ Ampa atherr apek *bump*-em-ilerrem apatwerrem. (Sa) *Two kids are bumping each other.* ◆ Mwetek atherr apatwerrek. (Sa) *Two cars collided.*

apawenhem, apay-unhem (E), **apaw-utnhem** (E) *vt.*
ask someone for something ◆ Thwengk apawenhem merneh apek kereh apek kwenh, angayel anthwerr kwenh. (N) *I am asking you for bread or meat because I am really hungry.* ◆ Arelh nhak apay-unhetyek lhay ngkwerlpek. (St) *Go and ask that woman for tobacco.*
SEE ALSO nhwem

apawerr (E) *n.*
everybody; everywhere, lots of, all over the place ◆ Apawerr yanh akarr-irretyenh *football*-warl. (Sa) *People from all over the place are going to get together for football.*
= apapeth
SEE ALSO apanp

apay-unhem (E) ask someone for something SEE UNDER **apawenhem**

apek *part.*
1. maybe, might, perhaps, probably. Used when the speaker is not sure if what he or she is saying is true or of the certainty of an event or action. ◆ Yapek apay apek unhey. (Sa) *Maybe [I'll] ask [them].* ◆ Tyerrty apek ankey apetyem kereh. (M) *[Those] people will probably come begging for meat.* ◆ Kwenyel apek ywerretyenh. (M) *He may die during the night.*
2. conditional; if (one action must happen before another can follow) ◆ Atnyenty-atnyentyan alhemey kel tyerrtyel apek anpem, alakenh rtapety anem irrerl-alhem. (St) *The* atnyenty-atnyenty *beetle goes along and if a person touches it curls up.* ◆ Angayel apek artang-iletyek, alhetyek apek. Artang-ilem tey apek mern apek. Tha apek artang-iletyek, ngkwengetyem athath, ntwa anem antyweyameng. *You might eat first if you're hungry, or go somewhere first. You might have tea or food first. I might drink before you, and then you drink.*
SEE ALSO thweng

apekap *n.*
1. crippled ◆ Arntety apekap alhetyangenh, apekap, alhetyakenh arntety. (Sa) *Somebody is sick and unable to walk, crippled.*
= apertap
2. unable to speak properly, having a speech

impediment ◆ Aleny apekap angkem, aleny ywarn angketyek. War apekap-irrek aleny. *Might* tywen-akert apek. (St) *Unable to speak properly, the tongue having difficulty in talking. Maybe there is a sore on the tongue.*
SEE ALSO akerter, apap

apekap-irrem *vi.*
1. become lame or crippled, get weak ◆ Arnerrerl antem anem apekap-irrem. (St) *Crippled and only able to crawl.*
= apertap-irrem
2. be unable to speak properly

apekath *n.*
1. a part-Aboriginal person (from English 'half-caste')
2. a bit light in colour (skin); light-skinned; a light brown colour ◆ Tyapwert-apwert, arlewatyerr akely-artek. *Little one* anert, ankert-ankert kwa. Apekath akelyarlap ra. (Sa) *The* tyapwert-apwert *lizard is like a little goanna. It has a small stomach, like* ankert-ankert. *It is a little light-coloured one.* • SEE ALSO alperrty, athethek

apekath-apekath *n.*
a bit light in colour (skin); a light brown colour ◆ Ayengan arelyerrty anep-anem, apekath-apekath. Apekath artek inngerr wal arelyerrty. (St) *I am light-skinned, a bit light in colour. A face that like that of a half-caste person is* arelyerrty.
SEE ALSO arelyerrty

apel[1] (E) *n.*
kidney fat from kangaroo. Also referred to as *anter apel* and *apel anter.* ◆ Apel tha kwern-aynetyek. Ultiperr, mpwerrketyel-arlengarl anem, ker anter. Apel, ker anter apel. (Sa) *I'm going to eat the kidney fat, from the side of the kangaroo, from around the kidneys.*
SEE ALSO anter

apel[2], **apelay** *part.*
Shows that something really is the way it is being described, or that a report of something is accurate and complete. Shows that the speaker wants to make a point of something so that the listener will take special note of it; really, truly, I know for a fact that . . . ◆ Arratyant-alkenty apelay ina *win*-em-ilek — tha arekay kwenh. (T) *It's really true that they won — I know for a fact because I saw them.* ◆ Tyerrty nhenh ankerl apelay, ywarn angkem nheng mern apek ker. 'Ker anthay.' '*No.*' Ankerlam tyerrty nhenh. *Everybody knows that this person is really greedy and [you] ask them in vain for bread or meat. 'Give me some meat.' 'No.' That person is greedy.* ◆ Kwer nhenh ltyernt apelay. (M) *I know for a fact that this kid is naughty.* ◆ Alangkw, mern aparl akerl-apek, mern akwerrk akerl-apek, akerl-apemel akerl-apemel. Rwewarn antem angernem, rwelap itetyam, mern aparl apel, rwel itetyam. Perrap *soft one* anthwerr, rwepenh. (N) *The young fruits of the bush banana were picked and then taken back to the fire to be cooked. They are really nice and soft after being cooked in the fire.*

apelinterr-interr (E) *n.*
rainbow bird, rainbow bee-eater (*Merops ornatus*) ◆ Apelinterr-interrel alhweng mpwarem kwartek ahern-itwek. (Sa) *The rainbow bird builds a nest for its eggs on the ground.*
= kwelinterr-interr, terr-terr

apelkel (W,T) *adv.*
1. (doing something) without reason or for no good reason; (doing something) without thinking ◆ Apelkel ayeng artwa yanhel atwek. (T) *That man hit me for no reason.* ◆ Artwang nhak atyeng unpart-irrekaw! Apelkel war. (T) *That man is getting sulky with me! For no reason.*
2. doing something for nothing (wasting your time) ◆ Apelkel alherrek kwenh. Apelkel alherrern ker-kwenh. Ker atwety-kweny apelkel ityel alperrey kwenh. (T) *They went for nothing. They went and there was no game. They didn't shoot anything at all and went back with nothing.* ◆ Anwern alhek *town*-warn maney inetyeh. Thang ywarek, maney-kweny. Apelkel war ayeng alhek. Thang *ring*-em *up*-ilemer arrwekel. (T) *We went to town to get money. I went in vain, there was no money. I went for nothing. I should have rung up first.*
SEE ALSO war, apal[2], arrangkw

apely *n.*
1. green (of foliage) ◆ Apely arna yanhaw. (St) *That tree is green.* ◆ Apelyek-amparr intem-penh antyerrk anem ra irrem. (St) *After being green it's drying up.*
2. wet, moist, soft or sloppy (of food)
SEE ALSO anthwel
CAN SOUND A BIT LIKE pely *'small loin cloth'*

apely-ilem *vt.*
make something wet or soft ◆ Kwaty thelemarl apely-ilem, item anem renh. (St) *Tipping water in to make it wet then cooking it.*

apem[1] (W,T) *vi.*
walk along, go along ◆ Tyerrty yanh aperl-anem. (M) *That person is going along.* ◆ Ngwath ayeng apep-apem. (M) *I keep walking about alone.*

SEE ALSO alhem, nthwem

apem[2] (E) *vt.*

paint someone with something or rub something onto someone ◆ Anterel apem. (Sa) *Rubbing with fat.* ◆ Ilpengkel apem. (Sa) *Rubbing someone with the* ilpengk *medicine.*

SEE ALSO pernem, pernelhem

apeng *n.*

desert kurrajong (*Brachychiton gregorii*). Tree to 8 m high, with smooth shiny leaves, pale yellow flowers, and woody fruits that hang in bunches. The roots of the kurrajong tree were scraped and used as a source of water. It also has edible seeds and a sweet resin which was eaten. ◆ Antyelty atnartengel anem, apeng rltwel. (Sa) *Sitting at the base of the big kurrajong tree.* ◆ Apeng ntha — kwaty-penh ampeny iwem anem, ntha renh. Kwaty arlkarl thelek-penh. (St) *The chips of wood from the kurrajong tree root — after the cool water has been poured off, the leftovers, the chips of wood, are thrown away. After the cool water has been poured off.*

SEE ALSO ntha, ngkweyang

apengeleytanenh (E) *n.*

canegrass dragon, blue-lined dragon (*Diporiphora winneckei*) (?) ◆ Apengeleytanenh war apeng-angkwerr alherl-anem apeng-warl ingwerel alhem apeng ingwerel alhem apeng ingwerel alhem urnterl-anem. (Sa) *The* apengeleytanenh *lizard just goes from one kurrajong tree to another, running between them.*

= arlanty

Apengarlayntem (T) *n.*

the name of a rockhole and the location of an outstation in the Utopia (Angarapa Aboriginal Land Trust) area (lit. 'where the desert kurrajong is lying'). Also spelt as Pungelindum. See map p. viii.

-apenh (W,T) *n.ending*

'Poor thing', 'Dear thing' (an expression of endearment)

SEE ALSO -amperl, -angwel-angwel, -angwen-angwen, -awern

akeweny-apenh (W,T)

'Poor thing'

= akeweny-amperl

SEE ALSO akeweny

apentem (T,E) *vt.*

1. follow someone or something; track someone or something ◆ Alewatyerr apek apentem apentem apentem atwemel, kel alhwengek. (Sa) *Following the goanna along and then killing it in its hole.* ◆ Ilekek unta ayenh apentem? (Sa) *Why are you following me?* ◆ Apentem unta ayeng ingkerneng, kel unta ayeng arety-alhem. (T) *You follow me from behind and then you see me.*

2. follow a particular belief or system of law ◆ War Altyerr apentemel, anpernem war. (Sa) *Just following the Dreaming, the kinship system.*

SEE ALSO ingkantem, antelhem, ampinem

+apenty Follows the name of an animal, plant or other thing to form the name of a place associated with that particular Dreaming. SEE UNDER **+apwenty**

-apeny (E) *ending*

1. resembles; is like (someone or something else); is similar to, is like this, it seems like ◆ Aperarntan thelelhetyel *honey*-**apeny**, aperel-arleng inngart. (Sa) *Actually, the* aperarnt *is found on the river red gum and it seeps out like honey.* ◆ Arremparreng-rnem. 'Ayeng-**apeny** arremparreng yanh kwenh. Inngerr ayeng-**apeny** kwenh, kwey nhenh aperley atyenh.' (Sa) *All the people who are very much alike. 'That person there closely resembles me. My grandchild has a face just like mine.'* ◆ Ker pwelh-irrem — ker *barbecue* arrtyerrenty pwelh-irrem, aperrk-irremel, pwelh-irrem. Irrpwerl-irrerl-anem aperrk-**apeny** irrem, pwelh. (Sa) *Meat gets burnt — meat that is cooked on the barbecue gets burnt and turns to charcoal. It goes black like charcoal, burnt.*

2. Goes on the end of verbs to show that something does an action in the way something else does it; like that. ◆ Arengk alta anetyakenh altelhey, perleyn. Weth altwerl nhakw perleyn anetyel-**apeny**, arengk artwampw weth. *Naked.* (Sa) *A dog with no hair is called* perleyn. *Like that old hairless male dog sitting over there. Naked.*

3. Following *+el* on nominals, *-apeny* shows that something else does an action in the way that particular thing does it. ◆ Mern anatyel tenh anyenem akern. Anaty artelhampwel inngel. Urrper-wem, urrper ra tetnh atnyenem irrkwenngel-**apeny**. (Sa) *The bush potato makes the earth lift right up. A really big bush potato. It makes the earth swell up and crack, like a native truffle does.*

SEE ALSO -artek

aper *n.*

river red gum (*Eucalyptus camaldulensis* var. *obtusa*). Large tree that grows on the banks and in the beds of watercourses. ◆ Aper lywangel tyerrty anerl-anetyeh. (N) *People sit in the shade of the river red gum.*

aper tyelk

inner bark of river red gum (tyelk *'flesh', 'inner part of something'*) ◆ Aper tyelkel, kapert alhewelhetyeh, annga arlka. (N) *The bark of the river red gum can be used to wash the head and the eyes.* ◆ Aper arntapel anwern atantherl-anem alhewelherl-anetyek, per kwa tyelk. Atanthem aper tyelk, kapert alhewelhetyeh, annga arlka. (N) *We use the bark of the river red gum for a washing medicine. We get the inside bark of the river red gum and use it to make a wash for our heads and our eyes.*

aper akwerrk
young river red gum (akwerrk[1] *'young'*) ◆ Aper akwerrkel tyerrty rlkert alhewelhem. (T) *[A mixture made of] young river red gum tree [leaves] is used as a medicinal wash for sick people.*

aperayt (E) *n.*
grub from the branch of the river red gum
SEE ALSO ingweneng, perlanty, aylperlayt, ngkenhar, mpaty[2], ahekwenayt

aperaley (W,T) *n.*
seed capsules of the river red gum
= aperrper

aperaly (W) *n.*
blossoms of the river red gum

aperarnt (T,E), **aperarntw** (E) *n.*
honey made by lerp insect living under the bark of the river red gum ◆ Aperarntan thelelhetyel *honey*-apeny, aperel-arleng inngart. (Sa) *Actually, the* aperarnt *is found on the river red gum and it seeps out like honey.*
= mamp

aperengengel (E), **aperengelengel** (E), **aperelayeng** (W) *n.* = **aperarnt**

aperelty, aperalty, aperilty (E) *n.*

white substance made by the lerp-scale insect on the leaf of the river red gum. Also referred to as *mern aperelty.* ◆ Mern aperelty. Mern arlkwenh arlkwenhap aperelty anthwerr, anganekarl. Mern aperelty akerl-apemel. Mern alakenharl ayernem aperelty. Arlpang artaly-wem, arlpang wem, *clean*-em arrernem. Kel arlkwem antem. Kelh antem mparem. (N) *The white substance made by the lerp-scale insect from the river red gum tree is edible — it's a traditional practice — going along and collecting* aperelty. *We rub the scale off the leaves like that, and then discard the leaves and then make the* aperelty *into a cake. Then we eat it.*

aperalhem (E) types of mistletoe SEE UNDER **pweralhem**

aperl, aperley *n.kin*
1. father's mother; grandmother
2. father's mother's brothers or sisters; great-aunt, great-uncle
3. a woman's son's child; grandchild, grandson, granddaughter
4. a person's sister's son's child; great-nephew, great-niece
5. particular relations with the same skin as your *aperl*
6. the country and Dreamings belonging to a person's *aperl.*
7. the husband or wife of someone who is not in the same generation moiety as oneself. For example, this would include a person's children's or nephew's and niece's husbands or wives, and a person's aunt's and uncle's husbands and wives. One's own parents could be referred to as *aperl-nheng.* In most cases if a person calls someone *aperl*, then they are called *aperl* back. • SEE ALSO arrkar, anew, ngwarr, -nheng

aperl-aperl, aperley-aperley (E) *n.kin*
father's mother; a woman's son's child, etc. This may be an affectionate or respectful way of talking to or about one's *aperl.* It is also used to talk to children about their *anew* 'potential husband or wife'. ◆ Atyankerney-apenh angetyetyart warntapelant mern atyankern arrwekeleny mapel. Aperl-aperl-rrpwerelaty menh-menh-rrpwerel arlka atyemeyel-rrpwer. *The olden-time people used to get mistletoe berries in bark containers. All my grandmothers, the old women.* ◆ 'Aperl-aperl ngkwenh, aperley ngkwenh.' Anewikw inngart ilem, ampa akelyek. 'Aperl-aperl' ilem anewikw ap. Aperl-aperlap ileman, kel 'anew' anem nhenh akngerretyekant anem anewan anem. *'There is your* aperl-aperl.*' That's what is said for* anew *to a little child. '*Aperl-aperl*' is what their [potential] husband/wife is called. Only when they get bigger is their spouse referred to as* 'anew'.
SEE ALSO anew

aperlaty *n.kin*
my/our *aperl*

aperlikw (E), **aperleyekw** (E) *n.kin*
his/her/their *aperl*

aperlengkw *n.kin*
your *aperl*

aperlwek (W,T) *n.kin*
1. your *aperl*
2. his/her/their *aperl*

aperl-nheng *n.kin*
1. a group of two or more people who are

related to each other as *aperl*
2. a group of two or more people, at least two of whom are a married couple in the opposite generation moiety to the speaker
aperl-intyerr *n.kin* = **aperl-nheng**
aperl-nheng-arey *n.kin*
a group of more than two people who are related to each other as *aperl*
aperl-nheng atherr *n.kin*
1. a person together with one of their *aperl* ◆ Aperl-nheng atherr yanh alherreperrem — kwey marl awenk then arelh ampwa then. (Sa) *Those two are going there, grandmother and grandchild — a teenage girl and an old woman.*
2. a married couple in the opposite generation moiety to the speaker ◆ Arelhel melikwel ilem mam ikwerenh artwethen, 'Aperl-nheng atherr yanh'. Anewart renh 'aperl-nheng' akem — mikwel, artwekenh mikwelan ilem aperl-nheng atherr akem, anherrikw then ampikw then. Arelh-kenh amikw mwerikwantarl ilem, 'ngwarr-nheng atherr' akem, arelh-kenh mikwan ngwarr-nheng atherr akem. (Sa) *The woman, the mother of the man, says of her son and his wife, 'There's those two, husband and wife,* aperl-nheng atherr'. *The man's mother calls the spousal couple* 'aperl-nheng' *— that's referring to her son and her daughter-in-law. The mother of the wife calls [her son-in-law]* mwer *and refers to the spousal couple as* 'ngwarr-nheng atherr'.
aperl-parety *n.kin*
respectful or 'sorry way' of talking about someone's *aperl*
SEE ALSO -parety
aperl-ankethenh *n.kin*
1. having a close *aperl* still alive
2. someone who is always with their *aperl*
SEE ALSO -ankethenh

aperler (W,T) *n.*
dark rain cloud ◆ Kwaty aperler apetyem, mwemengk angerr. (M) *Big dark rain clouds are coming.*

aperley father's mother; grandmother SEE UNDER aperl

aperlk-aperlk (T,E), **apeylk-apeylk** (E) *n.*
wet, sloppy, runny, a liquid or sloppy mixture. Some uses of this word are very rude.
SEE ALSO alyemp-alyemp[1]
aperlk-aperlk-ilem (T,E),
apeylk-apeylk-ilem (E) *vt.*
make something sloppy or runny ◆ Mern atyenh tha aperlk-aperlk ilek *dry* anetyanhan. '*Dry* atyeng anthey kwenh, mern tamp mpwaretyek.' (Sa) *I made this mixture wet, not dry. 'Give me some dry [flour] to make damper.'*

apernem *vt.*
paint or rub something on or into something ◆ Arelhel apernem rlkert kwer anterel apek *or medicine* pwety-arenyel apek. (T) *The woman is rubbing the sick child with fat or with bush medicine.*
CAN SOUND A BIT LIKE pernem *'chase something down and kill it'*
apernelhem *vi.*
rub something on self; paint up ◆ Anterel apernelheyaw. (St) *Rub yourself with fat.* ◆ Pwek-pwek, ampel apernelherl-anem arrwert lyapetyek, urrperl ilelhemel, arrkenel-arleng. (Sa) *The boys use the stalked puffball to paint themselves with, to make their beards grow, and to make themselves dark in colour, for fun.* ◆ Lyarwek apernelhenhelhenh akin. Lyarwek anthwerr. Arrkernk-areny. Arrkinty-kenh, apernelhetyek, rtety-rtety apek aremarl. Arrkernk renh kwa rnpwa lyarwek. (N) Lyarwek *is a rubbing medicine as well, from the bloodwood tree. If you have scabies or other lumps on your skin you can rub yourself with the resin from the bloodwood tree.*
SEE ALSO apem[2]

aperr (E) *n.*
a type of worm or caterpillar (?)
SEE ALSO ahaylengkeyler

aperrem (T) *vt.*
stop someone from going somewhere or from doing something ◆ Tyerrty nhak-kety aperrem! (T) *Stop that person [he's making trouble]!*
SEE ALSO arnpakem

aperrety-aperrety (T), **perety-perety** (T) *n.*
white-plumed honeyeater (?) (*Lichenostomus penicillatus*)
= tyelyapwerety

aperretyen (W,T) *n.*
plain flour (maybe from English 'half raising'). Also referred to as *mern aperretyen.* ◆ Aperretyen anyent payem-ilay *bucket* rnter-rnterel-ayeng. (M) *Buy one [container] of plain flour, in the red bucket.*
SEE ALSO thelperretyen, mern pelaw, arterrty, nmwenth, unmenth, warnp

aperrk *n.*
1. coals, hot coals ◆ Aperrk anem ra irrem, kel ura rnter-rnter urek-amperr ampeynepeynem, kel ilwem anem aperrk anem, urrperl-irrem anem. Urinp, aperrk urakert. Urinp urinp menty anep-anem. *Something* anem item kwerel, aperrkel. (St) *Then it turns to coals. The*

fire is red at first, burning, then it dies down and turns to coals, goes black. The coals are hot. When they are too hot you leave them for a while, then you can cook something on the coals.
2. charcoal, coal ◆ Amwekel kwer kwerenh apernem aperrkel tywen-akert. (T) *The mother is rubbing her child, who has sores, with charcoal.*
3. starter motor (of a car)
aperrk-irrem *vi.*
turn to charcoal

aperrper (E) *n.*
seed capsules of the river red gum (*Eucalyptus camaldulensis* var. *obtusa*)
= aperaley
SEE ALSO aper

aperrpert *n.*
(speaking) in a confused way; not speaking properly; (speaking) wrongly, stumbling over your words; (being) distracted or anxious ◆ Aleny aperrpert, angkem aperrpert war, *drunk*-artek war angkem. (Sa) *Talking in a confused way, talking like a drunk.*
SEE ALSO apap, alhwerrkert, tetherrp-tetherrp
aperrpert-ilem (W,T) *vt.*
bump into something; hit someone or something by mistake; push someone ◆ Aperrpert-ilek, apalelarl aperrpert-ilek ngenh. (T) *I didn't mean to bump into you.*
SEE ALSO apantelh-ilem
aperrpert-irrem *vi.*
1. (speak) in a confused way, not speaking properly, speak wrongly
2. be unable to do something, make a mistake while doing something, be unable to see properly ◆ Annga ayeng akeng aperrpert-irrekaw, arntety-irrenty kapert *headache*-irrenty, annga aperrpert-irrem. (Sa) *My eyes are no good and I can't see properly, I've got a headache and my eyes are no good.*
3. get lost, go the wrong way • SEE ALSO apant-irrem

-apert *n.ending*
having (something), associated with (something) ◆ Rlwek yanhel mwerrarl ilem *clean*-em ilelhem annga, *everything* alhewelhem artwengkenng-**apert**em mernt-**apert**, iteth-ilem. *The native pine is used to wash eyes and clean them and make them better and to wash a person all over and make them better if they have a cold or are sick.*
ilek-apert
'What's up?', 'What's wrong?' (ilek '*what?*') ◆ Ilek-they nga arnkelyan anetyel? Angketyakenh arnkely ahel. Ilelha atyengay. Ilek-**apert**arl ngan anep-anem tyernetyangan? Arntety apek nga awelhek apek ilelhetyang. (Sa) *Why are sitting there sulkily? You are sulky and angry and not saying anything. Tell me. Why are you sitting there and not answering? Maybe you felt sick and you're not saying anything about it.*
iwenh-apert
'What's up?', 'What's wrong?' (iwenh '*what?*') ◆ Iwenh-**apert** nga marakat-irrem? (M) *Why are you feeling tired?*

apert-atwem (E) *vt.*
crush, pound or smash something up, hammer something (atwem '*hit*') ◆ Apert-atwem ker apwert-warl, inpinp apert-atwem. (Sa) *Smashing up the marrow bone on a rock.* ◆ Apert-atwenhety-alpep-alpem mwetekay arlwepertaty *tyre flat*. (Sa) *The little round car with a flat tyre is going back, smashing up [the tyre] as it goes.*
SEE ALSO ulpilem, mweltyem, anthim-ilem, ngkwelty atwem, ngkwelty-ilem, ngkweltyelh-ilem, ngkweltyem

apertap (W,T) *n.*
quiet, weak, harmless, not dangerous, non-aggressive, crippled ◆ Ngkwanty-irretyakenh ra anem, apertaparl ra anem, apekaparl ra anem. (T) *That person doesn't get aggressive because they're weak and harmless.*
= apekap
SEE ALSO ameleth, angwang, anik
apertap-irrem (W,T) *vi.*
get weak, be unable to do things for yourself, become crippled or lame ◆ Ayeng apertap-irrem ngkwern atherr. (T) *My legs are crippled.*
= apekap-irrem

apertaynp (E), **apertaymp** (E) *n.*
fat in the flesh from the thigh of a kangaroo. Also referred to as *anter apertaynp*. ◆ Apertaynp, tyelkel-arlengarl anem, anter. Aherr-kenh. Iyleperel-arleng. (St) Apertaynp *is fat found in the flesh of the kangaroo. In the thigh.*
= iylpernk
SEE ALSO akepitelh, rtwarnp

apertem *vi.*
creep up on someone; stalk someone, sneak up on someone or something ◆ Apertenhemel apertenhemel kel atyerremel renh aker. (Sa) *Creeping along and creeping along and then shooting the kangaroo.* ◆ Aperterl-apem aperterl-apem ker *there* interl-anem. Apertem apertem atanthem irrtyartel. (N) *Stalking up on the kangaroo to where it is there lying down. Sneaking up on it and then spearing*

it with a spear. ◆ Mpwenyek apertem ingwel. (Sa) *Sneaking up to someone at night to have sex with them.*

apetherr (W) *n.* [RESPECT LANGUAGE]
eye
SEE ALSO annga

apetyem *vi.*
come ◆ Mer-warn apetyek ngangkay-akert inyang aretyeh. (M) *The traditional healer came to the home of the sick man to see him.* ◆ Artwang lwereny apetyekaw. (M) *A stranger came.*
apety-alhem *vi.*
come ◆ Apety-alhay, arelhay! (M) *Come here woman!* ◆ Unmernt rang apety-alhem aterel anthety-alhem tyerrtyan. (N) *The dust comes along and gives people a fright.* ◆ Tyerrty apekarl nheng apety-alhem alethang apek wal nheng renh mer akweteth akenh rltwatyarl irrerleng, nheng mer akweteth anep-anem rltwaty-irrem. '*Oh someone* lyet arratem kwenh.' (M) *If a person is coming, maybe a stranger, well the person who lives in the place all the time has a premonition about it. 'Oh, someone is going to arrive.'*
apety-alherrem *vi.*
come (two), come along in a pair
apetyewarrem *vi.*
come (more than two), come in a group ◆ Mern alangkw nhel arlpar athwenkarr anemek apetyewarray, anwengkerr aketyek. (T) *All of you come here to where the bush bananas are hanging in bunches, so that we can pick them.* ◆ Ampaty-intyarr ingkerreny apetyewarray! (P) *Come here all you kids!*
apety-alpem *vi.*
come back, return ◆ Nthwemel nthwemel apety-alpern aker-kweny itya, itya akwet. (M) *Walking and walking [I] came back without any meat, still nothing.* ◆ Mer atyenhek tha iwerl-alhern mantarr apek, kel ayeng apety-alpern. (St) *I just left the clothes at my place and then I came back.*

apetyepetyem (W,T) *n.*
rufous whistler (*Pachycephala rufiventris*) ◆ Thep rantem angkem, 'Apetyepetyem apetyepetyem'. (M) *Then the bird sings, 'Apetyepetyem apetyepetyem' ['coming along, coming along'].*
= kwarlpatengkelyengkely, ipeny apetyepetyem, artwang apetyepetyem, artwatherr apetyepetyem, tyenyepweny

apewarrng (W) *n.* [RESPECT LANGUAGE]
sleep
SEE ALSO ankwa

Apewenty (T) Plenty River SEE UNDER **Apiwenty**

apeyarrel alhem *vi.*
(women) hop or skip along showing intention to fight
= anwerntem
apeyarr-irrem *vi.* = **apeyarrel alhem**
SEE ALSO arrtyernem, meyl-meyl-irrem, antyatar-irrem

apeylk-apeylk (E) wet, sloppy, runny SEE UNDER **aperlk-aperlk**

apeynt (T,E) spring (water) SEE UNDER **apinty**

apeynt-apeynt (E) *n.*
emu blood ◆ *No* renh 'awerrp' akem — apeynt-apeyntarl ra. Ankerr, itnewem renh 'apeynt-apeynt', 'awerrp' aketyakenh. Antywem renh. (St) *You don't call it 'awerrp' — it's 'apeynt-apeynt'. Emu's blood is called 'apeynt-apeynt', not 'awerrp'. [We] drink it.*
SEE ALSO awerrp[1]

apinty (W,T), **apeynt** (T,E) *n.*
spring (water). Also referred to as *kwaty apinty*.
= ayay
SEE ALSO ulamp

Apiwenty (E), **Apewenty** (T) *n.*
Plenty River

apma (T) bud or flower of native tobacco etc. SEE UNDER **alpma**

apmakw (E) the back of the emu SEE UNDER **amakw**

Apmakweng (E) Central Mt Stuart SEE UNDER **Amakweng**

apmany-irrem (E) sigh or take a deep breath SEE UNDER **amany-irrem**

apmarl (E), **apmarley** (E) uncle (mother's brother) SEE UNDER **amarl**

apmarn (E) still, quiet, motionless SEE UNDER **amarn**

apmarrkel angem (E) carry something on the hip SEE UNDER **amarrkel angem**

apmatheng (E) orphan SEE UNDER **amatheng**

apmatheng-apmatheng (E) black-faced cuckoo-shrike SEE UNDER **amatheng-amatheng**

apmelerr (E) permanent, same, usual SEE UNDER **amelerr**

apmer (E) camp, home, house SEE UNDER **mer**

apmerrk (E) young boy about 10-12 years old SEE UNDER **amerrk**[1]

apmerrk (E) hot earth or ashes (used for cooking or healing) SEE UNDER **amerrk**[2]

apmewarr (E) *n.*
honey from a honeyant that has been split open ◆ Ngka tha awantyetyek apmewarr. (Sa) *Give me some honeyant honey to suck on.*
SEE ALSO yerramp, inkwareny, awert[1]

Apmewarr (E) *n.*
Bundey River
apmikw (E) native pine SEE UNDER **amikw**[1]
apmwa (E) snake SEE UNDER **amwa**[1]
apmwa (E) bad, no good SEE UNDER **amwa**[2]
apmwer (E) mint bush SEE UNDER **amwer**
apmwern-irrem (T,E) grow close together (of plants) SEE UNDER **mwern-irrem**
apmwerrk (E) yesterday SEE UNDER **amwerrk**
apmwethek (E) type of frog SEE UNDER **angwethek**
apur (E) shyness, shame, embarrassment SEE UNDER **apwer**
apwa (E) *n.*
1. emu feathers ◆ Ankerr-kenh apwa, artep-iperr. (Sa) *Emu's feathers, from the back of the emu.*
= artarr
SEE ALSO angkwely-angkwely, awenth-awenth
2. kurdaitcha's feather shoes, 'kurdaitcha boot'. Worn to disguise footprints.
apwirrpem (E) *vi.*
put on the kurdaitcha feather shoes (?) (irrpem *'put something on'*) ◆ Ingkarl apwirrpek mwak. (Sa) *The kurdaitcha put on the feather shoes.*
apwak (W) (eating something) before the main meal SEE UNDER **apak**
apwarrewerlker (E), **apwarrewerlkenh** (E) *n.*
1. emu (first-hatched of a brood) [SOME SPEAKERS] ◆ Apwarrewerlker itepelarl alhep-alhem weth, aletharr *that one, first time* rek-amparr anem kwart, atherneng. Marl *one or boy one.* Arlter-arlterarl ra. (St) *The first-hatched emu is the one that goes along on the side [of the group of emu hatchlings]. That's the first-born, that comes out of the egg first, either a female or a male. They are whitish in colour.*
2. old white-coloured male emu [SOME SPEAKERS]
SEE ALSO areyakeyarr, aletharr, apwa
apwart-apwart (E) *n.*
whistling kite (*Haliastur sphenurus*) (?)
SEE ALSO apwelanty, artapw-artapw, apwerl-apwerl
apwelanty, **apwelaynt** (E) *n.*
black kite (*Milvus migrans*) ◆ Apwelantyel ker arlkwenhem, atek arlka arlkwerl-anem. Alhem ra, inenhem. (N) *The black kite gets meat to eat as it flies along, including button quails. It flies and grabs them as it goes.* ◆ Apwelaynt ker arlkwenh-arlkwenh. Iwenh apekarl arlkwem, atanthem, kwen-irrenhemel inenhem. (St) *Black kites eat meat. Whatever they eat, they hunt with their claws, swooping down to get it.*
= apwerl-apwerl, artapw-artapw
apwelh *n.*
young men's ceremony, initiation ceremony ◆ Amparl alyep-alyem apwelhel. (St) *The* apwelh *ceremony is where the young boys are sung into manhood.*
SEE ALSO anmanty
CAN SOUND A BIT LIKE pwelh *'burnt'*
apwelh alkey (W)
the middle part of the initiation (young man) ceremony ground
= arawern
apwen *n.*
1. broom bush, desert cassia (*Senna artemisioides* ssp. *filifolia*)
SEE ALSO ngkwert
2. silver cassia (*Senna artemisioides* ssp. *alicia artemisioides*). Shrubs to about 2 m with narrow leaves and bright yellow flowers. • SEE ALSO manatwerrp, areyawarr
apwenayt (T,E), **apwetnayt** (E) *n.*
grub from the broom bush, desert cassia (and others (?))
apwen-apwen (E) *n.*
country where there are lots of cassias growing
+apwenty (T,E), **+apenty** *n.ending*
Follows the name of an animal, plant or other thing to form the name of a place associated with that particular Dreaming. ◆ Arnmanapwenty, Arlpmanapwenty *Long Range, Ti Tree/Stirling Station area* (arnman[2] *'honeyant'*) ◆ Urapenty, Rwapenty *Sandover River; Mt Hay* (ura *'fire'*)
apwer (W,T), **apur** (E) *n.*
1. shyness, shame, embarrassment
2. behaving with the appropriate degree of respect, or showing good manners in terms of Aboriginal Law
= nyerr
CAN SOUND A BIT LIKE pwer *'tail'*
apwer-irrem (W,T), **apur-irrem** (E) *vi.*
be nervous, shy, ashamed or embarrassed ◆ Tyerrty alethangeng apwer-irrem, arrpenharl apetyemeng, nyerr-irrem. (T) *Being embarrassed and shy because of strangers coming.*
= nyerr-irrem
SEE ALSO pwerep-irrem
apwer-apwer-irrem (W,T), **apur-irrem** (E) *vi.*
= **apwer-irrem** ◆ Wenh-apertam tyerrty yanhan apwer-apwer-irrem? (T) *Why is that person ashamed?*
apweralth (W,T), **apuralth** (E) *n.*
a person who is timid, shy, ashamed or embarrassed

= nyerralth
apwerel anthem (W,T), **apurel anthem** (E)
make someone feel shamed, shy or embarrassed (anthem *'give'*)
= nyerrel anthem

apwerety, apwerety-iteng (W) *n.* [RESPECT LANGUAGE]
big ◆ Nyewel apwerety-warl ahanenherl-wek tyety-ayerrek. (St) *[Your] son-in-law has gone hunting towards the big hill.*
SEE ALSO angerr[1]

apweretyapwer (W) brown songlark SEE UNDER **tyelyapwerety**

apwerl-apwerl *n.*
black kite (*Milvus migrans*) ◆ Thip apwerl-apwerl apetyem, alkerel akern apetyem, arerl-apemem. Ker tyerrty-henh apek intem inenhem. (N) *The black kite comes along, high in the sky, looking around. It might [fly down and] pick up people's meat.*
= apwelanty, artapw-artapw, inkwel

apwert *n.*
1. stone, rock, boulder ◆ Ntha arrerlp-iletyek yanh anthey apwert-warl tha arrerlp-iletyek. *Give that thing to me so that I can sharpen it on the rock.*
2. hill, mountain
3. money (especially coins) ◆ Apwert ayenh antheyaw. (Sa) *Give me some money.*
SEE ALSO irnta
4. car [RESPECT LANGUAGE] ◆ Mwerekatyenh mwetek wal 'apwert'. (St) *[I] call my son-in-law's car 'apwert'.* • = twertert-ayerr • SEE ALSO mwetek
5. unripe fruit of the native currant, native citrus (*Psydrax latifolia*)
6. A general word that goes before things made of stone, types of hill or mountain, or features of hills or mountains.
CAN SOUND A BIT LIKE apwert *'together', 'in a group'*
apwert artep (T,E)
mountain top, top of a hill (artep *'back'*)
apwert akern
mountain top, top of a hill (akern *'high', 'on top'*)
= irntang akern
apwert lterr (E)
side of a hill or mountain (lterr *'shin'*)
◆ Apwert akernel ayeng alhep-alhem, kel ayeng rlterr-angkwerr atnarnpenhem. (St) *I am going along the top of the hill, and then I come down the side of the hill.*
apwert arnka
cliff, cliff face (arnka *'cliff'*)
= irntang arnkang
apwert ngkwelty
money, small change, coins (ngkwelty *'bits and pieces'*)
apwert antha (E)
stone knife
= irntang arlter
SEE ALSO alywek
apwert ather
large flat rock, lower grinding stone (used for grinding seed)
= arlkwat
apwert alyer (E)
grinding stone (small one used for smashing things up); crushing or pounding stone
apwert artwert (E) = **apwert alyer**
apwert-arlkwenh (E), **apwert akwernenh** (E) *n.*
1. button grass, finger grass, toothbrush grass (*Dactyloctenium radulans*). A grass about 25 cm high.
2. the edible seeds of the button grass ◆ Ntang antywer. *Seed* an *yellow*-arl apwert-arlkwenh. Lherel kwenh arnkengeny wethel aneynetyel, atherrkenyel, kwaty-taym. Ntang apwert-arlkwenh mwerr-angker innga. (Sa) *A grass seed. The button grass seeds are yellow. There are lots found growing in the creek after rain. Button grass seed is really nice.*
= ngelyerr, talkwerrk

apwertek *n.*
hail, hailstone ◆ Kwaty apwertek-akert apetyem, arna arlka antyakenty-alhem, ngkwelty-ilem, war atwentyem. (N) *There's a hailstorm coming, that's going to uproot the trees as it comes this way, smash them up as it hits.*
◆ Apwertekel ahern iltewem. (M) *The hailstones are hitting the ground.*
= kwaty irntakert
SEE ALSO artarwerr

apwerterrerterr (W,T), **pwerterrerterrert** (W) *n.*
round in shape ◆ Mern anaty apwerterrerterr inyem. *Digging up the round bush potato tubers.*
= arlwa
SEE ALSO alkey[1]

apwet-apwet (E) *n.*
a type of dragon lizard (*Tympanocryptis tetraporophora* (?))
= angket-angket

Apwiperr (E) *n.*
place name, community at Ooratippra Station

arak (E) *n.*
black stone which is ground up and used for making ceremonial paint ◆ Apwert urrperl arak, apernelhenhelhenh. Arak ikwerel

apernelheman. Arelhak ateyak. (Sa) Arak *is a black stone used for rubbing on yourself. [You] rub yourself with it. Women and men [use it].*
= mwak[1]
SEE ALSO aperrk

arakakw (E) *n.*
fog, dust haze (seen after rain)
SEE ALSO alharrkw
= mwekelengk, rlweyang

aral-aral (W,T) *adv.*
going sideways, turning back, swinging back or returning (boomerang) ◆ Alyang apety-alpem aral-aral. (M) *The boomerang is swinging back.*
SEE ALSO irrepereperr

ararem (W,T) *vt.*
watch out for or look after someone
◆ Mwerram thwengk ararem, mwerr ntwa ananem thwengk ararem kwenh. (N) *You are sitting down and I'm looking after you properly.*
SEE ALSO arem

ararlk *n.*
loose, undone
ararlk-ilem *vt.*
untie or loosen something ◆ Thewak ararlk-ilem, iytekarl-irrek, iylwem — iylwetyel. (Sa) *Untie the swag that has been tied up — undo it.*
= tyek-ilem
SEE ALSO lywem[1], akap-rlwem

ararnt (W,T) *n.*
1. native tomato, potato bush, wild gooseberry (*Solanum ellipticum* var. *Foothills GJ Leach 1145*). Plant about 30 cm high, with velvety grey leaves, purple flowers, and edible fruits that are green with purplish stripes at first and then pale yellow when ripe.
2. edible fruit from the native tomato ◆ Mern ararnt aketyam, arlkwem, arlkwarlkerl-alpem atyerremel rwel, rtapwel atyerremel. Mern ararnt. Kwer-penh, angwel-irretyameh, manty kwetyetyam, kwetyetyam. Arlpang *self* akin. Mern ararnt arlpang. [Apwertel] ahernel *mixed up*, apwertel ahernel anem. *We collect the native tomatoes and eat the fruits. Native tomato. We cook them in the hot earth and then after that let them cool and collect them carefully. The* ararnt *plant has distinctive leaves and it grows in the hills and in the open country.*
= alperrantyey

ararr *n.*
light (not heavy); flimsy, soft or insubstantial (such as white bread); see-through or light-weight (of clothing) ◆ Arrwekeleny mapel mern awerant anaty arlkwerretyart. Ararr arlkwetyakenh. Ararran akeng *light one*-arl, *can't eat*-em. Angayakw akweteth anerl-anem. (Sa) *The olden-time people used to eat just substantial foods such as bush potatoes. They didn't eat 'light' foods. 'Ararr' are no good because they are light ones, you can't eat them. If you eat them, you'll always be hungry.*
◆ Petekwet-akert *light one* ararrek irrpem. *Can't* anyent-akert aperl, tyerrtyel arekety. Artwel apek arekety ararr-akert. (T) *Putting on a flimsy petticoat. You can't go around with just one [dress] on or people will see [through your clothes]. If you have light-weight clothes on men might see through them.*
SEE ALSO artaly-artaly
ker ararr (T)
'light' or 'soft' meats such as corned beef

ararrarlkanty (W) *n.*
car, motorcar (note Warlpiri *rarralykaji*)
= mwetekay

ararrkw (W) *n.*
a man with many wives
CAN SOUND A BIT LIKE Arrarrkw *'Pleiades'*

arathap, arethap (E) *n.*
1. newborn baby ◆ Ampa akely arethap akwek, akely lyetarl *born*-irrenty. Arethap. Aynterl-anem arethap akely. (Sa) *A little newborn baby that has just been born today. Newborn. The newborn is lying there.*
◆ Arathap, panthel intem akwek. (St) *The little newborn baby is lying in the coolamon.*
SEE ALSO panth-penh
2. helpless, unable to walk

araty (E) *n.kin* [RESPECT LANGUAGE]
A special way of referring to the mother's father and the mother's father's brothers and sisters of a person whom the speaker is in an avoidance relationship to. For example, a woman may use *araty* to refer to her son-in-law's mother's father, or a man may use *araty* to refer to his mother-in-law's mother's father.
SEE ALSO atyemey
aratyengkw (E) *n.kin*
your *araty*
aratyikw (E) *n.kin*
his/her/their *araty*
araty-nheng (E) *n.kin*
a group of two or more people related as grandparents (mother's father or their brothers and sisters) and grandchildren (a man's daughter's child or a person's brother's daughter's child). This is said by a woman if one of them is her son-in-law, or by a man if one of them is his mother-in-law.
◆ Araty-nheng ahanenhek. (St) *[My son-in-law]*

and his mother's father went [said by a woman].

araty-intyerr (E) *n.kin* = **araty-nheng**

araty-nheng atherr (E) *n.kin*

a grandparent (mother's father or their brothers and sisters) together with their grandchild (a man's daughter's child or a person's brother's daughter's child). This is said by a woman if one of them is her son-in-law, or by a man if one of them is his mother-in-law. ◆ Mpetyanel ilem renh-anteyan. 'Araty-nheng atherr kwenh ahanenhek. Pwerl then Ngwarray then.' Wal, araty-nheng atherrarl. (St) *A Mpetyan woman might say that. 'He [my son-in-law] and his mother's father went off together. A Pwerl and a Ngwarray.' Well, she calls them* 'araty-nheng atherr'.

SEE ALSO atyenheng atherr

aratyaperaty (W) *n.*

a type of bird ◆ 'Aratyaperaty aperaty aperaty', alakenh angkerl-apem. Kwaty-tayemarl angkem aratyaperaty. Kwaty renh irnmerr tyarr-inerl-anem kwaty. Kwaty irnmerr lernelhemel, thep ra. (N) *The* aratyaperaty *bird sings out like this,* 'Aratyaperaty aperaty aperaty'. *It brings the rain in, the raindrops in. In the rainy time it sings.*

arawern (W) *n.*

the middle part of the initiation (young man) ceremony ground. Also referred to as *arawern alkey*. ◆ *Road* akwek alkey mpwarem, *like grader*-el mpwarenhem-arteh. Alkey akwekem arawern yanh. (M) *There is a long little road made, just as if it's been graded. That is [what is called]* 'arawern'.

= apwelh alkey

SEE ALSO mwerlkenty, apwelh, anmanty

Arawerr (E) *n.*

Soapy Bore, Utopia (Angarapa Aboriginal Land Trust) area. The location of a small outstation. See map p. viii.

arawerrng *n.*

1. feeling unsettled, excitable, restless or preoccupied; feeling really angry or worked up ◆ Mpwenyek urtakwert arawerrng atarterl-wem. (Sa) *When [someone] is feeling excited about a lover their heart beats fast.* ◆ Arawerrngarl aterlpatem-ketyaw. Rtwakertarl aterlpatem arawerrngel. (Sa) *[I] am feeling really excited. My heart is beating with excitement.*

2. power, spirit, vitality, life-force ◆ Irrngerney rarl ap arawerrng ra. Irrngerney rarl arawerrng angkerl-anemel alhetyek ant anem. (Sa) *She is lively and has her spirit back. She's excited and feeling like going somewhere.* (?)

arawerrng-irrem *vi.*

get worked up, be frightened, excited or unsettled ◆ Arawerrng-irrek, nhenhel ayenh atnwerlkel anthek, ayeng arawerrng angkek. (St) *I got unsettled and frightened because that person startled me.*

arawerrng angkem

get worked up, be frightened or excited (angkem *'speak', 'talk'*) ◆ Ayeng ater arawerrng angkek yanh-kety. Yanhel ayenh aterel anthern. (St) *I got worked up because of that person. They just gave me a fright.* ◆ Ayeng arawerrng angkem ater, apmwekety apek ayeng. (St) *I am frightened because of the snake.*

arawerrng inem

become empowered; get worked up (for a fight); make oneself strong to protect oneself (inem *'get'*) ◆ Arrwekeleny mapel arawerrng inetyam alyelhemel atwerretyenheng-angent. (T) *The olden-time people used to empower themselves by singing themselves before they fought.* ◆ Ahel nheng atwerretyenheng arawerrng inem tyerrty arrpenh alenh-hety. (M) *When [they] were about to fight they used to get worked up to fight the other person.*

SEE ALSO arnkaty-ilelhem

arawerrng rakem (E)

take someone's power away, make someone feel overwhelmed or dispirited, disempower someone (rakem *'grab something off someone'*) ◆ Arawerrng rakenhem, *family* awemel. (St) *On hearing [bad news] about the family [my] spirit left me.* ◆ Arelh-they arawerrng rakem, tha apek rakem. (St) *I might take the power away from that woman.* ◆ Mwetek *new one buy*-em-ilek lyetant, arlka ngenh arawerrng rakem. (St) *[On seeing] the new car that somebody has just bought, your body feels overwhelmed [like something is coming out from you].*

arek-wem (W,T) *vt.*

mix tobacco into ashes; dip something into something; immerse something in liquid (e.g. a biscuit in tea) ◆ Ngkerlp aketyan arnmeny, arnmeny iterl-aneh ngkerlp kwerel arlkwerl-alhem alewatyerr-alewatyerr kwerel anem arlkwerl-alhem. Arekem wem, arlkwerl-alhemel alhem lyweny. (N) *Ashes are collected for chewing with tobacco. The broom bush leaves are cooked to make ashes and then they are mixed with tobacco, and chewed as people go along.* ◆ Mern tamp arek-wemel arlkwem

teyel-ayel. (T) *Damper is dipped into tea and eaten.* ◆ Ker pwelek *bucket*-el impetyeh arekwemel (T) *Leave the beef in the bucket to soak.*
SEE ALSO pwerlp-wem

arekar *n.*
sore, injured ◆ Arekar awelhem, lyekelarl atanthek, pwet anetyakenh atantherl-anem, aperl-anem twernel amperl-anem ingkang. (N) *[I] feel sore because the prickle spiked me when I didn't have any shoes on, going along with the heat of the sun burning my feet.*
arekar-irrem *vi.*
be in pain, ache, feel sore ◆ Ngkang atyengenh arekar-irrem. (M) *My feet feel sore.* ◆ Kapert arekar-irrem twernelarl ampempenh. Petyet atanthemel ayernemelhem kapert mwerrem irrem. (N) *My head is aching from the heat of the sun. I'll peel some bark to make a bandage to tie up my head and then it will feel better.*
= pwerep-irrem[1]
SEE ALSO arlkwem, arntem, kwarnelhem, rlkert intyem, antyernem[1]

arekel (E) *n.* [RESPECT LANGUAGE]
sun, heat of the sun (note Central Anmatyerr *arwekel* 'thirsty') ◆ Arekel-ayerr-ketyaw. Arekelel ampekerr kwenh, ngwarr-nheng. (Sa) *Watch out for the heat of the sun. The heat of the sun might burn my daughter and her husband.*
SEE ALSO utern

arekerr (T,E) *n.*
pituri bush, poison bush, emu plant, camel poison (*Duboisia hopwoodii*). Shrub to 2.5 m with white flowers and black fruit. Traditionally used to catch emus and other game by using it to poison waterholes. ◆ Arekerr pwelek ilwenh-ilwenh. Pwelekelarl arlkwem renh wal yang lwem. Pathen. (T) *The pituri bush kills cattle. If cattle eat it then they die. It's poisonous.*

arekwarr (E) *n.*
flock bronzewing (*Phaps histrionica*)
= arntep

arekwenth-kwenth (T,E) *n.*
really sick, in pain or suffering; having a hard time
SEE ALSO ntywekelywekely
arekwenth-kwenth-ilem (T,E) *vt.*
make someone upset or distressed, make someone sick ◆ Arekwenth-kwenth inngelarl arekwenth-kwenth-ilemel atwek. (Sa) *Somebody hit them and made them sick.*
SEE ALSO ntywekelywekely-ilem
arekwenth-kwenth-irrem (T,E) *vi.*
1. have a pain in the back, have a backache ◆ Artep ayeng arekwenth-kwenth-irrem. (Sa) *My back is aching.*
2. be suffering distress or hardship
SEE ALSO ntywekelywekely-irrem

arekwer (E) *n.*
bunch Paspalidium (*Paspalidium rarum*) (?). A grass about 20 cm high, which is often found around mulga.
SEE ALSO kwarrety, arlepenh, yakerr, akwetelh, nyetempwer

arelh[1] *n.*
1. woman (note: some regard the use of this word, particularly by men, as offensive in some contexts.) ◆ Arelhan arelharl — rarl ilkelhem-angkwarr. (St) *Women are women — [they do] whatever they feel like.* ◆ Arelhel atwek arnakertel angwely yenh. (M) *A woman hit the dog with a stick.*
2. person (Aboriginal person) ◆ Arelh nthakentyel yanhan angerrirretyel? *How many people are here?*
SEE ALSO arrwekety[1], tyerrty
3. wife (term used by a husband to refer to his wife) ◆ Mpa arelh alhey, ker-warl. (Sa) *Come on wife, let's go hunting.* • SEE ALSO interrkekety, ampeyamp
4. an adult female animal.
arelh ampwang (W,T), **arelh ampwa** (E)
old woman, senior woman (ampwang *'old'*) ◆ Ayeng aharlperr akin angkem arelh ampwekan. Anerl-anetyek ayeng aharlperr angkerl-anem awetyek-areny ra. (St) *I talk loudly to the old woman. I keep on talking loudly to her so that she can hear.*
arelh awenk
teenage girl (awenk *'teenage girl'*) ◆ Arelh awenk map anerl-anem arlwekerel angkety angkerrerl-anemel. (T) *The teenage girls are sitting around in the women's camp telling stories.*
arelheng-arelh (E) *n.*
'pretend' women, playing at being women ◆ Artwengartw rarey arrken-irrerl-anem, nyetyepel. Kenh arelheng-arelh arrpantey ampa marl-arey arrken-irrerl-anem nyetyepel akin. (St) *They [the boys] play at being men in the cubbyhouse. And the girls play at being women in their cubbyhouses as well.*
SEE ALSO artwengartw

-arelh[2] (E) *n.ending*
Goes on words for things to show that the thing is used for, or associated with, another thing in the sentence; is used for . . . , is for . . . This ending follows *+ek* or *+eh.*

◆ Kwatyek-**arelh** arranty wetharl yanhel iletyel, arrwekelenyel antywerretyart, *no billycan.* (Sa) *The kangaroo-skin waterbag is what the olden-time people used to drink out of, when they had no billycans.* ◆ Mwakelarl apernelhem, awelyek-**arelh** akin. (Sa) Mwak *is used for painting yourself up, and for women's ceremonies as well.* ◆ Interrk weth-rnem alyangkwek-**arelh**-rnem, alyangkwek rernem arraly-irretyel. (Sa) *Those Seven Sisters stars are associated with winter-time, they shine in the winter.*

arelty (E) *n.*
faint, hardly visible ◆ Arelty apetyem *someone* yanh kwenh. Apetyepetyem anwekantherr-wern. (St) *There is someone coming there but they are hardly visible. They are coming towards us*
SEE ALSO arrkay

arelty-arelty (E) *n.*
faint, hardly visible ◆ Arelty-arelty apetyetyel ilewerrelarl akern-ilek. (Sa) *[That person] that is coming there is hardly visible because of the mirage lifting them up.*
SEE ALSO arrkay-arrkay

arelyerrelyerr (W) *n.*
saltbush (*Atriplex* spp.)
= ilewerr-ilewerr

arelyerrty (T,E), **urelyerrty** (E) *n.*
light-skinned, reddish in colour ◆ Ayengan arelyerrty anep-anem, apekath-apekath. Apekath artek inngerr wal arelyerrty. (St) *I am light-skinned, a bit light in colour. A face that is like that of a half-caste person is* arelyerrty.
SEE ALSO apekath

arem *vt.*
1. see, be able to see ◆ Tha arrkay-arrkayarl arem, ingwemernt-artekarl arrkay anem tha arerl-anem, aretyakenhaw kwenh. (St) *My vision is blurred, and now when I look my eyesight is faded and it's as if everything is dark; I can't see.*
2. see something, look at something, watch something, watch out for something ◆ Aherrel arek pap irrtyart-akert. (M) *The kangaroo saw dad with the spear.* ◆ Alpek anwern ingkerrek *football* renty-penh. (M) *We all went back after watching football.* ◆ Wenh ntwa arem kwenh? (M) *What are looking at?* ◆ Kereh arerl-apay! (M) *Watch out for [edible] animals!*
3. see someone (i.e. meet someone) ◆ Arerl-alpaw! *Sister* atyenh apek arerl-alpem, arem apek unta, kel unta apety-alpem, *'He's all right'*. (St) *Go back and have a look! Go back and meet my sister, and if you see her then you can come back and say, 'She's all right'.*

arelhem *vi.*
1. look at your reflection, look at part of your body or something closely associated with your body ◆ Kelathel apek arelhem, *comb-*ilelhemel arelhem. (St) *Looking at yourself in the mirror, combing your hair.* ◆ Inngerr atyengenh arelhem ayeng. (M) *I am looking at my face.* ◆ Lywang rrpwamper arelhetyam kwenyel atayengarl Anengkerr. (M) *In the Dreaming the possum looked at its shadow cast by the moon.*
2. watch out for yourself, look after yourself ◆ Kwaty-kety ayeng arelhetyam, kel tha aremel arerr kwa atyeweyay akngerr apetyem. (St) *I was watching out for rain, and then I saw a huge storm coming closer.* ◆ Kwaty-kety aterel arelhepelhem. Amwekety aterel arelhepelhem, arep-arem. (St) *Fearfully looking out for yourself, because of a storm. Or looking out for yourself because of snakes.*

arerrem *vi.*
1. meet up with someone ◆ Rlkwerr apek arem, tyerrty apetyerleng arerrem. (N) *Halfway you might see people coming, meet up.*
2. look at each other ◆ Ulengerek ulengerek angkerreperrem, alak apek angketyek. Unta apek atyeng angkem, ayeng ngkweng angkem, ulengerek ulengerek angkerrem. Arratyant-arey weth-lkwer angkerrem alknga arerrem. (St) *Talking face to face. We two might talk. You might talk to me and I might talk to you, talk to each other face to face. Talk straight to each other, looking each other in the eye.*

arety-alhem *vt.*
go and find something ◆ Artekerr kwen antem rwang ampetyam. Lweren ratherr arety-alhek. (M) *The fire was burning in the root of the tree. That's what they went and found.*

aremay (E) short-tailed pygmy monitor (?) SEE UNDER **arwemay**

arementy (W) *n.*
a hide (especially for hunting emu)
◆ Arementyel atanthem irrtyartel. Intarlp angety-alpem mer-warl. (N) *The [emu] is speared from the hide. It is carried back to camp, slung around the [person's] shoulder.* ◆ Angey atyenharl athew anetyam arementyel, an atanthetyam ankerr. (M) *My father sat in the hide, and speared emus.*
SEE ALSO ipey, ntat

Arempey (W,T), **Arimpey** (W,T) *n.*
name of a place in the Pine Hill area.

Aremweng *n.*
1. Warumungu person or people
2. Warumungu language ◆ Awemarl tha

Aremweng angkerlek. (St) *I can understand people speaking Warumungu.*

aren pygmy mulga monitor SEE UNDER **arin**

-areng[1] *n.ending*

Indicates the number of times (on the end of a number word). ◆ Atherr-**areng** ayeng alhem. Atherr-**areng** akwey unta alhemay? (St) *I am going for two days. Are you going for two days?* ◆ Atherr-**areng** ayeng alhek *shop*-warn. (M) *I went to the shop twice.*

= -ingar

-areng (W) with someone, accompanied by someone, around someone SEE UNDER **-arleng**[2]

areng[2] *n.*

euro, wallaroo (*Macropus robustus*)

= areyneng, irntareny, lyerl-areny

Arengel Antywetyart (W) *n.*

name of a place north of the Mt Allan community (lit. 'the euro used to drink')

areng-areng (E) *n.*

native lemon grass, scented oilgrass (*Cymbopogon ambiguus*). A grass about 1 m high that usually grows in rocky areas. ◆ Areng-areng akemel kwaty-warl arrernem alhewelhetyek. (Sa) *Lemon grass is picked and put in water to use to wash yourself.*

= aherr-aherr

arengk *n.*

dog ◆ Rrtywerremelam arengk nhenh arlkwerrp-nhwerrerreperrem. (M) *These dogs are always barking at nothing.* ◆ Arengk akwekel kwaty antywep-antywem arwekel. (M) *The little dog keeps thirstily drinking water.*

= angwely

arengk arleny (E)

a dog with not much hair (arleny '*dry*') ◆ Arengk arleny alhay! (Sa) *Go away, hairless dog!*

arengk aleny *n.*

a part of the guts of animals such as cattle and kangaroos ◆ Arengk aleny antheyaw, ker tha arlkwetyek. (Sa) *Give me some* arengk aleny *meat to eat.* ◆ Kwenam arengk aleny, mwerlkel-ayel. (T) *The* arengk aleny *is inside [the guts], alongside the stomach.*

Arengkapert (W) *n.*

the name of a soakage in the Mt Wedge area

arengkatwepatwetyenh (W,T), **arengkatwepatwetyen** (W,T), **arengkartepatetyenh** (W,T), **arengkatwepatety** (W) *n.*

perennial yellowtop, tall yellowtop (*Senecio magnificus*) ◆ *Dreaming* angwely-kenh. Angwelyarl anngampelh-ilem. Angwely akely-amperl. *Dingo* akwek anngampelh-ilem annga. Arengkatwepatwetyenh angwely akwerrk anngampelh-ilem, annga. Arrken-irrem anem angwely akwek ra. Anngakert antem. *Yellow flower. Sun flower*-art. (N) *This plant is a Dreaming for dingoes. It makes the little pups open their eyes. The yellowtop plant makes the puppies open their eyes and then they start to play. It has a yellow flower like a sunflower.* ◆ Arengkatwepatwetyenh, arrken-henh. Awenk mapel arrken irretyart anwern pertipelaw kwer. (N) *The yellowtop plant is used for fun. When we were teenage girls we used to play with that pretty-flower.*

= ntweyentwerl

arengkerlpart, **arengkirlparert**, **arengkirlpart**, **arengkirlpahert** (W), **arengkeylpart** (E) *n.*

1. dog-eye bush tomato, bony-fruited bush tomato (*Solanum quadriloculatum*). A plant about 35 cm high, with soft grey-green leaves, purple flowers and angular shaped fruits. The fruits are poisonous and should NOT be eaten.

2. the inedible fruits of the dog-eye bush tomato ◆ Ankerrel arlkwem arengkirlparert yanh. Katyerrart arneng akin. Anety. (N) *Emus eat that dog-eye bush tomato. The plant is similar to bush raisin but the fruits are no good [to eat]. The fruits are not edible.*

= arntek-arntek

Arenpeng (E) Morning Star, Daylight Star, Venus SEE UNDER **Arwenpeng**

Arentyerrentyerr (W) *n.*

Crown Hill, north-east of Mt Allan community

-areny *ending*

1. belonging to or associated with a place; from a place, having traditional associations with a particular place ◆ Amey ikwerenh anem Arrwek-**areny**. (N) *His/her mother is from Arrwek.* ◆ Ingka aretyakenh arrangkw, merlalp war ra alhep-alhem. Mer-**areny**, mer akngganekarl-areny. (St) *You can't see the footprints of the* melarlp *spirits, they just go around. They are from the country, the country where they originated.*

2. living in a particular location or place, inhabitant of a place ◆ Ayeng *Ti Tree*-**areny**. (T) *I live at Ti Tree.* ◆ Warlekwertan arelh arlweker-**areny**arl — arlweker-warnarl irrek, anewekarl aparlp-ilek-arleng, warlekwertan ilem, arlweker-warn irrek. (T) *A widow lives in the single-women's camp — someone who has lost her husband, that's what a widow is.*

3. (something that is) usually found in a particular habitat or environment ◆ Perrpantyenan ker rlpwer-**areny**arl, ker arlkwenh-arlkwenh. (N) *The black-faced woodswallow lives in hollow trees and is edible.*
4. associated with a particular thing ◆ Ikalharr amirr-**areny**, amirr-warlarl arrernem ikalharr, atanthemel irrtyartel. Arreylp akely weth. Kel ikwereng atanthemel irrtyartel ker apek atanthemel. (Sa) Ikalharr *are found on woomeras, they are put on woomeras and then the woomera is used for throwing spears. That little sharp thing. From there the spear is thrown to spear animals.*
5. associated with a particular action, ability or quality ◆ Ayeng aharlperr akin angkem arelh ampwekan. Anerl-anetyek ayeng aharlperr angkerl-anem awetyek-**areny** ra. (St) *I talk loudly to the old woman. I keep on talking loudly to her so that she can hear.* ◆ *Baby one-*an arrakert arrangkwarl-**areny**, arntek anetyakenh. Ampa angerr irrem arntek-akert anem irrem, arratem apek, lyapem apek. (St) *Babies have empty mouths, they don't have any teeth. When they get bigger they get teeth, the teeth come out or grow.*

Arepalehenh (W) *n.*
name of place south of Coniston

arepampey (E) *n.*
hot weather, the middle of summer. Also referred to as *utern arepampey*. ◆ Ingka anem ampeynepeynem utern arepampeyel. (St) *[Your] feet burn in the hot weather.*
SEE ALSO utern

arepenngenkey (E), **arepengenkey** (E) *n.*
a type of fungus or puffball (?) ◆ Arwerlel ap renh atwenty, wal kwert urntemarl, arepenngenkeyan. (Sa) *If you hit the* arepenngenkey *fungus with a stick, then a cloud of smoky stuff comes up.*

areperlp (E) bush stone-curlew, bush thick-knee SEE UNDER **arepeylp**

areperreperr (W,T) *n.*
the winding path of a snake going fast ◆ Mpaty tyerrtyel arem, '*Eh,* areperreperr alhek kwenh'. (M) *The person sees the tracks [and says], 'Hey, [this snake] went flat out'.*

areperrk *n.*
old female animal. Mostly said of kangaroos and dogs, but occasionally of people. ◆ Arengk ahinpeny areperrk. (St) *An old female dog.*
SEE ALSO alkeperr

arepeylp (E), **areperlp** (E) *n.*
bush stone-curlew, bush thick-knee (*Burhinus grallarius*)
= mwelyar
CAN SOUND A BIT LIKE arreperlp *'king brown snake'*

arepilyerr (E) *n.*
young sand goanna, *arlewatyerr* or perentie, *ilkwert*; hatchling (sand goanna or perentie)
SEE ALSO kwentarreng

arepmay (E) short-tailed pygmy monitor (?) SEE UNDER **arwemay**

arepwelepwel *n.*
feeling tired, faint or dizzy from heat; feeling silly in the head; having a headache from sun or sickness ◆ Twern-penh arepwelwepel anem arrernelherl-arrernem, twernel ampem. (T) *After being burnt by the heat of the sun [you] feel dizzy and you go and sit yourself down.* ◆ Arratherrk kapert ayernelhenhelhenh. Arepwelepwelarl awelhem, wal kwerelam ayerlpengayernelhem, lweren. Awelhem wal *round*-arl irrem kapert renh, 'Arepwelepwelem irrem ayeng kwenh'. Nheng twern-penh *hot time* alakenh antem ilelhem, 'Ayeng kwenh kapert arepwelepwel-irrem terangk-terangk irrem *see* alakenh'. Lwerenel antem *tie*-em *up* ilelhem, arratherrkelem *tie em up* ilelhem, awelhem ilelhem mwerrem anem. *Tie*-em iletyam amwelt arlka, kapert arlka ingkerrek. (N) *The snake vine is used for binding the head. If you feel dizzy, then you tie the snake vine around your head. If you feel like your head is starting to spin, 'I'm feeling dizzy'. You know, particularly in the hot weather, you might say, 'My head is spinning and I feel like I am drunk'. Well then you tie your head up with that vine and then you'll feel better. People used to tie up their arms, and their heads as well.*
arepwelepwel-irrem *vi.*
feel dizzy or faint ◆ Arepwelepwel kapert-akert arntemarl ayeng. Arepwelepwel-irrem. (St) *My head is aching and I'm feeling dizzy. I'm feeling faint.*
SEE ALSO arert-arert-irrem

arernem (E) tie something SEE UNDER **ayernem**

arerr, **arirr** (T) *n.*
1. chest, breastbone
2. collarbone [SOME SPEAKERS]
SEE ALSO alkwert-alkwert, anirnterrm-irnterr

arerrk (W,T) *n.*
1. sandhill
2. sandy country
SEE ALSO twerrp

arerrth-arerrth (T,E) *adv.*
noisily ◆ Arerrth-arerrth apetyem, artwa apek,

kwenyel. (T) *The man is coming along noisily in the night.*
= aywerrty-aywerrty, ahenty-ahenty[2]

arerrty *n.*
dry, dried out (of country, clothes etc.)
= aherraty
SEE ALSO arleny

arert, ahert *n.*
1. deaf, not hearing properly ◆ Ntwa apek arert anep-anem, awetyakenh ayenh. (St) *Maybe you're deaf, and you can't hear me.* ◆ Iylpel tha awetyel — arert anetyang. (Sa) *I can hear with my ears — I'm not deaf.*
2. mad, stupid, crazy, silly, insane, out of control, heedless. Also referred to as *kapert arert.*
3. unconscious; (having) a fit ◆ Pew-ilem iylpa apek, arert apek iylpenkelh-ileman, kel renh akemel anem ilem, ra awem anem, iylpel inngart awem. (St) *You might be able to blow in the ears of someone who is unconscious, to revive them, and then this makes them get up and then they can hear again, with their ears.*
= arwengk

arert-arert, ahert-ahert *n.*
1. a bit deaf
2. not able to think properly; a bit silly; mad, confused, senile or stupid ◆ Arert-arert-kety mwanty-antey, arelhemel aney. Arert-arertel atwety-alhekerr. (Sa) *Be careful of that mad person, watch out for yourself. In case the mad one goes and fights [them].* ◆ Tyerrty arert-arert apant-irrem, apant-irremel alherl-apem. (N) *A person who is a bit silly in the head gets lost, gets lost as they go along.*

arert-irrem, ahert-irrem *vi.*
1. go deaf, become deaf ◆ Arert-irrekarl, nthakenh awetyakenh. Perrap *loud,* akngerrety arlkentyant ra awem. Akngerretyarl arlkem. Arnterr arlkenty weth-lkwer, renhant ra awem perrap *one.* (Sa) *He has gone deaf and can't hear. He can only hear if you shout out really loudly. If you shout loudly like that. That's all he can hear properly.*
2. go mad or crazy; get confused or silly, behave stupidly ◆ Arelh ampwirremel apek arert-irrem. (St) *When a woman gets old she might go silly.* ◆ Ahert-irrem arrwengkelth-penh *or* ahert-ahert apekarl *born*-irrek — kwer ahert-ahert apek. (T) *You might go mad after being sick, or you might be born mad — a child can be mad.* ◆ Amwek arlkety-alhem, 'Iwenham nta arna renh antyantyam akernan kwenh? Nhenham arertarl-irrek ntwa antyerl-anetyeh arna akerneh kwenh. *You want to* anerl-anerl arna antyetyal kwenh!' (N) *The mother sings out, 'What are you climbing that tree for? You must have gone mad to want to climb to the top of the tree. You should sit down and not climb trees!'*
= arwengk-irrem

arert-arert-irrem, ahert-ahert-irrem *vi.*
1. go a bit deaf
2. go a bit mad or crazy, get a bit confused or silly

arert-ilem, ahert-ilem *vt.*
1. make someone go deaf, deafen someone with noise ◆ Iylpa arert-ilem — alherl-wa arleng. (St) *Go a long way away — you're deafening me.*
2. make someone go mad or crazy, drive someone mad
= arwengk-ilem

arethap (E) newborn baby SEE UNDER **arathap**

aretharr *n.*
wind from north or west; north wind, west wind. Some speakers say that the *aretharr* wind can blow from the south as well.
◆ Aretharr nhel tyerrelh-ilem arlewatyerr. (N) *The* aretharr *wind makes the goannas come out.*
SEE ALSO alhwerrp

arety *n.*
top of the shoulder
SEE ALSO pwerlep, anpeth

Aretyerlker *n.*
Tinfish Well, south-east of Wilora (Stirling) community

arew-arew (E) *n.*
quarrion, cockatiel (*Nymphicus hollandicus*)
= newingk, kanaweylker, aneweylker

arewamp *n.*
1. weak and tired; feeling lazy, exhausted, sick and tired of something ◆ Pwerrk ayeng awelhem arewamp tyelk. (M) *My body feels weak and tired.*
= utelh-utelh
SEE ALSO parrk
2. unsuccessful at hunting ◆ Arewamp ayeng apety-alpek, ker-kwenh. (T) *I came back exhausted and unsuccessful from hunting, with no meat.*

arewamp-irrem *vi.*
1. become tired or weak, feel exhausted or sick and tired of something ◆ Arlka ayeng arewamp-irrem arntety-irremel. (Sa) *I am getting sick and my body is feeling weak.* ◆ Ayeng arewamp-irrem kwenyel, ankwang intemel, tyerrty maparl awemel. (T) *Listening to the people [talking] in the night when I was [trying to] sleep made me exhausted.*

SEE ALSO parrk-irrem, atnhakert-irrem
2. be unsuccessful at hunting

areweylker (E) cockatiel, quarrion SEE UNDER **aneweylker**

-arey[1] *n.ending*
Plural marker which shows that more than two are doing the verb action or are the object of the verb action; lots of, group of. ◆ Katyerr anwa *show*-em-iletyenh ikwer-**arey**, alangkw, ampa map kwerl *kid* mapek. (N) *We show them all bush tomatoes and bush bananas, show them to the school kids.* ◆ Amaty-**arey** panth-akert, anem-akert alherl-atherr-apetyart, tyap arlka akerl-apetyeh awenkel, ker alewatyerr renh atwerl-apetyeh. (N) *Our mothers used to walk along carrying their wooden dishes and their digging sticks, and together with the young girls they gathered grubs and killed goannas as they travelled along.* ◆ Ampa map akangkemel rltwampek, rltwampek-**arey** akangketyenheng anthwerr. (N) *The children really like sugarbag, they really enjoy all those things like sugarbag.* ◆ Ntheyelkwer-**arey** altyarey akin. (St) *The Ntheyelkwer mob are family as well.* ◆ Arreng-nheng-**arey** alhek itningkerr. (St) *All of the grandparents and grandchildren went.*
= -rnem

-arey[2] (E) *v.ending*
Shows that more than two people are being told, or ordered, to do the verb action. Follows *+enh* or *+enh+err.* ◆ Ampernem anerl-ayntenherr-**arey**, irrerarl alhem-ketyay, anerl-ayntenherr-**arey**. Ulyel anerl-ayntenherr-**arey**. (Sa) *All you kids, sit down, because [we] are going hunting. You all sit down in the shade.* ◆ Alerl athek-irrerl-iwerretyang arternpeng anenherr-**arey**. Mern arlkwetyek athek-irrerlarr-anetyang — yanhan atyenharl. *Wait, don't you all get excited and rush in, sit down quietly. Don't get over-excited about eating — that's my food.* ◆ Ker anthenherr-**arey**aw! Mern anthenherr-**arey**aw! (St) *[All of you] give me some meat! Give me some food!* ◆ Arrantherr irrkwaperl-anenh**arey**ay ayengan anyent irrkwapepapem-kety. (Sa) *All of you do some work, because I am working on my own.*
SEE ALSO +a, +erl-anerr+[2], +errirr+

areyakeyarr (W), **areyarrkeyarr** (W) *n.*
a whitish or grey-coloured emu ◆ Ankerr mperlker, yanh kwenh anwern ilem 'areyakeyarr'. (M) *A white-coloured emu is what we call* 'areyakeyarr'.
SEE ALSO apwarrewerlker, rntwely, ankerr

areyawarr (E), **areyawerr** (E) *n.*
oval-leaved cassia (*Senna artemisioides* ssp. *oligophylla*). A woody shrub to 0.5 m high, with broad leaves and broad papery pods. Has edible grub. Leaves used as a medicine. ◆ Apwenan arlpa arlpenty-arlpenty — rarl ilperr-ilperr *one* areyawerr. Apwert akern *too much.* (Sa) *The* apwen *has longish leaves and the* areyawerr *has flat ones. There are lots of them growing on top of the hills.*
= manatwerrp
SEE ALSO apwen
areyawarrayt (E) *n.*
grub from the oval-leaved cassia

areyneng (E) *n.*
euro (*Macropus robustus*)
= areng[2], irntareny, lyerl-areny
SEE ALSO arrwa

areytarr (E) *n.*
collecting food together (women gathering it into one container) (?) ◆ Mern apek anaty areytarr inek, atherramarl nyepenyem. (St) *The bush potatoes were collected into one container, the ones that two people were digging.*

arimpem (E) *vt.*
waste something ◆ Kwaty arimpetyal, uyerrekerr. (Sa) *Don't waste the water or it will run out.*
SEE ALSO ywerrelh-ilem, uyerrelh-ilem, intyarlkwem

Arimpey (W,T) name of a place in the Pine Hill area SEE UNDER **Arempey**

arin, **aren** (W) *n.*
pygmy mulga monitor (*Varanus gilleni*). Referred to by some as *ker arin.* Said to be a 'crazy or mad one'. ◆ Aren yanh akenh war nthwerl-alhem rlpwer-angkwerr. *The pygmy mulga monitor just moves around the hollows of trees.*
= ahert-ahert[2], arwangk

arirr (T) chest, breastbone SEE UNDER **arerr**

+arl *ending*
1. Goes in sentences in which there are more than one clause or 'idea' and links the two; that, while, which, when, as, because, who. ◆ Arnang nhenh tha mpwarem ltwakelhek**arl**. (M) *I am fixing this [thing] that was broken.* ◆ Awerr atherr yatherr angkety ilep-ilem amw**arl** yatherr atwek-penh. (M) *Now the two boys are telling their friends about how they killed the snake.* ◆ Irrtyart anem ipakert, alwerrngel**arl** ayernem, aherrel alwerrngel. (St) *Spears have a hook on them, that has been tied up with sinew, with kangaroo sinew.* ◆ Kerek uyarn unthem, arrangkw-antey apety-alpem

uyarn**arl** unthek-penh. Ayeng apek arlewatyerrek uyarn unthemel apety-alpem. (St) *Looking around in vain for meat, and coming back with nothing after searching in vain. Maybe I will look around for goannas and not find any and then return.* ◆ Ayeng nyerr-irrem tyerrtyel**arl** aremeng arnterr. (T) *I feel shamed when people stare hard at me.* ◆ Arrken utnherretyek alherl-iway, arlengel arrken-irretyek iylp**arl** arwengk-ilem-kety. (Sa) *All you go off and play, go and play a long way away, because you are driving us crazy.*

2. Provides emphasis or focus. ◆ Akngerr-awern**arl** ra. *It is a bit big.* ◆ Ahalper nhel aknganek**arl** ayeng. (Sa) *I came here from Ahalper.* ◆ Arelhan arelh**arl** — rarl ilkelhem-angkwarr. (St) *Women are women — [they do] whatever they feel like.* ◆ Artep**arl** arntem. Ayeng**arl** artep arntem, intem ayeng. (N) *My back is aching. My back is aching, and I'm lying down.* ◆ Terawath apek ngkwenh tyet**arl** atyeng. (St) *Your trousers might be too tight for me.*

+arl-penh, **+arl-iperr** *v.ending*
Goes on the end of verbs to show that something else happens after that verb action. ◆ Kwaty arrep-wem tyerrtyel, antywem**arl**-penh. (T) *The person spits the water out after drinking.* ◆ Awerr atherr alherl-aperretyam anyerrkentyem mer-warn, amwang yatherr atwek**arl**-penh. (M) *The two boys went home happy because they had killed a snake.*
SEE ALSO -penh, -iperr

arla[1], **arlang** (W,T) *n.*
the opening of an ant's nest or a honeyant's hole ◆ Yerramp-kenh apek arlarl ilem. Alhweng ikwerenh arla. Alakenh. Yerr-kenh arla altywer-altywer akwek — arla anem renh ilem. (St) *The honeyant's hole is called* 'arla'. *Ants' holes have small openings — they are called* 'arla'. ◆ Alhweng altywer yanh-lkwer, wal arlarl. Arlethey tyerrelhem yerr. (St) *'Arla' is the opening of the ants' nest. The ants come out of the opening in the nest.*
SEE ALSO alyap, inkwa, ahenty[1], wenty
CAN SOUND A BIT LIKE ala *'they (two)'*

arla[2] (T,E) *n.*
1. not having anything, without ◆ Arla ayeng *might* ampa anetyakenh ayeng *or husband*-kweny apek ayeng arla. Arla wart ayeng alhem. *Family* anetyakenh wart ayeng. (St) *I am* arla, *maybe because I haven't got any children, or I might not have a husband. I'm just going along without anything. I haven't got any family.*
SEE ALSO aleyak
2. having nothing to do with something, disassociating yourself from someone or something ◆ Ayeng arlaw, ngenh iltetyakenhaw. (Sa) *It's nothing to to with me, I didn't growl at you.* ◆ Ilekek unta angkek-angkek-ilety-alpek? Ayenhan arlan. Ayengarrparl anep-anem. (Sa) *Why did you go and try to make me talk? I've got nothing to do with it. I'm just sitting here minding my own business.* ◆ 'Arla wart ayeng alhem, anewelaty ayeng atwep-atwem alhengkemel. Arla apelkel wart ayeng alhem kwenh. Kel kwenh ayeng alhem, arla.' Kel ra alhem antem. (T) *'I've got nothing to do with my husband because he keeps hitting me and rubbishing me. I'm just going to go regardless. So I'm going, I've got nothing to do with him.' So then she goes.*
3. open (country where there are no restricted places)
CAN SOUND A BIT LIKE ala *'they (two)'*

arlangkwarr (E) *n.*
open country where there are no restricted places (-angkwarr *'by way of'*) ◆ Arlangkwarr alherl-anem kel mwerrarl, mer arlangkwarr. Mentyarl amek-amek. (Sa) *It's all right to travel round in the open country, where there aren't any restricted places. [You] don't go near the restricted places.* ◆ Ahelh arlangkwarr ayeng alhep-alhem amek-amek anetyakenh. (St) *I'm going along in the open country where there isn't any* amek-amek.
SEE ALSO amek-amek

arla[3], **arlang** (W,T) *n.*
stem, trunk of a tree ◆ 'Arla' atnewem artekerr-penh. (T) *'Arla' is what you call [the part which grows] from the root.*
CAN SOUND A BIT LIKE ala *'they (two)'*

arlakem (T,E) chase someone or something SEE UNDER **lwakem**

arlalalpirrenh (E), **arlalalpirreny** (E) *n.*
a type of ant found in mulga country
SEE ALSO arnman[2], arlekert, utern-utern

arlalherrk (W,T) Coonavittra wattle SEE UNDER **alalherrk**

arlalty *n.*
1. own, personal or private possession ◆ Mwetek atyengenh arlalty ltwaketyalay! (P) *Don't crash my private car!* ◆ Mer arlalty-warn irremel apety-alpetyek. Apety-alpem arlalty-warn, irrar-irrem ayeng mereh. Mer arlaltyeh. (St) *I've got to come back to my own country. I'm feeling homesick for my country and I want to come back.* ◆ Anmatyerr arlalty akwet angketyeh. (M) *Keep on talking [our] own*

Anmatyerr. (?)
2. close family or relations ◆ Arlalty atherr alherray! (M) *You two go, family!* ◆ Kwer atyengenh map nhenh arlalty map kwenh. Maney atyenhel tha *self*-el amangkelh-ilek. Maney arlalty-penh tha amangkelh-ilek. (P) *These kids here are my own family. I grew them up myself with my own money. I grew them up with my own private money.*
= altya
SEE ALSO pelty
arlalty-arey *n.*
close family or relations
= altyarey
arlalty-intyerr *n.*
all the family ◆ Arlalty-intyerr arrantherr anem kwenh. (M) *We are living here, all the close family.* ◆ Arlalty-intyerr alhetyeh. (M) *All the family can go.*
tyerrty arlalty map
family
mer arlalty (W,T)
your own country, place or camp
SEE ALSO mer, rinty

arlamarr, alamarr *n.*
lame, crippled ◆ Arlamarr akeweny-amperl anep-anem, nthwetyakenh. (T) *That poor thing is sitting down crippled, not able to walk around.*
SEE ALSO alpalth, anath, anenyirrp irrkweynar, apekap, apertap, arlwemeny, lim-lim, lyer, rnwerr, rnwerr-rnwerr, rtapety, yer
arlamarr-irrem, alamarr-irrem *vi.*
become lame or crippled ◆ Ngkwern ayeng alamarr-irrety-alpek, arlengelarl ayeng alhek. (St) *I came back lame, after going a long way.*
SEE ALSO rnwerr-irrem

arlan-irrem, arlatn-irrem (E) *vi.*
1. become quiet or still ◆ Arlan-irraw ker aherr yanh urntekerraw. (Sa) *Be still in case that kangaroo runs off.*
SEE ALSO ntert-irrem
2. have a fit; throw a tantrum or cry a lot; get paralysed ◆ Arlatn-irrerl-alhem ra arnethey akern-they atnyem. Kel renh irlpa atherr pew-ilem, akem anem ra irrenty-alpem. (N) *He/she is having a fit after falling from high up in the tree. If you blow in her ears she will get up again.* ◆ Kwer yanh arlan-irremeyay, rntert antem irrem paty anthemel. (M) *That child is throwing a tantrum but if [you] offer the breast he/she will quieten down.* • SEE ALSO atywaty-irrem[2], nthat-nthat-irrem, tyerrty-tyerrty internem, arlerlp-irrem

Arlanenty, Rlanenty (W,T) *n.*
1. a big river or watercourse [SOME SPEAKERS] ◆ Lpway angerr arlanentyarl, 'arlanenty' angerr. Kenh lpway akwek kenh akwek wararl — ilerrtyarl apetyem war. (T) *A large river is called* 'arlanenty'. *On the other hand small creeks are just small — where a small watercourse or gully comes along.*
2. Lander River (in the Willowra area and in the Ti Tree area)
CAN SOUND A BIT LIKE alanenty *'everything', 'everybody'*

arlang (W,T) the opening of an ant's nest or a honeyant's hole SEE UNDER **arla**[1]

arlang (W,T) stem; trunk of a tree SEE UNDER **arla**[3]

arlangkw (E) *n.*
a type of bloodwood (*Corymbia sphaerica*). The seed capsules are used to make necklaces.
CAN SOUND A BIT LIKE alangkw *'bush banana', 'silky pear'*

arlangkw-arlangkw (E) matted hair or knotted hair SEE UNDER **alangkw-alangkw**

arlanty *n.*
canegrass dragon, blue-lined dragon (*Diporiphora winneckei*)
= apengeleytanenh
CAN SOUND A BIT LIKE alanty *'waiting for someone'*

Arlanty *n.*
a star constellation; the Saucepan (part of Orion)
SEE ALSO Anterl, Arnkenty, Pwereytarr, Ingkapeny, Ingkartek
CAN SOUND A BIT LIKE alanty *'waiting for someone'*

arlap (E) *n.*
backbone; spine (of goanna). Also referred to as *ker arlap.*

arlarl-ilem (E) *vt.*
hammer, bang or knock something in; tighten something (e.g. axe handle) ◆ Ilep renh arlarl-iletyek, rlterrk ilem. *Tighten the axe to make it strong.* ◆ Antywa mpwaretyek, arlarl-ilem, rlterrk-ilemel, kerwepel anem aterlp-atanthemem ahern. (St) *Making a shelter and banging the ground with a crowbar to tighten it [the post].*
= kanth-atwem

arlarnt (E) *n.*
axe handle; short straight stick made of mulga wood ◆ Arlarnt arrperretyart arrwekelenyel-arey. Arlarnt ilep-warl akwernem. (Sa) *The olden-time people carved axe handles and then joined them to the axe head.*
SEE ALSO kwempalth, twererr, mwert

arlarrangkern (E) desert tree frog SEE UNDER **larrangkern**

arlarrernem (E) *vt.*
join parts of a spear together to make it longer
SEE ALSO aparr

arlatn-irrem (E) become quiet or still SEE UNDER **arlan-irrem**

arlatyey *n.*
1. pencil yam (*Vigna lanceolata* var. *latifolia*). Creeping plant with bright green leaves, yellow flowers and edible roots.

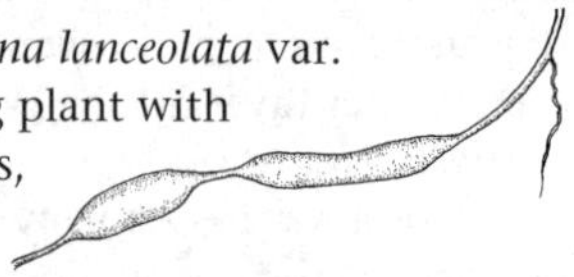

2. edible root of the pencil yam. Also referred to as *mern arlatyey*. ◆ Mern arlatyey anemel inyerlapetyart. 'Mern arlatyey aray, mwernenty map. Yekay mern mwernenty kwenh nhenh!' *We used to go along digging for* arlatyey *with digging sticks. 'Look at all these yams, all growing together. Look at all the yams!'* ◆ Aperrk atyerrem rwel arlatyey map an arlkwemem ampeng — mwerr anthwerr patartart. Rltar-rltar-irrem rwel patartart. (N) *The pencil yams are cooked in the coals and then eaten when they are cooked — they taste really nice, like potatoes. They make a hissing noise when they are cooking, like potatoes.*
SEE ALSO anwerlarr, arnamp, katywetarr

arlatyey-arlatyey (E) *n.*
a type of plant (no common name) ◆ Aherrel arlkwem renh, ngernemel. *Purple one flower.* Lywemp-lywemp-artek. Yerrakwerr-artek arlpa. *Kangaroos dig this [*arlatyey-arlatyey*] up and eat it. It has a purple flower. It is similar to parakeelya, and has leaves like a bush onion.*
SEE ALSO ilperntatherr

arlawarr (W) wedge-tailed eagle SEE UNDER **arlawerr**

arlawem (T), **arlewem** (T) *vt.*
put something away; hide something
◆ Maney apek arlawek. (T) *The money was hidden away.*
= alhengk-wem

arlawerr (W), **arlawarr** (W) *n.*
wedge-tailed eagle (*Aquila audax*)
= irrety
SEE ALSO apwelanty

-arlek, **-arleh** (W) *ending*
1. Shows where someone or something is put by the action of the verb, or where someone or something puts itself by the action of the verb; at, on, in, into, onto. The ending *-arlek* follows the *+ek* or *+eh* ending. ◆ Arengkel map iwelhem tyerrtyek-**arlek**, wal pwarn-ilem anem arlerlp irrem anem. (Sa) *The dogs throw themselves down on top of the people, and then people get squashed up and cramped, as there is not much room.* ◆ Waly akwek akerneng arrernem, arntap-el-arleng, yerrampek-**arlek**. (N) *A small branch is placed over the bark container, on top of the honeyants.* ◆ Aperel-arleng. Aperel ngkwarl larl-arteh awantyerl-apetyeh. Theweyet anthwerr. Ngkwarlel apel anwern amangkek kwerel, mampel-arleng. Ahelh-warn anyep-anyerl ahelhek kwetyemel, kwatyek-**arlek** arrernerl-apem. Antywem anem. (N) Mamp *is from the river red gum tree. We go along sucking on the sweet gum from the river red gum, just like lollies. Really sweet. We grew up on that sweet stuff, on* mamp. *When it drops to the ground we gather it up and put it into water and then drink it.* ◆ Tyirran atnwenthek-**arlek** irrkwem, kel anwenth iwem anem, tyirr-akert. (St) *Flies' eggs are laid in meat, then the maggoty meat is thrown away.*
2. Shows where something is got from.
◆ Ngwarrekengkw-**arlek** irrepetherl-wa aympelh-ayerr atyeng. (Sa) *Go and get some bush turkey from your husband for me [woman talking to her daughter].* ◆ Arna intel yerramp inerl-anem inkwek-**arlek**, ahern-warn anem anyep-anyem. (St) *With a stick called 'inta' the honeyants are poked out from where they are on the shelves in the nest, and then they fall to the ground.*
3. Indicates the reason for doing something; because. ◆ Mern antheyaw akewenyek angayelarl anem-**arlek**. (T) *Give some food to the poor thing because she's hungry.*
◆ Tyerrtyekant alhwarrp-irrem, *family*-ekant, atwerrem-**arlek** apek. (St) *[You] just get sorry for family, maybe because they are fighting.* ◆ Arelh arrangkem arltwaremel kwer mertarl alhek-**arlek** lyweny. (T) *The woman is crying for her husband because he didn't come back from hunting.* ◆ Nakelhem ayeng ker tha nhenh atwern-**arlek**. 'Inngelarl tha twekaw kwenh!' (St) *I praise myself because I have just killed some game. 'I really killed it!'* ◆ War apekarl atwerretyel arrkenty-ilerremel ilterretyel, mernek-arrngel apek. Alhek-**arlek**-arrngel apek. (St) *They are fighting and picking on each other and swearing at each other for no particular reason. Perhaps over food, or because somebody went.*
SEE ALSO +arl, +ek[2]

arlekert, **arlekert-arlekert** (W,T) *n.*
a type of big black ant ◆ Yerrampek-arneng arlekert, arlekert-arlekert alhem. (T) *The* arlekert *ant is closely related to the honeyant.*
◆ Arlekert-arlekertan yerr rrpwerl akin. Anwerlk-thayt alakenh alhem. Wal, *name*

arlekert-arlekert akwet. (M) *The* arlekert-arlekert *ant is black as well. It goes along with its backside like that [pointing up]. Well, its name is* arlekert-arlekert.
= atnangkerney, atna irrkert-irrkert
SEE ALSO atyank

Arlekert-arlekert (W) *n.*
Drakluder Dam, Mt Allan area

arlekety (W) *n.*
a type of spinifex resin. Found in spinifex that grows in the hills.
SEE ALSO tyalangk, arlwererrwengk

arlelty *adv.*
1. putting pressure on people for things
2. being stubborn, tough-minded, or refusing to budge ◆ Arlelty intep-intem, arleltyan nga intep-intem. Mwernt apekarl intep-intem. Angka atherr — 'mwernt', 'arlelty'. (St) *You are lying there and refusing to budge. You are lying there stubbornly. There are two words [for it] —* 'mwernt' *and* 'arlelty'. ◆ Arlelty interl-anem artwa nhenh kwenh arlelty antey interl-anem, akem-irretyakenh arlelty akwet ya intep-intem. Menty awerl-anemel (T) *This man is still lying there, not getting up and not moving. Just listening and not taking any notice.*
SEE ALSO mwernt
3. traditional executioner, kurdaitcha [SOME SPEAKERS] ◆ Artwang nhenh arlelty apetyem kwenh, atwetyek anwernantherr kwenh. (T) *The kurdaitcha is coming, coming to kill us.*
SEE ALSO ngkekern, urlaylp

arlelty-irrem *vi.*
1. put pressure on people for things, be persistent about something ◆ Terangk arlelty akin irrem. '*You* atyeng antherl parrp kwenh, thwengk atwekety kwenh!' (T) *Drunks put pressure on people. 'You give me that straight away or I'll hit you!'*
2. be stubborn; 'get hard' (not give things), be tough-minded ◆ Mwelek anywelek apek ilem, 'Wenhek nta arlelty-irrem kwenh?' '*No,* ayengan arlelty akwetam.' (M) *[The kid's] mother or father might say, 'Why are you being so stubborn?' 'No, I still want to do it,' says the kid.*
3. get sooky; throw a tantrum, cry hard till the need is satisfied ◆ Amparl arlelty-irrem artnemel ap arlelty-irrem, mernek apek *mother* kwerenhek apek. (St) *The child is throwing a tantrum and crying, maybe for food or for his mother.* ◆ Kwer akwek nhenhey arlelty-irrem. Inang nhak angkep anthety-alpangaw! Kwer arlelty-irremek. (T) *This little kid is crying. Give those things back to him! To the kid who's crying.*
4. try to fight someone, get angry
SEE ALSO mwernt-irrem, ahel-irrem, rrwampem, urrampem, yerrng-irrem

arlelty intem
lie without moving (intem[1] *'lie down'*) ◆ Arelh arrpenh rntwarr-ilem kenh arleltyarl interl-anem, arlelty intem arelh arrpenh. Kenh arelh arrpenh ilelherleng mer kwerenh, 'Ntwarr-irray, rntwarr intay!' (N) *Moving another woman out of the way, one who is lying there without moving. And then the other woman claims that it's her place and says, 'Move out of the way, sleep further away!'*

arlelty angkem
argue the point; talk all the time; humbug someone for something (angkem *'speak'*) ◆ Yanh arlelty angkep-angkem, akwetantarl angkem. Tha apek anthetyek antem. (St) *That person keeps on asking and asking, talking all the time. I'll have to give [it] to them.*
SEE ALSO tyety angkem, aker-aker-ilem, arnterr angkem, arrkwertep-irrem

arlelyek, alyelyek, arlelyerrk (T,E) *n.*

1. banana-flavoured bush tomato (*Solanum cleistogamum*). Plant with grey or blue-green leaves, thorns on stems, pale purple flowers and pale yellow fruits. Grows to about 25 cm high.
2. the edible fruit of the banana-flavoured bush tomato ◆ Mern *yellow one* arlelyek; *self*-arl anganek akin ararnt then, *self*-eley anganek. Wal, mern renh arlkwem akin. Rwel akin atyerrem renh. (N) *The fruit of the* alyelyek *is yellow; the* alyelyek *and the* ararnt *are both different and originated separately. Well, the fruit is eaten as well. It is cooked in the fire as well.* ◆ Mern arlelyek. Apwertel anem ant lpwayel anem. Manyemart arlelyekan anem, *same one*. Akwek alkey akwek, arlelyek arla. Mern theweyet anthwerr. (N) *The bush tomato. It grows in the hills and in the creeks. It is similar to the* manyem. *The* arlelyek *is a small plant. The fruit is really sweet.* ◆ Arlelyek ampengem arlkwem. Akemel angernemel rwelem item, mern atyerrety-alpem, rarrp rew-irrem. Kernt-irretyek arrernem, arlkwem renh alenyel war inem. (N) *The* arlelyek *fruit is eaten cooked. It is picked then taken back and then cooked in the fire so that it goes soft. Then it is put down to cool and then it's eaten, just*

with the tip of the tongue.
= manyem, tepernter
SEE ALSO rrwarlp[1]

arlemeny curled up, doubled up SEE UNDER **arlwemeny**

arleng[1] *n.*
1. far, distant, a long way away ◆ Arleng-warl ayeng alhetyek kerek apek. (St) *I'm going a long way, hunting for meat.* ◆ Arleng anthwerr ayeng alherl-apem. (T) *I'm going a really long way away.*
2. distant in time, a long time away
SEE ALSO rntwarr
arleng-awaty (T,E) *n.*
further, a bit further away ◆ Arleng-awaty anay — rlkert apek ayeng. (St) *Sit a bit further away — maybe I'm sick.*
arlengek-arleng (T,E) *n.*
further away, a bit further away from each other ◆ Arlengek-arleng aneyaw. *Sit a bit further away from each other.*
arleng-arlenty (T,E) *n.*
1. a long way ◆ Arleng-arlenty alhem. (St) *Travelling a long way.*
2. a long time, for a long time
arleng-areny (T,E) *n.*
someone from a distant place, a stranger (-areny '*inhabitant of*')
arleng-irrem (T,E) *vi.*
move away, go far away ◆ Kel arleng-irray! (T) *Move away!*
SEE ALSO rntwarr-irrem

-arleng[2], **-ayeng** (W,T), **-areng** (W) *n.ending*
1. with someone, accompanied by someone, around someone. Usually follows the *+el* ending. ◆ Awenk anetyam ayeng, awenkel *self* inetyart akin *salt*, angey atyenhel-**arleng** *mother* atyenhel-**arleng** ayeng anetyart. (N) *When I was a young girl I used to collect salt myself, along with my father and mother.* ◆ Arelhel-**arleng** alhem. (T) *Going with the woman.* ◆ Ayeng alhem arelh yanhel-**ayeng**. *I'm going with that woman there.*
2. together with something, in with something, in (a container), contained in something ◆ Mern angelth lpway-areny akin. Rwel atyerrewarretyart walyel-**arleng**, *roll*-em *up. Nice* anthwerr. (N) *Bush pears also grow in the creeks. Everybody used to cook them in the fire, rolling them up in leaves. They are really nice.*
3. on something, at something, from something ◆ Arnel-**arleng** ampekernem. (M) *Leaning on a stick.* ◆ Waly akwek akerneng arrernem, arntapel-**arleng**, yerrampek-arlek. (N) *A small branch is placed over the bark container, on top of the honeyants.* ◆ Akern artarnk anem kelkertel-**arleng**. (M) *On knees, sitting on heels.* ◆ Arelhel rltwamp atwep-atwem arnang ltyentyel-**ayeng**. (M) *The woman is chopping sugarbag from the beefwood tree.*
SEE ALSO -akert[2]

-arleng[3] *v.ending*
1. Goes on a verb to show that the person or thing doing the action of that verb is not the same as the person or thing doing the action of the other verb in the sentence; because of something, over. ◆ Anwengkerr ntert aneyaw angkety-kweny, yatenh angkem-**arleng**. (N) *We should sit down and not talk, because that person is talking.* ◆ Mwekernp-irrem tyerrtyel ayeng arnterr arem-**arleng**. (M) *I don't like people staring at me.* ◆ Alhernter yanh anpway, merarl irrpem-**arleng**. (M) *Tell that white person to go away, because they are going into the house.* ◆ Wenng-irrem iltem-**arleng** ayenh, iknga anem ayeng alhep-alhem, ilterlarl-apem nhenhel. (St) *I am keeping away because [someone] is swearing at me. So now I'm going around on my own, because this one is swearing at me.*
= +erleng, +erlek
2. because of something; over (the person or thing doing the action of both verbs may be the same) ◆ Rtapetyem anem, *too much* ayeng amper atherr anety-irrem-**arleng**, rtapetyem ayeng anem — alhekarl-penh ayeng amper atherr nhenh atherr kwern-irrety-alhek. (N) *I am sitting with my legs curled up because my two knees are no good — after walking around my knees became no good.*
= -ayeng

arlengarr (E) coolamon, wooden dish SEE UNDER **lengarr**

arlengarr-arlengarr (E) a type of beetle SEE UNDER **lengarr-lengarr**

arlengkety (W) *n.*
bad-tasting, not sweet, having a funny taste ◆ Mern arlengkety tha arlkwep-arlkwem kwenh — ikwa anetyakenh. (M) *My food is not sweet — it hasn't got any taste.*
SEE ALSO anetywek, tyekert[1]

arlenthem (T,E) *vt.*
lend something to someone; give something to someone ◆ *Toyota* nhenh war tha arlenthek, angety-alpem atyeng. (St) *I just lent this Toyota, and you'll bring it back to me [later].*

arlenty *n.*
hip (of animal or person) ◆ Arlentyel-arleng arrethaker anem. (M) *Lying curled up on the*

side. ◆ Arlenty-akert ayeng arrernelhey, arlentyarl arlkwem. (T) *I'm going to sit myself down because I've got a sore hip.*
= aneny
SEE ALSO anngarlp
arlenty annga (W)
point of the hip (annga *'eye', 'round thing'*)

arleny (E) *n.*
dry
= antyerrk
CAN SOUND A BIT LIKE aleny *'tongue'*
arleny-irrem (E) *vi.*
get dry, dry up ◆ Ahenty arleny-irrem. (Sa) *[My] throat is going dry.*
= antyerrk-irrem
SEE ALSO arerrty
arleny-ilem (E) *vt.*
make something dry
= arterrty-ilem, antyerrk-ilem
arengk arleny (E)
a dog with not much hair (arengk *'dog'*)
◆ Arengk arleny alhay! (Sa) *Go away, hairless dog!*

arlep (T,E), **arlwep** (W) *n.*
1. acacia bush, elegant acacia, bramble wattle (*Acacia victoriae* ssp. *arida*). Shrub up to 5 m high, with green or grey-green leaves and pale yellow flowers.
2. the edible seeds of the acacia bush. Referred to as *ntang arlep, anterrng arlep* or *mern arlep.* ◆ Arwenthelam aketyart arlwep renh. Kwer mapel nheng waram itetyart, rwa anngenthel kik-wemel, arnwety renh-perram. Kwerel antem arnwety renh arlkwetyart. (N) *They used to pick lots of* arlwep *seeds. Kids just used to cook them in the flame, peel off the skin and then eat them.* • SEE ALSO amper¹
arlepayt (E) *n.*
grub from the acacia bush
arlep ngkwarl (E)
edible resin from the acacia bush

arlepenh (T,E), **alepenh** (E) *n.*
1. desert Flinders grass, bunch panic (*Yakirra australiensis* var. *australiensis*). A grass about 15 cm high, with reddish-coloured leaves.
2. the edible seeds of the desert Flinders grass. Also referred to as *ntang arlepenh.* ◆ Arlepenh renh anterrngan athem, kel renh urel anem item, kel renh arlkwem anem. (T) *The* arlepenh *grass seed is ground up, then cooked and then eaten.*
= kwarrety, nyetempwer, arrepeny
SEE ALSO akwetelh

arleperlterrk (E) *n.*
1. spiny-leaved wattle, stiff wattle (*Acacia maitlandii*). Shrub up to 2 m high, with leaves which have a sharp spine at the tip.
2. the edible seeds of the spiny-leaved wattle. Also referred to as *ntang arleperlterrk.*
SEE ALSO patwert

arlepewem (W,T) *vt.*
1. copy someone or something, imitate ◆ Kwer alenhel apek arlepewem tyerrty alenh angkep-angkemel. (M) *That kid is copying what that other person is saying.* ◆ Thep arrpwerel arlepewem tyerrty. (M) *Magpies imitate people.*
2. taste or try something ◆ Kwaty apek arlepewem, anety apek. (M) *Try the water, it might be no good.* ◆ Atyengenh mern anthay tha arlepewetyeh. (M) *Give me some food so that I can taste it.*
3. try something out (to see if it works) ◆ War-atety arlepewa mwetek ywerr-angketyeh. (M) *Just see if the car starts.*
SEE ALSO arrkernem, warrernem
arlepewelhem (W,T) *vi.*
1. try yourself out at something, try to do something ◆ Akem-irrem wal ntang arlwepewelhetyeh, *'I like* alherl kwenh'. (M) *You might get up and try to move, [thinking] 'I'd like to go'.*
2. try something on ◆ Rrwek ayeng arlepewelhetyeh mantarr. (M) *Wait while I try this dress on.*
= arrkernelhem

arler, alyer, ayler (E) *n.*
smooth, slippery
arler-arler, alyer-alyer, ayler-ayler (E) *n.*
smooth, slippery ◆ Ahern arler-arler. (M) *Slippery ground.*
SEE ALSO alyelk-alyelk
arler-irrem, alyer-irrem, ayler-irrem (E) *vi.*
slip over ◆ Arnkarrel arler-irrem, anarnp-akerl, arnkarr angerrel arler-irrem kwenelak. (N) *Slipping downwards from the bank of the creek.* ◆ Kwer arler-irrem arnang akerneng. (T) *The child is slipping from the top of the tree.*
= alyelkelhem
SEE ALSO alyelk-irrem

arlerlk-arlerlk (T) Sandover lily SEE UNDER **alyerlk-alyerlk**

arlerlp¹ (E) *n.*
mound of earth made by animal such as goanna or rabbit
= rrngwa

arlerlp² *n.*
cramped, in pain, numb, paralysed, not moving ◆ Arlerlparl intep-intem, akngelhetyakenh. (St) *Lying down cramped and in pain, not moving.*

SEE ALSO arlelty, tharr, rtapety

arlerlp-irrem *vi.*

cramp up, get numb ◆ Iltya arlka arlerlp-irrem, tyerrty arlka ingkerrek arlerlp-irrem. Lwelty angerreng wal arlerlp-irrem. *Your hands can cramp up, and all of the body as well. Well, when there is a big frost you cramp up.* ◆ Arlerlp-irrek ayeng ngkwern. (St) *My legs have cramped up.* ◆ Ankwepenh an *one side*-el intem, wal ayeng arlerlp-irrem, intetyek arrpenh-angkwerr. (St) *I get numb from sleeping on one side and then I have to sleep on the other side.*

= impelhem, tharr-irrem

arlernem (W) *vt.*

leave something for later ◆ Thang arlernern ilep-kwenyel ngkwarl rltwamp. (M) *I left the sugarbag for later because I didn't have an axe.*

= arlwarrernem

arlerrk (E) *n.*

1. dry

= althalth

SEE ALSO arleny

2. solid bits of meat and sinew left when cooked fat has been poured off. Also referred to as *ker arlerrk.* ◆ Irrngwilem anter mpwank. Kel irrngwirrem anem ra, kel *milk tin*-warl apek, kel arlerrk anem ampeny anem. (St) *The fat is melted. When it melts, maybe in a milk tin, then the* arlerrk *is left over.*

arlerrk-irrem (E) *vi.*

dry out (food) ◆ Anter arlety-penh, wal arlerrk-irrem anem ampemarl. Arlerrk anem arengkek iwem. (St) *The uncooked fat gets dry as it cooks. Then the dry pieces of meat and fat are thrown to the dogs.*

arleth, arlweth *n.* [SENSITIVE LANGUAGE]

testicles

CAN SOUND A BIT LIKE aleth *'for good'*

arleth urrperl (T,E)

a type of ant (*Melophorus* sp. (reproductive and soldier)) (arleth *'testicles'*; urrperl *'dark-coloured'*)

arleth-arleth[1] (T,E) *n.*

1. hill mulga (*Acacia macdonnelliensis*). Has edible resin.

2. grub from the hill mulga • = arlethayerr

arlethayerr (E) *n.*

grub from the hill mulga (and other types of mulga (?)). Some speakers regard this grub as being edible and others do not.

arleth-arleth[2] *n.*

a type of Solanum plant (?) ◆ Arleth-arleth, mern areng-kenh, arengel arlkwenh-arlkwenh. *The* arleth-arleth *plant is euro food — they eat it.*

arlety[1] (T,E), **arlety-arlety** (T,E) *n.*

a type of small, aggressive ant ◆ Arlety akwek urrperl, wal ra ahelengkwarl, tyerrty utnhemel wangkem anem ra. (St) *The* arlety *ant is small and dark in colour. It is aggressive, and if it bites a person then the person will swell up.*

SEE ALSO atywer

arlety[2] *n.*

1. raw, uncooked ◆ Ker arlety — arnterr itetyakenh. Ura inemel weth iteyamel, antyerrk ilemel. (T) *[This] meat us raw — it hasn't been cooked properly. Get some wood to cook it some more and make it solid.*

2. raw, green, unripe ◆ Mern perlap arlety, ampeng-irrem anem. (St) *The conkerberry is unripe, then it ripens.*

= anka

arlety-antey *n.*

1. still raw or uncooked

2. still green or unripe

arlety-arlety *n.*

1. half cooked

2. not properly ripe

SEE ALSO pwarr, anthwerrk[1]

arlety-arlety (T,E) a type of ant SEE UNDER **arlety**[1]

arletyety (W) *n.*

1. spinifex which is found in the open desert country

2. wax or resin from this spinifex ◆ Arletyety rrkwalel irnerl-apem, kenh tyalangk akenh anem irntarenyarl — *self*-anteyarlam. Arletyety atwem aken, rwel mpwarem, mpwarem antem tamp-arteh. (M) Arletyety *is found in the open desert country, whereas* tyalangk *is found in the hilly country — they are different from each other. The* arletyety *spinifex is beaten as well, then the resin is heated on the fire and made into [a resin cake] a bit like a damper.*

SEE ALSO tyalangk, anker[1], aywert, rrkwal

-arlew (E) 'Where is (someone or something)?' SEE UNDER **-alew**[1]

arlewarr (W) *n.*

full, whole, uncut ◆ Apwert lyerl-warl akwernek ker arlewarr antey. Arrenty anengk arrpenh aken Pangkelang kwen antem inteyel, *rush*-irrek ina. (M) *[The man] had put the entire kangaroo carcass in a cave. There were a lot of Pangkelang monsters inside the cave and they rushed in to grab [the meat].*

SEE ALSO ampwerrk

arlewatyerr, alewatyerr *n.*

1. sand goanna, Gould's goanna, sand monitor (*Varanus gouldii*) ◆ Arrwernek tha alhweng arlewatyerr-kenh apek. (St) *I made a hole in the goanna's burrow.* ◆ Alewatyerr alhwel kwer tywen-akert apernem. (T) *A child who has sores can be rubbed with goanna blood.* ◆ Alewatyerr anterel apernelhem kapert rwernparl-irrem. (T) *If your head is hot you can rub yourself with goanna fat.*

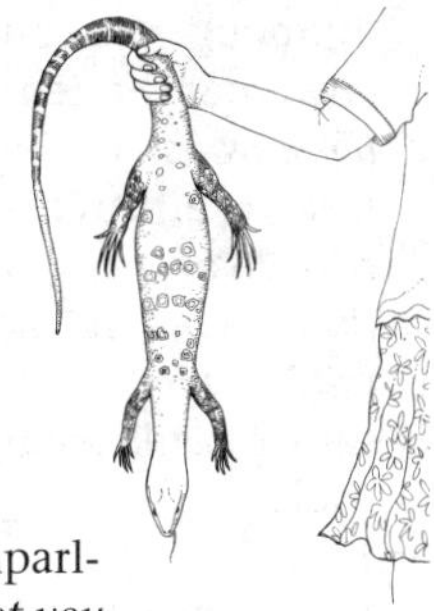

SEE ALSO kwentarreng
2. the edible flesh of the sand goanna. Also referred to as *ker arlewatyerr.*
3. fifty-dollar note. This word is used because the word 'fifty' is *kwementyay*, and because the note is coloured and patterned a bit like a goanna.
SEE ALSO karntewarr

arlewatyerr-arlewatyerr[1] (T,E), **alewatyerr-alewatyerr** (T,E) *n.*
yellow-faced whip snake (*Demansia psammophis*) (?)
SEE ALSO pwer arlewatyerr

arlewatyerr-arlewatyerr[2], **alewatyerr-alewatyerr** *n.*
broom bush (*Templetonia egena*) ◆ Ngkerlp aketyan arnmeny, arnmeny iterl-aneh ngkerlp kwerel arlkwerl-alhem alewatyerr-alewatyerr kwerel anem arlkwerl-alhem. Arekem wem, arlkwerl-alhemel alhem lyweny. (N) *The broom bush was picked and then burnt to make ashes. The tobacco was dipped into the broom bush ashes and then people would chew it as they went along hunting.*

arlewem (T) put something away, hide something SEE UNDER **arlawem**

arlewenp (T,E) *n.*
whole, unopened, not yet cut into pieces ◆ Ker nhenh ntwa atyeng anthek arlewenp — *never been cut*-em *up*, tyip-iletyakenh aker. Mern apek. Mern tamp apek arlewenp. *This meat that you gave me is whole — it hasn't been cut up yet. Damper can be* arlewenp *too, uncut.*
SEE ALSO ampwerrk

arlewent (E) *n.* [RESPECT LANGUAGE]
long way away, far, a bit distant ◆ Aheyleng mpwarewarraw arlewent. Arlewent ahanety-alperl-wemel. (St) *Go and make a camp a bit further away. Go and move back further away [said by a woman referring to her son-in-law]* ◆ Mey-mey atyenh arlewent-kwenyel ayepel-irrepirrem — arleng-anetyakenh kwenh. (St) *My son-in-law is sitting not very far away — not far.* ◆ Alal-werlentyarrey arlewent-kweny-kety. Arrer-kety. Arlewent-artek alal-wey. (Sa) *Go and make a camp a bit further away, because you're not very far away. Because you're [too] close.*
SEE ALSO arleng[1]

arlewent-kweny (E) *n.* [RESPECT LANGUAGE]
close, close together
SEE ALSO arrer

arley (W,T) *n.*
1. emu (*Dromaius novaehollandiae*)
= ankerr
2. baby emu, emu chick [SOME SPEAKERS] ◆ Arley, akwek map angernerl-apem pap kwerenhel, aperrk arlkwerl-apem lpway-angkwerr, rltar-rltarel arlka wanterl-apem, aperelty arlka, atyankern arlka. (N) *The father emu takes the little emu chicks along, eating charcoal along the creek, and feeding them on rattlepod fruits, mistletoe fruits and the white substance made by the lerp-scale insect from the river red gums.*
• = artelh[1]

arley kwart (W,T)
emu egg (kwart *'egg'*)
SEE ALSO atherneng

arleyakwerr (T,E) *n.*
nut bush (no common name) (?) (*Stylobasium spathulatum*). A shrub about 2 m high, with hard brown nuts about the size of a pea. The nuts are used for making necklaces.
= warrangkwer, ampweth-ampweth

arleyarr *n.*
young man who has just been through initiation (young man) ceremony, newly initiated man
SEE ALSO alyepelengkw, awerrty, arwekert, lyaty, amarleyarr, tyakwertekwert, lwekerleny, antingkar

arleytarr (T,E) *n.*
burrow ◆ Ker rapetel angernem arleytarr, alhweng akwek arleytarr. (T) *The rabbit digs a little burrow, an* arleytarr.
= alhweng
SEE ALSO arwerr

arleytarr-ilem (T,E) *vt.*
dig a burrow ◆ Rapetel arleytarr-ilem alhweng iltyel angernem. (St) *The rabbit digs a burrow with its front legs.*

arlinem *vt.*
1. fight with a person, hit someone or something ◆ Angwenharl arlinerl-iwerrek? (Sa) *Who was fighting?* ◆ Tyerrty arlinek akuny-amperl, ampikw apekarl arlinek — *someone*-el apek arlinek. (St) *Her child, the poor thing, was*

hit — someone had a fight with him.
2. fight with a person, hit someone or something [RESPECT LANGUAGE]
SEE ALSO atwem, kelthemartem, ulpakem

arlka[1] (T,E) *n.*
body ◆ Arlka apekarl awelhem rlkert, *pain* apek atanthepanthem. 'Arlka ayeng tyelk ingkerr akeng-irrekaw, arlka atyenh.' (St) *[Your] body might feel sick and the pain might be stabbing you. 'My whole body, my flesh is no good.'*
SEE ALSO tyerrty, tyelk

arlka[2] *ending*
too, as well as (something else), also, and. When describing a number of things or presenting a list of things *arlka* can go on the words for each of the things, on some of them, or on just one of them, typically the last item. This ending is written as a separate word. ◆ Artwa map apety-alpek ker aherr arlka akert. *[Finally the] men came back, with kangaroos too.* ◆ Mer nhenh arlka-atwety arrkwetyety *Coniston*-warn arlka ingkang alhetyart. (N) *We went as far as here [Napperby] and Coniston as well, on foot.* ◆ Iltya arlka arlerlp-irrem, tyerrty arlka ingkerrek arlerlp-irrem. Lwelty angerreng wal arlerlp-irrem. (T) *Your hands can cramp up, and all of the body as well. Well when there is a big frost you cramp up.* ◆ Kapert arlka ingkerr anwern arlkwetyart. (N) *We used to eat all of it, the top part [of the sugarbag] as well.* ◆ Pernelhetyeh kwer map, nhenh arrkenel alakenh *moustache* arlka mpwarerl-apetyeh, arralt arlka. *For kids to rub on themselves, for them to have fun going along and making moustaches and beards on themselves.*

arlkany intem, arlkany ayntem (E) *vi.*
lie resting propped up on hand or elbow (intem[1], ayntem '*lie down*') ◆ Amakel irrertety ayeng arlkany intem. (St) *I am lying using my elbow as a support.*

arlkany irnem (W,T)
lie resting propped up on hand or elbow (irnem '*stand*') ◆ *Tired* awelhem alakenh arlkany irnerl-anem. Kwereng akem-irremel anerl-anem. Wal kem antem irrem. (N) *When I'm feeling tired I rest using my arm as a support. Then I get up and sit. Then I get up.*

arlkarem *vt.*
make someone tired or exhausted, tire someone out, hassle or annoy someone, 'humbug' someone ◆ Kwer mapel anwernantherrenh arlkarem. (T) *The kids are hassling us.* ◆ *All night*-arrp rntwemaw, kwatyel arlkaremaw. Akwek-lkwer rntwetyakenh. (T) *It's raining all night and tiring us out. It's not just raining a little bit [it's raining a lot].*
SEE ALSO parrkel-anthem, arrkenty-ilem, arlelty angkem

arlkarl[1] *n.*
1. cool, cold ◆ Kwaty tha arlkarl antywetyek, *ice*-akert apek. (St) *I might drink some cold water with ice in it.*
2. cool, cold [RESPECT LANGUAGE]
SEE ALSO irrernt, anyel, kernt, anyartey, angwerl, angwerleny, atheperr

arlkarl-irrem (E) *vi.*
cool down, get cooler

arlkarl-ilelhem (E) *vi.*
make yourself cool, cool yourself down ◆ Kapert ayeng alhewelhetyek, tyerrty arlka ayeng alhewelhetyek, arlkarl-ilelhemel. (St) *I'm going to wash my head and my whole body to cool myself down.*
SEE ALSO irrernt

arlkarl[2] *n.*
1. new, flash, brand new ◆ Mwetek arlkarl inek. Anwengkerr lyweny aperlanetyek. (T) *He got a new flash car. We'll all go hunting.*
2. newborn baby ◆ Ampa akely apek alhewek apek, ampa arlkarl akwek mwerr-angker. (St) *The little baby has been washed, the lovely little newborn baby.* • SEE ALSO ampa rlternt, ampelyerrk, arathap, iylker

arlkarlker *n.*
sideways, leaning sideways, on one's side, tilted to one side ◆ Arlkarlkerel tha arek, tyerrty apek talkw alherlek apek. (St) *From the side I saw someone going across.* ◆ Arlkarlker intem kel impalkert then-wem. (St) *Lying on [your] side and then lying down on your back.* ◆ Ipertel ankert-iwek mwetekay arlkarlker-irrety-ayntek, atnyekarl. (Sa) *The hole made the car roll and it ended up on its side.*
SEE ALSO arrethaker

arlkarlker intem, arlkarlker ayntem (E)
lie on side

arlkarntar (W,T) *n.*
yellow fruit of the desert raisin and the banana-flavoured bush tomato (*Solanum centrale, Solanum cleistogamum*)
SEE ALSO katyerr, manyem, tweny, kwart, katyerr kwart

arlkarrkwatyerr (E) *n.* [RESPECT LANGUAGE]
goanna

SEE ALSO arlewatyerr

arlkarrpem (W) *vt.*
chop tree open for native honey or sugarbag ◆ Ngkwarl renh arlkarrpem ilepel. (M) *Chopping out the sugarbag with an axe.*

arlkem *vi.*
call out, sing out, yell out, shout, scream, cheer ◆ Tyerrtyek arrpenhek arlkem, ampek apek arlkem 'Apety-alpay, arleng alhetyal!' Alakenhant. (St) *Singing out to another person or to a child, 'Come back, don't go a long way away!' Like that.* ◆ Ywerntemeh arlkerrirretyam, arnterrkwetyam-arleh, kewelarl arrernek-arleh. (M) *We cheered for Yuendumu when they caught the ball, and someone kicked a goal.*

arlkelh-ilem *vt.*
sing out about something; shout out to let people know about something; call someone over ◆ 'Nhenhek apetyaw!' Alakenh angkem, arlkelh-ilem. (St) *'Come here!' Talking like that, shouting out to tell [the person].*
SEE ALSO antangkelhem

arlkemal *n.*
desert poplar (*Codonocarpus cotinifolius*). Tree up to 9 m high, with smooth pinkish or blue-grey bark, and leathery leaves. ◆ Arlkemaleh kwer tywenem, ampa akwek map tywenem. Ampa map tywenem antyenhetyek. Ra arlpenty-irretyenheng. Wal, amwelek amwelek inang intert atwetyart kwer arlpenty-irretyeh. Kwer amangkelh-ilemel. *No* mernt *anything* apek itya. (N) *The children are put there to climb the desert poplar, so that they will grow tall. Well, the mothers used to hit the base of the tree so that the child would grow tall. That was to grow the children up, and so that they wouldn't get sick or anything like that.*

arlkemalayt (E) *n.*
edible grub from the desert poplar

arlkemal-areny (T) *n.* = **arlkemalayt**

arlkenty (E) big mob, a lot, everyone SEE UNDER **irlkenty**

arlkeny *n.*
1. stripe, design, marking, groove (in boomerang, dish or shield) ◆ Awely apek arrernem arlkeny, awely. (St) *Putting on the designs for the* awely *ceremony.* ◆ Aylayl apek arlkeny arrernem. (St) *Putting grooves on the boomerang.*
SEE ALSO tyepety[1]
2. track ◆ Arlkeny wararl tha arek, rarl alhetyam. (St) *I just saw the track where he went.*

arlkeny-arlkeny *n.*
striped, stripey, patterned, grooved, multi-coloured ◆ Terreth apek mantarr arlkeny-arlkeny. (St) *A dress might be stripey.* ◆ Ker arrwerrperl apmwa. *Yellow and brown* arlkeny-arlkeny alakenh an kapertan urrperl ra arrwerrperl. (St) *The* arrwerrperl *snake has yellow and brown stripes and a dark-coloured head.*

arlkeny arrernem
draw, paint, make a design or mark on something (arrernem '*put*')

arlkeny-wem *vt.*
1. draw, paint, make a design or mark on something ◆ Kwer marlel arlkeny-wem twererr way-akertel. (T) *The girl is making designs on the music sticks with a wire.*
2. make a mark on the ground or on a tree to show where you have gone
SEE ALSO ingkwernem, arrernem, atanthem, intelh-ilem, mpaty-ilem, tyepety-wem, ahimperr-wem

arlkeny-werrem *vi.*
paint each other up with ceremonial designs (women)
= tyepety-werrem

arlkerl *n.*
1. small prickly plants
2. bindy-eye, cat-head, caltrop (*Tribulus terrestris* s. *lat*). A small plant with sharp prickles. ◆ Arlkerlelarl atanthem pwet anetyakenh ayeng ingka aketh. (Sa) *When my feet are bare and I haven't got any shoes the bindy-eyes stab my feet.*
3. buckbush, rolypoly, tumbleweed (*Salsola tragus*). Rounded plant about 1 m high which turns yellow when old and rolls along blown by the wind. ◆ Lyek arlkerl. Lyekam arlkerl yanh. Tyapeyay arlkerlel kwen intem, anyematy-artek akin. (N) *That buckbush has sharp spikes. There is a grub that lives in the base of the bush, like a witchetty grub.*
• = inkwert

arlkerlaty (W,T), **arlkerlayt** (T,E) *n.*
edible grub from the buckbush
= inkwert-areny, inkwertayt

ker arlkerl (E)
echidna, porcupine, anteater (*Tachyglossus aculeatus*)
= inap, inarleng

arlkernem (T,E) *vt.*
pick up, sort out or collect (of native currant, *Psydrax latifolia*) ◆ Ahakeyantarl arlkernem, ahelh-warlarl ywerrkem, 'arlkernem' anem renh, *not* 'kwetyem'. Arlkernem, arlkernem renh panth-warl apek arrernem. (St) 'Arlkernem' *is only said of bush plums. The tree is shaken and then the fruits are collected. You*

say 'arlkernem', *not* 'kwetyem'. *The bush plum fruits are collected and then put in wooden dishes.*
SEE ALSO kwetyem

arlkerrk[1] (T,E) *n.*
meat ant (*Camponotus* sp.) ◆ Arlkerrk, yerr akngerr, ahelengkw-ahelengkw. Arlkerrk *are big ants and they are a bit aggressive.*
SEE ALSO arrekarlkarlker, yerr

arlkerrk[2] (W,T) *n.*
shiny, sparkling (water, sunshine, glass) ◆ Kwaty arlkerrk intek. *The sparkling water was lying there.*
SEE ALSO merawarr

arlkerrk-wem (W,T) *vi.*
shine or sparkle (water, sunshine, glass) ◆ Kwaty kwenh arlkerrk-wem yanh arrwekel, kwaty aketh-penh. (M) *The water is shining there in front of us, water in the claypan.* ◆ Mwetekay kelath arlkerrk-wenty-alhem, apetyemel. Arnaremel, '*Eh,* arlkerrk-wenty-alhem kwenh kelath yanhel, kwatyel-artek'. (T) *The windows of the car are shining as it comes along towards us. Watching it coming we say, 'Hey, the car windows are shining, sparkling like water'.*
SEE ALSO mperlkem, amparrkem, alenm anyem

arlketh[1] (W,T) *n.*
wooden water dish
= rnwa
SEE ALSO atywekal, urety, kwerlintyerr, panth, lwengkart[2], irrkwely[2], alparr[1], irrkwa, lengarr

arlketh[2] (T,E) *n.*
snappy gum (*Eucalyptus leucophloia*). Tree to 5 m high, with white bark that is sometimes spotted with black. The bark is used to cure kangaroo skin for making into waterbags and the wood is used for making wooden dishes. ◆ Arntap renh iyltem kel kwaty-warl arrernem arntap. Karntey-artek anem ra irrem, alhwartek. Kel lyek-lyek apek alhewelhem rtety-rtetyarl irrem weth-lkwer. *The bark is peeled off and then it is put into water. Then it goes like Condy's crystals, like blood. Then you wash sores, lumpy skin or things like that with it.*

arlketh-arlketh (E) *n.*
a type of beetle
= perrk-perrk
SEE ALSO lengarr-lengarr, panth-panth

arlketyerr *n.*
1. various prickly plants
SEE ALSO lyek, thenkarr
2. dead finish (plant) (*Acacia tetragonophylla*). Shrub to about 3 m high, with sharp pointed leaves and curved seed pods. ◆ Tyap akert akin arlketyerr yanh tyer yanh. Arlkwenh-arlkwenh. Tyap anyematyart *same* akin. Aningk anthwerr artekerrel anem tyer. *It has edible grubs as well, the dead finish bush. They are similar to the witchetty grub. There are lots of them in the roots of the dead finish bush.*
• = tyer
3. parkinsonia (*Parkinsonia aculeata*)
4. types of prickle or burr (*Sclerolaena* spp.) ◆ Ingkarl atanthemel arlketyerran, *sharp one. Cheeky bugger,* ingkang awangkelh-ilenh-ilenh. 'Pwet kweny arekerr-irrem ayeng.' (T) *The* arlketyerr *prickle spikes your foot. It's a cheeky bugger and it makes your feet swell up. 'I haven't got any shoes and I'm in pain.'*

arlkngem (E) wipe, wash or clean something SEE UNDER **arnngem**

arlkwat (W,T) *n.*
large flat rock; lower grinding stone (used for grinding seed) ◆ Arlkwat ra akwel anterrng athenh-athenh, artety athenh-athenh. (T) *The* arlkwat *stone is used for grinding seeds, for grinding mulga seeds.*
= apwert ather
SEE ALSO pwerl

arlkwatelhem (W,T) *vi.*
moan, groan ◆ Rlkert ayeng arlkwatelhem. (M) *I am moaning because I'm sick.*

arlkwatem (W,T) *vt.*
1. throw something to the ground ◆ Ker aherr arlkwatety-alpem ahelh-warn. (T) *The kangaroo is brought back to camp and thrown to the ground.*
2. hit, knock or throw something against something else in order to break it up or kill it ◆ Rwang wety-alpem arlkwatem ahelh-warn. (T) *The firewood is brought back and thrown to the ground to break it up.* ◆ Lewatyerr pwer tayleng inemel arlkwatem. (N) *The goanna is grabbed by the tail and hit [against the ground] to kill it.*
SEE ALSO ntewem, ilatwem

arlkwaterrem (W,T) *vi.*
wrestle each other, 'play fight' ◆ Tyerrty atherr arlkwaterrem ahangel-ayeng. *The two people are wrestling each other angrily.*
= ntewerrem

arlkwem *vt.*
1. eat; feed on something ◆ Ker ankerr arlkwerl-anem kwer rrweyel. (M) *The boy is eating emu meat.* ◆ Arlkwem tha mern apek ker apek. (St) *I might eat bread or meat.* ◆ Kwer akwekel arlkwarlkw nthwepenthwem anwenth, arlkwerl-apep-apem, ntywel anerl-

apemel. (N) *The little child is going along eating meat, sitting on his/her mother's shoulders.*
2. chew something; chew (tobacco) ◆ Ngkwerlpan arlkwem antey, kelh mpwaremel, arnmenyel-arleng. (St) *Tobacco is chewed as well, made into lumps mixed with ashes.*
3. take (tablets) ◆ *Tablet* tha arlkwem. (St) *I am taking the tablets.*
4. hunt (get something to eat); use something to hunt with ◆ Rntwerarl akerrerl-anem maket yanh-lkwer, akngerrelan. Arlkwerretyel ap ikwerel rntwerel. (Sa) *'Rntwer' is what lots of people call guns and that sort of thing. People use guns to hunt with.*
5. ache, be in pain, be hurt by something ◆ Atnert ayenh arlkwemaw. Kapert then arlkwem ayenh, kapert ayeng arntem. (Sa) *My stomach is aching. My head is aching as well.* ◆ Ngkwern arlkwem. (T) *[My] leg is hurting.*
6. win, beat someone (in a race, game or a fight); perform impressively ◆ *Football*-el apekarl arrken-irreperrem ina, anyentel apek impek kel. Arlkwerrem-antey. 'Arlkwek anyentel.' *Winner* apek ra anem. Arlkwek, *Stirling* mapel apek arlkwek, Kwenthey-kwenthey mapel. (St) *They are playing football and one team won. 'One team beat the others.' And then they are the winners. Maybe Stirling mob won, the* Kwenthey-kwenthey *team [named after* Eremophila duttonii*].* ◆ Arrpel ilety-alpem, 'Kel arlkwerrekaw!' (T) *The other person goes back and tells them, 'They won the game!'* ◆ War arlkwerl-apetyenh kwey akengel. (T) *This fabulous little girl is going to bowl them over.*
arlkwerrem *vi.*
fight each other ◆ Ahel arlkwerrek, atwerrekarl-penh apek. *Might someone* apek ngkweng apek tha ilem, 'Ahel arlkwerrekaw'. Wararl ilterrek apek. Arlkwerreperrem. Ahel. (St) *[They] were arguing and fighting. Someone might tell you, or I might tell you, 'They had an angry fight'. Maybe they just swore at each other, or they were fighting, angrily.*

arlkwenhem *vt.*
fill something up; fill up a container with fruits, seeds, grubs etc. (not water) ◆ Yakweth atyenh arlkwenhem katyerrel, tha utnhek angerr. (St) *I am filling my bag with desert raisin fruits, I picked a lot.* ◆ Yakweth atyengenh arlkwenhek arreweh-atwety mern, rnwanenty apek. (M) *I have filled my bag to the brim with food and clothes.*
CAN SOUND A BIT LIKE alkwernem *'wait while others go'*

arlkwenth (E) *n.*
1. white-necked heron (*Ardea pacifica*)
2. white-faced heron (*Ardea novaehollandiae*)
= ntyar, kamparwengk, ulamp-areny
Arlkwenth (E) *n.*
the name of a waterhole near Aniltji outstation, Utopia (Angarapa Aboriginal Land Trust)

arlkwer *n.*
1. unsettled, walking around too much, being a nuisance ◆ Arelh nhenh arlkwer aperl-apem merarrp merarrp. (M) *This woman is unsettled and walking around from place to place.*
2. behaving in a flirtatious way ◆ Awenk yanh map arlkwer map. (M) *Those young girls are playing up.*
= **urlker** (E)
arlkwer-arlkwer *n.*
1. behaving in a flirtatious way, showing off ◆ Kwer arlkwer-arlkwer, arlkwer-arlkwer nthwem. (T) *That kid is going round showing off.*
2. in a hurry ◆ Arlkwer-arlkwerel arlkwem, parrp-parrpel. (T) *Eating in a hurry.*
= **urlker-urlker** (E)
arlkwer-ilem *vt.*
carry a baby around all the time and make it unsettled; make someone unsettled or upset; stir someone up; make someone tired ◆ Ampa arlkwer-iletyal akuny menty aney rlkert-irrekerr. (St) *Don't carry that baby round all the time and make it unsettled, leave the poor thing alone in case it gets sick.* ◆ Arlkwer-iletyal impay kwer akwek. (T) *Don't stir the baby up, leave him/her.*
SEE ALSO ingekelh-ilem, arwekar-ilem
arlkwer-irrem[1] *vi.*
become unsettled or upset ◆ Kwer nhenh arlkwer-irrem, atyernp anetyakenh. (M) *This child is upset, not settling down.*

arlkwer-irrem[2] (W) *vi.* [SENSITIVE LANGUAGE]
commit sexual indiscretion; commit adultery ◆ Awey amerrk rang arlkwer-irretyam marl kwerenhel-ayeng. (M) *Then that boy started to muck around with [his brother's] wife.*
SEE ALSO antay-wem

arlkwerrng *n.*
liquid honey, juice from meat, juice from fruits such as *ahakey* plums ◆ Arlkwerrng thelelhem ngkwarl ntyarleyarleng-penh. (M) *The honey is dripping down from the corkwood flowers.*
SEE ALSO awerrp[1]

arlkwerrpernem (W,T) *vt.*
bark or growl at somebody or something
= arntwerrem

arlkwerrpel-nhwem (W,T) *vt.*
= **arlkwerrpernem** (nhwem *'bite'*)
◆ Angwelyel arlkwerrpel-nhwem. (N) *The dog is barking at something.*
= parlkwem, arrpwarnt angkem
arlkwerrpel-angem (T) *vt.*
carry something in mouth (animal)

arlngem (E) wipe, wash or clean something SEE UNDER **arnngem**

arlpa[1] (E) *n.*
hot ashes or earth (used for cooking or healing) ◆ Arlpel ampernem arlewatyerr. (Sa) *Cooking the goanna in the hot ashes.*
= arnmeny, rtwap
SEE ALSO awerrth, atnmanth, ntyerlp[1], amerrk[2]
CAN SOUND A BIT LIKE irlpa *'ear'*

arlpa[2], **arlpang** (W,T), **aylpa** (E) *n.*
1. leaf, leaves ◆ Ahakeyan arlpang angerr. (N) *Bush plums have big leaves.* ◆ Arlpang waly akeyaw. (T) *Cut the leaves and branches.*
◆ Aylpa antyerrk-irrek. *The leaves have gone dry.*
= alperr
2. wing ◆ Arntep kwenyel apetyem, arlpang atherr rltar-irrem. *The bronzewing pigeon comes in the night and flaps its wings.*
3. feather
= arlpelh
CAN SOUND A BIT LIKE irlpa *'ear'*

arlpalh, arlpelh *n.*
hairstring, hairstring belt or waist band (men's). Made from the fur of animals such as rabbits, possums or spectacled hare-wallabies. The umbilical cord of a newborn baby was tied up with this and worn around the baby's neck to stop it from crying. ◆ Arlpalh wetyam altepenh, kapert anem ayernelhetyam alta nhelkwer. *Men*-elant. Kwarlp-penh apek mpwaremel wemel, kel kapert anem *string* mpwaremel. Alta yanh akwernelherl-anetyek, ayernerl-anetyek. (St) Arlpalh *was spun from hair, and then the head was bound up. Just men did it. The fur from the spectacled hare-wallaby was used for spinning, and then string was made for tying up the head, tying up the hair.*
SEE ALSO alyep[1], antyarn, irrkety, matyart, ngatywelarr, antingkar, antay

arlpalywerrng *n.*
small, red witchetty grub (*Xyleutes bipartii*). The witchetty grub is called *arlpalywerrng*, when it is small and red, that is, before it becomes mature and is called *anyematy*.
SEE ALSO anyematy, irrarl

arlpampem (E) *vi.*
be a red, pink or orange colour (especially of kangaroo and honeyant) ◆ Arlpampemarl intep-intem ker aherr, alta weth-lkwer arlpampepampem. (St) *The kangaroo lying there is a reddish colour, its fur is showing red.*

arlpang (W,T) leaf, leaves SEE UNDER **arlpa**[2]

arlpang (W,T) ear, ears SEE UNDER **irlpa**

arlpar (E) a type of bush potato SEE UNDER **irlpar**

arlparernem, aylparernem (E) *vi.*
hang down, dangle, swing from something (irnem, rnem *'stand'*) ◆ Pwarl arlparernep-rnem arnangel-ayel. (M) *The bush bananas are hanging in the tree.* ◆ Arnel kwer antyekarl-penh arlpar-arlparernem. Waram kanty-warl apetyem kanty-warl antyintyem *right up* antyinty-alhem wal nhenheng-lkwer arlparernem, kantyengem. (N) *The child is hanging from the tree after climbing up. She just climbed right along to the top of the tree and hung there, right from the end of the branches.*
SEE ALSO amaralty-anem
arlpar-arrernem, aylpar-arrernem (E) *vt.*
hang something up (arrernem *'put'*)
◆ Angwely-kety akern tywernem arlpar-arrernem antywerlan-kety. (N) *Put it up high because of the dogs, because the dogs might drink it.* ◆ Arnewarl aylpar-arrerney urrek tha arengk-kety *billycan* atyenh. (St) *Wait while I hang my billycan up in case the dogs get at it.* ◆ Mantarr apek tha atyenh *line*-warl aylpar-arrernem. (St) *I am hanging my clothes up on the line.*
SEE ALSO tek-wem
aylpar anyenem (E), **aylpar atnyenem** (E) *vt.*
hold something hanging from hand (anyenem *'hold'*) ◆ Aylper ra atnyenem, *bag* apek, iltyel aylper atnyenepenem. (St) *Holding the bag hanging from the hand.*
arlpar athwenkarr (W,T),
aylpar athwenkarr (E) *n.*
in a bunch, a lot of things hanging down in a group ◆ Katyerr apek arlpar athwenkarr anem, map. (T) *There are lots of desert raisins hanging in a bunch [from the plant].* ◆ Mern alangkw nhel arlpar athwenkarr anemek apetyewarray, anwengkerr aketyek. (T) *All of you come here to where the bush bananas are hanging in bunches, so that we can pick them.*
SEE ALSO anarnkw, iltyingk, rlkwangk

arlparlety (E) *n.*
water at the bottom of a soakage. Also referred to as *kwaty arlparlety.* ◆ Kwaty arlparlety, angernekarl iltyel — kwaty renh anem arratem arlparlety renh. Kel kwaty renh antywem. (Sa) *The water at the bottom of the soakage that has been dug out by hand — the the water, the* arlparlety *comes up. Then [you]*

drink the water.
SEE ALSO anthwerrng, antha[1], urta

arlpaty *n.*
ringneck parrot, Port Lincoln parrot (*Barnardius zonarius*). Also referred to as *ker arlpaty*. ◆ Ker arlpaty akwerrk anwern inerrirretyart rlpwerew, atwemel anwern inetyart *full* anwern atwetyart. Thewetam yanh perrap anper akin, atetherrart. (N) *We used to get baby ringneck parrots from the hollows in trees, kill them and collect lots of them. The meat is really lovely and sweet, like budgerigar meat.*
Arlpatyant (W,T) *n.*
name of a hill in the Anmatjira Range area (lit. 'only ringneck parrot'). See map p. viii.

arlpaty-antey-antey (W) *n.*
a type of beetle

arlpaw *n.*
waterless country; wide open space, clearing ◆ Alhetyek ayeng ahern arlpawel. (St) *I'm going through the wide open country.* ◆ Anantherr arlpawel intetyek, tyerrty arwenth. (T) *Lots of us are going to sleep in the clearing.*
SEE ALSO pwarn
arlpaw-irrem *vi.*
become wide, broaden out ◆ Tyet anem ra alhem lher wethel apek. Arlpaw anem ra irrem. (St) *The creek goes along narrowly, and then it becomes wider.*
arlpaw-ilem *vt.*
make something wide
lher arlpaw (E)
flat country beside a creek (lher *'creek', 'river', 'sand'*)

arlpelh[1] (T,E) *n.*
1. leaf, leaves
2. tea-leaves ◆ Tey arlpelh yaleng angetyay. (M) *Get me those tea-leaves from there.*
3. wing
4. feather
= aylpa
SEE ALSO aympelh

arlpelh[2] *n.*
hairstring, hairstring belt or waist band (men's) SEE UNDER **arlpalh**

arlpelhart *n.*
a type of mulga (*Acacia aneura* (broad leaf variety)) ◆ Arlpelhart anem *self* akin rnpwa. Theweyet. Rnpwang anem arlpelhartel. Awantyewarretyart. (N) *The* arlpelhart *tree is different again and has sweet resin. There is a sweet resin on the* arlpelhart *tree that they used to suck on.*

arlpenty, arlpwenty (E) *n.*
long, tall ◆ Uterrp-areny ap arrwelth-arrwelth. Mern kweny akeng, *name* ant. Alhewelhemel kwatyel, alta angkwelk-ilelhemel, alta angerr ilelhemel, alta awer anetyek arlpenty. *The* arrwelth-arrwelth *plant grows in the sandhills. It's not edible, it's just a plant. Mixed with water and used to wash yourself, it makes your hair thick, makes it grow long and thick.* ◆ Artwa ampwa arrwert arlpenty. (St) *The old man has a long beard.* ◆ Pentarlp atyeng anthay thang akern atwetyew — *whipstick*-artek arnang arlpenty. (N) *Get me a whipstick so that I can hit up high — a long stick like a whipstick.*
= alkey[1]
SEE ALSO karteng
arlpenty-arlpenty,
arlpwenty-arlpwenty (E) *n.*
longish, a bit tall ◆ Apwenan arlpa arlpenty-arlpenty rarl ilperr-ilperr *one* areyawerr. Apwert akern *too much.* (Sa) *The* apwen *has longish leaves and the* areyawerr *has flat ones. There are lots of them growing on top of the hills.*
= alkey-alkey
arlpenty-irrem, arlpwenty-irrem (E) *vi.*
get taller or longer, grow tall ◆ Arlkemaleh kwer tywenem, ampa akwek map tywenem. Ampa map tywenem antyenhetyek. Ra arlpenty-irretyenheng. Wal, amwelek amwelek inang intert atwetyart kwer arlpenty-irretyeh. Kwer amangkelh-ilemel. *No* mernt *anything* apek itya. (N) *The children are put there to climb the desert poplar, so that they will grow tall. Well, the mothers used to hit the base of the tree so that the child would grow tall. That was to grow the children up, and so that they wouldn't get sick or anything like that.*
= alkey-irrem

arlpenty-arlpenty (E) a type of small snake SEE UNDER **aylpenty-aylpenty**

Arlper[1], Aylper (E) *n.*
1. Warlpiri person or Warlpiri people ◆ Arlper map apetyepetyem, rareyant angkerrerl-anem. (T) *The Warlpiri are coming and they're just talking amongst themselves.*
2. the Warlpiri language ◆ Arlperan tha awetyakenharl alturleny ant, inekenh angkarrparl — Arlper. (St) *I can't understand Warlpiri, it's from the western side and it's just their language — Warlpiri.*

arlper[2] (W) *n.kin*
kin relationship between a person and their father or their son or daughter (if one of them is the mother's brother or the cross-cousin of the speaker) (?)

arlperengkw (W) *n.kin*
your *arlper*
arlperekw (W) *n.kin*
1. your *arlper*
2. his/her/their *arlper*
arlper-nheng (W) *n.kin*
a group of fathers and their sons or daughters (said by a person if one of them is their mother's brother or their cross-cousin)
arlper-intyerr (W) *n.kin* = **arlper-nheng**
arlper-nheng atherr (W) *n.kin*
a person and their father or their son or daughter (said by a person if one of them is their mother's brother or their cross-cousin)
◆ Lyweny alhek arlper-nheng atherr (M) *Father and child went hunting.*

arlperl, **aylperl** (E) *n.*
honeydew found on mulga, *artety* (made by the lerp-scale insect). Also referred to as *ngkwarl arlperl*. ◆ War thelelherl-anem irnmerr renh war amparrkerl-anerlek arerl-anem, arna anyent kwerel antem. Arlperl artety kwereng antem war thelelherl-anem. (N) *It just drips from the mulga tree and you can see it like drops of water sparkling on the branch of that particular tree. The* arlperl *just drips from the mulga tree.*

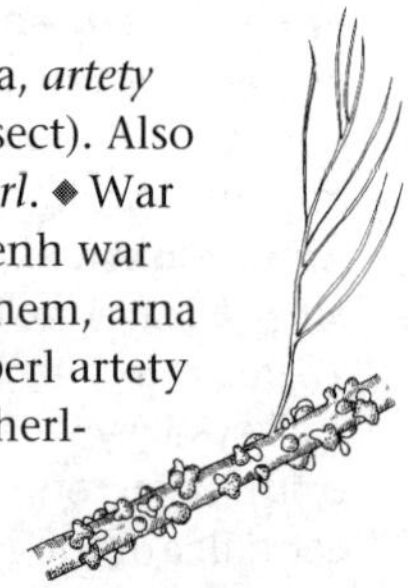

◆ Artetyayerr akenh anerleng rnpwangeyang, arlperl thelelherl-anem. Renh-perr arraw-ilemel walyel arraw-ilemel rnpwang arrernetyam, kelh arrernetyam. Artetyaywerrk. Rnpwang. (N) *The sweet resin comes from the mulga tree, and it seeps out. Then it is gathered together with a branch and made into a lump.*
SEE ALSO artetyaywerrk
CAN SOUND A BIT LIKE alperl *'pubic covering'*

arlperlp *n.*
1. kangaroo grass (*Themeda triandra*)
2. silky browntop, sugar grass (*Eulalia aurea*)
◆ Kernt mparetyam, arnam, arlperlp. Kwaty alakenh arrernetyam, arrwekel kwa, angernerlapetyam *olden time*-el rnwang rwetyel. (N) *The* arlperlp *grass was used to keep the water cool. It was put [on top] of the water in the wooden dish, and the olden-time mob used to carry it along like that.* ◆ Arlperlpel akwel intetyart antyamel arlperlpel. Antyam-wemel arlperlp renh wal intetyart, pelangket itya. (N) *People used to make beds of* arlperlp *grass. They'd lay out the grass and sleep on it, when there weren't any blankets.*

Arlperlp (E) *n.*
the name of the Hanson River area to the west of Wilora (Stirling) community

arlperr loud speech; a public speaking style SEE UNDER **aharlperr angkem**

arlperr *n.*
whitewood (*Atalaya hemiglauca*). Tree to 7 m high, with pale green leaves, creamy flowers and winged fruit.
CAN SOUND A BIT LIKE aylperr *'fish'*; alperr *'leaf'*
arlperrangkwarl *n.*
sweet gum from the whitewood
◆ Arlperrangkwarl apel theweyet anthwerr inelhapetyart, akap-rlwemel peleth, theweyet anthwerr. Awantyerlapetyeh. Lweren arlkwerl anwern amangkek, arlkwerl-apemel awantyerl-apemel — *everything* anthwerrel anwern amangkek. (N) *We used to collect the sweet resin from the whitewood tree — it's really sweet, I can tell you. We used to go along sucking on it. We'd eat those things and that's how we grew up, going along eating and sucking on the sweet whitewood resin — we grew up on all sorts of bush foods.*
arlperrampw (E) *n.* = **arlperrangkwarl**
arlperrayt (E), **arlperrenhayt** (T,E), **arlperretnhayt** (E) *n.*
whitewood grub
arlperreny (W), **arlperrenh** (W,T) *n.*
= **arlperrayt** ◆ Tyap arlperrenh inyerrirretyart. Arnka arlka arlkwem an rwewarn angerrirremel atyerremel arlkwetyenheng, arlperrenh yanh renh. Arnka arlka arlkwem nheng inyemel inyemel arlkwetyart. (N) *We used to dig out the grubs from the whitewood tree and eat them raw and also after cooking them in the fire. We ate them raw as we were going along digging.* ◆ Tyap arlperrenh, *olden time*-arl aketyam anyent renh, arlperrenh renh. Kapert angerr nheng-lkwer anyem-areny-arteh akin *different one*, kapert angerr. (N) *The whitewood grubs, that's what the olden-time people used to get. Their heads are big, a bit like the grub from the witchetty bush only larger.*

Arlperrakeny (W,T), **Arlperrakenh** (W,T) *n.*
the name of a rockhole near the Yuelamu (Mt Allan) community. The Mt Allan community store, *Alpirakina*, and the Yalpirakinu Aboriginal Land Trust are named after this place. See map p. viii.

arlperreh atwem (W), **arlperrek atwem** (T,E), **arlpirrek atwem** (E) *vt.*
1. fight on own, successfully take on many opponents (in a fight) (atwem *'hit', 'fight'*)
◆ Artwang yanhel arlperrek atwem, anyentel

akwet. (T) *That man is fighting all on his own.*
2. kill many animals on your own, get lots of game (meat) ◆ Arlewatyerr tha arlpirrek atwem, map apek. (St) *I am killing lots of goannas myself.*
SEE ALSO kwerremp-ilem

arlperrepwenty, aylperrepwenty (E) *n.*
someone who steps in to stop a fight or to diffuse trouble ◆ Tyerrty arrpenh atwetyek apekarl angkem wal arrpenhel arrngert angkemarl, impetyek. 'Arlperrepwenty' yanhan ilep-ilem. (St) *Somebody who is talking about fighting someone and another tries to talk them into stopping. That person who tries to stop them is called* 'arlperrepwenty'. ◆ Arlperrepwenty arrngert angkem arrpel atwekety. 'Impang akeweny kwenh. Menty aney kwenh.' Alakenharl ilem. (T) *The* arlperrepwenty *stops someone from fighting. 'Leave the poor thing. Settle down.' That's what they say.*
arlperr angkem (W), **arlperrepwenty angkem, aylperrepwenty angkem** (E) *vi.*
talk someone out of fighting; negotiate a dispute, sort out trouble
SEE ALSO aharlperr angkem

Arlperreyt (E) *n.*
the name of a soakage in the Hanson River, near Hanson Well south-west of Wilora (Stirling) community

arlperrty (T,E) *n.*
1. light-coloured
2. a part-Aboriginal person, half-caste
SEE ALSO athethek, apekath

arlpertey (E) *n.* [RESPECT LANGUAGE]
anger, angry
SEE ALSO aha
arlpertey-irrem (E) *vi.* [RESPECT LANGUAGE]
get angry or wild ◆ Arlpertey-irrepirremaw ngwarrengkw yanhenty kwenh. (St) *[Daughter], your husband over there is getting angry [said by the woman's mother].* ◆ Arlpertey-irrerlanekerr kwey ahaneynay. Ngenh lyet ulpakerl-iwerrem. (Sa) *Daughter, [your husband] might get angry, so go. Any minute he'll hit you [said by the woman's mother].*
SEE ALSO ahel-irrem

Arlperuneng (E), **Arlperweneng** (E) *n.*
name of a place in the Waite River Station homestead area

arlpetharlp (E) *n.*
flowers of the kurrajong tree (*Brachychiton gregorii*)
SEE ALSO apeng, alyalyarr, artwengarr, ngkweyang

arlpirrek atwem (E) fight on one's own SEE UNDER **arlperreh atwem**

arlpiwem (E) *vt.*
come out of hibernation (snake, goanna) ◆ Utern-taym arlpiwem arlewatyerrel, arlpiwenhem — arlkwetyekant anem, tyerrelhenhemel. (Sa) *In the summer the goanna comes out of hibernation — it comes out so that it can eat.*

arlpman (T,E) [RESPECT LANGUAGE] mother or the mother's brother SEE UNDER **arnman¹**

arlpman (T,E) honeyant worker SEE UNDER **arnman²**

arlpmeny (E) ashes SEE UNDER **arnmeny**

arlpwenty (E) long, tall SEE UNDER **arlpenty**

arlpwerr (E) *n.*
a special word used for food that is used during initiation (young man) ceremonies (note Warlpiri *yarlpurru* 'men initiated at same ceremony') ◆ Mern arlpwerr ngkernetyek alyey-tayem. Anthep-irremel. Mern arlety *dish*-elayeth. (Sa) *During the young men ceremony the* arlpwerr *food is put out. When people are dancing. Uncooked flour in a dish.*
SEE ALSO alyey², apwelh

arlpwerr atwem (W) *vt.*
beat rhythm on the ground (with a shield) at initiation (young man) ceremony (atwem '*hit*') ◆ Arlpwerr apel atwem anmantyarl, ayaterl-anem, alkwert yanh ahern-warl atwerl-anem, kenh marl map nthwerl-anerleng. (M) Arlpwerr atwem *is what [the men] do at the young men ceremonies, banging the rhythm on the ground with shields while the women dance.*

arlpwerrng atwelhem (E) beat rhythm on lap with cupped hands SEE UNDER **urlperrng atwelhem**

arlta¹, arltang (W,T) *n.*
day, daytime, daylight, a particular day ◆ Arlta ingwepenh *Tuesday*. (Sa) *Tomorrow is Tuesday.*
CAN SOUND A BIT LIKE alta '*hair*'
arltemarlt (T) *n.*
every day
arlta mpep (E)
daytime, midday (mpep '*middle*')
= aherrk angerr
arlta angerr (W,T), **arltang angerr** (W,T), **arlta angerrety** (E)
Sunday (angerr¹ '*big*') ◆ Arlta angerrel anantherr alhem tyaty-warn. (T) *On Sundays we go to church.*
arlta pwerrk (T)
Sunday (pwerrk '*tired*')

arlta² (E) *n.*
part of emu's guts (?)

SEE ALSO anwerl-anwerl

arltang (W,T) day, daytime, daylight, a particular day SEE UNDER **arlta**[1]

arltapwerlt-irrem (W), **arltaparlt-irrem** (W,T) *vi.* swell up or blister (skin raise up after being burnt by fire, sun or hot water) ◆ Kwer akwek rwepenh arltaparlt-irrek. (T) *The little child's skin has blistered from the fire.* ◆ Mern anaty arltaparlt-irrem rwepenh. (T) *The bush potato blisters from the fire.*

arltarrernem *vi.*
burp, belch ◆ Arltarrernem ayengaw arlkwekarl-penh, anerteng apek. Ngkwerlp-penh apek anterrk angkep-angkem, wal ampem anem ngkwerlp yanh, wal anterrk angkep-angkem. Arltarrerneman mern apekarl arlkwem-penh, akngerr, ker apek, kwaty apek. (St) *I am burping after eating, or if my stomach is full. I might burp after chewing tobacco, the tobacco burns and then you burp. You burp after eating a lot of food or meat, or after drinking.*
SEE ALSO anetyerrk-irrem, arnenthernem, anterrk angkem, anetyerrkernem

arlter *n.*
1. white, pale, light-coloured ◆ Arlteran ilem alhernter. Apwert 'arlter' ilem, arengk apek. Kapert 'arlter' akin, aywa. (Sa) *White people are called* 'arlter'. *Stones can be called* 'arlter', *or dogs. A person's head can be* 'arlter', *when the hair is grey.*
2. white person, non-Aboriginal person ◆ *'Uncle'* renhap amarl-amarl akem urrperl-angkwarr. *'Uncle'*-an yanhan arlter-kenh. (Sa) *'Uncle' is called* amarl-amarl *in Aboriginal way. 'Uncle' is white people's [language].*
= mperlker
SEE ALSO alhernter, warlpal

arlter-ayerr (E) *n.*
flour [RESPECT LANGUAGE]
= mperlker-ayerr

arlter-arlter *n.*
whitish, off-white, a bit light in colour ◆ Ntang iylaw. Arlter-arlter wetharl ngkweytek. *Grey-grey one-*arl iylaw. (St) *The munyeroo plant has edible seeds. The* ngkweytek *plant is whitish in colour. The* iylaw *plant is greyish.*

arlter-irrem *vi.*
go white, go pale ◆ Ngkwarl yerrekeyerr akerlkeperlkem, arlter-irrem. Ngkwarl aperelty apek akerlkem. (St) *The sweet stuff called 'yerrekeyerr' sparkles, goes white. The white substance, made by the lerp-scale insect from the river red gum tree, shines.*

annga arlter, alkngа arlter (E)
eyes that have whitened over with cataracts

arlterernternt (W) *n.*
yellow (native tobacco) after being put in ashes

arlterernternt-irrem (W) *vi.*
go yellow (native tobacco) after being put in ashes ◆ Ngkwerlp arlterernternt-irrem arnmeny-penh. (M) *The native tobacco goes yellow after being in the ashes.*
= atnmangkem

arlternkem (E) *vi.*
build up (clouds or rain-storm) ◆ Kwaty arlternkenhetyem arrer, arlternkem kwaty urntetyek. (Sa) *The storm clouds are building up and getting closer, building up to rain.*

arlterrng *n.*
warm ◆ Arlterrngelant urrek anwengkerr alhetyenheng. (T) *Let's wait till we get warm before we go.*

arlterrng-irrem *vi.*
get warm ◆ Urel apek arlterrng-irretyek, irrerntekarl irrem, arlterrng-irrem anem. (St) *Getting warm by the fire after being cold, getting warm then.*
= ntywety-irrem

arltwa, arltwang (W,T) *n.*
1. empty ◆ *Billycan* arltwa apek atyenh tnem, kwaty-kweny apek arltwarl tnem. (St) *My billycan is empty, it hasn't got any water in it and it's empty.* ◆ Kwey! Kwaty-kweny itya — *billycan* arltwang iney! (T) *Girl! We've got no water — get the empty billycan!*
2. empty, abandoned, deserted ◆ Mer arltwa tnem, ingkerrekarl alhekeng. (T) *The place is empty because everybody has gone.*

arltwerrem (W,T), **arltwirrem** (T,E) *vi.*
run out, become empty, become abandoned ◆ *Tobacco* atyenh arltwirrek arlpmenyant arltwa anem, arrangkw anem. (St) *My tobacco has run out and there's only ashes left.*
SEE ALSO ywerrem, uyerrem
CAN SOUND A BIT LIKE rltwerrem *'get bigger'*

arltwelem (W,T), **arltwilem** (E) *vt.*
empty something out ◆ Metheth nhakwel arltwilek alwerrng angkenh-angkenh, kel mwerr angketyek anem. (St) *That white woman emptied [the coins out of] the telephone and now we can talk [on the phone].*

arltwarem (W,T) *vt.*
look for something but not see it ◆ Arelh arrangkem arltwaremel kwer mertarl alhek-arlek lyweny. (T) *The woman is crying for her husband because he didn't come back from hunting.* ◆ Thang arltwarem, itya akwet. *I see*

nothing, nothing yet.

arltwelth (E) *n.*
toothache ◆ Arltwelthel angwarek ayenh arntek. (St) *I've got a toothache.*
SEE ALSO rtety[1], arntek, arranyenganyeng

arltwem (W,T) *vt.*
cover over; cover something up, block the way ◆ Alhek unmerntel arltwintyem, alhek unmerntel arltwem ingkerr, ahelh inkerr. Lwerenarl alker-irrenhem ingkerr anam-irrerl-alhem alhek unmernt ran. (N) *The dust haze comes towards you and covers everything over. Then it clears up and all the dust moves on.* ◆ Pelangketel kwer arltwem anyeleng. (T) *In the cold, cover the child with a blanket.* ◆ Kwatyel kwenh anwernenh arltwentyem. (T) *We're getting inundated with water.*
SEE ALSO artem, iparem

arltwelhem (W,T) *vi.*
cover yourself up, cover yourself with something ◆ Nyerreng arltwelhem. Tyelkatheng arltwelhem. (M) *Covering yourself over because you are shamed or because of the red-ochre men.*
SEE ALSO artelhem

arltwemp (W) *n.*
good hunter (said of a person or a dog)
SEE ALSO inngeny, kwerremp

arltwerlp (W,T) *n.*
swollen, bloated ◆ Arltwerlp tha arety-alhern ker. (T) *I went and saw the bloated carcass of an animal.*

arltwerlp-irrem (W,T) *vi.*
become swollen, bloated ◆ Ker aherr arltwerlp-irrem mwetekayelarl atwek. (T) *The kangaroo that was hit by a car becomes bloated.*

arltwerlpernem (W,T) *vi.*
blister (skin), rise up (of bread or damper) (irnem, rnem '*stand*') ◆ Ayenp arltwerlpernem rwepenh. (M) *Skin blisters [from being burnt] by the fire.* ◆ Mern tamp arltwerlpernem *baking powder* arrernenty-penh. (M) *The damper rises after the baking powder is put in [the mixture].*

arltwerrker-iwem (E) *vt.*
say that something bad will happen to someone, (say) 'you're dead' ◆ Marl arrpenh yanh akuny mwerrarl anepanem, arltwerrker-iwem. Atnimampel. Arelh yanh ilwetyenh. (St) *That poor woman was okay, but [someone] is saying that bad things are going to happen to her. She's cursed. That woman will die.*
SEE ALSO arrampewem[1]

arlurr-arlurr (E) curly, wavy (hair) SEE UNDER **arlwerr-arlwerr**

arlwa (T,E) *n.*
round in shape, circular
SEE ALSO apwerterrerterr, artwert-artwert, arlwepertaty, rlwatert

arlwelem (W,T), **arlwilem** (E) *vt.*
1. gather things together; round things up, muster ◆ Arelh yanhel ker map arlwelem. (T) *That woman is getting all the meat together.* ◆ Mern thwen ker thwen arlwelerl-apem. (T) *Collecting groceries [to take to the counter].* ◆ Arlwilem pwelek angerr apek. *Mustering lots of bullocks.*
SEE ALSO akarr-ilem, arraw-ilem, rwelemap-ilem
2. make something into a round shape ◆ Mern arlwilemel athem, kel ampernem. *Knead the damper into a round shape and then cook it.*

apwert arlwa (E)
round rock used for pounding things up (such as native tobacco)
= alyer

arlwar *n.*
swollen, round, puffed up, inflated
SEE ALSO arterrp

arlwar-ilenh-ilenh
1. baking powder
2. tyre pump (lit. 'that which makes something rise')

mern arlwar-ilenh
baking powder (mern '*food*'; arlwar-ilenh '*that which makes something rise*')

arlwar-irrem *vi.*
swell up, puff up, rise
SEE ALSO wangkem, amwerenthenng-irrem, alhapelhem

arlwar-ilem *vt.*
inflate something, pump something up, make something rise ◆ Arlwar-ilem, *pump*-em-ilemel. Arlwar-irrem akin tamp. (St) *Pumping it up to inflate it. Dampers rise up as well.*

arlwarernem *vi.*
rise up (of bread or damper); stomach swell up, become bloated (stomach of a dead animal) (irnem, rnem '*stand*') ◆ Kwaty akeng apekarl antywek wal atnertan arlwarernemarl. (St) *[Your] stomach swells up from drinking bad water.* ◆ Mern-warl arrernem *yeast* apek, arlwarernemarl ra. Kel arlwarernek mpwarem, mern arrernemel, ngkernem antey arlwarernetyek anteyarl. *If you put yeast into flour mixture, well it rises up. You put the mixture aside and then it rises.* ◆ Ker aherr arlwarernem mwetekayelarl atwek. (T) *The kangaroo that was hit by a car swells up.*
SEE ALSO wangkem

arlwarreng (E) *n.*
something that is left or saved for later ◆ Ngkwarl apek yerrekeyerr arlwarreng, arlwarrernekarl. Mern yerrakwerr apek ngkwarl apek, arwengalker, arlwarrengan yanh anep-anem atyenh. Arrangkw-antey war tha arekant. Neyel atwetyek ngkwarl — *save-*em-ilem. (St) *Perhaps the sweet* yerrekeyerr *might be left for later. The bush onions or the sugarbag that I am saving for later are over there. I've only looked at them. I'll chop the sugarbag out soon — I'm saving it.*
SEE ALSO arlwarrernem

arlwarrernem (T,E) *vt.*
leave something for later, save something for later ◆ Lyet renh itetyenh anem ker atharl arlwarrernek, arrernekarl ntwa. Ilenger apek ra ampetyenh? (St) *The meat that I left for later is going to be cooked today, the meat that you left. When is it going to be cooked?* ◆ Tha arlwarrernek, mern ampeng anem ra irrek, arlwarrernekarl. (St) *I left it for later, and now the fruit that I left has ripened.* ◆ Arlwarrernek, ilep anetyakenh. Ngkwarl arlwarrernentyek alhetyek, tharl arrernek. (St) *I didn't have an axe and so I left the sugarbag for later. Then I'll go for the sugarbag that I left.*
= arlernem
SEE ALSO arlwarreng

Arlwekarr (T,E) *n.*
Illoquara Waterhole and the name of country/estate in the Stirling Station area. See map p. viii.
CAN SOUND A BIT LIKE arlweker *'woman's camp'*

arlweker *n.*
1. women's camp, single-women's camp ◆ Arelh awenk map anerl-anem arlwekerel angkety angkerrerl-anemel. (T) *The teenage girls are sitting around in the women's camp telling stories.*
SEE ALSO arnkenty
2. an open expanse of country, typically where there is an abundance of bush foods ◆ Arlweker anthwerrek arety-alhem, katyerr renh arety-alhem. (T) *They go and see all the desert raisin plants right there on the spinifex plain.*
arlweker-areny *n.*
1. a single woman, or a woman who is on her own; unmarried woman, widow
2. a woman who lives in the women's camp (-areny *'inhabitant of'*)
SEE ALSO arnkenty-areny
arlweker-warn-irrem (W,T), **arlweker-warl-irrem** (E) *vi.*
become a widow (lit. 'go to the single-women's camp')
SEE ALSO arnkenty-warn-irrem, warlekwert-irrem, inpert-irrem
arlwekereng-arlweker *n.*
girl's cubbyhouse
= nyetyep
SEE ALSO arnkentyeng-arnkenty, mereng-amer, antyweng-antyweng, alyetyepengalyety

Arlwem (W), **Rlwem** (W), **Lwem** (W) *n.*
the name of a place in the Yuelamu (Mt Allan) area. Honeyant Dreaming place associated with Penangk/Pengart father–child pair of skin names. See map p. viii.

arlwemeny, arlemeny *adv.*
1. curled up, doubled up ◆ Amwang arlwemeny intem twernel. (T) *The snake is lying curled up in the sun.* ◆ Kwey arlemeny aynterl-anetyalay, akem-irray! (Sa) *Girl, don't lie there all curled up, get up!*
2. crippled, cramped
SEE ALSO arrepert, rtapety
arlwemeny-irrem, arlemeny-irrem *vi.*
1. curl up, clench up (fist), double up, make a fist ◆ Arlwemeny-irrem, kwer-penh intem rlkerremelhem, arlwemeny akin irrinty-alpem. (N) *Curling up, and then after that lying with legs straight out, and then curling back up again.*
2. become cramped up or disabled ◆ Tyerrty apek arlwemeny-irrekaw! (T) *That person has become cramped up.*
arlwemeny anem, arlemeny anem
sitting with legs curled up to the side

arlweng-rlpwerr (W) *n.*
a type of fish
SEE ALSO pety, irrpenng

arlwenth (E) *n.*
married, married couple ◆ Ampaty yanh arlwenth apekarl anep-anem. *Maybe my child is married.*
SEE ALSO iteng[1], marrert, mwarlenth
arlwenth-ilem (E) *vt.*
marry someone ◆ Unta arlwenth-ilek mwerengkw. *You married your son-in-law.*
arlwenth-irrem (E) *vi.*
get married
= iteng-irrem, marrert-irrem, merangk anem

arlwep (W) acacia bush, elegant acacia SEE UNDER **arlep**

arlwepertaty (T,E) *n.*
1. short and round in shape (someone or something) ◆ Mwanyem arlwepertaty, an katyerr. *Banana-flavoured bush tomatoes are round, and so are desert raisins.* ◆ Apwert arlwepertaty, tyerrty apek arlwa akwek, karteng *shorty one* akwek, 'Arlwepertaty

yanhan apetyem'. (St) *Rocks can be round, and of a small round short person [you can say], 'There is that* arlwepertaty *coming'.*
2. round part of guts, stomach organ ◆ Ker arlwepertaty, atniwemel kel ampernemel. Lyepelyepant iwemel. Arlwepertatyant ampernemel. (Sa) *The round part of the guts are cleaned out and then cooked. Just the intestines are thrown away. The* arlwepertaty *are cooked.*
SEE ALSO arlwa, urtety, karteng, rlwatert, akwek, apwerterrerterr, artwert-artwert

arlwer, **aylwer** (E), **aylur** (E) *n.*
a type of gecko (*Nephrurus* spp.) ◆ Arlwerel anngang arrkay-ilem. (T) *Geckoes make your eyesight fade.*
SEE ALSO irnar
CAN SOUND A BIT LIKE alywer[1] *'dogwood seed'; 'emu chick'*

arlwererrwengk (W) *n.*
a type of spinifex
SEE ALSO aywert

arlwernarr (E) *n.*
1. ceremonial poles, or 'long sticks', used during initiation (young men) ceremony ◆ Arlwernarr-akert urntetyek artwa map. (St) *The men are dancing with the long sticks.*
2. the dance in which the 'long sticks' are used
= arretyet, utemeny
SEE ALSO apwelh, anmanty

arlwerr-arlwerr, **arlurr-arlurr** (E) *n.*
curly, wavy (hair) ◆ Alta arlwerr-arlwerr. *Curly hair.*
kapert arlwerr-arlwerr, **kapert arlurr-arlurr** (E)
curly hair (kapert[1] *'head'*) ◆ Nta kwenh anem perrap kapert arlwerr-arlwerr mwerr angerr kwenh nta anem. (T) *You have really lovely curly hair.*
arlwerrelhem, **arlurrelhem** (E) *vi.*
double up, cramp up, clench up (fist) ◆ Iltya ayeng arlwerrelhem, war ayeng iltya arlwerrelhem alwerrng arrepert-irrem. (St) *My hands are clenching up, the tendons in my hands are doubling up.*
SEE ALSO arrepert-irrem, apwert-irrem, arlwemeny-irrem

arlweth testicles SEE UNDER **arleth**

arlwety[1] (E) *n.*
a type of grasshopper
SEE ALSO intelty, arwekert-arwekert, ntyerlkem

arlwety[2] (W,T) *n.* [RESPECT LANGUAGE]
A special word used by men to refer to certain men who are in a cross-cousin relationship to them, and by women to refer to their *perlawel*. Sometimes referred to in English as 'poison cousin'. ◆ Marlel ilem, 'Arlwety atyenharl apetyewarrem urrek ayeng anamirrenhey kwenh'. (T) *A woman says, 'My* arlwety *are coming, I'll wait a while'.*
= thampartey
SEE ALSO perlawel, alyakw, antewarety
arlwety-penh (W,T) *n.* [RESPECT LANGUAGE]
= **arlwety**[2]
arlwety-irrem (W,T) *vi.* [RESPECT LANGUAGE]
come (used by men to refer to certain other men who are in a cross-cousin relationship to them, and by women to refer to their *perlawel*) ◆ Artwang alenh arlwety-irrentyek. Mer arrpenheng artwang alenh arlwety-irrentyek. (T) *That man has come. My 'poison cousin' has come from another place.* ◆ Yanh kwenh lyengkwert arlwety-irrentyewarrern. (M) *My* perlawel *just came this way today.*
SEE ALSO thampartey-irrem, ahanety-alhem

Arlweyem (W,T) *n.*
the name of a place in the 20 Mile Waterhole area, east of Napperby Station homestead. See map p. viii.

+arn provides emphasis or focus SEE UNDER **+an**[2].

arna, **arnang** (W,T) *n.*
1. tree, bush, plant ◆ Ayeng rrpwamper. Ayengan arnang rlpwererl anem. Ayeng arrken-irrem rrpwamper map-akert arnel akern. (M) *I'm a possum. I live in the hollow log in the tree. I play with other possums, high up in the trees.*
2. A general word that can go before the word for a particular type of tree or plant ◆ Arna uyenper ankerl-kweny. Alyelkarl ra. (St) *The spearbush tree doesn't have any lumps on it. It's smooth.*
3. stick ◆ Arelhel atwek arnakertel angwely yenh. *A woman hit the dog with a stick.*
4. thing, something (not necessarily made out of wood) ◆ Arna ingwer-kenh imeyaw. *Leave that, it's someone else's.* ◆ Arnang nhenh tha mpwarem ltwakelhekarl. (M) *I am fixing this broken thing.*
SEE ALSO antyelty
arnang ayenp (W,T)
bark (of a plant) (ayenp *'skin', 'bark'*) ◆ Arnang ayenp akap-rlwelhem. (T) *The bark is peeling off.*
arna ngkwern (E)
stem, bare stick, tree trunk (ngkwern *'bone', 'stem'*)
arna kanty (E)
tip of branch, top of tree (kanty *'tail'*)
arna akwerrk (E)
young tree (akwerrk[1] *'young animal or plant'*)

arna utneng (E)
the inside part of a tree, centre part of a tree trunk (utneng *'spirit'*)
arna intert (E)
butt or base (of a tree) (intert *'base'*)
= arwerl intert
arneweth (E) *n.*
'What's-his-name' (weth *'that thing being referred to'*) ◆ Nthenh arneweth atyenh uyerrek? *Where's my what's-his-name disappeared to?*

arnakwerlkerl (E) *n.*
caterpillar or grub that eats native currant fruit
SEE ALSO ahakey

arnal-inem (W,T) lift something up SEE UNDER arnwal-inem

arnam *n.*
1. grass ◆ Arntep altywernerl-anem arnamel, arlpelh kwenel altywernerl-anem. Altywernem ra alhemem, nthwerl-apem ra. (N) *The bronzewing pigeon crouches in the grass, amongst the leaves. It crouches there and then it flies around.* ◆ Atek arnamel anenty-angerr. Atek arrtyanem arnam arrpenh-warn, ahelh-angkwarr. *The button quail is a grass-dweller. The quail runs across the ground from one clump of grass to another.*
2. A general word that goes before the name of a particular type of grass. ◆ Antyepanty-wetyam pelangket anetyakenh arnam war, antyepanty-wem arnam arlperlp, arlperlpel akwet intetyam antyamel. (N) *If [we] haven't got any blankets we just spread out grasses, such as the* arlperlp *grass, and then sleep on a blanket of grass.*
= antywer¹
SEE ALSO atherrk
CAN SOUND A BIT LIKE anam *'doing something for someone else'*
arnam werrk (W,T)
scrub (werrk *'scrub'*)
arnam antyerrk
dry grass (antyerrk *'dry'*)
arnam atherrk
fresh green grass (atherrk *'green'*)
arnam apely
fresh green grass, wet grass (apely *'soft'*, *'fresh'*)
arnam-areny (T) *n.*
a type of spirit (lit. 'something that lives in the grass')
= arnamarwengk, irrernt-areny
arnameng-ayerr (E) *n.*
a type of ant from flat ant bed (*akerrth*), flying stage of termite ant (*Amitermes meridionalis*) (lit. 'from the grass')
SEE ALSO ngkwepey

arnamarwengk (W,T) *n.*
a type of spirit
= irrernt-areny, arnam-areny

arnamp *n.*
1. a type of pencil yam (*Vigna lanceolata* var. *lanceolata*). Creeping plant with bright green leaves, yellow flowers and edible roots.
2. the edible root of this yam ◆ Arrwekelenyel arlkwetyam arnamp. (St) *People in the old days ate the* arnamp *pencil yams.*
SEE ALSO arlatyey, anwerlarr, kwatywetarr

arnang (W,T) tree, bush, plant SEE UNDER **arna**

arnang-ilem¹ (E) *vt.*
do something first; do something before someone else ◆ Untek-amperr arnang-ilay. (St) *You have some first.* ◆ Tha mernt arnang-ileyamel-kety ngkweng. (Sa) *I'm going to have some before you do.*
SEE ALSO artang-ilem, ahaylem

arnang-ilem² *vt.*
move someone or something out of the way, shift something ◆ Arna apekarl intep-intem, arnang-ilemel iwem. (St) *A tree that might be lying there is shifted out of the way.*
SEE ALSO anam-ilem, anamelh-ilem, rntwarr-ilem
arnangelh-ilem *vt.* = **arnang-ilem²**
arnang-irrem *vi.*
move over, shift away, move on, move out of the way ◆ Arengk-arey arnang-irrerrirray! (St) *Get out of the way all you dogs!* ◆ Arnang-irremel alhay atyeng *room* anthemel. (T) *Get out the way and give me some room.*
= anam-irrem

arnapar (W,T) *n.*
dingo (*Canis lupus dingo*) ◆ Arnapar akwek antyey anngampelh-ilem. *[It] makes the little dingo pups open their eyes.*
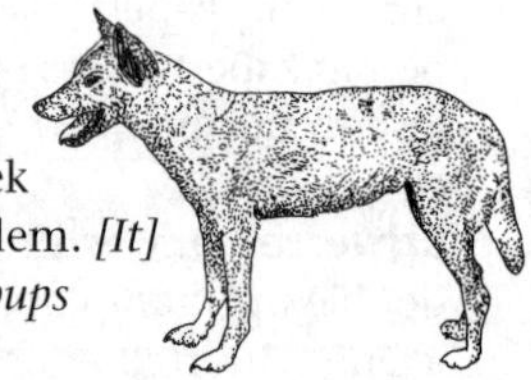
= arnwer¹
CAN SOUND A BIT LIKE arnaper *'deaf'*

arnaper (W,T) *n.*
deaf, unable to hear
= arert, ahert
CAN SOUND A BIT LIKE arnapar *'dingo'*
arnaper-irrem (W,T) *vi.*
go deaf ◆ Arelh ntwang arnaper-irrek — awetyakenh-irrek. (M) *Woman, you've gone deaf — you can't hear.*

arnarem *vt.*
watch someone or something coming towards you ◆ Yanh ulaneng-athek apetyepetyem, arnarem anem renh mer-they

apek arnarep-arem anerl-anemel. (St) *That person is coming in this direction and [I] am watching them come from where I am sitting down in camp.* ◆ Ker aherrel arnaretyam renh ikwer aperteynerlanenty atyerretyek. (Sa) *The kangaroo watched him sneaking up to shoot it.* ◆ Alha ayeng urltaty-irrem alethangek, alethang tha arnarem, arrer ra anem, yalengarl apetyem. Alha ayeng rltwar-irrem, urltaty-irrem. (St) *I have a feeling in my nose about a stranger, and then I see a stranger coming, and then they come closer, from over there. My nose clicks, as I have a premonition.* ◆ Kwerraly Arwenpeng, aremelarl renh aremel akem-irrem *early*-pal anem renh arem, anentyerlek anem renh arnarem. Kel aherrk anem irrentyem. *The Daylight Star is the one that you see early in the morning. You see it coming up and then the sun comes up.*
SEE ALSO atwarem, arnek-arnarem, arnek-irrem

arnarnk (W,T) *n.*
chest ◆ Artwang nhenh arnarnk aketh. (T) *This man has a bare chest.*
SEE ALSO uneng[1]

arnartew (W,T) *n.*
hungrily, with great appetite ◆ Angayel arlkwek arnartewek — arnterr arlkwek. (T) *[I] ate a real lot because I had such an appetite — I really ate.*

arnaty (W) *n.*
root of bush banana, silky pear (*Marsdenia australis*)
= artwey-artwey[1], atnety
SEE ALSO alangkw, parl

arnek-irrem *vi.*
go and meet someone; go towards someone who is approaching ◆ Yanhek arnek-irrerl-alha, ker-akertek arnek-irra — kerek aretyek. (Sa) *Go and meet that person, meet the person who has meat — go and see if there's meat.* ◆ *Hawker*-ek arnek-irrerl-alhem. (Sa) *Going to meet the hawker.*

arnek-arnarem *vi.* = **arnek-irrem** ◆ Artwang apetyem aker-akert, kwer map arnek-arnarirrem angayel. (T) *The man is coming with the kangaroo meat and the hungry kids are going to meet him.* ◆ Ayeng arnek-arnarirrem marnt-warn, yay atyengenharl apety-alpemek. *I am going to meet my big sister who is coming back on the bus.*

arnekarnar *n.*
meeting up with someone; going towards someone who is approaching ◆ Arnekarnar ayeng alhem apetyarr-alpemek apek. *I'm going to go and meet [the person] that is coming.*

arnekarnar alhem
go back and look for something (?); go and meet someone ◆ Ayeng alhem arnekarnar, mwetekay apekarl akelhekek. (St) *I'm going to go and meet [them] because the car might have broken down.* ◆ Arnekarnar alhem tyerrty arrpenharl uyerrekek. (St) *Going back to look for the person who has disappeared.*

arnelheng, artnelheng (E) *n.* [RESPECT LANGUAGE]
two ◆ Artnelhengarrp ahanenhek. Akngerrant alhetyang. (St) *Just the two of them went [at least one of whom is in a respect relationship to the speaker]. Not a lot of people went.*
SEE ALSO atherr[1]

arnem, artnem (E) *vi.*
1. cry, wail, bawl ◆ Arnem, alharrpelam arnemam, tyerrtyarl ywerremeng. (T) *Feeling sorry and crying because somebody has passed away.* ◆ Arelh map arnerlatherr-anem rlkerteng. (M) *Some women are crying for the sick man.* ◆ Kwer akwek arnem angayel. (T) *The baby is crying because she is hungry.*
2. howl, whine or make other crying sounds (animals) ◆ Arrpwarnt angkerreperrerl — *everywhere* arrpwarnt angkerrerl-anemel, iylpan arwengk-ilem, arengkel-rneman. Artnemel arlka. *The dogs are barking — everywhere the dogs are barking and howling and deafening our ears.* ◆ Arengk yanh tyarl-waw, mpwek apekarl arnep-arnem. *Let the dog go, because it's whining and might want to go to the toilet.*
= arrangkem
CAN SOUND A BIT LIKE anem[1] *'sit';* anem[2] *'now and then';* anem[3] *'digging stick'*

arnelh-ilem, artnelh-ilem (E) *vt.*
make someone cry ◆ Tha apek ngenh artnelh-ilety-alhem, arntety apekarl arrpenh intemeng. (St) *I might cause you to cry, over that person that is sick.* ◆ Ampa tha apekarl atwek, artnelh anem ilem. (St) *If I hit that kid then it will make them cry.*
= arrangkelh-angkelh-ilem

arnelh-ilerrem, artnelh-ilerrem (E) *vi.*
cry together (in mourning) ◆ Arnelh-ilerrem arelh atherr. (M) *The two women are crying in mourning.*

arnelh-arnelh-ilerrem, artnelh-artnelh-ilerrem (E) *vi.*
cry together in mourning (many people) ◆ Ayeng apek alhemel wal tha awerlpawem, artnelh-artnelh-ilerrerlek. (St) *I might go and then I start to hear all the people crying in mourning.*

arnemerr (T,E) *n.kin*
1. father-in-law

2. father-in-law's brothers (note Warlpiri *jarnimirri* 'relationship between a speaker's mother and their mother's mother')
SEE ALSO ahenterr, maly, maly-maly, ampwek, ampaty-ampaty
arnemerraty (T,E) *n.kin*
my/our *arnemerr*
CAN SOUND A BIT LIKE anemarraty *'type of plant'*
arnemerrwengk (T,E) *n.kin*
your *arnemerr* ◆ Arnemerrwengk akeweny yanh anep-anem. (T) *Your poor old father-in-law is sitting over there.* ◆ Yanh artwehenh ngkweng mert-henh anywek arnemerrwengkarl kwenh. Marlel ilem artwel apek ilem alakenh. (T) *Your spouse's father is your* arnemerr. *Both women and men say that.*
arnemerrikw (T,E) *n.kin*
his/her/their *arnemerr*
arnemerrekw (T) *n.kin*
1. your *arnemerr*
2. his/her/their *arnemerr* ◆ Arnemerrekw atherr apety-alherrek. (T) *Her two fathers-in-law came.* ◆ Arelh yanh arnemerrekwel-arleng alhern. (T) *That woman just went with her father-in-law.*
arnemerr-nheng (T,E) *n.kin*
a group of two or more people who are related to each other as *arnemerr*
arnemerr-intyerr (T,E) *n.kin* = **arnemerr-nheng**
arnemerr-nheng-arey (T,E) *n.kin*
a group of more than two people who are related to each other as *arnemerr*
arnemerr-nheng atherr (T,E) *n.kin*
someone together with their *arnemerr*
arnemerr-parety (E) *n.kin*
respectful or 'sorry way' of talking about someone's *arnemerr*
SEE ALSO -parety
arnemerr-ankethenh (E) *n.kin*
1. having a close *arnemerr* still alive
2. someone who is always with their *arnemerr*
SEE ALSO -ankethenh

-arneng *n.ending*
someone or something that is closely related to another person or thing (particularly said of siblings and cross-cousins). This ending always follows *+ek*, *+eh* or an equivalent pronoun (see below). ◆ Twern-twernan yerrampeh-arneng. (M) *The* twern-twern *ant is closely related to the honeyant.* ◆ Alparrantyey, ararnt, arlelyek — *different* ingkerr. Ararntek-arneng. Alparrantyey. Ntyer-areny. Alparrantyey, ararnt *and* arlelyek *are all different.* Alparrantyey *is closely related to the* ararnt. *It's found in the floodout country.* ◆ Atyeng-arneng ingkerr, atyeng ipelty-ipelty-rnem. (Sa) *These people are all my close relations, all my friends.* ◆ Atyeng-ayteyan atyeng-arnengarl. (Sa) *My younger brother or sister is my close relation.*
arneng-arneng (E) *n.*
relations
atyeng arneng
my close relations (especially siblings or cousins) (atyeng *'for me', 'to me'*) ◆ Atyeng arneng-rnem an atyenh *brother*-rnem anem *Stirling*-el. (Sa) *All my close relations are my brothers at Stirling.*
ngkweng-arneng
your close relations (especially siblings or cousins) (ngkweng *'for you', 'to you'*) ◆ Ngkweng-arneng alhek. (Sa) *Your brother/sister/cousin went.* ◆ Ngkweng-arneng-warl alhay! (St) *Go back to your relations!*
ikwer-arneng
his/her/their close relations (especially siblings or cousins) (ikwer *'for him/her', 'to him/her'*)

arnengerr *n.*

1. with hands held together behind your back; hands clasped behind back, with one hand holding on to the other arm behind the back ◆ Arelh arnengerr ntywem-atheh alhep-alhem. (M) *The woman is going away from me with her hands clasped behind her back.*
2. carrying something held behind one's back
arnengerr-ilem *vt.*
1. put someone's hands behind their back ◆ Arnengerr-ilem mpweny apek atwetyek apek. (Sa) *Putting [the person's] hands behind their back to race off with them or maybe to hit them.* ◆ Urlaylpelarl arnengerr-ilety-alhemel. (Sa) *The kurdaitcha goes and puts [the person's] hands behind their back.*
2. tie a perentie's legs behind its back (in order to cook it)

Arnengerr (W) *n.*
name of place north of Mt Allan community

arnenthernem (E), **artnenthernem** (E) *vi.*
burp, hiccough
= anetyerrkernem, anetyerrk-irrem, arltarernem

arnernkem *vi.*
1. say that you don't know about something; say that you have nothing to do with something; not know about something
◆ Ywarn kwer ayeng arnernkemarl. (T) *I don't know that person.* ◆ Arelh arrpel apek

apawenhem, wal ya arnernkem. 'Ayeng kwenh aretyakenh — arnernkem.' (T) *Another woman might ask her, and she says she doesn't know anything about it. 'I didn't see it — I don't know about it.'* ◆ Wenheh ntam ayeng apawenhay? Ayengan arnernkemam. (M) *Why are you asking me? It's nothing to do with me.*
2. get sick of something, dislike or be uninterested in something, be fed up ◆ Arnernkemel ayeng alpetyekeyay. (Sa) *I'm sick of this place and I want to go back home.*
SEE ALSO apatem

arnernkelhem (W) *vi.*
not say anything, not get involved ◆ Arelh yanh arnernkelhemel irnem. (M) *That woman is standing there not saying anything.*

arnernkey *n.*
sitting down in one place without doing anything; lazy, having no motivation, not wanting to do things, not really concentrating, being slow, taking your time to do things ◆ Ntwan arnernkey anem. (M) *You're not paying attention.*
SEE ALSO akwenp

arnernkey-irrem *vi.*
be sulky or uncooperative, not want to do something ◆ Kwer nhenh map arnernkey-irrem, kwerleng ina arnernkem. Ankwepenh *I think* ina arnernkey anerl-anem. (T) *These kids are being sulky about school, they're not interested in going to school. I think it's because they just got out of bed.*

arnerr, **artnerr** (E) *n.*
rockhole ◆ Tyerrtyel angkwey kwaty antywetyart arnerr-penh. (T) *In the olden days Aboriginal people used to drink from rockholes.*

arnerrem, **artnerrem** (E) *vi.*
crawl ◆ Kwer akwek arnerrem amwek-warn. (T) *The little baby is crawling towards his/her mother.* ◆ Amwek anerl-anem. Kwer akwek arnerrerl-apem arnerrerl-apem aweth apety-alpem, arnerrenty-alpem. (N) *His/her mother is sitting there. The child crawls along, crawls along and then comes back again, crawls back.*

arnerrenty, **artnerrenty** (E) *n.*
crawling baby, a baby of crawling age
SEE ALSO athathingk

arnerrenty-iperr (T,E), **artnerrenty-iperr** (E), **arnarrenty-iperr** (E) *n.* = **arnerrenty**
◆ Arnerrenty-iperr ampa akwek, lyetantarl artnerrerl-anem. (Sa) *A crawling baby, one that has just started crawling.*

arnerrekenty, **artnerrakenty** (E) *n.*
= **arnerrenty**

arnewem (W) *vt.*
throw hot soil or ashes at someone (in anger) ◆ Rwang rtwapel arnewem, apeth-warl wetyek, artwel anywelek. (M) *The father throws the hot ashes at the lap [of the woman].*
CAN SOUND A BIT LIKE anewem *'name something', 'to call somebody or something by a name'*

arneyel nhwerrem (W,T) *vi.*
rub chests together (at particular ceremonies) ◆ Arelh atherr arneyel nhwerrem ntwerlengarl ilerrem-penh. (M) *The two women are rubbing their chests together after becoming* ntwerleng *[special ceremonial relationship] for each other.*

arnka, **arnkang** (W,T), **artnka** (E) *n.*
cliff, steep rockface. Also referred to as *apwert arnka.* ◆ Arnkang irntang angerr, can't antyerl. (T) *An* arnkang *is a big rock that [you] can't climb up.* ◆ Ngkwerlp rnpwernp arnkelarl anem, inteyelarl anem. (T) *The rock pituri is the one that grows on steep rockfaces, and in caves.*

Arnka (W,T), **Arnkang** (W,T) *n.*
Mt Leichhardt. See map p. viii.

arnkarnp (T,E) *adv.*
being in a hurry to do something; rushing off and leaving things behind ◆ Arnkarnpelarl iwerl-alhek mern arlka *tea* arlka, arrewelhemel. (St) *She was in such a hurry to go she left the food and the tea behind.*
= ngwarrertakert
SEE ALSO arrewelhem

arnkarr *n.*
bank of a river or creek, riverbank, creekbank ◆ Arnkarr-angkwerr anarnpenhem lpway-warn kwaty arnwengk-iletyeh. (N) *[We] climb down the riverbank to the riverbed to dig a soakage.*
SEE ALSO lher twemper, lher twerr, twerr, akwerlp, arnka
CAN SOUND A BIT LIKE ankarr *'juice of bush plum'*

arnkarr-ilem (T,E) *vt.*
erode, wash earth away ◆ Arnkarr, kwatyelarl arnkarr-ilek. (St) *The bank of the creek, where the water has eroded it.*
SEE ALSO ilerrty-ilem, thalkerr-ilem

arnkarr-akem (W) *vt.* = **arnkarr-ilem**

arnkarr-akelhem (T) *vi.*
become eroded, get washed away (earth) ◆ Kwaty rew pwelap alhem arnkarran arnkarr-akelhem anem. (T) *A big flood goes along and the creekbank gets washed away.*

irntang arnkarr-arnkarr (W)
a gorge, steep rockface or cliff (irntang *'hill', 'rock'*)

SEE ALSO tyarrp-tyarrp, arnka

arnkarr-arnkarr aiming at something SEE UNDER **angkarr-angkarr**

arnkaty (T,E) *n.*
brave, fearless, confident ◆ Ayengan arnkaty atnew-atnew alhem aterek arrangkw. (Sa) *I'm brave and I go anywhere without being frightened.*
= anew-anew
SEE ALSO irrpelth, rrkwanth, alhewer, lywenpeny

arnkaty-ilelhem (T,E) *vt.*
become empowered; get worked up (for a fight), make oneself strong to protect oneself
SEE ALSO arawerrng inem

Arnkawenyerr (E) *n.*
name of place and outstation west of the Sandover River on the Alyawarra Aboriginal Land Trust. See map p. viii.

arnkely *n.*
sulky, silent, in a huff, 'proper wild' ◆ Ilek-they nga arnkelyan anetyel? Angketyakenh arnkely ahel. Ilelha atyengay. Ilek-apertarl ngan anep-anem tyernetyangan? Arntety apek nga awelhek apek ilelhetyang. (Sa) *Why are you sitting there sulkily? You are sulky and angry and not saying anything. Tell me. Why are you sitting there and not answering? Maybe you felt sick and you're not saying anything about it.* ◆ Ntarl atyeng tyel angkerneng, arnkely anem ayeng ngkweng anem. (St) *You talked behind my back and now I am sulky with you.*
SEE ALSO kewarr, kekart

arnkely-irrem *vi.*
get sulky, be in a huff ◆ Iwenhengakap atyeng arnkely-irrem? Amerneng apek, kereng apek, ngkweltyeng apek? (M) *Why are you in a huff with me? Is it over food, or meat, or money?*
SEE ALSO kekart-irrem, kewarr-irrem

arnkengeny (E) *n.*
many, a mob, a lot ◆ Arnkengeny akarr-irrem mer arrpanenh-they — mer arrpanenh-they apetyepety-alpem akarr-irrem. (Sa) *Lots of people are gathering together from all the different places — they are all coming together from all over the place.*
SEE ALSO alhirrel, map, anengk[1], angerr[1]

ingka arnkengeny (E)
centipede (lit. 'many feet'). This word is used because another word for centipede is *kwementyay* in the eastern Anmatyerr region.
= arnperrk, arrpanty, ingka

arnkenty *n.*
1. men's camp, single-men's camp, single-men's quarters ◆ Artwang map anerl-anem arnkentyel. (T) *The men are sitting in the single-men's camp.* ◆ Inpert-irrek, yanh arnkenty-warl irrek. (St) *That man has become a widower, has gone to the single-men's camp.*
SEE ALSO arlweker
2. a star constellation; the Saucepan (part of Orion) • SEE ALSO Anterl, Arlanty, Ingkapeny, Ingkartek, Pwereytarr

arnkenty-areny *n.*
1. single man; man without a wife, widower
2. a man who lives in the single-men's camp (-areny '*inhabitant of*') ◆ Artwa arnkentyel intep-intem mapam yanhan. Arnkenty-areny mapey apetyewarrem ankey. (T) *That mob over there are the men that sleep in the single-men's camp. All the men from the single-men's camp come up asking for things.*

arnkenty-warn-irrem (W,T),
arnkenty-warl-irrem (E) *vi.*
become a widower; lose wife (lit. 'go to the single-men's camp') ◆ Arnkenty-warn-irrek artwa. (M) *The man has become a widower.*
SEE ALSO arlweker-warn-irrem, warlekwert-irrem, inpert-irrem

arnkentyeng-arnkenty *n.*
boy's cubbyhouse ◆ Ampa urrey map anem arnkentyeng-arnkentyel, an marl map anerl-anem arlwekereng-arlwekerel. (T) *The boys are in the boys' cubbyhouse and the girls are in the girls' cubbyhouse.*
SEE ALSO mereng-amer, arlwekereng-arlweker, nyetyep, alyetyepengalyety, antyweng-antyweng

Arnkenty (W,T) *n.*
the name of a waterhole, 8 Mile Soak in the Napperby Creek

arnkerrth (T,E) *n.*
mountain devil, thorny devil (*Moloch horridus*)
= nywerr, mernerr

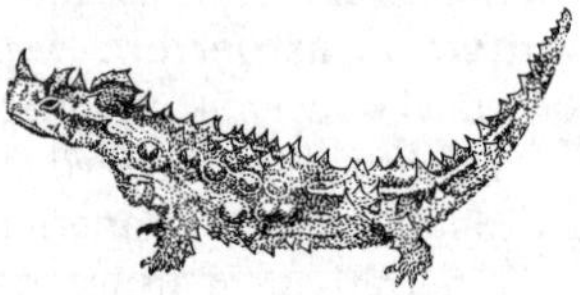

arnkety scarf, headscarf SEE UNDER **ankety**

arnkwa (E) *n.*
clothes and blankets, personal belongings
SEE ALSO rnwanenty, mantarr, irrpenh-irrpenh

arnkwayerr (E) *n.* [RESPECT LANGUAGE]
clothes, things ◆ Kwey arnkwayerr irrepetha, ngwarrekengkwenh. (Sa) *Daughter, go and get your husband's clothes [said by the mother of the woman].*

arnkwarn (E), **ankwarn** (E) *n.*
sleep (in the eyes when you wake up); pus in a sore ◆ Alknga ankwarn-ankwarnarl ayeng irrek-kety, utyen alknga ankwarn-ankwarn aretyakenh. Alknga ankwarn-akert. Utyenan

ankwarn anthwek. (Sa) *My eyes have gone all pussy, my eyes are sore and pussy and I can't see. My eyes have got pus in them. It's seeping from my sore eyes.*
= rrkwa

arnkwerrng (E) *n.*
cracked ground, a crack in the ground ◆ Arlewatyerr kwen anerl-anem arnkwerrngel. Intyer-ampeny *crack*-irretyel, arnkwerrngel anem ra anetyel. (Sa) *The goanna is living inside a crack in the ground. The ground cracks where the floodout is, and then the goanna lives there.*
SEE ALSO awal

arnkwert *n.*
crooked, bent, twisted, curved, bowed
arnkwert-arnkwert *n.*
crooked, bent, twisted, curved, bowed, not in a straight line ◆ Kel arnkwert-arnkwert kweny — arraty akwet alhem kwenh. (Sa) *Don't go crooked — keep going in a straight line.* (T) ◆ Amwa arrpenhem arratyeny alhem, kel amwa arrpenhem alhem arnkwert-arnkwert. (T) *Some snakes go along in a straight line and some follow a crooked path.*
= amper-amper, irrkert-irrkert, iylwerl-iylwerl, lew-lew, rtapety
SEE ALSO arratyeny
arnkwert alhem
go in a crooked line (alhem *'go'*)
arnkwert-ilem *vt.*
bend or twist something
arnkwertelhem *vi.*
be crooked, get bent or twisted ◆ Lpway yanh arnkwertelhem. (T) *That river is crooked.*

arnman[1], **arlpman** (T,E), **artnman** (E) *n.kin*
A respectful way of referring to the mother or the mother's brother of a person with whom the speaker is in an avoidance relationship. For example, a woman may use *arnman* to refer to her son-in-law's mother or mother's brother, or a man may use *arnman* to refer to his mother-in-law's mother or mother's brother. ◆ Mweraty Ngal. Rapek anewikw angkem, 'Arnmanekengkw-warl ahanenhaw, weyapelek atyeng'. (St) *My [woman speaking] son-in-law is Ngal. He might say to his wife, 'Go to your mother and get me some meat'.*
SEE ALSO marley, amey
arnmanikw, artnmanikw (E), **arlpmanikw** (E) *n.kin*
his/her *arnman* ◆ Urrerikw then arlpmanikw then arrepirrerr-ilentyarretyek ra. (Sa) *He is going to see his father and mother [said by a woman in reference to her son-in-law].*
arnmanengkw, arlpmanengkw (T,E), **artnmanengkw** (E) *n.kin*
your *arnman* ◆ 'Artnmanekengkw angkerlanetyal.' Math kwerenhel ilep-ilem, *daughter* kwerenhek. (St) *'Don't talk to your husband's mother.' A mother might say that to her daughter.*
arnman-nheng, arlpman-nheng (T,E), **artman-nheng** (E) *n.kin*
a group of two or more people related as mother and child, or maternal uncle and nephew or niece (said by a woman if one of them is her son-in-law, or by a man if one of them is his mother-in-law) ◆ Kemarr then Ngwarray then ap alhetyek. Petyarr then alhetyek ilak then Pwerl then. 'Arlpman-nheng.' Arelh mwerelikw ilem. (Sa) *A Kemarr person and a Ngwarray person might be going. Or a Petyarr and a Pwerl. 'Arlpman-nheng.' [That's] what his mother-in-law says [about her son-in-law and his mother or maternal uncle].* ◆ *Uncle* kwerenhel-arleng ra alhek, 'artnman-nheng' war ilem, marlelarl ilem. (St) *If he [the woman's son-in-law] has gone with his uncle, well the woman just says* 'artnman-nheng' *to refer to the two of them going together.*
arnman-nheng atherr, arlpman-nheng atherr (T,E), **artnman-nheng atherr** (E) *n.kin*
a mother and their child or a maternal uncle and their nephew or niece (said by a woman if one of them is her son-in-law, or by a man if one of them is his mother-in-law)

arnman[2], **arlpman** (T,E), **artnman** (E) *n.*
honeyant worker (black and yellow ants outside the honeyants' nest) ◆ Arnman nhenh apep-apem — anantherr arey kwenh. (T) *Here the honeyant workers are going along — we'll have a look.* ◆ Arnman nthwek yalengeng — arraty nhenh alhweng. (T) *The worker honeyant went along there — and here's the hole.*
SEE ALSO yerramp, inkwareny
Arnmanapwenty (T,E), **Arlpmanapwenty** (T) *n.*
Long Range, Ti Tree/Stirling Station area. See map p.viii. ◆ Mer Arnmanapwentyel anganek yerramp. (T) *The honeyants originated from Arnmanapwenty.*

arnmeny, arlpmeny (E) *n.*
ashes ◆ Arelhel item arnmeny ngkerlpek. (T) *The woman is cooking ashes for chewing with tobacco.* ◆ Tyerrtyel arwernp arlkwem arnmenyel-ayeng. (N) *People chew pituri with ashes.*
= ikwenty
SEE ALSO arlpa[1], atnmanth, awerrth, ntyerlp[1], amerrk[2], rtwap

arnmeny-irrem, arlpmeny-irrem (E) *vi.*
turn to ashes, burn down to ashes ◆ Aperrk-irremel, arnmeny anem irrem, pelaw-artek. (T) *[The fire] turns to coals, then burns down to ashes, like flour.* ◆ Rwang arnmeny-irrem. (N) *The fire is burning down to ash.*
arnmeny item, arlpmeny item (E)
prepare ashes for chewing with tobacco, 'cook' ashes (item '*cook something*')

arnngem, arlkngem (E), **arlngem** (E) *vt.*
wipe, wash or clean something; wipe something off something ◆ Kwer akwek apek arnngem annga. (M) *Wiping the child's eyes.* ◆ Arlkngemarl mernarl arlkwem-penh, ampeny. Manter atyenh tha arlkngetyek, *wash*-em-iletyek. (St) *Wipe the leftovers off after eating. I'll clean my clothes, wash them.* ◆ Alhang arnngelhetyeh anketyel, mernt-penh apek. Kwatyel war anngey, arnngelherl-wetyeh kwatyel, thwep-kwenyeng. (P) *[You can] wipe your nose with a rag if it's snotty. You can just clean it with water if you haven't got any soap.*
SEE ALSO irrarlkem, iparem, rrpwarem, urrparem
CAN SOUND A BIT LIKE angem *'take', 'carry'*
arnngelhem, arlkngelhem (E) *vi.*
wipe or clean yourself, wipe something off yourself ◆ Ahern apek inngerr-warl, inngerrek apek ahern ipekarl, wal arnngelhem. (St) *If there is dirt on your face, well then you can wipe it clean.* (M) ◆ Kwatyel ayeng arlkngelhetyek alknga. (St) *I am cleaning my eyes with water.*

arnpakem *vt.*
1. stop someone from going somewhere or from doing something ◆ Thwengk arnpakem. (N) *I am going to stop you from going.* ◆ Kwer yanh arnpakerl-alpay amwekety. Angerr mapant ina alhetyenheng. (T) *Go and stop that child from going, because of the snakes. Only the big kids can go.* ◆ Tyerrty yanh-areyarl atwerrem. Arnpakem anem renh. (T) *Those people over there are fighting. Then [someone] stops them.* ◆ Ngkwarl antywetyal anetyeh, arnpakerrem, *might* rlkert-irrerl. (M) *Stopping someone from going and drinking grog, in case they get sick.*
SEE ALSO ayakem, arrngert-irrem, akayak-ilem, apatel-anthem
2. trip someone up, trip someone over ◆ Atyeng-angkwerr alhem apal wal ngenh arnpakem anem atnyem anem. Ayenh apek unta rlkerr intemel arnpakem. (St) *If you are going past me without noticing, then I might trip you up and then you fall. If you are lying with your legs stretched out then you might trip me up.* ◆ Arengkel ayeng arnpakem. (St) *The dog tripped me up.*
SEE ALSO ankert-wem
arnpakelhem *vi.*
be tripped up by something ◆ Ingka-kenhel ayeng arnpakelhem (St) *The shoes tripped me up.*

arnpan (T,E) *n.*
bits of dark-coloured pollen found on the ground under a tree where a native beehive is ◆ Arnpan akely renh iwerl-anem ra arlkwerl-anem. Ameng yanhel-rnem iwerl-anem. Ahern-warl. Kel aremel alyangkwek apek kel aretyek altywernemel. 'Nhenh-antey kwang akern.' Urrperl ap ra. Arnpan, ampeny-ampeny. Arlkwetyelarl-penh. (Sa) Arnpan *are the small bits that the honey bee throws down after eating. (?) The honey bees throw it away, down to the ground. Then in the winter time the [person] bends down and sees it. 'Here it is [the native bee hive], up here.' It is dark in colour.* Arnpan *are the leftovers, after eating.*
= atyang[2]
Arnpan (T) *n.*
name of place and location of community, known as Six Mile or Ti Tree Six Mile. Also known as Pmara Jutunta. See map p. viii.

arnpem *vi.*
set out, head off, leave to go somewhere
CAN SOUND A BIT LIKE anpem *'touch something'*
arnperl-alhem *vi.*
set out, head off ◆ Awenhwek an anywek aweth arnperl-alhek. Petyarlerrek angketyeh aperlehekw. (M) *The auntie and father set out again. The two of them went to talk to the child's grandmother.*
arnpenhem *vi.*
set out, head off ◆ Inang arnpenhem, alpem ina mer kwer-warl. (N) *They are setting off, and going back to the place.*

arnperrk *n.*
centipede ◆ Arnperrk kwaty-taym arratem. (T) *Centipedes come out in the wet weather.*

= ingka arnkengeny, arrpanty

arnperrkenty (W,T) *n.*
small amount of running water after a flood. Also referred to as *kwaty arnperrkenty.* ◆ Kwaty yanh alhep-alhem arnperrkenty, akwekemek. (T) *There is just a little bit of floodwater running along.*
SEE ALSO rew

arntampernem (E) *vt.* [RESPECT LANGUAGE]
cook ◆ Arntampernetyel ngwarrelengkw. Ker arntampernem. (St) *[Daughter], your husband is*

cooking meat [said by the mother of the woman].
SEE ALSO angwey-ilem, irrkwertem, ulerrtyem, ampernem, item, ampem

arntap *n.*
bark (of a plant)
SEE ALSO arrngelh, ayenp
arntap iyltem (E)
peel bark off a plant or tree

arntap-arntap (W,T) *n.*
a type of insect (possibly sandfly) ◆ Arntap-arntapel arlkwem aherrkel. Arlkwem, atwelherl-anem atwelherl-anem atwelherl-anem — ankwa kweny. Kwaty-penhant war. (N) *The* arntap-arntap *bites you in the summer. They bite and you slap at them and slap at them — you don't get any sleep. This just happens after rain.*

arntarlkw V-shape, forked tree or stick SEE UNDER antarlkw

arntarlperrk, antarlperrk *n.*

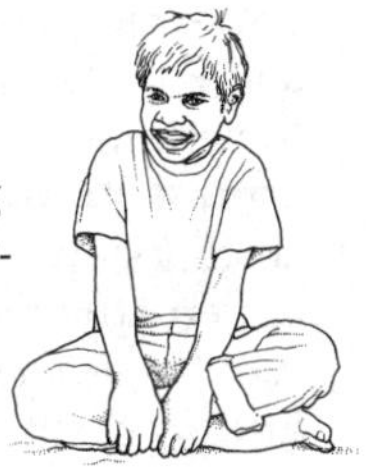

(sitting) cross-legged; doing something in a cross-legged position ◆ Antarlperrk ayeng anep-anem. *I am sitting cross-legged.* ◆ Arntarlperrkel mern iterl-anem. Ker arlka iterl-anem arntarlperrk anerl-anem. (N) *Sitting cross-legged and cooking food. Sitting cross-legged and cooking meat as well.*
= aymparrk anem

arntarnt-arem *vt.*
look after someone or something; watch out for someone; care for someone or something, mind someone or something ◆ Arntarnt-arerl-anem mwerr ntwang ayeng, arratyem anthem tey arlka kwenh, mern arlka, ker arlka. (N) *You are looking after me well, giving me tea and bread and meat.*
arntarnt-arelhem *vi.*
look after yourself, watch out for yourself ◆ Manty arntarnt-arelhem — arerl-anemel, irrerntel atwekety. (N) *Look after yourself — watch out, or the cold might get to you.*
SEE ALSO iwerr arelhem

arntarrk anem (W) squat (on toes or flat-footed) SEE UNDER **artarnk anem**

arntatherrk (E) slime SEE UNDER **arntwatherrk**[1]

arntay (W,T) *n.*
deep water, a big, wide waterhole. Also referred to as *kwaty arntay.* ◆ Twern-penh apetyemel, kwaty arntayek irrpem, irrpety-alpem, lyweny-penh. (T) *After hunting in the hot sun, [you] go swimming in the wide waterhole.*
SEE ALSO akern, kwaty kanty
CAN SOUND A BIT LIKE intay *'stallion'*
arntay-ilem (W,T) *vt.*
dig a hole out to make it wider ◆ Kwaty yanh arntay-ilay kwer akwek irrpetyeh. (T) *Dig that water [hole] wide for the little baby to swim in.* ◆ Mern anaty arntay-ilemel nyetyek. (T) *Dig the bush yam's hole wider.*

arntayl (E) *n.*
pigeon-toed. Also referred to as *ingka arntayl.*
SEE ALSO amper-amper, ingka
CAN SOUND A BIT LIKE antay *'rope of hairstring'*

arntek (T,E) *n.*
tooth, teeth ◆ *Baby one*-an arrakert arrangkwarl-areny, arntek anetyakenh. Ampa angerr irrem arntek-akert anem irrem, arratem apek, lyapem apek. (St) *Babies have empty mouths, they don't have any teeth. When they get bigger they get teeth, the teeth come out or grow.*
= rtety[1]
CAN SOUND A BIT LIKE antek *'wide'*
arntek arlkwem (T,E)
have a toothache
= rtety arekar-irrem, rtety arlkwem

arntek-arntek (E) *n.*
1. dog-eye bush tomato, bony-fruited bush tomato (*Solanum quadriloculatum*). A plant about 35 cm high, with soft grey-green leaves, purple flowers and angular shaped fruits. The fruits are poisonous and should NOT be eaten.
2. the inedible fruits of the dog-eye bush tomato
= arengkerlpart

arntekakarl (E), **arntekakel** (E), **arntekakal** (E) *n.*
a type of lizard (?)

arntem *vi.*
ache, be in pain ◆ Arteparl arntem. Ayengarl artep arntem, intem ayeng. (N) *My back is aching. My back is aching, and I'm lying down.* ◆ Kapert ayeng arntemaw! (St) *My head is aching!*

arnteng, arntengey (T,E) *n.kin*
1. a woman's sister-in-law (brother's wife or husband's sister)
2. a woman's sister-in-law's sisters
3. particular relations with the same skin as a woman's *arnteng.* If a woman calls another woman *arnteng,* then that woman calls her *arnteng* in return.
arnteng-arnteng *n.kin*
1. a woman's sister-in-law (brother's wife or husband's sister) etc.
2. a woman's sister-in-law (brother's wife or

husband's sister) etc. [BABY TALK]
arntengaty *n.kin*
my/our *arnteng*
arntengengkw *n.kin*
your *arnteng*
arntengikw (E), **arntengeyekw** (E) *n.kin*
her/their *arnteng*
arntengekw (W,T) *n.kin*
1. your *arnteng*
2. her/their *arnteng*
arnteng-nheng *n.kin*
a group of two or more people related to each other as *arnteng* ◆ Aylanth arnteng-nheng urrpety anerl-anem. Arnteng-nheng-arey, ingkerr. (Sa) *There's a few of us here who are related to each other as sisters-in-law to each other. We are all related like that.*
arnteng-intyerr *n.kin* = **arnteng-nheng**
arnteng-nheng-arey (T,E) *n.kin*
a group of more than two people related to each other as *arnteng*
arnteng-nheng atherr *n.kin*
a person together with their *arnteng*
arnteng-ankethenh *n.kin*
1. having a close *arnteng* still alive
2. someone who is always with their *arnteng*
SEE ALSO -ankethenh
arnteng-parety *n.kin*
respectful or 'sorry way' of talking about someone's *arnteng*
SEE ALSO -parety

arntep *n.*
common bronzewing, bronzewing pigeon (*Phaps chalcoptera*). Also referred to as *ker arntep* (note Warlpiri *ngarntipi*). ◆ Arntep altywernerl-anem arnamel, arlpelh kwenel altywernerl-anem. Altywernem ra alhemem, nthwerl-apem ra. (N) *The bronzewing pigeon crouches in the grass, amongst the leaves. It crouches there and then it flies around.* ◆ Arntep kwenyel apetyem, arlpang atherr rltar-irrem. *The bronzewing pigeon comes in the night and flaps its wings.*
= arekwarr (?)

arnteparl, **arntepwarl** (W) *n.*
black gidgee (*Acacia pruinocarpa*). Tree to 5 m high, with smooth grey bark, bluish green leaves and golden yellow flowers. ◆ Lywang irnem, anwern arnmeny renh akem, atyarnp-irrwengerr antey. Atyarnp arnmeny inem an arnteparl arnmeny inem. Anwern akemarl *seed* war alhernterek war anwa akem, alyapelh-iletyeh, *sell*-em-ilem anwern. (N) *The black gidgee is good shade, and we collect ashes from it as well. We get ashes from the ironwood and the gidgee. We collect the seeds just to sell to sell to whitefellas so that they can grow the trees.*
arnteparl altywer-ilenh (W,T), **arntepwarl altywer-ilenh** (W,T) *n.*
a type of insect that bores holes in the black gidgee (lit. 'that makes holes in the black gidgee')

arnterr *adv.*
(doing something) a lot; (doing something) forcefully or intensively, really (doing something)
arnterr arlkwem
eat a lot, eat greedily (arlkwem *'eat'*) ◆ Angayelarl arnterr arlkwetyek mern arlka aker arlka. (T) *Hungrily eating a lot of bread and meat.*
SEE ALSO nyant arlkwem, ahanthem, arrwer-ilem
arnterr untem (E), **arnterr ntwem** (W,T)
run fast (untem *'run'*)
arnterr angkem
talk a lot, talk excessively, talk loudly, say something loudly (angkem *'talk'*, *'speak'*)
arnterr atherrem
laugh loudly (atherrem *'laugh'*) ◆ Arelh yanh arnterr atherrem. (T) *That woman is killing herself laughing.*
arnterr arem
stare hard at something or somebody (arem *'look'*, *'see'*)

arntert, **arnteyt** (E) *n.*
1. rotten, stinking, bad (especially of meat) ◆ Ker arntert intyem. (St) *The meat smells off.*
SEE ALSO iynteng, akeng, aywek
2. something you don't like; awful, no good
CAN SOUND A BIT LIKE ntert *'quiet'*
arntert-irrem, **arnteyt-irrem** (E) *vi.*
decay, become rotten, go bad, go off (especially of meat) ◆ Ker arntert-irrekaw nhenhaw — iweyant anem. *This meat has gone off — just throw it away.* ◆ Ker uternelarl intemeng wal arntert anemarl irrem. Lywelarl intem *right* ker mwerr. (T) *Meat that is lying in the sun goes off. Meat that is left in the shade is all right.*

Arntertek (W) *n.*
name of a rockhole east of Brooks Soak, Mt Denison area

arntetherrk carpet python, diamond python SEE UNDER **antetherrk**

arntety (E) *n.*
sick, ill, sickness ◆ Arrengeparety arntetyaw. Anterel apek apernetyekaw. (Sa) *My poor old grandfather is sick. Maybe you can rub him with fat.* ◆ Arntety tha akareparem. Ngkwengan ayeng uyarnarl iwerr arelhepelhem, atherrel

akaretyek, arntety nhenh. (St) *I am looking after the sick person. I watched the road in vain for you to come so that the both of us could look after this sick person.*
SEE ALSO rlkert, mernt[1], inkwerr, arrwengkelth, pwenty[1]

arntety-irrem (E) *vi.*
get sick ◆ Pwenty arntetyarl mpwaretyel. Arntety-irreman ikwer-penh. Pwentyel arlarl atwek kel renh angkwerr-wentyelant pwenty renh inem iwetyek. (Sa) *Diseases make people sick. You get sick from that. If someone gets a disease then the only thing that will get rid of it is traditional massage and healing.* ◆ Uneng anetyangarl arntety-irrem. *Something*-el aterel anthek. Arengk arrpwarnt angkerremelarl aterel anthek, kel akem-irrenty alpem ankwepenh, utneng anetyang irremel. (Sa) *[If a person] has no spirit then they get sick. Something might have given them a fright. Dogs barking might give the person a fright, then they get up from sleep, and their spirit goes [away].*
= mernt-irrem, rlkert-irrem

arnteyn (E) wasp, hornet SEE UNDER **arntirn**

arnteyt (E) rotten, stinking, bad (especially of meat) SEE UNDER **arntert**

arntimerrk (E) *n.*
cross-legged, sitting with your legs crossed
SEE ALSO aymparrk anem

arntirn (T), **arnteyn** (E) *n.*
wasp, hornet

arntirrkwem (E) hold something SEE UNDER **arntwerrkem**

arntwa (W,T), **arntwang** (W,T) *n.*
a root with lots of grubs in it ◆ Arratyam nhenh kwenh arntwa anthwerr. (M) *There really are a lot of grubs here in this root.* ◆ Arntwa ntwa tyer-wem anyematy-akert. (M) *You poke with the crowbar for roots with grubs in them.* ◆ Rwernp-rwernpel mpwarerl-anem anaty, arntwang arrernerl-anem, *all night* angkerl-anemel. Angkerl-anem *crack*-em-ilem, an arntwang anem arrernem. (T) *The cricket goes along making the bush potatoes, putting the tubers under the ground by singing all night. They sing and crack [the earth open] and then place the tubers there.* (?)

arntwangkem (W,T) *vi.*
make a 'hollow' sound (that the earth makes when there is a grub or tuber underneath the surface and when the ground is tapped with a crowbar or digging stick) (angkem *'speak', 'talk', 'make characteristic noise'*) ◆ Arntwangkem. Ntwang ahelh tyer-wem, anyematy-akert apek — wal ahelh alenh arntwangkem, wal ntwang anyemem. (M) *Make a hollow sound. You tap the ground with a digging stick or crowbar, and maybe there is a witchetty grub underneath there — well then the ground makes a hollow sound, and then you dig [for the grub].*
= pwep-angkem
SEE ALSO tyer-wem

arntwaly (E) *n.* [RESPECT LANGUAGE]
water ◆ Urrem-iletyek kwey arntwaly-ayerr, ahanelh-ila. (Sa) *Daughter, give [your husband] some water, take [it] to him [said by the mother of the woman].* ◆ Arlkarl-ayerr arntwaly yanhentyak urrem-ileyaw, irrernt-ayerr. (Sa) *Give some of that cool water to your husband over there [said by a woman to her daughter].*
SEE ALSO kwaty

arntwang (W,T) a root with lots of grubs in it SEE UNDER **arntwa**

arntwatherrk[1] (E), **arntatherrk** (E) *n.*
slime ◆ Kwaty artnwepelarl anem wal arntatherrkel anem artem renh kwaty. (St) *The water that is lying in the swamp gets covered with slime.*
SEE ALSO nthwerrkamp, ntharrengarreng

arntwatherrk[2] (T,E) *n.*
1. raw emu meat ◆ Arntwatherrk-antey nhenh — ampetyek atyeng. (Sa) *This emu meat is still raw — cook it for me.*
2. green seeds of the dogwood tree (*Acacia sericophylla*) • = artwengarr

arntwelhem (E) *vi.*
be pleased about something you have done ◆ Kerarl tharl angety-alpek, arntwelhem ayeng. (St) *I am pleased that I have brought back lots of meat.* ◆ Man angerr ra *win*-em-ilek, arntwelhem anem ra. (St) *He was pleased with himself for winning a lot of money.*
SEE ALSO nakelhem, narlkwelhem

arntwem (W,T) *vi.*
grow, grow on something ◆ Mangarray arntwem arrkernkel-arleng. (M) *Bush coconuts grow on the bloodwood tree.*
SEE ALSO lyapem
CAN SOUND A BIT LIKE rntwem *'dance'*

arntwelh-ilem (W,T) *vt.*
grow (plants), cultivate plants ◆ Atherrk arntwelh-ilem, kel mern arlkwetyenheng. (T) *Growing the plants and then eating [the food from] them.*

arntwety-alpem (W,T) *vi.*
grow back (vegetation) ◆ Rlpwatel amparr rwel amparr antyerrk-ilem, wal arntwety-alpem atherrk-irrenty-alpem. (M) *The plants dry up at first from the fire, from being burnt out, and then they grow back again, grow back green*

again.

arntwer (W) cooking pit with hot rocks [SOME SPEAKERS] SEE UNDER **rntwer**[1]

Arntwer (W) *n.*
name of a hill south of Garden Bore and west of Tilmouth Well

arntwerlem (W,T) *vt.*
(birds) tell people that there is an abundance of bush plums (*Psydrax latifolia*) or honeyants ◆ Arrety-arretyel arntwerlem ahakey angerr-ilem. (T) *The spiny-cheeked honeyeater tells you that there's lots of bush plums.*
◆ Perrpantywenel yerramp arntwerlem. (T) *The wood swallow tells people that there's lots of honeyants.*
SEE ALSO akern-ilem, angerr-ilem, arntwem, arrmernem

arntwerr-arntwerr (E) *n.*
the western end of the initiation (young man) ceremony ground ◆ Rteyepertey arlkep-arlkemaw, altwerl apek arntwerr-arntwerrel arlkep-arlkem artwan. Arelhan nhakw *round-*el arlkep-arlkem. (St) *The* rteyepertey *women sing out, and from the western end of the ceremony ground the men sing out. The women go round calling out.*
SEE ALSO apwelh, anmanty

arntwerrem, antwerrem (T,E) *vi.*
1. to growl (dog) ◆ Angwely arntwerrem tyerrty arrpenharl aremarl. An angwelyeh arrpehekw arntwerrem. (T) *The dog is growling when it sees another person. And it growls at other dogs as well.* ◆ Arntwerreperremeyay arengk yanh ahel. (St) *That dog is growling angrily.* ◆ Arengk arntwerrem atyeng, utnhetyek apek ayenh. (St) *The dog is growling at me, and it might bite me.*
SEE ALSO parlkwem
2. to thunder ◆ Alenh arntwerrety-alhem kwaty. (T) *The rain storm is thundering as it goes along.*

arntwerrert *n.*

rock pigeon, plumed pigeon, spinifex pigeon (*Geophaps plumifera*)
◆ Thip arntwerrert irntel akern anem, irrkarlp akwek-akert. (M) *The rock pigeon has a small crest and lives on the top of rocks.* ◆ Aketh-angkwerr anerl-apem thep arntwerrert, nthwerl-atherr-anem kwaty-angkwerr. Arntwerrert irntel anerl-anem iterel ina. (N) *Rock pigeons live in the open places and, and they go around near water. They live on the side of rocks.*

= ntarrwerarrwer
SEE ALSO marekwerr

arntwerrkem, antwerrkem, arntirrkwem (E) *vt.*
1. hold or hang onto something; grab something; catch something ◆ Ampan arntwerrkem akin. Ampa akely alhekerr arntwerrkem, atnyekerr apek. (Sa) *[You] hold onto children as well. [You] hold onto a little baby in case it goes away or falls.* ◆ Man tha antwerrkem iltyel. (St) *I am holding the money in my hand.* ◆ Amwelteng arntwerrkem tyarr-inemel amwelteng arntwerrkem — mpwenyel angetyek. (N) *Grabbing the person by the arm and dragging them by the arm — racing them off.*
2. hold onto something; keep something ◆ Irrkwentyel antwerrkem mwetekay alenh. (M) *The policeman is keeping that car.*
SEE ALSO arterrkwem
3. arrest someone

arntwerrkerrem, arntirrkwerrem (E) *vi.*
shake hands ◆ Iltyang arntwerrkerrem arelh atherr. (T) *The two women are shaking hands.*

arntwerrkelhem, arntirrkwelhem (E) *vi.*
hold part of your body ◆ Artwa irnerl-anem akatemarengk, kapwert arntwerrkelhemel. (T) *The man is standing with his hands clasped behind his head, holding his head.*

arntwerrkenh-arntwerrkenh (E) *n.*
handle (e.g. of a shield)

arnwa, arnwang (W,T), **artnwa** (E) *n.*
1. emu fat (from back part of emu). Also referred to as *ker arnwang.* ◆ Ankerr artnwel apernelhem arntety-irrenty. (Sa) *[You] rub yourself with emu fat if you get sick.*
SEE ALSO artep lpway, artep ulpay
2. emu [RESPECT LANGUAGE] ◆ Ker *emu* kwa — arnwang, akemel antherrerl-anem tyerrty mapeh. (N) *Emu meat — emu fat called* arnwang *is cut up and handed out to people.*
• SEE ALSO anhelengkw-ayerr, ankerr

arnwelem (W) *vt.*
cut up emu fat ◆ Arnwelem ker ampeng antem. (M) *The emu fat is cut up when the animal is cooked.*

arnwal-inem (W,T), **arnal-inem** (W,T) *vt.*
lift something up ◆ Rwang irlpart arnwal-inem. (M) *Lifting the log up.* ◆ Kwer akwek alenh arnal-inemel angay. (M) *Lift that little kid up and take them.*
= anhwert inem

arnwalel angem
lift something up and carry it; hold someone or something clasped to chest (?) (angem *'take', 'carry'*)

arnwang (W,T) emu fat (from back part of emu) SEE UNDER **arnwa**

arnwekety (E) *n.*
1. conkerberry (*Carissa lanceolata*). Spiny shrub up to 2 m high, with white flowers and black berries.
2. the edible fruit of the conkerberry. Also referred to as *mern arnwekety* ◆ Mpa, mern arnwekety arnkengeny utnhetyek alherl-wey. (Sa) *Come on, let's go and pick lots of conkerberries.*
= perlap

arnwekety-arnwekety (E) *n.*
orange-naped snake, moon snake (*Furina ornata*) (?)
= perlap-perlap

arnwematy (W) mallee fowl SEE UNDER **anwematy**

arnweng-inem (W,T) *vt.*
dip or scoop up (water) ◆ Kwaty arnweng-inem kwaty arnwengkeng. (M) *The water is scooped up from the soakage.*
= athankwem
SEE ALSO thelem, inpem, arnwengk

arnwengk (W,T) *n.*
soakage that is dug in a creek
= thewekety
SEE ALSO angenty[1], arnweng-inem

arnwengk-ilem (W,T) *vt.*
make a soakage, dig a soakage ◆ Kwaty arnwengk-ilem. Angernem kwenh, aketh-ilem kwaty renh. (N) *Digging a soakage. Scraping away [the sand] and uncovering the water.* ◆ Kwaty lpway yanh arnwengk-ilay. (M) *Go and dig a soakage in that creek.*
SEE ALSO arnweng-inem

arnwengk arrernem (E)
make a soakage, dig a soakage ◆ Kwaty arnwengk arrernem ilpayek. (St) *Dig a soakage in the creek.*
= angenty arrernem

Arnwengk Kwaty (W) *n.*
the name of a place and the location of an outstation near Coniston (arnwengk '*soakage*'; kwaty '*water*')

arnwep, artnwep (E) *n.*
claypan, low-lying swampy area ◆ Kwaty arnwep weth antywetyek alheyaw. (Sa) *Let's go and drink from that claypan.*

arnwep-arnwep, artnwep-artnwep (E) *n.*
claypan, low-lying swampy area ◆ Arnwep-arnwep arerl-alhem, kwaty lpwertey interleng. Mentyel arerl-alhem arnwep-arnwep renh, kwatyelarl *mess* mpwarek ingkel arlka, pwelek atna arlka ulhemel. (N) *We'll go and see the claypan, where the muddied water is lying there. We'll go and see that claypan, but we'll leave it because the bullocks have messed up the water up with their hooves and by shitting in it.*

arnwer[1], artnwer (E) *n.*
dingo (*Canis lupus dingo*). Also referred to as *arengk arnwer* or *angwely arnwer.*
= arnapar

arnwer[2] *n.*
a humming noise ◆ Arnwer-akert alhay, arnwer-irretyek iyntwarray, ankweketyay. (St) *Go a long way away and make that humming noise, because [I'm] trying to sleep.*

arnwer-irrem *vi.*
hum, make a droning or humming noise; sing
SEE ALSO unyem, alyerrem

arnwety (W,T) *n.*
1. edible seed ◆ Arnwety, athenh-athenh, kelh arrernenhernenh, tamp-arteh mparenharenh kelh. (N) *This is a seed that is ground up and made into a seedcake, similar to a damper.* ◆ Anwerneh mpwaretyam alakenh amangkelh-ilek alakenhel-iperr, arnwety angwenh-akeyel-iperrel athep-atherl. *Not* mern perlawel — itya. (N) *They made it for us like that and that's how we grew up, from grinding those what-d'ye-call-it seeds. We didn't grow up on flour — not at all.*
2. a general word that can go before the name of a particular type of seed. In the Anmatyerr way of classifying foods most fruits and vegetables are known as *mern*, sweet things as *ngkwarl*, seeds as *anterrng, arnwety* or *ntang*, meats as *ker* and edible grubs as *tyap*.
= anterrng, ntang
3. damper or seedcake made from seeds • SEE ALSO kelh

arnwety-arnwety (W) *n.*
eight day grass (*Fimbristylis dichotoma*) ◆ Arnwety-arnwetyel awantyewarretyart mamp. Arnwety-arnwety akemel mampem arek-werremel awantyewarretyartem antywerrirretyart kwa. (N) *The sweet stuff from the bark of the river red gum used to be eaten by dipping the* arnwety-arnwety *grass in the honey and then sucking on it.*
= taty-taty[1]
SEE ALSO akwetelh

+arr+[1] (E) *v.ending*
Plural marker. Goes on some verbs to show that more than one person or thing is doing the action. Possibly goes only on the verbs *apetyem* 'come' and *irrepethem* 'get something (respect language)'. ◆ Arnekarnar ayeng alhem apetyarr-alpemek apek. *I am going to meet the people that are coming back.*

◆ Aywepem alperlewetyek. Angath apety**arr**-alhetyang — alperl-waw! (Sa) *Hunt them away. Don't you all come up close — go away!* ◆ Ahantherrek mern atyenh, ingkerrek-antey. Tey atyenh impen ingkerrek ahantherrek. Ahantherrek ingkerrek innga. Ker atyenh uyerrek, angayakwarl apety**arr**-alherrek. (Sa) *All of my food has been eaten, the whole lot. The only tea I have has been used up. Absolutely everything has gone. All of my meat has run out, eaten up by the hungry people who came.*
SEE ALSO +erl-w+2, +erl-warr+

+arr2 (W) *n.ending*
Shows the time or season when particular plants appear (?). ◆ Mern arlatyey**arr**, mern yerrakwerr**arr**, tywerrk**arr** apek. (M) *The time when pencil yams, bush onions or wild figs [are found].*

arra *n.*
mouth. A short form of the word *arrakert,* which often appears in compound words to do with the mouth.
= arrakert
arratyelk (E) *n.*
gums (in mouth) (tyelk '*flesh*')
= arra merrng
arremwar-mwar *n.*
loud talker, 'big mouth' (mwar '*wooden scoop*') ◆ Arremwar-mwar, arnterr angketyal! (Sa) *Stop talking so loud, big mouth!*
arrelthenp-lthenp *n.*
mouth (covered with something) (lthenp '*covered in dirty stuff*')
arrepwek-pwek (T,E) *n.*
1. a teenage boy's first facial hair (pwek-pwek '*stalked puffball*') ◆ Arrepwek-pwek, lyetantarl lyapepapem weth-lkwer ampa. (St) Arrepwek-pwek *is a boy's [whiskers] that are just starting to grow.*
2. a young teenage boy with facial hair just starting to grow. Young boys use the stalked puffball to paint themselves with pretend beards and moustaches.

arrak (E) *n.*
a type of small boomerang ◆ Aylayl arrak, aylaylap ra arnkwert-arnkwert, arrak. Artwekenhap ra. (Sa) *The* arrak *is a crooked type of boomerang. It belongs to the men.*
SEE ALSO aylayl, iylkwa1

arrakakwarl-kwarl (W) *n.*
a type of Solanum plant that emus eat (but NOT people)

arrakelakel (E) *n.*
lonely, sad, having no company, friendless, on one's own ◆ Arrakelakel anerl-anem, ikngа, anyent — anyent-areny ap arrakelakel anerl-anem. (Sa) *Sitting there lonely, without company, alone — sitting there sad and lonely on [my] own.* ◆ Ayengarl ilkwatherr-kweny amwerrk arrakelakel arep-arem, ikngа anep-anerl. (St) *Yesterday I didn't have any company and I was lonely, sitting on my own and watching out.*
SEE ALSO anyent, inga, ngwath, akalk

arrakerr *prn.*
you (more than two). This pronoun is used in the subject part of the sentence (i.e. representing the 'doers' of the verb action) when the people belong to the same patrimoiety and different generation moiety; for example, a person together with their fathers or father's sisters. See Appendix 1. ◆ Arrakerram alherrirra awenh-intyerr rwang inetyeh. (T) *You all go and get wood, all the aunties and nieces.*
SEE ALSO arrengkerr, arrantherr
arrenhakerrenh, arrenhakerr *prn.*
you (more than two). This pronoun is used in the object part of the sentence (i.e. representing those the verb action is 'done to').
arrehakerr (W,T), **arrekakerr** (E) *prn.*
for you, to you (more than two)
arrakerrenh (W), **arrehakerrenh** (W,T), **arrekakerrenh** (E) *prn.*
your, yours (belonging to more than two)
arrakerr-altyerr (E) *n.*
your sons-in-law; your mothers-in-law (closely related ones whose mothers come from the same country) ◆ Arrakerr-altyerr alhek kerek. (St) *Your sons-in-law went hunting.*
SEE ALSO -altyerr

arrakert *n.*
1. mouth ◆ Arrakert lthenp-lthenp ngkwerlp-penh ker-penh apek. Rarl [arengkel] arlkwem-penh *flour*-penh, wal arrelthenp-lthenp antey arl apety-alpem. (St) *[Your] mouth might be covered in stuff after chewing tobacco or eating meat. If a dog eats flour, well it comes back with its mouth covered in the stuff.*
2. beak ◆ Irretyel ker atanthem arrakertel. *The eaglehawk kills prey with its beak.*
= arra
arrakert ayenp
lips (ayenp '*skin*')
= arreyenp
arrakert angerr
pelican (*Pelecanus conspicillatus*) (angerr '*big*')
= pelekan2

arrakert rrpwerl (T)
a type of snake (?) (rrpwerl *'black'*)
= arrwerrperl
arrakert-kenh (T) *n.*
telephone (lit. 'belonging to the mouth')
= terlepawen, alwerrng angkenh-angkenh, irlpekenh
SEE ALSO alwerrng
arrakert-ilem (T,E) *vt.*
release a person from speech taboo or ceremonial ban on speaking ◆ Awenpan anem arelh warlekwert anewekarl aparlp-ilem *or* arelh ywerlt anem kwer kwerenharl aparlp-ilem. Kakey kwerenhel antem mern tyenkerrel arrakert-ilem angketyek. (T) *A woman who has lost her husband, or a woman who has lost her child is* awenp *and she is not allowed to talk. Later on her elder brother gives her some ceremonial food to release her from the ban on speaking.*
= ulypmakert-ilem, angkakert-ilem

arrakwerakwer (T,E) *n.*
1. spiny-cheeked honeyeater (*Acanthagenys rufogularis*)
2. singing honeyeater (*Lichenostomus virescens*)
= alpeyart-alpeyart, arrety-arrety

arrakwernem[1] (E) *vt.*
join something together; make things meet up ◆ Parrek arrakwernetyek. (St) *Joining the fence up.*
SEE ALSO pwit-ilem, anyentelh-ilem, irrtyernem

arrakwernem[2] (T,E) *vt.*
1. put something in mouth (to eat); feed someone ◆ Mern ra arlkwetyeh arrakwernemel. (T) *He's putting food in his mouth to eat.* ◆ War thwengk arrakwerney arlkwetyeh apek. (M) *I'll just put some food in your mouth and that might make you eat.* ◆ Ulpmerr-atwenhel uthipel arrakwernepernem yanh nyengk. Arrakwernem, atanthemel. Antyeltyek-arlek akwernem. (Sa) *The kestrel catches zebra finches and puts them in its beak. It hunts them and catches them, and then puts them on a branch.* (?)
2. (of native bees) put pollen and nectar into native bees' hive or sugarbag ◆ Lwerlkerel ngkwarl arrakwernepernem arnang kwenel. (T) *The native bees put the pollen into the hollow tree.*
SEE ALSO akwernem

arrakwernem[3] *vt.*
1. go and tell others about something that is happening (something that birds do) ◆ Tyerrty alethang apetyem, wal thep akwek ya apetyem *fly away*-irremel alkerel, wal ya arrakwernety-alhem, tyerrty arrpenh alenheh. Wal tyerrty alenhel *know*-em-ilem, 'Tyerrty kwenh apetyem'. (M) *A stranger might be coming, and a little bird comes and then flies away into the sky, and then goes and tells the other people what is happening. Then those people know, 'There's a person coming'.*
2. go and tell others about something that is happening ◆ Arrakwernem, arrpenharl arteny anemek ilety-alpemel arrakwernem. *Something*-arl arerl-alpem. Ilety-alpem. Tha ilety-alpem, ngkweng ilety-alpem, arrakwernety-alpemel. (Sa) *Going and telling the others that are staying at home what happened. Going back and telling them something that you saw. I'll go back and tell you, tell you what I saw.*

arralkem, arrarlkem (T) *vi.*
1. yawn ◆ Arralkem ankwek-irremel, ankwayntetyek. *Getting tired and yawning, wanting to go to sleep.* ◆ Ankwek arrarlkem ayeng, intetyek ankwa anem. Kel ayeng akem-irremel ayeng arrarlkety-ayntem akin. (St) *I am yawning because I want to lie down and sleep. Then when I get up I yawn again.*
2. open your mouth wide
arralkelh-ilem, arrarlkelh-ilem *vt.*
1. open something up ◆ Mwetek arralkelh-ilem, kwaty apek theletyek. (Sa) *Opening the car [bonnet] up, maybe to pour some water in.*
2. make someone or something open its mouth ◆ *Dentist*-el arralkelh-ilem. (Sa) *The dentist makes you open your mouth up wide.*

arralt *n.*
beard, moustache ◆ Artwelarl arralt irrkwem arrarnel. (T) *Men have beards on their chins.*
= arrwert
SEE ALSO arra, alta
arralt aywang (W,T)
grey beard (aywang *'old', 'grey'*)

arralthem (T,E) *vi.*
scream or shout, call out loudly ◆ Arralthem, 'Ampa atwerretyalay anerlanerray kwenh!' (St) *Shouting, 'You kids sit down and stop fighting!'*
SEE ALSO arrpwernem, arlkem
arralthelhem (T,E) *vi.*
scream or shout, call out loudly ◆ Arternp angkaw, arralthelherl-anetyang. Arralthelhetyang arternp angkay. (Sa) *Speak quietly, don't shout. Don't scream, talk quietly.*

arralty (T,E) *n.*
fright ◆ Arralty anem ap ayeng. (St) *I am frightened.*
SEE ALSO ater, ilkwel anthem

arralty arrernem (T,E) *vt.*
give someone or something a fright; make someone nervous (arrernem *'put'*) ◆ Arraltyarl arrernem-kety aterel antherl-anetyakenh, alpaw! Arlengel arlkerl-anetyek. (Sa) *Go away! Don't give us a fright and make us nervous. Go a long way away and shout.*
arralty anem (T,E)
feel frightened, scared or worried
◆ Ankwepenh arralty anem, ater-irrem. Akem-irrenty-alpemel, arralty anerl-anem. *Feeling frightened after being asleep. Getting up and feeling scared.* ◆ *Family*-ek arralty anem atwerrem-arlek. Anert arralty anerl-alhem. (T) *[You] feel worried about your family if they are fighting. You feel worried in your guts.*

arraltyaltyen (E), **arraltyalty** (T,E) *n.*
a type of edible grub found on mistletoe plants. Also referred to as *tyap arraltyaltyen* or *tyap arraltyalty*.
SEE ALSO akweltyayt, amar, atyankern, pweralhem, ngartangkern, ngkwerrm

arraly-arraly-irrem (T,E) *vi.*
1. shine, shimmer, sparkle, twinkle ◆ Utern arraly-arraly-irrem, *hot* innga. Arlengek arem renh arraly-arraly-irrerl-anenty utern, ulewerr-apeny inngart. Anengkel apek *no* alhwerrp, *no* alhwerrparl arraly-arraly-irrerl-anem, *no* irrernt. (Sa) *The heat is shimmering and it's really hot. You can see the heat shimmering in the distance, and it's like a mirage. When it's calm and there is no wind the heat shimmers, when it's really hot.* ◆ Ulyethey renh arerl-anem utern arraly-arraly-irrerl-anenty. (Sa) *From the shade [you] can see the heat shimmering.* ◆ Arraly-arraly-irrem kwerraly. Mwetek *light* apek arraly-arraly-irrem. Tyampet apek. (Sa) *Stars twinkle. Car lights shine. Billycans shine.*◆ Kwerraly arraly-arraly-irrepirrem. (St) *The stars are twinkling.*
2. flutter (wings) ◆ Ntelyapelyapan arraly-arraly-irrerl-anem. (T) *The butterflies are fluttering [their wings].*
SEE ALSO alharrkem, angap-angap-irrem

arramenty, **arramanty** *n.*
single-men's camp, 'single quarters' [RESPECT LANGUAGE] ◆ Arramanty-kety nhenh-ntyel-antey kwang nhel-antey ahanetyek. Arramanty yanh-kety. *Go this way because your son-in-law's camp is over there. Because of your son-in-law's camp [woman speaking].*
SEE ALSO arlweker, arnkenty, ahileng, irrewatyent

arramparreng (E) a person's spirit double SEE UNDER **arremparreng**

arramperrty (E) *n.*
deserted place or camp ◆ Merant arramperrty anem, mer ingkenyel anem anetyel. Ingkerrarl alhekek, arengkant unthem. (Sa) *The camp is deserted and there's nobody there. Because everybody's gone, and there's only dogs wandering around.*
SEE ALSO ampeny[1], ingkeny, arltwa

arrampewem[1] *vt.*
1. tease or mock someone, ridicule someone, make fun of someone ◆ Iwenhek unta ayenh arrampewem? Atyenh arrp unta arem arrampewemel. (T) *Why are you mocking me? You are staring at me and mocking me.* ◆ Arelh nywerrp apek nta arrkenel arrampewem. (M) *You can tease women who are in the opposite generation moiety to you — for fun.* ◆ Tyerrty yanhel anwernenh arrampewepewem. (T) *That person is teasing us.*
SEE ALSO kwanthem, ngkwanty-irrem, arntarrp-ilem, arlkarem, arrken-ilem, anngernt-irrem
2. joke about something serious; tell something that is not true, tell lies ◆ *Don't* mpwankel arrampewetyek, akwek nhakw mwerr akwet. (T) *Don't say that the worst has happened, that child is still all right.* ◆ Arelh yanhel arrampewem, arraty-iletyakenh. (T) *That woman is joking about something serious, not telling the truth.*

arrampewem[2] (E) *vt.*
have a feeling about wanting to go back to your country; feel homesick, worry for home
◆ Arrampewepewem. Arrampewem mer *Ti Tree*-warl apek ayeng alhem, wal arrampewem tha irrar-irremel. (St) *Feeling like going home. I might go to Ti Tree and then I get homesick and want to go home.* ◆ Arrampewepewem mer kwerenh, rarl aknganek. (St) *She is feeling homesick for the country where she came from.*
SEE ALSO irrar-irrem, alther-irrem
arrampewelhem (E) *vi.*
look out a long way; stare into the distance

arrang (E) *n.* [RESPECT LANGUAGE]
a term for teenage 'uncles' (*amarl*) ◆ Tha apek 'arrang' akem *uncle* atyenh. 'Arrang yanh apetyepetyemaw.' *That's uncle* atyenh tha ilem. Apmerrk map 'arrang' akemel. (St) *I might call my uncle* 'arrang'. *'There comes my* arrang.*' That's what I call my uncle. Teenage boys are referred to as* 'arrang'.
SEE ALSO awey amerrk, amarl
CAN SOUND A BIT LIKE arreng *'father's father'*

arrang-arem (E) *vt.*
take aim; get ready to strike, brandish a weapon

= angkarr arem
SEE ALSO akwanth-ilem, rtwely-inem

arrangk (E) *n.*
buck spinifex, bull spinifex (*Triodia longiceps*). A grass that grows in hummocks up to 1.5 m high, and has very sharp bluish green leaves. ◆ Arrangkan arreylp-arreylp ilkwa — arreylp rlterrk *one*. Antywer. Anker-akertan arrpenh. (Sa) *The buck spinifex is large and has sharp spikes — hard spikes. Other kinds [of spinifex] have spinifex wax.*
= ntwemerr, welyar
SEE ALSO alatyeyt

arrangkem *vi.*
1. cry, wail, bawl ◆ Kwer angayel ra arnem arnem arnem arrangkem arrangkem arrangkem kel kwer inetyenheng arrpantey mam kwerenhel apek, kel renh ntert anem iletyenheng. Ntert anem yang irrem. (T) *The child is hungry and crying and crying and crying, and then her mother pretends to get her something and then that makes her quieten down. She quietens down.*
2. howl, whine or make crying sounds (animals), miaow (cats)
= arnem
arrangkelh-ilem *vt.*
make someone cry
arrangkelh-angkelh-ilem *vt.* = **arrangkelh-ilem**
= arnelh-ilem
arrangkelh-ilerrem *vi.*
make each other cry

arrangketh *n.*
1. thirsty ◆ Arrangkethey alhep-alhem, kwaty-kweny. (T) *Travelling along thirsty, with no water.*
SEE ALSO parrety, arwekel, angkethakw
2. dry country, desert country, dry camp ◆ Arrangketh-kety alheyaw, kwaty-warl irrem iparrp. (Sa) *Let's keep going quickly to the place where there's water because this country is dry.*
• SEE ALSO aherraty, urrepert, rrwepert, ahepet

Arrangkey (W,T) *n.*
Garden Bore, Dingo dam. See map p. viii.

arrangkw *part.*
1. no (in answer to a question or a request) ◆ Arrangkweyay, mety. (Sa) *No, it's shut.*
2. nothing; none; not having a particular thing; a particular thing not being there ◆ Thep unernengk, rltimpelarl arrangkw-artekarl anerl-anem, artety rltimpel. (St) *The tawny frogmouth sits amongst the bits of bark and it's as if it isn't there, you can hardly see it.* ◆ Utyekel utyel, urrtyirretyel ntwa. Ngan urrtyirretyelarl atyeng, angka-arrpantey unta atyeng ilep-ilerl. Mern-arrpantey unta ilemel urrtyirretyel, nhenhan arrangkwarl. (Sa) *You're lying. You're lying to me, telling me some sort of story. You're pretending that there's food here, but there's nothing.* ◆ Kerek uyarn unthem, arrangkw-antey apety-alpem uyarnarl unthek-penh. Ayeng apek arlewatyerrek uyarn unthemel apety-alpem. (St) *Looking around in vain for meat, and coming back with nothing after searching in vain. Maybe I will look around for goannas but not find any, and then return.*
SEE ALSO itya
arrangkw akwet (W,T)
nothing yet; (there's still) nothing
= itya akwet
arrangkw-irrem *vi.*
die, pass away ◆ Arrangkw-irreman ulemarlel, *die*. Pwelekan kenh arrangkw-irremarl pwetyel, ilwemarl. (Sa) Arrangkw-irrem *is dying. Cattle pass away, die in the bush.* ◆ Ampa apek *might* iylpangkerl, '*Eh* iylpangketyalay akuny-amperl ywerrek-arlek — arrangkw-irrek-arlek'. (St) *A child might remind you of someone, 'Hey, don't remind me of that [person] — that poor thing has passed away.'*

arrantherr *prn.*
you (more than two). This pronoun is used in the subject part of the sentence (i.e. representing the 'doers' of the verb action) when the people belong to different patrimoieties; for example, a person together with their sisters-in-law or their cross-cousins. This form of the pronoun is also used when the kin relations are not specified or in reference to a group where there is a range of kin relations. See Appendix 1.
SEE ALSO +anth, arrengkerr, arrakerr
arrenhantherr, **arrenhantherrenh** *prn.*
you (more than two). This pronoun is used in the object part of the sentence (i.e. representing those the verb action is 'done to'). ◆ Thang arrenhantherrenh atwem. (M) *I am hitting you mob.*
arrehantherr (W,T), **arrekantherr** (T,E) *prn.*
for you, to you (more than two) ◆ Arrantherr anerrirra, tha ker itetyenheng arrehantherr. (M) *You all sit there while I cook you some meat.*
arrantherrenh (W,T), **arrehantherrenh** (W,T), **arrekantherrenh** (E) *prn.*
your, yours (belonging to more than two)
arrantherr-apakwey (E) *prn.*
you (belonging to the opposite generation moiety to the speaker) ◆ 'Akalk arrpemarl arrantherr-apakwey alherl-wa. Anwantherr-

apakwey ikngantey akalk arrpemarl alherl-wem akalk, *separate.'* Arrkenel kwantherrem. Nywerrp. (Sa) *'You [in the opposite generation moiety] all go separately. Us mob [in the same generation moiety] will go separately as well.' That's how we have fun teasing those people. The ones in the other generation group.*
SEE ALSO nywerrp, -apakwey, -apatherr, alanth-apakwey, ilernanth-apakwey, anwernantherr-apakwey, anantherr-apakwey

arranty[1] (W,T), **arrwanty** (W,T) *n.*
a type of snake (?)

arranty[2] (E) *n.*
kangaroo-skin waterbag ◆ Kwatyek-arelh arranty wetharl yanhel iletyel, arrwekelenyel antywerretyart, *no billycan.* Aherr-kenharl itna mpwaretyart, aherr pwalh-iwem, kel arranty anem itna mpwarem. Ngkwern atherr arrernem, kwaty-kenh antywerl-anetyek, irrernt-areny antywetyek. (Sa) *The kangaroo-skin waterbag is what the olden-time people used to drink out of, when they had no billycans. They used to make them from kangaroo [skin], skinning the kangaroo and then making the waterbag. The two legs were tied up, and then they were able to drink the cold water.*

arrantyakem (W,T) *vt.*
tell someone off, shout at someone or something ◆ Tyerrty arrantyakem — akeng mparek apek. (T) *Tell a person off — maybe for doing the wrong thing.* ◆ Thang arengk nhenh arrantyakem. 'Ntert-irra kwenh!' (T) *I am shouting at this dog. 'Shut up!'*
SEE ALSO iltem

arrantyeyantyeng, **arrantyetyantyeng** (W), **aherrantyeyantyeng** (E), **arrantyengantyeng** (T) *n.*
1. kangaroo's sleeping hole
2. kangaroo's salt lick or water hole [SOME SPEAKERS] ◆ Aherr-kenh mer ipert. Interl-anem ikwerel. *Salt*-kenh *separate* akin angernem. Itnan 'arrantyeyantyeng' ipertel interl-anek, angernerl-anem, ankwa anem iwelherl-arrernem. Aherr-kenhant. (Sa) *A kangaroo's sleeping hole. It sleeps there. It digs a separate hole for salt. The name of the hole that it digs and lies down to sleep in is* 'arrantyeyantyeng'. *These are just kangaroos' holes.*
SEE ALSO arrantywem

arrantywem *vt.*
kiss someone or something ◆ Marl kwerenh arrantywem artwel *or* angwelyel. (T) *The man kisses his wife, or a dog licks [someone].*
CAN SOUND A BIT LIKE awantyem *'lick', 'suck'*

arranyenganyeng (W,T) *n.*
a type of blind snake (*Ramphotyphlops endoterus*) ◆ Arranyenganyengel ngenh angwarem, arlkwem rtety. (M) *The blind snake gives you toothache.*
= rtety arlkwenh-arlkwenh, ahaylengkeyler
SEE ALSO aytwelth
Arranyenganyeng (W) *n.*
the name of a place west of Bluebush in the Mt Allan area

arrap-anem *vi.*
crouch down and hide behind something; lie in wait to ambush someone or give someone a fright, or to kill an animal
arrap-welhem, arrap-iwelhem (E) *vi.*
= **arrap-anem** ◆ Ayeng arrap-welhem arrpenhel arekety. (T) *I am crouching down and hiding in case someone sees me.* ◆ Untang arrap-welhem atyengay, atnwerlkel anthetyek. (T) *You are hiding from me, so that you can give me a fright.* ◆ 'Yanh thwengk arernam kwenh — *don't* arrap-welherl.' (M) *'I just saw you there — don't crouch down and hide.'*
arrap-intem = **arrap-anem** ◆ Arrap-intem, kwer arrpenh aterel-anthem. 'Waaaa.' Alakenh-irrem, arrap-interl-anemel. Kel ra aterarl-irrerleng. (T) *Lying in wait to give another kid a fright. 'Waaaa.' Going like that while you are lying waiting. Then the kid gets a fright.*
SEE ALSO alengk-welhem, ulernem

arrapayernem *vi.*
get in the way (particularly of hunting); rush in and grab things, crowd in on someone (irnem, rnem *'stand'*) ◆ Arrapayernem ankey inkemel, kerek apek mernek apek. (St) *Hanging around hoping to get something, maybe some meat or some food.* ◆ Arelh nhenh ankey arrapayernep-rnem. (T) *This lady is hanging round hoping to get food (no-one can get in front of her).*
SEE ALSO ankey, arrngen-welhem

arraper *n.*
bunched kerosene grass, mulga grass (*Aristida contorta*) ◆ Arraperel tyart ingkerr mwernetyenheng atanthetyenheng altywer-altywer-irremel. (N) *The kerosene grass will stick into your shirt and pierce it, and the shirt will get full of holes.*
SEE ALSO intwerrker

arrapert (T) curled up, doubled up SEE UNDER **arrepert**

Arrapey (W) name of place between Napperby and Coniston SEE UNDER **Irrapey**

arrarem *vi.*
miss out on a share of something; want something but not get it, go without ◆ Arrarem mernek. Ayengan arrarek angayakw-anteyarl ayeng, arrantherrantarl arlkwek mern. Kerekan ayeng angayakw. Arrarerl-alpekarl ayeng arrekantherr. Manek arrarem akin, ingwerelant kenh mern inemek. Anthetyakenhel. Arrarem. (Sa) *I am missing out on my share of the food. I wanted some but I am still hungry, because you all ate the food. I am hungry for meat. I went without and you got the lot. You can miss out on money too, and only the others buy food. Nobody gives you anything. You miss out.* ◆ Ayengarl arrarentyel ngkweng anep-anem. Arrpenh map ntwang anthep-anthem. (T) *I'm missing out. You're only giving things to the others.* ◆ Arraremarl-kety alpeyaw — yanhel anthetyakenh. Ngkwerlp apek utnanthemel arlkwep-arlkwem, arraremarl-kety alpeyaw. (St) *Let's go back because we're not getting any — that person is not giving us any. They are chewing on their tobacco and not sharing it.*
SEE ALSO kewarr-irrem, arrelharrp

arrarlernem (W,T) *vi.*
1. go downwards (in the air), fly down, descend (in the air) (irnem, rnem *'stand'*) ◆ Irrtyart arrarlernem kwenelak. (M) *The spear is going down.* ◆ *Aeroplane* kwenelak arrarlernem. (M) *The aeroplane is descending.*
2. face or slope downwards ◆ Irntang arrarlernem kwenelak. (M) *The hill is sloping downwards.* ◆ Mwetek nhenh kwenelak arrarlernem. (M) *This car is facing downwards.*
arrarl-arrarl (W) *n.*
swinging back (like a returning boomerang)

arrarletyel *adv.*
swearing, using bad language, being foul-mouthed, speaking roughly or rudely ◆ Ampa akely map arrarletyel ilterrem. (Sa) *The little kids are using bad language and swearing at each other.* ◆ Arrarletyel tha iltem arelh nhenh anhelhenty angerr. Iltek anem tha arrarletyel akuny-amperl. (St) *I am growling and swearing at this nasty woman. I swore at the poor thing.* ◆ Iwenhek ntwa ayeng iltem arrarletyek? (T) *Why are you growling and being rude to me?*
SEE ALSO iltem

arrarlkem (T) yawn SEE UNDER **arralkem**

Arrarlkw (T,E) the Seven Sisters or Pleiades SEE UNDER **Arrarrkw**

arrarlp-wem, arrarlp-iwem (E) *vt.*
throw something away, tip something out ◆ Mern ampeny arrarlp-iwem. Mantarr arruleny arrarlp-iwem rapety-warl. *Throw away the leftover food. Throw the old clothes away into the rubbish.* ◆ Arrarlp-wem pelangket iwem, urinparl ayeng irrem irrkwer anemarl-kety, arrarlp-wem. (St) *Throwing the blankets off, because I'm getting hot, feeling hot.*
SEE ALSO irranyent-iwem

arrarn (W,T) *n.*
1. chin
2. beard, whiskers, an animal's whiskers
= arrwert
arrarn-penh (W,T) *n.*
1. a man's child; son, daughter
2. a person's brother's child; nephew, niece (lit. 'from the beard')
= arrwert-penh
SEE ALSO alem-penh, anert-penh

arrarntenh (E) *n.*
1. native currant, native citrus (*Psydrax latifolia*). A shrub up to 3 m high, with broad deep green leaves, small white flowers and fruit which ripens to a black colour.
2. the edible fruit of the native currant
= ahakey, artapaly, antyern angerr

arrarntwer (W,T) *n.*
thunderstorm ◆ Kwaty alenh arrarntwer angerr apetyem. (M) *There is a big thunderstorm coming there.* ◆ Kwaty arrarntwerel anwernenh atwem. (T) *The thunderstorm is going to hit us.*

arrarrarrarr-irrem (T,E) *vi.*
(women) make *'arrarrarrarr'* sound at initiation (young man) ceremony
SEE ALSO apwelh, rteyepertey, anmanty

Arrarrkw (T,E), **Arrarlkw** (T,E) *n.*
a star constellation; the Seven Sisters or Pleiades. They are of the Peltharr skin.
= Interrk[1], Kwerraly Angerr, Peltharr Map, Alyang Rlkwang
CAN SOUND A BIT LIKE ararrkw *'a man with a lot of wives'*

arratem *vi.*
1. go out, come out, exit, emerge ◆ Mereng arratenhem. (N) *Coming out of the house.*
2. come up (sun, moon, stars) ◆ Aherrk arratenty-alhem lyetant. (St) *The sun has just come up.*
3. arrive, turn up ◆ Lyetant arratem akuny. Arrwekeleng aretyakenh rwengk anep-anem. Lyetant anem arratem ra, arratenty-alpem. (St) *The poor thing has just arrived today. We didn't see him/her before. Now she has just arrived, just returned.*
4. come out, appear (flowers and plants) ◆ Ngkwarl ntywey arratem twern-rlwer. (M) *Corkwood honey [flowers] come out in the*

summer.
SEE ALSO tyerrelhem
arratelhem (E) *vi.*
arrive, turn up
SEE ALSO arwem-irrem
arratelh-ilem *vt.*
take something out of something, bring something out, pull something out of something
= tyerrem
arratety-alhem (W,T)
turn up, arrive, come out ◆ Arratety-alhem tyerrty alenh alethang. (M) *That stranger is arriving.*

arrathenem (E) *vt.*
throw a spear using a woomera ◆ Amirr-warl irrtyart akwernemel arrathenem atanthem anem. (St) *Putting the spear in the woomera, throwing it and then spearing it [the target].*
= rtwely-ilem

arratherrk *n.*
snake vine (*Tinospora smilacina*). A woody vine that climbs trees and shrubs, has leaves like a bush potato, and inedible red fruits. ◆ Arratherrk kapert ayernelhenhelhenh. Arepwelepwelarl awelhem, wal kwerelam ayerlpengayernelhem, lweren. Awelhem wal *round*-arl irrem kapert, nheng twern-penh *hot time* alakenh antem ilelhem. 'Ayeng kwenh kapert arepwelepwel-irrem terangk-terangk-irrem *see* alakenh.' Lwerenel antem *tie*-em *up* ilelhem, arratherrkelem *tie em up* ilelhem, awelhem ilelhem mwerrem anem. (N) *The snake vine is used for tying round the head. If you feel dizzy, then you tie the snake vine around your head. You might feel like your head is starting to spin, particularly in the hot weather. 'My head is spinning and I feel like I am drunk.' Well then you tie your head up with that vine and you'll feel better.*
= anwerl
SEE ALSO alyep
arratherrkayt (E) *n.*
snake vine grub. This grub is not edible.

arratwek *n.*
seed of the pencil yam, *arlatyey*, *anwerlarr* (*Vigna lanceolata*)
= kam

arraty *n.*
1. straight (in shape or path), in a straight line
2. right, correct, true, proper, precisely, it's a fact that . . . ◆ Anewart arratyant-atherr anerretyel. Kemarr uthen Petyarr uthen. (Sa) *The husband and wife are right [skin] for each other. Kemarr and Petyarr.* ◆ Arratyarl ayeng angkem. (St) *I am saying the right thing.* ◆ Angank arwengkalth. Arraty. Nyenngel arlkwerl-anem akweteth akweteth ateram arrtyanetyenheng — pwerlt-irrem. (N) *Crows are robbers. True. They always sneak around and steal food to eat and then when something gives them a fright they fly off — they bolt.* ◆ Rrtywerrenty angerr nta mpwarerl-apem kwenh — *no* unta arraty akwet apek ayey ilem war — rrtywerremel nta iltem, ngkweng ngkwanty kwenharl alarterl-anem map kwenh. (N) *You are going along and telling big lies — you're just not telling the story properly — you're lying when you say that lots of people are picking on you.* ◆ Altwerl arraty. *Due west.*
3. really, actually (something happens); really, actually (do something) ◆ Anengkerr arerl, ankwa intemel. Wal arraty ina apetyem. (T) *Dreaming [about them] while lying asleep. Then they really come.* ◆ Maney atnewel antherlanetyang. Arraty anthay. (Sa) *Don't just pretend to give me money. Really give it to me.*
4. right-hand side, to the right
kapert arraty
knowledgeable or clever; a person who has good ideas (kapert[1] *'head'*)
akwarraty *n.*
1. right-hand side, the right hand
2. right-handed (akwa *'hand', 'arm'*)
◆ Akwarratyel arratyarl wemek, arratyarl wem. (St) *Throwing something with the right hand.*
SEE ALSO alyeng
arraty-angkwerr (T,E) *n.*
right-hand side (-angkwerr *'by way of'*)
= arratyakw
SEE ALSO alyeng
arratyakw (W) *n.* = **arraty-angkwerr**
arraty-antey (T,E)
keep on going in a straight path (?) ◆ Arraty-antey yanh-angkwerr alha. (Sa) *Go straight that way.*
arraty akwet (W,T)
in a straight line or path ◆ Kel arnkwert-arnkwert-kweny — arraty akwet alhem kwenh. (Sa) *Don't go in a crooked line — go straight.*
arraty-akey (W,T) *n.*
'Is it true?', 'Is that so?' ◆ Arraty-akey ntwang ilep-ilem nthakenharl irrek? (M) *Is what you're saying happened really true?* ◆ Arraty-akey unta arek? (T) *Is it true that you saw it?*
= tyathew, tyakey
SEE ALSO akwey

arraty ilem
tell the truth (ilem *'say', 'tell'*)
arraty-irrem *vi.*
1. go in a straight line or path
= akert-arraty-irrem, akertarreng-irrem
2. go forwards ◆ Atnepetheng-irrem, kel arratyek irrenhem anem. (St) *Go backwards, then go forwards again.*
3. become corrected or fixed up
4. become straightened out
arraty-akwer-irrem (W) *vi.*
line up, go along in a straight line ◆ Pwelek kwaty-warn arraty-akwer-irrem. (M) *The cattle are going in a straight line to the water.*
arraty-ilem *vt.*
1. straighten something out ◆ Antyelty arraty-ilemel arternem, *straight*-em-ilem, urel itemel, atnem. (Sa) *Straightening out the stick by heating it in the fire, the digging stick.* ◆ Kerwep amper-amper nhenh tha arraty-iletyek. (T) *I've got to straighten this crooked crowbar.*
SEE ALSO arternem2
2. make things level, line things up with each other
3. correct something, set things straight, sort out a problem
arraty-ilelhem *vi.*
justify yourself, set the record straight about yourself ◆ Arraty-ilelha, tyel-angkekarl. Arrpenhek iletyek arraty. (St) *Set the record straight about yourself, after another spoke badly about you. [You've] got to tell the others the right story.*

arratyeny, arratyeyn (E) *n.*
straight ◆ Arna apek arratyeny, irrtyart apek arratyeny. (St) *A straight tree, or a straight spear.* ◆ Kapert arratyeny arrpenhem, akwerl alkey. (T) *Some have straight hair, long straight hair.*
arratyeyn-antey (E) *n.*
in a line, in a straight position ◆ Iylaw aymperr, ngkweytekan arlpenty, arratyeny-antey tnetyenh, arratyeny arratyeny. *Straight one*-rnem. Urrperl arnterran ngkweytek. (St) *The* iylaw *plant is flat, whereas the* ngkweytek *plant is taller and stands up straight. [The seeds] are really dark in colour.* ◆ Arratyeyn-antey alherl-wetyel. *Going along in a line.*

arraw-irrem *vi.*
1. gather together, come together in a group, meet together ◆ Anmanty-warn tyerrty map arraw-irrem rntwetyek. (T) *Aboriginal people gather together to dance at the young men's ceremony.*
2. swarm (ants), start to move around, bustle around, mill around ◆ Ameng map arraw-irrem ker ampengel-ayel. (T) *There are lots of flies gathering around the cooked meat.* ◆ Arraw-irrem pwelek ulyethey, ker apek aherr. Arelh apek arraw-irrem, arraw-irrem *meeting* akngerr-they, alperrty anem irrem. (Sa) *The bullocks are starting to move out from the shade, or the kangaroos. Maybe the women are moving away from the big meeting and splitting up [to go home].*
SEE ALSO akarr-irrem
arraw-ilem *vt.*
1. sweep or gather things together, stoke a fire ◆ Rwang yanh anwekantherr arraw-ilay anwantherr ntywety anetyek. Irrerntek. (T) *Stoke that fire up for us so that we can sit down warm. It's cold.*
2. stir things up, make things unsettled
SEE ALSO akarr-ilem, arlwelem
arrawelh-ilem *vt.* = **arraw-ilem** ◆ Arelh yanhel arrawelh-ilem rwang rrwelty. (T) *The woman is gathering the pieces of firewood together.* ◆ Arelhel arna-akertel arrawelh-ilem rwang aperrk map. (T) *The woman is scraping the coals together with a stick.* ◆ Yerr akwek weth-lkwer arrawelh-ileman. Arrawelh-ilemel anwantherr apalel arrernety-alhemel. (St) *Stirring up little ants and things like that. We stir them up when we mistakenly sit ourselves down [on them].*

arrawel *n.kin*
a sympathetic or respectful word for father. This term may be used if the father referred to is sick or has died. The term may also be used respectfully by an auntie (*awenh*) when asking her nephew or niece (*aler*) about their father (i.e. her brother). ◆ Akeweny kwenh, arrawel rlkert-penh apety-alpern. (T) *The poor thing, [the] father just came back after being sick.* ◆ Arrawel-kweny irretyenh yanhanaw. (St) *That person is going to be without a father soon.*
SEE ALSO angey
arrawelaty *n.kin*
my/our *arrawel*
arrawelengk *n.kin*
your *arrawel* ◆ 'Arrawelengk-alew?' 'Nhak alhek.' (Sa) *'Where is your father?' 'He went over there.'*
arrawelikw (E) *n.kin*
his/her/their *arrawel.*
arrawelekw (W,T) *n.kin*
1. your *arrawel*
2. his/her/their *arrawel.*

arrawelp (W,T) *n.*
axe handle. Usually made from mulga or ironwood wood. ◆ Arrawelp angety-alpem

mer-warn arrperl-anetyek, arterrp-ilemel arrperl-anetyek, anker kwerel, kwempalthel. (T) *The axe handle is brought back to camp to be chiselled and smoothed, with an adze.*
= arlarnt

arrawenth-irrem *vi.*
whistle ◆ Ayeng arrawenth-irrem yanhek. Ayeng arrawenth-irrem ngkweng apek. (St) *I might whistle to that person over there. I might whistle to you.* ◆ Ngkekern arrawenth-irrerl-anem artwang. (N) *The kurdaitcha man whistles.*
= ilpwerlenty-rnem

arrawey (W,T) weapons (spears or boomerangs) SEE UNDER **irrawey**

arrayenp (E), **arreyenp** (E) *n.*
lips (arra *'mouth'*; ayenp *'skin'*)
= arrakert ayenp, arrenpenp
SEE ALSO arrakert

arraylem (E) use supernatural powers or magic on someone SEE UNDER **arrilem**

arrek (E) *n.*
emu apple, sour plum (*Owenia acidula*). A small tree with rough bark, dark-coloured leaves and red fruits about the size of an apricot.

arrekar-irrem (T) *vi.*
avoid a person; not like a person ◆ Tyerrty apek unpart, ayeng menty kwer aretyal aney, ayeng arrekar-irrem. (T) *If a person is sulky, then I don't want to see them and I avoid them.*

arrekarlkarlker (T,E) *n.*
types of ant (*Camponotus* sp.; *Iridomyrmex* sp.; *Rhytidoponera* sp. (?)) ◆ Artety-arenyarl ra. Ahelengkw. Alhweng ikwerenh *self*-anteyarl anep-anem arrekarlkarlker-kenhan akngerrarl — wetharl *heap*-em *up*. (St) *It lives in the mulga and it's aggressive. The* arrekarlkarlker *ant nest is large — those ones that are heaped up.*
SEE ALSO arlkerrk[1], yerr

arrekelyekely-wem (W) *vt.*
chase someone or something ◆ Angwelyel arrekelyekely-wem ker aherr. (M) *The dog is chasing the kangaroo.*
= alwernem, lwakem

arrekelyekely-werrem (W) *vi.*
chase each other

arrekelyekely-ilerrem (T) *vi.* = **arrekelyekely-werrem** ◆ Kwer atherram arrekelyekely-ilerreperrem mer kwenel. (T) *There are two kids chasing each other round inside the house.*

arrekwep-kwep (W) *n.*
stalked puffball (*Podaxis pistillaris*). Grows to about 10 cm high, on a long stalk. Powdery purplish black spores inside. (arra *'mouth'*; kwep-kwep[3] *'stalked puffball'*)
= pwek-pwek, pweng-pweng, anngarnt rrpwerl, kwep-kwep[3]

arrelh (E) colony wattle SEE UNDER **arrely**[1]

arrelharrp (W), **arreylarrp** (E) *adv.*
behaving in a one-sided way; paying attention to one person at the expense of another; ignoring someone, favouring some at the expense of others ◆ Arreylarrp angkep-angkem, ra apek angkep-angkem war apek ilep-ilem. Arreylarrp angkep-angkem arrpenhek. (St) *That person is talking and paying attention to the others [and ignoring me].*
◆ Arreylarrp arrkerenyel-iwemel, arreylarrp angayakwel arerl-anemek. Menty, kerel arntarnt-aretyangel anem rarrp, ingwer anem wanterl-anemel. *Abandoning the hungry person and not paying them any attention. Just leaving them to fend for themselves, and meanwhile feeding other people.*
SEE ALSO arrkerenyel-wem

arrelharrp anthem (W), **arreylarrp anthem** (E)
give something to some and not to others
◆ Arrelharrp ntwa anthem. Ayeng akenh itya anep-anem. (M) *You are giving the things to the others. I'm sitting here without any.*
◆ Arreylarrp ntwa anthetyel ayengan arrarentyarl anep-anem, arraretyelarl. Arreylap ntwa anthetyel ayeng angayakw arrarentyarl. Arrpenhek-areyarl ntwa anthetyel, arrpenh-arey ntwa wantetyel ayengan arrarentyarl. (Sa) *You are just giving [the food] to them and I am sitting here missing out. You are giving it to the others and I am hungry and missing out. You are giving food to the others, feeding them, and I'm not getting my share.*
SEE ALSO arrarem

arrelharrp alhem (W), **arreylarrp alhem** (E)
go across, cut across

arrelty[1] (T,E) *n.*
lungs ◆ Arrelty akeng-irrem, pwentyelarl atwem. (Sa) *The person's lungs are no good after they've been sick.*
= arrelyarn

arrelty arem (E)
be an omen of death, foretell death (lit. 'see the lungs'). The howling of dogs or the cawing of crows is believed to be a sign of the impending death of a person.
= arreltyarn arem

arrelty[2] *n.*
1. saliva, slobber ◆ Arengk yanh arrelty-akert ilantha! (M) *Shoo that slobbery dog away!*
SEE ALSO arrwek, iylkerr, pelh[1]

2. juice of the witchetty grub and other grubs ◆ Arrelty antywetyam. Arrengey tha arerl-apetyam atyenh, antywetyamarl rarey. Kwaty anetyakenhel ina antywetyam, war then antywemel. *No* altyewetyek arrangkwarl. (St) *[People] drank the juice of the witchetty grub. I saw all my grandparents drinking it. When they didn't have any water they just drank it. They didn't tip it out [and throw it away].* ◆ Tyap arrelty thelelhem tyampet-warn. (T) *The juice of the witchetty grub is leaking into the billycan.*

arrelty thelelhem
dribble, slobber, leak (juice of grub)
◆ Arrakerteng arrelty thelelhem. (M) *Saliva is dribbling from the mouth.*
= iylkerr thelelhem

arreltyarn (T) lungs SEE UNDER **arrelyarn**

arrely[1], **arrelh** (E) *n.*
1. colony wattle (*Acacia murrayana*). Shrub up to 3 m high, with bright yellow flowers and with edible seeds and grubs.
2. the edible seed of the colony wattle ◆ *Seed* map arrely map. Arnwety-akert arlkwenh-arlkwenh, mern arlkwetyart anwern. An akerl-apetyart arnwety kwer-akert. *The colony wattle has lots of edible seeds which we used to eat. We used to go along collecting the seeds.*

arrely[2], **arreyl** (E) *n.*
cheek (of face)
= rlkey

arrely ngkwern, arreyl ngkwern (E)
cheekbone, jawbone (ngkwern *'bone'*)
= rlkey ngkwern

arrely tyelk, arreyl tyelk (E)
cheek (fleshy part) (tyelk *'flesh'*)

arrely ayenp, arreyl ayenp (E)
= **arrely tyelk** (ayenp *'skin'*)

arrely-arrely weak from hunger or sickness, very old, thin, wrinkled SEE UNDER **arrwely-arrwely**

arrelyarn (W,T), **arreltyarn** (T) *n.*
lungs
= arrelty[1]

arreltyarn arem (T)
be an omen of death, foretell death (lit. 'see the lungs'). The howling of dogs or the cawing of crows is believed to be a sign of the impending death of a person. ◆ Arreltyelarl arem arengkel. Parrp atwerrirraw kwenh, arreltyarn aremeng kwenh. (T) *The dog is bringing an omen of death. Hit it quickly, because it's foretelling death.*
= arrelty arem

arrem (T,E) *n.*
1. louse, lice, nits
2. native bee larvae (used as medicine). The egg-like substance from the sugarbag nest is used to rub on aching heads.
SEE ALSO anma[1]

arremangkw (E) *part.* [RESPECT LANGUAGE]
no, nothing, having nothing
◆ Arremangkwarl akwel uyarerrerlentyarrek — *no* mern. Ahanety-alpek thew-ayerr-they. (Sa) *They [including respect kin] went looking in vain and there was nothing there — no food. They came back from the store.* ◆ Arremangkw-antey ker anetyakenh-antey. (Sa) *There's still nothing, no meat.* ◆ Tyanywengek arremangkw-antey. (Sa) *[My respect kin] has no tobacco.*
SEE ALSO arrangkw

arremangkw-irrem (E) *vi.*
pass away, die
SEE ALSO ilwem, arrangkw-irrem, alyent-artek-irrem, anengkan-irrem

arrematy rltey-rltey (T,E) *n.*
New Holland rattlepod (*Crotalaria novae-hollandiae*) ◆ Ankerrelarl arlkwem arrematy rltey-rlteyan. Ingkarl rltar-rltar atantherl-anem ampel apek arrkenel, arrematy rltey-rltey renh. (T) *The* arrematy rltey-rltey *plant is something that emus eat. Kids also enjoy themselves by stepping on the plant so that the pods make a popping sound.*
= rltey-rltey

Arremewern (E) *n.*
the name of a place west of Apengarlayntem, in the Utopia (Angarapa Aboriginal Land Trust) area. *Arrem* 'louse' Dreaming.

arremparreng, arramparreng (E) *n.*
1. a person's spirit double; the spitting image of someone; people with a very strong family resemblance to each other
2. a spirit friend ◆ Nyanyikwel ilem akin nyanyekikwel, 'Ngarremparrengarl yanh ngapenyarl'. (Sa) *Her granny might say, 'That person is* ngarremparreng, *the spitting image of you'.* ◆ Arremparreng-rnem. 'Ayeng-apeny arremparreng yanh kwenh. Inngerr ayeng-apeny kwenh, kwey nhenh aperley atyenh — arremparreng.' (Sa) *All the people who are very much alike. 'That person there closely resembles me. My grandchild has a face just like mine —* arremparreng.*'*

ayeng-arremparreng (E) *n.*
my *arremparreng*; someone who closely resembles me, my spirit friend (ayeng[1] *'I'*)

atyeng-arremparreng (W,T) *n.*
my *arremparreng*; someone who closely resembles me, my spirit friend (atyeng *'for me', 'to me'*)

ngarremparreng (E) *n.*
your *arremparreng;* someone who closely resembles you (nga *'you'*) ◆ Inngerr ngapeny anenty alanh, kwey ngkwenh ayteyengkw atherr. *Felicity* weth ngapeny inngerr — ngarremparreng. Rantey arremparreng, rarremparreng. Ingwerelan ilem, 'Rarremparrengarl yanh kwenh.' *Your two younger sisters have faces similar to yours. That Felicity has a face like yours —* ngarremparreng. *She looks like you. Other people say, 'She is the spitting image of her —* rarremparreng.*'*

ngkweng-arremparreng (W,T) *n.*
your *arremparreng;* someone who closely resembles you, your spirit friend (ngkweng *'to you', 'for you'*) ◆ Ngkweng-arremparreng — arety-kwenh ayenh, warant awerlanem. (T) *Your spirit friend — you can't see him, only hear him.*

rarremparreng (E) *n.*
his or her *arremparreng,* someone who closely resembles him or her (ra *'he', 'she'*)

ikwer-arremparreng (W,T) *n.*
his or her *arremparreng,* someone who closely resembles him or her, his or her spirit friend (ikwer *'for him/her', 'to him/her'*)

mpwel-arremparreng *n.*
your *arremparreng;* someone who closely resembles you (two) (mpwel *'you two'*) (St) ◆ Mpwel-arremparreng apetyek. (St) *The person who looks like you two came.*

arrantherr-arramparreng *n.*
your *arremparreng,* someone who closely resembles you (plural) (arrantherr *'you (more than two)'*)

anwakerr-arramparreng (T,E) *n.*
our *arremparreng,* someone who closely resembles us (plural)

anantherr-arramparreng (W,T) *n.*
our *arremparreng,* someone who closely resembles us (plural) (anantherr *'we (more than two)'*)

arrempelty (E), **urrempelty** (E) *n.*
1. a type of cloud that forms on top of a column of smoke, pyrocumulus cloud ◆ Arrempeltyel inem. Ura kwert imernt ampem, *bushfire* apek. Wal, ura kwert arratyeny apek ampem, wal arrempeltyel inem. (St) *The cloud gets the smoke. And then the bushfire burns. Well, the smoke burns straight up because the cloud has taken it.* (?)
2. an area of country that has been burnt before ◆ Ker arlewatyerr atwerl-anetyek alhem urrempelty-angkwerr. Urrempelty-irremelarl ampek-angkwerr. (Sa) *[We] go looking for goannas in the country that has been burnt. In the country that has been burnt.*
SEE ALSO urntem, rlpwat, lerranty

arrempelty-irrem (E), **urrempelty-irrem** (E) *vi.*
become burnt (country) ◆ Urrempelty-irrem antywerelarl ampek-angkwerr. (Sa) *The country where the bushfire burnt has been burnt out.*
SEE ALSO rlpwat-irrem

arremwar-mwar *n.*
loud talker, 'loud mouth', 'big mouth' (arra *'mouth'*; mwar *'wooden dish'*) ◆ Arremwar-mwar arlengel angketyek alhaw, arremwar-mwaray, irlparl arwengk-ilem-kety. (Sa) *Big mouth, go and talk a long way away, big mouth. You're deafening us.* ◆ 'Arremwar-mwaray, thwengk atweketyay!' Arrpenhem *swear*-irrem ikwer. (T) *'Big mouth, I'm going to hit you!' Others swear at him/her.*

arreng, arrengey (E) *n.kin*
1. father's father; grandfather
2. father's father's brother or sister; great-uncle, great-aunt
3. a man's son's child; grandchild; grandson, granddaughter
4. a person's brother's son's child; great-niece, great-nephew
5. particular relations with the same skin as a person's *arreng*
6. the country and Dreamings belonging to a person's *arreng.* If a person calls someone *arreng* then they will call them *arreng* back.

arreng-arreng *n.kin*
father's father, (man's) son's child, etc. This may be an affectionate or respectful way of talking to or about one's *arreng.* It is also the word used when talking to children about their *arreng.* ◆ Artwampw atyenh arreng-arreng uyerrek. (Sa) *My old grandfather passed away.* ◆ Arreng-arreng ampa akelyekarl ilerl-anem. Ampa akelyel awetyel. 'Arreng-arreng aray. Angey akely, angang.' (Sa) Arreng-arreng *is what you say to children. So that the child can hear. 'Look at your* arreng-arreng. *Your little grandfather.'*
SEE ALSO angang

arrengaty *n.kin*
my/our *arreng*

arrengengkw *n.kin*
your *arreng*

arrengikw (E), **arrengeyekw** (E) *n.kin*
his/her/their *arreng*
arrengwek (W,T) *n.kin*
1. your *arreng*
2. his/her/their *arreng*
arreng-nheng *n.kin*
a group two or more people related to each other as *arreng*
arreng-intyerr *n.kin* = **arreng-nheng**
arreng-nheng-arey *n.kin*
a group of more than two people related to each other as *arreng*
arreng-nheng atherr *n.kin*
a person together with one of their *arreng* ◆ Arreng-nheng atherr ilern. (M) *We two are related as grandparent and grandchild.*
arreng-parety *n.kin*
respectful or 'sorry way' of talking about someone's *arreng* ◆ Arreng-parety arntetyaw. Anterel apek apernetyekaw. (Sa) *Your poor old* arreng *is sick. Rub him/her with fat.*
SEE ALSO -parety
arreng-ankethenh *n.kin*
1. having a close *arreng* still alive
2. someone who is always with their *arreng*
SEE ALSO -ankethenh

arrengakw on the other side of something (to the speaker) SEE UNDER **arrwengak**

arrengarlp (W) *n.*
bull ant
= atyank, ntyeyapert, tyekarnparnp[1]

arrengey (E) father's father; grandfather SEE UNDER **arreng**

arrengker *adv.*
1. (doing something) quickly, being in a hurry ◆ Kwer akwek arrtyanem arrengker. (M) *The child is running fast.* ◆ Angkem ayeng arrengker, parrp-parrp. (St) *I am talking quickly.* ◆ Arrengker uremeny alhem, *lazy bugger* irretyang — uremeny alhetyek. (Sa) *That person is going along quickly, not being lazy and slow — going fast*
SEE ALSO uremeny, parrp, aher
2. being about to do something, having a go at something ◆ Artwang yanh arrengker anem warl atwetyek. (T) *The man tried to hit the house.*
3. feel ready to eat or drink ◆ Ker arlkwetyek ayeng arrengker anem anert atyenh. (T) *My stomach feels ready to eat meat.* ◆ Ayeng arrengker awelhem ker arlkwetyeh. (M) *I really feel like eating meat.*
CAN SOUND A BIT LIKE arrengkerr *'you (more than two)'*
arrengker anthem
give someone an appetite, make someone feel like eating or drinking (anthem *'give'*) ◆ Atnert arrengker anthemel, mern angerr arlkwetyek, alyemel. Arrengkerel anem arlkwem. (Sa) *Singing [the person] gives them their appetite back, and then they can eat lots of food. Then they feel like eating.* ◆ Yanhel ker arlkwep-arlkwem, ayeng arrengker-anthem. (M) *That person is eating meat and making me feel like eating.*
SEE ALSO arrernkelh-ilem
arrengker-irrem (W,T) *vi.*
1. go quickly, do something quickly, go fast
2. feel like eating or drinking, get appetite back
arrengker-ilem (W,T) *vt.*
1. make something go quickly or do something quickly, speed something up
2. make someone feel like eating or drinking

arrengkerr, **arringkerr** *prn.*
you (more than two). This pronoun is used in the subject part of the sentence (i.e. representing the 'doers' of the verb action) when the people are all in the same patrimoiety and the same generation moiety; for example, a person together with their sisters or brothers, their father's fathers or their mother's mothers. See Appendix 1. ◆ Arringkerr awenh-awenh map alherrirray. (T) *Off you go, all you aunties.*
SEE ALSO arrakerr, arrantherr
CAN SOUND A BIT LIKE arrengker *'do something quickly etc.'*
arrenh-ingkerrenh, **arrenh-ingkerr** *prn.*
you (more than two). This pronoun is used in the object part of the sentence (i.e. representing those the verb action is 'done to').
arreh-ingkerr (W,T), **arrek-ingkerr** (E) *prn.*
for you, to you (more than two)
arrengkerrenh (W,T), **arreh-ingkerrenh** (W,T), **arrek-ingkerrenh** (E) *prn.*
your, yours (belonging to more than two)
arrengkerr-altyerr (T), **arringkerr-altyerr** (E) *n.*
your sons-in-law; your mothers-in-law (closely related ones whose mothers come from the same country) ◆ Arringkerr-altyerr apetyewarray. *Come here all of you [brothers or sisters who call one county* altyerr*].*
SEE ALSO -altyerr

arrenkelh-ilem[1] (T) *vt.*
trick or deceive someone; falsely or mistakenly raise someone's expectations ◆ Tyerrty yanhel ngwenh arrenkelh-ilem ker-warn akwel alhetyek. (T) *That person is telling you that they might be going hunting but they*

were tricking you.
arrenkelh-anthem (T) *vt.* = **arrenkelh-ilem**1 ◆ Arelh yanhel ilem ngwenh arrenkelh-anthem amwang-kety. (T) *That woman is making out as if there is a snake there, to give you a fright.* ◆ Tyerrty nhenhel ayeng arrenkelh-anthek, ker aherr akwel atyerretyek. Rang apal arek — kerrertek. (T) *This person raised my expectations that I was going to shoot a kangaroo. He mistook an ant bed for a kangaroo.*

arrenkelh-ilem2 (T), **irrenkelh-ilem** (E) *vt.*
make someone feel as if something is crawling around or touching them, give someone a fright
= irraker-ilem
SEE ALSO inkerrelh-ilem, mpwarelh-ilem, aterel-anthem

arrenpenp (W,T), **arrimpimp** (E), **arreympeyemp** (E) *n.*
1. lips
2. beak (especially emu beak) ◆ Arrimpimpel iytarr-inemel arlkwerl-anemel ntywey, tharrkarr, intekw. (Sa) *With its beak [the emu] pulls down the corkwood flowers, the honey grevillea and the* intekw *plant to eat.*
SEE ALSO arra

arrenper (W) gap left in front teeth after a tooth has been knocked out (ceremonial) SEE UNDER **arrimper**

arrent (W,T), **arrint** (E), **arreynt** (E), **irreynt** (E) *n.*
toothpick ◆ Ker nheng tetyelarl mwernelhem, wal arnang arrent inem, atanthelhem. (M) *If there is meat stuck in your teeth you get a toothpick and poke it out.*
= irreyneper
SEE ALSO arra, inta
CAN SOUND A BIT LIKE Arrernt *'Arrernte people and language'*

arrenty *n.*
1. venomous animal, dangerous thing, creepy crawly ◆ Arrenty akely. Arrwekelenyelan ilerretyart 'arrenty'. Payteyan alhernter-kenhan. (Sa) *Little creepy crawlies. The old people used to call them '*arrenty*'. 'Bitey' is a word that white people use.*
2. the devil ◆ Ayeng anpwelhem arrenty-kety, *pray*-irremel. Altyerrek ayeng *pray*-irrem wal arrenty anpwemarl. (T) *I pray to keep the devil away. I pray to God and then the devil is chased away.* ◆ Arrentyel uternem, 'Wal, unta atyenh ana kwenh'. Renh apek tyerrty arrpenh atwetyek. (St) *The devil makes him do it, 'Well, you can be mine'. It makes the person kill another person.*
3. monster ◆ Kwer map rrtywerremel ilem kwenyel 'arrenty', wal ater-irrem kwereng. (T) *In the night the kids pretend and say 'monster', and then they get frightened from that.*
arrenty-arrenty *n.*
a sort of pretend monster ◆ Aterel-anthem kwer map, arrkenel war arrenty-arrentyel. (T) *Frightening the kids just for fun, pretending to be monsters.*
Arrenty-atherr (E) *n.*
a star constellation; Magellanic Clouds (lit. 'two devils')

arreny (W,T), **arreyn** (E), **arreytn** (E) *n.*
1. name, skin name, the name of a thing, the word for a thing ◆ Ilak arreyn? (Sa) *What name?* ◆ Arreytn ayeng ilelhem *self*. (St) *I am saying my name, myself.* ◆ Arreny-akert ingkerr anem, arreny-akert ingkerr tyerrty map alartem. Peltharram arreny ayeng anem. (N) *All of them have skin names, all the Aboriginal people have skin names. My skin name is Peltharr.* ◆ Mer arreny-akert, *Napperby* arreny-akert. (N) *The country has names — Napperby has names.* ◆ Tharl aparlp-ilek arreyn yanh. (Sa) *I have forgotten that name.*
SEE ALSO anpernenty
2. song, verse, tune ◆ Arreytn arrpenh ywerrem-arleng arreytn arrpenh anem alyelhetyek. (St) *When one verse finishes then you sing another.*
= ina2
arreny anewem (W,T), **arreyn inewem** (E)
call someone or something by a name, say something's or someone's name (anewem *'call someone by a name'*)
arreny anthem (W,T), **arreyn anthem** (E)
name something, give someone or something a name (anthem *'give'*) ◆ Arreny anthem — aperlelikw apek arreny anthem. (T) *Naming [the child] — maybe the grandparent will name him/her.*
arreny arrernem (W,T), **arreyn arrernem** (E)
name something, give someone or something a name (arrernem *'put'*)

arrenyanty (E) *n.*
spitfire larva (?). Green in colour and lives on the red mallee tree, red river gum, bloodwood etc. ◆ Alperr anpenhemel apal alhem kel urrampentyant awelhem. 'Arrenyantyel ayenh akekaw!' (Sa) *If you mistakenly touch a leaf as you are going past then you will feel the burning sting [of the spitfire]. 'The spitfire stung me!'*

arrep-ilem *vt.* [RESPECT LANGUAGE]
look, see ◆ Ampeyamp tha arrep-ilem kwenh.

(M) *I can see my son-in-law [coming].* ◆ Ngwarrekikw arrep-ilep-ilem. (St) *She [my daughter] is looking for her husband [said by a woman].*
SEE ALSO arem

arrep-wem, **arrep-iwem** (E) *vt.*
spit something out ◆ Apmwa antyakert, arntekelarl anyenem. Wal, apmwa antya anem arrep-wem. (St) *Snakes have poison, that they carry in their teeth. Well, the snake spits the poison out.* ◆ Kwaty arrep-wem tyerrtyel, antywemarl-penh. (T) *The person spits the water out after drinking.*
SEE ALSO pelh-wem

arrepeny (T) *n.*
1. desert Flinders grass (*Yakirra australiensis* var. *australiensis*). A grass about 15 cm high, with reddish-coloured leaves.
2. the edible seeds of the desert Flinders grass ◆ Rrkwalelarl anem arrepeny. (T) *The* arrepeny *grass is the one that grows in the desert country.*
= arlepenh, nyetempwer, kwarrety

arreper (T) western brown snake (?) SEE UNDER arriper

arreperlk (E) *n.* [RESPECT LANGUAGE]
snake ◆ Arreperlk-kety mwerrenganty ahanerlentyarretyek kwey tyanterlentyarr. (Sa) *Daughter, go and tell your husband to watch out for snakes when he goes [said by the mother of the woman].*
SEE ALSO urnem

arreperlp (W,T) *n.*
king brown snake, mulga snake (*Pseudechis australis*) ◆ Arreperlp anem ahangerr anthwerr. (T) *King brown snakes are really dangerous.*
= tyamparl
SEE ALSO ikwelengk
CAN SOUND A BIT LIKE arepeylp *'bush thick-knee'*

arrepert (E), **arrapert** (T) *n.*
curled up, doubled up ◆ Rlkerr apekarl intem, wal arlerlp-irrem arrepert-irrenty-alpem. Ngkwernarl akeng-irrem. (St) *Lying stretched out, and then [your] legs cramp up and double back up again. If your legs are no good.*
= arlwemeny
SEE ALSO rtapety

arrepert-irrem (E), **arrapert-irrem** (T) *vi.*
double up, curl up, become tight and twisted ◆ Iltya arrepert-irrem. (Sa) *[My] hand is doubled up.* ◆ Alwerrng ayeng arrepert-irrem, arrepert-irrek-ketyaw. (Sa) *My tendons have become doubled up and twisted.*
= arlwemeny-irrem
SEE ALSO apwert-irrem, arlwerrelhem

arrepwek-pwek (W) *n.*
1. a teenage boy's first facial hair
2. a young teenage boy with facial hair just starting to grow (arra *'mouth'*; pwek-pwek *'stalked puffball'*)
SEE ALSO arrepweng-pweng, pweng-pweng, pwengep, pwek-pwek, anngarnt rrpwerl, kwep-kwep³

arrepweng-pweng (E) *n.*
stalked puffball (*Podaxis pistillaris*) (arra *'mouth'*; pweng-pweng *'stalked puffball'*). Grows to about 10 cm high, on a long stalk. Has powdery purplish-black spores inside.
= pweng-pweng, pwengep, pwek-pwek, arrekwep-kwep, anngarnt rrpwerl, kwep-kwep³

arrer (T,E) *n.*
close, near ◆ Arrer nhenh anep-anem. Arlengan yanhan alhep-alhem. (St) *[This person] is sitting close. That person is going in the distance.* ◆ Arrer-artek ana. (St) *Sit a bit closer.* ◆ Arrer war anwengkerr alheyaw. (T) *We're not going very far, just close up.*
SEE ALSO angath, itwa, arleng¹, rntwarr
CAN SOUND A BIT LIKE arwerr *'hole', 'burrow'*

arrer-irrem (E) *vi.*
move or get closer to something
= itwirrem, itwang-irrem

arrer-ilem (E) *vt.*
make something closer
= itwilem, itwang-ilem

arrerelh-ilem (E) *vt.* = **arrer-ilem**

arrerenty (E) *n.*
near, close

arrer-antey (T,E) *n.*
near, close

arrerek-arrer (T,E) *n.*
1. things that are close to each other ◆ Arrerek-arrer aneyaw. (St) *Sit close to each other.*
2. things that are similar to each other ◆ Arrerek-arrer ratherr anem — 'arwerr' an 'arrer'. (St) *Those two [words] are similar to each other — 'arwerr' and 'arrer'.*
= rtwang-rtwang, itwek-itwa

arrerlang (T,E) *n.*
1. rat tails (a type of plant) (*Dysphania rhadinostachya*). A sticky herb about 25 cm high with flowers forming erect spikes, and with tiny, shiny black seeds.
2. the edible seed of the rat tails plant. *Arrerlang* is said to be the elder sister and *alpar* 'rat-tail goosefoot plant' the younger sister.
SEE ALSO alpar, parntentyarlp, mwelyeparnt-parnt
CAN SOUND A BIT LIKE rrwerleng *'honey grevillea'*

arrerlkart (T,E) *adv.*
feeling really hungry, feeling starving ◆ Anert urrelp-urrampem angayakw, arrerlkart ulthem — *right out* mernek angayakw, arlkwetyek anem arlkwem mern arnterr anem anert pwelap-ilelhemel. (Sa) *My stomach is starting to burn from hunger — I'm really starving, hungry for food so that I can eat a lot and fill my stomach up.*
arrerlkart-irrem (T,E) *vi.*
feel really hungry, feel starving
arrerlkart urntem (E) = **arrerkart-irrem** ◆ Ayeng atnert arrerlkart urntem angayel, arrerlkart anem. (St) *My stomach is really feeling hungry.*
arrerlkart pwem (E) = **arrerlkart-irrem**

arrerlker (E) *n.*
1. a light brown colour, pale colour
2. 'light' sound (of speech) ◆ Arrerlker Alyawarr apek. Arrerlker-artek angkep-angkem Ankerrapw thayt. (Sa) *Maybe Alyawarr sounds a bit 'light'. [People] over Utopia side talk in a 'light' way.* ◆ Ntheyelkwer map arrengker, akern-antey. Anmatyerr *little bit* ulthentyarl, itna akenh angkem arrerlker *light one.* (T) *Ntheyelkwer people speak fast, and with a 'high' pronunciation. Anmatyerr is a bit heavy in sound, whereas the Ntheyelkwer people speak in a 'light' way.*

arrerlp, **arreylp** (E) *n.*
sharp, pointed, prickly ◆ Ker kerl-aynetyek, mern apek kerl-aynetyek, *knife* arreylpel. (Sa) *Quickly cutting the bread or the meat with a sharp knife.*
arrerlp-arrerlp, **arreylp-arreylp** (E) *n.*
sharp, pointed, prickly ◆ Arreylp-arreylp ilkwa — arreylp rlterrk *one*. Antywer. Anker-akertan arrpenh. (Sa) *It is large and has sharp spikes — hard spikes. Different kinds [of spinifex] have spinifex wax.*
artwang arrerlp (W,T), **artwa arreylp** (E)
cowboy (lit. 'sharp man' because of the shape of his hat) ◆ Artwang arrerlp ananem yartel-ayeng. (N) *The cowboy is sitting on the fence.*
arrerlp-ilem, **arreylp-ilem** (E) *vt.*
sharpen something ◆ Ntha arrerlp-iletyek yanh anthey apwert-warl tha arrerlp-iletyek. *Give that thing to me so that I can sharpen it on the rock.* ◆ Yenper arternetyam, *clean* antem yarr-wetyam, arrerlp-iletyam, kel *clean*-ilemel arternemel arrernetyam. (N) *The spearwood was scraped and cleaned and then straightened and sharpened. When it was cleaned it was put in the fire to straighten and sharpen it.*

arrerlpank (W) *n.*
a bark container used for carrying things. Also referred to as *arntap arrerlpank*. ◆ Anewek akenh apety-alpetyart arety-alpetyart kwart pwelap ankerr akertel. Nheng arntap arrerlpank angerrelel-arleng angety-alpetyart. (M) *Her husband came back with a big load of emu eggs that he carried in a big bark container.*

arrerlpem (W,T), **arreylpem** (E) *vt.*
chew something, munch on something ◆ Mern arlkwemel arrerlpem. (M) *Chewing the food as [you] eat it.* ◆ Aleth-anteyelarl ntwan arreylpepeylpem — akwet-antey arlkwep-arlkwem arreylperl-anem aleth. (Sa) *You keep on chewing and chewing — you're always eating and chewing.*
SEE ALSO arlkwem, karlkwem
arreylpenh-iylpenh (E) *n.*
temple (on the side of the head) ◆ Mernarl arlkwem alakenh arreylpem arreylpem, wal nhenharl *move*-irrem. Mern arlkwemel arreylpem arlkwemel arlkwemel, arreylpemarl, wal nhenharl *move*-arl irrepirrem akngelhepelhem. Wal alhwarl warrk-irrem nhenh. Arreylpenh-iylpenh. (St) *When you eat food like that and chew on it, well this [the temple] moves. When you chew on food well this moves. The blood makes it work here [pointing to the temple].*

arrernem *vt.*
1. put something in place, put something down ◆ Rtak arrernetyek, irlkengey. (M) *[I] will set up a windbreak against the wind.* ◆ Tyerrty nhenhel rwang-warn tey arrernem. (N) *This person is putting the tea [in a billycan] on the fire.*
2. write, draw ◆ Pep-warn arrernem. (M) *Writing something in the book.* • SEE ALSO atanthem, mpaty-ilem, ingkwernem, intelh-ilem
3. lay eggs ◆ Kwetakwetel kwart arrernem arnamek. (St) *Spotted nightjars lay their eggs in the grass.*
4. appoint, give a job to
5. Goes with some other words to form verbs with the general meaning of 'put something in place or put something in some position'. For example, *arlpar-arrernem* 'hang something up'; *ayak-arrernem* 'tip things out and pile them up'; *rwelh-arrernem* 'squeeze something out of something else'; *tek-arrerenem* 'hang something up'. The first parts of these compounds do not seem to be used their own.
arrernelhem *vi.*
1. sit yourself down ◆ Arlenty-akert ayeng arrernelhey, arlentyarl arlkwem. (T) *I'm going to sit myself down because I've got a sore hip.*

2. land (bird or aeroplane) ◆ Irrarnt arlkerl-apem aningk, angkerrerl-apem. Akem-irremel aywerr angkemel arrernelhenhem irrarnt. Lyek arlkwerl-anem. (N) *Lots of red-tailed black cockatoos fly along screeching. They fly up and make a lot of noise and then land. They eat prickles.* ◆ Thep arrernelhem anwerlk-arleng, antywel-arleng. (N) *The bird settles down on its rump in the nest.* ◆ Yanh *aeroplane* arrernelhem. Uthip then yanh arrernelhem. Alethang apetyem, anwantherr kel arrernelhem. (Sa) *That aeroplane is landing. The bird is landing as well. A stranger comes and then we all sit down.*

3. arrive somewhere ◆ Artar yanh atyenh apety-alpetyel. Lyetant arrernelhenty-alhek. (Sa) *My son is coming back. He has just arrived back today.*

4. write (own name) ◆ Arreny arrernelhem. (M) *Write [your] name.*

5. put something on yourself, or put something close to part of yourself ◆ Angkwey alhetyamarl, artarr arrernelhetyam ingkern, wal alhetyam mpweny. (M) *In the olden days he [the man] went and put the emu feathers behind [his back], and then went off with his lover.* ◆ Iyterlarr arrernelhem awelyek-angent, anthep-irretyek-angent. (St) *Putting the headdress on before the* awely *ceremonies, before dancing.*

arrernkem (W,T), **arrirnkem** (T,E) *vi.*
feel hungry, want to eat something; really want a particular food ◆ Ayeng angayel arlkwetyek arrirnkem. (Sa) *I am hungry and I really want to eat.*
SEE ALSO arrerlkart urntem

arrernkelh-ilem (W,T), **arrirnkelh-ilem** (E) *vt.*
make someone want to eat, give someone an appetite ◆ Alyemel rlkert arrirnkelh-ilem, mern arlkwetyek. Artwampwel alyem, arrirnkelh-anthem mern. (Sa) *The sick person is sung to give them an appetite and make them eat. The old man sings them and makes them eat.*

arrernkelh-anthem (W,T), **arrirnkelh-anthem** (E) *vt.* = **arrernkelh-ilem**

Arrernt *n.*
1. an Arrernte person or people
2. the Arrernte language
CAN SOUND A BIT LIKE arrent *'wooden toothpick'*

arrernt-arrernt (W,T) *n.*
noisy ◆ Kwer map arrernt-arrernt. (M) *The kids are noisy.* ◆ Iy, arelh arrernt-arrernt mapel irlpa ahert-ilem. (T) *Hey, the noisy women are deafening us.*

arrernt-arrernt-irrem (W,T) *vi.*
make a noise

arrert *n.*
1. emu shinbone
2. meat from the emu shinbone. Also referred to as *ker arrert.* ◆ Ker arrert yanh tha arlkwetyek. (Sa) *I'm going to eat that meat from the emu shinbone.*
3. tool made from emu shinbone. Used in particular for cleaning out the bitter seeds of *anakety* (*Solanum chippendalei*). ◆ Arrertel ipem anakety. (M) *The tool made from the emu shinbone is used to clean the bitter seeds out from the bush tomato.*
SEE ALSO wetyeny, katyelarr

arrertarnk (T,E), **arrerternk** (E) *n.*
tail meat from goanna, perentie, or kangaroo. Also referred to as *ker arrertarnk.*
= rtwarnp
SEE ALSO anter

arrertewarrert-irrem (W,T) *vi.*
make a loud noise ◆ Kwer map arrertewarrert-irrepirrem werrkel-ayel. (T) *The kids are making a loud noise in the bush.* ◆ Thep map arrertewarrert-irrepirrem arnang anyentel-ayel. (T) *There are lots of birds singing loudly in the tree.*

arreth *n.*

hill fuchsia (*Eremophila freelingii*). Shrub to 1.5 m high, with soft bluish green leaves and lilac flowers. Usually grow on rocky hillsides. ◆ Wararl akemel *medicine* arl yanhan, tyerrtyarl alhewelhenhelhenh tyerrty, kapert arlka alhewelhenhelhenh arreth yenh. Itya, *can't* arlkwerl. (T) *It is just picked and used as a medicine. People use the* arreth *to wash their bodies and their heads. It's not edible.*

arrethaker *n.*
edge or side ◆ Arrethaker ankwang intem. (N) *Lying asleep with legs curled up.*

arrethaker-irrem *vi.*
lie on side with legs curled up

arrethaker intem
lie on side with legs curled up (intem[1] *'lie down'*)

arrethaker anyem
fall onto side (anyem *'fall'*)

arrethaker anem
sit on one side (e.g. on one buttock) (anem *'sit'*)

arrethaker-welhem *vi.*
shift oneself onto one side ◆ Arrethakerem welhem arrpenhem, interl-anetyeyem. (N) *Others shift themselves onto one side to sleep.*
arrethakerel atwem
hit something with the outer edge of something (e.g. the outer curved edge of a boomerang) (atwem '*hit*') ◆ Tyerrty apek atwem arrethakerel kaylel, arrerlp ampenyel. (St) *The person is hitting something with the outer edge of the boomerang, the sharp side.*

arrety-arrety (W,T) *n.*
1. spiny-cheeked honeyeater (*Acanthagenys rufogularis*)
2. singing honeyeater (*Lichenostomus virescens*) ◆ Arrety-arrety arntwerlem ngkwarl yerramp angerr-ilem. (N) *The spiny-cheeked honeyeater tells you that there's lots of honeyants.*
= alpeyart-alpeyart, arrakwerakwer

arretyem (W,T), **arreytem** (T,E) *vi.*
whisper, talk softly ◆ Tyerrty atherr apek ilerrerl-anem arretyemel. (T) *Two people are whispering to each other.*
arretyemel angkem (W,T), **arreytemel angkem** (T,E)
whisper, talk softly
SEE ALSO tyel angkem

arretyet (W,T) *n.*
1. ceremonial poles or 'long sticks' used during initiation (young men) ceremony. These are made of leaves tied onto a spear with hairstring, which are then tied onto the legs of the dancers. ◆ Artwang map rntwem arretyet-akert. (T) *The men are dancing with the 'long sticks'.*
2. the dance in which the 'long sticks' are used
= arlwernarr, utemeny
SEE ALSO apwelh, anmanty

arrew (W,T), **arriw** (T,E) *n.*
door, opening, entrance, exit, brim ◆ Kwer map arrew-angkwerr arrtyanem. (T) *The children are running through the door.*
◆ Yakweth atyengenh arlkwenhek arreweh-atwety mern, rnwanenty apek. (M) *I have filled my bag to the brim with food or clothes.*
SEE ALSO altywer

arrew-arrew-ilem (T,E) *vt.*
move something backwards and forwards; rock (baby in arms) ◆ Arrew-arrew-ilemel ankwathenem ampa akely inngart ankwathenem artnerl-anenty. (Sa) *Rocking a little crying baby to make him/her go to sleep.*
= angelh-angelh-ilem

arrewaly (E) dead body, corpse SEE UNDER **irrewaly**

arrewatyent (T,E) single-women's camp SEE UNDER **irrewatyent**

arrewelhem *vi.*
do something quickly or in a hurry; be in a hurry to do something ◆ Wenheh nta arrewelhepelhem? Arternp anantherr alhey. (M) *Why are you in such a hurry? Let's take it easy.* ◆ Arrewelhem ayeng *store*-warl alhetyek martelhekerr. (St) *I am hurrying to the store in case it closes.* ◆ Ker apek inetyek anem arrewelhem ayeng, arlkwetyek anem tha. (St) *I am in a hurry to get some meat to eat.*
SEE ALSO athek-irrem, arnkarnp, arrewem

arrewem *vi.*
shiver (with cold), shake, tremble ◆ Anyelel arrewem. (M) *Shivering with cold.* ◆ Ater apek ayeng arrewem, yanh-kety atwekerr ayenh. (St) *I am shaking with fear because that person might hit me.* ◆ Ura irrerntek arrtyey, irrerntekarl ayeng arrewem-kety. (Sa) *Light a fire because of the cold, because I'm shivering with cold.*
SEE ALSO arrewelhem
anert arrewem
stomach rumble or shake with hunger

arreweng ampey (W), **arriweng ampey** (T,E) *n.*
beard that is just starting to go grey ◆ 'Arriweng ampey', lyetantarl ampeynepeynem akwek, kel akngerr anem irrem. Mperlker ingkerrek anem ra irrem. (St) *'Arriweng ampey' is when the beard is just starting to go grey, then it all goes grey. The whole beard goes white.*
SEE ALSO aywa

arrey-arrey (E) *n.*
cicada ◆ Arrey-arrey ingwelarl angkerl-anem. Iylpa arwengk-ilemel angkerl-anem arrey-arrey. (Sa) *The cicadas make a noise in the night. The cicadas deafen you with their noise.*
= aterr, anngener

arreyeng-arrey (W,T) *n.*
chirping, chattering or twittering sound, loud noise (such as the sound made by cicadas) ◆ Arreyeng-arrey-irrem thip inang angkem, arreyeng-arrey angkerrem thip map, kweny-itweh, angkerrerl-anem. *The birds are singing and making a lot of noise in the night.* ◆ Arreyeng-arrey-kweny anwengkerr anetyeh, irlpang altywer awelhemel. (T) *We've got to sit down and not make a noise, and listen with open ears.* ◆ Arreyeng-arrey map angkerrem arnterr. (T) *People are talking really loudly.*
arreyeng-arrey-irrem (W,T) *vi.*
make a chirping, chattering or twittering

sound, make a loud noise (such as the sound made by cicadas) ◆ Arreyeng-arrey-irretyal anwengkerr aneyaw, angkety-kweny aneyaw, arreyeng-arrey-kweny. Irlpa apek anwengkerr akangkwerrey, iwenhek apek anwengkerr akangkwerrey, irlpel manty awerl-anemel. (N) *We shouldn't chatter, but sit down without talking, without making a noise. We'll pay attention and listen to whatever, listening carefully with our ears.* ◆ Kwer map arreyeng-arrey-irrepirrem kwen yanh warlel-ayeng. (M) *The children are being noisy inside that house over there.*

arreyenp (E) lips SEE UNDER **arrayenp**

arreyl (E) cheek SEE UNDER **arrely**[2]

arreyl-arreyl alhem (E) *vi.*
go across, cut across
arreyl-irrem (E) *vi.*
turn away

arreylarrp (E) behaving in a one-sided way SEE UNDER **arrelharrp**

arreylp (E) sharp, pointed, prickly SEE UNDER **arrerlp**

arreylpem (E) chew something, munch on something SEE UNDER **arrerlpem**

arreymper (E) gap left in front teeth after a tooth has been knocked out (ceremonial) SEE UNDER **arrimper**

arreympeyemp (E) lips SEE UNDER **arrenpenp**

arreyn (E) name, skin name SEE UNDER **arreny**

arreynem (E) *vt.*
scratch something
= irrkem
SEE ALSO angernem[1], alherrem[1], irrkernem
arreynelhem (E) *vi.*
scratch yourself
= angernelhem, irrkernelhem, ahinelhem, angernelhem

arreynt (E) toothpick SEE UNDER **arrent**

arreytem (T,E) whisper, talk softly SEE UNDER **arretyem**

arreytn (E) name, skin name SEE UNDER **arreny**

arrilem, arraylem (E) *vt.*
use supernatural powers or magic on someone; 'sing' someone. The use of these powers can have positive or negative consequences, and in some cases can even result in sickness or death. ◆ Ahenty-penhel arrilem kwer ahenty-anetyek. (T) *The one who desires her sings [her] to make her like [him].*
SEE ALSO alyem, artimperr-wem, arrwengkelthel alyem
arrilelhem, arraylelhem (E) *vi.*
sing oneself to get supernatural powers or magic ◆ Arelh yanh arrilelhem artwang yanh inetyek. (T) *That woman is singing herself so that she can get that man.*
arrilenty, arraylenty (E) *n.*
power associated with persons or objects that have been sung with special songs so that the person or object becomes irresistible to particular others ◆ Arrilentyel ilem, tyart apek alyem arrilenty-irremel artwa yanhek. Kel ra inem. Artwel alyelhem akin arrilenty ilelhem marl yanhek — kel renh inem. (St) *Making herself powerful, maybe singing a shirt to give her power over that man. Then she gets him. Men sing themselves as well to make themselves powerful and attractive to that woman — then he gets her.*
arrilenty-ilem (T,E), **arraylenty-ilem** *vt.*
= **arrilem**

arrimper (T,E), **arrenper** (W), **arreymper** (E) *n.*
gap left in front teeth after a tooth has been knocked out (ceremonial). In the west of the Anmatyerr area only men have this done to them, whereas in the eastern Anmatyerr area both women and men do. The practice of removing teeth is done by people in the opposite generation moiety to the person having the tooth removed. ◆ Rtety-kwenh arrimper-akert. Rtety anyent atwekarl, arrimper mpwarek. (T) *Teeth have a gap in the front. One tooth is knocked out to make the gap.*
= alyeneng
SEE ALSO tyekerr, arra
arrimper atwem (T,E), **arrenper atwem** (W), **arreymper atwem** (E)
remove a front tooth (ceremonial) (atwem '*hit*') ◆ Arrenper atwem artwant — marl akenh itya. (M) *Only men knock the front tooth out — women don't.*
= alyeneng atwem

arrimpimp (E) lips SEE UNDER **arrenpenp**

arringkerr you (more than two) SEE UNDER **arrengkerr**

arrint (E) toothpick SEE UNDER **arrent**

arrintety *n.*
healed over, joined together
SEE ALSO tywenmernt
arrintety-irrem *vi.*
heal over, (bones) mend, join back together
SEE ALSO arterrp-irrem, ltyerrem, tywenmernt-irrem, kwerrm-irrem, pwarn-irrem, urrmirrem
arrintety-ilem *vt.*
make things join back together or heal over ◆ Atnert arrintety-ilem alyemel, arntety. (Sa) *Singing the sick person's stomach to make it heal over.*

arriper (T,E), **arreper** (T) *n.*
western brown snake (*Pseudonaja nuchalis*) (?) ◆ Arriperan ahelengkw artelhampwarl. Irrewalyekan akenh-akenh arriperan ahelengkwarl. (Sa) *Western brown snakes are really big and dangerous. They are deadly and their bite can kill a person.*
= antywemp
SEE ALSO tyamparl, arreperlp

arrirnkem (T,E) feel hungry, really want a particular food SEE UNDER **arrernkem**

arrirnt (E) facing away, not looking at someone, sulky SEE UNDER **arrwernt**

arriw (T,E) door, opening, entrance, exit, brim SEE UNDER **arrew**

arriweng ampey (T,E) beard that is just starting to go grey SEE UNDER **arreweng ampey**

arrka (E) *n.*
part of kangaroo guts. Also referred to as *ker arrka*.
= anarrk

arrkar *n.kin*
the husband or wife of someone who is the same generation moiety as oneself. For example, one's cross-cousin's husband or wife, or one's sister's or brother's husband or wife. Also said of spousal relationships in grandparents' or grandchildren's generation. *Arrkar* cannot be used to refer to one's own husband or wife. (Note Warlpiri *marrkari* 'spousal relationship between own subsection and father's mother's subsection'.)
SEE ALSO aperl, anew

arrkarengkw *n.kin*
your *arrkar* ◆ 'Arrkarengkw nhak arlketyel.' Marlel ilem, arrwempelikw apek, kakey kwerenhel arlketyel-warl. 'Arrkarengkw-warl alha.' (Sa) *'Your husband is singing out.' A woman says that [to her sister-in-law] if her elder brother is singing out. 'Go to your husband.'*

arrkarikw, arrkareyekw (E) *n.kin*
his/her/their *arrkar*

arrkarekw (W,T) *n.kin*
1. your *arrkar*
2. his/her/their *arrkar*

arrkar-nheng *n.kin*
a group of two or more people, at least two of whom are a married couple in the same generation moiety as the speaker ◆ *Like* ntwa apekarl ilem altyeley ngkweng-wenh, 'Arrkar-nheng alherray'. (T) *Like you might say [about] your cross-cousin's [husband], 'You two go, husband and wife'.*

arrkar-intyerr *n.kin* = **arrkar-nheng** ◆ Arrkar-intyerr lyweny alhek. (T) *The husbands and wives went hunting.*

arrkar-nheng-arey *n.kin*
a group of more than two people, at least two of whom are a spousal couple in the same generation moiety as the speaker

arrkar-nheng atherr *n.kin*
a married couple in the same generation moiety as the speaker

arrkar-ankethenh *n.kin*
1. having a close *arrkar* still alive
2. someone who is always with their *arrkar*
SEE ALSO -ankethenh

arrkarlp crest (of bird) SEE UNDER **irrkarlp**

arrkay, irrkay (E) *n.*
dull, not bright, blurry, soft or faint (of sound), faint, faded, hardly visible ◆ Arrkayarl arerl-apem, alkngarl akeng-irremel. (St) *I can only see faintly, my eyes are going bad.* ◆ Irrkay akely-rnem-arey atham-areny-rnem. *The* atham-areny *spirits are hardly visible.*

arrkay-arrkay, irrkay-irrkay (E) *n.*
blurry ◆ Tha arrkay-arrkayarl arem, ingwemernt-artekarl arrkay anem tha arerl-anem — aretyakenhaw kwenh. (St) *My vision is blurred, and now when I look my eyesight is faded and it's as if everything is dark — I can't see.*

annga arrkay, alknga arrkay (E)
poor or faded eyesight (annga *'eye'*)

ahenty arrkay, ahenty irrkay (E)
faint voice (ahenty *'voice', 'throat'*) ◆ Ahenty irrkay angketyakenh, inkwerr-penh. (Sa) *[Your] voice fades and you can't talk, from having a cold.*

arrkay-irrem, irrkay-irrem (E) *vi.*
fade, become faint or blurry ◆ Ingwemernt ap ayeng anngan arrkay-irrenhemel an ingwemernt anem irrenhem, *can't look much now*. Irrkay-irrenhem anngan. (St) *I can't see much now because everything looks dark as my eyesight is fading. My eyesight is fading.*

arrkay-ilem, irrkay-ilem (E) *vt.*
make something fade, make something become faint or blurry ◆ Ingkerrkentyel arem twernel anngang arrkay-ilem-hety. (M) *Shading [your] eyes with your hand in case the sun makes your eyesight blurry.*

arrkaylp (E) crest (of bird) SEE UNDER **irrkarlp**

Arrkelth (T) *n.*
name of a soakage west of the Hanson River and north of Nturiya

arrkem (E) *vi.*
1. flash (lightning) ◆ Kwaty arrketyel arrer anem arrkep-arrkem kwaty arrketyel kwaty

arrer anem arrkeynetyepetyel. (Sa) *The lightning is flashing close now, the lightning storm is flashing as it goes along.*
2. tremble, shake or vibrate (parts of the body) ◆ Lyweper arrkep-arrkem. (Sa) *[The] thighs are shaking.*
SEE ALSO alharrkem, ngkwarrkem

arrken *n.*
happily, joyfully, in fun, playfully, not seriously
arrken-arrken *n.*
happily, joyfully, in fun, playfully, not seriously ◆ Ampa maparl arrken-arrkenel, irrtyarteng-irrtyart, atantherl-apem arrken nheng atantherremel lyentyel, ketyey map. (N) *The kids enjoy themselves going along spearing each other with the kangaroo grass, their pretend spears.*
arrken-kenh *n.*
1. for fun, in jest, for play (-kenh *'belonging to'*) ◆ Alyaper kwer mapel mparem alyeng-alya. Alyel anem akwel ina ltewerretyenh. Arrken-kenh war. (T) *The* alyaper *is a sort of toy boomerang that the kids make. Then they throw them at each other. It's just for fun.*
2. someone who is funny, playful or amusing
arrken angkem
joke, say something funny (angkem *'speak', 'talk'*)
arrken angerr, arrken akngerr (E)
a joker; a funny, playful or amusing person (angerr *'lots'*)
arrken nhwelhem (W,T)
have fun, play, enjoy oneself, muck around ◆ Kwer map arrken nhwelherl-anem, arrken-irremel, antywang akwekel nhwelherl-atherr anem, alwernererl-atherr anem. (N) *The children are playing around in the little humpy, playing and chasing each other around.*
arrken nhwerrem (W,T), **arrken unherrem** (E), **arrken utnherrem** (F) *vi.*
have fun, play, enjoy oneself, muck around (nhwerrem *'bite each other'*) ◆ Arrken utnherretyek alherl-iway, arlengel arrken-irretyek iylparl arwengk-ilem-kety. (Sa) *All you go off and play, go and play a long way away, because you are driving us crazy.*
arrken-irrem *vi.*
1. have fun, play, enjoy oneself, muck around ◆ Arrken-irrem kwer map thip-angkwerr. Thip ina ltewerl-apem kwer mapel, arrken-irrerl-apemel. (T) *The children are playing around the birds. They are going along shooting at birds, having fun.*
2. play (a game)
arrken-ilem *vt.*
1. make fun, play with something
2. tease or make fun of someone ◆ Ampa apek arrken-ilem. (St) *Teasing the child.* • SEE ALSO kwanthem, ngkwanty-irrem, arntarrp-ilem, arlkarem, anngernt-irrem, arrampewem[1]

arrkenty[1] (T), **irrkenty** (W), **arrkinty** (W) *n.*
skin rash, scabies, mange ◆ Angwely yanh arrkenty-akert. (T) *That dog is mangy.*
SEE ALSO rtety-rtety, altelhey, mentyey, irrkem

arrkenty[2] *adv.*
fighting, picking on, or ridiculing someone ◆ Arrkentyel atwem mey-mey apek wal urrparelhem arrkentyarl ilem-penh urrparelhem anem. (St) *If you have a fight with or ridicule your son-in-law, well, then you apologise.*
arrkenty-ilem *vt.*
pick on or tease someone, annoy someone, rubbish or ridicule someone ◆ War apekarl atwerretyel arrkenty-ilerremel ilterretyel — mernek-arrngel apek, alhek-arlek-arrngel apek. *They are fighting and picking on each other and swearing at each other for no particular reason — perhaps over food, or because somebody went somewhere.* ◆ Angerretyel-rnem, anyent arrkenty-ilem ina atwep-atwem, anyentan, ampa. (Sa) *The bigger ones are picking on and hitting one kid.* ◆ Alherl-way! Aywa map arrantherrarl arrkenty-ilerl-anem-kety! (T) *Go away! You mob are annoying the old people!*
SEE ALSO kwanthem, ngkwanty-irrem, arntarrp-ilem, arlkarem, arrken-ilem, anngernt-irrem, arrampewem[1]

arrkep, irrkep (E) *n.*
desert oak (*Allocasuarina decaisneana*). Tree to 10 m high, with rough thick bark, long needle-like leaves and heavy cones. Grows in spinifex sandplains and sandhills. ◆ Arrkep alhewelhenhelhenh — *not* arlkwenh-arlkwenh athew, *medicine* war. (N) *The desert oak is used as a washing medicine — it's not edible, it's just used as a medicine.*
= kwerrkar

arrkeper (W,T), **arrkiper** (E) *n.*
gum or kino from the bloodwood (*arrkernk*) or ghost gum (*pwernengk, ulemp*) ◆ Arrkiperan ulemp-areny. Alhewelhenhelhenh. Utyen alhewem, utyenarl ikwer alhewelhem utyen akngerr anenty, wal renh akem kel alhewelhemel anem. *The* arrkiper *comes from the ghost gum. It's a washing medicine. If you have a large sore, then you can collect it [the bloodwood gum] and use it to wash yourself with.*
SEE ALSO lyarwek, nthwarr

arrker *n.*
side of something (e.g. creek, road, hill) ◆ Lpwayel arrkerel ntwa alherl-apem. (M) *You are going along the side of the creek.*
SEE ALSO twerr
irntang arrker (W)
side of a hill

arrkereny-irrem *vi.*
desert or abandon someone; stop looking after someone; lose interest in somebody; ignore someone ◆ Ngarl arrkereny-irrek, atyengetyeng. Inpirremel arrkereny-irrenhemel inperrenhek, uyerrenhek. (Sa) *You abandoned me. You disappeared without trace and deserted me.* ◆ Atyengeng ntwa arrkereny-irrek. (T) *You didn't look after me.*
SEE ALSO reken-irrem, arrelharrp, arwekar-ilem
arrkerenyel-wem, arrkerenyel-iwem (E) *vt.*
desert or abandon someone; stop looking after someone; lose interest in somebody; ignore someone ◆ Akeweny akwek arrkerenyel-wek amwekel. (M) *The poor little thing was abandoned by its mother.* ◆ Arrkereny-irremel ra mentyarl aretyel, kerarl arntarnt-aretyang. Kerel arntarnt-aretyang. Arrkerenyel-iwek. Arrpenhel inngart. Renh akiwarrerl anem ilem, 'Ntwa arrkerenyel-iwek. Kerel ayenh arntarnt-aretyang.' *She is just watching but not taking an interest, not looking after that person by giving them meat. That person has deserted the other. And then the other person says sulkily to the other, 'You are ignoring me, and not looking after me by feeding me meat'.*
arrkereny-ilem (E) *vt.*
make someone desert or abandon someone else

arrkerlpangkwarl (W,T) bush coconut [SOME SPEAKERS] SEE UNDER **arrkipangkwarl**

arrkernem *vt.*
1. taste or try something to see what it's like ◆ Tha arrkernemel arlkwetyek ntha. (Sa) *Give me [this] so that I can taste it and eat it.*
2. attempt to do something, have a go at something, try to do something ◆ *Batik* tha arrkernetyek ingkwernerl-ayntetyek. Arrkernemel ingkwernetyek. Ingwer kaltyelan arrkernetyang ingkwernay. Ngka. Ayeng arrkernelhetyek. (Sa) *I'll try to paint batik. Those others who are knowledgeable don't have to try first — they can paint. Give it to me. I'll try myself out.* ◆ Mwetek arrkernemel mpwarerlanetyek, kwert-kenh arlka arrernemel. Ura apek akwek-irrekarl, arrangkw apek irrek. Ura aperrk apek arrangkw-irrekarl. Ankert-wetyek apek arrpenhel. (St) *Trying to fix the car, and putting in an exhaust pipe. Maybe the battery is a bit flat or the starter motor doesn't work. People might have to push the car.*
SEE ALSO arlepewem
arrkernelhem *vi.*
1. try yourself out at something
2. try something on
= arlepewelhem

arrkernk *n.*
bloodwood (*Corymbia opaca*). Tree to 12 m high, with brown scaly bark, pale yellow flowers and large seed capsules.

Arrkernk Amar-amar (W) *n.*
the name of a waterhole/swamp east of the Yuelamu (Mt Allan) community

arrkerr *n.*
barn owl (*Tyto alba*)
◆ Thep arrkerr annga angerr-akert. Arrkerr kwenyel angkerl-anem. (T) *The barn owl has big eyes. It sings out in the night.*

Arrkerreretyey (W) *n.*
name of a place in Mt Denison area

Arrkeyanem *n.*
Connors Well

arrkeyt (E) *n.*
yellow ochre
= marlalperr, karntewarr
SEE ALSO rlpwa, arwethenp, atywerlk, artep arlpenty, karntewarr, marlalperr
arrkeyt-arrkeyt (E) *n.*
yellow ◆ Pwet arrkeyt-arrkeyt. (Sa) *Yellow shoes.*
Arrkeytepwenty (E) *n.*
name of a place north of Antarrengeny, on the Alyawarra Aboriginal Land Trust

arrkilem (E) *vt.*
share things with other people; give things to other people; bring things back and give to other people ◆ Tha arrkilem mern apek tey apek. Arrpenhek anthem, arrangkw-kety. (Sa) *I'm giving food and tea to the other person. Giving things to the others because they haven't got any.*

arrkinty (W) skin rash, scabies, mange SEE UNDER **arrkenty**[1]

arrkipangkwarl, arrkerlpangkwarl (W,T), **irrkeylpangkwel** (E), **akerlpangkwarl** (T), **akerlpankwel** (W,T), **kirrpangkwel** (E) *n.*
1. gall on the bloodwood (*arrkernk*); bush coconut, bloodwood apple [SOME SPEAKERS]. Also referred to as *mern arrkipangkwarl*. Made by the female of a type of wasp (*Cystococcus*

pomiformis).
= mangarray, arrkwerlperlp
SEE ALSO kathip
2. seed capsules of the bloodwood • = mernperr

arrkiper (E) gum or kino from the bloodwood or ghost gum SEE UNDER **arrkeper**

arrkng SEE UNDER **arrng**

Arrkwel (E) *n.*
name of a soakage east of the Wilora (Stirling) community

arrkwelem (E), **arrkwilem** (E) *vt.*
cut up cooked meat
SEE ALSO artep ultatwem, tyep-ilem

arrkwer *n.*
showing off ◆ Arrkwer apety-alpep-alpem, mer arrernelhety-alpem kel tharemap-ilety-aynterleng, arrkwerelhemel. (N) *He is always coming back and showing off, coming back to camp and then stirring people up.* (?)
arrkwer-arrkwer *n.*
1. restless, agitated, moving round all over the place ◆ Tyerrty nhenh arrkwer-arrkwer anep-anem. (T) *This person is restless.* ◆ *No* intemel apek, itya. Intety-kwenh, *no* ankwang intety-kwenh, merel anety-kwenh — arrkwer-arrkwer war. (St) *[That person] doesn't sleep, doesn't stay home — they're just restless.*
2. showing off ◆ Arrkwer-arrkwer-akert alherray! Iyteny apety-alhetyal. (N) *Don't come round here flirting and showing off.*
annga arrkwer-arrkwer, **alknga arrkwer-arrkwer** (E)
1. someone who makes eyes at someone, acts flirtatiously or shows off ◆ *Larrikin*-el arem annga arrkwer-arrkwer. (M) *[Someone] who makes eyes at someone is* annga arrkwer-arrkwer.
2. eyes all over the place (not noticing the obvious) (?)
arrkwer-arrkwer-irrem (E) *vi.*
show off, behave flirtatiously ◆ Arelh nhenh arrkwer-arrkwer-irrem, ikwer anewikw — arem inngart, *everywhere*. (St) *This woman is showing off for her husband — looking all over the place.*
arrkwer-arrkwer-ilem *vt.*
make a fuss of someone, smother someone with attention ◆ Arrkwer-arrkwer-ilemel ntwang arrpenhek anthem. (T) *You're worrying too much about that kid; give him to someone else.*
arrkwerelhem *vi.*
1. showing off, acting, looking funny, giving oneself away in the eyes, roll eyes to get attention, looking round all over the place ◆ Kwer nhenh arrkwerelhepelhem mantarr *new one*-akert. (M) *This kid is showing off with their new clothes on.*
2. rush around in a hurried or agitated way ◆ Arelh yanh arrkwerelhem alhetyenheng-angent. (T) *That woman is rushing round in a hurry, getting ready to go.*
arrkwer-ilem (W,T) *vt.*
show off ◆ Ntwa arrkwer-ilem mantarr atyengenhek apek arrkwer-ilemel anthek. (M) *You're showing off by giving my things away.*

Arrkweray (E) *n.*
Buggy Camp, in the Spring Range area

arrkwerlperlp (E) *n.*
gall on the bloodwood (*arrkernk*); bush coconut, bloodwood apple
= mangarrey, arrkipangkwarl
SEE ALSO arrkernk, kathip

arrkwertep (W,T) *n.*
loud talk
arrkwertep-irrem (W,T) *vi.*
talk loudly (like a drunk) ◆ Terangk yanh arrkwertep-irrepirrem. Arrkwertep angketyek apetyern. (T) *That drunk is talking loudly. The drunk has just arrived to talk loudly.*
SEE ALSO irrkwerteth, arnterr angkem, aker-aker-ilem, arlelty angkem, tyety angkem

arrkwerteth (W) language or accent which is hard to understand SEE UNDER **irrkwerteth**

arrkwetyety, **irrkwetyety** (E), **irrkutyety** (E) *n.*
a respectful word used for a place where someone who lived there before has passed away; old or deserted camp (because of bereavement) ◆ Arleng-angkwerr alhetyek arrkwetyety-kety. (St) *Go round the long way because of the place where someone passed away.*

arrkwilem (E) cut up cooked meat SEE UNDER **arrkwelem**

arrmaly-arrmaly (T,E) *n.*
lightweight, flimsy, sickly, floppy, weak (in the body) ◆ Arntety arrmaly-arrmaly. Innga, ampa apek. Arntety anem nhenhan arrmaly-arrmaly anem. Atyet-atyet weth-lkwer. Rlterrk anetyang. *A sick person is* arrmaly-arrmaly. *An adult or a child. This person is weak and sick. A bit fragile. Not strong.*
SEE ALSO artaly-artaly, atyet-atyet, althalth, atyet[1]
arrmaly-arrmaly-irrem (T,E) *vi.*
become sickly, floppy, or weak (in the body)

arrmar *n.kin* [RESPECT LANGUAGE]
a respectful way for a woman to refer to her son-in-law's male cross-cousins or to her son's brother-in-law (i.e. her son-in-law)
SEE ALSO ankel[1], mpwern, pantyey
arrmarikw (E) *n.kin*

his/their *arrmar*
arrmarengkw *n.kin*
your *arrmar* ◆ Arrmarekengk-warl ahanenhaw. *Go back to your brother-in-law (said by a woman to her son).*
arrmarekw (W,T), **anmarekw** (W,T) *n.kin*
1. your *arrmar*
2. his/their *arrmar*
arrmar-nheng *n.kin*
a group of two or more people related as male cross-cousins or as brothers-in-law (said by a woman if one of them is her son-in-law) ◆ Mpwern-nheng, pantyey ikwerenh then, 'arrmar-nheng atherr'. Arrmar-nheng, melikw ilem. *Son* ikwerenh then alhetyek, 'Arrmar-nheng kwenh ahanenherra. *You fellas go.*' *Son* ikwerenh an *son-in-law* ikwerenh. Ateyel ilem, aynelikw, 'Mpwern-nheng mpwelanth alherraw'. (Sa) *A man and his brother-in-law, his* pantyey, *are called* 'arrmar-nheng atherr' *by the mother of the man. If her son and the other one go she says, 'You two go,* arrmar-nheng. *You two blokes go'. That's how she refers to her son and his brother-in-law together. The father of that man would say, 'You two go* mpwern-nheng *[using the word* mpwern-nheng *'brothers-in-law together' rather than* arrmar-nheng*]'.*
arrmar-intyerr *n.kin* = **arrmar-nheng**
SEE ALSO ankel-nheng, mpwern-nheng
arrmar-nheng atherr *n.kin*
a term used by a woman to refer to her son-in-law and his male cross-cousin together or to her son and his brother-in-law together ◆ Arrmar-nheng ahanerlentyarreyaw. Ankel-nheng atherr ap arrmar-nheng atherr. (Sa) *[My] son-in-law and his male cross-cousin are going.* Ankel-nheng atherr *['male cross-cousins together'] is* arrmar-nheng atherr. ◆ Anmar-nheng atherr ahanenhewarrern. (M) *Those two cousins went [said by a person who is in an avoidance relationship to either of them].* ◆ 'Arrmar-nheng atherran' ilem mwerikw-kety kertemwengk akemel. Mwerekikwety kertemwengk angkemel. 'Arrmar-nheng atherr yanh alhek kwenh.' Ankel-nheng atherr ilem. (St) 'Arrmar-nheng atherr' *is what is said by a woman in a way of not talking directly because of her son-in-law. 'Those two male cross-cousins went.' That's what she says of the two cousins, one of whom is her son-in-law.*

arrmernem, **anmernem** (W) *vt.*
hold an increase ceremony to make bush plants and animals abundant; create something; bring something into being ◆ Arrwekeleny mapel anmernetyam angkwey kwaty arlka kwa, mern arlka an ker. Ker arwenth anetyeh, anmernetyam. (M) *A long time ago the ancestors used to hold ceremonies to make rain, bush foods and meat abundant. So that there would be lots of meat.* ◆ Altyerrel arrmernek, thep, *everything. World* nhenh arrmernek. (T) *God made the birds and everything. He made this world.* ◆ Lyet anantherr ahelh nhenhel anem Altyerrelarl arrmernekarl, anwekantherr-kwenhel amparr. *Eve*-ek atherr *Adam*-ek atherr arrmernek. (T) *Now we live in this land that God created, before we existed. It was created for both of them, Eve and Adam.* ◆ Artwa ampwel arrmernem kel atherrkeny anem anem. (St) *The old men hold increase ceremonies and then everything is green.*
SEE ALSO intety-iwem, angerr-ilem
arrmernenty, **anmernenty** (W) *n.*
creation, something that has been created ◆ Mern annga apek arety-alhem, arlatyey arlka arem, wal ilem, 'Anmernentyam nhenh arlatyey nhenh amangkek, arlatyey nhenh map angerr-irrek kwenh, anmernekarl kwenh'. (M) *[You] might go and see some fruits or seeds, or pencil yams, and then you say, 'These pencil yams have been created, have grown up — there's lots of them here'.* ◆ Altyerreng anwantherr arrmernenty anek, everything. Mernak anwekantherr, ingkerr anwekantherr arratek, arrmernek. Tyap anyemayt, ker arlewatyerr, mern katyerr — everything, anwekantherr arrmernek, Altyerrel. (Sa) *In the Dreaming everything was created. All of the foods were created for us, and everything appeared. Witchetty grubs, goannas, desert raisins — God created everything for us.*

-arrngel *ending*
because of something; over. This ending goes on the word that is seen as being the cause or the trigger for an argument or dispute. It is preceded by the *+ek*, *+eh* or *+eng* ending ◆ War apekarl atwerretyel arrkenty-ilerremel ilterretyel — mernek-**arrngel** apek, alhek-arlek-**arrngel** apek. *They are fighting and picking on each other and swearing at each other for no particular reason — perhaps over food, or because somebody went somewhere.* ◆ Kereng-**arrngel** yanh atherr atwerrem. (T) *Those two are fighting each other over meat.* ◆ Marl yanhel alkngwenh-kerr ayenh, anewikweng, artwa yanhek-**arrngel**. (St) *That woman over there*

might get jealous of me, over her husband, over that man there.

arrngelh (W,T) *n.*
bark, dry leaves ◆ Tyapantarr arnel rnerl-anem akweteth. Rlpwerelam yanh irnanem arrngelhel. Arnethey yanh *jump*-irrerl-alhem nheng tyerrty-kety aterarl arem. (N) Tyapantarr *lizards always live in trees. They live in the hollows and amongst the bark. They jump in fright from the trees if they see people.*
SEE ALSO arntap

arrngent-wem, **angent-wem** (W,T), **arrngen-wem** (W,T) *vt.*
1. step in to stop a fight, intervene to stop people fighting ◆ Atyey-atyey atherram tha angent-wetyam ngkwarl-penhel. (M) *I stopped my two younger brothers from fighting when they were drunk.* ◆ Ratherr atwerreperremarl arwelthel, tha arrngent-wem. (St) *Those two were having a jealous fight, and I stopped them.* ◆ Arrngent-wetyek alheyaw. Yanharl atwerrem arrngent-wetyek alherl-iway. Arrngent-wetyek parrp untenherr-arey. Yanharl atwerremek alhenherr-arey arrngent-wetyek. (Sa) *Go and stop them. Those ones over there are fighting — go and stop them. Run quickly and stop them. Go and stop them fighting.*
2. stop or block someone from going somewhere or near something; get in the way of someone or something; take someone's place or spot ◆ Nta atyengety mer arrngen-wem, ayeng intetyenheng. Rntwarr-irra! (T) *You've taken my place, I want to lie down there. Shift out of the way!* ◆ Arengk atwem, arrngen-wemeng. (T) *Hitting the dog that's in the way.* ◆ Ayeng alhetyenheng — *don't* arrngen-werl kwenh. (M) *I'm about to go — don't stop me.*
SEE ALSO arrngert-wem, ayakem, ilpelhem

arrngen-welhem (W,T) *vi.*
get yourself in the way of someone or something (?) ◆ Ayeng arrngen-welhem ngkwengety. Rntwarr-irrem ayeng ngkwengety. (T) *I'm getting in your way. I'll shift out of your way.*
SEE ALSO arrapayernem

arrngern, **arrngwern** (W) *n.*
1. smooth spiderbush (*Clerodendrum floribundum*). Shrub about 2 m high, with bright green leaves, white flowers, and small, fleshy pink or purple fruit.
2. edible roots of the smooth spiderbush. Also referred to as *mern arrngern.*
= tywerlp

Arrngernangker (E) *n.*
Mt Swan

Arrngernangker Arlpaw (E) *n.*
the name of a place north of Adelaide Bore

arrngert, **angert** (W,T) *adv.*
being in a way that obstructs or blocks something off

arrngert-wem, **angert-wem** (W,T), **arrngert-iwem** (E) *vt.*
1. block something off, get in the way of something ◆ Arwerlel arrngert-iwem. Nthakenh alhetyang. *Road* arrngert-iwem arwerlelarl akek, alhwerrpel. Iwerr arrngert-iwek. *The tree is blocking the road. You can't go. The road is blocked by the tree broken by the wind. It blocked the road.* ◆ Kwatyel rewel arrngert-wem, ilpay. Tyerrty nthakenh alhetyakenh, amek anem arem. (St) *The flood water blocks off the creek. People can't go, they get blocked off.*
2. stop someone from doing something, stop a fight ◆ Arrngent-wetyek alhay. Arrngent-wetyek atwerremarl yanh untaw arrngent-wetyek. Parrp kwenh arrngent-wetyek alhay. *Run quickly and stop those people over there that are fighting each other. Go quickly and stop them.*
SEE ALSO arnpakem, arrngent-wem, ayakem, apatel-anthem, akayak-ilem

arrngert-welhem, **arrngert-iwelhem** (E) *vi.*
get in the way of someone or something, use your body to block someone off

arrngert-irrem, **angert-irrem** (W,T) *vi.*
interrupt, push or butt in; do something or get something before someone else; stop someone from doing something; block something off; get in the way ◆ Arelh kerek ankey angkem kwer yanh akenh angert-irrem ker kwerenhek. (T) *When the woman asked for the meat the child grabbed her meat before she got it.* ◆ Arelh map ayey ilerrerl-anem, kel artwang yanhel angert-irrety-alhem. (T) *The women are telling stories and that man goes across and interrupts them.* ◆ Nhenh angert-irrety-alpem mer antyam atyengenhek. (T) *This person came to lie down on my bed before me.* ◆ Nhenh angert-irremel arlkwem ker atyengenh, tharl imperl-alhek. (T) *This person is eating my meat that I left behind.*

arrngert-ilem *vt.*
block something off, get in the way of someone or something

angert arrernem (W) *vt.*
place something in the way to block something off ◆ Arrngert arrernay. (St) *Put*

something there to block it off. ◆ Tyerrtyel angert arrernem arnang yanh mwetekayeng. (M) *The person has put a tree across to block the car.*

arrngert intem *vi.*
be or lie in the way of something ◆ Arnang yanh angert intem rwertel. (M) *The tree is lying across the road and blocking it off.*

angert irnem (W,T) *vi.*
stand in the way of something (?)

arrnguntem (E) *vi.*
bleed ◆ Awey akely arrnguntem alhethey. (St) *The little boy is bleeding from the nose.*
= alhwuntem, alhwang thelelhem
SEE ALSO arrnga, untem

arrngunt-ilem (E), **arrnguntelh-ilem** (E) *vt.*
make something bleed

arrngwelty (E) tears SEE UNDER **anngwenty**

arrngwern (W) smooth spiderbush SEE UNDER **arrngern**

+arrp¹ *ending*
1. Goes on the end of pronouns to emphasise that the person or thing referred to is doing the action themself; do something by yourself or on your own; self (as opposed to someone else), (my)self, (your)self, (him)self, (her)self, etc. ◆ Ayeng**arrp**ey akeng mpwarenh *wrong.* (T) *I did the wrong thing myself.* ◆ Th**arrp** kwenh kwern-ilek. (M) *I, myself, have made a mistake.* ◆ Arranther**arrp** itang. (M) *You mob cook it yourselves.* ◆ Arlelyek ampengem arlkwem. Akemel angernemel rwelem item, mern atyerrety-alpem, r**arrp** rew-irrem. Kernt-irretyek arrernem, arlkwem renh alenyel war inem. (N) *The* arlelyek *fruit is eaten cooked. It is picked then taken back and then cooked in the fire so that it goes soft itself. Then it is put down to cool and then it's eaten, just with the tip of the tongue.* ◆ Menty ng**arrp** alhay — ayengan anetyelarl. Thanh alhetyang. *Forget it, you go yourself — I'm stopping. I am not going.*
2. only, just ◆ Arelh nhenh arlkwer aperl-apem mer**arrp** mer**arrp**. (M) *That woman never settles, she just walks around a lot, going from place to place.* ◆ Aylernanth, atherr**arrp** alherl-anem, amenheng. Amenheng aylernanth alherrem. *We two, just the two of us, are going, mother and child. Mother and child we two are going.*

arrp+²
Goes only with the endings *+aty*, *+engkw*, *+ikw* and *+ekw*, and shows that someone or something is the same as someone or something else in some way, particularly in terms of appearance, skin name, etc. This may be followed by endings such as *+el* or *+ek*/*+eh*. For example ***arrpelikw*** 'someone like him/her (is doing the action of the verb)'.

arrpaty *n.*
someone or something which is the same as me or us in some way ◆ Petyarr **arrp**aty nhak. *Over there is a Petyarr person, like me.* ◆ Atyeng-kety alwirremel untekaw. Ampa apek marl **arrp**aty apek. (St) *[They] ran away from me. A child or a woman like me.*
SEE ALSO +aty¹

arrpengkw *n.*
someone or something which is the same as you in some way ◆ Nthenhel Kemarr **arrp**engkw? (St) *Where is that person who is a Kemarr like you?*
SEE ALSO +engkw

arrpikw, **arrpekw** *n.*
someone or something which is the same as him/her/them in some way ◆ Angwely arntwerrem tyerrty arrpenharl aremarl. An angwelyeh **arrp**ehekw arntwerrem. (T) *The dog is growling when it sees another person. And it growls at other dogs as well.* ◆ Piwerretyel terangkant-arey. Terangk alhenty piwerl-alpem ingwer alpemel iteth rant imekel atwemek, terangkel **arrp**elikw. (Sa) *The drunks get themselves into trouble. The drunks go somewhere and one of them gets into trouble and then comes back alive after he's been nearly beaten to death by another drunk like him.* (?) ◆ Ayengan Kemarr **arrp**ikw. *I am a Kemarr like him/her.*
SEE ALSO +ikw

arrpanenh (E) *n.*
1. each, every, each and every one
2. all over the place; different (ones); lots of different ones ◆ Mer arrpanenh apawerr. Mer ingwer mer ingwer. Mer akngerr. Mer arrpanenh mpwareynerl-wetyel, alal-weynerlewepewem mer arrpanenh. *All over the place. In each and every place. Lots of places. They are making [communities] all over the place.* ◆ Ayeng alhek apmer arrpanenh-warl. (St) *I went to all the different places.* ◆ Arnkengeny akarr-irrem mer arrpanenh-they, mer arrpanenh-they apetyepety-alpem akarr-irrem. (Sa) *Lots of people are gathering together from all the different places, they are all coming together from all over the place.*
= arrpethet
SEE ALSO arrpenh

aherrk arrpanenh (E)
every day (aherrk '*sun*')

-arrpantey *ending*
1. something which is an imitation of the real thing; a pretend thing, a fake ◆ Ampengamp amarrkel angerl-wetyel ampel-rnem, *nappy*-akert. Amp**arrpantey**. *Bottle* angetyel ampa akwel *baby* akwel kwerenh, ampengamp. (Sa) *All the children carry the dolls, with nappies, around on their hips. They are pretend babies. They carry bottles and supposedly they are their babies.*
2. something that is not up to standard, something that is supposed to be something but is not; 'so-called' ◆ Warl-**arrpantey**arl artek akeng altywer-altywer. (T) *These so-called houses that were built are full of holes.*
SEE ALSO +eng-anyimp, -arrpatenty
3. make out as if (to do something); pretend to do something; shows that the verb action half happened or something a bit like it happened ◆ Utyekel utyel, urrtyirretyel ntwa. Ngan urrtyirretyelarl atyeng, angk**arrpantey** unta atyeng ilep-ilerl. Mern-**arrpantey** unta ilemel urrtyirretyel, nhenhan arrangkwarl. (St) *You're lying. You're lying to me, telling me some sort of story. You're pretending that there's food here, but there's nothing.* ◆ Riken-irretyel ntwa atyengety, mwetek *new one*-akert unta riken-irretyel atyengety. Ayenh anthetyakenh. Riken-**arrpantey** unta irretyel urrtyirrepirrerl, atyengety. (Sa) *You're showing off to me because you've got a new car. [You] didn't give me one. You're showing off in front of me and making out as if you're fantastic.* ◆ Kwer angayel ra arnem arnem arnem arrangkem arrangkem arrangkem kel kwer inetyenheng-**arrpantey** mam kwerenhel apek, kel renh ntert anem iletyenheng. Ntert anem yang irrem. (T) *The child is hungry and crying and crying and crying, and then her mother pretends to get her something and then that makes her quieten down. She quietens down.*
4. try to do something and fail

arrpanty (E) *n.*
centipede ◆ Arrpanty-kety pwertay! (St) *Look out for the centipede!*
= arnperrk, ingka arnkengeny

-arrpatenty (E) *n.ending*
1. something which is an imitation of the real thing; a pretend thing; a fake
2. something that is not up to standard; something that is supposed to be something but is not; 'so-called' ◆ Mern kwen anem anngarl ran, mern-**arrpatenty**. (St) *There is a seed underneath, a sort of food.*
SEE ALSO -arrpantey, +eng-anyimp

arrpayerr (E), **alpayerr** (E) *n.*
grub from the tar vine (*ayep*) (*Celerio lineata livornicoides*) ◆ Ipemel ipemel akert akemel kel renh arlkwerretyart. Arrpayerr ra then arlkwerretyart, arrwekeleny mapel — tharl aretyart, arrwekeleny-areyelarl arlkwetyart. (Sa) *They used to clean all the guts out, pulling the end off and then eating them. The olden-time people used to eat the tar vine grubs — I used to see them eating them.*
= ayep-areny, ayepaty
SEE ALSO antyarlk, unerrengayt

arrpelhem (E) *vi.*
talk too much about eating or drinking; really want to eat or drink something ◆ Arrpelhem ayeng mern arlkwetyek. (St) *I really want to eat.* ◆ Tyapek nga arrpelhepelhem. (Sa) *You really want to eat some witchetty grubs.*

arrpem *vt.*
scrape, carve or chisel something ◆ Arelhel arrpem panth kantyengarr-akertel. (T) *The woman is carving the wooden dish with an adze.*
SEE ALSO arterrp-ilem, yarr-wem

arrpenh *n.*
1. other, another, another thing, a different one ◆ Mer arrpenh-they apetyek alethang. Nyerr apek irrem ulereny-irrepirremarl yanh-ketyaw. Angketyakenh. (St) *A stranger came from another place. [People] were shy of him/her and didn't say a word.* ◆ Tha mpart-wem mern rtamp, arrpenh-thayt ampetyeh. (M) *I am turning the damper over to cook the other side.* ◆ Arrpenh atyeng angakang anyent apek. (M) *Pick another one out for me, maybe one.*
2. somebody, another person, other people, strangers, foreigners ◆ Mwetekayeng anngwenhem. Mwetekayeh-arteyel arrpenhel antyem wal anngwenhem, ltwakey-hety mwetekay. (T) *People get jealous over cars. The owner of the car might get jealous if another person gets in the car, in case they crash the car.* ◆ Kwer yanh ater-irrem arrentyeng *or* angwelyeng *or* tyerrtyeng arrpenh, terangkeng. (T) *That child is frightened of the monster, or of the dog, of other people, or of drunks.* ◆ Iwerrek ratherr, marl then artwethen apek. Wal ratherr iwerrek anem, arrpenh-akert anemarl ra. (St) *Those two split up, the woman and the man. They split up and*

he has another one now. ◆ Tyerrty arrpenh apertewarrarrem, kwenyel. (M) *Some people stalk other people at night.*
= ingwer

arrpenh-angkwerr (W) *n.*
in a different way, in another direction

alker arrpenh-areny *n.*
someone from a different country, someone from overseas (lit. 'something associated with another sky')

anyent arrpenh
a ceremonial term used between particular relatives of the young initiate (anyent *'one'*). The personal names of people related in this way should not be used by each other, and a*nyent arrpenh* is used instead. ◆ Anyent arrpenh-kety alhetyang anem. Arreytn iletyal. Mey-mey-artek akin. (St) Anyent-arrpenh *are a bit similar to sons-in-law in that you don't go near then and you don't say their name.*
SEE ALSO thampartey, perlal, ntwerleng, ntyangkwenng, rteyepertey, alyey[2], alyaperwarn, ywerlperr

arrpenh-irrem *vi.*
change into something else, look different, appear different ◆ Alta arrpenh-irrem — rnter-rnter apek irrem. (T) *[Her] hair looks different — perhaps it's gone [been dyed] red.* ◆ Arengk arrpenh-irrem, annga *different*-arl irrem. Rlkert apek anetyenheng. (T) *The dog looks different, its eyes look different. Maybe it is getting sick.*
= ingwer-irrem

arrpenhem *n.*
some, certain or particular things, other ones, 'some' as opposed to 'others' ◆ Lywang arrpenhem irrkerleng, arrpenhem lywerrng. (T) *Some shade areas are sparse, and others are thick.* ◆ Kerretherrengam ayeng. Ayeng tyatyel kerretherreng-irrek, *Napperby*-el. Kerretherreng-irretyakenh arrpenhem, itya, aheyen war. (M) *I am a Christian. I got baptised in the church at Napperby. Some people have not become Christians, they are just heathens.*
◆ Arrpenhemel ngkwerlp arlkwem, arrpenhemel kwert antywem. (St) *Some people chew tobacco and others smoke cigarettes.*

arrpentharrp (E), **arrpentharrp atherr** (E) *n.*
[RESPECT LANGUAGE]
two sons-in-law; two brothers (one of whom is the actual son-in-law of the woman speaking) ◆ Arrpentharrp atherrel amely-akety-alhek-ketyaw! (Sa) *My son-in-law and his brother went off drinking [said by a woman]!*
SEE ALSO mwer-nheng atherr, urtalty

arrpethet (W,T) *n.*
1. each, every, each and every one ◆ Inwek arrpethet alhek. (M) *Gone for days and days.*
2. all over the place; different (ones); lots of different ones ◆ Mer arrpethetel tyerrty map ananem. (M) *Aboriginal people are living all over the place.* ◆ Mer arrpethet alhem. (M) *Go from place to place.*
= arrpanenh

arrpm SEE UNDER **arrm**

arrpwarnt (T,E) *n.*
loud, noisy ◆ Arrpwarnt-arey alherl-wa! Ayeng angkep intetyeh kwenh! Arrantherr alhetyeh, ayeng intetyeh kwenh! (T) *You noisy mob leave! I want to go back to sleep! Go away so that I can sleep!*

arrpwarnt angkem (T,E) *vi.*
make a loud noise; bark (dog) ◆ Arrpwarnt angkerreperrerl — *everywhere* arrpwarnt angkerrerl-anemel, iylpan arwengk-ilem, arengkel-rneman. Artnemel arlka. *The dogs are barking — everywhere the dogs are barking and howling and deafening our ears.*
◆ Arengkan arrpwarntarl angkem, arrpwarnt angketyel ankwakel. (Sa) *The dogs are barking all through the night.*
= apangkem, arrpwernem, arlkwerrpel-nhwem

arrpwayl (E) *n.*
big male central netted dragon, *kaperl* (*Ctenophorus nuchalis*) ◆ Arrpwayl, kaperl urrey akngerr weth, arrpwaylarl ra. (St) Arrpwayl *is that big male* kaperl *lizard — that's what* arrpwayl *is.*
SEE ALSO arntekakarl

arrpwer *n.*

magpie (*Gymnorhina tibicen*) ◆ Arrpwerel arlepewem arreny tyerrty-henh. (M) *Magpies copy what people say.*

arrpwerek-arrpwer (W) *n.*
grey butcherbird (*Cracticus torquatus*)
= alpwertek-alpwert

arrpwernem *vt.*
sing out to someone to get their attention; shout or yell at someone or something to stop them or to warn them about danger; growl at someone ◆ Arrpwernemarl unta ayenh. *Might* ayeng apek alhem, wal arlkem, 'Waaaaa, apety-alpay!' (St) *You might sing out to get my attention. I might go away and you sing out, 'Waaaaa, come back!'* ◆ Arengk yanh ahakertel arrpwernepwernem. (T) *That dog is aggressive and it's growling.* ◆ Ampa arrpwernem apmwekety, 'Waaa'. (St) *I'm*

warning the child about the snake, 'Waaa'.
arrpwernelhem *vi.*
growl at someone or something to go away (?) ◆ Arrpwernelhem ayeng ampekety, ampa arrken angerrarl apetyek. (St) *I am growling at the kid to go away, at that joking kid that came.*
SEE ALSO alkwarrer-arrpwernenh, arralthem

arrth+ (E)
Goes before some verbs to show that the action was in vain, or that you were unable to do the action. ◆ Arrthawem. *Be unable to hear.*
= ath+, athem¹
SEE ALSO uyarn

arrthat (T), **arrtheth** (T) *n.*
unable to hear, a bit deaf, stubborn ◆ Artwang arrtheth, *can't* awerl. (T) *A stubborn man, he won't listen.*

arrthem (E) do something unsuccessfully; try to do something and fail SEE UNDER **athem¹**

arrtheth (T) unable to hear, a bit deaf, stubborn SEE UNDER **arrthat**

arrthwarrthw (E) *n.*
Australian owlet nightjar (*Aegotheles cristatus*)
= angkertakwertak, akwet-akwet
SEE ALSO nwernengk

arrtya¹, **arrtyel**, **arrtyang** (W,T) *adv.*
(women) doing a ritual hopping or skipping step in preparation for a fight ◆ Arrtyel alhem, kel amerl-amerl arrernem, kwaty-artek ngkwern atherr arrewem. (T) *[The woman] skips along, then shakes her legs, and her two legs vibrate like water.*
arrtyernem (T,E), **arrtyertnem** (E), **arrtyang irnem** (W) *vi.*
(women) hop or skip along showing intention to fight ◆ Kweter-akert arrtyernem. (T) *Dancing along with a nulla-nulla, ready to fight.* ◆ Ahel arrtyernem atwetyek ingwer. (Sa) *Dancing along angrily, ready to fight the other one.* ◆ Arelh apek arrtyernem ahel, iylweper atherr arrerlparrewem. Ngkwern atherr arrerlparrewem. Ampek-arrngel apek atwetyek arrtyernemel. (St) *The woman is skipping along angrily, shaking her two thighs and her two legs. She might be getting ready for a fight over a child.*
= anwerntem
SEE ALSO irnem, arrtyarnpem, antyatar-irrem, apeyarr-irrem, amerl-amerl arrernem, urrernter-irrem, rrwernter, urrernter¹
CAN SOUND A BIT LIKE arrtyenem *'shine brightly'*
arrtyel rntwem (W)
(women) hop or skip along showing intention to fight (rntwem *'dance'*)

arrtya² *n.*
ghost gum flower (*Corymbia aparrerinja*)
= ulemparrty
SEE ALSO ntewal, ulemp, pwernengk

arrtya³ (W), **arrtyang** (W) *n.*
small rocks or stones ◆ Irntang akwek 'arrtyang'. (M) *Small rocks are 'arrtyang'.*
= urrtyel, irrtyewat¹

arrtyanem *vi.*
1. run ◆ Kwer nhenh arrengkerr anthwerr arrtyanem. (N) *This child is running really fast.*
2. run away ◆ Alenh arlewatyerr ater arrtyanem. (N) *The goanna over there is running away frightened.*
= untem

arrtyang (W,T) a ritual hopping or skipping step that is done in preparation for a fight (of women) SEE UNDER **arrtya¹**

arrtyang (W) small rocks or stones SEE UNDER **arrtya³**

arrtyangk (W), **atyangk** (W) *n.*
clean honey (native honey). Also referred to as *ngkwarl arrtyangk.*
Arrtyangk (W) *n.*
the name of a soakage south of Coniston

arrtyarnpem (E) *vi.*
get ready for a fight (men), talk angrily ◆ Arrtyarnpeparnpem ahel, nhakw-areyarl ilterreperrem. Rareyarl anem-warl arrtyarnpeparnem. (St) *They are getting worked up and angry because those others over there are swearing at them. They are getting ready to go over and fight them.*
SEE ALSO arrtya¹

arrtyelh-ilem (T) ask someone to go with you SEE UNDER **irrtyelh-ilem**

arrtyem (E) *vt.*
1. light (a fire) ◆ Ura irrerntek arrtyey, irrerntekarl ayeng arrewem-kety. (Sa) *Light a fire because of the cold, because I'm shivering with cold.*
2. warm oneself by the fire or in the sun
3. cook something ◆ Ker arrtyem urel. (Sa) *Cooking the meat on the fire.* ◆ Apmerrkel ker arrtyem. (Sa) *The young fella is cooking meat.*
4. mix tobacco with ashes ◆ Urnpernp ahelengkw. Ngkwerlp arlkwentyan renh arlkwem arlpmenyel arrtyemel, wal antewarl irrem ikwer-penh, ahelengkw arnterr-penh. Mwerr ngkwerlp atherrk. (Sa) *The rock pituri is very strong. If you chew it after mixing it with ashes you might vomit, because it's really strong. Sandhill pituri is better.*
5. make the earth go a yellow or red colour (honeyants) ◆ Yerrampel arrtyeynem aleyaw.

Ahern aley arrtyeynemaw. (Sa) *This is where the honeyants are making the earth go a yellow or red colour.*
SEE ALSO item, atyerrem[1], ampeng-ilem, ampernem

arrtyelh-ilem (W) *vt.*
warm oneself by the fire or in the sun

arrtyelhem (T,E) *vi.*
mourn (cut hair), be in mourning, grieve. In the past the bereaved would burn their hair off. ◆ Ampikwek arrtyelhek. *Daughter* ikwerenhek arrtyelhem, amikw. Artnerl-anemel. *Lose*-emarl ilek ikwerenh, arrtyelhem. Aynikw arrtyelhem arrpemarl — anewart ratherr. (Sa) *The mother cut her hair off. In mourning for her daughter. Crying. If she loses her daughter she cuts her hair in grief. Her father cuts his hair as well — both the husband and the wife.*
= itelhem, anker-athek-irrem

arrtyenem (E) *vt.*
shine, shine brightly ◆ Arrtyenem ura arlengarl ampep-ampem *bushfire* apek alakenh, arrtyenepenem ingwel. Mwetek *light* arrtyenenty alhem ularr-athek apek apetyem. (St) *A bushfire burning in the distance might shine brightly at night. The car lights shine as the car is coming in this direction.*
= alhenem
CAN SOUND A BIT LIKE arrtyernem *'a way of moving when preparing for a fight (women)'*

arrul (T,E) *n.*
a long time ago; for a long time; for good, all the time ◆ Lyetant apetyety, mer ingwer-they, arrul aretyang. (Sa) *[We] haven't seen that person for a long time, they have just arrived from another place.*
= angkwey, ahenp
CAN SOUND A BIT LIKE arwerl *'tree'*

arruleny (T,E) *n.*
old, from a long time ago, a long time ago, for a long time, for good ◆ Mantarr arruleny arrarlp-iwem rapety-warl. (Sa) *Chuck the old clothes into the rubbish.*
= angkweyeny, arrwekeleny, ahenpeny

arrul innga (E)
a really long time ago (innga *'really'*)

arruneng (E), **arrutneng** (E) wild passionfruit SEE UNDER **arrweneng**

arrurrperl (E) black-headed python SEE UNDER **arrwerrperl**

arrurt (E), **arrurtn** (E) chin SEE UNDER **arrwert**

arrwa, arrwang (W,T) *n.*
black-footed rock-wallaby (*Petrogale lateralis*). Also referred to as *ker arrwa*.
SEE ALSO areng[2]

arrwanty (W,T) a type of snake SEE UNDER **arranty**[1].

arrwarlp (E) native tomato SEE UNDER **rrwarlp**[1].

arrwatnwer (E) *n.*
a type of native tobacco (*Nicotiana* sp.). Also referred to as *ngkwerlp arrwatnwer*.

arrwek (T,E) *n.*
saliva, dribble ◆ Pelh angerr-irrepirrem ayeng, arrwek thelelhetyek. (St) *I am dribbling a lot, the saliva is dribbling.*
= iylkerr, arrelty[2], pelh[1]

Arrwek (W,T) *n.*
the name of a place in the Coniston area. See map p. viii.

arrwekel *n.*
1. first, in front, ahead of others ◆ Arrwekel alhay, ayeng ingkern alheyamel. (St) *You go first, and then I'll go later.*
2. the front part of something ◆ Artep arrengakw-thayt, [werlaty] arrwekel-thayt. (Sa) *[Your] back is behind, and your breasts are on the front side.*
3. before, beforehand, earlier, first (before something else) ◆ Alhekarl apek ayeng wal unta apekarl alhirrkem apety-alpem apek, arrwekel ngan alhirrkem — urltaty apek nga irrem. (St) *I might have gone away, and then you have a feeling that I'm coming back. Beforehand you have a premonition about it — you might have a twitching feeling in the nose.*
◆ Arnmenyel apek marl yanh akerlkem. Tyerrty anengk apetyem kel arrwekel akerlkem ra. (T) *That woman is covering herself with ashes. Lots of people are coming so she covers herself first.*
SEE ALSO ahenp, angkwey

arrwekel-arrwekel *n.*
in front, first, ahead ◆ Arrwekel-arrwekel atweynetyel arrwekel atweynetyel ker alewatyerr. (Sa) *[She] is going along ahead killing goannas.*

arrwekel-ampeny *n.*
in front, first

arrwekeleny *n.*
1. olden-time people, people from long ago, ancestors ◆ Ker alhwet arlkwerretyart arrwekelenyel-rnem. (Sa) *The olden-time people used to eat the bettong.* ◆ Ntang ilkert, mwerr-angker renh athetyam arrwekelenyel, apwert tyengel athetyam. *The seed from the Halls Creek wattle is really nice and the olden-time people ground it up with a stone called* 'tyeng'.
2. eldest sibling, the first child
◆ 'Arrwekelenyan' angerr-patarl ilem. (St)

'Arrwekeleny' is what you call the eldest. ◆ Marl angerr-pat atyengenh arrwekeleny. (M) *My eldest daughter, the first one.*

arrwekel-irrem *vi.*
go in front, take the lead, go first ◆ Arrwekel-irray, ayeng ingkern-they alheyam — nyerrel arrwekel irray. (Sa) *You go first and then I'll go after you — I'm a bit shamed so you go first.*
SEE ALSO yel-irrem

arrwekel alhem = arrwekel-irrem

arrwekety[1] *n.*
1. woman ◆ Arrwekety artelhampw. (Sa) *A big solid woman.*
2. female animal ◆ Mpwenyerlpel mpweny iytarr-iytarr arrwekety, marl ikwerenh anewikw. Marlarl iytarr akngem ra, alhwengek akwernety-alpem. (Sa) *The* mpwenyerlp *mouse drags the female — its mate — off to have sex with her. He drags the female off and puts her in the burrow.*
SEE ALSO arelh[1]

arrwekety ampwang (W,T), **arrwekety ampwa** (E) *n.*
old woman (ampwa *'old'*)

arrwekety[2] (E) *n.*
leaves of the bush banana, *alangkw, parl* (*Marsdenia australis*), which are rolled up for cooking
SEE ALSO altyey, unelh

arrwekety-arrwekety[1] (E) *n.*
a type of plant (?)
= altyel-altyel

arrwekety-arrwekety[2] *n.*
a type of black beetle. When you put this beetle to your ear it makes a high-pitched whining sound, and it tells you where there are a lot of *anaty* (bush potatoes) or *katyerr* (desert raisins).

arrwelth-arrwelth (E) *n.*
1. desert fringed lily (*Thysanotus exiliflorus*). A plant about 25 cm high, with long shiny green leaves, purple lily-like flowers and swollen roots. ◆ Uterrp-areny ap arrwelth-arrwelth. Mern kweny akeng — *name* ant. Alhewelhemel kwatyel, alta angkwelk-ilelhemel, alta angerr ilelhemel, alta awer anetyek arlpenty. *The* arrwelth-arrwelth *plant grow in the sandhills. It's not edible — it's just a plant. Mixed with water and used to wash yourself, it makes your hair thick, makes it grow long and thick.*
= akwerl-akwerl
2. broad-leaf parakeelya (*Calandrinia balonensis*). A fleshy herb about 25 cm high with succulent leaves and purple flowers. ◆ Arrwelth-arrwelthel apernelhenh urinpel alhenh-penh. (Sa) *The parakeelya is used for rubbing on yourself after you have been travelling in the heat.* • = parrkely, lywemp-lywemp

arrwelth-ilem (E) *vt.*
melt something ◆ Ker tha anter arrwelth-ileyamel. *I'm going to melt the fat.*
= rew-ilem, irrngwilem

arrwelth-irrem (E) *vi.*
melt
= rew-irrem, irrngwirrem
SEE ALSO kwaty-irrem

Arrweltyapet (W,T) *n.*
1. Gidgee Bore
2. name of a soakage at Six Mile, Ti Tree area

arrwely-arrwely, arrely-arrely (W) *n.*
weak from hunger or sickness, very old, thin, wrinkled ◆ 'Arrely-arrely' apel anwern ilem artwa ampwa an arelh ampwa. Artwang ampwang arrely-arrelyem ananem anety-anetyem. *One place*-el altywernerl-anem, alhetyakenh. Antarl-areny, mer akweteth. *Half* pweng rang anem, annga arlka nheng anngwenty *all over.* Nheng iterrenty kwerenh aparlp antemarl ilek. Lwerenan ilerrirrem 'arrely-arrely'. (M) *'Arrely-arrely' is what we call a really old man or old woman. An old man might be really old and wrecked. Staying in one place and not going anywhere. They stay at home all the time. They might be half blind and their eyes all weepy. They might have lost their senses. That's what [we] call 'arrely-arrely'.*

arrwely-arrwely-irrem, arrely-arrely-irrem (W) *vi.*
become weak from hunger or sickness, grow old, lose weight ◆ Arrwely-arrwely angerr rlkert-penh, arrwely-arrwely angerr anem yanh. (St) *[That person] is really weak after being sick, they're really weak.*
SEE ALSO ampwerrem, alyemp-alyemp[1]

arrwemp *n.kin*
1. elder opposite gender sibling [SOME SPEAKERS] ◆ Mpetyanarl tha Mpetyan arrpatyarl 'arrwemp' akem. Arrwempaty yanh alhep-alhem. Kakey apek. (St) *I call Mpetyan people like myself* 'arrwemp'. *There goes my* arrwemp. *Maybe my elder brother [woman speaking].*
2. elder sister [SOME SPEAKERS]
3. younger opposite gender sibling [SOME SPEAKERS] ◆ Kakarl akem arrwekel-penh — 'kakey kwenh atyenh, arrwekeleny'. Ingkerneny atyey-atyeyarl akem. Arrwempaty atyey-atyey. (St) *The eldest brother is called 'kak'*

— *'my eldest brother'. The youngest is called* 'atyey-atyey'. *My* arrwemp *is the youngest.*
4. cross-cousin of opposite gender [SOME SPEAKERS]
SEE ALSO ngayekenh, angalthen, kak, angkwer, yay
arrwempaty *n.kin*
my/our *arrwemp* ◆ Arelh angerr-pat mapel iletyart, 'Arrwempatyam yanhan. Arrwempaty atyengenh, arrwempaty ngkwengenh, arrwempaty inekenh.' Marl mapel. Artwang mapel ilem ngayekenharl. Arelh ampwel ilem arrwempaty. (T) *The old women used to say, 'That's my* arrwemp. *My* arrwemp, *your* arrwemp, *their* arrwemp.*' The women said that. The men say* 'ngayekenh' *[sister]. The old women say* 'arrwempaty'.
arrwempengkw *n.kin*
your *arrwemp*
arrwempikw (T,E) *n.kin*
his/her/their *arrwemp*
arrwempekw (W,T) *n.kin*
1. your *arrwemp*
2. his/her/their *arrwemp*
arrwemp-nheng *n.kin*
a group of two or more people, one or more of whom is called *arrwemp* by the others ◆ Arrwemp-nhengan akem kakeyarl, marlel apek. 'Arrwempaty yanh alhep-alhemaw kwenh.' Atyeyekw apek. Atyeyekw thenarl 'arrwemp' akemam, marlel, artwa atherr. 'Arrwemp-nheng*' is what a woman calls her elder brothers. 'There goes my elder brother.' Or maybe her younger brother [might be called* 'arrwemp'*]. A woman calls both her younger and her elder brother* arrwemp.
arrwemp-intyerr *n.kin* = **arrwemp-nheng**
arrwemp-nheng-atherr *n.kin*
a person together with their *arrwemp*
arrwemp-ankenthenh *n.kin*
1. having *arrwemp* (still alive)
2. someone who is always with their *arrwemp*
SEE ALSO -ankethenh

arrwemper (W,T) *n.*
shovel spear. This was thrown from the hand rather than using a woomera. ◆ Artwel atanthem ker ankerr arrwemperel. (T) *The man is spearing an emu using a shovel spear.*
SEE ALSO irrtyart
= **urremper** (T,E)

arrweneng, arrutneng (E), **arruneng** (E) *n.*
1. wild passionfruit, caper bush (*Capparis spinosa* var. *nummularia*). Shrub about 1.5 m high, with delicate white flowers and fruits which turn yellow and split open when they are ripe.

2. edible fruits of the wild passionfruit ◆ Arrweneng tyarrp-irrem ampeng antem, kel arlkwem renh akemel. Ampengemey irrem arlkwem tyerrtyel. *The wild passionfruit splits open when it is ripe, then we pick it and eat it. Aboriginal people eat it when it's ripe.*

arrwengak, arrengakw *n.*
on the other side of something (to the speaker); behind something, on the back side or far side of something ◆ Tyerrty apek anep-anem arrwengak *side*. (St) *The people are sitting down there on the other side.* ◆ Artep arrengakw-thayt, werlaty arrwekel-thayt. (Sa) *[Your] back is behind, and your breasts are on the front side.* ◆ Arrengakwel anep-anem, rtakwel apek anep-anem arrengakw-thayt. (St) *Sitting on the other side, maybe on the other side of the windbreak.* ◆ Arrengakw tnepetnem, aretyakenharl anwantherr anep-anem. Iyntwarr-ampenyelantarl arep-areman. (St) *Standing on the other side, and we can't see [them]. We can only see people on this side.*
SEE ALSO irrweper, anwenger
arrwengak-irrem, arrengakw-irrem *vi.*
move to the other side of something (from the speaker); be on the other side of something ◆ Arrengakw-irrerl-anem arekerr. (Sa) *Going behind something in case [they] see you.*
= anwenger-irrem

-arrwengerr (T) those two; and (the other one)
SEE UNDER **-irrwengerr**

arrwengkelth *n.*
1. disease, sickness, illness ◆ Rlkert angerr intem arrwengkelth-penh. (M) *He is very sick from that disease.* ◆ Angwarekarl arrwengkelth. (St) *Catching a disease.*
SEE ALSO inkwerr, pwenty[1]
2. sickness resulting from traditional practices such as boning or singing ◆ Arrwengkelth yanhel akeng-ilek. Arrwekeleny map *clean*-arl ina anek — *no* arrwengkelth ina atnyenek *disease* apek *nothing*. Perrap *clean, only* artwekenhant arrwengkelthant ina alyerretyart. Alhernter maparl apetyek-tayman *worse* anem. (St) *That disease made him/her sick. The olden days people were free of disease — they didn't have any sickness. They lived a clean life and didn't have any sickness or disease. They just used to sing each other with men's things and with*

traditional arrwengkelth. *When white people came things got worse.*
3. something that is poisonous
arrwengkelthel alyem (E)
'sing' someone to make them sick (alyem '*sing someone*') ◆ Arrwengkelthel ap alyem tyerrty arrpenh renh. Kel arntety anem intem, awerlp-awelhemel. (St) *Somebody might be sung with* arrwengkelth. *Then they lie down and start to feel sick.*
SEE ALSO arrilem, arrilenty-ilem, artimperr-wem

arrwengkengk (E) *n.*
fleshy part just under the chin
◆ Arrwengkengk-they atwetyek tyerrty apek. (St) *Hitting somebody under the chin.*

arrwer-ilem1 (T,E) *vt.*
satisfy hunger or thirst, eat or drink quickly, really get stuck into food or drink ◆ Mern apek arlkwetyek tha arrwer-iletyek. Arrpenhel *might* atyeng anthem, anthem atyeng arrpenhel. 'Ngka tha arrwer-iletyek.' (St) *I want to satisfy my hunger by eating something. Another person might give me some [food]. 'Give me some, so that I can satisfy my hunger.'*
◆ Kwaty apek angkethel arrwer-iletyek tha. Mwerr anem ayeng awelhem arrwer-ilek tha. (St) *I'm thirsty and I'm going to satisfy my thirst. I feel better after satisfying my thirst.* ◆ Ngka, mern thang arlkwerl-alhetyeh arrwer-ilemel. (T) *Give me some, I want to eat quickly before I go.*
= antyetem
SEE ALSO nyant arlkwem, arnterr arlkwem, ahanthem, arrwer-ilem
arrwer-arrwer (T,E) *n.*
something that is really delicious (food); someone you really like, or someone who is desirable (?); a special person ◆ Ker arrwer-arrwer arlkwetyek. (T) *Eating the delicious meat.*
◆ Ampa akwek arrwer-arrwer. (T) *A gorgeous baby.*

arrwer-ilem2 *vt.*
1. drop something ◆ *Spanner* thang arrwer-ilek akerneng. (T) *I dropped the spanner from high up.*
2. leave something behind (?) ◆ Ityaw! Thang arrwer-ilemel parrpel alhek. (T) *No! I left it behind, leaving in too much of a hurry.*
arrwerelhem *vi.*
fall to the ground, fall, drop down ◆ Kwaty arrwerelhem. (N) *The rain is falling.*
◆ Ankerteng arrwerelhem kwaty. (M) *The rain is falling from the clouds.*
SEE ALSO anyem1, anhem

arrwernem *vt.*
make a hole in something, drill a hole in something ◆ Arrwernek tha alhweng arlewatyerr-kenh apek. (St) *I made a hole in the goanna's burrow.*
SEE ALSO thakem
CAN SOUND A BIT LIKE rrwernem, urrernem *'make trouble for someone'*

arrwernt, arrwirnt (E), **arrirnt** (E), **arrweynt** (E) *adv.*
facing away; not looking at someone; turning to face away; sulky ◆ Arrwernt anem ntywem-atheh arrpenh-kety. (T) *Facing away from the others.*
SEE ALSO nyerr, arnkely
arrwernt-irrem, arrwirnt-irrem (E), **arrweynt-irrem** (E), **arrirnt-irrem** (E) *vi.*
be sulky, sulkily face away from someone, turn your back on someone ◆ Ilek-kety unta arrwirnt-irretyel, irntwem-irrem? (Sa) *Why are you getting sulky and turning your back on me?*
◆ Arrwernt-irremel anem arnkely ngkweng, nhel-anyem mern unantherneng — arnkely anem ayeng ngkweng anem, arrwernt-irremel. Unanthek-arleng. (St) *Turning my back on you and getting sulky, because of this food that you didn't share — so then I get sulky with you and turn my back on you because you didn't share.*
SEE ALSO nyerr-irrem, irntwem-irrem

arrwerrperl (T,E), **arrurrperl** (E) *n.*
black-headed python (*Aspidites melanocephalus*) (arra '*mouth*'; rrpwerl '*dark-coloured*'). Also referred to as *ker arrwerrperl.*
◆ Ker arrwerrperl apmwa. *Yellow and brown* arlkeny-arlkeny alakenh an kapertan urrperl ra arrwerrperl. Rapet ra akwernemarl akuny, *anything* ikwer *stuck*-irrem, *finish.* Ampwerrk ra akwernem, arlewatyerr apek ker arlewatyerr apek. Ahelengkw anetyang. (St) *The black-headed python. It has yellow and brown stripes and a dark-coloured head. It swallows the poor rabbits, and anything that gets stuck in its gullet dies. It swallows goannas whole. Black-headed pythons are not dangerous [to people].* ◆ Ker arrwerrperl renh arlkwem. Ker mwerrarl ra. (St) *Black-headed pythons are edible. They are good meat.*
= antwerrkenh, arrakert rrpwerl, urayerrp, rwayerrp

arrwert (T,E), **arrurt** (E), **arrurtn** (E) *n.*
1. chin
2. beard, whiskers, an animal's whiskers
◆ Arrwertan lyapeman. Marl arrpenhemant arrwert-akert — aler-aler. *The beard grows. Some women have beards — called* aler-aler *[nephew or niece].*

= arralt
Arrwert (W) *n.*
name of hill between Mt Allan and Coniston
arrwert-penh (E) *n.*
a person's brother's child; nephew, niece (lit. 'from the beard')
= arrarn-penh
SEE ALSO rnwepenh
Arrurtepenh (E) *n.*
the name of a soakage east of Wilora (Stirling) community (-penh[1] *'from'*)
paty arrwert (W,T)
the shape of breasts when they are just starting to develop; pointy breasts (paty *'breast'*) ◆ Paty arrwert awenk. Anwengkerr paty ayenp. (M) *Teenage girls have pointy breasts. We [senior women] have saggy ones.*
= akarnterrng

arrwertem (W,T) *n.*
a low rise in the hills; hill with scrubby trees. Also referred to as *irntang arrwertem.*
arrwertem-arrwertem (W,T) *n.*
a low rise in the hills
SEE ALSO rrwelty-rrwelty

arrwety *n.*
dead body, corpse
SEE ALSO irrewaly, irrernng, aweyaw, ima

arrwety-akem (E) *vt.* [RESPECT LANGUAGE]
chase someone angrily ◆ Ngwarrelengkw arrwety-akety-alpem. Ahel-irremel. Atwetyekarl apetyem ilem, artwa ingwerek. Arrwety-akerlentyarremarl-ketyaw — ngwarrelengkw! Arrwety-akety-alhem yanh ngwarrelengkw ngenh. (Sa) *Your husband is angrily chasing that man. He's come to fight another man. Look out — your husband is angry! Your husband might get angry and chase you [woman talking to her daughter].*
SEE ALSO arlpertey, aha, alwernem

arrweynt (E), **arrwirnt** (E) facing away; not looking at someone; turning to face away; sulky SEE UNDER **arrwernt**

+art (W,T) *k.ending*
1. Goes on some kinship terms following the *-nheng* ending to show that there is a group of more than two people, one of whom is called *-nheng* that kinship term by the others. ◆ Amenheng**art** rrpwety alhem lyweny kerek. (T) *A group of mothers and their children went hunting.* ◆ Anyenheng**art** alhek. (M) *Fathers and their children went.*
2. With the kin term *anew* refers to two people together; a married couple. ◆ Anew**art** arratyant-atherr anerretyel. Kemarr uthen Petyarr uthen. (Sa) *The husband and wife are right [skin] for each other. Kemarr and Petyarr.*
SEE ALSO anew, -nheng[2], -rrpwer

+art (T) Goes on the end of the names of certain plants to form the name of the grub that is found on that plant. SEE UNDER **+aty**[2]

-art (W) be like, similar to or resemble someone or something else; seem like something else
SEE UNDER **-artek**

artakw *n.kin* [RESPECT LANGUAGE]
mother. This word is used in sympathy or in bereavement. The third person kin possessive form *artakikw,* and other proniminal kin forms with *artakw,* are not used by most Anmatyerr speakers. ◆ Artakwaty apek arleng anep-anem. Unta apek ilem, 'Artakw-kweny anemarl irrem, arrangkwarl ayeng, artakw-kweny anem'. (St) *My mother might be living a long way away. You might say, 'I haven't got a mother any more, I have nothing, no mother now'.*
SEE ALSO amey
CAN SOUND A BIT LIKE tak *'windbreak'*
artakwaty *n.kin*
my/our *artakw* ◆ Artakwaty akwey alhern kwenh? (St) *Did my poor old mother go?* ◆ 'Artakwaty-ayerr arrangkw. Ahern anengk. Artakwatyek arrangkw. *No mum.*' Alhwarrp-irremel an 'artakwaty' akem 'amaty' kwenh. (Sa) *'My poor old mum has passed away. I haven't got a mother.' When someone is grieving for their mother they refer to them as* 'artakwaty' *and not* 'amaty'.
SEE ALSO amaty
artakwengk *n.kin*
your *artakw* ◆ Artakwengk nhak alhernaw kwenh. Anyentarl ra alhern. (St) *Your mother just went over there. She went on her own.* ◆ Rtakwel anep-anemaw, artakwengk. (St) *Your mother is sitting behind the windbreak.*
SEE ALSO amwengk
artakwikw (E) *n.kin*
his/her/their *artakw*
artakw-nheng *n.kin*
a group two or more people, at least two of whom are related to each other as *artakw*
artakw-intyerr (E) *n.kin* = **artakw-nheng**
artakw-nheng atherr *n.kin*
a person together with one of their *artakw*
artakw-parety *n.kin*
respectful or 'sorry way' of talking about someone's *artakw*
SEE ALSO -parety
artakw-ankethenh *n.kin*
1. having a close *artakw* still alive
2. someone who is always with their *artakw*
SEE ALSO -ankethenh

artaly (W,T) *adv.*
throwing things around (?) ◆ Arrkenel artalyel imperretyart nywerrpek-nywerrp. (M) *People in the opposite generation moiety to each other used to have fun throwing things at each other.*
artaly-artaly (T,E) *n.*
1. lightweight, flimsy, loose, weak ◆ Irrtyart artaly-artaly — arterney urrek, rlterrk-iley. Uternel apek ampem rlterrk-irremel. (St) *The spear has become loose — wait while I straighten it and tighten it up. Maybe putting it in the sun to heat up will make it tight.*
SEE ALSO ararr, althalth, arrmaly-arrmaly, atyet[1]
2. unsteady, weak (of legs) ◆ Ngkwern atherr ayeng artaly-artaly. (St) *My legs are feeling weak.*
artaly-artaly alhem (T)
going along with weak legs, unsteady on your feet ◆ Arelh nhenh kwenh artaly-artaly alhep-alhem atyengety. Ngkwern artaly-artaly ya alhep-alhem. (T) *This woman is a bit unsteady on her feet because of me. She's going along with weak legs.* (?)
artaly-wem (W,T) *vt.*
throw something away; chuck something out; throw something around, throw things all over the place; throw something off ◆ Mantarr ngkwelty artaly-wem. (T) *Throwing the bits of clothes away.* ◆ Mern arlka ker arlka anwengkerr artaly-wem arengkel arlkwetyek. (N) *We are chucking the bread and the meat out for the dogs to eat.*
SEE ALSO iwem, altyewem, intyalp-wem, antarr-wem, arrarlp-wem
artaly-artaly-wem (T) *vt.* = **artaly-wem**
◆ Mern artaly-artaly-wem. (T) *Throwing the food all over the place.*
artang-ilem *vt.*
1. (do something) before someone else ◆ Angayel apek artang-iletyek, alhetyek apek. Artang-ilem tey apek mern apek. Tha apek artang iletyek, ngkwengetyem athath, ntwa anem antyweyameng. *You might [eat] first if you're hungry, or go [somewhere] first. You might have tea or food first. I might drink before you, and then you drink.* ◆ Artang-ilemel thek-amparr antywey, unta anem antywetyek ingkerrek. (St) *I'll drink first before you do, then you can drink the lot.*
2. give somebody half of something ◆ *Cool drink* atyeng artang-ilang! (T) *Give me half of the cool drink!*
= arnang-ilem[1]
Artangalherrp (W) *n.*
name of a place near a bore south of Tilmouth Well
artangaty *adv.*
doing things together; helping someone do something ◆ Artangatyel arlkwem ker apek, atherrel apek rrpwetyel apek. *Eating the meat together, two or three people.* ◆ Artangatyel pewetyem-iletyek mwetekay, anyentel pewetyem-ilekerr. (St) *Pushing the car together, so that one person doesn't have to push it on their own.* ◆ Artangatyel mpwareyaw, *painting*, parrp uyerrelh-iletyek. (St) *Doing the painting all together, so that it can be finished quickly.* ◆ Artangaty alhem ahel atwerretyeh. (M) *Going together to fight.*
artangaty-irrem *vi.*
help each other or do things together
artangatyel atwem
back someone up in a fight; gang up on someone, 'double bank' someone ◆ Rrpwetyel atwetyek anyent apek, artangatyel atwem. (St) *A few people might fight one person, ganging up.*
SEE ALSO ampak-irrem
artangk anem (W) squat (on toes or flat-footed)
SEE UNDER **artarnk anem**
artapaly (E) *n.*
1. native currant, native citrus (*Psydrax latifolia*). A shrub up to 3 m high, with broad, deep green leaves, small white flowers and fruit which ripen to a black colour.
2. edible fruit of the native currant
= ahakey, arrarntenh, antyern-angerr
artaper *n.*
a roll or bundle of something
SEE ALSO antyakwer, anhwert
Artaper (W) *n.*
the name of a place north-east of Napperby Station homestead
artaper-wem, artaper-iwem (E) *vt.*
roll or fold something up, make something into a bundle, wrap something up ◆ Mern apek ikwerenh artaper-wem akngwely-kety apek. (St) *She might roll up her food because of the dogs.* ◆ Altyey artaper-wem, mern ampem anem artaper anem. (St) *Bush banana leaves are rolled up and then they cook in a bundle.*
SEE ALSO anhwert-ilem, ayernem, akwengerr-werl-alhem, rwelemap-ilem
artaper-ilem *vt.* = **artaper-wem** ◆ Manteran artaper-ilem anteyarl, manter apek *swag* apek artaper-ilem. Pelangket artaper-ilem arengk-kety. (St) *Clothes and swags are rolled up. Blankets are rolled up because of the dogs.*
artapw-artapw (E) *n.*
black kite (*Milvus migrans*)
= apwelanty, apwerl-apwerl, inkwel
SEE ALSO apwart-apwart

artar *n.*
1. a young male (especially kangaroo) ◆ Ker aherr artar. (T) *A young male kangaroo.*
2. special word used by a mother to refer to her teenage son ◆ Artar yanh atyenh apety-alpetyel. Lyetant arrernelhenty-alhek. (Sa) *My son is coming back. He just came and arrived back today.* • SEE ALSO anthety
CAN SOUND A BIT LIKE artarr *'emu feathers'*
Artar *n.*
Mt Solitary, east of Ti Tree town. See map p. viii.

artarnk anem (W,T), **arntarrk anem** (W), **artangk anem** (W), **atangk anem** (E) *vi.*
squat (on toes or flat-footed); sit with arms wrapped around legs ◆ Artangk anerl-anem, rwang iterl-anemel, akem-irremel, an mern iterl-anem, artangk-artangkel mern item, artangk anemel item. (N) *Squatting down and lighting a fire, getting up and [then] cooking food, squatting down and cooking food.*

artarr *n.*
emu feathers (longer ones from the back of the emu) ◆ Artarran mpwenyekarl *use*-em-ilerretyart arrwekeleny *olden time*-el arey. Kwey awenkan mpwenyek artarrel ingkwernelhetyart artwa, kweyek mpwenyek alhemel, artarr-akert. (Sa) *The olden-time people used to use the emu feathers for eloping with people. The man used to decorate himself with emu feathers and then go to race off the young girl.* ◆ Angkwey artwang alhetyamarl, artarr arrernelhetyam ingkern, wal alhetyam mpweny. (M) *In the olden days he the man went and put the emu feathers behind [his back], and then went off with his lover.*
SEE ALSO apwa, angkwely-angkwely
Artarr *n.*
the name of a place in the Neutral Junction Station area. Also spelt as *Tara.*

artarrernem *vt.*
1. sool a dog onto someone or something ◆ Artwa anyentel arengk-rnem-akert ker aherr artarrernek — rarl apmwerrk alhekarl. (St) *A man with some dogs sooled them onto the kangaroo — he went yesterday.*
= ipernem
2. put a curse on someone, bone someone, make someone sick ◆ Pwentyel renh artarrernem arrmel urlaylpel, kel renh angkwerr-iwemel mwerrarl irrem, iteth anem alherl-anem pwenty inenty ngangkar-akertel. (Sa) *The kurdaitcha puts a curse on someone as well, and then the person gets better when they are massaged, they become lively again after the traditional healer gets the sickness out.*
SEE ALSO arrwengkelth, akwety-irrpenem, artimperr-wem, pew-ilem, rltwatyel atwem, urltatyel atwem

artart[1] (W) *n.*
handle of an adze
= arlarnt

artart[2] (W,T) *n.*
1. men's business, serious business ◆ *No* anwengkerr alhetyek artart-warn, artartel ineh anep-anem. (T) *We can't go over there where they're doing business.*
2. dead body; coffin ◆ Mwetekay yanh kwenh artart-akert apetyem. (St) *That car is coming on serious business (i.e. carrying a coffin).*
3. pregnant ◆ Arelh artart anem, nthat akeweny. (T) *That poor woman is pregnant.*

artartey (E) *n.kin*
1. mother's father; grandfather
2. mother's father's brother or sister; great-uncle, great-aunt
3. a man's daughter's child; grandchild, grandson, granddaughter
4. a person's brother's daughter's child; great-niece, great-nephew
5. particular relations with the same skin as a person's *artartey*
6. the country and Dreamings belonging to a person's *artartey.*
= atyemey
SEE ALSO rtartart
artartety (E) *n.kin*
my/our *artartey*
artartengkw (E) *n.kin*
your *artartey*
= atywengk
artartikw (E), **artarteyekw** (E) *n.kin*
his/her/their *artartey*
= atyikw
artartey-nheng (E) *n.kin*
a group of two or more people related to each other as *artartey*
= atyenheng
artartey-intyerr (E) *n.kin* = **artartey-nheng**
artartey-nheng atherr (E) *n.kin*
a person together with one of their *artartey*
= atyenheng atherr
artartey-parety (E) *n.kin*
respectful or 'sorry way' of talking about someone's *artartey*
= atyeparety
SEE ALSO -parety
artartey-ankethenh (E) *n.kin*
1. having a close *artartey* still alive
2. someone who is always with their *artartey*

= atyenkethenh
SEE ALSO -ankethenh

artarwerr (W,T) *n.*
thunder clouds building up; thunderstorm. Also referred to as *kwaty artarwerr.* ◆ Kwaty artarwerr intentyem. (M) *The thunderstorm is building up.*
SEE ALSO katyar, apwertek

-artek, **-arteh** (W,T), **-art** (W) *ending*
1. be like, similar to or resemble someone or something else; seem like something else ◆ Tyerrty yanh alhem mwerr-**artek**, rlkert anety kwenh. (T) *That person seems to be better, not sick any more.* ◆ Ampeng-ilemel angernetyart panth-**artek** yanh-lkwerel akin, arneng mpwaretyart. *When the goannas were cooked they used to take them back in dishes similar to* panth, *made from wood.* ◆ Alta werrp weth-**artek** mern weth-**artek** werrp altyey-apeny, aylep-aylep. (St) *Hair that is matted is like that food — tangled like the leaves of the bush bean.* ◆ Arnwety, athenh-athenh, kelh arrernenhernenh, tamp-**arteh** mparenharenh kelh. (N) *This is a seed that is ground up and made into a seedcake, similar to a damper.* ◆ Tyap mpaty lpway-areny, alher kwen-areny. Perlaty-**arteh** akin, arlkeny *same one*, tyap mwerr angerr. (N) *The* mpaty *grub is found in the creek, in the sand. It is similar to the* perlaty *grub, has the same markings, and is a really nice grub [to eat].*
2. do an action in a similar way to someone or something else, or in the same way something is done to another thing ◆ Tyerrtyelarl mpwarem-**artek** ra mpwarem antywa kwerenh kwerlakwekel. Antywa kwart . apek anem ra arrernem. Ura kwert-**artek**arl ra. (St) *The peaceful dove make its shelter, just like people do. Then it lays its eggs in the nest. It is like smoke [in colour].*

artek-wem (W,T) *vt.*
take someone halfway, accompany someone part of the way, drop someone off somewhere ◆ Arelh yanhel kwer akwek artek-werl-alpem kwer map-warn arrken-irretyeh. (T) *That woman is taking the child and leaving her to play with the other kids.*
= arteng-wem, twap anthem

artekernem (T,E), **tekernem** (E), **tekertnem** (E) *vi.*
1. cough
2. burp, hiccough
SEE ALSO arltarrernem, anetyerrkernem, anetyerrk-irrem, anterrk angkem, arnenthernem, ilwem

artekerr *n.*
root ◆ Artekerr-penh mpwarem ywekerrekerr. (T) *Dancing boards [for use in ceremonies] are made from roots.* ◆ Perlap artekerr alakenharl irretyart kwaty-warl arrernetyart alhewelhetyeh perlap, alhewelhenhelhenh akin artekerr. Artekerr alhewelhenhelhenh perlap, arrwekeleny map anetyam. Kikewetyamel alpweletyam irntelem, irntelem alpweletyam ayenp. Atewat arrernetyam. Alhewelhetyamem. (N) *The root of the conkleberry is put in water and used as a washing medicine. The olden-time people used it. The bark is peeled off the root and then the root is crushed with a stone and then put in hot water to make a washing medicine.*
Artekerr *n.*
1. name of a place near Alherramp (Laramba) community
2. 3 Bores (Angarapa Aboriginal Land Trust area)

artekw (W,E), **artikw** (E), **artik** (T), **artiw** (E) *n.*
mulgara (*Dasycercus cristicauda*) (?)
SEE ALSO ampwert
CAN SOUND A BIT LIKE atek *'button quail'*

artelh[1] (W,T) *n.*
baby emu, emu chick (just hatched) ◆ Artelh anywelek angernerl-anem — amwek akenh *somewhere*-arl. (N) *The father emu takes the chicks around — the mother is somewhere else.*
= alywer[1], ankerr akwek, ankerr akwerrk
SEE ALSO ankerr, arley

artelh[2] (T,E), **arteyl** (E) *n.*
anus, backside
= anaynp, anwerlk[2], alywel
artelh-irrkert-irrkert (E) *n.*
a type of ant that lifts its backside up (lit. 'bent or twisted backside')

artelh[3] (E) *n.*
big, huge ◆ Artelh innga. *Really big.*
artelhampw (E) *n.*
fat, heavy, solid, big ◆ Arrwekety artelhampw. (Sa) *A big solid woman.* ◆ Mern anatyel tetnh anyenem akern. Anaty artelh ampwel inngel. Urrper-wem, urrper ra tetnh atnyenem irrkwenngel-apeny. (Sa) *The bush potato makes the earth lift right up. A really big bush potato. It makes the earth swell up and crack, like a native truffle does.*
SEE ALSO angerrety, angerr[1], awer[1], ilkwa[2], rltwa, urlta, anter, anter angerr, awek, angerrety-pwek

artely-ilem (W,T) *vt.*
make a cut across the top part of the thighs of a cooked kangaroo ◆ Ker aherr artely-ilem irntang arlterel. (M) *Cutting the kangaroo's thighs with a stone knife.*
SEE ALSO tyep-ilem

artem *vt.*
1. cover something over ◆ Kwer yanh tha artem anyeleng. (M) *I'll cover that child over because of the cold.*
2. bury something
3. build or put something up, construct something ◆ Warlan artem tyerrty map warrken mapel. (T) *The working mob build houses.*
CAN SOUND A BIT LIKE aytem *'pick up firewood'*
artelhem *vi.*
1. cover part of yourself over ◆ Kapert artelhenhem, twernel inngerr ampekety. (N) *Going along with [your] head covered over in case it gets burnt by the sun.* ◆ Pelangketel ayeng artelheyamel, irrernt-kety. (St) *I'm going to cover myself with a blanket because of the cold.* ◆ Kapert artelhem arelhan akenty-penhan nyerr-irremel. (T) *The woman is covering her head after her hair has been cut because she's feeling shamed.*
2. be built, be constructed ◆ Warl artelhem. *The houses are being built.* ◆ Parrek ina artelhenhepenhem. Pwelek-kety an wethey-kety. (T) *They are building the fence along there. Because of the cattle and the horses.*
arteng (W), **rteng** (W) *n.*
bottom part of a native beehive or sugarbag hive
SEE ALSO mern
arteng-wem (T,E), **arteng-iwem** (E) *vt.*
take someone half way, accompany someone part of the way, drop someone off somewhere ◆ Urrek tha yanh arteng-werlewey. Ngenh apek *me might* arteng-werl *halfway*-irrem mer. *Highway*-they iyntwarr-ampeny-they apek arteng-werlewem ngenh. *Wait while I go part of the way with that [person]. I might accompany you halfway to the place. I might go as far as the other side of the highway with you.* ◆ Ngarrp alpetyek — tha ngenh arteng-iwem. (Sa) *You go back yourself — I'll go part of the way with you.*
= artek-wem
artengel-arem (T,E) *vt.*
argue or fight on behalf of somebody; back someone up; take someone's side in a fight or argument ◆ Artengel arem, arelh arrpenhel atwenty. (Sa) *Backing a person up if another woman is hitting them.* ◆ Nhenhel apek ayeng artengel arem. (St) *This person might back me up.* ◆ Artwa atherr wenh nhwerrem — *might be* artwang ankelekw apek atwem artwang anywek ankelekw. Kenh artengel-arerleng *might be* kelekw apek — *that's* ankwernem. Yatherr anem atwerrem. (M) *Two men might be fighting each other — maybe a man is fighting with his cousin or his cousin-father. And then his brother might step in and back him up, take his side — that's* ankwernem. *The two of them fight then — the man's brother and the cousin.*
SEE ALSO ankwernem
artengert arem (W) *vt.*
follow someone ◆ Kwer alenhel artengert arem, amwek apek, angey apek. (M) *The child is following her/his mother or father.*
artenh *n.*
following someone or something ◆ Tyerrty arrpenh ywerr-arleng kel artenheng alhem. (T) *If a person disappears then you follow them.*
artenh-irrem, artenheng-irrem *vi.*
follow someone or something ◆ Mwetekay artenh-irra, akengenty alhekerr. (Sa) *Follow that car in case it goes the wrong way.*
arteny[1] *adv.*
staying behind, stopping at home, not going anywhere ◆ Arteny-antey anerl-anetyang ayeng atywaty-irremel alhetyek. (Sa) *I'm not going to stay at home, I'll go and stretch my legs.* ◆ Arteny ntwa anerl-anem, alhety-kweny. (M) *You are staying at home, not going anywhere.*
SEE ALSO antarl, rlwemp, urlemp, rlwepety, urlepety
artenyem-arteny (E) *adv.* = **arteny**[1]
◆ Apmerel-antey anep-anem, artenyem-arteny. (St) *Staying at home and not going anywhere.*
arteny[2] (T,E) *n.*
middle of the day; dinnertime ◆ Aherrk artenyel ayeng anerl-anem. (St) *I am sitting down in the middle of the day.*
artep *n.*
1. back of a person or animal ◆ Kwer akwek amwekel-ayeng artepel anem. (N) *The child is sitting on his/her mother's back.*
2. the top of something (with the back or rounded part facing upwards) ◆ Warl artep. *The top of the house.*
artep ngkwern
backbone (ngkwern *'bone'*)
artep-akert *n.*
having a backache (lit. 'having a back') ◆ Artep-akert intem, arteparl arekar-irrerl-anem. (N) *Lying down with a backache, a back that is hurting.*
artepeng arem (E)
look back over shoulder
artepeng arelhem (E) = **artepeng arem**
= anngarelhem, angkep arem, angkep-athek arem

artep arrernem
turn or tip something upside down (so that the back part is facing up) (arrernem *'put'*)
= altywarrernem
apwert artep (T,E)
top of a hill (apwert *'hill'*) ◆ Arelh nhakway apwert akertnel alhep-alhem artepel, akertn alhep-alhem artep-angkwerr. (St) *That woman is going along the top of the hill, along the top of the hill.*
iltya artep (E)
the back of the hand (iltya *'hand'*)
SEE ALSO iltya anert
ingka artep, ingkang artep (W,T)
the top of the foot (ingka *'foot'*)
SEE ALSO ingka anert
artep nyerr
shamefully (nyerr *'shame'*)
artepelh-ilem *vt.*
1. leave something behind; turn your back on something; not bother with something
2. accidentally bump or step on someone ◆ Akeweny — thwengk artepelh-ilem, artep apek, ingka apek. (T) *Poor thing — I accidentally stepped on your back, or maybe your foot.* • SEE ALSO aperrpert-ilem, menty-ilem[1]
artep arlpenty (T,E)
red ochre (arlpenty *'long'*)
SEE ALSO rlpwa, arwethenp, atywerlk, ngwenty-ngwenty, karntewarr, marlalperr
artep irrpent (E)
pygmy desert monitor (*Varanus eremius*). Used to be eaten.
= irrpent
SEE ALSO tyalep, irrerlaly
artep lpway (W,T), **artep ulpay** (T,E) *n.*
1. emu fat (from the back of the emu) (lpway *'creek'*) ◆ Artep ulpay atyeng akwek akaw. (St) *Cut me a little bit of emu fat.* ◆ Artep ulpay ultakem, kwer-penh tyep-tyep-akem. (T) *Cut the emu fat into sections, then cut it into pieces.*
SEE ALSO arnwa
2. emu [SOME SPEAKERS]
Artep Lpway *n.*
the name of a place north of Mt Allan community
artep ultatwem (T,E) *vt.*
cut up meat along the backbone (particularly said of emu) ◆ Artep ultatwem ker ankerr, kel renh akalkelh-ilemel artep atherr kel renh tyep-ilemel iylweper atherr akemel anem akalk ant-atherr. (Sa) *Cut up the emu meat, then separate the two sides of the back, then cut the two thighs up, so that they are separate.*
SEE ALSO arrkwelem, ulta, atwem

arteperrk *n.*
kidney ◆ Arteperrk anyentarl ayeng. (T) *I've got one kidney.*
= mpwerrkety
SEE ALSO kwerrern
ker arteperrk
edible kidneys
arterlkwarr (E) button quail SEE UNDER **aterlkwarr**
arternem[1] (E) *vt.*
chop (wood), chop something out of a tree ◆ Ulya arternem. (Sa) *Chopping branches for a shade.* ◆ Arwengalker arelhel arternetyel ilepel. (Sa) *The woman is chopping sugarbag out with an axe.*
SEE ALSO atwem
CAN SOUND A BIT LIKE ayternem *'peep out from behind something'*
arternem[2] *vt.*
1. straighten something ◆ Artwel irrtyart arternem. (T) *The man is straightening the spear.* ◆ Anem arternem — rwel itemel an arnang ntarlkw nhelkwer-warl tyarrp-warl angem tyarrpel arternetyeh. (N) *Straightening a digging stick — heating it in the fire and then taking it to a forked tree, or that sort of thing, and straightening it in the crack.* ◆ Artep arternetyek ulperr ayntay. Artep ngenh arternetyek ulperr aynteyaw, ingkel ulthemel. (Sa) *Lie down on your stomach so that I can straighten your back. Lie down so that I can straighten your back by pressing down on it with my feet.*
SEE ALSO arraty-ilem
2. step on, tread on something ◆ Arelh ampwangel arternepernem arnwety mamperrk. (M) *The old woman is treading on the* mamperrk *seeds [to husk them].* ◆ Ingkang ayeng arternerl-alhem — arekarrarlay! (M) *Somebody is treading on my foot — it's hurting!* • SEE ALSO rlpwerrkem, rrwethem, lthwem, ulthem
CAN SOUND A BIT LIKE ayternem *'peep out from behind something'*
arternelhem *vi.*
stretch or straighten yourself ◆ Arternelhem ayeng, arteparl mwerr-irremel ayeng intem. (N) *I am stretching myself, so my back feels better and then I'll lie down.*
SEE ALSO irrketelhem
arternp, atyernp *adv.*
1. slowly, unhurriedly ◆ Angwelyan arternp akwet irrpek warl-warn, kwer-penh arterrkwek tywek-tywek anyent. (M) *The dog slowly entered the house and grabbed one of the little chickens.* ◆ Arternp alhem, arrengker-kweny. (Sa) *Go*

slowly, not quickly. ◆ Atyernp alhay! (M) *Go slowly!*
2. quietly, calmly, carefully ◆ Alerl athek-irrerl-iwerretyang arternpeng anenherr-arey. Mern arlkwetyek athek-irrerlarr-anetyang — yanhan atyenharl. *Wait, don't you all get excited and rush in, sit down quietly. Don't get over-excited about eating — that's my food.* ◆ Arternp angkaw. Arralthelherl-anetyang, arralthelhetyang arternp angkay. (Sa) *Speak quietly. Don't shout, don't scream — talk quietly.*
SEE ALSO manty, mwerranty
arternp-irrem, **atyernp-irrem** *vi.*
1. slow down, settle down
2. settle down (in a place) ◆ Ayeng atyernp-irrety-alpek mer nhelem. (M) *I came back and settled down in this place.* • SEE ALSO kwak-irrem
arternp-ilem, **atyernp-ilem** *vt.*
slow someone down; quieten someone down, settle someone or something down
SEE ALSO anngwanng-ilem, aparlp-parlp-ilem
arternpelh-ilem, **atyernpelh-ilem** *vt.*
= **arternp-ilem** ◆ Atyernp ra alhetyek atyenpelh-ilem. 'Atyernp-irray kwenh, ker aretyek atyernpel-artek kwenh.' Atyernpelh-ilemel renh, ker ingka apek aretyek. (St) *Slow her down so that she goes slowly. 'Slow down, watch carefully for the game'. Slow her down so that she can look for tracks.*

arterrk *n.*
umbrella bush (*Acacia ligulata*). Shrub up to 2.5 m high, which always grows where spinifex is. The leaves of the umbrella bush are used for 'smoking' babies. ◆ Kamwerlel arlkwerl-apek — arnwety anetyakenh. Arterrk yanh kamwerl-wenh antem. Kamwerl *seed* arlka arlkwenh-arlkwenh *self.* Tyerrtyel arlkwety itya. (N) *Camels eat it — it doesn't have any seeds that we eat. Arterrk is camels' food. Camels eat the seeds but Aboriginal people don't.*

arterrkwem (W) *vt.*
catch someone or something ◆ Angwelyan arternp akwet irrpek warl-warn, kwer-penh arterrkwek tywek-tywek anyent. (M) *The dog slowly entered the chook house and grabbed one of the little chickens.*
SEE ALSO arntwerrkem

arterrp *n.*
1. smooth, flat, level
2. plump, a bit fat ◆ Arengk arterrparl anem. (T) *The dog is a bit plump now.*
3. inflated ◆ Nhenh arterrp-antey, alpwely-irretyakenh. (St) *This thing is still inflated, it hasn't gone down.*
SEE ALSO arlwar, alyelk
arterrp-ilem *vt.*
1. smooth something, scrape something to make it smooth ◆ Alparr kantyengarrel arterrp-ilem. (M) *Scraping the wooden dish with an adze to make it smooth.*
SEE ALSO arrpem, yarr-wem
2. clean something ◆ Mer arterrp-ilem. (M) *Cleaning the camp.*
arterrp-irrem *vi.*
smooth over; heal over, heal up ◆ *Knife*-penh kwerrm-irrek anem. Urrmirrek anem. Utyen arterrp-irrek anem. Weth utyen anetyakenh. (St) *After [being cut with] a knife the wound healed over. The sore healed over, and then there wasn't a sore there.*
SEE ALSO urrmirrem, ltyerrem, tywenmernt-irrem

arterrty (T,E) *n.*
1. dry
= arleny, antyerrk
2. flour ◆ Arterrty atyeng antheyaw tha rlterrk-iletyek mern, rew-rewarl ilek — kwatyarl thelek *too much.* (St) *Give me some flour so that I can make this mixture thicker — it went runny because I poured too much water in.* • SEE ALSO nmwenth, warnp, perlaw
arterrty-irrem (T,E) *vi.*
get dry ◆ Mantarr tek-wem arterrty-irretyek. *Hang out the clothes to dry.* ◆ Ahelh apek arterrty-irrek. (St) *The ground might have dried up.*
= arleny-irrem, antyerrk-irrem
arterrty-ilem (T,E) *vt.*
make something dry ◆ Arterrty-iletyek tha mern nhenh. (St) *I'm going to make this mixture here dry.*
= arleny-ilem, antyerrk-ilem

artety *n.*
types of mulga (*Acacia aneura, A. paraneura*). Trees to 12 m high, with rough bark and yellow flowers. ◆ *Seed*-akert, atwem arnangel, ahern-warl atwem artety, arnwety, rwelam atyerrety-alpem, atyerrem rwel, anterrng athemam, rwel itemel. Rnpwarl anetyam larl-artek rnpwa. Kwer mapel arlkwerl-apetyart. (N) *The mulga tree has seeds which we hit to the ground and then cook in the fire. Then we grind up the seed. The mulga has an edible resin like a lolly that the kids go along eating.*

CAN SOUND A BIT LIKE rtety[1] *'tooth'*; tety *'step', 'foothold'*

artety akwerrk
young mulga trees (akwerrk[1] *'young'*). These are used to make spears from.
artetyayt (E) *n.*
grub found on mulga
= alethayerr, kepartart
SEE ALSO ulalthengayt
artetyaywerrk (W), **artetyayerrkw** (W) *n.*
honeydew on mulga (made by the lerp-scale insect, *Austrotachardia acaciae*)
◆ Ngkwarl artetyaywerrk awantyerl-apek, arna akemel rnpwang awantyerl-apek artetyaywerrk renh, larlartarl. (N) *We went along sucking on the sweet honeydew from the mulga, picking the branches and sucking on the resin, like a lolly.*
= arlperl
SEE ALSO alkeramp

Artetyarntweng (E) waterhole/swamp near the Aniltji/Sandover highway turn-off SEE UNDER **Artwetyarnteng**

artetyehenp (W) *n.*
a type of black ant ◆ Yerr angerr akin artetyehenp, rwert angerr mparerlapemel. Artetyel nthwerlapem, rwert mparerlapem. (M) *The* artetyehenp *is a big ant that makes wide tracks as it goes along. It makes tracks as it goes along through where the mulga trees are.*
SEE ALSO atywer

artetyerretyerr[1] *n.*

willie wagtail (*Rhipidura leucophrys*) ◆ Tyerrtyel ltewem artetyerretyerr kwaty angerrem anhem. (M) *If a person throws something at the willie wagtail then there will be a lot of rain.* ◆ Artetyerretyerrel kwaty tyarr-inem, rlkang angerr tyarr-inem. (T) *The willie wagtail brings rain and lots of wind.*
= tyenterr-tyenterr

artetyerretyerr[2] (E) *n.*
bush place where women and children camp during initiation (young men) ceremonies
◆ Artetyerretyerr-warl alpeyaw, anety-alpetyek marl map. (St) *All us women will go back to the* artetetyerretyerr *place to sit down.*
SEE ALSO apwelh, anmanty

artew *n.*

bush turkey, wild turkey, bustard (*Ardeotis australis*). Also referred to as *ker artew*.
◆ Artewan akerarlam. Altang althem altang althem kwerpenh ker renh atyerrem. Rlweth akem amwelt atherr an kapert rlweth akem. (N) *Bush turkey meat is edible. The feathers are plucked out and then after that the meat is cooked. The two legs and the head are split open.*
= arwengerrp, warterlk

Artew Irnem *n.*
the name of a swamp, Sullivan Well, Stuart Bluff Range area (artew *'bush turkey'*; irnem *'stand'*)

-artey *ending*
1. Goes on the end of words as a way of asking where someone or something is; 'Where is . . . ?' ◆ Manperl atyengenh-**artey**? (P) *Where is my stone knife?* ◆ Ngkwengenh-**artey**? *Where is yours?* ◆ Anherrey-**artey**? (St) *Where is my sister-in-law?*
= alew[1]
2. Makes a question out of a statement; 'What about . . . ?', 'What if . . . ?', 'How about . . . ?'

-artey (W,T) people related to a particular Dreaming; owners or 'bosses' of a particular Dreaming, place or story SEE UNDER **-artwey**

arteyl (E) anus, backside SEE UNDER **artelh**[2]

artik (T), **artikw** (E) mulgara (?) SEE UNDER **artekw**

artimperr-wem (T,E), **artimperr-iwem** (E) *vt.*
'sing' someone with supernatural powers or magic; put a curse on someone
◆ Arrwengkelthel apek renh alyetyek, artimperr-wetyek. Alha apek akeng-irrem. Arrwekelenyel artimperr-wetyam arrwengkelthel, amper apek, alknga apek, ahenty apek. (St) *[Somebody] might sing them with a traditional disease, put a curse on them. Their nose might get sore. Olden-time people put curses on others, on their knee or their eyes or maybe their throat.* ◆ Tha ngenh artimperr-iwekerr alha, arleng alha, arlengel arrken-irretyek. (Sa) *Go a long way away and play or I'll put a curse on you.*
SEE ALSO akwety-irrpenem, artarrernem, pew-ilem, rltwatyel atwem, urltatyel atwem, alyem, arrilem, arrilenty-ilem, arrwengkelthel alyem

artiw (E) mulgara (?) SEE UNDER **artekw**

artna (E) *n.*
scrub ◆ Artneketyaw! (Sa) *Look out for the scrub!*
SEE ALSO werrk, arnam

artnangk (E) *n.*
bilby (*Macrotis lagotis*)
= ahert, angkay

artnelheng (E) two [RESPECT LANGUAGE] SEE UNDER **arnelheng**

artnem (E) cry, wail, bawl SEE UNDER **arnem**

artnenthernem (E) burp, hiccough SEE UNDER **arnenthernem**

artnerr (E) rockhole SEE UNDER **arnerr**

artnerrem (E) crawl SEE UNDER **arnerrem**
artnka (E) cliff, steep rockface SEE UNDER **arnka**
artnman (E) mother or the mother's brother (respect term) SEE UNDER **arnman**[1]
artnman (E) honeyant worker SEE UNDER **arnman**[2]
artnwa (E) emu fat (from back part of emu) SEE UNDER **arnwa**
artnwep (E) claypan, low-lying swampy area SEE UNDER **arnwep**
artnwer (E) dingo SEE UNDER **arnwer**[1]
artuty (E) kangaroo bladder (?) SEE UNDER **artwety**
artwa, **artwang** (W,T) *n.*
1. man (initiated man) ◆ Artwa arnkentyel intep-intem mapam yanhan. Arnkenty-areny mapey apetyewarrem ankey. (T) *That mob over there are the men that sleep in the single-men's camp. All the men from the single-men's camp come up asking for things.* ◆ Anngarnt rrpwerlel kwer map apernelhem artwarteh apernelhem. (M) *Kids use the puffball to paint themselves and make themselves look like men.* ◆ Artwang atherr rtwang anerreperrem. (M) *The two men are sitting close to each other.*
2. man (any man including non-Aboriginal men)
3. a term used by women to refer to their husbands [SOME SPEAKERS]
4. Can go before other words that refer to men.
SEE ALSO alyakw
CAN SOUND A BIT LIKE itwa *'close'*
artwang akwerrk (W,T)
young man, young fellow (akwerrk[1] *'young'*)
artwang akwek (T), **artwa akwek** (E)
= **artwang akwerrk** (akwek *'small'*)
artwang anthety (W,T), **artwa anthety** (E)
= **artwang akwerrk** (anthety *'young man'*)
SEE ALSO amerrk[1]
artwampw (E), **artwang ampwang** (W,T) *n.*
old man (ampwa *'old'*)
artwa aywang (W,T), **artwang aywang** (W,T)
= **artwampw** (aywang *'old'*, *'grey'*)
artwang inenty (W,T), **artwa inenty** (E)
kurdaitcha (inenty *'kurdaitcha'*) ◆ Artwang inenty-kety anwengkerr arelhey. Mwantyel. (T) *We'll look out for the kurdaitcha man. Carefully.*
artwengartw *n.*
playing at being men ◆ Artwengartw rarey arrken-irrerl-anem, nyetyepel. Kenh arelheng-arelh arrpantey ampa marl-arey arrken-irrerl-anem nyetyepel akin. (St) *They play at being men in their cubbyhouses. And the young girls play at being women, pretend to be little women in their cubbyhouses.*
SEE ALSO arelheng-arelh
artwak (W,E) mother SEE UNDER **artakw**
artwang (W,T) man (initiated man) SEE UNDER **artwa**
artwang apetyepetyem (W) *n.*
rufous whistler (*Pachycephala rufiventris*) (lit. 'man coming')
= apetyepetyem, artwatherr apetyepetyem, kwarlpatengkelyengkely, ipeny apetyepetyem, tyenyepweny
artwarem (W,T), **irtwarem**, **iytwarem** (E) *vt.*
1. watch someone or something going away ◆ Arrpenh apekarl alhem anem irtwarem ingkern-they. Irtwarem, kel ra alhetyek menty. (St) *Someone might be going and you watch them from behind. And then they go off.* ◆ Tyerrty nhak-warl alhem — anwengkerr artwarerl-alpetyeh. (T) *The person is going over there — we're watching him.*
2. see someone off ◆ Ayeng alhek *Ti Tree*-warl, ampa atyenh irtwaretyek — irrepelayen lyet alhetyenh *hospital*-warl. (T) *I went to Ti Tree to see my child off — the aeroplane is going today to the hospital.* ◆ Tharrp iytwareyamel, tha anyentel. (St) *I'll see [them] off myself, just me.* ◆ Utnin arrernem awenng-warl, ra anem anem *Christmas* arrpenhekant. *All right* mer ikwerenhel anem iytwarem. Tywerreng ikwerenhel anem iytwarem. Utnin anem iwem anem, artem anem ingkerrek — *finish. Country* ikwerenh iytwaretyekant. (St) *The branches are put over the grave, and they stay there till the next Christmas. Then ceremonies are held to farewell the deceased person's country and their ceremonial business. Then the branches are thrown away, and the grave is covered over — that's the end. It's not over until his country has been farewelled.*
CAN SOUND A BIT LIKE atwarem *'approach someone'*, *'meet up'*
artwarelhem (W,T), **irtwarelhem**, **iytwarelhem** (E) *vi.*
1. watch someone or something going away
2. see someone off ◆ Ayeng artwarelhek ngkweng. (T) *I saw you off.*
artwatherr apetyepetyem (E) *n.*
rufous whistler (*Pachycephala rufiventris*) (lit. 'two men are coming')
= apetyepetyem, ipeny apetyepetyem, tyenyepweny, artwang apetyepetyem, kwarlpatengkelyengkely
SEE ALSO artwa, atherr, apetyem
artwek (W,T), **urtek** (E) *n.*
a type of tick found on perenties, euros or cattle

artweker *n.*
a boil ◆ Artweker wangkem iltyel-arleng. Altyerreng artwekeran anek. Arlewatyerr anterel apernelherl-anem, amwely anterel, ankerr anterel, aherr anterel. (Sa) *The boil is swelling up on the finger. Boils came from the Dreamtime. They are rubbed with goanna fat, cadney lizard fat, emu fat or kangaroo fat.* ◆ Atey ampwel apek alyem artweker ikwer, artweker antyerlparl-irrem. Alanh arrwekelenyan anek. (Sa) *The old man might sing the boil and it will burst. That's how the olden-time people lived.*
= tyapernp
SEE ALSO mantalyarrp
Artweker (E) *n.*
the name of a place near Aniltji (Boundary Bore), Utopia (Angarapa Aboriginal Land Trust) area. Location of an important soakage where people used to live.

-artwemeny *k.ending*
Respectful word which goes on the end of kin terms and is used when the particular relation referred to by the kin term has passed away. ◆ Mam-**artwemeny** ywerrek ingkwey-antey. (Sa) *My mother passed away a long time ago.* ◆ *No* arrengey ayeng anem. Arrengeyek arrangkw. Arreng-arreng-**artwemeny** arrwekel *pass away*-irrek. *No* aperley anem ayeng. Arrangkw anem aningkerr anetyel. Aperley anetyang. Aperley-**artwemeny**. *I've got no grandfather. My grandfather passed away before. I have no father's mother now. Now we have none of them left. No father's mother.*
SEE ALSO -ankethenh

artwengarr (T,E) *n.*
green seeds of the dogwood tree, *awenth, akerlperr* (*Acacia sericophylla*) and kurrajong tree, *apeng* (*Brachychiton gregorii*) ◆ Mern akely ngkweyang. Akely imernt ra anem, alpeyt-penh mern kel amangkemel ra, angwenh anem, artwengarr anem. Kel renh urelarl arrtyerl-anem karlkwerl-anem, apely. (Sa) *The kurrajong seed pod is small at first. It's small at first, then after flowering it grows, then it becomes* artwengarr. *Then it is cooked in the fire and eaten, when it's soft.*
SEE ALSO arntwatherrk[2], lyarr, alywer[1], alyalyarr, arlpetharlp, ntyerrm, apal[1], anma[1], kertaty

artwengkenng, artwengkelkng (E) *n.*
1. nasal mucus, snot, snotty nose, phlegm ◆ Alhethey apek thelelhepelhem artwengkenng. (St) *The snot is dripping out from the nose.*
2. a cold or flu ◆ Rlkert ayeng awelhem artwengkenng-akert. (St) *I am feeling sick with a cold.* ◆ Rlwek yanhel mwerrarl ilem *clean*-em ilelhem annga, *everything* alhewelhem artwengkenng-apertem mernt-apert, iteth-ilem. (N) *That native pine is used to wash eyes and clean them and make them better, to wash all over and to make people better if they have a cold or are sick.*
SEE ALSO rta, mernt[1], rlkert, arrwengkelth, inkwerr, artwengkenng, nkwanng, arntety
artwengkenng-akert, artwengkelkng-akert (E) *n.*
having a cold or the flu
= inkwerr-akert

artwep-artwep, twep-twep *adv.*
(doing something) while going around something ◆ Twep-twep alhay amwekety. (St) *Go around because of snakes.* ◆ Twep-twep alhetyek rewelarl arrngert-wek-kety. (St) *[You] have to go around because of the floodwater that has blocked the way.* ◆ Tyap anyemayt apek twep-twep angernem. (St) *Digging round and round [the tree] for witchetty grubs.* ◆ Mey-mey-kety twep-twep alhem. (St) *Going around because of your son-in-law or mother-in-law.* ◆ Twep-twep nthwem. (T) *Go round looking for someone.*
= **urtep-urtep** (E)
artwep-akem, twep-akem *vi.*
go around something ◆ Aweth arrpenh artwep-akemel akenhem akenhem akenhem, *right round* akem akem akem tyap renh kel akemem-irremel arrernem *billycan*-warn. Kel akem akem irrenhem. (N) *When we find a good spot we dig up the root and then go around to the next one and dig that up and keep going right round the tree, filling up the billycan with witchetty grubs. Then we get up again.*
artwep-akelhem, twep-akelhem *vi.*
go around and around; go round someone or something to avoid them; go round in circles ◆ Mey-mey-kety apek ayeng twep-akelhemel alhem. (St) *I am going around because of my son-in-law.*
= **urtep-akelhem** (E)
artwep-irrem, twep-irrem *vi.*
1. go back, turn round and go back, change direction ◆ Ayeng artwep-irremel alpem mer-warn. (T) *I am turning round and going back home.* ◆ Ker-kweny-antey artwep-irremel. Artwep-irremel ina alpem, rlkert-akert, artwepelh-ilem arelh merntel. (N) *[They] are turning back because they still haven't found any meat. They are turning back because they have a sick person with them, the sick woman*

made them turn back. ◆ Artwep-irrek mwetekay akeng-akert, arlkarenharl. (St) *We turned back as we got sick of the bad car.*
SEE ALSO angkep-irrem, aneyangketh-irrem, anepetheng-irrem, pert-irrem
2. stop what you're doing or not go along with the trip ◆ Ayeng artwep-irremel anem! (T) *I don't want to go. I'm staying here!*
= **urtep-irrem** (E)
artwep-artwep-irrem, twep-twep-irrem *vi.*
go round something; go round in circles
artwepelh-ilem, twepelh-ilem *vt.*
1. make someone or something turn round and go back ◆ Marl apekarl alhemeng wal ayeng artwepelh-iletyek arlkemarl ikwer, 'Pety-alpay!' (St) *The woman might be going and I sing out to her make her turn back, 'Come back!'* ◆ Tyerrty alenh apek alhetyeh ahenty-irrem wal nta artwepelh-ilem, 'Apety-alpa! Apety-alpa!' (M) *That person might want to go, and you try to make them turn back. 'Come back! Come back!'*
2. bring something back, return something ◆ Mantarr artwepelh-ilety-alpem arelh yanhel. (T) *That woman is bringing back the clothes.*
= **urtepelh-ilem** (E)
artwep-wem, twep-wem *vt.*
emerge from cover and run off (of some animals) ◆ Twep-wem arlewatyerrel alhweng-they apek. (St) *The goanna emerged from the hole and ran off.*
artwep-irrenty-alpem, twep-irrenty-alpem *vi.*
turn round and go back ◆ Artwep-irrenty-alpem ayeng alpemaw, mer-warl. (N) *I'm going to turn round and go back home.*

artweper (T,E) *adv.*
1. doing something secretly or surreptitiously (especially to avoid contact with certain respected kin); secretively. This is particularly said of men who call each other *thampartey* or *perlal.* ◆ Tyerrty yanhan artweper angkep-angkem. (T) *That person is talking secretly.*
2. something that is hidden or out of the way, out of site, the back way ◆ Tyey kwenh artweper-angkwerr intem. (T) *There is a back road.*
artweperek tywenem (E)
put something up out of sight (of certain restricted kin) (tywenem '*put something up somewhere*') ◆ Artwerepek tywenem thampartey, perlal ikwerenhek apek. Artweper anem ra alpem mer-warl. Kel perlal ikwerenhel inetyekarl alhem. *He can't* angkem. (St) *He puts the things there out of site for his* thampartey *or for his* perlal. *And then he goes back to camp, the back way. Then his* perlal *goes and gets the things. He can't talk to him directly.*

artwerel alhem (E) *vi.*
go across, cut across
= arreyl-arreyl alhem, arreylarrp alhem

artwert[1] *n.*
1. small round rock or stone
2. stone used for pounding or smashing seed or bone, etc. Also referred to as *irntang artwert* or *apwert artwert.* ◆ Irntang artwertel atwerl-anem. Apwert artwertel ker atwetyek ilep-kwenyel, ker ngkwern atwep-atwem. (T) *Hitting it with a small round rock. When people haven't got an axe they smash the meat bones up with a small round rock.*
= tyeng, alyer
artwert-artwert *n.*
small and round in shape ◆ Nyert-nyerteley kartelam irrarnp-irrarnp-ilerl-apem nyert-nyert yanhan artwert-artwert, irnngang ka nyert-nyert lweren athew yanh. (N) *The dung beetle is a sort of small round maggoty thing that [goes into] the shit and makes it scatter.*
SEE ALSO arlwepertaty, rlwatert, apwerterrerterr, arlwa

artwert[2] *n.* [SENSITIVE LANGUAGE]
vulva, vagina
SEE ALSO tyely, tyarrp, kep[2]

Artwert (W) *n.*
name of a place in the Coniston area

artwert-irrem (W,T) *vi.*
to thunder ◆ Kwaty yanh angath anem artwert-irrenty alhem. (T) *That rain storm is coming closer and it's thundering.* ◆ Kwaty yanhaw artwert-irrentyem, antywang artey. (T) *Build a shelter, there's a thunderstorm coming this way.*

-artwety up to (somewhere), as far as (something) SEE UNDER **-atwety**[2]

artwety (E), **artuty** (E) *n.*
kangaroo bladder (?)
SEE ALSO urtarnp
CAN SOUND A BIT LIKE atwety[1] *'young kangaroo';* -atwety[2] *'as far as';* urtety *'short'*

Artwetyarnteng (E), **Rtwetyarnteng** (E), **Artetyarntweng** (E) *n.*
waterhole/swamp near the Aniltji/Sandover highway turn-off

-artwey, -artey (W,T) *n.ending*
1. people related to a particular Dreaming; owners or 'bosses' of a particular Dreaming, place or story, custodian. This ending usually follows *+ek* or *+eh.* ◆ Artnangkek-**artwey** *mob*

might finish-irrek. Itna *finish again*-irrek. *Possum*-ek-**artwey** *finish*-irrek. (St) *Maybe the bosses for bilbies died out. They finished up as well. The bosses for possum finished up.* ◆ Mer atyengenh merek-**artwey** ayeng. Mer nhenh. Mer atyengenh. (P) *I am the boss for my country. This place. This is my country.* ◆ Angwely ap ilwemarl kwa, alharrp-irrem angwely-**artey** mapel alharrp-irrem. 'Angwely akeweny atyengenh kwenh, akeweny angwely.' (N) *If the dogs die then the owners of the dogs get sad. 'My poor dog, the poor dog.'* ◆ Mwetekayeng anngwenhem. Mwetekayew-**artey**el arrpenhel antyem wal anngwenhem, ltwakey-hety mwetekay. (T) *People get jealous over cars. The owner of the car might get jealous if another person gets in the car, in case they crash the car.*
2. relation, especially older relation; parents, grandparents, ancestors ◆ Amwek kwer-**artey**. (M) *His/her mother.* ◆ Atyeng-**artey** aywang. *My father.* ◆ Arrengey-henh yanham mer Arlwem. Atyengenh arrengey-henh, tharl arreng akek angey-henh, angeyeh-**artey**-henh, papeh-**artey**-henh, angey atyeng-**artwey**-henh. (N) *My grandfather's country is Arlwem [Mt Allan area]. That is the place that I am related to through my father's father and my father.*
3. having a particular relation ◆ Anewek-**artwey**arl ayeng alpep-alpem. Anew yanhel anep-anemek-**artwey**. (St) *I have a husband. I have that husband who is sitting over there.*
mereh-artwey (W,T), **apmerek-artwey** (E)
owner or boss of a place (mer *'country', 'place'*) ◆ Apmerek-**artwey** ayeng anem. Mer atyengek-**artwey** ayeng anem. Mer nhek-**artwey**arl ayeng. (St) *I am the boss for this place. I'm living in my place. I am the owner for this place.*
atyeng-artwey, **atyeng-artey** (W,T) *n.*
my family or relation (particularly father) (atyeng *'for me', 'to me'*) ◆ Atyeng-**artwey**el *all day* ultaketyam nantew. (St) *My father used to break in horses all the time.* ◆ Atyeng-**artwey** amarley atyenh. Akngey apek tha atyeng-**artwey** akem. (St) *My uncle is* atyeng-**artwey**. *I also call my father* atyeng-**artwey**.
ngkweng-artwey, **ngkweng-artey** (W,T) *n.*
your family or relation (ngkweng *'for you', 'to you'*) ◆ Anywek ngkweng-**artey** alhek. (P) *Your father went.*
kwer-artwey, **kwer-artey** (W,T) *n.*
his/her/their family or relation (kwer *'to him/her', 'for him/her'*) ◆ 'Kwelyalp kwelyalp kwelyalp.' Alakenh angkerl-anem irrety akwek an angerr *too*, amwek kwer-**artwey**. (M) *'Kwelyalp kwelyalp kwelyalp.' That's the sound that baby wedge-tailed eagles, and bigger ones too, make for their mother.*

artwey-artwey[1] *n.*
root of the bush banana, silky pear (*Marsdenia australis*). Also referred to as *mern artwey-artwey.* ◆ Ahelh akwen-arenyam artwey-artwey, kenh mern alangkw arlka akernarl arlparant anemel mern anteth arlka. Renh akenty-penhel wal artwey-artweyem inyem, alangkw arlka kel akekarl arnang akerneng, anteth an *all* ingkerr akekarl mern renh. Alangkw arlka. Artwey-artweyem inyem, rlweth akem rlweth akem inyerl-apem inyerl-apem rlweth akem, twep-akerl-akerlel akem twep-akerl-akerlel akem inyerl-anem, artwey-artwey renhem inerl-anem arrernerl-anem. Artwey-artwey arnkang arlkwety kweny — angernetyam rwewarn. (N) *The bush banana root is underground, whereas its fruit is found hanging high up, with the flowers as well. After picking them you dig up the roots, after picking the fruits from high up on the tree. You dig up the roots and break them in half and keep digging and digging, going round and round the tree and digging. The roots are not eaten raw — they are taken to the fire to cook.*
= atnety, arnaty

artwey-artwey[2] (W,T) *n.*
part of guts. Also referred to as *ker artwey-artwey.*
SEE ALSO lyep-lyep

Artweyamperlaneng (E) Coulters Camp, name of a soakage near Neutral Junction Station homestead SEE UNDER **Artweyelperlayneng**

artweyaty *n.kin*
1. my/our dog
2. a dog's owner (master, mistress)
SEE ALSO ngwarraty
artweyengk *n.kin*
your dog ◆ Artweyengkel arwengkel ker atyenh arlkwerl-alhern. (T) *Your dog just went and ate my meat.*
SEE ALSO ngwarrekw
artweyikw (E) *n.kin*
his/her/their dog
artweyekw (W,T) *n.kin*
1. your dog
2. his/her/their dog ◆ Arengk anyirrkem artweyekwek, pwath kwerenhek. Apety-alpem artweyekw, anyirrkem anem ra, tayl. (St) *The dog is wagging its tail excitedly for its boss. Its boss comes back and the dog wags its tail.*
artwey-nheng, **artew-nheng** (W,T) *n.kin*
a person together with two or more of their

dogs, a group of people with their dogs

artwey-intyerr (W,T), **artew-intyerr** (W,T) *n.kin* = **artwey-nheng** ◆ Artew-intyerr alherrirrem lyweny. Aywang an arengk anengk akert — artew-intyerr. (T) *The man and his dogs are going hunting. The old man and lots of his dogs — man and dogs together.*

artwey-nheng atherr, **artew-nheng** (W,T) *n.kin*
a person together with one of their dogs ◆ Artwey-nheng atherr, arengk thwen tyerrty thwen. (St) *The dog and his owner, the dog and the person.*
SEE ALSO ngwarr-nheng atherr

artwey-ankethenh, **artew-ankethenh** (W,T) *n.kin*
a dog who always accompanies its owner or master, a dog that really adores its master or owner ◆ Arengk yanh artwey-ankethenh intep-intem akwen yanh artweyikw irrpenhek. (St) *That dog is sleeping inside with its master.* ◆ Arengk yanh artwey-ankethenh apetyepetyem. (T) *That dog is coming along with its master.* ◆ Arengk yanh atyenh artew-ankethenh. (M) *My dog really loves me.*
SEE ALSO -ankethenh

Artweyelperlayneng (T,E), **Artweyamperlaneng** (E) *n.*
Coulters Camp, name of a soakage near Neutral Junction Station homestead

arwa[1] (E) *n.*
root of a witchetty bush which has a witchetty grub in it

arwakem, **arakem** *vt.*
lever something up, pull something up (especially witchetty bush root) (akem[1] *'cut'*) ◆ Tyap anyemayt apek artekerr arwaketyek, atnemel arwaketyek. (St) *Lever up the root with the witchetty grub in it with a digging stick.* ◆ *Tyre* then arwakem anyematy arwakem-artek antey. (St) *[You] lever tyres just like you do roots with witchetty grubs in them.*
= alpwarternem, ilpent-wem
CAN SOUND A BIT LIKE rakem *'take something away from someone'*

arwa[2], **arwang** (W,T) *n.*
the handle of a shield ◆ Alkwert arwang. Altywer-ilem altywer-ilem alkwert arwang altywer intem. Iltyem irrpem. Kel irrakeram wem, arwarl mpwarem-penh. (N) *The handle of a shield. You make a hole for the handle. Then your hand goes in the hole. Then, after making the handle, you make grooves on the shield.*
SEE ALSO alkwert
CAN SOUND A BIT LIKE rwa *'fire'*

arwangk (W,T) *n.*
1. deaf
= arert
2. pygmy mulga monitor (*Varanus gilleni*)
• = ahert-ahert[2], arin

arwekar (W,T) *n.*
lively, energetic, generous, happy ◆ Arwekarel anthetyeh parrp, tyerrty arrpenhek. (M) *Happily giving something to someone else, straightaway.* ◆ Arwekaram ayeng aneh. (M) *I was feeling happy.*
SEE ALSO irlpareth, ankerl

arwekar-ilem, **arweker-ilem** *vt.*
1. make someone lose interest in another, unsettle someone (?) ◆ Arweker-ilep-ilem ntwan ampa, *too much* angkep-angkem arnterr. (St) *You're talking to that kid too much and he might not want to know his [own] family.*
2. separate someone off from others ◆ Mekikwety arweker-ilem ampa akely perlelikw. (Sa) *The little child's grandmother is trying to separate the child from her mother.* ◆ Arweker-ilerreperrem yanh atherr, angkerreperrem — ikngekel ilerreperrem, *self* atherr alhetyek apek, ikngatherr alhetyek. (St) *Those two are talking to each other about going off separately — about going off on their own.*
SEE ALSO arlkwer-ilem, ingekelh-ilem, arrkereny-ilem

arweker-irrem (E) *vi.*
behave as if you are too good for people, be full of your own importance (?)
SEE ALSO arrkereny-irrem

arwekel (W,T) *n.*
1. thirsty ◆ Parretyarl awelhem arwekel antywem, angkethakw. (T) *Feeling thirsty and drinking thirstily.*
SEE ALSO angkethel, angkethakw, parrety, arrangketh
2. water ◆ Arwekel anthay antywetyew. (M) *Give me some water to drink.* ◆ Arwekel antywerl-alpetyeh ayeng angkethakw anem. (T) *I'll go back and drink some water, I'm thirsty now.*
CAN SOUND A BIT LIKE arrwekel *'first', 'in front'*

arwekel-irrem (W,T) *vi.*
get thirsty, feel thirsty
= angkethakw-irrem, parrety-irrem

arweker-ilem (E) make someone lose interest in another, unsettle someone (?) SEE UNDER arwekar-ilem

arwekert *n.*
young man who is in seclusion in the bush after initiation (young man) ceremony
SEE ALSO alyepelengkw, awerrty, lyaty, arleyarr,

amarleyarr, tyakwertekwert, lwekerleny, antingkar, apwelh, anmanty

Arwekert (E) *n.*
1. name of hill east of Stuart Highway, north of Ti Tree
2. name of place in Derry Downs area

Arwekert tharr (E) *n.*
the name of a place in the Mt Skinner Station area

arwekert-arwekert (E) *n.*
a type of grasshopper
SEE ALSO arlwety[1], intelty, ntyerlkem

arweketherwek (W,T) *n.*
rushing around; being being unsettled or unable to sit still; being annoying, making a lot of noise
= **urekethwerek** (E)

arweketherwek-ilem (W,T) *vt.*
stir things up, stir someone up; make things unsettled, argue all the time; create a disturbance; annoy or disturb people, by making a lot of noise ◆ Artwang ngkekenel arweketherwek-ilem tyerrty map. (M) *The kurdaitcha is making the people unsettled.* ◆ Tyerrty terangk map apetyem arweketherwek-iletyek anwernenh, ankwarl intemeng. (T) *The drunks come and disturb us when we are asleep.*
= **urekethwerek-ilem** (E)

arwelth (T,E) *n.*
jealous, envious (particularly over husband or wife) ◆ Arwelthel amwerrk atwerrek. Arwelth-rnem arelh arrpenh arwelth-rnem. Arelh arwelthel atwerrem ateyek-arrngel, anewek-arrngel. Atey-rnem atwerrem akin arwelthel arelhek-arrngel. (Sa) *There was a jealous fight yesterday. One woman was jealous of the other. Women have jealous fights over men, over husbands. Men have jealous fights over women as well.*

arwelth-rnem (E) *vi.*
be jealous or envious of someone (particularly over husband or wife)
SEE ALSO tyaleth-irrem, anngwenhem, mayel anngwenhem

arwelthel atwerrem (T,E)
have a jealous fight (particularly over husband or wife)
SEE ALSO mayel atwerrem

arwelthel arem (T,E)
look at someone jealously or enviously
SEE ALSO anngwenhem, mayel arem

arwem-irrem (T,E) *vi.*
arrive, turn up, appear ◆ Lyetantarl arwem-irrenhetyek, arrwelarl alpek, uyerrek. (Sa) *[Somebody] is just turning up today, after going away a long time ago, after disappearing.* ◆ Arwem-irrintyem arerr mwetekay yanh. (Sa) *That car is appearing closer as it comes in this direction.*
SEE ALSO arratem

arwemay, aremay (E), **arepmay** (E) *n.*
1. short-tailed pygmy monitor (*Varanus brevicauda*) (?)
2. the edible flesh of this lizard. Also referred to as *ker arwemay.* ◆ Lher-arenyarlap ra ker arwemay. Alhweng-areny arlewatyerr-artek antey. (St) *The* arwemay *lizard lives in the creek. They live in burrows like goannas do.* ◆ Arlewatyerran akely-rnem, ra arepmay. Rapet alhwengek atwerretyart, pet-pet-kenhek. Alkwert atwenh-kenh alhwengekarl atwerretyart ra rapet arepmay ra aylpetyart, urtety akely rnem. Ker arepmay. (Sa) *The* arepmay *is smaller than the sand goanna. We used to kill them in rabbits' burrows. They used to go into rabbits' burrows and we used to kill them. The* arepmay *are short.*
3. a large sand goanna (*arlewatyerr*) (*Varanus gouldii*) [SOME SPEAKERS] • SEE ALSO arlewatyerr

Arwemay (W) *n.*
the name of a soakage in the Mt Allan area

arweng[1] (E) *n.kin*
one's own personal Dreaming
SEE ALSO anganenty, altyerr[1]

arwengaty (E) *n.kin*
my/our *arweng* ◆ Anyemayt tha arlkwem — wal, arwengaty tha arlkwem. Ayeng antem arwengatyaw tha arlkwem, atyengarl anganek. (St) *I eat witchetty grubs — well, that's my own Dreaming that I am eating. Now I am eating my Dreaming, that was created for me.*

arwengengkw (E) *n.kin*
your *arweng* ◆ 'Arwengengkweyay arlkwep-arlkwem ntwa kwenh', arrpenhelarl ilem. 'Arwengaty tha arlkwem.' (St) *Another person might say, 'You are eating your Dreaming.' 'I'm eating my Dreaming.'*

arwengikw (E) *n.kin*
his/her/their *arweng* ◆ Arwengikw yalelarl arlkwep-arlkwem. (St) *That person over there is eating his/her Dreaming.*

arweng[2] (W) *n.kin*
husband

arwengaty (W) *n.kin*
my husband ◆ Nhenhan atyeng arwengatyam kwenh. (M) *This is my husband.*

arwengengk (W) *n.kin*
your husband

arweng-nheng atherr (W) *n.kin*
a person together with their husband
= anewart atherr

arwengalker *n.*
1. native honey, sugarbag, wild honey. Also referred to as *ngkwarl arwengalker*.
◆ Arrkernkel ngkwarl arwengalker anem. Atwem, arrpem anem ngkwarl renh tyampet-warl arntap-warl arrernem. Ankerrmernel arlka. (St) *Sugarbag is found in bloodwood trees. [You] chop the tree and pare back the wood and then put the honey in a tin or in a bark container. Sugarbag is also found in coolibah trees.*
2. the nest or hive made by native bees
= rltwamp

arwengerrp (T,E) *n.*
bush turkey, wild turkey, bustard (*Ardeotis australis*). Also referred to as *ker arwengerrp*.
◆ Yanh-antey ker alhep-alhem arwengerrp. Ra untemekarl. Alkerek-irrenhemarl alhem. (Sa) *There is the bush turkey going along. It runs. Then it flies up into the sky.*
= artew, warterlk

arwengk (T,E) *n.*
1. deaf
2. mad, stupid, crazy, silly
= arert

arwengk-arwengk (T,E) *n.*
a bit mad or silly ◆ Arwengk-arwengkarl yanhanaw. (T) *That person is a bit mad.*
= arert-arert

arwengk-irrem (T,E) *vi.*
1. go deaf, become deaf
2. go mad or crazy, become silly in the head
= arert-irrem

arwengk-ilem (T,E) *vt.*
1. make someone go mad or crazy, drive someone mad
2. make someone go deaf, deafen someone with noise ◆ Arrken atherretyalaw! Arnterr atherretyal — arrken atherrirremel iylpa arwengk-ilemeyay! Arleng atherrirretyek alherl-way, utnherretyekay. (Sa) *Don't laugh! Don't laugh loud — your laughing is deafening us. All of you go a long way away to laugh and play around.*
= arert-ilem

arwengkel *adv.*
sneakily, secretly, furtively, dishonestly, (doing something) without asking or behind someone's back
= anyenngel

arwengkel inem
steal something (inem *'get', 'take'*) ◆ Angank mer-warn apetyem arwengkel inerl-alhem mern. (N) *Crows come into the camp and steal food.*
= anyenngel inem

arwengkalth *n.*
a robber, thief ◆ Angank arwengkalth — arraty. Nyenngel arlkwerl-anem akweteth akweteth ateram arrtyanetyenheng, pwerlt-irrem. (N) *Crows are robbers — true. They always sneak around and steal food to eat and then when something gives them a fright they fly off, they bolt.*
= anyenngalth

arwenp, arwernp *n.*
sandhill pituri (*Nicotiana rosulata* ssp. *ingulba*). Herb about 45 cm high with smooth shiny leaves, and found in mulga and spinifex country. Also referred to as *ngkwerlp arwenp*. ◆ Arwenp, akemel akemel akemel angety-alpem, pwelap. Twernek wem ahatel ampetyek, lpwerretyek, renh antem inem. Lpwelemel. (N) *We pick the pituri and then bring back a load of it. Then we lay it out in the sun to dry, and then get it and grind it up.*
= ngkwerlp atherrk

Arwenpeng (E), **Arenpeng** (E) *n.*
Morning Star, Daylight Star, Venus
◆ Kwerraly Arwenpeng, aremelarl renh aremel akem-irrem *early*-pal anem renh arem, anentyerlek anem renh arnarem. Kel aherrk anem irrentyem. (St) *The Daylight Star is the one that you see early in the morning. You see it coming up and then the sun comes up.*
= Anthelper, Awelh, Kwerraly Angerr, Kwerraly Rltwa, Kwerraly Urlta

arwenth *n.*
many; a lot of things; plural (more than four or five people or things); a group of particular people or things ◆ Atyeng-akwerrkan arwenth, nhenh anem. (St) *I have lots of children, living here.* ◆ Tyerrty arwenth apetyemaw! (T) *Lots of people are coming!*
= map, anengk[1]

arwenth-irrem (W,T) *vi.*
get together, gather together (a lot of people or things)
= map-irrem, anengk-irrem

arwentyey (E) *n.*
an emu's neck
SEE ALSO ngkwemengk

ker arwentyey (E)
meat from the emu neck ◆ Ker arwentyey tha arlkweyew. *I'll eat some emu neck meat.*

arwerl (T,E) *n.*
1. stick, tree, branch, plant ◆ Arntek ayeng inelhetyek, antywer apek akem arntek inelhetyek, tyerretyek ker, kerarl arntek-warl aylperrek. Arwerl antywerel, arwerl tyepalel. (Sa) *I am going to pick my teeth, get a bit of grass to pick at my teeth and get the meat that is stuck in my teeth out. With a bit of grass or a stick.* ◆ Nthakenh renh atwetyakenh inangkal, ilpelhetyelarl. Ngkwern atwetyakenh perrap inangkal iyterrty ilpelhetyelarl ra arwerlel. (Sa) *He is really clever and can't be beaten because he is protecting himself. He is really invincible and can't be hit because he is shielding himself with a branch.*
2. Goes before the name of a particular type of plant.
= arna
SEE ALSO antyelty
arwerl kanty (E)
branch (of tree), top branches of a tree (kanty *'tip'*)
= arna kanty

arwerl-arwerl (E) *n.*
common brown snake, eastern brown snake (*Pseudonaja textilis*) (?)

arwerlk (E) *n.*
witchetty grub (*Xyleutes bipartii*) while still in the root
SEE ALSO anyematy

arwerlt *n.*
side of the body
Arwerlt Atwaty *n.*
Native Gap. See map p. viii.

arwernp sandhill pituri SEE UNDER **arwenp**.

arwerr *n.*
hole, burrow or tunnel (goanna's or rabbit's) ◆ Arwerrek ayeng urnteyaw ker arlewatyerrek kwen arwerrelarl intep-intemek. (St) *I've got to go and look round for a hole where a goanna is lying.* ◆ Ker alewatyerr-henh arwerrek apetyewarray, arwerrelarl intep-intem. Kerwep-akert apek anem-akert apek apetyemel atwetyek, irrpekarl arwerr-warl. Rapet-kenh 'alhweng', alewatyerr-kenh 'arwerr'. (St) *All of you come here where there is a goanna lying in its burrow. People come with crowbars or digging sticks to kill the goanna that has gone into it's hole. A rabbit burrow is called* 'alhweng' *and a goanna's hole is called* 'arwerr'.
SEE ALSO alhweng, arleytarr
arwerr-areny (E) *n.*
goanna (?)

arwethenp *n.*
a type of red ochre
SEE ALSO rlpwa, atywerlk, ngwenty-ngwenty, artep arlpenty, karntewarr, marlalperr

ata[1] (E) *n.*
mud, a lump of dirt or mud ◆ Ahern atel ayenh iwetyal! (Sa) *Don't throw mud at me!*
SEE ALSO urta, antha[1], anthwerrng, tert, atanty
atilem (E) *vt.*
make mud cakes (children) ◆ Merneng mern atilepilem ampel-areny. Ata anem anep-anem. (St) *The children are making pretend dampers out of mud.*

ata[2], **ahat** *n.*
hot (from English 'hot') ◆ Arwenp, akemel akemel akemel angety-alpem, pwelap. Twernek wem ahatel ampetyek, lpwerretyek, renh antem inem. Lpwelemel. (N) *We pick the pituri and then bring back a load of it. Then we lay it out in the sun to dry, and then get it up and grind it up.*
atewat, ahatewat *n.*
hot water (from English 'hot water')
ker atewat
hot soup with meat or vegetables ◆ Ker atewat antywetyeh. (M) *Drinking the hot soup.*
= ker thwep-thwep
atewat-ilem *vt.*
heat water up, make water hot ◆ Kwaty atewat-ilay. (M) *Heat the water up.*
atewat-irrem *vi.*
heat up (water), become hot (water) ◆ Kwaty atewat-irrem. (M) *The water is heating up.*
atewat-ayerr (E) *n.* [RESPECT LANGUAGE]
tea

atakem *vt.*
break through or into something; make something collapse; make a hole or soakage cave in, open something up ◆ Atakem tha arlewatyerr-kenh alhweng, atnemel. (Sa) *I am opening up the goanna's hole with a digging stick.*
atakelhem *vi.*
fall down, become dismantled, cave in, collapse ◆ Kwaty angenty atakemelhem. Wal atakelhem kenh imperl-alhem, angenty kwaty renh thewekety mpwarem, wal atakelhem alhem, wal imperl-alhem. (N) *The soakage caves in. Well then, when it caves in, you leave that soakage that you have made.* ◆ Antywa atakelhem, atakerl-alhem alhetyenh-arleng. (N) *The humpy is dismantled when [people] are about to move on.* ◆ Interrkelarl arlkwem-penh atakelhem warl. (Sa) *The house falls down after being eaten by white ants.*

ataltyakwerl, atantyakwerl (W,T) *n.*
mulga apple (a small gall made by the larva of various wasp species)

◆ Artetyel-ayel mern atantyakwerl akerl-apem. Akem, arwenth akem atantyakwerl renh an akem akem akem arlkwerlem apem, angayel-irremel, alherl-apemel lywenyel, atantyakwerl renh arlkwerl-apem. Arlkwemel arrernerl-apemel *billycan*-warn kwer mapeh arlka angety-alpetyeh ina. (N) *Mulga apples are picked from the mulga trees. Lots and lots of them are picked and eaten as people go along, as they get hungry when they are out hunting — they eat mulga apples as they go along. They eat them and put some in the billycan to take back to the children.*
SEE ALSO artety
Ataltyakwerl (T) *n.*
the name of a place in the Anningie Station area

atanem[1] (E) *vi.*
squat (on toes or flat-footed) ◆ Atanemel arlkwetyal. Nyerr anetyang atanetyal! (Sa) *Don't squat there eating. Don't squat — you've got no shame!*
= artarnk anem

atanem[2] (W,T) *vi.*
1. get stuck or bogged
2. be tight or constricted ◆ Arelh nhenh mantarr atanem. (M) *That woman has tight clothes on.*
3. choke on something • SEE ALSO twerl-akem
atanelhem (W,T) *vi.*
1. get bogged; get stuck on or in something ◆ Mwetek atanelhem lherel, anthwerrngel. (M) *The car is getting bogged in the creek, in the mud.*
2. be tight on someone or something ◆ Manterr nhenh atyengel-ayeng atanelhem. (M) *These clothes are tight on me.*
SEE ALSO mwernelhem, kerelty-welhem, uthinem

atangk anem (E) squat (on toes or flat-footed) SEE UNDER **artarnk anem**

atanthem *vt.*
1. stab or poke into something; pierce something with something sharp; make a hole in something with something sharp; puncture something ◆ Rltwar-rnkem *tube* apek arnel apekarl atanthek. Kel alpwely-irrenhem anem. (St) *The tyre tube bursts after being pierced by a stick. Then it goes flat.* ◆ Lyekel atanthemay, yekay ingka atanthem lyekel. (St) *The prickle is stabbing my foot. Ouch!* ◆ Warrangkwer nekeleth atanthewarretyart nekeleth ina mparetyart pwelap atanthewarretyart warrangkwer. (N) *[They] used to make necklaces by making holes in the seeds of the* warrangkwer *plant.*
2. hunt an animal using something sharp such as a spear, beak or claws ◆ Irretyel ker atanthem arrakertel. (N) *Eagles hunt meat with their beaks.* ◆ Uthipel ap irrkerlanty rnternerl-anem thip akely nyingk apek. Nyingkek unthemel atanthenhemel. Mperlker ap ra. (Sa) *The falcon goes along hunting small birds such as zebra finches. It looks for zebra finches and grabs them with its claws. They [falcons] are white in colour.*
3. hook something ◆ Tyap perlanty map, atantherl-apek, lywenkel inelh-apek perlanty renh, pwelap. (N) *We used to go along hooking the grubs from the branches of the river red gum with a grass hook.*
4. spear something ◆ Angkweyel ker irrtyartelarl atanthewarretyart. (M) *In the old days they speared game with spears.*
5. sew, mend ◆ Mantarr atyenh tyarrp-irrek, atanthetyakenh. (St) *My clothes have split open because they haven't been mended.*
6. write, draw or paint • SEE ALSO ingkwernem, arrernem, intelh-ilem, mpaty-ilem, arlkeny arrernem, arlkeny-wem
7. squash or crack nits or head lice ◆ Anyang kapert arlkwenh-arlkwenh arntert, anya, kwartarl ampenem wal tyerrtyel atantherrerl-anem alakenh. (N) *Lice are no good and they burrow into the head and lay eggs which people crack.*
8. have a sharp or stabbing pain ◆ Arlka apekarl awelhem rlkert, *pain* apek atanthepanthem. 'Arlka ayeng tyelk ingkerr akeng-irrekaw, arlka atyenh.' (St) *[Your] body might feel sick and the pain might be stabbing you. 'My whole body, my flesh is no good.'*
9. strip the bark off a tree or plant ◆ Arntap iterl-anem arnmeny akin, arnmeny ngkerlp-kenh antyerrkarl irrek arnmeny. Ankerrmern atanthem atanthem atanthem rwel item arnmeny mparem. (N) *The bark is burnt to make ashes, for tobacco. The dry bark is used for ashes. The bark is stripped from the coolibah tree and then burnt to make ashes.* ◆ Aper arntapel anwern atantherl-anem alhewelherl-anetyek, per kwa tyelk. Atanthem aper tyelk, kapert alhewelhetyeh, annga arlka. (N) *We use the bark of the river red gum for a washing medicine. We get the inner bark of the river red gum and*

use it to wash our heads and our eyes.
10. sting someone or something
= rnternem
atanthelhem *vi.*
1. hit yourself or spear yourself with something sharp ◆ Lyweper renh akem alhwarrpeng. Arelh anemel atanthelhem kapert. (St) *[People] cut their thighs when they are in mourning. Women hit themselves on the head with digging sticks.*
2. give yourself an injection

atanty *adv.*
(doing something) without taking notice of others; anyway, despite, heedless, regardless
= alanty
CAN SOUND A BIT LIKE tanty *'hard ground'*
atanty-atanty *adv.*
doing something while others are waiting ◆ Atanty-atanty anep-anem ayeng, warrkarl-irremek. (St) *I'm waiting while the others are working.* ◆ Marlel atanty-atanty arlkwep-arlkwem atyeng atanty. (St) *The girl is eating while I am waiting.*
= alanty-alanty
atanty anem
wait for someone while they are doing something; wait with someone, keep someone company (anem *'sit'*) ◆ Urrek ayeng ngkweng atanty anem. *I am waiting for you.* ◆ Itwernel ampek. Lywel ayeng atanty anem. (T) *The sun's hot. I'm waiting in the shade.*
= alanty anem
atanty alhem
go without caring about others or without waiting for others, leave someone behind; go away from someone, move or walk away from something not liked, go regardless of what people say (alhem *'go'*) ◆ Ngkweng-kety ayeng atanty alhetyek. (St) *I'm not waiting for you — I'm going.* ◆ Mpa! Anwern artwang nhak-kety atanty-alhem. (T) *Come on! We'll go away from that man.*
= alanty alhem
atanty anthem
give something to someone without taking notice of others (anthem *'give'*) ◆ Ngkwengety tha anthem *cool drink* nhenh kwer anyent-warl kwenh atanty anthem kwenh. Nta apek kelarl antywern kwenh. (T) *I'm going to give this kid some cool drink in spite of what you think. You've just had a drink.* (?)
= alanty anthem
atanty arlkwem (T,E)
eat without sharing, eat while another is waiting, eat greedily (not caring about others) (arlkwem *'eat'*) ◆ Atanty arlkwem tha angayel. (St) *I'm hungrily eating without giving any to others.*
= alanty arlkwem
atanty angem
take something away from someone (without asking) (angem *'take'*) ◆ Ker thang ngkwengety atanty angem, anyentel tha arlkwerlanetyek. (T) *I'm going to take the meat off you so that I can eat it on my own.* ◆ Atanty war tha arna nhenh ngkwenh akngem. (Sa) *I'm going to take this thing of yours without asking.*
= alanty angem
atanty angkem
1. say something in spite of what others say, talk to someone regardless of what others think (angkem *'talk', 'speak'*) ◆ Ayeng ngkwengety atanty angkem. (T) *I'm going to talk, regardless of what you think.* (?)
2. talk to someone on behalf of someone else, do the talking for someone else
= alanty angkem
atanty arem
watch while someone else does something (arem *'look', 'see'*)
= alanty arem

atantyakwerl (W,T) mulga apple SEE UNDER **ataltyakwerl**

atarlanenty, atarlepwenty (E) *n.*
full moon ◆ Atnyenty atarlanenty arratenty-alhem akngerr-penh wethan. (St) *That big full moon rises.*
= atay angerrety
SEE ALSO anyenty, atay[1], anyenty akwerrk, atay akwerrk

atatem (E), **atarterl-iwem** (E) *vi.*
beat (heart) ◆ Mpwenyek urtakwert arawerrng atarterl-wem. (Sa) *When [the person] is feeling excited about a lover their heart beats fast.*
SEE ALSO atem

atay[1] (W,T) *n.*
moon ◆ Atayam anentyem kwenyel, akern. (N) *The moon comes up at night, high in the sky.* ◆ Atay irrpenhem. Arratenty-alhem an irrpenhem altwerl-atheh. (M) *The moon goes down. It comes up, and then goes down in the west.*
= anyenty
atay akwerrk (W,T)
new moon (akwerrk[1] *'young', 'newly formed'*) ◆ Atay akwerrk kel apety-alpekew. *The new moon has already come back.*
= anyenty akwerrk
atay akwek (W,T)
new moon (akwek *'small'*)

atay angerrety (W,T)
full moon (angerrety *'big'*)
= atarlanenty
atay ampwang (W,T)
new moon (ampwang *'old'*)
atay parrk-irrem (W,T)
wane (moon) (lit. 'the moon is getting tired')
= aherrk parrk-irrem

atay2 (W) *n.*
small white grub, the larva of the Christmas beetle, cockchafer larvae (*Anoplognathus olivieri* sp.)
= anyenty-anyenty

atehepenh (T) whipstick wattle SEE UNDER **ateyepenh**

atek *n.*

button quail (*Turnix velox*) ◆ Atek arnamel anenty-angerr. Atek arrtyanem arnam arrpenh-warn, ahelh-angkwarr. (N) *The button quail is a grass-dweller. The quail runs across the ground from one clump of grass to another.* ◆ Atek aperl-apem mwelek-arleng. Arnamel altywernerl-anem. (N) *The button quail goes along with its mother, then sits crouched in the grass.* ◆ 'Mmmmm mmmmm' athew ra angkerl-anem atek. Ker akwel inarl arlkwetyart. Akely-amperl. Atek. (St) *The button quail makes a 'Mmmmm mmmmm' sound. Supposedly they [people] used to eat them. They are tiny little things. Quails.*
= iylpwerr, aterlkwarr

atek-kenh (E) *n.*
fontanelle. It is said that this part of the head hardens up when the child starts to talk. ◆ Atek-kenh atyet nhelkwer ampa akwekelarl atyet anyenem — wal atek-kenharl ilem Anmatyerrel. (St) *That soft part that little babies have on the top of their heads — well that's called* 'atek-kenh' *in Anmatyerr.*
= iylpwerr-iylpwerr, ahey-ahey
SEE ALSO atyet-atyet

atem *vi.*
1. burst, bust, split open ◆ Tyre apek aterl-alhem, nheng alhemel. (M) *The tyre might burst as [you] are going along.*
= rltar-rnkem
SEE ALSO antyelp-irrem, aterlkem, atem, aterlk-irrem
2. beat or thump (heart) ◆ Iylkert angerr kwenh unta urtakwert atem. (Sa) *Your heart is beating fast because you are really sick.* ◆ Untemarl-penh rtwakert atem. (Sa) *[Your] heart beats fast from running.*
SEE ALSO atartem

atemart angkem (E) *vi.*
stamp one's feet, make a knocking or thudding noise ◆ Nanth atemart angkemel unterl-wem. (Sa) *The horses make a thudding noise as they are galloping along.*
= nenty-nenty alhem
SEE ALSO ahenty-ahenty-irrem

ateng-ilem (W,T) *vt.*
warn somebody about something, tell somebody that something is about to happen (especially warning about aggression) ◆ Thwengk ateng-ilem, artwang yanh apetyepetyem ngwenh atwetyek. (T) *I am warning you about that man who is coming to fight with you.*
= anngarr-ilem
atengelh-ilem (W,T) *vt.* = **ateng-ilem**
◆ Yatenh-hety atengelh-ilem thwengk. (M) *I am warning you about that person.* ◆ Amwehety atengelh aken ilem. (M) *[You] warn people about snakes as well.* ◆ 'Kwer yanh irntakert arrtyanepanemeyay!' *That's* atengelh-ilem. Ahangeng atengelh-ilem. (M) *'That child is running along holding a rock!' That's warning someone. Warning them because the child is angry.*
= lyarnem

Atengakey (W) *n.*
name of place in the Woodforde River in the vicinity of Tinarkie Soak and Tinarkie Bore

atengkel (E) *adv.*
trying to do something and not succeeding
atengkel atanthem (E)
miss something when trying to spear it ◆ Atengkel atanthek irrtyartel. *Missing when trying to spear something.*
atengkel atwem (E)
miss something when trying to hit it ◆ Ker arlewatyerr atengkel anem tha atwek. (St) *I missed the goanna while trying to hit it.*
= athem1, arrthem
SEE ALSO uyarn, -arrpantey

ater *n.*
afraid, fright, fear ◆ Rntwarr irntangkwerr alhem, ater. (M) *When he is frightened he goes a long way into the hills.*
ateralth *n.*
1. frightened, cowardly ◆ Kwer yanh ateralth kwenyel. (T) *That child is not frightened.*
2. wild, not broken in, untamed
atna ateralth (E)
frightened, 'scared shitless' (lit. 'scared arse') ◆ Atna ateralthharl untepuntem yanh. (St) *That*

person is running away, scared shitless.

ater-kweny (W), **ater-kwenh** (T) *n.*
fearless, ready to fight

aterel-anthem *vt.*
frighten someone or something, give someone a fright (anthem *'give'*) ◆ Aterel-anthem kwer map, arrkenel war arrenty-arrentyel. (T) *Frightening the kids, just for fun, pretending to be monsters.* ◆ Ntwa ayenh aterel-anthek. (St) *You gave me a fright.* ◆ Aterel-anthek ayenh altyerrel, altyerr tha arek akeng. *I had a bad dream and it gave me a fright.*

ater-irrem *vi.*
be afraid, feel frightened ◆ Kwer yanh ater-irrem arrentyeng *or* angwelyeng *or* tyerrtyeng arrpenh, terangkeng. (T) *That child is frightened of the monster, or of the dog, of other people, or of drunks.* ◆ Anwern ater-irrem ngkekerneng. (M) *We are frightened of the kurdaitcha.*

aterlkem *vi.*
burst or bust, split open
SEE ALSO atem

aterlk-irrem *vi.*
burst or bust, split open ◆ Yerrampel aterlk-irrem, awert renh awantyem. (M) *The honeyant bursts and then [you] suck on the honey-soaked earth.*
= antyelp-irrem
SEE ALSO rltar-rnkem, atem

aterlk-ilem *vt.*
1. smash or bust something
2. hatch out from an egg
SEE ALSO iyltem, pelty-ilem
3. poke into something ◆ Anngang arnangel aterlk-ilem. (T) *The stick pokes you in the eye.*
• = antyelp-ilem

aterlkelhem *vi.*
be burst or split open by something

aterlkwarr (E), **arterlkwarr** (E) *n.*
button quail (*Turnix velox*)
= atek, iylpwerr

aterrng *n.*
dirty, grubby, messy
SEE ALSO alhwerrk, alkwemp-alkwemp, altelhey, iltelhey, alther, nywet-nywet[2]

aterrng-aterrng
a bit dirty, grubby or messy

aterrng-ilem *vt.*
make something dirty ◆ Ampernemay kwatyel aterrng-ilerl-irrerlanetyang anenherr-areyay, apety-alperleway. Kwatyel aterrng-ilemelarl alhwerrk-kety. Apety-alpenherr-arey! (Sa) *All you kids, don't mess up the water — come back and sit down. You'll make the water muddy. Come back all of you!*
= alhwerrk-ilem

aterrng-irrem *vi.*
get dirty ◆ Mantarr atyenh aterrng-irrekarl tha alhewetyek. (St) *I'll wash my clothes that have got dirty.*
SEE ALSO alhwerrk-irrem

aterr (W,E) *n.*
cicada (*Tropha* sp.) ◆ Aterr angkep-angkem arna wethel. (St) *The cicadas are singing in that tree.*
= anngener, arrey-arrey

atetherr *n.*
budgerigar (*Melopsittacus undulatus*) ◆ Ker atetherrel arlkwem arnwety kwarrety, lpway-areny. (M) *Budgerigars eat the* kwarrety *seeds that grow in the creek.* ◆ Ker atetherr rlpwereh inem. Atwem atwem atwem intyarr-wem intyarr-wem kelem anarnpenty-alhem ahern, *billycan*-warl pwelap inem. Ker mwerr anthwerr. Akwek map kart-akert inemel, kart-akert arlkwem. Angerr mapant iterleng rwel. (N) *[You] get budgerigars from hollow trees. You kill them and throw them to the ground and then climb down to the ground and fill up the billycans. The meat is really nice. The baby ones are eaten, guts and all. Only the bigger ones are cooked in the fire.*

atetherr arlkwenh *n.*
mulga snake, king brown snake (*Pseudechis australis*) (lit. 'budgerigar eater') ◆ Atetherr arlkwenhel atetherr angkerrerlek awem, wal antyenhem anem ra rlpwer-warl. Rlpwer-warl irrpety-alhem ra, kel utnhem ra, arlkwem anem ra — atetherr akuny akwek-akwek. (St) *The* atetherr arlkwenh *hears the budgerigars singing and then it climbs up to the hollow tree. It goes into the hollow, then it catches the budgie and eats it — the poor little budgie.*
= ikwelengk, kantharlkw, arreperlp, alhingk, tyamparl
SEE ALSO arriper

atetherr-atetherr *n.*
a type of prickle; cartwheel burr (*Sclerolaena cornishiana*) ◆ Atetherr-atetherr, atanthemarl ingka. (St) *The* atetherr-atetherr *prickles pierce [your] feet.*
SEE ALSO kapert angerr, kapert-kapert, arlketyerr, lyek

-atety *ending*
Used when asking questions, and in emphasising one thing or situation rather than another; instead, on the contrary (?).
◆ Angwenh-**atety** tyerrty yanh apetyem? (T) *Who is that person coming there?* ◆ Ipey

arrernem, alengk-iwelhem ankerr-kety aleth akwet kel tyeteng anem renh arnaremel — arraty-**atety** arratem kwaty-warl kwenh. (Sa) *[The hunter] makes a hide, and hides himself there from the emu, and stays there in the narrow space watching or the emu to come — and then the emu appears, coming towards the water.*

-atety (T) up to (somewhere), as far as (something) SEE UNDER **-atwety**[2]

atey (E) *n.*
man ◆ Ilengem-warl alhek atey-rnem. (St) *The men went to do their ceremonial business.*
= artwa

ateyarrp *n.* [RESPECT LANGUAGE]
1. son-in-law (of a woman)
2. mother-in-law (of a man) ◆ Ateyarrp then alpety-alperreperremaw. (Sa) *My son-in-law and his wife are coming back.* ◆ Ateyarrp, Napwerr, alhek *clinic*-warn. (T) *My mother-in-law, Napwerr [skin name], has gone to the clinic.*
SEE ALSO mwer, anherr

ateyepenh (W,T), **atehepenh** (T) *n.*
1. whipstick wattle (*Acacia adsurgens*). Shrub about 3 m high with narrow leaves and cylindrical yellow flowers.
2. edible seeds of the whipstick wattle. Also referred to as *anterrng ateyepenh* or *ntang ateyepenh.* ◆ Ateyepenh anterrng *heap* arrernetyam ahern-warl. Anterrng ateyepenh athetyam irntel, pwerlel panth-warn, *heap* arrernetyam, athetyam, awantyetyam, theletyam. *The seeds from the whipstick wattle were heaped up on the ground and then ground up using grinding stones. The seed paste was put into the wooden dishes and eaten.*
= antyweleny

Ateylimp (E) *n.*
the name of a creek east of Wilora (Stirling) community

ath+ (E)
Goes before some verbs to show that the action was in vain, or that you were unable to do the action. ◆ 'Thang **ath**arem. Thang **ath**arerl-apem.' Anngel ap nta arerlapem akwekel war. (M) *'I can only see a little bit. I can only see a bit as I go along.' [That's when] you can only see a little bit.* ◆ Tha **ath**awemarl tha — arert apekarl. **Ath**awemarl tha, awetyakenh. (St) *I can't hear — maybe I'm deaf. I can't hear.*
= arrth+, athem
SEE ALSO atharem, athawem, uyarn

atham *n.*
1. no fire
2. no light, in the dark ◆ 'Atham' *no light.* Mwetek atham *light* ilwek mpep-antey, athamel anem. (Sa) *'Atham' means no light. The car light died halfway, and now it is dark.* ◆ Athamel anem ayeng apek. Ura-kweny. *I might be sitting in the dark with no fire.*

atham-areny (T,E) *n.*
a type of spirit (-areny *'inhabitant of'*) ◆ Atham-arenyan athamelarl anep-anem ra alhep-alhem rwengk aretyakenh *no light, no ura apek*, atham-areny. Apetyek atyeng-warl. Tha renh arek utneng wararl arek, apetyem. (St) *The* atham-areny *spirits live in the dark place where there is no fire, and they travel around unable to see because they have no light and no fire. They came to me. I saw them coming, just the spirit.* ◆ Artwa akwel atham-areny, aretyakenh renh. Arelh thwen atham-areny. (St) *There are male and female* atham-areny *spirits, and you can't see them.* ◆ Atham-areny apetyem ankwa ayntenty aretyek angketyek. Angkety-alhetyek. Atyekelh-ilem atham-arenyel, kenh inngek-athen akem-irrenty-alhem atham-arenyek. *'Eh*, arrangkw kwenh, arrangkwarl ap nhenhan kwenh. Angwenh angkekay kwenh?' 'Aretyekarl apetyekay ayeng.' Atham-areny angkem alanh. (Sa) *The* atham-areny *spirits come to where a person is sleeping, to see them and talk to them. They wake the person up, and the person wakes up, thinking it was a real person. 'Hey, there's nobody, nobody here. Who was it that spoke?' 'I've come to see [you]'. That's what the* atham-areny *says.*
SEE ALSO anngirrenty, irrernt-areny

atham-atham *n.*
1. feeling worried and sorry ◆ Mekikw atham-atham, math ikwerenharl *pass* away-irrek. (Sa) *Feeling sad about his mother who passed away.*
SEE ALSO alharrp
2. kind, generous, compassionate ◆ 'Atham-atham' mwerr, *happy*. Atham-athamel unta mpwareparem, mwerr *look after*-em-ilem, arntarnt-arep-arem atham-athamel ntwa. (St) *'Atham-atham' is good or happy. You might do things in a kind way or look after someone properly.* ◆ Atham-athamel arntarnt-arem. (Sa) *Kindly looking after someone.* • SEE ALSO imeng, arwekar

atham-irrem *vi.*
1. go out (fire) ◆ Rwang atham-irrem. (M) *The fire is going out.*
= lwernelhem
2. feel sorry for someone or something; worry about someone, be kind or compassionate ◆ Yay atyenh apek rlkert-irrerleng ayeng

atham-irrem, alhwarrp-irremel. Atyey apek. (St) *If my elder sister or my younger sibling is getting sick then I feel sorry.* • SEE ALSO alharrp-irrem

athankwem (T,E) *vt.*
dip or scoop something up (water) ◆ Kwaty athankwem thewekety. (St) *Dipping up the soakage water.*
= arnweng-inem
SEE ALSO inpem

atharem *vt.*
be unable to see, see only a bit ◆ Athareparem nhenh-angkwerr, athareparem — nhenhel antel tha areman. Anper tha arem alknga anyentel. Nhenhel tha atharemarl. (St) *On this side I can't see properly — only with this [eye] can I see properly. I can only see properly with one eye. With this one [the other eye] I can't see much.* ◆ 'Thang atharem. Thang athareri-apem.' Anngel ap nta arerlapem akwekel war. (M) *'I can only see a little bit. I can only see a bit as I go along.' [That's when] you can only see a little bit.*
SEE ALSO arem, ath+

atharlkw (E) *n.*
nest
= antywa

-athath *ending*
(do something) before another thing happens; (do something) before someone else does; (something has to happen) before another thing happens; (something happens) before something else, in preparation (for something else), until (a particular time) ◆ Angayel apek artang-iletyek, alhetyek apek. Artang-ilem tey apek mern apek. Tha apek artang-iletyek, ngkwengetyem-**athath**, ntwa anem antyweyameng. *You might [eat] first if you're hungry, or go [somewhere] first. You might have tea or food first. I might drink before you, and then you drink.* ◆ Aherrkelam aherrkel alherl-anetyek, ingwirrek-irrem-**athath**. (St) *Going around all day, right up until it gets dark.*

athathel *adv.*
(doing something) quickly, in a rush or in a hurry; pushing in, not giving others a chance ◆ '*Eh*, athathel arlkwetyalay anwern apwertel arlkwetyeh kwenh!' Arelhel apek alakenh. (M) *'Hey, don't rush in to eat, we're all going to eat together!' A woman might tell [another one].* ◆ Athathel arlkwerrem. Maney ngkwelty ina *spend*-em-ilerrerl-anem athathel, arrwekel-antey, arrwekelam arrwekel. (St) *They eat in a rush. They spend all their small change in a big hurry, straight away.*

athathew-ilem (T) *vt.*
push in, try and go first

Athatheng (T,E) *n.*
the name of a place in the Woodgreen Station area. See map p. viii. Sometimes spelt as Atartinga.

athatheth *n.*
1. small baby
2. the noise that small babies make when they are crawling ◆ Ampa akwek 'atha atha atha' angkeynem arnerreynepeynerl mekikwel apek. 'Atha atha atha' angkeynepeynerl. Ampa akwek artnerrenty. (St) *A little baby says* 'atha atha atha' *as it crawls along towards its mother.* 'Atha atha atha.' *A little crawling baby.*
athathath-irrem *vi.*
(baby) make an *atha atha atha* sound
athath angkem = athathath-irrem

athathingk (E) *n.*
crawling baby (just about ready to walk)
SEE ALSO arnerrenty

athawem *vt.*
be unable to hear; hear only a bit, not hear properly ◆ Tha athawemarl tha, arert apekarl. Athawemarl tha, awetyakenh. (St) *I can't hear, maybe I'm deaf. I can't hear.* ◆ Arnterr atyeng angkay, tharl athawemeng. (St) *Talk to me loudly, because I can't hear properly.*
SEE ALSO athem[1], awem, ath+

-athek, -atheh (W) *n.ending*
in the general direction of; towards (a particular place or in a particular direction) ◆ Ananther alhem lpway-warn-**athek** *road* nhenh-angkwerr. (M) *We are going along this road towards the creek.* ◆ *Ti Tree*-warl-**athek** ayeng alhem, katyerr akerl-anetyek. (St) *I am going towards Ti Tree to collect desert raisins.* ◆ Angkern-**athek** anngarelhem, 'Lenh kwenh tyerrty apetyepetyem'. (N) *Looking backwards over your shoulder, 'There is a person coming'.* ◆ Artwang rlkert intep-intem rwewarn-**atheh**. (M) *The sick man is sleeping by the fire.* ◆ Mewarr arraty interl-apem talkw altwerl-**atheh**. (N) *The Milky Way lies straight across in a westerly direction.* ◆ Aherrk irrpem altwerl-atheh. Ingerreng apetyem aherrk anenty-alhem, altwerl-**atheh** irrpem. (N) *The sun goes down in the west. It comes from the east and goes down in the west.* ◆ Ulaneng-**athek** aretyel. *Looking this way.* ◆ Arelh yanh rnpepernem ntywem-**athek** arnengerr. (M) *The woman there is standing facing away with her hands clasped behind her back.* ◆ Ayenparl akernengan. Ayenp nhenh apetyem

amwelteng arlka. Kenh alhwarl kweneng *run-irrerl-anem*, ingkewarn-**athek**, iltyewarn-**athek**, alakenh kapert-warn-**athek.** (T) *Skin is on the surface. For example, there is skin all the way along the arm. Whereas blood runs on the inside, towards the feet, the hands and to the head.* ◆ Kwenel-**athek** atnarnpenhetyek arnkarreng apek. (St) *Maybe jumping downwards from the bank of the creek.*

lyet-athek, **lyet-atheh** (T)
nowadays (lyet *'today'*)

anker-athek-irrem (T,E) *vi.*
become bereaved; become bereaved of a son or daughter (anker *'spinifex resin'*; -irrem *'become something'*)
= ywerlt-irrem

nthakenh-athek
1. 'What's up?' (nthakenh *'how'*)
2. 'Which way?', 'Where?' ◆ Nthakenh-**athek** ntwa alhem? (T) *Which way are you going?* ◆ Nthakenh-**athek** ntwa mern item? Alturl-**athek** ayeng alhem, mern-akert. (T) *Where are you going to cook the food? I'm going to the west with the food.*

athek-athek-ilem *vt.*
tickle someone ◆ Athek-athek-iletyalay! (St) *Don't tickle [her]!* ◆ Ampa athek-athek-ilem, ampa arrken atherrem arnterr. (St) *[If] you tickle a child it will laugh really hard.*
= tyek-tyek-ilem, kert-kert-ilem

athek-irrem *vi.*
be in a hurry or a rush; get excited or happy (especially about food); rush in excitedly, be impatient ◆ Alerl athek-irrerl-iwerretyang arternpeng anenherr-arey. Mern arlkwetyek athek-irrerlarr-anetyang — yanhan atyenharl. *Wait, don't you all get excited and rush in, sit down quietly. Don't get over-excited about eating — that's my food.* ◆ Kwer map athek-irrem, 'Mamew, mamew apetyem kwenh mern-akert kwenh!' (N) *The children get excited and say, 'Mummy, mummy is coming with food!'* ◆ Kerek athek-irrety-ayntem, arlewatyerr *four*-pal apekarl atwek. (St) *Getting excited because of killing four goannas.*
SEE ALSO inkwerelhem, arrewelhem

athem[1] (E), **arrthem** (E) *adv.*
Goes before verbs to show that the action was done unsuccessfully or not very well; doing something unsuccessfully, trying to do something and failing.
= atengkel, ath+

athem rnternem (E), **arrthem rnternem** (E), **athem atanthem** (E), **arrthem atanthem** (E)
miss something when trying to spear it, miss a target when spearing it (rnternem *'spear something'*; atanthem *'spear something'*)
= atengkel atanthem

athem-wem (E), **arrthem-wem** (E) *vt.*
miss something when throwing something at it; miss a target when throwing something at it (wem *'hit something by throwing'*) ◆ Athem tha wek ngenh. *Not* tha ngenh *properly*, arnterr wetyakenh antey — athem-wek tha ngenh. (St) *I threw something at you but missed. I didn't hit you properly — I missed you.*
= atengkel wem

athem atwem (E), **arrthem atwem** (E)
miss something when trying to hit it (atwem *'hit'*) ◆ Athem atwek tha atnemel apek, arengk apek, *might* ker apek alewatyerr. Apmwa apekarl athem atwek tha untem anem. (St) *I struck out at the dog or the goanna with a digging stick but I missed. I might have tried to hit the snake but I missed and now it's slithering away.*
= atengkel atwem

athem-athem (E), **arrthem-arrthem** (E) *adv.*
do the verb action incompletely; do the verb action unsuccessfully or not very well ◆ Athem-athem atwem apek ampa. Athem-athem atweynem atweynem atweynem, athem-athem atweynem, arnel apek. Melikw apek. Ampa urntem arna kwerety — mekikwety. (St) *Hitting at the child. Maybe the mother goes along and tries to whack the child with a stick. Then the child runs away from the stick — from its mother.* ◆ Athem-athem tha antywerl-alhern, mwetek *too much* ayeng arrerarl tnetyam wal ayeng antyerl-alhern. (St) *I just drank a little bit before I went off because the car was too close, so I just drank and left.*

athem[2] *vt.*
1. grind something ◆ Arelh ampwel arnwety athep-athem. (N) *The old woman is grinding seeds.*
SEE ALSO ulpilem

2. knead, mix ◆ Arelhel mern tamp athep-athem. *The woman is kneading damper.*

-athen (E) *ending*
1. Goes on nominals to show that you mistake something for something else; mistakenly think that . . . , mistake something for . . . This ending always follows *+ek* or *+eh.* ◆ Arnek-**athen** unernengk renh arerl-anem, wararl altywernerl-anem, war arna then ra **then** lepwel. (St) *You see the tawny frogmouth just sitting there and you might think*

it is a branch because they are both similar to each other. ◆ 'Ankerringk' ap ra, ngkwerlpek-**athen**, ngkwerlp anem rarey ngkwerlp-kwenyel renh arlkwetyart, arnmenyel. Urrelty akemel anyem, renh itetyart. Arlkwetyart anem ina. (St) *It's called 'ankerringk' and it could be mistaken for tobacco. They mixed it with ashes and used it as a tobacco when they didn't have other sorts of tobacco. They cut the twigs and cooked them and then chewed it.* ◆ Ingwerek-**athen** ayenh atwekerr, mer nhareny ayeng alhetyel-kety. (Sa) *Because I'm from this country and they might mistake me for someone else and kill me.* ◆ Ilewerr. Kwatyek-**athen** arem ilewerrelarl akern-ilem. (St) *The mirage. You see where the mirage raises it up and you mistake it for water.*

2. Goes on the end of verbs to show that you want the verb action to happen, or thought that it might happen but it didn't. ◆ Alhetyekek-**athen** irrar-irreman irrkaw-irreman alhetyek irrar-irrem. (Sa) *You feel restless and homesick and really want to go (but you didn't).*

kelek-athen (E)
(you thought) that something had already happened but it hadn't ◆ Ayeng ngkweng atnew-irrek kelek-**athen**. *I thought you had already gone but you're still here.*

athenem *vt.*
1. lay someone or something down ◆ Ampa akwek tha intetyek athenem. (St) *I am laying the baby down to sleep.*
2. lay something across something ◆ *Rail* athenetyek arntarlkw-warl. (Sa) *The rail is laid across the forked sticks.*
3. knock someone down
SEE ALSO thelp-athenem
CAN SOUND A BIT LIKE athernem *'(water) lie on the ground'*

athen-wem = **athenem**

ankwa athenem
lay someone down to sleep (ankwa *'sleep'*) ◆ Kwer ankwa athenerl-alhem, ayeng arrken-irretyeh alhetyenheng kartel. (M) *I'm going to lay the child down to sleep and then I'm going to play cards.*

anenp athenem (T), **atninp athenem** (E)
lay someone right out (by fighting them), 'drop them dead', 'half murder' someone (lit. 'lay arse out') ◆ Atninp athenem renh atwem terangkel. (Sa) *The drunk is half murdering him.*
SEE ALSO nyant atwem

athelp-athenem *vt.*
drag something to the ground; knock someone down (athenem *'lay something down'*) ◆ Angwelyel athelp-athenem ker aherr nhenh. (M) *The dog is dragging the kangaroo to the ground.* ◆ Tyerrtyel athelp-athenek. (T) *The person knocked [someone] flat.*

atheng *n.*
ironwood (*Acacia estrophiolata*). Tree to 15 m high with drooping narrow leaves.
= athimp, atyarnp

athengarlperl (E) *n.*
edible gum from the ironwood
= atyarnpangkwarl, athimpangkwarl

atheng-atheng (W,T) *n.*
lower back, lumbar region
= urteth, antywert

atheperr (E) *n.*
cool, cold
SEE ALSO anyel, kernt, anyartey, irrernt, angwerl, angwerleny, arlkarl[1]

atheperr-irrem (E) *vi.*
cool down, get cold ◆ Tey urinp atheperr-irretyek rnkernem. (Sa) *Put the hot tea [somewhere] to cool down.*

atheperr-ilem (E) *vt.*
make something cool or cold

ather *n.*

1. large flat rock
2. lower grinding stone (used for seed). Also referred to as *apwert ather* or *irntang ather.* ◆ Irntang atherel arnwety athem. (N) *Seeds are ground up on the grinding stone.* ◆ Apwert ather, ikwer-warl apert-atwemel ntang. Ntyerrm arlka apert anem ulpilemel, kel aympernem anem. (Sa) *The seed is crushed on the grinding stone. Dogwood seed is ground up as well, and then it is winnowed.*
= arlkwat
SEE ALSO tyeng, alyer

ather-ayerr (E) *n.* [RESPECT LANGUAGE]
hill, rock
= nyewel
SEE ALSO irnta, apwert

ather-ather[1] (E) *n.*
1. fat
2. flat

ather-ather-irrem (E) *vi.*
get fat ◆ Mernarl angerr arlkwem-penharl ather-ather-irrem. (St) *Getting fat after eating lots of food.*
SEE ALSO alpwely-irrem

kapert ather-ather (W)
bald, bald headed (kapert[1] *'head'*)

ather-ather[2] (W) *n.*
not able to hear, deaf ◆ Irlpang ather-ather awety-kwenh. (M) *Not able to hear anything with [your] ears.*

athernem (E) *vi.*
(of water) lie on the ground ◆ Kwaty arnwepel athernem. (Sa) *The water is lying in the claypan.* ◆ Kwaty nhenh athernemaw angkethel antywetyek ant anem. (St) *The water is lying here and now we can drink it, because we are thirsty.*
CAN SOUND A BIT LIKE athenem *'lay someone or something down'*

atherneng (E) *n.*
emu egg ◆ Ankerr-kenhan athernengarl, arnam-warlarl arrernemarl irrkwal-warl ipert-ilemel. Atherrk-atherrkarl. (St) Atherneng *are emu's eggs, that are laid in the grass that has been hollowed out in the desert country. They are green.*
SEE ALSO ankerr, arley

athernt (W) *n.*
a large flat rock. Also referred to as *irntang athernt.*
SEE ALSO ather

Athernt (W) *n.*
the name of a rockhole east of Pine Hill Station

atherr[1] *n.*
1. two, both, a couple or pair of things ◆ Ngkwern atherr rlkerrelhem. (M) *Sitting with both legs straight out.* ◆ Awerr atherr alherl-aperretyam. (M) *Two boys were going for a walk.* ◆ Nantewan ingka atherr an iltya atherr akin. Arrwekel-thayt iltyarl, ingkern-thaytan ingkarl. (St) *Horses have two front hooves and two back hooves. The ones at the front are called 'iltya' and the ones behind 'ingka'.*
2. that person and the other person; that thing and the other thing; both of them (following a person's name or the name of a thing) ◆ Lyet anantherr ahelh nhenhel anem Altyerrelarl arrmernekarl, anwekantherr-kwenhel amparr. *Eve*-ek atherr *Adam*-ek atherr arrmernek. (T) *Now we live in this land that God created, before we existed. It was created for both of them, Eve and Adam.*
3. Goes on some kinship terms following the *-nheng* ending to show that there are two people, one of whom calls the other by that kinship term. ◆ Alanth alherrek amenheng atherr. (T) *Two went, mother and child.* ◆ Aperl-nheng atherr yanh alherreperrem, kwey marl awenk then arelh ampwa then. (Sa) *Grandmother and granddaughter are going along there, a teenage girl and an old woman.*
+ant-atherr *ending*
just them (the two of them); only the two of them ◆ Artep ultatwem ker ankerr, kel renh akalkelh-ilemel artep atherr kel renh tyep-ilemel iylweper atherr akemel anem akalkant-atherr. (Sa) *Cut up the emu meat, then separate the two sides of the back, then cut the two thighs up, so that they are separate.* ◆ Anewart arratyant-atherr anerretyel — Kemarr uthen Petyarr uthen. (Sa) *The husband and wife are right [skin] for each other — Kemarr and Petyarr.*
atherrengk-atherr (T,E) *adv.*
in pairs, two at a time, two by two, two each ◆ Kwer atherr warrk-irretyek atherrengk-atherr. (T) *The two children are working in a pair.*
atherrek-atherr (E) *adv.* = **atherrengk-atherr** ◆ Ntwang atherrek-atherr inek, atyeng anthety-kweny. (T) *You got both of them, and I wasn't given any.*
atherram-atherr (E) *adv.* = **atherrengk-atherr**
atherrelam atherrelam (T) = **atherrengk-atherr**
atherr-angkwerr *n.*
on both sides
atherr-antey *n.*
both of them, both ◆ Arlpenty arnterrarl anwerlarr, artelhampw tyelpetyerrem. Aylpa ra akely-akely, arlatyey-kenh aylpa awer-rnem. Pertipelawan *yellow one* ratherr atherr-antey. (Sa) *The* anwerlarr *yam is really long, and the big ones are pulled out [of the ground]. It has smallish leaves, whereas the* arlatyey *yam has big ones. Both of them have similar looking yellow flowers.* ◆ Ingkelthel atherr-antey — iltyekenh ingkelthel, ingkekenh ingkelthel. (Sa) *They are both* ingkelthel *— the nails on the hands and the nails on the feet.*
atherr-ingar (W,T), **atherr-inger** (E) *adv.*
1. twice
2. for two days, for two nights ◆ Unekel atherr-ingar alhem, kerek untherl-ayntetyek. (Sa) *Going camping out for two nights, hunting for two nights.*
atherr-areng *adv.* = **atherr-ingar**
atherrarrp-ingar (E), **atherrarrp-inger** (E) *adv.* = **atherr-ingar** ◆ Atherrarrp-ingerel aynterl-alpem. (Sa) *Going for two days.*

-atherr[2] *v.ending*
1. Goes in the middle of some compound verbs to show that more than two people or things are doing the verb action. ◆ Kwer map arrken nwelherl-anem, arrken-irremel, antywang akwekel nwelherl-**atherr**-anem,

alwernererl-**atherr** anem. (N) *The children are playing around, playing around in their little shelters, chasing each other around.* ◆ Rnpwang kwer mapel arlkwerl-**atherr**-apetyart. (N) *The kids used to come along eating the resin.* ◆ Anerl-**atherr** anem anwantherr arteny, anwantherr rrpwety war anerl-**atherr**-anem. (St) *We are staying home, a few of us are stopping.* ◆ Arelh map arnerl-**atherr**-anem rlkerteng. *Some women are crying for the sick man.* ◆ Amaty-arey panth-akert, anem-akert alherl-**atherr**-apetyart, tyap arlka akerl-apetyeh awenkel, ker alewatyerr renh atwerl-apetyeh. (N) *Our mothers walked along carrying their wooden dishes and their digging sticks, and together with the young girls they gathered grubs and killed goannas as they travelled along.* ◆ Aketh-angkwerr anerl-apem thep arntwerrert, nthwerl-**atherr**-anem kwaty-angkwerr. Arntwerrert irntel anerl-anem iterel ina. (N) *Rock pigeons go along in the open and look around the water. The rock pigeons live on the edge of the rocks.*
2. Goes in the middle of some compound verbs to show that more than two are being told to do the verb action. ◆ Antywerl-**atherr** alhay! Ayeng alhem-arleng. (T) *You all go and drink! I'm going.*

Atherrarliwek (E), **Atherralewek** (E) *n.*
waterhole to the south of the Sandover Highway, near Aniltji (Boundary Bore)

atherrem *vi.*
laugh, smile, giggle ◆ Ilekek nhenheyan atherreperrem ampwerrk ilwep-ilwem atyewey-rnem? Ilek ra nhengey? (Sa) *Why is this person killing themself laughing? What's it about?* ◆ Arrken atherrem — kwer arrpel arrken mpwarem atherretyek. (T) *Laughing — the other kid made her laugh.*

arrken atherrem
laugh (arrken *'fun', 'in fun'*) ◆ Yanhek arrken atherrem ayeng. (St) *I am laughing at that person over there.* ◆ Arrken atherretyalaw! Arnterr atherretyal — arrken atherrirremel iylpa arwengk-ilemeyay! Arleng atherrirretyek alherl-way, utnherretyekay. (Sa) *Don't laugh! Don't laugh loud — your laughing is deafening us! All of you go a long way away to laugh and play around.*

atherrk *n.*
1. grass, green grass, foliage, plants ◆ Irlpang map akeweny irnenhirrem atherrk arlkwerl-anem, ina angayakwel arlkwerl-anem, irlpa mapel kwenh. (T) *The poor old donkeys are standing and eating grass, the donkeys are hungry and are eating.*
2. green colour (a colour that includes green and some shades of yellow and blue)
3. hair that has not gone grey [SOME SPEAKERS] ◆ Ilkwa ampetyangel, alta atherrkarl. Alta atherrk nga. (Sa) *Hair that has not gone grey is called* 'atherrk'. *Your hair is not grey yet.*

alknga atherrk (E)
cat (alknga *'eye'*)

mern atherrk
vegetable food, grass, salad (mern *'food'*)

atherrkelhem (E) *vi.*
turn a greenish colour, go rotten (meat) ◆ Atherrkelhem, akeran, arntert-irremel ant atherrkelhek. (St) *The meat goes green, goes rotten and green.*

atherrk-atherrk (T,E) *n.*
1. green colour (a colour that includes green and some shades of yellow and blue) ◆ Ker mpwelengk. Perrak-artek akngerr-awatyarl ra. Akngerr-lkwerarl ra. Atherrk-atherrk, *yellow yellow.* (St) *The* mpwelengk *frog. It's like a frog only a bit bigger. It's a bit bigger. They are a greenish-yellow colour.*
2. ten dollar note; one hundred dollar note
3. someone who has married the 'wrong' way ◆ Alem atherrk-atherrk. *Someone who has married the 'wrong' way.* (alem *'belly', 'stomach'*) • = alem iyterrk-iyterrk

atherrk-atherrk-irrem *vi.*
1. be bruised
2. turn a greenish colour; go rotten ◆ Atherrk-atherrk-irreman tywenelarl rrkwem akengem-irrem atherrk-atherrkem irrem. Tywen-penh akengem irrem atherrk-atherrk, *clean*-em iletyakenh. (T) *If you have a wound that hasn't been cleaned then it can go bad, turn green. A sore that hasn't been cleaned can go rotten.* ◆ Kwaty atherrk-atherrk-irrek, arntwatherrkel artelhek. *The water has gone green from being covered with slime.* • SEE ALSO iynteng-irrem

alknga atherrk-atherrk (E)
someone who has married the 'wrong' way (alknga *'eye'*) ◆ Untam alknga atherrk-atherrk-irrek mwerekengkw, ampekengkw apek. Nyerrerl-itany. (St) *You married your son-in-law, or your son, even though it's shameful.*

atherrkeny *n.*
green or lush country; 'green time' (when plants grow abundantly after rain) ◆ Ayeng alhetyek atherrkenyel anem, arlewatyerr apek tha atwetyek, ker arlewatyerr ampwarl anek-penh, anter anem. (St) *I'm going hunting for goannas in the green time because the goannas are fat now, after being skinny.* ◆ Artwa ampwel

arrmernem kel atherrkeny anem anem. (St) *The old men hold increase ceremonies and then everything is green.* ◆ Mern atherrkenyarl anem perlap. Mern arlkwerl-apekarl perlap anthwerr, kwerelarl amangkenhek, perlapel. Alherl-apek lyweny, mern perlap akerl-anetyek. (N) *The conkerberry fruit comes out after rain. We grew up eating conkerberries. We'd go hunting and collect conkerberries.*

atherrkeny-irrem *vi.*
go green (country), become lush and vegetated

atherrkeny-ilem *vt.*
make the country go green ◆ Kwatyel anem atherrkeny anem ilek anwekantherrenh atherrkeny anem. (St) *The rain made our [country] green.*
SEE ALSO anyemwerr-ilem

athethek (W,T) *n.*
reddish-brown colour; half-caste
= rnter-rnter
SEE ALSO arlperrty, apekath

athethem (T,E) *vi.*
go reddish in colour ◆ Aherrk athethem. (T) *Red sunset.*
= rnterelhem, atyetyek-irrem

athew *part.*
1. 'Is it true?', 'Is that so?', 'Isn't that right?' An expression used by a speaker to ask the person listening to agree with or confirm what they are saying. ◆ Arraty athew tha ilep-ilem, thathew? (M) *I'm saying the right thing, aren't I?*
SEE ALSO tyakey, arraty-akey, tyathew
2. Provides emphasis for what has been said; contrasts the characteristics of one particular person or thing with another; whereas on the other hand . . . ◆ 'Mmmmm mmmmm' athew ra angkerl-anem atek. Ker akwel inarl arlkwetyart. Akely-amperl. Atek. (St) *The button quail makes a 'mmmmm mmmmm' sound. Supposedly they [people] used to eat them. They are tiny little things. Quails.* ◆ Mpwernatyan ilem artwelant athew, kenh anewekarl ilem marlel. 'Artwang yanhan anewaty.' (T) *'Mpwernaty' [my brother-in-law] is only said by men, whereas, on the other hand, women call [their brother-in-law]* 'anew'. *'That man is my brother-in-law.'*

athimp (T,E) *n.*
ironwood (*Acacia estrophiolata*). Tree to 15 m high with drooping narrow leaves. ◆ Arna athimp, ngkwerlp itenh-itenh. (St) *The ironwood is used for making ashes to chew with tobacco.*
= atheng, atyarnp

athimpangkwarl (E) *n.*
edible gum from the ironwood
= athengarlperl, atyarnpangkwarl

athwang (E) *part.*
Provides emphasis to what is being said (?). ◆ Ahanelh-ilenherr-areyay tyety-ayerr yanhentyakay. Weyapelek-uthek tyety-ayerr ahanelh-iley. 'Weyapel' ap ilem 'angayakw'. Angayakwek kwenh weyapelek-uthek kwenh. Weyapelek-uthekel mely-aketyek athwangang. (Sa) *All of you take the meat to that one over there. Take it to the one over there [my son-in-law] who is hungry. 'Weyapel' is what is said [in avoidance language] for 'angayakw' [hungry]. [Take the meat] for the hungry one. So that he can eat.*

athwenter, athwernter *n.*
1. flower of the dogwood (*Acacia sericophylla*)
SEE ALSO awenth, anteth
2. egg yolk (emu egg and others) ◆ Athwenter arlkwem renh ikiwemel, ayenp weth-lkwer iwem, ikareyan. (St) *The egg yolk is eaten after [the egg] has been peeled and the shell thrown away.* • SEE ALSO atherneng

atna (E) faeces, shit, excreta, droppings, poo SEE UNDER **ana**

atna irrkert-irrkert (E) *n.*
a type of big black ant (atna *'arse'*; irrkert-irrkert *'sticking out'*)
= arlekert, atnangkerney

atnakapeltherr (E) a type of cricket (insect) SEE UNDER **anwengkapeltharr**

atnal (E) house SEE UNDER **anal**

atnalharr (E) yellow fat from the emu's stomach SEE UNDER **analharr**

atnalpenty (E) a type of spirit SEE UNDER **analpenty**

atnalth (E) *n.*
a place where there are a lot of footprints or tracks

atnalth-ilem (E) *vt.*
1. make a mess, mess up tracks by walking all over the place ◆ Ingka angerr unthemel atnalth-ilem. (St) *Lots of people walking all over the place mess up the tracks.*
2. talk over the top of someone, talk across someone ◆ Mapel atnalth-ilemeng — *can't* awerl kwenh. (St) *People are talking over the top of one another — I can't hear.* • SEE ALSO anthakemel angkem

atnamp (E) *n.*
ripe native currants (or other fruits) that have fallen to the ground ◆ Ntyenpek-amparr ra irrem kel atnyem anem, atnamp anem ra

atnyem. (St) *[The* ahakey *fruits] get ripe and then they fall to the ground when they are* 'atnamp'.
SEE ALSO unemarnt
atnamp rnternem (E)
fall to the ground (native currants)

Atnangker (T,E) name of a place and of country/estate in the Utopia (Angarapa Aboriginal Land Trust), Mt Skinner Station area SEE UNDER **Anangker**

atnangkerney (E) *n.*
1. a type of big black ant
2. wasp, ant mimic
= arlekert, atna irrkert-irrkert

atnapert (E) larrikin, promiscuous person SEE UNDER **anapert**

atnarlt (E) *n.*
part of a bush turkey's guts; crop (of a bird) (?) ◆ Ker atnarlt artew-kenh kwen, anertel. Inem renh, arlkwem renh, atniwemel. (St) *The edible* atnarlt *meat is inside the stomach part of the bush turkey. [You] get it and eat it, after cleaning out the guts.*
SEE ALSO ana, mpurl
CAN SOUND A BIT LIKE anarlt *'track', 'pad or path of kangaroo or euro'*

atnarlt (T,E) track, pad or path of a kangaroo or euro SEE UNDER **anarlt**

atnarnkw (E) in a group or bunch (of particular fruits) SEE UNDER **anarnkw**

atnarnpem (E) jump down from something SEE UNDER **anarnpem**

atnarrk (E) part of kangaroo guts (stomach or large intestine) (?) SEE UNDER **anarrk**

atnarteng (E) the base or bottom of something SEE UNDER **anarteng**

atnath (T) unable to walk, handicapped, paralysed, crippled SEE UNDER **anath**

atnawert (E) native willow, apricot tree SEE UNDER **anawert**

atnaymp (E), **atnaynp** (E) buttocks, bum, backside SEE UNDER **anaynp**

atnaynenh (E) wrist SEE UNDER **anaynenh**

atnekapeltharr, anekapeltherrey (E) a type of cricket (insect) SEE UNDER **anwengkapeltharr**

atnelth (E) *n.*
diarrhoea, 'guts-ache'
= ampeltyey
SEE ALSO ana
atnelth-irrem (E) *vi.*
have diarrhoea or 'guts-ache' ◆ Ampa akwek nhenh atnelth-irrem, ra apekarl akeng apek arlkwek apek antywek apek. (St) *The little child here has guts-ache from eating or drinking something bad.* ◆ Katyerr apekarl arlkwem atnelth-irrem. (St) *Eating desert raisins can give you guts-ache.*
= ampeltyem, ampeltyey-irrem

Atneltyey (E) name of a place and the location of an outstation (Boundary Bore) west of Sandover River in the Utopia (Angarapa Aboriginal Land Trust) area SEE UNDER **Aneltyey**

atneltyey-irrem (E) have diarrhoea or 'guts-ache' SEE UNDER **aneltyey-irrem**

atnem (E) yam stick, digging stick SEE UNDER **anem**3

atnemarraty (W,T) caustic bush SEE UNDER **anemarraty**

atnemel pweyntengeynteng (E) a type of beetle SEE UNDER **anemel pweyntengeynteng**

atnemwernt (E) *n.*
someone who is not greedy or pushy; someone who lets other people eat first and doesn't demand anything ◆ Ankey angketyangel atnemwerntel menty arerl-anem, atnemwerntel arep-arerl anngelant. Kel renh anthem anem, yanhantarl arlkweman. (St) *Someone who is* atnemwernt *just watches and doesn't ask for anything. If someone gives them something then they'll eat it.*
◆ Atnemwerntel tha arerl-anem menty — menty itnarrp arlkwerlek. Atyeng apekarl anthem, yanhantarl tha arlkwem. (St) *I just watch — not pushing in greedily — while they eat. If they give me some, then I'll eat it, that's the only time I eat.*
SEE ALSO ana, mwernt1

atnengk (E) calm, no wind SEE UNDER **anengk**2

atnengkan (E) arriving somewhere too late for something SEE UNDER **anengkan**

atnenyerr (E) avoiding or staying away from trouble SEE UNDER **anenyerr**

atneperrk (E) fat-covered intestines of some animals SEE UNDER **aneperrk**

atnepetheng-irrem (E) go backwards, reverse SEE UNDER **anepetheng-irrem**

atnepeywenp (E) a big perentie, *ilkwert* SEE UNDER **anepeywenp**

atnepwart (E) a type of big louse SEE UNDER **anepwart**

atneraty (E) feeling happy about something SEE UNDER **anaraty**

atnerlangket (E) *n.* [RESPECT LANGUAGE]
blanket
SEE ALSO pelangket, pangkarr, antyam

atnerrk1 (E), **atnerrk-ayerr** (E) *n.* [RESPECT LANGUAGE]
bad, no good ◆ Artwa atnerrk ipmeyaw. Akeng artwa. (Sa) *Don't have anything to do with that bad man.*
SEE ALSO akeng

atnerrk-irrem (E) *vi.* [RESPECT LANGUAGE]
go bad, get sick, break down ◆ Twertert-ayerran anerrk-irrekarl yanhentyak atyewey-rnem mpwarerlentyarrenherr-areyay! Mpepel-antey atnerrk-irrety-alpek. (Sa) *[My son-in-law's] car broke down over there — for goodness sake why don't you all fix it! It broke down half way back.*
SEE ALSO ngkwerltelhem, akeng-irrem
atnerrk-ilem (E) *vt.* [RESPECT LANGUAGE]
spoil something, wreck something
◆ Mwetekayarl atnerrk-ilek-kety artwel. (Sa) *[Because] the man wrecked the car.*
SEE ALSO akeng-ilem

atnerrk2 (E) *n.*
personal belongings of the deceased (?)
SEE ALSO ampeny1

atnert (E) stomach area, belly, abdomen SEE UNDER **anert**

atnerwerrk (E), **atnerurrk** (E) ankle SEE UNDER **anewerrk**

atneth-akert (E) scorpion SEE UNDER **aneth-akert**

atnety (E) *n.*
root of the bush banana, silky pear (*Marsdenia australis*)
= artwey-artwey1
SEE ALSO alangkw, parl

atnetyelp (E) *n.*
1. dog (a word used when you are angry or cranky with a dog) ◆ Atnetyelp arert anem irrek. (St) *That wretched dog has gone mad.*
2. dog [RESPECT LANGUAGE]
SEE ALSO ana, arengk, angwely, rtwek-rtwek, wang-wang, tywetyety-ayerr

atnew-atnew (E) brave, fearless, confident SEE UNDER **anew-anew**

atnew-irrem (E) get excited or happy about something but then be let down SEE UNDER **anew-irrem**

atneyangketh-irrem (E) go backwards, reverse SEE UNDER **aneyangketh-irrem**

atneyarnteng (E) *n.* [RESPECT LANGUAGE]
behind, going after
= anengant
SEE ALSO ingkern

atnhakert (E) *n.*
weak, tired, exhausted ◆ Anem ayeng atnhakert. (St) *I am sitting down, exhausted.*
atnhakert-irrem (E) *vi.*
feel weak in the legs from hunger (?); feel exhausted, weak or lazy ◆ Atnert ayeng angayelarl irrem arlkwetyakenh-penh, ngkwern atnhakert-irrem. (St) *My stomach is hungry from not eating, and I'm feeling weak in the legs.*
SEE ALSO arewamp-irrem, parrk-irrem

atnhal (E) *n.*
heavy or steady rain
atnhal-irrem (E) *vi.*
rain steadily or heavily ◆ Atnhal-irrem kwaty. (St) *It's raining heavily.*

atnhem (E) fall (rain) SEE UNDER **anhem**

atnhwerrem (E) clear (the ground for a camp or to collect bush foods) SEE UNDER **anhwerrem**

atnhwert (E) folded up, in a bundle (?) SEE UNDER **anhwert**

atnik (E) quiet, non-aggressive, timid SEE UNDER **anik**

atnik (E), **atnik-atnik** (E) *n.*
cracked or split part of foot, hoof or paw
◆ Ker aherr ingka atnik-akert. (St) *The kangaroo has got cracked paws.*
CAN SOUND A BIT LIKE anik *'timid', 'harmless'*
ingka atnik-atnik (E)
cracked foot (ingka *'foot'*)
atnik-atnik-irrem (E) *vi.*
get cracked (hoof, foot or paw)
SEE ALSO tyarrp-irrem

atnimampel (E) someone who is cursed SEE UNDER **animampel**

atninem (E) gut (an animal) SEE UNDER **anenem**

atningk (E) many, lots of things SEE UNDER **anengk**1

atnirnterrm-irnterr (E) collarbone SEE UNDER **anirnterrm-irnterr**

atniwem (E) *vt.*
let someone or something go ◆ Mwetekayel apek yanh atniwenty-alpem, alhernter atniwenty-alpern. (St) *[Someone] in a car just dropped that white person off.* ◆ Arengk atniwem, *chain*-el apekarl ayerneng, kenh arengk atyenh atniwetyek anem alhetyek ra. Atniwem anem arengk renh. (St) *Let the dog go from the chain that was tying it up. Let my dog go so that it can go off.*
SEE ALSO tyarl-wem, ilanthem
CAN SOUND A BIT LIKE anewem *'name something'*

atnker-atnker (E) type of spinifex SEE UNDER **anker-anker**2

atnkerrmern (E) coolibah SEE UNDER **ankerrmern**

atnma (E) bud or flower of native tobacco SEE UNDER **alpma**

atnmangkem (E), **alpmangkem** (E) *vi.*
go yellow (native tobacco) after being put in ashes; gain strength or 'bite' (native tobacco)
◆ Ngkwerlp then anyentarl-ilem arlpmeny-warl akwernem ngkwerlp, atnmangkem anem ra. Ngkwerlp atnmangkem. Atnmangkem ahelengkwarl, mwerr — atnmangketyakenh akengarl. (St) *The native tobacco is mixed with*

the ashes and then it goes yellow. If it goes yellow, well that means that it is 'cheeky' or has a kick to it — if it doesn't then it's no good.
= arltererntern-irrem

atnmanth (E) *n.*
hot ashes or earth (used for cooking or healing) ◆ Ampernem renh atnmanthel ampernem, urel ampernemel-penh arlkwem, irrkwenng. (Sa) *Desert truffles are eaten after cooking them in the hot ashes.*
SEE ALSO arnmeny, arlpa[1], awerrth, ntyerlp[1], amerrk[2], rtwap

atnment (E) fire SEE UNDER **alpment**

atnurerrk (E) ankle SEE UNDER **anewerrk**

atnwalty (E) part of the guts (of kangaroos or cattle) SEE UNDER **anwalty**

atnwar (E) heel SEE UNDER **anwar**

atnwekert (E) bent over SEE UNDER **anwekert**

atnwengk a type of wallaby or bettong (?) SEE UNDER **anwengk**

atnwengk-atnwengk mulga native currant, narrow-leaved native currant SEE UNDER **anwengk-anwengk**

atnwenth (E) meat, flesh, game SEE UNDER **anwenth**

atnwer dry kangaroo droppings SEE UNDER **anwer**

atnwerl (E) snake vine SEE UNDER **anwerl**

atnwerl-atnwerl (E) emu's intestines or guts SEE UNDER **anwerl-anwerl**

atnwerlarr (E) pencil yam (narrow leaf variety) SEE UNDER **anwerlarr**

atnwerlk (E) fright, fear SEE UNDER **anwerlk**[1]

atnwerlk (E) buttocks, bum, backside, the rump of an animal SEE UNDER **anwerlk**[2]

atnwernt (E) stubborn, uncooperative SEE UNDER **anwernt**

atnwerrng (E) yellow fatty substance inside witchetty grubs SEE UNDER **anwerrng**

atnyaty (E) 'cousin-uncle' SEE UNDER **anyey**

atnyelh-ilem (E) drop someone or something SEE UNDER **anyelh-ilem**

atnyem (E) fall off something SEE UNDER **anyem**[1]

atnyem (E) witchetty bush SEE UNDER **anyem**[2]

atnyem anteth (E) part of guts (kangaroo) SEE UNDER **anyem anteth**

Atnyem Kwaty (E) Ryans Well SEE UNDER **Anyem Kwaty**

Atnyemamern (E) Goofy Bore, near the Sandover River on Mt Skinner station SEE UNDER **Anyemamern**

atnyemeylpar (E), **atnyemilparr** (E) south wind SEE UNDER **anyemilparr**

atnyenem (E) hold onto something; carry something SEE UNDER **anyenem**

atnyengkw (E) 'cousin-uncle' SEE UNDER **anyey**

atnyenheng (E) 'cousin-uncle' SEE UNDER **anyey**

atnyenheng atherr (E) 'cousin-uncle' SEE UNDER **anyey**

atnyenty (E) moon; moonlight SEE UNDER **anyenty**

atnyenty-atnyenty (E) small white grub SEE UNDER **anyenty-anyenty**

atnyer (T,E) supplejack SEE UNDER **anyer**

atnyerleng (T,E) turkey bush SEE UNDER **anyerleng**

atnyerr (E) running water; floodwater SEE UNDER **anyerr**

atnyey (E), **atnyikw** (E) 'cousin-uncle' SEE UNDER **anyey**

atnywa (E) *n.*
dry or old (of certain bush foods)
= pweynteng
atnywirrem (E) *vi.*
go dry, get old (of certain bush foods) ◆ Mern alangkw atnywa, aywa anemarl ampem, atnywirrek. (St) *The bush banana fruit is dry, it's got old and dried up.*
= pweynteng-irrem

atwakey *n.*
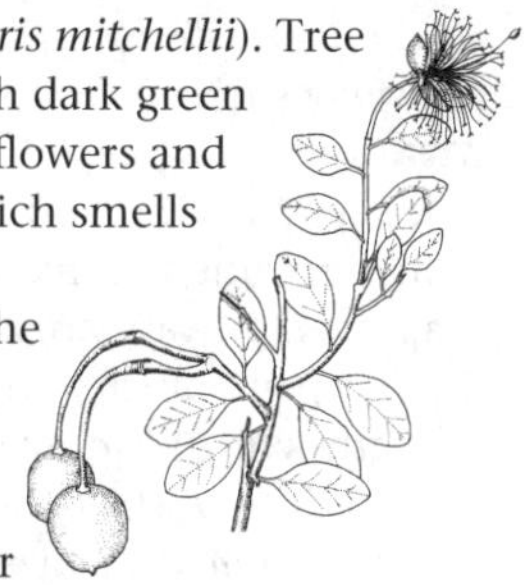
1. wild orange (*Capparis mitchellii*). Tree up to 3.5 m high, with dark green leaves, creamy white flowers and yellow-green fruit which smells nice when it's ripe.
2. the edible fruit of the wild orange. Also referred to as *mern atwakey*. ◆ Atwakey tha intyernem rntwarr angerr. (N) *I can smell the wild oranges from a long way away.* ◆ Arlkwem arrkernemel, kel pwelap-akertem alhem atwakey renh inelhem alhem, arlkwerl-apem nwenty-nwentyem alherl-apem. *We taste the wild orange fruits first, and then go and collect a whole lot of them, munching noisily as we go.*

atwarem *vt.*
1. approach someone; meet up with someone; go over to someone; go near someone ◆ Nhak tha atwarem, tyerrty arrpenh yanh apekarl anep-anem. (St) *I am going over to that person who is sitting over there.* ◆ Anew ngkwengenh ntwa atwarem. (M) *You are going to meet your husband.* ◆ Mweraty nthanh tha atwaretyang. Alerekikwenh thanh atwaretyangarl anek arrwekeleny. *Law way.* Akngey-ketyan ikirrenty akin. Amek-aremel. Thanh atwaretyang. Apmarlikwantarl atwarem. (Sa) *I don't go near my son-in-law. In the olden days it was not permitted for a person to go near their* aler *[nephew, niece; child of a man]. That was the Law. There were restrictions*

with regard to a person's father as well. They were avoided, and a person would not go near them. They were only allowed to go near their apmarl *[mother's brother].*
2. infect someone ◆ Artwengkelkng angerrel anem akertel. 'Tyampet atyenhel antywetyal, yenh atwarekerreng.' (St) *Somebody might have a bad cold or flu. 'Don't drink out of my cup, in case I catch it from you.'*
SEE ALSO angwarem
CAN SOUND A BIT LIKE artwarem *'watch someone or something going away', 'see someone off'*
atwarerrem *vi.*
meet up with each other

Atwarlk (W) *n.*
Milky Way (galaxy)
= Lpwararr, Mewarr

atwarteng (W) *n.*
a type of plant (?) ◆ Mern atwarteng, *carrot*-art. Ayep *self* akin, kenh angerrety anthwerr. Kwen inyemel, anemel. (N) *The* atwarteng *is like a carrot. It is different from the tar vine, a lot bigger. We dig it from the ground with a digging stick.*

atwaty *n.*
1. gap, gully, gorge ◆ Atwaty-angkwerr anwern alhem, arnkewarn, ngkwerlpek arerl-apetyek. Atwaty-angkwerr anarnpenhem. Kwer-penh atwaty arrpenhek anem anarnpem. (T) *We are going through the gully, towards the rockface, looking for native tobacco. We are climbing down the gully. After that we climb up another gap.*
2. gap or crack in something
irntang atwaty (W,T)
gorge, gap in hills (irntang *'hill', 'rock'*)
apwert atwaty (T,E)
gorge, gap in hills (apwert *'hill'*)
ingka atwaty (E)
gap between toes (ingka *'foot'*)
atwaty-atwaty *n.*
place where there are lots of gaps or cracks
atwaty-ilem *vt.*
make a gap in something ◆ Arntek atwaty-ilem alyeleng atwek. (Sa) *A tooth was knocked out to make a gap in the teeth.*

atwaylpaylp (E) *n.*
fruit hanging in a bunch (said particularly of bush bananas and wild oranges)
◆ Atwaylpaylp anep-anem mern alangkw. Anteth-penh alangkw akwerrk-irrem, atwaylpaylp anem ra anerl-anem arnel. (St) *Bush bananas are found in a bunch. After the flower, the young bush banana fruits develop, and then they hang in a bunch on the branch.*

atwayntem (E) *vi.*
go up something, climb, get onto something (e.g. a horse) ◆ Atwayntenhem akern-antep kel tharew ilenhem anem, kwenelak. (Sa) *Climbing up to the top then facing downwards again.*
= antyem
SEE ALSO anganem
atwayntenhem (E) *vi.*
climb up along something

Atwel (E) *n.*
name of country/estate which extends over parts of Bushy Park and Alcoota pastoral leases. See map p. viii.

atwem *vt.*
1. hit, slap, whack, bash or beat someone or something ◆ Arengk tha atwem. (St) *I am hitting the dog.* ◆ Arelhel atwek arnakertel angwely yenh. (M) *A woman hit the dog with a stick.*
2. chop or carve something ◆ Arwengalker tha atwem ilepel. (St) *I am chopping the sugarbag with an axe.* ◆ Inernteng alparr atwem. (M) *Carving a carrying dish from bean tree wood.*
3. kill someone or something; murder someone
4. kill or catch (an animal) ◆ Awerr atherr alherl-aperretyam anyerrkentyem mer-warn, amwang yatherr atwekarl-penh. (M) *The two boys went home happy because they had killed a snake.* • SEE ALSO arlinem, kwarterrem
5. play an instrument, such as a guitar
◆ Tyerrtyel atwem ketay. (M) *The person is playing the guitar.*
6. affect badly (of sickness or disease); make someone sick ◆ *Pneumonia*-el ayeng atwenhek. (Sa) *I caught pneumonia.* ◆ Annga alhap-irrem amengelarl atwem, atherrkeny apek. (St) *Eyes become bunged up when flies bite them, in the green time.* ◆ Manty arntarnt-arelhem, arerl-anemel, irrerntel atwekety. (N) *Look after yourself, watch out, or the cold might get to you.* ◆ Ngangkarel angkwerr-wem pwenty renh iwemel, pwentyelarl atwek kwenh — kel mwerrarl ra irrem. (Sa) *The traditional healer massages the patient to get rid of the sickness that has affected them — then the person gets better.*
7. hit, strike (of a storm or lightning)
◆ Apwertek-akertarl atwek kwatyel. (Sa) *Rain and hail struck [a place].*
8. fall (rain) ◆ Kwaty lthelel atwem. (M) *Steady rain is falling.*
atwenh-atwenh *n.*
a dangerous thing (lit. 'something that is used to hit with')

atwerrem *vi.*
fight or hit each other ◆ Artwang atherr ngkwantyel atwerreperrem. (M) *The two men are angrily fighting with each other.* ◆ Atwerremarl-ketyaw. Mernek-arrngel apek ratherr atwerrem. (St) *Look out, they're fighting. Maybe those two are fighting over food.*
imayel atwerrem (E)
have a jealous fight with each other ◆ Artwa atherr apek imayel atwerrem. (St) *The two men are having a jealous fight.*
atwelhem *vi.*
1. hit yourself, hit or slap at something that is on part of yourself; clap hands against part of your body ◆ Kapert ayeng atwelhem. (St) *I am hitting myself on the head.* ◆ Weny atwelhem antem. (N) *Slapping at the mosquitoes.*
2. have an accident and hurt or kill yourself
urlperrng atwelhem (E), **arlperrng atwelhem** (E)
beat rhythm on lap with cupped hands to accompany ceremonial dancing (women) ◆ Althartek apek urlperrng atwelhem. (St) *Beating the rhythm on the lap during the* althart *ceremony.*
iltya atwelhem (E)
clap hands (iltya '*hand*') ◆ Iltya ayeng atwelhem. (St) *I am clapping my hands.*
iltyel atwerl-apem (T)
swim (lit. 'go along hitting with hands') ◆ Kwaty iltyel atwerl-apem, irrpelherl-apemel atwerl-apemel iltyel. (T) *Swimming along in the water, going into the water and then swimming along.*
nyant atwem, **tnyant atwem** (E)
kill someone or something; nearly kill someone or something (nyant '*nearly kill*') ◆ Ahelarl tha nyant atwem, ayeng urrampemarl tha nyant atwem renh. Nthakenh apek ra irreyamel. (St) *I was so angry with that person that I practically killed them. I don't know what's going to happen to them.*
= nyey-nyey atwem
SEE ALSO anenp athenem
ingkel atwem (E)
kick something (ingka '*foot*') ◆ Artwel patepwerl ingkel atwem arrpenh alenh-warn. (T) *The man is kicking the football to the other one over there.*
rltar-rltar atwem (E)
make a banging or knocking noise (rltar-rltar '*banging noise*') ◆ Rltar-rltar atwem unta apek atyeng. (St) *You might be knocking [on something] for me.*
rlterrp atwem (E)
rattle boomerangs together (men) ◆ Althartek rlterrp atwep-atwem kayl. (St) *At the* lthart *ceremony [they] rattle the boomerangs together.*

atwemenh (E), **atwemeny** (E) ceremonial poles or 'long sticks' used during initiation (young man) ceremony SEE UNDER **utemeny**

atwenh-atwenh a dangerous thing SEE UNDER **atwem**

atwerneng (W,T) *n.*
edible grub from ant bed, winged termite (*Amitermes vitiosus*). Also referred to as *tyap atwerneng.*
= ngkwayt, ngkwepeyayt
SEE ALSO ngkwepey, kerrertek, arnameng-ayerr, interrk2

atwerrp (E) *n.*
afternoon, in the afternoon
= angwerrel, angwerr-angwerr
CAN SOUND A BIT LIKE twerrp *'sandhill'*
atwerrp-atwerrp (E) *n.*
very late afternoon (sun almost going down)
atwerrp-irrem (E) *vi.*
become late in the afternoon
= angwerr-irrem, ngway-ngway-irrem

atwertim (E) *n.*
black-breasted buzzard (*Hamirostra melanosternon*). Eats emu eggs, breaking them with stones dropped from its beak.
= aytwertek, lywerlperr

atwety1 *n.*
joey, young kangaroo ◆ Aherr aympelarl akngep-akngem atwety akwek. (St) *The young joey is carried along in the pouch.* ◆ Kwer akwek atwetyeh impa! *Little child, leave the joey alone!*
CAN SOUND A BIT LIKE urtety *'short'*

-atwety2, **-artwety**, **-atety** (T) *ending*
1. up to (somewhere), as far as (something). This ending can go on nominals and verbs. On nominals this ending usually follows the ending *+ek* or *+eh*, or dative pronouns such as *atyeng*, *ngkweng* or *ikwer*. On verbs it follows *+etyek* or *+etyeh*. ◆ Mer nhenh arlka-**atwety** arrkwetyety *Coniston*-warn arlka ingkang alhetyart. (N) *We went as far as here [Napperby]. Coniston as well, on foot.* ◆ Arwengalkerel anem, ankerel ap renh martem arwengalker, ikwer-**atwety** ngkwarl intem. (St) *In the sugarbag, the wax blocks off the sugarbag and the honey goes as far as there.*
2. until (a particular time) ◆ Rntwetyart rntwetyart anwern akwek map rntwetyart

rntwetyart rntwetyart, angwerr-angwerrek-**artwety**. (N) *Us little ones used to dance and dance and dance until evening.* ◆ Urrek anem *Tuesday*-ek-**atwety**. (St) *Wait till Tuesday.*
3. until (a particular thing happens), until (someone does something) ◆ Keran atanthem irrtyartelant — urremperan tyerrtyarl atanthetyam. Ilwetyek-**artwety** kel renh atanthetyam. (St) *Just kangaroos were speared with the hunting spear — people were speared with a shovel spear. They were speared to death.* ◆ Atyengant akwet untang aparelherl-anem kwenh. Thwengk anthetyeh-**atwety** unta aparelherl-anem. (T) *You always bludge off me. You wait around until I give you something.*

atweynterl (E) *n.*
desert spadefoot toad (*Notaden nichollsi*). Also referred to as *ker atweynterl.*
= kwep, pwerreparnt, kwep-kwep[2]
SEE ALSO mpwelengk, antyetyerr, perrak

+aty[1] *k.ending*
my relation; our relation. Goes on the end of kin terms and other words that are similar to kin terms. ◆ Aler**aty**-rnem-akert ayeng alhek, atyenh-akwerrk. (Sa) *I went with all my nephews and nieces, my family.* ◆ Aler**aty**-arey altyarey. Altyarey anteyarl ipmenh**aty**-arey. Arreng**aty**-areyan altyarey anteyarl. Anherr**aty**-areyan altyarey antey. (St) *My nephews and nieces are close family; my daughter's children are family as well, and my son's children are family, my sons' wives are family too.* ◆ Am**aty**-arey panth-akert, anem-akert alherl-atherr-apetyart, tyap arlka akerl-apetyeh awenkel, ker alewatyerr renh atwerl-apetyeh. (N) *Our mothers walked along carrying their wooden dishes and their digging sticks, and together with the young girls they gathered grubs and killed goannas as they travelled along.*
SEE ALSO +engkw, +ikw, +ekw

altyerraty (E) *n.kin*
my mother's country

arwengaty (E) *n.kin*
my/our personal Dreaming ◆ Anyemayt tha arlkwem wal arweng**aty** tha arlkwem. Ayeng antem arweng**aty**aw tha arlkwem, atyengarl anganek. (St) *I eat witchetty grubs, well I eat my personal Dreaming. I eat the Dreaming that I came from.* ◆ Arweng**aty** tha arlkwem aherr. (St) *I eat my Dreaming, kangaroo.*

+aty[2], **+ayt** (E), **+art** (T) *n.ending*
Goes on the end of the names of certain plants to form the name of the grub that is found on that plant. ◆ Ngkwert**aty** tyap. Kwen-areny artekerr kwen-areny, ngkwertel-arleng. (N) *The* ngkwertaty *grubs. They are found in the roots underneath the* ngkwert *bush.*

anyematy, anyemart (T), **anyemayt** (T,E), **atnyematy** (T,E) *n.*
witchetty grub (anyem '*witchetty bush*')

ayepaty, ayepayt (T,E) *n.*
grub from the tar vine (ayep '*tar vine*') ◆ Ayepaytan ayepel anep-anem. (St) *The* ayepayt *grub lives on the* ayep *plant.*

ankerrayt (T,E) *n.*
grub from the coolibah (ankerr '*coolibah*')

arlkerlayt (T,E) *n.*
grub from the buckbush, rolypoly, tumbleweed (arlkerl '*buckbush*')

atyanem (W) *vi.*
be busy, occupied; work doing something ◆ Ntwang rnwanentyeh akweteth atyanerl-anem. (M) *You're always busy sorting out clothes.*
SEE ALSO mpwarem, rrkwapem, warrk-irrem
CAN SOUND A BIT LIKE arrtyanem *'run'*

atyang[1] *adv.*
(doing something) for or on behalf of someone else. Goes with transitive verbs such as *item* 'cook', *inem* 'get', *atwem* 'hit, fight, kill etc.', *nyem* 'dig' and *apawenhem* 'ask'.

atyang-item (T) *vt.*
cook something for someone else ◆ Rrwek mpwelhemel anang. Ker ngkweng tyang-item, apety-alpemel arlkwety-alpem. (T) *Hold on, wait a while. I'm preparing food for you to eat when you come back.* ◆ Arelh yanhel ngkweng atyang-item. (T) *That woman is cooking for you.*

atyang-inem (T) *vt.*
1. get something for someone else ◆ Mern atyang-inerl-alpem. (T) *Going and getting food for someone else.*
2. make trouble for someone else, bring trouble for someone ◆ Nhel atyeng atyang-inem. (T) *This one is making trouble for me.* • SEE ALSO rrwernem, urrernem, nakepakel-ilem

atyang-atwem (T) *vt.*
hit or fight someone for someone else, kill something for someone else ◆ Arlewatyerr atyang-atwem ngkweng, ntwa arlkwetyeh. (T) *[I'm] killing the goanna for you so that you can eat it.*

atyang[2] (W) *n.*
small bits of yellow-coloured pollen (or resin) found at the base of a tree containing a native bees' hive or sugarbag
= arnpan
SEE ALSO rltwamp, arwengalker
CAN SOUND A BIT LIKE arrtya[1] *'ritual hopping or*

shuffling step'; arrtya[2] *'ghost gum flower'*; arrtya[3] *'small pieces of rock or stone'*

atyang ngkwern (T) *n.*
shinbone (ngkwern *'bone'*)

atyangk (W) clean honey (native honey) SEE UNDER **arrtyangk**

atyank *n.*
bull ant (*Myrmecia nigriceps* (reproductive)) ◆ Atyank, utnhenh-utnhenharl ra ahelengkw. Arrkernk intertelarl anem. (St) *Bull ants are really dangerous, they bite. They live at the base of bloodwood trees.*
= ntyeyapert, tyekarnparnp[1], arrengarlp

atyankern, aytankern (E) *n.*
1. types of mistletoe (*Amyema* spp.; *Lysiana murrayi*)
2. edible fruits of these types of mistletoe ◆ Panth-warn arrernerl-apem, atyankern map. Rnterelh-ilem peleth! *Red one* anem, an *yellow one* an *black one*, rrpwerl-irrerl, *self* akin inelh-apem, inelh-apetyam *long time*. Ityarlam lyetarr. Ityemarl. (N) *We gather the mistletoe berries in the coolamons. Some go red, please! And some turn yellow and others black. A long time ago we used to collect them all separately. Nowadays people don't [collect them].*
SEE ALSO ngkwerrm, pweralhem, amar, ngartangkern, peketyalkwarr

atyarleny (W) *n.*
dirty, unwashed (person or animal)
SEE ALSO aternng
CAN SOUND A BIT LIKE tyaheleny *'I', 'mine (?)'*

atyarnp *n.*
ironwood (*Acacia estrophiolata*). Tree to 15 m high with drooping narrow leaves. ◆ Atyarnp arnmeny itenh-itenh ra kwel. Arnmeny item, rnpwa akert renh-perr arnmeny iterl-anem, ngkwerlp-kenh, *not tobacco*-kenh athew, arwenp-kenh, ngkerlp-kenh. (N) *The ironwood tree is also used for ashes and we cook the ashes to use for native tobacco, not whitefella tobacco, for pituri.* ◆ *Medicine* kwen-penh atanthem. Alhwart artekerr-penh, arrernem kwaty-warl irrem rarrp alhwartey-irretyenheng *red* irretyenheng rarrp. Alhewelhenhelhenh annga renh arlka atyarnp yanh. Artekerr kwen-penh. Tyap arlka akert akin yanh kwen-penh, artekerrel-aleng atyarnp arlka akin inyerrirretyart artekerrel-arleng tyap. Tyap arlka akin anwa arlkwetyart. (N) *We get medicine from the roots of the ironwood tree. We put it in water and it goes red, like blood itself. We use the [mixture made from the] root of the ironwood for washing eyes. There is also an edible grub in the roots that was dug up. We used to eat the grub.*
= atheng, athimp

atyarnpangkwarl (W,T) *n.*
edible gum from the ironwood ◆ Ngkwarl rnpwa-akert *right* atyarnpan anem. Atyarnpangkwarl-akert war irnem atyarnp. Atyarnp rnpwa akert, arlkwenh-arlkwenh akert. Lweren arlka inetyeh, awantyem arlkwem, atyarnp. (N) *The ironwood tree has sweet edible resin called* 'atyarnpangkwarl'. *We collect that and suck on it.*
= athengarlperl, athimpangkwarl

atyaw-tyaw-ilem *vi.*
shoo flies away (from English 'shoo' (?)) ◆ Ameng atyaw-tyaw-ilem ayweperl-apemel ameng yanh-lkwer. (St) *Shooing and hunting the flies away.*

atyehenh (W,T) mine, my SEE UNDER **atyengenh**

atyek (E) *n.*
awake ◆ Ankwa intetyal — atyek anetyek. Arelhemel mwanty artwekety. Tyekel anem arem. (St) *Don't go to sleep — you've got to stay awake. And watch out carefully for men. Stay awake and watch.*
= karr

atyek-atyek (E) *n.*
awake

atyek-irrem (T,E) *vi.*
wake up ◆ Ankwa aynterlanetyang — atyek-irraw, akem-irraw! (Sa) *Don't go to sleep — wake up, get up!*
= karr-irrem

atyekelh-ilem (E) *vt.*
wake someone up
= karr-ilem, akemelh-ilem

atyelp, atyilp (T,E) *n.*
native cat, western quoll (*Dasyurus geoffroii*). These are now extinct in Central Australia.
= atyet[2]

Atyelpathek (T) *n.*
name of place south-east of Adelaide Bore. See map p. viii.

atyemey *n.kin*
1. mother's father; grandfather ◆ Atyemey atyenh. Mam-kenh *daddy* ikwerenh, atyemeyarl atyeng. *My grandfather. My mother's father is* atyemey *for me.*
2. mother's father's brother or sister; great-uncle, great-aunt
3. a man's daughter's child; grandchild, grandson, granddaughter

4. a person's brother's daughter's child; great-niece, great-nephew
5. particular relations with the same skin as a person's *atyemey*
6. the country and Dreamings belonging to a person's *atyemey*. If someone calls someone *atyemey* then they are called *atyemey* in return.
= artartey
SEE ALSO rtartart

atyengkw (T,E) *n.kin*
your *atyemey*

atyikw (E), **atyeyekw** (E) *n.kin*
his/her/their *atyemey*
CAN SOUND A BIT LIKE atyeyikw *'his/her younger sibling'*

atywek (W,T) *n.kin*
1. your *atyemey*
2. his/her/their *atyemey*

atyenheng *n.kin*
a group of more than two people, at least two of whom are related to each other as *atyemey*

atyenh-intyerr (T) *n.kin* = **atyenheng**

atyenheng-arey (E) *n.kin* = **atyenheng**

atyenhengart *n.kin* = **atyenheng**

atyenheng atherr *n.kin*
a person together with one of their *atyemey* ◆ Atyenheng atherr alhekaw. (St) *The grandparent and the grandchild went.*

atyenkethenh *n.kin*
1. having *atyemey* (still alive)
2. someone who is always with their *atyemey* ◆ Atyenkethenh ayeng, atyemey atyenh iteth. (Sa) *I have an* atyemey, *my* atyemey *is [still] alive.*
SEE ALSO -ankethenh

atyeparety *n.kin*
respectful or 'sorry way' of talking about someone's *atyemey* ◆ [Arrpenhel ilem], 'Atyeparety apetyem yanh'. (T) *[Another person says], 'There is your poor old grandfather coming'.*
SEE ALSO -parety

atyeneny *n.*
something belonging to a particular person, someone else's belongings ◆ Mern atyeneny — yanh impa atyeneny. (St) *Leave that food alone — it belongs to someone else.* ◆ Atyeneny, kerek-artweyekant mpwelheyaw, atyeneny kwenh. (St) *That belongs to someone else, wait for the owner of the meat.* ◆ *Don't* anyelkek-irretyek atyeneny imay. (Sa) *Don't steal that — leave it alone — it belongs to someone else.* ◆ Atyeneny kwerenh menty impeyaw. Rarrp anthety-alpetyek atyeneny kwerenh. (St) *Leave her things alone. She can give you some herself when she gets back (?).*
SEE ALSO atyenernkeny

atyenernkeny (E) *n.* [RESPECT LANGUAGE]
belonging to a particular person, someone else's belongings ◆ Atyenernkeny yanhentyak irrepetheyaw, ameram-ilerrekerr. Ameram-ilerrekerr atyenernkeny yanhentyak irrepethetyek alha kwey, ngwarrekengkwenh. (Sa) *Daughter, go and get your husband's things, in case he says something. Go and get your husband's things otherwise he might talk [said by a woman to her daughter].*
SEE ALSO atyeneny

atyeng *prn.*
1. for me, to me, at me, on me. See Appendix 1. ◆ Arrpenh atyeng angakang anyent apek. (M) *Pick another one out for me, maybe one.* ◆ Man apek tha atyenh alengk-wem, atyeng ankeyel inekerrel. *I'm going to hide my money in case somebody comes and asks me for it.* ◆ Atyeng alkngetherr anem angka, tha awerleng. (St) *Say it straight to my face and I'll listen to you.* ◆ Arnterr atyeng angkay, tharl athawemeng. (St) *Talk to me loudly, because I can't hear properly.*
2. my (with kin terms) ◆ Atyeng aler. (M) *My child [man speaking] or my brother's child.*
CAN SOUND A BIT LIKE tyeng *'hand held grinding stone'*

atyeng-artwey *n.*
my family

atyengenh, atyeng-henh (W,T), **atyehenh** (W,T) *prn.*
mine, my. See Appendix 1. ◆ Mern atyengenh. (M) *My food.* ◆ Arrengey-henh yanham mer Arlwem. Atyengenh arrengey-henh, tharl arreng akek angey-henh, angeyeh-artey-henh, papeh-artey-henh, angey atyeng-artwey-henh. (N) *My grandfather's country is Arlwem [Yuelamu (Mt Allan) area]. That is the place that I am related to through my father's father and my father.* ◆ Angwely ap ilwemarl kwa, alharrp-irrem angwely-artey mapel alharrp-irrem. 'Angwely akeweny atyengenh kwenh, akeweny angwely.' (N) *If the dogs die then the owners of the dogs get sad. 'My poor dog, the poor dog.'* ◆ Mer atyehenh-warn alherrey. (M) *Let's go to my camp.* ◆ Alenh kwaty atyehenh. (T) *There is my water.*
= atyenh
SEE ALSO atyeng

atyengkw SEE UNDER **atyemey** 'mother's father etc.'.

atyenh *prn.*
1. my, mine. See Appendix 1. ◆ Ngkang

atyenh arekar. *My foot is sore.* ◆ Yay atyenh apek rlkert-irrerleng ayeng atham-irrem, alhwarrp-irremel. (St) *If my elder sister gets sick then I feel sorry for her, feel sad.* ◆ Alerl athek-irrerl-iwerretyang arternpeng anenherr-arey. Mern arlkwetyek athek-irrerlarr-anetyang, yanhan atyenharl. *Wait, don't you all get excited and rush in, sit down quietly. Don't get over-excited about eating, that's my food.* ◆ Angwarlp-irrem nhenhan kel arna yanh-arey atyenh, kwaty-penh. (St) *After the rain these plants of mine have grown lush.*
2. my relation, family ◆ Atyenh-areyay, arleng alherl-way angketyekay. (St) *All my family, go a long way away to talk.*
= atyengenh
SEE ALSO atyeng

atyenh-intyerr SEE UNDER **atyemey** 'mother's father etc.'

atyenheng atherr SEE UNDER **atyemey** 'mother's father etc.'

atyenheng-arey SEE UNDER **atyemey** 'mother's father etc.'

atyenhengart SEE UNDER **atyemey** 'mother's father etc.'

atyenkethenh SEE UNDER **atyemey** 'mother's father etc.'

atyep-atyep *n.*
lively, energetic, happy, chirpy ◆ Ayeng atyep-atyep alherl-anem, purrk-irretyanan. Mernek apek warrk-irrem tey arrtyetyek warrk-irrem atyep-atyep akwet, irrngerney-antey. (Sa) *I go around energetically, I don't get tired. I work cooking food and making tea and I'm still lively and energetic.* ◆ Atyep-atyeparl anem, rlkert-kweny mwerrarl anem atyep-atyep. (St) *Being energetic, being lively and not sick.*
SEE ALSO irrngerney, arwekar, ampwengamp
CAN SOUND A BIT LIKE tyep-tyep *'bits and pieces'*

atyeparety SEE UNDER **atyemey** 'mother's father etc.'

atyepet (E) *n.* [RESPECT LANGUAGE]
boomerang
= iltyekenh-ayerr
SEE ALSO alya

atyernp slowly, unhurriedly SEE UNDER **arternp**

atyerrem[1] *vt.*
1. cook something ◆ Aperrk atyerrem rwel arlatyey map an arlkwemem ampeng — mwerr anthwerr patartart. (N) *The pencil yams are cooked in the coals and then eaten when they are cooked — they taste really nice, like potatoes.* ◆ Artewan akerarlam. Altang althem altang althem kwer-penh ker renh atyerrem. Rlweth akem amwelt atherr an kapert rlweth akem. (N) *Bush turkey meat is edible. The feathers are plucked out and then after that the meat is cooked. The two legs and the head are split open.*
2. make the earth go a yellow or red colour (of honeyants)
SEE ALSO item, arrtyem, ampeng-ilem, ampernem
CAN SOUND A BIT LIKE tyerrem *'pull something out'*
atyerrelhem (T,E) *vi.*
burn yourself ◆ Ayeng ingkang rwel atyerrelhek ker itemel. (T) *I burnt my foot while I was cooking meat.*
SEE ALSO item

atyerrem[2] *vt.*
1. shoot something ◆ Artwel atyerrem ker artew. (T) *The man is shooting the bush turkey.* ◆ Kel pwelert anem akwernem, maket yanhek-arlek. Kel ra arraty anem irrem — arraty akwet atyerrem. (T) *Then the bullet is put in the gun. Then the gun is aimed straight [at the animal] — then it's shot.*
2. go (shoot off somewhere) (?)
CAN SOUND A BIT LIKE tyerrem *'pull something out'*
ker atyerrenherrenh (W,T)
gun (lit. 'animal shooter')
= maket
atyerrelhem *vi.*
shoot yourself ◆ Ayeng atyerrelhek ingkang. (T) *I shot myself in the foot.*

atyerrp (E) *n.*
hibernation ◆ Atyerrparl urlelth ipelhem irrernt-taym. Urlelthel aynterl-anem kwen, nthanh tyerrelhetyanh. Amwantarl atyerrp aylpem. (Sa) *In the winter [the animal] digs itself into the ground to hibernate. It lies there under the ground, hibernating, and it doesn't come out. Only snakes hibernate.*
= ilka[1]
SEE ALSO urlelth, rlwelth, ilkeparr, urlelth ipem

atyet[1] *n.*
1. soft, flimsy, fragile ◆ Ahern kwaty-penh atyet. (St) *After the rain the ground is soft.* ◆ Atek-kenh atyet nhelkwer ampa akwekelarl atyet anyenem — wal atek-kenharl ilem Anmatyerrel. (St) *That soft part that little babies have on the top of their heads — well that's called 'atek-kenh' in Anmatyerr.*
SEE ALSO althalth, arrmaly-arrmaly, artaly-artaly
2. ripe • = thelty
CAN SOUND A BIT LIKE tyet *'narrow'*
atyet-atyet *n.*
1. soft, tender (meat) ◆ Ker atyet-atyet arlkwetyek. (St) *Eating tender meat.*
2. weak, fragile

atyet-irrem *vi.*
1. go soft ◆ Ker atyet-irrem. War apek aherrkel apek intep-intem anem arntert-irrem, atyet-irremel. Iwem anem renh. (St) *The meat is going soft. If it is just left lying in the sun it goes off, gets soft. Then [you] throw it away.*
2. get ripe. Especially of native citrus fruit, *ahakey* (*Psydrax latifolia*). ◆ Ahakey atyet-irrem. (St) *The* ahakey *fruits get ripe.*
= thelty-irrem

atyet2 (E) *n.*
native cat, western quoll (*Dasyurus geoffroii*)
= atyelp

atyet-atyet (T,E) *n.*
a toddler
atyet-atyet alhem (T,E)
toddle (learning to walk); stumble along (maybe from sickness) ◆ Ampa akwek atyet-atyet alhem. Atnyem ra, kel akem-irrerl-alhem kel alhem-anteyarl ra, atnyem-anteyarl ra. (St) *The small child toddles along. She falls then gets up and goes, then keeps going, then falls again.*

atyetyart *n.*
1. traditional boss, senior person, elder, leader ◆ Yanh kwenh anerl-anem atyetyart atyeng. (M) *That person is boss for me.* ◆ Atyetyart anthwerr anwerneh angerr-pat. (M) *The senior person is really our boss.*
2. really big, really fat (of a person or kangaroo)
SEE ALSO angerr1, angerrety, alkey1
atyetyart-irrem *vi.*
1. be like a boss, be in charge of something, become boss, rule over something, govern ◆ Tyerrty mapel renh arrernem, rang tyetyart-irretyeh. (T) *People will put him in to be boss.* ◆ Atyetyart-irremel anetyel, mpwelherl-anemel, merel atyetyart-irretyel angwenhel atwaretyek. (Sa) *Sitting down there at home like bosses, waiting to see who might go and meet [them].* (?)
2. skite, brag, big-note yourself, think that you are really important
3. get big or fat [SOME SPEAKERS] ◆ Tyerrty nhenh angerrety-irrek, atyetyart-irrek, arlkwemel arlkwemel. (M) *This person has got really fat from eating and eating.*

atyetyek (T,E) *n.*
red ◆ Ker arlety renh thanh than arlkwetyang, arletyarl atyetyekarl. (Sa) *I can't eat this raw meat, it's red-raw.*
= athethek, rnter-rnter
atyetyek-irrem (T,E) *vi.*
go red, become red
= rnterelhem, athethem
atyetyek-ilem (T,E) *vt.*
make something go red

atyetyem (E) *v.*
tell lies ◆ Urrtyirremel unta ilepilem, atyetyemel. (Sa) *You are telling lies.*
SEE ALSO rrtywerrem, urrtyirrem, urirrem2, rnter-irrem, arrampewem1, therlkem

atyew *n.kin*
1. what a man calls someone who has been through men's business at the same time as himself
SEE ALSO apwelh, anmanty
2. someone of the same age as a person; friend, mate; age-mate, twin ◆ Atyew atyenh aylern amangkek — *born*-irrek *level, just like twins.* Atyew-nheng aylernanth alhetyart *level.* (Sa) *Me and my friend grew up together — we were born at about the same time, just like twins. The two of us friends used to go around together, both of us the same age.*
SEE ALSO alyey2, pelty
atyew-atyew *n.kin*
friend, age-mate etc. ◆ Atyew-atyew arelh mapek anemarraty yanhey alyey-alyey. (T) *The* anemarraty *plant is a friend for the women, their spirit friend.*
atyewaty *n.kin*
my/our *atyew*
atyewengkw *n.kin*
your *atyew*
atyewikw *n.kin*
his/her/their *atyew*
atyewek (W,T) *n.kin*
1. your *atyew*
2. his/her/their *atyew*
atyew-nheng *n.kin*
a group of two or more people, one or more of whom are called *atyew* by the others ◆ Atyew-nheng aylernanth alhetyart lepwel. Ampa atyew-intyerr. *The two of us used to go around together as friends, about the same age. All of us kids were age-mates.*
atyew-intyerr *n.kin* = **atyew-nheng**
atyew-nheng atherr *n.kin*
a person together with their *atyew* ◆ Alethang map atyew-intyerr inang apetyem. (T) *They are coming, the strangers — all the friends.*
atyew-ankethenh *n.kin*
1. having a close *atyew* still alive
2. someone who is always with their *atyew*
SEE ALSO -ankethenh

atyeweyay (E) *part.*
an exclamation; 'For goodness sake!' ◆ Atyeweyay! Ayeng arteparl arntem-kety.

Atyeweyay ipmey ayenh ipmenherr-arey — pwerrkarl irrem! *For goodness sake! My back is aching. Won't you all leave me alone — I'm tired!* ◆ Akengentyenyant-atherr — mwer-nheng atherr menh-nheng atherr. Akengentyeny atherrarl anerretyelarl atyeweyay, mwer-nheng atherr, *wrong one* atherr! (Sa) *Those two are 'wrong way' for each other— mother-in-law and son-in-law, or grandchild and granny. For goodness sake! Those two are wrong for each other, mother-in-law and son-in-law.*

atyey, **aytey** (E) *n.kin*
1. younger brother or sister, younger sibling
2. other (junior) relations with the same skin as your *atyey*, such as your mother's younger sister's child or your father's younger brother's child. Whether or not a person is a junior or senior sibling to another can be calculated in terms of the relative ages of their parents.
CAN SOUND A BIT LIKE tyey[1] *'road'*; tyey[2] *'backwards and forwards'*

atyeyaty (W), **ayteyaty** (E) *n.kin*
my/our *atyey* ◆ Ayteyaty atyenh alhek. Ayeng mpwelhem ikwer, ayteyekaty atyenhek. Angkwerikw ayeng — angkwerikw. (Sa) *My younger sister went. I am waiting for her, for my little sister. I am her elder sister — her* angkwer.

atyeyengkw, **ayteyengkw** (E) *n.kin*
your *atyey*

atyeyikw (E), **atyeyeyekw** (E), **ayteyikw** (E), **ayteyeyekw** (E) *n.kin*
his/her/their *atyey*

atyeyekw (W,T) *n.kin*
1. your *atyey*
2. his/her/their *atyey*

atyey-atyey, **aytey-aytey** (E) *n.kin*
younger brother or sister, etc. This may be a more affectionate or respectful way of talking than using *atyey*. Some speakers use this word when speaking to children about their *atyey*.

atyey-nheng, **aytey-nheng** (E) *n.kin*
a group of two or more people related to each other as *atyey* and *kak*, *yay* or *angkwer* (younger siblings and elder siblings)

aytey-intyerr (E) *n.kin* = **atyey-nheng**

atyey-nheng-atherr, **aytey-nheng-atherr** (E) *n.kin*
a person together with their *atyey*

atyey-ankethenh, **aytey-ankethenh** (E) *n.kin*
1. having a close *atyey* still alive
2. someone who is always with their *atyey*
SEE ALSO -ankethenh

atyey-parety, **aytey-parety** (E) *n.kin*
respectful or 'sorry way' of talking about someone's *atyey*
SEE ALSO -parety

atyikw SEE UNDER **atyemey** 'mother's father etc.'

atyilp (T,E) native cat, western quoll SEE UNDER **atyelp**

atyur (E) a type of ant SEE UNDER **atywer**

atyurety (E) bean tree SEE UNDER **atywerety**

atywa, **atywang** (W,T) *n.*
calf (of leg), calf muscle
= pertarnp

atywaty-irrem[1] *vi.*
1. stretch or straighten yourself ◆ Rtapety interl-anem, alwerrngarl pwert-irrem, *cramp*-arl-irremeng, atywaty-irrememe. Atywaty amparr irrem kwer-penh rtapetyem interl-anem. (N) *Lying down cramped up, because your tendons have cramped up. Stretch out first and then lie there curled up.*
SEE ALSO althekalth-irrem, arternelhem
2. feel restless (?) ◆ Alhetyekek-athen irrar-irreman irrkaw-irreman alhetyek irrar-irrem. Alhetyek ayeng irrar-irrem atywaty-irremel ayeng alherl-ayntetyek. (Sa) *You feel restless and homesick and it's as if you yearn to go. I'm really restless and I want to get going.*

atywaty-irrem[2] (T,E) *vi.*
convulse, have a fit, take a fit ◆ *Wrong medicine* apekarl antywemel atywaty-irrem. (St) *[You] might take a fit from taking the wrong medicine.*
SEE ALSO arlan-irrem, nthat-nthat-irrem, tyerrty-tyerrty internem

atywaty-atywaty-irrem (T,E) *vi.*
throw a tantrum, have a fit ◆ Atywaty-irrem mekikwarl artnem, melikwarl iwerl-alhernekarl artnem, atywaty-atywaty-irrem. (St) *[He] is throwing a tantrum and crying for his mother because his mother dropped him off there and went.*

atywek SEE UNDER **atyemey** 'mother's father etc.'

atywek-atywek *n.*
yellowish, blond
= kapert tywelker, rnter-rnter

atywekal (W) *n.*
wooden water dish
SEE ALSO arlketh[1], rnwa, urna, urety, kwerlintyerr, panth, lwengkart[2], irrkwely[2], alparr[1], irrkwa, lengarr, mwar

atywekel-iwem (E) *vt.*
step on top of someone's tracks, walk in someone's footsteps
= ingkatyel-wem, lyekel-wem

atywekel-iwerrem (E) *vi.*
step in each other's tracks, walk in each other's footsteps ◆ Anyent arrpantey

atywekel-iwerrem, ingkatyel-iwerrem, anyent arrpantey anem alhemel. Anyent arrwekel alhem, ingwer ra ingkernel irrkaty ingka ikwerenhel akin. Ingkatyel-werrety-akerlem. (Sa) *Stepping in someone else's footsteps to make it look as if only one person is going along. One person goes in front, and the other goes along behind, stepping in the same foot tracks.*
= ingkatyel-wem

atywer, **atyur** (E) *n.*
a type of ant ◆ Urelarl artekarl item kwang atywer, ahelengkw wangkerl-ilenh-ilenh. Atyweran ahelengkw. Urrperl. Arrakert akwek rnter-rnter-awaty. (St) *The* atywer *ant is definitely aggressive makes you swell up and burn like fire [when it bites]. It is dark in colour and its mouth is a bit reddish.* ◆ Atywer weth ahelengkw atna atyetyek. Arleth atyetyek ap ra. (Sa) *The* atywer *ant is aggressive and it has a red backside.*
= arlety[1]
SEE ALSO tyekarnparnp[1]

atywerety, **atyurety** (E) *n.*
bean tree, bat's-wing coral tree (*Erythrina vespertilio*). Tree to 10 m high, with bright red flowers and shiny red and yellow seeds in clustered pods. ◆ Panth atwenh-atwenh, an *seed* inenh-inenh. Amern akwerrk-penh. Akwerrk inyemel, *carrot*-art. Arlkwem akwek mapan — angerrety map akenh ityarl, arlkwenh anetyakenh. (N) *The bean tree is used for making wooden dishes, and the seeds are collected. There is a root like a carrot which is eaten when it is small — the larger ones are not edible.*
= aparrty
SEE ALSO inernt

Atywerl (W,T) *n.*
20 Mile Waterhole, Napperby Station area

atywerlk (W,T), **aytwerlk** (E) *n.*
white clay which is mixed with water and used to paint up with, especially for sorry business; lime (?) ◆ Tyerrty apernelhem ikwerel aytwerlkel *anything wrong* apek apernelhemel alhem anem ra. Awelyek then aytwerlkel apernelhem. Aytwerlkan urlpa. Lpwelem renh kel athem anem renh. (St) *People paint themselves up with* aytwerlk *if there's anything wrong, and then they go [for finishing up business]. They paint themselves with* aytwerlk *for* awely *ceremonies as well.* Aytwerlk *is a kind of ochre. It's crushed up and ground up.*
SEE ALSO ngwenty-ngwenty, rlpwa, marlalperr, tywelker

atywerlkelhem (T) *vi.*
paint oneself with white clay (in mourning)

atywerlkel-ilelhem (W,T), **aytwerlkel-ilelhem** (E) *vi.*
paint oneself with white clay (in mourning)

atywerlk-ilem (T) *vt.*
make white paint

atywert-atywert (E) *n.*
native morning glory (*Ipomoea muelleri*). A vine with branches that creep along the ground and with pink trumpet-like flowers.
= rtwatyert, tatyetarr
SEE ALSO anely-pwet

atywertek (E) black-breasted buzzard SEE UNDER aytwertek

+aw, **+ew** *ending*
Goes on the end of a word to add emphasis to what you are saying. ◆ Artwang lwereny apetyek**aw**! (M) *A stranger has arrived!* ◆ Mpank**ew** ampeng-irretyakenh, rrwek**aw**! (M) *It's not ready, not yet cooked, just wait!* ◆ Antyam wetye**w**! (M) *Spread a ground-sheet out!* ◆ Alethang apek urrpety apetyek. 'Urrpety apetyawarrem yanh-kety**aw**!' (St) *There might be a few strangers coming. 'Look out, there's a few coming!'* ◆ *'Eh,* apetyeyaw awetyek**aw**, angkety iletyeh.' (P) *'Hey, come and listen, tell the story.'*

awakem *vt.*
save something (for somebody) ◆ Mern atyeng awakaw ker apek. (M) *Save me some food, or some meat.* ◆ Ker apek tha awakem, tyerrty arrpenh apek pelty atyenh. Ikwer tha awakemarl mern apek ker apek, antyalkenh apek mern katyerr apek, atnyemayt apek. (St) *I might save some meat for another person who is my friend. I might save them some bread, meat, bush potatoes, desert raisins or witchetty grubs.*

awakelhem *vt.*
1. put something away for yourself, save something for yourself ◆ Atyeng tha ker awakelhem (M) *I am putting some meat away for myself.*
2. keep something to yourself, keep a story to yourself ◆ Iletyakenh arrpenhek, alerekikw, ilelhetyakenh — awakelhek ntert-antey, rarrp angketyek. Ra ayeng aremel apek angkety-ayntetyek. (St) *[He] didn't say anything to anyone, to his sons or daughters — he kept it to himself and kept quiet so that he would just talk about it himself. He might talk to me about it when he sees me.*

awakerl-wem (E) *vt.*
go and get something for someone ◆ Ker atyeng awakerl-wem. (Sa) *Go and get some meat*

for me.
SEE ALSO inerl-wem

awal (W,T) *n.*
ground cracked from water, ground with small gullies and fissures in it ◆ Awal nheng yanh-warn ananthern alpey. (M) *Let's go back to that place over there where the ground is cracked from water.* ◆ Kwaty arratem awal ikwereng. Awal ikwer-warl anem arlewatyerr arlka, *dry time.* (T) *The water comes out of the cracks in the ground. In the dry-time goannas live there as well.*
SEE ALSO arnkwerrng
CAN SOUND A BIT LIKE warl *'house'*
kwaty awal (W,T)
water that is lying around in cracks in the ground

awangker Pacific black duck (?) SEE UNDER **awengker**

awantyem *vt.*
1. lick or suck something ◆ Tyampet awantyep-antyem yanh arengkel. (St) *That dog is licking the billycan.*
2. eat (of certain foods such as honeyants, sugarbag, corkwood honey, ground seeds and some fruit) ◆ Arwengalker apek tha awantyem, ngkwarl yerramp apek awantyem akin. Inpinpan awantyem arrpemarl, ltyantywem apek. (St) *I might suck on sugarbag, or on honeyants. Bone marrow is sucked on as well.* ◆ Untyeyel anem ngkwarl untyeyamp. Awantyem renh, *treacle*-artek rrpwerl mwerr-angker. (St) *The corkwood honey is found on the corkwood tree. It's nice and dark-coloured, like treacle, and you eat it.*
SEE ALSO ltyantywem, kwek-arem, arrantywem
CAN SOUND A BIT LIKE arrantywem *'kiss'*
awantyelhem *vi.*
lick or suck part of self (such as fingers) ◆ Iltya ngkwarl anpemarl anemarl-penh ngkwarl arwengalker apek, awantyelhem anem alakenh. (St) *[You] lick your fingers if they have honey on them from touching sugarbag.* ◆ Kwer akwek iltyang awantyelhem. (M) *The little child is sucking his/her fingers.* ◆ Arengkarl awantyelhem tywen. (T) *The dog is licking its wound.*

awarr *n.*
flood, floodwater, running water. Also referred to as *kwaty awarr.* ◆ Kwaty awarr alhem lpwayel. (M) *The floodwater is flowing along in the creek.*
SEE ALSO rew, urew, alay[1], anyerr

awatem *vt.*
make someone or something shiny or greasy with fat ◆ Anter-penharl awatem ker anter-penh. Yenh awatem, anterel apekarl apernelhem. (St) *[You] get shiny from fat. If I rub myself with fat then it makes me greasy and shiny.* ◆ Ker lyet tharl arlkwern, awatem arrakert apek. (St) *I have just eaten some meat and it's made my mouth all greasy.*
awatelhem *vi.*
become shiny or greasy from fat ◆ Ahern awatelherl-anem ker apekarl altyiwemelan awatemarl ra. (St) *The ground becomes shiny and greasy from the meat [juice] that has been tipped out.*

-awaty (T,E) *n.ending*
1. Emphasises the word it appears on (a bit like the 'er' in English 'long**er**', 'short**er**' or the 'ish' in 'small**ish**' etc.); a bit more of something, slightly greater (or lesser) degree, rather, somewhat ◆ Ker mpwelengk. Perrak-artek akngerr-**awaty**arl ra. Akngerr-lkwerarl ra. Atherrk-atherrk, *yellow yellow.* (St) *The* mpwelengk *frog. It's like a frog only a bit bigger. It's a bit bigger. They are a greenish-yellow colour.* ◆ Kartengarl nhenhaw — arlpenty-**awaty** inay. (St) *This one is short — get one that is a bit longer.* ◆ Nhenhan ker ampwang-**awaty** — nhenhan ker anter angerr-**awaty**. (T) *This meat is a bit lean — this meat is a bit fattier.* ◆ Mwerr-**awaty** irrem ayengaw. Mwerr-**awaty** ayeng alhep-alhem. (St) *I'm getting a bit better. I'm going around feeling a bit better.* ◆ Arleng-**awaty** anay, rlkert apek ayeng. (St) *Sit a bit further away, maybe I'm sick.*
2. Indicates that a situation continues for some time; still, while (there's still time). ◆ Uternek uternek alhey, mwerr-awaty aherrkel-**awaty**. (Sa) *[Let's] go in the daytime, when its a bit better and there's some daylight.* ◆ Ker antywantyw yanh antheyaw, antywantyw tha arlkwetyek urinp-**awaty**. (Sa) *Give me that hip-meat there, so that I can eat it while it's still a bit warm.* ◆ Alewatyerr wanmal anengk twerl-apem. Wanmal-**awaty**. (N) *Going along and killing lots of goannas. Rather a lot of them.*
SEE ALSO -lkwer

away (E) *n.kin*
1. elder brother
2. particular (senior) relations with the same skin as your *away*, for example your father's older brother's son or your mother's older sister's son. Whether or not a person is a junior or senior sibling to another can be calculated in terms of the relative ages of their parents.
= kak, kely
awayaty (E) *n.kin*
my/our *away*

awayengkw (E) *n.kin*
your *away*
= kengkw
awayikw, awayeyekw (E) *n.kin*
his/her/their *away*
= kikw

awek (T,E) *n.*
fat, in good condition
SEE ALSO anter, anter angerr, amperrk, angerrety-pwek, artelhampw
awek-irrem (T,E) *vi.*
get fat, put on weight
SEE ALSO anter-irrem, ampwerrem

Awekanty (E) *n.*
the name of a place east of Wilora (Stirling) community

awel-ilem (E) *vt.*
urinate or piss on something (dogs) ◆ Yanh arengkel awel-ilem thewak ngkwenh. (Sa) *That dog is pissing on your swag.*
= mpwerl-ilem

aweleth (E) *n.* [RESPECT LANGUAGE]
1. one
2. on own, alone ◆ Aweletharl ayepel-irrep-irrem-kety — ilkwangketh anem ahanenha. (St) *He is sitting down there all on his own — go over there and keep him [your husband] company [said by a woman to her daughter].*
SEE ALSO anyent
aweleth-irrem (E) *vi.*
end up on your own, become bereaved
SEE ALSO anyent-irrem

Awelh (E) *n.*
Daylight Star, Venus
SEE ALSO Alkerreylp[1], Anthelper, Arwenpeng, Kwerraly Angerr, Kwerraly Rltwa, Kwerraly Urlta
Awelh (E) *n.*
name of place near Adelaide Bore, Woolla Downs. See map p. viii.

awelhem 'listen, hear' SEE UNDER **awem**

awely *n.*
1. women's ceremony ◆ Analpentyel awely alyemel inngek, ankwa aynterl-anentyek. Awely renh alyerl-anemel. 'Alanh alanh kwenh arrekantherr aney.' Analpentyel alyerl-anem. Kel arlkeny arlka ingkwernelhemel, alyemel kel inngel anem alyemel. Innga anem ingkwernelherl-anem. (Sa) *The* analpenty *spirits sing* awely *ceremonies to people while they are asleep. They sing the* awely. *'This is how you've all got to do it.' The* analpenty *sing and then they paint themselves with ceremonial designs as well. Then the people sing and paint themselves up [in the way the spirits have shown them].*
2. the body designs and songs associated with women's ceremonies ◆ Arelh ampwel arrernem awely marl akwekew. (M) *The old woman is putting* awely *designs on the little girl.* ◆ Awely mernem, awely arlkeny-akert kel-akert, mernelhem, 'Kelaw, awely-akertam ayeng anem kwenh, kelaw awely kelarl wek-akertam ayeng anem kwenh.' (N) *Showing the women's ceremony. [The woman] who already has the ceremonial designs on shows herself. 'I already have the designs on — I've already been painted up.'*
SEE ALSO tyepety[1], ilpenty
awely anter
1. rubbing medicine, medicinal fat (anter *'fat'*)
2. fat used for painting up for women's *awely* ceremonies

awely-awely *n.*
lightning, thunder ◆ Awely-awelyel aterel-anthem. Awely-awelyel ltewerl-anem. Tyerrty arrtyanemel irrpenhem. (N) *The lightning frightens people. The lightning strikes and people run inside.* ◆ Awely-awely. Tyart atyetyekek irrpetyangarl — aterarl ap irrem tyart atyetyek ina iwem, iylwemel, rrpwerlekarl aylpemel. Awely-awelyel wem tyart atyetyek-akert. (Sa) *The lightning. [You] shouldn't wear red shirts — people get frightened and they take off red shirts and put on something dark-coloured. Lightning will strike someone who has a red shirt on.*
SEE ALSO kwaty pwer, ngkwarrkenty, angkeyawarr

awem *vt.*
1. hear something; listen to something ◆ Arrpenh apekarl angkep-angkem tha awem. (St) *I can hear someone talking.* ◆ Irlpel thwengk awem. (M) *I am listening to you with my ears.* ◆ Arelhan ankweperr intep-intem awetyakenh. *The woman went back to sleep again and she didn't hear a thing.*
2. understand something ◆ Tha awetyakenh. (Sa) *I can't understand.*
CAN SOUND A BIT LIKE wem[1] *'hit something by throwing something at it'*; wem[2] *'spin hairstring'*; iwem *'throw'*
awelhem *vi.*
1. hear something about yourself ◆ Arreny atyenh ayeng awelhem, tyerrty alenhel anewepewem. (M) *I can hear my name, that the person over there is saying.*
2. hear yourself saying something or talking ◆ Ayeng angkety awelhem *tape recorder*-el. (T) *I can hear myself talking on the tape recorder.* ◆ Rrwar atyengenh ayeng awelhek, *or* awek tha. (T) *I heard my echo.*

3. to feel, have a feeling or sensation ◆ Rlkert ayeng awelhem. Mwerr apekarl ayeng irrem, awelhem ayeng mwerr anemarl. (St) *I feel sick. If I get better, then I'll feel good.* ◆ Angayelemap awelhem. (M) *[I am] feeling hungry.* ◆ Ampwengamp awelhem alhetyeh ayeng. (M) *I really feel good about going.*

menty awelhem
ignore; not take notice of someone, not respond, not listen when someone is talking to you ◆ Menty awelhemel ayeng alhep-alhem, nhakwel atyeng tyel angkep-angkem — menty awelhemel ayeng alhep-alhem. (St) *I am going along ignoring that person who is running me down — I'm not taking any notice.* ◆ Menty awelhem ngenh apek iltenty. Mentyel unta awelhem. (Sa) *If someone swears at you then you can ignore it. You can ignore it.*

awempem (E) *vi.*
sweat, perspire, feel hot ◆ Antyey iylpem awempem. Awempemarl-kety iyntwarr-irray. (Sa) *I am feeling hot and sweaty. Move over a bit because I'm feeling hot.* ◆ Awempemarl-kety pelangket rntwarr-ileyaw. (Sa) *Move these blankets — I'm feeling hot.*
SEE ALSO antyey-irrem, antyey iylpem

awempey (E) *n.*
hot, warm to the touch
SEE ALSO irrkwer

awempey-irrem (E) *vi.*
get hot, feel hot

awengker, **awangker** *n.*
Pacific black duck (*Anas superciliosa*) (?) ◆ Awengker akwek map untherl-aperl kwaty-angkwerr. (N) *The* awengker *ducks swim round in the water.*
= pelyak (?)

awenh, **awenhey** (E) *n.kin*
1. father's sister; aunt
2. mothers's sister-in-law (mother's brother's wife)
3. particular relations with the same skin as your *awenh*
4. a person's great-grandfather's (father's father's father's) sister. If a person calls someone *awenh*, then they will be called *aler* in return.

awenhaty *n.kin*
my/our *awenh* ◆ Awenhaty anwernekingkerrenh anyent. Anyent anem *left*-irrem anwekingkerrenh. (Sa) *We all have one auntie. There is only one of ours left.*

awenhengkw *n.kin*
your *awenh* ◆ Awenhengkw-warl alhay. (P) *Go to your auntie.*

awenhikw (E), **awenheyekw** (E) *n.kin*
his/her/their *awenh*

awenhwek (W,T) *n.kin*
1. your *awenh*
2. his/her/their *awenh* ◆ Anywek alhek angketyeh awenhwehek. *The father went to talk to the child's auntie.*

awenh-awenh *n.kin*
father's sister; aunt etc.
This may be a more affectionate and casual way of talking than using the word *awenh*. ◆ Awenh-awenh then ayeng then irrer alherl-anem kerek tyap anyemayt-warl apek, tyap tyerrerl-alpetyek. (Sa) *Me and my auntie are going hunting to get meat and to dig for witchetty grubs.* ◆ Mam atyengenh-kenh *sister-in-law* 'awenh-awenh' ilem. (T) *I call my mother's sister-in-law 'awenh-awenh'.*

awenh-nheng *n.kin*
a group of two or more people who are related to each other as as aunties and nephews and nieces — as *awenh* and *aler*

awenh-intyerr *n.kin* = **awenh-nheng**
◆ Awenh-intyerr urlart-iperr alhek ina. Kemarr Pwerrerl awenh-intyerr urlart alhek. (P) *Just all the aunties and nephews or nieces went. Kemarr and Pwerrerl, just all the aunties and nieces went.*

awenh-nheng-arey *n.kin*
a group of more than two people who are related to each other as as aunties and nephews and nieces — as *awenh* and *aler*

awenh-nheng-atherr *n.kin*
a person together with their *awenh* or their *aler*; auntie and nephew or niece together

awenh-ankethenh *n.kin*
1. having a close *awenh* still alive
2. someone who is always with their *awenh* ◆ Ayeng awenh-ankethenh. (Sa) *I still have an auntie.*
SEE ALSO -ankethenh

awenk *n.*
teenage girl ◆ Awenk, ampa anetyakenh, marl awenk, werlaty-kweny. (St) *An* awenk *is a young girl, with no kids and no breasts.*
SEE ALSO marl, aleyak

awenk-irrem *vi.*
grow into a teenage girl

awenng *n.*
grave (person's), cemetery ◆ Awenng angernem rtwep, wal irrernng arrernem, ahelhelem artem. Artwel artem. (M) *You dig a hole for the grave, then put the corpse in, then cover it with earth. The men cover it.*
SEE ALSO utnin, ipert

awenp (W,T) *n.*
1. someone who is not allowed to talk because of bereavement ◆ Awenpan anem arelh warlekwert anewekarl aparlp-ilem *or* arelh ywerlt anem kwer kwerenharl aparlp-ilem. Kakey kwerenhel antem mern tyenkerrel arrakert-ilem angketyek. (T) *A woman who has lost her husband, or a woman who has lost her child is* awenp *— she's not allowed to talk. Later on her elder brother gives her some ceremonial food to release her from the ban on speaking.*
2. food given to release speech taboo. Also referred to as *mern awenp.* ◆ Mern awenp anthem arrempewek. Awenp-penh angkemem. (M) Awenp *food is given to his sister. Then, after not being allowed to talk, she can talk again.*
SEE ALSO angkakert-ilem, arrakert-ilem, ulypmakert-ilem, kertemwengk, akerter
awenth (E) *n.*
dogwood (*Acacia sericophylla*). Tree to 6 m high, with long grey-green leaves, pale yellow flowers and long twisted pods.
= akerlperr
SEE ALSO ntyerrm
awenthayt (E) *n.*
grub found on the dogwood. Also referred to as *tyap awenthayt.*
awenth-awenth (E) *n.*
emu's fluffy feathers
= angkwely-angkwely
SEE ALSO apwa, artarr
awenyey-awenyey (E), **winy-winy** (E) *n.* [BABY TALK]
auntie (father's sister)
SEE ALSO awenh
awer1 (E) *n.*
big, heavy, strong, solid ◆ Ampa awer artelh-ampw. (Sa) *A big fat kid.* ◆ Arna nhenh awer, rlpwer anetyakenh. (St) *This tree is solid, without hollows.*
SEE ALSO angerr1, angerrety, artelhampw, artelh3, ilkwa2, rltwa, urlta, rlterrk, twer
awer-awer (E) *n.*
big, heavy, strong, solid
awer2 (W,T) *n.*
bad smelling, stinking ◆ Ker awerarl intyem, arntert. (T) *The meat stinks, smells rotten.*
awerantyerrng (T,E) *n.*
whirlwind, willy-willy
= rrwep-rrwep, aharlparrengk2
SEE ALSO rwarr
-awern *n.ending*
1. Expresses sympathy, pity or sometimes affection; 'Poor (thing)', 'Dear (thing)'. ◆ Angketharrparl ra ahanenhek. Ahanenhek angketharrp. *Like* anyentarl alhek. Anyent-**awern**arl ra alhek. Mey-mey ikwerenhekarl angkep-angkem. (St) *He [her son-in-law] went on his own. He went on his own. The poor thing went, just one, on his own. [She] is talking about her son-in-law.*
SEE ALSO -amperl, -angwel-angwel, -angwen-angwen, -apenh
2. just a little, just a bit ◆ Apwenan arlpa akely-rnem. Areyawarran apwen arlpa ilperr-ilperr-**awern**, antek-**awern**, apwen yanh-lkwer arlpenty-antey. (Sa) *The* apwen *bush has small leaves. The* areyawarr *has flattish leaves, a bit wider, whereas the* apwen *leaves are longer.* ◆ Ngerr-angerr-**awern**. *A biggish one.*
awerr *n.*
boy ◆ Awerr atherr alherl-aperretyam. (M) *Two boys were going for a walk.*
awerr amerrk
big boy, teenage boy
awerr-malangk (T,E)
a lovely boy, a 'champion' (-malangk '*attractive*')
awerr-awerr1 (E) *n.*
a type of large ant bed
SEE ALSO ngkwepey, merntap, kerrth, merntap, pwentereng
awerr-awerr2 (E) *n.*
a type of plant (*Rhodanthe* sp. (?))
awerraty (E) dry waterless country SEE UNDER aherraty
awerreh-alyey-alyey (W,T), **awerrek-alyey-alyey** (W,T) *n.*
lamb's tail, pussy-tails, mulla-mulla (*Ptilotus exaltatus*) (awerr '*boy*'; alyey-alyey '*spirit friend*'). Plant about 60 cm high with smooth green leaves and pink flowers.
= mernteparn, rrweyek-alyey-alyey
SEE ALSO marlek-alyey-alyey, alyey-alyey
= **urreyek-alyey-alyey** (E)
awerreng-iylpwer (E), **awerreng-rlpwer** (E) *n.*
a type of male spirit
SEE ALSO atham-areny, irrernt-areny, aleperenty
awerrepweng (E), **aherrepweng** (E) *n.*
a type of rain cloud. Also referred to as *kwaty awerrepweng.*
SEE ALSO mwekelengk, rlweyang, kwaty akwerrk, kwaty angkarl, ankert1, aperler, akantyer
awerretyepwer (W,T) *n.*
fruit of the bush bean, *angerak* (*Rhyncharrhena linearis*) ◆ Mern angarak apel akwerrk arlkwerl-apem. Awerretyepwer anyent renh. 'Angarak' akenh arlparl. Kenh mern 'awerretyepwer'. (N) *The young pods of the bush*

bean are eaten. That's the same thing as awerretyepwer. *'Angarak' is what the leaves are called, and the edible part is 'awerretyepwer'.*
= werrp, aherretyepwer

awerrk-awerr *n.*
tired, weak, floppy or loose in the body
awerrkelhem *vi.*
feel tired or weak, stumble about weakly
◆ Awerrkelhem ayeng ankwa intetyek. Warrk nhenh-penh awerrkelhety-alpem ayeng, ankwa anem intetyek. Ampethen ap awerrk-awerr. (St) *I feel tired and I want to go to sleep. After this work I go back, feeling tired and weak, and I go to sleep. Tired now. Children can be* awerrk-awerr *as well.*
awerrk-irrem (T) *vi.*
feel tired or weak, stumble about weakly

awerrkem *vt.*
1. rub things against each other to get stuff off ◆ Mern apereltyan awerrkem awerrkem, akemel akemel waly-they. Waly mern-akert arrernem ngkwarl-akert, awerrkem anem, antyam-warl apek. (St) *The white substance made by the lerp-scale insect from the river red gum tree is rubbed off the leaves, the leaves that are picked. The branches with the sweet food on them are laid down, then the [leaves] are rubbed together, [so that the scale falls off] onto a blanket or groundsheet.*
2. twist or wring something out ◆ Mantarr alhewem awerrkem anem renh. Alhewemarl-penhan awerrkem. (St) *Clothes are washed and then they are wrung out. They are wrung out after being washed.*
3. choke someone, wring somebody's or something's neck, strangle someone ◆ Artwa urlaylp, apetyem ingwel atwetyek, awerrkem anem ternng. Urlaylp arwengk aretyakenh kwenh anwantherr. (St) *The kurdaitcha comes in the night to kill people, to wring their necks. We can't see the kurdaitcha.*
SEE ALSO ahenty twerl-akem, ahenty ltwakem, ahenty ultakem, itutnhem, ayenem, alyernem

awerrp[1] *n.*
blood and meat juice from cooked kangaroo. Also referred to as *ker awerrp.* ◆ Ker alhwarl rarl *gravy*-artek anem irrem. Ker aherr awerrp, alhwa. Item renh kel renh akem, kel ker awerrparl thelem apwert-warl apek, ipert angernemel, thelemel. (St) *The blood from the meat goes like gravy.* Awerrp *is kangaroo blood. The [kangaroo] is cooked then the blood is poured onto a stone or into a hole that has been dug.* ◆ Aherr awerrp tyerrty rlkertel antywem. (T) *Sick people drink kangaroo blood.* ◆ Alhwa pwelap-ilelhemel awerrpan antywemarl. (Sa) *[You] drink kangaroo blood to make your blood plentiful.*
SEE ALSO apeynt-apeynt
CAN SOUND A BIT LIKE werrp *'mulga bean'*

awerrp[2] (W) *n.*
a small amount of rain; a small amount of running water. Also referred to as *kwaty awerrp.*

awerrth (E) *n.*
hot ashes or earth (used for cooking or healing) ◆ Ampa akely awerrthel ampernem. (Sa) *The baby is being warmed in the hot ashes.*
= amerrk[2], rtwap
SEE ALSO untyety, arnmeny, arlpa[1], atnmanth, ntyerlp[1]

awerrty *n.*
young teenage boy who has just been 'caught' for ceremonial business ◆ Awerrty-awarr nhenh arratem kwenh. (M) *The young fellas who have been 'caught' for ceremonial business are arriving.*
SEE ALSO alyepelengkw, arwekert, lyaty, arleyarr, amarleyarr, tyakwertekwert, lwekerleny, antingkar

awert[1] *n.*
honey-soaked earth (from a honeyant that has burst open) ◆ Awert arlka awantyem. Aterlk-irrem wal awert yanham awantyerl-anem, arlkwerl-anem *anyway.* Anemel atanthem, aterlk, awanty-ilem anem awert. (N) *[You] suck on the* awert *as well. If the honeyant bursts then you suck on the honey-soaked earth. If you break the honeyant with the crowbar, then you suck on the honey-soaked earth.*
awert-irrem *vi.*
(earth) become soaked with honey from honeyant that has burst open
Awert *n.*
Bullocky Soak Bore, west of the Stuart Highway near Stirling

awert[2] (W), **iwert** (E) *n.*
burrowing bettong (*Bettongia lesueur*). These animals lived in burrows. They ate witchetty grubs and the grubs from the tar vine. People used to trap them by building a yard of spinifex round their holes. They hopped like kangaroos, and were found in salt lake country. No longer found in Central Australia.
= rtway
SEE ALSO alhwet

awertaw (E) *n.*
love grasses (*Eragrostis* spp.), a type of grass with edible seeds
Awertaw (E) *n.*
the name of a place south of Spring Range

aweth *adv.*

1. (doing something) some more; (doing something) again ◆ Aweth mpwaray. (M) *Do it again.* ◆ Aweth apety-alpay. (M) *Come back again.* ◆ Ker rapet alhwengeh atyerrem an twerl-akem renh. Weth artaly-wem aweth arrpenh tyarr-inem aweth twerl-akem rapet, twerl-akem ahenty. (N) *The rabbit is pulled out of its burrow and then its neck is wrung. It's thrown to the ground and then another one is pulled out and its neck is broken.* ◆ Amwek anerl-anem. Kwer akwek arnerrerl-apem arnerrerl-apem aweth apety-alpem, arnerrenty-alpem. (N) *His/her mother is sitting there. The child crawls along, crawls along and then comes back again, crawls back.*

2. more (of something)

CAN SOUND A BIT LIKE weth *'the one being referred to'*

aweth-antey *adv.*

once again, another time, another one ◆ Aweth-antey nthaw. *Give me another.*

aweth aken

once again, another time (aken *'again'*)

awethenty-antey (E) *adv.* [RESPECT LANGUAGE]

1. once again; another time, another one ◆ Yanhenty anem kel ahanerlentyarrety-alperl-wek, yanhenty-anyeman. Awethenty-antey ahanety-alpek. (Sa) *They [respect kin] have already gone back to there. They have gone back again.*

2. the same one, the same person

awey (T,E) *n.*

boy

= rrwey, awerr

awey amerrk (T,E)

young boy about 10–12 years old, teenage boy (before young man ceremonies) (amerrk *'teenage boy'*)

aweyaw *n.*

corpse, dead body

SEE ALSO irrernng, irrewaly, ima, arrwety

aweyek-alyey-alyey (E) *n.*

lamb's tail, pussy-tails, mulla-mulla (*Ptilotus exaltatus*) (awey *'boy'*; alyey-alyey *'spirit friend'*). Plant about 60 cm high with smooth green leaves and pink flowers.

= urreyek-alyey-alyey, mernteparn, awerreh-alyey-alyey

SEE ALSO marlek-alyey-alyey, alyey-alyey

+ay[1] *ending*

1. Goes on the end of a word to add emphasis to what you are saying. Often used when calling out, when trying to get someone's attention, or when telling someone what to do. ◆ Ilanthem apek, *grandmother*-el apek, *mother*-el apek, 'Alhang kwenh, kweray kwenh! *Don't* anngarenty-irrerl-anerl kwenh, ayerrp ilelhemel kwenh. *You* kwerl-warl alherl kalty-irretyeh unta kalty-irretyeh kwenh, Angkeleth unta kalty-irretyeh kwenh.' (N) *Their grandmother or mother might send them. 'Go child! Don't behave as if you don't want to and avoid it. You've got to go to school to learn, to learn English.'*

2. Goes on the end of a verb when someone is telling a person to do that action. ◆ Manterr nhenh-lkwer apek angwaremel angkem, 'Atyeng anth**ay** kwenh, mantarr mwerr kwenh!' *[If you] see a really nice dress and you would like one like it you might say, 'Give it to me, give me that lovely dress!'* ◆ Iltyel angern**ay**! (M) *Scoop it up with your hands!* ◆ Ayenp kekew**ay**! (M) *Peel the skin off!*

SEE ALSO +a, +erlanerr, +errirr, +ap

ay[2] (E) *part.*

'Hey!' ◆ *Ay*, apety-alperliwa ahern-kety! (Sa) *Hey, come back because of the dust!*

ayak-arrernem (W,T) *vt.*

pile things up in a heap, pile things on top of each other, tip things out and pile them up (arrernem *'put'*) ◆ Rnpwernp anwern apertarl akem, lyerl intey, inteyel anerl *everywhere* anerl. Apetyemel anwern arem, 'Nhenhey *everywhere* anem kwenh'. Ntywem akerl-apem akerl-apem akerl-apem, *heap* arrernem, intey kweram irrperlp-irrpenhemel akem ingkerr anthwerr. Ayak-arrernem. Ayak-arrernem akin. *We pick pituri in the hills — it grows in the caves and everywhere. We come along and see it and say, 'Here it is growing everywhere'. We go along picking it, heaping it up and then we go into the cave and pick the whole lot. Pile them up. We make a pile of pituri.* ◆ Rapety apek ayak-arrernem *drum*-warl apek, kel awetharl alpem kel aweth yak-arrernety-alpem. (T) *[You] might heap the rubbish up in a drum, then go back and get some more and then go back and pile some more in.*

SEE ALSO aharl arrernem, aharl-wem, lyernt arrernem, mpwer tywenem, antyakwer-wem, antarr-arrernem

ayakem *vt.*

stop someone from doing something ◆ Uyarn mwetek ayakem. Uyarn-antey ayakem renh mwetek. Uyarn ayakem *stop*-em ilemel, iltyirrem iltyirrem uyarn-antey, akwenp alhek. (St) *I tried in vain to stop the car. I tried to stop by waving at it. I waved and waved and tried to stop it, but [the people] kept on going without taking any notice.* ◆ Thwengk ayakem,

'Alhetyal anay'. (M) *I'm stopping you, 'Don't go — sit down'.* ◆ Tha ayakem ahel-irrerl-anekerr. 'Menty aneyaw iltetyal kwenh!' (St) *I stop them in case they start fighting. 'Leave it, sit down and don't swear!'* ◆ Parrp nthweyaw, ayaketyek! (T) *Run quickly and stop them [fighting]!*
SEE ALSO angernt-wem, arnpakem, arrngert-wem, akayak-ilem, apatel-anthem

Ayalpayalp (W) *n.*
the name of a place in the Coniston area

Ayamp (T,E) *n.*
1. the name of a place in the Arlwekarr area, Stirling Station
2. the name of a place in the Yambah Station area

ayang (T) grey hair, grey-headed SEE UNDER **aywa**

ayapay (E) *n.*
container made from a powdered-milk tin, saucepan, a little wooden dish, or bark. Used for collecting smaller quantities of bush foods which are then put into larger containers ◆ Ayapay tha akngerl-anem, *milk tin* tyampit apek tyampit atyenh, kel kerl-apem kwer-warl. *Alright* kel pwelap anem arrernenhem apek *bucket*-warl apek. Mern yerrakwerr inerl-alhem ayapay-warl. (St) *I'm carrying my little container along, my milk tin or my billycan, and I am collecting food in it. When it's full I put the food into a bucket. Collecting bush onions in a small container.*

ayarrty (E) *n.*
fire made to get rid of flies or mosquitos. Also referred to as *ura ayarrty*. ◆ Ameng-kety ayarrtyel anemel arlkweyaw, ura iterel. (St) *Sit beside the fire to eat, to get rid of the flies.*
ayarrty-rnem (E) *vi.*
shine in the distance (light or bushfire) ◆ Ayarrty-rnepernem arleng innga *bushfire*. (Sa) *The bushfire is shining a long way off in the distance.*
SEE ALSO ampem[1], ampem[2]

ayatwem, ayatem (T) *vt.*
sing (generally in a group), sing along; sing a ceremony; sing so that others can dance ◆ Arelh mapel arrpel map ayatem, arrpenh mapel rntwem — tyepety-akert, arlkeny-akert. (T) *Some of the other women sing, and others dance — the ones with the ceremonial designs on.* ◆ Ayatwem rarey artwa mapel, marl map anthep-irrerl-anem. (St) *The men sing, and the women dance.* ◆ Artwangel ayatwem anmanty. (M) *The man is singing the* anmanty *ceremony.*
SEE ALSO alyem, alyelhem

ayay (W,T) *n.*
spring (water)
= apinty
SEE ALSO intyang, angenty

ayemem (W,T) *vt.*
1. not recognise someone; behave as if you don't know about a person or thing ◆ 'Ayengem nta ayemepemem kwenh.' Arrpenh angkerleng, '*Ah, no* tha ngwenh ayemem kwenh, kwer yanham tha ayemem'. (M) *'You are pretending that you don't know me.' And then the other person says, 'Ah, it's not you that I don't recognise, it's that kid over there.'*
2. tell someone to go away ◆ Ayemem mereng anpwem. (M) *Hunting [the person] away from the camp.* • SEE ALSO alharlkwem, anpwem
3. get jealous or possessive about something ◆ Arelh yanhel ayemem ker kwerenheng. (T) *That woman is getting jealous over her meat.*
SEE ALSO yem
= **uyemem** (E)

ayenem (E) *vt.*
ask
SEE ALSO apawenhem
CAN SOUND A BIT LIKE ayernem *'tie something up'*

ayeng *prn.*
1. I. This pronoun is used as the subject of an intransitive verb action (i.e. representing the 'doer' of the verb action). *Tha* or *thang* is used with transitive verbs. See Appendix 1. ◆ Ngwath ayeng apep-apem. (M) *I keep walking about alone.* ◆ Anwerlkel angkem ayeng. (M) *I am speaking with fear.* ◆ Ayeng ahenty-anem marl yanh kwer. (T) *I like that girl over there.*
2. me. This pronoun can also be used in the object part of the sentence (i.e. representing the person or thing the verb action is 'done to') ◆ Apentem unta ayeng ingkerneng, kel unta ayeng arety-alhem. (T) *You follow me from behind and then you see me.* • SEE ALSO ayengenh, ayenh
3. my (of body parts) ◆ Kapert ayeng arntem, katyerr apek tepwerl-akert tharl arlkwek, kapert anem ayeng arntem, ahelhel iletyakenh. (St) *I have a headache after eating bush raisins that still had a bitter coating on them because they hadn't been cleaned on the ground.* ◆ Iltya ayeng wangkek. Ingka apek. Urepenh apek. Lyekel apek atanthek, arnel apek atanthek, wangkek. Kapert ayeng wangkem, atwekarl apek ayenh. (St) *My hands have swollen up. Or my feet. Maybe from the fire. Or maybe I was pierced by a prickle, or poked by a branch. My head is swelling up after I was hit.* • SEE ALSO atyenh, atyengenh

-ayeng (W,T) with someone, accompanied by someone SEE UNDER **-arleng**[2]

ayengey (E) [BABY TALK] father's father and his brothers and sisters SEE UNDER **angang**

ayenh, ayengenh (W,T) *prn.*
me. This pronoun is used in the object part of the sentence (i.e representing the person or thing the verb action is 'done to'). ◆ Ayenh angernay, artep ayenh angernay! (Sa) *Scratch me, scratch my back!* ◆ Rernem ayenh awenh-awenh akem, than aler-alerarl akem renh. (Sa) *They call me* 'awenh-awenh' *(auntie) and I call them* 'aler-aler' *(niece, nephew).* ◆ Alkngarr-ilek ayenh yanhel. (St) *That person warned me.* ◆ Artwang arawerrng-akertel ayengenh aterel-anthem, ayengenh akwet atwetyakenh; ayeng ater-irreperrem atwetyakenh. (T) *This powerful* (?) *man frightens me, always threatens to hit me; I'm always frightened of being hit.*
SEE ALSO ayeng

ayenp *n.*
1. bark; skin of fruits
= arntap
SEE ALSO rltimp[1]
2. skin (of a person or animal) ◆ Ayenparl akernengan. Ayenp nhenh apetyem amwelteng arlka. Kenh alhwarl kweneng *run*-irrerl-anem, ingkewarn-athek, iltyewarn-athek, alakenh kapert-warn-athek. (T) *Skin is on the surface. For example, there is skin all the way along the arm. Whereas blood runs on the inside, towards the feet, the hands and to the head.*
arna ayenp
bark (of a plant) (arna *'plant', 'tree'*)
paty ayenp (W,T)
flat or sagging breasts (paty *'breast'*)

ayep *n.*
tar vine (*Boerhavia schomburgkiana*). A creeping herb with stems trailing up to 1 m along the ground. ◆ Ayep, alewatyerrel arlkwerl-apem, anter angerr mparelhetyek. *Goannas eat tar vine to make themselves fat.* ◆ Ayep arlkwetyam, inyetyamey warek, arlatyeyart inyetyam ayep yenh, arlkwetyam atyerremel arlkwetyam ayep yenh. (N) *The tar vine roots were eaten, just dug up like a pencil yam and cooked and eaten.*
= irlperleny
CAN SOUND A BIT LIKE yep *'umbilical cord'*
ayep-areny (W), **ayepayt** (T,E), **ayepaty** *n.*
grub from the tar vine. Also referred to as *tyap ayepayt* or *tyap ayep-areny*. ◆ Ayepaytan ayepel anep-anem. (St) *The* ayepayt *grub lives on the tar vine.*

ayepel-irrem *vi.* [RESPECT LANGUAGE]
1. sit ◆ Ngwarrengkw nhakw ayepel-irretyel. (Sa) *Your husband is sitting over there [said by a woman to her daughter].* ◆ Ngwarrengkw twertertel-ayerr ayepel-irrepirrem. (St) *Your husband is sitting in the car [said by a woman to her daughter].* ◆ Ngwarr-nheng ayepel-irrepirrem ngkwelyel. (St) *My daughter and her husband are sitting in the shade [said by the mother of the woman].*
2. sit down, be seated
3. be, am, is, are, were, be (in a particular way)
4. live, stay (in a place)
ayepel-irrety-alpem *vi.*
come back and settle down in a place
SEE ALSO anem[1], angerr-irrem, anety-alpem

ayepert (E) *n.* [RESPECT LANGUAGE]
1. head
2. headache ◆ Ngwarrengkw kweyay ayepert-ayerr-akertek ahaneyna. (Sa) *Daughter, go to your husband who has a headache [said by a woman].*
SEE ALSO kapert[1], akamperrng

ayernem, arernem (E) *vt.*
1. tie or fasten something; roll something up ◆ Aherr alwerrngel ayernem. (M) *Tying it up with kangaroo sinew.* ◆ Ayernem mantarr, *swag* apek ayernem, akert atherr apek ayernem *swag*. Kel alhem anem. *Roll*-em *up* weth-lkwer ayernem. (St) *Rolling up the clothes, or maybe the swag, rolling up the two ends. Then heading off.* Ayernem *is rolling something up.* ◆ Ayernekarl apek — urrek tha irlwerl-alhey. (St) *It might have been tied up — wait while I untie it.*
SEE ALSO anhwert-ilem, artaper-ilem, artaper-wem, rwelemap-ilem
2. wring something out ◆ Kwaty-penh tha ayernetyek *wet* tek-arrernetyeh twern-warn. (M) *After washing it I'm going to wring it out and hang it in the sun to dry.* • SEE ALSO awerrkem
CAN SOUND A BIT LIKE ayenem *'ask'*
ayernelhem, arernelhem (E) *vi.*
tie something round yourself; tie something up that is on yourself ◆ Petyetel ingka atherr ayernelhem. (N) *Tying up the two feet with a* petyet *[bark] bandage.* ◆ Anketyel kapert ayernelhem. (M) *Tying the headscarf round your head.*
= irrtyernelhem

-ayerr *n.ending* [RESPECT LANGUAGE]
Goes on the end of some ordinary language words and some avoidance language words when the special respect register is being used. ◆ Atnem-**ayerr** irrepetherl-alhay ngwarr-nheng ahanetyek. *Go and get the digging stick so that my daughter and her husband can go.* ◆ Ngwarrekengkw ahanerl-

iletyek arlpmeny-**ayerr** then. (Sa) *Take the ashes and the other things to your husband.* ◆ Ntwerr-**ayerr**-akert kwey ngwarrengk ahanemay, tyety-**ayerr**ek, ker aherrek. (Sa) *Daughter, your husband is going hunting with a gun, for kangaroo.* ◆ Ngkwepey-**ayerr**el ayepelirrerliwerretyel yanhentyak, arrengakw-**ayerr**el. *They are all sitting over there on the other side amongst the ant hills.*

ayerrer *n.*
north, in a northerly direction ◆ Ayerrer-they ayeng apety-alpek. (St) *I came back from the north.*
SEE ALSO antekerr, altwerl, ingerr, angerrakw
ayerrer arraty
due north (arraty *'straight', 'correct'*)
ayerrel-penh (E), **aywerrel-penh** (E) *n.*
north ◆ Ayeng aywerrel-penh-they apety-alpek. *I came back from the north.*
ayerrer-ayerrer (E) *n.*
1. north-east
2. north-west [SOME SPEAKERS]
ayerrer altwerl
north-west (altwerl *'west'*)
ayerrer ingerr (W,T), **ayerrer ikngerr** (E)
north-east (ingerr *'east'*)
ayerrereng *n.*
north wind; from the north ◆ Rlkang apetyem ayerrereng angerr, alhem alakenh-atheh, antekerr-atheh. (N) *A big wind comes from the north, and blows that way, to the south.*

ayerrp-ilem *vt.*
keep something for yourself; don't give things to others; hold onto your things; take someone else's things (?) ◆ Ker apek atyenh mern apek atyenh, ayerrp-ilem. Arrpenh mapek anthetyang tha ayerrp-ilemel arlkwetyek. (St) *I'm hanging on to my meat and food myself. I'm not giving it to the others, I'm eating it myself.* ◆ Ayerrp-ilem, arrpenharl ankey nkem wal tha ayerrp-ilemarl, angayel anthety kweny. (St) *Others might ask me for [food], but I'm hungry and I'm not going to give them any.* ◆ Ilekety unta ayerrp-iletyel? Ayenh antha. Angayakw tha arlkwetyek. (Sa) *Why are you keeping it to yourself? Give some to me. I'm hungry and I want to eat.*
ayerrp ilelhem
1. say that you want to keep things to yourself
2. tell someone not to pester you; say you're not going somewhere ◆ 'Ayeng anetyek anyent — pwarrk anthetyal, apawenhenemel.' Ayerrp ilelhem. 'Pwarrkem ayeng imperrirra!' (T) *'I want to sit here on my own — don't tire me out asking for things.' Telling someone not to pester you. 'I'm tired so leave me alone!'*

ayet (E) *n.*
really fat, having rolls of stomach fat ◆ Mern angerr arlkwep-arlkwerl ayet angerr irrek. (St) *He'd eat lots of food and that's how he got really fat.*
ayet angerr (E)
having rolls of fat (angerr[1] *'lots of'*)
ayet-irrem (E) *vi.*
get fat, put on weight

-ayeth *n.ending*
On words for body parts, shows that this part is in contact with the surface on which the body rests. ◆ Ampwethel-**ayeth** anem. *Kneel [i.e. rest on knees].* ◆ Atnel-**ayeth** unta anetyel arrpenhek mpwelherl-anemel. (Sa) *You are sitting on your arse and waiting for other people [to do things].*

ayety-ilem (W) winnow seed (rapid sideways movement of coolamon) SEE UNDER **ahety-ilem**

ayew *n.*
waist, soft part above the hip

ayewarr (E) *n.*
bad, rotten (emu meat)
ayewarr-irrem (E) *vi.*
go off, become rotten (emu meat)

ayey (W,T) *n.*
news, story, message, conversation ◆ Kwerr akwek mapel ayey ilep-ilem. Kwerr akwek mapel ayey angernerl-apem, angerr map-warn angernerl-apem ayey kwenh, kwerr akwek nhel map kwenh. (N) *The little girls are telling stories. They are going and telling the stories to the grown-ups. That's what these little girls are doing.* ◆ Arrwekeleny, waram ina ayey iletyam, ilety-alpetyam, awetyarl-alpetyam-penharl arrpenh alenh, ayey ilety-alpetyam. (N) *In the olden days they used to tell the story, go to another place and when they heard the story they'd come back and tell the others.*
ayey ilem (W,T)
tell a story (ilem *'tell', 'say'*)
ayey ilelhem (W,T)
tell a story, tell a story about yourself (ilelhem *'say something about yourself'*)
ayeyalth (W,T) *n.*
someone who tells stories (true or untrue), a 'news-carrier'

ayla (E) we (we two) SEE UNDER **ila**

aylak (E) we (we two) SEE UNDER **ilak**

aylanth (E) we (we two) SEE UNDER **ilanth**

aylayl (E) *n.*
boomerang ◆ Artwel aylayl mpwaretyel ker aherr wetyek. (Sa) *Men make boomerangs to*

throw at kangaroos.
= alyang, kayl
SEE ALSO arrak
aylayl iylkwa (E)
hooked boomerang, number 7 boomerang
= alyang rlkwang
aylayl arrethaker (E)
outer sharp edge (or end) of a boomerang (arrethaker '*edge or side*')
aylayl ilperr (E)
inner edge of a boomerang (?) (ilperr '*flat*')
= kayl ilperr

aylem (E) sing SEE UNDER **alyem**

ayleng (E) left-handed SEE UNDER **alyeng**

aylep (E) hairstring belt or strap SEE UNDER **alyep**[1]

ayler (E) smooth, slippery SEE UNDER **arler**

aylern (E) we (we two) SEE UNDER **ilern**

aylern-ingkerr (E) we (we two) SEE UNDER **ilern-ingkerr**

aylernak (E) we (we two) SEE UNDER **ilernak**

aylernanth (E) we (we two) SEE UNDER **ilernanth**

aylernem (E) twist or wring something out SEE UNDER **alyernem**

aylpa (E) leaf, leaves SEE UNDER **arlpa**[2]

aylpar anenhem (E), **aylper anenhem** (E) *vi.*
set (sun) ◆ Aherrk aylpar anenhem. (St) *The sun is setting.*
SEE ALSO iltyem-anem

aylparernem (E) hang down, dangle, swing from something SEE UNDER **arlparernem**

aylpat-aylpat (E) *n.*
desert lantern, keeled lantern-bush (*Abutilon otocarpum*). A plant about 50 cm high with broad leaves and bright yellow flowers.

Aylpatyarlayntem (E) *n.*
name of a sandhill on the south side of the Sandover Highway, Utopia (Angarapa Aboriginal Land Trust) area (lit. 'where the breasts are lying')

aylpel-ayerr (E) *n.* [RESPECT LANGUAGE]
hairstring
SEE ALSO irrkety, alyep

aylpem (E) *vi.*
1. go in; enter; get into or go inside something; burrow into something
◆ Mwetek-warl ayeng aylpenheyaw kwenel anenhetyek. *I'm getting into the car so that I can sit inside as we go along.*
2. go to something; attend something
3. go underneath something ◆ Ahekwenaytan ahern-areny, aper intert-utek — *not* artekerrel — arwa ahernel aylpem. Artekerr angkwerr anperel ayntenhem, alhwengan ikwerenh. (Sa) *The* ahekwenayt *grub lives in the ground at the base of the river red gum tree — not in the roots — they just live underneath the ground. Their holes are found around beside the roots of the tree.*
4. swim
5. go down (sun or moon), set (sun or moon)
6. put on (clothes, shoes) ◆ *Shirt*-ek aylpetyel ayeng. Mwerr-angkerek. *I'm putting the shirt on. The nice one.* ◆ Awely-awely. Tyart atyetyekek irrpetyangarl aterarl ap irrem tyart atyetyek ina iwem, iylwemel, rrpwerlekarl aylpemel. Awely-awelyel wem tyart atyetyek-akert. (Sa) *The lightning. [You] shouldn't wear red shirts — people get frightened and they take off red shirts and put on something dark-coloured. Lightning will strike someone with a red shirt on.*
SEE ALSO irrpem

aylpenty-aylpenty (T,E), **arlpenty-arlpenty** (E) *n.*
a type of small snake (?)
= aylperl-aylperl

Aylper (E) a Warlpiri person or Warlpiri people SEE UNDER **Arlper**[1]

aylper anenhem (E) set (sun) SEE UNDER **aylpar anenhem**

aylperl (E) honeydew found on mulga SEE UNDER **arlperl**

aylperl-aylperl (E) *n.*
a type of snake (?)
= aylpenty-aylpenty

aylperlayt (T,E) *n.*
grub from the branch of the river red gum, *aper*, cossid moth grub (*Xyleutes* sp. (?))
= ingweneng, perlanty, ngkenhar, aperayt
SEE ALSO aper
Aylperlayt iwerr (E) *n.*
name of a place west of Arlwekarr, Stirling Station area (iwerr '*path*')

aylperleny (E) a type of plant SEE UNDER **irlperleny**

aylperr (E) *n.*
fish
= irrpenng, pety
CAN SOUND A BIT LIKE arlperr *'whitewood'*; alperr *'leaf'*

aylperrepwenty (E) someone who steps in to stop a fight or to diffuse trouble SEE UNDER **arlperrepwenty**

aylpmenh (E) mother's mother, granny SEE UNDER **ipmenh**

aylpmerrem (E) *vi.*
sleep a lot; lie around feeling sleepy, drowsy, lifeless, lazy or lethargic ◆ 'Aylpmerrerl-anetyang akem-irrenherr-arey ankwantey aleth aynterl-anetyang.' Ileman akemelh-ilem. 'Aylpmerrerl-anetyang akem-irrenherr-arey.' *'Don't you all lie round sleeping all the time, get up.' That's what [you] say to get people up. 'Get up — don't lie round sleeping all the time.'*
= rrwempem

aylpwar angem (T,E), **aylpwar akngem** (E), **aylpwer angem** (E) *vt.*
carry something on the shoulder (e.g. a kangaroo) ◆ Artwel ra ker aylpwerel angeynetyam ulyewarl. (Sa) *The man carried the kangaroo back to the shade, slung across his shoulder.*
SEE ALSO ntywel angem, alpalyel angem, intarlp angem, ntwarlp angem, anhwert angem, intwerl angem

aylur (E)**, aylwer** (E) a type of gecko SEE UNDER **arlwer**

aylwer (E) young seed pods of the dogwood SEE UNDER **alywer**[1]

aympa (E), **aynpa** (E) *n.*
1. pouch ◆ Aherr aympa. Ker apwert-areny aympakert ingkerrek. Arwangan aympakert arrpemarl anem. Aympan ikwerenh anem ampa akelyel ikwerel aynterl-apetyel. (Sa) *A kangaroo's pouch. Euros and all have pouches. Rock wallabies have pouches as well. [The young ones] lie in the little pouch [as the mother] goes along.*
= peth
SEE ALSO pewaty
2. groin or paunch of a person (?)
aympel angem
carry (baby animal) in pouch
= alhelth-angem

aymparrk anem (E), **aynparrk anem** (E) *vi.*
sit cross-legged ◆ Aymparrk anep-anem ayeng. (St) *I am sitting down cross-legged.*
= arntimerrk, arntarlperrk
aymparrk-aymparrk (E), **aynparrk-aynparrk** (E) *n.*
bandy legs ◆ Lyweper atherr aymparrk-aymparrk alhep-alhem. (St) *Going along with bandy legs.*

aymparrk-aymparr (E) *n.*
a type of bush medicine plant (?)

aympaymp (E) yellow-throated miner bird SEE UNDER **impaymp**

aympelh (E), **aynpelh** (T,E) *n.*
1. wing ◆ Aympelh angerrarl ikwerenh, arwengerrp-kenh. (St) *The bush turkey's wings are big.* ◆ Lthep-lthep akwekel manteran altywer-altywer-ilem, interrkel-artek arlkwem. Ingkan akwek akwek. Aympelh-akert anetyakenh. (St) *The little* lthep-lthep *beetle chews holes in clothes, eats them like a white ant does. They have small legs and no wings.*
2. feather
= arlpa[2]
aympelh-ayerr (E), **aynpelh-ayerr** (E) *n.* [RESPECT LANGUAGE]
bush turkey ◆ Ngwarrekengkw-arlek irrepetherl-wa aympelh-ayerr atyeng. (Sa) *Go and get some bush turkey from your husband for me [woman talking to her daughter].*
SEE ALSO artew, arwengerrp

aympernem (E), **aynpernem** (E), **iynpernem** (E) *vt.*
winnow seed (rapid sideways movement of coolamon); yandy. When winnowing seed the coolamon is also shaken in a vertical motion referred to as *ilpem*[1]. ◆ Panthel aynpernem. (St) *Winnowing [seeds] in a wooden dish.* ◆ Ahernarl iwemarl yanh, aympernemel, ilpemel yanh mern urlart anetyek. *Leaf* yanh iwemel arna arlka, ilpem ilpem. (St) *[Seed] is yandied to get rid of the dirt, it's winnowed so that just the clean seed remains. The leaves and sticks are thrown away.*
= ahety-ilem
SEE ALSO ilpem[1], irrkertert-wem

aymperr (E), **aynperr** (E) *n.*
flat, wide, roomy ◆ Aymperr-artek antyam weyaw, anetyek apek intetyek apek. (St) *Spread the blanket out wide to sit on, or to sleep on.*
SEE ALSO arlpaw, antek, ilperr
aymperr-irrem (E), **aynperr-irrem** (E) *vi.*
spread out wide
aymperr-ilem (E), **aynperr-ilem** (E) *vt.*
spread something out wide ◆ Aymperr-ilem tha antyam nhenh urrpety anetyek. (St) *I am spreading this blanket out wide so that a few people can sit on it.*
aymperrelh-ilem (E), **aynperrelh-ilem** (E) *vt.*
= aymperr-ilem
SEE ALSO antek-ilem

ayna (E) father SEE UNDER **anya**[1]

aynakerr (E) they (more than two) SEE UNDER **inakerr**

aynanelhem (E) make a fuss of someone SEE UNDER **anyanelhem**

aynantherr (E) they (more than two) SEE UNDER **inantherr**

aynaty (E) my/our father SEE UNDER **anya**[1] 'father'

aynelh-ilem (E) drop someone or something SEE UNDER **anyelh-ilem**

aynem (E) fall off something SEE UNDER **anyem**[1]

aynengkw (E) SEE UNDER **anya**[1] 'father'

aynenheng-nheng (E) SEE UNDER **anya**[1] 'father'

aynenkethenh (E) SEE UNDER **anya**[1] 'father'

ayneparety (E) SEE UNDER **anya**[1] 'father'

aynikw (E) SEE UNDER **anya**[1] 'father'

ayningkerr (E) they (more than two) SEE UNDER **inengkerr**

aynpa (E) pouch SEE UNDER **aympa**

aynparrk anem (E) sit cross-legged SEE UNDER **aymparrk anem**

aynpaynp (E) yellow-throated miner bird SEE UNDER **impaymp**
aynpekenh (E) small rockhole with a stone lid SEE UNDER **impekenh**
aynpelh (T,E) wing SEE UNDER **aympelh**
aynpernem (E) winnow seed (rapid sideways movement of coolamon); yandy SEE UNDER **aympernem**
aynperr (E) flat, wide, roomy SEE UNDER **aymperr**
ayntarrp-ilem (E), **antyarrp-ilem** (E) *vt.*
1. play a joke on someone, tease someone ◆ Ayeng ayntarrp-ilemel angkem ngkweng. Urrtyirremel war ayntarrp-ayntarrp. (St) *I am playing a joke on you. I am just making it up, joking.*
2. make a wrong suggestion about someone, tell untrue stories, lie ◆ Ayntarrp-ilem, ilenty arrpantey, *story* ilenty arrpantey ayntarrp-ilemel ilerl-anem, urrtyirremel. (Sa) *Making out as if to tell the [true] story, but not telling the truth, lying.* ◆ Akengenty-akengenty yal angkep-angkem, ayntarrp-ayntarrp angkep-angkem. (St) *That person is talking nonsense, not telling the truth.*
SEE ALSO urrtyirrem, ilpernem
ayntem (E) lie, lie down SEE UNDER **intem**
-ayntem verb action continues for some time SEE UNDER **+ety-aynt+**
aynwer (E), **aynur** (E), **iynwer** (E) *n.*
bee (or just the queen bee) (?)
SEE ALSO ameng
aypmenh (E), **aypmenhey** (E) mother's mother; grandmother, granny SEE UNDER **ipmenh**
aypmerr (E) drop or drip of water SEE UNDER **imerr**
+ayt (E) Goes on the end of the names of certain plants to form the name of the grub that is found on that plant. SEE UNDER **+aty**[2]
aytankern (E) types of mistletoe SEE UNDER **atyankern**
aytem (E) *vt.*
pick up firewood, collect firewood ◆ Ura aytem. (Sa) *Picking up firewood.*
SEE ALSO inem
CAN SOUND A BIT LIKE artem *'cover over'*
ayternem (E) *vt.*
peep out from behind something, look at something from behind something
= kert-arem, tyel-arem
CAN SOUND A BIT LIKE arternem[1] *'chop wood'*; arternem[2] *'straighten something'*
aytey (E) younger brother or sister SEE UNDER **atyey**
aytnakerr (E) they (more than two) SEE UNDER **inakerr**
aytnantherr (E) they (more than two) SEE UNDER **inantherr**
aytnem (E) fall off something SEE UNDER **anyem**[1]
aytningkerr (E) they (more than two) SEE UNDER **inengkerr**
aytwelth (E) *n.*
1. toothache
= kayltwelth
2. a type of small snake (?) • SEE ALSO arranyenganyeng
aytwelth-akert (E) *n.*
having a toothache
= kayltwelth-akert, rtety arlkwem
aytwerlk (E) white clay SEE UNDER **atywerlk**
aytwertek (E), **atywertek** (E) *n.*
black-breasted buzzard (*Hamirostra melanosternon*) ◆ Aytwertekel atherneng iyltem arrakertel. (Sa) *The black-breasted buzzard cracks emu eggs open with its beak.* ◆ Aytwertek angkerrerl-arerl-apem athernengek ra. Anwernekingkerrenharl ap ra. Arerl-anem anem ra arwengekikw, anyelkel inetyek. Ratherr ap anganekan Atnangkerel. (Sa) *The black-breasted buzzard goes around looking for emu eggs. It belongs to all of us [from Atnangker country. It goes around looking for its relations — the Dreaming that is closely related to it — so that it can steal them. Both of them [the black-breasted buzzard and the emu egg] originated at Atnangker.*
= lywerlperr, atwertim
aywa, **aywang** (W,T), **ayang** (T) *n.*
1. grey hair, grey-headed ◆ Ayengan aywa anemarl ampek. (St) *My hair is getting grey now.*
2. old or senior person ◆ Arelh ayang. *Old woman.* ◆ Artwang aywang. *Old man.* ◆ Lyetant ampeynepeynem ayeng aywa. (St) *I am getting old now.*
kapert aywa, kapert aywang (W,T), **kapert ayang** (T)
grey-headed (kapert[1] *'head'*)
aywa ampem, aywang ampem (W,T), **ayang ampem** (T)
1. go grey (hair), go white-headed (ampem[2] *'cook', 'heat up'*)
2. grow old ◆ Atherrkek-amparrarl anek-penh, ngartek alakenhek-amparr kel aywa anem ampem, mperlkem anem. (St) *At first the hair is not grey —* atherrk *— like you at first, and then the hair goes grey, goes white.*
aywerrem (W,T), **aywirrem** (E)
aywang-irrem (W,T), **ayang-irrem** (T) *vi.*
1. go grey (hair), go white-headed
2. grow old
aywek (E) *n.*
rotten
SEE ALSO arntert, iynteng

aywek-irrem (E) *vi.*
go rotten ◆ Ker nhenh aywekarl-irrekaw. (St) *This meat has gone rotten.*

aywek-aywek *adv.*
calling out to someone (?)
aywek-aywek-irrem *vi.*
1. make a sound to get someone's attention ◆ Aywek-aywek-irrem, ra awetyek. Mwerikwel awetyek, ampelikw apek. (St) *Making a sound so that they can hear. So that her son-in-law or nephew can hear.*
SEE ALSO unpernem, unpernelhem
2. set a story straight, say sorry (?)
aywek-aywek angkem (E)
ask someone to come out and face you; ask for an explanation (?) ◆ Aywek-aywek ywarn angkek, arratetyakenh awemel apek. (St) *I was calling out but he didn't come out to face me and listen to me.*

aywel (T,E) *n.*
sandhill grevillea, rattlepod grevillea (*Grevillea stenobotrya*). Shrub to 3 m high, with long narrow leaves and white or yellow bottlebrush flowers. Always grows on sandhills.

aywelernety (W), **aywelerneyt** (E), **aywelern** (E) *n.* [RESPECT LANGUAGE]
north ◆ Aywelernety ahanewarrem. (M) *They [respect kin] are going to the north.*
SEE ALSO ayerrer, altwerlernety, antwekenety, ngwelernety
aywelern-athek (E) *n.* [RESPECT LANGUAGE]
north, in a northerly direction ◆ Ahanenherl-wek aywelern-athek. (St) *[My son-in-law] went to the north.*

aywepem (T,E) *vt.*
hunt someone or something away; chase someone or something away, get rid of someone ◆ Aywepem alperlewetyek. 'Angath apetyarr-alhetyang alperlewaw.' (Sa) *Hunting them away so that they go back. 'Go back and don't come close.'* ◆ Arengk tha aywepem, kwaty atyenharl antywem. (St) *I am hunting away the dog that's been drinking my water.*
= anpwem
SEE ALSO alharlkwem
aywepelhem (T,E) *vi.*
chase someone or something away from yourself ◆ 'Ayeng aywepelhek artwang ngkwenh mert-hety, ayeng aywepelhek.' Marl arrpenhek ilelhem. 'Npwek tha kwenh.' (T) *'I chased your husband away, I sent him off.' Telling the other woman that that's what you did. 'I hunted him away.'*
= anpwelhem
SEE ALSO alharlkwelhem

aywerr *n.*
a whirring, whooshing or rumbling noise (such as that made by the wind or an engine); a howling or blowing sound (wind) ◆ Aywerr angkem, mwetek mwerr anem atyenh aywerr angkem. (St) *My car is all right now, it's making a whirring noise.* ◆ Iylka aywerr angkentyem. (T) *The wind is howling in this direction.*
aywerr angkem
make a whirring, whooshing or rumbling noise (such as that made by the wind or an engine); make a howling or blowing sound (wind) (angkem *'talk'*)
aywerr angerr
a loud noise (angerr[1] *'big'*)
aywerr angkenh-angkenh (E) *n.* [RESPECT LANGUAGE]
car (lit. 'noise maker')
SEE ALSO mwetekay

aywerrem SEE UNDER **aywa** 'grey-headed, old'

aywerrty-aywerrty (E) *adv.*
noisily (of a person moving) ◆ Aywerrty-aywerrty urlaylp apetyem ingwel. (Sa) *In the night the kurdaitcha comes noisily.* ◆ Akem-irremel awem, alerl aywerrty-aywerrty apetyek aweyaw. Kel akem-irremel awemel ankwarl aynterlanenty-iperr. (Sa) *[You] get up and hear the noise of footsteps coming. You get up and listen after being asleep.*
= arerrth-arerrth

aywert *n.*
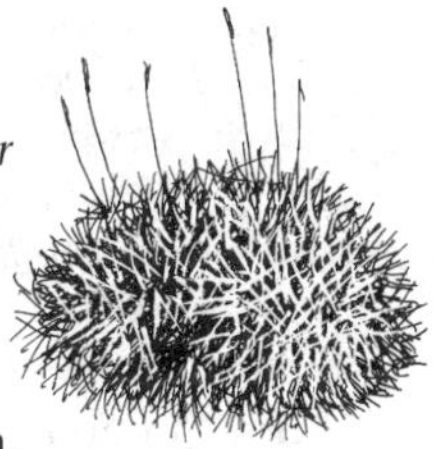
spinifex, porcupine grass (*Triodia basedowii and other Triodia* spp.). A hummock grass about 40 cm high with very sharp pointed greyish green leaves. ◆ Antywang artenh-artenh. *Tent*-kwenyel renh artetyam, aywert yanh. Kwaty-kety, *dry* antem anetyam kwen, aywert kwen, artekarlel antywa. Aywertel anetyam kwen *dry* kwaty-kety. (N) *Spinifex is used for building shelters. When people didn't have tents they built shelters out of spinifex to keep themselves from the rain, and then sat down dry inside the humpy. People kept dry inside spinifex shelters.*
Aywert (W) *n.*
10 Mile Bore. Name of a soakage and the location of a small outstation south-east of Yuelamu (Mt Allan) community. See map p. viii.

Ee

+ek[1], **+eh** (W) *v.ending*
Shows that the action of the verb has already happened and is completed. In the western part of the Anmatyerr region, following rounded consonants such as *tw*, *lw*, *nw* etc., this ending may sometimes sound like *+ew*. This is spelt as *+eh*. ◆ Kapert ayenh arelh yanhel atw**ek**. (St) *That woman hit me on the head.*
SEE ALSO +etyam, +etyart

+ekeng, **+eheng** (W) *v.ending*
because (of something that has happened); something happens because of something that someone else has done ◆ Mer arltwa tnem, ingkerrekarl alh**ekeng**. (T) *The place is empty because everybody has gone.* ◆ *Jail*-eng arratem rang, *policeman*-el apek angety-alhem renh *community* antyaper-warl *like Yuendumu* arlka kwer-warl, wal mapel renh atanthem irrtyartel. Irrtyartel atanthem ankwernem renh, tyerrty irrewalyek apek atw**ekeng**. Ankwernem ina renh, artwang renh ina atwem. Alakenham angkety Anmatyerr anwa ilem. (M) *He comes out of jail, and the policeman might bring him back to all the communities, to such places as Yuendumu and all, and then all the people spear him with spears. They spear him to 'pay him back', to pay back the person who has killed someone. They beat the person that did it, to pay him back. That's how we talk about it in Anmatyerr.*
SEE ALSO +eng[1]

+ek[2], **+eh** (W) *n.ending*
1. Goes on nominals or on clauses to show what the reason for or the purpose of an action is; for, for the purpose of. In the western part of the Anmatyerr region, following rounded consonants such as *tw*, *lw*, *nw* etc., this ending may sometimes sound like *+ew*. This is spelt as *+eh*. ◆ Inkem ntwa mern**eh** apek ker**eh** apek. (M) *You might ask someone for bread or meat.* ◆ Wenh**eh** ntwang apalenthwem? *What are you looking for?* ◆ Ker**ek** ipernem angwely. (M) *Sool the dogs onto the kangaroo.*
2. for, to see if something is there, to test for something ◆ Kwaty**ek** lyelyer-ipem thang. (M) *I'm poking around for water.* ◆ Tyap anyemayt**ek** angernem angernem angernem, kel ra arwerl-rnem akemel akemel, arlkwem anem tyap tyerremel. (Sa) *They dig and dig for the witchetty grubs and then break the roots, then pull the grubs out and eat them.*
3. Goes on the end of the word for the person or thing who is benefiting from an action, or on the end of the phrase describing that person or thing; for, beneficiary, for someone. ◆ Rwang angerr amperl-anem kwer rlkert**eh**. (M) *A big fire is burning for the sick man.* ◆ Angka yanhel ilelhenty angep-angemaw, tyerrty nhakwel anep-anem**ek**. Ilem ra kel arrpenhek anem ra ilety-alpem. (St) *He is going and telling that story to the others over there. He tells them and then goes back and tells others.*
4. Goes on the thing that a feeling or thought is directed towards. ◆ Ahenty anem ayeng ngkweng, artw**ek** apek unta ahenty-anem, *or* artwa apek marl**ek**. (St) *I like you, or maybe you like a man, or a man likes a woman.* ◆ Ilkelhem anem ayeng. Ker**ek** ayeng ilkelhem, mern**ek** ayeng ilkelhem, mantarr**ek** ayeng ilkelhem, warrk**ek** ayeng ilkelhem — angk**ek** ayeng ilkelhem. *I'm happy. I like meat, food, clothes and work — I like doing language [work].*
5. Shows the position, time or location that something is in when an action happens to it; on, at, in, out of, from, off. ◆ Arlewatyerran akely-rnem, ra arepmay. Rapet alhweng**ek** atwerretyart, pet-pet-kenh**ek**. Alkwert atwenh-kenh alhweng**ek**arl atwerretyart ra rapet aremay ra aylpetyart. (Sa) *The* arepmay *is smaller than the sand goanna. We used to kill then in rabbits' burrows. They used to go into rabbits' burrows and we used to kill them.* ◆ Ker atetherr rlpwereh inem. (N) *The budgerigars are got from the hollows in the trees.*
6. Goes in between some doubled-up words (nominals) to show that a relation between things applies both ways, i.e. from one thing to another and vice-versa; to/for/from/at each other. ◆ Anngetherr**ek**-anngetherr. *Facing each other, face to face.*
7. Goes in between doubled-up number words to show that (something is happening) bit by bit or in a numerical sequence. ◆ Anyent**ek**-nyent. (St) *One each, one at a time.* ◆ Atherr**ek**-atherr. (Sa) *Two at a time, in pairs, two each.*
8. Precedes certain other endings, including *-atwety*[2] 'up to (somewhere)', *-athen* 'mistaken belief', *-artwey* 'custodian', *-arlek* 'location', and *-arelh*[2] 'is used for'.

+ek-ahepel (W,T), **+ek-apel** *ending*
perhaps, maybe ◆ Nhakek-ahepel aretyeh alhang! (T) *Go over there to see — he might be*

there! ◆ Iwenhek-apel? *What is it?*
SEE ALSO apek

+ek-anternenh SEE UNDER **-anternenh**

+ek-apel perhaps, maybe SEE UNDER **+ek-ahepel**

+ek-arelh SEE UNDER **-arelh**

+ek-athen SEE UNDER **-athen**

+ekerr (E) *v.ending*
because (warning that the action may have bad consequences); one action is done (in order to avoid the negative consequences of another); for fear of, lest, in case ◆ Man apek tha atyenh alengk-wem, atyeng ankeyel in**ekerr**el. *I'm going to hide my money in case somebody comes and asks me for it.*
◆ Mwetekeng anarnpa, ntwa any**ekerr**. (St) *Get down from the car, in case you fall.*
SEE ALSO -kety

+ekw (W,T), **+wek** (W,T), **+weh** (W,T) *k.ending*
1. your relation
2. his/her/their relation
3. my/our relation [SOME SPEAKERS]. This ending goes on certain kin terms. ◆ Awenh**wek** an any**wek** aweth anperl-alhek. Apetyarlerrek angketyeh aperlehe**kw**. (M) *His auntie and father set out again. The two of them went to talk to the child's grandmother.* ◆ Anywek alhek angketyeh awenh**weh**ek. (M) *Her father went to talk to the child's auntie.*
SEE ALSO +ikw, +engkw, +aty[1]

+el[1] *n.ending*
Shows the person or thing that is the doer of the action of a transitive verb. This ending does not go on pronouns (I, you, we, them, etc.). With kin terms there is some variation as to the position of this ending in the word. For example, *mikwel* and *melikw* — 'his/her mother (does the verb action)' — are possible variations. If there are several words that describe this 'doer of the action' then the *+el* ending goes on the last of them. For example, *angwely* 'dog' *akwekel* 'little' — 'the little dog (does some action)'. Some speakers in the western part of the Anmatyerr region pronounce this ending as *+erl.* ◆ Arelh**el** atwek arnakertel angwely yenh. (M) *A woman hit the dog with a stick.* ◆ Kwaty lthel**el** atwem. (M) *Steady rain is falling ['hitting'].*
◆ Arelh**el** alparrel rrkwerl-anem kwer akwek. (M) *His wife is holding the baby in the baby-carrier.* ◆ Atwety akely, akwek-amperl alhelth angem ra, aympel, m**el**ikw. (St) *The little joey, its mother carries the little thing in her pouch.*

+el[2] *n.ending*
Shows the tool or instrument that an action is being done with or with which an activity is carried out; using (something), by means of (something). Some speakers in the western part of the Anmatyerr region pronounce this ending as *+erl.* ◆ Anaty arelhel inyem aneme**l**. (N) *The woman digs for the bush potato tubers with a digging stick.* ◆ Kwer urreyel irnte**l** ultewem thep. (T) *The boys are throwing stones at birds.* ◆ Iltye**l** angernay! (M) *Scoop it up with your hands!* ◆ Ker irrtyarte**l** atanthek. (M) *[He] speared some meat with a spear.* ◆ Arelhel atwek arnakerte**l** angwely yenh. (M) *A woman hit the dog with a stick.*

+el[3] *n.ending*
Shows where somebody or something is, or where an action happens; at, in, on, by, along. In sentences with verbs describing motion, for example *alhem* 'go', *+el*[3] shows the path along which someone or something travels. Some speakers in the western part of the Anmatyerr region pronounce this ending as *+erl.* ◆ Tyey irrkatye**l** alpetyek. (M) *[I/he/ . . .] will go back on the same road.*
◆ Alalherrk lpwaye**l**arl irnem. *The* alalherrk *bush grows in the creeks.* ◆ Thenkarr-kety lher-lhere**l** ayeng intem. (T) *I'm going to sleep in the little creek because of the prickles.* ◆ Angwely map altywernerl-anem antyame**l**. (M) *The dogs crouched on the bed.*

+el[4] *ending*
Goes on words that function as adverbs. Some speakers in the western part of the Anmatyerr region pronounce this ending as *+erl.* ◆ Anwerlk**el** angkem ayeng. (M) *I am speaking with fear.* ◆ Man apek tha atyenh alengk-wem, atyeng ankeye**l** inekerrarl. *I am going to hide my money in case someone wants to take it from me.*

+el[5] *n.ending*
Goes on the end of words for times of the day, seasons, etc. to show the time at which an action or event occurs; shows that some action happens within this time or for (that amount of time); in, at, during, through. Some speakers in the western part of the Anmatyerr region pronounce this ending as *+erl.* ◆ Tyerrtye**l** rwang irlpart arrernetyart kwenye**l** amperl-anetyek. (T) *People used to put a log there to burn through the night.* ◆ Thang rtak artem alhwerrpe**l**. (T) *I build a windbreak during the winter.* ◆ Angwerre**l** itna apety-alpem. (M) *Late in the evening they come back.*
◆ Malewik**el** apetyem *hawker.* (Sa) *The hawker comes during sit-down money week.*

+el[6] *n.ending*
Used in describing what language is being

used; in (the . . . language). Some speakers in the western part of the Anmatyerr region pronounce this ending as *+erl*. ◆ 'Atwakey' Anmatyerr**el** ilem. (T) *In Anmatyerr it is called* 'atwakey'.

+el[7] SEE UNDER **+emel**

+el-arleng SEE UNDER **-arleng**[1]

+el-ayeth SEE UNDER **-ayeth**

+elengkw *n.ending*

having the particular characteristic shown by the word it goes onto

ahelengkw

aggressive, something with a bite or a kick (ahel *'anger', 'angry'*) ◆ Pitherr, ahel**engkw**arl ra anep-anem apwert-arenyarl. *The* pitherr *plant has a bite to it and it grows in the hills.*

iytenyelengkw

a flirt; someone who fancies someone (iyteny *'flirtation', 'flirtaceous'*) ◆ Arrwengkelthel ina alyetyam alharlk. Alyetyam arelh iytenyel**engkw**an, alha then alakenh, tyarrp-ilemel alyetyam. *Too much lover girl* apek, *everywhere* untetyam. *Pretty girl* apek. (St) *They used to sing [a person's] nose with sorcery as well. They would sing a woman who was flirtatious, and make her nose split open. If she was a pretty girl who was too promiscuous and carried on all over the place.*

alyepelengkw, aylepelengkw (E)

young teenage boy who is going through ceremonial business (alyep *'hairstring belt or strap'*)

SEE ALSO awerrty, arwekert, lyaty, arleyarr, amarleyarr, tyakwertekwert, lwekerleny, antingkar

+elh+ *v.ending*

1. Goes on verbs to show that someone or something is doing the action to themself or to part of themself ◆ Arntap-arntapel arlkwem aherrkel. Arlkwem, atw**elh**erl-anem atw**elh**erl-anem atw**elh**erl-anem — ankwa-kweny. Kwaty-penhant war. (N) *The* arntap-arntap *bites you in the summer. They bite and you slap at them and slap at them — you don't get any sleep. This just happens after rain.* ◆ Manty arntarnt-ar**elh**em. (M) *Look after yourself.* ◆ Arlewatyerr rlwelth arrern**elh**em alhwerrpel. (M) *In the winter the goanna digs itself in to hibernate.* ◆ Arntek ayeng in**elh**etyek, antywer apek akem arntek in**elh**etyek, tyerretyek ker, kerarl arntek-warl aylperrek. Arwerl antywerel, arwerl tyepalel. (Sa) *I am going to pick my teeth, get a bit of grass to pick at my teeth and get the meat that is stuck in my teeth out. With a bit of grass or a stick.*

2. Shows that some action happens to someone or something (by itself) ◆ Ngkwern ltwak**elh**ek. (M) *The leg broke.* ◆ Mwetek ak**elh**ekaw! (St) *The car broke down!* ◆ Warl art**elh**em. (M) *A house is being built.* ◆ Kwaty thel**elh**em altywereng. (M) *The water is pouring out of the hole.*

3. Shows that the direction of the action is away from yourself ◆ 'Ayeng aywep**elh**ek artwang ngkwenh mert-hety, ayeng aywep**elh**ek.' Marl arrpenhek ilelhem. 'Npwek tha kwenh.' (T) *'I chased your husband away, I sent him off.' Telling the other woman that that's what you did. 'I hunted him away.'* ◆ Ngenh apek tha alharlkw**elh**em, ankeyarl apetyemeng. (St) *I'm hunting you away from me, because you're coming and asking for things.*

+elh-il+ *v.ending*

Goes on intransitive verbs to make them into transitive ones; make something happen, make someone or something a certain way or make them do something. For example, *amangkem* 'grow up', *amangk**elh-il**em* 'grow someone up'; *lyapem* 'grow', *lyap**elh-il**em* 'grow something' ◆ Tha akwek map amangk**elh-il**ek — wal urrpetyap anthwerrek amangk**elh-il**enh. Akwekeng-ntyel anenh tha amangk**elh-il**ek. (P) *I grew some children up — I grew up three altogether. I grew them up from when they were small.* ◆ Uyerr**elh-il**emel atyenh arlkwekaw ker ingkern, uyerr**elh-il**ek. Lyet tha yarety-alpek ker atyenh uyerr**elh-il**errirrek. (St) *They used up all my meat while I was away. I just came back and saw that my meat had all disappeared.*

SEE ALSO -il+

+elh-ilerr+ *v.ending*

Goes on intransitive verbs to make them into reciprocal ones; make each other a certain way or make each other do something; cause something to happen to each other. For example, *arrangkem* 'cry'; *arrangk**elh-ilerr**em* 'make each other cry'

SEE ALSO +err[2], -ilerr+

+elh-ilem SEE UNDER **-ilem**

+elp *v.ending*

Goes in the middle of partially doubled-up verbs to show that the action is just starting, is happening bit by bit or repeatedly, or to a lesser degree (than the normal action of the verb) ◆ Nga akenh akweteth — nga ampw**elp**ampw-irrek yanh-angkwerr. (St) *You are permanent [always there] — you've grown older and older in that area.*

◆ Alkngw**elp**alkngw-irretyek nga, tha ngenh

alkngwanngw-ilem, kel ayeng alwirremel ngkweng-kety. (St) *I keep on distracting you so that you'll start to lose attention, and then I'll run away from you.* ◆ Marl alenh arnkelyel wart aw**elp**awenhek ntywem akwet. (M) *That woman just kept going away in the other direction and didn't take any notice because she was sulky and in a bad mood.*

+elth Goes on certain nominals to describe someone or something that characteristically behaves in that way. SEE UNDER **+alth**

+em (W,T) Emphasises particular things. SEE UNDER **+am**[1]

+em[1] *v.ending*

1. Shows that the verb action is happening now (at the time of speaking). ◆ Pap alh**em** lyweny kereh. (M) *Father is going hunting.* ◆ Arelh akay arrangk**em** ayey anetyarl awekarl. (T) *The woman is wailing after hearing bad news.* ◆ Kapert arekar-irr**em** twernelarl amp**em**-penh. (N) *My head is hurting from the heat of the sun.*

2. Shows that the verb action is something that typically or usually happens. ◆ Aherrel arlkw**em** renh, ngernemel, *purple one flower*. Lywemp-lywemp-artek. Yerrakwerr-artek arlpa. *Kangaroos dig this up and eat it, it has a purple flower. It is similar to parakeelya. It has leaves like a bush onion.* ◆ Anyem apel antyw**em** merntel, antyw**em** *tea leaf* akwek arrernemel. *Stir-em up* ilemel item renh, *mixed up* amp**em**ey kel antyw**em**em. (N) *Witchetty bush leaves are drunk by sick people. The small leaves are put in water and stirred up and cooked, and then the liquid is drunk.*

3. Shows that the verb action will probably happen some time in the future or that the doer of the verb action intends the action to happen, or can do the verb action. ◆ Aleth akwet ayeng alh**em**. (T) *I am going away for good.*

SEE ALSO +etyel

+em-[2] *v.ending*

Follows an English transitive verb when used in Anmatyerr to make it into an Anmatyerr verb (from English 'him' via Kriol). The *+em*[2] ending is followed by *-ilem*. ◆ Anwernenh *show*-**em**-iletyart angerr-pat mapel. Lweren anwern arek arek arek awenkel. (N) *All the old people used to show us [about bush food]. That's what we saw all the time when we were teenagers.* ◆ *Choke*-**em**-iletyart anwern kwep angerrety, arrernetyart *billycan*-warl. (N) *We used to choke those big frogs called* kwep, *and put them in a billycan.*

SEE ALSO -ilem

+em-ilem SEE UNDER **-ilem**

+emeh (W) *ending*

Provides emphasis (?). ◆ Thang**emeh** angwely nhenh rrkwem. (M) *I'm the only one who will look after these dogs.* ◆ Ywerntem-areny kwenelak**emeh** alartetyam. (M) *The people from Yuendumu sat with their heads down in silence.*

+emel *v.ending*

Goes on the end of verb to show that that action is happening at about the same time as another action or several actions. The doer of the actions of both verbs, or of a series of verbs, is the same. Can be glossed as 'while' or ' . . . ing'. ◆ Aherran akem-irr**emel** arrtyanek itetheh. (M) *The kangaroo stood up and ran for its life.* ◆ Arrat**emel** alhay, aketh-warn! (M) *Go out into the open!* ◆ Kerek uyarn unthem, arrangkw-antey apety-alpem uyarnarl unthek-penh. Ayeng apek arlewatyerrek uyarn unth**emel** apety-alpem. (St) *Looking around in vain for meat, and coming back with nothing after searching in vain. Maybe I will look around for goannas and not find any and then return.* ◆ Ikngerr-ampeny-kenh 'yalkw' — anwern-kenh 'yerrakwerr'. Kik-w**emel** arlkwerl-apem inelhap**emel**. *The word 'yalkw' belongs to the people from the eastern region — ours is 'yerrakwerr'. We go along picking them and peeling them and eating them.* ◆ Yenper arternetyam, *clean* antem yarr-wetyam, arrerlp-iletyam. Kel *clean*-il**emel** artern**emel** arrernetyam. (N) *The spearwood was scraped and cleaned and then straightened and sharpened. When it was cleaned it was put in the fire to straighten and sharpen it.*

+emer *v.ending*

Goes on verbs and shows that the action might or could happen; if one thing happens then something else might happen; suppose that (something might happen); 'if only' (the action had happened or could happen), would; if (the action can happen if something else is the case). ◆ Ayeng apek alengk-welh**emer** ngkweng-kety, warrk-kety apek. (St) *I might hide myself from you, or hide myself from work.* ◆ Nheng mpwenyel apek angem ra. Wal arrpenh mapel apek ina ilt**emer**. 'Ankerl-ankerlam ntwan *wrong skin*-ek ntwa angwenhek-irrerl-anetyek, alperl-anetyek.' (P) *He might race off with her. Well then other people might growl at him. 'You are the wrong skin — you're doing whatever, going off with someone who is the wrong skin for you.'* ◆ *Policemen*-kety alengk-iwelhem. Ayeng apek

untemer alengk-iwenhemel anem ayeng untem *policeman*-kety. (St) *I might hide myself from the policeman. I might run away and hide from the police.*

+eng¹ *ending*

1. Shows where something is from, or where something moves from; away from, from the direction of. Often occurs preceding the ending *-ntyel*. ◆ Rlkang alturl**eng** apetyem aretharr. (M) *The* aretharr *wind comes from the west.* ◆ *Aileron*-**eng** nta alhem *Ti Tree*-warn. (M) *From Aileron you go on to Ti Tree.* ◆ Rrwep-rrwep-wety tyerrtyarl ater arrtyanewarrem antyw**eng** arratemel. 'Yanh arraty akwetarl apetyem kwenh!' (N) *Because of the whirlwind, people rush out of their humpies. 'It's coming straight [at us]!'* ◆ Alethang ilety-alhem, ilety-alhem ngkweng, 'Ayeng apetyek *Pine Hill*-**eng**, *or* Arrwek**eng** apek apetyek ayeng, *or Willowra*-**eng** apek'. (P) *The traveller says, says to you, 'I've come from Pine Hill, or Arrwek, or maybe from Willowra'.* ◆ Mer rntwarr**eng** tyerrty lwereny apetyem. (M) *The stranger came from a long way away.* ◆ Kwaty thelelhem altywer**eng**. (M) *The water is leaking out of the hole.*

2. Indicates what something is made of, indicates the source of something. ◆ Inernt**eng** alparr twem. (M) *Carving a carrying dish from bean tree wood.* ◆ Artweker wangkem iltyel-arleng. Altyerr**eng** artwekeran anek. Arlewatyerr anterel apernelherl-anem, amwely anterel, ankerr anterel, aherr anterel. (Sa) *The boil is swelling up on the finger. Boils came from the Dreamtime. They are rubbed with goanna fat, cadney lizard fat, emu fat or kangaroo fat.*

3. Indicates the cause or reason for something; because. In this sense, the *+eng*¹ ending occasionally goes on verbs (following other endings). ◆ Akikart-irrerl-anem, *anything* mern**eng** apek. Ker**eng** apek. Ker**eng** akikart-irrem. (St) *Getting upset over anything, such as food or meat. Getting upset about meat.* ◆ Ayeng nyerr-irrem tyerrtyelarl aremeng arnterr. (T) *I feel shamed when people stare hard at me.* ◆ Mwetekay**eng** anngwenhem. Mwetekayeh-arteyel arrpenhel antyem wal anngwenhem, ltwakey-hety mwetekay. (T) *People get jealous over cars. The owner of the car might get jealous if another person gets in the car, in case they crash the car.*

4. Shows the part of a body or thing which is involved in an action, or the part of something which is held. ◆ Amwelt**eng** arntwerrkem mpweny inem. (Sa) *Grabbing [the person] by the arm to race off with them.*

5. Indicates the location of the action (?). ◆ Waly akwek aker**neng** arrernem, arntap-el-arleng, yerrampek-arlek. (N) *A small branch is placed over the bark container, on top of the honeyants.*

6. Indicates a vehicle or other type of transport used to go somewhere; in, by, on. ◆ Marnt**eng** alhem, lyweny apek, apety-alpem, altywer-ilety-alpem, anarnpenty-alpem. (N) *We might go for a day trip in the bus, come back, open it, and get out.*

+eng-ntyel (W,T) *n.ending*
from, away from, from the direction of, from the time of etc. ◆ Awenk apel anwern rntwetyartel akwek**eng-ntyel** anwernenh apernetyart, apernetyart anwernenh. (N) *When we were teenage girls we used to dance, from when we were small they used to paint us up.* ◆ Rtey-rteyel mer mpwarem anthwerrng**eng-ntyel**. (N) *Mudlarks make their nests from mud.* ◆ Alhernter kwenh anpernerrenty itya, kenh tyerrty akenh Anengkerr**eng-ntyel** anpernerrem. Anengkerrel anpernek Anengkerr**eng-ntyel** anpernerrem kenh alhernter akenh anpernenty ityarl. Apal wararl alhernteran. (M) *White people don't have a skin system, whereas Aboriginal people get their skin system from the Dreaming. The Dreaming named everyone as relations, and people got the way of calling each other as relations from there. White people don't have a skin system. White people don't know.*
= +eng¹

+eng-anyimp (E), **+eng-anyemp** (E) *n.ending*
Shows something which is an imitation of the real thing; a pretend thing, something that is not up to standard, substandard, something that is supposed to be something but is not, 'so-called'. This ending always follows *+eng*³. ◆ Arengk**eng-anyemp** atyenh, akeng-akeng. (St) *This so-called dog of mine is not very good.* ◆ Mwetekay**eng-anyemp** atyenh, akengarl-irrek inngart mwetekay**eng-anyemp**. (St) *This so-called car of mine broke down, it's not much of a car.* ◆ Warl**eng-anyimp** atyenh, akeng-akeng artelhepelhem. (St) *My house is substandard, it wasn't built very well.*
= -arrpantey, -arrpatenty

+eng² *n.ending*
Goes in the middle of a doubled-up word for a thing to describe the 'pretend' or 'toy' thing that is used by children when playing.

◆ Alkwert**eng**-alkwert ina mpwaretyam ampa arrken-irrerretyek, wererrl-anetyek, alyaperel werrerl-anetyek, kayl**eng**-kayl, alyaperel, kalyel-arrpantey. (St) *The children make toy shields to play with, to use when they are throwing pretend boomerangs at each other.* ◆ Mer**eng**-amer ina mer mparem, pelangket an *all there* ina angem — *billycan*, tey apek angem, tey itemel, merel anerremel mer**eng**-amer kwerel. (P) *They makes cubbyhouses and they take blankets and all there — billycans and tea. They sit in the camp and make tea, in the cubbyhouse.*

+eng-arrngel SEE UNDER **-arrngel**

+eng-ayerr (E) *n.ending*
from, out of ◆ Rltimp atnkerrmern, aper rltimp-akert akin, artety arlka rltimp-akert ingkerrek. Akarntety-arntetyan rltimp**eng-ayerr**. Akarntety-arntety rltimpel-arlengarl anem. (St) *The coolibah tree has bits of dried bark, and the river red gum and mulga trees do as well. The* akarntety-arntety *lizard comes out from amongst the bits of dried bark. It lives amongst the dried bark.*
arnameng-ayerr (E) *n.*
a type of ant from flat ant bed (*akerrth*) (lit. 'from the grass')

+engkw, +angkw *k.ending*
your relation. Goes on the end of kin terms and other words that are similar to kin terms. ◆ Am**angkw**. *Your mother.* ◆ Arek arrengkerr atyey**engkw**? *Have you seen your younger brother or sister?* ◆ Amer altyerr**engkw**. *Your mother's country.*
SEE ALSO +aty[1], +ikw, +ekw

+enh[1] *prn.ending*
Goes on the end or in the middle of pronouns, and shows that the verb action is happening to the person or thing to whom the pronoun refers. For example *ra* 'he, she, it' becomes *renh* 'him, her, it' (as the object of the verb). Sometimes this ending may appear twice in a pronoun. See pronoun table, Appendix 1. ◆ Rntwetyart anwern, mer nhenh kwerel anwern rntwetyart kalty-anthetyart akngerr-pat mapel anwern**enh**. (N) *We used to dance, at this place here we danced, and the elders used to teach us.* ◆ Thang arr**enh**antherr**enh** atwem. (M) *I am hitting you mob.*
SEE ALSO ayenh, ngenh, renh, anwernenh, inenh etc.

+enh[2] *prn.ending*
1. Goes on the end of dative pronouns to form possessive pronouns. The use of *+enh*[2] on the pronouns *atyeng* ('for me') and *ngkweng* ('for you') to form *atyengenh/atyehenh* ('mine'), and *ngkwengenh/ngkwehenh/ngkweyenh* ('yours') seems to be particularly associated with Anmatyerr spoken at Ti Tree and to the west of there. The equivalent forms in the Eastern Anmatyerr region are *atyenh* and *ngkwenh*. ◆ Mern atyeng**enh**. (M) *My food.* ◆ Anew ngkweng**enh** ntwa atwarem. (M) *You are going to meet your husband.* ◆ Amey ikwer**enh** arrangkw-irrek. *His/her mother passed away.*
2. Part of the *-kenh* or *-henh* ending that goes on nominal pronouns to form possessive pronouns. The *+enh* part is often split off from the *+ek* or *+eh* part. ◆ Rapet arr**ek**antherr**enh**, arlter map-kenh. (Sa) *Rabbits are yours, whitefellas'.*
SEE ALSO -kenh

+enh+[3] *v.ending*
1. Shows that the verb action is happening while the person or thing that is doing the verb action is going past somewhere or moving along. This ending goes after the verb root and before the tense ending.
2. Shows that the verb action is happening along something. ◆ Kart map aneltyem. Aneltyem aneltyem aneltyem altywer-ilerl-apemel, kart nhenh map, atnarl arlwepelwem nheng map. Kel ip**enh**em ip**enh**em kel *finish clean*-em angem. (N) *Cleaning the intestines out. Cleaning the intestines and opening them out and cleaning out all the round pieces of shit. Then squeezing the shit out along the intestines and then, when it's finished, taking the clean intestines [back].* ◆ Kwaty rewel-ayeng akwemp-akwemp an**enh**em. (M) *The froth is on top of the floodwater as it goes along.*
SEE ALSO +eyn+

+enh[4] *v.ending*
Goes on some verbs to turn them into a nominal or 'thing' that is usually used to do the verb action, or has the action done to it. For example, *atwem* 'hit, kill', ***atwenh-atwenh*** 'a dangerous thing, a gun'; *arlkwem* 'eat', ***arlkwenh-arlkwenh*** 'edible'. Used with a partially reduplicated verb root. ◆ Lyarwek apernelh**enh**elh**enh** akin. Lyarwek anthwerr. Arrkernk-areny. (N) Lyarwek *is a rubbing medicine as well. It is from the bloodwood tree.* ◆ Alkart anterrng antem, arlkw**enh**-arlkw**enh**. Alkart, rwel antem atyerretyam ina alkart yanh kwa. Rwel it**enh**-it**enh**, wanty**enh**anty**enh**. Ath**enh**-ath**enh**. Athetyamarl awantyetyamarl, Anengkerr-

penh wart. (N) *The* alkart *seed is edible as well. They cook the* alkart *seed in the fire. It's cooked in the fire and then ground up and eaten. It comes from the Dreaming, of course.* ◆ Ingkarl atanthemel arlketyerran, arrerlp. *Cheeky bugger,* ingkang awangkelh-il**enh**-il**enh**. 'Pwet-kweny arekerr-irrem ayeng.' (T) *The* arlketyerr *prickle spikes your foot. It's a cheeky bugger and it makes your feet swell up. 'I haven't got any shoes and I'm in pain.'*
SEE ALSO +enty2

+enh+arey SEE UNDER **+arey**

+enh+atherr SEE UNDER **+atherr**

+enh+err+arey SEE UNDER **+arey**

+enp (E) along with, including, having, too, as well, also SEE UNDER **+inp**

+enty+1, **+inty+**, **+ety+** (E) *v.ending*

1. Goes on verbs to show that action is happening in a direction towards someone or something; do while coming this way, do coming hither. ◆ Mwetekay *light* alhenenh**ety**em. (Sa) *The car light is shining as it comes towards us.* ◆ Pwelek kwaty-warl akert-arraty-irr**inty**em, kwaty antywetyek. (St) *The cattle are coming this way in a straight line to drink water.* ◆ Alhek nmwerntel arltw**inty**em, alhek nmwerntel arltwem ingkerr, ahelh ingkerr. (N) *The dust haze comes towards you and covers everything over.* ◆ Mwetekay apek anty**inty**em, twerrp yanh-angkwerr. (St) *The car is climbing up that sandhill over there, as it comes this way.*

2. do something back to someone ◆ Ntwan atw**enty**eyam renh, ankwernang, ngenharl atwekarl-penh. (T) *You go and hit him, pay him back after he's hit you.*

3. become a certain way again, go back to the way it was before ◆ Akethamarl irr**enty**em anwern perempeth arlkwerremel rwang item mern item tey item mernam arlkwerrem. (N) *As it gets light again we light the fire, boil tea and cook and eat breakfast.*

+enty-alhem, **+inty-alhem** (E) *ending*

1. go along doing the action in a direction towards someone or something (alhem *'go'*) ◆ Artar yanh atyenh apety-alpetyel. Lyetant arrernelh**enty**-alhek. (Sa) *My son is coming back. He just came and arrived back today.* ◆ Mwetekay kelath arlkerrk-w**enty**-alhem, apetyemel. Arnaremel, *'Eh,* arlkerrk-wenty-alhem kwenh kelath yanhel, kwatyel-artek'. (T) *The windows of the car are shining as it comes along towards us. Watching it coming we say, 'Hey, the car windows are shining, sparkling like water'.* ◆ Kwaty apwertek-akert apetyem, arna arlka antyak**enty**-alhem, ngkwelty-ilem, war atw**enty**em. (N) *There's a hailstorm coming that's going to uproot the trees as it comes this way, smash them up as it hits.*

2. Describes the movement of weather and natural phenomena such as sun, moon, wind, clouds, rain etc. ◆ Rlkang pw**enty**-alhem antekerreng. (N) *The wind is blowing this way from the south.* ◆ Aherrk arrat**enty**-alhem lyetant. (St) *The sun has just come up.* ◆ Atay irrpenhem. Arrat**enty**-alhem an irrpenhem altwerl-atheh. (M) *The moon goes down. It comes up, and then goes down in the west.*

+enty-alpem, **+inty-alpem** (E) *ending*

1. do something on the way back; come back and do something (alpem *'go back'*) ◆ Artwep-irr**enty**-alpem ayeng alpemaw, mer-warl. (N) *I'm turning round and going back home.* ◆ Lyetant arratem akuny. Arrwekeleng aretyakenh rwengk anep-anem, lyetant anem arratem ra, arrat**enty**-alpem. (St) *The poor thing has just arrived today. We didn't see her before. Now she has just arrived, just returned.* ◆ Amwek anerl-anem. Kwer akwek arnerrerl-apem arnerrerl-apem aweth apety-alpem, arnerr**enty**-alpem. (N) *His/her mother is sitting there. The child crawls along, crawls along and then comes back again, crawls back.* ◆ Angenty akwen alakenh tety-wem, anarnpetyek kel anty**enty**-alpey akern-warl. (St) *Cut the steps down in the soakage like that, jump down and then climb back up again to the top.*

2. do something back to someone ◆ Waram tha ngkweng arlenthek, artelhetyek apek. Urnanenty apek *something* awenh apek, arlenthekarl tha. Kenh ntwa atyeng anth**enty**-alpeyamel. (St) *I just lent it to you, so that you could cover yourself up. Some clothes or whatever, I lent them to you. And then you will give them back to me later.*

+enty2 *v.ending*

1. Turns a verb into a noun which describes the action as a noun or which describes a person or thing who usually does that verb action. ◆ Rrkw**enty**. *Police, policeman, policewoman [i.e. a catcher]* (rrkwem *'hold', 'catch'*). ◆ Irrkwap**enty**. *Work* (irrkwapem *'work'*). ◆ Rrtywerr**enty**. *A lie* (rrtywerrem *'to lie'*). ◆ Kerrenty. *Rules associated with respect of particular kin, for example the avoidance of mothers-in-law by sons-in-law* (kerrem *'observe rules associated with respect of particular kin'* etc.).

2. Turns a verb into a noun which describes that action as an event. ◆ Alpek anwern

ingkerrek *football* arenty-penh. (M) *We all went back after watching football.* ◆ Akangkwerr**enty** (akangkwerrem *'pay attention'*) itya, kwer kwerl-areny map. Maneyekant angkerl-anem, maney akwel ngkwelty anthetyeh. (N) *They don't pay attention [i.e. have no attention], the school children. They just talk about money, and ask [us] to give them change.* ◆ Irrkwaperl-an**enty**-penh (irrkwaperl-anem *'work'*) ayeng purrk-irremeyay, purrk anem ayeng. *After work I am tired, I am tired.*
SEE ALSO +enh[4]

+enty-angerr *ending* = **+enty**[2] (angerr[1] *'lots'*) ◆ Atek arnamel an**enty-angerr** (anem *'be', 'live'*). Atek arrtyanem arnam arrpenh-warn, ahelh-angkwarr. *The button quail is a grass-dweller. The quail runs across the ground from one clump of grass to another.* ◆ Arrarletyel tha iltem arelh nhenh anhelh**enty-angerr** (anhelhem *'be nasty'*). Iltek anem tha arrarletyel akuny-amperl. (St) *I am growling and swearing at this nasty woman. I swore at the poor thing.* ◆ Rrtywerr**enty-angerr** (rrtywerrem *'to lie'*) nta mpwarerl-apem kwenh. (N) *You are going along and telling big lies.* ◆ Nhenhan tha ngkweng anthem arnam nty**enty-angerr** (ntyem *'give off a smell'*) ngwenh mwerr-iletyek. (T) *I am giving you this smelly grass to make yourself better.*
SEE ALSO +enh[4]

+enty[3] *n.ending*
Turns some nominals into adverbs.

akengenty (E) *adv.*
wrong, wrongly (*akeng* 'wrong, bad')
◆ Mwetekay artenh-irra, akengenty alhekerr. (Sa) *Follow that car in case it goes the wrong way.*

+eny *n.ending*
Goes on certain spatial and time words to describe a person or thing that is from that place or time.

arrwekeleny *n.*
from before, olden-time (*arrwekel* 'first', 'in front') ◆ Atyankerney-apenh angetyetyart warntapelant mern atyankern arrwekel**eny** mapel. Aperl-aperl-rrpwerelaty menh-menh-rrpwerel arlka atyemeyel-rrpwer. *The olden-time people used to get mistletoe berries in bark containers. All my grandmothers, the old women.*

ingkerneny *n.*
1. last (*ingkern* 'last', 'behind')
2. youngest one, younger ones
3. the next generation, the younger generation, people of today (ingkern *'behind'*)
◆ Ingkern**eny**, alhengk apek aretyenheng tywerreng mer arreng-kenh angey-kenh. Kalty apek anetyenheng. *The next generation might know about sacred things and about their grandparent's and father's land. Maybe they'll get to know about it.*
4. after, later

kantyeny (T,E) *n.*
last child in a group of siblings; middle child (?) (*kanty*[1] 'edge')

+ep- *v.ending*
1. (do something) continuously; the action is being repeated or keeps happening. Goes in the middle of partially doubled-up verbs.
◆ Artwang rlkert angerr rwangkwerr int**ep**-intem. (M) *A sick man keeps lying by the fire.*
◆ Arengk akwekel kwaty antyw**ep**-antywem lyweny-penh. (T) *The little dog keeps on drinking water after going hunting.* ◆ Aherr nhenhel aterel tyerrty ar**ep**-arem. (N) *This kangaroo is fearfully watching the person.* ◆ Anper anthwerr *story* nhenh anwern il**ep**-ilem. *Olden time* renh anwern *story* nhenh il**ep**-ilem anper — mwerr angerr, kerarl atanthetyam, kerelarl wantetyam. (N) *This is really good story that we keep on telling. It's the olden-time story that we continue to tell — it's really good. About the kangaroos that were speared, and the meat that we were fed on.* ◆ Angka irrkwerteth wararl angk**ep**-angkem. Arlper apek awetyakenh angkerl-anem, irrkwertetharl angk**ep**-angkem awetyakenh, *German* apek. Irrkwerteth-irrkwertetharl angkem. *They just keep on speaking a different language. They might speak Warlpiri which [I] don't understand. You can't understand [some] other languages. For example, German; they speak language that is not understandable.*
2. (do something) often or most of the time
◆ Ngwath ayeng ap**ep**-apem. (M) *I keep walking about alone.*
3. (do something) sporadically or every now and again ◆ *Olden time* ina aketyam. *Still* arlkw**ep**-antey arlkwem. (T) *They used to pick it in the old days. They still eat it occasionally.*

+erl[1] *v.ending*
1. Shows that the action of the verb is something that usually happens or would usually happen; would (do the verb action).
◆ Arlperrangkwarl apel theweyet anthwerr inelhapetyart, akap-rlwemel peleth, theweyet anthwerr. Awantyerlapetyeh. Lweren arlkw**erl** anwern amangkek, arlkwerl-apemel awantyerl-apemel — *everything* anthwerrel anwern amangkek. *We used to collect the sweet*

resin from the whitewood tree — it's really sweet, I can tell you. We used to go along sucking on it. We'd eat those things and that's how we grew up, going along eating and sucking on the sweet whitewood resin — we grew up on all sorts of bush foods. ◆ Mern angerr arlkwep-arlkw**erl** ayert angerr irrek. (St) *He'd eat lots of food and that's how he got really fat.*

2. Often used in Anmatyerr sentences in which the English words 'don't', 'can't', 'might' or 'gotta' have been incorporated. ◆ *Can't* thang ker apek ar**erl** kwenh — itya. (N) *I can't see the animal — nothing.*

+erl2 *v.ending*

Part of compound verbs formed with *apetyem* 'come', *alhem* 'go', *anem* 'sit', *alpem* 'go back', *apem* 'go'.

+erl-ap+ *v.ending*

Shows that the verb action happens continuously or over a period of time while in motion, or while going along (apem *'go'*). ◆ War ar**erl-ap**em. (M) *Just going along looking.* ◆ Amwerrk an**erl-ap**etyam mwetekayel anwantherr. (St) *Yesterday we came along in the car.* ◆ Amaty-arey panth-akert, anem-akert alh**erl**-atherr-**ap**etyart, tyap arlka ak**erl-ap**etyeh awenkel, ker alewatyerr renh atw**erl-ap**etyeh. (N) *Our mothers used to walk along carrying their wooden dishes and their digging sticks, and together with the young girls they gathered grubs and killed goannas as they travelled along.* ◆ Kwer akwek-akert *pram* anampartew**erl-ap**em. (T) *Pushing the little baby along in the pram.* ◆ Arlkwem arrkernemel, kel pwelap-akertem alhem atwakey renh inelhem alhem, arlkw**erl-ap**em nwenty-nwentyem alh**erl-ap**em. *We taste the wild orange fruits first, and then go and collect a whole lot of them, munching noisily as we go.* ◆ Amwek anerl-anem. Arnerr**erl-ap**em arnerr**erl-ap**em aweth apety-alpem, arnerrenty-alpem. (N) *His/her mother is sitting there. [The child] crawls along, crawls along and then comes back again, crawls back.* ◆ Mern arlatyey anemel iny**erl-ap**etyart. 'Mern arlatyey aray, mwernenty map. Yekay mern mwernenty kwenh nhenh!' *We used to go along digging for* arlatyey *with digging sticks. 'Look at all these yams, all growing together. Look at all the yams!'*

+erl-apety+ (W), **+erl-apetyem** *v.ending*

(do something) and come; come along (doing something) (apetyem *'come'*) ◆ Mern pwarl akwerrk, k**erl-apety**em ina, mwanyem tyampet-warn k**erl**-atherr-**apety**art. (M) *The children came along picking young bush bananas and bush tomato fruits, which they put in their billycans as they went along.*

+erl-alh+ *v.ending*

do something and then go; do something before going; go after doing something (alhem *'go'*) ◆ Mer atyenhek tha iw**erl-alh**ern mantarr apek, kel ayeng apety-alpern. (St) *I just left the clothes at my place and then I came back.* ◆ Ayeng akem-irr**erl-alh**ek aherlkenty-aherlkentyel. (St) *I got up and went early in the morning.* ◆ Arnwep-arnwep ar**erl-alh**em, kwaty lpwertey interleng. Mentyel ar**erl-alh**em arnwep-arnwep renh — kwatyelarl *mess* mpwarek ingkel arlka, pwelek atna arlka lhwemel. (N) *We'll go and see the claypan, where the muddied water is lying there. We'll go and see that claypan, but we'll leave it — where the bullocks have messed up the water up with their hooves and by shitting in it.*

+erl-alp+ *v.ending*

go back and do (the verb action); do (the verb action) and then go back; go and do (the verb action) and then come back (alpem *'go back'*) ◆ Antangkem, 'Apetyay teyekay, mern nhenh in**erl-alp**etyekay!' Antangkeyay tha kenh ngkweng. (N) *Calling you over, 'Come for tea, come and get this food to take back!' I am calling you over.* ◆ Ar**erl-alp**aw! *Sister* atyenh apek ar**erl-alp**em. Arem apek unta, kel unta apety-alpem, *'He's all right'*. (St) *Go back and have a look! Go back and see my sister. If you see her then you can come back and say, 'She's all right'.* ◆ Ura irlpart weth tha atyeng in**erl-alp**eyew, ura atyeng ampetyek irlpart. (St) *I'll go back and get that log for myself, so that I can burn it for myself.* ◆ Ntarl iw**erl-alp**ek nhakwek mantarr ngkwenh. Iltyant nga apety-alpern, nhenh ant iw**erl-alp**ek, mantarr ngkwenh. (St) *You went and dropped your clothes off over there. You came back empty-handed, you just dropped your clothes off.*

+erl-an+ *v.ending*

Shows that the verb action happens continuously or over a period of time; (do something) continuously; (do something) for a while (anem *'sit', 'be'*). ◆ Rwang angerr amp**erl-an**em kwer rlkerteh. (M) *A big fire is burning for the sick man.* ◆ Arelhel alparrel rrkw**erl-an**em kwer akwek. (M) *His wife is holding the baby in the baby-carrier.* ◆ Athem athem rnewarl alparr-warl apek, rwewarlam thel**erl-an**em alakenh, kel amp**erl-an**em, mern *nice* anthwerr kelh arlkw**erl-an**etyenheng. (N) *They were ground up into a* *wooden dish and then poured onto the fire. The seed would cook really nicely, into a seed cake, which was then eaten.*

+erl-anerr+[1] *v.ending*

Shows that two people are doing something continuously or doing something for a while (+err[1] *'two people doing verb action'*).

◆ Anawerr-nheng atherr al**herl-anerr**em apek an**erl-anerr**em apek. *The uncle and his nephews or nieces are going or maybe sitting down.*

+erl-arrern+ (E) *v.ending*

do something then place oneself in some bodily position (arrernem *'put'*) ◆ Aherr-kenh mer ipert. Interl-anem ikwerel. *Salt*-kenh *separate* akin angernem. Itnan 'arrantyeyantyeng' ipertel interl-anek, angernerl-anem, ankwa anem iwel**herl-arrern**em. Aherr-kenhant. (Sa) *A kangaroo's sleeping hole. It sleeps there. It digs a separate hole for salt. The name of the hole that it digs and lies down to sleep in is* 'arrantyeyantyeng'. *These are just kangaroos' holes.*

+erl-anerr+[2] (W,T) *v.ending*

Goes on the verb when two people are being ordered to do that action.

SEE ALSO +a, +errirr, -arey[2]

+erl-atherr+ SEE UNDER **-atherr**

+erl-ayn+ (E) *v.ending*

do something quickly, do something straight away ◆ Ker atnalharr yanh tha arlkw**erl-ayn**etyek. Ker atnalharr yanh antheyaw kely tha k**erl-ayn**emel arlkwerl-anetyek. (Sa) *I'm going to eat some emu stomach fat straightaway. Give me some of that* ker atnalharr *so that I can cut a bit off to eat.* ◆ Ker altywekerr tnep-tnem atw**erl-ayn**eyaw. Anter innga. (Sa) *Quickly kill that* altywekerr *lizard that's standing there. It's really fat.* ◆ Ker k**erl-ayn**etyek, mern apek k**erl-ayn**etyek, *knife* arreylpel. (Sa) *Quickly cutting the bread or the meat with a sharp knife.*

+erl-aynt+ (E) *v.ending*

Shows that the verb action happens continuously or over a period of time.

◆ Arlengel ampernem arrken-irretyek alherl-way, arrken utnherr**erl-aynt**etyek. (Sa) *You kids go off and play a long way away.* ◆ Alhetyekek-athen irrar-irreman irrkaw-irreman alhetyek irrar-irrem. Alhetyek ayeng irrar-irrem atywaty-irremel ayeng al**herl-aynt**etyek. (Sa) *You feel restless and homesick and really want to go (but you don't). I feel restless and want to get going.*

+erl-w+[1], **+erl-iw+** (T,E) *v.ending*

(do something) quickly; (do something) suddenly; (do something) only for a short time. ◆ Atnwenth ampakemel arlkwem, ampakemel arlkwem. Lyetant *knife* ant akngerr anemel ampakemel arlkwetyek. *Knife*-kwenyel ampakemel arlkwarlkw**erl-w**em. (St) *Meat is ripped apart and eaten. Nowadays knives are used to divide up the meat. If there is no knife the meat is torn apart and eaten quickly.* ◆ Ilpetyelam yanhelan in**erl-w**em, parrparl awerl-alhemel, ilpetyel in**erl-w**em — iwenh apek *swag* apek mern apek ker apek in**erl-w**em ilpetyel. (St) *That helpful person goes and gets things quickly — swags or food or meat or whatever — the helpful person gets them straightaway.* ◆ Yanh amperr arlkw**erl-w**ay! Parrp arlkw**erl-w**ay! (T) *Quickly eat that first! Eat it quickly!* ◆ Antywantyw**erl-w**ey urrek, teyek-amparr tha antywantyw**erl-w**ey, urinp nhenh. (St) *Wait while I drink this quickly, I'll quickly drink this hot tea first.* ◆ Ilpety mwerr alhem *swag* apek in**erl-w**etyek. (St) *The helpful person is good and goes and gets the swag quickly.*

+erl-w+[2] (T,E), **+erl-iw+** (T,E) *v.ending*

Shows that more than two are doing the verb action. ◆ Ayeng anyentarl alhem. Atherr alherremarl. Anwantherr al**herl-w**em. (St) *I am going, one. Two are going. We (more than two) are going.* ◆ Anengk al**herl-w**em. (T) *Lots of people are going.* ◆ Alperrty-irremel alperl-alp**erl-w**em, apmer-warl irremel. (St) *They all scattered and went back home.*

+erl-warr+ (T,E), **+erl-werr+** (T,E) *v.ending* = **erl-w+**[2]

Some Anmatyerr people regard this as an Eastern Arrernte way of talking, or a children's way of talking. ◆ Nhenhel an**erl-warr**ay! (T) *All of you, come and sit here!*

+erlek (E) *v.ending*

Goes on a verb to show that the person or thing doing the action of that verb is not the same as the person or thing doing the action of the main verb in the sentence. ◆ Alker yanh akernel alhem wal arem renh war arlter irrerl-ap**erlek**, *aeroplane* mperlkel-ap**erlek**ant. Alhem ra. Arrernelhety-alhem. Atnarnpem anem. (St) *When it [the aeroplane] is flying high in the sky, well it can just be seen going along, shining. It goes along and then it lands, comes down.* ◆ Alkngwa ayeng anetyam aretyakenh — tyerrty talkw-irr**erlek** aretyakenh. (St) *I was not paying attention and I didn't see them — I didn't see the person who went across.* ◆ Iltya rltety-irrem. Arwerl rltety-irrem akin arnan rltety-irrem antey. Tyerrty arrpenh apek alhemel rltety-irr**erlek** anem awem, *'Oh* yaleng rltety-irremaw kwenh'. Ingwel apek

rltety-irr**erlek**. (St) *Fingers make a cracking noise. Trees make a cracking noise as well. If a person is going along then you can hear the cracking sound, 'Oh, something over there is making a crackling sound'. Maybe making a cracking sound in the night.* ◆ Atyeng-warl apety**erlek** tha alharlkwem. War tha alharlkwem ankey angkenty akngerr. (St) *I hunt away somebody who came to me asking for things. I just hunt them away.*
= +erleng

+erleng *v.ending*
Goes on a verb to show that the person or thing doing the action of that verb is not the same as the person or thing doing the action of the main verb in the sentence. ◆ Yay atyenh apek rlkert-irr**erleng** ayeng atham-irrem, alhwarrp-irremel. (St) *If my elder sister gets sick then I feel sorry for her, feel sad.* ◆ Rlkwerr apek arem, tyerrty apety**erleng** arerrem. (N) *Halfway you might see people coming, meet up.* ◆ Thwengk awerl-anem, angkety yanh angkerl-an**erleng**, alhengk awep-awem. (N) *I can understand you, what you are saying, I can understand.* ◆ Arengk utnherr**erleng** anwantherr ater wartam arraw-irrem, arengk-kety. (St) *We move around, frightened of the dogs that are fighting.* ◆ Anwern ingkang arlkwetyart pwak-amparr ker alenh amp**erleng**. *We used to eat the feet first to satisfy our hunger while the meat was cooking there.* ◆ Renh-artekarl angkem urrar kwenh awem, arlk**erleng**, 'Aayyyyyyyyyyy.' (St) *It sounds like her talking. You can hear the echo singing out, 'Aayyyyyyyyyyy.'* ◆ Aherrk irrpem *supper* arlkwerr**erleng**. (N) *The sun goes down while people are eating supper.*
= +erlek
SEE ALSO -arleng[3]

+erlentyarr+ *v.ending* [RESPECT LANGUAGE]
Goes on verbs used in avoidance or respect language. This ending can go on verbs that are only used in ordinary language, as well as on those verbs that are only used in avoidance or respect contexts. It goes after the main part or the stem of the verb and before other endings. ◆ Ntyangkwelkngel tyety-ayerr nta ampern**erlentyarr**em ngwarrekengkw. *You are cooking the meat on the fire for your husband [said by a woman to her daughter].* ◆ Inp**erlentyarr**etyel arntwaly-ayerr angern**erlentyarr**etyel, angenty. *Digging a soakage to get some water.* ◆ Yanhenty anem kel ahan**erlentyarr**ety-alperl-wek, yanhenty-anyeman. Wethenty antey ahanety-alpek. (Sa) *That one [e.g. my son-in-law] has come back. That one has already come back.* ◆ Akalth**erlentyarr**eyaw amely-aketyek keraw, akaltheyaw. Kwey ngwarrekengkw akaltha. (Sa) *Cut up the meat to eat. Daughter, cut up the meat for your husband.*

+ern+[1] (W) *v.ending*
(do something) while going back somewhere, (move something) back (to somewhere). This ending goes on the verb *angem* 'take' to form *angernem* 'take back'. ◆ Ampeng-ilemel ang**ern**etyart panth-artek yanh-lkwerel kin. Arneng mpwaretyart. (N) *When [the goannas] were cooked they used to take them back in dishes made from wood.* ◆ Ker aherr ampwerrk ang**ern**em, merelant tyep-iletyeh. (M) *Take the whole kangaroo back, and then just cut it up back at camp.*

+ern[2] *v.ending*
Shows that the verb action just happened recently. ◆ Nthwemel nthwemel apety-alp**ern** aker-kweny itya — itya akwet. (M) *Walking and walking [I] just came back without any meat — still nothing.* ◆ Arengk yanh alwernay kerek-arrngel. Kerarl arlkwerl-alh**ern**eng. Alwernemel atway! (St) *Chase that dog away. It's just gone and eaten the meat. Chase it and hit it!* ◆ Kwaty urew, tharl amwerrk amek-arety-alh**ern** kwaty urew, ulpayek. *Shopping-ek alhek, amek-arerl-alpek.* (St) *Just yesterday I went and was blocked by the flood water in the creek. I went to go shopping and I was blocked off and came back.*

+ern[3] *prn.ending*
A marker on dual and plural first person pronouns that show that the person being spoken to is not included in the referent group. See Appendix 1.
SEE ALSO ilern, anwern

+err+[1] *v.ending*
Shows that two people or things are doing the verb action. ◆ Angkwey anetyam aherr akwerrk-akert. Kel yatherr alh**err**ek atherrk arlkwetyeh amenheng. (M) *A long time ago there lived a kangaroo with her baby. They used to go together to eat grass.* ◆ Ratherr apety-alp**err**em yanh. Ratherr anety-alp**err**em. (Sa) *Those two are coming back. Those two are coming back to sit down.*

+err+[2] *v.ending*
Shows that two people or things are doing the verb action to each other; each other, one another. ◆ Kereng-arrngel yanh atherr atw**err**em. (T) *Those two are fighting each other over meat.* ◆ Rlkwerr apek arem, tyerrty

apetyerleng ar**err**em. (N) *You might see someone halfway, meet each other halfway.* ◆ Ulengerek ulengerek angk**err**eperrem. Alak apek angketyek. Unta apek atyeng angkem, ayeng ngkweng angkem, ulengerek ulengerek angk**err**em. Arratyant-arey weth-lkwer angk**err**em alknga ar**err**em. (St) *Talking face to face. We two might talk. You might talk to me and I might talk to you, talk to each other face to face. Talk straight to each other, looking each other in the eye.* ◆ Arengk atherr utnh**err**em. (St) *The two dogs are fighting.*

+errirr+ (W,T) *v.ending*

1. Shows that more than two are doing the verb action. ◆ *Olden time* antywang, lwerenam *clean*-em-il**errirr**etyart antywang renh. (N) *The olden-time humpies, that's what they used to clean.* ◆ Tyap arlperrenh ny**errirr**etyart. Arnkarlk arlkwem an rwewarn ang**errirr**emel atyerremel arlkwetyenheng, arlperrenh yanh renh. Arnkarlk arlkwem nheng inyemel inyemel arlkwetyart. (N) *We used to dig up the grubs from the whitewood tree. We'd eat them raw and also after cooking them in the fire. We ate them raw as we were going along digging.*

2. Shows that more than two people or things are being told to do the verb action. ◆ Kwer map, akangkwirr**errirr**ay kwerl tetyekay! (T) *You kids, pay attention to the school teacher!* ◆ Tyerrty yanheh akeweny rnwanenty anth**errirr**ay. (T) *Why don't you all give the poor thing some clothes.* ◆ Ingkang mpatyam alherl-apem, ingkang mpaty aperl-apem. Mpaty renh arelhem, '*Eh*, nhel alhekaw! Ingkang mpaty yanh ar**errirr**ay!' (N) *There are footprints going along. When you see the track, 'Hey, this is where it went! All of you, look at the tracks!'* ◆ Arrakerram alh**errirr**a awenh-intyerr rwang inetyeh. (T) *You all go and get wood, all the aunties and nieces.*

SEE ALSO +a, +ay, +erl-anerr+^{2}, -arey^2

+ety+ (E) do an action in a direction towards someone SEE UNDER **+enty+**^{1}

+ety-akerlem SEE UNDER **-akerl**

+ety-alh+ *v.ending*

1. go and do verb action (alhem '*go*') ◆ 'Nthakenty-inger nga alhem?' 'Urrpety-arengek ayeng alhem, urrpety-inger int**ety-alh**etyek ayeng alhem.' (St) *'How long are you going for?' 'I am going for a few days, I'm going to camp there for a few days.'* ◆ *Might* nhenhel il**ety-alh**emer, alkngarr-il**ety-alh**ek ayenh, *might someone* apekarl apetyepetyem atwetyek atyeng. Alkngarr-il**ety-alh**ek anherrey atyenhel. *Maybe this one went and told me, went and warned me that somebody was coming to fight with me. My daughter-in-law warned me.* ◆ Arelh map ayey ilerrerl-anem, kel artwang yanhel angert-irr**ety-alh**em. (T) *The women are telling stories and that man goes across and interrupts them.* ◆ Ntwang in**ety-alh**ay rwang. (T) *You go and get the firewood.*

2. go like, become like something ◆ Ntywey arrernetyart, akem renh arrernetyart, twernel ampetyeh. Twernel ampetyek, akerl-anek akerl-anek ahern arrernerl-alhetyart. *Jam*-arteh am irr**ety-alh**em. (N) *We used to pick the corkwood flowers and lay them out in the sun to heat up. We'd lay them on the ground in the heat of the sun. Then the honey would go like jam.*

SEE ALSO +erl-alh+

+ety-alp+ *v.ending*

do the verb action and then go back; go back and do the verb action (alpem '*go back*') ◆ Alywelpel-ayel yerrekeyerr perrap kelh anthwerr, an perrap theweyet anthwerr. Akemel akemel akemel kel mer-warn ang**ety-alp**etyenheng theweyet anthwerr. (T) *There is a white substance made by the lerp-scale insect on the* alywelp *tree that is in lumps, and it is really sweet. It is picked and picked and picked and this really sweet stuff is taken back to camp.* ◆ Karnkw awantyetyam aketyam, awantyetyam, panth-warl iletyam, kwenty-kwenty angernetyam mer-warn, merelam ath**ety-alp**emel awantyetyam. *We used to pick the* karnkw *seeds and eat them, heap up the wooden dishes and take the seeds back to camp to grind them up.* ◆ Ker akngerr apek tha atwek, wal tnakelh**ety-alp**em ayeng. (St) *If I have killed a lot of meat, well I go back and skite about it.*

SEE ALSO +erl-alp+

+ety-aynt+ (T,E), **+ety-anty+** (W) *v.ending*

Shows that the verb action continues for some time; shows that the verb action happens after another action; and then (something else happens); because (of that something else happens). ◆ Kerek athek-irr**ety-aynt**em, arlewatyerr *four fella* apekarl atwek. (St) *Getting excited because of killing four goannas.* ◆ Ankwek arrarlkem ayeng, intetyek ankwa anem. Kel ayeng akem-irremel ayeng arrarlk**ety-aynt**em akin. (St) *I am yawning because I want to lie down and sleep. Then when I get up I yawn again.* ◆ Anyanelhem artweyekikw arengk-arey. Ahenparl alpetyam anyanelh**ety-aynt**em. (St) *All the dogs are*

excited about their owner who has come back after going away a long time ago. ◆ Anengkerr-anengkerr-irrem, 'Tyerrty map apetyemarl kwenh.' Kel kweny-itwek a**rety-aynt**em yanh kel apetyewarrem, tharl anengkerr-anengkerr arek-penh. (T) *Having a dream, 'The people are coming.' And then, during the night, seeing the people that you dreamt about coming.* ◆ Ampa nhenh kwerenhel ilety-antyetyart, 'Amatyel ayenh anthern, ankerr kwartam'. (M) *Well, his child came straight back to tell the story, 'My mother has just given me some emu eggs'.*
SEE ALSO +erl-aynt+

+ety-kweny SEE UNDER **-kweny**

+etyakenh *v.ending*
Shows that the action of the verb did not happen, is not happening now, or won't happen etc. ◆ Ayeng ilkelh**etyakenh** ngkweng. (St) *I do not like you.* ◆ Maney an**etyakenh** amparr. *No money* — arrangkw. (N) *There wasn't any money at first. No money — nothing.* ◆ Akwerr, Anmatyarr-kenh, pakwerran Kaytety-kenh. Atnwenth akwerr. Ar**etyakenh**arl ayeng. (St) *'*Akwerr*' is the Anmatyerr word, '*pakwerr*' is the Kaytetye one.* Akwerr *is an animal. I haven't seen one.* ◆ Urlepety-antey ayengan anep-anem, apmer arrpenh-kenh-warl alh**etyakenh**. (St) *I keep stopping in one place, I haven't been to other people's country.* ◆ Iylka atnengk-irrekaw, iylka an**etyakenh**. *The wind has died down, there is no wind.* ◆ Kwatyel rewel arrngert-wem, ilpay. Tyerrty nthakenh alh**etyakenh**, amek anem arem. (St) *The floodwater blocks off the creek. People can't go, they get blocked off.* ◆ Atham-areny ar**etyakenh**. (St) *You can't see the* atham-areny *spirits.* ◆ Ilpetyel ap ra item ker, anwernt-irr**etyakenh**el — ilpetyarl ra. (St) *She cooks the meat really quickly, without bailing up or sulking — she is helpful.* ◆ Mwetek urlaylp-akertarl yanh alhep-alhem pwetyel ant alhenh-alhenh. Ingkwern**etyakenh**. (St) *That person is going around with an unregistered car that can only go in the bush. It hasn't been registered.*
= +ety-kweny, +etyang

+etyal *v.ending*
Used when ordering or telling someone not to do something; don't (do the verb action)!; had better not (do the verb action).
◆ Atw**etyal** akeweny akwek! (T) *Don't hit the poor little thing!* ◆ Ker akeng arlkw**etyal**! (T) *Don't eat that rotten meat!* ◆ Anp**etyal** impa! *Don't touch it!* ◆ Ahekweny aneyaw, ahel angk**etyal** aneyaw. (St) *Sit down and stop being angry, don't talk angrily.* ◆ Arlkwer-il**etyal** impay kwer akwek. (T) *Don't stir the baby up, leave him.*
2. Shows that something is not usually done or shouldn't be done; 'You don't . . . ', 'You shouldn't . . . ' 'I don't . . . ' 'I shouldn't . . . ' etc. ◆ Alhewer ayeng angkem. Nyerr-irr**etyal** ayeng alhewer angkem, tyerrty arrpenhek. (St) *I am just talking anyway. I wouldn't get shamed, I just talk anyway to other people.* ◆ Amwek arlkety-alhem, 'Iwenham nta arna renh antyantyam akernan kwenh? Nhenham arertarl-irrek ntwa antyerl-anetyeh arna akerneh kwenh. *You want to* anerl-anerl arna anty**etyal** kwenh!' (N) *The mother sings out, 'What are you climbing that tree for? You must have gone mad to want to climb to the top of the tree. You should sit down and not climb trees!'* ◆ Arreyeng-arrey-irr**etyal** anwengkerr aneyaw, angkety-kweny aneyaw, arreyeng-arrey-kweny. Irlpa apek anwengkerr akangkwerrey, iwenhek apek anwengkerr akangkwerrey, irlpel manty awerl-anemel. (N) *We shouldn't chatter, but sit down without talking, without making a noise. We'll pay attention and listen to whatever, listening carefully with our ears.*

+etyam *v.ending*
1. was doing the verb action; were doing the verb action (action happened in the past over a period of time); the action of the verb continued for some time in the past
◆ Angkwey an**etyam** aherr akwerrk-akert. Kel yatherr alherrek atherrk arlkwetyeh amenheng. (M) *A long time ago there lived a kangaroo with her baby. They used to go together to eat grass.* ◆ Angayel ap**etyam** mern-kweny ker-kweny. (M) *He came hungry, with no meat and no food.* ◆ Awerr atherr alherl-aperr**etyam** anyerrkentyem mer-warn, amwang yatherr atwekarl-penh. (M) *The two boys went home happy because they had killed a snake.* ◆ Artwang arelh angwely map-akert anerr**etyam**. (M) *A man and a woman were sleeping with their dogs.* ◆ Tyerrty anyent an**etyam**arl-penh anengkem-irrek. (M) *After there had only been one person there were lots.*
2. Shows that the action of the verb usually used to happen. ◆ Anper anthwerr *story* nhenh anwern ilep-ilem. *Olden-time* renh anwern *story* nhenh ilep-ilem anper — mwerr angerr, kerarl atanth**etyam**, kerelarl want**etyam**. (N) *This is really good story that we keep on telling. It's the olden-time story that we continue to tell — it's really good, about the kangaroos that were speared, and the meat that*

we were fed on. ◆ Kernt mpar**etyam**, arnam, arlperlp. Kwaty alakenh arrern**etyam**, arrwekel kwa, angernerl-ap**etyam** *olden time-*el rnwang rwetyel. (N) *The* arlperlp *grass was used to keep the water cool. It was put [on top] of the water in the wooden dish, and the olden-time mob used to carry it along like that.*
◆ Alkwerteng-alkwert ina mpwar**etyam** ampa arrken-irrerretyek, wererl-anetyek, alyaperel wererl-anetyek, kayleng-kayl, alyaperel, kalyel-arrpantey. (St) *The children used to make toy shields to play with, to use when they were throwing pretend boomerangs at each other.*
◆ Anterrng athenh-athenh akin, arrwekelenyelarl arlkw**etyam**, ath**etyam**, awanty**etyam**. (T) *It is also a seed that is ground up, that the olden-time people ground up, ate and licked.*
SEE ALSO +ek[1], +etyart, -inkwern

+etyang (E) *v.ending*
1. Shows that the action of the verb did not happen, is not happening now, or won't happen etc. ◆ Rtetyant ra arlkwem ahaylengkeylerel, akwek, rtety ra arlkwem altywer-ilemel. Pwengarl ra ar**etyang**arl akeng. Irrpenhem ap ra ahernek anem. (St) *The* ahaylengkeyler *bites into your teeth and makes holes in them. They are blind and can't see. They burrow into the ground.* ◆ Nhenham ampwa akeng ampwa. Anter an**etyang**, weyang anetyakenh anter anetyakenh. (St) *This one is thin — it's no good. It's got no fat.*
◆ Ker apek atyenh mern apek atyenh, ayerrp-ilem. Arrpenh mapek anth**etyang** tha ayerrp-ilemel arlkwetyek. (St) *I'm hanging on to my meat and food myself. I'm not giving it to the others, I'm eating it myself.* ◆ Apwert thanh atwaynt**etyang**, akern, anyekerr apek ikwer-they. (Sa) *How could [you] climb that hill, it's too high and you might fall down.*
= +ety-kweny, +etyakenh
2. Is used when the speaker is telling someone or something not to do the verb action
◆ Uremeny apetyay, atyernp alherl-an**etyang**. (Sa) *Come quickly, don't go slowly.* • = +etyal

+etyart *v.ending*
Shows that the verb action used to happen or usually happened. ◆ Ampeng-ilemel angern**etyart** panth-artek yanh-lkwerel kin. Arneng mpwar**etyart**. (N) *When the goannas were cooked they used to take them back in dishes made from wood.* ◆ Amaty-arey panth-akert, anem-akert alherl-atherr-ap**etyart**, tyap arlka akerl-apetyeh awenkel, ker alewatyerr renh atwerl-apetyeh. (N) *Our mothers used to walk along carrying their wooden dishes and their digging sticks, and together with the young girls they gathered grubs and killed goannas as they travelled along.* ◆ Ker nanekwet arlkw**etyart** tyerrtyel angkwey. (T) *In the olden days Aboriginal people used to eat goat meat.*
◆ Alalherrk lpwayelarl irnem. Alalherrk rnpwang nhenh-lkwer arlkw**etyart**, larl-arteh rnpang. Awanty**etyart** larlarl awantyem-artek. Lwerenart. Intertelarl anem. (N) *The* alalherrk *bush grows in the creeks. We used to eat the sweet resin from the* alalherrk *bush, just like a lolly. Like that. We used to suck on it just like you suck lollies. It is found in the base of the tree.* ◆ Arlkemaleh kwer tywenem, ampa akwek map tywenem. Ampa map tywenem antyenhetyek. ra arlpenty-irretyenheng. Wal, amwelek amwelek inang intert atwetyart kwer arlpenty-irretyeh. Kwer amangkelh-ilemel. *No* mernt *anything* apek itya. (N) *The children are put there to climb the desert poplar, so that they will grow tall. Well, the mothers used to hit the base of the tree so that the child would grow tall. That was to grow the children up, and so that they wouldn't get sick or anything like that.*
SEE ALSO +ek[1], +etyam, -inkwern

+etyek, +etyeh (W,T) *v.ending*
1. Shows that the speaker believes that the action 'must' or 'ought' to happen or that the action is supposed to happen.
2. Shows the purpose or the reason for the action; in order to (do something); so that (something can happen), one action happens so that another can happen. ◆ Rwelam atyerrem tyap renh, arlkw**etyeh**. *The grubs are cooked in the fire so that they can be eaten.*
◆ Anywek alhek angk**etyeh** awenhwehek. (M) *The father went to talk to the child's auntie.*
◆ Angkwey anetyam aherr akwerrk-akert. Kel yatherr alherrek atherrk arlkw**etyeh** amenheng. (M) *A long time ago there lived a kangaroo with her baby. They used to go together to eat grass.* ◆ Arnang arrwelty aharl-way, rwang it**etyek**. (T) *Heap up the firewood so that we can light the fire.* ◆ Ikngw**etyek** alhem tyerrty arrpenh, kel apety-alpeyamel antey. (St) *Going and asking the other person, then coming back again.* ◆ Pernelh**etyeh** kwer map, nhenh arrkenel alakenh *moustache* arlka mpwarerl-ap**etyeh**, arralt arlka. *For kids to rub on themselves, for them to have fun going along and making moustaches and beards on themselves.*
3. Shows that the person or thing intends to

do the action or is about to do the action. ◆ Arleng-wern ayeng alh**etyek**. (St) *I've got to go a long way.* ◆ Irrngerney-irremel ayeng alh**etyek** mer arleng pwetyel untherl-ap**etyek**, kerek apek alewatyerr. (Sa) *I am happy to go a long way, looking round in the bush for game such as goannas.*
4. Shows the normal or usual way a thing is done. ◆ Ker arlewatyerr apek it**etyek**, mern apek it**etyek** tyerrkerel. (St) *Goannas or other sorts of food are cooked in a* tyerrker.

+etyel (E) *v.ending*
1. Shows that the verb action is happening now (at the time of speaking).
2. Shows that the verb action is something that typically happens.
3. Shows that the verb action will probably happen or that the doer of the verb action intends the action to happen.
4. Shows that the action is continuing for some time or will probably go on continuously. ◆ Ayeng an**etyel** ampaty atyenhel-rnem-arleng. (Sa) *I am living with my children.* ◆ War apekarl atwerr**etyel** arrkenty-ilerremel ilterr**etyel** — mernek-arrngel apek, alhek-arlek-arrngel apek. (St) *They are fighting and picking on each other and swearing at each other for no particular reason — perhaps over food, or because somebody went.*
SEE ALSO +em[1]

+etyenh *v.ending*
Shows that the verb action will happen or will probably happen; going to (do something), (do something) in the future, will (do the verb action). ◆ Kwenyel apek ywerr**etyenh**. (M) *He may die during the night.* ◆ Lyet nga alp**etyenh** angwerr-angwerr. (St) *You are going back today, in the afternoon.* ◆ Thang anth**etyenh** ker thwep-thwep. (M) *I will give him meat and soup.* ◆ Ayeng alh**etyenh** weth-warl-antey. (St) *I am going to go to that place.* ◆ Lyet renh it**etyenh** anem ker atharl arlwarrernek. Ilenger apek ra amp**etyenh**? (St) *The meat that I left for later is going to be cooked today. When is it going to be cooked?* ◆ Apawerr yanh akarr-irr**etyenh** *football*-warl. (Sa) *People from all over the place are going to get together for football.*
SEE ALSO +etyenheng, +eyam

+etyenheng (W,T) *v.ending*
Goes on a verb to show that this action happens after another action; (do this) after (doing something else), (do something else) so that (this) will (happen), (do something else) and then (do this). ◆ Athem athem rnewarl alparr-warl apek, rwewarlam thelerl-anem alakenh. Kel amperl-anem, mern *nice* anthwerr kelh arlkwerl-an**etyenheng**. (N) *They were ground up into a wooden dish and then poured onto the fire. The seed would cook really nicely, into a seed cake, which was then eaten.* ◆ Ntwamparr alha, alh**etyenheng** ingkern-angkwerr ayeng. (M) *You go first, and I'll go along behind later.* ◆ Arraperel tyart ingkerr mwern**etyenheng** atanth**etyenheng** altywer-altywer irremel. (N) *The kerosene grass will stick into your shirt and pierce it, and the shirt will get full of holes.* ◆ Ker kapert tyarrp-ilem kampely arlkw**etyenheng**. (N) *The head is split open and then the brains are eaten.* ◆ Tyap irrarl-irrem alh**etyenheng** thipem irrerl-alhem tyerrelhem alhem arlpakert. (N) *The grub transforms in the cocoon and then emerges as a moth with wings and then flies around.* ◆ Mangarray arrkernkel-arleng anem altywernem anyent, alakenh anem. Akemem renh tyarrp-ak**etyenheng**. (N) *The bloodwood gall grows on the bloodwood tree. We pick them and then split them open.* ◆ Angank arwengkalth — arraty. Nyenngel arlkwerl-anem akweteth akweteth ateram arrtyan**etyenheng**, pwerlt-irrem. (N) *Crows are robbers — that's true. They always sneak around and steal food to eat and then when they are frightened they fly off, clear out.*
SEE ALSO +eyam, +etyenh

+ew Adds emphasis to what someone is saying.
SEE UNDER **+aw**

+ewarr+ *v.ending*
Goes on verbs to show that more than two people are doing the verb action. ◆ Atyemey-rrpwer alherl-wetyam, menh-menh rrpwer alherl-wetyam. Ker arlka angety**ewarr**em aperl-aperlel-rrpwer, mern arlka *everything* — parl arlka angety**ewarr**em kwenh. *All my* atyemey *[mother's fathers] and my* menh-menh *[mother's mothers] used to go. They used to bring back everything — bush bananas, bush tomatoes.* ◆ Arna ra ulpayel tneyn**ewarr**eparrem anterrng-akertarl ra, ilkert ran. (T) *The* ilkert *trees grow along the creek, and they have seeds.* ◆ Arlpelhart anem *self* akin rnpwa. Theweyet. Rnpwang anem arlpelhartel. Wanty**ewarr**etyart. (N) *The* arlpelhart *tree is different again and has sweet resin. There is a sweet resin on the* arlpelhart *tree that they used to suck on.* ◆ Artwa arnkentyel intep-intem mapam yanhan. Arnkenty-areny mapey apety**ewarr**em ankey. (T) *That mob over there are the men that sleep in*

the single-men's camp. All the men from the single-men's camp come up asking for things. ◆ Rrwep-rrwep-wety tyerrtyarl ater arrtyan**ewarr**em antyweng arratemel. 'Yanh arraty akwetarl apety kwenh!' (N) *Because of the whirlwind people rush out of their humpies. 'It's coming straight [at us]!'*
SEE ALSO +err+[1], +errirr+, +erl-w+[2], +erl-warr+

+ey *v.ending*
1. Used in asking for or giving permission to do something, in the polite expression of intention to do something, or in suggesting that someone should do something; 'Can I (do this)?', 'Would you like . . . ?', 'Are they going to . . . ?', 'I'll (do something)', 'Let's (do something)', 'We'll (do something)' 'Let him (do something)' etc. ◆ Mer atyehenh-warn alherr**ey**. (M) *Let's go to my camp.* ◆ Ayeng alkngarelh**ey** urrek. *Wait, I'll look back.* ◆ Apakek amparr tha tey antyw**ey** arlkweyamel. (St) *I might drink some tea first then I'll eat later.* ◆ Ikngwetyek**ey**ay tha irrtyelh-il**ey** kwenh arelh nhakw kwenh irrer alhetyek irrtyelh-ilem alhetyek irrer. *'Come on, we go* kwenh.*'* (St) *I'll ask that woman over there to go hunting with me. 'Come on, let's go.'*
2. Goes on the end of word(s) for something you are asking about or checking on; 'Is it . . . ?', 'Isn't it?' ◆ Alhem**ey**? *Are you going?*

+eyam (E) *v.ending*
Goes on a verb to show that this action happens after another action; (do this) after (doing something else), (do something else) so that (this) will (happen), (do something else) and then (do this). This ending may be followed by either *+el* or *+eng*. ◆ Apakek amparr tha tey antywey arlkw**eyam**el. (St) *I might drink some tea first then I'll eat later.* ◆ Ikngwetyek alhem tyerrty arrpenh, kel apety-alp**eyam**el antey. (St) *Going and asking the other person, then coming back again.* ◆ Apmer althem, arnel apek atnemel althem. Arnam renh iwemel, akethel ilemel int**eyam**eng. (St) *Clearing the grass away from the camp, with a stick or a digging stick. Throwing away the grass and clearing it so that you can sleep there.* ◆ Irrer ayeng alhetyek ker arlewatyerrek, angwerrel ant apety-alp**eyam**. (St) *I am going hunting for goannas, and I will only come back in the afternoon.* ◆ Alharlkwem, ayeng an**eyam**eng. 'Ankey-akert alpeyaw!' Alharlkwem tha ikngel tha arlkw**eyam**eng. (St) *Chase (someone) away so that I can then sit down. 'Go back you bludger!' I hunt them away so that I can eat by myself.* ◆ Waram tha ngkweng arlenthek, artelhetyek apek. Newanenty apek *something* awenh apek, arlenthekarl tha. Kenh ntwa atyeng anthenty-alp**eyam**el. (St) *I just lent it to you, so that you could cover yourself up. Some clothes or whatever, I lent them to you. And then you will give them back to me later.* ◆ Angayel apek artang-iletyek, alhetyek apek. Artang-ilem tey apek mern apek. Tha apek artang-iletyek, ngkwengetyem athath, ntwa anem antyw**eyam**eng. *You might [eat] first if you're hungry, or go [somewhere] first. You might have tea or food first. I might drink before you, and then you drink.*
SEE ALSO +etyenheng, +etyenh

+eyaw *v.ending*
1. Goes on verbs to make a command or to tell someone (forcefully) that you want them to do something. ◆ Mern anth**eyaw** akewenyek angayelarl anem-arlek. (T) *Give some food to the poor thing who is hungry.* ◆ Rtwenk atyeng arrern**eyaw** ayeng intetyek. (St) *Put a head rest there for me so that I can sleep.* ◆ Arna ingwer-kenh im**eyaw**. *Leave that, it's someone else's.*
2. Goes on verbs to suggest that somebody must or should do the action. ◆ Anwengkerr ntert an**eyaw** angkety-kweny, yatenh angkem-arleng. (N) *We should sit down and not talk, because that person is talking.* ◆ Arwerrek ayeng urnt**eyaw** ker arlewatyerrek kwenh arwerrelarl intep-intemek. (St) *I've got to go and look round for a hole where a goanna is lying.*

+eyay *ending*
Goes on verbs and nominals to provide emphasis. ◆ Antangkem, 'Petyay teyekay, mern nhenh inerl-alpetyekay!' Antangk**eyay** tha kenh ngkweng. (N) *Calling you over, 'Come for tea, come and get this food to take back!' I am calling you over.* ◆ Lyek arlkerl. Lyekam arlkerl yanh. Tyap**eyay** arlkerlel kwen intem, anyematy-artek akin. (N) *The* arlkerl *bush has sharp spikes. There is a grub that lives in the base of the bush, like a witchetty grub.*

+eyekw (E) his or her kin relation; their kin relation SEE UNDER **+ikw**

+eyn+ (E) *v.ending*
1. Goes on verbs to show that the action is happening while the doer of the verb action is going past somewhere or moving along. ◆ Menyeynterl arwerlarl alth**eyn**erl-anemel, antywer anetyangarl ileynem. Menyeynterl akngerr anem alhem weth. Akngerrel alth**eyn**erl-anem alanh alpep-alpem. *The locusts are the ones that go along stripping the*

trees, go along wiping out the grass. Lots of locusts go along like that, stripping the foliage. ◆ Athem-athem atwem apek ampa. Athem-athem atw**eyn**em atw**eyn**em atw**eyn**em, athem-athem atw**eyn**em, arnel apek. Melikw apek. Ampa urntem arna kwerety — mekikwety. (St) *Hitting at the child. Maybe the mother goes along and tries to whack the child with a stick. Then the child runs away from the stick — from its mother.*

2. Shows that the verb action happens over a geographical area or along a path. ◆ Nhenh akwa pwerlep akwa int**eyn**em, amak-warl-athek. *Here the upper arm goes along towards the elbow.*

3. Shows that the action is performed or continues over a period of time. ◆ Nyerr anetyangel unta arnkatyel il**eyn**ep**eyn**em, nyerr apek ngkwenh anetyangel arnkatyel nyerr irretyang. (Sa) *You don't get embarrassed, you just keep on talking confidently. You don't get shamed.* ◆ Ina angwaremel akin arlkeny yanh arrernepernem. Nhenh unta atyenh arep-arem angwar**eyn**ep**eyn**em. (St) *They copy designs as well. You might look at mine and go along copying it.* ◆ Ntang antywer. *Seed* an *yellow*-arl apwert-arlkwenh. Lherel kwenh arnkengeny wethel an**eyn**etyel, atherrkenyel, kwaty-taym. Ntang apwert-arlkwenh mwerr-angker innga. (Sa) *A grass seed. The button grass seeds are yellow. There are lots found growing in the creek after rain. The button grass seed is really nice.* ◆ Antywerretyart angkethakwel, apeng-areny artekerr. Lyetarr kwaty ant anem anty**weyn**erl-wetyel — kwaty ant anem anty**weyn**etyel. (Sa) *They used to drink the liquid from the roots of the kurrajong tree when they were thirsty. Nowadays they just go along drinking water — they just drink water.*

SEE ALSO +enh+3

+eyneng (E) *k.ending* [RESPECT LANGUAGE]

Goes on the end of kin terms to make an ordinary kin term into a respect one. ◆ Ngwarrengkw ahanek arreng**eyneng** arrep-iletyek. (Sa) *Your husband has gone to see his grandfather [said by a mother to her daughter].* ◆ Ampweyampw**eyneng** ayepelirrerl-iwerretyel-kety. (Sa) *[Look out] for all the mothers-in-law sitting there [said by a son-in-law].*

+eytarr (E) *n.ending*

Goes on a few nominals, in particular *arlpenty* 'long, tall'. It seems to have no meaning of its own separate from the combined form.

Hh

-henh (W,T) belonging to, owned by SEE UNDER **-kenh**1

-hety (W,T) for fear of someone or something SEE UNDER **-kety**

Ii

ika (T,E) *n.*

1. wax (in ears) ◆ Ika arrngert-welhek ika nhenh irlpel-arleng. *The wax has blocked up the ear here.*

2. egg shell

3. the crust of bread ◆ Mern impen iwetyang anay — alhewerel arlkwetyek mern ikinp. (Sa) *Don't throw the last of the bread away — just eat the bread along with the crust.*

4. the skin of some fruits or bulbs ◆ Panth-warl mern yerrakwerr ikinp arlkwekerr thwerremarl renh, ilpem anem renh. Ika yanh map iltyelarl ikewepewem. (St) *The skins of the bush onion are rubbed off and then separated by yandying. The skins of the bush onion are peeled off with the fingers.*

SEE ALSO rta, ikewem, irrnya

ikalharr (E) *n.*

the hook on woomera ◆ Ikalharr amirr-areny — amirr-warlarl arrernem ikalharr, atanthemel irrtyartel. Arreylp akely weth. Kel ikwereng atanthemel irrtyartel ker apek atanthemel. (Sa) Ikalharr *are found on woomeras — they are put on woomeras and then the woomera is used for throwing spears. That little sharp thing. From there the spear is thrown to spear animals.*

SEE ALSO lywernk

ikanem (E) avoid particular relations SEE UNDER **kanem**

ikarl (T,E) *n.*

yabby or crab (*Cherax destructor*) (?). Also referred to as *ker ikarl*. ◆ Ker ikarl. Ker ikarl kwaty iterelarl aylpem. Angwenh-akwey-apeny, atneth-akert-apeny. (Sa) *Yabbies. They burrow into the sides of creeks and are like what's-its-names, scorpions.*

SEE ALSO kwertetyengetyeng

ikarl-ikarl (T,E) *n.*

cracked foot (?)

SEE ALSO tyarrp-tyarrp

ikelak *n.*

eagle (from English 'eaglehawk')

SEE ALSO irrety

ikelh a mass or lump of something SEE UNDER **kelh**

iker *n.*

1. clay, dried up soakage, soakage with clay on the bottom. Also referred to as *apwert iker.* ◆ Iker anem kwenaw. Angentyarl angernem, wal rltar-rnternepernem renh, uyarn anem angernepernem apwertarl, apwert iker anem. (St) *There's clay on the bottom. [If you are] digging a soakage it makes a banging noise when you thrust the crowbar into the creek, and it's hard to dig because there is rock there, clay at the bottom.*

2. a small amount of water, a sprinkle of water ◆ Kwaty akngerr anetyakenh, ikereyay. Thelelhepelhem kwenh. Angenty. Wal ikerarl thelelherl-anem, akwek-amperl. (St) *There's not much water in the soakage, just a little bit seeping out. A little bit of water is seeping out —* iker.

iker-irrem *vi.*

dry up (water or soakage) ◆ Itya, kwaty iker-irrek. (M) *There's nothing, the water has dried up.*

ikewem (E), **ikiwem** (E) *vt.*

skin or peel something; rub skin off fruit; shell an egg (ika *'shell', 'crust'*; iwem *'throw away'*) ◆ Panth-warl mern yerrakwerr ikinp arlkwekerr thwerremarl renh, ilpem anem renh. Ika yanh map, iltyelarl ikewepewem. (St) *The skins of the bush onion are rubbed off and then separated by yandying. The skins of the bush onion are peeled off with the fingers.* ◆ Ker kwart atyenh tha ikiwem. (St) *I am peeling my egg.* ◆ Alerl tha ikewey nhenh kwart apek, *orange same,* mern yerrakwerr apek. *Wait while I peel this egg, or an orange, or maybe a bush onion.*

= kek-wem

SEE ALSO irrnyewem

ikirrem (E) observe rules associated with respect of particular relations SEE UNDER **kerrem**

ikiwem (E) skin or peel something SEE UNDER **ikewem**

iknga (E) alone, by yourself SEE UNDER **inga**

ikngerr (E) east SEE UNDER **ingerr**

ikngerrakw (E) east SEE UNDER **angerrakw**

ikngeth (E) itchy grub SEE UNDER **ingeth**

ikngwem (E) ask someone for something SEE UNDER **ngwem**

ikngwer (E) other, another one SEE UNDER **ingwer**

+ikw, +eyekw (E) *k.ending*

his or her kin relation; their kin relation. Goes on the end of kin terms and other words that are similar to kin terms. ◆ Atwety akely, akwek-amperl alhelth angem ra, aympel, meli**kw**. (St) *The little joey, its mother carries the little thing in her pouch.* ◆ Arelhel meli**kw**el ilem mam ikwerenh artwethen, 'Aperl-nheng atherr yanh'. Anewart renh 'aperl-nheng' akem, mi**kw**el, artwekenh mi**kw**elan ilem 'aperl-nheng atherr' akem, anherri**kw** then ampi**kw** then. Arelh-kenh mi**kw** mweri**kw**antarl ilem, 'ngwarr-nheng atherr' akem, arelh-kenh mi**kw**an 'ngwarr-nheng atherr' akem. (Sa) *The woman, the mother of the man, says of her son and his wife, 'There's those two, husband and wife,* aperl-nheng atherr*'. The man's mother calls the spousal couple* 'aperl-nheng' *— that's referring to her son and her daughter-in-law. The mother of his wife calls him [her son-in-law]* 'mwer' *and refers to the spousal couple as* 'ngwarr-nheng atherr'.

SEE ALSO +aty[1], +engkw, +ekw

ikwa (T,E), **ikwang** (T) *n.*

1. skin name, subsection name (general term) ◆ Ikwa ilek ngan? *What skin are you?* ◆ Ilek-apatherr ngan ikwa ngkwenh? (Sa) *What is your skin name?* ◆ Ikwa ayeng Pwerl. *I am a Pwerl.* ◆ Ikwek arrangkw ikwa anpernerrenty anetyakenh, ikwek arrangkw 'alyelk'. Alhernter mapan ikwek arrangkw, 'alyelk'. *Not having a skin name is like not being related, not having a skin name is* 'alyelk'. *Non-Aboriginal people don't have skin names, they are* 'alyelk' *['without identity'].*

SEE ALSO -apatherr

2. body scent or smell, a person's or animal's scent. ◆ Ikwa ntyernekerr, rwarr-angkwarrarl alheman. Rwarr-angkwarr alhetyal, ikwa ntyernekerr, ikwa ntyernemel ra untemarl, aherr apek. Antyey apekarl intyem. (St) *The kangaroo might smell the scent of your body if you go upwind from it. Don't go upwind, in case it smells you and runs away. It might smell your sweat.*

3. the taste of something; flavour, a strong or 'good' taste ◆ Ker ikwakert. *Shop*-areny alyelk. (Sa) *[Bush] meat has taste. The meat from the shop is tasteless.* ◆ Ikwa anetyang ker apek pwelek — *no* alhwa. Aherrant mwerr. (Sa) *Beef has no taste — no blood. Only kangaroo is tasty.*

SEE ALSO kwang, ikwemey, anpernem

ikwarr (E) *n.*

types of skink (*Ctenotus* spp.). Also referred to as *ker ikwarr.*

SEE ALSO alyalkarr, lyengkarr, lyangkay-lyangkay

ikwelengk (T,E), **kwelengk** (T,E) *n.*

mulga snake, king brown snake (*Pseudechis australis*) ◆ Arrwekelenyel ikwelengk

arlkwetyam. (St) *The olden-time people ate mulga snakes.*
= atetherr arlkwenh, arreperlp, kantharlkw, alhingk, tyamparl
SEE ALSO arreperlp

ikwemey, kwemey *n.*
tasty food, sweet-tasting, sweet things
◆ Arwengalker kwemey anthwerr. (T) *Sugarbag is really sweet-tasting.* ◆ Ker tha mwerr arlkwetyeh, ilewerr-penh, ikwemey. (M) *I'm going to eat some nice tasty meat that has been salted. Goannas are tasty.*
SEE ALSO ikwa, alemeh
kwaty ikwemey-ilenh (E)
sugar (lit. 'that which makes water sweet')
ker ikwemey ilenh-ilenh (T)
salt (lit. 'that which makes meat tasty')
SEE ALSO thalt, melyek, ilewerr, ulewerr

ikwenty (E) *n.*
1. ashes used for chewing with tobacco
2. various plants that are burnt to make ashes for chewing with tobacco ◆ Arelhel ikwenty nthiletyel. (Sa) *The woman is burning [plants] to make ashes for tobacco.*
= arnmeny

ikwer for him/her/it SEE UNDER **kwer**[2]

-il+ *n.ending*
1. Goes on nominals and makes them into transitive verbs; make or cause (something to happen). For example, *akern* 'high', *akern-ilem* 'raise up'.◆ Kwaty-artek akern-**il**em. Mwetek apek akern-**il**em, mwetek akern anem arnarem, angentel akern-**il**em, apwert arlka. Ilewerr arlka. Ilewerr weth kwaty-artekarl yanhelarl akern-**il**em. (St) *It raises them up like water. It might lift up a car and you will see a car coming along, raised up by the mirage. Hills as well. Salt lakes as well. The mirage lifts up the salt lake and it looks like water.* ◆ Rlterrk-ilem. Aley apek angkep-angkem, 'Urrek tha rlterrk-**il**ey'. (St) *Tighten something. Someone there might say, 'Wait while I tighten it'.* ◆ Ampeng-**il**emel angernetyart panth-artek yanh-lkwerel kin. Arneng mpwaretyart. (N) *When the goannas were cooked they used to take them back in dishes made from wood.* ◆ Apmer aketh-**il**emel atnhwerrem, thenkarr-kety. (St) *The camp is cleared up, because of the prickles.* ◆ Amengel anngang tywen-**il**em. (T) *Flies make your eyes sore.*
2. Follows an English transitive verb when used in Anmatyerr to make it into an Anmatyerr verb. The English word often has the *+em-*[2] ending before *-ilem.* ◆ Yenper arternetyam, *clean* antem yarr-wetyam, arrerlp-**il**etyam. Kel *clean*-ilemel arternemel arrernetyam. (N) *The spearwood was scraped and cleaned and then straightened and sharpened. When it was cleaned it was put in the fire to straighten and sharpen it.*
◆ Anwernenh *show*-em-**il**etyart angerr-pat mapel. Lweren anwern arek arek arek awenkel. (N) *All the old people used to show us [about bush food]. That's what we saw all the time when we were teenagers.* ◆ *Salt*-arl anwern inetyart *sell*-em-**il**etyart, an pwelekam *salt*-em-**il**etyart anwenth pwelekam. (N) *We used to get the salt and sell it to make salted bullock meat.* ◆ *Choke*-em-**il**etyart anwern kwep angerrety, arrernetyart *billycan*-warl. (N) *We used to choke those big frogs called* kwep, *and put them in a billycan.*
SEE ALSO +elh-il+
ipert-ilem *vt.*
make a hole, dig a hole (ipert '*hole*')
mwerr-ilem *vt.*
make something better; fix something, heal someone (mwerr '*good*', '*well*')
altywer-ilem *vt.*
open something (up); make a hole in something (altywer '*opening*', '*hole*')

-ilerr+ *ending*
1. Goes on nominals and makes them into reciprocal verbs; make each other a certain way or make each other do something, cause something to happen to each other. ◆ War apekarl atwerretyel arrkenty-**ilerr**emel ilterretyel — mernek-arrngel apek, alhek-arlek-arrngel apek. (St) *They are fighting and picking on each other and swearing at each other for no particular reason — perhaps over food, or because somebody went.*
2. Follows an English transitive verb when used in Anmatyerr to make it into a reciprocal Anmatyerr verb. The English verb often has the *+em*[2] ending before *-ilerr+.*
◆ Ampa atherr apek *bump*-em-**ilerr**em apatwerrem. (Sa) *Two kids are bumping each other.*
SEE ALSO +elh-ilerr+, +err[2]

ila (E), **ayla** (E) *prn.*
we (we two). This pronoun is used in the subject part of the sentence (i.e. representing the 'doers' of the verb action). It is strictly used for people who are in the same patrimoiety and same generation moiety — for example, two sisters or two brothers, or a person together with their paternal grandfather — but it may also be used as a general term. The person being spoken to is

included. See Appendix 1. ◆ Kemarr atherran ila alherrem. *We two Kemarr are going.*
SEE ALSO ilengkerr, ilak, ilanth, ilern, ilern-ingkerr, ilernak, ilernanth

ilak (E) 'What?' SEE UNDER **ilek**

ilak, **aylak** (E) *prn.*
we (we two). This pronoun is used in the subject part of the sentence (i.e. representing the 'doers' of the verb action) when the two people belong to the same patrimoiety and different generation moiety; for example, a person together with their father or father's sister. The person being spoken to is included. See Appendix 1. ◆ Ilak alherretyek awenh-nheng atherr. (T) *We two are going, auntie and niece [or nephew].*
SEE ALSO ila, ilengkerr, ilanth, ilern, ilern-ingkerr, ilernak, ilernanth
ilenhak, **ilenhakenh**, **ilenhenhakenh**, **aylenhak** (E) *prn.*
us (two). This pronoun is used in the object part of the sentence (i.e. representing those the verb action is 'done to').
ilakeh (W,T), **ilahek** (W,T), **ilekak** (E), **aylakek** (E) *prn.*
for us, to us (two) ◆ Ilahek thang ker item. (M) *I am cooking meat for the two of us.*
ilahekenh (W,T), **ilekakenh** (E), **aylakakenh** (E) *prn.*
ours (belonging to us two)
ilak-akey (E), **aylak-akey** (E) *n.*
we (belonging to the same patrimoiety as each other)
SEE ALSO -akey, ilernak-akey, ilern-ingkerr-akey, anwern-akey, anwernakerr-akey, anakerr-akey
CAN SOUND A BIT LIKE alak-akey *'they (people belonging the opposite patrimoiety)'*

ilamwerrk (E) *n.* [RESPECT LANGUAGE]
yesterday ◆ Ilamwerrkel ahanerlentyarrety-alpek. (Sa) *They [respect kin] came back yesterday.*
= ahamwerrk
SEE ALSO amwerrk

ilanth, **aylanth** (E) *prn.*
we (we two). This pronoun is used in the subject part of the sentence (i.e. representing the 'doers' of the verb action) when the two people belong to different patrimoieties; for example, a person together with their husband or wife, their sister-in-law or their cross-cousin. The person being spoken to is included. See Appendix 1. ◆ Ilanth alherretyek anewart atherr. (T) *We two will go, husband and wife.*
SEE ALSO ila, ilengkerr, ilak, ilern, ilern-ingkerr, ilernak, ilernanth
ilenhanth, **ilenhenhanthenh**, **aylenhanth** (E) *prn.*
us (two). This pronoun is used in the object part of the sentence (i.e. representing those the verb action is 'done to').
ilehanth (W,T), **ilenhehanth** (W,T), **ilekanth** (T,E), **aylekanth** (E) *prn.*
for us, to us (two)
ilahenthenh (W,T), **ilanth-henh** (W,T), **ilekanthenh** (E), **aylekanthenh** (E) *prn.*
ours (belonging to us two)

ilanthem *vt.*
1. send someone away; send someone off to do something ◆ Ilanthem tha ra alpetyek. (St) *I'll send him back.* ◆ Ilanthem. 'Mern arlkwety alhang rntwarr kwenh — mer-warn kwenh. Alpang kwenh.' (N) *Sending someone off. 'Go and eat the food further away — go back to camp. Go back.'*
SEE ALSO atniwem, tyarl-wem
2. send something to someone, send a message, pass on a message ◆ Tharl ilanthem mantarr apek nhakwek, mern anaty apek ilanthem tha angkwerekaty apek kakeyek apek akngeyek apek. (St) *I might send some clothes to those over there, or some bush potatoes, to my elder sister, elder brother or to my father.* ◆ Tha angkety ilanthem tyerrty arrpenhel-ayeng ayeng inety apetyetyeh. (M) *I'm sending a message with someone else to tell someone to come and pick me up.* • SEE ALSO thwenem
3. let someone or something go ◆ Pwelek map *yard*-elarl irnem ilanthem atherrk-warn. (T) *The bullocks that are standing in the yard are let go [so they can go off] to the grass.* • SEE ALSO tyarl-wem
4. hunt or shoo something away
angkety ilanthem (W,T), **angka ilanthem** (E)
send a message, pass on a message (angkety *'story', 'word', 'message'*)

ilatwem *vt.*
throw something on the ground; push someone around; wrestle ◆ Tha ngenh ilatwekerr alhay! (Sa) *Go away or I'll flatten you.* ◆ Ker arlewatyerr apek ilatwem. *Throwing the goanna to the ground.*
SEE ALSO ntewem, arlkwatem, anampart-wem
CAN SOUND A BIT LIKE rlwatem *'meet someone'*
ilatwerrem *vi.*
wrestle; push each other around ◆ Kwer atherr ilatwerrem. Ilatwerrem ilatwerrem arrken-irrem, ilatwerrerl-anem ilatwerrerl-anem kwer atherr. 'Kwer mapay, rlkert-

irrekety kwenh! Ilatwerrerl-anety kweny. Kwer impay!' (N) *The two kids are wrestling. Wrestling and pushing each other around and enjoying themselves. 'Stop it you kids, or you'll get sick! Don't push each other around. Stop it you kids!'*

ilek (E), **ilak** (E) *n.*
'What?' ◆ Ilek angkarl untan? *What language do you speak?*
= wenh
SEE ALSO angwenh, nthakenh, nthanh
ilek-iperr (E)
'What's the matter?'
ilekay (E), **ilakay** (E)
'What?'
= wenhay
ilek-apert (E)
'What's wrong?', 'What's up?'
= wenh-apert
ilek-pat (E)
'What's-his-name'
ilekakwey (E)
'What's-his-name'
= wenhekwey
ilek-apatherr (E)
1. 'What skin?'
2. 'What's-his-name?'
= wenh-apatherr
ilekek (E)
'What for?', 'Why?' ◆ Ilekek nhenheyan atherreperrem ampwerrk ilwep-ilwem atyewey-rnem? Ilek ra nhengey? (Sa) *Why is [this person] killing themself laughing? What's it about?* ◆ Ilekek unta ayenh apentem? (Sa) *Why are you following me?*
= wenhek
ilek-kety (E)
'Why?', 'What for?', 'From what?' ◆ Ilek-kety unta arrwirnt-irretyel, irntwem-irrem? (Sa) *Why are you getting sulky and turning your back on me?*

ilem *vt.*
1. tell someone about something, explain something, give a message
2. say something, say something in a particular way ◆ Thang ilem, 'Ilern-apatherr alherretyeh, lyweny apek'. Mpetyan arrpaty, 'ilern-apatherr' ilem. (T) *I'll say, 'We in the same generation moiety will go hunting'. I call someone who is Mpetyan like me 'ilern-apatherr'.*
3. tell someone to do something ◆ 'Wapey-kety rntert-irray' — ampek ilem. (St) *'Be quiet because of the whitefella' — that's what you tell kids.*
4. tell a story ◆ *'Eh* apetyeyaw awetyekaw, angkety iletyeh.' (P) *'Hey, come and listen, tell the story.'*
5. call something by a particular word, call something by a name ◆ 'Alker anert' anwern ilem akern alker. (M) *'Alker anert' is what we call the high part of the sky.* ◆ Kalyeyampan ilem Kaytetyel. Alyeyamparl ananther ilem, Anmatyarrel. (St) *'Kalyeyamp' is what it's called in Kaytetye. In Anmatyerr we say 'alyeyamp'.*

ilelhem *vi.*
1. say something about yourself, tell a story about yourself, explain about yourself ◆ Nheng twern-penh *hot time* alakenh antem ilelhem. 'Ayeng kwenh kapert arepwelepwel-irrem terangk-terangk irrem *see* alakenh.' (N) *You know, particularly in the hot weather, you might say, 'My head is spinning and I feel like I am drunk'.* ◆ Ilek-they nga arnkelyan anetyel? Angketyakenh arnkely ahel. Ilelha atyengay. Ilek-apertarl ngan anep-anem tyernetyangan? Arntety apek nga awelhek apek ilelhetyang. (Sa) *Why are sitting there sulkily? You are sulky and angry and not saying anything. Tell me. Why are you sitting there and not answering? Maybe you felt sick and you're not saying anything about it.* ◆ Arelh arrpenh rntwarr-ilem kenh arleltyarl interl-anem, arlelty intem arelh arrpenh. Kenh arelh arrpenh ilelherleng mer kwerenh, 'Ntwarr-irray, rntwarr intay!' (N) *Moving another woman out of the way, one who is lying there without moving. And then the other woman claims that it's her place and says, 'Move out of the way, sleep further away!'*
2. say what you are doing, explain yourself to someone ◆ Ayeng tyerrty nhakwek ilelherl-alhem lywenyarl alhem. (T) *I'm going to tell that person that I'm going hunting.*
• SEE ALSO angkawelhem
3. call yourself by a particular word or name ◆ 'Iwenharlam ntwan anem anpernenty ngkwengenh arreny?' 'Ngwarray' arlka war ilelhem — anpernenty ra kwa, arreny. (N) *'What is your skin name?' [The person] might just say 'Ngwarray' — that's the skin name.* ◆ Anwengkerr ilem 'nywerrp' map, kenh anwengkerr ilelhem 'kweyekar'. (M) *We call [them] 'nywerrp' and we call ourselves 'kweyekar'.*
4. tell someone that you did something; apologise, confess, admit ◆ Ayeng ilelhety-alpem, mwetek ngkwengenh tha angek. (M) *I'm coming back to tell you that I took your car.* ◆ Ilelhetyek ayengaw, ayeng angkekarl-penh. (St) *I've got to tell [them] what I said.*
5. talk to yourself

SEE ALSO +elh

ilelhenty angem, ilelhenty akngem (E) tell story to others, take news to others (angem *'take', 'carry'*) ◆ Angka yanhel ilelhenty angep-angemaw, tyerrty nhakwel anep-anemek. Ilem ra kel arrpenhek anem ra ilety-alpem. (St) *[He] is going and telling that story to the others over there. He tells them and then goes back and tells others.* ◆ Urrtyirremel ilelhenty angep-angem. Kel arrpenh an ahel anem irrem. *'Eh,* yanhel ilelhenty angep-angem, urrtyirrentyel.' (St) *Going and telling an untrue story. Then someone else gets angry. 'Hey, that person is going around telling lies.'*

ilemey (E), **alemey** (E) *n.kin* [RESPECT LANGUAGE]
A way of referring to the father's father and the father's father's brothers and sisters of a person whom the speaker is in an avoidance relationship to. For example, a woman may use *ilemey* to refer to her son-in-law's father's father, or a man may use *ilemey* to refer to his mother-in-law's father's father.
SEE ALSO arreng

ilemey-nheng (E), **alemey-nheng** (E) *n.kin*
a group of two or more people related as grandparents (father's father or their brothers and sisters) and grandchildren (a man's son's child or a person's brother's son's child). This is said by a woman if one of them is her son-in-law, or by a man if one of them is his mother-in-law.
SEE ALSO arreng-nheng

ilemey-nheng atherr (E), **alemey-nheng atherr** (E) *n.kin*
a grandparent (father's father or their brothers and sisters) together with their grandchild (a man's son's child or a person's brother's son's child). This is said by a woman if one of them is her son-in-law, or by a man if one of them is his mother-in-law. ◆ Kerek untetyek alherrey, alemey-nheng atherr. Arreng-nheng atherr. (Sa) *Go and off and find some meat with your grandfather [said by someone who is in a respect relationship to the grandfather].*
SEE ALSO arreng-nheng atherr

ilengar (E) 'When?' SEE UNDER **lwengar**

ilengem (E), **ilenngem** (E) *n.*
1. something frightening, scary or unknown ◆ Ilenngem weth akenh arrenty nhenh apetyekarl anwekantherr-warl. (Sa) *That scary thing, that monster has come here where we are.*
SEE ALSO arrenty
2. an oblique way of referring to a ceremonial business place or thing ◆ Ilengem-warl alhek atey-rnem. (St) *The men went to do their ceremonial business.* ◆ Ilengem-angketyarr-kety mwanty alhetyek. (St) *Go carefully and watch out for all the business things.*
SEE ALSO amek-amek
3. 'What-d'ye-call-it', 'What's-his-name' ◆ Werlaty-angketyarrarl ahekwenayt, werlaty-akert. Werlaty akely-rnem. Werlaty-artek ilenngem akwey ikwerenh. (Sa) *The* ahekwenayt *grub has lots of 'breasts'. Little breasts. They are like — what-d'ye-call-it — like breasts.*

ilenger (T,E) 'when?' SEE UNDER **lwengar**

ilengkerr, ilingkerr *prn.*
we (two). This pronoun is used in the subject part of the sentence (i.e. representing the 'doers' of the verb action) when the two people are both in the same patrimoiety and the same generation moiety; for example, a person together with their sister or brother, or their father's father. The person being spoken to is included. See Appendix 1.
SEE ALSO ila, ilern-ingkerr, ilak, ilanth, ilern, ilernak, ilernanth

ilengkerrenh, ilingkerrenh, ilenh-ingkerrenh *prn.*
us (two). This pronoun is used in the object part of the sentence (i.e. representing those the verb action is 'done to').

ileh-ingkerr (W,T), **ilek-ingkerr** (E) *prn.*
for us, to us (two)

ileh-ingkerrenh (W,T), **ilek-ingkerrenh** (E) *prn.*
ours (belonging to us two)

ilenngem (E) something frightening, scary or unknown SEE UNDER **ilengem**

ilenty *n.*
galah (*Eolophus roseicapillus*) ◆ Thep ilentyel anterrng arlkwerl-apem. (T) *Galahs go along eating seeds.*
= kerlelkerlelp, uneng atyetyek

ilep[1] *n.*
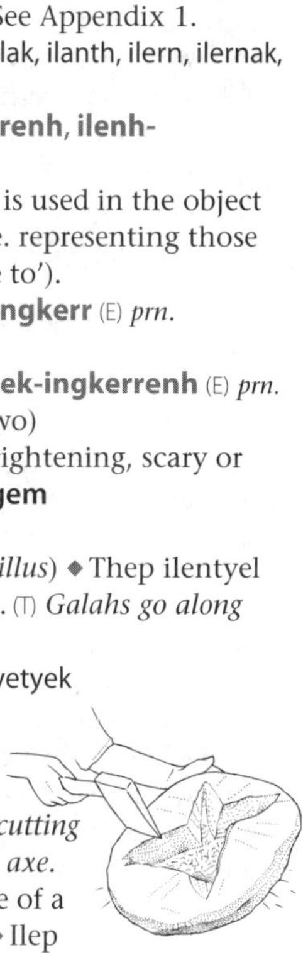
1. axe ◆ Artwangel ilepel atwem ngkwarl rltwamp. (T) *The man is cutting the sugarbag out with an axe.*
2. Goes before the name of a particular type of axe. ◆ Ilep martarrp. *Stone axe.*

ilep[2] (E) *n.*
emu liver ◆ Ilep tha arlkwem. (St) *I'm eating emu liver.*

Ilepampel (T) *n.*
Prowses Gap

ilern, aylern (E) *prn.*
we (we two, us two). This pronoun is used in

the subject part of the sentence (i.e. representing the 'doers' of the verb action). It is strictly used for people who are in same patrimoiety and same generation moiety — for example, two sisters or two brothers, or a person together with their paternal grandfather — but it may be used as a general term. The person being spoken to is not included. See Appendix 1. ◆ Ilern alherrey lyweny. (T) *We two [but not you] will go hunting.*
SEE ALSO ila, ilengkerr, ilak, ilanth, ilern-ingkerr, ilernak, ilernanth

ilernenh, **aylernenh** (E) *prn.*
us (us two). This pronoun is used in the object part of the sentence (i.e. representing those the verb action is 'done to').

ilerneh (W,T), **ilernek** (E), **aylernek** (E) *prn.*
for us (two)

ilern-henh (W,T), **ilern-kenh** (E), **alyern-kenh** (E) *prn.*
ours (belonging to us two)

ilern-apatherr, **aylern-apatherr** (E) *n.*
we two, who have the same skin name ◆ Thang ilem, 'Ilern-apatherr alherretyeh, lyweny apek'. Mpetyan arrpaty, 'ilern-apatherr' ilem. (T) *I'll say, 'We in the same generation moiety will go hunting'. I call someone who is Mpetyan like me* 'ilern-apatherr'.

ilern-altyerr, **aylern-altyerr** (E) *n.*
son-in-law; mother-in-law (closely related ones whose mothers come from the same country as the person speaking) (*altyerr* 'dream', 'mother's country' etc.). Two people may call each other *ilern-altyerr* if their mothers belong to the same country. Such kin are too 'close' to be called *mwer* (son-in-law, mother-in-law), and the rules of respect and avoidance that normally apply to one's *mwer* do not apply.The referent is singular in spite of the use of a dual pronoun. ◆ 'Aylern-altyerr' mwerey. *Like brother*-artekan. 'Aylern-altyerr', aylern altyerr akek anyent. Anyent altyerr akek mer anyent. *One country.* Altyerr anyent. *'Aylern-altyerr' is son-in-law. Like a brother. 'Aylern-altyerr' is we who call the same place* altyerr. *Our mothers were from the same country. One country. One* altyerr. ◆ 'Ilern-altyerr' ilem *son-in-law*. Ntap ilem Ngal, wal Kemarrel, 'ilern-altyerr', Pengart-henh *son*. Ngkwengenh Kemarr yanh ilem Pengartel 'ilern-altyerr'. Kenh rntwarr iter-penh mwerekwarl anem. Mwerek. Rntwarr-areny. Mer rntwarr-areny. Kenh *one country* akenh 'ilern-altyerr', mer anyent-areny 'ilern-altyerr' ilem. (M) 'Ilern-altyerr' *is what you call a son-in-law. A Kemarr like you calls a Ngal* 'ilern-altyerr', *a Pengart's son. And the Pengart woman calls your son* 'ilern-altyerr'. *On the other hand, those from further away, on the 'side', are referred to as* 'mwer', *those from country that is further away. Those from one country are called* 'ilern-altyerr'. ◆ Pwertam ananem ilern-altyerr, atyengel-arleng anem nheng apwert anerl-anem, kenh mwerekw kirrem. Mwerek-henh mer rntwarr-areny. Ilern-altyerr *free*-arl anem. Itwek-arteh ananem pwert. Mwerekant kirrem mwerek-hety, alert-hety. Rntwarr-areny. (M) *We live close together with our* ilern-altyerr, *whereas the people related as* mwer *are avoided and treated with respect. They are from more distant country.* Ilern-altyerr *are free [restrictions don't apply to interactions with them]. A person can be in close proximity to their* ilern-altyerr. *Sons-in-law and mothers-in-law, who are from country that is further away, are avoided.*
SEE ALSO altyerr1, mpwel-altyerr, mpwelak-altyerr, alaltyerr, alak-altyerr, arrengkerr-altyerr, arrakerr-altyerr, anwernakerr-altyerr

ilern-ingkerr, **aylern-ingkerr** (E) *prn.*
we (we two). This pronoun is used in the subject part of the sentence (i.e. representing the 'doers' of the verb action) when the two people are both in the same patrimoiety and the same generation moiety; for example, a person together with their sister or brother, or their father's father. The person being spoken to is not included. See Appendix 1. ◆ Ilern-ingkerr angkwer-nheng alherrem. (T) *We two sisters are going.*
SEE ALSO ila, ilengkerr, ilak, ilanth, ilern, ilernak, ilernanth

ilernenh-ingkerrenh, **aylernenh-ingkerrenh** (E) *prn.*
us (two). This pronoun is used in the object part of the sentence (i.e. representing those the verb action is 'done to').

ilerneh-ingkerr (W,T), **ilernek-ingkerr** (E), **aylernek-ingkerr** (E) *prn.*
for us, to us (two)

ilerneh-ingkerrenh (W,T), **ilernek-ingkerrenh** (E), **aylernek-ingkerrenh** (E) *prn.*
ours (belonging to us two)

ilern-ingkerr-akey (W,T) *prn.*
we (people belonging to the same patrimoiety as each other)
SEE ALSO -akey, ilernak-akey, ilak-akey, anwern-akey, anwern-akerr-akey, anakerr-akey

ilernak, **aylernak** (E) *prn.*
we (we two). This pronoun is used in the subject part of the sentence (i.e. representing the 'doers' of the verb action) when the two people belong to the same patrimoiety and different generation moiety; for example, a person together with their father or father's sister. The person being spoken to is not included. See Appendix 1. ◆ Ilernak alherrek lyweny kerek alewatyerrek, anherr-nheng atherr. (T) *We two, mother-in-law and daughter-in-law, went hunting for goannas.*
SEE ALSO ila, ilengkerr, ilak, ilanth, ilern, ilern-ingkerr, ilernanth
ilernakenh, **ilernenhakenh**, **ilernenhak**, **alyernenhak** (E) *prn.*
us (us two). This pronoun is used in the object part of the sentence (i.e. representing those the verb action is 'done to').
ilernehak, **ilernekak** (E), **aylernekak** (E) *prn.*
for us, to us (two)
ilernehakenh (W,T), **ilernekakenh** (E), **alyernekakenh** (E) *prn.*
ours (belonging to us two)
ilernak-akey, **aylernak-akey** (E) *n.*
we (people belonging to the same patrimoiety as each other) ◆ Aylernak-akeyan anwakerr. Alak-akey *mum*-rnemarl — Kemarr Pwerlarl — alak-akey. An aylernak-akey Petyarr Ngwarray. *'Aylernak-akey' is us. 'Alak-akey' are all our mothers — Kemarr people and Pwerl — they are* alak-akey. Aylernak-akey *are Petyarr and Ngwarray.*
SEE ALSO -akey, alak-akey, ilak-akey, ilern-ingkerr-akey, anwern-akey, anwernakerr-akey, anakerr-akey
ilernanth, **aylernanth** (E) *prn.*
we (we two). This pronoun is used in the subject part of the sentence (i.e. representing the 'doers' of the verb action) when the two people belong to different patrimoieties; for example, a person together with their husband or wife, their sister-in-law or their cross-cousin. The person being spoken to is not included. See Appendix 1. ◆ Ilernanth altyel-nheng alherrek alhewelhetyek. (T) *We two cousins went to wash ourselves.*
SEE ALSO ila, ilengkerr, ilak, ilanth, ilern, ilern-ingkerr, ilernak
ilernanthenh, **ilernenhanthenh**, **alyernanthenh** (E) *prn.*
us (us two). This pronoun is used in the object part of the sentence (i.e. representing those the verb action is 'done to').
ilernehanth (W,T), **ilernekanth** (E), **aylernekanth** (E) *prn.*
for us, to us (two)
ilernehanthenh (W,T), **ilernekanthenh** (E), **aylernekanthenh** (E) *prn.*
ours (belonging to us two)
ilernanth-apakwey (T,E), **aylernanth-apakwey** (E) *prn.*
we (belonging to different patrimoieties but the same generation moiety as each other) ◆ Ilernanth-apakwey alhetyenh lyweny. (T) *We, who are in the same generation moiety as each other, will go hunting.* ◆ Aylernanth-apakwey pwelty iwemel aylernanth-apakwey arrpenh-warl. Alanth-apakwey antwerrkemel mpep-they. (St) *We of the same generation team throw the ball towards the others in our team [i.e. people in the same generation moiety as us]. The others [those in the opposite generation moiety] get hold of the ball in the middle.*
SEE ALSO -apakwey, -apatherr, nywerrp, alanth-apakwey, arrantherr-apakwey, anwernantherr-apakwey, anantherr-apakwey
ilerrty *n.*
1. gutter, small creek, gully, small watercourse ◆ Ilerrty alhem kwaty alhem ikwerel, ulpay angerr-warl lher angerr-warl anem ra anyent-irrem. (St) *The water flows along the small watercourse and then it joins in with the big river.*
= intyer, mpwetyerr
SEE ALSO atwaty
2. wrinkled (face)
ilerrty-ilerrty *n.*
1. an area with a lot of small creeks or gullies
2. wrinkled, creased ◆ Ilerrty-ilerrty kwenh yanh apetyem antywekarl-penh, ilerrty-ilerrty angerr. (T) *[That person] coming along over there has a really wrinkled face from drinking [grog].*
SEE ALSO alyemp-alyemp[1]
ilerrty-ilem *vt.*
erode ◆ Kwatyelarl ilerrty-ilek, ilpay akwek. (St) *The water eroded the little creek.*
ilerrty-ilerrty-irrem (E) *vi.*
become wrinkled or creased ◆ Inngerr ilerrty-ilerrty-irrek anem. (St) *The face has gone wrinkled now.*
ilerrty-ilerrty-ilem (E) *vt.*
make something go wrinkled
iltya ilerrty (E)
wrinkled hand (iltya *'hand'*)
inngerr ilerrty (E)
wrinkled face (inngerr *'face'*)
ileway (W,T), **aleway** (W,T) *n.*
Stimson's python (*Antaresia stimsoni*) (?)
SEE ALSO ahenenh, nwey

ilewerr *n.*
1. mirage, heat haze ◆ Ilewerrel akern-ilep-ilem. *Might* unta arem arleng, akern anem. Ilewerrel akern-ilem mer, arwerl apek apwert apek, wal *you see em* arleng-they, Ilewerrel akern-ilem. (St) *The mirage raises [the ground] up. You might see it from a long way away. The mirage lifts up the ground, or trees or hills, and you can see it from afar.* ◆ Ilewerr. Kwatyek-athen arem ilewerrelarl akern-ilem. (St) *The mirage. You see where the mirage raises it up and you mistake it for water.*
= angent
2. a general name for salt lakes
3. salt, salty ◆ Ker tha mwerr arlkwetyeh, ilewerr-penh, ikwemey. (M) *I'm going to eat the nice meat, tasty after having salt put on it.* ◆ Kwaty arntert ilewerr. (M) *Salty bad-tasting water.* ◆ Ilewerr angetyay ker kwemey mpwaretyeh. (M) *Bring some salt to make the meat taste good.* • SEE ALSO ker ikwemey ilenh-ilenh, melyek, thalt
= **ulewerr**
ilewerr-ilewerr (W,T) *n.*
1. saltbush
= arelyerrelyerr
2. salty water
Ilewerr-ilewerr (W,T) *n.*
2 Mile Bore, Yuelamu (Mt Allan) area. Peltharr/Ngwarray *anyenheng.*

Ilewerr *n.*
1. Lake Lewis
2. the name of a swamp near Wilora (Stirling) community, Stirling Station. The name Wilora comes from Ilewerr. See map p. viii.
• SEE ALSO Wilora

ilhem (W,T) *vt.*
chase or hunt someone or something away ◆ Arengk yanh ilhay. (M) *Hunt that dog away.*
SEE ALSO ilanthem, anpwem
ilhelhem (W,T) *vi.*
chase or hunt something away from yourself ◆ Ameng yanh ilhelhay. (M) *Hunt those flies away from yourself.*
CAN SOUND A BIT LIKE ilelhem *'say about self'*

ilingkerr we (two) SEE UNDER **ilengkerr**

ilka[1] *n.*
1. hibernation
2. burrow where certain animals hibernate (?) ◆ Arlewatyerr ilka, ilkewem anem renh. Ilkewety-akerlem renh, arerl-apemel rtanty, altywer anem ra irrenhem. Ker anem renh atwem arlewatyerr, altywer-irrenhekarl, ilkepenh. (St) *The goanna is in hibernation, and then [you] open up its burrow. You go along opening it up and inspecting the mud [to see if its nose has poked out], and then the burrow opens up. Then you kill the goanna that has come out of hibernation.* ◆ Ilka kwen irrpek arlewatyerr. (St) *The goanna has gone into hibernation.*
= atyerrp
SEE ALSO rlweth, urlelth, ilkeparr
CAN SOUND A BIT LIKE rlka *'wind'*
ilkang intem (W,T), **ilkarl ayntem**, **ilka anem** (T)
hibernate, lie dormant (intem[1] *'lie down'*)
ilkewem *vt.*
poke into a burrow with a crowbar or digging stick to see if there is an animal there, open up a burrow (?) ◆ Ilkewem tha, *might* arem, arlewatyerr-kenh nhenh. Arrpenh-angkwarr tha ilkewem, ilkewetyek tha, *'Oh,* akengarl nhenh arrangkw'. Atnemel apek angerneynerl-anem, ilkeweynerl-anem. Altywer anem irrenhem, ker aley anem. (St) *I might poke around in the burrow, in the goanna's hole that I've seen. I'll poke round on the other side, 'Oh, this one is no good, there's nothing here'. I might dig along with a digging stick, poking at the hole. It gets opened up, and there's the animal.*
= ilkakem
SEE ALSO tyewentem, tyer-wem

ilka[2] (T,E) *n.*
tick, louse ◆ 'Arengk alhay, ilkakertay kwenh!' Aherr apek anem ilkakert ingkerrek. Anwantherr kwementyay-akert — alta arlkwenh-arlkwenh-akert. (St) *'Go away dog, you've got ticks!' Kangaroos and all might have ticks. We have* kwementyay *[lice] — the things that 'eat' hair.*
SEE ALSO artwek
CAN SOUND A BIT LIKE rlka *'wind'*

ilkakem, alkakem (W,T) *vt.*
1. open or uncover something; spread something out; sort through things to find something; open something or turn something over to look for something ◆ Angelth tha arlkwemem mern, rwel itemel, akemarl *roll*-em *up*-ilem atyerremem renh, rwel angelth renh, wal alkakemel arlkwemem. (N) *I eat the native pear fruits, cooking them in the fire, picking them, rolling them up and cooking them and then opening them out and eating them.* ◆ Yakweth atyenh ilkaketyal! (Sa) *Don't go through my handbag!* ◆ Rnwanenty ilkakem, lert apek ngkwerlp apek tha arrernekek. (T) *Turning the clothes over, looking for the tin or the tobacco that I put there.* ◆ Pep

ilkakerlapem pety aretyeh. (T) *Turning the pages over to look at the pictures.*
2. open up a goanna's hole ◆ Ker alewatyerr ilkang inang ilkaketyart, ipert mpwaremel. (T) *They used to dig up a goanna's burrow, making a hole.* • SEE ALSO ilkewem
SEE ALSO irrkerem

Ilkamp (W) *n.*
place name, Pine Hill area

ilkelhem *vi.*
1. enjoy yourself, feel happy about something ◆ Ilkelhem anem ayeng. Kerek ayeng ilkelhem, mernek ayeng ilkelhem, mantarrek ayeng ilkelhem, warrkek ayeng ilkelhem — angkek ayeng ilkelhem. *I'm happy. I like meat, food, clothes and work — I like doing language [work].*
2. want or like someone or something ◆ Ayeng ilkelhetyakenh ngkweng. (St) *I don't like you.*
3. want or like to do something, feel like doing something ◆ Ayeng alhetyek ilkelhemaw. *I'd like to go.* ◆ Arelhan arelharl, rarl ilkelhem-angkwarr. (St) *Women are women, [they do] whatever they feel like.*
4. like, love or fancy someone
= ahenty-irrem
SEE ALSO akangkem, anyerrkem, inkwerelhem, irrngerney-irrem, kwak-irrem

ilkelhey (W,T) *n.*
nice and green (country), a place that you like, a good place ◆ Mer ilkelhey anthwerr, kwaty-penh. (T) *The country is nice and green, after the rain.*
ilkelhey-irrem (T) *vi.*
go nice and green (country) ◆ Mer anety amparr arem, kel mer ikelhey-irrem, kel mwerram arerlanem. Kel anwern ilkelhey-warn atherrk-warn anem apety-alpem. (T) *The country is no good at first, and then it gets nice and green, and you can see how good it is. Then we come back to the nice green country.*
SEE ALSO anyemwerr-irrem

ilkeparr *n.*
hibernation ◆ Tyek untem tha ker ilkeparrel intep-intem. (St) *I am poking the ground for the [goanna] that is hibernating.*
= atyerrp, ilka1
SEE ALSO rlwelth, urlelth

ilkert (T,E) *n.*
Halls Creek wattle (?) (*Acacia cowleana*). Shrub up to 7 m high, with large, sickle-shaped leaves and cylindrical yellow flowers. ◆ Ntang ilkert, mwerr-angker renh athetyam arrwekelenyel, apwert tyengel athetyam. Urel ina itetyam, aynpernetyam panthel. *The seed from the Halls Creek wattle is really nice and the olden-time people ground it up with a stone called* tyeng. *They yandied the seed in a coolamon and cooked it in the fire.*
Has edible seeds and sweet resin.
= alkart
CAN SOUND A BIT LIKE rlkert *'sick'*

Ilkewarn (T,E) *n.*
name of country/estate which extends from parts of Ti Tree east to Alcoota pastoral lease. See map p. viii.

ilkngeny (E) (having) a lucky, successful feeling, especially for hunting SEE UNDER **inngeny**

ilkwa1 (T,E), **ilkwang** (W) *n.*
flower of the native currant, native citrus, *ahakey* (*Psydrax latifolia*) ◆ Ilkwa anem, kwer-penh irnta anem anem, kwer-penh rrpwerl anem anem. (T) *There is the flower, then after that the fruit, and then the fruit ripens.*
CAN SOUND A BIT LIKE iylkwa1 *'number seven boomerang'*; iylkwa2 *'armpit'*
ilkwenkem (E), **ilkwernkem** (E) *vi.*
to flower or blossom (native currant, native citrus) (nkem, rnkem *'emerge or come out from'*)
SEE ALSO ahakey

ilkwa2 (E) *n.*
big
= angerr1
SEE ALSO angerrety, artelhampw, artelh3, awer1, rltwa, urlta
CAN SOUND A BIT LIKE iylkwa1 *'number seven boomerang'*; iylkwa2 *'armpit'*
ilkwirrem (E) *vi.*
grow bigger, get bigger
= angerr-irrem
SEE ALSO amangkem

ilkwa3 (E) *n.*
white hair, grey hair ◆ Ilkwarl ampekarl, ingkerrarl ilkwa ampek. Aywa. Ingkerr mperlkemel. No atherrk. Atherrkarl ngkwenh. Ayengan ingkerr ampekarl ilkwa, arelh ampwa irremel. (Sa) *All the hair has gone grey. All of it has gone white. There is no non-grey hair left. Your hair is not grey. All of my hair has gone grey, as I became an old woman.*
= aywa, kapert aywang
ilkwamp ilkwang (E) *n.*
grey-headed, white-headed
ilkwa ampem (E) *vi.*
go grey, go white-headed, grow old (ampem2 *'cook', 'heat up'*)
= aywa ampem

ilkwangketh, **ilkwangkenty** (E) *adv.* [RESPECT LANGUAGE]
accompanying someone, go with someone to keep them company ◆ Ilkwangketh ahanenhay, ngwarrekengk-warl. (St) *Go and keep your husband company [said by a woman to her daughter].*
SEE ALSO ilkwatherr

ilkwanty (E), **ulkanty** (E) *n.*
flower of the bush banana, silky pear (*Marsdenia australis*)
SEE ALSO amwernt, alangkw, parl

ilkwart native gooseberry, ulcardo melon SEE UNDER **lkwart**

ilkwart-ilkwart (T,E) headache vine SEE UNDER **lkwart-lkwart**

ilkwatherr, **irlkwatherr**, **rlkwatherr** (W,T) *adv.*
1. accompanying someone, going with someone to keep them company ◆ Artwekety ilkwatherr alhetyek, rlwaylp-kety. (St) *We'll go together to keep each other company, because of the kurdaitcha.* ◆ Rlkwatherr anwengkerr alhem lyweny. (T) *We'll go hunting together.*
2. using something for protection, 'to save' self; something that is used to protect yourself with, such as a weapon ◆ Artwang ampwangel rrkwem alkwert irlkwatherr. (N) *The old man has a shield to protect himself.* ◆ Rlkwatherr rrkwem kweter arelhel atwerr-kety. (T) *The woman has a nulla-nulla to protect herself from fights.*
ilkwatherrek-uthek (E) *adv.*
friendless, by yourself, without companionship or company ◆ Ilkwatherrek-uthek unthepunthem ayeng. (St) *I am looking round for a good friend.* ◆ Ilkwatherrek-uthek ayeng anep-anem, anyent-areny. (St) *I am sitting on my own with no company.*
SEE ALSO ilkwangketh

ilkwem (E), **irlkwem** (E) *vi.*
1. twitch, flinch, take a fit, start (in fright) ◆ Ankwepenh ater irlkwem. Ampel apekarl atyekelh-ilem, irlkwem anem. (St) *After being asleep [I] get a fright. The child might wake me up and I get a fright.*
2. have a feeling (particularly about family members) ◆ Yay apek alakenh akin. Irlkwem lyweper irlkwem amper. Yay apek apetyem kakey apek apetyem. *It is the same for my elder sister. I have a feeling in my thigh or my knee. If my elder sister or elder brother is coming.*
SEE ALSO anwerlkem
CAN SOUND A BIT LIKE rlkwem *'foretell'*
ilkwel alhem (E)
get a fright, flinch ◆ Ankwepenhel ilkwel alhek. (St) *[The person] woke up in fright.*
ilkwel anthem (E)
give someone or something a fright

ilkwenng (E) *n.*
a type of mouse (?). Also referred to as *ker ilkwenng.* ◆ Anwantherr ampa mapel ker ilkwenng arlkwetyart. (St) *As kids we used to eat mice.*
SEE ALSO alepey, alwepay, thakey[2], thakwer, aherraty-anywertangey

ilkwernarr *n.*
1. waxy wattle (*Acacia melleodora*). Shrub to about 2.5 m high, with grey-green leaves with a whitish crust.
2. edible seed of the waxy wattle
= alhepalh
SEE ALSO patwert
ilkwernarrayt (E) *n.*
grub from waxy wattle
= alhepalhayt

ilkwert (E), **ulkert** (E) *n.*
perentie (*Varanus giganteus*)
= tywenp

ilpa, **ilpang** (W,T) *n.* [SENSITIVE LANGUAGE]
placenta
SEE ALSO tyelepelep

ilpang (W,T) placenta SEE UNDER **ilpa**

ilpankwer (E) *n.*
blue-tongue lizard (*Tiliqua multifasciata*). Also referred to as *ker ilpankwer.*
= lhwelk, ulhelk, lwengkart[1]

ilpay (E) creek, river, watercourse SEE UNDER **ulpay**

ilpem[1] *vt.*

winnow or yandy seed (upwards movement of coolamon). When winnowing seed the coolamon is also shaken in a backwards and forwards motion referred to as *ahety-ilem* or *aympernem.* ◆ Mern yerrakwerr ilpemarl panthel. Mern perlap ilpemel, aympernemel arlka renh. (St) *The bush onions are yandied in a coolamon. Conkerberries are yandied, and then shaken sideways in the wooden dish as well.*
SEE ALSO then-wem, aympernem, ahety-ilem, irrkertert-wem

ilpem[2] *vt.*
1. stop someone from doing something by putting yourself in the way; block a fight, obscure something ◆ Kweterel atwem, wal ilpem arrpenhel. Ilpelhem apek rarrp, tyerrty anpetyakenh. (St) *If someone is hitting someone*

with a nulla-nulla, well another one might step in to block it. Or the person themself might shield themself with something, so that they can't be touched.
2. cover something over, obscure something from view ◆ Materel atay ilpem. (M) *The cloud is covering the moon.*
ilpelhem *vi.*

place something in front of yourself for protection; go behind something; shield yourself with something, block something with part of yourself ◆ Artwel mpwarem alkwert arnang inernt-penh, alyang-kety ilpelhetyek. (T) *Men make shields from bean tree wood to protect themselves from boomerangs.* ◆ Tyerrty nhak ilang, rang apetyetyeh ilpelhetyek. (T) *Tell that person over there to come and block the fight.*
SEE ALSO wawely-irrem

ilpengk (T,E), **ilpengkw** (E) *n.*
gidgee fuchsia bush (*Eremophila dalyana*). A shrub to about 1.5 m high, with rough black bark, narrow grey-green leaves, and white flowers. ◆ Arlkwetyakenh wararl anterel-arleng anterek ulpilem, ulpilem ulpilem ulpilem renh *all right* anter-warl anem *mix*-em *up* ilem apernelherl-anetyek anem. *This plant is not edible, it is just ground up to make it soft then mixed with fat and used to rub on yourself.*
CAN SOUND A BIT LIKE iylpernk *'fat in kangaroo meat'*

ilpent-wem (E), **alpent-wem** (E) *vt.*
lever something up; make something crack or rise up ◆ Atnemel ilpent-wem, arwakem thamethengk, rlterrkarl-irrek. (Sa) *Using a digging stick to lever something up that is tight or hard.* ◆ Anatyel ahern ilpent-wem. (Sa) *The bush potato makes the ground rise up and crack.*
SEE ALSO arwakem, alpwarternem, urtep-wem, urrper-wem

ilpenty *n.*
1. women's ceremony [SOME SPEAKERS]
2. songs used to attract lovers, love song ◆ Ilpenty alyelhem. (M) *Singing a love song.*
SEE ALSO awely, tyepety1, irrenyankwerl

Ilpereny (W) *n.*
Arden Soak

ilperl1 (E) *n.*
1. stone knife ◆ Apwert ilperlel aketyek ker apek. (St) *Cutting the meat with a stone knife.*
2. a type of white rock (used for making stone knives)
SEE ALSO alywek, irntang arlter

ilperl2 *n.*
1. teatree, paperbark (*Melaleuca glomerata*). Shrub about 3 m high, with white papery bark, narrow leaves, and creamy yellow flowers. Grows around salt lakes, claypans or watercourses.
2. sandhill teatree (*Melaleuca lasiandra*). Shrub about 2.5 m high, with papery bark, silvery green leaves and creamy yellow flowers. Usually grows at the base of sandhills.
◆ Arrwekelenyel ilperl inetyam alywekek, mpwaretyan pewatyan kwerenh. (St) *The olden-time people collected teatree bark to make pouches for their stone knives.*
SEE ALSO thankw
CAN SOUND A BIT LIKE arlperl *'lerp scale on mulga'*
Ilperl Anyent (T) *n.*
the name of a place in the Ti Tree (Ahakeye Aboriginal Land Trust) area (anyent *'one'*)

ilperl3 (E), **ilperley** (E) *n.kin* [RESPECT LANGUAGE]
A respectful way of referring to the father's mother and the father's mother's brothers and sisters of a person whom the speaker is in an avoidance relationship to. For example, a woman may use *ilperl* to refer to her son-in-law's father's mother, or a man may use *ilperl* to refer to his mother-in-law's father's mother.
SEE ALSO aperl
ilperl-nheng (E), **ilperley-nheng** (E) *n.kin*
a group of two or more people related as grandparents (father's mother or their brothers and sisters) and grandchildren (a woman's son's child or a person's sister's son's child). This is said by a woman if one of them is her son-in-law, or by a man if one of them is his mother-in-law. ◆ Ilperl-nheng ahanenhekaw, aperley ikwerenharl, aperl-nheng atherrarl alhem. (St) *[My] son-in-law and his father's mother went, that's his* aperley, *he and his* aperley *going together.*
SEE ALSO aperl-nheng
ilperl-nheng atherr (E), **ilperley-nheng atherr** (E) *n.kin*
a grandparent (father's mother or their brothers and sisters) together with their grandchild (a woman's son's child or a person's sister's son's child). This is said by a woman if one of them is her son-in-law, or by a man if one of them is his mother-in-law.
SEE ALSO aperl-nheng atherr

ilperl4 (W) *n.*
a type of men's ceremonial headdress

SEE ALSO kwertar

ilperl-ilperl (E) *n.*
back of the neck ◆ Tha ngenh ilperl-ilperl atwekerr. (Sa) *[Watch out] or I'll hit you on the back of the neck.*
SEE ALSO temarl, tarnng, ntywa

ilperletyewenh (E) *n.*
a type of python (?). Also known as *ker ilperletyewenh.*
SEE ALSO kaperrkwelt, uney

ilperley (E) father's mother and her brothers and sisters (respect term) SEE UNDER **ilperl**3

ilperlp-irrem (W) *vi.*
sing (of bellbirds only)
= inmenm-irrem
SEE ALSO kwepalepal

ilperlper-wem, **ilperrper-wem** (E) *vt.*
shake something (especially said of bush plum tree) ◆ Arengkan ilperlper-wem kwatypenh. (T) *The dog is shaking off the water.*
= ywerrkem
ilperlper-welhem, **ilperrper-welhem** (E) *vi.*
shake self ◆ Arengk ilperlper-welhem atyengangkwerr. (St) *The dog is shaking itself over me.*
SEE ALSO awerrkem

ilpernem *vt.*
blame or accuse someone of something ◆ Ilpernety-alpem ayenharl, arengkelarl kwerenh arlkwerrek. Ayenh anem ankeyek ilpernety-alpek. (St) *He went and blamed me for the dog fighting his dog. So then he went and blamed me for it.* ◆ Irrkwentyel ilpernemantey, ilpernek apek irrkwentyel ayenh, tharl akwel inek. (St) *The police blamed me, supposedly because I took it.* ◆ Ntwa kwenh ayenh ilpernek. (M) *You blamed me.* ◆ Rrkwentyel ilpernem nyenngel inenty. (M) *The police accused them of stealing.*
SEE ALSO urrtyirrem, antyarrp-ilem
ilpernerrem *vi.*
blame or accuse each other of something ◆ Tyerrty atherr ilpernerremaw! Marl-warn apek alhek, rwengkel apek inek. (T) *The two people are accusing each other of doing the wrong thing! Maybe because one went after a woman or stole something.*

ilpernk (E) fat in the flesh from the thigh of a kangaroo SEE UNDER **iylpernk**

ilpernkeny (E) *n.*
smallest (of finger or toe)
iltya ilpernkeny (E)
little finger
ingka ilpernkeny (E)
little toe

ilperntatherr (T) *n.*
a type of plant (?). Similar to the pencil yam, it grows in creeks and has a yellow flower.
SEE ALSO arlatyey, arlatyey-arlatyey

ilperr (E) *n.*
flat
SEE ALSO aymperr
ilperr ayntem (E)
lie flat on stomach (ayntem *'lie'*)
= lpwerr intem, ulperr ayntem
ilperrelh-ilem (E) *vt.*
make something flat ◆ Tamp apek mpwaretyek. 'Urrek tha ilperrelh-iley, ilperrilperr iley.' (St) *Making damper. 'Wait, I'll make it flat.'*
ilperr-ilperr (E) *n.*
flat, flattish, round ◆ Apwert ilperr-ilperr, ngkwerlp anem ikwer-arleng athem. (St) *Native tobacco is ground up on a flat rock.* ◆ Ilperrilperr angetyang! *Bring the round thing [e.g. billycan].*
iltya ilperr-ilperr (E)
palm of the hand

ilperrk (W) *n.*
a small amount of rainwater lying around. Also referred to as *kwaty ilperrk.*
ilperrkenty (W) *n.*
a small amount of running water after a flood
SEE ALSO arnperrkenty

ilperrpayentyel (E) black-faced woodswallow SEE UNDER **perrpantywen**

ilperrper-wem (E) shake something (especially said of bush plum tree) SEE UNDER **ilperlper-wem**

ilpety (E) *n.*
helpful, cooperative ◆ Ilpety mwerr alhem *swag* apek inerlewetyek. (St) *The helpful person is good and goes and gets the swag quickly.* ◆ Ilpetyel ap ra item ker, anwernt-irretyakenhel, ilpetyarl ra. (St) *She cooks the meat really quickly, without bailing up or sulking, she is helpful.*
SEE ALSO irrngerney, irlpareth

ilpey, **ilpey-ilpey** (E) *n.*
needle bush, needlewood (*Hakea leucoptera* ssp. *leucoptera*). Shrub to about 3 m high, with needle-like leaves and white or yellow flowers. ◆ Akngerr weth arey apwertel. Arwerl weth tnenherretyel alhirrel, ilpey-ilpey. (Sa) *There are lots of those [trees] in the hills. Lots of those* ilpey-ilpey *trees grow there.*
= rrkwalty

ilpwerlenty-rnem (E), **ilpwerlenty-irrem** (E) *vi.*
whistle
= arrawenth-irrem

iltatwem (T,E) *vt.*
kill lots of something (game) ◆ Akngerr atwek, iltatwek anem ker. Iltatwek anem unta ker. *You killed lots of animals. You got lots of meat.*
SEE ALSO althinem, kwerremp-ilem, akwetyerretyerr-ilem

iltem *vt.*
swear or growl at somebody or something, tell someone off ◆ Tyerrty yanhel iltep-iltem ngkwantyel. (M) *That person is swearing and picking a fight.* ◆ Mernek-arrngel thwengk iltem. (T) *I'm growling at you over food.* ◆ Ngenh apek tha iltetyek. Nga apek atyeng tyel angkek, iltetyek ngenh. Ngarl tyel angkek-penh angayel apek ntwa arlkwek atyeng-kety. (St) *I might growl at you. If you run me down, then I'll growl at you. After you ran me down and ate [the food] behind my back.*
SEE ALSO arrantyakem
CAN SOUND A BIT LIKE iyltem *'break or crack something open'*
ilterrem *vi.*
swear or growl at each other, argue with each other ◆ Tyerrty atherr ilterrem. (M) *Two people are swearing at each other.*
CAN SOUND A BIT LIKE alterrem *'tear something up'*; altherrem *'burn away', 'catch alight'*

ilterrem (E) tear something, rip something open SEE UNDER **alterrem**

iltewem (E) smash or break something SEE UNDER **ultewem**

iltha (E) *n.*
humpy
SEE ALSO antywa, wak, warl

iltya, **iltyang** (W,T) *n.*
1. hand ◆ Anantherr iltyang atherr-akert anem. (T) *We have two hands.*
2. finger ◆ Iltya ngkwarl anpemarl anemarl-penh ngkwarl arwengalker apek, awantyelhem anem alakenh. (St) *[You] lick your fingers if they have honey on them from touching sugarbag.*
3. front hooves or paws of animals, foreleg, claw of birds ◆ Nantewan ingka atherr an iltya atherr akin. Arrwekel-thayt iltyarl, ingkern-thaytan ingkarl. (St) *Horses have two front hooves and two back hooves. The ones at the front are called* 'iltya' *[hand] and the ones behind* 'ingka' *[foot].*
4. a 'five' in cards
CAN SOUND A BIT LIKE altya *'family'*
iltya kanty (E)
finger tip (kanty *'tip'*)
iltya akwek-antyey (W)
little finger
iltya akwerreny (E)
little finger
iltya pwel-pwel (W,T), **iltyang pwel-pwel** (W,T), **iltyang pwel** (W,T)
thumb (pwel-pwel *'large'*)
= iltyang angerr, iltya amikw, iltya anywek, iltyilkw
iltya anywek (W), **iltyang anywek** (W) = **iltya pwel-pwel** (anywek *'father'*)
iltya amikw (E) = **iltya pwel-pwel** (amikw2 *'mother'*)
iltyilkw (E) *n.* = **iltya pwel-pwel** (ilkwa *'big'*)
iltya angerr, **iltyang angerr** (W,T), **iltya akngerr** (E)
1. thumb (angerr1 *'big'*)
= iltya anywek, iltya amikw, iltya pwel-pwel
2. large fingers (i.e. not little finger)
3. a big hand
iltya akely-rnem (E), **iltya akwerrk-rnem** (E)
fingers (not including thumb) (akely *'small'*; -rnem *'plural'*)
iltyang kwerrng (W)
fingers (not including thumb) (kwerrng *'small'*)
iltya mpep-iperr (E)
middle three fingers (mpep *'middle'*)
iltyang antarlkw-antarlkw (W)
gap between fingers (antarlkw *'forked'*)
= iltya tyarrp-tyarrp, iltya atwaty-atwaty, iltya ipert
iltya tyarrp-tyarrp (T) = **iltyang antarlkw-antarlkw** (tyarrp *'crack', 'gap'*)
iltya atwaty-atwaty (T) = **iltyang antarlkw-antarlkw** (atwaty *'gap'*)
iltya ipert (W) = **iltyang antarlkw-antarlkw** (ipert *'hole', 'hollow'*)
iltya anert, **iltya atnert** (E)
palm of the hand (anert *'stomach'*)
iltya artep
back of hand (artep *'back'*)
iltya ngkwern (W,T)
wrist (ngkwern *'bone'*)
= akwengkwern, amwelt anngang, anaynenh
iltya pwert-irrem (W,T) *n.*
clench fists (pwert-irrem *'curl into a ball'*)
iltyang atwelhem (W,T), **iltya atwelhem** (E)
clap hands (atwelhem *'hit part of self'*)
iltyang tywemar (W,T)
fingernails
SEE ALSO ingkelthel
iltya arlkeny (E), **iltyang arlkeny** (W,T)
lines on hand (arlkeny *'stripe', 'marking'*)

iltyang mpwetyerr-mpwetyerr (W)
lines on hand (mpwetyerr *'gully', 'small creek'*)
iltyang rrkwerrem (W,T)
shake hands (rrkwerrem *'hold each other'*)
iltyekenh-ayerr (E) *n.* [RESPECT LANGUAGE]
boomerang (lit. 'belonging to the hand')
= atyepet
SEE ALSO aylayl, alya, kayl
aherrk iltya (T), **aherrk iltyem-iltyem** (E)
the rays of the sun (when setting) (?) ◆ Aherrk iltyel-rwek ayeng arety-kwenh. (T) *I can't see anything because of the rays of the sun.* ◆ Aherrk iltyem-iltyem anenhem. Aherrk irrpenhetyek anem. (Sa) *The rays of the sun are showing. Then the sun goes down.* ◆ Aherrk iltyem-iltyemel akem-irrem ayeng. (Sa) *I get up when the first rays of the sun appear.*
SEE ALSO iltyem-iltyem
aherrk iltyem anem (E)
set (sun), go down (sun) ◆ Aherrk iltyem anem altwerl-athek. (Sa) *The sun sets in the west.*
aherrk iltyem anintyem (E)
rise (sun) ◆ Aherrk iltyem anintyem angerrakw-they. (Sa) *The sun rises in the east.*
SEE ALSO aylpar anenhem, iltya, urlem-anem
iltyel-ilem *vt.*
signal with hands, use handsigns, point
iltyel ikngwem (E)
beckon or signal to someone (ikngwem *'ask'*)

iltyampem, **ltyampem**, **ltyampwem** (E) *vi.*
blister from fire ◆ Urepenh iltyampekarl arnterrarl ampek. Ingka iltyampem akin urepenh. Urel ampenty. (Sa) *After being burnt by the fire [the skin] blisters. Feet can blister as well from being burnt in the fire.*
iltyampelh-ilem, **ltyampelh-ilem**, **ltyampwelh-ilem** (E) *vt.*
make something blister (?)

iltyang (W,T) hand SEE UNDER **iltya**

iltyant, **iltyantey** *n.*
empty-handed (+ant *'only', 'that and nothing else'*) ◆ Itya, iltyantey apety-alpem aker-kweny. (T) *Nothing, returning empty-handed with no meat.*
= rep

iltyarnm (W) *n.*
yabby (?), crab (?). Also referred to as *ker iltyarnm.*
SEE ALSO ikarl, kwertetyengetyeng, iltya

iltyarrng (W,T) *n.*
part of the guts (of kangaroos and cattle); milk gut
SEE ALSO aneperrk, lyep-lyep

iltyelay-irrem (W,T) *vi.*
1. have no food or money; run out of food or money ◆ Ayeng kwenh iltyelay-irrem, maney-kwenyel mern-kwenyel. (T) *I'm right out of supplies, no money or food.*
2. not get anything (when hunting), not win (at cards) ◆ Iltyelay akwet ayeng irrek, *win*-irretyakenh ngkweltyeh. (M) *I didn't win any money at cards.* ◆ Ker aherreh nta alhem lyweny. *No* ker arratek itya. Iltyant apety-alpek, iltyeley-irremel apety-alpek. (M) *You might go hunting for kangaroo. No kangaroos appear. You come back empty-handed, without anything.*
SEE ALSO iltya

iltyem (E) break or crack something open; hatch out from an egg SEE UNDER **iyltem**

iltyem-iltyem (W,T) *adv.*
signalling with hands, using handsigns ◆ Iltyem-iltyeman angkem alakenham: 'Amer-warn anwengkerr alpey kwenh, intetyeh kwenh, mern arlka arlkwetyeh kwenh'. (N) *Using handsigns you can say things like this: 'Let's go back to camp to sleep and to have something to eat'.* ◆ Iltyem-iltyemel ingwem, akerterel ingwem, angketyakenhel. (N) *Someone who can't talk, or is unable to speak because they are in mourning, uses handsigns to ask someone to do something.*

iltyerrem, **iltyirrem** (T,E) *vi.*
to wave, use handsigns, signal to someone (iltya *'hand'*; -irrem *'become'*) ◆ Tyerrty alenh iltyerreperrem. (M) *That person over there is waving.* ◆ Yanh iltyirrem, 'Apetya kwenh'. (Sa) *That person over there is signalling, 'Come here'.*
= akwerrem, iltyel-ilem
SEE ALSO iltya, iltyem-iltyem
CAN SOUND A BIT LIKE ltyerrem *'heal over'*

iltyingk (E) *n.*
in a bunch (of particular fruits)
= anarnkw
SEE ALSO rlkwangk, arlpar athwenkarr

iltyirrem (T,E) to wave; use handsigns SEE UNDER **iltyerrem**

iltywel-antey (E), **ultyel-antey** (E), **ultyel-ayerr** (E) *n.* [RESPECT LANGUAGE]
daylight, first light, daybreak ◆ Ultyel-ayerr ngwarr-nheng ahanekaw. (Sa) *My daughter and her husband went at first light [said by the mother of the woman].*
SEE ALSO ingwa

iltywelty (T,E) a type of cricket SEE UNDER **ltywelty**

iltywerrem (T) have a rest, have a spell SEE UNDER **ltywerrem**

Ilwek (T) *n.*
place name, Pine Hill area

ilwelty (E) frost, ice SEE UNDER **ulelty**

ilwem, lwem (W) *vi.*
1. die ◆ Arengk ilwekaw. (St) *The dog died.*
SEE ALSO nyerrem, uyerrem, ywerrem, ahap-irrem, arrangkw-irrem
2. cough ◆ Arrwengkelth-penh ayeng ilwem. (St) *I'm coughing because I'm sick.* • = artekernem
3. lose strength or intensity; die down (fire); finish (rain) ◆ Aperrk anem ra irrem, kel ura rnter-rnter urek-amperr ampeynepeynem, kel ilwem anem aperrk anem, urrperl-irrem anem. (St) *Then it turns to coals. The fire is red at first, burning, then it dies down and turns to coals, goes black.* ◆ Kwaty arrangkw anemaw, ilwek. (St) *There's no rain now, it's finished.* • SEE ALSO anmerrem
4. finish, run out ◆ Mern ywerrekarl, mern kel ilwekaw. Anwengkerr mern-warn irrem, mern ywerrek-arleng. (N) *The food has run out, it's finished. Let's go somewhere where there is food because [our food] has run out.*
CAN SOUND A BIT LIKE lwem^1 *'defecate'*; lwem^2 *'drip'*; lywem^1 *'take something off'*; lywem^2 *'poke'*
= **ulem** (T,E)
ampwerrk-ilwem (E) *vi.*
laugh really hard; kill yourself laughing
= nyant atherrem

ilwemp (T,E) ghost gum SEE UNDER **ulemp**

ilwengar (W,T) 'When?' SEE UNDER **lwengar**

ilwernem (E) put something out (fire or light) SEE UNDER **lwernem**

ilwernkernem (E) break or dislocate (an animal's leg) SEE UNDER **ulernkernem**

ilwerreny (E), **ulerreny** (E) *n.*
1. whipstick wattle (*Acacia adsurgens*) (?). Shrub about 3 m high with narrow leaves and cylindrical yellow flowers.
2. edible seed of the whipstick wattle
= antyweleny, ateyepenh
3. desert witchetty bush, bastard mulga (*Acacia stowardii*) (?). The seeds were ground up and eaten.

ilwerrk (E) eggs of honeyants and other species of ant SEE UNDER **lwerrk**

Ilwerrk (W) *n.*
the name of a place in the Yuelamu (Mt Allan) area

ilyartey, alyartey, iylartey (E) *n.*
green seed pods of the Georgina gidgee, *rrwenyenk/urrenyenk*
SEE ALSO kikarr

Ilyerl (W) name of a place west of Yuelamu (Mt Allan) community SEE UNDER **Lyerl**

ima (E) *n.*
dead body, corpse
imek atwem (E)
hit or beat someone to death (?) (atwem *'hit', 'kill'*)
SEE ALSO irrewaly, irrernng, aweyaw, arrwety

imarewanem (E) *vi.*
bounce back, bounce off something
◆ Apwertel apekarl tha wem wal imarewanem. (St) *I might throw a rock at something and it might bounce back.* ◆ Apwertel wentyan imarewanemarl, innga anem wemel. Urla apek artep apek wem, imarewanemel. (Sa) *When [you] throw a rock it might bounce back and hit someone on the forehead or on the back.* ◆ Iynteth an imarewanem arrpem. (Sa) *Sparks bounce back as well.*
SEE ALSO irrkarnpem

imarlew (E), **ipmarlew** (E) *n.*
a type of python (?)
SEE ALSO uney, ahenenh, ileway

imay (T), **may** (W) *part.*
'Hey, what's up?' (note Warlpiri *mayi*) ◆ Imay, mwerram ntwa? (T) *Hey, are you okay?* ◆ Imay, nthakenh-athek? (T) *Hey, where are you going?*
SEE ALSO ma^2

imayel (E) jealous (particularly over husband or wife) SEE UNDER **mayel**

imeng, ipmeng (T,E) *adv.*
generous, generously, sharing ◆ Ipmengel anthek ayeng, ngkwerlp apek ayeng anthek ipmengel. (St) *[The person] generously gave me some tobacco.* ◆ Ipmengel, wararl anthem arrpenhek. (St) *Generously, just giving things to another person.*
= atham-atham
imeng-irrem, ipmeng-irrem (T,E) *vi.*
1. be generous, share
2. get full of food, be sated with food, lose appetite ◆ Ipmeng-irrek anem ayeng, atnerteng anem. (Sa) *I haven't got any appetite now, I'm full of food.* ◆ Rlkert apek ayeng imeng-irrem, nheng mern arlkwety-kweny. (M) *I'm sick and I've lost my appetite, so I'm not eating.*

imenty 'Leave it', 'Don't worry about it' SEE UNDER **menty**

imernem, mernem (W,T) *vt.*
show something to someone ◆ Imernem ngkweng tha. (N) *I am showing you something.*
◆ Ngkwelty apek kwer imernem, mantarr apek. (N) *I might show him money or clothes.*
= nernem
SEE ALSO irlparrernem

imernelhem, mernelhem (W,T) *vi.*
show oneself, show something about yourself, bear witness ◆ Awely mernem, awely arlkeny-akert kel-akert, mernelhem. 'Kelaw, awely-akertam ayeng anem kwenh, kelaw awely kelarl wek-akertam ayeng anem kwenh.' (N) *Showing the women's ceremony. [The woman] who already has the ceremonial designs on shows herself. 'I already have the designs on — I've already been painted up.'*

imernt (E) at first, previously SEE UNDER **mernt**[2]

imerreynt (E) murderer; someone who is guilty of manslaughter SEE UNDER **merrenty**

imert (W) at first, previously SEE UNDER **mernt**[2]

Imertenng (E) *n.*
the name of a place to the east of Wilora (Stirling) community

imey (E) *n.* [RESPECT LANGUAGE]
1. back (of a person)
2. sore back (of a person) ◆ Imey-ayerraw kwey ngwarrengkw. Atnerrk-irrerlentyelarrekek imey-ayerr. Imey ahaneyna. Anterel apernerlentyarretyek ahaneyna. (Sa) *Daughter, your husband has a sore back. His back is no good. Go and rub him with fat [said by the mother of the woman].*
SEE ALSO artep

Imiwerr (E) Milky Way SEE UNDER **Mewarr**

impakemp-iwelhem (E) rub yourself in or on something SEE UNDER **impalerrp-welhem**

impakwert (E), **impakwart** (E) *n.*
the 'pipe' through which the witchetty grub (and other grubs) emerge from the ground
= akartw, akarternenty
SEE ALSO irrarl

impalerrp-welhem (W,T), **impakemp-iwelhem** (E), **imparrkemp-iwelhem** (E) *vi.*
rub yourself in or on something, roll around in something ◆ Arengk impalerrp-welhem antyamel, anety npwangerr. (M) *The smelly dog is rubbing itself on the blankets.* ◆ Nanth impalerrp-welhem ahelh-warn. (M) *The horse is rolling around on the ground.* ◆ Arengk *might* pelangket-warl impakemp-iwelhem. (St) *The dog might rub itself on the blanket.*
SEE ALSO ywer-welhem

impalkert, impalkart (W) *adv.*
lying on one's back ◆ Aherr impalkert ampem. (St) *Kangaroos are cooked lying on their backs.* ◆ Impalkertem intem, kwer-penh aweth angart-welhem. (N) *Lying on [your] back, then, after that, turning over again.*
impalkert intem, impalkart intem (W)
lie on one's back (intem[1] *'lie down'*) ◆ Artepel-ayel ayeng impalkart intem. (M) *I am lying on my back.*
SEE ALSO ulperr intem, arlkarlkar intem, akern-antep intem
impalkert-wem, impalkart-wem (W), **impalkert-iwem** (E) *vt.*
turn something onto its back; roll something over onto its back, lay someone or something on their back

impalt-ayerr (E) *n.* [RESPECT LANGUAGE]
hair
SEE ALSO alta, -ayerr

imparrkemp-iwelhem (E) rub yourself in or on something SEE UNDER **impalerrp-welhem**

impaty (E) footprint, track SEE UNDER **mpaty**[1]

impaymp (E), **aympaymp** (E), **aynpaynp** (E) *n.*
yellow-throated miner bird (*Manorina flavigula*)
= irnpernp

impekenh (T,E), **inpekenh** (E), **aynpekenh** (E) *n.*
small rockhole with stone lid
Impekenh (T,E) *n.*
the name of a rockhole south of Aniltji (Boundary Bore)

impelhem (E) *vi.*
cramp up, get numb ◆ Aneny impelhenty akngart-iwelhem. (Sa) *Turning yourself over if your hip is cramped.*
= arlerlp-irrem, tharr-irrem

impelty (E) *n.*
scar or mark ◆ Altyerr ampetyarl nhanyeman, kerarl atwek. Aherrarl atwekan impelty anerl-anem urrperl. Ulta apekarl atyerrek, ulta apekarl atanthek irrtyartel, wal impeltyarl anerl-anem, ampan. *Mark*-akert anem anerl-anem, urrperl. (Sa) *This is a birthmark from where the animal was hit. Where the kangaroo was shot is a dark-coloured mark. If it was shot in the side, or speared in the side, well there is a mark there on the child. The child has a dark-coloured mark.*
SEE ALSO mpaty

impem, ipmem (E) *vt.*
1. leave someone or something alone, reject something ◆ Mern atyenharrp yanh impeyaw. (St) *Leave that food there that belongs to me alone.* ◆ Kwaty yanh impang tha antywety-angent. *Leave that water for me, I'll drink it after.* ◆ Urraremel inem mantarr mwerr map ant mwerr angerr aremel — akeng-akeng impemel arrkay-arrkay. (St) *Sort through and just pick out the good clothes that you see — leave the no-good ones, the faded ones.* ◆ Mern impetyek atyeng, akertang arlkwemel. (St) *I am leaving the food and eating half.* ◆ Mwetekay angkweyeny yanh impa

anem kwenh. (T) *Leave that old motor car now.*
2. stop doing something, give something up ◆ Atwerlanetyang — ipmay! (Sa) *Don't fight — stop fighting!* ◆ *Paint* apek atyenh tha uyarn mpwarem, wal tha impemarl, uyarnarl mpwarem. (St) *I am having difficulty doing this painting, so I'm going to stop doing it, because it's too hard to do.*
3. win, beat someone in a race or a game ◆ Thang impern *Caroline* kartel-ayeng kwenyel akeweny-amperl. (M) *I beat poor old Caroline at cards last night.* ◆ *Football*-el apekarl arrken-irrep-irrem ina, anyentel apek impek kel. Arlkwerrem-antey. 'Arlkwek anyentel.' *Winner* apek ra anem. Arlkwek, *Stirling* mapel apek arlkwek, Kwenthey-kwenthey mapel. (St) *They are playing football and one team won. 'One team beat the others.' And then they are the winners. Maybe Stirling mob won, the* Kwenthey-kwenthey *team [named after* Eremophila duttonii*].*
SEE ALSO menty

imperrem[1], **ipmerrem** (E) *vi.*
1. split up, separate from each other ◆ Anewart atherr apek imperrem. (M) *That husband and wife might split up.*
2. stop doing something to each other ◆ Ipmerray — ahel atwerretyangenh. Ipmerrenherratherr! (Sa) *Leave it — stop fighting each other. Both of you stop it!*

impelhem, **ipmelhem** (E) *vi.*
stop doing something; give something up; leave someone, quit a job ◆ Anenty-penh impelh-anem kwaty, impelhenhem. (St) *It's been raining, and it's stopping.* ◆ Impelhetyek ayeng, warrk menty anem aney ayeng impelherl-alhey mer arrpenh-warl ayeng alhetyek. (St) *I'm going to stop, give up work and shift to another place.*
SEE ALSO ywerrem

imperl-alhem, **ipmerl-alhem** (E) *vt.*
leave someone or something behind ◆ Tha imperl-alhem atyeneny apek. Unta arntarnt-arelhanaw. (St) *I am leaving the things that might belong to someone else behind. You can look after them.*

impen *n.*
special, important, unique, favourite, precious, the last of something, the only one you've got ◆ Ngkwerlp impen atyenh. (St) *My special tobacco.* ◆ Impen ngkweng anyenay, akwek-amperl. (St) *Keep the last of that for yourself, there's just a little bit.* ◆ Angka weth-apeny impen anwekantherrenh — *we got to* angkerlanetyenh. Angka anwekantherrenharl impen Anmatyerrarl angkep-angkem. (St) *That language of ours is important — we've got to keep on talking it. The Anmatyerr language of ours that we talk is unique.* ◆ Althart, awely, impen. Tyerrtyelarl apmerinparl aknganekarlel. (St) Althart *and* awely *ceremonies are very important. They originated in the country.* ◆ Kwaty anthetyal — impen atyenh tnetyek. (St) *Don't give that water away — it's all I've got.*
= tyeperr

impen-irrem (T,E) *vi.*
save something for oneself, not share ◆ Mantarrek apek impen-irrem atyenhek. Manterr atyenhek ayeng impen-irrem. Anthetyakenh tha anyenem, impen. (St) *I'm keeping these clothes to myself. I'm keeping them and not giving them [to anyone else].* ◆ Impen-irrem arrpenh-kety. (St) *Save something for yourself because of the others.*

impen-impen (T,E) *n.*
greedy, not sharing ◆ Tha impen-impenel arlkwep-arlkwem anyentam-anyent impen-impen. Arrpenhek apek anthetyang. (St) *I'm greedily eating it, bit by bit. Without sharing it or giving it to another.*

impen-impen-irrem (E) *vi.*
be mean or greedy

impen awem (E)
listen carefully or pay attention to what someone is saying ◆ Impen awem tha, unta ayeng ilerlek, impenel tha awem ngenh. Impenel nga angkem atyeng. Impen kwenh tyeperr awem ngenh, untarl angkem. (St) *I am listening carefully to what you are telling me, I'm paying attention to you. You are telling me something important. I am listening carefully to what you are saying.*

impengemp (W) the smell of rain SEE UNDER **mpengemp**

impeny imperrk (W) *n.*
hard to see, camouflaged

impeny imperrk intem (W)
be hidden or camouflaged ◆ *'Eh, something here* kwenh, mer nhel kwenh inngelhem *like* kamern-akert-arteh.' Nwernengk nheng arnarteh impeny imperrk anthwerr interl. (M) *'Hey, there is something here, it seems as if something like my uncle is there.' The tawny frogmouth was hard to see and it looked very much like a branch.*

imperalker-ayerr (E) *n.* [RESPECT LANGUAGE]
sugarbag
= iylpweralker-ayerr, iylpwer-areny, rlpwer-areny, ngkwarl-ayerr

SEE ALSO arwengalker, rltwamp

imperrem[1] split up; stop doing something to each other SEE UNDER **impem**

imperrem[2] (E) *vi.*
go along on the top of water ◆ Urewap-imperr imperreperrem kwatyel. (St) *The dragon-fly goes along on the top of the water.*
SEE ALSO urewap-imperreny, kwaty-inperrenh

imperrty (W), **irnperrty** (W) *n.*
a mark or track (sometimes those from the Dreaming) ◆ Imperrty intem kwaty alhekarlpenh. (M) *There is a mark there from where the water flowed.*
SEE ALSO impelty

ina[1], **inang** (W,T), **itna** (E) *prn.*
they (more than two). This pronoun is used in the subject part of the sentence (i.e. representing the 'doers' of the verb action). It is generally used when the kin relations in the group being referred to are not specified. See Appendix 1. ◆ Angkwey inang ker pwethekat arlkwetyart. (T) *In the old days they used to eat cats.* ◆ Inang alhem lyweny. (T) *They are going hunting.*
SEE ALSO inengkerr, inakerr, inantherr

inenh, **itnenh** (E) *prn.*
them (more than two). This pronoun is used in the object part of the sentence (i.e. representing those the verb action is 'done to'). ◆ Thang atwem inenh. (M) *I am hitting them.*

ineh (W,T), **inek** (E), **itnek** (E) *prn.*
for them, to them (more than two)

inehenh (W,T), **inekenh** (E), **itnekenh** (E) *prn.*
their, theirs (belonging to more than two)

inant-inant, **itnant-itnant** (E) *n.*
more than two things that are the same as, or very similar to, each other ◆ Kwer akwek inant-inant, inngerr inant-inant. (T) *Those two kids are almost identical, their faces are the same.* ◆ Inant-inant alhep-alhem. Anwengkerr ingkern alherlapem. (T) *They, who are similar to each other, are just going together. We'll come along behind.* ◆ Inant-inant alhep-alhem kwenh — mantarr *same*-akert kwenh an inngerr *same* kwenh. Inant-inant. (M) *[They] look the same as each other — their clothes are the same and their faces are the same. Same as each other.*
= inantarrety
SEE ALSO rant-atherr

inantarrety (W,T) = **inant-inant**
more than two things that are the same as, or very similar to, each other
SEE ALSO rant-atherr

inant-inant atwerrem (T), **itnant itnant atwerrem** (E)
fight evenly

ina[2] (E), **itna** (E) *n.*
name
= arreny
SEE ALSO anewem[1]

ina (E) firewood that has been prepared by burning a tree down SEE UNDER **una**

inaheleny (W) *prn.*
they (are doing the verb action themselves) ◆ Inaheleny menty irrkwey. (M) *They can keep it themselves.* ◆ Inahelenyarrp itey, ayengan arrpenharlam. (M) *They can cook it themselves, I don't want anything to do with it.*
SEE ALSO tyaheleny, kwarleny, ngkewarl

inakerr, **itnakerr** (E), **aynakerr** (E), **aytnakerr** (E) *prn.*
they (more than two). This pronoun is used in the subject part of the sentence (i.e. representing the 'doers' of the verb action) when the people belong to the same patrimoiety and different generation moiety; for example, a person together with their fathers or father's sisters. See Appendix 1. ◆ Anyenhengart inakerr apetyem. *Fathers and sons are coming.*
SEE ALSO ina[1], inengkerr, inantherr

inenhakerrenh, **itnenhakerrenh** (E), **aynenhakerrenh** (E), **aytnenhakerrenh** (E) *prn.*
them (more than two). This pronoun is used in the object part of the sentence (i.e. representing those the verb action is 'done to').

inehakerr (W,T), **inakerreh** (W,T), **inekakerr** (E), **itnekakerr** (E), **aynekakerr** (E), **aytnekakerr** (E) *prn.*
for them, to them (more than two)

inakerr-henh (W,T), **inakerr-kenh** (E), **itnekakerrekenh** (E), **aynekakerrenh** (E), **aytnekakerrenh** (E) *prn.*
their, theirs (belonging to more than two)

inakerr-akey *prn.*
they (people in the opposite patrimoiety)
SEE ALSO -akey, alak-akey

inamen (W,T) *n.*
place where a lot of people are living ◆ Wal, alkereh-irretyam ra. Alkereh-irretyam rang mer inamen arrpenh irrety-alhetyam. (M) *Well, he flew into the sky. He flew up and then came to a place where lots of other people lived.*

inang (W,T) they (more than two) SEE UNDER **ina**[1]

inangkal *n.*
clever, knowledgeable, someone who is good at doing things, invincible ◆ Nthakenh renh

atwetyakenh inangkal, ilpelhetyelarl. Ngkwern atwetyakenh perrap inangkal iyterrty ilpelhetyelarl ra arwerlel. (Sa) *He is really clever and can't be beaten because he is protecting himself. He is really invincible and can't be hit because he is shielding himself with a branch.* ◆ Inangkal anthwerr ntwa anem kwenh, kalty anthwerr. (M) *You are really clever, really knowledgeable.*
SEE ALSO kalty, kapert altywer, kapert arraty, kwerathek, lywenpeny, wetyerretyerr2, weretyerretyerr

inangkal-irrem *vi.*
1. learn, become knowledgeable ◆ Kwer map inangkal-irrem kwerlel. (T) *The children learn at school.* ◆ Arelh inangkal-irrem awely wetyek. (T) *The woman is learning to paint the women's ceremonial designs.*
SEE ALSO kalty-irrem
2. dodge or duck out of the way ◆ Artwa inangkal-irrem kayl-kety. (Sa) *The man is dodging the boomerang.* ◆ Arnekety apek inangkal-irrem, atwekety apek inangkal irrenhem. (St) *Dodging the trees, or going along ducking to avoid being hit.* • SEE ALSO uremeny-irrem

inantherr, **itnantherr** (E), **aynantherr** (E), **aytnantherr** (E) *prn.*
they (more than two). This pronoun is used in the subject part of the sentence (i.e. representing the 'doers' of the verb action) when the people belong to different patrimoieties; for example, a person together with their sisters-in-law or their cross-cousins. See Appendix 1.
SEE ALSO ina1, inengkerr, inakerr

inenhantherrenh, **itnenhantherrenh** (E), **aynenhantherrenh** (E), **aytnenhantherrenh** (E) *prn.*
them (more than two). This pronoun is used in the object part of the sentence (i.e. representing those the verb action is 'done to').

inehantherr (W,T), **inantherreh** (W,T), **inekantherr** (E), **itnekantherr** (E), **aynekantherr** (E), **aytnekantherr** (E) *prn.*
for them, to them (more than two)

inehantherrenh (W,T), **inantherr-henh** (W,T), **inekantherrenh** (E), **itnekantherrenh** (E), **aynekantherrenh** (E), **aytnekantherrenh** (E) *prn.*
their, theirs (belonging to more than two)

inap (T,E) *n.*
echidna, anteater, 'porcupine' (*Tachyglossus aculeatus*). Also referred to as *ker inap.*
= inarleng, ker arlkerl
SEE ALSO lyek

inarleng *n.*
1. echidna, anteater, 'porcupine' (*Tachyglossus aculeatus*). Also referred to as *ker inarleng.* ◆ Inarlengel yerr arlkwerl-anem. (M) *Porcupines eat ants.*
= inap, ker arlkerl
2. spinifex (said by some young speakers)

inaty (W) *part.*
An expression of sympathy; 'Poor thing'.
= akeweny

inaty-amperl (W) *part.*
An expression of sympathy; 'Poor thing'. (-amperl '*an expression of endearment or sympathy*')
= akeweny-amperl
SEE ALSO -amperl, -angwel-angwel, -angwen-angwen, -apenh, -awern

inem *vt.*
get something, pick something up, take something ◆ Ker aherr atninem, kel renh lyep-lyep inemel arrernem akethek kel renh arna yanh renh interlp arrernem. (St) *The kangaroo is gutted, then the intestines are taken and laid out in the open, and then that stick, the skewer, is put into place to close the belly cavity.* ◆ Tyap lywernkel inem. Lywernk akwek *hook* yanh-lkwer mpwarerl-iwem, kel anem inem tyap anem, tyap ingweneng apek. (St) *[You] get grubs with a hook. You make a little hook [of grass] and then get grubs such as those from the river red gum.* ◆ Amwelyan karlkwem rtemarlel. Inemel, karlkwemel anem. Iteth-antey rtemarl karlkwem. (Sa) *The cadney lizard is bitten on the back of the neck. [You] get it and bite it on the back of the neck while. It is still alive when you do it.*
SEE ALSO inenty

inelhem *vi.*
1. pull something (such as a prickle) out of part of your body ◆ Arntek ayeng inelhetyek, antywer apek akem arntek inelhetyek, tyerretyek ker, kerarl arntek-warl aylperrek. Arwerl antywerel, arwerl tyepalel. (Sa) *I am going to pick my teeth, get a bit of grass to pick at my teeth and get the meat that is stuck in my teeth out. With a bit of grass or a stick.*
2. comb hair

inenhem *vt.*
1. pick or collect something as you go along ◆ Kwenthey-arenyam ngkwerrman, mern kwenthey-areny. Kwenthey akepakerl,

inenhepenherl iltyel war inenhepenherl. *This mistletoe grows on the Eremophila bush. We go and pick it by hand as we go along.*
SEE ALSO akem[1]
2. pick someone up from a place

inengkerr, iningkerr (W,T), **itningkerr** (E), **ayningkerr** (E), **aytningkerr** (E) *prn.*
they (more than two). This pronoun is used in the subject part of the sentence (i.e. representing the 'doers' of the verb action) when the people are all in the same patrimoiety and the same generation moiety; for example, a person together with their sisters or brothers, or their father's fathers. See Appendix 1. ◆ Iningkerr angkwer-intyerr anep-anem. (M) *They are there, all the sisters together.*
SEE ALSO ina[1], inakerr, inantherr
inengkerrenh, iningkerrenh, inenh-ingkerrenh (W,T), **itnenh-ingkerr** (E), **aynenh-ingkerrenh** (E), **aytnenh-ingkerrenh** (E) *prn.*
them (more than two). This pronoun is used in the object part of the sentence (i.e. representing those the verb action is 'done to'). It can sound like forms of the pronoun *ineh-ingkerrenh* 'their', 'theirs (belonging to more than two)'.
ineh-ingkerr (W,T), **inengkerreh** (W,T), **itnek-ingkerr** (E), **aynek-ingkerr** (E), **aytnek-ingkerr** (E) *prn.*
for them, to them (more than two)
ineh-ingkerrenh (W,T), **inengkerr-henh** (W,T), **itnek-ingkerrenh** (E), **aynek-ingkerrenh** (E), **aytnek-ingkerrenh** (E) *prn.*
their, theirs (belonging to more than two)
itningkerr-angkwer (E) *prn.* [RESPECT LANGUAGE]
they (more than two)

inenty *n.*
kurdaitcha, ritual executioner ◆ Artwa mer-areny. Inenty anem ra *act*-irrem — *like cowboy* akin. (P) *They are men from the land. They act like* inenty — *a bit like cowboys.*
= ngkekern, kwertaty, mwak[2], nwernternenty, rlwarlp, urlaylp
SEE ALSO atham-areny, inem

inernkelhem (W) *vi.*
say how you are related to someone, call someone by a kin term (?) ◆ Ayengarl ngkweng inernkelhem 'tyemey'. *I call you 'grandfather'.*

inernt *n.*
1. bean tree, bats-wing coral tree [SOME SPEAKERS]. Tree to 10 m high, with bright red flowers and shiny red and yellow seeds in clustered pods. ◆ Inernt-they-antey alkwert mpwarem. (St) *Shields are made from bean tree wood.*
◆ Tyerrtyel arlkwem inernt akwerrk rwangel itemel. (M) *People cook the young bean tree plants and eat them.*
= atywerety, aparrty
2. seeds of the bean tree, bats-wing coral tree ◆ Tyerrtyel inernt kwetyem nekeleth mparetyeh. *People collect bean tree seeds to makes necklaces.* • SEE ALSO nekeleth

Inernt irrpenh (W), **Nernterrpenh** (W) *n.*
Nintabrinna Bore, east of Anmatjira Range

inernt-inernt (T) *n.*
1. sharp, spiky [SOME SPEAKERS]
SEE ALSO arrerlp
2. having different colours [SOME SPEAKERS]

inewarr (E) *n.*
wispy clouds. Also referred to as *kwaty inewarr.*
SEE ALSO katyar, urrarl

inewem (T,E) name something SEE UNDER **anewem**[1]

Ineyarr (W) *n.*
the name of a hill west of Napperby

inga, ikngα (E) *n.*
alone, on your own, solitary, friendless, by yourself ◆ Ingang ayeng anyent untherl-apem. (M) *I am going around on my own.*
◆ Ikngan anem ayeng anep-anem, arengk-rnemant akert. (Sa) *I'm here all on my own, with just the dogs.*
SEE ALSO anyent, ngwath, akalk, arrakelakel
ingek-ingek (E), **ikngek-ikngα** (E) *n.*
separately (from each other or from others)
◆ Akalk-akalk anem apmer ikngek-ikngel, arrpenh anep-anem arrpenh, arrpenh anep-anem, war anem atwarirrem. (St) *[They] are living in separate places — some people live in one place and others in another, and they just meet up occasionally.*
ingareny, ikngareny (E) *n.*
someone who lives by themself; a friendless person, a loner ◆ Ayeng ingarenyam ananem. (M) *I'm sitting here on my own.* ◆ Ikngareny alhem aterek arrangkw. (Sa) *[That person] goes around on their own, they're not frightened.*
◆ Akuny-amperl *too* ayeng anep-anem ikngα. *No* ilkwatherr. Arengk-artekarl iwerrek. (Sa) *Poor me, I am all on my own. I have no company. They abandoned me like a dog.*
= anyent-areny
ingatherr, ikngatherr (E) *n.*
two people on their own (separate from others) (atherr[1] *'two'*) ◆ Atherrarrp alherrem, ikngatherr. (Sa) *Those two are going together, on their own.*
ingarey, ikngarey (T,E) *n.*
a group of people (more than two) on their

own (separate from others) (-arey *'plural'*) ◆ Anwantherr marl map-antey ikngarey anep-anem. (St) *Just all of us women are here on our own.*

ingirrem, ikngirrem (E) *vi.*
1. become solitary, be on one's own ◆ Ikngirremel anem ayeng alpetyek, iwerremarl-kety. (Sa) *I am going back on my own now, because we have split up.* (?)
2. become bereaved of a brother or sister ◆ Ikngirrek ayeng, *brother* apek tha aparlp-ilek. Iknga anem. *I lost my brother and now I'm on my own, alone.*

ingekelh-ilem, ikngekelh-ilem (E) *vt.*
separate a person from another, cut one out from the others ◆ Ampa akely tha ikngekelh-ilem *self* atherr anerlanetyek, mikwekety. (St) *I am separating that child from its mother so that the two of them can be apart.*
SEE ALSO arlkwer-ilem, arwekar-ilem, angakelh-ilem

inganem (E) climb up, go up something SEE UNDER **nganem**

-ingar, -inger *n.ending*
Goes on number words to show the number of times something happens; a number of nights or days, that many times. ◆ Anyent-**ingar** war intety-alhem. (M) *I just went and camped out for one night.* ◆ Rrpwety-**inger** ayeng alhek. (M) *I went three times.* ◆ Map-**ingar** anwern angkem. (M) *We are talking lots of times.* ◆ Thew-warn alhay anyent-**ingar** anem, map-**ingar** alhetyal. (T) *Go to the store once, don't go lots of times.* ◆ 'Nthakenty-**ingar** nga alhemay?' *You might* ilem, *'Four days* apek. Alakenty-**ingar** ayeng alhem atherr-atherr'. (St) *'How many days are you going for?' And you might say, 'Maybe for four days. That's how many days I am going for'.* ◆ Ayeng alhemaw urrpety-**inger** intetyek. Apawenhem ra apek unta apek ayenh, 'Nthakenty-**inger** nga alhem?' 'Urrpety-arengek ayeng alhem, urrpety-**inger** intety-alhetyek ayeng alhem.' (St) *I'm going to camp out for a few days. He might ask me or you might ask me, 'How long are you going for?' 'I'm going to go for a few days.'*
= -areng[1]

ingerr (W,T), **ikngerr** (E) *n.*
east ◆ Aherrk irrpem altwerl-atheh. Ingerreng apetyem aherrk anenty-alhem, altwerl-atheh irrpem. (N) *The sun goes down in the west. It comes from the east and goes down in the west.*
= angerrakw
SEE ALSO altwerl, ayerrer, antekerr

ingerr-penh (W,T) *n.*
from the east

ingerr arraty (W,T), **ikngerr arraty** (E)
due east

ingeth (T,E), **ikngeth** (E) *n.*

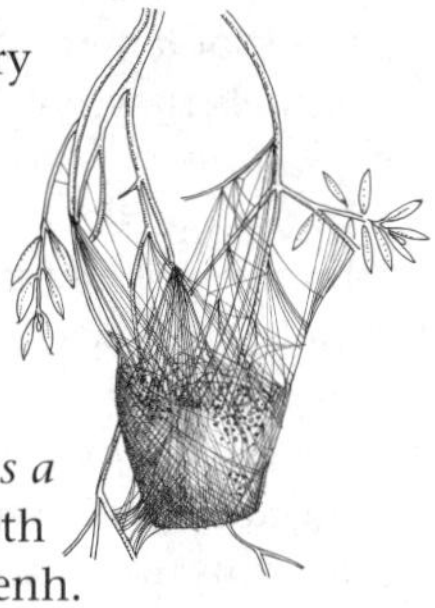

1. itchy grub, processionary caterpillar, larvae of the bag-shelter moth. This is the larvae of the bag-shelter moth. (*Onchrogaster* spp.) ◆ Yakweth ilkwa ikngeth-kenh. (Sa) *The itchy grub has a big nest, like a bag.* ◆ Ikngeth weth rtety-rtety-irrenh-irrenh. (Sa) *Those itchy grubs make you go lumpy.*
2. the nest of the itchy grub
SEE ALSO wep
3. fine hair on the seeds of the kurrajong tree, *ngkweyang*

ingka, ingkang (W,T) *n.*
1. foot, feet ◆ Ngkang atyenh arekar. *My foot is crippled.*
2. toe
3. track
4. back hooves or paws of animals ◆ Arengk iltya-akert. Alakenty iltya: iltya atherr ingka atherr. *A dog has front paws. That many front paws: two front paws and two back paws.* ◆ Nantewan ingka atherr an iltya atherr akin. Arrwekel-thayt iltyarl, ingkern-thaytan ingkarl. (St) *Horses have two front hooves and two back hooves. The ones at the front are called 'iltya' and the ones behind 'ingka'.*
CAN SOUND A BIT LIKE inka *'spirit'*

ingka akwerrk (E)
toes (other than big toe) (akwerrk[1] *'young'*)

ingkang kwerrng (W,T)
= **ingka akwerrk** (kwerrng *'small'*)

ingka amikw (E)
big toe (amikw[2] *'mother'*)
= inkang pwel-pwel, ingilkw, ingka angerrety

ingkang pwel-pwel (W,T), **ingka pwel-pwel** (E)
big toe (pwel-pwel *'large'*)

ingkilkw (E)
big toe (ilkwa *'big'*)

ingka angerrety (E)
big toe (angerrety *'big'*)

ingka akwerreny (E)
little toe (akwerreny *'smallest'*)

ingka alyeng, ingka ayleng (E)
left foot (alyeng *'left side'*)

ingka arraty
right foot (arraty *'straight', 'correct'*)

ingkang kwart (W)
barefooted (kwart *'egg'*)
ingka anert, **ingkang anert** (W,T), **ingka atnert** (E)
bottom of the foot, middle part of the sole of the foot (anert *'stomach'*) ◆ Ingka atnert ampekerraw! (Sa) *The bottom of [my] foot might get burnt!*
ingka ipert (E)
bottom of the foot, sole of the foot (ipert *'hole'*, *'hollow'*)
ingka artep, **ingkang artep** (W,T)
instep, top of foot (artep *'back'*)
ingka ingkelthel, **ingkang ingkelthel** (W,T)
toenails (ingkelthel *'toenails'*)
ingkang tywemar (W,T)
toenails (tywemar *'toenails'*)
ingka tyelk (E)
heel (tyelk *'flesh'*)
ingka amper-amper (E)
pigeon-toed (amper-amper *'crooked'*)
ingka arntayl (E)
pigeon-toed ◆ Ingka arntaylarl ingwerem, ingwerem amper-amper. Ingka arratyarl ingwer. (Sa) *Some people are splay-footed, others are pigeon-toed. Others have straight feet.*
ingkel atwem (W,T), **ingkel-wem** (T)
kick (atwem *'hit'*) ◆ Artwel patepwerl ingkel atwem arrpenh alenh-warn. (T) *The man is kicking the football to the other one over there.*
ingkekenh (E) *n.*
shoe (lit. 'belonging to the foot')
mwetekay-kenh ingka (T)
tyre (lit. 'the car's foot') ◆ Arelhel mwetekay-kenh ingka mpwarem alpwely-irrekarl. (T) *The woman is fixing the tyre that went flat.*
Ingkapeny (E), **Ingkartek** (E) *n.*
a star constellation; the Saucepan (part of Orion) (lit. 'like a foot')
SEE ALSO Anterl, Arlanty, Arnkenty, Pwereytarr
ingka arnkengeny (E)
centipede (lit. 'lots of feet'). Used as an alternative to the more common word for centipede, *arnperrk*, which is *kwementyay*.
= arnperrk
ingka iyntwem (E)
echidna, 'porcupine', anteater (iyntwem *'facing away'*)
SEE ALSO inap, inarleng

ingka-mwerney, **ingkang mwerney** (W) *n.*
life-saver burr, teddy bears arsehole (*Sida platycalyx*) (ingka *'foot'*; mwernem *'get stuck'*). Soft herb with large yellow flowers. Fruits are doughnut-shaped and prickly when dry. ◆ Angkwey anwa kwer akwek map anwern arrken-irretyart ingka-mwerney akwernetyart arnewarn, angwenh-akey-artek, nekeleth-artek, an *round one tyre* akwek-artek. Kel *roll*-em-ilem mpatyel anem, mwetekay-kwenhel. (T) *In the old days us kids used to play, threading the life-saver burrs onto sticks, like necklaces or little round tyres. Then we rolled them along and made tracks, when we didn't have any [toy] cars.*
= akeley-akeley, kwem, anmang

ingkang (W,T) foot, feet SEE UNDER **ingka**

ingkang mwerney (W) life-saver burr SEE UNDER ingka-mwerney

ingkantem (W,T), **ingkentem** (W,T) *vt.*
track someone or something, follow footprints or tracks ◆ Artwang nhenhel ingkanterl-apem ker ankerr. (N) *This man is tracking an emu.* ◆ 'Eh, nhenh arlewatyerr lyet alhern.' Ingkang apenterl-anerrem, ingkenterl-anerrem ingkenterl-anerrem. 'Alhweng nheteh irrpern.' (N) *'Hey, a goanna has just gone here recently.' [Then] we follow the footprints, track it along. 'Here is the hole it's just gone into.'* ◆ Rrwey ingkentem marlel, alhekarl ker atanthetyeh. (N) *The woman tracks the man who has gone to spear some meat.*
SEE ALSO ampinem, apentem, ingka

ingkart missionary, minister, priest, boss SEE UNDER **ngkart**

ingkatharrp (E) alone, on your own [RESPECT LANGUAGE] SEE UNDER **ingketharrp**

ingkatyel-wem *vt.*
step on top of someone's tracks, walk in someone's footsteps ◆ Ingkatyel-wek arrpenharl alhekel-arleng ingkatyel-wenhem. (St) *Walking along in the tracks where another person has gone.* ◆ Anewikwel ingkatyel-werl-alpem, urrpar-urrpar alpemel anewikw. (Sa) *Her husband is going back stepping in someone else's foot tracks, so that he disguises where he is going.*
= atywekel-iwem, lyekel-wem
SEE ALSO ingka

ingkaylt (E) new moon SEE UNDER **ngkarlt**

ingkel iylkenh (E) *n.*
Australian hobby (a type of bird) (*Falco longipennis*)
= nyengk rnternenh

ingkelarr alhem *vi.*
follow tracks or footprints, follow someone or something ◆ Ingkelarr alhep-alhey. (T) *Let's follow the track.*
SEE ALSO ingkantem, ingka
ingkelarr alwernem (W,T) = **ingkelarr alhem**

ingkelthel, ngkelthel *n.*
1. fingernails ◆ Anantherr anyenem ngkelthel iltyangel-ayel. (T) *We have fingernails on our fingers.*
2. toenails [SOME SPEAKERS]
3. claw (of bird)
= tywemar
SEE ALSO ingka, iltya, lthel

ingkem (E) *vi.*
be itchy, feel itchy ◆ Ayeng ikngeth-penh ngkelpengkem. (Sa) *I feel itchy from the itchy grub.*
SEE ALSO irrkem, ngkelpengkem

ingkentem (W,T) track someone or something SEE UNDER **ingkantem**

ingkeny *n.*
deserted or empty place or camp ◆ Mer ingkeny. Mer alhekarl tyerrty apekarl alhekarl wal mer ingkeny arety-alhem. (St) *An empty place. If the people have gone, well [you] see a deserted place.* ◆ Apmer ingkeny apek uyarem, alhek-arleng apek. (St) *[You] might look around the deserted place and see no-one, because they've gone.*
SEE ALSO ampeny1, arramperrty, arltwa

ingkep back, returning, backwards SEE UNDER **angkep**

ingkern *n.*
1. behind ◆ Ingkern apek alhep-alhem. (St) *Going along behind.* ◆ Ingkern nhak artepeng arelhay, ingkernarl arrpenh-arey apetyemek. (Sa) *Look behind there, where the others are coming along behind.*
2. the back part of something ◆ *He can* artep-warl irrem, artep-warl irrem, ingkern-thayt-warl irrem *kidney* renh nheng anwerlkemarl. (M) *It can go towards the back, the kidney can go towards the back if [the person] gets a fright.*
3. after, later ◆ *Something*, ker arlkarl arrernerl-alhem, *plastic*-elayeng — wal ingkern anety-irrem. (P) *Something such as meat that's left behind in plastic — well after that it goes off.* ◆ Arrwekel alhay, ayeng ingkern alheyamel. (St) *You go first, and then I'll go later.*
SEE ALSO arrwekel

ingkern-penh (W,T), **ingkern-iperr** (E)
from behind

ingkern-ilem (E) *vt.*
leave someone or something behind

ingkerneny *n.*
1. last
2. youngest one, younger ones
3. the next generation, the younger generation, people of today ◆ Ingkerneny, alhengk apek aretyenheng tywerreng mer arreng-kenh angey-kenh. Kalty apek anetyenheng. *The next generation might know about sacred things and about their grandparent's and father's land. Maybe they'll get to know about it.* ◆ Kwer ingkerneny mapel arlkwem mern aperelty. (M) *Today's children eat the white substance made by the lerp-scale insect from river red gum trees.*
4. after, later ◆ 'Alha kwenh rntwarr — alhangkwarr alhetyal!' Tyerrty apek. *Two fellas might talk* ingkerneny *tickley*-irremel. 'Iyntwarr-angkwerr alha kwenh!' (St) *'Go further away — don't go right in front of me!' People talk like that. Later those two people might get annoyed with each other. 'Go further away!'*
SEE ALSO arrwekeleny

ingkern alhem, ingkerneny alhem
1. follow or go behind ◆ Ingkern alherl-apem tyerrty alenh, ingkerneny alhem, tyerrty arrwekelarl alhekarl. Arrwekel alhekarl map artenheng-irreperrem ingkern nhenh ina, mer-warl. (N) *Those people are going along behind the others who are in front. They are following the ones who went ahead, back home.*
2. go later
CAN SOUND A BIT LIKE ngkernelhem *'stop something'*

ingkerney (W,T) *n.*
youngest child
= ingkerneny, akwerreny

ingkerr1, ingkerrek *n.*
all, everything, everybody, the whole lot, every one of them, all of them ◆ Mer irranyent-iwem arengkel. Mern, ingkerr arlkwerrek. Mernek akent-werreperrem irranyent-iwetyel. (Sa) *The dogs have gone through the place and messed everything up. They've eaten all the food. They've gone through everything looking for food and messed everything up.* ◆ Alpek anwern ingkerrek. *We all went back.* ◆ Tyelk ingkerrek ayeng akeng-irrek *pain*-angketyarr, arlkwemarl. Tyelk ingkerrek ayeng arlkwem. (St) *My whole body feels no good and I'm in pain all over. My whole body is aching.* ◆ Ahantherrek mern atyenh, ingkerrek-antey. Tey atyenh impen ingkerrek ahantherrek. Ahantherrek ingkerrek innga. Ker atyenh uyerrek, angayakwarl apetyarr-alherrek. (Sa) *All of my food has been eaten, the whole lot. The only tea I have has been used up. Absolutely everything has gone. All of my meat has run out, eaten up by the hungry people who came.*

ingkerrek-antey (T,E), **ingkerr-antey** *n.*
the whole lot, everybody, everything ◆ Mpa, ingkerr-antey alherl-wey. (Sa) *Come on, let's all*

go. ◆ Ingkerr-antey arlkwek angayakwel. (Sa) *The hungry person ate everything.*

ingkerreny *n.*
all, whole lot, all of them

+ingkerr[2] *prn.ending*
Goes on dual and plural pronouns and shows that the people being referred to are in the same patrimoiety and the same generation moiety as each other. For example, a person or persons along with their siblings, father's father, mother's mother, father's mother, mother's father or cross-cousins. ◆ Angkwer-nheng-arey arr**ingkerr** alhek? Yew. Ingkerr anw**ingkerr** apety-alperrek angkwer-intyerr. (Sa) *Have all of you sisters gone? Yes. All of us came back, all the sisters together.* ◆ Anwern**ingkerr** angkwer-intyerr alhem anwekel. (T) *All of us, all the sisters, are going camping out.*
SEE ALSO +ak[2], +anth

ingkerrek all, everything, everybody SEE UNDER **ingkerr**[1]

ingkerrkentyel arem (W) *vt.*
shade eyes with hand ◆ Ingkerrkentyel arem twernel anngang arrkay-ilem-hety. (M) *Shading [your] eyes with your hand in case the sun makes your eyesight blurry.*
SEE ALSO merlpeng

ingketharrp (E), **angketharrp** (E), **ingkatharrp** (E) *n.* [RESPECT LANGUAGE]
alone, on your own ◆ Angketharrp ahanenherl-wek. Iknga kwenh alhek, angketharrp. (St) *He went on his own. He really went alone, on his own [said by a woman referring to her son-in-law].* ◆ Angketharrparl ra ahanenhek. Ahanenhek angketharrp. *Like* anyentarl alhek. Anyent-awernarl ra alhek. Mey-mey ikwerenhekarl angkep-angkem. (St) *He [her son-in-law] went on his own. He went on his own. The poor thing went, just one, on his own. [She] is talking about her son-in-law.*
SEE ALSO aweleth, inga, anyent-areny

ingketharrp-irrem (E), **angketharrp-irrem** (E) *vi.* [RESPECT LANGUAGE]
become alone

ingkety *n.*
good, nice, lovely ◆ Ker ingkety, mentyarl arep-arem. (Sa) *[I'm] just looking at that lovely meat.* ◆ Ker ingkety thang rwernp arlkwem. (M) *I'm going to eat some lovely hot meat.* ◆ Ker mwerr anthwerr, ker ingkety. (M) *Really good meat, lovely meat.*
SEE ALSO alyerremey

ingkirrpem *vi.*
put on feather shoes (kurdaitcha) (ingka *'foot'*; irrpem *'put something on'*) ◆ Ingkirrpem ra kel ra apetyem, mer nthenh apekarl iterlarem, kel arraty atwety-alhem, rlwaylpel. (St) *The kurdaitcha puts on his feather shoes and then goes to whatever place he knows, and then kills [someone].*

ingkwarrkem (T,E) flash (lightning) SEE UNDER **ngkwarrkem**

ingkwayt (E) grub from ant bed, flying ant (?) SEE UNDER **ngkwayt**

ingkwerelhem (E) like someone or something, want SEE UNDER **inkwerelhem**

ingkwernem (T,E) *vt.*
1. write, paint, draw, make a mark or design on something ◆ Arelhel ingkwernem Anengkerr kampeth-warn. (T) *The woman is painting Dreamings on the canvas.* ◆ *Batik* tha arrkernetyek ingkwernerl-ayntetyek. Arrkernemel ingkwernetyek. Ingwer kaltyelan arrkernetyang ingkwernay. 'Ngka, ayeng arrkernelhetyek.' (Sa) *I'll try to paint batik. Those others who are knowledgeable don't have to try first — they can paint. 'Give it to me — I'll try myself out.'*
2. make something official; put something on a list; register a car ◆ Mwetek ingkwernekarl yanh, arrernekarl, rlwaylp-kwenyarl yanh. (St) *That car has been registered, it's not unregistered [lit. 'not a kurdaitcha'].*
SEE ALSO arrernem, atanthem, intelh-ilem, mpaty-ilem, arlkeny arrernem, arlkeny-wem

ingkwernelhem (T,E) *vi.*
1. make a mark on oneself, paint up, paint oneself ◆ Analpentyel awely alyemel inngek, ankwa aynterl-anentyek. Awely renh alyerl-anemel. 'Alanh alanh kwenh arrekantherr aney.' Analpentyel alyerl-anem, kel arlkeny arlka ingkwernelhemel, alyemel kel inngel anem alyemel. Innga anem ingkwernelherl-anem. (Sa) *The* analpenty *spirits sing* awely *ceremonies to people while they are asleep. They sing the* awely. *'This is how you've all got to do it.' The* analpenty *sing, and then they paint themselves with ceremonial designs as well. Then the people sing and paint themselves up.*
2. write or sign one's name

ingkwey (E) old SEE UNDER **angkwey**

ingwa (T,E) *n.*
1. night, night-time, darkness
2. a night ◆ Unekel alhem ingwa anyentel, ingwa anyentel interl-alpetyek. (St) *Going and camping out for one night and then coming back.*
= kweny[1]
SEE ALSO ngwemernt

ingwa mpep (E)
the middle of the night, midnight (mpep *'middle'*)
= kweny rlkwerr
ingwel-ingwel (T,E) *n.*
very early in the morning, daybreak
ingwel-ingwel arlkenh-arlkenh (E)
rooster (lit. 'that which sings out at daybreak')
ingwirrem (T,E) *vi.*
get dark, become night ◆ Ingwirrem-arleng alpemaw. (St) *Let's go back — it's getting late.*
= kweny-irrem
ingwepenh (E) *n.*
tomorrow, morning, in the morning (-penh[1] *'after'*) ◆ Ingwepenh apety-alpay. (Sa) *Come back tomorrow.*
= ngwenp, ngwenth
ingwelem (T,E) *n.*
early in the morning
SEE ALSO aherlkenty

ingwatentyel (T,E), **ingwartentyel** (T,E) *adv.*
in the night, all through the night, doing something all through the night
◆ Ingwartentyel arlkwep-arlkwem yanhel. (St) *That person is eating all night.*
◆ Ingwatentyelan ilekekel anem ankwa ayntetyakenhan? Ingwatentyel untherl-anem ankwel atwetyakenh. Ankwa aynteyaw! (Sa) *How come you are not sleeping through the night? Wandering around all night and not getting to sleep. Go to sleep!* ◆ Ingwartentyel ingkety alpem. (T) *Go back during the night on foot.*
SEE ALSO ankwakel

ingway-ingway (T,E) a little bit dark, dusk, early evening SEE UNDER **ngway-ngway**

ingwelenthel (E) tomorrow, tomorrow morning [RESPECT LANGUAGE] SEE UNDER **ngwelenthel**

ingwemernt (E) dark (night-time) SEE UNDER **ngwemernt**

ingweneng *n.*
1. grub from the branch of river red gum, *aper*, cossid moth grub (*Xyleutes* sp. (?))
2. grub from the coolibah, *ankerrmern* [SOME SPEAKERS]
= aylperlayt, perlanty, ngkenhar, aperayt
SEE ALSO mpaty[2]

ingwenp (W,T), **ingwenth** tomorrow SEE UNDER **ngwenp**

ingwer (E), **ikngwer** (E) *n.*
1. other, another one, a different one
◆ Lyetant arnarekerr, ingwer apetyenty mer ingwer-areny wal ikwer nyerrarl irrem. (Sa) *Because it is the first time that we have met up with that stranger from another place, we get shy of him.* ◆ Lyetant apetyety, mer ingwer-they, arrwel aretyang. (Sa) *[We] haven't seen that person for a long time, they have just arrived from another place.*
2. other person or people, strangers, foreigners, somebody else ◆ Arna ingwer-kenh imeyaw. *Leave that, it's someone else's.*
◆ Ingwerarl ayeng — arrekantherrek-artwey anetyang. (Sa) *I'm somebody else — I'm not related to you lot.* ◆ Kwaty antywetyek apek apay-unhem, angkethakwel tha antywetyek kwatyaw, apay-unhemel ingwer. (Sa) *I'm going to ask someone for water to drink, because I'm thirsty and I want to drink, I'm going to ask someone else.* ◆ Ingwerek-athen ayenh atwekerr. (Sa) *They might mistake me for a stranger and kill me.*
= arrpenh
ingwer-rnem (E), **ikngwer-rnem** (E) *n.*
others, other people
ingwer-angkwerr (E),
ikngwer-angkwerr (E) *n.*
in another direction; in another way ◆ Ipert-ipertel anaynpenherl-anem, ipert ingwer-angkwerr mwetek. (Sa) *The car is bumping along on the rough [road], from one hole to another.*
= arrpenh-angkwarr
ingwer-irrem (E) *vi.*
change into something else, look different, appear different
= arrpenh-irrem

ingwikw (E) *n.*
food or drink that is left over from the day before ◆ Ingwikw thamperl antywep-antywem. (St) *Poor old me is drinking tea from yesterday.* ◆ Arelhel kwaty ingwikw altyiwem, lyeteny ineyam. (St) *The woman is throwing out yesterday's water so that she can get some fresh water.*
SEE ALSO irrkweny

inka (W,T), **inkang** (W,T), **yenk** (T) *n.*
spirit, soul ◆ Inka ywerrem, wal tyerrty angketyakenh-irrem. (M) *If the spirit departs, then the person is unable to speak.*
= kwerrern
CAN SOUND A BIT LIKE ingka *'foot'*

inkely (E) *n.kin* [RESPECT LANGUAGE]
A respectful way of referring to the mother's mother and the mother's mother's brothers and sisters of a person whom the speaker is in an avoidance relationship to. For example, a woman may use *inkely* to refer to her son-in-law's mother's mother, or a man may use *inkely* to refer to his mother-in-law's mother's

mother. The term may also be used by a man to refer to his male cross-cousin's wife. (?)
= alywerr (?)
SEE ALSO ipmenh, nyany[2]
inkelyikw (E) *n.kin*
his/her/their *inkely*
inkelyengkw (E) *n.kin*
your *inkely*
inkely-nheng (E) *n.kin*
a group of two or more people related as grandparents (mother's mothers or mother's mother's brothers) and grandchildren (daughter's children or a person's sister's daughter's children). This is said by a woman if one of them is her son-in-law, or by a man if one of them is his mother-in-law.
SEE ALSO nyany-nheng
inkely-nheng atherr (E) *n.kin*
a grandparent (mother's mother or mother's mother's brother) together with their grandchild (daughter's child or a person's sister's daughter's child). This is said by a woman if one of them is her son-in-law, or by a man if one of them is his mother-in-law. ◆ Inkely-nheng atherr kwenh, ahanenhek. Anyany-nheng atherr. Wal, inkely-nheng atherr ilernenh ilemer, nyany-nheng atherrarl, Kemarr, Mpetyan. Artwa akenh ilerlek renh akin. 'Inkely-nheng atherr kwenh yanh.' (St) *Those two, granny and grandson, have gone hunting. Granny and grandson. Well, they might call us two Kemarr and Mpetyan, who are related as granny and granddaughter to each other* inkely-nheng atherr. *Men say that too. 'There's that granny and grandchild there.'*
SEE ALSO nyany-nheng atherr

inkem *vt.*
ask someone for something; demand something, beg for something ◆ Inkem ntwa merneh apek kereh apek. (M) *You might ask someone for bread or meat.* ◆ Ayeng inkety-alhem ngkweng kereh apek. (M) *I'm going to demand meat from you.*
ankey inkem = inkem (ankey *'asking for something'*) ◆ Ayeng ankey inkem ngkweng. (M) *I am asking you for something.*

inkenhar pinkish-coloured grub from the branch of the river red gum SEE UNDER ngkenhar

inkerrem *vi.*
make a rustling, rattling or scratching sound ◆ Inkerreperremaw — apmwa apek. (St) *[Something] is making a rustling sound — it might be a snake.*
inkerrelh-ilem, ankarrelh-ilem (W) *vt.*
1. make something rattle or rustle ◆ Inkerrelh-ilem waly artwel. (St) *The man is making the branches rustle.*
SEE ALSO rerrkelh-ilem
2. make someone feel as if something is crawling around on them or touching them ◆ Yerrel inkerrelh-ilem artep. (T) *The ant makes [me] feels like there is something crawling on my back.*
= mpwarelh-ilem
SEE ALSO arrenkelh-ilem[2], irraker-ilem
3. wake someone up (by passing a hand over their face) ◆ Iltyel anpem ankarrelh-ilemel, ankwang alenh intep-intem, alakenh ankarrelh-ilem iltyel, 'Kem-irrang kwenh'. (N) *Somebody is lying there sleeping, you wake them up by touching them with your hand, by passing your hand over their face, and saying, 'Get up'.*

inkwa, ankwang (W,T) *n.*
the chamber or shelf in a honeyant nest ◆ Yerramp-kenh, alhweng apmer ikwerenh, akwek map anem kwerel anem, inkwa ikwerel. (St) *The honeyants' nest is their home, and the little [honeyants] are there, in the chambers of the honeyant nest.*
inkwareny, ankwareny (W) *n.*
1. honeyant (*Camponotus inflatus*) (-areny *'inhabitant of'*) ◆ Inkwareny kwaty-rlwer anwern akern war inyem. (M) *In the rainy time we dig up honeyants just near the surface.*
= yerramp
SEE ALSO yerr
2. honeyant [SOME SPEAKERS, RESPECT LANGUAGE] ◆ Irrepetherl-wa inkwareny atyeng. (Sa) *Go and get me some honeyants [from my respect kin].*

inkwanng (E) *n.*
leaf of bush potato, desert yam [SOME SPEAKERS]

inkwartety (E) *n.*
stone knife (used for cutting meat) ◆ Ker-kenh inkwartety arrwekelenyel *knife* anetyangel arlkwerretyart. (Sa) *The stone knife was what the olden-time people used to cut up meat when they didn't have any [metal] knives.*
SEE ALSO alywek, apwert antha, kartamp, irntarlter, irntang arlter, werlamp

inkwel (E) *n.*
black kite (bird) (*Milvus migrans*)
= apwelanty, artapw-artapw, apwerl-apwerl

inkwerelhem (T,E), **ingkwerelhem** (E) *vi.*
like someone or something, want; feel happy about something; be pleased or excited (about something) ◆ Ayeng inkwerelhem ngkweng. *Happy*-irrem. Atnertinp inkwerelhem. (St) *I like you. I'm happy about you. I feel happy about you from the bottom of*

my heart [lit. 'stomach']. ◆ Tyerrty apetyemek inkwerelhem. (St) *I am happy about the people coming.* ◆ Inkwerelhetyel ampa akelyek. Inkwerelhety-ayntem ampa akely arrkenarl atherremek. (Sa) *Feeling happy about a little baby. Feeling happy about a little baby that is smiling and laughing.* ◆ Arengkan inkwerelhemarl artweyekikw, anyerrkem inngart tayl. (St) *The dog is pleased about its master, and it wags its tail.*
SEE ALSO anyerrkem, akangkem, anyanelhem, tywenelhem

-inkwern (E) *v.ending*
Shows that the verb action used to happen. This verb ending always follows *+ety*. ◆ Mer Ahert-kenh anwantherr arety-**inkwern**, *Harper Springs*. Ikwerel arlkwerretyart atnyemayt ahertel. Tyap renh iytnetyart, tyerremel arlkwemel. (St) *And we used to see them at* Ahert-kenh, *Harper Springs. That's where the bilbies used to eat the witchetties. They used to dig up the grubs and pull them out and eat them.*
SEE ALSO +etyart, +ek[1], +etyam

inkwerr (E) *n.*
1. snot, nasal mucus ◆ Artep apek irrarlkem anter-penh. Alha inkwerr-penh irrarlkem. (Sa) *Maybe wipe the back after it has been covered with fat, or wipe the snotty nose.*
2. a cold or flu ◆ Ahenty irrkay angketyakenh, inkwerr-penh. (Sa) *[Your] voice fades and you can't talk, from having a cold.*
SEE ALSO rta, mernt[1], rlkert, arrwengkelth, artwengkenng, nkwanng, arntety
CAN SOUND A BIT LIKE angkwerr *'type of ceremony'*

inkwerr-akert (E) *n.*
having a cold or flu
= artwengkenng-akert

inkwert (E) *n.*
buckbush, rolypoly, tumbleweed (*Salsola tragus*). Rounded plant about 1 m high which turns yellow when old and rolls along, blown by the wind.
= arlkerl

inkwert-areny (E) *n.*
buckbush grub
= inkwertayt, arlkerlaty

inkwertayt (E) *n.*
buckbush grub

inmelh (W), **irrmelh** (W) *n.*
fat from the side of the emu (near the kidney). Also referred to as *ker inmelh* or *anter inmelh.*

inmenm-irrem (W) *vi.*
sing (only of bellbirds)
= ilperlp-irrem
SEE ALSO kwepalepal

inmwernt (E) dust, dust haze, dust storm SEE UNDER **unmernt**

innga[1] (E) *part.*
right, sure, really (provides emphasis) ◆ Tyap mwerr-angker innga. *A really nice [tasting] grub.* ◆ Pwarrk-irrentyan aynterl-anem arleng alhenty, parrp innga ra aynterl-anem, awetyangel aynterl-anem. (Sa) *[She] is tired after travelling a long way, and she is lying down really quickly without listening [to anyone].*
SEE ALSO iyterrty
CAN SOUND A BIT LIKE irnnga *'maggot', 'worm'*

inngart (E) *part.*
really, of course, actually ◆ Apmer Alhalkerel, Alhalkerel, ikwerel inngart. Kel akely anem apetyarr-alpek *Utopia Station*-warl. (Sa) *At Alhalker, at Alhalker of course. Then [when I was small] we came back to Utopia Station.* ◆ Mey-mey ngkwenh. Ampa akelyek inngart ilem, 'Mey-mey ngkwenh'. (Sa) *Your son-in-law/mother-in-law. [We] just say, 'Your* mey-mey*' to little kids, of course.* ◆ Aperarntan thelelhetyel *honey*-apeny, aperel-arleng inngart. (Sa) *Actually, the* aperarnt *is found on the river red gum and it seeps out like honey.* ◆ Ker iylek, iylek-iylek inngart. Arrpemel anem renh. Tyelk anetyang anter. Ker iylek arlkwem. (Sa) *Of course the echidna is really prickly and it has its spines scraped off. They don't have flesh — just fat. We eat echidnas.*

innga[2] (E) *n.*
person ◆ Analpentyel awely alyemel inngek, ankwa aynterl-anentyek. Awely renh alyerl-anemel. 'Alanh alanh kwenh arrekantherr aney.' Analpentyel alyerl-anem, kel arlkeny arlka ingkwernelhemel, alyemel kel inngel anem alyemel. Innga anem ingkwernelherl-anem. (Sa) *The* analpenty *spirits sing* awely *ceremonies to people while they are asleep. They sing the* awely *song. 'This is how you've all got to do it.' The* analpenty *sing and then they paint themselves with ceremonial designs as well. Then the people sing and paint themselves up.*
CAN SOUND A BIT LIKE irnnga *'maggot', 'worm'*

inngernem (E) *n.*
people (-rnem *'plural'*) ◆ Inngernem yanh apetyek. (Sa) *Those people came.*
SEE ALSO tyerrty

inngelhem *vi.*
1. appear or seem to be there; be like someone, be recognisable, be familiar ◆ *'Eh*

something here kwenh, mer nhel kwenh inngelhem *like* kamern-akert-arteh.' Nwernengk nheng arnarteh impeny imperrk anthwerr intem. (M) *'Hey, there is something here that looks familiar, it seems as if something like my uncle is there.' The tawny frogmouth is hard to see and it looks very much like a branch.*
2. be beautiful or attractive, become 'right' ◆ Mer inngelhek anem kwaty-penh, atherrkeny anem. (St) *The country became right again, beautiful and green after the rain.* ◆ Rnwanenty yanh ngkweng inngelhem. (M) *Those clothes look right for you.* ◆ Mer nhenh atyeng inngelhepelhem. (M) *I feel comfortable [not homesick] in this place.*
inngelhey (E) *n.*
1. something that looks a bit like someone or something else; something faint and indistinguishable ◆ Rartekarl alhep-alhem inngelhey. (St) *There is something going along there that looks like him.*
2. beautiful, attractive (?)
inngelhey-ilem (E) *vt.*
make something beautiful or attractive
SEE ALSO innga1, innga2

inngeny, ilkngeny (E) *n.*
(having) a lucky, successful feeling, especially for hunting; (being) good at doing something ◆ Inngeny, kerek ayeng inngeny arlewatyerrek. Inngeny ayeng arlewatyerrek. Atwetyek apek tha inngenyel. Irreyakwerrek inngeny, arlatyeyek ayeng inngeny. *I am good at hunting goannas. I am good at killing them. I am good at collecting bush onions and pencil yams.* ◆ Ilkngenyarl arengk atyenhan ilkngeny kerarl aherr *find*-em-ilek, ker arlewatyerr apek. (St) *My dog is a very good hunter, good at finding kangaroos and goannas.* ◆ Ilkngeny-penharl ampwirrek anem pweng anem ra. (St) *That person used to be a very good hunter but now they are old and blind.* ◆ Inngenyel tha *painting* mpwarem. (St) *I am good at painting.*
inngeny-inngeny, ilkngeny-ilkngeny (E) *n.*
= **inngeny** ◆ Inngeny-inngeny ayeng alhetyek ayeng arrken mwerr-angkwerr inngenyel tha *win*-em-iletyek. (St) *I am feeling lucky and I am going to play and I'll be lucky and win.*
SEE ALSO lywenpeny
inngeny-irrem, ilkngeny-irrem (E) *vi.*
have a lucky or successful feeling, especially for hunting

inngerr *n.*
1. face ◆ Kwer mapel rlkwerrp arrkenel arrernelhem kapert-warn, inngerr-warn. (M) *The kids are enjoying themselves putting suds on their heads and faces.*
2. looks, appearance ◆ Kwer akwek rant-atherr, inngerr anyent akwet. (T) *These two kids are similar to each other, their faces are alike.*

inngwerr (T,E) *n.*
ceremonial trade/payment of items such as feathers, ochre and spears
SEE ALSO kwerapak, tyenkerr, tyewarrely

+inp (E), **+enp** (E) *n.ending*
associated with something, having a particular quality; along with; including; having; too; as well; also ◆ Alep**inp**el arrpenhel akngem, ikwerenh anem nthiletyek. (St) *Others go along taking a firestick, and they light their own [fires] then.* ◆ Ker anter**inp** arlkwem. (St) *Eating the meat along with the fat.*

inpa (E), **iynpa** (E) *part.*
1. used to say you don't know the answer to a question; 'I don't know'
= iy, ywek
2. 'I don't know (about something)' ◆ Mern iwerrarrkw arlkwety-inkwern. Inpa anem menty-irrek anem. (Sa) *They used to eat the gidgee wild orange. I don't know about nowadays — they've given it up I guess.*
inpirrem (E), **iynpirrem** (E) *vi.*
disappear without trace; go somewhere (but nobody knows where) ◆ Ngarl arrkereny-irrek, atyengetyeng. Inpirremel arrkereny-irrenhemel inperrenhek, uyerrenhek. (Sa) *You abandoned me. You disappeared without trace and deserted me.*

inpalel anem (W) *vi.* [RESPECT LANGUAGE]
sit
inpalety-alhem (W) *vi.* [RESPECT LANGUAGE]
go and camp somewhere

inpay (T) wire bush, tangled Lechenaultia SEE UNDER **unpay**

inpay-inpay (W,T) *n.*
mountain primrose, pinnate Goodenia (*Goodenia grandiflora*). Used as a washing medicine.
SEE ALSO unpay

inpekenh (E) small rockhole with stone lid SEE UNDER **impekenh**

inpem (T,E) *vt.*
scoop up or pour liquid, get petrol ◆ Mwarel kwatyarl angernem. Urtnewarl anem inpem. (Sa) Mwar *are used for digging for water and then for scooping the water into wooden dishes.*
SEE ALSO athankwem, thelem
CAN SOUND A BIT LIKE impem *'leave something'*

inpenp (E) bone marrow SEE UNDER **inpinp**

inperarr (W,T) *n.*
sharp or pointy hill. Also referred to as *irntang inperarr.*
= kwemper

inpert *n.*
widow, widower
= warlekwert
inpert-irrem *vi.*
become a widow or a widower ◆ Inpert-irrek, yanh arnkenty-warl irrek. (St) *That man has become a widower.*
= warlekwert-irrem
SEE ALSO arnkenty-warn-irrem, arlweker-warn-irrem

inpewem (E) *vt.*
rub desert raisins on the ground to remove the sticky bitter-tasting coating ◆ Ahelh-warl inpewerl-anem katyerr arlkwetyek. (Sa) *Rub the desert raisin fruits on the ground so that they can be eaten.*
SEE ALSO tewem, thwerrem, pwarr-wem, theweth-ilem

inpinp (E), **inpirnp** (E), **inpenp** (E) *n.*
bone marrow ◆ Aherr ngkwern inpenp atwetyek. (St) *Smash up the kangaroo leg for the marrow.*
CAN SOUND A BIT LIKE rnpwernp *'rock pituri'*

inta *n.*
1. spindle ◆ Arna inta, irrkety wenh-wenh. (St) *The spindle is used for spinning hairstring.*
= werintyerr
2. small stick used for poking honeyants out of their nests ◆ Arna intel yerramp inerl-anem inkwek-arlek, ahern-warn anem anyep-anyem. (St) *With a stick called 'inta' the honeyants are poked out from where they are on the shelves in the nest, and then they fall to the ground.*
SEE ALSO lywernk, interlp
3. the stem of a fruit

intahet (W) *n.* [RESPECT LANGUAGE]
head
SEE ALSO kapert[1]

intak (E) *n.*
the bit of the stem that holds Solanum fruits, calyx (?) ◆ Intak-akert ahelh-warl inpewem renh. *[Fruit] that has the stem attached is rubbed on the ground.*
intak rnternem (E)
skewer meat onto a stick so that it can be carried (rnternem *'spear or pierce something'*) ◆ Intak rnternem ker ampeng. (Sa) *Skewer the cooked meat onto a stick.*
= tyet-atanthem
SEE ALSO inta

intarlp angem (W,T), **ntwarlp angem** (E) *vt.*
carry something slung across the shoulders or over the shoulder (especially kangaroo) (angem *'carry', 'take'*) ◆ Arementyel atanthem irrtyartel. Intarlp angety-alpem mer-warl. (N) *[The emu] is speared from the hide. It is carried back to camp, slung around the person's shoulders.* ◆ Ker aherr yanh ntwarlp angety-alpem mereng itetyek, merelant itetyek angety-alpem. (St) *Bringing the kangaroo back slung over the shoulder, bringing it back to cook at camp.*

SEE ALSO ntywel angem, alpalyel angem, intwerl angem, anhwert angem, aylpwar angem
intarlpek-ilem (W,T), **ntwarlpek-ilem** (E) *vt.*
put something on the shoulder, lift or heft something onto the shoulder

intat rubbish or debris left by floodwater SEE UNDER **ntat**

intay *n.*
stallion (from English 'entire'). Also referred to as *nantew intay.*

intayerr-intayerr (E) *n.*
a type of medicinal plant (?) ◆ Intayerr-intayerr, anter-warl renh twetnhem renh *green one* inngap ra anem anem mwerr-angker innga. (Sa) Intayerr-intayerr *plant is crushed up with fat and it goes really lovely and green.*

intekw (E) *n.*
fan-flower (*Scaevola parvifolia*). A plant about 30 cm high, with hairy branches, small dark blue flowers in the shape of a fan, and pale orange fruits. ◆ Intekwan akely-akely arlpa akely-akely atherrk. Artetyel ap intekw ra anetyel. Pertipelaw arlter. Intekw. Mern kweny war atherrk — *name*-ant. Intekw ankerr-kenh mern. Rant arlkwenh-arlkwenh an *turkey*, uthip *everything*-el arlkwerrerl-anem. (Sa) *The* intekw *plant has small green leaves. It grows in mulga country. Its flower is white. It's not edible — it just has a name.* Intekw *is emu's food. Only the emu eats it, and bush turkeys and all sorts of other birds go along eating it.*

intelhem (W,T) *vt.*
make a design or mark on something; write, draw, paint
SEE ALSO ingkwernem, arrernem, atanthem, mpaty-ilem, arlkeny arrernem, arlkeny-wem
intelh-ilem (W,T) *vt.* = **intelhem** ◆ Pep-warn

intelh-ilem angkety yanh ingkerr. (M) *Writing all those words on paper.*
SEE ALSO atanthem, ngkwernem, mpwarem, arrernem

intelty *n.*
a type of grasshopper (*Monistria pustulifera* (?)) ◆ Intelty anarnperl-apem. (T) *The grasshopper is hopping along.*
SEE ALSO arwekert-arwekert, ntyerlkem, arlwety[1]

intelyapelyap (E) butterfly, moth SEE UNDER **antelyapelyap**

intem[1], **ayntem** (E) *vi.*
1. lie, lie down ◆ Ankwa ayeng intetyek. (St) *I am lying down to sleep.* ◆ Artwang rlkert angerr rwangkwerr intep-intem. (M) *A really sick man keeps lying by the fire.* ◆ Amakel irrertety ayeng arlkany intem. (St) *I am lying using my arm as a support.*
2. be positioned or lie in a horizontal direction; be, is, are, were. Particularly of things that are thought of as typically being in a lying position, such as hills, water, smoke, houses, roads etc. ◆ Road intenhem. (M) *The road lies along [there].* ◆ Rwang kwertarl intem. Rwa item, an kwert anem intem, kel altherrem anem, rwa ya ampem antem. (T) *The fire starts smoking. [You] light the fire, then it starts smoking, then it catches alight and then it burns.*
3. sleep, have a sleep ◆ Kwetyerretyerr intem kapert altwerl-atheh. (T) *It is bad luck to sleep with [your] head to the west.* ◆ *Mattress*-kweny ayeng intek akethel wal ayeng antywekelywekely-irrek. (St) *I slept outside without a mattress, and that made me feel unwell.*
4. be born
ankwang intem (W,T), **ankwa intem** (E), **ankwayntem** (E)
go to sleep (ankwa '*sleep*')

intem[2] (E) *adv.*
for good, for a long time
intem-antey (E) *adv.*
for good, for a long time ◆ Alethang arraty apety-alpek nhenh arlka intem-antey anem anetyek. (St) *The stranger really did come back and then stayed here for good.*
= twem, aleth, akwet
intengk (W,T) *n.*
sticky, solid (of honey or paint); tight, hard
SEE ALSO thelty
intengk-irrem (W,T) *vi.*
go solid, solidify
= kelh-irrem

interlp (T,E) *n.*
1. skewer used for closing the belly cavity of certain animals before cooking them ◆ Ker aherr atninem, kel renh lyep-lyep inemel arrernem akethek kel renh arna yanh renh interlp arrernem. (St) *The kangaroo is gutted, then the intestines are taken and laid out in the open, and then that stick, the skewer is put into place to close the belly cavity.*
= alemp, rltimp[2]
2. stick used for spinning hairstring ◆ Interlpel werl-anem alta. (Sa) *Spinning the hairstring on the spindle.* • = werintyerr
SEE ALSO inta

Internt Angkwerlp (W,T) *n.*
the name of a place south of Coniston

interr-interr (E) *n.*
hairless dodder-laurel (*Cassytha capillaris*). A twining plant with small, white, fleshy inedible fruits.

interrenty (T,E) *n.*
close together, matted together, stuck together ◆ Arna interrenty lyapek. (St) *The trees grew close together.*
interrenty-irrem *vi.*
grow back together, become closed over ◆ Kapert altywer, kapert mwerr anem ilek renh, altywerarl-irrek. Rlka aretharrel, rlka altwerlengarl apetyernel. Aretharrel renh akeng-ilek kapert, altywer-ilek. Mwerr anem ilemel interrenty-irrek. (T) *His head was no good after being 'opened up' by the west wind, but now it is better. The west wind was the thing that made his head no good, opened it up. Now it's been healed and it has closed over.*

Interrk[1] (E) *n.*
a star constellation; the Seven Sisters, Pleiades
= Arrarrkw, Kwerraly Angerr, Peltharr Map, Alyang Rlkwang

interrk[2] *n.*
white ant, termite (*Amitermes vitiosus*) ◆ Interrk ahelhel kwen anem, arnang kerrertekel-ayeng. Interrkel altywer-altywer-ilem kwen *side*. (M) *Termites live underground, in the flat ant bed. They make lots of holes in the underneath part.* ◆ Arna arlkwenh-arlkwenharl ra, arna anem interrkel arlkwerl-anem althalth-ilemel. (St) *The white ants eat trees, they eat trees and make them break up into bits.*

interrk-atherather (W,T), **interrk-atherratherr** (W,T) *n.*
1. banded lapwing (*Vanellus tricolor*) ◆ Interrk akwek map arlkwerl-apem, *that's why they call*-em 'interrk-atherather'. (M) *The lapwing*

goes along eating termites [interrk[2]*], that's why they call them* 'interrk-atherather'. ◆ Kwenyel angkerl-anem interrk-atherather, 'Interrk-atherather, interrk-atherather', angkerl-apem. Perlern arlka aketh nhel angkep-angkem. (N) *The lapwing sings out in the night,* 'Interrk-atherather, interrk-atherather'. *It sings out in the plain country and out in the open.*
2. red-kneed dotterel (?) (*Erythrogonys cinctus*)
SEE ALSO tyelkatherather, ampelyetyerrker, tartarrp

interrkekety (E) *n.*
a special word meaning 'woman' (especially senior women). This term appears to be used by both men and women and by most kin relations, with the exception of sons-in-law (and husbands). ◆ Interrkekety arey anep-anem yanh. Angkerreperrem apek rarey kwenh. (St) *The women are sitting down over there. Maybe they are talking.* ◆ Arrwempelikw ilem, 'Interrkekety kwenh. Marl yanh-arey kwenh.' Ikirrenty *way* angkem. 'Interrkekety yanh arey kwenh.' (St) *Her elder brother says, 'The women. All the women over there.' That's a respectful way of talking. 'There are all the women over there.'* ◆ Marlel ilem, 'Interrkekety yanh apetyem. Interrkekety apetyemaw, akuny. Arelh ampwa.' (St) *The woman says, 'The [senior] woman is coming here. The poor old woman is coming.'*
SEE ALSO ampeyamp, ngayekenh

interrpar-wem (E) *vi.*
grind (teeth); rub together (trees) ◆ Interrpar-wem arna apek, arntek apek. Ankwa apek interl-anem wal alakenh, interrpar-wep-wemarl yanh. (St) *Trees, or someone's teeth, might rub together. That person might be sleeping and grinding their teeth.* ◆ Arna interrpar-werrem. (St) *The trees are rubbing together.*
= irrpenper-wem

intert *n.*
1. at the bottom; underneath; the base of something ◆ Marl aper intertel anem. (N) *The women are sitting at the base of the river red gum.* ◆ Alalherrk lpwayelarl irnem. Alalherrk rnpwang nhenh-lkwer arlkwetyart, larl-art rnpang. Awantyetyart larlarl awantyem-artek. Lwerenart. Intertelarl anem. (N) *The* alalherrk *bush grows in the creeks. We used to eat the sweet resin from the* alalherrk *bush, just like a lolly. We used to suck on it just like you suck lollies. Like that. It is found in the base of the tree.* ◆ Artwang aywang arnang intertel ankwang interl-anem. (St) *The old man is sleeping under the tree.*
2. senior people, ancestors
SEE ALSO atnarteng
CAN SOUND A BIT LIKE ntert *'quiet'*

arwerl intert (E)
butt or base (of a tree) (arwerl *'tree'*) ◆ Arwerl intertel anerl-aneyaw, anyent-areny. (Sa) *One person, on their own, sitting at the base of the tree.*

arnang intert (W,T)
butt or base (of a tree) (arnang *'plant', 'tree'*)

aywang intert (W,T)
senior person, elder (aywang *'old', 'grey'*) ◆ Aywang intert map amarl-amarl. (M) Amarl-amarl *are the senior men.*

intertek-irrem, interteh-irrem (W) *vi.*
follow someone or something, go along behind ◆ Amwek intertek-irrem kwer akwekek. (T) *The mother is following the child.*

inteth-iwem (E) (men) perform traditional increase ceremonies to make plants and animals plentiful SEE UNDER **intety-iwem**

intety (T,E) *n.*
spark, sparks. Also referred to as *ura intety.* ◆ Ura intety item kel intety anem intety anem arrerlparratem. (St) *The fire is lit and then the sparks start to fly out.*
= ntyeth

intety-intety-irrem (E) *vi.*
spark up, jump out (spark)
= iynteth-iynteth-irrem, iynteth ngkem

intety-iwem (E), **inteth-iwem** (E) *vt.*
(men) perform traditional increase ceremonies to make plants and animals plentiful ◆ Arrwelarl intety-werretyart ker *everything* mern arlatyey mern arnwekety, artapaly. Alanh intety-iwerretyart arrwekelenyel. Pwetyel anerlanerl aylelherl-anemel. Intety-iwepewem, arlkeny mpwaremel alkwert-warl. (Sa) *In the old days [they] used to hold ceremonies for every sort of meat, and for pencil yams, conkerberries, and bush plums. The olden-time people used to hold increase ceremonies for those things. They used to sit in the bush singing to make everything plentiful, making designs on their shields.*
SEE ALSO angerr-ilem, arrmernem

intetyeng-intety (T,E), **iyntethengeynteth** (E) *n.*
spotted, patterned
SEE ALSO rtety-rtety

intey *n.*
cave ◆ Intey wak-apeny artelherl-anem kwaty-kety anenh-anenh kwenel inteyel. (Sa) *[Some] caves are formed like humpies, and they are used for sheltering in from the rain.* ◆ Inteyelarl angerretyart — *not* wak. Wakan lyetarrarl artek. Kel inteyel pwety-areny-rnem angerretyart, mern pwety-areny arlkwerreperrerl. (Sa) *People used to live in caves — not in houses. Houses were only built lately. The bush people used to live in caves, eating bush foods.* ◆ Perrpantyel irntelarl anem, wal anthwerrng akin arrernem, antywang akwek kwer artem, inteyel. (M) *Black-faced woodswallows live in the rocks and they make nests in caves out of mud.*
SEE ALSO lyerl
irntang intey (W), **apwert intey** (E)
cave
= irntang lyerl

inthwerey (E) *n.*
heap of flood refuse, leaf litter ◆ Inthwerey iwem kwatyel. (Sa) *The floodwater leaves leaf litter behind.*
SEE ALSO ntat, nthat, anthelk[1]

intirrkwer (E) curly wire grass, firegrass SEE UNDER **intwerrker**

intwerelh-ilem (T,E) *vt.*
mix things together, stir things together (seeds, leaves and fat)
SEE ALSO anyentelh-ilem

intwerl angem (E) *vt.*
carry someone on one's shoulders
SEE ALSO ntywel angem, alpalyel angem, intarlp angem, ntwarlp angem, anhwert angem, aylpwar angem

intwerrkenh (W) black-headed python SEE UNDER **antwerrkenh**

intwerrker, intirrkwer (E) *n.*
1. curly wire grass, firegrass (*Aristida inaequiglumis*). A grass which grows to about 1 m high, and has sharp seed heads. When this grass dries people know that the *ahakey* plums are ripening.
2. the sharp seed heads of this grass ◆ Intwerrker ahentyarl mwernepernem, *stuck*-irrem terreth-warl then, pelangket-warl apek. (St) *[The seeds of] the curly wire grass get stuck in your throat, or in clothes and blankets.* ◆ Intwerrker weth mantarr-warlarl aylperreman. Arraper ahelengkw akin, *same one* akin, arraper ahelengkw arrpemarl. (Sa) *That curly wire grass gets stuck in clothes. The* arraper *grass is another cheeky one, the same as the curly wire grass.*
SEE ALSO thenkarr, arraper

intwert-intwert (E) *n.*
a type of plant; tall verbine (*Cullen australasicum*)

intweth-intweth (E) a person who is neglected or on their own SEE UNDER **ntweth-ntweth**

+inty+ do an action in a direction towards someone SEE UNDER **+enty+**[1]

intyakwerlp (W) *n.*
a pile or heap of something (especially said of dirt)
intyakwerlp-wem (W) *vt.*
heap or pile something up ◆ Ahelh intyakwerlp-werl-apem *grader*-el. (M) *The grader is going along heaping the dirt up.*
intyakwerlp arrernem (W)
heap or pile something up

intyalhem (T,E) burst into flames SEE UNDER **intyelhem**

intyalp-wem (W,T) *vt.*
1. throw something away; chuck something out (just liquids)
2. throw something away, abandon someone or something, chuck something out [SOME SPEAKERS] ◆ Terangkel apek intyalp-wem kwer akwek. Arrpenh anem kwetyem. Arelh arrpenhel apetyemel anem kwetyerl-alhem. (T) *The drunk might abandon the little child. Then another person grows it up. Another woman comes along and grows the kid up.*
SEE ALSO artaly-wem, iwem, altyewem, antarr-wem, arrarlp-wem

intyang (W,T) *n.*
spring (water) ◆ Kwaty intyangel interl-anem kwelay — kwerenh kwaty, alhweng akwek. (N) *The rainbow snake lives in the spring — that's its water, its little burrow.*

intyaper (T) all (of something) SEE UNDER **antyaper**

intyar (W,T) white-necked heron SEE UNDER **ntyar**

intyarlkwem *vt.*
waste something ◆ Mern intyarlkwetyal! (M) *Don't waste the food!* ◆ Anherreyel intyarlkwern kwaty atyenh amwerrk. Tey atyenh apek intyarlkwem. (St) *My daughter-in-law wasted my water yesterday. Or maybe she wasted my tea.* ◆ Maney unta atyenh intyarlkwekaw, arrangkw anem ayeng aleyan anem. (St) *You wasted my money, and now I have nothing.*
SEE ALSO ywerrelh-ilem, uyerrelh-ilem, arimpem

-intyarr (W,T) a plural marker SEE UNDER **-intyerr**

intyarr (W,T) *n.*
scattered all over the place ◆ Rwang intyarr intem. (M) *The wood is lying everywhere.* ◆ Rnwanenty nhenh map intyarr intintem.

(M) *These clothes are lying all over the place.* ◆ Rapety apek intyarr interl-anemel *everywhere* nta arem. *You* arerl *everywhere shop*-el yanh, *cool drink* arlkarl antywek-penh intyarr intem. (M) *You can see the rubbish lying scattered everywhere. You can see it everywhere, empty cool-drink containers scattered around the shop there.*

intyarr-wem (W,T) *vt.*
scatter or throw things about ◆ Rwang intyarr-wem mereh, an rtak artem. (M) *Throwing the wood down at camp, and then making a windbreak.* ◆ Ker atetherr rlpwereh inem. Atwem atwem atwem intyarr-wem intyarr-wem kelem anarnpenty-alhem ahern, *billycan*-warl pwelap inem. Ker mwerr anthwerr. (N) *The budgerigars are got from the hollows in the trees. [You] kill them and kill them and then keep throwing them down and then you climb back down to the ground and fill the billycan up with them. They are really good meat.*
SEE ALSO iwem

intyarrkwer (E) neck bone, lower part of the back of the neck SEE UNDER **untyarrkwer**

intyelhem (W), **intyalhem** (T,E) *vi.*
burst into flames, flare up (fire) ◆ Ura intyalhem. (St) *The fire bursts into flames.*
= anngenth-irrem

intyelty (E) tree, bush, plant SEE UNDER **antyelty**

intyem[1] (E) *vi.* be in pain, ache. Only occurs with *rlkert* 'sickness'

rlkert intyem (E)
be in pain, ache ◆ Rlkert intyem ayeng. Amwelt apek ayeng rlkert intyem. (St) *I am in pain. Maybe my arm is aching.* ◆ Atnert ayeng rlkert intyem. (St) *My stomach is aching.*
SEE ALSO arntem

intyem[2], **iyntem** (E) *vi.*
smell (have a smell), give off a smell ◆ Ker arṇtert yanharl intyep-intyem. (M) *That rotten meat smells.* ◆ Mern kwen yaleng intyemel ampem. (St) *The food cooking inside there is smelling.* ◆ Ker apek mwerr-angker intyem. (St) *The meat smells really good.* ◆ Ura kwert intyem. (St) *The smoke smells.*
SEE ALSO intyernem

intyem intyerrk
the smell of fat or meat cooking ◆ Anwenth, ker apekarl item intyem intyerrk intyem. (N) *If meat is being cooked well [you] can smell it cooking.*
= parntewelyewely

intyemeny ruby saltbush SEE UNDER **ntyemeny**

intyen (E) butterfly bush SEE UNDER **intyern**

intyeng rrkwem (W,T) *vt.*
stop someone from doing something (particularly stop a woman going to her 'promised' husband, or a man going to a woman) (rrkwem *'hold'*) ◆ Ngkwarl-kety intyeng rrkwem thwengk, rlkert-irreketyeng. (T) *I am stopping you from drinking, in case you get sick.*

intyeng rrkwerrem (W,T) *vi.*
stop each other from doing something ◆ Arelh atherr intyeng rrkwerrem artwang alert-hety. (M) *Those two women are stopping each other from going with that man.* (?)
SEE ALSO alhelem, arnpakem, ayakem

intyengintyerl (E) *n.*
soft membrane between nasal cavities; septum ◆ Aherr-kenh ngkwernelarl atanthek, intyengintyerl yanh renh alha. (Sa) *The septum of the nose was pierced with a kangaroo bone.*
SEE ALSO urleynterr[1], alha ngkwern, ntyarl

intyer *n.*
small creek, gully, gutter or watercourse ◆ Kwatyelarl intyer mpwarek, alherl-anemel *all day*. (Sa) *The running water made gutters.* ◆ Intyer nhangkwerr atnarnpenheyaw. (Sa) *Climb down along this little gully.*
= ilerrty

intyerlp (E) hot ashes or earth (used for cooking or healing) SEE UNDER **ntyerlp**[1]

intyerlp (W,T) water in claypan (?) SEE UNDER **ntyerlp**[2]

intyern (E), **intyen** (E) *n.*
butterfly bush (*Petalostylis cassioides*). A shrub about 1.5 m high, with fern-like leaves and orange flowers. Has edible scale, *ngkwarl intyern*, made by a lerp insect.

intyernem, **iynternem** (E) *vt.*
smell something ◆ Atwakey tha intyernem rntwarr angerr. (N) *I can smell the wild oranges from a long way away.* ◆ Intyem intyerrkarl ampep-ampem aley intyernem. (St) *[I] can smell the meat cooking over there.*
SEE ALSO intyem[2]

-intyerr, **-intyarr** (W,T) *n.ending*
a plural marker ◆ 'Altyernem' amikw anyent-kenh *mother* anyent-kenh-rnem 'altyernem'. Rernem-antey, 'altyernem'. Angkwer-**intyerr**. (Sa) *'Family' are children who have one mother — they are close relations. They are close family, just them, all the sisters.* ◆ Anakerr alhem lyet lyweny, awenh-**intyerr**. (T) *We are all going hunting today, all the aunties.* ◆ Ntwa anperl-alhemel anwernekeng ntwa arratemel alhek, arrpenh-**intyarr**el-arleng. (T) *You left us and went to live with another mob.* ◆ Arrantherr

anety map kwer-**intyarr**. (M) *All you kids are no good.* ◆ Ampaty-**intyarr** ingkerreny apetyewarray! (P) *Come here all you kids!*

intyerrem, iynterrem (E) *vi.*
snore
CAN SOUND A BIT LIKE ntyerrm *'seed of dogwood'*

intyerrm (E) dogwood seeds SEE UNDER **ntyerrm**

intyeth sparks SEE UNDER **ntyeth**

intyew, intyewey solidified blood SEE UNDER **ntyew**

intyewarl (E) a type of bush tomato plant SEE UNDER **antyewarl**

intywa (E) *n.* [SENSITIVE LANGUAGE]
pubic hair
= antalt, altalt

intywem (E) facing away from someone or something SEE UNDER **untyem**[2]

intywert (W) lower back SEE UNDER **antywert**

intywetenty (E), **antywetenty** (E) *n.*
a type of plant that grows in swamps (?) ◆ Ilewerrel intywetenty arwenth anep-anem. (St) *There are lots of* intywetenty *plants growing in the salt lake country.*

inwanyerr anem (E) *vi.*
sit clasping legs with arms
SEE ALSO arlkarlker

inwek (E) (do something) overnight SEE UNDER **unek**

inweng (E) chest SEE UNDER **uneng**[1]

inwerl, anwerl (W,T) *n.*
barking spider

◆ Anwerl kwenyel angkerl-anem, 'Mmmm mmmm'. (T) *In the night the barking spider goes, 'Mmmm mmmm'.* ◆ Inwerl, kwen ra irrpenhem, ahelh kwenel ra anep-anem. Lthel-lthelarl ra. (St) *Barking spiders live under the ground. They are hairy.* ◆ Iltyang map-akert anwerl, *woolly one* angerrety. (M) *The barking spider is large and hairy and has lots of legs.*

inya (W), **inyang** (W) *n.*
sick person ◆ Tyerrty map apetyeh aretyeh inyang. (M) *A lot of people came to visit the sick man.*
SEE ALSO rlkert
CAN SOUND A BIT LIKE nya[1] *'louse'*

inyem, itnyem (E), **iytnem** (E) *vt.*
dig, dig for something ◆ Anyematy tha inyem anemel. (N) *I'm digging for witchetties with a digging stick.* ◆ Tyerrty map alhem mwetekayel anaty nyetyek. (T) *The people are going in the car to dig for bush potatoes.*
SEE ALSO angernem[1], ahinem

inyelhem, itnyelhem (E), **iytnelhem** (E) *vi.*
dig something out of yourself ◆ Itnyelhem ayeng lyek. (St) *I am digging the prickle out of myself.*

ipa (E) *n.*
hook on a woomera or spear. Made of wood and tied or bound to the spear or woomera with sinew. ◆ Irrtyart anem ipakert, alwerrngelarl ayernem, aherrel alwerrngel. (St) *Spears have a hook on them, which is tied with sinew, with kangaroo sinew.*
= ikalharr
SEE ALSO antha[2], lywernk

iparem (E) *vt.*
wipe something out; wipe something off something, rub out, scratch off ◆ Ingka iparem. (Sa) *Wipe out the footprints.*
SEE ALSO arnngem, rrpwarem, urrparem, irrarlkem

iparelhem (E) *vi.*
wipe something off yourself
SEE ALSO arnngelhem, irrarlkelhem, rrpwarelhem, urrparelhem

nyerr iparelhem (E)
make amends, apologise (lit. 'wipe out shame')
= nyerr urrparelhem
SEE ALSO arltwem

iparip (E), **parip** (E) *n.*
Burton's snake-lizard (*Lialis burtonis*)
◆ Apmwa parip. Rrweyan arlkeny-arlkeny. Marlan *yellow one yellow one* nteny-nteny war. *Whistle*-artekap ra irrerl-anem iparip. Rnwem-apenyarl ap ra. Atwemel renh wal urleth-urleth akelhemarl ra. Atwenty. Urnemek-athen atwenty, akuny-amperl. Kel ingkernant anem *sorry*-irremel. (St) *The* parip *snake-lizard. The male is stripey. The female is yellowish and just spotty. They are similar to snakes and they make a sort of whistling sound. If you hit one they break into bits. If you think the* parip *is [another sort of] snake and you kill the poor thing then you'll feel sorry later.*

iparrp quick, quickly SEE UNDER **parrp**

ipelhem (E) *vi.*
dig oneself into a hole or burrow (some animals)
SEE ALSO ipem
CAN SOUND A BIT LIKE ilpelhem *'shield self'*

urlelth ipelhem (E)
dig self into a hole or burrow (some animals); go into hibernation ◆ Atyerrparl urlelth ipelhem irrernt-taym. Urlelthel aynterl-anem kwen, nthanh tyerrelhetyanh. Urlelth ipelhenty. (Sa) *[Goannas] go into hibernation in the winter. They lie under the ground, and they*

don't come out.
= rlwelth arrernelhem, kelerr ipelhem
kelerr ipelhem (E) **= urlelth ipelhem**
◆ Amwely kelerr ipelhem atyerrp. (Sa) *Cadney lizards go into hibernation.*

ipelhip (E) *n.*
soft, mashed up ◆ Ipelhip anem arlkwetyek, arntek akeng. (Sa) *If [your] teeth are no good you have to eat mashed up food.*
ipelhip-ilem (E) *vt.*
crush or squash something, mash something up ◆ Ker aherr artep apert-atwemel ipelhip-ilem. Ngkwerlparl ipelhip-ilem. *Something* ipelhip-ilenhemel, alhemel ingkel ulthenhemel, ipelhip. (Sa) *The backbone of a kangaroo is smashed up to make it soft. Pituri is crushed up. [You] might crush something if you walk on it.* ◆ Ker arlewatyerr ipelhip-ilemel atanthem kwenel alhwengek. Ipelhip-ilem kwen-antey apmwek-athen. (St) *A goanna might be crushed when someone pokes at it when it's inside its hole. They might crush it, thinking it's a snake.*
SEE ALSO antyelp-ilem, mwely-ilem

ipelty friend, age-mate, relation SEE UNDER **pelty**

ipely (E) small loin cloth SEE UNDER **pely**

ipelyak (E)**, ipelyakw** (E) duck, grey teal SEE UNDER **pelyak**

ipem *vt.*
squeeze something out of something else (e.g. shit from intestines), clean something out of something ◆ Kart ipay! (M) *Clean out the guts!* ◆ Atna ipem. (St) *Cleaning out the guts.* ◆ Mern anakety ipem. (St) *Cleaning [the bitter black seeds out from] the* anakety *fruit.* ◆ Ker lyep-lyep ipangaw, anter-angerr! (St) *Squeeze out the really fatty intestines!*
SEE ALSO lhwerrp-ilem, ulherrpernem
CAN SOUND A BIT LIKE apem[1] *'walk along'*; apem[2] *'rub on'*

Ipementy *n.*
Poomingie Waterhole, on Utopia (Angarapa Aboriginal Land Trust) area near 3 Bores

-ipenh (E) because of something, after SEE UNDER **-penh**

ipeny apetyepetyem (W,T)**, ipenyang apetyepetyem** (W) *n.*
rufous whistler (*Pachycephala rufiventris*) (lit. 'a stranger is coming') ◆ Ipenyarl apetyemarl angkem thep ra, 'Ipeny apetyem ipeny apetyem, ipenyang apetyepetyem'. (N) *The whistler sounds like this, '*Ipeny apetyem ipeny apetyem, ipenyang apetyepetyem*'.*
= apetyepetyem, kwarlpatengkelyengkely, artwang apetyepetyem
SEE ALSO tyenyepweny

iper (E) *n.*
a type of spinifex (?). Also referred to as *antywer iper.* ◆ Antywer iper. Aywert-apeny. Iper. Intwerrker-artek. Iperap. Arreylp-arreylp uterrpelarl aneynetyel weth. (Sa) *The* iper *grass is similar to the* aywert *spinifex, and to the curly wire grass. It's that sharp one that grows in the sandhills.*
iper-iper (E) *n.*
country where there is lots of *iper* spinifex ◆ Iper-iperel anwern alhetyek. Antywer-angketyarrel. *We're going through the country where there is lots of spinifex.*

ipernem (W,T)**, pinem** (W) *vt.*
hunt something down using dogs, sool a dog onto someone or something ◆ Kerek ipernem angwely. (M) *Sool the dogs onto the kangaroo.*
= artarrernem

-iperr *ending*
1. after an event or after an action has been completed, after a certain situation. If the action is being described as an event, then *-iperr* follows a verb with the ending *+enty* on it. It can also go on verbs following the *+arl* ending. ◆ Arlewatyerr athem atwem, *miss*-em-ilemel. Ra unteman. Arlewatyerr untem. Kel athem atwenty-**iperr**, atwemarl ra arlewatyerr untem, ra alwernem anem renh. (Sa) *If she misses the goanna when trying to hit it, then it runs away. After missing the goanna it runs off and she chases it.*
SEE ALSO +arl-penh
2. because of something
3. Indicates the source or origin of something; from, out of. ◆ Angeynemel tywekety, kwatyan antywerretyart, an urnewarn thelewetyart kwaty, mwarel thelewarretyart. Kwaty angenty-**iperr.** (N) *Soakage water used to be taken back and drunk, and tipped into the water dishes using a wooden scoop. Water from soakages.* ◆ Irnker. Akern-**iperr** nanekwetel arlkwenh-arlkwenh yep-yepel arlkwenh arlkwenh, menty — *rubbish.* (N) *The mimosa bush. The top part is just used as tucker by goats and sheep — it's rubbish.*
SEE ALSO -penh[1]

-iperr something is obvious, of course SEE UNDER **-perr**

ipert *n.*
1. hole, ditch (including cooking hole) ◆ Ahern ipert, kwatyelarl angernenhek ipertem, ipert-ilenhek kwatyel, *or* inngel apek ipert angernek kerek aherrek, aherr ampernetyek ipert-warl akwernemel. (Sa) *A*

hole in the ground might be there from the rain, from the rain making a hole, or a person might dig a hole to cook kangaroo in. ◆ Ker ipertel item. (T) *Cooking the meat in a hole in the ground.*

2. grave (for an animal)

SEE ALSO awenng

iltya ipert (E)

palm of the hand (iltya '*hand*')

ipert-ipert *n.*

rough, bumpy (of a road) ◆ Ipert-ipertel anaynpemernerl-anem, ipert ingwer-angkwerr mwetek. (Sa) *The car is bumping along on the rough [road], from one hole to another.*

ipert-ilem *vt.*

make a hole, dig a hole ◆ Ipert-ilem ina ker ankerr atyerretyeh. (N) *They are digging a hole to cook the emu in.* ◆ Kwaty-kety ipert-iletyek *run*-irreyameng. (St) *Digging a hole to stop the water that is going to flow.*

ipert-irrem *vi.*

sink back (eyes in head) ◆ Alkngarl ipert-irrek, pweng irreynekarl, pwengarl irrek. *[He] has gone blind and his eyes are sunken.*

ipert angernem (W,T)

dig an oven or cooking hole (angernem[1] '*dig*')

ipey (E) *n.*

a place where hunters hide when they are hunting emus; a hide ◆ Ipey arrernem, alengk-iwelhem ankerr-kety aleth akwet kel tyerteng anem renh arnaremel — arraty-atety arratem kwaty-warl kwenh. (Sa) *[The hunter] makes a hide and hides himself there from the emu, and stays there in the narrow space watching or the emu to come — and then the emu appears, coming towards the water.*

= arementy

SEE ALSO ntat

ipmarlew (E) a type of python SEE UNDER **imarlew**

ipmayel (E) jealous (particularly over husband or wife) SEE UNDER **mayel**

ipmem (E) leave someone or something alone SEE UNDER **impem**

ipmeng (T,E) generous, sharing SEE UNDER **imeng**

ipmenh (E), **aypmenhey** (E), **aypmenh** (E), **aylpmenh** (E) *n.kin*

1. mother's mother; grandmother, granny ◆ Ayenh apek 'ipmenh' akem *daughter* atyenh-kenhel ayenh 'ipmenh' akem, 'nyany' akem. (St) *My daughter's [child] calls me 'ipmenh' or 'nyany'.*

2. mother's mother's brother or sister; great-uncle, great-aunt [SOME SPEAKERS]

3. a woman's daughter's child; grandchild; grandson, granddaughter

4. a person's sister's daughter's child; great-niece, great-nephew

5. cross-cousin's wife or husband, cross-cousin of husband or wife

6. particular relations with the same skin as a person's *ipmenh*

7. the country and Dreamings belonging to a person's *ipmenh.*

= menh-menh

SEE ALSO nyany[2]

ipmenhaty (E), **aypmenhaty** (E) *n.kin*

my/our *ipmenh* ◆ Kwey atyenhan ipmenhaty yanh ampa atyenh-kenh. *My* ipmenhaty *is my daughter's [child].*

ipmenhengkw (E), **aypmenhengkw** (E) *n.kin*

your *ipmenh*

ipmenhikw (E), **aypmenhikw** (E) *n.kin*

his/her/their *ipmenh*

ipmenh-nheng (E), **aypmenh-nheng** (E) *n.kin*

a group of two or more people related to each other as *ipmenh*

= ipmenh-intyerr

ipmenh-intyerr (E), **aypmenh-intyerr** (E) *n.kin*

= ipmenh-nheng

ipmenh-nheng-arey *n.kin*

a group of more than two people related to each other as *ipmenh*

ipmenh-nheng atherr (E), **aypmenh-nheng atherr** *n.kin*

a person together with one of their *ipmenh*

ipmenh-parety (E), **aypmenh-parety** (E) *n.kin*

respectful or 'sorry way' of talking about someone's *ipmenh*

SEE ALSO -parety

ipmenh-ankethenh (E), **aypmenh-ankethenh** (E) *n.kin*

1. having a close *ipmenh* still alive

2. someone who is always with their *ipmenh*

SEE ALSO -ankethenh

ipmenty (E) 'Leave it', 'Don't worry about it', 'Never mind' SEE UNDER **menty**

ipmerr (T,E) drop or drip of water SEE UNDER **imerr**

ipmerrng (E) palate, roof of the mouth SEE UNDER **merrng**

irlengarr (E) coolamon, wooden dish SEE UNDER **lengarr**

irlkenty (E), **arlkenty** (E) *n.*

big mob, a lot, everyone ◆ Irlkentyarl apetyem-kety! (Sa) *Look out, there's lots [of people] coming!*

irlkenty-ilem (E) *vt.*

gather a fighting force, gang up on someone

irlkngerr (E) sunset SEE UNDER **rlngerr**

irlkwatherr accompanying someone SEE UNDER **ilkwatherr**

irlkwem (E) twitch, flinch, start (in fright) SEE

UNDER **ilkwem**

irlkwer-irlkwer (E) a liquid or sloppy mixture SEE UNDER **rlkwer-rlkwer**

irlpa, irlpang (W,T), **arlpang** (W,T), **iylpa** (E) *n.*

1. ear, ears ◆ Irlpel thwengk awem. (M) *I am listening to you with my ears.* ◆ Iylpel tha awetyel — arert anetyang. (Sa) *I can hear with my ears — I'm not deaf.* ◆ Arreyeng-arrey-irretyal anwengkerr aneyaw, angkety-kweny aneyaw, arreyeng-arrey-kweny. Irlpa apek anwengkerr akangkwerrey, iwenhek apek anwengkerr akangkwerrey, irlpel manty awerl-anemel. (N) *We shouldn't chatter, but sit down without talking, without making a noise. We'll pay attention and listen to whatever, listening carefully with our ears.* ◆ Arlatn-irrerl-alhem ra arnethey akern-they atnyem. Kel renh irlpa atherr pew-ilem. Akem anem ra irrenty-alpem. (N) *He/she is having a fit after falling from high up in the tree. If you blow in her ears she will be revived.*

2. donkey ◆ Irlpang map akeweny irnenhirrem atherrk arlkwerl-anem, ina angayakwel arlkwerl-anem, irlpa mapel kwenh. (T) *The poor old donkeys are standing and eating grass, the donkeys are hungry and are eating.*

3. various things that are shaped like ears, for example the parts of a billycan that the wire goes through

CAN SOUND A BIT LIKE arlpa[1] *'hot ashes'*; arlpa[2] *'leaf'*

irlpa alhap (W,T)
blocked up (ear) (alhap *'shut', 'blocked off'*)

irlpa akwenp (E), **iylpekwenp** (E) *n.*
earwax (akwenp *'not taking notice'*) ◆ Irlpa akwenpel *shut*-em *up* ilem, aleth-antey martem. Kel irlpa akwenp *clean*-em ilem *doctor*-el apek yanhan awem anemarl. (St) *The earwax blocks up [the ear] for good. If the doctor cleans out the wax then the person can hear again.*
SEE ALSO rta

irlpa atyet-atyet (E), **iylpa atyet-atyet** (E), **iylpa atyet** (E)
soft part of the ear, earlobe (atyet[1] *'soft'*)

irlpa artep, irlpang artep (W,T), **iylpa artep** (E)
back of the ear (artep *'back'*) ◆ Iylpa nhenh artepel, wal ngkwerlparl arrernem, ngkwerlp atnyenem akngerl-anem nhenh kwerel, iylpa artepel. (St) *Here at the back of the ear, well that's where you put the tobacco wad, and you hold it there and carry it along there behind your ear.*

irlpalkey (W,T) *n.*
donkey (alkey *'long'*)
= tangkey, irlpangerr, irlpa urety

irlpangerr (W,T) *n.*
donkey (angerr[1] *'big'*) ◆ Nhenhan irlpangerr anety. (M) *This is a bad donkey.*
= tangkey, irlpalkey, irlpa urety

irlpa urety (E), **iylpa urety** (E)
donkey (urety *'water dish'*)
= tangkey, irlpalkey, irlpangerr

irlpekenh (T) *n.*
telephone (-kenh *'belonging to'*)
= alwerrng angkenh-angkenh, terlepawen
SEE ALSO alwerrng

irlpakert-ilem (E), **iylpakert-ilem** (E) *vt.*
revive someone by blowing in their ears (lit. 'make someone have ears')
= iylpenkelh-ilem

irlpang-alpem (W) *vi.*
go back to the place where you came from (alpem *'go back'*) ◆ Ankerr angkek, 'Yetyeng. Irlpang-alpa'. (M) *The emu said, 'No. Go back to the same place where you came from'.* ◆ Irlpang-alpem, rarl amangkek-warl, *or* alyelhek-warl apek. Iter arrpenh apekarl rang alhemel anerl-alpek-penh, *family* mob arrpenhel-arleng. (M) *He is going back to the place where he grew up or to the place where he went through the Law. He is going back after having gone to another country and stayed with another family.*

irlpang apety-alpem (W)
come back to the place where you came from (apety-alpem *'come back'*)

irlpang-irrpem (W) *vi.*
come back again to the same man or woman [SOME SPEAKERS] (irrpem *'go in'*) ◆ Artwa irlpang-irrpety-alpem, irrkaty kwerenh anewehek. (M) *The man came back again to his original wife.*

irlpangkem, iylpangkem (E) *vi.*
remember about someone or something; be reminded of something, talk about someone and so remind others of that person (?) ◆ Ampa apek iylpangkerl. *'Hey, iylpangketyalay akuny-amperl ywerrek-arlek, arrangkw-irrek-arlek.'* (St) *A child might remind you of someone. 'Hey, don't remind me of that [person], that poor thing has passed away.'*
SEE ALSO iterlarem, irlpa

irlpangkelh-ilem, iylpangkelh-ilem (E) *vt.*
make someone remember something, remind someone of something ◆ Thwengk irlpangkelh-ilem arneh nhenh nta aparlp-ilek mer alerteh kwenh. (M) *I'm reminding you about this thing that you lost over there.*

irlpar (E), **arlpar** (E), **iylpar** (E) *n.*
a type of bush potato (?) ◆ Mern iylpar arrwekelenyel antarl arlkwerrek. Than

itnyetyart akin renh. Altwerl-thayt, *Boundary Bore* angerrakw. Pertipelawan *orange one*. Mwerr-angker innga. Anaty-apeny antey pertipelaw. (Sa) *Only the olden-time people ate iylpar. I used to dig it up to the west side, east of Boundary Bore. It has a beautiful orange flower like a bush potato.*

irlpareth, **iylpareth** (E) *n.*
cooperative, helpful ◆ Iylparethel iparrp-iparrpel inerl-wem. (Sa) *A helpful [person] goes and gets things quickly.*
SEE ALSO ilpety, irrngerney
irlpareth-irrem, **iylpareth-irrem** (E) *vi.*
be helpful, cooperate
SEE ALSO ankerl

irlparrernem (W,T), **iylparrernem** (E) *vt.*
show something to someone, show the way, take someone and show them something ◆ Tyeyekel kwaty irlparrernem tyerrty mapeh. (M) *The zebra finches show people where the water is.*
SEE ALSO imernem, irlpa, nernem

irlpart, **iylpart** (E) *n.*
a log ◆ Ura irlpart weth tha atyeng inerl-alpeyew, ura atyeng ampetyek irlpart. (St) *I'll go back and get that log for myself, so that I can burn it for myself.*
rwang irlpart (W,T), **ura iylpart** (E)
a log of firewood ◆ Tyerrtyel rwang irlpart arrernetyart kwenyel amperl-anetyek. (T) *People used to put a log there to burn through the night.*

Irlpatherr *n.*
the name of a place near Brookes Soak

irlpekernem, **iylpekernem** (E) *vi.*
listen, pay attention ◆ Anwengkerr irlpekerneyay, tyerrtyarl angkerrem alenh, arratyep irlpekernem. Kel irlpekernem, kel awem antem. (T) *We'll listen to the people talking to one another there, pay attention to them properly. We'll pay attention to them and hear what they are saying.* ◆ Kwerltety arrekantherrenhek irlpekernenherr-areyay arrantherr! (Sa) *You all pay attention to your schoolteacher!*
SEE ALSO akangkwerrem, irlpa, awem

irlperleny (T,E), **aylperleny** (E) *n.*
a type of plant (*Boerhavia schomburgkiana*). A creeping herb with yellow flowers.
= ayep

irnar (W,T), **rnar** (W,T) *n.*
central netted dragon (*Ctenophorus nuchalis*)
= kelyaw, kaperl
SEE ALSO arrpwayl, arlwer

irnem, **rnem**, **tnem** (E) *vi.*
1. stand, stand up ◆ Tyerrty yanh irnem. (M) *A person is standing there.* ◆ Artwang yanh yapay irnem rwertel-ayel. (M) *That man over there is standing in the way on the road.* ◆ Pweney-pweney akwek amwekel-ayel irnem. *The little foal is standing with its mother.* ◆ Arelh yanh rnepernem ntywem-athek arnengerr. (M) *The woman there is standing facing away with her hands clasped behind her back.*
2. be, stand, is, are (of things thought to be in a vertical or upright position, or of things that are high up) ◆ Waly anetyakenh irrkerleng arna, walyarl ingkerrek atnyek. Irrkerleng anem ra tnepetnem, urreltyant-akert anem. (St) *A tree without leaves is* irrkerleng, *when all the leaves have fallen. Then the tree is just bare, only branches.* ◆ Kwaty apek ywerrem mpwelarr tnem, mpwelarr atherram apek, awely-artek mpwarelhem. (St) *When the rain finishes there might be a rainbow there, or maybe a double rainbow, looking like the [stripey] designs in women's ceremonies.*
3. be, grow, live (of plants) ◆ Mern angwarak lpwayel irnem. Arlpenty angerr. Altyeyart akin angwarak. (N) *The bush bean grows in creeks. It is a long plant. [The leaves] are similar to the leaves of the bush banana.*
4. strike (lightning) ◆ Lyweny-penh apety-alpemel awely-awely renh rnetyart ker akenh anwern-kenh nheng kwenel akwernetyart. (N) *When we returned from hunting, as the lightning was striking, we'd put all our meat inside the shelters.*
CAN SOUND A BIT LIKE anem *'sit'*; atnem *'digging stick'*; artnem *'cry'*

irnker (W,T) *n.*
mimosa bush (*Acacia farnesiana*). Shrub up to 5 m high, with fern-like leaves which have a spine at the base. ◆ Waram aketyam *medicine* antem, irnem tyelk, ityarlam arlkwety-henh. Arnang war anety *rubbish*-am irnerl-anem. Irnker. Kwen nheng irnem artekerrel, kenh akern-iperr nanekwetel arlkwenh-arlkwenh yep-yepel arlkwenh-arlkwenh, menty — *rubbish*. Artekerrel *medicine*, kwaty lpwelemel arrernetyeh, alhewelhem antem. Lyek akert akwel. (N) *The mimosa bush is just picked for medicine, the wood is not edible. The tree is useless. There is a root underneath, and the top part is just used as tucker by goats and sheep — it's rubbish. In the roots is the medicine, and it's crushed up in water and used as a wash. It has prickles.*

= alekw
SEE ALSO arlketyerr

irnmerr, iytnmerr (E), **iylpmerr** (E), **iypmerr** (E) *n.*
1. dew
2. a drop or drip of water, a raindrop. Also referred to as *kwaty irnmerr.* ◆ Irnmerr thelelhem altywereng. (M) *The water is seeping out of the hole.* ◆ Kwaty irnmerr kwenelak anyerl-anem, kwaty angerr. (T) *There are drops of water falling down, lots of rain.*

irnnga (W,T), **irnngang** (W,T) *n.*
maggot, worm ◆ Mweremwelk. Irnnga akwekem arrernem, mweremwelkel kerewarl, arntertem irrem. (M) *The blowfly. It leaves maggots in the meat and the meat goes off.*
= tyerr
CAN SOUND A BIT LIKE annga *'eye'*; innga[1] *'really'*; innga[2] *'person'*

irnpernp (W,T), **rnpernp** (W,T) *n.*
soldier bird, yellow-throated miner bird (*Manorina flavigula*) ◆ 'Irnpernp irnpernp', alakenh *early* angkem, akemelh-ilem tyerrty ingkerr. Wal, map akem-irrem. (M) *'Irnpernp irnpernp', that's the noise it makes early in the morning, making everybody get up. Well, then everybody gets up.*
= impaymp
CAN SOUND A BIT LIKE rnpwernp *'rock pituri'*

irnperrty (W) a mark or track SEE UNDER **imperrty**

irnta (W,T), **irntang** (W,T) *n.*
1. rock, stone ◆ Arnang atherr yatherr inek, an irntang atherr yatherr inek. (M) *Then each boy took a stick and a stone.*
2. hill, mountain ◆ Irntang angerr altywernerl-anem. Iter-angkwerr alhem arlewatyerrek. (T) *There is a big hill there. [We] go along the side looking for goannas.* ◆ Rrwarlpan irntareny. Mern akin an tyekert. Ampengant arlkwenh, wal tyekertarl yanh, mentyel anwa aretyart. (N) *The native tomato grows in the hills. It has a fruit but it is bitter and we only eat it if it's ripe. If it was bitter we used to just leave it.*
SEE ALSO apwert
3. the green, unripe fruit of the native currant, native citrus (*Psydrax latifolia*) ◆ Irntang mpank ahakey — ampeng-irretyakenh. (M) *The bush plum fruit is not ready — it hasn't ripened.* • = anthwerrk[1]

irntangerr (T) *n.*
rocky or stony ground (angerr[1] *'lots of'*) ◆ Irntangerreng nwengkerr aketh-warn irrey. (T) *Let's get out of the rocky country and go to the clear ground.*

irntang arnkang (W,T)
cliff, cliff face (arnkang *'cliff'*)
= apwert arnka

irntang artep (W,T)
the top of a hill (artep *'back'*)
= irntang rrpwang, irntang akern, apwert artep, apwert akern

irntang rrpwang (W,T) = **irntang artep** (rrpwang *'backbone'*)

irntang akern (W,T) = **irntang artep** (akern *'high', 'on top'*)

irntang atwaty (W,T)
gorge, gap in hills (atwaty *'gap'*)
= apwert atwaty

irntang lyerl (W)
cave (lyerl *'gravel'*)
= apwert intey

irntang arlkwat (W,T)
large flat rock; lower grinding stone (used for seed)
= apwert ather, irntang ather
SEE ALSO pwerl

irntang ather (W,T) = **irntang arlkwat** (ather *'flat rock'*)

irntang apwert (W)
round grinding stone held in hand

irntang artwert (W,T)
1. small round rocks or stones
2. grinding stone held in hand ◆ Arelhel irntang artwert-akertel ngkerlp athem. (T) *The woman is grinding up the tobacco with a small grinding stone.*
SEE ALSO apwert alyer

irntarlter (W,T), **irntang arlter** (W,T) *n.*
stone knife (used for cutting meat) (arlter *'white'*) ◆ Anwern irntang arlter akertel ker tyep-ilem. (T) *We cut up meat with a stone knife.* ◆ Artwel anenem ker aherr irntang arlter-akertel. (T) *The man guts the kangaroo with the stone knife.*
SEE ALSO apwert antha, kartamp, alywek, inkwartety, werlamp

Irntang Arlter (W,T) *n.*
name of a place near Pine Hill. See map p. viii.

irntareny (W,T) *n.*
euro, wallaroo (*Macropus robustus*) (-areny *'inhabitant of'*)
= areng[2], areyneng, lyerl-areny

irntar (W,T), **irntarel** (W,T) *n.*
midday, lunchtime. Also referred to as *aherrk irntar.* ◆ Irntarel arlkwem mern. (M) *At midday [we] eat.*
= aherrk akern

irntwer (E) cooking pit with hot rocks [SOME

SPEAKERS] SEE UNDER **rntwer**[1]
irntwer (E) spirit SEE UNDER **rntwer**[2]
irnwa (E) *n.*
a person's lap ◆ Ampa atyeng apetya — irnwel arrernelhetya, arternp anay. (Sa) *Child, come to me — sit yourself down on my lap and settle down.*
= rnwart
SEE ALSO rnwepenh
irnwepenh (E) a woman's child; a person's sister's child SEE UNDER **rnwepenh**
-irr+ *ending*
1. become something, turn into something ◆ Tyap irrarl-**irr**em alhetyenheng thipem **irr**erl-alhem tyerrelhem alhem arlpakert. (N) *The grub transforms in the cocoon and then emerges as a moth with wings and then flies around.*
2. become (some way); get (that way); go (that way), be (some way) ◆ Mer arrpenheng ayeng irrar-**irr**em. Ayeng irrar-**irr**em merwarn alpetyek. Mer arrpenheng irrar-**irr**em. (T) *When I am in another place I get homesick. I get homesick and want to go back home. I get homesick when I am in a different place.* ◆ Irrngwilem renh urel kel kernt ilem anem renh, ikelh anem renh ilenty-alpem, ikelh anem kernt-**irr**em, anker renh. (St) *You melt it on the fire and then it cools down and solidifies again. The spinifex resin solidifies when it cools.* ◆ Alyem awely arntety apek mwerr-**irr**etyek. Anter warel tha alyem, apernelhetyek ra mwerr-**irr**etyek, irrernt-**irr**etyek. (St) *A sick person is sung with* awely *to make them better. I just sing them with the fat, so that they can rub themselves with it and get better, cool down.*
3. make (a particular noise), go like (a particular sound) ◆ Nwernengk ker. 'Mmmmm mmmmm' **irr**erl-anem anem. *Tawny frogmouths are edible. They go like this, 'Mmmmm mmmmm'.*
4. Goes on the end of nominals to make them into intransitive verbs.
5. Goes on the end of some English verbs to turn them into intransitive verbs. ◆ Ayenparl akernengan. Ayenp nhenh apetyem amwelteng arlka. Kenh alhwarl kweneng *run*-**irr**erl-anem, ingkewarn-athek, iltyewarn-athek, alakenh kapert-warn-athek. (T) *Skin is on the surface. For example, there is skin all the way along the arm. Whereas blood runs on the inside, towards the feet, the hands and to the head.*
irraker *n.*
parallel grooved markings carved into boomerangs, wooden dishes or shields. In some areas the teeth of possums, or small stones, were used to make these markings. ◆ Aylayl then iylkwa then. Arrperrirretyel. Irrakerel. Kwempalthel imernt arrpemel arrpemel, kel irraker anem wem. *Boomerangs and the hooked boomerangs are chiselled. First they are chiselled with the adze and then the grooved markings are made.* ◆ Irraker-akert weth *flash one*. Irraker mwerr angerr. (T) *That flash one has grooved markings on it. Really nice markings.*
SEE ALSO arlkeny
irraker-wem *vt.*
make grooves or markings on wooden implements such as boomerangs, wooden dishes or shields ◆ Irraker-wem panth, mwar apek irraker-wem, kayl, urremper. (St) *Markings are made on wooden dishes, boomerangs and spears.* ◆ Panth apek irraker-wem kin, arlkeny akwek arrerneperrnerl. (St) *Grooves are made on wooden dishes as well, putting little stripes on them.*
irraker-ilem *vt.* = **irraker-wem**
irranty (W) *n.*
a type of snake (?)
irranyent-iwem (E) *vt.*
mess things up, rifle through things, throw things all over the place ◆ Mer irranyent-iwem arengkel. Mern, ingkerr arlkwerrek. Mernek akent-werreperrem irranyent-iwetyel. (Sa) *The dogs have gone through the place and messed everything up. They've eaten all the food. They've gone through everything looking for food and messed everything up.*
SEE ALSO akent-iwem
Irrapey (W), **Arrapey** (W) *n.*
name of a place between Napperby and Coniston
irrar[1] (E) *n.*
1. pirraru, shiny-leaved wattle (*Acacia ancistrocarpa*). Shrub about 2.5 m high, with shiny leaves and cylindrical flowers.
2. edible seed of the pirraru
= perrar
irrar[2] *n.*
feeling sadness, loneliness or homesickness ◆ Mer arrpenheng irrarel alpetyenheng. (M) *Being in another place and feeling homesick to go home.*
SEE ALSO alther, alharrp
irrar-irrem *vi.*
feel lonely, homesick or alone; miss someone or something, long for something, pine for someone or for something ◆ Mer arrpenheng

ayeng irrar-irrem. Ayeng irrar-irrem mer-warn alpetyek. Mer arrpenheng irrar-irrem. (T) *When I am in another place I get homesick. I get homesick and want to go back home. I get homesick when I am in a different place.* ◆ Ayeng irrar-irremel anep-anem, alpetyek anem apmerek irrar-irremek. (St) *I'm feeling homesick, and I want to go back to the place I'm longing for.* ◆ Kwerler-kwerler yanh kwer akwekeh arnerl-anem, kwer kwerenharl angekarl. Lweren arnerl-anem akeweny, 'Kwer akwek kwer akwek. Kwer atyenheng kwenh angkek kwenh'. Alakenh arnerl-anem, kwerler-kwerler. 'Kwaty alay-warl angekarl.' Lweren. Anywelekarl angekarl. Irrar-irrerl-anemel arnerl-anerl amwek. Kwer ikwer. (N) *That diamond dove is crying for its little child that was taken away. That's why the poor thing is crying, 'Little child, little child. My little child has been taken away to the sea'. Its father took it away, and the mother is feeling sorry and crying for the child.*
= alther-irrem

irrar-irrar *n.*
feeling lonely or unhappy, miss someone or something ◆ Irrar-irrar war kwenh ayeng anep-anem *son* atyenhek-arey. (Sa) *I'm missing my sons.*

irrarel anthem
make someone feel lonely or homesick (anthem *'give'*)

irrarl *n.*
the stage in the life cycle of a moth or butterfly when it is still in a cocoon; chrysalis. Also referred to as *tyap irrarl*. ◆ Kel ra iwenh anem irrem tyap, *ready* anem alhetyek anem. Tyap rlwaylp anem ra irrem, irrarl irrem anem. Irrarl arreyn anem arrengey atyenhan. Kel tyerrelhenhem, antelyapelyap anem ra alhem. (St) *Then the grub is ready to go. It turns into a* rlwaylp, *turns into a chrysalis.* Irrarl *was the name of my grandfather. Then the grub emerges and flies away as a moth.*
SEE ALSO rlwaylp, urlaylp, ngkekern

irrarl-irrem *vi.*
turn into a moth or butterfly, transform or metamorphose (grub) ◆ Tyap irrarl-irrem alhetyenheng thipem irrerl-alhem tyerrelhem alhem arlpakert. (N) *The grub transforms in the cocoon and then emerges as a moth with wings and then flies around.*
SEE ALSO akarternem, rlwarlp-irrem, urlaylp-irrem, ngkekern-irrem

irrarlkem (E) *vt.*
wipe something clean, wipe something off something ◆ Artep apek irrarlkem anter-penh. Alha inkwerr-penh irrarlkem. (Sa) *Maybe wipe the back after it has been covered with fat. Or wipe the snotty nose.* ◆ Atna yanh irrarlkaw! (Sa) *Wipe that bottom!* ◆ Akuny-amperl alknga arrngwelty-arrngweltyekarl atwerliwerreperremarl. Arrngwelty yanh irrarlkey. (St) *The poor thing was beaten till the tears came. Wipe the tears away.*
SEE ALSO arnngem, iparem, rrpwarem, urrparem
CAN SOUND A BIT LIKE arralkem *'yawn'*

irrarlkelhem (E) *vi.*
wipe something off yourself ◆ Ampa angerrety awenharl atna irrarlkelhemel impakemp-iwelherlanem. (Sa) *The big kid is cleaning the shit off herself by rubbing herself [on the ground].*
SEE ALSO arnngelhem, iparelhem, rrpwarelhem, urrparelhem

irrarnp-irrem (W,T) *vi.*
go in different directions; split up, disperse ◆ Tyerrty map irrarnp-irrem. Apwert amparr anerl-anem wal irrarnpem irrem. (M) *People are going in all directions. First of all they are together, then they split up.*
= akalk-irrem, alperrty-irrem

irrarnp-irrarnp-irrem (W,T) *vi.* = **irrarnp-irrem**

irrarnp-ilem (W,T) *vt.*
divide something up, separate something, split something up, share something among many

irrarnpelh-ilem (W,T) *vt.* = **irrarnp-ilem**
◆ Yanhel kwenh mer ingkerr irrarnpelh-ilek ratherr. Anwerneh antem *Jesus*-el anthek mer angakenty ingkerr. Anpernenty an *all* anwerneh anthek, tywerreng an *all* anwerneh anthek, mer an *all* anwerneh anthek. Wal, *same* anwern alhep-alhem lyet. (M) *The two of them divided up the world. And then Jesus gave us all of the country that had been divided up. He gave us the kinship system, and sacred objects or Law, and he gave us the land. Well, that's how we are still going along today.*
= akalkelh-ilem

irrarnp-irrarnp-ilem (W,T) *vt.*
make someone or something scatter or go in all directions ◆ Nyert-nyerteley kartelam irrarnp-irrarnp-ilerl-apem nyert-nyert yanhan atwert-atwert, irnngang ka nyert-nyert lweren athew yanh. (N) *The dung beetle is a sort of small round maggoty thing that [goes into] the shit and makes it scatter.*

irrarnp-wem (W,T) *vt.*
scatter things around
SEE ALSO alperrty-irrem

irrarnt *n.*
black cockatoo, red-tailed black cockatoo (*Calyptorhynchus banksii*) ◆ Irrarntel arlkwerl-apem tampewern. (N) *Red-tailed black cockatoos go along eating pie melons.* ◆ Irrarnt arlkerl-apem aningk, angkerrerl-apem. Akem-irremel aywerr angkemel arrernelhenhem irrarnt. Lyek arlkwerl-anem. (N) *Lots of red-tailed black cockatoos fly along screeching. They fly up and make a lot of noise and then land. They eat prickles.*

irrarnt-irrarnt (E) *n.*
1. upside-down plant (*Leptosema chambersii*). A grass-like plant about 35 cm high which has leafless stems and bright red flowers at the base of the plant.
2. fan-flower (*Scaevola parvifolia*) (?). A plant about 30 cm high, with hairy branches, small dark blue flowers in the shape of a fan, and pale orange fruits.

irrawey, arrawey (W,T) *n.*
lots of weapons (spears or boomerangs) ◆ Artwang yanh arrawey-akert apetyem, irrtyart map-akert. (T) *That man is coming with weapons, with lots of spears.*

irrekerr-ilem (E) *vt.*
1. make someone feel as if something is crawling around or touching them ◆ Irrekerr-ilep-ilem anem ayenh, yerrel apek. (St) *It might be an ant that is crawling around on me.*
2. give someone or something a fright, make them 'start' in fright
CAN SOUND A BIT LIKE irraker-ilem *'make grooves'*
irrekerr-irrem (E) *vi.*
1. feel something crawling on you
2. have a funny or strange feeling (as if somebody is coming) ◆ Rlwaylp-kety irrekerr-irrem. (Sa) *Having a strange feeling that a kurdaitcha is coming.* • = arrenkelh-ilem², mpwarelh-ilem
SEE ALSO inkerrelh-ilem, lyekarr anem

irreltyenng (E) *n.*
sparse, thin (of hair or shade) ◆ *No* ulya. Irreltyenng ulya anetyakenh. Uternel ampekerr irreltyennggel. Arwerlant. Arlenyarl-irrek, lernelhekarl arlperr irreltyenng. (Sa) *No shade. 'Irreltyenng' is when there is only thin shade. The sun might burn [you] when the shade is thin. There are just the branches, and all the leaves have dried up and fallen to the ground.*
SEE ALSO angkwelk, irrkerleng
irreltyenng-irrem (E) *vi.*
go bald, thin out (hair); fall out (leaves)

irrelywekelywek (E), **irrerlwekeylwek** (E) *n.*
a mess (?)
irrelywekelywek-ilem (E), **irrerlwekeylwek-ilem** (E) *vt.*
make a mess of something ◆ Arengkel irrelywekelywek-ilek mer. (St) *The dogs made a mess of the camp.*

irrengernt (E) *n.*
nose bone
SEE ALSO marrapernt, ntyarl, melyalker, ngerl

irrenkelh-ilem (E) make someone feel as if something is crawling around or touching them SEE UNDER **arrenkelh-ilem²**

irrenyankwerl (W) *n.*
love song
SEE ALSO ilpenty

irrep-akem *vt.*
go round something
= artwep-akem
irrep-akelhem *vi.*
go round and round something; go right round; go round the long way; hide behind something (?) ◆ Warl-angkwerr irrep-akelhem. (M) *Going around the houses.* ◆ Irrep-akelhakelh-ilerrerl-anem, *round* irrerl-anem, irrep-akelhakelh alwernirrerl-anem alwernirrerl-anem. Kwer-penhan angkem, '*Eh*, parrkarl anthemengay — irrep-akelhakelh-ilemel alwernerl-anetyalay kwenh, parrkemarl irremengay kwenh'. (N) *Going round and round, chasing each other round and around. After that saying, 'Hey, this is making me tired — don't chase [me] round and round, because it's making me tired'.* ◆ Ayeng irrep-akelhem arnang intertel. (M) *I am going round and round the base of the tree.* ◆ Mwey-mwey-kety apek-arl irrep-akelhemel alhem ikwer-angkwerr arlengel. (St) *Going right round the long way because of the son-in-law/mother-in-law.*
SEE ALSO amperelhem, amperelh-ilem

irrepayepay, irrepelayen *n.*
aeroplane (from English 'aeroplane')
= alkerel alhenh, alker-areny

irrepereperr *adv.*
going fast, going flat out or in a straight path along the ground ◆ Amwang irrepereperr alhem. (M) *The snake is going flat out along the ground.* ◆ Irrtyart nta rtwelyel wem, wal irrepereperr alhem, irrtyart. (M) *You might throw a spear, and it goes skidding along the ground.*
irrepereperr-wem *vt.*
throw something so that it slides or skids

along the ground ◆ Anem atyenh irrepereperr-wem arelh nhakwel. Ayeng alherl-apetyek rtwenk-akert. (T) *That woman is throwing my walking stick over to me along the ground. Then I can walk, leaning on my stick.*
= ahertety-iwem

irrepethem *vt.* [RESPECT LANGUAGE]
get something, bring something ◆ Irrepetherl-way mwerekatyety tyety. (Sa) *Go and get some meat from my son-in-law.*
◆ Ngwarrekengkwenh irrepetherl-wa angwely-ayerr, akwetyakw-ayerr yanhentyak. (Sa) *Go and get your husband's little dog from over there [said by a woman to her daughter].*
SEE ALSO inem, inerl-wem

irrer *n.*
a day trip, for the day
irrer alhem
go hunting; go for a day trip, for the day ◆ Irrer ayeng alhetyek ker arlewatyerrek, angwerrel ant apety-alpeyam. (St) *I am going hunting for goannas, and I will only come back in the afternoon.* ◆ Inngernem irrer alhem mwetekayel. (Sa) *The people are going hunting in a car.*
= lyweny alhem

irrerernk (E) *n.* [RESPECT LANGUAGE]
going hunting; going for a day trip ◆ Irrerernk ahanenhetyakenh, mwarlenth atherr, ayepel anem irrepirrem. (St) *The husband and wife haven't gone hunting, they're sitting there.*
SEE ALSO irrer alhem

irrerlaly (E) *n.*
a type of lizard; pygmy desert monitor (*Varanus eremius*) (?)
SEE ALSO artep irrpent, irrpent

irrerlkng (E) corpse, dead body; skeleton SEE UNDER **irrernng**

irrerlwekeylwek (E) a mess (?) SEE UNDER **irrelywekelywek**

Irrernng, irrerlkng (E) *n.*
1. corpse, dead body, skeleton ◆ Irrernngarl intep-intem pwelek, ilwekarl-penh. (St) *The bullock corpse is lying there, after the bullock has died.* ◆ Pwelekarl ilwekan ilem, 'Yanhaw akuny irrerlkng intep-intem'. (St) *About a dead bullock you can say, 'There is the poor thing lying there, the [dead] body'.*
2. people from long ago (who have since passed away); ancestors ◆ Irrernngel-arey iletyam arrwekeleny, ampwetyampwel irrernngel-arey. (St) *Those who have since passed away said that, the olden-time people, all the old women [who have since died].*
SEE ALSO aweyaw, irrewaly, ima, arrwety

irrernng atwem, irrerlkng atwem (E)
beat someone to death; hit someone very hard (atwem *'hit', 'kill'*) ◆ Kwarterrek kwenh, irrernng apek nheng atwekarl kwa, wal 'kwarterrem' ilem. (M) *If somebody is beaten to death, well that's called 'kwarterrem'.*
irrernng-pat, irrerlkng-pat (E) *n.*
people who have passed away; ancestors
= irrewaly-pat

irrernt (T,E) *n.*
1. cold weather ◆ Irrerntel kwenty weyaw! (T) *Make a windbreak because of the cold weather!*
2. cold, cool (the way a person or a thing feels) ◆ Irrerntekam ayeng, urel apek untyetyek. (St) *I'm cold and maybe I should warm myself by the fire.* ◆ Aretharr alturl-they pwem. Urinp *one.* Akngerrakw-they irrernt pwem, alhurrp irrernt. (Sa) *The* aretharr *wind blows from the west. The warm one. From the east blows the cold wind.*
SEE ALSO anyel, kernt, anyartey, angwerl, angwerleny, arlkarl[1], atheperr, alhwerrp
irrernt-irrem (T,E), **irrerntek-irrem** (E) *vi.*
get cold, cool down ◆ Alyem awely arntety apek mwerr-irretyek. Anter warel tha alyem, apernelhetyek ra mwerr-irretyek, irrernt-irretyek. (St) *A sick person is sung with* awely *to make them better. I just sing them with the fat, so that they can rub themselves with it and get better, cool down.*
= angwerleny-irrem
irrernt-ilem (T,E) *vt.*
make something cold, cool something down
= angwerleny-ilem
irrernt-ilelhem (T,E) *vi.*
make oneself cool or cold ◆ Kwatyel ayeng irrpelh-ilelhem irrernt-ilelhemel. (Sa) *I am wetting myself with water to make myself cool.*
irrernt-areny (T,E) *n.*
a type of spirit (-areny *'inhabitant of'*) ◆ Irrernt-areny, artwartekarl ra alhep-alhem aretyangarl ra. Ingka anetyakenh an *all.* (St) *The* irrernt-areny *spirits travel around like men, but [you] can't see them. They don't leave footprints either.*
= atham-areny

irrert (W,T) *n.*
pup, puppy
SEE ALSO akwerrk[1], tywetyety

irrert-irrem *vi.*
bleed, flow, leak or seep out (especially blood) ◆ Alhwa irrert-irrem ker-they apek. (St) *The blood flows out from the meat.* ◆ Alhwa irrert-irrem, arnelarl atanthem-

penh. (St) *The blood flows out from where the stick pierced.* ◆ Kwaty irrert-irremel akngem *billycan* altherrng-they apek, altywer akert-they. (St) *As you go along water leaks out from a billycan with a hole in it.*
SEE ALSO thelelhem

irrertety *n.*
1. something used for support or for leaning on, such as a walking stick ◆ Ayeng lyet irrertetyel apetyetyam, irrertety-akert. Amperarl ayeng akeng-irrek. (St) *Just now I came, leaning on a walking stick. My knees are no good.*
2. supported by something ◆ Amakel irrertety ayeng arlkany intem. (St) *I am lying using my arm as a support.* ◆ Atnemel irrertety alherlanetyek. (Sa) *Going along supported by a walking stick.*
SEE ALSO rtwenk
3. a platform made for storing food in a tree ◆ Irrertety mpwarem arnek-arlek kel ker apek arrernem irrertety ikwer. (St) *A platform is made in the tree and then the meat is put up on the platform.*
amperel irrertety
supported on knees (amper *'knee'*)

irrety *n.*
eaglehawk, wedge-tailed eagle (*Aquila audax*) ◆ Irrety anteth-akert, anteth kwerel wantelhem artwa. (N) *Eaglehawks have down, and the men decorate themselves with it.* ◆ Akern anem, mern rapet arlka angety-alpem, alker-angkwerrarl atanthemel ker tarlew arlka, irretyel. Ker angety-alpem akwerrk wantetyeh. (N) *The eaglehawk is high up in the sky, and it gets rabbits to take back, and from the sky it hunts kangaroos as well. It takes the meat back to feed its young.*

= arlawerr
Irrety Ingka (E), **Irrety-kenh Ingka** (E)
a star constellation; the Southern Cross (lit. 'eaglehawk's foot') ◆ Irrety-kenh Ingka, akern yanh. Kwerraly atherrarl anerrirreperrem, irrety artek ingka. (Sa) *High up in the sky are two stars called 'Irrety-kenh Ingka'. They look like an eaglehawk's foot.*

Irretyekwart (W) *n.*
name of a place in the Narwietooma area

Irretyepwenty (W) *n.*
name of a hill west of Aileron

irrewaly, arrewaly (E) *n.*
1. dead body, corpse
2. really sick, critically ill ◆ Arrewaly ayntetyelaw, alerl-antey akarr-iletyek. (Sa) *That person is really sick and people will gather up soon.*
irrewalyeh (W), **irrewalyek** (T,E), **arrewalyek** (E) *adv.*
(doing something) to the death, until death ◆ Arengk irrewalyek akek. (Sa) *The dog was bitten to death.* ◆ Arriperan ahelengkw artelhampwarl. Irrewalyekan akenh-akenh arriperan ahelengkwarl. (Sa) *Western brown snakes are really dangerous and big. They are deadly and their bite can be fatal to a person.*
irrewaly atwem, arrewaly atwem (E)
fight to the death
SEE ALSO kwarterrem, nyant atwem
irrewaly angerr, arrewaly angerr (E)
critically ill, close to death (*angerr* 'big', 'lots')
irrewaly intem
be critically ill, be close to death (*intem* 'lie down')
irrewaly-pat, arrewaly-pat (E)
people who have passed away, ancestors ◆ Tyerrty irrewaly-pat ywerrewarrek kwenh, akeweny-arey kwenh. (T) *All the ancestors have passed away, poor old things.*
= irrernng-pat
SEE ALSO aweyaw

irrewatyent, arrewatyent (T,E) *n.* [RESPECT LANGUAGE]
1. single-women's camp
2. married couple's camp (said by a man in reference to his mother-in-law and father-in-law's camp) ◆ Arrewatyentan mer ikwer-arenharl, anewartewart ikwer-arenh, arrewatyent. (Sa) Arrewatyent *is their camp, the married couple's camp.* ◆ Marlelan ilem, *boy*-el ilem, 'Irrewatyent-warl alpaw, ahaneynaw'. (Sa) *A woman might say, or a man might say, 'Go back to the* irrewatyent *camp'.*
SEE ALSO arlweker, arnkenty, ahileng, arramenty, ngwemay, anperr
irrewatyentel-irrem, arrewatyentel-irrem (T,E) *vi.* [RESPECT LANGUAGE]
become a widow ◆ Arrewatyentel-irrek ayeng. (St) *I have lost my husband [become bereaved].*
SEE ALSO arlweker-warn-irrem, inpert-irrem

irreyakwerr (E) *n.*
1. yalka, onion grass, nalgoo (*Cyperus bulbosus*). A grass with chocolate-brown-coloured seed heads, and small edible bulbs which are found underground.
2. the edible bulb of the onion grass. Also referred to as *mern irreyakwerr.*
= yerrakwerr, yalk

Irreyerr Kanty *n.*
name of a place in the Annas Reservoir area

irreyneper (T) *n.*
toothpick
= arrent
irreynm (E), **irrim** (E), **irrinm** (E) *n.*
desert cave cricket
SEE ALSO ltywelty, anwengkapeltharr
irreynt (E) toothpick SEE UNDER **arrent**
irrim (E) desert cave cricket SEE UNDER **irreynm**
irrimarnt (E) *n.*
a type of python (?). Also referred to as *ker irrimarnt.*
irrimper-irrem (T,E) *vi.*
dodge something (a spear or boomerang, or in a football game) ◆ Irrtyart-kety irrimper-irretyek. (St) *Dodging the spear.*
= irrkar-aytnem, wawely-irrem
irringk (E), **irrink** (E) *n.* [RESPECT LANGUAGE]
fearful, frightened, fearfully ◆ Irringkel-ayerr ahanenhay atyewey-rnem ayepel-irrerlanetyakenh. Irringkel akngerrarl apetyarr-alhemeng. (Sa) *For goodness sake, go back and don't just sit around. Lots of trouble [something frightening] is coming.*
SEE ALSO ater
irringk-irrem (E), **irrink-irrem** (E) *vi.* [RESPECT LANGUAGE]
become frightened
SEE ALSO ater-irrem
irrink (E) fearful, frightened, fearfully SEE UNDER **irringk**
irrinm (E) a type of cricket (?) SEE UNDER **irreynm**
irrkar-aytnem (T,E) *vi.*
dodge something (a spear or boomerang, or in a football game) ◆ Irrtyart-kety irrkar-aytnem. (Sa) *Dodging the spear.*
= irrimper-irrem, wawely-irrem
irrkarlp, arrkarlp, irrkaylp (E), **arrkaylp** (E) *n.*
1. crest (of a bird) ◆ Irrkarlp-akert thep kakepewey. (N) *Cockatoos have crests.*

2. feathers used for decoration, decorative headdress ◆ Arrkaylp-akert urntetyek. Arrkaylp rnkernem kapert-warl ra arrkaylp-akert urntetyek, anthep-irretyek. *[Women] dance with feather headdresses. They put the headdress in place on their heads and then they dance.*
irrkarnpem *vi.*
1. bounce away from something, jump away from something ◆ Amwekety ayeng irrkarnpem. (T) *I am jumping away from the snake.* ◆ Rwang aperrk irrkarnperl-alhem, rwang intyeth. (M) *The coals and the sparks bounce away [from the fire].* ◆ Irntang irrkarnpem, mwetek *wheel*-elarl atwenhemeng. (T) *The stones bounce away from the wheel as it runs over them.* ◆ Ker aherr irrkarnpem tyerrty-hety, maket-hety. (T) *The kangaroo jumps away from the person, because of the gun.*
SEE ALSO imarewanem
2. convulse, take a fit, twitch, jerk around, wriggle, writhe, thrash around ◆ Ayeng irrkarnpem, kwaty apek akeng tha antywek. (St) *I am convulsing after drinking bad water.*
• SEE ALSO atywaty-irrem2
irrkarnpety-alpem *vi.*
bounce back, bounce off something ◆ Arnang irrkarnpety-alpem irnta apek. Kwerel apek ltewem. (M) *The stone bounces back off the tree. Maybe the stone that the kid threw.*
irrkarnperl-apem (W,T) *vi.*
bounce along
irrkaty *n.*
the same, the same old thing, the same as always, the usual thing ◆ Irrkaty wetharl yanh apetyepetyem. (Sa) *That's that same old person coming along.* ◆ Irrkatyek angkerl-anetyang. Irrkaty wethek antey angkerl-anetyang. (Sa) *Don't talk about the same old thing. Don't talk about that same old thing over again.* ◆ Mer irrkatyel ayeng ananem, mer arrpenh-warl alhetyakenh. (M) *I am living in the same place, I haven't moved to another place.* ◆ Mwetekay-akert apek irrkaty-akertarl alhep-alhem. (St) *[That person] is travelling around in the same car as always.*
SEE ALSO marany, amelerr, akweteth, amperreny
irrkaw *adv.*
being restless, sleepless, or unable to sleep ◆ Ayeng ankwa akngerr intetyakenh war irrkawarl alhep-alhem, awemarl tha irlpel. (St) *I didn't have much sleep, I was wandering round restlessly and listening.* ◆ Ankwa intetyakenh irrkaw ayeng anep-anemaw. (St) *I can't get to sleep and I'm am just sitting here, unable to sleep.*
SEE ALSO ankwakel
irrkaw-irrem *vi.*
be restless, sleepless, be unable to sleep ◆ Tyerrty apetyem ingwenp, ayengarl irrkaw-irrep-irrem. (T) *Someone is coming tomorrow, and I'm worrying about it and unable to sleep.* ◆ Alhetyekek-athen irrar-irreman irrkaw-irreman alhetyek irrar-irrem. (Sa) *I feel restless and homesick and I want to go.*
irrkaw anthem
make someone restless, stop someone from sleeping ◆ Irrkaw-irrek ayeng alethangel apek ayenh ingwel irrkaw anthentyek, alethangel.

Irrkaw anem ayeng ankwa arlka intetyakenh anek. (St) *I was restless, perhaps because a stranger made me restless in the night. Then I couldn't sleep.*

irrkay (E) dull, faint, faded, hardly visible SEE UNDER **arrkay**

irrkaylp (E) crest (of a bird) SEE UNDER **irrkarlp**

irrkem *vi.*

1. be itchy, feel itchy ◆ Mantarr *dirty one*-ek irrpem, wal irrkem. (T) *If you put on dirty clothes, well you get itchy.*

SEE ALSO arreynem, ingkem, alhirrkem, irrkernem

2. have a feeling in a part of your body that tells you about certain relatives ◆ Aler-alerek apek ayeng urltaty-irrem — alha irrkem. (T) *I might have a premonition about my nephew/niece — my nose itches.*

irrkelh-irrkelh-anthem *vt.*

make someone itchy (anthem *'give'*)

SEE ALSO kert-kert-ilem

irrkelh-irrkelh-ilem *vt.* = **irrkelh-irrkelh-anthem**

SEE ALSO angernem[1], alherrem[1]

irrkenty (W) skin rash, scabies, mange SEE UNDER **arrkenty**[1]

irrkep (E) desert oak SEE UNDER **arrkep**

irrkerem *vt.*

1. uncover something, clear things away, sort through things to find something

◆ Yerrakwerr inyetyart irrkeremel irrkeremel inyetyart yerrakwerr renh, *billycan* pwelap inyetyart aweth inyetyart irrkeretyart irrkeretyart. Lpwelemel then-wetyart arlka arrernetyart pwelap kwetyemel, yerrakwerr yanh renh. (N) *We used to clear the ground and dig up the wild onions, filling up the billycans. We'd beat them to make them soft and then winnow them to clean them and then collect together all the wild onions that we had found.*

SEE ALSO akent-iwem

2. search through a house or place

irrkerlanty *n.*

1. brown falcon (*Falco berigora*)

2. grey falcon (*Falco hypoleucos*) (?) ◆ Uthipel ap irrkerlanty rnternerl-anem thip akely nyingk apek. Nyingkek unthemel atanthenhemel. Mperlker ap ra. (Sa) *The falcon goes along hunting small birds such as zebra finches. It looks for zebra finches and grabs them with its claws. It is white in colour.*

◆ Irrkerlanty-kety arrwert artelhemel, amparl, arrwert akeng-irrekerr, irrkerlerrk anekerr. (Sa) *Young boys cover their chins if they see a falcon, otherwise their beards will not grow very well — they will be thin and sparse.*

Irrkerlantyarneng (W) *n.*

the name of a creek in the Yuelamu (Mt Allan) area

irrkerleng, irrkerlerrk (E) *n.*

1. sparse or patchy shade ◆ Waly anetyakenh irrkerleng arna, walyarl ingkerrek atnyek. Irrkerleng anem ra tnepetnem, urreltyant-akert anem. (St) *A tree without leaves is* irrkerleng, *when all the leaves have fallen. Then the tree is just bare, only branches.*

◆ Lywang arrpenhem irrkerleng, arrpenhem lywerrng. (T) *Some shades are sparse, and some are thick.*

2. thin hair, hair with bald patches

◆ Arengkan irrkerlerrk. 'Arengk irrkerlerrk yanh aywepeyaw.' Alta anetyakenh *naked one.* (Sa) *Dogs can have hair with bald patches. 'Hunt that hairless dog away, the one with no hair, the naked one.'*

SEE ALSO lywerrng, irreltyenng

alta irrkerleng

not much hair, thin or sparse hair (alta *'hair'*)

kapert irrkerleng = alta irrkerleng (kapert[1] *'head'*)

lywang irrkerleng (W,T), **ulya irrkerleng** (E)

sparse or patchy shade (lywang *'shade'*)

= irreltyenng

irrkerleng-ilem, irrkerlerrk-ilem (E) *vt.*

strip bare (eat all the leaves off something)

◆ Arnarlam arlkwem interrkel. Arna ingkerrek irrkerleng-ilerl-apem arna ingkerrek irrkerleng-ilem. Arna antem irnem. (T) *The white ants eat the tree. They go along stripping the tree of leaves and then just the bare tree is left.*

irrkerlerrk (E) sparse or patchy shade SEE UNDER **irrkerleng**

irrkernem (W,T) *vt.*

scratch something

SEE ALSO irrkem, angernem[1], alherrem[1], arreynem

irrkernelhem (W,T) *vi.*

scratch yourself ◆ Ayew irrkernelhem irrkem-arlek. (M) *Scratching your side that is itching.*

◆ Tety-tety-akert irrkernelhem. (T) *Scratching yourself if you have sores.*

= angernelhem, arreynelhem, ahinelhem

irrkerrk-wem stick or poke into something else; press or lean into something SEE UNDER **kerrk-wem**

irrkert-irrkert *n.*

crooked, sticking out, bent ◆ Artep irrkert-irrkert. (Sa) *A bent back.* ◆ Karlayteng-ayteng apek — *chook-chook black one* — irrkert-irrkert. *Tail* ikwerenh. Irrkertelherl-alhem *tail* ikwerenh, irrkert-irrkert anem untem. (St) *The*

black-tailed native-hen — that black one that looks like a chook — has a tail that sticks out. It sticks its tail in the air and then runs off.
SEE ALSO amper-amper, arnkwert, arnkwert-arnkwert, iylwerl-iylwerl, lew-lew, rtapety, amper-amper

irrkertelhem (E) *vi.*
bend backwards to stretch your back
SEE ALSO arternelhem

irrkertem (W,E) cook something SEE UNDER **irrkwertem**

irrkertert-wem (E) *vt.*
winnow or yandy seed in a coolamon to separate dirt from seed (rapid sideways movement of coolamon). When winnowing seed the coolamon is also shaken in a vertical motion referred to as *ilpem1*. ◆ Irrkertert-wem ntang aympernemel. Irrkertert-wem weth-lkwer *clean*-em-ilemel, ahern-rnem iwemel. Ilpeman alanh, alanh aympernem, irrkertert-wem. (Sa) *The seed is yandied.* Irrkertert-wem *is cleaning the seed and throwing the dirt away. The action called* 'ilpem' *is like that [an up-and-down movement], yandying the seed like that.*
SEE ALSO ilpem1, ahety-ilem, aympernem
CAN SOUND A BIT LIKE irrkwertem *'cook'* [RESPECT LANGUAGE]

irrkertey *n.*
bitter-tasting, 'strong' (tea) ◆ Tampewenh yanh anety tyekert — irrkertey kwa. Arrakert itenh-itenh. (N) *The* tampewenh *melon is no good — bitter-tasting. It burns the mouth.*
SEE ALSO alyew-alyew

irrketem (E) *vi.*
feel really hungry
CAN SOUND A BIT LIKE irrkwertem *'cook'* [RESPECT LANGUAGE]

irrkety *n.*

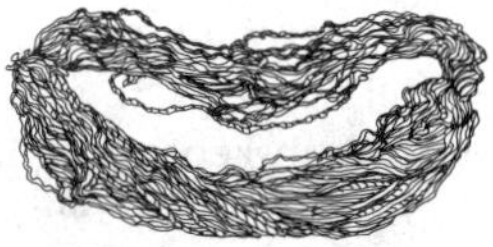

1. hairstring, string made from animal fur. Also referred to as *kapert irrkety*. ◆ Irrkety kapertek mpwarelhem, irrkety mpwarelhem *young fella*-ek apek kel arelh alyepel anem ayernem, kapert alta yanh ikwer-penh. (St) *Hairstring is made for tying round the head, it's made from hair and used for young fellas [during ceremony time].* ◆ Kapert altepenh rrpwamper-penh ina wetyart irrkety. (M) *They spun hairstring from human hair and from possum fur.*
2. hairstring waistband or headband
SEE ALSO alyep1, arlpalh, antyarn, antingkar, antay

irrkety-irrkety (T) *n.*
matted or knotted (hair)
= kelh-kelh

irrkety-wem *vt.*
spin string from hair or fur
= alyep mpwarem, wenty-ilem
SEE ALSO wem2

irrkng SEE UNDER **irrng**

irrkutyety (E) old or deserted camp (because of bereavement) SEE UNDER **arrkwetyety**

irrkwa (E) sleep (in the eyes when you wake up); pus SEE UNDER **rrkwa**

irrkwa (E) *n.*
small wooden carrying dish
SEE ALSO atywekal, urety, kwerlintyerr, panth, lwengkart2, irrkwely2, alparr1, lengarr, rnwa, urna, arlketh1

irrkwal (E) a type of spinifex SEE UNDER **rrkwal**

irrkwalty (W) needle bush, needlewood SEE UNDER **rrkwalty**

irrkwanth (T) brave, confident SEE UNDER **rrkwanth**

irrkwapem (E) be occupied doing something; work SEE UNDER **rrkwapem**

irrkwely1 (E) *n.*
woman

irrkwely akely (E)
baby girl (akely *'small'*)
= atnem-kenh

irrkwely2 (E) *n.*
a type of wooden dish
SEE ALSO atywekal, urety, kwerlintyerr, panth, lwengkart2, alparr1, irrkwa, lengarr, rnwa, urna, arlketh1

irrkwem (E) keep; hold onto something SEE UNDER **rrkwem**

irrkwenng (T,E), **urrkenng** (T,E) *n.*
native truffle, desert truffle (*Choiromyces aboriginum* (tentative taxonomy)). These are white and juicy when young, and yellow and wrinkled when older. Found in spinifex country. ◆ Ampernem renh atnmanthel ampernem, urel ampernemel-penh arlkwem, irrkwenng. (Sa) *Desert truffles are eaten after cooking them in the hot ashes.*
= akwerrerteth, pwerlantar
SEE ALSO pwek-pwek

irrkwenthey (E) red poverty bush SEE UNDER **kwenthey**

irrkweny (E) *n.*
food or meat that is left over from the day before ◆ Aherr irrkweny akety-ayntem, ingwelarl utyenety-alpek, ingwekety. Kety-ayntem anem renh irrkweny, ingwepenh-ingwepenh. (Sa) *Cutting up the leftover kangaroo meat from yesterday, the animal that was brought back and put away because it got dark. Then it is cut up early in the morning.*
SEE ALSO ingwikw

irrkwer (E) feeling hot SEE UNDER **rrkwer**
irrkwern (W) orphan SEE UNDER **rrkwern**
irrkwertem (E), **irrkertem, urrkertem** (E) *vt.*
[RESPECT LANGUAGE]
cook something ◆ Tey-ayerr irrkerta ngwarrekwengk. (St) *Make some tea for your husband [said by a woman to her daughter].* ◆ Ngwarrelengk tyety-ayerr irrkwertepertem. (St) *Your husband is cooking meat [said by a woman to her daughter].* ◆ Kwey irrkwerterlentyarretyek ahana, tyety-ayerr-akertarl ahanenhety-alpemek ngwarrekengkw — weyapelel irrkwerterlentyarra. *Daughter, go and cook the meat that has been brought back for your husband — go and cook for him because he's hungry.*
= angwey-ilem, ulerrtyem, arntampernem
SEE ALSO arrtyem, item, ampernem
CAN SOUND A BIT LIKE irrketem *'feel really hungry'*

irrkwerteth (T,E), **arrkwerteth** (W) *n.*
1. language or accent which is hard to understand ◆ Angka irrkwerteth wararl angkep-angkem. *Might* Arlper apek awetyakenh angkerl-anem, irrkwertetharl angkep-angkem awetyakenh, *German* apek. Irrkwerteth-irrkwertetharl angkem. *They just keep on speaking a different language. They might speak Warlpiri which [I] don't understand. You can't understand [some] other languages. For example, German; they speak language that is not understandable.*
2. someone who speaks a different language or has a speech impediment, someone who doesn't speak properly
SEE ALSO arrkwertep
irrkwerteth-irrkwerteth (T,E), **arrkwerteth-arrkwerteth** (W) *n.*
language or an accent which is hard to understand ◆ Irrkwerteth-irrkwerteth angkem, awetyakenh. (St) *[Someone] is talking in a strange way and [I] can't understand them.*

irrkwetyety (E) old or deserted camp (because of bereavement) SEE UNDER **arrkwetyety**
irrkweynar anem (E) *vi.*
sit on heels or haunches; sit with legs to the side
anenyirrp irrkweynar (E)
crippled, lame, limping, having a gammy leg ◆ Arelh ampwa anenyirrp irrkweynar apetyetyel-kety. (Sa) *The old woman is coming along, crippled and limping.*
SEE ALSO alpalth, aneny

irrmelh (W) fat from the side of the emu (near the kidney) SEE UNDER **inmelh**
irrmeng (E), **irrmerrng** (E) palate, roof of the mouth SEE UNDER **merrng**

irrngerney (E) *n.*
lively, happy, energetic, enthusiastic ◆ Irrngerney ayeng akem-irretyel *early.* (Sa) *I get up, lively and energetic, first thing in the morning.* ◆ *Lazy bugger*-irretyang — irrngerney. Irrngerney alherl-anemel, *no* purrk-irretyakenh. Irrngerney akwet. Warrk-irremel, mernek *everything*-ek tey arrtyemel. Irrngerney irrkwaperl anem mernek, urek ra alhemel kwatyarl inerl-wemel, kel irrngerneyarl akwetam arrtyemel. Mern themel irrngerneyel. Purrk-irretyang. (Sa) *[I] don't get lazy — I'm energetic. I walk around energetically and I don't get tired. I'm always lively. I do all sorts of work, cooking and making tea. I work energetically, and I go and get firewood and water, and then I light the fire. I enthusiastically make damper. I don't get tired.*
SEE ALSO atyep-atyep, irlpareth, ilpety, ampwengamp
irrngerney-irrem (E) *vi.*
liven up, feel happy or excited, be enthusiastic ◆ Irrngerney-irremel ayeng alhetyek mer arleng pwetyel untherl-apetyek, kerek apek alewatyerr. (Sa) *I am happy to go a long way, looking round in the bush for game such as goannas.*
SEE ALSO ahenty-irrem, akangkem, anyerrkem, inkwerelhem, kwak-irrem
irrngerney-ilem (E) *vt.*
make someone happy, liven someone up

irrngerrng (E) *n.*
sensitive, touchy or jumpy ◆ Arelh yanhan irrngerrng anep-anem. (St) *That woman is very touchy.*
= tyelety
irrngerrng-irrem (E) *vi.*
feel sensitive, touchy or jumpy ◆ Tyerrty arrpenh-kety ayeng irrngerrng-irrem. 'Ayenh anpetyalay!' (St) *I might get touchy because of another person. 'Don't touch me!'* ◆ Irrngerrng-irrem nantew, tywen-akert apek. (St) *The horse is touchy, maybe because it has a sore.*
= tyelety-irrem
SEE ALSO lyekarr anem, tikeley

irrngwa (T,E) mound of earth SEE UNDER **rrngwa**
irrngwa (E), **urrnga** (E) *n.*
a runny, liquid or sloppy mixture ◆ Kwatyarl arnterr unta thelek, irrngwa. Kwaty unta akngerr thelek. Irrngwa anem nhenhan pwelap. Irrngwilek. (Sa) *You poured too much water in, and the mixture is sloppy. You poured too much water in. Now this is really runny. It's gone runny.* ◆ Arelhel anterrng athem, irrngwa

thelelhem mwar-warl. (St) *The woman grinds the seeds, and the seed-paste mixture runs into the wooden dish.*

ngkwarl irrngwa (E)
liquid honey (ngkwarl *'sweet things'*)

ntang irrngwa (E), **anterrng irrngwa** (E)
seed paste (ntang, anterrng *'seed'*) ◆ Irrngwa weth awantyetyek angayakwel. (Sa) *Hungry people eat seed paste.*

irrngwelth (E) *n.*
sloppy, boggy, wet (ground)
SEE ALSO aperlk-aperlk, tert, urta

irrngwilem (E) *vt.*
melt something; make something go watery, sloppy or runny ◆ Anter atyenh tha irrngwilem. (St) *I am melting my fat [to cook with].* ◆ Irrngwilem renh urel kel kernt ilem anem renh, ikelh anem renh ilenty-alpem. Ikelh anem kernt-irrem, anker renh. (St) *You melt it on the fire and then it cools down and solidifies again. The spinifex resin solidifies when it cools.*
SEE ALSO arrwelth-ilem, rew-ilem

irrngwirrem (E) *vi.*
melt
SEE ALSO arrwelth-irrem, kwaty-irrem, rew-irrem

irrnya, **irrnyang** (W,T) *n.*
skin or husk on fruits or seeds; skin (of snake or lizard)

irrnyewem (W,T), **irrnyiwem** (E) *vt.*
peel or rub skin off fruit; shell an egg ◆ Mern yerrakwerr irrnyiwem, kwen-penh anem arlter inem. (St) *The bush onion is peeled and then [you] get the white bulb inside.*
SEE ALSO thwerrem

irrnyat-wem (W) *vt.*
husk or skin grass seeds before grinding them

irrnyewelhem (W,T), **irrnyiwelhem** (E) *vi.*
= **irrnyewelhem** ◆ Amwang irrnyewelhem, ayenp irlwelhem. (T) *The snake is shedding its skin.*

irrnyek ampwem (E)
shed skin (snakes and lizards) ◆ Ulkertarl irrnyek ampwem arrpemarl, irrnyant anem aynterl-anem. Tyerrelhenhem *clean* anem, irrnyiwekarl-kety. Inngelan aketharl arem, 'Irrnyek ampwekarl-kety urnem yanh-penh-kety'. (Sa) *Perenties shed their skins as well, and then just the skin is left lying there. They come out all clean, after shedding their skins. People see [the snake skin] and say, 'Look out, that snake has shed its skin'.*

irrnyengerrny, **irrnyangerr** (W) *n.*
turpentine bush (*Acacia lysiphloia*). Shrub up to 2 m with red curly bark and sticky seed pods. Has edible resin.
= ngkwern irrnyepirrny
SEE ALSO mwerlerr

irrnyang (W,T) skin or husk on fruits or seeds SEE UNDER **irrnya**

irrpamper (W,T) common brush-tailed possum SEE UNDER **rrpwamper**

irrparlerrp-wem, **rrpwarlerrp-wem** (W), **irrpaterrp-wem** (E) *vt.*
rub part of self on something ◆ Marl akwek 'atnem-akert', angwerrm-irrek — 'atnem-akert'. Alakenharl iletyam. *Granny* kwerenh then mern-akert apetyam, altywernetyam math kwerenh *grandmother* kwerenh, irrparlerrp-wetyam, war nheng *rub*-em, uneng-warl anem. Ampa akwek nhenh, iylpa atherr pewelhetyam. (St) *A little girl* 'atnem-akert' *was found/born* — 'atnem-akert'. *That's what they used to say. Her granny came with food and her mother and granny crouched down and rubbed their chests against each other. They blew in the little baby's ears.* ◆ Melikw irrpaterrp-iwem arlkemal-warl kel awer anem anem. Ampa akely awer-irretyek, irrpaterrp-wem. (Sa) *His/her mother rubs the child against the desert poplar tree to make the little child grow big.*

irrparlerrp-welhem, **rrpwarlerrp-welhem** (W), **irrpaterrp-iwelhem** (E) *vi.*
1. (women) rub chest on backs of new initiates when they have finished going through ceremonial business ◆ Artep irrparlerrp-welhem, *young fella* akwek map pwetyeng arratemek. Amwek map, awenhek map arlka, *granny* kwerenh map arlka. (T) *The mothers, the aunties and the grannies rub themselves on the backs of the young fellas who have just come out of the bush.*
2. rub self on coffin or on dead body

Irrpatyerrp (W) *n.*
Bloodwood Bore, Yuelamu (Mt Allan) area

irrpelth, **urrpelth** (E) *n.*
brave, fearless, courageous ◆ Apmwa apek irrpelthel arntwerrkem, ater anetyakenhel. (St) *Bravely holding onto the snake, without fear.*
SEE ALSO anew-anew, arnkaty, rrkwanth

irrpelth-irrem, **urrpelth-irrem** (E) *vi.*
get 'smart' or angry with someone; skite; look for trouble; be argumentative, provoke someone ◆ *Don't* atyeng irrpelth-irrerl-anerl, thang atwehety ngwenh. (M) *Don't get smart with me or I'll hit you.* ◆ Ayengap nhenhek irrpelth-irrem, ra angketyakenhek, *no* atyengel-arleng ra angkem apek — wal ayeng irrpelth-irrem yanhek. (St) *I am getting angry with that person because they haven't talked to*

me — so I am getting angry with them.
= anywerr-irrem
SEE ALSO anew-anew-irrem, urrtyirrem, tyel angkem

irrpem *vi.*
1. go in, enter, get into, go inside something ◆ Kwatyarl urntem-kety irrpenhem warl-warl. (Sa) *It's raining so [I] am going inside the house.* (N)
2. go to something; attend something ◆ *School*-warl inang irrpem, rrweyap marl inang irrpem. (N) *They go to school, the boys and the girls go.*
3. go underneath something ◆ Irrpenhem ayeng nhenh-angkwerr, tintey-angkwerr, kwen-irrenhem. (St) *I am bending down and going underneath the bent-over branch.*
4. swim (i.e. enter water) ◆ Irrpenng irrpenhem kwaty-warl. (Sa) *Fish swim along in the water.*
5. go down (sun or moon); set (sun or moon) ◆ Aherrk irrpem *supper* arlkwerrerleng. (N) *The sun goes down while [we] are eating supper.* ◆ Atay irrpenhem. Arratenty-alhem an irrpenhem altwerl-atheh. (M) *The moon goes down. It comes up, and then goes down in the west.*
6. put on (clothes, shoes); wear particular clothes, get into clothes ◆ Ingkekenhek irrperl-alhek, atyeng atyey. (St) *My younger sister put the shoes on and went.*
7. marry, enter into a relationship (?) ◆ Ankerlam untan kwenh. Mwerekangkwan kwenh, ankerlan untang irrek kwenh, mwerewekarl unta irrpek kwenh. (T) *You have married the wrong way. You married your son-in-law, got into a relationship with your son-in-law.*
SEE ALSO aylpem
CAN SOUND A BIT LIKE arrpem *'carve', 'chisel'*

irrpenh-irrpenh (E) *n.*
clothes
SEE ALSO mantarr, rnwanenty, urnanenty, arnkwa

kwatyek irrpem (T,E)
go swimming; have a bath (kwaty *'water'*) ◆ Kwatyek irrpetyek ayeng alhey. (St) *I'm going swimming.*

irrpelh-ilem *vt.*
1. put something on yourself; put something inside something else; cover yourself with something ◆ Tyaket mperlkerek ina irrpelh-ilem. 'Nta kwenh ngkart angerr.' (T) *They put a white coat on. 'You are an important priest.'*
2. put someone in (jail)
3. wet someone or something; water something ◆ Kwatyel irrpelh-iletyel kapert. Kapert ayenh irrpelh-iley kwatyel. *Garden* an irrpelh-ilemarl kwatyel irrpelh-ilem, lyapetyek atherrk. *Green one* anetyek, *dry*-arl anem-kety. *[You can] wet your head with water. I'll wet my head with water. Gardens are watered so that the grass grows. So that they will be green and not dry.* ◆ Atanthem aper tyelk, kapert alhewelhetyeh, annga arlka. Merntpenh kel irrpelh-ilem. (N) *We get the inside bark of the river red gum and use it to wash our heads and our eyes. You can wash yourself with it if you are sick.* • SEE ALSO tyeyepetyey atwem

irrpelh-apem *vi*
go along digging yourself into something. ◆ Kwatyarl ntyeny-ntyeny ahelhekarl irrpelh-apem ra, akely-amperl. (St) *The ant lion is a small creature that digs itself into the ground.*

irrpelh-ilelhem *vi.*
wet oneself to cool down ◆ Kwatyel ayeng irrpelh-ilelhem irrernt-ilelhemel. (Sa) *I am wetting myself with water to make myself cool.*
= akarl-welhem, anhelhem

irrpenng, **irrpeng** *n.*
fish ◆ Irrpenng kwatyel-ayeng anem. (M) *Fish live in the water.*
= pety, aylperr

ker irrpenng
edible fish

irrpenper-welhem (W) *vi.*
grind teeth; rub together (trees) ◆ Rtety irrpenper-welhem. (M) *Grinding [your] teeth together.* ◆ Arnang atherr irrpenper-welhem. (M) *The two branches are rubbing together.*
= interrpar-wem

irrpent (E) *n.*
pygmy desert monitor (*Varanus eremius*)
= artep irrpent
SEE ALSO arern

irrperrpantyel (E) black-faced woodswallow SEE UNDER **perrpantywen**

irrpeyl (E) *n.*
emu foot
= irrtyewat[2]

irrpwarem (E) wipe something out, rub out SEE UNDER **urrparem**

irrpwerl (E), **urrperl** (E) *n.*
1. black, dark in colour ◆ Ayeng irrpwerl, nga arlterarl. (St) *I'm black, you're white.* ◆ Apwert urrperl arak. Apernelhenhelhenh. Arak ikwerel apernelheman. Arelhak ateyak. (Sa) Arak *is a black stone used for rubbing on yourself. [You] rub yourself with it. Women and men.*
2. Aboriginal person, Aboriginal ◆ *'Uncle'*

renhap 'amarl-amarl' akem urrperl-angkwarr. *Uncle*-an yanhan arlter-kenh. (Sa) *'Uncle' is called* 'amarl-amarl' *in Aboriginal way. 'Uncle' is white people's [language].*
= **rrpwerl** (W,T)
irrpwerlayt (E), **urrperlayt** (E)
irrpwerl-irrpwerl (E), **urrperl-urrperl** (E) *n.*
a little bit dark (in colour); blackish
= **rrpwerl-rrpwerl** (W,T)
irrpwerl-awaty (E), **urrperl-awaty** (E) *n.*
a little bit dark (in colour); blackish
irrpwerl-irrem (E), **urrperl-irrem** (E) *vi.*
go dark in colour, darken, go black ◆ Ker pwelh-irrem, ker *barbecue* arrtyerrenty pwelh-irrem, aperrk-irremel, pwelh-irrem. Irrpwerl-irrerl-anem aperrk-apeny irrem, pwelh. (Sa) *Meat gets burnt, meat that is cooked on the barbecue gets burnt and turns to charcoal. It goes black like charcoal, burnt.*
= **rrpwerl-irrem** (W,T)
irrpwerl-ilem (E), **urrperl-ilem** (E) *vt.*
make something go dark or go black in colour
= **rrpwerl-ilem** (W,T)
Irrpwerl-kenh (E), **Urrperl-kenh** (E) *n.*
belonging to Aboriginal people
= Tyerrty-kenh

irrpwernp (E) country devoid of bushtucker SEE UNDER **urrpernp**

Irrthwet *n.*
name of a place in Coniston area

irrtny SEE UNDER **irrny**

irrtyart *n.*
spear ◆ Artwang yanh arrawey-akert apetyem, irrtyart map-akert. (T) *That man is coming with weapons, with lots of spears.* ◆ Irrtyart anem ipakert, alwerrngelarl ayernem, aherrel alwerrngel. (St) *Spears have a hook on them that has been tied up with sinew, with kangaroo sinew.*
CAN SOUND A BIT LIKE tyart *'shirt'*
irrtyarteng-irrtyart *n.*
pretend spear, toy spear ◆ Ampa maparl arrken-arrkenel, irrtyarteng-irrtyart, atantherl-apem arrken nheng atantherremel lyentyel, ketyey map. (N) *The kids enjoy themselves going along spearing each other with the kangaroo grass, their pretend spears.*
irrtyart-akert (E) *n.*
1. baby boy (newborn) (lit. 'having a spear') ◆ Ampa awey akwekarl *born*-irrem, wal ilem, arrwekelenyel iletyam, mparetyam, iteth-wetyam ina, 'Irrtyart-akertaw'. *Daddy* ikwerenhan ikirrentyarl anetyam, math kwerenh yanh kel. (St) *When a baby boy was born, the olden-time people used to say, to give the baby life,* 'Irrtyart-akert'. *His father had to keep a respectful distance, his mother was okay.* **2.** respectful word a father uses to refer to his son
= irrtyart-kenh
SEE ALSO atnem-akert
irrtyart-kenh (E) *n.*
baby boy (newborn) (lit. 'belonging to the spear')
= irrtyart-akert

irrtyelh-ilem, **arrtyelh-ilem** (T) *vt.*
ask someone to go with you
◆ Ikngwetyekeyay tha irrtyelh-iley kwenh arelh nhakw kwenh irrer alhetyek irrtyelh-ilem alhetyek irrer. *'Come on we go* kwenh.*'* (St) *I'll ask that woman over there to go hunting with me. 'Come on let's go.'* ◆ Tharl uyarn irrtyelh-iletyel atnwerntantarl irretyel. Anetyek akwel. (Sa) *I am trying in vain to get [her] to go with me but she is stubborn and wants to stay put. Supposedly she wants to stay.* ◆ Mpa, nwengkerr lyweny alhey! Anwern arrtyelh-ilemel alhey! Ker arlewatyerr-warn apek. (T) *Come on, let's go hunting! We'll go, taking others with us! Maybe we'll go and get goannas.*
= ngwelh-ilem

irrtyernem (E) *vt.*
tie something up
SEE ALSO ayernem, rlterrk-ilem
irrtyernelhem (E) *vi.*
tie something round yourself
= ayernelhem
SEE ALSO arrakwernem[1]

irrtyewat[1] (E) *n.*
small rocks or stones ◆ Apwert akely-rnem ahernel anetyel irrtyewat, akely-akely-rnem aneynetyel, 'irrtyewat' anem renh ilem apwert ra. (Sa) *Small rocks that are lying on the ground are called* 'irrtyewat'.
= arrtya[3], urrtyel

irrtyewat[2] (W,T) *n.*
emu foot
SEE ALSO irrpeyl

irrwelty kindling wood, scraps of wood SEE UNDER **rrwelty**

-irrwengerr (W,T), **-arrwengerr** (T) *n.ending*
those two; and (the other one), both of them
◆ Ameyan amwekek ilem, amwek-**irrwengerr** antey ilem anyent-antey ilem. (T) *Mothers are called both 'amwek' or 'amey', that's what they are called.* ◆ Mpweny yanh atherran alherrem, marl-**irrwengerr** artwang-**irrwengerr**. (T) *Those two went off together, the girl and the man.* ◆ Anterrng, wantyarlewarretyart. Lepwel anem artety-**irrwengerr** arlpelhart-

irrwengerr. Anterrngem, angkwey awantyetyart. (N) *People used to eat seeds. The mulga and the broad-leaved mulga are both similar to each other. They have edible seeds that people used to eat.*

irrwenyenk (E) Georgina gidgee SEE UNDER **urrenyenk**

irrweper (E), **urreper** (E) *n.*
on the other side of something (to the speaker); behind something; on the back or far side of something ◆ Urreperel alhetyek, arrpenhel arekety. *Going along on the other side in case someone sees [you].*
= arrwengak, anwenger

Irrwerlety *n.*
the name of a soakage in the Yuelamu (Mt Allan) area, near Uldirra Hill

irrwernem (E) make trouble for someone else SEE UNDER **urrernem**

irrwernter (E) hopping or skipping motion that indicates aggression (men) SEE UNDER **urrernter**[1]

irrwernter (E) red-backed kingfisher SEE UNDER **urrernter**[2]

irta (W,T)**, irtang** (W,T) hard part of a hoof or paw SEE UNDER **rta**

irtak (W,T) windbreak SEE UNDER **rtak**

irtety (W,T) tooth, teeth SEE UNDER **rtety**[1]

irtwarem watch someone or something going away SEE UNDER **artwarem**

ita (E) *n.*
1. throat
2. side of the neck (?); top part of the back of the neck ◆ Ita kelarl akeng-ilem, nhenh-lkwer ternng apek, twengkwelkel akeng-ilek ahenty — *no* itirretyakenh *eh.* Ahenty iter yanharl akeng-ilem, wal itirretyakenh anem arrangkw — aparlp-ilemarl. *You can't remember. Don't know — just like little baby* weth anep-anem. (St) *If your* ita *is not good, or the back of the neck just below the head, or if a flu has made your throat no good — well then, you can't think properly. If the side of the throat is no good, well then you can't think — you forget. You can't remember. You don't know — just like a little baby.*
SEE ALSO ahenty[1], iterrem, iterlarem

itepenh (E) *n.*
necklace ◆ Arrwekelenyel mapelarl atnyenek itepenh, angwenh-penh, akekarl-penh, alta-penh. *Rabbit,* tyerrty-kenh apek alakenh. (St) *The olden-time people had necklaces made from whatever, from hair. Rabbit hair or human hair.*
SEE ALSO akarl-ayntenh, ahenty-kenh

-itany (E) *ending*
even though . . . , despite the fact that . . . , regardless of the fact that . . . ◆ Untam alknga atherrk-atherrk-irrek mwerekengkw, ampekengkw apek. Nyerrel-**itany**. (St) *You married your son-in-law, or your son. Even though it's shameful.*

itekem (E) *vt.*
pinch (with fingers) ◆ Yenh iteketyalay! (St) *Don't pinch me!*
= lther-wem

itelh (E) *n.*
kneecap
SEE ALSO amper[2], kelkert, akepitelh, amper alkwert-alkwert, kelkert tyelh, kelkert ngkwern, tyelh

itely (E) *n.*
wart
= mwenth
SEE ALSO ankerl, amern-amern

item *vt.*
1. cook something, heat something up ◆ Arelhel arlewatyerr item urel. (T) *The woman is cooking the goanna in the fire.*
2. boil (tea or other liquids) ◆ Tey arlka itetyek ura mwenng atyeng inerl-way. (T) *Get me some kindling so that I can boil some tea.*
3. light a fire ◆ Ura tha itetyekaw. *I'm going to light a fire.*
4. warm a person in hot earth for healing purposes ◆ Untyetyel ampa item. Arrwekelenyel itetyam untyetyel. (St) *Babies were warmed in the hot earth. The olden-time people used to warm them up in the hot earth.*
5. burn something, cause a burning pain ◆ Urelarl artekarl item kwang atywer, ahelengkw wangkerl-ilenh-ilenh. Atyweran ahelengkw. Urrperl. Arrakert akwek rnter-rnter-awaty. (St) *The* atywer *ant is definitely aggressive and makes [you] swell up, and burn like fire [when it bites]. They are dangerous. They are dark in colour and their mouth is a bit reddish.*
6. burn patterns or designs on something ◆ Twererr rwel itep-item wayel. (M) *Burning patterns on the clapsticks with [hot] wire.*
7. make the earth go a yellow or red colour (honeyants) ◆ Ahelh nhenh *yellow one* ileynem. 'Nhenh anyem iteynetyam.' Yerrampel iteynepeynem, aretyakenharl ap ran, itekarl wararl apentem renh, irrkereynem irrkereynem, nhenh-anyem iteynetyam, anekarl anem angwerrm-ilem. Ilwerrk arlka anem angwerrm-ilem. Iteynepeynemarl yanh urelarl item-artek antey. *Yellow one* irrem

alakenh. (St) *The ground here is made yellow [by the honeyants]. 'Here is where the earth is yellow.' You can't see the honeyants but they make the earth go a yellow colour, and you follow along, clearing the ground where it has gone yellow. Then you find the honeyants and the honeyant eggs. The honeyant 'burns' the ground just like fire burns. And the ground goes a yellow or red colour.*

8. burn or 'cook' ashes for chewing with tobacco, reduce to ashes ◆ Atyarnp arnmeny itenh-itenh ra kwel. Arnmeny item, rnpwa akert renh-iperr arnmeny iterl-anem, ngkwerlp-kenh, *not tobacco*-kenh athew, rnpwenp-kenh, ngkerlp-kenh. (N) *The ironwood tree is also used for ashes and we cook the ashes to use for native tobacco, for* rnpwenp *— not whitefella tobacco.*

9. mix tobacco with ashes ◆ Ngkwerlp anem arnmeny-warn arrernem, item, item item kel arlkwem antem. Arnmenyekarl arrernem, ngkwerlp item arnmenyel-ayel. (T) *The tobacco is put into the ashes, and mixed together, then chewed. After putting it in the ashes, the tobacco is mixed with the ashes.*

SEE ALSO arrtyem, ampem[1], atyerrem[1], ampernem, ampeng-ilem

itelhem (E) *vi.*

1. warm oneself ◆ Itelhem uternel, irrernt-penh. *Warming [yourself] in the sun, after being cold.*

2. burn or cut hair in mourning, grieve ◆ Kwerenh ampikw *lose*-em-iletyam, itelhetyam anem ra kapert, alta. (St) *After losing her child, she cuts her hair in mourning.* ◆ Ampa ikwerenharl aparlp-ilekan itelhek, anker-athek-irremel. Altarl itelhem, arrwekelenyel itelhetyamarl. (St) *Because she has lost her child she cuts her hair in grief. In the old days parents who lost a child would burn their hair off.* • SEE ALSO akelhem, anker-athek-irrem

= arrtyelhem

iteng[1] (E) *n.*

married, together (a married couple) ◆ Arlwenth alherrek anewart kerek unthetyek. Iteng alherrek. (Sa) *The married couple went together, looking for meat.* ◆ Irrkwerrenty ananem iwetyangenh, purt antey, itengant-atherr. Itengant-atherr iwerretyang purt anerl-anem irrkwerrenty. (Sa) *The two of them are still together, they haven't split up. The two of them are still together.*

SEE ALSO arlwenth, marrert

iteng-irrem (E) *vi.*

get married, get together

= marrert-irrem, arlwenth-irrem, merangk anem

-iteng[2] *ending*

marks respect language words

itep *n.*

the side or the edge of something ◆ Itepel anep-anem ayeng. Unta anep-anem mpepelarl. (St) *I am sitting on the side. You are sitting in the middle.* ◆ Apwarrewerlker itepelarl alhep-alhem weth, aletharr *that one, first time* ra kamparr anem kwart, atherneng. Marl *one or boy one.* Arlter arlter arl ra. (St) *The first-hatched emu is the one that goes along on the side [of the group of emu hatchlings]. That's the first-hatched, the one that comes out of the egg first, either a female or a male. They are whitish in colour.*

= iter

SEE ALSO angath, mpep, akwerr[1], kanty[1], rlkwerr

itep-ampeny *n.*

on the side or the edge of something

= itep-thayt, iter-ampeny, iter-thayt

itep-thayt *n.* = **itep-ampeny**

itep-angkwerr *n.*

(along) the side

itep-penh (T,E) *n.*

the eldest in a group of siblings

SEE ALSO aletharr, arrwekeleny

itepenh throat SEE UNDER **ita**

iter *n.*

on the side or the edge of something ◆ Lher iterel alhem. (St) *Going along the side of the river.* ◆ Kwaty alay iter-areny lyet apetyem. (T) *The people from the coast are coming today.* ◆ Pwarlkeny kwenh anerl-anek, nheng *know*-em arlka iletyakenh, iwenh apekarl iter arrpenhel mpwarek. *Pass away* apekarl irrekarl apek anwern apal anek antem. Pwarlkeny wart anwern anerl-anek, awetyakenh. (M) *[We] were not told about it, we didn't know what happened on the other side. If people got killed then we didn't know about it. We were ignorant, we didn't hear about it.*

SEE ALSO itep, kanty[1], akwerr[1], arrethaker

CAN SOUND A BIT LIKE ater *'fright'*

iter-ampeny *n.*

on the side or the edge of something

= iter-thayt, itep-ampeny, itep-thayt

iter-thayt *n.* = **iter-ampeny**

iter-angkwerr *n.*

(along) the side

= itep-angkwarr

apwert iter

the side of a hill (apwert *'hill'*) ◆ Apwert iterel

untherl-anem akin, ker iylekek untherl-anemel, inteyel, intey areynepeynerl. (Sa) *Going along the side of the hill looking for echidnas, looking in the caves for echidnas.* = irntang arrker

iterlarem *vt.*

1. know about someone or something; recognise someone or something ◆ Atnew-atnewel tha mpwarem tharl iterlarem-angkwerr. (St) *I'm confident, I know what I'm doing.* ◆ Ampa akwek ra anem urrem-urrem. Kel angerr-awern irrem, angkakert anem irrem nhenh-lkwer rlterrk anem irreynepeynem, atyet-atyet weth. Rlterrk anem ra irreynepeynem, kel angkethen antey rlterrk-irrem. Iterlarem anem ra atyemey apek nyany apek, arrengey apek, mam apek akngey kwerenh. Urrem-urremek-amparr. (St) *Little babies do not understand properly at first. Then they get a bit bigger and they start to talk, and the soft part [the fontanelle] hardens up. That gets hard, and then their talking gets stronger as well. Then they know their mother's father, or their granny, or their father's father, their mother or their father. At first they don't know things properly.*

2. remember something ◆ Ntwa iterlarem nheng *time* anwern alhek Altywep-warn? (M) *You remember the time we went to Altywep?*

3. understand something

SEE ALSO ita, iterrem, irlpangkem

iterlarelhem *vi.*

think about something involving yourself; know something about yourself, think to yourself ◆ Iterlarelhem ayeng kapertel tha antwerrkem. (St) *I know about it and I'm keeping it in my head.* ◆ Iterlarelhem ayeng, angkekarl ayeng akengenty apek yanhek. (St) *I know that I spoke badly to that person there.*

iterleng-iterl-irrem (W) *n.*

lose memory

iterrem, itirrem (E) *vi.*

think; think about someone or something; think about doing something; reckon (think about something), think that . . . ; have an opinion about something ◆ Nthakenh ntwa itirrem? (M) *What do you think?* ◆ Iterrerl-anem ayeng alhetyeh, kwer-warn. *I keep thinking about going to him.* ◆ Iwenham ngan iterreperremay? Alhety akey? Nthenh-warn ntwa alhetyenh? (N) *What do you reckon? Are you going? Where to?* ◆ Lyet ayeng alherl-anetyek ayeng itirrepirrem. (St) *I'm thinking that I'll go today.* ◆ Ita kelarl akeng-ilem, nhenh-lkwer ternng apek, twengkwelkel akeng-ilek ahenty — *no* itirretyakenh *eh*. Ahenty iter yanharl akeng-ilem, wal itirretyakenh anem arrangkw — aparlp-ilemarl. *You can't remember. Don't know — just like little baby* weth anep-anem. (St) *If your ita is not good, or the back of the neck just below the head, or if a flu has made your throat no good — well then you can't think properly. If the side of the throat is no good, well then you can't think — you forget. You can't remember. You don't know — just like a little baby.*

SEE ALSO ita, iterlarem

iterrenty, itirrenty (E) *n.*

idea, thoughts, senses, knowledge, intellect ◆ Mwerr anetyek Altyerrel ilem. Altyerr iterlaremel, itirrenty anemel — *no* atwerretyek, *no* ilterretyek, *no* ilerretyek, urrtyel ilerretyek, urrtyirretyang — mwerr akwet anetyek. Altyerr iterlarenty anem, mwerr anetyek, ingkart way anetyek, atnert irrernt, arlka irrernt anetyek, altyerrant iterlaremel, ingkartant iterlaremel angerrirretyek. (Sa) *God tells us to be good. To know God and live with this knowledge — no fighting, no swearing, no telling lies, no lying — being consistently good. Knowing God and living well, in God's way, being good to each other and not getting angry [*lit. *'being with a cool stomach and cool body'], just thinking of God.* ◆ Artwang ampwang arrely-arrelyem ananem anety-anetyem. *One place*-el altywernerl-anem, alhetyakenh. Antarl-areny, mer akweteth. *Half* pweng rang anem, annga arlka nheng anngwenty *all over*. Nheng iterrenty kwerenh aparlp antemarl ilek. (M) *An old man might be really old and wrecked. Staying in one place and not going anywhere. They stay at home all the time. They might be half blind and their eyes all weepy. And they might have lost their senses.*

iteth *n.*

alive, living ◆ Alewatyerr iteth akwet arrtyanem atwekarl-penh. (M) *After being hit the goanna is still alive and it's running away.* ◆ Tyerrty iteth anem. (M) *The person is still alive.* ◆ Amwelyan karlkwem rtemarlel. Inemel, karlkwemel anem. Iteth-antey rtemarl karlkwem. (Sa) *The cadney lizard is bitten on the back of the neck. [You] get it, and bite it on the back of the neck. While it is still alive.*

itethek mpwarem (E)

keep someone from trouble; save someone's life (mpwarem *'make', 'do'*) ◆ Itethek mpwaremel ilem tha, *don't go* mer arrpenh-warl. (St) *To save your life I tell you not to go to another place.*

iteth-antey *n.*

still alive, lively ◆ Iteth-antey nga anep-anem, arntety anetyakenh. (St) *You are still lively, you haven't got sick.*

itethakenp *n.*

alive, having a long life ◆ Ingkerrek itethakenp-antey anep-anem, ilwetyakenh. (St) *Everybody is still alive, nobody's died.*

iteth-ilem *vt.*

make someone better; heal; liven someone up; revive someone ◆ Ngangkarel iteth-ilem, rlkertarl intep-intem. Kel ra akem-irrem anem. (St) *The traditional healer heals the person that is lying there sick. Then [the person] gets up.* ◆ Rlwek yanhel mwerrarl ilem *clean*-em ilelhem annga, *everything* alhewelhem artwengkenng-apertem mernt-apert, iteth-ilem. (N) *The native pine is used to wash eyes and clean them and make them better, to wash all over and to make people better if they have a cold or are sick.*

SEE ALSO mpwarem, mwerr-ilem, tangkelh-ilem, althekalth-ilem

iteth-wem *vt.*

1. assist in a birth, bring to life ◆ Thang iteth-wek kwer ampelyerrk. (M) *I helped [the woman] give birth to the newborn baby.* ◆ Ampa awey akwekarl *born*-irrem, wal ilem, arrwekelenyel iletyam, mparetyam, iteth-wetyam ina, 'Irrtyart-akertaw'. *Daddy* ikwerenhan ikirrentyarl anetyam — math kwerenh yanh kel. (St) *When a baby boy was born, the olden-time people used to say, to give the baby life, 'Irrtyart-akertaw ['having a spear']'. His father had to keep a respectful distance — his mother was okay.*

2. bring back to life, revive someone

iteth-irrem *vi.*

get better, liven up, recover (get better) ◆ Atwekarl-penh ayeng iteth-iteth-irrep-irrem. (St) *After being beaten I am getting a little bit better.* ◆ Rlkert angerr-penh iteth-irrem akwet. (M) *[He] has recovered after a big illness.*

itewem (E) clean or scrape burnt hair or skin off an animal SEE UNDER **tewem**

Ithew *n.*

Jesus (from old German 'Jesu')

SEE ALSO ngkart

ithweng (E) maybe, perhaps SEE UNDER **thweng**

itirrem (E) think SEE UNDER **iterrem**

itna (E) they (more than two) SEE UNDER **ina**[1]

itna (E) name SEE UNDER **ina**[2]

itnakerr (E) they (more than two) SEE UNDER **inakerr**

itnantherr (E) they (more than two) SEE UNDER **inantherr**

itnewem (E), **itniwem** (E) name something SEE UNDER **anewem**[1]

itningkerr (E) they (more than two) SEE UNDER **inengkerr**

itnwerreng (E) emu bush SEE UNDER **unerreng**

itnyem (E) dig, dig for something SEE UNDER **inyem**

itutnhem (E) *vt.*

choke something, screw or wring somebody's or something's neck, strangle someone (ita '*throat*'; utnhem '*bite*') ◆ Alewatyerr apek itutnhetyek rapet apek. Ita utnhem. (Sa) *Wringing the goanna's or the rabbit's neck. Wringing the neck.*

SEE ALSO twerl-akem, ahenty ltwakem, ahenty ultakem, ahenty ahenpem, alyernem, awerrkem

itwa, **itwang** (W,T), **rtwa** (W,T), **rtwang** (W,T) *n.*

close, near, close to something else ◆ Nta alhem *Napperby*-warn, rtwewarn. *Ti Tree*-warn *little bit* rntwarr-lkwer. (M) *You can go to Napperby, it's close. Ti Tree is a little bit further.* ◆ Artwang atherr rtwang anerreperrem. (M) *The two men are sitting close together.*

= arrer, angath

CAN SOUND A BIT LIKE artwa *'man'*

itwek-irrem, **rtwek-irrem** (W,T) *vi.*

move closer to something, get closer to something ◆ 'Ilwengar mer itwek-irretyenh?' 'Ngathemam', nta ilelhem, 'Ngathem kwenh, *close now.*' (M) *'When will the place get close [to us]?''It's close', you say, 'It's really close now.'*

= arrer-irrem

itwirrem (E), **itwang-irrem** (W,T) *vi.*

move closer to something, get closer to something

= arrer-irrem, angath-irrem

itwilem (E), **itwang-ilem** (W,T) *vt.*

move something closer to something

= arrer-ilem

itwerlker *n.*

quite close, reasonably close

itwang-itwang (W,T), **rtwang-rtwang** (W,T) *n.*

1. things that are close to each other ◆ Artwang map anep-anem rtwang-rtwang. (T) *The men are sitting close together.*

2. things that are similar to each other

= arrerek-arrer

itwek-itwek, **rtwek-rtwek** (W,T), **itwek-itwa** (E) *n.*

1. things that are close to each other

2. things that are similar to each other

= arrerek-arrer

tweket (W,T), **rtweket** (W,T) *n.*

close together ◆ Arelh map kwenyel intem

tweket. (T) *The women are sleeping close together at night.*
tweket-tweket (W,T), **rtweket-rtweket** (W,T) *n.*
close together ◆ Warl tweket-tweket. (T) *Houses that are close together.*
= arrerek-arrer

-itwek (T,E), **-rtwek** (T,E), **-utek** (E) *n.ending*
1. amongst, at, on, by ◆ Apelinterr-interrel alhweng mpwarem kwartek ahern-**itwek.** (Sa) *The rainbow bee-eater builds its nest for its eggs on the ground.* ◆ Ngkwarl aperelty aper arlpe**rtwek** anetyel. (Sa) *A sweet white substance made by the lerp-scale insect is found on the leaves of the river red gum.* ◆ Werrp-**rtwek** lyapem mern aherretyepwer. (Sa) *The bush bean fruit grows on the bush bean vine.*
2. during, in the time of ◆ Anengkerr-anengkerr-irrem. 'Tyerrty map apetyemarl kwenh.' Kel kweny-**itwek** arety-ayntem yanh kel apetyewarrem, tharl anengkerr-anengkerr arek-penh. (T) *Having a dream. 'The people are coming.' And then, during the night, seeing the people that you dreamt about coming.*

itwern (E) sun, sunshine SEE UNDER **utern**

itwert-itwert (E) *n.*
a type of grass (grows in swamps) (?)

itya (W,T) *part.*
no, nothing, not ◆ Awely aketh-akert, awely aketh war anwa alyelherl-anem, *not* kwen intem, itya. Aketh-akert anwa ananem, arreny-akert, awely-akert. (N) *We are singing our* awely *ceremony out in the open, not keeping it secret. We are still keeping our ceremony and song that goes with it.* ◆ Arety-kweny itya melarlp. (M) Melarlp *spirits are not visible.* ◆ Tyap-kweny itya kwa. Arnant war. Mern anetyakenh, rnpwa anetyakenh itya. *The [ghost gum] doesn't have any grubs, no edible food and no resin — its just a tree.* ◆ Tyathew ityakey ntwang arern? (M) *Is it true that you didn't see it?* ◆ Akangkwerrenty itya, kwer kwerl-areny map, maneyekant angkerl-anem, maney akwel ngkwelty anthetyeh. (N) *The school kids don't pay attention; apparently they just ask for money, ask to be given coins.* ◆ Kwenthey akerl-apek. *No rake,* an kwenthey war, kwentheyel mer *clean*-em-iletyeh war. *Not rake,* itya. *Olden time* arnel war *clean*-em-ilek kwentheyel. (N) *People used to go and cut* kwenthey *branches. No rake, they used to clean their camps with* kwenthey *branches. They didn't have any rakes. There were no rakes — nothing. In olden times they just used* kwenthey *branches for sweeping.* ◆ Kwey! Kwaty-kweny itya — *billycan* arltwang iney! (T) *Girl! We've got no water — get the empty billycan!* ◆ Nthwemel nthwemel apety-alpern akerkweny itya, itya akwet. (M) *Walking and walking [I] came back without any meat, still nothing.*
SEE ALSO arrangkw
ityilem (W,T) *vt.*
finish something off, kill someone ◆ Merrenty ineh-artey maparl arlkwek-penh map ingkerr arlperrek atwek. Ityilek — anyent-arenyel. (M) *He killed all of them who were guilty of eating his family. He finished them off — all on his own.*
itya-antey (W,T) *n.*
nothing yet, (there's still) nothing ◆ Itya-antey tyerrty ywerrek. (M) *That person is still missing.*
itya akwet (W,T)
nothing yet, (there's still) nothing ◆ Thang arltwarem, itya akwet. (T) *I see nothing, nothing yet.*
= arrangkw akwet

iwarlkw (E) *n.*
something that is closed in at one end, the end of a burrow, the corner (of a room etc.)
= mety-mety

iwarrernem (E) copy someone or something SEE UNDER **warrernem**

-iwelhem (E) Occurs in some compound verbs. SEE UNDER **-welhem**

iwelhem throw SEE UNDER **iwem**

iwem *vt.*
1. throw something; throw something off
2. throw something away ◆ Yanh iway. (St) *Throw that away.* ◆ Atnarrk ipem, atherrk iwemel, item anem renh. (St) *The green stuff inside the guts is cleaned out and thrown away, and then the guts are cooked.* ◆ Arwerl apek tha akeng-akeng yanh-lkwer lyapek, tyerretyek tha, tyerremel iwetyek. (St) *If I have grown some useless plants or that sort of thing, then I'll pull them out, pull them out and chuck them away.*
SEE ALSO artaly-wem
3. spread something out ◆ Antyam iwem. (St) *Spread out the blanket.*
4. Occurs in some compound verbs, may be pronounced as *-wem* or *-iwem*. The meaning of *-iwem* is sometimes not distinguishable from that of the compound verb as a whole; it frequently occurs in verbs with actions to do with placing something such as *arlkeny-wem* 'make a design or marking' or *irraker-wem* 'make grooves or markings'. • = -wem[3]
iwerrem *vi.*
1. divorce, split up (married couple) (lit.

throw each other away) ◆ Iwerrek ratherr, marl then artwethen apek. Wal ratherr iwerrek anem, arrpenh-akert anemarl ra. (St) *Those two split up, the woman and the man. They split up and he has another one now.*

2. become abandoned, be rejected ◆ Akuny-amperl *too* ayeng anep-anem ikngа. *No* ilkwatherr. Arengk-artekarl iwerrek. (Sa) *Poor me, I am all on my own. I have no company. [They] abandoned me like a dog.*

3. put ceremonial designs on each other, paint each other up

4. throw things to each other

iwelhem *vi.*

1. lie down, throw self down ◆ Arengk map iwelhem tyerrtyek-arlek, wal pwarn-ilem anem arlerlp irrem anem. (St) *When the dogs lie down to sleep on top of the people, well they squash the people and the people get cramped.* ◆ Ayeng iwelhem antyameh intetyeh. (M) *I am lying down on the blanket to sleep.*

2. comb or brush hair ◆ Iwelhem alta alakenh. (St) *Combing [your] hair like that.*

iwerl-alhem *vt.*

leave someone or something behind, drop someone or something off ◆ Iwerl-alhek wethek-antey, wethek-antey tha iwerl-alhek. (St) *I left it at that place.* ◆ Iwerl-alhek tha mer arrpenhek, ayengant anem apety-alpek, mer arrpenhek tha iwerl-alhek. (St) *I went and left [that person] at the other place and then I just came back myself.* ◆ Mer atyenhek tha iwerl-alhern mantarr apek. Kel ayeng apety-alpern. (St) *I just left the clothes at my place. Then I just came back.*

iwerl-wem (E) *vt.*

drop someone or something off ◆ Yanhan angkep-angkem iwerl-wetyek. (St) *That person is talking about being dropped off.*

iwerl-alpem *vt.*

drop someone or something off and then return, take someone or something somewhere and leave them there (then return) ◆ Ntarl iwerl-alpek nhakwek mantarr ngkwenh. Iltyant nga apety-alpern, nhenh ant iwerl-alpek, mantarr ngkwenh. (St) *You went and dropped your clothes off over there. You came back empty-handed, you just dropped your clothes off.*

pelh-wem, pelh-iwem (E) *vt.*

spit, spit something out

arlkeny-iwem (E) *vt.*

make a stripe, design or marking ◆ Awelyek apek tha awely apek iwetyek arlkeny, arlkeny-iwetyek. (St) *I might paint the ceremonial designs for the women's ceremonies.*

iwenh 'What?', 'Which one?' SEE UNDER **wenh**

iweny mosquito SEE UNDER **weny**

iwep spider SEE UNDER **wep**

iwer (E) *n.*

a type of animal, possibly the agile wallaby (?)

iwerr (E) *n.*

road, path, track, way ◆ Iwerr amper-amper. (St) *A crooked track.* ◆ Pwelek iwerrel ra alhep-alhem, kwaty-warl, iwerr kwerenhel. (St) *The bullock goes along its track, towards the water.* ◆ Iwerr arnangelh-ilemel rarrp imernt ineyam-kety mern. *Room* anetyang. Mwerekikw. Alkiwerr-kety. (Sa) *Clear a path for [that person] so that they can get their tucker first. There is no room [for her] because her son-in-law is there.* ◆ Apal alhemel therrert-irremel anem, iwerr ingwer-angkwerr anem. Iwerr ayeng alhetyek alhek ikwer-angkwerr kweny anem apal anem alhek. (Sa) *Going the wrong way and then getting lost, going along another track. I went to go on the track, but I went the wrong way.*

= tyey[1], rwert

iwerr arem (E)

watch the road for someone to come; wait for somebody to come (arem '*look*')

= tyey arem

iwerr arelhem (E) = **iwerr arem** ◆ Arntety tha akareparem. Ngkwengan ayeng uyarnarl iwerr arelhepelhem, atherrel akaretyek, arntety nhenh. (St) *I am looking after the sick person. I watched the road in vain for you to come so that the both of us could look after this sick person.*

SEE ALSO alkiwerr

iwerrarrkw *n.*

1. gidgee wild orange, narrow-leaf bumble (*Capparis loranthifolia*). Shrub to 3 m high, with rough bark and creamy flowers.

2. the edible fruit of the gidgee wild orange ◆ Mern iwerrarrkw arlkwety-inkwern. Inpa anem menty-irrek anem. (Sa) *They used to eat the gidgee wild orange. I don't know about nowadays, they've given it up.*

= angerterrk

iwerrem throw SEE UNDER **iwem**

iwert (E) *n.*

curly-pod wattle (*Acacia sessiliceps*). A shrub to about 2.5 m high, with narrow leaves, rough bark and curly pods.

CAN SOUND A BIT LIKE awert[2] *'burrowing bettong'*

iwert (E) burrowing bettong SEE UNDER **awert**[2]

iy *part.*

1. Shows that you think something is

distasteful, disgusting or repulsive; 'Yuk!', 'That's terrible!', 'Oh no!' ◆ Anenyerr anetyakenharl nga, nyerr-irretyakenh. Iy! (Sa) *You haven't got any shame, you don't get shamed. That's terrible!*
2. Used in answer to a question in the negative; 'I don't know'.
SEE ALSO inpa, ywek

iylalth (E) march fly SEE UNDER **lyalth**

iylarn (E), **iylarnayt** (E), **lyarnayt** (E), **larnayt** (E) *n.*
1. blue wattle, leather-leaved colony wattle (*Acacia validinervia*). Shrub about 1.5 m high, with smooth white bark and thick leathery bluish green leaves.
2. edible grub from the roots of the blue wattle
= ntwarnengayt

iylarnem (E) get someone's attention SEE UNDER **lyarnem**

iylarnt (E) circular pad for carrying things on the head SEE UNDER **lyarnt**

iylartey (E) green seed pods of the Georgina gidgee SEE UNDER **ilyartey**

iylaw (E) *n.*
1. munyeroo, pigweed, purslane (*Portulaca oleracea*). Fleshy herb that spreads along the ground, has small yellow flowers, pinkish stems and small black seeds.
2. edible seed of the munyeroo. Also referred to as *ntyang iylaw*. ◆ Ntang iylaw. Arlter-arlter wetharl ngkweytek. *Grey-grey one*-arl iylaw. Akemel, panth-warl apek renh lernem lernem lernem, kerl-apemel lernerl-apem, *all right*, aympernem anem renh. Iylaw. (St) *The munyeroo plant has edible seeds. The* ngkweytek *plant is whitish in colour. The* iylaw *plant is greyish. It is picked and the seeds are shaken in the wooden dish, the seeds are picked and then shaken into the dishes. Alright, after that they are yandied. Munyeroo.*
= akat
SEE ALSO ngkweytek

iylayempeylay (E) ribbon grass, spear grass SEE UNDER **lyayepelyay**

iylek (E) prickle, spike, thorn SEE UNDER **lyek**

iylekarr anem (E) get goose pimples or goose bumps SEE UNDER **lyekarr anem**

iylelkenng (E) Sandover lily SEE UNDER **lyelkenng**

iylelth (E) *n.*
leaves that have fallen to the ground
SEE ALSO lyerrk, anwerlarr

iylelty (E) *n.*
Sandover lily, desert lily (*Crinum flaccidum*). A plant with shiny leaves, white flowers and a large inedible onion-like bulb.
= alyerlk-alyerlk, lyelkenng

iylenty (E) swamp kangaroo grass SEE UNDER **lyenty**

Iylenty (E) *n.*
Mosquito Bore, Utopia (Angarapa Aboriginal Land Trust). Location of an outstation.

iylenyenp (E) *n.*
chocolate bush, firebush (*Senna pleurocarpa*). A shrub to about 0.5 m high, with yellow flowers. According to some it has edible white grubs in the roots. ◆ Anteth anem pertipelaw kwerel, arrkeyt-arrkeyt, kel ntang anem ra anem *brown*. Ankerr akwek akwekel aylwerel arlkwem ntang, pertipelaw *too* arlkwem, iylenyenp. (St) *It has yellow flowers and the seeds are brown. Young emus eat the seeds and the flowers of the chocolate bush.*

iyleper (E) thigh SEE UNDER **ulyeper**

iylerl (E) gravel, coarse sand SEE UNDER **lyerl**

Iylerl (E) *n.*
Gibbs Hole (Sandover area)

iylerlkarr (E), **iylwerlkarr** (E) *n.* [RESPECT LANGUAGE]
headband ◆ Iylerlkarr-ayerr arrerna ngwarrekengkw. (Sa) *Put the headband there for your husband [said by a woman to her daughter].*
SEE ALSO tyerlarr

iylernt arrernem (E) heap or pile something up SEE UNDER **lyernt arrernem**

iylka (E) wind SEE UNDER **rlka**

iylker (E) *n.*
newborn baby

iylkerr (E) *n.*
dribble, saliva
= pelh[1], arrelty[2], arrwek
CAN SOUND A BIT LIKE rlkerr *'stretched out', 'spread out'*
iylkerr-iylkerr (E) *n.*
slobbery, dribbly, covered in saliva ◆ Arengk arra iylkerr-iylkerr yanh aywepeyaw, tethet anthekerr! (Sa) *Chase that dog with the slobbery mouth away in case it makes us sick!*
iylkerr thelelhem (E)
dribble, slobber (thelelhem *'leak', 'pour or drip from'*) ◆ Arengk iylkerrant thelelhetyel. (Sa) *The dog is slobbering.*
arreylkerr-iylkerr (E) *n.*
slobbery mouth (arra *'mouth'*) ◆ *Eh*, tyampet atyenhel antywetyalay arreylkerr-iylkerr. (Sa) *Hey, slobbery mouth, don't drink out of my tin.*

iylkerr (E) stretched out, spread out SEE UNDER **rlkerr**

iylkert (E) sick, ill, sickness SEE UNDER **rlkert**

iylkwa (E) *n.*
1. armpit
= lhenp
2. number 7 boomerang, hooked boomerang.

Also referred to as *kayl iylkwa*.
SEE ALSO rlkwa
iylkwelhem (E) push (or 'wash') something down in throat (with water or tea) SEE UNDER **rlkwelhem**
iylkwem (E) foretell; cause someone to have a predictive dream SEE UNDER **rlkwem**
iylkwerr (E) middle, in the middle SEE UNDER **rlkwerr**
iylpa (E) ear, ears SEE UNDER **irlpa**
iylpangkem (E) remember about someone or something SEE UNDER **irlpangkem**
iylpar (E) a type of bush potato SEE UNDER **irlpar**
iylpareth (E) cooperative, helpful SEE UNDER **irlpareth**
iylparrernem (E) show something to someone SEE UNDER **irlparrernem**
iylpart (E) a log SEE UNDER **irlpart**
iylpekernem (E) listen, pay attention SEE UNDER **irlpekernem**
iylpel-irrem (E) *vi.*
forget ◆ Ngkweng-kety ayeng iylpel-irrek iterlaretyang. (Sa) *I forgot all about you.*
iylpel-wem (E), **iylpel-iwem** (E) *vt.*
leave something behind; forget something and leave it behind ◆ Alhemel pert-irrerl-alpemel, ngkwerlp iylpel-wentyek ngkwerlp inerlewetyek. (Sa) *Going and then turning back to get the tobacco that [you] left behind.* ◆ Menkethenh kweny. *Mummy*-ek alhampw — mam uyerrekeng. *No* menkethenh arey *no mum*, alhampw. Alhamp ayeng. *No* aynenkethenh. Akngey ingwerel arey ap ayenh arntarnt-aretyang. Anyentelarl ayenh iylpel-wek. (Sa) *[My] mother is not alive. I've lost my mother — she's passed away. I have no mother and no father still alive. My other fathers don't look after me. One left me behind.*
SEE ALSO irlpa
iylpenkelh-ilem (E) *vt.*
revive someone by blowing in their ears ◆ Pew-ilem iylpa apek, arert apek iylpenkelh-ileman, kel renh akemel anem ilem, ra awem anem, iylpel inngart awem. (St) *You might be able to blow in the ears of someone who is unconscious, to revive them, and then this makes them get up and then they can hear again, with their ears.*
= irlpakert-ilem
SEE ALSO pew-ilem, irlpa
iylpernk (E), **ilpernk** (E) *n.*
fat in the flesh from the thigh of a kangaroo
= apertaynp
SEE ALSO ulyelatanenh, anter tyelh, akepitelh
CAN SOUND A BIT LIKE ilpengk *'gidgee fuchsia bush'*

iylperr ngkwern (E) *n.*
pelvic bone (ngkwern *'bone'*)
iylperrem (E) *vt.*
clear (the ground to make a camp); grade (a road) ◆ *Road*-an iylperretyel. (Sa) *The road is being graded.* ◆ Mer iylperrem ankwa ayntetyek. (Sa) *Clear the place to go to sleep.*
= aketh-ilem, anhwerrem
iylpmerr (E) dew, drop of water SEE UNDER **irnmerr**
iylpmwa (E) word, language SEE UNDER **ulypma**
iylpwer (E) hollow log or tree SEE UNDER **rlpwer**
iylpwer-iylpwer (E) a type of plant with a hollow stem SEE UNDER **rlpwer-rlpwer**
iylpwerr (E) *n.*
button quail (*Turnix velox*)
= atek, aterlkwarr
iylpwerr-iylpwerr (E) *n.*
fontanelle (the soft part on top of a baby's head) ◆ Iylpwerr-iylpwerr kapert atyet-atyet nhelkwer. Iylperr-iylpwerr rlterrk-irretyakenh *that's why* ra akwek antey urrek angkerl-anem, *little bit* angkerl-anem. Nhenh rlterrk-irrem yanhan angka rlterrk anemarl ra angkem. (St) *The fontanelle is that soft part [in the middle] of the head. If the fontanelle hasn't hardened [closed over], then the child can only talk a little bit. When the fontanelle gets hard then the child starts to speak strongly.*
= kapert thelty, atek-kenh, ahey-ahey, thelty-thelty, kwerrk-kwerrk[1]
iyltem (E), **iltyem** (E) *vt.*
1. break or crack something open; hatch out from an egg ◆ Kwart-they arratemel, wal altywer-ilem akwek, iyltemarl ra kwart. Iyltepeyltem kweneng, kel arratenhem anem. (St) *[The chick] comes out of the egg, making a little opening. It cracks the egg open from inside and then hatches out.*
= pelty-ilem
SEE ALSO aterlk-ilem, apert-atwem, peltyem
2. peel bark off a plant or tree ◆ Arntap renh iyltem kel kwaty-warl arrernem arntap. Karntey-artek anem ra irrem, alhwartek. Kel lyek-lyek apek alhewelhem rtety-rtetyarl irrem weth-lkwer. (St) *The bark is peeled off and then it is put into water. Then it goes like Condy's crystals, like blood. Then you wash sores, lumpy skin or things like that with it.* • SEE ALSO akap-rlwem
3. chip something off (flakes from a rock) ◆ Alywek iyltem apwertel. Arrerlp-ilem alanh. (St) *The stone knife is chipped with a stone. Then it is sharpened like that.* • SEE ALSO mpalty-atwem, kek-wem
CAN SOUND A BIT LIKE iltem *'swear or growl'*

iyltelhem (E), **iltyelhem** (E) *vi.*
1. hatch out from an egg ◆ Thep iyltelhem rarrp. Alhek amparr arratepatem, kwer-penh iltya anem ra arratem. Arratenhem anem ra. (St) *The bird hatches out from the egg itself. At first its beak comes out, and after that its claws. Then [its whole body] comes out.*
2. peel off (bark from a tree)
3. chip off (flakes from a rock)
iyltenty (E) beefwood SEE UNDER **ltyenty**
iylwek (E) native pine SEE UNDER **rlwek**
iylwem (E) take something off something SEE UNDER **lywem**1
iylwenpeny (E) clever, smart, good at hunting SEE UNDER **lywenpeny**
iylweper (E) thigh SEE UNDER **ulyeper**
iylwer (E) sand SEE UNDER **urler**
iylwerl-iylwerl (E) *n.*
crooked, bent, round, winding
SEE ALSO amper-amper, arnkwert, arnkwert-arnkwert, irrkert-irrkert, lew-lew, rtapety
iylwerlkarr (E) headband SEE UNDER **iylerlkarr**
iylwernk (E) hook on woomera or spear SEE UNDER **lywernk**
iynpa (E) 'I don't know' SEE UNDER **inpa**
iynpernem (E) winnow seed (rapid sideways movement of coolamon) SEE UNDER **aympernem**
iyntem (E) smell (have a smell) SEE UNDER **intyem**2
iynteng (E) *n.*
rotten, stinking ◆ Atnert ultakemaw, atnertarl arlwar tnek. Ker iyntengarl arlkwek-penh. (Sa) *My stomach is hurting and has swollen up. From eating rotten meat.*
= arntert
SEE ALSO anety, aywek
iynteng-irrem (E) *vi.*
go off, become rotten
= arntert-irrem
SEE ALSO atherrk-atherrk-irrem
iynteng-iynteng (E) *n.*
1. apple bush (*Pterocaulon serrulatum*). Sticky herb avout 60 cm high, with hairy leaves and purplish flowers. When crushed its leaves smell like apples.
2. pintye-pintye, sweet pillow (*Stemodia viscosa*). A strong-smelling sticky herb with purple flowers that grows about 25–50 cm high. • = ntyapentyetyen
3. stink bug
Iynteper (E) *n.*
name of place south of Awertaw, Spring Range area
iynterlp (E) hot ashes or earth (used for cooking or healing) SEE UNDER **ntyerlp**1
iynterlpeny Richard's pipit, black-fronted dotterel SEE UNDER **ntyelpeny**
iynternem (E) smell something SEE UNDER **intyernem**
iynterrem (E) snore SEE UNDER **intyerrem**
iynteth (E), **iyntety** (E) sparks SEE UNDER **ntyeth**
iyntethengeynteth (E) spotted, patterned SEE UNDER **intetyeng-intety**
iyntwarr (E) far, a long way SEE UNDER **rntwarr**
iyntwem (E) facing away from someone or something SEE UNDER **ntywem**2
iyntwernem (E) *vt.*
chop something down, chop a tree
◆ Iyntwernem arna ilepel. (St) *Chopping the tree down with an axe.*
= lywewem
SEE ALSO atwem
iyntweth (E) *n.* [RESPECT LANGUAGE]
raw ◆ Iyntwetharl ahanelh-ilety-alpekaw, iyntweth-ayerr yanhentyak amperneyaw. (Sa) *[The meat] that they took back was raw, and they're going to cook it over there [said by a woman referring to her son-in-law].*
SEE ALSO arlety2
CAN SOUND A BIT LIKE antweth *'white silky stuff inside bush banana'*
iynwart (E) a person's lap SEE UNDER **rnwart**
iynwer (E) bee (or just the queen bee) (?) SEE UNDER aynwer
iynwerr (E) lame, crippled SEE UNDER **rnwerr**
iypmerr (E) dew SEE UNDER **irnmerr**
iytan-ilem (E) *vt.*
mix or stir something up
iytarr-angem (E) lead someone or something along SEE UNDER **tyarr-angem**
iytek (E) loose, slack SEE UNDER **tyek**
iyteny (E) *n.*
flirtation, flirtatious, romance, fancying someone
iyteny-iyteny (E) *n.*
flirtation, flirtatious, romance, fancying someone
iyteny-irrem (E) *vi.*
flirt with someone, desire or fancy someone
◆ Iyteny-irretyang anetyek, mwerr anetyek. (Sa) *Don't flirt, sit down and behave properly.*
= alherrem2
SEE ALSO ahenty-anem, ahenty-irrem
iytenyelengkw (E) *n.*
a flirt, someone who fancies someone ◆ Arelh yanh iytenyelengkw. *That woman is a 'lover girl'.*
= mpweny angerr, mpwenyartw-mpwenyartw
iytenyel arem (E)
flirt, makes eyes at someone
iyter (E) turpentine bush SEE UNDER **tyer**

iyterlarr (E) headband SEE UNDER **tyerlarr**
iyternem (E) limp, limp along SEE UNDER **tyernem**[2]
iyterrk (E) marrying 'wrong way' SEE UNDER **tyerrk**
iyterrty[1] (E) *part.*
really (provides emphasis) ◆ Nthakenh renh atwetyakenh inangkal, ilpelhetyelarl. Ngkwern atwetyakenh perrap inangkal iyterrty ilpelhetyelarl ra arwerlel. (Sa) *He is really clever and can't be beaten because he is protecting himself. He is really invincible and can't be hit because he is shielding himself with a branch.*
SEE ALSO innga[1]
iyterrty[2] *n.*
person (male) ◆ Iyterrty arrer apetyem. (Sa) *The person is coming close.*
SEE ALSO tyerrty, innga[2]
iytert-iytert (E) *n.*
a type of plant (no common name) (*Eremophila obovata*)
iytnem (E) dig, dig for something SEE UNDER **inyem**
iytnmerr (E) dew SEE UNDER **irnmerr**
iytwarem (E) watch someone or something going away SEE UNDER **artwarem**
iytwerr (E) *n.*
sinews going to the eye (?) ◆ Mantharrel utnhem alwerrng iytwerr ltwakenhem, kenh tyerrty ilwemarl. *If a person gets bitten by a death adder and the sinews going to the eye get broken, then they will die.* (?)
iytwerr-iytwerr (E) *n.*
a type of grass

Kk

k+ *n.kin*
A short form of the word for 'elder brother etc.' that precedes other endings. ◆ Kenh artengel-arerleng *might be* **k**elekw apek — *that's* 'ankwernem'. Yatherr anem atwerrem. (M) *And then his brother might step in and back him up, take his side — that's 'ankwernem'. The two of them fight then, the man's brother and the cousin.*
SEE ALSO kak
kak *n.kin*
1. elder brother
2. particular (senior) relations with the same skin as a person's *kak*; for example, their father's older brother's son or their mother's older sister's son. Whether or not a person is a junior or senior sibling to another can be calculated in terms of the relative ages of the parents.
= kely, away
kakey *n.kin*
1. elder brother etc.
2. elder brother [BABY TALK]
kakey angerr-pat
elder brother
kengkw *n.kin*
your *kak* ◆ Kengkw nhakw alhem. (St) *Your brother is going over there.*
kikw (T,E), **keyekw** (W,T) *n.kin*
his/her/their *kak*
kekw (W,T) *n.kin*
1. your *kak*
2. his/her/their *kak*
kenheng *n.kin*
a group of two or more people, at least two of whom are related to each other as *kak*
= kenheng-arey, kenhengart
kenheng-arey (T,E) *n.kin* = **kenheng**
kenhengart (W,T) *n.kin* = **kenheng**
kenheng atherr *n.kin*
a person together with their *kak*
kenkethenh, **kankethenh** *n.kin*
1. having *kak* (still alive)
2. someone who is always with their *kak*
SEE ALSO -ankethenh
keparety *n.kin*
respectful or 'sorry way' of talking about someone's *kak* ◆ Keparety akuny atwetyal menty aney. (St) *Don't hit your poor brother, leave him alone.*
SEE ALSO -parety

kaka (T) *n.* [BABY TALK]
toilet, shit etc.
SEE ALSO ana

kakapwerl *n.*
be ready to shoot or fight (maybe from English 'cock a gun') ◆ Tyerrty map kakapwerl inang anem atwerretyeh. (M) *The people are ready to fight.*

Kakatew (W,T) *n.*
name of a place in the Mt Denison area. Named after Cockatoo Creek. See map p. viii.
SEE ALSO Anartelh

kakelhelh (W,T) *n.*
type of cockatoo

kakepewey *n.*
cockatoo (from English 'cocky boy')
SEE ALSO angkwen

Kal ntheyelkwer, **Kal nthwelker**, **Ntheyelkwer**, **Nthwelker** (E) *n.*
an old type of Anmatyerr language spoken by some in the west of the Anmatyerr area. Some speakers say that this type of Anmatyerr has a 'heavy ' or 'deep' sound. The name seems to be based on the particular pronunciation, in that dialect, of the phrase *kel nthenh-lkwer* 'Okay, where is it' (?). ◆ Angkety twer Ntheyelkwer ina angkem. *The Ntheyelkwer language that they talk has a heavy sound.*

kalapel angem (W,T) *vt.*
carry someone on your back, piggyback someone (angem *'carry', 'take'*) ◆ Kwer akwek kalapel angep-angem. (T) *Piggybacking the little child.*
SEE ALSO ntywel angem

kalawerr (W,T), **kalewerr** (W,T) *n.*
a type of goanna (?)

kalayteng-ayteng (E) black-tailed native-hen SEE UNDER **karlayteng-ayteng**

kalikew *n.*
a camp sheet or piece of canvas (from English 'calico')

kalkareng holly-leaf grevillea SEE UNDER **kelkareng**

kalty *n.*
1. knowing; expert at doing something, clever, knowledgeable ◆ *Batik* tha arrkernetyek ingkwernerl-ayntetyek. Arrkernemel ingkwernetyek. Ingwer kaltyelan arrkernetyang ingkwernay. 'Ngka. Ayeng arrkernelhetyek.' (Sa) *I'll try to paint batik. Those others who are knowledgeable don't have to try first — they can paint. 'Give it to me. I'll try myself out at it.'* ◆ Ingkerneny, alhengk apek aretyenheng tywerreng mer arreng-kenh angey-kenh. Kalty apek anetyenheng. *The next generation might know about sacred things and about their grandparent's and father's land. Maybe they'll get to know about it.*
2. knowing a person, knowing about a thing or how to do something
SEE ALSO inangkal, kapert altywer, kapert arraty, kwerathek, lywenpeny, wetyerretyerr2, weretyerretyerr

kalty-anthem, **kaltyel-anthem** *vt.*
teach (anthem *'give'*) ◆ Anmatyerr tha kalty-anthem yang Anmatyerr angketyeh. (M) *I am teaching him Anmatyerr, so he can speak Anmatyerr.* ◆ Kalty-antherl-apem kwer map, alherl-apemel. 'Arrantherr atyengel-ayel aperlapay, ilerl-apem — atyengel-ayel apetyewarray!' (N) *[I] teach the kids as we go along. 'All you come along with me, and I'll tell you about things as we go — all of you come with me!'* ◆ Anwern kwer map kaltyem anthanthem. (M) *We are teaching the children.*

kalty-anthenh-anthenh, **kaltyel-anthenh-anthenh** (E) *n.*
teacher, pastor

kalty-irrem *vi.*
learn ◆ Lyetant kalty-irretyel, ampa nyerralth. *He's just started learning things [at school], he's very timid.*

kaly-kaly1 (T,E) *n.* [BABY TALK]
1. husband, wife, spouse
2. brother-in-law (note Warlpiri *kalyakalya* 'person in spousal relation with speaker's daughter, or speaker's daughter's husband') ◆ Kaly-kaly ngkwenh yanh apetyem. Kwer-penh 'mpwerney' akem anem ra. *There's your brother-in-law coming. After that he calls him* 'mpwerney'.
SEE ALSO arrkar, mpwern, anew, pantyey, ngwarr

kaly-kaly2 (W,T) *n.*
nauseated, nauseating (from eating too much meat or fat) (note Warlpiri *kalyilpa* 'nauseating smell, sickening odour, nauseating taste, sickening taste')

kaly-kaly-ilem (W,T) *vt.*
make someone feel sick or nauseated ◆ Tyap ankerrmern, mwerr angerr *too*, perrap anter angerr. Tyerrty kaly-kaly iletyeh, arraty. Ankerrmern-areny. (N) *Grubs from the coolibah tree are really good as well, really fatty. It is true that the grubs from the coolibah make people feel nauseated.*
SEE ALSO alyelk-alyelk, alyew-alyew, antewek-antew

kalyeyamp a type of frog (possibly Spencer's burrowing frog) SEE UNDER **alyeyamp**

kalyeyampel SEE UNDER **alyeyamp**

kam (T,E) *n.*
1. seed of the pencil yam, *arlatyey, anwerlarr* (*Vigna lanceolata*) ◆ Kaman renh-antey itniwem pertipelaw *seed* akely-akely weth-arey. Renharl ap anem. Mernan kwenarl. Mern pertipelaw ikwereng antey *seed* anem. Pertipelaweng-tyel antey, kam. Kaman ilem. (Sa) *'Kam' is what those flowers, those little seeds, are called. The edible part of the plant is underground. The seeds come after the plant has flowered, and they are called 'kam'.*
2. edible white pods of the pencil yam (found under the ground)
= arratwek

kamern (W,T) *n.*
1. uncle (mother's brother)
2. uncle (mother's brother) [BABY TALK]
◆ 'Kamern' akem kwerelant, kenh artwel akenh renh 'angerrety' ilem. 'Angerrety apetyay, nhenh-warlay.' 'Angerrety' akem, *he don't* 'kamern' anpernerl. (M) *Only children use the term 'kamern', whereas on the other hand men call [their mother's brother]* 'angerrety'. *'Come here* angerrety, *come here.' They call them* 'angerrety', *not 'kamern'.*
3. father's sister's husband
4. brother's daughter's husband. If a person calls someone *kamern* then they will be called *ampaty-ampaty* or *ampwek* in return.
◆ Kamernan ilem amwek-kenh *brother*. *'Kamern' is what you call your mother's brother.*
◆ Anywek awenhwek aperlekw inang anperl-alhek. Apetyek inang angketyeh kamerneh. (M) *Then the father and auntie and grandma set out again. They all went to speak to the child's uncle.*
SEE ALSO amarl

kamparwengk (E) *n.*
1. white-necked heron (*Ardea pacifica*)
2. white-faced heron (*Ardea novaehollandiae*)
◆ Kamparwengkan wetharl alha arlpenty, lterr arlpenty. *Blue one*-arl arrpenh, arrpenhan arlter. Ura kwert-apenyarl arrpenh. (St) *The heron is that one with the long beak and the long legs. Some are blue and some are white. Others are a greyish colour.*
= ulamp-areny, ntyar, arlkwenth

kampely[1] (W,T) *n.*
1. brain ◆ Ker kapert tyarp-ilem kampely arlkwetyenheng. (N) *The head is split open and then the brains are eaten.* ◆ Kampely ngkwengenheng ntwang iterretyeh mwerr. (St) *You think clearly when you use your brains.*
= akwerrng
2. crown of the head

ker kampely (W,T)
edible brains of some animals ◆ Ker kampely arlkwetyeh. (M) *Eating the brains.*
SEE ALSO aka

kampely[2] (E) *n.*
1. mother's mother, granny ('private', own, closely related — from the same country as a person's actual granny)
2. the country belonging to a person's *kampely* ◆ Kampely rarl apmerinparl nyany akemarl. Apmer then antey. Kampely. Kampely nyany atyenh. (St) *Your own close granny is called 'kampely', and the country where she comes from is called 'kampely' as well.*
3. own, personal or private possession [SOME SPEAKERS] ◆ Mwetek atyenh kampely. (Sa) *My private car.*
SEE ALSO ngwenyarr, aka

kamperarrp (W,T) *n.*
1. desert raisin (variety found in sandhill country) (*Solanum centrale*). Small plant about 30 cm high with purple flowers and fruit that is yellow and sticky when ripe (note Warlpiri *kampurarrpa*). The Anmatyerr regard the two varieties of *Solanum centrale* as being closely related. *Kamperarrp* has bigger fruits than *katyerr*.
2. the edible fruit of the desert raisin. Also referred to as *mern kamperarrp*. ◆ Wal, anwern walyel akin arrawelh-ilem, renh twenyan antyerrk, twenyarl irrek. *Bucket*-warn arrernem theweyet arlkwarlkwerl-alpemel, arlkwerl-apemel theweyet yenh arlkwerl-apemel. Mern kamperarrp, arlpang akwekarley. Katyerr rntwarr-lkwer, akern-lkwer. Alkey angerr. Arlkwenh-arlkwenh. Anganekarl. Katyerr, kamperarrp. (N) *Well, we sweep them together with a branch, the fruits that have become dry. We put them in a bucket and go along eating the sweet fruit. The* kamperarrp *has small leaves. In comparison the* katyerr *plant is taller and more erect. They're both edible. They both came from the country,* katyerr *and* kamperarrp.
SEE ALSO katyerr

kampeth *n.*
canvas (used for painting) (from English 'canvas') ◆ Arelhel ngkwernem Anengkerr kampeth-warn. (T) *The woman is painting Dreaming designs on the canvas.*

kamwerl *n.*
camel (*Camelus dromedarius*) (from English '*camel*')
= kawartewar

kanaweylker (E) *n.*
cockatiel, quarrion (*Nymphicus hollandicus*)
= aneweylker, arew-arew, newingk

kanem (W,T), **ikanem** (E) *vi.*
1. avoid particular relations
2. avoid talking about someone who has passed away ◆ Ikanem ayeng mey-mey-kety. (St) *I avoid my son-in-law.*
= kerrem

ikanelhem (E) *vi.*
avoid particular relations ◆ *Law*-akert ilkwarl ayengan, ikanelheyarl mwey-mwey-ketyarl. Arlengel amper-irrerlanetyek mwerekaty, ikanelhem. (Sa) *I've got that important Law, and I avoid my son-in-law. I avoid him and go the long way round.*

kanern-irrem *vi.*
be sneaky, shy away from doing what is asked of you (from English 'cunning')
SEE ALSO anwernt-irrem, mweny-irrem, anngarenty-irrem

kangkew *n.* [BABY TALK]
kangaroo (from English 'kangaroo')
SEE ALSO aherr

kank (W,E) *part.* [RESPECT LANGUAGE]
already, before ◆ Kank-ayerrel ahanerrekety ampeny-ayerr anem yanhentyak tawertant anem. (Sa) *They've already gone and their camp over there is empty now.*
SEE ALSO kel

kank-antey (E) *part.* [RESPECT LANGUAGE]
finished, (something) has already happened ◆ Kank-antey ahanerrek. (Sa) *They've already gone.*
SEE ALSO kel-antey

kanng anem (W) *vi.*
have something stuck in the throat ◆ Ker apek mern apek kanng anem ahentyel-arleng. (M) *The meat or the food might be stuck in the [person's] throat.*

kanth-atwem *vt.*
hammer, bang or knock something in; tighten something (e.g. axe handle) ◆ Parrek, *post* apek kanth-atwerl-apem, parrek nheng mparemel. (T) *Making a fence and going along banging in the posts.*
= arlarl-ilem
SEE ALSO akak-atwem[1], rlterrk-ilem

kantharlkw (W,E) *n.*
mulga snake, king brown snake (*Pseudechis australis*)
= atetherr arlkwenh, arreperlp, ikwelengk, alhingk, tyamparl

kanty[1] *n.*
1. edge or tip of something ◆ Aleny kanty. *The tip of the tongue.*
SEE ALSO itep, akwerr[1], iter, arrethaker
2. a small part of something ◆ Kanty war arlkway anengk-hety, map-hety. Akern-penh war antyway, artang-ilay. (M) *Just eat a bit of it, because there's lots of people. Just drink a bit and leave some for the others.*
3. tail (of some animals); tails with a tail-bone. Some Anmatyerr people say that birds and fish do not have *kanty*. Also referred to as *ker kanty*. ◆ Kanty mwatan arlewatyerr. (Sa) *Goannas have short fat tails.* ◆ Ker kanty tha tiwem tyepalel. (St) *I am cleaning the burnt hair off the kangaroo tail with a stick.* ◆ Pwel-pwel-penh ingkakert anem irrem — kantyan kelarl ikwerenh. Pwel-pwel weth kanty-akert ra anem, wal ingka atherr, iltya atherr. Kel *tail* apek arrangkw anem. (St) *The tadpole gets legs — it already has a tail. Those tadpoles have tails, and two hind legs and two forelegs. And then the tail disappears.*
4. younger, younger generations • SEE ALSO intert

iltya kanty, iltyang kanty (W,T)
finger tip (iltya '*finger*')

iltya kanty-rnem (E) *n.*
fingers (iltya '*finger*'; -rnem '*plural*')

ingka kanty, ingkang kanty (W,T)
end of toe (ingka '*foot*', '*toe*')

ingka kanty-rnem (E)
toes (ingka '*foot*', '*toe*'; -rnem '*plural*')

arnang kanty (W,T)
top of a tree (arnang '*plant*', '*tree*')

kanty-kanty *n.*
the very top of a tree ◆ Kanty-kanty-warl antyep-antyem arnewarl, akern kanty-kanty-warl. (St) *Climbing to the very top of the tree, high up to the very top.*
SEE ALSO waly

kantyeny (T,E) *n.*
1. the rest or remainder of something
2. the last in a group of siblings

kantyeny-ayerr (E) *n.* [RESPECT LANGUAGE]
young fellas, young men

aleny kanty
1. tip of the tongue (aleny '*tongue*') ◆ Aleny kantyel war tywen apek anep-anem. (St) *There might be a sore right on the tip of the tongue.*
2. (speaking) in a high tone of voice, (speaking) deceitfully (?) ◆ Aleny kanty warel angkep-angkem, akern-antey. Ahel apekarl irrek *or* iltekarl apek, aleny kanty warel angkep-angkem akern war. Mwerr-arrpantey. (St) *Speaking with the tip of the tongue, speaking high. Maybe because you are angry or because*

someone swore at you, talking with the end of the tongue, up high. Not really properly. ◆ Aleny kanty wararl angkep-angkem. *Might don't like* apek atyeng, mwerr-arrpantey, ra *still* ilkelhetyakenh apek *don't like me. Just speaking a bit deceitfully. Maybe the person doesn't like me, and they pretend to say the right things, but they don't like me all the same.* (?)
kwaty kanty (T)
1. running water on the side of the creek (kwaty *'water'*)
2. shallow water ◆ Kwer map kwaty kantyek irrpem. (T) *The kids are swimming in the shallow water.* • SEE ALSO kwaty arntay

kanty[2] *n.*
marijuana, cannabis, ganga, ganja (from English 'ganga'/'ganja')

kantyengarr (W,T), **kanyengarr** (E) *n.*
metal chisel, adze. Made from the leaf spring of a car. These are distinct from *tyalangk* and *anker*[1], which are made by attaching a stone chip to a wooden handle with spinifex resin. ◆ Artwel kantyengarr mpwarem arrpetyek panth. (T) *The man makes an adze to carve the wooden dish with.*

SEE ALSO tyalangk, anker[1], arlarnt, kwempalth

kap-ayerr (E) *n.* [RESPECT LANGUAGE]
hat (from English 'cap')
SEE ALSO mwekart

kaperl (T,E) *n.*
central netted dragon lizard (*Ctenophorus nuchalis*)
= kelyaw, irnar

kaperl-kaperl (T,E) *n.*
Australian (Richard's) pipit (*Anthus novaeseelandiae*) (?)
= aleraperap

kaperlantarlant (E) *n.*
a type of bird, perhaps red-browed pardalote (*Pardalotus rubricatus*) ◆ Kaperlantarlantel utern ilem. Utern ap ra iletyel. Utern arrer anem ileman ra. Akely, *yellow one* akely. Uternek angkerl-anem kaperlantarlant. Ileman ra, 'Utern arrer kwenh.' (Sa) *The* kaperlantarlant *bird tells you that the summer is coming, that the hot time is close. It is small and yellow. It talks to the summer. It says, 'The summer is close'.*

kaperrkwelt (E) *n.*
a type of python (?). Also known as *ker kaperrkwelt.*
SEE ALSO ilperletyewenh, uney

kapert atwenh-atwenh (W,T) stick insect, mantis SEE UNDER **kapert atwenh**

kapert[1], **kapwert** (T,E) *n.*
1. head ◆ Kapert artelhenhem, twernel inngerr ampekety. (N) *[You] cover your head as you go along in case the sun burns your face.* ◆ Alyep arrernem kapert-warn kwaty angernetyek. (T) *The head ring is put on the head to carry water.*
2. Goes with words that describe states of mind. • SEE ALSO kapert arraty, kapert altywer
3. hair ◆ Kapert kelh-kelh alhewelhety-kweny kapert. (M) *Matted hair is hair that hasn't been washed.*
4. the top part of the sugarbag or native bees' hive, which is made up of compacted yellow pollen. Also referred to as *ngkwarl kapert* or *rltwamp kapert.* ◆ Kapert arlka ingkerr anwern arlkwetyart. (N) *We used to eat all of it, the top part of the sugarbag as well.* ◆ Arwengalker kapert-akert — karntewarr-artek ra anem kapert. Mwerr-angker arlkwem renh. *The sugarbag has a part called 'kapert' — it's like yellow ochre [in colour]. It's good to eat.*
5. engine; the 'head' of a car. Also referred to as *mwetek kapert.*
kapert aketh
bald, shaved head, no hair (aketh *'open', 'clear'*) ◆ Artwang yanh kapert aketh, akelhekarl. (T) *That man has no hair after he cut it off.*
= kapert pweley, kapert ather-ather
kapert ather-ather (W,T) = **kapert aketh** (ather-ather *'flat'*)
kapert pweley = **kapert aketh** (pweley *'bald'*)
kapert twengk (W)
short hair (twengk *'short'*)
kapert kelh-kelh
knotted or matted hair (kelh-kelh *'knotted or matted hair'*)
= akalangkw-alangkw, aylep-aylep, akaylep-aylep
kapert aywang (W,T)
grey-headed (aywang *'old', 'grey'*) ◆ Kapert aywa anem ampemaw. (St) *Now [she] is going grey.*
kapert tywelker (W)
yellowish or blond hair (tywelker *'white'*)
kapert ahey-ahey (W)
fontanelle (the soft part on top of a baby's head)
= kapert thelty, atek-kenh, iylpwerr-iylpwerr
kapert thelty (W) = **kapert ahey-ahey** (thelty *'soft'*)
kapert ngkwern (T,E)
skull (ngkwern *'bone'*)

kapert arraty
knowledgeable or clever, a person who has good ideas (arraty *'straight', 'correct'*)
◆ Mwerrarl angkep-angkem yanh, kapert arraty, iterlarenty mwerr. (St) *That person over there is speaking well, they are knowledgeable and have good ideas.*
kapert altywer
1. knowledgeable; clever; a person who has good ideas, someone who learns quickly, brainy (altywer *'open'*) ◆ Arelh yanh kapert altywer anthwerram. (T) *That woman is really clever.*
2. sick from traditional curse or evil
◆ Kapwert altywer, nheng arrentyelarl altywer-ilek, aretharr urntemel. (T) *[The person] is sick because the evil spirit made a hole in their head when they were standing in the north wind.*
kapert rawen-irrem
have a headache; feel dizzy (from English 'round')
kapert arntem
have a headache; feel drowsy (arntem *'ache'*)
◆ Kapert ayeng arntem, katyerr apek tepwerl-akert tharl arlkwek, kapert anem ayeng arntem, ahelhel iletyakenh. (St) *I have a headache after eating bush raisins that still had a bitter coating on them because they hadn't been cleaned on the ground.*
kapert angerr (W,T) *n.*
1. a type of prickle (*Sclerolaena cornishiana*) (lit. 'big head')
= atetherr-atetherr, kapert-kapert
SEE ALSO lyek-lyek, kapert-kapert
2. dwarf bearded dragon (*Pogona minor*) (lit. 'big head') • = tyapantarr
kapert-kapert *n.*
a type of prickle (*Sclerolaena cornishiana*)
= atetherr-atetherr, kapert angerr
SEE ALSO kapert angerr, lyek
kapert atwenh (W,T),
kapert atwenh-atwenh (W,T) *n.*
stick insect, mantis (*Eurycnema osiris*) (lit. 'head-hitter') ◆ Unta anpem yanh yenh *and* kapert ngkwenhem *headache*-irrem. Kapert atwenh-atwenh nta anpemel. (M) *If you touch the stick insect then you'll get a headache. If you touch that stick insect.*
= antyekanty
kapert rnter-rnter (E) *n.*
red-capped robin (*Petroica goodenovii*) (lit. 'red head')
= akarl-atwerrey, alywerr-alywerr, uneng atyetyek

kapert2 *n.*
dragonfly (from English 'helicopter' or 'copter')
= urewap-imperreny
SEE ALSO kapert atwenh
kapertey *n.*
cup of tea (from English 'cup of tea')
kapertey-taym *n.*
tea-break
SEE ALSO arlpelh, tey
Kapety (W,T) *n.*
name of a place in the Pine Hill area. See map p. viii.
Kapetyew (W) *n.*
name of place near Anmatjira Range and east of Lander Bore
kapwert (T,E) head SEE UNDER **kapert**1
karerrem (W) *vi.*
froth (at the mouth); dribble, saliva accumulate in mouth ◆ Pelh karerrem arrakert. *[His] mouth is frothing [with] saliva.*
SEE ALSO arrelty
karl-irrkwely-irrkwely (T,E) domestic turkey SEE UNDER **kart-irrkwely-irrkwely**
karlarrangkern (E) *n.*
tree frog (*Litoria* spp.)
= antyetyerr, larrangkern
karlayteng-ayteng (E), **kalayteng-ayteng** (E) *n.*
black-tailed native-hen (*Gallinula ventralis*)
◆ Karlayteng-ayteng apek — *chook-chook black one* — irrkert-irrkert. *Tail* ikwerenh. Irrkertelherl-alhem *tail* ikwerenh, irrkert-irrkert anem untem. (St) *The black-tailed native-hen — that black one that looks like a chook — has a tail that sticks out. It sticks its tail in the air and then runs off.*
= narremantyerr
SEE ALSO angkeparr, kart-irrkwely-irrkwely, lhekethatethat, ngkwern rnter-rnter
karlkwem *vt.*
bite into something; munch or chew something ◆ Arengkel karlkwem ker ngkwern. (T) *The dog is chewing the bone.* ◆ Amwelyan karlkwem rtemarlel. Inemel, karlkwemel anem. Iteth-antey rtemarl karlkwem. (Sa) *The cadney lizard is bitten on the back of the neck. [You] get it, and bite it on the back of the neck while it is still alive.* ◆ Alewatyerr ngkwern arengkel karlkwep-arlkwem. (St) *The dog is chewing on the goanna bone.*
= akakwem
SEE ALSO arlkwem, arrerlpem
karlkwelhem *vi.*
1. bite part of yourself
2. poke tongue out between teeth (a gesture

made to little babies) ◆ Ntwang aleny karlkwelhem kwer akwek arem angkemel. (T) *When you see a baby talking you poke your tongue out between your teeth.*

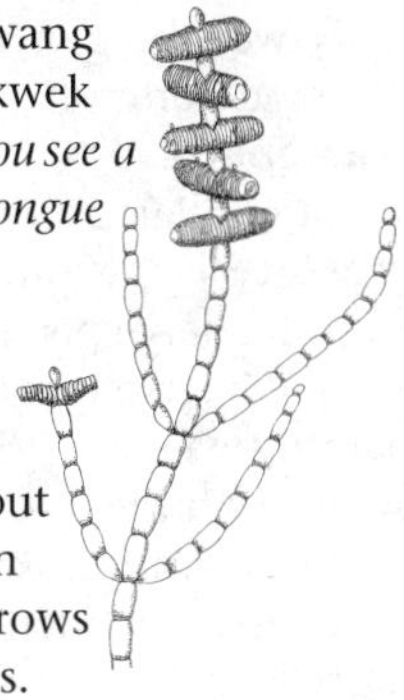

karnkw (W,T) *n.*
1. mungilypa, claypan samphire (*Tecticornia verrucosa*). Fleshy plant about 25 cm high with grey-green or purplish green stems. Grows in moist or salty conditions. Has edible grub in roots. ◆ Karnkw awantyetyam aketyam, awantyetyam, panth-warl iletyam, kwenty-kwenty angernetyam mer-warn, merelam athety-alpemel awantyetyam. (N) *We used to pick the* karnkw *seeds and eat them, heap up the wooden dishes and take the seeds back to camp to grind them up.* ◆ Arrpenh apel *medicine*, karnkw arrpenh. Rrweyam yanh, karnkw arrpenh, alhewelhenhelhenh. (N) *Another sort of* karnkw *is a medicine. That one is a male plant, the* karnkw *that is used as a washing medicine.* ◆ Rrweyan *medicine* alhewetyamelhem, alhewelhetyamarl aketyam. *Salt water* kwa karnkw yanh, alhewelhetyart mernt perrap nhenh ngkernetyenheng. (N) *The male plant is a medicine that is collected and used for washing yourself. It is salty and is used as a wash when people are really sick.*
2. slender glasswort (*Sclerostegia tenuis*)

karnt[1] (T,E) *n.*
a crack in the ground caused by a tuber or root underneath ◆ Nhek-antey, karntek apety-alpa kwenh angernetyek. (Sa) *Here is where the ground is cracked — come back and dig [here].*
= urrper, ahatyerr
karnt-wem (T,E) *vt.*
(tuber or root) make the ground crack and lift up ◆ Anatyel karnt-wem, urrper-wem then. Tyap anyemaytel urrper-wem arrpem karnt-wem arrpem. (Sa) *Bush potatoes make the ground crack. Witchetty grubs do as well.*
karnt anyenem (T,E) = **karnt-wem**
= tenh anyenem, urrper anyenem, ahatyerr-wem

karnt[2] (W,T) *n.*
circular pad for carrying things on the head ◆ Karntel kwaty angernewarretyart, urnel. (T) *[People] used to carry water in wooden dishes on the carrying pad.*
= lyarnt
SEE ALSO alyep

karntewarr, karntawarr *n.*
1. yellow ochre ◆ *Yellow one* irntang ilem 'karntawarr' tyerrtyel. Arlkenyek akin *use*-em-ilem rlpwa, karntawarr, tywelker, ntyengwenty. (T) *Aboriginal people call the yellow rock 'karntewarr'. It's used as well for making ceremonial designs, along with* rlpwa, tywelker *and* ntyengwenty *[red ochre and white ochres].*
= marlalperr, arrkeyt
SEE ALSO rlpwa, arwethenp, atywerlk, artep arlpenty, ngwenty-ngwenty
2. yellow colour
3. fifty dollar note [SOME SPEAKERS] • SEE ALSO arlewatyerr

karntey *n.*
Condy's crystals (from English 'Condy') ◆ Arntap renh iyltem kel kwaty-warl arrernem arntap. Karntey-artek anem ra irrem, alhwartek. Kel lyek-lyek apek alhewelhem rtety-rtetyarl irrem weth-lkwer. (St) *The bark is peeled off and then it is put into water. Then it goes like Condy's crystals, like blood. Then you wash sores or lumpy skin with it.*

karr *n.*
awake ◆ Karrarl intem artwekety. (T) *Lying awake because of the men.*
= atyek
CAN SOUND A BIT LIKE akarr *'liquid honey'*
karr-irrem *vi.*
wake up
= atyek-irrem
CAN SOUND A BIT LIKE akarr-irrem *'gather together'*
karr-ilem *vt.*
wake someone up
= akemelh-ilem, atyekelh-ilem
CAN SOUND A BIT LIKE akarr-ilem *'sweep things together'*

Karrenyarr (T) *n.*
name of hill north-east of Ti Tree town.

Karrwerlereny (E), **Akarralwereny** (E), **Karrwerleny** (E) *n.*
1. Karrwerlereny language. An Arandic dialect spoken to the east of the Plenty River area and in the Harts Range area.
2. Karrwerlereny person or people
= Akarr
SEE ALSO Kityarr

kart[1] (W,T) *n.*
1. faeces, shit, excreta, droppings, poo ◆ Kart lthenp kwer akwek. (M) *The little child is covered with shit.* ◆ Aneperrk kart twer map-akert iperl-apem. (T) *The intestines have solid bits of shit in them that are squeezed out.*
2. bitter seeds inside some fruits ◆ Kik-wem, kart wem, mern kart wem, *clean*-em-ilem

mern anakety rwel anem item. Arlkwem antem renh. (N) *The anakety fruits are split open and then the bitter seeds are cleaned out carefully. Then they are cooked and eaten.*
3. intestines, guts ◆ Kart ipay! *Clean out the guts!*
4. A general word for guts that goes before a particular term for part of the guts. ◆ Ker kart lyep-lyep atyeng anthang! (St) *Give me some intestine meat!*
= ana
kart tyarrp (W,T), **kart altywer** (W,T)
anus, arsehole (tyarrp *'crack', 'gap'*; altywer *'hole'*)
kart arnngem (W,T)
clean out guts (arnngem *'wipe'*)
kart ltwakem (W,T), **kart inkem** (W,T)
fart ◆ Kart inkem nyerrelay. (M) *It's shameful to fart.*
= atna rltwar-rnkem, atnernkem

kart2 *n.*
playing cards ◆ Thangemeh terlem-iley kart? (M) *Will I deal the cards?* ◆ Ayeng alhem kartel arrken-irretyeh. (M). *I'm going to go and play cards.*
= parlperrp
SEE ALSO kwernt1, peyenat

kart-irrkwely-irrkwely (W,T), **kart-irrkwelh-irrkwelh** (T), **karl-irrkwely-irrkwely** (T,E) *n.*
1. domestic turkey [SOME SPEAKERS] ◆ Ker kart-irrkwely-irrkwely warlpelel arlkwenh-arlkwenh. (T) *White people eat turkeys.*
= urrkely-urrkely
2. black-tailed native-hen (*Gallinula ventralis*)
• SEE ALSO narremantyerr, angkeparr, karlayteng-ayteng, lhekethatethat, ngkwern rnter-rnter

kartak (W,T), **kartakw** (W,T) *n.*
billycan (note Warlpiri *kartaku*)
= tyampet

kartamp (W,T) *n.*
stone knife ◆ Kartampel ker aherr aketyart. (M) *Kangaroo meat was cut up with stone knives.*
SEE ALSO apwert antha, alywek, inkwartety, irntarlter, irntang arlter, werlamp

Kartaty (W) *n.*
name of a waterhole and hill north-west of Yuelamu (Mt Allan) community

karteng *n.*
short ◆ Karteng anter angerr weth apetyepetyem. (St) *That short fat person is coming.* ◆ Kartengarl nhenhaw — arlpenty-awaty inay. (St) *This one is short — get one that is a bit longer.*
= twengk
SEE ALSO urtety

kartepel *n.*
caterpillar, grub (from English 'caterpillar')

Kartety (W,T), **Kaytety** (E) *n.*
1. Kaytetye person or people
2. Kaytetye language

kartey (W) *n.*
non-Aboriginal, European, white person (note Warlpiri *kardiya*)
SEE ALSO alhernter, mperlker, warlpal, tywelker

katety *n.*
bullet (from English 'cartridge') ◆ Katety antha, ker atyerrety-alhetyeh. (M) *Give me some bullets, I'm going hunting.*
= pwelert
SEE ALSO annga

kathet *n.*
video or audio cassette (from English 'cassette')

kathip (E) *n.*
1. gall on bloodwood, *arrkernk*; bush coconut, bloodwood apple [SOME SPEAKERS]. Made by the female of a type of wasp (*Cystococcus pomiformis*). ◆ Mern kathip arrkernkel lyapem. (Sa) *The bush coconut grows on the bloodwood tree.*
= mangarrey, arrkwerlperlp, arrkipangkwarl
2. wasp larvae inside gall on bloodwood ◆ Ngkwarl kathip arlkwem. (Sa) *The sweet wasp larvae inside the bush coconut are edible.*

katy *n.* [BABY TALK]
desert raisin (*Solanum centrale*)
SEE ALSO katyerr

katyar (W,T) *n.*
small, high wispy clouds (note Warlpiri *kajara*) ◆ Katyar awelhem akern-angkwarr. *Right* kwatyem irremey, anhemem kwaty. (N) *The* katyar *clouds form high up in the sky. Then it rains.*
SEE ALSO artarwerr, ankert1, urrarl, inewarr

katyelarr (W,T) *n.*
tool, made from an emu shinbone or from a stick, which is used for cleaning the bitter black seeds out of *Solanum chippendalei* fruits ◆ Anakety kart pemel wetyam, katyelarrel. (M) *The bush tomato fruits are cleaned out with the* katyelarr *tool, then the seeds are thrown away.*
SEE ALSO arrert, anakety

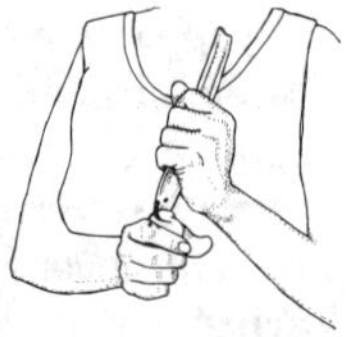

katyemap-ilem *vt.*
catch up with someone or something (from English 'catch them up') ◆ Aherr ingkanterl-

apekeeey katyemap-iletyeh-atety. Weth rang intek mpep, rang aweth kweny-rteh ra ingkantety-alhek. *'Eh* lyetenyam mpaty nhenh kwenh.' (M) *He kept on tracking [the kangaroo] till he caught up with it. He slept again and then in the daytime followed it further. 'Hey, these tracks are fresh,' he said.*

katyerr *n.*

1. desert raisin (*Solanum centrale*). Small plant about 30 cm high with purple flowers and fruit that is yellow and sticky when ripe.

2. western nightshade (*Solanum coactiliferum*). Small plant about 35 cm high, with grey-green leaves, purple flowers and yellow fruits.

3. the edible fruits of these plants ◆ Yerrakwerr apek tha kwakwel anem inerl-anem. Katyerr akerl-anem kwakwel, arternpel akerl-anetyek. (St) *I really enjoy collecting bush onions. I like picking bush raisins, picking them carefully.* ◆ Kapert ayeng arntem, katyerr apek tepwerl-akert tharl arlkwek, kapert anem ayeng arntem, ahelhel iletyakenh. (St) *I have a headache after eating bush raisins that still had a bitter coating on them because they hadn't been cleaned on the ground.*

katyerr kwart *n.*
fresh fruit of desert raisin (kwart *'egg'*)

katyerr alha *n.*
dry fruit of desert raisin (alha *'nose'*)

katyerr tweny (W,T), **katyerr uteny** (E)
dry fruit of desert raisin

katywetarr (W,T) *n.*

1. pencil yam (narrow leaf variety) (?) (*Vigna lanceolata* var. *filiformis*). Creeping plant with bright green leaves, yellow flowers and edible roots.

2. edible root of the pencil yam (narrow leaf variety) ◆ Katywetarr nyetyart kwen angerr angernemel inyetyart katywetarr renh. Katywetarr *self* akin lpwayel anem lpway-areny mern rtwatyert. (N) *[We] used to dig the* katywetarr *yams from really deep in the ground. The* katywetarr *yam is separate [from other yams] and it grows in creeks.*
= anwerlarr
SEE ALSO arlatyey, arnamp

kaw-kaw *n.*
crow (*Corvus bennetti*) (from English 'caw caw' or 'crow crow'). The usual word for crow, *angerl*, is *kwementyay*.
= kway-kway
SEE ALSO angerl, angep, angank

kawartewar (W,T) *n.*
camel (*Camelus dromedarius*) (note Warlpiri *kawartawara*'. This word is used because the word 'camel', or *kamwerl*, is *kwementyay*.)
= kamwerl

kayl (T,E) *n.*
boomerang ◆ Rwemeny-irrem ayeng alakenh, apwert-kety, *or* kayl-kety. (St) *I am dodging to avoid rocks, or boomerangs.* ◆ Athemewek tha kaylel. (St) *I threw the boomerang and missed.*
= alyang, aylayl

kayl iylkwa (E)
number 7 boomerang, hooked boomerang
= alyang rlkwang, aylayl iylkwa, iylkwa[1]

kayl ulyeper (E), **kayl iylweper** (E)
a type of boomerang (curved shape) (ulyeper *'thigh'*)
= alyang lyweper

kayl arrethaker (E)
outer sharp edge (or end) of a boomerang (arrethaker *'edge or side'*)
= aylayl arrethaker

kayl ilperr (E)
inner edge of boomerang (inner edge of curve) (ilperr *'flat'*)

kayleng-kayl (E) *n.*
pretend or toy boomerang ◆ Alkwerteng-alkwert ina mpwaretyam ampa arrken-irrerretyek, werrerl-anetyek, alyaperel werrerl-anetyek, kayleng-kayl, alyaperel, kalyel-arrpantey. (St) *The children used to make toy shields to play with, to use when they were throwing pretend boomerangs at each other.*
= alyang-alyang

kayltwelth (E) *n.*
toothache
= aytwelth
SEE ALSO arranyenganyeng

kayltwelth-akert (E) *n.*
having a toothache
= aytwelth-akert

Kaytety (E) Kaytetye person or people SEE UNDER **Kartety**

kek-wem, kik-wem (W,T) *vt.*
peel the skin off fruit or the bark off a stick; shell an egg ◆ Kik-wey ayenp arnang artety ayenp-penh. Ayenp iweyaw, yarr-wetyenheng. Ayenp renhan wetyeh, ayenp-amparr, yarram wetyenheng. (P) *The bark is peeled off the mulga. It is thrown away before the stick is scraped smooth. First of all the bark is discarded and then the [stick] is scraped smooth.* ◆ Mern yerrakwerr kekarl-werl-anem iltyel, arlter mpwaremel. Kel mern

arlkwetyenheng antem. (T) *The bush onions are peeled by hand, so that you can see the white bulb inside. Then the bulb is eaten.*
= ikewem

kekart (T), **akikart** (E) *n.*
sulky, in a huff, upset ◆ Akikartel unta iwerl-alhek ker apek atyengety. (St) *You were sulky with me and you left the meat at home.* ◆ Map ilerrirrek. Kwer-penh rang kekart alhek. Angwerl-irremel angkep apety-alpetyenh. (T) *Some people were talking. After that he went off upset. He'll return when he cools off.*
SEE ALSO arnkely, kewarr
kekart-irrem (T), **akikart-irrem** (E) *vi.*
get sulky, be in a huff, get upset about something ◆ Amerneng apek kereng kekart-irrem. Wal, arnkely anem ra anem. (T) *She is getting sulky over food or meat. Well, then she sits there in a huff.*
SEE ALSO arnkely-irrem, kewarr-irrem
kekartem-ilem (T) *vt.*
make someone wild, upset or angry

kekw SEE UNDER **kak** 'elder brother etc.'

kel *part.*
1. 'Okay', 'Alright', 'Ready' (often in response to a question about how things are going)
2. something is finished or completed; something has already happened ◆ Kel ker ampeng anemew. *The meat is already cooked.* ◆ Awely mernem, awely arlkeny-akert kel-akert, mernelhem. 'Kelaw, awely-akertam ayeng anem kwenh, kelaw awely kelarl wek-akertam ayeng anem kwenh.' (N) *Showing the women's ceremony, [the woman] who already has the ceremonial designs on shows herself. 'I already have the designs on, I've already been painted up.'*
3. and then (something else happened), well then (something else happened) ◆ Angkwey anetyam aherr akwerrk-akert. Kel yatherr alherrek atherrk arlkwetyeh menheng. (M) *A long time ago there lived a kangaroo with her joey. Then the two of them used to go together to eat grass.*
kelakey (W,T), **kelakwey** (E) *part.*
have you done it already? ◆ 'Kelakwey tha arlkwek?' *Another one might say*, 'Ya, ingkerrek unta arlkwek'. (St) *'Have I eaten already?' Another person might say, 'Yes, you ate the lot'.* ◆ Kelakey nta tywernek pelangket mwetekay-warn? (T) *Have you already put the blankets in the car?* ◆ Kelakey ntwa inek arnang lweren? (M) *Did you already get that thing?*
kel-antey (E) *part.*
something is finished or completed; 'Okay, it's finished'
= kelepenh
kelepenh *part.* = **kel-antey** ◆ Tha renh atwetyek anek, kelepenhay — athemel tha atwek. (St) *I was going to hit her, but it's finished now — I hit at her and missed.* ◆ Kelepenh nta antywekarl. (T) *You have already drunk it.* ◆ 'Kelepenham unta?' 'Ya, kel tharl arlkwek kwenh.' (T) *'Have you finished?' 'Yes, I have eaten.'*
kel mwerr
'Good'; 'Okay', 'Everything is fine'
kel anay
'Leave it', 'Forget it' (said to settle people down) ◆ Kel anay, menty. *Forget about it, leave it.*
kel-kety *part.*
An expression used for telling someone to hurry up because something might happen; 'Okay we're ready' (something is about to happen soon). ◆ Kel-kety alhetyek parrp. (Sa) *Come on, let's hurry up and go.* ◆ Kel-ketyaw, arrer anem ra apetyewarrem-kety. (St) *Hurry up, they're getting close now.* ◆ Pwelek ater alhem pwety-angkwerr. 'Kel-ketyay. Kel alhepalhetyekay kwenh. Kel pwelek yanharl arrtyanety-alhem kwenh.' Kel arrtyanem antem tyerrty map pwelek *cheeky bugger*-eng. (T) *The cattle are stampeding through the bush. 'Hurry up. We've got to get going. Those cattle are already running.' Then the people run away from the dangerous cattle.*

kelath *n.*
glass, mirror, glasses, spectacles, window (from English 'glass') ◆ Kelathel apek arelhem, *comb*-ilelhemel arelhem. (St) *Looking at yourself in the mirror and combing your hair.* ◆ Mwetekay kelath arlkerrk-wenty-alhem, apetyemel. Arnaremel. '*Eh*, arlkerrk-wenty-alhem kwenh kelath yanhel, kwatyel-artek.' (T) *The windows of the car are shining as it comes along towards us. Watching it coming we say, 'Hey, the car windows are shining, sparkling like water'.*

kelengwem (W,T) *vt.*
1. wave someone down to get their attention; nudge or tap someone to get their attention (ngwem '*ask for something*') ◆ Kelengwem, alhetyeh atherr, alherretyek. (M) *Wave someone down to get their attention so that the both of them can go together.*
2. paw at something or someone (as a dog does to get someone's attention)
SEE ALSO atengelh-ilem

kelerr ipelhem (E) *vi.*
hibernate; dig self in for hibernation (said of

snakes and lizards)
= urlelth ipelhem
SEE ALSO atyerrp, ipelhem

kelh, ikelh *n.*
a mass or lump of something, such as seed, spinifex resin, tobacco or earwax ◆ Ngkerlp tharl arrernek lertel atyenh anep-anem ikelh. (T) *The lump of tobacco that I put there is in my tin.*
kelh-kelh, ikelh-ikelh *n.*
matted or knotted hair. Also referred to as *kapert kelh-kelh.* ◆ Ikelh-ikelh kapert apek *anything*, ikelh-ikelharl irrem. Kapert ikelh-ikelh-irrek *might* anter-penh apek, aternng apek. (St) *Hair or anything can be matted, can become matted and frizzy. Hair might become matted from fat or if it's dirty.* ◆ Kapert ikelh-ikelh yanh alhewelheyaw. (T) *Wash that matted hair.*
SEE ALSO irrkety-irrkety
kelh-irrem, ikelh-irrem *vi.*
get hard, solidify, get matted or knotted (hair) ◆ Alhwa ikelh-irrem tywen-penh, rlterrk-irremel. (St) *Blood from a sore solidifies, gets hard.*
= intengk-irrem
ngkwerlp kelh, ngkerlp ikelh (W,T)
wad or lump of tobacco (ngkwerlp '*tobacco*')
tyalangk kelh (W,T), **tyalangk ikelh** (W,T)
lump of spinifex resin (tyalangk '*spinifex resin*')
= anker ikelh
anker ikelh (E)
lump of spinifex resin (anker '*spinifex resin*')
katyerr kelh, katyerr ikelh
lump or cake made of desert raisins which have been ground up (katyerr '*desert raisin*')
kelh-kelh atwelhem (T)
get bogged ◆ Anthwerrngek kelh-kelh atwelhem. Anthwerrngek irrpety-alhem mwetekay, kelh-kelh atwelhety-alhem. Kel arrpenh ilem tyarr-ilem mwetekay arrpenhel. (T) *Getting bogged in the mud. The car goes into the mud and gets bogged. Then another car pulls it out.*

kelkareng, kalkareng *n.*
holly-leaf grevillea (*Grevillea wickhamii* ssp. *aprica*). Shrub to 2.5 m high, with dull green holly-like leaves and bright red flowers. ◆ Mernarl kelkareng. Mernan ikwerel anemarl, ngkwarl-artek. Arlkwenh-arlkwenh. Arwerlel-arleng anem anthwem. Anwern arlkwerretyartel apert-atwemel. (Sa) *[Parts of] the holly leaf grevillea are edible. There is a sweet substance that is found on the tree that is edible. It seeps from the branches and we used to crush it up and eat it.*

kelkert (W,T) *n.*
knee ◆ Kelkert rtapety-irremel anep-anem. (M) *Sitting with bent knees.* ◆ Kwer nhenh anem kelkertel-ayel. (T) *This child is kneeling.*
= amper[2], ampweth
kelkert tyelh (W,T), **kelkert ngkwern** (W,T)
kneecap
kelkert kwen (W,T)
back of knee

kelthemartem (W,T) *vt.* [RESPECT LANGUAGE]
fight, hit ◆ Kelthemartem atyengenh marl. (T) *[My son-in-law] is hitting my daughter [said by a woman].*
SEE ALSO atwem, ulpakem, arlinem

kely (W,T) *n.*
1. elder brother
2. particular relations with the same skin as your *kak*; for example, your father's older brother's son or your mother's older sister's son
= kak, away

kely-kely-irrem (W,T) *vi.*
not wanting to move from a place or go to another place, not wanting to budge ◆ Anewelek iltem, 'Ntwam kely-kely-irrek *pub* nhenhel, ngkwarl antywerlanetyek.' (T) *His wife growls at him, 'You're always hanging round the pub drinking.'* ◆ Arengk yanh kely-kely-irrety-alpek mer nhenhel. (T) *That dog keeps coming back to this place.* ◆ Artwang yanh kely-kely-irrety-alpek marl awenkarl arekarl. (T) *That man keeps coming back and hanging around the young girl that he saw.*

kelyaw *n.*
central netted dragon (*Ctenophorus nuchalis*)
= irnar, kaperl
SEE ALSO arrpwayl

Kemarr *n.*
skin name, subsection name, marriage class. See diagram p. 744. ◆ Arelh Kemarrel anew akem artwang Pelthar. (T) *Kemarr women marry Peltharr men.*
SEE ALSO Tyakarr, Watyal, Nakarr, Nakakwet, Nakemarr, Tyakemarr

kengkw elder brother etc. SEE UNDER **kak**

-kenh[1], -henh (W,T) *n.ending*
1. Shows the person or thing that possesses or has an item; belonging to, owned by. Equivalent to **'s**, as in 'child**'s** shoe'. There is variation in the use of *-kenh* and *-henh* throughout the Anmatyerr region. Sometimes this ending sounds like *-wenh.* ◆ 'Akwerr', Anmatyerr-**kenh**, pakwerran Kaytety-**kenh**.

Atnwenth akwerr. Aretyakenharl ayeng. (St) *'Akwerr' is the Anmatyerr word, 'pakwerr' is the Kaytetye one.* Akwerr *is an animal. I haven't seen one.* ◆ Aympelh angerrarl ikwerenh, arwengerrp-**kenh**. (St) *The bush turkey's wings are big.* ◆ Urlepety-antey ayengan anep-anem, apmer arrpenh-**kenh**-warl alhetyakenh. (St) *I keep stopping in one place, I haven't been to other people's country.* ◆ Arrengey-**henh** yanham mer Arlwem. Atyengenh arrengey-**henh**, tharl arreng akek angey-**henh**, angeyeh-artey-**henh**, papeh-artey-**henh**, angey atyeng-artwey-**henh**. (N) *My grandfather's country is Arlwem. That is the place that I am related to through my father's father and my father.* ◆ Angwenh-**henh**am angwely yanhan? *Whose dog is that?*
2. something which is typically used for something or associated with something; for ◆ Ker-**kenh** inkwartety arrwekelenyel *knife* anetyangel arlkwerretyart. (Sa) *The stone knife was what the olden-time people used to cut up meat when they didn't have any [metal] knives.* ◆ Arengkatwepatwetyenh, arrken-**henh**. Anwernarl arlelthel alakenh, kapert pertipelaw anerl-apemel, arrken-**henh** kwa. (N) *The* arengkatwepatwetyenh *plant is used for fun. We used to enjoy ourselves putting the flowers on our heads.*

kenh2**, akenh** *part.*
Often indicates a change of focus or topic in the conversation; but, and, whereas, on the other hand. ◆ Mern lkwart anthwerr. Mern lkwart lpway-areny kenh lkwart arrpenh nhenh ker-kenh, *kangaroo*-arl arlkwenh-arlkwenh. (M) *The edible* lkwart *melon. One sort of* lkwart *is edible and grows in the creeks, and another sort is kangaroo food.* ◆ Waram tha ngkweng arlenthek, artelhetyek apek. Rnwanenty apek *something* awenh apek, arlenthekarl tha. Kenh ntwa atyeng anthenty-alpeyamel. (St) *I just lent it to you, so that you could cover yourself up. Some clothes or whatever, I lent them to you. And then you will give them back to me later.* ◆ Ayenparl akernengan. Ayenp nhenh apetyem amwelteng arlka. Kenh alhwarl kweneng *run*-irrerl-anem, ingkewarn-athek, iltyewarn-athek, alakenh kapert-warn-athek. (T) *Skin is on the surface. For example, there is skin all the way along the arm. Whereas blood runs on the inside, towards the feet, the hands and to the head.*

kenheng SEE UNDER **kak** elder brother etc.
kenheng atherr SEE UNDER **kak** elder brother etc.
kenheng-arey SEE UNDER **kak** elder brother etc.
kenhengart SEE UNDER **kak** elder brother etc.
kenkethenh SEE UNDER **kak** elder brother etc.

kentyentyelarr (T) *n.*
a type of lizard

kep1 (W,T) *n.*
firestick ◆ Arrngelh kep-akert, arntap-akert alhetyam, rwang itety-alhetyam. (T) *[They] went around with bark firesticks which they used to light fires with as they went.*
= alep, rwang lyenenty, uralep
rwakep (W,T), **rwang kep** (W,T) *n.*
firestick (rwa *'fire'*)
= uralep
kep-ilem (W) *vt.*
light fire with a firestick
= alep-ilem

kep2 (W) *n.* [SENSITIVE LANGUAGE]
vagina
SEE ALSO artwert2, tyarrp, tyely

keparety SEE UNDER **kak** elder brother etc.

kepartart *n.*
a type of grub found on mulga, *artety*
= alethayerr, artetyayt
SEE ALSO arrpayerr

ker *n.*
1. meat, flesh, game ◆ Angayel apetyam mern-kweny ker-kweny. (M) *He had no meat and no food. He walked around starving.*
2. animal, animal that is edible; an animal's prey
3. A general word that can go before the name of a particular type of edible animal. In the Anmatyerr way of classifying foods most fruits and vegetables are known as *mern*, sweet things as *ngkwarl*, seeds as *anterrng*, *arnwety* or *ntang*, meats as *ker* and edible grubs as *tyap*.
= anwenth
SEE ALSO tyelk
ker anter
edible fat (anter *'fat'*)
ker anthwerrk (E)
green, watery contents of a kangaroo's stomach (anthwerrk2 *'green, watery contents of a kangaroo's stomach'*)
ker artep
meat from the back of an animal (artep *'back'*)
ker tyekert (T,E)
tasteless meat (tyekert1 *'salty or sour-tasting'*)
ker tyelk
flesh (tyelk *'flesh'*)
ker awerrp
meat juice (awerrp1 *'meat juice'*)

ker arnwang (W,T), **ker arnwa** (E)
emu fat
ker-henh (W) *n.*
man (lit. 'the one that belongs to the meat'). This term is used when people are in mourning.
SEE ALSO kwaty-henh
ker kwaty
soup (lit. 'meat water') ◆ Ker kwaty tha antywetyek anert mwerr-iletyek. (T) *I'm going to drink some soup to make my stomach better.*
ker ngkwern[1]
a meaty bone or a bone with marrow in it (ngkwern *'bone'*) ◆ Ker ngkwern atwemel anter awantyetyek. (T) *Smashing up the bone to eat the marrow [inside].*
ker ngkwern[2] (E)
pimple
kerelty-welhem (W,T) *vi.*
1. get stuck on or in something ◆ Kerety aken welhem thenkarr antyamek, ingkek. (T) *Prickles get stuck on blankets or in your foot.* ◆ *Bubble gum* kerelty-welhem kapertek. (T) *Bubble gum gets stuck in the hair.* ◆ Lwelty aken anwerneh kerelty-welhek. *Might be* rwa anetyakenh apek, *little bit* nheng rwa apek kwen antem irrek. Wal, kerelty antem welhem kwer. (M) *Frost covers us over as well. Maybe there is no fire, or the fire burns down a little bit. Well, the ice sticks to everything.*
2. become stuffed up or congested (throat or chest) ◆ Ahenty kerelty-welhem tywen anem irrem. (T) *[A person's] throat becomes congested and then it gets sore.* ◆ Kereltyarl welhem rtwekert, mernt-penh, artwengkenng-penh. (T) *[The] chest gets congested from the cold or flu.*
SEE ALSO mwernelhem, kerrk-welhem
kerlelkerlelp (W,T) *n.* [SOME SPEAKERS]
galah (*Eolophus roseicapillus*) (note Warlpiri *kirlilkirlilpa*) ◆ Kerlelkerlelpelel arlkwem tampewern. (N) *Galahs eat paddy melons.*
= ilenty, uneng atyetyek
kerlp *n.*
scalp (from English 'scalp')
kerlpem-ilem *vt.*
scalp something
kerlpaty (W), **kerlpayt** (E) *n.*
a type of grub found in the roots of the gidgee tree, *rrwenyenk/urrenyenk,* and the witchetty bush, *anyem*
SEE ALSO urrenyenkayt, anyemayt, ulalthengayt
Kerlpaty (W) *n.*
Black Hill Bore, near the Anmatjira Range
kernt *n.*
cool, cold ◆ Angwerl-iletyeh kwaty kerntel tey. (N) *Cool the tea down with cold water.* ◆ Kernt mparetyam, arnam, arlperlp. Kwaty alakenh arrernetyam, arrwekel kwa, angernerl-apetyam *olden time*-el rnwang rwetyel. (N) *The* arlperlp *grass was used to keep the water cool. It was put [on top] of the water in the wooden dish, and the olden-time mob used to carry it along like that.* ◆ Kwatyinpenginpan rnwewarl angerl-apek arrwekel kernt anthwerr antywerl-apek. Kwatyinpenginpel ilerrirrepirrem rnwareny, kernt mpwarenharenh. (N) *Before, the* kwatyinpenginp *grass was carried along on the top of the water dish so that [we] could have really cold water to drink. The grass that is used for water dishes, for making the water cold, is called 'kwatyinpenginp'.*
SEE ALSO irrernt, angwerl, angwerleny, anyartey, anyel, arlkarl[1], atheperr
kernt-irrem *vi.*
cool down ◆ Irrngwilem renh urel kel kernt ilem anem renh, ikelh anem renh ilenty-alpem. Ikelh anem kernt-irrem, anker renh. (St) *You melt it on the fire and then it cools down and solidifies again. The spinifex resin solidifies when it cools.* ◆ Arlelyek ampengem arlkwem. Akemel angernemel rwelem item, mern atyerrety-alpem, rarrp rew-irrem. Kernt-irretyek arrernem, arlkwem renh alenyel war inem. (N) *The* arlelyek *fruit is eaten cooked. It is picked then taken back and cooked in the fire so that it goes soft. Then it is put down to cool and then it's eaten, just with the tip of the tongue.*
= angwerl-irrem, irrernt-irrem, anyel-irrem
kernt-ilem *vt.*
cool something down
= irrernt-ilem
kerr-kerr (W,T), **kirr-kirr** *n.*
rough-tailed goanna, ridge-tailed monitor (*Varanus acanthurus*). Also referred to as *ker kerr-kerr.* ◆ Kerr-kerr kerrertekel anem, an irntel anem. Lyek-akert tayl. (T) *The rough-tailed goanna lives amongst the ant hills and in the rocks. It has a spikey tail.* ◆ Ikwang arlewatyerr-arteh kerr-kerr. Mwerr anthwerr arlkwem. (M) *Rough-tailed goannas taste like the sand goannas. They are really good to eat.*
= antyerr
kerraney *n.*
granny (from English 'granny')
SEE ALSO menh-menh, nyany[2], ipmenh
kerrart (T) a type of puffball SEE UNDER **kwerrart**
Kerrekwaty (W) *n.*
name of a soakage at Yuendumu

kerrelhem (W) *vi.*
dress up, put on good clothes

kerrem (W,T), **kirrem, ikirrem** (E) *vi.*
observe rules associated with respect of particular relations; for example, the avoidance of mothers-in-law by sons-in-law and vice versa ◆ Mwey-mwey kerrem. Angey-kety, aler-aler-kety, kerrenty akin anem. (T) *[You] avoid your son-in-law. There are restrictions between you and your father and between you and your nephews or nieces [brother's children] as well.*
= kanem

kerrenty (W,T), **kirrenty, ikirrenty** (E) *n.*
1. rules associated with respect of particular kin ◆ Ikirrenty anetyakenh yanh alhewer alhem, mey-mey kwerenh, rtwalty kwerenh-angkwarr. Akengarlaw. (St) *That person does not respect the avoidance rules and just goes anywhere, near her son-in-law. It's really bad.* ◆ Kerrenty ananem angey-hety. Kerrenty-irrem paty arrwert, wal, rntwarrem ananem angey-hety. (M) *There are rules about a girl avoiding her father. When her breasts start to develop, well, she sits a distance away from her father.*
2. a person who follows the rules associated with respect of particular kin ◆ Ikirrenty. Ayeng ikirrenty anem. Ikirrem ayeng yanh-kety — mwer-kety. (St) *It's respectful. I follow the rules about avoiding particular relations. I avoid that person over there — I avoid my son-in-law.*

kerrertek *n.*
1. ant hill, ant bed, termite mound.. Some of these types of ant hill or ant bed are used to make a medicine for diarrhoea. ◆ Tyap ngkwepey kerrertek-areny angkwey arlkwetyart. (M) *In the old days people used to eat the grubs from the ant hill.*
2. flat ant bed [SOME SPEAKERS] ◆ Antywem renh ampa akwek ampa akngerrel apek marl akngerrel apek. Aketh kwen-penh inem, renh anem itemelel ngkwelty-ilem apek kel *boil*-em apek anem ilem, kel ngkernem anem, antywem anem renh. Mwerr-irrem anem. (St) *[The ant bed is made into a mixture] and drunk by little kids, big kids or big girls. You get it from out in the open, heat it up, smash it up or maybe boil it, put it aside for a bit, and then drink it. Then [the person] gets better.*
SEE ALSO ngkwepey, kerrth, merntap, awerr-awerr[1], pwentereng

Kerretherreng (T) *n.*
Christian (from English 'Christian') ◆ Kerretherrengam ayeng. Ayeng tyatyel kerretherreng-irrek, *Napperby*-el. Kerretherreng-irretyakenh arrpenhem, itya, aheyen war. (M) *I am a Christian. I got baptised in the church at Napperby. Some people have not become Christians, they are just heathens.*
SEE ALSO Pep-areny, aheyen, tyaty

kerretherreng-irrem (W), **kerretyen-irrem** (T) *vi.*
get baptised, become Christian

kerrk-wem, irrkerrk-wem *vt.*
1. stick or poke into something else; press or lean into something, get stuck ◆ Lyek kerrk-wem ingka, ulthemelarl alhem. (St) *Prickles stick to your feet when you tread on them.* ◆ Ntwa ayenh irrkerrk-wetyalay, irrkerrkarl-wem. Ayenharl irrkerrk-wem-kety iyntwarr-irray. Arrerant-atherr anem irrkerrk-wem. (Sa) *Don't lean on me. You're leaning on me. Move further away.* ◆ Ayenh irrkerrk-wetyalaw, impelhemarl. Ahern rlterrk-kety! (Sa) *Don't lean heavily on me — the ground is hard. Leave me alone!*
SEE ALSO atanthem
2. step on someone; run over something ◆ Tyerrty apek lthwem, kerrk-wem antem. (T) *Someone might tread on someone.*

kerrk-welhem, irrkerrk-welhem *vi.*
1. lean on or press down on someone ◆ Kerrk-welhetyal alhay kwenh, atyeng-arlek. Rntwarr anemelay! (T) *Don't lean on me. Move over!*
SEE ALSO alernelhem, rlpwerrkem, rrwethem
2. (something) press into, be tight on or cling to self ◆ Mantarr pwarn kerrkarl welhem atyeng. Ywarn tha kap-rlwem. (T) *These tight clothes are pressing into me. I can't get them off.*

kerrth (E) *n.*
flat ant bed
SEE ALSO ngkwepey, kerrertek, merntap, awerr-awerr[1], pwentereng

kert-arem *vt.*
peep (out from behind something); peer down into something ◆ Urrek tha kert-arerl-wey. (St) *Wait while I just have a quick peep.* ◆ Warl kwen-they kert-arem. Kert-arerl-wem. (St) *Peeping out from inside the house. Peeping out.* ◆ Tyerrty nhakwel ayeng kert-arep-arem. (T) *That person is peering at me.* ◆ Mwetekay kweneng yanh kert-arang! (T) *Look under the car!*
= tyel-arem, ayternem

kert-kert-ilem (W) *vt.*
tickle someone
= irrkelh-irrkelh-anthem, athek-athek-ilem, tyek-tyek-ilem

kertaty (E) *n.*
dark-coloured or dry seeds of the dogwood, *akerlperr, awenth* (*Acacia sericophylla*) ◆ Kertaty tek-wem utern-warl, kwer-penh urel anem item rerrkel. Kel aympernem anem renh. Kel pert-atwem anem renh, anterrng anem atherl-anem. (St) *The dark-coloured seeds of the dogwood tree are laid out in the son, and then after that they are cooked in the firepit. Then they are yandied. Then they are crushed up, and then the seed is ground up.*
= tartaty
SEE ALSO ntyerrm, artwengarr, anma[1]
CAN SOUND A BIT LIKE kwertaty *'kurdaitcha'*

kertemwengk *n.*
1. someone who is not allowed to talk (especially because of bereavement) ◆ Tyerrty nheng *pass* away irremeng kertemwengk ra anem. Iltya anem iltyerrerl-anetyenheng. (T) *If that person passes away then [she] doesn't talk. She just uses handsigns.*
= awenp
SEE ALSO akerter
2. not saying anything; not talking to someone; not back-talking or passing on gossip
3. a story that is secret, and the meaning cannot be freely disclosed; an indirect or oblique way of talking (for example, using respect language) ◆ Arrmar-nheng atherran ilem mwerikwekety kertemwengk akemel. Mwerekikwety kertemwengk angkemel. 'Arrmar-nheng atherr yanh alhek kwenh.' Ankel-nheng atherr ilem. (St) *'Arrmar-nheng atherr' is what is said by a woman in a way of not talking directly because of her son-in-law. 'Those two male cross-cousins went.' That's what she says of the two cousins, one of whom is her son-in-law.*
angkety kertemwengk (W,T)
1. a short version of a story, a summary of a story (angkety *'story', 'word'*) ◆ Artwangel angkety akwek war ilem, angkety kertemwengk, kwer mapel iterlaretyek. (T) *The man is just telling the children part of the story, so that they will know it.*
2. not the full story, not the real story

kertety (T) *adv.*
stepping over something
kertety alhem (T), **kertety arnpenhem** (T)
step over something (alhem *'go'*) (arnpem *'set out'*) ◆ Arneng irrweltyeng kertety arnpenhem, kel alhemem, anyekety. (T) *Stepping over the branches in case you fall, then going on.*

kerwep *n.*
crowbar (from English 'crowbar') ◆ Arelh lyweny alhetyeh kerwep-akert. (N) *The woman is going hunting with a crowbar.*
SEE ALSO anem[3]

ketay, ketar *n.*
guitar (from English 'guitar') ◆ Tyerrtyel atwem ketay. (M) *The person is playing a guitar.*

-kety, -hety (W,T) *ending*
1. Goes on nominals and signals something that should be watched out for or avoided; for fear of someone or something, look out for someone or something, beware of . . ., avoid someone or something, move away from something, keep away from something. On some pronouns the shortened form *+ety* is used. For example, *ikwerety* ('because of him/her/it'), *atyengety* ('because of me').
◆ 'Wapey-**kety** rntert-irray!' Ampek ilem. (St) *'Be quiet, because of the whitefella!' That's what you say to a child.* ◆ Kwer map, mwetekay-**kety**! (T) *Look out for the car all you kids!*
◆ Alethang apek urrpety apetyek. 'Urrpety apetyawarrem yanh-**kety**aw!' (St) *There might be a few strangers coming. 'Look out, there's a few coming!'* ◆ Ntwerrkenhan alhek. Tywenp apawenhwek, 'Alhweng ngkwengenh ayeng irrpey, tyerrty-**hety**?' 'Yetya. Alhweng akwekam yanh atyengenh.' (M) *The python went off. He asked a perentie, 'Can I come into your burrow to escape from the humans?' 'No. My burrow is too small.'* ◆ Ipert-ipert-**kety**aw mwetek yanhap mwerranty alhey kwenh. (St) *Drive that car slowly because of the bumps.*
◆ Alkiwerr-**kety**aw. Alkiwerr atyeng-**kety** arnang-irrey, ayeng irrpenheyamel warl-warl apek. Antywewarl apek. (St) *There is no room for me to go there because of avoidance relations. Because of that you go first, and I'll go into the house or the humpy later.*
2. Goes on the names of people or places to provide an explanation for why something shouldn't be said. For example, a word might not be spoken in front of a particular family or group, and a speaker can refer to this indirectly by naming a bereaved person and putting the ending *-kety* on the end of their name (Lucy-*kety* 'because of Lucy' etc.).
3. Goes on verbs to show that the speaker does not want a particular thing to happen; because of (something bad or unwanted), in case (something happens), lest (something is happening or something might happen).
◆ Ura yanh ilwerneyaw, alkngentharl angerr ampem-**kety**. Ura ilwernem tha. (St) *Put that*

fire out, because the flames are burning high. [So] I put the fire out. ◆ Anarnpa, arnel atwe**kety**. (M) *Jump down, in case the tree hits you.* ◆ Angwely-kety akern tywernem arlpar arrernem antywerlan-**kety**. (N) *Put it up high because of the dogs, because the dogs might drink it.*
4. Goes on verbs and provides an explanation for an action (not necessarily a frightening or unwanted one), provides an explanation for difficulty in doing something; because. ◆ Ampernem anerl-ayntenherr-arey, irrerarl alhem-**kety**ay, anerl-ayntenherr-arey. Ulyel anerl-ayntenherr-arey. (Sa) *All you kids, sit down, because [we] are going hunting. You all sit down in the shade.* ◆ Ayengan mentyarlaw. Ayeng anemarl-**kety**aw, ngarrp alhay. *I don't want to do it. I'm stopping, you go yourself.*
-ketyeng *ending* = **-kety** ◆ Anant-iperray, mernt-irrenh-**ketyeng**ay. Rlkert apek ane**ketyeng**. Arrwengkelth ine**ketyeng**. Anantay! (P) *Sit down, in case you get sick. In case you catch something. Sit down!* ◆ Angkeparr-ilem, arrpenhel artwel apek angkeparr-ilem arelh *mother*-an akerterel anetyel *family*-**ketyeng**. Kel renh angkeparr-ilemel marlel artwel. Angkemel anem anerl-anem. (Sa) *Another person, maybe a man, frees her so that she can talk, after she has been sitting down and not talking out of respect for the family. The man frees her to talk. Then she talks.*

ketyey (W) *n.*
child, children ◆ Ampa maparl arrken-arrkenel, irrtyarteng-irrtyart, atantherl-apem arrken nheng atantherremel lyentyel, ketyey map. (N) *The kids enjoy themselves going along spearing each other with the kangaroo grass, their pretend spears.*
SEE ALSO ampa, kwer

kewaleny (W) do action for oneself SEE UNDER **kwaleny**

kewan (E) *part.*
an exclamation used to hunt dogs away; 'Go on!' (from English 'go on')

kewarr (W,T), **akiwarr** (T,E) *n.*
sulky, bad-tempered, in a bad mood
= arnkely
SEE ALSO kekart
kewarr-irrem (W,T), **akiwarr-irrem** (T,E) *vi.*
get sulky, have a tantrum or lose your temper, be in a bad mood ◆ Ngkweng ayeng akiwarr-irrem, angayelek apek ayeng ngkweng akiwarr-irrek, ngkweltyek apek, ker apek anthetyakenh, ngkwelty apek anthetyakenh. (St) *I am in a bad mood with you because I am hungry and because of money, because you didn't give me any meat or money.* ◆ Akiwarr-irrem, mern apek ikwereng utnanthemel. (St) *She is sulky because they didn't share their food with her.*
SEE ALSO arnkely-irrem, kekart-irrem
kewarr alhem (W,T), **akiwarr alhem** (T,E)
go off sulkily, in a huff or in a bad mood ◆ Akiwarr ra alhek mern anthetyakenheng. (St) *She went off in a huff because she wasn't given any food.*

kewel *n.*
goal (from English 'goal') ◆ Ywerntemeh arlkerrirretyam, arnterrkwetyam-arleh, kewelarl arrernek-arleh. (M) *We cheered for Yuendumu when they caught the ball, and someone scored a goal.*

kewenyeweny (W) *n.*
mosquito (note Warlpiri *kiwinyi-winyi* 'swarm of mosquitoes')
= aheny, weny, angeylk

kewerrewerr (E) *n.* [RESPECT LANGUAGE]
all, everybody ◆ Kewerrewerr ahanerrek akngwelerneyt. (Sa) *They [respect kin] have all gone east.*
SEE ALSO alanenty, ingkerrek

key (T) *n.* [BABY TALK]
meat
SEE ALSO ker

key-key-irrem (E) *vi.* [BABY TALK]
go to the toilet, have a shit, defecate ◆ Key-key-irretyek alha. (Sa) *Go to the toilet [said to a baby].*

kik-wem (W,T) peel skin off fruit or bark off a stick SEE UNDER **kek-wem**

kikarr (E) *n.*
resin from the Georgina gidgee, *rrwenyenk/urrenyenk* (*Acacia georginae*)
SEE ALSO ilyartey

kikw SEE UNDER **kak** elder brother etc.

kimpwet *n.*
computer (from English 'computer')

kirr-kirr rough-tailed goanna SEE UNDER **kerr-kerr**

kirrem observe rules associated with respect of particular relations SEE UNDER **kerrem**

kirrpangkwel (E) bush coconut, bloodwood apple [SOME SPEAKERS] SEE UNDER **arrkipangkwarl**

Kngwarray (E) skin name SEE UNDER **Ngwarray**

kwa, kwang *part.*
Provides emphasis or stresses that something is definite or obvious; definitely, exactly, of course, you know that . . . ◆ Lweren kwa arrwekeleny map *live*-irrek. (N) *That's how the olden-time people lived.* ◆ Mern perlap kwa

anwa arlkwarlkwem angerram. *We definitely eat lots of conkerberries.* ◆ Kwaty-kety ayeng arelhetyam, kel tha aremel arerr kwa atyeweyay akngerr apetyem. (St) *I was watching out for rain, and then I saw a huge storm coming closer.* ◆ Urelarl artekarl item kwang atywer, ahelengkw wangkerl-ilenh-ilenh. Atyweran ahelengkw. Urrperl. Arrakert akwek rnter-rnter-awaty. (St) *The* atywer *ant is definitely aggressive and makes [you] swell up and burn like fire [when it bites]. It is dangerous. It is dark in colour and its mouth is a bit reddish.* ◆ Kel alhemel, warrk-irrety-alhemel, *breakfast* inety-alhemel arlkwety-alhemel — perempeth akeng kwang — mern *bread* akenty, *not* ampwerrk athew. (Sa) *Then we'd go, go to work and get breakfast to eat on the way — it was a really awful breakfast — a piece of bread that had been cut off, not a full loaf.*
SEE ALSO lweth

kwak, kwakw *adv.*
enjoying doing something; happily ◆ Yerrakwerr apek tha kwakwel anem inerl-anem. Katyerr akerl-anem kwakwel, arternpel akerl-anetyek. (St) *I really enjoy collecting bush onions. I like picking bush raisins, picking them carefully.* ◆ Kwakel arlkwerl-anem anyemayt. (T) *Enjoying eating witchetties.* ◆ Kwakel nta mpwarerl-anem. (M) *You enjoy doing this.*
kwak-irrem, kwakw-irrem *vi.*
1. get excited; enjoy doing something; feel pleased or happy; want to do something; be very enthusiastic about something ◆ Kwakw-irrem ayeng, mern apek arlkwetyek mwerr. Kwakwel arlkwerl-anem. (St) *I really enjoy eating good food. I get happy eating it.* ◆ Kwak-irrem mernarl akemeng. Arrpenhel ingweyameng 'Kwaty-kwenyel alpem, mer-warn'. '*No*, urrek nhenhek-amparr tha akeyaw mern, angerr-angerr.' (T) *I am really enjoying picking the bush foods. Another person might ask me, 'Let's go home, we haven't got any water'. [And I'll say] 'No, wait, I'm going to pick these fruits first, there's quite a lot of them.'*
SEE ALSO ahenty-anem, anyanelhem, anyerrkem, inkwerelhem, ahenty-irrem, akangkem, irrngerney-irrem
2. settle in a place, not move from a place, like a place and not want to go anywhere else ◆ Kwak-irrety-alpek mer nhenhel. (T) *He settled in this place.* ◆ Mer nhenhel akwet antem ra anety-alpek, kwak-irrety-alpek. (T) *He went and lived in this place permanently, settled down there.* • SEE ALSO kely-kely-irrem, arternp-irrem

kwaleny (W,T), **kewaleny** (W) *adv.*
doing an action for oneself. This goes with transitive verbs. ◆ Kwalenyel tharl ker atwerl-apek. (T) *I killed animals for myself, travelling along.*
SEE ALSO +arrp

Kwamparr (W), **Kwamper** (W) *n.*
name of a place near Claypan Bore (Stuart Bluff Range area)

kwang (W) *n.*
1. taste ◆ Kwang anetyam tey nhenh. (M) *This tea tastes bad.* ◆ Kwang mwerr angerr. (M) *A really nice taste.*
2. voice ◆ Kwang yanh thang awem. (M) *I can hear that voice.* ◆ Kwang ntwa alhengk-awem. (M) *I recognise that voice.*
3. a person's or animal's scent, body smell [SOME SPEAKERS] ◆ Ker aherr kwang ntyern-hety. (M) *Look out or the kangaroo will smell you.* • SEE ALSO npwa
= ikwa (E)

kwang definitely, exactly, of course SEE UNDER kwa

kwanth-kwanth (T) *n.*
bleed (a lot) ◆ Atwem renh, anyant atwem kwanth-kwanth kel kapert. Kwanth-kwanth alhwang thelelhem. (T) *The person is hit, just about killed, and their head bleeds a lot. The blood pours from their head.*
= anthwek-anthwek
CAN SOUND A BIT LIKE rrkwanth *'brave', 'confident'*; akwanth-akwanth *'take aim'*

kwanthem *vt.*
tease someone ◆ Ampa yanh kwanthetyalay! (St) *Don't tease that kid!* ◆ Nywerrp tha kwanthep-anthem. (St) *I am teasing people from the opposite generation moiety.*
SEE ALSO urrayerr, arrken-ilem, anngernt-irrem, arrampewem1, arrkenty-ilem

kwarlk (W) *n.* [SENSITIVE LANGUAGE]
lymph nodes at the top of the thighs (?); top of thighs where they join the torso
SEE ALSO kwart-kwart

kwarlp *n.*
spectacled hare-wallaby, sandhill wallaby (*Lagorchestes conspicillatus*) ◆ Kwarlpan atwety akwek-artek. (T) *Spectacled hare-wallabies are similar to little joeys.*
SEE ALSO lkwameny

kwarlpatengkelyengkely (E), **kwarlpatyatengkelyengkely** (E) *n.*
rufous whistler (*Pachycephala rufiventris*)
= apetyepetyem, artwang apetyepetyem,

artwatherr apetyem, ipeny apetyepetyem, tyenyepweny

kwarnem *vt.*
cause pain, hurt someone ◆ Tywenel ayeng kwarnem. (M) *My sore is hurting me.* ◆ Apalel thwengk kwarnem tywen. (M) *By accident I made your sore hurt.*
kwarnelhem *vi.*
feel hurt, ache, feel sore or in pain, have a pain ◆ Utyen apek ayeng kwarnelhem. (St) *My sore is hurting.* ◆ Atnert ayeng kwarnelhem. (St) *My stomach is aching.*
SEE ALSO arlkwem, arntem, arekar-irrem, rlkert intyem, antyernem[1]

kwarrernem *vt.* [RESPECT LANGUAGE]
listen, hear ◆ Kwarrernepernemarl yanhentyel arey. (St) *All of those people [including respect kin] over there are listening.* ◆ Kwarrernetyek ahanenherr-areyay. (Sa) *All of you [including respect kin], go and listen.* ◆ Kwarrernay, alenhel ngkweng angkep-angkem kwarrernang kwenh. (M) *Listen to that person who is talking to you.*
SEE ALSO awem

kwarrety (W,T) *n.*
1. desert Flinders grass, bunch panic (*Yakirra australiensis* var. *australiensis*). A grass about 15 cm high, with reddish-coloured leaves. = arlepenh, arrepeny, nyetempwer
2. bunch Paspalidium (*Paspalidium rarum*). A grass about 20 cm high, which is often found around mulga. • = nyetempwer, tywaynt
3. the edible seeds of these grasses ◆ Athetyamarl ina *olden time* mern anetyakenh. Kwarrety wararl atherlapek. Athetyam ina pwerlel. Irnta atherek arrernemel arnwety. Weth ina alhetyam mern ywerretyamam aweth akin ina kwarrety renh, nheng yerrelarl arrernem akethek. Arrernerl-apem, wal arerlapetyam, 'Nhenhey arrernek kwenh — atyeng-apenh kwenh'. Inelhalhetyam. Weth alhetyam arrpenhem *find*-em-iletyam. (N) *The olden-time people used to grind up the grass seeds before they had any whitefella food. They used to just go along grinding up* kwarrety *seeds. They ground them up with a stone called* 'pwerl'. *They put the seed on a flat stone called* 'ather'. *When the food ran out they used to go again for* kwarrety *seeds, where the ants had heaped them up in the open ground. They'd see that and say, 'Here's where the ants have heaped up the grass seeds — these are mine'. They'd go and collect them and then go looking for more.*

kwart *n.*
1. egg ◆ Tyerrty mapel ankerr kwart arlkwetyart. (M) *People used to eat emu eggs.* ◆ Kwentarreng alewatyerr akwek, kwart-penh. Nheng kwart-penh lyetantarl arratem. Angerr anetyakenh. Ilanthem rarrp angerr-irretyeh. Akwek anthwerr *can't* atwerl, akwek, akely-amperl. Ilanthem, ker angerr-irretyeh. (N) *A* kwentarreng *is a small goanna that has just hatched out of the egg. That has just come out of the egg. They are not very big. You leave them so that they grow up. You can't kill the little ones, the tiny little ones. You send them off so that they can grow bigger.*
2. unripe fruit of the desert raisin, *katyerr* (*Solanum centrale*). Also referred to as *katyerr kwart*. • = pwarr, urleynterr[2]
3. bulb of the wild onion, onion grass, nalgoo, *yerrakwerr* (*Cyperus bulbosus*). Also referred to as *yerrakwerr kwart*.
ker kwart
edible egg (ker '*meat*')
kwart ika (T,E)
egg shell (ika '*shell*', '*crust*')
alknga kwart (E), **anngang kwart** (W,T)
eyeball (alknga '*eye*')
ingkang kwart (W)
barefoot (ingkang '*foot*')
kwart-kwart *n.*
1. groin area; lymph nodes at top of thighs and under arms
SEE ALSO kwarlk
2. pregnant [SOME SPEAKERS] • = anert-anert

kwart-wem *vt.*
give something to someone when they are about to go somewhere ◆ Mern anthem kwart-wemel ra alpetyek anem, apmer-warl apmer kwerenh-warl anem, apmer arrpenh-they. (St) *Give something to that person who has come from another place, and then they go back home, back to their place.* ◆ Akeweny kwart-werleway, ngkwelty apekay. *Or* ker apekarl ngkwenh intep-intem nta antherl-wetyeh. (M) *Give the poor thing something before they go — some coins. Or maybe you could give them that meat that you have there.*
SEE ALSO anngwanngw-ilem

kwarterrem *vi.*
fight to the death; kill one another; beat each other to death ◆ Angwely atherr kwarterrem irrerlkng akwet. (T) *The two dogs are fighting to the death.* ◆ Tyerrty atherr kwarterrem, ahel atwerrem. (T) *The two people are angrily beating each other to death.* ◆ Kwarterrenty-ilerrem, terangkel apek. (T) *The drunks are murdering*

each other. ◆ Kwarterrek kwenh, irrernng apek nheng atwekarl kwa, wal 'kwarterrem' ilem. (M) *If somebody is beaten to death, well that's called* 'kwarterrem'.
SEE ALSO irrewaly atwem, nyant atwem, atwem, arlinem

kwatem *vi.*
moan, groan ◆ Kwatem ayeng, arntety apek. (St) *I am moaning, maybe because I am sick.*

kwaty *n.*
1. water
2. rain ◆ Intey wak-apeny artelherl-anem kwaty-kety anenh-anenh kwenel inteyel. (Sa) *[Some] caves are formed like humpies, and they are used for sheltering in from the rain.*
3. A general word that goes before the name of a particular type of water or water sources. ◆ Kwaty irnmerr lwerl-anem. (M) *Rain drops keep dripping down.*
4. petrol ◆ Ayeng nakepakel-irrek kwaty-kwenyel. (T) *I had a difficult time because I ran out of petrol.*

kwaty lpwert (W,T), **kwaty ulpert** (E)
muddy or dirty water (lpwert '*muddy or dirty water*')

kwaty lyeteny
fresh water (lyeteny '*recent*', '*fresh*') ◆ Kwaty lyeteny antywetyek. *Drinking fresh water.*

kwaty narwep (W,T)
fresh water, clean water, rainwater (narwep '*fresh water*')
= kwaty narengk

kwaty narengk (T) = **kwaty narwep** (narengk '*fresh water*')

kwaty arntay (W,T)
deep water, deep waterhole (arntay '*deep water*')

kwaty alay
sea, a large expanse of water (alay '*sea*') ◆ Kwaty alay iter-areny lyet apetyem. (T) *The people from the coast are coming today.*

kwaty irnmerr
a drop or drip of water (irnmerr, '*dew*', '*drop of water*') ◆ Kwaty irnmerr lwerl-anem. (M) *Raindrops keep dripping down.*

kwaty lthel
light rain, drizzle, a sprinkle of rain (lthel '*light rain*') ◆ Kwaty lthelel atwem. (M) *Light rain is falling.*

kwaty perler
steady rain, drizzle
= kwaty thawel

kwaty thawel (T) = **kwaty perler** (thawel '*steady rain*') ◆ Kwaty thawel rntwem. (T) *It's raining steadily.*

kwaty angkarl
rain cloud (angkarl '*rain cloud*') ◆ Kwaty angkarl kel apetyem kwaty angerrew-angent. (T) *The rain clouds come and then there will be lots of rain.*
SEE ALSO kwaty urla

kwaty pwer
lightning (pwer '*tail*')
= awely-awely, ngkwarrkenty
SEE ALSO angkeyawarr

kwaty irntakert (T)
hail, hailstone (irnta '*stone*'; -akert '*having*')
= apwertek

kwaty angkem
to thunder (angkem '*talk*') ◆ Kwaty angkem angkeyawarr. *The storm is thundering.*
SEE ALSO angkeyawarr

kwaty arrwerelhem
fall (rain), rain (to rain) (arrwerelhem '*fall to the ground*')
= anhem

kwatyeh irrpem (W,T), **kwatyek irrpem** (T,E)
swim, bathe, bogey (irrpem '*go in*')
SEE ALSO pwerlp-irrem

kwaty urrperl-ilenh (T,E)
tea (lit. 'that which makes the water dark-coloured')

kwaty-henh (W,T), **kwaty-kenh** (E) *n.*
1. woman. This word is used when people are in mourning (lit. 'belonging to the water').
2. radiator (of a car)

kwaty-irrenhenh (E) *n.* [RESPECT LANGUAGE]
a long beard (lit. 'that which goes into water') ◆ Alta weth-lkwer, arrwertel anem, arrwert-iperram yanh-lkwer. Wal, 'kwaty-irrenhenh', anem war ilem ikirrenty way. *Son* apek atyenh alakenh tha ilemer, 'Kwaty-irrenhenh-akert ayanhan'. 'Arrwert' aketyakenharl, kwaty-irrenhenhant. (St) *That hair, that grows on the chin. Well, in a respectful way it is just called* 'kwaty-irrenhenh'. *If I am talking about my son I might say, 'That man has got a long beard'. [His beard] is not called* 'arrwert', *it's just called* 'kwaty-irrenhenh'.
SEE ALSO arrwert

kwaty-irrem (W,T) *vi.*
go watery or runny, melt

kwaty-inperrenh (W,T), **kwaty-imperrenh** (E) *n.*
dragonfly (kwaty '*water*'; imperrem[1] '*go along the top of the water*') ◆ Kwaty-inperrenh kwatyelarl apem, arlpa-akert akwek. (M) *The dragonfly has small wings and flies around the water.*

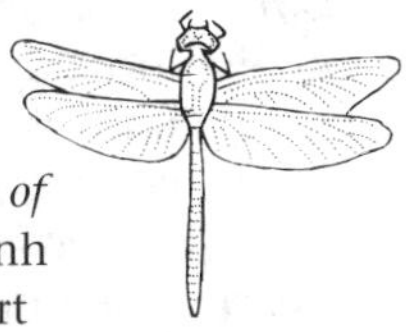

= urewap-imperreny, warepelh-pelh, rew inperrenh, kapert[2]

kwaty-kwaty[1] (W,T) *n.*
watery, sloppy, runny, weak, tasteless (of tea) ◆ Angwenhel renh tey itek kwaty-kwaty, *no tea-leaf* anengk arrernek, *strong* mpwaretyek? *Who made this weak tea, not putting lots of tea-leaves in to make it strong?*
= rew-rew

kwaty-kwaty-ilem (W,T) *vt.*
make something watery, sloppy or runny
= rew-rew-ilem

kwaty-kwaty[2] *n.*
1. soft part or hollow above the collarbone
2. collarbone [SOME SPEAKERS]
SEE ALSO anirnterrm-irnterr, arerr, alkwert-alkwert
3. Adam's apple [SOME SPEAKERS] • = ahenty amern-amern

kwatyarl iytey-iytey (E) mudlark, peewee SEE UNDER **kwatyarl rtey-rtey**

kwatyarl ntyeny-ntyeny (E) *n.*
ant lion (lacewing larvae) (*Neuroptera* spp.) (larvae) ◆ Kwatyarl ntyeny-ntyeny ahelhekarl irrpelh-apem ra, akely-amperl. (St) *The ant lion is a small creature that digs itself into the ground.*
= angkwerey-angkwerey
SEE ALSO mamerweterwet, kwaty

kwatyarl rtey-rtey (E), **kwatyarl iytey-iytey** (E) *n.*
mudlark, peewee (*Grallina cyanoleura*) ◆ Kwatyarl iytey-iyteyel mpwarem ahern ata atharlkw ikwer. (Sa) *The mudlark makes its nest out of mud.*
= rtey-rtey, ntwerleperl
SEE ALSO kwaty

kwatyempengemp (W,T), **kwatyimpengimp**, **kwatyinpenginp** (W), **kwatyengimpengimp** (E), **kwatyenginpenginp** (E) *n.*
cotton panic grass (*Digitaria brownii*). A type of grass used rolled up (like a sponge) for getting water from small soakages or rockholes, and for placing on the top of water containers to keep the water cool.
◆ Kwatyinpenginpan rnwewarl angerl-apek arrwekel kernt anthwerr antywerl-apek. Kwatyinpenginpel ilerrirreperrem rnwareny, kernt mpwarenharenh. (N) *Before, the* kwatyinpenginp *grass was carried along on the top of the water dish so that [we] could have really cold water to drink. The grass that is used for water dishes, for making the water cold, is called '*kwatyinpenginp*'.*
SEE ALSO kwaty

kway-kway (E) *n.*
the little crow (*Corvus bennetti*)
= angank, angerl, angep

kwek (E) *n.* [BABY TALK]
water ◆ Kwek antyway. (St) *Drink some water.*
= apa
SEE ALSO kwaty

kwek-arem (E) *vt.*
suck on something, suck something ◆ Kwek-arem *icy pole* ampeny. (St) *Sucking on the leftover icy pole.*
SEE ALSO awantyem, ltyantywem

kwekew (T) *n.* [BABY TALK]
southern boobook (*Ninox novaeseelandiae*)
SEE ALSO kwerrkwerrk, akekw

kwel-irrem (W,T) *vi.*
get sulky or upset (especially if you're missing out on something) ◆ Ayeng kwel-irrem, tyerrty alenhel arlkwerl-anem mern arlka ker arlka. Wal ayeng kwel-irrem, kwel-irremel alhem, anthetyakenheng. (M) *I am upset because that person is eating bread and meat, and I'm missing out. I'm going off in a sulk because I didn't get any.*

kwel-anyem (W,T) *vi.*
get sulky or upset (especially if you're missing out on something) ◆ Nta kwel-anyem merneng, mern arlatyeyeng apek. (M) *You are getting sulky about food, or maybe about pencil yams.*
SEE ALSO kewarr-irrem

kwelel arem (T)
be really dissappointed about something (arem *'look', 'see'*) ◆ Arelh yanhel kwelel arem ker ampwang. (T) *That woman is really dissappointed because the meat is not fatty.*

kwelay *n.*
rainbow snake, water-snake monster. Also referred to as *amwang kwelay*. This mythical snake is believed to have a head like a horse, and big eyes.
= akwerteyteng, kwelernarr

kwelengk (T,E) mulga snake, king brown snake SEE UNDER **ikwelengk**

kwelernarr (E) *n.*
rainbow snake, water-snake monster. This mythical snake is believed to have a head like a horse, and big eyes.
= akwerteyteng, kwelay

kwelinterr-interr (T,E), **kweleynterreynterr** (E) *n.*
rainbow bee-eater (*Merops ornatus*)
◆ Kweleynterreynterrel alhweng angernem *baby* anem ra mpwarem kwer-antey alhweng kwer-antey. Kel arraterl-alhep-alhem

arlewatyerr-artek. Arnam arrernem kel akwerrk map anem ra mpwarem. (St) *The rainbow bee-eater digs a burrow and has its babies there in the burrow. Then it comes out and goes around just like a goanna does. It puts grass there in the burrow and then it has its babies.*
= terr-terr, apelinterr-interr
SEE ALSO parlkenng

kwelteringk *n.*
soft drink or lemonade (from English 'cool drink')

kwelyalp *n.*
the sound that wedge-tailed eagles make ◆ 'Kwelyalp kwelyalp kwelyalp.' Alakenh angkerl-anem irrety akwek an angerr *too*, amwek kwer-artwey. (M) 'Kwelyalp kwelyalp kwelyalp.' *That's the sound that baby wedge-tailed eagles, and bigger ones too, make for their mother.*
kwelyalp-irrem *vi.*
make a '*kwelyalp*' sound, sing (wedge-tailed eagles)
SEE ALSO irrety

kwelyely-irrem *vi.*
chirp (budgerigars) ◆ Atetherr kwelyely-irrem rlpwer-angkwerr. (T) *The budgies are chirping in the hollow tree.*

kwem (W), **kwem-kwem** (W) *n.*
life-saver burr, teddy bears arsehole (*Sida platycalyx*) (from English 'comb'). Soft herb with large yellow flowers. Fruits are doughnut-shaped and prickly when dry.
= ingka-mwerney, akeley-akeley, anmang

kwemarn substitute name for the name of a person or thing SEE UNDER **kwenman**

kwementyay *n.*
1. substitute name for the name of a person or thing, the name of which name cannot be used due to a death of a person with that name or a similar sounding name ◆ Tyap ngkenhar, ingwenengek-arneng, kwementyayek-arneng. (Sa) *The* ngkenhar *grub is related to the* ingweneng *grub, to that kwementyay one.* ◆ Akampamp-angkwerr arem kwementyayek. (St) *You look around the crown of the head for kwementyay [lice].*
2. substitute name for the name of a person whose name cannot be used because the speaker has an avoidance or respectful relationship to that person ◆ Ayeng alhem ankey Kwementyay-warn mernek kerek ankey. (T) *I'm going to go and ask Kwementyay for bread and meat.*
= kwenman

kwemey tasty food, sweet-tasting SEE UNDER **ikwemey**

kwempalth (T,E) *n.*
chisel, adze ◆ Kwempalthel arrpetyam panth. (T) *Adzes were used to chisel wooden dishes.*
SEE ALSO kantyengarr, kanyengarr, anker[1], tyalangk, arlarnt

kwemper (W,T) *n.*
sharp or pointy hill ◆ Irntang kwemper alenh-warn alhey. (M) *Let's go to that sharp pointy hill over there.*
SEE ALSO akwerlp, inperarr
CAN SOUND A BIT LIKE akwemper *'small bush banana'*

kwen, **kwetn** (E) *n.*
1. inside, in
2. down, deep, deep down ◆ Kwen angerr ra angernem, wal kwaty kwenarl anem. (St) *He digs down deep and the water is there inside.* ◆ Kwaty kwen-kety. (St) *Beware of the deep water.* ◆ Kwaty kwetn akngerrek pwerlp-irrekerr, iterel pwerlp-irra. (Sa) *Swim on the side, not in the really deep water.*
3. under
SEE ALSO aketh
CAN SOUND A BIT LIKE akwen *'not knowing'*
kwen-angerr *n.*
1. deep water
2. water that is a long way down (in a hole, well or soakage)
kwen-antep *adv.*
downwards, down ◆ Kwen-antep atnarnpetyek, arnethey atnarnpem kwen-antep. (St) *Climbing down from the tree.*
= kwen-akerl, kwenel-athek
kwen-akerl *adv.* = **kwen-antep** ◆ Kwen-akerl ayeng atnarnpenhem. (St) *I am climbing down.*
kwenel-athek *adv.* = **kwen-antep** ◆ Kwenel-athek atnarnpenhetyek arnkarreng apek. (St) *Maybe jumping downwards from the bank of the creek.*
kwenelak *adv.*
facing or slanting downwards ◆ Kwenelak yanh pewetyem-ilenheyaw. Thar-warl ngkernetyek mwetek, kwenelak. Kwenelak thar-iwetyek, pewetyem-iletyek angkem, 'Kwenelak yanh-warl thar-warl pewetyem-iley'. (Sa) *Push that car downwards. Put it on a downwards slant. When you are talking about pushing a car you say, 'Push it so that it faces down that way'.* ◆ Aka kwenelak ayeng intek, rtwenk-kwenyel. (St) *Without a pillow I am sleeping with my head on a downwards slant.*
SEE ALSO akernelak
kwen-ampeny *n.*
under, on the underneath side

kwenameny (T) *n.*
hidden, secret, complex, underlying
secret talk ◆ Angkety kwenameny inteh yanh aketh-ilang! (T) *Explain that hidden story!* ◆ Akern war mern-penh angkek, kwenameny tyerrty-penharl angkek. (T) *On the surface [he] spoke about bread, but the underlying meaning was about people.*

kweneng *n.*
the underneath side of something, lower, bottom

annga kwenengeneng (T,E), **alknga kwenengeneng** (E) (annga *'eye'*)
looking at something with narrowed eyes, cautiously; look downwards

kweneng-apert (E) *n.*
lower, bottom
SEE ALSO kweneng

kwen-ilem *vt.*
pull something down ◆ Kwen-ilem arna, waly renh kwen-ilem rtakw artetyek. (St) *Pull the branch down so that [you] can make a windbreak.*

kwen-irrem *vi.*
1. bend down, stoop ◆ War ayeng yanh-kety kwen-irrem, arrpenhel ayenh arekerr. (St) *I am just bending down because of that one over there, in case somebody sees me.* ◆ Arnekety apek kwen-irrenhem. (St) *Stoop as [you] are going along, to avoid the branches.* ◆ Mwerekatyety kwen-irretyel. (Sa) *Bending down because of my son-in-law.*
2. die down (flames)

kwenemangkarr (T,E) *n.*
1. bush tomato (*Solanum chippendalei* (sandhill form)). Plant about 80 cm high (though it may grow to 1.5 m) with purple flowers and fruits which are pale yellow when ripe. The seeds inside the fruit are inedible, and are thrown away.
2. the edible fruits of this bush tomato
= unemangkerr, antyewarl, ngantyewarl
SEE ALSO anakety

kweng-kweng *n.*
rinsing mouth out with water; gargling ◆ Kweng-kweng ntwang antywem, an artaly-wem. (M) *You rinse your mouth out with water then spit it out.*
= ngkwengk

kwenh *part.*
1. Adds emphasis; really, definitely, clearly. ◆ Tharrp kwenh kwern-ilek. (M) *I have really made a mistake.* ◆ Thwengk apawenhem mern apek ker apek kwenh, angayel anthwerr kwenh. (N) *I am asking you for bread or meat because I am really hungry.* ◆ Tyerrty yanh akey arelh then yanh apetyemarl arrantherr alhengkem ara kwenh, yanharl apetyepetyem atherr kwenh, yatenh atherr kwenh. (N) *Look at those people there, that woman and the other one that are coming there, you'll all recognise them, those two that are coming.*
2. Used to indicate quoted speech. In this context *kwenh* does not necessarily provide emphasis. ◆ Mern tywerrkel anwern amangkek, arlkwerl-apekarl, ampeng-irremarl. Arnkang arerl-alhem mentyel. *'Ah* ampeng-irrekam nhenh kwenh, anwengkerr mern arlkwerl-aney kwenh.' (N) *We grew up on wild figs, going along and eating them when they were ripe. If we saw unripe ones we'd leave them. 'Ah, this one is ripe, let's eat these ones', we'd say.* ◆ Nhenhek apek ayeng tyel angkerl-anem: 'Nhenh arertarl irrek anem kwenh.' (St) *I might talk about this one behind their back: 'This one has gone mad now.'*
3. Used to encourage someone to say a particular thing; 'Say . . . !'
CAN SOUND A BIT LIKE -kweny[2] *'without', 'none', 'not having something'*; kwern *'bad', 'no good'*

-kwenh (T) without, none, not having something SEE UNDER **-kweny[2]**

kwenkart (E) *n.*
turkey bush, mulga fuchsia (*Eremophila gilesii*). A small shrub with narrow leaves and blue flowers. Always grows near mulga. Leaves used as a washing medicine.
= pwenkart

kwenman, kwemarn *n.*
substitute name for the name of a person or thing, the name of which name cannot be used due to a death of a person with that name or a similar sounding name
= kwementyay

kwenpay (E) *n.*
light cloud ◆ Aherlkelarl ampetyel, alker atnert-they — aketh, *no* kwenpay. (Sa) *The sun is shining from high up in the sky — it's clear, no clouds.*
SEE ALSO ankert[1], mater

kwentarreng *n.*
young sand goanna, Gould's goanna, sand monitor, goanna hatchling, *arlewatyerr* (*Varanus gouldii*) ◆ Kwentarreng alewatyerr akwek, kwart-penh. Nheng kwart-penh lyetantarl arratem. Angerr anetyakenh. Ilanthem rarrp angerr-irretyeh. Akwek anthwerr *can't* atwerl, akwek, akely-amperl. Ilanthem, ker angerr-irretyeh. (N) *A* kwentarreng *is a small goanna that has just hatched out of the egg. That has just come out of*

the egg. They are not very big. You leave them so that they grow up. You can't kill the little ones, the tiny little ones. You send them off, so that they can grow bigger.
SEE ALSO arepilyerr

kwenterarr (T,E) *n.*
1. burial platform in a tree ◆ Kwenterarr-warl tyerrty arrernetyam, ilwekarl-penh. Mpwaretyam renh atharlkw, kel itna arrernetyam *dead fella* apek. (St) *After they died the person was placed on a burial platform. They made a sort of 'nest' and the dead body was put there.*
2. tree house (?)
SEE ALSO wimperr, thanarnt, awenng

kwentharr *n.*
water found in the hollow trunks of some trees, such as the bloodwood and the ghost gum
= nthwarr

kwenthey, irrkwenthey (E) *n.*
red poverty bush (*Eremophila duttonii*). Sticky shrub to 2.5 m high, with narrow bright green leaves and red flowers. ◆ Kwenthey arlpang inemey, kwer itenh-itenharl. Lhwertel kwer itenh-itenh, kwer mwerr anetyeh. (N) *The leaves of the* kwenthey *are collected and used for smoking babies. They are used for smoking babies, so that they will be strong.* ◆ Kwenthey akerl-apek. *No rake*, an kwenthey war, kwentheyel mer *clean*-em-iletyeh war. *Not rake*, itya. *Olden-time* arnel war *clean*-em-ilek kwentheyel. *Olden-time* antywang, lwerenam *clean*-em-ilerrirretyart antywang renh. (N) *People used to go and cut* kwenthey *branches. They used to clean their camps with* kwenthey *branches as they didn't have any rakes. There were no rakes, nothing. In the olden-time they just used* kwenthey *branches for sweeping. The olden-time humpies, that's what they used to clean them.*
kwenthey-kwenthey (E) *n.*
a place where there are lots of *kwenthey* bushes (and things associated with such places) ◆ *Football*-el apekarl arrken-irrep-irrem ina, anyentel apek impek kel. Arlkwerrem-antey. 'Arlkwek anyentel.' *Winner* apek ra anem. Arlkwek, *Stirling* mapel apek arlkwek, Kwenthey-kwenthey mapel. (St) *They are playing football and one team won. 'One team beat the others.' And then they are the winners. Maybe Stirling mob won, the* Kwenthey-kwenthey *team [named after Eremophila duttonii].*

kwenty[1] *n.*
stacked up, packed in close together ◆ Mern kwenty ngkernek ra arlkwetyek anem. (St) *[She] has stacked all the food up to eat.* ◆ Nthenhel anem ayeng intetyenh, kwentyarl intem-kety? (St) *Where am I going to sleep? There's too many packed in here.*
kwenty-kwenty *n.*
lots of things heaped up or stacked up, close together, in a group ◆ Karnkw awantyetyam aketyam, awantyetyam, panth-warl iletyam, kwenty-kwenty angernetyam mer-warn, merelam athety-alpemel awantyetyam. (N) *We used to pick the* karnkw *seeds and eat them, heap up the wooden dishes and take the seeds back to camp to grind them up and eat them.*
kwenty atherr
1. things that are close together, side by side or level with each other (atherr[1] *'two'*) ◆ Ilingkerr anerrem kwenty atherr ipmenh-nheng atherr. (T) *We are sitting close together, grandmother and granddaughter.* ◆ Warl atherr kwenty atherrarl artelhem. (St) *The two houses are built side by side.*
2. (two people) of the same age as each other

kwenty[2] (W,T), **kwinty** (W,T) *n.*
windbreak ◆ Irrerntel kwenty weyaw! (T) *Make a windbreak because of the cold weather!*

= rtak, werrant

kweny[1] (W,T) *n.*
darkness, night, night-time ◆ Kwenyel kwerrkwerrk anep-anem arnangel. (N) *In the night the mopoke owl sits in the tree.* ◆ Kweny arrpenhel yatherr intek. (M) *A few nights later they were sleeping.*
= ingwa
SEE ALSO ngwemernt
kweny rlkwerr (W,T), **kweny rlkwerrel** (W,T)
the middle of the night (rlkwerr *'middle'*) ◆ Kweny rlkwerrel angkerl-anem. (T) *Talking in the middle of the night.*
= ingwa mpep, kweny lpwararr
kweny Lpwararr (T) = **kweny rlkwerr**
(Lpwararr *'Milky Way'*)
kweny-rtwek arlkenh-arlkenh (T)
chicken, rooster (lit. 'something that sings out in the night') ◆ Nhenh thep kweny-rtwek arlkenh-arlkenhel anwernenh akemelh-ilem. (T) *This rooster gets us up in the morning.*
= tywek-tywek
kweny-areny (W,T) *n.*
black goanna (*Varanus tristis*) (lit. 'something

associated with the night') ◆ Ker kweny-areny kwenyelarl aperl-apem, rlpwer-areny. (T) *The black goanna lives in hollow trees and it goes around at night.*
= altywekerr, pwer rrpwerl, kwenyel alhem
kwenyel alhem (T), **kwenyel alhenh** (T)
= **kweny-areny** (lit. 'something that goes around in the night')
kweny-irrem (W,T) *vi.*
become night, get dark
= ingwirrem

-kweny[2], **-kwenh** (T) *ending*
1. Goes on nominals to mean 'not having that thing'; without, none, not. ◆ Alkiwerr-**kweny**, alhetyakenharl ayeng, mey-mey atyenh-kety. (St) *There's no room there, so I can't go, because of my son-in-law.* ◆ Aleny ayeng antyerrk-irrek, kwaty-**kweny**el. (St) *Without water my tongue dried up.* ◆ Tyerrty twernelarl ampek, kwaty-**kwenh**. (T) *Without water, the sun burnt the person.* ◆ Angayel apetyam mern-**kweny** ker-**kweny**. (M) *He came hungry, with no meat and no food.* ◆ Aleyak arelh awenk, kwer-**kweny**. (T) Aleyak *is a young woman without children.* ◆ *Family* atyenh ayeng anngwirrek, alhekarl apek iyntwarr. Ayeng-**kweny** itnarl alhekarl, ayeng anngwirrek anem. (St) *I forgot about my family because they went a long way away. They went without me, and then I forgot.*
2. Goes on nominals to show that something is not a particular thing. ◆ Mwetek ingkwernekarlarl yanh, arrernekarl, urlaylp-**kweny**arl yanh. (St) *That car has been registered, it's not* urlaylp *[unregistered].* ◆ Kwer yanh ateralth-**kweny**el. (T) *That child is not frightened.*
3. Goes on kin terms to show that someone has recently lost (become bereaved of) that particular relative.
4. Goes on verbs to show that the action of the verb did not happen, is not happening now, or won't happen, etc. When this ending goes on verbs it always follows *+ety*. ◆ Ayeng alh**ety**-**kweny**. (M) *I am not going.* ◆ Kwer nhenh mangk**ety**-**kwenh** itya, akwek-antey anep-anem. (M) *This child has not grown, it is still small.* ◆ Anwengkerr ntert aneyaw angk**ety**-**kweny**, yatenh angkem-arleng. (N) *We should sit down and not talk, because that person is talking.*
= +etyakenh, +etyang

Kwenyemp (W) *n.*
name of a hill west of Pine Hill

kwep *n.*

desert spadefoot toad (*Notaden nichollsi*). Also known as *ker kwep*. ◆ Kwep mpwanth-areny. (M) *The desert spadefoot toad lives in the open ground.*
= atweynterl, kwep-kwep2, pwerreparnt

kwep-anem (E), **ngkwep-anem** (E) *vi.* [RESPECT LANGUAGE]
sing out, shout, yell out ◆ Kwep-ana atyeweyay alharrenty-ayerr yanhentyak-kety, paytey-kety. 'Kwep-anetyek', 'arlketyek' ilem. (Sa) *For goodness sake, sing out and warn [him] about that creepy crawly, that 'bitey' [said in reference to respect kin]. 'Kwep-anetyek' is what is said for* 'arlketyek'. ◆ Arntwaly-ayerrek kwep-anerliwerretyel. (Sa) *[My son-in-law] is singing out for water.* ◆ Alharrenty-kety ngkwep-anetyek. (St) *Singing out because of the snake.*
SEE ALSO ameram-irrem, arlkem

kwep-kwep[1] *n.*
1. caustic vine, milk bush, milk vine (*Sarcostemma viminale* ssp. *australe*). Shrub with leafless tangled branches, pale green flowers and milky sap. Very poisonous.
2. caustic weed, mat spurge (*Euphorbia drummondii*). A ground-hugging herb that has small flowers and leaves, and milky sap.
= amwekel-amwekel1
SEE ALSO merterr1

kwep-kwep[2] *n.*
desert spadefoot toad (*Notaden nichollsi*)
= kwep, atweynterl, pwerreparnt

kwep-kwep[3] (W,T) *n.*
stalked puffball (*Podaxis pistillaris*). Grows to about 10 cm high, on a long stalk. Powdery purplish-black spores inside. ◆ Kwep-kwepel pernelhetyeh kwer map, nhenh arrkenel alakenh *moustache* arlka mpwarerl-apetyeh, arralt arlka. Mern anetyakenh. (N) *The* kwep-kwep *is for kids to rub on themselves, for them to have fun going along and making moustaches and beards on themselves. It's not edible.*
= pwek-pwek, arrepweng-pweng, pweng-pweng, anngarnt rrpwerl, arrekwep-kwep

kwepalepal *n.*

crested bellbird (*Oreoica gutturalis*) ◆ Kwepalepal yanh ilperlp-irrerl-anem. Aterel anthem tyerrty. '*Eh*, artwel atwehety kwenh.' (N) *The bellbird whistles and gives people a fright. 'Hey, the man is going to kill you.'* ◆ 'Kwepalepal, kwepalepal kwepalepal'.

Arreny inewelhem. (M) 'Kwepalepal, kwepalepal kwepalepal'. *It calls its name.*
= pakw-pakw
Kwepalepal (W) *n.*
name of a soakage west of Yuelamu (Mt Allan) community

kwer[1] (W,T) *n.*
1. child, children ◆ Arelhel alparrel rrkwerl-anem kwer akwek. (M) *His wife is holding the baby in the baby-carrier.* ◆ Arelh Pwerrerlel anew akem artwang Penangk. Kwer kwer-atherrenh angwerrm-irrek Pengart map. (T) *A Pwerrerl woman's husband is Penangk. Their children will be born Pengart.* ◆ Amwekel kwer kwerenh apernem aperrkel tywen-akert. (T) *The mother is rubbing her child, who has sores, with charcoal.*
SEE ALSO ampa, ketyey
2. young (animal)
kwer akwek (W,T)
baby (akwek *'small'*)
kwer marl (W,T)
girl (marl *'girl'*)
kwer rrwey (W,T)
boy (rrwey *'boy'*)
kwer rrkwern (W,T)
orphan (rrkwem *'hold', 'have'*)
= alhamp
kwereng-akwer (W,T) *n.*
doll
= ampengamp
kwer-tayem *n.*
the time when initiation or young man ceremonies are held ◆ Lweren arlka nheng arrwekeleny mapelam atwetyart. Nheng alpety alakenh-iletyeh, nheng kwer-tayem. (N) *That's why the olden-time people used to kill them. So that they could use the bilby tails like this [swing the tails around] during initiation ceremony time.*
= alyey-tayem

kwer[2], **ikwer** *prn.*
1. for him/her/it. See Appendix 1. ◆ Kwer itetyek mern. (T) *Cook some food for him/her.*
2. to him/her/it ◆ Artwang angkem kwer ngangkay-akerteh. (M) *A man talks to the traditional healer.*
3. on or onto him/her/it ◆ Irrertety mpwarem arnek-arlek kel ker apek arrernem irrertety ikwer. (St) *A platform is made in the tree and then the meat is put on the platform.*
4. After a word referring to one person or thing, refers to something that has previously been mentioned; the (one), this (one), that (one). ◆ Irrety anteth-akert, anteth kwerel wantelhem artwa. (N) *Eaglehawks have down, and it's with that down that the men decorate themselves.*
kwerenh, ikwerenh *prn.*
his, her, hers, its ◆ Kwerenh mern yanh. (T) *That food is hers/his.* ◆ Aympelh angerrarl ikwerenh, arwengerrp-kenh. (St) *The bush turkey's wings are big.*
SEE ALSO ra, renh
kwer-atherr, ikwer-atherr *prn.*
for them, to them, on or onto them (the two of them) ◆ Arrpenh apek kwer-atherr atwerretyek, ratherr anem ankwerl-inerrem. (T) *Somebody might come to fight for those two, so they help one another.* ◆ Ngkekern kwer-atherr apertepertem. *The kurdaitcha is sneaking up on the two of them.*
SEE ALSO ratherr, renh-atherr
kwer-atherrenh, ikwer-atherrenh *prn.*
their, theirs (belonging to the two of them) ◆ Arelh Pwerrerlel anew akem artwang Penangk. Kwer kwer-atherrenh angwerrm-irrek Pengart map. (T) *A Pwerrerl woman's husband is Penangk. Their children will be born Pengart.*
SEE ALSO ratherr, renh-atherr
kwer-arey, ikwer-arey *prn.*
for them, to them, onto them (more than two)
SEE ALSO rarey, renh-arey
kwer-areyenh, ikwer-areyenh, ikwer-arenh (E) *prn.*
theirs, their (belonging to more than two) ◆ Alhernter-rnem uneng-akert arrma, uneng rlterrk-akert arl ikwer-areyenh. (Sa) *White people have a spirit as well, their spirit is strong.* ◆ Arrewatyentan mer ikwer-arenharl, anewartewart ikwer-arenh, arrewatyent. (Sa) *The* arrewatyent *is their camp, the camp belonging to the husband and wife.*
SEE ALSO rarey, renh-arey
kwer-penh, ikwer-penh *n.*
after that; and then, because of that, from that ◆ Kwer-penh alhek anyerrkentyem akwerrk-akert mer-warn. (M) *Then [the mother] happily went back home with her child.* ◆ Arrwekel ayeng ltywerrerl-alhey rtweth-akert, rntwarrarl alhek-penh. Kwer-penh akem-irrem, 'Mwerram ayeng awelhem'. (N) *I'm going to go and have a rest first because my lower back aches from walking a long way. After that I get up and say, 'I feel good'.*
kwerety, ikwerety *prn.*
because of him/her/that/it ◆ Rlwelty ikwerety ater-irrem anyelel arrewem. (N) *Frightened of the frost and shivering in the cold.* ◆ Wenng-irrem, anthetyang anem, antewarl irrem kety.

Ngkerlp anthetyang anem renh antewarl-irrem-kety. Mwerrek-athen tha anthetyam. Yanhap ikwerety. Ra ilwekarl, '*Ah ah ah*'. Artekernekan. Ayeng wenng-irrek ikwerety. Wenng-irrem, menty anerlanetyek. Ayeng wenng-irrek yanh anthetyakenh — apant antherlanekerr. (Sa) *I now know not to give [her] any in case she vomits, not to give her any tobacco in case she vomits. I gave her some, thinking it was all right, but because of it she started coughing, 'Ah ah ah', she coughed. Then I knew about the bad effect it had. I knew to avoid it, and not to give her any — not to give her the wrong thing.*
SEE ALSO -kety

kwereng, ikwereng *prn.*
1. from him/her, from there, from that, from (the thing that has previously been mentioned) ◆ Kwer map rrtywerremel ilem kwenyel 'arrenty', wal ater-irrem kwereng. (T) *In the night the kids pretend and say 'monster', and then they get frightened from that.* ◆ War thelelherl-anem irnmerr renh war amparrkerl-anerlek arerl-anem, arna anyent kwerel antem. Arlperl artety kwereng antem war thelelherl-anem. (N) *It just drips from the mulga tree and you can see it like drops of water sparkling on the branch of that particular tree. The* arlperl *just drips from the mulga tree.*
2. then, after that (the event that has previously been mentioned) ◆ Tyampernem ayeng, kwereng rlkerremelhem, ingkang angelherl-anem alakenh. (N) *I am lying with my knees up, and after that I stretch, move my legs like that.* ◆ Angkweyarl anwern pwerlp-irretyart, rewel pwerlp-irrenhem, irrpenhem, mer arrpelant arratenhetyam. Kwereng mer arrpelem irrpentyetyam, arratetyam mer arrpelant. Arnang tintey-angkwarr apek kel *jump*-irretyart anwern. (N) *We used to swim in the running water, going into the water at one spot and then coming out at another. Then we'd go in again and come out at yet another place. We used to jump in from the bent-down branches of trees.*

kwerakwek (W,T) peaceful dove SEE UNDER **kwerlekwek**

kwerapak (W) *n.*
ceremonial payment of food; food used as a gift for someone who performs a ceremony; food presented at important occasions such as the birth of a child
= tyenkerr, tyewarrely, inngwerr

kwerathek (W,T) *n.*
clever, expert at doing something ◆ Tyerrty yanhel kwerathekel arlkeny-wem. (T) *That person is expertly painting the designs.* ◆ Arelh nhenhel kwerathekel panth atwep-atwem. (T) *This woman is expertly making the coolamon.*
= tyak
SEE ALSO inangkal, kalty, kapert altywer, kapert arraty, lywenpeny, wetyerretyerr[2], weretyerretyerr

kwerert (W,T) *n.*
not allowed, out of bounds, a restricted place (e.g. sacred site) ◆ Artwang map-henh kwerert — artwehenhant war, arelh-kweny. (M) *Men's things are* kwerert *— they just belong to the men, not to women.*
= amek-amek
SEE ALSO mwekeny, mwekenh, mweketyey, mety-mety

kwerewarr *n.*
1. a person's own country
2. a ceremonial design ◆ Artwel apek kwerewarr wem arlkeny, an mer ilem antim, mer arlalty. Atyengenh apek kwerewarr, mer kwerewarr wenh apekarl anganek. Yatenh arlka anwern ilem, angkety Anmatyerrel. (M) *The men paint the ceremonial designs, and talk about the country, their own country. My own country, and the place where I originated from, is 'kwerewarr'. That's what we say in the Anmatyerr language.*
SEE ALSO altyerr[1], anganenty, anengkerr

kwerl *n.*
school (from English 'school')
kwerl tety *n.*
schoolteacher (from English 'schoolteacher') ◆ Kwerl tetyel kwer map kaltyel-anthem. (M) *The teacher teaches the kids.*

kwerlekwek, kwerlakwek, kwerler-kwerler, kwerakwek (W,T) *n.*
1. peaceful dove (*Geopelia striata*)
2. diamond dove (*Geopelia cuneata*) (note Warlpiri *kurlukuku, kurluru-kurluru*)
◆ Tyerrtyelarl mpwarem-artek ra mpwarem antywa kwerenh kwerlakwekel. Antywa kwart apek anem ra arrernem. Ura kwert-artekarl ra. (St) *The diamond dove makes a nest, just like people make humpies. It lays its eggs in the nest. It is a smoky grey colour.* ◆ Angkep-angkem, 'Kwey akwekaw, kwey akwekaw'. Kwey akwek angkethel anem parrety. (St) *It calls out like this, 'Little girl, little girl'. The little girl is thirsty and perishing.* ◆ Kwerler-kwerler yanh kwer akwekeh arnerl-anem, kwer kwerenharl angekarl, lweren arnerl-anem akeweny, 'Kwer akwek kwer akwek. Kwer atyenheng kwenh angkek kwenh.' Alakenh arnerl-anem,

kwerler-kwerler. 'Kwaty alay-warl angekarl.' Lweren. Anywelekarl angekarl. Irrar-irrerl-anemel arnerl-anerl amwek. Kwer kwer. (N) *That diamond dove is crying for its little child that was taken away, that's why the poor thing is crying, 'Little child, little child. My little child has been taken away to the sea.' Its father took it away, and the mother is feeling sorry and crying for the child.*
= urelyarr
SEE ALSO lerakwenty

kwerleparr (W,T) *n.*
central military dragon (*Ctenophorus isolepis*) ◆ Rlwehenhan alhek kwerleparr-warn, yang apawenhwek, 'Lyertan atyeng ntwang awely arrernem?' 'Yety. Akwenam ayengan.' Kwer-penh tywenpel arlkwek. (M) *Perentie then went to the little dragon lizard and asked him, 'Will you paint a design on me today?' 'No. I don't know how to paint.' So the Perentie ate up the little dragon lizard.*
= nyarl
SEE ALSO tyalep, lyengkarr

kwerler-kwerler (W,T) peaceful dove SEE UNDER kwerlekwek

kwerlintyerr *n.*
large wooden water dish (note Warlpiri *kurlinjirri*)
SEE ALSO urna, amar

kwerlt *n.*
colt (from English 'colt') ◆ Tyerrtyel nantew kwerlt ltwakem. (M) *The person is breaking the colt in.*
SEE ALSO nanth, nantew

kwern (W,T) *n.*
1. bad, no good, wrong, inappropriate
2. no good, useless, dysfunctional
3. sick, sore, unwell ◆ Kwern kwenh ayeng anerl-anem. (T) *I am not feeling very well.*
= anety, akeng
SEE ALSO amwa2
CAN SOUND A BIT LIKE akwen *'not knowing'*

kwern-kwern (W,T) *n.*
not too good, not very good, so-so, a bit unwell, a bit useless
= akeng-akeng

kwern-irrem (W,T) *vi.*
1. go off; become damaged or spoilt, get wrecked, break down
2. get sick ◆ Alhekarl-penh ayeng amper atherr nhenh atherr kwern-irrety-alhek. (N) *After walking around these two knees of mine are no good.*
= anety-irrem, akeng-irrem, amwirrem

kwern-ilem (W,T) *vt.*
1. wreck something, damage something, spoil something ◆ Mwetek atyenh yanhel kwern-ilek. (M) *That person wrecked my car.* ◆ Tharrp kwenh kwern-ilek. (M) *I have made a mistake, myself.*
2. make someone sick
= anety-ilem, akeng-ilem

kwernt1 *n.*
the name of a card game. Thought to have originated in the northern part of Australia.
SEE ALSO peyenat, kart2, parlperrp

kwernt2 (W,T) *n.*
1. they (people in the opposite matrimoiety). In Anmatyerr society there are two matrimoieties. In one are Kemarr, Mpetyan, Penangk and Ngwarray people, and in the other Pengart, Ngal, Peltharr/Petyarr and Pwerrerl/Pwerl. (Note: Warlpiri *makurnta* 'member or members belonging to other matrimoiety than that of the speaker'.) See Appendix 1. ◆ Kwernt atherr kwenh yanh apety-alherrem. Mwer-nheng atherr kwerntan ilem. (M) *There are two people coming who are in the opposite matrimoiety to each other. A person together with their* mwer. ◆ Kwernt-henh mer — *don't* apetyerl mer kwernt-henh-warn kwenh. Kwernt-henh mer menty irney kwenh. (T) *Don't go to the country belonging to the people in the other matrimoiety. Leave that place alone.*
2. brother-in-law, husband's brother, wife's brother

kwernt-thayt (W,T) *n.*
1. they (people in the opposite matrimoiety)
2. country belonging to people in the opposite matrimoiety to a person (-thayt '*side*')

kwernt-nheng atherr *n.*
a person together with someone from the opposite matrimoiety to themself; for example, two brothers-in-law together, a woman and her mother-in-law, a man and his mother-in-law's brother ◆ 'Kwernt-nheng atherr yanh apetyerrem kwenh.' Tyerrty arrpel ilem, arelhel apek ilem. 'Artwa mwer-nheng atherrarl apetyerrem kwernt-nheng atherr.' (T) *'There come two people who are from the opposite matrimoiety.' That's what another person will say, maybe what a woman says. 'Two men who are in the opposite matrimoiety to each other and related as* mwer *are coming along.'*

kwernt-nheng *n.*
a group of two or more people who are from the opposite matrimoiety to each other; for

example, two or more brothers-in-law together, two or more women and their mothers-in-law, two or more men with their mother-in-law's brothers
SEE ALSO mwer-nheng atherr, mpwern-nheng, anherr-nheng

kwerr (W,T) *n.*
girl
= kwey
kwerr-malangk *n.*
a lovely girl (-malangk '*attractive*')
= kwey-malangk

kwerraly *n.*
1. star, falling star (comet) ◆ Kwerraly anyem ahern-warn. (T) *The star is falling to the earth.* ◆ Kwerraly arraly-arraly-irrepirrem. (St) *The stars are twinkling.* ◆ Kwerraly urltant-atherr, Arwenpeng an Mwer-nheng ratherr. (Sa) *They are both big stars,* Arwenpeng *and* Mwer-nheng.
2. Goes before the name of a particular star constellation. ◆ Kwerraly Arwenpeng, aremelarl renh aremel akem-irrem *early fella* anem renh arem, anentyerlek anem renh arnarem. Kel aherrk anem irrentyem. (St) *The Daylight Star is the one that you see early in the morning. You see it coming up and then the sun comes up.*
Kwerraly Rltwa (W), **Kwerraly Urlta** (T,E) *n.*
Morning Star, Daylight Star, Venus (rltwa '*big*') ◆ Kwerraly Urlta anenhem altwerl-athek. Anenhem an ywerrem anem ra. (T) *The Daylight Star appears in the west. It rises and then it disappears.*
= Anthelper, Arwenpeng, Awelh, Kwerraly Angerr
Kwerraly Angerr *n.*
1. Seven Sisters (angerr[1] '*big*')
= Interrk[1], Peltharr Map
2. Morning Star, Daylight Star, Venus
• = Kwerraly Rltwa, Kwerraly Urlta, Anthelper, Arwenpeng, Awelh
kwerralyarl rnternem (T,E)
fall (shooting star) (rnternem '*spear*', '*pierce*')
Kwerraly (W) *n.*
name of a place south of 20 Mile Waterhole, east of Napperby Station homestead

kwerrart (W), **kerrart** (T) *n.*
a type of puffball (?). It grows around mulga and river red gum trees and has a yellow powdery substance inside.
SEE ALSO kwerrerteth

Kwerrentyey *n.*
1. Gurindji person or people
2. Gurindji language (note Warlpiri *Kuurrinji*)

kwerrern *n.*
1. spirit (of a living thing), soul ◆ Kwerrern ngkwengenh alhek. (M) *Your spirit went away.* ◆ Kwerrern-akert ananther anem an arrpenh lwem wal kwerrern alpem akern. (T) *We all have a spirit, and when someone dies, well the spirit goes back into the sky.* ◆ Aretyakenharl ra, kwerrern tyerrty-they alhem. (St) *The spirit leaves the body but you can't see it.* ◆ Kwerrern-akert kwenh anwengkerr ananem. Kwerrern alenh apek, wal anwerlkem anwern wal kwerrern nhenh alakenh-irrem, *slip*-irrem. Arteperrk-angkwarr anwengkerr anem kwerrern, arteperrkel-arleng. Wal, antyerrk-irrem. Wal, ngangkayel mparem, kwerrern alenh angety-alpem, arrernem, mwerrem irrem tyerrty. Artep-warn-irrem, arteperrkeng-ntyel. Wal, kwerrern apek artep-warn irrem anwerlkemel. Kwerrern apek *wrong* apek irrem, artep-warn-irrem. (M) *We all have a spirit. If we get a fright then the spirit 'slips'. Our spirit is located around the kidney area. Well, it can get dry. Well, then the traditional healer fixes the person, brings the spirit back and puts it in place, and then the person gets better. If a person gets a fright the spirit moves from the kidney and goes towards the back of the person. The spirit ends up in the wrong place, towards the back.*
= anngirrenty
SEE ALSO uneng[2], inka, tyarrenng, lthan, arrelty
2. kidney [SOME SPEAKERS] • = arteperrk, mpwerrkety

kwerrert-kwerrert (W) *n.*
a grub while still in a root (when it goes black and gets wings)
SEE ALSO irrarl, akarternenty

kwerrk-kwerrk[1] (T) *n.*
fontanelle
= thelty-thelty, ahey-ahey, atek-kenh, iylpwerr-iylpwerr, kapert ahey-ahey, kapert thelty

kwerrk-kwerrk[2] (E) *n.*
monster (said to frighten children) ◆ Kwerrk-kwerrk-kety rntert-irray. (St) *Be quiet or the monster will get you.*
SEE ALSO kwerrkwerrk

kwerrkar (W,T) *n.*
desert oak (*Allocasuarina decaisneana*). Tree to 10 m high, with rough thick bark, long needle-like leaves, and heavy cones. Grows in spinifex sandplains and sandhills. ◆ Kwerrkar *self*, mern anetyakenh, akern anthwerr renh arlpelh. (N) *The desert oak does not have edible fruits, and the leaves are really high up.*
= arrkep

kwerrkwerrk, kwerrkwerrp (W) *n.*
southern boobook (*Ninox novaeseelandiae*)

(note Warlpiri *kuurrkurrpa*)
◆ Kwerrkwerrk kwenyel merneh nthwerl-apem. Kwerrkwerrk kwenyel angkem, 'Kwerrkwerrk kwerrkwerrk'. (N) *The mopoke goes round at night looking for food. At night the mopoke sings out like this, 'Kwerrkwerrk, kwerrkwerrk'.*
= akekw
SEE ALSO kwekew

kwerrm (E) *n.*
scar
kwerrm-irrem (E) *vi.*
heal over ◆ Kel ayeng kwerrm-irrem mwerr anem ayeng, utyenarl ayeng akngerr anek-penh. (St) *After having a big wound I am better now, I have healed up.*
= urrmirrem
SEE ALSO arrintety-irrem, arterrp-irrem, ltyerrem, tywenmernt-irrem, pwarn-irrem

kwerrng (W,T) *n.*
small (of fingers and toes) ◆ Iltyang kwerrng. (M) *Small fingers (not including thumb).*
SEE ALSO akwerrk[1]

kwerrpar (T,E) *n.*
wooden object used by women and girls when dancing in ceremonies

kwert *n.*
1. smoke ◆ Rwang kwert arratem. (N) *The fire is smoking.* ◆ Rwang kwertarl intem. Rwa item, an kwert anem intem, kel altherrem anem, rwa ya ampem antem. (T) *The fire starts smoking. [You] light the fire, then it starts smoking, then it catches alight and then it burns.*
2. cigarette, smokes
rwang kwert (W,T), **ura kwert** (E)
smoke (rwang, ura *'fire'*)
kwert-henh (W,T), **kwert-kenh** (E) *n.*
exhaust pipe (of a car) (lit. 'belonging to the smoke')
kwert antywem
smoke (cigarettes) (antywem *'drink'*)
◆ Arrpenhemel ngkwerlp arlkwem, arrpenhemel kwert antywem. (St) *Some people chew tobacco and others smoke cigarettes.*
ura kwert-kwert (E)
blue or grey in colour, 'smoky' in colour (ura *'fire'*)
kwertel item (W,T)
'smoking' a young man or new baby for healing or strengthening purposes (item *'cook something'*) ◆ Kwertel item ampelyerrk map, lhwertel. (M) *Newborn babies are 'smoked' in the healing smoke.*
= lhwertel-ilem
SEE ALSO lhwert
kwertelh-ilem *vt.* = **kwertel item** ◆ Arelh ampwel kwertelh-ilem arelh an kwer akwek. (T) *An old woman or a child might be 'smoked'.*

kwert-kwert (W,T) *n.*
blunt-leaf cassia (*Senna artemisioides* ssp. *helmsii*). A woody shrub to about 0.5 m high, with broad leaves and broad papery pods. This plant is used for making ashes to chew with native tobacco. ◆ Kwer akwek tywen-akert alhewem kwert-kwertel. (T) *Little kids with sores are washed with [a mixture made from] blunt-leaf cassia.*
SEE ALSO ngkwert

kwertar, kwetar *n.*
men's ceremonial headdress. Made from grass and emu feathers. ◆ Artwang map rntwem althart kwetar-akert. (T) *The men are dancing the* althart *ceremony with ceremonial headdresses on.*
= ilperl[4]
SEE ALSO perety[1]
CAN SOUND A BIT LIKE kweter *'fighting stick'*

kwertaty (E) *n.*
kurdaitcha, kurdaitcha man, ritual executioner
= rlwarlp, urlaylp, inenty, nwernternenty, ngkekern
SEE ALSO melarlp, mwak[2]
CAN SOUND A BIT LIKE kertaty *'dark-coloured or dry seeds of the dogwood tree'*

kwertengerl *n.*
ceremonial role that a person has in relation to their mother's and mother's brother's country. Sometimes this role is glossed in English as 'manager', or 'offsider'.
◆ Kwertengerl anem, apmerarl altyerr akek, kwertengerl anem anem. (St) Kwertengerl *are the ones who are related to that particular country through their mothers, they call that place* 'altyerr'. ◆ Kwertengerlel apmer arntarnt-arem, iwenhek apek irrkwapem. (St) Kwertengerl *look after the country, and work doing various things.* ◆ Kwertengerl map inang rntwetyeh, arelh map. (T) *All the* kwertengerl, *the women, have to dance.*

kwertetyengetyeng *n.*
a type of crab (?)
SEE ALSO ikarl, iltyarnm

kwetang *n.*
a type of large rat (*Rattus villosissimus* (?))
◆ Kwetang angkweyarl anetyam rapet-artek. (T)

Kwetang *used to be [here] before, and they were similar to rabbits.*
SEE ALSO nyemal

kwetar men's ceremonial headdress SEE UNDER **kwertar**

kweter *n.*
fighting stick, nulla-nulla, women's ceremonial stick. These are usually made from mulga or dogwood. ◆ Arelhel mpwarem kweter ahel atwerretyek. (T) *Women make nulla-nullas to fight with.* ◆ Kweterel atwem, wal ilpem arrpenhel. Ilpelhem apek rarrp, tyerrty anpetyakenh. (St) *If someone is hitting someone with a nulla-nulla, well another one might step in to block it. Or the person themself might shield themself with something, so that they can't be touched.*
SEE ALSO anem[3]
CAN SOUND A BIT LIKE kwertar *'men's ceremonial headdress'*

kweth-kweth *n.*
1. dripping with blood, covered with blood ◆ Kweth-kweth akngerrek atwek akeweny. (T) *The poor thing was beaten till he was covered with blood.*
2. blood [RESPECT LANGUAGE] ◆ Atyeng urrem-iletyek kweth-kweth-ayerr apek. (St) *Give me some [kangaroo] blood [from my son-in-law].*
SEE ALSO alhwa

kwetn (E) inside, in SEE UNDER **kwen**

kwety-arem *vt.*
look after someone ◆ Thang rlkert kwety-arem. (M) *I am looking after the sick person.*
SEE ALSO kwetyakw-ilem, arntarnt-arem, akarem

kwety-arerrem (E) *vt.*
hold or embrace each other in mourning, express grief and sorrow. People of the same gender as each other hold each other chest to chest; men touch women on the back.
◆ Kwety-arerrem arelhel. (Sa) *The women are embracing each other in sorrow.*

kwetyakw-ilem (T,E) *vt.*
look after someone or something; raise someone or something (children), bring up a child ◆ Thang kwetyakw-ilem ampa rlkert. (T) *I am looking after the sick child.* ◆ Kwetyakw-ilay akeweny amwel renh nthwekerr. Mwanty arntarnt-arem. (T) *Look after the poor thing carefully in case she gets bitten by a snake. Look after her carefully.*
= amangkelh-ilem
SEE ALSO kwety-arem, mpwarem, arntarnt-arem

kwetyem *vt.*
1. gather, collect, pick something up
◆ Artwang nhenhel arrwelty kwetyerl-apem. (N) *This man is going along collecting kindling.*
◆ Inernt apek kwetyepetyem. (St) *Going along gathering bean tree seeds.* ◆ Rnwanenty apek ngkwenh anyekarl, nta kwetyem, anyemarl. (M) *You pick up your clothes which have fallen down.*
2. grow up or raise a child, adopt a child

kwetyenty *n.*
lost child, orphan (i.e. one that has been 'picked up')
SEE ALSO alhamp, rrkwern, amatheng

kwey (T,E) *n.*
girl, young woman, female person ◆ Kwey nhenh atherrel ayenh mwarrewetyel, pwerrkel anthetyel. (Sa) *These two girls are wearing me out, making me tired.*
= kwerr
SEE ALSO marl

kwey akarnterrng (T,E)
young teenage girl (with breasts starting to grow) (akarnterrng *'the shape of breasts when they are starting to develop'*)

kwey awenk (T,E)
big girl, teenage girl (awenk *'teenage girl'*)
◆ Tyepety ilelherl-anem, kwey awenk. (St) *The young women are telling a story in the sand.*

kwey-malangk (T,E)
a lovely girl (-malangk *'attractive'*)
= kwerr-malangk

kwey-kwey (W,T) *n.*
part of intestines (?). Also referred to as *ker kwey-kwey.*
SEE ALSO lyep-lyep, mwerlk[1]

kweyekar *n.*
those who are in the same generation moiety to the person or persons whose point of view you are taking. In one generation moiety are Pwerrerl (and Pwerl), Ngwarray, Penangk and Ngal people and in the other Kemarr, Mpetyan, Pengart and Peltharr (and Petyarr).
◆ Anwengkerr ilem 'nywerrp map', kenh anwengkerr ilelhem 'kweyekar'. (M) *We call [them] 'nywerrp' and we call ourselves 'kweyekar'.* ◆ Kweyekar mpwel atherr, nywerrp anyent ayeng. (M) *You two are in the same generation moiety, and I am in the opposite.*
SEE ALSO nywerrp, -apakwey, -apatherr, anantherr-apakwey, anwernanth-apakwey, anwernantherr-apakwey, ilernanth-apakwey

kweyepey (E) *n.*
stubble quail (*Coturnix pectoralis*)
SEE ALSO atek

kwinty (W,T) windbreak SEE UNDER **kwenty**[2]

Ll

lakem (W,T) chase someone or something SEE UNDER **lwakem**

lalthengayt (E) grub from the branches of the Georgina gidgee SEE UNDER **ulalthengayt**

lam-lam *n.*
lamb (from English 'lamb')

Lampetherr (W), **Rlampetherr** (W) *n.*
name of a hill in the Stuart Bluff Range area

lant-em-ilem *vt.*
1. lend something to someone
2. borrow something (from English 'lend')

larakwenty (W,T) diamond dove; peaceful dove (?) SEE UNDER **lerakwenty**

Laramba SEE UNDER **Alherramp**

larl *n.*
lolly, sweet (from English 'lolly') ◆ Alalherrk lpwayelarl irnem. Alalherrk rnpwang nhenh-lkwer arlkwetyart, larlart rnpwang. Awantyetyart larlarl awantyem-artek. Intertelarl anem. (N) *The* alalherrk *bush grows in the creeks. We used to eat the sweet resin from the* alalherrk *bush, just like a lolly. We used to suck on it just like you suck lollies. It is found in the base of the tree.*

larnayt blue wattle, leather-leaved colony wattle etc. SEE UNDER **iylarn**

Larnt (W,T) *n.*
name of a place in the Willowra area

larrangkern, arlarrangkern (E) *n.*
tree frog (*Litoria* spp.) ◆ Larrangkern rlpwerel angkem, kwaty akangkemel angkem. (T) *The tree frog sings out from hollow logs, it sings out because it's happy about the rain.*
= karlarrangkern, antyetyerr
SEE ALSO alyeyamp, mpwelengk, kwep

Latyaman (W,T), **Latyamaney** (T) *n.*
Lajamanu. The name of a Warlpiri community in the north-western part of the Northern Territory.

layempeylay (T,E) ribbon grass, spear grass SEE UNDER **lyayepelyay**

lengarr (E), **arlengarr** (E), **irlengarr** (E) *n.*
coolamon, wooden dish ◆ Lengarr mpwarem arwerl atywerety-penh. (Sa) *Coolamons are made from bean tree wood.*
= panth, alparr[1]
SEE ALSO atywekal, urety, kwerlintyerr, arlketh[1], lwengkart[2], irrkwely[2], irrkwa, rnwa, urna

lengarr-iperr (E), **arlengarr-iperr** (E), **irlengarr-iperr** (E) *n.*
baby at the stage when it is carried in a coolamon

lengarr-lengarr (E), **arlengarr-arlengarr** (E) *n.*
piedish beetle (*Helea* spp.)
SEE ALSO perrertety, panth-panth

lengk-lengk (W,T), **rlengk-rlengk** (W,T) *n.*
point of the jawbone
SEE ALSO arrely[2]

lepwel *n.*
1. level, even (from English 'level') ◆ Lepwel mer anetyangel tharel aynterl-anenty, kapwert thar. (Sa) *The place is not level, and [the person] is lying on a slant, with their head on a slant.*
2. similar, about the same (as something else) ◆ Atyew-nheng aylernanth alhetyart lepwel. Ampa atyew-intyerr. *The two of us used to go around together as friends, about the same age. All of us kids were age-mates.* ◆ Arnek-athen unernengk renh arerl-anem, wararl altywernerl-anem, war arna then ra then lepwel. (St) *You see the tawny frogmouth just sitting there and you might think it is a branch, just because they are both similar to each other.*
SEE ALSO kwenty atherr

lerakwenty (W), **larakwenty** (W,T) *n.*
1. diamond dove (*Geopelia cuneata*) (?)
2. peaceful dove (*Geopelia striata*) (?)
SEE ALSO kwerlekwek, kwerler-kwerler, urelyarr

lernem *vt.*
1. shake something out; shake, brush or beat something so that things on it fall off; brush off coals, ashes and sand ◆ Ntang iylaw. Arlter-arlter wetharl ngkweytek. *Grey-grey one-*arl iylaw. Akemel, panth-warl apek renh lernem lernem lernem, kerl-apemel lernerl-apem. *All right,* aympernem anem renh. Iylaw. (St) *The munyeroo plant has edible seeds. The* ngkweytek *plant is whitish in colour, whereas the* iylaw *plant is greyish. It is picked and the seeds are shaken in the wooden dish. Munyeroo. All right, after that they are yandied.*
2. fall (rain) ◆ Nyempant ap intyernem arleng, kwatyelarl lernem-penh. (St) *After the rain has fallen you can smell it from a distance.*
CAN SOUND A BIT LIKE alernem[1] *'shine;* alernem[2] *'lean against something', 'poke into something'*

lernelhem *vi.*
1. fall down, scatter, fall onto something ◆ Mern perlap ingkerrek lernelhek ahern-warl. (St) *All of the conkerberries have fallen to the ground.* ◆ Ahakey rwerrkem, ahelh-warnan lernelhem ahakey *seed* map. Renh anem kwetyerl-anem. (T) *[You] shake the bush plum tree so that the fruit falls to the ground. Then you go along and collect them.*
2. fall down (from part of your body)

◆ Anngethey, war arrngwelty lernelhem, irrerntel apek. (St) *In the cold weather the tears fall from [your] eyes.*
3. shake something off part of yourself
◆ Ayeng lernelhem ahern altethey. (St) *I am shaking the dirt from my hair.*
CAN SOUND A BIT LIKE alernelhem *'lean on something for support'*

lerranty (W,T), **lharranty** (T) *n.*
billowing smoke, cloud of smoke, pyrocumulus cloud ◆ Lerranty anem rwa, ankert anem kwerel-ayel anem. (T) *The smoke billows up from the fire and then the cloud forms on top of it.*
SEE ALSO arrempelty, angkarl

lerrenp *n.*
a type of cricket ◆ Lerrenp aretyakenh, war angkep-angkerlekant awem. (St) *You can't see the* lerrenp *crickets, you can only hear them making a noise.*
= irreynm

lert *n.*
small tin, such as those used to keep tobacco or ashes in (from English 'lid') ◆ Lert anthentyay ngkwerlp-akert. (T) *Give me back my tin which has tobacco in it.*
lert-lert *n.*
toy car that has tins for wheels ◆ Kwer mapel mpwarem lert-lert mwetek-mwetek. (T) *The kids are making toy cars.*

lew-lew (W,T), **liw-liw** (E) *n.*
bent, crooked ◆ Artep lew-lew. (M) *A bent back.*
◆ Ker arlewatyerr liw-liw irrkert-irrkert-ilemel ampek. (St) *The goanna twisted up and bent when it was cooking.*
SEE ALSO amper-amper, arnkwert, arnkwert-arnkwert, irrkert-irrkert, iylwerl-iylwerl, rtapety
lew-lew-irrem (W,T), **liw-liw-irrem** (E) *vi.*
get bent, get twisted ◆ Arlewatyerr rwepenh lew-lew-irrem. (T) *Goannas get twisted after being in the fire.*
SEE ALSO irrkert-irrkert

leyterr (E), **leytwerr** (E) *n.* [RESPECT LANGUAGE]
fat (used for healing, rubbing fat, cooking fat)
◆ Leyterrel aperneyaw arntety apek. (Sa) *Rubbing the sick person with healing fat.*
SEE ALSO anter

lharranty (T) billowing smoke, cloud of smoke
SEE UNDER **lerranty**

lhekethatethat (E) *n.*
a type of waterbird; black-tailed native-hen (*Gallinula ventralis*) (?) ◆ Lhekethatethatel antyarlkw mpwarem iylpwerek, antyelty akernek. (Sa) *The black-tailed native-hen makes its nest in hollows high up in trees.*
SEE ALSO angkeparr, karlayteng-ayteng, kart-irrkwely-irrkwely, narremantyerr, ngkwern rnter-rnter

lhelpengelhem (W,T) *vt.*
chase someone or something; frighten something away (birds or animals) (?) ◆ Kwer nhenh mapel lhelpengelhem ker aherr. (M) *These kids are frightening the kangaroo away.*
◆ Tyerrty lhelpengelhem kweter-akertel atwetyek. (T) *Chasing someone to fight them with a nulla-nulla.* ◆ Tyerrty alenhel lhelpengelhem tyerrty alenh atwetyew. Wal, tyerrty arrpenhel alakenh apek, 'Impang kwenh akeweny kwenh! Lhelpengelhetyal kwenh.' (M) *That person chases someone to give them a fright and hit them. Well, another person says, 'Leave the poor thing alone! Don't chase them and frighten them.'*
SEE ALSO aterel-anthem

lhenp *n.*
1. armpit
2. the part under the foreleg or front leg (of an animal) ◆ Tywenp anenem arrakerteng anem, kart, kenh arlewatyerr anenem lhenpengarl. (N) *Perenties are gutted through the mouth, whereas goannas are gutted from under their forelegs.*
ker lhenp
edible meat from under the foreleg of an animal (ker *'meat'*)
lhenp alta
armpit hair (alta *'hair'*)

lher *n.*
1. creek, river, watercourse ◆ Lher iterel alhem. (St) *Going along the side of the river.*
◆ Lher akngerr, alpep-alpem lher akngerr yanh. (St) *There is a big river flowing along there.*
2. creekbed, riverbed
3. sand, soft sand ◆ Lher atnertel ingka ampem ayeng uternelaw. Aper-warl iparrp alhey, ingkarl ampem-kety lherel. (Sa) *The heat of the sand in the middle of the creek is burning my feet. Let's go quickly to [the shade of] the river red gum, my feet are being burnt by the sand.*
lher twemper (T,E)
riverbank, side of a creek, drifts of sand left by floodwater (twemper *'side of a creek'*)
= lher twerr, arnkarr
lher twerr (W,T) = **lher twemper** (twerr *'side of a creek'*)
lher twerrp (W)
small sandy rise (twerrp *'sandhill'*)
lher pwarn
small or narrow creek (pwarn *'narrow'*)

SEE ALSO mpwetyerr, ilerrty

lher tyert (E) = **lher pwarn** (tyert *'narrow'*)

lher-lher[1] *n.*

1. small creek

2. the soft part in the middle of a creek; sandy country [SOME SPEAKERS] ◆ Thenkarr-kety lher-lherel ayeng intem. (T) *I'm going to sleep in the little creek because of the prickles.*

Lher Arrpant *n.*

name of a waterhole south of Yuelamu (Mt Allan) community. Location of an old station.

lher-lher[2] *n.*

soft fleshy part of the foot or hand ◆ Lher-lher-warl irrpek, ingka lher-lher-warl, lyek. Arna apek. (St) *A prickle, or a stick, went into the soft part of [my] foot.*

lherrm (T,E) *n.*

flame ◆ Lherrmelarl ampem. (T) *The flames are burning.*

= anngenth, aleny, anngenenty, lyenenty

lherrm-ilem (T,E) *vt.*

light a fire

= anngenth-ilem, nthilem

lherrm-irrem (T,E) *vi.*

catch alight ◆ Ura pew-ilem lherrm-irretyek. (Sa) *Blow the fire so that it catches alight.*

= alep-irrem, antant-irrem

Lherrm-penh (E) *n.*

1. a star or planet (possibly Mars)

2. something that has been burnt in the flames ◆ Lherrm-penh arlkwetyalay! (St) *Don't eat that [food] that has been burnt!*

lhwek-lhwek (W,T) *n.*

1. emu bush (*Eremophila longifolia*). Shrub to 4 m high, with green drooping leaves and red flowers which are pink inside. ◆ Akwerrk ampetyam akwerrk ampem alkey akwek *baby one* lhwertel ampetyam *baby one* lhwek-lhwekel. Angerr map *little bit* akwek tyelepelep kwenyem ananem yanh itetyam. Amwek amparr ampem akwekem ampem, arrernem rnwartel ampem amelekwel-ayel menhelekw-ayel apek. Menhelekw-ayel ampem akweran ampetyam lhwertel, lhwert akenh angerr anep-anerleng. (N) *Babies were smoked with the emu bush leaves. When they get a little bit bigger and the umbilical cord is not there any more, then they are smoked. The mother is smoked first and then the baby, the baby is put in the lap of its mother or granny. The baby might be smoked with the emu bush while sitting on its granny's lap.*

= unerreng

2. grub from the emu bush and some other Eremophilas ◆ Tyap arlkwetyenheng kwenthey-areny. Tyap lhwek-lhwek maparl intem kwentheyel, anwern arlkwetyart. (T) *We used to eat the grubs from the red poverty bush [Eremophila duttonii]. There are a lot of* lhwek-lhwek *grubs on the red poverty bush and we used to eat them.* • SEE ALSO unerrengayt, alwerrpent

lhwelk *n.*

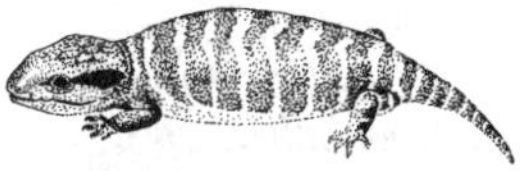

blue-tongue lizard (*Tiliqua multifasciata*). Also known as *ker lhwelk*. ◆ Arreyl atherr irrpwerl ker lhwelk ra. (St) *The blue-tongue lizard is dark-coloured on both its cheeks.*

= lwengkart[1], ilpankwer

= **ulhelk** (T,E)

lhwem (T) *vi.*

1. defecate, have a shit, go to the toilet

2. urinate ◆ Ayeng mpwang lhwem. (T) *I am urinating.*

3. lay an egg

= **ulhem** (T,E)

mpwelhem (T) *vi.*

have a piss, urinate (mpwa *'urine'*)

lhwerrp-ilem (T) *vt.*

squeeze something out of something else (e.g. shit from intestines); clean something out of something; blow something out (of nose) ◆ Kwer akwek apek mernt wal lhwerrp-ilem. Kel ra arratem *clean*-em ilemel wem. (T) *If a child has a snotty nose well [you] squeeze the snot out. It comes out and then you chuck it away and then [the nose] is clean.*

= ulherrpernem

lhwert *n.*

1. smoke used for healing and for particular ceremonies

2. leaves or other plant material that is burnt to make the healing smoke ◆ Kwenthey arlpang inemey, kwer itenh-itenharl. Lhwertel kwer itenh-itenh, kwer mwerr anetyeh. (N) *The leaves of the* kwenthey *are collected and used for smoking babies. They are used for smoking babies, so that they will be strong.* ◆ Ya, lhwertek arrernem ampa akwek, rlkert, lhwertel item, ampa akely, mwerr-ilemel. Lhwert arrernem ipertek, kel ura kweneng arrernem, lhwert anem arratem renhek anem arrernem ampa. Tyerrty akngerran arrernem akin, alakenh arrernelhem, rlkert. Lhwertel ampem. (St) *Yes,* *you put little kids, sick kids, in the healing smoke and 'smoke' them to make them better. You put the leaves in a hole, light a fire underneath and then, when the smoke starts coming up, you put the child in the smoke. Grown-ups are smoked as well, if they are sick. Smoked in the healing smoke.*

lhwertel-ilem *vt.*
'smoke' someone, put a person in the healing smoke
= kwertelh-ilem, kwertel item

lhwertel item = lhwertel-ilem (item *'cook something'*)

lhwertel ampem = lhwertel-ilem (ampem2 *'cook', 'heat up'*)

lhwert-irrem *vi.*
smoke or burn (from cooking) ◆ Ker apek lhwert-irrem, antyerrk-irremel lhwert-irrem. (St) *That meat is smoking and going dry.* ◆ Ker yanh lhwert-irrek, parrp ina. (T) *That meat is burnt, get it quickly.*

lim-lim (W) *n.*
lame, crippled (from English 'lame')
SEE ALSO anath, anenyirrp irrkweynar, apekap, apertap, arlamarr, arlwemeny, lyer, rnwerr, rnwerr-rnwerr, rtapety, yer

lim-lim-irrem (W) *vi.*
become lame or crippled

liw-liw (E) bent, crooked SEE UNDER **lew-lew**

lkwameny (W,T), **rlkwameny** (W,T), **lkwampeny** (T) *n.*
spectacled hare-wallaby (?) (*Lagorchestes conspicillatus*)
SEE ALSO kwarlp

lkwart (W,T), **ilkwart** *n.*

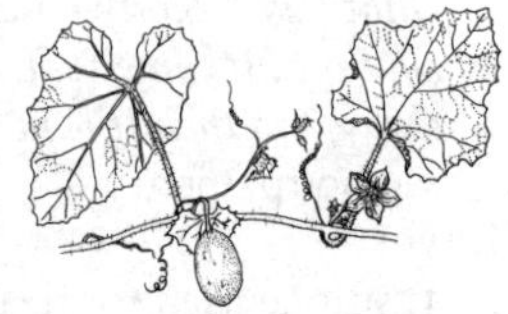

1. native gooseberry, ulcardo melon, native melon, native cucumber (*Cucumis melo* ssp. *agrestis*). A vine with yellow flowers and green fruits which turn yellow when ripe.
2. the edible fruits of the native gooseberry. Also referred to as *mern lkwart.* ◆ Mern lkwart anthwerr. Mern lkwart lpway-areny kenh lkwart arrpenh nhenh ker-kenh, aherrarl arlkwenh-arlkwenh. (M) *The edible* lkwart *melon. One sort of* lkwart *is edible and grows in the creeks, and another sort is kangaroo food.*
SEE ALSO lkwart-lkwart
= ulkart (T,E)

lkwart-lkwart (W,T), **ilkwart-ilkwart** (T,E) *n.*
1. headache vine (*Cucumis maderaspatanus*). A climbing vine that has fruits which change from green to yellow then bright red. ◆ Aherrel arlkwenh-arlkwenh, anter mpwarelhenhelhenh mern inekenh, ker aherr. (N) *It's kangaroos' food. It makes them fat — it's their tucker.* ◆ Lkwart-lkwartel anwern apernelherl-apek kapert twernel alherl-apemel, twernel ampem pwet kweny wart, wal anwern ingkang apernelherlapetyart ingkang. Kernt alhetyeh. Lkwart-lkwart yanh-lkwerel anwern apernelherlapetyart an kapert. Ker aherrel arlkwem akin renh, kenh anwern-kenh apernelherl-aperlek. (N) *We used to rub our heads with headache vine when were travelling about in the hot sun, when the hot sun was burning our heads and we didn't have any shoes on. Well we used to rub our feet as well, so that we could travel cool. We used to rub our heads with headache vine. Kangaroos eat it as well, and we used it for rubbing on ourselves.*
SEE ALSO aherr-arlweth ◆ *Olden-time*-el apernelhetyart lkwart-lkwart yanh, mern kwerenhel akwel apernelhem. Kapert arlka apernelhem. (N) *The olden-time people used to rub themselves with that* lkwart-lkwart, *with the fruit from that plant. They used to rub their heads as well.*
2. native gooseberry, ulcardo melon, native melon, native cucumber (*Cucumis melo* spp. *agrestis*) [SOME SPEAKERS]. A vine with yellow flowers and green fruits which turn yellow when ripe. • = lkwart

rlkwemen (W,T) old woman SEE UNDER **werlkemen**

-lkwer *n.ending*
1. Shows that something is a bit like something else; this type of thing, that type of thing, more-or-less (like this). ◆ Kwep angerrety nheng-**lkwer** anwern inyetyart ker renh, inyemel inyemel inyemel, inyetyart anwern, ker kwep. (N) *Those big frogs, we used to dig up things like that, dig and dig and dig them and get the* kwep *frogs.* ◆ Ker rrpwamper yanh-**lkwer**, ker rlpwerelarl anetyart, rrpwamper. Lweren arlka arlkwerretyart. (N) *They also used to eat possum meat and that sort of thing — animals that lived in hollow trees.* ◆ Wetharl unta mpwarek-artek mpwaray, weth-**lkwer** mpwaray. (St) *Make one like that one that you made, make that sort of thing.*
2. Used in making comparisons between things; a bit like **er** in English bigg**er**, small**er** etc. ◆ Ker mpwelengk. Perrak-artek akngerr-awatyarl ra. Akngerr-**lkwer**arl ra. Atherrk-atherrk, *yellow yellow.* (St) *The burrowing frog is like a frog only bigger. It's bigger. It's a yellowy green colour.* ◆ Ker angerr-**lkwer** akay! (T) *Cut more meat!*

nhenh-lkwer *n.*
this sort of thing, this type of thing (often while indicating or pointing to the thing) (nhenh *'this', 'here'*) ◆ 'Nhenh-**lkwer** angetyang.' Tyerrty alenh apek antangk-ilem. (M) *'Bring one like this.' Asking that person to get it.*

lpwa (W,T) *n.*
soft, crushed up or softened pieces of something (e.g. tobacco)
CAN SOUND A BIT LIKE rlpwa *'red ochre'*
= **ulpa** (E)

lpwelem (W,T) *vt.*
grind or smash something up to make it soft ◆ Yerrakwerr inyetyart irrkeremel irrkeremel inyetyart yerrakwerr renh, *billycan* pwelap inyetyart. Aweth inyetyart irrkeretyart irrkeretyart lpwelemel then-wetyart arlka arrernetyart pwelap kwetyemel, yerrakwerr yanh renh. (N) *We used to clear the ground and dig up the wild onions, filling up the billycans. We'd dig for more and clear the ground for more and then beat them to make them soft and then winnow them to clean them, collecting together all the wild onions that we had found.* ◆ Rlpwang lpwelem irntang ather-warn. (T) *Grinding the red ochre up on the grinding stone.*
SEE ALSO athem[2]
= **ulpilem** (E)

lpwanem (W,T), **ulpanem** (T,E) *vi.* [RESPECT LANGUAGE]
lie down; sleep ◆ Kwey ahaneyna, ngwarr-nheng ulpanerl-ayntetyek. (Sa) *Daughter, go and lie down with your husband [said by a woman].* ◆ Ngwarr-nheng ulpanep-anem ngkwelyel. (St) *My daughter and her husband are lying down in the shade [said by a woman].* ◆ 'Ankwang ulpanewarray.' Kerremel angkem. (M) *'Go to sleep [husband and wife].' That's respect talk.* ◆ Aletharl ulpanirretyel aherrkant akern irretyekarl ulpanirrerl-anem. Aherrkan akern anemarl irrek. (Sa) *They [my daughter and her son-in-law] are still sleeping, although the sun is already high in the sky. The sun is up.*
SEE ALSO intem[1], ankwa intem

Lpwararr (W,T), **Rlpwararr** (W,T) *n.*
Milky Way ◆ Lpwararr intem aherlkentyek-atwety, Lpwararr twarlk intem mpwank, aherlketyenheng. (T) *The Milky Way lies across [the sky] right up until daybreak.*
= Mewarr, Atwarlk

lpway (W,T) *n.*
1. creek, river, watercourse ◆ Anantherr alhem lpway-warn-athek *road* nhenh-angkwerr. (M) *We are going along this road towards the creek.* ◆ Mpwetyerr apetyem lpway angerr-warn. (M) *The small gullies come towards the big creek.*
2. creekbed, riverbed ◆ Arnkarr-angkwerr anarnpenhem lpway-warn kwaty arnwengk-iletyeh. (N) *[We] climb down the riverbank to the riverbed to dig a soakage.*
SEE ALSO lher
= **ulpay** (T,E)

lpwerr intem (W,T) *vi.*
lie on stomach ◆ Lyweny-penh apety-alpem lpwerr intem, angart-welhem, arrethakerem intem. (N) *After hunting, coming back and lying on [your] stomach, then turning yourself over and lying on your side with your legs curled up.*
= ilperr ayntem
= **ulperr intem** (E)

lpwerr-welhem (W,T) *vi.*
lie yourself on stomach
= **ulperr welhem** (E)

lpwerrem (W,T), **alpwerrem** (W,T) *vi.*
go rotten, stink, go off ◆ Ker ingkerrek nheng wal alpwerrem, arntert anem ra irrem, kel wetyenheng antem angwelyek. (T) *If all the meat has gone off, gone rotten, then [you] throw it to the dogs.* ◆ Uternel ampem, alpwerrem ker. (T) *Meat goes off in the heat of the sun.*
= arntert-irrem
= **ulpirrem** (E)

lpwert (W,T) *n.*
muddy or dirty water ◆ Kwaty lpwert mentyarl arerl-alheyaw. Arraty-iperr alhem anper. (N) *If you see muddy water you just leave it and go past.* ◆ Arnwep-arnwep arerl-alhem, kwaty lpwertey interleng. Mentyel arerl-alhem arnwep-arnwep renh, kwatyelarl *mess* mpwarek ingkel arlka, pwelek atna arlka ulhemel. (N) *We'll go and see the claypan, where the muddied water is lying there. We'll go and see that claypan, but we'll leave it — where the bullocks have messed up the water up with their hooves and by shitting in it.*
SEE ALSO alhwerrk
= **ulpert** (T,E)

lpwert-irrem (W,T) *vi.*
get muddied, get dirty
= **ulpert-irrem** (T,E)

lpwert-ilem (W,T) *vt.*
make water muddy or dirty
= **ulpert-ilem** (T,E)

lpwertelh-ilem (W,T) *vt.*
1. make water muddy or dirty
2. interrupt; make a noise, make a mess, stir people up • SEE ALSO apatel-anthem, apatelh-ilem, aparlp-ilem, aparlpelh-ilem
= **ulpertelh-ilem** (T,E)

ltar a banging, knocking, rattling or clicking

sound SEE UNDER **rltar**

ltar-rnkem burst, bust, come out through something etc. SEE UNDER **rltar-rnkem**

Ltarlpelt (E) name of a place in the Harts Range area SEE UNDER **Rltarlpelt**

Ltemp (W) hill near Garden Bore, Yuelamu (Mt Allan) area SEE UNDER **Rltemp**

ltengk-ltengk bell SEE UNDER **rltengk-rltengk**

lterlt (E), **lternt** (E) newborn SEE UNDER **rlternt**

lterr, **rlterr** *n.*
shin
lterr ngkwern, **rlterr ngkwern**
shinbone (ngkwern *'bone'*)
apwert lterr (E), **apwert rlterr** (E)
the end of a hill, foothill (apwert *'hill'*)
◆ Apwert akely irrenhemelarl ayntenhem yanh-lkwer. Apwert ilkwa menty, ran akely anem akely anem aynteynerl-anem, 'lterr'. Atherram an ra, 'tywerr' an 'lterr'. (Sa) *The hill gets smaller as it goes down. Not the high part of the hill, the part of the hill where it gets lower and lower is called* 'lterr'. *There are two names for it,* 'tywerr' *and* 'lterr'.
= tywerr

lterrk strong, forceful SEE UNDER **rlterrk**

lterrkem (E) rattle, clatter SEE UNDER **rlterrkem**

lterrp a rattling or banging noise SEE UNDER **rlterrp**

ltety a sharp cracking or clicking sound SEE UNDER **rltety**

ltewem (W,T) *vt.*
1. smash or break something
2. throw something at someone or something
◆ Alyel ltewang. (T) *Throw the boomerang.*
◆ Lteway arnel angwely yanh. (T) *Throw the stick at that dog.* ◆ Tyerrtyel ltewem artetyerretyerr kwaty angerrem anhem. (M) *If a person throws something at the willie wagtail then there will be a lot of rain.*
3. strike (of a storm or lightning), hit
◆ Awely-awelyel ltewem. (M) *The lightning is striking.* ◆ Apwertekel ahern ltewem. (M) *The hailstones are hitting the ground.*
SEE ALSO wem[1]
= **ultewem** (E)
ltewelhem (W,T) *vi.*
break, become broken or smashed up; split open

ltey-ltey (E) New Holland rattlepod SEE UNDER **rltey-rltey**

lthan (W,T) *n.*
1. ghost or spirit
2. skeleton
3. a skinny or boney person (an insult) ◆ Marl yanhan apetyem akeweny lthanam, antywekarl-penh. (T) *That poor woman coming there is just skin and bone from drinking grog.*
SEE ALSO anngirrenty, irrernng, akarnng[1]
= **ulthan** (E)

lthangkw (T,E), **ilthangkw** (E) *n.*
soaking wet
SEE ALSO anthwek-anthwek
lthangkw-lthangkw (T,E), **ilthangkw-ilthangkw** (E) *n.*
soaking wet ◆ Ilthangkw-ilthangkw ayeng alpemaw, kwaty-penh, anthwek-anthwek anem *wet*. Manter atyenh *wet*, wal ilthangkw-ilthangkw nhenh apety-alpem. *I'm going back, soaking wet from the rain. My clothes are wet, well I'm coming back wet.*
lthangkw-irrem (T,E), **ilthangkw-irrem** (E) *vi.*
get soaked ◆ Mantarr arlka ingkerr lthangkw-irrem, kel aketh-warl tek-arrernem. (T) *All the clothes have got soaked, so they are hung outside to dry.*

lthap-lthap, **rltap-rltap** (W) *adv.*
making a flapping, lapping, slurping, stomping, sloshing or stamping sound, such as the noise of footsteps ◆ Kwatyel-arleng lthap-lthap nthwerl-apem. (T) *Going along in the water, making a splashing noise.* ◆ Ker lthap-lthap apetyem aherr. (T) *The kangaroo is making a stomping sound as it comes.*
lthap-lthap-irrem, **rltap-rltap-irrem** (W) *vi.*
make a flapping, lapping, slurping, stomping or sloshing sound ◆ Werlaty yanh lthap-lthap-irrem anthep-irrem, rntwem. Brassier-kwenyel kel lthap-irrem. (T) *Her breasts are making a flapping sound as she is dancing. She hasn't got a bra on.*
lthap-lthap atwem (W)
splash water (atwem *'hit'*)
lthap-lthap antywem (T)
slurp or lap (liquid) (antywem *'drink'*)
◆ Angwelyel kwaty lthap-lthap antywem. (T) *The dog is lapping the water.*

lthel *n.*
light rain; a shower of rain; small amount of rain, a sprinkle of rain. Also referred to as *kwaty lthel*. ◆ Kwaty lthel akwek mapel war anhem. (M) *There is just a sprinkle of rain.*
SEE ALSO kwaty, arrarntwer

lthel-lthel *n.*
hair sticking up; messy hair; hairy, woolly, scruffy ◆ Ankwepenharl akem-irrem alta lthel-lthel. (St) *Getting up from sleeping, with messy hair.* ◆ Nwernengk arrakert angerr lthel-lthel an annga angerr. (M) *The tawny frogmouth has a big hairy beak and big eyes.* ◆ Iltelhey, akeng war alhep-alhem lthel-lthel war, mantarr akeng-akeng-akert iltelhey-iltelhey alhep-

alhem. Aternng-aternng mantarr atyenh — *clean* anetyakenh. Iltelhey akeng wararl alhep-alhem alhewelhetyakenh. (St) *[I] am just going along with raggedy, dirty clothes on. My clothes are dirty — they're not clean. I'm a bit scruffy and I haven't had a wash.*

ngkwern lthel-lthel
hairy leg (ngkwern *'bone', 'leg'*) ◆ Ngkwern lthel-lthel apek arrantherr. *Maybe you mob have hairy legs.*

lthel-lthel-ilem *vt.*
make hair stand on end (?) ◆ Iylkel apek lthel-lthel ilem. (St) *The wind makes your hair stand on end.*

lthel-arelhewelhem (E) *vi.*
hair stick up on end ◆ Arengk lthel-arelhewelhem artep, urlalyp apek arekarl. (Sa) *The hair on the dog's back stood up, maybe because it saw a kurdaitcha.*

lthelhey, lthelhey-lthelhey *n.*
hairy, woolly (especially of animals)

lthenp, lthinp *n.*
covered in dirty stuff ◆ Kart lthenp kwer akwek. (M) *The little child is covered with shit.*

lthenp-lthenp, lthinp-lthinp *n.*
mouth (covered with something)

arrelthenp-lthenp
mouth (covered with something) (arra *'mouth'*) ◆ Arengkelarl arlkwem-penh *flour*-penh, wal arrelthenp-lthenp-anteyarl apety-alpem. Arrelthenp-akert, lthenp-lthenp. (St) *After eating flour the dog comes back with its mouth covered in the stuff. Its mouth is all messy.*

lthep-lthep (E) *n.*
a type of beetle ◆ Akwek lthep-lthepel manteran altywer-altywer-ilem, interrkel-artek arlkwem. Ingkan akwek akwek. Aympelh-akert anetyakenh. (St) *The* lthep-lthep *beetle chews holes in clothes, eats them like a white ant does. They have small legs and no wings.*

lther-wem, lther-iwem (E) *vt.*
pinch (with fingers) ◆ Wenhek ntwa ayeng lther-wem? (M) *Why are you pinching me?* ◆ Thwengk lyet ltheremam wetyenh kwenh. (N) *I'm going to pinch you later.*
= itekem

ltherrp-ltherrp (W,T) *n.*
showing off, behaving in a flirtatious way

ltherrp-wem *vt.*
have diarrhoea or 'gutsache', have very watery shit ◆ Pwelek ltherrp-werlapem atherrk-penh. (T) *The bullock is going along shitting after eating the green grass.*

lthinp covered in dirty stuff SEE UNDER **lthenp**

lthwelth-ilem (W,T) *vt.*
1. tell someone you don't want something, knock back an offer of something ◆ Tha lthwelth-ilem arrantherr. Arrantherrarrp arlkwerram. (M) *I am knocking back your offer of [food]. You can all eat yourselves.* ◆ Arelh yanhel mern anthek. Arelh arrpenhel akenh lthwelth-ilek. 'Mern atyenh lthwelth-ilern yanhel, tharl antyetyeh-anern kwer.' (T) *That woman gave her some food. And the other woman knocked it back. [The first woman says] 'That woman just knocked back the food that I was going to give her.'*
2. tell someone to stay behind, tell someone to sit down and wait ◆ Anwern ngenh lthwelth-ilemel arrernerl-alhem — ntwa anetyeh. (T) *We're going to leave you here — you stay here.*
= menty-ilem
= **ulthelth-ilem** (E)

lthwem (W,T) *vt.*
1. step or tread on something; press or weigh down upon something; lean weight on something; be heavy
2. oppress someone; make someone feel weak, lazy or overwhelmed
= **ulthem** (E)

lthwenty (W,T) *n.*
heavy (weight) ◆ Lthwenty angerram yanh, menty intey. Artwelant ina inetyenheng. (T) *That one is really heavy, let's leave it. The men can get it later.*
= **ulthenty** (E)

lthwerrem (W,T) have a rest, have a spell SEE UNDER **ltywerrem**

ltimp (T,E) dry bits of bark SEE UNDER **rltimp**[1]

ltimp skewer used used for cooking SEE UNDER **rltimp**[2]

ltwa (W,T), **ltwang** (W,T) *n.*
the side of a person or animal, near ribs
SEE ALSO ayew
CAN SOUND A BIT LIKE arltwa *'empty'*; rltwa *'big'*
= **ulta** (T,E)

ltwakem (W,T) *vt.*
1. break or cut something, break something in half ◆ Rlkwerr ltwakem, mern tamp apek ltwakem. (M) *Break something in the middle, maybe break a damper.*
2. break a horse in ◆ Tyerrtyel nantew kwerlt ltwakem. (M) *The person is breaking the colt in.*
3. have a stomach-ache ◆ Ayeng ampeltyem, anertarl ltwakem. (M) *I've got diarrhoea and my stomach is hurting.*
SEE ALSO urleth-akem
= **ultakem** (E)

ltwakelhem (W,T) *vi.*
1. break a part of yourself ◆ Ayeng ngkwern ltwakelhek. (M) *I broke my leg.*
2. become broken, break down ◆ Arnang nhenh tha mpwarem ltwakelhekarl. (M) *I am fixing this thing that has broken.*
= **ultakelhem** (E)
angka ltwakem (T)
stop someone talking, interrupt someone talking (angka *'word', 'story'*)
kart ltwakem (W,T)
fart (kart *'shit', 'guts'*)
ahenty ltwakem (W,T)
choke or strangle someone or something, wring somebody's or something's neck (ahenty *'throat'*) ◆ Arelhel ahenty ltwakem ker rapet. (T) *The woman is wringing the rabbit's neck.* ◆ Kwer atherr arrkenel ltwakerrem ahenty. (M) *The two kids are strangling each other for fun.*

ltwamp-ltwamp (W,T), **rltwamp-rltwamp** (W,T), **rltamp-rltamp** (T) *n.*
a type of fly (?)
SEE ALSO yek-yek

ltwang (W,T) the side of a person or animal, near ribs SEE UNDER **ltwa**

ltyampem, ltyampwem (E) blister from fire SEE UNDER **iltyampem**

ltyantywem (T,E) *vt.*
suck or sip something, suck on something (antywem *'drink'*) ◆ Inpinpan awantyem arrpemarl, ltyantywem apek. Ngkwern inpinp yanh-lkwer. (St) *You suck on the marrow as well. That marrow from bones.* ◆ Ngkwarl ntyweyamp ltyantywem. (T) *Sipping on the corkwood honey.*
SEE ALSO awantyem, kwek-arem

ltyayerr (E) *n.* [RESPECT LANGUAGE]
kangaroo blood ◆ Ltyayerr atyengaw, kwey irrepetherl-wa. (Sa) *Daughter, go and get me some kangaroo blood [from your husband].*
SEE ALSO awerrp1

ltyenty, iyltenty (E) *n.*
beefwood (*Grevillea striata*). Tree to 10 m high, with rough bark and creamy white bottlebrush flowers. ◆ Ltyenty anwengkerr atwetyam rltwamp. (M) *We used to chop sugarbag from the beefwood tree.*
ltyentyarwek (E), **iyltentyarwek** (E) *n.*
medicinal gum or kino from the beefwood

Ltyenty (W) *n.*
name of a place south of 20 Mile (Napperby Station area)

Ltyenty Arlpenng *n.*
name of a place in Bushy Park Station area

ltyernt (W,T) *n.*
naughty ◆ Kwer nhenh ltyernt apelay. (M) *I know for a fact that this kid is naughty.*
SEE ALSO anhelhenty, anngernt
ltyernt-irrem (W,T) *vi.*
be naughty, misbehave ◆ Kwer maparl ltyerntel twerrerl-anem, ltyernt-irremel. 'Kwer map twerretyal!' Kwer angerr angerrel ilem, '*Don't* twerrerl ltyernt-irretyal anay!' (N) *The kids are being naughty and fighting. 'Don't fight you kids!' A bigger kid will say, 'Don't fight, settle down and don't be naughty!'*
= anngernt-irrem

ltyerrem (E), **ltyirrem** (E) *vi.*
heal over, heal up ◆ Ngkwern ltyerrek, akekarl-penh. (Sa) *The leg has healed after being cut.*
SEE ALSO arrintety-irrem, tywenmernt-irrem, arterrp-irrem, kwerrm-irrem, pwarn-irrem, urrmirrem
CAN SOUND A BIT LIKE iltyerrem *'wave'*; ltywerrem *'have a rest'*

ltyerrem (E), **ltyirrem** (E) have a rest, have a spell SEE UNDER **ltywerrem**

ltywelty, iltywelty (T,E), **ultyulty** (E) *n.*
a type of cricket ◆ Ankwakel angkerl-anem ingwel ltywelty. Itna atherr ap renh, intelty-apeny. Irreynm. Itna atherr akert. (Sa) *The cricket makes a noise all through the night. It is similar to a grasshopper and it has two names — irreynm and ltywelty. It has two names.*
SEE ALSO anwengkapeltharr, irreynm, anwengkapeltharr

ltywerrem (W,T), **ltyirrem** (E), **iltywerrem** (T), **lthwerrem** (W,T), **ltyerrem** (E) *vi.*
have a rest, have a spell ◆ Lywenyarl alhek-penh ltywerrem, arrernelhety-alpem. 'Arwengalker twekarl-penh urrek amparr ayeng ltywerrey.' Ltywerrerl-anem, arteparl antyernek. (N) *Going back and sitting down and having a rest after hunting. 'Wait while I have a rest from chopping sugarbag.' Having a rest because my back is aching.* ◆ Parrk ayeng lthwerrem lyweny alhek-penh. (M) *I am tired and having a rest after going hunting.* ◆ Arrwekel ayeng ltywerrerl-alhey rtweth-akert, rntwarraral alhek-penh. Kwer-penh akem-irrem, 'Mwerram ayeng awelhem'. (N) *I'm going to go and have a rest first because my lower back aches from walking a long way. After that I get up and say, 'I feel good'.*
ltyerrelh-ilem *vt.*
give something a rest, give something a spell ◆ Nantew ltyerrelh-ilem urrek apek. (St) *Give the horse a spell for a while.*

CAN SOUND A BIT LIKE iltyerrem *'wave'*

lwakem (W,T), **lakem** (W,T), **arlakem** (T,E) *vt.*
chase someone or something
= alwernem
CAN SOUND A BIT LIKE rlwakem *'dislocate animal's leg'*
lwakerrem (W,T), **lakerrem** (W,T), **arlakerrem** (E) *vi.*
run around; rush around, chase each other round, play around (a group of people or things) ◆ Kwer nhenh atherr lwakerreperrem. (M) *These two kids are chasing each other around.* ◆ Yanh arlakerrem tyerrty map — *something wrong* apek — urrek tha awetyek alhey. (Sa) *People are rushing round over there — maybe there is something wrong — wait while I go and listen to find out.* ◆ Ampa nyetyeng nyetyel arlakerretyel, arrken utnherretyel arlakerretyel. (Sa) *The kids are playing around in the cubbyhouses, playing and chasing each other round.*
SEE ALSO utnherrem, arrken-irrem, alwernerrem
lwakelhem (W,T), **lakelhem** (W,T), **arlakelhem** (E) *vi.* = **lwakerrem** ◆ Ampa atherr arlakelhepelhem arrken-irrep-irremel. (St) *The two children are playing and running all over the place.* ◆ Pwelek arlakelhem. *Something*-el apek aterel-anthek. (St) *The cattle are rushing around. Something must have given them a fright.*

lwaneng (T) facing or moving towards the speaker SEE UNDER **ulaneng**

lwarr (W,T) *adv.*
facing or moving towards the speaker ◆ Artwang lwarr apetyepetyem. (M) *The man is coming towards me.*
= ulaneng
SEE ALSO urla
= **ularr** (T,E)
lwarr-athek (W,T), **lwarr-atheh** (W,T) *adv.*
= **lwarr** ◆ Lwarr-athek aney alakenh, atyeng-warl-athek. Ntywem anetyal kwenh lwarr-athek anay. (T) *Sit facing in this direction, facing towards me. Don't face away, sit facing me.*
= ulaneng-athek
= **ularr-athek** (T,E)
lwarr-irrem (W,T) *vi.*
move in a direction towards the speaker ◆ Nta ntywem alhem, nta lwarr-athehem apety-alpem. (M) *You go in that direction and then come back in this direction.*
= ulaneng-irrem
SEE ALSO untyem-athek
= **ularr-irrem** (T,E)
lwarrek-lwarr (W,T) *adv.*
facing each other, face to face ◆ Anwengkerr ananem lwarrek-lwarr. (M) *We are sitting facing each other.*
= ulanengek-ulaneng
SEE ALSO untyem[1]
= **ularrek-ularr** (T,E)

lwarrpeny (E) *n.*
be the only sibling left in a family (others have passed away) ◆ Lwarrpeny anyent ikwerenh, kakey ikwerenharl aparlp-ilek. (Sa) *Her elder brother has passed away and she is the only one left.* (?)
lwarrpeny-irrem (E) *vi.*
become bereaved of one's siblings; be the only sibling left in a family ◆ Ayeng lwarrpeny-irrek, arrpenhem *pass away*-arl irrek. (St) *I am the only sibling left in the family, the others have passed away.*

lwekatat (W) *n.*
small round bark toy used by men and boys for target practice (with spears). Made of river red gum bark.
SEE ALSO alyaper

lwekerleny (W) *n.*
term used by women to refer to young teenage boys who are going through ceremonial business and who are in seclusion in the 'bush camp'
SEE ALSO amerrk[1]

lwelty (W,T), **rlwelty** (W,T) *n.*
frost, ice. Also referred to as *kwaty lwelty*. ◆ Rlwelty ikwerety ater-irrem anyelel arrewem. (N) *[People] are frightened of the frost and they shiver in the cold.* ◆ Kwaty rlwelty anyem. (M) *There is a frost.* ◆ Ankwang interleng map, wal lwelty anyem nta lweltyem arem, pelangketel nheng mperlkerel. (M) *When people are asleep and there is a frost you'll see the white frost on the blankets.* ◆ Rlwelty tamp-arteh intem. Akap-rlwem rlwelty renh, kwaty antywetyenheng. (T) *The ice is [solid] like a damper. You peel the ice [off the water] and then drink the water.*
= **ulelty** (E)

lwem (W) die SEE UNDER **ilwem**

Lwem (W) the name of a place in the Yuelamu (Mt Allan) area SEE UNDER **Arlwem**

lwem[1] (W) *vi.*
1. defecate, have a shit, go to the toilet
2. urinate
= lhwem, ulhem
mpwang lwem (W)
urinate
= mpwelhem[2]

lwem[2] (W,T) *vi.*
drip down ◆ Kwaty irnmerr lwerl-anem. (M)

Rain drops keep dripping down.
CAN SOUND A BIT LIKE ilwem *'die', 'cough'*

lwemar (W,T) *n.*
sugar. This word is used because the usual word for 'sugar' is *kwementyay*.
= tywek, kwaty ikwemey-ilenh

lwengar (W,T), **ilwengar** (W,T), **ilengar** (E), **ilenger** (T,E) *n.*
'When?' ◆ Ilwengar anwern alpetyenh merwarn? (M) *When are we going home?* ◆ Ilengar apek anwantherr man inetyenhay? (St) *When are we going to get paid?* ◆ Lyet renh itetyenh anem ker atharl arlwarrernek, arrernekarl ntwa. Ilenger apek ra ampetyenh? (St) *The meat that I left for later is going to be cooked today, the meat that you left. When is it going to be cooked?*
ilenger-lkwer *n.*
'About when?', 'Round about when?', 'About what time?' ◆ Ilengar-lkwer rarey apetyetyenh? (St) *About what time are they coming?*

lwengkart[1] (T) *n.*
blue-tongue lizard (*Tiliqua multifasciata*) (note Warlpiri *lungkarda*)
= lhwelk, ulhelk, ilpankwer

lwengkart[2] (W) *n.*
a type of carrying dish
SEE ALSO atywekal, urety, kwerlintyerr, panth, irrkwely[2], alparr[1], irrkwa, lengarr, arlketh[1], rnwa, urna

lweper *n.*
Aboriginal woman (maybe from Tasmanian Aboriginal language via English 'lubra') ◆ Arrwekeleny map tha wetyam ampel 'lweper' aketyam. (St) *I heard the olden-time people calling [them] 'lubra'.*

lweperr (E) blue mallee SEE UNDER **uleperr**

lweren (W,T) *n.*
'Like that', 'That's what it's like', 'That's how', 'That's when' ◆ Lweren kwa arrwekeleny map *live*-irrek. (N) *That's how the olden-time people lived.* ◆ Anngenth nhenh akwek-irrem, kwen-irrem, lwerenelarl nthekemarl wem rrweyel. (N) *When the flame becomes smaller, dies down, that's when the boy singes the hair off the animal.* ◆ Mern tywerrk. Mern tywerrkel anwern amangkek, arlkwerl-apekarl, ampeng-irremarl. Arnkang arerl-alhem mentyel. *'Ah* ampeng-irrekam nhenh kwenh, anwengkerr mern arlkwerl-aney kwenh.' Inerl-alhemel iltyel inerl-alhemel arlkwem anemarl. Lwerenarl yanh mern tywerrk, kwerel anwern amangkelhekarl. (N) *Wild figs. We grew up on wild figs, going along and eating them when they were ripe. If we saw unripe ones we'd leave them. 'Ah, this one is ripe, let's eat these ones', we'd say. We'd pick them by hand and them eat them. That's what it's like, the wild figs that we grew up on.*
SEE ALSO alakenh, alanh, alanh-anyem

lwereny (W,T) *n.*
1. a stranger ◆ Lwereny apetyek lyetant. (T) *A stranger came, just today.* ◆ Mer rntwarreng tyerrty lwereny apetyem. (M) *A stranger comes from a faraway place.*
= alethang
= **ulereny** (E)
2. non-Christian [SOME SPEAKERS]
tyerrty lwereny (W,T)
a stranger (tyerrty *'person'*)
lwereny-irrem (W,T) *vi.*
feel shy or shamed ◆ Ayeng lwereny-irrem tyerrtyelarl arnterr arem-arleng. (T) *I am feeling shamed because somebody is staring hard [at me].*
= nyerr-irrem
= **ulereny-irrem** (E)

lwerlker (W,T) *n.*
native bee (large one) ◆ Lwerlker *like* ameng-arteh akin. Wal *green one.* Nheng *show*-em-arteh ilemel *sugarbag* alenh. (M) Lwerlker *is like a fly. It's green in colour. It shows you where the sugarbag is.*
= ngarntarnt
SEE ALSO ameng, minekey, rltwamp, arwengalker

lwernem (W,T), **ilwernem** (E) *vt.*
put something out (fire or light), extinguish ◆ Ura yanh ilwerneyaw, alkngentharl angerr ampem-kety. (St) *Put that fire out, because the flames are burning too high.* ◆ Rwang yanh lwernay. (M) *Put that fire out.*
CAN SOUND A BIT LIKE alwernem *'chase something'*
= **ulernem** (E)
lwernelhem (W,T), **ilwernelhem** (E) *vi.*
go out (fire, light), become extinguished ◆ Man-kwenyel *light* ilwernelhem (St) *If there is no money [in the meter] the lights will go out.*
SEE ALSO atham-irrem

lwerrk (W,T), **ilwerrk** (E) *n.*
eggs of honeyants and other species of ant ◆ Yerramp-kenhan ilwerrkarl, kwart. (St) *Honeyants' eggs are called* 'ilwerrk'.

lwerrm (W) *n.*
a type of frog
SEE ALSO perrak, kwep, alheramp

Lweterreyn, Lweterrern *n.*
Lutheran

lweth (E) *part.*
Provides emphasis or stresses that something

is definite or obvious; definitely, exactly, of course (?). ◆ Rlengkayarl arrernelhem, arrernem ampa apek arrernem alakenh aretharrel lweth. Aretharr akngerrarl apetyemeng. Ampa akwek apek, rlkert-kety. (St) *The mark made with burnt bark from the corkwood tree is put on the foreheads of little children because of that north wind. When the north wind is blowing this mark is put on them so that they don't get sick.*
SEE ALSO kwa

lwethep *n.*
matches (from English 'lucifer', which was a word for a match) ◆ *No* lwethep — lyetarr anem lwethepan, urtnarl itna urtnetyarl ina nthiletyartan, urtnety-wemel. Atham alhemel kel urtnety-wety-alhemel. (Sa) *No matches — nowadays there are matches, whereas before they used to make fire using a firesaw. They'd go around with no fire and then make fire with a firesaw.* ◆ Lwethep anthety-alha rwang antant-iletyeh. (M) *Get me some matches so that I can light the fire.*

lyalth, **rlalth** (W,T), **iylalth** (E) *n.*
1. march fly ◆ Rlalth *cheeky one* akin ameng-artek angerr. (T) *March flies are similar to flies only bigger.* ◆ Aherr arlkarl aterel anthem iylalthel, unhenh-unhenh *cheeky one*, ahelengkw. (St) *March flies frighten kangaroos as well, they are aggressive and they bite.*
SEE ALSO mweremwenk
2. pallid cuckoo [SOME SPEAKERS] • = alkwarrer-arrpwernenh, lyweketweretwer

iylalth-atweng-atweng (T,E), **iylalth-atwenh-atwenh** (E), **iylalth-angkern** (E) *n.*
a type of bird (?) ◆ Ra ingwel arlkem iylalthek, angkep-angkem, arlkep-arlkem, iylalth-angkern. *Blue, grey.* (St) *In the night they sing out to the march flies. They are a blue-grey colour.*

lyangkay-lyangkay (E) *n.*
a type of skink (*Ctenotus schomburgkii* (?))
= alyalkarr, lyengkarr
SEE ALSO ikwarr

Lyanng (W) *n.*
name of a rockhole east of Yuelamu (Mt Allan) community

lyapem (T,E) *vi.*
grow (plants, hair, teeth). *Lyapem* is not used in reference to people. ◆ Arna akwek-akwek lyapem, lyetantarl ra lyapewarreparrem, kwatyel amangkelh-ilek lyapem lyet. (St) *The little plants are growing, just now they are starting to grow from the rain.* ◆ *Baby one*-an arrakert arrangkwarl-areny, arntek anetyakenh. Ampa angerr irrem arntek-akert anem irrem, arratem apek, lyapem apek. (St) *Babies have empty mouths, they don't have any teeth. When they get bigger they get teeth, the teeth come out or grow.* ◆ Werrp-rtwek lyapem mern aherretyepwer. (Sa) *The* aherretyepwer *fruit grows on the bush bean vine.*
= arntwem

lyapelh-ilem (T,E) *vt.*
grow something, make something grow

lyarnayt (E) blue wattle; leather-leaved colony wattle SEE UNDER **iylarn**

lyarnem (T,E), **iylarnem** (E) *vt.*
get someone's attention, touch someone to get their attention or to warn them ◆ Ngenh tha lyarnem. 'Yanh-ketyaw!' (St) *I am warning you. 'Look out from [that thing] there!'*
= atengelh-ilem
SEE ALSO anpem

lyarnt, **iylarnt** (E) *n.*
circular pad for carrying things on the head. This was made from rags or pieces of cloth, and in the old days bark from trees or certain types of grass. ◆ Lyarnt, kapertelarl angetyem kwaty *bucket*-el, lyarnt arrernelhewem kel kapertel kwaty angerl-apem. (T) *When water was carried on the head in a bucket, a carrying pad was put on the head and then the water was carried along.*
= karnt2
SEE ALSO alyep

lyarr (E) *n.*
seeds of the dogwood *akerlperr, awenth* (*Acacia sericophylla*) that have just gone dark and dry. These seeds are used to make a sweet drink. The seeds are mashed up in water, laid out to dry, and then they are pounded up.
= kertaty, tartaty
SEE ALSO ntyerrm

lyarr-irrem (E) *vi.*
go dry (dogwood seeds) ◆ Ntyerrm antyerrkarl-irrem ilem lyarr. 'Lyarr-irrek-ketyaw', antyerrkarl-irreman. (St) *Dogwood seeds that have gone dry are called 'lyarr'. Of those that have gone dry [we] say, 'Lyarr-irrek [they have dried]'.*
SEE ALSO antyerrk-irrem

lyarwek *n.*
gum or kino from the bloodwood, *arrkernk,* and from ghost gum, *pwernengk, ulemp* ◆ Lyarwek apernelhenhelhenh akin. Lyarwek anthwerr. Arrkernk-areny. Arrkinty-kenh, apernelhetyek, rtety-rtety apek aremarl. (N) Lyarwek *is a rubbing medicine as well. That's*

lyarwek. *It comes from the bloodwood tree. It's used for rubbing onto scabies or other skin diseases.*
SEE ALSO arrkeper, nthwarr

lyaty *n.*
1. baby ◆ Mwelek ilem, 'Lyaty akwek atyenh'. (T) *The mother says, 'My little baby'.*
SEE ALSO ampa, kwer
2. baby [RESPECT LANGUAGE]. This word is used when the baby is very young and the given name of the baby is not said. ◆ 'Lyaty' akem ampa akwek, akwek-amperl. Ikirrenty *way. Can't call-em name* arreny apek ampa apek aketyek. *Might sick* apek irrerl. (St) *'Lyaty' is what a small baby is called. That is a respectful way of talking. You can't say the name of that child. They might get sick.*
3. young man who is in seclusion in the bush after initiation (young man) ceremony [SOME SPEAKERS] ◆ 'Lyatyeh *something* ilanthewarray.' Nheng werrkel anem anmanty-penh. Lyaty akwekem ilem mathel. (M) *'You should all send something for the young fella.' The one that is in the bush after the* anmanty *ceremony. 'Lyaty akwek' is what his mother calls him.* • SEE ALSO alyepelengkw, awerrty, arwekert, arleyarr, amarleyarr, tyakwertekwert, lwekerleny, antingkar

lyayepelyay (W,T), **layempeylay** (T,E), **iylayempeylay** (E) *n.*
ribbon grass, spear grass (*Chrysopogon fallax*). A grass that grows to 1.5 m high, with long, narrow ribbon-like leaves. ◆ Lyayepelyay *use-em-ilem* awantyetyeh mamp, awantyewarretyart akwel arek-wemel awantyetyart. Kwak-ilem awantyewarretyart athew tyerrtyel — kwer mapel arlka anwern awantyetyart. (N) *We use ribbon grass to soak up the sweet stuff from the river red gum, the* mamp. *We used to dip it into the honey and then suck on it. Adults used to enjoy sucking on it — and us kids used to suck on it as well.*

lyek, iylek (E) *n.*
1. prickle, spike, thorn ◆ 'Yekay! Ingka atanthem lyekel!' (St) *'Ouch! The prickle is piercing my foot.'*
2. certain prickly plants such as bindy-eye, dead finish
SEE ALSO arlketyerr
3. echidna, porcupine, anteater. Also referred to as *ker lyek* or *ker iylek*. ◆ Ker iylek, iylek-iylek inngart. Arrpemel anem renh. Tyelk anetyang anter. Ker iylek arlkwem. (Sa) *Of course the echidna is really prickly. It has its spines scraped off. They don't have flesh — just fat. We eat echidnas.*
4. spine (of echidna) ◆ Inarlengel rrkwek irntel kwer akwek lyek-kweny. (M) *A mother echidna on a hill had a little baby that had no spines.*
iylek-ayerr (E) *n.* [RESPECT LANGUAGE]
echidna, porcupine
SEE ALSO inap, inarleng
lyekakapert (E), **lyekakapwert** (T,E) *n.*
bindy-eye, caltrop (*Tribulus terrestris*) (kapert[1] *'head'*)
lyek-lyek, iylek-iylek (E) *n.*
spiky, rough or lumpy skin ◆ Arntap renh iyltem kel kwaty-warl arrernem arntap. Karntey-artek anem ra irrem, alhwartek. Kel lyek-lyek apek alhewelhem rtety-rtetyarl irrem weth-lkwer. (St) *The bark is peeled off and then it is put into water. Then it goes like Condy's crystals, like blood. Then you wash sores or lumpy skin with it.*
SEE ALSO rtety-rtety
lyek-lyek-irrem, iylek-iylek-irrem (E) *vi.*
go rough or lumpy (skin)

Lyek-lyek (T) *n.*
the name of a rockhole east of Ti Tree town. See map p. viii.

lyekarr anem, iylekarr anem (E) *vi.*
1. get goose pimples or goose bumps; hair stand on end (from cold or fear) ◆ Alta lyekarr anem alhwerrpel. (M) *[You] get goose bumps in the cold.* ◆ Artwekety lyekarr anem alta tnenherrem anem, lyekarr anemel. Amwekety apek lyekarr anem. (St) *[You] might get goose bumps and your hair might stand on end because you are frightened of a man. Or you might get goosebumps because you're frightened of a snake.* ◆ Lyekarr apek anem kwaty irrernt-penh. Ater-penh *too* lyekarr anem anteyarl. (St) *[You] get goose bumps from cold water. And from being frightened.*
2. have a funny feeling, feel disgusted by something ◆ Tyerrty lyekarr anem ker antereng. (M) *The person feels disgusted by the fatty meat.*
lyekarr-irrem, iylekarr-irrem (E) *vi.*
get goose pimples or goose bumps, hair stand on end (from cold or fear)
SEE ALSO arraw-irrem

lyekel-wem (W) *vt.*
step on top of someone's tracks, walk in someone's footsteps ◆ Arrpenh apek ingka alhem, lyekel-wem arrpenh (M) *One person goes, and the other walks in their foot tracks.*
= ingkatyel-wem, atywekel-iwem

Lyekenaty (W,T) *n.*
Lake Nash (from English 'Lake Nash')

lyelkenng (E), **iylelkenng** (E) *n.*
Sandover lily, desert lily (*Crinum flaccidum*). A plant with shiny leaves, white flowers and a large inedible onion-like bulb. Used as a medicine in the Eastern Anmatyerr region. ◆ Ra anem *onion*-artek kwen anep-anem ahelhel. Pertipelaw *really white* mwerr-angker. (St) *The part that is under the ground is like an onion. The flower is really nice and white.*
= alyerlk-alyerlk, iylelty

lyely-lyely (W,T), **lyely-lyely-lyely** (W) *n.*
the sound of meat cooking; a sizzling or bubbling sound
lyely-lyely-irrem (T),
lyely-lyely-lyely-irrem (W) *vi.*
make a sizzling or bubbling sound (the high-pitched popping sound when the skin of an animal that is being cooked breaks open and steam or fat comes out)
= tyelyely-irrem

lyelyaw (E) *n.*
light rain, drizzle ◆ Kwaty lyelyaw, akwek-akwekelarl anhem. (St) *It's drizzling a bit.*
SEE ALSO lthel, irnmerr

Lyelyepweny (W), **Lyelyepwenh** (W) *n.*
name of a place and the location of a small outstation between Yuelamu (Mt Allan) and Yuendumu. See map p. viii.

lyelyer-ipem *vt.*
push or poke stick or crowbar into sand and move it backwards and forwards (to test for water) ◆ Kwatyek lyelyer-ipem thang. (M) *I'm poking around for water.*
lyelyer-wem *vt.* = **lyelyer-wem**
◆ Lyelyer-wem kwaty anem angwerrm-ilem. 'Kwaty angernem nhenh, kwaty akernarl lyelyer-wem tha.' (St) *Poking around for water and then finding some. 'I'm digging the water here, that I found close to the surface.'* ◆ Kwaty lyelyer-wek kel kwaty renh anpek anem renh kel angernem anem renh kel inpem anem renh. (T) *The crowbar was moved backwards and forwards to test for water, and then, when [you] touched water, it was dug up and scooped out.*
SEE ALSO tyer-wem, tyew-rntem

lyelyerr (E) *n.*
offshoot from main bush potato plant, *anaty* (*Ipomoea costata*) ◆ Lyelyerr alerikwarl nyetyam, urrper, alerikwarl. Urrper nhenhan angey kwerenh. Anthal alerikw. Mwerr iyterrtyarl yanh. (Sa) *The offshoot,* lyelyerr, *of the bush potato plant is the son or daughter of the main plant, the* urrper. *The* urrper *is their father. The young tuber is the son or daughter. That's really true.*
SEE ALSO urrper

lyenenty, **lyernenty** *n.*
1. light
2. flame ◆ Arlkwenh arlkwenh ntyerrp. Mern arlkwerl-apemel arna ilkakerl-apemel rwel iterl-apemel lyenentyel, ntyerrp. (N) *Dogwood seeds are edible. [We'd] go along eating them, peeling open the pods and cooking them in the flames of the fire.*
= anngenth
lyenenty-ilem, **lyernenty-ilem** *vt.*
light (a fire), set fire alight
= nthilem
lyenenty-irrem, **lyernenty-irrem** *vi.*
catch alight ◆ Ntang pew-ilem an lyenenty-irrem. (M) *You blow [the fire] and it catches alight.*

lyengkarr (W,T), **lyenkarr** (W,T) *n.*
a type of skink (*Ctenotus schomburgkii* (?))
= alyalkerr, lyangkay-lyangkay
SEE ALSO ikwarr

lyengkwert *n.* [RESPECT LANGUAGE]
today, a short while ago ◆ Lyengkwert ahanewarrern. (M) *They [including respect kin] have just gone today.* ◆ Ampeyamp-iteng lyengkwert ahanenty-alhek. (M) *My old mother-in-law came today [said by her son-in-law].* ◆ Nthenhenty-angkwerr lyengkwert ahanerrekay? (Sa) *Where did they [including respect kin] go today?* ◆ Lyengkwert ather-ayerr-warl nganetyekaw ngwarr-nheng nganerlentyarretyek. (Sa) *Today my daughter and her husband are going to climb the hill.*
SEE ALSO lyet
lyengkwerteny (E) *n.* [RESPECT LANGUAGE]
recent, fresh
SEE ALSO lyeteny

lyenkarr (W,T) a type of skink SEE UNDER **lyengkarr**

lyenty, **iylenty** (E) *n.*
swamp kangaroo grass, native oat grass (*Themeda avenacea*). A grass that grows to 2 m high, with long bluish green leaves. ◆ Ampa maparl arrken-arrkenel, irrtyarteng-irrtyart, atantherl-apem arrken nheng atantherremel lyentyel, ketyey map. (N) *The kids enjoy themselves going along spearing each other with the kangaroo grass, their pretend spears.*
CAN SOUND A BIT LIKE ilenty *'galah'*
= **iylenty** (E)
lyentyatayerr (E), **iylentyatayerr** (E) *n.*
grub from swamp kangaroo grass, native oat grass [SOME SPEAKERS]

lyentyelyeng, lyentyelyerr (W,T), **lyentyelerrng** (W), **lyentyeleng** (T), **lyentyelyaw** (E) *n.*
nankeen kestrel (*Falco cenchroides*) ◆ Thep lyentyelyeng rlpwerelarl anem. (N) *The* lyentyelyeng *is a bird that lives in hollow trees.*
= anthep-anthep, warakeparleparl, ulpmerr-atwenh
SEE ALSO alekaper

lyep-lyep *n.*
part of guts; milk gut, intestines. Also referred to as *ker lyep-lyep.* ◆ Ker lyep-lyep, aherr, pwelek. Anwantherr lyep-lyep-akert akin. (St) *Kangaroos and cattle have edible intestines. We have intestines as well.*

lyer (E) *n.*
crippled, unable to walk ◆ Alhetyakenh lyer. Alhetyang lyerarl anerl-anem. Arntety-penh apek ra lyeran anerl-anem — he *can't walk.* (Sa) Lyer *is someone who can't walk. They can't walk and they sit there. They might be crippled from sickness — can't walk.*
SEE ALSO anath, anenyirrp irrkweynar, apekap, apertap, arlamarr, arlwemeny, lim-lim, rnwerr, rnwerr-rnwerr, rtapety, yer

lyerl, iylerl (E) *n.*
1. gravel, very small rocks, coarse sand ◆ Lyerl akwek ulpayel aneynepeynem, lyerl akwek map, lyerl akwek weth-lkwer apwert akwek-akwek. (Sa) *There are little rocks in the creek, little tiny rocks.*
2. cave ◆ Tyerrty arrwekeleny anetyam lyerlel kwaty-kety. (M) *The olden-time people sheltered from the rain in caves.* ◆ Lyerlel ngkwerlp renh akem. (T) *Native tobacco is picked in caves.* • SEE ALSO intey
= **iylerl** (E)
lyerl-areny (W), **lyerl-iperr** (W) *n.*
wallaby, euro (*Macropus robustus*) (?) (lit. 'cave-dweller')
SEE ALSO areng[2], areyneng, irntareny

Lyerl (W), **llyerl** (W) *n.*
name of a place west of Yuelamu (Mt Allan) community

lyernenty light SEE UNDER **lyenenty**

lyernt arrernem (T,E), **iylernt arrernem** (E) *vt.*
heap or pile something up ◆ Lyernt arrernem mantarr apek ulyewarl, ulyewarl lyernt arrernety-alpem antyam ikwer, ikwerel interl-anetyek. (St) *Maybe pile the clothes up in the shade, take them back and heap them up on the blanket where [she] is going to sleep.* ◆ Anterrng akerlperr wal lyernt arrernemel atwem. Wal ra lernelhem. (T) *The dogwood seed pods are heaped up and then beaten [with a stick]. Then the seeds separate from the pods.*
SEE ALSO aharl arrernem, aharl-wem, mpwer tywenem, ayak-arrernem, antyakwer-wem, antarr-arrernem
lyernt-lyernt (E), **iylernt-iylernt** (E) *n.*
a big pile of something
lyernt-iwem (T,E), **iylernt-iwem** (E) *vt.*
pile or heap something up ◆ Lyernt-iwem tha ura apek. (St) *I might heap up the firewood.*

lyerr-lyerr, lyerretyelyerr (E) *n.*
types of wrens, including fairy-wrens and grasswrens (*Malurus* spp.; *Amytornis striatus*) ◆ Lyerr-lyerrel arlkwem mern ntyemeny. (N) *Wrens eat ruby saltbush fruit.*
= tyewelyerr-lyerr, pwerelyerr-lyerr

lyerrer (E) *n.*
thin, slender, skinny
SEE ALSO alkey[1], arlpenty, ampap-ampap
lyerrer-irrem (F) *vi.*
grow tall and slender

lyerretyelyerr (E) types of wrens SEE UNDER **lyerr-lyerr**

lyerrk *n.*
dry leaves, leaves that have fallen to the ground
SEE ALSO antyerrk, iylelth

lyerrp akely-akely (E) a type of lizard SEE UNDER **alhwerrp akely-akely**

lyet *n.*
1. now, soon
2. today ◆ Lyet nga alpetyenh angwerr-angwerr. (St) *You are going back today, in the afternoon.*
lyet innga (E)
right now, just now, immediately (innga '*really*')
lyetant *n.*
just now (after a time), now for the first time in a long time ◆ Amwek atherr lyetant apetyern. (M) *The two mothers have just come.* ◆ Arna akwek-akwek lyapem, lyetantarl ra lyapewarreparrem, kwatyel amangkelh-ilek lyapem lyet. (St) *The little plants are growing, just now they are starting to grow from the rain.* ◆ Lyetantarl antyerrk-irrerl-anem, arlpa, waly. Antyerrk-irremel anem anyem ahern-warl. (St) *The leaves and branches are just drying up lately. They dry up and then they fall to the ground.*
lyetengarl-iperr (E) *n.*
by and by, soon
lyet war
any minute now, very soon, in a moment, round about now, just a moment ago ◆ Angwerr-angwerr-irrem lyet war. (T) *Soon it*

will be late afternoon. ◆ Lyet war alhem. (T) *Going in a moment.*

lyet-athek (T), **lyet-atheh** (T)
nowadays, in the near future ◆ Amangkep-angkem lyet-atheh Pwerrerl akwek. (T) *Little Pwerrerl is growing up these days.*

lyeteny *n.*
new, fresh, from today, modern ◆ Angka lyeteny anetyakenh — ahinpenyant nhenh. (St) *This language is not from nowadays — it's olden-time language.* ◆ Mern lyeteny, lyetarl itern. (M) *[This] food is fresh, it's just been cooked.* ◆ Lyeteny mwetekayaw, amparrkey-amparrkey. (St) *This car is new and shiny.*

lyetarr *n.*
nowadays, in the recent past ◆ Angkwey anwern anemel nyetyam, lyetarr kerwepel aperl-apem. (M) *In the old days we dug with digging sticks, nowadays we go around with crowbars.* ◆ Lyetarr-lyetarr anwengkerr angkerrem. (T) *Nowadays we speak together.* ◆ Antywerretyart angkethakwel, apeng-areny artekerr. Lyetarr kwatyant anem antyweynerl-wetyel, kwatyant anem antyweynetyel. (Sa) *They used to drink the liquid from the roots of the kurrajong tree when they were thirsty. Nowadays they just go along drinking water, they just drink water.*

lyetarr-lyet (T) *n.*
recently ◆ Angkwey-pat mapelarl ahenp angkety ilek. Lyetarr-lyet anem angkety arratem. Arrwekel akwel *no* arratek. (T) *The olden-time people spoke old language. Recently the language started to come back. It didn't come out before, apparently* (?).

lyetarrpwerreny (E) *n.*
the first time, just now, recently

lyetyepengalyetyep (W) cubbyhouse SEE UNDER **alyetyepengalyety**

lywa (W,T), **lywang** (W,T) *n.*
1. shade, a shade or shade shelter, branches or things used to make a shade ◆ Aper lywangel tyerrty anerl-anetyeh. (N) *People sit in the shade of the river red gum.* ◆ Tyerrty mapel lywang mpwarem utern-kety. (T) *Aboriginal people make shades to protect themselves from the sun.* ◆ Lywang arrpenhem irrkerleng, arrpenhem lywerrng. (T) *Some shades are sparse and some are thick.*

2. shadow of something or somebody ◆ Lywang rrpwamper arelhetyam kwenyel atayengarl Anengkerr. (M) *In the Dreaming the possum looked at its shadow cast by the moon.*
= **ulya** (E)

Lywang Arelhetyam (W)
name of a rockhole east of Yuelamu (Mt Allan) community (lit. 'looking at shadow of self'). The place in the Dreaming where the possum looked at its reflection in the moonlight.

lyweketwertwer (W,T), **rlweketereter** (W,T) *n.*
pallid cuckoo (*Cuculus pallidus*)
◆ 'Lyweketwertwertwertwer', alakenh angkem. Ngwem akwel rlalth apetyeh. (M) *'Lyweketwertwertwertwer.' [The pallid cuckoo] calls out like this. Supposedly they are asking the march flies to come.*
= alkwarrer-arrpwernenh
SEE ALSO lyalth

lywem[1], **rlwem** (W,T), **iylwem** (E) *vt.*
1. take something off something, undo something, untie or loosen something
◆ Mantarr rlway, mantarr arrpenhek anem nta irrpetyenheng. (T) *Take those clothes off so that you can put some others on.* ◆ Iylwemarl arernekarl-penh. Mantarr iylwem alhewelheyam-kety, pwerlp-irreyam-kety. (Sa) *Untying something that has been tied up. Take off the clothes so that [you] can wash yourself, have a bath.* ◆ *Tyre* iylwetyek *tyre* yanh, alpwelyarl irrem. (St) *Take that tyre that has gone flat [off the rim].* ◆ Lit apek tha iylwem inngart altywer-ilemel ngkwerlp. (St) *I am taking the lid off to open the tobacco tin.*
◆ Thewak atyenh tha iylwem, ayernekarl-penh. (St) *I'm going to untie my swag that has been tied up.* ◆ Arntekan iylwem, tyerremel anem, *chuck*-em away. (Sa) *[You] loosen the tooth, then pull it out and throw it away.*
SEE ALSO akap-rlwem

2. husk seeds with one's feet
◆ Mamperrk lywerl-anem ingkel, *clean* anthwerr irrem-arleng. Ingkang nhenh anewerrk nhenhel, *clean*-emey anem, ahetyem-ilem. Ingkel lpwelem alakenh arrew alakenh. Lywemel lywem lywem, rlkwankem anem. (N) Mamperrk *seed is husked with the feet, so that it gets really clean. It's cleaned with the feet, with the heels then winnowed [in a wooden dish]. It is cleaned and softened till the seed is separated from the husks.* ◆ Iylwem kwenh alyatywereng, ingka atherr alanh ilem. Alyatywereng ahelhek-arlek iylwem. (Sa) *The woollybutt grass seed is husked, and your feet go*

like that, husking the woollybutt grass seed on the ground.
lywelhem, **rlwelhem** (W,T), **iylwelhem** (E) *vi.*
take something off self; undress; pull something out of part of your body, shed bark or skin, become undone ◆ Mantarr ayeng rlwelhem. (M) *I'm taking my clothes off.* ◆ Rtety ayeng rlwelhem. (M) *I'm pulling my tooth out.* ◆ Twer arrerna, lywelh-hety, mwetekay *wheel*. (M) *Put the car wheel on tightly so that it doesn't come off.* ◆ Amwang-kenh ayenp rlwelhem ilkarl intem-penh. (T) *The snake sheds its skin after hibernating.* ◆ *T-shirt* ayeng iylwelhem *naked* ayeng aneyamel. (Sa) *I'm going to take my T-shirt off and then I'll be naked.*
= rlpwerlem

lywem[2] (W,T) *vt.*
poke into something ◆ Anngang ayeng lywern. (M) *[It] just poked me in the eye.*
SEE ALSO atanthem

lywemp-lywemp *n.*
broad-leaf parakeelya (*Calandrinia balonensis*). A fleshy herb about 25 cm high with succulent leaves and purple flowers.
= parrkely
SEE ALSO arrwelth-arrwelth

lywenpeny, **iylwenpeny** (E) *n.*
clever, smart, good at hunting, skilled or expert at doing something ◆ Lywenpenyel arelh nhenhel nyep-nyem arlatyey. (M) *This women is very good at digging up pencil yams.* ◆ Arelh nhenhel kalty-anthem lywenpenyel. (M) *This woman is skilled at teaching.* ◆ Tyerrty lywenpeny ker atwenh-atwenh. Ker *him one shot* atwerl. (M) *That man is a skilled hunter. He'll get a kangaroo with one shot.*
SEE ALSO inangkal, kalty, kapert altywer, kapert arraty, kwerathek, wetyerretyerr[2], weretyerretyerr, tyak, arnkaty, alhewer, inngeny

lywenty (W) *n.* [RESPECT LANGUAGE]
shade ◆ Lywentyel yang ayepel-irrerlantyarrarreparrem, marl atyengenh. (M) *They are sitting in the shade, my daughter [and her husband].*
= ngkwely
SEE ALSO lywa

lyweny (W,T) *n.*
hunting, day trip ◆ Anakerr alhem lyet lyweny, awenh-intyerr. (T) *We are all going hunting today, all the aunties.* ◆ Alhem ayeng lyweny, ker-warl ayeng alhem, atyarnp arlka aketyeh. (N) *I am going hunting to get kangaroo and to get some ironwood twigs.*

lyweny alhem (W,T)
go hunting, go for a day trip, for the day ◆ Ker aherr-warn lyweny alhem. (T) *Going hunting for kangaroo.*
= irrer alhem

lyweper *n.*
1. thigh, thigh part of an animal ◆ Artwa akelhem alety lyweper alhwarrp. (St) *Men cut themselves on the thigh when they are in mourning.*
2. young seed pods of the dogwood (*Acacia sericophylla*) • = alywer[1]
= **ulyeper** (E)

alyang lyweper (W)
a type of boomerang (curved shape) (alyang '*boomerang*')
= kayl ulyeper

lywerlperr (W,T) *n.*
black-breasted buzzard (*Hamirostra melanosternon*) ◆ Lywerlperrel arlkwem ankerr kwart. Arety-alhemel, kwer-penh alkerem irrenhem. (N) *The black-breasted buzzard eats emu eggs. It goes and finds some and then after that it flies up into the sky.*
= aytwertek, atwertim
SEE ALSO apwerl-apwerl

lywernk, **iylwernk** (E) *n.*
the hook on a woomera or spear; barb (on a spear); hooked stick, hooked thing ◆ Artwel lywernk arrernem amirrel-ayel irrtyart antwerrketyek. (T) *The man puts a hook on the woomera so that it can hold the spear.* ◆ Tyap lywernkel inem. Lywernk akwek *hook* yanh-lkwer mpwarerl-iwem, kel anem inem tyap anem, tyap ingweneng apek. (St) *[You] get grubs with a hook. You make a little hook [of grass] and then get grubs, such as those from the river red gum.*
SEE ALSO ipa, ikalharr

lywerrng (W,T) *n.*
good solid shade, thick hair ◆ Lywerrngel ananther anerlaney. (T) *We'll sit down in the thick shade.* ◆ Lywang arrpenhem irrkerleng, arrpenhem lywerrng. (T) *Some shades are sparse and some are thick.*
SEE ALSO irrkerleng

alta lywerrng (W,T)
thick hair (alta '*hair*')
SEE ALSO kapert irrkerleng

lywerrp (E) son-in-law's brother (respect term) SEE UNDER **alyarrp**

lywewem *vt.*
chop something down, chop a tree ◆ Arwengalker lywewem ilepel, kel akem, kel ngkwarl anem arrpem, lywewekarl-penh. (St)

Chopping the sugarbag nest with an axe, then chopping the honey out. ◆ Arnang lywewem, ilepel atwem lywang artetyeh. (M) *Chopping the tree down with an axe to make a shade shelter.*
= iyntwernem
SEE ALSO lywa, ulya
= ulyewem (E)

lywey (W) *n.*
1. silver witchetty, pirli (*Acacia cuthbertsonii* ssp. *cuthbertsonii*). Shrub up to 3 m high, with silvery leaves and cylindrical flowers.
2. the edible seeds of the silver witchetty ◆ Lywey anwern aketyart aketyart aketyart yanh-lkwer mer-warn angety-alpetyeh. Pwelap-ilemel anwern aketyart rwelem anwern itetyart, mern arlkwetyart anwern, mern mwerr angerr. (N) *We used to pick the silver witchetty bush seeds and then take them back to camp. We used to fill up our containers, then cook the seeds in the fire, and then eat them. They taste good.*
= perley
SEE ALSO alhanker

Mm

m+ *n.kin*
a short form of the word for 'mother etc.' that precedes other endings ◆ Mankethenh angerr kwer nhenh. (M) *This kid is a real mummy's girl.*
SEE ALSO amey

ma[1] *part.*
'Here!', 'There!', 'Take it!' (when giving something to someone)

ma[2] (W) *part.*
'You see', 'You know', 'Isn't that true?' (probably from Warlpiri *mayi* 'isn't it?')
SEE ALSO imay

maket, makit (E) *n.*
gun, rifle (from English 'musket') ◆ Artwel atyerrem ker aherr maketel. (T) *The man is shooting the kangaroo with a gun.*

makwerl (E) *n.* [RESPECT LANGUAGE]
many, a lot (note Kaytetye *makwerle*) ◆ Makwerl-ayerr ayepel-irretyel. (Sa) *There are lots of people [including respect kin] sitting there.*
SEE ALSO angerr[1]

mal (W,T) *n.*
rufous or western hare-wallaby (*Lagorchestes hirsutus*)
SEE ALSO lkwameny, kwarlp

mal-mal *n.*
a meeting of families after someone has passed away; 'finishing up' or 'sorry business'; sorry camp ◆ Mal-mal-warn alhem, anyent-irretyeh. (T) *Gather to finish up, for sorry business.* ◆ Yanh kwenh ngkweng anyent-irretyek anep-anem mal-malek kwenh. Nta mel-irrkwerl-apetyem mal-malel kel mal-malel irrkwetyem amel-irrkwerrem antem. (T) *Those people are all gathered together for the sorry business. You come and embrace people to express your grief at the sorry camp.* ◆ Mal-mal atwarirrem ywerlt atherr. Ywerlt atherr atwarirrem mal-malel, parnparlarlem irrem. (M) *At the sorry camp the grieving parents meet up with everybody. They meet at the sorry camp and people embrace each other in mourning.*
SEE ALSO panparl

mal-mal alhem
go for 'finishing up' or 'sorry business' ◆ Mal-mal alhem mer arrpenh-warn, kel anyent-irrem. (T) *Going to another place to 'finish up', then getting together.*

malan (T,E) *n.*
1. pie melon (*Citrullus lanatus*). Spreading vine-like plant with melon-like fruit (from

English 'melon').
2. the edible fruit of the pie melon ◆ Malan pwety-areny ampernarlerretyart angayakw, angayakwel ampernerretyart lherek akerreperrerl. Artelhampw inngernem, *watermelon*-artek-rnem. Wal, uyerrerliwerrekarl ina. Arlkwenh-arlkwenh mwerr-angker ampernenty, theweyet. (Sa) *When we were hungry we used to collect pie melons in the creek and cook them. Some of them were really huge, like watermelons. Well, now they've disappeared. When they're cooked they're really good to eat, sweet.*
= payemalan

-malangk *n.ending*
lovely, attractive, gorgeous, nice, pleasant, good-looking ◆ Kwerr-malangk. *A lovely girl.*

malewik *n.*
sit-down money week, 'single week'; the week when people receive unemployment (as opposed to pension) benefits (from English 'mail week')

maly (E), **malyey** (E) *n.kin*
1. father-in-law
2. mother's mother's mother's brother
3. father's male cross-cousin
4. woman's brother's child's spouse (?)
SEE ALSO amarl, ampaty-ampaty, ahenterr, arnemerr

maly-maly (E) *n.kin*
father-in-law etc. This word is particularly used when talking to children about their *maly*. ◆ Ampekan ilem, 'Maly-maly aray ngkwenh'. (Sa) *To a kid you say, 'Look at your* maly-maly *there'.*

malyaty (E) *n.kin*
my/our *maly*

malyengkw (E) *n.kin*
your *maly*

malyikw (E), **malyeyekw** (E) *n.kin*
his/her/their *maly*

maly-nheng (E) *n.kin*
a group of two or more people related to each other as *maly*

maly-intyerr (E) *n.kin* = **maly-nheng**

maly-nheng-arey (E) *n.kin*
a group more than two people related to each other as *maly*

maly-parety (E) *n.kin*
a respectful or 'sorry' way of talking about someone's *maly*
SEE ALSO -parety

maly-ankethenh (E) *n.kin*
1. having a close *maly* still alive
2. someone who is always with their *maly*
SEE ALSO -ankethenh

malyanwek (W,T) *n.*
1. they (people in the opposite patrimoiety)
2. country that belongs to people in the opposite patrimoiety to the speaker. One patrimoiety has Ngwarray, Peltharr/Petyarr, Pengart and Penangk, and the other has Kemarr, Pwerrerl/Pwerl, Mpetyan and Ngal.
SEE ALSO alak-akey, maly, anakerrakey, ampaty

malyey (E) father-in-law SEE UNDER **maly**

mam *n.* [BABY TALK]
1. mother (from English 'mum')
2. father's mother
3. breast milk [SOME SPEAKERS]

mam-mam (W) *n.* [BABY TALK]
father's mother
SEE ALSO amey, papap[1], aperl-aperl, nyany[2], ipmenh

mamerweterwet (W,T), **mameyweteywet** (W) *n.*
ant lion (lacewing larvae) (?) (*Neuroptera* spp.)
SEE ALSO kwatyarl ntyeny-ntyeny, angkwerey-angkwerey

mamety (W,T) *n.*
behaviour that is socially unacceptable and will bring bad luck to people. For example, fighting between people who have been through business together, or elder siblings fighting. ◆ Tyew-nheng atherr mamety kwenh atwerretyek, pwelhelarl rntwem-penh. (T) *It will bring bad luck if two people who have been through ceremonial business together fight each other.* ◆ Kwer anay, kwerraly *count*-em-iletyalay. Mamety kwenh. (M) *Hey kid, don't count the stars. It'll bring bad luck.* ◆ Nywerrp atherr inerretyalay, mametyeng. (M) *Don't marry the person who is the wrong skin for you because it will bring you bad luck.*
SEE ALSO akwety-irrpenem, akwetyerretyerr, mawenng

mameyweteywet (W) ant lion (lacewing larvae) (?) SEE UNDER **mamerweterwet**

mamp (W,T) *n.*
honey made by lerp insect living under the bark of the river red gum, *aper* (*Eucalyptus camaldulensis* var. *obtusa*). Also referred to as *ngkwarl mamp*. ◆ Aperel-aleng. Aperel ngkwarl mamp larlart awantyerlapetyeh. Theweyet anthwerr. (N) *It is from the river red gum tree. We go along sucking on the honey from the river red gum, just like lollies. Really sweet.* ◆ Ngkwarl apel anwern amangkek kwerel, mampel-arleng. Ahelh-warn anyep-anyerl ahelhek kwetyemel, kwatyek-arlek arrernerl-apem. Antywem anem. (N) *We grew up on that sweet stuff, on* mamp. *When it drops to the*

ground we gather it up and put it into water. Then we drink it.
= aperarnt, aperengengel
SEE ALSO yerrekeyerr

Mamp (W,T) *n.*
name of place in old Coniston Homestead area. See map p. viii.

mamperrk (W,T) *n.*

1. summer grass, armgrass millet (*Urochloa piligera*)
2. the edible seeds of the summer grass
◆ Mamperrk lywerl-anem ingkel, *clean* anthwerr irrem-arleng. Ingkang nhenh anewerrk nhenhel, *clean*-emey anem, ahetyem-ilem. Ingkel lpwelem alakenh arrew alakenh. Lywemel lywem lywem, rlkwankem anem. Mamperrkan rlkwankem anem ahetyem-ilem, panthel antem. Arnwety awantyety antem *clean*-ilerl-anem. (N) Mamperrk *seed is husked with the feet so that it gets really clean. It's cleaned with the feet, with the heels. It is cleaned and softened, till the seed is separated from the husks. The separated seed is winnowed, in a wooden dish. After it is cleaned the seed is eaten.* ◆ Anterrng apel kelharl mparetyart, kelharl. Rwel itetyart, tamp-artey alakenh. Mamperrk kwa. (N) *The seed was made into a seed cake, and then cooked in the fire, like a damper. That's* mamperrk *seed.*

man, maney *n.*
money (from English 'money') ◆ Maney rrkwem mern inetyeh. (M) *[You] have money to buy food.*
SEE ALSO ngkwelty, apwert, tal

man-man (W,T) *n.*
bent stick or wire used by women and girls to tell stories by drawing on the ground
◆ Arelhel mpaty-ilem man-manel ahern-warn. (T) *The woman is telling stories on the ground with the* man-man *stick.*
man-man atwem (W,T)
tell stories by drawing on the ground with a bent stick or wire (women and girls) (atwem '*hit*')
SEE ALSO mpaty-ilem, tyepety ilem

manangkarr (W,T) *n.*
spinifex country, desert country (note Warlpiri *manangkarra*) ◆ Aherr yarn apalenthwek mereh, anetyeh manangkarr-angkwerr, artety nwanth-angkwerr, twerrp-angkwerr kwerem alpek. (M) *The kangaroo couldn't find a home, so he went back to the spinifex and mulga and sandhills for ever and ever.*
= rrkwal

manatwerrp *n.*
oval-leaved cassia (*Senna artemisioides* ssp. *oligophylla*). A woody shrub to 0.5 m high, with broad leaves and broad papery pods. Used as a washing medicine, and has an edible grub in the roots.
SEE ALSO areyawarr, apwen

maney money SEE UNDER **man**

mangarrey, mangarray (W,T), **mengarray** (W,T) *n.*

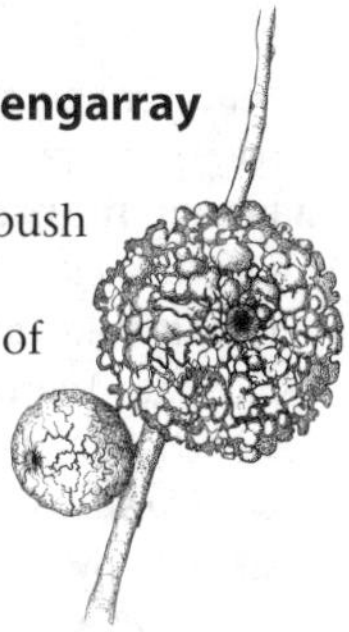

gall on bloodwood, *arrkernk*; bush coconut, bloodwood apple. Made by the female of a type of wasp (*Cystococcus pomiformis*). ◆ Mangarray arrkernkel-aleng anem altywernem anyent, alakenh anem. Akemem renh tyarrp-aketyenheng. Tyap-akert akwel akwek-akert nhenh, rnpwa akert — *nice one*. Anwa arlkwetyart akwel. (N) *The bloodwood gall grows on the bloodwood tree. We pick them and then split them open. They have a little grub inside — a nice-tasting one. We used to eat it.*
= arrkwerlperlp, arrkipangkwarl
SEE ALSO kathip

mangart[1] *n.*
1. quandong, native peach, peach tree (*Santalum acuminatum*). Tree to 4 m high, with rough bark, small green flowers and bright red fleshy fruits.
2. the edible fruit of the quandong
= mwerlp

mangart[2] (W,T) *n.*
the number eight

Mangker (E) name of place in the Murray Downs area SEE UNDER **Urrmangkerr**

mangw (E) *n.*
cat
= nyarrapeng, pwethekat, rlwatert, angay
SEE ALSO annga atherrk, meyaw-meyaw

manmarrp-irrem (W,T) feel dead tired or weak SEE UNDER **marrmarrp-irrem**

manpwerl (W,T), **manperl** (W,T) *n.*
blade on the end of an adze (joined to its handle by spinifex resin); stone knife
SEE ALSO kartamp

mantalyarrp, mantalyerrp (E) *n.*
a big boil with more than one opening or head (note Warlpiri *marntalyarrpa*)
◆ Mantalyarrpan arriw urrpety-akert. (Sa) *The* mantalyarrp *boil has several openings.* ◆ Aherr-

arlwethel apernelhetyam utyen, mwerr-irretyam kwer-penh. Mantalyerrp, artweker. Aherr-kenh atna weth-lkwer atherrk. Arlkwep-arlkwemarl ra, aherrel arlkwem, wal, kwaty weth anem *squish*-em ilem, apernelhem anem tywen anem. (St) *Sores were rubbed with the kangaroo balls vine, and that made them better. The boils are called* 'mantalyarrp' *and* 'artweker'. *The green stuff inside the kangaroo's stomach. After the kangaroo has eaten grass, well, the water is squeezed out and used to rub on sores.*
SEE ALSO tyapernp, artweker

mantarr, **manterr**, **mantar**, **manter** *n.*
clothes, clothing, dress ◆ Angkwey tyerrty manterr-kwenh rntwetyam. Lyet manterr-akertam tyerrty map. (T) *A long time ago Aboriginal people went around with no clothes on. Nowadays they have clothes.*
SEE ALSO rnwanenty, arnkwa, irrpenh-irrpenh
CAN SOUND A BIT LIKE mantharr *'desert death adder'*

mantharr *n.*
desert death adder (*Acanthophis pyrrhus*) ◆ Mantharr amwang ahangerr — nhwenh-nhwenh. (T) *The death adder is a dangerous snake — they bite.*

= antharr
CAN SOUND A BIT LIKE mantarr *'clothes'*

manty (W), **mwanty** (T,E), **mantyel** (W), **mwantyel** (T,E) *adv.*
carefully, slowly, cautiously. *Manty* or *mwanty* can also occur on its own as a command. ◆ Mwanty anerl-aynta. (Sa) *Be careful.* ◆ Manty alhetyeh atwewety *or* amwel apek nhwewety. (M) *Be careful in case you get into a fight or a snake bites you.* ◆ Ampa akwek yanh mwanty. 'Wawel ampekerr pepey!' (St) *Watch out for that baby over there. 'The fire will burn you baby!'* ◆ Arreyeng-arrey-irretyal anwengkerr aneyaw, angkety-kweny aneyaw, arreyeng-arrey-kweny. Irlpa apek anwengkerr akangkwerrey, iwenhek apek anwengkerr akangkwerrey, irlpel manty awerl-anemel. (N) *We shouldn't chatter, but sit down without talking, without making a noise. We'll pay attention and listen to whatever, listening carefully with our ears.*
SEE ALSO arternp

manty-manty (W), **mwanty-mwanty** (T,E) *adv.*
carefully, slowly, cautiously ◆ Mwanty-mwanty arengkel arlkwekerr. (Sa) *Be careful in case the dog bites you.* ◆ Mwanty-mwanty arrernerl-ayntaw, utyenemel, thewak. (Sa) *Put the swags up carefully.*

manty alhem (W), **mwanty alhem** (T,E)
go slowly and carefully, look out

manty-irrem (W), **mwanty-irrem** (T,E) *vi.*
be careful, watch out for something ◆ Manty-irraw tyerrty alert-hety. (M) *Watch out for that person.*

manty-manty-ilem (E), **mwanty-mwanty-ilem** (E) *vt.*
1. warn somebody about something, tell someone to be careful
2. look after someone or something, care for someone or something
= mwerranty-ilem

manyem, **mwanyem** *n.*
1. banana-flavoured bush tomato (*Solanum cleistogamum*). Plant with grey or blue-green leaves, thorns on stems, pale purple flowers and pale yellow fruits. Grows to about 25 cm high.
2. the edible fruit of the banana-flavoured bush tomato
= arlelyek, tepernter
SEE ALSO rrwarlp[1], alperrantyey

map *n.*
many; a lot of things; plural (more than four or five people or things), a group of particular people or things (from English 'mob') ◆ Map apetyemaw anwekantherr-warl. (St) *Lots of people are coming towards us.* ◆ Kwer map marnteng apetyem kwerl-warn. (M) *The kids come to school in the bus.* ◆ Tyerrty arrerlp map mwekartek irrpem. (T) *Cowboys wear hats.*
= anengk[1]
SEE ALSO arwenth, intyarr

map-irrem (W) *vi.*
get together, gather together (a lot of people or things)
= anengk-irrem

map-ingar *adv.*
(doing something) many times, lots of times ◆ Thew-warn alhay anyent-ingar anem, map-ingar alhetyal. (T) *Go to the store once, don't go lots of times.*

mar (W,T) small wooden shovel or scoop SEE UNDER **mwar**

marakat (W,T) *n.*
tired, lethargic, lazy, not energetic (note Warlpiri *marakata*)
= parrk

marakat-irrem (W,T) *vi.*
get tired, feel tired or lazy ◆ Iwenh-apert nga marakat-irrem? (M) *Why are you feeling tired?* ◆ Ayeng marakatem irrem parrk nthwerl-

apenty-penh. (M) *I'm feeling tired and lazy from walking around.*
= parrk-irrem

marany (T,E) *n.*
the same, the usual thing ◆ Marany-warl alhetyek kwaty-warl. (St) *[I] am going to the same place for water.* ◆ Marany ayeng antarl anerl-anem. (T) *I'm staying home as usual in the same place.*
SEE ALSO irrkaty, amperreny, akweteth, amelerr

marekwerr (W,T) *n.*
spinifex pigeon (*Geophaps plumifera*) (?)
SEE ALSO arntwerrert, ntarrwerarrwer

marl *n.*
1. female (person or animal), woman ◆ Marl nhenhel ahelh panthel inyem. (N) *This woman is digging the ground with a wooden scoop.* ◆ Marl yanhel alkngwenh-kerr ayenh, anewikweng, artwa yanhek-arrngel. (St) *That woman over there might get jealous of me, over her husband, over that man there.*
2. wife ◆ Marl apetyay! (St) *Come here wife!*
SEE ALSO kwey, kwerr, arelh[1], arrkwekety[1]

marl akwek
young girl, little girl (akwek '*small*')

marl awenk
young girl, teenage girl (awenk '*teenage girl*') ◆ Aperl-nheng atherr yanh alherreperrem, kwey marl awenk then arelh ampwa then. (Sa) *Grandmother and granddaughter are going along there, a teenage girl and an old woman.*

aherr marl
doe kangaroo, female kangaroo (aherr '*kangaroo*')

marlek-alyey-alyey, marleh-alyey-alyey (W), **marl-kenh-alyey-alyey** (W) *n.*
caustic bush, desert spurge (*Euphorbia tannensis*) (marl '*girl*'; alyey-alyey '*spirit friend*'). A small plant that grows along the ground, with milky sap and small flowers and fruit.
SEE ALSO anemarraty, rrweyek-alyey-alyey

marlalperr (T,E) *n.*
yellow ochre
= karntewarr, arrkeyt
SEE ALSO rlpwa, arwethenp, atywerlk, artep arlpenty, marlalperr, ngwenty-ngwenty

marnt *n.*
1. closed in, shut
SEE ALSO alhap, martelhenty, mety, mwernt[2]
2. bus ◆ Marnteng alhem, lyweny apek, apety-alpem, altywer-ilety-alpem, anarnpenty-alpem. (N) *We might go for a day trip in the bus, come back, open it, and get out.* ◆ Kwer map marnteng apetyem kwerl-warn. (M) *The kids come to school in the bus.* ◆ Ayeng arnekarnarirrem marnt-warn, yay atyengenharl apety-alpemek. (T) *I am going to meet my big sister, who is coming back on the bus.*

marnt-ilem (W,T) *vt.*
shut something, lock something up ◆ *Store* marnt-ilem, altywerem ilem, marntarl-ilem penh. (N) *The store is closed, and after being closed it will open.*
SEE ALSO martem

marnt-irrem (W,T) *vi.*
close down, become shut
SEE ALSO mwernt-irrem, martelhem

marnterlpel (W,T) *n.*
talking in a secretive way, talking in away so that others don't know what you are talking about

marrapernt (W,T) *n.*
nosebone made from kangaroo bone (note Warlpiri *marrapirnti*)
SEE ALSO ntyarl, melyalker, irrengernt, ngerl

marratyelpely (W,T), **marratyelperl** (T), **marretyelperr** (W) *n.*
a type of bird (?) (note Warlpiri *marra-jilpirli* 'dotterel')
SEE ALSO tyelyapwerety

marrawaty (T,E) *n.*
native walnut (*Owenia reticulata*). A tree up to 10 m tall, with dark rough bark, twisted leaves and walnut-sized fruit with a red or purplish covering. (note Warlpiri *marrawaji*)

marrert *n.*
married (from English 'married')
= arlwenth, iteng[1]

marrert-irrem *vi.*
get married
= iteng-irrem, arlwenth-irrem, merangk anem

marretyelperr (W) a type of bird SEE UNDER **marratyelpely**

marrmarrp-irrem, manmarrp-irrem (W,T) *vi.*
feel dead tired or weak ◆ Ngkwern atherr marrmarrp-irrem, rlkert apek, angayel apek. (M) *[My] legs are feeling dead tired, maybe because I'm sick or hungry.*

marrwelyenng (W), **marrwelyeng** (W), **marrwelyen** (T) *n.*
1. old camp (where people have died and been buried)
2. sickness that can be caught from going close to a place where people have died and been buried ◆ Akwek alenh unta angem mer-angkwerr angerrepat maparl anetyam-angkwerr, wal tyerrtyel ilem 'marrwelyenng'. 'Marrwelyenng alakenh *right round* angay,

akwek yanh rlkert irrerr-hety kwenh. Antelhem kwenh tywemar.' (M) *If you are taking a small child around near a place where the old people used to live before, then people call it 'marrwelyenng'. 'Take that little kid right round, in case it gets sick. In case it catches "fingernails".'*

-mart *ending*
Provides emphasis; really. ◆ Ankerl-**mart** arelh nhenh — anthetyakenh. (T) *This woman is really greedy — she doesn't give things to anybody.* ◆ Kwey rwanng-**mart** angkem. (Sa) *That girl we have all known for a really long time is talking.* ◆ 'Warlpal nhenhey — warlpal-kweny, arrenty. Arrenty-**mart** nhenh-rnem.' (Sa) *'It's a whitefella — no it's not a whitefella, it's a devil. These are really devils.'*

martarrp (W,T) *n.*
stone axe ◆ Ilep ina mparetyam martarrp, irntepenh mparetyam ina. (M) *They made axes, called 'martarrp', from stone.*
SEE ALSO ilep[1], mety
ilep martarrp (W,T)
stone axe (ilep *'axe'*)

martem (T,E) *vt.*
1. close or shut something, block something off ◆ Arwengalkerel anem, ankerel ap renh martem arwengalker, ikwer-atwety ngkwarl intem. (St) *In the sugarbag, the wax blocks off the sugarbag and the honey goes as far as there.*
2. turn off a tap or a switch etc.
martelhem (T,E) *vi.*
become closed or shut, close or shut yourself in ◆ Arrewelhem ayeng *store*-warl alhetyek martelhekerr. (Sa) *I am hurrying to the store in case it closes.*
SEE ALSO marnt-irrem, mwernt-irrem
martelhenty (T,E) *n.*
shut, closed ◆ Martelhenty yanh arlta pwarrkeng. (St) *[The store] is closed because it's Sunday.*
SEE ALSO altywer, marnt, alhap, mety, mwernt[2]

mater (T,E), **matay** (E) *n.*
cloud (note Warlpiri *matayi*)
= ankert[1]

math *n.*
mother (from English 'mother')
SEE ALSO amey, mam

matyart *n.*
hairstring belt or waist band (men's) ◆ Alta rrpwamper-penh anwengkerr matyart mpwarem. (T) *We make hairstring belts out of possum fur.*
= arlpalh, mawelyarr
SEE ALSO ngatywelarr

matyawenng (T,E) a curse, a bad omen SEE UNDER mawenng

matyekatyer *n.*
pied butcherbird (*Cracticus nigrogularis*) ◆ Arrpwer-arteh akin matyekatyer. Ker akwek map kwetyemel arlkwerl-apem. (M) *The pied butcherbird is similar to the magpie. We collect the baby ones and eat them.*
= pweretyetyer
SEE ALSO arrpwerek-arrpwer

matyekwel (E), **matyikwel** (E) *n.*
black-faced cuckoo-shrike (*Coracina novaehollandiae*)
= amatheng-amatheng

Maw (W) *n.*
Mau Hills

mawelyarr (W,T) *n.*
hairstring belt or waist band (men's)
= matyart
SEE ALSO arlpelh[2]

mawenng (T,E), **matyawenng** (T,E) *n.*
1. a curse, a bad omen, things or behaviour that are likely to bring a curse upon someone or make someone sick ◆ Mawenng angketyal! (St) *Don't say things that will bring bad luck!* ◆ Mawenng mer atyenh-warl atnarnpety-alhek. (St) *Something which was a bad omen landed in my place.* ◆ *'Don't* arrpenhek urarrernerl-anerl, matyawenng kwenh.' Kel ratherr imperrem antem. (T) *'Don't growl and talk badly to that person, it'll curse them.' Then the two of them leave off arguing.*
2. someone who is near death, is cursed, or is about to get into big trouble ◆ Akuny mawenng anep-anem, lyetek, lyetarl ngenh atwetyenh. (St) *You poor thing, you're cursed, and today they're going to beat you up.*
SEE ALSO mamety

may (W) 'Hey, what's up?' SEE UNDER **imay**

mayal ignorant, not knowing, inexperienced SEE UNDER **maywel**

mayel, imayel (E), **ipmayel** (E) *adv.*
jealous (particularly over husband or wife); jealously ◆ Artwang anyenteng mayel atwerrem, arelh atherr. (T) *Two women are having a jealous fight over one man.*
CAN SOUND A BIT LIKE mayal *'ignorant'*
mayel atwerrem, imayel atwerrem (E)
have a jealous fight (particularly over husband or wife) (atwerrem *'fight'*) ◆ Arelh atherr apek anew anyenteng anep-anem, wal imayel atwerrerl-anem. (St) *If two women are married to one man, well they might have jealous fights.* ◆ Mernek-arrngel ararl atwerremant. Artwek-arrngel imayel

atwerrem. (St) *They just fight over food. 'Jealous fights' are over men.*
mayel anngwenhem (W,T), **imayel alkngwenhem** (E)
get jealous (of or for someone), have a jealous fight (particularly over a husband or wife) (anngwenhem *'get jealous'*) ◆ Arelh alenhel mayel anngwenhem, arelh arrpekw. (M) *That woman is jealous of the other woman.*
mayel arem
get jealous (of or for someone), feel jealous (particularly over husband or wife) (arem *'look', 'see'*)

mayeth (T,E) *n.*
boss ◆ Waylpel mayeth apetyekaw! (T) *The whitefella boss has come!*

maywel, **mayal** *n.*
ignorant, not knowing, inexperienced (from English 'myall') ◆ Pwety-areny maywel. (T) *Ignorant people from the bush.*
CAN SOUND A BIT LIKE mayel *'jealous'*

mekelarey (W,T) *n.*
really good, fantastic, pretty, nice, lovely ◆ Mekelarey anwern ilep-ilem *story* nhenh. (N) *This is a really good story that we are telling here.* ◆ Awenh-awenh, atyeng anthay, mekelarey. (T) *Auntie, give me that lovely thing.* ◆ Mekelarey ntwa mpwarek, alkwert apek alya apek. (T) *You made a really nice one, a shield or a boomerang.*
SEE ALSO mwerr anthwerr, anper anthwerr

melarlp, **merlalp** *n.*
a type of spirit ◆ Melarlpan atham-areny ra. *Four*-pel *name*-akert ra. An irrernt-areny, *same one*. Renh-antey. Inenty an *same*. (Sa) Melarlp *are the same as* atham-areny. *They have four names —* irrernt-areny *are the same, and* inenty. ◆ Arety-kweny itya melarlp. (M) Melarlp *spirits are not visible.*
SEE ALSO mer akweteth, aleperenty, arnamarwengk, arnam-areny, irrernt-areny, atham-areny, inenty, urlaylp

meltyang angkem (W,T) *vi.*
whine (like a dog when it wants to go hunting)
SEE ALSO mwelty-mwelty angkem, urrmelty angkem

melyalker (W,T) *n.*
nosebone made from kangaroo bone
= marrapernt, ntyarl
SEE ALSO irrengernt, ngerl

melyek (E) *n.*
salt
SEE ALSO thalt, ker ikwemey ilenh-ilenh, ilewerr, ulewerr

melyerrkwer (W,T) *n.*
desert bandicoot (*Perameles eremiana*) (?)
SEE ALSO akwerr[2]

memp (W,T) *n.*
men's round headpiece (like a cap), made of emu feathers and hairstring ◆ Mempan inang mpwarem artwang ayang mapel althart rntwetyeh kwer map apek kalty-anthetyeh *or tourists* apek *or* mer apek. (T) *The old men make emu-feather hats for dancing the* althart *ceremonies, for teaching the children, for teaching about the country, or for tourists.*

meng (W) generous, sharing SEE UNDER **ipmeng**

mengarray (W,T) bush coconut, bloodwood apple SEE UNDER **mangarrey**

menh-menh (W,T), **menh** (W) *n.kin*
1. mother's mother; granny, grandmother
2. mother's mother's brother or sister; great-uncle, great-aunt
3. a woman's daughter's child; grandson, granddaughter
4. a person's sister's daughter's child
5. particular relations with the same skin as a person's *menh-menh*
6. the country and Dreamings belonging to a person's *menh-menh* ◆ Amwek-kenh mam ilem 'menh-menh'. (T) *[Your] mother's mother is called* 'menh-menh'.
menhaty (W,T) *n.kin*
my/our *menh-menh*
menhengkw (W,T) *n.kin*
your *menh-menh*
menhekw (W,T) *n.kin*
1. your *menh-menh*
2. his/her/their *menh-menh*
3. my/our *menh-menh* [SOME SPEAKERS]
menhenheng (W,T) *n.kin*
a group two or more people related to each other as *menh-menh*
CAN SOUND A BIT LIKE amenheng *'a group of two or more people related to each other as mother and child'*
menh-intyerr (W,T) *n.kin* = **menhenheng**
menhenheng-arey *n.kin* = **menhenheng**
menhenhengart (W,T) *n.kin* = **menhenheng** (P)
menh-nheng atherr (W,T) *n.*
a person together with their *menh-menh*
CAN SOUND A BIT LIKE amenheng atherr *'a person together with their mother'*

ment-ayerr (E) *adv.* [RESPECT LANGUAGE]
'Leave it!', leave (something) alone
SEE ALSO menty

menty, **imenty**, **ipmenty** (E) *adv.*
1. An expression used when you want to say that you're not interested in something, or

when you reject a suggestion; 'Leave it', 'Don't worry about it', 'Never mind', '[I] don't want it'. This word can occur on its own ◆ Menty impang! (M) *Leave it alone!* ◆ Ker arlewatyerr ampwa iwey apek menty, anter anetyakenh menty iwey. (St) *Leave that skinny goanna, throw it away because it hasn't got any fat.*
2. stop (doing an action) ◆ Tha ayakem ahel-irrerl-anekerr. 'Menty aneyaw iltetyal kwenh!' (St) *I stop them in case they start fighting. 'Leave it, sit down and don't swear!'* • SEE ALSO impem
3. be left out, left on own ◆ Ayengan mentyem anem — parrp antherrirretyakenh. Angayelarl arrarem. (T) *I am being left out — they didn't give me any straight away. I'm just hungrily watching the others eat.*
menty awelhem, ipmenty awelhem (E)
ignore or not take notice of what is happening; not answer someone back ◆ Ayeng menty awelhem ngkweng, tha atwekerreng-antey menty awelhepelhem ayeng, tha atwekerreng. (T) *I am ignoring you, I'm ignoring you otherwise I'll [have to] hit you.* ◆ Ngenh *somebody*-el atwetyam wal nta mentyel awelhem. *Next time* yang atwelhem ngwenh, wal, nta atwem akin, atwenhem antem. Kenh aweth apek ya atwety-apety-alpem, *that's the time* nta atwetyenheng akin. Mentyel amparr nta awelhem. (M) *If somebody fights you then you don't take any notice. The next time that they fight you, well, that's the time that you hit them back. If they come back again to fight, that's the time that you fight. At first you ignore them.*
mentyel awem, ipmentyel awem (E)
hear someone or something but take no notice; ignore, hear but not answer ◆ Mentyel awem, arrpenh nhakw apekarl atyeng angkem wal mentyel tha awem, rarrp angketyek. (St) *That person over there might talk to me, but I'm not taking any notice, [she] can just talk herself.*
mentyel arem, ipmentyel arem (E)
look at something but leave it alone; watch something happen but not be involved; keep away from someone or something ◆ Atnert pwelapel apek mentyel arem. (St) *I'm just looking because my stomach is full.* ◆ Mentyel tha arem maney anetyangan, ker apek mern apek yanh mentyel arem. (St) *I am just looking at that meat and bread because I haven't got any money.* ◆ Mwerekikwenh an mentyel arem artwel. Kweyarl anetyel ikwerel-arleng. Mwer-mwerek angketyenh arrangkwarl. (Sa) *A man keeps away from his mother-in-law. Her daughter is living with him. He doesn't talk to his mother-in-law at all.* ◆ Mwetekay akeng mentyel arem. Inetyang arrangkw. (St) *Leave that car. Don't get it, it's no good.* ◆ Tyerrty arrpek atwerrerlek mentyel arem. (T) *Watching other people fighting but not getting involved.*
menty-irrem, ipmenty-irrem (E) *vi.*
1. leave something alone; give something up; abandon something; leave something for someone else (?) ◆ Menty-irrek nga, mern nhenh kwenh. (St) *You left this food behind.* ◆ Mern iwerrarrkw arlkwety-inkwern. Inpa anem menty-irrek anem. (Sa) *They used to eat the gidgee wild orange. I don't know about nowadays, they've given it up.*
2. give away belongings to appropriate relations (when in mourning) ◆ Mwetek apek menty-irrem, rnwanenty, *swag* apek. Wal, kamernel inem. Ampewek, alem-penh-henh. *Not* mwelek. (M) *They give away the car and the clothes and the swag. Well, the uncle [of the deceased] gets them. Or the sister's children. Not the mothers.*
menty-ilem, ipmenty-ilem (E) *vt.*
1. refuse to do something, say you don't want something, knock something back; refuse something ◆ Rlkertel apek tha menty-ilem. (St) *If I'm sick I might refuse to do it.* ◆ Alhemarlel tha menty-ilerl-alhem. 'Mentyaw arlkwerlanaw kwenh — ayeng alhem-arleng.' (St) *If I'm going I might say I don't want any. 'Forget it, you all eat — because I'm going.'* ◆ Wenhek ntwang atyengety menty-ilek? (T) *Why did you tell me not to do it?*
2. leave something behind
menty ilem
say you don't want to do something
menty-menty, ipmenty-ipmenty (E) *n.*
surplus food, an over-abundance of food ◆ Menty-menty intep-intem ker, ker akngerr yanh. (St) *There's a lot of meat and it can't all be eaten.* ◆ Atnertengarl tha mern ipmenty-ipmenty arrernek ingwenthekant. (St) *I was full up and so I left the surplus food for tomorrow.*

mentyey (W,T) *n.*
mange (from English 'mange') ◆ Arengk angernelhem mentyey-akert. (T) *The mangy dog is scratching itself.*

meny (T,E) *n.* [BABY TALK]
food ◆ Meny akway. (St) *Eat [this] food.*
= nan[2], nyam-nyam, nyany[1]
SEE ALSO mern

menyarenyar (T) *n.*
the smell of rain ◆ Menyarenyar mwerr intyem kwenh. (T) *The rain smells good.*
= mpengemp, nyemp

menyeynterl (E), **menyinterl** (E) *n.*
locust ◆ Menyeynterl arwerlarl altheynerl-anemel, antywer anetyangarl ileynem. Menyeynterl akngerr anem alhem weth. Akngerrel altheynerl-anem alanh alpep-alpem. (Sa) *The locusts are the ones that go along stripping the trees, go along wiping out the grass. Lots of locusts go along like that. They go along like that, stripping the foliage.*
= tyarrerrey
SEE ALSO intelty

mer, **apmer** (E) *n.*
1. camp, home, house ◆ Mer atyengenh-warn alherrey. (M) *Let's go to my camp.* ◆ Thang mer akwek artetyek kwaty-kety. (T) *I'm going to make a little camp in case it rains.*
◆ Ntwerrkenh alhek. Thakwey apawenhwek, 'Mer ngkwengenh ayeng irrpey, tyerrtyeng?' 'Itya. Alhweng akwekam yanh atyengenh.' 'Yeway. Mer arrpenh-warn ayeng alhem.' (M) *The python went off. He asked a mouse, 'Can I come into your home to escape from the humans?' 'No. My burrow is too small.' 'All right. I will go to another place.'*
2. place, region, area, country ◆ Mer rntwarreng tyerrty lwereny apetyem. (M) *A stranger comes from a faraway place.*
3. Goes before the name of a particular place or country. ◆ Apmer Alhalkerel, Alhalkerel, ikwerel inngart. Kel akely anem apetyarr-alpek *Utopia Station*-warl. (Sa) *At Alhalker, at Alhalker of course. Then [when I was small] we came back to Utopia Station.*
mer arlalty (W,T)
a person's own country, own place or camp (arlalty *'own', 'personal or private possession'*)
◆ Mer arlaltyel intetyek. Rtakw arrernelhemel, ura itemel, itepek atherr. (T) *Sleeping in your own camp. Putting up a windbreak and lighting a fire on both sides.* ◆ Mer arlaltyel anem ayeng anerl-anem. Kwer-penh lyweny anwern alherl-anem, mer arlaltyengetyel. Kwer-penh apety-alpem mer arlalty-warn. (T) *I'm living at my place. From there I go hunting. After that I return to my place.*
meralty, **apmeralty** (E) *n.*
family, close relations ◆ Apmeralty ingkerrek anwantherr anep-anem, apmer anyent-areny. (St) *We are all close relations living here, from one country.*
SEE ALSO altya
mereh-artwey (W,T), **mereh-artey** (W), **merek-artwey**, **apmerek-artwey** (E) *n.*
owner or boss of a place (-artwey *'custodian'*)
◆ Mer atyengenh merek-artwey ayeng. Mer nhenh. Mer atyengenh. (P) *I am the boss for my country. This place. This is my country.*
mer akweteth (W,T)
1. staying in one place; someone who stays home all the time (akweteth *'permanent'*)
2. a type of spirit [SOME SPEAKERS] ◆ Mer akwetethel anety-ilem tyerrty. (M) *The* mer akweteth *spirits make people sick.* • SEE ALSO melarlp, irrernt-areny, atham-areny, akweteth
mer iteng-areny (E), **apmer iteng-areny** (E) *n.*
married person's camp (iteng[1] *'married'*)
merangk anem (E), **apmerangk anem** (E)
marry, be married
mereng-amer, **apmereng-apmer** (E) *n.*
cubbyhouse, children's pretend camp
◆ Mereng-amer ina mer mparem. Pelangket an *all there* ina angem — *billycan*, tey apek angem — tey itemel, merel anerremel mereng-amer kwerel. (P) *They make cubbyhouses. They take blankets and all there — billycans, tea — they boil tea sitting there in the cubbyhouse.*
= nyetyep
SEE ALSO arnkentyeng arnkenty, arlwekereng arlweker

merawarr (W,T), **merewarr** (W,T) *n.*
mirage, heat haze ◆ Merawarr intem, irntang akern-ilemel, mer arrpenheng. (N) *There is a mirage there, and from another place it [looks as if] it is lifting the hills up.* ◆ *Road* alherl-apem nta, merawarr *there like* kwaty akin, amparrkerl-anerleng. (N) *If you are going along a road there'll be a mirage there, sparkling like water.*
= angent
SEE ALSO ilewerr
CAN SOUND A BIT LIKE Mewarr *'Milky Way'*

merlalp a type of spirit SEE UNDER **melarlp**

merlk (T) *n.*
milk (from English 'milk')

merlpeng (W,T) *adv.*
shading eyes with hand
= urlengimar
merlpengel arem (W,T)
shade eyes with hand; look, while shading eyes with hand ◆ Merlpengel arem twerneng. (M) *Shading your eyes with your hand because of the sun.* ◆ Tyerrty alenh tha arep-arem merlpengel. (M) *Shading my eyes with my hand, I can see that person over there.*
= ingkerrkentyel arem

mern *n.*
1. food, tucker, food from plants ◆ Maney rrkwem mern inetyeh. (M) *[You] have money to buy food.* ◆ Mern apek ikwerenh artaper-wem akngwely-kety apek. (St) *She might roll up her food because of the dogs.*
2. A general word that can go before the name of a particular type of food. In the Anmatyerr way of classifying foods most fruits and vegetables are known as *mern*, sweet things as *ngkwarl*, seeds as *anterrng*, *arnwety* or *ntang*, meats as *ker* and edible grubs as *tyap*. ◆ Mern pelaw. *Flour.* ◆ Mern tywerrk. Mern tywerrkel anwern amangkek, arlkwerl-apekarl, ampeng-irremarl. (N) *Wild figs. We grew up on wild figs, going along and eating them when they got ripe.* ◆ Mern arlatyey anemel inyerlapetyart. 'Mern arlatyey aray, mwernenty map. Yekay mern mwernenty kwenh nhenh!' *We used to go along digging for* arlatyey *yams with digging sticks. 'Look at all these yams, all growing together. Look at all the yams!'*
3. the edible part of something ◆ Mern angarak apel akwerrk arlkwerl-apem. Awerretyepwer anyent renh. 'Angarak' akenh arlparl, kenh mern 'awerretyepwer'. (N) *The young pods of the bush bean are eaten. That's the same thing as* awerretyepwer. *'Angarak' is what the leaves are called, and the edible part is 'awerretyepwer'.*
4. edible white substance in sugarbag or native bees' hive
mern anwerrng
wet dough made by mixing boiling water with flour
SEE ALSO awerrp[1]
mern thwep-thwep (W) = **mern anwerrng**

mernem (W,T) show something to someone SEE UNDER **imernem**

mernerr (W,T) *n.*
mountain devil, thorny devil (*Moloch horridus*) (note Warlpiri *mirnirri*)
= arnkerrth, nywerr

mernperr *n.*
seed capsules of the bloodwood, *arrkernk*. Used for making necklaces (note Warlpiri *mirnpirri*). ◆ Mernperr ntewal anyent ra akwel. Mernperrarl *seed*-am pertipelaw kwer-penh mernperram irrem. Anyem antem ahelh-warl ingkerreny. Arrkernk-areny. (N) Mernperr *is from the bloodwood tree and it's the same as* ntewal. Mernparr *are the seed capsules that come after the flowers. Then they all fall to the ground. They are from the bloodwood tree.*
SEE ALSO ntewal, mangarrey, arrkipangkwarl

mernt[1] (W,T) *n.*
1. sick, sickness (note Warlpiri *miirnta* 'snot, head cold') ◆ Anant-iperray, mernt-irrenh-ketyengay. Rlkert apek aneketyeng. Arrwengkelth ineketyeng. Anantay! (P) *Sit down, in case you get sick. In case you get sick. In case you catch something. Sit down!*
2. a sick person ◆ Anyem apel antywem merntel, antywem *tea leaf* akwek arrernemel. *Stir*-em *up* ilemel item renh, *mixed up* ampemey kel antywemem. (N) *Witchetty bush leaves are used as a medicine for sick people. The small leaves are put in water, like tea-leaves, and stirred up and cooked, and then the liquid is drunk.*
3. nasal mucus, snot ◆ Kwer mernt-akert. (M) *The child has a snotty nose.* ◆ Artwengkenng mernt inelhem iltyel, alakenh, *clean*-em anem. (N) *Clean the snot out [from your nose] like that.*
SEE ALSO rlkert, arrwengkelth, inkwerr, artwengkenng, nkwanng, arntety
mernt-apert (W,T) *n.*
having a sickness, having a cold or flu ◆ Rlwek yanhel mwerrarl ilem *clean*-em ilelhem annga, *everything* alhewelhem artwengkenng-apertem mernt-apert, iteth-ilem. (N) *That native pine is used to wash eyes and clean them and make them better, to wash all over, to make people better if they have a cold or are sick.*
mernt-irrem (W,T) *vi.*
get sick
= arntety-irrem, rlkert-irrem
mernt-ilem (W,T) *vt.*
make someone or something sick

mernt[2] (T,E), **imert** (W), **imernt** (E), **amernt** (E) *part.*
(doing something first) and then something else happens; at first, previously ◆ Nga mernt arrwekel irray, ayeng ingkerneng. (Sa) *You go first and then I'll come later.* ◆ Mern mernt tha arlkwetyek. (St) *I'm going to eat first.* ◆ Kwempalthel imernt arrpemel arrpemel, kel irraker anem wem. (Sa) *First it is scraped with the adze then the grooves are made.* ◆ Iwerr arnangelh-ilemel rarrp imernt ineyam-kety mern. *Room* anetyang. Mwerekikw. Alkiwerr-kety. (Sa) *Clear a path for [that person] so that they can get their tucker first. There is no room [for her] because her son-in-law is there.*
SEE ALSO -amparr

merntap (W,T) *n.*
large ant hill or ant bed (note Warlpiri *mintapa*)

SEE ALSO kerrertek, ngkwepey, kerrth, awerr-awerr[1], pwentereng

merntepam (W), **merntepwarn** (W,T) *n.*
a type of plant; lamb's tail, pink mulla-mulla (*Ptilotus exaltatus*) (note Warlpiri *mintiparnu*). Plant about 60 cm high with smooth green leaves and pink flowers.
= awerreh-alyey-alyey, rrweyek-alyey-alyey
SEE ALSO alyey-alyey

merrenty (W), **merreynt** (E), **imerreynt** (E) *n.*
murderer; someone who is guilty of manslaughter ◆ Imerreynt irrkwentyel arntwerrkem. (Sa) *The policeman arrests the murderer.* ◆ Apetyewarray kwenh, merreynt yaleng alengk-iwelh-atherr anetyal angetyewarra kwenh, nhenhek atwetyek. Kel renh atwem anem renh merreynt renh. (St) *All of you come on, don't let that guilty people hide themselves — bring them here so that they can be punished. Then the guilty people are beaten.* ◆ Merrenty ineh-artey maparl arlkwek-penh map ingkerr arlperrek atwek. Ityilek, anyent-arenyel. (M) *He killed all of them who were guilty of eating his family. He finished them off, all on his own.*

merrert (T) *n.*
water from hollow trees (note Warlpiri *mirrirdi*). Also referred to as *kwaty merrert.*
= untharr

merreynt (E) murderer; someone who is guilty of manslaughter SEE UNDER **merrenty**

merrkel (T,E) *n.*
having sores or ringworm ◆ Arengk angernelhetyel — atway merrkel-apert. (Sa) *Belt that dog that is scratching itself — it's got ringworm.*

merrkwernerl (E) *n.* [RESPECT LANGUAGE]
shame, shamefully ◆ Merrkwernerl. Nthakenh ameram-ilerretyakenh mwerey-ayerrek. (Sa) *It's shameful. [You] are not supposed to talk to your son-law.* ◆ Merrkwernerl. Atay angkerlentyarretyang ayepel-irrerlayntenherrarey. Kweyay ayepel-irrerlayntetyek ntert-ayerr, merrkwernerl. (Sa) *It's shameful. Just sit down and don't talk so loudly. Daughter, sit down quietly and stop behaving shamefully.*
SEE ALSO nyerrel

merrng (E), **ipmerrng** (E), **irrmeng** (E), **irrmerrng** (E) *n.*
1. palate, roof of the mouth
2. gums (mouth). Also referred to as *arrakert merrng.* ◆ Arrakert merrng ayeng utyen-irrek. (Sa) *The gums in my mouth got sore.*
SEE ALSO tyelk
arntek merrng (E)
gums (in mouth) (arntek *'tooth'*)

mert (W,T), **meyt** (T,E) *n.*
1. sweetheart, girlfriend, boyfriend, lover
SEE ALSO ahenty-penh, anew, anew-anew
2. good friend, mate (from English 'mate')
mert-mert (W,T), **meyt-meyt** (T,E) *n.*
sweetheart, girlfriend, boyfriend, lover
◆ Yanh mert-mert ngkwengenham. (T) *There's your sweetheart.* ◆ Meyt-meyt yanh ngkwenh alhepalhem. (Sa) *There's your boyfriend going along there.*
SEE ALSO mpweny
atyeng mert (W,T), **atyeng meyt** (T,E) *n.*
my sweetheart/girlfriend/boyfriend (atyeng *'for me', 'to me'*)
ngkweng mert (W,T), **ngkweng meyt** (T,E) *n.*
your sweetheart/girlfriend/boyfriend (ngkweng *'for you', 'to you'*) ◆ Ngkweng mert apety-alpern. (N) *Your sweetheart just came back.*
kwer mert (W,T), **ikwer meyt** (E) *n.*
his or her sweetheart/girlfriend/boyfriend (kwer *'for him/her', 'to him/her'*)
ineh mert (W), **itnek meyt** (E) *n.*
their sweethearts/girlfriends/boyfriends (ineh *'for them', 'to them'*)
mert-mert-irrem (W,T), **meyt-meyt-irrem** (T,E) *vi.*
become sweethearts, become boyfriends/girlfriends/lovers
mert-mert-ilem (W,T), **meyt-meyt-ilem** (T,E) *vt.*
make someone your sweetheart/boyfriend/girlfriend ◆ Urrey mapel mert-mert-ilerrem awenk map. (T) *The boys are making the teenage girls their girlfriends.*
mert-mert mpwarem (W,T), **meyt-meyt mpwarem** (T,E) = **mert-mert-ilem** (mpwarem *'make', 'do'*) ◆ Mert-mert mpwarek rrwey an marl. (M) *The boy and the girl became sweethearts.*

merterr[1], **merterr-merterr** (W,T) *n.*
caustic weed, milk weed, mat spurge (*Euphorbia drummondii*). A ground-hugging herb that has small flowers and leaves, and milky sap. ◆ Merterr-merterrel alhewem kwer tyapernp-akert. (T) Merterr-merterr *is used to wash kids who have boils.*
= amwekel-amwekel[1], kwep-kwep[1]

merterr[2] (E) *n.*
women's ceremonial hairstring 'shirt' (worn around the chest)
SEE ALSO ngatywelarr

meth (W,T) *n.*
rib, ribs

= utyim
SEE ALSO ltwa
ker meth (W,T)
the edible meat from around the rib
metheth *n.*
white woman, European woman, non-Aboriginal woman (from English 'missus') ◆ Ntwan methetham. (T) *You are a white woman.*
= waterlweper
SEE ALSO alhernter
mety, **mwety** (W,T) *n.*
1. blunt ◆ Ilep nhenh metyarlaw. (Sa) *This axe is blunt.* (St) ◆ Irrtyart mwety. (M) *A blunt spear.*
SEE ALSO arrerlp
2. shut ◆ Arrangkweyay, mety. (Sa) *No, it's shut.* • SEE ALSO alhap, marnt, martelhenty, mwernt[2]
3. the closed-in end of a burrow, the corner of a room etc. ◆ Ker rapet mety-warl irrpek. (St) *The rabbit went into the end of the burrow.*
mety-mety *n.*
1. not allowed, restricted ◆ Artwant alhetyeh mety-mety-warl. (M) *Only men can go to restricted places.*
SEE ALSO amek-amek
2. the closed-in end of a burrow, the corner of a room etc.
mety-irrem, **mwety-irrem** (W,T) *vi.*
1. become blunt ◆ Anem atyenh mety-irrek, angernekarl-penh. (St) *My digging stick went blunt from digging.*
2. become closed off or blocked ◆ Alhweng mety-irrek, alhweng anetyakenh mety anem. (St) *The burrow became blocked off, and then there wasn't a burrow because it was closed.*
mety-ilem, **mwety-ilem** (W,T) *vt.*
make something blunt ◆ Tyerrtyel atwemel mwety-ilem ilep. (M) *The person made the axe blunt by chopping [with it].*
metyeletyel (W,T) *n.*
1. navel, umbilicus
2. umbilical cord
= tyelepelep
SEE ALSO yep
metyernk (W,T) rabbit SEE UNDER **mwetyernk**
mew-mew *n.* [BABY TALK]
cow, cattle (from English 'moo moo') ◆ War arrkenel 'mew-mew' akem. (St) *We just call them [cows], 'mew-mew', for fun.*
SEE ALSO pwelek
Mewarr (W), **Miwerr** (T,E), **Imiwerr** (E) *n.*
Milky Way ◆ Mewarr arraty interl-apem talkw altwerl-atheh. (N) *The Milky Way lies straight across in a westerly direction.*
= Lpwararr, Atwarlk
mey-mey[1], **mwey-mwey** (W) *n.*
1. a man's mother-in-law; a man's wife's mother
2. a man's mother-in-law's sisters and brothers
3. a woman's son-in-law; woman's daughter's husband
4. a woman's son-in-law's brothers
5. particular relations with the same skin as a person's *mwer*
6. a man's mother-in-law; a woman's son-in-law etc. This word is particularly used when talking to children about people related to them as sons-in-law or mothers-in-law etc.
◆ Mey-mey ngkwenh. Ampa akelyek inngart ilem, 'Mey-mey ngkwenh'. (Sa) *Your son-in-law/mother-in-law. [We] just say, 'Your* mey-mey*' to little kids of course.* ◆ 'Mey-mey ngkwenh aray' — alanh ilem ampa akelyek. (Sa) *'Look at your* mey-mey*' — that's what you say to little kids.*
SEE ALSO mwer, rtwalty, urtalty
mey-mey[2] (T) *n.* [BABY TALK]
cubbyhouse
SEE ALSO mer, mereng-amer, alyetyepengalyety, antyweng-antywa, nyetyep
Meyateng (T,E) *n.*
name of a hill in the Mt Solitary area
meyaw-meyaw *n.* [BABY TALK]
cat (from English 'miaow')
SEE ALSO rlwatert, mangw, nyarrapeng, pwethey, pwethekat, angay, annga atherrk
Meyekanty (W) *n.*
name of spring near old Mt Doreen Station
meyt (T,E) sweetheart, girlfriend, boyfriend, lover
SEE UNDER **mert**
minekey (W,T) *n.*
native bee (note Warlpiri *minikiyi*) ◆ Rltwamp minekey nta arety-alhem. (M) *You go and see the native bees.*
SEE ALSO lwerlker, ngarntarnt, arwengalker, rltwamp
Miwerr (T,E) Milky Way SEE UNDER **Mewarr**
mpa *part.*
'Come on', 'Let's go' ◆ Mpa anwengkerr alhetyek, rapet akwerrk aretyeh. (N) *Come on, let's go and look for baby rabbits.*
mpalernem (W), **mpal-inem** (W,T) *vt.*
break something into bits (wood, meat etc.); cut something up
SEE ALSO tyarrp-atwem, rlweth-akem, urleth-akem, mpalty-akem, ltwakem
mpal-akem (W,T) *vt.* = **mpalernem** ◆ Mpal-akem akin mern tamp iltyel. (T) *Break the damper up into bits with your hands.*

SEE ALSO ltwakem, urleth-akem

mpal-akelhem (W,T) *vi.*

split open, crack open ◆ Alparr mpal-akelhek. (M) *The coolamon split.*

= mpalty-akelhem

mpalth (E) high, open ground on the side of a creek, plain, level ground SEE UNDER **mpwanth**

mpalty (W,T) *n.*

pieces, little pieces

mpalty-irrem (W,T) *vi.*

break into bits and pieces

mpalty-akem (W,T) *vt.*

cut or break something into bits or pieces; cut something in half ◆ Ker mpalty-akem kel kwer anthem. (T) *Cut the meat up into bits and give it to her.*

= tyarrp-akem, mpal-akem

mpalty-akelhem (W,T) *vi.*

crack open, split in half (stone, coolamon, boomerang) ◆ Nheng irnta apek ltwakelhem *half*, mpalty-akelhem. Alyang apek mpalty-akelhem. (M) *A rock might break in half, split in half. A boomerang might split in half.*

= mpal-akelhem

mpalty-atwem (W,T) *vt.*

chip something off (flakes off a rock)

SEE ALSO iyltem

mpank (W,T), **mpwank** *n.*

1. full (unopened), whole (uncut), entire ◆ Ampwerrk mpank intem, ker tyep-iletyenh. (M) *The meat is still whole, it hasn't been cut up.*

SEE ALSO ampwerrk

2. not ready, not taken or used up ◆ Rrpwetyem mpwank akwet. (M) *There are only a few left.*

3. (something) that hasn't happened yet; (something) that hasn't been done yet ◆ Itya, mpwank akwet. *No* ina arratek. (M) *They are still away. They haven't turned up.* ◆ Mpank, amangkety-kwenh-antey. (T) *He is immature, he hasn't grown up yet.* ◆ Mpwankaw! *Wait!*

mpank-antey (W,T), **mpwank-antey** (W,T)

1. (something) hasn't happened yet

2. (something) is not ready

mpankeny (W,T), **mpwankeny** *n.*

1. a new or fresh place; place where people haven't been lately; fresh hunting country; pristine ◆ Mpankenyel aherr map anem. Anter angerr. (T) *In the fresh country there are plenty of kangaroos. Fat kangaroos.* ◆ *No* altywer-ilemel inyem — ahelh ampwerrk mpankeny. (M) *The ground hasn't had holes made in it from digging — it's still whole and fresh.* ◆ Tyerrtyel aretyakenh 'mpankeny'. (M) 'Mpankeny' *is a place that people haven't seen before.* ◆ Ker atwetyek apek alheyaw mpwankeny-angkwerr. (St) *Let's go hunting in the fresh country.*

2. an abundance of something (that hasn't been touched) ◆ 'Ker apek mpwankeny. Nhakw alheyaw ker mpwankeny-warl-areny. Nhenh apek *too much* maparl unthekarl.' (St) *'There might be still kangaroos there [that haven't been touched]. Let's go over there where there might be some kangaroos. Too many people have been looking round here.'*

mer mpwankeny (E)

a fresh camp, country that has not been used before ◆ Mpwankeny-angkwerr ntwa alhem. (M) *You are going through the fresh country.*

mpankeny-irrem (W,T), **mpwankeny-irrem** *vi.*

1. return to pristine or original state (country); grow back (vegetation) ◆ Mer nhenh mpankeny-irrem, angkweyantarl nyetyam. (M) *This place that was dug up a long time ago is growing over again.* ◆ Mer nhenh anwekantherrenh mpwankeny-irrek anem. (St) *This country of ours has now returned to its original state.*

2. get fresh or become renewed (country after sorry business)

mparem (W) make or create something SEE UNDER **mpwarem**

mparengareng (W) rule, Law, custom, tradition SEE UNDER **mpwarengareng**

mparlp-wem (W), **mpwarlp-wem** (W) *vt.*

turn something around, turn something over

mparlp-welhem (W), **mpwarlp-welhem** (W) *vi.*

turn yourself over ◆ Antyamel mparlp-welherl-anem arengk nhenh. Altakert. (M) *This dog has itchy skin and it's turning itself over and over on the blanket.*

= mpart-wem, angart-wem

mparnt, **mpwarnt** *n.*

1. middle

2. married person's camp ◆ Mer mparntan yanh anewartarl anep-anem-kenharl, *married*-kenharl ikwerenh, arlweker marl *single*-kenh, arlweker-areny-kenh. (St) Mer mparnt *is the place where the married couples live, whereas the* arlweker *is the single-women's camp.*

SEE ALSO arnkenty, arlweker

alhwerrp mparnt, **alhwerrp mpwarnt**

the middle of winter (alhwerrp *'winter'*) ◆ Alhwerrp mpwarnt mpepel anem, alhwerrp mpep anem irrenhem, mpep. *Really cold.* Mpwarnt. (St) Alhwerrp mpwarnt *is the middle of winter, when it's really cold.*

twern mparnt, **utern mparnt** (E)

the middle of summer (twern, utern *'sun'*,

'summer') ◆ Utern akwerrkek-amparr anek, utern mparnt anem irrem, ampem anem, ingka atherr arlka anem ampem. (St) *First there was the beginning of summer, then the middle of summer comes, and then everything burns, including the feet.*

mparrwekel *n.* [RESPECT LANGUAGE]
first, in front (of something) ◆ Mparrwekel ahanenherl-wekaw tyety-ayerrek. (St) *They [including my son-in-law] went on ahead, hunting.* ◆ Mparrwekel irrenherr-arey — ingkern-thaytarl anwantherr. (Sa) *You all [including my son-in-law] go ahead — we'll come along behind.*
SEE ALSO arrwekel
mparrwekel-irrem *vi.* [RESPECT LANGUAGE]
go first, go in front
SEE ALSO arrwekel-irrem

mpart-wem (W,T), **mpwart-wem** (W,T) *vt.*
turn someone or something over; tip something over ◆ Tha mpart-wem mern rtamp, arrpenh-thayt ampetyeh. (M) *I am turning the damper over to cook the other side.* ◆ Ker yanh mpart-way. (M) *Turn that meat over.* ◆ Ker *kangaroo* mpart-wem ker aketyenheng. (T) *Turning the kangaroo over to cut it up.*
SEE ALSO angart-wem, mparlp-wem
mpart anyem (W,T), **mpwart anyem** (W,T)
fall onto back or side; tip over (anyem *'fall'*) ◆ Mwetekay mpwart anyek. (M) *The car tipped over.*
mpart intem (W,T), **mpwart intem** (W,T)
be upside down (intem[1] *'lie down'*) ◆ Mwetek mpart intem, akern antep. (T) *The car is upside down.*
SEE ALSO impalkert-wem

mpaty[1], **impaty** (E) *n.*
1. footprint, track ◆ Nhenhel apmwa alhek, impaty nhenh. (St) *This track here is where the snake went.* ◆ Mpaty arem tert-penh. (T) *[You] can see the tracks in the mud.* ◆ Mpatyel alherl-anemel kel kwerel-antey mpatyel apety-alpeyam, mpaty aremel. Mpaty irrkatyel-anteyarl apety-alpeyamel. Arlaltyel-antey apety-alpem ingka, ingka mpatyel. *Miss*-kety. (T) *Going along [following] the tracks and then coming back again following the same tracks. Coming back following the same tracks. Following the same tracks in case you miss them [and get lost].* ◆ Ayeng mpaty arek unta? (T) *Did you see my tracks?*
2. marking or design on something ◆ Arelh mapel wem impaty ahern-warn an *canvas*-warn, tyepety-wem mer kwerenh. (T) *The women make designs on the ground and on canvas, drawing the designs from their country.*
3. scar
CAN SOUND A BIT LIKE ampaty *'child (of a woman)'*
ingka mpaty, ingkang mpaty (W,T)
footprint, track (ingka *'foot'*) ◆ Ingkang mpatyam alherl-apem, ingkang mpaty aperl-apem. Mpaty renh arelhem, *'Eh*, nhel alhekaw! Ingkang mpaty yanh arerrirray!' (N) *There are footprints going along. When you see the track, 'Hey, this is where it went! All of you, look at the tracks!'*
mwetekay mpaty
wheel track, car track (mwetekay *'car'*) ◆ Mwetek ngkekern-ngkekern impaty anetyakenh. (M) *The unregistered car doesn't leave any tracks.*
mpaty-ilem (W,T) *vt.*

1. tell a story by drawing on the ground (women and young girls) ◆ Arelhel mpaty-ilem man-manel ahern-warn. (T) *The woman is telling stories on the ground with the* man-man *stick.*
= tyepety ilem, man-man atwem
2. draw
3. make a mark on the ground or on a tree to show where you have gone
SEE ALSO ingkwernem, arrernem, atanthem, intelh-ilem, arlkeny arrernem, arlkeny-wem, tyepety-wem, ahimperr-wem, man-man

mpaty[2] (W,T) *n.*
grub from the root of the river red gum, *aper*, larvae of the hepialid moth (*Trictena argentata*) ◆ Mpaty yang anem per artekerrel. (M) Mpaty *grubs are found in the roots of the river red gum.* ◆ Inyemel inyemel ahern, inerl-apem war angerrety map, tyap mpaty. Artekerr kwen ahelh-areny. Anemel akwel inyem, *olden time.* (N) *You dig and dig in the ground and then get the larger* mpaty *grubs. They are in the roots in the ground. In the olden-time we dug them up with yam-sticks.* ◆ Rwelam atyerrem tyap renh, arlkwetyeh. (N) *The grubs are cooked in the fire so that they can be eaten.*
SEE ALSO ahekwenayt, perlanty, ingweneng, aylperlayt, ngkenhar

mpengemp (W), **impengemp** (W) *n.*
the smell of rain ◆ Mpengemp renh antyernem, wal tyerrtyel intyernem mer arrpenheh apek. *'Ah*, kwaty intyety-alhemaw, mpengemp kwenh.' (M) *People might smell the rain when they are in a particular place. 'Ah, the smell of rain is coming,* mpengemp.'
= nyemp, menyarenyar

mpep, mpwep (T) *n.*
middle, in the middle, in between, halfway (between one place and another) ◆ Alhek ayeng, mpepel intenhek. (St) *I went and camped halfway.* ◆ Kapert mpep apek atwem. (St) *Hitting the middle of the head.*
SEE ALSO rlkwerr
ingwa mpep (E)
middle of the night (ingwa *'night'*)
= kweny rlkwerr
arlta mpep (E)
middle of the day (arlta *'day'*) ◆ Arlta mpepel mern arlkwetyek anem. (St) *Eating in the middle of the day.*
= irntar
mpepel-areny (T)
something that is in the middle, or in between other things
mpep-penh, mpwep-penh (T) *n.*
1. middle (child or children)
= rlkwerr-penh
SEE ALSO ingkern-penh, arrwekeleny
2. something that is in the middle, or in between other things
mpep-iperr (E) *n.* = **mpep-penh**
mpepengel (E) *n.* = **mpep-penh**
mpepel-irrem (E), **mpwepel-irrem** (T) *vi.*
get caught in the middle of something ◆ Akeweny artwang nheng mpwepel-irrekaw! Inang renh atwek! (T) *That poor man was caught in the middle [of a fight]! They hit him!*
mpepek-ilem (E), **mpwepek-ilem** (T) *vt.*
put someone or something in the middle of or in between other things ◆ Ampa akwek mpepek-ilem tha amikw atherrel-arleng anetyek. (St) *I'm putting the little child to sit in the middle between the two mothers.*

mperlkem *vi.*
shine, look white or shiny; glisten ◆ Kapert mperlkem, aywang, rntwarreng. (M) *The grey hair shines in the distance.* ◆ Ngkwarl mamp mperlkem. (M) *The sweet honey on the river red gum is glistening.* ◆ Kwaty akngerr alharrkem, akngerrarl apetyem, ingwemernt irremel, alharrkenty-alpem. Mperlkemel ap alharrkenty-alpem arlter. (St) *There is a big thunderstorm, and it gets dark, and the lightning flashes. The lightning flashes white.*
SEE ALSO mperlker, akerlkem

mperlker *n.*
1. white, white in colour; pale in colour ◆ Ywerntemelan rrkwek rrpwerl mperlker. Latyamanel rrkwek rnter-rnter an mperlker. (M) *Yuendumu wore black and white. Lajamanu wore red and white.* ◆ Uthipel ap irrkerlanty rnternerl-anem thip akely nyingk apek. Nyingkek unthemel atanthenhemel. Mperlker ap ra. (Sa) *The falcon goes along hunting small birds such as zebra finches. It looks for zebra finches and grabs them with its claws. They [falcons] are white in colour.*
2. white person, whitefella, European people ◆ Tyerrty mperlker. Mperlker anwekantherrenh apetyem yanh. (St) *A white person. There is our whitefella is coming.*
SEE ALSO arlter, alhernter, tywelker, warlpal, rrpwerl
mperlker-mperlker *n.*
whitish, off-white
mperlker-ayerr (E) *n.* [RESPECT LANGUAGE]
flour ◆ Ankwerl-waw mperlker-ayerr atyeng tha thetyek. (Sa) *Go and get me some flour [from my respect kin] so that I can make [some damper].*
= arlter-ayerr
SEE ALSO pelaw

Mpetyakwert *n.*
female junior skin name, corresponding to Mpetyan. See diagram p. 744.
◆ Mpetyakwertan marl Mpetyan akwek. (T) *A Mpetyakwert is a young Mpetyan girl.*
SEE ALSO Mpetyan

Mpetyan *n.*
skin name, subsection name, marriage class. See diagram p. 744. ◆ Mpetyan-kenh alerekw Ngal. (T) *A Mpetyan [man's] children are Ngal.*
SEE ALSO Tyamperlk, Mpetyakwert, Nampetyenp, Ngampin, Tyampetyenp

mpetyan-mpetyan[1] (E) *n.*
yellow or white seeds from the bean tree, *inernt, atywerety* (*Erythrina vespertilio*)
SEE ALSO ngal-ngal

mpetyan-mpetyan[2] (E) *n.*
young bush turkey
SEE ALSO arwengerrp, artew

mpurl (E), **mpwerl** (E) *n.*
1. part of guts, stomach organ
SEE ALSO atnarlt
2. crop (of a bird). Also referred to as *ker mpurl.* ◆ Mpurl ikwer-warl mern arlkwetyel, artewel. (Sa) *When a bush turkey eats, the food goes into its* mpurl.
CAN SOUND A BIT LIKE mpwel *'you two'*

mpwa, mpwang (W,T) *n.*
1. urine, piss ◆ Mpwal-thaytel intem-kety, nhakw-angkwerr iylkangkwerr interl-anerray. *Someone* apek mpwa apek ulhetyenh-kety. Ampa apekel ulheyamel marlel apek. (St) *Lie down [with your head facing] the eastern side [wind side], not to the western side. Because*

someone might urinate there. A child might piss there, or perhaps a woman.
2. the little sack filled with liquid that is found inside the bush coconut gall
CAN SOUND A BIT LIKE ampwa *'old', 'thin'*
mpwa ulhem (E) *vi.*
urinate, have a piss (ulhem *'urinate'*)

mpwal foot-end of the bed SEE UNDER **mpwarl**

mpwalth (E) high, open ground on the side of a creek SEE UNDER **mpwanth**

mpwang (W,T) urine, piss SEE UNDER **mpwa**

mpwank full (unopened), whole (uncut), entire SEE UNDER **mpank**

mpwanth, mpwalth (E), **mpalth** (E) *n.*
1. high, open ground on the side of a creek; plain, level ground ◆ Kwep mpwanth-areny. (M) *The desert spadefoot toad lives in the open ground on the sides of creeks.* ◆ Ahern mpwanth. (M) *Level ground.*
2. the western end of the bed (where people urinate) ◆ Ura itetyel mpwanthek. (Sa) *Lighting a fire at the end of the bed.*
SEE ALSO twerr, mpwarl

mpwarelh-ilem (E) *vt.*
make someone feel as if something is crawling around or touching them; touch someone with something ◆ Yerrelarl mpwarelh-ilem ayenh artep. (Sa) *It feels like there is an ant crawling on my back.*
SEE ALSO arrenkelh-ilem, irrekerr-ilem

mpwarem, mparem (W) *vt.*
1. make or create something ◆ Artwel mpwarem alkwert arnang inernt-penh, alyang-kety ilpelhetyek. (T) *Men make shields from bean tree wood to protect themselves from boomerangs.* ◆ Alyep ina mpwaretyam pwelty anem ina arrken-irretyam. Than aretyart arrengey map, anawerr map. (St) *They made a hairstring ball and then they played* pwelty *[traditional football game]. I used to watch my grandfathers and my father's elder brothers.* ◆ Rtey-rteyel anthwerrng mpwarem mer antywang kwerenh. (M) *The magpie-lark makes its nest from mud.*
2. make something happen ◆ Atherrkeny mpwarem mpwelarrel. (St) *Rainbows make the country green.*
3. do something, prepare something
4. fix or mend something ◆ Arnang nhenh tha mpwarem ltwakelhekarl. (M) *I am fixing this thing that broke.* ◆ Tha mparem patyekel nhenh. (M) *I am fixing this bicycle.* ◆ Arelhel mwetekay-kenh ingka mpwarem alpwely-irrekarl. (T) *The woman is fixing the flat tyre.*
5. heal, cure somebody ◆ Ngangkerel mpwaretyek ngenh, mwerr-iletyek. (Sa) *The traditional healer will heal you and make you better.*
6. have (babies or offspring)
◆ Kweleynterreynterrel alhweng ra angernem *baby* anem ra mpwarem kwer-antey alhweng kwer-antey. Kel arraterl-alhep-alhem arlewatyerr-artek. Arnam arrernem kel akwerrk map anem ra mpwarem. (St) *The rainbow bee-eater digs a burrow and then it has its babies there in the burrow. Then it comes out and goes around just like a goanna does. It puts grass there in the burrow and then it has its babies.*
mpwarelhem, mparelhem (W) *vi.*
1. make something happen to yourself; make yourself a certain way ◆ War alyelherl-anem arrkenel nheng *happy* mpwarelherl-anemel alyelherl-anem, merel anerl-anemel. (N) *[People] just sing along to make themselves happy when they are sitting round at home.*
◆ Ayep, alewatyerrel arlkwerl-apem, anter angerr mparelhetyek. (N) *Goannas go along eating tar vine to make themselves really fat.*
2. heal yourself, make yourself better

mpwarengareng, mparengareng (W), **mpwarenharenh** (E) *n.*
1. codes of social behaviour which include showing respect for family and the land; rule, Law, custom, tradition ◆ Mpwarengarengel arraty ilem tyerrty. (T) *The Law tells people how to do the right thing.* ◆ *We can't partem/passem [?] that* anpernenty. Anpernenty yanh tyeperr ra. Mpwarengareng anthwerr. Tyeperr kwenh. (M) *We can't part with that kinship system. Kinship is very special. It is the Law. Really important.* ◆ Mpwarengareng ikwerenh-angkwerrel *policeman*-el *arrest*-em-ilem. *That's his law.* Artwehenh *law* 'mpwarengareng' renh anem ilem. (M) *The policeman uses his law to arrest people. That's his law. Aboriginal law is called 'mpwarengareng' as well.*
2. something that is used to do something or fix something ◆ Mpwarenh-arenh anetyakenh akwey mwetek nhenhan. (St) *There is nothing in this car to fix it with.*
3. somebody who is able to do things

mpwarl, mpwal *n.*
foot-end of the bed, western end of the bed (where people urinate). It is generally thought that the proper orientation for sleep is with the head to the east and the feet to the west. ◆ Angerrakw-thaytel iylka-thayt intetyek. Altwerl-thayt intetyek apek anetyek yanh ilem, 'Mpwal-thayt anem nga anep-

anem. Mpwal-angkwerr anem nga anep-anem. Ikngerrakw-angkwerr anetyakenh.' (St) *Sleeping [with your head to] the east side is lying in the direction that the wind comes from. About sleeping or sitting on the western side people say, 'You are sitting on the* mpwarl *side, not on the east'.* ◆ Mpwal-thaytel intem-kety, nhakw-angkwerr iylkangkwerr interl-anerray. *Someone* apek mpwa apek ulhetyenh-kety. Ampa apekel ulhweyamel marlel apek. (St) *Lie down [with your head facing] the eastern side [wind side], not to the western side. Because someone might urinate there. A child might piss there, or perhaps a woman.*
SEE ALSO mpwa, mpwanth

mpwarl-thayt, **mpwal-thayt** *n.*
foot-end of the bed, western end of the bed (where people urinate)
SEE ALSO rlkangkwerr

mpwarl-angkwerr, **mpwal-angkwerr** *n.*
sitting or lying with your head to the west; the western end of a bed

mpwarlp-wem (W) turn something around SEE UNDER **mparlp-wem**

mpwarnt middle SEE UNDER **mparnt**

mpwart-wem (W,T) turn someone or something over; tip something over SEE UNDER **mpart-wem**

mpwekaly (T) *n.*
a type of inedible solanum plant
SEE ALSO arengkerlpart

mpwekenh (T,E), **mpwepenh** (E) *n.*
types of frog (*Neobatrachus* spp.). Also referred to as *ker mpwekenh.*
= mpwelengk
SEE ALSO mpwa, angwethek

mpwel *prn.*
you (you two). This pronoun is used in the subject part of the sentence (i.e. representing the 'doers' of the verb action). It is usually used for people who are in same patrimoiety and same generation moiety — for example, a person together with their brother or sister or with their paternal grandfather — but it may be used as a general term. See Appendix 1. ◆ Kweyekar mpwel atherr nywerrp anyent ayeng. (M) *You two are in the same generation moiety, and I am in the opposite.*
SEE ALSO mpwelak, mpwelanth, mpwel-ingkerr
CAN SOUND A BIT LIKE mpurl *'crop (of a bird)'*

mpwelenh *prn.*
you (you two). This pronoun is used in the object part of the sentence (i.e. representing those the verb action is 'done to').

mpweleh (W,T), **mpwelek** (E) *prn.*
for you, to you (you two)

mpwel-henh (W,T), **mpwel-kenh** (E) *prn.*
yours (belonging to you two)

mpwel-altyerr *n.*
a special term for a closely related son-in-law or mother-in-law (whose mothers come from the same country) ◆ 'Mpwel-altyerr yanhan ngkweng.' Alakenh thwengk ilem. Mpwel-henh altyel-nheng atherrenh. (M) *'He/she is* mpwel-altyerr *for you.' That's what I tell you. You two are the children of two female cross-cousins.*
SEE ALSO mwer, altyerr[1], ilern, ilern-altyerr, mpwelak-altyerr, alaltyerr, alak-altyerr, arrengkerr-altyerr, arrakerr-altyerr, anwernakerr-altyerr

mpwel-ingkerr *prn.*
you (you two). This pronoun is used in the subject part of the sentence (i.e. representing the 'doers' of the verb action) when the two people are both in the same patrimoiety and the same generation moiety; for example, a person together with their sister or brother, their father's father or their mother's mother. See Appendix 1. ◆ Mpwel-ingkerr alherray angkwer-nheng atherray. (T) *Off you go, two sisters together.*
SEE ALSO mpwel, mpwelak, mpwelanth

mpwelenh-ingkerrenh, **mpwelenh-ingkerr** *prn.*
you (you two). This pronoun is used in the object part of the sentence (i.e. representing those the verb action is 'done to').

mpweleh-ingkerr (W,T), **mpwelek-ingkerr** (E) *prn.*
for you, to you (you two)

mpwel-ingkerrenh, **mpweleh-ingkerrenh** (W,T), **mpwelek-ingkerrenh** (E) *prn.*
yours (belonging to you two) ◆ Mpweleh-ingkerrenh ngkwerlp tha inerl-alpetyeh. (M) *I'll go and get the tobacco that belongs to the two of you.*

mpwelak *prn.*
you (you two). This pronoun is used in the subject part of the sentence (i.e. representing the 'doers' of the verb action) when the two people belong to the same patrimoiety and different generation moiety; for example, a person together with their father or father's sister. See Appendix 1. ◆ Mpwelak alherray kwaty inetyek, mpwelak awenh-nheng alherray. (T) *You two go and get the water, auntie and niece together.*
SEE ALSO mpwel, mpwelanth, mpwel-ingkerr

mpwelenhakenh, **mpwelenhak** *prn.*
you (you two). This pronoun is used in the

object part of the sentence (i.e. representing those the verb action is 'done to').

mpwelehak (W,T), **mpwelekak** (E) *prn.*
for you, to you (you two)

mpwel-kenh, mpwelehakenh (W,T), **mpwelekakenh** (E) *prn.*
yours (belonging to you two)
◆ Mpwelehakenh thang ngkwerlp arlkwetyeh. (M) *I'm chewing the tobacco that belongs to the two of you.*

mpwelak-akey *prn.*
you (belonging the opposite patrimoiety to me or us).
SEE ALSO -akey

mpwelak-altyerr (E) *n.*
a special term for a closely related son-in-law or mother-in-law (whose mothers come from the same country)
SEE ALSO -altyerr, ilern, mpwel-altyerr, ilern-altyerr, alaltyerr, alak-altyerr, arrengkerr-altyerr, arrakerr-altyerr, anwernakerr-altyerr

mpwelanth *prn.*
you (you two). This pronoun is used in the subject part of the sentence (i.e. representing the 'doers' of the verb action) when the two people belong to different patrimoieties; for example, a person together with their husband or wife, their sister-in-law or their cross-cousin. See Appendix 1. ◆ Mpwelanth alherray, rwang inetyek. (T) *You two go and get some firewood.*
SEE ALSO mpwel, mpwelak, mpwel-ingkerr

mpwelenhanthenh, mpwelenhanth *prn.*
you (you two) This pronoun is used in the object part of the sentence (i.e. representing those the verb action is 'done to').
◆ Mpwelenhanthenh thang atwem. (M) *I'm hitting the two of you.*

mpwelehanth (W,T), **mpwelekanth** (E) *prn.*
for you, to you (you two)

mpwelanth-henh (W,T), **mpwelekanthenh** (E) *prn.*
yours (belonging to you two)

mpwelarr *n.*
rainbow ◆ Atherrkeny mpwarem mpwelarrel. (St) *Rainbows make the country green.* ◆ Kwaty apek ywerrem mpwelarr tnem, mpwelarr atherram apek, awely-artek mpwarelhem. (St) *When the rain finishes there might be a rainbow there, or maybe a double rainbow, looking like the [stripey] designs in women's ceremonies.*

mpwelengk (E) *n.*
types of frog (*Neobatrachus* spp.) ◆ Ker mpwelengk. Angernem angernem arety-alhem, irrpekarl renh arem, angernem anem angernem angernem. *Choke*-em anem alakenh kapert-they. Kel renh atwemarl yanh. *Squash*-em, ilwetyek ra. Ker itemel anem renh arlkwem, anter mwerr-angker. (St) *The* mpwelengk *frog is edible. [You] dig and dig and dig till you see it, where it's burrowed into the ground. Then you choke it from the head part. Hit it. Squash it so that it dies. Then you cook it and eat it, they are nice and fatty.* ◆ *Medicine* mwerrarl ra, ntwa ikwerel apernelhemarl. Anterelarl apernelhem. Mpwelengk anterel apernelhem. (St) *They are good medicine and you can rub yourself with it. With the frog's fat.*
= mpwekenh
SEE ALSO alyeyamp, angwethek, larrangkern, atirrenty, kwep, perrak

mpwelhem[1] *vi.*
wait for someone or something ◆ Ayeng ngkweng mpwelhem. (St) *I am waiting for you.* ◆ Mpwelhem tyerrty yanhek. Tyerrty arrpenh yanhek mpwelhepelhem. (St) *Waiting for that person over there. Waiting for that other person.* ◆ Lywel mpwelherl-anem. (N) *Waiting in the shade.* ◆ Rntwarr alherrirray — ayeng mpwelhem anyent. (M) *All of you go further away — I'm waiting here on my own.*
= tywempelhem, akarelhem

mpwelhem[2] (T), **mpwulhem** (E) *vt.*
have a piss, urinate (mpwa '*urine*'; ulhem '*urinate*') ◆ Ayeng mpwelhetyek alhetyek aketh-warn. (T) *I am going to go and have a piss in the open ground.*

mpwelileng (T,E) cockroach (?) SEE UNDER **mpwerleyerleng**

mpwempew *n.* [BABY TALK]
car, vehicle
SEE ALSO mwetekay

mpweny *n.*
flirtatious or suggestive behaviour; (do something) in order to race someone off or have sex with them ◆ Mpwenyek apertem ingwel. (Sa) *Sneaking up on someone at night to have sex with them.* ◆ Alknga anyent-irrerl-alhekaw, mpweny ra alknga anyent-irrerl-alhek, mpweny, nhakw akwel alhetyek. (St) *He went and winked, making at eyes at someone, suggesting that they could race off together.* ◆ Angkwey artwang alhetyamarl, artarr arrernelhetyam ingkern, wal alhetyam mpweny. (M) *In the olden days the man went and put the emu feathers behind his back, and then went off with his lover.* ◆ Arelh weth mpweny alhek. (St) *That woman went and raced off with someone.*

mpweny angerr (E)
a flirt, a promiscuous person (angerr *'lots'*)
= iytenyelengkw, mpwenyartw-mpwenyartw
SEE ALSO anapert, annga atherrk-atherrk

mpwenyartw-mpwenyartw (T,E), **mpwenyart-mpwenyart** (T,E) = **mpweny angerr**

mpweny alhem
go off to become lovers; run off with someone; elope, go off intending to have sex (alhem *'go'*) ◆ Mpweny yanh atherran alherrem, marl-irrwengerr artwang-irrwengerr. (T) *Those two went off together, the girl and the man.*
SEE ALSO mert, mert-mert

mpweny-mpweny-irrem *vi.*
flirt, behave in a flirtatious way ◆ Mpweny-mpweny-irrem nanth yanhek. (St) *[The horse] is flirting with the other horse.*

mpwenyel inem
take someone off to become your lover or to have sex with them; race someone off (with the intent to have sex with them) (inem *'get', 'take'*) ◆ Yanh apetyem mpweny inerl-alhetyek antem arelh, an mpweny anem ratherr alhem artwa yanh apetyemarl inerl-anem alhem mpwenyarl. (T) *That man comes to race off with the woman, and then the two of them go off as lovers, after that man has come to get her.*

mpwenyel angem, **mpweny akngem** (E)
= **mpwenyel inem** (angem *'take'*) ◆ Arelh Kemarr mpwenyel angek artwa Peltharrel. (M) *The Peltharr man raced off with the Kemarr woman.* ◆ Mpweny akngem, mpwenyel ra inerl-alhek, arleng anem akngernem, mpweny kwerenh kwey. Arelhel mpweny akin akngem artwa. (Sa) *The man came and took the woman off, took his lover a long way away. Women race off with men as well.* ◆ Mpweny angem, mer arrpenh-warl, rwanng-iletyek. (Sa) *[He] takes her off to another place so that he can make her get used to it.*

mpweny iytarr-iytarr (E) *n.*
desert mouse (*Pseudomys desertor*) (?) (iytarr-angem *'drag along'*)
= mpwenyerlp
SEE ALSO alepey, thakwer, kwetang, mpweny

mpwenyerlp (E) *n.*
desert mouse (*Pseudomys desertor*) (?)
◆ Mpwenyerlpel mpweny iytarr-iytarr arrwekety, marl ikwerenh anewikw. Marlarl iytarr akngem ra, alhwengek akwernety-alpem. (Sa) *The* mpwenyerlp *mouse drags the female, its mate, off to have sex with her. He drags the female off and puts her in the burrow.*
= mpweny iytarr-iytarr
SEE ALSO alepey, thakwer, kwetang, mpweny

mpwep (T) middle, in between SEE UNDER **mpep**

mpwepenh (E) types of frog SEE UNDER **mpwekenh**

Mpwer (T,E) *n.*
name of a soakage in the Mt Harper area

mpwer tywenem (T,E) *vt.*
heap something up (e.g. rubbish) (tywenem *'put something up'*)
SEE ALSO aharl arrernem, aharl-wem, lyernt arrernem, ayak-arrernem, antyakwer-wem, antarr-arrernem

Mpwerarneng (W,T), **Mpwereneng** (W,T) *n.*
Long Waterhole, near Coniston

mpwerl *n.*
dog's piss or urine ◆ Angwely-wenh mpwerl lhwem, tyerrty-warn apek mpwerl lhwem, angwelyan. (M) *The dog might urinate on the person.*
CAN SOUND A BIT LIKE mpwel *'you two'*; mpurl *'part of guts', 'stomach organ'*

mpwerl-ilem *vt.*
piss or urinate on something (dogs)
◆ Arengkel mpwerl-ilem. Antyam atyenh mpwerl-ilem. (St) *The dog is urinating. Urinating on my swag.*
= awel-ilem

mpwerl lhwem, **mpwerl ulhem** (E)
= **mpwerl-ilem** ◆ Mpwerl ulhem arengkel. (T) *The dog is urinating.*
SEE ALSO mpwa, mpwelhem

mpwerl (E) part of guts, stomach organ SEE UNDER **mpurl**

mpwerleyerleng, **mpwerlerleng** (W), **mpwerleyarleng** (W), **mpwerl-ilenh-ilenh** (E), **mpwelileng** (T,E) *n.*
striped desert cockroach (*Desmozosteria cincta*)
◆ Mpwerleyarleng unta anpem wal arntert unta intyernem. (M) *If you touch the cockroach then it smells bad.* ◆ Mpwelileng, mpwel antem lhwerl-alhem, kel rang arrtyanem antem. (T) *The cockroach urinates and then runs away.*
SEE ALSO mpwerl

mpwern, **mpwerney** *n.kin*
1. a man's brother-in-law
2. a man's brother-in-law's brother
3. particular male relations with the same skin as a man's *mpwern*
SEE ALSO pantyey, anew, arnteng

mpwern-mpwern *n.kin*
1. a man's brother-in-law etc.
2. a man's brother-in-law etc. [BABY TALK]
◆ 'Mpwern-mpwern kwaty ayeng anthay

mern apek anthay, angayakwengay.' (P) *'Brother-in-law, get me some water and some food, I'm hungry.'*
SEE ALSO kaly-kaly[1]
mpwernaty *n.kin*
my/our *mpwern* ◆ Mpwernatyan ilem artwelant athew, kenh anewekarl ilem marlel. (T) 'Mpwernaty' *is only said by men, whereas, on the other hand, women call [their brother-in-law]* 'anew'.
mpwernengkw *n.kin*
your *mpwern*
mpwerneyekw (E), **mpwernikw** (T,E) *n.kin*
his/their *mpwern* ◆ Mpwernikwan ateyant-atherrel akerrem. Pantyey inngart mpwerney. (Sa) *Only men call each other* 'mpwernikw'. Pantyey *is the same as* mpwerney.
mpwernekw (W,T) *n.kin*
1. your *mpwern*
2. his/their *mpwern*
mpwern-nheng *n.kin*
a group of two or more people related to each other as *mpwern*
mpwern-intyerr *n.kin* = **mpwern-nheng**
mpwern-nheng-arey *n.kin*
a group of more than two people related to each other as *mpwern*
mpwern-nheng atherr *n.kin*
a person together with one of their *mpwern*
mpwern-ankethenh *n.kin*
1. having a close *mpwern* still alive
2. someone who is always with their *mpwern*
SEE ALSO -ankethenh
mpwern-parety *n.kin*
respectful or 'sorry way' of talking about someone's *mpwern* ◆ Arrpenh alenhel ilem, 'Mpwern-parety alenh akeweny arrangkw'. (M) *Another one says, 'That poor old brother-in-law is no longer with us'.*
SEE ALSO -parety, anew, arnteng, pantyey

mpwerrkety (T,E) *n.*
kidney
ker mpwerrkety (T,E)
edible kidneys of some animals
= arteperrk

mpwetyerr (W,T) *n.*
gully, gutter, small creek ◆ Mpwetyerr apetyem lpway angerr-warn. (M) *The small gullies come towards the big creek.* ◆ Mpwetyerr-angkwerr *run*-irrem kwaty akwek, lpway angerr-warlam anyent-anyent-irrerl-anem mpwetyerr then. (N) *A little bit of water runs in the gully, and then it joins together with the big creek.*
= ilerrty, intyer
SEE ALSO arnkarr, atwaty
mpwetyerr-mpwetyerr (W,T) *n.*
country with small gullies going through it
SEE ALSO ilerrty

mpwulhem (E) have a piss, urinate SEE UNDER **mpwelhem**[2]

mwak[1] (E) *n.*
black powder made from charcoal and used for body painting ◆ Mwakelarl apernelhem, awelyek-arelh akin. (Sa) Mwak *is used for painting yourself up, and for women's ceremonies as well.*
= arak
SEE ALSO arrkeyt, karntewarr, marlalperr

mwak[2] (E) *n.*
kurdaitcha, kurdaitcha man, ritual executioner. Also referred to as *artwa mwak.* ◆ Ingkarl apwirrpek mwak. (Sa) *The kurdaitcha put on the feather shoes.*
= urlaylp, ngkekern
SEE ALSO melarlp

mwanty (T,E), **mwantyel** (T,E) carefully, slowly, cautiously SEE UNDER **manty**

mwanyem banana-flavoured bush tomato SEE UNDER **manyem**

mwar, **mar** (W,T), **pmwar** (E) *n.*
small wooden shovel or scoop ◆ Mwarel kwatyarl angernem. Urtnewarl anem inpem. (Sa) Mwar *are used for digging for water and for scooping the water into wooden dishes.* ◆ Mwar akwek ipert angernenhernenh, yerrampekarl angernem mwarel. (T) *Small* mwar *are used for digging holes, and for digging for honeyants.*
mwareng-mwar *n.*
toy wooden bowl or dish
SEE ALSO pantheng-panth
arremwar-mwar *n.*
loud talker, 'big mouth' (arra '*mouth*')

mwarlenth *n.* [RESPECT LANGUAGE]
married couple (term used by a woman to refer to her daughter and her son-in-law) ◆ Mwarlenth ahanenhek ngwarr-nheng irrerernk tyety-ayerrek. (St) *My daughter and her husband have gone hunting for kangaroo [said by the mother of the woman].* ◆ Mwarlenth-ayerr ahanerlentyarr-irrerl-werretyek ingkerr-antey. *Whole lot* mwerikw-arey alhetyek. Mwarlenth. *Brother*-rnem ikwerenh rnem. (Sa) *All of the married couples are going. All of my sons-in-law and their wives. My son-in-law and his brothers [said by a woman].*
SEE ALSO ngwarr-nheng, arlwenth, iteng[1]
mwarlenth-mwarlenth (E) *n.*
several married couples (term used by a woman to refer to her sons-in-law and their

wives), a man with several wives (term used by a woman to refer to her son-in-law and his wives)

mwarrewem (E) *vt.*
make someone tired ◆ Kwey nhenh atherrel ayenh mwarrewetyel, pwerrkel anthetyel. (Sa) *These two girls are wearing me out, making me tired.*
SEE ALSO arlkwer-ilem

mwat (E) *n.*
short and fat, thick ◆ Kanty mwatan arlewatyerr. (Sa) *Goannas have short fat tails.* ◆ Ingka mwat, ingkarl wangkek mwat. (Sa) *A foot that has swollen up is* mwat.

mwekart *n.*
hat ◆ Tyerrty arrerlp map mwekartek irrpem. (T) *Cowboys wear hats.*
SEE ALSO memp

mwekelengk (W,T), **mwekeleng** (W,T) *n.*
a type of rain cloud, fog or mist following rain ◆ Mwekelengk ankert akwek apetyem, irrernt. (T) *The small rain clouds come, and it's cold.*
= rlweyang, arakakw

mwekeny, **mwekenh** *n.*
something of a sensitive or restricted nature; (something that is) not allowed; 'tickley' [dangerous], secret or serious business (something that can't be played around with or trifled with) ◆ *No* mwekenh apek anem pep nhel intem — angkety war intem. (M) *There's nothing restricted about what's in this book — it's just language.*
SEE ALSO kwerert, mety-mety, npwart, amek-amek, tikeley

mweketyey (W,T) *n.* = **mwekeny** ◆ Mweketyey anem — *can't* ilerl. (T) *It's serious business — I can't talk about it.*

mwekeny-irrem, **mwekenh-irrem** *vi.*
get annoyed, upset, angry or become offended about things (especially to do with restricted sites etc.); don't like, feel shamed over something (?) ◆ Mwekeny-irrem arrpenhel apek arnterr aremeng. 'Ayeng akwet arerl-anety-kweny kwenh, nyerrel kwenh.' (St) *[People] get upset if someone stares at them hard. 'Don't keep staring at me, it's making me shamed.'* ◆ Anwern mwekenh-irrem angkety yanheng arlka. (T) *We get upset over that kind of language [e.g. swearing].* ◆ Ayeng mwekeny-irrem tyerrty yanheng. (M) *I am really upset with that person.* ◆ Mwekeny-irrem mwerew-kety. (M) *[A person] feels shamed because of their son-in-law or mother-in-law.*
= mwekernp-irrem

mwekernp-irrem (W,T) *vi.* = **mwekeny-irrem** ◆ Mwekernp-irrem tyerrtyel ayeng arnterr arem-arleng. (M) *I don't like people staring at me.*

mwelper, **pmwelper** (E) *n.*
the part of the throat including windpipe, inside part of throat, trachea ◆ Ahenty mwelper, kwaty akwernenhernenh. (Sa) *The* mwelper *is what pushes the water down [the throat].*

mwelper kwaty-kwaty (W,T)
soft part between the collarbones

mwelty-mwelty angkem (T), **urrmelty angkem** (E) *vi.*
whine (dog)
SEE ALSO meltyang angkem

mweltyem (W,T) *vt.*
smash something up; crack something open ◆ Anywelek ankerr kwart mweltyem. (T) *The father [emu] cracks open the emu egg.* ◆ Mwetekay apek mweltyem. (M) *[You] might smash up the car.*
SEE ALSO ngkwelty-ilem, anthim-ilem, ngkweltyem, apert-atwem, mwely-ilem

mwely, **pmwely** (E) *n.*
squashed, crushed, dented
SEE ALSO ipelhip-ilem
CAN SOUND A BIT LIKE amwely *'cadney lizard'*

mwely-mwely, **pmwely-pmwely** (E) *n.*
squashed, crushed, dented

mwely-ilem, **pmwely-ilem** (E) *vt.*
squash, crush or dent something ◆ Tyampet atyenh mwely-ilekan, atyeneny apek atyenh amek-aretyakenh. Impen atyenh mwely-ilek. (Sa) *[Somebody] squashed my billycan, they didn't avoid [stepping on it]. My special billycan is dented.*
SEE ALSO mweltyem

mwely-irrem, **pmwely-irrem** (E) *vi.*
become squashed, crushed or dented ◆ Pelekan mwely-irrem ulthemel ingkel. (St) *The billycan gets crushed if [somebody] treads on it with their foot.*

mwelyar, **mweylar** (E), **pmwelyar** (E), **pmweylar** (E) *n.*
bush thick-knee, stone-curlew (*Burhinus grallarius*) ◆ Thep mwelyar kwenyel angkerl-anem, 'Werlperlp werlperlp werlperlp'. Alakenh angkerl-anem thep yanh. (N) *The stone-curlew sings out in the night like this,* 'Werlperlp werlperlp werlperlp'. *That's what that bird sounds like.* ◆ Arlkerl-anem ap mweylar ingwel. (Sa) *The stone-curlew sings out at night.*
= arepeylp

mwelyeparnt-parnt (T), **mwenyeparnt-parnt** (W), **ngwelyeparnt-parnt** (T) *n.*
1. rat-tail goosefoot, green crumbweed (?) (*Dysphania* sp.). A sticky herb about 25 cm high with flowers forming erect spikes, and with very small shiny black seeds.
2. the edible seeds of the rat-tail plant
SEE ALSO parntentyarlp, arrerlang, alpar

mwemengk (W,T) *n.*
pitch dark, no light ◆ Mwemengk amparr anem. Atay arratenty-alhem. Atayel parrtyelh-ilem. (M) *It is pitch dark at first. The moon comes up. The moon lights things up.*
SEE ALSO kweny[1]

mwemengk-irrem (W,T) *vi.*
get dark, become night
= ngwemernt-irrem, kweny-irrem

mwemper (W) *n.*
young fruit of the bush banana, silky pear, *alangkw, parl* (*Marsdenia australis*)
= akwemper, amwernt, ngwemper, twemper[1]

mwenkerr (E) *n.* [RESPECT LANGUAGE]
good, well (note Alyawarr *mwenkerr*)
◆ 'Mwenkerr-ayerrang ngwarrengkway?' 'Ya, mwenkerr.' (Sa) *'Is your husband [my son-in-law] well?' 'Yes, he's well.'*
SEE ALSO mwerr, alhengerr

mwenng *n.*
kindling, wood chips, twigs. Also referred to as *ura mwenng* or *rwang mwenng*. ◆ Tey arlka itetyek ura mwenng atyeng inerl-way. (T) *Get me some kindling so that I can boil some tea.* ◆ Ura mwenng kwetyetyek. (St) *Collecting kindling wood.*
= mwenthenng
SEE ALSO ngkwelty, rrwelty, urrelty

mwenth (E) *n.*
wart, lump or gall on tree
= itely, amern-amern
SEE ALSO ankerl

mwenth-mwenth (E) *n.*
lumpy

mwenthenng (E) *n.*
pieces of kindling or wood chips, twigs. Also referred to as *ura mwenthenng*. ◆ Ura mwenthenng ineyaw. (Sa) *Get some kindling wood.*
= mwenng
SEE ALSO ngkwelty, rrwelty, urrelty

mweny-irrem *vi.*
1. not want to do something or go somewhere; feel shamed and want to stay in one place; stay behind ◆ Arelh yanh mweny-irrem lyweny-kety. (T) *That woman doesn't want to go hunting.* ◆ Marl arrpenhel ngwem, 'Alherrey kwenh'. Kenh ra mweny-irrerleng, 'Ntwarrp alhay ayeng anerleng'. (T) *Another woman asks her, 'Let's go'. And she doesn't want to go and says, 'You go yourself, I'm stopping'.*
= anwernt-irrem
2. sit with legs close together (women) ◆ Mweny-irremel anay, map-kety kwenh. (St) *Sit with your legs together, there's lots of people.* ◆ Mweny-irrem ayeng, arlpawarl anetyam-penh ayeng mweny-irrem anem. (St) *After sitting with my legs wide I put them together.*
• SEE ALSO pwarn-irrem

mwenyent (T,E) *n.*
gutless, cowardly, frightened
SEE ALSO alkwemp

mweny rrkwem, mweny irrkwem (E)
1. want to give something to someone but change your mind ◆ Nta arrpenh alenheh anthety ahenty-irrem, wal mwenyem nta rrkwem, nta anthety ahenty-kwenyem. Nta *think* amparr irrem anthetyeh, wal mwenyem nta rrkwem. (M) *You want to give something to the other person, and then you decide that you don't want to give it to the other person. At first you think you'll give it and then you don't want to give it.*
2. keep a story to yourself, keep something secret from others ◆ Ilay kwenh atyengay kwenh — mweny-rrkwetyalay kwenh. (M) *Tell me [the story] — don't keep it secret.*
3. put hand over mouth to hide laughter; giggle behind hand ◆ Arnterr ayeng atherrekerr, mweny irrkwey tha arrken. (St) *In case I laugh too loud I put my hand over my mouth to hide the laughter.* ◆ Iwenh-penh nhenh arrken mweny rrkwem? (M) *Why is this person giggling behind their hand?*

mweny-mweny rrkwem, mweny-mweny irrkwem (E)
put hand over mouth to hide laughter; giggle behind hand ◆ Iyteny-irremel mweny-mweny-irrkwem, artwek apek akwel. (T) *Flirting with a man and giggling behind your hand.*

mweny-mweny-irrem *vi.*
1. smile ◆ Mweny-mweny-irrem, weth arrken atherremel. (T) *That person is smiling and laughing.*
2. not want to do something or go somewhere; feel shamed and want to stay in one place; stay behind ◆ Ayeng mweny-mweny-irrem, menty impeyaw! (T) *I'm staying behind, leave me!*

mwenyar (W), **rrmwenyar** (W,T) *adv.*
with legs curled back or bent
SEE ALSO rtapety-irrem, arntarlperrk

= **urrmenyar**
mwenyar alhem (W), **rrmwenyar alhem** (W,T)
walk along with legs tight together (maybe because of a sore)

mwenyeparnt-parnt (W) rat-tail goosefoot (?) SEE UNDER **mwelyeparnt-parnt**

mwer, mwerey (E) *n.kin*
1. a man's mother-in-law; a man's wife's mother
2. a man's mother-in-law's sisters and brothers
3. a woman's son-in-law; woman's daughter's husband
4. a woman's son-in-law's brothers
5. particular relations with the same skin as a person's *mwer*
SEE ALSO rtwalty, mey-mey[1], ilern-altyerr
mwer-mwer *n.kin*
a man's mother-in-law; a man's wife's mother etc. This may be a more affectionate or respectful way of talking than using *mwer*. ◆ Mwerekikwenh an mentyel arem artwel. Kweyarl anetyel ikwerel-arleng. Mwer-mwerek angketyenh arrangkwarl. (Sa) *A man keeps away from his mother-in-law. Her daughter is living with him. He doesn't talk to his mother-in-law at all.*
SEE ALSO mey-mey[1]
mweraty *n.kin*
my/our *mwer* ◆ Mwerekatyety kwen-irretyel. (Sa) *Bending down because of my son-in-law.*
mwerengkw *n.kin*
your *mwer* ◆ Mwerekengkwety kwen-irra! (Sa) *Bend down because your son-in-law is there!*
mwerekw (W,T) *n.kin*
1. your *mwer*
2. his/her/their *mwer*
mwerikw (E), **mwereyekw** (E) *n.kin*
his/her/their *mwer* ◆ Mwer-mwer ikwerenh-kety anerl-anem artwa arlengel kweyek, kenh mam-kety. Kwey-kenh mam an mwerikwan ikwerenh. (Sa) *A man sits at some distance away from his mother-in-law, from his wife's mother. That girl's mother is his mother-in-law.*
mwer-nheng *n.kin*
a group of two or more people related to each other as *mwer*
mwer-intyerr *n.kin* = **mwer-nheng**
mwer-nheng-arey *n.kin*
a group of more than two people related to each other as *mwer*
mwer-nheng-atherr *n.kin*
1. a person together with their *mwer* ◆ Mwer-nhengek-atherrety kwen-irraw. (Sa) *Bend down because of the two sons-in-law/mothers-in-law.* ◆ 'Kwernt-nheng atherr yanh apetyerrem kwenh.' Tyerrty arrpel ilem, arelhel apek ilem. 'Artwa mwer-nheng atherrarl apetyerrem kwernt-nheng atherr.' (T) *'There come two people who are from the opposite matrimoiety.' That's what another person will say, maybe what a woman says. 'Two men who are in the opposite matrimoiety to each other and related as* mwer *are coming along.'*
2. a pair of stars
mwer-ankethenh *n.kin*
1. having a close *mwer* still alive
2. someone who is always with their *mwer*. (Generally a person avoids their *mwer*.) ◆ Akweteth apek ratherr mwer-nheng aperl-anem, wal *someone*-el ilem, artwang arrpel apek ilem, 'Yanhan mwer-ankethenham kwenh'. *Like friends* yatherr aperl-anem. (M) *If that person is always going around with their* mwer*, then another person will say, or another man might say, 'That person is always hanging round with their* mwer*'. It's like they are always going around together as friends.*
SEE ALSO -ankethenh
mwer-parety *n.kin*
respectful or 'sorry' way of talking about someone's *mwer*
SEE ALSO -parety

mweremwenk (T,E), **mweremwelk** (W,T), **mweremwerlk** (W,T) *n.*
blowfly ◆ Mweremwenkelan ker-warl kwartarl irrkwem, tyerr anem anem. (Sa) *Blowflies lay eggs in meat, and then there's maggots.*
SEE ALSO lyalth

mwerey (E) a man's mother-in-law etc. SEE UNDER **mwer**

mwerlerr (E) *n.*
hill turpentine (*Acacia monticola*). A shrub about 2 m high with greyish green leaves.
mwerlerrayt (E) *n.*
grub from the hill turpentine

mwerlk[1] *n.*
large intestine, guts, stomach organ ◆ Mwerlk kwenh arekar-irrem ayeng. (T) *My guts are aching.* ◆ Mwerlk anert kwenel-ayel. (T) *The* mwerlk *is inside the belly.*
ker mwerlk
edible stomach organ of some animals
SEE ALSO kwey-kwey, lyep-lyep, anert

mwerlk[2] (E) *n.*
round (and hollow) in shape ◆ Arlengarr mwerlk, mwerlk-ilemelarl arrpek. Arlketh mwerlk mwerr akngerr. (Sa) *A round-shaped wooden dish that has been carved out to make it hollow. A really nice hollow wooden water dish.*

mwerlk-ilem (E) *vt.*
hollow or carve something out
SEE ALSO rtwep-ilem, urtep-ilem

mwerlkenty *n.*
1. the first part of the dancing at initiation (young man) ceremonies. This part of the ceremony is 'open' (i.e. not restricted). ◆ Mwerlkentyel ina arraw-irrem, *all night*-ek-angent. (T) *They are gathering together for the first part of the young men's ceremony, and they will be there all night.*
2. a singalong; any kind of singing or get-together
SEE ALSO arawern, apwelh, anmanty

mwerlp *n.*
1. quandong, native peach, peach tree (*Santalum acuminatum*). Tree to 4 m high, with rough bark, small green flowers and bright red fleshy fruits. The round fruits are used as marbles.
2. the edible fruit of the quandong.
= mangart

mwern-irrem, **apmwern-irrem** (T,E) *vi.*
1. grow close together (of plants) ◆ Mern anaty mwern-irrem. (T) *The bush potatoes are growing close together.*
SEE ALSO mwernenty
2. sit close together [SOME SPEAKERS] ◆ Apmwern-irremel anem irrerntek. (St) *Sitting close together in the cold.*

mwernem *vt.*
stick or catch onto something, attach to something ◆ Arraperel tyart ingkerr mwernetyenheng atanthetyenheng altywer-altywer irremel. (N) *The kerosene grass will stick into your shirt and pierce it, and the shirt will get full of holes.*
mwernelhem *vi.*
get stuck or caught on something; get bogged ◆ Arlewatyerr apek mwernelhetyel rlpwerel. (Sa) *The goanna might be stuck in the hollow tree.* ◆ Ker apek mwernelhety-alhem ahentyel. (Sa) *Meat might get stuck in one's throat.* ◆ Altel-arleng tyewen kamp mwernelhem, ampelarl iwek. (Sa) *The chewing gum that the kid threw is stuck in her hair.*
SEE ALSO atanem[2], atanelhem, kerelty-welhem, uthinem
ingka-mwerney (T,E), **ngkemwerney** (T), **ingkang mwerney** (W) *n.*
life-saver burr, teddy bears arsehole (*Sida platycalyx*) (ingka '*foot*'). Soft herb with large yellow flowers. Fruits are doughnut-shaped and prickly when dry.
= akeley-akeley, anmang, kwem

mwernenty *n.*
1. white tubers of the pencil yam, *arlatyey*, *anwerlarr* (*Vigna lanceolata*), and the bush potato, *anaty*, *anek* (*Ipomoea costata*) ◆ Mern arlatyey mwernenty. (T) *The white tubers of the pencil yam.*
2. yam roots where they have grown thickly and close together ◆ Mern anaty mwernenty akin anem. (M) *Bush potatoes have roots that grow thickly together.*
SEE ALSO mwern-irrem

mwernt[1] (T,E) *adv.*
keeping on doing something, doing something persistently ◆ Ampa nhenh mwernt artnep-artnemaw. (St) *This child keeps on crying.* ◆ Pwerlel mwerntel apayenhwepenhwem ngkweltyek apek. (St) *Pwerl keeps on asking for money.*
SEE ALSO arlelty, anwernt, atnemwernt
mwernt-irrem (T,E) *vi.*
don't like something; don't want to do something; be stubborn or uncooperative; refuse to do something ◆ Pwerrkarl awelhem mwernt-irrem. (T) *[I] don't want to do it because I'm tired.*
SEE ALSO anwernt-irrem, mweny-irrem, arlelty-irrem, ankerl-irrem
mwerntel anthem (T,E)
really want to give someone something; force something on someone ◆ Mwerntel antherl-anetyal, kelarl anert angerr anem anemeng. (T) *Don't force [more food] on me, my stomach is already full.*
mwerntel inem (T,E)
get something (by being forceful or applying pressure) (?) ◆ Mwerntel mern inem angayakwel. (Sa) *The hungry person makes sure they get some food.*

mwernt[2] (W,T) *n.*
shut, turned off
SEE ALSO marnt, alhap, martelhenty, mety
mwernt-irrem (W) *vi.*
become closed or shut
SEE ALSO marnt-irrem, martelhem

mwerr *n.*
1. well, healthy, better (after being sick) ◆ Mwerrem artwang arrenhan anep-anem rlkert angerr-penh. (M) *The man is all right now after being sick.* ◆ Arrwekel ayeng ltywerrerl-alhey rtweth-akert, rntwarrarl alhek-penh. Kwer-penh akem-irrem, 'Mwerram ayeng awelhem'. (N) *I'm going to go and have a rest first because I have lower-back ache from walking a long way. After that I get up and say, 'I feel good'.* ◆ Mwerr-awaty irrem ayengaw.

Mwerr-awaty ayeng alhep-alhem. (St) *I'm getting a bit better. I'm going around feeling a bit better.*
2. good, nice, well-behaved, pleasant, enjoyable, non-aggressive, functional
◆ Nhenhan angwely mwerr. (M) *This is a good dog.* ◆ Manterr mwerrek akent-wetyel, terreth mwerrek. Tha akent-wetyel. (Sa) *I am sorting through to find good clothes, a nice dress.*
◆ Nhenhan kwer mwerr map. (M) *These children are well-behaved.*
mwerr anthwerr (W,T)
really good, fantastic, splendid (anthwerr '*really*') ◆ Ntheteh ntwang inek? Mwerr anthwerr yanh. (M) *Where did you get that? It's really good.*
mwerr angerr (W,T)
good, nice, pleasant, enjoyable, beautiful (angerr[1] '*lots*')
mwerr-angker (E) *n.* = **mwerr angerr**
◆ Mern mwerr-angker. (Sa) *Really nice food.*
mwerr-irrem *vi.*
heal up, become good, get better, improve
◆ Aherr-arlwethel apernelhetyam utyen, mwerr-irretyam kwer-penh. (St) *Sores were rubbed with the kangaroo balls vine, and they got better after that.*
mwerr-ilem *vt.*
make something better, fix something, heal or cure somebody ◆ Akwepenhan anthetyam arntetyek, mwerr-iletyam. (St) *Blood from the arm was given to sick people, to make them better.*
mwerranty *adv.*
(doing something) carefully or properly
◆ Mwerranty utyerna, atnyekerr. (Sa) *Put it up carefully in case it falls.* ◆ Mwerranty tha mern item, pwelh-iletyang. (Sa) *I am cooking this food carefully and not burning it.*
mwerrenganty (E) *adv.* [RESPECT LANGUAGE]
(doing something) carefully or properly
◆ Alharrenty-ketyaw, mwerrenganty apek. (St) *Be careful and look out for the monster.*
SEE ALSO manty, mwerranty
mwerranty-ilem *vt.*
1. warn somebody about something; tell someone to be careful
2. look after someone or something
= manty-manty-ilem
mwerrakey (W,T)
'Is it all right?', 'Is it okay?'
kel mwerr
'Good', 'Okay', 'It's all right'
mwerr-kweny (E) *n.* [RESPECT LANGUAGE]
sick (-kweny '*without*')

mwert (W,T) *n.*
1. short throwing stick, like a *kweter* (nulla-nulla)
2. axe handle
mwetekay, mwetek *n.*
car, motorcar, vehicle (from English 'motorcar') ◆ Tyerrty map alhem mwetekayel anaty nyetyek. (T) *The people are going in the car to dig for bush potatoes.*
Mweteng (E) *n.*
name of a well east of Wilora (Stirling) community.
mwety (W,T) blunt SEE UNDER **mety**
Mwetyek (W,T) *n.*
Wurmbrandts Rock
mwetyernk (W), **metyernk** (W,T), **mwetyingk** (W) *n.*
rabbit (note Warlpiri *mujunyku, mujurnku*)
= rapet, alkwert atwenh, pet-pet
mwey-mwey (W) a man's mother-in-law etc. SEE UNDER **mey-mey**[1]
mweylar (E) bush thick-knee, stone-curlew SEE UNDER **mwelyar**
mweyntenng (E) *n.*
kangaroo bone (underneath bladder) (?)
◆ Mweyntenng apert-atwetyek inpernp arlkwetyek. (Sa) *Smashing up the kangaroo bone to eat the marrow.*
SEE ALSO pwer

Nn

na *part.*
no (from English 'no')
SEE ALSO arrangkw, itya, new

nak *n.*
men's loin cloth (from Wuna (language east of Darwin) *naga* 'dress, covering')
SEE ALSO ngatywelarr

Nakakwet *n.*
female junior skin name, corresponding to Kemarr (note Warlpiri *Nakakutu* 'diminutive of *Nakamarra*'). See diagram p. 744.
= Nakarr
SEE ALSO Kemarr, Nakemarr

Nakarr (W,T) *n.*
female junior skin name, corresponding to Kemarr (note Warlpiri *Nakarra* 'diminutive of *Nakamarra*'). See diagram p. 744. ◆ Nakarran marl Kemarr akwek. (T) *A Nakarr is a young Kemarr girl.*
= Nakakwet
SEE ALSO Kemarr, Nakemarr

nakem, tnakem (E) *vt.*
praise someone or something; talk well of someone; be grateful to someone ◆ Akngey tha tnakem. (St) *I am praising God.* ◆ Nakem renh, kerarl antherl-alpew, nakemarl renh. (T) *Being grateful to someone for bringing meat to give [us].* ◆ Tyerrty yanh thang mwerr nakeh. (M) *I praised that person well.* ◆ Mernarl ayenh anthem anyent, nhel wal tha nakem renh. (St) *That person gave me a loaf of bread, so I am grateful to them.* ◆ Thwengk apek nakem nta mwerr apekarl *anything* rrkwapenty anem, wal thwengk nakemel. (M) *I might praise you if you're doing good work or doing something well.* ◆ Altyerr renh kwenh nakem anwern. (M) *We are praising God.*
= narlkwem

nakelhem, tnakelhem (E) *vi.*
praise yourself; be proud of self; say good things about yourself; brag, skite ◆ Ker akngerr apek tha atwek, wal tnakelhety-alpem ayeng. (St) *If I have killed a lot of meat, well I go back and skite about it.*
= narlkwelhem
SEE ALSO arntwelhem, tyenkarl-irrem, tywenelhem, utyenelhem

Nakemarr *n.*
female skin name, corresponding to Kemarr (note Warlpiri *Nakamarra*). See diagram p. 744.
SEE ALSO Kemarr, Nakakwet, Nakarr

nakepakel (W,T) *n.*
having a hard time, being mistreated ◆ Tyerrty arrpenhel ayengenh nakepakel mpwarem. (T) *Someone is giving me a hard time.*

nakepakel-ilem (W,T) *vt.*
make trouble for someone, make things difficult, mistreat someone
SEE ALSO atyang-inem, rrwernem, urrernem

nakepakel-irrem (W,T) *vi.*
have a difficult time, struggle to do things, be mistreated ◆ Ayeng nakepakel-irrek kwaty-kwenyel. (T) *I had a difficult time because I ran out of petrol.* ◆ Akweteth apel ayeng akwet nakepakel-irrem anyent akwet. (M) *I am always struggling to get things right.*

nalal (E) *n.*
flower of the bush potato, *anaty* (*Ipomoea costata*)

Nampetyenp *n.*
female skin name, corresponding to Mpetyan (note Warlpiri *Nampijinpa*). See diagram p. 744.
SEE ALSO Mpetyan

Nampin (T) female junior skin name corresponding to Mpetyan SEE UNDER **Ngampin**

nan[1] (W,T) *n.* [BABY TALK]
granny, mother's mother (from English 'nanna')

nan-nan (E), **nyanyany** (E) *n.* [BABY TALK]
granny, mother's mother
SEE ALSO nyany[2]

nan angkwey (W,T)
senior granny, senior mother's mother (angkwey *'old'*)

nan[2] (E) *n.* [BABY TALK]
food
= nyany[1]
SEE ALSO mern

nanekwet, nanikwet (E) *n.*
goat (from English 'nanny goat') ◆ Ker nanekwet arlkwetyart tyerrtyel angkwey. (T) *In the olden days Aboriginal people used to eat goat meat.*

Nangal (W,T) *n.*
female skin name, corresponding to Ngal (note Warlpiri *Nangala*). See diagram p. 744.
SEE ALSO Ngal

Nangaley *n.*
female junior skin name, corresponding to Ngal (note Warlpiri *Nangali* 'diminutive of *Nangala*'). See diagram p. 744.
= Ngangkal
SEE ALSO Ngal

nanikwet (E) goat SEE UNDER **nanekwet**

nantew *n.*
horse
= nanth
SEE ALSO wethey

nantew kwerlt
colt (from English 'colt') ◆ Tyerrtyel nantew kwerlt ltwakem. (M) *The person is breaking the colt in.*
= nanth

nanth *n.*
horse ◆ Nanth nhenh tywepelhem artwang antyetyeh. (N) *This horse is waiting for the man to mount it.*
= nantew
SEE ALSO wethey

Nanty (W), **Rnanty** (W) *n.*
Dunja Bore, south-east of Laramba community

Napeltyarr *n.*
female skin name, corresponding to Peltharr or Petyarr (note Warlpiri *Napaljarri*). See diagram p. 744.
SEE ALSO Peltharr, Petyarr

Napenangk *n.*
female skin name, corresponding to Penangk (note Warlpiri *Napanangka*). See diagram p. 744.
SEE ALSO Penangk

Napengart *n.*
female skin name, corresponding to Pengart (note Warlpiri *Napangardi*). See diagram p. 744.
SEE ALSO Pengart

napey *n.*
without horns (from English 'knobby' (?)) ◆ Napey pwelek *horn*-kweny. (T) Napey *is a cow with no horns.*

Napwerr *n.*
female junior skin name, corresponding to Pwerrerl (note Warlpiri *Napurru* 'diminutive of *Napurrurla*'). See diagram p. 744.
= Ngampwerl
SEE ALSO Pwerrerl

Napwerrerl *n.*
female skin name, corresponding to Pwerrerl (note Warlpiri *Napurrurla, Napurrula*). See diagram p. 744.
SEE ALSO Pwerrerl

narengk (T), **narengkw** (T) *n.*
fresh water, clean water, rainwater. Also referred to as *kwaty narengk*.
= narwep, aparew, kwaty lyeteny

narlkwem (E), **tnarlkwem** (E) *vt.*
praise someone or something; talk well of someone, be grateful to someone ◆ Tyerrty arrpenhel ilem, 'Unta tnarlkway'. (St) *One person says, 'You praise them'.*
= nakem

narlkwelhem (E), **tnarlkwelhem** (E) *vi.*
praise yourself; be proud of self; say good things about yourself; brag, skite
= nakelhem
SEE ALSO tyenkarl-irrem, tywenelhem, utyenelhem

narremantyerr (W,T), **nwarremantyerr** (W) *n.*
black-tailed native-hen (*Gallinula ventralis*)

◆ Narremantyerr arrtyanem ngkwern rnter-rnter. Kwer map-kety arrtyanerl-apem kwer mapel arrken rlwaketyam. Kwart akenh anengk, ilperl intertel intem, arnamel. (N) *The black-tailed native-hen runs along and has red legs. They run away from children who are chasing them. They have lots of eggs which they lay at the base of tea trees and in the grass.*
SEE ALSO karlayteng-ayteng, kart-irrkwely-irrkwely, angkeparr, lhekethatethat, ngkwern rnter-rnter

narwep (W,T) *n.*
fresh water, clean water, rainwater. Also referred to as *kwaty narwep*.
= narengk, aparew, kwaty lyeteny

nathat (T) flower of the mulga and the witchetty bush SEE UNDER **nwathet**

natyaker, nwatyaker (E), **unatyaker** (E), **utnatyaker** (E) *n.*
type of lizard (?)
SEE ALSO ankert², amwely

nek-nek plug tobacco, black twist tobacco SEE UNDER **nikey-nikey**

nekeleth, nikeleth *n.*
necklace (from English 'necklace') ◆ Arlangkw-areny 'ntewal' akin, nekeletharl mpwarerl-anem. (Sa) *Those that are found on the bloodwood are called 'ntewal' as well, and they are used to make necklaces.* ◆ Tyerrtyel inernt kwetyem nekeleth mparetyeh. (N) *People collect bean tree seeds to make necklaces.*

nenty-nenty (T,E), **nwenty-nwenty** (W,T) *adv.*
noisily

nenty-nenty-irrem (T,E), **nwenty-nwenty-irrem** (W,T) *vi.*
make a galloping, thudding or stomping sound

nenty-nenty alhem (T,E), **nwenty-nwenty alhem** (W,T)
go along making a galloping, thudding or stomping sound ◆ Arlkwem arrkernemel, kel pwelap-akertem alhem atwakey renh inelhem alhem, arlkwerl-apem nwenty-nwentyem alherl-apem. (N) *We taste the wild orange fruits first, and then go and collect a whole lot of them, munching noisily as we go.* ◆ Anwern pwelek nenty-nenty alherlek awem. (St) *We can hear the cattle making a noise as they go.*

SEE ALSO atemart angkem, ahenty-ahenty-irrem

nep-nep *n.*
scissors (from English 'snip snip')

nernem (E), **tnernem** (E) *vt.*
show something to someone ◆ Nern atyeng tha aretyek. (Sa) *Show me, so that I can have a look.* ◆ Tha ngkweng nerney. (Sa) *I'll show you.*
= imernem

Nernterrpenh (W) Nintabrinna Bore, east of Anmatjira Range SEE UNDER **lnernt irrpenh**

nerrkempwany (W,T) *n.*
brolga (*Grus rubicunda*) (?)

nerrty (E) *n.*
white-backed swallow (*Cheramoeca leucosternus*)
SEE ALSO urrernter2

new *part.*
no (from English 'no')
SEE ALSO itya, arrangkw, na

new-irrem *vi.*
say 'no' (from English 'no')

newingk (W,T), **neweyingk** (W,T) *n.*
cockatiel, quarrion (*Nymphicus hollandicus*) ◆ Ker newingk anwern inetyart. Rlpwereh anwern inetyart, akwerrk map. Angety-alpetyart anthety-alpetyam ker renh. (N) *We used to get cockatiels to eat. We got the baby ones from hollow trees. We used to take the meat back home to give [to the others].*
= aneweylker, arew-arew, kanaweylker
CAN SOUND A BIT LIKE anewengk *'your spouse'*

ney-ney, **tney-tney** (E) *n.*
early in the morning, daybreak ◆ Tney-tney anem arratintyem 'mwer-nheng atherr'. (Sa) *The two stars called* 'mwer-nheng atherr' *appear early in the morning.* ◆ Ayeng ney-ney akem-irrenh-irrenh. (Sa) *I am an early riser.*
SEE ALSO alartetherrker, aherlkenty, aketh-irrem

neyel (E), **tneyel** (E) *n.*
soon ◆ Tneyel apety-alpetyek, *two week* apek anetyek. Tneyel ayeng apety-alpem, urrek ayeng anerl-anem. (Sa) *I'm coming back soon, maybe staying two weeks. I'm going to stay there for a while then come back soon.*
= lyet war

nga *prn.*
you. *Nga* is a singular pronoun used in the subject part of the sentence (i.e. representing the 'doer' of the verb action). It is usually used in sentences which have an intransitive verb. Those with a transitive verb use *ntwa* or *unta*, although some people use *ntwa* or *unta* for both types of verb. See Appendix 1. ◆ Iwenh-apert nga marakat-irrem? (M) *Why are you feeling tired?* ◆ Ayeng alhemaw urrpety-inger intetyek. Apawenhem ra apek unta pek ayenh, 'Nthakenty-inger nga alhem?' Urrpety-arengek ayeng alhem, urrpety-inger intety-alhetyek ayeng alhem. (St) *I am going for a couple of days. He might ask me, or you might ask me, 'How long are you going for?' I am going to go and stay there for a couple of days.* ◆ Nga akenh akweteth, nga ampwelpampw-irrek yanh-angkwerr. (St) *Whereas you have always been here, you have grown old in that country.*

Ngal *n.*
skin name, subsection name, marriage class. See diagram p. 744. ◆ Arelh Ngwarray ahenty-irrem artwang Ngal anew aketyek. (T) *Ngwarray women like to marry Ngal men.*
SEE ALSO Tyangkarl, Ngangkal, Nangaley, Tyangaley, Nangal, Tyangal

ngal-ngal *n.*
red seeds from the bean tree, *inernt, atywerety* (*Erythrina vespertilio*)
SEE ALSO mpetyan-mpetyan

ngaleny (E) *n.* [RESPECT LANGUAGE]
1. hand ◆ Ahaneynaw. Ngaleny-ayerrarl ultakelherlentyarrekek kweyay. (Sa) *Go daughter, because your husband has broken his hand [said by a woman].*
2. finger
SEE ALSO iltya

ngalepwerr (E) *n.* [RESPECT LANGUAGE]
1. forehead
2. headache
SEE ALSO urla, ayepert

ngalepwerr-akert (E) [RESPECT LANGUAGE]
having a headache ◆ Ngalepwerr-akert ayepel-irrepirrem. (St) *[My son-in-law] has a headache [said by a woman].*

Ngalwerrty (W), **Ngarlwerrty** (W), **Ngalwerrp** (T) *n.*
name of hill in Mt Wedge/Tilmouth Roadhouse area. See map p. viii.
SEE ALSO Rnkwer

Ngalyerr, **Ngalyarr** *n.*
female junior skin name, corresponding to Peltharr (note Warlpiri *Ngalyarri*, diminutive of *Napaljarri*). See diagram p. 744. ◆ Ngalyarran marl Peltharr akwek. (T) *A Ngalyarr is a little Peltharr girl.*
SEE ALSO Peltharr, Tyapaly

Ngaman, **Ngamen** (T,E) *n.*
female junior skin name, corresponding to Penangk (note Warlpiri *Ngamana*, diminutive of *Napanangka*). See diagram p. 744.
SEE ALSO Penangk, Tyanam

ngamarwengk (T) *n.*
a type of waterbird

SEE ALSO kamparwengk, ntyar

Ngamen (T,E) female junior skin name, corresponding to Penangk SEE UNDER **Ngaman**

Ngampart, Ngampeyart (E) *n.*
female junior skin name, corresponding to Pengart (note Warlpiri *Ngampayardi* and *Naparti*, diminutive of *Napangardi*). See diagram p. 744. ◆ Ngampartan marl Pengart akwek. (T) *A Ngampart is a little Pengart girl.*
SEE ALSO Pengart, Tyapart

Ngampekwel *n.*
female junior skin name, corresponding to Ngwarray (note Warlpiri *Ngampukulu*, diminutive of *Nungarrayi*). See diagram p. 744. ◆ Ngampekwelan marl Ngwarray akwek. (T) *A Ngampekwel is a young Ngwarray girl.*
SEE ALSO Ngwarray

Ngamperl (E) female junior skin name, corresponding to Pwerrerl SEE UNDER **Ngampwerl**

Ngampeyart (E) female junior skin name, corresponding to Pengart SEE UNDER **Ngampart**

Ngampin (T), **Ngampeyen** (T), **Nampin** (T) *n.*
female junior skin name corresponding to Mpetyan (note Warlpiri *Ngampin* and *Nampin*, diminutive of *Nampijinpa*). See diagram p. 744.

Ngampwerl, Ngampwel, Ngamperl (E) *n.*
female junior skin name, corresponding to Pwerrerl (note Warlpiri *Ngampurla*, diminutive of *Napurrurla*). See diagram p. 744. ◆ Ngampwerlan marl Pwerrerl akwek. (T) *A Ngampwerl is a young Pwerrerl girl.*
= Napwerr
SEE ALSO Pwerl, Tywerlam, Pwerrerl

ngampwerrp (W) *n.*
really (want to do something) (note Warlpiri *ngampurrpa* 'desirous, want, need') ◆ Ayeng ngampwerrp awelhem alhetyeh. *I really want to go.* ◆ Thang ngampwerrpel arlkwem. *I really feel like eating.* ◆ Ayeng ngampwerrp awelhem, thang atwetyeh. *I really feel like hitting [that person].*
SEE ALSO ampwengampw

nganem (E), **inganem** (E) *vi.*
climb up, go up something, get onto something, mount an animal ◆ Apwert-warl nganenhem. (Sa) *Climbing the hill.* ◆ Nantewek nganem. (Sa) *Mount the horse.*
SEE ALSO antyem, atwayntem, antyan-akelhem

Ngangkal, Ngangkarl *n.*
female junior skin name, corresponding to Ngal (note Warlpiri *Ngangkarla*, diminutive of *Nangala*). See diagram p. 744. ◆ Ngangkalan marl Ngal akwek. (T) *A Ngangkal is a young Ngal girl.*
SEE ALSO Ngal, Tyangkarl

ngangkar, ngangkay *n.*
1. traditional healer, doctor, sorcerer ◆ Ngangkarel amwelt atherr angkwerr-wem, arlka ingkerr angkwerr-wem atheperr-ilemel. (Sa) *The traditional healer massages both of the arms and all of the body to make it cool.* ◆ Ngangkarel iteth-ilem, rlkertarl intep-intem. Kel ra akem-irrem anem. (St) *The traditional healer heals the person that is lying there sick. Then the person gets up.*
2. the healing powers that a traditional healer has
SEE ALSO angkwerr-wem
3. a type of worm found in a kangaroo's stomach • SEE ALSO antya[1]
ngangkar-akert, ngangkay-akert *n.*
= **ngangkar** ◆ Arelh alhep-alhem inetyeh ngangkay-akert. (M) *A woman goes to get a traditional healer.* ◆ Ngangkay-akertarl *old man* yanh anep-anem. (St) *That old man sitting over there has healing powers.*

Ngangkarl female junior skin name, corresponding to Ngal SEE UNDER **Ngangkal**

ngangkay traditional healer, doctor, sorcerer SEE UNDER **ngangkar**

ngantyewarl (W,T) *n.*
1. bush tomato (*Solanum chippendalei* (sandhill form)). Plant about 80 cm high (though it may grow to 1.5 m) with purple flowers and fruits which are pale yellow when ripe. The seeds inside the fruit are inedible, and are thrown away. Anmatyerr distinguish two types of *Solanum chippendalei*. One, the *ngantyewarl*, grows on the sandplains. The plant is larger and has less seeds than the *anakety*, which is found in the hills (note Warlpiri *nganjawarli*).
2. edible fruits of the bush tomato
= antyewarl, unemangkerr, kwenemangkarr
SEE ALSO anakety

ngapalhwerrk (W) *n.*
red nectar from the flat-leaved hakea and the fork-leaved corkwood, *ntyarleyarleng*. Also referred to as *ngkwarl ngapalhwerrk*.
SEE ALSO tyan

Ngapert (T,E), **Ngapet** (T,E) *n.*
female junior skin name, corresponding to Ngwarray (note Warlpiri *Ngapita*, diminutive of *Nungarrayi*). See diagram p. 744.
SEE ALSO Ngwarray, Tywekertay

Ngapet (T,E) female junior skin name, corresponding to Ngwarray SEE UNDER **Ngapert**

ngarakwerr-irrem (E) *vi.*
go through the air and double back, spin

back, vibrate (of bark boomerang, boomerang or spear) ◆ Aylayl alkerel-artek alhem, kel ngarakwerr-irrenhem. (St) *The boomerang flies though the air and then doubles back.*

ngarlaleny, ngarlarleny *n.*
uvula (the small fleshy appendage that hangs down at the back of the throat)
= angerl-angerl

Ngarlew (W) *n.*
Red Hill, Yuelamu (Mt Allan) area; name of a rockhole in the Red Hill area

Ngarleyekwerlang (W,T) *n.*
name of a place north of Yuendumu. Emu Dreaming. See map p. viii.
SEE ALSO arley

Ngarlwerrpernt Ngalurbindi hills SEE UNDER **Alwerrpent**

Ngarlwerrty (W) name of a hill in the Mt Wedge/Tilmouth Roadhouse area SEE UNDER **Ngalwerrty**

Ngarnkerrety (W) *n.*
name of a place in the Haasts Bluff area

ngarntarnt (T,E), **ngarntart** (T,E) *n.*
native bee (large one) ◆ Ngarntarntel akwernepernem arwengalker, arnpan-arey, arnpan kwerenh, altywer akwek-warl. (St) *The native bee puts all the pollen, all the sugarbag pollen, inside the little hole [in the tree].*
= lwerlker
SEE ALSO ameng, minekey, rltwamp, arwengalker

ngarntatyarr (W,T), **ngarntatyar** (W) *n.*
1. northern wild orange (*Capparis umbonata*). Shrub up to 3.5 m high, with rough dark bark, white flowers and yellow or reddish fruits which hang down on stalks (note Warlpiri *ngarntajari*).
2. the edible fruits of this wild orange
◆ *Orange*-artam ayenp an arrernem ahelh ampeng-irretyeh akwernem arrernem rarrp ampeng-irretyeh, ngarntatyar. Inem antem arlkwetyeh ngarntatyar. (N) *The northern wild orange has a skin like an orange, and the fruit is put in the ground so that it goes ripe itself. Then [you] get the northern wild orange fruits and eat them.*
= akarlety

ngartangkern (W) *n.*
1. type of mistletoe (*Amyema maidenii*). A bunched plant with greyish leaves, greenish flowers, and yellow fruit (note Warlpiri *ngardanykinyi/ngardarnkirni*).
2. the edible fruit of this mistletoe plant. Also referred to as *mern ngartangkern.* ◆ Mern ngartangkern atyankernart akin. Artetyel anyemel arlka. *Yellow one* ampeng. (N) *The* ngartangkern *is like the* atyankern *mistletoe. It grows on mulga and on witchetty bushes. When it's ripe it's yellow.*
= peketyalkwarr
SEE ALSO atyankern, amar

ngatywelarr (T,E) *n.*
women's hairstring skirt ◆ Arrwekel-warl arrernelhem ngatywelarr yanh. (Sa) *The women's hairstring skirt is worn on the front.*
= matyart
SEE ALSO arlpalh, merterr2

ngay *part.*
'Truly', 'Really', 'Is that so?' (note Warlpiri *ngayi*) ◆ '*Waite River*-warl alhek-ketyaw.' 'Ngay?' (Sa) *'Because [they] have gone to Waite River.' 'Really?'* ◆ 'Weth alherl-wek kel-antey.' 'Ngay?' (Sa) *'They have already gone.' 'True?'*
SEE ALSO alew2

ngayekenh (W,T), **ngayekety** (E) *n.* [RESPECT LANGUAGE]
1. a man's sister
2. woman (word used by men)
◆ Ngayekenhan ilem kakeyel apek *or* atyeyel apek. *Not allowed* rang arreny anewetyeh, *or* 'ayay' aketyeh. 'Ngayekenh' war ina ilem. (T) *Her older brother or younger brother calls her* 'ngayekenh'. *They are not allowed to say her name or call her* 'yay' *[elder sister]. They have to just say* 'ngayekenh'.
SEE ALSO interrkekety, ampwa, arelh1

ngelyerr (E) *n.*
1. button grass, finger grass, toothbrush grass (*Dactyloctenium radulans*). A grass about 25 cm high.
2. the edible seeds of the button grass
◆ Ngelyerr, athenh-athenharl yanh. Apwert-warl atherl-anemarl ra. (Sa) *The* ngelyerr *seeds are ground up. They are ground up on the grinding stone.*
= talkwerrk
SEE ALSO apwert-arlkwenh

ngenh, ngwenh (W,T) *prn.*
you. This is a singular pronoun used in the object part of the sentence (i.e. representing the person or thing the verb action is 'done to'). See Appendix 1. ◆ Rang ngwenh atwem. (M) *He is hitting you.* ◆ *You got to* akangkwerrerl tyerrtyel ngenh apawenherl, *not* rntert anerl-anety unta. Tyerrtyel ngenh apawenhetyenheng, 'Iwenh-apert apek ntwa akarntemel anep-anem? Akangkwerretyeh, irlpel awemel'. (N) *You have to pay attention to what people are asking you, you shouldn't sit there silently. Or the person will ask you, 'Why are you sitting there quietly? Pay attention, listen*

with your ears.' ◆ Awem tha ngenh angkerlek, iylpel. (St) *I can hear you talking, with my ears.* ◆ Ngenh tha alhengk-arem. (St) *I recognise you.* ◆ Urrek tha yanh arteng-werlewey. Ngenh apek *me might* arteng-werl *halfway*-irrem mer. *Highway*-they iyntwarr-ampeny-they apek arteng-werlewem tha ngenh. (St) *Wait while I go part of the way with that [person]. I might accompany you halfway to the place. I might go as far as the other side of the highway with you.* SEE ALSO nga

-nger (W,T) Goes on number words to show the number times something happens. SEE UNDER **-ingar**

ngerl (E) *n.*
nosebone
SEE ALSO ntyarl, melyalker, irrengernt, marrapernt

ngerrng (E) *n.*
young shoots of the native tobacco (*Nicotiana* spp.) ◆ Ngerrng ngkerlp lyapetyang — ngerrng akely-antey, lyapetyakenh-antey. Lyetant tha lyapenty arerl-alpek ngerrng-antey. (Sa) Ngerrng *is tobacco that hasn't grown up yet — still just young shoots. Just now I went and saw that the native tobacco is just sprouting.*
= antyanp², akerrng, rrngwaly

ngka *part.*
1. 'Give it here!' ◆ 'Ngka! Atyeng anthay!' (M) *'Here! Give it to me!'*
SEE ALSO ma¹
2. 'Get out of the way!' ◆ 'Ngka, rntwarr-irray!' (M) *'Out of the way, move over!'*

ngkarlt (E), **ingkaylt** (E) *n.*
new moon. Also referred to as *anyenty ngkarlt*.
= anyenty akwerrk

ngkarrp (W,T) *adv.*
drinking or eating half of something and saving the rest for someone else ◆ Ngkarrp arlkwa atyeng, tha anem arlkwetyenheng. (T) *You eat half of it and save some for me, and then I'll eat.* ◆ Atyeng ngkarrp antywang. (M) *You drink first and save me half.*
ngkarrp-ilem (W,T) *vt.*
drink or eat half of something and save the rest for someone else ◆ Urrek tha ngkarrp-iley ngkweng. (M) *Wait while I have some and then I will give the rest to you.*
SEE ALSO artang-ilem, awakem

ngkart, ingkart *n.*
missionary, minister, priest, boss ◆ Ingkart, kaltyel-anthenh-anthenh. (T) *Priests are teachers.* ◆ Ngkartel anwernenh anyentelh-ilenty-alpem. *Priest mapel.* (M) *The priests came along and put us all in together. The priests did.*

ngkart-irrem, ingkart-irrem *vi.*
become a priest, be ordained as a minister ◆ Artwa apek ngkart-irrem yenh arrernem. Urlamperreny antyaperel anem renh arrernem. Tyaket mperlkerek ina irrpelh-ilem. 'Nta kwenh ngkart angerr.' (T) *The man is put there to be ordained as a minister. The whole congregation places him there. They put the white robe on him. '[Now] you are an important priest,' [they say].*
ngkartel arem (E), **ingkartel arem** (E)
'Really, truly, true to God', 'Cross my heart' (lit. 'God will see it')
= altyerrel arem
SEE ALSO werl-arem

ngkekern (W,T), **ngkeken** (W,T) *n.*
1. kurdaitcha, ritual executioner ◆ Ngkekenel aterel-anthem tyerrty map. *The kurdaitcha gives Aboriginal people a fright.*
= inenty, artwang inenty, kwertaty, mwak², nwernternenty, rlwarlp, urlaylp
2. black phase of the witchetty grub. Also referred to as *tyap ngkekern*. • SEE ALSO kwerrert-kwerrert
ngkekern-ngkekern (W,T), **ngkeken-ngkeken** (W,T) *n.*
unregistered vehicle. ◆ Mwetek ngkekern-ngkekern impaty anetyakenh. (M) *The unregistered car doesn't leave any tracks.*
mwetek ngkekern (W,T), **mwetek ngkeken** (W,T) *n.*
unregistered vehicle
= mwetek urlaylp
ngkekern-irrem (W,T), **ngkeken-irrem** (W,T) *vi.*
1. turn into a kurdaitcha
2. turn into a moth or butterfly; transform or metamorphose (grub) ◆ Tyap anyematy ngkekern-irrem. (T) *The witchetty grub turns into a moth.*
SEE ALSO akarternem, irrarl-irrem, rlwarlp-irrem, urlaylp-irrem

ngkelthel fingernails SEE UNDER **ingkelthel**

ngkenhar (E), **inkenhar** (E) *n.*
pinkish-coloured grub from the branch of the river red gum, *aper* (*Eucalyptus camaldulensis* var. *obtusa*) ◆ Tyap ngkenhar, ingwenengek-arneng, kwementyayek-arneng. (Sa) *The* ngkenhar *grub is related to the* ingweneng *grub, to that* kwementyay *one.*
= ingweneng, perlanty, alyperlayt, aperayt
SEE ALSO mpaty²

ngkep-ilem (T,E) *vt.* [RESPECT LANGUAGE]
give something back
SEE ALSO angkep

ngkerlp (W,T) wild tobacco, native tobacco SEE UNDER **ngkwerlp**

ngkernem *vt.*
1. put something in place; stand something up; erect or put something up ◆ Mwetekay ulyewarl ngkernay. (St) *Put the car in the shade.* ◆ Atnem impen tha ngkernek anyelk-kety. (Sa) *I put my only crowbar somewhere in case someone steals it.* ◆ Lywang yanh map ngkernay. (M) *Put that shade up.*
2. plant something (a plant)
3. stop something moving
ngkernelhem *vi.*
stop moving (when moving along), stop moving (along) ◆ Ngkernelhay! (M) *Stop!* ◆ Mwetek ngkernelhem. Kel kwer map antyetyenheng. (T) *The car stops. Then the kids get in.*

ngkewarl (W,T), **ngkewarleny** (W,T) *prn.*
you (can do verb action yourself) ◆ Ker yanh ngkewarl itay. (M) *You cook that meat yourself.* ◆ Menty ngkewarl rrkwa. (M) *You can have it.* ◆ Ngkwarl atway ntarrpay — ngkewarlay, rltwampay. (M) *You chop it yourself — the honey, the sugarbag.* ◆ Arrpenhel ilem, 'Ker ngkewarl itay, angayel apek nta awelhemay'. (M) *Another person says, 'You can cook the meat yourself, you're feeling hungry'.* ◆ Ngkewarleny ker ngkwengenh nhenh impey, ngkewarleny ntwarl atwerl-alpek. (T) *Leave this meat for yourself, you killed it for yourself as you were travelling along.* ◆ Ngkewarleny alhewelhay tyerrty. (T) *You wash yourself.* ◆ Ngkewarlenyarrp ngkwarl yanh antyway. (M) *You drink that grog yourself.*
SEE ALSO kwarleny, inaheleny, tyaheleny
CAN SOUND A BIT LIKE ngkwarl *'honey'*

ngkwank (W) glands inside the mouth or under the jaw SEE UNDER **ankwa**[2]

ngkwanty (W,T) *n.*
aggressive, looking for a fight ◆ Kwer map ngkwantyel atwerrem. (M) *The children are fighting aggressively.*
SEE ALSO anngernt
ngkwanty-irrem (W,T) *vi.*
pick a fight with someone; growl ◆ Kwer yanh ngkwanty-irrek kwer arrpenh nhakaw! Kwer ngkwengenh yakay! (T) *That kid is picking on the other one over there! Stop your kid!*
SEE ALSO ahel-irrem
ngkwantyel atwerrem (W,T)
pick a fight with someone
= anngernt-irrem
SEE ALSO anhelhem, arrkenty-ilem

ngkwarl *n.*
1. sweet things
2. grog, wine, beer, alcohol, booze, cool drink ◆ Artwang atherr atwerrem ngkwarl-penh. (T) *Two men are fighting because they are drunk.* ◆ *Town*-kety ayeng wenng-irrem, ngkwarl-kety, *family*-el antherl-anekerr, terangkem-ilem anem. (St) *I keep away from town because of the grog, and because family give you grog and make you drunk.*
3. A general word that can go before the name of a particular sweet thing. In the Anmatyerr way of classifying foods most fruits and vegetables are known as *mern*, sweet things as *ngkwarl*, seeds as *anterrng*, *arnwety* or *ntang*, meats as *ker* and edible grubs as *tyap*. ◆ Ngkwarl ntywey arratem twern-rlwer. (M) *Corkwood honey comes out in the summer.* ◆ Arrkernkel ngkwarl arwengalker anem. Atwem, arrpem anem ngkwarl renh tyampet-warl arntap-warl arrernem. Ankerrmernel arlka. (St) *Sugarbag is found in bloodwood trees. [You] chop the tree and pare back the wood and then put the honey in a tin or in a bark container. Sugarbag is also found in coolibah trees.*
ngkwarl antywem
drink alcohol (antywem *'drink'*)
ngkwarl-ayerr (T,E) *n.* [RESPECT LANGUAGE]
sugarbag
SEE ALSO rltwamp, arwengalker

Ngkwarlemayntey (T,E) *n.*
name of a sandhill south of Wilora (Stirling) community (note Kaytetye *ngkwarlemaynteye 'Solanum cleistogamum'*)

Ngkwarlerlanem (T,E) *n.*
name of a place and outstation west of the Sandover River on the Alyawarra Aboriginal Land Trust. See map p. viii.

ngkwarrkem (W,T), **ingkwarrkem** (T,E) *vi.*
1. flash (lightning)
2. sparkle, twinkle ◆ Kwerraly ngkwarrkem. (T) *Stars twinkle.*
SEE ALSO alharrkem, arrkem
ngkwarrkenty (W,T), **ingkwarrkenty** (T,E) *n.*
lightning ◆ Tyerrty ater-irrem ngkwarrkemarl ikwereng. 'Kwaty angerr atwewety anwernenhantherr. Ngkwarrkenty angerrarl apetyepetyem.' (N) *People get frightened of the [lightning] flashing. 'A big storm is going to hit us. There's a lot of lightning coming.'*
= awely-awely, kwaty pwer
SEE ALSO angkeyawarr

ngkwarteh (W) *n.*
as soon as (something happens) ◆ Ngkwarteh

rang antyentyelirrek artwang akekw rang, arnang alkerel-irrek, ikwer-akert. (M) *As soon as he climbed up the tree, the tree flew away into the sky with him in it.* ◆ Ngkwarteh thang ker alenh arlkwek, ayeng antew-irrek. (M) *As soon as I ate that meat I vomited.*

ngkwayt (T,E), **ngkwaty** (T,E), **ingkwayt** (E) *n.*
grub from ant bed, winged termite (*Amitermes vitiosus*) ◆ Ngkwaty tyap ngkwepey akngerr-areny. Arlkwenh-arlkwenharl ra tyap. Arlkwetyam arrwekelenyel. (St) Ngkwaty *are grubs from the big ant hills. They are edible. People used to eat them in the old days.*
= atwerneng, ngkwepeyayt
SEE ALSO interrk², ngkwepey, kerrertek, arnameng-ayerr

ngkwehenh (W,T) your, yours SEE UNDER **ngkwenh**

Ngkwelay (E) *n.*
Kurrajong Bore. Location of an outstation east of the Sandover river on the Angarapa Aboriginal Land Trust. See map p. viii.

ngkwelty *n.*
1. bits and pieces of something, fragments of something ◆ Ura ngkwelty kwetyetyek. (St) *Collecting pieces of wood.*
2. small change, coins. Also referred to as *apwert ngkwelty*. ◆ Rlkwerrp tha antywetyek. Rlkwerrp antywetyek ayeng alhem, ngkwelty apek anthay? (St) *I'm going off to drink beer. Can you give me some small change?*
SEE ALSO apwert

ngkwelty-ayerr (E) *n.* [RESPECT LANGUAGE]
money

ngkwelty-ngkwelty *n.*
bits and pieces, fragments of something, chips of wood ◆ Arna apek ultakelhem ngkwelty-ngkwelty anem intem. (St) *The tree breaks up and then there's bits and pieces lying there.*

ngkwelty-ilem *vt.*
smash something into bits, smash something up ◆ Ngkwern apek atwem ngkwelty-ilemel. (M) *Hit the bone to break it into bits.* ◆ Ura apek anwantherr ngkwelty-ilemel atwep-atwem, ura akwek-akwek-ilem. (St) *We smash up the wood into bits, to make it smaller.*
SEE ALSO ulpilem, mweltyem, tyep-ilem, anthim-ilem, ngkweltyem, apert-atwem

ngkweltyelh-ilem *vt.* = **ngkwelty-ilem**

ngkweltyem (W,T) *vt.* = **ngkwelty-ilem**

ngkwelty atwem
smash something into bits, smash something up

ngkwelty-irrem *vi.*
get smashed up, get broken into small pieces ◆ Aherr apek ilepel atwem ngkwelty-irrem. (M) *If a kangaroo is hit with an axe it gets smashed up.*

ngkwely *n.* [RESPECT LANGUAGE]
shade ◆ Ngwarr-nheng ayepel-irrepirrem ngkwelyel. (St) *My daughter and her husband are sitting in the shade [said by the mother of the woman].*
= lywenty
SEE ALSO ulya

ngkwemengk (W) *n.*
emu crop (?) ◆ Ngkwemengk kwer-warn kwaty antywem ankerrel. Kwaty ya angerlapem kwerel — *basin*-artek rtwep akwek. (M) *The emu drinks water and it goes into its* ngkwemengk. *It carries the water along in that — it's small and hollow like a basin.*
SEE ALSO arwentyey

ngkweng *prn.*
for you, to you, at you. See Appendix 1. ◆ Nhenhan tha ngkweng anthem arnam ntyenty angerr ngwenh mwerr-iletyek. (T) *I am giving you this smelly grass to make yourself better.* ◆ Ulengerek-ulengerek angkerreperrem, ilak apek angketyek. Unta apek atyeng angkem, ayeng ngkweng angkem, ulengerek-ulengerek angkerrem. Arratyant-arey weth-lkwer angkerrem alknga arerrem. (St) *Talking face to face. The two of us might talk. You might talk to me and I might talk to you, talk to each other face to face. Talk straight to each other, looking each other in the eye.* ◆ Nthenh-angkwerr nga uyerreperrem. Ayengarl ngkweng uyarn-antey ayeng mpwelhek, untan alhep-alhemant, uyerreperremarl nga. (St) *Where did you get to? I kept waiting for you in vain and you kept going, disappeared.*
SEE ALSO nga

ngkwengenh *prn.*
your, yours (belonging to one). See Appendix 1. ◆ Yatenh inay arnang ngkwengenh. (M) *Get that thing of yours.* ◆ 'Iwenharlam ntwan anem anpernenty ngkwengenh arreny?' 'Ngwarray' arlka war ilelhem — anpernenty ra kwa, arreny. (N) *'What is your skin name?' [The person] might just say 'Ngwarray' — that's the skin name.* ◆ Kampely ngkwengenheng ntwang iterretyeh mwerr. (St) *You think clearly when you use your brains.*
= ngkwenh

ngkwengk (E), **ngkwengkel** (E) *adv.*
cleaning mouth out with water; gargling ◆ Ngkwengkel thelem. Arrakert-they thelem, ngkwengkel iwemel ahelh-werl. Arrakert *clean*-ilelhemel *clean* antyweyam-kety. (Sa) *Clean the mouth out with water. Rinse the mouth and then spit it out on to the ground. [This]*

makes the mouth clean so that you can drink.
= kweng-kweng
SEE ALSO ngkwerrmengkwerr ilelhem
ngkwengk-irrem (T,E) *vi.*
clear throat; make a small coughing noise
◆ Angwenh yanhel ngkwengk-irrenty-alhek? (St) *Who is that who just made a small coughing sound over there?*
SEE ALSO ilwem
Ngkwengk (W) *n.*
name of a place in the Glen Helen Station area
ngkwenh (T,E), **ngkwinh** (T,E), **ngkweyenh** (W,T), **ngkwehenh** (W,T) *prn.*
your, yours. (belonging to one person). See Appendix 1. ◆ Terawath apek ngkwenh tyetarl atyeng. (St) *Your trousers might be too tight for me.* ◆ Apmer ngkwenhel kwenh waylpel warl artelhetyel. (St) *Whitefellas are building houses on your land.* ◆ Ntwerrkenhan alhek. Rapet apawenhwek, 'Alhweng ngkwehenh ayeng irrpey tyerrtyeng?' 'Yeway. Alhweng angerr yanh atyengenh.' (M) *The python went off. He asked a rabbit, 'Can I come into your burrow to escape from the humans?' 'Yes. My burrow is a big one.'*
= ngkwengenh
ngkwep-anem (E) sing out, shout, yell out SEE UNDER **kwep-anem**
ngkwepey *n.*
1. ant hill, ant bed, termite hill [SOME SPEAKERS] ◆ Ngkwepeyel-ayel anem arnang angwenh-akey, yerr map. Yerr angerr map. Interrk-artek akin. (T) *In the ant hill live what's-his-name, lots of ants. Big ants. They are similar to termites.*
SEE ALSO kerrertek, kerrth, merntap, awerr-awerr[1], pwentereng
2. the grub from the ant hill or ant bed, winged termite (*Amitermes vitiosus*) [SOME SPEAKERS] ◆ Tyap ngkwepey kerrertek-areny. (M) *The* ngkwepey *grub lives in the ant hill.*
• = ngkwepeyayt • SEE ALSO atwerneng
ngkwepeyayt (E) *n.*
the edible grub from the ant hill or ant bed, winged termite (*Amitermes vitiosus*). Also referred to as *tyap ngkwepeyayt* or *tyap ngkwepey*.
= atwerneng, ngkwayt
ngkwerengkw-irrem (E) *vi.* [RESPECT LANGUAGE]
ask for something ◆ Weyapelek ngkwerengkw-irretyek. (St) *Asking for meat [from respect kin].* ◆ Rltwaty-ayerr ngkwerengkw-irretyek tyety-ayerr ulpaketyek. (St) *Ask for a gun to shoot some kangaroos [from respect kin].*
SEE ALSO apawenhem
ngkwerlp, ngkerlp (W,T) *n.*
1. wild tobacco, native tobacco, pituri (*Nicotiana* spp.). This is mixed with ash and chewed.
2. any sort of tobacco. ◆ Ngkwerlp anthenherr-arey atyeweyay. (Sa) *Give me some tobacco for goodness sake.*
ngkwerlp rnpwernp (W), **ngkwerlp urnpernp** (E), **ngkwerlp rnpernp** (T,E)
rock pituri (*Nicotiana gossei*). Herb about 60 cm high (though sometimes growing to 3 m), with white flowers. Found in hills and caves. ◆ Arelh ampwang mapel ngkwerlp rnpwernp aketyart irntangel-ayeng. (N) *The old women used to pick rock pituri in the hills.* ◆ Rnpwernp anwern apertarl akem, lyerl intey, inteyel anerl *everywhere* anerl. Apetyemel anwern arem, 'Nhenhey *everywhere* anem kwenh'. Untyem akerl-apem akerl-apem akerl-apem, *heap* arrernem, intey kweram irrperlp-irrpenhemel akem ingkerr anthwerr. Ayak-arrernem. Ayak arrernem akin. 'Thamparr arnmeny inemel arlkwerl-wey nhenh.' Arlpangeyang arlkwem, arek-wemey, arlkwememeyang, kel *tie*-em *up*-em ilem ngkerlp renh. (N) *We pick pituri in the hills, it grows in the caves and everywhere. We come along and see it and say, 'Here it is growing everywhere'. We go along picking it, heaping it up and then we go into the cave and pick the whole lot. We make a pile of pituri. 'I'll get some ashes and get some of the leaves and dip them in ashes and chew it straight away.' We chew some of the leaves, after rolling them in ashes, and then we tie all the tobacco up into a bundle.*
ngkwerlp arwenp (W,T)
sandhill pituri (*Nicotiana rosulata* ssp. *ingulba*). Herb about 45 cm high with smooth shiny leaves. Found growing in mulga and spinifex country.
= ngkwerlp atherrk
ngkwerlp atherrk = ngkwerlp arwenp
(atherrk *'green'*)
ngkwerlp akwerrk (W), **ngkerlp akwerrk** (W)
young shoots of the native tobacco, young native tobacco plants (akwerrk[1] *'young'*)
◆ Ngkerlp akwerrk alyelk mpank. (M) *The native tobacco is just starting to grow.*
= akerrng, antyanp[2]
ngkwerlp ampeng (W), **ngkerlp ampeng** (W)
a wad or lump of tobacco (ampeng *'cooked', 'ripe', 'ready to eat'*) ◆ Ngkerlp ampeng

arrakert-penh inemel irlpeh arrernem. (M) *After the wad of tobacco has been in your mouth you get it and put it behind your ear.*
= ngkwerlp kelh, warn
ngkwerlp kelh (W,T), **ngkerlp kelh** (W)
= ngkwerlp ampeng (kelh *'lump'*)
ngkwerlp arlkwem, ngkerlp arlkwem (W,T)
chew tobacco (arlkwem *'eat'*)

ngkwerlpay-ayerr (E) *n.* [RESPECT LANGUAGE]
creek, river
= angkeway
SEE ALSO lher, lpway

ngkwerltem (E) *vt.* [RESPECT LANGUAGE]
1. cut ◆ Ngwarrelengk tyewarrelh-ayerr ngkwerltetyek. (St) *Your husband is going to cut up the meat.*
2. pick, collect
SEE ALSO akem[1]
ngkwerltelhem (E) *vi.*
1. cut yourself
2. break down, fall apart
SEE ALSO akelhem, atnerrk-irrem

ngkwern *n.*
1. bone ◆ Ngkwern ltwakelhek. (M) *The bone is broken.*
2. shin, leg ◆ Ngkwern atherr rlkerrelhem. (M) *Sitting with both legs straight out.*
3. Goes with the names of particular types of bones. ◆ Pwerlep ngkwern. (Sa) *Shoulderblade.*
4. the stem of a plant or the trunk of a tree. Also referred to as *arna ngkwern*.
ngkwern alyang (W,T)
bandy, crooked or bent legs (alyang *'boomerang'*)
ngkwern amper-amper (W,T)
bandy, crooked or bent legs (amper-amper *'crooked'*)
ngkwernant
skinny, really thin, skin and bone, bony ◆ Pwelek iteth alhem alkngirrenty, ngkwernant — *no* anter *no* tyelk *no* alhwa. (St) *The bullock goes around alive, just skin and bone — no fat, no flesh and no blood.*
2. only the bone
ngkwern-ngkwern *n.*
skinny, really thin, skin and bone, bony ◆ Ngkwern-ngkwern alhep-alhem akuny nhenh. (St) *This poor thing is skin and bone.*
ngkwern-ngkwern-irrem *vi.*
get thin, get skinny
ngkwern-kweny-irrem
show off, flirt, act sexily; go 'weak at the knees' (lit. 'go without legs') ◆ Marl apek tywenap-tywenap irrem, ngkwern-kweny-irrem alyemp-alyemp, artwel akwel renh aretyek, tywenap-irrem. (St) *The girl might be showing off, acting flirtatiously and making her legs go all limp, so that the man can see her showing off.*
SEE ALSO awerrek-awerr

ngkwern irrnyepirrny (E) *n.*
turpentine bush (*Acacia lysiphloia*). Shrub up to 2 m with red curly bark and sticky seed pods.
= irrnyengerrny

ngkwern rnter-rnter (W,T) *n.*
1. mint bush (*Prostanthera striatiflora*) (lit. 'red stem'). Shrub to 2 m high, with shiny green leaves, which smell nice when crushed, and white flowers. ◆ *Medicine* inang waly akenhem ngkwern rnter-rnter. (N) *They pick the branches of the mint bush as they go along, for medicine.*
= amwer
2. black-tailed native-hen [SOME SPEAKERS] (lit. 'red leg' • SEE ALSO angkeparr, karlayteng-ayteng, kart-irrkwely-irrkwely, narremantyerr, lhekethatethat

ngkwernateylp (E) *n.*
mulga native currant, narrow-leaved native currant (*Psydrax suaveolens*). A shrub up to 3 m high, with narrow leaves, small white flowers and fruit which ripens to a black colour.
= ngkwernelyerr, antenh-antenh, anwengk-anwengk
SEE ALSO anngey-anngey

ngkwernelyerr *n.*
1. mulga native currant, narrow-leaved native currant (*Psydrax suaveolens*). A shrub up to
3 m high, with narrow leaves, small white flowers and fruit which ripens to a black colour.
2. edible fruits of the mulga native currant ◆ Ngkwernelyerrap mern anwern-henharl. Anwernarl aketh-ilem, ahakeyart akin antyen angerrart anwern aketh-ilem, ywerrkem. Ywerrkem anwern, an kwetyerl-apem anwern, an akwernerl-apem. Arlpang akwek, akwek anthwerr. Ahakey akenh angerr-lkwer. (N) *The mulga native currant is our food. As we do for the* ahakey *plum, we clear the ground and shake the tree. Then we collect the fruit and eat it. It has small leaves, whereas the* ahakey *plum has larger ones.*
= ngkwernateylp, anngey-anngey, antenh-antenh, anwengk-anwengk

ngkwernerrp[1] (E) *n.*
1. a respectful word for sons-in-law (young ones or old ones who are closely related)

2. mother's mother's father, woman's daughter's son's child; woman's mother's mother's brother's son; father's mother's mother ◆ Ngkwernerrp akwek. Mey-mey kelarl, mey-meyarl perrap *one*. Kel ngkwernerrp akem 'ngwenyarr' akem. 'Ngkwernerrp' anwantherrarl ilem. (St) *A little* ngkwernerrp. Mey-mey *are there okay, they are the proper ones [i.e. actual sons-in-law]. And then* ngkwernerrp *are what are also called* 'ngwenyarr'. *We say* 'ngkwernerrp'.
= ngwenyarr
SEE ALSO akwetyerr, mey-mey[1]

ngkwernerrp[2] (E), **ngkwernirrp** (E) *n.*
a 'strong' type of native tobacco ◆ Ngkwerlp ngkwernerrp, ahelengkwarl irrek ngkwernerrp. Akem renh tek-weynerl-anemel tek-weynerl-anemel. (Sa) *The* ngkwernerrp *tobacco is one that is very strong. It is picked and then spread out in the sun to dry.*

ngkwerrm, **ngkwerrpm** (E) *n.*
1. a type of mistletoe plant (*Amyema* spp.)
2. the fruit of this mistletoe plant; 'snotty gobbles' ◆ Kwenthey-arenyam ngkwerrman, mern kwenthey-areny. Kwenthey akep-akerl, inenhepenherl iltyel war inenhepenherl. Ngkwerrm *too* anwern-henh mern atyankernart akin. (N) *This mistletoe grows on the Eremophila bush. We go and pick it by hand as we go along.* Ngkwerrm *is one of our foods, and it is similar to* atyankern.
SEE ALSO atyankern, pweralhem, amar, ngartangkern, peketyalkwarr

ngkwerrmengkwerr ilelhem (E) *vi.*
clean one's mouth out with water; gargle
SEE ALSO kweng-kweng, ngkwengk

ngkwerrpm (E) a type of mistletoe plant SEE UNDER **ngkwerrm**

ngkwert (W,T) *n.*
1. type of senna bush (*Senna artemisioides* ssp. *petiolaris*)
2. desert cassia, broom bush (*Senna artemisioides* ssp. *filifolia*) ◆ Tyap-akert ngkwert angerr, pertipelaw-akert. Wal, tyap kwen intem. Anyematy-arteh akin, ngkwert angerrel. (N) *The* ngkwert *bush has grubs as well, and flowers. Well, the grubs are in the roots underneath. The* ngkwert *grubs are like witchetty grubs.*
SEE ALSO apwen, kwert-kwert

ngkwertaty (W,T) *n.*
grub from some types of Senna bush ◆ Ngkwertaty tyap, kwen-areny artekerr kwen-areny, ngkwertel-aleng. Ketyam angkwey. (N) *The grubs are called* 'ngkwertaty' *and they are found in the roots underneath the* ngkwert *bush.*

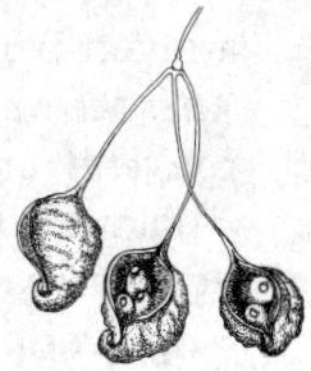

ngkweyang *n.*
seed of the desert kurrajong (*Brachychiton gregorii*). Also referred to as *mern ngkweyang*.
SEE ALSO apeng

ngkweyenh (W,T) your, yours SEE UNDER **ngkwenh**

ngkweytek (E) *n.*
1. slender pigweed (*Portulaca filifolia*)
2. the edible seeds of the slender pigweed ◆ Iylaw aymperr, ngkweytekan arlpenty, arratyeny-antey tnetyenh, arratyeny arratyeny. Urrperl arnterran ngkweytek. (St) *The* iylaw *plant is flat, whereas the* ngkweytek *plant is taller and stands up straight. [The seeds] of the* ngkweytek *are really dark in colour.*
SEE ALSO akat, iylaw

ngkwinh (T,E) your, yours SEE UNDER **ngkwenh**

ngwarr[1] (T,E) *n.kin* [RESPECT LANGUAGE]
1. woman's (or her sister's) daughter's husband
2. woman's son's brother-in-law

ngwarraty (T,E) *n.kin*
my/our *ngwarr*

ngwarrengkw (T,E) *n.kin*
your *ngwarr* ◆ Ngwarrengkw-warl alha. *Go to your husband.* ◆ Thapek ilem *daughter* atyenh, 'Ngwarrengkw ila, alkiwerr atyeng-kety'. Mey-mey atyenhek ayeng angkem. (St) *I might say to my daughter, 'Tell your husband that there's no room [to go there] because of me'. I am talking about my son-in-law.*

ngwarrikw (E) *n.kin*
his/her/their *ngwarr*

ngwarrekw (T) *n.kin*
1. your *ngwarr*
2. his/her/their *ngwarr*

ngwarr-nheng (T,E) *n.kin*
1. a group of two or more people, at least two of whom are husband and wife (said by a woman of her daughter and her husband)
2. a group of two or more people, at least two of whom are related as brothers-in-law (said by a woman of her son and his brother-in-law) ◆ Ngwarr-nheng marlel ant ilem urtalty ikwerenh then *daughter* ikwerenh then. (Sa) *Women just say* ngwarr-nheng, *about their sons-in-law and their daughters together.*
◆ Arelhel melikwel ilem mam ikwerenh artwethen, 'Aperl-nheng atherr yanh'. Anewart renh 'aperl-nheng' akem, mikwel, artwekenh mikwelan ilem 'aperl-nheng atherr' akem, anherrikw then ampikw then. Arelh-kenh amikw mwerikwantarl ilem,

ngwarr-nheng atherr akem, arelh-kenh mikwan 'ngwarr-nheng atherr' akem. (Sa) *The woman, the mother of the man, says of her son and his wife, 'There's those two, husband and wife,* aperl-nheng atherr'. *The man's mother calls the spousal couple* 'aperl-nheng', *that's referring to her son and her daughter-in-law. The mother of the wife calls [her son-in-law]* 'mwer' *and refers to the spousal couple as* 'ngwarr-nheng atherr'. ◆ Arelh atherr anewart ratherr anerretyel mwerengkw then, wal, 'ngwarr-nheng' akin ratherr. Mpwern-nheng atherr artwant-atherr anem, 'ngwarr-nheng' atherr arrpem. (Sa) *If two women are married with your son-in-law, well, the two of them together with the son-in-law are called* 'ngwarr-nheng'. *Two men who are related as brother-in-law to each other, well they are* 'ngwarr-nheng' *as well.*
SEE ALSO aperl-nheng, arrkar-nheng

ngwarr-intyerr (T,E) *n.kin* = **ngwarr-nheng**

ngwarr-nheng atherr (T,E) *n.kin*
1. a married couple (said by a woman of her daughter and her husband)
2. brothers-in-law together (said by a woman of her son and his brother-in-law)

ngwarr-ankethenh (T,E) *n.kin*
1. having *ngwarr* still alive
2. someone who is always with their *ngwarr* ◆ Ngwarr-ankethenharl yanh. (Sa) *That one has a husband.*
SEE ALSO -ankethenh

ngwarr[2] (W) *n.kin*
dog

ngwarraty (W) *n.kin*
my/our dog ◆ Ngwarraty atyenh-artey? (M) *Where is my dog?*

ngwarrengkw (W) *n.kin*
your dog

ngwarrekw (W) *n.kin*
1. your dog
2. his/her/their dog ◆ Arrpenhel ngwenh ilem, 'Ngwely ngwarrekw ngkwengenh-artey?' 'Oh, merel kwenh interl-atherr-anem.' (M) *Another person might say to you, 'Where are your dogs?' 'Oh, they are sleeping at camp.'*

Ngwarray, Kngwarray (E) *n.*
skin name, subsection name, marriage class. See diagram p. 744. ◆ Arelh Ngwarray ahenty-irrem artwang Ngal anew aketyek. (T) *A Ngwarray woman likes to marry a Ngal man.*
SEE ALSO Tywekertay, Ngampwekel, Ngapert, Nwengarray, Tywengarray

ngwarray-ngwarray *n.*
velvet tobacco, rubbish pituri, and other types of native tobacco plant (*Nicotiana velutina* and *Nicotiana* spp.). Herb about 40 cm high. Highly toxic to stock, and NOT chewed by people.
= pengart-pengart[2]

ngwarrertakert (W,T) *adv.*
getting very excited about something; being in a hurry to do something; rushing off and leaving things behind ◆ Arelh yanh alhek ngwarrertakertel mern map imperl-alhek kethek. (T) *That woman rushed off in a hurry and left her food outside.* ◆ Artwang yanh ngwarrertakert alhek mwetekay kwarl inetyeh *buy*-em-iletyeh *garage*-eng. (M) *That man went off excitedly to buy himself a car from the garage.*
= arnkarnp

ngwath (W) *n.*
on your own, alone ◆ Ngwath ayeng apep-apem. (M) *I keep walking about alone.*
= inga
SEE ALSO anyent, akalk, arrakelakel

Ngwatyeng (W) *n.*
No 1 Bore. Location of the old Mt Allan Station homestead.

ngway-ngway (W), **ingway-ingway** (T,E) *n.*
a little bit dark, early evening, dusk ◆ Ingway-ingway anemarl irrem. Ingwel anem lyet artety-alhetyenh ingwa angerrel, ingwa angerr. (St) *It's got a little bit dark now. Soon it will be really dark.*
SEE ALSO ngwemernt, angwerr-angwerr, aherlkenty

ngway-ngway-irrem (W), **ingway-ingway-irrem** (T,E) *vi.*
get dark, become evening
SEE ALSO angwerr-angwerr-irrem, atwerrp-irrem

ngwelenthel (E), **ingwelenthel** (E) *n.* [RESPECT LANGUAGE]
tomorrow, tomorrow morning
◆ Ingwelenthel ahanenherl-wem warrk-ayerr-warl. (St) *Tomorrow [my son-in-law] is going to work.*
SEE ALSO ngwenth

ngwelernety (W), **ngwelern** (E), **akngwelern** (E), **ngwelerneyt** (E), **akngwelerneyt** (E) *n.* [RESPECT LANGUAGE]
east
SEE ALSO angerrakw, ingerr, aywelernety, antwekenety

ngwelernety-athek (W), **ngwelern-athek** (E), **akngwelerneyt-athek** (E) *n.* [RESPECT LANGUAGE]
east, in an easterly direction

ngwelyeparnt-parnt (T) rat-tail goosefoot, green crumbweed (?) SEE UNDER **mwelyeparnt-parnt**

ngwem, ikngwem (E) *vt.*
1. ask someone for something ◆ Ayeng ngwety-alhem kereh apek. (M) *I'm going to go and ask for meat.*
2. ask someone to do something or go somewhere ◆ Tha ngwem anwern alhetyeh kwaty-warn. (M) *I am asking if we can go to the river.* ◆ Atnwernt-irrem atyengety yanh, uyarn tha ikngwem. (St) *I've asked that person in vain but they don't want to do it.*
SEE ALSO antangkem
ngwelh-ilem, ikngwelhem (E) *vt.*
ask someone to do something or to go somewhere
= irrtyelh-ilem

ngwemay (E) *n.* [RESPECT LANGUAGE]
married person's camp ◆ Ngwemay-warl ahaneynek. (St) *They [respect kin] went back to camp.*
SEE ALSO rrwarlp2, arlweker, arnkenty, ahileng, arramenty

ngwemernt (W,T), **ingwemernt** (E) *n.*
1. dark (night-time) ◆ Ingwemernt anem irrenhem-ketyaw, aherrk. (St) *Look out, it's getting dark now, the sun.*
2. dark in colour; dull, not clear, clouded over ◆ Tha arrkay-arrkayarl arem, ingwemernt-artekarl arrkay anem tha arerl-anem, aretyakenhaw kwenh. (St) *My vision is blurred, and now when I look my eyesight is faded and it's as if everything is dark, I can't see.*
3. shade, a shade or shade shelter ◆ Ngwemernt artang! (M) *Build a shade!*
ngwemernt-ngwemernt (W,T), **ingwemernt-ingwemernt** (E) *n.*
half dark, dusk, half-light
SEE ALSO ngway-ngway
ngwemernt-ilem (W,T), **ingwemernt-ilem** (E) *vt.*
make something go dark, turn off a light ◆ *Light* yanh ingwemernt-iletyek. (st) *Turn that light off.*
ngwemernt-irrem (W,T), **ingwemernt-irrem** (E) *vi.*
1. get dark, darken over (sky) ◆ Kwaty akngerr alharrkem, akngerrarl apetyem, ingwemernt-irremel, alharrkenty-alpem. Mperlkemel ap alharrkenty-alpem arlter. (St) *There is a big thunderstorm, and it gets dark, and the lightning flashes. The lightning flashes white.*
2. go dark (in colour) ◆ Mern perlap apek *you might cooked one* arerl ingwemernt-irrekaw. (St) *You might see ripe conkerberries that have gone dark in colour.*
3. blackout (go dizzy or faint); become blurry or faded (vision) ◆ Alknga ingwemernt-irrek. (St) *[My] vision became blurred.*

ngwemper (W), **ngwerremp** (W), **ngwempey** (W) *n.*
1. young fruits of the bush banana, silky pear (*Marsdenia australis*) ◆ Ngwempey akwek, anteth-penh arratem. (M) *The small bush banana fruits come out after the flowers.*
= akwemper, amwernt, mwemper, twemper1
2. sharp or pointed breasts [SOME SPEAKERS]
• = paty arrwert

ngwenh (W,T) you SEE UNDER **ngenh**

ngwenp (W,T), **ingwenp** (W,T) *n.*
tomorrow, tomorrow morning ◆ Ngwenp ayeng alhetyenheng. (M) *I'm going tomorrow.*
= ngwenth, ingwepenh
SEE ALSO ngwerrew, amwerrk
ngwenpel (E) *n.*
early in the morning
= ingwepenh

ngwenth (W,T), **ingwenth** *n.*
tomorrow, tomorrow morning
= ngwenp, ingwepenh
SEE ALSO lyet
ngwenth-ngwenth, ingwenth-ingwenth *n.*
first light, break of day, daylight ◆ Kwerraly Angerr apetyem, aherlkenty alhetyenheng, ngwenth-ngwenth. (M) *The Daylight Star comes, before the sun rises, at first light.*
SEE ALSO aherlkenty
ngwenth-ngwenth-irrem (W,T), **ingwenth-ingwenth-irrem** *vi.*
become daylight, become first light, become daybreak
SEE ALSO aketh-aketh-irrem
ingwenth anyent-ingar (E)
one day soon (anyent-ingar *'once'*)
ngwenth arrpenh, ingwenth arrpenh
the day after tomorrow (arrpenh *'another'*)
ngwenth war, ingwenth war (T,E)
sometime soon (war *'just'*)

ngwenty (T) tears, watery eyes SEE UNDER **anngwenty**

ngwenty-ngwenty (T,E), **ntyengwenty** *n.*
whitish yellow ochre ◆ Yellow *one* irntang ilem 'karntawarr' tyerrtyel. Arlkenyek akin *use*-em-ilem rlpwa, karntawarr, tywelker, ntyengwenty. (T) *Aboriginal people call the yellow rock 'karntewarr'. It's used as well for making ceremonial designs, along with* rlpwa *[red ochre and white ochres],* tywelker *and* ntyengwenty.
SEE ALSO rlpwa, arwethenp, atywerlk, artep arlpenty, karntewarr, marlalperr, atywerlk, karntewarr, rlpwa, arwethenp

ngwenyarr (W,E) *n.*
1. a respectful word for sons-in-law (young ones or old ones who are closely related)
2. mother's mother's father, woman's daughter's son's child; woman's mother's mother's brother's son; father's mother's mother (note Warlpiri *ngunyarri* 'speaker calls male who is his mother's mother's father')
= ngkwernerrp

Ngwenyenp (W,T) name of a large hill in the Pine Hill area SEE UNDER **Anngwenyenp**

ngwerr (W,T), **ngwerreh** (W,T) *n.*
yesterday ◆ Ngwerreh thang ywarerl-alpern mernek. (T) *Yesterday I went to look for bread and there was none there.* ◆ Ngwerreh war alhek ayeng mer arrpenh-warn. (M) *Yesterday I just went somewhere else.*
= amwerrk
SEE ALSO ngwenp, ngwenth

ngwerreheny (W,T) *n.*
from yesterday, from before ◆ Ker ngwerreheny. (M) *Meat from yesterday.*
= amwerrkeny

ngwerreh arrpenh (W,T), **ngwerrek arrpenh** (T) *n.*
1. the day before yesterday, a few days ago (arrpenh '*another*') ◆ Lyweny anwern alhek ngwerreh arrpenh. (M) *We went hunting the day before yesterday.*
= amwerrkel arrpenh-ingar
2. another day, another time ◆ Ngwerreh arrpenh artew rang alherl lyweny aken, marl ra akenh akwer akwek ra anpenhek lpwayel antem. (M) *Another time the bush turkey man went hunting again, and the woman and boy set off along the creek.*

ngwerremp (W) young fruits of the bush banana SEE UNDER **ngwemper**

ngwerrty (W) hungry, want to eat without sharing SEE UNDER **rrngwerrty**

nh+ *n.*
A shortened form of *nhenh* ('here', 'this', 'this one') which rarely occurs on its own. It is usually followed by other endings such as *+el* or *+el-perr*.
= nhenh
SEE ALSO nhanyem, nhangkwerr, nhatherr, nhelkwer, nhareny, nhel-ayemy, nhantey

nhakw, **nhak** (E) *n.*
1. over there, there (a fair distance away) ◆ Tyerrty nhak-warl alhem, anwengkerr artwarerl-alpetyeh. (T) *The person is going over there, we're watching him.* ◆ 'Aylernemel' — alakenh inan ilem nhakw-thayt Arrernt-thayt. 'Alakenh aylernetyekaw.' 'Awerrketyekarl' anwantherr ilem Anmatyerrel. (St) 'Aylernemel' *— that's what they say over there on the Arrernte side.* 'Alakenh aylernetyekaw.' 'Awerrketyek' *is what we say in Anmatyerr.* ◆ Ntarl iwerl-alpek nhakwek mantarr ngkwenh. Iltyant nga apety-alpern, nhenh ant iwerl-alpek, mantarr ngkwenh. (St) *You went and dropped your clothes off over there. You came back empty-handed, you just dropped your clothes off.*
2. that (person or thing); those (persons or things) ◆ Arelh nhak apay-unhetyek alhay ngkwerlpek. *Go and ask that woman for tobacco.* ◆ Nhakw apekarl angkerreperrem, alhengk-awemarl tha, tyerrtyarl angkerremarl. (St) *Those people talking over there, well I know the sound of their voices, of those people talking.* ◆ Tha kak akem nhakw-arey. (St) *I call those people over there older brother.*
= alenh

nhangkwerr SEE UNDER **nhenh**

nhanyem SEE UNDER **nhenh**

nhatherr SEE UNDER **nhenh**

nhel-anyem SEE UNDER **nhenh**

nhelkwer SEE UNDER **nhenh**

nheng[1] *n.*
Indicates a particular person, place, event or thing that both the speaker and the hearer know is being referred to; 'You know the one', 'That one', 'This one', 'That thing', 'That place' etc. ◆ Arelh nheng kel alpek. (T) *That women has already gone back.* ◆ Apalenthwety-alhay, arnang nheng ntwarl *lose*-em-ilekarlekay. (M) *Go and look for that thing that you lost.*
2. Indicates uncertainty; supposedly, so they say, reportedly. ◆ Rlngerr-rlngerr weth akwekarl angkep-angkem, nheng aherrk apek irrperl-alhem, wal ra anem *red one* apek *show*-irrem. Wal rlngerr-rlngerrarl angkem akwek-akwek. Rwengkarl angkep-angkem anwantherr aretyakenh. (St) *That* rlngerr-rlngerr *is a small creature that sings out, supposedly when the sun is going down, and when the sunset becomes red. Well the little* rlngerr-rlngerr *sings out. It makes a noise but we can't see them.*

nheng-lkwer *n.*
like or similar to (the one that has been referred to); something (like that), that sort of thing ◆ Tyap arlperrenh, *olden time*-arl aketyam anyent renh, arlperrenh renh. Kapert angerr nheng-lkwer anyem-areny-arteh akin *different one*, kapert angerr. (N) *The whitewood grubs, that's what the olden-time*

people used to get. Their heads are big, like that thing, they are a bit like the grub from the witchetty bush but their heads are larger. ◆ Mern anakety akem arrernem *clean*-em-ilem arna arrert nheng-lkwerel alakenhel *clean*-em-ilem. *Seed* renhan antarram wemel *clean* anthwerr mparem. (N) *The bush tomato is picked and then the seeds are cleaned out using a tool called 'arrert', with a thing like that. All the seeds are cleaned out and thrown away.*

nheng-antey (E) *n.*
somewhere round there

nhengentyak-antey (E) *n.* [RESPECT LANGUAGE]
somewhere round there ◆ Nhengentyak-antey angwenharl apetyek? (Sa) *Who is that over there who came [said by someone who might be in a respect relationship to that person]?*
SEE ALSO nheng-antey

-nheng2 *k.ending*
Goes on most kin terms and marks a group of two or more people who are related to each other in a particular way; a person 'together' with their complementary relation or relations. For example, when added to the kin term *awenh* 'auntie' it forms the word *awenh-nheng* 'an auntie together with her nephews or nieces' (or 'several aunties with a nephew or niece'). With *altyel* 'female cross-cousin' it forms *altyel-nheng* 'a group of two or more people who are related to each other as female cross-cousins'. For some kin terms, such as *mey* 'mother' and *kak* 'brother', -*nheng* goes directly onto the shortened forms of these words to form the words *menheng* and *kenheng* respectively.
SEE ALSO +art, -rrpwer

-nheng atherr *k.ending*
Goes on most kin terms and marks a group of two people who are related to each other in a particular way; a person 'together' with a particular relation. For example, *aperl-nheng atherr* 'a person together with their father's mother (or equivalent kin)' (*aperl* 'father's mother etc.)

-nheng-arey *k.ending*
Goes on most kin terms and marks a group of more than two people who are related to each other in a particular way; a person 'together' with particular relations. (-arey '*plural*')

-nheng-rnem *k.ending* = **-nheng-arey**

-nheng-nheng (E) *k.ending* = **-nheng-arey**

nhenh *n.*
1. here (in close proximity to the speaker). ◆ Lyet ayeng apety-alpek nhenh-warl. (St) *I came back here today.* ◆ Mern payemalan arlkwerrerl-apek, lpway nhenhel. Atetherr atwerl-apemel. Arntap-warn arrernetyart. (N) *We went along eating pie melons in the creek here. We went along killing budgerigars. We used to put them in bark containers.* ◆ Rntwetyart anwern, mer nhenh kwerel anwern rntwetyart kalty-anthetyart akngerr-pat mapel anwernenh. (N) *We used to dance, at this place here, we danced, and the elders used to teach us.*
2. this (person or thing); these (persons or things) ◆ Nhenhan tha ngkweng anthem arnam ntyenty angerr ngwenh mwerr-iletyek. (T) *I am giving you this smelly grass to make yourself better.* ◆ Nhenhan nyany atyengenh. (T) *This is my granny.* ◆ Nhenhan ker ampwang-awaty — nhenhan ker anter angerr-awaty. (T) *This meat is a bit lean — this meat is a bit fattier.*
SEE ALSO nhetenh, yatenh, alert, alertenh, alenh

nhatherr *n.*
these two (atherr1 '*two*') ◆ Mert-mert ilerrirrem tyerrty nhatherr, werrk-angkwerr. (M) *These two have gone off into the scrub to become lovers.*
SEE ALSO nh+

nhangkwarr (E) *n.*
this way, in this direction
SEE ALSO -angkwarr, nh+, nhenh-angkwarr

nhenh-lkwer, nhelkwer *n.*
this sort of thing, this type of thing; that sort of thing, that type of thing (often while indicating or pointing to the thing) ◆ 'Nhenh-lkwer angetyang.' Tyerrty alenh apek antangk-ilem. (M) *'Bring one like this.' Asking that person to get it.* ◆ Atek-kenh atyet nhelkwer ampa akwekelarl atyet anyenem, wal, atek-kenharl ilem Anmatyerrel. (St) *That soft part that little babies have on the top of their heads, well that's called 'atek-kenh' in Anmatyerr.* ◆ Anem arternem, rwel itemel an arnang ntarlkw nhelkwer-warl tyarrp-warl angem tyarrpel arternetyeh. (N) *Straightening a digging stick, heating it in the fire and then taking it to a forked tree, or that sort of thing, and straightening it in the crack.*
SEE ALSO -lkwer, nh+

nhenh-anyem (E), **nhanyem** (E) *n.*
this one here ◆ Alknga ayeng alhwer-alhwer-irrek nhanyem amengel apekarl utnhek. Alhwer-alhwer-irrek. (St) *This eye of mine here has bunged up, probably because flies bit it. Bunged up.*
SEE ALSO -anyem, nh+

nhetenh (W,T) *n.*
1. here ◆ Nhetenh irnep-irnem mwetek atyengenh. (T) *My car is standing here.*
2. this (person or thing), these (persons or things); that (person or thing), those (persons or things) ◆ Nhetenh inay atyeng. (M) *Get me that thing.* ◆ Artwangel tyerrty nhetenh atwem. (M) *The man is hitting that person.*
SEE ALSO nhenh, alert, alertenh, yatenh

nhey-nhey (E) *n.* [BABY TALK]
1. woman's mother-in-law
2. woman's daughter-in-law ◆ Akngerrety-rnem ilerrem. Ampa akelyek ilem *too.* 'Anherr-anherr aray. Nhey-nhey ngkwenh.' (Sa) *Grown ups say that. It is said to little kids as well. 'Look at your* anherr-anherr. *Your* nhey-nhey.*'*
SEE ALSO anherr

nhwem (W,T) *vt.*
1. bite someone or something ◆ Arengk nhenhel ngkwern nhwem. (N) *This dog is biting the [person's] leg.*
2. sting (insect) ◆ Aneth-akertel tyerrty nhwem, kwaty-taym. (T) *Scorpions bite people during the rain time.*
3. kill (something by biting it); catch (food with mouth).
4. pick, collect
= **utnhem** (E)
nhwerrem (W,T) *vi.*
1. bite each other
2. fight or argue with each other (lit. 'bite each other') ◆ Angwely arrpenhek anem angwely atherr anem nhwerrem *properly* anthwerr ratherr nhwerrem, kel pwath *one*-el renh-atherr atwem atwem kenh akwenpel atherr nhwerreperrerleng. Kel ratherr imperrem antem, kel *cut*-em *out* anem iletyenheng. (T) *The two dogs are really fighting each other hard, and then the boss of the dogs belts them and they keep on fighting each other regardless, ignoring him. Then the two of them give up, and they are separated from each other.*
= **utnherrem** (E)
ahel nhwerrem (W,T)
fight, argue (ahel *'anger', 'angrily'*)
arrkenel nhwerrem (W,T)
to play (arrken *'for fun'*) ◆ Kwer alenh arrkenel nhwerreperrem. (M) *Those kids are playing.*
= arrkenel utnherrem
nhwelhem (W,T) *vi.*
to play ◆ Kwer map arrken nhwelh-atherr anem. (M) *The children are playing.*
= arrken-irrem

nikeleth necklace SEE UNDER **nekeleth**

nikey-nikey, nek-nek *n.*
plug tobacco, black twist tobacco (from Australian pidgin *nicki-nicki* 'black twist tobacco, nigger tobacco'). Tobacco used to be available in solid dark-coloured lumps.

nkem (E) emerge or come out from chrysalis SEE UNDER **rnkem**

nkwanng (T) *n.*
bad cold
SEE ALSO rta, mernt[1], rlkert, arrwengkelth, inkwerr, artwengkenng, arntety

nmwenth (W,T) *n.*
flour ◆ Mern nmwenth-artey? (M) *Where's the flour?*
= pelaw
SEE ALSO arterrty, warnp, aperretyen, thelperretyen
= **unmenth** (E)

nmwernt (W,T) *n.*
dust, dust haze, dust storm ◆ Nmwerntarl apem aretharr *time.* (T) *The dust blows when the west wind blows.* ◆ Nmwernt rang apety-alhem aterel anthety-alhem tyerrtyan. (N) *The dust storm comes along and gives people a fright.*
= **unmernt** (T,E)

nparnpetyenh (W), **rnparnpetyenh** (W) *n.*
1. a type of bush tomato (*Solanum* sp.) (?)
2. the edible fruits of this bush tomato. Also known as *mern nparnpetyenh.*
◆ Rnparnpetyenh angerrety anthwerr, arlpang angerr. Mern *yellow one* irretyenh. (N) *The* rnparnpetyenh *is really large, it has big leaves. The fruit goes yellow when it is ripe.*
SEE ALSO manyem

npart sulky, sooky, angry, resentful SEE UNDER **npwart**

npwa (W,T), **npwang** (W,T) *n.*
smelly (of a person or dog); having a bad smell ◆ Arengk impalerrp-welhem antyamel, anety npwangerr. (M) *The smelly dog is rubbing itself on the blankets.*
CAN SOUND A BIT LIKE rnpwa *'edible gum from plant'*
= **unpa** (E)
npwakert (W,T) *n.*
smelly (-akert *'having'*)
= **unpakert** (E)
npwangerr (W,T) *n.*
smelly (angerr[1] *'lots'*)
= **unpangerr** (E)

npwart (W,T), **npart** (W,T) *n.*
sulky, in a huff, unsociable, not mixing with other people or talking to other people
◆ Wenh-penh arelh alenh npwart alhek? (T) *Why did that woman go off sulkily?* ◆ Arelh awenk yanh alhem npwart, ngkweltyek uyarn

angkek-penh. (T) *That teenage girl went off in a huff, after asking for money and not getting any.*
SEE ALSO **arnkely**
= **unpart** (T)
alha npwart (W,T)
sulky
npwart-irrem (W,T), **npart-irrem** (W,T) *vi.*
get sulky, angry or resentful ◆ Alhang nta atyeng npwart-irrerl, thwengk arrarem kwenh. (M) *You're getting sulky with me and I'm missing out on my share.*
SEE ALSO **arnkely-irrem**
= **unpart-irrem** (T)

npway-npway (W,T) *n.*
wire bush, tangled Lechenaultia (*Lechenaultia divaricata*) (?). Leafless tangled shrub about 50 cm high.
SEE ALSO **unpay**

nta you (one person) SEE UNDER **ntwa**

ntalwerrk (W) button grass SEE UNDER **talkwerrk**

ntang (E) *n.*
1. edible seed ◆ Weth ntangarl athep-athemarl. Ntangarl atherl-anemarl, tyengel. Alyerarl yanhan apert-atwep-atwemarl, mern katyerr arlka ikelh-ilem kwerel alyerelan. Tyengan yanh anterrngarl athemel. (St) *That's that thing that's used for grinding seed. Seed is ground with the* tyeng *stone. The* alyer *stone is used for crushing foods, such as the desert raisin, which is made into a seed cake. The* tyeng *stone is used for grinding seed.*
2. A general word that can go before the name of a particular type of seed. In the Anmatyerr way of classifying foods most fruits and vegetables are known as *mern*, sweet things as *ngkwarl*, seeds as *anterrng*, *arnwety* or *ntang*, meats as *ker* and edible grubs as *tyap*. ◆ Ntang ilkert, mwerr-angker renh athetyam arrwekelenyel, apwert 'tyengel' athetyam. Urel ina itetyam, aynpernetyam panthel. (Sa) *The seed from the Halls Creek wattle is really nice, and the olden-time people ground it up with a stone called 'tyeng'. They yandied the seed in a coolamon and cooked it in the fire.*
= **arnwety**, **anterrng**
CAN SOUND A BIT LIKE **irnta** *'rock', 'hill'*

ntarrwerarrwer (W) *n.*
rock pigeon, plumed pigeon, spinifex pigeon (*Geophaps plumifera*)
= **arntwerrert**
SEE ALSO **marekwerr**

ntat, **intat** *n.*
1. rubbish or debris left by floodwater ◆ Anthelk aper-penh ntat. (T) *The bits and pieces of river red gum left by the floodwater.*
SEE ALSO **anthelk**[1]
2. a hide (especially for hunting emu) ◆ Ker ankerrekarl anem ntatel. Irrtyartel anem renh atanthem ker ankerr, ker ankerr apetyerlek. (T) *[They] sit down in the hide waiting for emus. Then they spear the emu when it comes.* (T) • SEE ALSO **armenty**, **ipey**
CAN SOUND A BIT LIKE **nthat** *'blocked', 'full (stomach)'*
ntat-wem, **intat-wem**, **ntat-iwem** (E) *vt.*
leave a mass of flood refuse or debris ◆ Ntat-iwenhem, kwatyel urewel. (St) *The floodwater leaves debris as it goes along.*

ntekentyenarr (W) ring-tailed dragon (?) SEE UNDER **tekentyenarr**

nteny-nteny (E) *n.*
spotted, spotty, covered in spots ◆ Apmwa parip. Rrweyan arlkeny-arlkeny. Marlan *yellow one yellow one* nteny-nteny war. *Whistle*-artekap ra irrerl-anem iparip. Rnwem-apenyarl ap ra. (St) *The* parip *snake. The male is stripey. The female is yellowish and spotty. They are similar to snakes and they make a sort of whistling sound.*
nteny-nteny-ilem (E) *vt.*
dot something, make something spotty

nter (E) greedy SEE UNDER **rnter**

nter-rnter red SEE UNDER **rnter-rnter**

ntererrpererrp (W,T) a type of wasp (?) SEE UNDER **rntererrpererrp**

nternem spear or pierce something with a sharp object SEE UNDER **rnternem**

ntert, **rntert** *n.*
quiet ◆ Ntert-ntert anetyek, tyerrty arwenthari awekety, ntert-ntert anerl-anetyek. (T) *Sitting down quietly in case all the people hear us.* ◆ Anwengkerr ntert aneyaw angkety-kweny, yatenh angkem-arleng. (N) *We should sit down and not talk, because that person is talking.* ◆ Ngkekern yanhengarl arrawenth-irrety-alhemeng anwengkerr ntert aney kwenh. Irlkwatherr rwang yanh ilwernewarray, artarrern-ketyay, atwewetyay. (N) *We've all got to sit down quietly because of the kurdaitcha that is whistling there. For goodness sake, put out that fire in case he puts a curse on us.* (?)
CAN SOUND A BIT LIKE **intert** *'base of something'*; **arntert** *'rotten', 'stinking'*
ntert-ilem, **rntert-ilem** *vt.*
quieten someone or something down, turn volume down, stop a car
ntertelh-ilem, **rntertelh-ilem** *vt.* = **ntert-ilem**
ntert-irrem, **rntert-irrem** *vi.*
become quiet, quieten down ◆ Kwer nhenh

arrangkepangkem. 'Kwer ntert-irray!' (M) *This kid is crying. 'Quieten down child!'* ◆ 'Wapey-kety rntert-irray' — ampek ilem. (St) *Be quiet because of the whitefella' — that's what [you] tell kids.*

ntewal *n.*

1. flowers of the bloodwood, *arrkernk, arlangkw* ◆ Ntewal arrkernk-areny akerlkewarranem. (M) *The flowers from the bloodwood tree shine.*

2. seed capsules of the bloodwood ◆ Ntewal ikwereng atanthepanthem nikeleth anemarl. (St) *Necklaces are made from bloodwood seed capsules.*

SEE ALSO mernperr

ntewem (E) *vt.*

1. beat or bash an animal against something (in order to kill it) ◆ Alewatyerr ntewem. Alhweng-they tyarr-inemel, ntewem. (St) *You pull the goanna from its hole and then beat it against something.* ◆ Ker renh arlewatyerr angernemel, ntewem anem renh. 'Hey, arnterr ntewetyalaw, anter apek ulpirrekerr!' (St) *You dig up the goanna and then beat it against the ground. 'Hey, don't beat it too hard, you'll smash up all the fat!'*

2. knock someone to the ground ◆ Tyerrty apek ntewem, tyerrty arrpenhel, ingkel apek arnpakem renh. (St) *One person might knock another to the ground by tripping them up with their foot.*

SEE ALSO arlkwatem, ilatwem

ntewelhem (E) *vi.*

throw yourself to the ground ◆ Ampa apek artnep-artnem, ntewelhemel artnep-artnem, mathek apek. (St) *The child might cry and then throw herself to the ground, maybe crying for her mother.*

ntewerrem (W) *vi.*

throw each other around; wrestle each other ◆ Ntewerrem kwer atherr. (M) *The two kids are wrestling.*

= arlkwaterrem

CAN SOUND A BIT LIKE antew-irrem *'vomit'*

ntewerrk (T,E) *n.*

1. dry fruit of the native currant, native citrus (*Psydrax latifolia*)

2. a type of native currant (?) ◆ Ahakeyek-arneng, ntewerrk. Ingerr-thayt arlka apwertel anem, ahelhel arlka anem. (T) *The* ntewerrk *tree is closely related to the* ahakey *plum. It grows in the east, in the hills and on the plains.*

SEE ALSO ahakey

Ntewerrk (E) *n.*

name of a place near Atnwarl (Huckitta)

ntha (E), **untha** (E) *n.*

chips of wood left over after carving; the bits of wood that are left over after scraping the kurrajong tree root (for use as a source of water) ◆ Apeng ntha — kwaty-penh ampeny iwem anem, ntha renh. Kwaty arlkarl thelek-penh. (St) *The chips of wood from the kurrajong tree root — after the cool water has been poured off the leftovers, the chips of wood, are thrown away. After the cool water has been poured off.*

nthakenh *adv.*

1. 'How?', 'What?', 'What's up?', 'How come?' *Nthakenh* can occur on its own. ◆ Nthakenh ntwa itirrem? (M) *What do you think?* ◆ Nthakenhay? (M) *What's happening?*

2. can't (do verb action), unable (to do verb action), how could someone or something (do the verb action). In this sense *nthakenh* accompanies a verb which has a negative ending on it. ◆ Kwatyel rewel arrngert-wem, ilpay. Tyerrty nthakenh alhetyakenh, amek anem arem. (St) *The floodwater blocks off the creek. People can't go, they get blocked off.* ◆ Yer, nthakenh alhetyakenh, atnathan anerl. *A person who is crippled can't walk and just sits.* ◆ Nthakenh renh atwetyakenh inangkal, ilpelhetyelarl. Ngkwern atwetyakenh perrap inangkal iyterrty ilpelhetyelarl ra arwerlel. (Sa) *He is really clever and can't be beaten because he is protecting himself. He is really invincible and can't be hit because he is shielding himself with a branch.*

= nthanh

SEE ALSO wenh, ilek

nthakenh-irrem *vi.*

'What's happening?', 'What's someone doing?' ◆ Arraty-akey ntwang ilep-ilem nthakenharl irrek. (M) *Is what you're saying happened really true?*

nthakenty *n.*

'How many?', 'How much?' ◆ Arelh nthakentyel yanhan angerrirretyel? (Sa) *How many people are there?* ◆ Nthakenty arrantherr apetyern? Rrpwety. (M) *How many of you came? A few.*

nthakenty-ingar

'How many times?', 'For how long?', 'For how many days?' (-ingar *'times'*) ◆ 'Nthakenty-ingar nga alhemay?' *You might* ilem, *'Four days* apek. Alakenty-ingar ayeng alhem atherr-atherr'. (St) *'How many days are you going for?' And you might say, 'Maybe for four days. That's how many days I am going for'.*

nthangkwerr *n.*

'Where to?', 'Which way?'

= nthenh-angkwerr

nthanh (E), **thanh** (E) *n.*
1. 'How?', 'What?', 'What's up?', 'How come?'
2. can't (do verb action), unable (to do verb action), how could someone or something (do the verb action)? In this sense *nthanh* accompanies a verb which has a negative ending on it.
= nthakenh

Ntharey *n.*
Hermannsburg. Also spelt as Ntaria.

ntharr (T), **nthwarr** (T) *n.*
1. burnt hair or fur
2. the smell of hair or fur burning
= utharr
CAN SOUND A BIT LIKE nthwarr *'gum or kino from bloodwood'*

ntharr (T) gum or kino from bloodwood, *arrkernk* SEE UNDER **nthwarr**

ntharrengarreng (W,T), **ntyarrengarreng** (W), **nthayarrengarreng** (W) *n.*
slime on water ◆ Ntharrengarreng inta, kwaty renh menty kwenh, ntharrengarreng-akert kwenh. (T) *Leave that slimy water alone.*
SEE ALSO nthwerrkamp, arntwatherrk[1]

nthat *n.*
1. blocked up; full (stomach)
2. pregnant
SEE ALSO alhap
CAN SOUND A BIT LIKE ntat *'flood refuse', 'a hide'*

nthat-irrem *vi.*
1. be blocked up or congested; be full (stomach) ◆ Alha nthat-irrem, alha altywer anetyakenh. (St) *The nose is blocked up and there's no hole [to breathe through].* ◆ Atnertarl ulthem akwel, nthat-irrem, atnerteng ulthem, arlkwemarl-penh, nthat anem irrem, nthat-irrem. (St) *[Your] stomach is heavy and full from eating, blocked up.*
2. sob, groan or moan; breathe heavily

nthat-ilem *vt.*
block something up, make something congested ◆ Alha nthat-ilem atwengkenngel. (St) *The mucus is blocking the nose.*

nthat-nthat *n.*
sob, a choking sound when crying

nthat-nthat-irrem *n.*
sob, throw a tantrum, cry a lot ◆ Ampa nthat-nthat-irrem rlkert, nthat-nthat-irremel artnep-artnem. (St) *The sick child is sobbing.* ◆ Kwer nthat-nthat-irrem, kwer arrpenhelarl atwem. Wal *pain* awelhemeng nthat-nthat-irrem. (T) *The child is sobbing because another child hit her. She is sobbing because she is in pain.*
SEE ALSO arlan-irrem

nthayarrengarreng (W) slime on water SEE UNDER ntharrengarreng

nthek-wem *vt.*
throw animal carcass on fire to singe off hair, fur or scales ◆ Nthek-wemem ker renh, aherr renh nthek-wem, aweth tyarr-inemel arnngem arnngem walyel arnngem walyel arnngem, kwer-penh aweth nthek-wem pwer-thayt. (N) *The kangaroo is thrown on the fire to singe the fur off, and then pulled out again and cleaned with a branch, then after that put on the fire again to singe the fur off the tail side.*
SEE ALSO pwerlp-wem

nthelem (W,T), **nthilem** *vt.*
light a fire, set fire alight ◆ Arrngelhel rwang nthelem. (T) *Lighting the fire with dried bark.* ◆ Rrwelty akem rwa nthiletyenheng. (T) *Cut some kindling to light the fire.* ◆ Ura nthilem, alkngenth ra ampetyek. (St) *Lighting the fire, and then the flames start burning.*
= antant-ilem, anngenth-ilem

nthenh *n.*
1. 'Where?', 'Which place?' ◆ Kwaty alyerremwey nthenhek anwantherr antywey kwenh? (T) *Where are we going to get some nice-tasting water to drink?* ◆ Nthenhel Kemarr arrpengkw? (St) *Where is that person who is a Kemarr like you?* ◆ Nthenhel anem ayeng intetyenh? Kwentyarl intem-kety. (St) *Where am I going to sleep? There's too many packed in here.*
2. whatever place, whichever place, the place where, somewhere, some place ◆ Ingkirrpem ra kel ra apetyem, mer nthenh apekarl iterlarem, kel arraty atwety-alhem, rlwaylpel. (St) *The kurdaitcha puts on his feather shoes and then goes to whatever place he knows, and then kills someone.*

nthenh-nthenh *n.*
from wherever, from all over the place, from whichever place ◆ Artwa nthenh-nthenh. (M) *A person from wherever.*

nthenh-iperr (E), **nthenh-they** (E)
'From where?'

nthenh-penh (W,T), **nthenheng** (W,T)
= **nthenh-iperr**

nthenh-warn (W,T), **nthenh-warl** (E)
'Where to?', 'Which way?'

nthenh-angkwerr
'Where to?', 'Which way?' ◆ Nthenh-angkwerr nga alhep-alhem? (St) *Which way are you going?*
= nthangkwerr

nthenhenty-angkwerr (E) [RESPECT LANGUAGE]
'Where to?', 'Which way?' ◆ Ngwarrengkw

ahanenhek nthenhenty-angkwerr? (St) *Which way did your husband go [said by a woman to her daughter]?* ◆ Nthenhenty-angkwerr lyengkwert ahanerrekay? (Sa) *Where did they [including respect kin] go today?*
SEE ALSO nthenh-angkwerr

Ntheyelkwer an 'old' type of Anmatyerr language SEE UNDER **Kal ntheyelkwer**

nthilem light a fire SEE UNDER **nthelem**

Nthurey (W,T) name of place in Ti Tree (Ahakeye Aboriginal Land Trust) area SEE UNDER **Nthwerey**

nthwarr (W), **ntharr** (T) *n.*
1. gum or kino from bloodwood, *arrkernk* (*Corymbia opaca*) ◆ Nthwarr rnpwa arrkernk-areny. *Medicine* waram yanh, apernelhenhelhenh tywen. Kwaty arrernem *soak*-irretyeh, rwa item rwel nthwarr yanh ampem, kel lweren inem apernelherl-anem alhewelhemel, nthwarr-iperram. *Red*-irrem, *red* anthwerr. (N) Nthwarr *is the gum from the bloodwood tree. It's just a medicine, used for rubbing on sores. You put it in water to soak it, boil the mixture on the fire, then use it to wash yourself and rub on yourself. It goes a really red colour [in the water].*
SEE ALSO lyarwek, arrkeper
2. water found in the trunk of the bloodwood
• = kwentharr, untharr
CAN SOUND A BIT LIKE ntharr *'burnt hair or fur'*

nthwarr (T) burnt hair or fur SEE UNDER **ntharr**

Nthwelker (E) an 'old' type of Anmatyerr language SEE UNDER **Kal ntheyelkwer**

nthwem (W,T) *vt.*
1. walk around ◆ Rtwenk-akert nthwerl-apem. (M) *Walking along with a walking stick.*
2. look around for something; go around looking for something ◆ Nthwemel nthwemel ayeng apety-alpern ker-kweny itya, itya akwet. (M) *Walking and walking I came back without any meat, still nothing.*
SEE ALSO apem[1]
CAN SOUND A BIT LIKE anthwem *'seep or ooze out'*
= **unthem** (E)
nthwelh-ilem (W,T) *vt.*
make someone go somewhere
= **unthelh-ilem** (E)

nthwenharr (E) a type of cloud (after rain has finished) SEE UNDER **antwenharr**

Nthwerey, **Nthurey** (W,T) *n.*
name of a place in the Ti Tree (Ahakeye Aboriginal Land Trust) area, west of the Stuart Highway. See map p. viii.

nthwerrkamp (E) *n.*
slime
SEE ALSO ntharrengarreng, arntwatherrk[1]

ntwa, **ntwang** (W,T), **nta** (W) *prn.*
you (one person). Generally used as the subject of both transitive and intransitive verbs, although some speakers, particularly those on the east, use *nga* as the subject pronoun with intransitive verbs. See Appendix 1. ◆ Ntwang inety-alhay rwang. (T) *You go and get the firewood.* ◆ Ntwang tyel angkem atyeng. (T) *You're saying bad things about me behind my back.* ◆ Alharlkwemarl alpem. Ntwa apekarl ayeng alharlkwem, mern-they apek ayeng alharlkwek. (St) *Hunt someone away and send them back home. You might hunt me away because of food.*
◆ Mpwankeny-angkwerr ntwa alhem. (M) *You are going through the fresh country.*
= **unta** (E)

ntwarlp (E) (carrying something) slung across or over the shoulder SEE UNDER **intarlp**

ntwarneng (E) *n.*
flying-saucer bush (*Acacia hilliana*)
SEE ALSO pwentarnengayt

ntwarnengayt (E) *n.*
1. blue wattle, leather-leaved colony wattle (*Acacia validinervia*). Shrub about 1.5 m high, with smooth white bark and thick, leathery bluish green leaves.
2. grub from blue wattle [SOME SPEAKERS]
= iylarn

ntwat (W,T) *n.*
1. good-looking person, good-looking young man or woman, handsome, beautiful
◆ Nwernengk arrpenh artwang ntwat anetyam. Artwang ntwatel arrwekety mpwenyel inerl-alhek. (M) *There was another handsome tawny frogmouth man. The handsome tawny frogmouth man came and ran off [with the tawny frogmouth woman].*
2. light-skinned, albino

ntwely-ntwely-irrem (W,T) *vi.*
getting dark, dusk

ntwemerr (T,E), **untemerr** (T,E) *n.*
buck spinifex, bull spinifex (*Triodia longiceps*). A grass that grows in hummocks up to 1.5 m high, and has very sharp bluish green leaves.
◆ Arlter, arrerlp-arrerlp untemerr akngerr. (St) *Buck spinifex is large, white in colour and sharp.*
= welyar, arrangk

ntwerleng (W,E) *n.*
one of the special relationships between people made through ceremony. People in this relationship avoid direct contact with each other.
ntwerleng-ilerrem
become *ntwerleng* for each other (?) ◆ Arelh

atherr arneyel nhwerrem ntwerlengarl ilerrem-penh. (M) *The two women are rubbing their chests together after becoming* ntwerleng *for each other.* (?)
SEE ALSO anyent arrpenh, perlal, thampartey, ntyangkwenng, rteyepertey, alyey², alyaper-warn, ywerlperr

ntwerleperl (W), **rtwerleperl** (W,T), **ntwerleperleng** (W), **rtwerleperlep** (W) *n.*
magpie-lark (*Grallina cyanoleuca*)
= rtey-rtey, kwatyarl rtey-rtey

ntwerlk (T) *n.*
cross (Christian cross) ◆ Ingkart *Jesus* alenh ntwerlkel anwernek ilwek. (T) *The Lord Jesus died for us on the cross.*
SEE ALSO antarlkw

Ntwerrperl (W,T) *n.*
Yundurbulu Range

ntwertety (W,T) *n.*
taking a short-cut ◆ Ntwertety arelh nhakw alhem, arelh arrpenh apek *catch*-em *up*-iletyek. (T) *That woman is taking a short-cut so that she can catch up with the other woman.*
= akwerterrp
= **untertety** (E)
ntwertety alhem (W,T)
take a short-cut, go the most direct way
= akwerterrp alhem
= **untertety alhem** (E)

ntweth-ntweth (W,T), **intweth-intweth** (E) *n.*
1. a person who is neglected or on their own with no family; a person who feels rejected by others ◆ Alhamp akwek ntweth-ntweth aperl-anem. (T) *That little orphan is neglected.* ◆ Ntweth-ntweth ayeng ananem tyerrtyel alhengk-aretyakenh, ntweth-ntweth ingareny war anyent-areny-iperr ananem. (M) *I am feeling neglected, and nobody is taking any notice of me, I'm all on my own.*
2. something that has been discarded or thrown away by others
SEE ALSO arla²

ntweyentwerl (E), **ntweyenterl** (E) *n.*
perennial yellowtop, tall yellowtop (*Senecio magnificus*)
= arengkatwepatwetyenh

ntyangkwenng, ntyangkwelkng (E) *n.*
1. female cousins who are related in a special way to each other through initiation (young man) ceremony; mother and mother-in-law of the inititate. As a mark of respect women related in this way continue to call each other *ntyangkwenng* rather than using personal names for each other. ◆ 'Anyent arrpenh' ntyangkwelkng ilem. (St) Ntyangkwelkng *are also called* 'anyent arrpenh'. ◆ Ntyangkwelkng atyenh nhenharl anep-anem ampwarrp, marl arrpaty ntyangkwelkng anep-anem. (St) *Here is my old* ntyangkwelkng *sitting down, a woman like me, my* ntyangkwelkng. ◆ *We can't* arreyn itniwerl arrangkw. Arrpenhel-arey arreyn itniwetyek. Nyerrerl. Ikirrem ap ntyangkwelkng. (Sa) *We can't call their names. Other people can use their names. It's shameful [to say the name of your* ntyangkwelkng*].* Ntyangkwelkng *are treated with respect.*
SEE ALSO thampartey, anyent arrpenh, perlal, ntwerleng, rteyepertey, alyey², alyaper-warn, ywerlperr, akerlkem
2. a ceremonial firestick (of supplejack wood) that women look after at initiation (young man) ceremonies ◆ Arnang anyer ntyangkwenng — *not any* arna, itya — anyer anyent 'ntyangkwenng' akem. (M) *The ceremonial firestick comes from the supplejack tree — not just from any tree — it is only the supplejack that is called* 'ntyangkwenng'.
3. a substitute word for 'fire' or 'firestick' ◆ Arlterrng-irrerlentyarretyek ahanelh-ila atyeweyay ntyangkwelkng yanh. (Sa) *For goodness sake, take the firestick over there so that you can get warm.*
ntyangkwenng-irrem, ntyangkwelkng-irrem (E) *vi.*
become mother-in-law for a man through initiation (young man) ceremony ◆ *Young fella* atyenhek ntyangkwelkng-irrem wal ntyangkwelkng tha ilem. (St) *If she becomes the mother-in-law for my young fella [my son], well I call [her]* ntyangkwelkng.
SEE ALSO anyent arrpenh-irrem

ntyapentyetyen (W,T) *n.*
pintye-pintye, sweet pillow (*Stemodia viscosa*). A strong-smelling sticky herb with purple flowers that grows about 25–50 cm high. ◆ *Medicine*, alhewelhetyeh, anterel lpwelemel anterel apernelhetyeh. Alhewelhenhelhenh rlkert, artwengkwenng-apert. (N) *This plant is a washing medicine, and it is also mixed up with fat and used as a rubbing medicine. It is used as a washing medicine for people who maybe have colds.*
= iynteng-iynteng

ntyar (W,T), **intyar** (W,T) *n.*
1. white-necked heron (*Ardea pacifica*)
2. white-faced heron (*Ardea novaehollandiae*) ◆ Thep ntyarel arlkwem pwel-pwel. (T) *Herons eat tadpoles.*
= arlkwenth, kamparwengk, ulamp-areny

ntyarl (W,T), **ntyerl** (T,E) *n.*
1. kangaroo leg bone
2. nosebone (worn through the septum) ◆ Ntyerlarl akwernetyart arrwekel. Alharlan altywer-ilem, kel ntyerl anem arrernem. Arelhel inngart. (Sa) *In the old days they used to put a nosebone there. After making a hole in the nose, they'd put a nosebone in the hole. Women did it.*
3. bone used for 'boning' or sorcery ◆ Aherr-penh ntyerl. Renh ultaketyam arrerlp-iletyam. *Law* akngerr ra anek. (St) *The* ntyerl *was from the kangaroo. It was broken [from the kangaroo bone] and sharpened. There was a lot of Law associated with it.*
SEE ALSO marrapernt, melyalker, irrengernt, ngerl
4. stone point in the handle of a woomera

ntyarleyarleng, ntyarleyarley (W) *n.*
1. flat-leaved Hakea, dogwood Hakea (*Hakea macrocarpa*). Tree to 5 m high, with twisted branches, corky fissured bark and flat leathery leaves.
2. fork-leaved corkwood, long-leaved corkwood (*Hakea divaricata*). Tree to 7 m high, with twisted branches, corky fissured bark and yellow-green flowers. Leaves are branched or forked.
3. the flower of various Hakeas [SOME SPEAKERS]. Also referred to as *ngkwarl ntyarleyarleng*. ◆ *Self* akin ntyarleyarley, kenh ntywey akenh *self* akin. Ntyarleyarley anwengkerr akerl-alhek. Ngkwarl. Kenh ntywey akenh ahakeyart arlkwerrng, thelelherl-anem. Lweren anthwerr athew. (N) *The flat-leaved Hakea is different from the corkwood — they are both distinct. We get honey from the Hakea. The corkwood has sweet juice like the* ahakey *plum, that drips down. That's how it really is.*
SEE ALSO ngapalhwerrk, ntywey

ntyarrengarreng (W) slime on water SEE UNDER **ntharrengarreng**

ntyarrkwer (W,T) *n.*
neck bone, lower part of the back of the neck. Also referred to as *ker ntyarrkwer*. ◆ Tha ngwenh ntyarrkwer ltwaketyenh! (T) *I'll break your neck!*
SEE ALSO untyarrkwer

ntyarrng-anyem (E), **ntyarrng-aynem** (E)
sneeze SEE UNDER **ntyerrng-anyem**

-ntyel, -tyel (W) *ending*
1. Shows where something moves from, is moved from, or comes from; away from, off, from, out of, out from. Often follows the *+eng* ending. ◆ Yanh-**tyel** arelh map ina alhek alewatyerr apalenthwetyek. (M) *From there the women went to look for sand goannas.*
2. from the time of, since ◆ Awenk apel anwern rntwetyartel akwekeng-**ntyel** anwernenh apernetyart, apernetyart anwernenh. (N) *When we were teenage girls we used to dance, from when we were small they used to paint us up.*
3. Shows what something is made of or the source or origin of something. ◆ Rtey-rteyel mer mpwarem anthwerrngeng-**ntyel**. (N) *Mudlarks make their nests from mud.* ◆ Alhernter kwenh anpernerrenty itya, kenh tyerrty akenh Anengkerreng-**ntyel** anpernerrem. Anengkerrel anpernek Anengkerreng-**ntyel** anpernerrem kenh alhernter akenh anpernenty ityarl. Apal wararl alhernteran. (M) *White people don't have a skin system, whereas Aboriginal people get their skin system from the Dreaming. The Dreaming named [everyone] as relations, and people got the way of calling each other as relations from there. White people don't have a skin system. White people don't know.*
SEE ALSO -they
+eng-ntyel (W,T) = **-ntyel**

ntyelpeny (W,T), **ntyerlpeny** (W,T), **iynterlpeny** (E) *n.*
1. Richard's pipit (*Anthus novaeseelandiae*)
2. black-fronted dotterel (*Elseyornis melanops*)
• SEE ALSO kaperl-kaperl, aleraperap

ntyemeny, intyemeny *n.*
1. ruby saltbush (*Enchylaena tomentosa*). Soft greyish shrub which grows about 70 cm high and which has bright yellow or red fruits.
2. the edible fruits of the ruby saltbush ◆ Anwern arlkwetyart *red one* akwek map. *Seed.* Anwern arlkwerl-apetyart arlkwerl-apetyart arrkenel. Kapert *red one* ilenh-ilenharl arrpenh. Intyemeny apel mern arlkwenh-arlkwenh. (N) *We used to eat the little red fruits. We used to go along eating them for fun. Another [similar] one is used as a red hair dye.* Intyemeny *fruits are edible.*

ntyengwenty whitish yellow ochre SEE UNDER **ngwenty-ngwenty**

ntyenp *n.*
dry fruit of the native currant, native citrus, *ahakey* ◆ Ahakey, antyerrkarl irrek renh ilem, 'ntyenp'. (T) *Bush plum fruits that have gone dry are called* 'ntyenp'.
SEE ALSO unemarnt, ahakey
ntyenp-irrem *vi.*
go dry (fruit of native currant, native citrus)

ntyeny (E) *n.*
red mallee (*Eucalyptus pachyphylla*). A tree to

6 m high, with smooth pink bark, red buds and yellow flowers. Grows in spinifex country.
CAN SOUND A BIT LIKE antyeny *'old person'*
ntyenyengkwarl (E) *n.*
honey from the red mallee
ntyer (T) *n.*
seeds of the dogwood, *awenth, akerlperr*
ntyererlk-akem (E) *vt.*
gut an emu
SEE ALSO anenem
ntyerl (T,E) kangaroo leg bone SEE UNDER **ntyarl**
ntyerlkem (W) *n.*
a type of grasshopper
SEE ALSO arwekert-arwekert, intelty, arlwety[1]
Ntyerlkem (W) *n.*
name of a place and the location of an outstation on Amburla Station
ntyerlp[1], **intyerlp** (E), **iynterlp** (E) *n.*
hot ashes or earth (used for cooking or healing) ◆ Ura intyerlpel itetyek, mern apek item intyerlpel. (St) *Food is cooked in the hot ashes.* ◆ Mern arrtyem iynterlpel. (Sa) *Cooking the food in the hot ashes.*
= rtwap
SEE ALSO arnmeny, arlpa[1], atnmanth, awerrth, amerrk[2]
= **iynterlp** (E)
ntyerlp-irrem, **intyerlp-irrem** (E), **iynterlp-irrem** (E) *vi.*
burn down (fire) ◆ Rrwek amparr ntyerlp-irrey rwang. (M) *Wait till the fire burns down.* ◆ Ntyerlp-irrekeyay kel ntyerlpel itetyek anem kwenh. (St) *The fire has burned down, so now things can be cooked in the hot ashes.*
ntyerlp-ilem, **intyerlp-ilem** (E), **iynterlp-ilem** (E) *vt.*
make a fire, stoke up a fire ◆ Ura tha ntyelp-ilek mernek. (St) *I am stoking the fire up to cook the food.* ◆ Yerrakwerrek ntyerlp-ilem. Kel ntyerlp anem yanh kwenh mern itey ant anem. (St) *Stoking the fire up to cook the bush onions. And then, when it has burned down, [we'll] cook the food.*
CAN SOUND A BIT LIKE antyelp-ilem *'bust something'*
ntyerlp[2] (W,T), **intyerlp** (W,T) *n.*
water in a claypan (?); drop or drip of water (note Warlpiri *yinjirlpi*). Also referred to as *kwaty ntyerlp.* ◆ Kwaty intyerlp anyep-anyem warleng akerneng apek. (T) *Water is dripping from the house, maybe from the roof.*
= awal
SEE ALSO irnmerr
ntyerlpeny (W,T) Australian (Richard's) pipit SEE UNDER **ntyelpeny**
Ntyerrkekenh (E) *n.*
name of a rockhole near Aniltji (Boundary Bore)
ntyerrm, **intyerrm** (E), **ntyerrp** (W) *n.*
1. seeds of the dogwood, *awenth, akerlperr* ◆ Intyerrm apert-atwemel apwert alyerel, mern apeng-areny weth-lkwer, ngkweyang, alyer. (Sa) *The dogwood tree seed is crushed with a grinding stone called* 'alyer'*, and that edible seed from the kurrajong tree,* ngkweyang, *is too.* ◆ Akerlperr akenh arlkwerrarlirretyart rwelarl atyerremel, atyerrewarretyartarl akerlperr akemel arnkan. Kenh ntyerrp akenh *self* akin. Ntyerrp nhenh antywerrkarlewarretyartam. Akerlperr alyaly atwetyart, irntel apwertel atwerl-anek. Anterrng *milk*-arteh *nice one.* Athemem athetyartem mwerr angerr anthwerr. Lweren kwa arrwekeleny map *live*-irrek. (N) *The green seeds of the dogwood tree were cooked in the fire after they had been picked raw. The* ntyerrp *is separate again. The* ntyerrp *used to be mixed up with water. The* akerlperr *was smashed up with a rock. It goes like milk and tastes really good. It was ground up. That's how the olden-time people lived.*
2. dry dogwood seeds
3. sweet milky drink made from dogwood seeds
SEE ALSO atnma, apal[1], artwengarr, kertaty, alyaly, tartaty, lyarr
4. old thin emu ◆ Intyerrm ampwirremarl ilem — *no* anter. Intyerrm anem irrem. Ankerr ra ampwirrenty 'intyerrm'. Arwerl ikwerenh inngart — ratherrarl akngkanek mer anyent ikwerel. Ankerr ampwirrenty, 'intyerrm' renh ilem. (Sa) Intyerrm *is what you call an old, thin emu — no fat. An emu that has got old is 'intyerrm'. That's the emu's tree [the dogwood] — in the creation time they both came from the same place. [So] an old emu is called* 'intyerrm'. ◆ Iwenheng ker nhenh unta ntyerrman angetyek, ker anter angetyakenh? (T) *Why did you bring this skinny emu, why didn't you get a fat one?*
Ntyerrmekwerlang (T), **Ntyerrpekwerlang** (T) *n.*
Yindjirbi Range (note Warlpiri *-kurlangu* 'belonging to'). Dogwood seed Dreaming. See map p. viii.
ntyerrng-anyem, **ntyarrng-anyem** (E), **ntyarrng-aynem** (E) *vi.*
sneeze. It is believed that people may sneeze if a stranger is coming. ◆ Alha arrwengkelth-penh ikelh-ikelh-ilem wal ntyarrng-anyem. (St) *If [your] nose is blocked up with snot from a*

cold, well you sneeze.
SEE ALSO rltwaty, anyem1

ntyerrp (W) dogwood seeds SEE UNDER **ntyerrm**

ntyeth (W), **intyeth**, **iynteth** (E), **iyntety** (E) *n.*
spark, sparks. Also referred to as *rwang ntyeth, ura iynteth* etc. ◆ Iynteth ura unarnpemarl-ketyaw. *Look out for the sparks which are flying out.*
= intety
SEE ALSO lyenenty
iynteth ngkem (E), **iynteth rnkem** (E)
spark up, spark jump out
= intety-intety-irrem
iynteth-iynteth-irrem (E), **iyntety-irrem** (E) *vi.*
= **iynteth ngkem**

ntyew, **ntyewey**, **intyew**, **intyewey** *n.*
solidified blood, coagulated blood, blood clot, scab. Also referred to as *ker ntyewey.* ◆ Ker alhwang ntyew antywetyeh. (M) *Drinking the clotted [kangaroo] blood.* ◆ Arlkwem renh, mwerr akngerr. Alhwa rarl purt-irrekarl ntyewey. Ker mwerr angerr renh arlkwem. (St) *It is really nice to eat. Blood that has gone into a solid lump is* ntyewey. *It is really good to eat.*
= tewey
SEE ALSO awerrp1, alhwa
ntyew-irrem, **ntyewey-irrem**, **intyew-irrem**, **intyewey-irrem** *vi.*
coagulate, solidify (blood), clot ◆ Arengkel apek utnhemarl, irrtyartel apek atanthem, wal ntyeweyel anem artem. Ntyewey-ntyewey anem irrem. Rlterrk anem irrem ntyewey-ntyewey anem. (St) *If a person gets bitten by a dog, or speared with a spear, then a scab forms over the wound. The blood solidifies and goes hard.*

ntyeyapert (E) *n.*
bull ant (*Myrmecia nigriceps* (reproductive))
= arrengarlp, atyank, tyekarnparnp1

ntyurtenty (E), **ntywertenty** (E) *n.*
old man saltbush (*Atriplex nummularia*)

ntywa (W,T), **ntywang** (W,T) *n.*
back of the neck, nape of neck, top of the shoulder ◆ Mwelek angep-angem ntywel rrwey akwek. (M) *The mother is carrying the little boy on the top of her shoulders.* ◆ Artwang nhenhel ntywangel angety-alpem ker. (N) *This man is carrying the kangaroo home around the back of his neck.*
= **untya** (E)
ker ntywang (W,T)
meat from the back part of a kangaroo's neck
ntywel angem (W,T), **ntywangel angem** (W)
carry something on the top of the shoulder or round the back of the neck (angem *'carry', 'take'*)
SEE ALSO intwerl angem, alpalyel angem, intarlp angem, ntwarlp angem, anhwert angem, aylpwar angem
= **untyel angem** (E)

Ntywelarlangem (W) *n.*
name of a place south of Yuelamu (Mt Allan) airstrip

ntywem1 (W,T) *vi.*
warm oneself by the fire or in the sun ◆ Rwel ntywem nyerlel. (M) *Warming [yourself] by the fire in the cold weather.*
SEE ALSO ampem2
CAN SOUND A BIT LIKE antywem *'drink'*
= **untyem**1 (E)
ntywelh-ilem (W,T) *vt.*
warm something up, heat something up ◆ Ker ntywelh-ilem rwel arelh yanhel. (T) *The woman is warming the meat up on the fire.*

ntywem2 (W,T), **iyntwem** (E) *adv.*
facing away from someone or something; going in a direction away from or opposite to someone or something ◆ Arelh arrtyanem ntywem-athek. (M) *The woman is running away [from me].* ◆ Nta ntywem alhem, nta lwarr-athehem apety-alpem. (M) *You go in a direction away from me and then you come back towards me.*
SEE ALSO ularr
CAN SOUND A BIT LIKE antywem *'drink'*
= **untyem**2 (E)
ntywem-irrem (W,T), **iyntwem-irrem** (E) *vi.*
turn away, turn your back on someone; face away from someone or something ◆ Artwang ntywem-irrek artwang arrpenh-kety. (T) *The man turned his back on the other man.* ◆ Ilek-kety unta arrwirnt-irretyel, iyntwem-irrem? (Sa) *Why are you getting sulky and turning your back on me?*
= **untyem-irrem** (E)
ntywem-ilem (W,T), **iyntwem-ilem** (E) *vt.*
make someone or something go backwards
= **untyem-ilem** (E)
ntywem-athek (W,T), **iyntwem-athek** (E) *adv.*
facing away from someone or something; going in a direction away from or opposite to someone or something
= **untyem-athek** (E)
ntywemek-ntywem (W,T), **iyntwemek-iyntwem** (E) *adv.*
back-to-back, facing away from each other ◆ Ntywemek-ntywem anwengkerr arlkwetyeh ker, mern. (M) *We are all eating the meat and the food back-to-back, facing away from each other.*

= **untyemek-untyem** (E)
ntywemarrel (W,T) *adv.*
without looking back ◆ Ntywemarrel alhep-alhem, *no* anngarelhem apek. (T) *[He] goes without looking back.*

ntywenart (W) *n.*
heavy-soil handflower, tobacco handflower (*Goodenia lunata*). A herb about 10 cm high with yellow flowers and leaves shaped a bit like an emu's foot.
= ankerringk, ankerr-ankerr

ntywerr (T) water SEE UNDER **untyerr**

ntywerr anyenem (E) mash certain types of fruit up with water SEE UNDER **untyerr atnyenem**

ntywerrkem *vt.*
mash certain types of bush fruits up with water ◆ Ahakey ntywerrkem antey. Atyetarl irreman, *not really cooked one no* — atyet-irremarl. Ahakeyan. Renh anem kwatyel-anteyarl ilem renh. Kwatyel ilem, Ntyerrkwem renh kwatyek. Ntyerrkwem antey ankwerleyan. (St) *The* ahakey *bush plum is mashed up in water. When it gets a little bit soft — not really ripe — soft. It is mixed with water and mashed up. The* ankwerley *plum bush fruit is mashed up as well.*
= untyerr anyenem

ntywert (T) *n.*
skewer used for cooking bush tomato fruit (*Solanum chippendalei*)
= pernampal

ntywertenty (E) old man saltbush SEE UNDER **ntyurtenty**

ntywety (W,T) *n.*
hot earth, warmth, warm ◆ Rwang yanh anwekantherr arraw-ilay anwantherr ntywety anetyek. Irrerntek. (T) *Stoke that fire up for us so that we can sit down warm. It's cold.* ◆ Aherr angkek, 'Nthenh-warn ayeng alhey ntywety-warn?' (M) *The kangaroo said, 'Where can I find a warm place?'*
SEE ALSO awerrth
= **untyety** (E)
ntywety-irrem (W,T) *vi.*
get warm or hot (person or place) ◆ Tyerrty ntywety-irrem rwangel — rwel anem nyelarl arrewem-penh ntywety-irrem anem. (T) *People get warm by the fire — they get warm sitting by the fire after shivering with cold.*
SEE ALSO irrernt-irrem
= **untyety-irrem** (E)
ntywety-ilem (W,T) *vt.*
make something hot, warm something up
= **untyety-ilem** (E)

ntywey *n.*
1. northern corkwood, bootlace tree (*Hakea chordophylla*). Tree to 5 m high, with twisted branches, corky fissured bark and yellow flowers.
2. fork-leaved corkwood, long-leaved corkwood (*Hakea divaricata*). Tree to 7 m high, with twisted branches, corky fissured bark and yellow-green flowers. Leaves are branched or forked.
3. honey from the northern corkwood and the fork-leaved corkwood [SOME SPEAKERS]
◆ Ngkwarl ntywey arratem twern-rlwer. (M) *Corkwood honey [flowers] come out in the summer.* ◆ Ntywey arrernetyart, akem renh arrernetyart, twernel ampetyeh. Twernel ampetyek, akerl-anek akerl-anek ahern arrernelhalhetyart. *Jam*-arteh am irrety-alhem. Arlkwetyetyart arntap-warn thelelherlapetyart, awantyerlapetyart. Ngkwarl ntywey apel ntywey, ntyey. Anganekarl. Awantyerl-apek awantyerl-apek peleth! (N) *We used to pick the corkwood flowers and lay them out in the sun to heat up. We'd lay them on the ground in the heat of the sun. Then the honey would go like jam. We used to eat it out of bark containers. The corkwood came from the country. We go along sucking on the honey, please!*
SEE ALSO ntyarleyarleng
ntyweyamp *n.*
honey from the northern corkwood. Also referred to as *ngkwarl ntyweyamp*.
= ntyweyangkwarl
SEE ALSO tyan
ntyweyangkwarl (W) *n.* = **ntyweyamp**
ntywey aperrk *n.*
burnt bark of the northern corkwood (aperrk '*charcoal*'). The burnt bark of the corkwood tree is used to rub on babies to stop them from sweating and to rub on their foreheads to stop them burping. ◆ Ntywey aperrkel apernem kwer akwek ahenty tywen-akert. (T) *Little kids with sore throats are rubbed with burnt corkwood bark.*

nwanth (W,T) *n.*
scrub
SEE ALSO werrk
= **utnanth** (E)
nwanth-nwanth (W,T) *n.*
scrubby country
= **unanth-unanth**
artety nwanth (W,T)
mulga scrub (artety '*mulga*') ◆ Artety nwanth-angkwerr anwengkerr alhey yerrampeh. (M) *Let's go through the mulga scrub looking for*

honeyants.
= **artety utnanth** (E)

nwanthem (W,T) *vt.*
not share food or drink; eat or drink greedily ◆ Anyentel arlkwem wal nwanthem nta tyerrty arrpenh nwanthem. (M) *You might be eating on your own and not sharing with others.* ◆ Atyengety nta nwanthemel arlkwem anthety-kwenyel, ankerlel. (T) *You're eating greedily and not sharing anything with me.*
SEE ALSO ahanthem, ankeyel arlkwem
= **unanthem** (E)
nwanthelhem (W,T) *vi.*
eat or drink everything so there is nothing left, not save anything; finish food or drink in one sitting ◆ Nwanthelhem kwenh, ker arrernetyakenh. (T) *Eating everything and not putting any meat aside.*
= **unanthelhem** (E)

nwarremantyerr (W) black-tailed native-hen SEE UNDER **narremantyerr**

nwathet (W), **nathat** (T) *n.*
flower of the mulga, *artety,* and of the witchetty bush, *anyem*
= **utnathat** (E)

nwatyaker (E) type of lizard SEE UNDER **natyaker**

Nwengarray *n.*
female skin name corresponding to *Ngwarray* (note Warlpiri *Nungarrayi*). See diagram p. 744.
SEE ALSO Ngwarray

nwenty-nwenty (W,T) noisily SEE UNDER **nenty-nenty**

nwernengk, unernengk (E), **nwerningk** (E) *n.*
tawny frogmouth (*Podargus strigoides*) ◆ Thep nwernengk kwenyel angkerl-anem, *'Hmmmm hmmmm'*. (M) *The tawny frogmouth sings out in the night, 'Hmmmm hmmmm'.* ◆ Nwernengk yanh mern pwarl arlka arlkwem, yatenhel, mern altyey arlka. (N) *The tawny frogmouth eats bush bananas, that sort of thing, and bush banana leaves.* ◆ Arrakert angerr lthel-lthel an annga angerr. (M) *It [the tawny frogmouth] has a big hairy beak and big eyes.* ◆ Thep unernengk, rltimpelarl arrangkw-artekarl anerl-anem, artety rltimpel. (St) *The tawny frogmouth sits amongst the bits of bark, and it's as if they aren't there, you can hardly see them.*

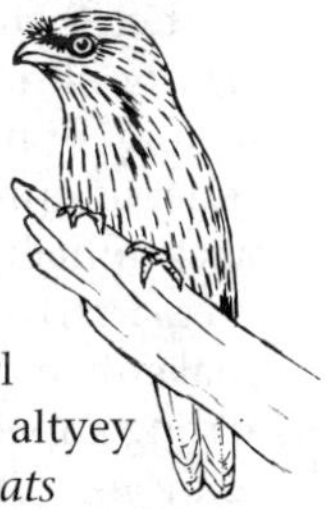

= uring
SEE ALSO arrthwarrthw
Nwernengk (W,T) *n.*
name of a hill in the Anmatjira Range area. See map p. viii.

nwernp (W) red-backed kingfisher SEE UNDER **rlwernp**

nwernternenty (W,T) *n.*
kurdaitcha, kurdaitcha man, ritual executioner ◆ Nwernternenty, artwang apetyem atwetyew. Nwernternenty ra antem apetyem, ahelheh irrpety-alhem, *and* mer arrpenhant arratem. *Magic one* kwa. Aheh akwel apetyem, atwetyeh tyerrty alenh, mer arrpenh atwerl-alpem, *and* alpemek. (M) *The* nwernternenty *is a man who comes to kill people. He comes along, goes underground and then comes out at another place. He's a magic one. He comes to fight, to kill particular people at another place, and then goes back again.*
= ngkekern, rlwarlp, urlaylp, inenty

Nwert (W) *n.*
name of a place east of Yuelamu (Mt Allan) community

nwertal (T) *n.*
ten dollar note (maybe from English 'new dollar')

nwey (T) *n.*
woma, sandhill python (*Aspidites ramsayi*)
= ahenenh
SEE ALSO ileway
= **uney** (E)

nya, tnya (E) *n.*
1. dead
2. almost dead
SEE ALSO nyerrem
CAN SOUND A BIT LIKE anya[1] *'father'*; anya[2] *'louse'*
nyant, tnyant (E) *adv.*
1. (doing something) to the death; killing someone or something
2. (doing something) almost to the death
3. (doing something) a lot or excessively
nyekant, tnyekant (E) *adv.* = **nyant**
◆ Ker apek tha atwek tnyekant. Tnyant atwem. (St) *I hit the animal till it was dead. I killed it.*
nyant atwem, tnyant atwem (E)
1. kill someone; fight to the death (atwem *'hit', 'kill'*)
2. just about kill someone; fight almost to the death ◆ Nyant atwem artwel anewelekw. (M) *Her husband practically killed her.* ◆ Nyant atwem alhwewarn, alhwa irret anem irrem, kapetarl atwem. (T) *Just about killing that person, hitting them on the head till the blood comes, till the blood flows.*
= nyey-nyey atwem
SEE ALSO irrewaly atwem, kwarterrem

nyant atherrem, **tnyant atherrem** (E)
kill yourself laughing (atherrem *'laugh'*)
◆ Nan angkweyek atherrek, nyant. (T) *[We] killed ourselves laughing at old granny.*
◆ Arrkenel nyant atherrem, tyerrty arrpenhek apek nyant atherrem. (T) *Killing [yourself] laughing, maybe at another person.*
= ampwerrk-ilwem

nyant arlkwem, **tnyant arlkwem** (E)
overeat, eat a lot after feeling hungry, stuff yourself with food (arlkwem *'eat'*) ◆ 'Angayel tha nyant arlkwern', alakenh ilelhem. 'Ker tha angayel nyant arlkwern, mern arlka. Angayel angerr ayeng awelhirrem.' (M) *'I really stuffed myself with food', that's what you say. 'I ate a lot of meat and bread because I was feeling very hungry.'* ◆ Ayengarl angayak-irrekarl — thang nyant arlkwetyew. (T) *I'm so hungry — I'm going to stuff myself.*
SEE ALSO nyerrem, arnterr arlkwem, ahanthem, arrwer-ilem

nyek-nyek-ilem (T,E), **tnyek-tnyek-ilem** (E) *vt.*
nearly kill someone; (fight) almost to the death ◆ Nyek-nyek-ilem, nyant atwemel, kapert tyarrp-ilemel. Ankwa anem ra intem, rlkert ra awelhemel. (T) *[Somebody] almost beats him to death, and splits his head open. Then he lies down, because he's feeling sick.*
◆ Ampa akwek tnyek-tnyek-ilemel atwem ampa akwekel yanh. 'Akuny kwenh — rlkert-rlkert-ilemel atwetyal impa.' (St) *That little kid is almost killing the other little kid. 'The poor thing — leave her alone, don't hit her and make her sick.'*

nyam-nyam *n.* [BABY TALK]
food (from English 'yum yum' (?))
= meny, nan2, nyany1
SEE ALSO mern

nyany1 *n.* [BABY TALK]
1. food
2. meat
3. water
= meny, nan2, nyam-nyam
SEE ALSO mern, kwaty, ker

nyany2 *n.kin*
1. mother's mother; grandmother, granny
2. mother's mother's brother or sister; great-uncle, great-aunt
3. a woman's daughter's child; grandchild; grandson, granddaughter
4. a person's sister's daughter's child; great-niece, great-nephew
5. cousin's wife or husband, cousin of husband or wife
6. particular relations with the same skin as a person's *nyany*
7. the country and Dreamings belonging to a person's *nyany*
8. mother's mother etc. [BABY TALK] ◆ Nhenhan nyany atyengenh. (T) *This is my granny.* ◆ Tha apek ngenh anpernem nyany — Mpetyan uthen Kemarr uthen apek. (St) *I might call you granny — a Mpetyan and a Kemarr [i.e. Mpetyan talking to Kemarr].* ◆ Tyap-rnem mperlker-rnem. Than aretyart nyanyel-rnem aperleyel-rnem arlkwerrerl-anenty, tyerremp-arey. (Sa) *The grubs are white. I used to see my grannies and my father's mothers eating the tyerremp.* ◆ Ampa akwek ra anem urrem-urrem. Kel angerr-awern irrem, angkakert anem irrem nhenh-lkwer rlterrk anem irreynepeynem, atyet-atyet weth. Rlterrk anem ra irreynepeynem, kel angkethen antey rlterrk-irrem. Iterlarem anem ra atyemey apek nyany apek, arrengey apek, mam apek akngey kwerenh. Urrem-urremek-amparr. (St) *Little babies do not understand properly at first. Then they get a bit bigger and they start to talk, and the soft part [the fontanelle] hardens up. That gets hard, and then their talking gets stronger as well. Then they know their mother's father, or their granny, or their father's father, their mother or their father. At first they don't know things properly.*
SEE ALSO menh-menh, ipmenh

nyanyengkw (E) *n.kin*
your *nyany* ◆ Nyanyengkw-warl alhay. (St) *Go to your granny.*

nyanyikw (E), **nyanyeyekw** (E) *n.kin*
his/her/their *nyany*

nyany-nheng (E) *n.kin*
a group of two or more people related to each other as *nyany* ◆ Kenh tha ngenh apawenhem, 'Ntwa iwenharl kwenh?' 'Kemarrarl ayeng kwenh.' Ntwan ilelhem. Alakenh anpernerremarlan. Wal nyany-nheng anpernerrem. (St) *And then I [Mpetyan] ask you, 'What [skin] are you?' 'I am a Kemarr.' That's what you say. That's how people call each other as relations. Well we call each other granny and grandchild.*

nyany-intyerr (E) *n.kin* = **nyany-nheng**

nyany-nheng-arey (E)
a group of more than two people related to each other as *nyany*

nyany-nheng atherr (E) *n.kin*
a person together with one of their *nyany*

nyany-ankethenh (E) *n.kin*
1. having a close *nyany* still alive
2. someone who is always with their *nyany*

SEE ALSO -ankethenh

nyany-parety (E) *n.kin*

respectful or 'sorry' way of talking about someone's *nyany*

SEE ALSO -parety

nyarew *n.*

Horsfield's bronze-cuckoo (*Chrysococcyx basalis*) ◆ Nyarew angkerl-anem rlpwerel, rlpwerel arnerl-apem, arnang antarlkwel apek. Kwenyel *all night* angkerl-anem nyarew, aherlkelh-ilem nyarewel. (N) *The Horsfield's bronze-cuckoo sings out from hollow trees, or maybe from a forked branch. The cuckoo sings out all night, and makes the daylight come.*

= anatyelepwerray

SEE ALSO urrempen urrempen

nyarl (W,E) *n.*

military dragon lizard (*Ctenophorus isolepis*)

= kwerleparr

SEE ALSO tyalep

nyarrapeng (T,E) *n.*

cat

= pwethekat, mangw, rlwatert, angay

SEE ALSO annga atherrk, meyaw-meyaw

nyek-nyek-ilem SEE UNDER **nya** 'dead, almost dead'

nyely-ilem (T,E) *vt.*

show something to someone, lift something up to show someone ◆ Nhenh apek tha atyenh mantarr apek nyely-ilem, *show*-em-ilemel. (St) *I'm showing my clothes.*

CAN SOUND A BIT LIKE anyelh-ilem *'drop something'*

nyemal (E) *n.*

long-haired rat (*Rattus villosissimus*)

SEE ALSO thakwer, kwetang

Nyemanyem (W) *n.*

name of a hill in the Stuart Bluff Range area

nyemp (E) *n.*

the smell of rain ◆ Nyempant ap intyernem arleng, kwatyelarl lernem-penh. (St) *After the rain has fallen you can smell it from a distance.*

nyengk, nyingk (E) *n.*

zebra finch, waxbill (*Taeniopygia guttata*) ◆ Nyengk angkerreperrem kwatyel-arleng. Tyerrtyel awerlp-awem renh, nyengkarl angkem. (St) *Zebra finches make a twittering sound near water. People hear them twittering.*

= tyeyek

nyengk rnternenh (E) *n.*

Australian hobby (a type of bird) (*Falco longipennis*) (lit. 'zebra finch hunter')

= ingkel iylkenh

SEE ALSO alekaper, anthep-anthep

nyengk-nyengk (W) *n.*

fat from the lower body of the emu; an emu that is fatty in the lower part of the body ◆ Ker ankerr nyengk-nyengk. (M) *The emu is fat in the lower part of its body.*

SEE ALSO ankerr

Nyengkweleny (W) *n.*

name of a very small rockhole to the west of Aileron

Nyepwart, Nyepwat (W) *n.*

name of a hill in the Stuart Bluff Range area

nyerlp (E) *n.* [RESPECT LANGUAGE]

axe

= alenyakenyak, iylpwer arternenh

SEE ALSO ilep[1]

nyerr *n.*

1. shyness, shame, embarrassment ◆ Nyerr anetyangel unta arnkatyel ileynepeynem. Nyerr apek ngkwenh anetyangel arnkatyel nyerr-irretyang. (Sa) *You don't get embarrassed, you just keep on talking confidently. You don't get shamed.*

2. behaving with the appropriate degree of respect, or showing good manners in terms of Aboriginal Law

= apwer

SEE ALSO lwereny, alhewer

artep nyerr

shamefully (artep *'back'*)

nyerrel *n.*

something that makes people feel shamed or embarrassed; bad manners ◆ Nyerrel ayeng anem, menty. (St) *I'm feeling shamed, I'm not going to do it.* ◆ Nyerrel-ayerr apwer-irrerlentyarr arem-kety ayeng kwenh. (Sa) *It's shameful that [those avoidance kin of mine] are looking at me.* ◆ Nyerrelay, alhernterel arem-arleng arlkwerlek. (M) *It's shameful for white people to see you eating.*

nyerr-irrem *vi.*

be nervous, shy, ashamed, or embarrassed ◆ Tyerrty alethangeng nyerr-irrem, lwereny-kety. (T) *Feeling shy because of the strangers.* ◆ Artep ayeng nyerr-irrem, arnterrarl arerrirreperrem. Tharl atwek-penh ayeng nyerr-irrem anem artep. (St) *I am feeling shamed [in my back], because [people] are staring hard at me. After I had a fight I am feeling shamed.* ◆ Nyerr-irrem kwenh ayeng arrakertarl aremeng arrpenh yanhel. (St) *I'm feeling shamed because that person over there is staring at my mouth.*

= lwereny-irrem, apwer-irrem, pwerep-irrem

nyerralth *n.*
a person who is timid, shy, ashamed or embarrassed ◆ Lyetant kalty-irretyel, ampa nyerralth. (Sa) *He's just started learning things [at school], he's very timid.* ◆ Tyerrty yanh nyerralth, angketyakenh arrpenhek nyerralthar! irreynepeynem. (St) *That person is shy, they don't talk to others because they get shy.* ◆ Tyerrty yanh nyerralth, war alhewer alherl-anetyakenh, nyerralth. Kwenel-antey anep-anem. (St) *That person is shy, they don't just go about freely. They're shy and they sit down inside all the time.*
= pweralth

nyerrel anthem
make someone feel shamed, shy or embarrassed (anthem '*give*') ◆ Unta ayeng nyerrel anthem, aremel unta nyerrel anthem. Wal ayeng nyerr-irrem ngkwengety. (St) *You are making me feel shamed by looking at me. Well I'm feeling shy of you.*
= pwerel anthem

nyerr rrpwarelhem (W,T), **nyerr urrparelhem** (E), **nyerr iparelhem** (E)
make amends, apologise (?) (rrpwarelhem '*wipe something off self*') ◆ Ayeng apekarl ahel-irrek, nyerr tha iparem ngkweltyel anem. Nyerr iparelhem ayeng, ngkwelty anem tha anthem, ayengarl ahel angkek-penh. (St) *Supposing I got angry, then I can make amends by giving the person some money. I apologise and give the person some money, after I have spoken angrily.* ◆ Nyerr nta rrpwarelhem thametheng apek nta inemarl-penh. Mern apek *or* ker apek nta inemarl-penh. Nta rrpwarelhem antey ilelhem. 'Iy ayeng — ityam *no* tha anyenngel-inek kwenh.' Angkety alenh *turn*-em-ilem, rrpwarelhemem. (M) *You apologise maybe after you have got something. Maybe you got some food or some meat. Then you apologise for yourself. 'I don't know — I didn't steal anything.' You set the story straight.* ◆ Nyerrel urrparelhey, nyerrarl irrem-kety. Nyerrel urrparelhetyek alha. Angketyek arrpenhek, 'Arrangkw kwenh ayeng. Nyerrel ayeng urrparelhetyek apetyek ilelhetyek'. Mwerr anem, *friend* anem. (Sa) *Make amends so that you don't feel shamed. Go and make amends. Go and talk to the other one and say, 'It wasn't me. I've come to tell you and to apologise'. Then they're friends again and everything is fine.*
SEE ALSO rlwaty angkem, urlaty angkem

nyerrem (W,T) *vi.*
pass away, die ◆ Aherr nyerrem, nyerrem pwety-angkwarr an tyerrtyel atwem. *Self* yang nyerrem akin. Anwantherr nyerrem akin. (T) *Kangaroos die in the bush, if a person has wounded them. They die of their own accord as well. We die too.*
SEE ALSO nya, ilwem, uyerrem, ywerrem, ahap-irrem, arrangkw-irrem

Nyerrey (E) *n.*
name of waterhole north of Wilora (Stirling) community

nyert-nyert *n.*
dung beetle (?) ◆ Nyert-nyerteley kartelam irrarnp-irrarnp-ilerl-apem nyert-nyert yanhan atwert-atwert, irnngang kwa nyert-nyert lweren athew yanh. (N) *The dung beetle is a sort of small round maggoty thing that [burrows into] the shit and makes it scatter.*

nyetempwer (W) *n.*
1. desert Flinders grass, bunch panic (*Yakirra australiensis* var. *australiensis*). A grass about 15 cm high, with reddish-coloured leaves.
= kwarrety, arlepenh, arrepeny
2. bunch Paspalidium (*Paspalidium rarum*). A grass about 20 cm high, which is often found around mulga. ◆ Nyetempwer arnwety athenh-athenh, kelh arrernenhernenh, tamp-arteh mparenharenh kelh. (N) Nyetempwer *is a seed that is ground up and made into a seedcake, similar to a damper.* ◆ Yerr mapel akwel nyetempwer kwetyerl-apem. (N) *Supposedly ants collect the* nyetempwer *seeds.*
• = kwarrety, tywaynt

nyetyep (T,E), **nyetyeng** (E), **nyetyep-nyetyep** (T,E), **nyety-nyety** (E), **nyetyeng-anyety** (E), **nyetyepeng-anyety** (T), **nyetyepeng-anyetyep** (W,T) *n.*
cubbyhouse ◆ Nyety-nyetyel anwantherran anetyart, nyety-nyetyek mern arlkwerreperrerl. (Sa) *We used to sit in our cubbyhouses, eating food.* ◆ Arnkentyan inekenh *self*-arl nyetyep-nyetyep *that one,* arrkenel ina. Arlweker *self* anteyarl, arnkentyan akwel inekenh *self* anteyarl. Arnkenty nyetyep war. (St) *They [the boys] had their own separate 'single boys' cubbyhouse where they played. The 'single girls' camp was separate as well, and the boys' cubbyhouse was separate.*
= alyetyepengalyety
SEE ALSO antyweng-antywa, mereng-amer, arnkentyeng-arnkenty, arlwekereng-arlweker, mey-mey[2]

nyew tyam *n.*
somebody who has recently arrived in a place and is inexperienced, someone who doesn't

know things (from English 'new chum') ◆ Iterlaretyakenh — ayeng nyew tyam anem. (T) *I don't know — I'm inexperienced.*
SEE ALSO akwen

nyewel (E) *n.* [RESPECT LANGUAGE]
hill ◆ Nyewel-warl ahanenhekaw tyety-ayerrek apek. (St) *They [respect kin] have gone to the hills looking for game.*
= ather-ayerr
SEE ALSO apwert

nyewel-areny (E) *n.* [RESPECT LANGUAGE]
euro ◆ Altwerlerneyt ahanenhek tyety-ayerrek, nyewel-areny apek aretyek, arrep-iletyek. (St) *[They] have gone to the hills in the west looking for meat, maybe for euros [said by a women referring to her son-in-law].*
SEE ALSO areng²

nyey-nyey atwem (W) *vt.*
just about kill someone; (fight) almost to the death ◆ Nyey-nyey atwem, rlkert-irretyeh tyerrty alenh, wal 'nyey-nyey atwem' Anmatyerrel ilem. (M) *If the person is beaten so much that they get sick, well that's called* 'nyey-nyey atwem' *in Anmatyerr.*
= nyant atwem
SEE ALSO nya²

nyeyepenyey (W) *n.*
light rain, a sprinkle of rain, drizzle
= tyeyepetyey

nyingk (E) zebra finch SEE UNDER **nyengk**

nywemerranty (W) *n.* [RESPECT LANGUAGE]
good
SEE ALSO mwerr, mwerranty

Nywepart (W) *n.*
name of place near Patty Hill, Napperby Station area

nywerr (W,T) *n.*
mountain devil lizard, thorny devil (*Moloch horridus*) ◆ Nywerrel yerr arlkwerl-apem. Ker kweny — ankerl-akert yanh. Yerrarl arlkwerl-apem. (M) *The mountain devil goes along eating ants. They're not edible — they've got lumps on them. They eat ants.*
= arnkerrth, mernerr

nywerrp *n.*
those who are in the opposite generation moiety to the person or persons whose point of view you are taking. In one generation moiety are Pwerrerl/Pwerl, Ngwarray, Penangk and Ngal people and in the other Kemarr, Mpetyan, Pengart and Peltharr/Petyarr. Relationships between some kin who are *nywerrp* to each other are characterized by teasing and joking. See Appendix 1. ◆ Nywerrp nhenhel atyeng. (St) *This person is in the opposite generation moiety to me.* ◆ Ayeng-amperl anyent anep-anem nywerrp. Arrantherrant akngerr, kweyekar map. (St) *There's only poor old me in the opposite generation moiety [to all of you]. There's lots of you, in the same generation moiety as each other.* ◆ Anwengkerr ilem 'nywerrp' map, kenh anwengkerr ilelhem 'kweyekar'. (M) *We call them* 'nywerrp', *and we call ourselves* 'kweyekar'. ◆ Nhenh apek tha *tease*-em-ilem nywerrp (St) *I am going to tease this person because they are* nywerrp *to me.* ◆ Mpwelanth atherr antem altyel-nheng atherr apek nywerrp atherram. Kenh ilern apek Ngwarray-irrwengerr kweyekar atherr. Penangk ap Ngwarray ap, Pwerrerl ap — *that's* kweyekar map anwern. Kenh arrantherr akenh anem Peltharr ap Kemarr ap Pengart ap Mpetyan, *that's* nywerrp maparl arrantherr. (M) *You two female cross-cousins [of one another] are in the opposite generation moiety [to us]. And we two Ngwarray are* kweyekar. *Penangk, Ngwarray, and Pwerrerl — we are* kweyekar, *in the same group as each other. And all of you — Peltharr, Kemarr, Pengart and Mpetyan — you're all* nywerrp *for us, in the other group.*
SEE ALSO kweyekar, alanth-apakwey, arrantherr-apakwey

nywerrpek-nywerrp *n.*
being in the opposite generation moiety to each other; people who are *nywerrp* to each other doing something backwards and forwards to each other ◆ Arrkenel artalyel imperretyart nywerrpek-nywerrp. (M) *People in the opposite generation moiety to each other used to have fun throwing things at each other.*

nywertep (E) *n.*
part of guts (of animal such as cattle). Also referred to as *atna nywertep.*

nywet-nywet¹ (W) *n.*
a type of grass (?)

nywet-nywet² (T) *n.*
messy, scruffy ◆ Kapert nywet-nywet nhenhan, *no comb*-em-ilelhem. (T) *This one has scruffy hair, he doesn't comb it.*
SEE ALSO aternng, alhwerrk, alkwemp-alkwemp, altelhey, iltelhey, alther, nywet-nywet²

nyweter-nyweterrp (W,T) *n.*
knotty or curly hair
= kapert arlwerr-arlwerr
SEE ALSO lthel-lthel

Pp

pa (W) *part.*
and

pakerey (W,T) *n.*
headband made of material (generally white) (from English 'puggaree')
SEE ALSO tyerlarr, memp, irrkarlp

pakw-pakw (W) *n.*
crested bellbird (*Oreoica gutturalis*) (note Warlpiri *pakupaku*). This name is based on the sound that the bird makes.
= kwepalepal

pakweth *n.*
box (from English 'box')

-pal, -pel *n.ending*
Goes on the end of English number words. Especially used by younger speakers. (from Creol/English 'fellow') ◆ Kenhengart *three*-**pel** alhek. Rrpwetyap alhek. (P) *Three brothers went. Three went.*
pew-pal *n.*
four (from English 'four')

pal-irrem *vi.*
boil (to boil) (from English 'boil')

paleken (E) pelican SEE UNDER **pelekan**[2]

palthet, palthat (E) *n.*
pocket ◆ Ngkwerlp apek palthetek arrernek. (St) *The tobacco might have been put in the pocket.* ◆ Arelh ampwang mapel ilem, 'palthet'. (T) *Old ladies say* 'palthet'.

palty atwem (E) *vt.*
punch, smack or whack someone or something ◆ Iyntwarr-iletyek tha arengk palty atwem. (St) *I'm whacking the dog to make it move away.*
= apar atwem, anampart atwem

pampew *n.*
didgeridoo (from Creol/English 'bamboo')

paneken cup SEE UNDER **paniken**

pang (E) *part.*
Gives emphasis to what you are saying. ◆ Ankerr innga angerrety, 'urrekek'. Angerrety weth. Urrey pang weth artwa ampwa. (Sa) *An emu that is really large is called* 'urrekek'. *Those big ones. Those big male ones.* ◆ Pweltak pang inngek-arelh, arreynelhetyek mpwarem *scratch*-em ilelhem. Ayengan akwerrp pweltak ikwer *clean*. (Sa) *The* pweltak *louse is found on people, and they make people scratch themselves. I haven't had much experience with lice, I'm clean.*

pangkarr *n.*
blanket ◆ Pangkarr alenh atyeng anthay, ayeng artelhetyeh. (M) *Give me that blanket over there so that I can cover myself.*
= pelangket
SEE ALSO antyam, antyepanty, panty

pangkat (T) *n.* [BABY TALK]
blanket (from English 'blanket')
SEE ALSO pelangket, antyam, antyepanty, pangkarr, panty

pangkelang (W) *n.*
a type of monster. Also referred to as *arrenty pangkelang.* ◆ Artwel apwert lyerl-warl akwernek ker alewarr antey. Arrenty anengk arrpenh aken pangkelang kwen antem inteyel, *rush*-irrek ina. (M) *The man had put the entire kangaroo carcass in a cave. There were a lot of pangkelang monsters inside the cave and they rushed in to grab [the meat].*
SEE ALSO arrenty

paniken, paneken *n.*
cup (from English 'pannikin')

panipak *n.*
something odd or strange (from English 'funny bugger')

Panmaparnt (T) *n.*
name of a place and location of houses at Mt Barkly

panparl (W,T) *n.*
a gathering of people for sorry business (note Warlpiri *panparla* 'holding one another around shoulders with extended arms as people who are in mourning')
panparl-irrem (W,T) *vi.*
hold or embrace someone in an expression of mourning
SEE ALSO mal-mal, anyent-irrem
parnparl-ilerrem (W,T) *vi.*
hold or embrace one another in an expression of mourning ◆ Parnparl-ilerrem arelh anengk. (M) *Lots of women are holding each other in grief.*
SEE ALSO arnerl-ilerrem, mel-irrkwem

pantety *n.*
bandage (from English 'bandage')

panth *n.*

wooden bowl or dish, coolamon, wooden scoop or shovel ◆ Arelhel kwer akwek angerl-apem panthel. (M) *The woman is carrying the baby along in the coolamon.* ◆ Marl nhenhel ahelh panthel inyem. (N) *This woman is digging the ground with a wooden scoop.*
= alparr[1], lengarr
SEE ALSO atywekal, urety, kwerlintyerr, lwengkart[2], irrkwely[2], irrkwa, arlketh[1]

pantheng-panth *n.*
toy wooden bowl or dish ◆ Marl akwek mapel arntap iltyemelarl angerl-wetyart arntap mwareng-mwar pantheng-panthel. (St) *The young girls used to peel bark off trees and carry the bark around as pretend wooden dishes.*
SEE ALSO mwareng-mwar

panth-penh (E) *n.*
young baby who is still in the coolamon

panth-panth (E) *n.*
piedish beetle (*Helea* spp.)
SEE ALSO lengarr-lengarr

panty (T,E) *n.*
blanket, groundsheet
= antyepanty, antyam, pangkarr

panty-wem (T,E) *vt.*
spread out a bed, blanket or groundsheet; spread out leaves to cut meat on
= antyepanty-wem, antyam-wem

pantyey *n.*
brother-in-law, my brother-in-law (probably from English 'fancyman')
SEE ALSO mpwern

pap *n.* [BABY TALK]
dad (from English 'papa') ◆ Kalty-irrek kwerlel, papan akerrirrem. (P) *They learn to say 'pap' in school.* ◆ Pap apety-alpem ker arlewatyerr-akert. (M) *Dad came back with goannas.*
SEE ALSO angey

pap aywa (W), **pap aywang** (W)
1. great-grandfather (father's father's father)
2. father's elder brother (aywa *'old', 'grey-headed'*). If a person calls someone *pap aywa* then they call that person *aler* back.
SEE ALSO aler

pap anawey (W)
father's elder brother; uncle (anawey *'father's elder brother or sister'* [BABY TALK])

papap[1] (E) *n.* [BABY TALK]
grandmother, father's mother
SEE ALSO aperl, mam, mam-mam

papap[2] (T) *n.*
dog (from English 'pup')
SEE ALSO angwely, arengk

-paraty your relation (respectful or 'sorry' way of talking) SEE UNDER **-parety**

parerr (E) *n.* [RESPECT LANGUAGE]
1. eye ◆ Parerr-ayerrarl anerrk-irrekeketyaw, ahaneyna kwey ngwarrekengkw. (Sa) *Daughter, go to your husband, his eye is no good [said by a woman to her daughter].*
2. blind, having a sore eye ◆ Ngwarrengkw parerr ayepelirrem (St) *Your husband is blind [said by a woman to her daughter].*
= angapanty
SEE ALSO apal-apal, pweng, aparrng, annga

parety thirsty SEE UNDER **parrety**

-parety, **-paraty** *k.ending* [RESPECT LANGUAGE]
your relation. Goes on the end of kin terms, and is used by others to refer to that relation. It is not used as a form of address. Respectful or 'sorry' way of talking ◆ 'Awenh-**parety** akeweny arety-alha rlkert apek interl-anem.' Alakenh ilem Anengkerr-penh. (M) *'Go and see your poor old auntie who is lying there sick.' That way of talking comes from the Dreaming.* ◆ Awenh-**parety** ngkwengenh anep-anem. (T) *Your poor old auntie is sitting there.* ◆ *If* nta apekarl arelh Pwerrerl, 'Awenh-**parety** alenh arety alhang kwenh, akeweny kwenh, rlkert apekarl interl-anem'. Alakenh ngwenh ilem. Arrpenhel ilem. Mathel apek ngwenh ilem Penangkel. (M) *If you are a Pwerrerl woman [someone might say], 'Go and see your auntie, the poor thing, she's sick'. That's what they say to you. Another person says that to you. A Penangk woman, your auntie's mother, might say that to you.* ◆ *Friend-***parety** ngkwengenh apetyem. (T) *Your poor old friend is coming.* ◆ Anye**parety** yanh apetyern. Kel apetyern akeweny lyet-akey kwenh. (T) *Your poor old father has just arrived. He just came today, the poor thing.*

parip (E) Burton's snake-lizard SEE UNDER **iparip**

parl (W,T), **pwarl** (W,T) *n.*

1. bush banana, silky pear (*Marsdenia australis*). A winding vine which climbs other trees and shrubs and has creamy flowers and oblong edible fruits.
2. the edible fruit of the bush banana ◆ Pwarl arlparernep-rnem arnangel-ayel. (M) *The bush banana fruits are hanging in the tree.* ◆ Nwernengk yanh mern pwarl arlka arlkwem, yatenhel, mern altyey arlka. (N) *The tawny frogmouth eats bush bananas, that sort of thing, and bush banana leaves.* ◆ Alangkw, mern aparl akerl-apek, mern akwerrk akerl-apek, akerl-apemel akerl-apemel. Rwewarn antem angernem, rwel ap itetyam, mern aparl apel, rwel itetyam. Perrap *soft one* anthwerr, rwepenh. (N) *The young fruits of the bush banana were picked. Then they were taken back to the fire to be cooked. They are really nice and soft after being cooked in the fire.*
= alangkw, alkwarrer
SEE ALSO altyey

parlarlweker (E) *n.*
a type of leech (?)
parlaw flour SEE UNDER **perlaw**
parlk (E) something loose and baggy SEE UNDER **parlkw**
parlk (W), **pwarlk** (W,T) *n.*
in ignorance, not knowing about something ◆ Pwarlkel ayeng anek. (T) *I didn't know what was going on.*
SEE ALSO apal[2]
parlkel anem (W), **pwarlkel anem** (W,T)
not knowing what is happening ◆ Pwarlk anwern anetyam — apal war nheng iterlant aretyam irlpangelant, rarrp nthwerl-apetyam inarrp atwetyew, kwarterretyeh nthwerl-apetyam. (N) *We didn't know what was happening — we only knew from what we heard, that he was going around himself killing them.*
parlkeny (W), **pwarlkeny** (W,T) *n.*
not knowing about something; not being informed about something ◆ Pwarlkeny kwenh anerl-anek, nheng *know*-em arlka iletyakenh, iwenh apekarl iter arrpenhel mpwarek. *Pass away* apekarl irrekarl apek anwern apal anek antem. Pwarlkeny wart anwern anerl-anek, awetyakenh. (M) *[We] were not told about it, we didn't know what happened on the other side. If people got killed then we didn't know about it. We were ignorant, we didn't hear about it.*
= akwenpeny
parlkem (W) bark (dog) SEE UNDER **parlkwem**
parlkenng (E) *n.*
red-backed kingfisher (*Todiramphus pyrrhopygia*) ◆ Parlkenngel mpwarem kwen arnkarrek apek, kel ra akwerrk anem irrkwem kel ra alhem anem akwerrk. (St) *The red-backed kingfisher makes its nest in the banks of creeks, then it has its young there, and then they fly away.*
= rlwernp, urrernter[2]
SEE ALSO kwelinterr-interr
parlkw, parlk (E) *n.*
1. something loose and baggy
2. large bag or sack (such as hessian bag, flour bag, potato or onion bag, chaff bag or (imperial weight) 100 lb bag) ◆ *Coat*-arrpantey ina mpwaretyam parlkw-penh, *corner* atherr-they akemel, ahentyek akemel, altywer-ilemel, kel irrpemel. (St) *They made sort of coats from big sacks, cutting the two corners and making a hole for the neck and then putting it on.* • SEE ALSO yakweth, pewaty
parlkw-parlkw *n.*
something loose, baggy and worn out
ana parlkw-parlkw (E),
atna parlkw-parlkw (E)
baggy skin, baggy arse (ana *'arse'*)
SEE ALSO alyemp-alyemp[1]
parlkw-parlkw-irrem (E) *vi.*
go loose or slack, become baggy
parlkwem (T,E), **parlkem** (W) *vt.*
bark (dog) ◆ Arengkel parlkwem arengkarrpikw. (St) *The dog is barking at another dog.* ◆ Arengk nhel-arey parlkwep-arlkwem ingwatentyel. (St) *These dogs are barking all night.*
parlperrp *n.*
playing cards (note Warlpiri *parlpirr(pa)* 'branch, fork, playing cards') ◆ Parlperrpel anwern arrken-irrey ngkweltyek-wem. (M) *We're going to play cards, chucking in some small change.* ◆ Parlperrp-warl ayeng alhem arrken-irretyeh. (T) *I'm going to go and play cards.*
= kart[2]
SEE ALSO kwernt[1], peyenat
parn (W,T) narrow, tight, cramped SEE UNDER **pwarn**
parntar (W,T) *n.*
a bright fire or light. Also referred to as *rwa parntar* (note Warlpiri *parntaru* 'fire used to signal presence at night') ◆ Rwang parntar ampem. (T) *The fire is burning brightly.* ◆ Parntar yanh ampentyem mwetek *light.* (T) *The car light is shining brightly as it comes this way.* ◆ Mer arrpenheng ntwa arem parntar amperleng. (M) *You can see the lights shining brightly from the other place.*
SEE ALSO mperlkem, alhenem
parntentyarlp (W) *n.*
1. rat-tail goosefoot, green crumbweed (*Dysphania kalpari*). A sticky herb about 25 cm high with flowers forming erect spikes, and with very small shiny black seeds.
2. the edible seeds of the rat-tail goosefoot plant
= alpar, mwelyeparnt-parnt
SEE ALSO arrerlang
parntewelyewely (W,T) *n.*
1. fire (placed to stop sickness) (?)
2. the smell of fat or meat cooking (note Warlpiri *parnti* 'odour') ◆ Ker anterarl ampem, parntewelyewely-kety anwengkerr arnang-irretyeh iter-warn. (T) *Because of the smell of fatty meat burning we'll move to the side.*
= intyem intyerrk
parr-iwem (E) *vt.*
use healing massage on someone ◆ Parr-iwetyek ayenh anpetyek. (St) *Touching me and using healing massage.*

= angkwerr-wem

parray (E) *n.*
sagging (of breasts) ◆ Werlaty parray. (Sa) *Sagging breasts.*
SEE ALSO alhwemperemper, akarnterrng

parrek, parrik *n.*
fence, boundary (from English 'paddock') ◆ Thang arem thep parrekel akern anem. (T) *I can see birds sitting on top of the fence.*
SEE ALSO way

parrelyarrely (W) *n.*
blind ◆ Arelh ampwang akeweny parrelyarrely, anngang pweng. (M) *That poor old woman is blind.*
= pweng

parrety, parety *n.*
thirsty (from English 'perish') ◆ Wethey nhenh kwaty-kwenh parrety ilwek. (N) *Without water this horse perished and died.*
= angkethakw, angkethel, arwekel
parrety-irrem, parety-irrem *vi.*
be thirsty
= arwekel-irrem, angkethakw-irrem

parrewem (T) *vt.*
clean husks or skin off a bush onion

parrik fence, boundary SEE UNDER **parrek**

parrk (W,T), **pwarrk** (T,E), **pwerrk** (T), **purrk** (E) *n.*
weak, tired ◆ Pwarrk ra interl-anem apenty-penh. (T) *She is lying down, tired after travelling.*
parrk-irrem (W,T), **pwarrk-irrem** (T,E), **pwerrk-irrem** (T), **purrk-irrem** (E) *vi.*
get tired, feel tired ◆ Pwarrk-irrem, atyenp apek ayeng anetyek. Pwarrk anthek arrpenhel ayeng. (St) *I'm tired and I'm going to sit down quietly. Other people made me tired.*
parrk awelhem (W,T), **pwarrk awelhem** (T,E), **pwerrk awelhem** (T), **purrk awelhem** (E)
= **parrk-irrem**
parrkel anthem (W,T), **pwarrkel anthem** (T,E)
make someone tired (anthem *'give'*)
parrk-parrk-ilem (W,T), **pwarrk-pwarrk-ilem** (T,E) *vt.* = **parrkel anthem**
aherrk parrk-parrk-irrem (W)
wane (moon) (?) (lit. 'the sun (*aherrk*) is getting tired')
arlta pwerrk (T)
Sunday (lit. 'tired day' or 'day of rest')

parrkely *n.*
broad-leaf parakeelya (*Calandrinia balonensis*). A fleshy herb about 25 cm high with succulent leaves and purple flowers.

◆ Parrkelyel arrakert apelyelh-iletyam arrakert antyerrk. (M) *Parakeelya was used to moisten the mouth if it was dry.* ◆ Parrkelyel ngkwern atherr apernelhem kwaty-kwenyel. (N) *If you haven't got any water you can rub your legs with parakeelya.*
= lywemp-lywemp
SEE ALSO arrwelth-arrwelth

parrp, iparrp *adv.*
quick, quickly, fast, being in a hurry, straight away, rapidly. *Parrp* can also be used on its own as a command. ◆ Parrp inety-alhay kwaty. (T) *Quickly go and get the water.* ◆ Parrp alhetyeh lyweny. (M) *Let's go hunting straightaway.* ◆ Ker yanh parrp atway, arekerr ngenh. Parrp atway! (St) *Kill that animal quickly or it will see you. Hurry up and kill it!* ◆ Arrngent-wetyek alheyaw. Yanharl atwerrem arrngent-wetyek alherl-iway. Arrngent-wetyek parrp untenherr-arey. Yanharl atwerremek alhenherr-arey arrngent-wetyek. (Sa) *Go and stop them. Those ones over there are fighting — go and stop them. Run quickly and stop them. Go and stop them fighting.*
SEE ALSO arternp, uremeny, aher, arrengker
parrp-parrp, iparrp-iparrp *adv.*
quick, quickly, fast, being in a hurry, straight away, rapidly ◆ Parrp-parrp alha kwenh, mwetekarl *ready*-irremeng, alhetyek. Parrp-parrp untay. (St) *Hurry up and go, because the car is ready to go. Run quickly.* ◆ Parrp-parrp ahey-angkerl-anem rtwekert. (T) *The heart is beating rapidly.*

parrty, pwarrty (T) *n.*
1. moonlight
SEE ALSO anyenty, atay[1]
2. falling star, shooting star, a bright light in the night sky (?). Shooting stars are seen as a sign or omen of bad things. ◆ *Eh* parrty yanh anyekay kwenh. Ingwel arrken-irretyalay ampareyay. (St) *Hey, that shooting star fell down. Don't you kids play around in the night.*
• SEE ALSO kwerraly
parrtyel, pwarrtyel (T)
in the moonlight ◆ Parrtyel akwet ntwa nthwerl-apem. (M) *You're still going round in the moonlight.*
= anyentyel
parrtyelh-ilem (W,T), **pwarrtyelh-ilem** (T) *vt.*
make light, light things up (sun or moon) ◆ Aherrkel parrtyelh-ilem. (T) *The sun makes it light.* ◆ Mwemengk amparr anem. Atay arratenty-alhem. Atayel parrtyelh-ilem. (M) *It is pitch dark at first. The moon comes up. The*

moon lights things up.
SEE ALSO aketh-irrem

-pat *n.ending*
An ending that goes on a few words such as *angerr* 'big', *irrewaly* 'dead body' and *angkwey* 'old' to form words with the general meaning of 'senior people', 'ancestors' etc. (see below)
angerr-pat, akngerr-pat (E) *n.*
1. elder, senior person
2. eldest (in a family group or a group of siblings) ◆ Kakey angerr-**pat**. *Older brother.* ◆ Marl angerr-**pat** atyengenh arrwekeleny. (M) *My eldest daughter, the first one.*
irrewaly-pat *n.*
people who have passed away; ancestors, olden-time people ◆ Tyerrty irrewaly-**pat** ywerrewarrek kwenh, akeweny-arey kwenh. (T) *All the ancestors have passed away, poor old things.*
angkwey-pat (T) = **irrewaly-pat** ◆ Angkwey-**pat** mapelarl ahenp angkety ilek. Lyetarr-lyet anem angkety arratem. Arrwekel akwel *no* arratek. (T) *The olden-time people spoke old language. Nowadays the language started to surface. It didn't come out before, apparently* (?).

patart *n.*
potato (from English 'potato')

patepwerl (T) football SEE UNDER **pweteperl**

paterl *n.*
bottle (from English 'bottle')

patey (W), **paytey** (T,E) *n.*
creepy crawly, small insect or bug that 'bites', bitey (from English 'bitey') ◆ Arrenty akely, arrwekelenyelan ilerretyart arrenty. Payteyan alhernter-kenhan. (Sa) *Little creepy crawlies, the old people used to call them* 'arrenty'. *'Bitey' is a word that white people use.*
patey-patey (W), **paytey-paytey** (T,E) *n.*
creepy crawly, small insect or bug that 'bites' ◆ Paytey-paytey yanh-kety — ngenh utnhekerr. (T) *Look out for that creepy crawly — it'll bite you.*

pathekel, patyekel *n.*
bicycle (from English 'bicycle')

pathem (W) *n.*
possum (from English 'possum')
= rrpwamper, antenh

pathen (W,T) *n.*
poison, poisonous (from English 'poison') ◆ Arekerr pwelek ilwenh-ilwenh. Pwelekelarl arlkwem renh wal yang lwem. Pathen. (T) *The pituri bush kills cattle. If cattle eat it then they die. It's poisonous.*
pathenem-ilem (W,T) *vt.*
poison someone or something

patimalan (E) *n.*
paddy melon (from English 'paddy melon')
SEE ALSO malan

patwert (W,T) *n.*
1. waxy wattle (*Acacia melleodora*). Shrub to about 2.5 m high, with grey-green leaves with a whitish crust.
= alhepalh, ilkwernarr
2. spiny-leaved wattle, stiff wattle (*Acacia maitlandii*). Shrub up to 2 m high, with leaves which have a sharp spine at the tip.
• = arleperlterrk
3. the edible seeds of these acacias ◆ Arnwetyam yanh patwert, arlkwenh-arlkwenh. Intertel rnpwa map, patwert kwerelarl. (N) *The* patwert *bush has edible seeds. There is resin found at the base of the shrub.*

paty (W,T) *n.*
1. breast, teat
2. milk
= werlaty
paty antywem (W,T)
suck on the breast, drink from the breast (antywem *'drink'*) ◆ Paty antywem kwer akwekel. (T) *The little baby is drinking from the breast.*
= werlaty antywem
paty anthem (W,T)
breastfeed (anthem *'give'*) ◆ Paty antherl-anem kwer akwekeh. (M) *Breastfeeding the little baby.*
= werlaty anthem
paty arrwert (W,T)
sharp or pointed breasts ◆ Paty arrwert amparr angkwey anem, paty ayenpem irrem. (M) *At first the breasts are pointy, then they sag.*
= ngwemper
paty ayenp (W,T)
flat or sagging breasts (ayenp *'skin'*) ◆ Kwerel antywek, paty ayenp mpwarek. (M) *The child drank from the breasts and made them sag.*
paty alha (W,T)
nipple (alha *'nose'*)
= werlaty alha
paty antyerrk-ilenh (T)
the last child in a family (lit. 'the one that dries the breast up')
= werlaty ilwernenty

patyekel bicycle SEE UNDER **pathekel**

Patyimp (E) *n.*
a star constellation

Patyimp-kenh (E) *n.*
name of a place east of Stirling Station homestead

Paw (W,T) *n.*
Bau Range, Mt Barkly. See map p. viii.

paw-arlkem (T) *vi.*
sing out to someone ◆ Paw-arlkerl-apem tyerrty arrpenhek arlkerl-apem. (T) *Singing out to another person.*

pay *part.*
an exclamation; 'I'm here!', 'Here I am!' ◆ Apant-irremel arlkerl-apem, 'Nthenh tyerrty mapay? Pay! *Might* ayeng apant apek irrek kwenh.' (N) *Getting lost and singing out, 'Where is everybody? Here I am! I might be lost.'*

pay-arlkem (W) *vt.*
make a particular call during initiation (young man) ceremonies (women). This sounds a bit like *pay pay pay* or *pey pey pey*.
pay-arlkenty-iwem (E) *vi.* = **pay-arlkem**
= payakayak anem
SEE ALSO rteyepertey, tyarewarn

pay-pay *n.* [BABY TALK]
sleep (from English 'bye bye')
SEE ALSO ankwa
pay-pay-irrem *vi.* [BABY TALK]
go to sleep

payakayak anem (T,E) *vi.*
make a particular call during initiation (young man) ceremonies (women). This sounds a bit like *pay pay pay* or *pey pey pey*. ◆ Payekayak anem, arlkerl-arlkerl-ilererl-anem, 'Pey pey pey'. Teyeperteyel arlkerl-anem, *daylight*-ekatety arlkerl-anem, arelh. (T) *Singing out and making that particular sound during the young fella ceremonies, 'Pey pey pey'. The* teyepertey *women sing out like that, right up to daylight.*
payakayak-irrem (T,E) *vi.* = **payakayak anem**
= pay-arlkem, pay-arlkenty-iwem
SEE ALSO rteyepertey, tyarewarn

payem-ilem *vt.*
buy something or pay for something (from English 'buy', 'pay')

payemalan *n.*
1. pie melon (*Citrullus lanatus*). Spreading vine-like plant with melons.
2. the edible fruit of the pie melon (from English 'melon' or 'pie melon'). Also referred to as *mern payemalan.* ◆ Mern payemalan arlkwerrerl-apek, lpway nhenhel. Atetherr atwerl-apemel. Arntap-warn arrernetyart. Arlkwetyart anwern perrap mwerr anthwerr. (N) *We went along eating pie melons in the creek here, and killing budgerigars. We used to put them in bark containers. We used to eat them and they tasted really good.*
= malan

paytey (T,E) creepy crawly, bitey SEE UNDER **patey**

pek-pek (W,T) *n.*
pig (from English 'pig') ◆ Nhenh ker pek-pek, anthwerrngek irrpenh-irrpenh. (T) *This is a pig, they mess around in the mud.*
= wangk-wangk, pingkey

peketyalkwarr (T,E), **peketyalkarr** (E) *n.*
1. pale-leaf mistletoe (*Amyema maidenii*)
2. edible fruit of the pale-leaf mistletoe
= ngartangkern
SEE ALSO amar, akweltyayt

-pel Goes on the end of English number words.
SEE UNDER **-pal**

pelangket (W,T), **pwelangket** (E) *n.*
blanket, swag (from English 'blanket')
SEE ALSO antyam, antyepanty, pangkarr, panty

pelekan[1] (W), **perlekan** (W), **pilikan** (E) *n.*
billycan (from English 'billycan')
SEE ALSO tyampet

pelekan[2] (W), **paleken** (E) *n.*
pelican (*Pelecanus conspicillatus*) (from English 'pelican') ◆ Irnngang map arlkwerl-apem, nthwerl-apemel pelekan angerrel. (N) *Pelicans go round eating, eating worms.*
= arrakert angerr

peleth *part.*
'Really!', 'For goodness sake!' (said when you feel excited or happy about something) (from English 'please') ◆ Mern mwanyem aray peleth! (N) *For goodness sake, look at all banana-flavoured bush tomatoes!* ◆ Arlperrangkwarl apel theweyet anthwerr inerl-apetyart, akap-rlwemel peleth, theweyet anthwerr. Awantyerl-apetyeh. (N) *We used to go and collect the sweet resin from the whitewood tree, peeling it off from the branch. It's really sweet, I can tell you. We used to go along sucking on it.*

pelh[1] *n.*
saliva, spit, spittle
SEE ALSO arrelty[2], arrwek, iylkerr
pelh-pelh (T,E) *n.*
froth on lips, dribble ◆ Ayeng pelh-pelh urntep-urntem. Iwenh apekarl arlkwek-penh. Katyerr tyatyarlkwerr apek tharl arlkwek. Tyatyarlkwerr katyerr-artek anteyarl. Pelh-pelh anem ayeng urntem. (St) *I'm dribbling from eating something. Maybe it was that* tyatyarlkwerr *fruit that I ate. The* tyatyarlkwerr *is similar to the desert raisin plant. Now I'm dribbling.*
pelh-wem, pelh-iwem (E) *vt.*
spit, spit something out ◆ Pelh-iwetyalay atyeng-warn! (T) *Don't spit in my direction!*

pelhel-iwenh-iwenh (E) *n.*
a type of gecko (sandplain or northern spiny-tailed) (*Diplodactylus stenodactylus* (?); *Strophurus ciliaris* (?)) (lit. 'spitter')
= akarntety-arntety, rltimp-areny

pelh[2] (W,T) *n.*
non-fatty meat of a kangaroo; lean (of kangaroo) ◆ Pelhant kwenh, anter anetyakenh ampwang. (M) *This kangaroo meat is not fatty, it's thin and there's no fat.*
SEE ALSO ampwa

pelker *n.*
crested pigeon (*Ocyphaps lophotes*) ◆ Pelkeran aker. Mern an *all* ina arlkwem tyerrty map-henh, an irnngang akwek ina arlkwerl-apem. (N) *Crested pigeons are edible. They eat all sorts of food that people eat, and they go along eating little worms.*

pelp (E) *n.*
fast asleep ◆ Iynterremel aynterl-anem ankwa pelp. (Sa) *Lying fast asleep and snoring.*
SEE ALSO ankwa[1], ankwa angerr, ankwa alert

pelp-ayntem *vi.*
be fast asleep, be in a deep sleep (ayntem '*lie*')

Peltharr *n.*
skin name, subsection name, marriage class. See diagram p. 744. ◆ Kemarr anew akek Peltharrel. (St) *The Peltharr married the Kemarr.*
SEE ALSO Petyarr, Tyapaly, Ngalyerr, Napeltyarr, Tyapeltyarr

Peltharr Map (W,T)
a star constellation; Seven Sisters, Pleiades ◆ Peltharr Map anentyem, kwerraly. (T) *The Seven Sisters come up.*
= Arrarrkw, Interrk[1], Kwerraly Angerr, Alyang Rlkwang

pelty, ipelty *n.*
friend, age-mate, relation ◆ Pelty atherr yanh atherr kwey atherran alherretyel, atyew-nheng atherr pelty atherr. Pelty atherr alherl-anerrem kwenh. (Sa) *Those two girls are friends, round about the same age. They hang round together.* ◆ Pelty apetyem yanh atyengenh. (M) *My friend is coming there.*
SEE ALSO atyew, alyey[2], rwanng

atyeng pelty (T,E) *n.*
my friend/age-mate/relation (atyeng '*for me*', '*to me*')
= atyeng-arneng

ngkweng pelty (T,E)
your friend/age-mate/relation (ngkweng '*for you*', '*to you*') ◆ Ngkweng pelty yanh apetyem. (St) *Your friend is coming there.*
= ngkweng-arneng

kwer pelty (T,E)
his or her friend/age-mate/relation (kwer '*for him/her*', '*to him/her*')
= kwer-arneng

pelty-irrem, ipelty-irrem *vi.*
become friends ◆ Lwereny arelh apetyem arrpenh. Wal yanhan lwereny-penh pelty-irrerl-anem arelh arrpenhek. (St) *A woman who is a stranger comes along. Well then, after being a stranger, she becomes friends with another woman.*

pelty-ilem, ipelty-ilem *vt.*
1. make friends with someone
2. make up, make friends (after an argument) ◆ Pelty-ileynem tha, tha apek renh iltekarl-penh. (St) *I am making friends again, after I growled at him.*

peltyem (W,T) *vt.*
1. break or crack something open; hatch out from an egg ◆ Thep akwekel peltyem, tyerrelhem antem. (T) *The baby bird cracks [the egg] open and then hatches out.* ◆ Kwartarl anem. Amwelek-antey peltyem. Lweren arratem *pretty* antem, lyentyelyerr. (T) *There's the egg there. Then the mother cracks it open. Then the pretty* lyentyelyerr *bird comes out.*
2. chip something off (flakes from a rock) ◆ Thang irntang peltyem alywek mpwaretyeh, ker akerlanetyek. (T) *I am chipping flakes off the rock to make a stone knife to cut meat up with.*
SEE ALSO iyltem, akap-rlwem, ampwatem

pelty-ilem (W,T), **peltyelh-ilem** (W,T) *vt.*
break or crack something open; hatch out from an egg ◆ Arrakertel kwart yenh atanthem, mathel, peltyelh-ilem. Wal akwekey arratenhem kwart alenh akenh impememarl. (M) *The mother cracks the egg open with her beak. Well then the little [bird] comes out of the egg and leaves it behind.*
SEE ALSO iyltem, terlk-ilem

pely (E), **ipely** (E) *n.*
small loin cloth
SEE ALSO matyart
CAN SOUND A BIT LIKE apely *'green', 'wet', 'moist'*

pelyak (W,T), **pelyakw** (T,E), **ipelyak** (E), **ipelyakw** (E) *n.*
duck, grey teal (*Anas gracilis*) ◆ Thip pelyakw kwatyelarl alhep-alhem, urrperl, kerarl arlkwerrerl-anem ina. (St) *The grey teal swims around in the water, is dark in colour and people eat them.* ◆ Pelyakan ker mwerr. (T) *Grey teals*

are good meat.
= tyepelyakw

Penangk *n.*
skin name, subsection name, marriage class. See diagram p. 744. ◆ Arelh Penangk lyweny alhem ampwek Kemarr map-akert. (T) *The Penangk woman is going hunting with her Kemarr children.*
SEE ALSO Tyanam, Ngaman, Napenangk, Tyapenangk

Pengart *n.*
skin name, subsection name, marriage class. See diagram p. 744. ◆ Artwang Pengartel anew akem Mpetyan. Kwer kwerenh map anem Penangk map. (T) *A Pengart man marries a Mpetyan. Their children are Penangk.*
SEE ALSO Tyapart, Ngampart, Napengart, Tyapengart

pengart-pengart[1] *n.*
a type of cricket (note Warlpiri *japangardi japangardi*)

pengart-pengart[2] (W) *n.*
velvet tobacco, rubbish pituri (*Nicotiana velutina* and other *Nicotiana* spp.). Herb about 40 cm high. Highly toxic to stock, and NOT chewed by people. ◆ Apaleh-athen ngkerlpew-athen pengart-pengart akeh. (M) *I picked some rubbish pituri, mistaking it for native tobacco.*
= ngwarray-ngwarray

Pengerr (W) *n.*
name of a soakage west of Mt Denison Station

-penh[1], **-ipenh** (E) *ending*
1. Shows that an event happens after another event or action has been completed; because of something; after a certain situation. If the action is being described as an event, then *-penh* follows a verb with the ending *+enty* or *+arl* on it. The ending *-penh* can also follow straight after the tense ending on a verb. ◆ Awerr atherr alherl-aperretyam anyerrkentyem mer-warn, amwang yatherr atwekarl-**penh**. (M) *The two boys went home happy because they had killed a snake.* ◆ Pew-ilem ntwa ampwerretyeh. Tyerrty alenh pew-ilem wal ampwerremarl alenh pew-ilenty-**penh**. (M) *You put a curse on someone to make them thin. If you put a curse on someone then they will get thin after that.* ◆ Awantyem-**penh** ampeny anem awem. (T) *After sucking on it then throw away what's left.* ◆ Arengkelarl antywem-**penh**, altyewa! (T) *Chuck it out, because the dog's been drinking it!* ◆ Lyweny-**penh** apety-alpemel awely-awely renh rnetyart ker akenh anwern-kenh nheng kwenel akwernetyart. (N) *When we returned from hunting, as the lightning was striking, we'd put all our meat inside the shelters.*
2. because of something; from (the cause of) ◆ Rlkert angerr intem arrwengkelth-**penh**. (M) *He is very sick because he was boned [cursed].*
3. from, out of, indicates the source or origin of something ◆ Alwerrng ker aherr-**penh**el kwa. (N) *Sinews are from kangaroos.* ◆ Ngkwarl rnpwang yanh anyerleng-**penh** anyem pertipelaw kwer-**penh** *red one* kwer-**penh** anyem, renh-iperr arraw-ilem arraw-ilemel arlkwetyam — awantyem akwel arlkwem arlka. (N) *The honey drips from the flowers, from the red flowers on the* anyerleng *bush, and we used to gather it together and eat it — suck it and eat it.* ◆ Mern artwey-artwey rwel itetyeh. Altyey-**penh** mern artwey-artwey, arlatyeyart akin intentyem. (N) *The roots of the bush banana are cooked in the fire. The roots are a bit like pencil yams and they go down from where the leaves are.*

kwer-penh, **ikwer-penh**, **kwer-ipenh** (E) *n.*
after that, and then, because of that, from that ◆ Arrwekel ayeng ltywerrerl-alhey rtweth-akert, rntwarrarl alhek-**penh**. Kwer-**penh** akem-irrem, 'Mwerram ayeng awelhem'. (N) *I'm going to go and have a rest first because my lower-back is aching from walking a long way. After that I get up and say, 'I feel good'.*
SEE ALSO kwer

wenh-penh (W,T), **iwenh-penh** *n.*
1. 'Why?' ◆ Wenh-**penh** arelh alenh npwart alhek? (T) *Why did that woman go off sulkily?*
2. from whatever, because of whatever ◆ Alta ayeng rnter-rnter akwet. Alta rnter-rnter-irrek anem ayeng iwenh-**penh**, ayeng apernelhek. (St) *My hair is still red. It went red after I did whatever, dyed it.*

-penh[2], **-pwenh** *n.ending*
1. Goes on words for compass directions; from that direction. ◆ Ayerrer-they ayeng apety-alpek. Aywerrel-penh. Ayeng aywerrel-**penh**-they apety-alpek. (Sa) *I came back from the north. I came back from the north.* ◆ Altwerl-**penh** apetyem tyerrty alethang apek. (M) *A stranger might come from the west.*
2. Goes on words for compass directions; in that direction. [SOME SPEAKERS] ◆ Altwerl-**penh** alhekaw. Ayeng altwerl-**penh** alhekaw nhenh-they ayeng alhek altwerl-**penh**. (St) *I went to the west. I went to the west from here.* ◆ Artwang altwerl-**pwenh** alpem. (M) *The man went back to the west.*

SEE ALSO altwerl, antekerr, ayerrer, ingerr, angerrakw

penng (E) *n.*
sandhill canegrass (*Zygochloa paradoxa*)

Pentapey (W) Pintupi person or people SEE UNDER **Pintwepey**

pentarlp (T,E) *n.*
whipstick, small stick ◆ Pentarlp atyeng anthay thang akern atwetyew — *whipstick*-artek arnang arlpenty. (N) *Get me a whipstick so that I can hit up high — a long stick like a whipstick.*

pentyengeyengey (E), **pwentyengeyengey** (E) *n.*
moustache, facial hair above the lips
SEE ALSO arralt

pep, pip (E) *n.*
1. paper; things made from paper such as books, documents, letters etc. ◆ Ayeng pep-warn intelh-ilerl-apem. (T) *I'm writing on paper.* ◆ Rwer-welhem ampa apek, ahernel *dry*-ilelhem, ampekenharl alakenh. Pep-kwenyel atna rwer-welherl-alhem. (St) *A child might rub themselves on the ground to make themselves dry. If they haven't got any paper they might rub themselves on the ground to get the shit off their bottoms.*
2. church service; funeral (from English 'paper')
SEE ALSO tyaty

Pep-areny *n.*
Christian (-areny '*associated with*') ◆ Ayengan Pep-areny. (T) *I'm Christian.* ◆ Aheyen maparl arrpenhan, arrpenh mapan Pep-arenyarl Kerretyen maparl. Aheyenan anem Pep-areny-kweny. (T) *Some people are non-Christians and others are church-goers, Christians.* Aheyen *are people who are not Christians.*
= Kerretherreng, Kerretyen
SEE ALSO aheyen

pep-warn alhem
go to a funeral; go to church (lit. 'go to the paper')

pepey *n.* [BABY TALK]
baby (from English 'baby') ◆ Pepey tyety arlkway. (St) *Baby, eat the meat.* ◆ Ampa akwek yanh mwanty. 'Wawel ampekerr pepey!' (St) *Watch out for that baby over there. 'The fire will burn you baby!'*
SEE ALSO arathap

peraty *n.*
a brush (from English 'brush')

Perawey (W) *n.*
Berowie Bore, Yuelamu (Mt Allan) area

perempeth (W), **perimpeth** (T,E) *n.*
breakfast (from English 'breakfast')
SEE ALSO altyerr[1]

perety[1] (E) *n.*
1. men's ceremonial headdress (made from tea-tree bark). Nowadays this may also be made from cardboard. Shorter than *kwertar.*
SEE ALSO kwertar
2. pouch made from tea-tree bark (?)

perety[2] *n.*
bridge (from English 'bridge')

perety-perety (T) white-plumed honeyeater (?) SEE UNDER **aperrety-aperrety**

perimpeth (T,E) breakfast SEE UNDER **perempeth**

perlal a respectful term used by men and women to refer to particular men who have a special role in men's ceremonies SEE UNDER **perlawel**

perlanty (W,T), **perlaty** (W,T) *n.*
grub from the branch of the river red gum, *aper*, the cossid moth grub (*Xyleutes* sp. (?)) ◆ Tyap perlaty, arlkwenh-arlkwenh anthwerr. (N) *The grubs from the river red gum are really edible.* ◆ Tyap perlanty map, atantherl-apek, lywenkel inelh-apek. (N) *We used to go along hooking the grubs from the branches of the river red gum with a grass hook.*
= ingweneng, aylperlayt, ngkenhar, aperayt
SEE ALSO mpaty[2]

perlap *n.*

1. conkerberry, conkleberry (*Carissa lanceolata*). Spiny shrub up to 2 m high, with white flowers and black berries.
2. the edible fruit from the conkerberry. Also referred to as *mern perlap.* ◆ Mern atherrkenyarl anem perlap. Mern arlkwerl-apekarl perlap anthwerr, kwerelarl amangkenhek, perlapel. Alherl-apek lyweny, mern perlap akerl-anetyek. (N) *The conkerberry fruit comes out after rain. We grew up eating conkerberries. We'd go hunting and collect conkerberries.* ◆ Perlap artekerr kwaty-warl arrernetyart alhewelhetyeh perlap. Artekerr alhewelhenhelhenh perlap, arrwekeleny map anetyam, kik-wetyamel lpweletyam irntelem, irntelem lpweletyam ayenp. Atewat arrernetyam, alhewelhetyamem. (N) *The root of the conkerberry used to be put into water and used as a washing medicine. The olden-time people used to peel the root and then soften it by beating it with a stone. Then they put it in hot water and used it to wash themselves.*
= arnwekety

perlap arlwelenh (W), **perlap arlwenhenh** (W)
a type of dragon lizard (?) (lit. 'conkerberry

gatherer')
perlap-areny (W) *n.*
a type of dragon lizard (?) (-areny *'inhabitant of'*)
perlap arraw-ilenh (W) *n.*
the vestigial wings of an emu (lit. 'conkerberry gatherer'). These have a small hook on the end which the emu uses for pulling down certain of its foods such as conkerberries, corkwood and grevillea honeys, and mistletoe berries.
= angkangk iytarr-inenh, perlap tyarr-inenh
perlap tyarr-inenh (E) = **perlap arraw-ilenh**
= angkangk iytarrinenh (tyarr-inem *'pull'*)
perlap-perlap (E) *n.*
orange-naped snake (*Furina ornata*) (?)
= arnwekety-arnwekety

perlaty (W,T) grub from the branch of the river red gum SEE UNDER **perlanty**

perlaw, parlaw *n.*
flour (from English 'flour')
SEE ALSO unmenth, arterrty, nmwenth, unmenth, warnp, aperretyen, thelperretyen

perlawel (E), **perlal** *n.*
1. a respectful term used by men and women to refer to particular men who have a special role in men's ceremonies. Close relations of the 'young fella' who is going through the Law will call these men *perlawel.*
2. a respectful term used by women to refer to particular men who have a special role in men's ceremonies for their close male kin. This term is used instead of actual names between kin who are related to each other in this way. (Note: Warlpiri *pirlaali, pirlawali* 'special ceremonial relationships between men'.) ◆ Perlawel atyenh kwenh, perlawel atyenh yanh-kety kwenh. (T) *There is my* perlawel, *look out for my* perlawel *there.* ◆ Perlawel atyenh arlwety-irrerrepirrem — ayeng rntwarr-angkwerr alhetyek. (T) *My* perlawel *is coming — I'll go further away.* ◆ Yanh akenh *me call him* 'perlawel'*, brother* atyenhekarl thampartey-irrek. (St) *I call that man who became* thampartey *for my brother* 'perlawel'.
SEE ALSO thampartey, anyent arrpenh, ntwerleng, ntyangkwenng, rteyepertey, alyey[2], alyaper-warn, ywerlperr
perlawel-irrem (E), **perlal-irrem** *vi.*
become related as *perlawel* to someone in ceremony

perlekan (W) billycan SEE UNDER **pelekan**[1]

perler *n.*
steady rain, drizzle. Also referred to as *kwaty perler.* ◆ Kwaty aperler anem irrety-alpek, akwet anhep-anhem. (St) *The steady rain came back, and it keeps raining and raining.*
= kwaty thawel

perlern, perleyn (E) *n.*
1. plain, open country; open ground (from English 'plain') ◆ Arnam-kety perlern nhel aneyaw, aketh mwerr-angkerel. (T) *Sit on this nice open ground, because of all the grass.* ◆ Perlern angerr nta arem, aketh arna anetyakenh. (M) *You can see the big plain, open country with no trees.*
2. hairless, bald ◆ Arengk alta anetyakenh altelhey, perleyn. Weth altwerl nhakw perleyn anetyel-apeny, arengk artwampw weth. *Naked.* (Sa) *A dog with no hair is called* perleyn. *Like that old hairless male dog sitting over there. Naked.*

perley (W,T), **peyley** (E), **pirley** (E) *n.*
1. silver witchetty (*Acacia cuthbertsonii* ssp. *cuthbertsonii*). Shrub up to 3 m high, with silvery leaves and cylindrical flowers.
2. the edible seed of the silver witchetty
CAN SOUND A BIT LIKE aperley *'mother's father'*

perleyn (E) plain, open country, open ground SEE UNDER **perlern**

perlkarr (T) *n.*
golden bandicoot (*Isoodon auratus*) (note Warlpiri *piilkarra*)

perlp-perlp (W,T), **peylp-peylp** (E) *adv.*
making a splashing or lapping noise
perlp-perlp alhem (W,T), **peylp-peylp alhem** (E)
go along splashing
perlp-perlp atwem (W,T), **peylp-peylp atwem** (E)
splash water (with hand or foot) ◆ Peylp-peylp anem atwerl-apem, kwaty. (St) *Going along splashing the water.*
perlp-perlp antywem (W,T), **peylp-peylp antywem** (E)
make a lapping sound ◆ Peylp-peylp akngerrel antywep-antywem arengkel. (St) *The dog is making a loud lapping noise as it drinks.*
SEE ALSO lthap-lthap antywem

pernampal (T) *n.*
skewer used for cooking bush tomatoes (*Solanum chippendalei*)
= ntywert

pernem (W,T) *vt.*
chase something down and kill it ◆ Ahenp arengkel ker aherr pernetyart. (T) *Long ago the dogs used to chase kangaroos down and kill them.*
CAN SOUND A BIT LIKE apernem *'paint', 'rub on'*

pernernpernernp, pernernpernern (W) *n.*
dotterel (?) ◆ Pernernpernernp kwaty alay-angkwerr nthwerl-apem rew-angkwerr, arlkwerl-apem thep irnngang. (N) *The* pernernpernernp *bird goes around large areas of water and floodwater eating worms.*

-perr (W,T), **-iperr** *ending*
Shows that something is obvious to the listener; of course (?). ◆ Anant-**iperr**ay, mernt-irrenh-ketyengay. Rlkert apek aneketyeng. Arrwengkelth ineketyeng. Anantay! (P) *Sit down, in case you get sick. In case you catch something. Sit down!*

perrak, perrak-perrak *n.*
frog (from English 'frog')
SEE ALSO atweynterl, antyetyerr, kwep, larrangken, alemerr, akalarrangkern

perral *n.*
bridle (from English 'bridle')

perram *n.*
Brahman cow (from English 'Brahman')

perrameth *n.*
promised husband or wife (from English 'promise')

perrap *n.*
1. really (from English 'proper') ◆ Mern payemalan arlkwerrerl-apek, lpway nhenhel. Atetherr atwerl-apemel. Arntap-warn arrernetyart. Arlkwetyart anwern perrap mwerr anthwerr. (N) *We went along eating pie melons in the creek here. And killing budgerigars. We used to put them in bark containers and eat them. They tasted really good.* ◆ Kwey nheng lim-limel aperl-anem kwenh akeweny rnwerr, perrap rnwerr anthwerr akeweny aperl-anetyenheng kel anety-alpem antem merel interl-anem. An rnwerrarl awelhem. (T) *That poor girl is really lame and crippled, she's really crippled when she walks, and then she goes and sits down, lies down at camp. Feeling crippled.*
2. the right one, the correct one, the actual one, the proper one ◆ Ngkwernerrp akwek. Mey-mey kelarl, mey-meyarl perrap *one.* Kel ngkwernerrp akem 'ngwenyarr' akem. (St) *A little* ngkwernerrp. Mey-mey *are there all right, they are the proper ones [i.e. actual sons-in-law]. And then* ngkwernerrp *are what are also called* 'ngwenyarr'.

perrar (W,T), **pirrar** *n.*
1. pirraru, shiny-leaved wattle (*Acacia ancistrocarpa*). Shrub about 2.5 m high, with shiny leaves and cylindrical flowers.
2. the edible seeds of the pirraru
= irrar

perrertern (E) *n.*
a type of duck (?)

perrertety (E) *n.*
a type of beetle
SEE ALSO lengarr-lengarr, panth-panth

perrk-perrk (W,T), **pwerrk-pwerrk** (E) *n.*
a type of black beetle, dung beetle (?)
◆ Akwekarl ra pwerrk-pwerrk akely, atnek irrpem aherrek apek, alperrty anem irrerl-anem. (St) *The* pwerrk-pwerrk *beetle is small and it burrows into kangaroo dung and makes a mess of it.*
SEE ALSO nyert-nyert
CAN SOUND A BIT LIKE parrk *'tired'*

perrpantywen (W,T), **perrpantyen** (W), **perrpantywel** (E), **perrpantyel, perrpantywerl** (E), **ilperrpayentyel** (E), **irrperrpantyel** (E) *n.*

1. black-faced woodswallow (*Artamus cinereus*)
2. masked woodswallow (*Artamus personatus*)
◆ Perrpantyenan ker rlpwer-arenyarl, ker arlkwenh-arlkwenh. (N) *Black-faced woodswallows are edible and they live in hollow trees.* ◆ Yerramparl akern-ilep-ilem perrpantywerlel. (St) *The black-faced woodswallow is what makes the honeyants come up [closer to the surface of the ground].*
◆ Perrpantyel irntelarl anem, wal anthwerrng akin arrernem, antywang akwek kwer artem, inteyel. (M) *Black-faced woodswallows live in the rocks, and they make nests out of mud in caves.*

perrtyeny (E) *n.* [RESPECT LANGUAGE]
1. foot
2. (going) on foot ◆ Lyengkwert ahanekaw perretyeny-ayerr kwey ngwarrengkw. (Sa) *Daughter, today your husband went off on foot [said by a woman].*
SEE ALSO ingka

pert-irrem (E) *vi.*
turn round and go back; return ◆ Alhemel pert-irrerl-alpemel, ngkwerlp iylpel-wentyek ngkwerlp inerlewetyek. (Sa) *Going and then turning back to get the tobacco that [you] left behind.*
= urtep-irrem, artwep-irrem

pertarnp (W) *n.*
calf (of leg)

pertipelaw *n.*
flower, blossom (from English 'pretty flower')

◆ Utern, arem anwantherr mern atwakey interlek pertipelaw wal utern anemarl irrem. (St) *When we see the flowers of the wild orange, then we know that the summer is coming.* ◆ Arengkatwepatwetyenh, arrken-henh. Anwernarl arlelthel alakenh, kapert pertipelaw anerl-apemel, arrken-henh kwa. Awenk mapel arrken irretyart anwern pertipelaw kwer. (N) *The* arengkatwepatwetyenh *plant is used for fun. We used to enjoy ourselves putting the flowers on our heads. When we were teenage girls we used to play with that flower.*

pet-pet (E) *n.*
rabbit ◆ Ker pet-pet yanh untepuntem. Ker alwerney atyeweyay! (Sa) *There is a rabbit running along. Chase it for goodness sake!*
= rapet, alkwert atwenh, mwetyernk, metyernk

petekwet *n.*
petticoat (from English 'petticoat') ◆ Petekwet-akert *light one* ararrek irrpem. *Can't* anyent-akert aperl, tyerrtyel arekety. Artwel apek arekety ararr-akert. (T) *You wear a petticoat when you have a flimsy dress on. You can't go along with just one dress on or people will see. Maybe the men will see if you have a lightweight dress on [and no petticoat].*

peth *n.*
1. pouch ◆ Alhelth-angem pethel, peth kwerenhel, atwety akwek alhelth-angem kwerenh pethel. (St) *[The kangaroo] carries its joey in its pouch.*
2. the lap or crotch of a person
= aympa
SEE ALSO rnwart, irnwa

petherr (W,T), **pitherr** (E) *n.*
a type of white louse (found in body hair and clothes)
= pweltak
SEE ALSO nya[1]
CAN SOUND A BIT LIKE pitherr *'rock isotomc (?)'*

petheth (W,T) *n.*
piece of rag or cloth (from English 'pieces') ◆ Petheth atanthem. Petheth akwek war tyep-tyep tha atanthem. (T) *I am sewing the rags. I am just sewing up the little bits of rag.*

pety *n.*
fish (from English 'fish') ◆ Pety tha arlkwetyek. *I'm going to eat fish.*
= irrpenng

Petyapety *n.*
1. Pitjantjatjara person or people
2. Pitjantjatjara language
= Petyentyarr

Petyarl (T) *n.*
name of a place on the Hanson River north-west of Ti Tree town. Location of a small outstation. See map p. viii.

Petyarr (E) *n.*
skin name, subsection or section name, marriage class. See diagram p. 744.
SEE ALSO Peltharr

Petyentyarr (E) *n.*
1. Pitjantjatjara person or people
2. Pitjantjatjara language
= Petyapety

petyet (W) *n.*
a kind of bush bandage made from bark ◆ Petyetel ingka atherr ayernelhem. (N) *Tying up the two feet with the bush bandage.*
SEE ALSO arratherrk

Petyey (E) *n.*
name of a soakage to the west of Wilora (Stirling) community

pew-ilem *vt.*
1. blow on something (with mouth) ◆ Ura pew-ilem lherrm-irretyek. (Sa) *Blow the fire so that it catches alight.* ◆ Thang arrakertel rwang pew-ilem nthelh-iletyek. (T) *I am blowing the fire with my mouth to make it light.* ◆ Iylpa pew-pew-ilem renh pew-ilem, iylpel anem ra awemel akem-irremel. Akem-irrem anem ra awem. (St) *Blowing in the ears, and then the person can hear and they get up. They get up and they can hear now.*
2. put a curse on someone, make someone sick ◆ Pew-ilem ntwa ampwerretyeh. Tyerrty alenh pew-ilem wal ampwerremarl alenh pew-ilenty-penh. (M) *You put a curse on someone to make them thin. If you put a curse on someone then they will get thin after that.* ◆ Arengk yanh tha pew-ilep-ilem kwenh, arlkenty-akert kwenh, ankwekwenyarl ilem. (M) *I am putting a curse on the noisy dog that keeps us awake.*
SEE ALSO akwety-irrpenem, artarrernem, artimperr-wem, rltwatyel atwem, urltatyel atwem

pewaty *n.*
small bag, purse, money bag (from English 'pouch')
SEE ALSO yakweth

pewem, piwem (T,E) *vt.*
1. sweep an area or camp where someone has passed away with branches; 'finish up' after a death ◆ Waly-akertel angety-alhem math map pewem antem. Nthwerl-anetyenh *anyway* antem. (M) *The mothers [of the deceased] come and bring branches to sweep the place where the person passed away. Then [people] can go*

around there without restriction.
2. put someone in danger; do something that allows something bad to happen to someone; be responsible for something bad that happens to a person or animal ◆ Arengk apek tha pewek, apmwarl anem utnhek. (St) *I let my dog get into danger, and then it got bitten by a snake.*

pewelhem, piwelhem (T,E) *vi.*
take a risk or put yourself in danger; bring trouble on yourself ◆ Rantey pewelhek terangk apekarl irrek. (St) *He brought trouble on himself by getting drunk.* ◆ Yarrp alhem mwerr antywetyew, wal tyerrty alenhel apek atwem, irrernng apek atwem — wal pewelhem. Yarrp. (M) *He might go himself to drink grog and then that person fights him, maybe even kills him — well that's trouble that he brought upon himself.* ◆ Rarrp kwenh pewelhek. Apal-pal angkerl-apenh, ahel-ahel akerl-apemel. (T) *He brought trouble on himself. By talking rubbish, and going around angrily.* ◆ *Town*-warl apek ayeng alhem. Atwety-ayntem apek. Pewelhek ayeng-antey. (St) *If I go to town and then run into a fight, then I have put myself in danger.*

pewerrem, piwerrem (T,E) *vi.*
get each other into trouble ◆ Piwerretyel terangkant-arey. Terangk alhenty piwerl-alpem ingwer alpemel iteth rant imekel atwemek, terangkel arrpelikw. (Sa) *The drunks get themselves into trouble. The drunks go somewhere and one of them gets into trouble and then comes back alive after he's been nearly beaten to death by a person who is drunk like him.* (?)

pewerl-alpem, piwerl-alpem (T,E) *vt.*
go somewhere and get into trouble, take someone or something somewhere where they get into trouble ◆ Artwa map irrer alhek, anyent apek piwerl-alpek. (St) *The men went hunting and one of them got into trouble.* ◆ Arengk atyenh tha pewerl-alpek. Ilwek kel. Amwel apek unhek. (St) *I let my dog get into danger. And then it died. Maybe it got bitten by a snake.* ◆ Pewek ampa akwek nhenhaw. Pewerl-alpek tha. Ayengarl alhek irrer, wal akwek nhenh atyeng antelhekarl. Akwek renh arnekarl antyety-alhek, kel arnel atanthek renh. Akuny — tha akngetyek irrer kerek-arrpantey. (St) *I let this little kid get into trouble. I went and they got into trouble. I went hunting and this little one followed me. The child went and climbed a tree and then got cut by a branch. The poor thing — I just meant to take her hunting.*

pewetyam (W,T), **pewetyem** (W) *n.*
fox. Also referred to as *angwely pewetyam.*

pewetyem-ilem (T) *vt.*
push someone or something (from English 'push')

peyaw (E) *part.*
an exclamation made when chasing goannas, perenties, and other animals ◆ Arlewatyerr athem atwem, *miss*-em-ilemel, ra unteman. Arlewatyerr untem. Kel athem atwenty-iperr, atwemarl ra arlewatyerr untem, ra alwernem anem renh, 'Ker atyenh untem, peyaw peyaw peyaw peyaw peyaw'. 'Peyaw peyaw', akemel. 'Pepepepepep', alakenh. (Sa) *If she misses the goanna when trying to hit it, then it runs away. After missing the goanna it runs off and she chases it, singing out, 'My meat is running away,* peyaw peyaw peyaw peyaw peyaw*'. She sings out,* 'peyaw peyaw'. *Like that,* 'pepepepepep'.
SEE ALSO arrpwernem

peyenat *n.*
the name of a card game (from English 'spear and heart' (?))
SEE ALSO kwernt[1], kart[2], parlperrp

peyley (E) silver witchetty SEE UNDER **perley**

pilal (T,E), **peylarl** (E) *n.*
ground-up seeds of the dogwood, *awenth, akerlperr* (?)

pilikan (E) billycan SEE UNDER **pelekan**[1]

pimpart (E) *n.*
1. a dog whose owner has died
2. ownerless (of other things apart from dogs)

pimpart-irrem (E) *vi.*
become ownerless (dog)
SEE ALSO ampeny[1]

pinem (W) hunt something down using dogs SEE UNDER **ipernem**

pingkey (E) *n.*
pig (from English 'pinky'). Another word for pig, *pek-pek*, is *kwementyay.*
= wangk-wangk, pek-pek

Pintwepey, Pentapey (W) *n.*
1. Pintupi person or people
2. Pintupi language

pip (E) paper, things made from paper SEE UNDER **pep**

pirley (E) silver witchetty SEE UNDER **perley**

pirrar pirraru, shiny-leaved wattle SEE UNDER **perrar**

pitepwerl (E) football SEE UNDER **pweteperl**

pitherr (T,E), **piterr** (T) *n.*
rock isotome (*Isotoma petraea*). A small plant about 30 cm high with soft green leaves and pale blue flowers. It grows around rocks and in caves. It is very poisonous and can cause blindless. Some people say that small

amounts were chewed along with native tobacco to increase its potency.
SEE ALSO anterernp
CAN SOUND A BIT LIKE petherr *'a type of white louse'*

pitherr (E) a type of white louse SEE UNDER **petherr**

piwem (T,E) 'finish up' after a death SEE UNDER **pewem**

Pmara Jutunta *n.*
Six Mile or Ti Tree Six Mile. From *Ywerternt* 'name of a place near Aileron'.
SEE ALSO Ywerternt

pmwar (E) small wooden shovel or scoop SEE UNDER **mwar**

pmwelper (E) part of the throat including the windpipe SEE UNDER **mwelper**

pmwely (E) squashed, crushed, dented SEE UNDER **mwely**

pmwelyar (E), **pmweylar** (E) bush thick-knee, stone-curlew SEE UNDER **mwelyar**

Pulardi SEE UNDER **Pwelartey**

Pungelindum SEE UNDER **Apengarlayntem**

purl (E) male SEE UNDER **pwel**[3]

purrk (E) weak, tired SEE UNDER **parrk**

purt (T,E) together, in a group SEE UNDER **pwert**

pwalh-iwem (E) *vt.*
skin an animal ◆ Kwatyek-arelh arranty wetharl yanhel iletyel, arrwekelenyel antywerretyart, *no billycan*. Aherr-kenharl itna mpwaretyart, aherr pwalh-iwem, kel arranty anem itna mpwarem. Ngkwern atherr arrernem, kwaty-kenh antywerl-anetyek, irrernt-areny antywetyek. (Sa) *The kangaroo-skin waterbag is what the olden-time people used to drink out of, when they had no billycans. They used to make them from kangaroo [skin], skinning the kangaroo and then making the waterbag. The two legs were tied up, and then they were able to drink the cold water [from the waterbag they made].*
SEE ALSO irrnyewem

pwarl (W,I) bush banana SEE UNDER **parl**

pwarleng (T) *n.*
in ignorance, not knowing ◆ Pwarleng anwern alartewerretyam. (T) *We were sitting down ignorant and we didn't know.*

pwarlk (W,T) in ignorance SEE UNDER **parlk**

pwarn, **parn** (W,T) *n.*
narrow, tight, jammed in close together, cramped ◆ *Road* yanh pwarn akwek mwetek alhetyek. (T) *The road is narrow, the car can't get through.* ◆ Pwarn nhenh mer, arlpaw anetyang. (St) *This place is too cramped, there is not enough room.* ◆ Pwet pwarn, uyarnarl irrpem. (T) *[I] can't get into these tight shoes.*
SEE ALSO tyert, arlpaw

pwarn-pwarn (E) *n.*
a bit narrow or tight

pwarn-irrem, **parn-irrem** (W,T) *vi.*
1. shrink, get narrow or tight ◆ Pwarn-irrem mantarr apek pwarn, ayeng irrpetyakenh. Alhewenty-penh, mantarr arnterrarl alhewekarl-penh irrpetyek ayeng tha inenh, pwarn-irrekarl. (St) *These clothes are tight and I can't get into them. After washing them too much I got them to put on but they'd shrunk.* ◆ Ahenty pwarn-irrem ayeng, arrkay akwel ahenty pwarn-irrem kwaty kwenyel. (St) *My throat is tight and my voice is faint because I haven't had any water to drink.* ◆ Mantarr atyenh angerrety-penh pwarn-irrek, atewatelarl alhewek. (T) *My clothes, that used to be big, have shrunk after being washed in hot water.*
2. heal over, close over (wound) ◆ Utyen pwarn-irrem. Arnterrek-amperr anem altywer wal pwarn-irrenty-alpem, ampwerrk-irremel anem, kel arrangkw anem. (St) *The sore heals over. It was open at first, but then it closes back over again, heals up and now there's nothing there.* • SEE ALSO arrintety-irrem, arterrp-irrem, ltyerrem, tywenmernt-irrem, kwerrm-irrem, urrmirrem

pwarn-ilem, **parn-ilem** (W,T) *vt.*
1. squash someone up, take up their space or room ◆ Tyerrty yanhel atyeng-kety pwarn-ilem mwetekay. (T) *That person is taking my space in the car.* ◆ Arengkarl intep-intemel apek pwarn-ilem ayenh, arengkel. (St) *The dogs that are sleeping here are squashing me.*
2. close something up, make narrow

pwarr (T,E) *n.*
1. unripe desert raisin fruit, *katyerr* = urleynterr[2]
SEE ALSO kwart
2. the bitter-tasting coating found on Solanum fruits and on the mulga apple ◆ Mern pwarr tiwem ahernel, kapert arntekety. Mern renh arlkwem anem. Pwarrinp arlkwem kapertan arntem. Renhengarl pwarr-iwem. (St) *The unripe desert raisin fruits are rubbed on the earth, so that you don't get a headache. Then you can eat the fruit. You'll get a headache if you eat the fruit with the bitter coating on it. That's why you rub it off.*
• SEE ALSO anka, tepwerl

pwarr-wem (T,E), **pwarr-iwem** (E) *vt.*
rub desert raisins on the ground to clean off the *pwarr*, the bitter-tasting coating
SEE ALSO tewem, thwerrem, inpewem, theweth-ilem

pwarrk (T,E) weak, tired SEE UNDER **parrk**
pwarrty (T) moonlight SEE UNDER **parrty**
pwarrtyelhem (E) *vt.*
eat till you are satisfied, feed yourself
SEE ALSO wantelhem
pwath *n.*
boss (from English 'boss')
pwek-pwek *n.*
stalked puffball (*Podaxis pistillaris*). Grows to about 10 cm high, on a long stalk. Powdery purplish-black spores inside. ◆ Pwek-pwek, ampel apernelherl-anem arrwert lyapetyek, urrperl ilelhemel, arrkenel-arleng. (Sa) *The boys use the stalked puffball to paint themselves with, to make their beards grow, and to make themselves dark in colour, for fun.*

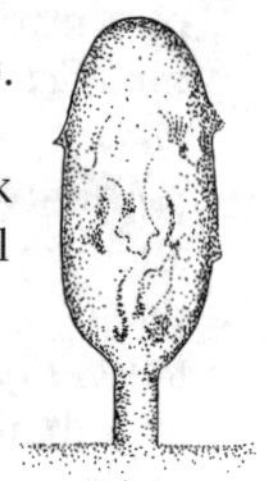

= anngarnt rrpwerl, arrepweng-pweng, arrekwep-kwep, kwep-kwep[3], pweng-pweng
pwel[1] *n.*
bull (from English 'bull')
pwel[2], **pwelap** *n.*
full, a lot of something (from English 'full', 'full up') ◆ Atnert pwelapel apek mentyel arem. (St) *I'm just looking because my stomach is full.* ◆ Yerrakwerr inyetyart irrkeremel irrkeremel inyetyart yerrakwerr renh, *billycan* pwelap inyetyart aweth inyetyart irrkeretyart irrkeretyart lpwelemel then-wetyart arlka arrernetyart pwelap kwetyemel, yerrakwerr yanh renh. (N) *We used to clear the ground and dig up the wild onions, filling up the billycans. We'd beat them to make them soft and then winnow them to clean them and then collect together all the wild onions that we had found.*
pwel-ilem, pwelap-ilem *vt.*
fill something up ◆ Arrpenh-warn alhemel aweth arntap arrpenh inemel angerretyem inem aweth, pwel-iletyart anwern pwel-iletyart anwern pwel-iletyart. Anyerrkemel. (N) *We used to fill up the bark containers and then move on to another tree and then fill another container, we filled them up. We enjoyed doing it.* ◆ Alhwa pwelap-ilelhemel awerrpan antywemarl. (Sa) *[You] drink kangaroo blood to make your blood plentiful.*
pwelap-irrem *vi.*
become full, fill yourself up
pwel[3] (W,T), **purl** (E) *n.*
male
aherr purl (E)
old male kangaroo (aherr *'kangaroo'*)
= aherr ampelaherr
pwel-pwel (W,T), **purl-purl** (E) *n.*
large ◆ Iltya pwel-pwel. *Thumb.* ◆ Ingka pwel-pwel. *Big toe.*
pwel-pwel *n.*
tadpole ◆ Pwel-pwel-penh ingkakert anem irrem, kantyan kelarl ikwerenh. Pwel-pwel weth kanty-akert ra anem, wal ingka atherr, iltya atherr. Kel *tail* apek arrangkw anem. (St) *The tadpole gets legs, it already has a tail. Those tadpoles have tails, and two hind legs and two forelegs. And then the tail disappears.* ◆ Ingka anetyakenhek-amparr anem perrak anem ra irrenhem. (St) *At first they don't have any legs and then they turn into frogs.*

= tyekepwelepwel, pwepely
pwelangket (E) blanket, swag SEE UNDER **pelangket**
pwelap full, a lot of something SEE UNDER **pwel**[2]
Pwelapert (W) *n.*
name of soakage south of Yuelamu (Mt Allan) community
Pwelartey (W,T) *n.*
Desert Bore. Location of an outstation on Yalpirakinu Aboriginal Land Trust (Mt Allan). Also spelt as Pulardi. See map p. viii.
pwelek *n.*
cattle, bullock, cow (from English 'bullock')
pwelerntar (W,T) native truffle SEE UNDER **pwerlantar**
pwelert *n.*
bullet (from English 'bullet') ◆ Maket-warl pwelert arrernem. (Sa) *Put the bullets in the gun.* ◆ 'Ngka, pwelertek, annga anthetyek, urrpety apek.' Kel renh inerl-alhem. Ker angwerrm atwety-alheyamel. (T) *'Give me a few bullets.' Then [he] gets them and goes off. Then he goes and shoots the game that he finds.*
= anngang atyerrenherrenh
SEE ALSO katety, annga
pweley *n.*
bald (from English 'baldy')
SEE ALSO kapert pweley
pwelh (E) *n.*
burnt (from too much cooking), charred
SEE ALSO antyerrk
CAN SOUND A BIT LIKE apwelh *'type of ceremony'*
pwelh-irrem (E) *vi.*
get burnt ◆ Ker pwelh-irrem, ker *barbecue* arrtyerrenty pwelh-irrem, aperrk-irremel, pwelh-irrem. Irrpwerl-irrerl-anem aperrk-apeny irrem, pwelh. (Sa) *Meat gets burnt, meat that is cooked on the barbecue gets burnt and*

turns to charcoal. It goes black like charcoal, burnt.

pwelkanty (T,E) *n.*
a type of dragon lizard (?) ◆ Amwely-artek pwelkanty akely ra. (Sa) *The* pwelkanty *lizard is like a little Cadney lizard.* ◆ Uterrpel ap alhetyel-rnem pwelkanty, ampekernerl-anem aretharrel, pwelkanty. Amwelyan ilkwarl, ra akely *one*. Ker arlkwenh-arlkwenh. (Sa) Pwelkanty *lizards go around in the sandhills, and they stand up when the north wind blows. The Cadney lizard is bigger, and the* pwelkanty *is smaller. They are edible.*
SEE ALSO amwely, ankert[2]

pweltak *n.*
a type of louse (found in clothes) ◆ Pweltak pang inngek-arelh, arreynelhetyek mpwarem *scratch*-em ilelhem. Ayengan akwerrp pweltak ikwer *clean*. Arrwelan angerrirretyart pweltak. Petherr ra. (Sa) *The* pweltak *louse is found on people, and they make [the people] scratch themselves. I haven't had much experience with lice, I'm clean. There used to be a lot of* pweltak *lice a long time ago. They are also called* petherr.
= petherr
SEE ALSO nya[1], artwek

pwelty *n.*
traditional football game played by men and children. A ball made of rags or hairstring was used, and the teams were arranged in opposing generation moieties [i.e. those that were *nywerrp* to each other]. ◆ Alyep ina mpwaretyam pwelty anem ina arrken-irretyam. Than aretyart arrengey map, anawerr map. (St) *They made a hairstring ball and then they played* pwelty. *I used to watch my grandfathers and my father's elder brothers.*
SEE ALSO nywerrp

pwely (E) *n.*
thick scrub ◆ Pwely-angkwerran alhem arnangkwerr, arna *too much* angkwerr, pwely, nthanh aretyanh. (Sa) *[We] are going though all the thick scrub, where there are too many trees, and you can't see anything.*
SEE ALSO werrk

Pwely (W) *n.*
name of a hill east of Coniston

pwem *vi.*
blow (wind) ◆ Rlkang pwem. (M) *The wind is blowing.* ◆ Alhurrp pwetyel akngerrakw-they. Ayerrer-theyarl aretharr pwetyel, alturl-they arlka. (Sa) *The* alhurrp *wind blows from the east. The* aretharr *wind blows from the north and the west.* ◆ Rlkang pwenty-alhem antekerreng. (N) *The wind is blowing from the south.*

pwenarr *n.*
bow and arrow (from English 'bow and arrow') ◆ Pwenarrel atanthem. (M) *Shooting with the bow and arrow.*

pweney-pweney *n.*
foal, pony (from English 'pony') ◆ Pweney-pweney akwek amwekel-ayel irnem. (T) *The little foal is standing with its mother.*

pweng *n.*
1. blind. Also referred to as *annga pweng* or *alkngа pweng*. ◆ Arelh ampwang anngang pweng arnerrerl-apem. (M) *The old blind woman is crawling along.* ◆ Pweng aretyakenh. Alkngа pweng aretyakenh. (St) *[I] am blind and I can't see. My eyes can't see.*
2. with eyes shut ◆ Arengk akwerrk pweng anem. Kel annga antem anngampem. (T) *The puppies are blind. Then their eyes open.* ◆ Ankwepenh apek pwengek-amperr intep-intem kel alkngerlkenty alhem. (St) *After being asleep you lie there with your eyes shut and then you open them.*
3. an affectionate term for women or girls ◆ Arelh awenk 'pweng' akep-akem-antey. 'Pweng akelyek, pweng akwekek.' Alerelikw, ampikwel apek, mathel apek. 'Pweng akwek nhenhaw.' War 'pweng' akem. (St) *A teenage girl might be called* 'pweng' *as well. 'Little blind one.' Her nephew might call her that or her niece, or her mother. 'This little blind one.' They are just called* 'pweng' *for no particular reason.* ◆ 'Pweng' arrpenh-antey arrkenel. Wararl ilem, *meaning*-arl. 'Pwengay. Pweng nhenh-warl apety aretyek.' 'Pwengay nga apek alhay yanh awetyek. Arntengengkw apek awetyek.' Alkngа mwerrarl kel, wararl ilem yanh, mpwerneleyekw apek ilem, wararl ilem, *sister-in-law* ikwerenh ilem. Mwerr way wararl angkem. (St) *'Pweng' is just said for fun. It doesn't mean anything in particular. 'Blind one. Come and see this.' 'Blind one, you should go and listen to that person over there. To your sister-in-law.' Her eyes are good all right, but it's just something that is said, maybe by a brother-in-law to his sister-in-law. It's okay to just talk like that.*
4. an old honeyant nest

pweng-irrem *vi.*
1. go blind
2. blink, close eyes

annga pweng-irrem, **alkngа pweng-irrem** (E)
blink, go blind (annga *'eye'*)

pwengentem (W,T) *n.*
close (eyes)

pweng-pweng (W), **pwengep** (W) *n.*
stalked puffball (*Podaxis pistillaris*). Grows to

about 10 cm high, on a long stalk. Powdery purplish-black spores inside.
= pwek-pwek, anngarnt rrpwerl, kwep-kwep[3], arrepweng-pweng, arrekwep-kwep

-pwenh Goes on words for compass directions; from that direction. SEE UNDER **-penh[2]**

pwenkart *n.*
turkey bush (*Eremophila gilesii*). A small shrub with narrow leaves and blue flowers. Always grows near mulga. ◆ Pwenkart angwerrm, *medicine,* alhewelhenhelhenh, ant lpwelenhelenh, lpwelem, *green* mparemel. Apwertel. Anter-warl arrernem. (T) *The turkey bush is used as a medicine, a washing medicine. It is also crushed up with a stone till it is green and then mixed with fat.*
= kwenkart

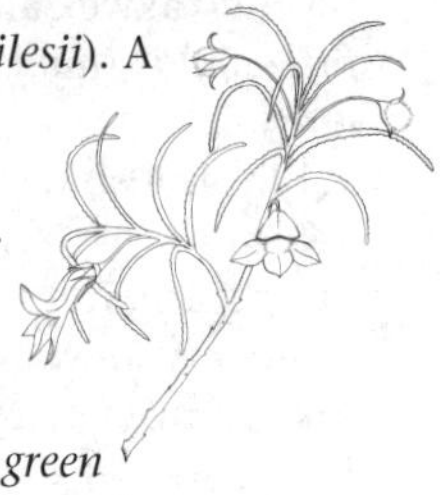

pwenkel anem (T,E) *vi.* [RESPECT LANGUAGE]
stay in one place and not go anywhere because of mourning ◆ Ayeng pwenkel aney, menty kwenh, *self.* Atwaretyal. (T) *I am sitting down here grieving on my own. Not meeting up with anyone.* (?) ◆ Alyent-artek ahern anengkanel anwantherr pwenkel aney. Pwenkel aney anwantherr alyent-artekel. (Sa) *We are sitting down in one place in mourning.* (?)

pwentarnengayt (E) *n.*
grub from the flying-saucer bush, *ntwarneng*

pwentereng (E) *n.*
large ant bed or ant hill. *Pwentereng are usually only found in the northern areas of Central Australia.*
SEE ALSO ngkwepey, kerrertek, merntap, awerr-awerr[1]

pwenty[1] (E) *n.*
disease or sickness ◆ Alhernteran arntety-irrem arrmel wethey pwenty-penh. Pwenty alanhel anyem angetyetyel aretharrel atwenhem, kel ra arntety-irremel, angkwerr-wenty apek ra mwerrarl-irrem. Arrwengkelth anyent rantey. (Sa) *White people get sick as well from that* pwenty. *It's the* aretharr *wind that brings that sickness, then the person gets sick, and they get better after being treated with traditional massage.* Arrwengkelth *is the same as* pwenty. ◆ Pwentyel artarrernem, urlaylpel apek artarrernem, urlaylpel apek artarrernem pwenty yal, kel arntety-irrem ra ikwer-penh. Kel ngangkerelant angkwerr-iwem. (Sa) *The kurdaitcha might send the sickness onto someone, and then they get sick after that. Only the traditional healer can cure them with the healing massage.*
SEE ALSO arrwengkelth

pwenty[2] (E) *n.*
a type of ceremony
SEE ALSO althart, ilpenty

pwentyengeyengey (E) moustache, facial hair above lips SEE UNDER **pentyengeyengey**

pwep-angkem *vi.*
make a hollow sound (ground). This is generally said of the noise that indicates the presence of a tuber or hollow root (containing a grub) beneath the surface of the ground. ◆ Ahelh pwep-angkem. Ntap kerwepel atanthem atanthem wal pwep-angkem ahelh alenh. Anyematy-akert apek. (M) *The ground makes a hollow sound. You might go along stabbing the ground with a crowbar and then the ground makes a hollow sound. Maybe there is a witchetty grub there.* ◆ Pwep-angkenty awem aketh-antey, 'Mern nhenhaw kwenh'. Kel angernemel. Tyer-wem anemel apek renh tyer-wem. Kel renh angernemel angernemel. 'Pweparl angkek arraty kwenh anaty nhenh.' (Sa) *When you clearly hear that hollow sound you say, 'This is where the tuber is'. Then you dig. You might poke around at it with the digging stick. And then dig and dig, dig it up. [Then you say]. 'It really did make that hollow sound, here's the bush potato.'*
SEE ALSO rltar-irrem, urrper

Pwepany (W,T) *n.*
Papunya

pwepely *n.*
tadpole
= pwel-pwel, tyekepwelepwel

pwer *n.* [SENSITIVE LANGUAGE]
1. tail of an animal ◆ Aherr pwer. (M) *Kangaroo tail.* ◆ Kwer-penh aweth anthek-wem pwer-thaytem. Ngkwern atherr ltwakem ingka atherr, pwer ltwakem. (N) *Then you singe the kangaroo on the tail side. The two legs are broken, and the two feet, and the tail.*
2. lightning. Also referred to as *kwaty pwer.* ◆ Kwaty pwerel ltewetyam arrwekeleny. (T) *People used to get hit by lightning.* ◆ Kwaty angkentyem pwer-akert. (T) *A thunderstorm is coming, with lightning.* • = awely-awely
3. penis
CAN SOUND A BIT LIKE apwer *'shame'*

ker pwer
tail-meat of a kangaroo

pwer rrpwerl (W,T)
black goanna (*Varanus tristis*) (lit. 'black tail')
= kweny-areny, alpangwerr, altywekerr,

kwenyel alhem
pwer arlewatyerr, pwer arlewatyerr-arlewatyerr (E)
yellow-faced whip-snake (*Demansia psammophis*) (lit. 'goanna tail')
SEE ALSO arlewatyerr-arlewatyerr[1]
pwer arlpenty-arlpenty (W)
a type of snake (?) (lit. 'long tail')

pwerakart *n.*
meat from the back part of the emu

Pwerakart (W), **Pwerakert** (W) *n.*
name of a soakage and creek east of old Coniston Homestead

pweralhem (E), **aperalhem** (E) *n.*
1. types of mistletoe (*Amyema* spp.; *Lysiana* spp.)
2. the edible fruits of these mistletoes ◆ Arwerl arlperr-areny, amarelap ra anetyel pweralhem. (Sa) *The* pweralhem *fruits are found on the mistletoe which grows on the whitewood.*
SEE ALSO atyankern, amar, ngartangkern, peketyalkwarr, ngkwerrm

pwerelyerr-lyerr (W,T) *n.*
types of wren (?) (*Malurus* spp.)
SEE ALSO lyerr-lyerr

pwerep-irrem *vi.*
1. feel sore or tender; be in pain, hurt; feel sensitive, touchy or jumpy ◆ Lyekel atanthem wal ingkan pwerep-irrem. (St) *Feet are hurting from being spiked by prickles.* ◆ Arntety apek ayeng pwerep-irrem. (St) *I'm in pain because I'm sick.*
2. feel shamed or uncomfortable ◆ Ayeng pwerep-irrem mwerew-kety. (M) *I feel shamed because of my son-in-law.*
SEE ALSO nyerr-irrem, apwer-irrem, lwereny-irrem

pweretyetyer (W), **pweretyety** (W,T), **pweretyetyey** (T) *n.*
pied butcherbird (*Cracticus nigrogularis*)
= matyekatyer
SEE ALSO arrpwerek-arrpwer, rtey-rtey

Pwereytarr (E) *n.*
a star constellation; the Saucepan (part of Orion)
SEE ALSO Anterl, Arnkenty, Arlanty, Ingkapeny, Ingkartek

pwerl *n.*
small grinding stone used for seeds ◆ 'Pwerl', arnwetyarl athem, awantyetyek, athem anemey. Anterrng athem awantyem, pwerl yal. Pwerlel athemek, irntang atherarl. (N) *The stone called* 'pwerl' *is used to grind up seeds so that they can be eaten. That* pwerl *is used to grind the seeds up on the large flat grinding stone.* ◆ Ateyepenh, anterrng, *heap* arrernetyam ahern-warl. Anterrng ateyepenh athetyam irntel, pwerlel panth-warn, *heap* arrernetyam, athetyam, awantyetyam, theletyam. (N) *The seeds from the whipstick wattle are heaped up on the ground. Then they are ground up using grinding stones. The seed paste is put into the wooden dishes and eaten.*

SEE ALSO ather, artwert[1], tyeng
CAN SOUND A BIT LIKE pwel[1] *'bull'*; pwel[2] *'full'*

Pwerl *n.*
skin name, subsection or section name, marriage class. See diagram p. 744.
SEE ALSO Pwerrerl

pwerlantar (T), **pwelerntar** (W,T) *n.*
native truffle, desert truffle (*Choiromyces aboriginum* (tentative taxonomy)). These are white and juicy when young, and yellow and wrinkled when older. Found in spinifex country.
= akwerrerteth, irrkwenng

pwerlep *n.*
shoulder, shoulderblade ◆ Maket annga akwernem, thak yanhan alernem pwerlep-warl, kel atyerrem anem. (St) *You put the bullet in the gun, rest the stock against your shoulder and then shoot.*
pwerlep annga (W,T)
point or top of the shoulder; shoulder joint (annga *'eye', 'round thing'*)
pwerlep ngkwern (E)
shoulderblade (ngkwern *'bone'*)
SEE ALSO rrpwa, alkwert-alkwert

pwerlp-irrem *vi.*
1. swim; dive into water; get into water ◆ Artwang lyweny-penh kwaty-warn pwerlp-irrem anyartey-ilelhetyek. (T) *After going hunting the man dives into the water to cool himself down.* ◆ Kwaty kwetn akngerrek pwerlp-irrekerr, iterel pwerlp-irra. (Sa) *Swim on the side [of the creek], not in the really deep water.* ◆ Angkweyarl anwern pwerlp-irretyart, rewel pwerlp-irrenhem, irrpenhem, mer arrpelant arratenhetyam. Kwereng mer arrpelem irrpentyetyam, arratetyam mer arrpelant. Arnang tintey-angkwarr apek kel *jump*-irretyart anwern. (N) *We used to swim in the running water, going into the water at one spot and then coming out at another. Then we'd go in again and come out at yet another place. We used to jump in from the bent-down branches of trees.*
2. have a shower, a bath or a wash [SOME SPEAKERS]
SEE ALSO irrpem

pwerlp-wem (T,E), **pwerlp-iwem** (E) *vt.*
1. mix tobacco with ashes ◆ Pwerlp-wem arnmeny-warl ngkwerlp atyenh. (St) *I'm mixing my tobacco with ashes.*
= arek-wem
2. put animal carcass on a fire to singe off hair, fur or scales ◆ Alkngenth ampem, ker anem pwerlp-iwem aherr apek arlewatyerr apek. (St) *When the flames are burning you throw the kangaroo or the goanna onto the fire to singe it.* • = nthek-wem
3. bathe somebody ◆ Ampa akelyan pwerlp-wem. (Sa) *Bathing the little baby.*

pwerlt-irrem *vi.*
run off; clear out, go away in a hurry (from English 'bolt') ◆ Angank arwengkalth — arraty. Nyenngel arlkwerl-anem akweteth akweteth ateram arrtyanetyenheng, pwerlt-irrem. (N) *Crows are robbers — that's true. They always sneak around and steal food to eat and then when they are frightened they fly off, clear out.*
SEE ALSO arrtyanem

pwernengk (W,T) *n.*
ghost gum (*Corymbia aparrerinja*). Tree to 15 m high, with smooth white trunk and drooping branches.
= ulemp

pwernkem[1] (W) *vi.*
(men) make a noise with the lips to indicate the presence of certain kin; warn them of your presence. For example, men make this special sound with their lips to indicate the presence of their *thampartey*, with whom they have a special respect relationship.
SEE ALSO unpernem, thampartey
pwernkelhem (W) *vi.* = **pwernkem**

pwernkem[2] (E) *vi.*
split open
= tyarrp-irrem

Pwerray (T) *n.*
name of a place in the Ti Tree (Ahakeye Aboriginal Land Trust) area. See map p. viii.
SEE ALSO Nthwerey

pwerrenperrenp (W,T) *n.*
a type of prickle (?)
SEE ALSO arlketyerr, thenkarr, kapert angerr, lyek

pwerreparnt (W,T) *n.*
desert spadefoot toad (*Notaden nichollsi*) (note Warlpiri *purru-parnta*)
= kwep-kwep[2], atweynterl, kwep

pwerrer anyem (E), **pwerrer atnyem** (E) *vi.*
(lots of things) fall down (anyem *'fall'*); pwerrer (?) ◆ Mern atwakey pwerrer atnyek arwerl-they. (St) *Lots of wild oranges fell from the tree.*
pwerrer atwem (E)
hit something so that lots of things fall down (atwem *'hit'*) ◆ Mern kathip pwerrer atwetyek arnel. (St) *Hit the bush coconuts with a stick so that lots of them fall down.*

Pwerrerl *n.*
skin name, subsection name, marriage class. See diagram p. 744. ◆ Arelh Pwerrerlel anew akem artwang Penangk. Kwer kweratherrenh angwerrm-irrek Pengart map. (T) *A Pwerrerl woman's husband is Penangk. Their children will be born Pengart.*
SEE ALSO Pwerl, Tywelam, Ngampwerl, Napwerr, Napwerrerl, Tyweperr, Tyweperrerl

pwerrk (T) weak, tired SEE UNDER **parrk**

pwerrk-pwerrk (E) a type of black beetle SEE UNDER **perrk-perrk**

pwerrtyel atwem (W) *vt.*
1. hit or bump somebody or something ◆ Ingkern anyerl-anem tyerrtyarl pwerrtyel atwenheman. (M) *[Somebody] falls over after a person has bumped into them as they went past.*
2. punish someone straight away without waiting to talk (?); fight without consideration for kinship; fight somebody in a rage ◆ Ilterrekarl-penh rang pwerrtyelam renh atwek. (T) *After arguing, he hit him straight away (i.e. didn't wait to talk).* • = pwethel atwem

pwert (W,T), **purt** (T,E) *n.*
together, in a group ◆ Pwert anwengkerr ananetyeh. (M) *We are all sitting here together.* ◆ Purt anwantherr anerl-anem *whole lot.* (St) *We are all sitting down together, the whole lot of us.* ◆ Pwert ingkerrek anantherr anerl-anem, alhetyakenh. (T) *We are all sitting down together, not going anywhere.* ◆ Thakeman pwertant-arey anwern warrk-irretyart. (T) *We used to work together as stockmen.*
◆ Irrkwerrenty ananem iwetyangenh, purt antey, itengant-atherr. Itengant-atherr iwerretyang purt anerl-anem irrkwerrenty. (Sa) *The two of them are still together, they haven't split up. The two of them are still together.*
CAN SOUND A BIT LIKE pwet *'shoe'*; apwert *'rock', 'hill'*
pwert-irrem (W,T), **purt-irrem** (E) *vi.*
1. get together, get into a group ◆ 'Anwengkerr pwert-irrey.' Tyerrty ina angkem, pwert-irretyeh. (M) *'Let's get together.' People talk like that, about getting together.*
2. cramp or tighten up; curl into a ball ◆ Iltya purt-irrem arlerlp-irrenty irrerntek. (Sa) *Fingers curl up when they are cramped from the cold.*
◆ Rtapety interl-anem, alwerrngarl pwert-

irrem, *cramp*-arl-irremeng, atywaty-irrememem. Atywaty amparr irrem kwer-penh rtapetyem interl-anem. (N) *Lying down cramped up, because your tendons have cramped up. Stretch out first and then lie there curled up.* • SEE ALSO arrepert-irrem, arlwerrelhem

3. turn into a lump ◆ Arlkwem renh, mwerr akngerr. Alhwa rarl purt-irrekarl 'ntyewey'. Ker mwerr angerr renh arlkwem. (St) *It is really nice to eat. Blood that has gone into a solid lump is called* 'ntyewey'. *It is really good to eat.*

pwert-ilem (W,T), **purt-ilem** (E) *vt.*

1. make something into a lump ◆ Iltyel amparr inetyart pwertem iletyart perrap theweyet rnpwang *mixed* akwel anyerleng ra. (N) *First [you] used to collect it with your hands and then the sweet stuff was made into a lump, mixed with [the flowers of] the turkey bush.*

2. get things together into a group

pwertay (E) *part.*

an exclamation used when warning people; 'Be careful', 'Watch out!', 'Look out!' ◆ Pwertay! Iyntwarr-iyntwarr ana! (Sa) *Look out! Shift a bit further away!*

= alay[2]

pwerterleng *n.*

heart ◆ Pwerterleng anem kwen-thayt, rtwekertel-ayel. (M) *The heart is inside the chest.*

SEE ALSO rtwekert

pwerterrerterrert (W) round in shape SEE UNDER apwerterrerterr

pwet *n.*

boot, shoe (from English 'boot') ◆ Ingkarl atanthemel arlketyerran, *sharp one. Cheeky bugger*, ingkang awangkelh-ilenh-ilenh. 'Pwet-kweny arekerr-irrem ayeng.' (T) *The* arlketyerr *prickle spikes your foot. It's a cheeky bugger and it makes your feet swell up. 'I haven't got any shoes and I'm in pain.'*

SEE ALSO thangey

pweteperl, **patepwerl** (T), **pitepwerl** (E) *n.*

football (from English 'football') ◆ Artwel patepwerl ingkel atwem arrpenh alenh-warn. (T) *The man is kicking the football to the other one over there.*

pwetew *n.*

photo, photograph (from English 'photo')

pwetewem-ilem *vt.*

take a photo

pweth-irrem (E) *vi.*

get really angry or wild

= urrampem

SEE ALSO ahel-irrem

pwethekat, **pwetyekat** (E) *n.*

cat (from English 'pussy cat'). Also referred to as *ker pwethekat.* ◆ Angkwey inang ker pwethekat arlkwetyart. (T) *In the old days they used to eat cats.*

SEE ALSO rlwatert, mangw, nyarrapeng, pwethey, angay, annga atherrk, meyaw-meyaw

pwethel atwem (W,T), **pwetyel atwem** (T) *vt.*

punish someone straight away without waiting to talk (?); fight without consideration for kinship; fight somebody in a rage

= pwerrtyel atwem

pwethey (E) *n.*

cat, pussy (from English 'pussy')

SEE ALSO pwethekat, rlwatert, mangw, nyarrapeng, angay, annga atherrk, meyaw-meyaw

pwety *n.*

bush (from English 'bush')

pwety-areny *n.*

things from the bush

pwety-ilem (T), **pweyt-ilem** (E) *vt.*

join something together; mix something; mend something that is broken

SEE ALSO anyent-ilem, anyentelh-ilem, arrakwernem[1]

pwetyelh-ilem (T), **pweytelh-ilem** (E) *vt.*

= **pwety-ilem** ◆ Panth pweytelh-ilem arrkiper ilwemp-arenyel. (St) *Mending the coolamon by joining it together with the resin from the ghost gum.*

pwety-irrem (T), **pweyt-irrem** (E) *vi.*

join together, get back together, mix together ◆ Tyerrty atherr pweyt-irrem. Kel ratherr anem *friend* anem alhep-alhem. (St) *The two people get back together. Then the two of them go around as friends now.*

SEE ALSO anyent-irrem

pwetyekat (E) cat SEE UNDER **pwethekat**

pwetyel atwem (T) punish someone straight away without waiting to talk (?) SEE UNDER **pwethel atwem**

pweynteng (E) *n.*

dry, old (especially of certain bush foods) ◆ Alkwarrer pweyntengarl irrek. (Sa) *The bush banana has gone dry.*

= atnywa

pweynteng-irrem (E) *vi.*

go dry, get old (of certain bush foods)

= atnywirrem

Rr

ra, rang (W,T), **ya** (W,T), **yang** (W,T) *prn.*
he, she, it. This pronoun is used in the subject part of a sentence (i.e. representing the 'doer' of the verb action) with both transitive and instransitive verbs. See Appendix 1.
SEE ALSO renh, kwer, kwerenh

rantey (E) *prn.*
1. something is similar to, or the same as, something else ◆ Urrar arlkem wal ranteyarl arlkem, ra arlkem tyerrtyek kenh nhakw urrar tyernelhekarl. (St) *The echo calls out in the same way as the person calls out, the person sings out to someone and the echo answers back.*
◆ Alhernteran arntety-irrem arrmel wethey pwenty-penh. Pwenty alanhel anyem angetyetyel aretharrel atwenhem, kel ra arntety-irremel, angkwerr-wenty apek ra mwerrarl-irrem. Arrwengkelth anyent rantey. (Sa) *White people get sick as well from that* pwenty. *It's the* aretharr *wind that brings that sickness, then the person gets sick, and they get better after being treated with traditional massage.* Arrwengkelth *is the same as* pwenty.
2. emphasises that someone did an action themselves ◆ Rantey pewelhek terangk apekarl irrek. (St) *He brought trouble on himself by getting drunk.*

ratherr, yatherr (W,T) *prn.*
they (two), those two, the two of them. This pronoun is used in the subject part of a sentence (i.e. representing the 'doer' of the verb action) with both transitive and instransitive verbs. See Appendix 1. ◆ Ratherr alherrek. (T) *Those two went.* ◆ Atwerremarl-ketyaw. Mernek-arrngel apek ratherr atwerrem. (St) *Look out, they're fighting. Maybe those two are fighting over food.* ◆ Awerr atherr alherl-aperretyam anyerrkentyem mer-warn, amwang yatherr atwekarl-penh. (M) *The two boys went home happy because they had killed a snake.*
SEE ALSO ra, atherr[1], renh-atherr, kwer-atherr, kwer-atherrenh

ratherr-apeny (E) *n.*
the same as those two

rant-atherr, yant-atherr (W,T)
two things that are the same as, or very similar to, each other; two identical things
◆ Tyampet nhenh atherr rant-atherr. (T) *These two billycans are the same.* ◆ Arlewatyerr nhenh atherr rant-atherr, arlkeny rant-atherr. (T) *These two goannas are the same, they have the same markings.* ◆ Kwer akwek rant-atherr, inngerr anyent akwet. (T) *These two kids are similar to each other, their faces are alike.*
SEE ALSO inant inant

rarey, yarey (W,T) *prn.*
they (more than two) (-arey '*plural*'). This pronoun is used in the subject part of a sentence (i.e. representing the 'doers' of the verb action) with both transitive and instransitive verbs. See Appendix 1.
◆ Alhengkey-ilemarl ayenh iltep-iltem rarey. (St) *They are growling and making me feel not wanted.*
= rernem
SEE ALSO renh-arey, kwer-arey, kwer-areyenh

rernem (E) *prn.* = **rarey** (-rnem '*plural*')
◆ Apwertel rernem anetyel. Rwekwenyel athamel. (Sa) *They are living in the hills. In the dark without fire.*

rakem *vt.*
take something away from someone; grab something off someone; steal, snatch ◆ Ker arlewatyerr arengkel nhwem, kel tyerrty rakem kel angernem itetyeh. (T) *The dog bites the goanna, and then the person grabs the goanna and takes it back to cook.* ◆ Tyerrty arrpenh alert-hety nta rakem pweteperl apek, or mern apek rakem nta. (M) *You might grab the football, or some food, off that person.*
CAN SOUND A BIT LIKE arwakem *'lever up root'*

rakerrem *vi.*
grab things off each other; take things off each other ◆ Ampa akely atherr rakerrem, rakemel ampa ikngwer mern apek ker apek, rakerrem. 'Ampa atherr yanh rakerremaw!' Alanhel ilerrem. (Sa) *The two little kids are grabbing things off each other, one of them is taking the meat or the food off the other. 'Those two kids are taking things off each other!' That's what people say.*

rang (W,T) he, she, it SEE UNDER **ra**

rang-rang (W,T) *n.*
crooked, the wrong way round (from English 'wrong') ◆ Mantarrek ntwang irrpek rang-rang. (T) *You have put your clothes on the wrong way round.*
SEE ALSO arnkwert-arnkwert

raperap-irrem (W) *vi.*
become silly in the head; get a headache, be driven mad ◆ Raperapem ayeng irrem kapert, ahert-ahert-irrem kwer nhenhel ahert-ahert mpwarem. (M) *I'm going silly in the head, this kid is driving me mad.*
= akeleraperap-irrem

rapet *n.*
rabbit (from English 'rabbit')
= pet-pet, alkwert atwenh, mwetyernk, metyernk

rapety *n.*
rubbish, garbage (from English 'rubbish') ◆ Mantarr arrweleny arrarlp-iwem iwem rapety-warl. (Sa) *Chuck the old clothes into the rubbish.* ◆ Rapety tha aharl arrerney. (St) *I'll make a pile of rubbish.*

rarrp SEE UNDER **+arrp**

ratherr SEE UNDER **ra**

rawenyerr-ilem (E) make a nuisance of self SEE UNDER **urawenyerr-ilem**

rayerrp (T,E) black-headed python SEE UNDER **rwayerrp**

reken-irrem (W,T), **riken-irrem** (E), **reken-reken-irrem** (W,T) *vi.*
show off, brag, think you're smart, reckon you're something (from English 'reckon') ◆ Riken-irretyel ntwa atyengety, mwetek *new one*-akert unta riken-irretyel atyengety. Ayenh anthetyakenh. Riken-arrpantey unta irretyel urrtyirrepirrerl, atyengety. (Sa) *You're showing off to me because you've got a new car. You didn't give me one. You're showing off in front of me and making out as if you're fantastic.* ◆ Kwer yanh reken-reken-irrerlapem, artwang anthwerr. (T) *That little child is going round showing off, he reckons he's a big man.*
SEE ALSO arrkereny-irrem, tyenkarl-irrem

rempereng (W) a type of bird, possibly the mulga parrot SEE UNDER **urimpering**

reng inem (W,T), **reng-reng inem** (W,T) *vt.*
sort things out; separate one thing out from another ◆ Reng inay, mwerr mapay. (M) *Sort out the good ones.* ◆ Arelh yanhel mantarr reng-reng inepinem. (T) *That woman is sorting out the clothes.* ◆ Artwang yanhel reng-reng arrernepernem ker aherr map, ker anter-angerr, ker ampwang map. (T) *That man is sorting out the kangaroo meat, the fatty meat and the lean meat.*
= angakem

rengalengal (E) *n.* [RESPECT LANGUAGE]
shield
SEE ALSO alkwert

renh, **yenh** (W,T) *prn.*
him, her, it. This is a singular pronoun used in the object part of the sentence (i.e. representing the person or thing the verb action is 'done to'). See Appendix 1. ◆ Thang renh atwem. (M) *I hit him/her/it.* ◆ Ayenh thang arern. (M) *I just saw her.* ◆ Ker atnarlt artew-kenh kwen, anertel. Inem renh, arlkwem renh, atna iwemel. (St) *The edible* atnarlt *meat is inside the stomach part of the bush turkey. [You] get it and eat it, after cleaning out the guts.* ◆ Arrkernkel ngkwarl arwengalker anem. Atwem, arrpem anem ngkwarl renh tyampet-warl arntap-warl arrernem. Ankerrmernel arlka. (St) *Sugarbag is found in bloodwood trees. [You] chop the tree and pare back the wood and then put the honey in a tin or in a bark container. Sugarbag is also found in coolibah trees.*
= renhenh
SEE ALSO ra

renhenh (W,T), **yenhenh** (W,T) *prn.* = **renh** [SOME SPEAKERS] ◆ Ampelam tha renhenh arek, Coniston side. (M) *As a child I saw him over Coniston way.*
SEE ALSO ra

renh-atherr, **yenh-atherr** (W,T), **yenh-atherrenh** (W,T) *prn.*
them (the two of them). This is a dual pronoun used in the object part of the sentence (i.e. representing the two the verb action is 'done to'). See Appendix 1. ◆ Yenh-atherr thang atwem. (M) *I'm hitting the two of them.* ◆ Artwang atherr atwerrem, an arelhel akalkelh-ilem renh-atherr. (T) *Two men are fighting each other, and the woman splits them up.*
SEE ALSO ratherr, ra, atherr[1]

renh-arey, **yenh-arey** (W,T) *prn.*
them (more than two). This is a plural pronoun used in the object part of the sentence (i.e. representing those the verb action is 'done to'). See Appendix 1.
SEE ALSO ra, rarey, kwer-arey, kwer-areyenh

rep (E) *adv.*
going along empty-handed, without anything
= iltyant

rernem SEE UNDER **ra**

rernp-rernp (W) a type of cicada or cricket (?) SEE UNDER **rwernp-rwernp**

rerrk (T,E), **yerrk** (W,T) *n.*
old fireplace, cooking spot, fire pit ◆ Kerarl ampem-penh rerrk. 'Rerrk yanh irrkatyek-antey angerney, aherr ampeyameng.' (St) *The fireplace is there from cooking meat. 'Dig up that same old fire pit so that we can cook the kangaroo meat.'* ◆ Ker-kenh rerrk akweteth. Aherr apek akngety-alpem rerrk anyent yanh ikwerel iterl-anetyek, ipert anyentel iterl-anetyek. (St) *A* rerrk *is a permanent cooking place. You might bring the kangaroo back to that one place to cook it, to cook it in the same hole.*

rerrkem *vi.*
make a rustling, rattling or scratching sound ◆ Apmwa apek rerrkem, kwen apek rerrkelh-ilem anthelk, rerrkelh-ilenhem anem, arnam apek rerrkelh-ilenhem apmwel. (St) *The snake might making a rustling sound, underneath the scraps of grass, making the grass rustle as it goes along.*
rerrkelh-ilem *vt.*
make something rattle or rustle
SEE ALSO inkerrelh-ilem

retyeperety (T,E) *n.*
a type of bird (?)

rew *n.*
flowing water, flood, running water. Also referred to as *kwaty rew*. ◆ Rew rlkwerrp-akert apetyem. (T) *The floodwater, with froth on it, is coming.*
SEE ALSO awarr
= **urew** (E)
rew inperrenh (W)
dragonfly (rew '*flood*'; imperrem '*go along the top of water*' (?))
= kwaty-inperrenh, urewap-imperreny, warepelh-pelh, kapert[2]
rew-irrem *vi.*
go soft (fruits); melt, turn into a liquid ◆ Arlelyek ampengem arlkwem. Akemel angernemel rwelem item, mern atyerrety-alpem, rarrp rew-irrem, kernt-irretyek arrernem, arlkwem renh alenyel war inem. (N) *The* arlelyek *fruits are eaten when they are ripe. They are picked, taken back home and cooked so that they go soft, laid out to cool down, and then eaten.*
SEE ALSO thelty-irrem, arrwelth-irrem, irrngwirrem, kwaty-irrem
rew-ilem *vt.*
melt something; make something wet
SEE ALSO arrwelth-ilem, irrngwilem
rew-rew *n.*
wet, sloppy, watery, runny
= aperlk-aperlk, kwaty-kwaty[1]
rew-rew-irrem *vi.*
go watery or runny
rew-rew-ilem *vt.*
make something watery, sloppy or runny ◆ Arterrty atyeng antheyaw tha rlterrk-iletyek mern — rew-rewarl ilek, kwatyarl thelek *too much.* (St) *Give me some dry flour so that I can make this mixture more solid — I made it runny by tipping too much water in.*
= kwaty-kwaty-ilem

rewap-imperr (E) dragonfly SEE UNDER **urewap-imperreny**

rewelyerr (T,E), **rewelyey** (E), **rewelyek** (E) *n.*
horn (of an animal) ◆ Rewelyek-akert nanekwet — yep-yep rewelyek akert-antey. (St) *Goats have horns — sheep have horns as well.*
= yerewelyek, yarwelyem, ahiwelhem, napey

riken-irrem (E) show off, brag SEE UNDER **reken-irrem**

ring-irrem (E) *vi.*
ring (make a ringing sound) (from English 'ring')
= rltengk-rltengk-irrem

rinty (E) *n.*
home, familiar place ◆ 'Rinty' akeman apmer-warl irremel alpetyek. Mer rinty-warl irremel alpetyek. Mer-warl irremel, aknganekarl-warl. (St) *'*Rinty*' is what going back home is called. Going back home to the familiar place. Going back to the place where you originated from.* ◆ Mer rinty-warl ayeng alpetyek, rintyel anety-alpetyek, rwanng-warl. (Sa) *I want to go back home, go back and stay in the familiar place, the place that I'm used to.*
SEE ALSO arlalty, uranng

rirrkwem (E) shake bush plum or native citrus tree, *ahakey*, to make the fruit fall down SEE UNDER **ywerrkem**

ritak (E) *n.* [RESPECT LANGUAGE]
red ochre (from English 'red ochre') ◆ Ritak-ayerr yanhentyak ayeng apernelherlentyarretyek irrepethenherrarey, aperlentyarretyek, arlter-ayerr yanhentyak. (Sa) *Go and get me some red ochre [from my respect kin] so that I can paint myself up, and some white ochre.*
SEE ALSO urlpa

rlalth (W,T) march fly SEE UNDER **lyalth**

Rlampetherr (W) name of a hill in the Stuart Bluff Range area SEE UNDER **Lampetherr**

Rlanenty (W,T) a big river or watercourse [SOME SPEAKERS] SEE UNDER **Arlanenty**

rlengk-rlengk (W,T) point of the jawbone SEE UNDER **lengk-lengk**

rlengkay (E) a mark made on the foreheads of small children to protect them from the *aretharr* wind SEE UNDER **rlwengkay**

rleynterr (E) ridge of the nose between the eyes SEE UNDER **urleynterr**[1]

rlka (W,T), **rlkang** (W,T), **iylka** (E) *n.*
wind ◆ Rlkang pwem. (M) *The wind is blowing.* ◆ Rlkangel arnang map angelh-angelh-ilem. (M) *The wind is making the trees shake.* ◆ Rlkang pwenty-alhem antekerreng. (N) *The wind is blowing from the south.* ◆ Rlkang angerrarl apety-arleng rtak aretyeh. (T) *When there is a big wind [we] look for a windbreak.*

CAN SOUND A BIT LIKE ilka[1] *'burrow for hibernation'*; ilka[2] *'tick', 'louse'*

rlkangkwerr (W,T), **iylkangkwerr** (E) *n.*
with head to the prevailing wind (often east); to the wind side ◆ Mpwal-thaytel intem-kety, nhakw-angkwerr iylkangkwerr interl-anerray. *Someone* apek mpwa apek ulhetyenh-kety. Ampa apekel ulheyamel marlel apek. (St) *Lie down [with your head facing] the eastern side [wind side] — not to the western side. Because someone might urinate there. A child might piss there, or perhaps a woman.*
= rlkang-ampeny, rlkampeny
SEE ALSO mpwarl

rlkang-ampeny (W,T), **iylkampeny** (E) *n.*
= **rlkangkwerr** ◆ Iylkampeny, iylkel intetyek, iylkangkwerr intaw! (St) *Sleep with your head to the wind!* ◆ Iylkan alakenh atakwarl artemarl yanh iylkekety *stop*-em-ilem. Iylkampeny rtakw artem, an mpwarl-ampeny ura ampem. (St) *The windbreak is built to stop the wind. The windbreak is built to the prevailing wind and on the foot end (the western side) of where a fire burns.*

rlkang angerr (W,T), **iylka angerr** (E), **iylka akngerr** (E)
strong wind, storm (angerr[1] *'big'*) ◆ Rlkang angerr apetyemew. (M) *A big storm is coming.*

iylker anthem (E) *vt.*
winnow seed, yandy seed with hands (lit. 'give to the wind') ◆ Iylker anthem, iylkel arnam akwek-akwek renh akngetyek, urlart anem ra aneyameng. (St) *Winnow the seed, so that the wind takes all the little bits of grass and just the clean [seed] is left.*
= then-wem
SEE ALSO ilpem[1], ahety-ilem

rlkerr, **iylkerr** (E) *adv.*
stretched out, spread out

rlkerr-welhem, iylkerr-welhem (E) *vi.*
1. stretch yourself out
2. spread out in all directions (e.g. a plant) ◆ Mern anaty iylkerr-welhem, mern arlatyey apek. (St) *The bush potato plant or the pencil yam plant spreads out in all directions.*

rlkerr intem, iylkerr-intem (E) *vi.*
sit with legs straight out
= tywerr intem

rlkerrelhem, iylkerrelhem (E) *vi.*
stretch one's legs straight out ◆ Ngkwern atherr rlkerrelhem. (M) *Sitting with both legs straight out.* ◆ Rlkerrelhemel anem, alhekarl-penh, atwaty-irremel. (N) *Sitting with legs straight out, after travelling, stretching out.*

rlkerremp-rlkerr anem, iylkerr-iylkerr anem (E) *vi.*
sit with legs straight out ◆ Lyweper atherr rlkerremp-rlkerr anem alakenh, atywaty-irremel, aweth rtapety inenty-alpem. (N) *Sitting with your two thighs straight out, like that, stretching, then curling your legs up again.*

rlkerremp-rlkerr alhem (T,E), **iylkerremp-iylkerr alhem** (E) *vi.*
go along dragging one's legs ◆ Angkethakw apek ra iylkerremp-iylkerr alhek, akuny-amperl. Kwatyek antywetyek. Iylkerremp-iylkerr anem ra. (St) *The poor thing went along thirstily, dragging their legs. Wanting to have a drink of water, dragging her legs.*

rlkert, **iylkert** (E) *n.*
1. sick, ill, sickness ◆ Artwang rlkert angerr rwangkwerr intep-intem. (M) *A really sick man keeps lying by the fire.* ◆ *Don't* rlpwerrkerl, nta rlkert mpwarekety. War arntwerrkay. (T) *Don't squeeze [her] tight or you'll make her sick. Just hold her.* ◆ Mwerrem aneh rlkert-penh, akeweny atyengenh. Tharl aparlp-ilety anek! (T) *My relative is better now, after being sick. I nearly lost him!*
2. a sick or injured person ◆ Rwang angerr amperl-anem kwer rlkerteh. (M) *A big fire is burning for the sick man.* ◆ Ker-kweny-antey artwep-irremel. Artwep-irremel ina alpem, rlkert-akert, artwepelh-ilem arelh merntel. (N) *[They] are turning back and they still haven't found any meat. They are turning back because they have a sick person with them, the sick woman made them turn back.*
= mernt, arntety

rlkert-irrem, iylkert-irrem (E) *vi.*
become sick or injured, be in pain ◆ Yay atyenh apek rlkert-irrerleng ayeng atham-irrem, alhwarrp-irremel. (St) *If my elder sister gets sick then I feel sorry for her, feel sad.*
= mernt-irrem, arntety-irrem

rlkert-ilem, iylkert-ilem (E) *vt.*
make someone sick, hurt someone ◆ Ampa akwek tnyek-tnyek-ilemel atwem ampa akwekel yanh. 'Akuny kwenh rlkert-rlkert-ilemel atwetyal impa.' (St) *That little kid is almost killing the other little kid. 'The poor thing, leave her alone, don't hit her and make her sick.'*

rlkert intyem
feel hurt or in pain (intyem[1] *'be in pain'*) ◆ Ingka ayenh ulthetyalay, rlkertek. Ulthem, ingka arrpenhel ngkwenhel, ntwa ayenh ulthem, rlkert intyem. (St) *Don't tread on my foot. If you tread on me with your foot it will hurt.*

rlkey (W,T) *n.*
cheek (of face) (note Warlpiri '*wirlki*')
= arrely[2]
rlkey ngkwern (W,T) *n.*
cheekbone (ngkwern '*bone*')
= arrely ngkwern

rlkwa (W,T), **rlkwang** (W,T) *n.*
hooked boomerang, number 7 boomerang. Also referred to as *alyang rlkwang*. ◆ Artwangel alyang rlkwang mparem artety-penh. (N) *Men make hooked boomerangs from mulga wood.*

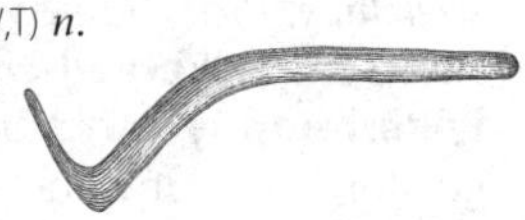

SEE ALSO iylkwa, alya, kayl

rlkwameny (W,T) spectacled hare-wallaby (?) SEE UNDER **lkwameny**

rlkwang (W,T) hooked boomerang, number 7 boomerang SEE UNDER **rlkwa**

rlkwangk (W,T) *n.*
thick, in a bunch (of particular fruits) ◆ Rlkwangkel anem. Perlap rarl rlkwangk anem. Atyankern anem, rlkwangk. (T) *In a bunch. Conkerberries hang in a bunch. Mistletoe berries are in a bunch.*

rlkwank (W,T) *n.*
seed that is prepared by being cleaned and husked
rlkwank-ilem (W,T) *vt.*
clean seed, separate clean seed from dirt and fragments of plant matter ◆ Arnwety panthel rlkwank-ilem. (T) *Seeds are cleaned in the coolamon.* ◆ Akat anterrng anwern awantyerl-apek, athemel. Panth-warn, atwerl-apek, rrpwerl anthwerr kwenh. Ahety-ilem ahety-ilem, rlkwank-ilem alakenh arrernem *clean.* (N) *The munyeroo is a seed that we eat, after grinding it up and putting it in the wooden dish. It's really black in colour. We winnow the seed and separate it out and then put the clean seed to one side.*
SEE ALSO ilpem[1], ahety-ilem

rlkwatherr (W,T) accompanying someone, going with someone to keep them company SEE UNDER **ilkwatherr**

rlkwelhem (W,T), **iylkwelhem** (E) *vi.*
push or 'wash' something down in the throat (with water or tea) ◆ Iylkwelhemel antywem, mwernarlelhek ker. Kwatyelarl renh iylkwenhem, anert-warl anem. (Sa) *Drinking to push the meat that's got stuck [in the throat]. The water will push it down towards the stomach.*

rlkwem (T,E), **iylkwem** (E) *vt.*
foretell, cause someone to have a predictive dream ◆ Altyerr kwerenh tha arek. Iylkwerl-alhek ra. Lyet apek ra apetyem. Iylkwek altyerr. (Sa) *I saw her in a dream. She caused me to dream about her. Maybe she is coming today.* ◆ Ampelikw altyerr iylkwem amikw uternelhem. (Sa) *Her child caused her mother to dream about [her].*
SEE ALSO rltwaty-irrem, urltaty-irrem, alhel arem, alhirrkem
CAN SOUND A BIT LIKE ilkwem *'start in fright'*

rlkwemen (W,T) old woman, senior woman SEE UNDER **werlkemen**

rlkwer-rlkwer (E), **irlkwer-irlkwer** (E) *n.*
wet, sloppy, runny, a liquid or sloppy mixture
SEE ALSO aperlk-aperlk, rew-rew
CAN SOUND A BIT LIKE arlkwer *'unsettled'*

rlkwerr, **iylkwerr** (E) *n.*
middle, in the middle, in between, halfway (between one place and another) ◆ Kwer map anem rlkwerrel. (M) *The children are sitting in the middle.* ◆ Ilkwatherrel ayeng rlkwerrel ayeng atherrel-arleng intetyek. Mpepel ayeng intetyek. (St) *For company I'm going to sleep in the middle of these two. I'm going to sleep in the middle.* ◆ Rlkwerr nta arem tyerrty, wal nta anper akwet alhem. (M) *If you see someone halfway, well you [should] go straight past them.*
SEE ALSO mpep, itep
rlkwerr-rlkwerr *n.*
somewhere in the middle, somewhere in between
rlkwerr ltwakem (W,T), **rlkwerr ultakem** (E), **iylkwerr ultakem** (E)
split or cut something in half (ltwakem '*break*')
= urleth-akem
rlkwerr arerrem (W,T)
meet someone halfway (arerrem '*see each other*') ◆ Rlkwerr apek arem, tyerrty apetyerleng arerrem. (N) *You might see someone halfway, meet each other halfway.*
rlkwerramerrenty (W,T), **iylkwerramerrenty** (E) *n.*
middle child or children
rlkwerr-penh (W,T), **rlkwerr-pwenh** (W) *n.*
1. middle child or children
2. something that is in the middle or between other things
= mpep-penh
rlkwerrel-irrem *vi.*
come between people (?) ◆ Akwek atherr apek atwerrem alenh atherr. Wal kwer alenh rlkwerrel-irrem. Rlkwerrel-irrem, amwek atherram atwerrem. (M) *Those two kids might be fighting. Well, that kid causes trouble for the mothers and then they start fighting.*

rlkwerrelh-ilem (W,T) *vt.*
make trouble between people (?) ◆ Akwek atherr atwerrem. Akwek alert-henh math, an akwek arrpenh alenh-henh math, wal yatherr atwerrememem, akwek kwer atherreng. Akwek atherr atwerrem an amwek atherram atwerrem — 'rlkwerrelh-ilem' ilem, anyentelh-ilem atwerretyeh. (M) *Two kids are fighting. Well that child's mother, and the other little child's mother start fighting because of the two little kids. The two kids are fighting and the two mothers are fighting — that's called* 'rlkwerrelh-ilem', *when they are made to come together to fight.*

rlkwerrp *n.*
1. frothy things such as suds, soap powder, foam ◆ Kwer mapel rlkwerrp arrkenel arrernelhem kapert-warn, inngerr-warn. (M) *The kids are enjoying themselves putting suds on their heads and faces.* ◆ Kwaty rlkwerrp apetyem akwemp-akwemp, apetyemel anper alhem. Arerl-anem tyerrtyel talkwek kwaty rlkwerrp renh. Kwaty arrwekel nthwerl-apem rlkwerrp. (N) *The frothy floodwater is coming along and going past. People watch the frothy water from the edge. The frothy floodwater runs first.*
2. beer [SOME SPEAKERS] ◆ Rlkwerrp tha antywetyek. Rlkwerrp antywetyek ayeng alhem, ngkwelty apek anthay? (St) *I'm going off to drink beer — can you give me some coins?*
= **urlkerrp** (E)
rlkwerrp-rlkwerrp *n.*
frothy, foaming
SEE ALSO akwemp-akwemp
= **urlkerrp-urlkerrp** (E)
rlkwerrp-irrem *vi.*
get frothy, froth up
= **urlkerrp-irrem** (E)

rlkwetherlkweng (E) *n.*
a type of plant (*Ptilotus incanus*)
SEE ALSO ahert-ahert[1]

rlngerr (E), **irlkngerr** (E) *n.*
sunset. Some people say that this is 'old' language.
rlngerr-rlngerr (E), **irlkngerr-irlkngerr** (E) *n.*
a type of cricket (?) ◆ Rlngerr-rlngerr weth akwekarl angkep-angkem, nheng aherrk apek irrperl-alhem, wal ra anem *red one* apek *show*-irrem. Wal rlngerr-rlngerrarl angkem akwek-akwek. Rwengkarl angkep-angkem anwantherr aretyakenh. (St) *That* rlngerr-rlngerr *is a small creature that sings out, supposedly when the sun is going down, and when the sunset becomes red. Well the little* rlngerr-rlngerr *sings out. It makes a noise but we can't see them.*
rlkngerr akwernenh (E), **irlkngerr akwernenh** (E)
a type of bird (?) (lit. 'the one that puts the sunset in')

rlpwa (W,T), **rlpwang** (W,T), **rlpa** (T), **rlpang** (T) *n.*
red ochre ◆ Rlpwang lpwelem irntang ather-warn. (T) *Red ochre is ground up on a flat stone.*
SEE ALSO arwethenp, atywerlk, ngwenty-ngwenty, artep arlpenty, karntewarr, marlalperr
CAN SOUND A BIT LIKE ulpa *'soft'*
= **urlpa** (E)
rlpwang rnter-rnter (W,T)
red ochre (rnter-rnter *'red'*)
= urlpa atyetyek
rlpwapert (W,T) *n.*
covered in red ochre

Rlpwararr (W,T) Milky Way SEE UNDER **Lpwararr**

Rlpwarraty (W) *n.*
New Well (just west of the Tanami Road, and south of Tilmouth Roadhouse)

rlpwat (W,T) *n.*
clear country that has been burnt, a large expanse of burnt country ◆ Rlpwatel amparr rwel amparr antyerrk-ilem, wal arntwety-alpem atherrk-irrenty-alpem. (M) *The plants dry up at first from the fire, from being burnt out, and then they grow back again, grow back green again.*
= **urlpat** (T,E)
rlpwat-ilem (W,T) *vt.*
1. singe fur, hair or scales off an animal ◆ Pwelek kapert rlpwat-ilem. (T) *Singeing the hair off the bullock head.*
SEE ALSO nthek-wem
2. burn grass, burn country to clean it ◆ Tyerrtyel angkwey rlpwat-iletyart arnam atherrkeny mpwaremel. (T) *Aboriginal people used to burn the grass to make the country green.*
= **urlpat-ilem** (T,E)

rlpwentyem (W,T) *vt.*
pull something out of something; squeeze something out of something else ◆ Mwetek rlpwentyem anthwerrngeh irrpekarl. (M) *Pulling out the car that got stuck in the mud.* ◆ Kwer akwek alhang rlpwentyem. (T) *Squeezing the [snot] out of the little kid's nose.* ◆ Arlatyey apek inyem inyem, nta rlpwentyem arlatyey yenh. (M) *You dig and dig the pencil yam, and then you pull it out [of the ground].* ◆ *Tyre* nheng rlpwentyem, angetyem aketh-warn, *patch*-el arrernem, martem. (T) *Pull the tube out of the tyre, bring it into the open, put on the patch and then close the hole.*
= **urlpentyem** (E)

rlpwer, **iylpwer** (E) *n.*
1. hollow log or tree; a hollow in a log or tree ◆ Atetherr rlpwerel anerl-anem. (T) *Budgerigars live in hollow trees.* ◆ Inap irrpem rlpwerek. (St) *The echidna is going into the hollow.*
2. the hollow part of other things
3. thin, without fat (of emu)
apwert iylpwer (E)
gun (apwert *'stone'*)
arnang rlpwer (W,T)
hollow log or tree (arnang *'plant'*, *'tree'*)
iylpwer arternenh (E) [RESPECT LANGUAGE]
axe (lit. 'hollow tree chopper')
= alenyakenyak, nyerlp
SEE ALSO ilep[1]
iylpweralker-ayerr (E), **iylpweralker** (E), **iylpwer-areny** (E), **rlpwer-areny** (W) *n.* [RESPECT LANGUAGE]
sugarbag ◆ *Sugarbag* 'iylpwer-areny' ilem. Mwerekikw ilem, 'Kwey, iylpweralker ahanelh-ila, ngwarrekengkw'. (Sa) *Sugarbag is called* 'iylpwer-areny'. *When talking about her son-in-law she says, 'Daughter, take the sugarbag to your son-in-law'.*
SEE ALSO imperalker-ayerr, ngkwarl-ayerr, arwengalker, rltwamp
apwert iylpwer (E) *n.*
gun (apwert *'stone'*) ◆ Apwert iylpwer ineyaw. (St) *Get the gun.*

rlpwer-rlpwer, **iylpwer-iylpwer** (E) *n.*
a type of plant with a hollow stem; long pussy-tails (plant) (*Ptilotus polystachyus* spp.). Children play with these by blowing through the hollow stem. ◆ Pelh-iwerl-anetyeh *pipe* renhant rlpwer-rlpwer, kwaty-akert. Pelhem iwerl-anem kwerel arrkenel. Arelh angerrel arlka arrkenenh, wal pelh iwerl-anem kwerel rlpwer-rlpwer renh. (N) *Children play with the* rlpwer-rlpwer, *making it like a pipe and blowing water through it. Women play with it too, blowing water through it.*
SEE ALSO rlpwer

rlpwerrkem (W,T) *vt.*
stamp or stand on someone or something; tread on something, press down on something; squeeze or squash something (hard) ◆ Iltya rlpwerrkek irntel. (M) *The rock squashed the hand.* ◆ Apal nta arrernelhem, wal rlpwerrkem tyerrty alenh. (M) *If you sit yourself down without thinking or looking properly then you'll squash that person.* ◆ *Don't* rlpwerrkerl, nta rlkert mpwarekety. War arntwerrkay. (T) *Don't squeeze [her] tight or you'll make her sick. Just hold her [gently].*
= rrwethem
SEE ALSO arternem[2], kerrk-welhem

rlpwerrng atwelhem *vi.*

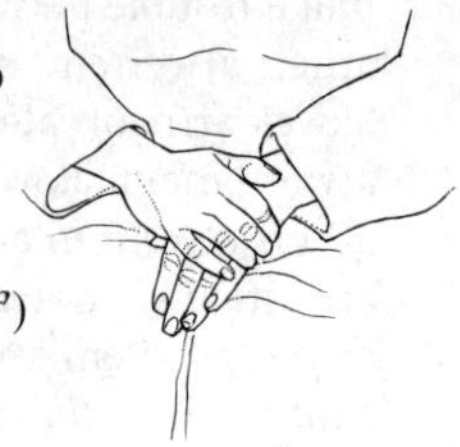

beat a rhythm on the lap with cupped hands to accompany ceremonial dancing (women) (atwelhem *'hit part of self'*) ◆ Ampel arlkan aretyart, arrkenel-arleng alakenh irreperrem. Arrpenhem alyerl-anem, arrpenhem rntertarl anerl-anem, arrpenhem rlpwerrng atwerl-anem. (St) *Children used to watch for fun as well, watch people going in for the* althart *ceremony, enjoying themselves doing it like that. Some would sing, others would sit quietly, and others would beat the rhythm on their laps.*
= **urlperrng atwelhem** (E)

rltamp (W) native honey, sugarbag SEE UNDER **rltwamp**

rltamp-rltamp (T) a type of fly (?) SEE UNDER **ltwamp-ltwamp**

rltap-rltap (W) a flapping, lapping, slurping, stomping or sloshing sound SEE UNDER **lthap-lthap**

rltar, **ltar** *n.*
making a banging, knocking, rattling or clicking sound ◆ Rltar away! (Sa) *Listen to the banging noise!*
SEE ALSO rltety
rltar-rltar[1], **ltar-ltar** *adv.*
making a banging, knocking, rattling or clicking sound ◆ Rltar-rltar alhep-alhem pwet-akert kwer yanh. (M) *That child with shoes on is walking along making a banging sound.*
rltar-rltar[2] (W,T), **rltwar-rltwar** (W) *n.*
1. a type of plant; desert rattlepod (*Crotalaria eremaea*). The name of this plant comes from the noise — *rltar* — that it makes when the seed pods are trodden on. ◆ Ingkelarl lthwerl-anem ingkel, rltar-rltar apel anem lthwerl-anem lthwerl-anem kwer map arlka arrken-irrem, rltar-rltar yanhek. (T) *The rattlepod plant is the one that the children go along treading on, squashing [the seeds] for fun.* ◆ Ankerrel arlkwerl-apemel mern rltar-rltar. Kwetyerl-apemel arlkwerl-apemel akerl-apemel, ankerrel. (T) *Emus go along eating* rltar-rltar. *They go along picking it and eating it.*
= rltwayep-rltwayep
SEE ALSO rltey-rltey, arrematy rltey-rltey
2. a type of inedible Solanum (?) (*Solanum* sp.)
rltar-atwem, **ltar-atwem** *vt.*
knock or bang something so that it makes a noise

rltar-irrem, **ltar-irrem** *vi.*
make a clicking, cracking, banging, rattling or knocking sound; click fingers or other joints in body ◆ Ayeng akem-irrenhem, wal ayeng rltar-irrenhem amper atyenhenh atherr. Rltar-irremel anem ayeng alhem kel mwerr anem irrenhem. (T) *When I get up I crack my knees. After cracking them then I walk around and feel better.* ◆ Arntek rltar-rltar-irrem, arrewemel. (Sa) *Shivering, [her] teeth are chattering.*
SEE ALSO urltaty-irrem, rltwar-rnkem

rltar-wem, **ltar-wem** *vt.*
crack something (e.g. whip); go off (gun) ◆ *Whip* tha rltar-wetyek. Rltar-wetyart tha *whip* pwelek arrengker alhetyek, rltar-wem *whip*-el, nantew apek arraty-ilenhemel apek. Alakenh anetyam. Ayeng *stockman*-kamparr. (St) *I'll crack the whip. I used to the crack the whip so that the cattle would go fast or so that the horses would go along in a straight line. That's how it was. I was a stockwoman at first.* ◆ Maketan rltar-wem arleng, ker apek atyerrek. (St) *The gun goes off in the distance, maybe shooting kangaroo.*

rltar-rnkem (E), **rltwar-rnkem**, **ltar-rnkem** (E) *vi.*
1. burst, bust, come out through something ◆ Rltwar-rnkem *tube* apek arnel apekarl atanthek. Kel alpwely-irrenhem anem. (St) *The tyre tube bursts after being pierced by a stick. Then it goes flat.* ◆ Artweker rltwar-rnkem, kel irrkwa anem thelelhem. (St) *The boil bursts and then the pus comes out.* ◆ Ker arlewatyerr apekarl ampem, mern tamp apek, kel rltwar-rnkem, *bust*-em ilemel. (T) *The goanna or the damper is cooking, and then it bursts.*
2. go off, explode, go 'bang' (gun) ◆ Maket nhak rltwar-rnkem. (T) *That gun over there has just gone off.* ◆ Ker aherr apekarl atyerrek rltwar-rnkem maket. (St) *The gun goes bang when the kangaroo is shot.*
3. make a clicking, cracking, banging, rattling or knocking sound
SEE ALSO atem, aterlk-irrem, aterlkem, antyelp-irrem, rnkem
= **urltar-rnkem** (E)

Rltarlpelt (E), **Ltarlpelt** (E) *n.*
the name of a place in the Harts Range area

Rltemp (W), **Ltemp** (W) *n.*
name of a hill near Garden Bore, Yuelamu (Mt Allan) area

rltengk-rltengk, **ltengk-ltengk** *n.*
bell (from English 'dingle')

rltengk-rltengk-irrem, **ltengk-ltengk-irrem** *vi.*
make a ringing sound ◆ War *supper*-taym apek arrwekeleny *whitefella mob* rltengk-rltengk-irretyam. (St) *Just at suppertime the olden-time whitefellas rang the bell.*
= ring-irrem

rltengk-rltengk-ilem, **ltengk-ltengk-ilem** *vt.*
ring something (e.g. bell) ◆ Rltengk-rltengk-iletyalaw, irlpant arwengk-ilem-kety. (Sa) *Don't ring that [thing], you're deafening [us].*

rlternt (E), **lternt** (E), **lterlt** (E) *n.*
newborn ◆ Ampa akely rlternt. Akely-amperl innga. Lyetant arl *born*-irrepirrem, ampa rlternt. (Sa) *A little newborn baby. A really small one. It was just born today.*
= ampelyerrk
SEE ALSO arathap, arlkarl[2], iylker

rlterr shin SEE UNDER **lterr**

rlterrk, **lterrk** *n.*
1. strong, forceful ◆ Angka rlterrkarl yanhan angkep-angkem. (St) *That person is speaking strongly.* ◆ Alhernter-rnem uneng-akert arrma, uneng rlterrk-akert arl ikwer-areyenh. (Sa) *White people have a spirit as well, their spirit is strong.*
2. hard (to the touch), sturdy; tough (of meat) ◆ Ayenh irrkerrk-wetyalaw, impelhemarl — ahern rlterrk-kety! (Sa) *Don't lean heavily on me — the ground is hard. Leave me alone!* ◆ Ker nhenh rlterrk *knife* atyeng anthey alywek apek, akemel tha arlkwetyek. (St) *This meat is tough, give me a knife or a stone knife so that I can cut some and eat it.*
SEE ALSO twer, awer[1]
3. mean, hard, hard-nosed, not generous ◆ Angayel anthetyakenh rlterrk akngerr. Man anthetyakenh rlterrk akngerr. Rlterrk-irremarl ra. (St) *[Someone] who doesn't give any food is mean. Someone who doesn't give money is mean. They get hard.*

rlterrk-irrem, **lterrk-irrem** *vi.*
1. become solid, harden ◆ Mern nhenhan rlterrk anem irrek — anwengkerrem arlkwetyew. (T) *This food is cooked solid now — we can eat it.* ◆ Iylpwerr-iylpwerr kapert atyet-atyet nhelkwer. Iylperr-iylpwerr rlterrk-irretyakenh *that's why* ra akwek antey urrek angkerl-anem, *little bit* angkerl-anem. Nhenh rlterrk-irrem yanhan angka rlterrk anemarl ra angkem. (St) *The fontanelle is that soft part [in the middle] of the head. If the fontanelle hasn't hardened [closed over], then the child can only talk a little bit. When the fontanelle gets hard then the child starts to speak strongly.*

2. get 'hard'; be mean; not want to do something or help someone; refuse to do something ◆ Tyerrty alenh rlterrk-irremel anem. (M) *That person is refusing [to do something].* ◆ Lterrk-irretyalay, mwetek atyeng anthay. (T) *Don't be mean, give me the car.*

rlterrk-ilem, **lterrk-ilem** *vt.*
tighten something; make something strong; make something solid; tie something up ◆ Rlterrk-ilem. Aley apek angkep-angkem 'Urrek tha rlterrk-iley'. (St) *Tighten something. That person is saying, 'Wait while I tighten it'.* ◆ Arterrty atyeng antheyaw tha rlterrk-iletyek mern, rew-rewarl ilek, kwatyarl thelek *too much*. (St) *Give me some flour so that I can make this mixture thicker, it went runny because I poured too much water in.*
SEE ALSO twer-ilem

rlterrkelh-ilem, **lterrkelh-ilem** *vt.* = **rlterrk-ilem**

rlterrkem (E), **lterrkem** (E) *vi.*
rattle, clatter

rlterrkelh-ilem (E), **lterrkelh-ilem** (E) *vt.*
rattle something, make something clatter ◆ Tyampet apek rlterrkelh-ilem. (St) *Making the billycan rattle.*
SEE ALSO rltar, rlterrp

rlterrp, **lterrp** *n.*
a rattling or banging noise ◆ Rlterrp-rlterrp alhep-alhem *billycan*-akert. (T) *Rattling a billycan as he goes along.*

rlterrp-wem, **lterrp-wem** *vt.*
make something bang or rattle ◆ Rlterrp-wem alyang. (M) *Rattling the boomerangs.*

rlterrpelh-ilem, **lterrpelh-ilem** *vt.* = **rlterrp-wem** ◆ Rlterrpelh-iletyalay, *bucket* apek, ankwekety. (St) *Don't bang the buckets, [people] are trying to sleep.*

rlterrpel atwem, **lterrpel atwem**
make something rattle (especially boomerangs) ◆ Rlterrp atwem angwenh, kayl apek, alakenh akin ilem, althartek apek. (St) *[They] rattle the what's-his-name, the boomerangs, at the* althart *ceremony.*

rlterrp rrkwem (W,T), **rlterrp irrkwem** (E), **lterrp rrkwem** (W,T)
make something rattle (especially boomerangs) ◆ Artwangel rlterrp rrkwerl-anem alyang. (M) *The men are rattling the boomerangs.*
SEE ALSO rltar, rlterrkem

rltety, **ltety** *n.*
a sharp cracking or clicking sound ◆ Rltety tha awekaw ltwakekarl. (St) *I heard the sharp crack of it breaking.*
SEE ALSO rltar

rltety-irrem, **ltety-irrem** *vi.*
make a cracking or clicking sound ◆ Iltyang ntwa rltety-irrem. (M) *You can crack your fingers.* ◆ Iltya rltety-irrem. Arwerl rltety-irrem akin arnan rltety-irrem antey. Tyerrty arrpenh apek alhemel rltety-irrerlek anem awem, *'Oh* yaleng rltety-irremaw kwenh'. Ingwel apek rltety-irrerlek. (St) *Fingers make a cracking noise. Trees make a cracking noise as well. If a particular person is going along then you can hear the cracking sound, 'Oh, something over there is making a cracking sound'. Maybe making a cracking sound in the night.*
SEE ALSO rltar, rlterrp, rlterrkem

rltey-rltey (E), **ltey-ltey** (E) *n.*
New Holland rattlepod (*Crotalaria novae-hollandiae*)
= arrematy rltey-rltey

rltimp[1] (T,E), **ltimp** (T,E) *n.*
dry bits of bark ◆ Arlpmenyek tha itetyek rltimp inerl-anem. Rltimp impenarl arlpmeny-kenh. (St) *I am collecting dry bits of bark to burn to make ashes. Dry bits of bark are really important for ashes [for chewing with tobacco].* ◆ Rltimp atnkerrmern, aper rltimp-akert akin, artety arlka rltimp-akert ingkerrek. Akarntety-arntetyan rltimpengayerr. Akarntety-arntety rltimpel-arlengarl anem. (St) *The coolibah tree has bits of dried bark, and the river red gum and mulga trees do as well. The* akarntety-arntety *lizard comes out from amongst the bits of dried bark. It lives amongst the dried bark.* ◆ Thep unernengk, rltimpelarl arrangkw-artekarl anerl-anem, artety rltimpel. (St) *The tawny frogmouth sits amongst the bits of bark, and it's as if it isn't there, you can hardly see it.*
SEE ALSO arntap, ayenp

rltimp-areny (E), **ltimp-areny** (E) *n.*
a type gecko (sandplain or northern spiny-tailed) (?) (*Diplodactylus stenodactylus*); *Strophurus ciliaris*). Lives amongst the dry bark on trees. (-areny *'inhabitant of'*).
= akarntety-arntety, pelhel-iwenh-iwenh

rltimpat-arrweremarrwer (E), **ltimpat-arrweremarrwer** (E) *n.*
a type of lizard (?)
SEE ALSO akarntety-arntety

rltimp[2] (T), **ltimp** (T) *n.*
skewer used used for closing the belly cavity of certain animals before cooking them
= alemp, interlp

rltwa (W,T), **rltwang** (W,T) *n.*
1. big, large, important ◆ Aper rltwa. (M) *A big river red gum tree.*
2. boss, senior person, spokesperson, elder ◆ Tyerrty mereh-artey rltwang angerr. (T) *The traditional owners are big bosses.*
SEE ALSO angerr^1, angerrety, artelhampw, artelh^3, awer, ilkwa^2
CAN SOUND A BIT LIKE ulta, ltwa *'side'*; arltwa *'empty'*
= **urlta** (E)
arnang rltwang (W,T)
a big tree (arnang *'plant'*, *'tree'*)
= **arna urlta** (E)
Kwerraly Rltwa (W)
Morning Star, Daylight Star, Venus (kwerraly *'star'*) ◆ Kwerraly Angerr anentyem *early*, nheng aherlkenty alhem ka, lweren — wal 'Kwerraly Rltwa' anwern ilem. (M) *There's a large star that comes up early, early in the morning — well we call that star 'Kwerraly Rltwa'.*
= Anthelper, Arwenpeng, Awelh, Kwerraly Angerr, Kwerraly Urlta
rltwerrem (W,T) *vi.*
1. get bigger
2. be in charge, become boss of something
CAN SOUND A BIT LIKE arltwerrem *'run out', 'get empty'*

rltwamp (W,T), **rltamp** (W), **urltamp** (T) *n.*
1. native honey, sugarbag. Also referred to as *ngkwarl rltwamp*. ◆ Arelhel rltwamp atwep-atwem arnang ltyentyel-ayeng. (M) *The woman is chopping sugarbag from the beefwood tree.* ◆ Ngkwarl rltwamp alemeh awantyem. (M) *Sugarbag is eaten for the sweet taste.*
2. the nest or hive made by native bees
= arwengalker
rltwamp alha (W,T)
the entrance to native bees' nest or hive (alha *'nose'*)
= arwengalker alha
rltwamp kapert (W,I)
the top part of the sugarbag or native bees' hive, which is made up of yellow compacted pollen (kapert^1 *'head'*)
= ngkwarl kapert

rltwamp-rltwamp (W,T) a type of fly (?) SEE UNDER **ltwamp-ltwamp**

rltwang (W,T) big, large, important SEE UNDER **rltwa**

rltwar-rltwar (W) desert rattlepod SEE UNDER **rltar-rltar**

rltwaty (W,T) *n.*
1. a premonition or feeling about something that is going to happen (often in the form of a twitch or click in the nose)
2. gun
= **urltaty** (E)
rltwaty-irrem (W,T) *vi.*
have a premonition; have a feeling (in your nose) that something is going to happen ◆ Tyerrty apekarl nheng apety-alhem alethang apek wal nheng renh mer akweteth akenh rltwatyarl irrerleng, nheng mer akweteth anep-anem rltwaty-irrem. '*Oh someone* lyet arratem kwenh.' (M) *If a person is coming, maybe a stranger, well the person who lives in the place all the time has a premonition about it. 'Oh, someone is going to arrive.'*
SEE ALSO alhirrkem, rltar-irrem, rlkwem, alhel arem
= **urltaty-irrem** (E)
rltwatyel atwem (W,T)
1. put a curse on someone or something; wish something bad to happen to someone or something ◆ Rltwatyel atwem kwenh thwengk. *Something* nthakenh-atety irretyenh nta kwenh, thwengk rltwatyarl atwek kwenh. (T) *I'm going to put a curse on you. Something is going to happen to you after I put a curse on you.*
2. have a premonition or feeling about something that is going to happen
SEE ALSO akwety-irrpenem, artarrernem, artimperr-wem, pew-ilem
= **urltatyel atwem** (E)

rltwayep-rltwayep (E) *n.*
a type of plant; desert rattlepod (*Crotalaria eremaea*)
= rltar-rltar^2

rltwernt (W,T) *n.*
limestone
= **urlternt** (E)
rltwernt-rltwernt (W,T) *n.*
limestone country
= **urlternt-urlternt** (E)

rlwa (W,T), **rlwang** (W,T) *n.*
1. forehead
2. clean honey from the native bees' nest or sugarbag. Also referred to as *ngkwarl rlwa*. ◆ Ngkwarl kapert, ant rlwang, ngkwarl rlwang *clean one*. Rlwang renhem inem *spoon*-el apek inem inem inemel arrernem *billycan*-warn arntap-warn apek arrernem pwelap. Awantyem [rlwang], kapert arlkwem. (N) *The top part of the sugarbag and the clean honey.* Rlwang *is the clean part. It is spooned into a billycan or into a container made of bark. [We] suck on the* rlwang *and eat the top part [made of yellow compacted pollen].*
3. the first or front part of something
4. Used to form some words based on 'forehead'. For example, *rlweng apeltyey* 'honeyant queen' (lit. 'friend of the

forehead')
= **urla** (E)
alhwerrp rlwa (W,T)
the beginning of winter (alhwerrp *'winter'*)
= **alhwerrp urla** (E)
twern rlwa (W,T)
the beginning of summer (twern *'sun', 'summer'*)
= **utern urla** (E)
mwetekay rlwa (W,T)
car bonnet (mwetekay *'car'*) ◆ Mwetekay rlwel kwer akwek akern anerl-anem. (T) *The child is sitting on the car bonnet.*
rlwatherr atwerrem (W,T)
bump into each other (atherr *'two'*; atwerrem *'hit each other'*) ◆ Kwer yanh atherr rlwatherr atwerrern. (M) *Those two kids just bumped into each other.*
rlwather-ather (W,T) *n.*
a person with a wide or broad forehead, or with a balding or receding hairline (ather-ather[1] *'flat', 'fat'*)
= **urlather-ather**

rlwakem (W,T) *vt.*
dislocate kangaroo's leg joints before cooking it ◆ Ingkang rlwakem artwel. (M) *The man is dislocating the [kangaroo] foot.* ◆ Ker aherr rlwang mpwankem intey — rlwakay. (M) *The kangaroo hasn't had its legs dislocated yet — dislocate the legs [before cooking it].*
= ulernkernem
CAN SOUND A BIT LIKE lwakem *'chase'*

Rlwampetherr (W) *n.*
name of a hill in the Mt Wedge/Tilmouth Roadhouse area

rlwang (W,T) forehead SEE UNDER **rlwa**

rlwang arrernem (W,T) *vt.*
dislocate kangaroo's legs so that they spread out (before cooking) ◆ Rlwang arrernem ker aherrek, nheng ker lyweper nheng tyep-ilem kenh lyweper arlpaw akwet interlek — kenh rlwang arrernetyakenh akenh pwarn akwekarl intem. (M) *The legs of the kangaroo are dislocated, the thighs are cut so that they are wide and spread out — if they weren't cut then they would remain tight.*
SEE ALSO rlwakem

Rlwang Npwer (W) *n.*
hill near Kadaitcha Dam, east of Yuelamu (Mt Allan) community

rlwank anyem (E), **rlwank atnyem** (E), **urlank-anyem** (E), **urlank-atnyem** (E) *vi.*
become drowsy, nod off to sleep (anyem *'fall'*) ◆ Rlwank atnyep-atnyem ankwa. (St) *Dropping off to sleep.* ◆ Ankwa urlank-anerlapem, anerlapemel alhemel apek. 'Ankwa urlank-atnyetyaleyay.' (Sa) *Going along and nodding off to sleep, as you are sitting [in a car] or going along. 'Don't drop off to sleep.'*
SEE ALSO rlwa

rlwant-rlwant (W,T) *n.*
spying on someone, peeping out at someone
SEE ALSO kert-arem
= **urlant-urlant** (T,E)

rlwarel (E), **urlarel** (E) *adv.*
1. taking over or intervening in a situation (when you think someone else is not acting appropriately) ◆ Rlwarel tha atwem ngkweng-kety, ntwa akwetan angkem-kety. (St) *I am going to just go and hit him because you keep on talking too much [and you're not going to do it].* ◆ Tha rlwarel ngkweng-kety anthek. Untan arengk-rnem wantepantem mernel. (St) *I gave that bread to someone else because you keep on feeding your dogs with it.* ◆ Rlwarel tha *drive-em*-iletyek mwetekay. Mwetekayek-artwey terangk. (St) *I'm going to take over and drive the car because the owner of the car is drunk.*
2. doing something to avoid bad consequences ◆ Ker tha rlwarel itek, ankey angkem-kety. (St) *I cooked all the meat in case people came and asked me for it.*

rlwarlp (W,T), **rlwaylp** (T,E) *n.*
kurdaitcha, kurdaitcha man, ritual executioner
= ngkekern, kwertaty
SEE ALSO melarlp, mwak[2]
= **urlaylp** (E)
rlwarlp-irrem (W,T), **rlwaylp-irrem** (W,T) *vi.*
1. turn into a kurdaitcha
2. turn into a moth or butterfly; transform or metamorphose (grub)
SEE ALSO akarternem, irrarl-irrem, ngkekern-irrem
= **urlaylp-irrem** (E)

rlwarrkany (W,T) *n.*
snake that lives in the bottom of the honeyant nest (?)
SEE ALSO rlweng apeltyey, yerramp

rlwart (W,T) *n.*
1. a group of only one kind of thing (with nothing else); entirely, mostly, only, just ◆ Artwang rlwart alhem. (M) *Just the men are going.*
2. clean, pure (not mixed up with anything else)
= **urlart** (E)
rlwart-ilem (W,T) *vt.*
sort things out, separate one thing out from another

rlwart-irrem (W,T) *vi.*
become clear, become separated

rlwatert *n.*
1. something short and round in shape ◆ Rlwatert akwek apetyem kwenh, mwetekay yanh kwenh. (T) *There's a little round car coming there.*
SEE ALSO rlwa, arlwa, apwerterrerterr, arlwepertaty, artwert-artwert
2. bush cat, feral cat • SEE ALSO rlwa, mangw, nyarrapeng, pwethey, pwethekat, angay, annga atherrk, meyaw-meyaw

rlwatwem (W) *vt.*
meet someone
CAN SOUND A BIT LIKE ilatwem *'bang on ground'*
= **urlatwem** (E)

rlwaty angkem (W,T) *vi.*
apologise for behaviour, say sorry, face up to a person you have wronged, pacify, placate, admit guilt in a situation, face up to ritual punishment (?) (angkem *'speak'*) ◆ Ayeng rlwaty angkem ngkweng, apal apek ayeng angkek-penh. 'Apal ayeng angkek — ngkwarl-penh kwenh.' (M) *I might apologise to you after I have said the wrong thing to you. 'I said the wrong thing — I was drunk.'* ◆ Ayeng ngkweng rlwaty angkem. (T) *I'll give you a good explanation [to someone who wants to hit you].*
SEE ALSO nyerr rrpwarelhem
= **urlaty angkem** (E)

rlwaylp (T,E) kurdaitcha SEE UNDER **rlwarlp**

rlwek apeltyey (W) honeyant queen SEE UNDER **rlweng apeltyey**

rlwek (W,T), **iylwek** (E) *n.*
native pine (*Callitris glaucophylla*). Tree to 6 m high, with rough bark, blue-green leaves and woody fruit. Grows in hilly country.
◆ Kwatyel item, rwel item, *green*-irremey, *soapy water* thelem, *naked*-em ilelhem, alhewelhem. Anngartel. Arnang. Walyel. Arlpelhel war alhewelhem. Arreny atherram, 'anngart', 'rlwek'. (N) *It is boiled in water till it goes green and then you strip off and wash yourself with the soapy water. With the native pine, just with the leaves. It has two names —* 'anngart' *and* 'rlwek'.
= anngart, amikw[1]

rlweketereter (W,T) pallid cuckoo SEE UNDER **lyweketweretwer**

rlwelth (W,T) *n.*
dug into the ground, in hibernation underground ◆ Arlewatyerr rlwelth anem. (T) *The goanna is hibernating.*
SEE ALSO atyerrp, ilka[1], ilkeparr
= **urlelth** (E)

rlwelth arrernelhem (W,T) *vi.*
dig self into a hole or burrow (some animals); dig self into the earth; hibernate (arrernelhem *'put self somewhere'*) ◆ Arlewatyerr rlwelth arrernelhem alhwerrpel. (M) *The goanna hibernates in winter.*
= urlelth ipelhem

rlwelty (W,T) frost, ice SEE UNDER **lwelty**

rlwem (W,T) take something off something; undo something, untie or loosen something SEE UNDER **lywem**[1]

Rlwem (W) the name of a place in the Yuelamu (Mt Allan) area SEE UNDER **Arlwem**

rlwem-anem (W,T) *vi.*
1. watch out for something; poke head out and look out for something; peep out from behind something ◆ Tyerrty antywangkwerr rlwem-anem. (T) *The person is peeping out from the humpy.* ◆ Amwang alhwengel rlwem-anem. (T) *The snake is peeping out from its hole.* ◆ Merel apek tyerrty rlwem-anem. (M) *The person is watching out from the house.*
2. rise (sun) ◆ Aherrk ingerreng rlwem-anenty-alhem. (M) *The sun rises in the east.*
= **urlem-anem** (E)

rlwemp *adv.*
staying home, staying in one place
SEE ALSO urlert, arteny[1], rlwemp, rlwepety, urlepety
CAN SOUND A BIT LIKE ulemp *'ghost gum'*
= **urlemp** (E)

rlweng peltyey (W), **rlwek peltyey** (W) *n.*
honeyant queen (lit. 'friend of the forehead') (*pelty* 'friend'). Children play with them and burst them. This is done to increase the number of honeyants. ◆ Rlweng peltyey yanh apel ilem *empty one. Just like a balloon.* Ra anem *empty, no* ngkwarl *long that white one* itya. Anwern arrkenel *use*-em-iletyart rlwewarteh *bang*-em-ilemel arrken — rlwang peltyelh-iletyeh. Rang anem *empty, no juice* ngkwarl apek kwerel anem *only empty one just like* a *balloon* rang anem. An amwang anem kwen akenh *last end* anthwerrel. (M) Rlweng peltyey *is what we call that empty one [honeyant]. It's just like a balloon. It's empty and white in colour and there's no honey in it. We used to play with them and bang them against our foreheads — to make friends. It is empty, it has no juice or honey in it, and it's just empty like a balloon. And there is a snake there right at the end [of the honeyant hole].*
= rlwetantyey
SEE ALSO rlwarrkany, arnman[2], yerramp, inkwareny, rlwa

rlwengemar (T), **rlwengimar** (E) shading eyes with hand SEE UNDER **urlengimar**

rlwengkay (E), **rlengkay** (E) *n.*
a mark made with the burnt bark of the corkwood tree and rubbed on the foreheads of small children to protect them from the *aretharr* wind. ◆ Rlengkayarl arrernelhem, arrernem ampa apek arrernem alakenh aretharrel lweth. Aretharr akngerrarl apetyemeng. Ampa akwek apek, rlkert-kety. (St) *The mark made with burnt bark from the corkwood tree is put on the foreheads of little children because of the north wind. When the north wind is blowing. This mark is put on them so that they don't get sick.*

rlwenngelhem (W) *vi.*
fall down, fall out of something ◆ Rwang aperrk rlwenngelhem tyerrty ingkewarn, antyam-warn. (M) *The sparks are falling onto the person's foot, and onto the swag.* ◆ Tyerrty alenh tyety ingkerr rlwenngelhek, tyelkant-akert. (M) *This person's teeth have all fallen out, and they only have gums.*
SEE ALSO lernelhem

rlwentyerr (W,T) *n.*
furrow between the eyes; ridge of the nose between the eyes; bridge of the nose
SEE ALSO rlwa
= **urleynterr**[1] (E)

rlweny (W) *n.*
in half ◆ Ker rlweny atherr akem. (M) *Cut the meat in half.*
rlweny akem (W)
cut something in half

rlwepety (W,T) *adv.*
staying home, staying in one place ◆ Rlwepety antarl merel anerlanetyeh. (M) *Staying in one place, at home.*
SEE ALSO urlert, urlemp, antarl, arteny[1], rlwemp, urlemp
= **urlepety** (E)
rlwepety anem (W,T)
stay home, stay in one place ◆ Ayeng rlwepety ananem irrkwenty-hety. (T) *I am staying in one place because of the police.*
= **urlepety anem** (E)

-rlwer (W,T) *n.ending*
1. at some particular time; during, while. This ending often occurs on words that describe weather; wind, rain, sun etc. ◆ Anngener aperel-ayeng angkerl-anem twern-**rlwer**. (M) *Cicadas sing in the river red gums in the summer time.* ◆ Ngkwarl ntywey arratem twern-**rlwer**. (M) *Corkwood honey comes out in the summer.* ◆ Inkwareny kwaty-**rlwer** anwern akern war inyem. (M) *In the rain time we dig up honeyants just near the surface.* ◆ Kwer akwek akert alhwerrp-**rlwer** anay, kwen anay. (T) *Sit down inside, in the winter time. You've got a little child.*
2. through something, in the midst of something ◆ Ntwan nmwernt-**rlwer** apetyepetyem. *You're making a big dust as you come along.* ◆ Iwenh ntwan apetyem kwaty-**rlwer**? *Why are you coming along in the rain?*
= -rwek

rlwernp (W,T), **nwernp** (W) *n.*
red-backed kingfisher (*Todiramphus pyrrhopygia*) ◆ Kwen anem thep rlwernp arlewatyerr-arteh. Arrkenel anwern nyetyart thep akwek inetyehek. (M) *The red-backed kingfisher lives underground like a goanna. We used to dig them up for fun, to get the baby birds.*
= parlkenng, urrernter[2]

Rlwernpakwerlang *n.*
name of a place in the Mt Doreen area

rlwerrker (W,T) *adv.*
1. (doing something) backwards and forwards; (doing something) back to someone
2. (doing something) face to face ◆ Atwerrem angkwer-nheng atherr rlwerrkerant-atherr atwerrem. (T) *The two sisters are fighting each other face to face (?).*
SEE ALSO ularr, akepenh
= **urlerrker** (E)
rlwerrkerek-rlwerrker (W,T), **rlwerrkereng-rlwerrkereng** (T) *adv.*
face to face; 'square and square' (for example, two brothers-in-law who are married to each other's sisters); (do something) backwards and forwards to each other ◆ Rlwerrkerek-rlwerrkereng atwerrem. (T) *Fighting face to face.*
SEE ALSO ulengerek-ulenger, ularrek-ularr, ulanengek-ulaneng
= **ulerrkerek-urlerrkerek** (E)
rlwerrkerek-rlwerrker antherrem (W,T)
give things to each other reciprocally
= **ulerrkerek-urlerrkerek antherrem** (E)

rlwert-rlwert (W,T) *n.*
part of guts ◆ Ker aherr arlka anem rlwert-rlwert. (T) *Kangaroos have* rlwert-rlwert *as well [as some other animals].*

rlwertantyey (W,T) *n.*
honeyant queen. Children play with them and burst them. This is done to increase the number of honeyants.
= rlweng peltyey

rlweth-akem (W,T) *vt.*
break something up into bits, break

something in half, split (a log); cut something up ◆ Mern tamp rlweth-akem. (T) *Cutting up the damper.* ◆ Ker rlweth-akem. (M) *Cutting the meat up.*
= rlkwerr ltwakem
SEE ALSO mpalernem, mpal-inem, mpal-akem, mpalty-akem
= **urleth-akem** (E)
rlweth atwem (W,T)
chop or cut something into bits
= **urleth atwem** (E)
rlweth-wem (W,T) *vt.*
break something with a missile
= **urleth-wem** (E)
rlweth-ampem (T), **rlweth-item** (W)
burn something so that it breaks ◆ Rwang antyerrk rlweth-ampem. (T) *Burning the dry tree so that it falls down.*
SEE ALSO unewem

rlwetyarr (W) *n.* [RESPECT LANGUAGE]
meat
SEE ALSO ker

rlweyang (W) *n.*
a type of rain cloud; fog or mist following rain ◆ Kwaty-penh *wet*, rlweyang altywernem. (M) *After the rain the fog hangs there.* ◆ Rwa kwert-arteh arem rlweyang, kwatyarl anenty-penh. (M) *After the rain [you] see the fog that is like smoke from a fire.*
= mwekelengk, arakakw

Rnanty (W) Dunja Bore, south-east of Laramba community SEE UNDER **Nanty**

rnar (W,T) central netted dragon SEE UNDER **irnar**

rnem stand, stand up SEE UNDER **irnem**

+rnem[1] *v.ending*
Forms intransitive compound verbs, in which part of the meaning describes a vertical or standing position, or motion in an upwards direction. In some instances the word that this ending goes onto form the verb does not have a separate meaning of its own. In Central Anmatyerr this ending may sound like *-irnem* and in Eastern Anmatyerr like *-rtnem*, *-tnem* or *-nem*.
arlparernem *vi.*
hang down; dangle, swing from something
arlwarernem *vi.*
rise up (of bread); stomach swell up or get bloated, swell up (like a dead cow) (arlwar 'round')
ampekernem *vi.*
stand leaning against someone or something
anetyerrkernem (W,T) *vi.*
burp, hiccough

-rnem[2] (E) *n.ending*
Plural marker; shows that more than two are doing the verb action or are the object of the verb action; lots of, group of. ◆ Anewartewart-**rnem** alherl-iwep-iwem. Anewart nhel-arey ker anthetyangarl. (Sa) *All the husbands and wives are going along. These couples didn't give [me] any meat.* ◆ Atey-**rnem** atwerrem akin arwelthel arelhek-arrngel. (Sa) *Men have jealous fights as well, over women.* ◆ Aleraty-**rnem**-akert ayeng alhek. Atyenh-akwerrk. (Sa) *I went with my nieces and nephews. My family.* ◆ Ampengamp amarrkel angerl-wetyel ampel-**rnem**, *nappy*-akert. Amparrpantey. *Bottle* angetyel ampa akwel *baby* akwel kwerenh, ampengamp. (Sa) *All the children carry the dolls, with nappies, around on their hips. They are pretend babies. They carry bottles and supposedly they are their babies.*
= -arey[1]

rnkem, nkem (E) *vi.*
1. emerge or come out from chrysalis; fly away (moths and butterflies) ◆ Anyematy rnkem arnang artekerreng. (M) *Witchetty moths come out of the roots of the bush.*
2. Goes on some nominals to form words with the general meaning of 'bursting out from'. For example, *rltar* 'banging, knocking, rattling or clicking sound', *rltar-rnkem* 'burst, bust, come out through something, go off, explode etc.'; *atna* 'faeces, shit etc.' *atnernkem* 'fart'.

rnkwang (W,T) glands inside the mouth or under the jaw SEE UNDER **ankwa**[2]

rnkwenem (W) take sides in a fight, help someone in a fight SEE UNDER **ankwernem**

Rnkwer (W) *n.*
name of place in the Central Mt Wedge area
SEE ALSO Ngalwerrty

rnparnpetyenh (W) a type of bush tomato (?) SEE UNDER **nparnpetyenh**

rnpernp (T,E) rock pituri SEE UNDER **rnpwernp**

rnpernp (W,T) soldier bird; yellow-throated miner bird SEE UNDER **irnpernp**

rnpwa (W,T), **rnpwang** (W,T) *n.*
sweet gum, kino or resin from plants. Also referred to as *ngkwarl rnpwang.* ◆ Alalherrk rnpwang nhenh-lkwer arlkwetyart, larlart rnpang. Awantyetyart larlarl awantyem-artek. Lwerenart. Intertelarl anem. (N) *We used to eat the sweet resin from the* alalherrk *bush, like a lolly. Like that. We used to suck on it just like you suck lollies. It is found in the base of the tree.* ◆ Ngkwarl rnpwang yanh anyerleng-penh anyem pertipelaw kwer-penh *red one*

kwer-penh anyem, renh-iperr arraw-ilem arraw-ilemel arlkwetyam. (N) *The honey drips from the flower on the* anyerleng *bush and we gather it together and eat it, suck it and eat it.* ◆ Ngkwarl artetyaywerrk awantyerl-apek, arna akemel rnpwang awantyerl-apek artetyaywerrk renh, larlartarl. (N) *We went along sucking on the sweet honeydew from the mulga, picking the branches and sucking on the resin, like a lolly.*

CAN SOUND A BIT LIKE npwa *'smelly (of person or dog)'*

rnpwer (W,T) *n.*

1. hard, strong; heavy (of language or speaking style); difficult ◆ Rnpwer anthwerr angkety angkem. (M) *Talking really strongly, making a big noise.* ◆ Angkety yanh rnpwer anem. (T) *That language is hard to understand.*

2. heavy (weight) ◆ Aherr rnpwer angerr kwenh. Itya kwenh tywenemel angem. (T) *The kangaroo is really big and heavy. I can't carry it.*

SEE ALSO rlterrk, twerr

rnpwernp (W,T), **rnpernp** (T,E) *n.*

rock pituri (*Nicotiana gossei*). Herb about 60 cm high (though sometimes growing to 3 m) with white flowers. Found in hills and caves. Also referred to as *ngkwerlp rnpwernp*.

SEE ALSO arwenp, ngkwerlp, ngkwerlp atherrk

CAN SOUND A BIT LIKE irnpernp *'soldier bird'*; inpinp *'marrow'*

= urnpernp (T,E)

rnter (E), **nter** (E) *n.*

greedy ◆ Mern atyenh rnterel arlkwetyal. Ankey angerrarl irremel rnterel arlkwetyal. (St) *Don't greedily eat all my food. Don't get really greedy and eat it.*

SEE ALSO ankey, ankerl

rnter-irrem (E), **nter-irrem** (E) *vi.*

1. be greedy

2. tell lies (?) • SEE ALSO rrtywerrem, urrtyirrem, urirrem2, therlkem, arrampewem1, atyetyem

rnter-rnter, **nter-rnter** *n.*

1. red ◆ Alta ayeng rnter-rnter akwet. Alta rnter-rnter-irrek anem ayeng iwenh-penh, ayeng apernelhek. (St) *My hair is still red. It went red after I did whatever, dyed it.* ◆ Rnter-rnter anem irrenhem aherrk irrpetyekant anem. (St) *It goes red and then the sun sets.*

= athethek, atyetyek

2. twenty dollar note

rnter-rnter-ilem, **nter-rnter-ilem** *vt.*

make something go red

= atyetyek-ilem

rnterelhem, **nterelhem** *vi.*

go red; make part of yourself red ◆ Rnterelhenhem altwerl-athek, rnterelhentyem angerrakw-they. (St) *It [the sun] goes red in the west and it goes red in the east.* ◆ Aherrk rnterelherl-alhem altwerl-atheh. (M) *The sun is showing red as it sets in the west.* ◆ Kapert ayeng rnterelhem. (M) *I am making my hair go red.*

= atyetyek-irrem, athethem

rntererrpererrp (W,T), **ntererrpererrp** (W,T) *n.*

a type of wasp (?) ◆ Kwatyel aperl-apem rntererrpererrp — nhwenh-nhwenh, *cheeky bugger*. (N) *The* rntererrpererrp *goes around water — they are aggressive and they bite.*

SEE ALSO anngener

rnternem, **nternem** *vt.*

1. spear or pierce something with a sharp object ◆ Irrtyartel rnternem. (M) *Spearing with a spear.* ◆ Yep aketyek ampa akwek, atnemel rnternem, atanthem ampa akwekek-arlek yep. (Sa) *The umbilical cord of a child is cut with a digging stick.*

2. hunt an animal using something sharp such as a spear, or beak or claws ◆ Uthipel ap irrkerlanty rnternerl-anem thip akely nyingk apek. Nyingkek unthemel atanthenhemel. (Sa) *The falcon goes along hunting small birds such as zebra finches. It looks for zebra finches and grabs them with its claws.*

SEE ALSO atanthem

rntert quiet SEE UNDER **ntert**

rntwarr, **iyntwarr** (E) *n.*

1. far, a long way, further away ◆ Arrwekel ayeng ltywerrerl-alhey rtweth-akert, rntwarrarl alhek-penh. Kwer-penh akem-irrem, 'Mwerram ayeng awelhem'. (N) *I'm going to go and have a rest first because my lower-back is aching from walking a long way. After that I get up and say, 'I feel good'.* ◆ Rntwarr-lkwer intaw. (N) *Lie down a bit further away.*

2. on the other side of something

3. later on, afterwards ◆ Utnanthelhem anem ayeng, *me might finish*-em ker apek, arrangkw anem iyntwarr. (St) *I might finish off all the meat and then there won't be any later.*

SEE ALSO angath, arleng1, arrer

rntwarr-rntwarr, **iyntwarr-iyntwarr** (E) *n.*

a bit further away ◆ Pwertay! Iyntwarr-iyntwarr ana! (Sa) *Look out! Shift a bit further away!*

rntwarr-irrem, **iyntwarr-irrem** (E) *vi.*

move over, move away, shift out of the way

◆ Ntwa ayenh irrkerrk-wetyalay, irrkerrkarl-wem. Ayenharl irrkerrk-wem-kety iyntwarr-irray. (Sa) *Don't lean on me. You're leaning on me, move further away.* ◆ Rntwarr-irray, ankwang intetyenheng, ayeng intetyenheng parrk — apenty-penh, alhekarl-penh. (N) *Move out of the way — I'm tired from travelling and I want to go to sleep.* ◆ Arelh arrpenh ntwarr-ilem kenh arleltyarl interl-anem, arlelty intem arelh arrpenh. Kenh arelh arrpenh ilelherleng mer kwerenh, 'Rntwarr-irray, rntwarr intay!' (N) *Moving another woman out of the way, one who is lying there without moving. And then the other woman claims that it's her place and says, 'Move out of the way, sleep further away!'*
SEE ALSO angath-irrem, arleng-irrem

rntwarr-ilem, iyntwarr-ilem (E) *vt.*
move something away ◆ Awempemarl-kety pelangket rntwarr-ileyaw. (Sa) *Move these blankets, I'm feeling hot.*
SEE ALSO anam-ilem, anamelh-ilem, arnang-ilem[2], arnangelh-ilem

rntwarr-angkwerr, iyntwarr-angkwerr (E) *n.*
further away, round the long way ◆ Iyntwarr-angkwerr alhetyek, iyntwarr-angkwerr alhay, mwerekangkwety apek. (St) *You go round the long way, maybe because of your son-in-law.*

rntwarr-ampeny, iyntwarr-ampeny (E) *n.*
on the other side of something ◆ Urrek tha yanh arteng-werlewey. Ngenh apek *me might* arteng-werl *halfway*-irrem mer. *Highway*-they iyntwarr-ampeny-they apek arteng-werlewem ngenh. (Sa) *Wait while I go part of the way with that [person]. I might accompany you halfway to the place. I might go as far as the other side of the highway with you.*

rntwely (W) *n.*
a black-coloured emu
SEE ALSO areyakerarr, ankerr

rntwem (W,T) *vi.*
1. to dance ◆ Rntwetyart anwern, mer nhenh kwerel anwern rntwetyart kalty-anthetyart akngerr-pat mapel anwernenh. (N) *We used to dance, at this place here we danced, and the elders used to teach us.*
SEE ALSO anthep, anmanty, apwelh
2. rain, fall (rain) ◆ Kwaty ankerteng rntwem. (M) *The rain is falling from the clouds.*
= anhem
3. smoke (fire)
CAN SOUND A BIT LIKE arntwem *'grow'*
= **urntem** (T,E)

Rntwem (T) Yuendumu SEE UNDER **Ywerntem**

rntwer[1], irntwer (E), **arntwer** (W) *n.*
1. cooking pit with hot rocks [SOME SPEAKERS] ◆ Rntwerel itetyek aker, apwert urinp-ilemel, ker anem arrernem. (St) *Cooking the meat in a pit, heating up the rocks and then putting the meat in.* ◆ Rntwerek akwernem ker ankerr renh. Ampem ra, inetyenh renh. Kapertek amperr rlweth akem, artep ultatwem. (St) *The emu is put in the cooking pit with hot rocks. It cooks and then [you] get it. At first the head is split open then the meat is cut up along the back.*
2. gun, rifle [SOME SPEAKERS] ◆ Rntwerarl akerrerl-anem maket yanh-lkwer, akngerrelan. Arlkwerretyel ap ikwerel rntwerel. (Sa) Rntwer *is what lots of people call guns and that sort of thing. People use guns to hunt with.*
3. gun, rifle [RESPECT LANGUAGE] ◆ Rntwer-ayerr-akert kwey ngwarrengkw ahanemay. Tyety-ayerrek, ker aherrek. (Sa) *Daughter, your husband has gone off hunting with a gun. For meat, for kangaroo [said by a woman].* • SEE ALSO maket

rntwer[2], irntwer (E) *n.*
spirit ◆ Irntwer ngenh tha arek altyerr. (St) *In my dream I saw your spirit.* ◆ Akwek nhenh apek rlkert-irrek. 'Rntwer-kwenyarl ilerrirrek, *too much*-arl angkerrek kwenyel.' Wal rntwer ya alhem antemarl. Ngangkayel akin renh arraty-ilem. (T) *A child might have become sick. 'Their spirit has gone from too much talking at night.' The spirit has gone. The traditional healer can put it right.*
SEE ALSO uneng[2], anngirrenty, kwerrern

rnwa (W,T), **rnwang** (W,T) *n.*
wooden water dish

◆ Arelhel kwaty thelem rnwang-warn. *The woman is pouring water into the wooden water dish.* ◆ Angeynemel tywekety, kwatyan antywerretyart, an rnwewarn thelewetyart kwaty, mwarel thelewarretyart. Kwaty angenty-iperr. (N) *Soakage water used to be taken back and drunk, and tipped into the water dishes using a wooden scoop. Water from soakages.*
SEE ALSO atywekal, urety, kwerlintyerr, panth, lwengkart[2], irrkwely[2], alparr[1], irrkwa, lengarr, arlketh[1]
= **urna** (T,E)

rnwanenty *n.*
things, possessions, swag, clothes ◆ Yakweth atyengenh arlkwenhek arreweh-atwety mern, rnwanenty apek. (M) *I have filled my bag to the brim with food and clothes.* ◆ Ayeng rnwanenty mwerreh alherrem. (M) *I want those nice clothes.* ◆ Rnwanenty tha atyenh inerl-alheyay. (St) *I'm going to go and get my things.*

◆ Rnwanenty alhewem. (T) *Washing clothes.*
SEE ALSO mantarr
= **urnanenty** (E)
rnwanenty atyeneny (W,T)
(atyeneny *'someone else's things'*) someone else's things

rnwang (W,T) wooden water dish SEE UNDER **rnwa**

rnwart, iynwart (E) *n.*
1. a person's lap ◆ Kwer akwek nhenh rnwartel anem atyengel-arleng. (T) *This little kid is sitting on my lap.* ◆ Ampa akwek apetyay iynwart nhewarl anetyek. (St) *Come here child, and sit on my lap.*
2. the front part of the body, chest (?)
◆ Iynwart iltyel antirrkwemel angem mantarr, atnyeketyeng. *Holding the clothes and carrying them clasped to the front of your body in case they fall.*
= irnwa
SEE ALSO aympa, peth
rnwart-areny, iynwart-areny (E) *n.*
a sook, someone who is always sitting in someone's lap (lit. 'belonging to the lap')
◆ Rnwartel anetyal kwenh rntwarr alhay. Rnwart-areny-kwenyay. (T) *Don't sit on my lap, move further away. Don't be a sook.*
rnwartel anyenem, rnwartel atnyenem (E), **iynwartel anyenem** (E)
hold on lap (anyenem *'have', 'hold'*)

rnwek-werrem (W,T) *vi.*
be related as close female cousins
rnwek-werrenty (W,T) *n.*
two close female cousins (their children could marry one another) ◆ Arelh ampwel ilem alakenh, 'Atyengenhaw yatherr iperr rnwekarl-werrek atherr apetyerrem'. Arelh ampwel ilem, awenhelikw ilem. (T) *The old lady says, 'There's my two, those two close female cousins coming'. That's what the old woman, the auntie [of one of them] says.*
SEE ALSO altyel akerrem
= **urnek-iwerrenty** (E)

rnwem (E) snake (a general word for snakes) SEE UNDER **urnem**

rnwepenh (W,T), **irnwepenh** (E) *n.*
a woman's child; a person's sister's child; nephew, niece (lit. 'from the lap') ◆ Irnwepenh ampatyey kwerenh, atnertel akwel atnyenem kwerenh — ampekikw. (Sa) Irnwepenh *is her child, that is, from her stomach — her child.*
◆ Irnwepenh atyenharl yanh apetyem. (St) *That's my sister's child coming there.*
= anert-penh
SEE ALSO alem-penh, ampwek, ampa, rnwart

rnwerr, iynwerr (E) *n.*
lame, crippled ◆ Kwey nheng lim-limel aperl-anem kwenh akeweny rnwerr, perrap rnwerr anthwerr akeweny aperl-anetyenheng kel anety-alpem antem merel interl-anem. An rnwerrarl awelhem. (T) *That poor girl is really lame and crippled — she's really crippled when she walks — and then she goes and sits down, lies down at camp. Feeling crippled.*
SEE ALSO anath, anenyirrp irrkweynar, apekap, apertap, arlamarr, arlwemeny, lim-lim, lyer, rtapety, yer
rnwerr-rnwerr (W,T) *n.*
lame, crippled
rnwerr-irrem, iynwerr-irrem (E) *vi.*
become crippled or lame
SEE ALSO arlamarr-irrem

rrkng SEE UNDER **rrng**

rrkwa (W,T), **rrkwang** (W,T), **irrkwa** (E) *n.*
sleep (in the eyes when you wake up); pus
◆ Tyapernpam rrkwakertan, an irlpang tywen rrkwakert. (T) *Boils have pus, and sore ears have pus.* ◆ Annga rrkwakert tyerrty nhenh. (M) *This person has sleep in their eyes.*

rrkwal (W,T), **irrkwal** (E) *n.*
1. a type of spinifex (*Triodia schinzii*)
2. spinifex country, desert country ◆ Arletyety rrkwalel irnerlapem, kenh tyalangk akenh anem irntarenyarl. *Self*-anteyarlam. Arletyety atwem aken, rwel mpwarem, mpwarem antem tamp-arteh. (M) Arletyety *is found in the open desert country, whereas* tyalangk *is found in the hilly country. They are different from each other. The* arletyety *spinifex is beaten as well, then the resin is heated on the fire and made into [a resin cake] a bit like a damper.* ◆ Ankerr-kenhan athernengarl, arnam-warlarl arrernemarl irrkwal-warl ipert-ilemel. Atherrk-atherrkarl. (St) Atherneng *are emu's eggs which are laid in the grass [nest] that has been hollowed out in the desert country. They are green.* • = manangkarr

rrkwalty (W,T), **irrkwalty** (W) *n.*
needle bush, needlewood (*Hakea leucoptera* ssp. *leucoptera*). Shrub to about 3 m high, with needle-like leaves and white or yellow flowers. ◆ Arnang rrkwalty lyek-akert. (M) *The needlebush has spikes.*
= ilpey

rrkwang (W,T) sleep (in the eyes when you wake up); pus SEE UNDER **rrkwa**

rrkwanth (W,T), **irrkwanth** (T) *n.*
brave, confident, not scared ◆ Ater-kwenh rrkwanth tyerrty nhenh. (M) *This person is not frightened, they're brave.*

SEE ALSO akaty-akaty, anew-anew, arnkaty, irrpelth

rrkwanth-rrkwanth (W,T), **irrkwanth-irrkwanth** (T) *n.*
brave, confident, not scared
CAN SOUND A BIT LIKE kwanth-kwanth *'bleed (a lot)'*

rrkwapem (W,T), **irrkwapem** (E) *vi.*
do things; be occupied doing something; work ◆ Aylanth ap irrkwapepapem, angkek angketyel aylanth. (Sa) *We two are working, talking language.* ◆ Irrkwaperl-anenty-penh ayeng purrk-irremeyay, purrk anem ayeng. Mernek ayeng kwaty tharl inerl-iwem, ura tharl inemel ayeng purrk anem irremel ayengant anyent irrkwaperl-anenty. Arrantherr irrkwaperl-anenh-areyay ayengan anyent irrkwapepapem-kety. (Sa) *I'm tired after working — I'm tired now. I got the food and the water, and I got the wood and now I'm tired as I was the only one working. You all go and do some work as I'm the only one who has been doing anything.*
SEE ALSO atyanem, mpwarem, warrk-irrem

rrkwapenty (W,T), **irrkwapenty** (E) *n.*
work

rrkwapenh-apenh (T) *n.*
worker, employee

rrkwem (W,T), **irrkwem** (E) *vt.*
1. keep, hold onto something, carry something ◆ Amarrkel rrkweperrkwem amwelek kwer rrwey. (M) *His mother is carrying the baby boy on her hip.* ◆ Arelhel alparrel rrkwerl-anem kwer akwek. (M) *His wife is holding the baby in the baby-carrier.*
2. have something, possess something ◆ Artwang ampwangel rrkwem alkwert irlkwatherr. (N) *The old man has a shield to protect himself.* ◆ Artwelarl arralt irrkwem arrarnel. (T) *Men have beards on their chins.*
3. give birth to (of animals); lay (an egg) ◆ Arengkel irrkwety-alhek merek. (Sa) *The dog went and had its pups at the camp.* ◆ Mweremwenkelan ker-warl kwartarl irrkwem, tyerr anem anem. (Sa) *Blowflies lay their eggs in meat, and then there's maggots.*
SEE ALSO anyenem

rrkwenty (W,T), **irrkwenty** (E), **irrkwenh-irrkwenh** (E) *n.*
police, policeman, policewoman (lit. 'holder')

irrkwenty-akely (E) *n.*
a type of ant (lit. 'little policeman').

rrkwerrem (W,T), **irrkwerrem** (E) *vi.*
hold each other, hold parts of each other ◆ Iltyang rrkwerrem. (M) *Shaking hands.* ◆ Yanh kwenh ngkweng anyent-irretyek anep-anem mal-malek kwenh. Nta mel-irrkwerl-apetyem mal-malel kel mal-malel irrkwetyem amel-irrkwerrem antem. (T) *Those people are all gathered together for the sorry business. You come and embrace people to express your grief at the sorry camp.*

rrkwerrenty (W,T), **irrkwerrenty** (E) *n.*
together, with each other; close or joined together ◆ Irrkwerrenty ananem iwetyangenh, purt antey, itengant-atherr. Itengant-atherr iwerretyang purt anerl-anem irrkwerrenty. (Sa) *The two of them are still together, they haven't split up. The two of them are still together.* ◆ Irrkwerrenty waly yanh-arey, uleperr yanh. (St) *The leaves of the blue mallee are close together.*

rrkwer (W), **irrkwer** (E) *n.*
feeling hot ◆ Arrarlp-wem pelangket iwem, urinparl ayeng irrem irrkwer anemarl-kety, arrarlp-wem. (St) *Throwing the blankets off, because I'm getting hot, feeling hot.* ◆ Rwang yanh rntwarr-ileyaw, irrkwerarl anemeng tyerrty ayeng kwenh. (M) *Move that fire further away, my body is feeling hot.*
SEE ALSO awempem

Rrkwer (W) *n.*
Brookes Soak, Mt Denison area

rrkwern (W,T), **irrkwern** (W) *n.*
orphan, someone whose parents have died ◆ Kwer rrkwern. (M) *An orphan child.* ◆ Ayengan rrkwern akin. Mam atyenh tha aparlp-ilekarl. (P) *I am an orphan as well. I lost my mother.*
SEE ALSO alhamp, kwetyenty, amatheng

rrkwern-irrem (W,T), **irrkwern-irrem** (W,T) *vi.*
become an orphan

rrmwa (W,T), **rrmwang** (W,T) *n.*
ceremonial scars on chest, stomach and arms (men's and women's) ◆ Wararl akelhek rrmwang arrwekeleny tyerrty arrwekeleny rrmwang akelhenty, nhenh-angkwerr aketyam rrmwang alhwang anthetyam alhwekweny. (T) *The olden-time people just cut themselves round here [chest etc.] so that they could give some blood [for healing].*
SEE ALSO urrma

rrmwangk-rrmwangk (W,T) *n.*
a thumping or thudding noise; the sound of footsteps ◆ Rrmwangk-rrmwangk arrtyanem. (T) *Running along making a thudding sound.*
= ahenty-ahenty², twerlepwelh-pwelh, anenty-anenty

rrmwarl-wem (W,T) *vt.*
make fire using a firesaw; make fire by rubbing a hard

piece of wood against another softer one, or against a shield or carrying dish
◆ Arrwekeleny mapel rrmwarl-wetyam, alkwert-warn, amerrel. Rwem arratetyam. (M) *The olden-time people used to make fire using a firesaw, on a shield or a woomera. And then the fire would start.*
= urtnety-wem
SEE ALSO nthilem, rrmwa, wem[2]

rrmwenyar (W,T) sit with legs curled back or bent SEE UNDER **mwenyar**

rrngwa (W,T), **rrngwang** (W,T), **irrngwa** (T,E) *n.*
mound of earth made by an animal such as a goanna or rabbit ◆ Ahelh rrngwa angernem arlewatyerrel. Arlewatyerrel angernem alhweng mpwarem. Kel ra alhweng kwerenhel intem ankwa anem. Tyerrtyel arem rrngwa *there* anem arlewatyerr-kenh *new one* kwenh. Kel atwem. (T) *Goannas dig mounds of dirt when they are making a hole. Then they go to sleep in the hole. People see the fresh mound of dirt made by the goanna, then they kill the goanna.* ◆ Alhweng angernemel irrngwa iwepiwem. (St) *Digging a burrow and throwing out a heap of dirt.*
= arlerlp[1]

rrngwaly (W) *n.*
young shoots of the native tobacco. As this stage the tobacco is tasteless.
= ngkwerlp akwerrk, antyanp[2], akerrng, ngerrng
SEE ALSO ngkwerlp

rrngwang (W,T) mound of earth made by an animal such as a goanna or rabbit SEE UNDER **rrngwa**

rrngwerrty (W,T), **ngwerrty** (W) *n.*
hungry, want to eat without sharing, greedy
◆ Rrngwerrty kwenh ayeng awelhem kereh. (M) *I really feel like eating some meat.*
SEE ALSO angayel, ankey

rrngwerrty-irrem (W,T), **ngwerrty-irrem** (W) *vi.*
be very hungry, have a big appetite, eat too much
SEE ALSO ankey-irrem

rrpm SEE UNDER **rrm**

rrpwa (W,T), **rrpwang** (W,T) *n.*
1. backbone (animal or person). Also referred to as *rrpwang ngkwern.* ◆ Rrpwang ngkwern, rrpwang artep. Tyelkarl artep, kenh rrpwarl intenhem ngkwern. (T) *The backbone. The back is fleshy, and the* rrpwa *that lies along the back is the boney part.*
SEE ALSO artep ngkwern
2. meat from the back of an animal. Also referred to as *ker rrpwang.* ◆ Ker rrpwangaw! Thang lpwelemel atwetyew. (T) *Meat from the backbone! I'll smash it [the backbone] into bits.*
3. the top of a hill. Also referred to as *irntang rrpwang.*

rrpwamper (W,T), **irrpamper** (W,T) *n.*
common brush-tailed possum (*Trichosurus vulpecula*). Also referred to as *ker rrpwamper.* ◆ Ker rrpwamper yanh-lkwer, ker rlpwerelarl anetyart, rrpwamper. Lweren arlka arlkwerretyart. (N) *They also used to eat possum meat and that sort of thing. Animals that lived in hollow trees.*

◆ Kapert altepenh rrpwamper-penh ina wetyart irrkety. (M) *They spun hairstring from human hair and from possum fur.*
= antenh, pathem

rrpwang (W,T) backbone (animal or person) SEE UNDER **rrpwa**

rrpwarem (W,T) *vt.*
1. wipe or rub something out; wipe something off something; scratch off
◆ Rlkang angerrel rrpwarek aherr-kenh mpaty, tyerrty-kenh mpaty arlka. (T) *The big wind wiped out the tracks of the kangaroo, and the people's tracks as well.* ◆ Tyerrty mpaty alenhel anem rrpwarem. (M) *Wiping out the person's footprints.*
SEE ALSO iparem, irrarlkem, arnngem
2. wipe out a debt
3. apologise ◆ Kel angkety nhenh-penh rrpwarem antem. (T) *After talking they made up.*
SEE ALSO arltwem
= **urrparem** (T,E)

rrpwarelhem (W,T) *vi.*
1. wipe something off yourself
SEE ALSO arnngelhem, iparelhem, irrarlkelhem
2. wipe out footprints, take off or erase name from a paper
3. apologise ◆ Nyerr nta rrpwarelhem thametheng apek nta inemarl-penh. Mern apek or ker apek nta inemarl-penh. Nta rrpwarelhem antey ilelhem. 'Iy ayeng, ityam *no* tha anyenngel-inek kwenh.' Angkety alenh *turn*-em-ilem, rrpwarelhemem. (M) *You apologise [lit. 'wipe off shame'] maybe after you have got something. Maybe you got some food or some meat. Then you apologise for yourself. 'I don't know, I didn't steal anything.' You set the story straight.*
4. hold each other in mourning
= **urrparelhem** (T,E)

rrpwarlerrp-wem (W) rub part of self on something SEE UNDER **irrparlerrp-wem**

-rrpwer (W,T) *k.ending*
a lot, plural, all of them. This ending seems to go only on kin terms. ◆ Atyankerney-penh angetyetyart warntapelant mern atyankern arrwekeleny mapel. Aperl-aperl-**rrpwer**elaty menh-menh-**rrpwer**el arlka atyemeyel-**rrpwer**. (N) *The olden-time people used to get mistletoe berries in bark containers. All my grandmothers, the old women.* ◆ Atyemey-**rrpwer** alherl-wetyam, menh-menh-**rrpwer** alherl-wetyam. Ker arlka angetyewarrem aperl-aperlel-**rrpwer**, mern arlka *everything*; parl arlka angetyewarrem kwenh. (N) *All my mother's fathers and my mother's mothers used to go. They used to bring back everything; bush bananas, bush tomatoes.* ◆ Yayel-**rrpwer** ker arlewatyerr angetyam. (T) *My elder sister and all of them brought back goanna meat.*
SEE ALSO -intyerr, map, -nheng[2]

rrpwerl (W,T) *n.*
1. black, dark in colour ◆ Arntap-warn anwa antywerrketyart, arntap-warn. Awantyetyart anwern, *seed*-an wetyartan. Mpank, perrap rrpwerl anthwerr akin ahakeyart. Ankwerlay. (N) *We used to mash it up in water in the bark containers. Then we'd suck on the juice, discarding the seeds. The* ankwerlay *is a really black colour like the* ahakey *plum.*
2. Aboriginal person
= **irrpwerl** (E)
tyerrty rrpwerl (W,T)
Aboriginal person (tyerrty '*person*')
rrpwerl-rrpwerl (W,T) *n.*
a little bit dark (in colour)
= **irrpwerl-irrpwerl** (E)
rrpwerl-irrem (W,T) *vi.*
darken; go dark in colour; blacken ◆ Tyampet rrpwerl-irrem. (M) *The billycan is going black.*
= **irrpwerl-irrem** (E)
rrpwerl-ilem (W,T) *vt.*
make something go dark in colour
= **irrpwerl-ilem** (E)

rrpwernp (W,T) *adv.*
1. country that doesn't give up any food, meat etc. to the hunter; country devoid of bushtucker
2. being unlucky or unsuccessful in hunting; coming back with nothing (from hunting) ◆ Rrpwernp apem — ker angwerrm-ilety-kweny, mern arlka arlatyey arlka apek itya apem — rrpwernp anthwerr. Iltyant angayel alpem, lyweny-angkwerr. (T) *Going along and not getting anything — not finding any meat, or food such as pencil yams — getting nothing at all. Coming back empty-handed and hungry from the hunting trip.*
= **urrpernp** (E)
rrpwernp-ilem (W,T) *vt.*
cause someone to be unsuccessful at hunting, frighten off game
= **urrpernp-ilem** (E)
rrpwernp anthem (W,T) = **rrpwernp-ilem** (anthem '*give*') ◆ Rrpwernp anthem ingkern-angkwerr alhemel arrpenh. (M) *A person coming along behind frightens off the game.*
= **urrpernp anthem** (E)

rrpwety (W,T) *n.*
1. a few, several
2. the number three, three of something ◆ Iltyang rrpwety. (T) *Three fingers.* ◆ Ampaty atyenh rrpwety. (T) *I have three children.*
= **urrpety** (E)
rrpwetyarrp (W,T) *adv.*
three, just a few, several ◆ Rrpwetyarrp war alhek. (T) *Just a few people went.*
= **urrpetyarrp** (E)
rrpwetyelam rrpwetyelam (T),
rrpwetyek-rrpwety (W) *adv.*
in threes or in small groups
rrpwety-ingar (W,T) *adv.*
a few times, several times, for a few days ◆ Rrpwety-inger ayeng alhek. (M) *I went three times.*
= **urrpety-inger** (E)
rrpwety-ilem (W,T) *vt.*
make something into a few bits or pieces ◆ Ker rrpwety-ila! Ker rrpwety akay! (T) *Cut the meat up into a few bits! Make the meat into bits!*
rrpwety-irrem (W,T) *vi.*
split or separate off into threes, a few split off from a larger group ◆ Aherr map arrtyanem. Angakelhemel rrpwety-irrem. (T) *The kangaroos are running away. Then a few of them split themselves off from the group.*

rrpwey (W,T) *n.*
1. message, news
2. messenger, someone with a message, (coming) with a message ◆ Tyerrty yenh angkety-akert, rrpwey apetyem, tyerrtyelarl angkety ilanthek. (M) *That person's coming with a message that a person sent.*
= **urrpey** (T,E)
rrpwey alhem (W,T)
take a message to someone (alhem '*go*') ◆ Rrpwey alhem tyerrty alerteh. (M) *Taking a message to that person over there.*

rrtny SEE UNDER **rrny**

rrtywekelh-ilem (T) *vt.*
trick or deceive someone; tell lies, pretend

◆ Tyerrty yanhel ayengenh rrtywekelh-ilek. (T) *That person was tricking me.*
= rrtywerrem, therlkem

rrtywerrem (W,T) *vi.*
trick or deceive someone; tell lies, pretend ◆ Rrtywerremel ayeng ilerl-alhek. (T) *[She] told me lies.*
SEE ALSO therlkem, rrtywekelh-ilem, urirrem², rnter-irrem
= **urrtyirrem** (E)
rrtywerrenty (W,T) *n.*
a lie, a liar ◆ Rrtywerrenty angerr nta mpwarerl-apem kwenh — *no* unta arraty akwet apek ayey ilem war — rrtywerremel nta iltem, ngkweng ngkwanty kwenharl alarterl-anem map kwenh. (N) *You are going along and telling big lies — you're just not telling the story properly — you're lying when you say that lots of people are picking on you.* ◆ Ntwang rrtywerrenty angerr anek. (T) *You were a big liar.* ◆ Arelh yanh rrtywerrenty mantarr anthetyeh. (T) *That woman lies about giving the clothes.*
rrtywerremel ilem (W,T)
tell lies (ilem *'say', 'tell'*)
= **urrtyirremel ilem** (E)
rrtyweng-rrtyweng (W,T), **tyweng-tyweng** *n.*
pretend, fake, not real
= **urrtyeng-urrtyeng** (E)

rrwalyek (W) *n.*
a type of tree, possibly *Eucalyptus* sp.

rrwampem (W) *vi.*
1. get angry with someone; become annoyed, hot, agitated, or upset
SEE ALSO ahel-irrem, arlelty-irrem, yerrng-irrem
2. feel really hungry, really want to eat something; stomach (burn from hunger); be starving for something ◆ Anert ayeng rrwampem angayel apek ahel apek. (M) *My stomach is burning from hunger, or maybe from anger.*
= **urrampem** (T,E)

rrwar (W,T) *n.*
echo ◆ Rrwar atyengenh ayeng awelhek, *or* awek tha. (T) *I heard my echo.* ◆ Rrwar tyaheleny awelhek. (M) *I heard my echo.*
= **urrar** (T,E)

rrwarlp¹ (T), **arrwarlp** (E), **urrarlp** (E) *n.*
1. native tomato (*Solanum ellipticum* var. *Ranges DE Albrecht 5807*)
2. the edible fruit of the native tomato ◆ Rrwarlpan irntareny. Mern akin an tyekert. Ampengant arlkwenh, wal tyekertarl yanh, mentyel anwa aretyart. (N) *The native tomato grows in the hills. It has a fruit but it is bitter and we only eat it if it's ripe. If it was bitter we used to just leave it.*
SEE ALSO manyem, rtwengkerr, alperrantyey, katyerr, ararnt

rrwarlp² (W), **rwarlp** (W) *n.* [RESPECT LANGUAGE]
married person's camp; son-in-law's or mother-in-law's camp ◆ Rrwarlp-warl ahanenha anewek-warl. (M) *Go to your husband's camp [said by a woman to her daughter].*
SEE ALSO mparnt, ngwemay, arlweker, arnkenty, ahileng, arramenty

rrwayerr (T) behaving in a teasing or joking way with people who belong to the opposite generation moiety SEE UNDER **urrayerr**

rrwek (W,T) *adv.*
1. 'Wait on!', 'Just a minute!', 'Hang on!'. *Rrwek* can occur on its own as a command. ◆ Rrwek tywempelhaw, ingkang atanth-kety alyekel. (N) *Hang on, wait for me, I've been stabbed in the foot by a prickle.*
2. waiting till something has happened ◆ Rrwek amparr ntyerlp-irrey rwang. (M) *Wait till the fire burns down.* ◆ Rrwek ana. (M) *Sit down and wait.* ◆ Mpankew ampeng-irretyakenh, rrwekaw! (M) *It's still raw, not yet cooked, just wait!*
= alerl
= **urrek** (T,E)
rrwek-antey (W,T) *adv.*
'Wait a minute', 'Hang on a moment', 'Wait a while'
= alerl-antey
= **urrek-antey** (T,E)
rrwek-mernt (W,T) *adv.* = **rrwek-antey**
= alerl-mernt

rrwelty (W,T), **irrwelty** *n.*
1. kindling wood, scraps of wood, wood chips, twigs ◆ Ura akely-akely inetyek alhay, irrwelty. (Sa) *Go and get some small bits of wood, some kindling.* ◆ Rrwelty akem rwa nthiletyenheng. (T) *Cut some kindling to light the fire.*
SEE ALSO ngkwelty, mwenng, mwenthenng
2. wood that is put on top of a grave ◆ Angkwey ayang mapel anwern-kwenhel arnel amparr atwetyart, tyerrtyarl lwetyartan, rrweltyam akerneng wetyart alhengk-aretyek kwer akwek mapel. (T) *In the old days, before our time, the old people used to chop branches to put on top of the grave of someone who had passed away, so that the children would recognise the grave.*
= **urrelty** (T,E)
arnang rrwelty (W,T)
kindling wood (arnang *'plant'*)

rwang rrwelty (W,T)
kindling wood (rwang *'fire'*)

rrwelty-rrwelty (W,T) *n.*
1. small stones or rocks
2. a flat scrubby hill. Also referred to as *apwert rrwelty-rrwelty*.
SEE ALSO arrwertem

Rrweltyapet (W) *n.*
name of a place near Gidyea Bore (west of Napperby station homestead)

rrwem-ilem (W,T) *vt.* [RESPECT LANGUAGE]
1. give something to someone ◆ Mern apek rrwem-iletyeh, kwaty apek. (M) *Giving the food or the water [to respect kin].*
2. take something to someone
SEE ALSO anthem, angernem2
= **urrem-ilem** (E)

rrwem-rrwem (W,T) *n.*
not understanding properly; being silly in the head; forgetful ◆ Rrwem-rrwem anerl-anem, awetyakenh. (M) *Sitting down, not hearing.* ◆ Arelh rrwem-rrwemel ker akethek arrernerl-alhek yatyerr alhemel. (T) *The woman forgetfully left the meat out in the open when she went visiting.*
= **urrem-urrem** (T,E)
rrwem-rrwem-irrem (W,T) *vi.*
become silly in the head or forgetful; go a bit mad
= **urrem-urrem-irrem** (T,E)

rrwempem (W,T) *vi.*
sleep a lot; lie around; become sleepy, drowsy, lifeless, lazy or lethargic ◆ Iwenh-apert yanh rrwempewempem? (M) *How come that person is still asleep?* ◆ Tyerrty yanh rrwemperl-anem. (T) *That person sleeps all day.*
rrwempel anem (W) = **rrwempem** ◆ Rrwempel anetyang akem-irray! Wenheh nta rrwempel anetyenh? (M) *Don't lie around, get up! Why are you lying around sleeping?*

rrwenyenk (W,T) *n.*
Georgina gidgee (*Acacia georginae*). Twisted tree to about 5 m, with grey leaves and broad flat pods. The seeds are very poisonous.
= **urrenyenk** (E)

rrwep-rrwep (W,T), **rrwepeng-rrwep** (W) *n.*
whirlwind, willy-willy ◆ Rrwep-rrwep-wety tyerrtyarl ater arrtyanewarrem antyweng arratemel. 'Yanh arraty akwetarl apetyem kwenh!' (N) *Because of the whirlwind people rush out of their humpies. 'It's coming straight at us!'*
= awerantyerrng, aharlparrengk2

rrwepert (T) dry, dry place, dry country SEE UNDER **urrepert**

rrwerleng (W,T) *n.*

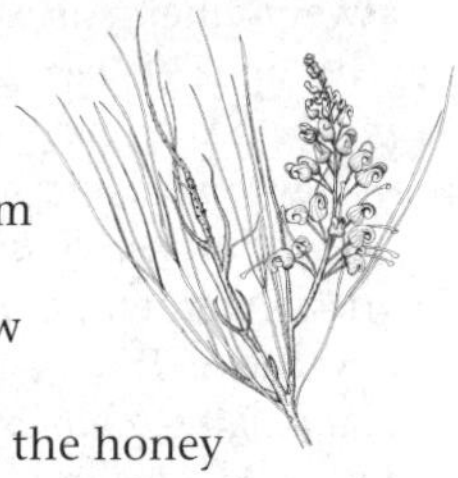

1. honey grevillea (*Grevillea juncifolia* ssp. *juncifolia*). Shrub to 3.5 m high, with thin pointy leaves and golden-yellow flowers.
2. the sweet nectar from the honey grevillea. Also referred to as *ngkwarl rrwerleng.* ◆ Rrwerleng ap mern ngkwarlarl, alkey angerr *anyway* twakemel lywenkel arlka akerrirretyart. Tek arrernem akin renh, *red one* nheng. (N) *The honey grevillea tree is tall and has edible honey, which we pick by pulling the branches down with a hooked stick. We lay flowers out in the sun as well, those red flowers.* ◆ Ntyweyart awantyem, ntyweyart rrwerleng anem, awantyem. (N) *We suck on the [honey grevillea] honey as we do on the corkwood honey.*
= tharrkarr

Rrwerlety (W), **Rrwerlenty** (W) *n.*
place name, Yuelamu (Mt Allan) area

rrwerlkem (W,T) *vt.*
round up game, hunt animals in a certain direction; flush game out into the open ◆ Anwengkerr ker irntareny rrwerlkem kwenelak irntang akerneng. (T) *We are chasing the euros down from the top of the hill.*
rrwerlkenty (W,T) *n.*
animals that have been frightened or flushed out into the open (?) ◆ 'Ker aherr rrwerlkenty apetyem, tyerrty alenhel wart aremel ipenem.' Lwerenarl aterel anthem, arrpenhel anem arem, *'Eh* nhenh-warn apetyem rrwerlkenty kwenh'. (T) *'The animals are running frightened in this direction, the ones that the person saw and hunted out.' The person might frighten the game, and then another sees it and says, 'Hey, the frightened animals are coming this way'.*

rrwernem (W,T) *vt.*
1. make trouble for someone else; get someone into trouble (especially close family such as a son, daughter or mother) ◆ Tyerrty atherr atwerrem. Arrpenh anem rrwernem, artwang atherr atwerrerleng. (T) *Two people might be fighting. Then this one makes trouble for other people, from the fight that the two men are having.* ◆ Marl yanhel atyeng rrwernek. Ayengem *wrong one* inek arrkwentyel. Kenh yatherr atwerrekarl. (T) *That woman got me into trouble. The police arrested me by mistake. It was those two who were fighting.* ◆ Tyerrty atherr atwerrem artwang atherr apek terangk, wal arrpenh nhakel rrwernem, amwekem

atwety-alhem, artwang nhak-henh amwek, *sister* apek. (T) *Two people may be fighting, maybe two drunken men, well another one makes trouble and goes and fights the mother of one of the men, or his sister.* ◆ Ngkwantyel apek rrwernem, amewek apek anyewek apek rrwernem. *Trouble* mpwarem. (M) *Getting angry and making trouble, for their mother or their father. Making trouble.*
SEE ALSO atyang-inem, nakepakel-ilem
2. blame someone for something they didn't do
CAN SOUND A BIT LIKE arrwernem *'make a hole in something'*
= **urrernem** (E)
rrwernelhem (W,T) *vi.*
get yourself into trouble

rrwernter (W,T) *adv.*
(men) doing a ritual dancing, hopping or skipping motion that indicates aggression
= **urrernter**[1] (E)
rrwernter-irrem (W,T) *vi.*
dance, hop or skip along showing intention to fight ◆ Artwang map rrwernter-irrem ankerr-akert, artarr-akert. (M) *The men dance along with the emu tail feathers [held behind their backs].*
SEE ALSO arrtyernem
= **urrernter-irrem** (E)
rrwernter alhem (W,T) = **rrwernter-irrem**
= **urrernter alhem** (E)

rrwethem (T) *vt.*
1. stamp or stand on someone or something; tread on something, press down hard on something; squeeze or squash something ◆ Artwang yanhel ingkel rrwethem arlewatyerr. (T) *That man is treading on the goanna.*
2. suppress, trample on ◆ Tyerrty merek-artwey waylpelel ingkel rrwethem. (T) *The whitefella is trampling [riding roughshod] over the Aboriginal landowners.*
= rlpwerrkem
SEE ALSO alernelhem, kerrk-welhem

rrwey (W,T) *n.*
1. boy. Also referred to as *kwer rrwey.* ◆ Amarrkel rrkweperrkwem amwelek kwer rrwey. (M) *His mother is carrying the baby boy on her hip.*
= **urrey** (E)
2. man. In some contexts it would be seen as very insulting to call a man *rrwey.* ◆ Rrwey nhenh anewek anpem, kemelh-ilem renh, 'Kem-irray! Ilanth alperretyekay!' (N) *The man touches his wife to wake her up and says, 'Get up! We two are going back!'* ◆ Arelh yanh ahenty-irrem rrwey yanhek. (T) *That woman likes that bloke.*
3. male (of a species) ◆ Rrweyan *medicine* alhewetyamelhem, alhewelhetyamarl aketyam. *Salt water* kwa karnkw yanh, alhewelhetyart mernt perrap nhenh ngkernetyenheng. (N) *The male plant is a medicine that is collected and used for washing yourself. It is salty and is used as a wash when people are really sick.* ◆ Apmwa parip. Rrweyan arlkeny-arlkeny. Marlan *yellow one yellow one* nteny-nteny war. *Whistle*-artekap ra irrerl-anem parip. Rnwem-apenyarl ap ra. (St) *The* parip *snake. The male is stripey. The female is yellowish and just spotty. They are similar to snakes and they make a sort of whistling sound.*
= **urrey** (E)

rrweyek-alyey-alyey (W,T), **rrweyeh-alyey-alyey** (W,T) *n.*
pussy-tails, mulla-mulla, lamb's tail (*Ptilotus exaltatus*) (rrwey *'boy'*; alyey-alyey *'spirit friend'*). Plant about 60 cm high with smooth green leaves and pink flowers.
= aweyek-alyey-alyey, awerreh-alyey-alyey, mernteparn
SEE ALSO alyey-alyey, marlek-alyey-alyey
= **urreyek-alyey-alyey** (E)

rta, **irta** (W,T), **ta**, **rtang** (W,T), **irtang** (W,T), **tang** (W,T) *n.*
1. hard part of a hoof or paw
2. dried nasal mucus, snot; dried-up crust on something ◆ Rtakert, rta alakenh inelhem alhang, alhang altywer atherr, an rtang inelhem alakenh, *clean* antem anem. Kwer map ingkerrek alhang rtakert akin *dirty* map. (N) *[Noses] have dried-up snot that is picked out from the two nostrils, and then the nose is clean. All the kids have dirty snotty noses.*
SEE ALSO tewem, ika, artwengkenng

rtak (W,T), **tak** (W,T), **irtak** (W,T), **rtakw** (E) *n.*
windbreak, something that shelters people from the wind ◆ Rtak angerr yatherr arrernek an rwang yatherr itek. (M) *They made a big windbreak and lit the fire.* ◆ Rtakw artetyek. Ankwa ayeng intetyek. (St) *I'll build a windbreak. Then I'll go to sleep.*
= kwenty[2]

rtamp flour, damper SEE UNDER **tamp**

rtang (W,T) hard part of a hoof or paw SEE UNDER **rta**

rtanty lump of dirt; hard (ground) SEE UNDER **tanty**

rtapety, **tapety**, **rtwapety** (T,E) *n.*
cramped, bent or doubled up; curled up (hand or leg); have crossed legs; crippled ◆ Rtapety interl-anem alakenh, amper

rlkerrelhenty-penh. Rlkerrelhemem wal rtapetyem-irrem, ankweng antemarl. Arlwemenyarl intem, alakenh-artek. (N) *Lying down curled up after stretching the knees out. Stretching out and then bending up again, and sleeping, curled up.* ◆ Atnyenty-atnyentyan alhemey kel tyerrtyel apek anpem, alakenh rtapety anem irrerl-alhem. (St) *The* atnyenty-atnyenty *beetle goes along and if a person touches it it curls up.* ◆ Rtapety interl-anem, alwerrngarl pwert-irrem, *cramp*-arl-irremeng, atywaty-irrememem. Atywaty amparr irrem kwer-penh rtapetyem interl-anem. (N) *Lying down cramped up, because your tendons have cramped up. Stretch out first and then lie there curled up.*
SEE ALSO arlerlp[2], tharr, arlwemeny, arrepert

rtapety anem, **tapety anem**, **rtwapety anem** (T,E)
sit with legs curled back or bent (anem '*sit*') ◆ Rtapety-irrem, ngkwernarl rlkert awelheman wal rtapety anem anerl-apem akeweny, rtapety anerl-apem ngkwern anetyan. Kel ra lkerrelhem, rtapety-penh. (T) *The poor thing is sitting with legs curled back because her legs hurt, her legs are no good. Then, after that, she stretches her legs out.*

rtapety intem, **tapety intem**, **rtwapety intem** (T,E)
lie in a curled up position (intem[1] '*lie down*') ◆ Rtapety intem irrernt-kety. (St) *Lying curled up because of the cold.*

rtapety-irrem, **tapety-irrem**, **rtwapety-irrem** (T,E) *vi.*
cramp up, curl up; bend legs to one side; sit cross-legged ◆ Kelkert rtapety-irremel anep-anem. (M) *Sitting with bent knees.*

rtapety-ilem, **tapety-ilem**, **rtwapety-ilem** (T,E) *vt.*
make something cramp or curl up

Rtar-rtar (W) name of a hill in the Mt Wedge/Tilmouth Roadhouse area SEE UNDER **Tar-tar**

rtarl (E) lump of wax or resin-like substance at the base of the native bees' hive SEE UNDER **tarl**

Rtarl (E) name of a soakage east of Wilora (Stirling) community SEE UNDER **Tarl**

rtarnng (W,T) the back of the head where it joins the neck SEE UNDER **tarnng**

rtartart, **tartart** *n.*
1. mother's father; grandfather
2. mother's father's brother or sister; great-uncle, great-aunt
3. a man's daughter's child; grandchild; grandson, granddaughter
4. a person's brother's daughter's child; great-niece, great-nephew
5. particular relations with the same skin as a person's *rtartart*
6. the country and Dreamings belonging to a person's *rtartart.*
7. mother's father (and equivalent kin) [BABY TALK]
SEE ALSO artartey, atyemey

rtartaty (E), **tartaty** (E) *n.*
dark-coloured or dry seeds of the dogwood tree, *awenth*
= kertaty, lyarr
SEE ALSO ntyerrm, alyaly

rtaty, **taty** *n.*
pig-footed bandicoot (*Chaeropus ecaudatus*) (?). This animal is now extinct in Central Australia.

rtek (E) burrow or nest made on top of the ground from grass or spinifex SEE UNDER **tek**

rtemarl (E) back of the head where it joins the neck, nape SEE UNDER **temarl**

rteng (W) bottom part of a native beehive or sugarbag hive SEE UNDER **arteng**

rtepernter (W) banana-flavoured bush tomato SEE UNDER **tepernter**

rtern (T,E) a big place, large camp, crowded place SEE UNDER **tern**

rternng (E) the back of the head where it joins the neck SEE UNDER **tarnng**

rterr-rterr (W,T) rainbow bee-eater SEE UNDER **terr-terr**

rtert mud, wet ground SEE UNDER **tert**

rtety[1], **tety**, **irtety** (W,T) *n.*
tooth, teeth ◆ Arranyenganyengel ngenh angwarem, arlkwem rtety. (M) *The blind snake gives you toothache.* ◆ Rtety-kwenh arrimper-akert. Rtety anyent atwekarl, arrimper mpwarek. (T) *Teeth have a gap in the front. One tooth is knocked out to make the gap.* ◆ Ayeng rtetyarl akeng-irrem. (St) *My teeth have gone rotten.*
= arntek
CAN SOUND A BIT LIKE artety '*mulga*'

rtety arekar-irrem, **irtety arekar-irrem** (W,T), **tety arekar-irrem**
have a toothache (arekar-irrem '*be in pain*')

rtety arlkwem, **tety arlkwem**, **irtety arlkwem** (W,T)
have toothache (arlkwem '*eat*', '*be in pain*') ◆ Rtety arlkwem ayenh. (St) *My teeth are aching.*

= arntek arlkwem
SEE ALSO aytwelth-akert
rtety arlkwenh-arlkwenh (W), **tety arlkwenh-arlkwenh** (W) *n.*
a type of blind snake (*Ramphotyphlops endoterus*) (lit. 'tooth eater')
= arranyenganyeng, ahaylengkeyler

rtety2 (W), **tety** (W), **rtetyep** (E), **tetyep** (E) *n.*
step, foothold ◆ Antyemarl-penh rtety ikwerel antyeynem antyeynem-penh atwem renh ker alewatyerr apek arwengalker apek ra atwem, kel atnarnpem rtety ikwerel akin. *After climbing up the steps [you] kill the goanna or get the sugarbag, and then you go down, using the steps again.*
rtety-wem, **rtety-iwem** (E) *vt.*
cut steps, cut footholds ◆ Angenty akwen alakenh rtety-wem, anarnpetyek kel antyenty-alpey akern-warl. (St) *Cut the steps down in the soakage like that, jump down and then climb back up again to the top.* ◆ Arna alyelk rtety-wemel anem antyem, arntarlkw anetyakenh. (St) *[You] cut footholds in a smooth tree that doesn't have any forks, then you climb up.* ◆ Tetyewa arna yanh, arwengalkerek apek arna antyetyek akern. (St) *Cut footholds in that tree so that [you] can climb up to get the sugarbag.*
rtety-ipem (E) *vt.* = **rtety-wem**
rtety-rtety, **tety-tety** *n.*
goose pimples, itchy lumps, scabies, rough or lumpy skin ◆ Arengk rtety-rtety, tyerrty apek rtety-rtety, *scabies*-apeny weth-lkwer rtety-rtety. (St) *A dog or a person might have itchy lumps, like scabies.*
SEE ALSO lyek-lyek
rtety-rtety-irrem, **tety-tety-irrem** *vi.*
get lumps, go lumpy ◆ Wenyel anhwem an rtety-rtety-irrem. (M) *When a mosquito bites [you] go lumpy.*
SEE ALSO iylek-iylek

rtewey (E) clotted, sticky, thickened or coagulated blood SEE UNDER **tewey**

rtey-rtey, **tey-tey** *n.*
magpie-lark (*Grallina cyanoleuca*) ◆ Rtey-rteyel anthwerrng mpwarem mer antywang kwerenh. (M) *The magpie-lark makes its nest from mud.* ◆ *Him* alakenh angkerl-anem, 'Rteyartey rteyartey rteyartey'. (T) *They make a sound like this, 'Rteyartey rteyartey rteyartey'.*

= ntwerleperl, kwatyarl rtey-rtey

rteyepertey, **teyepertey** *n.*
1. sisters of the initiate or 'young fella'
2. a particular way that the sisters of the initiate or 'young fella' call out during the initiation (young man) ceremony
◆ Rteyepertey arlkep-arlkemaw, altwerl apek arntwerr-arntwerrel arlkep-arlkem artwan. Arelhan nhakw *round*-el arlkep-arlkem. (St) *The* rteyepertey *women sing out, and from the western end of the ceremony ground the men sing out. The women go round calling out.*
SEE ALSO alyaper-warn, thampartey, anyent arrpenh, perlal, ntwerleng, ntyangkwenng, alyey2, ywerlperr, anmanty, apwelh

rtirr-rtirr (T) rainbow bee-eater SEE UNDER **terr-terr**

rtnwanenty (E) things; possessions, swag, clothes SEE UNDER **urnanenty**

rtwa (W,T) close, near SEE UNDER **itwa**

rtwakert (E) chest SEE UNDER **rtwekert**

rtwalty *n.*
1. a man's mother-in-law; man's wife's mother
2. a woman's son-in-law; woman's daughter's husband ◆ Ntwang anthem rtwalty ngkwengenh ngkweng rtwaltyem anem. (T) *If you give [your daughter] to your son-in-law, then he is* rtwalty *for you.*
3. certain other relations who are related to each other by marriage (for example, two cross-cousins will call each other *rtwalty* if their children are married to each other)
◆ Rtwalty-nheng atherr — rrwey ngkwengenhel apek *son* ngkwengenh *married*-em-ilem, altyelewengkwenh, wal rtwaltyem ngkweng anem. (M) *Two people are* rtwalty *to each other — maybe your son married your female cross-cousin's [daughter], well then your cousin is* rtwalty *for you.*
SEE ALSO mey-mey1, mwer, ampeyamp
= **urtalty** (E)
rtwalty-nheng atherr *n.*
a person together with their *rtwalty*
rtwaltyek-rtwalty (W,T) *n.*
be related as *rtwalty* to each other ◆ *Like* Kemarr apek apety-alpem *niece* atyengenh-akert, ayeng akenh kwerenh *niece*-akert akin anerleng. Alakenh rtwaltyek-rtwalty antem atherr anem. (M) *For example, a Kemarr might come back married to my niece [sister's child] and I am married to his niece as well. That's what it means to be* rtwaltyek-rtwalty *[Ngal man speaking].*
SEE ALSO rlwerrkerek-rlwerrker
rtwalty-irrem (W,T) *vi.*
become mother-in-law/son-in-law for someone

rtwang apetyepetyem (W) rufous whistler SEE UNDER **artwang apetyepetyem**

rtwang (W,T) close, near SEE UNDER **itwa**

rtwanng *n.*
a barrier or trench to stop floodwater or running water ◆ Kwaty apek antyewarn irrpehety, irrpentyetyam, wal rtwanng arrernetyam, *dry* anetyenheng alenh-thayt. (M) *If it looked like water was going to come into the shelter, or if the water was already coming in, then a trench or a barrier was made to so that the other side would be dry.* ◆ Tha rtwanng arrernetyek ipmerrarl atnyep-atnyem-kety, kwaty rew apek apetyekerr. (St) *I am making a trench because the raindrops are falling, and because the running water might come in.*
SEE ALSO urtanng
rtwanng-rtwanng *n.* = **rtwanng**
SEE ALSO angert arrernem

rtwap *n.*
hot earth or ashes (used for cooking or healing). Also referred to as *rwang rtwap.* ◆ Ker rtwapel itetyek, aperrk iwemel. (St) *Cooking the meat in the hot ashes, throwing away the coals.*
SEE ALSO arerrk
= **urtap** (T,E)

Rtwapert (W) *n.*
Aunty Marys Dam, north of Yuelamu (Mt Allan) community

rtwapety (T,E) cramped, bent or doubled up SEE UNDER **rtapety**

rtwarnp *n.*
fat on lower stomach or upper thighs (person, kangaroo); a large paunch or belly. Also referred to as *ker rtwarnp.* ◆ Arelh arrpenhel ilem, '*Oh* rtwarnp angerr yanhey, arelh yanh apetyepetyem. Rtwarnpek-anternenh'. (T) *Another woman might say, 'Oh look at that woman with the really fat stomach coming. A really fat stomach'.* ◆ Ker aherr anter 'rtwarnp' anwern ilem. (T) *We call a fat kangaroo* 'rtwarnp'.
SEE ALSO apel[1], atnwerlk, arrertarnk, apertaynp
= **urtarnp** (E)

rtwaty (E) *n.*
carrying strap made from hairstring
SEE ALSO irrkety, alyep, alyepengantay

rtwatyert (W,T) *n.*
a type of yam; native morning glory (*Ipomoea muelleri*). A vine with branches that creep along the ground and pink trumpet-like flowers. Also referred to as *mern rtwatyert.* ◆ Mern rtwatyert apel, mern inyemel arlkwerl-apem, rwel itemel, rtwatyert. Inyemel inyemel inyemel anemel inyemel anem. Inyerl-apek inyerl-apek, rwelem atyerrem mern arlatyeyartek arlkwem. (N) *The* rtwatyert *is a food that is dug up and then cooked in the fire. We dig and dig and dig and then cook the roots in the fire and then eat them like we do pencil yams.*
= atywert-atywert, tatyetarr

rtway (W,T) *n.*
burrowing bettong (*Bettongia lesueur*) ◆ Rtwayel yerrakwerr arlkwem. (N) *Burrowing bettongs eat bush onions.*
= awert[2]
SEE ALSO alhwet

-rtwek (T,E) amongst, at, on, by SEE UNDER **-itwek**

rtwek-rtwek (T,E) *n.* [RESPECT LANGUAGE]
1. a sympathetic word for 'dog'. This word may be used for a dog belonging to someone who has passed away, or for a dog that has passed away or is sick. ◆ 'Rtwek-rtwek' ilem angwely, nheng 'rtwek-rtwek' ilem irrernng tyerrty alert-henh, tyerrtyarl *pass away*-henh. 'Rtwek-rtwek yanh imperrirray atwetyal kwenh.' (M) *'Rtwek-rtwek' is what the dog who belonged to someone who has passed away is called. 'Leave that poor dog alone and don't hit it.'* ◆ Rtwek-rtwek atyenh kwenh utnherrirrek. Ker-kenh. Ker arlewatyerr-kenh kwenh atyenh impen utnherrirrek rtwek-rtwek atyenh. (St) *My poor dog was in a fight. My hunting dog. My special goanna dog was in a fight.* ◆ Akely atyenh rtwek-rtwek uyerrek. (Sa) *My poor little dog died.*
2. a woman's son-in-law's dog ◆ Rtwek-rtwek yanhenty aywepey. (St) *Hunt that dog [belonging to my son-in-law] away.*
= wang-wang
SEE ALSO angwely, arengk, tywetyety

rtwekert (W,T), **rtwakert** (E) *n.*
1. chest ◆ Kereltyarl welhem rtwekert, mernt-penh, artwengkenng-penh. (T) *The chest gets congested from the cold or flu.*
2. heart ◆ Rtwekert-akertarl parrk-irrem. Rtwekert ahey-angkentyeh rrwem *shaking* antem. Kel renh parrp *medicine* anthem, wal mwerram antem. (N) *With heart disease a person gets tired. Then their heart beats fast. If they are given medicine quickly then they get better.* ◆ Rtwakert ayeng akeng-irrek. Ngkwerlpel apek ayeng ampek. (St) *My heart is no good. Maybe tobacco burnt me.*
SEE ALSO pwerterleng, arnarnk
= **urtakwert** (E)
rtwekert ngkwern (W,T), **rtwakert ngkwern** (E) breastbone

rtwely, **rtweyl** (E) *adv.*
throwing a spear; throwing a spear with a woomera ◆ Irrtyart nta rtwelyel wem, wal irrepereperr alhem, irrtyart. (M) *You might throw a spear, and it goes skidding along the ground.* ◆ Amerr-warl irrtyart akwernem, rtweyl anem ra irrem, atanthetyek anem. (St) *[You] put the spear in the woomera, then throw the spear, and then it spears [the animal].*
rtwely-wem, **rtweyl-wem** (E) *vt.*
throw a spear; throw a spear with a woomera ◆ Amerreng rtwely-way! Amerreng rtwely atanthetyeh! (M) *Throw [it] with the woomera! Throw the spear with the woomera!*
rtwely-ilem, **rtweyl-ilem** (E) *vt.* = **rtwely-wem** ◆ Amerr-warl ra akwernem irrtyart, kel rtweyl-ilem anem ra. (St) *He puts the spear in the woomera, then he throws the spear.*
= arrathenem
rtwely-inem, **rtweyl-inem** (E) *vt.*
aim a spear at something
SEE ALSO arrang-arem, akwanth-ilem, angkarr arem
SEE ALSO atanthem

rtwengkerr (W,T) *n.*
1. native tomato, potato bush, potato weed (*Solanum ellipticum* var. *Ranges DE Albrecht 5807*) (?)
2. edible fruit of the native tomato
= rrwarlp[1]

rtwenk *n.*
something that is used for support or to lean on, such as a pillow, headrest or walking stick ◆ Rtwenk atyeng arrerneyaw ayeng intetyek. (St) *Put a headrest there for me so that I can sleep.* ◆ Rtwenk-akert nthwerl-apem. (M) *Walking along with a walking stick.*

rtwep (W,T) *n.*
1. hole ◆ Awenng angernem rtwep, wal irrernng arrernem, ahelhelem artem. Artwel artem. (M) *Dig a hole for the grave, then put the corpse in, then cover it with earth. The men cover it.*
2. a hole for cooking in ◆ Rtwep angernem. (M) *Digging a cooking hole.* • SEE ALSO rtwap
3. the inside hollow part of something • SEE ALSO urtep
rtwep-ilem (W,T) *vt.*
1. dig a hole, make a hole ◆ Arnang rnkernetyeh rtwep-ilem. (M) *Dig a hole to put the plant in.*
2. hollow out or carve something out ◆ Panth rtwep-ilem ilepel, rtwep mpwarem. (T) *The wooden dish is carved out to make a hollow.* ◆ Tyerrtyel rtwep-ilemel arrpek, rtwepem anem. (M) *The person carved [it] out to make it really hollow.*
= mwerlk-ilem

rtwerleperl (W,T), **rtwerleperlep** (W) magpie-lark SEE UNDER **nterlepwerl**

rtwerlp (W), **alhang rtwerlp** (W)
a nasal sound; blocked nose ◆ Alhang rtwerlp angkem mernt-penh. (M) *Speaking with a nasal sound from having a blocked nose.*

rtweth *n.*
1. lower back; small of the back ◆ Rtweth ayeng akeng-irrek. (St) *My lower back is no good.* ◆ Arrwekel ayeng ltywerrerl-alhey rtweth-akert, rntwarrarl alhek-penh. Kwer-penh akem-irrem, 'Mwerram ayeng awelhem'. (N) *I'm going to go and have a rest first because I have lower-back ache from walking a long way. After that I get up and say, 'I feel good'.*
= antywert, atheng-atheng
= **urteth** (E)
2. kangaroo meat (portion from near the tail). Also referred to as *ker rtweth.*

Rtwetherr (W) *n.*
name of a well south of Lake Lewis

Rtwetyarnteng (E) waterhole/swamp near the Aniltji/Sandover Highway turn-off SEE UNDER **Artwetyarnteng**

rtweyl (E) throwing a spear, throwing a spear with a woomera SEE UNDER **rtwely**

rwa (W,T), **rwang** (W,T) *n.*
1. fire ◆ Rwang antant-ilem rrmwarl-wemel. (N) *Lighting the fire using a firesaw.* ◆ Rwang angerr amperl-anem kwer rlkerteh. (M) *A big fire is burning for the sick man.* ◆ Rwang kel altherremew. (M) *The fire is already burning.*
2. firewood ◆ Rwang tyarrp atwem ilepel. (T) *Splitting the firewood with an axe.*
3. matches
4. A general word that goes before things to do with fire.
5. battery (of a car)
= **ura** (E)
rwang kep (W,T)
firestick (kep '*firestick*'). Made from dogwood (*akerlperr*), ironwood (*atheng, atyarnp, athimp*) or supplejack wood (*anyer*). ◆ Rwang kep nta inem rwang itetyeh. (M) *You get a firestick to light the fire with.* ◆ Tyerrty map lyweny nthwetyart rwang kep-akert. (T) *People used to carry firesticks when they went hunting.*
rwang lyenenty (W,T)
firestick, light, torch (lyenenty '*light*')
rwang kwert (W,T)
smoke (*kwert* 'smoke') ◆ Rwang kwertarl

intem. Rwa item, an kwert anem intem, kel altherrem anem, rwa ya ampem antem. (T) *The fire starts smoking. [You] light the fire, then it starts smoking, then it catches alight and then it burns.*

rwang kwert-arteh (W,T)
blue colour (lit. 'like smoke')

rwang ngkwelty (W,T), **rwa ngkwelty** (T)
kindling wood (ngkwelty *'bits and pieces'*)

rwang rrwelty (W,T)
kindling wood (rrwelty *'kindling'*)

rwang irlpart (W,T)
a log (irlpart *'log'*) ◆ Tyerrtyel rwang irlpart arrernetyart kwenyel amperl-anetyek. (T) *People used to put a log there to burn through the night.*
SEE ALSO ura iylpart

rwang inem (W,T)
collect firewood (inem *'get'*)

rwampey (T) hot SEE UNDER **urrampey**

rwanenty *n.*
resting place, shady place, base camp, resting place on the way home ◆ Rwanentyel arrwekel ayeng mpwelhety-alpem, ulyel anety-alpem, rwanentyel. Mern katyerr apek ikwer-warl angety-alpem rwanenty-warl. Rwanenty-they alpey. Mpa! Mer-warl. Rwanenty-warl ngkernem kwaty apek. (St) *I'm going to wait at that resting place ahead there, sit down in the shade. [I] might take some desert raisins there to the resting place. From there we'll go back home. Come on! [We] might put the water there, in the base camp.*
SEE ALSO rerrk

rwanenty-wem *vt.*
leave things somewhere while going hunting ◆ Lywewarl rwanenty-wem, nta apek arrernerl-alhem, rwanenty-werl-alhem. Lywang angerr aremel, rwanenty-wem. Lyweny alhetyenheng rwanenty-werl-alhem. (M) *[You] might leave things there in the shade and then keep going. If you see a nice shade, then you leave your things there and then go hunting.*
SEE ALSO alal-wem

rwang (W,T) fire SEE UNDER **rwa**

rwang arrernem (W) *vt.*
swear at somebody; talk badly to someone; argue all the time ◆ Tyerrty nhenhel atyeng rwang arrernek. Iwenheng? (M) *This person swore at me. Why?*
= urarrernem
CAN SOUND A BIT LIKE rwang arrernem *'put fire'*

rwanng *n.*
1. a familiar place, home ◆ Mer rwanng-warn apety-alpek. (T) *Coming back to the old familiar place.* ◆ Mer rwanngel ayeng ananem, nthenhem-warn ayeng alhemer. Mer rwanngel ayeng anerl-anem? (M) *I am staying home in the familiar place. Where else am I going to go?*
2. a familiar person, good friend, someone who has been associated with a place for a long time and is well liked
SEE ALSO pelty
CAN SOUND A BIT LIKE rwa *'fire'*
= **uranng** (E)

rwanng-ilem *vt.*
make friends; make someone get used to a place; familiarise someone with a person or place
= **uranng-ilem** (E)

rwanng-irrem *vi.*
get used to something; get used to a place; become familiar with a place or a person ◆ Arengk rwanng-irrem tyerrtyek. (T) *The dog is getting used to the person.*
= **uranng-irrem** (E)

rwarlp (W) married person's camp; son-in-law's or mother-in-law's camp SEE UNDER **rrwarlp**[2]

rwarr (E) *n.*
wind from the east

rwarr-angkwerr alhem (E), **rwarr-angkwarr alhem** (E)
go upwind from something (lit. 'go by way of the wind') ◆ Ikwa ntyernekerr, rwarr-angkwarrarl alheman. Rwarr-angkwarr alhetyal, ikwa ntyernekerr, ikwa intyernemel ra untemarl, aherr apek. Antyey apekarl intyem. (St) *The kangaroo might smell the scent of your body if you go upwind from it. Don't go upwind, in case it smells you and runs away. It might smell your sweat.*

rwayerrp (T), **rayerrp** (T,E) *n.*
black-headed python (*Aspidites melanocephalus*) ◆ Ker rayerrp arlkwerretyart atwemel arrwekeleny mapel. (Sa) *The olden-time people used to kill and eat the black-headed python.*
= arrwerrperl, antwerrkenh
= **urayerrp** (E)

-rwek (T) *n.ending*
1. at some particular time; during. This ending often occurs on words that describe weather or seasons. It follows the *+el*[5] ending.
2. through something, in the midst of something ◆ Arelh rlkel-**rwek**, irrernt angerrel-**rwek** apetyem. (T) *The woman is coming along in the wind, in the cold.* ◆ Iwenheh ntwan apetyem kwatyel-**rwek**? (T) *Why are you coming when it's raining?* ◆ Aherrk

iltyel-**rwek** ayeng arety-kwenh. (T) *I can't see because of the rays of the sun.*
= -rlwer

rwekar (T) *n.*
a bit tired, listless ◆ Thang ngwenh rwekar arep-arem. (T) *I see that you are tired.* ◆ Ayengan rwekar-kweny mwerram. (T) *I'm not tired, I'm okay.*

rwekarlp (E) *n.*
fruit of native currant, native citrus, *ahakey* (when red in colour)

rwekem-ilem *vt.*
cheat someone; steal something (from English 'rook') ◆ Atyengenh ntwa rwekem-iletyal. (T) *Don't steal my things.*
SEE ALSO ankey
rwekey pak
a thief; a cheat (from English 'rook; bugger') ◆ Thakey akwek-akwek mern arlkwenh-arlkwenh. Kwenyel apertemarl arlkwerl-anem. *Him* rwekey pak. (T) *Little mice eat food. They sneak up in the night and eat. They are thieves.*

rwelemap-ilem *vt.*
roll something up; gather things together (from English 'roll-em up')
= artaper-ilem
SEE ALSO ayernem

rwelh-ilem (W,T) *vt.*
get something down from something; make someone get down from somewhere ◆ Rnwanenty apek mwetekayeng rwelh-ilem. (M) *Getting the things down off [the top of] the car.*
SEE ALSO anarnpelh-ilem
rwelh-rwelh-ilem (W,T) *vt.* = **rwelh-ilem**
rwelh-arrernem *vt.*
1. squeeze something out of something else; blow something out (of nose) ◆ Artangk anem rwelh-arrernay — ampa apek. (St) *Squat down and squeeze hard — maybe [said to a] child.*
= ulherrpernem
SEE ALSO pewelhem
2. get something down from something • SEE ALSO anarnpelh-ilem

rwemeny (E) fast, quickly, being in a hurry SEE UNDER **uremeny**

rwempereng (E) a type of bird, possibly the mulga parrot SEE UNDER **urimpering**

Rwepenty (W) *n.*
Mt Hay
SEE ALSO rwa

rwer-welhem (E) rub yourself in or on something SEE UNDER **ywer-welhem**

Rwerlengerleng (W) *n.*
name of a hill north of Yuelamu (Mt Allan) community

rwernelhem (W,T) *vi.*
go out of sight behind something; hide behind something ◆ Ayeng rwernelhem arnangkwerr. (M) *I am going out of sight behind the trees.* ◆ Anngarenty-irrem, ahenty-kwenh artweh. Marl alwernemel alwernemel alwernetyam ityantey. Arrtyanetyam marl ikwerety rwernelhemel. (N) *She doesn't want to go with the man because she doesn't like him. [The man] keeps on chasing the girl but she doesn't change her mind. The girl runs away from him and hides herself from him, behind something.*
= **ureynelhem** (E)

rwernp (W,T) *n.*
1. hot, warmth, heat
2. hot weather
= urinp
rwernp-irrem (W,T) *vi.*
get hot, warm up ◆ Twern-penh ayeng rwernp-irrem ingka. (T) *My feet are getting hot in the sun.*
= urinp-irrem
rwernp-ilem (W,T) *vt.*
heat something up; warm something up
= **urinp-ilem** (E)

rwernp-rwernp (W,T), **rernp-rernp** (W) *n.*
a type of cicada or cricket (?) ◆ Ahelheh irrpem kwen, arnameh, wal, 'Rwernp-rwernpem' angkerl-anem. Nheng angkem *all night, early* arlka angkety-antyem. 'Rwernp rwernp' alakenh. (M) *It goes under the ground, or in the grass, and then it makes a 'Rwernp-rwernp' noise. It sings out all night and also early in the morning. 'Rwernp-rwernp', like that.* ◆ Kwenyel angkerl-anem rwernp-rwernp. (M) *The* rwernp-rwernp *sings out at night.* ◆ Rwernp-rwernpel mpwarerl-anem anaty, arntwang arrernerl-anem, *all night* angkerl-anemel. Angkerl-anem *crack*-em-ilem, an arntwang anem arrernem. (T) *The cricket goes along making the bush potatoes, putting the tubers under the ground by singing all night. They sing and crack [the earth open] and then place the tubers there.* (?)

rwerrem (W,T) *vi.*
go behind something or through something and come out the other side ◆ *Gate*-angkwarr anwengkerr rwerrenhey. (T) *We'll go through the gate.* ◆ Mwetek rwerrenty-alhem altywer arrpenh-angkwerr, kenh arratenty-alhemem. (M) *The car is going through the gap and then*

coming out the other side.
= **urirrem** (E)

rwerrkem (T) shake bush plum or native citrus tree, *ahakey*, to make the fruit fall down SEE UNDER **ywerrkem**

rwert, **rwet** *n.*
road (from English 'road') ◆ Rwert nhenhan angerrety. (M) *This road here is big.*
rwertath *n.*
roadhouse (from English 'roadhouse')

Rwety anem (W) *n.*
name of a soakage west of Yuelamu (Mt Allan) community

rwimpereng (E) a type of bird, possibly the mulga parrot SEE UNDER **urimpering**

Tt

ta hard part of a hoof or paw SEE UNDER **rta**

tak windbreak SEE UNDER **rtak**

tal *n.*
money, dollar (from English 'dollar') ◆ Tal apek ywerrem, *form* apek *sign*-em-ilety-kweny. (T) *The money will run out if [you] don't sign the form.*
SEE ALSO man, maney, ngkwelty

talew (W,T) kangaroo SEE UNDER **tarlew**

talkw *adv.*
1. across something; the long way around; sideways ◆ Alhem tyerrtyan, kel arnel arnpakety-antyerleng talkwel intemel. Kel anyemem. (T) *A person might be walking along, and a tree that is lying across trips them up. Then they fall.* ◆ Lpwararr intem aherlkentyek-atwety, Lpwararr talkw intem mpwank, aherlketyenheng. (T) *The Milky Way lies across [the sky] right up until daybreak.*
2. one-sided; favouring some at the expense of others ◆ Talkwel ntwang ker arrpenh mapeh anthep-anthem. Ayeng ngkweng arrarentyarl. (T) *You are favouring the others and giving them meat. I'm missing out because of you.*
talkw alhem
go the long way around; go across (alhem *'go'*) ◆ Talkw alhem mwerek-kety arlka. (N) *Going round the long way because of [your] son-in-law.* ◆ Ahileng-kety, talkw alhem. (T) *[You] go around the side way because of your son-in-law's camp.*
talkw-irrem *vi.*
go across (in front of something); cut across ◆ Tyerrty alenh talkw-irrem *somewhere*-warn-atheh. Nthenh-warnek-aperl? (M) *That person is going across, heading for somewhere. Where are they going?* ◆ Yanh talkw-irremel alhep-alhem. (T) *That one is going past [our place].*

talkwelanyey (W) *n.*
a type of solanum (?) ◆ Ankerrel arlkwerl-apem talkwelanyey yanh renh, mern kwerenh arlkwerl-apem *self. Can't* tyerrtyel arlkwem. (N) *Emus go along eating the* talkwelanyey, *that's their food that they eat themselves. People don't eat them.*

talkwerrk (W), **talwerrk** (W), **ntalwerrk** (W) *n.*
1. button grass, finger grass, toothbrush grass (*Dactyloctenium radulans*). A grass about 25 cm high.
2. the edible seed of the button grass ◆ Talkwerrk mwarel ilpemem ilpem ilpem

kwer-penh arnam ingkerr anyenhem anyenhem. Arrernemem athetyehem, arrernelhem athemem athemem athemem lweren athetyam. (N) *The button grass seed is winnowed in the wooden dish, and after that all the bits of grass fall down. Then the seed it put there and ground up.*
= ngelyerr, apwert-arlkwenh

talwek (W) kangaroo SEE UNDER **tarlew**

talwerrk (W) button grass SEE UNDER **talkwerrk**

tamp, **rtamp** *n.*
flour, damper (from English 'damper')
anyenty tamp (T,E)
full moon (lit. 'damper moon')

tampewern (W,T), **tampewenh** (W,T) *n.*
a type of melon (?) ◆ Anety pwelekel arlkwerl-anenh-anenh. Anety wart tyekert kwa. Tankeyel arlka arlkwenh-arlkwenh. Irlpa alkeyel arlka arlkwenh-arlkwenh. Tampewenh yanh anety tyekert, irrkertey kwa — arrakert itenh-itenh. (N) *The* tampewenh *melon is no good and it's eaten by cattle. It's bitter-tasting. Donkeys eat it as well. The* tampewenh *melon is bitter — it burns your mouth.*

tangkelh-ilem (W,T) *vt.*
save, heal or cure someone ◆ Ngkartel ngenh tangkelh-ilem mernt apek. (M) *Jesus will heal you if you are sick.* ◆ Altyerray anwernenh tangkelh-ilay, anwern apetyek-arleng ngkweng-warn. (M) *God, save us, because we are coming to be with you.*
SEE ALSO mpwarem, mwerr-ilem, iteth-ilem, althekalth-ilem

tangkey, **tankey** *n.*
donkey (from English 'donkey')
= irlpa urety, irlpalkey, irlpangerr

tanty, **rtanty** *n.*
lump of dirt, hard (ground), dried mud
◆ Rtantyel tha wem ngenh apek. (St) *I might hit you by throwing dried mud at you.*
SEE ALSO ata[1]
CAN SOUND A BIT LIKE atanty *'wait'*
tanty-ilem, **rtanty-ilem** *vt.*
make something muddy

tapak *n.*
tobacco (from English 'tobacco')
SEE ALSO ngkwerlp

tapety cramped, bent or doubled up SEE UNDER **rtapety**

Tar-tar (W), **Rtar-rtar** (W) *n.*
name of a hill in the Mt Wedge/Tilmouth Roadhouse or Tilmouth Well area

tarl (E), **rtarl** (E) *n.*
1. lump of wax or resin-like substance at the base of the native bees' hive
2. lumps of dry snot ◆ Arwengalkerel anem — ankerel ap renh martem arwengalker, ikwer-atwety ngkwarl intem. Tarlarl arrernem, aman mpepel anem kel ngkwarl. Kapert an weth. (Sa) *[It] is there in the native bees' nest — the wax blocks off the nest, and the honey goes as far as there. There is a sort of wax plug there, the ama in the middle, then the honey, and the compacted pollen, the 'head'.*

Tarl, **Rtarl** (E) *n.*
name of a soakage east of Wilora (Stirling) community

tarlew (W,T), **talew** (W,T), **talwek** (W) *n.*
kangaroo
= aherr

tarnng (W,T), **rtarnng** (W,T), **ternng** (E), **rternng** (E) *n.*
the back of the head where it joins the neck; the back of the neck at the base of the skull
= temarl
SEE ALSO ntyarrkwer
ternng ultakem (E), **rternng ultakem** (E)
break someone's neck (ultakem *'break'*)
ternng anyenem (E), **rternng anyenem** (E)
choke someone or something (anyenem *'have', 'hold'*)

tartarrp (E) *n.*
banded lapwing (*Vanellus tricolor*) (?)
SEE ALSO ampeltyetyerrker, interrk-atherather, tyelkatherather

tartart mother's father; grandfather etc. SEE UNDER **rtartart**

tartaty (E) dark-coloured or dry seeds of the dogwood tree SEE UNDER **rtartaty**

taty pig-footed bandicoot (?) SEE UNDER **rtaty**

taty-taty[1] *n.*
1. five-minute grass, rye beetle grass (*Tripogon lolliformis*) (?)
2. eight-day grass (*Fimbristylis dichotoma*)
• = arnwety-arnwety
3. lukarrara (*Fimbristylis oxystachya*) (?). A grass about 30 cm high. ◆ Taty-tatyarl arlkwem aherrel. (St) *Kangaroos eat* taty-taty *grass.* ◆ Kwaty urntem taym, taty-taty imerntarl arratem *first*. Ra imernt antyerrk-irrem. *Just* atherrk war. (St) *When it rains, it is the* taty-taty *grass that comes out first. Then it withers. It's just a grass.* • SEE ALSO akwetelh

taty-taty[2] (T) *n.*
a type of spear ◆ Irrtyart taty-taty ineyaw! (T) *Get the spear!*

Taty-taty (E) *n.*
name of a place; location of Red Gum store on New MacDonald Downs pastoral lease

tatyetarr *n.*
a type of yam; native morning glory (*Ipomoea muelleri*). A vine with branches that creep along the ground, and pink trumpet-like flowers.
= rtwatyert, atywert-atywert

tawel-tawel (E) *n.*
part of a bullock's guts
= anwalty

tawert *n.* [RESPECT LANGUAGE]
a respectful word used for a place or a 'camp' whose proper name shouldn't be said. This might be a woman's son-in-law's camp, a man's mother-in-law's camp, or a place where people have passed away ◆ Ampa kwerenh ilem, 'Tawert-warl ahanenhetyek'. (St) *She tells her daughter, 'You have to move to another camp [you and your husband]'.* ◆ Tawert-warn ahanety-alpek. (T) *[The son-in-law] returned to his camp.* ◆ 'Tawert-warn ahanay.' Alakenh apek *mother-in-law*-el ilanthem *daughter* alenh. (M) *'Go over to the camp where your husband is.' That is how the mother-in-law [of the man] tells that daughter [of hers] to go.*
SEE ALSO arrkwetyety, irrewatyent, arlweker

-tayem, **-taym** *n.ending*
'time'; during a particular season or event; the time when something happens (from English 'time') ◆ Lweren arlka nheng arrwekeleny mapelam atwetyart. Nheng alpety alakenh-iletyeh, nheng kwer-**tayem**. (N) *That's why the olden-time people used to kill them. So that they could use the bilby tails like this [swing them around] during initiation ceremony time.* ◆ Alakenh arnerl-alhem, *'Boo, boo, boo'*, arlkerl-anemel kwaty-**tayem**. (N) *Rain time they [the frogs] sing out like this, 'Boo, boo, boo'.* ◆ Mweremwenk-artek akngerr, utnhem anem ra, atherrkeny-**taym**. (St) *It is like a big blowfly, and it bites, in the green time after rain.*

tayl (E) *n.*
tail (from English 'tail'). Also referred to as *ker tayl.*
= kanty[1]
SEE ALSO pwer

tayl-ayerr (E) *n.* [RESPECT LANGUAGE]
tail

-taym 'time'; during a particular season or event; the time when something happens SEE UNDER **-tayem**

tek (E), **rtek** (E) *n.*
burrow or nest made on top of the ground from grass or spinifex ◆ Rtekel anep-anem rapet, ker kwarlp apek. (St) *Rabbits and spectacled hare-wallabies live in nests made of grass.*
CAN SOUND A BIT LIKE atek *'button quail'*

tek-wem, **tek-iwem** (E) *vt.*
hang something up; lay or spread something out to dry in the sun ◆ Manterr tek-wem tek-ampetyeh. (M) *Hang the clothes up to dry.* ◆ Mantarr apek uternek arrernem tek-iwetyek, tek-ampetyek uternel. Ntang tek-iwem akin, uternel antyerrk-irretyek. (St) *Clothes are hung out it in the sun to dry. Seeds are laid out to dry as well, so that the sun can make them dry.*
= tek-arrernem

tek-arrernem *vt.* = **tek-wem** (arrernem *'put'*) ◆ Ngkerlp akem, kel tek-arrernem twernek. (T) *The native tobacco is picked, then laid out in the sun to dry.*
= tek-wem

tek-ampem *vi.*
be layed or spread out to dry in the sun (ampem[2] *'cook', 'heat up'*) ◆ Tekem iwety-alpem yanh ngkerlp yanh. Iwety-alpem. Tekem ampem ngkerlp yanh. (N) *The native tobacco is taken back to be laid out in the sun to dry.* ◆ Tek-ampetyek twernel mantarr. (St) *The clothes are drying in the sun.*

tek-anem *vi.*
sit drying out or getting warm in the sun

tekentyenarr (W), **ntekentyenarr** (W) *n.*
ring-tailed dragon (*Ctenophorus caudicinctus*) (?)

tekernem (E), **tekertnem** (E) cough SEE UNDER **artekernem**

temarl (E), **rtemarl** (E) *n.*
1. back of the head where it joins the neck; nape ◆ 'Arlewatyerr yanh rtemarl atweyaw!' Kel *finish*-em-ilemel atwem rtemarl. Ker aherr apek rtemarl atwetyek. (St) *'Hit that goanna on the back of the head!' Hitting it on the back of the head will finish it off [kill it]. Kangaroos can be hit on the back of the head.* ◆ Amwelyan karlkwem rtemarlel. Inemel, karlkwemel anem. Iteth-antey rtemarl karlkwem. (Sa) *The cadney lizard is bitten on the back of the neck. [You] get it, and bite it on the back of the neck. Bite it while it is still alive.*
= tarnng
2. pillow [SOME SPEAKERS] • = rtwenk

tempety *n.* [RESPECT LANGUAGE]
personal belongings of the deceased. This word is especially used by close relations such as the mothers and mother's brothers of the deceased. Others use the word *ampeny*.
SEE ALSO ampeny[1]

tenh (E), **tetnh** (E) *n.*
earth that is lifted up by a swollen tuber underneath
SEE ALSO urrper
tenh-wem (E), **tetnh-wem** (E) *vt.*
cause the earth to raise or swell up; make the earth crack (by a swollen root or tuber)
tenh anyenem (E), **tetnh anyenem** (E)
= **tenh-wem** (anyenem *'have', 'hold'*) ◆ Mern anatyel tenh anyenem akern. Anaty artelhampwel inngel. Urrper-wem, urrper ra tetnh atnyenem irrkwenngel-apeny. (Sa) *The bush potato makes the earth lift right up. A really big bush potato. It makes the earth swell up and crack, like a native truffle does.*
= urrper anyenem, karnt anyenem
SEE ALSO urrper-wem

tent, **tint** (E) *n.*
canvas used for shelter; tent, swag (from English 'tent') ◆ *Tent*-kwenyel renh artetyam, aywert yanh. Kwaty-kety. (Sa) *When people didn't have canvas they made shelters from the rain out of spinifex.*
SEE ALSO kalikew

tentey, **tintey**, **tentey-tentey**, **tintey-tintey** *n.*
a bent branch; tree with low-hanging branches ◆ Tinteyan arna, ankerrmern apek aper apek. (St) *A coolibah or a river red gum might have low-hanging branches.*
◆ Angkweyarl anwern pwerlp-irretyart, rewel pwerlp-irrenhem, irrpenhem, mer arrpelant arratenhetyam. Kwereng mer arrpelem irrpentyetyam, arratetyam mer arrpelant. Arnang tintey-angkwarr apek kel *jump*-irretyart anwern. (N) *We used to swim in the running water, going into the water at one spot and then coming out at another. Then we'd go in again and come out at yet another place. We used to jump in from the bent down branches of trees.*

Tepanteng (W) *n.*
name of a hill in the Stuart Bluff Range area

tepernter (W), **rtepernter** (W) *n.*
1. banana-flavoured bush tomato (*Solanum cleistogamum*). Plant with grey or blue-green leaves, thorns on stems, pale purple flowers and pale yellow fruits. Grows to about 25 cm high.
2. the edible fruit of the banana-flavoured bush tomato (note Warlpiri *yipirntiri*)
◆ Arreny atherram, rtepernter an manyem, kel atherrarrp ratherr, mern arlkwenh-arlkwenh atherr. (N) *There are two names,* rtepernter *and* manyem, *and they are both separate species, both edible.*
= manyem, arlelyek

tepwerl (E) *n.*
bitter-tasting coating found on desert raisin fruits and on mulga apples. This is usually removed by rubbing the fruit on the ground.
◆ Kapert ayeng arntem, katyerr apek tepwerl-akert tharl arlkwek, kapert anem ayeng arntem, ahelhel iletyakenh. (St) *I have a headache after eating bush raisins that still had a bitter coating on them because they hadn't been cleaned on the ground.*
SEE ALSO inpewem, katyerr, ataltyakwerl, pwarr

terangk *n.*
drunk, drunken person, a drunk (from English 'drunk') ◆ Kwer yanh ater-irrem arrentyeng *or* angwelyeng *or* tyerrtyeng arrpenh, terangkeng. (T) *That child is frightened of the monster, or of the dog, of other people, or of drunks.*
terangk-terangk *n.*
a bit drunk, light-headed, dizzy, faint
◆ Nheng twern-penh *hot time* alakenh antem ilelhem, 'Ayeng kwenh kapert arepwelepwel-irrem terangk-terangk irrem *see* alakenh'. (N) *You know, particularly in the hot weather, you might say, 'My head is spinning and I feel like I am drunk'.*
terangk-irrem *vi.*
get drunk ◆ Tyerrty yanh terangkemart irrirrem. (M) *Those people are getting drunk.*
terangkem-ilem *vt.*
make someone drunk ◆ Tyerrty arrpenhel renh terangkem-ilem. (M) *Another person is making him drunk.*

terarl *n.*
kangaroo's path or track ◆ Terarlan ker aherr-henh, rwert kwa, atyey, terarl akwek war. Terarl kwerel alherl-apem. (N) *A terarl is a kangaroo's road or path, a little track which it goes along.*
SEE ALSO tyey[1], anarlt

teraty (T,E) *n.*
calm, no wind, windless
SEE ALSO anengk[2]
teraty-irrem (T,E) *vi.*
calm down, settle down (wind) ◆ Teraty, rlka nhenh akngerr apetyem, wal teraty anem irrem. Rlka-kweny anem irrem, teraty. (St) *There might be a big wind blowing, well then it calms down. There is no wind, it's calm.*
= anengk-irrem

terawath, **terraweth** *n.*
trousers, pants (from English 'trousers')
◆ Terawath apek ngkwenh tyetarl atyeng. (St) *Your trousers might be too tight for me.*

terekerr *n.*
little corella, white cockatoo (*Cacatua sanguinea*)
terlem-ilem *vt.*
deal cards (from English 'deal') ◆ Thangemeh terlem-iley kart? (M) *Will I deal the cards?*
terlapak *n.*
dilly bag (from English 'dilly bag')
terlepawen *n.*
telephone (from English 'telephone')
= alwerrng angkenh-angkenh, arrakert-kenh, irlpekenh
tern (T,E), **rtern** (T,E) *n.*
a big place, large camp, crowded place
◆ Tyerrty map tern kwerel alartewarreperrem. (T) *Lots of people are living at that big place.*
ternng (E) the back of the head where it joins the neck SEE UNDER **tarnng**
terr-terr (W,T), **rterr-rterr** (W,T), **tirr-tirr** (T), **rtirr-rtirr** (T) *n.*
rainbow bee-eater (*Merops ornatus*) ◆ Rterr-rterrel alhweng mpwarem arnkarrel-ayeng. (N) *Rainbow bee-eaters make their nests in the banks of creeks.*

= kwelinterr-interr, apelinterr-interr
SEE ALSO rlwernp
terraweth trousers, pants SEE UNDER **terawath**
terrenth, tirrenth (T,E) *n.*
trilling frog (*Neobatrachus centralis*)
◆ Tirrenth, '*Trrr trrrrr trrrr*', alakenh angkep-angkem. (St) *The trilling frog goes, 'Trrr trrrrr trrrr', that's the sound it makes.*
SEE ALSO alyeyamp
terreth *n.*
dress (from English 'dress')
SEE ALSO mantarr
terrth (W) *n.*
shallow water, a small amount of water
◆ Kwaty terrth anem, kwaty-kweny itya. (M) *There's no water, only just a little bit.*
SEE ALSO iker
tert, rtert *n.*
mud, wet ground ◆ Ahern tert, ahern kwaty-penh. (St) *The ground is wet after rain.*
SEE ALSO anthwerrng, ata[1], urta, antha[1]
tert-irrem, rtert-irrem *vi.*
get wet (ground, camp)
tert-ilem, rtert-ilem *vt.*
make ground wet ◆ Kwatyel anhem ahelh tert-iletyek. (St) *The rain falling makes the ground wet.*

terweth *n.*
tourist (from English 'tourist')
tetherrp-tetherrp *adv.*
1. talking nonsense, speaking in a confused way ◆ Tyerrty yanhan urrtyalth tetherrp-tetherrp angkep-angkem. (T) *That lying person is talking nonsense.*
2. being confused, going in all directions
◆ Tetherrp-tetherrp alhepalhem therrert-therrert. Apal-apal alhepalhem. Ingka arnpenhem therrert-therrert tetherrp-tetherrp. (Sa) *[That person] is stumbling around all over the place. They don't know where they are going. They are heading off in all directions.*
SEE ALSO alhwerrkert, therrert-therrert, apal-apal[2], aperrpert
tetherrp-ilem (T) *vt.*
talk nonsense
tethet *n.*
disease, sickness (from English 'disease')
◆ Arengk arra iylkerr-iylkerr yanh aywepeyaw, tethet anthekerr! (Sa) *Chase that dog with the slobbery mouth away in case it makes us sick!*
tetnh (E) earth that is lifted up by a swollen tuber underneath SEE UNDER **tenh**
tety tooth, teeth SEE UNDER **rtety**[1]
tety (W) step, foothold SEE UNDER **rtety**[2]
tewem, tiwem (E), **itewem** (E) *vt.*
1. clean or scrape burnt hair or skin off an animal; pull hard piece off a kangaroo's paw; scrape burnt skin off a tuber ◆ Ker kanty tha tiwem tyepalel. (St) *I am cleaning the burnt hair off the kangaroo tail with a stick.* ◆ Mern tywerlp tyiparlel tewetyam, *clean*-ilemel *clean*-ilemel. (N) *The roots of the spiderbush are scraped and cleaned with a stick.* ◆ Ingka rta tiwetyek. *Scrape the hard crust off the foot.*
2. rub desert raisins on the ground to remove the sticky bitter-tasting coating ◆ Katyerr tewem ahernel. (N) *Desert raisins are cleaned on the ground.* ◆ Katyerr aketyam mern akem theweyet. Tyekert akin, wal tewerl-anem, tewetyam *bucket*-el akem akem akem. Anwern tewetyam anem ahern inyemel, ahern inyem tewerl-anemam. (N) *We picked the sweet desert raisin fruits. The ones that were bitter were rubbed in the earth and then put into buckets. We'd dig up the earth and rub them in the dirt.*
• SEE ALSO pwarr-wem, inpewem, thwerrem, theweth-ilem, rta
tewelhem (W,T), **tiwelhem** (E) *vi.*
scrape skin off yourself, have a scrub ◆ Ayeng tewelhem amparr kwatyel. (T) *I am going to scrub myself with water first.*

tewenhem (E), **twetnhem** (E) *vt.*
crush or pound something up (native tobacco or other plants) using a grinding stone ◆ Ilpengk tewenhem apert-atwemel, apert-atwem apert-atwem kel renh tewenhemel anem ulpilemel *smash*-em ilemel. (Sa) *The* ilpengk *plant is crushed and then ground up, crushed then ground up to make it into small pieces.* ◆ Intayerr-intayerr, anter-warl renh twetnhem renh *green one* inngap ra anem anem mwerr-angker innga. (Sa) *The* intyayerr-intayerr *plant is crushed up with fat and it goes really lovely and green.*
SEE ALSO ulpilem, apert-atwem

tewey (E), **rtewey** (E) *n.*
clotted, sticky, thickened or coagulated blood. Also referred to as *ker tewey.*
= ntyew
SEE ALSO awerrp[1]
tewey-irrem (E), **rtewey-irrem** (E) *vi.*
coagulate, clot (blood) ◆ Ker tewey-irrenty arlkwem, ampeng-irrenty, ampeng mwerr-angker. (Sa) *Clotted blood is eaten, when it's cooked, and it tastes really good.*
= ntyewey-irrem

teweyat *n.*
truck, Toyota (from English 'Toyota')

tey *n.*
tea (from English 'tea')
SEE ALSO arlpelh
teyelep *n.*
tea, tea-leaves (from English 'tea-leaves')

tey-tey magpie-lark SEE UNDER **rtey-rtey**

teyepertey sisters of the initiate or 'young fella' SEE UNDER **rteyepertey**

tha, **thang** (W,T) *prn.*
I. This pronoun is used as the subject of a transitive verb action (i.e. representing the 'doer' of the verb action). *Ayeng* is used with intransitive verbs. See Appendix 1.
◆ Arwengalker tha atwem ilepel. (St) *I am chopping the sugarbag with an axe.* ◆ Kwer akwek thang arem. (T) *I can see the child.*
◆ Thang anthetyenh ker thwep-thwep. (M) *I will give him meat and soup.* ◆ Thang arem rwang kwert rntwarr amperl-anerlek. (T) *I can see the smoke from the fire in the distance.*
SEE ALSO ayeng

thak *n.*
butt of a rifle, stock of a rifle (from English 'stock') ◆ Maket annga akwernem, thak yanhan alernem pwerlep-warl, kel atyerrem anem. (St) *You put the bullet in the gun, rest the stock against your shoulder, and then shoot.*

thakem (E) *vt.*
make a hole in something, open a burrow ◆ Anemel tha thakek alhweng, rlpwer apek. Altywer anem ilem. *I opened up the burrow, or the hollow, with a digging stick. Made it open.*
thakelhem (E) *vi.*
cave in (hole or burrow)
= arrwernem, atakelhem

thakeman *n.*
stockman, stockwoman (from English 'stockman') ◆ Yanh apetyem thakeman-arey. (St) *There are all the stockmen coming.*
◆ Artwang thakeman alhem nanth arlweletyek. (T) *The stockman is going to round up the horses.*

thakey[1] (W) *part.*
'Will I (do something)?' ◆ Thwengk ikwer anthey, thakey? (M) *I'll give him some, will I?*
SEE ALSO akwey

thakey[2] (W,T), **thakwey** (W), **thakwer** (T,E) *n.*
a type of mouse (?) ◆ Thakey akwek-akwek mern arlkwenh-arlkwenh. Kwenyel apertemarl arlkwerl-anem. *Him* rwekey pak. (T) *Little mice eat food. They sneak up in the night and eat. They are thieves.*
SEE ALSO alwepay, alepey, ilkwenng, aherraty-anywertangey

Thaleng *n.*
Stirling (from English 'Stirling')

thalh (W,T) *n.*
1. heap or load of cooked meat (especially kangaroo) ◆ Ker thalh angetyem. Ker ampeng thalh. Ker aherr apek thalh angetyem. Ker arlewatyerr thalh angetyem. (N) *Bringing a load of cooked meat. Bringing a load of cooked kangaroo meat. Bringing a load of cooked goanna meat.*
2. a heap ◆ Yerr map thalh anep-anem. (M) *The ants are in a heap.* • SEE ALSO aharl, antyakwer

thalkerr (W,T), **tharlkerr** (W,T) *n.*
hard ground, clay
= arnkarr
thalkerr-ilem (W,T) *vt.*
make creek or gully; erode (?) ◆ Kwatyel thalkerr-ilem. (T) *The water is eroding the earth.*
SEE ALSO arnkarr-akelhem, arnkarr-ilem, ilerrty-ilem

thalt, **thaltw** (E) *n.*
salt (from English 'salt') ◆ Kwaty thalt-akert. (T) *Salty water.*
SEE ALSO ker ikwemey ilenh-ilenh, melyek, ilewerr, ulewerr

thampartey *n.* [RESPECT LANGUAGE]
a respectful term used by men to refer to particular men who have a special role in

men's ceremonies. This term is used instead of actual names between kin who are related to each other in this way (perhaps from English 'somebody') (note Warlpiri *jampartiyi*).
SEE ALSO anmanty, apwelh, anyent arrpenh, perlal, ntwerleng, ntyangkwenng, rteyepertey, alyey[2], alyaper-warn, ywerlperr
thampartey-irrem *vi.*
become related as *thampartey* for someone in ceremony

thametheng (E), **thamethengk** (E) *n.*
something or other (from English 'something') ◆ Altyerr-altyerr angkep-angkem yanh. Thametheng atham-arenyelarl altyerr-altyerr mpwarek. (Sa) *That person is talking in her sleep. Something or other, the* atham-areny *spirits made her talk in her sleep.*

thanarnt *n.*
1. platform made for storing food in a tree ◆ Thanarntarl arrernek, mern anem utyenem. Arnel. (St) *Putting a platform in a tree and then putting the food up there.* ◆ Akern arrernang ker mern arlka, arengkel arlkwehety thanarnt-warn. (T) *Put the meat and the food up in the tree in case the dogs eat it.*
2. burial platform in a tree ◆ Angkwey irrernng ina thanarnteh arrernetyam. (M) *In the old days they used to place dead bodies on a platform in a tree.*
SEE ALSO wimperr, kwenterarr
thanarnt-wem *vt.*
1. make a platform in a tree for storing food on ◆ Thanarntel-wek ker anem utyenetyam arrwekelenyel. (St) *The olden-time people made platforms in trees and then stored food up there.*
2. make a platform in a tree for a corpse

thang (W,T) I SEE UNDER **tha**

thangenh *prn.*
I (will do/am doing/have done) something to you. This pronoun is made up of *tha* 'I' and *ngenh* 'you'. ◆ Thangenh apay-unhey. *I want to ask you a question.*
= thwengk
SEE ALSO tha, ngenh, ngkweng, thweker

thangey *n.*
thong (from English 'thong') ◆ Thangey aparlp-ilern atyengenh. (M) *I've lost my thongs.*
SEE ALSO pwet

thanh (E) 'How?', 'What?', 'What's up?' SEE UNDER **nthanh**

thankw (E) *n.*
tea-tree (?) (*Melaleuca lasiandra*)
SEE ALSO ilperl[2]

thap *n.*
supper, the evening meal (from English 'supper')

thar *n.*
facing or slanting downwards; on a slope or an angle
thar-thar *n.* = **thar**
tharew (W) *n.*
facing or slanting downwards; on a slope or an angle ◆ Atwayntenhem akern-antep kel tharew ilenhem anem, kwenelak. (Sa) *Climbing upwards and then going downwards.*
thar-irrem (E) *vi.*
1. go downwards ◆ Ipertel thar-irrenhemel alhem kwenelak. (Sa) *Going downwards along the steep slope.*
2. go a long way away ◆ Ayeng ingwenth thar-irremel alhem. (St) *Tomorrow I am going a long way away.*
thar intem
lie facing or slanting downwards (intem *'lie'*)
thar irnem (W,T)
be tipped onto side or on an angle (irnem *'stand'*) ◆ Mwetekay thar irnem ipertel. (T) *The car is tipped on an angle in the hole.*
thar-wem, **thar-iwem** (E) *vt.*
1. put something on an angle; tip something over ◆ Kwenelak yanh pewetyem-ilenheyaw. Thar-warl ngkernetyek mwetek, kwenelak. Kwenelak thar-iwetyek, pewetyem-iletyek angkem, 'Kwenelak yanh-warl thar-warl pewetyem iley'. (Sa) *Push that car downwards. Put it on a downwards slant. When you are talking about pushing a car you say, 'Push it so that it faces down that way'.*
2. tip all of a liquid into something ◆ Kwaty thar-wem parretyel, ingkerrekarl antywem. (T) *Perishing from thirst and tipping all of the water [into the mouth], drinking the lot.* ◆ *Petrol* alenh mwetek alenh apek *empty* irnem, wal nta thar-wem ingkerr. (M) *If the car has got no petrol, then you tip the whole lot in.*

tharlkerr (T) hard ground; clay SEE UNDER **thalkerr**

tharr *n.*
numb, cramped
SEE ALSO arlerlp[2], rtapety
tharr-irrem *vi.*
get numb, go numb, get cramped
SEE ALSO arlerlp-irrem, impelhem

tharr-tharr (E) a type of bird SEE UNDER **utharr-utharr**

tharremap-ilem *vt.*
rush around, create a disturbance (from English 'stir-em up')
SEE ALSO arweketherwek-ilem

tharrkarr (T,E) *n.*
1. honey grevillea (*Grevillea juncifolia* ssp. *juncifolia*). Shrub to 3.5 m high, with thin pointy leaves and golden-yellow flowers.
2. the sweet nectar from the honey grevillea. Also referred to as *ngkwarl tharrkarr*.
◆ Arrimpimpel iytarr-inemel arlkwerl-anemel ntywey, tharrkarr, intekw. (Sa) *With its beak [the emu] pulls down the corkwood flowers, the honey grevillea and the* intekw *fruits to eat.*
= rrwerleng

tharrkarr-tharrkarr (E) *n.*
a type of snake (?) ◆ Apmwa tharrkarr-tharrkarr-kety mwantyaw. (St) *Look out for the* tharrkarr-tharrkarr *snake.*

that-irrem *vi.*
start, begin (from English 'start')

thathew 'Is it true?', 'Is that so?' SEE UNDER **tyathew**

thawel (T) *n.*
steady rain, drizzle. Also referred to as *kwaty thawel*. ◆ Kwaty thawel rntwem. *It's raining steadily.*
= thew-thew, kwaty perler
SEE ALSO tyeyepetyey, lthel-lthel

thayengarr (E) *n.*
1. a type of ceremony
2. brush shelter used at *angkwerr* ceremonies

-thayt *n.ending*
side, area (from English 'side') ◆ Alak-akey-kenh ayerrer-**thayt**. Angerrakw-**thayt**arl alak-akey ingwerek-areyenh, aylernak-akeyenh altwerl-**thayt**arl. *The north side belongs to people from the other moiety, and the east side belongs to another group of people from the opposite moiety to us. The western side belongs to people from the same moiety as us.*
◆ Alyengel-**thayt**el mpwarem. Ayengan akwarraty. *Making things with the left hand. I am right-handed.* ◆ Artep arrengakw-**thayt**, [werlaty] arrwekel-**thayt**. (Sa) *[Your] back is behind, and your breasts are on the front side.*
SEE ALSO -ampeny[2]
ingwer-thayt (E) *n.*
on the other side

thekaret *n.*
cigarette, smokes (from English 'cigarette')
◆ Ngkwerlpek urrampemarl ayeng, thekaret antywetyek. (Sa) *I really feel like smoking a cigarette.*
SEE ALSO kwert, ngkwerlp

thelem *vt.*
pour a liquid out of or into something; fill something (with a liquid) ◆ *Petrol* thelem mwetek-warn. (M) *Filling the car with petrol.*
◆ Kwaty, tey-warl tha anyentelh-ilem thelern. (St) *I poured some [cold] water into the tea.*
◆ Arterrty atyeng antheyaw tha rlterrk-iletyek mern, rew-rewarl ilek, kwatyarl thelek *too much*. (St) *Give me some flour so that I can make this mixture thicker, it went runny because I poured too much water in.*
thelelhem *vi.*
leak or pour out; (liquid) run out of; drip down from; seep out from something
◆ Kwaty thelelhem altywereng. (M) *The water is leaking out of the hole.* ◆ Alhwang thelelhem irrtyart-penh. (M) *The blood is running out from the spear [wound].* ◆ Kanthwek-anthwek thelelhem marl arrpenhelarl atwek kweterel. (T) *Her head is pouring with blood because another woman hit her with a nulla-nulla.*
◆ War thelelherl-anem irnmerr renh war amparrkerl-anerlek arerl-anem, arna anyent kwerel antem. Arlperl artety kwereng antem war thelelherl-anem. (N) *It just drips from the mulga tree and you can see it like drops of water sparkling on the branch of that particular tree. The* arlperl *just drips from the mulga tree.*
SEE ALSO anthwem

thelperretyen (W,T) *n.*
self-raising flour (from English 'self-raising')
SEE ALSO arterrty, nmwenth, unmenth, warnp, aperretyen

thelty (W,T), **therrty** (W,T) *n.*
soft ◆ Mern atwakey theltyek anpem. (T) *Feel the wild orange to see if it's soft.*
= atyet[1]
thelty-irrem (W,T) *vi.*
go soft
= atyet-irrem
SEE ALSO rew-irrem
kapert thelty (W,T)
fontanelle (kapert[1] *'head'*)
thelty-thelty (T) *n.*
fontanelle
= kwerrk-kwerrk[1], ahey-ahey, atek-kenh, iylpwerr-iylpwerr

them (E) *vt.*
poke into something ◆ Alknga ayenh thekaw arna nhenhel. (St) *This stick poked me in the eye.*

then and, as well as SEE UNDER **thwen**

-then away from, off, from, out of, out from SEE UNDER **-they**

then-wem *vt.*
winnow seed ◆ Arelh ampwang atherrel mamperrk then-wem. (N) *The two old women*

are winnowing summer-grass seeds. ◆ Ntyerrm apek then-wem antey renh, iylkel *blow*-em-iletyek. (St) *Dogwood seeds are winnowed as well, so that the wind can blow [the rubbish] away.*
= iylker-anthem
SEE ALSO ilpem[1], ahety-ilem

thenayek (E) *n.*
snake (from English 'snake')
SEE ALSO amwa, urnem

thenkarr *n.*
types of prickles; bindy-eye (*Calotis hispidula*) ◆ Thenkarr-kety lher-lherel ayeng intem. (T) *I'm going to sleep in the little creek because of the prickles.*
SEE ALSO lyek, arlketyerr

thep (W,T) *n.*
1. bird. The word *thep* is usually only used of birds that fly, and so does not include emus. ◆ Kwer amerrk tyangar-akert alhem thep ltewetyek. (T) *The teenage boys are going to hunt birds with shanghais.* ◆ Thep map arrertewarrert-irrepirrem arnang anyentel-ayel. (T) *There are lots of birds singing loudly in the tree.*
2. other creatures that fly, such as bats, grasshoppers, beetles etc.
3. Goes before the name of a particular kind of bird or flying creature. ◆ Thep alekaperel intelty arlkwem. (T) *The sparrowhawk eats grasshoppers.*
4. other small creatures (not necessarily ones that fly) ◆ Pernernpernernp kwaty alay-angkwerr nthwerl-apem rew-angkwerr, arlkwerl-apem thep irnngang. (N) *The* pernernpernernp *bird goes around large areas of water and floodwater eating worms.*
= **uthip** (E)
thep-thep (W,T) *n.* [BABY TALK]
bird

therlkem (W,T) *vi.*
tell lies ◆ Arelh yanh therlkem, *no* ayeng arraty ilek kwenh. (M) *That woman is lying, she didn't tell me straight.* ◆ Kwer nhenh map therlketyam. (M) *These kids lied.*
= rrtywerrem, urrtyirrem, urirrem[2], rnter-irrem, arrampewem[1], atyetyem

therrang *n.*
strong in taste, not sweet (especially said of tea without sugar) (from English 'strong')

therrert-irrem (E) *vi.*
1. get lost ◆ Apal alhemel therrert-irremel anem, iwerr ingwer-angkwerr anem. Iwerr ayeng alhetyek alhek ikwer-angkwerr kweny anem apal anem alhek. (Sa) *Going the wrong way and then getting lost, going along another track. I went to go on the track, but I went the wrong way.*
2. make a mess or mistake, get confused
SEE ALSO apalekalek-irrem, apant-irrem, aperrpert-irrem
therrert-therrert (E) *adv.*
being confused, going off in all directions ◆ Tetherrp-tetherrp alhepalhem therrert-therrert. Apal-apal alhepalhem. Ingka arnpenhem therrert-therrert tetherrp-tetherrp. (Sa) *[That person] is stumbling around all over the place. They don't know where they are going. They are heading off in all directions.*
alknga therrert-irrem (E)
be unable to see properly, feel dizzy (alknga *'eye'*) ◆ Alknga therrert-irrem ayeng angayakw. (Sa) *I am feeling dizzy and I can't see properly because I'm hungry.*

therrty (W,T) soft SEE UNDER **thelty**

theth *n.*
nurse, health sister (from English 'sister') ◆ Thethel tyerrty rlkert map mpwarem. (T) *The nurse cures sick people.*

thew *n.*
store, shop (from English 'store') ◆ Thew-warn alhay anyent-ingar anem, map-ingar alhetyal. (T) *Go to the store once, don't go lots of times.*

thew-thew[1] (W,T) *n.*
steady rain, drizzle ◆ Kwaty thew-thewel anherl-anem lthel. Lthelarl anherl-anem, akwet anyerl-anem, alker-irretyakenh. (N) *It's raining steadily. The rain keeps falling and it's not clearing up.*
= thawel, kwaty perler
SEE ALSO tyeyepetyey, lthel-lthel

thew-thew[2] (T) *n.* [BABY TALK]
sore (from English 'sore')
SEE ALSO tywen

thewak *n.*
swag, bedding (from English 'swag')
SEE ALSO antyam

thewekety (T), **theweketh** (T), **tywekety** *n.*
soakage (from English 'soakage')
= angenty, arnwengk

theweth-ilem (W) *vt.*
rub desert raisins on the ground to remove the sticky bitter-tasting coating ◆ Katyerr theweth-ilem ahelh-warn. (M) *The desert raisin fruits are rubbed on the ground to remove the sticky substance.*
SEE ALSO tewem, thwerrem, pwarr-wem, inpewem

theweyet *n.*
sweet-tasting, sweet things (from English

'sweet') ◆ Katyerr aketyam mern akem theweyet. Tyekert akin, wal tewerl-anem, tewetyam *bucket*-el akem akem akem. Anwern tewetyam anem ahern inyemel, ahern inyem tewerl-anemam. (N) *We picked the sweet* katyerr *fruits. The ones that were bitter were rubbed in the earth and then put into buckets. We'd dig up the earth and rub them in the dirt.*
SEE ALSO ikwemey

-they (E), **-then** (T) *n.ending*
1. shows where something moves from, is moved from, or comes from; away from, off, from, out of, out from ◆ Ayerrer-**they** ayeng apety-alpek. (Sa) *I came back from the north.* ◆ Mer arrpenh-**they** apetyek alethang. Nyerr apek irrem ulereny-irrep-irremarl yanh-ketyaw, angketyakenh. (St) *A stranger came from another place. [People] were shy of him/her and didn't say a word.* ◆ Alhwa irrert-irrem ker-**they** apek. (St) *The blood is flowing from the meat.* ◆ Kwaty alhwerrk-alhwerrkek-amparr thelelhem kwaty angenty-**they**. (St) *First of all the muddy water comes out of the soakage.* ◆ Alewatyerr ntewem. Alhweng-**they** tyarr-inemel, ntewem. *Banging the goanna against something. Pulling it out of the hole and banging it.* ◆ Irrar-irrek ayeng *Indonesia*-**they**, mer-**they** kwer-**they**an ayeng irrar-irrek, apety-alpetyek. *Indonesia*-**they** irrar-irrem, nhenh-warl apety-alpetyek, mer rinty-warl irremel apety-alpetyek, nhenh-warl. (St) *From Indonesia I got homesick, from there I got homesick and wanted to come back. From Indonesia I got homesick to come back here, to come back to the familiar old place here.*
2. shows the reason for something; because of something, over ◆ Alharlkwemarl alpem. Ntwa apekarl ayeng alharlkwem, mern-**they** apek ayeng alharlkwek. (St) *Hunt someone away and send them back home. You might hunt me away because of food.*
3. shows the part of a body or thing which is involved in an action ◆ Arrpenh apek pweng apek yel-akngep-akngem amwelt-**they**. (St) *Somebody who is blind is led along by the arm.*
4. shows what something is made of or the source or origin of something
5. refers to the language being used ◆ Ulpme**they**arl angkem, innga yanhaw. (Sa) *That person is talking [Aboriginal] 'language'.*
SEE ALSO -ntyel

ilek-they (E)
'Why?' ◆ Ilek-**they** nga arnkelyan anetyel? Angketyakenh arnkely ahel. Ilelha atyengay. Ilek-apertarl ngan anep-anem tyernetyangan? Arntety apek nga awelhek apek ilelhetyang. (Sa) *Why are you sitting there sulkily? You are sulky and angry and not saying anything. Tell me. Why are you sitting there and not answering? Maybe you felt sick and you're not saying anything about it.*

nthenh-they (E)
'From where?'

thip (E) bird SEE UNDER **uthip**

thweker (W,T) *prn.*
I (will do/am doing/have done) him/her/it. This pronoun is made up of *tha* 'I' and *kwer* 'him, her, it'. ◆ Thweker akayak-ilem, arneng apek anyekety, arnekarl antyem tenteyek, aperek apek. Wal akayak-ilem, 'Unta anyekety kwenh'. (T) *I might warn him about falling from the tree when he is climbing up onto the overhanging branch, maybe of a river red gum. Well, then I warn him, 'You'll fall down'.*
SEE ALSO tha, kwer[2], thangenh, thwengk

thwen, **then** *part.*
and, as well as, (this thing) and something else as well. This word cannot go on its own, and it usually occurs after each item in a list of similar things. ◆ Artwey-nheng atherr, arengk thwen tyerrty thwen. (St) *The dog and his owner, the dog and the person.* ◆ *Plate* wetyerrpetyerrp ker thwen mern thwen angetyem anwehengkerr. (T) *Bring us a plate full of meat and vegetables.*
= uthen (E)

thwenem (E), **uthenem** (E) *vt.*
send something to someone
= ilanthem

thweng (T), **ithweng** (E) *part.*
Indicates uncertainty about the facts; maybe, perhaps. ◆ Apek ithweng. (St) *Maybe.* ◆ Thwengam apek alhekaw? (T) *Did he go?*
SEE ALSO apek

thwengk (W,T) *prn.*
I (will do/am doing/have done) something to you ◆ Thwengk atwem. (M) *I am hitting you.* ◆ Thwengk awerl-anem, angkety yanh angkerl-anerleng, alhengk awep-awem. (N) *I can understand you, what you are saying, I can understand.*
= thangenh
SEE ALSO tha, ngkweng, ngenh, thweker

thwep *n.*
soap (from English 'soap')

thwep-thwep *n.*
soup (from English 'soup')
SEE ALSO anwerrng

ker thwep-thwep
soup with meat or vegetables (*ker* 'meat')

◆ Thang anthetyenh ker thwep-thwep. (M) *I will give him meat and soup.*
= ker atewat
mern thwep-thwep (W)
wet dough made by mixing boiling water with flour (*mern* 'food')
= mern anwerrng
SEE ALSO awerrp[1]
thwerray (W,T) *n.*
a type of bird (?)
thwerrem *vt.*
clean bush onions, rub skins off bush onions; shake bush onions in wooden dish to clean skins off ◆ Panth-warl mern yerrakwerr ikinp arlkwekerr thwerremarl renh, ilpem anem renh. Ika yanh map. Iltyelarl ikewepewem. (St) *Bush onions are cleaned and winnowed in wooden dishes so that you don't eat the skins. Those skins. You throw the skins away by hand.*
SEE ALSO tewem, inpewem, tewem, kek-wem
thwerremp-irrem (T,E) *vi.*
1. make a mark to show where you have gone (?); walk making clear tracks for someone to follow ◆ Thwerremp-irrem ap ingka. Rwert apekarl intem wal thwerremp-irrem, 'Nhel ra alhek kwenh'. Renh anem arety-alhem, kel ampinemarl. (Sa) *Walking along making clear tracks. There might be a road there, well [you] make clear footprints, [and another person will say], 'This is where she went'. Seeing the tracks, the other person then follows them.*
SEE ALSO ahimperr-wem, arlkeny-wem, mpaty-ilem
2. drag feet as you go along ◆ Mey-mey-kety tha urrparenhem, ingkekety, thwerremp-irrenhem. (St) *I am wiping out the tracks of my son-in-law, dragging my feet as I go along and wiping out his tracks.*
thwerremp-thwerr (T,E) *n.*
lame, shuffling, dragging feet
Thwerrkethet (W) *n.*
name of a place near Laramba community
thwerrp alhem (W,T) *vi.*
run into trouble without knowing; go somewhere and not know that there is some sort of trouble waiting for you there; be unaware of impending danger
◆ Thwerrpemarl alhek-penh apety-alpem mer-warl, rlkertem irrenty-alpem. (M) *After going somewhere, unaware that you are going to get sick, you come back home and get sick* (?).
SEE ALSO pewelhem
thwinem (E) get stuck onto something SEE UNDER **uthinem**
tikeley *n.*
troublesome, problematic, of a sensitive or restricted nature (from English 'tickly')
tikeley-irrem *vi.*
get upset about something
tint (E) canvas used for shelter; tent, swag SEE UNDER **tent**
tintey a bent branch SEE UNDER **tentey**
tirr-tirr (T) rainbow bee-eater SEE UNDER **terr-terr**
tirrenth (T,E) trilling frog SEE UNDER **terrenth**
titey *n.*
breast (from English 'titty')
SEE ALSO werlaty, paty
titey paterl
baby's bottle (from English 'titty bottle')
tithem-ilem *vt.*
tease someone or something (from English 'tease them')
SEE ALSO therlkem, urrtyirrem, iltem, kwanthem
tiwem (E) clean or scrape burnt hair or skin off an animal SEE UNDER **tewem**
tnakem (E) praise someone or something SEE UNDER **nakem**
tnarlkwem (E) praise someone or something SEE UNDER **narlkwem**
tnem (E) stand, stand up SEE UNDER **irnem**
tnernem (E) show something to someone SEE UNDER **nernem**
tney-tney (E) early in the morning SEE UNDER **ney-ney**
tneyel (E) soon SEE UNDER **neyel**
tnya (E) dead SEE UNDER **nya**
tul-akem (E) choke someone or something SEE UNDER **twerl-akem**
tul-irrem (E) rumble (thunder) SEE UNDER **twerl-irrem**
turr (T,E) side of a creek SEE UNDER **twerr**
twa (W,T) close, near SEE UNDER **itwa**
twakem (W,T) *vt.*
pull down a branch ◆ Rrwerleng ap mern ngkwarlarl, alkey angerr *anyway* twakemel lywernkel arlka akerrirretyart. (N) *The honey grevillea tree has edible honey, and we used to just pull the branches of the tall trees down with a hooked stick and break them off.*
twant arem (W,T) *vt.*
stare at someone, look hard at someone
◆ Tyerrty alenhel ayeng twant arep-arem an nyerr-irrem ayeng. (M) *That person is staring at me and I'm getting shamed.*
SEE ALSO arnterr arem
twap-anthem (W,T) *vt.*
1. take someone and leave them halfway; follow someone halfway and then come back
= artek-wem, arteng-wem

2. leave something with someone ◆ Ker twapanthay! (T) *Leave the meat (with someone)!*

twem (W,T) *n.*
for good, for a long time ◆ Akeweny-amperl alhem twemeh apek. (M) *That poor thing has gone, maybe for good.*
= intem², akwet, aleth
SEE ALSO akweteth

twemper¹ (W) *n.*
young fruit of the bush banana, silky pear, *alangkw, parl* ◆ Parl twemper, twemper akwek. Anteth-penh akwek twemper irrem, angerrem ra irrem. (N) *A small bush banana. After it flowers the small fruit develops, then the fruit gets bigger.*
= akwemper, amwernt, mwemper, ngwemper

twemper² (T,E) *n.*
side of a creek, riverbank, sandbank, high mound of sand in the middle of creek
SEE ALSO lher twerr, twerr, akwerlp
atna twemper (E)
having a protruding arse (atna *'arse'*) ◆ Atna atwemper yanhan alhep-alhem (St) *[That person] walking along over there has an arse that sticks out.*
SEE ALSO irrkert-irrkert
twemper-twemper (W) *n.*
1. curly windmill grass, umbrella grass, spider grass (*Enteropogon acicularis*)
2. creek windmill grass, curly windmill grass (*Enteropogon ramosus*). Clumped grasses about 1 m high which are usually found on the edges of watercourses. These grasses are used to make hooks for hooking grubs out of trees ◆ Arnam twemper-twemperel perlanty inem. (M) *Grubs from the river red gum are pulled out with a grass hook.*
SEE ALSO lywernk

twengk (W) *n.*
short
= karteng
kapert twengk (W)
short hair (kapert¹ *'head'*)

Twenkerr (W) *n.*
name of a hill in the Stuart Bluff Range area

tweny *n.*
dry fruit of the desert raisin, *katyerr* ◆ Katyerr tweny. An mern kwart. Kwart mperlker anwern akerl-anem akin mern, tweny *mixed* anwern akem. Kwer-penh angety anem alpem. (T) *The dried fruits of the desert raisin. And the white-coloured fruits. We go along picking a mixture of both the white fruits and the dried fruits. Then after that we take them back home.*
SEE ALSO arlkarntar, alha²
= **uteny** (E)
tweny-irrem *vi.*
go dry (of desert raisin fruit)
= **uteny-irrem** (E)

twep-twep going around something SEE UNDER **artwep-artwep**

twer (W,T) *n.*
1. strong, healthy ◆ Ayeng tweram anerlanem, rlkert-kweny twer. (T) *I'm strong now, not sick but healthy.* ◆ Kwer akwek nhak angkety twer angkem. (T) *That little baby there is speaking strongly now.*
2. solid, heavy, hard, tight, hard to cut or break ◆ Thang arnang twer rnkernetyeh. (M) *I'm going to put a strong piece of wood there.* ◆ Twer arrerna, lywelh-hety, mwetekay *wheel*. (M) *Put the car wheel on tightly so that it doesn't come off.* ◆ Ywarn apek akem arnang twer angerr. (T) *It's difficult to cut a really solid tree.*
SEE ALSO rlterrk, awer¹
twer-ilem (W,T) *vt.*
1. make something strong; tighten something up ◆ Twer angerr ayernay! (M) *Tie it up really tight!*
2. make a person healthy or strong ◆ Tyerrty twer-ilem *baptise* anthemel, twerem-ilem Altyerrem naketyek arrenty-kety twer-ilem. (T) *Baptising people makes them strong, makes them strong to praise God and resist the devil.* ◆ Kwer twer-ilem mern mwerr anthemel. (T) *Making the child strong by giving them good food.*
SEE ALSO rlterrk-ilem
twer-irrem (W,T) *vi.*
1. get strong or healthy ◆ Kwer akwek twerirrem. (T) *The little child is getting stronger.*
2. be 'hard' or tough-minded ◆ Marl yanh tha ywarn awern, wal ya twer-irremelarl anek, atyengety ya twer-irremelarl anek. Rlterrk-arl ra irrern twerarl irrek atyengety (T) *I didn't hear that woman properly, and then she got tough with me. She just got hard and tough with me.*

twerelh-ilem (T) *vt.*
bring somebody back ◆ Renh twerelh-ilerlalpang! Angkep apety-alpetyeh. (T) *Go and stop him! He's got to come back.*
twer-irrem *vi.*
turn back

twererr *n.*
clapsticks, music sticks. These are usually made of mulga wood. ◆ Twererr rltar-atwem arrkenel kwer map *song* alyelhemel. (T) *The kids are enjoying themselves banging the*

clapsticks as they sing a song. ◆ Wayel iterl-anem twererr map. (T) *[Patterns] are burnt on the music sticks with a wire.*

twerl-akem (W,T), **tul-akem** (E) *vt.*
choke (someone or something); wring somebody's or something's neck; break neck; twist neck ◆ Ker rapet alhwengeh atyerrem an twerl-akem renh. Weth artaly-wem aweth arrpenh tyarr-inem aweth twerl-akem rapet, twerl-akem ahenty. (N) *The rabbit is pulled out of its burrow and then its neck is wrung. It's thrown to the ground and then another one is pulled out and its neck is broken as well.*
= itutnhem, ahentyel-akem, tywekem-ilem

twerl-irrem (E), **tul-irrem** (E) *vi.*
rumble (thunder) ◆ Kwaty angkekarl-kety tul-irremel. (Sa) *Look out, the thunder is rumbling.*

twerl-twerl (W,T) *n.*
part of guts

twerlepwelh-pwelh (W,T) *adv.*
(making) a thudding or galloping noise; the sound of hoofbeats (horses or cattle)
◆ Twerlepwelh-pwelh arrtyanem nanth ater. (M) *The horses are galloping off in fear.*
= rrmwangk-rrmwangk, ahenty-ahenty[2], anenty-anenty
SEE ALSO lthap-lthap

twern (W,T) *n.*
1. sun, sunshine, sunlight ◆ Tyerrty twernelarl ampek, kwaty-kwenh. (T) *Without water, the sun burnt the person.*
2. heat, hot weather, heat of the sun, summer
◆ Twern angerr kwenh apetyem — *we can't* aperl. Ingka then ampemarl, twern angerrarl apetyemeng. (T) *It's going to get very hot — we can't walk around. Our feet and everything will get burnt from the hot weather.*
SEE ALSO aherrk
= **utern** (E)

twern angerr (W,T)
1. hot weather, the middle of summer
2. midday, the middle of the day (angerr[1] '*big*') • SEE ALSO irntar

twern mpep (W,T) = **twern angerr** (mpep '*middle*')

twern rlwang (W,T)
1. the beginning of summer (rlwang '*forehead*')
2. the end of summer (?)
= **utern urla** (E)

twern-tayem (W,T) *n.*
hot weather, summer
= **utern-tayem** (E)

twern akwek (W,T)
not too hot (weather) (akwek '*small*')

twernakak (W) *n.*
in the hot weather

twern-twern, itwern-itwern *n.*
Bagot's furnace ant (*Melophorus bagoti*)
◆ Twern-twern anwern nyetyart. Anwern awantyetyart *like* yerramp-arteh akin. (M) *We used to dig up the* twern-twern *ants. We used to suck on them like we do honeyants.*
SEE ALSO yerramp, inkwareny
= **utern-utern** (E)

twernem *vt.*
tell someone to do something; make someone do something; force someone to do something ◆ Thang kwer nhak twernern arwengkel inetyek. (T) *I made that kid steal something.* ◆ Thwengk twernern kwaty nta inetyeh atyeng. (T) *I told you to go and get me some water.*
= **uternem** (E)

twernelhem *vi.*
declare or 'tell yourself' that you are going to hit or growl at somebody; say that you are going to talk to someone about something
◆ Arelh yanh twernelhem ngwenh iltetyek. (T) *That girl is telling herself that she's going to growl at you.*
= **uternelhem** (E)

twernk (W,T) *n.*
boss ◆ Merek-artwey twernk mer intyaperek. (T) *The landowner is boss for the whole place.*
SEE ALSO tyetyart

twerr (T,E), **turr** (T,E) *n.*
side of a creek, riverbank, sandbank, high mound of sand in the middle of a creek
◆ Twerr akwek kwatyel mpepel anem. (St) *There is a sandbank in the middle of the water.*
◆ Kwaty atwerl-apem atwerl-apem wal twerr-warn anem arratenhem. (T) *Swimming along in the water then coming out at the riverbank.*
= twemper[2]
SEE ALSO akwerlp

twerrp *n.*
sandhill ◆ Twerrp kwer-warl anwern alhalhem katyerr akerl-anetyeh. (N) *We're going to the sandhill to pick desert raisins.*
SEE ALSO arerrk
CAN SOUND A BIT LIKE atwerrp '*late afternoon*'
= **urterrp** (E)

lher twerrp (W)
small sandy rise (lher '*creek*', '*river*', '*sand*')

twertert-ayerr (E) *n.* [RESPECT LANGUAGE]
car, vehicle ◆ Twertert-ayerr yanhentyak anyem, angwenthangw-kenh? Angwenthangwelarl angetyek? Angwenthangwel irrepetherl-alhek yanhan?

Kantyeny-ayerrel-rnem. (Sa) *Whose is that vehicle over there? Who brought it? It must have been the young fellas who brought it [said by a woman in a respect relationship to one of them].*
= aywerr-angkenh-angkenh, urnayerr
SEE ALSO mwetekay, apwert

twetnhem (E) crush or pound something up SEE UNDER **tewenhem**

tyak (E) *n.*
clever, cleverly, skilfully ◆ *Painting* yanh arlka tha tyakel mparek aray. (St) *Look at that painting that I cleverly did.*
= kwerathek
SEE ALSO lywenpeny

Tyakarr *n.*
male junior skin name, corresponding to Kemarr (note Warlpiri *Jakarra*). See diagram p. 744. ◆ Tyakarran urrey Kemarr akwek. (T) *A* Tyakerr *is a little* Kemarr *boy.*
SEE ALSO Watyal, Kemarr

Tyakemarr *n.*
male skin name, corresponding to Kemarr (note Warlpiri *Jakamarra*). See diagram p. 744.
SEE ALSO Kemarr

tyakert with knees up SEE UNDER **tyakwert**

tyaket *n.*
jacket, coat (from English 'jacket')

tyakey (W,T) *part.*
'Is that right?', 'True?', 'Really?', 'Is that so?'
= tyathew, arraty-akey
SEE ALSO akwey

tyakwart with knees up SEE UNDER **tyakwert**

tyakwerl (W) *n.*
shell ◆ Tyakwerl yanh anek, *not* nhenh *area*, ayerrer thayt nheng inang antherrirretyart. *Hand*-em *over to other person.* Arrpenham akwek arrpenham angerr. (M) *Shells were not from this area. In the north they used to hand them over to [trade with] other people. Some were small and some were large.*

tyakwert, **tyakwart**, **tyakert** *n.*
with knees up
tyakwert intem, **tyakwart intem**, **tyakert intem**
lie with the knees up, or with one bent over the other in a number 4 shape (intem[1] *'lie down'*)

◆ Tyakwart intep-intemarl yanhan. *Number 4*-artek ra intep-inteman. (St) *That person is lying down with their knees up. They are lying [with their legs in] a position like the number 4.*
tyakwert anem, **tyakwart anem**, **tyakert anem**
sit with the knees up, or with legs crossed in a number 4 shape (anem *'sit'*)
tyakwert irnem, **tyakwart irnem**, **tyakert irnem**
with the knees up, or with one bent over the other in a number 4 shape (irnem *'stand'*)
= tyampernem

tyakwertekwert (W) *n.*
teenage boy travelling around just prior to initiation (young man) ceremony
SEE ALSO apwelh, anmanty, alyepelengkw, awerrty, arwekert, lyaty, arleyarr, amarleyarr, lwekerleny, antingkar

tyalangk (W,T) *n.*
1. spinifex resin (*Triodia pungens*) ◆ Aywert-penh tyalangk, twetyam. Kelh mparetyam.Tyalangk atwem, arnel atwem, arnel atwem aywert antyakemel angem, arrernetyeh. Aweth inetyam atwetyam arnelem atwetyam, akelhem mpwaretyam arnel alakenh. Tamp-art ra intetyam. Angerrety. Rwang ampetyam irntang, irntang arrernetyam. Irntelem athetyam, arnel alakenh rrkwemel. (N) *The spinifex resin comes from the spinifex grass. It was made into a resin cake. We beat the spinifex with sticks, and then collect the resin and them beat some more spinifex and them make a cake of resin like a big damper. We heat the rocks in the fire and them work the resin, holding onto the stick and pushing the rocks backwards and forwards.*
= anker[1]
SEE ALSO arletyety
2. adze made from a metal blade with a wooden handle attached to it with spinifex resin ◆ Tyalangkel anwern arrpem rnwang. Ilepel amparr atwem, tyalangkelem arrpem. (M) *We use the adze to carve wooden dishes. At first we chop [the wood] with an axe and then we chisel it with the adze.* • SEE ALSO kanyengarr, kantyengarr, kwempalth
3. thick, strong tea or a bitter drink
tyalangk kelh (W,T)
a lump of spinifex resin (kelh *'lump'*)
= anker kelh
arwengalker tyalangk (T)
a lump of wax or resin-like substance at the base of a native bees' hive (arwengalker *'sugar bag', 'native bee hive'*) ◆ Tyalangk alakenh altywerel arlparernerl-anem, rrpwerl akwek. Wal ameng map irrperl-anem arnewarn kwen, rltwamp alenh mpwaretyeh. Ameng akwek mapel arrernekarl, arrakertel apek ina

arrernerl-anem. Tyalangk inety-alhem mer arrpenheng, *might be* aywerteng apek. (M) *The* tyalangk *is a small dark-coloured thing that hangs there in the hole of the bees' nest. Well, the bees go inside the tree to make that honey. The honey is what they put there, maybe with their mouths. They go and get the* tyalangk *resin from somewhere else, maybe from spinifex.*

tyalatywerrp (T,E) *n.*
chiming wedgebill (*Psophodes occidentalis*)

tyalep, **tyalwep** (W), **tyalip** (E) *n.*
central military dragon (*Ctenophorus isolepis*) (?). Also referred to as *ker tyalep.*
SEE ALSO kwerleparr, nyarl, irrpent, artep irrpent

tyaleth *n.*
jealous (from English 'jealous')
tyaleth-irrem *vi.*
be jealous, get jealous
SEE ALSO anngwenhem, arwelth-rnem, mayel anngwenhem

tyalip (E), **tyalwep** (W) central military dragon (?) SEE UNDER **tyalep**

tyamem-ilem (E) *vt.*
block someone off (in a card game) (from English 'jam them')

tyamp-tyamp (E) *n.*
bumpy (of a road) (from English 'jump jump')

tyampap *n.*
a sharp hump or rise in a road (from English 'jump up') ◆ Tyampap-angkwerr mwetek antyenty-alhem. (M) *The car is climbing up the rise.*

tyamparl (T) *n.*
mulga snake, king brown snake (*Pseudechis australis*) (note Warlpiri *jamparli*)
= arreperlp, atetherr arlkwenh, kantharlkw, ikwelengk, alhingk

tyampart (W) pannikin, tin SEE UNDER **tyampet**

Tyamperlk *n.*
male junior skin name, corresponding to Mpetyan. See diagram p. 744. ◆ Tyamperlkan urrey Mpetyan akwek. (T) *A* Tyamperlk *is a young* Mpetyan *boy.*
SEE ALSO Mpetyan, Mpetyakwert

tyampernem (W,T) *vi.*
lie with the knees up; sit with legs crossed in a number 4 shape (irnem, rnem *'stand'*) ◆ Tyampernem ayeng, kwereng rlkerremelhem, ingkang angelherl-anem alakenh. (N) *I am lying with my knees up, and after that I stretch, move my legs like that.*
= tyakwert irnem
SEE ALSO arlkany irnem

tyampet, **tyampert**, **tyampart** (W), **tyampit** (E) *n.*
pannikin, tin, container used for drinking out of (from English 'jam pot') ◆ Tey antywenh-antywenh tyampet. (T) *A pannikin is used for drinking tea.* ◆ Tyampet altywarrernetyeh kwenelak angwelyel awantyeh-hety. (M) *Turn the tin up side down in case the dog licks it.*
ker tyampet
tinned meat, tin of meat (ker *'meat'*)
tyampet way-akert
billycan (lit. 'tin with a wire handle')

Tyampetyenp *n.*
male skin name, corresponding to Mpetyan (note Warlpiri *Jampijinpa*). See diagram p. 744.
SEE ALSO Mpetyan

Tyampeyat (E) male junior skin name, corresponding to Pengart SEE UNDER **Tyapart**

tyampit (E) pannikin, tin SEE UNDER **tyampet**

tyan (W,T) *n.*
yellow-coloured honey from the northern corkwood tree, *ntywey* (*Hakea chordophylla*). Also referred to as *ngkwarl tyan.* The yellow-coloured honey is called *tyan* and the dark-coloured honey *ntywey.*
SEE ALSO ntyweyamp, ntyweyangkwarl, ankarr

Tyanam (T,E) *n.*
male junior skin name, corresponding to Penangk. See diagram p. 744.
SEE ALSO Penangk, Ngaman

Tyangal (W,T), **Tyangaley** *n.*
male skin name, corresponding to Ngal (note Warlpiri *Jangala*). See diagram p. 744.
SEE ALSO Ngal, Ngangkal, Tyangkarl

tyangar (W,T), **tyangay** (E) *n.*
shanghai, slingshot, catapult (from English 'shangai') ◆ Kwer amerrk tyangar-akert alhem thep ltewetyek. (T) *The teenage boys are going to hunt birds with shanghais.* ◆ Tyangay, theparl ampel werrerl-anem tyangayel. Ina mpwarem wenhakwey-penh *tube*-penh. (St) *Kids shoot at birds with shanghais. They make them from [tyre] tubes.*

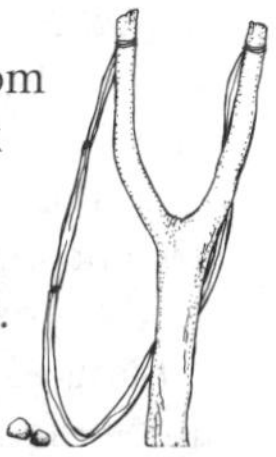

Tyangkarl, **Tyangkal** *n.*
male junior skin name, corresponding to Ngal. See diagram p. 744. ◆ Tyangkarlan urrey Ngal akwek. (T) *A* Tyangkarl *is a young* Ngal *boy.*
SEE ALSO Ngangkal, Ngal, Tyangal

tyangkay (T,E) *n.* [RESPECT LANGUAGE]
single-men's camp (note Warlpiri *jangkayi*) ◆ Tyangkayel mey-mey ayepel-irrepirrem. (St)

My son-in-law is sitting down in the single-men's camp [said by a woman].
SEE ALSO arnkenty, ahileng, irrewatyent

tyantem (E), **tyantel-wem** (E) *vt.* [RESPECT LANGUAGE]
tell ◆ Ngwarrengk tyantetyek ahanenhaw. (St) *Go and tell your husband [said by a woman to her daughter].* ◆ Tyantel-iwerrem yanhentyak ilenngem-ayerr akwel nhengentyak. Arrep-ilenherr-arey. Tyanterlentyarretyel-rnem. Arrep-ilenherr-arey nhengentyak. (Sa) *They are talking about that business over there. Go and have a look. Go and see what they are talking about.* (?)
SEE ALSO ilem

tyantelhem *vi.*
1. say something about yourself, tell a story about yourself
2. say what you are doing ◆ Ngwarrekengkw tyantelherl-wa ilanth amenheng atherr alherretyek. (St) *Go and tell your husband that we two, mother and daughter, are going.*
SEE ALSO ilelhem

tyantwerr (E) *n.* [RESPECT LANGUAGE]
meat, kangaroo
SEE ALSO ker, aherr, urla alkey

tyanyweng (E) *n.* [RESPECT LANGUAGE]
tobacco (note Kaytetye *tyanywenge* 'native tobacco') ◆ Tyanyweng-ayerr atyengaw, irrepetherl-waw. (Sa) *Go and get me some tobacco [from my son-in-law].*
= tyekert[2]
SEE ALSO ngkwerlp

tyap *n.*
1. edible grub ◆ Rwelam atyerrem tyap renh, arlkwetyeh. (N) *The grubs are cooked in the fire so that they can be eaten.*
2. Goes before the name of a particular kind of edible grub. In the Anmatyerr way of classifying foods most fruits and vegetables are known as *mern*, sweet things as *ngkwarl*, seeds as *anterrng*, *arnwety* or *ntang*, meats as *ker* and edible grubs as *tyap*. ◆ Tyap ankwerrenh, ankerrmern inetyenheng tyap renh arlkwetyenheng. Anyematyart akin ankwerrenh. Lywernkel tyarr-inetyart. Tyap ankwerrenh, mwerr angerr *too* — perrap anter angerr. (N) *The grub called* 'ankwerrenh' *is collected from the coolibah tree and then eaten. It is similar to a witchetty grub. We used to pull them out with a grass hook. The coolibah grubs taste really good — they're really fatty.*
3. witchetty grub

tyap ayep (W)
tar vine grub

tyap-tyap *n.*
a sort of a grub, a grub that is barely edible

Tyapaly *n.*
male junior skin name, corresponding to Peltharr (note warlpiri *Japalyi*). See diagram p. 744. ◆ Tyapalyan urrey Peltharr akwek. (T) *A* Tyapaly *is a young* Peltharr *boy.*
SEE ALSO Peltharr, Ngalyerr

Tyapaney *n.*
Japanese (from English 'Japanese') ◆ Tha awetyakenh, irrkwerteth angwenh apekarl angkep-angkem, Tyapaney apek, angkep-angkem awetyakenh, alhwerrkert. (St) *I can't understand Italian or Japanese or whatever they're talking — it sounds all mixed up to me.*

tyapantarr (W,T) *n.*
dwarf bearded dragon (*Pogona minor*) (note Warlpiri *japantarra*) ◆ Tyapantarr arnel irnerl-anem akweteth. Rlpwerelam yanh irnanem arrngelhel. Arnethen yanh *jump*-irrerl-alhem nheng tyerrty-kety aterarl arem. Lyek-lyek tyapantarr. Kapert angerr. Kapert angerr irnerl-anem. Ankert artek nheng-lkwer kapert. (N) *Bearded dragon lizards always live in trees. They live in the hollows and amongst the bark. They jump from the trees in fright if they see people. They are spiky. They have big heads. Their heads are a bit like the* ankert *lizard.*
= kapert angerr

Tyapart, Tyampeyat (E), **Tyapeyart** (E) *n.*
male junior skin name, corresponding to Pengart. See diagram p. 744. ◆ Tyapartan urrey Pengart akwek. (T) *A* Tyapart *is a young* Pengart *boy.*
SEE ALSO Pengart, Ngampart

Tyapartem Ngkwerrm (W) *n.*
name of a plain south of Coniston

Tyapeltyarr *n.*
male skin name, corresponding to Petyarr or Peltharr (note Warlpiri *Japaljarri*). See diagram p. 744.
SEE ALSO Peltharr, Petyarr

Tyapenangk *n.*
male skin name, corresponding to Penangk (note Warlpiri *Japanangka*). See diagram p. 744.
SEE ALSO Penangk

Tyapengart *n.*
male skin name, corresponding to Pengart (note Warlpiri *Japangardi*). See diagram p. 744.
SEE ALSO Pengart

tyapernp, tyapwenp (E) *n.*
a boil ◆ Tyapernp-akert ayeng menty aney. Kwartarl arlkwem. Arlewatyerr kwart akwetarl arlkwem awangkem tyapernp. (St) *I've got boils and I'm not going anywhere. From eating eggs; if*

you always eat goanna eggs then you can get boils.
SEE ALSO mantalyarrp, artweker

Tyapeyart (E) male junior skin name, corresponding to Pengart SEE UNDER **Tyapart**

tyapwenp (E) a boil SEE UNDER **tyapernp**

tyapwert-apwert (E) *n.*
a type of small lizard (?) ◆ Tyapwert-apwert, arlewatyerr akely-artek. *Little one* anert, ankert-ankert kwa. Apekath akelyarl ap ra. (Sa) *The* tyapwert-apwert *lizard is like a little goanna. It has a small stomach, like* ankert-ankert *lizards. It is a little light-coloured one.*

tyarl (W,T) *prn. (?)*
do something (for, by) myself ◆ Thang tyarl inek. (T) *I got it for/by myself.* ◆ Thang tyarl angwerrm-ilek. (T) *I found it by myself.*
tyaheleny (W) *prn.*
I, mine (?) ◆ Urrar tyaheleny awelhek. (M) *I heard my echo.* ◆ Ayeng tyaheleny arntarnt-arelhem. (M) *I am looking after myself.* ◆ Kelathel tyaheleny arelhek. (M) *I saw myself in the mirror.* ◆ Irntang inemel tyaheleny atwelhem. (M) *I am getting a rock and hitting myself.* ◆ Mantarr tyaheleny angetyeh anyelel. Atyengenh anthay — tyahelenyam yanh. (M) *I am getting some clothes myself in the cold weather. Give me my clothes — those ones are mine.*
SEE ALSO ayeng, atyengenh, inaheleny, kwarleny, ngkewarl
CAN SOUND A BIT LIKE atyarleny *'dirty', 'unwashed'*

tyarl-wem (E), **tyarl-iwem** (E) *vt.*
let someone or something go, release something ◆ Arengk yanh tyarl-waw, mpwek apekarl arnep-arnem. (St) *Let the dog go, it's whining and might want to go to the toilet.*
SEE ALSO ilanthem, atniwem

tyarr-angem, **tyarr-akngem** (E), **iytarr-angem** (E) *vt.*
lead, drag or pull someone or something along ◆ Pelangket apek tyarr-akngeynem. (St) *Drag the blankets.*
tyarr-inem, **iytarr-inem** (E) *vt.*
pull or drag something out of something ◆ Tyap ankwerrenh, ankerrmern inetyenheng tyap renh arlkwetyenheng. Anyematyart akin ankwerrenh. Lywernkel tyarr-inetyart. Tyap ankwerrenh, mwerr angerr *too* — perrap anter angerr. (N) *The grub called* 'ankwerrenh' *is collected from the coolibah tree and then eaten. It is similar to a witchetty grub. We used to pull them out with a grass hook. The coolibah grubs taste really good — they're really fatty.* ◆ Alhweng-they tyarr-inemel arlewatyerr ntewem. (St) *The goanna is dragged from the hole and them beaten on the ground [to kill it].*

tyarralpenty (W) *n.*
talkative

tyarrenng (W,T), **tyerrenng** (T) *n.*
skeleton
ngkwern tyarrenng (W), **ngkwern tyerrenng** (T)
skeleton (ngkwern *'bone'*)
SEE ALSO irrernng

tyarrerrey (T) *n.*
locust (?) ◆ Tyarrerreyel arlkwerl-apem mern ingkerrek, arnant anem rnkernem. Intelty-artek-antey, akwek-akwek. (T) *The locusts go along eating everything, till only the trees are left standing. They are small, like grasshoppers.*
= menyeynterl

tyarrp *n.* [SENSITIVE LANGUAGE]
1. a crack or split in something
2. vagina • SEE ALSO artwert[2], kep[2], tyely
tyarrp-tyarrp *n.*
having lots of cracks; cracked, fissured ◆ Ingkan tyarrp-tyarrp. *Cracked feet.*
tyarrp-ilem *vt.*
split something in half; split something open ◆ Ker kapert tyarrp-ilem kampely arlkwetyenheng. (N) *The head is split open and then the brains are eaten.* ◆ Ura nhenh althalth tha tyarrp-ilem. (St) *I'm going to split up this light wood.*
= tyarrp-atwem, tyarrp-akem
tyarrp-atwem *vt.* = **tyarrp-ilem** ◆ Rwang tyarrp atwem ilepel. (T) *Splitting the firewood with an axe.*
tyarrp-akem *vt.* = **tyarrp-ilem**
tyarrp-irrem *vi.*
split open, crack open ◆ Mantarr atyenh tyarrp-irrek, atanthetyakenh. (St) *My clothes have split open, they haven't been mended.* ◆ Alwerr apek iltewelhem, tyarrp-irrem. (St) *The split-jack splits open, cracks open.*
tyarrp inkem (W)
split or crack open (rock)

Tyarrwerr (W), **Tyarwerr** (W) *n.*
the name of a place north of Napperby Station homestead

tyart, **tyat** *n.*
shirt (from English 'shirt') ◆ Tyarteh irrpay! (M) *Put a shirt on!*
CAN SOUND A BIT LIKE irrtyart *'spear'*

Tyarwerr name of a place north of Napperby Station homestead SEE UNDER **Tyarrwerr**

tyat shirt SEE UNDER **tyart**

tyathew, **thathew** *part.*
An expression used by a speaker to ask the

person listening to agree with what they are saying;'Is it true?', 'Is that so?', 'Isn't that right?' ◆ Tyathew ityakey ntwang arern? (M) *Is it true that you didn't see it?* ◆ Arraty athew tha ilep-ilem thathew? (M) *I'm saying the right thing aren't I?*
= tyakey, arraty-akey
SEE ALSO athew

tyaty *n.*
church (from English 'church') ◆ Arlta angerrel anantherr alhem tyaty-warn. (T) *On Sundays we go to church.*
Tyaty-areny *n.*
Christian
= Kerretyen, Pep-areny

tyaty atwem (W,T) *vt.*
teach, advise strongly
SEE ALSO kalty-anthem, kaltyel-anthem

tyatyarlkwerr (E) *n.*
a type of Solanum (*Solanum* sp.) ◆ Ayeng pelh-pelh urntep-urntem, iwenh apekarl arlkwek-penh. Katyerr tyatyarlkwerr apek tharl arlkwek. Tyatyarlkwerr katyerr-artek anteyarl. Pelh-pelh anem ayeng urntem. (St) *I'm dribbling from eating something. Maybe it was that* tyatyarlkwerr *fruit that I ate. The* tyatyarlkwerr *is similar to the desert raisin plant. Now I'm dribbling.*

Tyatyenepalepweng (W) *n.*
a gap in the Anmatjira Range

tyatyey (T) horse SEE UNDER **tyey-tyey**

tyaynt (E) bunch Paspalidium SEE UNDER **tywaynt**

tyek (E), **iytek** (E) *n.*
loose, slack, not tight ◆ Arntek ayeng iytek. (Sa) *My teeth are loose.*
tyek-ilem (E), **iytek-ilem** (E) *vt.*
loosen something ◆ Iytekarl-ilem arwerl rlterrkan iytekel iytekel-ilem, kel tyerremel ant anem. (Sa) *A solid tree is loosened and loosened and then just pulled out.*
= ararlk-ilem
tyek-irrem (E), **iytek-irrem** (E) *vi.*
get loose

tyek-tyek-ilem1 (E) *vt.*
tickle someone
= athek-athek-ilem

tyek-tyek-ilem2 (W) *vt.*
shake someone or something; make something move ◆ Rlkel *move*-em-ilemel tyek-tyek-ilem, rlkang angerr apek apetyerleng. (M) *The big wind coming along makes it move.*
SEE ALSO angelh-angelh-ilem

tyek-tyek-irrem (W,T) *vi.*
nod head in agreement (or disagreement) ◆ Kapert tyek-tyek-irrem tyerrtyelarl ngwenh apawenhem. (M) *[You] nod your head when someone asks you something.*
= akak-atwem2

tyek-untem (E) stab or poke the ground with a digging stick or crowbar, searching for a burrow or animal SEE UNDER **tyewentem**

tyekarnparnp1 (E) *n.*
bull ant (*Myrmecia nigriceps* (reproductive)) ◆ Uremeny ap ra atnarnp-atnarnp-alpem tyekarnparnp, ahelengkw. (Sa) *The bull ant jumps along quickly, they're aggressive.*
= atyank, ntyeyapert

tyekarnparnp2 (E) *n.*
a type of bird

tyekepwelepwel (E) *n.*
tadpole
= pwel-pwel, pwepely

tyekerr (E) *n.*
gap left in front teeth after a tooth has been knocked out (ceremonial)
= arrimper, alyeneng

tyekert1 *n.*
salty, bitter or sour-tasting; not sweet (of food) ◆ Mern tyekert akeng. Tey tywek anetyakenh tyekert. (St) *Sour-tasting food. Tea without sugar is bitter.* ◆ Tampewenh yanh anety tyekert, irrkertey kwa, arrakert itenh-itenh. (N) *The* tampewenh *melon is no good, bitter-tasting, it burns the mouth.* ◆ Rrwarlpan irntareny. Mern akin an tyekert. Ampengant arlkwenh, wal tyekertarl yanh, mentyel anwa aretyart. (N) *The native tomato grows in the hills. It has a fruit but it is bitter and we only eat it if it's ripe. If it was bitter we used to just leave it.*
= arrerlkart, irrkertey

tyekert2 (T,E) *n.* [RESPECT LANGUAGE]
tobacco, cigarettes, grog ◆ 'Arrkengekw tyekert-ayerr ahanelh-ila.' Kel kweyel ra inerl-alhem ngkwerlp anamerl anewekikw anthetyek. Tyekertarl ngkwerlp. (Sa) *'Go and get some tobacco for your husband.' Then the girl goes quickly and gets the tobacco and gives it to her husband. 'Tyekert' is what 'tobacco' is called [in respect language].* ◆ Tyekert-ayerrek ngkwerengkw-irretyek. (St) *Go and ask your husband for some tobacco [said by a woman referring to her son-in-law].*
= tyanyweng
SEE ALSO ngkwarl, ngkwerlp

-tyel (W) shows where something moves from, is moved from, or comes from SEE UNDER **-ntyel**

tyel angkem *vi.*
talk about someone behind their back; run someone down; speak badly of someone

(angkem *'speak', 'talk'*) ◆ Nhenhek apek ayeng tyel angkerl-anem. 'Nhenh arertarl irrek anem kwenh.' (St) *I might talk about this one behind their back. 'This one has gone mad now.'* ◆ Ntwang tyel angkem atyeng. (T) *You're saying bad things about me behind my back.* ◆ Ntarl atyeng tyel angkerneng, arnkely anem ayeng ngkweng anem. (St) *You talked behind my back and now I am sulky with you.* ◆ Menty awelhemel ayeng alhep-alhem, nhakwel atyeng tyel angkep-angkem — menty awelhemel ayeng alhep-alhem. (St) *I am going along ignoring that person who is running me down — I'm not taking any notice.*
SEE ALSO anywerr-irrem

tyel-arem (W,T) *vt.*
peep out from behind something (arem *'look', 'see'*) ◆ Warl kweneng tyel-ararerl-anem interl-anemel. (N) *Peeping out from where you are lying in the house.*
= kert-arem, ayternem

tyelalwernenh (W,T) *n.*
a type of marsupial mouse

tyelepelep, tyelapetyel (W,T), **tyelepetyel** (W,T), **tyelepey** (E) *n.*
1. navel, umbilicus
2. umbilical cord ◆ Atnem arrerlpel atanthetyart tyelepelep renh. (St) *Umbilical cords used to be cut with a sharp digging stick.*
= metyeletyel
SEE ALSO ilpa, ayep

Tyelepetyel (W) *n.*
name of a soakage and hill in the Crown Creek area north-east of Yuelamu (Mt Allan) community

tyelety (E) *n.*
sensitive, touchy or jumpy
= irrngerrng
tyelety-irrem (E) *vi.*
feel sensitive, touchy or jumpy
= irrngerrng-irrem

tyelewerr (W,T) *n.*
in fun, playing a trick, joking (note Warlpiri *jiliwirri*)
= urrayerr
SEE ALSO arrken

tyelh *n.*
kneecap
SEE ALSO amper alkwert-alkwert, itelh, kelkert tyelh, kelkert ngkwern
anter tyelh (W)
the fat from under the kneecap (of a kangaroo) (anter *'fat'*)
= akepitelh, ulyelatanenh
SEE ALSO apertaynp, iylpernk

tyelk *n.*
1. the body ◆ Tyelk ingkerrek ayeng akeng-irrek *pain*-angketyarr, arlkwemarl. Tyelk ingkerrek ayeng arlkwem. (St) *My whole body feels no good and is paining all over. My whole body is aching.*
SEE ALSO arlka
2. fleshy parts of humans or animals; flesh, meat, gums ◆ Pwelek iteth ra alhem alkngirrenty, ngkwernant — *no* anter *no* tyelk *no* alhwa. (St) *The bullock goes around alive, just skin and bone — no fat, no flesh and no blood.* ◆ Ker iylek, iylek-iylek inngart, arrpemel anem renh. Tyelk anetyang anter. Ker iylek arlkwem. (Sa) *Of course the echidna is really prickly and it has its spines scraped off. They don't have flesh, just fat. We eat echidnas.* ◆ Ayenp akern nhenh, tyelk kwen. (M) *The skin is on top and the flesh is underneath.*
SEE ALSO ker, anwenth
3. the inner part of things such as trees ◆ Atanthem aper tyelk, kapert alhewelhetyeh, annga arlka. Mernt-penh kel irrpelh-ilem. Aper tyelk lpwelem, *hot water*-em ampem, kwerel ap alhewelhem, waly arlka item *mixed*, waly aper. (N) *We get the inside bark of the river red gum and use it to wash our heads and our eyes. You can wash yourself with it if you are sick. The bark is beaten till it's soft, then cooked in water along with the leaves, and then used as a wash.*
ker tyelk
flesh, meat (ker *'meat'*)
arrakert tyelk
gums (in mouth) (arrakert *'mouth'*)
rtety tyelk (E)
gums (in mouth) (rtety[1] *'teeth'*)
alker tyelk *n.*
high in the sky (where something is hardly visible) (alker *'sky'*) ◆ Alker tyelkel alhem akern. Akernarl alhem aretyakenh — *that's* alker tyelkel alhem. *Might see*-em ywarn anem. *Might* alker tyelkel nhakw ra alhem akwek-amperl. *Really high.* (St) *Going along high up in the sky. Going along very high where you can't see [it] — that's going along in the* alker tyelk. *You might be just able to see [it]. Something [that looks] really small might be going along high up in the sky. Really high.*

tyelk-aperrety-aperrety (T), **tyelk-aperrertety** (E) *n.*
brown songlark (*Cincloramphus mathewsi*)
= tyelyapwerety

tyelkath (W), **tyelkaty** (T) *n.*
a group of men travelling around in

preparation for particular ceremonies; 'business' men, red ochre men. Women are not supposed to see the red ochre men or travel on the same route as them. ◆ Nyerreng arltwelhem. Tyelkatheng arltwelhem. (M) *Covering yourself over because you are shamed. Or because of the red ochre men.*

tyelkatherather, tyelkatherratherr (E) *n.*
1. banded lapwing (*Vanellus tricolor*)
2. red-kneed dotterel (*Erythrogonys cinctus*) ◆ Uthip tyelkatherratherr, *white one* iterelan anem, *brown.* 'Tyelkatherratherr tyelkatherratherr', arlkerl-anem. (Sa) *The* tyelkatherratherr *bird is brown with white on its sides. It sings out,* 'Tyelkatherratherr, tyelkatherratherr'.
SEE ALSO tartarrp, interrk-atherather, ampelyetyerrker

tyelkaty (T) a group of men travelling around in preparation for particular ceremonies SEE UNDER **tyelkath**

tyelpaperretyaperrety (T) brown songlark SEE UNDER **tyelyapwerety**

tyelper-tyelper (W,T), **tyelperr-tyelperr** (T) *n.*
a type of green bird that nests on the ground

tyelpetyerrem *vt.*
pull something out ◆ Arlpenty arnterrarl anwerlarr, artelhampw tyelpetyerrem. Aylpa ra akely-akely, arlatyey-kenh aylpa awer-rnem. Pertipelawan *yellow one* ratherr atherr-antey. (Sa) *The* anwerlarr *yam is really long, and the big ones are pulled out. It has smallish leaves, whereas the* arlatyey *yam has big ones. Both of them have similar looking yellow flowers.*
SEE ALSO tyerrem

tyely (W,T) *n.* [SENSITIVE LANGUAGE]
vagina
SEE ALSO artwert², kep², tyarrp

tyely-irrem (E) make a sizzling or bubbling sound SEE UNDER **tyelyely-irrem**

tyely-tyely *n.*
part of guts (of kangaroos and cattle). Also referred to as *ker tyely-tyely.*

tyelyapwerety (W), **tyelyapweretyapwerety** (W,T), **tyelyapwerretyapwerrety** (T), **tyelpaperretyaperrety** (T), **apweretyapwer** (W) *n.*
brown songlark (*Cincloramphus mathewsi*) ◆ Alakenh angkem, 'Tyelyapwerretyapwer tyelyapwerretyapwer'. (T) *It sings out like this,* 'Tyelyapwerretyapwer tyelyapwerretyapwer'.
= tyelk-aperrertety-aperrertety

tyelyely-irrem (E), **tyely-irrem** (E) *vi.*
make a sizzling or bubbling sound, like the high-pitched popping sound when the skin of an animal that is being cooked breaks open and steam or fat comes out ◆ Ker tyelyely-irremel ampem. (St) *The meat is sizzling and popping as it cooks.*
= lyely-lyely-irrem

tyemurrely (E) *n.* [RESPECT LANGUAGE]
1. leg, parts of leg ◆ Tyemurrely-akertaw. Rlkertarl irrek. Awempekarl akwel alherlanenty arlengel. Arlewent-penh ahanerretyel-penh tyemurrely atnerrk-irrek. (Sa) *[My son-in-law] has a sore leg. He's sick. Supposedly he got really hot after travelling a long way. After going a long way [his] leg has become sore.*
2. bone ◆ Apert-atweyaw tyety tyemurrelyaw. (Sa) *Crush up the meat bone.*
SEE ALSO ngkwern, ampweth

tyen (W,T) *n.*
feeling happy after being reunited with family ◆ Tyenem akeweny ananem. (M) *That person is sitting down happy now (because their family has come back).*
tyen-irrem (W,T) *vi.*
1. feel happy after being reunited with family ◆ Ayeng arengk anyent-arteh anerlanem. Tyenem akey ayeng irrek. (M) *I was sitting down on my own like a dog. Then my family came back and I felt better.* ◆ Tyen-irrem ntwang ananem. (M) *You're happy now that you're back with your family.* ◆ Tyerrty yanh angwely-arteh anek anyent-areny. Tyen-irrek antem mapel-ayeng. (M) *That person was alone like a dog. Now the families have come and they are glad.*
SEE ALSO altyirrem
2. settle down after an argument, fight or sickness

tyenelhem¹ (T,E) *vi.*
go backwards, reverse ◆ Tyenelhem mwetekay yanh. (St) *That car is reversing.*
= angkep-irrem, anepetheng-irrem, aneyangketh-irrem, anwengentyengenty-irrem

tyenelhem² (W) *vi.*
go out into the open ◆ Mapelareng amparr nta irnerlanem, wal nta tyenelherl-alhem, kethel nta irnetyeh. *Hot*-eng apek nta arraterl-alhem, nyentem, tyenelherl-alhem nta nyentem anem. (M) *At first you might be standing there with lots of people, and then you go out into the open to stand there. You might be getting too hot and that's why you go out into the open to be on your own.*
SEE ALSO ampay-irrem

tyeng (T,E) *n.*
small grinding stone used for seeds ◆ Weth

ntangarl athep-athemarl. Ntangarl atherl-anemarl, tyengel. Alyerarl yanhan apert-atwep-atwemarl, mern katyerr arlka ikelh-ilem kwerel alyerelan. Tyengan yanh anterrngarl athemel. (St) *That's that thing that's used for grinding seed. Seed is ground with the* tyeng *stone. The* alyer *stone is used for crushing foods, such as the desert raisin which is made into a seed cake. The* tyeng *stone is used for grinding seed.*
= pwerl
SEE ALSO ather, alyer
CAN SOUND A BIT LIKE atyeng *'for me'*

Tyengel *n.*
1. Jingili person or people
2. Jingulu language

tyenkarl-tyenkarl (W,T) *n.*
showing off, behaving like you're pretty good ◆ Arelh tyenkarl-tyenkarl, mantarr mwerr-akertarl alhem. (M) *That woman with the pretty dress on is showing off.*
tyenkarl-irrem (W,T) *vi.*
show off, brag, think you're pretty good ◆ Ntwang tyenkarl-irrem mantarr arlkarl-akert. (T) *You think you're smart with your new clothes.* ◆ Mwetek *new one*-akert ntwa tyenkarl-irrem atyengety. (T) *You're showing off in front of me with your new car.*
SEE ALSO arrkereny-irrem, reken-irrem, nakelhem, narlkwelhem, tywenelhem, utyenelhem

tyenkerr *n.*
ceremonial payment of food; food used as a gift for someone who performs a ceremony; food presented at important occasions such as the birth of a child ◆ Tyenkerran mpwarem mern mpwarem tyenkerr, an *young fella*-arl aketh-warn irrety-alpem *or* tyenkerr mpwarem arelh awenkew, anew kwerenharl *promise* inem. (T) *Ceremonial food might be made for a young fella who has completed going through business, or it might be made for a young woman who has been promised to a man.* ◆ Tyenkerr angkwey arrernetyam ker aherr. (M) *In the old days they used to present kangaroo meat as ceremonial payment.*
= tyewarrely, kwerapak, inngwerr

Tyenkerrakwerr (E), **Tywenkerangerr** (T) *n.*
name of a place in the Tennant Creek area, and an Aboriginal organisation based in Tennant Creek — Jurnkurakurr.

tyenperarr *n.*
a type of mulga (*Acacia* sp.) ◆ Anem mpwarenharenh. Arnarl atwem anem mpwaretyeh, tyenperarr. Arna war atwem anem. (N) *This plant is just used for making digging sticks. We cut* tyenperarr *wood to make digging sticks.*

tyenterr-tyenterr (W) *n.*
willie wagtail (*Rhipidura leucophrys*) (note Warlpiri *jintirr-jintirrpa*)
= artetyerretyerr[1]

Tyentyaw (E) *n.*
name of a place south of New Store

tyentyentyelarr (W) *n.*
a type of small lizard

tyenyepweny (E) *n.*
rufous whistler (*Pachycephala rufiventris*)
= artwatherr apetyepetyem, artwang apetyepetyem, ipeny apetyepetyem, kwarlpatengkelyengkely

tyep[1], **tyip** (E) *n.*
bits and pieces ◆ Ker tyep anem akngeynetyek. (St) *Taking the bits of meat back then.*
tyep-tyep, **tyip-tyip** (E) *n.*
bits and pieces ◆ Petheth atanthem. Petheth akwek war tyep-tyep tha atanthem. (T) *I am sewing the rags. I am just sewing up the little bits of rag.*
CAN SOUND A BIT LIKE atyep-atyep *'lively', 'energetic'*
tyep-ilem, **tyip-ilem** (E) *vt.*
cut something up into pieces (especially meat) ◆ Ker aherr tyep-ilem irntang arlterel, lwerenarl akerl-anem ker renh. (N) *Kangaroo meat is cut up with a stone knife, that's how you cut up the meat.*
= tyep-akem
SEE ALSO ngkwelty-ilem, tyarrp-atwem, urleth atwem, akem[1]
tyep-tyep-ilem, **tyip-tyip-ilem** (E) *vt.*
cut something up into pieces (especially meat) ◆ Ura apek ilepel akwek-akwek-ilem tyip-tyip-ilem. (St) *The firewood is cut up into small pieces with an axe.*
tyep-akem, **tyip-akem** (E) *vt.* = **tyep-ilem**
◆ Artep ulpay ultakem, kwer-penh tyep-tyep-akem. (T) *Cut the emu [fat] into sections, then cut it into pieces.*
tyep-akelhem, **tyip-akelhem** (E) *vi.*
fall apart, fall to pieces ◆ Mantarr apek tyep-akelhem. (M) *The clothes might fall to bits.*

tyep[2], **tyipey**, **tyepey** *n.*
sheep (from English 'sheep')
= yep-yep

tyepal *n.*
small stick used for cleaning things out, or for making a 'brush' for painting up for ceremonies ◆ Ker kanty tha tiwem tyepalel. (St) *I am cleaning the burnt hair off the kangaroo tail with a stick.* ◆ Mern anakety akem

arrernem *clean*-em-ilem arna tyepal nhenglkwerel alakenhel *clean*-em-ilem *seed* renhan antarram wemel *clean* anthwerr mparem. Atanthem atanthemel wem kart renh *clean*-em mern aperrk war arrernem arlkwemem. (N) *The bush tomato is picked and then the seeds are cleaned out using a stick called 'typepal'. All the seeds are cleaned out and thrown away and then [the fruits] are cooked on the coals and eaten.*

tyepelyakw (W), **tyepelywek** (W), **tyepelyak** (W), **tyepelyey** (E) *n.*
1. grey teal (*Anas gracilis*)
2. plumed whistling duck (?) (*Dendrocygna eytoni*) (note Warlpiri *jipilyaku*)
= pelyak
SEE ALSO awengker

tyeperr *n.*
main thing, special one, important
◆ Anpernenty, *we tied up in that one. We can't part-em that* anpernenty. Anpernenty yanh tyeperr ra. Mpwarengareng anthwerr. Tyeperr kwenh. (M) *We are tied up with the kinship system. We can't part with that kinship system. Kinship is very special. It is the Law. Really important.* ◆ Tyeperr atyeng intem, mwetekay apek, pelangket apek. (M) *The car, or the blanket, might be very important to me.* ◆ *No,* tyeperr nhenhan! Menty! (T) *No, that's the main one! Leave it!*
= impen

tyepety[1] *n.*
1. women's painting, body paint or ceremonial designs (Central Anmatyerr)
◆ Arelh map tyepety arrernelhem patyel-ayel. (T) *The women are painting their breasts up with ceremonial designs.*
SEE ALSO arlkeny, awely
2. a story (particularly a Dreaming story) that is told by drawing designs on the ground (women or girls) (Eastern Anmatyerr)

tyepety ilem (E)
tell a story by drawing on the ground (women and young girls) (ilem *'say', 'tell'*)
◆ Tyepety ilelherl-anem, kwey awenk. (St) *The young women are telling a story (in the sand).*
◆ Tha ngkweng tyepety iley. (Sa) *I'll tell you a story.*
= mpaty-ilem

tyepety-wem (W,T) *vt.*
paint someone up, paint or draw a ceremonial design (women) ◆ Tyepety-wem arnarnk-warn arelh Anengkerr kwerenh ra rntwetyek kwer akwekek. (T) *The woman is being painted up on her chest with her Dreaming designs so that she can dance for the little kids.* ◆ Arelh mapel wem impaty ahern-warn an *canvas*-warn, tyepety-wem mer kwerenh. (T) *The women make designs on the ground and on canvas, drawing the designs from their country.*
SEE ALSO mpaty-ilem, arlkeny-wem, altyerr ilem

tyepety-werrem (W,T) *vi.*
paint each other up with ceremonial designs (women) ◆ Arelh rntwetyek-angent tyepety-werrem. (T) *The women are painting each other up before they dance.*
= arlkeny-werrem

Tyepety (E) *n.*
name of a place on Stirling Station where the *tyepety* stories originated from

tyepety[2] (E) *n.*
bits and pieces, leftover bits ◆ Ampeny-ampeny arlkwem, tyepety arlkwep-arlkwem. (St) *Eating the leftovers.* ◆ Tyepety antywep-antywem war. Akwek war imperl-alhek. (St) *Just drinking what is left over. A little bit was left.*
SEE ALSO ampeny[1]

tyepey (W) sheep SEE UNDER **tyep**[2]

tyer[1] (W,T) *n.*
dead finish (plant) (*Acacia tetragonophylla*). Shrub to about 3 m high, with sharp pointed leaves and curved seed pods. ◆ Tyer arlkwetyam, rwel atyerretyam, kwer mapel, arlkwetyam tyer yanh akemel, arlkwetyam. Tyap akert akin arlketyerr yanh tyer yanh. Arlkwenh arlkwenh. Tyap anyematyart *same* kin. (N) *We ate* tyer *seeds, picking them and then cooking them in the fire, all us kids. That* tyer *bush also has edible grubs, just like witchetty grubs.*
= arlketyerr

tyer[2] (E), **iyter** (E) *n.*
turpentine bush, Sturt's desert fuchsia (*Eremophila sturtii*). A sticky shrub about 2 m high, with narrow leaves and white, pink or mauve flowers.

tyer-wem, **tyer-iwem** (E) *vt.*

tap a digging stick or crowbar on the ground to listen for the hollow sound which tells you that there is a grub or an animal's burrow there; stab or poke the ground with a digging stick or crowbar ◆ Arelhel tyer-wem ker arlewatyerr-kenh alhweng. (T) *The woman is poking around the goanna's hole.* ◆ Anemel tyer-wem arlewatyerreh apek, wal arraty arrwernem. (M) *Poking around for a goanna, then the crowbar goes right into the hole.* ◆ Pwep-angkenty awem aketh-antey, 'Mern nhenhaw kwenh!'

Kel angernemel. Tyer-wem anemel apek renh tyer-wem. Kel renh angernemel angernemel. 'Pweparl angkek arraty kwenh anaty nhenh.' (Sa) *When you clearly hear that hollow sound you say, 'This is where the tuber is!' Then you dig. You might poke around at it with the digging stick, and then dig and dig, dig it up. [Then you say,] 'It really did make that hollow sound, here's the bush potato.'*
SEE ALSO thakem

tyerlarr, **iyterlarr** (E) *n.*
headband ◆ Arelh tyerlarr arrernelhem anthep-irretyek. (T) *The woman puts on the headband so that she can dance.*

SEE ALSO pakerey, irrkarlp

tyernem[1] *vt.*
1. answer someone, reply, respond, answer back ◆ Nga angkem, tha ngenh tyernemel. (St) *You talk, then I answer back.*
2. echo back ◆ Urrar tyernepernem apwertel arlkerlek, *someone*-ek apek arlkerlek, kel urrarel ra tyerneman arlkenty. Apwert yanh rntwarr apek arlkem, kel ra tyernem artek arrpenharl artekel tyernem. (St) *The echo answers back if [someone] sings out in the hills, if you sing out to someone then the echo answers back. It answers back as if it's another person.*
tyernelhem *vi.* = **tyernem**[1] (?) ◆ Urrar arlkem wal ranteyarl arlkem, ra arlkem tyerrtyek kenh nhakw urrar tyernelhekarl. (St) *The echo calls out in the same way as the person calls out, the person sings out to someone and the echo answers back.*

tyernem[2], **iyternem** (E) *vi.*
limp, limp along ◆ Tyernerl-apem ingka utyen-akert. (St) *Limping along with a sore foot.* ◆ Ingka utyen iyternetyel, marl apek, arwerlelarl atanthek, arwerlelarl atanthek ingka utyen anem iyternetyel. (Sa) *The woman is limping with a sore foot, it got stabbed by a stick.*

tyerr (T,E), **tyirr** (E) *n.*
maggot, maggots ◆ Ker nhenh tyerr-akert anem, iwey, rntert anem. (St) *This meat has got maggots in it now, chuck it away, it's gone rotten.* ◆ Mweremwenkelan ker-warl kwartarl irrkwem, tyerr anem anem. (Sa) *Blowflies lay eggs in meat, and then there's maggots.*
= irnnga

tyerr-tyerr (W), **tyerr-tyerrey** (W), **tyerrepert** (W) *n.*
inland dotterel (*Charadrius australis*) ◆ 'Tyerr-tyerr, tyerr-tyerr', angkerl-apem. Arrakert rnter-rnter. Atek-arteh arlkeny mwerr anthwerr. *It makes a* 'Tyerr-tyerr, tyerr-tyerr' *sound as it goes along. It has a red beak. And pretty markings like a button quail.*

tyerrem *vt.*
pull something out of something ◆ Arwerl apek tha akeng-akeng yanh-lkwer lyapek, tyerretyek tha, tyerremel iwetyek. (St) *If I have grown some useless plants or that sort of thing, then I'll pull them out, pull them out and chuck them away.* ◆ Lyek tyerrem ingkethey. (St) *Pulling the prickle out of the foot.*
= arratelh-ilem
CAN SOUND A BIT LIKE atyerrem[1] *'cook'*; atyerrem[2] *'shoot'*
tyerrelhem *vi.*
1. pull something (such as a prickle) out of part of your body ◆ Lyek ayeng ingkewarl tyerrelhetyek. Lyekel ayenh atanthekarl. Tyerrelhetyek ayeng. (St) *I'm going to pull the prickle out of my foot. The prickle went into my foot. I'm going to pull it out.* ◆ Aleraty ayeng tyerrelhem. (St) *I am pulling out the hairs [symbolising my brother's children] from my chin.* ◆ Rrwey akwek artwengkwenng tyerrelhem. (M) *The little boy is blowing the snot out [of his nose].*
2. come out, go outside, emerge from something; hatch out of an egg ◆ Arelh tyerrelhem aketh-warn. (M) *The woman is going outside.* ◆ Thep akwekel peltyem, tyerrelhem antem. (T) *The baby bird cracks [the egg] open and then hatches out.* ◆ Urlaylp tyerrelhem akartw-angkwerr, kel ra alhem intelyapelyap anem. (St) *The witchetty grub comes out through the* akartw, *and then it flies around as a moth.* ◆ Ker alewatyerr tyerrelhenhem atyerrp-penh. (Sa) *The goanna comes out after hibernating.* ◆ Ulkertarl irrnyek ampwem arrpemarl, irrnyant anem aynterl-anem. Tyerrelhenhem *clean* anem. Irrnyiwekarl-kety. Inngelan akethari arem, 'Irrnyek ampwekarl-kety urnem yanh-penh-kety'. (Sa) *Perenties shed their skins as well, and then just the skin is left lying there. They come out all clean, after shedding their skins. People see [the snake skin] and say, 'Look out, that snake has shed its skin'.*
3. come up, rise (sun, moon, stars) ◆ Aherrk tyerrelhem akngerrakw-they. (Sa) *The sun comes up in the east.*
SEE ALSO arratem
tyerrelh-ilem *vt.*
make something come out of something else ◆ Aretharr nhel tyerrelh-ilem arlewatyerr. (N) *The* aretharr *wind makes the goannas come out.*

tyerremp (T,E), **tyerrwemp** (T) *n.*
1. spinifex ant (*Ochetellus* sp.). These ants make nests and tunnels from the resin of the soft spinifex (*Triodia pungens*).
2. medicinal substance made by these ants and found in the base of soft spinifex and in some other grass species. Also used as a mosquito repellent. ◆ Tyerrwempan yerrel mpwarem, ahern-arteh. Arem tyerrtyel lyeteny inemel, lpwelemem itemem. Anterel-arleng *or* kwatyel amparr alhewem item, anter-warn anem arrernem. (T) *Ants make the* tyerrwemp, *and it's like earth. If a person sees some fresh* tyerrwemp, *well they get it and crush it up and cook it. It's washed and cooked with fat, then mixed with fat.* ◆ Tyap an ikwerel anem *white one*-rnem, arrwekelenyelant arlkwerrek tyap, tyap akely-akely weth-lkwer, arlkwerretyart, tyerrempek-arlek. Tyap-rnem mperlker-rnem. Than aretyart nyanyel-rnem aperleyel-rnem arlkwerrerl-anenty. Tyerremp-arey. (Sa) *There is a white grub there that the olden-time people ate, a little sort of a grub that is found in the* tyerremp. *The grubs are white. I saw my grannies and my father's mothers eating the* tyerremp.
SEE ALSO alatyeyt
tyerremp kwart (T,E), **tyerrwemp kwart** (T)
the eggs of the spinifex ant (kwart *'egg'*)
◆ Tyerremp, kwart renh arrwekelenyelan aynpernemel kel apemelarl kwart tyerremp ikwerel. (Sa) *The olden-time people yandied the eggs of the spinifex ant and then used them to rub on themselves.* ◆ Kwartan arlkwemel, ulpilemel arlkwem. (St) *The eggs are eaten, crushed up and eaten.*

tyerremper (E), **tyerreymper** (E) *n.*
fairy martin (*Hirundo ariel*) ◆ Tyerreymperel artep-artem apwert akertnek inteyek. (St) *Fairy martins build [their nests] high up in caves.*

tyerrenng (T) skeleton SEE UNDER **tyarrenng**

tyerrepert (W) inland dotterel SEE UNDER **tyerr-tyerr**

tyerreymper (E) fairy martin SEE UNDER **tyerremper**

tyerrk (W,T), **iyterrk** (E) *n.*
1. marrying 'wrong way'; marrying, sleeping with, or acting flirtatiously towards inappropriate kin (someone who is not related to the person in the proper way under Aboriginal Law) ◆ Ankerl tyerrk. Anetywek atherrarl inerrek — arrwemp-nheng apek mwer-nheng, amenheng apek inerrek, tyerrk. (M) Tyerrk *is when two people marry the wrong way — maybe they get married with their 'brother' or 'sister', their 'son-in-law' or 'mother-in-law', or a 'mother' and 'child' get married.* ◆ Anherrikw apek anew akem, wal iyterrkarl ra. (St) *Someone who marries their mother-in-law is* iyterrk.
SEE ALSO akengentyeny
2. someone who is really hard, tough or greedy ◆ Tyerrkam ra, mern anthetyakenh, ker anthetyakenh, ankerl. (M) *That person is greedy, not giving food or meat.* ◆ Iyterrkel arlkwep-arlkwem yanhel anthetyakenhel, akwenpety akwenpel. *That person is greedily eating and not giving anything to others, without caring a bit.*
3. being stubborn or uncooperative, keeping on doing something ◆ Ampa nhenh iyterrkarl arnep-arnem. (St) *This child keeps on crying all the time.*
SEE ALSO ankerl
tyerrk-tyerrk (W,T), **iyterrk-iyterrk** (E) *n.*
1. acting flirtatiously towards inappropriate kin (someone who is not related in the proper way under Aboriginal Law) ◆ Ankerl-ankerl angwenh-akwey-irrerl-anemel, tyerrk-tyerrk anemel. Marl an rrweyarl alherremel, mapel-aleng uyarn ilemel. 'Ankerl angerr tyerrk-tyerrkay kwenh.' (P) Ankerl-ankerl *is someone who behaves flirtatiously [towards the wrong kin]. A girl and a boy might go together, and other people tell them in vain. 'You two are really wrong for each other.'*
2. someone who is really hard, tough or greedy
= ankerl-ankerl
iyterrk-irrem (E) *vi.*
be greedy
= ankerl-irrem
alem iyterrk-iyterrk (T,E)
someone who has married the 'wrong' way (alem *'belly', 'stomach'*)
= atna iyterrk-iyterrk, akengentyeny, alem atherrk-atherrk
atna iyterrk-iyterrk (E) **= alem iyterrk-iyterrk**
(ana, atna *'arse'*)

tyerrker (E) *n.*
a small wooden shovel or scoop made from a hollow branch and used for handling hot coals, cooking food, or getting a damper out of the fire ◆ Ker arlewatyerr apek itetyek, mern apek itetyek tyerrkerel. (St) *Goannas or other sorts of food are cooked using a* tyerrker.
= antyanp[1]
SEE ALSO mwar

tyerrty *n.*
1. person, people, human being ◆ Ikngwetyek alhem tyerrty arrpenh, kel apety-alpeyamel

antey. (St) *Going and asking the other person, then coming back again.* ◆ Ayeng nyerr-irrem tyerrtyelarl aremeng arnterr. (T) *I feel shamed when people stare hard at me.* ◆ Tyerrty yanh apetyepetyem. (St) *That person is coming.* ◆ Wenh-apatherr tyerrty ra? (M) *What skin is that person?*
2. Aboriginal person ◆ Tyerrtyam yanhan. Ntwan tywelkeram. (T) *That's an Aboriginal person. You are a white person.* ◆ Anmanty-warn tyerrty map arraw-irrem rntwetyek. (T) *Aboriginal people gather together to dance at the young men's ceremony.*
3. body ◆ Tyerrty ayeng akeng-irrek ngkwern nhenhel arlkwek tyerrty anem ingkerrek anem akeng-irrenhek. (St) *My body is no good, my leg here is hurting and my whole body is no good.* ◆ Apmwer, *medicine*-arl mpwarem renh apmwer. Antyerrk-ilemel anem renh apmwer mpwarem anterel-arleng. Apernelhem tyerrty ingkerrek. (T) *The mint bush is made into a medicine. It is dried and then mixed with fat. It is used to rub over the whole body.*
SEE ALSO arlka[1], iyterrty
tyerrty rrpwerl (W,T), **tyerrty irrpwerl** (E)
Aboriginal person (rrpwerl '*dark-coloured*') ◆ Tyerrty urrperlarl ayeng. (St) *I am an Aboriginal person.*
tyerrty-kenh
belonging to Aboriginal people
= lrrpwerl-kenh
tyerrty arlter (E)
white person, European person, non-Aboriginal person (arlter '*white*') ◆ Tyerrty arlterarl nga. (St) *You are a white person.*
tyerrty angerr
an adult (angerr[1] '*big*')
tyerrty ampwerrk (W,T)
body, the whole body (ampwerrk '*whole*')

tyerrty-tyerrty internem (W), **tyerrty-tyerrty irnternem** (W) *vi.*
convulse, have a fit, take a fit

tyerrwemp (T) spinifex ant SEE UNDER **tyerremp**

tyert (T,E), **tyet** (T,E) *n.*
narrow, tight (as clothes) ◆ Terawath apek ngkwinh tyetarl atyeng. Pwet apek tyet. (St) *Your trousers are too tight for me. The boots might be tight.* ◆ Tyet anem ra alhem lher wethel apek. Arlpaw anem ra irrem. (St) *That creek goes along narrowly. Then it widens out.*
= pwarn
CAN SOUND A BIT LIKE atyet[1] '*soft*', '*flimsy*', '*fragile*'; atyet[2] '*native cat*'
tyert-irrem (T,E), **tyet-irrem** (T,E) *vi.*
get narrow or tight

tyet-atanthem (W) *vt.*
skewer something onto a stick (atanthem '*pierce something*') ◆ Anakety tyet-atanthem tyetyaty-warn. (M) *The bush tomato fruits are skewered onto a stick.*
= intak rnternem

tyetaty *n.*
1. small spear, toy spear. Made from the stems of the spearbush, *yenper* (*Pandorea doratoxylon*).
SEE ALSO irrtyart, arrwemper
2. a stick used for carrying skewered meat on, or for skewering fruits such as *anakety* (*Solanum chippendalei*) ◆ Ker aherr angem tyetatyel, lyweny-penh angernem, an akwek map ina tyetaty mpwarem irrtyart. (T) *Kangaroo meat is carried back home on a wooden skewer called 'tyetaty', and the kids make toy spears called 'tyetaty'.* ◆ Anakety tyet-atanthem tyetyaty-warn. (M) *The bush tomato fruits are skewered onto a stick.*
3. small stick used in women's dances

tyetep (W,T) *n.*
tall desert rose, native cotton (*Gossypium australe*)

tyetepayen *n.*
sheet of iron, corrugated iron (from English 'sheet of iron')

tyetepetep (W,T) *n.*
piercing or spearing something right through ◆ Ingkang arnangel atanthek tyetepetep. (T) *The stick went right through my foot.*
= wetyerretyerr[1]

tyety (E) *n.* [RESPECT LANGUAGE]
1. meat ◆ Tyety-ayerr urrem-iletyek, tyety-ayerr ahanenh-ilety-alpem. (St) *Giving the meat [to someone], getting the meat and bringing it back.*
2. meat [BABY TALK] ◆ Pepey, tyety arlkway. (St) *Baby, eat the meat.*
tyety-ayerr (E) *n.* [RESPECT LANGUAGE]
meat ◆ Tyety-ayerr tha urrem-ilem. (St) *I am giving the meat [e.g. to my son-in-law].*
SEE ALSO ker, tyewarrelh

tyety angkem (T,E) *vi.*
talk loudly or without stopping; talk excessively ◆ Tyety angkerrem, ntert apek anetyakenh ankwarl arrpenh ayntemeng. (Sa) *Talking without stopping, not shutting up when other people are sleeping.*
SEE ALSO arnterr angkem, aker-aker-ilem, arlelty angkem, arrkwertep-irrem

tyety-tyety nternem (W,T) *vi.*
have a fit, convulse
SEE ALSO atywaty-irrem

tyetyel-wem (E) *vt.*
sprinkle (rain), shower (rain), drizzle
tyetyen-ilem, tyetyeny-ilem (T) *vt.*
point to a person or a thing (with the hand); point to something in the sky ◆ 'Alenh kwenh.' Iltyel tyetyen-ilem. (M) *'There it is.' Pointing with your hand.*
tyetyey (T) horse SEE UNDER **tyey-tyey**
tyew (W,T) *n.*
thin, skinny
SEE ALSO ampwa
= **utyew** (E)
tyew-irrem (W,T) *vi.*
get thin, lose weight
= ampwerrem, ngkwern-ngkwern-irrem
= **utyew-irrem** (E)
tyew-tyew (E) *n.*
traditional healer (from English 'shoo shoo')
SEE ALSO ngangkar
tyew-tyew-ilem (E) *vt.*
use healing massage [BABY TALK]
SEE ALSO angkwerr-wem, parr-iwem
tyewakety *n.*
grey-crowned babbler, happy family (bird) (*Pomatostomus temporalis*) ◆ 'Tyewakety tyewakety', alakenh angkerl-anem. (N) *'Tyewakety tyewakety', that's the sound it makes.* ◆ Tyewaketyel mpwarem antywang angerr. (T) *Babblers make big nests.*
tyewarrelh (E) *n.* [RESPECT LANGUAGE]
meat ◆ Ngwarrelengk tyewarrelh-ayerr ngkwerltetyek. (St) *Your husband is going to cut up the meat [said by a woman to her daughter].*
SEE ALSO ker, tyety
tyewarrely (W,T) *n.*
ceremonial payment; food used as a gift for someone who performs a ceremony; food presented at important occasions such as the birth of a child ◆ Tyewarrely-akert rang alpem. Alakenh kwenh arrwekelenyan anek. *Can't* war *free* alperl. Mern arlatyey-akert *or* mern yerrakwerr-akert apek. (M) *The person goes back after ceremonies with a gift of food. That's how the olden-time people were. You couldn't just go back with nothing. There'd be a gift of pencil yams, or maybe bush onions.*
= tyenkerr, kwerapak, inngwerr
tyewelyerr-lyerr (W) *n.*
types of wren (*Malurus* spp.)
= lyerr-lyerr
SEE ALSO pwerelyerr-lyerr
tyewen kamp *n.*
chewing gum (from English 'chewing gum') ◆ Tyewen kamp mwernelhety-alhek atyengel-arleng. Altel-antey mwernelhek. (Sa) *The chewing gum went and got stuck to me. Got stuck in my hair.*
tyewentem (W), **tyek-untem** (E), **tywek-untem** (E) *vt.*
stab or poke the ground with a digging stick or crowbar, searching for a burrow or animal ◆ Arlewatyerrek tyek-untem, kel renh thakem kel renh ntewem anem. Atnemel tyek untem, kel ntewem anem renh. (St) *Poking the ground with a crowbar, looking for a goanna, and then a hole is made in the burrow [and you get the goanna] and then bash the goanna against the ground. [You] use a crowbar or digging stick to poke the ground [and when you find the goanna] you bash it on the ground to kill it.*
= tyer-wem
tyewerr (E) *n.*
the end of a hill, foothill. Also referred to as *apwert tyewerr.* ◆ Apwert tyewerr-angkwerr alhetyekaw, kerek irrer. (Sa) *[Let's] go hunting along the foothills.*
= apwert lterr
tyey[1] (W,T) *n.*
road, track, pathway ◆ Tyey yanh-angkwerr alhay. (M) *Go along that road.* ◆ Mer-warl alpetyeh tyey arratyel, apant-irrehety. (N) *Follow the right track back home, in case you get lost.* ◆ Tyey anyent kwerel tyey anerl-anem. (M) *[He] is going backwards and forwards on the same track.* ◆ Arnang intertel akwerr *live*-irretyart meran kwerenh — ahern ipert angernekarl an arnamem ya arrernetyart. Tyey apel kwerenh angerr *like* nheng aherr nheng tyey anem-arteh, nheng lywang arrpenh-warl. (M) *The desert bandicoots make their nests at the bottom of trees — they dig a hole and line it with grass. Their paths that go from shade to shade are wide, like those of kangaroos.*
= iwerr, rwert
CAN SOUND A BIT LIKE atyey *'younger brother or sister'*
tyey-irrem (W,T) *vi.*
go along the same road or track
tyey arem (W)
watch the road for someone to come; wait for somebody to come (arem *'look', 'see'*)
= iwerr arem
tyey[2] (W) *n.*
backwards and forwards ◆ Ntwa tyey anerl-anem rwertel. (M) *You are going up and down the road.* ◆ Tyey anerl-anetyal, ntwa anerl-anetyeh. (M) *Don't go backwards and forwards, stay in one place.*

tyey-angem (W,T) *vt.*
lead someone or something along (angem '*take*') ◆ Arelh pweng nhenh thang tyey-angem. (T) *I'm leading this blind woman along.* ◆ Nantew-arteyel apek tyey-angem, perraleng. (M) *The owner of the horse is leading it by the bridle.*
SEE ALSO tyarr-angem, yel-angem

tyey-tyey, **tyatyey** (T), **tyetyey** (T) *n.* [BABY TALK]
horse (from English 'gee gee')
SEE ALSO nanth, nantew, wethey

tyeyek (W,T) *n.*
zebra finch, waxbill (*Taeniopygia guttata*) ◆ Tyeyek akwekey alhem, nheng unta arem, kwatyengkw *show*-em-ilem. Parrety apek unta anep-anem wal unta tyeyek akwek nhenh map arem. Tyeyek akwek ina antem anengk anthwerr anem arnerl-ayel, kwaty yanh aremel. (M) *When you see zebra finches flying along, well they show you where the water is. If you are perishing from thirst, well you might see some little zebra finches. Lots of them will be perching on the branches, looking at the water.*
= nyengk

tyeyepetyey (W) *n.*
light rain, a sprinkle of rain, drizzle ◆ Kwaty tyeyepetyey atwem. (M) *It's raining a little bit.*
= nyeyepenyey
SEE ALSO irrpenh-ilem
tyeyepetyey atwem (W)
rain a little bit, sprinkle (rain) (atwem '*hit*')

tyeylp (E) *n.*
new moon ◆ Atnyenty altwerlelarl intety-alpem tyeylp akwekarl. (St) *The moon that is going down in the west is a new moon.*
= ngkarlt

tyeyt (E) *n.*
shade (from English 'shade')
SEE ALSO ulya

tyimp (E) *n.*
emu's nest ◆ Ankerrel mpwarem tyimp werrk artnek. (Sa) *The emu makes its nest in the scrub.*

tyip (E) bits and pieces SEE UNDER **tyep**[1]

tyipey (W) sheep SEE UNDER **tyep**[2]

tyirr (E) maggot SEE UNDER **tyerr**

tyurr-iwelhem (E) stretch legs straight out SEE UNDER **tywerr-iwelhem**

tywa (T), **tywang** (T) *n.*
dark rainstorm, rain in the distance
= **utya** (E)

tywaynt (E), **tyaynt** (E) *n.*
1. bunch Paspalidium (*Paspalidium rarum*). A grass about 20 cm high, which is often found around mulga.
2. the edible seed of this grass. Also known as *ntang tywaynt.*
= kwarrety, nyetempwer
SEE ALSO arlepenh, yakerr, akwetelh

tywek *n.*
sugar (from English 'sugar') ◆ Ayengan tywek akwek. (T) *I do not have much sugar [in my blood].*
= kwaty ikwemey-ilenh, lwemar

tywek-tywek *n.*
chook, chicken (from English 'chook') ◆ Tywek-tywek akwek map ankwang intetyam merel amweh-kenhel. (M) *The little chickens are sleeping with their mother in their home.*
= kweny-rtwek arlkenh-arlkenh

tywek-untem (E) stab or poke the ground with a digging stick or crowbar, searching for a burrow or animal SEE UNDER **tyewentem**

tywekem-ilem *vt.*
wring or twist somebody's or something's neck, break neck, choke something (from English 'choke')
= twerl-akem

tyweker *n.*
not liking something
SEE ALSO anwernt
tyweker-irrem *vi.*
not like someone or something; get fed up with something and leave it
SEE ALSO anyurr-irrem

tywekerl[1] (W,T) *n.*
1. native pear (bush cabbage) (*Cynanchum floribundum*). Shrub up to 1 m high, with twining branches and milky sap. Usually grows near watercourses.
2. edible seed pods and leaves of the native pear ◆ Tywekerl mern arlkwemarl renh. Mern tywekerlel anwernenh amangkelh-ilek mern yanhel *now*. (N) *The native pear plant is edible. They grew us up on that food.*
= angelth

tywekerl[2] (W) *n.* [RESPECT LANGUAGE]
foot
SEE ALSO ingka

Tywekertay *n.*
male junior skin name, corresponding to Ngwarray (Warlpiri *Jukartayi*). See diagram p. 744. ◆ Tywekertayan rrwey Ngwarray akwek. (T) *A* Tywekertay *is a young* Ngwarray *boy.*
SEE ALSO Ngwarray, Ngapert

tywekety soakage SEE UNDER **thewekety**

Tyweleng (W), **Tywel** (W) *n.*
name of place east of Laramba community

tywelker *n.*
1. white
2. white clay ◆ *Yellow one* irntang ilem

'karntawarr' tyerrtyel. Arlkenyek akin *use*-emilem rlpwa, karntawarr, tywelker, ntyengwenty. (T) *Aboriginal people call the yellow rock 'karntewarr'. It's used as well for making ceremonial designs, along with* rlpwa *[red ochre and white ochres]* tywelker *and* ntyengwenty.
3. white person, European person, non-Aboriginal person ◆ Tyerrtyam yanhan. Ntwan tywelkeram. (T) *That's an Aboriginal person. You are a white person.*
SEE ALSO mperlker, atywerlk, arlter, kartey, alhernter
marl tywelker
white woman (marl '*female*')
= metheth
artwa tywelker
white man (artwa '*man*')

tywelyely (W) *n.*
a type of bird. Small and brown/yellow/grey in colour.

tywemar (W,T) *n.*
fingernails, toenails, claw (of birds)
= ingkelthel

tywempelhem (W,T) *vi.*
wait for someone ◆ Urrek tywempelhay atyeng. (M) *Wait for me.* ◆ Tywempelhay, mwetek arrpenh yanharl ingkern apetyepetyem-arleng. (M) *Wait, there's another car coming along there behind.*
= akarelhem, mpwelhem[1]

tywemperr-tywemperr (W) *n.*
creek windmill grass, curly windmill grass (*Enteropogon ramosus*). Clumped grass about 1 m high which is usually found on the edges of watercourses.

tywen *n.*
1. a sore, rash or wound ◆ Aleny kantyel war tywen apek anep-anem. (St) *There might be a sore right on the tip of the tongue.*
2. sore, inflamed ◆ Tyapernpam rrkwakertan, an irlpang tywen rrkwakert. (T) *Boils have pus, and sore ears have pus.* ◆ Anyem antywem ahenty tywen-akertel. (St) *You can drink the witchetty bush leaf mixture if you have a sore throat.*
SEE ALSO alety, urrma
= **utyen** (E)
tywen-irrem *vi.*
get sore
= **utyen-irrem** (E)
tywen-ilem *vt.*
make something sore ◆ Amengel anngang tywen-ilem. (T) *Flies make your eyes sore.*
= **utyen-ilem** (E)

tywenap (T,E), **tywenap-tywenap** (T,E) *n.*
showing off (from English 'showing off')
◆ Tywenap-tywenap urntep-urntem marl yanh apek. (St) *That girl is running round showing off.*
tywenap-irrem (T,E), **tywenap-tywenap-irrem** (T,E) *vi.*
show off ◆ Marl apek tywenap-tywenap irrem, ngkwern-kweny-irrem alyemp-alyemp, artwel akwel renh aretyek, tywenap-irrem. (St) *The girl might be showing off, acting flirtatiously and making her legs go all limp, so that the man can see her showing off.*
= reken-irrem

tywenem, tywernem *vt.*
put something up high; lift something up onto something; put something away
◆ Artwang nhenhel *box* tywernem *Toyota*-warn. (N) *This man is putting the box into the truck.* ◆ Antarlkw-warn tywenem ker aherr. (T) *Putting the kangaroo meat in the fork of the tree.*
= tywenelh-ilem
= **utyenem** (E)
tywenelh-ilem, tywernelh-ilem *vt.*
= **tywenem**
tywenelhem, tywernelhem *vi.*
1. put yourself up onto something, lift yourself up onto something ◆ Mwetek akernel ayeng tywernelhem. (St) *I am lifting myself up onto the top of the car.*
2. show off, brag, skite, boast, put yourself on a pedestal, feel happy about yourself
◆ Tyerrty yanh tywenelhem. (T) *That person is showing off.* ◆ Artwang yanh tywenelhem mwetekay *new one*-akert. (T) *That man is boasting because he has a new car.*
SEE ALSO inkwerelhem, nakelhem, narlkwelhem, tyenkarl-irrem

Tywengarray *n.*
male skin name, corresponding to Ngwarray (note Warlpiri *Jungarrayi*). See diagram p. 744.
SEE ALSO Ngwarray

Tywenkerangerr (T) name of a place in the Tennant Creek area SEE UNDER **Tyenkerrakwerr**

tywenmernt (T) *n.*
healed over
SEE ALSO arrintety
tywenmernt-irrem (T) *vi.*
heal over, heal up ◆ Aletyarl akem-penh tywenmernt-irrem ra, kel mwerr anem ra anem tywenmerntem. (T) *After being wounded [it] heals over and then it is all right again, healed.*
SEE ALSO ltyerrem, arterrp-irrem, arrintety-irrem, kwerrm-irrem, pwarn-irrem, urrmirrem

tywenp *n.*

perentie (*Varanus giganteus*). Also referred to as *ker tywenp*. ◆ Angernemel arlkwem rapet, tywenpel. (M) *Perenties dig up rabbits to eat.*
= ilkwert
SEE ALSO anepeywenp

tywent-tywenterrp (W), **tywenterr-tywenterr** (W) *n.*
yellow
SEE ALSO ngwenty-ngwenty

Tyweperr (W,T) *n.*
male junior skin name, corresponding to Pwerrerl. See diagram p. 744.
= Tywerlam
SEE ALSO Pwerrerl, Tyweperrerl

Tyweperrerl *n.*
male skin name, corresponding to Pwerrerl (note Warlpiri *Jupurrurla*). See diagram p. 744.
SEE ALSO Pwerrerl

tywerengk anthem (W,T) *vt.*
pretend to give something to somebody (then take it back) (anthem *'give'*) ◆ Ntwa apek atyeng ker anthemel, wal ayeng tywerengk anthem. (T) *You might give me meat, and then take it back again (for fun).*
= atnewel anthem, ulang anthem

tywererr (W) *n.* [RESPECT LANGUAGE]
on own, alone ◆ Tywererr-penh ahanety-atherr alhern kwenh. (M) *The two of them [including respect kin] went off on their own.*
SEE ALSO aweleth, anyent

Tywerlam *n.*
male junior skin name, corresponding to Pwerrerl. See diagram p. 744. ◆ Tywerlaman urrey Pwerrerl akwek. (T) *A* Tywerlam *is a young* Pwerrerl *boy.*
= Tyweperr
SEE ALSO Pwerrerl

tywerlp (W,T) *n.*
1. smooth spiderbush (*Clerodendrum floribundum*). Shrub about 2 m high, with bright green leaves, white flowers, and small fleshy pink or purple fruit.
2. the edible roots of the smooth spiderbush. Also referred to as *mern tywerlp*. ◆ Tyepalel yarr-wetyam, tyarrp akemel. Ampetyam. Mernem arlkwetyam, perrap anper anthwerr. (N) *[The* tywerlp *roots] were cleaned with a stick after being split in half. Then they were cooked. [We] ate the roots, and they tasted really good.*
= arrngern

tywernem put something up high SEE UNDER tywenem

tywerr-arem (W,T) *vt.*
inspect something, look something over, look at something to see if you want it ◆ Nta tywerr-arem, 'Thakey mantarr nhenh iney?' Tywerr-aremel, wal nta ahenty-kwenyel impemem. (M) *You look it over and say to yourself, 'Will I get these clothes?' You inspect them and, if you don't like them, you leave them.* ◆ Arnang arlka nta tywerr-arem, alparr atwetyeh-angent. 'Mwerr nhenh — arratyenyarl irnep-irnem kwenh.' (M) *You inspect trees too, that you might want to chop for making a wooden dish. 'This one is good — it's growing tall and straight.'* ◆ Ayeng *shop*-warn alhep-alhem, mwekart apek pelangket apek tywerr-arerl-alpetyeh. *I'm going to the shop to pick out a hat and a blanket.*
tywerr-arelhem (W,T) *vi.*
inspect part of yourself, check your appearance, look at your reflection ◆ Tyerrty rang alhem tywerr-arelherl-apem. (T) *The person is going along, looking at their reflection.*

tywerr-iwelhem (E), **tyurr-iwelhem** (E) *vi.*
1. stretch your legs straight out
2. spread out in all directions
= rlkerr-welhem
tywerr intem (E)
stretch out, sit with your legs straight out (intem *'lie'*)
= rlkerr intem

tywerreng *n.*
1. sacred objects
2. secret, sacred
3. Law, Dreaming ◆ Akampwerrk, tywerreng iterlaretyakenh. (St) *[Somebody] who is* akampwerrk *doesn't know about the Law.* ◆ Tywerreng angey atyenh-henh. (M) *My father's Dreamings.*
SEE ALSO anmanty

tywerrk (W,T) *n.*

1. wild fig, desert fig (*Ficus brachypoda*). Spreading tree up to 4 m high, with glossy green leaves, and fruits that change from yellow to red–brown as they ripen. Grows in hills.
2. the edible fruit of the wild fig. Also referred to as *mern tywerrk*. ◆ Mern tywerrk. Mern tywerrkel anwern amangkek, arlkwerl-apekarl, ampeng-irremarl. Arnkang arerl-alhem mentyel. *'Ah,* ampeng-irrekam nhenh kwenh, anwengkerr mern arlkwerl-aney kwenh.' Inelh-alhemel iltyel inelh-alhemel

arlkwem anemarl, lwerenarl yanh mern tywerrk, kwerel anwern amangkelhekarl. (N) *Wild figs. We grew up on wild figs, going along and eating them when they were ripe. If we saw unripe ones we'd leave them. 'Ah, this one is ripe, let's eat these ones.' We'd pick them by hand and them eat them. That's the wild fig that we grew up on.*
= **utyerrk** (E)

Tyweteyeng (W) *n.*
name of a rockhole in the Yuelamu (Mt Allan) area

tywetyerrng *n.*
1. someone who has died; skeleton (?). Also referred to as *aweyaw tywetyerrng.*
◆ Ngkwernant tywetyerrng anem ra alherl-anem — ngkwern-rnem, utyim, artep, iltya kanty-rnem ingka — tywetyerrng. Inngepenh, antey tywetyerrng anem ra alherl-anem, inngan ikwerenh tyelk-rnem uyerrekarl, lernelherrek, tywetyerrngant anem. (St) *Then [the body] just goes around as a skeleton — the bones, ribs, back, fingers and toes —* tywetyerrng. *After being a person [they] go about as a skeleton. All the person's flesh has disappeared, fallen away, and there's just the skeleton.* (?)
SEE ALSO angirrenty, aleperenty, aweyaw
2. a type of insect or bird (?). The sound of this insect (or bird) is a sign that someone has passed away. ◆ Kwenyel angkety-alhem tywetyerrng. (M) *The* tywetyerrng *sings out in the night.*

tywetyety *n.*
1. dog, pup, puppy [BABY TALK] ◆ Tywetyety utnhekerr. (St) *Look out or the dog will bite you.*
SEE ALSO irrert
2. dog [RESPECT LANGUAGE] ◆ Tywetyety-ayerr ngwarrekengkwenh artnep-artnem. Kwey, irrepetherl-alpa. (Sa) *Your husband's dog is howling. Daughter, go and get it [said by a woman].*
3. a word that is used when calling out to a dog
tywetyety-ayerr (E) *n.* [RESPECT LANGUAGE]
dog
SEE ALSO atnetyelp, angwely, arengk

Uu

ulalthengayt (E), **lalthengayt** (E) *n.*
grub from the branches of the Georgina gidgee, *awenth*

ulamp (E), **urlamp** (E) *n.*
a large expanse of water. Also referred to as *kwaty ulamp.*
SEE ALSO pirnt, alay[1]
ulamp-areny (E), **urlamp-areny** (E), **ulamparrwek** (E), **urlamparrwek** (E) *n.*
1. white-necked heron (*Ardea pacifica*) (-areny *'inhabitant of'*)
2. white-faced heron (*Ardea novaehollandiae*)
= kamparwengk, arlkwenth, ntyar

ulanem (E) sort things out, pick something out
SEE UNDER **urlanem**

ulaneng (E), **lwaneng** (T) *adv.*
facing or moving towards the speaker
◆ Ulaneng anem apety-alpem. (St) *Coming back this way now.* ◆ Ulaneng unta ayenh arep-arem. (St) *You are looking in my direction.*
= lwarr, ularr
SEE ALSO untyem[2]
ulaneng-athek (E), **lwaneng-athek** (T) *adv.*
= **lwaneng** ◆ Yanh ulaneng-athek apetyepetyem, arnarem anem renh mer-they apek arnarep-arem anerl-anemel. (St) *That person is coming in this direction and [I] am watching them come from where I am sitting down in camp.*
= lwarr-athek, ularr-athek
SEE ALSO untyem-athek
ulaneng-irrem (E), **lwaneng-irrem** (T) *vi.*
move in a direction towards the speaker
= lwarr-irrem, ularr-irrem
ulanengek-ulaneng (E), **lwanengek-lwaneng** (T) *adv.*
facing each other; face to face
◆ Alkngetherrek alkngetherr atwerretyek ulanengek-ulaneng. (St) *[They] are fighting face to face.*
= ularrek-ularr, lwarrek-lwarr
SEE ALSO anngetherrek-anngetherr

ulang anthem (E) *vt.*
pretend to give something to somebody (and then take it back) (anthem *'give'*)
= atnewel anthem, tywerengk anthem

ularr (T,E) *adv.*
facing or moving towards the speaker ◆ Ularr apetyepetyem. (St) *[That person] is coming in this direction.*
= ulaneng
= **lwarr** (W,T)

ularr-irrem (E) *vi.*
come towards (the speaker); move towards (the speaker); turn to face (the speaker)
= ulaneng-irrem
ularr-athek (T,E) *adv.*
facing towards the speaker; motion in a direction towards the speaker ◆ Mwetek *light* arrtyenenty alhem ularr-athek apek apetyem. (St) *The car lights are coming in this direction.* ◆ Ularr-athek apety-alpa. (St) *Come back in this direction.*
= ulaneng-athek
= **lwarr-athek** (T)
ularrek-ularr (T,E) *adv.*
facing each other, face to face ◆ Ularrek-ularrarl anep-anem anwakerran. (St) *We are all sitting facing each other.*
= ulanengek ulaneng
= **lwarrek-lwarr** (W,T)

ulelty (E), **ilwelty** (E) *n.*
frost, ice
= **lwelty** (W,T)

ulem (T,E) *vi.*
1. die
2. cough
3. lose strength or intensity; die down (fire); finish (rain)
4. finish, run out
= ilwem, lwem

ulemp (T,E), **ilwemp** (T,E) *n.*
ghost gum (*Corymbia aparrerinja*). Tree to 15 m high, with smooth white trunk and drooping branches.
= pwernengk
CAN SOUND A BIT LIKE urlemp *'stay home', 'stay in one place'*
ulemparrty (E), **ilwemparrty** (E) *n.*
1. honey from ghost gum bark ◆ Ngkwarl renh anem iltyel inem, ulemparrty renh, arlkwem war. (St) *You get the honey with your fingers, the honey from the ghost gum, and just eat it.*
= yerrkengal
2. seeds of the ghost gum
ulemp-ulemp (T,E), **ilwemp-ilwemp** (T,E) *n.*
country where there are lots of ghost gums ◆ Ulemp-ulemp-angkwerr ayeng alhem. (St) *I'm going through the country where there are lots of ghost gums.*

Ulempatnew *n.*
Nine Mile Waterhole (west of the Stuart Highway), Stirling Station

ulengerek-ulenger (E), **urlengerek-urlenger** (E) *adv.*
(doing something) face to face; (doing something) backwards and forwards to each other ◆ Ulengerek-ulenger alakenh atwerrem kweterel. *No chance* apek arrpenh apek irrpelhetyek. Atwem unta, atwem unta ayenh. (St) *Hitting [each other] backwards and forwards with the nulla-nulla. No chance for anyone else to step in and stop us. I hit you, and you hit me.* ◆ Ulengerek-ulenger anthem. Unta ayenh mern apek anthem, tha ngenh anthem. (St) *Giving backwards and forwards to each other. You might give me some food and I give you some back.* ◆ Ulengerek-ulengerek angkerreperrem. Ilak apek angketyek. Unta apek atyeng angkem, ayeng ngkweng angkem, ulengerek-ulengerek angkerrem. Arratyant-arey weth-lkwer angkerrem alknga arerrem. (St) *Talking face to face. The two of us might talk. You might talk to me and I might talk to you, talk to each other face to face. Talk straight to each other, looking each other in the eye.*
= lwarrek lwarr, ularrek ularr, rlwerrkerek-rlwerrker
SEE ALSO anngetherr

uleperr (E), **lweperr** (E) *n.*
blue mallee (*Eucalyptus gamophylla*). Tree about 3 m high, with bluish green leaves. Grows in spinifex country. Some people say that the seeds are edible.
= alhelp

ulereny (E) *n.*
a stranger ◆ Nyerr-irrem ayeng ulereny-kety, yanh aretyakenh ayeng alhengk-aretyakenh. (St) *I get shy of strangers, I've never seen that person and don't recognise them.*
= alethang
= **lwereny** (W,T)
ulereny-irrem (E) *vi.*
feel shy or shamed
= nyerr-irrem
= **lwereny-irrem** (W,T)

ulernem (E) *vt.*
put something out (fire or light); extinguish
= **lwernem** (W,T)

ulernkernem (E), **urlenkernem** (E), **ilwernkernem** (E) *vt.*
break or dislocate (an animal's leg) by twisting it ◆ Ker aherr ulernkernem. (St) *Dislocating the kangaroo's legs.*
= rlwakem

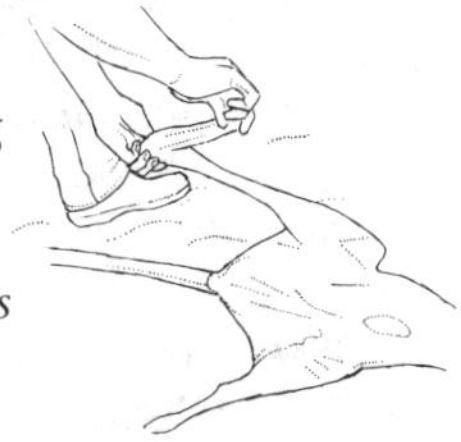

ulerreny (E) whipstick wattle (?) SEE UNDER **ilwerreny**

Ulerrperl (E) name of a waterhole in the Alhalker/Atnangker area SEE UNDER **Urlerrperl**

ulerrtyem (E) *vt.* [RESPECT LANGUAGE]

1. cook something; boil something ◆ Lyep-lyep ulerrtyem ngwarrelengkw — kwey atyeng irrepetherl-wa. (Sa) *Daughter, your husband is cooking* lyep-lyep *guts — go and get me some [said by a woman].* ◆ Kwey, ngwarrelengkw atewat-ayerr ulerrtyeperrtyem-warl alha. Atyeng ankwerl-wa. (Sa) *Girl, go over there to where your husband is boiling tea. Go and get me some [said by a woman].*

2. cook lots of meat

SEE ALSO angwey-ilem, irrkwertem, arntampernem, arrtyem, ampernem, item

ulewerr (E) *n.*

1. mirage, heat haze

= angent[1]

2. a general name for salt lakes

3. salt, salty

= **ilewerr**

ulhelk (T,E) *n.*

blue-tongue lizard (*Tiliqua multifasciata*) ◆ Tyerrtyel arlkwem ker ulhelk. (St) *People eat blue-tongue lizards.*

= lwengkart[1], ilpankwer

= **lhwelk** (W,T)

ulhem (T,E) *vt.*

1. defecate, have a shit, go to the toilet, urinate ◆ Kart ulhem. (T) *Having a shit.* ◆ Mpwang ulhem. (T) *Urinating.* ◆ Mpwal-thaytel intem-kety, nhakw-angkwerr iylkangkwerr interl-anerray. *Someone* apek mpwa apek ulhetyenh-kety. Ampa apekel ulhweyamel marlel apek. (St) *Lie down [with your head facing] the eastern side [wind side], not to the western side. Because someone might urinate there. A child might piss there, or perhaps a woman.*

2. lay an egg ◆ Arlewatyerrel kwart ulhem, arlewatyerr alkeperrel kwa. (St) *Goannas lay eggs, old goannas.* ◆ Thip anem akwek-akwekel ulhem akin ra atna apek kwerenh kwart apek ra ulhetyek. Ulhem akwel ra [*chooks*] atnarl ulhem artek-antey. Antywewarl, kwart ra ulhem. (St) *Little birds go to the toilet as well, they go to the toilet, or they lay eggs. Chooks lay eggs, in a similar way to they way that they go to the toilet. They lay eggs in nests.*

SEE ALSO irrkwem

= **lhwem** (T)

mpwelhem[2] (T) *vi.*

have a piss, urinate (mpwa *'urine'*)

ulherrpernem (E) *vt.*

squeeze something out of something else (e.g. shit from intestines); clean something out of something; blow something out (of nose) ◆ Ulherrpernetyek tha artweker apek. (St) *I might squeeze the boil.*

= rwelh arrernem, ipem, lhwerrp-ilem

ulilem (E) *vt.*

chase someone away; send someone away

ulilelhem (E) *vi.*

avoid someone, avoid particular relations; keep someone at a distance ◆ Arnerrwelty yanh-theyarl ap ayeng ayntety-alhemel ayeng ikirrenty irrety-alpek anem apety-alpemel Ankerrapw-warl. *Daddy* atyenh ulilelhek. 'Kel kwenh. Angerrety anem.' (Sa) *At about the age when I had to start respecting the kinship avoidance rules, I came back from over there at* Arnerrwelty *to* Ankerrapw. *My father avoided me. 'Okay. You're a big girl now.'*

ulkanty (E) flower of the bush banana SEE UNDER **ilkwanty**

ulkart (T,E) *n.*

1. native gooseberry, ulcardo melon, native melon, native cucumber (*Cucumis melo* ssp. *agrestis*). A vine with yellow flowers and green fruits which turn yellow when ripe.

2. the edible fruits of the native gooseberry. Also referred to as *mern ulkart.*

= **lkwart** (W)

ulkert (E) perentie SEE UNDER **ilkwert**

ulpa (T,E) *n.*

soft (ground etc.); crushed up or softened pieces of something (e.g. tobacco) ◆ Ahern ulpel anetyek. (St) *Sitting on the soft ground.* ◆ Ngkwerlp ulpa arrernem yakweth-warn, ulpilekarl. (T) *Putting the soft tobacco that has been ground up into the bag.*

CAN SOUND A BIT LIKE urlpa, rlpwang *'red ochre'*

= **lpwa** (W,T)

ulpilem (T,E) *vt.*

grind or crush something up to make it soft ◆ Ker tha ulpiletyek apwertel. (St) *I am crushing up the meat with a stone.* ◆ Ulpilem ker inpernp apek aherr. (Sa) *Smashing up the kangaroo bones [with marrow in them].* ◆ Ngkwerlp ulpilem apwert alyerek-arlek. (St) *Grinding up the native tobacco on the grinding stone.*

SEE ALSO athem[2]

= **lpwelem** (W,T)

ulpakem (E) *vt.* [RESPECT LANGUAGE]

1. hit, fight ◆ Kweth-kwethek akamperrng ulpakek. (St) *[My son-in-law's] head was hit until it bled [said by a woman].* ◆ Ulpaketyek-

antey ameram-irrepirrem. (St) *They [including respect kin] are talking about fighting.*
2. kill, shoot ◆ Rltwaty-ayerr ngkwerengkwirretyek tyety-ayerr ulpaketyek. (St) *Ask for a gun [from respect kin] to shoot some kangaroos.* ◆ Ngwarrelengkw ulpakerlantyerrek tyety-ayerr. (St) *Your husband shot some kangaroos [said by a woman to her daughter].*
SEE ALSO atwem, atyerrem
ulpakerrem (E) *vi.* [RESPECT LANGUAGE]
fight, hit each other
ulpakelhem *vi.* [RESPECT LANGUAGE]
1. hit yourself, hit or slap at something that is on part of yourself; clap hands against part of your body
2. have an accident and hurt or kill yourself

ulpanem (T,E) lie down, sleep [RESPECT LANGUAGE] SEE UNDER **lpwanem**

ulpatewelhem (E) *vi.*
build up (storm) ◆ Kwaty urrarl ulpatewelhem-kety — kwenek aylpey. (Sa) *Look out, the storm is building up — let's go inside.*

ulpay (T,E), **ilpay** (E) *n.*
creek, river, watercourse ◆ Kwaty urew, tharl amwerrk amek-arety-alhern kwaty urew, ulpayek. *Shopping*-ek alhek, amek-arerl-alpek. (St) *Just yesterday I went and was blocked by the floodwater in the creek. I went to go shopping and I was blocked off and came back.* ◆ Ilerrty alhem kwaty alhem ikwerel, ulpay angerr-warl lher angerr-warl anem ra anyent-irrem. (St) *The water flows along the small watercourse and then it joins in with the big river.*
SEE ALSO lher
= **lpway** (W,T)

ulpelp (E) *n.*
flower of sennas (broom bush, desert cassia). The flowering of sennas is a sign that kangaroos are getting fat. ◆ Apwen ulpelp lyetantarl arratem. (St) *The broom bush flowers have just come out.*
SEE ALSO apwen, ngkwert

ulperr intem (T,E), **ulperr ayntem** (E) *vi.*
lie flat on stomach (intem, ayntem *'lie'*) ◆ Ulperr intem. Alewatyerr apek ulperr intenhem. Tyerrty apek atnertel-arleng ulperr intemel. (St) *Lying on the stomach. A goanna might lie on its stomach. A person might lie on their stomach.*
SEE ALSO impalkert intem, arlkarlkar intem
= **lpwerr intem** (W,T), **ilperr ayntem**
ulperr-wem (T,E), **ulperr-iwem** (E) *vt.*
lie someone on their stomach
ulperr-welhem (T,E), **ulperr-iwelhem** (E) *vi.*
lie on your stomach
= **lpwerr-welhem** (W,T)

ulpert (T,E) *n.*
muddy or dirty water ◆ Kwaty ulpert, pwelekel ulpert-ilemarl, aherrel. Ampel apek pwerlp-irrerl-anem ulpert-ilem. (St) *Dirty water that cattle or kangaroos have muddied. Children swimming might make the water dirty.*
ulpert-ulpert (T,E) *n.*
a bit muddy or dirty (water) ◆ Kwaty ulpert-ulpert, angenty apek. Urrek tha altyewey, kwaty mwerr-ilem, ulpert-ulpert-kety. (St) *The water in a soakage might be a bit muddy. Wait while I tip out the muddy water to make the water clean.*
= alhwerrk-alhwerrk
SEE ALSO aperlk-aperlk
ulpert-irrem (T,E) *vi.*
get muddied or dirty (water)
ulpert-ilem (T,E) *vt.*
make water muddy or dirty ◆ Mew-mewel ulpert-ilek kwaty. (St) *The cattle made the water dirty.*
ulpertelh-ilem (T,E) *vt.*
1. make water muddy or dirty (stir it up)
2. interrupt; make a noise, mess or disturbance; stir people up ◆ Ampa arnterr angkerremel tyerrty-arey angkerreperrerlek ulpertelh-ilem, angka. Arengkel parlkwemel ulpertelh-ilem. (St) *Kids talking loudly while adults are talking interrupts the conversation. Dogs barking makes a noise.* ◆ Unmernt angerr ilem, ulpertelh-ilem. 'Ntwarr alhay, ulpertelh-iletyalay.' (T) *They are raising lots of dust and making a mess. 'Go further away, don't make a mess.'* • SEE ALSO apatel-anthem, apatelh-ilem, aparlp-ilem, aparlpelh-ilem

ulpirrem (E) *vi.*
1. get smashed up or crushed ◆ Ker renh arlewatyerr angernemel, ntewem anem renh. 'Hey, arnterr ntewetyalaw, anter apek ulpirrekerr!' (St) *So the goanna is dug up and then bashed against the ground to kill it. 'Hey, don't bash it too hard, or the fat will get smashed up!'*
2. go rotten, stink, go off ◆ Amwerrkeny ulpirrekarl, iweyaw, ulpirrekarl amwerrkeny. Tyelkarl ulpirrek. Iynteng-irretyek. (Sa) *That meat from yesterday has gone off, throw it away. The flesh has gone rotten. It's stinking.*
SEE ALSO akeng-irrem, ulpilem, arntert-irrem
= **lpwerrem** (W,T)

ulpma (E) word SEE UNDER **ulypma**

ulpmenth (E) flour SEE UNDER **unmenth**

ulpmernt (T,E) dust, dust haze, dust storm SEE UNDER **unmernt**

ulpmerr (E) *n.*
soft dirt, soft earth. Also referred to as *ahern ulpmerr.*
SEE ALSO unmernt
ulpmerr-atwenh (E), **ulpmerr-atwenh-atwenh** (E) *n.*
nankeen kestrel, Australian kestrel (*Falco cenchroides*) (lit. 'soft earth beater')
= lyentyelyaw, warakeparleparl, anthep-anthep

ulta (T,E) *n.*
1. the side of a person or animal, near the ribs ◆ Altyerr ampetyarl nhanyeman, kerarl atwek. Aherrarl atwekan impelty anerl-anem urrperl. Ulta apekarl atyerrek, ulta apekarl atanthek irrtyartel, wal impeltyarl anerl-anem, ampan. *Mark* akert anem anerl-anem, urrperl. (Sa) *This is a birthmark on the child from where the animal [associated with the child's place of quickening or where the child was 'found'] was hit. Where the kangaroo was shot is a dark-coloured mark. If it was shot in the side, or speared in the side, well there is a corresponding mark there on the child. The child has a dark-coloured mark.*
2. shirt ◆ *Blouse*-ek irrpeyaw, ultek. (T) *Put the blouse on, the shirt on.*
CAN SOUND A BIT LIKE urlta *'big'*
= **ltwa** (W,T)

ultakem (E) *vt.*
1. break or cut something; break something in half ◆ Ker ultakem tyelk. (St) *Cut up the meat.*
2. break a horse in ◆ *Quiet*-arl ileman, ultakem-antey. Nantew yanh tha ultaketyek, *quiet*-ilemel. Atyeng-artweyel *all day* ultaketyam nantew. (St) *Break a horse in to make it quiet. I'm going to break that horse in to make it quiet. My father used to break in horses all the time.*
3. have a stomach-ache ◆ Atnert ultakemaw, atnertarl arlwar tnek. Ker iyntengarl arlkwek-penh. (Sa) *My stomach is hurting and has swollen up. From eating rotten meat.*
SEE ALSO urleth-akem
= **ltwakem** (W,T)
ultakelhem (E) *vi.*
1. break a part of yourself ◆ *Not* akern *jump*-irretyeh ahelh-warl ngkwern ultakelh-kety. (N) *Don't jump high or you'll [fall] to the ground and break your leg.* ◆ Arna apek ultakelhem ngkwelty-ngkwelty anem intem. (St) *The tree breaks up and then there's bits and pieces lying there.*
2. become broken, break down ◆ Mwetek yanh ultakelhek. (St) *That car broke down.*
= **ltwakelhem** (W,T)
angka ultakem (E)
break off talk, stop a conversation (angka *'word', 'story'*) ◆ Angka tha ultakek, aweth angketyakenh — menty anetyek. *Meeting*-el apekarl angka *keep going* angkep-angkem. Wal aweth angketyal. Angka ultakekarl *finish.* (St) *I've broken off talking, and I'm not going to talk anymore — I'll just leave it. The talk is going on and on in the meeting. Well I'm not going to say anything else. I've finished with talking.*

ulteketh *part.*
really, very, extremely (from English 'altogether') ◆ *Oh,* kwer akenh yang anek kwer akenh kwerenh anngerrek anengk ulteketh akwel anengk. Kwer an kwerenh anngerrek, awey amerrk kwerenhan. (M) *Oh, he had so many children, a really large number of children. The young fella had a lot of children.*

ultewem (T,E), **iltewem** (E) *vt.*
1. smash or break something
2. throw something at someone or something ◆ Kwer urreyel irntel ultewem thep. (T) *The boy is throwing stones at birds.*
3. strike, hit (of a storm or lightning)
SEE ALSO wem[1]
= **ltewem** (W,T)
ultewelhem (T,E), **iltewelhem** (E) *vi.*
break, become broken or smashed up; split open ◆ Iltewelhek atyenh panth. (St) *My wooden dish broke.* ◆ Alwerr apek iltewelhem, tyarrp-irrem. (St) *The split-jack splits open, cracks open.*
= **ltewelhem** (W,T)

ulthan (E) *n.* [SOME SPEAKERS]
1. ghost or spirit
2. skeleton
3. a skinny or boney person (an insult)
SEE ALSO anngirrenty, irrernng, akarnng[1]
= **lthan** (W,T)

ulthelth-ilem (E) *vt.*
1. tell someone you don't want something, knock back an offer of something
2. stop someone from going somewhere, tell someone to sit down and wait ◆ Ulthelth-ilem tha, menty aney anetyek, ahel irrety-alhekerr. (St) *I am telling that person not to go and to just sit down, in case they get angry.* ◆ Tyerrty arleng-theyel ayeng ulthelth-ilenty-alhek anem, alhetyekan anek. (St) *The people from another place came, and I was ready to go but they stopped me.*
= **lthwelth-ilem** (W,T)

ulthem (E) *vt.*
step on or tread on something; press or weigh down upon something; lean weight on something; be heavy ◆ Ingka ayenh ulthetyalay, rlkertek. Ulthem, ingka arrpenhel ngkwenhel, ntwa ayenh ulthem, rlkert intyem. (St) *Don't tread on my foot. If you tread on me with your foot I'll get sick.* ◆ Ingkel apek ulthenhem. Apmwa apek ulthenhem. Ker arlewatyerr apek ulthem alakenh ingkel, kel renh inem tayleng, kel ntewem anem renh. (St) *Stepping on something as you go along. Treading on a snake. You might step on the goanna with your foot, then grab it by the tail, then beat it on the ground.* ◆ Atnertel ulthem, atnert akngerr *too much*. Atnertel anem renh ulthem *he can't run*. (St) *His stomach is heavy, weighing down upon him — it's too big. He can't run because his stomach is too heavy.*
= **lthwem** (T)
annga ankwel lthwem (W,T), **annga ankwel ulthem** (E), **alknga ankwel ulthem** (E)
be very tired, have heavy eyelids (lit. 'sleep pressing on eyes') ◆ Ankwa intetyekan ulthem [*eyes*]. Ankwel ulthem alknga. (St) *I'm really sleepy. My eyes are heavy with sleep.*
ulthenty (E), **ulthinty** (E) *n.*
1. heavy (weight) ◆ Tyerrty apek ulthintyaw. Ywarnarl inem. Ywarn ayeng tywernelh-ilem. (St) *A heavy person. Too hard to lift up. I am unable to lift them up.*
2. heavy (of language or speaking style) ◆ Ntheyelkwer map arrengker, akern-antey. Anmatyerr *little bit* ulthentyarl, *heavy one*. Itna akenh angkem arrerlker *light one*. (St) *The* Ntheyelkwer *people speak fast, and high. Whereas [the other sort of] Anmatyerr is a little bit heavy. They speak in a 'light' way.*
= **lthwenty** (T)

ultyel-antey (E), **ultyel-ayerr** (E) [RESPECT LANGUAGE]
daylight, first light SEE UNDER **iltywel-antey**

ultyitywelty (E), **ultyetyulty** *n.*
a type of worm found in a kangaroo's stomach
= antya[1]
SEE ALSO ngangkar

ultyulty (E) a type of cricket SEE UNDER **ltywelty**

ulya (E) *n.*
1. shade, a shade or shade shelter, branches or things used to make a shade ◆ Ulya tha waly yanh-arey atwetyek alhey, ulya aketyek. (St) *I'm going to go and cut those branches, cut those branches to make a shade.* ◆ Uterneng ulyewarl irrpetyek alhetyek, ulyel anetyek, utern-kety ampemarl-kety. (St) *In the heat of the day [people] go under the shade, they sit in the shade so that the sun won't burn them.* ◆ Ulya angwarlp yanh-warl alheyew angerr-warl. (St) *Let's go to that thick shade over there.*
2. shadow (of something or somebody) ◆ Ulya akngerrakw-athek alpem ra arraty, akngerrakw anem irreynem. (St) *The shadow goes back due east, it goes towards the east.*
= **lywa** (W,T)

ulyelatanenh (E) *n.*
edible fat from a kangaroo's kneecap and leg ◆ Ulyelatanenh ampwethel-arleng anem. Ker anter akely weth. Ampweth iylwem, kel renh arlkwerl-anemel akemel. (Sa) *The* ulyelatanenh *is that small bit of fat that is found around the knee. The knee [cap] is lifted up and then the fat is cut out and eaten.*
SEE ALSO iylpernk, akepitelh, anter tyelh, apertaynp

ulyeper (E), **iylweper** (E), **iyleper** (E) *n.*
1. thigh
2. young seed pods of the dogwood, *awenth*
• = alywer[1]
= **lyweper**
kayl ulyeper (E), **kayl iylweper** (E)
a type of boomerang (curved shape) (kayl *'boomerang'*)
= alyang lyweper

ulyewem (E) *vt.*
chop something down, chop a tree
= **lywewem**

ulypma (E), **iylpmwa** (E), **ulpma** (E) *n.*
1. word
2. language (particularly an Aboriginal language) ◆ Ulypma angkerrerl-anemel. (Sa) *Speaking 'language' [i.e. an Aboriginal language].*
3. message, story
4. voice
5. Goes before the name of a particular language.
= angka[1], angkety
ulypma ilanthem (E)
send a message, pass on a message (ilanthem *'send'*)
= angka ilanthem
ulypma angkem (E)
speak an Aboriginal language (angkem *'speak'*)
= angka angkem
ulypma apekap (E)
unable to speak properly, having a speech impediment
= angka apekap
ulypmakert-ilem (E) *vt.*
release a person from speech taboo or

ceremonial ban on speaking; free someone to talk after silence (from mourning) (lit. 'make a person have speech') ◆ Artwel ulypma-akert-ilem akerter-iperr. (Sa) *The man is letting [the woman] talk after she has been silent because of sorry business.*
= angkeparr-ilem, angkakert-ilem, arrakert-ilem
ulypma ultakem (E), **iylpmwa ultakem** (E)
interrupt someone who is talking; stop talking; break up an argument (ultakem '*break*') ◆ Ulypma ultakem, atwetyekarl angkerrem-kety. *Break up the argument in case they start fighting.*
= angka ultakem

una (E), **ina** (E) *n.*
firewood that has been prepared by burning a tree down. Also referred to as *ura una.*
unewem (E), **inewem** (E) *vt.*
burn a tree down to make it fall so that it can be used for firewood ◆ Ura inewek tha, kel akelhetyenh ra. Kel tha inetyenh anem ura. (St) *I set fire to the tree, and then it will burn and break itself. Then I'll collect the wood and light a fire.*
SEE ALSO rlweth-ampem

unanth (T,E), **utnanth** (E) *n.*
scrub ◆ Werrk angerr kwa. *Can't* alherl mwetekay-akert, itya. Unanth angerrel. *Tyre* apek atanthek-athen. (T) *[There's] lots of scrub. [We] can't go with a car through the dense scrub. We might puncture a tyre.*
= **nwanth** (W,T)
artety unanth (T,E), **artety utnanth** (E)
mulga scrub (artety '*mulga*')
= **artety nwanth** (W,T)
unanth-unanth (T,E), **utnanth-utnanth** (E) *n.*
scrubby country

unanthem (E), **utnanthem** (E) *vt.*
not share food or drink; eat or drink greedily ◆ Arraremarl-kety alpeyaw, yanhel anthetyakenh. Ngkwerlp apek utnanthemel arlkwep-arlkwem, arraremarl-kety alpeyaw. (St) *Let's go back because we're not getting any, that person is not giving us any. They are chewing on their tobacco and not sharing it.* ◆ Unta atyeng utnanthek, wal ayeng akiwarr anem ngkweng anerl-anem, *too much* unta utnanthekarl mern atyeng-kety. (St) *You are not sharing with me, well I'm in bad mood with you because you didn't share your food with me.*
= **nwanthem** (T)
unanthelhem (E), **utnanthelhem** (E) *vi.*
eat or drink everything so there is nothing left; not save anything; finish food or drink in one sitting ◆ Utnanthelhem anem ayeng, *me might finish*-em ker apek, arrangkw anem iyntwarr. (St) *I might finish off all the meat and then there won't be any later.*
= **nwanthelhem** (T)

unarnpem (E) *vi.*
1. jump
2. bounce off, shoot off (sparks) ◆ Iyntetyan unarnpekarl ampem kwang yanh. (St) *The sparks that flew out are burning over there.*
unarnp-unarnp-alpem (E) *vi.*
hop or bound along (like a kangaroo)
◆ Aherrarl unarnp-unarnp-ketyaw. (Sa) *The kangaroo is bounding along.*
SEE ALSO anarnpem, intety-intety-irrem

unatyaker (E) type of lizard SEE UNDER **natyaker**

unek (E), **inwek** (E) *n.*
an overnight trip; camping out or staying somewhere for a night or a few nights
◆ Inwek atherrel apek ayeng alhetyek. (St) *I might go for two nights.*
= **anwek** (W,T)
unekel (E), **inwekel** (E) *adv.*
(doing something) overnight; camping out or staying somewhere for a night or for a few nights ◆ Alhem unekel, interl-alpem unek atherrel. Irrer unterl-alpem, apety-alpem angwerrel. (St) *Going camping out for two nights. Going hunting and then coming back in the evening.* ◆ Unekel alhetyelarl-kety, arteny anerl-ayntenherr-arey. (Sa) *[I'm] going to camp out, you all stay home.* ◆ Katyerr akerlanetyek unekel. (St) *Going and camping out to collect desert raisins.*
= **anwekel** (W,T)
unekel atherr-ingar (E),
inwekel atherr-ingar (E)
going for two nights, a two-night trip (atherr-ingar '*twice*') ◆ Unekel atherr-ingar alhem, kerek untherl-ayntetyek. (Sa) *Going camping out for two nights, hunting for two nights.*

unelh (E) *n.*
leaf of the bush banana, *alangkw, alkwarrer*
= altyey, ahertety[2]

unemangkerr (E), **unemangkarr** (E), **anemangkerr** (T,E), **anemangkarr** (E) *n.*
1. bush tomato (*Solanum chippendalei* (sandhill form)). Plant about 80 cm high (though it may grow to 1.5 m) with purple flowers, and fruits which are pale yellow when ripe. The seeds inside the fruit are inedible, and are thrown away.
2. edible fruit of the bush tomato
= kwenemangkarr, antyewarl, ngantyewarl
SEE ALSO anakety

unemarnt (E) *n.*
fruit of the native currant, *ahakey*, that has fallen to the ground
SEE ALSO ntyenp, atnamp

uneng[1] (E), **utneng** (E), **inweng** (E) *n.*
chest ◆ Uneng ayeng akeng-irrem. (St) *My chest is no good.* ◆ Utneng ayeng atwetyalaw. (Sa) *Don't hit me on the chest.*
= arnarnk
uneng atyetyek (E)
1. red-capped robin (*Petroica goodenovii*) (atyetyek *'red'*)
= akarl-atwerrey, alywerr-alywerr, kapert rnter-rnter
2. crimson chat (*Epthianura tricolor*) • SEE ALSO akarl-atwerrey
3. galah (*Eolophus roseicapillus*) • = ilenty, kerlelkerlelp

uneng[2] (E), **utneng** (E) *n.*
spirit of a person or living thing; soul
◆ Uneng anetyangarl arntety-irrem. *Something*-el aterel anthek. Arengk arrpwarnt angkerremelarl aterel anthek, kel akem-irrenty alpem ankwepenh, utneng anetyang irremel. (Sa) *[If a person] has no spirit then they get sick. Something might have given them a fright. Dogs barking might give the person a fright, then they get up from sleep, and their spirit goes [away].* ◆ Alewatyerr uneng-akert, ulkert uneng-akert, ker aherr uneng-akert, intelyapelyap an *all* akely-akely ingkerrek. Paytey akely-akely an *all*. (Sa) *Goannas have a spirit, perenties have a spirit, kangaroos have a spirit. Butterflies and all, all the little creepy crawlies [have a spirit].* ◆ Alhernter-rnem uneng-akert arrma, uneng rlterrk-akert arl ikwer-areyenh. (Sa) *White people have a spirit as well, their spirit is strong.*
SEE ALSO kwerrern, arrelty, rntwer[2]

unerlewem (E) *vt.*
ignore, not take notice of anyone
◆ Unerlewemel anem. Ngenh tha irrtyelh-ilemel unta unerlewem wal unta anerlanem. Mwernt-irremel anem. (Sa) *Sitting down and not taking any notice. I'm asking you to go but you are ignoring me. You're sitting there and refusing [to move].*
SEE ALSO arnernkey, mwernt-irrem, anwernt-irrem

unernengk (E) tawny frogmouth SEE UNDER nwernengk

unerreng (E), **utnerreng** (E), **itnwerreng** (E) *n.*
emu bush (*Eremophila longifolia*). Shrub to 4 m high, with green drooping leaves and red flowers which are pink inside. Leaves used as a washing medicine and for smoking babies.
= anwerreng (W)
unerrengayt (E), **utnerrengayt** (E), **itnwerrengayt** (E) *n.*
grub from the emu bush. Some regard this grub as being inedible. ◆ Tyap utnerrengayt. Utnerrengaytel arlkwem arna, arnarrp nhenhel arlkwep-arlkwem, atnyerleng ra arlkwem, utnerreng ra arlkwem. (St) *The emu bush grub. The grub from the emu bush eats the emu bush plant and the* atnyerleng *plant.*
SEE ALSO lhwek-lhwek, alwerrpent

uney (E), **utney** (E) *n.*
woma, sandhill python (*Aspidites ramsayi*)
= ahenenh, ahelh-ahelh
SEE ALSO ileway
= **nwey** (T)

uneynt (E), **utneynt** (E) *n.*
spear wattle, mulyati (*Acacia jensenii*). A shrub about 2.5 m high, with wide papery pods and edible seeds and grubs. ◆ Irrtyartel ap renh mpwarem. Tyapan anem akin ikwerel. Tyap anem artekerrel. Tyap utneynt. Atnyemayt-artek ra mperlker ra anem. Arlkwerretyart, atyerremel. Nyanyel-arey aperleyel then. Ntang kel anem, athem ampernemel. (Sa) *Spears are made from it. There is a grub there as well, in the roots. The spear wattle grub. They are white like witchetty grubs. [My] grannies and my father's mothers used to cook and eat them. There is a seed too, that was yandied and ground up.*

uneyntem (E) *vi.*
give off a strong smell ◆ Mern atwakey apek uneyntem anemaw, mwerr. (St) *The wild oranges are giving off a nice strong smell.*
SEE ALSO intyem[2]

Uneyntepwenty (E), **Utneyntepwenty** (E) *n.*
name of a place north of Spring Range

unhem (E), **utnhem** (E) *vt.*
1. bite someone or something ◆ Alknga ayeng alhwer-alhwer-irrek nhanyem amengel apekarl utnhek. (St) *This eye of mine here has bunged up, probably because flies bit it.* ◆ Arlety akwek urrperl, wal ra ahelengkwarl, tyerrty utnhemel wangkem anem ra. (St) *The* arlety *ant is small and dark in colour. It is aggressive, and if it bites a person then they will swell up.*
2. sting (insect)
3. pick, collect (of fruit) ◆ Katyerr, mwanyem utnhem renh, urtnewarl *fill*-em *up* ilem. (St) *Picking the bush tomatoes, the* katyerr *and the* mwanyem, *filling up the wooden dish.*
◆ Yakweth atyenh arlkwenhem katyerrel, tha utnhek angerr. (St) *I am filling my bag with desert raisin fruits, I picked a lot.*

4. kill (something by biting it); catch (food with mouth) ◆ Atetherr arlkwenhel atetherr angkerrerlek awem, wal antyenhem anem ra rlpwer-warl. Rlpwer-warl irrpety-alhem ra, kel utnhem ra, arlkwem anem ra — atetherr akuny akwek-akwek. (St) *The* atetherr arlkwenh *snake hears the budgerigars singing and then it climbs up to the hollow tree. It goes into the hollow, then it catches the budgie and eats it — the poor little budgie.*
= **nhwem** (W,T)

unherrem (E), **utnherrem** (E) *vi.*
1. bite each other
2. fight, argue ◆ Arengk atherr utnherrem. (St) *Two dogs are fighting.* ◆ Arengk utnherrerleng anwantherr ater wartam arraw-irrem, arengk-kety. (St) *We move around, frightened of the dogs that are fighting.* ◆ Tyerrty-arey utnherrem-antey. (St) *The people are still fighting.* ◆ Rtwek-rtwek atyenh kwenh utnherrirrek. Ker-kenh. Ker arlewatyerr-kenh kwenh atyenh impen utnherrirrek rtwek-rtwek atyenh. (St) *My poor dog was in a fight. My hunting dog. My special goanna dog was in a fight.*
= nhwerrem

unhelhem (E), **utnhelhem** (E) *vi.*
1. cut yourself ◆ Artwa utnhelhem rapekarl aparlp-ilekarl. (St) *The man is cutting himself in mourning because he has lost a relative.*
= akelhem
2. to play ◆ Ampa akwek map utnhelhepelhem. (St) *The little children are playing around.*

ahel unherrem (E), **ahel utnherrem** (E)
fight, argue with each other (ahel *'anger', 'angrily'*)
= **ahel nhwerrem** (W,T)

arrkenel unherrem (E), **arrkenel utnherrem** (E)
to play (arrken *'fun', 'in fun'*) ◆ Arlengel ampernem arrken-irretyek alherl-way, arrken utnherrerl-ayntetyek. (Sa) *You kids go off and play a long way away.*
= arrken-irrem
= **arrkenel nhwerrem** (W,T)

unkil-ilem (E) *vt.*
1. take sides in a fight; help someone in a fight; fight on behalf of someone
2. hit someone back; 'pay' someone back (for what they did wrong); 'square' someone back ◆ *Jail*-eng arraterleng, wal renh atwem unkil-ilemel arrpenhel arey. Unkil-iletyayntem renh atwemel, *jail*-eng ra arratenty. (Sa) *When he comes out of jail the others punish him to pay him back [for what he did wrong]. They pay him back when he comes out of jail.*
= ankwernem
SEE ALSO artengel-arem

unkinem (E), **inkwinem** (E) *vt.* = **unkil-ilem**

unkilelhem (E), **inkwinelhem** (E) *vi.*
1. submit yourself for 'payback' or traditional punishment
2. pay someone back (administer traditional punishment)
SEE ALSO anthelhem, ankwernelhem

unmely (E) *n.*
squashed, crushed, dented
SEE ALSO ipelhip-ilem
CAN SOUND A BIT LIKE amwely *'cadney lizard'*
= **mwely** (T,E)

unmely-ilem (E) *vt.*
squash, crush or dent something ◆ Tyampet atyenh nta unmely-ilem, amek-aretyakenhel. Ingkel ulthemel ap atyenh unmely-ilck nta tey-kenh impen. (St) *You squashed my billycan, you didn't avoid it. You trod on and crushed my special tea-making billycan.*
= **mwely-ilem** (T,E)

unmely-irrem (E) *vi.*
get squashed, crushed or dented
= **mwely-irrem** (T,E)

unmenth (E), **ulpmenth** (E) *n.*
flour ◆ Ulpmenth aweth arrerneyaw. (St) *Put some more flour in.*
SEE ALSO unmernt
= **nmwenth** (W,T)

unmernt (T,E), **ulpmernt** (T,E), **inmwernt** (E) *n.*
dust, dust haze, dust storm ◆ 'Ulpmerntarl artem-kety. Ahern ulpmernt-kety, rtakwel aney, ulpmernt akngerrarl pwem-kety alhurrp.' (Sa) *'The dust will cover us over. Look out for the dust, sit behind the windbreak because a big dust storm is blowing up.'*
= **nmwernt** (W,T)

unpa (E) *n.*
smelly (of a person or dog); having a bad smell
= **npwa** (W,T)

unpakert (E) *n.*
smelly (-akert *'having'*)
= **npwakert** (W,T)

unpangerr (E) *n.*
smelly (angerr[1] *'lots'*)
= **npwangerr** (W,T)

unpart (T)
sulky, sooky, angry, resentful
= **npwart** (W,T)

unpart-irrem (T) *vi.*
get sulky, angry or resentful ◆ Artwang nhak atyeng unpart-irrekaw! Apelkel war. (T) *That*

man is getting sulky for me! For no reason.
◆ Tyerrty nhenh unpart nthwep-nthwem, *no* rwekar-rwekar apek irrem. (T) *This person is sulky, not cheerful.*
SEE ALSO arnkely-irrem
= **npwart-irrem** (W,T)

unpay (E), **inpay** (T) *n.*
1. wire bush, tangled Lechenaultia (*Lechenaultia divaricata*). Leafless tangled shrub about 50 cm high.
2. narrow-leaved Goodenia (*Goodenia armitiana*)
SEE ALSO inpay-inpay, npway-npway

unpernem (E) *vi.*
make signs to show that particular relations with whom you have a respect or avoidance relationship are close; warn them of your presence. Women slap their hands on their thighs to show that their *ntyangkwelkng* are close by, and men make a special sound with their lips to indicate the presence of their *thampartey*.
SEE ALSO pwernkem[1]
unpernelhem (E) *vi.* = **unpernem**
◆ Ntyangkwelkng-kety unpernelhem. (St) *Women slap their hands on their thigh if their* ntyangkwelkng *is close.*
SEE ALSO pwernkelhem
CAN SOUND A BIT LIKE anpernem *'call someone or something a particular relation'*

unta (E) *prn.*
you (one person). Generally used as the subject (i.e. representing the 'doer' of the verb action) of both transitive and intransitive verbs. Some speakers, particularly those on the east, use *nga* as the subject of intransitive verbs. ◆ Irrernteng rwel anem untyem. Irrernt-kety artep unta untyem. (St) *In the cold you warm yourself by the fire. Because of the cold you warm your back.* ◆ Apentem unta ayeng ingkerneng, kel unta ayeng arety-alhem. (T) *You follow me from behind and then you see me.*
= **ntwa** (W,T)

untem (E) *vi.*
1. run, hurry along ◆ *Something* arlewatyerr. 'Arnterr alwernay kwenh, unta kwenh. Parrp untay kwenh!' (St) *There might be something there like a goanna. 'Chase it quickly. Run fast!'* ◆ Yanhel untetyewarrem-kety anwekantherr-warl. (St) *Those people are running towards us.*
2. (snakes) slither, crawl away
3. run away ◆ Untem tyerrty arrpenh-kety apek untem anem ra. (St) *She might be running away from another person.*
= arrtyanem
4. run out, flow out (liquids) ◆ Ayeng pelh-pelh untep-untem, iwenh apekarl arlkwek-penh. Katyerr tyatyarlkwerr apek tharl arlkwek. Tyatyarlkwerr katyerr-artek anteyarl. Pelh-pelh anem ayeng untem. (St) *I'm dribbling from eating something. Maybe it was that* tyatyarlkwerr *fruit that I ate. The* tyatyarlkwerr *is similar to the desert raisin plant. Now I'm dribbling.*
CAN SOUND A BIT LIKE urntem *'dance', 'rain', 'smoke'*
untelh-ilem (E) *vt.*
run off with someone or something ◆ Arelhel untelh-ilem mern apek ker apek, arrpenhel alwernemarl. (St) *The woman might run off with the food or the meat, and the others chase her.* ◆ Artwel mpwenyel inerl-alhek, untelh-ilek anem. (St) *The man got the woman and raced off with her.*

untemerr (T,E) buck spinifex, bull spinifex SEE UNDER **ntwemerr**

unteng atwem (E) *vt.*
make a thumping noise; thump someone (on the back) ◆ Artep unteng atway. (Sa) *Thump [her] on the back.*
SEE ALSO ntewem, nenty-nenty

untertety (E) *n.*
short cut ◆ Untertety-angkwerr alhem arengk-kety. (St) *Taking a short cut because of the dogs.*
= **ntwertety** (W,T)
untertety alhem (E)
take a short cut; go the most direct way; meet up with someone (?) (alhem *'go'*)
◆ Untertetyel alhem, marl arrpenh nhenhel alhek-warl. (St) *Taking a short cut, going the way that other woman went.*
= akwerterrp alhem
= **ntwertety alhem** (W,T)

untha (E) chips of wood left over after carving SEE UNDER **ntha**

untharr (E) *n.*
water found in the trunk of the bloodwood tree, *arrkernk*, and the ghost gum, *ilwemp*
◆ Arrkernk-penh. Atwemel ilepel apek atwem, kwaty thelelhem, arntap apek ngkernem, kel thelelhem, antywem anem. Kwaty mwerr, *waterbag like cold water.* (Sa) *From the bloodwood tree. You might chop it with an axe and the water pours out and then you drink it. It's good water, cold like from a waterbag.*
= **nthwarr** (W)

unthem (E) *vt.*
1. walk around
2. look around for something, go around looking for something ◆ Uthipel ap irrkerlanty rnternerl-anem thip akely nyingk

apek. Nyingkek unthemel atanthenhemel. Mperlker ap ra. (Sa) *The falcon goes along hunting small birds such as zebra finches. It looks for zebra finches and grabs them with its claws. They are white in colour.* ◆ Kerek uyarn unthem, arrangkw-antey apety-alpem uyarnarl unthek-penh. Ayeng apek arlewatyerrek uyarn unthemel apety-alpem. (St) *Looking round in vain for meat and returning home with nothing, after looking and finding nothing. I might come back after looking in vain for a goanna.* ◆ Ker arlewatyerr arraty tha atwek untherl-anemel. (St) *I went round looking for a goanna and I really got one.*
SEE ALSO apem
CAN SOUND A BIT LIKE anthwem *'seep or ooze out'*
= **nthwem** (W,T)
unthelh-ilem (E) *vt.*
make someone go somewhere ◆ Ingwerel unthelh-ilem, alhetyek apek *show*-warl. (Sa) *The other person is making me go to the show.*

untya (E) *n.*
back of the neck; nape of the neck, top of the shoulders ◆ Untya ampa akngenh-akngenh. Ker aherr akngenh-akngenh, ker aherr akngem untyel. Untya nhelkwerel ap atnhwert akngem ker aherr. (St) *The back of the neck is for carrying children. And carrying kangaroos. Kangaroos are carried around the top of the shoulders. Round the top of the shoulders here is where [you] carry a curled up kangaroo.* ◆ Atwem renh untya, tnyantel renh atwem. (St) *If someone is hit on the back of the neck it can kill them.*
= **ntywa** (W,T)
untyel angem (E), **untyel akngem** (E)
carry something on the top of the shoulder; carry something round the back of the neck (angem *'carry'*) ◆ Untyel akngetyek, ampa tha atyenh untyel inerl-alhetyek. (St) *I'm carrying my child along on my shoulders.*
= anhwert angem
= **ntywel angem** (W,T)

untyarrkwer (E), **intyarrkwer** (E) *n.*
neck bone, lower part of the back of the neck. Also referred to as *ker untyarrkwer*. ◆ Kerek aherrek ayeng angkem. 'Untyarrkwer angetyenh, ker tha arlkwetyenh untyarrkwer kwenh.' (St) *I might talk about kangaroo meat. 'Bring some neck bone, I'll eat some neck bone meat.'*
= **ntyarrkwer** (W,T)

untyem[1] (E) *vi.*
warm oneself by the fire or in the sun ◆ Irrernteng rwel anem untyem. Irrernt-kety artep unta untyem. (St) *In the cold [you] warm yourself by the fire. Because of the cold you warm your back.* ◆ Untetyek ayeng urel apek untyem-athek anerlek apek untyetyek. Uternel untetyek akin. Artep apek ayeng untyetyek, iltya apek ayeng untyetyek irrernteng. Urel. (St) *I'll warm myself by the fire, facing away from the fire. I might warm myself in the sun as well. When it's cold I might warm my back or my hands by the fire.*
SEE ALSO ampem[2]
CAN SOUND A BIT LIKE antywem *'drink'*
= **ntywem**[1] (T)

untyem[2] (E), **intywem** (E) *adv.*
facing away from someone or something; going in a direction away from or opposite to someone or something
SEE ALSO ularr
CAN SOUND A BIT LIKE antywem *'drink'*
= **ntywem**[2] (W,T)
untyem-irrem (E) *vi.*
turn away; turn your back on someone; face away from someone or something ◆ Arlkwep-arlkwem untyem-irremel, ankeyel, *might* anthekerr arrpenhek. (St) *Eating facing away from others, in case you have to give [some food] to them.*
= **ntywem-irrem** (W,T)
untyem-ilem (E) *vt.*
make someone or something go backwards
= **ntywem-ilem** (W,T)
untyem-athek (E) *adv.*
facing away from someone or something; going in a direction away from or opposite to someone or something ◆ Ulaneng anetyang untyem ra anep-anem. Untyem-athek ra anep-anem. Untyemel-athek anep-anem. (St) *[He] is not sitting facing (the speaker) — he's sitting with his back turned.*
= **ntywem-athek** (W,T)
untyemek-untyem (E) *adv.*
back to back; facing away from each other
= **ntywemek-ntywem** (W,T)

untyerr (E), **ntywerr** (T) *n.* [RESPECT LANGUAGE]
water ◆ Untyerr-ayerr ahanelh-ilay. (St) *Take the water to your husband [said by a woman to her daughter]*
SEE ALSO kwaty

untyerr anyenem (E), **untyerr atnyenem** (E), **ntywerr anyenem** (E) *vt.*
mash certain types of fruit up with water ◆ Ntyerrm apek untyerr atnyenem, antyerrk, kwatyel anem. (St) *The dry seeds of the dogwood are mashed up in water.*
= ntywerrkem

untyety (E) *n.*
hot earth, warmth, warm things ◆ Untyetyel ampa item. Arrwekelenyel itetyam untyetyel. (St) *Babies were warmed in the hot earth. The olden-time people used to warm them up in the hot earth.*
SEE ALSO awerrth
= **ntywety** (W,T)
untyety-irrem (E) *vi.*
get warm (person or place) ◆ Mantarr *warm one*-ek irrpemel untyety-irrem, untyetyek irrpemel. (St) *[I'm] going to get into some warm clothes to warm up.* ◆ Uternel untyety-irremel ampem. (Sa) *Warming [yourself] up in the sun.*
SEE ALSO irrernt-irremk
= **ntywety-irrem** (W, T)
untyety-ilem (E) *vt.*
make a person or place warm; warm something up
= **ntywety-ilem** (W,T)
untyey (E) *n.*
1. northern corkwood, bootlace tree (*Hakea chordophylla*). Tree to 5 m high, with twisted branches, corky fissured bark and yellow flowers.
2. fork-leaved corkwood, long-leaved corkwood (*Hakea divaricata*). Tree to 7 m high, with twisted branches, corky fissured bark and yellow-green flowers. Leaves are branched or forked.
3. honey from the northern corkwood and the fork-leaved corkwood [SOME SPEAKERS].
SEE ALSO ntyarleyarleng
= **ntywey** (W,T)
untyeyamp (E) *n.*
honey from corkwoods. Also referred to as *ngkwarl untyeyamp*. ◆ Untyeyel anem ngkwarl untyeyamp. Awantyem renh, *treacle*-artek rrpwerl mwerr-angker. (St) *The corkwood honey is found on the corkwood tree. It's nice and dark-coloured, like treacle, and you eat it.*
= ntyweyangkwarl
SEE ALSO tyan
= **ntyweyamp** (T,E)
untyey aperrk (E)
burnt bark of the northern corkwood (aperrk '*charcoal*'). This is used to rub on babies to stop them from sweating and to rub on their foreheads to stop them burping.
untyeyapert (E) *n.*
a type of ant
unyem (E) *vi.*
make a droning or humming noise ◆ Thep unernengk unyep-unyerl. (St) *Tawny frogmouths make a humming sound.*
SEE ALSO arnwer-irrem, alyerrem
unyenem (E), **utnyenem** (E) *vt.*
look up for something, look upwards ◆ Tha ngkwarl arwengalkerek apek utnyenepenem. (St) *I am looking upwards for sugarbag.*
ura (T,E) *n.*
1. fire ◆ Urel mern item. (T) *Cooking on the fire.* ◆ Ura pew-ilem lherrm-irretyek. (Sa) *Blow the fire so that it catches alight.* ◆ Ura irrerntek arrtyey, irrerntekarl arrewem-kety. (Sa) *Light a fire because of the cold, because [I'm] shivering with cold.* ◆ Urepenh iltyampekarl arnterrarl ampek. Ingka iltyampem akin urepenh. Urel ampenty. (Sa) *After being burnt by the fire [the skin] blisters. Feet can blister as well from being burnt in the fire.*
2. firewood ◆ Lyernt-wem tha ura apek. (St) *I might heap up the firewood.*
3. matches
4. A general word that goes before things to do with fire.
5. battery (of car)
= **rwa** (W,T)
uralep (E) *n.*
1. firestick ◆ Uralep-akert alhetyam, rltimp weth-lkwer itemel, renh-akertarl alhetyam kerek apek. Artety-penh, rltimp weth-lkwer, uralep anem renh akngem, arrernemel, renh-akert alhetyart arrwel. (St) *In the old days people went round with firesticks, lighting bits of bark and things like that, and taking them with them when they went hunting. Bits of bark from the mulga tree, that's the sort of thing that was used for the firesticks that people carried with them before.*
2. a group of stars
ura ngkwelty (E)
kindling wood (ngkwelty '*bits and pieces*')
ura irlpart (E)
a log (irlpart '*log*') ◆ Ura irlpart weth tha atyeng inerl-alpeyew, ura atyeng ampetyek irlpart. (St) *I'll go back and get that log for myself, so that I can burn it for myself.*
ura kwert (E)
smoke (kwert '*smoke*')
ura kwert-kwert (E)
blue or grey in colour, 'smoky' in colour
Urapenty, Rwapenty *n.*
1. Sandover River
2. Mt Hay
Both of these places are associated with *ura* 'fire' Dreaming
uranng (E) *n.*
1. a familiar place, home place
2. a familiar person, good friend, someone

who has been associated with a place for a long time and is well liked ◆ Merelarl anyent-antey ipelty angerr-irrek kel ra mer ingwer-warl alpemel aleth, *two years* apek alpenty-penh kel ra apety-alpem, 'Nhantey pelty atyenhan uranng apety-alpek kwenh'. (Sa) *If a person makes a lot of friends in one place, and then they go away to another place for two years or so and then they come back [people say], 'Here my friend, my dear friend has come back'.*
• SEE ALSO pelty, akeweny
CAN SOUND A BIT LIKE rwang *'fire'*
= **rwanng**
uranng-ilem (E) *vt.*
make friends; make someone get used to a place; familiarise someone with a person or place ◆ Ipelty mpwarem, uranng mpwarem, ampa akely apek war arengk apek. Uranng-ilem. (Sa) *Making friends, a child or a dog. Familiarising them with something.*
= **rwanng-ilem**
uranng-irrem (E) *vi.*
get used to something; get used to a place; become familiar with a place or a person ◆ Uranng mer ingwer-they apetyenty uranng-irrety-alhemel anetyam. (Sa) *The familiar person who came from another place went and got used to the place.* (?)
= **rwanng-irrem**
urarrernem (T,E) *vt.*
swear or growl at someone; talk badly to someone; argue all the time ◆ Alhengkey-ilemel ilterrem. Urarrernetyal, mawenng. (T) *Swearing at the person and making them feel not wanted. Don't growl at them, it brings bad luck.* ◆ Urarrernek unta atyeng. (St) *You growled at me.*
= rwang arrernem
SEE ALSO iltem, urarrey ilem, alhengkelh-ilem
urarrey ilem (E) *vt.*
really swear at someone; call someone very bad names
urarreytnelhem (E), **urarretnyelhem** (E) *vt.*
= **urarrey ilem**
urarreytnelhemel iltem (E) = **urarrey ilem**
SEE ALSO alhengkelh-ilem, urarrernem, iltem
urawenyerr-ilem (E), **rawenyerr-ilem** (E) *vt.*
make a nuisance of oneself; disturb or interrupt someone ◆ Terangkel-rnem urawenyerr-iletyel ankwa ayntetyakenh. (Sa) *The drunks disturb us and stop us from sleeping.*
urayerrp (E) *n.*
black-headed python (*Aspidites melanocephalus*) ◆ Ker urayerrp arlkwerretyartarl ap renh, ampernemel arlkwerretyart renh. (Sa) *The black-headed python used to be eaten, cooked and eaten.*
= antwerrkenh, arrwerrperl
= **rwayerrp** (T)
urekethwerek (E) *n.*
rushing around, being unsettled or unable to sit still, being annoying, making a lot of noise
= **arweketherwek** (W,T)
urekethwerek-ilem (E) *vt.*
stir things up, stir someone up; make things unsettled, argue all the time; create a disturbance; annoy or disturb people; make a lot of noise ◆ Lyet apekarl itna alhem antywetyek apek, kwer-penh apety-alpem urekethwerek angkety-alperl-anem. (St) *They are going off today to drink, then after that they'll come back and stir everyone up.*
= **arweketherwek-ilem** (W,T)
urelh-urelh-ilem (E) *vt.*
block something off with earth
urelyarr (E) *n.*
diamond dove (*Geopelia cuneata*)
= kwerlekwek, kwerler-kwerler
SEE ALSO lerakwenty
urelyerrty (E) light-skinned, reddish in colour SEE UNDER **arelyerrty**
uremeny (E), **rwemeny** (E) *adv.*
fast, quickly, being in a hurry ◆ Uremeny apetya arternp alherlanetyang! (Sa) *Come here quickly, don't be slow!* ◆ Uremeny ap ra atnarnp-atnarnp-alpem tyekarnparnp, ahelengkw. (Sa) *The bull ant jumps along quickly, they're aggressive.*
= arrengker
SEE ALSO parrp, aher
uremeny-irrem (E), **rwemeny-irrem** (E) *vi.*
dodge, move sideways ◆ Rwemeny-irrem ayeng alakenh, apwert-kety, *or* kayl-kety. (St) *I am dodging to avoid rocks, or boomerangs.*
SEE ALSO inangkal-irrem
urengenty (E) *n.*
aggressive, dangerous ◆ Urengentyarl apetyem. Ahelengkw-ahelengkw yanh apetyem-kety. (St) *Look out, that person is coming along aggressively.*
= ahelengkw, ahangerr
urety (E) *n.*
wooden water dish
SEE ALSO atywekal, kwerlintyerr, panth, lwengkart[2], irrkwely[2], alparr[1], irrkwa, lengarr, rnwa, urna, arlketh[1]
urew (E) *n.*
flood, floodwater, running water. Also referred to as *kwaty urew.* ◆ Kwaty urew, tharl amwerrk amek-arety-alhern kwaty urew,

ulpayek. *Shopping*-ek alhek, amek-arerl-alpek. (St) *Just yesterday I went and was blocked by the floodwater in the creek. I went to go shopping and I was blocked off and came back.*
SEE ALSO aleny
= rew

urewap-imperreny (E), **urewap-imperrenh** (E), **urewap-imperr** (E), **rewap-imperr** (E) *n.*
dragonfly (imperrem[1] *'go along the top of the water'*)
= rew inperrenh, kwaty-inperrenh, warepelh-pelh, kapert[2]
SEE ALSO arntirn

ureynelhem (E) *vi.*
go out of sight behind something; hide oneself behind something ◆ Ureynelhek, alengk-iwelhek. Marl nhak atyengety alengk anemarl iwelh arnel nheng arrengakw, arnel arrengakw. (St) *Going behind something to hide yourself. That woman is hiding herself from me on the other side of those trees.*
= **rwernelhem**

urimpering (E), **rwempereng** (E), **rwimpereng** (E), **rempereng** (W) *n.*
1. a type of bird, possibly the mulga parrot (*Psephotus varius* (?)) ◆ Urimpering arlpaty-apeny *colour*-an anem *green one yellow one yellow one.* (Sa) *The mulga parrot is similar in colour to the ring necked parrot, green and yellow.*
2. princess parrot (*Polytelis alexandrae*) (?)
SEE ALSO anenperetyarr

uring (E) *n.*
tawny frogmouth (*Podargus strigoides*)
= nwernengk
SEE ALSO arrthwarrthw

urinp (E) *n.*
1. warmth, hot, heat
2. hot weather ◆ Antywantywerl-wey urrek, teyek-amparr tha antywantywerl-wey, urinp nhenh. (St) *Wait while I drink this quickly, I'll quickly drink this hot tea first.* ◆ Arrarlp-wem pelangket iwem, urinparl ayeng irrem irrkwer anemarl-kety, arrarlp-wem. (St) *Throwing the blankets off, because I'm getting hot, feeling hot.*
= **rwernp**

urinp-irrem (E) *vi.*
get hot, warm up ◆ Urinp-irrem ayengaw, urrampemarl kwang arlka ayeng. (St) *I'm getting really hot, my body is burning.*
= **rwernp-irrem**

urinp-ilem (E) *vt.*
heat something up; warm something up ◆ Rntwerel itetyek aker, apwert urinp-ilemel, ker anem arrernem. (St) *Cooking the meat in a pit, heating up the rocks and then putting the meat in.*
= **rwernp-ilem**

uripem (E) *vi.*
move backwards and forwards against someone or something in a sexual fashion
= ahetyem

urirrem[1] (E) *vi.*
go behind something or through something and come out the other side
= **rwerrem** (W,T)

urirrem[2] (E) *vi.*
tell lies ◆ Unta apek urirrepirrem, urrtyirrem. (St) *You are telling lies.*
= urrtyirrem

urit (E), **rwet** (T), **urit-urit** (E), **rwet-rwet** (T) *n.*
a bluish-coloured kangaroo

urla (E) *n.*
1. forehead ◆ Apwertel wentyan imarewanemarl, innga anem wemel. Urla apek artep apek wem, imarewanemel. (Sa) *When [you] throw a rock it might bounce back and hit someone. Bounce back and hit someone on the forehead or on the back.*
2. clean honey from the native beehive or sugarbag
3. the first or front part of something ◆ Urla, mwetek *Toyota* yanh tnepetnem ularr-athek. Arrwekel-penh yanh anem ilep-ilem urlan. (St) *That Toyota is standing there facing this way. The front part there is called* urla.
= **rlwa** (W,T)

kwaty urla (E)
the front or lighter part of an approaching storm (kwaty *'water'*)

alhwerrp urla (E)
the beginning of winter (alhwerrp *'winter'*) ◆ Alhwerrp urla, irrerntarl irrety-alhem anem alhwerrp. Arrewerl-anetyek anem, alhwerrp urlel — lyetant irrernt-irrek. (St) *In the beginning of winter it starts to get cold. Then [people] start to shiver in the beginning of winter — when it has just got cold.*
= **alhwerrp rlwa** (W,T)

utern urla (E)
the beginning of summer (utern *'sun', 'summer'*)
= **twern rlwa** (W,T)

urlather-ather (T,E) *n.*
a person with a wide or broad forehead, or with a balding or receding hair-line (ather-ather *'flat'*)
= **rlwather-ather** (W,T)

urla alkey [RESPECT LANGUAGE]
kangaroo (alkey *'long'*)

SEE ALSO aherr, tyantwerr

urlamp (E) a large expanse of water SEE UNDER **ulamp**

urlamp (T) stone knife (used for cutting meat) SEE UNDER **werlamp**

urlamparrwek (E) white-necked heron SEE UNDER **ulamparrwek**

urlamperrenty (E), **urlamperreny** (T) the congregation (of a church); a gathering, a lot of people, everybody SEE UNDER **werlamperrenty**

urlanem (E), **ulanem** (E) *vt.*
sort things out; pick something out
= angakem, urrarem

urlank-anyem become drowsy, nod off to sleep SEE UNDER **rlwank anyem**

urlant-urlant (T,E) *n.*
spying on someone; peeping out at someone ◆ Urlantel-urlantel arem tyerrty arrpenh werrkeng. (T) *Spying on someone from the scrub.*
SEE ALSO kert-arem
= **rlwant-rlwant** (W,T)

urlarel (E) taking over or intervening in a situation (when you think someone else is not acting appropriately) SEE UNDER **rlwarel**

urlart (E) *n.*
1. a group of one kind of thing, with nothing else; entirely, mostly, only, just ◆ Marlant-arey alhem urlart, marl map, urlart-antey alhem marlant angerr. (St) *Just all the women are going, just lots of women.*
2. clean, pure (not mixed up with anything else)
= **rlwart** (T, W)
urlart-ilem (E) *vt.*
sort things out, separate one thing out from another
= **rlwart-ilem** (W,T)
urlart-irrem (E) *vi.*
become clear, become separated
= **rlwart-irrem** (W,T)

urlatwem (E) *vt.*
meet someone ◆ Urlatwek tha ngenh nhenhek, untarl apetyek. (St) *You came and I met you here.*
CAN SOUND A BIT LIKE ilatwem *'bang something on the ground'*
= **rlwatwem** (W)

urlaty angkem (E) *vi.*
apologise for behaviour, say sorry, face up to a person you have wronged, pacify, placate, admit guilt in a situation, face up to ritual punishment (?) (angkem *'speak'*) ◆ Urlaty angketyek — urlaty ilelhetyek, ra apekarl akengenty angkek. Iltekarl apek ra. Arrarletyel apek ra iltek. Urlaty anem ra ilelhem. 'Arratyaw, ayeng terangkel ngkweng angkek. Unta anem ayenh iltaw.' (St) *Apologising — apologising for himself, after he had said something bad. Or after he has sworn at someone or growled at someone. Then he says he's sorry. 'It's true that when I swore at you I was drunk. Now you can swear at me.'*
SEE ALSO nyerr urrparelhem
= **rlwaty angkem** (W,T)

urlaylp (E) *n.*
1. kurdaitcha, kurdaitcha man, ritual executioner ◆ Artwa urlaylp, apetyem ingwel atwetyek, awerrkem anem ternng. Urlaylp arwengk aretyakenh kwenh anwantherr. (St) *The kurdaitcha comes in the night to kill people, to wring their necks. We can't see the kurdaitcha.* ◆ Pwentyel renh artarrernem arrmel urlaylpel, kel renh angkwerriwemel mwerrarl irrem, iteth anem alherl-anem pwenty inenty ngangkar-akert. (Sa) *The kurdaitcha puts a curse on someone as well, and then the person gets better when they are massaged, they become lively again after the traditional healer gets the sickness out.*
= ngkekern, inenty, kwertaty, nwernternenty
SEE ALSO melarlp, arlelty
2. black phase of a witchetty grub ◆ Tyap ra tyerrelhek urlaylp anem. Aympelh-akert ra alhem antelyapelyap anem, urlaylparl intek-penh. Urlaylp-irrek, urrperl-irrek. *Then the grub comes out as* urlaylp *then. Then it has wings and is a moth, after lying there as* urlaylp. *It transforms and gets darker.*
= **rlwarlp** (W,T)
mwetekay urlaylp (E)
unregistered car or vehicle (mwetekay *'car'*) ◆ Mwetekay urlaylp-akertarl yanh alhep-alhem pwetyel ant alhenh-alhenh. Ingkwernetyakenh. (St) *That person is going around with an unregistered car that can only go in the bush. It hasn't been registered.*
= mwetekay ngkekern
tyap urlaylp (E)
the chrysalis stage of a grub (tyap *'grub'*)
= tyap ngkekern
urlaylp-irrem (E) *vi.*
1. turn into a kurdaitcha
2. turn into a moth or butterfly; transform or metamorphose (grub) ◆ Urlaylparl-irrem kwerel. Anyemayt urlaylp-irrem. Mperlkerek-amparr ra intem, kel urlaylp anem ra irrem, kel tyerr anem irrem, nkem anem. (St) *The grub turns into a moth there. The witchetty grub transforms. At first it is white, then it turns into a moth, then it comes out [of the hole in the*

ground].
= ngkekern-irrem
SEE ALSO irrarl-irrem, akarternem
= **rlwarlp-irrem** (W,T)

urlelth (E) *n.*
dug into the ground; in hibernation underground ◆ Urlelth arrernem kel ra tyerrelhemel alhem, urlelthan arrernekarl arlewatyerrel. (St) *The goanna digs itself into the ground and then it comes out and goes, after hibernating.*
SEE ALSO atyerrp, ilka[1]
= **rlwelth** (W,T)
urlelth ipelhem (E) *vi.*
dig self into a hole or burrow (some animals); dig self into the ground; hibernate
◆ Arlewatyerr urlelth ipelhem, an alhem anem ra tyerrelhemel. Awelhemel, angayel arlkwetyek. (St) *Goannas dig themselves into the ground, and then they come out and go round. If they feel hungry they get something to eat.*
◆ Atyerrparl urlelth ipelhem irrernt-taym. Urlelthel aynterl-anem kwen, nthanh tyerrelhetyanh. Urlelth ipelhenty. (Sa) *[Animals] dig themselves into the ground to hibernate during the cold weather. They lie there underground and they don't come out.*
SEE ALSO ipelhem, kelerr ipelhem

urlem-anem (E) *vi.*
1. watch out for something; poke head out and look out for something; peep out from behind something ◆ Uthip akwerrk-rnem urlem urlem-ananem akernel, iylpwerel, urlem-ananem mam ikwerenhek arntarnt-arelherl-anem. (Sa) *The baby birds are peeping out from high up in the hollow tree, watching out for their mother who looks after them.*
◆ Urlem-ayntetyel arrpem rtakwelan, urlem-anemel arerl-anem. (Sa) *[You] peep out from behind the windbreak as well, sitting and watching out.*
SEE ALSO urlant-urlant
2. rise (sun) ◆ Utern urlem-anentyem ingwepenh angerrakw-they. (St) *In the morning the sun rises in the east.*
SEE ALSO urla
= **rlwem-anem** (W,T)

urlemp (E) *adv.*
staying home; staying in one place ◆ Urlemp ayeng anerl-anem arteny nhenhel-antey, arleng alhetyakenh. (St) *I am staying here at home, and not going far.*
SEE ALSO urlert, arteny[1], antarl, rlwepety, urlepety
CAN SOUND A BIT LIKE ulemp *'ghost gum'*
= **rlwemp** (W)

urlengerek-urlenger (E) (doing something) face to face SEE UNDER **ulengerek-ulenger**

urlengimar (E), **rlwengimar** (E), **rlwengemar** (T) *adv.*
shading eyes with hand ◆ Urlengimarel alakenh arep-arem. 'Apetyepetyemaw rntwarr yanh.' (St) *Looking out and shading your eyes. 'There they are coming in the distance over there.'*
= merlpeng

urlenkernem (E) break or dislocate (an animal's leg) SEE UNDER **ulernkernem**

urlepety (E) *adv.*
staying home; staying in one place
SEE ALSO arteny[1], antarl, rlwemp, urlemp, urlert
= **rlwepety** (W)
urlepety anem (E)
stay home; stay in one place ◆ Urlepety-antey ayengan anep-anem, apmer arrpenh-kenh-warl alhetyakenh. (St) *I am still staying in one place, I'm not going to anyone else's place.*
= **rlwepety anem** (W,T)

urler (T,E), **iylwer** (E) *n.*
1. sand
2. sandhill country, sandy country. Also referred to as *ahern urler.* ◆ Anemangkarr apwertel then urlerel then anem. (Sa) *The bush tomato grows in the hills and in the sandy country.* ◆ Kwatyelarl iylwer-ilek ap renhey ahelh apmer mwerr-angker anem, iylwer ant anem. (St) *It was the rain that made the place all sandy, just sand.*

urlernem (E), **urlertnem** (E) *vi.*
wait to ambush somebody; lie in wait for someone or something ◆ Kerek ayeng urlernemel aney, ntatel. Ker ankerr apek apetyem, arerl-anemey, arnarem ra. Ker renh anem atyerrem maketel, irrtyartel. (St) *I am lying in wait for the emu, in the hide. The emu comes along, and I see it. Then I shoot the emu with a gun, or spear it.*
SEE ALSO mpwelhem[1], arrap-anem

urlerrker (E) *adv.*
1. (doing something) backwards and forwards; (doing something) back to someone ◆ Urlerrker ratherr apay-unherrem. Aylern apay-unha, kenh tha ngenh urlerrker apay-unheyam arrpemarl. Urlerrkerant-atherr. (Sa) *Those two are asking each other things. [You] ask us, and then I ask you back again. Backwards and forwards to each other.*
2. do something face to face
SEE ALSO ularr, akepenh
= **rlwerrker** (W,T)

urlerrker-urlerrkerek (E) *adv.*
face to face; 'square and square' (for example, two brothers-in-law who are married to each others' sisters); (doing something) backwards and forwards to each other
SEE ALSO ulengerek-ulenger, ularrek-ularr, ulanengek-ulaneng
= **rlwerrkerek-rlwerrkerek** (W,T)
urlerrkerek-urlerrker antherrem (E)
give things to each other reciprocally, give things backwards and forwards to each other
= **rlwerrkerek-rlwerrkerek antherrem** (W,T)

Urlerrperl (E) *n.*
name of a waterhole in the Alhalker/Atnangker area

urlert (E) *adv.*
staying in one place; being on your own; keeping to yourself ◆ Apmer anyentel anep-anem urlert. (St) *Staying in one place.*
SEE ALSO urlemp, urlepety, rlwepety, arteny[1], antarl

urlertnem (E) wait; wait to ambush somebody SEE UNDER **urlernem**

urleth-urleth (T,E) *n.*
bits and pieces ◆ Apmwa parip. Rrweyan arlkeny-arlkeny. Marlan *yellow one yellow one* nteny-nteny war. *Whistle*-artekap ra irrerl-anem iparip. Rnwem-apenyarl ap ra. Atwemel renh wal urleth-urleth akelhemarl ra. Atwenty. Urnemek-athen atwenty, akuny-amperl. Kel ingkernant anem *sorry*-irremel. (St) *The* parip *snake. The male is stripey. The female is yellowish and just spotty. They are similar to snakes and they make a sort of whistling sound. If you hit one they break into bits. If you think the* parip *is [another sort of] snake and you kill the poor thing then you'll feel sorry later.*
urleth-akem (T,E) *vt.*
break something up into bits, break something in half, split (a log); cut something up (akem *'cut'*)
= rlkwerr ltwakem
SEE ALSO mpalernem, mpal-inem, mpal-akem, mpalty-akem
= **rlweth-akem**
urleth atwem (T,E)
chop or cut something into bits (atwem *'hit'*) ◆ Ker urleth atwem akwek-ilemel, akwek anem arlkwetyenheng. (T) *Cutting the meat up into bits and making it smaller, and then eating the smaller bits.*
= **rlweth atwem**
urleth-wem (T,E) *vt.*
break something with a missile
SEE ALSO ultakem
= **rlweth-wem**

urleympeymp (E) hairline; top of the forehead SEE UNDER **urlimpimp**

urleynterr[1] (E), **urlintyerr** (E), **rleynterr** (E) *n.*
ridge of the nose between the eyes; bridge of the nose
= **rlwentyerr** (T)

urleynterr[2] (E) *n.*
unripe fruit of the desert raisin, *katyerr*
= pwarr
SEE ALSO kwart

urlimpimp (E), **urleympeymp** (E) *n.*
hairline, top of the forehead, hair just above forehead

urlintyerr (E) ridge of the nose between the eyes SEE UNDER **urleynterr**

urlker (E) *n.*
1. unsettled, walking around too much, being a nuisance ◆ Urlker arternp anetyakenh, talkwant alherl-wetyel. (Sa) Urlker *is not settling down, going backwards and forwards.*
2. behaving in a flirtatious way, showing off
= **arlkwer**
urlker-urlker (E) *n.* = **urlker**
= **arlkwer-arlkwer**

urlkernem (E) *vt.*
rinse something out to clean it ◆ Tyampet urlkernay, tey antywetyek. (Sa) *Rinse out the tin so that [you] can drink tea from it.*
urlkernelhem (E) *vi.*
dissociate yourself from your family; say that you are not someone's relation ◆ 'Ayengan ikngwerarlaw — ayengan arrekantherrenh anetyakenharl.' Urlkernelhem, aywepelhem. (Sa) *'I am different, another person — not your relation.' [That's]* urlkernelhem, *telling people to leave you alone.*

urlkerrp (E) *n.*
1. froth, suds, soap powder
2. beer [SOME SPEAKERS]
= **rlkwerrp**
urlkerrp-urlkerrp (E) *n.*
frothy
SEE ALSO akwemp-akwemp
= **rlkwerrp-rlkwerrp**
urlkerrp-irrem (E) *vi.*
get frothy, froth up
= **rlkwerrp-irrem**

urlpa (E) *n.*
red ochre
SEE ALSO arwethenp, atywerlk, ngwenty-ngwenty, karntewarr
CAN SOUND A BIT LIKE ulpa *'soft'*
= **rlpwa** (W,T)

urlpa atyetyek (E)
red ochre (atyetyek *'red'*)
= rlpwang rnter-rnter

urlpat (T,E) *n.*
clear country that has been burnt; a large expanse of burnt country ◆ Urlpatel urntetyek alewatyerrek apek. (St) *Going round the burnt country looking for goannas.* ◆ Urlpat-ilem, urlpat angerr anem mpwarem. Kel akethel anem renh kerek anem aretyek alhem, arlewatyerrek apek urlpatel. (T) *Burning the country to make a big burnt area. Then going looking for goannas on the burnt area.*
= **rlpwat** (W,T)

urlpat-ilem (T,E) *vt.*
1. singe fur, hair or scales off an animal ◆ Ker aherr urlpat-ilem alta. (St) *Singeing the fur off the kangaroo.* ◆ Ker tha iweyam urlpat-iletyek. Ker nhenh inemel aherr apek, ker rapet apek, alewatyerr apek, urlpat-iletyek tha. Urlpat-ilem alta. (St) *I'm throwing the animal [on the fire] to singe the fur off. I might get this kangaroo, rabbit, or goanna, and then I'll singe the fur or scales off. Burn the hair off.*
2. burn grass, burn country to clean it ◆ Arnam urlpat-ilem amwekety, urel alepel nthilemel urlpat-ilem. (St) *Burning the grass because of snakes, lighting the grass with a firestick and burning it off.* ◆ Arnam angerr urlpat-ilek. (St) *Lots of grass was burnt.*
= **rlpwat-ilem** (W,T)

urlpat-ilelhem (E) *vt.*
cut one's hair (in mourning)
= akampwerr-ilelhem
SEE ALSO arrtyelhem

urlpat-irrem (E) *vi.*
become burnt (country), become cleared by burning
SEE ALSO urrempelty-irrem

urlpentyem (E) *v.*
pull something out of something; squeeze something out of something else
= **rlpwentyem** (W,T)

urlperrng atwelhem (E), **arlpwerrng atwelhem** (E) *vi.*
beat rhythm on lap with cupped hands to accompany ceremonial dancing (women) (atwelhem *'hit self'*)
= **rlpwerrng atwelhem**

urlta (E) *n.*
1. big, large ◆ Kwerraly urltant-atherr, Arwenpeng an Mwer-nheng ratherr. (Sa) *They are both big stars, the Daylight Star and the stars called 'Mwer-nheng'.* ◆ Arwerl urlta. *A big tree.*
2. boss, senior person, spokesperson, elder ◆ Urltarl yanh, akngerr-pat. (St) *That's the boss there, the senior person.*
SEE ALSO angerr[1], angerrety, artelhampw, artelh[3], awer, ilkwa[2]
CAN SOUND A BIT LIKE ulta *'side'*
= **rltwa** (W,T)

urltirrem (E) *vi.*
be in charge, become boss of something ◆ Apmer arrpenhel urltirrepirrem. (St) *[That person] is in charge of another place.*

urltamp (T) native honey, sugarbag SEE UNDER **rltwamp**

urltar-rnkem (E) *vi.*
1. burst, bust, come out through something
2. go off, explode, go 'bang' (gun)
3. make a clicking, cracking, banging, rattling or knocking sound
= **rltar-rnkem** (E)

urltaty (E) *n.*
1. a premonition or feeling about something that is going to happen (often in the form of a twitch or click in the nose)
2. a type of worm found in a kangaroo's nose (which warns it of danger) ◆ Urltaty ikwerel-arleng anem ngangker, wal aterarl arem ra, urntem anem anem. Urltatyel anep-anem weth ngangker kwerenh, *worm* akely-artek, kel urntem anem aterel aremel [aherr]. (St) *The kangaroo has its worm, its* ngangker, *and when the kangaroo gets a fright it runs away. The* urltaty *is that thing like a little worm.* • SEE ALSO ngangkar, ultyitywelty
3. an indirect way of referring to a gun, or to a gun belonging to a person who has passed away ◆ 'Urltaty atyeng antheyaw.' *Policeman*-ketyarl. (St) *'Give me an* urlalty.*' For fear of the policeman you don't say 'gun'.* ◆ Maket apek urltaty, angketheyan ilem 'urltaty'. (St) *A gun is called* 'urltaty'*, that's what it's called in language.* • SEE ALSO maket
= **rltwaty** (W,T)

urltaty-ayerr (E) *n.* [RESPECT LANGUAGE]
gun ◆ Urltaty-ayerr ngkwerengkw-irretyek tyety-ayerr ulpaketyek. (St) *Ask for a gun [from respect kin] to shoot some kangaroos.*
SEE ALSO maket

urltaty-irrem (E) *vi.*
have a premonition; have a feeling (in your nose) that something is going to happen ◆ Urltaty-irremarl aherr, artwekety, artwa yanh ikwer apertepertem-kety. *Might* ameng ra antyernem, tyerrty-theyarl apetyem. Arlengel anem ra anep-anem arep-arem, nthenh-angkwerr ra arratetyenh. (St) *The*

kangaroo has a feeling about the man that is stalking it. Maybe it smells a fly that has come from the person. It stands in the distance and watches to see which direction the man will appear from. ◆ Urltaty-irrem ayeng *someone*-arl apetyemek, arrpenh apekarl apetyemeng. Kel arraty ra arnaremel apetyerlek aleth. (St) *I have a feeling about somebody coming. Then [he] sees that person coming.* ◆ Alha ayeng urltaty-irrem alethangek, alethang tha arnarem, arrer ra anem, yalengarl apetyem. Alha ayeng rltwar-irrem, urltaty-irrem. (St) *I have a feeling in my nose about a stranger, and then I see a stranger coming, and then they come closer, from over there. My nose clicks, I have a premonition.*
SEE ALSO alhirrkem, rltar-irrem, rlkwem, alhel arem
= **rltwaty-irrem** (W,T)

urltatyel atwem (E)
1. put a curse on someone or something; wish something bad to happen to someone or something (*atwem* 'hit') ◆ Arrpenhel apek urltatyel atwem mantarr atyenh, arntety apek ayeng irretyenh. (St) *If someone puts a curse on my clothes, then I might get sick.* ◆ Urltatyel atwemekety ngenhaw — mwanty alhaw, ngenharl urltatyel atwem. (Sa) *Be careful in case someone puts a curse on you— go carefully.* ◆ Mwetek urltatyel atwem, kel ra apekarl akelhety alhetyenh. (St) *If a curse is put on a car, then it might crash.*
2. have a premonition or feeling about something that is going to happen
SEE ALSO akwety-irrpenem, akety-urrpenem, artarrernem, artimperr-wem, pew-ilem
= **rltwatyel atwem** (W,T)

urlternt (E) *n.*
limestone
= **rltwernt** (W,T)

urlternt-urlternt (E) *n.*
limestone country ◆ Urlternt-urlterntel ayeng alhemaw. (St) *I am going through the limestone country.*
= **rltwernt-rltwernt** (W,T)

urna (T,E), **urtna** (E) *n.*
1. wooden water dish ◆ Urnel angetyem. Arnam arlperlp arrernemel irrernt-angkarreny. Arnam arlperlp anem arrernetyam kwaty kwer-arlek. (T) *Carrying [the water] in the wooden dish. Putting the* arlperlp *grass on top of the water so that it stays cold.* ◆ Akarntel kwaty angernewarretyart, urnel. (T) *[People] used to carry water in wooden dishes on the* akarnt, *the carrying pad.*
SEE ALSO atywekal, urety, kwerlintyerr, panth, lwengkart[2], irrkwely[2], alparr[1], irrkwa, lengarr, arlketh[1]
2. car [RESPECT LANGUAGE] ◆ Mwerekikwenhan ilem 'urna' mwetekay. (Sa) *Her son-in-law's car is called 'urna'.*
= **rnwa** (W,T)

urnayerr (E), **urtnayerr** (E) *n.* [RESPECT LANGUAGE]
car (lit. 'wooden dish')
= twertert-ayerr
SEE ALSO mwetekay, apwert

urnakw (E), **urtnakw** (E) *n.*
kangaroo's windbreak or sleeping place (where they sleep in the sun)

urnanenty (E), **rtnwanenty** (E) *n.*
things, possessions, swag, clothes
◆ Urnanenty akent-iwetyal atyenhaw. (Sa) *Don't go through all my things.*
= **rnwanenty**

urnanenty atyeneny (E), **rtnwanenty atyeneny** (E)
someone else's things

urnek-iwerrem (E) *vi.*
be related as close female cross-cousins
SEE ALSO altyel akerrem
= **rnwek-werrem** (W,T)

urnek-iwerrenty (E), **urtnek-iwerrek** (E) *n.*
two close female cross-cousins (their children could marry one another) ◆ Urtnek-iwerrek ratherr, ratherr urtnek-iwerrek alhep-alhem altyel-nheng atherr. (St) *Those two going along there are very close female cousins.*

urnelth-irrem (E) *vi.*
groan or cry out in pain

urnem (E), **urtnem** (E), **rnwem** (E) *n.*
snake (a general word for snakes) ◆ Urnem nhenh arlemeny ayntetyel. (Sa) *This snake is lying there curled up.* ◆ Alenyenp-iwem, aleny arratem. 'Alenyenp-wetyelarl-kety yanh-ketyaw!' Urnemel alenyenp-iwetyel. (Sa) *Flicking the tongue out, the tongue comes out. 'Look out [for that thing] that's flicking its tongue out!' Snakes flick their tongues out.*
◆ Rnwem tnyekant akenh-akenh. (Sa) *Snakes bite to the death.*
= amwa

urnem arlkeny (E)
snake track (arlkeny *'stripe', 'marking'*)
= amwang mpaty

urnety (T,E), **urtnety** (E) *n.*
the process of making fire by rubbing a hard piece of wood against another softer one, or against a shield; making fire by using a firesaw

urnety-wem (T,E), **urtnety-wem** (E) *vt.*
make fire by rubbing a hard piece of wood against another softer one, or against a shield;

make fire using a firesaw ◆ Urtnety-werretyart, kel kwert urntemel kel nthilemel antywer-warl arrernemel. Urtnety. Tyarrp anemel tyarrp kel alanh anem wemel ura akwertarl urntemek, arwerlel tyepalel. Wemel wemel wemel. Nthilerretyart. *Matches* anetyangel, urtnetyarl werretyart. Kel ura nthilemel, ura lherrm ampem. (Sa) *[People] used to light fires by using a firesaw, then the fire would start smoking and then they'd put some grass there. The stick called the* tyepal *was rubbed and rubbed against the crack [in the other bit of wood] until it started smoking, until it was alight. Rubbed and rubbed until it ignited. When people didn't have any matches they used to use the firesaw to light fires. The fire caught alight, and then the flames started burning.*
= urrmarl-wem, rrmwarl-wem
SEE ALSO wem[2]

urnpernp (T,E) *n.*
rock pituri (*Nicotiana gossei*). Herb about 60 cm high (though sometimes growing to 3 m), with white flowers. Found in hills and caves. Also referred to as *ngkwerlp urnpernp*. ◆ Urnpernp ahelengkw. Ngkwerlp arlkwentyan renh arlkwem arlpmenyel arrtyemel, wal antewarl irrem ikwer-penh, ahelengkw arnterr-penh. Mwerr ngkwerlp atherrk. (Sa) *The rock pituri is very strong. If you chew it after mixing it with ashes you might vomit as it's really strong. Sandhill pituri is better.*
SEE ALSO arwenp, ngkwerlp, ngkwerlp atherrk
CAN SOUND A BIT LIKE irnpernp *'soldier bird'*; inpinp *'marrow'*
= **rnpwernp** (W,T)

urntem (T,E) *vi.*
1. to dance ◆ Arelhan urntem awelyek — artwan urntem althartek. (Sa) *Women dance at the* awely *ceremonies — men dance the* althart.
SEE ALSO anthep
2. to rain ◆ Kwatyarl urntem-kety ayeng irrpenhem warl-warl. (Sa) *It's raining so I am going inside the house.* ◆ Alker-they kwaty urntem. (Sa) *It's raining from the sky.* • = anhem
3. to smoke (fire) ◆ Urtnety-werretyart, kel kwert urntemel kel nthilemel antywer-warl arrernemel. (Sa) *[People] used to light fires by using a firesaw, then the fire would start smoking and then they'd put some grass there.*
CAN SOUND A BIT LIKE arntwem *'grow'*; untem *'run', 'hurry along'*; unthem *'look for something'*
= **rntwem** (W,T)
urntelh-ilem (E) *vt.*
make something shake or move ◆ Ampel apek arrkenel urntelh-urntelh-ilem waly. (St) *The child is enjoying herself shaking the branch.*

urrampem (T,E) *vi.*
1. get angry with someone; become annoyed, agitated, or upset; get heated (angry) ◆ Anert urrampetyel, anert urinp-irrerl-anemel inngart ahel. Anert urrampem ayeng, atwetyek ahel apek. (Sa) *My stomach is feeling hot with anger. I'm feeling agitated and I might go and fight.* ◆ Arelh alerteh ayeng urrampem. (T) *I am getting angry with that woman.* ◆ Urrampem anert urrampem, kel ra atwemel irrerntarl ra mpwarelhem, anert irrernt-ilelhemel. (Sa) *[His] stomach is burning with anger, then he goes and fights and makes himself cool down, cools his stomach down.*
SEE ALSO ahel-irrem, arlelty-irrem, yerrng-irrem
2. feel really hungry; really want to eat something; stomach (burn from hunger); be starving for something ◆ Kerek urrampemel arlkwem aneperrk. (Sa) *I really want to eat some meat, some intestines.* ◆ Anert urrelp-urrampem angayakw, arrerlkart ulthem, *right out* mernek angayakw, arlkwetyek anem arlkwem mern arnterr anem anert pwelap-ilelhemel. (Sa) *My stomach is starting to burn from hunger — I'm really starving, hungry for food so that I can eat a lot and fill my stomach up.* ◆ Ngkwerlp ayenh antheyaw — ngkerlpek ayeng urrampemarl. (Sa) *Give me some tobacco — I'm starving for tobacco.*
SEE ALSO urrampey, urranem
= **rrwampem** (W)

urrampey (W), **rwampey** (T) *n.*
hot ◆ Kwenyel rwampey anem — ayeng kwenh rwampey. Ywarn wenh iterrem. (T) *It's really hot at night — I'm really hot. I couldn't think.*
SEE ALSO urranem, urrampem

urranem (W,T) *vi.*
be hot, feel hot ◆ Urranem-arleng lyewarl alhey. (T) *[I'm] feeling really hot, so let's go into the shade.* ◆ Rwang yanh rntwarr-ileyaw, urranem-arleng. (M) *Shift that fire further away, it's hot.*
SEE ALSO urrampey, urrampem

urrar (T,E) *n.*
echo ◆ Urrar tyernepernem apwertel arlkerlek, *someone*-ek apek arlkerlek, kel urrarel ra tyerneman arlkenty. (St) *The echo answers back when [someone] calls out in the hills.*
= **rrwar** (W,T)

urrarem (T,E) *vt.*
pick out good things; sort things out; draft (cattle) into separate groups ◆ Mantarr mwerr

map inem urraremel, urraremel inem mantarr mwerr-arey ant. Akeng-akeng impemel arrkay-arrkay. (St) *Sorting out the clothes, just picking out the good ones. Leaving the not so good ones, the faded ones.*
SEE ALSO angakem, urlanem

urrarl (E) *n.*
wispy clouds. Also referred to as *kwaty urrarl.* ◆ Kwaty urrarl ulpatewelhem-kety — kwenek aylpey. (Sa) *Look out, the storm is building up — let's go inside.*
SEE ALSO kwenpay, inewarr, katyar, antwenharr

urrarl-irrem (E) *vi.*
clouds build up ◆ Kwenpay urrarl-irrek nthwenharr. *The clouds have built up.*

urrarlp (E) native tomato SEE UNDER **rrwarlp**[1]

urrarn (T) *n.*
guilty, culpable, responsible for a misdeed ◆ Atwenh-atwenh 'urrarn', tyerrtyarl atwek-penh. (T) *A person who kills another is 'urrarn'.*

urrartn (E) *n.*
a type of cloud
SEE ALSO antwenharr

urraty (E) *n.*
small hollow made in a flat ant bed into which seeds are placed for husking with the feet ◆ Arelh ampwel iylwepeylwem ntang alyatywereng urratyek. (Sa) *The old lady is husking the woollybutt grass seed with her feet in the hole.*
SEE ALSO lywem[1]

urrayerr (T,E), **rrwayerr** (T) *adv.*
behaving in a teasing or joking way with people who belong to the opposite generation moiety. Joking in this way is accepted, and is in fact expected between relations of this sort. ◆ Urrayerrel arrantherr ayenhant ilerl-anetyek anyent. Nywerrp anyent arrantherr ayenh ilep-ilem urrayerrel. (St) *You are all just teasing me, one person. You are all teasing me, the only one who is in the opposite generation moiety to the rest of you.* ◆ Nywerrpel arrernetyam ker-warl arlewatyerr-warl rapet-warl apek ker antenh-warl apek, yanh ina tyenkerr ina atwetyam, wal ina lyekarl arrernetyam. Mwerikwel apek arlkwety-ayntetyek. Urrayerrel. Angkwerr-taym apek. (St) *The people in the other generation moiety prepared ceremonial food, and they put prickles in with the goanna meat, or the rabbit, or the possum meat. Maybe their son-in-law came along to eat it. That was the sort of joking behaviour that happened during the* angkwerr *ceremonies.*
SEE ALSO kwanthem, tyelewerr, nywerrp

urrayerr-irrem (T,E), **rrwayerr-irrem** (T) *vi.*
tease or joke around with people who belong to the opposite generation moiety

urrek (T,E) *adv.*
1. 'Wait on!', 'Just a minute!', 'Hang on!'. *Urrek* can occur on its own as a command.
2. waiting till something has happened ◆ Urrek mpwelh atyeng. (St) *Wait for me.* ◆ Urrekek-amparr aney. (St) *Wait for a little while first.* ◆ Althekalth-irrey ayengaw, urrek. Artep apekarl ayeng arntem. Althekalth-irrey. (St) *Wait while I stretch myself. Maybe my back is aching. I'll stretch myself.* ◆ Nantew ltyerrelh-ilem urrek apek. *Give the horse a spell for a while.*
= alerl
= **rrwek** (W,T)

urrek-antey (T,E) *adv.*
'Wait a minute', 'Hang on a moment', 'Wait a while' ◆ Urrek-antey anerlaney. (T) *Wait for a while.*
= alerl-antey
= **rrwek-antey** (W,T)

urrekatyakenh (E), **urrekatyalkenh** (E) *adv.*
[RESPECT LANGUAGE]
'Wait a minute', 'Hang on a moment', 'Wait a while' ◆ Urrekatyakenh amely-wepewem. (St) *Wait while [my son-in-law] is eating [said by a woman].* ◆ Urrekatyakenh ulpanep-anem. (St) *Wait while [my son-in-law] is sleeping [said by a woman].*
SEE ALSO alerl

urrekaty-antey (E) [RESPECT LANGUAGE]
= **urrekatyakenh**

urrekek (E) *n.*
a big male emu ◆ Ankerr innga angerrety, urrekek. Angerrety weth. Urrey pang weth artwa ampwa. (Sa) *An emu that is really large is called 'urrekek'. Those big ones. Those big male ones.*
SEE ALSO ankerr

Urrelenty (E) *n.*
Ooralingie Bore, east of Wilora (Stirling) community

urrelty (T,E) *n.*
1. kindling wood ◆ Urrelty mwenng akwek inetyek, urrelty, nthiletyek ura. (St) *Get some little bits of kindling wood to light the fire.*
2. wood put on top of a grave
SEE ALSO mwenng
= **rrwelty** (W,T)

urrem-ilem (E) *vt.* [RESPECT LANGUAGE]
give something to someone ◆ Anthetyekan urrem-ilem, mey-meyek apek. Urrem-ilek tha. (St) Urrem-ilem *means 'give', maybe to [your]*

son-in-law. I gave him something. ◆ Atyeng urrem-iletyek kweth-kweth-ayerr apek. (St) *Give me some [kangaroo] blood [from my son-in-law's kangaroo].* (?)
SEE ALSO anthem, angernem2
= **rrwem-ilem** (W,T)

urrem-urrem (T,E) *n.*
not understanding properly, silly in the head, forgetful, heedless ◆ Ampa akwek ra anem urrem-urrem. Kel angerr-awern irrem, angkakert anem irrem nhenh-lkwer rlterrk anem irreynepeynem, atyet-atyet weth. Rlterrk anem ra irreynepeynem. Kel angkethen antey rlterrk-irrem. Iterlarem anem ra atyemey apek nyany apek, arrengey apek, mam apek akngey kwerenh. Urrem-urremek-amparr. (St) *Little babies do not understand properly at first. Then they get a bit bigger and they start to talk, and the soft part [the fontanelle] hardens up. That gets hard. Then their talking gets stronger as well. Then they know their mother's father, or their granny, or their father's father, their mother or their father. At first they don't know things properly.* ◆ Urrem-urremel angkep-angkem, akengentyarl angkep-angkem. Arraty-anteyarl angkep-angkem kapert altywer. (St) *Talking in a silly way, talking the wrong way. [Someone] who is knowledgeable talks the right way.*
= **rrwem-rrwem** (W,T)
urrem-urrem-irrem (T,E) *vi.*
become silly in the head or forgetful; go a bit mad ◆ Utern-penh ant urrem-urrem-irreman arraty, urrem urrem anem irrenhemel, iylpa arlka arert-arert irrenhel. Ampwerneman urrem-urremarl. *Some of them.* (St) *It's true that you get a bit silly in the head from the heat of the sun, you go a bit silly and your ears go a little bit mad. Some old people are a bit mad.*
= **rrwem-rrwem-irrem** (W,T)

urrempelty (E) a type of cloud that forms on top of a column of smoke SEE UNDER **arrempelty**

urrempen urrempen (E) *n.*
Horsfield's bronze-cuckoo (*Chrysococcyx basalis*) (?)
SEE ALSO anatyelepwerray, nyarew

urremper (T,E) *n.*
shovel spear. This was carried in the hand and used as a parrying weapon, rather than thrown using a woomera. ◆ Tyerrty apekarl atanthetyam urremperel. Kerarl atanthetyam irrtyartelant, amerr-akertel. (T) *People might have been speared with a shovel spear. Animals were speared with* irrtyart, *used with a woomera.*
SEE ALSO irrtyart
= **arrwemper** (W,T)

urreny (T) *n.*
edible seed of the coolibah tree, *ankerrmern*

urrenyenk (E), **irrwenyenk** (E) *n.*
Georgina gidgee (*Acacia georginae*). Twisted tree to about 5 m high, with grey leaves and broad flat pods. The seeds are very poisonous.
= awenth
= **rrwenyenk** (W,T)
urrenyenkayt (E), **irrwenyenkayt** (E) *n.*
grub from the Georgina gidgee roots
= kerlpaty
SEE ALSO ulalthengayt

urreper (E) on the other side of something (to the speaker) SEE UNDER **irrweper**

urrepert (E), **rrwepert** (T) *n.*
dry, dry place, dry country ◆ Kwaty kwenyel urrepert anem mer — arna arlka ingkerrek mer urrepert. (St) *A place without water is* urrepert — *all the trees and everything is dry.*
SEE ALSO antyerrk, arrangketh, aherraty, ahepet
urrepert-irrem (E), **rrwepert-irrem** (T) *vi.*
get dry ◆ Alta urrepert anem irrek alhewelhetyek ayeng. Arrangkw apek irrek atherrk yanh, wal kel ra urrepertarl ra irrek, antyerrk-irremel. Arwerl apek urrepert-irrek, *might* ayeng apek alta urrepert-irrek. (St) *My hair has gone dry so I'd better wash it. Maybe that grass has died, well, it's already dried up. Trees might have dried up, or my hair might have gone dry.*
SEE ALSO antyerrk-irrem

urrer *n.kin* [RESPECT LANGUAGE]
a respectful way for a woman to refer to her son-in-law's father or her daughter's child's father (i.e. her son-in-law), and for a man to refer to his mother-in-law's father (i.e. his mother's mother's brother)
SEE ALSO angey, aler
urrerengkw *n.kin*
your *urrer* ◆ Urrerengkw-warl ahaneyna. Alpay, urrerekengk-warl. Ipmenhey ahaneyna. Yanhentyakel ayepel-irretyel-warl urrekengkw-warl. Ilkwangketh-ayerr. (Sa) *Go to your father. Go back, to your father. Grandchild [daughter's daughter], go. Go to where your father is sitting down there. To keep him company [said by a woman who is the mother-in-law of the child's father].* ◆ Nheng *grandmother*-el apek ilem, 'Urrerengk-warn alhay, urrer-intyerr-arreng alhetyekay. Lyweny apek arrantherr alhetyek urrer-intyerr'. (T) *The child's grandmother [mother's mother] might say to her, 'Go to your father, so that all the fathers and*

children can go hunting together'.

urrerikw (E) *n.kin*
his/her/their *urrer*

urrerek (W,T) *n.kin*
1. your *urrer*
2. his/her/their *urrer*

urrer-nheng *n.kin*
a group of two or more people related as fathers and children (said by a woman if one of them is her son-in-law, or by a man if one of them is his mother-in-law)
SEE ALSO anyenheng[1]
= urrer-intyerr

urrer-intyerr *n.kin* = **urrer-nheng** ◆ Urrer-intyerr alherl-wetyel. Aynenheng map, urrpety. Marl ingwerel ilem. Mwerelikw. (Sa) *A group of fathers and their sons are going. A few groups of fathers and sons. Another woman says that. The mother-in-law of one of them.*

urrerenheng atherr *n.kin*
a father and his child (said by a woman if one of them is her son-in-law or by a man if one of them is his mother-in-law) ◆ Marlel ilem mwerikw then ipmenhikw then, 'Urrer-nheng atherr kwenh'. (St) *A woman says of her son-in-law and her daughter's child, 'Urrer-nheng atherr'.*
SEE ALSO anyenheng atherr

urrer-ankethenh *n.kin*
1. having a close *urrer* still alive ◆ 'Urrer-ankethenharl yanhan aynankethenharl.' Ilem aynikwek-artwey. (Sa) *'His father is still alive.' That is what is said about the son [by his mother-in-law].*
2. someone who is always with their *urrer*
SEE ALSO -ankethenh

urrer-ampeny (W), **urrerek-thayt** (W,T) *n.*
country that is associated with the same patrimoiety as the speaker, or the person being referred to, but with the other patricouple (i.e. father–child pair of skin names). This patricouple, or pair of skin names, includes the one that the speaker is in an avoidance or respect relationship to. For example, a Penangk person calls country belonging to Ngwarray/Peltharr *urrer-ampeny*. A Penangk person is in a respect relationship to particular Peltharr people. A Kemarr person calls country belonging to Ngal/Mpetyan people *urrer-ampeny*. A Kemarr person is in a respect relationship to particular Ngal people. ◆ Urrerek-thayt angey alert-henh mer *country*. 'Wal, urrerengkw-thayt nhenh kwenh.' Ngkweng apek ilemer arrpenhel. (M) *That person's father's country is your* urrerek *side. 'Well, this is your* urrer *country [belonging to your respect kin].' That's what someone might tell you.*
SEE ALSO inakerr-akey

urrerewem (E) *vt.*
dislike something, reject something (?) ◆ Urrerewem. Urraretyelarl. Alparr-alparr. 'Menty kwenh ayeng *light one*-ek alparr-alparrek aylpetyangel, menty.' (Sa) *Rejecting the ones you don't like as you sort them out. 'This one is too light. I don't want that one because I don't wear flimsy [clothes].'*

urrerl-ilem (E) *vt.*
stoke up fire, lift up firewood to make it burn, lift something out of the fire ◆ Ura atyeng urrerl-ilaw, irrerntek. (Sa) *Stoke that fire up for me, it's cold.* ◆ Mern anaty urrerl-ilem atnemel, kel aweth ampernemel anem. (Sa) *Lifting the bush potato up out of the fire with a digging stick, and then it cooks some more.*

urrernem (T,E), **irrwernem** (E) *vt.*
1. make trouble for someone else; get someone into trouble (especially close family, such as a son or daughter or a mother) ◆ Urrernemarl ampelikw. (Sa) *Her child is making trouble for her.*
SEE ALSO atyang-inem, nakepakel-ilem
2. blame someone for something they didn't do
CAN SOUND A BIT LIKE arrwernem *'make a hole in something'*
= **rrwernem** (W,T)

urrernelhem (E) *vi.*
get yourself into trouble ◆ Iltep-iltem apek unta arrpenh, wal, urrernelhek anem nga. (St) *If you growl at another person, well, you might get yourself into trouble.*

urrernter[1] (E), **irrwernter** (E) *adv.*
doing a particular traditional kind of dancing, hopping or skipping motion to show aggression (men) ◆ Artwa yanham urrernter anem arl irrep-irrem kwenh. Atwerretyek urrernterarl apetyerlek artwa ahel. Atwetyek artwa arrpenh. Irrwernter apetyem. (St) *That man is dancing along showing how angry he is. The angry man has come to fight the other man. He's coming along, dancing and jumping around in an aggressive way.*
= **rrwernter** (W,T)

urrernter-irrem (E), **irrwernter-irrem** (E) *vi.*
hop or skip along showing intention to fight (men)
SEE ALSO arrtyernem
= **rrwernter-irrem** (W,T)

urrernter alhem (E), **irrwernter alhem** (E)
= **urrernter-irrem**
= **rrwernter alhem** (W,T)

urrernter2 (E), **irrwernter** (E) *n.*
red-backed kingfisher (*Todiramphus pyrrhopygia*)
= rlwernp, parlkenng

urrey (T,E) *n.*
1. boy ◆ Urrey akwek arrkenel antyem arnewarn. (T) *The little boy is climbing the tree for fun.* ◆ Tyakarran urrey Kemarr akwek. (T) *A* Tyakerr *is a little* Kemarr *boy.*
2. man. In some contexts it would be seen as very insulting to call a man *urrey*.
3. male (of a species) ◆ Arrpwayl, kaperl urrey akngerr weth, arrpwaylarl ra. (St) Arrpwayl *is that big male* kaperl *lizard, that's what* arrpwayl *is.*
= **rrwey** (W,T)

urreyek-alyey-alyey (T,E) *n.*
pussy-tails, mulla-mulla, lamb's tail (*Ptilotus exaltatus*) (urrey '*boy*'; alyey-alyey '*spirit friend*'). Plant about 60 cm high with smooth green leaves and pink flowers.
= merntepam, awerreh-alyey-alyey, rrweyek-alyey-alyey
SEE ALSO marlek-alyey-alyey, alyey-alyey

urreylk (E) *n.*
march fly
= rlalth

urrkely-urrkely (E) *n.*
domestic turkey (?)
= kart-irrkwely-irrkwely

urrkenng (T,E) native truffle SEE UNDER **irrkwenng**

urrkertem (E) cook something SEE UNDER **irrkwertem**

urrkng SEE UNDER **urrng**

urrma (T,E) *n.*
scars on chest, stomach and arms (men's and women's ceremonial)
SEE ALSO amarr, alety, tywen, utyen
= **rrmwa** (W,T)

urrmirrem (T,E) *vi.*
heal over ◆ Urrmirrek tywen-penh. Tywen-penhan *shut*-em-ilem urrmirrek, urrma anem irrek. (St) *After the sore has healed over. It has closed over and healed.*
= kwerrm-irrem
SEE ALSO arrintety-irrem, arterrp-irrem, ltyerrem, tywenmernt-irrem, pwarn-irrem

Urrmangkerr (E), **Mangker** (E) *n.*
name of a place in the Murray Downs area

urrmarl-wem (T,E) *vt.*
make a fire using a firesaw; make fire by rubbing a hard piece of wood against another softer one, or against a shield or carrying dish
= rrmwarl-wem, urtnety-wem
SEE ALSO nthilem, urrma

urrmelty angkem (E) whine (dog) SEE UNDER **mwelty-mwelty angkem**

urrmenyar (E), **urrmeynar** (E) *adv.*
with legs curled back or bent
SEE ALSO rtapety-irrem, arntarlperrk
= **mwenyar**

urrnga (E) a runny, liquid or sloppy mixture SEE UNDER **irrngwa**

urrparem (T,E), **irrpwarem** (E) *vt.*
wipe something out; wipe, rub or scratch something off something ◆ Tyerrty ingkarl alhek apek urrparem walyel. (St) *Wiping out the footprints where someone went, with a branch.* ◆ Mey-mey-kety tha urrparenhem, ingkekety, thwerremp-irrenhem. (St) *I am wiping out the tracks of my son-in-law, dragging my feet as I go along and wiping out his tracks.*
SEE ALSO iparem, irrarlkem, arnngem
= **rrpwarem** (W,T)

urrparelhem (T,E), **irrpwarelhem** (E) *vi.*
1. wipe something off yourself ◆ Arlkeny urrparelhay! (Sa) *Wipe the designs off yourself!*
SEE ALSO iparelhem, arnngelhem
2. wipe out footprints or take your name off a paper, resign ◆ Ayeng urrparelhek warrk atyenh-they. (St) *I resigned from my job.*
3. apologise ◆ Arrkentyel atwem mey-mey apek, wal urrparelhem arrkentyarl ilem-penh urrparelhem anem. (St) *If you have a fight with or ridicule your son-in-law, well then you apologise.*
= **rrpwarelhem** (W,T)

nyerr urrparelhem (E) *vi.*
make amends, apologise, 'square up' or make up after trouble (lit. 'wipe out shame') ◆ Nyerrel urrparelhey, nyerrarl irrem-kety. Nyerrel iparelhetyek alha. Angketyek arrpenhek, 'Arrangkw kwenh ayeng. Nyerrel ayeng urrparelhetyek apetyek ilelhetyek'. Mwerr anem, *friend* anem. (Sa) *Make amends so that you don't feel shamed. Go and make amends. Go and talk to the other one and say, 'It wasn't me. I've come to tell you and to apologise'. Then they're friends again and everything is fine.*
= nyerr iparelhem

urrpelth (E) brave, fearless, courageous SEE UNDER **irrpelth**

urrper (E) *n.*
1. a swollen tuber under the ground. Also referred to as *mern urrper*. ◆ Lyelyerr alerikwarl nyetyam, urrper, alerikwarl. Urrper nhenhan

angey kwerenh. Anthal alerikw. Mwerr iyterrtyarl yanh. (Sa) *The offshoot,* lyelyerr *of the bush potato plant, is the son or daughter of the main plant, the* urrper. *The* urrper *is their father. The young tuber is the son or daughter. That's really true.*
2. a crack in the ground caused by a tuber or root underneath ◆ Anatyarl urrper-wem. Anaty urrper yanh. Urrper yanh angernay. (Sa) *Bush potatoes make the earth lift up. That's a crack from a bush potato. Dig up where that crack is.*
= ahatyerr
SEE ALSO tyarrp, tenh, karnt, pwep-angkem
urrper-wem (E), **urrper-iwem** (E) *vt.*
(tuber or root) make the ground crack and lift up ◆ Urrper-iwem kwenh mern apekarl urrper-iwem tyap apek. *Crack*-arl irrem an urrperarl iwem. Mern anaty apek urrper-iwem. 'Urrper-iwek yanhan kwenh!' Arlatyeyan arrangkw. *Only* anatyant urrper-iwenh-iwenh. (St) *Certain types of food or grubs make the earth swell up. Make the earth crack and swell up. Bush potatoes make the earth raise up. 'There's where the earth has risen up!' Pencil yams don't make that happen. Only bush potatoes do it.*
= ahatyerr-wem
urrper inkem (E), **rrpwer inkem** (T)
1. (tuber or root) make the ground crack and lift up
2. make a hollow sound that indicates the presence of a tuber or swollen root below the surface of the ground (?) ◆ 'Nhenhaw rrpwer inkern tha rrwek nyey kwenh.' Arraty inyemel inem. (T) *'The earth has made a hollow sound here, wait while I dig.' Then [you] dig and get [the yam] right there.*
rrpwer-irrem (T) *vi.*
raise, crack or swell up (earth), because of a swollen root or tuber underneath

urrperl (E) black, dark in colour SEE UNDER **irrpwerl**

urrpernp (E), **irrpwernp** (E) *n.*
1. country that doesn't give up any food, meat etc. to the hunter; country devoid of bushtucker ◆ Mern apek ker apek arratetyakenh. Anyent apek atwetyakenh arrangkw akwet, mer urrpernp-angkwerr ayeng alhek. (St) *No bush tucker or game appeared. I didn't even kill a thing. I went through the* urrpernp *country and there was no bushtucker.*
2. unlucky or unsuccessful in hunting; come back with nothing (from hunting) ◆ Apmer urrpernp, ker anthetyakenh arrangkw. (St) *A place that is* urrpernp *doesn't give any meat [to the hunter].* ◆ Urrpernp ayeng alhek, ker apek arratetyakenh. Iltyant ayeng apety-alpek. Mer urrpernp-angkwerr ayeng alhek, anthetyakenh arrangkw ankeyarl yanh. (St) *I went hunting and came back with nothing — no animals appeared. I came back empty-handed. I went through country where there was no bushtucker, mean country that didn't give anything up.*
3. missing the target animal when hunting ◆ Ker urrpernp arrangkw atyerretyakenh. (T) *[I] missed the animal [after a shot].*
= **rrpwernp** (W,T)
urrpernp-ilem (E) *vt.*
cause someone to be unsuccessful at hunting, frighten off game ◆ Ampelarl urrpernp-ilem-ketyaw, ker-ketyaw. (Sa) *Look out, those kids are frightening off the kangaroos.*
= **rrpwernp-ilem** (W,T)
urrpernp anthem (E) *vt.* = **urrpernp-ilem** (anthem *'give'*)
= **rrpwernp anthem** (W,T)

urrpety (E) *n.*
1. a few, several
2. the number three, three of something ◆ Alethang apek urrpety apetyek. Urrpety apetyawarrem yanh-ketyaw. (St) *A few strangers came. Look out for those few [strangers] coming.* ◆ Atnyenty anyentel alhem kel atnyenty arrpenh tnety-alhem, urrpety-ingar, atnyenty urrpety apek. (St) *Going for one month, then another month passes, or several months.* ◆ Mantalyarrpan arriw urrpety-akert. (Sa) *The* mantalyarrp *boil has several openings.*
= **rrpwety** (W,T)
urrpety-ingar (E), **urrpety-inger** (E) *adv.*
a few times, several times, thrice, for a few days ◆ 'Nthakenty-inger nga alhem?' 'Urrpety-arengek ayeng alhem, urrpety-inger intety-alhetyek ayeng alhem.' (St) *'How long are you going for?' 'I am going for a few days, I'm going to camp there for a few days.'*
= **rrpwety-inger** (T)
urrpety-areng (E) *adv.* = **urrpety-inger**
urrpetyarrp (E), **urrpetyarrp-inger** (E) *adv.*
just a few, several, three
= **rrpwetyarrp** (T)
urrpetyek-urrpety (E) *adv.*
in threes or in small groups
urrpety-atherr (E) *n.*
the number five, five of something
urrpety-irrem (E) *vi.*
split or separate off into threes, a few split off from a larger group

urrpety-ilem (E) *vt.*
make something into a few bits or pieces

urrpey (T,E) *n.*
1. message, news
2. messenger, someone with a message; (coming) with a message ◆ Ayengarl ngkweng urrpey apetyek, man inerl-alpetyek. (T) *I've come with a message for you, to get money to take back.* ◆ Tyerrty apetyek urrpey, angka akngerr-akert. (St) *The person came with a message, with an important message.*
= **rrpwey** (T)
urrpey alhem (T,E)
take a message to someone; go and ask others something (?) (alhem *'go'*)
= **rrpwey alhem** (T)

urrpm SEE UNDER **urrm**

urrtha (E) *n.*
fragments of wood and dirt in a hollow tree left by white ants (?) ◆ Urrthakert kwenh, ngkwarl nhenh arwengalker nhenh. *Clean*-em ineyaw, urrthakert-kety. (St) *This sugarbag honey has bits of wood in it. Clean it, because it's got bits of wood in it.*
SEE ALSO althalth

urrtya (E) *n.*
a lie
urrtyirrem (E) *vi.*
trick or deceive someone; tell a lie; pretend; act untruthfully ◆ Urrtyirremel ilek kerek atyeng akngetyetyek, rarl alkngwirrelhek anem, urrtyirremel. (St) *[She] lied about bringing me some meat — she forgot.* ◆ Riken-irretyel ntwa atyengety, mwetek *new one*-akert unta riken-irretyel atyengety. Ayenh anthetyakenh. Riken-arrpantey unta irretyel urrtyirrepirrerl, atyengety. (Sa) *You're showing off to me because you've got a new car. You didn't give me one. You're showing off in front of me and making out as if you're fantastic.*
◆ Urrtyirremel ilelhenty angep-angem. Kel arrpenh an ahel anem irrem. *'Eh,* yanhel ilelhenty angep-angem, urrtyirrentyel.' (St) *Going and telling an untrue story. Then someone else gets angry. 'Hey, that person is going around telling lies.'*
SEE ALSO therlkem, urirrem², rnter-irrem, arrampewem¹, atyetyem
= **rrtywerrem** (W,T)
urrtyeng-urrtyeng (E) *n.*
pretend, fake, not real ◆ Urrtyeng-urrtyeng war artnep-artnem ampa. (St) *The child is just pretending to cry.*
= utyek-utyel
= **rrtyweng-rrtyweng** (W,T)
urrtyalth (T,E) *n.*
a liar
urrtyirremel ilem (E)
tell lies (ilem *'say', 'tell'*)
= therlkem
= **rrtywerremel ilem** (W,T)

urrtyel (E) *n.*
small rocks or stones. Also referred to as *apwert urrtyel.*
= arrtya³, irrtyewat¹

urta (E) *n.*
wet (ground), mud ◆ Mwetekay urtewarl aylpek. (Sa) *The car got bogged.*
SEE ALSO anthwerrng, antha¹, tert
urtilem (E) *vt.*
wet the ground ◆ Kwatyel urtilek ahern nhenh. (Sa) *The rain wet the ground here.*

urtakwert (E) *n.*
heart
= **rtwekert**

urtalty (E) *n.*
1. a man's mother-in-law; man's wife's mother
2. a woman's son-in-law; woman's daughter's husband
3. certain other relations who are related to each other by marriage (for example, two cross-cousins will call each other *urtalty* if their children are married to each other)
◆ Urtalty-ayerr-kety ahanenherr-areyaw. Urtalty arrekingkerrenh-kety ahanenherr-arey. (Sa) *You all have to shift because of your son-in-law. Move away because of the sons-in-law belonging to all of you.*
SEE ALSO mey-mey¹, mwer, ampeyamp
= **rtwalty**
urtalty-nheng atherr (E) *n.*
a person together with their *urtalty*
= **rtwalty-nheng atherr**
urtalty-irrem (E) *vi.*
become mother-in-law or son-in-law for someone (through ceremony) ◆ Urtalty-irrem ra arelh yanh. Urtalty-irrem anem ra *young fella* yanhek. Urtalty kwerenh anem ra anem. Marl anem ra anthem urtalty kwerenhek. (St) *That woman has become the mother-in-law for that young fella. Now she is his* urtalty. *She gives the girl [her daughter] to her son-in-law.*

urtanng (T,E), **urtanng-urtanng** (T,E) *n.*
a barrier or trench to stop floodwater or running water ◆ Urtanng arrernem tha kwaty-kety, urew-kety urtanng-urtanng arrernem. (St) *I am making a trench to stop the water, to stop the running water.*
= **rtwanng**

urtap (T,E) *n.*
hot earth or ashes (used for cooking or healing) ◆ Urtapel item, ker arlewatyerr. Aherr item urtapel, ker antyerrk-irrekerr. (St) *Cook the goanna in the hot ashes. Kangaroos are cooked in the hot ashes so that the meat doesn't get dried up.*
SEE ALSO ayerrk, arerrk
= **rtwap**

urtarnp (E) *n.*
fat from the lower stomach and inner thigh of a kangaroo
SEE ALSO apel[1], atnwerlk
= **rtwarnp** (T,E)

urtatyel angem (E) *vt.*
carry something in a sling or with a carrying strap
= antayel angem, alyepel angem

urtek (E) a type of tick found on perenties, euros or cattle SEE UNDER **artwek**

urtep (E) *n.*
inside or hollow part of something; something that is hollow ◆ Mwar atyenh urtep nhenh. (St) *My digging scoop is hollow.*
= **rtwep**
urtep-ilem (E) *vt.*
hollow or carve something out ◆ Mwar tha urtep-ilem ilepel. (St) *I am hollowing out the digging scoop with an axe.*
= **rtwep-ilem**

urtep-urtep (E) *n.*
going round something
= **artwep-artwep** (W,T)
urtep-akem (E) *vt.*
go around something; go round and around something
= **artwep-akem** (W, T)
urtep-akelhem (E) *vi.*
go around and around; go around someone or something to avoid them; go round in circles
= **artwep-akelhem** (W,T)
urtep-irrem (E) *vi.*
go back; turn round and go back; change direction
= **artwep-irrem** (W,T)
urtep-urtep-irrem (E) *vi.*
go round something; go round in circles
urtepelh-ilem (E) *vt.*
make someone or something turn round and go back; be made to turn back from halfway
urtep-wem (E) *vt.*
emerge from cover and run off (of some animals) ◆ Urtep-wem arlewatyerrel alhweng-they apek. (St) *The goanna emerges from its hole and runs.*
urtep-irrenty-alpem (E) *vi.*
turn round and go back
= **artwep-irrenty-alpem** (W, T)

urterrp (T,E), **uterrp** (T,E) *n.*
sandhill
SEE ALSO arerrk
= **twerrp**

Urterrp (T,E), **Uterrp** (T,E) *n.*
name of a place and country/estate in Neutral Junction Station area. Redbank Waterhole ◆ Mer Uterrp tha akem altyerr akem math-kenh. (St) *Uterrp is the place I call* 'altyerr', *my mother's country.*

urtert-iwem (E) push someone or something SEE UNDER **urturt-iwem**

urteth (T,E) *n.*
1. lower back, small of the back ◆ Urteth ayeng arntemaw! (Sa) *My lower back is aching!*
= antywert
= **rtweth** (W,T)
2. kangaroo meat (portion from near the tail). Also referred to as *ker urteth.*
urtethem-urteth-irrem (E) *vi.*
disappear into the distance

urtety (E) *n.*
short ◆ Arwerl urtety. (Sa) *Stump of a tree.* ◆ Arlewatyerran akely-rnem, ra arepmay. Rapet alhwengek atwerretyart, pet-pet-kenhek. Alkwert atwenh-kenh alhwengekarl atwerretyart ra rapet aremay ra aylpetyart, urtety akely rnem. (Sa) *The* arepmay *lizard is smaller than the sand goanna. We used to kill them in rabbits' burrows. They used to go into rabbits' burrows and we used to kill them. The* arepmay *are short little things.*
SEE ALSO karteng
CAN SOUND A BIT LIKE artwety *'kangaroo bladder'*

urtna (E) wooden water dish SEE UNDER **urna**

urtnakw (E) kangaroo's windbreak or sleeping place (where they sleep in the sun) SEE UNDER **urnakw**

urtnem (E) snake (a general word for snakes) SEE UNDER **urnem**

urtnety (E) making fire using a firesaw SEE UNDER **urnety**

urtntem (E) to dance SEE UNDER **urntem**

urturt-iwem (E), **urtert-iwem** (E) *vt.*
push someone or something ◆ Apwert urtert-iwem. Ker apek tnyepetnyerleng apwert urtert-iwem. (St) *Pushing the rock. Pushing the rock out of the way because there might be an animal there.*
SEE ALSO ankert-wem

-utek amongst, at, on, by SEE UNDER **-itwek**

utelh (E) *n.*
soft
utelh-utelh (E) *n.*
soft
= arewamp
utemeny (E), **atwemeny** (E), **atwemenh** (E) *n.*
1. ceremonial poles or 'long sticks' used during *apwelh* (young men) ceremony ◆ Utemeny-akert urntem *boy*-rnem urntem utemeny-akert. Arlpwenty-arlpwenty utemenyarl. (Sa) *The men dance with the* utemeny *sticks. They are long.*
2. the dance in which the 'long sticks' are used
= arretyet, arlwernarr
uteny (E) *n.*
dry fruit of the desert raisin, *katyerr* (*Solanum centrale*)
SEE ALSO arlkarntar, alha2
= **tweny**
uteny-irrem (E) *vi.*
go dry (desert raisin)
= **tweny-irrem**
utepeng-utep (E) *n.* [RESPECT LANGUAGE]
scorpion ◆ Ngwarrengkw utepeng-utepel akekaw. (Sa) *The scorpion bit your husband [said by a woman to her daughter].*
SEE ALSO aneth-akert, anem atherr-akert
utern (T,E), **itwern** (E) *n.*
1. sun, sunshine, sunlight ◆ *No* ulya. Irreltyenng ulya anetyakenh. Uternel ampekerr irreltyenngel. (Sa) *No shade.* Irreltyenng *is when there is only thin shade. The sun might burn [you] when the shade is thin.*
2. heat, hot weather, heat of the sun, summer ◆ Tyerrtyel awem akwet-akwet-irremel, wal arengkek akwel ra angkem, arengk akwerrkek. Uternek anem ra angkem. Utern akwerrkel anem, utern urla. (St) *When people hear the spotted nightjar singing, well supposedly they are singing to the dogs, to the puppies. And to the summer, to the beginning of summer.* ◆ Lher atnertel ingka ampem ayeng uternelaw. Aperwarl iparrp alhey, ingkarl ampem-kety lherel. (Sa) *The heat of the sand in the middle of the creek is burning my feet. Let's go quickly to [the shade of] the river red gum, my feet are being burnt by the sand.* ◆ Utern, arem anwantherr mern atwakey interlek pertipelaw wal utern anemarl irrem. (St) *When we smell the flowers of the wild orange, then we know that the summer is coming.*
SEE ALSO alhwerrp
= **twern** (W,T)
uternek (E) *n.*
daytime, in the daytime
uternek uternek (E)
1. all day, all through the day
2. in the daytime ◆ Uternek uternek alhey, mwerr-awaty aherrkel-awaty. (Sa) *[Let's] go in the daytime, when it's a bit better and there's some daylight.*
= aherrkelam aherrkel
utern urla (E)
the beginning of summer; the end of summer (?) (lit. 'forehead of the summer')
= utern akwerrk
= **twern rlwang** (W)
utern akwerrk (T,E)
the beginning of summer (akwerrk1 *'young', 'newly made'*)
= utern urla
utern mpep (E), **utern mpepel** (E)
1. midday, the middle of the day
2. the middle of summer (mpep *'middle'*)
utern mparnt (E)
the middle of summer (mparnt *'middle'*) ◆ Utern akwerrkek-amparr anek, utern mparnt anem irrem, ampem anem, ingka atherr arlka anem ampem. (St) *First there was the beginning of summer, then the middle of summer comes, and then everything burns, including the feet.*
utern-tayem (E) *n.*
hot weather, summer
= **twern-tayem**
utern-kenh iwerr (E)
a white streak in the sky (in the west in the evening in September) (lit. 'the path of the sun')
utern-utern (E), **itwern-itwern** (E) *n.*
Bagot's furnace ant (*Melophorus bagoti*) ◆ Ngkwarl utern-utern. Ngkwarl yerramp-artekarl ra anem. Inkwel anem yerramp-artek. Awantyem renh. (St) *Bagot's ants are like honeyants. They live in a nest like honeyants do. [We] suck on them.*
SEE ALSO yerramp, inkwareny
= **twern-twern** (W,T)
uternem (E) *vt.*
tell someone to do something; make someone do something; force someone to do something ◆ Ngenh tha uternek ker apek atwetyek alhetyek. (St) *I told you to go hunting.* ◆ Uternek tha kwey *Julie*, atyeng *bag* inerlalpetyek tha uternek. Yanh anem ra akngetyalpem atyeng. (St) *I told Julie to go and get that bag for me. And there she is bringing it back for me.* ◆ Arrentyel uternem, 'Wal unta atyenh

ana kwenh'. Renh apek tyerrty arrpenh atwetyek. (St) *The devil makes him do it, 'Well, you can be mine'. Makes the person go and kill another person.*
= **twernem** (T,E)
uternelhem (E) *vi.*
declare that you are going to hit or growl at somebody; say that you are going to talk to someone about something ◆ Ayeng apekarl uternelhek, angketyek nhakwek. (St) *I am telling you that I am going to talk to that person over there.* ◆ Uternelhem ayeng, tha apek artwa nhakw atwetyek. (St) *I am saying that I'm going to hit that bloke.*
= **twernelhem**
altyerr uternelhem (E)
have a predictive dream about a relation (altyerr[1] *'dream'*)
uterrp (T,E) sandhill SEE UNDER **urterrp**
utharr (E) *n.*
1. burnt hair or fur ◆ Utharr renh arlkngem anem, *clean*-ilem anem alta rarl ampek-penh. (St) *Then [you] clean off the burnt hair, clean off the hair that has been burnt.*
2. the smell of hair or fur burning ◆ Utharr intety-alhemaw — *someone*-el ker itep-item. Utharr intyem. Urlpat-ilem alta. (St) *The smell of burnt hair is coming this way — someone is cooking meat. Singeing off the hair.*
= nthar
SEE ALSO intyem intyerrk
utharr-utharr (E), **tharr-tharr** (E) *n.*
a type of bird
-uthek (E) *n.ending*
without, not having (something). This ending always follows *+ek*. ◆ Manek-**uthek**arl anep-anem ayeng — man anetyangarl ayeng. (Sa) *I'm broke — I haven't got any money.*
uthen (E) *part.*
and, as well as, (this thing) and something else as well. This word cannot go on its own, and it usually occurs after each item in a list of similar things. ◆ Anewart arratyant-atherr anerretyel. Kemarr uthen Petyarr uthen. (Sa) *The husband and wife are right [skin] for each other. Kemarr and Petyarr.* ◆ Ntang atherretyart ap yanh, apwertel athemel awantyemel, arlpar uthen arrerlang uthen. (Sa) *That is a seed that used to be ground up, ground up with a stone, the* arlpar *and the* arrerlang.
= **thwen** (W,E)
uthenem (E) send something to someone SEE UNDER **thwenem**
uthinem (E), **thwinem** (E) *vi.*
get stuck onto something ◆ Ingkelarl lyek uthinenhekarl-ketyaw. (Sa) *The prickles got stuck to my feet as I went along.* ◆ Lyek uthinekarl antyamel. (Sa) *The prickle got stuck on the blanket.* ◆ *Billycan* apek akwet anem uthelp-uthinem, arwengalkerel. (St) *The sugarbag might be stuck permanently to the billycan.* ◆ Mernel apek uthelp-uthinem iltya. (St) *The damper mixture gets stuck to [your] hands.*
SEE ALSO atanelhem, mwernelhem, kerelty-welhem
uthip (E), **thip** (E) *n.*
1. bird. *Uthip* is generally only used of birds that fly, and so does not include emus.
2. other small creatures that fly, such as grasshoppers, beetles etc.
3. Goes before the name of a particular kind of bird or flying creature.
= **thep** (W,T)
uthip-uthip (E), **thip-thip** (E) *n.*
bird [BABY TALK]
utnanth (E) scrub SEE UNDER **unanth**
utnanthem (E) not share food or drink; eat or drink greedily SEE UNDER **unanthem**
utnathat (T,E) *n.*
flower of the mulga, *artety*, and the witchetty bush, *anyem* ◆ Utnathat artetyel anem, kwer-penh anterrng antem ra anem. (T) *The mulga tree flowers, and after that the seeds come out.*
= **nwathet** (W)
utnatyaker (E) type of lizard SEE UNDER **natyaker**
utneng (E) chest SEE UNDER **uneng**[1]
utneng (E) spirit of a person or living thing, soul SEE UNDER **uneng**[2]
utnerreng (E) emu bush SEE UNDER **unerreng**
utney (E) woma, sandhill python SEE UNDER **uney**
utneyn (E) branches put over a grave SEE UNDER **utnin**
utneynt (E) spear wattle SEE UNDER **uneynt**
utnhem (E) bite someone or something SEE UNDER **unhem**
utnin (E), **utneyn** (E) *n.*
branches put over a grave ◆ Utnin arrernem awenng-warl, ra anem anem *Christmas* arrpenhekant. *All right* mer ikwerenhel anem iytwarem. Tywerreng ikwerenhel anem iytwarem. Utnin anem iwem anem, artem anem ingkerrek — *finish. Country* ikwerenh iytwaretyekant. (St) *The branches are put over the grave, and they stay there till the next Christmas. Then ceremonies are held to farewell the deceased person's country and their ceremonial business. Then the branches are thrown away, and the grave is covered over — that's the end. It's not over until the person's*

country has been farewelled.
SEE ALSO awenng

utnyenem (E) look up for something, look upwards SEE UNDER **unyenem**

utya (E) *n.*
dark rain storm; rain in the distance. Also referred to as *kwaty utya.* ◆ Kwaty arlengek arem kwaty utya. Kwaty utyekety, kwaty utyakert yanh apetyemaw. (St) *[You] can see the rain in the distance. Look out for the rain storm that is coming.*
= **tywa** (T)

utyek-utyel (E) *n.*
pretend, fake, not real ◆ Utyekel utyel, urrtyirretyel ntwa. Ngan urrtyirretyelarl atyeng, angka-arrpantey unta atyeng ilep-ilerl. Mern-arrpantey unta ilemel urrtyirretyel, nhenhan arrangkwarl. (Sa) *You're lying. You're lying to me, telling me some sort of story. You're pretending that there's food here but there's nothing.*
SEE ALSO urrtya, rrtywerrem

utyen (E) *n.*
1. a sore, rash or wound ◆ Amarr ra akelhem ampa akely apekan utyen anentyek, kel apernemel ra ikwerel amarrel. Arelh akelhem, amarr akelhem, kel alhwa thelelhemel, kel annga anem ikwerel aperneman, utyen, annga utyen-irrenty. (Sa) *She cuts herself on the arm and then rubs a child who has sores with the blood. Women cut themselves and then the blood seeps out and then they used the blood to rub on the eyes, eyes that have got sore.*
2. sore, inflamed ◆ Arwerl ayenh alherrek utyen mpwaremel. (St) *The stick rubbed me and made me sore.*
SEE ALSO alety, urrma
= **tywen**

utyen-irrem (E) *vi.*
get sore
= **tywen-irrem** (W,T)

utyen-ilem (E) *vt.*
make something sore
= **tywen-ilem** (W,T)

utyenem (E) *vt.*
put something up high; lift something up onto something; put something up somewhere or in something; put something away ◆ Thanarntarl arrernek, mern anem utyenem. Arnel. (St) *Putting a platform in a tree and then putting the food up there.* ◆ Aherr irrkweny akety-ayntem, ingwelarl utyenety-alpek, ingwekety. Akety-ayntem anem renh irrkweny, ingwepenh-ingwepenh. (Sa) *Cutting up the leftover kangaroo meat from yesterday, the animal that was brought back and put away after dark. Then it is cut up early in the morning.*
= **tywenem** (W,T)

utyenelh-ilem (E) *vt.* = **utyenem**

utyenelhem (E) *vi.*
1. put yourself up onto something; lift yourself up onto something
2. show off, brag, skite; boast; put yourself on a pedestal; feel happy about yourself • SEE ALSO tyenkarl-irrem, nakelhem, narlkwelhem, reken-irrem

utyerrk (E) *n.*
1. wild fig, desert fig (*Ficus brachypoda*). Spreading tree up to 4 m high, with glossy green leaves and fruits that change from yellow to red-brown as they ripen. Grows in hills.
2. the edible fruit of the wild fig
= **tywerrk** (W,T)

utyew (E) *n.*
thin, skinny
= **tyew** (T)

utyew-irrem (E) *vi.*
get thin, lose weight
= ampwerrem
= **tyew-irrem** (T)

utyim (T,E), **utyipm** (E) *n.*
ribs, rib bone. Also referred to as *ker utyim.* ◆ Ker utyipm atwetyekaw arlkwetyek. (St) *Get some rib bones to eat.*
= meth, ker meth
SEE ALSO ulta, ltwa

uyarem (T,E) *vt.*
look around for something but not find it; look for something but not see it; see that something is not there; search in vain
SEE ALSO uyarn
= **yarem** (W)

uyarelhem (T,E) *vi.*
1. look around for something ◆ Iwenhek apekarl aparlp-ilekek uyarelhem. 'Nthenhek apek tha aparlp-ilern kwenh, uyarelheman. Urrek ayeng itirrey nthenhek tha aparlp-ilerl-alhern. Uyarelhety-alhem, merel apek. Merel uyarelhety-alhem.' (St) *Looking round for something I've lost. 'Where did I lose it? Wait while I think about where I left it. Maybe I'll go and look around the camp.'*
2. look for someone who has gone away from you (?)
= **yarelhem** (W)

uyarn (E) *adv.*
can't (do something); couldn't (do something); try in vain; try to do something

and fail; be unable to do something; have difficulty doing something ◆ Uyarn tha ikngwerl-alhek, ra atnwerntarl irrek, anerl-anem akwel ra. (St) *I went and tried to ask her, but she doesn't want to go; she must want to stay.* ◆ Uyarn-antey ayeng angkem, anthetyakenh. Ra rlterrk-irremel mentyel awerl-anemel. (St) *I am asking in vain, and she's not giving me any. She's just getting really hard and not taking any notice of what I'm saying.* ◆ *Paint* apek atyenh tha uyarn mpwarem, wal tha impemarl, uyarnarl mpwarem. (Sa) *I am having difficulty doing this painting so I'm going to stop doing it, it's too hard to do.* ◆ Kerek uyarn unthem, arrangkw-antey apety-alpem uyarnarl unthek-penh. Ayeng apek arlewatyerrek uyarn unthemel apety-alpem. (St) *Looking round in vain for meat and returning home with nothing, after looking and finding nothing. I might come back after looking in vain for a goanna.*
= **ywarn** (W,T)
uyarn ahey-angkem (E)
have difficulty breathing (ahey-angkem *'breathe'*)

uyemem (E), **uyimem** (E) *vt.*
not recognise someone or something; behave as if you don't know a person or thing ◆ Uyemetyel untan alhengk-aretyangenhel, kwey atyenh. Alhengk-aretyangel unta uyemetyel. (Sa) *You are behaving as if you don't know my daughter. Not recognising her.* ◆ Ulyewarl ayeng apety-alpem — uyememel anetyalay. (St) *I've come back to the shade — don't behave like you don't know me.* ◆ Uyimemel-artekarl arnterr arep-arem, arep-arem, uyimep-imem uyimep-imem. Ayeng ngkweng-artweyarl apety-alpep-alpem. (St) *Looking really hard and staring [at me] as if you don't know who I am. I am your own relation that is returning.*
SEE ALSO **yem, apal-arem**
= **ayemem** (W)

uyenper (E) *n.*
spearbush, spearwood (*Pandorea doratoxylon*). A shrub to 5 m high, with creamy brown flowers and canoe-shaped pods. Grows in rocky hills. ◆ Arna uyenper ankerl-kweny. Alyelkarl ra. (St) *The spearbush tree doesn't have any lumps on it. It's smooth.*
= **yenper**

uyerrem (E) *vi.*
1. get lost, go missing, disappear out of sight; go away, be away from somewhere ◆ Nthenh-angkwerr nga uyerreperrem. Ayengarl ngkweng uyarn-antey ayeng mpwelhek, untan alhep-alhemant, uyerreperremarl nga. (St) *Where did you get to? I kept waiting for you in vain and you kept going, disappeared.* ◆ Lyetantarl arwem-irrenhetyek, arrwelarl alpek, uyerrek. (Sa) *[Somebody] is just turning up today, after going away a long time ago, after disappearing.*
2. finish; run out, get used up, end ◆ Ahantherrek mern atyenh, ingkerrek-antey. Tey atyenh impen ingkerrek ahantherrek. Ahantherrek ingkerrek innga. Ker atyenh uyerrek, angayakwarl apetyarr-alherrek. (Sa) *All of my food has been eaten, the whole lot. The only tea I have has been used up. Absolutely everything has gone. All of my meat has run out, eaten up by the hungry people who came.* ◆ Kwaty uyerlp-uyerrem akin artnwepel, antyerrk anem kwenh uyerlp-uyerrem anem. (Sa) *Water in the claypan starts to run out, and then it gets dry.*
SEE ALSO **arltwerrem**
3. pass away, die ◆ Arrangkw — uyerrerliwerrek. *Everybody* uyerrek. Rapet arlka. Rapetant nhak *side*-antel anem. (Sa) *Nothing — they've all disappeared. Everybody passed away. And rabbits disappeared as well. There's only rabbits over there on that side.*
SEE ALSO **ilwem, nyerrem, ahap-irrem, arrangkw-irrem**
= **ywerrem**
uyerrerl-alhem (E) *vi.*
go out of sight, disappear, get away
uyerrelh-ilem (E) *vt.*
waste something; make something run out, use something up ◆ Uyerrelh-ilemel atyenh arlkwekaw ker ingkern, uyerrelh-ilek. Lyet tha yarety-alpek ker atyenh uyerrelh-ilerrirrek. (St) *[They] used up all my meat while I was away. I just came back and saw that my meat had all disappeared.*
= **intyarlkwem, arimpem**
= **ywerrelh-ilem**

uyetherrk angkem (E) say things that you shouldn't say or that will upset people SEE UNDER **ywetherrk angkem**

uyimem (E) not recognise someone or something; behave as if you don't know a person or thing SEE UNDER **uyemem**

Ww

wak (E) *n.*
humpy, shelter ◆ Kwaty arrer angkenhetyem; wakek aylpeyaw. (Sa) *The thunder is coming closer; go inside the shelter.* ◆ Intey wak-apeny artelherl-anem kwaty-kety anenh-anenh kwenel inteyel. (Sa) *[Some] caves are formed like humpies, and they are used for sheltering in from the rain.*
= antywa, iltha
SEE ALSO warl

Wakay *n.*
1. Wakaya person or people
2. Wakaya language

wal *part.*
well, and so (from English 'well')

walarnp (W,T), **walaymp** (E), **walaynp** (E) *n.*
1. fighting hook or pick (maybe from Warlpiri *walanypa* 'native pickaxe, native pick')
2. the sharp stone point of a fighting hook or pick. This is attached to a wooden handle by spinifex resin. ◆ Walarnp arnewarnarl arrernetyam. Renhel anem atwerretyam, tyerrty atherr atwerretyam. (T) *The* walarnp *was attached to a stick. That's what people used to fight with, if two people were fighting.*
= alany

waly *n.*
branch, leafy branch, foliage ◆ Waly akeyaw kerek. (St) *Cut some leafy branches for the meat.* ◆ Waly akeyaw, mern apereltyek. (T) *Cut some leafy branches [so we can get] some white substance made by the lerp-scale insect.*
SEE ALSO arlpa²

waly-waly¹ (W,T) *n.*
the very end of a branch, the very top of a tree ◆ 'Waly-waly' ilem akern anthwerr. Arlewatyerr antyem arna waly-waly-warn. (M) *'Waly-waly' is what the really high part of the tree is called. The goanna climbs to the very top of the tree.*

waly-waly² *n.*
1. hair (bereavement term) ◆ 'Waly-waly' renh altarl ilem. Wemarl renh. Interlpel werl-anem. (Sa) *'Waly-waly' is what hair is called. It is spun on the spinning stick.*
2. hairstring and things made of hairstring that belonged to a deceased person (particularly men's things)
3. the red headbands worn by *tyelkath* men (i.e. men on ceremonial business)
SEE ALSO alta, ampeny¹

wamper-wamper (E) *n.*
a type of prickle or grass seed (?)
SEE ALSO intwerrker

wang-wang *n.*
dog (deceased); sympathetic word for dead dogs or dogs that are very sick ◆ Wang-wang atyenh ilwek, akuny. Ipert angernern tha akwernern. (St) *My dog died, poor thing. I just dug a hole and buried it.*
= rtwek-rtwek
SEE ALSO angwely, arengk, tywetyety

Wangerlakwerlang (W) *n.*
Wangala Hills (note Warlpiri *wangarla* 'crow')
= Angank

wangk-wangk (E) *n.*
pig (from English 'oink oink'). Another word for pig, *pek-pek*, is *kwementyay*.
= pingkey, pek-pek

wangkem *vi.*
swell up ◆ Ingka atherr ayeng wangkek. (St) *My two feet have swollen up.* ◆ Iltya ayeng wangkek. Ingka apek. Urepenh apek. Lyekel apek atanthek, arnel apek atanthek, wangkek. Kapert ayeng wangkem, atwekarl apek ayenh. (St) *My hands have swollen up. Or my feet. Maybe from the fire. Or maybe I was pierced by a prickle, or poked by a branch. My head is swelling up after I was hit.* ◆ Ankwa wangkem arntety-irremel, tyerrtyarl arntety-irrem, wangkemarl ra. (St) *When a person gets sick the glands inside their mouth swell up.*
SEE ALSO alhapelhem, arlwar-irrem, amwerenthenng-irrem

wangkelh-ilem *vt.*
make something swell up ◆ Ingkarl atanthemel arlketyerran, *sharp one. Cheeky bugger*, ingkang awangkelh-ilenh-ilenh. 'Pwet-kweny arekerr-irrem ayeng.' (T) *The* arlketyerr *prickle spikes your foot. It's a cheeky bugger [i.e. it hurts] and it makes your feet swell up. 'I haven't got any shoes and I'm in pain.'*

wangkethel (E), **weng angkethel** (E) *n.* [RESPECT LANGUAGE]
1. water
2. thirsty ◆ 'Weng angkethel anthetyek alha weng angkethel ngwarrengkw.' (Sa) *'Go and give some water to your thirsty husband [said by a woman to her daughter].'*
= angkethek-uthek
SEE ALSO angkethel, kwaty

wanmal (W,T) *n.*
lots of people or things, a big mob ◆ Alewatyerr wanmal anengk twerl-apem. Wanmal-awaty. (N) *Going along and killing lots of goannas. Rather a lot of them.* ◆ Artwang

wanmal map apetyem. (T) *Lots of men are coming.*

SEE ALSO anengk[1], angerr[1]

wantem *vt.*

1. feed someone or something ◆ Amwelek wantem kwer kwerenh mern pwety-arenyel. (T) *The mother is feeding her child on bush foods.* ◆ Kwer ngkwenh wantay. (M) *Feed your child.*

2. hunt (get something to eat); use something to hunt with ◆ Irrtyartel war wantetyart. (M) *Just using spears to hunt with.*

wantelhem *vi.*

1. feed yourself ◆ Angayel wantelhem ayeng. (St) *I'm hungry and I'm feeding myself.* ◆ Kel nta wantelha, kwer angerr wart. (M) *Feed yourself, you're a big kid now.*

2. provide your own food ◆ Ayeng anyent mernel wantelh-ilem. (M) *I get my own food myself.*

3. paint up (men) ◆ Irrety anteth-akert, anteth kwerel wantelhem artwa. *Pretty* mpwaremel alakenh. (N) *Men paint themselves up with eaglehawk feathers. They [make themselves] pretty like that.*

Wanty (W) *n.*

name of soakage west of Yuelamu (Mt Allan) community

wap-anem *vi.*

be blocked off, shut or closed ◆ Arrewarl wap-anek. (T) *The door was shut.* ◆ Ngkwarl rltwamp kweny-rtwek waparl-anem. Angwerr-lkwer altywer-irrem. (T) *In the night the hole in the sugarbag nest is closed. In the afternoon it opens.* (?)

SEE ALSO arrngert anem, martem

wap-arrernem *vt.*

block something off; shut something, close something (arrernem '*put*') ◆ Arrew yanh wap-arrernay. (M) *Shut that door.* ◆ *Flat tyre* nheng wap-arrernem antem *patch*-el. (T) *Patch that flat tyre [i.e. block the hole with a patch].* ◆ Arlewatyerreh wap-arrernem, arnang waly map akemel wapem arrernem rlpwer alenh. Kel altywer-ilemel atwem, tyerrem. (T) *Cutting some branches and blocking the goanna off in the hollow log. Then opening the log up, killing the goanna, and pulling it out.* ◆ Ankerr map ina kwaty-warn apetyem, antywetyek. Tyerrty nhak intatel anep-anem, wap-arrernekarl. Ankerrel arety-kwenh. Alakenh akwel irrtyartel ker inenh atwetyart, amerrel. (T) *The emus come to the water to drink. That person is sitting in the emu hide, blocked off from sight. The emu can't see him. That's how people used to kill emus, with a spear and woomera.*

wap-arrernelhem *vi.*

1. become blocked off, shut or closed ◆ Mpank-antey, wap-arrernelhekarl. (T) *It's not ready, [the hole] is still blocked off [said of sugarbag].*

2. use part of self to block something off ◆ Wap-arrernelhaw ngkwarl pwelaparl thelelhemekaw. Wap-arrernelhay, iltyay. (Sa) *Use your hand to block off all that sugarbag honey that is pouring out [of the hive]. Block it with your hand.*

wap-irrem *vi.*

close in on something

wapey (E) *n.* [BABY TALK]

whitefella, white person ◆ 'Wapey-kety rntert-irray.' Ampek ilem. (St) *'Be quiet because of the whitefella.' That's what you tell kids.*

war *part.*

1. (doing something) a little bit, nearly ◆ Akwek war rntwarr-irray! (M) *Move just a little bit!* ◆ Inkwareny kwaty-rlwer anwern akern war inyem. (M) *In the rain time we dig up honeyants just near the surface.*

2. only, just that (and nothing else) ◆ *No* mwekenh apek anem pep nhel intem — angkety war intem. (M) *There's nothing restricted about what's in this book — it's just language.* ◆ Lpway angerr arlanentyarl, arlanenty angerr. Kenh lpway akwek kenh akwek wararl — ilerrtyarl apetyem war. (T) *A large river is called 'arlanenty'. On the other hand small creeks are just small — where a small watercourse or gully comes along.*

3. (doing something) for no particular reason; (doing something) light-heartedly; 'It's not a big deal', 'It's unimportant' ◆ War ayeng angkep-angkem arrkenel-arleng. (St) *I'm talking about nothing in particular, just for fun.* ◆ Warek-amparr ayeng alhem, lyetant apety-alpetyenh. (St) *I'll just go first, and then come back soon.* ◆ War ayengarrp alhep-alhem. (St) *I'm just going around by myself.* ◆ War akarntemel ayeng anep-anem angayakw kwenh. (N) *I am just sitting down quietly because I'm hungry.* ◆ War apekarl atwerretyel arrkenty-ilerremel ilterretyel — mernek-arrngel apek, alhekarlek-arrngel apek. (St) *They are fighting and picking on each other and swearing at each other for no particular reason — perhaps over food, or because somebody went.*

4. 'Nothing', 'Nothing much' (in answer to a question such as 'What's up?')

lyet war

any minute now, round about now, just now,

any moment; soon; almost immediately, not long ago (lyet *'today'*) ◆ 'Alhekaw angey ngkwengenhan? Ilwengerekay?' *'No,* lyet war apety-alpem.' (P) *'Did your father go? Till when?' 'No, he's coming back any minute.'*

war anthem
lend something to someone (anthem *'give'*) ◆ War thwengk anthern, angety-alpang antey. (M) *I just lent it to you and you can bring it back later.*

warakeparleparl (W,T) *n.*
nankeen kestrel (*Falco cenchroides*) ◆ Warakeparleparl akern amparr wenhek irrem, kwenelak irrenhem inenhem arnarem, kelyaw antem. (N) *The nankeen kestrel is high up in the sky at first, then it swoops down and catches* kelyaw *lizards.*
= anthep-anthep, lyentyelyeng, lyentyelyaw, ulpmerr-atwenh
SEE ALSO irrkerlanty

Waramwengk (W), **Waramweng** (W) *n.*
1. Warumungu person or people
2. Warumungu language
= Arwemeng

warepelh-pelh (T), **wareng-pelh-pelh** (T), **warek-pelh-pelh** (T) *n.*
dragonfly
= urewap-imperreny, rew inperrenh, kapert^2, kwaty-inperrenh

Warey-warey (W,T) *n.*
name for Yuelamu (Mt Allan) community
SEE ALSO Arlperrakeny

warl *n.*
house, shelter ◆ Ayeng alhem warl-warn kwaty inetyek. (T) *I'm going to the house to get some water.* ◆ Apmer ngkwenhel kwenh waylpel warl artelhetyel. (St) *Whitefellas are building houses on your land.*
SEE ALSO antywa, wak
CAN SOUND A BIT LIKE awal *'cracked ground'*

-warl shows the direction of the motion towards or to something SEE UNDER **-warn**

warlekwert (W,T) *n.*
widow, widower ◆ Warlekwertan arelh arlweker-arenyarl, arlweker-warnarl irrek, anewekarl aparlp-ilek-arleng. Warlekwertan ilem, arlweker-warn irrek. (T) Warlekwert *is a woman who is in the single-women's camp, one who has lost her husband. She is called* 'warlekwert' *because her husband has died.*
= inpert

warlekwert-irrem (W,T) *vi.*
lose husband or wife; become a widow or a widower
= inpert-irrem, anker-athek-irrem

warlpal, waylpel (E), **warlpel** (E) *n.*
white man, white person, European person, non-Aboriginal person (from English 'whitefella')
= alhernter
SEE ALSO arlter, mperlker, tywelker, wapey

warn (E) *n.*
a wad or lump of tobacco ◆ Warn anyenem arrakertel. (St) *The tobacco wad is carried in the mouth.*
= ngkwerlp ampeng
SEE ALSO kelh

warn-ilem (E) *vt.*
make a wad of tobacco by grinding it up and mixing it with ashes ◆ Ngkerlp warn-ilemel arlkwem. (Sa) *Making the tobacco into a wad to chew.*

-warn (W,T), **-wern** (W,T), **-warl**, **-werl** *n.ending*
1. Shows the direction of the action towards or to something; towards, to, at, into, onto, (go) somewhere, (go) in a particular direction. ◆ Ahakey ra lernelhem ahelh-**warn**. *The native currant falls to the ground.* ◆ Urlepety-antey ayengan anep-anem, apmer arrpenh-kenh-**warl** alhetyakenh. (St) *I keep stopping in one place, I haven't been to other people's country.* ◆ Twerrp kwer-**warl** anwern alhalhem katyerr akerl-anetyeh. (N) *We're going to the sandhills to pick desert raisins.* ◆ Ayeng alhetyenh weth-**warl**-antey. (St) *I am going to go to that place.* ◆ Aherr angkek, 'Nthenh-**warn** ayeng alhey ntywety-**warn**?' (M) *The kangaroo said, 'Where can I find a warm place?'* ◆ Arratemel alhay, aketh-**warn**! (M) *Go out into the open!* ◆ Inpert-irrek, yanh arnkenty-**warl** irrek. (St) *That man has become a widower, has gone to the single-men's camp.*
2. Shows that the direction of the action is towards the place where particular things are; (go) for a particular purpose, for (something), to get (something). ◆ Ker aherr **warn** lyweny alhem. *Going hunting for kangaroo.*
3. Shows that the action is done into or on something; in, on, into. ◆ Athem athem rnewarl alparr-**warl** apek, rwewarlam thelerl-anem alakenh. Kel amperl-anem, mern *nice* anthwerr kelh arlkwerl-anetyenheng. (N) *They were ground up into a wooden dish and then poured onto the fire. The seed would cook really nicely, into a seed cake, which was then eaten.* ◆ Mern ahakey inerl-alpek arntap-**warn**. *We collected the native currant fruits in bark containers.* ◆ Artwel irrtyart arrernetyam amirr-**warn** ker atanthetyek. (T) *The man put the spear in the woomera to spear the kangaroo.*

◆ Arelhel ingkwernem Anengkerr kampeth-**warn.** (T) *The woman is painting Dreaming designs on the canvas.*

4. (facing or pointing) towards (something); in that direction

warnp (W,T) *n.*
cooked damper; ripe fruit or tuber; flour. Also referred to as *mern warnp.* ◆ Mern katyerr warnp. (T) *Ripe desert raisins.* ◆ Warnp kwer-warn kwaty thelem. (M) *Pouring the water into the flour.* ◆ Mern warnp ampeng, mern itemarl-penh. (M) Warnp *is damper that is cooked, after it has been cooked.*

warr (E) *n.*
emu's back. Also referred to as *ker warr.* ◆ Ker warr antheyaw tha arlkwetyek. (Sa) *Give me some meat from the emu's back to eat.*
= amakw

warrakwelakwel (W,T) *n.*
rock nightshade (*Solanum petrophilum*) (?). The fruits are poisonous.

warrangkwer (W,T), **warrenkwer** (W,T) *n.*
a type of plant (no common name) (*Stylobasium spathulatum*). A shrub about 2 m high, with hard, brown nuts about the size of a pea (note Warlpiri *warrurnkura*).
◆ Warrangkwer renh kwetyetyart angety-alpetyart rwangem itetyart atanthemewarratyart nekeleth mparetyeh. (N) *The* warrangkwer *seeds used to be collected and brought back and then holes were pierced in them [with hot wires] to make necklaces.*
= arleyakwerr, ampweth-ampweth

warrernem (E), **iwarrernem** (E) *vt.*
copy someone or something; imitate
◆ Warrernem arrkenel. Ahel apek unta apek angkep-angkem, wal ayeng angkep-angkem *same way* akin — warrernepernem tha ngenh. (St) *Imitating for fun. You might talk in an angry way, and then I talk the same way again — I copy you.*
SEE ALSO arlepewem

warrert-irrem (T,E) *vi.*
line up, go along in a line, go along in Indian file ◆ Ayeng warrert-irremel untherl-apem. (St) *I am going along in a line [with the others].*

warrk *n.*
work, job (from English 'work') ◆ Ayeng apek alengk-welhemer ngkweng-kety, warrk-kety apek. (St) *I might hide myself from you, or hide myself from work.*

warrk-irrem *vi.*
1. work, do a job ◆ Ayeng atyep-atyep alherl-anem, purrk-irretyanan. Mernek apek warrk-irrem tey arrtyetyek warrk-irrem atyep-atyep akwet, irrngerney-antey. (Sa) *I go around energetically, I don't get tired. I work cooking food and making tea and I'm still lively and energetic.* ◆ Thakeman pwertant-arey anwern warrk-irretyart. (T) *We used to work together as stockmen.*
2. function, be in working condition
SEE ALSO rrkwapem, mpwarem, atyanem

warrken map
the workers, employed people (map *'plural'*)
◆ Warlan artem tyerrty map warrken mapel. (T) *The working mob build houses.*

warrk-warrk alhem (W) rush along; flow quickly (water) SEE UNDER **werrk-werrk alhem**

wart *part.*
of course, obviously, really, as you should know ◆ Awenk wart anngarenty, *no* arrwekel ra artwa arek, artwa aretyakenh-penh, lyetantarl amangkek. (N) *Of course teenage girls who have not seen men before, and who have just grown up are* anngarenty, *they don't like to go with men.* ◆ Ker wart arlkwem angayel. (T) *Of course you eat meat if you're hungry.*
◆ Nhenh wart ayeng alhem. (T) *Of course I'm going over there.* ◆ Anew-anew anthwerr artwang angkety-alhem, arnkarr apek angkety-alhem — terangkel wart. (M) *That man comes up and argues, and just about hits [the person] — he's drunk of course.* ◆ Ntwang wart, kwer rrkwety-kwenh. (M) *You're the one who didn't look after the kid.*

wartay[1] (W,T) *part.*
'What's up?', 'How are you?', 'What's going on?' ◆ Ngenh apek apawenhem, 'Wartay?' (M) *[Someone] might ask you, 'What's up?'*
= wenhek

wartay[2] (E) *adv.*
wailing or crying in mourning (men)
◆ Watay-irrep-irreman artwarl, marlan akayelarl artnep-artnem. (St) *The word for men crying in mourning is* 'wartay-irrem', *whereas for women it is* 'akayel artnem'.

wartay-irrem (E) *vi.*
wail or cry in mourning (men)
SEE ALSO akayel arnem

warterlk (W) *n.*
bustard, bush turkey, plains turkey (*Ardeotis australis*) (note Warlpiri *wardilyka*)
= artew, arwengerrp

waterlweper *n.*
white woman, European woman, non-Aboriginal woman (from English 'white'; Tasmanian Aboriginal language 'lubra')
= metheth
SEE ALSO warlpal, alhernter, arlter, kartey,

mperlker, tyerrty arlter, tywelker

wath (E) *adv.* [RESPECT LANGUAGE]
1. (do something) a little bit
2. only, just that (and nothing else) ◆ Wath anerl-anetyek ayeng. (St) *I am just sitting down [in mourning].*
SEE ALSO war

Watyal (E) *n.*
female junior skin name, corresponding to Kemarr (note Kaytetye *Watyale*). See diagram p. 744.
SEE ALSO Kemarr, Tyakarr

watyepatyep (W) *n.*
really hungry, really starving ◆ Ntang lyweny alhem *somewhere*, ker arlka apek angwerrmelh-iletyakenh nta apety-alpem watyepatyep angayel anthwerr. (M) *You might go hunting somewhere and you don't find any meat or anything and you return home really starving.*

waw *n.* [BABY TALK]
1. fire
2. hot ◆ Ampa akwek yanh mwanty. 'Wawel ampekerr pepey!' (St) *Watch out for that baby over there. 'The fire will burn you baby!'*
SEE ALSO rwa, rwernp

wawely-irrem (W,T) *vi.*
dodge or ward off (a spear) ◆ Irrtyart-hety wawely-irrem. (M) *Dodging the spear.* ◆ Wawely-irrem ater, atanth-kety renh. Ra wawely-irremel impem, ahelh-warl anyem arnang yanh. (N) *He dodges it in case it spears him. He dodges it and then that thing falls to the ground.*
SEE ALSO irrkar-aytnem, irrimper-irrem

way *n.*
1. wire (from English 'wire') ◆ Twererr rwel itep-item wayel. (M) *Burning patterns on the clapsticks with [hot] wire.*
2. things made of wire, such as handles or fences ◆ Parrek way-akert. (T) *The paddock has a fence.* ◆ Tyampet way-akert akwek. *The tin has a small wire handle.*
SEE ALSO parrek
wayem-ilem *vt.*
ring up on the telephone (from English 'wire')

wayeleth *n.*
wireless, radio, tape recorder (from English 'wireless') ◆ Kwer rrwey wayeletheng angkerl-anem. (T) *The boy is talking on the radio.*

waylpel (E) European person, non-Aboriginal person SEE UNDER **warlpal**

wekel (E) *adv.* [RESPECT LANGUAGE]
(doing something) overnight; camping out or staying somewhere for a night or for a few nights ◆ Wekelang arrantherr ahanenhemay? (St) *Are you all [including respect kin] going camping out?* ◆ Wekel-ayerr akwel ahaneynem, tyety-ayerrek. (Sa) *Supposedly they [including respect kin] have gone camping out, hunting.*
SEE ALSO unekel

weken (E) edible grub found in the ground at the base of the river red gum SEE UNDER **ahekwenayt**

wel-arem (E) *vt.*
see that meat is not fat (?)

-welhem, -iwelhem (E) *v.ending*
Occurs in some compound verbs. Although the meaning of *-welhem* is sometimes not distinguishable from that of the compound verb as a whole, it frequently occurs in verbs with actions to do with placing the self on something or in some location.
SEE ALSO -iwem
irrpenper-welhem *vi.*
grind teeth; rub together (trees) ◆ Tety irrpenper-welhem. (M) *Grinding [your] teeth together.*
ilperlper-welhem (T,E), **ilperrper-welhem** *vi.*
shake self
impalerrp-welhem (W) *vi.*
rub self on something ◆ Arengk impalerrp-welhem antyamel, anety npwangerr. (M) *The smelly dog is rubbing itself on the blankets.*
kerrk-welhem (W,E) *vi.*
stick or poke into something

welterr (E) *n.*
native willow, apricot tree (*Pittosporum angustifolium*). Tree to 7 m high, with drooping leaves, pale yellow flowers and orange fruits which have sticky red seeds. ◆ Kwey awenk werlatyant artelhem welterr-kety, akely anekerr, artelhenhem. (Sa) *Young girls cover their breasts [when they are close to] the native willow, in case their breasts remain small.*
= anawert

welyar (W,T) *n.*
buck spinifex, bull spinifex (*Triodia longiceps*). A grass that grows in hummocks up to 1.5 m high, and has very sharp bluish green leaves. ◆ Angerrety, aywertart. Aywert angerr. Tyalangk kweny. Ulpayel anenhepenhem, welyar ra. (T) *The* welyar *spinifex is big like* aywert. *It doesn't have any resin. It grows along the creeks.*
= ntwemerr, arrangk

welyeyerlp (W), **welyerlp** (W), **welyererlp** (W) *n.*
a type of bird (maybe a parrot). This bird looks a bit like a ring-neck parrot, and lives in hollow trees.
SEE ALSO mwelyar

wem[1] *vt.*
1. hit something by throwing something at it ◆ Wem tha arengk, arnel apek. Arnel tha wem arengk alpetyek. (St) *I am hitting the dog, maybe by throwing a stick at it. I'm throwing a stick at the dog to make it go back.* ◆ Atantyel tha wem ngenh apek. (St) *I might pelt you with dried mud.*
2. strike or hit (lightning) ◆ Awely-awelyel arwerl wekarl. (Sa) *The lightning hit a tree.*
3. blow (wind) ◆ Werenyel wem akerneng, arnang akwek angetyeh. (N) *A strong wind is blowing and carrying small things along with it.*
SEE ALSO ltewem
CAN SOUND A BIT LIKE awem *'hear'*; iwem *'throw'*

wem[2] *vt.*
1. spin hair or fur to make hairstring ◆ Wem tha alta. (St) *I am spinning hair.* ◆ Arlpalh wetyam altepenh, kapert anem ayernelhetyam alta nhelkwer. *Men*-elant. Kwarlp-penh apek mpwaremel wemel, kel kapert anem *string* mpwaremel. Alta yanh akwernelherl-anetyek, ayernerl-anetyek. (St) Arlpalh *was spun from hair, and then the head was bound up with it. Just men did it. The fur from the spectacled hare-wallaby was used for spinning, and then string was made for tying up the head, tying up the hair.*

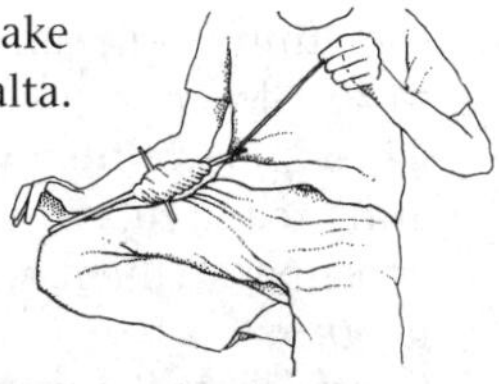

= irrkety-wem, alyep mpwarem, wenty-ilem
2. make fire using firesaw; make fire by rubbing a hard piece of wood against another softer one, or against a shield or carrying dish • = rrmwarl-wem

-wem[3], **-iwem** (E) *v.ending*
Occurs in some compound verbs. Although the meaning of *-wem* is sometimes not distinguishable from that of the compound verb as a whole, it frequently occurs in verbs with actions to do with placing or putting something somewhere or on something; for example, *arlkeny-wem* 'make a design or marking'; *irraker-wem* 'make grooves or markings'.
SEE ALSO iwem
anewem *vt.*
name something, call something a name
alhengk-wem (E) *vt.*
hide (something)
arrngert-wem *vt.*
block something off
rrmwarl-wem (W) *vt.*
make fire by rubbing

wemey (W) *n.*
a fun way to refer to someone that anyone listening would know; 'You know the one'; 'We all know who we are talking about'
SEE ALSO antyeny

weng angkethel (E) water [RESPECT LANGUAGE] SEE UNDER **wangkethel**

wenh (W,T), **iwenh** *n.*
1. 'What?', 'Which one?' ◆ Wenh intyem? (M) *What is smelling?*
2. something or other, whatever (used when the speaker is not being specific) ◆ Alengk-welhem ayeng tyerrty yanh-kety iwenhek apek apay-unhekerr. (St) *I am going to hide from that person in case they ask me for something or other.* ◆ Apwelaynt ker arlkwenh-arlkwenh. Iwenh apekarl arlkwem, atanthem, kwen-irrenhemel inenhem. (St) *Black kites eat meat. Whatever they eat, they hunt with their claws, swooping down to get [it].*
3. 'Who?' [SOME SPEAKERS]
SEE ALSO ilek, angwenh, nthakenh, nthanh
wenhay (W,T), **iwenhay**
'What?'
= ilekay
wenhek (W,T), **wenheh** (W), **iwenhek**
1. 'What for?', 'Why?' ◆ Wenheh apalenthwem? (M) *What [are you] looking for?* ◆ Wenhek ntwa ayeng lther-wem? (M) *Why are you pinching me?*
2. for whatever, for some reason (speaker is not being specific) ◆ Arreyeng-arrey-irretyal anwengkerr aneyaw, angkety-kweny aneyaw, arreyeng-arrey-kweny. Irlpa apek anwengkerr akangkwerrey, iwenhek apek anwengkerr akangkwerrey, irlpel manty awerl-anemel. (N) *We shouldn't chatter, but sit down without talking, without making a noise. We'll pay attention and listen to whatever, listening carefully with our ears.*
= ilekek
wenheng (W,T), **iwenheng**
'What for?', 'Why?', 'Because of what?' ◆ Iwenheng ker nhenh unta ntyerrman angetyek, ker anter angetyakenh? (T) *Why did you bring this skinny emu, why didn't you get a fat one?* ◆ Tyerrty nhenhel atyeng rwang arrernek. Iwenheng? (M) *This person swore at me. Why?*
wenh-wenh (W,T), **iwenh-iwenh** *n.*
various things, whatever ◆ Iwenh-iwenh tha inerl-alhetyek atyenh. (St) *I'll go and get various things of mine.* ◆ Ayeng irrkwapepapem iwenh-iwenh, iwenh ilep-ilem-kety ayeng irrkwapem. (St) *I work along at whatever, at*

whatever people tell me.
SEE ALSO angwenh-angwenh
CAN SOUND A BIT LIKE awenh-awenh *'auntie* 'father's sister'

wenh-apatherr (W,T), **iwenh-apatherr**
1. 'What skin name?', 'What is [a person's] skin name?' (-apatherr *'what skin'*) ◆ Wenh-apatherr tyerrty ra? (M) *What skin is that person?* ◆ Wenh-apatherram nta? (M) *What skin are you?*
2. whatever it is, what's-his-name, thingummyjig
= ilek-apatherr, angwenh-apatherr

wenh-apert (W,T), **iwenh-apert**
'What's the matter?', 'What's up?', 'What's wrong?' ◆ Wenh-apertay kweray? Ntwan rlkertam? (M) *What's the matter with you child? Are you sick?* ◆ Akarntemel anem iwenh-apert anemay? Iwenhengay? (N) *Why are you sitting down quietly? What's happened?*
= ilek-apert

wenhekwey (W,T), **wenhakwey** (W,T), **wenhakey** (T), **iwenhakwey** *n.*
what's-his-name, thingummyjig, something or other (said when the speaker is not sure of the name of something or has temporarily forgotten it)
= angwenh-akwey, ilekakwey

wenh-artek (W,T), **wenh-arteh** (W,T), **iwenh-artek**
1. 'What is it like?'
2. what something is like, what something resembles ◆ Altyerrarl akek-warn alhetyek, maty-kenh, tha aretyek, mer iwenh-artek kwenh. (T) *I want to go and see my mother's country to see what it's like.*

wenh-penh (W,T), **iwenh-penh**
1. 'Why?', 'For what reason?' ◆ Wenh-penh arelh alenh npwart alhek? (T) *Why did that woman go off sulkily?*
2. from whatever, because of whatever ◆ Alta ayeng rnter-rnter akwet. Alta rnter-rnter-irrek anem ayeng iwenh-penh, ayeng apernelhek. (St) *My hair is still red. It went red after I did whatever, dyed it.*

wenh-athew
'What is it?', 'What's its name?' (when trying to remember something)
= angwenh-athew

wenh-tety (W,T)
'What's that?'

wenng-irrem (T,E) *vi.*
keep away from trouble; avoid trouble or bad situations; shy away from something you've had a bad experience with ◆ Wenng-irrem iltem-arleng ayenh. Iknga anem ayeng alhep-alhem, ilterlarl-apem nhenhel. (St) *I am keeping away because [someone] is swearing at me. So now I'm going around on my own, because this one is swearing at me.* ◆ *Town*-kety ayeng wenng-irrem, ngkwarl-kety, *family*-el antherl-anekerr, terangkem-ilem anem. (St) *I keep away from town because of the grog, and because family give you grog and make you drunk.* ◆ Wenng-irrem, anthetyang anem, antewarl irrem kety. Ngkerlp anthetyang anem renh antewarl-irrem-kety. Mwerrek-athen tha anthetyam. Yanhap ikwerety. Ra ilwekarl, *'Ah ah ah'*. Artekernekan. Ayeng wenng-irrek ikwerety. Wenng-irrem, menty anerlanetyek. Ayeng wenng-irrek yanh anthetyakenh — apant antherlanekerr. (Sa) *I now know not to give [her] any in case she vomits. Not to give her any tobacco in case she vomits. I gave her some, thinking it was all right, but because of it she started coughing, 'Ah ah ah'. Then I knew about the bad effect it had. I knew to avoid it, and not to give her any — not to give her the wrong thing.* ◆ Wenng-irrem ayeng, unta apek ayenh iltekarl. (St) *I am going away to keep out of trouble, because you growled at me.*
CAN SOUND A BIT LIKE awenng *'grave'*

wenngel anthem (T,E) *vt.*
make someone dissatisfied, make someone want to avoid you (anthem *'give'*) ◆ Arelh apek artwel atwemel wal wenngel anthem, ikwer anewelikw apek wenngel anthem. (Sa) *The man might hit the women and this makes her dissatisfied, her husband might make her want to leave him.*

wenty (W,T), **winty** (W,T) *n.*
tunnel in honeyant nest
SEE ALSO inkwa

wenty-ilem (E) *vt.*
spin hair or fur to make hairstring ◆ Wenty-ilerl-anem renh, renh-lkwer, arna arntwerrkerl-anemel. (St) *Spinning it [hair], holding onto the stick.*
= irrkety-wem, alyep mpwarem
SEE ALSO wem2

weny, iweny *n.*
mosquito ◆ Alhem ayeng rwewarn, wenyeng. Yakay! (M) *I'm going to the fire to escape from the mosquitoes. Oh no!*
= aheny, angeylk, kewenyeweny

wep, iwep *n.*
1. spider
2. spider web [SOME SPEAKERS] ◆ Inwerl angerr wepel-ayeng arlparernem. Anarnpemel, ahelh kwerenh-warn irrpem lert-akert-warn. (M) *The*

big spider is hanging in the web. It climbs down and then goes into its [hole] in the ground, into its hole which has a lid.

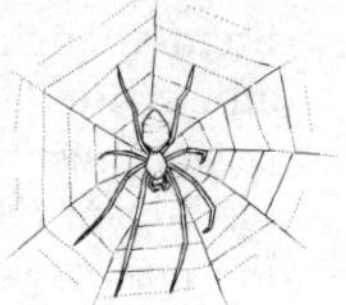

3. itchy grub, processionary caterpillar; larvae of the bag-shelter moth (*Onchrogaster* spp.) [SOME SPEAKERS] ◆ Wepel rtety-rtety mpwarem. (T) *Itchy grubs make you go lumpy.*

4. the nest of the itchy grub; processionary caterpillar, bag-shelter moth ◆ Wep yanh akenh perrap mwerr angerr *medicine*. Rwepenh arrernewarretyart. Alety-warl, kapert atwerrekarl penh-warl manty arrernenhernenh yanh renh. *Good medicine* kwenh. Wep renh kart alernem alernem. Kart renh *clean*-em-ilem *clean*-em-ilem *soak*-ilem alhewem wep renh. Kwatyel alhewem kwatyel *soap*-em ilem alhewem tekarl wem renh. *Right dry*-am renh inem, *something* angwenh-akwey kwer apek *medicine* kwer arrernem, anter apek. Alety-penh *bandage*-em akin ilem arnang kwerel. *Bandage* arrernem alakenh. *Finish* aretyenheng irrkatyartehem. Lwerenarl yanh. Mantyelarl alhewerl-anemel weth akin arrernetyenheng arrpenhemarl, alakenh. (N) *That* wep *is really good medicine. It was used as a bandage for burns and for bandaging up wounds or for tieing up heads that had been injured after a fight. It's really good medicine. The inside part of the itchy grub nest is shaken out. Then the web is washed till it's clean. Then it is hung out to dry. When it's dry you get it and maybe put some medicine on it, such as fat. Then you use it to bandage up the wound, and you'll see it heal up till it is just like it was before. Then you can wash it carefully and use it again for another wound.*
SEE ALSO ingeth

werengerr (E), **werrengerr** (E) *n.*
a type of plant (no common name) (*Muehlenbeckia florulenta*)

werengkerr (W,T), **weringkerr** (T) *n.*
spindle (note Warlpiri *wiringkirri, wirinykurru*) ◆ Arna akwek atherr alakenh, *windmill*-artek mpwarem. Arratyeny arna akwekarl irnem, renh-warnarl akwernem. Kel renhek-arlekan *tie*-up ilemel anem renh mpwarerl-anem. Ayernelherl-anetyek rarrp, alta map. (T) *There are two sticks that are made into a sort of windmill shape. The small stick is straight across and that's where you put the string. The hair is spun around that and it winds itself around the stick.*
= inta, werintyerr

wereny *n.*
strong wind ◆ Werenyel wem akerneng, arnang akwek angetyeh. (N) *A strong wind is blowing and carrying small things along with it.*
SEE ALSO rlkang, rrwep-rrwep, awerantyerrng, alhwerrp

wererr (E), **wurerr** (E) *n.*
twisted stem of the bush banana, silky pear, *alangkw, alkwarrer* (*Marsdenia australis*) ◆ Wererr. Arnel ra ayerlpayernenhem wererr anem anem akern. Alangkw anem ikwerel atwaylpaylp anem wererrel. (St) *The stem of the bush banana. It winds itself around, high up in the tree. The bush banana fruits hang in bunches from the stem.*
SEE ALSO altyey

werety (T) *n.*
a type of plant (no common name) (*Zornia albiflora*)

weretyerretyerr clever, knowledgeable, having a good memory SEE UNDER **wetyerretyerr**[2]

weringkerr (T) spindle SEE UNDER **werengkerr**

werintyerr (W,T) *n.*
spindle ◆ Irrkety wepewem werintyerr-warn. (M) *Hairstring is spun on the spindle.*
= werengkerr
SEE ALSO inta

-werl Shows the direction of the motion towards or to something; towards; to; at; into; onto; (go) somewhere, or in a particular direction. SEE UNDER **-warn**

werlamp (T), **urlamp** (T) *n.*
stone knife (used for cutting meat)
SEE ALSO antha[2], apwert antha, alywek, kartamp, inkwartety, irntarlter, irntang arlter

werlamperrenty (W,T), **werlamperreny** (W,T), **urlamperreny** (T), **urlamperrenty** (E) *n.*
the congregation (of a church); a gathering, a lot of people, everybody ◆ Tyerrty map anthwerr, 'werlamperrentyem' ilem. Tyerrty anengk, werlamperrenty, Altyerr-henh nheng *pray*-irrem, nheng tyaty-warn alhemel. (M) *A real lot of people, that's what is called* werlamperrenty. *Lots of people, going to church and praying to God.* ◆ Tyerrty map urlamperreny tyaty-warn alhem. (T) *All the people are going to church.* ◆ Urlamperrenyel arrernem mantarr tywelkerek. (T) *The congregation puts the white robes on [the priest].* ◆ Artwa apek ngkart-irrem yenh arrernem. Urlamperreny antyaperel anem renh arrernem. Tyaket mperlkerek ina irrpelh-ilem. 'Nta kwenh ngkart angerr.' (T) *The man is put there to be ordained as a minister. The whole congregation places him there. They put the white robe on him. '[Now]*

you are an important priest,' [they say].

werlaty (T,E) *n.*

1. breast, teat ◆ Werlaty alpwely-irrem antywekarl-penh. (St) *The breasts have gone slack from [the baby] drinking.* (St) ◆ Apetyem ampa akwek apek awenk werlaty-kweny apetyem, wal atnawert yanh aremelan artelhemarl. Ra werlaty-akert aneyamel, kenh arrangkwan-kety. (St) *A child coming along, or a young teenage girl who hasn't got any breasts yet, well when they see the native willow they cover themselves. That's so that their breasts will grow, whereas if they don't then their breasts won't grow.*

2. milk

= paty

werlaty akarnterrng (E)

breasts of an adolescent girl (akarnterrng *'the shape of breasts when they are starting to develop'*)

werlaty antywem (T,E)

suck breast, drink from the breast (antywem *'drink'*)

= paty antywem

werlaty anthem (T,E)

breastfeed (anthem *'give'*) ◆ Mikwel werlaty antherl-anem. (Sa) *The mother is breastfeeding.*

werlaty alha (T,E)

nipple (alha *'nose'*)

werlaty ilwernenty (E)

last child in a group of siblings (ilwernem *'extinguish something'*)

= paty antyerrk-ilenh

ker werlaty (E)

breast meat (of emu) (ker *'meat'*)

werlkemen, rlkwemen (W,T) *n.*

senior woman, old woman (probably from English 'old woman')

= arelh ampwa

werlkng (E) *n.*

mound of earth on top of a grave

= awenng

werltey *part.*

at the time, frequently (from English 'all day')

-wern (W,T) Shows the direction of the motion towards or to something. SEE UNDER **-warn**

wernem *vt.*

blow (wind), blow on someone ◆ Rlkang angerrel wernem. Rlkang angerrarl apety-arleng tak artelhey. (M) *There is a big wind blowing. Build a windbreak because there is a big wind coming.* ◆ Rlkangel ayeng anyartetyew, aketh-warn ayeng alhem. Rlkel ayenh wernetyeh. (M) *I'm going outside so that the wind can blow on me and cool me down. So that the wind will blow on me.* ◆ Rlkel arelh wernem. (T) *The wind is blowing the woman.*

SEE ALSO pwem

wernelhem (E) *vi.*

sit in the wind to cool down; have a breeze blow on you ◆ Iylkel wernelhem anem utern-kety. (Sa) *Because of the heat [I'm] sitting in the wind to cool down.*

wernman *n.*

senior man, old man (from English 'old man')

= artwampw, artwa aywang

wernpernp (W) *n.*

a type of cricket or cockroach

werrant (W) *n.*

windbreak

= rtak, kwenty[2]

werrengerr (E) a type of plant (no common name) SEE UNDER **werengerr**

werrk *n.*

scrub, thick plant growth ◆ Werrkel anem alengk-welhepelhem, waly akwekarl irrpety-alhek. (St) *I went in amongst the small bushes to hide myself in the scrub.* ◆ Werrkel ayeng apant-irrek. (St) *I got lost in the scrub.* ◆ Werrk yanh-kety kwenh aketh-angkwerr alhey. (St) *[Let's] go in the open country to avoid all that scrub over there.*

arnam werrk (W,T), **arnang werrk** (W,T)

scrub

werrk-werrk alhem (W,T), **warrk-warrk alhem** (W) *vi.*

rush or flow quickly (water)

(werrk-werrk (?))

werrk-werrk alpem (W,T), **warrk-warrk alpem** (W) *vi.* = **werrk-werrk alhem** ◆ Kwaty rew warrk-warrk alhem lpwayel. (M) *The floodwater is rushing along the creek.*

werrp (E), **wirrp** (E) *n.*

1. mulga bean, bush bean (*Rhyncharrhena linearis*). Climbing vine with long green bean-like pods. Often climbs up mulga trees.

= angerak

2. fruit of bush bean • = aherretyepwer, awerretyepwer

3. matted, frizzy, knotted or tangled hair ◆ Alta werrp weth-artek mern weth-artek werrp altyey-apeny, aylep-aylep. (St) *Matted or frizzy hair is like that plant, tangled like the leaves of the bush bean plant.* • = alangkw-alangkw • SEE ALSO lthel-lthel, kelh-kelh

CAN SOUND A BIT LIKE awerrp[1] *'blood and meat juice from cooked kangaroo'*; awerrp[2] *'small amount of rain'*

weth *n.*

Refers to the person, place or thing that both the speaker and the hearer know is being

discussed; that, you know the one etc. ◆ Arelh weth apety-alpek artwep-irremel. (St) *That woman turned round and came back.* ◆ Iwerl-alhek wethek-antey, wethek-antey tha iwerl-alhek. (St) *I went and left it at that place (you know the one).* ◆ Yerr, akwek-akwek weth, arlkerrk, urrperl angerr weth. (St) *That smallish ant, the meat ant, that large black one.* ◆ Ayeng alhetyenh weth-warl-antey. (St) *I am going to go to that place.*
SEE ALSO nheng
CAN SOUND A BIT LIKE aweth *'(do something) some more', '(do something) again'*
weth-lkwer *n.*
that sort of thing; something like (the one being referring to) ◆ Arntap renh iyltem kel kwaty-warl arrernem arntap. Karntey-artek anem ra irrem, alhwartek. Kel lyek-lyek apek alhewelhem rtety-rtetyarl irrem weth-lkwer. (St) *The bark is peeled off and then it is put into water. Then it goes like Condy's crystals, like blood. Then you wash sores, lumpy skin or things like that with it.* ◆ Wetharl unta mpwarek-artek mpwaray, weth-lkwer mpwaray. (St) *Make one like that one that you made, make that sort of thing.*

wethel-irrem (T,E) *vi.*
whistle (from English 'whistle')
= arrawenth-irrem

wethey (W) *n.*
horse (from English 'horsey') ◆ Parrek ina artelhenhepenhem. Pwelek-kety an wethey-kety. (T) *They are building the fence along there. Because of the cattle and the horses.*
wetheth-ayerr (E) *n.* [RESPECT LANGUAGE]
horse (from English 'horse')
SEE ALSO nanth, nantew

wetyeny (E) *n.*
emu shinbone

wetyerretyerr[1] (W) *n.*
piercing or spearing something right through
= tyetepetep

wetyerretyerr[2] (W), **weretyerretyerr** (W,T) *n.*
clever, knowledgeable, having a good memory
kapert wetyerretyerr (W,T)
someone who is clever or knowledgeable (kapert[1] *'head'*)
SEE ALSO inangkal, kalty, kapert altywer, kapert arraty, kwerathek, lywenpeny

wetyerrpetyerrp (T) *n.*
full, lots of (?) ◆ *Plate* wetyerrpetyerrp ker thwen mern thwen angetyem anwehengkerr. (T) *Bring us a plate full of meat and vegetables.*

weyang (E) *n.*
really fatty meat (just kangaroo, bullock)

weyapel *n.* [RESPECT LANGUAGE]
1. food
2. hungry ◆ 'Weyapel ahanelh-ilem kweyay.' Mwey-mwey atyenh-kety ayeng angkem. (St) *'Take the food, daughter.' I am talking that way because of my son-in-law [said by a woman].* ◆ Weyapel irrkertetyek. (St) *They [respect kin] are going to cook the food.* ◆ Weyapel amely-wepewem. (St) *They [respect kin] are eating the food.*
SEE ALSO mern, angayakw
weyapelek-uthek (E) *n.* [RESPECT LANGUAGE]
hungry ◆ Ayepel-irretyel ngwarrengkwan weyapelek-uthekarl. (Sa) *Your husband is sitting there hungry [said by a woman to her daughter].* ◆ Ahanelh-ilenherr-areyay tyety-ayerr yanhentyakay. Weyapelek-uthek tyety-ayerr ahanelh-iley. 'Weyapel' ap ilem 'angayakw'. Weyapelek-uthekel amely-aketyek athwangang. (Sa) *All of you take the meat to that one over there. Take it to the one over there [e.g. my son-in-law] who is hungry. 'Weyapel' is what is said [in respect language] for 'angayakw'. The hungry one can eat.*
weyapel-irrem *vi.*
feel hungry ◆ Weyapel-irrem ayeng kwenh (M) *I'm getting hungry.*
SEE ALSO angayakw-irrem

weylkerr atwem (E), **wirlkerr atwem** (E) *vt.*
cut a small hole in a tree to listen for the sound of native bees

weymperr (E) burial platform SEE UNDER **wimperr**

Wilora (E) *n.*
the name of the Aboriginal community on Stirling Station. This name is based on *Ilewerr*, the name of a swamp near the community.
SEE ALSO Ilewerr

wimperr (E), **weymperr** (E) *n.* [SENSITIVE LANGUAGE]
burial platform ◆ Wimperr-warl arrernetyam, tywenetyam, wimperr mpwaretyam, *pass away* irretyam tyerrty, yanh-warl anem arrernetyam, walyel-antey. (St) *When a person passed away they were put there on the burial platform, amongst the branches.*
SEE ALSO kwenterarr, thanarnt, awenng

winty (W,T) tunnel in honeyant nest SEE UNDER **wenty**

winy-winy (E) auntie (father's sister) [BABY TALK] SEE UNDER **awenyey-awenyey**

wirlkerr atwem (E) cut a small hole in a tree to listen for the sound of native bees SEE UNDER **weylkerr atwem**

wirrp (E) mulga bean, bush bean SEE UNDER **werrp**

wurerr (E) twisted stem of bush banana SEE UNDER **wererr**

Yy

ya (W,T) he, she, it SEE UNDER **ra**
ya, **yaw**, **yew**, **yeway** (W,T), **yew-yew** (T,E) *part.*
yeah, yes ◆ Ntwerrkenhan alhek. Rapet apawenhwek, 'Alhweng ngkwehenh ayeng irrpey tyerrtyeng?' 'Yeway. Alhweng angerr yanh atyengenh.' (M) *The python went off. He asked a rabbit, 'Can I come into your burrow to escape from the humans?' 'Yes. My burrow is a big one.'*
Yakakwerlp (W) *n.*
name of waterhole north of Yuelamu (Mt Allan) community
yakay (W) An exclamation of surprise; 'Oh!', 'Wow!' SEE UNDER **yekay**
yakerr (E) *n.*
1. a type of grass (no common name) (*Yakirra australiensis* (?))
2. the edible seed of this grass
yakerray (W,T), **yakerr** (W,T) *part.*
An exclamation of surprise, excitement or pain; 'Goodness!', 'Look at that!' ◆ Yakerr! Arlewatyerr angerr atwek. (M) *Look at that! [She] killed a big goanna.*
SEE ALSO yekay
Yakwetey (W) *n.*
name of a soakage and hill west of Yuelamu (Mt Allan) community
yakweth *n.*
bag, dilly bag, handbag (women's) ◆ Arelhel yakweth-warn arrernem mern arlatyey. (T) *The woman is putting the pencil yams in the bag.*
SEE ALSO parlkw, pewaty
yaleng *n.*
over there, from over there, somewhere round there ◆ Tey arlpelh yaleng angetyay. (M) *Get me those tea-leaves from there.* ◆ Alha ayeng urltaty-irrem alethangek, alethang tha arnarem, arrer ra anem, yalengarl apetyem. Alha ayeng rltwar-irrem, urltaty-irrem. (St) *I have a feeling in my nose about a stranger, and then I see a stranger coming, and then they come closer, from over there. My nose clicks, I have a premonition.*
SEE ALSO yanh
yalk (W,T), **yalkw** (W,T) *n.*
1. wild onion, onion grass, nalgoo (*Cyperus bulbosus*). A grass with chocolate-brown seed heads and small edible bulbs underground.
2. the edible bulbs of the wild onion
= yerrakwerr, irreyakwerr
yalk-ayerr (E) *n.* [RESPECT LANGUAGE]
wild onion ◆ Yalk-ayerr irrepetherl-wa. (Sa) *Go and get some wild onions.*
yalkwerr (T) *n.*
underground cave ◆ Ker arlewatyerr yalkwerr kwenel intem. (T) *The goanna is lying inside the underground cave.*
= aharlkwerr
yang (W,T) he, she, it SEE UNDER **ra**
Yangatyerr (W) *n.*
name of waterhole between Yuelamu (Mt Allan) community and Yuendumu
yanh *n.*
1. there, over there (in the middle distance; not very far away) ◆ Artwang yanh yapay irnem rwertel-ayel. (M) *That man over there is standing in the way on the road.*
2. that, those (persons or things that are in the middle distance; not very far away) ◆ Angwenh-henham angwely yanhan? (M) *Whose dog is that?* ◆ Angwenham yanhan? Ayengam. (M) *Who is that? It's me.* ◆ Antelhey ayeng yanhel-arleng. (St) *I'm going to follow that person.*
3. that (thing that you are referring to or has already been mentioned) ◆ Rlwek yanhel mwerrarl ilem *clean*-em ilelhem annga — *everything* alhewelhem artwengkenng-apertem mernt-apert, iteth-ilem. (N) *That native pine is used to wash the eyes and clean them and make them better — to wash all over and to make people better if they have a cold or are sick.*
SEE ALSO alenh
= yatenh
yanh-lkwer (E) *n.*
that sort of thing, that kind of thing ◆ Arwerl apek tha akeng-akeng yanh-lkwer lyapek, tyerretyek tha, tyerremel iwetyek. (St) *If I have grown some useless plants, or that sort of thing, then I'll pull them out, pull them out and chuck them away.* ◆ Ker rrpwamper yanh-lkwer, ker rlpwerelarl anetyart, rrpwamper. Lweren arlka arlkwerretyart. (N) *They also used to eat possum meat and that sort of thing — animals that lived in hollow trees.*
yanh-tyel (W), **yanh-ntyel** (W,T), **yanh-they** (E) *n.*
from there
yanh-angkwerr *n.*
that way, in that direction
yanhenty (E) *n.* [RESPECT LANGUAGE]
there, over there (in the middle distance; not very far away) ◆ Amerrkwernerliwerretyel yanhentyak-antey. (Sa) *They are singing over*

there [people including someone the speaker is in a respect relationship to].

yapaty (W,T), **yapety** (W,T) *part.*
An exclamation of pain, something you say when you are in pain; 'Ouch!' (note Warlpiri *yapaja*) ◆ Yapetyay, arekerr awelhemeng. (M) *Oh, I'm really in pain.*
SEE ALSO yekay
yapaty-irrem (W,T), **yapety-irrem** (W,T) *vi.*
groan or cry out in pain ◆ Yapety! Ngkwern ayeng ltwakelhek, yapaty-irrerl-anem ngkwern akert. 'Yapetyay, apetyewarray atyeng. Yapaty ayeng apenhay kwenh.' (N) *Ouch! My leg is broken, and I'm groaning in pain with the sore leg. 'Ahh, why don't you all come to me. I am in pain.'*
SEE ALSO yekay-irrem

Yapay Irran (W) *n.*
Yippee Dam, Yuelamu (Mt Allan) area

yapek
maybe, perhaps, that might be so ◆ Yapek apay apek unhey. (Sa) *Maybe [I'll] ask [them].*
SEE ALSO apek, ya

yapety (W,T) An exclamation of pain; 'Ouch!' SEE UNDER **yapaty**

yar-yar (E) *n.*
good solid shade, big shade; lush growth
= angwarlp

yarem (W), **ywarem** (T) *vt.*
look around for something but not find it; look for something but not see it; see that something is not there; search in vain for somebody or something ◆ Kwer yanhel lyet ywarem mam kwerenhek. (T) *That child is searching in vain for his/her mother.*
◆ Ngwerrew thang ywarerl-alpern mernek. (T) *Yesterday I went to look for bread and there was none there.* ◆ Lyet yarerl-alpek, mernarl ingkerrekan arlkwern katyerr aherrel. Ywarern anantherr arnang anyentarl inenhem kwenh. (T) *We just came back after not finding any food — the kangaroos had eaten all the desert raisins. We couldn't find much and only got one or two.*
◆ Mer ingkeny yarem. 'Ityam nhenh kwenh.' (M) *Going and seeing that the place is empty. 'There's nobody here.'*
= **uyarem** (T,E)
yarelhem (W), **ywarelhem** (T) *vi.*
1. look round for somebody or something
2. look for someone who has gone away from you; wait in vain for someone who has gone away (?) ◆ Kwer yanh ywarelhem amwekek, lyweny alhek-arleng. (T) *That kid is looking round in vain for his mother who has gone hunting.* ◆ Ayeng ywarelhek *jack* atyengenhek. Arrpenhel inekarl. (T) *I went looking for my [car] jack in vain. Somebody had taken it.*
= **uyarelhem** (T,E)

yarn (W) can't (do something) SEE UNDER **ywarn**

yarr-wem *vt.*
sandpaper or scrape something to make it smooth, or to sharpen it ◆ Yarr-wem, atnem apek tha arterrp-ilemel yarr-werl-alhem alyelk-ilemel. Apwertel apek, apwert ilep-arrpantey *knife*-arrpanteyel. *Knife*-el anem lyetarr yarr-wepewem. (St) *I am scraping the digging stick to make it smooth. I might scrape it with a stone, or with a stone axe or some sort of knife. Nowadays people use knives to scrape things smooth.* ◆ Irrtyart yarr-wem, arrerlp-ilemel yarr-wem yarr-wem yarr-wem. Arrerlpem antem. (N) *The spear is scraped to make it sharp, scraped and scraped. Then it's sharp.*
SEE ALSO arrpem, arterrp-ilem

yarrert angkem (E) *vi.*
pant (dog) (angkem '*speak*') ◆ Arengk yarrert angkerl-anem. (Sa) *The dog is panting.*

Yartepetyey (W) *n.*
Direct Action Bore, south-west of Yuelamu (Mt Allan) community

yartey (W) *part.*
An exclamation of satisfaction (?).

yarwelyem (W), **yawelywem** (W), **yaywelyem** (W) *n.*
horn (of an animal) ◆ Pwelek kapert yarwelyem atherr-akert. (M) *The bullock has two horns on its head.*
SEE ALSO ahiwelhem, yerewelyek, rewelyerr, napey

yatenh (W,T) *n.*
1. there, over there (in the middle distance; not very far away) ◆ Yatenh alhep-alhem aywang rang. (T) *The old man is walking over there.*
2. that, those (persons or things in the middle distance; not very far away) ◆ Yatenh inay arnang ngkwengenh. (M) *Get that thing of yours.* ◆ Artwangel tyerrty yatenh atwem. (M) *The man is hitting that person.*
3. that (thing that you are referring to or has already been mentioned)
= yanh
SEE ALSO alenh, alert1, alertenh, nhenh, nhetenh

yatyarr *adv.*
visit, go visiting, on a visit ◆ Arelh alhem yatyarr arlweker-warn. (T) *The woman is going visiting to the women's camp.* ◆ Yatyarr ayeng alhem *Barrow Creek*-warl. Ampekarey-warl ayeng alhem yatyarr. (St) *I'm going to Barrow Creek. To visit the children.*

yatyarr alhem
go visiting

yaw yeah, yes SEE UNDER **ya**

yawelywem (W) horn (of an animal) SEE UNDER **yarwelyem**

yawerrang (W), **yawerr** (T) *n.*
a big male kangaroo
SEE ALSO aherr, ampelaherr, aharlparrengk[1], artar

yay *n.*
1. senior or elder sister ◆ Yay atyenh apek rlkert-irrerleng ayeng atham-irrem, alhwarrp-irremel. (St) *If my elder sister gets sick then I feel sorry for her, feel sad.* ◆ Ayeng arnekarnarirrem marnt-warn, yay atyengenharl apety-alpemek. (T) *I am going to meet my big sister who is coming back on the bus.*
2. mother's elder sister's daughter or father's elder brother's daughter; cousin
3. particular (senior) relations with the same skin as your *yay*. Whether or not a person is a junior or senior sibling to another can be calculated in terms of the relative ages of their parents.
4. elder sister (baby talk) [SOME SPEAKERS]
SEE ALSO angkwer

yaywelyem (W) horn (of an animal) SEE UNDER **yarwelyem**

yek-yek (E) *n.*
a type of fly
SEE ALSO ltwamp-ltwamp

yekay, **yakay** *part.*
1. An exclamation of surprise; 'Oh!', 'Wow!'
2. An exclamation of pain, something you say when you are in pain; 'Ouch!'
SEE ALSO yapaty, yakerr
yekay-irrem, **yakay-irrem** *vi.*
groan in pain or cry out in surprise
SEE ALSO yapaty-irrem

yel-irrem (E) *vi.*
lead the way, take the lead, go first ◆ Yel-irrem ayengaw, arrpenhan atyeng antelhenhem iter-they. (St) *I'm going to lead the way, and the others can follow me from the side.*
SEE ALSO arrwekel-irrem
yel-angem (E), **yel-akngem** (E) *vt.*
lead someone along ◆ Arrpenh apek pweng apek yel-akngep-akngem amwelt-they. (St) *Somebody who is blind is led along by the arm.*
SEE ALSO tyarr-angem, tyey-angem

yelk (E) *n.*
bush camp, ceremonial camp (for young men)
= akew

yem (W) *adv. (?)*
not recognising someone, behave as if you don't know about a person or thing
yem-irrem (W,T) *vi.*
not recognise someone, behave as if you don't know about a person or thing
SEE ALSO ayemem, uyemem

yemay (W,T) *part.*
'What's up?', 'What's happening?', 'Are you all right?', 'Hey!'

yenarrk (W) *n.*
a type of spider (note Warlpiri *yinarrki*)
SEE ALSO wep, ingeth

yenh (W,T) him, her, it SEE UNDER **renh**

yenk (T) spirit, soul SEE UNDER **inka**

yenper, **ywenper** (E) *n.*
spearbush, spearwood (*Pandorea doratoxylon*). A shrub to 5 m high, with creamy brown flowers and canoe-shaped pods. Grows in rocky hills. ◆ Yenper arternetyam, *clean* antem yarr-wetyam, arrerlp-iletyam, kel *clean*-ilemel arternemel arrernetyam. Rwel itetyam, arternetyam, arternem wetyam, arrerlp-iletyam. Yatenh yenper, irrtyart anthwerr. Apwert nheng iterel irnerl-apem. (N) *The spearwood was scraped and cleaned and then straightened and sharpened. When it was cleaned it was put in the fire to straighten and sharpen it. That's* yenper, *it's really for making spears. They grow on the sides of the hills.*
= uyenper (E)

yep (E) *n.*
umbilical cord ◆ Yep aketyek ampa akwek, atnemel rnternem, atanthem ampa akwekek-arlek yep. (Sa) *The umbilical cord of a child is cut with a digging stick.*
SEE ALSO metyeletyel, tyelepelep
CAN SOUND A BIT LIKE ayep *'tar vine'*

yep-yep *n.*
sheep ◆ Arntarnt-aretyart war arraty, yep-yep. (St) *That's true that [we] used to look after sheep.*

yer (E) *n.*
unable to walk; crippled ◆ Yer, nthakenh alhetyakenh, atnathan anerl. (Sa) *A person who is crippled can't walk and just sits.*
= anath
yer-irrem (E) *vi.*
become crippled or lame

yer-welhem (T) rub yourself in or on something SEE UNDER **ywer-welhem**

yerewelyek (E) *n.*
horn (of animal)
SEE ALSO yarwelyem, rewelyerr, ahiwelhem, napey

yernt, **ywernt** (E) *n.*
1. native currant (narrow leaved variety) (*Psydrax ammophila*)
2. fruit of the native currant ◆ Arlkwenh-

arlkwenh akin, wantyarlewarretyart kwa. War inelh-alpemel arlkwem ahakeyart akin yernt yanh. Ahakeyart antywerrketyeh. Ntyenp akert akin. Inem akin renh. Yerntan arlpa alkey akwek. Ahakeyan arlpang angerr. (N) *The* yernt *native currant is edible as well, we used to eat [the sweet fruit]. We'd just go along picking them and eating them, the same way we did the* ahakey *plums. The fruits are mashed up like the* ahakey *fruits are. The dry fruits are also collected. The* yernt *plant has small long leaves. The* ahakey *plant has big leaves.*
SEE ALSO ngkwernelyerr

yerr *n.*
types of ants (particularly small black ones) (*Camponotus* spp. and *Iridomyrmex* spp.)
◆ Yerrelap arlkwem tyerrtyarl. Merel intety-alperl arlkwem, merel apek antyam werlek: '*Eh,* yekay — yerr-hety anwek alpey kwenh'. Yerr *cheeky bugger,* akakwenhakwenh. Akwek anthwerrarl. (N) *Ants bite people. When they are lying down in camp, where they have thrown down a blanket: 'Hey, ouch — let's move away from the ants'. Ants can be cheeky buggers, biters. Some of them are really small.*
SEE ALSO yerramp

yerrakwerr *n.*

1. wild onion, onion grass, nalgoo (*Cyperus bulbosus*). A grass with chocolate-brown seed heads and small edible bulbs.
2. the edible bulb of the wild onion ◆ Ikngerr-ampeny-kenh 'yalkw' — anwern-kenh 'yerrakwerr'. Kik-wemel arlkwerl-apem inelhapemel. (M) *The word 'yalkw' belongs to the people from the eastern region — ours is 'yerrakwerr'. We go along picking them and peeling them and eating them.* ◆ Yerrakwerr inyetyart irrkeremel irrkeremel nyetyart yerrakwerr renh, *billycan* pwelap nyetyart aweth nyetyart irrkeretyart irrkeretyart lpwelemel then-wetyart arlka arrernetyart pwelap kwetyemel, yerrakwerr yanh renh. Rwel atyerrety-alpem, thwerremel arlkwerl-anetyek panthel-ayel. Thwerrem, kwart ant anem arlkwerl-anetyeh mwerr anthwerr arlkwerl-anetyeh kwart arlkwemel arlkwemel arrernem. (N) *We used to dig up the wild onions, clearing the ground and digging the wild onions up and filling up the billycans. Then we'd dig some more. We'd go back and cook them in the fire and then clean the skins off in the wooden dishes. We'd clean the skins off and then just eat the bulb. They are really nice to eat.*
= irreyakwerr, yalk

yerrakwerr kwart *n.*
bulb of the wild onion, onion grass, nalgoo (kwart '*egg*')

yerramp *n.*
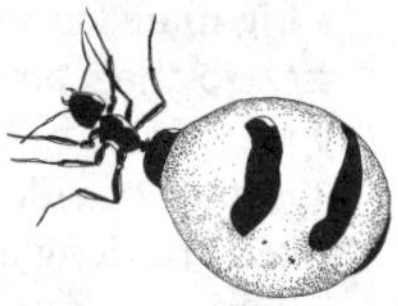
honeyant (*Camponotus inflatus*). Also referred to as *ngkwarl yerramp.*
◆ Yerramp-kenh, alhweng apmer ikwerenh, akwek map anem kwerel anem, inkwa ikwerel. (St) *The honeyants' nest is their home, and the little [honeyants] are there, in the chambers of the honeyant nest.* ◆ Waly akwek akerneng arrernem, arntap-el-arleng, yerrampek-arlek. (N) *A small branch is placed over the bark container, on top of the honeyants.* ◆ Yerrampel aterlk-irrem, awert renh awantyem. (M) *The honeyant bursts and then [you] suck on the honey-soaked earth.*
= inkwareny
SEE ALSO inkwa, yerr

Yerrekelyerr (W) *n.*
name of a waterhole in the Coniston area

yerrekeyerr (T,E) *n.*
sweet white substance made by the lerp-scale insect found on the Normanton box, *alywelp, alhelp* ◆ Alywelpel-ayel yerrekeyerr perrap kelh anthwerr, an perrap theweyet anthwerr. Akemel akemel akemel kel mer-warn angety-alpetyenheng theweyet anthwerr. (T) *There is a white substance made by the lerp-scale insect found on the* alywelp *tree that is in lumps, and it is really sweet. It is picked and picked and picked and this really sweet stuff is taken back to camp.*
SEE ALSO aperelty, mamp

Yerrekwaty *n.*
Dneiper

yerrk (W,T) old fireplace, cooking spot, fire pit SEE UNDER **rerrk**

yerrkengal (T) *n.*
honey from ghost gum bark
= ulemparrty

yerrng-irrem (W,T) *vi.*
1. show someone that you don't like them; be rude to someone, give them a dirty look; dislike someone or something, get angry, get touchy ◆ Tyerrty arrpenhek yerrng-irrem. (T) *Not liking another person.* ◆ Tyerrty angkety anety ngkweng angkek, mwerr apek ntwang. Ntwang yerrng-irremel renh ilterl-alhek. (T) *Somebody said bad things about you that were*

not true. So you went and angrily growled at them.
2. tell someone to get out or keep out
3. not want someone to touch your things
SEE ALSO anywerr-irrem, arnkely-irrem, ahel-irrem, arlelty-irrem, rrwampem, urrampem

yew, yew-yew (T,E)**, yeway** (W,T) yeah, yes SEE UNDER **ya**

Yuelamu *n.*
Mt Allan community
SEE ALSO Arlwem

ywarem (T) look around for something but not find it SEE UNDER **yarem**

ywarn, yarn (W) *adv.*
can't (do something); failing to (do something); trying in vain; trying to do something and fail; being unable to do something; having difficulty doing something ◆ Aleny apekap angkem, aleny ywarn angketyek. War apekap-irrek aleny. *Might* tywen-akert apek. (St) *Unable to speak properly, the tongue having difficulty in talking. Maybe there is a sore on the tongue.* ◆ Ywarn ahey-angkem. (St) *Having difficulty breathing.* ◆ ✎Aherr yarn apalenthwek mereh, anetyeh manangkarr-angkwerr, artety nwanth-angkwerr, twerrp-angkwerr kwerem alpek. (M) *The kangaroo couldn't find a home, so he went back to the spinifex and mulga and sandhills for ever and ever.*
= **uyarn** (E)

ywek, ywekaw *part.*
Used to answer a question in the negative; 'I don't know' ◆ Ywek, aretyakenh tha. (St) *I don't know, I haven't seen it.*
= iy^2
SEE ALSO inpa

ywekerrekerr *n.*
oval wooden board used by women in initiation (young man) ceremonies
◆ Artekerr-penh mpwarem ywekerrekerr. (T) *Dancing boards are made from roots.*

ywenper (E) spearbush, spearwood SEE UNDER **yenper**

ywep-arrernem (W,T) *vt.*
deny that you have something, pretend you haven't got something when you really have ◆ Wenheng ntwang ywep-arrernepernem? Mern arlka apek ker arlka apek. *You gotta* antherl! (T) *Why are you hiding stuff? Food or meat. You have to give it [to others]!*
SEE ALSO itya

Ywepentywern (W) *n.*
name of waterhole west of Yuelamu (Mt Allan) community

ywer-welhem (W), **yer-welhem** (T), **rwer-welhem** (E) *vi.*
rub yourself in or on something; roll around in something ◆ Pwelek anel-ayeng angwely ywer-welhem. (M) *The dog is rolling around in the bullock shit.* ◆ Rwer-welhem ampa apek, ahernel *dry*-ilelhem, ampekenharl alakenh. Pip-kwenyel atna rwer-welherl-alhem. (St) *A child might rub themselves on the ground to make themself dry. If they haven't got any paper they might rub themselves on the ground to get the shit off their bottoms.*
SEE ALSO impalerrp-welhem, impakemp-iwelhem

ywer-ywer arem (W,T) *vt.*
see something that is faintly visible; see something illusory; imagine that you see something
SEE ALSO arrkay, aherr arem

ywerlarr (T) *n.*
a person loaded with weapons

ywerlperr (W,T) *n.*
close upper generation family of the initiate (young man going through ceremony), including mothers, fathers, mother's brothers, father's sisters
SEE ALSO thampartey, anyent arrpenh, perlal, ntwerleng, ntyangkwenng, rteyepertey, alyey^2, alyaper-warn

ywerlt (W,T) *n.*
someone whose child has died; bereaved parent ◆ Awenpan anem arelh warlekwert anewekarl aparlp-ilem *or* arelh ywerlt anem kwer kwerenharl aparlp-ilem. Kakey kwerenhel antem mern tyenkerrel arrakert-ilem angketyek. (T) *A woman who has lost her husband, or a woman who has lost her child, is* awenp*; she's not allowed to talk. Later on her elder brother gives her some ceremonial food to release her from the ban on speaking.*
ywerlt-irrem (W,T) *vi.*
lose a child; become bereft of a child
= anker-athek-irrem

ywernt (E) native currant (narrow leaved variety) SEE UNDER **yernt**

Ywerntem, Rntwem (T), **Ywerntemew** *n.*
Yuendumu (rntwem *'to dance'*). See map p. viii. ◆ Anwern impek Ywerntem-areny map pwerreperlel. (T) *We beat Yuendumu at football.*

ywerrem *vi.*
1. get lost, go missing, disappear out of sight; go away, be away from somewhere ◆ Ywerrek, apant apekarl irrek tyerrty. (N) *The person disappeared, got lost.*
SEE ALSO apant-irrem
2. finish, run out, get used up, end ◆ Kwaty

nhenh ywerrekam. (M) *This water has run out.* (T) ◆ Tal apek ywerrem, *form* apek *sign*-em-ilety-kweny. (T) *The money will run out, if [I] don't sign the form.* ◆ Mern ywerrekarl, mern kel ilwekaw. Anwengkerr mern-warn irrem, mern ywerrek-arleng. (N) *The food has run out, it's finished. Let's go somewhere where there is food because [our food] has run out.* • SEE ALSO arltwerrem

3. pass away, die ◆ Tyerrtyan ywerrek. (T) *The people have died out.* ◆ Kwenyel apek ywerretyenh. (M) *He may die during the night.* • SEE ALSO ilwem, nyerrem, ahap-irrem, arrangkw-irrem

= **uyerrem** (E)

ywerrelh-ilem *vt.*

1. waste something, make something run out, use something up ◆ Atyengenh akwet ntwa ywerrelh-ilem anyentak akwet — tey apek mern apek. (M) *You are always wasting my things, so that there is hardly any left — tea or bread.*

= intyarlkwem, arimpem

2. turn something off (?)

= **uyerrelh-ilem** (E)

ywerrenhem *vi.*

disappear into the distance

ywerrengerreng (T) *n.*

people who have passed away

ywerrkem, rwerrkem (T), **rirrkwem** (E) *vt.*

shake bush plum or native citrus tree, *ahakey*, to make the fruit fall down ◆ Ywerrkem ahakey ahern-warl atnyetyek. (St) *[You] shake the bush plum tree so that the fruit falls to the ground.* ◆ Ahakey rwerrkem, ahelh-warnan lernelhem ahakey *seed* map. Renh anem kwetyerl-anem. (T) *[You] shake the bush plum tree so that the fruit falls to the ground. Then you go along and collect them.*

SEE ALSO lernem, ilperlper-wem

Ywerternt (T) *n.*

name of place west of Aileron. See map p. viii.

SEE ALSO Pmara Jutunta

ywetherrk angkem (T,E),

uyetherrk angkem (E) *vi.*

say things that you shouldn't say or that will upset people (for example, saying the names of deceased people instead of using the word *kwementyay*); say stupid things ◆ Ywetherrk nta angkep-angkem atyengel-ayel. 'Kwementyay' ilang atyengel-ayel. (T) *You are saying things in front of me that you shouldn't. Say 'kwementyay' in front of me.* ◆ Ntwa atyeng ywetherrk angkety-alpek. (St) *You came and said silly things to me.* ◆ Ywetherrk angketyal anay. (T) *Don't say all sorts of inappropriate things.* ◆ Uyetherrkarl angkerrem-ketyaw, atwetyek. (Sa) *They are going to fight over the stupid things that are being said.*

ywetherrk-irrem (T,E), **uyetherrk-irrem** (E) *vi.*

do silly things, behave stupidly

◆ Mpwenyekarl angkem-kety uyetherrk-irrem. (Sa) *[You] are behaving stupidly, talking about getting a boyfriend.*

SEE ALSO unerlewem

Ywetyeteng (W), **Ywetyertey** (W) *n.*

name of rockhole west of Yuelamu (Mt Allan) community

English *to* Central and Eastern Anmatyerr
Finder

The English to Central and Eastern Anmatyerr Finder is not a dictionary and should only be used to help you find the word you need in the main dictionary. You should always check back in the main dictionary to make sure you understand the meaning of the word fully so as to lessen the risk of making mistakes in translation.

List of abbreviations

(?) there is a degree of uncertainty about the word
SP only used by some speakers
E Eastern Anmatyerr communities
T Ti Tree
W communities west of the Stuart Highway, including Mt Allan, Laramba and Desert Bore

The finder list is meant as a guide to assist the reader in searching for entries in the main dictionary. The English headwords are arranged in alphabetical order. The general principles behind the ordering of the sub-entries in the finder are as follows.

Where there is a group of sub-entries under a main English headword entry these are arranged so that the most common word or generic Anmatyerr word comes first; for example, the general word for 'snake' comes before any words for particular species of snake. In a list of specific terms (say, for types of snake) they are ordered alphabetically: death adder, mulga snake etc. The most obscure things are at the bottom of the list and the most common at the top.

The general word is followed by special register equivalents such as 'respect' and 'baby talk'. However, if these special register words match other words that are further down the list they are paired together.

Within the sub-entries nominals usually come first followed by verbs—generally the intransitive ones first then the transitive. In part this ordering reflects the derivation of Anmatyerr words; for example, under the reversal headword 'healthy' the sub-entry 'well, healthy' *mwerr* is followed by 'get well' *mwerr-irrem* and then by 'make someone better' *mwerr-ilem*.

The dialect of Anmatyerr that a particular word comes from is shown by the abbreviations listed above.

Aa

a, an
one of a thing .... anyent
abandoned
empty .... arltwa, arltwang (W,T)
of places and houses .... ampeny[1]
become abandoned, empty .... arltwerrem (W,T), arltwirrem (T,E)
make someone desert or abandon someone else .... arrkereny-ilem (E)
abandon something .... menty-irrem
abdomen .... alem, anert
Aboriginal
Aboriginal person .... Tyerrty, Tyerrty rrpwerl (W,T), Tyerrty irrpwerl (E), Rrpwerl (W,T), Irrpwerl (E)
Aboriginal woman (from English) .... lweper
part-Aboriginal person .... arlperrty (T,E)
part-Aboriginal person (from English) .... apekath
belonging to Aboriginal people .... Tyerrty-kenh, Irrpwerl-kenh (E)
non-Aboriginal person .... alhernter, arlter, kartey (W), mperlker, tyerrty arlter (E), tywelker
non-Aboriginal person (from English) .... warlpal
non-Aboriginal woman (from English) .... waterlweper, metheth
above
on top .... akern, akerneng-ampeny (T,E), akern-ampeny (W)
abundant
abundance of (something) .... -angketyarr (E)
acacia bush, elegant acacia .... arlep (T,E), arlwep (W)
grub from .... arlepayt (E)
edible resin from .... arlep ngkwarl (E)
accidentally .... apal[2], apal-apal[2], apalel
accompany
accompanying someone .... ilkwatherr
accompanying someone (respect language) .... ilkwangketh
accompany someone part of the way .... artek-wem (W,T), arteng-wem (T,E)
accuse
someone of something .... ilpernem
each other of something .... ilpernerrem
ache .... arekar-irrem, arlkwem, arntem, kwarnelhem, rlkert intyem (E)
across something .... talkw
Adam's apple .... ahenty amern-amern (E), kwaty-kwaty[2] (SP)
admit .... ilelhem
adult .... tyerrty angerr, tyerrty angerrety
adze .... kantyengarr (W,T), tyalangk (W,T), kanyengarr (E), kwempalth (T,E)
adze handle .... artart[1] (W)
adze with handle joined on with spinifex wax .... anker[1] (E)
aeroplane .... alker-areny, alkerel alhenh
aeroplane (from English) .... irrepayepay (W)
affectionate
be affectionate to someone .... anyanelhem
afraid .... ater
after
an event happens after another event or action .... -penh[1], -ipenh (E), -iperr
after that .... kwer-penh, kwer-ipenh (E)
later .... ingkern
something that came later or after .... ingkerneny
afternoon
mid afternoon (about 3 o'clock) .... angwerr
in the mid afternoon .... angwerrel, atwerrp (E)
late afternoon .... angwerr-angwerr
become late in the afternoon .... angwerr-angwerr-irrem, atwerrp-irrem (E)
afterwards, later on .... rntwarr
again
(doing something) again (from English) .... aken
action or state of affairs has continued for some time .... -antey
once again .... aweth aken, aweth-antey
once again (respect language) .... awethenty-antey (E)
against
stand leaning against someone or something .... ampekernem
sit leaning against someone or something .... ampek-anem
lie leaning against someone or something .... ampek-intem
lean up against something .... alernelhem (T,E), anert-iwelhem (E), ampek-welhem

age, grow old .... ampwerrem
age group
people who grew up together or were born at around the same time .. atyew, alyey²
age mate .... atyew, pelty
aggression .... aha, ahang (W,T)
aggressively .... ahel
aggressive .... ahangerr, ahelengkw (E), ngkwanty (W,T), urengenty (E)
bit aggressive .... ahelengkw-ahelengkw (E)
non-aggressive .... ahekweny, angwang
agitated
be angry .... ampem²
agitated, restless .... arrkwer-arrkwer
agree
let someone go ahead with something .... anaraty-irrem (W,T) (?), aneraty-irrem (T,E) (?)
ahead .... arrwekel, arrwekel-arrwekel
aim
aim a spear at something .... rtwely-inem
take aim .... angkarr arem, arrang-arem (E), akwanth-ilem (E)
taking aim .... akwanth-akwanth
Akarre
language and people .... Akarr
alcohol .... ngkwarl
drink alcohol .... ngkwarl antywem
Alcoota .... Alkwert, Engawala
Alice Springs
(from English) .... Aletheperreng
alive .... iteth
liven up .... iteth-irrem
still alive, lively .... iteth-antey
alive, having a long life ... itethakenp
all
all of them .... ingkerr¹, ingkerrek, ingkerr-antey, ingkerreny
all (respect language) ..... kewerrewerr (E)
all at once .... anyent-ingar
all of something .... alewarr (W,T), antyaper
all over the place .... arrpethet (W,T), arrpanenh (E)
all sorts of (things) .... alhwengkelty
all right
'Is it all right?' .... mwerrakey (W,T)
'It's all right' .... kel mwerr
allowed
(something that is) not allowed .... mwekeny, mwekenh, mweketyey (W,T), kwerert (W,T), mety-mety

alone
on your own .... anyent, inga, ngwath (W), akalk, arrakelakel (E)
being on one's own, keeping to yourself .... urlert (E)
someone who is on their own .... anyent-areny, ingareny
person who is neglected or on their own with no family .... ntweth-ntweth (W,T), intweth-intweth (E)
be on one's own .... ingirrem
on your own (respect language) .... ingketharrp (E)
become alone (respect language) .... ingketharrp-irrem (E)
alpara *(plant)* .... alpar
already .... kel
already (respect language) .... kank (W,E)
have you done it already? .. kelakey (W,T), kelakwey (E)
'Alright' .... kel
also
as well, too .... arlka²
also, again, as well as (from English) .... aken, akin
always .... akwet, akweteth
Alyawarr
language and people .... Alyawarr
am *(go to 'be')*
ambush
lie in wait to ambush ...... arrap-anem, arrap-intem, arrap-welhem, urlernem (E)
amongst .... -itwek (T,E)
ampurta .... ampwert (E) (?)
ancestors .... angkwey-pat (T), arrwekeleny, irrernng, irrernng-pat, irrewaly-pat
ancestral being .... altyerr¹
and .... arlka², thwen, uthen (E)
and (from English) .... an¹, aken, akin
and then (something else happened) .... kel
anger .... aha, ahang (W,T)
angrily .... ahel
angrily (respect language) .. arlpertey (E)
get angry .... ahel-irrem, arlelty-irrem, rrwampem (W), urrampem (T,E), yerrng-irrem (W,T)
get angry (respect language) .... arlpertey-irrem (E)
angry, sulky .... rnpart (W,T), urnpart (T)
get sulky or angry .... rnpart-irrem (W,T), urnpart-irrem (T)
feel angry or sick .... anert ampem

feeling really angry or worked up ..... arawerrng
get 'smart' with someone ..... irrpelth-irrem
get really angry or wild ..... pweth-irrem (E)
make someone wild, upset or angry ..... kekartem-ilem (T)

angle
put something on an angle ..... thar-wem

animal
edible ..... anwenth, ker
old female animal ..... alkeperr, areperrk

ankle ..... anewerrk

Anmatyerr
language, people ..... Anmatyerr
type of 'old' Anmatyerr language ..... Kal ntheyelkwer, Ntheyelkwer

annoy
being annoying ..... arweketherwek (W,T), urekethwerek (E)
annoy or disturb people ..... arweketherwek-ilem (W,T), urekethwerek-ilem (E)
annoy someone ..... arlkarem, arrkenty-ilem
become annoyed, agitated or upset ..... rrwampem (W)

another
another one, another person ..... arrpenh, ingwer (E)
on another side, to another person ..... arrpenh-angkwerr, ingwer-angkwerr (E)
another time ..... aweth aken, aweth-antey
another time, another one (respect language) ..... awethenty-antey (E)

answer
answer someone ..... tyernem[1], tyernelhem (T,E)
not answer someone ..... menty awelhem

ant, ants
small black ones ..... yerr
Bagot's furnace ant ..... twern-twern, utern-utern (E)
bull ant ..... arrengarlp (W), atyank, ntyeyapert (E), tyekarnparnp[1] (E)
honeyant ..... yerramp, inkwareny
type of small, aggressive ant ..... arlety[1] (T,E), arlety-arlety (T,E)
type of ant found in mulga country ..... arlalalpirrenh (E)
type of ant that lifts its backside up ..... artelh-irrkert-irrkert (E)
type of big black ant ..... arlekert, arlekert-arlekert (W,T), atna irrkert-irrkert (E), atnangkerney (E)
eggs of honeyants and other species of ant ..... lwerrk (W,T), ilwerrk (E)
other types of ..... antyalyerrkwereny (E), arleth urrperl (T,E), arlkerrk[1] (T,E), artetyehenp (W), atywer, irrkwenty-akely (E), untyeyapert (E), arrekarlkarlker (T,E), arnameng-ayerr (E)

ant bed, ant hill ..... kerrertek, ngkwepey
types of large ant bed ..... awerr-awerr[1] (E), pwentereng (E), merntap (W,T)
flat ant bed ..... kerrertek, kerrth (E)
edible grub (from termite) ..... atwerneng (W,T), ngkwayt (T,E), ngkwepeyayt (E), ngkwepey (SP), arnameng-ayerr (E)

ant mimic ..... atnangkerney (E)

ant lion *(lacewing larvae)* ..... kwatyarl ntyeny-ntyeny (E), angkwerey-angkwerey (E), mamerweterwet (W,T)

anteater ..... inarleng, inap (T,E), ingka iyntwem (E), ker arlkerl (E), lyek

anus ..... kart altywer (W,T), atna altywer (E), kart tyarrp (W,T), artelh[2] (T,E)

anything ..... alhwengkelty

anyway
without taking notice of others ..... atanty, alanty

apart ..... akalkew-akalk

apologise ..... ilelhem, rrpwarelhem (W,T), urrparelhem (T,E)
'make up' after trouble ..... nyerr rrpwarelhem (W,T), nyerr urrparelhem (E)
apologise for behaviour ..... rlwaty angkem (W,T), urlaty angkem (E)

appear
appear or seem to be there ..... inngelhem
appear different ..... arrpenh-irrem, ingwer-irrem (E)
arrive ..... arwem-irrem (T,E)

appetite
get appetite back ..... arrengker-irrem (W,T)
give someone an appetite ..... arrengker anthem, arrernkelh-anthem (W,T), arrirnkelh-anthem (E), arrernkelh-ilem (W,T), arrirnkelh-ilem (E)
with great appetite ..... arnartew (W,T)

apple bush ..... iynteng-iynteng (E)

appoint, give a job to ..... arrernem
approach *(someone)* ..... atwarem
apricot tree ..... anawert, welterr (E)
Arden Soak ..... Ilpereny
are ..... anem[1], intem[1], ayntem (E)
area ..... -ampeny[2], -thayt
argue ..... ahel nhwerrem (W,T), ahel unherrem (E), aywek-aywek-irrem
argue with each other ..... ahel-ahel akerrem (E), ilterrem
argue over something ..... aker-aker-ilerrem (W)
argue all the time ..... rwang arrernem (W), urarrernem (T,E)
argue the point ..... arlelty angkem
argument
argumentative ..... anngernt (T,E)
be argumentative ..... anew-anew-irrem (W), irrpelth-irrem
break up an argument ..... angka ultakem (T,E), angkety ltwakem (W,T), ulypma ultakem (E)
arm ..... akwa, akwang (W,T), amwelt
left arm ..... akwang alyeng (W,T), akwalyeng (T,E), akwang anety (W,T)
right arm ..... akwang arraty (W,T), akwarraty (T,E)
armband ..... akwelayntenh (E)
men's armband (decoration) ..... akwelty
armgrass millet ..... mamperrk (W,T)
armpit ..... lhenp, iylkwa (E)
armpit hair ..... lhenp alta
around ..... amper[3] (E)
Arrernte
language and people ..... Arrernt
arrest someone ..... arntwerrkem
arrive ..... arratelhem (E), arratem, arratety-alhem (W,T), arrernelhem, arwem-irrem (T,E)
arrogant ..... anew-anew
set yourself apart from others ..... amerrelhem (W)
arse *(go to 'backside')*
artery ..... alwerrng
ashamed *(go to 'shame')*
ashes ..... arnmeny
used for chewing with tobacco ..... arnmeny, ikwenty (E)
prepare ashes for chewing with tobacco, 'cook' ashes ..... arnmeny item
turn to ashes ..... arnmeny-irrem
mix tobacco with ashes ..... arek-wem (W,T), pwerlp-wem (T,E)
hot ashes or earth (used for cooking or healing) ..... rtwap, urtap (T,E), arlpa[1] (E), atnmanth (E), awerrth (E), ntyerlp[1], amerrk[2] (E)
ask
ask for something ..... apawenhem, apay-unhem (E), ayenem (E)
ask for something (respect language) ..... ngkwerengkw-irrem (E)
ask for permission to do something ..... angkawelhem
ask, demand ..... ankey inkem, ankey-irrem (E), aparelhem (T,E)
ask for something on someone else's behalf ..... alhelem (W,T), alhilem (T,E)
ask someone to do something or to go somewhere ..... ngwem, ngwelh-ilem, irrtyelh-ilem
go and ask others something ..... rrpwey alhem (W,T), urrpey alhem (T,E)
ask for things all the time ..... aker-aker-ilem
someone who is always asking for something ..... ankeyalth
asleep *(go to sleep)* ..... ankwa[1], ankwang (W,T)
associated
belonging to or associated with a place ..... -areny
at *(go to Appendix 2)*
attempt
have a go at something ..... arrkernem
attend
go to something ..... irrpem, aylpem (E)
attention
pay attention ..... akangkwerrem (W,T), irlpekernem
pay attention to someone, notice ..... alhengk-arem
not paying attention ..... anngwa
not pay attention ..... anngwerrem (W,T), anngwirrem (E)
get someone's attention ..... lyarnem (T,E)
paying attention to one person at the expense of another ..... arrelharrp (W), arreylarrp (E)
attractive ..... -malangk
aunt
father's sister ..... awenh
father's sister (baby talk) ..... awenyey-awenyey (E)
mother's sister ..... amey
father's elder brother or sister ..... anawerr

father's elder brother or sister (baby talk) .... anawerr-anawerr, anawey, anawey-anawey (E)
great-aunt (father's father's sister) .... arreng
great-aunt (father's mother's sister) .... aperl
great-aunt (mother's father's sister) .... atyemey, artartey (E), rtartart
great-aunt (mother's mother's sister) .... menh-menh (W,T), nyany², ipmenh (E)

Aunty Marys Dam .... Rtwapert
Australian (Richard's) pipit .... kaperl-kaperl (T,E) (?)
Australian hobby
type of bird .... ingkel iylkenh (E), nyengk rnternenh (E)
Australian kestrel .... ulpmerr-atwenh (E), ulpmerr-atwenh-atwenh (E)
Australian owlet nightjar .... arrthwarrthw (E)
avoid
avoid particular relations .... kanem (W,T), ikanem (E), ikanelhem (E), amek-arem, ulilelhem (E)
person who follows the rules associated with respect of particular kin .... kerrenty (W,T), kirrenty, ikirrenty (E)
person who is of an age when they have to follow avoidance rules .... amek-arenty-penh (E), amek-arenty-iperr (E)
avoidance of certain relatives .... alkiwerr (E), alkewerr (T)
doing things separately (because of kinship restrictions) .... alewal (W,T)
avoid something .... amek-arem
avoiding or staying away from trouble .... anenyerr
avoid trouble .... anenyerr-irrem, wenng-irrem (T,E)
goes on respect verbs .... +erlentyarr
goes on respect nominals .... -ayerr
avoiding someone or something .... -kety
awake .... atyek (E), atyek-atyek (E), karr
half awake .... ankwapaperr (T,E)
away
away from (ending) .... +eng-ntyel (W,T), +eng¹, -ntyel, -they (E)
awful .... kwern (W,T), anety (W,T), akeng (T,E), amwa² (E), arntert
axe .... ilep¹
axe (respect language) .... alenyakenyak, iylpwer arternenh (E) nyerlp (E)
axe handle .... arlarnt (E), arrawelp (W,T), mwert (W,T)

Bb

babbler
grey-crowned babbler, happy family (bird) .... tyewakety
baby .... kwer akwek (W,T), ampa akely (E), ampa akwek (E)
baby (from English) .... pepey
baby (respect language) .... lyaty
newborn .... ampa rlternt (E), ampelyerrk, arathap, iylker (E), arlkarl²
small baby .... athatheth, athathingk (E)
baby at the stage when it is carried in coolamon .... lengarr-iperr (E), panth-penh (E)
baby boy .... irrtyart-akert (E), irrtyart-kenh (E)
baby girl .... atnem-akert (E), atnem-kenh (E), irrkwely akely (E)
baby of crawling age .... arnerrekenty, arnerrenty, arnerrenty-iperr (T,E), athathingk (E)
pretend or toy baby .... ampengamp (E), ampeng-ampeng (E)
baby's bottle
(from English) .... titey paterl
back
back part of something .... ingkern
back of a person or animal .... artep
back of a person (respect language) .... imey (E)
lower back .... rtweth, urteth (T,E), antywert (W,T), atheng-atheng (W,T)
upper back between shoulderblades .... ahenty-ahenty¹ (E)
upper back .... akerlak (E), angka² (E)
back of hand .... iltya artep (E)
back of neck .... ntywa (W,T), ntywang (W,T), untya (E)
with hands held together behind back .... arnengerr
look back over shoulder .... artepeng arelhem (E), artepeng arem (E)

turn back on something, not bother with something ..... artepelh-ilem
back-to-back ..... ntywemek-ntywem (W,T), untyemek-untyem (E)

back *(go back)*
going back ..... angkep-athek
be made to turn back from halfway ..... artwepelh-ilem, urtepelh-ilem (E)
do something on the way back ..... +enty-alpem
without looking back ..... ntywemarrel (W,T)

back *(do back)*
(doing something) back to someone ..... akepenh, rlwerrker (W,T), urlerrker (E)

back *(back up)*
back someone up, take someone's side in fight or argument ..... artengel-arem (T,E)

backache
have a backache ..... arekwenth-kwenth-irrem (T,E)
having a backache ..... artep-akert

backbone ..... artep ngkwern, rrpwa (W,T), rrpwang (W,T)
of goanna ..... arlap (E)

backside, arse ..... anwerlk^{2} (W,T), artelh^{2} (T,E), alywel (E), anaynp (E)

backwards ..... angkep, angkep-athek, anwengentyengenty (W,T)
go backwards ..... angkep-irrem, anepetheng-irrem, aneyangketh-irrem (E), anwengentyengenty-irrem (W,T), tyenelhem^{1} (T,E)
make something go backwards ..... anepetheng-ilem, aneyangketh-ilem (E), angkep-ilem, angkepelh-ilem, ntywem-ilem (W,T), untyem-ilem (E)

backwards and forwards ..... tyey^{2} (W)
(doing something) backwards and forwards ..... rlwerrkerek-rlwerrker (W,T), ulengerek-ulenger (E)

bad ..... kwern (W,T), akeng (T,E), amwa^{2} (E), anety (W,T)
no good (respect language) ..... atnerrk^{1} (E), atnerrk-ayerr (E)
badly ..... akengenty, anetyengwerl (W)
go bad ..... kwern-irrem (W,T), anety-irrem (W,T), akeng-irrem (T,E), amwirrem (E)
go bad (respect language) ..... atnerrk-irrem (E)
go bad, go off (especially of meat) ..... arntert-irrem
bring 'bad luck' on yourself ..... akwety-irrpenem (T,E), akety-urrpenem (E)
behaviour that will bring bad luck ..... akwetyerretyerr (T,E)

bad cold ..... mernt, artwengkenng, inkwerr (E), nkwanng (T)

bad luck *(go to 'sorry business')*

bad-smelling ..... awer^{2} (W,T)

bad-tasting ..... anety (W,T), anetywek (W), arlengkety (W)

bad, rotten
emu meat ..... ayewarr (E)

bad-tempered ..... ahangerr, ahelengkw (E), kewarr (W,T), akiwarr (T,E)

bag ..... yakweth
large bag ..... parlkw
small bag (from English) ..... pewaty

bag-shelter moth
nest, larvae ..... wep, ingeth (T,E)

baggy
something loose, baggy and worn out ..... parlkw-parlkw
go loose or slack, become baggy ..... parlkw-parlkw-irrem (E)
'baggy arse' ..... ana parlkw-parlkw (E)

Bagot's furnace ant ..... twern-twern, utern-utern (E)

baking powder ..... arlwar-ilenh-ilenh, mern arlwar-ilenh

bald
bald headed ..... akalyer (E), akalyer-alyer (E), akalyer kwart (E), aketh, kapert aketh, kapert ather-ather (W,T)
bald (from English) ..... akapweley (T,E), akeperleyn (E), pweley, kapert pweley

balls
testicles (sensitive language) ..... arleth

banana *(go to 'bush banana')*

banana-flavoured
bush tomato ..... arlelyek, manyem, tepernter (W)
yellow fruit ..... arlkarntar (W,T)

bandage
a kind of bush bandage made from bark ..... petyet (W)
bandage (from English) ..... pantety

banded lapwing ..... ampelyetyerrker (E), interrk-atherather (W,T), tyelkatherather, tartarrp (E) (?)

bandicoot, rabbit-eared ahert (T,E), angkay (W,T), artnangk (E)
bandy-legged aymparrk-aymparrk (E), ngkwern alyang (W,T), ngkwern amper-amper (W,T)
bang
banging or rattling sound rltar, rltar-rltar[1], rlterrp
make a banging or rattling sound rltar-irrem, rltar-rnkem (E), rltwar-rnkem, urltar-rnkem (E)
go 'bang' (gun) rltar-rnkem (E), rltwar-rnkem, urltar-rnkem (E)
make something bang or rattle rlterrp-wem, rlterrpelh-ilem, rltar-atwem
bang (something) in akak-atwem[1] (E)
bank *(river or creek)* arnkarr, akwerlp
baptised
get baptised kerretherreng-irrem (W), kerretyen-irrem (T)
barb *(on a spear)* lywernk
bare aketh
barefoot ingkang kwart (W)
bark *(of plant)* ayenp, arna ayenp, arnang ayenp (W,T), arntap, arrngelh (W,T)
dry bits of bark rltimp[1] (T,E)
bark container used for carrying arrerlpank (W)
peel bark off plant or tree arntap iyltem (E)
small round bark toy used by men and boys for target practice (with spears) lwekatat (W)
bark *(at something)* arlkwerrpel-nhwem (W,T), arlkwerrpernem (W,T), apangkem (W,T), arrpwarnt angkem (T,E), parlkwem (T,E), parlkem (W)
barking spider inwerl
barn owl arrkerr
barrier
trench to stop floodwater rtwanng, rtwanng-rtwanng, urtanng (T,E), urtanng-urtanng (T,E)
in a way that obstructs or blocks something off arrngert
base *(of something)* intert, anarteng
base *(of a tree)* arnang intert (W,T), arwerl intert (E)
bash
animal against something (in order to kill it) ntewem (E)
bash someone up atwem

bastard coolibah alhelp (W,T)
bastard mulga ilwerreny (E) (?)
bat antyepey (W,T), antyeper (T,E), antyiper (E)
bath
have a bath or a wash kwatyeh irrpem (W,T), kwatyek irrpem (T,E), pwerlp-irrem (SP)
bathe or wash oneself alhewelhem
bathe somebody alhewem, pwerlp-wem (T,E)
batik wax anker[1] (E)
bats-wing coral tree atywerety, aparrty (E), inernt (SP)
battery *(of a car)* rwa (W,T), rwang (W,T), ura (E)
Bau Range Paw
bawl arnem, arrangkem
be *(am, are, is, was, were)* anem[1], intem[1], ayntem (E)
be in a particular way anem[1], intem[1], ayntem (E)
be somewhere alartem (W,T), anerl-anem
is, are (of things thought to be in horizontal position) intem[1], ayntem (E)
is, are (of things thought to be in vertical or upright position, or of things that are high up) irnem
be (of a hill) altywernem
beak arrakert
especially emu beak arrenpenp (W,T), arrimpimp (E)
bean *(go to 'bush bean')*
bean tree atywerety, aparrty (E), inernt (SP)
flower akalapantherrty (T), akenty (W,T), akeynt (E)
red seeds ngal-ngal
yellow or white seeds mpetyan-mpetyan[1] (E)
beard arralt, arrarn (W,T), arrwert (T,E)
long beard (respect language) kwaty-irrenhenh (E)
grey beard arralt aywang (W,T)
beard that is just starting to go grey arreweng ampey (W), arriweng ampey (T,E)
beat
beat or hit someone or something atwem
beat someone to death irrernng atwem
beat an animal against something (in order to kill it) ntewem (E)
beat each other to death kwarterrem
hit or beat something akatwem (E)
beat something so that things on it fall off lernem

beat *(rhythm)*
beat rhythm on lap .... rlpwerrng atwelhem, urlperrng atwelhem (E)
beat rhythm on ground (with a shield) .... arlpwerr atwem (W)
beat *(heart)* .... ahey-angkem, atatem (E), atarterl-iwem (E), atem
beat someone
in a race, game or fight ... impem, arlkwem
beautiful .... mwerr angerr (W,T), mwerr-angker (E)
good-looking person .... ntwat (W,T)
be beautiful or attractive .. inngelhem
make something beautiful or attractive .... inngelhey-ilem (E)
because
'Because of what?' .... wenheng (W,T), iwenheng
because of him/her/that/it .... kwerety
because of that .... kwer-penh, kwer-ipenh (E)
because of something ...... -arrngel, -iperr, -penh, -ipenh (E), -they (E), +eng[1]
warning that action may have bad consequences .... +ekerr (E), -kety
become *(something)* .... -irr+
bedding .... antyam
swag (from English) .... thewak
bee
queen sugarbag bee .... aynwer (E) (?)
bee-eater *(rainbow)* .... apelinterr-interr (E), kwelinterr-interr (T,E), terr-terr (W,T)
beefwood .... ltyenty
medicinal gum or kino .... iyltentyarwek (E)
beer .... ngkwarl, rlkwerrp, urlkerrp (E)
beetle
small creatures that fly ... thep, uthip (E)
dung beetle .... nyert-nyert (?)
piedish beetles .... lengarr-lengarr (E), lthep-lthep (E), panth-panth (E)
type of black beetle .... arrwekety-arrwekety[2], perrk-perrk (W,T), pwerrk-pwerrk (E)
types of beetle .... arlpaty-antey-antey (W), anemel pweyntengeynteng (E), perrertety (E), arlketh-arlketh (E)
before
beforehand .... arrwekel
from before .... arrwekeleny
(doing something) before someone else .... artang-ilem
(doing something) before another thing happens (something happens) before the verb action .... -athath
(something happens) before the verb action ...... -angent
beg *(for something)* .... inkem, ankey inkem
begin *(from English)* .... that-irrem
behind .... ingkern
on the back or far side of something .... arrwengak, irrweper (E), anwenger (E)
from behind .... ingkern-penh (W,T), ingkern-iperr (E)
look behind .... angkep arem, angkep-athek arem
(doing something) behind someone's back .... anyenng, anyenngel, arwengkel
go along behind .... intertek-irrem
going after or behind (respect language) .... anengant (W), atneyarnteng (E)
go behind something or through something .... rwerrem (W,T), urirrem[1] (E)
go out of sight behind something .... rwernelhem (W,T), ureynelhem (E)
belch .... arltarrernem
bell *(from English)* .... rltengk-rltengk
bellbird .... kwepalepal, pakw-pakw (W)
sing .... ilperlp-irrem (W), inmenm-irrem (W)
belly .... alem, anert
belong
belonging to .... -kenh[1], -henh (W,T)
belongings
personal belongings .... arnkwa (E)
personal belongings of the deceased .... tempety
someone else's belongings .... atyeneny
someone else's belongings (respect language) .... atyenernkeny (E)
below .... kwen
bend
bend over .... altywernem
make someone bend over .. altywarrernem
bend or twist something .. arnkwert-ilem
get bent or twisted .... arnkwertelhem
bend legs to one side ...... rtapety-irrem
bend self backwards to stretch one's back .... irrkertelhem (E)
bent .... amper-amper, arnkwert, arnkwert-arnkwert, irrkert-irrkert, iylwerl-iywerl (E), lew-lew (W,T), liw-liw (E), rtapety
bent over .... anwekert

bent branch .... tentey, tentey-tentey
bereavement *(go to 'sorry business')*
Berowie Bore .... Perawey
beside
being beside (someone or something) .... anper[1]
better
better (after being sick) .... mwerr
get better .... iteth-irrem, mwerr-irrem
get better (respect language) .... alhengerr-irrem (E)
better, good quality, really .... -angkarreny (W,T)
bettong, burrowing .... alhwet (E) (?), anwengk[1] (E) (?)
beware
for fear of, beware of .... -kety, +ekerr (E)
between, in the middle .... mpep, rlkwerr
bicycle *(from English)* .... pathekel, patyekel
big .... angerr[1], angerrety, artelhampw (E), artelh[3] (E), awer-awer (E), awer[1] (E), ilkwa[2] (E), rltwa (W,T), rltwang (W,T), urlta (E)
big (respect language) .... apwerety, apwerety-iteng (W)
really big and solid .... ampwerrk angerr
get bigger .... angerr-irrem[1], ilkwirrem (E)
make something bigger .... angerr-ilem
big mob, a lot .... anengk[1] (W,T), atningk (E), angerr[1], arwenth, map, alhirrel (E), arnkengeny (E), irlkenty (E)
big person .... tyerrty angerrety (W,T)
big place, large camp, crowded place .... tern (T,E)
very large thing .... angerrety-pwek (W,T)
really fat (of person or kangaroo) .... atyetyart
get big or fat .... atyetyart-irrem (SP)
very big, enormous .... -anternenh
bilby .... ahert (T,E), angkay (W,T), artnangk (E)
white tail tip of .... alpety (W,T), alpeyt (T,E)
billycan .... kartak (W,T), tyampet way-akert
billycan (from English) .... pelekan[1] (W), perlekan (W), pilikan (E)
bindy-eye .... arlkerl, lyekakapert (E), lyekakapwert (T,E), thenkarr
bird .... thep (W,T), uthip (E), alker-areny
bird (baby talk) .... thep-thep (W,T), uthip-uthip (E)
birth
be born .... intem[1], ayntem (E)
assist in a birth .... iteth-wem
give birth to (of animals) .... rrkwem (W,T), irrkwem (E)
birthmark .... altyerr ampety (E), anengkerr (W,T), anger (W)
bit
a bit of something .... akwek
(doing something) a little bit .... akwek war
bit by bit, one at a time, two at a time etc. .... +am[2]
bits and pieces .... alhwengkelty, ngkwelty, ngkwelty-ngkwelty, tyep-tyep, tyepety[2] (E), tyep[1], urleth-urleth (T,E)
make something break into bits .... althalth-ilem
bite
bite someone or something .... akem[1], nhwem (W,T), unhem (E)
bite into something .... karlkwem, akakwem
bite each other .... akerrem, nhwerrem (W,T), unherrem (E)
bite part of yourself .... karlkwelhem
bitter-tasting .... irrkertey
black
dark in colour .... rrpwerl (W,T), irrpwerl (E)
blackish .... irrpwerl-awaty (E), urrperl-awaty (E), rrpwerl-rrpwerl (W,T), irrpwerl-irrpwerl (E)
go black .... rrpwerl-irrem (W,T), irrpwerl-irrem (E), angerl-irrem (E)
make something go black .... rrpwerl-ilem (W,T), irrpwerl-ilem (E)
black powder for body painting .... mwak[1] (E)
black stone for making ceremonial paint .... arak (E)
black cockatoo .... irrarnt
black gidgee .... arnteparl
black goanna .... kweny-areny (W,T), kwenyel alhem (T), pwer rrpwerl (W,T)
Black Hill Bore .... Kerlpaty
black kite .... apwelanty, apwerl-apwerl, artapw-artapw (E), inkwel (E)
black-breasted buzzard .... aytwertek (E), lywerlperr (W,T)
black-eared cuckoo .... anatyelepwerray (E) (?)
black-faced cuckoo-shrike .... amatheng-amatheng (T,E), matyekwel (E)
black-faced woodswallow .... perrpantywen (W,T), perrpantywel (E)

black-footed rock wallaby ... arrwa, arrwang (W,T)
black-fronted dotterel ... ntyelpeny (W,T), iynterlpeny (E)
black-headed monitor ... alpangwerr (W), altywekerr
black-headed python ... antwerrkenh (W,T), arrwerrperl (T,E), rwayerrp (T), rayerrp (T,E), urayerrp (E)
black-tailed native-hen ... angkeparr (W,T), karlayteng-ayteng (E), kart-irrkwely-irrkwely (W,T), karl-irrkwely-irrkwely (T,E), narremantyerr (W,T), lhekethatethat (E) (?), ngkwern rnter-rnter (W,T) (SP)
black out
go dizzy or faint ... annga ingwemernt-irrem, annga alkerelhem, ngwemernt-irrem (W), ingwemernt-irrem (E)
blade
on the end of an adze ... manpwerl (W,T)
blame
blame someone for something ... ilpernem
blame each other for something ... ilpernerrem
blame someone for something they didn't do ... rrwernem (W,T), urrernem (T,E)
bland ... alyelk
blanket ... antyam, antyepanty (W,T), pangkarr, panty (T,E)
blanket (from English) ... pelangket (W,T), pwelangket (E)
blanket (baby talk, from English) ... pangkat (T)
blanket (respect language) ... atnerlangket (E)
spread out a bed, blanket or groundsheet ... antyam-wem
bleed ... alhuntem (E), alhwa thelelhem, alhwang thelelhem (W,T), arrnguntem (E), irrert-irrem
bleeding a lot ... kwanth-kwanth (T)
make something bleed ... arrngunt-ilem (E), arrnguntelh-ilem (E)
hit someone so that their head bleeds ... akanthwek-anthwek atwem, akanthwel-anthwel atwem (W,T), akanthwek-anthwek-ilem, akanthwel-anthwel-ilem (W,T)
blind ... pweng, annga pweng, parrelyarrely (W)
blind (respect language) ... aparrng (E), parerr (E), angapanty (E)
go blind ... pweng-irrem, annga pweng-irrem
go blind (respect language) ... aparrng-irrem (E)
blink ... annga pweng-irrem, annga anyent-irrem
blister
skin blister up ... arltapwerlt-irrem (W), arltaparlt-irrem (W,T), arltwerlpernem (W,T), iltyampem
make something blister ... iltyampelh-ilem
bloated ... arltwerlp (W,T)
become swollen, bloated ... arltwerlp-irrem (W,T), arlwarernem
block
blocked up, congested, blocked off ... nthat, alhap
blocked nose ... alha nthat (T,E), alhang rtwerlp (W), alhap
be blocked up or congested ... nthat-irrem, alhap-irrem
be blocked or stopped by something ... amek-arem
be blocked off, shut or closed ... wap-anem, wap-arrernelhem
block something up ... alhap-ilem, nthat-ilem
block something off ... arrngert-ilem, arrngert-irrem, arrngert-wem, angert arrernem (W), arrngert anyem (W,T), martem (T,E), wap-arrernem, arltwem (W,T)
block someone off (in a card game) (from English) ... tyamem-ilem (E)
block a fight ... ilpem[2]
block something off with earth ... urelh-urelh-ilem (E)
use part of self to block something off ... wap-arrernelhem
blond ... atywek-atywek
blood ... alhwa, alhwang (W,T)
used by women for healing ... amarr
used by men as a medicine ... akwepenh (T,E)
blood and meat juice from cooked kangaroo ... awerrp[1]
blood (respect language) ... kweth-kweth
clotted, sticky, thickened or coagulated ... ntyew, ntyewey, tewey (E)

coagulate ntyew-irrem, ntyewey-irrem, tewey-irrem (E)
(head) dripping or pouring with blood akanthwek-anthwek, akanthwel-anthwel (W,T)
blood vessel alwerrng
bloodwood arrkernk
type of arlangkw (E)
buds of antyepey (W,T) (?), antyeper (T,E) (?)
flowers of ntewal
seed capsules of mernperr, ntewal, arrkipangkwarl
gum or kino of arrkeper (W,T), arrkiper (E), nthwarr (W), ntharr (T), lyarwek
bloodwood apple mangarrey, arrkwerlperlp (E), kathip (E), arrkipangkwarl
water found in the trunk kwentharr, nthwarr (W), ntharr (T), untharr (E)
Bloodwood Bore Irrpatyerrp
blossom anteth, alpety (W,T), alpeyt (T,E), alpety-alpety (W,T), alpeyt-alpeyt (T,E)
to flower or blossom alpety-alpety-irrem (W,T), alpeyt-alpeyt-irrem (T,E)
blow
wind blow pwem, wem[1], wernem
have a breeze blow on you wernelhem (E)
blow on something (with mouth) pew-ilem
blow something out (of nose) lhwerrp-ilem (T), rwelh-arrernem, ulherrpernem (E)
blowfly mweremwenk (T,E), mweremwelk (W,T)
bludge
bludge off someone aparelhem (T,E)
bludging off someone ankey
blue
blue or grey in colour ura kwert-kwert (E), rwang kwert-arteh (W,T)
blue mallee alhelp (W,T), uleperr (E)
blue wattle iylarn (E), iylarnayt (E), ntwarnengayt (E)
grub from iylarn (E), iylarnayt (E), ntwarnengayt (E) (SP)
blue-lined dragon arlanty, apengeleytanenh (E) (?)
blue-tongue lizard lhwelk, ilpankwer (E), lwengkart[1] (T)
blunt mety
become blunt mety-irrem
make something blunt mety-ilem
blunt-leaf cassia kwert-kwert (W,T)
blurry arrkay, arrkay-arrkay
become blurry or faded (vision) ngwemernt-irrem (W,T), ingwemernt-irrem (E)
boast tywenelhem, utyenelhem (E)
body tyelk, tyerrty, angwerrm, arlka[1] (T,E)
the whole body tyerrty ampwerrk (W,T)
body scent or smell ikwa (T,E), ikwang (T)
body paint
women's painting, body paint or ceremonial designs tyepety[1], arlkeny
bogey *(swim)* kwatyeh irrpem (W,T), kwatyek irrpem (T,E)
bogged
get bogged atanelhem (W,T), atanem[2] (W,T), kelh-kelh atwelhem (T), mwernelhem
boggy *(ground)* irrngwelth (E)
boil
a boil artweker, tyapernp
big boil with more than one opening or head mantalyarrp
boil
boil tea or other liquids item
boil something (from English) pal-irrem
boil something (respect language) ulerrtyem (E)
bone ngkwern
bone (respect language) tyemurrely (E)
bone used for 'boning' (sorcery) ntyarl (W,T), ntyerl (T,E)
bone marrow inpinp (E)
bony ngkwernant, ngkwern-ngkwern
bony part of the nose alha ngkwern
bony-fruited bush tomato arengkerlpart, arntek-arntek (E)
boomerang alya, alyang (W,T), aylayl (E), kayl (T,E)
(respect language) atyepet (E), iltyekenh-ayerr (E)
hooked boomerang, number 7 boomerang rlkwa (W,T), rlkwang (W,T), alyang rlkwang (W,T), kayl iylkwa (E)
curved type alyang lyweper (W), kayl ulyeper (E)
small type of boomerang arrak (E)
toy boomerang alyang-alyang (W,T), kayleng-kayl (E)

toy boomerang used in ceremonies ... alyaper
inner edge (inner edge of curve) ... kayl ilperr (E), aylayl ilperr (E)
outer sharp edge (or end?) ... aylayl arrethaker (E), kayl arrethaker (E)
boomerang going sideways, turning back, swinging back ... aral-aral (W,T)
boot *(from English)* ... pwet
bootlace tree ... ntywey (W,T), untyey (E)
honey ... ntyweyamp (W,T), untyeyamp (E)
booze ... ngkwarl
bored, feel bored ... anatem
born
be 'found' or spiritually conceived in a particular place or country ... anganem
be born ... intem[1], ayntem (E)
borrow something
(from English) ... lant-em-ilem
boss ... alkwert, mayeth (T,E), ngkart, rltwa (W,T), urlta (E), rltwang (W,T), twernk (W,T)
boss (from English) ... pwath
owner or boss of a place ... mereh-artwey (W,T), merek-artwey
become boss of something ... urltirrem (E)
be like a boss ... atyetyart-irrem
both ... atherr[1]
on both sides ... atherr-angkwarr
the both of them ... atherr-antey
bottle *(from English)* ... paterl
baby's bottle (from English) ... titey paterl
bounce
away from something ... irrkarnpem, imarewanem (E), irrkarnpety-alpem
bouncing along the ground ... ahertety[1] (E)
bounce off
shoot off (sparks) ... unarnpem (E), anarnpem
boundary *(from English)* ... parrek
bow and arrow
(from English) ... pwenarr
bowed ... arnkwert, arnkwert-arnkwert
bower bird *(western)* ... akerrk, ahern-areny (E)
box
(from English) ... pakweth
boy ... rrwey (W,T), urrey (T,E), awerr, awey (T,E), kwer rrwey (W,T)
newborn ... irrtyart-akert (E), irrtyart-kenh (E)
big boy, teenage boy ... amerrk[1], awey amerrk (T,E), awerr amerrk
young teenage boy who is going through ceremonial business ... alyepelengkw
become a teenage boy (before initiation ceremonies) ... amerrk-irrem
boyfriend ... ahenty-penh (W,T), anew, anew-anew (E), mert (W,T), meyt (T,E) mert-mert (W,T), meyt-meyt (T,E)
become boyfriends/ girlfriends ... mert-mert mpwarem (W,T), meyt-meyt mpwarem (E), mert-mert-ilerrem (W,T), meyt-meyt-ilerrem (E), mert-mert-irrem (W,T), meyt-meyt-irrem (E)
brag ... nakelhem, narlkwelhem (E), tyenkarl-irrem (W,T), tywenelhem, utyenelhem (E)
brag (from English) ... reken-irrem (W,T), riken-irrem (E)
Brahman cow
(from English) ... perram
brain ... kampely[1] (W,T), akwerrng (T,E), akakwerrng (E)
brainy ... kapert altywer
bramble wattle ... arlep (T,E), arlwep (W)
branch *(of a tree)* ... waly, arwerl (T,E), arwerl kanty (E), arna kanty (E)
very end of a branch ... waly-waly[1] (W,T), arna kanty (E), arwerl kanty (E)
branch put over a grave ... utnin (E)
branch used to make a shade ... lywa (W,T), lywang (W,T), ulya (E)
branch out (tree) ... antarlkw-Irrem
brandish
a weapon ... angkarr arem, arrang-arem (E)
brave ... anew-anew, arnkaty (T,E), irrpelth, rrkwanth (W,T), rrkwanth-rrkwanth (W,T)
bread ... mern
break
break or cut something ... ltwakem (W,T), ultakem (E), ultewem (T,E)
break a piece off something ... akem[1]

break something up into bits ... mpalernem (W), mpal-inem (W,T), mpal-akem (W,T), rlweth-akem (W,T), urleth-akem (T,E), mpalty-akem (W,T)
break something with a missile ... rlweth-wem (W,T), urleth-wem (T,E)
break or crack something open ... pelty-ilem (W,T), peltyelh-ilem (W,T), peltyem (W,T), iyltem (E)
dislocate (an animal's leg) by twisting ... ulernkernem (E)
break up an argument ... angka ultakem (T,E)
break in a horse ... ltwakem (W,T), ultakem (E)
break through something ... atakem
become broken or smashed up ... ltwakelhem (W,T), ultakelhem (E), ultewelhem (T,E)
break into bits ... anhwemp-anhwemp-irrem (W,T)
get broken into small pieces ... ngkwelty-irrem, mpalty-irrem (W,T)
break part of yourself ... ampakelhem (W,T)

break *(of day)* ... aketh, ngwenth-ngwenth
break down ... akelhem, akeng-irrem (T,E), kwern-irrem (W,T)
break down (respect language) ... atnerrk-irrem (E), ngkwerltelhem
breakfast *(from English)* ... perempeth (W), perimpeth (T,E)
eat something for breakfast ... altyerrek arlkwem, anengkerrek arlkwem
drink something for breakfast ... altyerrek antywem, anengkerrek antywem
not having had breakfast ... altyerrakw (E), altyerrinp (E)
breasts ... paty (W,T), werlaty (T,E)
breast (from English) ... titey
breastfeed ... paty anthem (W,T), werlaty anthem (T,E)
drink from the breast ... paty antywem (W,T), werlaty antywem (T,E)
sharp or pointed breasts ... paty arrwert (W,T), ngwemper (W)
breasts that are just starting to grow ... alhwemperemper (E), alhwetepwet (T)
breasts of adolescent girl ... werlaty akarnterrng (T,E), akarnterrng (T,E)
flat or sagging breasts ... paty ayenp (W,T)
breastbone ... arerr, rtwekert ngkwern (W,T), rtwakert ngkwern (E)

breast meat *(of emu)* ... ker werlaty (E)
breast milk *(from English)* ... mam
breathe ... ahey-angkem
breathe heavily ... nthat-irrem
have difficulty breathing ... ywarn ahey-angkem (W,T), uyarn ahey-angkem (E)
take a deep breath because of tiredness, fear, sorrow or relief ... amany-irrem
bridge
bridge (from English) ... perety[2]
bridge of the nose ... rlwentyerr (W,T), urleynterr[1] (E)
bridle *(from English)* ... perral
brim
edge of a container ... arrew (W,T), arriw (T,E)
bring
bring something, get something ... angetyem
bring something (respect language) ... irrepethem
bring something back ... angety-alpem, artwepelh-ilem
bring something out ... arratelh-ilem
bring somebody back ... twerelh-ilem (T)
bring something down from somewhere ... anarnpelh-ilem
bring something into being (ceremonial) ... arrmernem
bring up
bring up a child ... amangkelh-ilem, kwetyakw-ilem (T,E)
broad-leaf parakeelya ... lywemp-lywemp, parrkely
broaden out ... arlpaw-irrem
broken down ... althalth
brolga ... nerrkempwany (W,T) (?)
bronzewing pigeon ... arntep
Brookes Soak ... Rrkwer
Brooks Well ... Altywep
broom bush ... apwen, arlewatyerr-arlewatyerr[2], ngkwert (W,T)
grub from ... apwenayt (T,E)
brother
elder brother ... kak, kakey angerr-pat, kely (W,T), away (E)
elder brother (baby talk) ... kakey
eldest brother ... aletharr (T,E)
younger brother ... atyey
two brothers (respect language) ... arrpentharrp (E), arrpentharrp atherr (E)

father's elder brother or sister ... anawerr
father's elder brother or sister (baby talk) ... anawerr-anawerr

brother-in-law
man's brother-in-law ... mpwern
brother-in-law (from English) ... pantyey
husband's brother ... anew
man's brother-in-law (baby talk) ... mpwern-mpwern, kaly-kaly[1] (T,E)

brown
light brown colour ... apekath, apekath-apekath, arrerlker (E)
brownish in colour ... ahern-ahern, ahelh-ahelh

brown falcon ... irrkerlanty

brown snake
common brown snake ... arwerl-arwerl (E) (?)

bruise
be bruised ... atherrk-atherrk-irrem

brush
brush off coals or ashes and sand ... lernem
brush hair ... iwelhem
a brush (from English) ... peraty

bubble
make a sizzling or bubbling sound (meat) ... tyelyely-irrem (E), tyely-irrem (E)

buck spinifex ... ntwemerr (T,E), welyar (W,T), arrangk (E)

buckbush ... arlkerl, inkwert (E)
grub from ... arlkerlaty (W,T), arlkerlayt (T,E), inkwert-areny (E), inkwertayt (E)

budgerigar ... atetherr
chirp (budgerigars) ... kwelyely-irrem

Buggy Camp ... Arrkweray

build
build something ... artem
be built ... artelhem
building ... warl

build up
clouds or rain storm ... arlternkem (E), ulpatewelhem (E)

bulb *(of a plant)* ... annga, anngang (W,T)
bulb of wild onion, onion grass, nalgoo ... kwart

bull *(from English)* ... pwel[1]

bull spinifex ... ntwemerr (T,E), welyar (W,T), arrangk (E)

bull ant ... arrengarlp (W), atyank, ntyeyapert (E), tyekarnparnp[1] (E)

bullet ... annga, anngang (W,T), anngang atyerrenherrenh (T)
bullet (from English) ... pwelert, katety (W)

bullock, cow
(from English) ... pwelek

bum ... alywel (E), anaynp (E), anwerlk[2] (W,T)

bump
bump into something ... aperrpert-ilem (W,T), apatwem (E)
accidentally bump or step on someone ... artepelh-ilem
bump into each other ... apatwerrem (E), rlwatherr atwerrem (W,T)

bumpy *(of a road)* ... ipert-ipert
bumpy (from English) ... tyamp-tyamp (E)

bunch
in a bunch (of particular fruits) ... anarnkw, iltyingk (E), rlkwangk (W,T), arlpar athwenkarr (W,T), aylpar athwenkarr (E)
fruit hanging in a bunch (particularly bush bananas and wild oranges) ... atwaylpaylp (E)
gather things into a bunch ... anarnkw-ilem

bunch Paspalidium
type of grass ... kwarrety (W,T), nyetempwer (W), tywaynt (E)

Bundey River ... Apmewarr

bundle
in a bundle ... anhwert, antyakwer (E), artaper
make something into a bundle ... anhwert-ilem, antyakwer-wem (E), artaper-ilem, artaper-wem

bung-eye ... alhap

burial platform
(sensitive language) ... thanarnt, wlmperr (E), kwenterarr (T,E)

burn
burn something ... ampem[1], item
be burning ... ampem[2]
'cook' ashes for chewing with tobacco ... item
burn patterns or designs on something ... item
burn yourself ... atyerrelhem (T,E)
get burnt ... pwelh-irrem (E)
burn down to ashes ... arnmeny-irrem
burn away (fire) ... altherrem
burn down (fire) ... ntyerlp-irrem

burn high (fire) ..... aleny-aleny-irrem (W,T), aleny-aleny-wem (W)
burn from hunger (stomach) ..... rrwampem (W), anert ampem
burnt (from too much cooking) ..... pwelh (E)
something that has been burnt ..... lherrm-penh (E)
large expanse of burnt country ..... rlpwat (W,T), urlpat (T,E)
burn country to clean it ..... rlpwat-ilem (W,T), urlpat-ilem (T,E)
an area of country that has been burnt before ..... arrempelty (E)
become burnt (country) ..... arrempelty-irrem (E), urlpat-irrem (E)
burnt *(hair or fur)* ..... ntharr (T), utharr (E)
burp ..... anetyerrk-irrem (W,T), anetyerrkernem (W,T), anterrk angkem (E), arltarrernem, arnenthernem (E), artekernem (T,E)
burr
types of prickle or burr ..... arlketyerr
burrow ..... alhweng, arleytarr (T,E), arwerr
nest made on ground from grass or spinifex ..... tek (E)
where certain animals hibernate ..... ilka[1] (?)
dig a burrow ..... arleytarr-ilem (T,E)
burrow into something ..... irrpem, aylpem (E)
burrowing bettong ..... awert[2] (W), iwert (E), rtway (W,T), alhwet (E) (?)
burst ..... antyelp-irrem (E), atem, aterlk-irrem, aterlkem, rltar-rnkem (E), rltwar-rnkem, urltar-rnkem (E)
be burst or split open by something ..... aterlkelhem
make something burst or bust ..... antyelp-ilem (E)
Burton's snake-lizard ..... iparip (E)
bury *(something)* ..... akwernem, artem, ipertek akwernem
bus ..... marnt
bush ..... arna, arnang (W,T), antyelty (E)
bush (from English) ..... pwety
things from the bush ..... pwety-areny
bush banana ..... parl (W,T), alangkw, alkwarrer (E)
bush banana (respect language) ..... amernt-ayerr (E)
flower of ..... ilkwanty (E)
leaf of ..... altyey, ahertety[2] (E), unelh (E)
leaves rolled up for cooking ..... arrwekety[2] (E)
root of ..... arnaty (W), artwey-artwey[1], atnety (E)
twisted stem of ..... wererr (E)
young fruit of ..... akwemper (T), akwerrk[1], amwernt (T,E), mwemper (W), ngwemper (W), twemper[1] (W)
white inner skin of fruit ..... alhwer (E)
white silky substance inside fruit ..... antweth (E)
green seeds inside fruit ..... alwerremp (W,T), alurremp (E)
bush bean vine ..... angerak
fruit of ..... aherretyepwer (T,E), awerretyepwer (W,T), werrp (E), angerak
bush cabbage ..... tywekerl[1] (W,T)
bush camp
ceremonial camp (for young men) ..... akew (W,T), akiw (E), yelk (E)
bush coconut ..... arrkipangkwarl, arrkwerlperlp (E), kathip (E), mangarrey
bush onion ..... yalk (W,T), yerrakwerr, irreyakwerr (E)
bush onion (respect language) ..... yalk-ayerr (E)
bulb of ..... kwart, yerrakwerr kwart
flower of ..... akenty (W,T), akeynt (E)
white-coloured seed heads ..... akarnkw (W)
clean husks or skin off bush onion ..... parrewem (T)
shake in wooden dish to clean skins off ..... thwerrem
bush plum *(go to 'native currant')*
bush potato ..... anaty, anek (W,T)
flower of ..... nalal (E)
large, dark-coloured tuber ..... akngwert (E) (?)
white tubers ..... mwernenty
young tuber ..... akwerrk[1], anthal (T,E)
leaf of ..... inkwanng (E) (SP)
offshoot from main plant ..... lyelyerr (E)
type of bush potato, yam ..... antyalkenh (T,E), antyalkeny (W,T)
bush stone-curlew, bush thick-knee ..... arepeylp (E), mwelyar
bush tobacco *(go to 'native tobacco')*

bush tomato
banana-flavoured
bush tomato .... arlelyek
bush tomato (hill form)... anakety
bush tomato
(sandhill form).......... kwenemangkarr (T,E), ngantyewarl (W,T), antyewarl (T,E), unemangkerr (E), anemangkerr (T,E)
dog-eye bush tomato, bony-fruited bush tomato .... arengkerlpart, arntek-arntek (E)
native tomato .... alperrantyey, ararnt (W,T), rrwarlp[1] (T), arrwarlp (E), urrarlp (E), rtwengkerr (W,T)
types of bush tomato ...... antyewarl (T,E), nparnpetyenh (W)
bush turkey .... artew, arwengerrp (T,E), warterlk (W)
bush turkey
(respect language).......... aympelh-ayerr (E)
young bush turkey .... mpetyan-mpetyan[2] (E)
part of bush turkey guts ..atnarlt (E)
bushfire.......... antywer[1] (T,E)
bushy
bushy plants.......... angkwelk (E)
grow thick or bushy
(hair or plants).......... angkwelk-irrem (E), angwarlp-irrem (T,E)
make something grow
thick or bushy.......... angkwelk-ilem (E)
business.......... *(see 'ceremony')*
bust
come out through
something .... rltar-rnkem (E), rltwar-rnkem, urltar-rnkem (E)
split open .... atem
bust something .... aterlk-ilem
bustard *(go to 'bush turkey')*
bustle around.......... arraw-irrem
busy
be busy .... atyanem (W)
butcherbird
grey butcherbird .... arrpwerek-arrpwer (W), alpwertek-alpwert (E)
pied butcherbird.......... matyekatyer, pweretyetyer (W), pweretyety (W,T)
butt *(of a tree)*.......... arnang intert (W,T), arna intert (E), arwerl intert (E)
butt in, interrupt .... arrngert-irrem
butt *(of a rifle)*
(from English) .... thak
butter.......... anter
butterfly.......... antelyapelyap
when still in a cocoon..... irrarl
turn into a moth
or butterfly .... irrarl-irrem, ngkekern-irrem (W,T), urlaylp-irrem (E)
butterfly bush .... intyern (E)
buttocks.......... alywel (E), anaynp (E), anwerlk[2] (W,T)
button grass.......... apwert-arlkwenh (E), apwert akwernenh (E), ngelyerr (E), talkwerrk (W), ntalwerrk (W)
button quail .... atek, aterlkwarr (E), iylpwerr (E)
buy something
(from English).......... payem-ilem
buzzard
black-breasted.......... atwertim (E), aytwertek (E), lywerlperr (W,T)
by *(go to Appendix 2)*

Cc

cadney lizard.......... amwely, ankert[2] (W,T)
cake
of desert raisins which
have been ground up....... katyerr kelh
calf *(of leg)*.......... atywa, atywang (W,T), pertarnp (W)
call
call somebody or
something by a name...... ilem, anewem[1] (W,T), inewem (T,E), arreny anewem (W,T), arreny inewem (T,E)
call someone a
particular relation .... anpernem, akem[2]
call each other particular
relations.......... anpernerrem, akerrem
call each other's names... anewerrem (W), inewerrem (T,E)
call something after
yourself.......... anewelhem (W), inewelhem (T,E)
call yourself by a
particular word or name..ilelhem
call someone very
bad names .... urarrey ilem (E), urarreytnelhem (E), urarreytnelhemel iltem (E)
call out .... arlkem, arralthem (T,E), arralthelhem (T,E)
call over
call someone over .... antangkelhem, antangkem, arlkelh-ilem

calm
non-aggressive .... ahekweny
no wind .... anengk[2] (E), teraty (T,E)
become calm (wind) .... anengk-irrem (E)
calmly .... arternp
caltrop
type of prickle .... lyekakapert (E), lyekakapwert (T,E)
camel .... kawartewar (W,T)
(from English) .... kamwerl
camouflaged
be hidden or camouflaged .... impeny imperrk intem (W)
camp .... mer
one's own place or camp, women's camp, ... mer arlalty (W,T)
single-women's camp .... arlweker
single-women's camp (respect language) .... irrewatyent, anperr (E)
single-men's camp .... arnkenty
single-men's camp (respect language) .... arramenty, tyangkay (T,E)
married person's camp .... mer iteng-areny (E)
married person's camp (respect language) .... ngwemay (E), rrwarlp[2] (W)
woman's son-in-law's camp, man's mother-in-law's camp .... ahileng (T,E), ampeny-ampeny (SP)
old camp (where people have died and been buried) .... marrwelyenng (W)
old or deserted camp (because of bereavement) .... arrkwetyety
respectful word used for a 'camp' .... tawert
shady place, base camp .... rwanenty
make camp, find a place to camp .... alal-wem
camp out
camping out or staying somewhere for a night or for a few nights .... anwek (W,T), unekel (E)
camping out (respect language) .... wekel (E)
camp sheet
(from English) .... kalikew
can't *(do something)* .... ywarn, uyarn (E)
canegrass dragon .... arlanty, apengeleytanenh (E) (?)
cannabis *(from English)* .... kanty[2]
canvas *(from English)* .... kampeth
canvas used for shelter (from English) .... tent
caper bush .... arrweneng

car
car .... ararrarlkanty (W)
car (from English) .... mwetekay, mwetek
car (baby talk) .... mpwempew
car (respect language) .... apwert, twertert-ayerr (E), urnayerr (E)
toy car .... lert-lert
unregistered car .... mwetekay ngkekern (W,T), mwetekay urlaylp (E)
car bonnet .... mwetekay rlwa (W,T)
car track .... mwetekay mpaty
carcass .... angwerrm
card game
types of card game .... kwernt[1], peyenat
cards
playing cards .... kart[2], parlperrp
playing cards (respect language) .... alperr-ayerr (E)
deal cards .... terlem-ilem
care
care for someone or something .... arntarnt-arem, manty-manty-ilem (E)
careful
'Be careful' .... pwertay (E)
be careful .... manty-irrem (W), mwanty-irrem (T,E)
tell someone to be careful .... manty-manty-ilem (E), mwerranty-ilem
carefully .... arternp, manty (W), mwanty (T,E), mantyel (W), mwantyel (T,E), manty-manty (W), mwanty-mwanty (T,E)
(doing something) carefully .... mwerranty
(doing something) carefully (respect language) .... mwerrenganty (E)
carney lizard .... amwely, ankert[2] (W,T)
carpet python .... antetherrk
carry
carry or take someone or something .... angem
carry or hold something .... anyenem (T,E), rrkwem (W,T), irrkwem (E)
carry something on the hip .... amarrkel angem, amarrkel rrkwem (W,T)
carry something round the back of the neck .... ntywel angem (W,T), ntywangel angem (W), untyel angem (E), intwerl angem (E)

carry something slung across shoulder (especially kangaroo) ...... alpalyel angem, intarlp angem (W,T), ntwarlp angem (E), anhwert angem, aylpwar angem (T,E)
carry someone on your back ...... kalapel angem (W,T)
carry something in a sling or with a carrying strap ...... alyepel angem, antayel angem (T,E), urtatyel angem (E)
carry a baby animal in a pouch ...... alelth angem (T), alhelth-angem (E), aympel angem
circular pad for carrying things on the head ...... karnt[2] (W,T), lyarnt
carrying strap made from hairstring ...... alyepengantay (W,T), alyepelentenh (W), antay (T,E), rtwaty (E)

cartwheel burr ...... atetherr-atetherr
carve something ...... arrpem, atwem
cash a cheque ...... altywer-ilem
cassette
video or audio cassette (from English) ...... kathet
cassia
oval-leaved cassia ...... areyawarr (E)
grub from oval-leaved cassia ...... areyawerrayt (E)
cassia flowers ...... ulpelp (E)
country where there are lots of cassias growing ...... apwen-apwen (E)
cat ...... annga atherrk, angay (W), mangw (E), nyarrapeng (T,E)
bush cat, feral cat ...... anngarrkwer (W,T), rlwatert
cat (from English) ...... pwethekat, pwethey (E)
cat (baby talk, from English) ...... meyaw-meyaw
catapult *(from English)* ...... tyangar (W, T), tyangay (E)
catch
catch something ...... arntwerrkem, arterrkwem (W)
catch food with mouth ...... nhwem (W,T), unhem (E)
become infected with sickness or disease ...... antelhem, angwarem
catch alight ...... alep-irrem (T,E), altherrem, antant-irrem (W,T), lherrm-irrem (T,E)
catch up
catch up with someone or something (from English) ...... katyemap-ilem

caterpillar
caterpillar (from English) ...... kartepel
caterpillar that eats native currant fruit ...... arnakwerlkerl (E)
types of ...... antyarlk (E), aperr (E)
cattle *(from English)* ...... pwelek
caustic bush ...... alyey-alyey (W,T), anemarraty (W,T), marlek-alyey-alyey
caustic weed ...... amwekel-amwekel[1] (E), amwekel (E), kwep-kwep[1], merterr[1], merterr-merterr (W,T)
cautiously ...... manty (W), mwanty (T,E), mantyel (W), mwantyel (T,E), manty-manty (W), mwanty-mwanty (T,E)
cave ...... intey, irntang intey (W), apwert intey (E), irntang lyerl (W), lyerl
underground cave ...... aharlkwerr, yalkwerr (T)
cave in ...... atakelhem, thakelhem (E)
make a hole or soakage cave in ...... atakem
cemetery ...... awenng
centipede ...... arnperrk, arrpanty (E), ingka arnkengeny (E)
Centipede Dam ...... Alawenng
central bearded dragon ...... amwely, ankert[2] (W,T)
Central Mt Stuart ...... Amakweng
central netted dragon ...... kaperl (T,E)
ceremony
initiation ceremony, young man ceremony ...... anmanty (W,T), apwelh
time when initiation or young man ceremonies are held ...... alyey-tayem, kwer-tayem
first part of the dancing at young man ceremonies ...... mwerlkenty
other types of ceremony ...... althart, pwenty[2] (E), angkwerr[1] (T,E), thayengarr (E)
women's ceremony ...... awely, ilpenty (SP)
women's dance at initiation (young man) ceremonies ...... anthep (T,E)
women's painting, body paint or ceremonial designs ...... tyepety[1]
ceremonial poles, 'long sticks', and the dance in which they are used ...... arlwernarr (E), arretyet (W,T), utemeny (E)

oval wooden board used by women in initiation (young man) ceremonies..ywekerrekerr
wooden object used by women and girls when dancing in ceremonies.....kwerrpar (T,E)
special word used for food used during initiation (young man) ceremonies..arlpwerr (E)
words used to refer to young men before, during and after initiation (young man) ceremony....alyepelengkw, awerrty, arwekert, lyaty, arleyarr, amarleyarr (W), tyakwertekwert (W), lwekerleny (W), antingkar (E)
sing a ceremony............ayatwem
role that a person has in relation to their mother's and mother's brother's country...........kwertengerl
respectful terms used between particular relatives of the young initiate..........................thampartey, anyent arrpenh, perlal, ntwerleng (W,E), ntyangkwenng, rteyepertey, alyey², alyaper-warn (E), alyey-alyey (W,T), ywerlperr (W,T)
become related to someone in a particular way though ceremony.....ntyangkwenng-irrem, perlal-irrem, thampartey-irrem
(men) perform traditional ceremonies to make plants and animals plentiful, perform increase ceremony......................intety-iwem (E), arrmernem, angerr-ilem
beat rhythm on the ground (with a shield) at ceremony..................arlpwerr atwem (W)
dance (women) ....anthep-irrem (T,E)
beat rhythm on lap with cupped hands to accompany ceremonial dancing (women) ....rlpwerrng atwelhem
have feathers or eaglehawk down put on the head (initiate's mother-in-law)..............akerlkem
put feathers or eaglehawk down on the head of the initiate's mother-in-law during ceremony............akerlkelh-ilem
make a particular call during initiation (young man) ceremonies (women).......................pay-arlkem (W), pay-arlkenty-iwem (E), payakayak anem (T,E), payakayak-irrem (T,E)
make 'arrarrarrarr' sound at initiation (young man) ceremony (women) ....arrarrarrarr-irrem (T,E)
make a special hand movement when calling out to particular relatives during a ceremony (women).........amayernem (E)
make a particular dancing movement and hand gesture when young initiate is brought back from the bush (women)...ankey-ankey-irrem
paint each other up with ceremonial designs (women).......................tyepety-werrem (W,T), arlkeny-werrem
paint someone up (women).......................tyepety-wem (W,T), arlkeny-wem
rub chests together (at particular ceremonies).....arneyel nhwerrem (W,T)

ceremonial ground

place where initiation (young man) ceremony is held..........................alyey²
middle part of the initiation (young man) ceremony ground...........apwelh alkey (W), arawern (W)
western end of the initiation (young man) ceremony ground...........arntwerr-arntwerr (E)
bush camp, ceremonial camp (for young men).....yelk (E)
bush place where women and children camp during (young men) ceremonies..artetyerretyerr² (E)
place where a son went through the ceremonial business........ahileng (T,E)
brush shelter used at angkwerr *ceremonies*......thayengarr (E)

ceremonial payment
food used as a gift for someone who performs a ceremony ...... kwerapak (W), tyenkerr, tyewarrely (W,T), inngwerr (T,E)
certain
particular things ...... arrpenhem
chafe ...... alherrem[1] (E)
Chambers Leptosema
(plant) ...... irrarnt-irrarnt (E)
change
into something else ...... angart-welhem, arrpenh-irrem, ingwer-irrem (E)
change into a different form (caterpillars) ...... akarternem (W,T)
change direction ...... artwep-irrem, urtep-irrem (E)
charcoal ...... aperrk
turn to charcoal ...... aperrk-irrem
charge
be in charge ...... rltwerrem (W,T), urltirrem (E)
accuse or blame someone for something ...... ilpernem
accuse or blame someone for something they didn't do ...... rrwernem (W,T), urrernem (T,E)
charred ...... pwelh (E)
chase
chase someone or something ...... anpwem (W,T), aywepem (T,E), ilhem (W,T), alwernem, arrekelyekely-wem (W), lhelpengelhem (W,T), lwakem (W,T), arlakem (T,E), anelhem (T,E), ulilem (E)
chase each other round ...... alwernerrem, lwakelhem (W,T), arlakelhem (E), lwakerrem (W,T), arlakerrem (E), arrekelyekely-ilerrem (T), arrekelyekely-werrem (W)
chase someone or something away from yourself ...... anpwelhem (W,T), aywepelhem (T,E), ilhelhem (W,T), alharlkwelhem
chase someone angrily (respect language) ...... arrwety-akem (E)
chase something down and kill it ...... pernem (W,T)
chatter
chattering sound ...... arreyeng-arrey (W,T)
make a chattering sound ...... arreyeng-arrey-irrem (W,T)
cheat
a cheat (from English) ...... rwekey pak
cheat someone (from English) ...... rwekem-ilem
check your appearance ...... tywerr-arelhem (W,T)
cheek *(face)* ...... arrely[2], rlkey (W,T)
cheek (fleshy part) ...... arrely ayenp, arrely tyelk
cheekbone ...... arrely ngkwern, rlkey ngkwern (W,T)
cheeky
liable to cause harm ...... ahangerr, ahelengkw (E)
cheer ...... arlkem
chest ...... arerr, arnarnk (W,T), rtwekert (W,T), rtwakert (E), uneng[1] (E)
chew
chew something ...... arlkwem, arrerlpem (W,T), arreylpem (E), karlkwem, akakwem
chew (tobacco) ...... arlkwem
chewing gum
(from English) ...... tyewen kamp
chick
emu chick ...... artelh[1] (W,T), alywer[1] (T,E), ankerr akwek (W,T), ankerr akwerrk (W,T), arley (W,T) (SP)
chicken
hen, chook ...... tywek-tywek, kweny-rtwek arlkenh-arlkenh (T)
child ...... ampa, kwer[1] (W,T), ketyey (W), akely (E), akwek, akwerrk[1]
small child ...... kwer akwek (W,T), ampa akely (E), ampa akwek (E)
child just starting to walk ...... ampa alhenty-iperr (E)
man's child or a person's brother's child ...... aler, arrarn-penh (W,T), arrwert-penh (T,E)
woman's child or a person's sister's child ...... ampa, rnwepenh (W,T), irnwepenh (E), alem-penh
smallest or youngest child ...... ingkerney (W,T), akwerreny (E)
last child in a group of siblings ...... kantyeny (T,E), werlaty ilwernenty (E), paty antyerrk-ilenh (T)
become bereft of a child ...... ywerlt-irrem (W,T)
chiming wedgebill ...... tyalatywerrp (T,E)
chin ...... arrarn (W,T), arrwert (T,E)
fleshy part just under the chin ...... arrwengkengk (E)
Chinese person or people ...... annga alhap (E)
chip
chip flakes from a rock ...... iyltem (E), peltyem (W,T), ampwatem (W), mpalty-atwem (W,T)

chips of wood........ngkwelty-ngkwelty
chips of wood left over after carving........ntha (E)
chip off flakes from a rock........iyltelhem (E)

chirp
chirping sound........arreyeng-arrey (W,T)
make a chirping sound....arreyeng-arrey-irrem (W,T)
chirp (budgerigars)........kwelyely-irrem

chirpy, lively........atyep-atyep

chisel........kwempalth (T,E)
chisel something........arrpem

chocolate bush........iylenyenp (E)

choke
choke on something........atanem^2 (W,T)
choke someone or something........ahenty ahenpem (W), ahenty ltwakem (W,T), ahenty ultakem (E), alyernem, awerrkem, itutnhem (E), ternng anyenem (E), twerl-akem (W,T), tul-akem (E)
choke someone or something (from English)........tywekem-ilem

chook *(from English)*........tywek-tywek

choose things........angakem

chop
chop something........akalthem (E), atwem, arternem^1 (E)
chop something down, chop a tree........iyntwernem (E), lywewem, ulyewem (E)
chop something out of a tree........arternem^1 (E)
chop tree open for native honey or sugarbag........arlkarrpem (W)
cut something into bits....rlweth atwem (W,T), urleth atwem (T,E)

Christian........Pep-areny, Tyaty-areny
Christian (from English)..Kerretherreng (W), Kerretyen (T)
become Christian........Kerretherreng-irrem (W), Kerretyen-irrem (T)
non-Christian (maybe from English)........aheyen (W,T), aheytn (E), lwereny (W,T) (SP)

Christmas beetle *(larva)*...anyenty-anyenty (E), atay^2 (W)

chrysalis........irrarl, tyap urlaylp (E)

chuck
chuck something out........artaly-wem (W,T)
chuck something out (just liquids)........intyalp-wem (W,T)

church
church (from English).....tyaty
church service (from English)........pep
go to a funeral, go to church........pep-warn alhem

cicada........anngener, arrey-arrey (E), aterr (W,E)
type of cicada or cricket....rwernp-rwernp (W,T) (?)

cigarette........kwert
cigarette (from English)...thekaret
cigarette (respect language)........tyekert^2 (T,E)

circle
in a circle........amper^3 (E)
go round in circles........artwep-akelhem, urtep-akelhem (E), artwep-artwep-irrem, urtep-urtep-irrem (E)

circular........apwerterrerterr (W,T), arlwa (T,E)

clap
clap hands........iltyang atwelhem (W,T), iltya atwelhem (E)
clap hands against part of your body........atwelhem
clap hands against part of your body (respect language)........ulpakelhem

clapsticks........twererr

clatter........rlterrkem (E)

claw *(of bird)*........iltya, iltyang (W,T), ingkelthel, tywemar (W,T)

clay........thalkerr (W,T)
dried up soakage, soakage with clay on the bottom........iker
white clay used for sorry business........atywerlk (W,T), aytwerlk (E)

claypan
low-lying swampy area...arnwep, arnwep-arnwep

claypan samphire........karnkw (W,T)

clean
pure (not mixed up with anything else)........rlwart (W,T), urlart (E)
clean water (not dirty).....narwep (W,T)
wipe something off something........arnngem
clean yourself........arnngelhem
clean up........aketh-ilem, antarr-wem
clean a place up........anyemwerr-ilem (T,E)
clean something out of something........ipem, lhwerrp-ilem (T), ulherrpernem (E)
clean one's mouth out with water........ngkwerrmengkwerr ilelhem (E)

cleaning mouth out with water ..... kweng-kweng, ngkwengk (E)
clean bush onions, rub skins off bush onions ..... thwerrem
clean out guts ..... aneltyem (W), kart arnngem (W,T)
clean seed ..... rlkwank-ilem (W,T)

clear
open space ..... aketh, arlpaw
clear the ground for a camp or to collect bush foods ..... anhwerrem, iylperrem (E)
clear away grass ..... althem
clear something up ..... aketh-ilem
clear things away ..... irrkerem

clear *(sky)* ..... aketh-aketh (T,E), alker, alker anert
clear (water) ..... aketh
make something light or clear ..... aketh-ilem
clear up (rain) ..... akelhem, aketh-irrem, alker-irrem[1], alkerelhem (E)

clear out
run away (from English) ..... pwerlt-irrem

clearly
really, definitely ..... kwenh

clench up *(fist)* ..... arlwemeny-irrem, arlwerrelhem, iltya pwert-irrem (W,T)

clever ..... inangkal, kalty, kapert altywer, kapert arraty, kwerathek (W,T), lywenpeny, wetyerretyerr[2] (W), weretyerretyerr (W,T)

clever, cleverly ..... tyak (E)

click
banging, knocking, rattling or clicking sound ..... rltar, rltar-rltar[1], rltety
make a cracking or clicking sound ..... rltar-irrem, rltar-rnkem (E), rltwar-rnkem, urltar-rnkem (E), rltety-irrem

cliff
steep rockface or cliff ..... apwert arnka, arnka, arnkang (W,T), irntang arnkang (W,T), antherrty

climb
climb up ..... antyem, nganem (E), atwayntem (E), antyan-akelhem (W)
climb down from something ..... anarnpem

close *(nearby)*
nearby ..... angath, arrer (T,E), arrer-antey (T,E), arrerenty (E), itwa, itwang (W,T), kwenty atherr
bit close, a bit closer ..... angath-angath, itwerlker
close or joined together ..... rrkwerrenty (W,T), irrkwerrenty (E)
close together ..... interrenty (T,E), twek-twek (W,T), itwek-itwa (E), tweket (W,T), tweket-tweket (W,T)
close together (respect language) ..... arlewent-kweny (E)
move closer to something ..... arrer-irrem (E), itwek-irrem, itwirrem (E), itwang-irrem (W,T), angath-irrem
make something closer, move something closer to something ..... arrer-ilem (E), arrerelh-ilem (E), itwilem (E), itwang-ilem (W,T)
close in on something ..... wap-irrem, wap-arrernelhem

close *(shut)*
close or shut something ..... martem (T,E), wap-arrernem
become closed or shut ..... martelhem (T,E), mwernt-irrem (W), marnt-irrem (W,T)
become blocked off, shut or closed ..... mety-irrem
close or shut yourself in ..... martelhem (T,E)
close over (wound) ..... pwarn-irrem
close something up, make narrow ..... pwarn-ilem
closed, closed in ..... martelhenty (T,E), marnt
something that is closed in at one end ..... mety, mety-mety, iwarlkw (E)

clot
clotted or coagulated blood ..... ntyew, ntyewey, tewey (E)
get solid (blood) ..... ntyewey-irrem, tewey-irrem (E)

cloth
that hasn't been sewn ..... alparr[2]

clothes ..... mantarr, rnwanenty, urnanenty (E), arnkwa (E), irrpenh-irrpenh (E)
clothes (respect language) ..... arnkwayerr (E)
clothes and blankets ..... arnkwa (E)

cloud ..... mater (T,E), matay (E)
types of rain cloud ..... awerrepweng (E), mwekelengk (W,T), rlweyang (W), kwaty akwerrk (E), kwaty angkarl
dark rain cloud ..... aperler (W,T)
rain cloud (white) ..... ankert[1]

thick rain cloud ..... akantyer (E)
light cloud ..... kwenpay (E)
wispy clouds ..... inewarr (E), katyar (W,T), urrarl (E)
type of cloud that forms on top of a column of smoke, pyrocumulus cloud ..... arrempelty (E), lerranty (W,T)
type of cloud (after rain has finished) ..... antwenharr (E), urrartn (E)
clouds gather together or build up ..... alernkem (T), urrarl-irrem (E)
clouds clear up ..... alker-irrem[1], alkerelhem (E)

cooperative
cooperative ..... irlpareth, ilpety (E)
cooperate ..... irlpareth-irrem

coagulated
coagulated blood ..... ntyew, ntyewey, tewey (E)
blood coagulate ..... ntyewey-irrem, tewey-irrem (E)

coal
charcoal, hot coals ..... aperrk

coat *(from English)* ..... tyaket

cockatiel ..... aneweylker (E), areweylker (E), arew-arew (E), kanaweylker (E), newingk (W,T)

cockatoo
black cockatoo, red-tailed black cockatoo ..... irrarnt
Major Mitchell's cockatoo ..... angkwen
white cockatoo ..... terekerr
type of cockatoo ..... kakelhelh (W,T)
cockatoo (from English) ..... kakepewey

cockchafer larvae ..... anyenty-anyenty (E), atay[2] (W)

cockroach
striped desert cockroach ..... mpwerleyerleng
type of cricket or cockroach ..... wernpernp (W)

coconut *(go to 'bush coconut')*

cocoon
butterfly or moth when still in a cocoon ..... irrarl

coffin ..... artart[2] (W,T)

coins ..... ngkwelty, apwert

cold, cool ..... angwerl, angwerleny, kernt, anyartey (W,T), anyel (W,T), irrernt (T,E), arlkarl[1], atheperr (E)
cool down ..... angwerleny-irrem, anyatwem (W,T), anyel-irrem (W,T), kernt-irrem, antyernem[2] (T,E), anyartey-irrem (W,T), atheperr-irrem (E), irrernt-irrem (T,E), arlkarl-irrem (E)
cool something down ..... angwerl-ilem, angwerleny-ilem anyartey-ilem (W,T), irrernt-ilem (T,E), kernt-ilem, atheperr-ilem (E)
make self cool or cold ..... anyatelhem (W,T), arlkarl-ilelhem (E), irrernt-ilelhem (T,E)

cold *(or flu)* ..... mernt, artwengkenng, inkwerr (E), nkwanng (T)
having a cold or flu ..... artwengkenng-akert, inkwerr-akert (E), mernt-apert (W,T)

cold weather ..... alhwerrp, alyangkw (E), irrernt (T,E)
start of the cold weather ..... alhwerrp akwerrk, alhwerrp alhang (T), alhwerrp urla, alhwerrp rlwang (W,T)
cold wind ..... alhwerrp

collapse
make something collapse ..... atakem
collapse in on self ..... atakelhem

collarbone ..... alkwert-alkwert, anirnterrm-irnterr (E), kwaty-kwaty[2] (SP)
soft part between the collarbones ..... kwaty-kwaty[2], mwelper kwaty-kwaty (W,T)

collared sparrowhawk ..... alekaper (?)

collect
collect or gather things ..... inem, kwetyem, akalthem (E)
collect fruit ..... nhwem (W,T), unhem (E)
collect (native currants) ..... arlkernem (T,E)
collect firewood ..... aytem (E), rwang inem (W,T)
collect things together (one by one, bit by bit) ..... antelh-ilem (T,E)
collecting food together (women gathering into one container) ..... areytarr (E) (?)

collide ..... apatwerrem (E)

colony wattle ..... arrely[1]

colour
having different colours ..... inernt-inernt (T) (SP)
light-coloured ..... arlperrty (T,E)

colt *(from English)* ..... kwerlt, nantew kwerlt

comb *(hair)* ..... inelhem, iwelhem

come ..... apetyem, apety-alhem
come (two) ..... apety-alherrem
come (more than two) ..... apetyewarrem
come from a particular place or country ..... angwerrm-irrem, anngirrem, anngerrem
come (respect language) ..... ahanety-alhem, ahanenty-alhem (W), arlwety-irrem (W,T)

come together in a group .. akarr-irrem (T,E)
towards (the speaker) ...... ularr-irrem (E)
come back and do something .... +enty-alpem
come back, return .... apety-alpem
come back (respect language) .... ahanety-alpem
come back to same man or woman .... irlpang-irrpem (W)
come to the place where you came from .... irlpang apety-alpem (W)
come back and settle down in a place (respect language) .. ayepel-irrety-alpem
come between people .... rlkwerrel-irrem (?)
Come on! .... mpa
come out
emerge .... arratem, arratety-alhem (W,T), tyerrelhem
appear (flowers and plants) .... arratem
come out or emerge from chrysalis (moths and butterflies) .... rnkem
make something come out of something else ...... tyerrelh-ilem
come out (sun) .... aketh-aketh-irrem
come up *(sun or moon)* ..... arratem, tyerrelhem, aherlkenty alhem
company
keep someone company ... atanty anem
going with someone to keep them company .... ilkwatherr
going with someone to keep them company (respect language) .... ilkwangketh
without companionship or company .... ilkwatherrek-uthek (E)
compassionate, kind .... atham-atham
completed
something is finished or completed .... kel
completely .... anthwerr (W,T)
computer *(from English)* .. kimpwet
conceived
be 'found' or spiritually conceived in a particular place or country .... anganem, angwerrm-irrem, anngirrem
the spirit of a person, which comes from the place where they were 'found' .... anngirrenty (E)
concentrate
not really concentrating ... arnernkey
Condy's crystals
(from English) .... karntey

confess .... ilelhem
confident .... anew-anew, arnkaty (T,E), rrkwanth (W,T), rrkwanth-rrkwanth (W,T)
confidently, without (social) restrictions .... alhewer
confused .... arert-arert
being confused .... apalekalek
be confused .... apatem
become lost or confused ... apalekalek-irrem, therrert-irrem (E)
get a bit confused or silly .. arert-irrem, arert-arert-irrem
make someone confused .. aparlp-ilem, aparlpelh-ilem (E)
congested
be blocked up or congested .... nthat-irrem
make something congested .... nthat-ilem
become stuffed up or congested (throat or chest) .... kerelty-welhem (W,T)
congregation *(church)* ..... werlamperrenty (W,T), urlamperreny (T), urlamperrenty (E)
conkerberry .... perlap, arnwekety (E)
construct
construct something .... artem
be constructed .... artelhem
contained
in (a container) .... -arleng[2]
container
used for collecting smaller quantities of bush foods which are then put into larger containers ...... ayapay (E)
container used for drinking out of (from English) .... tyampet
continue
continuing to do something for a long time .... aleth-antey
conversation .... ayey (W,T), angka
convulse
take a fit .... atywaty-irrem[2] (T,E), tyerrty-tyerrty internem (W), irrkarnpem
cook
cook something .... item, atyerrem[1], arrtyem (E), ampeng-ilem, ampernem (E)

cook something (respect language)..........angwey-ilem (E), irrkwertem (E), irrkertem, ulerrtyem (E), arntampernem (E)
become cooked..........ampem², ampeng-irrem
cook something for someone else..........atyang-item (T)
cooking pit with hot rocks..........rntwer¹ (SP)
cooking spot, hearth..........rerrk (T,E), yerrk (W,T)
cooked..........ampeng
half-cooked..........arlety-arlety
cooked damper..........warnp (W,T)
cool *(go to 'cold')*
cool drink..........kwelteringk, ngkwarl
coolamon
types of..........alparr¹ (W,T), lengarr (E), panth
coolibah..........ankerrmern
edible grub found in the trunk of..........ankwerrern (E), ankwerrernayt (T), ankerrayt (T,E), anwerrngaty (W), ingweneng (SP)
edible seed of..........aley¹, ankwerrern (E), ankwerrernayt (T), urreny (T)
bastard coolibah..........alhelp (W,T)
Coonawittra wattle..........alalherrk (W,T)
coot *(Eurasian)*..........anker-anker¹ (E)
cop, police..........rrkwenty (W,T), irrkwenty (E), irrkwenh-irrkwenh (E)
copy
copy someone or something..........angwarem, arlepewem (W,T), warrernem (E)
corkwood
fork-leaved corkwood..........ntyarleyarleng, ntywey (W,T), untyey (E)
northern corkwood, bootlace tree..........ntywey (W,T), untyey (E)
honey of..........ntyweyamp (T,E), untyeyamp (E)
yellow-coloured honey..........tyan (W,T)
red nectar of..........ngapalhwerrk (W)
burnt bark of..........ntywey aperrk, untyey aperrk (E)
corner
of a room or burrow..........iwarlkw (E)
corpse..........arrwety, aweyaw, ima (E), irrernng, irrewaly
correct..........arraty
become corrected or fixed up..........arraty-irrem
correct something..........arraty-ilem
cossid moth grub..........aylperlayt (T,E), ingweneng, perlanty (W,T)
cotton panic grass..........kwatyempengemp (W,T), kwatyimpengimp
cough..........artekernem (T,E), ilwem, ulem (T,E)
make a small coughing noise..........ngkwengk-irrem (T,E)
couldn't *(do something)*..........ywarn, uyarn (E)
Coulters Camp..........Artweyelperlayneng
country *(place)*..........mer, ahelh, ahern
one's own country..........mer arlalty (W,T)
country where a person comes from or where they came into being..........anganenty
mother's country..........altyerr¹
be related to a place or a Dreaming through your mothers and mother's brothers..........altyerr akem, anengkerr akem (W,T)
someone from a different country..........alker arrpenh-areny (E)
country *(environment)*
open country, plain country..........alkwererlp (T), alkwerilp (E)
open country where there are no restricted places..........arlangkwarr (E), arla² (T,E)
country devoid of bushtucker..........rrpwernp (W,T), urrpernp (E)
country with small gullies going through it..........mpwetyerr-mpwetyerr (W,T)
dry waterless country..........aherraty
green, verdant country..........ilkelhey (W,T)
become verdant and green..........ilkelhey-irrem (T), anyemwerr-irrem (T,E)
make country green..........anyemwerr-ilem (T,E)
(of country) return to pristine or original state..........mpankeny-irrem (W,T), mpwankeny-irrem
large expanse of burnt country..........rlpwat (W,T), urlpat (T,E)
couple
two or a pair of things..........atherr¹
married couple..........anewart, anewart atherr, arlwenth (E)
married couple (respect language)..........mwarlenth
married couple (said by a woman of her daughter and his husband)..........ngwarr-nheng atherr (T,E)
married couple in the opposite generation moiety to the speaker..........aperlenheng atherr

married couple in the same generation moiety as the speaker ... arrkar-nheng atherr
courageous ... irrpelth, urrpelth (E)
cousin
female cross-cousin (father's sister's or mother's brother's daughter) ... altyel, altyel-altyel
male cross-cousin (father's sister's or mother's brother's son) ... ankel[1], ankel-ankel
cross-cousin of opposite gender ... arrwemp (SP)
be full female cross-cousins to each other ... altyel akerrem (W,T)
two close female cross-cousins ... rnwek-werrenty (W,T), urnek-iwerrenty (E)
be full male cross-cousins to each other ... ankel akerrem
father's cross-cousin ... amarl, amarl-amarl, maly (E)
'cousin-mother' ... amikw altyeley (E)
'cousin-uncle' ... anyey
cover
cover something over ... arltwem (W,T), artem
cover yourself with something ... arltwelhem (W,T), artelhem, irrpelh-ilem
cow
cow (from English) ... pwelek
cow (baby talk, from English) ... mew-mew
cowardly ... ateralth, atna anik (E), mwenyent (T,E)
cowboy ... artwang arrerlp (W,T), artwa arreylp (E)
crab
types of ... kwertetyengetyeng (?), ikarl (T,E) (?), iltyarnm (W) (?)
crack
cracked, fissured ... tyarrp-tyarrp, anhwerrm-anhwerr (W)
cracked ground ... arnkwerrng (E)
place where there are lots of gaps or cracks ... atwaty-atwaty
crack in the ground caused by tuber or root underneath ... ahatyerr (W,T), karnt[1] (T,E), urrper (E), tenh (E), antwerlperlp (W,T)
make the ground crack and lift up (tuber or root) ... ahatyerr-wem (W,T), karnt anyenem (T,E), karnt-wem (T,E), urrper inkem (E), rrpwer inkem (T), urrper-wem (E), tenh anyenem (E), tenh-wem (E)
cracked part of foot, hoof or paw ... atnik (E), atnik-atnik (E), ingka atnik-atnik (E), ikarl-ikarl (T,E)
get cracked (hoof, foot or paw) ... atnik-atnik-irrem (E)
make something crack or rise up ... ilpent-wem (E)
crack open ... mpal-akelhem (W,T), mpalty-akelhem (W,T), tyarrp-irrem
crack open (rock) ... tyarrp inkem (W)
crack something open ... pelty-ilem (W,T), peltyem (W,T), peltyelh-ilem (W,T), mweltyem (W,T)
crack *(sound)*
sharp cracking or clicking sound ... rltety
make a cracking or clicking sound ... rltety-irrem
crack a whip ... rltar-wem
cramp
cramped, tight ... arlerlp[2], rtapety, tharr
cramped, crowded ... pwarn
become cramped ... anam-irrem[2] (W,T), arlerlp-irrem, arlwerrelhem, arlurrelhem (E), rtapety-irrem
cramp or tighten up ... pwert-irrem (W,T), purt-irrem (E)
get cramped or numb ... tharr-irrem, impelhem (E)
make something cramp or curl up ... rtapety-ilem
crave
something that you really crave for ... alyerremwey
crawl ... arnerrem
feel something crawling on you ... irrekerr-irrem (E)
make someone feel as if something is crawling around or touching them ... arrenkelh-ilem[2] (T), irrenkelh-ilem (E), irrekerr-ilem (E), mpwarelh-ilem (E)
crawl back to someone after rubbishing them ... tyen-irrem (W,T)
crawling baby ... arnerrekenty, arnerrenty, arnerrenty-iperr (T,E)

crazy arert, arwengk (T,E)
creased ilerrty-ilerrty
creation
something that has been created arrmernenty
creation time altyerreng (E)
creek lher, lpway (W,T), ulpay (T,E)
creek (respect language) angkeway, ngkwerlpay-ayerr (E)
creekbank akwerlp
small creek, or gully mpwetyerr (W,T), ilerrty, lher-lher[1] (SP)
small creek, gutter intyer
small or narrow creek lher pwarn, lher tyert (E)
middle of a creek lher anert, lher-lher[1]
high mound of sand in the middle of a creek twerr (T,E), twemper[2] (E)
erode, make creek or gully thalkerr-ilem (W,T)
creek windmill grass twemper-twemper (W)
creep up *(on someone)* apertem
creepy crawly
bugs and insects arrenty
creepy crawly (from English) patey (W), paytey (T,E), patey-patey (W), paytey-paytey (T,E)
crest *(of a bird)* irrkarlp
of Major Mitchell's cockatoo akenty (W,T), akeynt (E)
crested bellbird kwepalepal, pakw-pakw (W)
crested pigeon pelker
cricket
desert cave cricket irreynm (E)
types of anwengkapeltharr (W,T), anakapeltherr (E), pengart-pengart[1], lerrenp, ltywelty, rlngerr-rlngerr (E) (?)
type of cricket or cockroach wernpernp (W)
crimson chat uneng atyetyek (E), akarl-atwerrey (T,E) (?)
crippled anath (W,T), anenyirrp irrkweynar (E), apekap, apertap (W,T), arlamarr, arlwemeny, lim-lim (W), lyer (E), rnwerr, rnwerr-rnwerr (W,T), rtapety, yer (E)
become crippled arlamarr-irrem, lim-lim-irrem (W), apekap-irrem, apertap-irrem (W,T), rnwerr-irrem, yer-irrem (E)

crooked
crooked, bent amper-amper, arnkwert, arnkwert-arnkwert, irrkert-irrkert, iylwerl-iywerl (E), lew-lew (W,T), liw-liw (E)
crooked (from English) rang-rang (W,T)
bent legs ngkwern alyang (W,T), ngkwern amper-amper (W,T)
be crooked arnkwertelhem
crop *(of a bird)* mpurl (E), atnarlt (E) (?)
cross *(Christian cross)* antarlkw, ntwerlk (T)
cross-cousin *(go to 'cousin')*
crouch
crouch down altywernem
crouch down and hide behind something arrap-anem, arrap-intem, arrap-welhem
crow *(little)* angank, angep, angerl (E), kway-kway (E)
(from English) kaw-kaw
crowbar *(from English)* kerwep
crowd
crowd in on someone arrapayernem
Crown Hill Arentyerrentyerr
crown *(of the head)* akamer (E), akampwep (W,T), akampep (T,E), kampely[1] (W,T)
cruel ahangerr, ahelengkw (E), anhelhenty
crumbly althalth
make something crumble up althalth-ilem
crush
crushed, dented mwely, mwely-mwely, unmely (E)
crushed up or softened pieces of something (tobacco) lpwa (W,T), ulpa (T,E)
become crushed mwely-irrem, unmely-irrem (E)
get smashed up or crushed ulpirrem (E)
crush or dent something mwely-ilem, unmely-ilem (E)
crush or smash something up apert-atwem (E)
crush or squash something ipelhip-ilem (E)
crush something (with stone axe or rock) anthim-ilem (T,E)
crush something up to make it soft lpwelem (W,T), ulpilem (T,E)
crush something up using a grinding stone tewenhem (E)

crust
dried up crust on something ..... rta, rtang (W,T)
crust of bread ..... ika (T,E)

cry ..... arnem, arrangkem
cry (respect language) ..... akey-irrem (E)
cry a lot ..... arlan-irrem, nthat-nthat-irrem
cry hard till the need is satisfied ..... arlelty-irrem
cry out in pain ..... ampangkem (T,E), yapaty-irrem (W,T)
cry out in surprise ..... yekay-irrem
make someone cry ..... arnelh-ilem, arrangkelh-ilem, arrangkelh-angkelh-ilem
make each other cry ..... arrangkelh-ilerrem
wailing or crying in mourning (men) ..... wartay[2] (E), wartay-irrem (E)
wailing or crying in mourning (women) ..... akay, akayel arnem
cry together (in mourning) ..... arnelh-ilerrem

cubbyhouse ..... alyetyepengalyety (W), angetyepengangety (W), antyweng-antywa (T,E), antyweng-antyweng (W), mereng-amer, nyetyep (T,E), nyety-nyety (E), anyetyepeng-anyety (T), anyetyepeng-anyetyep (W,T), nyetyeng (E)
boy's cubbyhouse ..... arnkentyeng-arnkenty
girl's cubbyhouse ..... arlwekereng-arlweker
cubbyhouse (baby talk) ..... mey-mey[2] (T)

cuckoo
black-eared cuckoo ..... anatyelepwerray (E) (?)
Horsfield's bronze-cuckoo ..... nyarew, anatyelepwerray (E) (?), urrempen urrempen (E)
pallid cuckoo ..... alkwarrer-arrpwernenh (E), lyweketweretwer (W,T), rlweketereter (W,T)

cuckoo-shrike *(black-faced)* ..... amatheng-amatheng (T,E), matyekwel (E), matyikwel (E)

cultivate plants ..... arntwelh-ilem (W,T)

cup *(from English)* ..... paniken

cup of tea *(from English)* ..... kapertey

cure *(someone)* ..... tangkelh-ilem (W,T)

curl
curled up ..... rtapety, arlwemeny, arrepert (E), arrapert (T)
curl up ..... rtapety-irrem, pwert-irrem (W,T), purt-irrem (E), arlwemeny-irrem, arrepert-irrem (E), arrapert-irrem (T)
make something cramp or curl up ..... rtapety-ilem

curlew *(go to 'stone-curlew')*

curly hair ..... arlwerr-arlwerr, kapert arlwerr-arlwerr

curly windmill grass ..... twemper-twemper (W)

curly wire grass ..... intwerrker

curly-pod wattle ..... iwert (E)

currant *(go to 'native citrus')*

curry wattle ..... anker-anker[2] (E)

curse
bad omen ..... mawenng (T,E), matyawenng (T,E)
someone who is cursed ..... animampel (T,E)
put a curse on someone ..... akwety-irrpenem (T,E), akety-urrpenem (E), artarrernem, artimperr-wem (T,E), pew-ilem, rltwatyel atwem (W,T), urltatyel atwem (E)

curved ..... arnkwert, arnkwert-arnkwert

custom ..... mpwarengareng, mpwarenharenh (E)

cut
a cut or wound ..... alety
cut something ..... akem[1]
cut something (respect language) ..... ngkwerltem (E)
cut something, break in half ..... ltwakem (W,T), ultakem (E)
cut something up ..... rlweth-akem (W,T), urleth-akem (T,E), akalthem (E)
cut something in half or into bits or pieces ..... mpalty-akem (W,T), mpal-akem (W,T), mpalernem (W), mpal-inem (W,T)
cut or break food up ..... ampakem
cut something up into pieces (especially meat) ..... tyep-akem, tyep-ilem, tyep-tyep-ilem
cut up cooked meat ..... arrkwelem (E)
make a cut across the top part of the thighs of a cooked kangaroo ..... artely-ilem (W,T)
cut up meat along the backbone (particularly said of emu) ..... artep ultatwem (T,E)
cut up emu fat ..... arnwelem (W)
cut each other ..... akerrem
cut yourself ..... akelhem, unhelhem (E)

cut yourself (respect language).......... ngkwerltelhem (E)
cut yourself (men in mourning).......... alety-akelhem

cut across
go across.......... talkw-irrem, arrelharrp alhem (W), arreylarrp alhem (E), arreyl-arreyl alhem (E), artwerel alhem (E)
short cut.......... akwerterrp (T,E), ntwertety (W,T), untertety (E)
take a short cut.......... akwerterrp alhem (T,E), ntwertety alhem (W,T), untertety alhem (E)

cut out
draft out (e.g. bullock from a mob).......... angakem

Dd

dad (see also 'father')
dad (baby talk, from English).......... pap

daisy
types of daisies, including Tietkin's daisy.......... anteth-anteth (W)

damage
become damaged or spoilt.......... akeng-irrem (T,E), anety-irrem (W,T), kwern-irrem (W,T)
damage something.......... akeng-ilem (T,E), kwern-ilem (W,T), anety-ilem (W,T)

damper *(from English)*.......... rtamp
made from seeds.......... arnwety (W,T)

dance
to dance.......... rntwem (W,T), urntem (T,E)
to dance (women).......... anthep-irrem (T,E)
to dance (respect language).......... anwerrtyem (E), anwerrty-irrem (E)
women's dance at initiation (young man) ceremonies.......... anthep (T,E)
dance for son-in-law (women).......... alpment-irrem (E) (SP)

danger
put someone in danger.......... pewem
put yourself in danger.......... pewelhem
be unaware of impending danger.......... thwerrp alhem (W,T)

dangerous.......... ahangerr, ahelengkw (E), amwa[2] (E), urengenty (E)
a bit dangerous.......... ahelengkw-ahelengkw (E)
dangerous thing.......... arrenty, atwenh-atwenh

dangle.......... arlparernem

dark *(night-time)*
darkness.......... ingwa (T,E), kweny[1] (W,T), ngwemernt (W,T), ingwemernt (E)
half dark.......... ngwemernt-ngwemernt (W,T), ingwemernt-ingwemernt (E)
pitch dark.......... mwemengk (W,T)
in the dark.......... atham
get dark, become night.......... ingwirrem (T,E), kweny-irrem (W,T), mwemengk-irrem (W,T)
getting dark, dusk.......... ntwely-ntwely-irrem (W,T)
get dark, darken over (sky).......... ngwemernt-irrem (W,T), ingwemernt-irrem (E)

dark *(in colour)*.......... rrpwerl (W,T), irrpwerl (E)
go dark in colour, blacken.......... rrpwerl-irrem (W,T), irrpwerl-irrem (E)
make something go dark in colour.......... rrpwerl-ilem (W,T), irrpwerl-ilem (E)

daughter
daughter (man's child).......... aler
daughter (woman's child).......... ampa
respectful word a father uses to refer to his daughter.......... atnem-akert (E)

daughter-in-law
woman's daughter-in-law.......... anherr, anherr-anherr
woman's daughter-in-law (baby talk).......... nhey-nhey (E)
man's daughter-in-law.......... ahenterr (E) (?)

dawn (go to 'daybreak')

day.......... arlta[1], arltang (W,T)
middle of the day.......... arlta mpep (E), arteny[2] (T,E)
all day, all through the day, in the daytime.......... aherrkelam aherrkel (E), uternek uternek (E)
every day.......... aherrk arrpanenh (E), arltemarlt (T)
a few days ago.......... amwerrk, amwerrkel, ngwerreh arrpenh (W,T)
one day soon.......... ingwenth anyent-ingar (E)
day after tomorrow.......... ngwenth arrpenh

daytime.......... arlta[1], arlta mpep (E), arltang (W,T)
in the daytime.......... aherrkel, uternek (E)

day trip.......... irrer, lyweny (W,T)
go for a day trip, for the day.......... irrer alhem, lyweny alhem (W,T)

day trip, for the day (respect language) ... irrerernk (E)

daybreak, dawn ... aherlkenty, aherlkentyel, aherrk ney-ney, ney-ney

daybreak (respect language) ... iltywel-antey (E), ultyel-antey (E), ultyel-ayerr (E)

when it is just getting light ... aketh-aketh (T,E), ngwenth-ngwenth

dawn, become daybreak ... aherlkem, aherrk aketh-irrem, aketh-irrem, ngwenth-ngwenth-irrem

daydream

being in a world of one's own, not thinking about anyone else ... ankwaty (W,T)

Daylight Star

Morning Star, Daylight Star, Venus ... Anthelper (W,T), Arwenpeng (E), Awelh (E), Kwerraly Angerr, Kwerraly Rltwa (W), Kwerraly Urlta (T,E)

dead ... nya

dead body ... arrwety, artart^{2} (W,T), aweyaw, ima (E), irrernng, irrewaly

dead finish *(plant)* ... arlketyerr, tyer^{1} (W,T)

deaf ... arert, arert-arert, arnaper (W,T), arwangk (W,T), arwengk (T,E), ather-ather^{2} (W)

a bit deaf ... arrthat (T), arrtheth (T)

go deaf ... arert-irrem, arnaper-irrem (W,T), arwengk-irrem (T,E)

go a bit deaf ... arert-arert-irrem

make someone go deaf, deafen someone with noise ... arert-ilem, arwengk-ilem (T,E)

dear

'Dear thing' (word endings) ... -amperl (E), -angwel-angwel (E), -angwen-angwen (T,E), -apenh (W,T), -awern

'Dear thing' ... akeweny (W,T), akuny (T,E), akeweny-amperl (W,T), akuny-amperl (T,E), akeweny-apenh (W,T), antyeny (T,E)

death

(doing something) to the death or almost to the death ... nyant, nyekant, irrewalyeh (W), irrewalyek (T,E)

fight to the death ... irrewaly atwem

debris

left by floodwater ... ntat

decay *(especially of meat)* ... arntert-irrem

deceive

trick or deceive someone ... rrtywerrem (W,T), urrtyirrem (E), arrenkelh-anthem (T), arrenkelh-ilem^{1} (T), rrtywekelh-ilem (T)

deep ... kwen, kwetn (E)

deep water ... arntay (W,T), kwen-angerr

deep waterhole ... kwaty arntay (W,T)

deep sleep ... ankwang angerr (W,T), ankwa angerr (E)

defecate ... lhwem (T), lwem^{1} (W), ulhem (T,E)

defecate (baby talk) ... key-key-irrem (E)

definitely ... kwa, kwang, kwenh, lweth (E)

deflated ... alpwely

become deflated ... alpwely-irrem

delay

delay or stop someone from doing something ... anngangem (E)

delicious *(food)* ... arrwer-arrwer (T,E)

demand

be demanding ... ankey-irrem (E)

demand something of somebody ... inkem, ankey inkem

dented ... mwely, mwely-mwely, unmely (E)

become crushed or dented ... mwely-irrem, unmely-irrem (E)

dent or crush something ... mwely-ilem, unmely-ilem (E)

deny

deny having something (that you have stolen) ... anyenng artelhem (T), anyelk artelhem (E)

deny that you have something ... ywep-arrernem (W,T)

depressed ... alharrp (W,T), alhwarrp (T,E), altarrp (W,T)

descend

climb down, get down ... anarnpem

descend (in the air) ... arrarlernem (W,T)

desert *(abandon someone)* ... arrkereny-irrem, arrkerenyel-wem

desert bandicoot ... akwerr^{2}, melyerrkwer (W,T)

Desert Bore ... Pwelartey

desert broom bush ... anngey-anngey

desert cassia ... apwen, ngkwert (W,T)

grub from ... apwenayt (T,E)

desert country ... manangkarr (W,T), rrkwal (W,T), irrkwal (E), arrangketh

desert death adder ... mantharr, antharr (E)

desert fig ... tywerrk (W,T), utyerrk (E)
desert Flinders grass ... arlepenh (T,E), arrepeny (T), kwarrety (W,T), nyetempwer (W)
desert fringed lily ... akwerl-akwerl (W,T), arrwelth-arrwelth (E)
desert kurrajong ... apeng
  seed of ... ngkweyang
desert lantern *(plant)* ... aylpat-aylpat (E)
desert lily ... iylelty (E) lyelkenng (E), iylelkenng (E), alyerlk-alyerlk (W), arlerlk-arlerlk (T)
desert oak ... arrkep, kwerrkar (W,T)
desert poplar ... arlkemal
  grub from ... arlkemal-areny (T), arlkemalayt (E)
desert raisin ... katyerr
  desert raisin (baby talk) ... katy
  sandhill variety ... kamperarrp (W,T)
  fresh fruit of ... katyerr kwart
  unripe fruit of ... kwart, pwarr (T,E), urleynterr[2] (E)
  yellow fruit of ... arlkarntar (W,T)
  dry fruit of ... alha[2], alhang (W,T), katyerr alha, katyerr tweny (W,T), katyerr uteny (E), tweny, uteny (E)
  go dry (fruit) ... tweny-irrem, uteny-irrem (E)
  bitter-tasting coating on fruit ... tepwerl (E)
  clean fruits by rubbing them on the ground ... pwarr-wem (T,E), inpewem (E), theweth-ilem (W), tewem
desert rattlepod ... rltar-rltar[2] (W,T), rltwar-rltwar (W), rltwayep-rltwayep (E)
desert spadefoot toad ... atweynterl (E), kwep, kwep-kwep[2], pwerreparnt (W,T)
desert spurge ... alyey-alyey (W,T), anemarraty (W,T), marlek-alyey-alyey
desert tree frog ... antyetyerr, karlarrangkern (E), larrangkern
desert truffle ... akwerrerteth (E), irrkwenng (T,E), pwerlantar (T), pwelerntar (W,T)
desert yam *(go to 'bush potato')*
deserted
  place or camp ... ampeny[1], arramperrty (E), ingkeny, arltwa, arltwang (W,T)
design ... arlkeny, mpaty[1]
  women's painting, body paint or ceremonial designs ... tyepety[1] (W,T), arlkeny (E)
  make a design or mark on something ... arlkeny arrernem, arlkeny-wem, intelhem (W,T), intelh-ilem (W,T)
  put ceremonial designs on each other ... iwerrem
desirable
  someone you really like, or someone who is desirable ... arrwer-arrwer (T,E) (?)
desire
  desire or fancy someone ... alherrem[2] (W,T), alhirrem, iyteny-irrem (E), ahenty-irrem, ahenty-anem
despite
  without taking notice of others or events ... atanty, alanty
  even though . . . , despite the fact that . . . ... -itany (E)
devil
  the Devil ... arrenty
  Devil, monster (respect language) ... alharrenty
dew ... irnmerr
diamond dove ... kwerlekwek, kwerler-kwerler (W,T), kwerakwek (W,T), urelyarr (E), lerakwenty (W) (?), larakwenty (W,T) (?)
diarrhoea ... ampeltyey (W,T), atnelth (E)
  have diarrhoea or guts-ache ... ampeltyem, ampeltyey-irrem (W,T), aneltyey-irrem (E), atnelth-irrem (E), ltherrp-wem
didgeridoo
  (from English/Creol) ... pampew
die ... ilwem, nyerrem (W,T), ulem (T,E), uyerrem (E), ywerrem, ahap-irrem (E), arrangkw-irrem
  die (respect language) ... alyent-artek-irrem (E), arremangkw-irrem (E), anengkan-irrem
  people who have passed away ... ywerrengerreng (T)
die down *(flames)* ... anmerrem (W,T), ilwem, ulem (T,E)
different
  a different one ... arrpenh, ingwer (E)
  in a different way ... arrpenh-angkwerr, ingwer-angkwerr (E)
  lots of different ones ... arrpethet (W,T), arrpanenh (E)

difficult
with difficulty ... ywarn, uyarn (E)
have a difficult time ... nakepakel-irrem (W,T)
make things difficult ... nakepakel-ilem (W,T)

dig
dig for something ... inyem, angernem1, ahinem (E)
dig a hole ... ipert-ilem, rtwep-ilem (W,T), ipert angernem (W,T)
dig a soakage ... angenty arrernem (E), angenty-ilem (E), arnwengk arrernem (E), arnwengk-ilem (W,T)
dig a hole out to make it wider ... arntay-ilem (W,T)
dig a burrow ... arleytarr-ilem (T,E)
dig something out of yourself ... inyelhem
dig self into a hole or burrow (some animals) ... kelerr ipelhem (E), rlwelth arrernelhem (W,T), urlelth ipelhem (E), ipelhem (E)

digging stick ... anem3

dilly bag ... yakweth
(from English) ... terlapak

dingo ... arnapar (W,T), arnwer1

Dingo dam ... Arrangkey

dinnertime ... arteny2 (T,E)

dip
dip something into something ... arek-wem (W,T), pwerlp-wem (T,E)
dip something up (water) ... athankwem (T,E), arnweng-inem (W,T), inpem (T,E)

direct
go the most direct way ... ntwertety alhem (W,T), untertety alhem (E)

Direct Action Bore ... Yartepetyey

direction
facing or pointing towards something (ending) ... -warn (W,T), -warl
in another direction ... arrpenh-angkwerr
towards or as far as particular place (ending) ... -athek
'Where to?', 'Which way?' ... nthenh-angkwerr, nthangkwerr, nthenh-warn (W,T), nthenh-warl (E)

dirt ... ahelh, ahern
lump of dirt or mud ... ahern ata (E), ata1 (E)
soft dirt ... ulpmerr (E)
wet or damp dirt or sand ... amel1

dirty ... aternng, alkwemp-alkwemp, altelhey (W,T), iltelhey (T,E), alther (T,E)
covered in dirty stuff ... lthenp
unwashed (person or animal) ... atyarleny (W)
dirty water ... lpwert (W,T), ulpert (T,E), alhwerrk (E)
get dirty ... aternng-irrem
get dirty or muddy (water) ... lpwert-irrem (W,T), ulpert-irrem (T,E), alhwerrk-irrem (E)
make something dirty ... aternng-ilem
make water muddy or dirty ... lpwert-ilem (W,T), ulpert-ilem (T,E), alhwerrk-ilem (E)

disappear
out of sight, go away ... ywerrem, uyerrem (E)
without trace, go somewhere (but nobody knows where) ... inpirrem (E)

disappointed
feel disappointed or let down (by someone) ... ahentyel-akem (T,E)

disassociate
disassociating yourself from someone or something ... arla2 (T,E)
dissassociaate yourself from your family ... urlkernelhem (E)

disbelieve
disbelieve or mistrust someone who breaks promises ... anew-irrem (T,E)

discard
discard something ... arntarr-wem (W,T)
something that has been discarded or thrown away by others ... ntweth-ntweth (W,T), intweth-intweth (E)

disease ... arrwengkelth, pwenty1 (E)
disease (from English) ... tethet

disgusted
feel disgusted by something ... lyekarr anem

dish
wooden water dish ... arlketh1 (W,T), atywekal (W), rnwa (W,T), rnwang (W,T), urety (E), urna (T,E), kwerlintyerr
types of dish ... panth, lwengkart2 (W), irrkwely2 (E), alparr1 (W,T), irrkwa (E), lengarr (E)
small wooden shovel or scoop ... mwar

toy wooden bowl or dish mwareng-mwar, pantheng-panth
dishonestly anyenng, arwengkel
dislike
showing someone that you don't like them anywerr-anywerr
dislike somebody or something ahenty-kwenh (W,T), anywerr-irrem, yerrng-irrem (W,T)
dislike or be uninterested in something arnernkem
dislocate
(an animal's leg) by twisting it rlwakem (W,T), rlwang arrernem (W,T), ulernkernem (E)
disperse akalk-irrem, irrarnp-irrem (W,T)
distant
a long way away arleng[1]
a long time away arleng[1]
someone from a distant place arleng-areny (T,E)
distract
distract or confuse someone apatel-anthem (T,E), apatelh-ilem
distract someone, keep someone occupied anngwanng-ilem, anngwelem, aparlp-ilem, aparlpelh-ilem, akwenpeny-ilem
distract yourself (take your mind off something) anngwanng-ilelhem
become distracted anngwerrem (W,T), anngwirrem (E)
disturb
create a disturbance arweketherwek-ilem (W,T), urekethwerek-ilem (E)
disturb, interrupt someone urawenyerr-ilem (E), rawenyerr-ilem (E)
ditch ipert
dive into water pwerlp-irrem
divide *(something up)* angakem, irrarnp-ilem (W,T), irrarnpelh-ilem (W,T), akalk-ilem, akalkelh-ilem
divorce
split up (married couple) iwerrem
dizzy
feel dizzy arepwelepwel-irrem, kapert rawen-irrem (W,T), annga ingwemernt-irrem, annga therrert-irrem (E), annga alkerelhem
Dneiper Yerrekwaty
do
do something, make something mpwarem
do things, be occupied doing something rrkwapem (W,T), irrkwapem (E), atyanem (W), mpwarem
do something quickly or in a hurry arrewelhem
be unable to do something, be at a loss as to what to do apatem
do something first or before someone else arnang-ilem[1] (E)
(doing something) a lot arnterr
(doing something) for or on behalf of someone else atyang[1], anam
(doing something) another time aweth aken
(doing something) without thinking, for no good reason apelkel (W,T)
(doing something) while others are waiting atanty-atanty, alanty-alanty
dodder-laurel *(plant)* interr-interr (E)
dodge
dodge, duck out of the way inangkal-irrem, uremeny-irrem (E)
dodge something (a spear or boomerang, or in a football game) irrimper-irrem (T,E), irrkar-aytnem (T,E)
dodge or ward off (a spear) wawely-irrem (W,T)
doe kangaroo aherr marl
dog angwely, arengk
dog (from English) papap[2]
dog (respect language) tywetyety-ayerr (E), atnetyelp (E) (SP)
dog (baby talk) tywetyety
dog with not much hair arengk arleny (E)
female dog that's had pups alkeperr
sympathetic words for a dog wang-wang, rtwek-rtwek (T,E)

dog whose owner has died .... pimpart (E)
a word used when you are angry or cranky with a dog .... atnetyelp (E) (SP)
word that is used when calling out to a dog .... tywetyety
my dog .... artweyaty, ngwarraty (W)
his/her/their dog .... artweyek (W,T), artweyikw (E), ngwarrekw (W)
your dog .... artweyek (W,T), artweyengk, ngwarrekw (W), ngwarrengkw (W)
dog who always accompanies its owner or master .... artwey-ankethenh, artew-ankethenh (W,T)
person together with one of their dogs .... artwey-nheng atherr
person together with two or more of their dogs .... artwey-intyerr (W,T), artwey-nheng
dog's piss or urine .... mpwerl
urinate (dog) .... mpwerl lhwem, mpwerl ulhem (E), mpwerl-ilem

dog-eye bush tomato .... arengkerlpart, arntek-arntek (E)

dogwood .... akerlperr (W,T), awenth (E)
flower of .... athwenter
young seedpods of .... alywer[1] (T,E), lyweper
seeds of .... akerlperr (W,T), ntyer (T), ntyerrm, alyaly (W)
green seeds of .... artwengarr (T,E), arntwatherrk[2] (T,E)
dark-coloured or dry seeds of .... kertaty (E), rtartaty (E), lyarr (E)
sweet milky drink made from seeds .... ntyerrm, apal[1] (E)
ground up seeds .... pilal (T,E) (?)
crush seeds .... alyaly atwem (W)
grub from .... awenthayt (E)

dogwood Hakea .... ntyarleyarleng

doll .... kwereng-akwer (W,T), ampengamp (E), ampeng-ampeng (E)

dollar *(from English)* .... tal

don't
don't (do the verb action) .... +etyal

don't know
behave as if you don't know a person or thing .... ayemem (W,T), uyemem (E)
something you say when you don't know about something .... ywek, ywekaw, inpa (E)

don't like
don't like something, don't want to do something .... mwernt-irrem (T,E)
don't like something, feel shamed over something .... mwekeny-irrem (?), mwekernp-irrem (W,T) (?)

donkey .... irlpa urety (E), irlpalkey (W,T), irlpangerr (W,T)
donkey (from English) .... tangkey

door .... arrew (W,T), arriw (T,E)

dot
make dots on something .... nteny-nteny-ilem (E)

dotterel .... pernernpernernp (?)
black-fronted dotterel .... ntyelpeny (W,T), iynterlpeny (E)
inland dotterel .... tyerr-tyerr (W), tyerr-tyerrey (W), tyerrepert (W)
red-kneed dotterel .... tyelkatherather, interrk-atherather (W,T) (?)

double back
go through the air and double back, spin back, vibrate (of bark boomerang, boomerang or spear) .... ngarakwerr-irrem (E)

double bank
'double bank' someone .... artangatyel atwem

doubled up
twisted, cramped .... arlwemeny, arrepert (E), rtapety
be doubled up .... arlwemeny-irrem, arlwerrelhem, arrepert-irrem (E)

dough
wet dough made by mixing boiling water with flour .... anwerrng, mern thwep-thwep (W)

dove
diamond dove .... kwerlekwek, kwerler-kwerler (W,T), kwerakwek (W,T), urelyarr (E)
peaceful dove .... kwerlekwek, kwerler-kwerler (W,T), kwerakwek (W,T), lerakwenty (W) (?), larakwenty (W,T) (?)

down .... kwen
bend down .... kwen-irrem
get down off something, go down .... anarnpem
get something down from something .... rwelh-ilem (W,T), rwelh-rwelh-ilem (W,T), kwen-ilem, anarnpelh-ilem
go downwards .... thar-irrem (E)

go downwards (in the air) … arrarlernem (W,T)
lie facing or slanting downwards … thar intem
doing an action down or along something … -akerl
(down)wards … -antep
facing down … kwen-akerl, kwen-antep, kwenel-athek, kwenelak, thar, thar-thar

draft *(cattle)* … angakem, urrarem (T,E)

drag
pull something along … tyarr-angem
pull something out … tyarr-inem
pull something to the ground … athelp-athenem alpalth (E), thwerremp-thwerr (T,E)
drag feet as you go along … thwerremp-irrem (T,E), rlkerremp-rlkerr alhem (T,E)

dragon lizard … irnar (W,T), kelyaw
dwarf bearded dragon … kapert angerr (W,T), tyapantarr (W,T)
type of dragon lizard … perlap arlwelenh (W), perlap-areny (W)

dragonfly … kwaty-inperrenh (W,T), kwaty-imperrenh (E), rew inperrenh (W), urewap-imperreny (E), warepelh-pelh (T)
dragonfly (from English) … kapert[2] (W)

Drakluder Dam … Arlekert-arlekert

draw *(something)* … arrernem, atanthem, ingkwernem (T,E), intelh-ilem (W,T), intelhem (W,T), mpaty-ilem (W,T), arlkeny arrernem, arlkeny-wem

dream
a dream … anengkerr (W,T), altyerr[1]
have a dream … altyerr arem, anengkerr arem (W,T)
nightmare … anengkerr-anengkerr (W,T), altyerr-altyerr
have a bad dream or nightmare … altyerr-altyerr arem, anengkerr-anengkerr arem (W,T)
have a predictive dream about a relation … altyerr uternelhem (E)
make someone have a predictive dream … altyerr iylkwem (E)

Dreaming
totem, ancestral being … Altyerr[1], Anengkerr (W,T), Anganenty
Dreaming from a person's mother's country … altyerr[1], anengkerr (W,T)
own personal Dreaming … arweng[1] (E)
from the Dreaming or creation time … altyerr-penh (E), altyerreng (E), anengkerr-penh (W,T), anengkerreng (W,T), Anengkerrant-alkenty (W,T)
people related to a particular Dreaming … -artwey
be created (in the Dreaming) … anganem
tell Dreaming stories … altyerr ilem, anengkerr ilem (W,T)

drenched … anthwek-anthwek
drench or soak something … anthwek-anthwek-ilem

dress … mantarr
dress (from English) … terreth

dribble
to dribble … arrelty thelelhem, arrwek (T,E), karerrem (W), pelh-pelh (T,E), iylkerr (E), iylkerr thelelhem (E)

drill
drill a hole in something … arrwernem

drink
drink something … antywem
drink something (respect language) … amely-wem, amely-akem (E)
drink to quench thirst … alywer-irrem
drink from the breast … werlaty antywem (T,E), paty antywem (W,T)
drink alcohol … antywem
eat or drink quickly … antyetem (E), arrwer-ilem[1] (T,E)
drink greedily without sharing … nwanthem (W,T), ahanthem (E), unanthem (E), ankeyel arlkwem
drink half of something and save the rest for someone else … ngkarrp-ilem (W,T)
make someone feel like eating or drinking … arrengker-ilem (W,T)

drip
a drip or drop of water … irnmerr, kwaty irnmerr, ntyerlp[2] (W,T)
drip down … lwem[2] (W,T), thelelhem

dripping
drenched … anthwek-anthwek
with blood, covered with blood (respect language) … kweth-kweth

drizzle
fine rain .... kwaty lthel, kwaty perler, lyelyaw (E), nyeyepenyey (W), perler, thawel (T), kwaty thawel (T), thew-thew[1] (W,T), tyeyepetyey (W)
to drizzle .... tyetyel-wem (E)

drop
drop down .... anyem[1], arrwerelhem
drop something .... arrwer-ilem[2], anyelh-ilem
drop off to sleep .... rlwank-anyem (E), rrwempem (W,T), rrwempel anem (W)
drop someone off somewhere .... artek-wem (W,T), arteng-wem (T,E), iwerl-alhem, iwerl-wem (E)
drop someone or something off (respect language) .... alpiwerl-alpem (E)

droppings .... ana, anang (W,T), kart[1] (W,T)

drought-stricken
(of country) .... arrangketh, aherraty, urrepert (E), rrwepert (T), ahepet (E)

drowsy
become drowsy .... rlwank anyem (E), rrwempem (W,T), rrwempel anem (W)
lie around feeling drowsy, lazy or lethargic .... aylpmerrem (E)

drunk
drunken person, a drunk (from English) .... terangk
bit drunk, light-headed, dizzy, faint .... terangk-terangk
get drunk .... terangk-irrem
make someone drunk .... terangkem-ilem

dry .... antyerrk, arleny (E), arlerrk (E), arterrty (T,E), arerrty
dry country .... arrangketh, urrepert (E), rrwepert (T), ahepet (E), aherraty
dry up (country or vegetation) .... aherraty-irrem, ahepet-irrem (E), urrepert-irrem (E), rrwepert-irrem (T)
dry damper or seed mixture .... akapw (E)
dry leaves .... arrngelh (W,T)
dry or old (of certain bush foods) .... atnywa (E), pweynteng (E)
dry kangaroo droppings .... anwer (E)
dried mud .... tanty
get dry .... antyerrk-irrem, arleny-irrem (E), arterrty-irrem (T,E), alyempelhem, alpwely-irrem
dry out (food) .... arlerrk-irrem (E)
get dry (of damper or seed mixture) .... akapw-irrem (E)
go dry, get old (of certain bush foods) .... atnywirrem (E), pweynteng-irrem (E)
dry up (water or soakage) .... iker-irrem
dry something .... antyerrk-ilem, arleny-ilem (E), arterrty-ilem (T,E)
lay or spread something out to dry .... tek-arrernem, tek-wem, tek-ampem

duck
Pacific black duck .... awengker (?)
plumed whistling duck .... tyepelyakw (W) (?), tyepelyey (E) (?)
types of .... pelyak (W,T), pelyakw (T,E), ipelyak (E), angkwer[2] (W), angkeparr (W,T), perrertern (E)

dull
blurry, not bright .... arrkay
not clear, dark .... ngwemernt (W,T), ingwemernt (E)

dumb
unable to speak (physical impediment) .... apekap, akerter, apap (W)

dung beetle .... nyert-nyert (?), perrk-perrk (W,T) (?), pwerrk-pwerrk (E) (?)

Dunja Bore .... Nanty

dusk .... ngwemernt-ngwemernt (W,T), ingwemernt-ingwemernt (E)

dust
dust haze, dust storm .... nmwernt (W,T), unmernt (T,E)
dust haze seen after rain .... alharrkw (E)
dust storm (before rain) .... alhek nmwernt (W,T), alhek unmernt (T,E)

dysfunctional .... anety (W,T), akeng (T,E), kwern (W,T)

Ee

eagle *(from English)* .... ikelak (E)
wedge-tailed eagle .... arlawerr (W)
eaglehawk .... irrety

ear, ears .... irlpa, irlpang (W,T), arlpang (W,T)
back of the ear .... irlpa artep, irlpang artep (W,T)

soft part of the ear, earlobe .... iylpa atyet (E), irlpa atyet-atyet (E)
earwax .... irlpa akwenp (E)
blocked up ears .... irlpa alhap (W,T)

earlier .... arrwekel

early
in the morning .... aherlkenty, aherlkentyel, ingwelem (T,E)

earth *(see also 'dirt')* .... ahelh, ahern
the Earth .... ahelh, ahern
the colour of the earth .... ahelh-ahelh, ahern-ahern
hot earth .... ntywety (W,T), untyety (E)

east .... angerrakw, ingerr (W,T)
east (respect language) .... ngwelernety (W), ngwelern (E), ngwelerneyt (E), akngwelern (E)
due east .... angerrakw arraty, ingerr arraty (W,T)
north-east .... ayerrer ingerr (W,T), ayerrer ikngerr (E), ayerrer-ayerrer (E)
south-east .... antekerr ingerr
on the eastern side .... angerrakw-ampeny

eat .... arlkwem
eat (respect language) .... amely-akem (E), amely-wem
eat (baby talk) .... akwem
honeyants, sugarbag, corkwood honey, ground seeds and some fruit (eating something) .... awantyem
before the main meal .... apak
eat or drink greedily or quickly .... arnterr arlkwem, ahanthem (E), antyetem (E), arrwer-ilem[1] (T,E), nwanthem (W,T), unanthem (E)
eat without sharing or while another is waiting .... atanty arlkwem (T,E), alanty arlkwem (E)
eat fast, gobble food up .... akwern-akwern-wem (E)
eat a lot after feeling hungry, overeat .... nyant arlkwem
eat or drink everything so there is nothing left .... nwanthelhem (W,T), unanthelhem (E)
eat half of something and save the rest for someone else .... ngkarrp-ilem (W,T)
feel like eating or drinking .... arrengker-irrem (W,T)
make someone feel like eating or drinking .... arrengker anthem, arrengker-ilem (W,T)

echidna .... inap (T,E), inarleng, ingka iyntwem (E), ker arlkerl (E), lyek
echidna (respect language) .... iylek-ayerr (E)
back of echidna, meat from back of echidna .... angkwer[1]

echo .... rrwar (W,T), urrar (T,E)
echo, bounce back .... tyernem[1], tyernelhem (T,E)

edge
edge or side of something .... itep, kanty[1], akwerr[1] (E), iter, arrethaker
on the side or the edge of something .... itep-ampeny, itep-thayt, iter-ampeny

edible
the edible part of something .... mern

egg .... kwart
eggshell .... ika (T,E), kwart ika (T,E)
egg white .... alker-alker, alkerey-alkerey (E)
egg yolk (emu egg and others) .... athwenter
emu egg .... atherneng (E)
eggs of honeyants and other species of ant .... lwerrk (W,T), ilwerrk (E)
eggs of the spinifex ant .... tyerremp kwart (T,E)

eight .... mangart[2] (W,T)

eight-day grass .... taty-taty[1], arnwety-arnwety (W)

elbow .... amak
point of the elbow .... amak annga (W,T)

elder .... angerr-pat, angerrety, atyetyart, aywang intert (W,T), rltwa (W,T), rltwang (W,T), urlta (E)
eldest sibling .... aletharr (T,E), arrwekeleny, itep-penh (T,E)
make a child the eldest (by having another one) .... aletharr-ilem (T,E) (?)

elephant grub .... antyarlk (E)

embarrassment .... apwer (W,T), apur (E), nyerr
person who is ashamed or embarrassed .... apweralth (W,T), apuralth (E), nyerralth
be embarrassed .... apwer-irrem (W,T), apur-irrem (E), nyerr-irrem
make someone feel shamed, shy or embarrassed .... apwerel anthem (W,T), apurel anthem (E), nyerrel anthem

embrace
in an expression of mourning ...... amel-rrkwem (W,T)
embrace each other ...... amel-rrkwerrem (W,T), kwety-arerrem (E)
emerge
emerge from something or somewhere ...... arratem, tyerrelhem
emerge from cover and run off (of some animals) ...... artwep-wem, urtep-wem (E)
emerge (moths and butterflies) ...... rnkem
emphasis
adds emphasis to what someone is saying .. +ay[1], +aw, +ew
employee ...... warrken map, rrkwapenh-apenh (T)
empty ...... arltwa, arltwang (W,T)
of places and houses ...... ingkeny, ampeny[1]
become empty ...... arltwerrem (W,T), arltwirrem (T,E)
empty something out ...... arltwelem (W,T), arltwilem (E)
empty-handed ...... iltyant, rep (E)
emu ...... ankerr, arley (W,T)
emu (respect language) ...... anhelengkw-ayerr (E), arnwa, arnwang (W,T)
baby emu, emu chick ...... artelh[1] (W,T), alywer[1] (T,E), aylwer (E), ankerr akwek (W,T), ankerr akwerrk (W,T), arley (W,T) (SP)
first born of a brood ...... apwarrewerlker (E) (SP)
big male emu ...... urrekek (E)
black-coloured emu ...... rntwely (W)
whitish or grey-coloured emu ...... areyakeyarr (W), apwarrewerlker (E) (SP)
old thin emu ...... ntyerrm
emu foot ...... irrpeyl (E), irrtyewat[2] (W,T)
emu heart ...... angka[2] (E)
emu crop ...... ngkwemengk (W) (?)
emu blood ...... apeynt-apeynt (E)
emu liver ...... ilep[2] (E)
emu intestines or guts ...... anwerl-anwerl (E), alyep[2] (W)
emu neck ...... arwentyey (E)
emu shinbone ...... arrert, wetyeny (E)
back of the emu ...... amakw (E), warr (E)
vestigial wings ...... angkangk iytarr-inenh (E), perlap arraw-ilenh (W), perlap tyarr-inenh (E)
emu nest ...... tyimp (E)
emu egg ...... arley kwart (W,T), atherneng (E)
emu meat
meat from the back ...... pwerakart
raw emu meat ...... arntwatherrk[2] (T,E)
bad, rotten (emu meat) ... ayewarr (E)
go off, become rotten (emu meat) ...... ayewarr-irrem (E)
gut an emu ...... ntyererlk-akem (E)
cut up meat along the backbone ...... artep ultatwem (T,E)
emu feathers ...... apwa (E)
longer feathers from back of emu ...... artarr
soft feathers, down ...... angkwely-angkwely (W), awenth-awenth (E)
emu fat
from the back ...... arnwa, arnwang (W,T), artep lpway (W,T), artep ulpay (T,E)
from the belly ...... ampatherr (W)
from the side (near the kidney) ...... inmelh (W)
yellow fat from stomach .. analharr (E)
emu that is fatty in lower part of body ...... nyengk-nyengk (W)
cut up emu fat ...... arnwelem (W)
emu apple ...... arrek (E)
emu bush ...... anwerreng (W), lhwek-lhwek (W,T), unerreng (E)
grub from ...... alwerrpent (W), alwerrpaty (W), lhwek-lhwek (W,T), unerrengayt (E)
end
something is finished or completed ...... kel, kel-antey (E), kelepenh
end, finish, run out ...... ywerrem, uyerrem (E), ilwem
end of a burrow ...... iwarlkw (E)
end or edge of something .. akert[1] (T,E)
energetic ...... ampwengamp, arwekar (W,T), atyep-atyep, irrngerney (E)
engine
the 'head' of a car ...... kapert[1]
English ...... Angkeleth
enjoy *(doing something)* ..... kwak-irrem, ilkelhem
enjoyable ...... mwerr, mwerr angerr (W,T), mwerr-angker (E)
enormous ...... -anternenh
enter ...... irrpem, aylpem (E)
enthusiastic ...... irrngerney (E)
be enthusiastic ...... kwak-irrem, irrngerney-irrem (E)
entire
complete, whole ...... mpank (W,T), mpwank
entirely
entirely one thing and not another, pure ...... rlwart (W,T), urlart (E)
entrance ...... arrew (W,T), arriw (T,E)
envious *(go to 'jealous')*

erode .... arnkarr-akem (W), arnkarr-ilem (T,E), ilerrty-ilem, thalkerr-ilem (W,T)
escape .... alwerrem
Eurasian coot .... anker-anker[1] (E)
euro .... areng[3], areyneng (E), irntareny (W,T)
euro (respect language) .... nyewel-areny (E)
European person
non-Aboriginal .... mperlker, alhernter, kartey (W), tyerrty arlter (E), tywelker
non-Aboriginal (from English) .... warlpal
European woman (from English) .... waterlweper, metheth
even
level, equal (from English) .... lepwel
evening
early evening .... angwerr-angwerr
little bit dark, early evening .... ngway-ngway (W), ingway-ingway (T,E)
get dark, become evening .... angwerr-angwerr-irrem, ngway-ngway-irrem (W), ingway-ingway-irrem (T,E)
every .... arrpanenh (E), arrpethet (W,T)
every day, frequently .... aherrk arrpanenh (E)
every now and then .... anyentam-anyent, anyentek-anyent
everybody
everybody, everything .... ingkerr-antey, ingkerr[1], ingkerrek, ingkerrek-antey (T,E)
everybody, everything (respect language) .... alanenty (E), kewerrewerr (E)
everything
all sorts of (things) .... alhwengkelty
everywhere
all over the place .... alperrty (T,E), apapeth, apawerr (E), apanp, arrpethet (W,T)
excessively
(doing something) a lot or excessively .... nyant, nyekant
excited
feel pleased or excited .... anyanelhem, anyerrkem, kwak-irrem
feel happy (especially about food) .... athek-irrem
be frightened, unsettled or excited .... arawerrng angkem, arawerrng-irrem
getting very excited about something .... ngwarrertakert (W,T)
exclamation
'For goodness sake!' .... atyeweyay (E)
exclamation of pain .... yapaty (W,T), yekay
exclamation made when chasing goannas, perenties, and other animals .... peyaw (E)
excreta .... ana, anang (W,T), kart[1] (W,T)
exhaust pipe *(of a car)* .... kwert-henh (W,T), kwert-kenh (E)
exhausted
feel exhausted or sick and tired of something .... arewamp-irrem, atnhakert-irrem (E)
exit
door, opening .... arrew (W,T), arriw (T,E)
go out .... arratem
expert
expert at doing something .... kalty, kwerathek (W,T), lywenpeny
explain
explain something .... ilem
explain yourself to someone .... angkawelhem, ilelhem
explode .... rltar-rnkem (E), rltwar-rnkem, urltar-rnkem (E)
extinguish
put something out .... lwernem (W,T), ilwernem (E)
become extinguished .... lwernelhem (W,T), ilwernelhem (E)
extremely .... angerr[1]
eye .... annga, anngang (W,T)
eye (respect language) .... angapanty (E), apal-apal[1] (E), parerr (E)
bung-eye .... annga alhwer-alhwer (W,T) annga alhap (E)
pupil, iris .... annga rrpwerl (W,T), annga urrperl (E)
sinews going to the eye .... iytwerr (E) (?)
white of the eye .... alker-alker, alkerey-alkerey (E)
cross-eyed, eyes that have whitened over with cataracts .... annga alker-alker (T,E), annga arlter
red eyes .... anngang rnter-rnter
eyes that are a blue-green in colour .... annga atherrk-atherrk
weepy, dirty or pussy eyes .... annganthwerr-anthwerr (W,T)
eyes fade or whiten over .... alkerelhem (E)
eyes shut .... annga pweng
eyes sink back in head .... annga ipert-irrem, ipert-irrem

open eyes ...... anngampem (W,T), anngerlkem (T,E)
make someone or something open their eyes ...... anngampelh-ilem, anngerlkelh-ilem (T,E)
shade eyes with hand ...... merlpeng (W,T), merlpengel arem (W,T)
shading eyes with hand ...... urlengimar (E), rlwengimar (E), rlwengemar (T)
eye socket ...... annga iylpwer (E)
eyeball ...... annga kwart, anngang kwart (W,T)
eyebrow ...... anngarnt, anngaty (W,T), annga urreyt (E), anngarnt alta
eyelash ...... anngarnpelh
eyelid ...... annga artep, annga tyelk
eyesight ...... annga, anngang (W,T)
poor or faded eyesight ...... annga arrkay
eyesight fade ...... annga ingwemernt-irrem, annga alkerelhem

Ff

fabric
that hasn't been sewn ...... alparr[2]
face ...... inngerr
to one's face, in public ...... anngetherr, anngetherrek-anngetherr
facing towards the speaker ...... lwarr-athek (W,T), ularr-athek (T,E)
(doing something) face-to-face ...... rlwerrker (W,T), urlerrker (E), lwarrek-lwarr (W,T), ularrek-ularr (T,E) rlwerrkerek-rlwerrker (W,T), urlerrker-urlerrkerek (E), ulanengek-ulaneng (E), lwanengek-lwaneng (T), ulengerek-ulenger (E)
facing away from someone or something ...... ntywem[2] (W,T), untyem[2] (E), ntywem-athek (W,T), untyem-athek (E)
turning to face away ...... arrwernt
face away from someone or something ...... ntywem-irrem (W,T), untyem-irrem (E)
facing away from each other ...... ntywemek-ntywem (W,T), untyemek-untyem (E)
face up to a person you have wronged ...... rlwaty angkem (W,T), urlaty angkem (E)
face or slope downwards ...... arrarlernem (W,T)
fact
it's a fact that... ...... arraty
fade
faded, faint ...... arrkay
become faded, faint or blurry ...... arrkay-irrem
make something fade ...... arrkay-ilem
fade (voice) ...... ahenty arrkay-irrem
faeces ...... ana, anang (W,T), kart[1] (W,T)
faint
feeling tired, faint or dizzy from heat ...... arepwelepwel
feel faint, dizzy ...... arepwelepwel-irrem, kapert rawen-irrem (W,T), annga ingwemernt-irrem, annga therrert-irrem (E), annga alkerelhem
faint *(visibility)*
hardly visible ...... arelty (E), arelty-arelty (E)
fairy martin ...... tyerremper (E)
fake
not the real thing ...... rrtyweng-rrtyweng (W,T), tyweng-tyweng, urrtyeng-urrtyeng (E), utyek-utyel (E)
falcon
peregrine falcon ...... aleraperap (E) (?)
brown falcon ...... irrkerlanty
fall
fall off something ...... anyem[1]
fall (rain) ...... anhem, anyem[1], kwaty arrwerelhem
something fall down (from part of your body) ...... lernelhem
fall onto back or side ...... mpart anyem (W,T), arrethaker anyem
fall out of something ...... rlwenngelhem (W)
fall to the ground ...... arrwerelhem
fall to the ground (native currants) ...... atnamp rnternem (E)
fall apart ...... tyep-akelhem
fall in, collapse ...... atakelhem
fall (lots of things) ...... pwerrer anyem (E)
fall out
hair or fur ...... altelhem, althelhem
falling star ...... parrty
fall (shooting star) ...... kwerralyarl rnternem (T,E)
familiar
a familiar place, home place, person, good friend ...... rwanng, uranng (E)
become familiar with a place or a person ...... rwanng-irrem, uranng-irrem (E)

familiarise someone with a person or place ..... rwanng-ilem, uranng-ilem (E)
be familiar or recognisable ..... inngelhem

family
close family or relations .. arlalty, arlalty-arey, tyerrty arlalty map, altya, altyarey, altyernem (E)
my family or relation (particularly father) .... atyeng-artwey, atyeng-artey (W,T)
your family or relation .... ngkweng-artwey
his/her/their family .... kwer-artwey
people with a very strong family resemblance to each other ..... arremparreng
feel happy, particularly about one's family ..... altyirrem

fan-flower ..... intekw (E), irrarnt-irrarnt (E) (?)

fancy
fancying someone ..... ahenty[2], iyteny (E), iyteny-iyteny (E)
desire or fancy someone ... alherrem[2] (W,T), alhirrem, iyteny-irrem (E)

fantastic
really good ..... anper[2] (W,T), mekelarey (W,T), anper anthwerr (W,T), mwerr anthwerr (W,T)

far ..... arleng[1], rntwarr
a bit distant (respect language) ..... arlewent (E)
as far as (something) ..... -atwety[2]

fart ..... atna rltwar-rnkem (E), atnernkem (E), atna anengkem (E), kart ltwakem (W,T), kart inkem (W,T)

fast ..... aher, parrp, parrp-parrp, uremeny (E)
go flat out or in a straight path along the ground ..... irrepereperr
really fast ..... alpent-alpent (W)

fasten *(something)* ..... ayernem

fat *(see also 'emu' and 'kangaroo')* ..... anter
fat, big ..... ampwerrk, anter, artelhampw (E), ather-ather[1] (E), ampwerrk angerr, angerrety-pwek (W,T)
fat, in good condition ..... anter, anter angerr, awek (T,E)
fat, particularly around the legs and stomach area ..... antwerlperlp-antwerlperlp (W,T)
having rolls of fat ..... ayet (E), ayet angerr (E)
on lower stomach or upper thighs (person, kangaroo) . rtwarnp
edible fat ..... ker anter
medicinal fat ..... awely anter
for painting up for women's awely *ceremonies* ..... awely anter
for healing, rubbing fat, cooking fat (respect language) ..... leyterr (E)
get fat ..... anter-irrem, awek-irrem (T,E), ayet-irrem (E), ather-ather-irrem (E)
make someone or something shiny or greasy with fat ..... awatem
become shiny or greasy from fat ..... awatelhem
fatty meat ..... anthetyingk (T,E)
really fatty meat (just kangaroo, bullock) ... weyang (E)
see that meat is not fat ... wel-arem (E) (?)

fat-tailed antechinus ..... alepey (E) (?)

father *(see also Appendix 1)* ..... angey, anya[1]
sympathetic or respectful word for father ..... arrawel

father-in-law *(see also Appendix 1)* ..... ahenterr (E), arnemerr (T,E), maly (E), maly-maly (E)
senior father-in-law ..... amarl, amarl-amarl
father-in-law (young) ..... ampwek (W,T)
woman's father-in-law .... ampaty-ampaty
father-in-law (baby talk) .. ahentey-ahentey (E)

favourite ..... impen

fear *(go to 'fright')*

feather ..... arlpa[2], arlpang (W,T), arlpelh[1] (T,E), aympelh (E), aynpelh (T,E)
feather (down) ..... anteth, alta, altang (W,T)
used for decoration, decorative headdress ..... irrkarlp
emu feathers ..... apwa (E), artarr, angkwely-angkwely (W), awenth-awenth (E)
feather shoes, 'kurdaitcha boot' ..... apwa (E)
put on feather shoes (kurdaitcha) ..... ingkirrpem, apwirrpem (E)

feather-top spinifex ..... antywer iper (E)

feature
having a particular part or feature .... -akert[2]
fed up
get fed up with something and leave it .... tyweker-irrem
feed
feed on something .... arlkwem
feed someone .... wantem, arrakwernem[2] (T,E)
feed yourself .... wantelhem
feed someone up .... anhwerlk-ilem (W,T)
feel
have a feeling or sensation .... awelhem
feel hot .... awempem (E)
feel sore .... arekar-irrem
have a feeling in a part of your body that tells you about certain relatives .... irrkem
have a funny or strange feeling (as if somebody is coming) .... irrekerr-irrem (E)
feel *(touch)*
touch or feel someone or something .... anpem
feet .... ingka, ingkang (W,T)
female
adult female animal .... arelh[1], arrwekety[1]
female (person or animal) .... marl
female kangaroo .... aherr marl
fence *(from English)* .... parrek, parrik
fetch .... inem
few
a few .... rrpwety (W,T), urrpety (E)
just a few .... rrpwetyarrp (W,T), urrpetyarrp (E), urrpetyarrp-ingar (E)
a few times .... rrpwety-ingar (W,T), urrpety-areng (E), urrpety-ingar (E)
(a few) split off from a larger group .... rrpwety-irrem (W,T), urrpety-irrem (E)
make something into a few bits or pieces .... rrpwety-ilem (W,T), urrpety-ilem (E)
fidget .... angelhem
fifty dollar note .... arlewatyerr, karntewarr (SP)
fig *(go to 'wild fig')*
fight
a fight .... aha, ahang (W,T)
to fight .... atwerrem, nhwerrem (W,T), unherrem (E), ahel nhwerrem (W,T), ahel unherrem (E), ngkwanty-irrem (W,T)
fight, hit each other (respect language) .... kelthemartem (W,T) ulpakem (E), ulpakerrem (E), arlinem
fight, argue .... akerrem
challenge someone to fight with you .... ankey angkem (W)
fight a lot of people .... lyernt-iwem (T,E)
fight almost to death .... nyek-nyek-ilem (T,E), nyant atwem, nyey-nyey atwem (W)
fight to the death .... irrewaly atwem, kwarterrem, nyant atwem
fight on one's own .... arlperreh atwem (W), arlperrek atwem (T,E), arlpirrek atwem (E)
fight somebody in a rage or without consideration for kinship .... pwethel atwem (W,T), pwetyel atwem (T), pwerrtyel atwem (W)
pick a fight with someone .... anngernt-irrem (T,E), ngkwanty-irrem (W,T), ngkwantyel atwerrem (W,T)
gang up on a person .... ampak-irrem (W,T)
back someone up in a fight .... artangatyel atwem
fight on behalf of someone .... ankwerl-atwem (W,T), ankwerl-inem (W,T), ankwernem, unkil-ilem (E), artengel-arem (T,E)
hit or fight someone for someone else .... atyang-atwem (T)
have a jealous fight .... mayel anngwenhem, mayel atwerrem, imayel atwerrem (E)
get worked up (for a fight) .... arawerrng inem, arnkaty-ilelhem (T,E), arrtyarnpem (E)
ritual dancing, hopping or skipping motion that indicates aggression (men) .... rrwernter (W,T), urrernter[1] (E)
dance, hop or skip along showing intention to fight (men) .... rrwernter alhem (W,T), rrwernter-irrem (W,T), urrernter alhem (E)
ritual hopping or skipping step that is done in preparation for a fight (women) .... arrtya[1], arrtyang (W,T)

go along vibrating or shaking the legs when preparing for a fight (women) .... anwerntenty alhem (W,T), amerl-amerl arrernem (W,T), ameyl-ameyl arrernem (E), anwerntem (W,T)
hop or skip along showing intention to fight (women) .... apeyarr-irrem, apeyarrel alhem, arrtyel rntwem (W), arrtyernem (T,E), arrtyang irnem (W), antyatar-irrem
someone who steps in to stop a fight or to diffuse trouble .... arlperrepwenty
step in to stop a fight .... arrngent-wem
talk someone out of fighting .... arlperr angkem (W), arlperrepwenty angkem

fighting hook or pick .... alany (E), walarnp (W,T), walaymp (E)

fighting stick .... kweter

fill
fill something with a liquid .... thelem
fill up a container with fruits, seeds, grubs etc. (not water) .... arlkwenhem
fill up a container with something (such as food, petrol) .... antelh-ilem (T,E)
fill something up .... ampwerrk-wem (E)
fill something in .... ampwerrk-ilem (E)

finch *(zebra)* .... nyengk, tyeyek (W,T)

find
something that is found in a place .... angwerrm
find something .... angwerrm-ilem, angwerrmelh-ilem
go and find something .... arety-alhem
be 'found' (ie spiritually conceived) in a place .... angwerrm-irrem, anngirrem
'find' a child in a place .... angwerrm-ilem, angwerrmelh-ilem

finger, fingers .... iltya, iltyang (W,T),
finger (respect language) .... ngaleny (E)
fingers (not including thumb) .... iltyang kwerrng (W), iltya akely-rnem (E), iltya akwerrk-rnem (E), iltya kanty-rnem (E)
large fingers (i.e. not little finger) .... iltya angerr, iltyang angerr (W,T)
middle three fingers .... iltya mpep-iperr (E)
gap between fingers .... iltya atwaty-atwaty (T), iltya ipert (W), iltya tyarrp-tyarrp (T), iltyang antarlkw-antarlkw (W)
little finger .... iltya akwek-antyey (W), iltya akwerreny (E), iltya ilpernkeny (E)
finger tip .... iltya kanty, iltyang kanty (W,T)
fingernails .... ingkelthel, tywemar (W,T), iltyang tywemar (W,T)

finger grass .... ngelyerr (E), talkwerrk (W)

finish *(completed)*
something is finished or completed .... kel, kel-antey (E), kelepenh
finished (respect language) .... kank-antey (E)
finish, run out .... ywerrem, uyerrem (E), ilwem
finish (rain) .... ilwem

finish *(kill)*
finish something off, kill someone .... ityilem (W,T), atwem

finish up
'finishing up' or 'sorry business' .... mal-mal
go for 'finishing up' or 'sorry' business .... mal-mal alhem

fire .... rwa (W,T), rwang (W,T), ura (T,E)
fire (baby talk) .... waw
fire (respect language) .... anyengk (W), alpment (E), ntyangkwenng
bright fire or light .... parntar (W,T)
fire made to get rid of flies or mosquitos .... ayarrty (E)
fire placed to stop sickness .... parntewelyewely (W,T) (?)
no fire .... atham
light a fire .... nthelem (W,T), nthilem, alep-ilem (T,E), annngenth-ilem, antant-ilem (W,T), item, lherrm-ilem (T,E), lyenenty-ilem
stoke a fire up .... ntyerlp-ilem
making fire with a firesaw .... urnety (T,E)
make fire using a firesaw .... rrmwarl-wem (W,T), urrmarl-wem (T,E)
fire catch alight .... alep-irrem (T,E), antant-irrem (W,T), lherrm-irrem (T,E), lyenenty-irrem, lyernenty-irrem

burst into flames ... intyelhem (W), intyalhem (T,E)
fire spread out of control .. altherrem
fire burn down ... ntyerlp-irrem
fire go out ... atham-irrem, lwernelhem (W,T), ilwernelhem (E)
an area of country that has been burnt before ... arrempelty (E), urrempelty (E)
become burnt (country) ... arrempelty-irrem (E), urrempelty-irrem (E)

fire pit
old fireplace ... rerrk (T,E), yerrk (W,T)

firebush ... iylenyenp (E)

firegrass ... intwerrker

firestick ... alep (T,E), kep[1] (W,T), rwakep (W,T), rwang kep (W,T), rwang lyenenty (W,T), uralep (E)
ceremonial firestick (respect language) ... ntyangkwenng
light fire with a firestick .. kep-ilem (W)

firewood ... rwa (W,T), rwang (W,T), ura (T,E)
firewood (respect language) ... alpment (E), anyengk (W)
collect firewood ... rwang inem (W,T), aytem (E)
firewood that has been prepared by burning a tree down ... una (E)
burn a tree down so that it can be used for firewood ... unewem (E)

first
first, in front ... arrwekel
first, in front (respect language) ... mparrwekel
go first, in front (respect language) ... mparrwekel-irrem
(doing something first) and then something else happens ... mernt[2] (T,E), imert (W)
do something first (before others do it) ... arnang-ilem[1] (E), ahaylem (E)
lead the way, go first ... arrwekel alhem, arrwekel-irrem, yel-irrem (E)
let someone do something first ... alkwernem
for the first time, just now ... lyetarrpwerreny (E)
do something first (before some other action) .-amparr

fish ... irrpenng, aylperr (E)
type of fish ... arlweng-rlpwerr (W)
fish (from English) ... pety

fissured ... tyarrp-tyarrp

fit
have a fit ... arlan-irrem, atywaty-irrem[2] (T,E), tyerrty-tyerrty internem (W), irrkarnpem

five ... urrpety-atherr (E)
a 'five' in cards ... iltya, iltyang (W,T)

five-minute grass ... taty-taty[1]

fix something ... mpwarem, mwerr-ilem

flame ... anngenth, aleny, anngenenty (T), lherrm (T,E), lyenenty
die down (of flame) ... anmerrem (W,T)

flap
flapping sound ... lthap-lthap, rltap-rltap (W)
make a flapping sound ... lthap-lthap-irrem, rltap-rltap-irrem (W)

flare up *(fire)* ... aleny-aleny-irrem (W,T), aleny-aleny-wem (W), intyelhem (W), intyalhem (T,E)

flash
flash, shine ... amparrkem
flash at something (like a camera flash) ... amparrkerl-wem (E)
really flash, dressed up ... angart-angart (W)

flash *(lightning)* ... alharrkem, arrkem (E), ngkwarrkem (W,T), ingkwarrkem (T,E)

flat ... aymperr (E), ilperr (E), ilperr-ilperr (E)
make something flat ... ilperrelh-ilem (E)
go flat ... alpwely-irrem

flat-leaved hakea ... ntyarleyarleng
red nectar of ... ngapalhwerrk (W)

flavour *(see also 'taste')*
the taste of something ... kwang (W), ikwa (T,E), ikwang (T)
tasteless, flavourless ... alyelk, anetywek (W)

flesh ... tyelk, anwenth, ker, ker tyelk

flick tongue out ... alenyenp-wem (T,E)

flimsy ... althalth, arrmaly-arrmaly (T,E), artaly-artaly (T,E), atyet[1]
become light or flimsy ... althalth-irrem
flimsy (of fabric) ... alparr-alparr (E)
soft or insubstantial (such as white bread) ... ararr

flirt
flirtatious or suggestive behaviour ... mpweny, iyteny (E), iyteny-iyteny (E)
a flirt ... iytenyelengkw (E), mpweny angerr (E), mpwenyartw-mpwenyartw (T,E)

behaving in a flirtatious way .... arlkwer, arlkwer-arlkwer, ltherrp-ltherrp (W,T), urlker (E), urlker-urlker (E)
flirt with someone .... mpweny-mpweny-irrem, iyteny-irrem (E), iytenyel arem (E)
someone who makes eyes at someone or acts flirtatiously .... annga arrkwer-arrkwer
show off or act sexily .... ngkwern-kweny-irrem

flock bronzewing .... arekwarr (E)

flood
flood, floodwater .... alay[1], awarr, rew, urew (E), anyerr (E)
front part of floodwater, head of the flood .... kwaty aleny
flood refuse, debris .... anthelk[1], inthwerey (E)
leave a mass of flood refuse or debris .... ntal-wem
barrier or trench to stop floodwater .... rtwanng, rtwanng-rtwanng

floppy .... arrmaly-arrmaly (T,E)

flour .... arterrty (T,E), nmwenth (W,T), unmenth (E), warnp (W,T)
flour (from English) .... perlaw
plain flour (from English) .... aperretyen (W,T)
self-raising flour (from English) .... thelperretyen (W,T)
flour, damper (from English) .... tamp
flour (respect language) .... arlter-ayerr (E), mperlker-ayerr (E)

flow
flow (water) .... alhem, alpem
flow quickly (water) .... werrk-werrk alhem (W,T), werrk-werrk alpem (W,T)
flow, seep out (especially blood) .... irrert-irrem
flow freely (blood) .... althekalth-irrem

flower .... anteth, alpety (W,T), alpeyt (T,E), alpety-alpety (W,T), alpeyt-alpeyt (T,E)
of bean tree .... akalapantherrty (T), akenty (W,T), akeynt (E)
of bloodwood .... ntewal
of bush banana, silky pear .... ilkwanty (E)
of bush potato .... nalal (E)
of cassias .... ulpelp (E)
of dogwood .... athwenter
of acacia, elegant acacia, bramble wattle .... amper[1] (E)
of ghost gum .... arrtya[2]
of kurrajong .... arlpetharlp (E)
of mulga and witchetty bush .... nwathet (W), nathat (T), utnathat (T,E)
of native currant, native citrus .... ilkwa[1] (T,E), ilkwang (W)
of native tobacco .... alpma (T,E)
of wild onion, onion grass, nalgoo .... akenty (W,T), akeynt (E)
to flower or blossom .... alpety-alpety-irrem (W,T), alpeyt-alpeyt-irrem (T,E)
to flower or blossom (native currant, native citrus) .... ilkwenkem (E)

flu *(a cold)* .... artwengkenng, inkwerr (E), mernt (W,T)
having a cold or flu .... mernt-apert (W,T), artwengkenng-akert, inkwerr-akert (E)

flush
flush game out into open .... rrwerlkem (W,T)

flutter
flutter wings or other parts of the body .... alharrkem, angap-angap-irrem (E), arraly-arraly-irrem (T,E)

fly
to fly .... alker-irrem[2], alkerek-irrem, alkerel alhem
flying creatures such as bats, grasshoppers, beetles etc. .... thep (W,T), uthip (E)
fly down .... arrarlernem (W,T)
fly out (sparks) .... unarnpem (E), anarnpem
fly away (moths and butterflies) .... rnkem

fly *(insect)* .... ameng
types of fly .... ltwamp-ltwamp (W,T) (?), yek-yek (E) (?)

flying-saucer bush .... anker-anker[2] (E), ntwarneng (E)
grub .... pwentarnengayt (E)

foal *(from English)* .... pweney-pweney

foam, foaming .... rlkwerrp, rlkwerrp-rlkwerrp

fog
mist following rain .... mwekelengk (W,T), rlweyang (W), arakakw (E)

fold
folded up .... anhwert
fold something up .... artaper-wem, artaper-ilem

foliage .... atherrk, waly

follow
follow or go behind ... apentem (T,E), ingkern alhem, ingkerneny alhem, anharrel alhem (T), artengert arem (W), ingkelarr alwernem (W,T), intertek-irrem, artenh-irrem, artenheng-irrem
copy what someone is doing ... antelhem
follow a particular belief or system of law ... apentem (T,E)
follow someone (usually when they don't want you to) ... antelhem

fontanelle ... ahey-ahey (W), atek-kenh (E), iylpwerr-iylpwerr (E), kapert ahey-ahey (W), kapert thelty (W,T), thelty-thelty (T), kwerrk-kwerrk[1] (T)

food
food from plants ... mern
food (baby talk) ... meny (T,E), nan[2] (E), nyam-nyam, nyany[1]
food (respect language) ... weyapel
plenty of food ... anthwely-anthwely (T)
without food, not having any food ... annger (W)
food leftover after meal ... ampeny[1]
special word for food used during 'young man' ceremonies ... arlpwerr (E)
gift for someone who performs a ceremony ... kwerapak (W), tyenkerr, tyewarrely (W,T)
collect plenty of food ... anthwely-anthwely-ilem (T)

foot ... ingka, ingkang (W,T)
foot (respect language) ... perrtyeny (E)
top of the foot, instep ... ingka artep, ingkang artep (W,T)
bottom of the foot, sole ... ingka anert, ingkang anert (W,T), ingka ipert (E)
left foot ... ingka alyeng
right foot ... ingka arraty
cracked foot ... ingka atnik-atnik (E)
soft fleshy part of foot ... lher-lher[2]
barefoot ... ingka aketh, ingkang aketh (W,T), ingkang kwart (W)
pigeon-toed ... arntayl (E), ingka arntayl (E)

football
traditional football game ... pwelty
football (from English) ... pweteperl

foot end *(of bed)* ... mpwarl, mpwarl-thayt

foothill ... apwert lterr (E), tyewerr (E)

foothold ... rtety[2] (W), rtetyep (E)

footprint ... mpaty[1], ingka mpaty, ingkang mpaty (W,T)
follow footprints or tracks ... ingkantem (W,T)
messed up or obscured with footprints ... altha (E)

footsteps
sound of footsteps ... ahenty-ahenty[2] (W,T), anenty-anenty, rrmwangk-rrmwangk (W,T)

for *(see also Appendix 2)*
for me ... atyeng
for you ... ngkweng
for him/her/it ... kwer[2]
for them, to them, on or onto them (the two of them) ... kwer-atherr
for them, to them, onto them (more than two) ... kwer-arey

force
force someone to do something ... twernem, uternem (E)
force something on someone ... mwerntel anthem (T,E)
forceful ... rlterrk

forearm ... akwa, akwang (W,T), amwelt

forehead ... rlwa (W,T), rlwang (W,T), urla (E)
forehead (respect language) ... ngalepwerr (E)
person with a wide or broad forehead ... rlwather-ather (W,T), urlather-ather (T,E)
top of forehead, hair just above forehead ... urlimpimp (E)

foreigner ... arrpenh, ingwer (E)

foreleg *(of animals)* ... akwa, akwang (W,T), amwelt, iltya, iltyang (W,T)

foretell ... rlkwem (T,E)
be an omen of death ... arrelty arem (E), arreltyarn arem (T)

forever ... akwet, akwetant, aleth

forget
forget something ... anngwerrem (W,T), anngwirrem (E), aparlp-ilem, iylpel-irrem (E), angwang-irrem (T)
forget something and leave it behind ... iylpel-wem (E)
make yourself forget about something ... angwang-ilelhem (W,T), anngwanng-ilelhem

forgetful ... rrwem-rrwem (W,T), urrem-urrem (T,E)

become silly in the head or forgetful .... rrwem-rrwem-irrem (W,T), urrem-urrem-irrem (T,E)

fork
of a tree .... antarlkw
fork out (tree) .... antarlkw-irrem

four *(from English)* .... pew-pal

fowl
chook, hen .... kweny-rtwek arlkenh-arlkenh (T), tywek-tywek
malleefowl .... anwematy (W)

fox .... pewetyam (W,T)

fragile .... atyet[1]

fragments *(of something)* .. alhwengkelty, ngkwelty, ngkwelty-ngkwelty

freckled monitor .... altywekerr, alpangwerr (W)

freeze
quieten down, freeze (of animal) .... amarn-irrem
cause an animal to become mesmerised or 'freeze' .... amarn-ilem

frequently .... akweteth

fresh .... lyeteny
fresh water .... kwaty lyeteny, narwep (W,T), aparew (E)
fresh hunting country ..... mpankeny (W,T), mpwankeny

friend .... atyew, pelty
friend (from English) ...... mert (W,T), meyt (T,E)
a familiar person, good friend .... rwanng, uranng (E)
become friends .... pelty-irrem
make friends with someone .... pelty-ilem
make friends, make someone get used to a place .... rwanng-ilem, uranng-ilem (E)
friendless .... arrakelakel (E)
friendless, by yourself ..... inga, ingareny, ilkwatherrek-uthek (E)

fright .... ater, anwerlk[1], arralty (T,E)
fearful .... ateralth, atna ateralth (E), mwenyent (T,E)
fearless, not frightened .... akaty-akaty, anew-anew, arnkaty (T,E), irrpelth, urrpelth (E), ater-kweny (W), ater-kwenh (T)
for fear of, beware of .... -kety, +ekerr (E)
feel frightened, be afraid .. ater-irrem, arralty anem (T,E)
get a fright or shock .... anwerlkem
twitch, flinch, start (in fright) .... ilkwem (E), ilkwel alhem (E)
give someone a fright ...... aterel-anthem, anwerlkel anthem[2], anwerlkelh-ilem, arralty arrernem (T,E), arrenkelh-ilem[2] (T), irrenkelh-ilem (E), ilkwel anthem (E), irrekerr-ilem (E), anelhem (T,E)
fear, fearful (respect language) .... irringk (E)
become frightened (respect language) .... irringk-irrem (E)

frizzy hair .... werrp (E)

frog
frog (from English) .... perrak, perrak-perrak
desert spadefoot toad ...... atweynterl (E), kwep, kwep-kwep[2], pwerreparnt (W,T)
Main's frog .... alheramp (W, T) (?)
Spencer's burrowing frog .. alyeyamp (E) (?), kalyeyamp (T) (?)
tree frogs .... antyetyerr, karlarrangkern (E), larrangkern
trilling frog .... terrenth
water-holding frog .... angwethek (T), akngwethek (E), alemerr (E)
types of .... amwekel-amwekel[2] (E), lwerrm (W), mpwekenh (T,E), mpwepenh (E), mpwelengk (E),

frogmouth *(tawny)* .... nwernengk, unernengk (E), nwerningk (E), uring (E)

from *(also see Appendix 2)*
belonging to or associated with a place, from a place .... -areny
from him/her .... kwereng
from that .... kwer-penh, kwer-ipenh (E)

front
in front, first .... arrwekel, arrwekel-ampeny, arrwekel-arrwekel
first or front part of something .... rlwa (W,T), rlwang (W,T), urla (E)
(doing something) right in front of someone .... anngetherr

front leg
foreleg, arm .... akwa, akwang (W,T), iltya, iltyang (W,T)

frost .... lwelty (W,T), ulelty (E)

froth .... rlkwerrp, urlkerrp (E)
frothy .... rlkwerrp-rlkwerrp, urlkerrp-urlkerrp (E)
froth on floodwater .... akwemp-akwemp (W,T)
froth on lips .... pelh-pelh (T,E)

get frothy, froth up .... rlkwerrp-irrem, urlkerrp-irrem (E)
froth (at the mouth) .... karerrem (W)

frown
to frown .... altyekelhem

fruit .... annga, anngang (W,T)
fruit hanging in a bunch (said particularly of bush bananas and wild oranges) .... atwaylpaylp (E)

full
full (unopened) .... ampwerrk, mpank (W,T), mpwank
a lot of something (from English) .... pwel², pwelap
be full (stomach) .... anert anhwerlk (W,T), anhwerlk (W,T), anerteng (E), nthat, alywer² (?)
become full .... pwelap-irrem, nthat-irrem
fill something up .... pwel-ilem, pwelap-ilem
get full of food, lose appetite .... imeng-irrem

full moon .... atarlanenty, atarlepwenty (E)

fun
for fun, in jest, for play ... arrken-kenh, tyelewerr (W,T)
in fun .... arrken, arrken-arrken
have fun (respect language) .... alyenteng-irrem (E)
have fun, play, enjoy oneself .... arrken-irrem, arrken nhwelhem (W,T), arrken nhwerrem (W,T), arrken unherrem (E)
make fun of someone .... arrampewem¹, arrken-ilem
a funny, playful or amusing person .... arrken angerr (E), arrken-kenh
say something funny .... arrken angkem

function
be in working condition ... warrk-irrem

functional .... mwerr

funeral *(see also 'sorry business')*
(from English) .... pep
go to a funeral, go to church .... pep-warn alhem

fungus
type of fungus or puffball .... arepenngenkey (E) (?)

fur
hair or fur of an animal .. alta, altang (W,T)
burnt hair or fur .... ntharr (T), utharr (E)

furrow
between the eyes .... rlwentyerr (W,T)
furrowed .... altyek-altyek

further
a bit further away .... arleng-awaty (T,E), rntwarr-rntwarr
further away, a bit further away from each other .... arlengek-arleng (T,E)
round the long way .... rntwarr-angkwerr

furtively .... anyenng, anyenngel, arwengkel

fuss
make a fuss of someone .. anyanelhem, arrkwer-arrkwer-ilem

future *(see Appendix 2)*

Gg

galah .... ilenty, kerlelkerlelp, uneng atyetyek (E)

game *(animal)* .... anwenth, ker
lot of game .... akwerremp
get lots of game (meat) .... akwerremp-ilem, akwetyerretyerr-ilem, akwetyerretyerr atwem, arlperreh atwem (W), arlperrek atwem (T,E)

game *(go to 'fun', 'football')*

gang
gang up on someone .... artangatyel atwem, ampak-irrem (W,T)

ganga *(from English)* .... kanty²

gap
gap or crack in something .... atwaty
place where there are lots of gaps or cracks .... atwaty-atwaty
gap in hills .... irntang atwaty (W,T), apwert atwaty (T,E), irntang arnkarr-arnkarr (W)
gap between toes .... ingka atwaty (E)
gap left in front teeth after a tooth has been knocked out (ceremonial) .. alyeneng (T,E), alyeleng (E), arrimper (T,E), arrenper (W), tyekerr (E)
make a gap in something .. atwaty-ilem

garbage *(from English)* .... rapety

Garden Bore .... Arrangkey

gargle .... ngkwerrmengkwerr ilelhem (E)
gargling .... kweng-kweng, ngkwengk (E), ngkwengkel (E)

gather
collect things .... kwetyem
come together in a group .. akarr-irrem (T,E), arraw-irrem

gather things together (from English) .... rwelemap-ilem
sweep or gather things together .... akarr-ilem (T,E), akarrelh-ilem (T,E), arraw-ilem, arrawelh-ilem, arlwelem (W,T), arlwilem (E)
a gathering .... werlamperrenty (W,T), urlamperreny (T), urlamperrenty (E)

gecko
sand-plain or northern spiny-tailed .... akarntety-arntety (E), pelhel-iwenh-iwenh (E), rltimp-areny (E) (?)
type of gecko .... arlwer

generation
the next generation, the younger generation .... ingkerneny

generous .... arwekar (W,T), atham-atham, imeng
be generous, share .... imeng-irrem, atham-irrem

genitals
penis (sensitive language) .... pwer
vagina (sensitive language) .... artwert[2], kep[2] (W), tyarrp, tyely (W,T)

gentle .... angwang

get
get something .... inem, angetyem
get something (respect language) .... irrepethem
get something for someone else .... atyang-inem (T)
go and get something for someone (respect language) .... awakerl-wem (E), ankwerl-wem (E), akelawerl-wem (E), aleper-ankwerl-wem (E), ankwerl-alhem (E)
get something down from something .... rwelh-arrernem
get yourself in the way of someone or something ..... arrngen-welhem (W,T), arrapayernem
get onto something .... antyem, nganem (E), atwayntem (E)
get into, go inside something .... irrpem, aylpem (E)
get down from something .... anarnpem

get together .... anyent-irrem, anengk-irrem (W,T), atningk-irrem (E)

get up .... akem-irrem
make someone or something get up .... akemelh-ilem

ghost .... lthan (W,T), ulthan (E)

ghost gum .... pwernengk (W,T), ulemp (T,E)
country where there are lots of ghost gums ..... ulemp-ulemp (T,E)
flower of .... arrtya[2]
seeds of .... ulemparrty (E)
gum or kino of .... arrkeper (W,T), arrkiper (E), lyarwek
honey from bark of .... ulemparrty (E), yerrkengal (T)
water found in trunk of ... untharr (E)

gidgee
black gidgee .... arnteparl
Georgina gidgee .... rrwenyenk (W,T), urrenyenk (E)
green seedpods of Georgina gidgee .... ilyartey
grub found in roots of Georgina gidgee .... urrenyenkayt (E), kerlpaty (W), kerlpayt (E)
grub on branches of Georgina gidgee .... ulalthengayt (E)
resin from Georgina gidgee .... kikarr (E)

Gidgee Bore .... Arrweltyapet

gidgee fuchsia bush .... ilpengk (T,E)

gidgee wild orange .... angerterrk (E), iwerrarrkw

gift
food used as a gift for someone who performs a ceremony .... kwerapak (W), tyenkerr, tyewarrely (W), tyawerrely (T), inngwerr (T,E)

giggle .... atherrem
giggle behind hand .... mweny rrkwem, mweny-mweny rrkwem

girl .... kwerr (W,T), kwey (T,E), kwer marl (W,T), marl akwek
lovely girl .... kwerr-malangk, kwey-malangk (T,E)
baby girl .... atnem-akert (E), atnem-kenh (E), irrkwely akely (E)
teenage girl .... awenk, arelh awenk, kwey akarnterrng (T,E), kwey awenk (T,E), marl awenk
young girls with breasts just starting to develop .... akarnterrng (T,E)
grow into a teenage girl ... awenk-irrem

girlfriend .... ahenty-penh (W,T), anew, anew-anew (E), mert (W,T), meyt (T,E), mert-mert (W,T), meyt-meyt (T,E) *become boyfriends/ girlfriends* ..... mert-mert mpwarem (W,T), meyt-meyt mpwarem (T,E), mert-mert-ilerrem (W,T), meyt-meyt-ilerrem (T,E), mert-mert-irrem (W,T), meyt-meyt-irrem (T,E)

give

'Give it here!' ..... ngka
give something to someone ..... anthem
give something to someone (respect language) ..... rrwem-ilem (W,T), urrem-ilem (E)
give things to each other ..... antherrem
give things to each other reciprocally ..... rlwerrkerek-rlwerrker antherrem (W,T), urlerrkerek-urlerrker antherrem (E)
give something back (respect language) ..... ngkep-ilem (T,E)
give something to some and not to others ..... arrelharrp anthem (W), arreylarrp anthem (E)
give something to someone by mistake ..... apantel anthem (W,T)
give something to someone when they are about to go somewhere ..... kwart-wem
give something to someone without taking notice of others ..... atanty anthem, alanty anthem
pretend to give something to somebody ..... tywerengk anthem (W,T), ulang anthem (E)
really want to give someone something ..... mwerntel anthem (T,E)

give away belongings to appropriate relations (in mourning) ..... menty-irrem
give someone or something a name ..... arreny anthem (W,T), arreyn anthem (E), arreny arrernem (W,T), arreyn arrernem (E)
give yourself up for payback (for traditional punishment) ..... anthelhem
give something up, stop doing it ..... impelhem, impem, menty-irrem

glands

inside mouth or under jaw ..... ankwa[2]

glass, glasses

(from English) ..... kelath

glasswort

brown-head glasswort ..... akwely-akwely (E)

glint ..... amparrkem

glisten ..... akerlkem, mperlkem

go

go, go along ..... alhem, apem[1] (W,T)
go (respect language) ..... ahanem
go around looking for something ..... nthwem (W,T), unthem (E)
go, shoot off somewhere ..... atyerrem[2]
set out, head off ..... arnpem, arnpenhem, arnperl-alhem

get into something and go ..... antyerl-alhem
go along on the top of water ..... imperrem[2] (E)
go inside something ..... irrpem
go over to someone ..... atwarem
going towards someone who is approaching ..... arnekarnar
go towards someone who is approaching ..... arnek-arnarem, arnek-irrem

make someone go somewhere ..... nthwelh-ilem (W,T), unthelh-ilem (E)
go forwards ..... arraty-irrem
go first, go in front ..... arrwekel alhem, arrwekel-irrem, yel-irrem (E)
go first, go in front (respect language) ..... mparrwekel-irrem
go along behind others and not get anything (when hunting) ..... ampenyel alhem
go behind something ..... ilpelhem
go downwards ..... thar-irrem (E)
go up something ..... antyem, atwayntem (E) nganem (E)
go in a crooked line ..... arnkwert alhem, amperelhem (E)

go underneath something ..... irrpem, aylpem (E)
go in a straight line or path ..... arraty-irrem, akert-arraty-irrem, akertarreng-irrem (E)

going flat out or in a straight path along the ground ..... irrepereperr
go fast ..... arrengker-irrem (W,T)

go slowly and carefully, look out .... manty alhem (W), mwanty alhem (T,E)
go without caring about others .... atanty alhem, alanty alhem
go the wrong way .... apant-irrem, aperrpert-irrem
going right in front of somebody (too close) .... alhangkwarr
going in a direction away from or opposite to someone or something .... ntywem² (W,T), untyem² (E), ntywem-athek (W,T), untyem-athek (E)
go in different directions .... irrarnp-irrem (W,T), irrarnp-irrarnp-irrem (W,T), akalk-irrem
go to something, attend something .... irrpem, aylpem (E)

go *(let go)*
let something go .... anelhem (T,E) anewem² (T)

go *(do)*
go like that (while showing someone) .... alanh-irrem

go across .... talkw alhem, talkw-irrem, arrelharrp alhem (W), arreylarrp alhem (E), arreyl-arreyl alhem (E), artwerel alhem (E)

go away .... alpem
go away, go away for good .... aleth-irrem, alethek-irrem (T,E), aleth alhem
go far away .... arleng-irrem (T,E)
go away in a hurry (from English) .... pwerlt-irrem

go back .... alpem, artwep-irrem, urtep-irrem (E)
go back (respect language) .... ahanenhem, ahaneynem (E)
go back to the place where you came from .... irlpang-alpem (W)
turn round and go back .... artwep-irrenty-alpem (W,T), urtep-irrenty-alpem (E)
go back and look for something, go and meet someone .... arnekarnar alhem

go down *(sun or moon)* .... irrpem, aylpem (E)

go home .... alpem

go off *(gun)* .... rltar-wem

go out *(exit)* .... arratem

go out *(fire, light)* .... lwernelhem (W,T), ilwernelhem (E), atham-irrem

go past, go across .... anper alhem

go round *(something)* .... artwep-akem, urtep-akem (E), artwep-artwep-irrem, irrep-akem, urtep-urtep-irrem (E), irrep-akelhem
go round the long way .... irrep-akelhem, talkw alhem

goal *(from English)* .... kewel

goanna
sand goanna .... arlewatyerr
large sand goanna .... arwemay (SP), aremay (E) (SP)
young sand goanna .... kwentarreng, arepilyerr (E)
black goanna .... kweny-areny (W,T), kwenyel alhem (T)
other types of goanna .... kalawerr (W,T), arwerr-areny (E) (?)
goanna (respect language) .... arlkarrkwatyerr (E)
tail meat .... arrertarnk (T,E)
said to a goanna when it is being beaten against the ground .... akwetyerretyerr (T,E)

goat *(from English)* .... nanekwet

gobble
gobble food up .... akwern-akwern-wem (E)

God .... Altyerr¹, Angey

good .... mwerr, mwerr angerr (W,T), mwerr-angker (E), ingkety, anyemwerr
good (respect language) .... alhengerr (E), mwenkerr (E)
really good .... anper anthwerr (W,T), anper² (W,T), mwerr anthwerr (W,T), mwerrant-alkenty (W,T)
'Good', 'Okay' .... kel mwerr
be good at doing something .... inngeny, inngeny-inngeny
become good .... mwerr-irrem
not too good, not very good .... anety-anety (W,T), kwern-kwern (W,T), akeng-akeng (T,E)

good-looking .... -malangk, ntwat (W,T)

good *(for good)*
for good, for a long time .... akwetant, aleth, twem (W,T), intem² (E)
(doing something) for good, for a long time .... akwet-antey, aleth-antey, intem-antey (E)

goodness!
'Goodness!' (exclamation of surprise) .... yakerray (W,T)

Goofy Bore .... Anyemamern

goose pimples
lumps .... rtety-rtety
get goose pimples or goose bumps .... lyekarr anem, lyekarr-irrem

gorge *(gap)* … apwert atwaty (T,E), atwaty, irntang atwaty (W,T), irntang arnkarr-arnkarr (W)
gorgeous … alyerremwey, -malangk
govern … atyetyart-irrem
grab
grab something … arntwerrkem
grab something off someone … rakem
grab things off each other … rakerrem
grade *(a road)* … aketh-ilem, anhwerrem, iylperrem (E)
grandchild
man's daughter's child … atyemey, rtartart, artartey (E)
man's son's child … arreng
woman's daughter's child … menh-menh (W,T), ipmenh (E), nyany[2]
woman's son's child … aperl
great-grandchild (woman's daughter's daughter's children) … amarl, amey
granddaughter *(see 'grandchild')*
grandfather
father's father … arreng
father's father (baby talk) … angang (E), angey (T,E), ahangey (T,E)
mother's father … atyemey, rtartart, artartey (E)
mother's father (baby talk) … rtartart
great-grandfather (father's father's father) … pap aywa (W), pap aywang (W), aler
grandmother
father's mother … aperl
father's mother (baby talk) … mam, mam-mam (W), papap[1] (E)
granny, mother's mother … menh-menh (W,T), ipmenh (E), nyany[2]
granny, mother's mother (baby talk) … nan-nan (E), nyanyany (E), nyany[2], nan[1]
granny (from English) … kerraney
mother's mother (closely related granny) … kampely[2] (E)
senior granny, senior mother's mother … nan angkwey (W,T)
great-grandmother (mother's mother's mother) … ahenterr (E), amarl
grandson *(see 'grandchild')*
grass … arnam, atherrk, antywer[2] (E), mern atherrk
dry grass … arnam antyerrk
fresh green grass … arnam apely, arnam atherrk
bunch paspalidium … arekwer (E) (?)
bunched kerosene grass, mulga grass … arraper
button grass, finger grass, toothbrush grass … apwert-arlkwenh (E), apwert akwernenh (E)
cotton panic grass … kwatyempengemp (W,T), kwatyimpengimp
desert Flinders grass, bunch panic … arlepenh (T,E), arrepeny (T)
eight-day grass … arnwety-arnwety (W)
five-minute grass, rye beetle grass … taty-taty[1]
love grasses … awertaw (E)
ribbon grass, spear grass … lyayepelyay (W,T), layempeylay (T,E)
summer grass, armgrass millet … mamperrk (W,T)
swamp kangaroo grass, native oat grass … lyenty
woollybutt grass … antyey[1] (W,T), alyatywereng (E)
type that grows in swamps … itwert-itwert (E)
grasshopper
types of … arlwety[1] (E), arwekert-arwekert (E), intelty, ntyerlkem (W)
small creatures that fly … thep (W,T), uthip (E)
grateful
be grateful to someone … nakem, narlkwem (E)
grave
a person's … awenng
for an animal … ipert
mound of earth on top … werlkng (E)
branches put over a grave … utnin (E)
gravel … lyerl
grease … anter
greasy
make someone or something shiny or greasy with fat … awatem
become shiny or greasy from fat … awatelhem
great, really good … anper[2] (W,T)
great-aunt *(see 'aunt')*
great-uncle *(see 'uncle')*
greedy … alyemp-alyemp[2] (W), ankerl, rnter (E), ankeyalth
not sharing … impen-impen (T,E)

be mean or greedy .... impen-impen-irrem (E)
be greedy .... ankerl-irrem (W,T), iyterrk-irrem (E), rnter-irrem (E)
eat or drink greedily .... ahanthem (E), nwanthem (W,T), unanthem (E), ankeyel arlkwem
someone who is not greedy or pushy .... atnemwernt (E)

green
a colour that includes green and some shades of yellow and blue .... atherrk, atherrk-atherrk (T,E)
turn a greenish colour .... atherrk-atherrk-irrem, atherrkelhem (E)
green grass .... atherrk
green or lush country .... atherrkeny
go green (country) .... atherrkeny-irrem
make country green and lush .... atherrkeny-ilem, anyemwerr-ilem (T,E)
green (of foliage) .... apely
green (unripe) .... anka, ankang (W,T), arlety[2]

green crumbweed .... alpar, parntentyarlp (W), mwelyeparnt-parnt (T) (?), mwenyeparnt-parnt (W) (?)

grey
grey hair, grey-headed .... aywa, aywang (W,T), ilkwa[3] (E), aherlkey (W,T), ilkwamp ilkwang (E), kapert aywa, kapert aywang (W,T), antyeny (T,E)
go grey, go white-headed .... ampem[2], ilkwa ampem (E)

grey butcherbird .... alpwertek-alpwert (E), arrpwerek-arrpwer (W)

grey falcon .... irrkerlanty (?)

grey teal .... pelyak (W,T), pelyakw (T,E), tyepelyakw (W), tyepelyey (E)

grey-crowned babbler .... tyewakety

grind
grind something .... athem[2]
grind something up to make it soft .... lpwelem (W,T), ulpilem (T,E)
grind (teeth) .... irrpenper-welhem (W), interrpar-wem (E)

grinding stone
lower grinding stone (used for seed) .... ather, irntang ather (W,T), apwert ather, arlkwat (W,T), irntang arlkwat (W,T)
small grinding or pounding stones .... pwerl, tyeng (T,E), alyer (E), irntang apwert (W), apwert alyer (E), irntang artwert (W,T), apwert artwert (E)

groan *(in pain)* .... ampangkem (T,E), anpelhem (E), apangkem (W,T), arlkwatelhem (W,T), kwatem, urnelth-irrem (E), yapaty-irrem (W,T), yekay-irrem

grog *(alcohol)* .... ngkwarl

groin area .... kwart-kwart

groin or paunch of a person .... aympa (E) (?)

groove
in boomerang, dish or shield .... irraker, arlkeny
grooved .... arlkeny-arlkeny
make grooves or markings on wooden implements such as dishes, shields or boomerangs .... irraker-ilem, irraker-wem

ground, earth .... ahelh, ahern
cracked from water .... awal (W,T), arnkwerrng (E)
ground get wet .... tert-irrem
make ground wet .... tert-ilem, urtilem (E)

groundsheet .... antyam, antyepanty (W,T), panty (T,E)
spread out a bed, blanket or groundsheet .... antyam-wem

group
large group of particular people or things .... arwenth, angerr
of particular people or things (from English) .... map
in small groups .... rrpwetyelam rrpwetyelam (T), rrpwetyek-rrpwety (W), urrpetyek-urrpety (E)
get things together into a group .... pwert-ilem (W,T), purt-ilem (E)

grow
grow on something .... arntwem (W,T), lyapem (T,E)
grow, live (of plants) .... irnem
grow close together (of plants) .... mwern-irrem
grow, cultivate (plants) .... arntwelh-ilem (W,T), lyapelh-ilem (T,E)
grow back (vegetation) .... arntwety-alpem (W,T), mpankeny-irrem (W,T), mpwankeny-irrem
grow back together, become closed over .... interrenty-irrem
grow bigger, grow up .... amangkem, angerr-irrem[1]
grown up .... angerrety
grow up in a place, be brought up in a place .... amangkem
grow up on something (e.g. food) .... amangkem

grow up or raise a child, adopt a child .... kwetyem, amangkelh-ilem

growl
be angry .... ahel-irrem, ngkwanty-irrem (W,T)
at somebody or something .... iltem, arrpwernem, alhengkem (T,E) (?)
at each other .... ilterrem
declare that you are going to hit or growl at somebody .... twernelhem
growl (dog) .... arntwerrem, arlkwerrpel-nhwem (W,T), unhem (E), arlkwerrpernem (W,T)

grub
edible grub .... tyap
grub that is barely edible .... tyap-tyap
grub (from English) .... kartepel
ending on names of certain plants for the name of the grub found on that plant .... +aty², +ayt (E)
root with lots of grubs in it .... arntwa (W,T), arntwang (W,T)
'pipe' through which witchetty grub (and other grubs) emerge from ground .... akartw (E), akarternenty (W,T)
metamorphosed form of a grub .... akartw (E), akarternenty (W,T)
grub while still in root (when it goes black and gets wings) .... kwerrert-kwerrert (W)
insides of some edible grubs .... anwerlk (E)
witchetty grub .... anyematy, tyap
juice of witchetty grub and other grubs .... arrelty²

grub types *(go to entries for individual plants)*

grubby .... aternng
bit dirty, grubby or messy .... aternng-aternng

guitar *(from English)* .... ketay, ketar

gully .... atwaty, ilerrty, mpwetyerr (W,T)
small creek or gully .... intyer

gum *(resin)*
sweet gum from plants .... rnpwa (W,T), rnpwang (W,T)
soft honey or sweet gum .... akaly (W,T)
from beefwood .... iyltentyarwek (E)
from bloodwood .... nthwarr (W), ntharr (T)
from bloodwood or from ghost gum .... arrkeper (W,T), arrkiper (E), lyarwek
from ironwood .... athengarlperl (E), athimpangkwarl (E), atyarnpangkwarl (W,T)
from supplejack .... anyerampw, anyerangkwarl
from witchetty bush .... ampwerrty (E), anyemampwerrty (E), anyemangkwarl (W), anyemaywerrk (W)
from whitewood .... arlperrampw (E), arlperrangkwarl

gums *(in mouth)* .... arntek merrng (E), arrakert tyelk, arratyelk (E), merrng (E), rtety tyelk (E), tyelk, arra merrng (E)

gun .... apwert iylpwer (E), ker atyerrenherrenh (W,T), rltwaty (W,T)
gun (from English) .... maket
gun (respect language) .... rntwer¹, urltaty, urltaty-ayerr (E)

Gurindji
language, person or people .... Kwerrentyey

gut *(an animal)*
gut an animal .... anenem (W,T), aninem, atniwem (E)
gut an emu .... ntyererlk-akem (E)
clean out guts .... aneltyem (W), kart arnngem (W,T)

gutless *(cowardly)* .... alkwemp, mwenyent (T,E)

guts .... ana, anang (W,T), anert, kart¹ (W,T), mwerlk¹
stomach .... mpurl (E)
part of guts .... arengk aleny, artwey-artwey² (W,T), lyep-lyep, rlwert-rlwert (W,T), twerl-twerl (W,T)
part of guts (of kangaroos and cattle) .... anwalty (T,E), tyely-tyely, iltyarrng (W,T), nywertep (E)
part of kangaroo guts .... anarrk (E), arrka (E)
part of bullock's guts .... tawel-tawel (E)
emu's intestines or guts .... anwerl-anwerl (E), arlta² (E) (?)
part of bush turkey's guts .... atnarlt (E)

guts-ache
diarrhoea .... ampeltyey (W,T), atnelth (E)
have diarrhoea or guts-ache .... ampeltyem, ampeltyey-irrem (W,T), aneltyey-irrem (E)

gutter
gutter, channel .... mpwetyerr (W,T), ilerrty

Hh

hail, hailstone .... apwertek, kwaty irntakert (T)

hair
on body or head .... alta, altang (W,T)
hair on head .... akalt (E), kapert[1]
hair (respect language) .... impalt-ayerr (E)
armpit hair .... lhenp alta
pubic hair (sensitive language) .... antalt (W), altalt (W,T), intywa (E)
yellowish or blond hair .... kapert tywelker (W), atherrk (SP)
white hair, grey hair .... ilkwa[3] (E), ilkwamp ilkwang (E), aherlkey (W,T)
go grey, go white-headed .... ampem[2], aywa ampem, aywang ampem (W,T), aywang-irrem (W,T), ilkwa ampem (E)
long hair .... akwerl, kapert akwerl (W,T)
lots of hair (of a dog) .... altelhey (W,T), iltelhey (T,E)
grow long (hair) .... angkwelk-irrem (E), angwarlp-irrem (T,E)
thick hair .... alta lywerrng (W,T), lywerrng (W,T)
short hair .... kapert twengk (W)
short hair (that has been cut in mourning) .... akampwerr (E), ampwerr (E)
hair (bereavement term) .... waly-waly[2]
cut hair in mourning .... akampwerr-ilelhem (E), urlpat-ilelhem (E), itelhem (E)
thin or sparse hair .... irrkerleng, alta irrkerleng, kapert irrkerleng, irrkerlerrk (E), altherrp
without hair .... akementhwerlk (W), aketh, altelhey (W,T), iltelhey (T,E), kapert aketh, kapert ather-ather (W,T), kapert pweley
matted or knotted hair .... alangkw-alangkw (E), alyep-alyep[1], kelh-kelh, alperrty-alperrty (E), akalangkw-alangkw (E), akaylep-aylep (E), kapert kelh-kelh, nyweter-nyweterrp (W,T)
unwashed or messy hair .... lthel-lthel, alteperety (E)
teenage boy's first facial hair .... arrepwek-pwek (T,E), arrepwek-pwek (W)
burnt hair or fur .... ntharr (T), nthwarr (T), utharr (E)
fine hair on the seeds of the kurrajong tree .... ingeth (T,E)
hair stand on end (from cold or fear) .... lyekarr anem, lyekarr-irrem, lthel-arelhewelhem (E)
make hair stand on end .... lthel-lthel-ilem (?)

hairline .... urlimpimp (E)

hairstring
hairstring belt or strap .... alyep[1], antingkar (E), antyarn (E), arlpalh, irrkety, antay (T,E)
hairstring (respect language) .... aylpel-ayerr (E)
women's ceremonial hairstring 'shirt' .... merterr[2] (E), ngatywelarr (T,E)
hairstring belt (men's) .... matyart, mawelyarr (W,T)
hairstring skirt (men's and women's) .... anma (W,T), anmang (W,T)
hairstring things that belonged to a deceased person .... waly-waly
spin hairstring .... wem[2], irrkety-wem, alyep mpwarem, wenty-ilem (E)

hairy .... lthel-lthel, lthelhey, lthelhey-lthelhey
hairy leg .... ngkwern lthel-lthel

half .... akertang (T,E)
in half .... rlweny (W)
split or cut something in half .... rlkwerr ltwakem (W,T), rlkwerr ultakem (E), rlweny akem (W)

half-caste .... arlperrty (T,E), athethek (W,T)
half-caste (from English) .... apekath

halfway
in between .... mpep, rlkwerr
take someone halfway .... artek-wem (W,T), arteng-wem (T,E)

Halls Creek wattle .... alkart (W,T), ilkert (T,E) (?)

hammer
bang or knock something in .... arlarl-ilem (E), kanth-atwem
hammer or crush something .... apert-atwem (E)

hand .... iltya, iltyang (W,T)
hand (respect language) .... ngaleny (E)
left-hand, left-handed .... akwang alyeng (W,T), akwalyeng (T,E), akwang anety (W,T)
left-handed (respect language) .... akwangeny-ayerr (E)
right-hand, right-handed .... akwang arraty (W,T), akwarraty (T,E)
back of the hand .... iltya artep
palm of the hand .... iltya anert, iltya ipert (E)

lines on palm of hand ..... iltya arlkeny (E), iltyang arlkeny (W,T), iltyang mpwetyerr-mpwetyerr (W)
soft fleshy part of hand ... lher-lher[2]
empty-handed .... iltyant, rep (E)
shake hands .... arntwerrkerrem, iltyang rrkwerrem (W,T)
clap hands .... iltyang atwelhem (W,T), iltya atwelhem (E)
use handsigns to communicate .... iltyel-ilem (E), iltyem iltyem angkem, iltyerrem
hands clasped behind back, with one hand holding on to the other arm behind the back .... arnengerr
put someone's hands behind their back .... arnengerr-ilem
hands clasped behind head .... akatemarengk

handbag *(women's)* .... yakweth
handicapped .... anath (W,T)
handkerchief
tied round head (from English) .... ankety
handle .... arntwerrkenh-arntwerrkenh (E)
handle (from English) ..... anterl (T,E)
of a shield .... arwa[2], arwang (W,T)
of an adze .... artart[1] (W)
handsome .... ntwat (W,T)
hang
hang something up .... tek-arrernem, tek-wem, arlpar-arrernem
hang down .... arlparernem
a lot of things hanging down in a group .... arlpar athwenkarr (W,T), aylpar athwenkarr (E)
hang on!
'Hang on a moment' .... rrwek-antey (W,T), urrek-antey (T,E)
'Hang on a moment' (respect language) .... urrekaty-antey (E), urrekatyakenh (E)
hang onto
hang onto something ...... arntwerrkem
Hanson River .... Alarnenty, Akweranty
happen
something happens in a particular way .... -irr+
happy
happily .... arrken, arrken-arrken, kwak
happy, lively .... ampwengamp, arwekar (W,T), atyep-atyep, irrngerney (E)
feel happy about something .... akangkem, ilkelhem
feel happy or excited .... anyerrkem, inkwerelhem (T,E), irrngerney-irrem (E), kwak-irrem
feel confident or happy about something happening or someone doing something .... anaraty-irrem (W,T), aneraty-irrem (T,E)
feel happy about family .. tyen-irrem (W,T), altyirrem
get excited or happy about something but then be let down .... anew-irrem (T,E)
make someone happy or excited .... irrngerney-ilem (E)

happy family *(bird)* .... tyewakety
hard
hard to the touch .... rlterrk, twer (W,T)
hard (ground) .... tanty, thalkerr (W,T)
strong .... rnpwer (W,T)
someone who is really hard or tough .... rlterrk, tyerrk (W,T), iyterrk (E), tyerrk-tyerrk (W,T), iyterrk-iyterrk (E)
become solid, harden ...... rlterrk-irrem, twer-irrem
get 'hard', be mean .... rlterrk-irrem, twer-irrem
get hard, solidify .... kelh-irrem
Hardons Soak .... Altywep
harmless
not dangerous .... ameleth, angwang, anik (E), apertap (W,T)
Harper Springs .... Ahert-kenh
hassle *(someone)* .... arlkarem
hat .... mwekart
hat (respect language, from English) .... kap-ayerr (E)
hatch
out from an egg .... aterlk-ilem, iyltem (E), pelty-ilem (W,T), peltyelh-ilem (W,T), peltyem (W,T), tyerrelhem, iyltelhem (E)
hatch out eggs .... altywernelh-ilem
hatchling
sand goanna .... kwentarreng
sand goanna or perentie .. arepilyerr (E)
have
have (something) .... rrkwem (W,T), irrkwem (E)
not having something ..... -kweny[2]
have babies or offspring .. mpwarem
hawk
eaglehawk .... irrety
collared sparrowhawk ..... alekaper (?)
type of hawk .... alywerlp (W) (?)
he
he, she, it .... ra, rang (W,T)

head ... aka, kapert[1]
head (respect language) ... akamperrng (E), ayepert (E)
back of head ... tarnng (W,T), ternng (E), temarl (E), kapert akarnng
top of head ... akamer (E), akampwep (W,T), akampep (T,E)
supporting head with hands ... akatemarengk
with head to the prevailing wind (often east) ... rlkang-ampeny (W,T)
be arrogant or big-headed ... amerrelhem (W)
head dripping or pouring with blood ... akanthwek-anthwek, akanthwel-anthwel (W,T)
make someone's head bleed ... akanthwek-anthwek-ilem, akanthwel-anthwel-ilem (W,T)

head ring ... alyep[1]

headache
get a headache ... akarntem[1] (E), akeleraperap-irrem (E), kapert arntem, kapert rawen-irrem (W,T)
having a headache from sun or sickness ... arepwelepwel
headache (respect language) ... ayepert (E), ngalepwerr (E)
having a headache (respect language) ... ngalepwerr-akert (E)

headache vine ... lkwart-lkwart (W,T), ilkwart-ilkwart (T,E)

headband ... tyerlarr
headband (respect language) ... iylerlkarr (E)
made of material (generally white) ... pakerey (W,T)
the red headbands worn by red-ochre men ... waly-waly (W)

headdress
feathers used for decoration, decorative headdress ... irrkarlp
men's ceremonial headdress ... ilperl[4] (W), kwertar
men's ceremonial headdress (made from tea-tree bark) ... perety[1] (E)
head piece made of emu-feathers and hairstring (men's) ... memp (W,T)
women's headdress ... akel-intenh (T), akel-ayntenh (E), akel-anenh (E)

headrest, pillow ... akertemarl (W,T), rtwenk

headscarf *(from English)* ... ankety

heal
cure somebody ... mpwarem, mwerr-ilem, iteth-ilem, tangkelh-ilem (W,T), althekalth-ilem
put a person in the healing smoke ... lhwertel ampem, lhwertel item, lhwertel-ilem
use healing massage ... angkwerr-wem, tyew-tyew-ilem (E)
heal yourself ... mpwarelhem
healed over ... arrintety, tywenmernt (T)
heal over, heal up ... arrintety-irrem, arterrp-irrem, ltyerrem (E), tywenmernt-irrem (T), kwerrm-irrem (E), pwarn-irrem, urrmirrem (T,E)
make things join back together or heal over ... arrintety-ilem

healer
traditional healer, healing powers ... ngangkar, ngangkay, ngangkar-akert, ngangkay-akert
traditional healer (from English) ... tyew-tyew (E)

healthy ... mwerr, mwerr-angker (E), twer (W,T)
get strong ... mwerr-irrem, twer-irrem (W,T)
make a person healthy or strong ... mwerr-ilem, twer-ilem (W,T)

heap
a heap ... aharl, antyakwer (E), thalh (W,T)
lots of things heaped up or stacked up ... kwenty-kwenty
heap of something (especially said of dirt) ... intyakwerlp (W)
heap something up (especially said of dirt) ... intyakwerlp arrernem (W), intyakwerlp-wem (W)
heap something up ... aharl arrernem (E), aharl-wem, lyernt arrernem (T,E), mpwer tywenem (T,E), ayak-arrernem (W,T), antyakwer-wem (E), antarr-arrernem

hear
hear something ... awem
hear (respect language) ... kwarrernem
hear yourself saying something or talking ... awelhem
hear something about yourself ... alhengk-awelhem, awelhem
be unable to hear, not hear properly ... athawem

hear but take no notice.... mentyel awem
not hearing or paying attention .... irlpa akwenp
unable to hear.......... arert, arert-arert, arnaper (W,T), arwangk (W,T), arwengk (T,E), akwerrk-akwerrk (W,T), arrthat (T), arrtheth (T), ather-ather² (W)
heart .... pwerterleng, rtwekert (W,T), rtwakert (E), urtakwert (E)
'Cross my heart'.......... altyerrel arem (W), ngkartel arem (E)
hearth
cooking spot, hearth .... rerrk (T,E), yerrk (W,T)
heat.......... rwernp (W,T), twern (W,T), urinp (E)
heat of the sun.......... aherrk, utern (T,E)
heat of the sun (respect language).......... arekel (E)
heat haze .... angent¹ (T,E), merawarr (W,T)
heat up .... ampem²
heat something up.......... item, ntywelh-ilem (W,T), rwernp-ilem (W,T), urinp-ilem (E)
heat up (water) .... atewat-irrem
heat water up.......... atewat-ilem
heaven .... Alker
heavy .... angerrety, artelhampw (E), awer-awer (E), awer¹ (E), twer (W,T)
be heavy.......... lthwem (W,T), ulthem (E)
heavy (weight), 'heavy' language or speaking style.......... lthwenty (W,T), ulthenty (E), rnpwer (W,T)
heavy-soil handflower .... ankerr-ankerr (W), ankerringk (T,E), ntywenart (W)
heedless .... arert, urrem-urrem (T,E)
without taking notice of others.......... atanty, alanty
heel *(of foot)*.......... anwar (E), ingka tyelk (E), anewerrk
help
helping someone do something .... artangaty
help each other .... artangaty-irrem
not want to do something or help someone .... rlterrk-irrem
help someone in a fight... unkil-ilem (E)
helpful .... irlpareth, ilpety (E)
be helpful.......... irlpareth-irrem
her
(something done to) her... renh, renhenh (W,T)
hers, belonging to her...... kwerenh
her relation.......... +ekw (W,T), +ikw (E)

here
in close proximity to the speaker .... nh+, nhenh, nhetenh (W,T)
'Here!' (when giving something to someone).... ma¹
Hermannsburg .... Ntharey
heron
white-faced, white-necked.......... arlkwenth (E), kamparwengk (E), ntyar (W,T), ulamp-areny (E), ulamparrwek (E)
Hey!.......... ay² (E), yemay (W,T)
hibernation
in hibernation underground .... rlwelth (W,T), urlelth (E), atyerrp (E), ilka¹, ilkeparr
hibernate.......... ilkang intem (W,T), ilkarl ayntem, ilka anem (T), kelerr ipelhem (E), rlwelth arrernelhem (W,T), urlelth ipelhem (E)
come out of hibernation (snake, goanna) .... arlpiwem (E)
hiccough .... anetyerrk-irrem (W,T), anterrk angkem (E), arnenthernem (E), artekernem (T,E)
hidden.......... kwenameny (T)
hide
hide something .... alengk-wem, arlawem (T)
hide something from others .... anyenng artem (T), anyelk artem (E)
hide yourself.......... alengk-welhem
hide yourself behind something .... rwernelhem (W,T), ureynelhem (E)
play hide-and-seek.......... alengk-alengk-welhem
a hide (especially for hunting emu).......... arementy (W), ntat, ipey (E)
high.......... akern
high up .... akerneng-ampeny, akern-ampeny
high ground
open ground on the side of a creek .... mpwanth
hill.......... apwert, irnta (W,T), irntang (W,T)
hill (respect language)..... ather-ayerr (E), nyewel (E)
side of a hill, foothill...... apwert iter, apwert lterr (E), irntang arrker (W), tyewerr (E)

top of a hill .... apwert akern, apwert artep (T,E), irntang akern (W,T), irntang artep (W,T), irntang rrpwang (W,T)
flat scrubby hill .... rrwelty-rrwelty (W,T)
low rise in the hills .... arrwertem (W,T), arrwertem-arrwertem (W,T)
sharp or pointy hill .... inperarr (W,T), kwemper (W,T)
hill fuchsia .... arreth
hill turpentine .... mwerlerr (E)
grub from .... mwerlerrayt (E)
him .... renh, renhenh (W,T)
hip *(of animal or person)* ... aneny, arlenty
point of the hip .... arlenty annga (W)
hip meat of an animal .... ker aneny, ker antywantyw (E)
hipbone .... anngarlp (T,E), antyarlk ngkwern (T), antywantyw (E)
his .... kwerenh
his relation .... +ekw (W,T), +ikw (E)
hit .... atwem
hit something by throwing something at it .. wem[1]
hit (respect language) ...... kelthemartem (W,T), ulpakem (E)
hit yourself .... atwelhem
hit yourself (respect language) .... ulpakelhem
hit or spear yourself with something sharp ..... atanthelhem
hit something against something to break it up or kill it .... arlkwatem (W,T), ntewem (E)
hit or beat something ...... akatwem (E)
hit someone very hard ..... irrernng atwem
hit someone so they bleed .... akanthwek-anthwek atwem, akanthwel-anthwel atwem (W,T)
beat something to death .. imek atwem (E)
be about to hit someone .. angkarr arem
make out as if to strike or hit someone .... angkarr atwem
hit or bump somebody or something .... pwerrtyel atwem (W)
hit or fight someone for someone else .... atyang-atwem (T)
hit someone back, pay them back .... ankwernem (W,T), unkil-ilem (E), unkinem (E)
hit someone or something by mistake ..... aperrpert-ilem (W,T), amenty-ilem (T,E)
hit something so that lots of things fall down ... pwerrer atwem (E)

hive
made by native bees .... arwengalker, rltwamp (W,T)
entrance to native bees' hive .... rltwamp alha (W,T), arwengalker alha (T,E)
hold
hold something .... arntwerrkem
hold onto something, have something .... anyenem (T,E), rrkwem (W,T), irrkwem (E)
hold something hanging from hand .... aylpar anyenem (E)
hold someone or something clasped to chest .... arnwalel angem (?)
hold each other .... rrkwerrem (W,T), irrkwerrem (E)
hold each other in mourning .... kwety-arerrem (E), rrpwarelhem (W,T)
hold part of your body ..... arntwerrkelhem, arntirrkwelhem (E)
hold onto your things, don't give things to others .... ayerrp-ilem
hold *(an event)*
hold (a meeting or ceremony) .... anyenem (T,E)
hole .... altywer, ipert, rtwep (W,T), althwerrk (W)
full of holes, holey .... altywer-altywer, altherrng (E)
shallow hole dug for cooling down .... amel[1]
burrow (a burrow) .... arwerr
hole for cooking in .... rtwep (W,T), urtep (E)
small hollow made in flat ant bed where seeds are husked with feet .... urraty (E)
hole made through septum of nose or through rock .... alhalker (E)
make a hole in something .... altywer-ilem, arrwernem
make a hole in something with something sharp ..... atanthem
make a hole in something, open a burrow .... thakem (E)
hollow
inside hollow part of something .... rtwep (W,T), urtep (E)
hollow or carve something out .... rtwep-ilem (W,T), urtep-ilem (E), mwerlk-ilem (E)
hollow log or tree .... arnang rlpwer (W,T), rlpwer
holly-leaf grevillea .... kelkareng
home .... mer
home, familiar place .... mer arlalty (W,T), rinty (E)

someone who stays home all the time .... mer akweteth (W,T)
staying at home, not going anywhere .... antarl (W,T), artenyem-arteny (E), arteny[1], rlwemp, urlemp (E), rlwepety (W,T), urlepety (E)
stay at home, not go anywhere .... antarl-irrem (W,T), rlwepety anem (W,T), urlepety anem (E)

homesick
feeling of sadness, loneliness or homesickness .... irrar[2], alther (T,E)
feel homesick .... irrar-irrem, alther-irrem (T,E), arrampewem[2] (E)
feel homesick, lonely or confused .... apatem
feel homesick or sad .... altarrp awelhem (W,T), alpwely-irrem
make someone feel lonely or homesick .... irrarel anthem

honey
liquid honey .... ngkwarl, akarr (T,E), arlkwerrng, ngkwarl irrngwa (E)
clean honey (native honey) .... arrtyangk (W)
soft honey or sweet gum .. akaly (W,T)
honey-soaked earth from honeyant that has burst open .... awert[1]
honey from honeyant that has been split open .. apmewarr (E)
(earth) become soaked with honey from honey-ant that has burst open ... awert-irrem
from corkwood .... ntywey (W,T), untyey (E), untyeyamp (E), ntyweyamp, ntyweyangkwarl (W)
liquid honey from corkwood flowers .... ankarr (T,E)
from ghost gum bark ...... ulemparrty (E), yerrkengal (T)
from red mallee .... ntyenyengkwarl (E)
from under river red gum bark .... aperarnt (T,E), aperengengel (E), aperelayeng (W), mamp (W,T)

honey grevillea .... rrwerleng (W,T), tharrkarr (T,E)

honeyant .... yerramp, inkwareny
honeyant (respect language) .... inkwareny
worker (black and yellow ants outside honeyants' nest) .... arnman[2]
queen .... rlweng apeltyey (W), rlwertantyey (W,T)
nest or hole .... alyap
chamber or shelf in nest .. inkwa
tunnel in nest .... wenty (W,T)
old honeyant nest .... pweng
opening of nest .... ahenty[1], arla[1], arlang (W,T)
eggs of honeyants and other species of ant .... lwerrk (W,T), ilwerrk (E)
honey from honeyant that has been split open .. apmewarr (E)
honey-soaked earth from honeyant that has burst open .... awert[1]
(earth) become soaked with honey from honeyant that has burst open .... awert-irrem
make earth go yellow or red colour (honeyants) ..... atyerrem[1], item, arrtyem (E)
snake (?) that lives in bottom of nest .... rlwarrkany (W,T)

honeyeater
singing, spiny-cheeked ..... alpeyart-alpeyart (E), arrakwerakwer (T,E), arrety-arrety (W,T)
white-plumed .... aperrety-aperrety (T)

hoof
back hooves or paws of animals .... ingka, ingkang (W,T)
front hooves or paws of animals .... iltya, iltyang (W,T)
hard part of hoof or paw .. rta, irta (W,T), rtang (W,T), irtang (W,T)

hoofbeats *(sound of)* .... twerlepwelh-pwelh (W,T)

hook
on woomera or spear .... ipa (E), lywernk, ikalharr (E)
fighting hook or pick .... walarnp (W,T), walaymp (E)
hooked stick .... lywernk
hooked boomerang .... rlkwa (W,T), rlkwang (W,T), iylkwa (E), alyang rlkwang (W,T), aylayl iylkwa (E)
hook something .... atanthem

hop along .... anarnperl-apem, unarnp-unarnp-alpem (E)

horn *(of animal)* .... ahiwelhem (T), rewelyerr (T,E), yarwelyem (W), yerewelyek (E)
without horns (from English) .... napey

hornet .... arntirn (T), arnteyn (E)

horse .... nantew, nanth, wethey (W)
horse (baby talk) .... tyey-tyey, tyatyey (T)

horse (respect language) .. wetheth-ayerr (E)
Horsfield's
bronze-cuckoo .... nyarew, anatyelepwerray (E) (?), urrempen (?)
hot .... rwernp (W,T), urinp (E), ampay (W)
hot (baby talk) .... waw
hot (from English) .... ata², ahat
hot, warm to the touch .... awempey (E)
feeling hot .... rrkwer (W), irrkwer (E)
become hot .... ampem², rwernp-irrem (W,T), urinp-irrem (E), awempey-irrem (E)
be hot, feel hot .... urranem (W,T)
make something hot .... ampem¹, ntywety-ilem (W,T)
hot ashes or earth .... ntyerlp¹, untyety (E), amerrk² (E), rtwap, urtap (T,E), arlpa¹ (E), atnmanth (E), awerrth (E)
hot weather *(go to 'summer')*
house .... mer, warl
house (respect language) .. anal (E)
how
'How?' .... nthakenh, nthanh (E), thanh (E)
this is how (while showing someone) .... alakenh
'How many?' .... nthakenty
'How come?' .... nthakenh, nthanh (E), thanh (E)
'How are you?' .... wartay¹ (W,T)
howl
make crying or howling sounds .... arnem, arrangkem
howling or blowing sound (wind) .... aywerr
make a howling or blowing sound (wind) .... aywerr angkem
huff, sulk
in a huff .... arnkely, npwart (W,T), unpart (T)
hug
hug someone .... amel-rrkwem (W,T)
hug each other .... amel-rrkwerrem (W,T)
hold or embrace one another in an expression of mourning ... parnparl-ilerrem (W,T)
huge .... -anternenh, artelh³ (E)
hum
humming noise .... arnwer²
make a droning or humming noise .... arnwer-irrem, unyem (E), alyerrem
human being .... tyerrty
humbug
'humbug' or annoy someone .... arlkarem, arlelty angkem
hump
sharp hump or rise in a road (from English) ...... tyampap
humpy .... antywa, antywang (W,T), iltha (E), wak (E)
hungry .... angayakw, angayel, anert angayel, anert altywer, anert arltwang (W,T)
hungry (respect language) .... weyapel, weyapelek-uthek (E)
hungrily .... arnartew (W,T)
feel hungry .... angayakw-irrem, angayel-irrem
feel hungry (respect language) .... weyapel-irrem
feeling really hungry .... arrerlkart (T,E), watyepatyep (W)
feel really hungry .... arrerlkart pwem (E), arrerlkart urntem (E), arrerlkart-irrem (T,E), irrketem (E), rrwampem (W), urrampem (T,E)
want to eat without sharing, greedy .... rrngwerrty (W,T)
be very hungry, have a big appetite .... rrngwerrty-irrem (W,T)
really want a particular food .... arrernkem (W,T), arrirnkem (T,E)
hungry, not having had breakfast .... altyerrakw (E), altyerrinp (E)
hunt
go hunting .... irrer alhem, lyweny alhem (W,T)
going hunting .... lyweny (W,T)
going hunting (respect language) .... irrererrnk (E)
hunt an animal using something sharp (e.g. spear, beak or claws) .... atanthem, rnternem
hunt (get something to eat) .... arlkwem, wantem
hunt something down using dogs .... ipernem (W,T)
leave things somewhere while going hunting .... rwanenty-wem
separate while hunting .... anpaty-irrem (T), anpert-irrem (T)
good at hunting .... lywenpeny, arltwemp (W)
get lots of game (meat) .... akwetyerretyerr-ilem, akwetyerretyerr atwem

someone not good at hunting or collecting food .... anik (E)
unsuccessful at hunting ... arewamp
be unsuccessful at hunting .... arewamp-irrem
coming back with nothing (from hunting) .... rrpwernp (W,T), urrpernp (E)
cause someone to be unsuccessful at hunting, frighten off game .... rrpwernp anthem (W,T), rrpwernp-ilem (W,T), urrpernp anthem (E), urrpernp-ilem (E)
hunt someone away, get rid of someone .... anpwem (W,T), aywepem (T,E), alhengkem (T,E), alharlkwem

hurry
be in a hurry .... arrewelhem, athek-irrem
being in a hurry .... arnkarnp (T,E), arrengker, parrp, parrp-parrp, uremeny (E), rwemeny (E), ngwarrertakert (W,T), aher, arlkwer-arlkwer, urlker-urlker (E)
doing something in a rush, in a hurry .... athathel

hurt
feel hurt or in pain .... kwarnelhem, rlkert intyem, antyernem[1] (W,T)
be hurt by something ...... arlkwem
hurt self .... atwelhem
hurt self (respect language) .... ulpakelhem
hurt someone .... kwarnem, rlkert-ilem

husband
spouse .... anew, arweng[2] (W)
term used by women to refer to their husbands ..... artwa, artwang (W,T)
husband (baby talk) .... kaly-kaly[1] (T,E)
husband and wife .... anewart, anewart atherr
husband of someone in the same generation moiety as oneself .... arrkar
husband of someone not in the same generation moiety as oneself .... aperl

husk
husk on fruits or seeds .... irrnya, irrnyang (W,T)
husk seeds with feet .... lywem[1], rlwem (W,T), iylwem (E)
husk grass seeds before grinding .... irrnyat-wem (W)

Ii

I .... ayeng, tha, thang (W,T)
I (will do/am doing/have done) something to him/her/it .... thweker (W,T)
I (will do/am doing/have done) something to you ... thangenh, thwengk (W,T)

ice .... lwelty (W,T), ulelty (E)
hailstone .... apwertek, kwaty irntakert (T)

idea .... iterrenty

identical *(see also 'same')*
two things that are the same as, or very similar to, each other .... rant-atherr
more than two things that are the same as, or very similar to, each other .... inant-inant, inantarrety (W,T)

if, maybe .... apek

ignorant
not knowing, inexperienced .... akwen, akwerrp (E)
not knowing, inexperienced (from English) .... maywel
not knowing about something (especially country) .... akampwerrk (E)
in ignorance, mistakenly .. apal[2], apal-apal[2], apalel, parlk (W), pwarlk (W,T)

ignore
not take notice of someone .... unerlewem (E)
ignore or not take notice of what is happening ...... menty awelhem
hear but not answer .... mentyel awem
ignoring or not paying attention to things .... akwenpeny
ignoring someone and paying attention to others instead .... arrelharrp (W), arreylarrp (E)
lose interest in somebody .. arrkereny-irrem, arrkerenyel-wem

ill .... mernt (W,T), arntety (E), rlkert
illness .... arrwengkelth
critically ill .... irrewaly

Illoquara Waterhole .... Arlwekarr

imagine
imagine that you see something .... aherr arem, aherr-aherr arem, ywer-ywer arem (W,T)

imitate someone .... angwarem, arlepewem (W,T), warrernem (E)

an imitation of the real thing .... -arrpantey, -arrpatenty (E)
immediately .... lyet innga (E)
almost immediately .... lyet war
immerse
something in liquid (e.g. a biscuit in tea) .... arek-wem (W,T)
impatient
rush in excitedly, be impatient .... athek-irrem
important .... angerr[1], impen, rltwa (W,T), rltwang (W,T), tyeperr
think that you are really important .... atyetyart-irrem
improve .... mwerr-irrem
in, on *(see Appendix 2)*
inappropriate .... anety (W,T), akeng (T,E), kwern (W,T)
increase
increase in number or size .... angerr-irrem[1], anengk-irrem (W,T), atningk-irrem (E)
increase the number or size of something .... angerr-ilem, anengk-ilem (W,T), atningk-ilem (E)
incubate
hatch out eggs .... altywernelh-ilem
inexperienced .... akwen
(from English) .... nyew tyam
infect
become infected with sickness or disease .... angwarem, antelhem
infect someone .... atwarem
inflamed .... tywen, utyen (E)
inflated .... arlwar, arterrp
inflate something .... arlwar-ilem
initially
(do something) first, before some other action .... -amparr
initiation ceremony
(see also 'ceremony') .... anmanty (W,T), apwelh
injection
give someone an injection .... atanthem
give yourself an injection .... atanthelhem
injured .... arekar
insane .... arert
insect
insect or bug that 'bites' (from English) .... patey (W), paytey (T,E), patey-patey (W), paytey-paytey (T,E)
small flying insects .... thep, uthip (E)
type of (possibly sandfly) .... arntap-arntap (W,T)
type of (maybe wasp) .... rntererrpererrp (W,T)
that bores holes in black gidgee .... arnteparl altywer-ilenh (W,T)
inside, in .... kwen
inside or hollow part of something .... rtwep (W,T), urtep (E)
inspect
inspect something .... tywerr-arem (W,T)
inspect part of yourself .... tywerr-arelhem (W,T)
instep .... ingkang artep (W,T), ingka artep (E)
intellect .... iterrenty
interest
make someone lose interest in another .... arwekar-ilem
interpret
(change something over) .... angart-wem
interrupt
interrupt someone to get their attention .... anthakem (E), anthakemel angkem (E)
make a noise, create a disturbance .... apatel-anthem (T,E), apatelh-ilem, lpwertelh-ilem (W,T), ulpertelh-ilem (T,E), aparlp-ilem, aparlpelh-ilem (E)
interrupt, block the way .... arrngert-irrem
interrupt someone talking .... angka ultakem (T,E), angkety ltwakem (W,T), ulypma ultakem (E)
intestines .... lyep-lyep, ana, anang (W,T), kart[1] (W,T)
fat-covered intestines of some animals .... aneperrk
large intestine .... mwerlk[1]
part of intestines .... kwey-kwey (W,T) (?)
invincible .... inangkal
invisible .... arrkay
iris *(of eye)* .... annga rrpwerl (W,T), annga urrperl (E)
iron
sheet of iron (from English) .... tyetepayen
ironwood .... atheng, athimp (T,E), atyarnp
edible gum .... athengarlperl (E), athimpangkwarl (E), atyarnpangkwarl (W,T)
is *(see 'be')* .... anem[1]
of things in a horizontal position .... intem[1], ayntem (E)
of things in a vertical position .... irnem
of hills .... altywernem

'Is that right?' … tyathew, tyakey, athew, alew[2] (W,T), alew-alew (W,T)

it
when 'it' is doing an action … ra, rang (W,T)
when 'it' is having the action done to it … renh, renhenh (W,T)
belonging to 'it' … kwerenh

itchy
be itchy, feel itchy … irrkem, ingkem (E)
make someone itchy … irrkelh-irrkelh-anthem, irrkelh-irrkelh-ilem

itchy grub … ingeth (T,E), wep (SP)
itchy-grub nest … wep

Jj

jacket *(from English)* … tyaket

jail
put someone in jail … irrpelh-ilem

jammed in close together … pwarn

Japanese … Tyapaney

jawbone … arrely ngkwern, arreyl ngkwern (E)
point of jawbone … lengk-lengk (W,T)

jealous
jealous (from English) … tyaleth
be jealous of someone or over something … anngwenhem, tyaleth-irrem
be jealous of each other … anngwenherrem
be jealous or envious of someone (particularly over husband or wife) … arwelth-rnem (E), mayel anngwenhem
jealous, particularly over husband or wife … arwelth (T,E), mayel
have a jealous fight (particularly over husband or wife) … arwelthel atwerrem (T,E), mayel anngwenhem, mayel atwerrem
look at someone jealously or enviously … arwelthel arem (T,E), mayel arem

Jesus … Altyerr[1], Angey
Jesus (from old German) … Ithew

jew lizard … amwely, ankert[2] (W,T)

Jingili
language or person … Tyengel

job
work (from English) … warrk
do a job … warrk-irrem

joey … atwety[1]

join
join together, become joined … anyent-irrem, pwety-irrem (T), pweyt-irrem (E)
join something together … anyentelh-ilem, pwety-ilem (T), pwetyelh-ilem (T), pweyt-ilem (E), pweytelh-ilem (E), arrakwernem[1] (E)
joined together, healed over … arrintety
make things join back together or heal over … arrintety-ilem

joke
say something funny … arrken angkem
funny, playful or amusing person … arrken angerr
play a joke on someone … ayntarrp-ilem (E)
in fun, playing a trick, joking … tyelewerr (W,T)
behaving in a teasing or joking way with people in the opposite generation moiety … urrayerr (T,E)
behave in a teasing or joking way with people in the opposite generation moiety … urrayerr-irrem (T,E)
joke (inappropriately) about something serious … arrampewem[1]

joyfully … arrken, arrken-arrken

juice
juice from meat, fruits … arlkwerrng
of native citrus or bush plum fruit … ankarr (T,E)
of witchetty grub and other grubs … arrelty[2]

jump
jump down from something … anarnpem
jump along … anarnperl-apem
jump over something … anarnperl-alhem
jump away from something … irrkarnpem
jump in fright … anwerlkem
(sparks) jump out … unarnpem (E), intety-intety-irrem (E), anarnpem

jumpy
sensitive, touchy or jumpy … irrngerrng (E), tyelety (E)
be sensitive, touchy or jumpy … irrngerrng-irrem (E), tyelety-irrem (E)

just
just one thing and not another … rlwart (W,T), urlart (E)
just now (after a time) … lyetant

just them (the two of them) .... +ant-atherr
just a few .... rrpwetyarrp (W,T), urrpetyarrp (E)
'just a minute' .... rrwek (W,T), urrek (T,E), alerl (E)
justify yourself .... arraty-ilelhem

Kk

kalkardi *(plant)* .... alkart (W,T)
kalpari *(plant)* .... alpar
kangaroo
red kangaroo .... aherr
kangaroo .... tarlew (W,T)
kangaroo (respect language) .... tyantwerr (E), urla alkey
kangaroo (baby talk, from English) .... kangkew
male kangaroo .... aherr rrwey (W,T)
big male kangaroo .... yawerrang (W), yawerr (T), ampelaherr (E)
big male red kangaroo .... aharlparrengk[1] (E)
old male kangaroo .... aherr ampelaherr (E), aherr purl (E)
young male kangaroo .... artar[1], aherr artar
bluish-coloured kangaroo .... urit (E), rwet (T), urit-urit (E), rwet-rwet (T)
female kangaroo, doe .... aherr marl
female kangaroo with joey .... aherr areperrk (T,E)
old female kangaroo .... aherr alkeperr (T,E)
young female .... aherr aympa ampwerrk (E)
young kangaroo .... atwety[1]
blood and meat juice from cooked kangaroo .... awerrp[1]
kangaroo blood (respect language) .... ltyayerr (E)
lower back of kangaroo .... antywert (W,T), intywert (W)
kangaroo leg bone .... ntyarl (W,T), ntyerl (T,E)
kangaroo bladder .... artwety (E) (?)
kangaroo bone (underneath bladder) .... mweyntenng (E)
part of guts .... anarrk (E), anyem anteth (E)
green watery contents from a kangaroo's stomach .... anthwerrk[2] (T,E)
worm found in stomach .... antya[1] (E)
dry kangaroo droppings .... anwer (E)
non-fatty meat of kangaroo .... pelh[2] (W,T)
make a cut across the top part of the thighs of a cooked kangaroo .... artely-ilem (W,T)
kangaroo's path or track .... terarl
kangaroo's salt lick or waterhole .... arrantyeyantyeng, aherrantyeyantyeng (E)
kangaroo's windbreak or sleeping place .... urnakw (E)
kangaroo-skin waterbag .... arranty[2] (E)
(kangaroo) make a thudding noise .... anerlpem
kangaroo fat
from kneecap and leg .... anter tyelh (W), akepitelh (E), ulyelatanenh (E)
from lower tail and scrotal area of kangaroo .... anwerlk (E), aherr-anwerlk (E)
from lower stomach .... urtarnp (E)
from the lower back .... aherr anwerlk (T,E), aherr-anwerlk (E)
in the flesh from the thigh .... apertaynp (E), iylpernk (E)
kidney fat .... apel[1] (E)
kangaroo tail .... aherr pwer, kanty[1]
meat (portion from near the tail) .... rtweth, urteth (T,E)
tail meat .... arrertarnk (T,E)
upper part of kangaroo tail .... anartelh (W)
kangaroo balls vine .... aherr-arlweth (T,E), aherr-arleth (E)
kangaroo grass .... arlperlp
Karrwerlereny
language or people .... Karrwerlereny
Kaytetye
language or people .... Kartety (W,T), Kaytety (E)
keeled lantern-bush .... aylpat-aylpat (E)
keep
keep something, have something .... rrkwem (W,T), irrkwem (E), anyenem (T,E)
keep something for yourself, don't give things to others .... ayerrp-ilem
keep something to yourself, keep a story to yourself .... awakelhem, mweny rrkwem
keep away from somebody or something .... anenyerr-irrem, mentyel arem
keeping on doing something regardless of anything .... akwenp
keeping someone company .... alanty
kestrel *(nankeen)* .... anthep-anthep (E)
kick someone or something .... ingkel atwem (W,T), ingkel-wem (T)

kidney .... arteperrk, mpwerrkety (T,E), kwerrern (SP)

kill
someone or something ..... atwem
kill, shoot (respect language) .... ulpakem (E)
a large 'kill' (game) .... akwerremp
kill lots of something (game) .... akwerremp-ilem, althinem (T,E), iltatwem (T,E)
kill something by biting it .... nhwem (W,T), unhem (E)
kill many animals on your own .... arlperreh atwem (W), arlperrek atwem (T,E)
kill something for someone else .... atyang-atwem (T)
kill one another .... kwarterrem
just about kill someone ... nyant atwem, nyey-nyey atwem (W)
kill self .... atwelhem
kill yourself laughing ..... ampwerrk-ilwem (E), nyant atherrem

kind .... akangkenty, atham-atham
be kind or compassionate .... atham-irrem

kindling .... rrwelty (W,T), urrelty (T,E), ngkwelty, arnang rrwelty (W,T), mwenng, mwenthenng (E), rwang ngkwelty (W,T), rwang rrwelty (W,T), ura ngkwelty (E)

king brown snake .... alhingk (E), arreperlp (W,T), atetherr arlkwenh, ikwelengk (T,E), kantharlkw (W,E), tyamparl (T)

kingfisher *(red-backed)* ..... parlkenng (E), rlwernp (W,T), urrernter² (E)

kinship system .... anpernerrenty
(see also 'skin name')

kiss .... arrantywem (W,T), arrwantyem

kite *(bird)*
black kite .... apwelanty, apwelaynt (E), inkwel (E)
whistling kite .... apwart-apwart (E) (?)

Kityarr
language or person .... Akityarr

knead, mix .... athem²

knee .... amper², ampweth (E), kelkert (W,T)
with knees up .... tyakwert, akartwernem (E), tyakwert irnem
supported on knees .... amperel irrertety
knee joint .... akarlwarl (E)
kneecap .... akarlwarl (E), amper alkwert-alkwert (T), itelh (E), kelkert tyel (W,T), kelkert ngkwern (W,T), tyelh

kneel .... ampwethel-ayeth anem (E)

knife
stone knife .... alywek, apwert antha (E), kartamp (W,T), inkwartety (E), irntarlter (W,T), irntang arlter (W,T), werlamp (T)

knock
bang or knock something in .... arlarl-ilem (E), kanth-atwem
knock someone down ...... athenem, athelp-athenem
knock something against something else in order to break it up or kill it ..... arlkwatem (W,T), ntewem (E)

knock back
knock back an offer of something .... lthwelth-ilem (W,T), ulthelth-ilem (E), menty-ilem

knot
knot in wood .... ankerl

knotted
matted or knotted together .... interrenty (T,E)
matted or knotted hair .... akalangkw-alangkw (E), alangkw-alangkw (E), akaylep-aylep (E), irrkety-irrkety (T), kapert kelh-kelh, werrp (E)
become matted or knotted (hair) .... akalangkw-alangkw-irrem (E), alyep-alyep-irrem², kelh-irrem

know
know about someone or something .... iterlarem
know something about yourself .... iterlarelhem
know someone, recognise someone .... alhengk-arem
not knowing about something .... akwen, akwerrp (E), parlkeny (W), pwarlkeny (W,T), apal², apalekalek, apal-apal², apalel
not know (about something) .... apatem, anatem
not know what to do .... apalekalek-irrem
'I don't know' .... inpa (E), iy, ywek, ywekaw

knowledge .... iterrenty

knowledgeable .... kalty, kapert altywer, kapert arraty, wetyerretyerr² (W), weretyerretyerr (W,T)

someone who is good at doing things........inangkal
kurapuka *(wattle)*........ampwey (E)
kurdaitcha........artwang inenty (W,T), artwa inenty (E), inenty, kwertaty (E), mwak[2] (E), ngkekern (W,T), nwernternenty (W,T), rlwarlp (W,T), urlaylp (E), arlelty (SP)
feather shoes, 'kurdaitcha boot'........apwa (E)
(kurdaitcha) put on feather shoes........ingkirrpem, apwirrpem (E)
turn into a kurdaitcha........ngkekern-irrem (W,T), rlwarlp-irrem (W,T), urlaylp-irrem (E)
kurrajong
desert kurrajong........apeng
flowers........arlpetharlp (E)
green seeds........artwengarr (T,E)
small green seed pods........alyalyarr (E)
Kurrajong Bore........Ngkwelay

Ll

Lajamanu........Latyaman
lake
large expanse of water........alay[1], kwaty alay, ulamp (E)
Lake Lewis........llewerr
Lake Nash *(from English)*........Lyekenaty
lamb *(from English)*........lam-lam
lamb's tail *(plant)*........alyey-alyey (W,T), awerreh-alyey-alyey (W,T), aweyek-alyey-alyey (E), merntepam (W), merntepwarn (W,T), rrweyek-alyey-alyey (W,T), urreyek-alyey-alyey (T,E)
lame........rnwerr, rnwerr-rnwerr (W,T), alpalth (E), anenyirrp irrkweynar (E), arlamarr, lim-lim (W), thwerremp-thwerr (T,E)
go lame........arlamarr-irrem, lim-lim-irrem (W), rnwerr-irrem
land, ground........ahelh, ahern
land *(bird or aeroplane)*........arrernelhem
language........angka[1] (E), angkety, ulypma (E)
accent which is hard to understand........irrkwerteth (T,E), arrkwerteth (W), irrkwerteth-irrkwerteth (T,E), arrkwerteth-arrkwerteth (W)
someone who speaks a different language........irrkwerteth (T,E), arrkwerteth (W)
lap
lapping sound........lthap-lthap, rltap-rltap (W)
make a lapping sound........lthap-lthap-irrem, rltap-rltap-irrem (W), perlp-perlp antywem (W,T), peylp-peylp antywem (E)
lap
person's lap........rnwart, peth, irnwa (E)
hold on lap........rnwartel anyenem
lapwing *(banded)*........ampelyetyerrker (E), interrk-atherather (W,T), tyelkatherather, tartarrp (E) (?)
Laramba community........Alherramp
large........rltwa (W,T), rltwang (W,T), urlta (E), angerr
very large thing........angerrety-pwek (W,T)
larrikin
promiscuous person (sensitive language)........anapert (T,E)
last........ingkerneny
last in a group of siblings........kantyeny (T,E)
late
get late in the day........angwerr-irrem, angwerrel-irrem
later
go later, go last........ingkern alhem, ingkerneny alhem
laugh........atherrem, arrken atherrem
kill yourself laughing........nyant atherrem, ampwerrk-ilwem (E)
laugh loudly........arnterr atherrem
put hand over mouth to hide laughter........mweny rrkwem, mweny irrkwem (E), mweny-mweny rrkwem (W,T), mweny-mweny irrkwem (E)
Laura Yard........Alewer
Law
custom, tradition, rule........mpwarengareng, tywerreng
lay
lay something out........antyepanty-wem (W,T)
lay someone down to sleep........ankwa athenem
lay someone or something down, lay something across something........athenem, athen-wem
lay someone out (by hitting them)........anenp athenem (T), atninp athenem (E)
lay an egg........lhwem (T), rrkwem (W,T), irrkwem (E), ulhem (T,E)

lazy
feeling lazy, exhausted .... arewamp, marakat (W,T)
having no motivation ..... arnernkey
be lazy or lethargic .... rrwempel anem (W), rrwempem (W,T), marakat-irrem (W,T)
lie around feeling lazy or lethargic .... aylpmerrem (E)
lazy person .... anam-athek (T,E), anam-kenh (T,E), anam-henh (W,T), anamek (T,E)

lead
lead someone along .... tyarr-angem, tyey-angem (W,T), yel-angem (E)
take the lead, go first ...... arrwekel alhem, arrwekel-irrem, yel-irrem (E)

leader .... atyetyart

leaf, leaves .... alperr (E), arlpa[2], arlpang (W,T), arlpelh[1] (T,E)
leafy branch .... waly
leaves that have fallen to the ground .... iylelth (E), lyerrk
of bush banana .... altyey, unelh (E), ahertety[2] (E)
of bush potato .... inkwanng (E) (SP)

leak out .... thelelhem
seep out (especially blood) .... irrert-irrem

lean
something used for support or for leaning on .... irrertety
lean up against something .... alernelhem (T,E), anert-iwelhem (E), ampek-welhem
lean or press weight on something .... lthwem (W,T), ulthem (E), kerrk-wem, anert-wem (E)
stand leaning against someone or something ..... ampekernem
sit leaning against someone or something ..... ampek-anem
lie leaning against someone or something ..... ampek-intem

lean *(not fat)* .... ampwa, ampwang (W,T)
lean (not fat) of kangaroo .... pelh[2] (W,T)

learn .... kalty-irrem, inangkal-irrem
someone who learns quickly .... kapert altywer

leather-leaved colony wattle .... iylarn (E), iylarnayt (E), ntwarnengayt (E)
grub from .... ntwarnengayt (E) (SP)

leave
set off, leave to go somewhere .... arnpem, arnperl-alhem, alhem
leave something alone, reject something .... impem, menty-irrem
leave something behind, forget something .... anngwerrem (W,T), anngwirrem (E), aparlp-ilem, imperl-alhem, ingkern-ilem (E), iwerl-alhem, iylpel-wem (E), menty-ilem, arrwer-ilem[2] (?)
leave something behind, turn your back on something .... artepelh-ilem
leave something with someone .... twap-anthem (W,T)
leave things somewhere while going hunting .... alal-wem, rwanenty-wem
leave something for later .. arlernem (W), arlwarrernem (T,E)
take someone and leave them halfway .... twap-anthem (W,T)
leave someone, give them up .... impelhem
'Leave it' .... menty
'Leave it' (respect language) .... ment-ayerr (E)

leaves *(go to 'leaf')*

leech
type of .... parlarlweker (E) (?)

left-hand side .... alyeng, alyeng-ampeny
left-handed .... akwang alyeng (W,T), akwa alyeng (T,E), akwang anety (W,T)
left-handed (respect language) .... akwangeny-ayerr (E)
left foot .... ingka alyeng

leftovers .... ampeny[1], ampeny-ampeny
food or drink left over from the day before .... ingwikw (E), irrkweny (E)
leftover bits and pieces .... tyepety[2] (E)

leg .... ngkwern
leg (respect language) ...... tyemurrely (E)
sit with legs close together (women) .... mweny-irrem

Leichhardt Bore .... Anpetyety

lemon grass
native lemon grass .... aherr-aherr, areng-areng (E)

lemonade *(from English)* .. kwelteringk

lend
something to someone ..... arlenthem (T,E), war anthem
something to someone (from English) .... lant-em-ilem

lerp scale
on the Normanton box …… yerrekeyerr (T,E)
on the leaf of the river red gum …… aperelty

let
someone or something go …… ilanthem, atniwem (E), tyarl-wem (E)

'Let's go' …… mpa

lethargic …… marakat (W,T)
feel tired or lazy …… marakat-irrem (W,T)
lie around feeling lazy or lethargic …… aylpmerrem (E)

level
level, even, equal (from English) …… lepwel
make ground level …… anhwerrem
make things level …… arraty-ilem

lever something up …… arwakem, alpwarternem (E), ilpent-wem (E)

liar
a liar, a lie …… rrtywerrenty (W,T), urrtyalth (T,E), urrtya (E)

lice …… anya[2] (W,T), anyang (W,T), arrem (T,E)

lick …… arrantywem (W,T), arrwantyem, awantyem
part of self (such as fingers) …… awantyelhem

lie
lie down …… intem[1], ayntem (E)
lie (of hills) …… altywernem
lie (respect language) …… lpwanem (W,T), ulpanem (T,E)
throw self down …… iwelhem
lie flat on stomach …… lpwerr intem (W,T), ilperr ayntem (E), ulperr intem (T,E)
lie someone on their stomach …… lpwerr-wem (W,T), ulperr-wem (T,E)
lie yourself on stomach …… lpwerr-welhem (W,T), ulperr-welhem (T,E)
lie on back …… akern-antep intem, impalkert intem
lay someone or something on its back …… impalkert-wem
lie on side …… arlkarlker intem
lie curled up …… altywernem, rtapety intem
lie on side with legs curled up …… arrethaker intem, arrethaker-irrem
lie with knees up or bent over one another …… tyakwert intem, tyampernem (W,T)
lie propped up on hand or elbow …… arlkany intem, arlkany irnem (W,T)
lying with head to the west …… mpwarl-angkwerr
lie without moving …… arlelty intem
lie in wait for someone or something …… urlernem (E), arrap-anem, arrap-intem, arrap-welhem
lie on the ground (of water) …… athernem (E)

lie
a liar, a lie …… rrtywerrenty (W,T), urrtyalth (T,E), urrtya (E)
tell lies …… rrtywerrem (W,T), urrtyirrem (E), arrampewem[1], atyetyem (E), rrtywekelh-ilem (T), rrtywerremel ilem (W,T), therlkem (W,T), urirrem[2] (E), urrtyirremel ilem (E), rnter-irrem (E) (?)

life
alive …… iteth
alive, having a long life …… itethakenp
bring back to life …… iteth-wem
bring to life (assist in a birth) …… iteth-wem

life-saver burr …… ingka-mwerney, ingkang mwerney (W), akeley-akeley (T,E), anmang (W)
life-saver burr (from English) …… kwem (W), kwem-kwem (W)

lift
lift something up …… arnwal-inem (W,T), arnal-inem (W,T)
lift something up onto something …… tywenem, utyenem (E), tywenelh-ilem
lift yourself up onto something …… tywenelhem, utyenelhem (E)
lift something up to show someone …… nyely-ilem (T,E)
lift something onto shoulder …… intarlpek-ilem (W,T), ntwarlpek-ilem (E)
lift up someone who is old and infirm …… akem-arrernem (E)

light
a light …… anngenth, lyenenty, rwang lyenenty (W,T), alernenty, alhenenty
bright fire or light …… parntar (W,T)
no light, in the dark …… atham
a bit light in colour …… arlter-arlter, arlperrty (T,E), arlter
light-skinned …… arelyerrty (T,E), urelyerrty (E)

half-light (sky) ngwemernt-ngwemernt (W,T), ingwemernt-ingwemernt (E)
get light, day break aherlkem, aherrk aketh-irrem, aketh-aketh-irrem
make light, light things up (sun or moon) parrtyelh-ilem (W,T), pwarrtyelh-ilem (T)
make something light or clear aketh-ilem

light a fire item, nthelem (W,T), nthilem, anngenth-ilem, antant-ilem (W,T), arrtyem (E), lherrm-ilem (T,E)
light fire with a firestick kep-ilem (W), alep-ilem (T,E)

light *(not heavy)* althalth, ararr, arrmaly-arrmaly (T,E), artaly-artaly (T,E)
become light or flimsy althalth-irrem
'light' sound (of speech) arrerlker (E)
light (of fabric) alparr-alparr (E)
light, soft or insubstantial (such as white bread) ararr

light-hearted
(doing something) light-heartedly war

lightning awely-awely, pwer, kwaty pwer, ngkwarrkenty (W,T), ingkwarrkenty (T,E)

like
liking or wanting something ahenty²
like someone or something, like to do something ahenty-anem, ahenty-irrem, akangkem, ilkelhem, inkwerelhem (T,E)
really like or want something alherrem² (W,T), alhirrem
place that you like ilkelhey (W,T)
like a place and not want to go anywhere else kwak-irrem
disliking somebody or something ahenty-kwenh (W,T), tyweker, amperr (W,T)
not like someone or something tyweker-irrem

like *(similar)*
two things that are like each other rant-atherr
more than two things that are like each other inant-inant, inantarrety (W,T)
resembles, is like (someone or something else) -apeny (E), -artek

like that, thus
like that, that's how, that's when alakenh, alanh, lweren (W,T)
something (like that), that sort of thing nheng-lkwer
do something like that alakenh-irrem, alanh-irrem

lily
desert fringed lily akwerl-akwerl (W,T)
Sandover lily alyerlk-alyerlk (W), arlerlk-arlerlk (T), iylelty (E), lyelkenng (E)

lime atywerlk (W,T) (?), aytwerlk (E) (?)

limestone rltwernt (W,T), urlternt (E)
limestone country rltwernt-rltwernt (W,T), urlternt-urlternt (E)

limp
limp along tyernem²
limping anenyirrp irrkweynar (E)
hanging loose alyemp-alyemp¹
go limp alpwely-irrem

line
in a line akert-arraty, arratyeyn-antey (E)
line things up with each other arraty-ilem
line up, go along in a line akert-arraty-irrem, warrert-irrem (T,E), arraty-akwer-irrem (W), akertarreng-irrem (E)

lips arrakert ayenp, arrayenp (E), arrenpenp (W,T), arrimpimp (E)

liquid
watery kwaty-kwaty¹ (W,T), rew-rew
liquid honey akamp (W,T), akampw (E), akarr (T,E)

listen awem, irlpekernem
listen (respect language) kwarrernem
listen to someone, pay attention akangkwerrem (W,T), impen awem (E)
not listen when someone is talking to you menty awelhem

little akwek, akely (E)
really little akely-amperl (E), akwek-amperl (T,E), akwek-antyey (W), akwek-antywey (W,T)
(doing something) a little bit war
(do something) a little bit (respect language) wath anem (E)

little corella terekerr

live

living in a particular location or place ... -areny

live (in a place) ... anem[1], angerr-irrem[1]

live in a place (respect language) ... ayepel-irrem

lively ... ampwengamp, arwekar (W,T), atyep-atyep, irrngerney (E)

feel lively ... ampwengamp-irrem, irrngerney-irrem (E)

liven someone up ... iteth-ilem, irrngerney-ilem (E)

liver ... alem

emu liver ... ilep[2] (E)

living, alive ... iteth

lizard

black goanna ... pwer rrpwerl (W,T)

sand goanna ... arlewatyerr

type of goanna ... kalawerr (W,T)

black-headed monitor, freckled monitor ... alpangwerr (W)

blue-tongue ... lhwelk, ulhelk (T,E), ilpankwer (E), lwengkart[1] (T)

Burton's snake-lizard ... iparip (E)

canegrass dragon, blue-lined dragon ... arlanty, apengeleytanenh (E) (?)

central military dragon ... kwerleparr (W,T), tyalep (?)

central netted dragon ... irnar (W,T), kaperl (T,E), kelyaw

big male central netted dragon lizard ... arrpwayl (E)

dwarf bearded dragon ... kapert angerr (W,T), tyapantarr (W,T)

military dragon lizard ... nyarl (W,E)

types of dragon lizard ... angket-angket (E), apwet-apwet (E), perlap arlwelenh (W), perlap-areny (W), pwelkanty (T,E)

mountain devil, thorny devil ... arnkerrth (T,E), mernerr (W,T)

perentie ... tywenp, ilkwert (E)

pygmy desert monitor ... artep irrpent (E), irrpent (E), irrerlaly (E) (?)

pygmy mulga monitor ... ahert-ahert[2] (W), arin, arwangk (W,T)

ring-tailed dragon ... tekentyenarr (W) (?), ntekentyenarr (W) (?)

rough-tailed goanna, ridge-tailed monitor ... kerr-kerr (W,T), kirr-kirr

short-tailed pygmy monitor ... arwemay (?)

spiny-tailed monitor ... antyerr (E)

types of gecko ... akarntety-arntety (E), pelhel-iwenh-iwenh (E), rltimp-areny (E) (?)

types of skink ... ameng irrkwenh-irrkwenh, lyengkarr (W,T), ikwarr (E)

other types of lizard ... ahalyepweng (E), alhwerrp akely-akely (E), ankwang (W), arntekakarl (E), kentyentyelarr (T), rltimpat-arrweremarrwer (E), natyaker, tyapwert-apwert (E), tyentyentyelarr (W)

lock

lock something up ... marnt-ilem (W,T)

locust ... menyeynterl (E), tyarrerrey (T) (?)

log ... irlpart

a log of firewood ... rwang irlpart (W,T), ura iylpart (E)

loin cloth ... nak

small loin cloth ... pely (E)

lolly, sweet *(from English)* ... larl

lonely

lonely ... alharrp (W,T), alhwarrp (T,E), alharrp-alharrp (W,T), alhwarrp-alhwarrp (T,E), altarrp (W,T), altarrp-altarrp (W,T), arrakelakel (E)

feel lonely ... alharrp-irrem (W,T), alhwarrp-irrem (T,E), altarrp awelhem (W,T), altarrp-irrem (W,T), alther-irrem (T,E), apatem, irrar-irrem

feeling sadness, loneliness or homesickness ... irrar[2], alther (T,E)

make someone feel lonely or homesick ... irrarel anthem

long

long, tall ... alkey[1] (W,T), arlpenty

longish, a bit long or tall ... alkey-alkey (W,T), arlpenty-arlpenty

get taller or longer ... alkey-irrem (W,T), arlpenty-irrem

long (of hair) ... akwerl, kapert akwerl (W,T)

long, yearn

long for something ... alther-irrem (T,E), irrar-irrem

long time

continuing to do something for a long time ... aleth-antey

long way away ... arleng[1], arleng-arlenty (T,E)

long way away (respect language) ... arlewent (E)

long pussy-tails *(plant)* ... rlpwer-rlpwer

Long Range ... Arnmanapwenty

long-leaved corkwood ntyarleyarleng, ntywey (W,T), untyey (E)

look

look at something arem

look (respect language) arrep-ilem

look at each other arerrem

look at your reflection arelhem, tywerr-arelhem (W,T)

look for something nthwem (W,T), unthem (E), apalenthwem (W,T), apalunthem (T,E)

look round for somebody or something, look for someone who has gone away from you yarelhem (W), ywarelhem (T), uyarelhem (T,E)

look up for something, look upwards unyenem (E)

look at something from behind something ayternem (E)

look out of the corner of your eye annga intyemel arem

look while shading eyes with hand merlpengel arem (W,T)

look back, look back over shoulder angkep arem, angkep-athek arem, anngarem (W,T), artepeng arelhem (E), artepeng arem (E), anngarelhem

looking over shoulder all the time anngaremp-anngar

looking downwards annga kwenengeneng (T,E)

look something over, inspect something tywerr-arem (W,T)

look hard at someone twant arem (W,T)

stare into the distance arrampewelhem (E)

look around for something but not find it uyarem (T,E), yarem (W), ywarem (T), arltwarem (W,T)

look at something but leave it alone mentyel arem

looks *(appearance)* inngerr

look different, appear different arrpenh-irrem, ingwer-irrem (E)

look after

look after someone ararem (W,T), arntarnt-arem, kwety-arem, manty-manty-ilem (E), akarem, kwetyakw-ilem (T,E), mwerranty-ilem

look after yourself arntarnt-arelhem, arelhem

'Look at that!'

exclamation of surprise yakerray (W,T)

'Look out!' alay[2] (W,E), pwertay (E)

loose alpwely, ararlk, artaly-artaly (T,E), tyek (E)

hanging loosely alyemp-alyemp[1]

something loose and baggy parlkw, parlkw-parlkw

able to move easily althekalth

get loose tyek-irrem (E)

go loose or slack, become baggy parlkw-parlkw-irrem (E)

loosen something ararlk-ilem, tyek-ilem (E)

loosen and break something antyakem

lose

lose something aparlp-ilem

lose a family member (become bereaved) aparlp-ilem

get lost apant-irrem, aparlp-irrem, aperrpert-irrem, therrert-irrem (E), ywerrem, uyerrem (E)

lots of *(something)* anengk[1] (W,T), atningk (E), angerr[1], alhirrel (E), arnkengeny (E)

lots of different ones, all over the place arrpethet (W,T), arrpanenh (E), apawerr (E)

loud arrpwarnt (T,E)

loud talker, 'big mouth' arremwar-mwar

make a loud noise (such as the sound made by cicadas) arreyeng-arrey-irrem (W,T)

louse anya[2] (W,T), anyang (W,T), arrem (T,E), ilka[2] (T,E)

type of big louse anepwart

type of louse (found in clothes) pweltak

type of white louse (found in body hair and clothes) petherr (W,T), pitherr (E)

louse eggs anyang kwart (W,T)

love

fall in love with (someone), love someone ahenty-anem, ahenty-irrem, ilkelhem

be pleased or excited anyerrkem

feel compassion, be generous atham-irrem

lover ahenty-penh (W,T), anew, mert (W,T), meyt (T,E), mert-mert (W,T), meyt-meyt (T,E)

become sweethearts, become boyfriends/ girlfriends ..... mert-mert mpwarem (W,T), meyt-meyt mpwarem (E), mert-mert-ilerrem (W,T), meyt-meyt-ilerrem (E), mert-mert-irrem (W,T), meyt-meyt-irrem (E)
take someone off to become your lover ..... mpwenyel angem, mpwenyel inem
go off to become lovers ..... mpweny alhem

love song ..... ilpenty, irrenyankwerl (W)

lovely ..... alyerr (W), ingkety, mekelarey (W,T), -malangk
lovely (of a person) ..... alyerremwey
lovely boy, a 'champion' ..... awerr-malangk (T,E)

lower
bottom, base ..... kweneng

lucky
lucky feeling (especially for hunting) ..... inngeny, inngeny-inngeny
have a lucky or successful feeling, especially for hunting ..... inngeny-irrem

lukarrara *(grass)* ..... akwetelh (E), taty-taty[1]

lump
lump of dirt ..... tanty
lump of something (e.g. seed, spinifex resin, tobacco or ear wax) ..... kelh
lump of spinifex resin ..... anker ikelh (E), tyalangk kelh (W,T)
lump of tobacco ..... ngkwerlp kelh, warn (E), ngkwerlp ampeng (W)
lump or gall on a tree ..... amern-amern (E), ankerl, mwenth (E)
covered in knots or lumps ..... ankerl-ankerl
turn into a lump ..... pwert-irrem (W,T), purt-irrem (E)
make something into a lump ..... pwert-ilem (W,T), purt-ilem (E)
lumpy ..... lyek-lyek, mwenth-mwenth (E)
go lumpy ..... lyek-lyek-irrem, rtety-rtety-irrem

lunchtime ..... irntar (W,T), irntarel (W,T)

lungs ..... arrelty[1] (T,E), arrelyarn (W,T), arreltyarn (T)

Luritja
language or person ..... Alweraty

lush growth ..... angwarlp (T,E), yar-yar (E)
lush, green (after being dry) ..... anyemwerr

lust
lust after someone ..... alherrem[2] (W,T), alhirrem

Lutheran ..... Lweterreyn

lymph nodes
at the top of the thighs ..... kwarlk (W) (?)
at the top of the thighs and under the arms ..... kwart-kwart

Mm

mad
insane, crazy ..... arert, arwengk (T,E)
a bit mad ..... arert-arert, arwengk-arwengk (T,E)
go mad or crazy, be driven mad ..... arert-irrem, arwengk-irrem (T,E), akeleraperap-irrem (E), raperap-irrem (W)
go a bit mad ..... rrwem-rrwem-irrem (W,T), urrem-urrem-irrem (T,E)
go a bit mad or crazy ..... arert-arert-irrem, arwengk-arwengk-irrem (T,E)
make someone go mad or crazy ..... arert-ilem, arwengk-ilem (T,E)

Magellanic Clouds ..... Antyekanty-atherr (E), Arrenty-atherr (E)

maggot ..... irnnga (W,T), irnngang (W,T), tyerr (T,E)

magic
use supernatural powers or magic on someone ..... arrilem, arrilenty-ilem (T,E)

magpie ..... arrpwer

magpie-lark ..... rtey-rtey, ntwerleperl (W), rtwerleperl (W,T), kwatyarl rtey-rtey

main thing ..... tyeperr

Major Mitchell's cockatoo ..... angkwen
crest ..... akenty (W,T), akeynt (E)

make
make something ..... mpwarem
make something happen to yourself, make yourself a certain way ..... mpwarelhem
make someone or something better ..... mwerr-ilem, iteth-ilem
make something really well (especially said of wooden tools) ..... anyemp unhem (E)
make someone do something ..... twernem, uternem (E)

make amends ..... nyerr rrpwarelhem (W,T), nyerr urrparelhem (E), nyerr iparelhem (E)

make up
make friends (after an argument) … pelty-ilem

male *(of a species)* … rrwey (W,T), urrey (T,E)
a young male (especially kangaroo) … artar

mallee
blue mallee … alhelp (W,T)

malleefowl … anwematy (W)

man
any man, including non-Aboriginal men … artwa, artwang (W,T), atey (E), rrwey (W,T), urrey (T,E)
initiated man … artwa, artwang (W,T)
man (respect language) … alyakw, antewarety, arlwety-penh (W,T), arlwety[2] (W,T)
man (bereavement term) … ker-henh (W)
old man … artwa aywang (W,T), artwang aywang (W,T), artwampw (E), artwang ampwang (W,T)
old man (from English) … wernman
young man, young fellow … anthety (E), artwang akwek (T), artwa akwek (E), artwang akwerrk (W,T), artwang anthety (W,T), artwa anthety (E)
group of men travelling around in preparation for particular ceremonies … tyelkath (W), tyelkaty (T)
men's camp … arnkenty
who lives in the single-men's camp … arnkenty-areny
ceremonial camp (for young men) … akew (W,T), akiw (E)
men's ceremonial business, serious business … artart[2] (W,T)
young man who is in seclusion in the bush after initiation (young man) ceremony … arwekert
young man who has just been through initiation (young man) ceremony … arleyarr, amarleyarr (W)
playing at being men … artwengartw

mange
mange, mangy … arrkenty[1] (T), irrkenty (W), altelhey (W,T), iltelhey (T,E)
mange (from English) … mentyey (W,T)

mantis … antyekanty (T,E), kapert atwenh (W,T), kapert atwenh-atwenh (W,T)

many … anengk[1] (W,T), atningk (E), angerr[1], arwenth, map, arnkengeny (E), alhirrel (E)
many, a lot (respect language) … makwerl (E)
many times … angerr-ingar, map-ingar (W,T)
this/that many (while showing how many) … alakenty

march fly … urreylk (E)

marijuana *(from English)* … kanty[2]

mark
mark, design … arlkeny, mpaty[1]
grooved markings on boomerangs, wooden dishes or shields … irraker
mark or track (sometimes from the Dreaming) … imperrty (W)
make a design or mark on something … arlkeny arrernem, arlkeny-wem, ingkwernem (T,E),
make grooves on dishes, shields or boomerangs … irraker-ilem, irraker-wem
make a mark to show where you have gone … ahimperr-wem (E), arlkeny-wem, mpaty-ilem (W,T), thwerremp-irrem (T,E) (?)
put a mark on self … ingkwernelhem (T,E)

marrow … inpinp (E)

marry
married … arlwenth (E), iteng[1] (E)
married (from English) … marrert
get married, be married … iteng-irrem (E), marrert-irrem, arlwenth-irrem (E), merangk anem (E)
married couple … anewart, anewart atherr, arlwenth (E)
married couple (respect language) … mwarlenth
married couple (said by a woman of her daughter and her husband) … ngwarr-nheng atherr (T,E)
married couple in opposite generation moiety … aperlenheng atherr
married couple in same generation moiety … arrkar-nheng atherr
married person's camp … mparnt, mer iteng-areny (E)
married person's camp (respect language) … rrwarlp[2] (W)
marry the 'wrong' way … ankerl-irrem (W,T)

someone who has married the 'wrong' way .... anetywek (W), tyerrk (W,T), iyterrk (E), akengentyeny (E), alem atherrk-atherrk (T,E), alem iyterrk-iyterrk (T,E), annga atherrk-atherrk, ankerl, ankerl-ankerl, ankerl angerr (W), ankerlewarr, atna ankerl-ankerl (E), atna iyterrk-iyterrk (E)
woman who doesn't want to get married or go with a man .... anngarenty (W,T)
Mars .... Alkerreylp (E)
martin
fairy martin .... tyerremper (E)
mash
mash certain types of bush fruits up with water .... ntywerrkem, untyerr anyenem (E)
mash something up .... ipelhip-ilem (E)
masked woodswallow .... perrpantywen (W,T), perrpantywel (E)
mass
mass of something (e.g. seed, spinifex resin, tobacco or ear wax) .... kelh
massage
use healing massage .... angkwerr-wem, parr-iwem (E)
mat
bed, blanket .... antyam
mat spurge *(plant)* .... amwekel-amwekel[1] (E), amwekel (E), kwep-kwep[1], merterr[1], merterr-merterr (W,T)
matches .... lwethep, rwa (W,T), rwang (W,T), ura (T,E)
mate
friend, age-mate .... atyew, pelty
mate (from English) .... mert (W,T), meyt (T,E)
material
that hasn't been sewn ..... alparr[2]
matted *(go to 'knotted')*
mature *(of a person)* .... angerr[1]
Mau Hills .... Maw
maybe .... apek, thweng (T), ithweng (E)
that might be so .... yapek
me .... ayeng, ayenh, ayengenh (W,T)
for me, to me, at me, on me .... atyeng
mean, tough .... anhelhenty, anngernt (T,E), rlterrk

meat .... ker, anwenth, ker tyelk, tyelk
meat (respect language) ... tyety (E), tyety-ayerr (E)
meat (baby talk) .... key (T), nyany[1], tyety (E)
fatty meat .... anthetyingk (T,E)
meat from the back of an animal .... ker artep, rrpwa (W,T), rrpwang (W,T)
really fatty meat (just kangaroo, bullock) ... weyang (E)
tasteless meat .... ker tyekert (T,E)
meaty bone or bone with marrow .... ker ngkwern[1]
heap or load of cooked meat (especially kangaroo) .... thalh (W,T)
solid bits of meat and sinew left when cooked fat has been poured off ... arlerrk (E)
the smell of meat cooking .... parntewelyewely (W,T)
the sound of meat cooking .... lyely-lyely (W,T), lyely-lyely-lyely (W)
meat juice .... awerrp[1], ker awerrp, akarr (T,E) (?)
meat ant .... arlkerrk[1] (T,E)
medicine
traditional medicine .... awely, awely anter
blood used by men as a medicine .... akwepenh (T,E)
blood used by women for healing .... amarr
medicinal substance made by spinifex ants ..... tyerremp (T,E)
meet
meet together .... anyent-irrem, akarr-irrem (T,E), arraw-irrem
meet someone .... rlwatwem (W), urlatwem (E), arerrem
go and meet someone who is coming .... arnek-arnarem, arnek-irrem
meet up with someone, go over to someone .... atwarem
meet someone halfway .... rlkwerr arerrem (W,T)
melon
native melon .... lkwart (W,T), ilkwart, ulkart (T,E), lkwart-lkwart (W,T) (SP), ilkwart-ilkwart (T,E) (SP)
pie-melon .... malan (T,E), payemalan
type of melon .... tampewern (W,T)
melt .... arrwelth-irrem (E), irrngwirrem (E), kwaty-irrem (W,T), rew-irrem

melt something .... irrngwilem (E), rew-ilem, arrwelth-ilem (E)

memory

having a good memory .... wetyerretyerr[2] (W), weretyerretyerr (W,T)

remember about someone or something .... irlpangkem, iterlarem

lose memory .... iterleng-iterl-irrem (W)

mend

something .... mpwarem, pwety-ilem (T), pwetyelh-ilem (T), pweyt-ilem (E), pweytelh-ilem (E)

mess

a bit dirty, grubby or messy .... aternng-aternng

messy .... altelhey (W,T), iltelhey (T,E), aternng, nywet-nywet[2] (T)

make a mess of something .... irrelywekelywek-ilem (E), irranyent-iwem (E)

mess up tracks by walking all over the place . atnalth-ilem (E)

message .... angka[1] (E), angkety, ayey (W,T), rrpwey (W,T), urrpey (T,E), ulypma (E)

messenger .... rrpwey (W,T), urrpey (T,E)

send a message .... angka ilanthem (E), angkety ilanthem (W,T), ulypma ilanthem (E)

take a message to someone .... rrpwey alhem (W,T), urrpey alhem (T,E)

metal chisel .... kantyengarr (W,T), kanyengarr (E)

metamorphose

turn into a moth or butterfly .... akarternem (W,T), irrarl-irrem, rlwarlp-irrem (W,T), urlaylp-irrem (E), ngkekern-irrem (W,T)

miaow *(cats)* .... arrangkem

midday .... aherrk akern, aherrk angerr, aherrk mpep (E), arlta mpep (E), irntar (W,T), irntarel (W,T), twern angerr (W,T), twern mpep (W,T), utern mpep (E)

middle

in the middle .... mpep, rlkwerr

middle of something .... mparnt

somewhere in the middle .. rlkwerr-rlkwerr

centre part of something .. anert

middle of the night .... ingwa mpep (E), kweny lpwararr (T), kweny rlkwerr (W,T), kweny rlkwerrel (W,T)

middle of summer .... twern mparnt, utern mparnt (E)

middle of winter .... alhwerrp mparnt

middle child or children .. mpep-iperr (E), mpep-penh, mpepengel (E), rlkwerr-penh (W,T), rlkwerr-pwenh (W), rlkwerramerrenty (W,T), iylkwerramerrenty (E)

get caught in the middle of something .... mpepel-irrem (E), mpwepel-irrem (T)

put someone or something in the middle of or in between other things .... mpepek-ilem (E), mpwepek-ilem (T)

middle-aged .... angerrety-iteng (E), ampwa, ampwang (W,T)

midnight .... kweny rlkwerrel (W,T), ingwa mpep (E), kweny lpwararr (T), kweny rlkwerr (W,T)

might, maybe .... apek

military dragon lizard .... nyarl (W,E)

milk .... ama (W), paty (W,T), werlaty (T,E)

milk (from English) .... merlk (T)

milk gut .... lyep-lyep, iltyarrng (W,T)

milk vine .... amwekel-amwekel[1] (E), amwekel (E), merterr[1], merterr-merterr (W,T), kwep-kwep[1]

Milky Way .... Atwarlk (W), Lpwararr (W,T), Mewarr (W), Miwerr (T,E), Imiwerr (E)

mill around .... arraw-irrem

mimosa bush .... irnker (W,T), alekw (E)

mind

mind, brains .... kampely[1] (W,T), akwerrng (T,E), akakwerrng (E)

mind *(look after)*

mind someone or something .... arntarnt-arem, akarem

mine, my .... atyengenh, atyeng-henh (W,T), atyehenh (W,T), atyenh

miner *(bird)*

yellow-throated miner ..... impaymp (E)

minister

priest .... ngkart, kalty-anthenh-anthenh

be ordained as a minister .. ngkart-irrem

mint bush .... ngkwern rnter-rnter (W,T), amwer (E)

mirage .... angent[1] (T,E), ilewerr, merawarr (W,T), ulewerr (E)

mirror *(from English)* .... kelath

misbehave .... anngernt-irrem (T,E), ltyernt-irrem (W,T)

miss
miss when throwing something .... athem-wem (E), arrthem-wem (E)
miss when trying to hit something .... atengkel atwem (E), athem atwem (E), arrthem atwem (E)
miss when trying to spear something .... atengkel atanthem (E), athem rnternem (E), athem atanthem (E)
miss something when trying to spear or shoot it . anerrk-ilem (W)
missing target animal when hunting .... urrpernp (E)
miss, pine for
miss someone or something .... alther-irrem (T,E)
miss out
on share of something ..... arrarem
missing
go missing .... ywerrem, uyerrem (E)
missionary .... ngkart
mistake
mistakenly .... apal[2], apant (W,T)
not knowing what you are doing .... apalekalek
give something to someone by mistake .... apantel anthem (W,T)
hit someone or something by mistake .... aperrpert-ilem (W,T), amenty-ilem (T,E)
throw something mistakenly or in the wrong direction .... apal-wem
mistletoe
types of mistletoe .... atyankern, pweralhem (E), amar, ngartangkern (W), ngkwerrm
grub found on .... akweltyayt (E), arraltyaltyen (E), arraltyalty (T,E)
pale-leaf mistletoe .... peketyalkwarr (T,E)
mix
mix or stir things together .... anyentelh-ilem, pwety-ilem (T), pwetyelh-ilem (T), pweyt-ilem (E), pweytelh-ilem (E), iytan-ilem (E)
mix things together .... intwerelh-ilem (T,E)
mix tobacco with ashes ... arek-wem (W,T), arrtyem (E)
moan .... ampangkem (T,E), apangkem (W,T), arlkwatelhem (W,T), kwatem, anpelhem (E)
mob, group
lots of (something) .... anengk[1] (W,T), atningk (E), angerr[1], arwenth, map, alhirrel (E), arnkengeny (E)
mock
tease or mock someone .... arrampewem[1]
modern .... lyeteny
moiety *(see also Appendix 2)*
we (belonging to same patrimoiety) .... ilernak-akey, anakerr-akey (T,E), anwern-akey (T), anwernakerr-akey (W), ilak-akey (E), ilern-ingkerr-akey (W,T)
they (people in opposite patrimoiety) .... alak-akey, inakerr-akey, malyanwek (W,T)
you (in opposite patrimoiety to me or us) .. mpwelak-akey
country associated with same patrimoiety as speaker, but other patricouple .... urrer-ampeny (W), urrerek-thayt (W,T)
people in the same generation moiety .... kweyekar
people in the opposite generation moiety .... nywerrp
behave in a teasing or joking way with people in opposite generation moiety .... urrayerr-irrem (T,E), rrwayerr-irrem (T)
we (in same generation moiety) .... anantherr-apakwey, anwernanth-apakwey (E), anwernantherr-apakwey (E), ilernanth-apakwey (T,E)
you (in opposite generation moiety) .... arrantherr-apakwey (E)
they (in opposite generation moiety) .... alanthapakwey
they (in opposite matrimoiety) .... kwernt[2] (W,T), kwernt-thayt (W,T)
moist *(of food)* .... apely
money *(from English)* ...... man, maney, tal
small change, coins .... apwert ngkwelty, ngkwelty
money (respect language) .. ngkwelty-ayerr (E)
ten dollar note .... atherrk-atherrk (T,E), nwertal (T)
twenty dollar note .... rnter-rnter
fifty dollar note .... arlewatyerr, karntewarr (SP)
one hundred dollar note .. atherrk-atherrk (T,E)
money bag
(from English) .... pewaty

monitor
black-headed monitor ..... alpangwerr (W), altywekerr
Gould's goanna, sand monitor ..... arlewatyerr
pygmy mulga monitor ..... ahert-ahert[2] (W), arin, arwangk (W,T)
ridge-tailed monitor ..... kerr-kerr (W,T), kirr-kirr
spiny-tailed monitor ..... antyerr (E)
monster ..... arrenty
monster (respect language) ..... alharrenty
monster (said to frighten children) ..... kwerrk-kwerrk[2] (E)
water-snake monster ..... kwelay, akwerteyteng (E), kwelernarr (E)
type of monster ..... pangkelang (W)
month
'moon' ..... anyenty (T,E)
one month ..... anyenty anyent (T,E)
two months ..... anyenty atherr (T,E)
mood
be in a bad mood ..... kewarr-irrem (W,T), akiwarr-irrem (T,E)
moon ..... anyenty (T,E), atay[1] (W,T)
moon (respect language) ..... alkent (E)
full moon ..... anyenty tamp (T,E), atarlanenty, atarlepwenty (E), atay angerrety (W,T), anyenty anert angerr (E)
new moon ..... anyenty akwerrk (T,E), anyenty ngkarlt (E), atay akwek (W,T), atay akwerrk (W,T), atay ampwang (W,T), ngkarlt (E), tyeylp (E)
rise (moon) ..... aherlkenty alhem
wane (moon) ..... aherrk parrk-irrem (W,T), atay parrk-irrem (W,T)
moonlight ..... anyenty (T,E), parrty
in the moonlight ..... anyentyel (T,E), parrtyel
more
(doing something)
some more ..... aweth
make a lot, make bigger, make more, ... anengk-ilem (W,T), atningk-ilem (E), angerr-ilem
morning
early in the morning ..... aherlkenty, aherlkentyel, ingwelem (T,E), ney-ney (T,E), ngwenpel (E), ingwepenh (E)
very early in the morning ..... aherlkenty-aherlkenty
morning glory
native morning glory ..... atywert-atywert (E), rtwatyert (W,T), tatyetarr

Morning Star ..... Anthelper (W,T), Arwenpeng (E), Kwerraly Angerr, Kwerraly Rltwa (W), Kwerraly Urlta (T,E)
mosquito ..... aheny (E), angeylk (E), kewenyeweny (W), weny
Mosquito Bore ..... lylenty
moth ..... antelyapelyap, intelyapelyap (E)
mother ..... amey
mother (from English) ..... math
mother (respect language) ..... artakw
baby talk (from English) ..... mam
mother-in-law
man's mother-in-law ..... mey-mey[1], mwer, rtwalty, urtalty (E), ateyarrp
senior son-in-law or mother-in-law ..... ampweyampw, ampeyamp
woman's mother-in-law .. anherr
woman's mother-in-law (baby talk) ..... nhey-nhey (E)
become mother-in-law/ son-in-law for someone ... urtalty-irrem (E)
man's mother-in-law's camp ..... ahileng (T,E), rrwarlp[2] (W), rwarlp
motionless ..... amarn
be immobile or 'rooted' to the spot ..... amarn-irrem
motorcar ..... ararrarlkanty (W)
car (from English) ..... mwetekay, mwetek
mound
of earth made by animal such as goanna or rabbit .. arlerlp[1] (E), rrngwa (W,T), rrngwang (W,T), irrngwa (T,E)
mount
something such as a car, horse or bicycle ..... antyem
Mt Swan ..... Arrngernangker
mountain ..... apwert, irnta (W,T), irntang (W,T)
mountain top ..... apwert akern, apwert artep (T,E)
mountain devil ..... arnkerrth (T,E), mernerr (W,T), nywerr (W,T)
mountain primrose ..... inpay-inpay (W,T)
mourn *(go to 'sorry business')*
mouse
desert mouse ..... mpweny iytarr-iytarr (E), mpwenyerlp (E) (?)
fat-tailed antechinus ..... alepey (E) (?)
type of marsupial mouse ..... tyelalwernenh (W,T)

types of .... alwepay (W,T), ilkwenng (E), thakey[2] (W,T), thakwer (T,E), aherraty-anywertangey (E)

moustache .... arralt, pentyengeyengey (E)

mouth .... arra, arrakert

mouth (respect language) .. ameng ulpma (E)

roof of the mouth .... arrakert merrng (E)

mouth (covered with something) .... arrelthenp-lthenp, lthenp-lthenp

open your mouth wide ..... arralkem

make someone or something open its mouth .... arralkelh-ilem

move

move around, move yourself .... angelhem

move away .... rntwarr-irrem, arleng-irrem (T,E)

move closer to something .. angath-irrem

move towards (the speaker) .... ularr-irrem (E)

move over .... anam-irrem[1], arnang-irrem, rntwarr-irrem

move sideways .... uremeny-irrem (E)

move to another place ..... aleth-irrem, alethek-irrem (T,E)

move to the other side of something .... anwenger-irrem (E), arrwengak-irrem

not wanting to move from a place .... kely-kely-irrem (W,T)

be able to move easily ..... althekalth-irrem

move someone or something out of the way .... anam-ilem, anamelh-ilem, arnang-ilem[2], arnangelh-ilem, rntwarr-ilem

move something closer .... angath-ilem

move something backwards and forwards .. angelh-angelh-ilem, arrew-arrew-ilem (T,E)

make something move ..... tyek-tyek-ilem[2] (W)

Mt Esther .... Alhather

Mt Hay .... Urapenty, Rwapenty

Mt Leichhardt .... Arnka, Arnkang

Mt Solitary .... Artar

mucus

nasal mucus .... inkwerr (E)

mud .... tert, urta (E), ahern ata (E), antha[1] (E), anthwerrng (W,T), anthurrng (E), ata[1] (E)

make mud cakes (children) .... atilem (E)

muddy

dirty water .... lpwert (W,T), ulpert (T,E), kwaty lpwert (W,T), kwaty ulpert (E), alhwerrk (E)

get dirty or muddy (water) .... lpwert-irrem (W,T), ulpert-irrem (T,E), alhwerrk-irrem (E)

make water muddy or dirty .... alhwerrk-ilem (E), lpwert-ilem (W,T), lpwertelh-ilem (W,T), ulpert-ilem (T,E), ulpertelh-ilem (T,E), tanty-ilem

mudlark .... rtey-rtey, ntwerleperl (W), rtwerleperl (W,T), kwatyarl rtey-rtey

mulga .... artety

young mulga trees .... artety akwerrk

flower of .... nwathet (W), nathat (T), utnathat (T,E)

honeydew .... arlperl, artetyaywerrk (W)

type of grub found on mulga .... kepartart, artetyayt (E)

resin from .... alkeramp

mulga scrub .... artety nwanth (W,T), artety unanth (T,E)

hill mulga .... arleth-arleth[1] (T,E)

grub from hill mulga ...... arleth-arleth[1] (T,E), arlethayerr (E)

type of .... arlpelhart, tyenperarr

mulga apple .... ataltyakwerl, atantyakwerl (W,T)

bitter-tasting coating on mulga apple .... tepwerl (E), pwarr (T,E)

mulga bean .... werrp (E)

mulga fuchsia .... kwenkart (E)

mulga native currant ...... anngey-anngey, antenh-antenh (E), anwengk-anwengk (E), ngkwernateylp (E), ngkwernelyerr

mulga parrot .... urimpering (E), rempereng (W) (?)

mulga snake .... alhingk (E), arreperlp (W,T), atetherr arlkwenh, ikwelengk (T,E), kantharlkw (W,E), tyamparl (T)

mulgara .... artekw (W,E) (?), artikw (E) (?), ampwert (E) (?)

mulla-mulla *(see 'lamb's tails')*

multiply

get more numerous .... anengk-irrem (W,T), atningk-irrem (E)

mulyati *(plant)* .... uneynt (E)

munch
on something — arrerlpem (W,T), arreylpem (E), karlkwem
mungilypa *(plant)* — karnkw (W,T)
munyeroo — akat, iylaw (E)
murder
murder someone — atwem
murderer — merrenty (W), merreynt (E)
music sticks — twererr
mustard bush — angerak-angerak (W)
muster — arlwelem (W,T), arlwilem (E)
mute — akerter
my, mine — atyenh, atyengenh, atyeng-henh (W,T), atyehenh (W,T),
my (of body parts) — ayeng
my family or relation — atyeng-artwey, atyeng arneng
my relation — +aty[1]
myself
do something (for, by) myself — tyarl (W,T)

Nn

nail
fingernails — ingkelthel, tywemar (W,T), iltyang tywemar (W,T)
toenails — tywemar (W,T), ingkelthel, ingka ingkelthel, ingkang ingkelthel (W,T), ingkang tywemar (W,T)
naked — aketh
nalgoo *(see 'bush onion')*
name — arreny (W,T), arreyn (E), ina[2] (E)
name something — anewem[1] (W,T), inewem (T,E), arreny anthem (W,T), arreyn anthem (E), arreny arrernem (W,T), arreyn arrernem (E)
say each other's names — anewerrem (W), inewerrem (T,E)
skin name, subsection name (general term) — ikwa (T,E), ikwang (T)
substitute name for name of a person or thing whose name cannot be used due to a death of a person with that name — kwementyay, kwenman, kwemarn
nankeen kestrel — anthep-anthep (E), lyentyelyeng, ulpmerr-atwenh (E), warakeparleparl (W,T)
nape of neck — ntywa (W,T), ntywang (W,T), untya (E)
Napperby community — Alherramp
narrow — pwarn, tyert (T,E)
get narrow or tight — pwarn-irrem, tyert-irrem (T,E)
narrow-leaf bumble — angerterrk (E), iwerrarrkw (W,E)
narrow-leaved goodenia — unpay (E), inpay (T)
narrow-leaved native currant — antenh-antenh (E), anwengk-anwengk (E), ngkwernateylp (E), ngkwernelyerr, anngey-anngey (SP)
nasal sound — alhang rtwerlp (W)
nasty — anhelhenty
native bee *(go to 'sugarbag')*
native cat — atyelp, atyet[2] (E)
native cotton — tyetep (W,T)
native cucumber — lkwart (W,T), ilkwart, ulkart (T,E), lkwart-lkwart (W,T) (SP), ilkwart-ilkwart (T,E) (SP)
native currant — ahakey, antyern angerr (T), arrarntenh (E), artapaly (E)
flower of — ilkwa[1] (T,E), ilkwang (W)
green unripe fruit — anthwerrk[1] (T,E), irnta (W,T), irntang (W,T)
newly ripened fruit — alwernp (W), akenp (T,E)
fruit when red in colour — rwekarlp (E)
fruit that has fallen to the ground — unemarnt (E), atnamp (E)
dry fruit — ntewerrk (T,E), ntyenp
go dry (of fruit) — ntyenp-irrem
respectful word for fruit — angayel
to flower — ilkwenkem (E)
mulga native currant, narrow-leaved native currant — antenh-antenh (E), anwengk-anwengk (E)
native currant (narrow leaved variety) — yernt
Native Gap — Arwerlt Atwaty
native gooseberry — lkwart (W,T), ilkwart, ulkart (T,E), lkwart-lkwart (W,T) (SP), ilkwart-ilkwart (T,E) (SP)
native hen
black-tailed native-hen — angkeparr (W,T), karlayteng-ayteng (E), kart-irrkwely-irrkwely (W,T), karl-irrkwely-irrkwely (T,E), narremantyerr (W,T), lhekethatethat (E) (?), ngkwern rnter-rnter (W,T)
native honey *(go to 'sugarbag')*
native millet — altywart
native oat grass — lyenty

grub from ... lyentyatayerr (E) (SP)
native peach ... mangart[1], mwerlp
native pine ... amikw[1] (E), anngart (W), akngart (W,T), rlwek (W,T), iylwek (E)
native tobacco *(go to 'tobacco')*
native tomato ... alperrantyey, ararnt (W,T), rrwarlp[1] (T), arrwarlp (E), urrarlp (E), rtwengkerr (W,T)
native truffle ... akwerrerteth (E), irrkwenng (T,E), pwerlantar (T), pwelerntar (W,T)
native walnut ... marrawaty (T,E)
native willow ... anawert, welterr (E)
naughty ... anhelhenty, anngernt (T,E), ltyernt (W,T)
be naughty ... anngernt-irrem (T,E), ltyernt-irrem (W,T)
nauseating ... alyelk-alyelk, alyew-alyew (E), antewek-antew (T), kaly-kaly[2] (W,T)
feel nauseous or sick ... alyelk-irrem, antyernem[1] (W,T)
make someone feel sick or nauseated ... kaly-kaly-ilem (W,T)
navel, belly button ... metyeletyel (W,T), tyelepelep
near ... arrer (T,E), arrer-antey (T,E), arrerenty (E), itwa, itwang (W,T), angath
neck
back of neck ... ilperl-ilperl (E), tarnng (W,T), ternng (E), akerlak (E)
neck bone, lower part of the back of neck ... ntyarrkwer (W,T), untyarrkwer (E)
break someone's neck ... ternng ultakem (E)
neckband
made of hairstring ... ahenty-henh (W,T), ahenty-kenh (E), ahentyel-intenh (W,T), itepenh (E)
necklace *(from English)* ... nekeleth
nectar or sap ... akamp (W,T), akampw (E)
needle bush, needlewood ... ilpey, ilpey-ilpey (E), rrkwalty (W,T)
neglected ... alhengkey, ntweth-ntweth (W,T), intweth-intweth (E)
negotiate a dispute ... arlperrepwenty angkem
nephew
person's brother's child ... aler, aler-aler, arrarn-penh (W,T), arrwert-penh (E)
person's sister's child ... ampa, ampaty-ampaty, alem-penh, anert-penh, rnwepenh (W,T), irnwepenh (E)
younger brother's child ... anawerr
younger brother's child (baby talk) ... anawerr-anawerr
great-nephew (brother's daughter's child) ... artartey (E), atyemey, rtartart
great-nephew (brother's son's child) ... arreng
great-nephew (sister's daughter's child) ... menh-menh (W,T), nyany[2], ipmenh (E)
great-nephew, a person's sister's son's child ... aperl
nest
a nest ... alhweng, antywa, antywang (W,T), atharlkw (E)
a nest in a burrow ... antyarlkw (E) (?)
hive made by native bees ... arwengalker, rltwamp (W,T), urltamp (T)
nest made on top of the ground from grass or spinifex ... tek (E)
nest of the itchy grub ... ingeth (T,E)
'Never mind' ... menty
new ... lyeteny
flash, brand new ... arlkarl[2]
fresh place ... mpankeny (W,T), mpwankeny
New Holland rattlepod ... arrematy rltey-rltey (T,E), rltey-rltey (E)
new moon ... anyenty akwerrk (T,E), atay akwerrk (W,T), ngkarlt (E)
New Well ... Rlpwarraty
newborn baby ... rlternt (E), ampa rlternt (E), ampelyerrk, arathap, arlkarl[2], iylker (E)
news ... ayey (W,T), rrpwey (W,T), urrpey (T,E)
Ngalurbindi Hills ... Alwerrpent, Ngarlwerrpernt
nice ... mwerr, mwerr angerr (W,T), mwerr-angker (E), alyerr (W), anyemwerr, ingkety, mekelarey (W,T),
niece
person's brother's child ... aler, aler-aler, arrarn-penh (W,T), arrwert-penh (E)
person's sister's child ... alem-penh, ampa, ampaty-ampaty, anert-penh, rnwepenh (W,T), irnwepenh (E)
younger brother's child ... anawerr
younger brother's child (baby talk) ... anawerr-anawerr
great-niece (brother's daughter's child) ... artartey (E), atyemey, rtartart

great-niece (brother's son's child) ... arreng
great-niece (sister's son's child) ... aperl
great-niece (sister's daughter's child) ... menh-menh (W,T), nyany[2], ipmenh (E)

night ... ingwa (T,E), kweny[1] (W,T)
become night, get dark ... kweny-irrem (W,T), ingwirrem (T,E)
middle of the night ... ingwa mpep (E), kweny lpwararr (T), kweny rlkwerr (W,T), kweny rlkwerrel (W,T)
in the night, all through the night ... ingwatentyel (T,E)

nightjar
Australian owlet nightjar .. arrthwarrthw (E)
spotted nightjar ... akwet-akwet, angkertakwertak (W,T)

nightmare ... altyerr-altyerr, anengkerr-anengkerr (W,T)
have a bad dream or nightmare ... altyerr-altyerr arem, anengkerr-anengkerr arem (W,T)

Nintabrinna Bore ... lnernt irrpenh, Nernterrpenh

nipple ... paty alha (W,T), werlaty alha (T,E)

nits ... anyang kwart (W,T), anya[2] (W,T), anyang (W,T), arrem (T,E)

no
in answer to a question or a request ... arrangkw, itya (W,T)
no, nothing (respect language) ... arremangkw (E)
say 'no' (from English) ... new-irrem

no good ... anety (W,T), kwern (W,T), akeng (T,E), alkwemp, amwa[2] (E)

nod
nod head in agreement (or disagreement) ... tyek-tyek-irrem (W,T), akak-atwem[2] (E), akek-atwem (E)
nod off to sleep ... rlwank anyem (E)

noise
loud noise ... aywerr angerr
noise of footsteps, thumping or thudding noise ... lthap-lthap, rltap-rltap (W), ahenty-ahenty[2] (W,T)
noise of lots of people talking, buzz, hubbub ... alyalk-alyalk (T)

noisily ... arerrth-arerrth (T,E), nenty-nenty (T,E), nwenty-nwenty (W,T), aywerrty-aywerrty (E), arrernt-arrernt (W,T), arrpwarnt (T,E), arweketherwek (W,T), urekethwerek (E)
(of animals) make their usual noise ... angkem
make a loud noise ... arrertewarrert-irrem (W,T), arrpwarnt angkem (T,E)
make a noise ... alyerrem, arrernt-arrernt-irrem (W,T)
make a noise, interrupt ... ulpertelh-ilem (T,E)
make a thumping or thudding noise ... ahenty-ahenty-irrem (W,T), atemart angkem (E)
make a thudding noise (kangaroo) ... anerlpem
make a whirring, whooshing or rumbling noise ... aywerr angkem
make a noise with the lips to indicate presence of certain kin (men) ... pwernkem[1] (W)

non-Aboriginal ... kartey (W), arlter, tywelker, alhernter
non-Aboriginal woman (from English) ... metheth

none ... itya (W,T), arrangkw

Normanton box ... alhelp (W,T), alywelp
lerp from Normanton box ... yerrekeyerr (T,E)

north ... ayerrer, ayerrel-penh (E), aywerrel-penh (E)
north (respect language) .. aywelernety (W), aywelerneyt (E), aywelern (E), aywelern-athek (E)
due north ... ayerrer arraty
from the north ... ayerrereng
north-east ... ayerrer ingerr (W,T), ayerrer ikngerr (E), ayerrer-ayerrer (E)
north-west ... altwerl-altwerl, ayerrer altwerl, ayerrer-ayerrer (E) (SP)
north wind ... aretharr

northern corkwood *(go to 'corkwood')*

northern wild orange ... akarlety, akarley (E), ngarntatyarr (W,T)

nose ... alha[1], alhang (W,T)
tip of nose ... alha kanty
nasal bone (soft part inside nose) ... alhwengkengk (W)
bony part of nose ... alha ngkwern (T,E)
blocked nose ... alha nthat (T,E)

soft membrane between nasal cavities ... intyengintyerl (E)

hole in nose (through septum) ... alha altywer, alhang altywer (W,T), alhalker (E)

have a feeling (in your nose) that something is going to happen ... rltwaty-irrem (W,T), urltaty-irrem (E)

nasal mucus, snot ... artwengkenng, mernt[1] (W,T)

dried nasal mucus ... rta, irta (W,T), rtang (W,T), irtang (W,T)

no ... itya (W,T), arrangkw, na, new

say 'no' ... new-irrem

nosebone

worn through septum ... marrapernt (W,T), melyalker (W,T), irrengernt (E), ngerl (E), ntyarl (W,T), ntyerl (T,E)

nostril ... alha altywer, alhang altywer (W,T), alha arrenpenp (W,T)

not ... itya (W,T), arrangkw

not having anything, having nothing to do with something ... arla[2] (T,E)

not ready ... mpank (W,T), mpwank

nothing ... arrangkw, itya (W,T)

'Nothing much' ... war

(doing something) for nothing, for no good reason, in vain ... apelkel (W,T)

(there's still) nothing ... arrangkw akwet (W,T), itya akwet (W,T), itya-antey (W,T)

notice

not taking notice ... akwenp-akwenp (T), akwenpety-akwenp, angweyep-angwey, anngwa

take no notice of others ... anerlpewem

take notice of someone ... alhengk-arem

give people notice of what you are doing ... angkawelhem

now ... aley[2] (T,E), anem[2], lyet

any minute now, round about now ... lyet war

right now, just now ... lyet innga (E), lyetarrpwerreny (E)

something is starting to happen now ... lyet-athek (T)

nowadays ... aley[2] (T,E), lyet-athek, lyetarr

nudge

nudge or tap someone to get their attention ... kelengwem (W,T)

nuisance

make a nuisance of self ... urawenyerr-ilem (E)

nulla-nulla ... kweter

numb ... arlerlp[2], tharr

go numb ... arlerlp-irrem, impelhem (E), tharr-irrem

number

a lot of times ... angerr-ingar

this/that many, this/that much (while showing how many) ... alakenty

this many, that many, this many times ... alakenty-ingar

number 7 boomerang ... alyang rlkwang (W,T), iylkwa (E), aylayl iylkwa (E), kayl iylkwa (E)

nurse *(from English)* ... theth

nut bush ... arleyakwerr (T,E) (?)

Oo

oak

desert oak ... arrkep, kwerrkar (W,T)

obey ... akangkwerrem (W,T)

oblivious ... anngwa, anaraty (W,T), aneraty (T,E)

be uncaring, oblivious or unconcerned ... anaraty-irrem (W,T), aneraty-irrem (T,E)

obscure

obscure something ... ilpem[2]

obviously ... wart

occasionally ... anyentam-anyent, anyentek-anyent

occupied

be occupied, busy ... atyanem (W)

ochre

types of red ochre ... rlpwa (W,T), rlpwang (W,T), urlpa (E), rlpwang rnter-rnter (W,T), urlpa atyetyek (E), arwethenp, artep arlpenty (T,E)

red ochre (from English) ... ritak (E)

white/yellow ochre ... ngwenty-ngwenty (T,E), ntyengwenty

yellow ochre ... karntewarr, marlalperr (T,E)

covered in red ochre ... rlpwapert (W,T)

of

belonging to ... -kenh[1]

off

rotten, off ... arntert, aywek (E), iynteng (E)

turn something off (a tap or a switch etc.) ... martem (T,E), ywerrelh-ilem

off *(away from) (see Appendix 2)*

offensive ... kwern (W,T), anety (W,T), akeng (T,E), amwa[2] (E)

official
make something official, put something on a list ... ingkwernem (T,E)
often ... akweteth
'Oh yeah?' ... alew² (W,T), alew-alew (W,T)
'Oh no!' ... yekay
oil
fat, grease ... anter
oilgrass
scented oilgrass ... aherr-aherr, areng-areng (E)
okay ... kel, kel mwerr
'Is it okay?' ... mwerrakey (W,T)
old
old person or animal ... ampwa, ampwang (W,T)
old or senior person ... aywa, aywang (W,T), antyeny (T,E), ampwety-ampweyneng (E)
old woman ... akelty ampwa (E)
old woman (from English) ... werlkemen
old man ... artwa aywang (W,T), artwang aywang (W,T), artwampw (E), artwang ampwang (W,T)
old man (from English) ... wernman
old weak person ... aherrantyerr (E)
thin, wrinkled, really old man or woman ... arrwely-arrwely
old female animal ... areperrk
old, from a long time ago, olden-time things ... ahenpeny, angkweyeny (W,T), ingkweyeny (E), arruleny (T,E), arrwekeleny
in the olden days ... angkwey (W,T), ingkwey (E), arrwekel, ahenp
grow old ... ampwerrem, angerr-pat-irrem, angkweyeny-irrem (W,T), ingkweyeny-irrem (E), arrwely-arrwely-irrem, aywa ampem, aywang ampem (W,T), aywang-irrem (W,T), ilkwa ampem (E)
be older than someone ... anngarelhem
old man saltbush ... ntyurtenty (E)
omen
bad omen ... mawenng (T,E), matyawenng (T,E)
be an omen of death ... arrelty arem (E), arreltyarn arem (T)
on *(see Appendix 2)*
on the other side ... arrpenh-thayt, ingwer-thayt (E)
once ... anyent-ingar
once again ... aweth aken
one ... anyent
one (respect language) ... aweleth (E)
one by one, one at a time, one each ... anyentam-anyent, anyentek-anyent
one hundred dollar note .. atherrk-atherrk (T,E)
one-sided
being one-sided, not sharing things with others ... anyentak (W), arrelharrp (W), arreylarrp (E)
oneself
do action for oneself ... kwaleny (W,T)
onion grass *(go to 'bush onion')*
only
just that (and nothing else) ... rlwart (W,T), urlart (E)
only the two of them ... +ant-atherr
onto ... -warn (W,T), -warl
Ooralingie Bore ... Urrelenty
Ooratippra ... Apwiperr

open
open place, clear place ... ahererr (E)
open *(not closed)* ... altywer
opening or door ... arrew (W,T), arriw (T,E)
open up, become open ... altywer-irrem
open something ... altywer-ilem, arralkelh-ilem, arrarlkelh-ilem, atakem
open or uncover something ... ilkakem
open up a goanna's hole .. ilkewem, ilkakem
open *(in the open)* ... aketh
doing something out in the open or in public ... anngetherr
come out into the open ... aketh-irrem
come out into the open, bring a young man out (after ceremonial business) ... aketh-ilem
open country ... alkwererlp (T), alkwerilp (E)
open ground (from English) ... perlern
country where there are no restricted places ... arla² (T,E), arlangkwarr (E)
opinion
have an opinion about something ... iterrem
oppress someone
make someone feel weak, lazy or overwhelmed ... lthwem (W,T), ulthem (E)
orange *(go to 'wild orange')*
orange-naped snake ... perlap-perlap (E) (?)
order
order someone to do something ... ilem, twernem, uternem (E)

two people being ordered to do verb action +erl-anerr+ (W,T)
more than two people being ordered to do verb action +errirr+ (W,T), -arey[2] (E)
don't (do verb action) +etyal, +etyang (E)

originate
come from (a place) anganem

orphan alhamp, rrkwern (W,T), amatheng (E), kwer rrkwern (W,T), kwetyenty
become an orphan alhamp-irrem, rrkwern-irrem (W,T)

other
another one, others arrpenh, ingwer (E), arrpenhem
in another direction, in another way arrpenh-angkwerr, ingwer-angkwerr (E)
other people arrpenh, ingwer-rnem (E)

'Ouch!' yekay, yapaty (W,T)

ought
ought to do the verb action +etyek, +etyeh (W,T)

our, ours *(belonging to us two)*
(go to Pronoun table, p 747)

our, ours *(belonging to more than two)*
(go to Pronoun table, p 747)
our relation +aty[1]

outside aketh
go outside tyerrelhem

outskirts
of town or camp akert[1] (T,E)

oval-leaved cassia manatwerrp, areyawarr (E)
grub areyawarrayt (E)

over
because of -arrngel

overnight
(doing something) overnight anwekel (W,T), unekel (E)
doing something overnight (respect language) wekel (E)

overseas
someone from overseas alker arrpenh-areny

owl
barn owl arrkerr
southern boobook kwerrkwerrk, akekw (E) (?)

own *(possess)*
own or have something anyenem (T,E), rrkwem (W,T), irrkwem (E)
own personal or private possession arlalty
owned by -kenh[1]
owner or boss of a place merek-artwey
owners or 'bosses' of a particular Dreaming -artwey

own
on one's own anyent, inga, ngwath (W), akalk, arrakelakel (E)

Pp

Pacific black duck awengker (?)

pacify rlwaty angkem (W,T), urlaty angkem (E)

pack things up akwengerr-werl-alhem

paddle *(along)* alyeyamp-irrem (E), kalyeyamp-irrem (T,E), alyeyampel alhem (E), kalyeyampel alhem (T,E)
paddling alyeyampel (E), kalyeyampel (T,E)

paddy melon
(from English) patimalan (E)

pain
be in pain antyernem[1] (W,T), arekar-irrem, arntem, pwerep-irrem, rlkert intyem (E), antywekelywekely-irrem, kwarnelhem, akalthem (E)
be hurt by something arlkwem
feeling sick or in pain antywekelywekely, arlerlp[2], arekwenth-kwenth (T,E)
have a stomach-ache ltwakem (W,T), ultakem (E)
cause pain kwarnem
cause a burning pain item
Ouch! (something said when in pain) yapaty (W,T), yekay

paint
paint something ingkwernem (T,E), intelh-ilem (W,T), intelhem (W,T)
paint or rub someone with something apernem, apem[2] (E)
paint up (paint self) apernelhem, ingkwernelhem (T,E)
draw ceremonial design, paint someone up (women) tyepety-wem (W,T), arlkeny arrernem, arlkeny-wem
paint each other up with ceremonial designs (women) tyepety-werrem (W,T), iwerrem
paint up (men) wantelhem
paint oneself with white clay (in mourning) atywerlkel-ilelhem (W,T), aytwerlkel-ilelhem (E), atywerlkelhem (T)

pair
couple or pair of things atherr[1]

person 'together' with a particular relation .... -nheng[2]
in pairs .... atherram-atherr (E), atherrek-atherr (E), atherrelam atherrelam (T), atherrengk-atherr (T,E)
palate *(of mouth)* .... merrng (E)
pale
pale in colour .... arlter, arrerlker (E), mperlker
go pale .... arlter-irrem
pallid cuckoo .... alkwarrer-arrpwernenh (E), lyweketweretwer (W,T), rlweketereter (W,T)
palm *(of the hand)* .... iltya anert, iltya ilperr-ilperr (E), iltya ipert (E)
pannikin *(from English)* .... tyampet, paniken
pant
breathe heavily .... ahey-angkem
pant (dog) .... yarrert angkem (E)
pants *(from English)* .... terawath
paper *(from English)* .... pep
paperbark .... ilperl[2]
Papunya .... Pwepany
parakeelya *(broad-leaf)* .... parrkely, arrwelth-arrwelth (E)
paralysed .... anath (W,T), arlerlp[2]
pardalote
red-browed pardalote .... kaperlantarlant (E) (?)
parent *(see 'father', 'mother')*
parkinsonia *(plant)* .... arlketyerr
parrot
budgerigar .... atetherr
cockateil .... aneweylker (E), areweylker (E), arew-arew (E), kanaweylker (E), newingk (W,T)
mulga parrot .... urimpering (E) (?), rempereng (W) (?)
ringneck parrot .... arlpaty
part of something .... akert[1] (T,E)
partially .... akertang (T,E)
pass
passing by (someone or something) .... anper[1]
pass by (someone or something) .... anper alhem
pass away
die .... arrangkw-irrem, ywerrem, uyerrem (E), ahap-irrem (E)
die (respect language) .... alyent-artek-irrem (E), arremangkw-irrem (E)
pass away (respectful way of talking) .... anengkan-irrem
passionfruit
wild passionfruit .... arrweneng
past *(time) (see Appendix 2)*
pastor .... ngkart, kalty-anthenh-anthenh
path, pathway .... tyey[1] (W,T), iwerr (E)
go along same pathway .... tyey-irrem (W,T)
patterned .... arlkeny-arlkeny, intetyeng-intety (T,E), iyntethengeynteth (E)
paunch
large paunch or belly .... rtwarnp
paw
back hooves or paws of animals .... ingka, ingkang (W,T)
front hooves or paws of animals .... iltya, iltyang (W,T)
hard part of hoof or paw .... rta, irta (W,T), rtang (W,T), irtang (W,T)
as a dog does to get someone's attention .... kelengwem (W,T)
pay
pay for something (from English) .... payem-ilem
payback
hit someone back, 'pay' them back .... unkil-ilem (E)
submit yourself for 'payback' or traditional punishment .... ankwernelhem (W,T), unkilelhem (E)
peaceful dove .... kwerlekwek, kwerler-kwerler (W,T), kwerakwek (W,T), lerakwenty (W) (?)
peach tree .... mangart[1], mwerlp
pear
native pear .... angelth, tywekerl[1] (W,T)
peel
peel bark off a plant or tree .... arntap iyltem (E), iltyem (E), alherrem[1] (E)
peel skin off fruit or bark off a stick .... kek-wem, irrnyewem (W,T), irrnyiwem (E)
peel something off something else .... akap-rlwem (W,T), akap-irlwem
peel something off self .... akap-rlwelhem (W,T), akap-irlwelhem
peel off (bark from a tree) .... iyltelhem (E)
peep
peeping out at someone .... rlwant-rlwant (W,T), urlant-urlant (T,E)
peer out from behind something .... tyel-arem (W,T), ayternem (E), kert-arem, rlwem-anem (W,T), urlem-anem (E)

peer
peer down into something ... kert-arem
peewee *(go to 'mudlark')*
pelican ... arrakert angerr
pelican (from English) ... pelekan² (W), paleken (E)
pelvic bone, pelvis ... antyarlk ngkwern (T), iylperr ngkwern (E), anngarlp (T,E) (?)
pencil yam ... arlatyey
pencil yam (narrow leaf variety) ... anwerlarr (E), katywetarr (W,T) (?)
type of ... arnamp
seed ... arratwek, kam (T,E)
white tubers ... mwernenty
penis *(sensitive language)* ... pwer
people *(go to 'person')*
peregrine falcon ... aleraperap (E) (?)
perennial yellowtop ... arengkatwepatwetyenh (W,T), ntweyentwerl (E)
perentie ... tywenp, ilkwert (E)
big perentie ... anepeywenp (E)
young sand goanna or perentie ... arepilyerr (E)
tail meat of ... arrertarnk (T,E)
perhaps
maybe ... apek, thweng (T), ithweng (E)
that might be so ... yapek
permanent ... akweteth, amelerr (T,E)
permanent soakage ... altywen (W)
permission
ask for permission to do something ... angkawelhem
persistent
be persistent about something ... arlelty-irrem
person, people ... tyerrty, innga² (E), inngernem (E), iyterrty² (E)
Aboriginal person ... arelh¹, tyerrty
non-Aboriginal person ... alhernter, kartey (W), arlter, tywelker
non-Aboriginal (from English) ... warlpal
someone from a different country ... alker arrpenh-areny
a lot of people, everybody ... werlamperrenty (W,T), urlamperreny (T), urlamperrenty (E)
olden-time people ... angkwey-pat (T), irrewaly-pat, arrwekeleny, irrernng, irrernng-pat
various people ... angwenhant angwenh
perspire , sweat ... antyey-irrem, antyey iylpem (E), awempem (E)
perspiration, sweat ... antyey²

petrol ... kwaty
petticoat *(from English)* ... petekwet
phlegm ... artwengkenng
phone ... alwerrng angkenh-angkenh (E), alwerrng
photo, photograph
(from English) ... pwetew
take a photo ... pwetewem-ilem
pick
pick something up ... inem, kwetyem
pick fruit ... nhwem (W,T), unhem (E), akalthem (E), akem¹
pick or collect something as you go along, pick someone up from a place ... inenhem
pick or sort something out ... angakem, urlanem (E), urrarem (T,E)
pick up (of native currant) ... arlkernem (T,E)
pick up firewood ... rwang inem (W,T), aytem (E)
pick on someone ... alhengkem (T,E), arrkenty-ilem
pie melon *(from English)* ... malan (T,E), payemalan
piece
of rag or cloth (from English) ... petheth (W,T)
little pieces ... mpalty (W,T), ngkwelty
fall to pieces ... tyep-akelhem
cut something up into pieces (especially meat) ... tyep-akem, tyep-ilem, tyep-tyep-ilem
make something into a few bits or pieces ... rrpwety-ilem (W,T), urrpety-ilem (E)
pied butcherbird ... matyekatyer, pweretyetyer (W), pweretyety (W,T)
pierce
something with something sharp ... atanthem
piercing something right through ... tyetepetep (W,T), wetyerretyerr¹ (W)
pig *(from English)* ... pek-pek (W,T), wangk-wangk (E), pingkey (E)
pig-footed bandicoot ... rtaty (?)
pigeon
common bronzewing, bronzewing pigeon ... arntep
crested pigeon ... pelker
flock bronzewing ... arekwarr (E)
rock pigeon, plumed pigeon, spinifex pigeon ... arntwerrert
spinifex pigeon ... ntarrwerarrwer (W) (?), marekwerr (W,T) (?)

pigeon-toed .... arntayl (E), ingka amper-amper (E), ingka arntayl (E)
piggyback someone .... kalapel angem (W,T)
pigweed .... akat, iylaw (E)
pile .... aharl
big pile of something .... lyernt-lyernt (E)
pile of something (especially dirt) .... intyakwerlp (W)
pile something up (especially dirt) .... intyakwerlp arrernem (W), intyakwerlp-wem (W)
pile something up .... aharl arrernem (E), aharl-wem, ayak-arrernem (W,T), lyernt arrernem (T,E), lyernt-iwem (T,E)
gather things into a pile .. anarnkw-ilem
pillow .... akertemarl (W,T), rtwenk, temarl (E)
pimple .... ker ngkwern[2] (E)
pinch *(with fingers)* .... itekem (E), lther-wem
pine
for someone or for something .... alther-irrem (T,E), irrar-irrem, anthwerrng-irrem (T)
pine
native pine .... amikw[1] (E), anngart (W), akngart (W,T)
pink mulla-mulla .... mernteparn (W), merntepwarn (W,T)
pinnate goodenia .... inpay-inpay (W,T)
Pintupi
language and people .... Pintwepey
pintye-pintye *(plant)* .... iynteng-iynteng (E), ntyapentyetyen (W,T)
pipit
Australian (Richard's) pipit .... kaperl-kaperl (T,E) (?)
pirli *(plant)* .... alhanker (E), lywey (W)
pirraru *(plant)* .... irrar[1] (E), perrar (W,T), pirrar
piss, urine .... mpwa, mpwang (W,T)
have a piss .... mpwa ulhem (E), mpwelhem[2] (T), mpwulhem (E)
urinate on something (dogs) .... mpwerl lhwem, mpwerl ulhem (E), mpwerl-ilem
Pitjantjatjara
language and people .... Petyapety, Petyentyarr
pituri .... anwengk[2], arekerr (T,E), ngkwerlp
rubbish pituri .... ngwarray-ngwarray, pengart-pengart[2] (W)
placate .... rlwaty angkem (W,T), urlaty angkem (E)
place .... mer
familiar place, home place .... rwanng, uranng (E)
good place .... ilkelhey (W,T)
sacred place, restricted place .... anganty (W,T), amek-amek
place where a lot of people are living .... inamen (W,T)
deserted place .... arramperrty (E)
place where someone who lived there before has passed away .... arrkwetyety
place where there's lots of footprints or tracks .... atnalth (E)
place where people haven't been lately .... mpankeny (W,T), mpwankeny
placenta
(sensitive language) .... ilpa, ilpang (W,T)
plain country .... alkwererlp (T), alkwerilp (E)
plain, open country (from English) .... perlern
plains turkey *(see 'bush turkey')*
plant .... arna, arnang (W,T), arwerl (T,E), antyelty (E), atherrk
food from plants .... mern
plant something (a plant) .... ngkernem
plant something (put something somewhere) .... akwernem
platform
made for storing food in a tree .... irrertety, thanarnt
make a platform in a tree .... thanarnt-wem
play
playfully .... arrken, arrken-arrken
playfully (respect language) .... alyenteng-ayerr (E)
for fun, in jest, for play ... arrken-kenh
have fun, play, enjoy oneself .... arrken-irrem, arrken nhwelhem (W,T), arrken nhwerrem (W,T), arrken unherrem (E)
play (respect language) .... alyenteng-irrem (E)
make fun, play with something .... arrken-ilem
playing a trick .... tyelewerr (W,T)
play (a group of people or things) .... lwakelhem (W,T), arlakelhem (E), lwakerrem (W,T), arlakerrem (E)
play an instrument such as a guitar .... atwem
playing at being women .. arelheng-arelh (E)
play hide-and-seek .... alengk-alengk-welhem

playing cards .... parlperrp
pleasant .... mwerr, mwerr angerr (W,T), mwerr-angker (E)
pleased
feel pleased or excited .... akangkem, ilkelhem, anyanelhem, arntwelhem (E)
Pleiades
Seven Sisters .... Arrarrkw (T,E), Interrk[1] (E), Peltharr Map (W,T)
plenty, lots .... anengk[1] (W,T), atningk (E), angerr[1], alhirrel (E), arnkengeny (E)
plenty of food .... anthwely-anthwely (T)
collect plenty of food .... anthwely-anthwely-ilem (T)
Plenty River .... Apiwenty, Apewenty
pluck
feathers from a bird .... althem
pluck, pick (fruit) .... nhwem (W,T), unhem (E), akalthem (E), akem[1]
plug tobacco .... nikey-nikey
plum bush .... alkwa (E), ankwerlay (W,T), ankwerley (T,E)
plumed pigeon .... arntwerrert, ntarrwerarrwer (W)
plumed whistling duck .... tyepelyakw (W) (?), tyepelyey (E) (?)
plump *(of a person)* .... anter, anter angerr
plural
more than four or five people or things .... arwenth, map
plural ending (especially for kin terms) .... -intyerr
more than two (doing verb action) .... +erl-warr+ (T,E), +errirr+ (W,T), +ewarr+, +erl-w+[2] (T,E)
more than two (doing verb action or the object of the verb action) .... -arey[1], -rnem[2] (E), -rrpwer (W,T)
pocket .... palthet
point *(indicate)*
signal with hands .... iltyel-ilem
point to a person or a thing .... tyetyen-ilem
point *(end)*
pointed .... arrerlp, arrerlp-arrerlp
point of something .... akert[1] (T,E)
sharp piece on spear .... alart
poison
something poisonous .... arrwengkelth
snake venom .... antya[2] (T,E)
something poisonous (from English) .... pathen (W,T)
poison someone or something .... pathenem-ilem (W,T)
poke
poke into something .... alernem[2] (T,E), aterlk-ilem, kerrk-wem, lywem[2] (W,T), them (E)
poke head out and look out for something .... rlwem-anem (W,T), urlem-anem (E)
poke the ground with a digging stick or crowbar .... tyer-wem, tyewentem (W), tyek-untem (E)
poke into a burrow with a crowbar .... ilkewem
poke stick or crowbar into sand (to test for water) .... lyelyer-ipem, lyelyer-wem
poke out tongue .... alenyenp-wem (T,E)
poke tongue out between teeth (gesture made to little babies) .... karlkwelhem
police .... rrkwenty (W,T), irrkwenty (E), irrkwenh-irrkwenh (E)
pollen
put pollen in native bee nest (native bee) .... amakwernem (W,T) (?)
pony *(from English)* .... pweney-pweney
poo .... ana, anang (W,T), kart[1] (W,T)
Poomingie Waterhole
on Utopia (Angarapa Aboriginal Land Trust) .... Ipementy
'Poor thing'
'Poor bugger', 'Poor thing' (expression of endearment) .... akeweny (W,T), akuny (T,E), akeweny-amperl (W,T), akuny-amperl (T,E), akeweny-apenh (W,T), inaty (W), inaty-amperl (W)
expression of endearment (endings) .... -amperl (E), -angwel-angwel (E), -angwen-angwen (T,E), -apenh (W,T), -awern
'Poor thing' (an expression of sympathy) .... anthelk[2] (E)
'porcupine', echidna .... inap (T,E), inarleng, ingka iyntwem (E), ker arlkerl (E), lyek
back of 'porcupine', meat from back of 'porcupine' .... angkwer[1]
'porcupine', echidna (respect language) .... iylek-ayerr (E)
porcupine grass .... aywert
Port Lincoln parrot .... arlpaty
possess
possess something .... rrkwem (W,T), irrkwem (E)
things, possessions .... rnwanenty, urnanenty (E)

someone else's things ...... rnwanenty atyeneny (W,T), urnanenty atyeneny (E)

possum

common brush-tailed ...... antenh, rrpwamper (W,T)

possum (from English) .... pathem

possum's track or path .... antywerreng (E)

potato *(from English)* .... patart

potato bush

native tomato .... alperrantyey, ararnt (W,T), rtwengkerr (W,T)

pouch

animal's pouch .... peth, aympa (E)

carry baby animal in a pouch .... pethel angem, aympel angem (E)

made from tea-tree bark .. perety[1] (E) (?)

pound

crush or smash something up .... apert-atwem (E)

something up using a grinding stone .... tewenhem (E)

pour

liquid out of or into something .... thelem

pour out of something ..... thelelhem

powdery .... althalth

power .... arawerrng

power associated with persons or objects that have been sung .... arrilenty

become empowered .... arawerrng inem

take someone's power away .... arawerrng rakem (E)

praise

praise someone or something .... nakem, narlkwem (E)

praise yourself .... nakelhem, narlkwelhem (E)

pray .... angkem

praying mantis .... antyekanty (T,E), kapert atwenh (W,T), kapert atwenh-atwenh (W,T)

precious .... impen

predict *(go to 'premonition')*

pregnant .... anert-anert, artart[2] (W,T), nthat, kwart-kwart (SP)

be pregnant .... anert-anert-irrem

premonition

a feeling about something that is going to happen ... rltwaty (W,T), urltaty (E)

have a predictive dream about a relation .... altyerr uternelhem (E)

have a premonition .... alhirrkem, alhang irrkem (W,T), rltwaty-irrem (W,T), rltwatyel atwem (W,T), urltaty-irrem (E), urltatyel atwem (E), alhel arem (T)

cause someone to have predictive dream .... rlkwem (T,E)

preoccupied .... angweyep-angwey

prepare

something .... mpwarem

present *(present time) (go to Appendix 2)*

present *(ceremonial payment)* .... kwerapak (W), tyenkerr, tyewarrely (W,T)

press

press down on something .. alernelhem (T,E), rlpwerrkem (W,T), rrwethem (T), kerrk-welhem

press into something .... kerrk-wem

weigh down upon something .... lthwem (W,T), ulthem (E)

pretend .... rrtywerrem (W,T), urrtyirrem (E), rrtywekelh-ilem (T)

pretend to give something to somebody (then take it back) .... anewel anthem (T,E), tywerengk anthem (W,T), ulang anthem (E)

pretend you haven't got something when you really have .... ywep-arrernem (W,T)

pretend shield .... alkwerteng-alkwert

a pretend thing, pretend to do something .... -arrpantey, -arrpatenty (E)

a pretend thing, something which is an imitation of the real thing .... +eng-anyimp (E)

pretty .... amparrkey, amparrkey-amparrkey, mekelarey (W,T)

previously .... mernt[2] (T,E), imernt (E)

prey

an animal's prey .... anwenth, ker

prickle

prickly .... arrerlp, arrerlp-arrerlp

certain prickly plants ...... lyek

life-saver burr, teddy bears arsehole .... ingka-mwerney, akeley-akeley (T,E), anmang (W)

types of .... thenkarr, arlketyerr, arlkerl, atetherr-atetherr, kapert angerr (W,T), kapert-kapert, pwerrenperrenp (W,T), wamper-wamper (E)

priest .... ngkart

become a priest .... ngkart-irrem

princess parrot .... urimpering (E) (?), rempereng (W) (?)

pristine .... mpankeny (W,T), mpwankeny

private
own, personal or private possession .... arlalty, kampely[2] (E) (SP)
probably .... apek
problematic
(from English) .... tikeley
processionary caterpillar .... ingeth (T,E)
processionary caterpillar nest .... wep
promiscuous person .... anapert (T,E), annga atherrk-atherrk, mpweny angerr (E), mpwenyartw-mpwenyartw (T,E)
promise
promise to give something to someone .... alhelem (W,T), alhilem (T,E)
promise someone in marriage .... alhelem (W,T), alhilem (T,E)
someone or something that is promised to someone (e.g. wife) .... alhelenty (W,T), alhilenty (T,E)
promised wife .... akwerrk-penh (E), akepenh (?)
promised husband or wife (from English) .... perrameth
prop
prop something up on something else .... alernem[2] (T,E)
proper
correct or true .... arraty
(doing something) carefully or properly .... mwerranty
(doing something) carefully or properly (respect language) .... mwerrenganty (E)
not properly, improperly .... apant (W,T), apal[2]
protect
using something for protection, 'to save' self .... ilkwatherr
place something in front of yourself for protection .... ilpelhem
proud
be proud of self .... nakelhem, narlkwelhem (E)
provoke
be argumentative .... irrpelth-irrem, urrpelth-irrem (E)
Prowses Gap .... Ilepampel
pubic covering .... alperl
pubic hair
(sensitive language) .... antalt (W), altalt (W,T), intywa (E)
public
doing something out in open or in public .... anngetherr
speak loudly, talk loudly in public .... aharlperr angkem (T,E), arlperr angkem

puddle .... aparew (E)
puffed up .... arlwar
puff up .... arlwar-irrem
puffed up (eyes or other parts of body) .... alhwer-alhwer
puff up (eyes or other parts of body) .... alhwer-alhwer-irrem
puffball
stalked puffball .... arrekwep-kwep (W), arrepweng-pweng (E), kwep-kwep[3] (W,T), pwek-pwek, pweng-pweng (W), anngarnt rrpwerl (W,T)
other types of .... kwerrart (W), kerrart (T), arepenngenkey (E)
pull
pull down a branch .... twakem (W,T)
pull seeds or resin off plant .... antyakem
pull something up .... arwakem
pull something out of something .... arratelh-ilem, rlpwentyem (W,T), tyarr-inem, tyerrem, urlpentyem (E)
pull something out of part of your body .... inelhem, lywelhem, tyerrelhem
pulse *(blood)* .... ahey-angkem
pump
pump something up .... arlwar-ilem
punch
someone or something .... anampart atwem (W), palty atwem (E), apar atwem (T,E)
puncture
puncture something .... atanthem
pup, puppy .... irrert (W,T), tywetyety
pupil *(of eye)* .... annga rrpwerl (W,T), annga urrperl (E)
purse *(from English)* .... pewaty
purslane *(plant)* .... akat, iylaw (E)
pus .... rrkwa (W,T), rrkwang (W,T), irrkwa (E), arnkwarn (E)
push *(from English)* .... pewetyem-ilem
push someone around .... ilatwem
push someone or something .... anampart-wem (W,T), ankert-wem, urturt-iwem (E), aperrpert-ilem (W,T)
push something down in throat (with water or tea) .... rlkwelhem (W,T), iylkwelhem (E)
push something into or onto something .... kerrk-wem

push something out of the way or to the side ...... antarr-wem, antarr-arrernem
push in ...... arrngert-irrem
crowd in on someone ...... apapeth-irrem
push in and try and go first ...... athathel, athathew-ilem (T)
pussy *(from English)* ...... pwethey
pussy-tails *(plant)* ...... alyey-alyey (W,T), aweyek-alyey-alyey (E), awerreh-alyey-alyey (W,T), rrweyek-alyey-alyey (W,T), urreyek-alyey-alyey (T,E)
put
put something down ...... arrernem
put something in place ...... arrernem, ngkernem
put something on shoulder ...... intarlpek-ilem (W,T), ntwarlpek-ilem (E)
put something on something else ...... ampek-arrernem
put something inside something else ...... akwernem, irrpelh-ilem
put something up high ...... tywenelh-ilem, tywenem, utyenem (E)
put something up out of sight (of certain restricted kin) ...... artweperek tywenem (E)
put something in a hole ...... ipertek akwernem
put something away ...... arlawem (T)
put something up, construct something ...... artem
put on clothes, shoes ...... irrpem, aylpem (E)
put something on yourself ...... arrernelhem, irrpelh-ilem
put yourself up onto something ...... tywenelhem, utyenelhem (E)
put something in mouth (to eat) ...... arrakwernem[2] (T,E)
put something out (fire or light) ...... lwernem (W,T), ilwernem (E)
pygmy mulga monitor ...... ahert-ahert[2] (W), arin, arwangk (W,T)
python
black-headed python ...... arrwerrperl (T,E)
carpet python ...... antetherrk
Stimson's python ...... ileway (W,T) (?)
woma, sandhill python ...... ahelh-ahelh (W), ahenenh, aheneny (T,E), nwey (T),
types of ...... imarlew (E), kaperrkwelt (E) (?), ilperletyewenh (E), irrimarnt (E) uney (E)

Qq

quail
button quail ...... atek, aterlkwarr (E), iylpwerr (E)
stubble quail ...... kweyepey (E)
quandong ...... mangart[1], mwerlp
quarrion ...... aneweylker (E), areweylker (E), arew-arew (E), kanaweylker (E), newingk (W,T)
queen *(ant, bee)*
honeyant queen ...... rlweng apeltyey (W), rlwertantyey (W,T)
queen sugarbag bee ...... aynwer (E) (?)
quench thirst ...... alywer-irrem
quick, quickly ...... aher, parrp, parrp-parrp, uremeny (E)
doing something quickly, in a hurry ...... arrengker
do something quickly ...... arrengker-irrem (W,T)
make something go quickly or do something quickly ...... arrengker-ilem (W,T)
(do something) quickly ...... +erl-w+[1], +erl-iw+ (T,E)
quiet
quiet, silent ...... ntert
quiet, still ...... amarn
quiet, non-aggressive ...... ahekweny, angemang (W,T), anik (E), alyerremwey, ameleth, apertap (W,T)
quietly, carefully ...... arternp
become quiet, quieten down ...... ntert-irrem, arlan-irrem
be quiet or still ...... amarn-irrem
sit down quietly and thoughtfully ...... akarntem[2]
quieten someone or something down ...... arternp-ilem, arternpelh-ilem, ntert-ilem, ntertelh-ilem
quieten something down (kangaroo or euro) ...... amarn-ilem
quit a job ...... impelhem
quiver
wings or others parts of the body ...... alharrkem
quoll
western quoll ...... atyelp, atyet[2] (E)

Rr

rabbit ...... alkwert atwenh (E), mwetyernk (W), metyernk (W,T), pet-pet (E)

rabbit (from English) ...... rapet
rabbit-eared bandicoot .. ahert (T,E)
radiator *(of car)* .... kwaty-henh (W,T), kwaty-kenh (E)
radio *(from English)* .... wayeleth
ragged .... alhengkey, alkwemp-alkwemp, altelhey (W,T), iltelhey (T,E), althalth
rain .... kwaty
light rain, shower of rain .. lthel, kwaty lthel, lyelyaw (E), nyeyepenyey (W), tyeyepetyey (W), awerrp[2] (W)
steady rain .... perler, thawel (T), atnhal (E), kwaty perler, kwaty thawel (T), thew-thew[1] (W,T)
rain in the distance .... tywa (T), tywang (T), utya (E)
the smell of rain .... menyarenyar (T), mpengemp (W), nyemp (E)
rain clouds .... angkarl, kwaty akwerrk (E), kwaty angkarl, aperler (W,T)
rain *(to rain)* .... anhem, kwaty arrwerelhem, rntwem (W,T), urntem (T,E)
rain a little bit .... tyeyepetyey atwem (W)
rain steadily or heavily .... atnhal-irrem (E)
rainbow .... mpwelarr
rainbow bee-eater .... rterr-rterr (W,T), apelinterr-interr (E), kwelinterr-interr (T,E)
rainbow snake .... akwerteyteng (E), kwelay, kwelernarr (E)
raindrop .... irnmerr
rainwater .... aparew (E), kwaty narengk (T), kwaty narwep (W,T), narwep (W,T)
raise
raise or lift something up .. akern-ilem
raise someone or something (children) .... kwetyakw-ilem (T,E), amangkelh-ilem
rapidly .... parrp, parrp-parrp
rat
long-haired rat .... kwetang, nyemal (E)
type of .... aherraty-anywertangey (E) (?)
rat tails *(plant)* .... alpar, arrerlang (T,E), mwelyeparnt-parnt (T), mwenyeparnt-parnt (W), ngwelyeparnt-parnt (T), parntentyarlp (W)
rattle
banging, knocking, rattling or clicking sound .. rltar, rltar-rltar[1], rlterrp
make a clicking, banging, rattling or knocking sound .... rltar-irrem, rltar-rnkem (E), rltwar-rnkem, urltar-rnkem (E), rlterrkem (E), lterrkem (E)
make something bang or rattle .... rlterrp-wem, rlterrpelh-ilem, rlterrp rrkwem (W,T), rlterrp irrkwem (E), lterrp rrkwem (W,T), rlterrpel atwem, rlterrkelh-ilem (E)
make a rustling, rattling or scratching sound .... inkerrem, rerrkem
make something rattle or rustle .... inkerrelh-ilem, rerrkelh-ilem
rattle boomerangs together (men) .... rlterrp atwem (E)
rattlepod grevillea .... aywel (T,E)
raw .... anka, ankang (W,T), arlety[2]
raw (respect language) .... iyntweth (E)
rays *(of the sun)* .... aherrk iltya (T), aherrk iltyem-iltyem (E)
ready
'okay, we're ready' .... kel-kety
(something is) ready to eat .... ampeng
(something) is not ready .. mpank-antey (W,T)
real
not real .... rrtyweng-rrtyweng (W,T), tyweng-tyweng, urrtyeng-urrtyeng (E), utyek-utyel (E)
really
really, very, extremely ..... angerr[1], anthwerr (W,T), ulteketh
really, truly .... arraty, arratyant-alkenty (W,T)
really, definitely .... kwenh
really, of course .... wart, inngart (E)
'Really!' (provides emphasis) .... innga[1] (E), iyterrty[1] (E), peleth
really (do something), do something intensively ..... arnterr
'Really?', 'Is that so?' ...... ngay, tyakey (W,T), tyathew, thathew, arraty-akey
'Really, truly, true to God' .... Altyerrel arem (W), Ngkartel arem (E)
reason
(doing something) for no particular reason .... war
(doing something) without reason .... apelkel (W,T)
'For what reason?' .... wenh-penh (W,T), iwenh-penh

recent
recent, fresh .... lyeteny
recent (respect language) .. lyengkwerteny (E)
not recent or fresh .... amwerrkeny (E)
reciprocal
something that is given to another person to 'square them up', something given reciprocally .... akepenh
give reciprocally .... akepenh anthem
reckon *(you're something)*. *(from English)* .... reken-irrem (W,T), riken-irrem (E)
they reckon, supposedly ... akwel
recognise
recognise someone or something .... alhengk-arem, iterlarem
be recognisable .... inngelhem
recognise yourself (in someone else) .... alhengk-arelhem
not recognise someone ..... apal-arem, uyemem (E), ayemem (W,T), yem-irrem (W,T)
recover *(get better)* .... iteth-irrem, mwerr-irrem
red .... rnter-rnter, atyetyek (T,E), athethek (W,T)
reddish in colour .... arelyerrty (T,E), urelyerrty (E)
go red .... rnterelhem, atyetyek-irrem (T,E), athethem (T,E)
make something go red .... rnter-rnter-ilem, atyetyek-ilem (T,E)
show red, pink or orange colour (especially of kangaroo and honeyant) .. arlpampem (E)
red mallee .... ntyeny (E)
honey of .... ntyenyengkwarl (E)
red ochre .... rlpwa (W,T), rlpwang (W,T), urlpa (E), rlpwang rnter-rnter (W,T), artep arlpenty (T,E), urlpa atyetyek (E)
red ochre (from English) .. ritak (E)
red-ochre men .... tyelkath (W), tyelkaty (T)
red poverty bush .... kwenthey
red-backed kingfisher ..... parlkenng (E), rlwernp (W,T), nwernp (W), urrernter[2] (E)
red-browed pardalote .... kaperlantarlant (E) (?)
red-capped robin .... akarl-atwerrey (T,E), alywerr-alywerr (W,T), kapert rnter-rnter (E), uneng atyetyek (E)
red-kneed dotterel .... tyelkatherather, interrk-atherather (W,T) (?)
red-tailed black cockatoo .... irrarnt
refuse *(to do something)* ..... ankerl-irrem (W,T), anwernt-irrem, mwernt-irrem (T,E), rlterrk-irrem
refuse or reject something .. menty-ilem
regardless
go off regardless .... anerlpewem
without taking notice of others .... atanty, alanty
region .... ahelh, ahern, mer
area, vicinity .... -ampeny[2]
register a car .... ingkwernem (T,E)
rejected
person who feels rejected by others .... ntweth-ntweth (W,T), intweth-intweth (E)
reject someone .... alhengkey-ilem
become abandoned, be rejected .... iwerrem
relation
close family or relations .. altya, altyarey, altyernem (E), arlalty, arlalty-arey, meralty, atyenh, pelty, arneng-arneng (E)
my family or relation ...... atyeng-artwey, atyeng-artey (W,T), atyeng arneng
your family or relation .... ngkweng-artwey, ngkweng-arneng
his/her/their relation .... kwer-artwey, ikwer-arneng
someone or something closely related (particularly siblings and cross-cousins) .... -arneng
kinship system, skin name .... anpernenty, anpernerrenty
call someone a particular relation .... akem[2], anpernem
be related to each other in a particular way .... akerrem, anpernerrem
say that you are not someone's relation .... urlkernelhem (E)
having a particular close kin relation (still alive) .... -ankethenh
respectful word used for relation who has passed away .... -artwemeny
your relation (respectful or 'sorry' way of talking) .. -parety
release
someone (from jail) .... althekalth-ilem (SP)
release something .... tyarl-wem (E)
relieved
feel confident or happy about something .... anaraty-irrem (W,T), aneraty-irrem (T,E)
remains
the rest of something ...... kantyeny (T,E), ampeny[1], ampeny-ampeny
Rembrandt Rock .... Akarntey

remember
remember about someone or something ..... irlpangkem, iterlarem

remind
remind someone of something ..... irlpangkelh-ilem

repeat
action is repeated or keeps happening ..... +ep-

reply, answer back ..... tyernem[1], tyernelhem

reportedly
'So they say' ..... akwel

resemble
be like, be similar to or resemble someone or something ..... -artek, -apeny (E)

resentful
get sulky or angry ..... rnpart-irrem (W,T), urnpart-irrem (T)

resign
take name off paper ..... urrparelhem (T,E)
quit a job ..... impelhem

resin
from plants ..... rnpwa (W,T), rnpwang (W,T)
from acacia bush ..... arlep ngkwarl (E)
from Georgina gidgee ..... kikarr (E)
from mulga ..... alkeramp
spinifex wax or resin ..... tyalangk (W,T), anker[1] (E), arletyety (W)

respect
rules associated with respect for particular relations, a person who follows the rules ..... kerrenty (W,T), kirrenty, ikirrenty (E)
observe rules associated with respect for particular relations ..... kerrem (W,T), kirrem, ikirrem (E)
make signs to show that relations with whom you have a respect relationship are close by ..... unpernelhem (E), unpernem (E)
behaving with the appropriate degree of respect, or showing good manners in terms of Aboriginal Law ..... apwer (W,T), apur (E), nyerr

respond
answer someone ..... tyernem[1], tyernelhem
not answer someone ..... menty awelhem

rest
have a rest, have a spell ..... ltywerrem (W,T), ltyirrem (E), lthwerrem (W,T)
give something a rest, give something a spell ..... ltyerrelh-ilem
rest something against something ..... alernem[2] (T,E), ampekernem, ampek-anem, ampek-intem
resting place ..... rwanenty

rest *(remainder)*
the remainder of something ..... kantyeny (T,E)

restless ..... arrkwer-arrkwer, irrkaw
feeling unsettled, excitable, restless ..... arawerrng
be restless ..... irrkaw-irrem
make someone restless ..... irrkaw anthem

restricted ..... mety-mety
something of a sensitive or restricted nature ..... mwekeny, mwekenh, mweketyey (W,T), amek-amek, tikeley
restricted place (e.g. sacred site) ..... kwerert (W,T), amek-amek
not allowed, out of bounds ..... akayak, kwerert (W,T)
'no room', because of certain relations that a person should avoid direct contact with ..... alkey-kweny (E), alkiwerr-kweny (E)
room to go (absence of restriction caused by the presence of certain relations, restricted places etc.) ..... alkey[2] (E)
not feeling restricted ..... alhewer, alhalhek (E)

retreat ..... anenyerr-irrem

return
go back, go home ..... alpem, apety-alpem, pert-irrem (E)
return something ..... artwepelh-ilem
returning ..... angkep

reverse
go backwards ..... anepetheng-irrem, aneyangketh-irrem (E), anwengentyengenty-irrem (W,T), tyenelhem[1] (T,E)
make something go backwards ..... anepetheng-ilem, aneyangketh-ilem (E), angkep-ilem, angkepelh-ilem

revive
revive someone ..... iteth-ilem, iteth-wem
be revived ..... akem-irrem
revive someone by blowing in their ears ..... irlpakert-ilem (E), iylpenkelh-ilem (E)

ribbon grass ..... lyayepelyay (W,T), layempeylay (T,E), iylayempeylay (E)
ribs ..... meth (W,T), meth anngarlp (T), utyim (T,E)
edible meat from ribs ..... ker meth (W,T), ker utyim (T,E)
Richard's pipit ..... ntyelpeny (W,T), iynterlpeny (E)
ride
a horse, bike etc. ..... antyem
ridge-tailed monitor ..... kerr-kerr (W,T), kirr-kirr
ridicule
ridicule someone ..... arrkenty-ilem, arrampewem[1]
rifle *(from English)* ..... maket
rifle (respect language) ..... rntwer[1]
rifle through things ..... irranyent-iwem (E)
right
correct ..... arraty, innga[1] (E)
'Isn't that right?' ..... athew, tyathew, thathew
right foot ..... ingka arraty (E)
right hand
right-handed, right arm ..... akwang arraty (W,T), akwarraty
right-hand side ..... arraty, arraty-angkwerr (T,E), arratyakw (W)
ring
make a ringing sound (from English) ..... rltengk-rltengk-irrem, ring-irrem (E)
ring something (e.g. bell) ..... rltengk-rltengk-ilem
ring up on the telephone (from English) ..... wayem-ilem
ringneck parrot ..... arlpaty
rinse
rinse mouth out with water ..... kweng-kweng
rinse something out to clean it ..... urlkernem (E)
rip
rip something open ..... alterrem
become ripped or torn ..... alterrelhem
ripe ..... ampeng, atyet[1]
not properly ripe ..... arlety-arlety
ripe fruit or tuber ..... warnp (W,T)
get ripe ..... ampeng-irrem, atyet-irrem
make something ripe ..... ampeng-ilem
rise *(sun)* ..... aherlkem, anenty-alhem (W,T), aherrk anintyem (T), aherrk iltyem anintyem (E), aherrk itenty-alhem (W), aherrk tyerrelhem (T,E), aherrkenety-alhem (E), rlwem-anem (W,T), urlem-anem (E)

rise up *(of bread or damper)* ..... arlwarernem, arltwerlpernem (W,T), arlwar-irrem
make something rise ..... arlwar-ilem
sharp hump or rise in a road (from English) ..... tyampap
risk *(take a risk)* ..... pewelhem
river ..... lher, lpway (W,T), ulpay (T,E)
river (respect language) ..... angkeway (W,E), ngkwerlpay-ayerr (E)
big river or watercourse ..... arlanenty (SP)
riverbank ..... arnkarr, lher twemper (T,E), lher twerr (W,T), twerr (T,E), akwerlp
river red gum ..... aper
blossoms of ..... aperaly (W)
seed capsules ..... aperaley (W,T), aperrper (E)
grub from the branch ..... ingweneng, perlanty (W,T), perlaty (W,T), aylperlayt (T,E), ngkenhar (E), aperayt (E)
grub from the root ..... mpaty[2] (W,T)
grub from the base ..... ahekwenayt (E)
honey from under the bark ..... aperarnt (T,E), mamp (W,T), aperengengel (E), aperelayeng (W)
white substance made by the lerp scale insect on the leaf ..... aperelty
inner bark ..... aper tyelk
young river red gum ..... aper akwerrk
road ..... tyey[1] (W,T), iwerr (E)
road (from English) ..... rwert
go along the same road ..... tyey-irrem (W,T)
roadhouse *(from English)* ..... rwertath
robber ..... anyenngalth, arwengkalth
robin *(red-capped)* ..... akarl-atwerrey (T,E), alywerr-alywerr (W,T), kapert rnter-rnter (E), uneng atyetyek (E)
rock *(stone)* ..... apwert, irnta (W,T), irntang (W,T)
rock (respect language) ..... ather-ayerr (E)
large flat rock ..... ather, apwert ather, irntang ather (W,T), arlkwat (W,T), irntang arlkwat (W,T), alkamp (E)
rocky ground ..... irntangerr (T)
small round rock or stone ..... artwert[1]
type of white rock ..... ilperl[1] (E)
small stones or rocks ..... arrtya[3] (W), arrtyang (W), irrtyewat[1] (E), urrtyel (E), lyerl
rock *(baby in arms)* ..... angelh-angelh-ilem, arrew-arrew-ilem (T,E)

rock isotome .... anterernp, pitherr (T,E)
rock pigeon .... arntwerrert, ntarrwerarrwer (W)
rock pituri .... rnpwernp (W,T), rnpernp (T,E), urnpernp (T,E), ngkwerlp rnpwernp (W), ngkwerlp rnpernp (T,E), ngkwerlp urnpernp (E)
rockface
steep rockface or cliff .... antherrty, arnka, arnkang (W,T), irntang arnkarr-arnkarr (W)
rockhole .... arnerr
small rockhole with stone lid .... impekenh (T,E)
roll
a bundle .... artaper
roll something up .... anhwert-ilem, artaper-ilem, artaper-wem, ayernem, akwengerr-werl-alhem
roll something up (from English) .... rwelemap-ilem
roll something along .... ankert-wem
roll around in something .... impalerrp-welhem (W,T), impakemp-iwelhem (E), ywer-welhem (W), yer-welhem (T), rwer-welhem (E)
rolypoly *(buckbush)* .... arlkerl, inkwert (E)
romance .... iyteny (E), iyteny-iyteny (E)
roof of the mouth .... merrng (E)
room
room to go (absence of restriction caused by the presence of certain relations, restricted places etc.) .... alkey[2] (E)
'no room', lack of social space .... alkey-kweny (E), alkiwerr-kweny (E)
roomy .... aymperr (E)
rooster .... ingwel-ingwel arlkenh-arlkenh (E), kweny-rtwek arlkenh-arlkenh (T)
root .... artekerr
of bush banana, silky pear .... artwey-artwey[1], atnety (E)
of witchetty bush which has a witchetty grub in it .... arntwa (W,T), arntwang (W,T), arwa[1] (E)
rope *(hairstring)* .... antay (T,E)
rotten *(meat)* .... arntert, aywek (E), iynteng (E)
rotten (wood) .... althalth
go off, become rotten .... arntert-irrem, iynteng-irrem (E), lpwerrem (W,T), ulpirrem (E), atherrk-atherrk-irrem, aywek-irrem (E)
go off, become rotten (emu meat) .... ayewarr-irrem (E)
rough
rough or lumpy skin .... lyek-lyek, rtety-rtety
rough (of a road) .... ipert-ipert
go rough or lumpy (skin) .. lyek-lyek-irrem
rough-tailed goanna .... kerr-kerr (W,T), kirr-kirr
round
round in shape .... apwerterrerterr (W,T), arlwa (T,E)
round and hollow .... mwerlk[2] (E)
round, crooked .... amper-amper, iylwerl-iywerl (E)
round, flat .... ilperr-ilperr (E)
round, puffed up .... arlwar
short and round in shape arlwepertaty (T,E), artwert-artwert, rlwatert
small round things .... annga, anngang (W,T)
make something into a round shape, round things up .... arlwelem (W,T), arlwilem (E)
going around something .. artwep-artwep, urtep-urtep (E)
go round someone or something .... amper-irrem (E), artwep-akelhem, urtep-akelhem (E), artwep-akem
turn round and go back ... artwep-irrem, urtep-irrem (E)
the long way around .... talkw
round up game
hunt animals in a certain direction .... rrwerlkem (W,T)
rub
chafe or scratch something .... alherrem[1] (E)
rub something on or into something .... apernem, apem[2] (E)
rub something on self .... apernelhem
rub something out .... rrpwarem (W,T), urrparem (T,E), iparem (E)
rub things against each other to get stuff off .... awerrkem
rub yourself in or on something .... impalerrp-welhem (W,T), impakemp-iwelhem (E), ywer-welhem (W), yer-welhem (T), rwer-welhem (E)

rub part of self on something ..... irrparlerrp-wem, rrpwarlerrp-wem (W), irrpaterrp-wem (E)
rub chests together (at particular ceremonies) ..... arneyel nhwerrem (W,T)
rub self on coffin ..... irrparlerrp-welhem, rrpwarlerrp-welhem (W), irrpaterrp-iwelhem (E)
rub skin off fruit ..... irrnyewem (W,T), irrnyiwem (E)
rub desert raisins on the ground to remove the sticky bitter-tasting coating ..... pwarr-wem (T,E), inpewem (E), theweth-ilem (W), tewem
rub together (trees) ..... interrpar-wem (E), irrpenper-welhem (W)

rubbing medicine ..... awely anter

rubbish
garbage (from English) ..... rapety
rubbish left by floodwater ..... ntat
rubbish or ridicule someone ..... arrkenty-ilem

ruby saltbush ..... ntyemeny

rude
being rude to someone ..... anywerr-anywerr
mean, rude ..... anhelhenty
be rude or mean ..... anhelhem
be rude to someone, give them a dirty look ..... anywerr-irrem, yerrng-irrem (W,T)

rufous whistler ..... apetyepetyem (W,T), artwang apetyepetyem (W), artwatherr apetyepetyem (E), ipeny apetyepetyem (W,T), kwarlpatengkelyengkely (E), tyenyepweny (E)

rule ..... mpwarengareng
rules about avoiding particular kin ..... kerrenty (W,T), kirrenty, ikirrenty (E), mek-arenty (E)
rule over something, govern ..... atyetyart-irrem

rumble *(thunder)* ..... angkem, kwaty angkem, arntwerrem, artwert-irrem (W,T), twerl-irrem (E)

rumbling
whirring, whooshing or rumbling noise ..... aywerr
make a whirring, whooshing or rumbling noise ..... aywerr angkem

rump *(of an animal)* ..... anwerlk[2] (W,T)

run
run, run away ..... arrtyanem, ntwem (W,T), untem (E)
run (from English) ..... pwerlt-irrem
run away from someone or something ..... alwerrem
run around ..... lwakelhem (W,T), arlakelhem (E), lwakerrem (W,T), arlakerrem (E)
make someone run away ..... alwerrelh-ilem
emerge from cover and run (of some animals) ..... urtep-wem (E)
run off with someone, elope ..... mpweny alhem

run out
get used up ..... arltwerrem (W,T), arltwirrem (T,E), ywerrem, uyerrem (E)
make something run out ..... ywerrelh-ilem, uyerrelh-ilem (E)
run out, flow out (liquids) ..... ntwem (W,T), untem (E)

run over
run over something ..... kerrk-wem

running water ..... anyerr (E), awarr, rew, urew (E)

runny
liquid or sloppy mixture ..... aperlk-aperlk (T,E), irrngwa (E), kwaty-kwaty[1] (W,T), rew-rew, rlkwer-rlkwer (E)
go watery or runny ..... kwaty-irrem (W,T), rew-rew-irrem
make something go runny ..... aperlk-aperlk-ilem (T,E), rew-rew-ilem, irrngwilem (E), kwaty-kwaty-ilem (W,T)

rush
doing something in a rush, in a hurry ..... athathel, arweketherwek (W,T), urekethwerek (E)
rushing off and leaving things behind ..... arnkarnp (T,E), ngwarrertakert (W,T)
rush around ..... lwakelhem (W,T), arlakelhem (E), lwakerrem (W,T), arlakerrem (E), anarrkenelhem (W,T), arrkwerelhem
rush in excitedly, be impatient ..... athek-irrem
rush in and grab things ..... ampak-irrem (W,T), arrapayernem
rush along (water) ..... werrk-werrk alhem (W,T), werrk-werrk alpem (W,T)

rush around and create a disturbance (from English) .... tharremap-ilem

rustle

make a rustling, rattling or scratching sound .... inkerrem

make something rattle or rustle .... inkerrelh-ilem

Ryans Well .... Anyem Kwaty

rye beetle grass .... taty-taty[1]

Ss

sacred objects .... tywerreng

sacred place .... amek-amek, anganty (W,T)

sad

feeling sad or sorry .... alharrp (W,T), alhwarrp (T,E), alharrp-alharrp (W,T), alhwarrp-alhwarrp (T,E), altarrp (W,T), arrakelakel (E), alther (T,E), alem altywer (W,T), anert altywer, anert arltwang (W,T)

feeling sadness, loneliness or homesickness .... irrar[2]

feel sad .... alharrp-irrem (W,T), alhwarrp-irrem (T,E), altarrp awelhem (W,T), altarrp-irrem (W,T), alpwely-irrem

feel sad or upset over men (women) .... anthwerrng-irrem (T)

safe

feeling safe or protected from something .... akaty-akaty

sag

get wrinkled, skin go slack or loose .... altyek-altyek-irrem, altyekelhem, alyemp-alyemp-irrem

sagging (of breasts) .... parray (E)

salad .... mern atherrk

saliva .... arrelty[2], arrwek (T,E), iylkerr (E), pelh[1]

salt .... ker ikwemey ilenh-ilenh (T), melyek (E), ilewerr, ulewerr (E)

salt (from English) .... thalt

salty, bitter, sour-tasting .... tyekert[1], alyelk, alyew-alyew (E)

salty water .... ilewerr-ilewerr (W,T)

salt lake .... ilewerr, ulewerr (E)

saltbush .... arelyerrelyerr (W), ilewerr-ilewerr (W,T)

(the) tall saltbush .... anngey-anngey

same

something that is the same as something else, the same thing .... anyent akwet, rantey (E)

the same old thing, same as always .... irrkaty, amperreny (E), marany (T,E)

two things that are the same as, or very similar to, each other .... rant-atherr

more than two things that are the same as, or very similar to, each other .... inant-inant, inantarrety (W,T)

samphire .... akwely-akwely (E)

sand .... lher, urler (T,E)

sandy country .... arerrk (W,T), lher-lher[1] (SP)

coarse sand .... lyerl

drifts of sand left by floodwater .... twemper[2] (T,E), twerr (T,E), lher twemper (T,E)

small sandy rise .... lher twerrp

sand goanna *(Gould's)* .... arlewatyerr

sandalwood .... ankwerlay (W,T), ankwerley (T,E)

sandhill .... arerrk (W,T), twerrp, urterrp (T,E)

sandhill country .... urler (T,E)

sandhill canegrass .... penng (E)

sandhill grevillea .... aywel (T,E)

sandhill pituri .... arwenp, ngkwerlp arwenp (W,T), ngkwerlp atherrk

sandhill python .... ahelh-ahelh (W), ahenenh, aheneny (T,E), nwey (T), uney (E)

sandhill wallaby .... kwarlp

Sandover lily .... alyerlk-alyerlk (W), iylelty (E), lyelkenng (E)

Sandover River .... Urapenty

sandpaper

sandpaper something to make it smooth .... yarr-wem

satisfied

feeling satisfied (from eating) .... anhwerlk (W,T), anert anhwerlk (W,T), anerteng (E)

feel satisfied from eating .... anhwerlk-irrem (W,T), anerteng-irrem (E)

satisfy hunger or thirst .... antyetem (E), arrwer-ilem[1] (T,E)

exclamation of satisfaction .... yartey (W) (?)

Saucepan *(star constellation)* Ingkapeny (E), Ingkartek (E), Pwereytarr (E)

savage ahangerr, ahelengkw (E)

save

save someone tangkelh-ilem (W,T)

save someone's life, revive itethek mpwarem (E)

save something for someone awakem

save something for someone (respect language) akelawerl-wem (E)

save something for oneself awakelhem

something that is left or saved for later arlwarreng (E)

save something for later arlwarrernem (T,E)

save something for oneself, not share impen-irrem (T,E)

say angkem

say something loudly arnterr angkem

say inappropriate things, say the wrong thing akengenty angkem, apal angkem

say something in a particular way ilem

say something about yourself ilelhem, tyantelhem

say the name of someone or something anewem[1] (W,T), inewem (T,E)

say each other's names anewerrem (W,T), inewerrem (T,E)

say your own name anewelhem (W,T), inewelhem (T,E)

say that something bad will happen to someone arltwerrker-iwem (E)

say that you are going to talk to someone about something twernelhem, uternelhem (E)

say that you don't know about something arnernkem

say that you want to keep things to yourself ayerrp ilelhem

say you will give someone something and then not do it anwerlkel anthem[1] (W,T)

say you don't want to do something menty ilem

say you will do something anaraty-ilem (T,E)

scab ntyew, ntyewey

scabies arrkenty[1] (T), irrkenty (W), rtety-rtety

scalp *(from English)* kerlp

scalp something kerlpem-ilem

scar kwerrm (E), mpaty[1], impelty (E)

scar on chest, stomach and arms (ceremonial) rrmwa (W,T), rrmwang (W,T), urrma (T,E)

scar on women's upper arm and breasts amarr

scared ater, atna anik (E), atna ateralth (E)

feel scared arralty anem (T,E), ater-irrem

scarf *(from English)* ankety

scatter

scattered all over the place intyarr (W,T), alperrty (T,E), akalk, apanp

get scattered all over the place apanp-irrem, akalk-irrem, alperrty-irrem (T,E)

scatter things around alperr-wem (T,E), alperrty-wem (T,E), irrarnp-wem (W,T), intyarr-wem (W,T), irrarnp-irrarnp-ilem (W,T)

scatter, fall down lernelhem

scent

a person's or animal's scent ikwa (T,E), ikwang (T), kwang (W)

scented oilgrass aherr-aherr, areng-areng (E)

school *(from English)* kwerl

schoolteacher (from English) kwerl tety

scissors *(from English)* nep-nep

scoop

small wooden shovel or scoop mwar, tyerrker (E)

scoop used for handling hot coals, cooking food antyanp[1] (E)

scoop something up (water) athankwem (T,E), arnweng-inem (W,T)

scoop up or pour liquid, get petrol inpem (T,E)

scorpion anem atherr-akert (W), aneth-akert

scorpion (respect language) utepeng-utep (E)

scrape

scrape something to make it smooth arrpem, yarr-wem, arterrp-ilem

scrape burnt hair or skin off an animal or skin off a tuber tewem

scrape food to make soft alywelenhem (E)

scraper *(stone)* alywek

scratch
scratch someone ..... angernem[1], alherrem[1] (E), arreynem (E), irrkernem (W,T)
scratch something off something ..... rrpwarem (W,T), urrparem (T,E), iparem (E)
scratch yourself ..... ahinelhem (E), angernelhem, arreynelhem (E), irrkernelhem (W,T)
scream ..... arlkem, arralthelhem (T,E), arralthem (T,E)
screw
something's neck ..... itutnhem (E)
frown, screw up face ..... altyekelhem
scrub ..... werrk, arnam werrk (W,T), arnang werrk (W,T), artna (E), nwanth (W,T), unanth (T,E)
scrubby country ..... nwanth-nwanth (W,T), unanth-unanth (T,E)
thick scrub ..... pwely (E)
scrub wattle ..... ampwey (E)
scruffy ..... altelhey (W,T), iltelhey (T,E), nywet-nywet[2] (T)
become scruffy ..... altelhem
sea ..... alay[1], kwaty alay
search
search for something ..... apalenthwem (W,T), apalunthem (T,E)
search in vain ..... uyarem (T,E), yarem (W), ywarem (T)
search through a house or place ..... irrkerem
season
beginning of seasons ..... akwerrk[1], rlwa (W,T), rlwang (W,T), urla (E)
secret ..... kwenameny (T)
secret, sacred ..... tywerreng
story that is secret ..... kertemwengk
talking in a secretive way ..... marnterlpel (W,T)
keep something secret from others ..... mweny rrkwem
secretly ..... anyenng, anyenngel, arwengkel
eat secretively ..... ankeyel arlkwem
sedge *(plant, type of)* ..... anker-anker[2] (E)
see
see, look ..... arem
see (respect language) ..... arrep-ilem
be unable to see, see only a bit ..... atharem
not see anyone (when you arrive at a place) ..... ampenyel alhem
see someone coming ..... arnarem, analty arem (W)
see someone off ..... artwarem (W,T), irtwarem
see something that is faintly visible ..... ywer-ywer arem (W,T)
see someone do something ..... anngel arrernem (T,E) (?)
see-through
light-weight (of clothing) ..... ararr
seed ..... annga, anngang (W,T)
edible seed ..... anterrng, arnwety (W,T), ntang (E)
seed paste ..... ntang irrngwa (E), anterrng irrngwa (E)
bitter seeds inside some fruits ..... kart[1] (W,T)
coolibah seed ..... aley[1], ankwerrern (E), ankwerrernayt (T)
desert kurrajong seeds ..... ngkweyang
dogwood seeds ..... ntyer (T)
dry seeds (especially of the dogwood) ..... alyaly (W)
green seeds of the dogwood and kurrajong ..... artwengarr (T,E)
ghost gum seeds ..... ulemparrty (E)
pencil yam seeds ..... arratwek, kam (T,E)
red seeds from the bean tree ..... ngal-ngal
yellow or white seeds from the bean tree ..... mpetyan-mpetyan[1] (E)
small hollow made in flat ant bed where seeds are placed for husking ..... urraty (E)
lay seedpods out so that they can be beaten ..... alyent arrernem (W,T)
beat seedpods with a stick (especially said of mulga and dogwood) ..... alyent atwem (W,T)
crush seeds with a round rock ..... alyaly atwem (W)
seed capsules
of bloodwood ..... ntewal, arrkipangkwarl
of river red gum ..... aperaley (W,T), aperrper (E)
seedlings ..... akwerrk[1]
seedpods
of kurrajong ..... alyalyarr (E)
seep
ooze out of something ..... anthwem (T,E), thelelhem
self
Goes on verbs to show that someone or something is doing the action to themself ..... +elh+
self-raising flour ..... thelperretyen (W,T)
send
send something to someone ..... ilanthem, thwenem (E)

send someone away, send someone off to do something ..... ilanthem, alharlkwem, ulilem (E)
send a message for someone to come ..... antangkelhem, antangkem

senile
a bit senile; stupid ..... arert-arert

senior person ..... angerr-pat, angerr[1], angerrety atyetyart, aywang intert (W,T), rltwa (W,T), rltwang (W,T), tyerrty angerrety (W,T), urlta (E), angerrety-iteng (E)

senses ..... iterrenty

sensitive ..... irrngerrng (E), tyelety (E), tikeley
feel sensitive, touchy or jumpy ..... irrngerrng-irrem (E), tyelety-irrem (E) pwerep-irrem

separate
on one's own ..... akalk, anyent, inga
spread apart ..... akalkew-akalk, akalk-akalk (E)
two people on their own (separate from others) ..... ingatherr
group of people (more than two) on their own (separate from others) ..... ingarey
doing things separately (because of kinship restrictions) ..... alewal (W,T)
become separate ..... akalk-irrem, rlwart-irrem (W,T), urlart-irrem (E)
separate one thing out from another ..... reng inem (W,T), reng-reng inem (W,T), rlwart-ilem (W,T), urlart-ilem (E), akalk-ilem, akalkelh-ilem
separate while hunting ..... anpaty-irrem (T), anpert-irrem (T)
separate self out from other people ..... angakelhem
separate a person from another ..... angakelh-ilem, ingekelh-ilem, arwekar-ilem

septum ..... intyengintyerl (E)

serious
serious law or business (something that can't be played around with) ..... mwekeny, mwekenh, mweketyey (W,T)

set *(sun or moon)* ..... irrpem, aylpem (E)

set *(sun)* ..... aherrk aylpenhem (E), aherrk iltyem anem (E), aherrk irrpem, aherrk irrpenhem, aylpar anenhem (E)

settle
settle down (in a place) ..... arternp-irrem, kwak-irrem
settle down after argument or fight or sickness ..... angemang-irrem (W,T), tyen-irrem (W,T)
settle someone down ..... anngwanng-ilem, aparlp-parlp-ilem (W), arternp-ilem, arternpelh-ilem
'Settle down' ..... kel anay

Seven Sisters *(constellation)*
Pleides ..... Arrarrkw (T,E), Kwerraly Angerr, Peltharr Map (W,T), Alyang Rlkwang (W,T) (?)

several ..... rrpwety (W,T), rrpwetyarrp (W,T), urrpety (E), urrpetyarrp (E), urrpetyarrp-ingar (E)
several times ..... rrpwety-ingar (W,T), urrpety-ingar (E), urrpety-areng (E)

sew, mend ..... atanthem

sex
have sex with someone (sensitive language) ..... anternem
have sex with someone else's husband or wife ..... antay-wem (W,T), arlkwer-irrem[2] (W)

shade ..... lywa (W,T), lywang (W,T), ulya (E)
shade (from English) ..... tyeyt
shade (respect language) ..... lywenty (W), ngkwely
good solid shade ..... angkwelk (E), angwarlp (T,E), lywerrng (W,T), yar-yar (E)
sparse or patchy shade ..... irrkerleng, irrkerlerrk (E), lywang irrkerleng (W,T), ulya irrkerleng (E)
shading eyes with hand ..... merlpeng (W,T), urlengimar (E), rlwengemar (T)
shade eyes with hand ..... ingkerrkentyel arem (W), merlpengel arem (W,T)

shadow ..... lywa (W,T), lywang (W,T), ulya (E)

shake
shake, shiver ..... arrewem
shake head in disagreement ..... akak-atwem[2] (E)
shake hands ..... arntwerrkerrem, iltyang rrkwerrem (W,T)
shake someone or something ..... tyek-tyek-ilem[2] (W)
shake parts of the body ..... arrkem (E)

shake legs when preparing for a fight (women) .... anwerntem (W,T)
shake self .... ilperlper-welhem, ilperrper-welhem (E)
shake something out .... lernem
shake something off part of yourself .... lernelhem
shake bush plum tree to make the fruit fall down .. ywerrkem, rwerrkem (T), ilperlper-wem

shallow .... akern
shallow water .... kwaty kanty (T), kwaty akern

shame .... apwer (W,T), apur (E), nyerr, nyerrel
shamefully .... artep nyerr
shame, shamefully (respect language) .... merrkwernerl (E)
person who is ashamed or embarrassed .... apweralth (W,T), apuralth (E), nyerralth
having an appropriate degree of modesty or shame .... anenyerr
being shamed because you know you have behaved badly .... anenyerr
without feeling shamed ... alhalhek (E), alhewer
be ashamed, feel shy or shamed .... apur-irrem (E), apwer-irrem (W,T), nyerr-irrem, apwer-apwer-irrem (W,T), lwereny-irrem (W,T), ulereny-irrem (E)
feel shamed or uncomfortable .... pwerep-irrem
make someone feel shamed, shy or embarrassed .... apwerel anthem (W,T), apurel anthem (E), nyerrel anthem

shanghai, catapult *(from English)* .... tyangar (W,T), tyangay (E)

share
generous, sharing .... imeng, atham-atham
be generous, share .... imeng-irrem, atham-irrem
share things out .... alperrty-ilem (T,E), alperrtyelh-ilem (T,E), arrkilem (E)
not share food or drink .... nwanthem (W,T), unanthem (E)

sharp .... arrerlp, arrerlp-arrerlp, inernt-inernt (T) (SP)
sharpen something .... arrerlp-ilem

shave *(have a)* .... althelhem

shaved head .... kapert aketh, kapert ather-ather (W,T), kapert pweley

she .... ra, rang (W,T)

shed *(bark or skin)* .... akap-rlwelhem (W,T), akap-irlwelhem, lywelhem, rlwelhem (W,T)

shed *(building)* .... warl

sheep .... yep-yep
sheep (from English) .... tyep²

sheet of iron *(from English)* .... tyetepayen

shell .... tyakwerl (W)
eggshell .... ika (T,E), kwart ika (T,E)
shell an egg .... ikewem (E), irrnyewem (W,T), irrnyiwem (E), kek-wem

shelter .... antywa, antywang (W,T), wak (E), warl
a shade or shade shelter .. lywa (W,T), lywang (W,T)

shield .... alkwert
shield (respect language) .. rengalengal (E)
handle of a shield .... arwa², arwang (W,T)
pretend shield, toy shield .. alkwerteng-alkwert
shield yourself with something .... ilpelhem

shift
shift camp .... alal-wem
shift out of the way .... rntwarr-irrem, anam-irrem¹, arnang-irrem
shift self onto one side .... arrethaker-welhem
shift something .... anam-ilem, anamelh-ilem, arnang-ilem², arnangelh-ilem

shimmer .... arraly-arraly-irrem (T,E)

shin .... lterr, ngkwern

shinbone .... atyang ngkwern (T), lterr ngkwern

shine
shiny .... alenm-alenm, amparrkey, amparrkey-amparrkey
sparkling (water, sunshine, glass) .... arlkerrk² (W,T)
shine, sparkle .... alenm anyem, alenm-alenm-irrem, amparrkem, arraly-arraly-irrem (T,E), arlkerrk-wem (W,T), ngkwarrkem (W,T), ingkwarrkem (T,E)
shine brightly .... arrtyenem (E)
look white or shiny, sparkle or shine white ..... mperlkem, akerlkem
shine in the distance (light or bushfire) .... ayarrty-rnem (E)
shine a light on something, shine (sun) .... alernem¹, alhenem

shiny-leaved wattle .... irrar¹ (E), perrar (W,T), pirrar

shirt .... ulta (T,E)
shirt (from English) .... tyart

shit ... ana, anang (W,T), kart[1] (W,T)
shit (baby talk) ... kaka (T)
have a shit ... lhwem (T), lwem[1] (W), ulhem (T,E), atna ulhem (E)
have a shit (baby talk) ... key-key-irrem (E)
shiver *(with cold)* ... arrewem
shock
give someone a shock ... anwerlkel anthem[2], anwerlkelh-ilem
shoe ... ingkekenh (E)
shoe (from English) ... pwet
shoo flies away
(from English) ... atyaw-tyaw-ilem
shoot
shoot something ... atyerrem[2]
shoot yourself ... atyerrelhem
shooting star ... parrty
shop, store ... thew
short ... akert[1] (T,E), karteng, twengk (W), urtety (E)
short and fat ... mwat (E)
something short and round in shape ... rlwatert
short cut ... akwerterrp (T,E), ntwertety (W,T), untertety (E)
take a short cut ... akwerterrp alhem (T,E), ntwertety alhem (W,T), untertety alhem (E)
short hair ... kapert twengk (W)
shoulder ... pwerlep, arety
point of the shoulder ... anpeth (E), pwerlep annga (W,T)
top of the shoulder, back of the neck ... ntywa (W,T), ntywang (W,T)
carry something on the top of the shoulder ... untyel angem (E)
carry something slung across shoulder ... alpalyel angem, intarlp angem (W,T), ntwarlp angem (E)
shoulder joint ... pwerlep annga (W,T)
shoulderblade ... pwerlep, pwerlep ngkwern (E), alkwert-alkwert (SP)
shout ... arlkem, arrantyakem (W,T)
shout (respect language) .. kwep-anem (E), ngkwep-anem (E)
shout to let people know about something ... arlkelh-ilem
shout to warn about danger ... arrpwernem
shovel
small wooden shovel or scoop ... tyerrker (E), antyanp[1] (E)
shovel spear ... arrwemper (W,T), urremper (T,E)
show
show something to someone ... irlparrernem (W,T), iylparrernem (E), imernem, nernem (E), nyely-ilem (T,E)
show the way ... irlparrernem (W,T), iylparrernem (E)
show self, show something about yourself ... imernelhem
show off
showing off ... arlkwer-arlkwer, arrkwer, arrkwer-arrkwer, urlker-urlker (E), ltherrp-ltherrp (W,T), tyenkarl-tyenkarl (W,T), tywenap (T,E), tywenap-tywenap (T,E)
show off ... tyenkarl-irrem (W,T), tywenelhem, utyenelhem (E), arrkwerelhem
show off, act sexily ... ngkwern-kweny-irrem
show off (from English) ... reken-irrem (W,T), riken-irrem (E), tywenap-irrem (T,E), tywenap-tywenap-irrem (T,E)
shower
have a shower ... pwerlp-irrem
shower of rain, small amount of rain ... lthel, kwaty lthel, lyelyaw (E), nyeyepenyey (W), tyeyepetyey (W), awerrp[2] (W)
shower (rain) ... akarl-wem (W,T), tyetyel-wem (E)
shrike-thrush ... alerterrperterrp (?)
shrink ... pwarn-irrem
shrivelled ... alpwely, alyemp-alyemp[1]
shrivel up ... alpwely-irrem, alyempelhem
shrivel up (desert raisin fruit) ... alhirrem, alherrem (W,T)
shuffling ... thwerremp-thwerr (T,E)
shut ... alhap, marnt, martelhenty (T,E), mety, mwernt[2] (W,T)
become shut ... marnt-irrem (W,T), mwernt-irrem (W)
shut something ... marnt-ilem (W,T), martem (T,E), wap-arrernem
be blocked off, shut or closed ... wap-anem, wap-arrernelhem
shy *(go to 'shame')*
shy away
shy away from doing what is asked of you (from English) ... kanern-irrem

shy away from something you've had a bad experience with ..... wenng-irrem (T,E)

sick

a sick or injured person ... kwern (W,T), mernt[1] (W,T), rlkert, akeng (T,E), anety (W,T), arntety (E), inya (W), inyang (W)

a bit unwell .... akeng-akeng (T,E), kwern-kwern (W,T), anety-anety (W,T)

sickly .... arrmaly-arrmaly (T,E)

feeling sick in the stomach .... anert anety (W,T), anert akeng (E)

critically ill, really sick .... irrewaly angerr, irrewaly, arekwenth-kwenth (T,E)

feeling really sick .... antywekelywekely

get sick or injured .... rlkert-irrem, akeng-irrem (T,E), arntety-irrem (E), kwern-irrem (W,T), mernt-irrem (W,T)

get sick (respect language) .... atnerrk-irrem (E)

become sickly, floppy, or weak (in the body) ...... arrmaly-arrmaly-irrem (T,E)

be critically ill .... irrewaly intem

feel nauseous or sick .... alyelk-irrem

feel unwell or in pain ...... antywekelywekely-irrem

make someone sick .... akeng-ilem (T,E), anety-ilem (W,T), arekwenth-kwenth-ilem (T,E), kwern-ilem (W,T), rlkert-ilem, mernt-ilem (W,T), antywekelywekely-ilem

sick of something, fed up arnernkem

sickness .... arrwengkelth, pwenty[1] (E)

sickness (from English) ... tethet

sickness caused by traditional practices such as boning or singing .... arrwengkelth

sickness that can be caught from going close to a place where people have died and been buried .... marrwelyenng (W), marrwelyen (T)

side

of something .... arrker, itep, iter, itep-ampeny, itep-thayt, iter-ampeny

edge or side .... arrethaker

area, vicinity .... -ampeny[2]

side (from English) .... -thayt

of a creek .... twemper[2] (E), twerr (T,E)

(along) the side .... itep-angkwerr, iter-angkwerr

this side of something (on the speaker's side) ..... angath, angath-ampeny

on the other side of something .... anwenger (E), arrwengak, irrweper (E), rntwarr, rntwarr-ampeny

be on or move to the other side of something ... anwenger-irrem (E), arrwengak-irrem

of a person or animal ...... ltwa (W,T), ltwang (W,T), ulta (T,E)

of the neck .... ita (E) (?)

on one's side .... arlkarlker

take sides in a fight .... unkil-ilem (E)

sideways .... talkw

sigh .... amany-irrem

sign *(one's name)* .... ingkwernelhem (T,E), arrernelhem

signal

signalling with hands ..... iltyem-iltyem (W,T)

signal or wave to someone .... akwerrem (W,T), iltyerrem, iltyirrem (T,E)

use handsigns .... iltyel-ilem (E), iltyem iltyem angkem

significant .... angerr[1], impen

silent

in a huff .... arnkely

silky browntop *(grass)* ..... arlperlp

silky pear *(go to 'bush banana')*

silly .... akwerrk-akwerrk (W,T), arert, arert-arert, arwengk (T,E), rrwem-rrwem (W,T), urrem-urrem (T,E), arwengk-arwengk (T,E)

become silly in the head .. akeleraperap-irrem (E), arwengk-irrem (T,E), raperap-irrem (W), rrwem-rrwem-irrem (W,T), urrem-urrem-irrem (T,E)

do silly things .... ywetherrk-irrem (T,E), uyetherrk-irrem (E)

silver cassia .... apwen

silver witchetty .... alhanker (E), lywey (W), perley (W,T), peyley (E)

similar

be like, be similar to or resemble someone or something else .... -artek, -apeny (E)

be like someone .... inngelhem

things that are similar to each other .... arrerek-arrer (T,E), rtwang-rtwang (T), twek-twek (W), itwek-itwa (E)

something is similar to or the same as something else ... rantey (E)
two things that are the same as or very similar to each other, two identical things ... rant-atherr
more than two things that are the same as, or very similar to, each other ... inant-inant, inantarrety (W,T)

sinew ... alwerrng

sing *(people)*
sing a song or ceremony .. alyelhem, alyem, alyerrem
sing (generally in a group), sing along ... ayatwem
sing (respect language) ... amerrkwernem (E)
'sing' someone or something with supernatural powers or magic ... alyem, arrilem, arrilenty-ilem (T,E), artimperr-wem (T,E), arrwengkelthel alyem (E)
'sing' each other with supernatural powers or magic ... alyerrem
'sing' oneself to get supernatural powers or magic ... arrilelhem, alyelhem
make a humming noise ... arnwer-irrem
'singalong', any kind of singing get-together ... mwerlkenty

sing *(birds)* ... angkem
sing (just of bellbirds) ... ilperlp-irrem (W), inmenm-irrem (W)

sing out
yell out ... arlkem
sing out (respect language) ... ameram-irrem, kwep-anem (E), ngkwep-anem (E)
sing out to someone to get their attention ... arrpwernem, paw-arlkem (T), arlkelh-ilem

singe
singe fur, hair or scales off an animal ... rlpwat-ilem (W,T), urlpat-ilem (T,E)
put animal carcass on fire to singe off hair, fur or scales ... pwerlp-wem (T,E)

single
single man, man without a wife, widower .. arnkenty-areny
single woman, or a woman who is on her own ... arlweker-areny

single-men's camp ... arnkenty
single-men's camp (respect language) ... arramenty, tyangkay (T,E)

single-women's camp ... arlweker
single-women's camp (respect language) ... irrewatyent, anperr (E)

sip *(something)* ... ltyantywem (T,E)

sister
elder sister ... angkwer[3], yay, arrwemp (SP)
elder sister (baby talk) ... yay (SP)
eldest sister ... aletharr (T,E)
younger sister ... atyey
younger sister of a man ... angalthen (E)
man's sister (respect language) ... ngayekenh (W,T), ngayekety (E)
health sister (from English) ... theth

sister-in-law
woman's sister-in-law ... arnteng, arnteng-arnteng
woman's sister-in-law (baby talk) ... arnteng-arnteng
wife's sister ... anew

sit
sit down, be seated ... anem[1]
sit down, be seated (respect language) ... ayepel-irrem
sit in a group ... angerr-irrem[1]
sit yourself down ... arrernelhem
kneel ... ampwethel-ayeth anem (E)
sit bent over ... anwekert-anem
sit cross-legged ... arntarlperrk, arntimerrk (E), aymparrk anem (E), rtapety-irrem
sit on heels or haunches .. amper irrertety anem (T,E), irrkweynar anem (E)
sit on one side (e.g. on one buttock) ... arrethaker anem
sit with arms wrapped around legs ... artarnk anem (W,T), atangk anem (E), inwanyerr anem (E)
sit with knees up ... anel-ayeth anem (E)
sit with legs crossed in a number 4 shape ... tyampernem (W,T), tyakwert anem
sit with legs curled back or bent ... akalker anem (E), mwenyar (W), arlwemeny anem, rtapety anem, irrkweynar anem (E)

sit with legs straight out .. rlkerr intem, rlkerremp-rlkerr anem, iylkerr-iylkerr anem (E), tywerr intem (E)
sit drying out or getting warm in the sun .... tek-anem
sit quietly and thoughtfully .... akarntel anem (W,T)
sit in the wind to cool down .... wernelhem (E)
sit not moving, sit on 'arse' .... atnel-ayel (T), atnerlayeth (E)

sit-down money week
(from English) .... malewik

Six Mile .... Pmara Jutunta

sizzle
make a sizzling or bubbling sound (meat) .... tyelyely-irrem (E), tyely-irrem (E), lyely-lyely-irrem (T), lyely-lyely-lyely-irrem (W)

skeleton .... irrernng, lthan (W,T), tyarrenng (W,T), tyerrenng (T), ngkwern tyarrenng (W), ngkwern tyerrenng (T)
skeletal .... anngirrenty (E), anngerrenty (E)

skewer
used for closing the belly cavity of animals before cooking .... alemp (W,T), interlp (T,E), rltimp^2 (T)
used for cooking Solanum chippendalei .... ntywert (T), pernampal (T)
skewer something onto a stick .... tyet-atanthem (W), intak rnternem (E)

skid .... alyelk-irrem, alyelkelhem
skidding along the ground .... ahertety^1 (E)
throw something so that it slides or skids along the ground .... irrepereperr-wem

skilled .... lywenpeny, tyak (E)

skin
of a person or animal .... ayenp
of a snake or lizard .... irrnya, irrnyang (W,T)
on fruits or seeds .... ayenp, irrnya, irrnyang (W,T)
skin light in colour (from English) .... apekath, apekath-apekath
shed skin (snakes and lizards) .... irrnyek ampwem (E), irrnyewelhem (W,T), irrnyiwelhem (E)
skin or peel something .... ikewem (E)
skin an animal .... pwalh-iwem (E)

skin and bone .... anngirrenty (E), ngkwern-ngkwern, ngkwernant

skin name .... arreny (W,T), arreyn (E), ikwa (T,E), ikwang (T), anpernenty, anpernerrenty
skin names (see diagram p. 744) .... Kemarr, Mpetyan, Ngal, Pwerl, Pwerrerl, Peltharr, Petyarr (E), Pengart, Penangk, Ngwarray, Kngwarray (E)
ending used when asking a person what their skin name is .... -apatherr
'What is (a person's) skin name?' .... angwenh-apatherr (W,T), wenh-apatherr (W,T), iwenh-apatherr
someone who is the same skin as oneself .... ilern-apatherr (E)

skink
types of .... alyalkarr (T,E), ameng irrkwenh-irrkwenh (W,E), ameng irrkweny-irrkweny (T,E), lyangkay-lyangkay (E), ikwarr (E)

skinny .... ampwa, ampwang (W,T), ampwetyampw (E), lyerrer (E), ngkwern-ngkwern, ngkwernant, tyew (W,T), utyew (E), ampweyampw, ampeyamp
skinny or bony person (an insult) .... lthan (W,T), ulthan (E) (SP)
get skinny .... ampwerrem

skite
brag, big-note yourself .... irrpelth-irrem, urrpelth-irrem (E), nakelhem, tywenelhem, utyenelhem (E), atyetyart-irrem, narlkwelhem (E)

skull .... akarnng^1 (E), kapert ngkwern (T,E)

sky .... alker
high in the sky (where something is hardly visible) .... alker anert, alker tyelk

slack
loose .... alpwely, tyek (E)
go slack or loose .... alpwely-irrem, alyempelhem, alyemp-alyemp-irrem, tyek-irrem (E)

slap .... atwem

sleep .... ankwa^1, ankwang (W,T)
'sleep' (in the eyes when you wake up) .... arnkwarn (E), rrkwa (W,T), rrkwang (W,T), irrkwa (E)

sleep (baby talk, from English) ... pay-pay
go to sleep ... ankwang intem (W,T), ankwa intem (E)
get sleepy, fall asleep ... ankwek-irrem (E), ankwerrem, annga lthwem (W,T), annga ulthem (E)
go to sleep (respect language) ... lpwanem, ulpanem (E)
half asleep ... ankwapaperr (T,E)
deep sleep, fast asleep ... ankwang angerr (W,T), ankwa angerr (E), ankwa alert (E), pelp (E)
be fast asleep, be in a deep sleep ... pelp-ayntem
sleep a lot ... rrwempel anem (W), rrwempem (W,T), aylpmerrem (E)
drop off to sleep ... rlwank-anyem (E)
being unable to sleep ... irrkaw, ankwakel (E)
be unable to sleep ... irrkaw-irrem
send someone to sleep ... ankwathenem, ankwelem
lay (baby) down to sleep ... ankwathenem
sleep talk ... altyerr-altyerr, anengkerr-anengkerr (W,T)
talk in sleep ... altyerr-altyerr angkem, anengkerr-anengkerr angkem (W,T)

slender ... lyerrer (E), ampap-ampap (E)
grow tall and slender ... lyerrer-irrem (E)

slender glasswort *(plant)* ... karnkw (W,T)

slender pigweed *(plant)* ... ngkweytek (E)

slice, cut something ... akem[1]

slide *(on something)* ... alyelk-irrem, alyelkelhem

slime ... arntwatherrk[1] (E), nthwerrkamp (E), ntharrengarreng (W,T)
slimy ... alyelk

slingshot *(from English)* ... tyangar (W,T), tyangay (E)

slip over ... alyelk-irrem, alyelkelhem, arler-irrem

slippery ... alyelk, alyelk-alyelk, arler, arler-arler

slobbery ... iylkerr-iylkerr (E)
slobbery mouth ... arreylkerr-iylkerr (E)
slobber ... arrelty thelelhem, arrelty[2], iylkerr thelelhem (E)

slope
of a hill, etc. ... akwerlp
on a slope, on an angle ... thar, thar-thar
lie on a slope, on an angle ... thar intem
slope downwards ... arrarlernem (W,T)

sloppy
watery or runny ... aperlk-aperlk (T,E), rlkwer-rlkwer (E), rew-rew
liquid or sloppy mixture ... irrngwa (E), kwaty-kwaty[1] (W,T)
sloppy (ground) ... irrngwelth (E)
sloppy (of food) ... apely
make something go watery, sloppy or runny ... irrngwilem (E), aperlk-aperlk-ilem (T,E), kwaty-kwaty-ilem (W,T), rew-rew-ilem

slosh
sloshing sound ... lthap-lthap, rltap-rltap (W)
make a sloshing sound ... lthap-lthap-irrem, rltap-rltap-irrem (W)

slow
slowly, carefully ... arternp, manty (W), mwanty (T,E), mantyel (W), mwantyel (T,E), manty-manty (W), mwanty-mwanty (T,E)
slow down ... arternp-irrem
slow someone down ... arternp-ilem, arternpelh-ilem

slurp
slurping sound ... lthap-lthap, rltap-rltap (W)
make a slurping sound ... lthap-lthap-irrem, rltap-rltap-irrem (W)
slurp or lap (liquid) ... lthap-lthap antywem (T)

smack
give someone a smack ... apar atwem (T,E), palty atwem (E)

small ... akwek, akwek-akwek, akely (E), akely-akely (E)
really small ... akwek-amperl (T,E), akwek-antyey (W,T), akely-amperl (E)
small (respect language) ... akwetyakw (E)
small and round in shape ... artwert-artwert
a bit of something, a small amount of something ... akwek, akely (E)
small amount, something smaller ... akwek-awaty (T,E), akely-awaty (E)
make something smaller ... akwek-ilem

small of the back ... rtweth, urteth (T,E)

smart ... lywenpeny

smash
get smashed up ... ngkwelty-irrem
smash or break something ... ltewem (W,T), ultewem (T,E)

crush or smash something up..........mweltyem (W,T), apert-atwem (E), anthim-ilem (T,E), ngkwelty atwem, ngkwelty-ilem, ngkweltyelh-ilem, ngkweltyem (W,T)
smash or bust something..aterlk-ilem
smash something up to make it soft..........lpwelem (W,T), ulpilem (T,E)

smell
have a smell, give off a smell..........intyem[2]
give off a strong smell.....uneyntem (E)
smell something..........intyernem
having a bad smell..........npwa (W,T), npwang (W,T), unpa (E), npwakert (W,T), npwangerr (W,T), unpakert (E), unpangerr (E)
a smell or taste that makes you feel sick..........alyelk
the smell of fat or meat cooking..........intyem intyerrk, parntewelyewely (W,T)
the smell of hair or fur burning..........ntharr (T), utharr (E)
the smell of rain..........menyarenyar (T), mpengemp (W), nyemp (E)

smile..........atherrem, mweny-mweny-irrem

smoke..........kwert, rwang kwert (W,T), ura kwert (E)
smoky in colour..........ura kwert-kwert (E)
billowing cloud above smoke..........lerranty (W,T)
cloud of smoke..........angkarl
smoke from bushfire in distance..........antywer[1] (T,E)
smoke used for healing and for particular ceremonies..........lhwert
to smoke (fire)..........rntwem (W,T), urntem (T,E)
smoke or burn (from cooking)..........lhwert-irrem
'smoke' someone..........lhwertel ampem, lhwertel item, lhwertel-ilem, kwertelh-ilem, kwertel item (W,T)

smokes, cigarettes..........kwert
smokes (from English).....thekaret
smoke a cigarette..........kwert antywem

smoke bush..........ahert-ahert[1] (T,E)

smooth..........alyelk, alyelk-alyelk, arler, arler-arler
flat, level..........arterrp
make something smooth..alyelk-ilem, arterrp-ilem
smooth over, heal over....arterrp-irrem

smooth spiderbush..........arrngern, tywerlp (W,T)

snack
having a snack..........apak

snake
general words for snake...amwa[1], amwang (W,T), urnem (E)
snake (respect language)..arreperlk (E)
snake (from English)..........thenayek
snake venom..........antya[2] (T,E)
snake track..........amwang mpaty (W,T), urnem arlkeny (E)
winding path of a snake going fast..........areperrereperr (W,T)
black-headed python..........antwerrkenh (W,T), intwerrkenh (W), rwayerrp (T), rayerrp (T,E), urayerrp (E)
common brown snake.....arwerl-arwerl (E) (?)
desert death adder..........mantharr, antharr (E)
king brown snake..........arreperlp (W,T), tyamparl (T)
mulga snake..........atetherr arlkwenh, ikwelengk (T,E), kantharlkw (W,E), alhingk (E)
orange-naped snake..........perlap-perlap (E) (?), arnwekety-arnwekety (E) (?)
rainbow snake, water snake..........kwelay, akwerteyteng (E), kwelernarr (E)
western brown snake.....antywemp (T,E) (?), arriper (T,E) (?)
woma, sandhill python...ahelh-ahelh (W), ahenenh, aheneny (T,E), nwey (T), uney (E)
yellow-faced whip snake..arlewatyerr-arlewatyerr[1] (T,E), pwer arlewatyerr, pwer arlewatyerr-arlewatyerr (E)
types of blind snake..........ahaylengkeyler (E), arranyenganyeng (W,T), rtety arlkwenh-arlkwenh (W)
type of python..........irrimarnt (E)
types of snake..........arrakert rrpwerl (T), arranty[1] (W,T), arrwanty (W,T), aylperl-aylperl (E), irranty (W), tharrkarr-tharrkarr (E), ankwepenh (E), aylpenty-aylpenty (T,E), arlpenty-arlpenty (E), pwer arlpenty-arlpenty (W)

snake vine..........alyep[1], anwerl (E), arratherrk
snake vine grub..........arratherrkayt (E)

snappy gum..........arlketh[2] (T,E)

snatch *(something)*..........rakem

sneak
sneak up on someone or something..........apertem

sneakily .... anyenng, anyenngel, arwengkel
be sneaky (from English) .. kanern-irrem
sneeze .... ntyerrng-anyem
snore .... intyerrem
snot .... artwengkenng, inkwerr (E), mernt[1] (W,T)
lumps of dry snot .... tarl (E)
snotty gobbles *(fruit)* ...... ngkwerrm
snout .... alha[1], alhang (W,T)
so-so .... kwern-kwern (W,T), akeng-akeng (E)
soak
water soak into the ground .... antyernem[3] (W)
soakage .... angenty
soakage (from English) .... thewekety (T), theweketh (T), tywekety
very old soakage .... altywen (W)
soakage that is dug in a creek .... arnwengk (W,T)
water at the bottom of a soakage .... arlparlety (E)
dig a soakage .... angenty arrernem (E), angenty-ilem (E), arnwengk arrernem (E), arnwengk-ilem (W,T)
soaked .... anthwek-anthwek
soap *(from English)* .... thwep
soap powder .... rlkwerrp, urlkerrp (E)
Soapy Bore .... Arawerr
sob
choking sound when crying .... nthat-nthat
groan or moan .... nthat-irrem, nthat-nthat-irrem
soft
soft to the touch .... atyet[1], ipelhip (E), lpwa (W,T), ulpa (T,E), thelty (W,T), therrty (W,T), utelh (E), utelh-utelh (E)
soft (of food) .... anthwel (T,E), apely, anhwemp-anhwemp (W,T), anhamp-anhamp (T)
soft, tender (meat) .... atyet-atyet
soft inside part of fruits or damper .... alhwer (E)
soft fleshy part of the foot or hand .... lher-lher[2]
soft or faint (of sound) .... arrkay
go soft .... atyet-irrem, thelty-irrem (W,T)
go soft (fruits) .... rew-irrem
go soft from cooking .... anthwel-irrem (T,E)
make something go soft by cooking it .... anthwel-ilem (T,E)
soft drink *(from English)* .. kwelteringk
soft spinifex .... alatyeyt (E)
soldier bird .... impaymp (E), irnpernp (W,T)
sole *(of the foot)* .... ingka anert, ingkang anert (W,T), ingka ipert (E)
solid
solid, big .... ampwerrk, angerrety, artelhampw (E), awer-awer (E), awer[1] (E), twer (W,T)
sticky, solid (of honey or paint) .... intengk (W,T)
solidified blood .... ntyew, ntyewey
become solid, harden ...... rlterrk-irrem
go solid, solidify .... intengk-irrem (W,T), kelh-irrem
solitary .... anyent, inga
become solitary, be on one's own .... ingirrem, anyent-irrem
some
'some' as opposed to 'others' .... arrpenhem
somebody *(else)* .... arrpenh, ingwer (E)
someone or something
the same as me or us in some way .... arrpaty
the same as you in some way .... arrpengkw
the same as him/her/ them in some way .... arrpikw, arrpekw
something else
(this thing) and something else as well ..... thwen, then
something like
the one we are referring to .... weth-lkwer
something or other .... wenh (W,T), iwenh
something or other (from English) .... thametheng
when trying to remember something .... wenhekwey (W,T), iwenhakwey
somewhere
somewhere round there ... nheng-antey (E)
son
man's child .... aler
woman's child .... ampa
special word used by a mother to refer to her teenage son .... artar
son-in-law
woman's son-in-law .... mey-mey[1], mwer, rtwalty, urtalty (E)
man's son-in-law and daughter-in-law .... ahenterr (E) (?)
senior son-in-law or mother-in-law .... ampweyampw (SP), ampeyamp (SP)

son-in-law (young or closely related) ngkwernerrp[1] (E), ngwenyarr (W,E)
woman's son-in-law (respect language) ateyarrp
woman's young son-in-law (respect language) akwetyerr (T,E)
woman's son-in-law or a man's mother-in-law (respect language) alpment-penh (E)
two sons-in-law (respect language) arrpentharrp (E), arrpentharrp atherr (E)
woman's son-in-law's camp (respect language) ahileng (T,E), ampeny-ampeny (SP), rrwarlp[2] (W)
become mother-in-law/ son-in-law for someone rtwalty-irrem (W,T), urtalty-irrem (E)

song arreny (W,T), arreyn (E)
love song ilpenty
body designs and songs associated with women's ceremonies awely

songlark *(brown)* tyelk-aperrety-aperrety (T), tyelk-aperrertety (E), tyelyapwerety (W), tyelyapweretyapwerety (W,T), apweretyapwer (W)

sook
a sook rnwart-areny
sooky, sulky rnpart (W,T), urnpart (T)
get sooky arlelty-irrem, rnpart-irrem (W,T), urnpart-irrem (T)

sool
a dog onto someone or something artarrernem, ipernem (W,T)

soon lyet, alerl (E), neyel (E)
very soon, in a moment, by and by lyet war, lyetengarl-iperr (E)
sometime soon ngwenth war

sore
a sore, rash tywen, utyen (E)
having sores or ringworm merrkel (T,E)
feeling sore arekar, kwern (W,T), tywen, utyen (E)
sore (baby talk, from English) thew-thew[2]
get sore tywen-irrem, utyen-irrem (E)
feel sore or tender pwerep-irrem
make something sore tywen-ilem, utyen-ilem (E)

sorry (see also 'sad')
feel sorry for someone or something atham-irrem
say sorry, apologise rlwaty angkem (W,T), urlaty angkem (E)

sorry business
sorry camp mal-mal
meeting of families after someone has passed away mal-mal, panparl (W,T)
go for 'finishing up' or 'sorry' business mal-mal alhem
become bereaved, lose a family member aparlp-ilem, alhamp-irrem
someone whose child has died ywerlt (W,T)
'lose' a child ywerlt-irrem (W,T), anker-athek-irrem (T,E)
become a widow or a widower inpert-irrem, warlekwert-irrem (W,T)
become bereaved (especially of son or daughter) ankerel-irrem (E)
become bereaved of one's siblings lwarrpeny-irrem (E), ingirrem
respectful word which goes on kin terms when the particular relation has passed away -artwemeny
in mourning (respect language) alyent-artek (E)
substitute name kwementyay, kwenman, kwemarn
'finish up', sweep an area or camp where someone has passed away pewem
wail or cry in mourning (women) akayel arnem
wail or cry in mourning (men) wartay-irrem (E)
short hair (that has been cut in mourning) akampwerr (E), ampwerr (E)
cut hair in mourning akampwerr-ilelhem (E), urlpat-ilelhem (E), arrtyelhem (T,E)
cut yourself (men in mourning) alety-akelhem
cover self with ashes akerlkem
hold or embrace each other in mourning parnparl-ilerrem (W,T), panparl-irrem (W,T), kwety-arerrem (E), amel-rrkwem (W,T)
paint oneself with white clay (in mourning) atywerlkel-ilelhem (W,T), aytwerlkel-ilelhem (E), atywerlkelhem (T)

hairstring (belongings of the deceased) ..... waly-waly[2]
personal belongings (of the deceased) ..... ampeny[1], tempety
give away belongings to appropriate relations ... menty-irrem
someone who is not allowed to talk (because of bereavement) ..... akerter, kertemwengk, awenp (W,T)
food given to release speech taboo ..... awenp (W,T)
release a person from speech taboo ..... arrakert-ilem (T,E), ulypmakert-ilem (E), angkakert-ilem (E), angkeparr-ilem (E)

sort
sort things out, pick something out ..... angakem, urlanem (E), urrarem (T,E), reng inem (W,T), reng-reng inem (W,T), rlwart-ilem (W,T), urlart-ilem (E)
sort through things to find something ..... akent-wem (E), ilkakem, irrkerem
set things straight, sort out a problem ..... arraty-ilem
this sort of thing, this type of thing ..... nhenh-lkwer, nhelkwer
that sort of thing ..... weth-lkwer (T,E), yanh-lkwer (E)
'sort of', not up to standard ..... +eng-anyimp (E), -arrpantey, -arrpatenty (E)

soul, spirit ..... inka (W,T), inkang (W,T), yenk (T), kwerrern, uneng[2] (E)

sound
whirring, whooshing or rumbling noise ..... aywerr
make a whirring, whooshing or rumbling noise ..... aywerr angkem
make a hollow sound (ground) ..... antwerlperlp-wem (W,T), arntwangkem (W,T), pwep-angkem, urrper inkem (E), rrpwer inkem (T)
sound that wedge-tailed eagles make ..... kwelyalp

soup ..... ker kwaty
soup (from English) ..... thwep-thwep
hot soup with meat or vegetables ..... ker atewat, ker thwep-thwep

sour
salty, bitter or sour-tasting ..... tyekert[1]

sour plum ..... arrek (E)

south ..... antekerr, antekerr-penh (W,T), antekerr-pwenh (E)
south (respect language) .. antwekenety (W), antwekeneyt (E)
due south ..... antekerr arraty
south-west ..... antekerr altwerl
south-east ..... antekerr ingerr
southerly ..... antekerr-antekerr
south, from the south ..... antekerr-penh (W,T), antekerr-pwenh (E), antekerreng (W,T)
south wind ..... antekerreny (W,T), anyemilparr (E)

southern boobook ..... kwerrkwerrk, akekw (E) (?)
southern boobook (baby talk) ..... kwekew (T)

Southern Cross
(constellation) ..... Irrety Ingka (E), Irrety-kenh Ingka (E)

sow *(seeds)* ..... alpent-wem (T)

spark, sparks ..... ntyeth (W), intyeth, intety (T,E), iyntety (E)

spark up
spark jump out ..... iynteth ngkem (E), iynteth-iynteth-irrem (E), iyntety-irrem (E), intety-intety-irrem (E), unarnpem (E), anarnpem

sparkle *(go to 'shiny')*

sparrowhawk *(collared)* .... alekaper (?)

sparse
hair or shade ..... irreltyenng (E)

speak ..... angkem
speak a particular language ..... angkem
speak an Aboriginal language ..... angkety angkem (W,T), angka angkem (E), ulypma angkem (E)
speak (respect language) .. ameram-irrem
being unable to speak properly ..... akerter, apap (W), apekap, aleny apekap, angka apekap (E), ulypma apekap (E)
someone who doesn't speak properly ..... irrkwerteth (T,E), arrkwerteth (W)
speaking in a confused way ..... aperrpert, alhwerrkert, tetherrp-tetherrp
speak in a confused way, not speaking properly ..... aperrpert-irrem

not saying anything .... kertemwengk
speak badly of someone ... tyel angkem
speaking deceitfully .... aleny kanty (?)
speak loudly,
talk loudly in public .... aharlperr angkem (T,E), arlperr angkem
speak wrongly,
say the wrong thing .... apal angkem, apant angkem (W,T)
speak roughly or rudely ... ahel-irrem
speaking roughly
or rudely .... arrarletyel
say things that you
shouldn't say or
that will upset people ...... ywetherrk angkem (T,E), uyetherrk angkem (E)
release a person from
speech taboo or ceremonial
ban on speaking .... angkakert-ilem (E), ulypmakert-ilem (E), angkeparr-ilem (E), arrakert-ilem (T,E)

spear .... irrtyart
shovel spear .... arrwemper (W,T), urremper (T,E)
spear (respect language) .. altyerrper (E)
type of spear .... taty-taty² (T)
pretend spear, toy spear ... irrtyarteng-irrtyart
small spear, toy spear ..... tyetaty
spear-thrower .... amirr
extra piece of wood
added to end of spear ...... aparr
point or sharp piece
on the end of spear .... alart
join parts of a spear together
to make it longer .... arlarrernem (E)
small round bark toy
used by men and boys
for target practice
(with spears) .... lwekatat (W)
spear something,
pierce something with
a sharp object .... rnternem, atanthem
throwing a spear
with a woomera .... rtwely
throw a spear
with a woomera .... rtwely-wem
spearing something
right through .... tyetepetep (W,T), wetyerretyerr¹ (W)
spear yourself with
something sharp .... atanthelhem

spear grass .... lyayepelyay (W,T), layempeylay (T,E)

spear wattle .... uneynt (E)

spearbush, spearwood ... yenper, uyenper (E)

special .... impen, tyeperr

spectacled hare-wallaby .. kwarlp, lkwameny (W,T) (?)

spectacles, eyeglasses
(from English) .... kelath

speech
loud speech, a public
speaking style .... aharlperr (T,E), arlperr

Spencer's burrowing
frog .... angwethek (T), akngwethek (E), mpwekenh (T,E), mpwepenh (E), mpwelengk (E)

spew, vomit .... antew
to spew or vomit .... antew-irrem, alyelkelhem

spider .... wep
spider web .... wep (SP)
barking spider .... inwerl
type of spider .... yenarrk (W)

spider grass .... twemper-twemper (W)

spike .... lyek
spiky .... lyek-lyek, inernt-inernt (T) (SP)

spill
spill out .... altyewelhem
throw or tip
something out .... altyewem

spin
spin hair of fur to
make hairstring .... wem², alyep mpwarem, wenty-ilem (E), irrkety-wem
spin back, vibrate
(of boomerang or spear) ... ngarakwerr-irrem (E)
spin around .... amper-irrem (E)

spindle .... inta, werengkerr (W,T), werintyerr (W,T)

spine *(of goanna)* .... arlap (E)

spine *(of echidna)* .... lyek

spine-leaf wattle .... anker-anker² (E)

spiny-leaved wattle .... patwert (W,T), arleperlterrk (E)

spinifex .... aywert
buck spinifex,
bull spinifex .... arrangk (E)
feather-top spinifex .... antywer iper (E)
soft spinifex .... alatyeyt (E)
spinifex found in open
desert country .... arletyety (W)
spinifex (said by some
young speakers) .... inarleng
types of .... anker-anker² (E), arlwererrwengk (W), iper (E), rrkwal (W,T), irrkwal (E)
spinifex country .... manangkarr (W,T), rrkwal (W,T), irrkwal (E)
spinifex resin .... anker¹ (E), tyalangk (W,T), tyalangk kelh (W,T)

resin from spinifex found in open desert country ..... arletyety (W), arlekety (W)
spinifex ant ..... tyerremp (T,E)
spinifex ant eggs ..... tyerremp kwart (T,E)
medicinal substance made by these ants ..... tyerremp (T,E)
spinifex pigeon ..... arntwerrert, ntarrwerarrwer (W)
spiny-cheeked honeyeater ..... alpeyart-alpeyart (E), arrakwerakwer (T,E), arrety-arrety (W,T)
spiny-tailed monitor ..... antyerr (E)
spirit
spirit of a person or living thing ..... kwerrern, uneng^2 (E), inka (W,T), inkang (W,T), yenk (T), rntwer^2
types of spirit ..... analpenty (E), irrernt-areny (T,E), anngirrenty (E), arnam-areny (T), arnamarwengk (W,T), atham-areny (T,E), melarlp, mer akweteth (SP)
type of female spirit ..... aleperenty (E)
type of male spirit ..... awerreng-iylpwer (E)
person's spirit double ..... arremparreng
spirit of a person, from their conception place or the place where they were 'found' ..... anngirrenty (E)
make someone feel over-whelmed or dispirited ..... arawerrng rakem (E)
spit, spittle ..... pelh^1
spit something out ..... arrep-wem, pelh-wem
spitfire larva ..... arrenyanty (E) (?)
splash
go along splashing water ..... perlp-perlp alhem (W,T), peylp-peylp alhem (E)
splash water ..... lthap-lthap atwem (W), perlp-perlp atwem (W,T), peylp-peylp atwem (E)
splendid ..... mwerr anthwerr (W,T), mwerr angerr, mwerr-angker (E)
split
a split in something (sensitive language) ..... tyarrp
split something ..... akalthem (E), ampwatem (W), tyarrp-akem, tyarrp-atwem, tyarrp-ilem
split (a log) ..... rlweth-akem (W,T), urleth-akem (T,E)
split or cut something in half ..... rlkwerr ltwakem (W,T), rlkwerr ultakem (E)
split open ..... atem, aterlk-irrem, aterlkelhem, aterlkem, mpal-akelhem (W,T), pwernkem^2 (E), tyarrp-irrem, ultewelhem (T,E)
split open (rock) ..... tyarrp inkem (W)
split in half (such as stone, coolamon, boomerang) ..... mpalty-akelhem (W,T)
split, fork out (tree) ..... antarlkw-irrem
split up
split or divide things up ... alperrty-ilem (T,E), alperrtyelh-ilem (T,E), akalk-ilem, akalkelh-ilem
go in different directions .. akalk-irrem, alperrty-irrem (T,E)
split, separate from each other ..... imperrem^1
split-jack *(plant)* ..... alwerr
unripe fruit of ..... anker^2 (E)
spoil
spoil something ..... anety-ilem (W,T), akeng-ilem (T,E), kwern-ilem (W,T)
spoil something (respect language) ..... atnerrk-ilem (E)
spokesperson ..... rltwa (W,T), rltwang (W,T), urlta (E)
sporadically ..... anyentam-anyent, anyentek-anyent
spotted ..... intetyeng-intety (T,E), iyntethengeynteth (E), nteny-nteny (E)
make something spotty ... nteny-nteny-ilem (E)
spotted nightjar ..... akwet-akwet, angkertakwertak (W,T)
spouse ..... anew
husband or wife of someone in opposite generation moiety ..... aperl
husband or wife of someone in same generation moiety ..... arrkar
spread
spread apart, out wide, all over the place ..... akalkew-akalk, akalk-akalk (E), alperrty (T,E), antek (T,E), apapeth
spread something out ..... antek-ilem (T,E), antyepanty-wem (W,T), ilkakem, iwem
spread things out, scatter things ..... alperrty-ilem (T,E), alperrtyelh-ilem (T,E)
spread something out wide ..... aymperr-ilem (E), aymperrelh-ilem (E)

spread out a bed, blanket or groundsheet .... antyam-wem, panty-wem (T,E)
spread out in all directions .... rlkerr-welhem, tywerr-iwelhem (E)
spread out wide .... aymperr-irrem (E)
spread seeds .... alpent-wem (T)

spring *(water)* .... apinty (W,T), apeynt (T,E), intyang (W,T), ayay (W,T)

Spring Range .... Alyew

sprinkle
a sprinkle of rain .... kwaty lthel, lthel, nyeyepenyey (W), tyeyepetyey (W)
sprinkle (rain) .... akarl-wem (W,T), tyetyel-wem (E), tyeyepetyey atwem (W)

spy *(on someone)* .... rlwant-rlwant (W,T), urlant-urlant (T,E)

square
'square and square' (for example, two brothers-in-law who are married to each other's sisters) .... rlwerrkerek-rlwerrker (W,T), rlwerrkereng-rlwerrkereng (T), urlerrker-urlerrkerek (E)
'square' someone back .... ankwernem, unkil-ilem (E)

squash
squashed .... mwely, mwely-mwely, unmely (E)
become squashed .... mwely-irrem, unmely-irrem (E), anhwemp-anhwemp-irrem (W,T)
squash someone up, take up their room .... pwarn-ilem
squash something .... anhwemp-anhwemp-ilem (W,T), mwely-ilem, unmely-ilem (E)

squat
squat on toes or flat-footed .... atanem[1] (E), artarnk anem (W,T), atangk anem (E)

squeeze
squash something (hard) .. rlpwerrkem (W,T), rrwethem (T)
squeeze something out of something else .... ipem, lhwerrp-ilem (T), rlpwentyem (W,T), rwelh-arrernem, ulherrpernem (E), urlpentyem (E)
squeeze something out from something (e.g. pus from a boil) .... anthwelh-ilem (T,E), antyelp-ilem (E)

stab
poke into something .... atanthem
stab the ground with a digging stick or crowbar .. tyer-wem, tyewentem (W), tyek-untem (E)

stack
packed in close together ... kwenty[1]
lots of things heaped up or stacked up .... kwenty-kwenty

stagger
stagger about (as if drunk) .... anyelpanyem

stalk *(someone)* .... apertem
track someone or something (follow tracks) .... apentem (T,E), ingkantem (W,T), ampinem (E), ingkelarr alhem, ingkelarr alwernem (W,T)

stalked puffball .... anngarnt rrpwerl (W,T), arrekwep-kwep (W), arrepweng-pweng (E), kwep-kwep[3] (W,T), pwek-pwek, pweng-pweng (W)

stallion *(from English)* .... intay

stamp
a stamping sound .... lthap-lthap, rltap-rltap (W)
stamp feet .... atemart angkem (E)
stamp or stand on someone or something .... rlpwerrkem (W,T), rrwethem (T)

stand, stand up .... irnem
stand bent over .... anwekerternem
stand in the way of something .... angert irnem (W,T) (?)
stand leaning against someone or something .... ampekernem
stand something up .... akem-ilem, ngkernem

star .... kwerraly
falling star .... parrty
Magellanic Clouds .... Antyekanty-atherr (E), Arrenty-atherr (E)
Milky Way .... Atwarlk (W), Lpwararr (W,T), Mewarr (W), Miwerr (T,E)
Morning Star, Venus .... Anthelper (W,T), Arwenpeng (E), Kwerraly Angerr, Kwerraly Rltwa (W), Kwerraly Urlta (T,E)
Saucepan (part of Orion) .. Anterl (T,E), Arlanty, Arnkenty, Ingkapeny (E), Ingkartek (E), Pwereytarr (E)
Seven Sisters, Pleiades .... Arrarrkw (T,E), Interrk[1] (E), Kwerraly Angerr, Peltharr Map (W,T)
group of stars near the Seven Sisters .... anem[3] (?)

Southern Cross .... Irrety Ingka (E), Irrety-kenh Ingka (E)
other star names .... Uralep (E), Mwer-nheng-atherr, Patyimp (E)
a star or planet (possibly Mars) .... Lherrm-penh (E)

stare
someone who stares a lot .. anngaparek (T,E)
stare at someone .... anngerlkelh-ilem (T,E), twant arem (W,T), arnterr arem

start
start (from English) .... that-irrem
start something up (e.g. a car or an engine) ... angkelh-ilem, angkelh-angkelh-ilem

starter motor *(of car)* .... aperrk

starving
be starving for something .. urrampem (T,E)
feel starving .... arrerlkart pwem (E), arrerlkart urntem (E), arrerlkart-irrem (T,E)

stay *(in a place)* anem1
stay somewhere, be somewhere .... alartem (W,T), anerl-anem
staying home, staying in one place .... arteny1, antarl (W,T), rlwemp, urlert (E), artenyem-arteny (E)
stay in one place .... akwet-irrem (T), antarl-irrem (W,T), amarn-irrem
someone who stays in one place .... mer akweteth (W,T)
stay in one place and not go anywhere because of mourning (respect language) .... pwenkel anem (T,E)

steal
steal something .... anyenngel inem, arwengkel inem
steal something (from English) .... rwekem-ilem
grab something .... rakem

stem .... arla3, arlang (W,T), arna ngkwern (E), ngkwern
stem of a fruit .... inta, intak (E)

step
foothold .... rtety2 (W), rtetyep (E)
cut steps, cut footholds .... rtety-ipem (E), rtety-wem
step on something .... arternem2, lthwem (W,T), ulthem (E)
step over something .... kertety alhem (T), kertety arnpenhem (T)
step in each other's tracks .... atywekel-iwem (E), atywekel-iwerrem (E), ingkatyel-wem, lyekel-wem (W)

stick
a stick, piece of wood ...... arna, arnang (W,T), antyelty (E), arwerl (T,E)
short straight stick .... arlarnt (E)
short throwing stick .... mwert (W,T)
small stick .... pentarlp (T,E)
small stick used for poking honeyants out of their nests .... inta
small stick used in women's dances or for carrying skewered meat on .... tyetaty
stick used by women and girls to tell stories by drawing on the ground .... man-man (W,T)
stick used for cleaning things out, or for use as a brush for painting up for ceremonies .... tyepal
stick used for spinning hairstring .... interlp (T,E)

stick into *(something else)* .. kerrk-wem

stick onto *(something)* ...... mwernem

stick insect .... antyekanty (T,E), kapert atwenh (W,T), kapert atwenh-atwenh (W,T)

sticking out .... irrkert-irrkert

sticky
solid (of honey or paint) .. intengk (W,T)

stiff wattle .... arleperlterrk (E), patwert (W,T)

still
not moving .... akwet, amarn
become quiet or still .... arlan-irrem
action or state of affairs has continued for some time .... -antey
still (doing an action) ..... akwet-antey

Stimson's python .... ileway (W,T) (?)

sting *(insect)* .... nhwem (W,T), unhem (E)

stink
stinking .... awer2 (W,T), iynteng (E)
stinking (especially meat) .... arntert
stink, go off .... lpwerrem (W,T)

stink bug .... iynteng-iynteng (E)

stir
mix or stir things together .... anyentelh-ilem, arrawelh-ilem, intwerelh-ilem (T,E), iytan-ilem (E)
stir people up, make things unsettled .... lpwertelh-ilem (W,T), ulpertelh-ilem (T,E), arlkwer-ilem, arraw-ilem, arweketherwek-ilem (W,T), urekethwerek-ilem (E)
Stirling .... Thaleng
stockman, stockwoman *(from English)* .... thakeman
stoke a fire .... arraw-ilem, arrawelh-ilem, ntyerlp-ilem
stomach
stomach area .... alem, anert
stomach organ .... mwerlk[1]
stomach-ache .... anert akeng (E), anert anety (W,T)
having a full stomach .... anert anhwerlk (W,T), anerteng (E)
stomach burn from hunger .... urrampem (T,E), anert ampem
stomach rumble or shake with hunger .... anert arrewem
become full (stomach) .... anhwerlk-irrem (W,T)
feel funny or cold in the stomach after eating fatty meat .... antyernem[1] (W,T)
stomach swell up .... arlwarernem
stomp
a stomping sound .... lthap-lthap, rltap-rltap (W)
go along making a galloping, thudding or stomping sound .... nenty-nenty alhem (T,E), nwenty-nwenty alhem (W,T)
make a stomping sound .... lthap-lthap-irrem, rltap-rltap-irrem (W), nenty-nenty-irrem (T,E), nwenty-nwenty-irrem (W,T)
stone .... apwert, irnta (W,T), irntang (W,T)
small stones or rocks .... arrtya[3] (W), arrtyang (W), irrtyewat[1] (E), rrwelty-rrwelty (W,T)
grinding stones .... alyey[1] (W), ather, irntang ather (W,T), apwert ather, arlkwat (W,T), irntang arlkwat (W,T), pwerl, tyeng (T,E), alyer (E), irntang apwert (W), irntang artwert (W,T), apwert alyer (E), apwert artwert (E)
stone point in handle of a woomera .... antha[2], anthang (W)
stone axe .... ilep martarrp (W,T), martarrp (W,T)
stone knife .... alywek, antha[2], anthang (W), apwert antha (E), ilperl[1] (E), kartamp (W,T), manpwerl (W,T), inkwartety (E), irntarlter (W,T), irntang arlter (W,T), werlamp (T)
stone-curlew .... mwelyar, arepeylp (E)
stoop down .... kwen-irrem
stop
stopping (doing an action) .... menty
stop doing something, give up .... impelhem, impem
stop moving (when moving along) .... ngkernelhem
stop what you are doing, leave off (e.g. hunting) .... ampakelhem (W,T)
stop each other from doing something .... intyeng rrkwerrem (W,T)
stop someone from doing something .... apatel-anthem (T,E), apatelh-ilem, arnpakirrem (W), arrngert-irrem, arrngert-wem, ayakem, arnpakem, akayak-ilem
stop someone from doing something (particularly stop a woman going to her 'promised' husband, or a man going to a woman) .... intyeng rrkwem (W,T)
stop or block someone from going somewhere or near something .... arrngent-wem, arrngert-wem
stop a fight .... arrngent-wem, arrngert-wem
stop someone from doing something by putting yourself in the way .... ilpem[2]
store, shop *(from English)* .... thew
storm .... rlkang angerr (W,T), iylka angerr (E)
dark rain storm .... tywa (T), tywang (T), utya (E)
dust storm (before rain) .... alhek nmwernt (W,T), alhek unmernt (E)
the front or lighter part of an approaching storm .... kwaty urla (E)
story .... ayey (W,T), altyerr[1], angka[1] (E), angkety, ulypma (E)
right, true or correct Dreaming story .... altyerr arraty

short version of a story, not the full story ... angkety kertemwengk (W,T)
stories that are told for fun ... altyerreng-altyerr
tell a story ... ayey ilelhem (W,T), ayey ilem (W,T), angka ilem (E), ulypma ilem (E)
spread a story around ... alpent-wem (T)
tell a story about yourself .. ilelhem, tyantelhem
story that is told by drawing designs on the ground (women or girls) ... tyepety[1]
tell a story by drawing on the ground (women or girls) ... mpaty-ilem (W,T), tyepety ilem (E), man-man atwem (W,T)
bent stick or wire used by women and girls to tell stories on the ground ... man-man (W,T)

straight
straight (in shape or path) ... arraty, arratyeny
in a straight line or path .. akert-arraty, arraty akwet (W,T)
go along in a straight line ... akert-arraty-irrem, akertarreng-irrem (E)
straighten something ... arternem[2], arraty-ilem
become straightened out .. arraty-irrem
set things straight, sort out a problem ... arraty-ilem
set the record straight about yourself ... arraty-ilelhem

straight away ... parrp, parrp-parrp

strange
something odd or strange (from English) ... panipak

stranger
a stranger ... alethang, arleng-areny (T,E), lwereny (W,T), tyerrty lwereny (W,T), ulereny (E)

strangle
choke or strangle somebody or something ... ahenty ltwakem (W,T), ahenty ultakem (E), ahenty twerl-akem (W), ahenty ahenpem (W), alyernem, awerrkem, itutnhem (E)

stretch
stretched out ... rlkerr
stretch yourself out ... rlkerr-welhem
stretch legs straight out ... rlkerrelhem, tywerr-iwelhem (E)
stretch yourself ... althekalth-irrem, arternelhem, atywaty-irrem[1]

strike
strike (of a storm or lightning) ... ltewem (W,T), ultewem (T,E), wem[1]
getting ready to strike ... akwanth-akwanth
get ready to strike, brandish a weapon ... arrang-arem (E), akwanth-ilem (E)

string
made from animal fur ... alyep[1]

strip
foliage from plants, eat bare ... althem, irrkerleng-ilem, irrkerlerrk-ilem (E)
strip bark off a tree or plant ... atanthem

stripe ... arlkeny
stripey ... arlkeny-arlkeny
make a stripe, design, marking ... arlkeny-wem

stroke along *(in water)* ... alyeyamp-irrem (E), kalyeyamp-irrem (T,E), alyeyampel alhem (E), kalyeyampel alhem (T,E)

strong
strong, tough ... rlterrk, twer (W,T), awer-awer (E), awer[1] (E)
strong or biting in taste ... ahelengkw (E)
strong in taste (from English) ... therrang
'strong' (tea) ... irrkertey
get strong ... twer-irrem (W,T)
make a person healthy or strong ... twer-ilem (W,T)
make something strong ... rlterrk-ilem, rlterrkelh-ilem, twer-ilem (W,T)
make oneself strong to protect oneself ... arawerrng inem, arnkaty-ilelhem (T,E)

struggle *(to do things)* ... nakepakel-irrem (W,T)

stubble quail ... kweyepey (E)

stubborn ... ankerl, anwernt, arrthat (T), tyerrk (W,T), iyterrk (E), ankerl-ankerl
be stubborn, tough-minded or uncooperative .. ankerl-irrem (W,T), anwernt-irrem, mwernt-irrem (T,E), arlelty-irrem

stuck
get stuck on or in something ... atanem[2] (W,T), atanelhem (W,T), mwernelhem, kerelty-welhem (W,T), uthinem (E)

have something stuck in the throat ..... kanng anem (W)
stuck together ..... interrenty (T,E)

stuff
stuff yourself with food ... nyant arlkwem

stumble
stumble along (from sickness) ..... atyet-atyet alhem (T,E)

stupid ..... arert, arwengk (T,E)
behave stupidly ..... arert-irrem, arwengk-irrem (T,E), ywetherrk-irrem (T,E), uyetherrk-irrem (E)
say stupid things ..... ywetherrk angkem (T,E), uyetherrk angkem (E)

sturdy ..... rlterrk

Sturt's desert fuchsia ..... tyer² (E)

substandard
not up to standard ..... +eng-anyimp (E), -arrpantey, -arrpatenty (E)

subsection *(go to 'skin name')*

successful
a successful feeling (especially for hunting) ... inngeny, inngeny-inngeny
have a lucky or successful feeling (especially for hunting) ... inngeny-irrem

suck
suck on something ..... awantyem, ltyantywem (T,E), kwek-arem (E)
suck part of self (such as fingers) ..... awantyelhem
suck on breast ..... paty antywem (W,T), werlaty antywem (T,E)

suds ..... rlkwerrp, urlkerrp (E)

sugar ..... kwaty ikwemey-ilenh (E), lwemar (W,T)
sugar (from English) ..... tywek

sugar grass ..... arlperlp

sugarbag ..... rltwamp (W,T), urltamp (T), arwengalker
sugarbag (respect language) ..... imperalker-ayerr (E), iylpweralker-ayerr (E), iylpwer-areny (E), rlpwer-areny (W), ngkwarl-ayerr (T,E)
clean honey ..... arrtyangk (W), rlwa (W,T), rlwang (W,T), urla (E)
top part of hive ..... kapert¹, rltwamp kapert (W,T)
bottom part of hive ..... arteng (W)
newly made hive ..... alhakwerrk (W,T), alhang akwerrk (W,T)
entrance to hive ..... alha¹, alhang (W,T), arwengalker alha (T,E), rltwamp alha (W,T)
yellow substance at bottom of hive ..... ama (T,E), alpma (T,E)
lump of wax or resin-like substance at base of hive .. anker¹ (E), arwengalker tyalangk (T), tarl (E)
bits of dark-coloured pollen on ground under a tree where a native bee hive is ..... arnpan (T,E), atyang² (W)
native bee ..... lwerlker (W,T), ngarntarnt (T,E), ameng, minekey (W,T)
native bee larvae (used as medicine) ..... arrem (T,E)
put pollen and nectar into hive (native bee) ..... arrakwernem² (T,E)
chop tree open for native honey or sugarbag ..... arlkarrpem (W)
cut a small hole in a tree to listen for the sound of native bees ..... weylkerr atwem (E)

sulky ..... arnkely, arrwernt, kekart (T), akikart (E), kewarr (W,T), akiwarr (T,E), npwart (W,T), unpart (T), alha npwart (W,T)
be sulky or uncooperative .. arnernkey-irrem, arnkely-irrem, kewarr-irrem (W,T), akiwarr-irrem (T,E), npwart-irrem (W,T), unpart-irrem (T), kekart-irrem (T), akikart-irrem (E), kwel-anyem (W,T), kwel-irrem (W,T)
be sulky, sulkily face away from someone, turn your back on someone ..... arrwernt-irrem
go off in a huff or a bad mood ..... kewarr alhem (W,T), akiwarr alhem (T,E)

Sullivan Well ..... Artew Irnem

summer ..... twern (W,T), twern-tayem (W,T), utern (T,E), utern-tayem (E)
beginning of summer ..... aherrk akwerrk, utern akwerrk (T,E), twern rlwa (W,T), twern rlwang (W,T), utern urla (E)
end of summer ..... twern rlwang (W,T) (?)
middle of summer ..... arepampey (E), twern angerr (W,T), twern mparnt, utern mparnt (E), twern mpep (W,T), utern mpep (E)

summer grass ..... mamperrk (W,T)

sun, sunshine, sunlight ... aherrk, twern (W,T), utern (T,E)
sun (respect language) ..... arekel (E)
with the sun out ..... aketh

rays of the sun .... aherrk iltya (T), aherrk iltyem-iltyem (E)
(sun) beat down on something .... ampem[1]
(sun) rise .... aherrk anintyem (T), aherrk itenty-alhem (W), aherrk tyerrelhem (T,E), aherrkenety-alhem (E), anenty (W,T), anenty-alhem (W,T), aherlkenty alhem
(sun) set .... aherrk irrpem, aherrk irrpenhem, aherrk aylpenhem (E), aherrk iltyem anem (E), angwerr-irrem, angwerrel-irrem
sunset (old language) .... rlngerr (E)

Sunday .... arlta angerr (W,T), arltang angerr (W,T), arlta angerrety (E), arlta pwerrk (T)

superior, really good .... anper[2] (W,T), mekelarey (W,T), anper anthwerr (W,T), mwerr anthwerr (W,T), mwerr-angker (E)

supper, evening meal
(from English) .... thap

supplejack, suplejack .... anyer
gum from .... anyerampw, anyerangkwarl

support
something used for support or for leaning on, supported by something .... irrertety

suppose
that (something might happen) .... +emer

supposedly
'so they say' .... akwel

surface
on the surface, near the surface .... akern

surplus
food, an over-abundance of food .... menty-menty, ampeny[1], ampeny-ampeny

surprise, exclamation .... yekay

swag .... antyam, rnwanenty, urnanenty (E)
swag (from English) .... thewak, pelangket (W,T), pwelangket (E)
swag canvas (from English) .... tent

swallow *(something)* .... akwernem

swallow *(bird)*
white-backed swallow .... nerrty (E)

swamp .... alkerr (E)

swamp kangaroo grass .... lyenty
grub from .... lyentyatayerr (E) (SP)

swap things .... antherrem

swarm *(ants)* .... akarr-irrem (T,E), arraw-irrem

swear
arguing, talking roughly or swearing at someone .... aywek-aywek, arrarletyel
swear or growl at somebody or something .... iltem, rwang arrernem (W), urarrernem (T,E)
swear at each other .... ilterrem, aywek-aywek-irrem
really swear at someone .... alhengkelh-ilem (E), alhengkem (T,E), urarrey ilem (E), urarreytnelhem (E), urarreytnelhemel iltem (E)

sweat .... antyey[2]
to sweat, perspire .... antyey-irrem, antyey iylpem (E)
sweat, feel hot .... awempem (E)

sweep
sweep an area or camp where someone has passed away with branches .... pewem
sweep or gather things together .... akarr-ilem (T,E), akarrelh-ilem (T,E)

sweet
sweet things .... ngkwarl
sweet-tasting, sweet things (from English) .... theweyet
sweet-tasting, sweet things .... ikwemey
for the taste, sweet, something eaten after the main meal .... alemeh (W,T), alemek (T,E)
not sweet .... anetywek (W)

sweet pillow *(plant)* .... ntyapentyetyen (W,T), iynteng-iynteng (E)

sweetheart .... mert (W,T), meyt (T,E), mert-mert (W,T), meyt-meyt (T,E)
become sweethearts, boyfriends/girlfriends .... mert-mert mpwarem (W,T), meyt-meyt mpwarem (E), mert-mert-irrem (W,T), meyt-meyt-irrem (E), mert-mert-ilerrem (W,T), meyt-meyt-ilerrem (E)

swell
swollen .... amwerenthenng (E), arltwerlp (W,T), arlwar, alhwer-alhwer
swell up .... wangkem, alhapelhem (W), amwerenthenng-irrem (E), arlwar-irrem

swell up (eyes or other parts of the body) ... alhwer-alhwer-irrem
skin raise up after being burnt by fire, sun or hot water ... arltapwerlt-irrem (W), arltaparlt-irrem (W,T)
become swollen, bloated .. arltwerlp-irrem (W,T)
make something swell up ... wangkelh-ilem
make the earth swell up (by a swollen root or tuber underneath) ... antwerlperlp arrernem (W,T)

swim ... irrpem, aylpem (E), kwatyeh irrpem (W,T), kwatyek irrpem (T,E), pwerlp-irrem, iltyel atwerl-apem (T)
swim along ... alyeyamp-irrem (E), kalyeyamp-irrem (T,E), alyeyampel alhem (E), kalyeyampel alhem (T,E)

swing
swinging back (like a returning boomerang) ... arrarl-arrarl (W)
swing from something ... amaralty-anem (E), arlparernem

swollen *(go to 'swell')*

sympathy
an expression of sympathy, 'Poor thing', 'Poor bugger', 'Dear one' . akeweny (W,T), akuny (T,E), akeweny-amperl (W,T), akuny-amperl (T,E), akeweny-apenh (W,T)
endings that show sympathy ... -angwen-angwen (T,E), -amperl (E), -angwel-angwel (E)

Tt

tadpole ... pwel-pwel, pwepely, tyekepwelepwel (E)

tail
tail of an animal ... kanty[1], pwer
tail (respect language) ... tayl-ayerr (E)
tail (from English) ... tayl (E)
tail tip of a bilby ... alpety (W,T), alpeyt (T,E)

tail meat
from goanna, perentie, or kangaroo ... arrertarnk (T,E)
of a kangaroo ... ker pwer

take
take someone or something somewhere ... angem
take something somewhere (respect language) ... ahanelh-ilem
take something, get ... inem
bring something back ... angernem[2] (W,T), akngirnem (E)
take something back ... angety-alpem
take something to someone (respect language) ... rrwem-ilem (W,T), urrem-ilem (E)
take someone back (respect language) ... alpiwerl-alpem (E)
take (drink) medicine, tablets ... antywem
take something away from someone ... rakem, alanty angem, atanty angem
take something without asking ... anyenngel inem
take someone off to become your lover ... mpwenyel angem, mpwenyel inem
take someone's place or spot ... arrngen-wem
take something out of something ... arratelh-ilem
'Take it!' (when giving something to someone) ... ma[1]

take aim ... angkarr arem

take notice ... akangkwerrem (W,T)

take off
take something off something ... lywem[1]
take something off self ... lywelhem
take off clothes ... akap-rlwem (W,T), akap-irlwem
take something off someone (because you don't like what they might do with it) ... anenyerrel angem
take things off each other .. rakerrem
take off into the air, ascend ... antyan-akelhem (W), alker-irrem[2], alkerek-irrem

talk
talk (to someone) ... angkem
talk (respect language) ... ameram-irrem
talk to each other, talk (a group of people) ... angkerrem
indirect or oblique way of talking ... kertemwengk
being unable to speak properly ... aleny apekap, angka apekap (E)

someone who is not allowed to talk (especially because of bereavement) .. akerter, kertemwengk, awenp (W,T)
someone who talks up front or who talks strongly .... alkwert
loud talk .... arrkwertep (W,T)
loud talker, 'big mouth' ... arremwar-mwar (T,E)
someone who talks a lot, talkative .... tyarralpenty (W)
talking nonsense .... tetherrp-tetherrp
speak loudly, talk loudly in public .... aharlperr angkem (T,E), arlperr angkem
talk a lot, talk excessively or loudly .... arnterr angkem, aker-aker-ilem, arlelty angkem, arrkwertep-irrem (W,T), tyety angkem (T,E)
talk over the top of someone .... anthakemel angkem (E), atnalth-ilem (E)
interrupt someone talking .... angka ltwakem (T)
talk the wrong way .... akengenty angkem
talk about somebody behind their back .... anywerr-irrem, tyel angkem
talk badly to someone .... urarrernem (T,E)
talk in sleep .... altyerr-altyerr angkem, anengkerr-anengkerr angkem (W,T)
talk to someone on behalf of someone else .... alanty angkem (E)
make someone talk, ask someone to tell a story .... angkelh-ilem, angkelh-angkelh-ilem, angkek-angkek-ilem (E)
free someone to talk after silence (from mourning) .... angkakert-ilem (E), angkeparr-ilem (E), ulypmakert-ilem (E), arrakert-ilem (T,E)

tall .... alkey[1] (W,T), arlpenty
tall (of people) .... ampap-ampap (E)
a bit tall .... alkey-alkey (W,T), arlpenty-arlpenty
grow tall .... alkey-irrem (W,T), arlpenty-irrem

tall desert rose .... tyetep (W,T)

tall verbine *(plant)* .... intwert-intwert (E)

tall yellowtop *(plant)* .... arengkatwepatwetyenh (W,T), ntweyentwerl

tame
untamed .... ateralth
tame, break in a horse .... ltwakem (W,T), ultakem (E)

tangled *(hair)* .... werrp (E)

tangled lechenaultia .... unpay (E), inpay (T), npway-npway (W,T) (?)

tantrum
throw a tantrum .... arlan-irrem, arlelty-irrem, atywaty-atywaty-irrem (T,E), nthat-nthat-irrem

tap
tap digging stick or crowbar on the ground to listen for the hollow sound .... tyer-wem

tape recorder
(from English) .... wayeleth

tar vine .... ayep
grub from .... arrpayerr (E), ayep-areny (W), ayepayt (T,E), ayepaty, tyap ayep (W)

taste
the taste of something .... kwang (W), ikwa (T,E), ikwang (T)
a strong or 'good' taste .... kwang (W), ikwa (T,E), ikwang (T)
nice-tasting, lovely (of food or water) .... alyerremwey
tasty food .... ikwemey
bitter-tasting .... irrkertey
salty, bitter, sour-tasting . tyekert[1], alyelk, alyew-alyew (E)
for the taste, sweet, something eaten after the main meal .... alemeh (W,T), alemek (T,E)
strong or biting in taste ... ahelengkw (E)
not sweet, having a funny taste .... arlengkety (W)
tasteless .... alyelk, anetywek (W)
taste or try something .... arlepewem (W,T), arrkernem

tattered .... alkwemp-alkwemp

tawny frogmouth .... nwernengk, unernengk (E), uring (E)

tea .... kwaty urrperl-ilenh (T,E)
tea (respect language) .... atewat-ayerr (E)
tea (from English) .... tey
cup of tea (from English) .. kapertey
tea-leaves .... arlpelh[1] (T,E)
tea-leaves (from English) .. teyelep
tea-break (from English) .. kapertey-taym

teach .... kalty-anthem, kaltyel-anthem, tyaty atwem (W,T)
teacher .... kalty-anthenh-anthenh
schoolteacher (from English) .... kwerl tety

teal *(grey teal bird)* … tyepelyakw (W), tyepelyey (E)

tear

tear meat apart … ampakem

tear something … alterrem

tears *(in eyes)* … anngwenty (W,T), arrngwelty (E)

teary … anngwenty-anngwenty, arrngwelty-arrngwelty (E)

tease

tease, mock someone … arrkenty-ilem, kwanthem, arrken-ilem, anngernt-irrem (T,E), arrampewem[1]

tease (from English) … tithem-ilem

tease someone, play a joke on someone … ayntarrp-ilem (E)

behave in a teasing or joking way with people who belong to the opposite generation moiety … urrayerr-irrem (T,E), rrwayerr-irrem (T)

teat … paty (W,T), werlaty (T,E)

tea-tree *(sandhill)* … ilperl[2], thankw (E) (?)

teddy bears arsehole

(a burr) … ingka-mwerney, ingkang mwerney (W)

teddy bears arsehole (from English) … kwem (W), kwem-kwem (W)

teenage

teenage girl … awenk, marl awenk, kwey akarnterrng (T,E), arelh awenk, kwey awenk (T,E)

teenage boy (before young man ceremonies) … amerrk[1], awerr amerrk, awey amerrk (T,E)

teenage boy travelling around just before young man ceremonies … tyakwertekwert (W)

become a teenage boy (before young man ceremonies) … amerrk-irrem

teeth … rtety[1], arntek (T,E)

telephone … alwerrng angkenh-angkenh (E), alwerrng, arrakert-kenh (T), irlpekenh (T)

telephone (from English) … terlepawen

ring up on the telephone (from English) … wayem-ilem

television … altyerr[1] (SP)

tell

tell someone about something, give a message … ilem

tell (respect language) … tyantem (E), tyantel-wem (E)

tell a story by drawing on the ground (women and young girls) … mpaty-ilem (W,T)

tell a story to others, take news to others … ilelhenty angem

tell someone that you did something … ilelhem

tell someone what you are doing … angkawelhem

tell someone to do something … ilem, twernem, uternem (E)

tell someone to get out or keep out … yerrng-irrem (W,T)

tell the truth … arraty ilem

tell someone they are not allowed to do something … akayak-ilem

tell someone not to pester you … ayerrp ilelhem

tell someone to go away and leave you alone … alharlkwelhem

tell someone off … arrantyakem (W,T), iltem

tell someone to keep away from private belongings … akayak-ilem

tell someone that something is about to happen (especially warning about aggression) … ateng-ilem (W,T), atengelh-ilem (W,T)

tell someone to sit down and wait … lthwelth-ilem (W,T), ulthelth-ilem (E)

tell someone you don't want something … lthwelth-ilem (W,T), ulthelth-ilem (E)

tell something that is not true … arrampewem[1]

(birds) go and tell others about something that is happening … arrakwernem[3]

(birds) tell people that there is an abundance of bush plums or honeyants … arntwerlem (W,T)

temper

have a tantrum or lose your temper … kewarr-irrem (W,T), akiwarr-irrem (T,E)

temple *(body part)* … arreylpenh-iylpenh (E)

Ten Mile Bore … Aywert

ten dollar note … atherrk-atherrk (T,E), nwertal (T)

tendon … alwerrng

tent *(from English)* … tent

termite … interrk[2], ngkwepeyayt (E), ngkwepey (SP), ngkwayt (T, E), atwerneng (W, T) *flying stage of termite* ..... arnameng-ayerr (E)

termite-hill

types of ..... kerrertek, ngkwepey (E) awerr-awerr[1] (E), pwentereng (E), merntap (W,T), kerrth (E)

testicles

(sensitive language) ..... arleth

that

that person or thing (close) ..... nhenh, nhetenh (W,T)

that person or thing (middle distance) ..... yatenh (W,T), yanh, yaleng

that person or thing (not close) ..... alenh (W,T), alert [1], nhakw, alertenh (W,T), alertekwenh, aley[2] (T,E)

because of that, from that ..... kwer-penh

like that, that's how (something is done) ..... lweren (W,T), alakenh, alanh, alanh-anyem (E)

that one, that thing (that is being referred to) ..... nheng[1], weth

that sort of thing ..... weth-lkwer (T,E), yanh-lkwer (E)

that way ..... yanh-angkwerr

their

their relation ..... +ekw (W,T), +ikw (E)

their, theirs *(belonging to two) (go to pronoun table p. 747)*

their, theirs *(belonging to more than two) (go to pronoun table p. 747)*

them, for them, to them *(the two of them) (go to pronoun table p. 747)*

them, for them, to them *(more than two) (go to pronoun table p. 747)*

then

after that (the event that has previously been mentioned) ..... kwereng

then (something else happens) ..... antem (W,T), anem[2]

there

there (close) ..... nhenh, nhetenh (W,T),

there (middle distance) ..... yatenh (W,T), yanh, yaleng

over there (middle distance) (respect language) ..... yanhenty (E)

there (not close) ..... alenh (W,T), alert [1], nhakw, alertenh (W,T), alertekwenh, aley[2] (T,E)

from there ..... yanh-ntyel (W,T), yanh-they (E)

'There!' (when giving something to someone) ..... ma[1]

these

these two ..... nhatherr

they *(two) (go to pronoun table p. 747)*

they *(more than two) (go to pronoun table p. 747)*

thick ..... mwat (E)

thief ..... anyenngalth, arwengkalth

(from English) ..... rwekey pak

thigh ..... lyweper, ulyeper (E)

thin ..... ampwa, ampwang (W,T), ampwetyampw (E), tyew (W,T), utyew (E), ampweyampw (SP), ampeyamp (SP)

thin (of people), slender ..... ampap-ampap (E), lyerrer (E)

really thin ..... ngkwern-ngkwern, ngkwernant

thin (hair or shade) ..... irreltyenng (E), irrkerleng, irrkerlerrk (E)

get thin, lose weight, get skinny ..... ampwerrem, ampweyampw-irrem (E), tyew-irrem (W,T), utyew-irrem (E), ngkwern-ngkwern-irrem

make someone thin or skinny ..... ampwelem

go bald, thin out (hair) ..... irreltyenng-irrem (E)

thing

something, a thing ..... arna, arnang (W,T), antyelty (E)

things, possessions ..... rnwanenty, urnanenty (E)

someone else's things ..... rnwanenty atyeneny (W,T)

personal belongings of the deceased ..... atnerrk[2] (E) (?)

personal belongings (respect language) ..... arnkwayerr (E)

thingummybob, thingummyjig ..... angwenh-akwey, wenh-apatherr (W,T), iwenh-apatherr, wenhekwey (W,T), iwenhakwey

think

think, about doing something ..... iterrem

think about something involving yourself ..... iterlarelhem

sit down thoughtfully ..... akarntem[2]

not able to think properly ..... arert-arert

thirsty, thirstily ..... angkethakw (T,E), angkethel (E), arrangketh, arwekel (W,T)

thirsty (respect language) ..... angkethek-uthek (E), wangkethel (E), weng angkethel (E)

thirsty (from English) ..... parrety

get thirsty ...... angkethakw-irrem (T,E), arwekel-irrem (W,T), parrety-irrem

this

this (person or thing) ...... nhenh, nhetenh (W,T), nh+

this sort of thing, this type of thing ...... nhenh-lkwer, nhelkwer

like this, this is how (something is done) ...... lweren (W,T), alakenh, alanh, alanh-anyem (E)

this way, in this direction ...... nhenh-angkwerr, nhangkwarr (E)

thong *(from English)* ...... thangey

thorn ...... lyek

thorny devil ...... mernerr (W,T), nywerr (W,T), arnkerrth (T,E)

those two ...... ratherr

thoughts ...... iterrenty

threaten

threaten to strike or hit someone ...... angkarr arem, angkarr atwem

three ...... rrpwety (W,T), urrpety (E)

just a few, three ...... rrpwetyarrp (W,T), urrpetyarrp (E)

in threes ...... rrpwetyelam rrpwetyelam (T), rrpwetyek-rrpwety (W), urrpetyek-urrpety (E)

three times ...... rrpwety-ingar (W,T), urrpety-ingar (E), urrpety-areng (E), urrpetyarrp-ingar (E)

split or separate off into threes ...... rrpwety-irrem (W,T), urrpety-irrem (E)

Three Bores ...... Artekerr

throat ...... ahenty[1], ita (E)

part of throat, including windpipe ...... mwelper

throw

throw something ...... iwem

throw something at someone or something ...... ltewem (W,T), ultewem (T,E)

throw something away ...... antarr-wem, arrarlp-wem, artaly-wem (W,T), iwem, artaly-artaly-wem (T)

throw or tip something out ...... altyewem

throw something away (just liquids) ...... intyalp-wem (W,T)

throw something off ...... iwem

throw something on the ground ...... ilatwem, arlkwatem (W,T)

throw things all over the place ...... artaly-artaly-wem (T), artaly-wem (W,T), irranyent-iwem (E)

throw a spear using a woomera ...... rtwely-wem, arrathenem (E), rtwely-ilem

throw animal carcass on fire to singe off hair, fur or scales ...... nthek-wem

throw hot soil or ashes at someone ...... arnewem (W)

throw something mistakenly or in the wrong direction ...... apal-wem

throw something so that it slides or skids along the ground ...... irrepereperr-wem, ahertety-iwem (E)

throw water over someone ...... akarl-wem (W,T)

throw things to each other ...... iwerrem

throw each other around ...... ntewerrem (W)

throw yourself to the ground ...... ntewelhem (E)

throw up, vomit ...... antew-irrem, alyelkelhem (?)

thrush *(grey shrike-thrush)* ...... alerterrperterrp (?)

thud

thumping or thudding noise ...... rrmwangk-rrmwangk (W,T), ahenty-ahenty[2] (W,T), twerlepwelh-pwelh (W,T), anenty-anenty

go along making a galloping, thudding or stomping sound ...... nenty-nenty alhem (T,E), nwenty-nwenty alhem (W,T), nenty-nenty-irrem (T,E), nwenty-nwenty-irrem (W,T)

make a knocking or thudding noise ...... atemart angkem (E), unteng atwem (E)

make a thudding noise (kangaroo) ...... anerlpem

thumb ...... iltya amikw (E), iltya angerr, iltyang angerr (W,T), iltya anywek (W), iltyang anywek (W), iltya pwel-pwel (W,T), iltyang pwel-pwel (W,T), iltyang pwel (W,T), iltyilkw (E)

thump

thump someone (on the back) ...... unteng atwem (E)

thunder .... angkeyawarr (E), awely-awely
thunderstorm .... arrarntwer (W,T)
thunder clouds building up .... artarwerr (W,T)
thunder (to thunder) .... angkem, kwaty angkem, arntwerrem, artwert-irrem (W,T), twerl-irrem (E)
Ti Tree Six Mile .... Pmara Jutunta
tick (insect) .... ilka[2] (T,E)
type of tick found on perenties, euros or cattle .. artwek (W,T), urtek (E)
tickle *(someone)* .... athek-athek-ilem, kert-kert-ilem (W), tyek-tyek-ilem[1] (E)
tickweed .... angerak-angerak (W)
tie
tie something .... ayernem
tie something round yourself .... ayernelhem, irrtyernelhem (E)
tie something up .... irrtyernem (E), rlterrk-ilem, rlterrkelh-ilem
tie a perentie's legs behind its back (to cook it) .... arnengerr-ilem
tight
tight (of clothes) .... tyert (T,E)
tight, not much room ...... pwarn
be tight or constricted ...... atanem[2] (W,T)
(something) press into, be tight on or cling to self ..... kerrk-welhem
tighten something .... rlterrk-ilem, rlterrkelh-ilem, twer-ilem (W,T)
tighten something (e.g. axe handle) .... arlarl-ilem (E), kanth-atwem
tilted
to one side, leaning sideways .... arlkarlker
time
a long time ago .... ahenp, ahenpeny, angkwey (W,T), ingkwey (E), angkwey-antey (W,T), ingkwey-antey (E), arrul (T,E), arruleny (T,E), arrul innga (E)
for a long time .... aleth, arleng-arlenty (T,E), akwet, akwetant
during a particular season or event (from English) .... -tayem
taking your time to do things .... arnernkey
times
'How many times?' .... nthakenty-ingar
lots of times, many times .. map-ingar
the number of times (on the end of a number word) .... -areng[1], -ingar
on the end of English number words .... -pal
timid
timid, shy .... apweralth (W,T), apuralth (E), nyerralth
timid (from English) .... ameleth
non-aggressive .... anik (E)
tin *(from English)* .... tyampet
tin such as those used to keep tobacco or ashes in (from English) .... lert
tinned meat, tin of meat .. ker tyampet
Tinfish Well .... Aretyerlker
tiny .... akely-amperl (E), akwek-amperl (T,E), akwek-antyey (W,T)
tip *(end)*
tip of something .... kanty[1], akert[1] (T,E)
tip of the tongue .... aleny kanty
tip *(over, out)*
tip over .... mpart anyem (W,T)
be tipped onto side or on an angle .... thar irnem (W,T)
tip something out .... arrarlp-wem, alperr-wem (T,E)
tip something over .... anampart-wem (W,T), ankert-wem, mpart-wem (W,T), thar-wem
tip things out and pile them up .... ayak-arrernem (W,T)
tip something upside down (so the back part is facing up) .... altywarrernem, artep arrernem
tip all of a liquid into something .... thar-wem
tired .... parrk (W,T), pwarrk (T,E), purrk (E), alyep-alyep[2] (W,T), alywep-alywep (T), atnhakert (E), marakat (W,T)
a bit tired, listless, weak .. arewamp, rwekar (T)
feeling tired, faint or dizzy from heat .... arepwelepwel
weak, floppy or loose in the body .... awerrk-awerr
feel tired .... parrk awelhem (W,T), pwarrk awelhem (T,E), purrk awelhem (E), parrk-irrem (W,T), pwarrk-irrem (T,E), purrk-irrem (E), alyep-alyep-irrem[2] (W,T), alywep-alywep-irrem (T)
feel dead tired or weak .... marrmarrp-irrem, manmarrp-irrem (W,T), arewamp-irrem
feel tired or lazy .... marakat-irrem (W,T)

feel tired or weak ... awerrk-irrem (T), awerrkelhem
be very tired, have heavy eyelids ... annga ankwel lthwem (W,T), annga ankwel ulthem (E)
make someone tired ... parrk-parrk-ilem (W,T), pwarrk-pwarrk-ilem (T,E), parrkel anthem (W,T), pwarrkel anthem (T,E), alyep-alyep-ilem (W,T), arlkwer-ilem, mwarrewem (E), arlkarem

to *(see also Appendix 2)* ... -warn (W,T), -warl
to, up to (somewhere) ... -atwety[2], -artwety

toad *(desert spadefoot)* ... atweynterl (E), kwep, kwep-kwep[2], pwerreparnt (W,T)

tobacco ... ngkwerlp
tobacco (respect language) ... tyanyweng (E), tyekert[2] (T,E)
tobacco (from English) ... tapak
smokes, cigarettes ... kwert
plug tobacco ... nikey-nikey
wad of tobacco ... warn (E), ngkwerlp kelh
make a wad of tobacco ... warn-ilem (E)
mix tobacco with ashes ... arek-wem (W,T), pwerlp-wem (T,E)
smoke tobacco ... kwert antywem
chew tobacco ... ngkwerlp arlkwem, ngkerlp arlkwem
native tobacco ... ngkwerlp
sandhill pituri ... arwenp
type of native tobacco ... arrwatnwer (E)
type of 'strong' native tobacco ... ngkwernerrp[2] (E)
type of very strong bush tobacco ... antererrnp (?)
bud or flower of native tobacco ... alpma (T,E)
young shoots of native tobacco ... akerrng (E), antyanp[2] (T,E), ngerrng (E), ngkwerlp akwerrk (W), rrngwaly (W)
native tobacco go yellow after being put in ashes ... arlterernternt-irrem (W), atnmangkem (E)
dried native tobacco ... akeyarr (E)
go dry (native tobacco) ... akeyarr-irrem (E)

tobacco handflower ... ankerr-ankerr (W), ankerringk (T,E), ntywenart (W)

today ... lyet
today (respect language) ... lyengkwert

toddle *(learn to walk)* ... atyet-atyet alhem (T,E)

toddler ... atyet-atyet (T,E)

toe ... ingka, ingkang (W,T)
big toe ... ingka amikw (E), ingka angerrety (E), ingkang pwel-pwel (W,T), ingka pwel-pwel (E), ingkilkw (E)
little toe ... ingka akwerreny (E), ingka ilpernkeny (E)
toes (other than big toe) ... ingka akwerrk (E), ingkang kwerrng (W,T), ingka kanty-rnem (E)

toenails ... tywemar (W,T), ingkelthel, ingka ingkelthel, ingkang ingkelthel (W,T), ingkang tywemar (W,T)

together
together (in a group) ... pwert (W,T), purt (T,E)
together (a married couple) ... iteng[1] (E)
person together with a particular relation ... -nheng[2]
together with something ... -arleng[2]
always be together with someone ... antyert
get together, get into a group ... pwert-irrem (W,T), purt-irrem (E)
doing things together ... artangaty
do things together ... artangaty-irrem
gather together (a lot of people or things) ... arwenth-irrem (W,T), map-irrem (W)
get back together ... pwety-irrem (T), pweyt-irrem (E)

toilet
go to the toilet ... lhwem (T), lwem[1] (W), ulhem (T,E)
have a shit, defecate ... atna ulhem (E)
have a piss, urinate ... mpwa ulhem (E), mpwelhem[2] (T), mpwulhem (E)
go to the toilet (baby talk) ... key-key-irrem (E)
toilet, shit (baby talk) ... kaka (T)

tomorrow ... ingwepenh (E), ngwenp (W,T), ngwenth (W,T)
tomorrow (respect language) ... ngwelenthel (E)

tongue ... aleny
side of the tongue ... aleny iter
tip of the tongue ... aleny kanty
poke out tongue, flick tongue out ... alenyenp-wem (T,E)

tonight *(see 'night')*

too, as well as ... arlka[2], thwen, uthen (E)

tooth, teeth ... rtety[1], arntek (T,E)

gap left after a front tooth has been knocked out (ceremonial) ... alyeneng (T,E), alyeleng (E), arrimper (T,E), arrenper (W), tyekerr (E)
remove a front tooth (ceremonial) ... alyeneng atwem (T,E), alyeleng atwem (E), arrimper atwem (T,E), arrenper atwem (W)

toothache ... arltwelth (E), kayltwelth (E)
having a toothache ... aytwelth-akert (E), kayltwelth-akert (E)
have a toothache ... rtety arekar-irrem, rtety arlkwem, arntek arlkwem (T,E)

toothbrush grass ... ngelyerr (E), talkwerrk (W), ntalwerrk (W)

toothpick ... arrent (W,T), arrint (E), irreyneper (T)

top
on top ... akern, akerneng-ampeny (T,E), akern-ampeny
top of something (with the back or rounded part facing upwards) ... artep
top of foot ... ingka artep
top of hill ... akwerlp, apwert artep (E)
top of tree ... arnang kanty (W,T), arwerl kanty (E), kanty-kanty, waly-waly (W,T), arna kanty (E)

torch ... rwang lyenenty (W,T)

torn
become ripped or torn ... alterrelhem

totem *(go to 'Dreaming')*

touch *(someone or something)* ... anpem
touch someone to get their attention or to warn them ... lyarnem (T,E)
touch someone with something, make someone feel as if something is crawling around on them ... inkerrelh-ilem, mpwarelh-ilem (E)

touchy ... irrngerrng (E), tyelety (E)
feel sensitive, touchy or jumpy ... irrngerrng-irrem (E), pwerep-irrem, tyelety-irrem (E)

tough
someone who is really hard or tough ... rlterrk, tyerrk (W,T), iyterrk (E), tyerrk-tyerrk (W,T), iyterrk-iyterrk (E)
be 'hard' or tough-minded ... twer-irrem (W,T), rlterrk-irrem

tourist *(from English)* ... terweth

towards ... -warn (W,T), -warl
in the general direction of, as far as ... -athek
facing or moving towards the speaker ... lwarr (W,T), ularr (T,E), ulaneng (E), lwaneng (T), ulaneng-athek (E), lwaneng-athek (T), ularr-athek (T,E)
move in a direction towards the speaker ... lwarr-irrem (W,T), ularr-irrem (E), lwaneng-irrem (T), ulaneng-irrem (E)

toy
toy boomerang ... alyang-alyang (W,T), kayleng-kayl (E)
toy car ... lert-lert
toy wooden bowl or dish .. mwareng-mwar, pantheng-panth
toy shield ... alkwerteng-alkwert
bow and arrow (from English) ... pwenarr

Toyota *(from English)* ... teweyat

track
footprint, track ... mpaty[1], ingkang mpaty (W,T), ingka mpaty (E), ingka, ingkang (W,T)
path ... iwerr (E), tyey[1] (W,T)
place where there are a lot of footprints or tracks .. atnalth (E)
pad or path of a kangaroo or euro ... anarlt
possum's track or path ... antywerreng (E)
go along the same track ... tyey-irrem (W,T)
track someone or something ... apentem (T,E), ingkantem (W,T), ampinem (E), ingkelarr alhem, ingkelarr alwernem (W,T)
step on top of someone's tracks ... lyekel-wem (W), atywekel-iwerrem (E), atywekel-iwem (E), ingkatyel-wem

tradition, rule, Law ... mpwarengareng

traditional boss ... atyetyart

translate ... angart-wem

travel ... alhem

traveller ... alethang

tray *(of a vehicle)* ... alparr[1] (W,T)

tread *(on something)* ... rlpwerrkem (W,T), rrwethem (T), ulthem (E), arternem[2]

tree ... arna, arnang (W,T), arwerl (T,E), antyelty (E)
very top of a tree ... arnang kanty (W,T), arna kanty (E), arwerl kanty (E), kanty-kanty, waly-waly (W,T)
with low hanging branches ... tentey, tentey-tentey
young tree ... arna akwerrk
tree house ... kwenterarr (T,E) (?)
tree litter ... anthelk[1]
tree trunk ... arla[3], arlang (W,T), arna ngkwern (E), ngkwern
tremble
shake, shiver ... arrewem
shake parts of the body ... arrkem (E)
shake wings or others parts of the body ... alharrkem
trench
trench to stop floodwater ... urtanng (T,E), urtanng-urtanng (T,E)
trick
deceive someone ... rrtywerrem (W,T), urrtyirrem (E), arrenkelh-anthem (T), arrenkelh-ilem[1] (T), rrtywekelh-ilem (T)
be tricked by someone ... anew-irrem (T,E)
trilling frog ... terrenth
trip
trip someone up ... ankert-wem, arnpakem
be tripped up by something ... arnpakelhem
trouble ... aha, ahang (W,T)
bring trouble on yourself ... pewelhem, rrwernelhem (W,T), urrernelhem (E)
get each other into trouble ... pewerrem
go somewhere and get into trouble ... pewerl-alpem
run into trouble without knowing ... thwerrp alhem (W,T) (?)
look for trouble ... irrpelth-irrem, urrpelth-irrem (E)
make trouble between people ... rlkwerrelh-ilem (W,T) (?)
make trouble for someone else ... atyang-inem (T), rrwernem (W,T), urrernem (T,E), nakepakel-ilem (W,T)
keep away from trouble ... wenng-irrem (T,E)
someone who steps in to stop a fight or to diffuse trouble ... arlperrepwenty
sort out trouble ... arlperr angkem (W), arlperrepwenty angkem
someone who is going to get into trouble ... animampel (T,E)

troublesome
(from English) ... tikeley
trousers *(from English)* ... terawath
truck *(from English)* ... teweyat
true, correct ... arraty
tell the truth ... arraty ilem
'Is it true?', 'Is that so?' ... arraty-akey (W,T), athew, tyathew, thathew, tyakey (W,T), ngay, ma[2] (W)
'Truly!' ... alew[2] (W,T), alew-alew (W,T)
truffle
native truffle, desert truffle ... akwerrerteth (E)
trunk *(of a tree)* ... arla[3], arlang (W,T), arna ngkwern (E), ngkwern
try
have a go at something ... arrkernem
taste or try something ... arrkernem, arlepewem (W,T)
try something on ... arlepewelhem (W,T), arrkernelhem
try something out (to see if it works) ... arlepewem (W,T)
try yourself out at something ... arlepewelhem (W,T), arrkernelhem
trying to do something and failing ... -arrpantey, athem[1] (E), arrthem (E), uyarn (E), ywarn, atengkel (E)
tucker ... mern
tumbleweed ... arlkerl, inkwert (E)
tune ... arreny (W,T), arreyn (E)
tunnel *(goanna or rabbit)* ... arwerr
turkey *(domestic)* ... kart-irrkwely-irrkwely (W,T), karl-irrkwely-irrkwely (T,E), urrkely-urrkely (E)
turkey bush ... anyerleng, kwenkart (E), pwenkart
turn
turn someone or something over ... mpart-wem (W,T), altywarrernem, mparlp-wem (W), mpwarlp-wem (W), angapety-iwem (E), angart-wem, ankert-wem
turn something onto its back ... impalkert-wem
turn something upside down (hollow shape down) ... altyewem
turn something over to look for something ... ilkakem
turn yourself around, turn yourself over ... angapety-iwelhem (E), angart-welhem, mparlp-welhem (W)

turn your back on someone ...... arreyl-irrem (E), ntywem-irrem (W,T), untyem-irrem (E)
turn away from people, go off in own direction ...... ampakelhem (W,T)

turn back
turn round and go back ...... aneyangketh-irrem (E), artwep-irrenty-alpem, pert-irrem (E), urtep-irrenty-alpem (E), twer-irrem

turn into *(something)* ...... -irr+, angart-welhem

turn off
turn something off (a tap, switch etc.) ...... martem (T,E), ywerrelh-ilem
turned off, shut ...... alhap, marnt, martelhenty (T,E), mety, mwernt² (W,T)

turn on
turn on (a light, a tap etc.) ...... altywer-ilem

turn up, arrive ...... arratelhem (E), arratem, arratety-alhem (W,T), arwem-irrem (T,E)

turpentine bush ...... irrnyengerrny, irrnyangerr (W), ngkwern irrnyepirrny (E), tyer² (E)

Twenty Mile Waterhole ...... Atywerl

twenty dollar note ...... rnter-rnter

twice ...... atherr-areng, atherr-ingar, atherrarrp-ingar (E)

twin ...... atyew

twinkle ...... arraly-arraly-irrem (T,E), ngkwarrkem (W,T), ingkwarrkem (T,E)

twist
twisted ...... arnkwert, arnkwert-arnkwert
get twisted ...... lew-lew-irrem (W,T), liw-liw-irrem (E)
twist or wring something out ...... alyernem, awerrkem
twist yourself up in something ...... alyernelhem
become twisted or swollen ...... amernelhem (E)

twitch
take a fit, start (in fright) ...... ilkwem (E)

twitter ...... arreyeng-arrey-irrem (W,T)
twittering ...... arreyeng-arrey (W,T)

two ...... atherr¹
two (respect language) ...... arnelheng
only the two of them ...... +ant-atherr
for two days, twice ...... atherr-areng, atherr-ingar
two at a time, two each ...... atherram-atherr (E), atherrek-atherr (E), atherrengk-atherr (T,E)
two by two ...... atherrelam atherrelam (T), atherrengk-atherr (T,E)

tyre ...... mwetekay-kenh ingka (T)

tyre pump ...... arlwar-ilenh-ilenh

Uu

ulcardo melon ...... lkwart (W,T), ilkwart, ulkart (T,E), lkwart-lkwart (W,T) (SP), ilkwart-ilkwart (T,E) (SP)

umbilical cord, umbilicus ...... metyeletyel (W,T), tyelepelep, yep (E)

umbrella bush ...... arterrk

umbrella grass ...... twemper-twemper (W)

unable
be unable to do something ...... ahentyel-arem (T,E), aperrpert-irrem
be unable to do something or go somewhere because of something ...... amek-arem
trying to do something and failing ...... -arrpantey, athem¹ (E), arrthem (E), uyarn (E), ywarn, atengkel (E)

unaware ...... akwen, akwerrp (E)

uncle
mother's brother ...... amarl, kamern (W,T)
father's brother ...... angey, anya¹, ayna (E), anywek-anywek (W,T), anawerr
father's elder brother ...... pap anawey (W), pap aywa (W)
father's elder brother (baby talk) ...... anawerr-anawerr, anawey, anawey-anawey (E)
uncle (from English) ...... angkel
respectful word for mother's brother (used by men) ...... angerrety
teenage mother's brothers (respect language) ...... arrang (E)
great-uncle (father's mother's brother) ...... aperl
great-uncle (father's father's brother) ...... arreng
great-uncle (mother's father's brother) ...... atyemey, rtartart, artartey (E)
great-uncle (mother's mother's brother) ...... menh-menh (W,T), nyany², ipmenh (E)

unconcerned ...... anaraty (W,T), aneraty (T,E)

be uncaring, oblivious or unconcerned … anaraty-irrem (W,T), aneraty-irrem (T,E)

unconscious

not taking notice … arert

uncooked … anka, ankang (W,T), arlety[2]

uncooperative … ankerl, anngarenty (W,T), anwernt, tyerrk (W,T), iyterrk (E)

uncover

peel off something … akap-rlwem (W,T), akap-irlwem, akap-iylwem (E)

uncover something … akent-wem (E), aketh-ilem, irrkerem

under … kwen

at the bottom, underneath … intert, anarteng

on the underneath side … kwen-ampeny, kweneng

underground cave … aharlkwerr, yalkwerr (T)

understand

understand something … awem, iterlarem

recognise sound of someone or something … alhengk-awem

not understand something … apatem

undo

undo something … lywem[1], akap-rlwem (W,T), akap-irlwem, ararlk-ilem

become undone … lywelhem

undress … lywelhem

unhurriedly … arternp, manty (W), mwanty (T,E), mantyel (W), mwantyel (T,E), manty-manty (W), mwanty-mwanty (T,E)

unique … impen, tyeperr

unite … anyent-irrem

unknowing … akwen, akwerrp (E)

unload something … anarnpelh-ilem

unlucky

unsuccessful in hunting … rrpwernp (W,T), urrpernp (E)

unmarried

unmarried man … arnkenty-areny

unmarried woman … arlweker-areny

unopened … ampwerrk

not yet cut into pieces … arlewenp (T,E)

unregistered *(vehicle)* … mwetek ngkekern (W,T), mwetekay urlaylp (E), ngkekern-ngkekern (W,T)

unripe … anka, ankang (W,T), arlety[2]

unripe fruit of the native currant, native citrus (respect language) … apwert

unsettled … arlkwer, urlker (E)

become unsettled or upset … arlkwer-irrem[1]

being unable to sit still … arweketherwek (W,T), urekethwerek (E)

carry a baby around all the time and make it unsettled … arlkwer-ilem

make things unsettled … arweketherwek-ilem (W,T), urekethwerek-ilem (E), arwekar-ilem

unsociable

not mixing with other people or talking to other people … arnkely, arrwernt, kekart (T), akikart (E), kewarr (W,T), akiwarr (T,E), npwart (W,T), unpart (T), alha npwart (W,T)

unsteady *(of legs)* … artaly-artaly (T,E)

unsuccessfully

doing something unsuccessfully … -arrpantey, athem[1] (E), arrthem (E), uyarn (E), ywarn, atengkel (E)

untidy … alhengkey

until

until (a particular thing happens), until (a particular time) … -atwety[2]

unwell *(see also 'sick')* … anety (W,T), kwern (W,T), akeng (T,E), altarrp (W,T)

feeling unwell … antywekelywekely

up

(up)wards … -antep

facing or pointing upwards, going upwards, moving upwards … akern-antep, akernelak

get up, move upwards … akern-irrem

lift something up … akern-ilem

uproot

uproot something (such as grass) … antyakem

upset … kekart (T), akikart (E)

get upset about something … kekart-irrem (T), akikart-irrem (E), tikeley-irrem

get sulky or upset … kwel-anyem (W,T), kwel-irrem (W,T)

get annoyed, upset, angry or become offended about things (especially to do with restricted sites etc.) … mwekeny-irrem, mwekenh-irrem

feel upset about something (women) … anthwerrng-irrem (T)

become unsettled or upset … arlkwer-irrem[1]

become annoyed, agitated, or upset .... rrwampem (W), urrampem (T,E)
be suffering distress or hardship .... arekwenth-kwenth-irrem (T,E)
say things that you shouldn't say or that will upset people .... ywetherrk angkem (T,E), uyetherrk angkem (E)
make someone unsettled or upset .... arlkwer-ilem
make someone upset or distressed .... arekwenth-kwenth-ilem (T,E)
make someone wild, upset or angry .... kekartem-ilem (T)

upside down
be upside down .... mpart intem (W,T)
tip something upside down (so that the back part is facing up) .... altywarrernem, artep arrernem

upside-down plant .... irrarnt-irrarnt (E)

urine .... mpwa, mpwang (W,T)
urinate .... lhwem (T), ulhem (T,E), lwem[1] (W), mpwa ulhem (E), mpwang lwem (W), mpwelhem[2] (T), mpwulhem (E)
dog's urine .... mpwerl
urinate on something (dogs) .... mpwerl lhwem, mpwerl ulhem (E), mpwerl-ilem, awel-ilem (E)

us, for us, to us *(two) (go to pronoun table p. 747)*

us, for us, to us *(more than two) (go to pronoun table p. 747)*

use
use something up .... ywerrelh-ilem, uyerrelh-ilem (E)
using something to do an action .... -akert[2]

used to
added to verbs to show that the verb action used to happen or usually happened .... +etyart

useless
no good, useless .... kwern (W,T), akeng (T,E), anety (W,T)
a bit useless .... kwern-kwern (W,T), akeng-akeng (T,E), anety-anety (W,T)
not able to do something (from English) .... ameleth
ragged, tattered .... alkwemp

usual .... akweteth, amperreny (E), marany (T,E)
something or somebody who is always there .... amelerr (T,E)
(something that is) usually found in a particular habitat or environment .... -areny

usually
added to verbs to show that the verb action used to happen or usually happened .... +etyart

uvula .... angerl-angerl (T,E), ngarlaleny

Vv

vagina
(sensitive language) .... artwert[2], kep[2] (W), tyarrp, tyely (W,T)

various things .... wenh-wenh (W,T), iwenh-iwenh

vegetable food .... mern atherrk

vehicle
vehicle (from English) .... mwetekay, mwetek
vehicle (respect language) .... twertert-ayerr (E)
vehicle (baby talk) .... mpwempew

vein .... alwerrng

velvet hill wattle .... ampwey (E)

velvet tobacco .... ngwarray-ngwarray, pengart-pengart[2] (W)

venom *(snake)* .... antya[2] (T,E)

venomous animal .... arrenty

Venus .... Anthelper (W,T), Arwenpeng (E), Awelh (E), Kwerraly Angerr, Kwerraly Rltwa (W), Kwerraly Urlta (T,E)

verse .... arreny (W,T), arreyn (E)

very .... angerr[1], anthwerr (W,T), ulteketh

via
by way of, through something, via .... -angkwerr[2]

vibrate
vibrate parts of the body .... arrkem (E)
shake legs when preparing for a fight (women) .... amerl-amerl arrernem (W,T), ameyl-ameyl arrernem (E)

vicinity
in the vicinity of .... -ampeny[2]

video or audio cassette
(from English) .... kathet

vine
kangaroo balls vine .... aherr-arlweth (T,E), aherr-arleth (E)

violent .... ahangerr, ahelengkw (E)

visible
hardly visible ..... arrkay
vision
have a vision ..... aherr arem, aherr-aherr arem
visit
go visiting ..... yatyarr, yatyerr alhem
visitor ..... alethang
voice ..... ahenty[1], angka[1] (E), angkety, ulypma (E)
faint voice, soft or low voice ..... ahenty arrkay, ahenty akwek, ahenty kwen
loud voice ..... ahenty angerr
voice fade ..... ahenty arrkay-irrem
volume
turn volume down ..... ntert-ilem, ntertelh-ilem
vomit ..... antew
to vomit ..... antew-irrem, alyelkelhem

Ww

wad
lump of tobacco ..... ngkwerlp ampeng (W), ngkwerlp kelh, warn (E)
make a wad of tobacco ... warn-ilem (E)
wag tail *(dog)* ..... anyerrkem
wail ..... arnem, arrangkem
wailing or crying in mourning (men) ..... wartay[2] (E), wartay-irrem (E)
wailing or crying in mourning (women) ..... akay, akayel arnem
waist
soft part above hip ..... ayew
waist band
men's hairstring waist band or belt ..... arlpelh[2], matyart, mawelyarr (W,T)
wait
'Wait a minute', 'Wait a while', 'Just a minute!', 'Hang on!' ..... rrwek (W,T), urrek (T,E), alerl (E), rrwek-antey (W,T), urrek-antey (T,E), alerl-antey (E), alerl-mernt (E), rrwek-mernt (W,T)
'Wait a minute' (respect language) ..... urrekaty-antey (E), urrekatyakenh (E)
waiting for someone to do something, waiting with someone ..... alanty, atanty
wait for someone or something ..... akarelhem (W,T), mpwelhem[1], tywempelhem (W,T)
wait for someone, wait with someone ..... akarem
hang round waiting for someone to give something to you ..... aparelhem (T,E)
keep someone waiting ..... anngangem (E)
wait to ambush somebody ..... arrap-anem, urlernem (E)
wait in vain for someone who has gone away ..... yarelhem (W) (?), ywarelhem (T) (?)
wait while others go ..... alkwernem
wait for someone to go and come back ..... alkwernem
wait for somebody to come ..... iwerr arelhem (E), iwerr arem (E), tyey arem (W)
waiting for someone else to do things for you ..... anam
someone who waits for someone else to do things for them ..... anam-athek (T,E), anam-kenh (T,E), anam-henh (W,T), anamek (T,F)
Wakaya
language or people ..... Wakay
wake *(see also 'awake')*
wake up ..... akem-irrem, atyek-irrem (T,E), karr-irrem
wake someone up ..... atyekelh-ilem (E), karr-ilem
wake someone up (by passing a hand over their face) ..... inkerrelh-ilem, ankarrelh-ilem (W)
walk
walk along ..... apem[1] (W,T), alhem
walk around ..... nthwem (W,T), unthem (E)
walk away from a fight ... anenyerr-irrem
walk away from someone, go off in own direction .... ampakelhem (W,T)
walk in someone's footsteps ..... ingkatyel-wem, lyekel-wem (W), atywekel-iwerrem (E), atywekel-iwem (E)
walk making clear tracks for someone to follow ..... thwerremp-irrem (T,E)
walking quickly, purposefully and resolutely (often with intent to fight) ..... antyatar-antyatar, antyatar-irrem

walking along with legs tight together (maybe because of a sore) ... mwenyar alhem (W), rrmwenyar alhem (W,T)

unable to walk ... anath (W,T), anenyirrp irrkweynar (E), apekap, apertap (W,T), arlamarr, arlwemeny, lim-lim (W), lyer (E), rnwerr, rnwerr-rnwerr (W,T), rtapety, yer (E)

walking stick ... rtwenk

wallaby

black-footed rock-wallaby ... arrwa, arrwang (W,T)

spectacled hare-wallaby .. kwarlp, lkwameny (W,T) (?)

wallaby, euro ... lyerl-areny (W) (?), lyerl-iperr (W) (?)

type of wallaby ... anwengk[1] (E) (?)

Wallaby Bore ... Alart

wallaroo ... areng[3], irntareny (W,T)

wane *(moon)* ... aherrk parrk-irrem (W,T), aherrk pwarrk-irrem (W,T), atay parrk-irrem (W,T)

Wangala Hills ... Wangerlakwerlang, Angank

want

liking or wanting something ... ahenty[2]

not wanting to do something ... ahenty-kwenh (W,T), amperr (W,T), anwernt

want someone or something ... ahenty-anem, ahenty-irrem, ilkelhem, akangkem, kwak-irrem

really like or want something ... alherrem[2] (W,T), alhirrem

want something, feel happy about something ... inkwerelhem (T,E)

want something (similar to the thing you see) ... angwarem

want to eat something, really want a particular food ... arrernkem (W,T), arrirnkem (T,E)

make someone feel not wanted ... alhengkey-ilem

not want to do something or go somewhere ... mweny-irrem, mweny-mweny-irrem, anwernt-irrem

want to give something to someone but change your mind ... mweny rrkwem

want something but not get it, go without ... arrarem

Warlpiri

language or people ... Arlper[1]

warm, warmth ... rwernp (W,T), urinp (E), ntywety (W,T), untyety (E), arlterrng

get warm (person or place) ... ntywety-irrem (W,T), untyety-irrem (E), arlterrng-irrem, rwernp-irrem (W,T), urinp-irrem (E)

warm oneself by the fire or in the sun ... ntywem[1] (W,T), untyem[1] (E), arrtyem (E), arrtyelh-ilem (W), alhenelhem (T,E), itelhem (E)

warm something up ... ntywelh-ilem (W,T), ntywety-ilem (W,T), untyety-ilem (E), urinp-ilem (E)

warn

warn somebody about something ... akayak-ilem, ateng-ilem (W,T), atengelh-ilem (W,T), mwerranty-ilem, anngarr-ilem, manty-manty-ilem (E)

Warrabri ... Alekareng

wart ... ankerl, itely (E), mwenth (E)

Warumungu

language or person ... Aremweng, Waramwengk

was *(go to 'be')*

wash

wash something ... alhewem

wash oneself ... alhewelhem

wipe something off something ... arnngem

wash earth away ... arnkarr-akem (W), arnkarr-ilem (T,E)

get washed away (earth) .. arnkarr-akelhem (T)

wasp ... arntirn (T), arnteyn (E), atnangkerney (E)

type of wasp ... rntererrpererrp (W,T) (?)

waste something ... intyarlkwem, uyerrelh-ilem (E), ywerrelh-ilem, arimpem (E)

watch

'Watch out!' ... alay[2], pwertay (E)

watch something ... arem

watch someone or something coming towards you ... arnarem, analty arem (W)

watch someone or something going away ... artwarem (W,T), irtwarem

watch out for or look after someone ... ararem (W,T), arntarnt-arem

watch out for yourself ... arntarnt-arelhem, arelhem

watch out for something, peer out ... rlwem-anem (W,T), urlem-anem (E)
watch the road for someone to come ... iwerr arelhem (E), iwerr arem (E), tyey arem (W)
watch something happen but not be involved ... mentyel arem

water ... kwaty, arwekel (W,T)
water (respect language) ... arntwaly (E), untyerr (E), ntywerr (T), wangkethel (E), weng angkethel (E)
water (baby talk) ... apa (W,T), kwek (E), nyany[1]
fresh water ... kwaty lyeteny, narengk (T), kwaty narengk (T), kwaty narwep (W,T)
muddy or dirty water ... lpwert (W,T), ulpert (T,E), kwaty lpwert (W,T), kwaty ulpert (E)
salty water ... ilewerr-ilewerr (W,T)
sparkling water ... arlkerrk[2] (W,T)
drop or drip of water ... irnmerr, kwaty irnmerr, ntyerlp[2] (W,T)
deep water ... kwaty arntay (W,T), kwen-angerr
shallow water ... kwaty kanty (T), terrth (W)
large expanse of water ... alay[1], kwaty alay, ulamp (E)
small amount of running water ... awerrp[2] (W), arnperrkenty (W,T), ilperrkenty (W)
running water on the side of the creek ... kwaty kanty (T)
small amount of water, a sprinkle of water ... iker
small amount of rain water lying around ... ilperrk (W)
water at the bottom of a soakage ... arlparlety (E)
water lying around in cracks in the ground ... kwaty awal (W,T)
water found in the hollow of tree trunks ... nthwarr (W), ntharr (T), untharr (E), kwentharr, merrert (T), angenty
water in claypan ... ntyerlp[2] (W,T) (?)
water lie on the ground ... athernem (E)
water get muddied, get dirty ... lpwert-irrem (W,T), ulpert-irrem (T,E)
make water muddy or dirty ... lpwert-ilem (W,T), lpwertelh-ilem (W,T), ulpert-ilem (T,E), ulpertelh-ilem (T,E)
hot water (from English) ... atewat, ahatewat
become hot (water) ... atewat-irrem
heat water ... atewat-ilem
water something ... irrpelh-ilem

waterbird
types of waterbird ... lhekethatethat (E), ngamarwengk (T)

water dish *(wooden)* ... arlketh[1] (W,T), atywekal (W), rnwa (W,T), rnwang (W,T), urety (E), urna (T,E), kwerlintyerr

waterbag
kangaroo-skin waterbag ... arranty[2] (E)

watercourse ... lher, lpway (W,T), ulpay (T,E)

waterhole *(big, wide)* ... arntay (W,T)

waterless *(country)* ... arlpaw, arrangketh, aherraty, urrepert (E), rrwepert (T), ahepet (E)

watery ... kwaty-kwaty[1] (W,T), rew-rew
go watery or runny ... kwaty-irrem (W,T), rew-irrem
make something watery ... kwaty-kwaty-ilem (W,T), rew-rew-ilem
watery (eyes) ... anngwenty (W,T), arrngwelty (E), anngwenty-anngwenty, arrngwelty-arrngwelty (E)

wave
to wave ... akwerrem (W,T), iltyerrem
wave someone down to get their attention ... kelengwem (W,T)

wax *(in ears)* ... ika (T,E)

waxbill *(bird)* ... nyengk, tyeyek (W,T)

waxy wattle ... alhepalh (E), ilkwernarr, patwert (W,T)
grub from ... alhepalhayt (E), ilkwernarrayt (E)

way
a long way ... rntwarr
by way of, through something, via ... -angkwerr[2]
get in the way of someone or something ... arrngen-welhem (W,T), arrngert-ilem, arrngert-welhem, arrngert-wem, angert irnem (W,T)
in this way, in that way ... alakenh, alanh, alanh-anyem (E), alakenh-anyem (E)

we *(we two)* *(go to pronoun table p. 747)*

we *(more than two)* *(go to pronoun table p. 747)*

weak ... apertap (W,T), artaly-artaly (T,E), atnhakert (E), parrk (W,T), pwarrk (T,E), purrk (E)
weak (in the body) ... arrmaly-arrmaly (T,E), artaly-artaly (T,E), arrwely-arrwely
become weak from hunger or sickness ... arrwely-arrwely-irrem, atnhakert-irrem (E)

feel dead tired or weak .... marrmarrp-irrem, manmarrp-irrem (W,T)
become sickly, floppy, or weak (in the body) ...... armaly-arrmaly-irrem (T,E)
get weak, unable to do things for yourself ...... apertap-irrem (W,T)
stumble about weakly ..... awerrk-irrem (T), awerrkelhem

weak *(tasteless)*
tasteless (of tea) .... kwaty-kwaty[1] (W,T)

weak, fragile .... atyet-atyet

weapons
loaded with weapons ...... ywerlarr (T)
lots of spears or boomerangs .... irrawey

weather
hot weather, summer ..... twern (W,T), twern-tayem (W,T), utern (T,E), utern-tayem (E), rwernp (W,T), urinp (E)
start of summer .... aherrk akwerrk (W), twern rlwa (W,T), twern rlwang (W,T), utern akwerrk (T,E), utern urla (E)
cold weather .... alhwerrp, alyangkw (E), irrernt (T,E)
start of cold weather .... alhwerrp akwerrk, alhwerrp alhang (T), alhwerrp urla, alhwerrp rlwang (W,T)

web *(spider)* .... wep (SP)

wedgebill *(chiming)* .... tyalatywerrp (T,E)

wedge-tailed eagle .... irrety, arlawerr (W)
sing, make a sound like (wedge-tailed eagles) .... kwelyalp-irrem

weep *(of wounds)* .... anthwem (T,E)

weight
put on weight .... anter-irrem, awek-irrem (T,E), ayet-irrem (E)
get thin, lose weight .... althalth-irrem,, ampwerrem, ampweyampw-irrcm (E), arrwely-arrwely-irrem, utyew-irrem (E)
make someone lose weight .... ampwelem

well, and so .... wal

well, healthy .... mwerr
well (respect language) .... alhengerr (E), mwenkerr (E)

well-behaved .... mwerr

were .... anem[1], intem[1], ayntem (E)

west .... altwerl
west (respect language) .... altwerlernety (W), altwerlerneyt (E)
due west .... altwerl arraty, altwerl arratyeny (T)
north-west .... altwerl-altwerl, ayerrer altwerl, ayerrer-ayerrer (E) (SP)
south-west .... antekerr altwerl
from the west .... altwerl-iperr (T,E), altwerl-penh, altwerleng (W,T)
in a westerly direction ..... altwerl-altwerl, altwerl-iperr (T,E), altwerl-penh
in a westerly direction (respect language) .... altwerlenety-athek (W), altwerlerneyt-athek (E)
west wind .... aretharr
western end of the bed (where people urinate) ..... mpwanth, mpwarl, mpwarl-thayt (W,T)

western bower bird .... akerrk

western brown snake ..... antywemp (T,E) (?), arriper (T,E) (?)

western nightshade .... katyerr

western quoll .... atyelp, atyet[2] (E)

wet .... antyet-antyet (T,E), aperlk-aperlk (T,E), apeylk-apeylk (E), rew-rew, rlkwer-rlkwer (E)
soaking wet .... lthangkw (T,E), lthangkw-lthangkw (T,E)
wet (ground) .... irrngwelth (E), tert, urta (E)
wet, sloppy (of food) .... apely
wet (clothes) .... anthwek-anthwek
get wet (ground, camp) .... tert-irrem
get soaked .... lthangkw-irrem (T,E)
wet oneself to cool down .. akarl-welhem (W,T), anhelhem, irrpelh-ilelhem
wet the ground .... tert-ilem, urtilem (E)
wet the ground (water) .... antyernem[3] (W)
wet someone or something .... antyet-antyet-ilem (T,E), rew-ilem, irrpelh-ilem
make something soaked .. anthwek-anthwek-ilem
make something wet or soft .... apely-ilem
wet someone, throw water over someone .... akarl-wem (W,T)

whack
give something a whack .. apar atwem (T,E), atwem

what
'What?' .... nthakenh, nthanh (E), thanh (E), wenh (W,T), iwenh, ilek (E), wenhay (W,T), iwenhay, ilekay (E)
'What thing, 'Which person?' .... angwenh, wenh (W,T), iwenh, ilek (E)
'What about . . . ?', 'What if . . . ?' .... -artey, -alew[1] (E)

'What for?' ... wenhek (W,T), iwenhek, wenheng (W,T), iwenheng, ilek-kety (E), ilekek (E)
'What is it like?' ... wenh-artek (W,T), iwenh-artek
'What is it?' (when trying to remember something) ... wenh-athew, angwenh-athew (W,T)
'What skin?' ... angwenh-apatherr (W,T), ilek-apatherr (E)
'What's up?', 'What's the matter?', 'What's going on?' ... nthakenh, nthanh (E), thanh (E), wartay[1] (W,T), wenh-apert (W,T), iwenh-apert, yemay (W,T), ilek-apert (E), nthakenh-athek, nthakenh-irrem
What's-his-name? (when trying to remember something) ... wenhekwey (W,T), iwenhakwey, angwenh, angwenh-akwey (W,T), angwenh-apatherr (W,T), arneweth (E), ilek-pat (E), ilekakwey (E), ilengem (E), wenh-apatherr (W,T), iwenh-apatherr, ilek-apatherr (E)

wheel track ... mwetekay mpaty (T)
when? ... lwengar (W,T), ilengar (E)
where?
'Where?', 'Which place?' ... nthenh
'From where?' ... nthenh-penh (W,T), nthenheng (W,T), nthenh-iperr (E), nthenh-they (E)
'Where is . . . ?' ... -artey, -alew[1] (E)
'Where to?', 'Which way?' ... nthangkwerr (W), nthenh-angkwerr, nthenh-warn (W,T), nthenh-warl (E)
'Where to?', 'Which way?' (respect language) ... nthenhenty-angkwerr (E)
from wherever, from all over the place ... nthenh-nthenh

which? *(see also 'what')*
whichever people ... angwenhant angwenh

while *(see also Appendix 2)*
while something is happening ... -rlwer (W,T), -rwek (T)

'Wait a minute', 'Wait a while' ... rrwek (W,T), urrek (T,E), alerl (E), rrwek-antey (W,T), urrek-antey (T,E), alerl-antey (E), alerl-mernt (E), rrwek-mernt (W,T)

whine
make crying sounds (animals) ... arnem, arrangkem
whine (dog) ... mwelty-mwelty angkem (T), urrmelty angkem (E), meltyang angkem (W,T)

whipstick ... pentarlp (T,E)
whipstick wattle ... antyweleny (T,E), ateyepenh (W,T), ilwerreny (E) (?)
whirlwind ... aharlparrengk[2] (E), awerantyerrng (T,E), rrwep-rrwep (W,T), rrwepeng-rrwep (W)

whirring
whirring, whooshing or rumbling noise ... aywerr
make a whirring, whooshing or rumbling noise ... aywerr angkem

whiskers ... arrarn (W,T), arrwert (T,E)
whisper ... arretyem (W,T), arreytem (T,E), arretyemel angkem (W,T), arreytemel angkem (T,E)
whistle ... arraweth-irrem, ilpwerlenty-rnem (E), ilpwerlenty-irrem (E)
whistle (from English) ... wethel-irrem (T,E)
whistler *(rufous)* ... apetyepetyem (W,T), artwang apetyepetyem (W), artwatherr apetyepetyem (E), ipeny apetyepetyem (W,T), kwarlpatengkelyengkely (E), tyenyepweny (E)
whistling kite ... apwart-apwart (E) (?)
white ... arlter, mperlker, tywelker
whitish, off-white ... arlter-arlter, mperlker-mperlker
go white ... arlter-irrem
whitish yellow ochre ... ngwenty-ngwenty (T,E), ntyengwenty
white clay ... tywelker

white ant ... interrk[2]
white cockatoo ... terekerr
white person ... alhernter, arlter, kartey (W), mperlker, tyerrty arlter (E), tywelker
white person (from English) ... warlpal
white person (baby talk) ... wapey (E)

white woman ... marl tywelker
white woman (from English) ... metheth, waterlweper
white man ... artwa tywelker, warlpal
white-backed swallow ... nerrty (E)
white-faced heron, white-necked heron ... arlkwenth (E), kamparwengk (E), ntyar (W,T), ulamp-areny (E), ulamparrwek (E)
white-headed ... aherlkey (W,T), ilkwa^{3} (E), ilkwamp ilkwang (E)
white-plumed honeyeater ... aperrety-aperrety (T) (?)
whitewood ... arlperr
sweet gum of ... arlperrampw (E), arlperrangkwarl
grub of ... arlperrayt (E), arlperrenhayt (T,E), arlperreny (W), arlperrenh (W,T)
who? ... angwenh, wenh (W,T) (SP), iwenh (SP)
who? (respect language) ... angwenthangw
whoever ... angwenhant angwenh
whole
the whole thing ... alewarr (W,T), antyaper
whole (uncut) ... ampwerrk, arlewenp (T,E), mpank (W,T), mpwank
why? ... ilek-kety (E), ilek-they (E), ilekek (E), wenh-penh (W,T), iwenh-penh, wenhek (W,T), iwenhek, wenheng (W,T), iwenheng
wide ... antek (T,E), aymperr (E)
wide open space ... arlpaw
become wide ... arlpaw-irrem
make something wide ... antek-ilem (T,E), arlpaw-ilem
dig a hole out to make it wider ... arntay-ilem (W,T)
widow, widower ... inpert, warlekwert (W,T)
become a widow or a widower ... inpert-irrem, warlekwert-irrem (W,T)
become a widow ... arlweker-warn-irrem (W,T), arlweker-warl-irrem (E)
become a widow (respect language) ... irrewatyentel-irrem
become a widower ... arnkenty-warn-irrem (W,T), arnkenty-warl-irrem (E)
wife ... anew, marl
wife (baby talk) ... kaly-kaly^{1} (T,E)
promised wife ... akwerrk-penh (E)
term used by a husband to refer to his wife) ... arelh^{1}
wife of someone not in the same generation moiety ... aperl
wife of someone in the same generation moiety ... arrkar
wild *(see also 'angry')*
not broken in ... ateralth
wild fig ... tywerrk (W,T), utyerrk (E)
wild gooseberry ... alperrantyey, ararnt (W,T)
wild honey *(go to 'sugarbag')*
wild onion *(go to 'bush onion')*
wild orange ... atwakey
northern wild orange ... akarley (E), akarlety, ngarntatyarr (W,T)
gidgee wild orange ... angerterrk (E)
wild passionfruit ... arrweneng
wild plum ... alkwa (E), ankwerlay (W,T), ankwerley (T,E)
wild tobacco *(go to 'tobacco')*
wild turkey ... artew, arwengerrp (T,E)
will
'Will I (do something)?' ... thakey^{1} (W)
will (do the verb action) ... +etyenh
willie wagtail ... artetyerretyerr^{1}, tyenterr-tyenterr (W)
willy-willy ... aharlparrengk^{2} (E), awerantyerrng (T,E), rrwep-rrwep (W,T), rrwepeng-rrwep (W)
win
beat someone in a race or a game ... impem
really win in a race, game or a fight ... arlkwem
wind ... rlka (W,T), rlkang (W,T), iylka (E)
blow (wind) ... wernem
strong wind ... rlkang angerr (W,T), iylka angerr (E), wereny
calm, no wind ... teraty (T,E), anengk (E)
cold wind ... alhwerrp
north or west wind ... aretharr
east wind ... rwarr (E)
south wind ... anyemilparr (E)
go upwind from something ... rwarr-angkwerr alhem (E)
with head to the prevailing wind ... rlkang-ampeny (W,T), iylkampeny (E), rlkangkwerr (W,T), iylkangkwerr (E)
wind calm down, settle down ... anengk-irrem (E), teraty-irrem (T,E)
sit in the wind to cool down ... wernelhem (E)
windbreak ... kwenty^{2} (W,T), rtak (W,T), rtakw (E), werrant (W)

wind something round yourself .... alyernelhem
winding .... amper-amper, iylwerl-iywerl (E)
window *(from English)* ..... kelath
windpipe .... ahenty mwelper
wine .... ngkwarl
wing .... arlpa², arlpang (W,T), aylpa (E), arlpelh¹ (T,E), aympelh (E)
wink .... annga anyent-irrem
winnow seed
winnow seed with hands .. iylker anthem (E), then-wem
winnow seed (upwards movement of coolamon) .. ilpem¹
winnow seed in coolamon (rapid sideways movement of coolamon) .. ahety-ilem (W,T), ayety-ilem (W), aympernem (E), irrkertert-wem (E)
winter .... alhwerrp
beginning of winter .... alhwerrp akwerrk, alhwerrp alhang (T), alhwerrp rlwa (W,T), alhwerrp rlwang (W,T), alhwerrp urla
middle of winter .... alhwerrp mparnt, alhwerrp mpep (E), alhwerrp rlkwerr (W,T), alhwerrp artep (T)
wipe
wipe something clean ...... arnngem, irrarlkem (E)
wipe something off something .... iparem (E), irrarlkem (E), rrpwarem (W,T), urrparem (T,E)
wipe something off yourself .... arnngelhem, iparelhem (E), irrarlkelhem (E), rrpwarelhem (W,T), urrparelhem (T,E)
wipe out footprints or take your name off a paper ..... rrpwarelhem (W,T), urrparelhem (T,E)
wipe out (kill lots of animals) .... akwerremp-ilem
wipe out a debt .... rrpwarem (W,T), urrparem (T,E), iparem (E)
wire *(from English)* .... way
wire bush .... npway-npway (W,T), unpay (E), inpay (T)
wireless *(from English)* ..... wayeleth
witchetty bush .... anyem²
witchetty bush (respect language) .... alyempetayt (E)
flower of .... nwathet (W), nathat (T), utnathat (T,E)
gum of .... anyemampwerrty (E), anyemangkwarl (W), anyemaywerrk (W), ampwerrty (E)
root with a witchetty grub in it .... arwa¹ (E)
witchetty grub .... anyematy, anyemayt (T,E), tyap
witchetty grub (respect language) .... alyempetayt (E)
small red witchetty grub .. arlpalywerrng
black stage of witchetty grub .... ngkekern (W,T), urlaylp (E)
yellow stage (before it goes black) .... akerurrurr (E)
witchetty grub while still in the root .... arwerlk (E)
yellow fatty substance inside .... anwerrng
type of grub from witchetty bush .... kerlpaty (W), kerlpayt (E)
'pipe' through which witchetty (and other grubs) emerge from the ground ... impakwert (E)
with
with someone, accompanied by someone .... -akert², -arleng²
with something, having (something) .... -akert²
wither *(vegetation)* .... aherraty-irrem, antyerrk-irrem
withered
not green (of vegetation) .. antyerrk
without
without, not having something .... arla² (T,E), alther (T,E), -kweny², -uthek (E)
without family .... alhamp-alhamp
without taking notice of others .... atanty, alanty
(doing something) without thinking, for no good reason .... apelkel (W,T)
want something but not get it, go without ...... arrarem
witness something .... anngel arrernem (T,E)
woma snake
sandhill python .... ahelh-ahelh (W), ahenenh, aheneny (T,E), nwey (T), uney (E)
woman .... arelh¹, arrwekety¹, irrkwely¹ (E), marl

old woman ..... akelty (E), akelty ampwa (E), arelh ampwa, arelh ampwang (W,T), arrwekety ampwang (W,T), arrwekety ampwa (E)
old woman (from English) ..... werlkemen
white woman (from English) ..... metheth
woman who has not had children ..... aleyak
special word for woman .. interrkekety (E)
woman (respect language used by men) ..... ngayekenh (W,T), ngayekety (E)
a single woman, or a woman who is on her own ..... arlweker-areny
young woman ..... arelh akwerrk (W,T)
'pretend' women ..... arelheng-arelh (E)
woman (bereavement term) ..... kwaty-henh (W,T), kwaty-kenh (E)
women's camp ..... arlweker
women's camp (respect language) ..... irrewatyent
women's ceremonial stick ..... kweter
women's ceremony ..... awely, ilpenty (SP)
women's hairstring garments ..... merterr[2] (E), ngatywelarr (T,E)

won't *(do something)* ..... +etyakenh, +ety-kweny, +etyang (E)

wood
firewood ..... rwa (W,T), rwang (W,T), ura (T,E)
kindling, wood chips, twigs ..... mwenng, mwenthenng (E)
fragments of wood and dirt in hollow tree left by white ants ..... urrtha (E) (?)
wood put on top of a grave ..... rrwelty (W,T), irrwelty, urrelty (T,E)

Wood Duck Swamp ..... Antyay

wooden dish ..... arlketh[1] (W,T), urna (T,E), lengarr (E)
wooden scoop or shovel ... mwar, panth

woodswallow
black-faced woodswallow, masked woodswallow ..... perrpantywen (W,T), perrpantywel (E)

Woolla Downs ..... Awelh

woolly ..... lthel-lthel, lthelhey, lthelhey-lthelhey

woollybutt grass ..... alyatywereng (E), antyey[1] (W,T)

woomera ..... amirr
hook on woomera ..... ikalharr (E)
stone point in handle ..... ntyarl (W,T), ntyerl (T,E)
throw a spear with a woomera ..... arrathenem (E), rtwely-ilem

word ..... angka[1] (E), angkety, ulypma (E)
the word for a thing, name ..... arreny (W,T), arreyn (E)

work
a job ..... rrkwapenty (W,T), irrkwapenty (E), warrk-irrem
work (from English) ..... warrk
be occupied doing something ..... rrkwapem (W,T), irrkwapem (E), atyanem (W)
worker ..... rrkwapenh-apenh (T), warrken map

worm ..... irnnga (W,T), irnngang (W,T)
type of worm ..... aperr (E) (?)
worm found in kangaroo's nose ..... urltaty
worm found in kangaroo's stomach ..... antya[1] (E), ngangkar, ngangkay, ultyitywelty (E), ultyetyulty

worried ..... alharrp (W,T), alhwarrp (T,E), altarrp (W,T)
feeling worried and sorry .. atham-atham
worry about someone ..... atham-irrem
worry about something .... akarntem[2] (SP)

wound
sore or wound ..... tywen, utyen (E), alety
wound something ..... alety-akem

wow! ..... yekay

wrap *(something up)* ..... artaper-ilem

wreck
get wrecked ..... akeng-irrem (T,E), anety-irrem (W,T), kwern-irrem (W,T)
wreck something ..... akeng-ilem (T,E), kwern ilem (W,T), anety-ilem (W,T)
wreck something (respect language) ..... atnerrk-ilem (E)

wren
types including fairy-wrens and grasswrens ..... lyerr-lyerr, lyerretyelyerr (E), tyewelyerr-lyerr (W), pwerelyerr-lyerr (W,T)

wrestle ..... ilatwem
push each other around ... ilatwerrem, arlkwaterrem (W,T), ntewerrem (W)

wring
wring somebody's or something's neck ... ahenty ltwakem (W,T), ahenty ultakem (E), awerrkem, itutnhem (E), twerl-akem (W,T), tul-akem (E), ahenty twerl-akem (W), tywekem-ilem
wring something out ... alyernem, ayernem
wrinkled ... altyek-altyek, alyemp-alyemp[1], ilerrty-ilerrty
wrinkled face ... inngerr ilerrty (E), ilerrty
become wrinkled, creased, limp ... alyempelhem, altyek-altyek-irrem, altyekelhem, ilerrty-ilerrty-irrem (E), alyemp-alyemp-irrem
wrist ... akwengkwern (E), amwelt anngang (W), anaynenh (E), iltya ngkwern (W,T)
write ... arrernem, atanthem, ingkwernem (T,E), intelh-ilem (W,T), intelhem (W,T)
write or sign your name ... ingkwernelhem (T,E), arrernelhem
wrong ... akeng (T,E), amwa[2] (E), anety (W,T), kwern (W,T)
feeling as if something is wrong ... anert altywer, anert arltwang (W,T)
someone who has married the 'wrong' way ... akengentyeny (E), alem atherrk-atherrk (T,E), alem iyterrk-iyterrk (T,E), atherrk-atherrk (T,E)
the wrong way ... apantantenh (W)
the wrong way round (from English) ... rang-rang (W,T)
wrongly ... akengenty, anetyengwerl (W), apal-apal, apalel, apal[2], apant (W,T)
not knowing what you are doing ... apalekalek
Wurmbrandts Rock ... Mwetyek

Yy

yabby ... ikarl (T,E) (?), iltyarnm (W) (?)
yalka *(go to 'bush onion')*
yam
bush potato ... anek (W,T), anaty
pencil yam ... arlatyey
type of ... rtwatyert (W,T)
type of bush potato, yam ... antyalkenh (T,E), antyalkeny (W,T)
yam roots that have grown thickly and close together ... mwernenty
yam stick ... anem[3]
yandy *(go to 'winnow')*
yawn ... arralkem, ankwang arralkem (W,T)
yeah ... ya, yaw, yew, yeway (W,T), yew-yew (T,E)
yellow ... arrkeyt-arrkeyt (E), karntewarr, tywent-tywenterrp (W)
yellowish ... atywek-atywek
yellow native tobacco after being put in ashes ... arlterernternt (W)
yellow ochre ... arrkeyt (E), karntewarr, marlalperr (T,E)
yellow-faced whip-snake ... pwer arlewatyerr, pwer arlewatyerr-arlewatyerr (E)
yellow-throated miner ... impaymp (E), irnpernp (W,T), rnpernp (W,T)
yelp ... apangkem (W,T)
yes ... ya, yaw, yew, yeway (W,T), yew-yew (T,E)
yesterday ... amwerrk, amwerrkel, amwerrkarr (E), ngwerr (W,T), ngwerreh (W,T)
yesterday (respect language) ... ahamwerrk (E), ilamwerrk (E)
from yesterday ... amwerrkeny (E), ngwerreweny (W,T)
the day before yesterday ... amwerrkel arrpenh-ingar (E), ngwerreh arrpenh (W,T)
Yindjirbi Range ... Ntyerrmekwerlang, Ntyerrpekwerlang
Yippee Dam ... Yapay Irran (W)
you *(one person)*
(you) doing the action ... ntwa, ntwang (W,T), unta (E)
(you) having the action done to you ... nga, ngenh, ngwenh (W,T)
for you, to you, at you ... ngkweng
you, for you, to you
(you two) *(go to pronoun table p. 747)*
you, for you, to you
(more than two) *(go to pronoun table p. 747)*
young
young person or animal ... akwek, kwer[1] (W,T), akwerrk[1], akely (E)
newly grown (of plants) ... akwerrk[1]
smallest or youngest child ... akwerreny (E)
younger ones, the younger generation ... ingkerneny, kanty[1]

your, yours *(belonging to one person)* ..... ngkwengenh, ngkwenh (T,E), ngkweyenh (W,T), ngkwehenh (W,T)
your relation ..... +engkw
your, yours *(belonging to more than two)* *(go to pronoun table p. 747)*
yours *(belonging to you two)* *(go to pronoun table p. 747)*
yourself
you (can do verb action yourself) ..... ngkewarl (W,T), ngkewarleny (W,T)
Yuendumu ..... Ywerntem
Yundurbulu Range ..... Ntwerrperl

Zz

zebra finch ..... nyengk, tyeyek (W,T)

Scientific names finder

Plants

Abutilon otocarpum	aylpat-aylpat (E)
Acacia acradenia	ampwey (E)
Acacia adsurgens	antyweleny (T,E), ateyepenh (W,T)
Acacia adsurgens	ilwerreny (E) (?)
Acacia ancistrocarpa	irrar[1] (E), perrar (W,T), pirrar
Acacia aneura	artety
flower	nwathet (W), nathat (T), utnathat (T,E)
grub	alethayerr, artetyayt (E), kepartart
honeydew	arlperl, artetyaywerrk (W)
mulga apple	ataltyakwerl
resin	alkeramp
Acacia aneura *(broad leaf variety)*	arlpelhart
Acacia colei	alkart (W,T)
Acacia cowleana	alkart (W,T), ilkert (T,E)
Acacia cuthbertsonii ssp. cuthbertsonii	perley (W,T), peyley (E), lywey (W), alhanker (E) (?)
Acacia elachantha	alkart (W,T)
Acacia estrophiolata	atheng, athimp (T,E), atyarnp
gum	athengarlperl (E), athimpangkwarl (E), atyarnpangkwarl (W,T)
Acacia farnesiana	irnker (W,T), alekw (E)
Acacia georginae	rrwenyenk (W,T), urrenyenk (E)
green seed pods	ilyartey
resin	kikarr (E)
grub found in roots	kerlpaty (W), kerlpayt (E), urrenyenkayt (E)
grub found on branches	ulalthengayt (E)
Acacia hilliana	ntwarneng (E)
grub	pwentarnengayt (E)
Acacia jennerae	alalherrk (W,T)
Acacia jensenii	uneynt (E)
Acacia kempeana	anyem[2]
flower	nwathet (W), nathat (T), utnathat (T,E)
gum	anyemampwerrty (E), anyemangkwarl (W), anyemaywerrk (W), ampwerrty (E)
grub	anyematy
root with grub in it	arwa[1] (E)
Acacia ligulata	arterrk
Acacia lysiphloia	irrnyengerrny (W,T) (E), irrnyangerr (W), ngkwern irrnyepirrny (E), tyer[2] (E)
Acacia macdonnelliensis	arleth-arleth[1] (T,E)
grub	arleth-arleth[1] (T,E), arlethayerr (E)
Acacia maitlandii	patwert (W,T), arleperlterrk (E)
Acacia melleodora	ilkwernarr, patwert (W,T), alhepalh (E)
grub	ilkwernarrayt (E), alhepalhayt (E)
Acacia monticola	mwerlerr (E)
grub	mwerlerrayt (E)
Acacia murrayana	arrely[1]
Acacia paraneura	artety
Acacia pruinocarpa	arnteparl
Acacia sericophylla	akerlperr (W,T), awenth (E)
flower	athwenter
young seed pods	lyweper, alywer[1] (T,E)
seeds	akerlperr (W,T), ntyer (T), ntyerrm, alyaly (W)
green seeds	arntwatherrk[2] (T,E), artwengarr (T,E)
dry seeds	ntyerrm, alyaly (W), kertaty (E), tartaty (E), lyarr (E)
ground-up seeds	pilal (T,E) (?)
seeds go dry	lyarr-irrem (E)
ripe seeds	apal[1] (E)
sweet milky drink made from seeds	ntyerrm, apal[1] (E)
grub	awenthayt (E)
Acacia sessiliceps	iwert (E)
Acacia spondylophylla	anker-anker[2] (E)
Acacia stipuligera	ampwey (E)
Acacia stowardii	ilwerreny (E) (?)
Acacia tenuissima	antyweleny (T,E) (?)
Acacia tetragonophylla	arlketyerr, tyer[1] (W,T)
Acacia validinervia	iylarn (E), iylarnayt (E), ntwarnengayt (E)
grub	iylarn (E), iylarnayt (E), ntwarnengayt (E) (SP)
Acacia victoriae ssp. arida	arlep (T,E), arlwep (W)
flower	amper[1] (E)
edible resin	arlep ngkwarl (E)
grub	arlepayt (E)
Allocasuarina decaisneana	arrkep, kwerrkar (W,T)
Amyema spp.	atyankern, ngkwerrm, pweralhem (E)
grub	akweltyayt (E)

Amyema spp. and
Lysiana spp. ... amar
Amyema maidenii ... ngartangkern (W), peketyalkwarr (T,E)
Anthobolus leptomerioides ... anngey-anngey
Aristida contorta ... arraper
Aristida inaequiglumis ... intwerrker
Atalaya hemiglauca ... arlperr
gum ... arlperrangkwarl, arlperrampw (E)
grub ... arlperrayt (E), arlperrenhayt (T,E), arlperreny (W), arlperrenh (W,T)
Atriplex spp. ... arelyerrelyerr (W)
Atriplex nummularia ... ntyurtenty (E)
Austrobryonia centralis ... aherr-arlweth (T,E), aherr-arleth (E)
Boerhavia schomburgkiana ... ayep, irlperleny (T,E)
Boerhavia spp.
grub ... ayepaty, arrpayerr (E), ayep-areny (W)
Brachychiton gregorii ... apeng
flower ... arlpetharlp (E)
seed ... ngkweyang
small green seed pods ... alyalyarr (E), artwengarr (T,E)
fur on seeds ... ingeth (T,E)
Calandrinia balonensis ... parrkely, arrwelth-arrwelth (E), lywemp-lywemp
Callitris glaucophylla ... amikw[1] (E), anngart (W), akngart (W,T), rlwek (W,T)
Calotis hispidula ... thenkarr
Canthium *(go to 'Psydrax')*
Capparis lasiantha ... alwerr
unripe fruit ... anker[2] (E)
Capparis loranthifolia ... angerterrk (E), iwerrarrkw (W,E)
Capparis mitchellii ... atwakey
Capparis spinosa var. **nummularia** ... arrweneng
Capparis umbonata ... akarlety, akarley (E), ngarntatyarr (W,T)
Carissa lanceolata ... perlap, arnwekety (E)
Cassytha capillaris ... interr-interr (E)
Choiromyces aboriginum *(tentative taxonomy)* ... akwerrerteth (E), irrkwenng (T,E), pwerlantar (T)
Chrysopogon fallax ... lyayepelyay (W,T), layempeylay (T,E)
Citrullus lanatus ... malan (T,E), payemalan (W,T)
Cleome viscosa ... angerak-angerak (W)
Clerodendrum floribundum ... arrngern, tywerlp (W,T)
Codonocarpus cotinifolius ... arlkemal
grub ... arlkemal-areny (T), arlkemalayt (E)
Corymbia aparrerinja ... pwernengk (W,T), ulemp (T,E)
flower ... arrtya[2]
seeds ... ulemparrty (E)
honey from bark ... ulemparrty (E), yerrkengal (T)
gum or kino ... arrkeper (W,T), arrkiper (E), lyarwek
Corymbia opaca ... arrkernk
buds ... antyepey (W,T) (?), antyeper (T,E) (?)
flowers ... ntewal
seed capsules ... mernperr, ntewal, arrkipangkwarl
gall ... mangarrey, arrkwerlperlp (E), kathip (E), arrkipangkwarl
gum or kino ... arrkeper (W,T), arrkiper (E), nthwarr (W), ntharr (T), lyarwek
water found in the trunk ... kwentharr, nthwarr (W), ntharr (T), untharr (E)
Corymbia sphaerica ... arlangkw (E)
flowers ... ntewal
Crinum flaccidum ... alyerlk-alyerlk (W), iylelty (E), lyelkenng (E)
Crotalaria eremaea ... rltar-rltar[2] (W,T), rltwayep-rltwayep (E)
Crotalaria novaehollandiae ... arrematy rltey-rltey (T,E), rltey-rltey (E)
Cucumis maderaspatanus ... lkwart-lkwart (W,T), ilkwart-ilkwart (T,E)
Cucumis melo ssp. **agrestis** ... lkwart (W,T), ilkwart, ulkart (T,E), lkwart-lkwart (W,T) (SP), ilkwart-ilkwart (T,E) (SP)
Cullen australasicum ... intwert-intwert (E)
Cymbopogon ambiguus ... aherr-aherr, areng-areng (E)
Cynanchum floribundum ... angelth, tywekerl[1] (W,T)
Cyperus bulbosus ... yalk (W,T), yerrakwerr, irreyakwerr (E)
bulb ... kwart, yerrakwerr kwart
flower ... akenty (W,T), akeynt (E)
white-coloured seed heads akarnkw (W)
Cyperus ixiocarpus ... anker-anker[2] (E)
Cystococcus pomiformis *(larvae)* ... kathip (E)
Dactyloctenium radulans ... apwert-arlkwenh (E), apwert akwernenh (E), ngelyerr (E), talkwerrk (W), ntalwerrk (W)
Digitaria brownii ... kwatyempengemp (W,T), kwatyimpengimp
Duboisia hopwoodii ... arekerr (T,E)

Dysphania sp. — mwelyeparnt-parnt (T) (?), mwenyeparnt-parnt (W) (?), ngwelyeparnteparnt (T) (?)
Dysphania kalpari — alpar, parntentyarlp (W)
Dysphania rhadinostachya — alpar, arrerlang (T,E)
Enchylaena tomentosa — ntyemeny
Enteropogon acicularis — twemper-twemper (W),
Enteropogon ramosus — twemper-twemper (W)
Eragrostis spp. — awertaw (E)
Eragrostis eriopoda — antyey[1] (W,T), alyatywereng (E)
Eremophila dalyana — ilpengk (T,E)
Eremophila duttonii — kwenthey
Eremophila freelingii — arreth
Eremophila gilesii — pwenkart, kwenkart (E)
Eremophila latrobei — anyerleng
Eremophila longifolia — lhwek-lhwek (W,T), anwerreng (W), unerreng (E)
  grub — lhwek-lhwek (W,T), alwerrpent (W), unerrengayt (E)
Eremophila obovata — iytert-iytert (E)
Eremophila sturtii — tyer[2] (E)
Erythrina vespertilio — atywerety, aparrty (E), inernt (SP)
  flower — akalapantherrty (T), akenty (W,T), akeynt (E)
  seeds — inernt
  red seeds — ngal-ngal
  yellow or white seeds — mpetyan-mpetyan[1] (E)
Eucalyptus camaldulensis var. obtusa — aper
  blossoms — aperaly (W)
  seed capsules — aperaley (W,T), aperrper (E)
  honey from under the bark — aperarnt (T,E), mamp (W,T), aperengengel (E), aperelayeng (W)
  white substance made by the lerp scale insect on leaf — aperelty
  grub found at the base of the tree — ahekwenayt (E)
  grub from branch — ingweneng, perlanty (W,T), perlaty (W,T), aylperlayt (T,E), ngkenhar (E), aperayt (E)
  grub from root — mpaty[2] (W,T)
  inner bark — aper tyelk
Eucalyptus coolabah ssp. arida — ankerrmern
  seed — aley[1], ankwerrern (E)
  grub — ankerrayt (T,E), ankwerrern (E), anwerrngaty (W)
Eucalyptus gamophylla — alhelp (W,T), uleperr (E)
Eucalyptus intertexta — alhelp (W,T)
Eucalyptus leucophloia — arlketh[2] (T,E)
Eucalyptus normantonensis — alhelp (W,T), alywelp
  sweet substance made by the lerp scale insect on leaves — yerrekeyerr (T,E)
Eucalyptus pachyphylla — ntyeny (E)
  honey — ntyenyengkwarl (E)
Eulalia aurea — arlperlp
Euphorbia drummondii — amwekel-amwekel[1] (E), amwekel (E), kwep-kwep[1], merterr[1], merterr-merterr (W,T)
Euphorbia tannensis — alyey-alyey (W,T), anemarraty (W,T), marlek-alyey-alyey
Ficus brachypoda — tywerrk (W,T), utyerrk (E)
Fimbristylis dichotoma — arnwety-arnwety (W), taty-taty[1]
Fimbristylis oxystachya — akwetelh (E), taty-taty[1] (?)
Goodenia armitiana — unpay (E), inpay (T)
Goodenia grandiflora — inpay-inpay (W,T)
Goodenia lunata — ankerr-ankerr (W), ankerringk (T,E), ntywenart (W)
Gossypium australe — tyetep (W,T)
Grevillea juncifolia ssp. juncifolia — rrwerleng (W,T), tharrkarr (T,E)
Grevillea stenobotrya — aywel (T,E)
Grevillea striata — ltyenty
  medicinal gum or kino — iyltentyarwek (E)
Grevillea wickhamii ssp. aprica — kelkareng
Hakea chordophylla — ntywey (W,T), untyey (E)
  honey — ntyweyamp (T,E), ntyweyangkwarl (W), untyeyamp (E), ankarr (T,E)
  yellow-coloured honey — tyan (W,T)
Hakea divaricata — ntyarleyarleng, ntyarleyarley (W), ntywey (W,T), untyey (E)
  honey — untyeyamp (E)
  red nectar — ngapalhwerrk (W)
Hakea leucoptera ssp. leucoptera — ilpey, ilpey-ilpey (E), rrkwalty (W,T)
Hakea macrocarpa — ntyarleyarleng
  red nectar — ngapalhwerrk (W)
Halosarcia indica — akwely-akwely (E)
Ipomoea costata — anaty, anek (W,T)
  flower — nalal (E)
  leaf — inkwanng (E)
  off shoot from main plant — lyelyerr (E)
  tuber — mwernenty
  young tuber — akwerrk, anthal (T,E)

Ipomoea muelleri atywert-atywert (E), tatyetarr (W,T), rtwatyert (W,T)
***Ipomoea* sp. Stirling** antyalkenh (T,E), antyalkeny (W,T)
Isotoma petraea antererrnp, pitherr (T,E)
Lechenaultia divaricata unpay (E), inpay (T), npway-npway (W,T) (?)
Leptosema chambersii irrarnt-irrarnt (E)
***Lysiana* sp.** pweralhem (E)
Lysiana murrayi atyankern
Marsdenia australis alangkw, alkwarrer (E), parl (W,T)
  flower ilkwanty (E)
  leaf altyey, ahertety[2] (E), unelh (E)
  leaves rolled up for cooking arrwekety[2] (E)
  young fruit akwemper (T), akwerrk[1], amwernt (T,E), mwemper (W), ngwemper (W), twemper[1] (W)
  white silky substance inside fruit antweth (E)
  white inner skin of fruit alhwer (E)
  green seeds inside fruit alwerremp (W,T), alurremp (E)
  twisted stem wererr (E)
  root arnaty (W), artwey-artwey[1], atnety (E)
Melaleuca glomerata ilperl[2]
Melaleuca lasiandra ilperl[2], thankw (E) (?)
Muehlenbeckia florulenta werengerr (E), werrengerr (E)
***Nicotiana* spp.** ngkwerlp
  bud or flower alpma (T,E)
  young shoots akerrng (E), antyanp[2] (T,E), ngerrng (E), ngkwerlp akwerrk (W), rrngwaly (W)
  dried native tobacco akeyarr (E)
***Nicotiana* spp.** arrwatnwer (E), antererrnp (?)
Nicotiana excelsior anwengk[2]
Nicotiana gossei rnpwernp (W,T), rnpernp (T,E), urnpernp (T,E), ngkwerlp rnpwernp (W), ngkwerlp rnpernp (T,E), ngkwerlp urnpernp (E)
Nicotiana rosulata* ssp. *ingulba arwenp, ngkwerlp arwenp (W,T), ngkwerlp atherrk
***Nicotiana velutina* and *Nicotiana* spp.** ngwarray-ngwarray, pengart-pengart[2] (W)
Owenia acidula arrek (E)
Owenia reticulata marrawaty (T,E)
Pandorea doratoxylon yenper
Panicum decompositum altywart
Parkinsonia aculeata arlketyerr
Paspalidium rarum kwarrety (W,T), nyetempwer (W), tywaynt (E)
Paspalidium rarum arekwer (E) (?)
Petalostylis cassioides intyern (E)
Pittosporum angustifolium anawert, welterr (E)
Podaxis pistillaris anngarnt rrpwerl (W,T), arrekwep-kwep (W), arrepweng-pweng (E), kwep-kwep[3] (W,T), pwek-pwek, pweng-pweng (W)
Portulaca filifolia ngkweytek (E)
Portulaca oleracea akat, iylaw (E)
Prostanthera striatiflora ngkwern rnter-rnter (W,T), amwer (E)
Psydrax ammophila yernt
Psydrax latifolia ahakey, antyern angerr (T), arrarntenh (E), artapaly (E)
  flower ilkwa[1] (T,E), ilkwang (W)
  unripe fruit anthwerrk[1] (T,E), irnta (W,T), irntang (W,T)
  newly ripened fruit alwernp (W), akenp (T,E)
  fruit when red in colour rwekarlp (E)
  dry fruit ntewerrk (T,E)
  dry fruit still on tree ntyenp
  fruit that has fallen to the ground unemarnt (E)
  juice from fruit ankarr (T,E)
  respectful word for fruit angayel
  to flower ilkwenkem (E)
  fruit go dry ntyenp-irrem
Psydrax suaveolens anngey-anngey, antenh-antenh (E), atnwengk-atnwengk (E), ngkwernelyerr, ngkwernateylp (E)
Pterocaulon serrulatum iynteng-iynteng (E)
Ptilotus exaltatus alyey-alyey (W,T), aweyek-alyey-alyey (E), awerreh-alyey-alyey (W,T), rrweyek-alyey-alyey (W,T), urreyek-alyey-alyey (T,E)
Ptilotus incanus rlkwetherlkweng (E)
Ptilotus obovatus ahert-ahert[1] (T,E)
***Ptilotus polystachyus* spp.** rlpwer-rlpwer (W,T), iylpwer-iylpwer (E)
Rhagodia eremaea anngey-anngey
***Rhodanthe* sp.** awerr-awerr[2] (E) (?)
***Rhodanthe tietkensii* and other *Rhodanthe* spp.** anteth-anteth (W)
Rhyncharrhena linearis angerak, werrp (E)
  fruit aherretyepwer (T,E), awerretyepwer (W,T), werrp (E)

Salsola tragus .... arlkerl, inkwert (E)
grub .... inkwert-areny (E), inkwertayt (E), arlkerlaty (W,T), arlkerlayt (T,E)
Santalum acuminatum .... mangart[1], mwerlp
Santalum lanceolatum .... alkwa (E), ankwerlay (W,T), ankwerley (T,E)
Sarcostemma viminale ssp. australe .... amwekel-amwekel[1] (E), amwekel (E), kwep-kwep[1]
Scaevola parvifolia .... intekw (E), irrarnt-irrarnt (E) (?)
Sclerolaena cornishiana .... atetherr-atetherr, kapert angerr (W,T), kapert-kapert
Sclerostegia tenuis .... karnkw (W,T)
Senecio magnificus .... arengkatwepatwetyenh (W,T), ntweyentwerl (E)
Senna artemisioides ssp. alicia artemisioides .... apwen
Senna artemisioldes spp.
flower .... ulpelp (E)
grub .... apwenayt (T,E)
Senna artemisioides ssp. filifolia .... apwen, ngkwert (W,T)
Senna artemisioides ssp. helmsii .... kwert-kwert (W,T)
Senna artemisioides ssp. oligophylla .... manatwerrp, areyawarr (E)
grub .... areyawerrayt (E)
Senna artemisioides ssp. petiolaris .... ngkwert (W,T)
grub .... ngkwertaty (W,T)
Senna pleurocarpa .... iylenyenp (E)
Sida platycalyx .... akeley-akeley (T,E), anmang (W), ingka-mwerney (T,E), ingkang mwerney (W), kwem (W), kwem-kwem (W)
Solanum centrale .... katyerr
baby talk .... katy
unripe fruit .... kwart, pwarr (T,E), urleynterr[2] (E)
fresh fruit .... katyerr kwart
yellow fruit .... arlkarntar (W,T)
dry fruit .... alha[2], alhang (W,T), katyerr alha, katyerr tweny (W,T), katyerr uteny (E), tweny, uteny (E)
fruit go dry .... tweny-irrem, uteny-irrem (E)
variety found in sandhill country .... kamperarrp (W,T)
Solanum chippendalei *(hill form)* .... anakety
Solanum chippendalei *(sandhill form)* .... unemangkerr (E), anemangkerr (T,E), kwenemangkarr (T,E), ngantyewarl (W,T), antyewarl (T,E)
Solanum cleistogamum .... arlelyek, manyem, tepernter (W)
yellow fruit .... arlkarntar (W,T)
Solanum coactiliferum .... katyerr
Solanum ellipticum var. Foothills GJ Leach 1145 .... alperrantyey, ararnt (W,T)
Solanum ellipticum var. Ranges DE Albrecht 5807 .... rrwarlp[1] (T), arrwarlp (E), rtwengkerr (W,T) (?)
Solanum orbiculatum ssp. orbiculatum .... ankerr-ankerr (W) (?)
Solanum petrophilum .... warrakwelakwel (W,T) (?)
Solanum quadriloculatum .... arengkerlpart, arntek-arntek (E)
Solanum spp. (?) .... arleth-arleth[2], rltar-rltar[2] (W,T), tyatyarlkwerr (E), mpwekaly (T), nparnpetyenh (W), talkwelanyey (W)
Stemodia viscosa .... iynteng-iynteng (E), ntyapentyetyen (W,T)
Stylobasium spathulatum .... ampweth-ampweth (E), arleyakwerr (T,E), warrangkwer (W,T)
Tecticornia verrucosa .... karnkw (W,T)
Templetonia egena .... arlewatyerr-arlewatyerr[2]
Themeda avenacea .... lyenty
grub .... lyentyatayerr (E) (SP)
Themeda triandra .... arlperlp
Thysanotus exiliflorus .... akwerl-akwerl (W,T), arrwelth-arrwelth (E)
Tinospora smilacina .... anwerl (E), arratherrk, alyep[1] (SP)
grub .... arratherrkayt (E)
Tribulus terrestris .... lyekakapert (E), lyekakapwert (T,E)
Tribulus terrestris s. lat .... arlkerl
Triodia basedowii and other *Triodia* spp. .... aywert
Triodia longiceps .... arrangk (E), ntwemerr (T,E), untemerr (T,E), welyar (W,T)
Triodia pungens .... alatyeyt (E)
resin .... anker[1] (E), tyalangk (W,T)
Triodia schinzii .... antywer iper (E), rrkwal (W,T), irrkwal (E)
Triodia triaristata .... anker-anker[2] (E) (?)
Tripogon lolliformis .... taty-taty[1] (?)
Urochloa piligera .... mamperrk (W,T)

Ventilago viminalis .... anyer
gum .... anyerampw, anyerangkwarl
Vigna lanceolata var. latifolia .... arlatyey
edible white pods .... kam (T,E)
seed .... arratwek, kam (T,E)
tuber .... mwernenty
Vigna lanceolata var. filiformis *(narrow leaf variety)* .... anwerlarr (E), katywetarr (W,T)
Vigna lanceolata var. lanceolata .... arnamp
Yakirra australiensis .... yakerr (E) (?)
Yakirra australiensis var. australiensis .... arlepenh (T,E), arrepeny (T), kwarrety (W,T), nyetempwer (W)
Zornia albiflora .... werety (T)
Zygochloa paradoxa .... penng (E)

Mammals

Bettongia lesueur .... rtway (W,T), awert[2] (W), iwert (E), alhwet (E) (?)
Camelus dromedarius .... kamwerl, kawartewar (W,T)
Canis lupus dingo .... arnwer[1], arnapar (W,T)
Chaeropus ecaudatus .... taty (?)
Dasycercus cristicauda .... artekw (W,E) (?), artikw (E) (?), ampwert (E) (?)
Dasycercus hillieri .... ampwert (E) (?)
Dasyurus geoffroii .... atyelp, atyet (E)
Isoodon auratus .... perlkarr (T)
Lagorchestes conspicillatus .... kwarlp, lkwameny (W,T) (?)
Lagorchestes hirsutus .... mal (W,T)
Macropus robustus .... areng[2], lyerl-areny, irntareny (W,T), areyneng (E)
Macropus rufus .... aherr
Macrotis lagotis .... angkay (W,T), ahert (T,E), artnangk (E)
Perameles eremiana .... akwerr (?)
Petrogale lateralis .... arrwa
Phascogale macdonellensis .... alepey (E) (?)
Pseudomys desertor .... mpweny iytarr-iytarr (E) (?), mpwenyerlp (E) (?)
Rattus villosissimus .... nyemal (E), kwetang (?)
Tachyglossus aculeatus .... inarleng, inap (T,E), ker arlkerl (E)
Trichosurus vulpecula .... antenh, rrpwamper (W,T)

Birds

Acanthagenys rufogularis .... arrety-arrety (W,T), alpeyart-alpeyart (E), arrakwerakwer (T,E)
Accipiter cirrhocephalus .... alekaper (?)
Aegotheles cristatus .... arrthwarrthw (E)
Amytornis striatus .... lyerr-lyerr
Anas gracilis .... pelyak (W,T), pelyakw (T,E), ipelyak (E), tyepelyakw (W), tyepelyey (E)
Anas superciliosa .... awengker (?)
Anthus novaeseelandiae .... ntyelpeny (W,T), iynterlpeny (E), kaperl-kaperl (T,E) (?)
Aquila audax .... irrety, arlawerr (W)
Ardea novaehollandiae and pacifica .... ntyar (W,T), arlkwenth (E), kamparwengk (E), ulamp-areny (E), ulamparrwek (E)
Ardeotis australis .... artew, arwengerrp (T,E), warterlk (W)
Artamus cinereus and personatus .... perrpantywen (W,T), perrpantywel (E)
Barnardius zonarius .... arlpaty
Burhinus grallarius .... mwelyar, arepeylp (E)
Cacatua leadbeateri .... angkwen
Cacatua sanguinea .... terekerr
Calyptorhynchus banksii .... irrarnt
Charadrius australis .... tyerr-tyerr (W), tyerr-tyerrey (W), tyerrepert (W)
Cheramoeca leucosternus .... nerrty (E)
Chlamydera guttata .... akerrk, ahern-areny (E)
Chrysococcyx basalis .... nyarew, anatyelepwerray (E), urrempen urrempen (E) (?)
Chrysococcyx osculans .... anatyelepwerray (E) (?)
Cincloramphus mathewsi .... tyelyapweretyapwerety (W,T), tyelyapwerety (W), tyelk-aperrety-aperrety (T), tyelk-aperrertety (E), apweretyapwer (W)
Colluricincla harmonica .... alerterrperterrp (?)
Coracina novaehollandiae .... amatheng-amatheng (T,E), matyekwel (E)
Corvus bennetti .... angank, angep, angerl (E), kway-kway (E), kaw-kaw (E)
Coturnix pectoralis .... kweyepey (E)
Cracticus nigrogularis .... matyekatyer, pweretyetyer (W), pweretyety (W,T)
Cracticus torquatus .... arrpwerek-arrpwer (W), alpwertek-alpwert (E)

Cuculus pallidus .... lyweketweretwer (W,T), rlweketereter (W,T), alkwarrer-arrpwernenh (E), lyalth, rlalth (W,T), iylalth (E)
Dendrocygna eytoni .... tyepelyakw (W), tyepelyey (E)
Dromaius novaehollandiae .... ankerr, arley (W,T)
Elseyornis melanops .... ntyelpeny (W,T), iynterlpeny (E)
Eolophus roseicapillus .... ilenty, kerlelkerlelp (W,T), uneng atyetyek (E)
Epthianura tricolor .... akarl-atwerrey (T,E) (?), uneng atyetyek (E) (?)
Erythrogonys cinctus .... tyelkatherather, interrk-atherather (W,T)
Eurostopodus argus .... akwet-akwet, angkertakwertak (W,T)
Falco berigora .... irrkerlanty
Falco cenchroides .... lyentyelyeng, warakeparleparl (W,T), ulpmerr-atwenh (E), anthep-anthep (E)
Falco hypoleucos .... irrkerlanty (?)
Falco longipennis .... ingkel iylkenh (E), nyengk rnternenh (E)
Falco peregrinus .... aleraperap (E) (?)
Fulica atra .... anker-anker[1] (E)
Gallinula ventralis .... narremantyerr (W,T), angkeparr (W,T), ngkwern rnter-rnter (W,T) (SP), kart-irrkwely-irrkwely (W,T), karl-irrkwely-irrkwely (T,E), karlayteng-ayteng (E), lhekethatethat (E) (?)
Geopelia cuneata .... kwerlekwek, kwerler-kwerler (W,T), kwerakwek (W,T), urelyarr (E), lerakwenty (W) (?)
Geopelia striata .... kwerlekwek, kwerler-kwerler (W,T), kwerakwek (W,T), lerakwenty (W) (?)
Geophaps plumifera .... arntwerrert, ntarrwerarrwer (W), marekwerr (W,T) (?)
Grallina cyanoleuca .... rtey-rtey, kwatyarl rtey-rtey (E), ntwerleperl (W), rtwerleperl (W,T)
Grus rubicunda .... nerrkempwany (W,T) (?)
Gymnorhina tibicen .... arrpwer
Haliastur sphenurus .... apwart-apwart (E) (?)
Hamirostra melanosternon .... lywerlperr (W,T), atwertim (E), aytwertek (E)
Hirundo ariel .... tyerremper (E)
Leipoa ocellata .... anwematy (W)
Lichenostomus penicillatus .... aperrety-aperrety (T)
Lichenostomus virescens .... arrety-arrety (W,T), arrakwerakwer (T,E), alpeyart-alpeyart (E)
Malurus spp. .... lyerr-lyerr, tyewelyerr-lyerr (W), lyerretyelyerr (E), pwerelyerr-lyerr (W,T) (?)
Manorina flavigula .... irnpernp (W,T), rnpernp (W,T), impaymp (E)
Melopsittacus undulatus .... atetherr
Merops ornatus .... terr-terr (W,T), kwelinterr-interr (T,E), apelinterr-interr (E)
Milvus migrans .... apwelanty, apwerl-apwerl, artapw-artapw (E), inkwel (E)
Ninox novaeseelandiae .... kwerrkwerrk, akekw (E) (?)
Nymphicus hollandicus .... newingk (W,T), aneweylker (E), areweylker (E), arew-arew (E), kanaweylker (E)
Ocyphaps lophotes .... pelker
Oreoica gutturalis .... kwepalepal, pakw-pakw (W)
Pachycephala rufiventris .... apetyepetyem (W,T), artwang apetyepetyem (W), artwatherr apetyepetyem (E), ipeny apetyepetyem (W,T), kwarlpatengkelyengkely (E), tyenyepweny (E)
Pardalotus rubricatus .... kaperlantarlant (E) (?)
Pelecanus conspicillatus .... pelekan[2] (W), paleken (E), arrakert angerr
Petroica goodenovii .... alywerr-alywerr (W,T), akarl-atwerrey (T,E), kapert rnter-rnter (E), uneng atyetyek (E)
Phaps chalcoptera .... arntep
Phaps histrionica .... arekwarr (E)
Podargus strigoides .... nwernengk, unernengk (E), uring (E)
Polytelis alexandrae .... urimpering (E) (?), rempereng (W) (?)
Pomatostomus temporalis .... tyewakety
Psephotus varius .... anenperetyarr (W) (?), urimpering (E) (?), rempereng (W) (?)
Psophodes occidentalis .... tyalatywerrp (T,E)
Rhipidura leucophrys .... artetyerretyerr[1], tyenterr-tyenterr (W)
Taeniopygia guttata .... nyengk, tyeyek (W,T)
Todiramphus pyrrhopygia .... rlwernp (W,T), nwernp (W), parlkenng (E), urrernter[2] (E)
Turnix velox .... atek, aterlkwarr (E), iylpwerr (E)
Tyto alba .... arrkerr

Vanellus tricolor .... tyelkatherather, interrk-atherather (W,T), ampelyetyerrker (E), tartarrp (E) (?)

Snakes & lizards

Acanthophis pyrrhus .... mantharr, antharr (E)
Antaresia stimsoni .... ileway (W,T) (?)
Aspidites melanocephalus .... antwerrkenh (W,T), arrwerrperl (T,E), rayerrp (T,E), urayerrp (E)
Aspidites ramsayi .... ahenenh, aheneny (T,E), ahelh-ahelh (W), nwey (T), uney (E)
Ctenophorus caudicinctus . tekentyenarr (W) (?), ntekentyenarr (W) (?)
Ctenophorus isolepis .... kwerleparr (W,T), nyarl (W,E), tyalep (?)
Ctenophorus nuchalis ...... kelyaw, irnar (W,T), kaperl (T,E)
big male .... arrpwayl (E)
Ctenotus spp. .... ikwarr (E)
Ctenotus schomburgkii .... lyengkarr (W,T) (?), alyalkarr (T,E) (?), lyangkay-lyangkay (E) (?)
Demansia psammophis ... pwer arlewatyerr, pwer arlewatyerr-arlewatyerr (E), arlewatyerr-arlewatyerr[1] (T,E) (?)
Diplodactylus stenodactylus .... akarntety-arntety (E) (?), rltimp-areny (E) (?), pelhel-iwenh-iwenh (E) (?)
Diporiphora winneckei .... arlanty, apengeleytanenh (E) (?)
Furina ornata .... arnwekety-arnwekety (E) (?), perlap-perlap (E) (?)
Lialis burtonis .... iparip (E)
Moloch horridus .... nywerr (W,T), mernerr (W,T), arnkerrth (T,E)
Morelia spilota ssp. bredli .... antetherrk
Morethia sp. .... ankwang (W) (?)
Nephrurus spp. .... arlwer
Pogona minor .... kapert angerr (W,T), tyapantarr (W,T)
Pogona vitticeps .... ankert[2] (W,T), amwely
Pseudechis australis .... atetherr arlkwenh, arreperlp (W,T), kantharlkw (W,E), tyamparl (T), ikwelengk (T,E), alhingk (E)
Pseudonaja nuchalis .... antywemp (T,E) (?), arriper (T,E) (?)
Pseudonaja textilis .... arwerl-arwerl (E) (?)
Ramphotyphlops endoterus .... arranyenganyeng (W,T), rtety arlkwenh-arlkwenh (W), ahaylengkeyler (E)
Strophurus ciliaris .... akarntety-arntety (E) (?), rltimp-areny (E) (?), pelhel-iwenh-iwenh (E) (?)
Tiliqua multifasciata .... lhwelk, ulhelk (T,E), lwengkart[1] (T), ilpankwer (E)
Tympanocryptis tetraporophora .... angket-angket (E) (?), apwet-apwet (E) (?)
Varanus acanthurus .... kerr-kerr (W,T), antyerr (E)
Varanus brevicauda .... arwemay (?)
Varanus eremius .... irrpent (E), artep irrpent (E), irrerlaly (E) (?)
Varanus giganteus .... tywenp, ilkwert (E)
hatchling .... arepilyerr (E)
big .... anepeywenp (E)
Varanus gilleni .... arin, ahert-ahert[2] (W), arwangk (W,T)
Varanus gouldii .... arlewatyerr
hatchling .... kwentarreng, arepilyerr (E)
Varanus tristis .... altywekerr, kweny-areny (W,T), kwenyel alhem (T), alpangwerr (W), pwer rrpwerl (W,T)

Frogs

Cyclorana australis .... angwethek (T), akngwethek (E), apmwethek (E)
Cyclorana maini .... alheramp (W,T) (?)
Cyclorana platycephalus . angwethek (T), akngwethek (E), apmwethek (E), alemerr (E) (?)
Litoria spp. .... antyetyerr, larrangkern, karlarrangkern (E)
Limnodynastes spenceri .. alyeyamp (E), kalyeyamp (T)
Neobatrachus spp. .... mpwekenh (T,E), mpwelengk (E), terrenth
Notaden nichollsi .... kwep-kwep[2], kwep, pwerreparnt (W,T), atweynterl (E), amwekel-amwekel (E) (?)

Insects

Amitermes meridionalis ... arnameng-ayerr (E)
Amitermes vitiosus ... interrk[2], ngkwepey (SP), ngkwepeyayt (E), ngkwayt (T,E), atwerneng
Anoplognathus olivieri sp. ... anyenty-anyenty (E), atay[2] (W)
Camponotus inflatus ... yerramp, inkwareny
Camponotus spp. ... yerr, arlkerrk[1] (T,E), arrekarlkarlker (T,E)
Celerio lineata livornicoides ... arrpayerr (E)
Desmozosteria cinta ... mpwerleyerleng, mpwerl-ilenh-ilenh (E)
Eurycnema osiris ... kapwert atwenh (W,T), antyekanty
Helea spp. ... lengarr-lengarr (E), panth-panth (E)
Iridomyrmex sp. ... arrekarlkarlker (T,E), yerr
Melophorus sp.
reproductive and soldier .. arleth urrperl (T,E)
Melophorus bagoti ... twern-twern, utern-utern (E)
Monistria pustulifera ... intelty (?)
Musca vetustissima ... ameng
Myrmecia nigriceps
reproductive ... atyank, tyekarnparnp[1] (E), ntyeyapert (E)
Neuroptera spp. ... mamerweterwet (W,T), kwatyarl ntyeny-ntyeny (E)
Neuroptera spp.
larvae ... kwatyarl ntyeny-ntyeny (E), angkwerey-angkwerey (E)
Ochetellus sp. ... tyerremp (T,E)
Onchrogaster spp. ... ingeth (T,E), wep (SP)
Rhytidoponera mayri gp (?) ... arrekarlkarlker (T,E)
Trictena argentata ... mpaty[2] (W,T)
Tropha spp. ... aterr (W,E), ahekwenayt (E) (?)
Xyleutes bipartii ... anyematy, anyemayt (T,E), tyap
when it is small and red in colour ... arlpalywerrng
while still in root ... arwerlk (E)
yellow stage before it goes black ... akerururr (E)
Xyleutes sp. ... ingweneng (?)

Appendices

Appendix 1 The Anmatyerr kinship system

For Anmatyerr people, kinship is a central part of social and cultural life. The kinship system not only encodes relationships between people, but also extends to encompass those between people and their traditional country, the plants and animals that originate in that country, and many other fundamental aspects of the Anmatyerr social world. The principles of this kinship system are very different from the English kinship system. In Anmatyerr there are many different words for family or relations — words for mother, father, uncle, cousin etc. — but the meanings of these words don't always closely match their equivalent English words. Some examples are given below.

One of the key differences is that the Anmatyerr system is an extended or 'classificatory' one which describes not only closely related people but also relationships between people who are not necessarily connected by birth links or by marriage. One of the consequences of this is that the terms used for genealogically distant relatives are the same as those used for close ones. Another is that groups of people who are related to a person in a similar way are all referred to using the same kin term. For example, a person uses the term *amey* or *amwek* to refer not only to their own 'private' biological mother, but also to their mother's sisters, and to their mother's mother's sister's daughters and so on.

In English, a person calls their father's brother's children or their mother's sister's children *cousin*, whereas in Anmatyerr the same words are used for these kinds of cousins as are used for brothers and sisters. In Anmatyerr there are different words for *cross-cousins* (a person's parents' opposite gender siblings' children), such as a mother's brother's children.

While in English the words *grandfather* and *grandmother* are used regardless of whether the grandparent in question is on a person's mother's side or on their father's side, in Anmatyerr there are separate words for each of the four kinds of grandparent: mother's mothers, mother's fathers, father's fathers and father's mothers. (Some of the relations called by the *grandparent* words in Anmatyerr are called *great-aunt* and *great-uncle* in English.) The terms for the four grandparents are also used for that grandparent's brothers and sisters. They are 'two-way', so grandparents of a particular type and their grandchildren call each other by the same kin term. For example, a person calls their father's father (and his brothers and sisters) *arreng*. That person also calls his or her grandchildren (a man's son's children or a woman's brother's son's children) *arreng*.

Children of sisters are classed together and distinguished from the children of brothers, and so a person has two kinds of children: maternal and paternal. A woman's children (regardless of their gender) and a person's sister's children are called *ampa*; a man's children, and a person's brother's children, are called *aler*. The small part of a family tree or genealogical diagram overleaf shows this difference, firstly from the point of view of a man (Figure 1) and then from the point of view of a woman (Figure 2). It also shows how the words *ampa* and *aler* overlap with English *son*, *daughter*, *nephew* and *niece*. Keep in mind that this is only a fragment of the total system.

Figure 1: Part of an Anmatyerr family tree from a male perspective

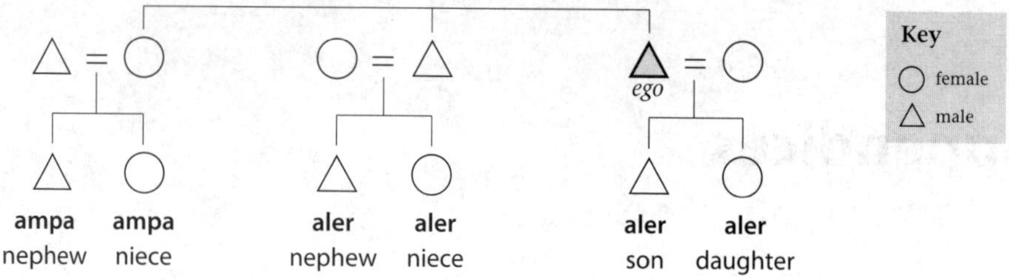

Figure 2: Part of an Anmatyerr family tree from a female perspective

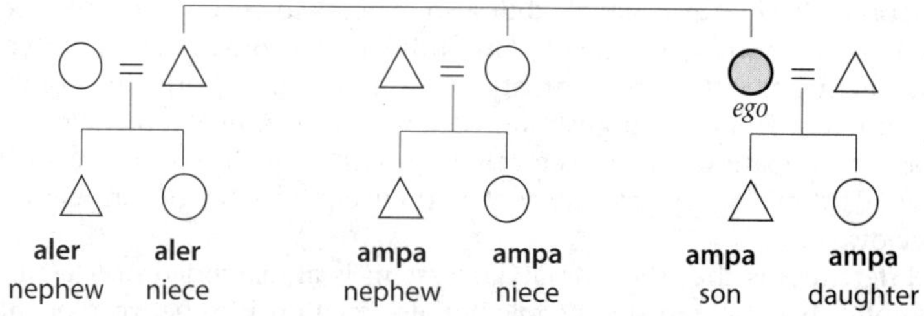

There is a symbolic association between paternal links and the beard or chin and between maternal links and the stomach. In spoken language a person's brother's child is referred to as *arrwert-penh* or *arrarn-penh* (literally 'from the beard') and a person's sister's child as *alem-penh* (literally 'from the stomach'). The handsigns for these particular types of kin also reflect this symbolism; the handsign for *aler* articulates with the chin, and that for *ampa* with the stomach.

The terms for kin are cyclical. Generally, a person uses the same terms for equivalent types of kin in the second generation above and the second generation below and in the first generation above and below, and this principle extends through genealogical time for each successive level of odd and even generations (though in practice it is much more complex than that). In English the prefixing of 'great', once or several times, to grandparent and grandchild (and uncle and aunt) terms is an example of a different way of doing things.

As mentioned above, kin terms are also used to describe the relationship between a person and their country and the Dreamings from that country. So in Anmatyerr it is quite normal for a person to call a particular place *arreng* (father's father) or *atyemey* (mother's father), depending on how they are related to that country. If a major Dreaming for that place is, for example, *yerramp* 'honeyant' then the person would be related to the honeyant in the same way as they are to the country where the ancestral honeyant came from, and so they would also call both the place and the honeyant *arreng* or *atyemey* accordingly.

Kin terms form a grammatical class because they have their own particular set of word endings (see Appendix 2). There are also some other words in Anmatyerr that behave grammatically like kin terms because they take the endings that ordinary kin terms do. One example of this is the word *altyerr*, which has a range of meanings including 'dream', 'Dreaming' and 'mother's country' (see pages 57–59 for more details). There are also some kin terms that behave differently from other kin terms because they do *not* take the kin term endings; for example, the word *yay* 'elder sister'.

Skin names

All Anmatyerr people are born into one of eight 'skin' groups (also called 'subsections') and so, in addition to their personal names, they have a 'skin name' which partly defines their relationship to all other people within their family and language group and to others beyond.

These names provide a system of labelling for a complex system of relationships and responsibilities between people. Knowing a person's skin name helps you to work out what relationship they are to you. Key Anmatyerr terms that refer to this system are *anpernem* 'call each other a particular relation' (page 124), *anpernenty* 'skin name or subsection name (page 124) and *ikwa* 'skin name or subsection name' (page 303).

The skin name a person has depends on the skin names of each of their parents, but is not the same as that of either parent. A person has the same skin name as, for example, their brothers and sisters, their father's father, and their father's brother's children. A person has a different skin name from their mothers, fathers, children, and their husband or wife.

Table 2 below shows the Central and Eastern Anmatyerr skin names, and also the skin names used by neighbouring groups such as the Arrernte, Alyawarr, Kaytetye and Warlpiri.

Table 2: Skin names in some Arandic languages and in Warlpiri

Central Anmatyerr	Eastern Anmatyerr	Central & Eastern Arrernte	Western Arrernte	Alyawarr	Kaytetye	Warlpiri
Peltharr	Petyarr	Peltharre	Peltharre	Apetyarr	Kapetye	Japaljarri Napaljarri
Pengart	Pengart	Pengarte	Pengarte		Pengarte	Japangardi Napangardi
Kemarr	Kemarr	Kemarre	Kemarre	Akemarr	Kemarre	Jakamarra Nakamarra
Mpetyan	Mpetyan	Ampetyane Mpetyane	Mpetyane		Ampetyane	Jampijinpa Nampijinpa
Ngwarray	Kngwarray Ngwarray	Kngwarraye	Kngwarreye	Kngwarrey Ngwarrey	Kngwarreye	Jungarrayi Nungarrayi
Penangk	Penangk	Penangke	Penangke		Penangke	Japanangka Napanangka
Pwerrerl	Pwerl	Perrurle	Pwerrerle	Pwerl	Pwerle	Jupurrurla Napurrurla
Ngal	Ngal	Angale	Ngale		Thangale	Jangala Nangala

A comparison of the skin names for these different languages shows a lot of similarities and some differences. For example, Warlpiri distinguishes between male and female in the skin names by the addition of the prefixes '*Ja*' of '*Ju*' (for male) and '*Na*' or '*Nu*' (for female). In the Anmatyerr region there are male and female junior or diminutive skin names (generally, but not always, used for young people) which are very similar to those used by Warlpiri (see Figure 3 below). In the western part of the Anmatyerr area people use the eight Anmatyerr skin names shown in Table 2 but, as the Warlpiri are close neighbours, they might also use Warlpiri skin names. Table 2 also shows that the Alyawarr system has a set of four names rather than the eight used by the other languages in the Arandic group. In reality a person may well have relatives from different language groups. The differences in the skin names do not stop people understanding their place in the social system, and Aboriginal people are versatile at switching between these systems and calculating complex social relations between groups of people, for which the skin names are but one of a set of guiding cues.

Some minor differences in the skin names can be accounted for by differences in spelling. The spelling of Aboriginal languages in Central Australia has gone through many phases and refinements. It began with early documents compiled by missionaries, linguists and others, who in some cases brought to the task their own idiosyncratic ways of spelling which reflected the sounds that they thought they heard. This resulted in much variation in spelling, and the spelling of skin names is no exception. This is partly because many of these were written down prior to the publication of Aboriginal language dictionaries. However, there are also variations in the way that some of these words are pronounced, and so, for example, many words in Arandic languages may be pronounced either with or without the initial *a* vowel, and with or without the final vowel which is written as *e* in some of the Arandic languages. The skin name spelt variously as *Mpetyan*, *Mpetyane*, or *Ampetyane* is a good example. Although this skin name essentially sounds the same in Anmatyerr, Arrernte and Kaytetye, some decided to write it starting with *M* and others with *A*, and some decided not to write a final *e* on the end of the word (see introduction, page xvii). Some people may also have their own preferred spelling of their own skin name, just like some English surnames have alternative conventional spellings for words that are pronounced the same way.

Figure 3 below shows the Anmatyerr skin names and some of the ways that people with a particular skin name might be related to each other. For example, it shows that if a person is *Kemarr*, their father will be *Pwerrerl*, their mother *Penangk* and their husband or wife will ideally be *Peltharr* or *Petyarr*. The children of a *Kemarr* woman are *Ngwarray* and those of a *Kemarr* man *Pwerrerl*. Figure 3 also shows skin names that are typically used for younger people (though they may also be used for adults). These 'diminutive' forms of the kin terms are not used much in the Eastern Anmatyerr region.

Figure 3: Anmatyerr skin names

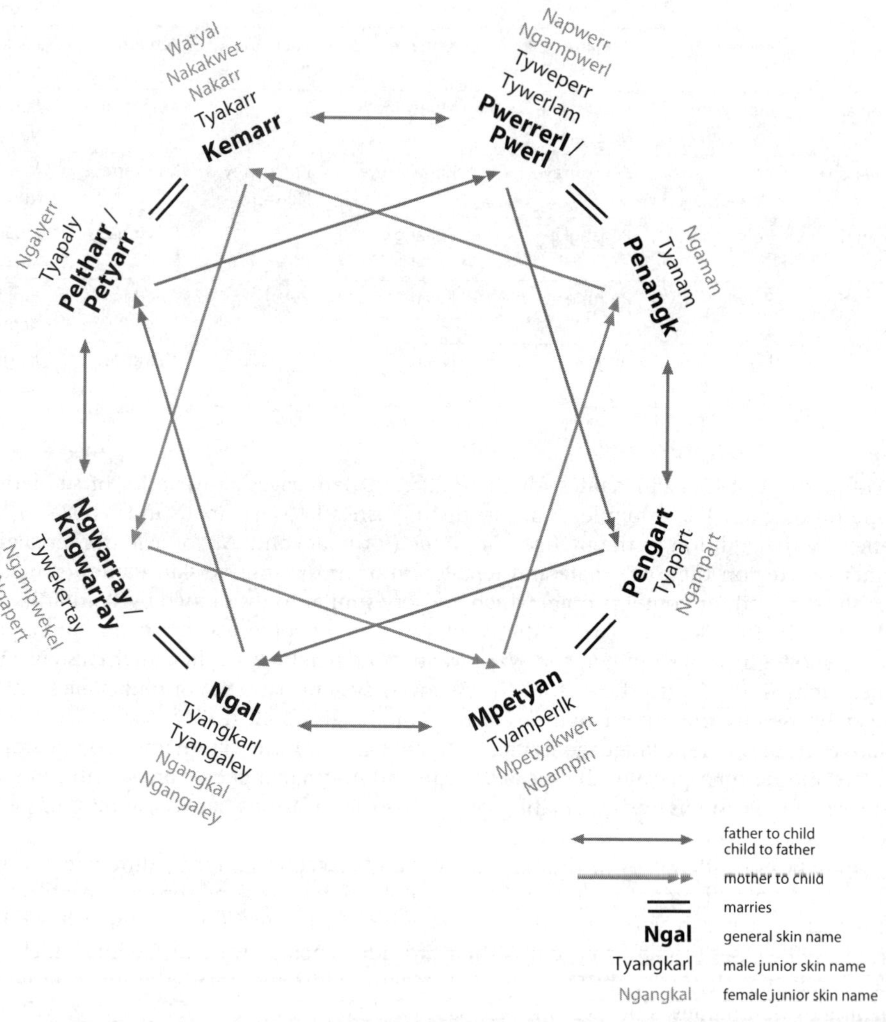

One aspect of the complexity of the kinship system which is reflected in the grammar of the Anmatyerr language, and in that of the pronouns in particular, is the way that people are divided into groups or 'moieties' ('moiety' means 'half'). Anmatyerr society may be divided into moieties in two main ways: patrimoieties and generation moieties. In the underlying structure of the kinship system it is partly these divisions that give rise to the skin name categories discussed above. The divisions into moieties are reflected in certain aspects of social behaviour, in law and ceremony, and in relationships to land. The division into patrimoieties reflects descent through male lines as follows:

Patrimoiety 1	**Patrimoiety 2**
Kemarr	Peltharr/Petyarr
Pwerrerl/Pwerl	Ngwarray/Kngwarray
Mpetyan	Pengart
Ngal	Penangk

Every person belongs to the same patrimoiety to kin which include their actual and classificatory fathers, their brothers and sisters, their fathers' fathers and their brothers' children. A person is also in the same patrimoiety as their mother's mother, their mothers-in-law and their sons-in-law. Every individual belongs to the opposite patrimoiety to that of their mother, their mother's father, their mother's brothers and sisters, their father's mother and their cross-cousins. The ending *-akey* goes on some dual and plural pronouns to form terms which refer to the patrimoiety divisions. The most commonly used of these are *alak-akey* 'they (people in the opposite patrimoiety as me or us)' and *ilernak-akey* 'we (people in the same patrimoiety as each other)'.

The second division is into generation moieties:

Generation moiety 1	**Generation moiety 2**
Kemarr	Pwerrerl/Pwerl
Mpetyan	Ngal
Peltharr/Petyarr	Ngwarray/Kngwarray
Pengart	Penangk

A person belongs to the same generation moiety as their actual and classificatory brothers and sisters, their cross-cousins, and their husbands or wives. Their grandparents and grandchildren are also in the same generation moiety. In the opposite generation moiety are a person's parents, parents-in-law, children, sons-in-law, and sisters-in-law. Communication with some kin in the opposite generation moiety is circumspect and oblique, and in some cases avoided altogether. For other types of kin in the opposite generation moiety the traditional style of communication can involve teasing and playing jokes. Marriage is ideally with someone of the same generation moiety and opposite patrimoiety. For example, a Kemarr is supposed to marry a Peltharr or a Petyarr.

The term *kweyekar* is used for those who are in the same generation moiety to the person or persons whose point of view you are taking, and *nywerrp* for those in the opposite generation moiety. The ending *-apakwey* goes on some dual and plural pronouns (referring to people not in the same patrimoiety) to form names which refer to generation moiety divisions. When the ending *-apakwey* goes on words that mean 'we' it forms words meaning 'we who are in the same generation moiety as each other', and when it goes on words meaning 'you' or 'they' it forms words that mean 'you, who are in the opposite generation moiety to me' or 'they, who are in the opposite generation moiety to me'. For example, *anwernantherr-apakwey* 'we (belonging to the same generation moiety as each other)' and *arrantherr-apakwey* 'you (belonging to the opposite generation moiety to me)'.

Anmatyerr pronouns

In Anmatyerr there is no distinction made between male and female in the pronoun system so, for example, the pronoun *ra* can mean 'he' or 'she' (and 'it'). However, other aspects of the

Anmatyerr pronoun system can seem to be very complicated to those not familiar with it. Not only are there different singular, dual and plural pronouns (unlike English, which only has singular and plural), but the form of these pronouns changes depending on what groups of kin are being referred to (in terms of which patrimoiety and generation moiety they belong to or, in other words, what skin groups the people in the group belong to). There is one set of dual and plural pronouns for people who are in the same patrimoiety and generation moiety, another for people of the same patrimoiety and opposite generation moiety, and another for people of the opposite patrimoiety. In the table below these three groups are called KinI, KinII and KinIII. Table 3 shows the parts that are added to the pronoun word to show these differences in kin relations.

Table 3: Pronoun endings that show kin relations

	KinI	KinII	KinIII
Word part	**ø, +ingkerr**	**+ak**	**+anth**
Patrimoiety	same	same	opposite
Generation moiety	same	opposite	either
Some types of kin	sibling father's father mother's mother father's mother mother's father	father aunt (father's sister) brother's child son-in-law mother-in-law	spouse cross-cousin sibling-in-law mother uncle (mother's brother) woman's child father-in-law

If there is no ending (ø) or the *+ingkerr* ending (KinI), this shows that the members of the group referred to by the pronoun are in the same patrimoiety and the same generation moiety (for example, a person together with their siblings); the ending *+ak* (KinII) shows membership of the same patrimoiety and opposite generation moiety (for example, a person together with their father or father's sister); and *+anth* (KinIII) shows opposite patrimoiety (for example, a person together with their mother). Plural pronouns marked with *+anth* appear to be the unmarked forms; that is to say, the ones that are used when kin relations between the members of the group are not specified. As an exception it seems that all pronouns referring to grandparents and grandchildren are marked as if they are in KinI group, even though a person's father's mothers and mother's fathers actually belong to the opposite patrimoiety.

In the first person (i.e. words for 'we', 'us' etc) there are also different forms of Anmatyerr pronouns depending on whether or not the person being spoken to is included in the group. The word part *+ern* is added to pronouns to show that the person being spoken to is *not* included. Thus, there is a different pronoun for 'we (including you who is being spoken to)' and for 'we (excluding you who is being spoken to)'. Such fine distinctions between the relationships of the speaker to the people listening and to the people being referred to are not possible in the English pronoun system.

The different columns in Table 4 below show the pronouns that have different grammatical functions in the sentence, such as the difference between 'we', 'us', 'for us' and 'our' in English. The rows show the pronouns that are used depending on the number of people being referred to, the kin relations, and whether or not the person being spoken to is included or not.

All this may seem a bit daunting, but remember that it takes many years, and a thorough knowledge of Anmatyerr society, to learn to use these pronouns fluently.

Table 4: Anmatyerr pronouns

1st = 1st person (I, me, my, we, us, ours etc.)
2nd = 2nd person (you, your etc.)
3rd = 3rd person (he, she, it, they, them, theirs etc.)

incl = inclusive (including the person being spoken to)
excl = exclusive (not including the person being spoken to)

	Nominative Shows the person or thing that is the 'doer' of the action of an intransitive verb.	**Ergative** Shows the person or thing that is the 'doer' of the action of a transitive verb.	**Accusative** Shows that the verb action is happening to the person or thing represented by the pronoun.	**Dative** Shows what the reason for or the purpose of an action is; *for* or *to* the person or thing represented by the pronoun.	**Possessive** Belonging to the person or thing represented by the pronoun.
Singular (one)	**I, you**	**I, you**	**me, you, him, her, it**	**for me, to me, for you, to him, for her, for it etc.**	**my, mine, your, yours, his, her, hers, its**
1st	ayeng	tha, thang (W,T)	ayeng, ayenh, ayengenh (W,T)	atyeng	atyenh, atyengenh, atyehenh (W,T), atyeng-henh (W,T)
2nd	nga	ntwa, ntwang (W,T), unta (E)	ngenh, ngwenh (W,T)	ngkweng	ngkwengenh, ngkwenh (T,E), ngkwinh (T,E), ngkweyenh (W,T), ngkwehenh (W,T)
	Nominative				
	he, she, it				
3rd	ra, rang (W,T), ya (W,T), yang (W,T)		renh, yenh (W,T), renhenh (W)	kwer, ikwer	kwerenh, ikwerenh
Dual (two)	**we (two), you (two), they (two)**		**us (two), you (two), them (two)**	**for us (two), for you (two), for the two of you, for them (two), for those two, etc.**	**our, ours (belonging to us two), your, yours (belonging to you two), their, theirs (belonging to those two)**
1st KinI (incl)	ilengkerr, ilingkerr, ila (E), ayla (E)		ilengkerrenh, ilingkerrenh, ilenh-ingkerrenh	ileh-ingkerr (W,T), ilek-ingkerr (E)	ileh-ingkerrenh (W,T), ilek-ingkerrenh (E)
1st KinII (incl)	ilak, aylak (E)		ilenhak, ilenhakenh, ilenhenhakenh, aylenhak (E)	ilakeh (W,T), ilahek (W,T), ilekak (E), aylakek (E)	ilahekenh (W,T), ilekakenh (E), aylakakenh (E)
1st KinIII (incl)	ilanth, aylanth (E)		ilenhanth, ilenhenhanthenh, aylenhanth (E)	ilehanth (W,T), ilekanth (T,E), aylekanth (E)	ilahenthenh (W,T), ilanth-henh (W,T), ilekanthenh (E), aylekanthenh (E)
1st KinI (excl)	ilern, aylern (E), ilern-ingkerr, aylern-ingkerr (E)		ilernenh, aylernenh (E) ilernenh-ingkerrenh, aylernenh-ingkerrenh (E)	ilerneh (W,T), ilernek (E), aylernek (E), ilerneh-ingkerr (W,T), ilernek-ingkerr (E), aylernek-ingkerr (E)	ilern-henh (W,T), ilern-kenh (E), alyern-kenh (E), ilerneh-ingkerrenh (W,T), ilernek-ingkerrenh (E), aylernek-ingkerrenh (E)

Table 4: Anmatyerr pronouns continued

Dual (two)	**we (two), you (two), they (two)**	**us (two), you (two), them (two)**	**for us (two), for you (two), for the two of you, for them (two), for those two, etc.**	**our, ours (belonging to us two), your, yours (belonging to you two), their, theirs (belonging to those two)**
1st KinII (excl)	ile-nak, aylernak (E)	ilernakenh, ilernenhakenh, ilernenhak, alyernenhak (E)	ilernehak (W,T), ilernekak (E), aylernekak (E)	ilernehakenh (W,T), ilernekakenh (E), alyernekakenh (E)
1st KinIII (excl)	ile-nanth, aylernanth (E)	ilernanthenh, ilernenhanthenh, alyernanthenh (E)	ilernehanth (W,T), ilernekanth (E), aylernekanth (E)	ilernehanthenh (W,T), ilernekanthenh (E), aylernekanthenh (E)
2nd KinI	mpwel, mpwel-ingkerr	mpwelenh, mpwelenh-ingkerrenh, mpwelenh-ingkerr	mpweleh (W,T), mpwelek (E) mpweleh-ingkerr (W,T), mpwelek-ingkerr (E)	mpwel-henh (W,T), mpwel-kenh (E), mpwel-ingkerrenh, mpweleh-ingkerrenh (W,T), mpwelek-ingkerrenh (E)
2nd KinII	mpwelak	mpwelenhakenh, mpwelenhak	mpwelehak (W,T), mpwelekak (E)	mpwel-kenh, mpwelehakenh (W,T), mpwelekakenh (E)
2nd KinIII	mpwelanth	mpwelenhanthenh, mpwelenhanth	mpwelehanth (W,T), mpwelekanth (E)	mpwelanth-henh (W,T), pwelekanthenh (E),
3rd	ratherr, yatherr (W,T)	renh-atherr, yenh-atherr (W,T), yenh-atherrenh (W,T)	kwer-atherr, ikwer-atherr	kwer-atherrenh, ikwer-atherrenh
3rd KinI	ala, alengkerr, alingkerr	alenh, alengkerrenh, alingkerrenh	aleh (W,T), alek (E), aleh-ingkerr (W,T), alek-ingkerr (E)	alehenh (W,T), alekenh (E) aleh-ingkerrenh (W,T), alek-ingkerrenh (E), alengkerr-henh (W,T)
3rd KinII	alak	alenhak	alahek (W,T), alekak (E)	alehakenh (W,T), alekakenh (E)
3rd KinIII	alanth	alenhanth	alehanth (W,T), alekanth (E)	alehanthenh (W,T), alekanthenh (E)

Table 4: Anmatyerr pronouns continued

Plural (more than two)	**we (more than two), you (more than two), they (more than two)**	**us (more than two), you (more than two), them (more than two)**	**for us (more than two), for you (more than two), for them (more than two) etc.**	**our, ours (belonging to more than two), your, yours (belonging to more than two), their, theirs (belonging to more than two)**
1st (incl)	anwa		anwekenh (E)	
1st KinI (incl)	anwengkerr, anwingkerr, aningkerr (E)	anwengkerrenh, anwingkerrenh, aningkerrenh (E)	anweh-ingkerr (W,T), anwek-ingkerr (E), anek-ingkerr (E)	anweh-ingkerrenh (W,T), anwek-ingkerrenh (E), anek-ingkerrenh (E)
1st KinII (incl)	anakerr, anwakerr (T,E)	anenhakerrenh anwenhakerrenh (E)	anehakerr (W,T), anekakerr (E), anwekakerr (E)	anakerrenh, anehakerrenh (W,T), anwekakerrenh (E)
1st KinIII (incl)	anantherr, anwantherr (E)	anantherrenh, anwantherrenh (E)	anehantherr (W,T), anekantherr (E), anwekantherr (E)	anantherrenh, anwekantherrenh (E)
1st (excl)	anwern	anwernenh	anwerneh (W,T), anwernek (E)	anwern-henh (W,T), anwern-kenh (E)
1st KinI (excl)	anwern-ingkerr	anwernenh-ingkerrenh	anwerneh-ingkerr (W,T), anwernek-ingkerr (E)	anwerneh-ingkerrenh (W,T), anwernek-ingkerrenh (E), anwern-ingkerrenh (E)
1st KinII (excl)	anwernakerr	anwernenhakerrenh, anwernenhakerr	anwernehakerr (W,T), anwernekakerr (E)	anwernehakerrenh (W,T), anwernekakerrenh (E)
1st KinIII (excl)	anwernantherr	anwernantherrenh, anwernenhantherr	anwernehantherr (W,T), anwernekantherr (E)	anwernehantherrenh (W,T), anwernekantherrenh (E)
2nd KinI	arrengkerr, arringkerr	arrenh-ingkerrenh, arrenh-ingkerr	arreh-ingkerr (W,T), arrek-ingkerr (E)	arrengkerrenh (W,T), arreh-ingkerrenh (W,T), arrek-ingkerrenh (E)
2nd KinII	arrakerr	arrenhakerr, arrenhakerrenh	arrehakerr (W,T), arrekakerr (E)	arrakerrenh (W), arrehakerrenh (W,T), arrekakerrenh (E)

Table 4: Anmatyerr pronouns continued

Plural (more than two)	**we (more than two), you (more than two), they (more than two)**	**us (more than two), you (more than two), them (more than two)**	**for us (more than two), for you (more than two), for them (more than two) etc.**	**our, ours (belonging to more than two), your, yours (belonging to more than two), their, theirs (belonging to more than two)**
2nd KinIII	arrantherr	arrenhantherr, arrenhantherrenh	arrehantherr (W,T), arrekantherr (T,E)	arrantherrenh (W,T), arrehantherrenh (W,T), arrekantherrenh (E)
3rd	rarey, yarey (W,T), rernem (E)	renh-arey, yenh-arey (W,T)	kwer-arey, ikwer-arey	kwer-areyenh, ikwer-areyenh, ikwer-arenh (E)
3rd	ina[1], inang (W,T), itna (E)	inenh, itnenh (E)	ineh (W,T), inek (E), itnek (E)	inehenh (W,T), inekenh (E), itnekenh (E)
3rd KinI	inengkerr, iningkerr, itningkerr (E), ayningkerr (E), aytningkerr (E)	inengkerrenh, iningkerrenh, inenh-ingkerrenh (W,T), itnenh-ingkerr (E), aynenh-ingkerrenh (E), aytnenh-ingkerrenh (E)	ineh-ingkerr (W,T), inengkerreh (W,T), itnek-ingkerr (E), aynek-ingkerr (E), aytnek-ingkerr (E)	ineh-ingkerrenh (W,T), inengkerr-henh (W,T), itnek-ingkerrenh (E), aynek-ingkerrenh (E), aytnek-ingkerrenh (E)
3rd KinII	inakerr, itnakerr (E), aynakerr (E), aytnakerr (E)	inenhakerrenh, itnenhakerrenh (E), aynenhakerrenh (E), aytnenhakerrenh (E)	inehakerr (W,T), inakerreh (W,T), inekakerr (E), itnekakerr (E), aynekakerr (E), aytnekakerr (E)	inakerr-henh (W,T), inakerr-kenh (E), itnekakerrekenh (E), aynekakerrenh (E), aytnekakerrenh (E)
3rd KinIII	inantherr, itnantherr (E), aynantherr (E), aytnantherr (E)	inenhantherrenh, itnenhantherrenh (E), aynenhantherrenh (E), aytnenhantherrenh (E)	inehantherr (W,T), inantherreh (W,T), inekantherr (E), itnekantherr (E), aynekantherr (E), aytnekantherr (E)	inehantherrenh (W,T), inantherr-henh (W,T), inekantherrenh (E), itnekantherrenh (E), aynekantherrenh (E), aytnekantherrenh (E)

Appendix 2 Anmatyerr word endings

The hyphen ('-') shows that the ending is usually hyphenated to the word (unless it is a short or monosyllabic word, in which case it will follow straight after it).

The plus sign ('+') shows that the ending is not usually hyphenated to the word, but rather goes straight onto it.

Endings followed by a '+' or '-' always have another ending or word part after them.

Some people prefer to write endings as separate words; there are also some 'words' that could be written as endings. Dialect codes are used in this appendix as they are in the rest of the dictionary.

Ending	Types of words the ending goes on*	Gloss†
+a	verb	order, command
+ak[1] (E)	nominal	an extra thing; something else or someone else; and, as well as
+ak[2]	pronoun	same patrimoiety but opposite generation moiety
-akerl+	verb	do action down or along something; do action from one end to the other; right along, down
-akert[2]	nominal	**1.** with something, having (something) **2.** having (a feeling or emotion) **3.** having something wrong with a particular part of the body **4.** using something to do an action; with **5.** with someone, accompanied by someone **6.** following a word that identifies a person, refers to their husband or wife **7.** shows the thing that a story, conversation or meeting is about
+akey	pronoun	forms words which refer to patrimoiety divisions
-akwerrk[2]	pronoun	family, relation
-alew[1] (E), -arlew (E)		'Where is (someone or something)?', 'What about (someone or something)?'
-alkenty		GO TO *+ant-alkenty*
-alpem		GO TO *+ety-alp+*
+alth, +elth	nominal	describes someone or something that characteristically behaves in the way indicated by the word it goes on
-altyerr[2]	pronoun	forms a word which refers to closely related sons-in-law or mothers-in-law
+am[1] (W,T), +em (W,T)		**1.** adds emphasis **2.** used (with question words) to form questions
+am[2]	nominal	in the middle of doubled-up words that describe number or amount, shows that something happens gradually or in stages; bit by bit, one at a time, two at a time etc.
+amel[2] (E)	verb	(the verb action) will happen soon
+amp, +ampw	nominal	goes on the end of nominals (usually plant names) to refer to the types of sweet resin or honey often found on that plant
-amparr, -amperr (W)	ending	(doing something) first (before some other action); (someone does something) first (before doing something else); initially
-ampeny[2]	nominal	side, area, region, in the vicinity of
-amperl (E)	nominal	**1.** an expression of endearment or sympathy; 'poor thing', 'poor bugger', 'dear thing' **2.** really, extremely
-amperr (W)		GO TO *-amparr*

* unmarked endings go on a range of word types   † see main entries for more details and for example sentences

Ending	Types of words the ending goes on*	Gloss†
+ampw		GO TO *+amp*
+an[2] (W), +arn		provides emphasis or focus
+ang (W,T)		goes on the end of most short words in the western and central parts of the Anmatyerr region
-angent[2], -anngernt (T)		**1.** (something happens) before the verb action, before, awaiting **2.** for, on behalf of
-angerr[2]	nominal	shows that there is a lot of that thing, characteristic or quality
-angkarreny (W,T), -angkerreny (W)	nominal	**1.** more (of a quality) **2.** in spite of the fact that . . . , even though . . . , contrary to expectations
-angker (E)	nominal	shows that there is a lot of that thing, characteristic or quality
-angketyarr (E)	nominal	**1.** shows that there is plenty of, lots of, or an abundance of (that thing) **2.** a place where there is lots of that particular thing
+angkw		GO TO *+engkw*
-angkwer[4] (E)	pronoun	shows that the speaker is in a respect relationship to the people referred to
-angkwerr[2], -angkwarr		**1.** the path or direction something goes along; by way of, through something, this way, in the direction of, across, via **2.** with someone or something, close to someone **3.** in comparison to **4.** on verbs it indicates that the action happens in a particular way, manner or fashion
-angwel-angwel (E), angwen-angwen (T,E)	nominal	an expression of sympathy or endearment; 'poor thing', 'poor bugger', 'dear thing'
-ankel[2] (E)	nominal	when, in that time, at that time.
-ankethenh	kin term	**1.** shows that the speaker, or the person being referred to, still has that particular close kin relation (i.e. that relation is still alive) **2.** shows that the person being referred to is together with that particular relation all the time
-anngernt (T)		GO TO *-angent[2]*
+ant		only, just, just that and nothing else, only this and nothing else, precisely, particularly, exclusively
+ant-alkenty		**1.** everybody **2.** provides emphasis; really
+ant-arey (T,E)	nominal	just the group of them, those in particular
+ant-atherr	nominal	just the two of them, those two in particular
-antep	nominal	(up)wards, down(wards)
-anternenh	nominal	very big, enormous, huge
-antey		**1.** an action or state of affairs has continued for some time; always; again; still; yet; keep on (doing action) **2.** with negative verbs, an action hasn't yet happened **3.** emphasises the similarity between things; too, as well, also, is similar to.
+anth	pronoun	**1.** opposite patrimoiety marker **2.** unspecified kin relations marker
-antyem[2]		GO TO *+ety-aynt+*
-anyem[3] (E)	nominal	just, exactly, precisely
-anyimp		GO TO *+eng-anyimp*
+ap		adds emphasis
-apakwey	pronoun	same or opposite generation moiety marker

* unmarked endings go on a range of word types   † see main entries for more details and for example sentences

Ending	Types of words the ending goes on*	Gloss†
-apatherr (W,T)	pronoun	**1.** used when asking a person what their skin name or subsection name is **2.** something said when the speaker is not sure of the name of something; 'what's-his-name', 'what-d'ye-call-it', **3.** with pronouns, shows whether or not people are in the same or in the opposite generation moiety to the person speaking
-apenh (W,T)	nominal	'poor thing', 'dear thing' (an expression of endearment)
+apenty		GO TO *+apwenty*
-apeny (E)		**1.** resembles; is like (someone or something else); is similar to, is like this, it seems like **2.** on verbs it shows that something does an action in the way something else does it; like that **3.** following *+el* on nominals, *-apeny* shows that something else does an action in the way that particular thing does it
-apert	nominal	having (something), associated with (something)
+apwenty (T,E), +apenty	nominal	follows the name of an ancestral animal, plant or other thing to form the name of a place associated with that particular Dreaming.
-arelh² (E)	nominal	shows that the thing is used for, or associated with; another thing in the sentence; is used for . . . , is for . . .
-areng¹	nominal	the number of times something happens (on the end of a number word)
-areng (W)		GO TO *-arleng²*
-areny		**1.** belonging to or associated with a place; from a place **2.** living in a particular location or place, inhabitant of a place **3.** (something that is) usually found in a particular habitat or environment **4.** associated with a particular thing **5.** associated with a particular action
-arey¹	nominal	plural marker; more than two are doing the verb action or are the object of the verb action; lots of, group of
-arey² (E)	verb	more than two people are being told, or ordered, to do the action
+arl		**1.** goes in sentences in which there is more than one clause or 'idea' and is used to link the two; that, while, which, when, as, because, who **2.** provides emphasis or focus
+arn		GO TO *+an²*
-arlek, -arleh (W)		**1.** shows where someone or something is put by the action of the verb, or where someone or something puts itself by the action of the verb; at, on, in, into, onto **2.** shows where something is got from **3.** indicates the reason for doing something; because
-arleng², -ayeng (W,T), -areng (W)	nominal	**1.** with someone, accompanied by someone, around someone **2.** together with something; in with something; in (a container), contained in something **3.** on something; at something, from something
-arleng³	verb	**1.** the person or thing doing the action of that verb is not the same as the person or thing doing the action of the other verb in the sentence; because of something, over **2.** because of something; over (person or thing doing the action of both verbs may be the same)
-arlew (E)		GO TO *-alew¹*
arlka²		too, as well as, also, and
+arl-penh, +arl-iperr	verb	shows that something else happens after that action
-arneng	nominal	someone or something that is closely related to another person or thing
+arr+¹ (E)	verb	plural marker; shows that more than one is doing the action
+arr² (W)	nominal	shows the time or season when particular plants appear (?)
-arrngel		because of something; over
+arrp¹		**1.** emphasises that the person or thing referred to is doing the action themself **2.** only, just

* unmarked endings go on a range of word types † see main entries for more details and for example sentences

Ending	Types of words the ending goes on*	Gloss†
-arrpantey		**1.** something which is an imitation of the real thing **2.** something that is not up to standard **3.** make out as if (to do something); pretend to do something **3.** try to do something and fail
-arrpatenty (E)	nominal	something which is an imitation of the real thing; a pretend thing; a fake, something that is not up to standard; something that is supposed to be something but is not, 'so-called'
+art (W,T)	kin term	**1.** following *-nheng* shows that there is a group of more than two people, one of whom is called by that kinship term by the others **2.** with the kin term *anew* refers to two people together: a married couple
+art (T)		GO TO *+aty*²
-artek, -arteh (W,T), -art (W)		**1.** be like, similar to or resemble someone or something else **2.** do an action in a similar way to someone or something else
-artey		**1.** a way of asking where someone or something is; 'Where is . . . ?' **2.** makes a question out of a statement; 'What about . . . ?', 'What if . . . ?', 'How about . . . ?'
-artey (W,T)		GO TO *-artwey*
-artwemeny	kin term	respectful word which goes on the end of kin terms and is used when the particular relation referred to by the kin term has passed away
-artwety		GO TO *-atwety*²
-artwey, -artey (W,T)	nominal	**1.** people related to a particular Dreaming; owners or 'bosses' of a particular Dreaming, place or story, custodian **2.** relation, especially older relation; parents, grandparents, ancestors **3.** having a particular relation
-atety		used when asking questions, and in emphasising one thing or situation rather than another; instead, on the contrary (?)
-atety (T)		GO TO *-atwety*²
-athath		(do something) before another thing happens; (do something) before someone else does; (something has to happen) before another thing happens
-athek, -atheh (W)	nominal	in the general direction of; towards (a particular place or in a particular direction)
-athen (E)		**1.** mistakenly think that . . . , mistake something for . . . **2.** shows that you want the verb action to happen, or thought that it might happen, but it didn't
-atherr²	verb	**1.** shows that more than two people or things are doing the verb action **2.** shows that more than two are being told to do the verb action
-atwety², -artwety, -atety (T)		**1.** up to (somewhere), as far as (something). **2.** until (a particular time) **3.** until (a particular thing happens), until (someone does something)
+aty¹	kin term	my relation; our relation
+aty², +ayt (E), +art (T)	nominal	goes on the end of the names of certain plants to form the name of the grub that is found on that plant
+aw, +ew		goes on the end of a word to add emphasis to what is said
-awaty (T,E)	nominal	**1.** adds emphasis; a bit more of something, slightly greater (or lesser) degree, rather, somewhat **2.** indicates that a situation continues for some time; still, while (there's still time)
-awern	nominal	**1.** 'poor thing', 'dear thing' **2.** just a little, just a bit
+ay¹		**1.** adds emphasis **2.** goes on verbs when someone is telling a person to do that action

* unmarked endings go on a range of word types † see main entries for more details and for example sentences

Ending	Types of words the ending goes on*	Gloss†
-ayeng (W,T)		GO TO *-arleng*[2]
-ayerr	nominal	goes on the end of some ordinary language words and some avoidance language words when the respect register is being used
-ayeth	nominal	on words for body parts it shows that this part is in contact with the surface on which the body rests
-ayntem		GO TO *+ety-aynt+*
+ayt (E)		GO TO *+aty*[2]
+ek[1], +eh (W)	verb	action has already happened and is completed
+ek[2], +eh (W)	nominal	**1.** shows the reason for an action; for, for the purpose of **2.** for, to see if something is there, to test for something **3.** goes on the end of the word for the person or thing who is benefiting from an action; for, beneficiary, for someone **4.** goes on the thing that a feeling or thought is directed towards **5.** shows the position, time or location that something is in when an action happens to it; on, at, in, out of, from, off **6.** goes in between some doubled-up words (nominals) to show that a relation between things applies both ways **7.** goes in between doubled-up number words to show that (something is happening) bit by bit or in a numerical sequence
+ek-ahepel (W,T), +ek-apel		perhaps, maybe
+ek-anternenh		GO TO *-anternenh*
+ek-arelh		GO TO *-arelh*[2]
+ek-athen		GO TO *-athen*
+ekeng, +eheng (W)	verb	because (of something that has happened)
+ekerr (E)	verb	because (warning that the action may have bad consequences); for fear of, lest, in case
+ekw (W,T), +wek (W,T), +weh (W,T)	kin term	**1.** your relation **2.** his/her/their relation **3.** my/our relation
+el[1]	nominal	shows the person or thing that is the 'doer' of the action of a transitive verb
+el[2]	nominal	shows the tool or instrument that an action is being done with or with which an activity is carried out; using (something), by means of (something)
+el[3]	nominal	shows where somebody or something is, or where an action happens; at, in, on, by, along
+el[4]		goes on words that function as adverbs
+el[5]	nominal	on the end of words for times of the day, seasons, etc. it shows the time at which an action or event occurs, shows that some action happens within this time or for (that amount of time); in, at, during, through
+el[6]	nominal	used in describing what language is being used; in (the . . . language)
+el[7]		GO TO *+emel*
+el-arleng		GO TO *-arleng*[2]
+el-ayeth		GO TO *-ayeth*
+elengkw	nominal	having the particular characteristic shown by the word it goes onto
+elh+	verb	**1.** someone or something is doing the action to themself or to part of themself **2.** some action happens to someone or something (by itself) **3.** the direction of the action is away from yourself

* unmarked endings go on a range of word types † see main entries for more details and for example sentences

Ending	Types of words the ending goes on*	Gloss†
+elh-il+	verb	goes on intransitive verbs to make them into transitive ones; make something happen, make someone or something a certain way or make them do something
+elh-ilerr+	verb	goes on intransitive verbs to make them into reciprocal ones; make each other a certain way or make each other do something; cause something to happen to each other
+elp+	verb	shows that the action is just starting, is happening bit by bit or repeatedly, or to a lesser degree (than the normal action of the verb)
+elth		GO TO *+alth*
+em[1]	verb	action is happening now (at the time of speaking)
+em-[2]	verb	follows an English transitive verb when used in Anmatyerr to make it into an Anmatyerr verb
+em (W,T)		GO TO *+am[1]*
+emeh (W)		emphasis (?)
+emel	verb	action is happening at about the same time as another action or several actions; the 'doer' of the actions of both verbs, or of a series of verbs, is the same; 'while' or '. . . ing'
+emer	verb	action might or could happen
+em-ilem		GO TO *-il+*
+eng[1]		**1.** shows where something is from, or where something moves from; away from, from the direction of etc. **2.** what something is made of **3.** cause or reason **4.** part of body used in action **5.** location of action (?) **6.** type of transport used to go somewhere
+eng[2]	nominal	goes in the middle of a doubled-up word for a thing to describe the equivalent 'pretend' or 'toy' thing
+eng-anyimp (E)	nominal	imitation of the real thing
+eng-arrngel		GO TO *-arrngel*
+eng-ayerr (E)	nominal	from, out of
+engkw, +angkw	kin term	your relation
+eng-ntyel (W,T)		from, away from
+enh[1]	pronoun	pronoun is the object of the verb action
+enh[2]	pronoun	forms possessive pronouns from dative ones
+enh+[3]	verb	**1.** action is happening while going past somewhere or moving along. **2.** action is happening along something
+enh[4]	verb	turns verb into a nominal or 'thing' that is usually used to do the verb action, or has the action done to it
+enh+arey		GO TO *+arey[2]*
+enh+atherr		GO TO *+atherr[2]*
+enh+err+arey		GO TO *+arey[2]*
+enp (E)		GO TO *+inp*
+enty+[1], +inty+, +ety+ (E)	verb	do while coming this way, do coming hither
+enty[2]	verb	turns a verb into a noun which describes the action as a noun or which describes a person or thing who usually does that verb action
+enty[3]	nominal	turns some nominals into adverbs
+eny	nominal	goes on certain spatial and time words to describe a person or thing that is from that place or time

* unmarked endings go on a range of word types † see main entries for more details and for example sentences

Ending	Types of words the ending goes on*	Gloss†
+ep-	verb	**1.** (do something) continuously **2.** (do something) often **3.** (do something) sporadically
+erl[1]	verb	action is something that usually happens or would usually happen; would (do the verb action)
+erl-[2]	verb	part of compound verbs formed with *apetyem* 'come', *alhem* 'go', *anem* 'sit', *alpem* 'go back', *apem* 'go'
+erl-alh+	verb	do something and then go; do something before going; go after doing something
+erl-alp+	verb	go back and do (the verb action); do (the verb action) and then go back; go and do (the verb action) and then come back
+erl-an+	verb	action happens continuously or over a period of time; (do something) continuously; (do something) for a while
+erl-anerr+[1]	verb	two people (doing something) continuously or (doing something) for a while
+erl-anerr+[2] (W,T)	verb	two people are being ordered to do the action
+erl-ap+	verb	action happens continuously or over a period of time while in motion, or while going along
+erl-apety+	verb	(do something) and come; come along (doing something)
+erl-arrern+ (E)	verb	do something then place oneself in some bodily position
+erl-atherr+		GO TO *-atherr*[2]
+erl-ayn+ (E)	verb	do something quickly, do something straight away
+erl-aynt+ (E)	verb	action happens continuously or over a period of time
+erlek (E), +erleng	verb	shows that the person or thing doing the action of that verb is not the same as the person or thing doing the action of the main verb in the sentence
+erlentyarr+	verb	makes respect-language verbs
+erl-w+[1], +erl-iw+ (T,E)	verb	(do something) quickly; (do something) suddenly; (do something) only for a short time
+erl-w+[2] (T,E), +erl-iw+ (T,E), +erl-warr+ (T,E), +erl-werr+ (T,E)	verb	more than two are doing the action
+ern+[1] (W)	verb	(do something) while going back somewhere, (move something) back (to somewhere)
+ern[2]	verb	action just happened recently
+ern[3]	pronoun	shows that the person being spoken to is not included in the referent group
+err+[1]	verb	shows that two people or things are doing the verb action
+err+[2]	verb	shows that two people or things are doing the action to each other; each other, one another
+errirr+ (W,T)	verb	**1.** more than two are doing the action. **2.** more than two people or things are being told to do the action
+ety+ (E)		GO TO *+enty*[1]
+etyakenh	verb	action did not happen, is not happening now, or won't happen etc.
+ety-akerlem		GO TO *-akerl+*
+etyal	verb	**1.** used when ordering or telling someone not to do something; don't (do the verb action)!; had better not (do the verb action) **2.** something is not usually done or shouldn't be done

* unmarked endings go on a range of word types † see main entries for more details and for example sentences

Ending	Types of words the ending goes on*	Gloss†
+ety-alh+	verb	**1.** go and do action **2.** go like, become like something
+ety-alp+	verb	do the action and then go back; go back and do the action
+etyam	verb	**1.** was doing the action; were doing the verb action (action happened in the past over a period of time); the action of the verb continued for some time in the past **2.** shows that the action usually used to happen
+etyang (E)	verb	**1.** action did not happen, is not happening now, or won't happen etc. **2.** the speaker is telling someone or something not to do action
+etyart	verb	action used to happen or usually happened
+ety-aynt+ (T,E), +ety-anty+ (W)	verb	action continues for some time; shows that the action happens after another action; and then (something else happens); because (of that something else happens)
+etyel (E)	verb	**1.** action is happening now (at the time of speaking) **2.** action is something that typically happens **3.** action will probably happen or the actor intends the action to happen **4.** action is continuing for some time or will probably go on continuously
+etyek, +etyeh (W,T)	verb	**1.** action must, ought or is supposed to happen **2.** shows the purpose or the reason for the action; in order to (do something); so that (something can happen) **3.** person or thing intends to do the action or is about to do the action **4.** shows the normal or usual way a thing is done
+etyenh	verb	action will happen or will probably happen, going to (do something), (do something) in the future, will (do the verb action)
+etyenheng (W,T)	verb	action happens after another action; (do this) after (doing something else), (do something else) so that (this) will (happen), (do something else) and then (do this)
+ety-kweny		GO TO *-kweny*[2]
+ew		GO TO *+aw*
+ewarr+	verb	more than two people are doing the action
+ey	verb	**1.** used in asking for or giving permission to do something **2.** goes on the end of word(s) for something you are asking about or checking on
+eyam (E)	verb	shows that this action happens after another action; (do this) after (doing something else), (do something else) so that (this) will (happen), (do something else) and then (do this)
+eyaw	verb	**1.** makes a command or is used to tell someone (forcefully) that you want them to do something. **2.** somebody must or should do the action
+eyay		emphasis
+eyekw (E)		GO TO *+ikw*
+eyn+ (E)	verb	**1.** action is happening while the 'doer' of the verb action is going past somewhere or moving along **2.** action happens over a geographical area or along a path **3.** action is performed or continues over a period of time
+eyneng (E)	kin term	makes an ordinary kin term into a respect one
+eytarr (E)	nominal	added to a few nominals, in particular *arlpenty* 'long, tall'; (it seems to have no meaning of its own, separate from the combined form)
-henh (W,T)		GO TO *-kenh*[1]
-hety (W,T)		GO TO *-kety*
+ikw, +eyekw (E)	kin term	his or her kin relation; their kin relation

* unmarked endings go on a range of word types † see main entries for more details and for example sentences

Ending	Types of words the ending goes on*	Gloss†
-il+	nominal	**1.** makes transitive verbs; make or cause (something to happen) **2.** makes an English transitive verb into an Anmatyerr verb (following *+em-2*)
-ingar, -inger	nominal	on number words to show the number of times something happens; a number of nights or days, that many times
-ingkerr2	pronoun	same patrimoiety and same generation moiety
-inkwern (E)	verb	action used to happen
+inp (E), +enp (E)	nominal	associated with something, having a particular quality; along with; including; having; too; as well; also
+inty+		GO TO *+enty+1*
-intyerr, -intyarr (W,T)	nominal	plural marker
-ipenh (E)		GO TO *-penh1*
-iperr		**1.** after an event or after an action has been completed, after a certain situation **2.** because of something **3.** indicates the source or origin of something; from, out of
-iperr		GO TO *-perr*
-irr+		**1.** become something, turn into something. **2.** become (some way); get (that way); go (that way), be (some way) **3.** make (a particular noise), go like (a particular sound) **4.** goes on the end of nominals to make them into intransitive verbs **5.** goes on the end of some English verbs to turn them into intransitive verbs
-irrwengerr (W,T)	nominal	those two; and (the other one), both of them
-itany (E)		even though . . . , despite the fact that . . . , regardless of the fact that . . .
-iteng2		marks respect language words
-itwek (T,E), -rtwek (T,E), -utek (E)	nominal	**1.** amongst, at, on, by **2.** during, in the time of
-iwem		GO TO *-wem3*
-iwelhem		GO TO *-welhem*
-kenh1, -henh (W,T)	nominal	**1.** shows the person or thing that possesses or has an item; belonging to, owned by **2.** something which is typically used for something or associated with something; for
-kety, -hety (W,T)		**1.** signals something that should be avoided; for fear of someone or something, look out for someone or something; avoid someone or something, move away from something **2.** on the names of people or places it provides an explanation for why something shouldn't be said **3.** on verbs it shows that the speaker does not want a particular thing to happen; because of (something bad or unwanted), in case (something happens) **4.** on verbs it provides an explanation for an action (not necessarily a frightening or unwanted one), provides an explanation for difficulty in doing something; because
-kweny2, -kwenh (T)		**1.** on nominals it means not having that thing; without, none, not **2.** on nominals it shows that something is not a particular thing **3.** on kin terms it shows that someone has recently lost that particular relative **4.** on verbs it shows that the action of the verb did not happen, is not happening now, or won't happen etc.
-lkwer	nominal	**1.** this type of thing, that type of thing, more-or-less (like this) **2.** used in making comparisons between things, a bit like 'er' in English 'bigger', 'smaller' etc.

* unmarked endings go on a range of word types † see main entries for more details and for example sentences

Ending	Types of words the ending goes on*	Gloss†
-malangk	nominal	lovely, attractive, gorgeous, nice, pleasant, good-looking
-mart		emphasis; really
-nheng2	kin term	together with complementary relation or relations
-ntyel, -tyel (W)	nominal	**1.** shows where something moves from, is moved from, or comes from; away from, off, from, out of, out from **2.** from the time of, since **3.** shows what something is made of or the source or origin of something
-pal, -pel	nominal	goes on the end of English number words
-parety, -paraty	kin term	your relation (respectful or 'sorry' way of talking)
-pat	nominal	goes on a few words — such as *angerr* 'big', *irrewaly* 'dead body' and *angkwey* 'old' — to form words with the general meaning of 'senior people', 'ancestors' etc.
-pel		GO TO *-pal*
-penh1, -ipenh (E)		**1.** an event happens after another event or action has been completed; because of something; after a certain situation **2.** because of something; from (the cause of) **3.** from, out of, indicates the source or origin of something
-penh2, -pwenh	nominal	**1.** goes on words for compass directions; from that direction **2.** goes on words for compass directions; in that direction
-perr (W,T), -iperr		something is obvious to the listener; of course (?)
-rlwer (W,T)	nominal	**1.** at some particular time; during, while **2.** through something, in the midst of something
-pwenh		GO TO *-penh2*
+rnem1	verb	forms intransitive compound verbs, in which part of the meaning describes a vertical or standing position, or motion in an upwards direction
-rnem2 (E)	nominal	plural marker; shows that more than two are doing the verb action or are the object of the verb action; lots of, group of
-rrpwer (W,T)	kin term	a lot, plural, all of them
-rtwek (T,E)		GO TO *-itwek*
-rwek (T)	nominal	**1.** at some particular time; during **2.** through something, in the midst of something
-tayem, -taym	nominal	'time'; during a particular season or event; the time when something happens
-thayt	nominal	side, area
-they (E), -then (T)	nominal	**1.** shows where something moves from, is moved from, or comes from; away from, off, from, out of, out from **2.** shows the reason for something; because of something, over **3.** shows the part of a body or thing which is involved in an action **4.** shows what something is made of or the source or origin of something **5.** refers to the language being used
-tyel (W)		GO TO *-ntyel*
-utek (E)		GO TO *-itwek*
-uthek (E)	nominal	without, not having (something)
-warn2 (W,T), -wern (W,T), -warl, -werl	nominal	**1.** shows the direction of the action towards or to something; towards, to, at, into, onto, go somewhere, go in a particular direction **2.** shows that the direction of the action is towards the place where particular things are; go for a particular purpose, for (something), to get (something) **3.** shows that the action is done into or on something; in, on, into **4.** (facing or pointing) towards (something); in that direction

* unmarked endings go on a range of word types   †, see main entries for more details and for example sentences

Ending	Types of words the ending goes on*	Gloss†
+wek (W,T), +weh (W,T)		GO TO *+ekw*
-welhem, -iwelhem (E)	verb	occurs in some compound verbs
-wem[3], -iwem (E)	verb	occurs in some compound verbs

* unmarked endings go on a range of word types † see main entries for more details and for example sentences